MOST ACCURATE. MOST CURRENT. MOST TRUSTED.

MW00339736

Table of Contents

MAPSCO Directory Lists

MAPSCO Street Index

MAPSCO Detail Maps

Tell us what you think.

Go to www.mapsco.com/comments and fill out our online survey.
Your comments help us improve maps year after year.

For advertising information, please contact Mapsco at (972) 450-9319.

Although the information in this Mapsco product is based on the most up-to-date information and has been checked for accuracy, Mapsco does not guarantee or warrant the accuracy of any information in this product and shall not be liable in any respect for any errors or omissions.
If you find any errors or omissions, please promptly bring them to our attention so that corrections may be made in future editions.

Published by MAPSCO, Inc. • 4181 CENTURION WAY • ADDISON, TX 75001 • (972) 450-9300
© Copyright 2009 by MAPSCO, Inc. All rights reserved. AUSTIN MAP - 80009

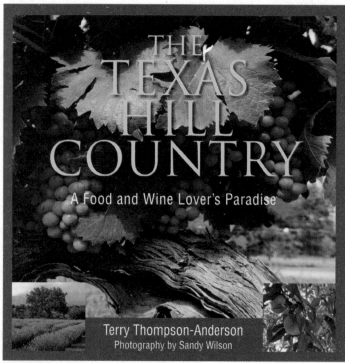

EXPLANATION of MAP SYMBOLS
Explicación de Simbologia del Mapa

INTERSTATE HIGHWAY NUMBER
Número de Carretera Interestatal — `35`

INTERSTATE HIGHWAY NUMBER (Business Route)
Número de Carretera Interestatal
(Curva Hacia el Centro Comercial) — `BUS 35`

U.S. HIGHWAY NUMBER
Número de Carretera de EE.UU. (Estados Unidos) — `183`

STATE HIGHWAY NUMBER
Número de Carretera Estatal — `71`

FARM TO MARKET ROAD NUMBER
Número del Camino entre Granja y Mercado — `FM 973`

RANCH TO MARKET ROAD NUMBER
Número del Camino entre Rancho y Mercado — `RM 620`

STATE LOOP NUMBER
Número de Lazo Estatal — `LOOP 275`

STATE SPUR NUMBER
Número de Espuela Estatal — `SPUR 69`

BLOCK NUMBER 1700
Número de Cuadra 1700 — *17*

CONTROLLED ACCESS HIGHWAY / TOLLWAY
Carretera de Acceso Controlado /
Autopista de Peaje — MOPAC EXPWY `130`

MAJOR ARTERIAL
Arteria Mayor — LEANDER RD

SECONDARY STREET
Calle Secundaria — CAMERON RD

RESIDENTIAL STREET
Calle Residencial — FOUST DR

PRIVATE STREET
Calle Privada — Buckskin Tr

CUL-DE-SAC
Calle Sin Salida — SMITH CIR

ONE-WAY STREET
Calle de Un Solo Sentido — →

RAILROAD
Ferrocarril — AUSTIN & NW RR

BRIDGE
Puente

BARRICADE
Barrera — B

UNDER CONSTRUCTION, PROPOSED STREET
Calle Bajo Construcción — HEEP DR

DAM
Presa

WATER FEATURES
Facciones de Agua

MUNICIPAL NAME
Nombre de Municipio — AUSTIN

MUNICIPAL BOUNDARY
Limite Municipal

COUNTY BOUNDARY
Limite de Condado

ZIP CODE BOUNDARY
Limites del Código Postal — 78723

AIRPORT, MILITARY BASE
Aeropuerto, Base Militar — *Landing Strip*

CEMETERY
Cementerio — Brown Cemetery

PARK, GOLF COURSE
Parque, Campo de Golf — Comal Park

POINT OF INTEREST
Punto de Interés — ● Symphony Square

ELEMENTARY SCHOOL
Escuela Primaria — ES Pillow

JUNIOR HIGH SCHOOL
Escuela Secundaria — JH Martin

MIDDLE SCHOOL
Escuela Secundaria — MS Burnet

HIGH SCHOOL
Preparatoria — HS Anderson

UNIVERSITY, COLLEGE
Universidad, Colegio — St Edwards University

COUNTY AREA
Área del Condado

INCORPORATED CITIES
Ciudades Incorporadas

Note: White area indicates
Austin incorporated city area
Noticia: Espacio de color
blanco indicar el area
de incorporar de Austin

SUBDIVISION NAME
Nombre de Subdivisión — *PARKVIEW ESTATES*

CITY HALL
Municipio de la Cuidad — CH

POLICE DEPARTMENT
Comisaria de Policia — PD

FIRE STATION
Estación de Bomberos — FS

METRO RAIL STATION
Estación de Tren Metro — MR

CHAMBER OF COMMERCE
Camara de Comercio — CC

POST OFFICE
Oficina Postal/Correo — PO

HOSPITAL
Hospital — ✚ Leander Hospital

LIBRARY
Biblioteca — LIB

COMMUNITY NAME
Nombre de Comunidad — Jollyville

LIST OF ABBREVIATIONS

AL .... Alley	CV .... Cove	N. .... North	SQ. .... Square
AVE. .... Avenue	DR. .... Drive	PKWY. .... Parkway	ST. .... Saint
BLVD. .... Boulevard	E. .... East	PL. .... Place	ST. .... Street
CIR. .... Circle	EXPWY. ...... Expressway	PLZ. .... Plaza	TERR. .... Terrace
CRES. .... Crescent	HW. .... Hollow	PT. .... Point	TR. .... Trail
CRSG. .... Crossing	HWY. .... Highway	RD. .... Road	W. .... West
CT. .... Court	LN. .... Lane	S. .... South	WAY. .... Way
	MT. .... Mount	SKWY. .... Skyway	

From Flowers to Freeways...

It was 1948 and Milton Boyd Keith owner of several Dallas florist shops, was frustrated. The Dallas maps were sadly out of date and his floral delivery drivers were constantly getting lost, orders were being delayed, and some were even cancelled. Keith's attempt to appeal to the local government entities did not help. Not even the city government had a map that could be called official.

Determined to find a solution to his costly problem, Keith sought aid from the Building Inspection Division of Dallas, the only source of accurate and up-to-date maps of the city. Armed with the proper resources, Keith and his store manager, Lily Kendrick, researched, designed, and indexed hand-drawn maps that anyone could use. Keith began creating more and more maps out of his Oak Lawn flower shop. After the City of Dallas purchased 300 guides for their fire and ambulance workers, it was official. Everyone wanted a MAPSCO Street Guide.

In 1952, the first commercial edition of MAPSCO Street Guide was published. As the metroplex grew, MAPSCO, under the leadership of Lily Kendrick and her son, expanded its potential. In 1971, the Fort Worth Street Guide was pub-

lished, igniting a MAPSCO flame that spread across Texas. After a half century of map creation, MAPSCO has gained the reputation of being the most accurate, most current, and most trusted maps in the industry. The MAPSCO commitment to excellence is apparent in every map made. In fact, the University of Texas at Arlington is the official archive of the MAPSCO company, and has preserved over five decades of valuable mapping.

In the age of the Internet, MAPSCO continues to surpass online mapping services, offering the most exact and up-to-date information possible. Period. Every street is displayed on the simple, unique MAPSCO - making it so easy for you to find your way. MAPSCO uses the latest, most accurate data to publish the most up-to-date map data available.

Today MAPSCO produces Street Guides, wall maps, fold maps, software, and custom maps for the Dallas, Fort Worth, Austin, San Antonio and El Paso, Texas areas, Louisville, Kentucky, Las Cruces and Almogordo, New Mexico and Denver, Colorado. A chain of retail Map & Travel Centers is located in Addison, Dallas, Frisco, Fort Worth, Austin, and San Antonio, Texas and Denver, Colorado.

The MAPSCO commitment to accuracy and quality has gained the trust of travelers, trekkers, commuters and more. As long as people need to find the way accurately and simply, MAPSCO will continue to be there.

Mapsco Contributors

ALBRIGHT, MICHAEL	FOX, NANCY	ISBELL, JOHN	MORRIS, JIM	SPARKS-FULLER, FRAN
BABB, PAUL	FRANCIS, STACEY	JOHNSON, DAVID	MORROW, MICHAEL	STOUT, CALVIN
BROWN, BRUCE	GARZA-PENA, GORDON	JOHNSON-SMITH,	MOYA, NORMA	THOMPSON, SHENEISHA
CAMPBELL, STEVE	GEARY, KEVIN	NANCY	PITTS, JR., THOMAS	TIMMONS, ANNA
CARNINE, GEORGIA	GERRISH, BEV	JONES, GEORGE	PRIDDY, TONA	TOLEDO, CAYETANA
CASTOR, TRACIE	GIBBS, RETT	KARON, CHRIS	PRYOR, MATT	TOLSTYKA, SHARON
COKER, DOROTHY	GIRVAN, JOHN	KASNER, LARRY	RICHARDS, RYAN	TRAGER, ROBERT
COZART, JUSTIN	HADOVSKY, DAVID	KLINE, MIKE	RICHARDSON, LAURA	VINSON, ROBERT
CRUMPTON, PETE	HARRELSON, BRIAN	LAABS, MICHAEL	RITCHIE, LEE	WALLACE, KIM
DAWSON, LORI	HARRIS, MICHAEL	LECOMPTE, MARITA	ROBERSON, TOMEKI	WILLCOT, MADELYN
DIAS, JARED	HATCHER, DAVID	LEWIS, PATRICK	SANTILLAN, RICARDO	WILLIAMSON,
DOUGLAS, DON	HERNANDEZ, DEBBIE	MARCUM, CHUCK	SANTOS, PAUL	KATHERINE
EASTLICK, BRAD	HERNANDEZ, OLIVA	MATHUR, NEIL	SCHERER, LIBBY	
ESPINOZA, JOSE	HOLTZ, ROLAND	MCKINNEY, MARCUS	SMITH, JENNIE	
EUBANKS, TRACY	HOWARD, DENNIS	MILLAR, SUE	SMITH, LYNN	

The Texas Country Reporter Hacienda
Bob Phillips' Hill Country Resort and Spa

Escondida is your escape from everyday life. Enjoy our luxurious rooms, gourmet food and world class spa that defines Texas hospitality. We are nestled among breathtaking views, abundant wildlife and the natural beauty of the Hill Country,

Escondida is the ultimate romantic getaway. You will find Escondida 14 miles south of Kerrville, Texas on State Highway 16 North.

For reservations
call toll-free at 1-888-589-7507
or log on to www.escondidaresort.com.

ESCONDIDA

The hard part isn't getting here. It's leaving.

MOST ACCURATE. MOST CURRENT. MOST TRUSTED.

The Austin Mapsco Book has been continuously revised and published on a yearly basis since 1993. Mapsco not only serves its customers basic need for up-to-date street maps, but also provides an effective resource tool with its comprehensive Numerical/Alphabetical Street Index with Zip Codes, and convenient lists of Major Buildings, Emergency Clinics, Public Schools and Shopping Centers.

HOW TO USE MAPSCO

COMPOSITE MAP: Shows "Map Page Areas" into which the Austin area has been divided and the "Map Page Number" assigned to each area. Also shown are major streets which may be used for travel from one area to another. The total Area Coverage Composite Map appears on the inside front cover. The Austin Mapsco Composite Maps appear on pages 18-19.

DIRECTORY OF STREETS: Numerical/Alphabetical listings of all streets in Travis County, and listings for selected areas of adjacent Counties.

TYPICAL LISTINGS

STREET NAME	CITY or COUNTY	MAP GRID	AUSTIN GRID	ZIP CODE	BLOCK RANGE	O/E
①	②	③	④	⑤	⑥	⑦
ADAMS AVE...................................Austin	555B	MJ-27	78756	5600-5799		
ADAMS CV...........................Lago Vista	459A	WW-36	78645	4100-4199		
ADAMS ST ....Taylor	352C	MZ-48	76574	1400-1899		

Each listing is comprised of:
① **Street Name**
② **City or county in which the street is located.**
③ **Mapsco Grid**   Area Map Number and Grid Letter needed to locate street name on map.
④ **Austin Grid**   Provided as a reference for users who may have a need to correlate the MAPSCO Grid with existing City of Austin Grid data. This grid number is not needed to actually locate the street.
⑤ **Zip Code**   Indicates appropriate Zip Code for block ranges shown.
⑥ **Block Range**   Indicates the range of street address block numbers shown on the map.
⑦ **O/E**   In most instances this column will be blank, indicating that the block ranges shown are all within the city and zip code shown. However, if only the odd or even block numbers are applicable, then either an "E" (for even numbers only) or an "O" (for odd numbers only) will appear.

ALPHABETIZATION FORMAT

Mapsco utilizes a strict alphabetical system which places each street in sequence based on the first letter of the first name of the street. Each subsequent letter of the street name (except for the "Suffix") is then used without regard to punctuation, abbreviation or spacing between words to further place the street in its appropriate order. The "Suffix" (i.e. Ave, Ct, Frwy, Ln...etc) is then used as the next level of alphabetization. When two or more streets are spelled exactly the same, including the "suffix", the streets are placed in alphabetical order based on the name of the city in which the street is located.

AREA MAPS

These area maps include all publicly dedicated streets and many private-use streets within Travis County & selected areas of adjacent counties. The maps are arranged in numerical order and start with map number 192. Occasionally you will experience a "gap" in the numerical sequence of the maps. These "gaps" are planned for future map coverage area expansion. The map areas that are currently included are shown on the "Austin Area Composite Maps" (see pages 18 through 19). On the margin of each area map, the adjoining map (if one exists) is indicated by the reference "Continued on Map _____". This allows you to readily locate the required map area when a street extends from one map area to another. Street address block numbers have been placed on most major streets at intervals, and in many cases on other streets to facilitate the location of specific sections of streets.

El Austin Mapsco Book (Libro de Mapsco para Austin) es revisado continuamente y publicado en forma anual desde 1993. Mapsco no sólo satisface las necesidades básicas que tienen sus clientes de poder contar con mapas de calles actualizadas sino que proporciona también un instrumento de recurso eficaz mediante su indice numérico alfabético de calles con códigos postales y sus listas muy útiles de los edificios importantes, las clínicas de urgencias, las escuelas públicas y los centros comerciales.

COMO UTILIZAR MAPSCO

MAPA COMPUESTO: Muestra zonas en las que se ha dividido Austin y el número asignado a cada una de ellas. También se muestran las calles principales que se pueden utilizar para ir de una zona a otra. El Mapa compuesto está en las páginas 18-19.

DIRECTORIO DE CALLES: Listas numéricas y alfabéticas de todas las calles del condado de Travis y de áreas seleccionadas de condados a contiguo.

LISTA TIPICA

STREET NAME	CITY or COUNTY	MAP GRID	AUSTIN GRID	ZIP CODE	BLOCK RANGE	O/E
①	②	③	④	⑤	⑥	⑦
ADAMS AVE	Austin	555B	MJ-27	78756	5600-5799	
ADAMS CV	Lago Vista	459A	WW-36	78645	4100-4199	
ADAMS ST	Taylor	352C	MZ-48	76574	1400-1899	

Cada lista esta compuesta de:

① **Nombre de la calle.**

② **Ciudad ó condado en el cual esta localizada.**

③ **Cuadrícula de Mapsco**   Número de el area del mapa y la letra de la cuadricula necesaria para localizar el nombre de la calle.

④ **Cuadrícula de Austin**   Se mantiene como referencia para usarios quienes puedan necesitar correlacionar la cuadrícula de MAPSCO con los datos existentes de la cuadrícula de la Ciudad de Austin. Este número de cuadrícula no es necesario actualmente para localizar la calle.

⑤ **Codigo Postal**   Indica el codigo postal apropiado para la cuadra mostrada.

⑥ **Alcanse de la Cuadra**   Indica el alcanse de direcciones de calles y números de cuadras mostradas en el mapa.

⑦ **O/E**   En la mayoría de los casos ésta columna estara en blanco indicando que el alcanse de la cuadra mostrada esta dentro de la ciudad y el codigo postal mostrada. De cualquier manera si nadamas los números impar ó números par de cuadras son aplicable, entonces cualquiera de los dos se mostradan, "E" (para los números de par) ó "O" (para los números impar).

FORMATO ALFABETICO: Mapsco utiliza un sistema alfabético estricto que coloca cada calle en secuencia basada sobre la primera letra del primer nombre de la calle. Cada letra subseguiente del nombre de la calle (excluiendo el sufijo...como Avenida, Hwy etc....) se utiliza sin tener en cuenta puntuacion, abreviación ó los espacios entre palabras para ademas colocar la calle en su orden apropiado. Cuando dos ó mas calles se deletrean exactamente igual, el sufijo se usa como el siguiente nivel alfabético. Cuando dos calles se deletrean igual incluiendo el sufijo las calles entonces son alfabetizadas basados en como se deletrea la ciudad ó condado en cual están colocadas.

MAPAS DE ZONAS: Los mapas de área incluyen todas las calles dedicadas publicamente y calles privadas colocadas en el condado de Travis y áreas seleccionadas de condados a contiguo. Los mapas están compuestos en orden numérico y empiezan con el mapa número 192. De vez en cuando se encuentra un vacío en la secuencia numérica de los mapas, estos vacíos son planeados para extensiónes futuras. Las áreas incluidas en mapa son mostradas en el "Mapa Compuestos de Austin - MAPSCO - Cubriendo el Area Total" (vea paginas numeros 18-19). En el margen de cada mapa de area, el mapa contiguo (si existe uno) se indica por referencia (Continued on Map ___.) Esto le permite localizar rapidamente la pagina del mapa cuando una calle se extiende de un mapa a otro. Direcciones de calles en las cuadras han sido mostradas por mayor parte en las calles mayores y en muchos casos en otras calles para facilitar la colocacion de direcciónes especificos.

AUSTIN CENTRAL BUSINESS DISTRICT

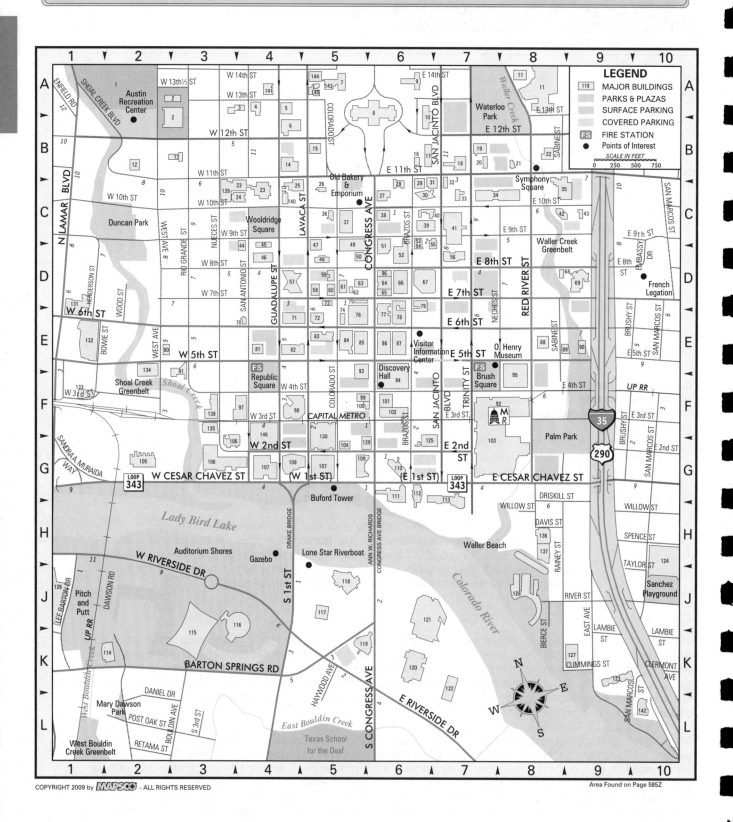

Area Found on Page 585Z

Alphabetical

Numerical

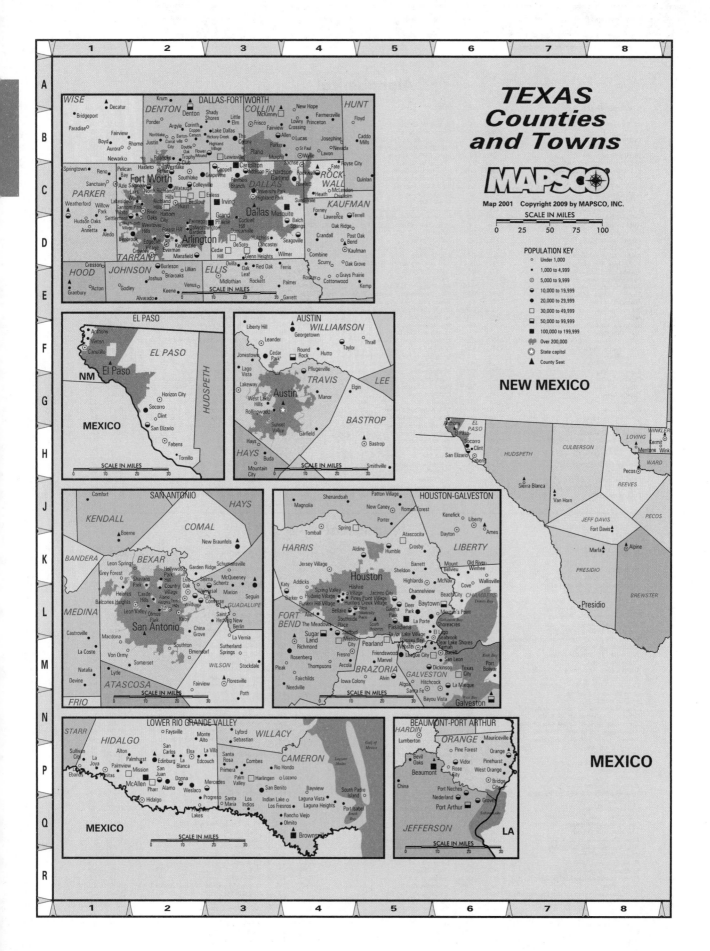

TEXAS
Counties
and Towns

MAPSCO

Map 2001 Copyright 2009 by MAPSCO, INC.

SCALE IN MILES

0   25   50   75   100

POPULATION KEY

○ Under 1,000
• 1,000 to 4,999
⊙ 5,000 to 9,999
⊖ 10,000 to 19,999
● 20,000 to 29,999
▫ 30,000 to 49,999
□ 50,000 to 99,999
■ 100,000 to 199,999
▬ Over 200,000
✪ State capitol
▲ County Seat

NEW MEXICO

MEXICO

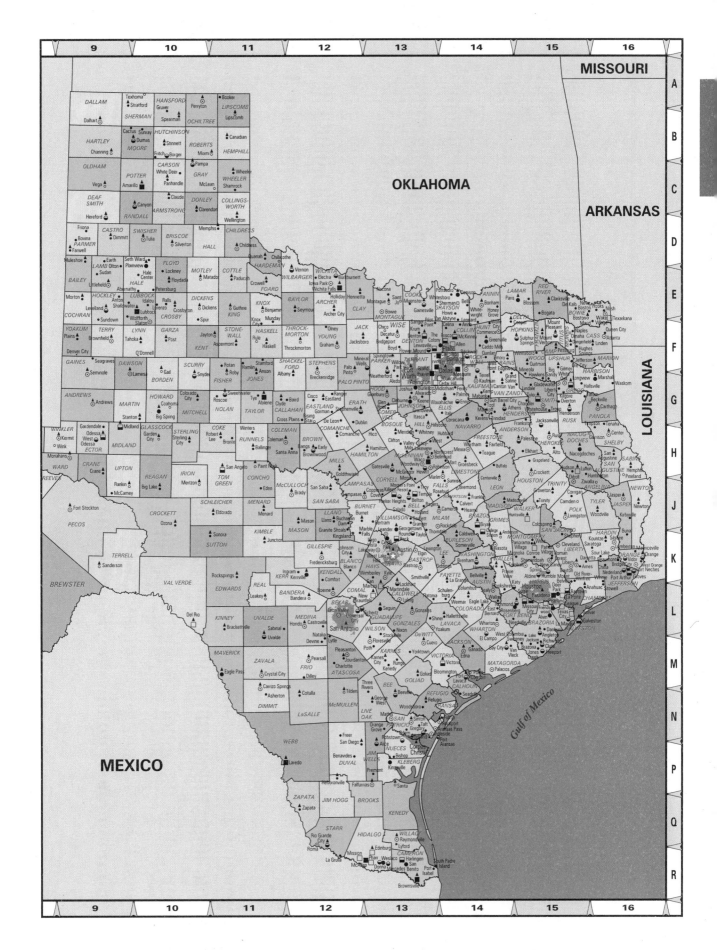

Texas Counties and Towns Index

CITIES

CITY	COUNTY	POP	GRID
Abernathy	Hale Co.	2,839	E9
Abilene	Taylor Co.	115,930	G11
Addison	Dallas Co.	14,166	C3
Alamo	Hidalgo Co.	14,760	P2
Alamo Heights	Bexar Co.	7,319	L2
Albany	Shackelford Co.	1,921	G11
Aldine	Harris Co.	13,979	K15
Aledo	Parker Co.	1,726	G13
Alice	Jim Wells Co.	19,010	P13
Allen	Collin Co.	43,554	F14
Alpine	Brewster Co.	5,786	K8
Alto	Cherokee Co.	1,190	H15
Alton	Hidalgo Co.	4,384	P1
Alvarado	Johnson Co.	3,288	G13
Alvin	Brazoria Co.	21,413	L15
Amarillo	Potter Co.	173,627	C10
Ames	Coryell Co.	1,079	K15
Anahuac	Chambers Co.	2,210	L15
Anderson	Grimes Co.	257	K14
Andrews	Andrews Co.	9,652	G9
Angleton	Brazoria Co.	18,130	L15
Anna	Collin Co.	1,225	F14
Annetta	Parker Co.	1,108	D1
Anson	Jones Co.	2,556	G11
Anthony	El Paso Co.	3,850	G6
Anton	Hockley Co.	1,200	E9
Aransas Pass	Aransas Co.	8,138	N13
Archer City	Archer Co.	1,848	E12
Arcola	Fort Bend Co.	1,048	M4
Argyle	Denton Co.	2,365	B2
Arlington	Tarrant Co.	332,969	G13
Asherton	Dimmit Co.	1,342	N11
Aspermont	Stonewall Co.	1,021	F11
Atascocita	Harris Co.	35,757	K5
Athens	Henderson Co.	11,297	G14
Atlanta	Cass Co.	5,745	F16
Aurora	Wise Co.	853	B1
Austin	Travis Co.	656,562	K13
Azle	Tarrant Co.	9,600	C1
Bacliff	Galveston Co.	6,962	M6
Baird	Callahan Co.	1,623	G12
Balch Springs	Dallas Co.	19,375	D4
Balcones Heights	Bexar Co.	3,016	L2
Ballinger	Runnels Co.	4,243	H11
Bandera	Bandera Co.	957	L12
Bangs	Brown Co.	1,620	H12
Barrett	Harris Co.	2,872	K5
Bartlett	Williamson Co.	1,675	J13
Bartonville	Denton Co.	1,093	B2
Bastrop	Bastrop Co.	5,340	K13
Bay City	Matagorda Co.	18,667	M14
Bayou Vista	Galveston Co.	1,644	N6
Baytown	Harris Co.	66,430	L15
Bayview	Cameron Co.	323	P4
Beach City	Chambers Co.	1,645	L6
Beaumont	Jefferson Co.	113,866	K16
Beckville	Panola Co.	752	G16
Bedford	Tarrant Co.	47,152	C2
Beeville	Bee Co.	13,129	N13
Bellaire	Harris Co.	15,642	L4
Bellmead	McLennan Co.	9,214	H13
Bells	Grayson Co.	1,190	E14
Bellville	Austin Co.	3,794	K14
Belton	Bell Co.	14,623	J13
Benavides	Duval Co.	1,686	P12
Benbrook	Tarrant Co.	20,208	D2
Benjamin	Knox Co.	264	E11
Bertram	Burnet Co.	1,122	J13
Bevil Oaks	Jefferson Co.	1,346	P5
Big Lake	Reagan Co.	2,885	J10
Big Sandy	Upshur Co.	1,288	G15
Big Spring	Howard Co.	25,233	G10
Bishop	Nueces Co.	3,305	P13
Blanco	Blanco Co.	1,505	K12
Bloomington	Victoria Co.	2,562	M13
Blossom	Lamar Co.	1,439	E15
Boerne	Kendall Co.	6,178	L12
Bogata	Red River Co.	1,396	E15
Bonham	Fannin Co.	9,990	E14
Booker	Lipscomb Co.	1,315	A11
Borger	Hutchinson Co.	14,302	B10
Boston	Bowie Co.	200	E16
Bovina	Parmer Co.	1,874	D9
Bowie	Montague Co.	5,219	E13
Boyd	Fannin Co.	1,099	F13
Brackettville	Kinney Co.	1,876	L11
Brady	McCulloch Co.	5,523	J12
Brazoria	Brazoria Co.	2,787	M15
Breckenridge	Stephens Co.	5,868	G12
Bremond	Robertson Co.	876	J14
Brenham	Washington Co.	13,507	K14
Briaroaks	Johnson Co.	493	E2
Bridge City	Orange Co.	8,651	K16
Bridgeport	Wise Co.	4,309	F13
Bronte	Coke Co.	1,076	H11
Brookshire	Waller Co.	3,450	L14
Brownfield	Terry Co.	9,488	F9
Brownsville	Cameron Co.	139,722	R13
Brownwood	Brown Co.	18,813	H12
Bryan	Brazos Co.	65,660	J14
Buchanan Dam	Llano Co.	1,688	J12
Buda	Hays Co.	2,404	H3
Buffalo	Leon Co.	1,804	H14
Buna	Jasper Co.	2,269	K16
Bunker Hill Village	Harris Co.	3,654	L4
Burkburnett	Wichita Co.	10,927	E12
Burleson	Johnson Co.	20,976	G13
Burnet	Burnet Co.	4,735	J12
Cactus	Moore Co.	2,538	B9
Caddo Mills	Hunt Co.	1,149	F14
Caldwell	Burleson Co.	3,449	K14
Calvert	Robertson Co.	1,426	J14
Cameron	Milam Co.	5,634	J14
Canadian	Hemphill Co.	2,233	B11
Canton	Van Zandt Co.	3,292	G14
Canutillo	El Paso Co.	5,129	F1
Canyon	Randall Co.	12,875	C10
Carrizo Springs	Dimmit Co.	5,655	N11
Carrollton	Dallas Co.	109,576	F14
Carthage	Panola Co.	6,664	G16
Castle Hills	Bexar Co.	4,202	L2
Castroville	Medina Co.	2,664	L12
Cedar Hill	Dallas Co.	32,093	G14
Cedar Park	Williamson Co.	26,049	K13
Celina	Collin Co.	1,861	F14
Center	Limestone Co.	5,678	H16
Centerville	Leon Co.	903	J14
Chandler	Henderson Co.	2,099	G15
Channelview	Harris Co.	29,685	L5
Channing	Hartley Co.	356	B9
Charlotte	Atascosa Co.	1,637	M12
Chico	Wise Co.	947	F13
Childress	Childress Co.	6,778	D11
Chillicothe	Hardeman Co.	798	D11
China	Jefferson Co.	1,112	K16
China Grove	Scurry Co.	1,247	L2
Cisco	Eastland Co.	3,851	G12
Clarendon	Donley Co.	1,974	C10
Clarksville	Red River Co.	3,883	E15
Claude	Armstrong Co.	1,313	C10
Cleburne	Johnson Co.	26,005	G13
Cleveland	Liberty Co.	7,605	K15
Clifton	Bosque Co.	3,542	H13
Clint	El Paso Co.	980	H6
Clute	Brazoria Co.	10,424	M15
Clyde	Callahan Co.	3,345	G11
Coahoma	Howard Co.	932	G10
Cockrell Hill	Dallas Co.	4,443	D3
Coldspring	San Jacinto Co.	691	J15
Coleman	Coleman Co.	5,127	H11
College Station	Brazos Co.	67,890	K14
Colleyville	Tarrant Co.	19,636	C2
Colorado City	Mitchell Co.	4,281	G10
Columbus	Colorado Co.	3,916	L14
Comanche	Comanche Co.	4,482	H12
Combes	Cameron Co.	2,553	P3
Combine	Kaufman Co.	1,788	D4
Comfort	Kendall Co.	2,358	K12
Commerce	Hunt Co.	7,669	F14
Conroe	Montgomery Co	36,811	K15
Converse	Bexar Co.	11,508	L3
Cooper	Delta Co.	2,150	F14
Coppell	Dallas Co.	35,958	C3
Copper Canyon	Denton Co.	1,216	B2
Copperas Cove	Coryell Co.	29,592	J13
Corinth	Denton Co.	11,325	B2
Corpus Christi	Nueces Co.	277,454	P13
Corral City	Denton Co.	89	B2
Corrigan	Polk Co.	1,721	J15
Corsicana	Navarro Co.	24,485	G14
Cottonwood	McLennan Co.	181	E4
Cotulla	La Salle Co.	3,614	N12
Cove	Chambers Co.	323	L6
Crandall	Kaufman Co.	2,774	D4
Crane	Crane Co.	3,191	H9
Crockett	Houston Co.	7,141	H15
Crosby	Harris Co.	1,714	K5
Crosbyton	Crosby Co.	1,874	E10
Cross Plains	Callahan Co.	1,068	G12
Crowell	Foard Co.	1,141	E11
Crowley	Tarrant Co.	7,467	D2
Crystal City	Zavala Co.	7,190	M11
Cuero	DeWitt Co.	6,571	M13
Daisetta	Liberty Co.	1,034	K15
Dalhart	Dallam Co.	7,237	B9
Dallas	Dallas Co.	1,188,580	F14
Danbury	Brazoria Co.	1,611	L15
Dayton	Liberty Co.	5,709	K15
De Kalb	Bowie Co.	1,769	E15
De Leon	Comanche Co.	2,433	G12
Decatur	Wise Co.	5,201	F13
Deer Park	Harris Co.	28,520	L15
Del Rio	Val Verde Co	33,867	L10
Denison	Grayson Co.	22,773	E14
Denton	Denton Co.	80,537	F13
DeSoto	Dallas Co.	37,646	D3
Devine	Medina Co.	4,140	M12
Diboll	Angelina Co.	5,470	J15
Dickens	Dickens Co.	332	E10
Dickinson	Galveston Co.	17,093	M6
Dilley	Frio Co.	3,674	M12
Dimmitt	Castro Co.	4,375	D9
Donna	Hidalgo Co.	14,768	R13
Double Oak	Denton Co.	2,179	B2
Dublin	Erath Co.	3,754	G12
Dumas	Moore Co.	13,747	B10
Duncanville	Dallas Co.	36,081	G14
Eagle Lake	Colorado Co.	3,664	L14
Eagle Pass	Maverick Co.	22,413	M11
Early	Brown Co.	2,588	H12
Earth	Lamb Co.	1,109	D9
East Bernard	Wharton Co.	1,729	L14
Eastland	Eastland Co.	3,769	G12
Edcouch	Hidalgo Co.	3,342	P2
Eden	Nacogdoches Co.	2,561	J11
Edgecliff Vllge.	Tarrant Co.	2,550	D2
Edgewood	Van Zandt Co.	1,348	F14
Edinburg	Hidalgo Co.	48,465	R12
Edna	Jackson Co.	5,899	M14
El Campo	Wharton Co.	10,945	M14
El Lago	Harris Co.	3,075	L5
El Paso	El Paso Co.	563,662	H6
Eldorado	Schleicher Co.	1,951	J11
Electra	Wichita Co.	3,168	E12
Elgin	Johnson Co.	5,700	K13
Elkhart	Anderson Co.	1,215	H15
Elmendorf	Bexar Co.	664	M2
Elsa	Hidalgo Co.	5,549	P2
Emory	Rains Co.	1,021	F14
Ennis	Ellis Co.	16,045	G14
Euless	Tarrant Co.	46,005	C2
Everman	Tarrant Co.	5,836	D2
Fabens	El Paso Co.	8,043	H6
Fairchilds	Fort Bend Co.	678	M4
Fairfield	Freestone Co.	3,094	H14
Fairview	Collin Co.	2,644	M2
Falfurrias	Brooks Co.	5,297	P12
Farmers Branch	Dallas Co.	27,508	C3
Farmersville	Collin Co.	3,118	B4
Farwell	Parmer Co.	1,364	D9
Fate	Rockwall Co.	497	C4
Faysville	Hidalgo Co.	348	N2
Ferris	Ellis Co.	2,175	G14
Flatonia	Fayette Co.	1,377	L13
Floresville	Wilson Co.	5,868	M13
Flower Mound	Denton Co.	50,702	F13
Floydada	Floyd Co.	3,676	E10
Forest Hill	Tarrant Co.	12,949	D2
Forney	Kaufman Co.	5,588	F14
Fort Davis	Jeff Davis Co.	1,050	J8
Fort Stockton	Pecos Co.	7,846	J9
Fort Worth	Tarrant Co.	534,694	F13
Franklin	Robertson Co.	1,470	J14
Frankston	Anderson Co.	1,209	G15
Fredericksburg	Gillespie Co.	8,911	K12
Freeport	Brazoria Co.	12,708	M15
Freer	Duval Co.	3,241	N12
Fresno	Fort Bend Co.	6,603	M4
Friendswood	Galveston Co.	29,037	L15
Friona	Parmer Co.	3,854	D9
Frisco	Collin Co.	33,714	F14
Fritch	Hutchinson Co.	2,235	B10
Fulton	Aransas Co.	1,553	N14
Gail	Borden Co.	202	F10
Gainesville	Cooke Co.	15,538	E13
Galena Park	Harris Co.	10,592	L5
Galveston	Galveston Co.	57,247	L15
Ganado	Jackson Co.	1,915	M14
Garden City	Glasscock Co.	293	H10
Garden Ridge	Comal Co.	1,882	K2
Gardendale	Ector Co.	1,197	H9
Garfield	Travis Co.	1,660	H4
Garland	Dallas Co.	215,768	F14
Garrett	Ellis Co.	448	E4
Garrison	Nacogdoches Co.	844	H15
Gatesville	Coryell Co.	15,591	H13
George West	Live Oak Co.	2,524	N13
Georgetown	Williamson Co.	28,339	J13
Giddings	Lee Co.	5,105	K14
Gilmer	Upshur Co.	4,799	F15
Gladewater	Gregg Co.	6,078	G15
Glen Rose	Somervell Co.	2,122	G13
Glenn Heights	Dallas Co.	7,224	D3
Godley	Johnson Co.	879	E1
Goldthwaite	Mills Co.	1,802	H12
Goliad	Goliad Co.	1,975	M13
Gonzales	Gonzales Co.	7,202	L13
Gorman	Eastland Co.	1,236	G12
Graham	Young Co.	8,716	F12
Granbury	Hood Co.	5,718	G13
Grand Prairie	Dallas Co.	127,427	F13
Grand Saline	Van Zandt Co.	3,028	G14
Grandview	Johnson Co.	1,358	G13
Granger	Williamson Co.	1,299	J13
Granite Shoals	Burnet Co.	2,040	J12
Grapeland	Houston Co.	1,451	H15
Grapevine	Tarrant Co.	42,059	C2
Grays Prairie	Kaufman Co.	296	E4
Greenville	Hunt Co.	23,960	F14
Gregory	San Patricio Co.	2,318	N13
Grey Forest	Bexar Co.	418	K1
Groesbeck	Limestone Co.	4,291	H14
Groves	Jefferson Co.	15,733	K16
Groveton	Trinity Co.	1,107	J15
Gruver	Hansford Co.	1,162	B10
Guthrie	King Co.	160	E11
Hale Center	Hale Co.	2,263	E10
Hallettsville	Lavaca Co.	2,345	L14
Hallsville	Harrison Co.	2,772	G15
Haltom City	Tarrant Co.	39,018	D2
Hamilton	Hamilton Co.	2,977	H13
Hamlin	Jones Co.	2,248	F11
Harker Heights	Bell Co.	17,308	J13
Harlingen	Cameron Co.	57,564	R13
Haskell	Haskell Co.	3,106	F11
Haslet	Tarrant Co.	1,134	C2
Hawkins	Wood Co.	1,331	G15
Hays	Hays Co.	233	H3
Hearne	Robertson Co.	4,690	J14
Heath	Rockwall Co.	4,149	C4
Hebbronville	Jim Hogg Co.	4,498	P12
Hedwig Village	Harris Co.	2,334	L4
Helotes	Bexar Co.	4,285	L1
Hemphill	Sabine Co.	1,106	H16
Hempstead	Waller Co.	4,691	K14
Henderson	Medina Co.	11,273	G15
Henrietta	Clay Co.	3,264	E12
Hereford	Deaf Smith Co.	14,597	D9
Hewitt	McLennan Co.	11,085	H13
Hickory Creek	Denton Co.	2,078	B3
Hico	Hamilton Co.	1,341	H13
Hidalgo	Hidalgo Co.	7,322	Q2
Highland Park	Dallas Co.	8,842	C3
Highland Village	Denton Co.	12,173	B3
Highlands	Harris Co.	7,089	L5
Hill Country Village	Bexar Co.	1,028	L2
Hillsboro	Hill Co.	8,232	H13
Hilshire Village	Harris Co.	720	L4
Hitchcock	Galveston Co.	6,386	M5
Holland	Bell Co.	1,102	J13
Holliday	Archer Co.	1,632	E12
Hollywood Park	Bexar Co.	2,983	K2
Hondo	Medina Co.	7,897	L12
Honey Grove	Fannin Co.	1,746	E14
Hooks	Bowie Co.	2,973	E15
Horizon City	El Paso Co.	5,233	G2
Houston	Harris Co.	1,953,631	L15
Howe	Grayson Co.	2,478	E14
Hubbard	Hill Co.	1,586	H14
Hudson	Angelina Co.	3,792	H15
Hudson Oaks	Parker Co.	1,637	D1
Hughes Springs	Cass Co.	1,856	F15
Humble	Harris Co.	14,579	K15
Huntington	Angelina Co.	2,068	J15
Huntsville	Walker Co.	35,078	J15
Hurst	Tarrant Co.	36,273	C2
Hutchins	Dallas Co.	2,805	D3
Hutto	Williamson Co.	1,250	F4
Idalou	Lubbock Co.	2,157	E10
Indian Lake	Cameron Co.	541	Q3
Ingleside	San Patricio Co.	9,388	N13
Ingram	Kerr Co.	1,740	K12
Iowa Colony	Brazoria Co.	804	M4
Iowa Park	Wichita Co.	6,431	E12
Irving	Dallas Co.	191,615	F13
Italy	Ellis Co.	1,993	G14
Itasca	Hill Co.	1,503	G13
Jacinto City	Harris Co.	10,302	L5
Jacksboro	Jack Co.	4,533	F12
Jacksonville	Cherokee Co.	13,868	G15
Jasper	Jasper Co.	8,247	J16
Jayton	Kent Co.	513	F10
Jefferson	Marion Co.	2,024	F16
Jersey Village	Harris Co.	6,880	K4
Johnson City	Blanco Co.	1,190	K12
Jones Creek	Brazoria Co.	2,130	M15
Jonestown	Travis Co.	1,681	F3
Josephine	Collin Co.	594	B4
Joshua	Johnson Co.	4,528	G13
Jourdanton	Atascosa Co.	3,732	M12
Junction	Kimble Co.	2,618	K11
Justin	Denton Co.	1,891	B2
Karnes City	Karnes Co.	3,457	M13
Katy	Harris Co.	11,775	L15
Kaufman	Kaufman Co.	6,490	G14
Keene	Johnson Co.	5,003	G13
Keller	Tarrant Co.	27,345	C2
Kemah	Galveston Co.	2,330	M6
Kemp	Kaufman Co.	1,133	G14
Kenedy	Karnes Co.	3,487	M13
Kenefick	Liberty Co.	667	J6
Kennedale	Tarrant Co.	5,850	D2
Kerens	Navarro Co.	1,681	G14
Kermit	Winkler Co.	5,714	H9
Kerrville	Kerr Co.	20,425	K12
Kilgore	Gregg Co.	11,301	G15
Killeen	Bell Co.	86,911	J13
Kingsland	Llano Co.	4,584	K12
Kingsville	Kleberg Co.	25,575	P13
Kirby	Bexar Co.	8,673	L2
Kirbyville	Jasper Co.	2,085	J16
Knox City	Knox Co.	1,219	F11
Kountze	Hardin Co.	2,115	K16
Krum	Denton Co.	1,979	F13
Kyle	Hays Co.	5,314	K13
La Blanca	Hidalgo Co.	2,351	P2
La Grange	Fayette Co.	4,478	L13
La Grulla	Starr Co.	1,211	R12
La Joya	Hidalgo Co.	3,303	P1
La Marque	Galveston Co.	13,682	L15
La Porte	Harris Co.	31,880	L15
La Vernia	Wilson Co.	931	L3
La Villa	Hidalgo Co.	1,305	P2
Lacy-Lakeview	McLennan Co.	5,764	H13
Lago Vista	Travis Co.	4,507	K13
Laguna Heights	Cameron Co.	1,990	Q4
Laguna Vista	Cameron Co.	1,658	Q4
Lake Dallas	Denton Co.	6,166	B3
Lake Jackson	Brazoria Co.	26,386	M15
Lake Worth	Tarrant Co.	4,618	C2
Lakeside	San Patricio Co.	333	C1
Lakeside	San Patricio Co.	1,040	C1
Lakeway	Travis Co.	8,002	K13
Lamesa	Dawson Co.	9,952	G9
Lampasas	Lampasas Co.	6,786	J12
Lancaster	Dallas Co.	25,894	D3
Laredo	Webb Co.	176,576	P12
Lavon	Collin Co.	387	B4
League City	Crosby Co.	45,444	L15
Leakey	Real Co.	387	L11
Leander	Williamson Co.	7,596	K13
Leon Valley	Bexar Co.	9,239	L12
Leonard	Fannin Co.	1,846	F14
Levelland	Hockley Co.	12,866	E9
Lewisville	Denton Co.	77,737	F13
Lexington	Lee Co.	1,178	K13
Liberty	Liberty Co.	8,033	K15
Liberty City	Gregg Co.	1,935	G15
Liberty Hill	Williamson Co.	1,409	F3
Lindale	Smith Co.	2,954	G15
Linden	Cass Co.	2,256	F16
Lipscomb	Lipscomb Co.	44	B11
Little Elm	Denton Co.	3,646	B3
Littlefield	Lamb Co.	6,507	E9
Live Oak	Bexar Co.	9,156	L2
Livingston	Polk Co.	5,433	J15
Llano	Llano Co.	3,325	J12
Lockhart	Caldwell Co.	11,615	L13
Lockney	Floyd Co.	2,056	E10
Longview	Gregg Co.	73,344	G15
Lorenzo	Crosby Co.	1,372	E10
Los Ebanos	Hidalgo Co.	403	P1
Los Fresnos	Cameron Co.	4,512	Q3
Los Indios	Cameron Co.	1,149	Q3
Lowry Crossing	Collin Co.	1,229	B4
Lozano	Cameron Co.	324	P4
Lubbock	Lubbock Co.	199,564	E10
Lucas	Collin Co.	2,890	B4
Lufkin	Angelina Co.	32,709	H15
Luling	Caldwell Co.	5,080	L13
Lumberton	Hardin Co.	8,731	K16
Lyford	Willacy Co.	1,973	R13
Lytle	Atascosa Co.	2,383	M12
Mabank	Kaufman Co.	2,151	G14
Madisonville	Madison Co.	4,159	J14
Magnolia	Montgomery Co	1,111	K14
Malakoff	Henderson Co.	2,257	G14
Manor	Travis Co.	1,204	G4
Mansfield	Tarrant Co.	28,031	D2
Manvel	Brazoria Co.	3,046	M5
Marble Falls	Burnet Co.	4,959	K12
Marfa	Presidio Co.	2,121	K8
Marion	Guadalupe Co.	1,099	L3
Marlin	Falls Co.	6,628	H13
Marshall	Harrison Co.	23,935	G16
Mart	McLennan Co	2,273	H14
Martindale	Caldwell Co.	953	L13
Mason	Mason Co.	2,134	J12
Matador	Motley Co.	740	E10
Mathis	San Patricio Co	5,034	N13
Maud	Bowie Co.	1,028	F15
Mauriceville	Orange Co.	2,743	K16
McAllen	Hidalgo Co.	106,414	R13
McCamey	Upton Co.	1,805	J9
McGregor	McLennan Co	4,727	H13
McKinney	Collin Co.	54,369	F14
McLean	Gray Co.	830	C11
McQueeney	Guadalupe Co.	2,527	K3
Memphis	Hall Co.	2,479	D11
Menard	Menard Co.	1,653	J11
Mentone	Loving Co.	50	H8
Mercedes	Hidalgo Co.	13,649	R13
Meridian	Bosque Co.	1,491	H13
Mertzon	Irion Co.	839	J10
Mesquite	Dallas Co.	124,523	G14
Mexia	Limestone Co.	6,563	H14
Miami	Roberts Co.	588	B10
Midland	Midland Co.	94,996	H9
Midlothian	Ellis Co.	7,480	G13
Mineola	Wood Co.	4,550	G15
Mineral Wells	Palo Pinto Co.	16,946	F12
Mission	Hidalgo Co.	45,408	R12
Missouri City	Fort Bend Co.	52,913	L15
Monahans	Ward Co.	6,821	H9
Montague	Montague Co.	400	E13
Monte Alto	Hidalgo Co.	1,611	N2
Moody	McLennan Co.	1,400	J13
Morgan's Point	Harris Co.	336	L6
Morgan's Point Resort	Bell Co.	2,989	J13
Morton	Cochran Co.	2,249	E9
Mount Pleasant	Titus Co.	13,935	F15
Mount Vernon	Franklin Co.	2,286	F15
Mountain City	Hays Co.	671	H3
Muenster	Cooke Co.	1,556	E13
Muleshoe	Bailey Co.	4,530	D9
Munday	Knox Co.	1,527	F11
Murphy	Collin Co.	3,099	B4
Naples	Morris Co.	1,410	F15
Nash	Ellis Co.	2,169	E16
Nassau Bay	Harris Co.	4,170	M5
Natalia	Medina Co.	1,663	M12
Navasota	Grimes Co.	6,789	K14
Nederland	Jefferson Co.	17,422	K16
Needville	Fort Bend Co.	2,609	L15
Nevada	Collin Co.	563	B4

Population figures are based on 2000 Census Data

CITIES

COUNTIES

Population figures are based on 2000 Census Data

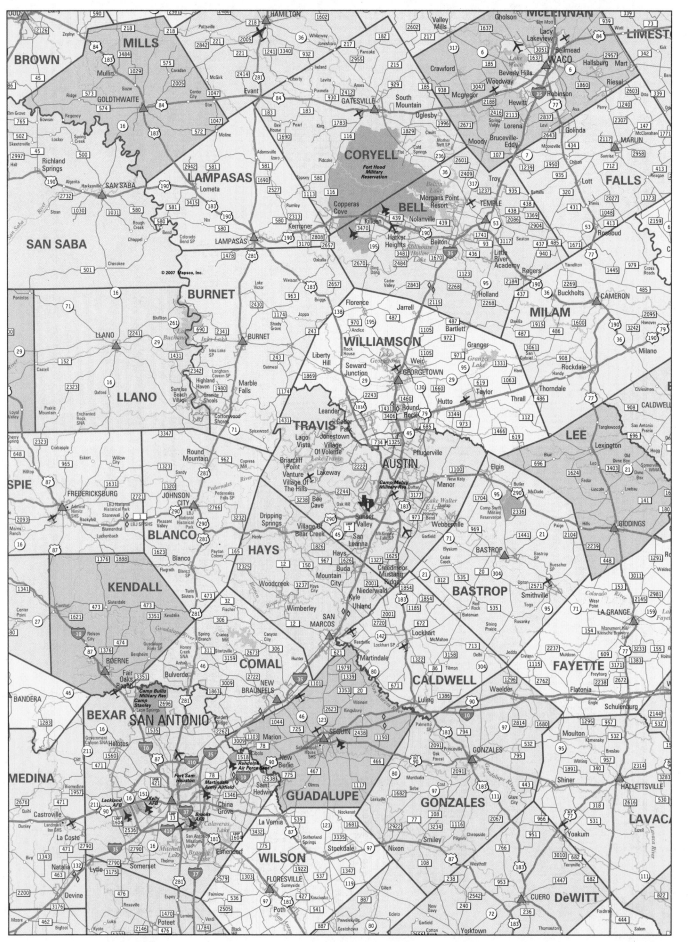

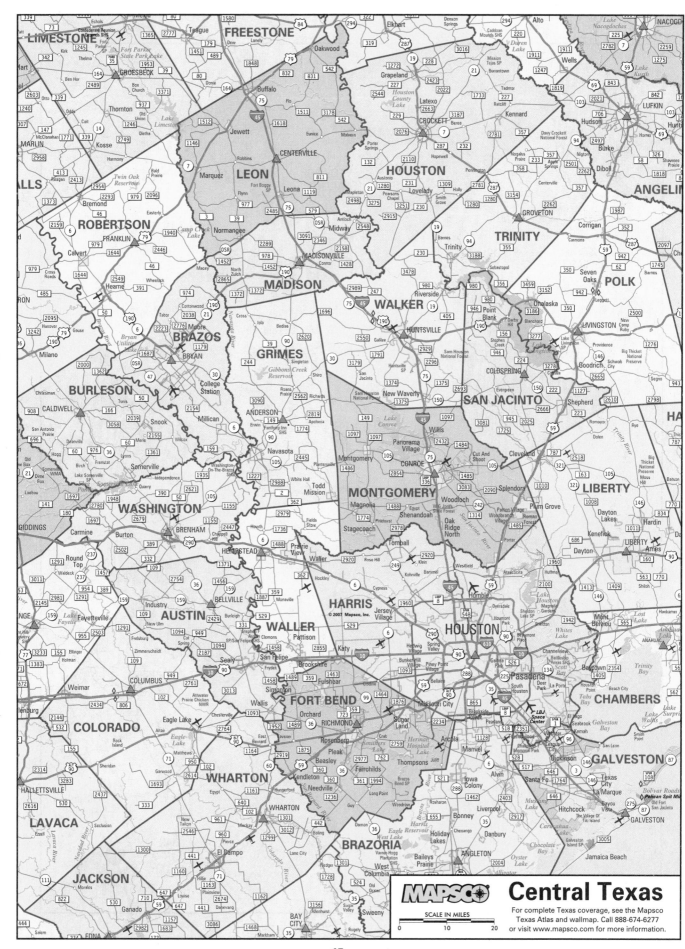

Central Texas

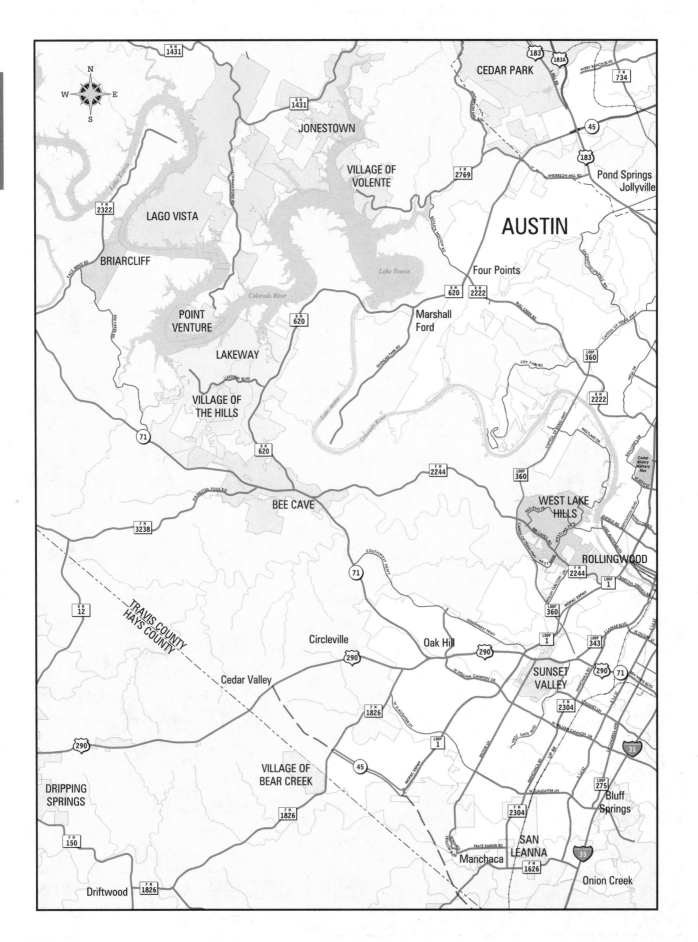

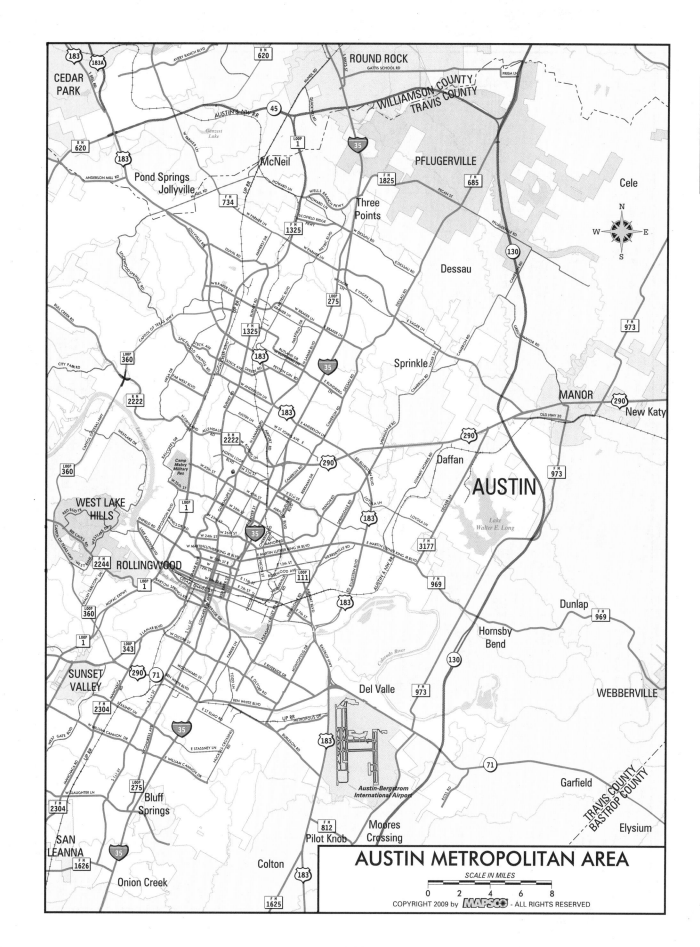

AUSTIN METROPOLITAN AREA

SCALE IN MILES

0 2 4 6 8

WEST AREA COMPOSITE MAP

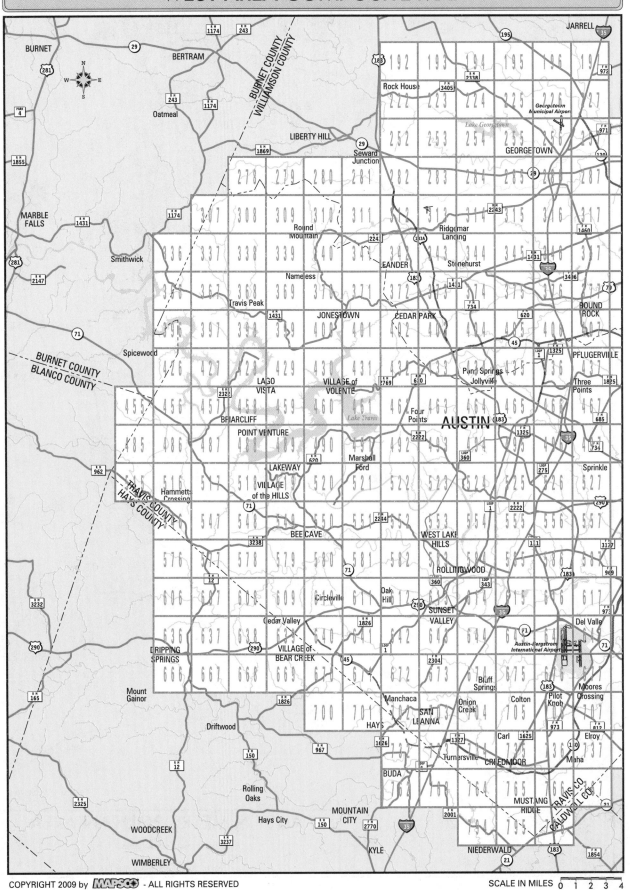

SCALE IN MILES   0 1 2 3 4

EAST AREA COMPOSITE MAP

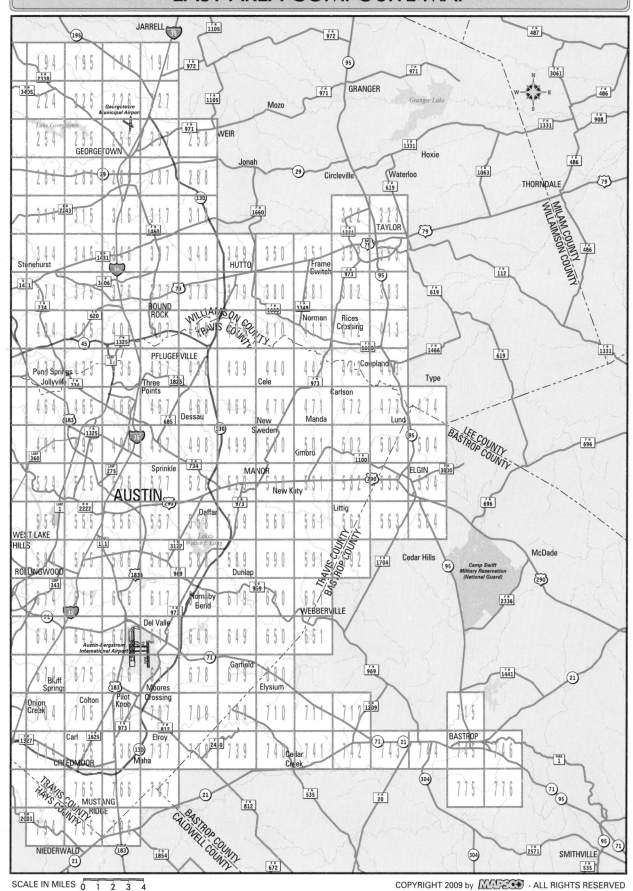

SCALE IN MILES 0 1 2 3 4

WEST AUSTIN ZIP CODE BOUNDARIES

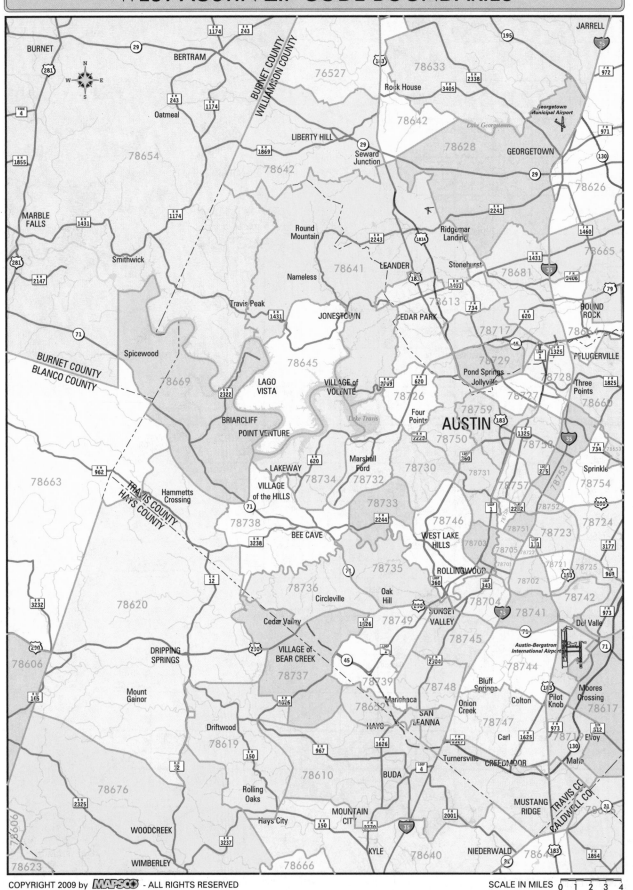

SCALE IN MILES 0 1 2 3 4

EAST AUSTIN ZIP CODE BOUNDARIES

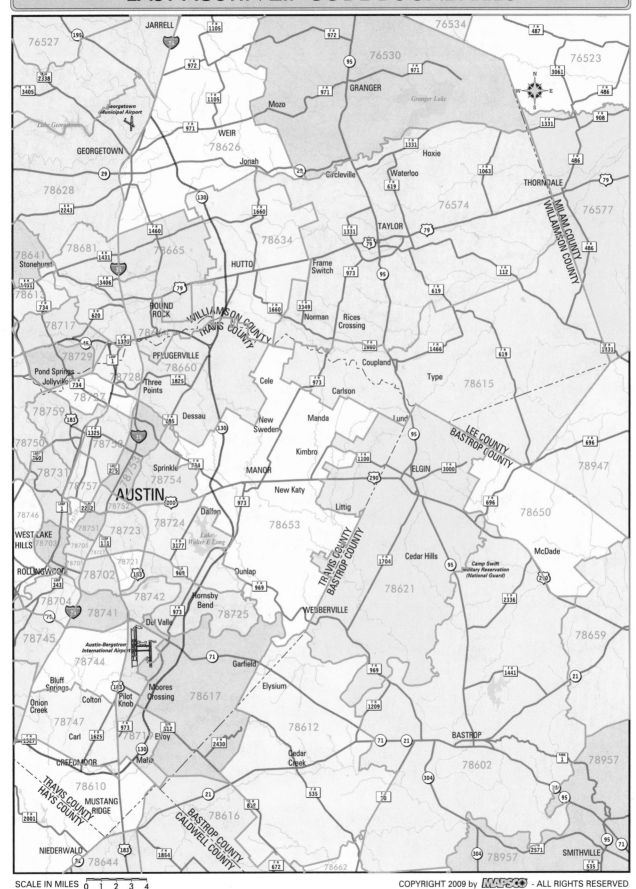

SCALE IN MILES 0 1 2 3 4

BURNET
BERTRAM
29
281
N
W E
S
BURNET ISD
Oatmeal
PARK 4
243
1174
243
1174
LIBERTY HILL ISD
LIBERTY HILL
1869
1855
1431
1174
MARBLE FALLS
Smithwick
2147
MARBLE FALLS ISD
Travis Peak
1431
71
Spicewood
BURNET COUNTY
BLANCO COUNTY
JOHNSON CITY ISD
962
LAGO VISTA ISD
LAGO VISTA
2322
BRIARCLIFF
POINT VENTURE
Hammetts Crossing
LAKEWAY
620
VILLAGE of the HILLS
71
TRAVIS COUNTY
HAYS COUNTY
LAKE TRAVIS ISD
3238
BEE CAVE
DRIPPING SPRINGS ISD
12
3232
290
DRIPPING SPRINGS
Mount Gainor
165
Driftwood
BLANCO ISD
12
WIMBERLEY ISD
2325
COMAL ISD
WOODCREEK
3237
WIMBERLEY
VILLAGE of Bear Creek
45
Cedar Valley
1826
Circleville
Village of BEAR CREEK
1826
Rolling Oaks
150
Hays City
150
MOUNTAIN CITY
2770
KYLE
967
HAYS ISD
BUDA
1626
FLORENCE ISD
183
Rock House
3405
2338
JARRELL
195
JARRELL ISD
35
972
GEORGETOWN ISD
Georgetown Municipal Airport
Lake Georgetown
GEORGETOWN
971
29
130
Kittie Hill Airport
2243
Round Mountain
2243
183A
Ridgemar Landing
LEANDER
LEANDER ISD
183
Stonehurst
1431
1431
734
Nameless
JONESTOWN
CEDAR PARK
620
2769
620
ROUND ROCK ISD
45
1325
LOOP 1
PFLUGERVILLE
1460
35
3406
79
ROUND ROCK
Pond Springs
Jollyville
Three Points
1825
VILLAGE of VOLENTE
Lake Travis
Four Points
AUSTIN
183
PFLUGERVILLE ISD
35
734
2222
LOOP 360
LOOP 275
1325
Sprinkle
MANOR ISD
290
Marshall Ford
2222
LOOP 1
EANES ISD
WEST LAKE HILLS
2244
LOOP 111
3177
183
969
71
AUSTIN ISD
Oak Hill
ROLLINGWOOD
LOOP 360
LOOP 343
Del Valle
973
290
SUNSET VALLEY
35
Austin-Bergstrom International Airport
71
LOOP 1
2304
Bluff Springs
183
Moores Crossing
Manchaca
Onion Creek
Colton
Pilot Knob
973
812
Elroy
SAN LEANNA
Carl
1625
130
Maha
1327
Turnersville
CREEDMOOR
LOOP 4
2001
DEL VALLE ISD
MUSTANG RIDGE
TRAVIS CO.
CALDWELL CO.
21
LOCKHART ISD
NIEDERWALD
183
21
1854
BURNET COUNTY
WILLIAMSON COUNTY
Seward Junction
29

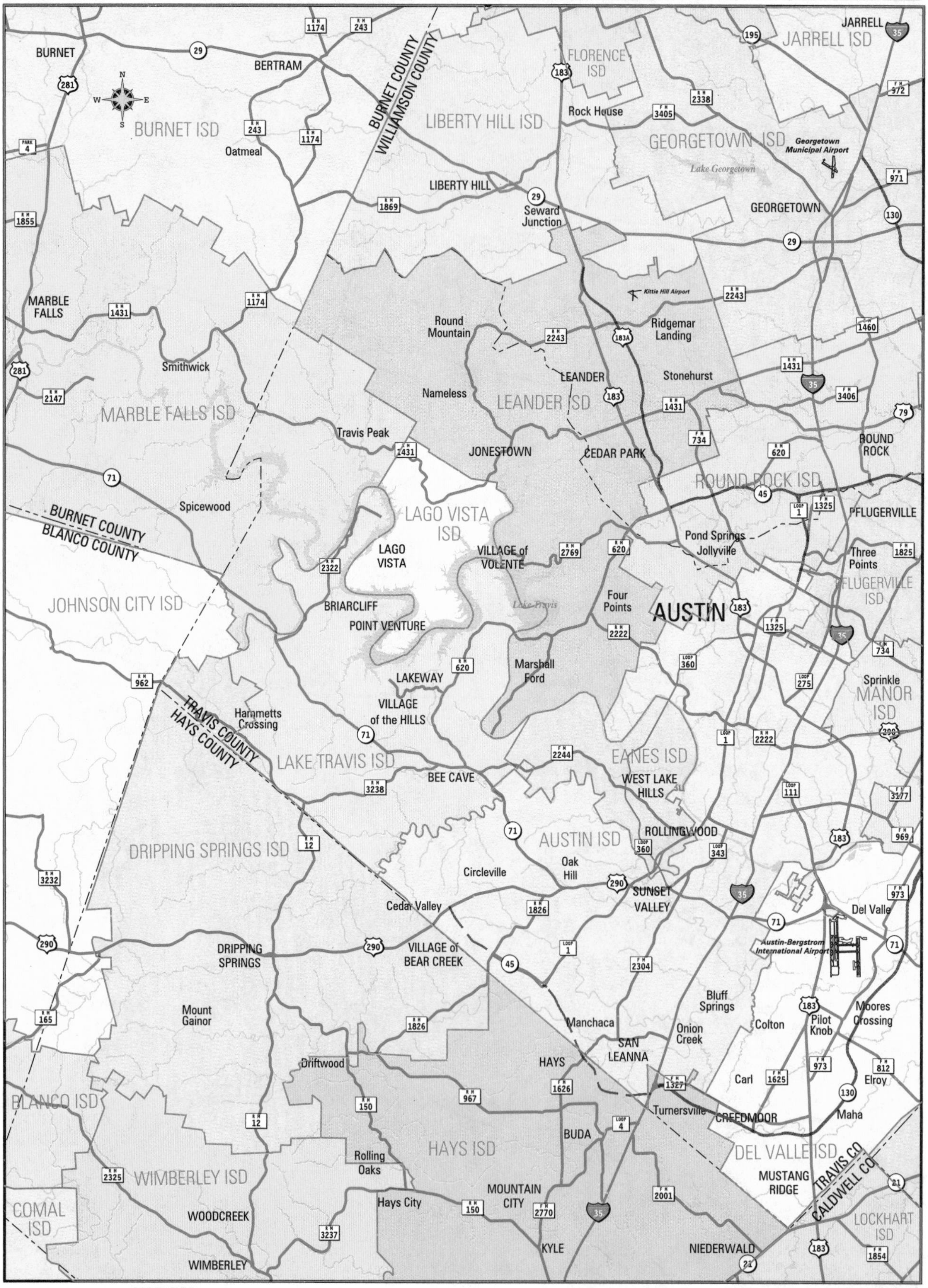

SCALE IN MILES 0 1 2 3 4

EAST AUSTIN ISD BOUNDARIES

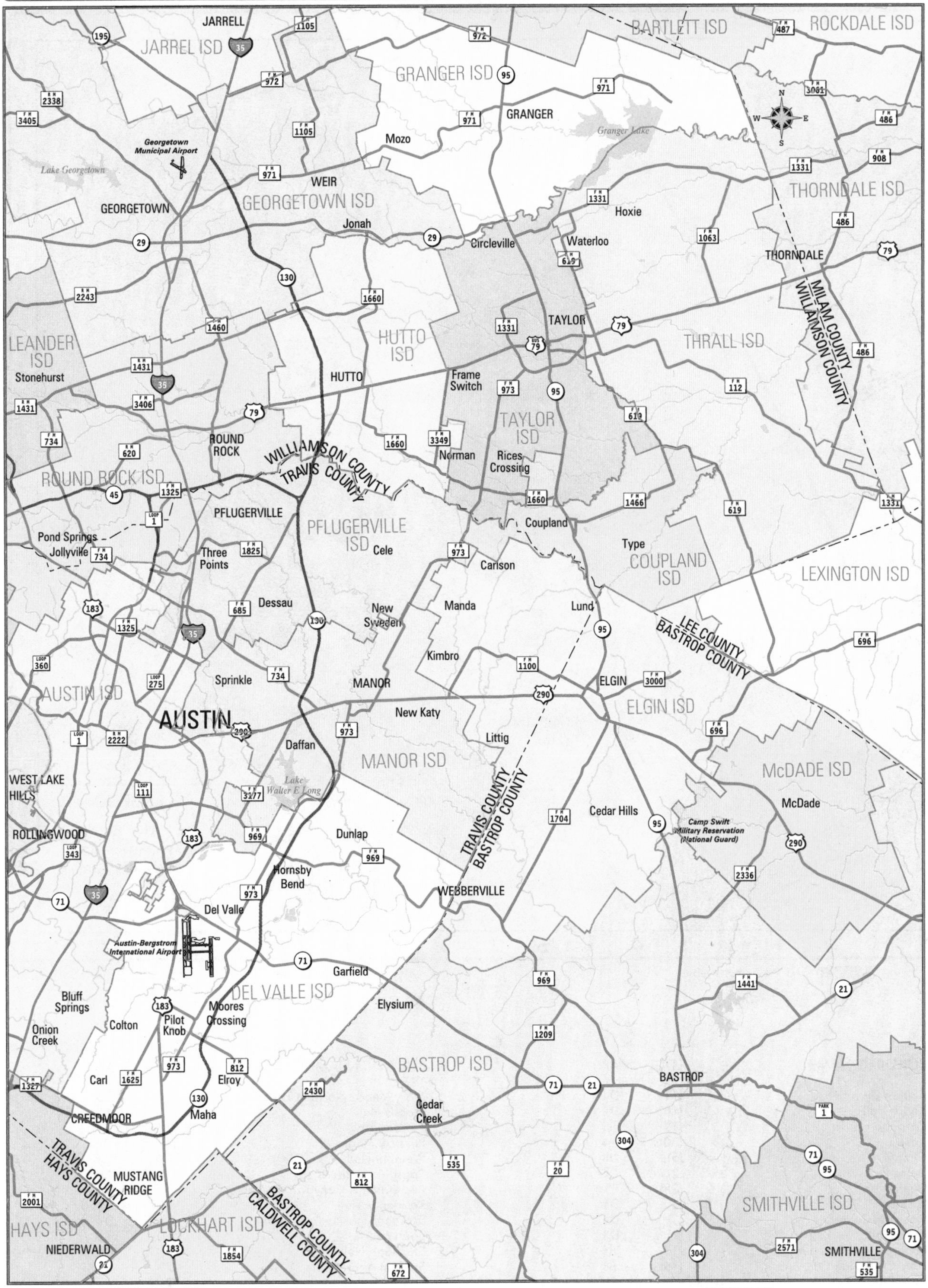

JARRELL
JARREL ISD
BARTLETT ISD
ROCKDALE ISD
GRANGER ISD
GRANGER
Granger Lake
Mozo
Georgetown Municipal Airport
Lake Georgetown
WEIR
GEORGETOWN ISD
GEORGETOWN
Jonah
Hoxie
THORNDALE ISD
Circleville
Waterloo
THORNDALE
MILAM COUNTY
WILLIAMSON COUNTY
TAYLOR
LEANDER ISD
Stonehurst
HUTTO ISD
HUTTO
THRALL ISD
Frame Switch
TAYLOR ISD
ROUND ROCK
WILLIAMSON COUNTY
TRAVIS COUNTY
Norman
Rices Crossing
ROUND ROCK ISD
PFLUGERVILLE
Coupland
Pond Springs
Jollyville
Three Points
PFLUGERVILLE ISD
Cele
Carlson
Type
COUPLAND ISD
LEXINGTON ISD
Dessau
New Sweden
Manda
Lund
LEE COUNTY
BASTROP COUNTY
Kimbro
Sprinkle
MANOR
ELGIN
ELGIN ISD
AUSTIN ISD
AUSTIN
New Katy
Littig
Daffan
MANOR ISD
McDADE ISD
WEST LAKE HILLS
Lake Walter E. Long
TRAVIS COUNTY
BASTROP COUNTY
Cedar Hills
McDade
ROLLINGWOOD
Dunlap
Camp Swift Military Reservation (National Guard)
Hornsby Bend
WEBBERVILLE
Del Valle
Austin-Bergstrom International Airport
Garfield
Bluff Springs
DEL VALLE ISD
Moores Crossing
Elysium
Onion Creek
Colton
Pilot Knob
Carl
Elroy
BASTROP ISD
BASTROP
CREEDMOOR
Maha
Cedar Creek
TRAVIS COUNTY
HAYS COUNTY
MUSTANG RIDGE
BASTROP COUNTY
CALDWELL COUNTY
SMITHVILLE ISD
HAYS ISD
LOCKHART ISD
NIEDERWALD
SMITHVILLE

SCALE IN MILES 0 1 2 3 4

ST EDWARD'S UNIVERSITY CAMPUS

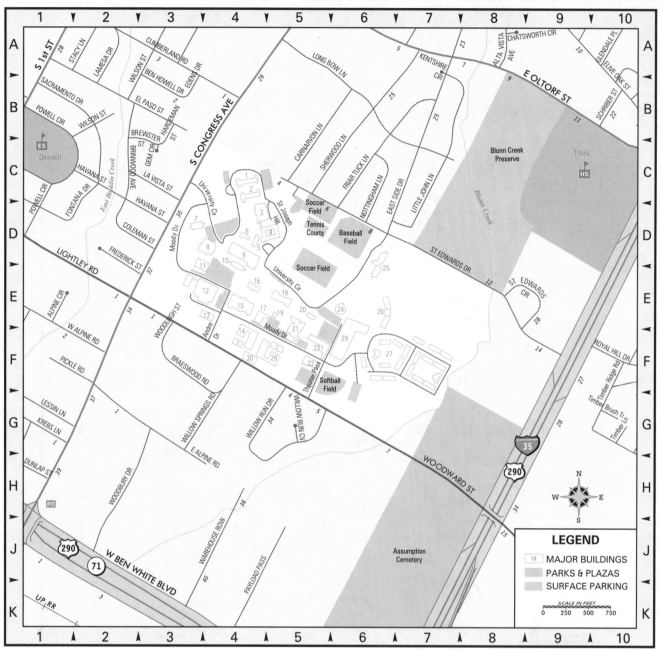

COPYRIGHT 2009 by **MAPSCO** - ALL RIGHTS RESERVED

Campus Found on Page 614Z

BUILDING NAME	BLDG.	MAP
Alumni Gym	(11)	D4
Andre Hall	(10)	D4
Carriage House	(19)	E5
Casa	(30)	F4
Chapel	(5)	D4
Doyle Hall	(2)	C4
Dujarie Hall	(28)	F5
East Hall	(25)	D6
Fine Arts Center	(3)	D4
Fleck Hall	(7)	D3
Fondren Hall Campus Store	(17)	E4
Holy Cross Hall	(16)	E4
John Brooks Williams Natural Sciences Center	(23)	F5
Main Building	(18)	E5
Mang House	(6)	D4

BUILDING NAME	BLDG.	MAP
Mary Moody Northen Theatre	(24)	E6
Moody Hall	(21)	E5
Moreau Hall	(14)	E4
Physical Plant - PP	(13)	E4
Premont Hall	(1)	C4
Ragsdale Center	(15)	E4
Recreation & Convocation Center	(12)	E4
Residence Hall	(29)	F6
Scarborough-Phillips Library	(8)	D4
Sorin Hall	(20)	E5
St Joseph Hall	(4)	D5
Student Apartments	(27)	F6
Teresa Hall	(26)	E6
Trustee Hall	(9)	D4
Woodward Office Building	(22)	F5

SOUTHWESTERN UNIVERSITY CAMPUS

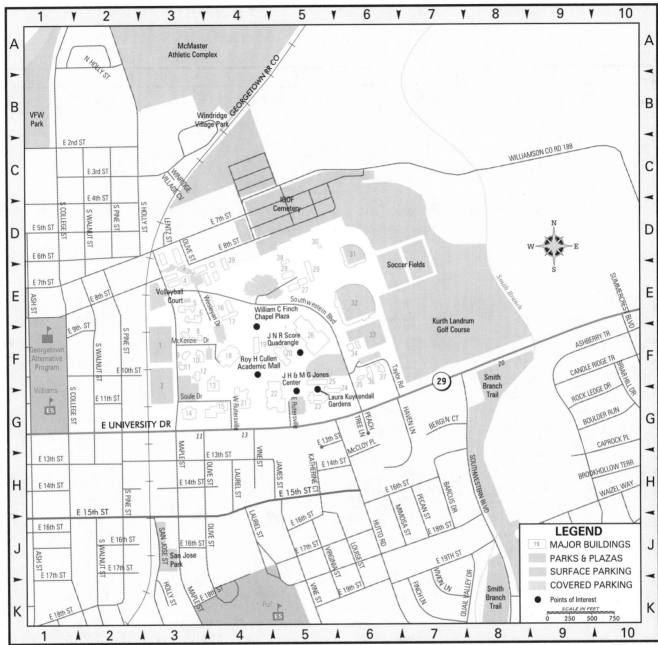

Campus Found on Page 286M

BUILDING NAME	BLDG.	MAP
A Frank Smith, Jr Library Center	(21)	G4
Alma Thomas Fine Arts Center	(22)	G5
Brown-Cody Residence Hall	(25)	F5
Central Chilling Station	(12)	F4
Charline Hamblin McCombs Residential Hall	(16)	E4
Corbin J Robertson Center	(26)	F5
Dorothy Manning Lord Residential Center	(39)	E4
Ernest L Kurth Residence Hall	(24)	F6
F W Olin Building	(20)	F5
Field House (Campus Police)	(11)	F3
Fondren-Jones Science Hall	(15)	G4
Fountainwood Observatory	(30)	D5
Greenhouse	(38)	D5
Grogan & Betty Lord Residence Hall	(3)	E3
Herman Brown Residence Hall	(6)	E3
J E & L E Mabee Residence Hall	(23)	G5
Joe S Mundy Hall	(27)	E5
Julie Puett Howry Center	(34)	F6
Kappa Alpha House	(9)	F3
Kappa Sigma House	(8)	F3

BUILDING NAME	BLDG.	MAP
Kyle E White Building	(36)	F6
Lois Perkins Chapel	(19)	F4
Martin Ruter Residence Hall	(17)	E4
Marvin D Henderson, Sr Tennis Courts	(33)	F6
McCook-Crain Building	(35)	F6
Mood-Bridwell Hall	(13)	F4
Moody-Shearn Residence Hall	(5)	E3
Phi Delta Theta House	(10)	F3
Physical Plant Building & Warehouse	(29)	E5
Pi Kappa Alpha House	(7)	F3
Red & Charline McCombs Campus Center	(18)	F4
Robert K Moses, Jr Field	(1)	F3
Rockwell Baseball Field	(32)	E6
Roy & Lillie Cullen Building	(14)	G3
Rufus Franklin Edwards Studio Arts Building	(28)	E5
Sharon Lord Caskey Community Center	(4)	E3
Snyder Athletic Field	(2)	F3
Taylor-Sanders Softball Field	(31)	D6
Turner-Fleming House	(37)	F6

25

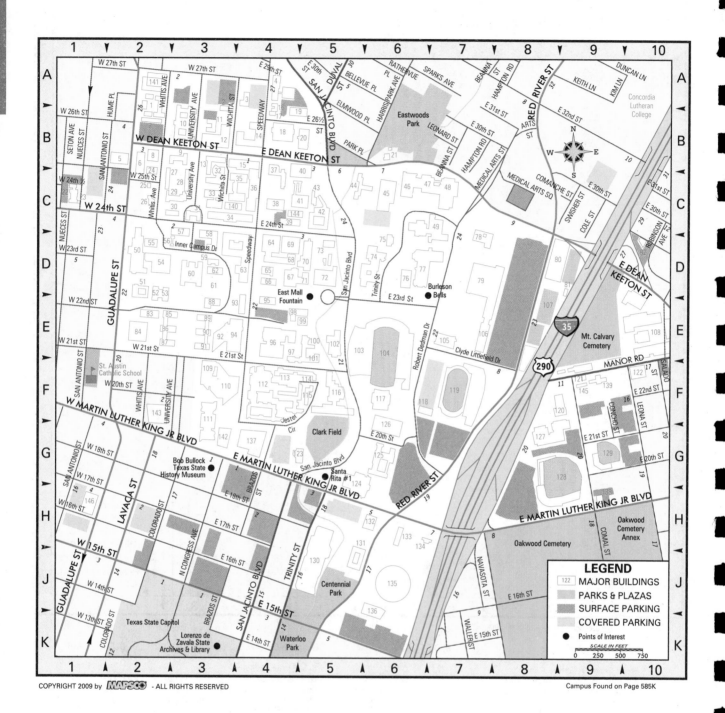

Campus Found on Page 585K

UNIVERSITY of TEXAS CAMPUS INDEX

Alphabetical

BUILDING NAME	BLDG.	MAP
2609 University Ave - UA9	(11)	B3
2616 Wichita (Instructional Assessment & Evaluation) - BWY	(2)	A3
2617 Speedway - SW7	(16)	B4
Academic Annex - ACA	(144)	C4
Almetris Duren Hall - ADH	(141)	A2
Andrews Dormitory - AND	(29)	C3
Animal Resources Center - ARC	(4)	A4
Anna Hiss Gymnasium - AHG	(35)	C4
Applied Computational Engineering & Sciences Building - ACE	(64)	D4
Arno Nowotny Building - ANB	(134)	H6
Art Building & Museum - ART	(74)	D6
Athletic Fields Pavilion - AFP	(81)	D9
AT&T Executive Education and Conference Center - EEC	(143)	F2
Battle Hall - BTL	(53)	D2
Batts Hall - BAT	(89)	E3
Beauford H Jester Center - JES	(112)	F4
Benedict Hall - BEN	(91)	E3
Bernard & Audre Rapoport Building - BRB	(95)	E4
Biological Greenhouse - BOT	(56)	D2
Biological Laboratories - BIO	(57)	C3
Biomedical Engineering Building - BME	(13)	B3
Blanton Dormitory - BLD	(28)	C3
Blanton Museum of Art - BMA	(137)	G4
Brackenridge Hall Dormitory - BHD	(113)	F4
Burdine Hall - BUR	(32)	C3
Calhoun Hall - CAL	(86)	E2
Carothers Dormitory - CRD	(27)	C3
Central Chilling Station 2 - CS2	(65)	D4
Central Chilling Station 3 - CS3	(123)	G5
Central Chilling Station 4 - CS4	(45)	C6
Central Chilling Station 5 - CS5	(19)	B4
Central Receiving Building - CRB	(120)	F9
Chemical & Petroleum Engineering Building - CPE	(18)	B4
Chemical Transfer Building - CTB	(43)	C5
Child Development Center - CML	(139)	F9
Collections Deposit Library - CDL	(132)	H6
Comal Child Development Center Annex - CDA	(121)	F9
Computation Center - COM (underground)	(61)	D3
Continuing Engineering Education - CEE	(17)	B4
Darrell K Royal Texas Memorial Stadium - STD	(104)	E6
Denton A Cooley Pavilion - DCP	(136)	J5
Development Office Building - DEV	(82)	D10
Dorothy H Gebauer Building - GEB	(59)	D3
Edgar A Smith Building - EAS	(142)	G3
E P Schoch Building - EPS	(66)	D4
E William Doty Fine Arts Building - DFA	(76)	D6
Engineering Teaching Center II - ETC	(20)	B5
Engineering-Science Building - ENS	(41)	C5
Ernest Cockrell, Jr, Hall - ECJ	(40)	C5
Etter-Harbin Alumni Center - UTX	(102)	E5
Experimental Science Building - ESB	(34)	C4
Facilities Complex Area - FC1-8	(108)	E10
F Loren Winship Drama Building - WIN	(72)	D5
Frank C Erwin, Jr, Special Events Center - ERC	(135)	J6
Frank Denius Fields - FDF	(107)	E8
Garrison Hall - GAR	(88)	E3
Geography Building - GRG	(30)	C3
Geology Building - GEO	(67)	D4
George I Sanchez Building - SZB	(111)	F3
Goldsmith Hall - GOL	(51)	D2
Graduate and International Admissions - GIA	(7)	B2
Graduate School of Business Building - GSB	(92)	E3
Gregory Gymnasium - GRE	(96)	E4
Hal C Weaver Power Plant - PPL	(70)	D5
Hal C Weaver Power Plant Annex - PPA	(73)	D5
Hal C Weaver Power Plant Expansion - PPE	(69)	D4
Harry Ransom Center - HRC	(84)	E2
Hill Hall Dormitory - HHD	(100)	E5
Hogg Memorial Auditorium - HMA	(55)	D2
Homer Rainey Hall - HRH	(87)	E2
Indoor Practice Facility - IPF	(80)	D9
J Frank Dobie House - FDH	(21)	B6
J T Patterson Laboratories Building - PAT	(38)	C4
Jesse H Jones Communication Center A - CMA	(8)	B2
Jesse H Jones Communication Center B - CMB	(6)	B2
Jesse H Jones Communication Center C - CMC	(24)	C2
Jesse H Jones Hall - JON	(46)	C6
Joe C Thompson Conference Center - TCC	(78)	D7
John B Connally Center for Justice - CCJ	(48)	C7
John W Hargis Hall - JHH	(133)	H6
Kinsolving Dormitory - KIN	(10)	B3
L Theo Bellmont Hall - BEL	(103)	E5
Laboratory Theatre Building - LTH	(71)	D5
Lee & Joe Jamail Texas Swimming Center - TSC	(124)	G5
Littlefield Carriage House - LCH	(25)	C2
Littlefield Dormitory - LTD	(9)	B3
Littlefield Home - LFH	(26)	C2
Living Learning Center - LLC	(1)	A2
Louise & James R Moffett Molecular Biology Building - MBB	(36)	C4
Lyndon B Johnson Library - LBJ	(79)	D7
Mail Services Building - MSB	(145)	F9
Main Building & Tower - MAI	(60)	D3
Mary E Gearing Hall - GEA	(31)	C3
McCombs School of Business - CBA	(94)	E4
Mezes Hall - MEZ	(90)	E3
Mike A Myers Track & Soccer Stadium - MMS	(119)	F7
Moncrief-Neuhaus Athletics Center - MNC	(117)	F6
Moore-Hill Dormitory - MHD	(101)	F5
Music Building East & Music Building/Recital Hall - MRH	(49)	C7
Nano Science and Technology Building - NST	(140)	C3
Neural Molecular Science Building - NMS	(15)	B4
North Office Building - NOA	(3)	A4
Nursing School - NUR	(131)	H5
OFPC Field Staff Office - FPC	(138)	H9
Parlin Hall - PAR	(85)	E2
Penick-Allison Tennis Center - TTC	(130)	J5
Performing Arts Center - PAC	(77)	D6
Perry-Castaneda Library (Main Library) - PCL	(110)	F3
Peter T Flawn Acedemic Center - FAC	(54)	D2
Pharmacy Building - PHR	(33)	C3
Prather Hall Dormitory - PHD	(115)	F5
Printing & Press Building - PPB	(127)	G8
Recreational Sports Center - RSC	(126)	G6
Red & Charline McCombs Field - SBS	(129)	G9
Robert A Welch Hall - WEL	(63)	D5
Robert Lee Moore Hall - RLM	(37)	C4
Roberts Hall Dormitory - RHD	(114)	F5
ROTC Rifle Range Building - RRN	(99)	E5
Russell A Steindam Hall - RAS	(98)	E4
San Jacinto Residence Hall - SJH	(116)	F5
Sarah M & Charles E Seay Building - SEA	(14)	B4
School of Social Work Building - SSW	(125)	G6
Service Building - SER	(42)	C5
Sid Richardson Hall - SRH	(106)	E7
Simkins Hall Dormitory - SHD	(44)	C5
Student Services Building - SSB	(12)	B3
Sutton Hall - SUT	(83)	E2
T S Painter Hall -PAI	(58)	D3
T U Taylor Hall - TAY	(68)	D4
Texas Memorial Museum - TMM	(75)	D6
Townes Hall - TNH	(47)	C6
Track/Soccer Field House - TSF	(118)	F6
UFCU Disch-Falk Field - DFF	(128)	G9
Union Building - UNB	(50)	D2
University Interscholastic League - UIL	(122)	F10
University Police Building - UPB	(105)	E7
University Teaching Center - UTC	(109)	F3
UT Administration Building - UTA	(146)	H1
UT Student Child Care Center - SCC	(23)	C1
Varsity Center - VRC (underground)	(97)	E4
W R Woolrich Laboratories - WRW	(39)	C4
Waggener Hall - WAG	(93)	E4
Walter Webb Hall - WWH	(5)	B2
West Mall Office Building - WMB	(52)	D2
Will C Hogg Building - WCH	(62)	D3
Woolridge Hall - WOH	(22)	C1

Numerical

BUILDING NAME	BLDG.	MAP
Living Learning Center - LLC	(1)	A2
2616 Wichita (Instructional Assessment & Evaluation) - BWY	(2)	A3
North Office Building - NOA	(3)	A4
Animal Resources Center - ARC	(4)	A4
Walter Webb Hall - WWH	(5)	B2
Jesse H Jones Communication Center B - CMB	(6)	B2
Graduate and International Admissions - GIA	(7)	B2
Jesse H Jones Communication Center A - CMA	(8)	B2
Littlefield Dormitory - LTD	(9)	B3
Kinsolving Dormitory - KIN	(10)	B3
2609 University Ave - UA9	(11)	B3
Student Services Building - SSB	(12)	B3
Biomedical Engineering Building - BME	(13)	B3
Sarah M & Charles E Seay Building - SEA	(14)	B4
Neural Molecular Science Building - NMS	(15)	B4
2617 Speedway - SW7	(16)	B4
Continuing Engineering Education - CEE	(17)	B4
Chemical & Petroleum Engineering Building - CPE	(18)	B4
Central Chilling Station 5 - CS5	(19)	B4
Engineering Teaching Center II - ETC	(20)	B5
J Frank Dobie House - FDH	(21)	B6
Woolridge Hall - WOH	(22)	C1
UT Student Child Care Center - SCC	(23)	C1
Jesse H Jones Communication Center C - CMC	(24)	C2
Littlefield Carriage House - LCH	(25)	C2
Littlefield Home - LFH	(26)	C2
Carothers Dormitory - CRD	(27)	C3
Blanton Dormitory - BLD	(28)	C3
Andrews Dormitory - AND	(29)	C3
Geography Building - GRG	(30)	C3
Mary E Gearing Hall - GEA	(31)	C3
Burdine Hall - BUR	(32)	C3
Pharmacy Building - PHR	(33)	C3
Experimental Science Building - ESB	(34)	C4
Anna Hiss Gymnasium - AHG	(35)	C4
Louise & James R Moffett Molecular Biology Building - MBB	(36)	C4
Robert Lee Moore Hall - RLM	(37)	C4
J T Patterson Laboratories Building - PAT	(38)	C4
W R Woolrich Laboratories - WRW	(39)	C4
Ernest Cockrell, Jr, Hall - ECJ	(40)	C5
Engineering-Science Building - ENS	(41)	C5
Service Building - SER	(42)	C5
Chemical Transfer Building - CTB	(43)	C5
Simkins Hall Dormitory - SHD	(44)	C5
Central Chilling Station 4 - CS4	(45)	C6
Jesse H Jones Hall - JON	(46)	C6
Townes Hall - TNH	(47)	C6
John B Connally Center for Justice - CCJ	(48)	C7
Music Building East & Music Building/Recital Hall - MRH	(49)	C7
Union Building - UNB	(50)	D2
Goldsmith Hall - GOL	(51)	D2
West Mall Office Building - WMB	(52)	D2
Battle Hall - BTL	(53)	D2
Peter T Flawn Acedemic Center - FAC	(54)	D2
Hogg Memorial Auditorium - HMA	(55)	D2
Biological Greenhouse - BOT	(56)	D2
Biological Laboratories - BIO	(57)	C3
T S Painter Hall -PAI	(58)	D3
Dorothy H Gebauer Building - GEB	(59)	D3
Main Building & Tower - MAI	(60)	D3
Computation Center - COM (underground)	(61)	D3
Will C Hogg Building - WCH	(62)	D3
Robert A Welch Hall - WEL	(63)	D5
Applied Computational Engineering & Sciences Building - ACE	(64)	D4
Central Chilling Station 2 - CS2	(65)	D4
E P Schoch Building - EPS	(66)	D4
Geology Building - GEO	(67)	D4
T U Taylor Hall - TAY	(68)	D4
Hal C Weaver Power Plant Expansion - PPE	(69)	D4
Hal C Weaver Power Plant - PPL	(70)	D5
Laboratory Theatre Building - LTH	(71)	D5
F Loren Winship Drama Building - WIN	(72)	D5
Hal C Weaver Power Plant Annex - PPA	(73)	D5
Art Building & Museum - ART	(74)	D6
Texas Memorial Museum - TMM	(75)	D6
E William Doty Fine Arts Building - DFA	(76)	D6
Performing Arts Center - PAC	(77)	D6
Joe C Thompson Conference Center - TCC	(78)	D7
Lyndon B Johnson Library - LBJ	(79)	D7
Indoor Practice Facility - IPF	(80)	D9
Athletic Fields Pavilion - AFP	(81)	D9
Development Office Building - DEV	(82)	D10
Sutton Hall - SUT	(83)	E2
Harry Ransom Center - HRC	(84)	E2
Parlin Hall - PAR	(85)	E2
Calhoun Hall - CAL	(86)	E2
Homer Rainey Hall - HRH	(87)	E2
Garrison Hall - GAR	(88)	E3
Batts Hall - BAT	(89)	E3
Mezes Hall - MEZ	(90)	E3
Benedict Hall - BEN	(91)	E3
Graduate School of Business Building - GSB	(92)	E3
Waggener Hall - WAG	(93)	E4
McCombs School of Business - CBA	(94)	E4
Bernard & Audre Rapoport Building - BRB	(95)	E4
Gregory Gymnasium - GRE	(96)	E4
Varsity Center - VRC (underground)	(97)	E4
Russell A Steindam Hall - RAS	(98)	E4
ROTC Rifle Range Building - RRN	(99)	E5
Hill Hall Dormitory - HHD	(100)	E5
Moore-Hill Dormitory - MHD	(101)	F5
Etter-Harbin Alumni Center - UTX	(102)	E5
L Theo Bellmont Hall - BEL	(103)	E5
Darrell K Royal Texas Memorial Stadium - STD	(104)	E6
University Police Building - UPB	(105)	E7
Sid Richardson Hall - SRH	(106)	E7
Frank Denius Fields - FDF	(107)	E8
Facilities Complex Area - FC1-8	(108)	E10
University Teaching Center - UTC	(109)	F3
Perry-Castaneda Library (Main Library) - PCL	(110)	F3
George I Sanchez Building - SZB	(111)	F3
Beauford H Jester Center - JES	(112)	F4
Brackenridge Hall Dormitory - BHD	(113)	F4
Roberts Hall Dormitory - RHD	(114)	F5
Prather Hall Dormitory - PHD	(115)	F5
San Jacinto Residence Hall - SJH	(116)	F5
Moncrief-Neuhaus Athletics Center - MNC	(117)	F6
Track/Soccer Field House - TSF	(118)	F6
Mike A Myers Track & Soccer Stadium - MMS	(119)	F7
Central Receiving Building - CRB	(120)	F9
Comal Child Development Center Annex - CDA	(121)	F9
University Interscholastic League - UIL	(122)	F10
Central Chilling Station 3 - CS3	(123)	G5
Lee & Joe Jamail Texas Swimming Center - TSC	(124)	G5
School of Social Work Building - SSW	(125)	G6
Recreational Sports Center - RSC	(126)	G6
Printing & Press Building - PPB	(127)	G8
UFCU Disch-Falk Field - DFF	(128)	G9
Red & Charline McCombs Field - SBS	(129)	G9
Penick-Allison Tennis Center - TTC	(130)	J5
Nursing School - NUR	(131)	H5
Collections Deposit Library - CDL	(132)	H6
John W Hargis Hall - JHH	(133)	H6
Arno Nowotny Building - ANB	(134)	H6
Frank C Erwin, Jr, Special Events Center - ERC	(135)	J6
Denton A Cooley Pavilion - DCP	(136)	J5
Blanton Museum of Art - BMA	(137)	G4
OFPC Field Staff Office - FPC	(138)	H9
Child Development Center - CML	(139)	F9
Nano Science and Technology Building - NST	(140)	C3
Almetris Duren Hall - ADH	(141)	A2
Edgar A Smith Building - EAS	(142)	G3
AT&T Executive Education and Conference Center - EEC	(143)	F2
Academic Annex - ACA	(144)	C4
Mail Services Building - MSB	(145)	F9
UT Administration Building - UTA	(146)	H1

FRANK C. ERWIN EVENTS CENTER

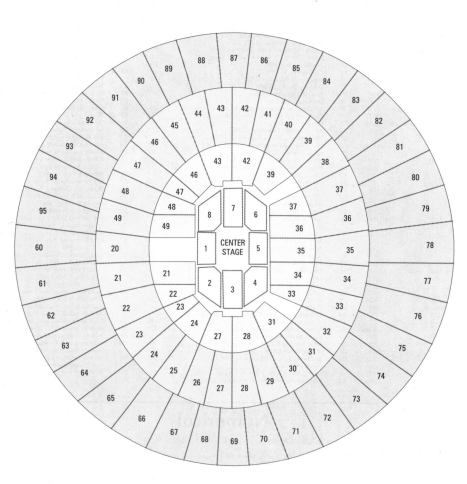

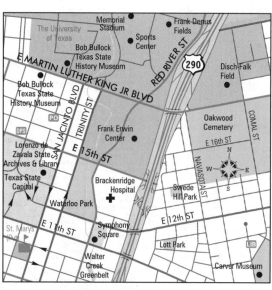

The Frank C. Erwin Events Center (aka the "Superdrum") is the prime sports and entertainment venue on the campus of the University of Texas at Austin. Built in 1977 at a cost of $34 million, the center is home court for both men's and women's Longhorn basketball, large concerts and other events.

Located just off IH-35 at 1701 Red River St (Mapsco 585P), the center is within walking distance of downtown Austin and the University campus.

AUSTIN-BERGSTROM INTERNATIONAL AIRPORT

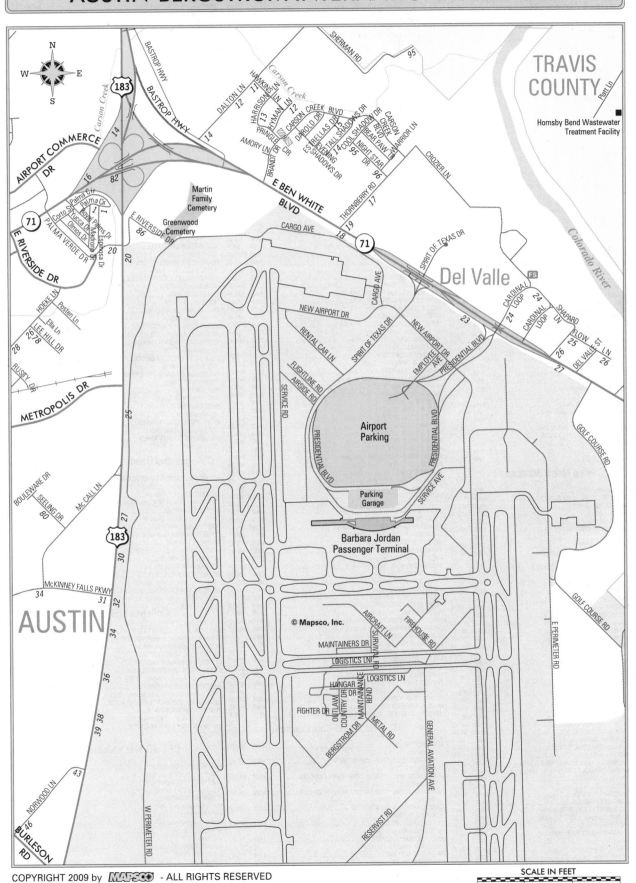

TRAVIS COUNTY

Hornsby Bend Wastewater Treatment Facility

Del Valle

AUSTIN

Martin Family Cemetery

Greenwood Cemetery

Airport Parking

Parking Garage

Barbara Jordan Passenger Terminal

© Mapsco, Inc.

SCALE IN FEET
0   1000   2000   3000

Airports and Military Bases

AUSTIN-BERGSTROM INTERNATIONAL AIRPORT *Austin* 646Q MM-17
BIRDS NEST AIRPORT *Travis Co* 499B MS-33
BREAKAWAY PARK LANDING STRIP *Williamson Co* 374T MG-43
CAMP MABRY MILITARY RESERVATION *Austin* 554L MH-26
GEORGETOWN MUNICIPAL AIRPORT *Georgetown* 256G MM-57
KITTIE HILL AIRPORT *Williamson Co* 313K ME-50
LAKEWAY AIR PARK *Lakeway* 519J WW-29
LANDING STRIP *Williamson Co* 343E ME-48
RUSTY ALLEN AIRPORT *Lago Vista* 399C WX-42
SPICEWOOD AIRPORT *Burnet Co* 396W WQ-40
TAYLOR MUNICIPAL AIRPORT *Taylor* 352F MY-48

Athletic Fields, Stadiums and Complexes

AUSTIN HIGH TENNIS CENTER *Austin* 584Q MH-23
BASEBALL COMPLEX *Round Rock* 378A MQ-45
BASEBALL/SOFTBALL FIELDS *Round Rock* 377H MP-45
BECK STADIUM *Austin* 612L MD-20
CASWELL TENNIS CENTER *Austin* 584H MH-24
CHAPARRAL ICE ARENA *Travis Co* 466D MM-36
CHAPARRAL STADIUM *West Lake Hills* 583P ME-23
CONNALLY STADIUM *Austin* 466M MM-35
CRUSADER STADIUM *Travis Co* 581H MB-24
DARRELL K ROYAL TEXAS MEMORIAL STADIUM *Austin* 585K MJ-23
DELCO CENTER (AISD) *Austin* 557J MN-26
DELL DIAMOND BASEBALL FIELD, THE *Round Rock* 377M MP-44
DEL VALLE FIELDS *Travis Co* 647U MP-16
DISCH-FALK FIELD *Austin* 585L MK-23
DOAK FIELDS *Taylor* 353J EA-47
DOWNS/MABSON FIELDS *Austin* 585R MK-23
DRAGON STADIUM *Round Rock* 376X ML-43
ELLIE NOACK SPORTS COMPLEX (AISD) *Travis Co* 557K MN-26
ERHARD STADIUM *Bastrop* 745B EE-9
FRANK DENIUS FIELD *Travis Co* 553B ME-27
HAVINS BALLFIELDS *Austin* 466Y MM-34
HAWKS STADIUM *Pflugerville* 438H MR-39
HIPPO STADIUM *Hutto* 349Z MT-46
HOUSE PARK *Austin* 585N MJ-23
KRIEG FIELD COMPLEX *Austin* 615M MK-20
KUEMPEL STADIUM *Pflugerville* 437V MP-37
LAKE TRAVIS ISD STADIUM *Lakeway* 549H WX-27
MEMORIAL FOOTBALL STADIUM *Taylor* 323W EA-49
MIKE A MYERS TRACK AND SOCCER STADIUM *Austin* 585K MJ-23
MUSTANG STADIUM *Manor* 529K MS-29
McMASTER ATHLETIC COMPLEX *Georgetown* 286D MM-54
NELSON ATHLETIC STADIUM *Austin* 556F ML-27
ONION CREEK SPORTS COMPLEX *Austin* 675J MJ-14
REX KITCHENS YOUTH COMPLEX *Travis Co* 703L MF-11
ROUND ROCK ISD STADIUM *Austin* 404K MG-41
RUSTY REYNOLDS BALL FIELD *Bastrop* 715T EE-10
SISEMORE FIELD *Lago Vista* 399Y WX-40
SNYDER ATHLETIC FIELD *Georgetown* 286M MM-53
SOCCER FIELDS *Round Rock* 377D MP-45
SOUTH AUSTIN TENNIS CENTER *Austin* 614Q MH-20
SOUTHWEST SOCCER COMPLEX *Travis Co* 641U MB-16
TIGER STADIUM *Dripping Springs* 636S WQ-16
TONY BURGER ACTIVITY CENTER *Sunset Valley* 613Y MF-19
UNIVERSITY OF TEXAS INTRAMURAL FIELDS *Austin* 555L MK-26
VETERANS STADIUM *Travis Co* 678K MQ-14
WILDCAT STADIUM *Elgin* 503X EA-31
WILLIAMS FIELD *Austin* 584V MH-22

Capital Metro Stations

BURNET STATION *Austin* 495H MK-33
CONVENTION CENTER - DOWNTOWN STATION *Austin* 585X MJ-22
HIGHLAND MALL STATION *Austin* 555H MK-27
LAKELINE STATION *Austin* 404S MG-40
LEANDER STATION *Leander* 312T MC-49
MARTIN LUTHER KING, JR STATION *Austin* 585M MK-23
MOPAC STATION *Austin* 435V MK-37
NORTH LAMAR STATION *Austin* 525U MK-28
PLAZA SALTILLO - COMAL STATION *Austin* 585Y MK-22

Cemeteries

ALLEN CEMETERY *Buda* 732Z MD-7
ALLEN-McNEIL CEMETERY *Travis Co* 522Q MD-29
ANDERSON CEMETERY *Williamson Co* 222P MC-59
ANTIOCH CEMETERY *Hays Co* 762B MC-6
ASSUMPTION CEMETERY *Austin* 645A MJ-18
AUSTIN MEMORIAL PARK CEMETERY *Austin* 524Z MH-28
AUSTIN MEMORIAL PARK CEMETERY *Austin* 554D MH-27
AVERY CEMETERY *Williamson Co* 412T MY-40
BAGDAD CEMETERY *Williamson Co* 342A MC-48
BARTON CEMETERY *Hays Co* 762S MC-4
BEE CAVE CEMETERY *Bee Cave* 550P WY-26
BERRY CREEK CEMETERY *Georgetown* 227A MN-60
BETHANY CEMETERY *Austin* 586L MM-23
BETHLEHEM CEMETERY *Travis Co* 473X EA-34
BLUE HOLE CEMETERY *Georgetown* 286G MM-54
BROWN CEMETERY *Travis Co* 590T MU-22
BROWN CEMETERY *Travis Co* 703S ME-10
BROWN CEMETERY *Travis Co* 590V MV-22
BULLION CEMETERY *Williamson Co* 223Q MF-59
BURDETT PRAIRIE CEMETERY *Austin* 616T ML-19
BURLESON CEMETERY *Bastrop Co* 744C ED-9
CAPITOL MEMORIAL PARK CEMETERY *Austin* 467A MN-36
CARL CEMETERY *Travis Co* 734H MH-9
CHAPEL HILL MEMORIAL PARK CEMETERY *San Leanna* 703K ME-11
CITIZENS MEMORIAL GARDEN CEMETERY *Williamson Co* 286J ML-53
CITY CEMETERY *Round Rock* 376T ML-43
CITY CEMETERY *Taylor* 353B EA-48
COMANCHE CEMETERY *Travis Co* 649M MT-17
COMANCHE CEMETERY *Travis Co* 649R MT-17
CREEDMOOR COMMUNITY CEMETERY *Mustang Ridge* 765G MK-6
DARTER CEMETERY *Travis Co* 520D WZ-30
DAVIS CEMETERY *Williamson Co* 313W ME-49
DECKER FREE CHURCH CEMETERY *Travis Co* 558C MR-27
DE MARIA CEMETERY *Austin* 674B MG-15
DESSAU CEMETERY *Pflugerville* 468F MQ-36
EASLEY CEMETERY *Travis Co* 590Z MV-22
ELGIN CEMETERY *Elgin* 533R EB-29
ELGIN LATIN CEMETERY *Bastrop Co* 534W EC-28
EVERGREEN CEMETERY *Austin* 586N ML-23
FAIRVIEW CEMETERY *Travis Co* 370Q WZ-44
FALL CREEK CEMETERY *Travis Co* 456N WQ-35
FISKVILLE CEMETERY *Austin* 526L MM-29
FITZHUGH CEMETERY *Hays Co* 608K WU-20
FORE CEMETERY *Williamson Co* 223A ME-60
FOREST OAKS MEMORIAL PARK *Austin* 612T MC-19
FOWLER CEMETERY *Bastrop Co* 680K MU-14
GARFIELD CEMETERY *Travis Co* 679A MS-15
GEORGETOWN MEMORIAL CEMETERY *Williamson Co* 257P MN-56
GLASSCOCK CEMETERY *Travis Co* 620F MU-21
GREEN CEMETERY *Williamson Co* 225U MK-58
GREGG CEMETERY *Travis Co* 498P MQ-32
GUADALUPE CEMETERY *Taylor* 353R EB-47
GUADALUPE CITY CEMETERY *Williamson Co* 257S MN-55
HAYNIE CEMETERY *Travis Co* 679C MT-15
HAYNIE FLATS CEMETERY *Burnet Co* 426G WR-39
HENSEL CEMETERY *Travis Co* 368W WU-43
HILL CEMETERY *Bastrop Co* 651D MX-18
HILL CEMETERY *Travis Co* 498V MR-31
HISTORIC SLAVE CEMETERY *Round Rock* 376T ML-43
HOG EYE CEMETERY *Bastrop Co* 563V EB-25
HOPEWELL CEMETERY *Williamson Co* 278C WV-54
HORNSBY CEMETERY *Travis Co* 618A MQ-21
HUDDLESTON CEMETERY *Travis Co* 310G WZ-51
HUNT CEMETERY *Williamson Co* 223S ME-58
HUTTO CITY CEMETERY *Williamson Co* 379R MT-44
IMMANUEL CHURCH CEMETERY *Williamson Co* 352S MY-46
INGRAM CEMETERY *Travis Co* 679Y MT-13
INTERNATIONAL CEMETERY *Austin* 586R MM-23
I.O.O.F. CEMETERY *Georgetown* 287E MN-54
JONES CEMETERY *Travis Co* 619E MS-21
KIMBRO CEMETERY *Travis Co* 501L MX-32
KIMBRO CEMETERY *Williamson Co* 411J MW-41
LIVE OAK CEMETERY *Travis Co* 703T ME-10
LOCKWOOD CEMETERY *Travis Co* 590M MV-23
LOWER CEDAR CREEK CEMETERY *Bastrop Co* 740Y MV-7
MANDA CEMETERY *Travis Co* 502E MY-33
MANOR CEMETERY *Manor* 529R MT-29
MANOR HILL CEMETERY *Webberville* 621X MW-19
MARTIN CEMETERY *Hays Co* 794P MG-2
MASONIC CEMETERY *Austin* 674F MG-15
MEMORIAL HILL PARK CEMETERY *Austin* 466H MM-36
MERRELLTOWN CEMETERY *Travis Co* 436P ML-38
MILLER CEMETERY *Williamson Co* 311B MA-51
MT. CALVARY CEMETERY *Austin* 585L MK-23
MOUNT OLIVE CEMETERY *Bastrop Co* 742L MZ-8
NELSON CEMETERY *Travis Co* 737G MP-9
NEW HOPE CEMETERY *Cedar Park* 372H MD-45
NIEDERWALD CEMETERY *Mustang Ridge* 796S ML-1
OAK GROVE CEMETERY *Austin* 463R MF-35
OAKWOOD CEMETERY *Austin* 585Q MK-23
OAKWOOD CEMETERY ANNEX *Austin* 585Q MK-23
OLD SHILOH CEMETERY *Williamson Co* 410E MU-42
OLIVER CEMETERY *Travis Co* 610X WY-19
PENNINGTON CEMETERY *Williamson Co* 257M MP-56
PERYEAR CEMETERY *Hays Co* 576P WQ-23
PFLUGER CEMETERY *Travis Co* 469R MT-35
PHILIPS CEMETERY *Dripping Springs* 666R WR-14
PLUMMERS CEMETERY *Austin* 586P ML-23
POND SPRINGS CEMETERY *Austin* 434A MG-39
PRAIRIE HILL CEMETERY *Travis Co* 440Z MV-37
PREECE CEMETERY *Travis Co* 493Y MF-31
PRESBYTERIAN CEMETERY *Georgetown* 286U MM-52
PUCKETT CEMETERY *Travis Co* 619K MS-20
ROBERT'S CEMETERY *Travis Co* 551Y MB-25
ROCKY HOLLOW *Williamson Co* 193M MF-62
ROGERS HILL CEMETERY *Austin* 587L MP-23
ROSEHILL CEMETERY *Travis Co* 500X MU-31
ST. MARY'S CEMETERY *Taylor* 323X EA-49
ST. MARY'S CEMETERY *Williamson Co* 409D MT-42
ST. JOHNS CEMETERY *Williamson Co* 317S MN-49
SALYER-MILLARD CEMETERY *Williamson Co* 197A MN-63
SANTA MARIA CEMETERY *Pflugerville* 437V MP-37
SAUL CEMETERY *Williamson Co* 410G MV-42
SCHILLER CEMETERY *Travis Co* 502Z MZ-31
SHILOH CEMETERY *Bastrop Co* 743Z EB-7
SHILOH CEMETERY *Williamson Co* 410J MU-41
SIMPSON CEMETERY *Travis Co* 459U WX-34
SMITH CEMETERY *Bastrop Co* 504X EC-31
STATE CEMETERY *Austin* 555L MK-26
TECK CEMETERY *Travis Co* 490F WY-33
TEXAS STATE CEMETERY *Austin* 585Y MK-22
TUCKER CEMETERY *Travis Co* 583X ME-22
UNION HILL CEMETERY *Williamson Co* 317X MN-49
UPCHURCH CEMETERY *Williamson Co* 283W ME-52
VASQUEZ CEMETERY *Travis Co* 795G MK-3
WALLACE MOUNTAIN CEMETERY *Hays Co* 667A WS-15
WALNUT CREEK CHURCH CEMETERY *Austin* 496G MM-33
WELLS CEMETERY *Leander* 282V MD-52
WESTBROOK MEMORIAL GARDEN *Bastrop Co* 534L ED-29
WHITE ROCK CEMETERY *Bee Cave* 549R WX-26
WHITLEY CEMETERY *Williamson Co* 284U MH-52
WILLIAMSON CREEK CEMETERY *Austin* 644U MH-16
WOODS CEMETERY *Webberville* 621N MW-20
WOODS CEMETERY *Webberville* 650C MV-18
WRIGHTS CEMETERY *Bastrop Co* 741L MX-8

City Halls and Courthouses

AUSTIN CITY HALL 585W MJ-22
301 W 2nd St *78701*
AUSTIN MUNICIPAL COURT-DOWNTOWN 585T MJ-22
700 E 7th St *78701*
AUSTIN MUNICIPAL COURT-NORTH SERVICE CENTER 466P ML-35
12425 Lamplight Village Ave *78758*
AUSTIN MUNICIPAL COURT-SOUTH SERVICE CENTER 643M MF-17
5700 Manchaca Rd *78745*
BASTROP COUNTY COURTHOUSE 745K EE-9
804 Pecan St *78602*
BEE CAVE CITY HALL 550T WY-25
4000 Galleria Pkwy *78738*
BEE CAVE MUNICIPAL COURT 550T WY-25
13333-A W State Hwy 71 *78738*
BRIARCLIFF CITY HALL 457R WT-35
402 Sleat Dr *78669*
BUDA CITY HALL 762D MD-6
121 N Main St *78610*
CEDAR PARK CITY HALL 373S ME-43
600 N Bell Blvd *78613*
CEDAR PARK COURTHOUSE 373N ME-44
911 Quest Pkwy *78613*
DRIPPING SPRINGS CITY HALL 637W WS-16
550 E US Hwy 290 *78620*
ELGIN CITY HALL 534J EC-29
310 N Main St *78621*
GEORGETOWN CITY HALL 286H MM-54
113 E 8th St *78626*
GEORGETOWN COURTHOUSE 286G MM-54
101 E 7th St *78626*
HUTTO CITY HALL 379D MT-45
401 W Front St *78634*
JONESTOWN CITY HALL 400M WZ-41
18649 RM Rd 1431 *78645*
LAGO VISTA CITY HALL 429P WW-38
5803 Thunderbird *78645*
LAKEWAY CITY HALL 519B WW-30
1102 Lohmans Crossing *78734*
LAKEWAY JUSTICE CENTER 519B WW-30
104 Cross Creek *78734*
LEANDER CITY HALL 312X MC-49
200 Willis St *78641*
MANOR CITY HALL 529U MT-28
201 E Parsons St *78653*
MUSTANG RIDGE CITY HALL 796B ML-3
12800 S US Hwy 183 *78610*
PFLUGERVILLE CITY HALL 438W MQ-37
100 E Main St *78660*
PFLUGERVILLE MUNICIPAL COURT 438P MQ-38
1611 Pfennig Ln *78691*
ROLLINGWOOD CITY HALL 584N MG-23
403 Nixon Dr *78746*
ROUND ROCK CITY HALL 376Y MM-43
221 E Main Ave *78664*
ROUND ROCK MUNICIPAL COURT 406C MM-42
301 W Bagdad Ave *78664*
SUNSET VALLEY CITY HALL 613Y MF-19
3205 Jones Rd *78745*
TAYLOR CITY HALL 353E EA-48
400 Porter St *76574*
TAYLOR MUNICIPAL COURT 353E EA-48
109 W 5th St *76574*
TRAVIS COUNTY COURT HOUSE 585N MJ-23
1000 Guadalupe St *78701*
UNITED STATES COURT HOUSE 585S MJ-22
Congress Ave *78701*
VILLAGE OF THE HILLS OFFICES 519J WW-29
102 Trophy Dr *78738*
VILLAGE OF VOLENTE CITY OFFICES 461B MA-36
15403 Hill St *78641*
WEIR CITY HALL 258D MR-57
450 FM Rd 1150 *78674*
WEST LAKE HILLS CITY HALL 583D MF-24
911 Westlake Dr *78746*
WILLIAMSON COUNTY ANNEX 376G MM-45
211 Commerce Cove *78664*
WILLIAMSON COUNTY ANNEX 373S ME-43
350 Discovery Blvd *78613*

Colleges and Universities (Austin Community)

ACC DISTRICT ADMINISTRATIVE OFFICES 555H MK-27
5930 Middle Fiskville Rd (Austin) *78752*
CYPRESS CREEK CAMPUS 402V MD-40
1555 Cypress Creek Rd (Cedar Park) *78613*
EASTVIEW CAMPUS 586S ML-22
3401 Webberville Rd (Austin) *78702*
NORTHRIDGE CAMPUS 466W ML-34
11928 Stonehollow Dr (Austin) *78758*
PINNACLE CAMPUS 611Z MB-19
7748 W US Hwy 290 (Austin) *78736*
RIO GRANDE CAMPUS 585N MJ-23
1212 Rio Grande (Austin) *78701*
RIVERSIDE CAMPUS 616S ML-19
1020 Grove Blvd (Austin) *78741*
SOUTH AUSTIN CAMPUS 643H MF-18
1820 W Stassney Ln (Austin) *78745*

Colleges and Universities

CONCORDIA UNIVERSITY TEXAS 462R MD-35
11400 Concordia University Dr (Austin) *78726*
HUSTON-TILLOTSON UNIVERSITY 585Y MK-22
900 Chicon St (Austin) *78702*
JJ PICKLE RESEARCH CAMPUS (UT) 495L MK-32
ST. EDWARD'S UNIVERSITY 614Z MH-19
3001 S Congress Ave (Austin) *78704*
SOUTHWESTERN UNIVERSITY 287J MN-53
1001 E University Ave (Georgetown) *78626*
TEXAS STATE UNIVERSITY-ROUND ROCK
HIGHER EDUCATION CNTR 347F MN-48
1555 University Blvd (Williamson Co) *78664*
UNIVERSITY OF TEXAS AT AUSTIN 585K MJ-23
78712

DPS - Driver's License Offices

AUSTIN NORTH CONGRESS 585N MJ-23
1500 N Congress Ave *78701*
AUSTIN NORTH LAMAR 555C MK-27
6121 N Lamar Blvd *78752*
AUSTIN NORTHWEST 433M MF-38
13730 Research Blvd *78750*
AUSTIN SOUTH 644L MH-17
4719 S Congress Ave *78745*
BASTROP 745J EE-8
305 Eskew St *78602*
GEORGETOWN 286H MM-54
515 Pine St *78626*
TAYLOR 353 EEA-48
412 Vance St *76574*

Fire Departments

AUSTIN FD

FIRE ACADEMY 676A ML-15
4800 Shaw Ln Travis Co *78744*

STATION #1 585X MJ-22
401 E 5th St Austin *78701*

STATION #2 585J MJ-23
506 W Martin Luther King Jr Blvd Austin *78705*

STATION #3 585B MJ-24
201 W 30th St Austin *78705*

STATION #4 584V MH-22
1000 Blanco St Austin *78703*

STATION #5 586Q MM-23
1201 Webberville Rd Austin *78721*

STATION #6 614M MH-20
1705 S Congress Ave Austin *78704*

STATION #7 615C MK-21
201 Chicon St Austin *78702*

STATION #8 495Y MK-31
8989 Research Blvd Austin *78758*

STATION #9 555U MK-25
4301 Speedway Austin *78751*

STATION #10 584C MH-24
3009 Windsor Rd Austin *78703*

STATION #11 614G MH-21
1611 Kinney Ave Austin *78704*

STATION #12 555E MJ-27
2109 Hancock Dr Austin *78756*

STATION #14 555Z MK-25
4305 Airport Blvd Austin *78722*

STATION #15 616F ML-21
829 Airport Blvd Austin *78702*

STATION #16 525U MK-28
7000 Reese Ln Austin *78757*

STATION #17 644B MG-18
4128 S 1st St Austin *78745*

STATION #18 556K ML-26
6311 Berkman Dr Austin *78723*

STATION #19 524Z MH-28
5211 Balcones Dr Austin *78731*

STATION #20 643Q MF-17
6601 Manchaca Rd Austin *78745*

STATION #21 494Z MH-31
4201 Spicewood Springs Rd Austin *78759*

STATION #22 615Z MK-19
5309 E Riverside Dr Austin *78741*

STATION #23 526L MM-29
1330 E Rundberg Ln Austin *78753*

STATION #24 675A MJ-15
5811 Nuckols Crossing Rd Austin *78744*

STATION #25 465N MJ-35
5228 Duval Rd Austin *78727*

STATION #26 587D MP-24
6702 Wentworth Dr Austin *78724*

STATION #27 612Y MD-19
5401 McCarty Ln Austin *78749*

STATION #28 466N ML-35
2410 W Parmer Ln Austin *78727*

STATION #29 642Y MD-16
3703 Deer Ln Austin *78759*

STATION #30 496P ML-32
1021 W Braker Ln Austin *78758*

STATION #31 524E MG-30
5507 RM Rd 2222 Austin *78732*

STATION #32 584W MG-22
2804 Montebello Rd Austin *78746*

STATION #33 494C MH-33
9409 Bluegrass Dr Austin *78759*

STATION #34 434A MG-39
10041 Lake Creek Pkwy Austin *78729*

STATION #35 645L MK-17
5500 Burleson Rd Austin *78744*

STATION #36 673M MF-14
400 Ralph Ablanedo Dr Austin *78748*

STATION #37 611G MB-21
8660 W State Hwy 71 Austin *78735*

STATION #38 433U MF-37
10111 Anderson Mill Rd Austin *78750*

STATION #39 462Z MD-34
7701 River Place Blvd Austin *78726*

STATION #40 497B MN-33
12711 Harrisglen Dr Austin *78753*

STATION #41 528P MQ-29
11205 Harris Branch Pkwy Austin *78754*

STATION #42 647E MN-18
2454 Cardinal Loop Austin *78617*

STATION #43 671F MA-15
11401 Escarpment Blvd Austin *78739*

STATION #44 464B MG-36
11612 Four Iron Dr Austin *78750*

BASTROP FD

STATION #1 745F EE-9
802 Chestnut St Bastrop *78602*

STATION #2 746N EG-8
120 Corporate Dr Bastrop *78602*

BUDA VFD

STATION #1 762G MD-6
209 Jack C Hays Trail Buda *78610*

STATION 2 763P ME-5
Tom Green School Rd and Old West Trail Hays Co *78610*

CE - BAR VFD

CENTRAL STATION 552E MC-27
353 S Commons Ford Rd Travis Co *78733*

CEDAR PARK FD

STATION #1 403B ME-42
220 S Old Hwy 183 Cedar Park *78613*

STATION #2 403S ME-40
1570 Cypress Creek Rd Cedar Park *78613*

STATION #3 372Q MD-44
1311 Highland Dr Cedar Park *78613*

STATION #4 374Q M-44
150 Church Park Rd Cedar Park *78613*

ELGIN VFD

STATION #1 534N EC-29
107 N Avenue C Elgin *78621*

GEORGETOWN FD

STATION #1 286U MM-53
301 Industrial Ave Georgetown *78626*

STATION #2 256U MM-55
204 W Central Dr Georgetown *78628*

STATION #3 225D MK-60
5 Texas Dr Georgetown *78628*

STATION #4 226Z MM-58
4200 Airport Rd Williamson Co *78628*

HUDSON BEND FD

STATION #1 490G WZ-33
15516 General Williamson Dr Travis Co *78734*

STATION #2 519G WX-30
1211 Lohmans Crossing Rd Lakeway *78734*

STATION #3 550T WY-25
13333 W State Hwy 71 Bee Cave *78738*

STATION #4 492E MC-33
6500 Comanche Trail Travis Co *78732*

STATION #5 491Y MB-31
3048 Steiner Ranch Blvd Travis Co *78732*

HUTTO VFD

HUTTO FIRE STATION 349Y MT-46
501 Exchange Blvd Hutto *78634*

JOLLYVILLE FD

STATION #1 434N MG-38
9218 Anderson Mill Rd Williamson Co *78729*

STATION #2 433M MF-38
12507 Mellow Meadow Dr Williamson Co *78750*

LAGO VISTA FIRE & RESCUE

STATION #1 458D WV-36
3605 Allegiance Ave Lago Vista *78645*

STATION #2 429P WW-38
20503 Dawn Dr Lago Vista *78645*

STATION #3 489N WW-32
400 Venture Dr Point Venture *78645*

LEANDER FD

CENTRAL STATION 312X MC-49
201 N Brushy St Leander *78641*

STATION #2 342W MD-45
1950 Crystal Falls Pkwy Leander *78641*

STATION #3 342G MD-48
701 Leander Dr Leander *78641*

MANCHACA VFD

STATION #501 702M MD-11
1310 FM Rd 1626 Travis Co *78652*

STATION #502 673N ME-14
2301 Riddle Rd Austin *78748*

STATION #503 672X MC-13
11902 Brodie Ln Travis Co *78739*

STATION #505 733B ME-9
13420 Onion Creek Dr Travis Co *78652*

STATION #506 701Q MB-11
2900 Chapparal Rd Hays Co *78652*

MANOR VFD

STATION #1 529U MT-28
405 W Parsons Rd Manor *78653*

NORTH HAYS CO VFD

CENTRAL STATION 636Y WR-16
400 Sportsplex Dr Dripping Springs *78620*

EAST STATION 638Z WV-16
14121 W US Hwy 290 Hays Co *78620*

NORTH STATION 607L WT-22
16716 Fitzhugh Rd Hays Co *78620*

NORTH LAKE TRAVIS FIRE & RESCUE

STATION #1 400M WZ-41
18300 Park Dr Jonestown *78645*

OAK HILL FD

STATION #1 610R WZ-20
9211 Circle Dr Travis Co *78736*

STATION #2 581M MB-23
4111 Barton Creek Blvd Travis Co *78735*

PEDERNALES EMERGENCY SERVICES

STATION #1 457Y WT-34
801 Bee Creek Rd Briarcliff *78669*

STATION #2 487W WS-31
22404 State Hwy 71 W Travis Co *78669*

STATION #3 426Y WR-37
311 N Paleface Ranch Rd Travis Co *78669*

PFLUGERVILLE FD

STATION #1 438W MQ-37
203 E Pecan St Pflugerville *78660*

STATION #2 436Q MM-38
15300 Bratton Ln Travis Co *78728*

STATION #3 438D MR-39
2301 Kelly Ln Pflugerville *78660*

STATION #4 437D MP-39
911 Pflugerville Loop Pflugerville *78660*

ROUND ROCK FD

CENTRAL STATION 376G MM-45
203 Commerce Blvd Round Rock *78664*

STATION #2 406C MM-42
200 W Bagdad Ave Round Rock *78664*

STATION #3 406L MM-41
1991 Rawhide Dr Round Rock *78681*

STATION #4 407H MP-42
3300 Gattis School Rd Round Rock *78664*

STATION #5 406A ML-42
350 Deep Wood Dr Round Rock *78681*

STATION #6 377Q MP-44
2919 Joe DiMaggio Blvd Round Rock *78664*

STATION #7 346Q MM-47
2811 Oakmont Dr Round Rock *78664*

SAM BASS FD

STATION #1 375T MJ-43
1001 Great Oaks Dr Williamson Co *78681*

STATION #2 405K MJ-41
16248 Great Oaks Dr Williamson Co *78681*

TAYLOR FD

CENTRAL STATION 353E EA-48
200 Washburn St Taylor *76574*

NORTHWEST STATION 322T MY-49
905 NW Carlos G Parker Blvd Taylor *76574*

VICTORIA ST STATION 352D MZ-48
910 Victoria St Taylor *76574*

TRAVIS CO FIRE & RESCUE

STATION #1 707Z MP-10
9019 Elroy Rd Travis Co *78617*

STATION #2 735X MJ-7
FM Rd 1625 Creedmoor *78610*

VOLENTE VFD

VOLENTE FIRE STATION 461B MA-36
15406 FM Rd 2769 Village of Volente *78641*

WEIR FD

STATION 1 258D MR-57
450 N FM Rd 1105 Weir *78626*

WESTLAKE FD

STATION 1 583D MF-24
1109 Westlake Dr West Lake Hills *78746*

STATION 2 583P ME-23
1295 S Capital of Texas Hwy West Lake Hills *78746*

STATION 3 584N MG-23
403 Nixon Dr Rollingwood *78746*

WESTLAKES 583L MF-23
3636 Bee Cave Rd West Lake Hills *78746*

Golf Courses and Country Clubs

AUSTIN COUNTRY CLUB (PVT) *Travis Co*	523V	MF-28
BALCONES COUNTRY CLUB (PVT) *Austin*	433Y	MF-37
BAR-K GOLF COURSE *Lago Vista*	399T	WW-40
BARTON CREEK COUNTRY CLUB *Travis Co*	582F	MC-24
BERRY CREEK COUNTRY CLUB (PVT) *Georgetown*	226M	MM-59
BLACKHAWK GOLF CLUB *Pflugerville*	439A	MS-39
BLUEBONNET HILL GOLF COURSE *Travis Co*	558E	MQ-27
BUTLER PARK PITCH AND PUTT *Austin*	584Z	MH-22
CIMARRON HILLS GOLF COURSE *Williamson Co*	283D	MF-54
CIRCLE C GOLF COURSE *Travis Co*	671E	MA-15
COLOVISTA COUNTRY CLUB *Bastrop Co*	776Y	EH-4
CRYSTAL FALLS GOLF COURSE *Leander*	371H	MB-45
FALCONHEAD GOLF CLUB *Travis Co*	549H	WX-27
FAZIO CANYONS AT BARTON CREEK *Travis Co*	581R	MB-23
FLINT ROCK AT HURST CREEK GOLF COURSE *Lakeway*	519X	WW-28
FOREST CREEK GOLF COURSE *Round Rock*	378Y	MR-43
GEORGETOWN COUNTRY CLUB (PVT) *Georgetown*	286A	ML-54
GOLF CLUB AT AVERY RANCH, THE *Austin*	404C	MH-42
GOLF CLUB STAR RANCH, THE *Williamson Co*	409A	MS-42
GREAT HILLS GOLF COURSE (PVT) *Austin*	464Y	MH-34
HANCOCK GOLF COURSE *Austin*	555Y	MK-25
HIGHLAND LAKES COUNTRY CLUB *Lago Vista*	458H	WV-36
HILLS OF LAKEWAY GOLF COURSE (PVT) *Village of the Hills*	519K	WW-29
JIMMY CLAY GOLF COURSE *Austin*	675C	MK-15
KURTH-LANDRUM GOLF COURSE *Georgetown*	287E	MN-54
LAGO VISTA COUNTRY CLUB (PVT) *Lago Vista*	428V	WV-37
LAKECLIFF ON LAKE TRAVIS GOLF COURSE *Travis Co*	427K	WS-38
LEGACY HILLS GOLF CLUB *Georgetown*	225H	MK-60
LIONS MUNICIPAL GOLF COURSE *Austin*	584F	MG-24
LIVE OAK GOLF COURSE (PVT) *Lakeway*	489X	WW-31
LOST CREEK COUNTRY CLUB *Travis Co*	582K	MC-23
LOST PINES GOLF COURSE *Bastrop*	746E	EG-9
MARSHALL RANCH GOLF COURSE (PVT) *Lago Vista*	429Z	WX-37
MORRIS WILLIAMS GOLF COURSE *Austin*	586F	ML-24
MUSTANG CREEK GOLF COURSE *Taylor*	353N	EA-47
ONION CREEK CLUB (PVT) *Travis Co*	704J	MG-11
PALMER LAKESIDE - BARTON CREEK *Travis Co*	426G	WR-39
PEDERNALES COUNTRY CLUB *Briarcliff*	487D	WT-33
PINE FOREST GOLF COURSE *Bastrop Co*	776N	EG-5
POINT VENTURE GOLF COURSE *Point Venture*	488M	WV-32
POLO COUNTRY CLUB *Hays Co*	638Q	WV-17
RIVER PLACE GOLF COURSE *Travis Co*	492X	MC-31
RIVERSIDE GOLF COURSE *Austin*	616S	ML-19
ROY KIZER GOLF COURSE *Austin*	675K	MJ-14
SHADOW GLEN GOLF CLUB *Manor*	529L	MT-29
SPANISH OAKS GOLF CLUB *Travis Co*	550X	WY-25
TERAVISTA GOLF COURSE *Williamson Co*	346D	MM-48

TWIN CREEKS COUNTRY CLUB *Travis Co*		432B	MC-39
UNIVERSITY OF TEXAS GOLF CLUB *Travis Co*		521G	MB-30
WHITE WING GOLF CLUB *Georgetown*		195Y	MK-61
WOLFDANCER GOLF CLUB *Bastrop Co*		711D	MX-12
YAUPON GOLF COURSE (PVT) *Lakeway*		519D	WX-30

Hospitals

AUSTIN DIAGNOSTIC MEDICAL CENTER	12221 N Mopac Expwy Austin 78758	466S	ML-34
CEDAR PARK REGIONAL MEDICAL CENTER	1401 Medical Pkwy Cedar Park 78613	373F	ME-45
DELL CHILDREN'S MEDICAL CENTER OF CENTRAL TEXAS	4900 Mueller Blvd Austin 78723	556S	ML-25
HEART HOSPITAL OF AUSTIN	3801 N Lamar Blvd Austin 78756	555S	MJ-25
JOHNS COMMUNITY HOSPITAL	305 Mallard Ln Taylor 76574	323N	EA-50
LAKESIDE HOSPITAL AT BASTROP	3201 HWY 71 E Bastrop 78602	745R	EF-8
ST. DAVID'S GEORGETOWN HOSPITAL	2000 Scenic Dr Georgetown 78626	286T	ML-52
ST. DAVID'S MEDICAL CENTER	919 E 32nd St Austin 78705	585G	MK-24
ST. DAVID'S NORTH AUSTIN MEDICAL CENTER	12221 N Mopac Expwy Austin 78758	466S	ML-34
ST. DAVID'S ROUND ROCK MEDICAL CENTER	2400 Round Rock Ave Round Rock 78681	375Z	MK-43
ST. DAVID'S SOUTH AUSTIN HOSPITAL	901 W Ben White Blvd Austin 78704	644B	MG-18
SCOTT & WHITE UNIVERSITY MEDICAL CAMPUS	300 University Blvd Round Rock 78664	346L	MM-47
SETON MEDICAL CENTER	1201 W 38th St Austin 78705	555S	MJ-25
SETON MEDICAL CENTER WILLIAMSON	201 Seton Pkwy Round Rock 78665	347F	MN-48
SETON NORTHWEST	11113 Research Blvd Austin 78759	465W	MJ-34
SETON SHOAL CREEK HOSPITAL	3501 Mills Ave Austin 78731	555S	MJ-25
SETON SOUTHWEST HEALTHCARE CENTER	7900 FM Rd 1826 Austin 78737	641C	MB-18
UNIVERSITY MEDICAL CENTER AT BRACKENRIDGE	601 E 15th St Austin 78701	585P	MJ-23

Libraries

A. FRANK SMITH, JR. LIBRARY CENTER	1001 E University Ave (Georgetown) 78626	287J	MN-53
AUSTIN HISTORY CENTER	810 Guadalupe Rd (Austin) 78701	585S	MJ-22
BASIL ANTHONY MOREAU MEMORIAL LIBRARY	303 N Main Rd (Buda) 78610	762D	MD-6
BASTROP PUBLIC LIBRARY	1100 Church Rd (Bastrop) 78602	745F	EE-9
BEE CAVE PUBLIC LIBRARY	13333-A W State Hwy 71 (Bee Cave) 78783	550T	WY-25
CARVER BRANCH LIBRARY	1161 Angelina St (Austin) 78702	585U	MK-22
CEDAR PARK LIBRARY	550 Discovery Blvd (Cedar Park) 78613	373S	ME-43
CEPEDA BRANCH LIBRARY	651 N Pleasant Valley Rd (Austin) 78702	615D	MK-21
DRIPPING SPRINGS COMMUNITY LIBRARY	501 Sportsplex Dr (Dripping Springs) 78620	636Y	WR-16
ELGIN PUBLIC LIBRARY	404 N Main Rd (Elgin) 78621	534J	EC-29
FAULK CENTRAL LIBRARY	800 Guadalupe St (Austin) 78701	585S	MJ-22
GEORGETOWN PUBLIC LIBRARY	402 W 8th St 78626	286L	MM-53
HAMPTON BRANCH AT OAK HILL	5125 Convict Hill Rd (Austin) 78749	642F	MC-18
HARRY RANSOM CNTR	Guadalupe St (Austin) 78705	585J	MJ-23
HOWSON BRANCH LIBRARY	2500 Exposition Blvd (Austin) 78703	554Y	MH-25
HUTTO PUBLIC LIBRARY	205 West St (Hutto) 78634	349Z	MT-46
JONESTOWN LIBRARY	18649 RM Rd 1431 78645	400M	WZ-41
LAGO VISTA COMMUNITY LIBRARY	5803 Thunderbird (Lago Vista) 78645	429P	WW-38
LAKE TRAVIS COMMUNITY LIBRARY	2300 Lohmans Spur, Ste 100 78738	519U	WX-27
LBJ LIBRARY	2313 Red River St (Austin) 78705	585F	MJ-24
LEANDER PUBLIC LIBRARY	1011 S Bagdad Rd (Leander) 78641	342P	MC-47
LITTLE WALNUT CREEK BRANCH LIBRARY	835 W Rundberg Ln (Austin) 78758	526A	ML-30
LORENZO DE ZAVALA STATE ARCHIVES/LIBRARY	W 14th St (Austin) 78701	585N	MJ-23
MANCHACA ROAD BRANCH LIBRARY	5500 Manchaca Rd (Manchaca) 78745	643H	MF-18
MANOR PUBLIC LIBRARY	601 W Carrie Manor Rd (Manor) 78653	529T	MS-28
MILWOOD BRANCH LIBRARY	12500 Amherst Dr (Austin) 78727	465M	MK-35
NORTH VILLAGE BRANCH LIBRARY	2139 W Anderson Ln (Austin) 78757	525K	MJ-29
OAK SPRINGS BRANCH LIBRARY	3101 Oak Springs Dr (Austin) 78702	586S	ML-22
OLD QUARRY BRANCH LIBRARY	7051 Village Center Dr (Austin) 78731	524M	MH-29
PFLUGERVILLE COMMUNITY LIBRARY	102 10th St (Pflugerville) 78660	437Z	MP-37
PLEASANT HILL BRANCH LIBRARY	211 E William Cannon Dr (Austin) 78745	644X	MG-16
ROUND ROCK LIBRARY	216 E Main Ave (Round Rock) 78664	376Y	MM-43
RUIZ BRANCH LIBRARY	1600 Grove Blvd (Austin) 78741	616W	ML-19
ST. JOHN BRANCH LIBRARY	7500 Blessing Ave (Austin) 78752	526X	ML-28
SOUTHEAST AUSTIN COMMUNITY BRANCH LIBRARY	5803 Nuckols Crossing Rd (Austin) 78744	675A	MJ-15
SPICEWOOD SPRINGS BRANCH LIBRARY	8637 Spicewood Springs Rd (Austin) 78759	464B	MG-36
TAYLOR PUBLIC LIBRARY	801 Vance St 76574	353A	EA-48
TERRAZAS BRANCH LIBRARY	1105 E Cesar Chavez St (Austin) 78702	615B	MJ-21
TWIN OAKS BRANCH LIBRARY	2301 S Congress Ave (Austin) 78704	614R	MH-20
UNIVERSITY HILLS BRANCH LIBRARY	4721 Loyola Ln (Austin) 78723	557N	MN-26
WESTBANK COMMUNITY LIBRARY	1309 Westbank Dr (West Lake Hills) 78746	583Q	MF-23
WINDSOR PARK BRANCH LIBRARY	5833 Westminster Dr (Austin) 78723	556P	ML-26
YARBOROUGH BRANCH LIBRARY	2200 Hancock Dr (Austin) 78756	555E	MJ-27

Major Office Buildings

3M	6801 River Place Blvd 78730	492H	MD-33
6TH & LAMAR	501 N Lamar Blvd 78703	584V	MH-22
100 CONGRESS	100 Congress Ave 78701	585W	MJ-22
300 W 6TH ST	300 W 6th St 78701	585S	MJ-22
301 CONGRESS AVE	301 Congress Ave 78701	585W	MJ-22
301 SUNDANCE PKWY	301 Sundance Pkwy 78681	406U	MM-40
816 CONGRESS	816 Congress Ave 78701	585S	MJ-22
1005 CONGRESS OFFICE BLDG	1005 Congress Ave 78701	585S	MJ-22
3307 NORTHLAND BLDG	3307 Northland Dr 78731	524Z	MH-28
8100 CAMERON	8100 Cameron Rd 78753	526Y	MM-28
8303 N MOPAC EXPWY	8303 N Mopac Expy 78759	495W	MJ-31
9500 ARBORETUM BLVD	9500 Arboretum Blvd 78759	494H	MH-33
ABBOTT LABORATORIES	3900 Howard Ln 78723	436W	ML-37
ADVANCED MICRO DEVICES	5204 E Ben White Blvd 78741	645L	MK-17
AMBER OAKS	9301 Amberglen Blvd 78729	434B	MG-39
ARBORETUM PLAZA I & II	9442 N Capital of Texas Hwy 78759	495J	MJ-32
ATRIUM OFFICE CENTRE	8701 Mopac Expy 78759	495T	MJ-31
AUSTIN CENTRE	701 Brazos St 78701	585S	MJ-22
AVALON I - IV	10415 Morado Cir 78759	494D	MH-33
BALCONES OFFICE PARK	3303 Northland Dr 78731	524Z	MH-28
BARTON CREEK PLAZA I - III	3755 S Capital Of Texas Hwy 78704	613R	MF-20
BARTON OAKS PLAZA I - V	901 S Mopac Expwy 78746	584W	MG-22
BARTON SKYWAY I-IV	1301 S Mopac Expy 78746	614A	MG-21
BERGSTROM TECHNOLOGY CENTER	6800 Burleson Rd 78744	646S	ML-16
BRAKER CENTER	2100 Kramer Ln 78758	495M	MK-32
BRAZOS PLACE	800 Brazos 78701	585S	MJ-22
BRIDGEPOINT PLAZA	5914 West Courtyard Dr 78730	523M	MF-29
BRIDGEPOINT SQUARE	6300 Bridge Point Pkwy 78730	523M	MF-29
CAPITAL VIEW CENTER	1301 S Capital Of Texas Hwy 78746	583P	ME-23
CAPITOL CENTER	919 Congress Ave 78701	585S	MJ-22
CAPITOL TOWER	206 E 9th St 78701	585T	MJ-22
CARBO MEDICS INC	1300 E Anderson Ln 78752	526X	ML-28
CENTENNIAL TOWERS	505 E Huntland Dr 78752	555D	MK-27
CHASE BANK TOWER	700 Lavaca 78701	585S	MJ-22
CHASE NORTHCROSS	7600 Burnet Rd 78757	525K	MJ-29
CHASE PARK OFFICE CENTER	7600 Chevy Chase 78752	526S	ML-28
CHASE TOWER	221 W Sixth St 78701	585S	MJ-22
CIELO CENTER	1250 S Capital Of Texas Hwy 78746	583K	ME-23
COMPUADD COMPUTER CORP	12303 Technology Blvd 78727	464D	MH-36
DELL COMPUTER CORP	9505 Arboretum Blvd 78759	494H	MH-33
DOMAIN	11400 Burnet Rd 78758	495C	MK-33
ECHELON, THE	9430 Research Blvd 78759	495J	MJ-32
ESCALADE, THE	4301 Westbank Dr 78746	583P	ME-23
EXCHANGE PARK	7800 Shoal Creek Blvd 78757	525E	MJ-30
FISHER CONTROL INTERNATIONAL INC	8301 Cameron Rd 78753	526U	MM-28
FROST BANK TOWER	401 Congress Ave 78701	585W	MJ-22
GREAT HILLS CORPORATE CENTER	9020-I Capital Of Texas Hwy N 78759	494M	MH-32
GREAT HILLS PLAZA	9600 Great Hills Trl 78759	494H	MH-33
GREYSTONE PLAZA	7200 N Mopac Expy 78731	525E	MJ-30
HARTLAND PLAZA	1717 W 6th St 78703	584Q	MH-23
HEWLETT-PACKARD	14321 Tandem Blvd 78728	436T	ML-37
IBM	11500 Burnet Rd 73758	495C	MK-33
JEFFERSON BLDG	1600 W 38th St 78731	555S	MJ-25
LAKEVIEW PLAZA	4516 Seton Center Pkwy 78759	495A	MJ-33
LAKEWOOD ON THE PARK	7600 N Capital of Texas Hwy 78731	494S	MG-31
LAS CIMAS OFFICE PARK	807 Las Cimas Pkwy 78746	583E	ME-24
LITTLEFIELD CONGRESS CENTER	106 E 6th St 78701	585S	MJ-22
MCC	3500 W Balcones Center Dr 78759	495F	MJ-33
MEDICAL OAKS PAVILION	12201 Renfert Way 78758	466S	ML-34
MET CENTER	7901 E Riverside Dr 78744	646F	ML-18
MILLENNIUM, THE	6504 Bridge Point Pkwy 78730	523L	MF-29
MOTOROLA INC	3501 Ed Bluestein Blvd 78721	586V	MM-22
NORTH LAMAR OFFICE PARK	7701 N Lamar 78752	525R	MK-29
NORTHPOINT CENTER I & II	6850 Austin Center Blvd 78731	524M	MH-29
NORTHVIEW BUSINESS CENTER	9001 N IH-35 78753	526F	ML-30
NORWOOD TOWER	114 W 7th St 78701	585S	MJ-22
OLD TOWN SQUARE	1 Chisholm Trl 78681	376T	ML-43
ONE AMERICAN CENTER	600 Congress Ave 78701	585S	MJ-22
ONE CONGRESS PLAZA	111 Congress Ave 78701	585W	MJ-22
ONE TEXAS CENTER	505 Barton Springs Rd 78704	615A	MJ-21
OVERWATCH CAMPUS	5301 Southwest Pkwy 78735	612R	MD-20
PARK 22	8601 RM Rd 2222 78730	493P	ME-32
PARK NORTH	8200 N Mopac Expy 78759	495W	MJ-31
PARKWAY AT OAK HILL	4801 Southwest Pkwy 78735	612R	MD-20
PARMER BUSINESS PARK	5300 Riata Park Ct 78727	465B	MJ-36
PAVILIONS AT TECH RIDGE, THE	E Parmer Ln @ McCallen Pass 78753	467W	MN-34
PERRY BROOKS BLDG	720 Brazos 78701	585S	MJ-22
PLAZA ON THE LAKE	5000 Plaza On The Lake 78746	523R	MF-29
PROMINENT POINTE OFFICE BLDG	8310 N Capital Of Texas Hwy 78759	494Q	MH-32
QUARRY LAKE BUSINESS CENTER	4515 Seton Center Pkwy 78759	495A	MJ-33
RESEARCH PARK PLACE I & II	12515 Research Blvd 78759	464H	MH-36
RESEARCH PARK PLAZA	12401 Research Blvd 78759	464H	MH-36
RESERVE AT BULL CREEK	7501 N Capital of Texas Hwy 78731	494S	MG-31
REUNION PARK	8501 N Mopac Expwy 78759	495W	MJ-31
RIATA GATEWAY	12007 Research Blvd 78759	464M	MH-35
SAN JACINTO CENTER	96 San Jacinto Bld 78701	585W	MJ-22
SCARBROUGH OFFICE BLDG	101 W 6th St 78701	585W	MJ-22
SEMATECH	2706 Montopolis Dr 78741	645H	MK-18
SETON MEDICAL PARK TOWER	1301 W 38th St 78705	555S	MJ-25
SOUTHFIELD OFFICE BLDG	4000 S IH 35 78704	644H	MH-18
SOUTHWEST TOWER BLDG	211 E 7th St 78701	585S	MJ-22
STONEBRIDGE PLAZA I & II	9606 N Mopac Expy 78759	495K	MJ-32
STRATUM EXECUTIVE CENTER	11044 Research Blvd 78759	465W	MJ-34
SUMMIT, THE	Hesters Crossing Rd @ La Frontera Blvd 78681	406Q	MM-41
TELLABS TEXAS INC	601 Jeffrey Way 78664	376B	ML-45
TEXAS INSTRUMENTS	12501 Research Blvd 78759	464H	MH-36
TRACOR INC	6500 Tracor Ln 78725	587N	MN-23
TRAVIS OAKS	5113 Southwest Pkwy 78735	612R	MD-20
TWIN TOWERS	1106 Clayton Ln 78723	556J	ML-26
UNIVERSITY BUSINESS CENTER	3019 Alvin Devane 78741	645G	MK-18
VISTA RIDGE	912 S Capital of Texas Hwy 78746	583E	ME-24
WELLS FARGO BANK BLDG	2028 E Ben White Blvd 78741	645E	MJ-18
WELLS FARGO BANK TOWER	400 W 15th St 78701	585N	MJ-23
WESTECH 360	8911 N Capital of Texas Hwy 78759	494M	MH-32
WESTGATE BLDG	1122 Colorado 78701	585N	MJ-23
WILD BASIN I & II	108 S Wild Basin Rd 78746	553S	ME-25

Malls and Shopping Centers

1890 RANCH 373K ME-44
E Whitestone Blvd & US Hwy 183A Cedar Park 78613
ANDERSON MILL SHOPPING CENTER 433M MF-38
13780 Research Blvd Austin 78750
ANDERSON SQUARE SHOPPING CENTER 525M MK-29
8002 Research Blvd Austin 78758
ARBORETUM AT GREAT HILLS 495E MJ-33
10000 Research Blvd Austin 78759
ARBORETUM MARKET 494H MH-33
9722 Great Hills Trl Austin 78759
BALCONES WOODS SHOPPING CENTER 465W MJ-34
11150 Research Blvd Austin 78759
BARTON CREEK SQUARE MALL 613C MF-21
2901 Capital of Texas Hwy Austin 78746
BARTON RIDGE SHOPPING CENTER 613V MF-19
4544 S Lamar Blvd Austin 78745
BOARDWALK SHOPPING CENTER 406V MM-40
2701 S IH-35 Round Rock 78664
BRODIE OAKS SHOPPING CENTER 613V MF-19
4141 S Capital Of Texas Austin 78704
CAPITAL PLAZA SHOPPING CENTER 556J ML-26
5400 N IH 35 Austin 78723
CENTRAL PARK SHOPPING CENTER 555S MJ-25
4001 N Lamar Blvd Austin 78756
CENTURY SOUTH SHOPPING CENTER 674B MG-15
701 E William Cannon Dr Austin 78745
DOBIE MALL 585J MJ-23
2021 Guadalupe St Austin 78705
DOMAIN, THE 495C MK-33
11410 Century Oaks Terrace Austin 78758
ESCARPMENT VILLAGE 641V MB-16
Escarpment Blvd @ W Slaughter Ln Austin 78749
GATEWAY MARKET AND COURTYARD 495J MJ-32
9607 Research Blvd Austin 78759
GATEWAY SQUARE 495J MJ-32
9503 Research Blvd Austin 78759
GREAT HILLS MARKET 495E MJ-33
9828 Great Hills Trail Austin 78759
GREAT HILLS STATION 495E MJ-33
10225 Research Blvd Austin 78759
GREENLAWN CROSSING SHOPPING CENTER 407P MN-41
603 Louis Henna Blvd Round Rock 78664
HANCOCK CENTER 555Y MK-25
1000 E 41st Austin 78751
HIGHLAND MALL 555D MK-27
6001 Airport Blvd Austin 78752
HILL COUNTRY GALLERIA 550P WY-26
Galleria Pkwy Bee Cave 78738
HOMESTEAD, THE 403Z MF-40
14010 US Hwy 183 Austin 78613
LA FRONTERA VILLAGE 406Q MM-40
Sundance Pkwy & Parker Dr Round Rock 78681
LAKE CREEK FESTIVAL 433H MF-39
13729 Research Blvd Austin 78750
LAKEHILLS PLAZA 613V MF-19
4211 S Lamar Blvd Austin 78704
LAKELINE MALL 433C MF-39
11200 Lakeline Mall Dr Austin 78613
LAKELINE PLAZA 433D MF-39
11066 Pecan Park Blvd Austin 78613
LAMAR OAKS 613V MF-19
4001 S Lamar Blvd Austin 78704
LAMAR PLAZA SHOPPING CENTER 614G MH-21
1120 S Lamar Blvd Austin 78704
MARKET AT PARMER LN, THE 466N ML-35
2501 Parmer Ln Austin 78727
MARKET AT ROUND ROCK, THE 406M MM-41
110 N IH 35 Round Rock 78681
MARKET AT WELLS BRANCH, THE 436X ML-37
13717 Burnet Rd Austin 78727
McNEIL CROSSING 435W MJ-37
6001 W Parmer Ln Austin 78727
NORTHCROSS MALL 525F MJ-30
2525 W Anderson Ln Austin 78757
NORTHFORK PLAZA SHOPPING CENTER 433D MF-39
13945 N Hwy 183 Austin 78613
NORTH HILLS TOWN CENTER 465S MJ-34
1131 N Hwy 183 Austin 78759
NORTH PARK SHOPPING CENTER 526B ML-30
9616 N Lamar Blvd Austin 78753
NORTH STAR HOME CENTER 525K MJ-29
7719 Burnet Rd Austin 78757
NORTH VILLAGE CENTER 525K MJ-29
2103 W Anderson Ln Austin 78757
PARKLINE SHOPPING CENTER 403V MF-40
11301 Lakeline Blvd Austin 78717
RENAISSANCE SQUARE 406L MM-41
1601 S IH-35 Round Rock 78664
RIVERY TOWNE CROSSING 286B ML-54
1103 Rivery Blvd Georgetown 78628
ROUND ROCK CROSSING 406V MM-40
117 Louis Henna Blvd Round Rock 78664
ROUND ROCK PREMIUM OUTLETS 346K ML-47
4401 N IH 35 Round Rock 78664
ROUND ROCK TOWN CENTRE 407K MN-41
2051 Gattis School Rd Round Rock 78664
ROUND ROCK WEST SHOPPING CENTER 376T ML-43
1100 N IH 35 Round Rock 78681
SHOPS AT ARBOR WALK, THE 495F MJ-33
N Mopac Expwy Austin 78759
SHOPS AT THE GALLERIA 550T WY-25
W State Hwy 71 Bee Cave 78738
SOUTHPARK MEADOWS 674S MG-13
S IH 35 & W Slaughter Ln Austin 78748
SOUTHRIDGE PLAZA 524Z MH-28
502 W William Cannon Dr Austin 78745
SOUTH TOWNE SQUARE 613T ME-19
4970 W Hwy 290 Austin 78735
SPRINGDALE SHOPPING CENTER 557J MN-26
7112 Ed Bluestein Blvd Austin 78723
SUNSET VALLEY MARKETFAIR 613X ME-19
5400 Brodie Ln Austin 78745
SUNSET VALLEY VILLAGE 613X ME-19
5601 Brodie Ln Austin 78745
TANGLEWOOD VILLAGE SHOPPING CENTER 673J ME-14
2110 W Slaughter Ln Austin 78748
TOWN & COUNTRY MALL 406V MM-40
2800 S IH 35 Round Rock 78681
TWIN OAKS SHOPPING CENTER 614M MH-20
1902 S Congress Ave Austin 78704
UNIVERSITY OAKS SHOPPING CENTER 346P ML-47
N IH-35 & University Blvd Round Rock 78665
VILLAGE AT WESTLAKE, THE 583A ME-24
Bee Cave Rd & Loop 360 West Lake Hills 78746
VILLAGE SHOPPING CENTER, THE 525F MJ-30
2700 W Anderson Ln Austin 78757
VISTA RIDGE SHOPPING CENTER 519V WX-28
2303 S RM Rd 620 Lakeway 78734
WALDEN PARK SHOPPING CENTER 403Z MF-40
10900 Lakeline Mall Dr Austin 78717
WEST ANDERSON PLAZA 525F MJ-30
2438 W Anderson Ln Austin 78757
WESTBANK MARKET 583R MF-23
3300 Bee Caves Rd West Lake Hills 78746
WESTGATE SHOPPING CENTER 613Z MF-19
4477 S Lamar Blvd Austin 78745
WESTWOODS SHOPPING CENTER 583R MF-23
3215 Bee Caves Rd Austin 78746
WOLF RANCH TOWN CENTER 286K ML-53
IH 35 & State Hwy 29 Georgetown 78628

Marinas

ANDERSON MILL MARINA *Travis Co* 461D MB-36
AUSTIN YACHT CLUB *Travis Co* 460M WZ-35
BRIARCLIFF MARINA *Briarcliff* 457R WT-35
COMMANDER'S POINT YACHT BASIN *Travis Co* 491A MA-33
CYPRESS CREEK MARINA *Travis Co* 461D MB-36
DODD STREET DOCKS *Volente* 431S MA-37
EAGLE RIDGE MARINA *Travis Co* 460B WY-36
EASY STREET MARINA *Jonestown* 400V WZ-40
EMERALD POINT MARINA *Travis Co* 460B WY-36
HIGHLAND LAKES MARINA *Volente* 431S MA-37
HURST HARBOR MARINA *Travis Co* 489V WX-31
ISLAND OF LAKE TRAVIS MARINA *Lago Vista* 428Y WV-37
KELLER MARINA *Travis Co* 460M WZ-35
LAGO VISTA MARINA *Lago Vista* 429E WW-39
LAKE TRAVIS LODGES *Travis Co* 460H WZ-36
LAKEWAY MARINA *Lakeway* 489T WW-31
MARSHALL FORD MARINA *Travis Co* 491H MB-33
PARADISE COVE MARINA *Travis Co* 460K WY-35
POINT VENTURE MARINA *Point Venture* 489N WW-32
RIVIERA MARINA *Travis Co* 461H MB-36
ROCK MARINA *Travis Co* 460S WY-34
SIESTA SHORES *Travis Co* 488L WV-32
VOLENTE BEACH CLUB *Travis Co* 431W MA-37
YACHT HARBOR MARINA *Travis Co* 489R WX-32

Museums

ALMA THOMAS FINE ARTS CENTER 287J MN-53
E University Ave 78626
AUSTIN CHILDREN'S MUSEUM 585W MJ-22
201 Colorado St 78701
AUSTIN MUSEUM OF ART AT LAGUNA GLORIA 554P MG-26
3809 W 35th St 78703
AUSTIN MUSEUM OF ART-DOWNTOWN 585S MJ-22
823 Congress Ave 78701
BLANTON MUSEUM OF ART, THE 585K MJ-23
MLK at Congress Ave 78701
BOB BULLOCK TEXAS STATE HISTORY MUSEUM 585K MJ-23
1800 N Congress Ave 78701
ELISABET NEY MUSEUM 555U MK-25
304 E 44th St 78751
FRENCH LEGATION MUSEUM 585X MJ-22
802 San Marcos 78702
GEORGE WASHINGTON CARVER MUSEUM 585U MK-22
1165 Angelina St 78702
MAYFIELD HOUSE AND PRESERVE 554Q MH-26
Old Bull Creek Rd 78703
MOODY MUSEUM 353A EA-48
114 W 9th St 76574
NEILL-COCHRAN HOUSE MUSEUM 585E MJ-24
2310 San Gabriel St 78705
O. HENRY MUSEUM 585X MJ-22
409 E 5th St 78701
OLD BAKERY AND EMPORIUM 585S MJ-22
1006 Congress Ave 78701
TEXAS MEMORIAL MUSEUM 585F MJ-24
2400 Trinity St 78705
TEXAS MILITARY FORCES MUSEUM 554Q MH-26
2200 W 35th St 78731
UMLAUF SCULPTURE GARDEN 584Y MH-22
605 Robert E Lee Rd 78704
WILLIAMSON COUNTY HISTORICAL MUSEUM 286G MM-54
716 S Austin Ave 78626

Parks

84 LUMBER PARK *Georgetown* 286Z MM-52
ADAMS-HEMPHILL PARK *Austin* 585B MJ-24
ALAMO PARK AND RECREATION CENTER *Austin* 585L MK-23
ALLEN PARK *Austin* 524V MH-28
ANDERSON MILL PARK *Williamson Co* 433L MF-38
ANDREWS PLAYGROUND *Austin* 556L MM-26
ARKANSAS BEND PARK *Travis Co* 490A WY-33
ARMADILLO PARK *Austin* 644S MG-16
AUDITORIUM SHORES *Austin* 584Z MH-22
AUSTIN'S COLONY PARK *Travis Co* 618Z MR-19
BAGDAD PARK *Cedar Park* 372R MD-44
BAILEY PARK *Austin* 555W MJ-25
BALCONES DISTRICT PARK *Austin* 465U MK-34
BARK PARK *Georgetown* 286D MM-54
BAR-K RECREATIONAL AREA (PVT) *Lago Vista* 429A WW-39
BARRINGTON PLAYGROUND *Austin* 526B ML-30
BARROW PRESERVE *Austin* 494Y MH-31
BARTHOLOMEW DISTRICT PARKS *Austin* 556T ML-25
BARTON CREEK GREENBELT EAST *Austin* 613M MF-20
BARTON CREEK GREENBELT EAST *Austin* 614A MG-21
BARTON CREEK GREENBELT WEST *Austin* 583S ME-22
BARTON CREEK GREENBELT WEST *Austin* 613B ME-21
BARTON CREEK WILDERNESS PARK *Austin* 613A ME-21
BARTON HILLS PLAYGROUND *Austin* 614E MG-21
BASTROP STATE PARK *Bastrop Co* 746L EH-8
BATHING BEACH PARK *Round Rock* 376T ML-43
BATTLEBEND PARK *Austin* 644L MH-17
BEDFORD PARK *Georgetown* 225Z MK-58
BEE CREEK PRESERVE *Austin* 584A MG-24
BENBROOK ATHLETIC COMPLEX *Leander* 311V MB-49
BEN E FISHER PARK *Travis Co* 529T MS-28
BERRY CREEK PARK *Georgetown* 226U MM-58
BERRY SPRINGS PARK AND PRESERVE *Williamson Co* 227Y MP-58
BEVERLY S. SHEFFIELD NORTHWEST DISTRICT PARK *Austin* 525N MJ-29
BIG STACY PARK *Austin* 615N MJ-20
BIG WALNUT CREEK GREENBELT *Austin* 466W ML-34
BIG WALNUT CREEK GREENBELT *Austin* 496G MM-33
BIG WALNUT CREEK GREENBELT *Austin* 497S MN-31
BIG WALNUT CREEK GREENBELT *Austin* 587X MN-22
BIG WALNUT CREEK GREENBELT *Travis Co* 527E MN-30
BIG WALNUT CREEK GREENBELT *Travis Co* 527X MN-28
BIG WALNUT CREEK PRESERVE *Travis Co* 557P MN-26
BLACK LOCUST PARK *Travis Co* 437G MP-39
BLOWING SINK PRESERVE *Austin* 642Y MD-16
BLUE HOLE PARK *Georgetown* 286C MM-54
BLUNN CREEK GREENBELT *Austin* 615J MJ-20
BLUNN CREEK PRESERVE *Austin* 615S MJ-19
BOB BRYANT PARK *Bastrop* 744D ED-9
BOB WENTZ PARK AT WINDY POINT *Travis Co* 461T MA-34
BOGGY CREEK GREENBELT *Austin* 585V MK-22
BOHLS PARK *Pflugerville* 468B MQ-36
BONITA VISTA PARK *Buda* 762H MD-6
BOWMAN PARK *Round Rock* 376M MM-44
BRADFIELD PARK *Buda* 762D MD-6
BRADFORD PARK *Round Rock* 408E MQ-42
BRENTWOOD PARK *Austin* 525T MJ-28
BROOKHOLLOW PARK *Pflugerville* 438N MQ-38
BRUSH SQUARE *Austin* 585X MJ-22
BRUSHY CREEK GREENBELT *Austin* 374Z MH-43
BRUSHY CREEK GREENBELT *Austin* 404A MG-42
BRUSHY CREEK GREENBELT *Hutto* 379K MS-44
BRUSHY CREEK LAKE PARK *Cedar Park* 404B MG-42
BRUSHY CREEK RECREATION PARK *Cedar Park* 404B MG-42
BUCK EGGER PARK *Round Rock* 406D MM-42
BULL BRANCH PARK *Taylor* 322V MZ-49
BULL CREEK DISTRICT PARK *Austin* 494W MG-31
BULL CREEK GREENBELT LOWER *Austin* 494P MG-32
BULL CREEK GREENBELT UPPER *Austin* 464J MG-35
BULL CREEK GREENBELT UPPER *Travis Co* 494F MG-33
BUTLER DISTRICT PARK *Austin* 584Z MH-22
BUTLER SHORES *Austin* 584Y MH-22
BUTTERCUP CREEK CAVE PRESERVE *Cedar Park* 402H MD-42
BUTTERCUP CREEK NATURAL AREA *Cedar Park* 403A ME-42
BUTTERCUP CREEK PARK *Cedar Park* 403A ME-42
BUTTERMILK BRANCH GREENBELT *Austin* 526X ML-28
CAMBRIDGE HEIGHTS PARK *Travis Co* 407X MN-40
CAMBRIDGE HEIGHTS ZOLA PARK *Travis Co* 407X MN-40
CAMP TEXLAKE (PVT) *Travis Co* 428C WV-39
CANYONLANDS PARK *Lakeway* 519N WW-29
CARRIAGE HILLS PARK #1 *Cedar Park* 372P MC-44
CARRIAGE HILLS PARK #2 *Cedar Park* 372P MC-44
CARRIAGE HILLS PARK #3 *Cedar Park* 372U MD-43
CARRIAGE HILLS PARK #5 *Cedar Park* 372K MC-44
CEDAR BREAKS PARK *Williamson Co* 255J MJ-56
CHAMPION PARK *Williamson Co* 374Z MH-43
CHANDLER CROSSING PARK *Round Rock* 376D MM-45
CHANDLER PARK *Georgetown* 256T ML-55
CHATAUQUA PARK *Georgetown* 286G MM-54
CHERRY CREEK PARK *Austin* 672C MD-15
CHESTNUT PARK *Austin* 585R MK-23
CHIMNEY SWIFT PARK *Cedar Park* 433B ME-39
CHISHOLM TRAIL CROSSING PARK *Round Rock* 376X ML-43
CHISHOLM VALLEY PARK *Round Rock* 406G MM-42
CHURCHILL FARMS PARK *Georgetown* 287L MP-53
CIRCLE C RANCH METROPOLITAN PARK *Travis Co* 641V MB-16
CIRKIEL COMMONS GREENBELT *Round-Rock* 377S MN-43
CITY CENTER BUSINESS PARK *Round Rock* 406C MM-42
CITY PARK *Buda* 762D MD-6
CITY PARK *Lakeway* 489V WX-31
CITY PARK *Manor* 529Q MT-29
CIVITAN PARK *Austin* 616T ML-19
CLARKSVILLE PARK *Austin* 584L MH-23
CLAY MADSEN PARK *Round Rock* 407E MN-42
CLUCK CREEK PARK *Cedar Park* 403J ME-41
COLONY PARK *Austin* 557Y MP-25
COLORADO RIVER GREENBELT *Austin* 587X MN-22
COLORADO RIVER PRESERVE *Austin* 616K ML-20
COMAL PARK *Austin* 615C MK-21
COMMONS FORD METROPOLITAN PARK *Austin* 521U MB-28
CONVICT HILL QUARRY *Austin* 612W MC-19
COOK PLAYGROUND *Austin* 496S ML-31
COUNTRY ESTATES PARK *Hutto* 379G MT-45
CREEKBEND GREENBELT *Round Rock* 375L MK-44
CREEKMONT WEST PARK *Round Rock* 406E ML-42
CREEKSIDE PARK *Cedar Park* 402H MD-42
CREEKSIDE PARK *Hutto* 380A MU-45
CREEKSIDE PARK *Pflugerville* 467D MP-36
CREEKSIDE PLAZA PARK *Round Rock* 376X ML-43
CRYSTAL KNOLL PARK *Georgetown* 257J MN-56
CUNNINGHAM PLAYGROUND *Austin* 643L MF-17
CYPRESS BEND PARK *Cedar Park* 402U MD-40
CYPRESS CREEK PARK *Travis Co* 462A MC-36
DAVE REED PARK *Travis Co* 430H WZ-39
DAVIS HILL PARK *Austin* 642Z MD-16
DAVIS/WHITE NORTHEAST *Austin* 557S MN-25
DAYNA LAWSON PARK *Cedar Park* 372U MD-43
DEEPWOOD PARK *Round Rock* 406A ML-42
DEERBROOK PARK *Williamson Co* 433L MF-38
DEER PARK AT MAPLE RUN PARK *Austin* 642P MC-17
DEL VALLE FIELDS *Travis Co* 647U MP-16
DEVINE LAKE PARK *Leander* 311Z MB-49
DICK NICHOLS DISTRICT PARK *Austin* 642K MC-17
DINK PEARSON PARK *Travis Co* 489K WW-32
DITTMAR PARK & REC CENTER *Austin* 673G MF-15
DOTTIE JORDAN PARK & RECREATION CENTER *Austin* 556R MM-26
DOVE SPRINGS DISTRICT PARK *Austin* 675B MJ-15
DOVE SPRINGS PARK *Williamson Co* 287M MP-53
DRAGON PARK *Lakeway* 518D WV-30
DRINKARDS LANDING PARK *Round Rock* 377S MN-43

WALLER CREEK GREENBELT *Austin* ...585T MJ-22
WALNUT CREEK GREENBELT *Austin* ...557W MN-25
WALNUT CREEK GREENBELT *Austin* ...587F MN-24
WALNUT CREEK METROPOLITAN PARK *Austin* ...496C MM-33
WALNUT CREEK SPORTS PARK *Austin* ...557H MP-27
WALSH BOAT LANDING *Austin* ...554W MG-25
WATERLOO PARK *Austin* ...585P MJ-23
WEBBERVILLE PARK *Travis Co* ...651J MW-17
WELLS CREEK GREENBELT *Austin* ...466L MM-35
WELLS POINT PARK *Pflugerville* ...437X MN-37
WEST AUSTIN PARK *Austin* ...584R MH-23
WEST BOULDIN CREEK GREENBELT *Austin* ...614G MH-21
WEST BULL CREEK GREENBELT *Austin* ...493Q MF-32
WEST CAMP PRESERVE *Travis Co* ...515Y WP-28
WESTENFIELD PARK *Austin* ...584G MH-24
WILD BASIN WILDERNESS PRESERVE *Travis Co* ...553P ME-26
WILDROSE PARK *Cedar Park* ...403E ME-42
WILLIAMS DRIVE POOL AND PARK *Georgetown* ...256P ML-56
WILLIAMSON COUNTY REGIONAL PARK *Williamson Co* ...344Q MH-47
WILLIAMSON CREEK GREENBELT CENTRAL *Austin* ...644F MG-18
WILLIAMSON CREEK GREENBELT EAST *Austin* ...644Y MH-16
WILLIAMSON CREEK GREENBELT WEST *Austin* ...642D MD-18
WILLIAMS PLAYGROUND *Austin* ...673H MF-15
WINDMILL RUN PARK *Austin* ...611U MB-19
WINDRIDGE VILLAGE PARK *Georgetown* ...287A MN-54
WINDY TERRACE PARK *Round Rock* ...406M MM-41
WOLF RANCH PARK *Georgetown* ...286P ML-53
WOODLAKE PARK *Georgetown* ...255C MK-57
WOODS PARK *Round Rock* ...376J ML-44
WOOLDRIDGE PLAYGROUND *Austin* ...525D MK-30
WOOLDRIDGE SQUARE *Austin* ...585S MJ-22
WOOTEN PARK *Austin* ...525L MK-29
WUTHRICH PARK *Pflugerville* ...468E MQ-36
YATES PARK *Austin* ...616S ML-19
YETT CREEK PARK *Austin* ...465F MJ-36
ZILKER BOTANICAL GARDENS *Austin* ...584T MG-22
ZILKER METROPOLITAN PARK *Austin* ...584U MH-22
ZILKER NEIGHBORHOOD PARK *Austin* ...614F MG-21

Performing Arts Theatres

CHICAGO HOUSE ...585W MJ-22
607 Trinity St 78701
DOUGHERTY ARTS CENTER ...614D MH-21
1110 Barton Springs Rd 78704
HYDE PARK THEATRE ...555T MJ-25
511 W 43rd St 78751
LONG CENTER FOR THE PERFORMING ARTS ...614D MH-21
701 W Riverside Dr 78704
MARY MOODY NORTHEN THEATRE ...614Z MH-19
Lightsey Rd 78704
PALACE THEATRE, THE ...286L MM-53
810 S Austin Ave 78626
PARAMOUNT THEATRE ...585S MJ-22
713 Congress Ave 78701
PERFORMING ARTS CENTER ...585F MJ-24
E Campus Dr 78705
SAM BASS THEATRE ...376Y MM-43
600 N Lee St 78664
STATE THEATRE COMPANY ...585S MJ-22
719 Congress Ave 78701
VORTEX REPERTORY CO ...585M MK-23
2307 Manor Rd 78722
WAY OFF BROADWAY COMMUNITY PLAYERS THEATRE ...343G MF-48
10960 E Crystal Falls Pkwy 78641
ZACHARY SCOTT THEATRE (ARENA STAGE) ...584Z MH-22
1510 Toomey Rd 78704
ZACHARY SCOTT THEATRE (KLEBURG STAGE) ...584Z MH-22
1421 W Riverside Dr 78704
ZILKER HILLSIDE THEATRE ...584X MG-22
William Barton Dr 78746

Points of Interest

AUSTIN CONVENTION CENTER *Austin* ...585X MJ-22
AUSTIN MUSIC HALL *Austin* ...585W MJ-22
AUSTIN NATURE CENTER *Austin* ...584T MG-22
AUSTIN STATE HOSPITAL *Austin* ...555T MJ-25
BARTON SPRINGS POOL *Austin* ...584Y MH-22
CANYON VISTA POOL *Austin* ...464E MG-36
CEDAR PARK EVENT CENTER *Cedar Park* ...373B ME-45
CHAMBER OF COMMERCE *Georgetown* ...256Z MM-55
DEEP EDDY POOL *Austin* ...584P MG-23
DISCOVERY HALL *Austin* ...585W MJ-22
EMMET SHELTON BRIDGE *Austin* ...584A MG-24
FRANK ERWIN CENTER *Austin* ...585P MJ-23
GOVERNOR'S MANSION *Austin* ...585S MJ-22
HAMILTON POOL *Travis Co* ...515V WP-28
HEALTHCARE REHABILITATION CENTER *Austin* ...673C MF-15
HUMANE SOCIETY *Austin* ...526N MK-29
INNER SPACE CAVERNS *Georgetown* ...316B ML-51
KENNEMER POOL *Austin* ...526E MK-30
KIDDIE ACRES AMUSEMENT PARK *Travis Co* ...435V MK-37
LADY BIRD JOHNSON WILDFLOWER CENTER *Austin* ...672A MC-15
LAKEWAY SKATE PARK *Lakeway* ...519J WW-29
LONGHORN DAM *Austin* ...615H MK-21
MAIN BUILDING & TOWER (UT) *Austin* ...585E MJ-24
MANOR DOWNS *Travis Co* ...529E MS-30
MANSFIELD DAM *Austin* ...491F MA-33
MEXICAN AMERICAN CULTURAL CENTER *Austin* ...615A MJ-21
MICKI KREBSBACH POOL *Round Rock* ...376W ML-43
MURCHISON POOL *Austin* ...524M MH-29
NORTH FORK SAN GABRIEL DAM *Williamson Co* ...255L MK-56
OAKS TREATMENT CENTER, THE *Austin* ...643M MF-17
OUR LADY OF GUADALUPE CONVENT *Austin* ...585Y MK-22
PALMER EVENTS CENTER *Austin* ...614D MH-21
ROCK'N RIVER FAMILY AQUATIC CENTER *Round Rock* ...377M MP-44
RODEO GROUNDS *Taylor* ...352F MY-48
ROUND ROCK, THE *Round Rock* ...376X ML-43
STARNES ISLAND *Travis Co* ...430Z WZ-37
SWIM CENTER *Austin* ...519J WW-29
SYMPHONY SQUARE *Austin* ...585T MJ-22
TERRACE, THE *Austin* ...615E MJ-21
TEXAS BAPTIST CHILDREN'S HOME *Round Rock* ...376Q MM-44
TEXAS DEPARTMENT OF HEALTH *Austin* ...555K MJ-26
TEXAS DEPARTMENT OF MHMR *Austin* ...555P MJ-26
TEXAS DEPARTMENT OF PUBLIC SAFETY *Austin* ...555C MK-27

TEXAS STATE CAPITOL *Austin* ...585N MJ-23
TEXAS UNION *Austin* ...585E MJ-24
TOM MILLER DAM *Austin* ...584A MG-24
TRAVIS COUNTY EXPOSITION CENTER *Austin* ...588A MQ-24
WILLIAMSON COUNTY JUSTICE CENTER *Georgetown* ...286G MM-54

Police Departments

AUSTIN POLICE ACADEMY ...676A ML-15
4800 Shaw Ln Travis Co 78744
AUSTIN POLICE DEPARTMENT EAST SUBSTATION ...616A ML-21
812 Springdale Rd Austin 78702
AUSTIN POLICE DEPARTMENT HEADQUARTERS STATION ...585X MJ-22
715 E 8th Rd Austin 78701
AUSTIN POLICE DEPARTMENT NORTH SUBSTATION ...466P ML-35
12425 Lamplight Village Ave Austin 78758
AUSTIN POLICE DEPARTMENT SOUTH SUBSTATION ...673M MF-14
404 Ralph Ablanedo Dr Austin 78748
BASTROP POLICE DEPARTMENT ...745J EE-8
104 Grady Tuck Ln Bastrop 78602
BEE CAVE POLICE DEPARTMENT ...550T WY-25
13333-A W State Hwy 71 Bee Cave 78738
CEDAR PARK POLICE DEPARTMENT ...373N ME-44
911 Quest Pkwy Cedar Park 78613
ELGIN POLICE DEPARTMENT ...534N EC-29
202 Depot St Elgin 78621
GEORGETOWN POLICE DEPARTMENT ...286L MM-53
809 Martin Luther King St Georgetown 78626
HUTTO POLICE DEPARTMENT ...379D MT-45
401 W Front St Hutto 78634
LAGO VISTA POLICE DEPARTMENT ...399X WA-40
7207 Bar K Ranch Rd Lago Vista 78645
LAKEWAY POLICE DEPARTMENT ...519B WW-30
104 Cross Creek Lakeway 78734
LEANDER POLICE DEPARTMENT ...342G MC-49
705 Leander Dr Leander 78641
MANOR POLICE DEPARTMENT ...529U MT-28
201 E Parsons St Manor 78653
MUSTANG RIDGE POLICE DEPARTMENT ...796B ML-3
12800 S US Hwy 183 Mustang Ridge 78610
PFLUGERVILLE POLICE DEPARTMENT ...438P MQ-38
1611 E Pfennig Ln Pflugerville 78660
ROUND ROCK POLICE DEPARTMENT ...376B MM-43
2701 N May St Round Rock 78665
SUNSET VALLEY POLICE DEPARTMENT ...613Y MF-19
2 Lone Oak Tr Sunset Valley 78745
TAYLOR POLICE DEPARTMENT ...353J EA-47
500 S Main St Taylor 76574

Post Offices

BALCONES STATION ...464M MH-35
11900 Jollyville Rd Austin 78759
BASTROP POST OFFICE ...745F EE-9
1114 Main Rd Bastrop 78602
BLUEBONNET STATION ...496E ML-33
1822 W Braker Ln Austin 78758
BUDA POST OFFICE ...762C MD-6
100 S Main St Buda 78610
CAPITOL STATION ...585P MJ-23
111 E 17th Rd Austin 78711
CEDAR CREEK POST OFFICE ...741W MW-7
1167 W State Hwy 21 Bastrop Co 78612
CEDAR PARK POST OFFICE ...373N ME-44
500 E Whitestone Blvd Cedar Park 78613
CENTRAL PARK POST OFFICE ...555S MJ-25
3507 N Lamar Blvd Austin 78705
CHEVERON POST OFFICE ...640A WY-18
10900 W US Hwy 290 Austin 78737
CHIMNEY CORNERS STATION ...524M MH-29
3575 Far West Blvd Austin 78731
CPL. STEVEN P GILL POST OFFICE ...376T ML-43
797 Sam Bass Rd Round Rock 78681
COUPLAND POST OFFICE ...443L EB-38
13701 S State Hwy 95 Coupland 78615
DEL VALLE STATION ...647P MN-17
2883 E State Hwy 71 Austin 78617
DOWNTOWN STATION ...585S MJ-22
510 Guadalupe St Austin 78701
DRIPPING SPRINGS POST OFFICE ...636Z WR-16
300 W Mercer St Dripping Springs 78620
EAST AUSTIN STATION ...615C MK-21
1914 E 6th St Austin 78702
ELGIN POST OFFICE ...534N EC-29
21 N Avenue C Elgin 78621
GEORGETOWN POST OFFICE ...286L ML-52
2300 Scenic Dr Georgetown 78626
HUTTO POST OFFICE ...349Z MT-46
101 Anthony St Hutto 78634
LAKE TRAVIS STATION ...519V WX-28
2110 S RM Rd 620 Lakeway 78734
LEANDER POST OFFICE ...342G MD-48
801 S US Hwy 183 Leander 78641
MAIN POST OFFICE ...526Z MM-28
8225 Cross Park Dr Austin 78710
MANCHACA POST OFFICE ...703J ME-11
780 W FM Rd 1626 Manchaca 78652
MANOR POST OFFICE ...529U MT-28
109 N Burnet St Manor 78653
McNEIL STATION ...435L MK-38
14005 McNeil Rd Travis Co 78728
MOCKINGBIRD STATION ...643U MF-16
7310 Manchaca Rd Austin 78745
NORTH AUSTIN STATION ...555T MJ-25
4300 Speedway Austin 78751
NORTHCROSS STATION ...525F MJ-30
7700 Northcross Dr Austin 78757
NORTHEAST STATION ...526W MM-28
900 Blackson Ave Austin 78752
NORTH LAKE TRAVIS POST OFFICE ...399Y WA-40
8027 Bronco Ln Lago Vista 78645
NORTH PARK STATION ...466T MM-34
1700 W Parmer Ln Austin 78727
OAK HILL STATION ...612U MD-19
6104 Old Fredericksburg Rd Austin 78749
ROUND ROCK FRONTIER POST OFFICE ...407K MN-41
2250 Double Creek Dr Round Rock 78664

SGT. BYRON W NORWOOD POST OFFICE ...437U MP-37
301 S Heatherwilde Blvd Pflugerville 78660
SGT. HENRY YBARRA III POST OFFICE ...644C MH-18
3903 S Congress Ave Austin 78704
SOUTH AUSTIN STATION ...614L MH-20
1806 S 5th St Austin 78704
SOUTHEAST STATION ...645K MJ-17
4516 Burleson Rd Austin 78744
TAYLOR POST OFFICE ...353E EA-48
202 W 4th St Taylor 76574
TOWN NORTH FINANCE UNIT ...525D MK-30
8557 Research Blvd Austin 78758
UNIVERSITY STATION ...585E MJ-24
West Mall Office Bldg Univ of Texas Austin 78712
WEIR POST OFFICE ...258H MR-57
200 FM Rd 1105 Weir 78626
WEST AUSTIN STATION ...554Y MH-25
2418 Spring Ln Austin 78703
WESTLAKE STATION ...583V MF-22
3201 Bee Caves Rd Austin 78746

Public Schools

Austin ISD

ACES ...614H MH-21
906 W Milton (Becker Elem) 78704
ADMINISTRATION CENTER, CARRUTH ...584V MH-22
1111 W 6th St 78703
ALTERNATIVE LEARNING CENTER ...585V MK-22
901 Neal St 78702
BAKER CENTER ...555T MJ-25
3908 Ave B 78751
LUCY READ PRE-K SCHOOL ...525K MK-29
2608 Richcreek Dr 78757
ROSEDALE ...555J MJ-26
2117 W 49th St 78756

Austin Elementary Schools

ALLAN ...616B ML-21
4900 Gonzales Rd 78702
ALLISON ...616T ML-19
515 Vargas Rd 78741
ANDREWS ...556L MM-26
6801 Northeast Dr 78723
BARANOFF, TIMY ...702C MD-12
12009 Buckingham Gate Rd 78748
BARRINGTON ...526F MK-30
400 Cooper Dr 78753
BARTON HILLS ...614E MG-21
2108 Barton Hills Dr 78704
BECKER ...614H MH-21
906 W Milton St 78704
BLACKSHEAR ...585Y MK-22
1712 E 11th St 78702
BLANTON ...556I ML-25
5408 Westminster Dr 78723
BLAZIER, JOHN C ...674Z MH-13
8601 Vertex Blvd Travis Co 78747
BOONE ...642R MD-17
8101 Croftwood Rd 78749
BRENTWOOD ...525T MJ-28
6700 Arroyo Seco 78757
BROOKE ...616E ML-21
3100 East 4th St 78702
BROWN ...525R MK-29
505 W Anderson Ln 78752
BRYKER WOODS ...554V MH-25
3309 Kerbey Ln 78703
CAMPBELL ...585M MK-23
2613 Rogers Ave 78722
CASEY, BERTHA ...673K ME-14
9400 Texas Oaks Dr 78748
CASIS ...554U MH-25
2710 Exposition Blvd 78703
CLAYTON, NAN ...641W MA-16
7525 La Crosse Ave 78739
COOK, KATHERINE A. ...496S ML-31
1511 Cripple Creek Dr 78758
COWAN ...673A ME-15
2817 Kentish Dr 78748
CUNNINGHAM ...643L MF-17
2200 Berkeley Ave 78745
DAVIS, WILL ...465N MJ-35
5214 Duval Rd 78727
DAWSON ...614U MH-19
3001S 1st St 78704
DOSS, LEONA ...524G MH-30
7005 Northledge 78731
GALINDO, EMMA H. ...614X MG-19
3800 S 2nd St 78704
GOVALLE ...586W ML-22
3601 Govalle Ave 78702
GRAHAM ...496Z MM-31
11211 Tom Adams Dr 78753
GULLETT ...525N MJ-29
6310 Treadwell Blvd 78757
HARRIS, THOMAS G. ...556K ML-26
1711 Wheless Ln 78723
HART ...526T ML-28
8301 Furness Dr 78753
HIGHLAND PARK ...554D MH-27
4900 Fairview Rd 78731
HILL ...495S MJ-31
8601 Tallwood Dr 78759
HOUSTON ...644Z MH-16
5409 Ponciana Dr 78744
JORDAN, BARBARA ...557X MN-25
6711 Johnny Morris Rd 78745
JOSLIN ...614W MG-19
4400 Manchaca Rd 78745
KIKER ...641T MB-16
5913 La Crosse Ave 78739
KOCUREK ...672M MD-14
9800 Curlew Dr 78748

LANGFORD 674G MH-15
2206 Blue Meadow Dr 78744
LEE 585C MK-24
3308 Hampton Rd 78705
LINDER 645B MJ-18
2800 Metcalfe St 78741
MAPLEWOOD 585D MK-24
3808 Maplewood Ave 78722
MATHEWS 584Q MH-23
906 West Lynn St 78703
McBEE 496P ML-32
1001 W Braker Ln 78758
MENCHACA 702M MD-11
12120 Manchaca Rd 78652
METZ 615G MK-21
84 Robert T Martinez Jr St 78702
MILLS 641M MH-17
6201 Davis Ln 78749
NORMAN 586R MM-23
4001 Tannehill Ln 78721
OAK HILL 612T MC-19
6101 Patton Ranch Rd 78735
OAK SPRINGS 586S ML-22
3601 Webberville 78702
ODOM 644N MG-17
1010 Turtle Creek Blvd 78745
ORTEGA 586U MM-22
1135 Garland Ave 78721
OVERTON, VOLMA 557Y MP-25
7201 Colony Loop Dr 78724
PALM 675S MJ-13
7601 Dixie Dr 78744
PATTON 612Y MD-19
6001 Westcreek Dr 78749
PEASE 585N MJ-23
1106 Rio Grande St 78701
PECAN SPRINGS 556V MM-25
3100 Rogge Ln 78723
PEREZ, NICHOLAS 674R MH-14
7500 S Pleasant Valley Rd 78744
PICKLE, JJ 526X ML-28
1101 Wheatley Ave 78752
PILLOW 495X MJ-31
3025 Crosscreek Dr 78757
PLEASANT HILL 644X MG-16
6405 Circle S Rd 78745
REILLY 555C MK-27
405 Denson Dr 78752
RIDGETOP 555R MK-26
5005 Caswell Ave 78751
RODRIGUEZ 645S MJ-16
4400 Franklin Park Dr 78744
ST. ELMO 644B MG-18
600 W St Elmo Rd 78745
SANCHEZ 615B MJ-21
73 San Marcos Rd 78702
SIMS 586L MM-23
1203 Springdale Rd 78721
SUMMITT 465R MK-35
12207 Brigadoon Ln 78727
SUNSET VALLEY 613Y MF-19
3000 Jones Rd 78745
TRAVIS HEIGHTS 615N MJ-20
2010 Alameda Dr 78704
WALNUT CREEK 496U MM-31
401 W Braker Ln 78753
WIDEN 675A MJ-15
5605 Nuckols Crossing Rd 78744
WILLIAMS 674E MG-15
500 Mairo Rd 78745
WINN 557J MN-26
3500 Susquehanna Ln 78723
WOOLDRIDGE 525D MK-30
1412 Norseman Terrace 78758
WOOTEN 525L MK-29
1406 Dale Dr 78758
ZAVALA 615C MK-21
310 Robert T Martinez Jr St 78702
ZILKER 614F MG-21
1900 Bluebonnet Ln 78704

Austin Middle Schools

ANN RICHARDS SCHOOL FOR YOUNG WOMEN LEADERS 614S MG-19
2206 Prather Dr 78704
BAILEY, GORDON A. 672S MC-13
4020 Lost Oasis Hollow 78739
BEDICHEK 644W MG-16
6800 Bill Hughes Rd 78745
BURNET 525C MK-30
8401 Hathaway Dr 78757
COVINGTON 642M MD-17
3700 Convict Hill Rd 78749
DOBIE 526L MM-29
1200 E Rundberg Ln 78753
FULMORE 614M MH-20
201 E Mary St 78704
GARCIA, GUSTAVO L. 557Q MP-26
7414 Johnny Morris Rd 78724
KEALING JR HIGH 585U MK-22
1607 Pennsylvania Ave 78702
LAMAR 525W MJ-28
6201 Wynona 78757
MARTIN 615F MJ-21
1601 Haskell St 78702
MENDEZ 675A MJ-15
5106 Village Square 78744
MURCHISON 524M MH-29
3700 North Hills Dr 78731
O. HENRY 584F MG-24
2610 W 10th St 78703
PAREDES 673Q MF-14
10100 S Mary Moore Searight Dr 78748
PEARCE 556Q MM-26
6401 N Hampton Dr 78723
SMALL, CLINT 612V MD-19
4801 Monterey Oaks Blvd 78749

WEBB 526W ML-28
601 E St Johns Ave 78752

Austin High Schools

AKINS 703H MF-12
10701 S 1st St 78748
ANDERSON 494V MH-31
8403 Mesa Dr 78759
AUSTIN 584U MH-22
1715 W Cesar Chavez St 78703
BOWIE 672B MC-15
4103 Slaughter Ln 78749
CLIFTON CAREER DEVELOPMENT 556C MM-27
1519 Coronado Hills Dr 78752
CROCKETT, DAVID 643M MF-17
5601 Manchaca Rd 78745
EASTSIDE MEMORIAL 616C MM-21
1012 Arthur Stiles Rd 78721
GARZA, GONZALO INDEPENDENCE 585Q MK-23
1600 Chicon St 78702
HEALTH SCIENCES INSTITUTE OF AUSTIN 526E ML-30
1201 Payton Gin Rd Lanier 78758
INSTITUTE OF HOSPITALITY & CULINARY ARTS 615S MJ-19
1211 E Oltorf (Travis H.S.) 78704
INTERNATIONAL 616C MM-21
1012 Arthur Stiles (Johnston H.S.) Austin 78721
JOHNSON, LYNDON BAINES 557N MN-26
7309 Lazy Creek Dr 78724
LANIER 526E ML-30
1201 Payton Gin Rd 78758
LIBERAL ARTS & SCIENCE ACADEMY 557N MN-26
7309 Lazy Creek Dr (Johnson H.S.) Austin 78724
McCALLUM 555F MJ-27
5600 Sunshine Dr 78756
McCALLUM FINE ARTS ACADEMY 555F MJ-27
5600 Sunshine Dr McCallum 78756
REAGAN 556F ML-27
7104 Berkman Dr 78752
TRAVIS, WILLIAM B. 615S MJ-19
1211 E Oltorf St 78704

Bastrop ISD

ADMINISTRATION OFFICES 745F EE-9
906 Farm St 78602
BASTROP HIGH 745C EF-9
1614 Chambers St 78602
BASTROP INTERMEDIATE 744H ED-9
509 Old Austin Hwy 78602
BASTROP MIDDLE 744H ED-9
709 Old Austin Hwy 78602
BLUEBONNET ELEM 712U MZ-10
416 FM Rd 1209 78612
CEDAR CREEK ELEM 740Z MV-7
5582 FM Rd 535 Bastrop Co 78612
CEDAR CREEK INTERMEDIATE 741T MW-7
151 Voss Pkwy Bastrop Co 78612
CEDAR CREEK MIDDLE 741T MW-7
125 Voss Pkwy Bastrop Co 78612
EMILE ELEM 745L EF-8
601 MLK Jr Dr 78602
GATEWAY 745T EE-7
1019 Lovers Ln 78602
GENESIS HIGH 745B EE-9
1200 Cedar St 78602
MINA ELEM 745F EE-9
1203 Hill St 78602
SPECIAL EDUCATION CO-OP 745L EF-8
1507 Pine St 78602

Coupland ISD

COUPLAND 443Q EB-38
620 S Commerce 78615

Del Valle ISD

ADMINISTRATION BLDG, EDWARD A. NEAL 678K MQ-14
5301 Ross Rd 78617
BATY ELEM 615Z MK-19
2101 Faro Dr Austin 78741
CREEDMOOR ELEM 735Y MK-7
5604 FM Rd 1327 Travis Co 78610
DEL VALLE ELEM 678J MQ-14
5400 Ross Rd 78617
DEL VALLE HIGH 678K MQ-14
5201 Ross Rd 78617
DEL VALLE JR HIGH 678N MQ-14
5500 Ross Rd 78617
DEL VALLE OPPORTUNITY CENTER 647U MP-16
3311 FM Rd 973 S Austin 78617
HILLCREST ELEM 675T MJ-13
6910 E William Cannon Dr Austin 78744
HORNSBY-DUNLAP ELEM 618M MR-20
13901 FM Rd 969 78724
OJEDA, JOHN P. JR HIGH 675D MK-15
4900 McKinney Falls Pkwy 78744
POPHAM ELEM 677Y MP-13
7014 Elroy Rd 78617
SMITH ELEM 645Z MK-16
4209 Smith School Rd Austin 78744

Dripping Springs ISD

ADMINISTRATION BLDG. 636Z WR-16
510 W Mercer Rd 78620
DRIPPING SPRINGS ELEM 607T WS-19
29400 RM Rd 12 78620
DRIPPING SPRINGS HIGH 636S WQ-16
111 Tiger Ln 78620
DRIPPING SPRINGS MIDDLE 636Y WR-16
940 W US Hwy 290 78620
ROOSTER SPRINGS ELEM 639X WW-16
1001 Belterra Dr Hays Co 78737
WALNUT SPRINGS ELEM 636Y WR-16
300 Sportsplex Dr 78620

Eanes ISD

ADMINISTRATION BLDG. 583P ME-23
601 Camp Craft Rd West Lake Hills 78746
BARTON CREEK ELEM 551V MB-25
1314 Patterson Rd Travis Co 78733
BRIDGE POINT ELEM. 523U MF-28
6401 Cedar St Austin 78746
CEDAR CREEK ELEM 583U MF-22
3301 Pinnacle Rd Austin 78746
EANES ELEM 583L MF-23
4101 Bee Caves Rd West Lake Hills 78746
FOREST TRAIL ELEM 583K ME-23
1203 Loop 360 S West Lake Hills 78746
HILL COUNTRY MIDDLE 583U MF-22
1300 Walsh Tarlton Ln Travis Co 78746
VALLEY VIEW ELEM. 583K ME-23
1201 Loop 360 S West Lake Hills 78746
WESTLAKE 9TH GRADE CENTER 583Q MF-23
3800 Westbank Dr 78746
WESTLAKE HIGH 583P ME-23
4100 Westbank Dr Travis Co 78746
WEST RIDGE MIDDLE 551V MB-25
9201 Scenic Bluff Dr Travis Co 78733

Elgin ISD

ADMINISTRATION BLDG. 533M EB-29
1002 N Avenue C 78621
ELGIN ELEM. 533M EB-29
1005 W 2nd St 78621
ELGIN HIGH 533B EA-30
14000 County Line Rd Travis Co 78621
ELGIN MIDDLE 533R EB-29
902 W 2nd St 78621
NEIDIG ELEM 533E EA-30
13700 County Line Rd 78621
PHOENIX HIGH 533M EB-29
1002 N Ave C 78621
WASHINGTON, BOOKER T ELEM 534S EC-28
510 MLK Blvd 78621

Georgetown ISD

BENOLD, DOUGLAS MIDDLE 256K ML-56
3407 Northwest Blvd 78628
CARVER, GEORGE WASHINGTON ELEM 286Q MM-53
1200 W 17th St 78628
CENTRAL ADMINISTRATION OFFICE 256K ML-56
603 Lakeway Dr 78628
COOPER, PATRICIA WEBB ELEM 257P MN-56
1921 NE Inner Loop 78626
FORBES, CHARLES A. MIDDLE 257P MN-56
1911 NE Inner Loop 78626
FORD, JO ANN ELEM 225Y MK-58
210 Woodlake Dr 78633
FROST, JACK ELEM 256K ML-56
711 Lakeway Dr 78628
GEORGETOWN ALTERNATIVE PROGRAM 286M MM-53
508 E 8th St 78626
GEORGETOWN CAMPUS-NINTH GRADE 257N MN-56
2295 N Austin Ave 78626
GEORGETOWN HIGH 257N MN-56
2211 N Austin Ave 78626
GEORGETOWN NINTH GRADE CENTER 288E MQ-54
4490 E Hwy 29 Georgetown 78626
McCOY, RAYE ELEM 256Y MM-55
1313 Williams Dr 78628
MITCHELL, JIM ELEM 287U MP-52
1601 CR 110 78626
PICKETT, DELL ELEM 286X ML-52
1100 Thousand Oaks Blvd 78628
PURL, ANNIE ELEM 287N MN-53
1700 Laurel St 78626
RICHARTE, CHIP HIGH 256R MM-56
2201 Old Airport Rd 78626
TIPPIT, JAMES MIDDLE 286W ML-52
1601 Leander Rd 78628
VILLAGE ELEM 225R MK-59
400 Village Commons Blvd 78633
WILLIAMS ELEM 286M MM-53
507 E University Ave 78626
WILLIAMSON CO ACADEMY 287U MN-52
1821 SE Inner Loop Williamson Co 78626

Hays Consolidated ISD

BUDA ELEMENTARY DOWNHILL CAMPUS 762C MD-6
500 FM Rd 967 Buda 78610
BUDA ELEMENTARY UPHILL CAMPUS 762C MD-6
300 San Marcos St Buda 78610
ELM GROVE ELEM 732W MC-7
801 FM Rd 1626 Hays Co 78610
GREEN ELEM 763P ME-5
1301 Old Goforth Rd Buda 78610

Hutto ISD

ADMINISTRATION BLDG. 349Z MT-46
200 College St 78634
COTTONWOOD CREEK ELEM 349R MT-47
3160 Limmer Loop Hutto 78634
FARLEY MIDDLE SCHOOL 379V MT-43
300 CR 137 Hutto 78634
HUTTO ELEM 350S MU-46
100 Mager Ln 78634
HUTTO HIGH 379C MT-45
101 FM Rd 685 78634
HUTTO MIDDLE 349U MT-46
1005 Exchange Blvd 78634
JOHNSON, NADINE ELEM 379G MT-45
955 Carl Stern Dr 78634
RAY ELEM 380S MU-43
225 Swindoll Ln Hutto 78634
VETERANS HILL ELEM 348L MR-47
555 Limmer Loop Williamson Co 78665

Lago Vista ISD

ADMINISTRATION BLDG. 399U WX-40
  8039 Bar K Ranch Rd 78645
LAGO VISTA ELEM 429P WW-38
  20311 Dawn Dr 78645
LAGO VISTA HIGH 399U WX-40
  8039 Bar K Ranch Rd 78645
LAGO VISTA MIDDLE 399U WX-40
  20801 FM Rd1431 78645

Lake Travis ISD

ADMINISTRATION BLDG. 549D WX-27
  3322 RM Rd 620 S 78734
BEE CAVE ELEM 549R WX-26
  14300 Hamilton Pool Rd Bee Cave 78738
HUDSON BEND MIDDLE 490G WZ-33
  15600 Lariat Trail Travis Co 78734
LAKE POINTE ELEM 550M WZ-26
  11801 Sonoma Dr Travis Co 78738
LAKE TRAVIS ELEM 490X WY-31
  15303 Kollmeyer Dr 78734
LAKE TRAVIS HIGH 549C WX-27
  3324 RM Rd 620 S 78738
LAKE TRAVIS MIDDLE 549D WX-27
  3328 RM Rd 620 S 78738
LAKEWAY ELEM 519L WX-29
  1701 Lohmans Crossing 78734
SERENE HILLS ELEM 519N WW-29
  3301 Serene Hills Dr Lakeway 78738

Leander ISD

ADMINISTRATION BLDG. 342C MD-48
  204 W South St 78641
BAGDAD ELEM 311Z MB-49
  800 Deercreek Ln 78641
BLOCK HOUSE CREEK ELEM 373A ME-45
  401 Creek Run Dr 78641
BUSH, LAURA WELCH ELEM 521B MA-30
  12600 Country Trails Travis Co 78732
CANYON RIDGE ELEM 521B MA-30
  12601 Country Trails Travis Co 78732
CEDAR PARK HIGH 402Y MD-40
  2150 Cypress Creek Rd Cedar Park 78613
CEDAR PARK MIDDLE 402Z MD-40
  2100 Sun Chase Blvd Cedar Park 78613
COX ELEM 403C MF-42
  1001 Brushy Creek Rd Cedar Park 78613
CYPRESS ELEM 432H MD-39
  2900 El Salido Pkwy Cedar Park 78613
DEER CREEK ELEM 402U MD-40
  2420 Zeppelin Dr Travis Co 78613
FAUBION, ADA MAE ELEM 403N ME-41
  1209 Cypress Creek Rd Cedar Park 78613
GIDDENS ELEM 372Q MD-44
  1500 Timberwood Dr Cedar Park 78613
GRANDVIEW HILLS ELEM 462Q MD-35
  12024 Vista Parke Dr Austin 78726
HENRY, ARTIE MIDDLE 374N MG-44
  100 N Vista Ridge Blvd Cedar Park 78613
KNOWLES ELEM 372E MC-45
  2101 Cougar Country Dr Cedar Park 78613
LEANDER EXTENDED OPPORTUNITY CENTER 342B MC-48
  300 S West St 78641
LEANDER HIGH 372C MD-45
  3301 S Bagdad Rd 78641
LEANDER MIDDLE 342C MD-48
  410 S West St 78641
MASON, C.C. ELEM 372P MC-44
  1501 N Lakeline Blvd Cedar Park 78613
NAUMANN ELEM 403W ME-40
  1201 Brighton Bend Ln Cedar Park 78613
NEW HOPE HIGH 342B MC-48
  401 S West St 78641
PARKSIDE ELEM 344C MH-48
  301 Garner Park Dr Williamson Co 78628
PLAIN ELEM 312S MC-49
  501 South Brook Dr
PLEASANT HILL ELEM 342R MD-47
  1800 Horizon Park Blvd 78641
RIVER PLACE ELEM 492H MD-33
  6500 Sitio Del Rio Blvd Austin 78730
ROUSE HIGH 343F ME-48
  1501 CR 271 78641
RUNNING BRUSHY MIDDLE 372K MC-44
  2303 N Lakeline Blvd Cedar Park 78613
RUTLEDGE ELEM 403H MF-42
  11501 Staked Plains Dr 78717
STEINER RANCH ELEM 491R MB-32
  4001 N Quinlan Park Rd Travis Co 78732
VISTA RIDGE HIGH 374S MG-43
  200 S Vista Ridge Blvd Cedar Park 78613
WESTSIDE ELEM 402C MD-42
  300 Ryan Jordan Ln Cedar Park 78613
WHITESTONE ELEM 342W MC-46
  2000 Crystal Falls Pkwy 78641
WILEY MIDDLE 343F ME-48
  1701 CR 271 78641
WINKLEY ELEM 372A MC-45
  2100 Pow Wow 78641

Manor ISD

ADMINISTRATION BLDG. 529Q MT-29
  312 W Murray Ave 78653
BLAKE MANOR ELEM 560S MU-25
  18010 Blake Manor Rd Travis Co 78653
BLUEBONNET TRAIL ELEM 528J MQ-29
  11316 Farmhaven Rd Austin 78754
DECKER ELEM 558N MQ-26
  8500 Decker Ln Travis Co 78724
DECKER MIDDLE 558N MQ-26
  8104 Decker Ln 78724
EXCEL HIGH SCHOOL 529V MT-28
  600 E Parsons St 78653

MANOR ELEM 529L MT-29
  12904 Gregg Manor Rd 78653
MANOR HIGH 529L MT-29
  12700 Gregg Manor Rd 78653
MANOR MIDDLE 529L MT-29
  12900 Gregg Manor Rd 78653
MANOR NEW TECH HIGH SCHOOL 529S MS-28
  10323 E Hwy 290 78653
OAK MEADOWS ELEM 587L MP-23
  5600 Decker Ln 78724
PRESIDENTIAL MEADOWS ELEM 530K MU-29
  13252 George Bush St Manor 78653

Pflugerville ISD

BROOKHOLLOW ELEM 438N MQ-38
  1200 N Railroad Ave 78660
CALDWELL ELEM 437B MN-39
  1718 Picadilly Dr 78664
CENTRAL ADMINISTRATION OFFICE 437D MP-37
  1401 W Pecan St 78660
CONNALLY HIGH 466R MM-35
  13212 N Lamar Blvd Austin 78753
COPPERFIELD ELEM 497J MN-32
  12135 Thompkins Dr Austin 78753
DELCO PRIMARY 497C MP-33
  12900 A Dessau Rd Austin 78753
DESSAU ELEM 497C MP-33
  1501 Dessau Ridge Ln Austin 78754
DESSAU MIDDLE 497C MP-33
  12900 Dessau Rd Austin 78754
HENDRICKSON HIGH 438H MR-39
  2905 FM Rd 685 78660
HIGHLAND PARK ELEM 408S MQ-40
  428 Kingston Lacy 78660
KELLY LANE MIDDLE 438H MR-39
  18900 Falcon Point Blvd 78660
MURCHISON ELEM 438D MR-39
  2215 Kelly Ln 78660
NORTHWEST ELEM 466H MM-36
  14014 Thermal Dr Travis Co 78728
OPPORTUNITY CENTER 437U MP-37
  1401 W Pecan 78660
PARK CREST MIDDLE 438J MQ-38
  1500 N Railroad Ave 78660
PARMER LANE ELEM 466P ML-35
  1806 W Parmer Ln Austin 78727
PFLUGERVILLE ELEM 468F MQ-36
  701 Immanuel Rd 78660
PFLUGERVILLE HIGH 437V MP-37
  1301 W Pecan St 78660
PFLUGERVILLE MIDDLE 437Y MP-37
  1600 W Settlers Valley Dr 78660
RIVER OAKS ELEM 466U MM-34
  12401 Scofield Farms Dr Austin 78758
ROWE LANE ELEM 409X MS-40
  3112 Speidel Dr Travis Co 78660
SPRING HILL ELEM 437Y MP-37
  600 S Heatherwilde Blvd 78660
TIMMERMAN ELEM 438W MQ-37
  700 W Pecan 78660
WESTVIEW ELEM 466P ML-35
  1805 Scofield Ln Austin 78727
WIELAND ELEM 467L MP-35
  900 Tudor House Rd Travis Co 78660
WINDERMERE ELEM 437G MP-39
  1100 Piccadilly Travis Co 78660
WINDERMERE PRIMARY 437F MN-39
  1330 Grand Avenue Pkwy Travis Co 78660

Round Rock ISD

ADMINISTRATION BLDG. 376X ML-43
  1311 Round Rock Ave 78681
ANDERSON ELEM 433Q MF-38
  10610 Salt Mill Hollow Williamson Co 78750
BERKMAN ELEM 376Y MA-43
  400 West Anderson Rd 78664
BLACKLAND PRAIRIE ELEM 407D MP-42
  2105 Via Sonoma Trail 78664
BLUEBONNET ELEM 406P MA-41
  1010 Chisholm Valley Dr 78681
BRUSHY CREEK ELEM 375X MA-43
  3800 Stonebridge Dr Williamson Co 78681
CACTUS RANCH ELEM 375C MK-45
  2901 Goldenoak Cir 78681
CALDWELL HEIGHTS ELEM 346M MM-47
  4010 Eagles Nest St 78664
CALLISON, NEYSA ELEM 407E MN-42
  1750 Thompson Trl Round Rock 78664
CANYON CREEK ELEM 463A ME-36
  10210 Ember Glen Dr Austin 78726
CANYON VISTA MIDDLE 464E MG-36
  8455 Spicewood Springs Rd Austin 78759
CARAWAY ELEM 464Q MH-35
  11104 Oak View Dr Austin 78759
CEDAR VALLEY MIDDLE 405K MJ-41
  8139 Racine Trail Williamson Co 78717
CHISHOLM TRAIL MIDDLE 406A MJ-42
  500 Oakridge Dr 78681
DEEP WOOD ELEM 406F ML-42
  705 St Williams Dr 78681
DEERPARK MIDDLE 434P MG-38
  8849 Anderson Mill Rd Williamson Co 78729
DOUBLE FILE TRAIL ELEM 377F MN-45
  2400 Chandler Creek Blvd Williamson Co 78664
FERN BLUFF ELEM 375U MA-43
  17815 Park Valley Dr Williamson Co 78681
FOREST CREEK ELEM 378X MQ-43
  3805 Forest Creek Dr 78664
FOREST NORTH ELEM 434A MG-39
  13414 Broadmeade Ave Austin 78729
FULKES, C.D. MIDDLE 376Y MA-43
  300 West Anderson Rd 78664
GATTIS ELEM 407G MP-42
  2920 Round Rock Ranch Blvd 78664

GREAT OAKS ELEM 405F MJ-42
  16455 Great Oaks Dr Williamson Co 78681
GRISHAM MIDDLE 433L MF-38
  10805 School House Ln Williamson Co 78750
HOPEWELL MIDDLE 347S MN-46
  1535 Gulf Way 78664
JOLLYVILLE ELEM 434V MH-37
  6720 Corpus Christi Dr Austin 78729
LAUREL MOUNTAIN ELEM 464S MG-34
  10111 D K Ranch Rd Austin 78759
LIVE OAK ELEM 434P MG-38
  8607 Anderson Mill Rd Williamson Co 78729
McNEIL HIGH 435T MJ-37
  5720 McNeil Rd Travis Co 78729
OLD TOWN ELEM 376E ML-45
  2200 Chaparral Dr 78681
POND SPRINGS ELEM 434U MH-37
  7825 Elk Horn Mountain Trail Austin 78729
PURPLE SAGE ELEM 433K ME-38
  11801 Tanglebriar Trail Williamson Co 78750
RIDGEVIEW MIDDLE 407D MP-42
  2000 Via Sonoma Trail 78664
ROBERTSON ELEM 377N MN-44
  1415 Bayland St 78664
ROUND ROCK HIGH 376X ML-43
  300 Lake Creek Dr 78681
ROUND ROCK OPPORTUNITY CENTER 346Z MM-46
  931 Luther Peterson Pl 78664
SOMMER ELEM 404D MH-42
  16200 Avery Ranch Rd Austin 78717
SPICEWOOD ELEM 433U MF-37
  11601 Olson Dr Austin 78750
STONY POINT 9TH GRADE CENTER 376M MM-44
  1901 Sunrise Rd 78664
STONY POINT HIGH 377J MN-44
  1801 Bowman Rd 78664
SUCCESS EAST 377J MN-44
  1801 E Bowman Rd Stony Point 78664
SUCCESS WEST 433M MF-38
  12515 Mellow Meadow Dr 78750
TERAVISTA ELEM 347A MM-48
  4419 Teravista Club Dr Round Rock 78665
UNION HILL ELEM 347S MN-46
  1511 Gulf Way 78664
VOIGT, XENIA ELEM 406H MM-42
  1201 Cushing Dr 78664
WALSH MIDDLE 375F MJ-45
  3850 Walsh Ranch Blvd Round Rock 78681
WELLS BRANCH ELEM 436T ML-37
  14650 Merriltown Dr Travis Co 78728
WESTWOOD HIGH 433M MF-38
  12400 Mellow Meadow Dr Williamson Co 78750

Taylor ISD

ADMINISTRATION BLDG. 353A EA-48
  602 W 12th St 76574
EAST WILLIAMSON COUNTY COOPERATIVE 322U MZ-49
  2501 North Dr 76574
JOHNSON, T.H. ELEM 322R MZ-50
  3100 Duck Dr 76574
NORTHSIDE ELEM 322V MZ-49
  1004 Dellinger St 76574
PASEMANN, NAOMI ELEM 322U MZ-49
  2809 North Dr 76574
TAYLOR HIGH 323N EA-50
  3101 N Main St 76574
TAYLOR MIDDLE 322L MZ-50
  304 NW Carlos Parker Blvd 76574

Charter Schools

AMERICAN YOUTH WORKS CHARTER SCHOOL 585W MJ-22
  216 E 4th St Austin 78701
AMERICAN YOUTH WORKS CHARTER SCHOOL-SOUTH CAMPUS .. 645J MJ-17
  1901 E Ben White Blvd Austin 78741
AUSTIN CAN ACADEMY CHARTER SCHOOL 585V MK-22
  2406 Rosewood Ave Austin 78702
AUSTIN DISCOVERY SCHOOL 587Q MP-23
  8509 FM Rd 969 Austin 78724
CEDARS INTERNATIONAL ACADEMY 526P ML-29
  8416 IH 35 N Austin 78753
EDEN PARK ACADEMY 643L MF-17
  6215 Manchaca Rd Austin 78745
GEORGE M KOMETZKY SCHOOL 616W ML-19
  1515A Grove Blvd Austin 78741
HARMONY ELEMENTARY-AUSTIN 495D MK-33
  11800 Stonehollow Rd Austin 78758
HARMONY SCIENCE ACADEMY-AUSTIN ...526G MM-30
  930 E Rundberg Ln Austin 78753
KIPP AUSTIN COLLEGE PREP 587Q MP-23
  8509 FM Rd 969 Austin 78724
KIPP AUSTIN COLLEGE PREP 2 ....587Q MP-23
  8509 FM Rd 969 Austin 78724
NYOS CHARTER SCHOOL 496C MM-33
  12301 N Lamar Blvd Austin 78753
NYOS-MAGNOLIA McCUKKOUGH CAMPUS ..496N ML-32
  1605 N Kramer Ln Austin 78758
OAKS TREATMENT CENTER, THE 644J MG-17
  1407 Stassney Ln Austin 78745
OLYMPIC HILLS 763N ME-5
  222 Park 35 CV Buda 78610
PREMIER HIGH SCHOOL OF AUSTIN. 614W MG-19
  1701 W Ben White Blvd Austin 78704
SAILL CHARTER SCHOOL 526Y MM-28
  1611 Headway Cir Austin 78754
SETTLEMENT HOME 525D MK-30
  1600 Payton Gin Rd Austin 78758
STAR CHARTER SCHOOL 436V MM-37
  1901 Fleisher Dr Travis Co 78728
TEXAS EMPOWERMENT ACADEMY 586V MM-22
  3613 Bluestein Dr Austin 78721
TEXAS NEUROREHABILITATION CENTER CAMPUS ..673C MF-15
  1106 W Dittmar Rd Austin 78745
UNIVERSITY OF TEXAS ELEMENTARY CHARTER SCHOOL ..615D MK-21
  2200 E 6th ST Austin 78702

Recreation and Activity Centers

ALLEN R. BACA CENTER *Round Rock* 406C MM-42
AMERICAN LEGION HALL *Taylor* 323W EA-49
AUSTIN RECREATION CENTER *Austin* 585N MJ-23
CLAY MADSEN RECREATION CENTER *Round Rock* 407E MN-42
COMACHO ACITVITY CENTER *Austin* 615L MK-20
CONLEY-GUERRERO SENIOR ACTIVITY CENTER *Austin* 585Z MK-22
CREATIVE PLAYSCAPE *Georgetown* 256Z MM-55
CREST HAVEN CHILDREN'S CENTER *Austin* 644F MG-18
DOVE SPRINGS MULTI-PURPOSE CENTER *Austin* 645W MJ-16
FIREMANS HALL *Taylor* 323W EA-49
GUS GARCIA RECREATION CENTER *Austin* 526L MM-29
HANCOCK RECREATION CENTER *Austin* 555Y MK-25
KNIGHTS OF COLUMBUS HALL *Taylor* 353C EB-48
LAKEWAY ACTIVITY CENTER *Lakeway* 519B WW-30
McBETH RECREATION CENTER *Austin* 584X MG-22
NORTHWEST RECREATION CENTER *Austin* 524Z MH-28
OUR LADY OF GUADALUPE RECREATION CENTER *Taylor* 352M MZ-47
RECREATIONAL SPORTS CENTER *Austin* 585K MJ-23
SAN GABRIEL COMMUNITY CENTER *Georgetown* 256Z MM-55
SENIOR ACTIVITY CENTER *Austin* 585A MJ-24
SENIOR CITIZEN CENTER *Taylor* 352H MZ-48
SPJST HALL *Williamson Co* 323V EB-49
STONEHAVEN SENIOR CENTER *Georgetown* 286Q MM-53
TAYLOR NEIGHBORHOOD CENTER *Taylor* 353K EA-47
TONY BURGER ACTIVITY CENTER (AISD) *Sunset Valley* 613Y MF-19
TRAVIS COUNTY EAST RURAL COMMUNITY CENTER *Travis Co* 529T MS-28
YMCA COMPLEX *Round Rock* 347Z MP-46
YOUTH ACTIVITY CENTER *Georgetown* 256P ML-56
ZILKER CLUB HOUSE *Austin* 584T MG-22

Sheriffs' Offices

BASTROP COUNTY 745Q EF-8
200 Jackson St Bastrop 78602
HAYS COUNTY SUBSTATION-BUDA 762G MD-6
500 Jack C. Hays Trl Buda 78610
HAYS COUNTY SUBSTATION-DRIPPING SPRINGS 636Z WR-16
101 Old Fitzhugh Rd Dripping Springs 78620
TRAVIS COUNTY-CENTRAL 555M MK-26
5555 Airport Blvd Austin 78751
TRAVIS COUNTY-EAST COMMAND 590X MU-22
7811 Burleson Manor Rd Travis Co 78653
TRAVIS COUNTY-WEST COMMAND 490C WZ-33
3800 Hudson Bend Rd Travis Co 78734
WILLIAMSON COUNTY-EAST SUBSTATION 353E EA-48
412 Vance St Taylor 76574
WILLIAMSON COUNTY-HEADQUARTERS 286G MM-54
508 S Rock St Georgetown 78626
WILLIAMSON COUNTY-WEST SUBSTATION 373S ME-43
350 Discovery Blvd Cedar Park 78613

State and Private Schools

AUSTIN STATE SCHOOL 554U MH-25
2203 W 35th St 78703
BANNOCKBURN ELEM 643J ME-17
7100 Brodie Ln 78745
BRENTWOOD CHRISTIAN SCHOOL 496G MM-33
11908 N Lamar Blvd 78753
HILL COUNTRY CHRISTIAN SCHOOL OF AUSTIN 433F ME-39
12124 N RM Rd 620 78750
HOLY FAMILY CATHOLIC SCHOOL 404Q MH-41
9400 Neenah Ave 78717
HYDE PARK BAPTIST SCHOOLS 555X MJ-25
3901 Speedway 78751
KIRBY HALL SCHOOL 585A MJ-24
306 W 29th St 78705
REDEEMER LUTHERAN SCHOOL 525L MK-29
1500 W Anderson Ln 78757
REGENTS SCHOOL OF AUSTIN 612G MD-21
3230 Travis Country Cir 78735
ROUND ROCK CHRISTIAN ACADEMY 376X ML-43
301 N Lake Creek Dr 78681
SACRED HEART CATHOLIC SCHOOL 556V MM-25
5911 Reicher Dr 78723
ST. ANDREWS EPISCOPAL SCHOOL 555W MJ-25
1112 W 31st St 78705
ST. ANDREWS EPISCOPAL SCHOOL 612L MD-20
5901 Southwest Pkwy 78735
ST. AUSTIN CATHOLIC SCHOOL 585J MJ-23
1911 San Antonio St 78705
ST. DOMINIC SAVIO CATHOLIC HIGH 404R MH-41
Neenah Ave 78729
ST. FRANCIS 555D MK-27
300 E Huntland Dr 78752
ST. GABRIEL'S CATHOLIC SCHOOL 582A MC-24
2500 Wimberly Ln 78735
ST. IGNATIUS MARTYR SCHOOL 614R MH-20
120 W Oltorf St 78704
ST. LOUIS CATHOLIC SCHOOL 525K MJ-29
2114 St Joseph Blvd 78757
ST. MARYS CATHEDRAL 585T MJ-22
910 San Jacinto Blvd 78701
ST. MARY'S CATHOLIC SCHOOL 353B EA-48
520 Washburn St 78660
ST. MICHAEL'S CATHOLIC ACADEMY 582E MC-24
3000 Barton Creek Blvd 78735
ST. PAUL LUTHERAN SCHOOL 585C MK-24
3407 Red River St 78705
ST. STEPHENS EPISCOPAL SCHOOL 553B ME-27
2900 Bunny Run Rd 78746
ST. THERESA'S SCHOOL 524P MG-29
4311 Small Dr 78731
SAN JUAN DIEGO CATHOLIC HIGH 614Q MH-20
800 Herndon Ln 78704
SHORELINE CHRISTIAN SCHOOL 436K ML-38
15201 Burnet Rd 78728
SUMMIT CHRISTIAN ACADEMY 342M MD-47
1303 Leander Dr 78641
SUMMIT CHRISTIAN ACADEMY 402Y MD-40
2121 Cypress Creek Rd 78613
TEXAS SCHOOL FOR THE BLIND & VISUALLY IMPAIRED 555K MJ-26
1100 W 45th St 78756
TEXAS SCHOOL FOR THE DEAF 614H MH-21
1102 South Congress Ave 78704
TRINITY EPISCOPAL SCHOOL 583L MF-23
3901 Bee Caves Rd 78746

Subdivisions

AIR COUNTRY ESTATES *Georgetown* 226Z MM-58
ALLANDALE *Austin* 525S MJ-28
ALLANDALE ESTATES *Austin* 495W MJ-31
ALTA MIRA *Austin* 641S MA-16
ANCIENT OAKS *Williamson Co* 192N MC-62
ANDERSON MILL ESTATES *Williamson Co* 433T ME-37
ANDERSON MILL WEST *Williamson Co* 432C MD-39
APACHE OAKS *Round Rock* 377P MN-44
APPALOOSA RUN *Travis Co* 670C WZ-15
APPLE SPRINGS *Travis Co* 341K MA-47
AQUA MONTE *Travis Co* 522N MC-29
AQUA VERDE *Travis Co* 523Q MF-29
ARBOLAGO *Lakeway* 490S WY-31
ARBORS AT DOGWOOD CREEK, THE *Bastrop Co* 564Z ED-25
ARBORS AT GREAT HILLS, THE *Austin* 494B MG-33
ASHFORD PARK *Buda* 763A ME-6
AUSTIN HILLS *Austin* 464Z MH-34
AUSTIN LAKE ESTATES *Travis Co* 522K MC-29
AUSTIN LAKE HILLS *Travis Co* 522S MC-28
AUSTIN'S COLONY *Travis Co* 618R MR-20
AUSTIN SKYLINE *Travis Co* 766K ML-5
AVALON *Travis Co* 439F MS-39
AVERY MORRISON *Williamson Co* 404D MH-42
AVERY RANCH *Austin* 404E MG-42
AVERY RANCH FAR WEST *Williamson Co* 404E MG-42
AVERY RANCH NORTH *Williamson Co* 404C MH-42
BAKER ESTATES *Williamson Co* 282F MC-54
BALCONES OAKS *Austin* 464F MG-36
BALCONES PARK *Austin* 554C MH-27
BALCONES VILLAGE *Austin* 433V MF-37
BALCONES WEST *Austin* 495W MJ-31
BALCONES WOODS *Austin* 465X MJ-34
BARCLAY WOODS *Travis Co* 583J ME-23
BARKER HILLS *Travis Co* 560E MU-27
BARON, THE *Travis Co* 707E MN-12
BARTON CREEK LAKESIDE *Burnet Co* 426K WQ-38
BARTON CREEK PRESERVE *Travis Co* 580L WZ-23
BARTON HOLLOW *Austin* 614C MH-21
BASTROP COUNTY WEST *Bastrop Co* 711T MW-10
BATTLE BEND SPRINGS *Austin* 644M MH-17
BAUERLE RANCH *Austin* 672R MD-14
BEAR CREEK OAKS *Village of Bear Creek* 670L WZ-14
BEE CAVE WOODS *Austin* 583V MF-22
BEHRENS RANCH *Round Rock* 375G MK-45
BEHRENS RANCH *Round Rock* 375H MK-45
BELLA LAGO *Travis Co* 522P MC-29
BELLA MONTAGNA *Lakeway* 520E WY-30
BELL FARMS *Manor* 530T MU-28
BELL MEADOWS *Williamson Co* 318G MR-51
BELTERRA *Hays Co* 639T WW-16
BENBROOK RANCH *Leander* 312W MC-49
BENT TREE *Round Rock* 375H MK-45
BERDOLL FARMS *Travis Co* 678K MQ-14
BERRY CREEK *Georgetown* 226G MM-60
BIRDLIP *Travis Co* 551D MB-27
BLOCK HOUSE CREEK *Williamson Co* 343S ME-46
BLUEBELL RIDGE *Travis Co* 735A MJ-9
BLUEBONNET ACRES *Bastrop Co* 711Y MX-10
BLUE RIDGE *Dripping Springs* 667J WS-14
BLUFF AT OAKLANDS, THE *Round Rock* 376S ML-43
BLUFFS AT EANES CREEK, THE *Travis Co* 522T MC-28
BLUFFS OF UNIVERSITY HILLS *Austin* 557S MN-25
BLUFFS, THE *Austin* 464E MG-36
BLUFFS, THE *Jonestown* 430N WY-38
BOHLS PLACE *Pflugerville* 468B MQ-36
BOULDER RIDGE *Travis Co* 468T MQ-34
BOULDERS AT CRYSTAL FALLS, THE *Leander* 342X MC-46
BRADFIELD VILLAGE *Austin* 763A ME-6
BRANGUS RANCH *Georgetown* 226R MM-59
BRATTON PARK *Travis Co* 436P ML-38
BRIARCREEK *Travis Co* 560J MU-26
BRIARWOOD *Georgetown* 256K ML-56
BRIDGES AT BEAR CREEK *Austin* 702L MD-11
BROOKFIELD ESTATES *Travis Co* 467M MP-35
BROOKHOLLOW *Pflugerville* 438N MQ-38
BROOKS HOLLOW *Travis Co* 489M WX-32
BRUSHY BEND PARK *Williamson Co* 374H MH-45
BRUSHY CREEK *Williamson Co* 405J MJ-41
BRUSHY CREEK ACRES *Travis Co* 441G MX-39
BRUSHY CREEK MEADOWS *Hutto* 379R MT-44
BRUSHY CREEK NORTH *Williamson Co* 375B MJ-45
BRUSHY CREEK SOUTH *Williamson Co* 375P MJ-44
BRUSHY CREEK VILLAGE *Austin* 375W MJ-43
BRUSHY SLOPE *Round Rock* 376U MM-43
BRYKER WOODS *Austin* 554U MH-25
BUCKINGHAM ESTATES *Austin* 673Q MF-14
BUCKINGHAM RIDGE *Austin* 644W MG-16
BULL CREEK BLUFF ESTATES *Austin* 464R MH-35
BUTTERCUP CREEK *Cedar Park* 402L MD-41
CABALLO RANCH *Cedar Park* 344S MG-46
CAMELOT *Travis Co* 582D MD-24
CAMERON PARK *Austin* 556E ML-27
CANTERBURY TRAILS *Austin* 673W ME-13
CANYON CREEK *Austin* 463A ME-36
CANYON CREEK *Austin* 462H MD-36
CANYON MESA *Travis Co* 463R MF-35
CANYON RIDGE *Austin* 493G MF-33
CAPITOL VIEW ESTATES *Travis Co* 704M MH-11
CARDINAL HILLS *Travis Co* 520J WY-29
CARDINAL HILLS ESTATES *Travis Co* 490L WZ-32
CAROL MEADOWS *Hutto* 350S MU-46
CARRIAGE HILLS *Cedar Park* 372P MC-44
CARRIAGE HILLS *Manor* 530T MU-28
CARRINGTON RANCH, THE *Williamson Co* 252A MC-57
CARVER HILLS *Travis Co* 588P MQ-23
CASA LOMA *Williamson Co* 225N MJ-59
CAT HOLLOW *Williamson Co* 405C MK-42
CAVALIER PARK *Austin* 587A MN-24
CEDAR PARK TOWN CENTER *Cedar Park* 373F ME-45
CHANDLER CREEK *Williamson Co* 377D MP-45
CHAPEL HILL NORTH *Round Rock* 376G MM-45
CHARRO ESTATES *Bastrop Co* 739B MS-9
CHATEAU AT ONION CREEK *Austin* 674Q MH-14
CHERRY CREEK *Austin* 643N ME-17
CHERRY CREEK *Austin* 672D MD-15
CHIMNEY HILL *Austin* 557B MN-27
CHIMNEY OAKS *Travis Co* 427R WT-38
CHISHOLM VALLEY *Round Rock* 406Q MM-41
CHURCHILL FARMS *Williamson Co* 287L MP-53
CIELO VISTA RANCH *Bastrop Co* 738Q MR-8
CIMARRON *Round Rock* 406S ML-40
CIMARRON HILLS *Williamson Co* 283D MF-54
CIRCLE C RANCH *Travis Co* 641L MB-17
CIRCLE C RANCH *Travis Co* 671G MB-15
CLARKS CROSSING *Hutto* 350T MU-46
CLEARVIEW *Williamson Co* 316Q MM-50
CLIFFBROOK ESTATES *Travis Co* 735M MK-8
CLUB AT WELLS POINT, THE *Pflugerville* 437Y MP-37
COLD SPRINGS *Leander* 343L MF-47
COLDWATER *Travis Co* 523F ME-30
COLONIAL PLACE *Travis Co* 527U MP-28
COLONY PARK *Austin* 557U MP-25
COLONY, THE *Bastrop Co* 712V MZ-10
COLORADO CROSSING *Austin* 646T ML-16
COLORADO RIVER ESTATES *Travis Co* 650Y MV-16
COMANCHE CANYON RANCH *Travis Co* 462N MC-35
COMMONS, THE *Travis Co* 409P MS-41
COPPERFIELD *Austin* 497F MN-33
COPPER OAKS *Austin* 643R MF-17
CORONADO HILLS *Austin* 556G MM-27
CORRIDOR PARK *Round Rock* 406Y MM-40
COSTA BELLA *Travis Co* 490J WY-32
COTTONWOOD CREEK *Williamson Co* 349B MS-48
COULVER ESTATES *Travis Co* 735G MK-9
COUNTRY CLUB ACRES *Georgetown* 256X ML-55
COUNTRY CLUB ESTATES *Lago Vista* 428Y WV-37
COUNTRY CLUB GARDENS *Austin* 616N ML-20
COUNTRY ESTATES *Hutto* 379D MT-45
COUNTRY LIVING ESTATES *Williamson Co* 280A WY-54
COUNTRYSIDE *Austin* 613D MF-21
COUNTRY VIEW ESTATES *Williamson Co* 348R MR-47
COUNTRY WEST *Williamson Co* 255H MK-57
COUNTY GLEN *Leander* 342V MD-46
COVERED BRIDGE *Austin* 611L MB-20
COVES OF CIMARRON *Hays Co* 732L MD-8
COVES ON LAKE TRAVIS, THE *Travis Co* 458Y WV-34
CRAIGWOOD *Austin* 587J MN-23
CREEK BEND *Austin* 674D MH-15
CREEK BEND *Hutto* 379M MT-44
CREEK BEND *Round Rock* 375R MK-44
CREEKMONT WEST *Round Rock* 406A ML-42
CREEKSIDE ESTATES *Hutto* 380A MU-45
CREEKVIEW *Cedar Park* 373V MF-43
CREEKWOOD RANCHETTES *Travis Co* 708U MR-10
CROSS CREEK *Travis Co* 371Q MB-44
CROSSWIND *Travis Co* 518B WU-30
CRYSTALBROOK *Austin* 557T MN-25
CRYSTAL KNOLL TERRACE *Williamson Co* 257E MN-57
CYPRESS BEND *Cedar Park* 402V MD-40
CYPRESS CANYON *Travis Co* 402T MC-40
CYPRESS CREEK *Cedar Park* 402Z MD-40
CYPRESS MILL *Cedar Park* 403J ME-41
CYPRESS MILL *Williamson Co* 433F ME-39
CYPRESS RIDGE *Travis Co* 704F MG-12
DAVENPORT RANCH *Austin* 553C MF-27
DAVENPORT WEST *Travis Co* 523U MF-28
DAVENPORT WEST *Travis Co* 553E ME-27
DAVIS HILL ESTATES *Austin* 673F ME-15
DAVIS SPRING *Austin* 404L MH-41
DEERFIELD VILLAGE *Austin* 642J MC-17
DEER PARK AT MAPLE RUN *Austin* 642P MC-17
DEERWOOD *Travis Co* 678J MQ-14
DELWOOD *Austin* 556N ML-26
DOMINION HILL *Travis Co* 551T MA-25
DOVE CREEK *Round Rock* 406D MM-42
DOVE SPRINGS *Williamson Co* 287R MP-53
DRIPPING SPRINGS HEIGHTS *Dripping Springs* 636X WQ-16
EAGLES LANDING *Elgin* 503T EA-31
EANES PLACE *Austin* 583Y MF-22
EAST TRAVIS HILLS *Travis Co* 709J MS-11
EDGEWATER BEACH *Travis Co* 458Z WV-34
EDINBURGH GARDENS *Austin* 498S MQ-31
EGGER ACRES *Round Rock* 376Q MM-44
ELM CREEK *Travis Co* 532Q MZ-29
ELM RIDGE *Bastrop Co* 709M MT-11
EL RANCHO ESTATES *Travis Co* 766G MM-6
ELROY ACRES *Austin* 707H MP-12
EMERALD FOREST *Austin* 644E MG-18
EMORY FARMS *Hutto* 349T MS-46
ENCHANTED ROCK *Bastrop Co* 711K MW-11
ENCLAVE AT BRUSHY CREEK, THE *Hutto* 379F MS-45
ENFIELD *Austin* 584M MH-23
ESCALERA RANCH *Williamson Co* 314F MG-51
ESCONDIDO ESTATES *Bastrop Co* 739K MS-8
ESTATES AT SETTLERS PARK *Round Rock* 348S MQ-46
ESTATES AT WILBARGER CREEK *Travis Co* 592E MY-24
ESTATES OF BAUERLE RANCH, THE *Austin* 672U MD-13
ESTATES OF BLACKHAWK, THE *Travis Co* 409Q MT-41
ESTATES OF BRENTWOOD *Austin* 433S ME-37
ESTATES OF LAKEWAY *Lakeway* 518D WV-30
ESTATES OF SHADY HOLLOW *Travis Co* 702A MC-12
ESTATES OF SOUTHLAND OAKS *Travis Co* 672W MC-13
ESTATES OF WESTLAKE *Williamson Co* 224U MH-58
EUBANK ACRES *Austin* 496M MM-32
FAIRWAY RIDGE *Austin* 675B MJ-15
FAIRWAYS OF BLACKHAWK *Pflugerville* 439A MS-39
FAIRWAYS, THE *Leander* 342W MC-46
FALCON POINTE SUBDIVISION *Pflugerville* 439J MS-38
FAWN HILL *Travis Co* 400G WZ-42
FERN BLUFF *Williamson Co* 375T MJ-43
FLINT ROCK AT HURST CREEK *Lakeway* 519X WW-28
FOOTHILLS AT BARTON CREEK, THE *Travis Co* 582P MC-23
FOREST AT COLORADO CROSSING, THE *Bastrop Co* 711B MW-12
FOREST BLUFF *Travis Co* 619A MS-21
FOREST CREEK *Round Rock* 378U MR-43
FOREST LAKE *Bastrop Co* 739P MS-8
FOREST NORTH ESTATES *Williamson Co* 434B MG-39
FOREST OAKS *Cedar Park* 403C MF-42
FOREST RIDGE *Round Rock* 378S MQ-43

FOREST, THE *Austin* 464A MG-36
FOUNTAINWOOD ESTATES *Williamson Co* 225N MJ-59
FOUR T RANCH *Williamson Co* 224D MH-60
FRANKLIN PARK *Austin* 645S MJ-16
FRIENDSHIP RANCH *Hays Co* 670N WY-14
GABRIEL ESTATES *Williamson Co* 225U MK-58
GABRIELS GROVE *Williamson Co* 194X MG-61
GABRIELS OVERLOOK *Williamson Co* 283L MF-53
GANN RANCH *Cedar Park* 372J MC-44
GARDEN VALLEY *Travis Co* 647D MP-18
GASTON-SHELDON *Travis Co* 467Q MP-35
GATLINBURG *Pflugerville* 468F MQ-36
GEORGETOWN VILLAGE *Georgetown* 225V MK-58
GEORGIAN ACRES *Austin* 526N ML-29
GLEN HEATHER *Travis Co* 519Q WX-29
GLENLAKE *Travis Co* 522G MD-30
GLENWOOD *Hutto* 380N MU-44
GOLDEN OAKS *Georgetown* 256Q MM-56
GRACYWOODS *Austin* 496F ML-33
GRANADA ESTATES *Travis Co* 641F MA-18
GRANADA HILLS *Travis Co* 611X MA-19
GRAND MESA *Leander* 341Y MB-46
GRAND OAKS *Austin* 673B ME-15
GRANDVIEW TERRACE *Jonestown* 430B WY-39
GREAT HILLS *Austin* 494H MH-33
GREAT OAKS *Austin* 554H MH-27
GREAT OAKS *Williamson Co* 375K MJ-44
GREENBURY *Manor* 530K MU-29
GREENHILL *Round Rock* 376L MM-44
GREENLAWN *Round Rock* 407J MN-41
GREEN PARK *Travis Co* 524W MG-28
GREEN RIDGE *Williamson Co* 255V MK-55
GREENSLOPES *Round Rock* 406H MM-42
GREENSLOPES AT LAKE CREEK *Round Rock* 407A MN-42
GREGG POINT *Jonestown* 400V WZ-40
HAMILTON POINT *Manor* 529Z MT-28
HARMON HILLS *Hays Co* 636E WQ-18
HARRIS BRANCH *Austin* 528K MQ-29
HARRIS RIDGE *Austin* 467X MN-34
HAWES RANCH *Williamson Co* 223C MF-60
HEATHERWILDE *Travis Co* 437H MP-39
HEIGHTS OF DEERFIELD, THE *Williamson Co* 378H MR-45
HERITAGE OAKS *Bastrop Co* 740U MV-7
HERITAGE OAKS *Georgetown* 225Y MK-58
HERITAGE PARK *Cedar Park* 372F MC-45
HERMITAGE, THE *Round Rock* 376K ML-44
HEWLETT *Georgetown* 346C MM-48
HIDDEN ESTATES *Austin* 466A ML-36
HIDDEN GLEN *Round Rock* 346W ML-46
HIDDEN HILLS *Travis Co* 518B WU-30
HIDDEN LAKE ESTATES *Travis Co* 560P MU-26
HIDDEN SPRINGS RANCH *Hays Co* 636P WQ-17
HIDDEN VALLEY *Austin* 523M MF-29
HIDDEN VALLEY *Austin* 587G MP-24
HIELSCHER, THE *Austin* 671A MA-15
HIGH COUNTRY *Round Rock* 408J MQ-41
HIGH GABRIEL EAST *Williamson Co* 282X MC-52
HIGH GABRIEL WEST *Williamson Co* 282W MC-52
HIGHLAND PARK *Pflugerville* 438E MQ-39
HIGHLAND PARK NORTH *Pflugerville* 408T MQ-40
HIGHLANDS AT CRYSTAL FALLS *Leander* 372E MC-45
HIGH MEADOW ESTATES *Williamson Co* 313L MF-50
HIGH MEADOWS *Austin* 587L MP-23
HIGH MEADOWS *Cedar Park* 372D MD-45
HIGH RIVER RANCH *Williamson Co* 279K WW-53
HILL COUNTRY *Travis Co* 611F MA-21
HILL CREEK WEST *Hays Co* 577Z WT-22
HILLCREST *Austin* 672Z MD-13
HILLS OF LAKEWAY, THE *Village of the Hills* 519P WW-29
HILLS OF MUSTANG CREEK *Taylor* 352R MZ-47
HILLS OF TEXAS ESTATES *Hays Co* 670K WY-14
HILLS OF TEXAS, THE *Hays Co* 670P WY-14
HISTORIC ACRES *Williamson Co* 226L MM-59
HOLLOWS AT NORTHSHORE, THE *Jonestown* 430P WY-38
HOMESTEAD ON HOBBS CREEK, THE *Bastrop Co* 741T MW-7
HORIZON PARK *Georgetown* 286V MM-52
HORIZON PARK *Leander* 342R MD-47
HORNSBY BEND *Travis Co* 589P MS-23
HORSESHOE BEND *Austin* 613H MF-21
HORSESHOE VILLAGE *Williamson Co* 252S MC-55
HUDSON BEND COLONY *Travis Co* 460C WZ-36
HUNTERS CHASE *Williamson Co* 434X MG-37
HUNTERS CROSSING *Bastrop* 744K EC-8
HUNTER'S GLEN *Cedar Park* 402Z MD-40
HUNTERS RIDGE *Travis Co* 735J MJ-8
HUNTINGTON TRAILS *Williamson Co* 408D MR-42
HUTTO HIGHLANDS *Hutto* 350J MU-47
HUTTOPARKE *Hutto* 349H MT-48
HUTTO SQUARE *Hutto* 349U MT-46
HYDE PARK *Austin* 555T MJ-25
IMPERIAL VALLEY *Travis Co* 588S MQ-22
INDIAN CREEK *Williamson Co* 287H MP-54
INDIAN HILLS *Travis Co* 674M MH-14
INDIAN RIDGE *Round Rock* 346M MM-47
INDIAN RIDGE *Round Rock* 347J MN-47
INVERNESS POINT *Travis Co* 488X WU-31
INWOOD HILLS *Austin* 614E MG-21
JACK'S POND *Travis Co* 436Q MM-38
JESTER ESTATES *Austin* 493V MF-31
JESTER POINT AT LAKEWOOD *Austin* 493C MF-33
JOHNSTON TERRACE *Austin* 616C MM-21
JONESTOWN HILLS *Jonestown* 400D WZ-42
KATY CROSSING *Georgetown* 257T MN-55
KATYMEAD *Pflugerville* 438P MQ-38
KENNEDY RIDGE ESTATES *Travis Co* 619B MS-21
KENSINGTON PLACE *Round Rock* 406R MM-41
KEY RANCH AT THE POLO CLUB *Hays Co* 638V WV-16
KIMBRO ROAD ESTATES *Travis Co* 530R MV-29
KINGSBURY PARK *Travis Co* 591K MW-23
KIRBY SPRINGS RANCH *Hays Co* 667G WT-15
KNOLLS, THE *Austin* 703G MF-12
LAGUNA VISTA *Travis Co* 457A WS-36
LA HACIENDA ESTATES *Travis Co* 460Q WZ-35
LAKECLIFF ON LAKE TRAVIS *Travis Co* 427J WS-38
LAKE CREEK *Round Rock* 406C MM-42
LAKE CREEK WEST *Round Rock* 406B ML-42
LAKE FOREST *Round Rock* 408A MQ-42
LAKE GEORGETOWN ESTATES *Williamson Co* 224Y MH-58
LAKEHURST *Travis Co* 488X WU-31
LAKELAND HILLS *Travis Co* 460M WZ-35
LAKELINE OAKS *Williamson Co* 403S ME-40
LAKELINE RANCH *Leander* 372B MC-45
LAKE OAK ESTATES *Travis Co* 490X WY-31
LAKE POINTE *Travis Co* 550M WZ-26
LAKE RIDGE *Round Rock* 376D MM-45
LAKE RIDGE ESTATES *Travis Co* 551D MB-27
LAKE SANDY *Jonestown* 401E MA-42
LAKES AT NORTHTOWN *Travis Co* 467E MN-36
LAKES AT WELLS BRANCH, THE *Travis Co* 436Q MM-38
LAKESHORE *Travis Co* 554S MG-25
LAKESHORE RANCH *Travis Co* 459M WX-35
LAKESIDE *Austin* 557Z MP-25
LAKESIDE *Round Rock* 346Z MM-46
LAKESIDE ESTATES *Williamson Co* 409B MS-42
LAKESIDE HILLS *Austin* 587D MP-24
LAKEWOOD *Austin* 494N MG-32
LAKEWOOD COUNTRY ESTATES *Williamson Co* 343U MF-46
LAKEWOOD ESTATES *Travis Co* 458T WU-34
LAKEWOOD ESTATES *Williamson Co* 225E MJ-60
LAMPLIGHT VILLAGE *Austin* 466K ML-35
LARSON ESTATES *Travis Co* 610T WY-19
LAS CIMAS *Austin* 557P MN-26
LAZY RIVER ACRES *Bastrop Co* 651Q MX-17
LEANDER HEIGHTS *Leander* 342L MD-47
LEGEND OAKS *Austin* 642D MD-18
LEGEND OAKS *Williamson Co* 285R MK-53
LEGENDS OF HUTTO *Hutto* 379H MT-45
LEGENDS VILLAGE *Round Rock* 377K MN-44
LEGEND'S WAY *Austin* 704P MG-11
LEWIS MOUNTAIN RANCH *Travis Co* 641J MA-17
LEXINGTON PARKE *Travis Co* 678E MQ-15
LICK CREEK RANCH *Travis Co* 486L WR-32
LINDA VISTA *Travis Co* 677S MN-13
LIVE OAK RANCH *Williamson Co* 281X MA-52
LODGE ACRES *Travis Co* 459V WX-34
LONG CANYON *Travis Co* 493T ME-31
LONG HOLLOW ESTATES *Travis Co* 430G WZ-39
LOOKOUT AT BRUSHY CREEK, THE *Williamson Co* 410J MU-41
LOOKOUT POINT *Travis Co* 641K MA-17
LOS CIELOS *Austin* 677V MP-13
LOST CREEK *Travis Co* 582G MD-24
LOST CREEK AT GAINES RANCH *Austin* 613A ME-21
LOST CREEK ESTATES *Travis Co* 582J MC-23
LOST RIVER *Williamson Co* 254Y MH-55
MADRONE RANCH *Travis Co* 577C WT-24
MAHA ESTATES *Mustang Ridge* 766T ML-4
MAJESTIC HILLS RANCHETTES *Travis Co* 519S WW-28
MANOR VILLA ESTATES *Travis Co* 530U MV-28
MAPLE RUN *Austin* 642C MD-18
MARSHALL'S HARBOR *Lago Vista* 459D WX-36
MARTINSHAW *Travis Co* 646W ML-16
MARTIN'S MEADOW *Bastrop Co* 742S MY-7
MASON CREEK *Leander* 342T MC-46
MASON CREEK NORTH *Leander* 342F MC-48
MAYFIELD RANCH *Round Rock* 345S MJ-46
McKNOWNVILLE *Travis Co* 641N MA-17
McNEIL ESTATES *Austin* 466A ML-36
McSHEPHERD RANCHES *Williamson Co* 441D MX-39
MEADOW CREEK *Austin* 674E MG-15
MEADOW LAKE *Round Rock* 347S MN-46
MEADOW OAKS *Hays Co* 636P WQ-17
MEADOWS AT BERDOLL *Austin* 678N MQ-14
MEADOWS AT BLUFF SPRINGS *Austin* 674G MH-15
MEADOWS AT CHANDLER CREEK *Williamson Co* 377C MP-45
MEADOWS OF BLACKHAWK *Pflugerville* 409S MS-40
MEADOWS OF BRUSHY CREEK, THE *Williamson Co* 405A MJ-42
MEADOWS OF HOBBS CREEK, THE *Bastrop* 741K MW-8
MERIDIAN *Austin* 670D WZ-15
MESA PARK *Austin* 465P MJ-35
MESA PARK *Round Rock* 377J MN-44
MESA RIDGE *Round Rock* 377N MN-44
MILWOOD *Austin* 465M MK-35
MILWOOD *Williamson Co* 434R MH-38
MONTERREY HILLS *Bastrop Co* 738X MQ-7
MORNINGSIDE MEADOWS *Williamson Co* 408K MQ-41
MOUNTAIN CREEK EAST *Pflugerville* 468E MQ-36
MOUNTAIN SHADOWS *Austin* 611G MB-21
MOUNTAIN VIEW *Travis Co* 490H WZ-33
MOUNT BONNELL TERRACE *Austin* 554F MG-27
MUSTANG MESA *Mustang Ridge* 765R MK-5
NAMANNS CAMP *Travis Co* 457B WS-36
NORTH ACRES *Travis Co* 526D MM-30
NORTH CREEK *Leander* 341D MB-48
NORTH FORTY *Dripping Springs* 636V WR-16
NORTH LAKE *Williamson Co* 193Z MF-61
NORTHLAKE ESTATES *Williamson Co* 224A MG-60
NORTH LAKEWAY VILLAGE *Lakeway* 490W WY-31
NORTH OAKS *Austin* 496M MM-32
NORTH PARK *Pflugerville* 437J MN-38
NORTH PARK ESTATES *Austin* 496L MM-32
NORTHRIDGE ACRES *Williamson Co* 436C MM-39
NORTHRIDGE PARK *Austin* 557K MN-26
NORTH RIM *Travis Co* 401B MA-42
NORTH SAN GABRIEL RANCHES *Williamson Co* 222J MC-59
NORTH SHEILDS *Austin* 466E ML-36
NORTH SHORE COLONY *Travis Co* 459Q WX-35
NORTHSHORE ON LAKE TRAVIS *Jonestown* 430T WY-37
NORTH STAR *Austin* 466N ML-35
NORTHTOWN *Travis Co* 467K MN-35
NORTHTOWN PARK *Travis Co* 467Q MP-35
NORTHVIEW HILLS *Austin* 464J MG-35
NORTHWOOD *Austin* 465D MK-36
NORWOOD PARK *Austin* 526T ML-28
OAK AT TWIN CREEKS, THE *Austin* 673Y MF-13
OAK BLUFF ESTATES *Round Rock* 378L MR-44
OAK BROOK *Williamson Co* 375S MJ-43
OAK COUNTRY ESTATES *Austin* 611M MB-20
OAK CREEK *Round Rock* 375V MK-43
OAK CREEK ESTATES *Travis Co* 590L MV-23
OAK CREEK PARKE *Austin* 672F MC-15
OAK CREST *Travis Co* 558J MQ-26
OAK CREST ESTATES *Williamson Co* 256J ML-56
OAK CREST RANCHETTES *Williamson Co* 256W ML-55
OAK FOREST *Austin* 464L MH-35
OAKLANDS, THE *Round Rock* 375Z MK-43
OAKLAND VILLAGE *Austin* 641H MB-18
OAKMONT FOREST *Cedar Park* 402C MD-42
OAK RIDGE *Leander* 342H MD-48
OAK SPRINGS *Dripping Springs* 667P WS-14
OAK SPRINGS *Round Rock* 376N ML-44
OAKWOOD GLEN *Williamson Co* 433E ME-39
ODELIA TERRACE *Travis Co* 708J MQ-11
OLD BISHOP PLACE *Williamson Co* 257B MN-57
OLDE OAK ESTATES *Williamson Co* 225T MJ-58
OLD FERRY *Travis Co* 457J WS-35
OLD TOWN MEADOWS *Round Rock* 376T ML-43
OLD TOWN VILLAGE *Leander* 342B MC-48
OLYMPIC HEIGHTS *Austin* 702D MD-12
ONION CREEK *Travis Co* 704F MG-12
ONION CREEK FOREST *Austin* 675J MJ-14
OVERLOOK AT RIVER PLACE, THE *Travis Co* 492X MC-31
OVERLOOK ESTATES *Leander* 342D MD-48
OWEN ACRES *Webberville* 650H MV-18
PADDOCK AT COMMONS FORD, THE *Travis Co* 521Z MB-28
PAINTED BUNTING *Travis Co* 432V MD-37
PALEFACE HOMESTEAD *Travis Co* 456S WQ-34
PALEFACE RANCH *Travis Co* 486D WR-33
PALOMA LAKE *Williamson Co* 348P MQ-47
PAMELA HEIGHTS *Travis Co* 436R MM-38
PANORAMIC HILLS *Travis Co* 400L WZ-41
PARADISE MANOR *Travis Co* 366Y WR-43
PARK AT BLACKHAWK, THE *Travis Co* 409T MS-40
PARK AT BRUSHY CREEK *Hutto* 379T MS-43
PARK AT SPICEWOOD SPRINGS, THE *Travis Co* 464E MG-36
PARKCREST *Pflugerville* 438J MQ-38
PARKE, THE *Travis Co* 462K MC-35
PARK PLACE *Cedar Park* 373P ME-44
PARK RIDGE *Austin* 673R MF-14
PARKSIDE AT MAYFIELD RANCH *Williamson Co* 344B MG-48
PARKVIEW ESTATES *Georgetown* 257S MN-55
PARKWOOD *Austin* 673C MF-15
PARSONS MEADOWS *Travis Co* 560L MV-26
PECAN BRANCH NORTH *Georgetown* 257K MN-56
PECAN TERRACE *Jonestown* 401A MA-42
PENNINGTON PLACE *Williamson Co* 257R MP-56
PERKINS VALLEY *Travis Co* 674T MG-13
PFLUGERVILLE ACRES *Travis Co* 408U MR-40
PFLUGERVILLE ESTATES *Travis Co* 467H MP-36
PFLUGERVILLE NORTHWEST *Travis Co* 437F MN-39
PICADILLY RIDGE *Travis Co* 437C MP-39
PINNACLE, THE *Georgetown* 317F MN-51
PIONEER CROSSING *Austin* 497W MN-31
PIONEER CROSSING *Round Rock* 378B MQ-45
PIONEER CROSSING EAST *Austin* 527G MP-30
PIONEER CROSSING WEST *Austin* 497T MN-31
PIONEER HILL *Austin* 527J MN-29
PLAIN VIEW ESTATES *Travis Co* 619J MS-20
PLANTATION, THE *Round Rock* 375M MK-44
PLEASANT VALLEY *Georgetown* 286Y MM-52
POLO CLUB AT ROOSTER SPRINGS, THE *Hays Co* 639N WW-17
POST OAK, THE *Travis Co* 560U MV-25
POUNDHOUSE HILLS *Hays Co* 636M WR-17
PRESERVE AT STONE OAK *Round Rock* 345N MJ-47
PRESERVE ESCALERA RANCH, THE *Williamson Co* 314K MG-50
PRESERVE, THE *Hays Co* 667B WS-15
PRESERVE, THE *Travis Co* 554A MG-27
PRESIDENTIAL MEADOWS *Travis Co* 530F MU-30
PRESTON OAKS *Austin* 465H MK-36
QUAIL CREEK *Austin* 526E ML-30
QUAIL CREEK WEST *Austin* 495V MK-31
QUAIL HOLLOW *Austin* 495H MK-33
QUAIL MEADOW *Georgetown* 256P ML-56
QUAIL VALLEY *Georgetown* 287S MN-52
QUARRY OAKS *Cedar Park* 372Y MD-43
RABBIT HOLLOW *Williamson Co* 316D MM-51
RAINTREE *Georgetown* 287P MN-53
RANCH AT BRUSHY CREEK, THE *Cedar Park* 374Q MH-44
RANCH AT CYPRESS CREEK, THE *Cedar Park* 402V MD-40
RANCH AT DEER CREEK *Travis Co* 402X MC-40
RANCHO ALTO *Austin* 702H MD-12
RANCH, THE *Bastrop Co* 739N MS-8
RAVINE, THE *Travis Co* 523Z MF-28
REATA TRAILS *Georgetown* 256F ML-57
RED OAKS *Cedar Park* 403K ME-41
RED WAGON RANCHETTES *Travis Co* 401L MB-41
REMUDA RANGE *Travis Co* 531Q MX-29
RESERVE AT BERRY CREEK, THE *Georgetown* 226K ML-59
RESERVE AT SOUTHPARK MEADOWS, THE *Austin* 673V MF-13
RESERVE AT TWIN CREEKS, THE *Travis Co* 432K MC-38
RESERVE AT WEST CREEK, THE *Travis Co* 439R MT-38
REYNERO *Travis Co* 737X MN-7
RIATA *Austin* 465E MJ-36
RIDGE AT ALTA VISTA, THE *Lakeway* 520W WY-29
RIDGE AT STEEDS CROSSING, THE *Travis Co* 409E MS-42
RIDGE AT THOMAS SPRINGS, THE *Travis Co* 610H WZ-21
RIDGE, THE *Travis Co* 582B MC-24
RIDGEWOOD ESTATES *Williamson Co* 224C MH-60
RIDGMAR LANDING *Williamson Co* 343C MF-48
RIDGMAR LANDING ON BRUSHY CREEK *Williamson Co* 313Y MF-49
RIVER BEND *Georgetown* 256P ML-56
RIVER COVE *Travis Co* 554E MG-27
RIVERCREST *Travis Co* 523T ME-28
RIVER DANCE *Travis Co* 520R WZ-29
RIVER HILLS *Georgetown* 286B ML-54
RIVER OAKS *Bastrop Co* 712P MY-11
RIVER PLACE *Travis Co* 492Q MD-32
RIVER RANCH *Travis Co* 497G MP-33
RIVER RIDGE *Georgetown* 286S ML-52
RIVER RIDGE *Travis Co* 704G MH-12
RIVERS CROSSING *Williamson Co* 350E MU-48
RIVERSIDE GROVE *Bastrop* 744C ED-9
RIVER TIMBER *Travis Co* 650K MU-17
RIVERVIEW ESTATES *Georgetown* 285Z MK-52
RIVERWALK *Hutto* 379Q MT-44
ROB ROY *Travis Co* 552M MD-26
ROCKING M RANCHETTES *Travis Co* 767G MP-6
ROLLING HILLS *Williamson Co* 409F MS-42
ROLLING HILLS WEST *West Lake Hills* 583Q MF-23
ROLLING MEADOWS *Travis Co* 409P MS-41
ROLLING RIDGE *Williamson Co* 407M MP-41
ROLLINGWOOD *Rollingwood* 583V MF-22

39

Austin, 2009

Interstate Highways

STREET NAME	CITY or COUNTY	MAPSCO GRID	AUSTIN GRID	ZIP CODE	BLOCK RANGE O/E
IH 35 N	Austin	**615F**	MJ-21	78702	1-199 O
	Austin	**615F**	MJ-21	78701	2-198 E
	Austin	**585L**	MK-23	78701	200-1798 E
	Austin	**585L**	MK-23	78702	201-1799 O
	Austin	**585L**	MK-23	78705	1800-3798 E
	Austin	**585L**	MK-23	78722	1801-3799 O
	Austin	**585L**	MK-23	78751	3800-4098 E
	Austin	**555V**	MK-25	78751	4100-5098 E
	Austin	**555V**	MK-25	78722	4101-4399 O
	Austin	**555V**	MK-25	78723	4401-5099 O
	Austin	**556J**	ML-26	78751	5100-6098 E
	Austin	**556J**	ML-26	78723	5101-6099 O
	Austin	**556A**	ML-27	78752	6100-7199
	Austin	**526K**	ML-29	78752	7200-7899
	Austin	**526K**	ML-29	78753	7900-10299
	Austin	**496U**	MM-31	78753	10300-12399
	Austin	**466R**	MM-35	78753	12400-13699
	Austin	**466R**	MM-35	78728	13700-14598 E
	Austin	**466R**	MM-35	78660	13701-14599 O
	Austin	**436Z**	MM-37	78728	14600-15198 E
	Austin	**436Z**	MM-37	78660	14601-15199 O
	Austin	**436Z**	MM-37	78660	15201-15499 O
	Georgetown	**256V**	MM-55	78626	100-1598 E
	Georgetown	**256V**	MM-55	78628	101-1599 O
	Georgetown	**257E**	MN-57	78626	1600-2698 E
	Georgetown	**257E**	MN-57	78628	1601-2699 O
	Georgetown	**227T**	MN-58	78626	2700-5098 E
	Georgetown	**227T**	MN-58	78628	2701-3999 O
	Georgetown	**227T**	MN-58	78633	4001-5099 O
	Georgetown	**197L**	MP-62	78626	5100-6398 E
	Georgetown	**197L**	MP-62	78633	5101-6399 O
	Pflugerville	**437N**	MN-38	78728	15500-15998 E
	Pflugerville	**437N**	MN-38	78660	15501-15999 O
	Round Rock	**376K**	ML-44	78681	300-3298 E
	Round Rock	**376K**	ML-44	78664	301-3299 O
	Round Rock	**376K**	ML-44	78665	2401-3299 O
	Round Rock	**346K**	ML-47	78681	3300-5498 E
	Round Rock	**346K**	ML-47	78665	3301-5499 O
	Travis Co	**436Z**	MM-37	78728	15200-15498 E
	Travis Co	**436D**	MM-39	78728	16000-16598 E
	Travis Co	**436D**	MM-39	78660	16001-16499 O
	Travis Co	**436D**	MM-39	78664	16501-16599 O
	Williamson Co	**197L**	MP-62	78626	6400-7998 E
	Williamson Co	**197L**	MP-62	78633	6401-7999 O
IH 35 S	Austin	**615F**	MJ-21	78741	1-3099 O
	Austin	**615F**	MJ-21	78704	2-3098 E
	Austin	**645A**	MJ-18	78704	3100-3898 E
	Austin	**645A**	MJ-18	78741	3101-3899 O
	Austin	**644H**	MH-18	78704	3900-4098 E
	Austin	**644H**	MH-18	78741	3901-4099 O
	Austin	**644R**	MH-17	78745	4100-6498 E
	Austin	**644R**	MH-17	78744	4101-6499 O
	Austin	**674B**	MG-15	78745	6500-9098 E
	Austin	**674S**	MG-13	78744	6501-10099 O
	Austin	**674S**	MG-13	78748	9100-10098 E
	Austin	**703V**	MF-10	78748	10100-11098 E
	Austin	**703H**	MF-12	78747	10101-11099 O
	Austin	**703V**	MF-10	78747	11100-12699
	Buda	**733L**	MF-8	78610	14700-15499
	Georgetown	**286F**	ML-54	78626	100-3298 E
	Georgetown	**286F**	ML-54	78628	101-3299 O
	Georgetown	**316C**	MM-51	78628	3300-7698 E
	Georgetown	**316T**	ML-49	78628	3301-7699 O
	Hays Co	**733L**	MF-8	78610	14200-14699
	Hays Co	**763J**	ME-5	78610	15500-16999
	Hays Co	**762Z**	MD-4	78610	17000-17599
	Round Rock	**406V**	MM-40	78681	300-3298 E
	Round Rock	**406V**	MM-40	78664	301-3399 O
	Round Rock	**406V**	MM-40	78728	3300-3398 E
	Travis Co	**733L**	MF-8	78747	12700-13299
	Travis Co	**733L**	MF-8	78610	13300-14199
IH 35 BUSINESS N	Georgetown	**286C**	MM-54	78626	100-799
See.. Austin Ave N					
	Georgetown	**256V**	MM-55	78626	800-2499
	Georgetown	**257J**	MN-56	78626	2500-2999
IH 35 BUSINESS N	Round Rock	**376Q**	MM-44	78664	100-2399
IH 35 BUSINESS S	Georgetown	**286Y**	MM-52	78626	100-2299
See.. Austin Ave S					
IH 35 BUSINESS S	Round Rock	**406H**	MM-42	78664	100-2299

Toll Roads

STREET NAME	CITY or COUNTY	MAPSCO GRID	AUSTIN GRID	ZIP CODE	BLOCK RANGE O/E
LOOP 1	Austin	**436A**	ML-39	78727	None
	Austin	**466N**	ML-35	78727	None
	Travis Co	**436A**	ML-39	78728	None
	Williamson Co	**406W**	ML-40	78728	None
	Williamson Co	**436A**	ML-39	78728	None
STATE HWY 45 N	Austin	**404Y**	MH-40	78717	None
	Pflugerville	**408N**	MQ-41	78660	None
	Round Rock	**406X**	ML-40	78664	None
	Round Rock	**407P**	MN-41	78664	None
	Williamson Co	**404Y**	MH-40	78717	None
	Williamson Co	**405Y**	MK-40	78717	None
	Williamson Co	**406X**	ML-40	78681	None
	Williamson Co	**406X**	ML-40	78717	None
	Williamson Co	**406X**	ML-40	78728	None
STATE HWY 45 SE	Creedmoor	**734J**	MG-8	78610	None
	Creedmoor	**735W**	MJ-7	78610	None
	Creedmoor	**765B**	MJ-6	78610	None
	Mustang Ridge	**765C**	MK-6	78610	None
	Mustang Ridge	**766B**	ML-6	78610	None
	Travis Co	**733H**	MF-9	78610	None
	Travis Co	**734J**	MG-8	78610	None
	Travis Co	**735W**	MJ-7	78610	None
	Travis Co	**765B**	MJ-6	78610	None
STATE HWY 130	Austin	**528H**	MR-30	78653	None
	Austin	**559E**	MS-27	78653	None
	Austin	**677L**	MP-14	78617	None
	Georgetown	**227X**	MN-58	78626	None
	Georgetown	**257U**	MP-55	78626	None
	Georgetown	**287H**	MP-54	78626	None
	Georgetown	**288T**	MQ-52	78626	None
	Hutto	**379E**	MS-45	78634	None
	Mustang Ridge	**736R**	MM-8	78610	None

Continued on next column

STREET NAME	CITY or COUNTY	MAPSCO GRID	AUSTIN GRID	ZIP CODE	BLOCK RANGE O/E
STATE HWY 130 (Cont'd)					
	Mustang Ridge	**766C**	MM-6	78610	None
	Pflugerville	**408R**	MR-41	78660	None
	Pflugerville	**438H**	MR-39	78660	None
	Pflugerville	**468D**	MR-36	78660	None
	Travis Co	**408R**	MR-41	78660	None
	Travis Co	**409A**	MS-42	78660	None
	Travis Co	**469W**	MS-34	78653	None
	Travis Co	**499J**	MS-32	78653	None
	Travis Co	**528H**	MR-30	78653	None
	Travis Co	**559E**	MS-27	78653	None
	Travis Co	**588R**	MR-23	78724	None
	Travis Co	**589E**	MS-24	78653	None
	Travis Co	**618K**	MQ-20	78724	None
	Travis Co	**618K**	MQ-20	78725	None
	Travis Co	**648J**	MQ-17	78617	None
	Travis Co	**648J**	MQ-17	78725	None
	Travis Co	**677L**	MP-14	78617	None
	Travis Co	**707S**	MN-10	78617	None
	Travis Co	**707S**	MN-10	78719	None
	Travis Co	**736R**	MM-8	78719	None
	Travis Co	**737A**	MN-9	78719	None
	Williamson Co	**288T**	MQ-52	78634	None
	Williamson Co	**318G**	MR-51	78634	None
	Williamson Co	**349E**	MS-48	78634	None
	Williamson Co	**379E**	MS-45	78634	None
	Williamson Co	**409A**	MS-42	78634	None
TOLL ROAD 183A	Austin	**403Q**	MF-41	78717	None
	Cedar Park	**373P**	ME-44	78613	None
	Cedar Park	**403Q**	MF-41	78613	None
	Leander	**312Q**	MD-50	78641	None
	Leander	**343P**	ME-47	78641	None
	Williamson Co	**312Q**	MD-50	78641	None
	Williamson Co	**343P**	ME-47	78641	None
	Williamson Co	**373P**	ME-44	78641	None
	Williamson Co	**403Q**	MF-41	78717	None

U.S. Highways

STREET NAME	CITY or COUNTY	MAPSCO GRID	AUSTIN GRID	ZIP CODE	BLOCK RANGE O/E
US HWY 79	Round Rock	**377S**	MN-43	78664	1200-4299
See.. Palm Valley Blvd E					
	Round Rock	**378G**	MR-45	78664	4300-4599
	Round Rock	**376U**	MM-43	78664	None
See.. Palm Valley Blvd W					
	Taylor	**352K**	MY-47	76574	None
	Taylor	**352Q**	MZ-47	76574	None
See.. SW Carlos G. Parker Blvd					
	Taylor	**353L**	EB-47	76574	None
See.. SE Carlos G. Parker Blvd					
	Williamson Co	**378G**	MR-45	78664	4600-4899
	Williamson Co	**378G**	MR-45	78634	4900-6799
	Williamson Co	**379B**	MS-45	78634	6800-7499
	Williamson Co	**350V**	MV-46	78634	10400-11299
	Williamson Co	**351S**	MW-46	78634	11300-12399
	Williamson Co	**351S**	MW-46	76574	12400-13799
	Williamson Co	**353D**	EB-48	76574	None
US HWY 79 E	Hutto	**349Z**	MT-46	78634	100-299
	Hutto	**350W**	MU-46	78634	300-1299
	Williamson Co	**350W**	MU-46	78634	300-1299
US HWY 79 W	Hutto	**379C**	MT-45	78634	100-799
US HWY 79 BUSINESS E	Taylor	**353C**	EB-48	76574	100-2399
US HWY 79 BUSINESS W	Taylor	**352H**	MZ-48	76574	100-799
	Taylor	**353E**	EA-48	76574	800-2599
US HWY 183	Austin	**616G**	MM-21	78721	200-2799
See.. Ed Bluestein Blvd					
	Austin	**556C**	MM-27	78752	1500-2699
	Austin	**586R**	MM-23	78721	2800-4899
	Austin	**587A**	MN-24	78724	4900-5799
See.. Ed Bluestein Blvd					
	Austin	**557S**	MN-25	78723	5800-7499
	Austin	**556H**	MM-27	78723	7500-7799
	Caldwell Co	**796X**	ML-1	78610	None
	Cedar Park	**373N**	ME-44	78613	100-1299
	Cedar Park	**372H**	MD-45	78613	1300-2799
	Williamson Co	**252W**	MC-55	78642	1-199
	Williamson Co	**282T**	MC-52	78641	200-2999
US HWY 183 N	Austin	**526Y**	MM-28	78752	100-1499
See.. Anderson Ln E					
	Austin	**525H**	MK-30	78758	7900-8799
See.. Research Blvd					
	Austin	**495U**	MK-31	78758	8800-9299
	Austin	**495E**	MJ-33	78759	9300-10899
	Austin	**465J**	MJ-35	78759	10900-11999
	Austin	**464G**	MH-36	78759	12000-12799
	Austin	**464G**	MH-36	78750	12800-12999
	Austin	**434S**	MG-37	78750	13000-13599
	Austin	**433M**	MF-38	78750	13600-13899
	Austin	**433D**	MF-39	78717	13900-13999
	Austin	**403F**	ME-42	78717	14000-14099
	Leander	**312T**	MC-49	78641	100-999
	Williamson Co	**312B**	MC-51	78641	3000-4999
US HWY 183 S	Austin	**616U**	MM-19	78742	1-799 O
See.. Bastrop Hwy					
	Austin	**616U**	MM-19	78741	2-798 E
	Austin	**616U**	MM-19	78742	800-1199
	Austin	**646C**	MM-18	78741	1200-1399
	Austin	**646C**	MM-18	78744	1500-3898 E
	Austin	**646C**	MM-18	78719	1501-3899 O
	Austin	**676C**	MM-15	78744	3900-4798 E
	Austin	**676C**	MM-15	78719	3901-4799 O
	Cedar Park	**403F**	ME-42	78613	100-2699
	Leander	**342L**	MD-47	78641	100-2799
	Mustang Ridge	**736P**	ML-8	78719	9600-10598 E
	Mustang Ridge	**736P**	ML-8	78747	9601-10999 O
	Mustang Ridge	**736P**	ML-8	78610	10600-10998 E
	Mustang Ridge	**766K**	ML-5	78747	11000-11898 E
	Mustang Ridge	**766K**	ML-5	78610	11001-11899 O
	Mustang Ridge	**766K**	ML-5	78610	11900-12699
	Mustang Ridge	**796F**	ML-3	78610	None
	Travis Co	**676T**	ML-13	78744	4800-6898 E
	Travis Co	**676T**	ML-13	78719	4801-6899 O
	Travis Co	**706K**	ML-11	78744	6900-7898 E
	Travis Co	**706K**	ML-11	78719	6901-8199 O
	Travis Co	**706K**	ML-11	78747	7900-8198 E
	Travis Co	**736P**	ML-8	78719	8200-9598 E
	Travis Co	**736P**	ML-8	78747	8201-9599 O
US HWY 183A	Austin	**403Q**	MF-41	78717	None
See.. Toll Road 183A					
US HWY 290	Austin	**555V**	MK-25	78722	None
	Austin	**555V**	MK-25	78751	None
	Austin	**585L**	MK-23	78701	None
	Austin	**585L**	MK-23	78702	None
	Austin	**585L**	MK-23	78705	None
	Austin	**585L**	MK-23	78722	None
	Austin	**585L**	MK-23	78751	None
	Austin	**615P**	MJ-20	78701	None
	Austin	**615P**	MJ-20	78702	None
See.. IH 35 N					
	Austin	**615P**	MJ-20	78704	None
	Austin	**615P**	MJ-20	78741	None
See.. IH 35 S					
	Austin	**644C**	MH-18	78704	None
See.. Ben White Blvd E					
	Austin	**644H**	MH-18	78704	None
	Austin	**644H**	MH-18	78741	None
	Austin	**645A**	MJ-18	78704	None
	Austin	**645A**	MJ-18	78741	None
	Bastrop Co	**534Y**	ED-28	78621	200E-399E
	Bastrop Co	**564D**	ED-27	78621	400E-699E
	Bastrop Co	**533K**	EA-29	78621	500W-699W
	Elgin	**534S**	EC-28	78621	100E-298E E
	Elgin	**533R**	EB-29	78621	200W-499W
	Travis Co	**640A**	WY-18	78736	10100W-11199W
	Travis Co	**640A**	WY-18	78737	10100W-11199W
	Travis Co	**533K**	EA-29	78653	18300W-18899W
	Travis Co	**533K**	EA-29	78621	18900W-19099W
US HWY 290 E	Austin	**556E**	ML-27	78723	6100-7599
	Austin	**556D**	MM-27	78724	7600-8099
	Austin	**557A**	MN-27	78724	8100-9599
	Austin	**558A**	MQ-27	78754	9600-9699
	Austin	**528Y**	MR-28	78724	9700-9999
	Austin	**528Y**	MR-28	78653	10000-10199
	Dripping Springs	**636Z**	WR-16	78620	100-599
	Hays Co	**637Y**	WT-16	78620	600-2699
	Hays Co	**638X**	WU-16	78620	2700-4399
	Manor	**529P**	MS-29	78653	10300-11999
	Manor	**530N**	MU-29	78653	12000-13299
	Manor	**530M**	MV-29	78653	13300-14098 E
	Manor	**531K**	MW-29	78653	14100-15498 E
	Manor	**531K**	MW-29	78621	15500-16398 E
	Travis Co	**529P**	MS-29	78653	10200-10299
	Travis Co	**530M**	MV-29	78653	13301-14099 O
	Travis Co	**531K**	MW-29	78653	14101-15499 O
	Travis Co	**531K**	MW-29	78621	15501-16399 O
	Travis Co	**532K**	MY-29	78621	16400-18299
US HWY 290 W	Austin	**644C**	MH-18	78704	100-599
See.. Ben White Blvd W					
	Austin	**614W**	MG-19	78704	600-2499
	Austin	**613T**	ME-19	78745	4400-4599
See.. State Hwy 71 W					
	Austin	**613S**	ME-19	78735	5000-5199
	Austin	**612T**	MC-19	78735	5200-6999
	Austin	**611Z**	MB-19	78736	7000-7999
	Dripping Springs	**636T**	WQ-16	78620	100-1299
	Hays Co	**636T**	WQ-16	78620	1300-2799
	Hays Co	**639Q**	WX-17	78737	12000-13599
	Hays Co	**638Z**	WV-16	78737	13600-14499
	Sunset Valley	**613T**	ME-19	78745	4600-4799
See.. State Hwy 71 W					
	Sunset Valley	**613S**	ME-19	78735	4800-4999
	Travis Co	**611S**	MA-19	78736	8000-8799
	Travis Co	**610V**	WZ-19	78736	8800-10599
	Travis Co	**640A**	WY-18	78736	10600-10899
	Travis Co	**639Q**	WX-17	78737	10900-11999

Loops (State Highways)

STREET NAME	CITY or COUNTY	MAPSCO GRID	AUSTIN GRID	ZIP CODE	BLOCK RANGE O/E
LOOP 1	Austin	**584X**	MG-22	78746	100-1299
See.. Mopac Expwy S					
	Austin	**584D**	MH-24	78703	100-2599
See.. Mopac Expwy N					
	Austin	**613D**	MF-21	78746	1400-4099
	Austin	**554R**	MH-26	78703	2600-3499
	Austin	**554R**	MH-26	78731	3500-5099
	Austin	**613P**	ME-20	78735	4100-5099
	Austin	**524R**	MH-29	78731	5100-6899
See.. Mopac Expwy					
	Austin	**613P**	ME-20	78749	5100-5999
	Austin	**643A**	ME-18	78749	6000-6299
	Austin	**642G**	MD-18	78749	6900-9599
	Austin	**525E**	MJ-30	78731	6900-7799
	Austin	**495F**	MJ-33	78759	8200-11499
	Austin	**642W**	MC-16	78739	9600-10199
	Austin	**465Y**	MK-34	78759	11500-11999
	Austin	**465Y**	MK-34	78758	12000-12099
	Austin	**466N**	ML-35	78758	12100-12499
	Austin	**466N**	ML-35	78727	12500-12799
	Austin	**671H**	MB-15	78739	None
LOOP 4 S	Hays Co	**762Q**	MD-5	78610	100-2499
See.. Main St S					
LOOP 111	Austin	**616B**	ML-21	78702	1-1099
See.. Airport Blvd					
	Austin	**586N**	ML-23	78702	1100-1899
	Austin	**586N**	ML-23	78722	1900-4099
	Austin	**555Z**	MK-25	78722	4300-4499
LOOP 150	Bastrop	**745H**	EF-9	78602	600-1999
	Bastrop	**745F**	EE-9	78602	None
	Bastrop	**746J**	EG-8	78602	None
LOOP 212	Manor	**529U**	MT-28	78653	None
	Travis Co	**530N**	MU-29	78653	None
LOOP 275 N	Austin	**525M**	MK-29	78753	8000-8299
See.. Lamar Blvd N					
	Austin	**526E**	ML-30	78753	8300-9799
	Austin	**496X**	ML-31	78753	9800-12299
	Austin	**466U**	MM-34	78753	12300-13699
LOOP 275 S	Austin	**644G**	MH-18	78745	4000-6799
See.. Congress Ave S					
	Austin	**674J**	MG-14	78745	6800-9099
LOOP 343	Austin	**585W**	MJ-22	78701	100-699
See.. Cesar Chavez St W					
LOOP 360 N	Austin	**523M**	MF-29	78746	3400-4999
See.. Capital of Texas Hwy N					

Continued on next page

STREET NAME	CITY or COUNTY	MAPSCO GRID	AUSTIN GRID	ZIP CODE	BLOCK RANGE O/E
LOOP 360 N (Cont'd)	Austin	524E	MG-30	78731	6100-6599
	Austin	494T	MG-31	78731	6600-8399
	Austin	494M	MH-32	78759	8400-9299
	Austin	495K	MJ-32	78759	9300-10099
	Travis Co	553F	ME-27	78746	100-3399
	See.. Capital of Texas Hwy N				
	Travis Co	523M	MF-29	78731	5000-6099
LOOP 360 S	Austin	613V	MF-19	78746	3300-3699
	Austin	613V	MF-19	78704	3700-4299
	Travis Co	553S	ME-25	78746	100-599
	See.. Capital of Texas Hwy S				
	Travis Co	583K	ME-23	78746	600-2599
	Travis Co	613B	ME-21	78746	2600-3299

Spurs (State Highways)

STREET NAME	CITY or COUNTY	MAPSCO GRID	AUSTIN GRID	ZIP CODE	BLOCK RANGE O/E
SPUR 69	Austin	555H	MK-27	78752	None

State Highways

STREET NAME	CITY or COUNTY	MAPSCO GRID	AUSTIN GRID	ZIP CODE	BLOCK RANGE O/E
STATE HWY 21	Bastrop	744M	ED-8	78602	200-499
	See.. State Hwy 71				
	Bastrop Co	742N	MY-8	78612	100-699
	Bastrop Co	744E	EC-9	78602	500-799
	Bastrop Co	743E	EA-9	78602	700-1299
	Hays Co	795Z	MK-1	78610	12600-13899
	Mustang Ridge	796T	ML-1	78610	None
	Niederwald	795Z	MK-1	78610	None
STATE HWY 21 E	Bastrop	745H	EF-9	78602	100-199
	Bastrop Co	746A	EG-9	78602	200-399
STATE HWY 21 W	Bastrop Co	741V	MX-7	78612	700-1199
	Bastrop Co	740W	MU-7	78612	1200-1699
	Bastrop Co	739Z	MT-7	78612	1700-1799
	Bastrop Co	767Z	MP-4	78616	2700-2899
STATE HWY 29 E	Georgetown	286M	MM-53	78626	100-1099
	See.. University Ave E				
	Georgetown	287K	MN-53	78626	1100-3199
	Georgetown	287H	MP-54	78626	3200-3899
	Williamson Co	288D	MR-54	78626	4200-6699
STATE HWY 29 W	Georgetown	286M	MM-53	78626	100-999
	See.. University Ave W				
	Georgetown	286K	ML-53	78628	1000-1699
	Liberty Hill	252X	MC-55	78642	10300-11199
	Williamson Co	285K	MJ-53	78628	1700-3499
	Williamson Co	284J	MG-53	78628	3500-6199
	Williamson Co	283F	ME-54	78628	6200-8599
	Williamson Co	282H	MD-54	78628	8600-10299
STATE HWY 45	Austin	671E	MA-15	78739	5200-7599
	Austin	670D	WZ-15	78737	7600-8299
	Austin	640Z	WZ-16	78739	None
STATE HWY 71	Bastrop	744M	ED-8	78602	200-499
	See.. State Hwy 21				
	Bastrop	745M	EF-8	78602	100E-399E
	Bastrop	746N	EG-8	78602	400E-599E
	Bastrop	745J	EE-8	78602	100W-299W
	Bastrop Co	744E	EC-9	78602	500-699
	See.. State Hwy 21				
	Bastrop Co	743E	EA-9	78602	700-1299
	Bastrop Co	742D	MZ-9	78602	1300-1399
	Bastrop Co	712T	MY-10	78612	1400-1899
	Bastrop Co	711A	MW-12	78612	1900-2499
	Bastrop Co	746Z	EH-7	78602	600E-999E
STATE HWY 71 E	Austin	646H	MM-18	78742	1500-1999
	Austin	647J	MN-17	78719	2000-2998 E
	Austin	647J	MN-17	78617	2001-2999 O
	Austin	647J	MN-17	78617	3000-3399
	Austin	644H	MH-18	78704	None
	See.. Ben White Blvd E				
	Austin	645E	MJ-18	78741	None
	Austin	646F	ML-18	78741	None
	Travis Co	647V	MP-16	78617	3400-3899
	Travis Co	648W	MQ-16	78617	3900-4199
	Travis Co	678D	MR-15	78617	4200-4899
	Travis Co	679A	MS-15	78617	4900-5399
	Travis Co	680E	MU-15	78612	5400-5599
	See.. Ben White Blvd E				
STATE HWY 71 W	Austin	644C	MH-18	78704	100-599
	Austin	614X	MG-19	78704	600-2499
	Austin	613U	MF-19	78745	4400-4599
	See.. US Hwy 290 W				
	Austin	613S	ME-19	78735	5000-5199
	Austin	612T	MC-19	78735	5200-6999
	See.. US Hwy 290 E				
	Austin	611R	MB-20	78735	7000-9399
	Bastrop Co	680V	MV-13	78612	None
	See.. Ben White Blvd E				
	Bee Cave	550S	WY-25	78738	11900-13699
	Bee Cave	549R	WX-26	78738	13700-15199
	Blanco Co	455G	WP-36	78620	None
	Burnet Co	455G	WP-36	78669	None
	Sunset Valley	613U	MF-19	78745	4600-4799
	See.. US Hwy 290 W				
	Sunset Valley	613S	ME-19	78735	4800-4999
	Travis Co	581N	MA-23	78736	9400-10299
	Travis Co	580D	WZ-24	78736	10300-11599
	Travis Co	550S	WY-25	78738	11600-11899
	Travis Co	549J	WW-26	78738	15200-16499
	Travis Co	548G	WV-27	78738	16500-18199
	Travis Co	518W	WU-28	78669	18200-19099
	Travis Co	517Q	WT-29	78669	19100-22199
	Travis Co	487S	WS-31	78669	22200-23099
	Travis Co	486H	WR-33	78669	23100-24499
	Travis Co	456Y	WR-34	78669	24500-26899
	Travis Co	455G	WP-36	78669	26900-27099
STATE HWY 95	Bastrop	746N	EG-8	78602	400-599
	Bastrop	745L	EF-8	78602	100N-299N
	Bastrop	715Y	EF-10	78602	300N-499N
	Bastrop Co	504J	EC-32	78621	300-799
	Bastrop Co	746Z	EH-7	78602	600-999
	Bastrop Co	715F	EE-12	78602	500N-899N
	Bastrop Co	564K	EC-26	78621	100S-799S
	Taylor	323N	EA-50	76574	None
	See.. Main St N				
	Taylor	353J	EA-47	76574	None
	See.. Main St S				
	Travis Co	473M	EB-35	78615	16300-17699
	Williamson Co	353W	EA-46	76574	7000-7499
	Williamson Co	473M	EB-35	78615	14700-16199
STATE HWY 95 N	Bastrop Co	474W	EC-34	78621	800-999
	Elgin	533R	EB-29	78621	100-299
	Elgin	534A	EC-30	78621	300-399
STATE HWY 95 S	Taylor	322H	MZ-51	76574	3800-4599
	See.. Main St N				
	Williamson Co	322H	MZ-51	76574	2400-3099
	See.. Main St N				
	Williamson Co	383F	EA-45	76574	7500-10599
	Williamson Co	413T	EA-40	76574	10600-12199
	Williamson Co	443F	EA-39	78615	12200-16099
STATE HWY 165	Austin	585Y	MK-22	78702	1500-1599
STATE HWY 195	Georgetown	227E	MP-60	78633	100-1298 E
	Georgetown	227E	MP-60	78628	101-1299 O
	Georgetown	197W	MN-61	78628	1300-2099
	Williamson Co	196E	ML-63	78628	2100-5799
	Williamson Co	195D	MK-63	78633	5800-6199
STATE HWY 304	Bastrop	744L	ED-8	78602	100-199
	Bastrop Co	744L	ED-8	78602	200-499

Farm To Market Roads

STREET NAME	CITY or COUNTY	MAPSCO GRID	AUSTIN GRID	ZIP CODE	BLOCK RANGE O/E
FM RD 20	Bastrop Co	744J	EC-8	78602	100-199
	Bastrop Co	743V	EB-7	78602	200-599
FM RD 112	Taylor	353L	EB-47	76574	None
	See.. Walnut St E				
	Williamson Co	353M	EB-47	76574	1800-2499
FM RD 397	Taylor	322M	MZ-50	76574	100-899
	See.. NW Carlos G. Parker Blvd				
	Taylor	352F	MY-48	76574	900-1299
FM RD 535	Bastrop Co	740M	MV-8	78612	5500-6199
	Bastrop Co	710X	MU-10	78612	6200-6499
	Bastrop Co	709R	MT-11	78612	6500-6799
FM RD 619	Williamson Co	353D	EB-48	76574	5900-6799
	Williamson Co	353M	EB-47	76574	7100-7199
FM RD 685	Pflugerville	438X	MQ-37	78660	100-2799
	Pflugerville	408Z	MR-40	78660	19200-19699
	Travis Co	408Z	MR-40	78660	19700-20199
	Travis Co	409A	MS-42	78660	20200-20799
	Travis Co	409A	MS-42	78634	20800-21499
	Williamson Co	379K	MS-44	78634	1-2499
	Williamson Co	409A	MS-42	78634	2500-2799
FM RD 734 E	Austin	467W	MN-34	78753	100-799
	Austin	497B	MN-33	78753	800-1699
	Austin	497Q	MP-32	78754	1700-4599
	Austin	498W	MQ-31	78653	5200-6799
	Austin	528M	MR-29	78653	8800-9499
	See.. Parmer Ln E				
	Travis Co	497Q	MP-32	78754	4600-4799
	Travis Co	498W	MQ-31	78653	4800-5199
	Travis Co	528M	MR-29	78653	6800-8799
	See.. Parmer Ln E				
	Travis Co	529N	MS-29	78653	9500-9599
FM RD 734 W	Austin	466N	ML-35	78753	100-1099
	Austin	466N	ML-35	78727	1100-3399
	See.. Parmer Ln W				
	Austin	465B	MJ-36	78727	3400-5599
	Austin	435S	MJ-37	78727	5600-6099
	Austin	435S	MJ-37	78729	6100-7499
	See.. Parmer Ln W				
	Austin	434H	MH-39	78729	7500-7999
	Austin	404Y	MH-40	78717	9200-10799
	Cedar Park	404Y	MH-40	78613	10800-11099
	See.. Parmer Ln W				
	Cedar Park	374T	MG-43	78613	11100-13099
	Williamson Co	434H	MH-39	78729	8000-8999
	Williamson Co	404Y	MH-40	78729	9000-9199
FM RD 812	Bastrop Co	738P	MQ-8	78617	2500-2899
	Bastrop Co	738P	MQ-8	78617	2900-2999
	Travis Co	676Y	MM-13	78719	8600-10099
	Travis Co	706D	MM-12	78719	10100-10399
	Travis Co	706H	MM-12	78617	10400-11098 E
	Travis Co	706H	MM-12	78719	10401-11099 O
	Travis Co	707J	MN-11	78617	11100-12899
	Travis Co	707Y	MP-10	78719	12900-13299
	Travis Co	707Y	MP-10	78617	13300-13999
	Travis Co	737D	MP-9	78617	14000-14899
	Travis Co	738P	MQ-8	78617	14900-17099
FM RD 969	Austin	586K	ML-23	78702	2900-3099
	See.. Martin Luther King Jr Blvd				
	Austin	586K	ML-23	78721	3100-6099
	Austin	587J	MN-23	78724	6100-9299
	Bastrop Co	744A	EC-9	78602	100-299
	Bastrop Co	651C	MX-18	78621	2200-2599
	Travis Co	587V	MP-22	78724	9300-10099
	Travis Co	588W	MQ-22	78724	10100-10599
	Travis Co	618H	MR-21	78724	10600-14499
	Travis Co	619J	MS-20	78724	14500-16299
	Travis Co	619H	MT-21	78653	16300-17699
	Travis Co	620K	MU-20	78653	17700-19199
	Travis Co	651C	MX-18	78653	20300-20999
	Webberville	650D	MV-18	78653	19200-19499
	Webberville	621W	MW-19	78653	19500-20299
	Webberville	620Z	MV-19	78653	None
FM RD 971	Georgetown	256V	MM-55	78626	1-199
	Georgetown	257P	MN-56	78626	200-2299
	Georgetown	258F	MQ-57	78626	3700-3799
	Weir	258F	MQ-57	78626	3900-5699
	Williamson Co	257P	MN-56	78626	2300-3799
	Williamson Co	258F	MQ-57	78626	3200-3699
	Williamson Co	258F	MQ-57	78626	3800-3899
FM RD 972	Williamson Co	197V	MP-61	78626	1-5199
FM RD 973	Taylor	352Y	MZ-46	76574	1-499
	Williamson Co	352Y	MZ-46	76574	500-899
	Williamson Co	382B	MY-45	76574	900-3599
	Williamson Co	412E	MY-42	76574	3600-5099
	Williamson Co	411Z	MX-40	76574	5100-6099
	Williamson Co	441D	MX-39	76574	6100-6899
FM RD 973 N	Austin	559K	MS-26	78653	10100-11398 E
	Manor	559C	MT-27	78653	11800-11999
	Manor	529Y	MT-28	78653	12000-12499
	Manor	530N	MU-29	78653	12800-13299
	Travis Co	617Z	MP-19	78725	2400-2599
	Travis Co	618N	MQ-20	78725	2600-4599
	Travis Co	618B	MQ-21	78724	4600-4999
	Travis Co	588U	MR-22	78724	5000-7799
	Travis Co	589B	MS-24	78724	7800-9098 E

Continued on next column

STREET NAME	CITY or COUNTY	MAPSCO GRID	AUSTIN GRID	ZIP CODE	BLOCK RANGE O/E
FM RD 973 N (Cont'd)	Travis Co	589B	MS-24	78653	7801-9099 O
	Travis Co	559K	MS-26	78653	9100-10099
	Travis Co	559K	MS-26	78653	10101-11399 O
	Travis Co	559K	MS-26	78653	11400-11799
	Travis Co	530N	MU-29	78653	12700-12799
	Travis Co	530A	MU-30	78653	13300-14199
	Travis Co	500K	MU-32	78653	14200-16399
	Travis Co	470R	MV-35	78653	16400-17999
	Travis Co	471B	MW-36	78653	18000-18399
	Travis Co	471B	MW-36	78615	18400-18699
	Travis Co	441U	MX-37	78615	18700-20399
FM RD 973 S	Austin	647G	MP-18	78617	2900-3299
	Austin	647Y	MP-16	78617	3300-4099
	Austin	677B	MN-15	78617	4100-6199
	Travis Co	617Z	MP-19	78725	800-1199
	Travis Co	647G	MP-18	78725	1200-2899
	Travis Co	677W	MN-13	78617	6200-7199
	Travis Co	706D	MM-12	78719	7200-7398 E
	Travis Co	706D	MM-12	78617	7201-7399 O
	Travis Co	706L	MM-11	78719	7700-9099
	Travis Co	736B	ML-9	78719	9100-9599
FM RD 1100	Elgin	533G	EB-30	78621	1300-1599
	See.. Main St N				
	Elgin	533A	EA-30	78621	18900-18999
	Travis Co	531F	MW-30	78653	13100-13899
	Travis Co	501U	MX-31	78653	13900-15199
	Travis Co	502T	MY-31	78621	15200-17599
	Travis Co	533A	EA-30	78621	17600-18899
FM RD 1105	Weir	258D	MR-57	78626	1-899
FM RD 1209	Bastrop Co	742G	MZ-9	78612	100-199
	Bastrop Co	712M	MZ-11	78602	200-799
FM RD 1325	Austin	495L	MK-32	78758	9000-11599
	Austin	465Z	MK-34	78758	11600-12099
	Austin	466S	ML-34	78758	12100-12499
	Austin	466E	ML-36	78727	12500-13899
	Round Rock	406Y	MM-40	78728	16500-16599
	Travis Co	436W	ML-37	78728	13900-14599
	See.. Burnet Rd				
	Travis Co	436B	ML-39	78728	14600-15299
	Williamson Co	436B	ML-39	78728	15300-15799
	Williamson Co	406Y	MM-40	78728	15800-16499
FM RD 1327	Austin	733H	MF-9	78610	100-999
	Creedmoor	734R	MH-8	78610	3100-3999
	Creedmoor	735S	MJ-7	78610	4000-5299
	Mustang Ridge	735Y	MK-7	78747	6100-6199
	Mustang Ridge	736W	ML-7	78747	6200-7199
	Travis Co	734E	MG-9	78610	1000-3099
	Travis Co	735Y	MK-7	78610	5300-6099
FM RD 1431	Williamson Co	345U	MK-46	78681	2401-3399 O
	Williamson Co	345U	MK-46	78681	3400-3499
FM RD 1460	Georgetown	286V	MM-52	78626	500-999
	Round Rock	377F	MN-45	78664	700-3099
	Round Rock	347Q	MP-47	78665	4400-4999
	Williamson Co	286V	MM-52	78626	800-1499
	Williamson Co	286V	MM-52	78626	1000-1399
	Williamson Co	316D	MM-51	78626	1400-1699
	Williamson Co	317J	MN-50	78626	1700-3999
	Williamson Co	347Q	MP-47	78665	3100-4399
	Williamson Co	347B	MP-47	78665	4000-4399
FM RD 1466	Williamson Co	443M	EB-38	78615	400-1199
FM RD 1625	Creedmoor	735X	MJ-7	78747	11400-12399
	Creedmoor	735X	MJ-7	78610	12400-12499
	Creedmoor	765B	MJ-6	78610	12500-12899
	See.. Turnersville Rd				
	Travis Co	706J	ML-11	78744	7500-7799
	Travis Co	706J	ML-11	78747	7800-9199
	Travis Co	705Z	MK-10	78747	9200-9899
	Travis Co	735D	MK-9	78747	10400-11399
FM RD 1626 E	Travis Co	703M	MF-11	78748	100-799
FM RD 1626 N	Hays	732A	MC-9	78610	1600-1799
	Hays	702T	MC-10	78610	1800-1999
	Hays Co	732A	MC-9	78610	100-1599
	Hays Co	702T	MC-10	78652	2000-2299
FM RD 1626 S	Hays Co	732S	MC-7	78610	100-1099
	Hays Co	762A	MC-6	78610	1100-2599
FM RD 1626 W	San Leanna	703J	ME-11	78748	400-699
	Travis Co	703M	MF-11	78748	100-399
	Travis Co	703J	ME-11	78748	700-1099
	Travis Co	702M	MD-11	78748	1100-1999
	Travis Co	702M	MD-11	78652	2000-2299
FM RD 1660	Hutto	379M	MT-44	78634	8100-9999
	Williamson Co	349D	MT-48	78634	4800-6399
	Williamson Co	380S	MU-43	78634	10000-11199
	Williamson Co	410C	MV-42	78634	11200-12599
	Williamson Co	411J	MW-41	76574	12600-15299
	Williamson Co	412W	MY-40	76574	15300-17399
	Williamson Co	413W	EA-40	76574	17400-18699
FM RD 1660 N	Hutto	349V	MT-46	78634	100-699
FM RD 1660 S	Hutto	379D	MT-45	78634	100-299
FM RD 1704	Bastrop Co	564A	EC-27	78621	1300-1399
	Bastrop Co	563R	EB-26	78621	1400-1799
	Elgin	534W	EC-28	78621	1200-1299
	See.. Main St S				
FM RD 1825	Austin	437W	MN-37	78660	14600-15599
FM RD 1825 W	Pflugerville	437U	MP-37	78660	600-2699
	See.. Pecan St W				
	Travis Co	437W	MN-37	78660	2700-2999
	See.. Pecan St				
FM RD 1854	Mustang Ridge	796V	MM-1	78610	None
FM RD 2001	Hays Co	763K	ME-5	78610	100-2799
	See.. Old Goforth Rd				
	Hays Co	794P	MG-2	78610	3600-5499
	See.. Niederwald Strasse Rd				
	Niederwald	794P	MG-2	78610	5500-7199
	Niederwald	795W	MJ-1	78610	7200-8599
FM RD 2244	Bee Cave	550U	WZ-25	78733	11700-12599
	Rollingwood	583V	MF-22	78746	2900-3199
	See.. Bee Caves Rd				
	Travis Co	583A	ME-24	78746	6000-6499
	See.. Bee Caves Rd				
	Travis Co	552V	MD-25	78746	6500-8999
	Travis Co	552K	MC-26	78733	9000-9599
	Travis Co	551N	MA-26	78738	9600-11299
	Travis Co	551N	MA-26	78738	11300-11699
	West Lake Hills	583V	MF-22	78746	3200-5999
	See.. Bee Caves Rd				

STREET NAME	CITY or COUNTY	MAPSCO GRID	AUSTIN GRID	ZIP CODE	BLOCK RANGE O/E
FM RD 2304	Austin	614S	MG-19	78704	2800-4399
	Austin	614S	MG-19	78745	4400-4699
	Austin	643Q	MF-17	78745	4700-8099
	Austin	673F	ME-15	78745	8100-8599
See.. Manchaca Rd					
	Austin	673F	ME-15	78748	8600-11299
	Austin	703A	ME-12	78748	11300-12299
FM RD 2430	Bastrop Co	738Q	MR-8	78617	8900-10199
See.. Mesa Dr					
FM RD 2770	Buda	762G	MD-6	78610	100-1499
	Hays Co	762T	MC-4	78610	1500-3099
See.. Plum St					
FM RD 3000	Bastrop Co	534G	ED-30	78621	100-1199
FM RD 3177	Austin	558W	MQ-25	78724	7000-7399
See.. Decker Ln					
	Travis Co	587M	MP-23	78724	5200-6999
See.. Decker Ln					
	Travis Co	558K	MQ-26	78724	7400-10799
	Travis Co	528Y	MR-28	78724	10800-11999
FM RD 3349	Williamson Co	351X	MW-46	76574	1-1499
	Williamson Co	381W	MW-43	76574	1500-4299
	Williamson Co	411E	MW-42	76574	None
FM RD 3405	Williamson Co	224K	MG-59	78633	1-2099
	Williamson Co	223J	ME-59	78633	2100-3999
	Williamson Co	222L	MD-59	78633	4000-6499
	Williamson Co	222L	MD-59	78642	6500-7499
FM RD 3406	Round Rock	376F	ML-45	78681	100-1999
	Round Rock	375M	MK-44	78681	2000-2799
See.. Old Settler's Blvd W					
FM RD 3406 E	Round Rock	376D	MM-45	78665	100-1299
See.. Old Settler's Blvd E					

Ranch To Market Roads

STREET NAME	CITY or COUNTY	MAPSCO GRID	AUSTIN GRID	ZIP CODE	BLOCK RANGE O/E
RM RD 12	Dripping Springs	666D	WR-15	78620	26000-27499
	Dripping Springs	636M	WR-17	78620	27500-29099
	Hays Co	666V	WR-13	78620	24300-25999
	Hays Co	636M	WR-17	78620	29100-29499
	Hays Co	637A	WS-18	78620	29500-29799
	Hays Co	607T	WS-19	78620	29800-32199
	Hays Co	577T	WS-22	78620	32200-33399
	Travis Co	577T	WS-22	78620	33400-33599
RM RD 150 W	Dripping Springs	666V	WR-13	78620	13500-14098 E
	Dripping Springs	666V	WR-13	78619	13501-14099 O
	Dripping Springs	667W	WS-13	78620	23300-23498 E
	Dripping Springs	667W	WS-13	78619	23301-23499 O
	Hays Co	667W	WS-13	78620	20900-23298 E
	Hays Co	667W	WS-13	78619	20901-23299 O
RM RD 620	Round Rock	376W	ML-43	78681	700-1999
See.. Round Rock Ave					
	Round Rock	375Z	MK-43	78681	2000-2499
	Williamson Co	405S	MJ-40	78717	15300-16699
	Williamson Co	405G	MK-42	78681	16700-17599
RM RD 620 N	Austin	492F	MC-33	78732	6700-7099
	Austin	462L	MD-35	78726	7100-9599
	Austin	433D	MF-39	78750	12700-13099
	Austin	433D	MF-39	78717	13100-13299
	Austin	434A	MG-39	78717	13300-13599
	Austin	404X	MG-40	78717	13600-14299
	Lakeway	520A	WY-30	78734	100-199
	Lakeway	490T	WY-31	78734	200-1799
	Travis Co	490G	WZ-33	78734	1800-4299
	Travis Co	491E	MA-33	78734	4300-4399
	Travis Co	491L	MB-32	78732	4400-5399
	Travis Co	492F	MC-33	78732	5400-6699
	Travis Co	462L	MD-35	78726	9600-10499
	Williamson Co	433S	ME-37	78726	10500-11599
	Williamson Co	433F	ME-39	78750	11600-12699
	Williamson Co	404V	MH-40	78717	14300-15299
RM RD 620 S	Bee Cave	550J	WY-26	78738	3700-4099
	Lakeway	520A	WY-30	78734	100-699
	Lakeway	519V	WX-28	78734	700-3099
	Lakeway	549D	WX-27	78734	3100-3399
	Travis Co	549D	WX-27	78738	3400-3499
	Travis Co	550J	WY-26	78738	3500-3699
RM RD 967	Buda	762C	MD-6	78610	100-699
	Hays Co	732Y	MD-7	78610	700-3099
RM RD 1174	Burnet Co	307A	WS-51	78654	None
	Burnet Co	336A	WQ-48	78654	None
RM RD 1431	Burnet Co	336T	WQ-46	78654	None
	Burnet Co	366L	WR-44	78654	None
	Cedar Park	373L	MF-44	78613	100-1699
	Cedar Park	372S	MC-43	78641	15700-16699
	Cedar Park	371T	MA-43	78641	16700-16999
	Cedar Park	344Z	MH-46	78641	None
See.. Whitestone Blvd E					
	Cedar Park	374B	MG-45	78613	None
	Cedar Park	374B	MG-45	78641	None
	Jonestown	371T	MA-43	78641	18000-18399
	Jonestown	401A	MA-42	78645	18200-18499
	Jonestown	400W	WY-40	78645	18500-19799
	Lago Vista	399Z	WX-40	78645	19800-21599
	Round Rock	346N	ML-47	78681	100-1799
	Round Rock	345U	MK-46	78681	1800-2399
	Round Rock	345U	MK-46	78681	2400-3398 E
	Travis Co	371T	MA-43	78641	17000-17999
	Travis Co	399F	WW-42	78645	21600-21699
	Travis Co	399F	WW-42	78641	21700-23199
	Travis Co	398C	WV-42	78641	23200-23999
	Travis Co	398C	WV-42	78654	24000-24499
	Travis Co	368W	WU-43	78654	24400-25799
	Travis Co	367P	WS-44	78654	25800-27999
	Travis Co	366L	WR-44	78654	28000-29599
	Williamson Co	344Z	MH-46	78681	3500-3999
RM RD 1826	Austin	640V	WZ-16	78737	11700-12098 E
	Austin	640V	WZ-16	78739	11701-12099 O
	Austin	670C	WZ-15	78737	12100-12199
	Hays Co	670S	WY-13	78737	12600-13199
	Hays Co	670S	WY-13	78737	13200-14899
	Hays Co	669Z	WX-13	78737	14900-15399
	Travis Co	641N	MA-17	78737	7900-10799
	Travis Co	640V	WZ-16	78737	10800-11698 E
	Travis Co	640V	WZ-16	78739	10801-11699 O
	Travis Co	670C	WZ-15	78737	12200-12599
	Travis Co	611Y	MB-19	78737	None
RM RD 1869	Williamson Co	279B	WW-54	78642	None

STREET NAME	CITY or COUNTY	MAPSCO GRID	AUSTIN GRID	ZIP CODE	BLOCK RANGE O/E
RM RD 2222	Austin	555B	MJ-27	78751	100-799
See.. Koening Ln E					
	Austin	555B	MJ-27	78757	800-2099
See.. Koening Ln W					
	Austin	525X	MJ-28	78757	2100-2899
See.. Allandale Rd					
	Austin	524Z	MH-28	78757	2900-3199
See.. Northland Dr					
	Austin	524N	MG-29	78731	3200-5799
	Austin	523D	MF-30	78730	5800-6798 E
	Austin	523D	MF-30	78750	5801-6799 O
	Austin	493E	ME-33	78730	6800-7599
	Austin	493E	ME-33	78730	7601-8499 O
	Austin	493E	ME-33	78730	8500-9999
	Austin	492G	MD-33	78730	10000-11599
	Travis Co	493E	ME-33	78730	7600-8498 E
RM RD 2243	Georgetown	286U	MM-52	78626	500-899
See.. Leander Rd					
	Georgetown	286T	ML-52	78628	900-1699
	Georgetown	316A	ML-51	78628	1700-1899
	Georgetown	315G	MK-51	78628	1900-2299
	Leander	312Y	MD-49	78641	9700-11099
	Leander	342A	MC-48	78641	11100-12199
	Leander	341F	MA-48	78641	12200-12899
See.. Broade St					
	Williamson Co	315G	MK-51	78628	2300-4999
	Williamson Co	314L	MH-50	78628	5000-5999
	Williamson Co	313R	MF-50	78628	6000-7999
	Williamson Co	313X	ME-49	78641	8000-9499
	Williamson Co	312Y	MD-49	78641	9500-9699
	Williamson Co	341F	MA-48	78641	12900-13899
See.. Nameless Rd					
RM RD 2244	Austin	584W	MG-22	78746	2500-2599
	Rollingwood	584W	MG-22	78746	2600-2899
RM RD 2322 N	Travis Co	457M	WT-35	78669	100-1899
See.. Pace Bend Rd N					
	Travis Co	428W	WU-37	78669	1900-5999
See.. Pace Bend Rd N					
RM RD 2322 S	Travis Co	457Y	WT-34	78669	100-1099
See.. Pace Bend Rd S					
	Travis Co	487F	WS-33	78669	1100-3699
	Travis Co	486M	WR-32	78669	None
RM RD 2338	Georgetown	256U	MM-55	78628	1100-3499
See.. Williams Dr					
	Georgetown	256E	ML-57	78628	3501-3999 O
	Georgetown	225T	MJ-58	78633	4500-4899
See.. Williams Rd					
	Williamson Co	256E	ML-57	78628	4000-4099
See.. Williams Dr					
	Williamson Co	255D	MK-57	78628	4100-4499
See.. Williams Rd					
	Williamson Co	225T	MJ-58	78633	4900-5899
	Williamson Co	224C	MH-60	78633	5900-7199
	Williamson Co	194N	MG-62	78633	7200-9299
	Williamson Co	193G	MF-63	78633	9300-11299
RM RD 2769	Travis Co	433J	ME-38	78726	11800-12399
	Travis Co	432T	MC-37	78726	12400-13899
	Travis Co	461D	MB-36	78641	13900-14999
	Village of Volente	461B	MA-36	78641	15000-15399
See.. Volente Rd					
	Village of Volente	431W	MA-37	78641	15400-16099
RM RD 3238	Bee Cave	549U	WX-25	78738	14100-15299
	Travis Co	549S	WW-25	78738	15300-15799
	Travis Co	548Z	WV-25	78738	15800-16199
	Travis Co	578C	WV-24	78738	16200-17699
	Travis Co	577H	WT-24	78738	17700-20499

County Roads

STREET NAME	CITY or COUNTY	MAPSCO GRID	AUSTIN GRID	ZIP CODE	BLOCK RANGE O/E
BASTROP CO RD 75	Bastrop Co	563Q	EB-26	78621	100-299
See.. Monkey Rd					
	Bastrop Co	562D	MZ-27	78621	300-699
BASTROP CO RD 79	Bastrop Co	742P	MY-8	78612	100-699
See.. Mt Olive Rd					
BASTROP CO RD 87	Bastrop Co	503H	EB-33	78621	100-199
See.. Lund Rd					
	Bastrop Co	504E	EC-33	78621	200-299
BASTROP CO RD 127	Bastrop Co	563N	EA-26	78621	200-799
See.. Upper Elgin River Rd					
	Bastrop Co	562Z	MZ-25	78621	800-1199
	Bastrop Co	621Z	MX-19	78621	2100-2199
	Bastrop Co	651D	MX-18	78621	2200-2299
BASTROP CO RD 364	Bastrop Co	738H	MR-9	78617	100-199
BLANCO CO RD 302	Blanco Co	485A	WN-33	78620	5800-6399
	Blanco Co	455W	WP-34	78620	6400-7699
BLANCO CO RD 303	Blanco Co	455J	WN-35	78620	3300-4499
BLANCO CO RD 312	Blanco Co	455L	WP-35	78620	200-1599
BURNET CO RD 328	Burnet Co	307K	WS-50	78654	100-2099
BURNET CO RD 345	Burnet Co	396A	WQ-42	78654	None
BURNET CO RD 404	Burnet Co	426K	WQ-38	78669	None
BURNET CO RD 414	Burnet Co	426B	WQ-39	78669	100-1399
	Burnet Co	396X	WQ-40	78669	1400-2899
BURNET CO RD 420	Burnet Co	426F	WQ-39	78669	100-1399
See.. Shady Creek					
HAYS CO RD 101	Hays Co	607F	WS-21	78620	100-1699
See.. Fitzhugh Rd W					
	Hays Co	606B	WQ-21	78620	1700-2999
	Hays Co	608V	WV-19	78736	13200-15199
See.. Fitzhugh Rd					
	Hays Co	608Q	WV-20	78620	15200-15798 E
	Hays Co	608Q	WV-20	78736	15201-15799 O
	Hays Co	607F	WS-21	78720	15800-16899
HAYS CO RD 104	Hays Co	733T	ME-7	78610	1600-1899
See.. Manchaca Springs Rd					
HAYS CO RD 105	Hays Co	733U	MF-7	78610	1300-1499
HAYS CO RD 106	Hays Co	764K	MG-5	78610	14600-15999
See.. Turnersville Rd S					
HAYS CO RD 107	Hays Co	763V	MF-4	78610	100-599
	Hays Co	764T	MG-4	78610	600-3499
	Hays Co	794G	MH-3	78610	3500-6099
See.. Satterwhite Rd					
HAYS CO RD 117	Buda	763A	ME-6	78610	400-699
	Buda	733X	ME-7	78610	700-899
	Buda	733X	ME-7	78610	15200-15499
	Hays Co	733T	ME-7	78610	900-1699
HAYS CO RD 118	Buda	733Y	MF-7	78610	None
	Hays Co	763G	MF-6	78610	100-1799
	Hays Co	733Y	MF-7	78610	None

STREET NAME	CITY or COUNTY	MAPSCO GRID	AUSTIN GRID	ZIP CODE	BLOCK RANGE O/E
HAYS CO RD 119	Hays Co	763T	ME-4	78610	700-1799
See.. Old Goforth Rd					
HAYS CO RD 120	Hays Co	794L	MH-2	78610	100-1199
See.. Williamson Rd					
	Hays Co	764Z	MH-4	78610	1200-1799
HAYS CO RD 121	Hays Co	794P	MG-2	78610	100-599
See.. Martin Church Rd					
HAYS CO RD 123	Hays Co	794S	MG-1	78610	1300-2399
See.. Mathias Ln					
HAYS CO RD 126	Hays Co	794X	MG-1	78610	100-1799
See.. Rohde Rd					
HAYS CO RD 132	Hays Co	762U	MD-4	78610	100-499
See.. Cement Plant Rd					
HAYS CO RD 133	Hays Co	763S	ME-4	78610	100-2199
See.. Hillside Terrace					
HAYS CO RD 148	Hays Co	762A	MC-6	78610	100-2299
See.. Cole Springs Rd					
HAYS CO RD 157	Hays Co	794N	MG-2	78610	6300-7299
See.. Goforth Rd					
HAYS CO RD 163	Hays Co	639Y	WX-16	78737	12300-12999
See.. Nutty Brown Rd					
	Hays Co	669R	WX-14	78737	13000-14599
	Hays Co	670S	WY-13	78737	14600-14699
HAYS CO RD 164	Hays Co	639W	WW-16	78737	13800-14299
See.. Sawyer Ranch Rd					
	Hays Co	668R	WV-14	78737	14300-16698 E
	Hays Co	668R	WV-14	78620	14301-16699 O
HAYS CO RD 169	Hays Co	606S	WQ-19	78620	2400-4699
	Hays Co	636E	WQ-18	78620	4700-5399
See.. Bell Springs Rd					
HAYS CO RD 185	Hays Co	608X	WU-19	78737	12000-12699
	Hays Co	638L	WV-17	78620	12700-14198 E
	Hays Co	638L	WV-17	78737	12701-14199 O
HAYS CO RD 190	Dripping Springs	666B	WQ-15	78620	100-1199
	Hays Co	666E	WQ-15	78620	1200-3199
HAYS CO RD 205	Hays Co	763W	ME-4	78610	5300-5999
HAYS CO RD 211	Hays Co	795Y	MK-1	78610	100-1799
See.. Schubert Ln					
HAYS CO RD 212	Hays Co	794A	MG-3	78610	100-599
See.. Turnersville Rd S					
	Hays Co	764W	MG-4	78610	600-1199
HAYS CO RD 220	Hays Co	666J	WQ-14	78620	100-2099
HAYS CO RD 228	Buda	762H	MD-6	78610	100-799
	Buda	763E	ME-6	78610	800-1199
See.. Goforth Rd W					
HAYS CO RD 236	Hays Co	732V	MD-7	78610	100-1099
HAYS CO RD 300	Hays Co	795T	MJ-1	78610	100-1099
See.. Engelke Rd					
HAYS CO RD 302	Hays Co	794V	MH-1	78610	100-1599
See.. Graef Rd					
HAYS CO RD 320	Dripping Springs	636T	WQ-16	78620	100-699
HAYS CO RD 354	Hays Co	669H	WX-15	78737	10100-10799
	Hays Co	639Y	WX-16	78737	10800-11199
HAYS CO RD 355	Hays Co	639Q	WX-17	78737	10600-10999
See.. Kit Carson					
HAYS CO RD 367	Hays Co	670X	WY-13	78610	14000-14699
	Hays Co	700B	WY-12	78610	14700-14899
TRAVIS CO RD 290	Travis Co	341J	MA-47	78641	200-999
	Travis Co	340M	WZ-47	78641	1000-1199
WILLIAMSON CO RD 100					
	Williamson Co	288D	MR-54	78626	1-699
WILLIAMSON CO RD 101					
	Williamson Co	351K	MW-47	76574	4900-6999
WILLIAMSON CO RD 103					
	Williamson Co	258X	MQ-55	78626	1-499
	Williamson Co	258P	MQ-56	78626	500-1899
	Williamson Co	258U	MR-55	78626	1900-2099
	Georgetown	288S	MQ-52	78626	1200-2099
WILLIAMSON CO RD 104					
	Williamson Co	288F	MQ-54	78626	1-1199
	Williamson Co	317D	MP-51	78626	2400-2499
	Williamson Co	318A	MQ-51	78634	2599-3299
WILLIAMSON CO RD 105					
	Williamson Co	318E	MQ-51	78626	1-399
	Williamson Co	318C	MR-51	78634	400-1799
	Williamson Co	288Z	MR-52	78634	1800-2599
WILLIAMSON CO RD 105 SPUR					
	Williamson Co	318B	MQ-51	78634	700-799
WILLIAMSON CO RD 106					
	Williamson Co	288L	MR-53	78626	1-1899
WILLIAMSON CO RD 107					
	Williamson Co	318Q	MR-50	78626	1-1099
	Williamson Co	318Q	MR-50	78634	1100-1399
	Williamson Co	318M	MR-50	78634	1400-1999
WILLIAMSON CO RD 107 SPUR					
	Williamson Co	318R	MR-50	78634	1-399
WILLIAMSON CO RD 108					
	Williamson Co	349A	MS-48	78634	1-899
	Williamson Co	379A	MS-45	78634	900-2899
	Williamson Co	348L	MR-47	78634	900-1399
	Williamson Co	349J	MS-47	78634	1400-2099
	Georgetown	287Y	MP-52	78626	1300-2299
WILLIAMSON CO RD 110					
	Williamson Co	287T	MN-52	78626	1-999
	Williamson Co	317M	MP-50	78626	2300-3699
	Williamson Co	318N	MQ-50	78626	3700-6499
	Williamson Co	348B	MQ-48	78665	5900-7599
	Williamson Co	378C	MR-45	78665	7600-9199
WILLIAMSON CO RD 111	Georgetown	316Y	MM-49	78626	1-899
	Georgetown	317L	MP-50	78626	2200-3899
	Williamson Co	316Y	MM-49	78626	900-2199
WILLIAMSON CO RD 112					
	Williamson Co	347Q	MP-47	78665	1-1099 O
	Williamson Co	347Q	MP-47	78665	2-1098 E
	Williamson Co	348E	MQ-48	78665	1100-2299
	Williamson Co	347K	MN-47	78665	None
WILLIAMSON CO RD 113	Round Rock	348W	MQ-46	78665	None
See.. Kiphen Rd					
WILLIAMSON CO RD 114	Round Rock	346L	MM-47	78665	1-299
See.. Chandler Rd					
	Williamson Co	346L	MM-47	78665	700-799
See.. Chandler Rd					
	Williamson Co	347E	MN-48	78665	800-999
WILLIAMSON CO RD 116	Georgetown	316L	MM-50	78626	None
	Williamson Co	316L	MM-50	78626	1-1599
WILLIAMSON CO RD 117					
	Williamson Co	347R	MP-47	78665	1-599
	Williamson Co	348S	MQ-46	78665	600-1399

STREET NAME	CITY or COUNTY	MAPSCO GRID	AUSTIN GRID	ZIP CODE	BLOCK RANGE O/E
WILLIAMSON CO RD 118					
	Williamson Co	**318Z**	MR-49	78634	300-1399
	Williamson Co	**348D**	MR-48	78634	1400-1799
	Williamson Co	**349A**	MS-48	78634	1800-2199
WILLIAMSON CO RD 119					
	Williamson Co	**349G**	MT-48	78634	1100-2099
WILLIAMSON CO RD 120	Weir	**258H**	MR-57	78626	1700-2199
	Williamson Co	**348T**	MQ-46	78665	1000-1099
	Williamson Co	**348P**	MQ-47	78665	1100-2299
WILLIAMSON CO RD 123					
	Williamson Co	**378K**	MQ-44	78664	3700-4599
	Williamson Co	**378M**	MR-44	78664	4600-4999
WILLIAMSON CO RD 129					
	Williamson Co	**410V**	MV-40	76574	1-1199
	Williamson Co	**411W**	MW-40	76574	1200-2099
WILLIAMSON CO RD 132					
	Williamson Co	**349H**	MT-48	78634	1-299
	Williamson Co	**350E**	MU-48	78634	300-3199
	Williamson Co	**380B**	MU-45	78634	3200-6099
	Williamson Co	**381E**	MW-45	78634	None
WILLIAMSON CO RD 133					
	Williamson Co	**350B**	MU-48	78634	900-1499
WILLIAMSON CO RD 134					
	Williamson Co	**380L**	MV-44	78634	1-2199
	Williamson Co	**410C**	MV-42	78634	None
WILLIAMSON CO RD 135					
	Williamson Co	**379R**	MT-44	78634	1-599
WILLIAMSON CO RD 137	Hutto	**379Z**	MT-43	78634	100-1099
	Williamson Co	**409H**	MT-42	78634	1100-2299
WILLIAMSON CO RD 138	Pflugerville	**409E**	MS-42	78634	2-298 E
	Williamson Co	**409E**	MS-42	78634	1-299 O
	Williamson Co	**409L**	MT-41	78634	300-2099
WILLIAMSON CO RD 139					
	Williamson Co	**409H**	MT-42	78634	1-1299
	Williamson Co	**410N**	MU-41	78634	1300-2199
WILLIAMSON CO RD 142					
	Williamson Co	**197R**	MP-62	78726	200-1399
WILLIAMSON CO RD 143					
	Williamson Co	**197P**	MN-62	78628	1-1799
	Williamson Co	**196V**	MM-61	78628	1800-2099
WILLIAMSON CO RD 144					
	Williamson Co	**197D**	MP-63	78626	1-899
WILLIAMSON CO RD 146					
	Williamson Co	**197A**	MN-63	78628	1-1999
WILLIAMSON CO RD 147					
	Williamson Co	**196L**	MM-62	78628	1-1899
	Williamson Co	**197J**	MN-62	78628	1900-2399
WILLIAMSON CO RD 150					
	Williamson Co	**227L**	MP-59	78626	1-1799
WILLIAMSON CO RD 151	Georgetown	**257J**	MN-56	78626	1-499
	Williamson Co	**257J**	MN-56	78626	500-999
WILLIAMSON CO RD 152	Georgetown	**257K**	MN-56	78626	1-1299
	Williamson Co	**257K**	MN-56	78626	1300-1399
	Williamson Co	**227Z**	MP-58	78626	1400-3099
WILLIAMSON CO RD 160					
	Williamson Co	**350C**	MV-48	78634	None
WILLIAMSON CO RD 163					
	Williamson Co	**410A**	MU-42	78634	1-1199
	Williamson Co	**380W**	MU-43	78634	None
WILLIAMSON CO RD 165					
	Williamson Co	**379B**	MS-45	78634	1-899
	Williamson Co	**349X**	MS-46	78634	None
WILLIAMSON CO RD 166					
	Williamson Co	**317J**	MN-50	78626	1-699
	Williamson Co	**316M**	MM-50	78626	None
WILLIAMSON CO RD 168					
	Williamson Co	**408E**	MQ-42	78664	3800-3999
WILLIAMSON CO RD 169					
	Williamson Co	**407Q**	MP-41	78664	1800-1899
WILLIAMSON CO RD 172					
	Williamson Co	**406T**	ML-40	78681	2200-3199
WILLIAMSON CO RD 175					
	Williamson Co	**313V**	MF-49	78641	1-899
	Williamson Co	**314W**	MG-49	78641	900-1599
	Williamson Co	**344F**	MG-48	78641	1600-4499
WILLIAMSON CO RD 176					
	Williamson Co	**314X**	MG-49	78628	1-2299
	Williamson Co	**344A**	MG-48	78628	None
WILLIAMSON CO RD 177	Leander	**343H**	MF-48	78641	700-1299
	Williamson Co	**344A**	MG-48	78641	1-699
WILLIAMSON CO RD 178	Cedar Park	**374B**	MG-45	78613	1-499
WILLIAMSON CO RD 179					
	Williamson Co	**344J**	MG-47	78641	1-799
	Williamson Co	**343M**	MF-47	78641	800-1399
WILLIAMSON CO RD 180					
	Williamson Co	**343Z**	MF-46	78641	1-599
	Williamson Co	**373C**	MF-45	78641	600-2799
WILLIAMSON CO RD 181					
	Williamson Co	**373F**	ME-45	78641	1-999
WILLIAMSON CO RD 182	Cedar Park	**403S**	ME-40	78613	100-1399
	Cedar Park	**402Y**	MD-40	78613	1400-2599
WILLIAMSON CO RD 186					
	Williamson Co	**317X**	MN-49	78665	1-999
WILLIAMSON CO RD 189					
	Williamson Co	**258V**	MR-55	78626	1-699
WILLIAMSON CO RD 194					
	Williamson Co	**258F**	MQ-57	78626	100-1499
WILLIAMSON CO RD 195					
	Williamson Co	**377Q**	MP-44	78665	100-399
WILLIAMSON CO RD 196					
	Williamson Co	**227C**	MP-60	78626	1-699
WILLIAMSON CO RD 197					
	Williamson Co	**379Y**	MT-43	78634	1-899
WILLIAMSON CO RD 198					
	Williamson Co	**410X**	MU-40	78634	1-799
WILLIAMSON CO RD 199					
	Williamson Co	**380A**	MU-45	78634	1-999
WILLIAMSON CO RD 234					
	Williamson Co	**196R**	MM-62	78628	1-799
	Williamson Co	**197E**	MN-63	78628	800-2199
WILLIAMSON CO RD 245					
	Williamson Co	**194X**	MG-61	78633	1-1299
	Williamson Co	**194F**	MG-63	78633	1300-2099
WILLIAMSON CO RD 247					
	Williamson Co	**193Q**	MF-62	78633	1-799
WILLIAMSON CO RD 248					
	Williamson Co	**193F**	ME-63	78633	1-1699
WILLIAMSON CO RD 249					
	Williamson Co	**193C**	MF-63	78633	1500-2299
WILLIAMSON CO RD 255					
	Williamson Co	**222B**	MC-60	78633	1-1299
	Williamson Co	**192T**	MC-61	78633	1300-2499
	Williamson Co	**192L**	MD-62	78633	2500-3499
WILLIAMSON CO RD 256					
	Williamson Co	**222K**	MC-59	78642	1-1199
	Williamson Co	**222N**	MC-59	78642	1200-1699
WILLIAMSON CO RD 257					
	Williamson Co	**222N**	MC-59	78642	1-1099
	Williamson Co	**222J**	MC-59	78642	1100-1399
WILLIAMSON CO RD 258					
	Williamson Co	**252B**	MC-57	78642	1-3399
	Williamson Co	**222R**	MD-59	78633	3400-6299
	Williamson Co	**222Z**	MD-58	78642	None
	Williamson Co	**223N**	ME-59	78633	None
WILLIAMSON CO RD 259					
	Williamson Co	**282B**	MC-54	78641	1-799
WILLIAMSON CO RD 260					
	Williamson Co	**252N**	MC-56	78642	1-1599
WILLIAMSON CO RD 261					
	Williamson Co	**223M**	MF-59	78633	1-999
WILLIAMSON CO RD 262					
	Williamson Co	**224T**	MG-58	78633	1-1899
	Williamson Co	**254C**	MH-57	78633	1900-2199
WILLIAMSON CO RD 263					
	Williamson Co	**281H**	MB-54	78642	1-799
	Williamson Co	**282A**	MC-54	78641	1-799
WILLIAMSON CO RD 264					
	Williamson Co	**313K**	ME-50	78628	1-399
WILLIAMSON CO RD 266					
	Williamson Co	**282K**	MC-53	78628	1-2399
WILLIAMSON CO RD 267					
	Williamson Co	**282M**	MD-53	78628	1-1899
WILLIAMSON CO RD 268	Leander	**313Q**	MF-50	78628	2600-4499
	Williamson Co	**283N**	ME-53	78628	1-2599
WILLIAMSON CO RD 269					
	Williamson Co	**313N**	ME-50	78641	1-1299
	Williamson Co	**312V**	MD-49	78641	1300-1899
	Williamson Co	**282Y**	MD-52	78641	1-199
WILLIAMSON CO RD 270					
	Williamson Co	**312M**	MD-50	78641	1-2199
	Leander	**343F**	ME-48	78641	800-1899
WILLIAMSON CO RD 271					
	Williamson Co	**312Z**	MD-49	78641	1-399
WILLIAMSON CO RD 272	Cedar Park	**374B**	MG-45	78641	1-199
	Cedar Park	**344W**	MG-46	78641	200-699
	Williamson Co	**344W**	MG-46	78641	700-1399
WILLIAMSON CO RD 273	Leander	**312Y**	MD-49	78641	100-299
	Leander	**342H**	MD-48	78641	300-1699
WILLIAMSON CO RD 276					
	Williamson Co	**312A**	MC-51	78641	1-499
WILLIAMSON CO RD 278					
	Williamson Co	**281F**	MA-54	78642	1-999
WILLIAMSON CO RD 279	Leander	**281T**	MA-52	78641	3100-3699
	Leander	**311G**	MB-51	78641	3700-6399
	Williamson Co	**281F**	MA-54	78642	1100-2199
	Williamson Co	**281T**	MA-52	78641	2200-3099
WILLIAMSON CO RD 280	Leander	**311K**	MA-50	78641	1-2199
	Travis Co	**310M**	WZ-50	78641	2200-3199
WILLIAMSON CO RD 281					
	Williamson Co	**281S**	MA-52	78641	1-999
	Williamson Co	**280Q**	WZ-53	78641	1000-2599
WILLIAMSON CO RD 282					
	Williamson Co	**280K**	WY-53	78642	900-2299
	Williamson Co	**280P**	WY-53	78641	2300-3699
WILLIAMSON CO RD 283					
	Williamson Co	**280J**	WY-53	78641	1-799
WILLIAMSON CO RD 284					
	Williamson Co	**280E**	WY-54	78642	1-999
	Williamson Co	**279N**	WW-53	78642	1000-4099
	Williamson Co	**278H**	WV-54	78642	4100-4999
WILLIAMSON CO RD 285					
	Williamson Co	**279E**	WW-54	78642	300-1999
	Williamson Co	**278H**	WV-54	78642	2000-2599
WILLIAMSON CO RD 286					
	Williamson Co	**278C**	WV-54	78642	1-699
WILLIAMSON CO RD 286 SPUR					
	Williamson Co	**278B**	WU-54	78642	1-899
WILLIAMSON CO RD 287					
	Williamson Co	**278J**	WU-53	78642	1-3599
WILLIAMSON CO RD 289					
	Williamson Co	**192Q**	MD-62	78633	400-499
	Williamson Co	**192V**	MD-61	78633	500-1599
	Williamson Co	**193W**	ME-61	78633	1600-2099
WILLIAMSON CO RD 289 S					
	Williamson Co	**223F**	ME-60	78633	2100-3099
WILLIAMSON CO RD 290					
	Williamson Co	**341E**	MA-48	78641	100-599
WILLIAMSON CO RD 345	Burnet Co	**366W**	WQ-43	78654	300-1499
WILLIAMSON CO RD 365					
	Williamson Co	**322D**	MZ-51	76574	1800-2199
WILLIAMSON CO RD 366	Leander	**322E**	MY-51	76574	3700-4199
	Williamson Co	**322E**	MY-51	76574	2300-2799
WILLIAMSON CO RD 367	Taylor	**322K**	MY-50	76574	2-798 E
	Williamson Co	**322K**	MY-50	76574	1-799 O
WILLIAMSON CO RD 369					
	Williamson Co	**322J**	MY-50	76574	2500-3299
WILLIAMSON CO RD 373					
	Williamson Co	**351M**	MX-47	76574	1-999
	Williamson Co	**351D**	MX-48	76574	1000-1599
WILLIAMSON CO RD 374					
	Williamson Co	**322A**	MY-51	76574	1-1099
WILLIAMSON CO RD 395					
	Williamson Co	**351G**	MX-48	76574	1-1399
WILLIAMSON CO RD 398	Taylor	**322X**	MY-49	76574	None
	Williamson Co	**322X**	MY-49	76574	1-1799
	Williamson Co	**351D**	MX-48	76574	None
	Williamson Co	**352A**	MY-48	76574	None
WILLIAMSON CO RD 400					
	Williamson Co	**383A**	EA-45	76574	1-399
WILLIAMSON CO RD 401					
	Williamson Co	**352W**	MY-46	76574	1-1099
	Williamson Co	**382A**	MY-45	76574	1100-1599
WILLIAMSON CO RD 403	Taylor	**352K**	MY-47	76574	1-2399
WILLIAMSON CO RD 404					
	Williamson Co	**381L**	MX-44	76574	100-2999
	Williamson Co	**382E**	MY-45	76574	3000-4899
	Williamson Co	**383A**	EA-45	76574	4900-5799
	Williamson Co	**353W**	EA-46	76574	5800-6399
WILLIAMSON CO RD 405					
	Williamson Co	**382M**	MZ-44	76574	1-1499
	Williamson Co	**412T**	MY-40	76574	1500-4199
WILLIAMSON CO RD 406					
	Williamson Co	**383J**	EA-44	76574	1-2299
	Williamson Co	**412V**	MZ-40	76574	2300-5099
	Williamson Co	**382Z**	MZ-43	76574	None
WILLIAMSON CO RD 407					
	Williamson Co	**413A**	EA-42	76574	1-1199
	Williamson Co	**412D**	MZ-42	76574	None
WILLIAMSON CO RD 408					
	Williamson Co	**322D**	MZ-51	76574	1-99
WILLIAMSON CO RD 409					
	Williamson Co	**323K**	EA-50	76574	1800-3499
WILLIAMSON CO RD 411					
	Williamson Co	**323B**	EA-51	76574	1-899
WILLIAMSON CO RD 412					
	Williamson Co	**323R**	EB-50	76574	1-1999
WILLIAMSON CO RD 452					
	Williamson Co	**353Y**	EB-46	76574	1000-2099
	Williamson Co	**383L**	EB-44	76574	2100-3399
WILLIAMSON CO RD 453					
	Williamson Co	**413G**	EB-42	76574	1-1699
WILLIAMSON CO RD 454					
	Williamson Co	**413T**	EA-40	76574	1-1399
WILLIAMSON CO RD 456					
	Williamson Co	**413V**	EB-40	76574	1-3199
	Williamson Co	**443H**	EB-39	78615	None
WILLIAMSON CO RD 457					
	Williamson Co	**443F**	EA-39	78615	1-899
WILLIAMSON CO RD 458					
	Williamson Co	**443N**	EA-38	78615	1-1399
	Williamson Co	**442R**	MZ-38	78615	1400-2299
WILLIAMSON CO RD 459					
	Williamson Co	**443S**	EA-37	78615	1-899
WILLIAMSON CO RD 460					
	Williamson Co	**443M**	EB-38	78615	1-2499
	Williamson Co	**474P**	EC-35	78615	2500-4499
WILLIAMSON CO RD 461					
	Williamson Co	**474J**	EC-35	78615	1-1799
WILLIAMSON CO RD 462					
	Williamson Co	**474F**	EC-36	78615	1-899
WILLIAMSON CO RD 463					
	Williamson Co	**474R**	ED-35	78615	1800-5499
WILLIAMSON CO RD 466					
	Williamson Co	**474D**	ED-36	78615	1-999
WILLIAMSON CO RD 483					
	Williamson Co	**383U**	EB-43	76574	1-2199
	Williamson Co	**413D**	EB-42	76574	None
WILLIAMSON CO RD 485					
	Williamson Co	**411H**	MX-42	76574	1-599
	Williamson Co	**412E**	MY-42	76574	None
WILLIAMSON CO RD 495					
	Williamson Co	**413M**	EB-41	76574	None
WILLIAMSON CO RD 497					
	Williamson Co	**382V**	MZ-43	76574	1-899

Numbered Streets

STREET NAME	CITY or COUNTY	MAPSCO GRID	AUSTIN GRID	ZIP CODE	BLOCK RANGE O/E
1ST AVE	Taylor	**353L**	EB-47	76574	100-199
1ST ST	Lago Vista	**399Y**	WX-40	78645	20500-20599
1ST ST E	Austin	**585X**	MJ-22	78701	100-799
See.. Cesar Chavez St E					
	Austin	**615H**	MK-21	78702	800-3199
	Austin	**616E**	ML-21	78702	3200-5299
1ST ST E	Elgin	**534N**	EC-29	78621	100-499
1ST ST E	Taylor	**353E**	EA-48	76574	100-399
	Taylor	**353F**	EA-48	76574	None
1ST ST N	Pflugerville	**438W**	MQ-37	78660	100-499
1ST ST S	Austin	**615A**	MJ-21	78704	1-499
	Austin	**614M**	MH-20	78704	500-3999
	Austin	**644F**	MG-18	78745	4000-7199
	Austin	**674A**	MG-15	78745	7200-7899
	Austin	**673M**	MF-14	78748	7900-10099
	Austin	**703G**	MF-12	78748	10100-11199
1ST ST S	Pflugerville	**438W**	MQ-37	78660	100-599
1ST ST W	Austin	**585W**	MJ-22	78701	100-699
	Austin	**584U**	MH-22	78703	700-2399
1ST ST W	Elgin	**534N**	EC-29	78621	100-399
1ST ST W	Taylor	**353E**	EA-48	76574	100-399
	Taylor	**352H**	MZ-48	76574	900-1099
2ND AVE	Taylor	**353L**	EB-47	76574	100-199
2ND ST	Travis Co	**703J**	ME-11	78652	600-699
2ND ST E	Austin	**585W**	MJ-22	78701	100-399
	Austin	**615B**	MJ-21	78702	800-3399
2ND ST E	Elgin	**534J**	EC-29	78621	100-899
See.. FM Rd 3000					
2ND ST E	Georgetown	**286H**	MM-54	78626	100-899
2ND ST E	Taylor	**353E**	EA-48	76574	100-599
2ND ST N	Pflugerville	**438W**	MQ-37	78660	100-499
2ND ST S	Austin	**614H**	MH-21	78704	900-1099
	Austin	**614M**	MH-20	78704	1600-2499
	Austin	**614Q**	MH-20	78704	2600-2799
	Austin	**614X**	MG-19	78704	3300-3999
	Austin	**644F**	MG-18	78745	4400-4699
2ND ST S	Pflugerville	**438W**	MQ-37	78660	100-499
	Pflugerville	**468A**	MQ-36	78660	500-599
2ND ST W	Austin	**585W**	MJ-22	78701	100-599
	Elgin	**533R**	EB-29	78621	None
2ND ST W	Elgin	**534N**	EC-29	78621	None
2ND ST W	Georgetown	**286G**	MM-54	78626	100-499
2ND ST W	Taylor	**353E**	EA-48	76574	100-799
	Taylor	**352H**	MZ-48	76574	800-4099
2ND 1/2 ST E	Austin	**615C**	MK-21	78702	2200-2299
3RD ST E	Austin	**585W**	MJ-22	78701	100-599
	Austin	**585X**	MJ-22	78701	600-799
	Austin	**585X**	MJ-22	78702	800-1199
	Austin	**615C**	MK-21	78702	1200-2199
	Austin	**615H**	MK-21	78702	2500-3099
3RD ST E	Elgin	**534J**	EC-29	78621	None
	Elgin	**534K**	EC-29	78621	None
3RD ST E	Georgetown	**286H**	MM-54	78626	100-1499

STREET NAME	CITY or COUNTY	MAPSCO GRID	AUSTIN GRID	ZIP CODE	BLOCK RANGE O/E
3RD ST E	Taylor	353E	EA-48	76574	100-899
3RD ST N	Pflugerville	438W	MQ-37	78660	100-499
3RD ST S	Austin	614D	MH-21	78704	500-699
	Austin	614H	MH-21	78704	1000-1499
	Austin	614M	MH-20	78704	1500-2499
	Austin	614Q	MH-20	78704	2600-2799
	Austin	644F	MG-18	78745	4400-4599
3RD ST S	Pflugerville	438W	MQ-37	78660	100-599
3RD ST W	Austin	585W	MJ-22	78701	100-699
	Austin	584V	MH-22	78703	800-1099
	Austin	584U	MH-22	78703	1400-1599
3RD ST W	Elgin	534N	EC-29	78621	None
3RD ST W	Georgetown	286G	MM-54	78626	100-499
3RD ST W	Taylor	353E	EA-48	76574	100-799
	Taylor	352H	MZ-48	76574	800-2099
4TH ST E	Austin	585X	MJ-22	78701	100-799
	Austin	585X	MJ-22	78702	800-1399
	Austin	615C	MK-21	78702	1400-2199
	Austin	615D	MK-21	78702	2500-2799
	Austin	615H	MK-21	78702	2800-3199
	Austin	616E	ML-21	78702	3300-3599
4TH ST E	Elgin	534J	EC-29	78621	200-599
4TH ST E	Georgetown	286H	MM-54	78626	100-899
4TH ST E	Taylor	353E	EA-48	76574	100-2699
4TH ST N	Pflugerville	438W	MQ-37	78660	100-499
4TH ST S	Austin	614Q	MH-20	78704	2300-2999
	Austin	614U	MH-19	78704	3000-3099
4TH ST S	Pflugerville	438W	MQ-37	78660	100-699
4TH ST W	Austin	585W	MJ-22	78701	100-699
	Austin	584V	MH-22	78703	1200-1299
4TH ST W	Elgin	533M	EB-29	78621	200-299
4TH ST W	Georgetown	286G	MM-54	78626	100-699
4TH ST W	Taylor	353E	EA-48	76574	100-799
	Taylor	352H	MZ-48	76574	800-1799
5TH ST E	Austin	585X	MJ-22	78701	100-799
	Austin	585X	MJ-22	78702	800-1599
	Austin	615D	MK-21	78702	1600-3099
	Austin	616E	ML-21	78702	3100-5299
	Austin	616F	ML-21	78702	None
5TH ST E	Elgin	534J	EC-29	78621	200-599
5TH ST E	Georgetown	286H	MM-54	78626	100-899
5TH ST E	Taylor	353E	EA-48	76574	100-699
5TH ST N	Pflugerville	438S	MQ-37	78660	300-399
5TH ST S	Austin	614L	MH-20	78704	900-3399
5TH ST S	Pflugerville	437Z	MP-37	78660	100-699
5TH ST W	Austin	585S	MJ-22	78701	100-799
	Austin	584V	MH-22	78703	800-1999
5TH ST W	Georgetown	286G	MM-54	78626	100-599
5TH ST W	Taylor	353E	EA-48	76574	100-699
	Taylor	352H	MZ-48	76574	700-1099
6TH ST E	Austin	585S	MJ-22	78701	100-799
	Austin	585Y	MK-22	78702	800-1899
	Austin	615C	MK-21	78702	1900-2699
6TH ST E	Elgin	534J	EC-29	78621	400-599
6TH ST E	Georgetown	286H	MM-54	78626	100-899
6TH ST E	Taylor	353A	EA-48	76574	100-599
6TH ST S	Austin	614H	MH-21	78704	1100-1499
	Austin	614L	MH-20	78704	1600-2199
	Austin	614Q	MH-20	78704	2400-2599
6TH ST S	Pflugerville	437Z	MP-37	78660	300-699
6TH ST W	Austin	585S	MJ-22	78701	100-799
	Austin	584V	MH-22	78703	800-2099
6TH ST W	Georgetown	286G	MM-54	78626	100-699
6TH ST W	Taylor	353A	EA-48	76574	100-699
	Taylor	352H	MZ-48	76574	700-1799
6TH 1/2 ST W	Austin	584Q	MH-23	78703	1400-1499
7TH ST E	Austin	585S	MJ-22	78701	100-799
	Austin	585Y	MK-22	78702	800-2099
	Austin	615C	MK-21	78702	2100-2799
	Austin	616E	ML-21	78702	2800-5299
7TH ST E	Elgin	534J	EC-29	78621	100-599
7TH ST E	Georgetown	286H	MM-54	78626	100-1199
7TH ST E	Taylor	353A	EA-48	76574	100-599
7TH ST S	Austin	614G	MH-21	78704	1500-1699
	Austin	614L	MH-20	78704	2000-2099
7TH ST S	Pflugerville	437Z	MP-37	78660	300-499
7TH ST W	Austin	585S	MJ-22	78701	100-799
	Austin	584R	MH-23	78703	1100-1199
	Austin	584L	MH-23	78703	1900-2699
7TH ST W	Elgin	534J	EC-29	78621	None
7TH ST W	Georgetown	286G	MM-54	78626	100-499
7TH ST W	Taylor	353A	EA-48	76574	100-599
	Taylor	352D	MZ-48	76574	600-1899
8TH ST E	Austin	585T	MJ-22	78701	100-799
	Austin	585X	MJ-22	78702	800-1299
	Austin	585Y	MK-22	78702	1600-2599
8TH ST E	Elgin	534E	EC-30	78621	100-799
8TH ST E	Georgetown	286H	MM-54	78626	100-1199
8TH ST E	Taylor	353A	EA-48	76574	100-399
8TH ST S	Austin	614G	MH-21	78704	1000-1199
8TH ST S	Pflugerville	437Z	MP-37	78660	300-499
8TH ST W	Austin	585S	MJ-22	78701	100-799
	Austin	584R	MH-23	78703	1200-1299
	Austin	584Q	MH-23	78703	1600-1699
	Austin	584L	MH-23	78703	1800-1899
	Austin	584K	MG-23	78703	2300-2699
8TH ST W	Georgetown	286G	MM-54	78626	100-899
8TH ST W	Taylor	353A	EA-48	76574	100-799
	Taylor	352D	MZ-48	76574	800-899
9TH ST E	Austin	585T	MJ-22	78701	100-799
	Austin	585Y	MK-22	78702	900-1699
	Austin	585Z	MK-22	78702	1900-2599
9TH ST E	Elgin	534E	EC-30	78621	400-599
9TH ST E	Georgetown	286M	MM-53	78626	100-799
9TH ST E	Taylor	353A	EA-48	76574	100-299
9TH ST S	Pflugerville	437Z	MP-37	78660	300-499
9TH ST W	Austin	585S	MJ-22	78701	100-799
	Austin	584R	MH-23	78701	800-899
	Austin	584R	MH-23	78703	900-1699
	Austin	584K	MG-23	78703	2200-2599
9TH ST W	Elgin	533M	EB-29	78621	None
9TH ST W	Georgetown	286L	MM-53	78626	100-999
9TH ST W	Taylor	353A	EA-48	76574	100-599
9TH 1/2 ST W	Austin	584R	MH-23	78703	1200-1399
	Austin	584Q	MH-23	78703	1600-1699
10TH ST E	Austin	585T	MJ-22	78701	100-799
	Austin	585T	MJ-22	78702	800-1299
	Austin	585Y	MK-22	78702	1600-1699
	Austin	585Z	MK-22	78702	1900-2599
10TH ST E	Elgin	533M	EB-29	78621	100-199
	Elgin	533H	EB-30	78621	300-399
	Elgin	534E	EC-30	78621	500-799
10TH ST E	Georgetown	286M	MM-53	78626	100-899
10TH ST E	Taylor	353A	EA-48	76574	100-299
10TH ST S	Pflugerville	437Z	MP-37	78660	100-599
	Pflugerville	467D	MP-36	78660	600-1299
10TH ST W	Austin	585N	MJ-23	78701	100-799
	Austin	584R	MH-23	78701	800-899
	Austin	584R	MH-23	78703	900-1599
	Austin	584L	MH-23	78703	1600-1899
	Austin	584L	MH-23	78703	2100-2699
10TH ST W	Elgin	533M	EB-29	78621	100-199
	Elgin	533R	EB-29	78621	None
10TH ST W	Georgetown	286L	MM-53	78626	100-999
10TH ST W	Taylor	353A	EA-48	76574	100-699
11TH ST E	Austin	585T	MJ-22	78701	100-799
	Austin	585Y	MK-22	78702	800-2599
11TH ST E	Elgin	533M	EB-29	78621	100-299
	Elgin	533H	EB-30	78621	300-399
11TH ST E	Georgetown	286M	MM-53	78626	100-899
11TH ST E	Taylor	353A	EA-48	76574	100-299
11TH ST S	Pflugerville	437Z	MP-37	78660	300-499
11TH ST W	Austin	585N	MJ-23	78701	100-799
	Austin	584R	MH-23	78703	1000-1199
	Austin	584L	MH-23	78703	1600-1899
	Austin	584L	MH-23	78703	2100-2399
11TH ST W	Elgin	533M	EB-29	78621	None
11TH ST W	Georgetown	286L	MM-53	78626	100-699
11TH ST W	Taylor	353A	EA-48	76574	100-699
	Taylor	352D	MZ-48	76574	700-799
11TH 1/2 ST W	Austin	584M	MH-23	78703	1600-1699
12TH ST E	Austin	585T	MJ-22	78701	100-799
	Austin	585R	MK-23	78702	800-2899
	Austin	586N	ML-23	78702	2900-3299
	Austin	586P	ML-23	78721	3300-4199
	Austin	586Q	MM-23	78721	4600-4799
12TH ST S	Pflugerville	437Z	MP-37	78660	100-499
12TH ST W	Austin	585N	MJ-23	78701	200-899
	Austin	584R	MH-23	78703	900-1699
	Austin	584G	MH-24	78703	2100-2699
12TH ST W	Taylor	353A	EA-48	76574	100-699
13TH ST E	Austin	585P	MJ-23	78701	200-399
	Austin	585R	MK-23	78702	800-2899
	Austin	586N	ML-23	78702	2900-3199
13TH ST E	Georgetown	286M	MM-53	78626	300-1199
	Georgetown	287J	MN-53	78626	1200-1399
13TH ST W	Austin	585N	MJ-23	78701	200-699
	Austin	584M	MH-23	78703	1200-1599
13TH ST W	Georgetown	286L	MM-53	78626	600-799
13TH 1/2 ST W	Austin	585N	MJ-23	78701	700-799
14TH ST E	Austin	585P	MJ-23	78701	200-399
	Austin	585R	MK-23	78702	800-2899
	Austin	586N	ML-23	78702	2900-3199
14TH ST E	Georgetown	286M	MM-53	78626	300-1199
	Georgetown	287J	MN-53	78626	1600-1699
14TH ST W	Austin	585N	MJ-23	78701	200-799
	Austin	584M	MH-23	78703	1600-1699
14TH ST W	Georgetown	286L	MM-53	78626	400-799
14TH 1/2 ST E	Austin	586N	ML-23	78702	3000-3199
	Austin	586N	ML-23	78721	3200-3299
14TH TEE DR	Austin	433Z	MF-37	78750	9400-9499
15TH ST E	Austin	585P	MJ-23	78701	100-799
	Austin	585P	MJ-23	78702	900-1099
15TH ST E	Georgetown	286M	MM-53	78626	200-1199
	Georgetown	287J	MN-53	78626	1200-1699
15TH ST W	Austin	585N	MJ-23	78701	100-899
	Austin	584M	MH-23	78701	900-999
	Austin	584M	MH-23	78703	1000-1199
15TH ST W	Georgetown	286L	MM-53	78626	600-999
16TH ST E	Austin	585P	MJ-23	78701	100-299
	Austin	585Q	MK-23	78702	800-999
	Austin	585R	MK-23	78702	1700-2899
	Austin	586N	ML-23	78702	2900-2999
	Austin	586J	ML-23	78702	3000-3199
	Austin	586J	ML-23	78721	3200-3299
	Austin	586K	ML-23	78721	3800-3999
16TH ST E	Georgetown	286R	MM-53	78626	100-899
	Georgetown	287N	MN-53	78626	1400-1599
	Georgetown	287J	MN-53	78626	1700-1899
16TH ST W	Austin	585J	MJ-23	78701	100-999
16TH ST W	Georgetown	286Q	MM-53	78626	100-1099
17TH ST E	Austin	585P	MJ-23	78701	100-499
	Austin	585Q	MK-23	78702	1700-1799
	Austin	585R	MK-23	78702	1900-2999
	Austin	586J	ML-23	78702	3000-3099
	Austin	586J	ML-23	78721	3200-3399
	Austin	586K	ML-23	78721	3400-3599
17TH ST E	Georgetown	286R	MM-53	78626	200-1199
	Georgetown	287N	MN-53	78626	1300-1799
17TH ST W	Austin	585J	MJ-23	78701	100-1099
17TH ST W	Georgetown	286Q	MM-53	78626	100-1099
17TH 1/2 ST E	Georgetown	286R	MM-53	78626	200-499
18TH ST E	Austin	585K	MJ-23	78701	100-399
	Austin	585Q	MK-23	78702	1700-1999
	Austin	585M	MK-23	78702	2100-2899
	Austin	586J	ML-23	78702	3000-3099
	Austin	586J	ML-23	78721	3100-3299
18TH ST E	Georgetown	286Q	MM-53	78626	100-799
	Georgetown	287N	MN-53	78626	1300-2099
18TH ST W	Austin	585J	MJ-23	78701	100-999
18TH ST W	Georgetown	286Q	MM-53	78626	200-999
18TH 1/2 ST E	Austin	586J	ML-23	78702	3000-3099
19TH ST E	Georgetown	286R	MM-53	78626	100-999
	Georgetown	287N	MN-53	78626	1400-2099
19TH ST W	Georgetown	286Q	MM-53	78626	700-999
19TH 1/2 ST E	Georgetown	286R	MM-53	78626	300-399
20TH ST E	Austin	585K	MJ-23	78705	500-699
	Austin	585L	MK-23	78722	1500-2299
20TH ST E	Georgetown	286R	MM-53	78626	100-999
20TH ST W	Austin	585J	MJ-23	78705	100-399
21ST ST E	Austin	585K	MJ-23	78705	100-399
	Austin	585L	MK-23	78722	1500-2399
21ST ST E	Georgetown	286V	MM-52	78626	100-399
	Georgetown	286R	MM-53	78626	400-599
21ST ST W	Austin	585J	MJ-23	78705	100-999
21ST ST W	Georgetown	286U	MM-52	78626	100-599
22ND ST E	Austin	585L	MK-23	78722	1700-2699
	Austin	585M	MK-23	78722	2700-2899
22ND ST E	Georgetown	286R	MM-53	78626	900-999
22ND ST W	Austin	585E	MJ-24	78705	400-1099
	Austin	584H	MH-24	78705	1100-1399
22ND ST W	Georgetown	286U	MM-52	78626	200-799
22ND 1/2 ST W	Austin	585E	MJ-24	78705	700-999
	Austin	584H	MH-24	78705	1100-1299
23RD ST E	Austin	585F	MJ-24	78705	300-599
23RD ST W	Austin	585E	MJ-24	78705	400-1099
24TH ST E	Austin	585F	MJ-24	78705	100-399
24TH ST W	Austin	585E	MJ-24	78705	100-1599
24TH ST W	Georgetown	286U	MM-52	78626	200-299
24TH 1/2 ST W	Austin	585E	MJ-24	78705	600-799
25TH ST W	Austin	585E	MJ-24	78705	300-1099
	Austin	584H	MH-24	78705	1100-1399
25TH 1/2 ST W	Austin	585E	MJ-24	78705	1000-1099
26TH ST W	Austin	585E	MJ-24	78705	400-1099
26TH 1/2 ST E	Austin	585F	MJ-24	78705	200-399
27TH ST E	Austin	585B	MJ-24	78705	100-199
27TH ST W	Austin	585A	MJ-24	78705	100-599
28TH ST E	Austin	585G	MK-24	78722	1200-1499
28TH ST W	Austin	585A	MJ-24	78705	500-899
28TH 1/2 ST W	Austin	585A	MJ-24	78705	500-899
29TH ST E	Austin	585G	MK-24	78722	1200-1499
29TH ST W	Austin	585A	MJ-24	78705	300-899
	Austin	554Z	MH-25	78703	1300-1899
	Austin	585B	MJ-24	78705	None
29TH 1/2 ST W	Austin	585A	MJ-24	78705	600-699
30TH ST E	Austin	585B	MJ-24	78705	100-499
	Austin	585G	MK-24	78705	800-1099
	Austin	585G	MK-24	78722	1100-1499
30TH ST W	Austin	585B	MJ-24	78705	100-599
	Austin	555W	MJ-25	78705	600-999
	Austin	554Z	MH-25	78703	1400-1999
30TH 1/2 ST W	Austin	555W	MJ-25	78705	800-999
31ST ST E	Austin	585B	MJ-24	78705	100-799
	Austin	585G	MK-24	78705	800-1099
	Austin	585G	MK-24	78722	1100-1799
31ST ST W	Austin	585B	MJ-24	78705	100-299
	Austin	555W	MJ-25	78705	600-1299
	Austin	554V	MH-25	78703	1500-1599
	Austin	554Z	MH-25	78703	1700-1799
31ST 1/2 ST W	Austin	555W	MJ-25	78705	600-699
32ND ST E	Austin	585G	MK-24	78705	100-1099
	Austin	585H	MK-24	78722	1100-1799
32ND ST W	Austin	555S	MJ-25	78705	100-1199
	Austin	554V	MH-25	78703	1500-1999
32ND 1/2 ST E	Austin	585C	MK-24	78705	800-899
33RD ST E	Austin	585B	MJ-24	78705	100-499
33RD ST W	Austin	555X	MJ-25	78705	100-699
	Austin	555S	MJ-25	78705	1000-1299
	Austin	554V	MH-25	78703	1500-1999
34TH ST E	Austin	555X	MJ-25	78705	100-499
	Austin	585H	MK-24	78722	1400-1799
34TH ST W	Austin	555S	MJ-25	78705	100-1399
	Austin	554V	MH-25	78703	1600-1999
35TH ST E	Austin	555X	MJ-25	78705	100-499
35TH ST W	Austin	555X	MJ-25	78705	100-799
	Austin	555S	MJ-25	78705	1000-1499
	Austin	554Q	MH-26	78703	1500-3999
36TH ST W	Austin	554R	MH-26	78731	1800-1999
37TH ST E	Austin	555X	MJ-25	78705	100-199
	Austin	585C	MK-24	78705	800-999
	Austin	585D	MK-24	78722	1400-1599
37TH ST W	Austin	555X	MJ-25	78705	300-699
	Austin	555S	MJ-25	78705	800-1099
	Austin	554R	MH-26	78731	1800-1999
38TH ST E	Austin	555Y	MK-25	78705	100-899
	Austin	585C	MK-24	78705	900-1099
	Austin	585H	MK-24	78722	1700-1799
	Austin	586E	ML-24	78723	1900-1999
38TH ST W	Austin	555S	MJ-25	78705	100-1399
	Austin	555S	MJ-25	78703	1400-1499
	Austin	554R	MH-26	78731	1800-1999
38TH 1/2 ST E	Austin	555X	MJ-25	78751	500-599
	Austin	585C	MK-24	78705	800-1099
	Austin	585D	MK-24	78722	1100-1799
	Austin	586E	ML-24	78722	1800-1899
38TH 1/2 ST W	Austin	555T	MJ-25	78751	100-599
39TH ST E	Austin	555X	MJ-25	78751	100-599
	Austin	585C	MK-24	78751	900-1099
	Austin	585D	MK-24	78722	1800-1899
39TH ST W	Austin	555T	MJ-25	78751	100-599
	Austin	555S	MJ-25	78756	1000-1199
	Austin	554R	MH-26	78731	1800-1999
39TH 1/2 ST W	Austin	555N	MJ-26	78756	1000-1699
40TH ST E	Austin	555T	MJ-25	78751	100-599
	Austin	555Y	MK-25	78751	900-1099
	Austin	585D	MK-24	78722	1700-1899
40TH ST W	Austin	555T	MJ-25	78751	100-599
	Austin	555N	MJ-26	78756	1000-1799
	Austin	554R	MH-26	78731	1900-1999
41ST ST E	Austin	555T	MJ-25	78751	100-499
	Austin	555Y	MK-25	78751	500-1099
41ST ST W	Austin	555T	MJ-25	78751	100-599
	Austin	555N	MJ-26	78756	1000-1799
	Austin	554M	MH-26	78731	1900-1999
42ND ST E	Austin	555T	MJ-25	78751	100-699
42ND ST W	Austin	555T	MJ-25	78751	100-599
	Austin	555N	MJ-26	78756	1000-1799
	Austin	554M	MH-26	78731	1900-1999
43RD ST E	Austin	555T	MJ-25	78751	100-1099
43RD ST W	Austin	555T	MJ-25	78751	100-599
	Austin	555N	MJ-26	78756	1000-1799
44TH ST E	Austin	555U	MK-25	78751	100-1099
44TH ST W	Austin	555P	MJ-26	78751	100-599
	Austin	555J	MJ-26	78756	1000-1799
	Austin	554M	MH-26	78731	2800-2999
45TH ST E	Austin	555U	MK-25	78751	100-1099
45TH ST W	Austin	555Q	MK-26	78751	100-999
	Austin	555J	MJ-26	78756	1000-2599
	Austin	554M	MH-26	78731	2600-2999

STREET NAME	CITY or COUNTY	MAPSCO GRID	AUSTIN GRID	ZIP CODE	BLOCK RANGE O/E
45TH 1/2 ST E	Austin	555U	MK-25	78751	700-899
46TH ST E	Austin	555U	MK-25	78751	100-1099
46TH ST W	Austin	555Q	MK-26	78751	100-599
	Austin	555K	MJ-26	78756	600-999
	Austin	555J	MJ-26	78756	1400-1899
47TH ST E	Austin	555Q	MK-26	78751	100-1099
47TH ST W	Austin	555K	MJ-26	78756	700-899
	Austin	555J	MJ-26	78756	1400-1899
48TH ST E	Austin	555Q	MK-26	78751	100-699
	Austin	555R	MK-26	78751	800-999
48TH ST W	Austin	555J	MJ-26	78756	2100-2199
	Austin	555E	MJ-27	78731	2600-2699
48TH 1/2 ST E	Austin	555V	MK-25	78751	900-999
49TH ST E	Austin	555Q	MK-26	78751	100-1099
49TH ST W	Austin	555E	MJ-27	78756	1000-2399
	Austin	555E	MJ-27	78731	2500-2699
49TH 1/2 ST E	Austin	555R	MK-26	78751	900-999
49TH 1/2 ST W	Austin	555K	MJ-26	78756	1200-1299
	Austin	555E	MJ-27	78731	2600-2799
50TH ST E	Austin	555L	MK-26	78751	100-799
	Austin	555R	MK-26	78751	900-1099
50TH ST W	Austin	554D	MH-27	78731	2800-3099
50TH 1/2 DR E	Austin	555L	MK-26	78751	100-199
51ST ST E	Austin	555R	MK-26	78751	100-1099
	Austin	556X	ML-25	78723	1100-2899
	Austin	586C	MM-24	78723	2900-5699
51ST ST W	Austin	555L	MK-26	78751	100-799
	Austin	555F	MJ-27	78756	1200-1499
52ND ST E	Austin	555L	MK-26	78751	100-1099
	Austin	556N	ML-26	78723	1100-1399
53RD ST E	Austin	555R	MK-26	78751	200-1099
	Austin	556N	ML-26	78723	1100-1199
53RD 1/2 ST E	Austin	555R	MK-26	78751	800-1099
54TH ST E	Austin	555M	MK-26	78751	100-999
55TH ST E	Austin	555M	MK-26	78751	100-999
55TH ST W	Austin	555G	MK-27	78751	100-599
55TH 1/2 ST E	Austin	555M	MK-26	78751	900-999
55TH 1/2 ST W	Austin	555G	MK-27	78751	100-499
56TH ST E	Austin	555H	MK-27	78751	100-499
	Austin	555M	MK-26	78751	700-799
	Austin	555M	MK-26	78751	900-999
56TH ST W	Austin	555G	MK-27	78751	100-299
56TH 1/2 ST E	Austin	555M	MK-26	78751	900-999
221 DR	Buda	733X	ME-7	78610	100-299
1000 OAKS	Williamson Co	374C	MH-45	78681	5300-5499

A

STREET NAME	CITY or COUNTY	MAPSCO GRID	AUSTIN GRID	ZIP CODE	BLOCK RANGE O/E
A LN	Austin	584H	MH-24	78703	2100-2299
AARON ROSS CV	Round Rock	347V	MP-46	78665	2800-2899
AARON ROSS WAY	Round Rock	347Z	MP-46	78665	2100-2199
	Round Rock	348W	MQ-46	78665	2200-2399
ABACO LN	Williamson Co	405F	MJ-42	78681	16100-16199
ABACO HARBOUR CV	Pflugerville	437C	MP-39	78664	1300-1399
ABACO HARBOUR LN	Pflugerville	437B	MN-39	78664	17300-17499
ABAMILLO CT	Hutto	380N	MU-44	78634	300-399
ABBATE CIR	Austin	586T	ML-22	78721	3600-3699
ABBEY CIR	Austin	466P	ML-35	78727	2000-2099
ABBEY DR	Hays Co	639X	WW-16	78737	100-399
ABBEY LN	Cedar Park	372P	MC-44	78613	1600-1699
ABBEY RD	Round Rock	406F	ML-42	78681	1000-1499
ABBEY GLEN LN	Austin	497J	MN-32	78753	12100-12299
ABBEYGLEN CASTLE DR	Pflugerville	408T	MQ-40	78660	600-1099
ABBOTSBURY DR	Travis Co	432P	MC-38	78613	3100-3599
ABBOTT DR	Hays Co	639X	WW-16	78737	100-399
ABBY ANN LN	Austin	704L	MH-11	78747	5600-5999
ABELIA DR	Austin	465L	MK-35	78727	4500-4599
ABERDEEN CIR	Austin	644F	MG-18	78745	4900-4999
ABERDEEN CT	Hays Co	639X	WW-16	78737	100-199
ABERDEEN DR	Austin	644F	MG-18	78745	4800-5199
ABERDEEN DR	Round Rock	376L	MM-44	78664	1800-1999
ABERDEEN WAY	Austin	526L	MM-29	78753	9300-9899
ABERNATHY	Manor	529T	MS-28	78653	None
ABILENE CV	Austin	642J	MC-17	78749	8500-8599
ABILENE LN	Williamson Co	344F	MG-48	78628	100-399
ABILENE TRL	Austin	642E	MC-18	78749	5400-6199
	Austin	641H	MB-18	78749	6200-6599
ABINGDON PL	Austin	556N	ML-26	78723	5300-5399
ABNEY DR	Williamson Co	434T	MG-37	78729	12300-12399
ABOVE STRATFORD PL	Austin	584E	MG-24	78746	3100-3199
ABRAHAM LINCOLN ST	Travis Co	530L	MV-29	78653	13500-13599
ABRAHAMSON CT	Travis Co	531G	MX-30	78653	None
ABRAHAMSON RD	Travis Co	531M	MX-29	78653	14000-14599
ABRAMS RD	Williamson Co	254C	MH-57	78633	500-599
ABYSSINIAN LN	Williamson Co	405B	MJ-42	78681	16900-16999
ACACIA DR	Williamson Co	344P	MG-47	78641	6200-7299
ACACIA WAY	Georgetown	225P	MJ-59	78633	100-199
ACACIA BUD DR	Travis Co	551P	MA-26	78733	1500-1899
ACADEMY DR	Austin	615E	MJ-21	78704	100-699
ACADEMY PL	Round Rock	407T	MN-40	78664	1600-1699
ACADIA CT	Hays Co	669F	WW-15	78737	100-199
ACADIAN TRL	Austin	465A	MJ-36	78727	12700-12799
ACANTHUS ST	Pflugerville	437M	MP-38	78660	1000-1299
ACAPULCO CT	Lakeway	489U	WX-31	78734	100-199
ACAPULCO DR	Lakeway	489U	WX-31	78734	1-299
ACCOMAC DR	Travis Co	672X	MC-13	78748	3100-3399
ACE PASS	Austin	466N	ML-35	78758	2400-2499
ACEQUIA PASS	Austin	495G	MK-33	78758	10700-10999
ACERS LN	Travis Co	619N	MS-20	78725	4400-4699
ACKER RD	Williamson Co	225U	MK-58	78633	200-299
ACORN CT	Cedar Park	403A	ME-42	78613	900-999
ACORN CV	Austin	645W	MJ-16	78744	5100-5299
ACORN DR	Burnet Co	426E	WQ-39	78669	200-299
ACORN LN	Cedar Park	372Y	MD-43	78613	900-1099
ACORN CREEK TRL	Williamson Co	433K	ME-38	78750	11800-12199
ACORN GROVE CT	Austin	645X	MJ-16	78744	5000-5099
ACORN OAKS DR	Austin	643Z	MF-16	78745	900-1099
ACROPOLIS CT	Austin	465T	MJ-34	78727	4300-4399
ACTON DR	Travis Co	611Y	MB-19	78736	8000-8199
ACUARELA CT	Travis Co	581V	MB-22	78735	8600-8799
ACUNA CT	Bastrop Co	738P	MQ-8	78617	100-199
ADA CT	Austin	675S	MJ-13	78744	6100-6199
ADA LN	Round Rock	377E	MN-45	78664	2200-2299
ADAGIO PL	Williamson Co	345X	MJ-46	78681	4200-4299
ADAK CV	Williamson Co	434V	MH-37	78729	12900-12999
ADALEE AVE	Austin	556U	MM-25	78723	6100-6299
ADAM CV	Round Rock	345T	MJ-46	78681	3000-3099
ADAMAE LN	Hutto	379M	MT-44	78634	100-199
ADAM L CHAPA SR ST	Austin	615C	MK-21	78702	100-299
ADAMS AVE	Austin	555A	MJ-27	78756	5600-5799
ADAMS CV	Lago Vista	459A	WW-36	78645	4100-4199
ADAMS ST	Bastrop Co	534X	EC-28	78621	600-799
ADAMS ST	Taylor	352C	MZ-48	76574	1400-1899
ADDIE LN	Georgetown	256N	ML-56	78628	2900-3099
ADDIE ROY RD	Travis Co	552R	MD-26	78733	200-399
ADDISON AVE	Austin	525N	MJ-29	78757	2400-2799
ADEL CV	Austin	642D	MD-18	78749	6200-6299
ADELAIDE DR	Austin	640Z	WZ-16	78739	7800-7999
ADELANTO CT	Travis Co	550Q	WZ-26	78733	3300-3399
ADELEN LN	Round Rock	408J	MQ-41	78664	2800-2899
ADELFA DR	Williamson Co	408K	MQ-41	78664	100-299
ADELPHI CV	Austin	465L	MK-35	78727	12400-12499
ADELPHI LN	Austin	465M	MK-35	78727	3000-4799
ADEN CT	Austin	671B	MA-15	78739	11300-11399
ADEN LN	Austin	671B	MA-15	78739	6400-6699
ADENA LN	Leander	372C	MD-45	78641	2800-2999
ADINA ST	Austin	586L	MM-23	78721	1700-1899
ADIRONDACK CV	Austin	494Q	MH-32	78759	8500-8599
ADIRONDACK TRL	Austin	494Q	MH-32	78759	8300-8599
ADIRONDACK SUMMIT DR	Bee Cave	549K	WW-26	78738	4300-4499
ADKINS CV	Georgetown	257T	MN-55	78626	300-399
ADLER AVE	Austin	464Q	MH-35	78759	11200-11299
ADLER FALLS LN	Round Rock	377Z	MP-43	78665	700-799
ADMIRAL NIMITZ CT	Williamson Co	344F	MG-48	78628	100-199
ADMIRAL'S PARK DR	Jonestown	430P	WY-38	78645	None
ADOBE TRL	Lago Vista	399Y	WX-40	78645	20400-20899
ADOBE TRL	Travis Co	641F	MA-18	78737	7700-7899
ADOLPH ALLEY	Austin	495J	MJ-32	78759	None
ADONIS DR	Williamson Co	434F	MG-39	78729	13200-13299
ADRIAN DR	Leander	342X	MC-46	78641	2200-2299
ADRIAN WAY	Travis Co	430E	WY-39	78645	19100-19599
	Travis Co	429D	WX-39	78645	19600-19999
ADRIANA LN	Hutto	349R	MT-47	78634	100-299
ADRIANE DR	Austin	586K	ML-23	78721	1600-1899
ADRIATICO WAY	Travis Co	432L	MD-38	78613	2900-3099
ADVENTURE LN	Williamson Co	374W	MG-43	78613	800-1099
ADVENTURER	Lakeway	489U	WX-31	78734	100-199
AEMILIAN WAY	Travis Co	523W	ME-28	78730	7300-7399
AERIE CV	Austin	464Q	MH-35	78759	11100-11199
AERO LN	Georgetown	226Z	MM-58	78628	3700-3999
AFFIRMED DR	Austin	678P	MQ-14	78617	13300-13399
AFGHAN PATH	Williamson Co	377A	MN-45	78664	1200-1299
AFTON LN	Austin	645P	MJ-17	78744	4100-4299
AFTON RIDGE RD	Travis Co	704F	MG-12	78747	None
AFTONSHIRE WAY	Austin	672H	MD-15	78748	2600-3099
AGAPE LN	Austin	582Z	MD-22	78735	3600-3999
AGARITA CV	Travis Co	491A	MA-33	78734	4600-4799
AGARITA DR	Lago Vista	429F	WW-39	78645	20500-20699
AGARITA PL	Travis Co	491A	MA-33	78734	4400-4599
AGARITA RD	Travis Co	491A	MA-33	78734	14400-14799
AGARITA TRL	Williamson Co	377K	MN-44	78665	2100-2499
AGARITO LN	Travis Co	517E	WS-30	78669	21700-21999
AGATE CV	Austin	494H	MH-33	78759	4900-4999
AGATHA CIR	Austin	587F	MN-24	78724	5300-5699
AGAVE CV	Austin	493V	MF-31	78750	6900-6999
AGAVE LN	Austin	465Y	MK-34	78758	3400-3499
AGAVE LN	Georgetown	225L	MK-59	78633	100-199
AGAVE LOOP	Round Rock	375C	MK-45	78681	2900-3099
AGGIE LN	Austin	525R	MK-29	78757	1000-1099
	Austin	525Q	MK-29	78757	1200-1999
AGNES ST	Bastrop	744M	ED-8	78602	400-599
AGUA CALIENTE CV	Austin	645W	MJ-16	78744	5400-5499
AGUA FRIO DR	Travis Co	429Q	WX-38	78645	19400-19999
AGUA VISTA	Travis Co	490N	WY-32	78734	16000-16199
AGUILA CIR	Travis Co	490C	WZ-33	78734	4100-4199
AGUILAR DR	Hutto	379H	MT-45	78634	100-199
AGUJA CT	Lakeway	518M	WW-29	78738	300-399
AHUMOA DR	Bastrop Co	746W	EG-7	78602	100-199
AHUPU LN E	Bastrop Co	775G	EF-6	78602	100-199
AHUPU LN W	Bastrop Co	775G	EF-6	78602	100-199
AIEA CT	Bastrop Co	775D	EF-6	78602	100-199
AIKEN DR	Leander	311R	MB-50	78641	900-1099
AINEZ DR	Austin	675B	MJ-15	78744	5600-5899
AINSWORTH ST	Austin	644P	MG-17	78745	100-299
AIRCRAFT LN	Austin	646V	MM-16	78719	10000-10099
	Austin	647W	MN-16	78719	10100-10299
AIRE LIBRE DR	Austin	463R	ME-36	78726	9500-9699
AIRLINE TERRACE	Travis Co	676X	ML-13	78719	8600-8899
AIROLE WAY	Austin	614P	MG-21	78704	1800-2199
AIROSO CV	Austin	644N	MG-17	78745	900-999
AIRPORT BLVD	Austin	616B	ML-21	78702	1-1099
	Austin	586X	ML-22	78702	1100-1899
	Austin	586A	ML-24	78722	1900-4099
	Austin	555Z	MK-25	78722	4100-4499
	Austin	555V	MK-25	78751	4500-5699
	Austin	555H	MK-27	78752	5700-6599
	Austin	525Z	MK-28	78752	6600-7099
AIRPORT DR	Taylor	352F	MY-48	76574	1-399
AIRPORT DR	Williamson Co	313K	ME-50	78641	1-299
AIRPORT RD	Georgetown	226Z	MM-58	78628	None
	Georgetown	256H	MM-57	78628	None
	Williamson Co	226Z	MM-58	78628	None
AIRPORT COMMERCE DR	Austin	646B	ML-18	78741	1300-1999
AIRSIDE RD	Austin	646M	MM-17	78719	9300-9499
AIR STRIP DR	Bastrop Co	745X	EE-7	78602	100-199
	Bastrop Co	775A	EE-6	78602	200-299
AIRSTRIP RD	Burnet Co	396S	WQ-40	78669	100-599
AJUGA CT	Lakeway	489Y	WX-31	78734	100-199
AKALA LN	Bastrop	746S	EG-7	78602	100-199
AKALOA DR	Bastrop Co	746W	EG-7	78602	100-199
	Bastrop Co	776A	EG-6	78602	200-399
	Bastrop Co	775M	EF-5	78602	400-499
AKRON CV	Austin	556L	MM-26	78723	2400-2499
ALABAMA DR	Austin	643X	ME-16	78745	8200-8499
ALABASTER CV	Williamson Co	375B	MJ-45	78681	3900-3999
ALABASTER DR	Hays Co	763S	ME-4	78610	100-199
ALABASTER LN	Williamson Co	375B	MJ-45	78681	3900-3999
ALAMEDA DR	Austin	615N	MJ-20	78704	1100-2199
ALAMEDA TRACE CIR	Austin	465A	MJ-36	78727	12300-12499
ALAMO CV	Lago Vista	459A	WW-36	78645	3700-3799
ALAMO ST	Austin	585V	MK-22	78702	1100-1199
	Austin	585R	MK-23	78702	1200-1699
	Austin	585L	MK-23	78722	1900-2299
ALAMO ST E	Elgin	534N	EC-29	78621	100-599
ALAMO ST W	Elgin	533V	EB-28	78621	None
	Elgin	534S	EC-28	78621	None
ALAMO BOUND	Leander	372A	MC-45	78641	1700-1999
ALAMO PLAZA DR	Cedar Park	373E	ME-45	78613	600-798 E
ALAMOSA DR	Austin	465X	MJ-34	78759	4500-4599
ALAMOSA DR	Georgetown	317J	MN-50	78626	300-399
ALASAN CV	Travis Co	493T	ME-31	78730	6400-6599
ALATA CV	Austin	494G	MH-33	78759	5700-5799
ALAU CT	Bastrop Co	776B	EG-6	78602	100-199
ALAZAN CIR	Travis Co	490C	WZ-33	78734	3800-3899
ALAZAN CV	Williamson Co	377E	MN-45	78664	1500-1699
ALBACETE LN	Williamson Co	405B	MJ-42	78681	7000-7099
ALBANIA WAY	Williamson Co	434M	MH-38	78729	13400-13599
ALBATA AVE	Austin	525P	MJ-29	78757	2500-2699
ALBERT RD	Austin	643Y	MF-16	78745	7200-7799
ALBERTA CV	Austin	671F	MA-15	78739	6600-6699
ALBERTA DR	Austin	671F	MA-15	78739	11500-11599
ALBERTA RIDGE TRL	Austin	462K	MC-35	78726	12500-12799
ALBERT BROWN DR	Travis Co	679C	MT-15	78617	5100-5299
ALBERT VOELKER RD	Travis Co	562C	MZ-27	78621	17600-17899
	Travis Co	532N	MY-29	78621	17900-18899
ALBURY CV	Austin	496A	ML-33	78758	1900-1999
ALCANZA DR	Austin	670H	WZ-15	78739	12200-12599
ALCORN CIR	Austin	673H	MF-15	78748	8200-8299
ALCOTT CV	Austin	672M	MD-14	78748	10100-10199
ALCOTT LN	Austin	672M	MD-14	78748	2600-2899
ALCOVE CT	Austin	525X	MJ-28	78757	1700-1799
ALDAMA DR	Travis Co	672N	MC-14	78739	4100-4299
ALDEA DR	Austin	643U	MF-16	78745	7200-7399
ALDEN DR	Austin	525H	MK-30	78758	1000-1199
ALDENBURGH CT	Travis Co	640V	WZ-16	78737	11100-11199
ALDER CV	Austin	493R	MF-32	78750	6900-6999
ALDERBROOK DR	Austin	466S	ML-34	78758	12200-12499
ALDERMINISTER LN	Travis Co	467Q	MP-35	78660	14300-14499
ALDERWOOD CV	Williamson Co	375S	MJ-43	78717	9000-9099
ALDERWOOD DR	Austin	643P	ME-17	78745	2700-2899
ALDFORD CIR	Austin	643K	ME-17	78745	6500-6699
ALDFORD DR	Austin	643L	ME-17	78745	2300-2699
ALDING VALLEY DR	Travis Co	497C	MP-33	78754	2000-2099
ALDRICH ST	Austin	556W	ML-25	78723	1700-1999
ALDRIDGE DR	Travis Co	526R	MM-29	78754	1700-1799
ALDWORTH DR	Travis Co	432C	MD-39	78613	2200-2399
ALDWYCHE DR	Austin	614T	MG-19	78704	3300-3499
ALEGRE PASS	Austin	674G	MH-15	78744	7000-7299
ALEGRIA RD	Austin	525Y	MK-28	78757	1000-1699
ALEGRO DR	Austin	495B	MJ-33	78759	11100-11199
ALELE DR	Bastrop Co	776B	EG-6	78602	100-299
ALEMAN CV	Round Rock	406K	ML-41	78681	1401-1599 O
ALEPPO PINE TRL	Travis Co	532Q	MZ-29	78621	17800-18099
ALETHA LN	Austin	673D	MF-15	78745	700-799
ALEX AVE	Travis Co	466C	MM-36	78728	1900-2099
ALEX LN	Austin	673V	MF-13	78748	9600-9799
ALEXANDER AVE	Austin	585R	MK-23	78702	1200-1499
	Austin	585M	MK-23	78702	1700-1899
	Austin	585M	MK-23	78722	1900-2299
ALEXANDER CT	Round Rock	377Z	MP-43	78665	2500-2599
ALEXANDER DR	Williamson Co	343W	ME-46	78641	2700-2899
ALEXANDER ST	Taylor	352D	MZ-48	76574	900-1099
ALEXANDER VALLEY CV	Round Rock	407H	MP-42	78665	3300-3399
ALEXANDRA LN	Cedar Park	433A	ME-39	78613	None
	Williamson Co	403W	ME-40	78613	2400-2599
ALEXANDRIA DR	Austin	642Q	MD-17	78749	3500-4499
ALEXANDRIA WAY	Round Rock	378E	MQ-45	78665	1100-1199
ALEXANDRITE WAY	Williamson Co	375F	MJ-45	78681	3300-3699
ALEXIS CV	Austin	615Z	MK-19	78741	5400-5499
ALEXIS CV	Pflugerville	468K	MQ-35	78660	900-999
ALEXS LN	Austin	703E	ME-12	78748	11700-11799
ALF AVE	Austin	586T	ML-22	78721	4600-5099
ALFALFA DR	Lago Vista	429L	WX-38	78645	None
	Travis Co	429L	WX-38	78645	19500-20399
ALFRED ST	Austin	672R	MD-14	78748	10200-10399
ALGARITA AVE	Austin	615N	MJ-20	78704	800-1399
ALGARITA CV	Williamson Co	193B	ME-63	78633	100-199
ALGARITA DR	Bastrop Co	709P	MS-11	78617	1-199
ALGERITA DR	Georgetown	256F	ML-57	78628	300-599
ALGERITA TERRACE	Travis Co	733B	ME-9	78652	13000-13299
ALGREG ST	Pflugerville	408V	MR-40	78660	20000-20299
ALGUNO RD	Austin	525X	MJ-28	78757	1200-1999
ALHAMBRA DR	Austin	465X	MJ-34	78759	11000-11399
ALHAMBRA DR	Georgetown	226U	MM-58	78628	600-999
ALI CV	Austin	587B	MN-24	78724	6800-6899
ALICE AVE	Austin	647Q	MP-17	78617	3100-3299
ALICIA DR	Travis Co	592E	MY-24	78621	23100-23399
ALICIA DR	Williamson Co	288C	MR-54	78626	100-199
ALIMONY CV	Austin	466F	ML-36	78727	2300-2399
ALISON ANN CT	Pflugerville	408Z	MR-40	78660	None
ALISON PARKE TRL	Williamson Co	433P	ME-38	78750	11000-11199
AL JONES ST	Bastrop Co	744D	ED-9	78602	100-199
	Bastrop Co	745A	EE-9	78602	None
ALLANDALE RD	Austin	525W	MJ-28	78757	2100-2899
ALLBRIGHT ST	Bastrop	745A	EE-9	78602	1600-1699
ALLEGHANY DR	Austin	615W	MJ-19	78741	1700-1799
ALLEGIANCE AVE	Lago Vista	458D	WV-36	78645	3600-3699
ALLEGRO LN	West Lake Hills	583B	ME-24	78746	200-499
ALLEGRO LUGAR	Austin	643E	ME-18	78749	3500-3899
ALLEN CIR	Williamson Co	225N	MJ-59	78633	100-499
ALLEN RD	Travis Co	583P	ME-23	78746	1300-1599
ALLEN ST	Austin	616A	ML-21	78702	300-799
ALLENDALE ALLEY	Austin	525W	MJ-28	78756	None
ALLENWOOD DR	Travis Co	460R	WZ-35	78734	15800-15999
ALLERFORD CT	Travis Co	432G	MD-39	78613	2900-2999
ALLERTON AVE	Austin	641L	MB-17	78749	6800-7199
ALLEY ST	Buda	762H	MD-6	78610	100-199
ALLEY A	Elgin	534N	EC-29	78621	400-599
	Elgin	533R	EB-29	78621	600-699
ALLISON CV	Austin	645C	MK-18	78741	4800-4999
ALLISON CV	Elgin	534X	EC-28	78621	100-199
ALLISON DR	Austin	645G	MK-18	78741	2800-2999
ALLISON DR	Taylor	353C	EB-48	76574	200-299
ALLISON WAY	Cedar Park	402L	MD-41	78613	None
ALLIUM DR	Travis Co	551Q	MB-26	78733	1700-1899
ALLOWAY DR	Briarcliff	457V	WT-34	78669	100-399
ALLRED DR	Austin	673N	ME-14	78748	2000-2499
ALLSTON LN	Travis Co	554N	MG-26	78746	2400-2699
ALLWOOD DR	Austin	614F	MG-21	78704	2100-2199
ALLWOOD PATH	Austin	672X	MC-13	78748	11800-11899
ALLYSON CT	Austin	645S	MJ-16	78744	5000-5099

STREET NAME	CITY or COUNTY	MAPSCO GRID	AUSTIN GRID	ZIP CODE	BLOCK RANGE O/E
ALLYSON LN	Williamson Co	318A	MQ-51	78634	100-399
ALMA DR	Austin	497N	MN-32	78753	1300-1499
ALMADEN DR	Austin	374Z	MH-43	78717	16200-16399
ALMARION DR	Rollingwood	584N	MG-23	78746	300-499
ALMARION WAY	Rollingwood	584N	MG-23	78746	100-299
ALMELO DR	Williamson Co	405F	MJ-42	78681	6000-6099
ALMIRANTE CV	Travis Co	580C	WZ-24	78738	4700-4799
ALMOND CV	Austin	494N	MG-32	78750	7600-7699
ALMONDSBURY LN	Austin	673H	MF-15	78748	8100-8199
ALMQUIST ST	Hutto	349H	MT-48	78634	100-399
ALNWICK CASTLE DR	Pflugerville	408X	MQ-40	78660	18600-19099
ALOE CV	Austin	493H	MF-33	78750	8200-8299
ALOE VERA CV	Williamson Co	433K	ME-38	78750	11700-11799
ALOE VERA TRL	Williamson Co	433K	ME-38	78750	11800-11999
ALOHA LN	Bastrop	746P	EG-8	78602	100-199
	Bastrop Co	746P	EG-8	78602	None
ALOMAR CV	Austin	678N	MQ-14	78617	5400-5599
	Austin	678N	MQ-14	78617	5600-5999
ALOMAR ST	Austin	678S	MQ-13	78617	5900-5999
ALONDRA LN	Austin	587G	MP-24	78724	7300-7499
ALONG CREEK CV	Austin	374Z	MH-43	78717	16400-16599
ALOPHIA DR	Austin	670D	WZ-15	78739	7800-8699
ALOYSIA DR	Travis Co	672T	MC-13	78748	11300-11499
ALPHA COLLIER DR	Travis Co	436U	MM-37	78728	14600-14999
ALPHEUS AVE	Austin	465P	MJ-35	78727	11800-11999
ALPINE CIR	Austin	614Y	MH-19	78704	3500-3599
ALPINE CT	Georgetown	225P	MJ-59	78633	100-199
ALPINE DR	Travis Co	708S	MQ-10	78617	8400-8699
ALPINE RD	Travis Co	462E	MC-36	78726	8100-8299
ALPINE RD E	Austin	644D	MH-18	78704	100-499
ALPINE RD W	Austin	614Y	MH-19	78704	100-599
ALPINE MOUNTAIN DR	Leander	372B	MC-45	78641	1300-1399
ALPS DR	Travis Co	708N	MQ-11	78617	14600-14999
ALSACE TRL	Austin	587F	MN-24	78724	5700-5999
ALSATIA DR	Austin	672Y	MD-13	78748	2600-2999
ALTA CT	Austin	554F	MG-27	78731	3600-3699
ALTA LOMA DR	Austin	642P	MC-17	78749	4500-4999
ALTA MESA	Austin	494V	MH-31	78759	8300-8499
ALTAMONT ST	Hutto	379P	MS-44	78634	100-399
ALTA MONTE DR	Travis Co	402Y	MD-40	78613	2400-2499
ALTA VERDE DR	Austin	494V	MH-31	78759	8300-8499
ALTA VISTA	Blanco Co	455L	WP-35	78620	200-1599
	Travis Co	455L	WP-35	78669	100-199
ALTA VISTA	Lago Vista	429F	WW-39	78645	6600-6799
ALTA VISTA AVE	Austin	615N	MJ-20	78704	1000-2399
ALTA VISTA CV	Williamson Co	318G	MR-51	78634	100-199
ALTA VISTA DR	Leander	341M	MB-47	78641	500-699
ALTERRA PKWY	Austin	495C	MK-33	78758	11100-11699
	Austin	465Y	MK-34	78758	11700-11999
ALTHEA CT	Austin	497S	MN-31	78753	1300-1399
ALTOGA DR	Austin	557F	MN-27	78724	8100-8199
ALTONA WAY	Austin	404Q	MH-41	78717	9400-9599
ALTUM ST	Austin	616C	MM-21	78721	1100-1199
ALTUS CV	Austin	494Q	MH-32	78759	8600-8699
ALUM ROCK CV	Austin	705A	MJ-12	78747	6500-6599
ALUM ROCK DR	Austin	675X	MJ-13	78747	7800-7999
	Austin	705B	MJ-12	78747	8000-8799
ALVA DR	Briarcliff	457U	WT-34	78669	500-599
ALVERSTONE WAY	Austin	494M	MH-32	78759	8500-8699
ALVIN	Austin	584P	MG-23	78703	None
ALVINA WOLFF CT	Austin	704S	MG-10	78747	5500-5599
ALVIN DEVANE BLVD	Austin	645L	MK-17	78741	2800-3299
ALVIN HIGH LN	Williamson Co	434L	MH-38	78729	8300-8599
ALWIN DR	Williamson Co	375Y	MK-43	78681	17600-17699
ALYSHEBA DR	Austin	678P	MQ-14	78617	13300-13699
ALYSSA DR	Williamson Co	224L	MH-59	78633	100-399
ALYSSA LN	Travis Co	437L	MP-38	78660	16500-16599
AMALFI CV	Austin	465M	MK-35	78759	3400-3499
AMANDA CIR	Bastrop Co	742J	MY-8	78612	100-399
AMANDA CV	Round Rock	406K	ML-41	78681	2300-2399
AMANDA DR	Williamson Co	434F	MG-39	78729	9100-9299
AMANDA ELLIS CT	Austin	642F	MC-18	78749	5400-5499
AMANDA ELLIS WAY	Austin	642F	MC-18	78749	7400-7799
AMANDAS WAY	Buda	732U	MD-7	78610	100-299
AMANDA'S WAY	Williamson Co	312A	MC-51	78641	100-299
AMARANTH LN	Austin	528P	MQ-29	78754	11000-11299
AMARILLO AVE	Travis Co	435S	MJ-37	78729	13000-13199
	Williamson Co	435S	MJ-37	78729	13200-13299
AMARRA DR	Travis Co	581V	MB-22	78735	4300-4799
AMARYLIS DR	Pflugerville	437H	MP-39	78660	1500-1599
AMARYLLIS AVE	Cedar Park	372H	MD-45	78613	500-699
AMARYLLIS TRL	Travis Co	532L	MZ-29	78621	13000-13099
AMASIA CV	Williamson Co	434L	MH-38	78729	8200-8299
AMASIA DR	Williamson Co	434R	MH-38	78729	13200-13399
AMBER PASS	Austin	643R	MF-17	78745	6100-6299
AMBER ST	Austin	585U	MK-22	78702	1100-1199
AMBER DAWN CT	Travis Co	529M	MT-29	78653	None
AMBER DAY DR	Pflugerville	437H	MP-39	78660	1400-1599
AMBERGLEN BLVD	Williamson Co	434C	MH-39	78729	8800-9699
AMBERGLOW CT	Round Rock	347Z	MP-46	78665	2700-2799
AMBERJACK CT	Williamson Co	196S	ML-61	78628	100-199
AMBERLY PL	Austin	464U	MH-34	78759	6100-6499
AMBER OAK CV	Austin	672L	MD-14	78748	10200-10299
AMBER OAK DR	Austin	672L	MD-14	78748	3200-3299
AMBER SKYWAY CV	Round Rock	407G	MP-42	78665	1700-1799
AMBERWOOD CV	Austin	494H	MH-33	78759	9200-9299
AMBLESIDE DR	Austin	465R	MK-35	78759	3400-3699
AMBLEWOOD WAY	Travis Co	496Z	MM-31	78753	10800-11199
AMBLING TRL	Cedar Park	372T	MC-43	78613	1400-1599
AMBLING TRL	Travis Co	409P	MS-41	78660	2300-2499
AMBROSE DR	Pflugerville	467H	MP-36	78660	100-1099
AMBUSH CV	Lago Vista	399U	WX-40	78645	20700-20799
AMBUSH CANYON	Leander	342W	MC-46	78641	2200-2499
AMELIA CV	Austin	493G	MF-33	78750	8100-8199
AMELIA DR	Cedar Park	402C	MD-42	78613	1500-1699
AMEN CORNER RD	Pflugerville	409W	MS-40	78660	2300-2599
AMENO DR	Lakeway	519V	WX-28	78734	100-199
AMERICAN CV	Lago Vista	458F	WU-36	78645	21600-21699
AMERICAN DR	Lago Vista	458C	WV-36	78645	1900-3499
AMERICAN WAY	Dripping Springs	638W	WU-16	78620	100-299
AMERICAN KESTREL DR	Bee Cave	549H	WX-27	78738	None
AMERICAN LEGION DR	Bastrop	745M	EF-8	78602	1-99
AMERICAN ROBIN PATH	Pflugerville	437R	MP-38	78660	1100-1199
AMES CT	Austin	641Y	MB-16	78739	6300-6399
AMES LN	Austin	641Y	MB-16	78739	10500-10699
AMESBURY LN	Austin	525V	MK-28	78752	600-699
AMESITE TRL	Austin	463A	ME-36	78726	11100-11199

STREET NAME	CITY or COUNTY	MAPSCO GRID	AUSTIN GRID	ZIP CODE	BLOCK RANGE O/E
AMESLEY CV	Austin	465P	MJ-35	78727	4800-4899
AMESWOOD DR	Austin	556Y	MM-25	78723	5500-5699
AMESWOOD DR	Round Rock	376L	MM-44	78664	200-499
AMESWOOD PL	Round Rock	376L	MM-44	78664	500-599
AMETHYST TRL	Williamson Co	433K	ME-38	78750	11200-11299
AMETHYST STONE LN	Travis Co	436L	MM-38	78728	3000-3199
AMHERST DR	Austin	465M	MK-35	78727	12000-12599
AMIGO WAY	Travis Co	339H	WX-48	78641	None
AMIS AVE	Travis Co	490N	WY-32	78734	1700-1899
AMIS CT	Travis Co	490N	WY-32	78734	15900-15999
AMISTAD CV	Round Rock	347N	MN-47	78665	3500-3599
AMISTAD DR	Travis Co	408H	MR-42	78664	1300-1399
	Williamson Co	408H	MR-42	78664	1200-1299
AMISTAD WAY	Round Rock	347N	MN-47	78665	1200-1399
AMMUNITION DR	Travis Co	672U	MD-13	78748	3000-3199
AMORY LN	Austin	646D	MM-18	78742	1400-1499
AMOS DR	Village of Volente	461A	MA-36	78641	15700-15899
AMPEZO TRL	Austin	642U	MD-16	78749	8700-8999
AMUR DR	Austin	643G	MF-18	78745	2000-2699
AMWELL CV	Travis Co	551D	MB-27	78733	10200-10299
AMY CIR	Austin	494V	MH-31	78759	3900-4099
AMY FRANCIS ST	Travis Co	618V	MR-19	78725	14500-14599
AMY LYNN LN	Cedar Park	372F	MC-45	78613	2200-2399
ANACACHO CV	Round Rock	377X	MN-43	78664	3100-3199
ANACACHO DR	Williamson Co	408K	MQ-41	78664	100-199
ANACAPO CV	Austin	466F	ML-36	78727	13400-13499
ANACONDA LN	Travis Co	492U	MD-31	78730	5200-5399
ANAHUAC TRL	Austin	704A	MG-12	78747	9900-10399
ANAHULU LN	Bastrop Co	775H	EF-6	78602	100-199
ANAQUA DR	Austin	493V	MF-31	78750	7000-7599
ANAROSA LOOP	Austin	466F	ML-36	78727	13400-13599
ANATOLE CT	Austin	672Y	MD-13	78748	11600-11699
ANCHOR DR	Williamson Co	224K	MG-59	78633	300-499
ANCHOR LN	Austin	586E	ML-24	78723	1800-2199
ANCHUSA TRL	Austin	611A	MA-21	78736	9500-9799
ANCONA TRL	Williamson Co	375T	MJ-43	78681	8000-8199
ANDALUSIA DR	Austin	465X	MJ-34	78759	4300-4699
ANDENWOOD DR	Austin	433X	ME-37	78726	11000-11299
ANDERSON AVE E	Round Rock	376Y	MM-43	78664	100-499
ANDERSON DR	Elgin	533M	EB-29	78621	100-199
ANDERSON LN E	Austin	526X	ML-28	78752	100-1499
	Austin	556D	MM-27	78752	1500-2699
ANDERSON LN W	Austin	525R	MK-29	78752	100-599
	Austin	525L	MK-29	78757	800-3399
ANDERSON RD	Travis Co	500F	MU-33	78653	15700-16199
ANDERSON ST	Hutto	349U	MT-46	78634	100-299
ANDERSON ST W	Round Rock	376Y	MM-43	78664	100-599
ANDERSON TRL	Travis Co	309R	WX-50	78641	24500-24999
ANDERSON CROSSING	Travis Co	374G	MH-45	78613	1-99
ANDERSON MILL RD	Austin	434S	MG-37	78729	9300-9699
	Austin	433V	MF-37	78750	10000-10498 E
	Austin	433P	ME-38	78750	10500-10699
	Cedar Park	372X	MC-43	78613	16100-16199
	Cedar Park	372T	MC-43	78613	16300-16699
	Travis Co	433P	ME-38	78750	10700-11699
	Travis Co	432C	MD-39	78613	13000-13799
	Travis Co	402Y	MD-40	78613	None
	Williamson Co	434L	MH-38	78729	7600-9299
	Williamson Co	433V	MF-37	78750	9700-9999
	Williamson Co	433V	MF-37	78750	10001-10499 O
	Williamson Co	433P	ME-38	78750	11700-11799
	Williamson Co	402F	MC-42	78613	None
ANDERSON SQUARE	Austin	525M	MK-29	78757	7900-8099
ANDERSON VILLAGE DR					
	Williamson Co	434E	MG-39	78729	9700-9799
ANDES CV	Austin	494Q	MH-32	78759	8500-8599
ANDICE PATH	Round Rock	346W	ML-46	78681	3200-3299
ANDORA DR	Austin	404K	MG-41	78717	10100-10299
ANDOVER CV	Round Rock	376M	MM-44	78664	500-599
ANDOVER DR	Round Rock	376M	MM-44	78664	600-2199
ANDOVER PL	Austin	556S	ML-25	78723	5200-5299
ANDRE DR	Austin	614Z	MH-19	78704	None
ANDREA WAY	Round Rock	407J	MN-41	78664	1600-1699
ANDREA RIDGE CV	Travis Co	550R	WZ-26	78733	2700-2799
ANDREAS CV	Austin	494Q	MH-32	78759	8500-8599
ANDREA WOODS CV	Austin	674L	MH-14	78744	2400-2599
ANDRES WAY	Round Rock	408J	MQ-41	78664	2600-2699
ANDREW CV	Cedar Park	402H	MD-42	78613	1200-1299
ANDREW DR	Travis Co	456H	WR-36	78669	24700-25299
ANDREWS LN	Austin	494R	MH-32	78759	8400-8599
ANDREW ZILKER RD	Austin	584T	MG-22	78746	2000-2499
ANDROMEDA CV	Austin	465G	MK-36	78727	12600-12699
ANDROSS CT	Hutto	380N	MU-44	78634	6000-6099
ANDTREE BLVD	Travis Co	557E	MN-27	78724	3400-3599
ANEMONE CIR	Georgetown	226A	ML-60	78633	100-199
ANEMONE CV	Austin	494B	MG-33	78759	6100-6199
ANEMONE WAY	Georgetown	226A	ML-60	78633	100-199
ANGEL DR	Austin	677R	MP-14	78617	5700-5899
ANGEL BAY DR	Travis Co	488D	WV-33	78669	19700-19999
ANGELFIRE LN	Austin	583Z	MF-22	78746	2900-2999
ANGEL HILL RD	Niederwald	795P	MJ-2	78610	100-199
ANGELIA DR	Bastrop Co	741C	MX-9	78612	100-299
ANGELICO CV	Williamson Co	345X	MJ-46	78681	3000-3099
ANGELICO LN	Williamson Co	345X	MJ-46	78681	4200-4399
ANGELINA CV	Georgetown	195N	MJ-62	78633	100-199
ANGUS DR	Briarcliff	457V	WT-34	78669	22100-22199
ANGELINA DR	Williamson Co	348P	MQ-47	78665	2800-2999
ANGUS RD	Austin	465N	MJ-35	78759	11500-11799
ANGELINA ST	Austin	585U	MK-22	78702	1100-1199
	Austin	585Q	MK-23	78702	1200-1499
ANGELIQUE CT	Leander	342R	MD-47	78641	1900-2099
ANGEL LIGHT DR N	Travis Co	458Y	WV-34	78669	100-899
ANGEL LIGHT DR S	Travis Co	488C	WV-33	78669	100-899
ANGEL MOUNTAIN DR	Jonestown	371S	MA-43	78641	18700-18999
ANGEL OAK ST	Austin	673Y	MF-13	78748	300-499
ANGEL SIDE DR	Jonestown	371P	MA-44	78641	12800-12899
ANGEL SONG CV	Travis Co	458Y	WV-34	78669	300-399
ANGEL SPRING DR	Jonestown	371N	MA-44	78641	12800-13099
ANGEL VALLEY	Jonestown	371T	MA-43	78641	18100-18499
ANGEL WING	Jonestown	371N	MA-44	78641	18600-18699
ANGELWYLDE DR	Travis Co	551R	MB-26	78733	9700-9799
ANGLETON CV	Austin	673X	ME-13	78748	800-999
ANGLIN LN	Hays Co	639V	WX-16	78737	1-99
ANGUS TRL	Lago Vista	399V	WX-40	78645	8300-8499
ANIKA CV	Georgetown	227A	MN-60	78628	30400-30499
ANIKAWI DR	Travis Co	554E	MG-27	78746	4500-4699
ANIMAS DR	Georgetown	317J	MN-50	78626	100-299

STREET NAME	CITY or COUNTY	MAPSCO GRID	AUSTIN GRID	ZIP CODE	BLOCK RANGE O/E
ANISE DR	Austin	646B	ML-18	78741	1200-1799
ANITA DR	Austin	614F	MG-21	78704	1800-1999
ANITA MARIE LN	Travis Co	436Y	MM-37	78728	14200-14399
ANJOU LN	Williamson Co	405B	MJ-42	78681	16700-16799
ANKARA CT	Travis Co	492U	MD-31	78730	5300-5399
ANKEN DR	Austin	615Y	MK-19	78741	2300-2599
ANN PL	Travis Co	466H	MM-36	78728	13700-13899
ANNA CT	Cedar Park	402H	MD-42	78613	1200-1399
ANNA ST	Austin	673R	MF-14	78748	8900-9099
ANNABELLE DR	Travis Co	591R	MX-23	78621	8300-8499
ANNADALE DR	Cedar Park	373Y	MF-43	78613	900-999
ANNA KATE CT	Pflugerville	438D	MR-39	78660	None
ANNA PALM WAY	Round Rock	378B	MQ-45	78665	1200-1399
ANNAPOLIS CV	Lago Vista	459A	WW-36	78645	3800-3899
ANN ARBOR AVE	Austin	614F	MG-21	78704	1800-2599
ANNETTE CV	Austin	587F	MN-24	78724	7300-7499
ANNIE ST	Taylor	352H	MZ-48	76574	200-699
ANNIE ST E	Austin	615J	MJ-20	78704	100-599
ANNIE ST W	Austin	614M	MH-20	78704	100-1199
ANNIE OAKLEY TRL	Austin	496X	ML-31	78753	10100-10399
ANNIKA WAY	Bastrop	744D	ED-9	78602	700-799
ANN JENE CT	Austin	645U	MK-16	78744	5800-5899
ANN SHOWERS DR	Travis Co	591P	MW-23	78621	21100-22399
ANN TAYLOR DR	Austin	673D	MF-15	78745	700-799
ANSELM CT	Austin	671G	MB-15	78739	5800-5899
ANSONIA TRL	Williamson Co	405C	MK-42	78681	3100-3199
ANTELOPE CIR	Austin	643V	MF-16	78745	6600-6699
ANTELOPE CV	Cedar Park	403C	MF-42	78613	700-799
ANTELOPE LN	Caldwell Co	767X	MN-4	78616	1-99
ANTELOPE TRL	Bastrop	744P	EC-8	78602	None
ANTELOPE RIDGE	Cedar Park	403C	MF-42	78613	800-1299
ANTELOPE RUN	Austin	672L	MD-14	78748	10400-10599
ANTERO DR	Austin	494V	MH-31	78759	8400-8499
ANTHONY CT	Cedar Park	402H	MD-42	78613	1500-1599
ANTHONY ST	Austin	615G	MK-21	78702	1-99
ANTHONY ST	Hutto	349Z	MT-46	78634	100-199
ANTIETAM DR	Elgin	533G	EB-30	78621	None
ANTIETAM TRL	Elgin	533G	EB-30	78621	None
ANTIETAM TRL	Travis Co	672X	MC-13	78748	11500-11599
ANTIGO LN	Austin	671F	MA-15	78739	6200-6699
ANTIGUA DR	Austin	464G	MH-36	78759	11500-11599
ANTIQUE FINISH DR	Travis Co	467G	MP-36	78660	14900-15099
ANTIQUE HERITAGE DR	Travis Co	467C	MP-36	78660	900-1099
ANTLER DR	Austin	615T	MJ-19	78741	1700-1799
ANTLER DR	Williamson Co	314U	MH-49	78628	100-199
ANTLER LN	Travis Co	433P	ME-38	78726	11200-11599
ANTLER BEND RD	Travis Co	639G	WX-18	78737	11400-11699
ANTLERS TRL	Williamson Co	281K	MA-53	78641	1-499
ANTOINE CIR	Austin	675N	MJ-14	78744	7200-7299
ANTOINETTE PL	Austin	465L	MK-35	78727	12200-12399
ANTONE ST	Austin	586A	ML-24	78723	1800-2299
ANTONIO WAY	Lakeway	490W	WY-31	78734	None
AOSTA LN	Williamson Co	346L	MM-47	78665	4100-4199
AOUDAD TRL	Austin	642P	MC-17	78749	8500-8599
APACHE	Lago Vista	429W	WW-37	78645	4800-4899
APACHE CV	Pflugerville	437Y	MP-37	78660	1400-1499
APACHE PASS	Austin	613Z	MF-19	78745	4500-4599
APACHE PASS	Williamson Co	410T	MU-40	78634	100-499
APACHE TRL	Leander	342Y	MD-46	78641	200-899
APACHE TRL	Round Rock	407C	MP-42	78665	1700-1999
APACHE TRL	Williamson Co	223D	MF-60	78633	100-199
APACHE CREEK CV	Austin	612M	MD-20	78735	5300-5499
APACHE FOREST DR	Travis Co	672P	MC-14	78739	3500-3799
APACHE MOUNTAIN LN	Georgetown	195S	MJ-61	78633	100-599
	Georgetown	194V	MH-61	78633	600-999
APACHE OAKS DR	Round Rock	377K	MN-44	78665	1000-1099
APACHE PLUM LN	Travis Co	409P	MS-41	78660	20800-21199
APACHE SPRINGS CIR	Travis Co	641C	MB-18	78737	8500-8599
APLOMADO FALCON CV	Bee Cave	549G	WX-27	78738	None
APOLLO CIR	Round Rock	377A	MN-45	78664	1000-1799
APOLLO DR	Austin	496K	ML-32	78758	1000-1199
APOLLO LN	Cedar Park	372G	MD-45	78613	1100-1199
APPALACHIAN DR	Austin	494Q	MH-32	78759	8300-8699
APPALOOSA CT	Mustang Ridge	765R	MK-5	78610	100-7199
APPALOOSA TRL	Lago Vista	399U	WX-40	78645	20600-20799
APPALOOSA WAY	Hays Co	795J	MJ-2	78610	100-199
APPALOOSA CHASE DR	Travis Co	491W	MA-31	78732	13200-13299
	Travis Co	521A	MA-30	78732	None
APPALOOSA RUN	Travis Co	670C	WZ-15	78737	8200-9099
APPENNINI CV	Travis Co	432Q	MD-38	78613	2900-2999
APPENNINI WAY	Travis Co	432L	MD-38	78613	3000-3299
APPERSON ST	Travis Co	677X	MN-13	78617	6800-7299
	Travis Co	707C	MP-12	78617	7300-7599
APPLE CARRIE CV	Austin	643W	ME-16	78745	8500-8599
APPLE CREEK DR	Georgetown	256V	MM-55	78626	300-399
APPLE CROSS DR	Travis Co	437C	MP-39	78660	1000-1099
APPLEGATE CIR	Williamson Co	346Z	MM-46	78665	1-99
APPLEGATE DR E	Austin	496Y	MM-31	78753	100-399
	Travis Co	496Y	MM-31	78753	800-999
	Travis Co	526D	MM-30	78753	1000-1499
APPLEGATE DR W	Austin	496X	ML-31	78753	100-799
APPLEGREEN CT	Village of the Hills	519S	WW-28	78738	1-99
APPLEGREEN LN	Village of the Hills	519S	WW-28	78738	1-99
APPLE ORCHARD LN	Austin	645T	MJ-16	78744	5300-5799
APPLE ROCK	Leander	342X	MC-46	78641	900-1199
APPLE SPRINGS CIR	Travis Co	341K	MA-47	78641	15400-15599
APPLE SPRINGS DR	Travis Co	341F	MA-48	78641	19100-19999
APPLE SPRINGS HOLLOW	Travis Co	341P	MA-47	78641	14900-15499
APPLETREE LN	Austin	433W	ME-37	78726	11100-11299
APPLE VALLEY CIR	Austin	704J	MG-11	78747	2400-2499
APPLE VISTA CIR	Travis Co	408L	MR-41	78660	3700-3799
APPLEWOOD CT	Village of the Hills	519S	WW-28	78738	1-99
APPLEWOOD DR	Austin	496J	ML-32	78758	11000-11299
APPLEWOOD DR	Bastrop Co	711F	MW-12	78612	100-199
APPLEWOOD DR	Pflugerville	438S	MQ-37	78660	100-899
APPOMATTOX DR	Austin	643X	ME-16	78745	7900-8199
APRICOT GLEN DR	Austin	613C	MF-21	78746	1700-2299
APRIL DR	Austin	497S	MN-31	78753	11300-11699
AQUA LN	Round Rock	344R	MH-47	78681	3800-3899
AQUA AZUL CT	Travis Co	521Z	MB-28	78733	10200-10299
AQUA AZUL PATH	Travis Co	490N	WY-32	78734	16000-16099
AQUA BELL	Leander	342B	MC-48	78641	500-599
AQUADUCT AVE	Pflugerville	409E	MS-42	78660	1700-1799
AQUAFREDDA CV	Travis Co	523K	ME-29	78730	None
AQUALINE CV	Round Rock	406F	ML-42	78681	1000-1199
AQUALUX CV	Travis Co	765M	MK-5	78610	10600-10799
AQUAMARINE DR	Williamson Co	375B	MJ-45	78681	3400-3699

STREET NAME	CITY or COUNTY	MAPSCO GRID	AUSTIN GRID	ZIP CODE	BLOCK RANGE O/E
AQUAPLEX DR	Travis Co	765H	MK-6	78610	12300-12899
AQUA VERDE CT	Travis Co	521Z	MB-28	78733	10200-10299
AQUA VERDE DR	Travis Co	523Q	MF-29	78746	4100-4599
AQUIFER CV	Austin	583U	MF-22	78746	1500-1599
AQUILA CT	Williamson Co	405C	MK-42	78681	3100-3299
AQUITAIINE DR	Pflugerville	408S	MQ-40	78660	None
ARABIAN TRL	Austin	464M	MH-35	78759	11800-11999
ARAGON CT	Williamson Co	226U	MM-58	78628	800-899
ARAGON DR	Austin	465X	MJ-34	78759	11100-11199
ARALIA DR	Austin	493H	MF-33	78750	8100-8199
ARALIA RIDGE DR	Austin	670H	WZ-15	78739	12200-12399
ARANSAS CV	Georgetown	225G	MK-60	78633	100-199
ARANSAS CV	Williamson Co	377F	MN-45	78664	1000-1099
ARAPAHO TRL	Lago Vista	399Y	WX-40	78645	7900-8199
ARAPAHO TRL	Leander	342Z	MD-46	78641	2400-2699
ARAPAHO TRL	Williamson Co	223D	MF-60	78633	100-199
ARAPAHOE PASS	Austin	613Z	MF-19	78745	4700-4799
ARAPAHOE TRL	Austin	643D	MF-18	78745	4600-4699
ARAX CV	Austin	494X	MG-31	78731	5000-5099
ARBOL CV	Williamson Co	345X	MJ-46	78681	4000-4099
ARBOLE CV	Austin	640V	WZ-16	78739	11000-11099
ARBOLEDA CV	Austin	643Y	MF-16	78745	7500-7599
ARBOR CIR	Austin	644K	MG-17	78745	600-699
ARBOR CT	Round Rock	375G	MK-45	78681	500-599
ARBOR DR	Round Rock	375G	MK-45	78681	2400-2599
ARBOR LN	Austin	644K	MG-17	78745	400-599
ARBOR PATH	Round Rock	375G	MK-45	78681	2400-2499
ARBOR CENTER DR	Dripping Springs	636Y	WR-16	78620	100-199
ARBOR DOWNS RD	Austin	672Y	MD-13	78748	11400-11999
ARBORETUM BLVD	Austin	494H	MH-33	78759	9300-9799
ARBOR GLEN WAY	Austin	494Z	MH-31	78731	3900-3999
ARBOR HILL CV	Travis Co	529D	MT-30	78653	13500-13699
ARBOR LAKE CV	Travis Co	521E	MA-30	78732	12800-12999
ARBOR OAK DR	Taylor	322Q	MZ-50	76574	4100-4199
ARBOR OAKS CV	Austin	494G	MH-33	78759	9000-9099
ARBOR PLACE DR	Round Rock	405C	MK-42	78681	None
ARBOR RIDGE CT	Austin	674L	MH-14	78744	7700-7799
ARBORS CIR	Bastrop Co	564Z	ED-25	78621	400-599
ARBORSIDE LN	Austin	527E	MN-30	78754	1900-2699
ARBOR VIEW LN	Travis Co	529H	MT-30	78653	None
ARBORVITA PL	Bastrop Co	776Y	EH-4	78602	100-199
ARBUTUS CV	Travis Co	523Z	MF-28	78746	5300-5399
ARCADIA AVE	Austin	525Y	MK-28	78757	1000-1599
ARCANA CV	Travis Co	522F	MC-30	78730	10300-10399
ARCHDALE DR	Austin	673X	ME-13	78748	10500-10699
ARCHER CV	Lago Vista	399V	WX-40	78645	20400-20499
ARCH HILL CIR	Austin	433V	MF-37	78750	9400-9499
ARCH HILL DR	Austin	433V	MF-37	78750	11900-11999
ARCHSTONE DR	Austin	640Z	WZ-16	78739	11300-11499
ARCH TERRACE	Austin	463D	MF-36	78750	11000-11199
ARCTIC CT	Travis Co	557Q	MP-26	78724	7400-7499
ARDASH LN	Austin	494R	MH-32	78759	8400-8499
ARDATH ST	Austin	525N	MJ-29	78757	6900-7099
ARDEN CT	Round Rock	376S	ML-43	78681	500-599
ARDEN DR	Austin	644E	MG-18	78745	1200-1299
ARDENWOOD RD	Austin	555Z	MK-25	78722	1100-1399
ARDISIA DR	Pflugerville	437L	MP-38	78660	17100-17399
	Travis Co	437L	MP-38	78660	16900-17099
ARDMORE CIR	Austin	674Q	MH-14	78744	7800-7999
ARENA DR	Austin	615Q	MK-20	78741	1300-1499
ARENA DR	Bastrop	745M	EF-8	78602	1-99
ARENA PATH	Lago Vista	399U	WX-40	78645	8300-8399
ARGENTIA RD	Austin	525N	MJ-29	78757	6600-6699
ARGENTO PL	Travis Co	432Q	MD-38	78613	3100-3299
ARGONNE FOREST CV	Austin	464G	MH-36	78759	6900-6999
ARGONNE FOREST TRL	Austin	464G	MH-36	78759	11600-11999
ARGOS LN	Austin	494Q	MH-32	78759	4500-4599
ARGYLE DR	Austin	641R	MB-17	78749	9500-9599
ARI CT	Austin	645C	MK-18	78741	4500-4599
ARIA CV	Williamson Co	345X	MJ-46	78681	4500-4599
ARIA DR	Lakeway	549D	WX-27	78734	100-199
	Lakeway	520W	WY-28	78734	200-499
ARIA RIDGE	Lakeway	549D	WX-27	78734	100-299
ARIELLA DR	Cedar Park	372J	MC-44	78613	2100-2199
ARIES LN	Austin	557Y	MP-25	78724	6700-7099
ARIKARA ST	Buda	762H	MD-6	78610	200-499
ARIKARA RIVER DR	Austin	703B	ME-12	78748	10700-10899
ARIOCK CV	Austin	641X	MA-16	78739	6600-6699
ARIOCK LN	Austin	671B	MA-15	78739	10800-11099
ARION CIR	Travis Co	523W	ME-28	78730	2400-2799
ARISTOCRAT DR	Travis Co	587Z	MP-22	78725	4500-4699
ARIZONA MESA CV	Round Rock	377N	MN-44	78664	1300-1399
ARIZONA OAK LN	Travis Co	619E	MS-21	78724	14900-15199
ARLA CV	Williamson Co	405J	MJ-41	78717	15900-15999
ARLINGTON CV	Lago Vista	459A	WW-36	78645	3700-3799
ARMADILLO CV	Travis Co	489M	WX-32	78734	16900-16999
ARMADILLO LN	Bastrop Co	743T	EA-7	78602	100-299
ARMADILLO RD	Austin	643V	MF-16	78745	900-1699
ARMADILLO TROT	Burnet Co	426F	WQ-39	78669	101-199 O
ARMAGA CV	Austin	466F	ML-36	78727	13200-13299
ARMAGA SPRINGS RD	Austin	466F	ML-36	78727	13100-13399
ARMATRADING DR	Travis Co	402T	MC-40	78613	2500-2699
ARMSTRONG AVE	Travis Co	530P	MU-29	78653	12800-13099
ARMSTRONG AVE	Travis Co	619E	MS-21	78724	15400-15499
ARMSTRONG DR	Georgetown	195T	MJ-61	78633	100-899
ARMSTRONG DR	Williamson Co	343S	ME-46	78641	2500-2699
ARNHAMN LN	Travis Co	500P	MU-32	78653	11700-12199
ARNHEM CV	Austin	678N	MQ-14	78617	6000-6099
ARNIE LN	Round Rock	378U	MR-43	78664	2300-2399
ARNOLD DR	Austin	556R	MM-26	78723	6200-6599
ARNOLD LN	San Leanna	703K	ME-11	78748	11800-11899
ARONA CV	Travis Co	492U	MD-31	78730	5300-5399
ARPDALE ST	Austin	614K	MG-20	78704	2000-2499
ARREN TERRACE	Village of Volente	430R	WZ-38	78641	8000-8099
ARRONIMINK CIR	Travis Co	583U	ME-23	78746	1200-1399
ARROW DR	Austin	642U	MD-16	78749	3800-8499
ARROWEYE TRL	Travis Co	521V	MB-28	78733	700-1199
ARROW HEAD	Williamson Co	375X	MJ-43	78681	400-499
ARROWHEAD CIR	Williamson Co	375K	MJ-44	78681	3300-3799
ARROWHEAD DR	Austin	524U	MH-28	78731	3500-3699
ARROWHEAD DR	Lago Vista	429S	WW-37	78645	4800-5699
ARROWHEAD DR	Travis Co	461F	MA-36	78641	14700-14999
ARROW HEAD DR	Travis Co	310Q	WZ-50	78641	16100-16599
ARROWHEAD LN	Georgetown	256F	ML-57	78628	100-299
ARROWHEAD LN	Williamson Co	194Y	MH-61	78633	100-199
ARROWHEAD PASS	Austin	434V	MH-37	78729	12800-12899
	Williamson Co	434V	MH-37	78729	None
ARROWHEAD PT	Lago Vista	428U	WV-37	78645	21500-21699
ARROWHEAD ST	Hays Co	669D	WX-15	78737	None
ARROWHEAD TRL	Cedar Park	374U	MH-43	78613	100-899
ARROWMOUND CV	Travis Co	707B	MN-12	78617	7400-7499
ARROWMOUND PASS	Travis Co	707B	MN-12	78617	11400-11899
ARROWOOD PL	Round Rock	377Z	MP-43	78665	600-799
ARROWPOINT CV	Austin	464Q	MH-35	78759	6800-6899
ARROW POINT DR	Cedar Park	373H	MF-45	78613	1100-1399
ARROWWOOD CIR	Georgetown	226S	ML-58	78628	1000-1299
ARROWWOOD DR	Austin	465L	MK-35	78727	12000-12399
ARROW WOOD RD	Cedar Park	374L	MH-44	78613	3700-4099
ARROYO AVE	Lago Vista	399Y	WX-40	78645	7900-8299
ARROYO CIR	Williamson Co	282U	MD-52	78641	100-199
ARROYO DR	Williamson Co	195R	ML-62	78633	None
ARROYO RD	Travis Co	460R	WZ-35	78734	5500-5699
ARROYO BLANCO CV	Austin	702C	MD-12	78748	2700-2799
ARROYO BLANCO DR	Austin	672Y	MD-13	78748	11400-11799
ARROYO BLUFF LN	Round Rock	345K	MJ-47	78681	3200-3299
ARROYO CANYON DR	Travis Co	580H	WZ-24	78736	11000-11099
ARROYO CLARO	Lakeway	490S	WY-31	78734	100-199
ARROYO DOBLE DR	Travis Co	703W	ME-10	78652	12700-13199
ARROYO ELENA PLAZA	Austin	495C	MK-33	78758	3200-3299
ARROYO GRANDE	Leander	342W	MC-46	78641	2200-2499
ARROYO SECO	Austin	555B	MJ-27	78756	5700-5899
	Austin	525T	MJ-28	78757	5900-7299
ARROYO VISTA DR	Travis Co	703S	ME-10	78652	300-699
ARTEMESIA WAY	Georgetown	314G	MH-51	78628	1700-1999
ARTERIAL A	Round Rock	377L	MP-44	78665	900-1099
ARTERIAL H	Round Rock	344R	MH-47	78681	None
	Round Rock	345J	MJ-47	78681	None
ARTESIA BEND	Williamson Co	345S	MJ-46	78681	3900-3999
ARTESIAN CIR	Austin	525H	MK-30	78758	1200-1299
ARTHUR CIR	Williamson Co	281Y	MB-52	78641	4200-4299
ARTHUR LN	Austin	614F	MG-21	78704	1900-2099
ARTHUR ST	Elgin	534E	EC-30	78621	600-699
ARTHUR STILES RD	Austin	616C	MM-21	78721	1000-1299
ARUBA CT	Lakeway	518D	WV-30	78734	None
ARUSHA ST	Pflugerville	437B	MN-39	78664	1500-1699
ARVIN DR	Travis Co	550Q	WZ-26	78733	3500-3599
ASA DR	Austin	675S	MJ-13	78744	6100-6399
ASBURY DR	Austin	557Y	MP-25	78724	7000-7199
ASBURY PARK	Williamson Co	347B	MN-48	78665	2100-2199
ASCENCO RD	Travis Co	522S	MC-28	78733	None
ASCENT CV	Pflugerville	437K	MN-38	78660	16300-16399
ASCHER ST	Williamson Co	443Q	EB-38	78615	100-299
ASCOT CV	Austin	523V	MF-28	78746	6000-6099
ASCOT LN	Cedar Park	372L	MD-44	78613	1700-1999
ASCOT ST	Georgetown	287L	MP-53	78626	1100-1399
ASCOT WAY	Travis Co	677G	MP-15	78617	4700-4999
ASH CV	Austin	496V	MM-31	78753	1100-1199
ASH CV N	Hutto	349X	MS-46	78634	1000-1099
ASH CV S	Hutto	349X	MS-46	78634	2000-2099
ASH PASS	Cedar Park	403E	ME-42	78613	500-599
ASH ST	Buda	762D	MD-6	78610	100-399
ASH ST	Georgetown	286H	MM-54	78626	500-1999
ASHBAUGH ST	Cedar Park	372K	MC-44	78613	1000-1099
ASHBERRY DR	Austin	556K	ML-26	78723	1500-1699
ASHBERRY TRL	Georgetown	287K	MN-53	78626	1200-2099
ASHBROOK DR	Travis Co	703L	MF-11	78652	11200-11599
ASHBROOK PL	Village of the Hills	519S	WW-28	78738	1-99
ASHBURNHAM DR	Travis Co	408H	MR-42	78634	20900-20999
	Williamson Co	408H	MR-42	78634	21000-21099
ASHBURY DR	Leander	342V	MD-46	78641	200-499
ASHBY AVE	Austin	614C	MH-21	78704	1600-1999
	Austin	614B	MG-21	78704	2000-2199
ASHCROFT CT	Austin	642F	MC-18	78749	5300-5399
ASHDALE DR	Austin	525B	MJ-30	78757	2400-2999
ASHERTON CV	Austin	493H	MF-33	78750	8100-8199
ASHEVILLE PL	Austin	642H	MC-17	78749	9200-9299
ASHFORD PARK BLVD	Buda	763E	ME-6	78610	100-299
ASH GLEN LN	Williamson Co	344V	MH-46	78681	3100-3299
ASH JUNIPER WAY	Burnet Co	307A	WS-51	78654	100-599
ASHLAND CIR	Austin	556V	MM-25	78723	6500-6599
ASHLAND DR	Austin	557S	MN-25	78723	6600-6799
ASHLEAF CV	Austin	464P	MG-35	78759	7600-7699
ASHLEY DR	Round Rock	346R	MM-47	78665	1300-1499
ASHLEY DR	Williamson Co	224E	MG-60	78633	100-199
ASHLEY WAY	Austin	674L	MH-14	78744	2400-4599
ASHLEY WORTH BLVD	Travis Co	551N	MA-26	78738	2500-2599
ASHMERE CV	Williamson Co	344V	MH-46	78681	3400-3499
ASHMERE LOOP	Williamson Co	344V	MH-46	78681	3500-3599
ASHSPRINGTON CV	Austin	528P	MQ-29	78754	11400-11499
ASHSPRINGTON LN	Austin	528K	MQ-29	78754	6600-6899
ASHTON CV	Austin	463H	MF-36	78750	10700-10799
ASHTON RIDGE	Austin	463H	MF-36	78750	9200-9599
ASHTON WOODS CIR	Travis Co	436W	ML-37	78727	13600-14099
ASHTON WOODS DR	Travis Co	436W	ML-37	78727	4300-4399
ASH TREE CT	Travis Co	703L	MF-11	78652	100-199
ASH TREE CT	Williamson Co	346H	MM-48	78665	1200-1299
ASHWOOD CT	Round Rock	407A	MN-42	78664	1400-1599
ASHWOOD LN	Williamson Co	256W	ML-55	78628	300-399
ASHWOOD RD	Austin	585D	MK-24	78722	1400-1599
ASHWORTH DR	Rollingwood	584N	MG-23	78746	100-299
ASMARA CT	Austin	493L	MF-32	78750	8200-8299
ASMARA DR	Austin	493L	MF-32	78750	8000-8499
ASOMBRA LN	Williamson Co	345X	MJ-46	78681	3000-3099
ASPEN CV	Cedar Park	373Y	MF-43	78613	300-399
ASPEN DR	Bastrop Co	745V	EF-7	78602	100-199
ASPEN DR	Hays Co	639Y	WX-16	78737	100-699
ASPEN DR	Travis Co	522W	MC-28	78733	800-1099
ASPEN DR	Williamson Co	408F	MQ-42	78664	100-199
ASPEN ST	Austin	496S	ML-31	78758	10100-10299
ASPEN TRL	Georgetown	257E	MN-57	78626	100-199
ASPEN TRL E	Williamson Co	408F	MQ-42	78664	200-299
ASPEN TRL W	Williamson Co	408F	MQ-42	78664	100-199
ASPEN BROOK DR	Austin	646T	ML-16	78744	7400-7599
ASPEN CREEK PKWY	Austin	672F	MC-15	78749	3500-3899
ASPENDALE CV	Austin	465U	MK-34	78727	3700-3799
ASPENDALE DR	Austin	465U	MK-34	78727	11900-12099
ASPEN GLENN BLVD	Austin	646T	ML-16	78744	7400-7599
ASPEN LEAF	Williamson Co	344V	MH-46	78681	3500-3699
ASPEN MEADOW RD	Leander	372C	MD-45	78641	2400-2699
ASTER CIR	Georgetown	226A	ML-60	78633	100-199
ASTER CV	Hays Co	732K	MC-8	78610	100-199
ASTER PASS	Williamson Co	432D	MD-39	78613	1800-2999
ASTER WAY	Williamson Co	377K	MN-44	78665	1800-2199
ASTOR PL	Austin	586K	ML-23	78721	1300-1899
ASTORIA DR	Bee Cave	550V	WZ-25	78733	11600-11899
ASTRO VIEW DR	Austin	557Y	MP-25	78724	7000-7199
ATASCOSA DR	Austin	645W	MJ-16	78744	5300-5499
ATEN LOOP	Round Rock	378A	MQ-45	78665	3000-3199
ATHENS ST	Manor	529X	MS-28	78653	11800-12299
ATHENS TRL	Williamson Co	434M	MH-38	78729	13400-13499
ATHLETIC DR	Austin	556F	ML-27	78752	6600-6899
ATKIN ST	Leander	342C	MD-48	78641	100-299
ATKINSON RD	Austin	556A	ML-27	78752	900-1199
ATLANTA ST	Austin	584Q	MH-23	78703	300-699
ATLANTA PARK DR	Williamson Co	344F	MG-48	78628	100-699
ATLANTIC	Lakeway	489W	WW-31	78734	100-399
ATLANTIS DR	Travis Co	587Z	MP-22	78725	4500-4699
ATLAS CV	Travis Co	522B	MC-30	78730	3600-3699
ATTAR CV	Austin	464G	MH-36	78759	7400-7499
ATTAYAC ST	Austin	585X	MJ-22	78702	100-699
ATTERBURY LN	Austin	497K	MN-32	78753	1300-1499
ATWATER CV	Hays Co	639U	WX-16	78737	100-199
ATWATER CV	Travis Co	552F	MC-27	78733	9000-9199
ATWOOD ST	Austin	616P	ML-20	78741	6000-6199
AUAU CT	Bastrop Co	745Z	EF-7	78602	100-199
AUBURN DR	Austin	556Q	MM-26	78723	6300-6499
AUBURNDALE	Austin	556R	MM-26	78723	6500-6699
AUBURNHILL	Austin	556Q	MM-26	78723	6500-6599
AUCKLAND CT	Austin	641L	MB-17	78749	6800-6899
AUCKLAND DR	Austin	641L	MB-17	78749	6800-7099
AUCTION OAK DR	Austin	673Y	MF-13	78748	10100-10299
AUDANE DR	Austin	465F	MJ-36	78727	12300-12499
AUDRA LN	Williamson Co	224R	MH-59	78633	100-199
AUDRA ST	Cedar Park	372Q	MD-44	78613	900-1099
AUDREY CT	Austin	614T	MG-19	78704	1000-1099
AUDREY DR	Austin	614X	MG-19	78704	800-999
AUDUBON PL	Austin	615W	MJ-19	78741	2400-2799
AUGER CV	Travis Co	517H	WT-30	78669	20200-20299
AUGER LN	Travis Co	517H	WT-30	78669	20300-22399
AUGUST DR	Austin	496V	MM-31	78753	1100-1199
	Austin	497S	MN-31	78753	1200-1399
AUGUSTA AVE	Austin	584Q	MH-23	78703	600-799
AUGUSTA CIR	Point Venture	488R	WV-32	78654	600-799
AUGUSTA CT	Georgetown	226H	MM-60	78628	30100-30199
AUGUSTA CT	Round Rock	375M	MK-44	78681	1901-1999 O
AUGUSTA CV	Point Venture	489N	WW-32	78645	300-399
AUGUSTA DR N	Point Venture	489J	WW-32	78645	200-299
AUGUSTA DR S	Point Venture	489N	WW-32	78645	200-299
AUGUSTA BEND DR	Travis Co	408H	MR-42	78634	1400-1699
	Williamson Co	408H	MR-42	78634	1100-1399
AUGUSTA NATIONAL CV	Travis Co	582H	MD-24	78746	6300-6399
AUGUSTA NATIONAL DR	Travis Co	582H	MD-24	78746	6200-6599
AUK RD	Travis Co	409U	MT-40	78660	20500-20599
AURORA CIR	Austin	555C	MK-27	78757	900-999
AURORA DR	Austin	555F	MJ-27	78756	5300-5499
	Austin	555C	MK-27	78757	5900-6099
AUS-TEX ACRES LN	Travis Co	528P	MQ-29	78653	11000-11699
AUSTIN AVE E	Hutto	379D	MT-45	78634	100-299
AUSTIN AVE E	Round Rock	376Z	MM-43	78664	100-1199
AUSTIN AVE N	Georgetown	286C	MM-54	78626	100-799
	Georgetown	256Z	MM-55	78626	800-2499
	Georgetown	257J	MN-56	78626	2500-2999
AUSTIN AVE S	Georgetown	286G	MM-54	78626	100-2299
	Georgetown	316C	MM-51	78626	None
AUSTIN AVE W	Hutto	379D	MT-45	78634	100-399
AUSTIN AVE W	Round Rock	376Y	MM-43	78664	100-499
AUSTIN BLVD	Lago Vista	459C	WX-36	78645	18400-19699
	Travis Co	459M	WX-35	78645	17900-18399
AUSTIN CV	Lago Vista	459A	WW-36	78645	3700-3799
AUSTIN DR	Jonestown	400H	WZ-42	78645	18300-18599
AUSTIN LN	Austin	495C	MK-33	78758	2900-3099
AUSTIN ST	Bastrop	745K	EE-8	78602	700-1299
AUSTIN ST E	Elgin	534N	EC-29	78621	200-299
AUSTIN ST N	Buda	762C	MD-6	78610	100-499
AUSTIN ST N	Williamson Co	443L	EB-38	78615	100-599
AUSTIN ST S	Buda	762C	MD-6	78610	100-399
	Elgin	533V	EB-28	78621	None
	Elgin	534N	EC-29	78621	None
AUSTIN CENTER BLVD	Austin	524M	MH-29	78731	6800-6899
AUSTIN CENTER DR	Austin	524M	MH-29	78731	3400-3499
AUSTIN CHALK WAY	Lakeway	519J	WW-29	78738	100-299
AUSTIN ELAINE DR	Williamson Co	223D	MF-60	78633	100-199
AUSTIN HIGHLANDS BLVD	Austin	643R	MF-17	78745	900-1299
AUSTIN PARK LN	Austin	496K	ML-32	78758	11300-11899
AUSTIN'S COLONY BLVD	Travis Co	618V	MR-19	78725	3100-4199
AUSTIN WOODS DR	Austin	494V	MH-31	78759	3900-4099
AUSTRAL CV	Austin	641Z	MB-16	78739	10000-10099
AUSTRAL LOOP	Austin	641Z	MB-16	78739	5200-5499
AUSTRALIS CV	Travis Co	521E	MA-30	78732	1500-1599
AUSTRINA PASS	Travis Co	521E	MA-30	78732	1500-1599
AUTREY DR	Williamson Co	342Z	MD-46	78641	2400-2599
AUTUMN TRL	Georgetown	287L	MP-53	78626	300-699
AUTUMN ASH DR	Travis Co	703L	MF-11	78652	11200-11599
AUTUMN BAY DR	Austin	646T	ML-16	78744	3300-4099
	Austin	646W	ML-16	78744	4000-4099
AUTUMN BEND LN	Cedar Park	403K	ME-41	78613	400-599
AUTUMN FIRE CV	Williamson Co	402V	MD-40	78613	1500-1599
AUTUMN FIRE DR	Williamson Co	402U	MD-40	78613	1700-2099
AUTUMNLEAF HOLLOW	Austin	524T	MG-28	78731	4500-4599
AUTUMN MIST	Travis Co	437K	MN-38	78660	16500-16599
AUTUMN OAKS DR	Village of the Hills	519S	WW-28	78738	1-99
AUTUMN OAKS PL	Village of the Hills	519S	WW-28	78738	1-99
AUTUMN RIDGE DR	Austin	464L	MH-35	78759	11500-11699
AUTUMN SAGE WAY	Pflugerville	407Z	MP-40	78660	600-899
AUTUMN WOOD DR	Bastrop Co	746W	EG-7	78602	100-199
AVA LN	Austin	587K	MN-23	78724	6300-6599
AVALANCHE AVE	Georgetown	317F	MN-51	78626	100-399
AVALON AVE	Austin	674H	MH-15	78744	4800-4899
	Austin	675E	MJ-15	78744	4900-5099
AVANTE DR	Cedar Park	372L	MD-44	78613	1700-1999
AVARANCHE WAY	Williamson Co	405F	MJ-42	78681	16500-16599
AVATAR CV	Austin	523Z	MF-28	78746	3700-3799
AVEBURY CIR	Austin	526L	MM-29	78753	1400-1499
AVELLA DR	Williamson Co	434M	MH-38	78729	8100-8199
AVENAL DR	Travis Co	550R	WZ-26	78733	3200-3399
AVENA VALLEY DR	Pflugerville	437H	MP-39	78660	17500-17599
AVENDALE DR	Bee Cave	550V	WZ-25	78733	3500-3699
AVENIDA ANN DR	Lago Vista	429K	WW-38	78645	6500-6799
AVENUE A	Austin	555P	MJ-26	78751	4000-4699
AVENUE A N	Elgin	534N	EC-29	78621	100-299
	Elgin	534J	EC-29	78621	None

STREET NAME	CITY or COUNTY	MAPSCO GRID	AUSTIN GRID	ZIP CODE	BLOCK RANGE O/E
AVENUE A S	Elgin	534N	EC-29	78621	100-599
AVENUE B	Austin	555P	MJ-26	78751	3800-4699
AVENUE B N	Elgin	534N	EC-29	78621	100-299
	Elgin	533M	EB-29	78621	None
AVENUE B S	Elgin	534N	EC-29	78621	100-499
AVENUE C	Austin	555P	MJ-26	78751	3900-4699
	Austin	555G	MK-27	78752	5700-5799
AVENUE C N	Elgin	533M	EB-29	78621	800-1599
	Elgin	534J	EC-29	78621	None
AVENUE C S	Elgin	534S	EC-28	78621	None
AVENUE D	Austin	555P	MJ-26	78751	3900-4699
	Austin	555G	MK-27	78752	5700-5799
AVENUE D N	Elgin	534J	EC-29	78621	None
AVENUE D S	Elgin	534S	EC-28	78621	300-599
AVENUE E N	Elgin	534J	EC-29	78621	None
AVENUE F	Austin	555L	MK-26	78751	3800-5699
	Austin	555H	MK-27	78752	5700-5899
AVENUE F N	Elgin	534J	EC-29	78621	100-499
	Elgin	533H	EB-30	78621	None
AVENUE G	Austin	555L	MK-26	78751	3800-5699
	Austin	555H	MK-27	78752	5700-5899
	Austin	526S	ML-28	78752	7400-7599
AVENUE G N	Elgin	534J	EC-29	78621	100-499
AVENUE H	Austin	555M	MK-26	78751	3800-5599
AVENUE H N	Elgin	534E	EC-30	78621	None
AVENUE I	Travis Co	466C	MM-36	78728	13800-13999
AVENUE J N	Elgin	534J	EC-29	78621	100-599
AVENUE K	Travis Co	466C	MM-36	78728	13700-13999
AVENUE N	Austin	466C	MM-36	78758	2200-2499
	Travis Co	466C	MM-36	78727	2000-2199
AVERING LN	Austin	528P	MQ-29	78754	11100-11399
AVERY DR	Taylor	353K	EA-47	76574	200-599
AVERY CLUB DR	Austin	404G	MH-42	78717	10200-10299
	Austin	404C	MH-42	78717	10300-10599
AVERY ELISSA LN	Cedar Park	402V	MD-40	78613	1500-1599
AVERY ISLAND AVE	Austin	465A	MJ-36	78727	5700-6299
	Austin	434Z	MH-37	78727	6300-6499
AVERY RANCH BLVD	Austin	403M	MF-41	78717	13000-13999
	Austin	404D	MH-42	78717	14000-16399
	Austin	405A	MJ-42	78717	16400-16699
	Cedar Park	403Q	MF-41	78613	2100-2299
AVERY RESERVE DR	Austin	404B	MG-42	78717	1-99
AVERY WOODS LN	Cedar Park	374L	MH-44	78613	3800-4099
AVIAN ST	Austin	672R	MD-14	78748	10500-10599
AVIARA DR	Austin	611R	MB-20	78735	6200-6599
AVIARY CV	Austin	675E	MJ-15	78744	6100-6299
AVIATION DR	Georgetown	256D	MM-57	78628	200-299
AVIGNON DR	Williamson Co	405F	MJ-42	78681	7000-7299
AVIS RD	Caldwell Co	767W	MN-4	78616	12500-13999
	Mustang Ridge	766R	MM-5	78610	12000-12099
	Travis Co	767N	MN-5	78616	12100-12299
AVISPA WAY	Bee Cave	549P	WW-26	78738	5100-5399
AVIAPA BONITA	Bee Cave	549P	WW-26	78738	5000-5099
AVOCET DR	Austin	643W	ME-16	78745	8100-8499
AVOCET DR	Hays Co	732A	MC-9	78610	300-399
AVON PL	Austin	556S	ML-25	78723	5200-5299
AVONDALE DR	Cedar Park	403P	ME-41	78613	1600-1699
AVONDALE RD	Austin	615J	MJ-20	78704	800-1099
AWALT DR	Travis Co	460R	WZ-35	78734	15700-16199
AWEHI CT	Bastrop Co	775A	EE-6	78602	100-199
AWEHI LN	Bastrop Co	776A	EG-6	78602	100-199
A. W. GRIMES BLVD N	Round Rock	377P	MN-44	78664	100-3099
	Round Rock	347F	MN-48	78665	4400-4999
	Williamson Co	347F	MN-48	78665	3100-4399
A. W. GRIMES BLVD S	Pflugerville	407Y	MP-40	78664	2900-3099
	Round Rock	377T	MN-43	78664	100-899
	Round Rock	407A	MN-42	78664	900-1199
	Round Rock	407K	MN-41	78664	1700-2799
	Williamson Co	407A	MN-42	78664	1200-1699
	Williamson Co	407T	MP-40	78664	2800-2899
AXEL LN	Austin	586R	MM-23	78721	3600-3799
AXELL LN	Travis Co	471S	MW-34	78653	16800-17499
AXIS DR	Austin	642P	MC-17	78749	8400-8699
AXIS RD	Hays Co	762E	MC-6	78610	200-499
AXIS DEER CV	Williamson Co	344D	MH-48	78628	100-199
AXIS DEER TRL	Williamson Co	378H	MR-45	78634	100-399
AXTELLON CT	Austin	641L	MB-17	78749	9300-9399
AYALA DR	Travis Co	618V	MR-19	78725	3900-4099
AYES CT	Cedar Park	372G	MD-45	78613	2400-2499
AYLESBURY LN	Austin	643T	ME-16	78745	2600-2699
AYLFORD CT	Austin	671D	MB-15	78739	5900-5999
AYRES DR	Austin	553K	ME-26	78746	6300-6399
AZALEA CIR	Hays Co	732F	MC-9	78610	12700-12799
AZALEA DR	Cedar Park	402U	MD-40	78613	1400-1899
AZALEA DR	Williamson Co	257K	MN-56	78626	1-199
AZALEA TRL	Austin	495S	MJ-31	78759	8600-8899
AZALEA BLOSSOM DR	Austin	672L	MD-14	78748	3300-3499
AZORES DR	Travis Co	467R	MP-35	78660	1600-1799
AZTEC DR	Austin	584C	MH-24	78703	2500-2599
AZTEC TRL	Lago Vista	399U	WX-40	78645	8100-8199
AZTEC FALL CV	Travis Co	554E	MG-27	78746	3200-3299
AZUL CT	Williamson Co	226X	ML-58	78628	4200-4299
AZUL CV	Williamson Co	345T	MJ-46	78681	4600-4699
AZUR LN	Round Rock	345N	MJ-47	78681	3800-3899
AZURE AVE	Lago Vista	458J	WU-35	78645	21900-22099
AZURE HIGHLAND RD	Burnet Co	366Q	WR-44	78654	None
	Travis Co	366Q	WR-44	78654	6600-7399
AZURE SHORES CT	Travis Co	521S	MA-28	78732	12000-12299
AZZURO WAY	Travis Co	432L	MD-38	78613	2700-2799

B

STREET NAME	CITY or COUNTY	MAPSCO GRID	AUSTIN GRID	ZIP CODE	BLOCK RANGE O/E
BABBLING BROOK DR	Travis Co	436Q	MM-38	78728	14900-15099
BABE DIDRIKSON LN	Austin	702C	MD-12	78748	2700-2799
BACH	Leander	311Z	MB-49	78641	1500-1599
BACH DR	Austin	498J	MQ-32	78660	3400-3599
BACHELOR GULCH	Leander	371B	MA-45	78641	3500-3599
BACK CT	Austin	524E	MG-30	78731	5800-5899
BACK BAY CT	Austin	671G	MB-15	78739	5800-5899
BACK BAY LN	Austin	671C	MB-15	78739	5700-6799
BACKBONE CREEK CROSSING LOOP					
	Travis Co	518X	WU-28	78669	None
BACK OF THE MOON	Travis Co	460V	WZ-34	78734	15100-15399
BACKSTROKE DR	Austin	523M	MF-29	78731	5600-5699
BACKTRAIL DR	Austin	524A	MG-30	78731	4900-5399
BACON CV	Lago Vista	459J	WW-35	78645	20100-20199
BACON STRIP	Travis Co	707F	MN-12	78617	None

STREET NAME	CITY or COUNTY	MAPSCO GRID	AUSTIN GRID	ZIP CODE	BLOCK RANGE O/E
BADEN LN	Austin	527E	MN-30	78754	10200-10399
BADGER BEND	Austin	612Y	MD-19	78749	5300-5499
BAFFIN CV	Williamson Co	377E	MN-45	78664	1400-1499
BAGBY DR	Travis Co	587H	MP-24	78724	8100-8599
BAGDAD AVE E	Round Rock	376Z	MM-43	78664	100-799
BAGDAD AVE W	Round Rock	406C	MM-42	78664	100-399
BAGDAD RD	Cedar Park	372M	MD-44	78613	1000-2499
BAGDAD RD N	Leander	342A	MC-48	78641	100-499
	Leander	312W	MC-49	78641	500-799
BAGDAD RD S	Leander	342U	MD-46	78641	100-2699
	Leander	372C	MD-45	78641	2700-3399
BAGDAD ST	Leander	312X	MC-49	78641	100-499
BAGGINS CV	Travis Co	672S	MC-13	78739	3800-3899
BAHAMA RD	Travis Co	522P	MC-29	78733	2200-2499
BAHAN DR	Austin	678J	MQ-14	78617	5200-5499
BAHIA CIR	Austin	645B	MJ-18	78741	2200-2299
BAILEY LN	Austin	555S	MJ-25	78705	3300-3399
	Austin	555S	MJ-25	78756	3900-3999
BAILEY JEAN DR	Williamson Co	405F	MJ-42	78681	16800-16899
BAIN RD	Travis Co	707A	MN-12	78617	7200-7499
BAINBRIDGE LN	Williamson Co	433M	MF-38	78750	12300-12399
BAIRD LN	Austin	614Q	MH-20	78704	1000-1099
BAIRD LN	Dripping Springs	636Y	WR-16	78620	100-699
BAJA CV	Austin	464K	MG-35	78759	7600-7799
BAKER CIR N	Williamson Co	282E	MC-54	78641	500-699
BAKER CIR S	Williamson Co	282E	MC-54	78641	600-699
BAKER CIR W	Williamson Co	282E	MC-54	78641	100-199
BAKER LN	Williamson Co	312H	MD-51	78641	1-799
BAKER ST	Austin	586L	MM-23	78721	5000-5099
BAKER ST	Round Rock	406G	MM-42	78664	700-899
BAKERS CV	Hutto	379M	MT-44	78634	1000-1099
BAKERS LN	Hutto	379M	MT-44	78634	200-399
BAKERS WAY	Cedar Park	372F	MC-45	78613	2200-2399
BALAMOS DR	Williamson Co	434R	MH-38	78729	13400-13499
BALANCED ROCK PL	Round Rock	345N	MJ-47	78681	1000-1099
BALBOA LN	Austin	465Q	MK-35	78727	4100-4399
BALBOA RD	Travis Co	522P	MC-29	78733	2200-2399
BALCH RD	Bastrop Co	592G	MZ-24	78621	300-599
BALCONES DR	Austin	554G	MH-27	78731	3500-5099
	Austin	524V	MH-28	78731	5100-6399
BALCONES WAY	Austin	433Z	MF-37	78750	11700-11899
BALCONES CENTER DR	Austin	495F	MJ-33	78759	3500-3599
BALCONES CLUB DR	Austin	434W	MG-37	78750	8500-8999
	Austin	433V	MF-37	78750	9000-9199
	Austin	434S	MG-37	78750	9200-9299
BALCONES SPRINGS DR	Burnet Co	336N	WQ-47	78654	100-699
BALCONES WOODS CIR	Austin	465W	MJ-34	78759	11100-11199
BALCONES WOODS CV	Austin	465W	MJ-34	78759	11200-11299
BALCONES WOODS DR	Austin	465W	MJ-34	78759	3700-5199
BALD CYPRESS CV	Travis Co	402U	MD-40	78613	1500-1599
BALDRIDGE DR	Austin	673M	MF-14	78748	400-499
BALDWIN DR	Travis Co	587H	MP-24	78724	6100-6399
BALDWIN ST	Hutto	379T	MS-43	78634	100-399
BALES ST	Travis Co	498S	MQ-31	78653	4800-5199
BALFOUR FALLS LN	Austin	672U	MD-13	78748	2900-2999
BAL HARBOR RD	Travis Co	522K	MC-29	78733	9700-9999
BALI LN	Travis Co	467M	MP-35	78660	14900-15099
BALLENTINE CT	Hutto	379R	MT-44	78634	400-499
BALLENTON CT	Austin	641Z	MB-16	78739	5700-5799
BALLENTON LN	Austin	641Z	MB-16	78739	5500-5699
BALLERSTEDT RD	Travis Co	561C	MX-27	78621	12000-12199
	Travis Co	531Y	MX-28	78621	12200-13199
BALLIMAMORE DR	Austin	404E	MG-42	78717	14500-14699
BALLINGER DR	Travis Co	426M	WR-38	78669	1800-2299
BALL PARK RD	Elgin	534E	EC-30	78621	900-999
BALLYBUNION PL	Austin	704P	MG-11	78747	10900-11099
BALLYCASTLE TRL	Austin	404J	MG-41	78717	14100-14699
BALLYCLARC DR	Austin	404E	MG-42	78717	14500-14699
BALMORAL CASTLE CT	Pflugerville	408X	MQ-40	78660	900-999
BALMORHEA CT	Pflugerville	407Y	MP-40	78664	17700-17799
BALMORHEA LN	Pflugerville	407Y	MP-40	78664	1400-1699
BALSAM ST	Hutto	350J	MU-47	78634	100-199
BALSAM WAY	Williamson Co	377K	MN-44	78665	1400-2199
BALSAM HOLLOW	Austin	524P	MG-29	78731	5900-5999
BALSORA CV	Georgetown	285P	MJ-53	78628	100-199
BALTUS DR	Austin	496J	ML-32	78758	11000-11199
BALTUSROL DR	Austin	704J	MG-11	78747	2100-2299
BAMBOO TRL	Cedar Park	402D	MD-42	78613	100-199
BAMFIELD CV	Round Rock	408A	MQ-42	78665	1500-1599
BAMFORD DR	Austin	494Y	MH-31	78731	4200-4399
BANBRIDGE TRL	Austin	404E	MG-42	78717	14500-15099
BANBURY BEND	Austin	644A	MG-18	78745	4500-4599
BANCROFT TRL	Williamson Co	434K	MG-38	78729	8900-9099
BANCROFT WOODS CV	Austin	434Z	MH-37	78729	12800-12899
BANCROFT WOODS DR	Austin	434V	MH-37	78729	6700-7099
BANDA LN	Travis Co	618V	MR-19	78725	3500-3699
BANDERA CV	Georgetown	287G	MP-54	78626	100-199
BANDERA CV	Round Rock	408A	MQ-42	78665	1900-1999
BANDERA PATH	Round Rock	407D	MP-42	78665	2100-2199
BANDERA RD	Austin	586L	MM-23	78721	4600-4999
BANDERA CREEK TRL	Austin	612M	MD-20	78735	5100-5299
BANDERA RANCH TRL	Austin	493E	ME-33	78750	7300-7399
BANDERA WOODS BLVD	Elgin	533F	EA-30	78621	100-499
BANDICE LN	Travis Co	439P	MS-38	78660	3700-4499
BANDITTI DR	Austin	463C	MF-36	78750	10000-10099
BANDON DR	Austin	404G	MH-42	78717	15300-15699
BANDSTAND LN	Cedar Park	373Q	MF-44	78613	300-499
BANGOR BEND	Austin	525M	MK-29	78758	8400-8499
BANISTER LN	Austin	614X	MG-19	78704	800-1299
	Austin	614X	MG-19	78704	3900-4099
	Austin	644A	MG-18	78745	4100-4799
BANKS CT	Austin	641Z	MB-16	78739	10200-10299
BANKSIDE ST	Austin	672Q	MD-14	78748	3300-3599
BANNER AVE	Leander	342B	MC-48	78641	100-399
BANNING LN	Travis Co	587H	MP-24	78724	6200-6399
BANNOCK LN	Travis Co	675W	MJ-13	78747	7900-8099
BANNOCKBURN DR	Austin	643J	ME-17	78749	3500-3599
	Austin	642H	MD-18	78749	3600-3899
BANPASS LN	Austin	611T	MA-19	78736	7600-7799
BANTOM WOODS BEND	Austin	587V	MP-22	78724	5000-5399
BANTON RD	Austin	585H	MK-24	78722	3400-3599
BANYAN CV	Cedar Park	403A	ME-42	78613	200-299
BANYON ST	Austin	525V	MK-28	78757	800-999
BARANCO WAY	Leander	341M	MB-47	78641	1800-1899
BARASINGA TRL	Austin	642P	MC-17	78749	8500-8699
BARB RD	Travis Co	650Y	MV-16	78612	19300-19399
BARBARA ST	Austin	525L	MK-29	78757	1500-2099

STREET NAME	CITY or COUNTY	MAPSCO GRID	AUSTIN GRID	ZIP CODE	BLOCK RANGE O/E
BARBARA WAY	Bastrop	744D	ED-9	78602	600-699
BARBARA JORDAN BLVD	Austin	555V	MK-25	78723	1100-1299
	Austin	556S	ML-25	78723	1300-1499
BARBERA PASS	Travis Co	702G	MD-12	78748	2600-2699
BARBERGALE ST	Travis Co	437S	MN-37	78660	1300-1599
BARBERRY DR	Travis Co	429C	WX-39	78645	6900-7699
BARBERRY DR	Williamson Co	257F	MN-57	78626	100-299
BARBIE CT	Lakeway	519C	WX-30	78734	100-199
BARBROOK CV	Austin	463A	ME-36	78726	11400-11499
BARBROOK DR	Austin	463A	ME-36	78726	9900-10199
BARBUDA DR	Lakeway	488Z	WV-31	78734	None
BARCELONA CT	Williamson Co	226V	MM-58	78628	5400-5499
BARCELONA CV	Austin	556C	MM-27	78752	7600-7699
BARCELONA DR	Austin	556C	MM-27	78752	7300-7599
BARCELONA DR	Williamson Co	226V	MM-58	78628	5300-5399
BARCHETTA DR	Austin	496F	ML-33	78758	11600-11799
BARCHETTA DR	Williamson Co	347B	MN-48	78665	4300-4599
BARCLAY DR	Austin	583N	ME-23	78746	1300-1799
BARCLAY DR	Leander	311V	MB-49	78641	1000-1199
BARCLAY LN	Bastrop Co	741V	MX-7	78612	100-199
BARCLAY HEIGHTS CT	Austin	583N	ME-23	78746	4900-4999
BARCUS DR	Georgetown	287J	MN-53	78626	1500-1699
BARDOLINO LN	Williamson Co	343N	ME-47	78641	3300-3399
BAREFOOT CV	Austin	523T	ME-28	78730	7100-7199
BAREFOOT CV	Round Rock	377Z	MP-43	78665	800-899
BAREFOOT LN	Round Rock	377Z	MP-43	78665	2700-2899
BARETTA DR	Georgetown	226S	ML-58	78628	100-199
BARGAMIN DR	Austin	611P	MA-20	78736	8400-8599
BARGE ST	Austin	643Q	MF-17	78745	1900-1999
BAR HARBOR CV	Williamson Co	375Q	MK-44	78681	6000-6099
BAR HARBOR BEND	Williamson Co	375Q	MK-44	78681	16800-16999
BARHILL DR	Austin	614E	MG-21	78704	2500-2599
BARILLA MOUNTAIN TRL	Pflugerville	437B	MN-39	78664	1700-1899
BAR K DR	Buda	733W	ME-7	78610	100-199
BARKBRIDGE TRL	Austin	674M	MH-14	78744	4800-4999
BAR K CLUBHOUSE CT	Lago Vista	429A	WW-39	78645	6600-6799
BARKDALE CT	Austin	674Q	MH-14	78744	7600-7699
BARKER ST	Taylor	353K	EA-47	76574	400-599
BARKER HILLS DR	Travis Co	560E	MU-27	78653	11800-12099
BARKER HOLLOW CV	Travis Co	702A	MC-12	78739	12400-12599
BARKER HOLLOW PASS	Travis Co	702A	MC-12	78739	3200-3499
BARKER RIDGE CV	Austin	464V	MH-34	78759	10600-10699
BARKER RIDGE DR	Austin	464V	MH-34	78759	5500-5799
BARKER VISTA CV	Austin	464V	MH-34	78759	10600-10699
BARKLEY DR	Travis Co	436W	ML-37	78727	4300-4399
BAR K RANCH RD	Lago Vista	429A	WW-39	78645	6700-7099
	Lago Vista	399T	WW-40	78645	7100-8199
	Lago Vista	399G	WX-42	78645	8200-8999
BARK RIDGE TERRACE	Georgetown	287K	MN-53	78626	2400-2499
BARKS CT	Austin	497J	MN-32	78753	None
BARKSDALE DR	Travis Co	618V	MR-19	78725	3100-3499
BARKWOOD DR	Austin	673E	ME-15	78748	2500-2699
BARLETTA RD	Williamson Co	405B	MJ-42	78681	6000-6699
BARLEY CV	Austin	493R	MF-32	78750	7300-7399
BARLEY FIELD PASS	Pflugerville	438H	MR-39	78660	2500-2599
	Pflugerville	439J	MS-39	78660	2600-2999
BARLOW DR	Williamson Co	405G	MK-42	78681	4000-5099
BARNARD LN	Cedar Park	374A	MG-45	78641	1-299
BARN DANCE CV	Georgetown	225C	MK-60	78633	100-199
BARNETT DR	Cedar Park	372J	MC-44	78613	1900-2399
BARNETT GLEN RD	Travis Co	518A	WU-30	78669	20200-20299
BARNEY DR	Travis Co	490T	WY-31	78734	1400-1899
BARNHILL DR	Austin	496P	ML-32	78758	10600-10899
BARN OWL DR	Austin	527C	MP-31	78754	11100-11299
BARN OWL LOOP	Williamson Co	282E	MC-54	78641	100-199
BARNSDALE WAY	Austin	643Z	MF-16	78745	7000-7399
BARNSLEY DR	Austin	643N	ME-17	78745	3100-3299
BARN SWALLOW DR	Austin	583Y	MF-22	78746	1500-1799
BARON LN	Cedar Park	373S	ME-43	78613	500-799
BARONET'S TRL	Austin	497N	MN-32	78753	1300-1499
BARON'S CT	Travis Co	557B	MN-27	78754	8900-8999
BARR LN	Travis Co	527L	MP-29	78754	10300-10699
BARRANCA CIR	Austin	554G	MH-27	78731	3400-3499
BARRAS BRANCH DR	Travis Co	702G	MD-12	78748	12200-12399
BARREL BEND	Austin	702B	MC-12	78748	12000-12299
BARRETT LN	Travis Co	552G	MD-27	78733	400-799
BARRHALL DR	Round Rock	376L	MM-44	78664	100-499
BARRHEAD CV	Austin	375W	MJ-43	78717	16600-16699
BARRICKS CV	Austin	465M	MK-35	78727	12600-12699
BARRIE DR	Lakeway	520J	WY-29	78734	900-1099
	Lakeway	520J	WY-29	78734	15000-15599
	Travis Co	520J	WY-29	78734	1100-1199
BARRILLA ST	Cedar Park	402Q	MD-41	78613	1600-1699
	Williamson Co	402Q	MD-41	78613	1700-1799
BARRINGTON CV	Austin	526H	MM-30	78753	10000-10099
BARRINGTON DR	Austin	526H	MM-30	78753	1200-1399
BARRINGTON WAY	Austin	464F	MG-36	78759	11100-12099
BARRINGTON FARM CT	Georgetown	195P	MJ-62	78633	300-399
BARROW AVE	Austin	555U	MK-25	78751	4100-4499
BARROW GLEN LOOP	Austin	642P	MC-17	78749	8600-8899
BAR RYDER TRL	Williamson Co	282X	MC-52	78641	100-199
BARRYKNOLL ST	Williamson Co	434K	MG-38	78729	9100-9199
BARSANA AVE	Hays Co	670W	WY-13	78610	100-299
BARSANA RD	Hays Co	669Z	WX-13	78610	100-699
BARSHAM CT	Travis Co	432C	MD-39	78613	2100-2199
BARSTOW AVE	Austin	641L	MB-17	78749	9100-9399
BARSTOW DR	Austin	641H	MB-18	78749	8800-8899
BARTHOLDI ST	Austin	497B	MN-33	78753	12700-12899
BART HOLLOW DR	Austin	433Z	MF-37	78750	9500-9899
BARTLETT ST	Austin	614R	MH-20	78704	101-199 O
BARTLETT PEAK DR	Georgetown	225E	MJ-60	78633	100-499
BARTLEY DR	Williamson Co	314F	MG-51	78628	100-199
BARTON BLVD	Austin	584Y	MH-22	78704	500-899
BARTON LN	Bastrop Co	740Z	MV-7	78612	100-199
BARTON PKWY	Austin	614E	MG-21	78704	1800-2399
BARTON BEND	Hays Co	606G	WR-21	78620	100-699
BARTONCLIFF DR	Austin	614A	MG-21	78704	1700-1799
BARTON CLUB DR	Travis Co	582F	MC-24	78735	7800-8399
BARTON CREEK BLVD	Travis Co	552Y	MD-25	78746	500-1399
	Travis Co	582E	MC-24	78735	1400-3299
	Travis Co	581Q	MB-23	78735	3300-5399
BARTON CREEK CIR	Hays Co	607K	WS-20	78620	100-199
BARTON CREEK DR	Hays Co	607K	WS-20	78620	100-1299
BARTON HILLS DR	Austin	614B	MG-21	78704	1000-2399
	Austin	613H	MF-21	78746	2400-2699
BARTON MEADOW DR	Hays Co	636F	WQ-18	78620	100-399
BARTON POINT CIR	Travis Co	581B	MA-24	78733	3000-3199

STREET NAME	CITY or COUNTY	MAPSCO GRID	AUSTIN GRID	ZIP CODE	BLOCK RANGE O/E
BARTON POINT DR	Travis Co	551Y	MB-25	78733	2700-3099
	Travis Co	581B	MA-24	78733	3100-3599
BARTON RANCH CIR	Hays Co	607J	WS-20	78620	100-299
BARTON RANCH RD	Hays Co	607P	WS-20	78620	100-499
BARTON'S PASS	Hays Co	607P	WS-20	78620	100-199
BARTON'S BLUFF CT	Austin	613H	MF-21	78746	2500-2599
BARTON'S BLUFF LN	Austin	613H	MF-21	78746	2700-2899
BARTONS CROSSING	Buda	762G	MD-6	78610	100-199
BARTON SKYWAY	Austin	614U	MH-19	78704	900-1299
	Austin	614J	MG-20	78704	2200-2799
	Austin	614A	MG-21	78746	2800-2999
BARTON SPRINGS RD	Austin	614D	MH-21	78704	600-1499
	Austin	584Y	MH-22	78704	1500-1999
	Austin	584Y	MH-22	78746	2000-2899
BARTON VIEW DR	Austin	613U	MF-19	78735	3200-3299
BARTON VILLAGE CIR	Austin	614J	MG-20	78704	2300-2399
BARWOOD PARK	Austin	526P	ML-29	78753	600-799
BAR-X DR	Austin	465K	MJ-35	78727	12100-12399
BASAL CT	Lakeway	518M	WV-29	78738	400-499
BASALT CV	Williamson Co	375F	MJ-45	78681	3300-3399
BASEBALL LN	Bastrop Co	745T	EE-7	78602	None
BASFORD RD	Austin	585H	MK-24	78722	3500-3899
BASIE BEND	Travis Co	402P	MC-41	78613	600-699
BASIL CV	Austin	493R	MF-32	78750	7600-7699
BASIL DR	Austin	493R	MF-32	78750	7600-7799
BASIL DR	Buda	763A	ME-6	78610	600-699
BASIN BROOK DR	Austin	582Z	MD-22	78735	3700-3799
BASIN LEDGE	West Lake Hills	553V	MF-25	78746	1800-1899
BASIN LEDGE E	West Lake Hills	553V	MF-25	78746	2-98 E
BASKET FLOWER CV	Travis Co	532Q	MZ-29	78621	12800-12899
BASKET FLOWER BEND	Travis Co	532L	MZ-29	78621	17800-18499
BASS LOOP	Round Rock	347S	MN-46	78665	3600-3699
BASS ST	Georgetown	226A	ML-60	78633	100-199
BASSINGTON CT	Pflugerville	468E	MQ-36	78660	800-899
BASSWOOD LN	Austin	586C	MM-24	78723	5200-5599
BASTIAN CV	Austin	671A	MA-15	78739	11400-11499
BASTIAN LN	Georgetown	257S	MN-55	78626	1-399
BASTOGNE LOOP	Austin	641W	MA-16	78739	11100-11399
BASTROP DR	Williamson Co	344B	MG-48	78628	100-199
BASTROP HWY	Austin	616U	MM-19	78742	1-799 O
	Austin	616U	MM-19	78741	2-798 E
	Austin	616Y	MM-19	78742	800-1299
	Austin	646C	MM-18	78742	1300-1599
BASTROP ST	Manor	529Y	MT-28	78653	11800-12199
BASTROP ST	Williamson Co	443L	EB-38	78615	300-399
BASTROP ST N	Manor	529U	MT-28	78653	100-999
BASTROP ST S	Manor	529U	MT-28	78653	100-399
BATAK LN	Austin	642S	MC-16	78749	5400-5499
BATAVIA DR	Travis Co	437K	MN-38	78660	1100-1399
BATES CV	Travis Co	437K	MN-38	78660	16300-16399
BATES DR	Leander	342R	MD-47	78641	100-199
BAT FALCON DR	Bee Cave	549L	WX-26	78738	4300-4699
BATH WAY	Austin	497E	MN-33	78753	900-999
BAT HAWK CIR	Bee Cave	549L	WX-26	78738	15100-15499
BATIK LOOP	Austin	467Q	MP-35	78660	14000-14299
BATLEY LN	Austin	615X	MJ-19	78741	2700-2799
BATON ROUGE DR	Austin	465A	MJ-36	78727	5900-6099
BATTENBURG TRL	Travis Co	467L	MP-35	78660	600-1299
BATTLE BEND BLVD	Austin	644Q	MH-17	78745	300-1299
BATTLE BRIDGE DR	Austin	702C	MD-12	78748	11900-12199
BATTLECREEK LN	Leander	341D	MB-48	78641	500-799
BATTLEGROUND CIR	Williamson Co	382D	MZ-45	76574	200-299
BATTLEGROUND CV	Williamson Co	382D	MZ-45	76574	100-199
BATTLESHIP DR	Williamson Co	314X	MG-49	78628	100-299
BAUERLE AVE	Austin	614G	MH-21	78704	1600-1799
BAVARIA LN	Austin	642S	MC-16	78749	9300-9399
BAXENDALE ST	Hutto	350J	MU-47	78634	100-399
BAXTER CIR	Travis Co	610W	WY-19	78736	10800-10899
BAXTER DR	Austin	643L	MF-17	78745	2500-2699
BAXTER LN	Travis Co	610X	WY-19	78736	9900-10299
BAXTER SPRINGS RD	Austin	673C	MF-15	78745	8000-8099
BAY CIR	Travis Co	488L	WV-32	78669	800-899
BAY LN	Round Rock	407S	MN-40	78664	3000-3099
BAYBERRY CT	Cedar Park	403A	ME-42	78613	500-599
BAYBERRY DR	Austin	494Z	MH-31	78759	4100-4199
BAYFIELD DR	Austin	466Q	MM-35	78727	13100-13299
BAY HILL CT	Georgetown	226G	MM-60	78628	29000-29099
BAY HILL CV	Travis Co	583N	ME-23	78746	5500-5599
BAY HILL DR	Travis Co	582M	MD-23	78746	1400-1499
	Travis Co	583N	ME-23	78746	1500-1899
BAY HILL LN	Round Rock	378U	MR-43	78664	3200-3299
BAYLAND ST	Round Rock	377N	MM-44	78664	1400-1899
BAY LAUREL TRL	Austin	464J	MG-35	78750	10700-10799
BAYLISS ST	Hutto	380S	MU-43	78634	100-199
BAYLOR ST	Austin	584V	MH-22	78703	300-1299
BAYLOR MOUNTAIN CV	Georgetown	194Z	MH-61	78633	100-199
BAYOU BEND	Austin	464G	MH-36	78759	11700-11799
BAYOU BEND DR	Buda	732W	MC-7	78610	100-699
BAYRIDGE CV	Austin	464Q	MH-35	78759	10700-10799
BAYRIDGE TERRACE	Austin	464Q	MH-35	78759	6800-6999
BAYSIDE DR	Austin	645S	MJ-16	78744	4700-4999
BAYSWATER GARDEN	Williamson Co	434B	MG-39	78729	13500-13599
BAYTHORNE DR	Austin	705A	MJ-12	78747	6200-6799
BAYTON DR	Travis Co	550U	WZ-25	78733	3600-3799
BAYTON LOOP	Austin	643C	MF-18	78745	5600-5699
BAYWOOD DR	Austin	525A	MJ-30	78759	7900-8199
BEACH RD	Travis Co	459R	WX-35	78645	4000-4099
BEACH RD	Travis Co	401J	MA-41	78641	10700-11399
BEACHAM CT	Austin	671C	MB-15	78739	10900-10999
BEACHMONT CT	Austin	671D	MB-15	78739	5600-5699
BEACHMONT LN	Austin	671D	MB-15	78739	10800-10899
BEACH MOUNTAIN CV	Georgetown	195S	MJ-61	78633	100-199
BEACH PLUM CV	Travis Co	409P	MS-41	78660	2800-2899
BEACON CIR	Travis Co	460M	WZ-35	78734	5900-6099
BEACON CV	Hutto	379P	MS-44	78634	1000-1099
BEACON DR	Travis Co	460V	WZ-34	78734	5100-5199
BEACONCREST DR	Austin	674J	MG-14	78748	8100-8399
BEACON POINT CV	Lago Vista	458B	WU-36	78645	22000-22099
BEACONSDALE CIR	Austin	465M	MK-35	78727	12600-12699
BEACONSDALE DR	Austin	465H	MK-36	78727	3800-4099
BEANNA ST	Austin	585F	MJ-24	78705	2900-2999
	Austin	585B	MJ-24	78705	3200-3299
BEAR RD	Lago Vista	459A	WW-36	78645	20300-20599
BEAR CANYON DR	Travis Co	703W	ME-10	78652	300-699
BEAR CLAW	Leander	371B	MA-45	78641	3500-3599
BEAR CREEK DR	Leander	341C	MB-48	78641	2000-2099
BEAR CREEK DR	Village of Bear Creek	670F	WY-15	78737	8000-9099
BEAR CREEK PASS	Hays Co	670T	WY-13	78610	14000-14699
	Hays Co	700B	WY-12	78610	14700-14899
BEARD AVE	Austin	672R	MD-14	78748	10200-10799
BEARDSLEY CV	Travis Co	552Q	MD-26	78746	8000-8099
BEARDSLEY LN	Travis Co	552U	MD-25	78746	300-799
BEAR HOLLOW	Austin	554P	MG-26	78731	None
BEAR HOLLOW CV	Travis Co	702A	MC-12	78739	12400-12499
BEAR PAW LN	Georgetown	285P	MJ-53	78628	1000-1199
BEAR PAW TRL	Austin	646D	MM-18	78742	9500-9699
BEARS DEN CT	Travis Co	702A	MC-12	78739	12500-12599
BEAR SPRINGS TRL	Austin	702F	MC-12	78748	2600-2899
BEARTRAP LN	Austin	434Y	MH-37	78729	12300-12399
	Williamson Co	434Y	MH-37	78729	12400-12499
BEARTREE CIR	Travis Co	523T	ME-28	78730	3400-3599
BEATRICE CV	Austin	495H	MK-33	78758	2300-2399
BEATTY CT	Austin	641L	MB-17	78749	8900-8999
BEATTY DR	Austin	641L	MB-17	78749	6800-6999
BEAUCHAMP SQUARE	Williamson Co	434B	MG-39	78729	9700-9799
BEAUFORD DR	Austin	494S	MG-31	78750	6500-6699
	Austin	493V	MF-31	78750	6700-7199
BEAUMONT ST	Travis Co	490H	WZ-33	78734	3700-3999
BEAUREGARD CIR	Austin	643X	ME-16	78745	7700-7899
BEAUREGARD DR	Village of Volente	431N	MA-38	78641	8100-8199
BEAUTY BERRY CV	Pflugerville	439E	MS-39	78660	2500-2599
BEAUTYBERRY LN	Georgetown	314G	MH-51	78628	1900-1999
BEAUTYBUSH CIR	Georgetown	226E	ML-60	78633	100-199
BEAUTYBUSH PASS	Hays Co	669T	WW-13	78737	100-199
BEAUTYBUSH TRL	Georgetown	226E	ML-60	78633	100-199
BEAVER CIR	Taylor	322R	MZ-50	76574	1000-1099
BEAVER RD	Bastrop Co	563V	EB-25	78621	100-299
	Bastrop Co	564W	EC-25	78621	300-499
BEAVER ST	Austin	526J	ML-29	78753	100-799
BEAVER TRL	Travis Co	583Q	MF-23	78746	1000-1099
	West Lake Hills	583Q	MF-23	78746	900-999
BEAVER BROOK LN	Austin	673H	MF-15	78748	8000-8399
BEAVER CREEK DR	Austin	465T	MJ-34	78759	4500-4899
BEAVER HEAD CV	Travis Co	517D	WT-30	78669	None
BEAVER PELT CV	Austin	497X	MN-31	78754	2100-2199
BECCA TEAL PL	Round Rock	376A	ML-45	78681	1300-1399
BECK CIR	Austin	495V	MK-31	78758	9500-9899
BECKER AVE	Austin	555Y	MK-25	78751	3900-3999
BECKER LN	Travis Co	737U	MP-7	78617	10200-10399
	Travis Co	737T	MN-7	78617	10400-10699
BECKETT CIR	Austin	642B	MC-18	78749	5300-5399
BECKETT RD	Austin	642B	MC-18	78749	6600-9399
BECKETT ST	Austin	525G	MK-30	78757	1400-1599
BECK FARM RD	Pflugerville	439S	MS-37	78660	17800-18299
BECKWOOD DR	Austin	433W	ME-37	78726	10600-10899
BECKWOOD TRL	Williamson Co	377F	MN-45	78665	2100-2399
BECKY LN	Travis Co	427C	WT-39	78654	25600-25699
BECKYS WAY	Hays Co	668H	WV-15	78620	100-399
BEDFORD CT	Georgetown	225Z	MK-58	78628	800-899
BEDFORD DR	Burnet Co	396S	WQ-40	78669	100-399
BEDFORD ST	Austin	586S	ML-22	78702	700-1199
BEDOUIN CT	Pflugerville	437F	MN-39	78664	1500-1599
BEDROCK CT	Cedar Park	374Y	MH-43	78613	3700-3799
BEDROCK TRL	Austin	465L	MK-35	78727	12300-12499
BEE CIR	Travis Co	640D	WZ-18	78737	None
BEE ST	Jonestown	401A	MA-42	78645	11500-11699
BEEBRUSH LN	Austin	673K	ME-14	78748	1500-1599
BEE CAVE PKWY	Bee Cave	550P	WY-26	78738	12200-13599
BEE CAVES RD	Austin	584S	MG-22	78746	2500-2599
	Rollingwood	584S	MG-22	78746	2600-2899
	Rollingwood	583R	MF-23	78746	2900-3199
	Travis Co	583A	ME-24	78746	6000-6499
	West Lake Hills	583R	MF-23	78746	3200-5999
BEE CAVE WOODS RD	Rollingwood	583V	MF-22	78746	1000-1099
BEECH DR	Austin	525H	MK-30	78758	8400-8599
BEECH ST	Bastrop	745F	EE-9	78602	700-1099
	Bastrop	745G	EF-9	78602	1300-1399
BEECH ST	Taylor	353N	EA-47	76574	1100-1199
BEECHER LN	Travis Co	552M	MD-26	78746	1-99
BEECHMOOR DR	Austin	586C	MM-24	78723	5200-5399
BEECHNUT CV	Williamson Co	432D	MD-39	78613	1800-1899
BEECHNUT DR	Austin	673K	ME-14	78748	9100-9699
BEECHNUT TRACE	Williamson Co	432D	MD-39	78613	2600-2899
BEECHWOOD HOLLOW	Austin	524P	MG-29	78731	4600-4699
BEE CREEK CT	Georgetown	195N	MJ-62	78633	100-199
BEE CREEK RD	Travis Co	487H	WT-33	78669	1000-2699
	Travis Co	488W	WU-31	78669	2700-3199
	Travis Co	518E	WU-30	78669	3000-4099
	Travis Co	518T	WU-28	78669	4100-5299
BEE HILL CIR	Travis Co	488W	WU-31	78669	20300-20599
	Travis Co	487Z	WT-31	78669	20600-20999
BEE HIVE LN	Travis Co	487Z	WT-31	78669	20600-20899
BEEHOLLOW CT	Travis Co	487Z	WT-31	78669	20500-20599
BEEKEEPER DR	Travis Co	487Z	WT-31	78669	3100-3199
BEELEIGH CT	Travis Co	432C	MD-39	78613	2400-2499
BEE TREE CIR	Travis Co	583M	MF-23	78746	400-599
BEGONIA CIR	Austin	616S	ML-19	78741	6100-6199
BEGONIA TERRACE	Austin	616S	ML-19	78741	1100-1399
BEHRENS PKWY	Round Rock	375G	MK-45	78681	2900-3299
BEHRENS PKWY	Williamson Co	375G	MK-45	78681	3300-3699
BEINVILLE CV	Austin	642R	MD-17	78749	7600-7699
BELAFONTE BLVD	Travis Co	619A	MS-21	78724	15400-15699
BEL AIR DR	Taylor	322V	MZ-49	76574	2100-2399
BELAIRE CIR	Round Rock	406M	MM-41	78664	100-199
BELCARA PASS	Travis Co	521N	MA-29	78732	400-499
BELCARA PL	Travis Co	521N	MA-29	78732	12500-12799
BELCLAIRE CIR	Austin	673M	MF-14	78748	8200-8399
BELCLAIRE LN	Austin	673H	MF-15	78748	8000-8399
BELFALLS DR	Georgetown	195Y	MK-61	78633	100-199
BELFAST DR	Austin	556P	ML-26	78723	5300-6299
BEL FAY LN	Austin	612X	MC-19	78749	6000-6099
BELFIELD LN	Travis Co	619N	MS-20	78725	4400-4699
BELFIN DR	Austin	404L	MH-41	78717	15400-15899
BELFORD DR	Austin	525G	MK-30	78757	1700-2099
BELFRY PASS	Travis Co	560K	MU-26	78653	18000-18499
BELGRADE DR	Austin	611D	MB-21	78735	5500-5599
BELGRAVE FALLS LN	Austin	672U	MD-13	78748	2900-3299
BELINDA CT	Bastrop	744D	ED-9	78602	300-399
BELINDA CT N	Bastrop	744D	ED-9	78602	400-499
BELINDA LN	Webberville	651E	MW-18	78653	20000-20199
	Webberville	650D	MV-18	78653	None
BELL AVE	Austin	464R	MH-35	78759	11400-11899
	Austin	465J	MJ-35	78727	11900-12099
	Austin	464H	MH-36	78727	12100-12299
BELL BLVD N	Cedar Park	373S	ME-43	78613	100-1499
	Cedar Park	372D	MD-45	78613	1500-2899
BELL BLVD S	Cedar Park	373X	ME-43	78613	100-299
	Cedar Park	403U	MF-40	78613	300-2699
BELL CV	Lago Vista	459E	WW-36	78645	3400-3499
BELL DR	Austin	611C	MB-21	78735	5700-5899
BELL LN	Buda	763E	ME-6	78610	100-199
BELL LN	Lago Vista	459E	WW-36	78645	20200-20499
BELLA PKWY	Manor	530T	MU-28	78653	None
BELLA CIMA DR	Lakeway	490N	WY-32	78734	100-199
	Travis Co	490N	WY-32	78734	200-299
BELLAGIO DR	Lakeway	490W	WY-31	78734	100-399
BEL LAGO CV	Lakeway	520A	WY-30	78734	100-199
BELLAIRE DR	Austin	615P	MJ-20	78741	1500-1599
BELLAIRE DR	Georgetown	225V	MK-58	78628	100-199
	Georgetown	226S	ML-58	78628	200-699
BELLAIRE OAKS DR	Pflugerville	468A	MQ-36	78660	400-699
BELLA MAR TRL	Travis Co	521N	MA-29	78732	12400-12799
BELLA MONTAGNA CIR	Lakeway	520E	WY-30	78734	100-199
	Lakeway	519D	WX-30	78734	200-399
	Lakeway	520A	WY-30	78734	400-599
BELLANCIA DR	Travis Co	547Z	WT-25	78738	8100-8599
BELLA RIVA DR	Travis Co	490J	WY-32	78734	200-299
BELLA STRADA CV	Lakeway	490N	WY-32	78734	None
BELLA VISTA	Williamson Co	224L	MH-59	78633	100-199
BELLA VISTA CV	Travis Co	490J	WY-32	78734	200-299
BELLA VISTA TRL	Travis Co	641K	MA-17	78737	7500-7699
BELLEHAVEN CT	Austin	674L	MH-14	78744	7700-7799
BELLEMEADE BLVD	Travis Co	437Q	MP-38	78660	400-799
BELLEMONT ST	Austin	584Q	MH-23	78703	1400-1499
BELLERIVE DR	Travis Co	409S	MS-40	78660	20200-20999
BELLE STAR CT	Austin	496X	ML-31	78753	200-299
BELLEVUE PL	Austin	585B	MJ-24	78705	500-699
BELLFLOWER CV	Austin	464P	MG-35	78759	7600-7699
BELLMAR DR	Round Rock	377N	MN-44	78664	1400-1499
BELL MEADOWS DR	Williamson Co	318B	MQ-51	78634	100-399
BELL MOUNTAIN DR	Travis Co	493T	ME-31	78730	7800-9699
BELLO CIR	Williamson Co	226X	ML-58	78628	200-399
BELLO DR	Leander	341D	MB-48	78641	300-499
BELLOWS FALLS AVE	Austin	672U	MD-13	78748	11200-11499
BELL ROCK CIR	Pflugerville	438T	MQ-37	78660	1200-1299
BELL SPRINGS RD	Hays Co	576N	WQ-23	78620	1000-2199
	Hays Co	606N	WQ-20	78620	2400-4699
	Hays Co	636J	WQ-17	78620	4700-5399
	Travis Co	576D	WR-24	78620	700-999
BELLVIEW AVE W	Round Rock	406C	MM-42	78664	400-699
	Round Rock	406K	ML-41	78681	700-999
BELLVUE AVE	Austin	555N	MJ-26	78756	4200-4499
BELLWOOD CV	Village of the Hills	519P	WW-29	78738	1-99
BELMONT CIR	Austin	555W	MJ-25	78705	3000-3099
BELMONT DR	Georgetown	287L	MP-53	78626	100-799
BELMONT PKWY	Austin	555W	MJ-25	78705	1100-1399
BELMONT PARK DR	Austin	523Z	MF-28	78746	3700-4199
BELMOOR DR	Austin	556P	ML-26	78723	5800-5899
BELO HORIZONTE CIR	Austin	524K	MG-29	78731	6300-6399
BELT DR	Travis Co	560E	MU-27	78653	17700-17799
BELTERRA DR	Hays Co	639T	WW-16	78737	100-1199
	Hays Co	669A	WW-15	78737	1200-1799
BELTEX DR	Travis Co	530U	MV-28	78653	12600-13099
BELTON LAKE CV	Travis Co	560K	MU-26	78653	11700-11799
BELVEDERE ST	Austin	524J	MG-29	78731	4800-4899
BELVERDE PL	Round Rock	407D	MP-42	78665	1600-1699
BENBROOK DR	Austin	495X	MJ-31	78757	2700-3999
BENCH MARK DR	Travis Co	466G	MM-36	78728	1600-1999
BENCHMARK ST	Georgetown	257S	MN-55	78626	100-199
BEN CRENSHAW WAY	Travis Co	582L	MD-23	78746	1500-1799
BEND CV	Austin	613M	MF-20	78704	2600-2699
BENDER DR	Austin	642R	MD-17	78749	7400-7699
BENDING TRL	Austin	644Z	MH-16	78744	2300-2499
BENDING BOUGH TRL	Austin	496J	ML-32	78758	11100-11299
BENDING OAK DR	Hays Co	638J	WU-17	78620	500-699
BENDING OAK RD	Austin	612W	MC-19	78749	7000-7299
BEND OF THE RIVER DR	Travis Co	582R	MD-23	78746	6100-6299
BEN DORAN CT	Travis Co	432F	MC-39	78613	2500-2599
BENDRIDGE TRL	Austin	674H	MH-15	78744	2300-2399
BENECIA CT	Travis Co	550R	WZ-26	78733	3400-3499
BENELVA DR	Austin	585B	MJ-24	78705	3100-3199
BENEVENTO WAY	Travis Co	432L	MD-38	78613	2700-2799
BENGAL DR	Pflugerville	437B	MN-39	78664	1600-1799
BEN GARZA LN	Austin	643A	ME-18	78749	3500-4099
BENGSTON ST	Austin	586S	ML-22	78702	3200-3499
BEN HOWELL DR	Austin	614V	MH-19	78704	100-399
BENJAMIN ST	Austin	645B	MJ-18	78741	2200-2399
BENJIE LN	Hays Co	636E	WQ-18	78620	100-399
BEN MILAM DR	Travis Co	733B	ME-9	78652	12900-13199
BENNEDICT LN	Travis Co	554N	MG-26	78746	3900-4399
BENNETT AVE	Austin	555Y	MK-25	78751	4200-4699
	Austin	555M	MK-26	78751	4900-5699
	Austin	556A	ML-27	78752	6900-7399
	Austin	526W	ML-28	78752	7400-7699
BENNETT CV	Hutto	379C	MT-45	78634	100-199
BENNETT-POKORNEY LN	Travis Co	499D	MT-33	78653	9400-10199
BENNETT RIDGE DR	Travis Co	497C	MP-33	78754	1900-1999
BEN NEVIS RD	Austin	498T	MQ-31	78653	12400-12499
BENNEY LN	Dripping Springs	636Y	WR-16	78620	100-299
BENNING DR	Pflugerville	438D	MR-39	78660	None
BENNINGTON LN	Austin	467X	MN-34	78753	13100-13399
BENSON WAY	Travis Co	677G	MP-15	78617	4600-4899
BENT PATH	Williamson Co	346G	MM-48	78665	4400-4498 E
BENT BOW CV	Williamson Co	402Y	MD-40	78613	2000-2099
BENT BOW DR	Travis Co	402Y	MD-40	78613	2300-2399
	Williamson Co	402Y	MD-40	78613	2100-2299
BENT BROOK DR	Round Rock	378X	MQ-43	78664	3800-3899
BENT CEDAR CV	Williamson Co	433G	MF-39	78750	12300-12399
BENTLEY DR	Austin	672R	MD-14	78748	10400-10499
BENTLEY GARNER LN	Austin	673V	MF-13	78748	9200-9399
BENT OAK CIR	Austin	642C	MD-18	78749	7000-7099
BENT OAK CV	Leander	342T	MC-46	78641	1800-1899
BENTON ST	Austin	642Z	MD-16	78745	3200-3299
BENTONITE CV	Lakeway	518H	WV-30	78738	100-199
BENTSEN LN	Austin	586H	MM-24	78723	5500-5699
BENT TREE CT	Round Rock	375M	MK-44	78681	2100-2199
BENT TREE CT	West Lake Hills	583M	MF-23	78746	200-399
BENT TREE CV	Bastrop Co	741K	MW-8	78612	100-199

B

STREET NAME	CITY or COUNTY	MAPSCO GRID	AUSTIN GRID	ZIP CODE	BLOCK RANGE O/E
BENT TREE CV	Round Rock	375M	MK-44	78681	3100-3199
BENT TREE DR	Georgetown	285Z	MK-52	78628	100-199
BENT TREE DR	Round Rock	375H	MK-45	78681	2000-2099
BENT TREE LOOP	Round Rock	375M	MK-44	78681	2000-3099
BENT TREE RD	Austin	495W	MJ-31	78759	8200-8499
BENT WOOD CT	Williamson Co	346G	MM-48	78665	4200-4299
BENT WOOD DR	Leander	342F	MC-48	78641	400-699
BENT WOOD PL	Williamson Co	346G	MM-48	78665	700-899
BENTWOOD RD	Austin	555V	MK-25	78723	1100-1499
BEN WHITE BLVD E	Austin	644C	MH-18	78704	100-1599
	Austin	645E	MJ-18	78741	1600-6499
	Austin	646J	ML-17	78741	6500-8499
	Austin	646H	MM-18	78742	None
	Bastrop Co	680J	MU-14	78612	None
	Travis Co	680J	MU-14	78612	5400-5599
BEN WHITE BLVD W	Austin	644C	MH-18	78704	100-599
	Austin	614W	MG-19	78704	600-2499
BENWICK CIR	Austin	556L	MM-26	78723	2100-2199
BERARDI PL	Travis Co	432G	MD-39	78613	None
BERDOLL LN	Bastrop Co	680D	MV-15	78612	400-599
BERDOLL LOOP	Bastrop Co	680U	MV-13	78612	100-199
BERENE AVE	Austin	586L	MM-23	78721	1400-1699
BERENSON LN	Travis Co	554N	MG-26	78746	2500-2799
BERESFORD TRL	Austin	673G	MF-15	78748	8500-8599
BERGAMONT DR	Pflugerville	437H	MP-39	78660	1500-1599
BERGER ST	Austin	586T	ML-22	78721	1100-1199
BERGFIELD DR	Austin	645X	MJ-16	78744	4700-4999
BERGIN CT	Georgetown	287J	MN-53	78626	1400-1499
BERGSTROM DR	Austin	647W	MN-16	78719	3500-3799
	Austin	676D	MM-15	78719	3800-4099
BERING CV	Austin	464G	MH-36	78759	7300-7399
BERKELEY AVE	Austin	643Q	MF-17	78745	1800-1999
	Austin	643L	MF-17	78745	2100-2699
BERKELEY CV	Austin	643L	MF-17	78745	6300-6399
BERKETT CV	Austin	643L	MF-17	78745	6200-6299
BERKETT DR	Austin	643L	MF-17	78745	2000-2799
BERKLEY RAYE LN	Austin	673R	MF-14	78748	400-499
BERKMAN DR	Austin	586A	ML-24	78723	4000-4399
BERKMAN DR	Austin	556P	ML-26	78723	5100-6899
	Austin	556B	ML-27	78752	6900-7599
BERKSHIRE DR	Austin	556K	ML-26	78723	1300-1499
BERMUDA	Lakeway	489X	WW-31	78734	600-999
BERMUDA DR	Travis Co	733A	ME-9	78652	100-199
BERMUDA LN	Hays Co	732K	MC-8	78610	200-299
BERN DR	Travis Co	708S	MQ-10	78617	14600-14999
BERNARD ST	Village of Volente	430R	WZ-38	78645	8000-8099
	Village of Volente	431N	MA-38	78641	8100-8299
BERNARDINO CV	Travis Co	436T	ML-37	78728	2900-3099
BERNOULLI DR	Austin	672H	MD-15	78748	9300-9499
BEROL DR	Pflugerville	407Y	MP-40	78660	18100-18299
BERRY CV	Georgetown	226M	MM-59	78628	100-199
BERRY LN	Williamson Co	287D	MP-54	78626	1-1299
BERRY BEND PATH	Round Rock	407A	MN-42	78664	900-1099
BERRYCONE CV	Austin	493R	MF-32	78750	7600-7699
BERRY CREEK DR	Georgetown	227J	MN-59	78628	30000-30299
	Georgetown	226H	MM-60	78628	30300-30899
BERRYESSA PASS	Travis Co	521S	MA-28	78732	200-299
BERRY HILL CIR	Austin	643G	MF-18	78745	2300-2399
BERRY HILL DR	Austin	643G	MF-18	78745	5600-5799
BERRYHILL WAY	Austin	524U	MH-28	78731	3900-3999
BERRYLAWN CIR	Austin	556V	MM-25	78723	3100-3199
BERRYLINE CV	Austin	587M	MP-23	78724	9000-9099
BERRYLINE WAY	Austin	587R	MP-23	78724	5700-5899
BERRYWOOD DR	Austin	496R	MM-32	78753	800-1099
BERRYWOOD LN	Williamson Co	225F	MJ-60	78633	6600-6699
BERT AVE	Austin	614S	MG-19	78704	2000-2099
BERTHOUND DR	Austin	496S	ML-31	78758	10500-10799
BERTRAM LN	Travis Co	487Y	WT-31	78669	21000-21299
BERTRAM ST	Jonestown	400H	WZ-42	78645	11400-11499
BERWICK CV	Round Rock	376A	ML-45	78681	2400-2499
BERWICK DR	Round Rock	376A	ML-45	78681	2300-2399
BERWYN CIR	Austin	643G	MF-18	78745	2500-2599
BERWYN LN	Austin	643G	MF-18	78745	2300-2499
BERYL OAK DR	Austin	645X	MJ-16	78744	5100-5299
BESCOTT DR	Travis Co	436V	MM-37	78728	14700-14999
BESS LN	Austin	672V	MD-13	78748	2600-2699
BESSEMER CV	Lago Vista	459E	WW-36	78645	20200-20299
BESSIE AVE	Austin	647Q	MP-17	78617	3100-3299
BEST WAY	Travis Co	619T	MS-19	78725	4500-4699
BETH DR	Travis Co	592N	MY-23	78621	22800-23099
BETH LN	Round Rock	377J	MN-44	78664	1200-1499
BETHEL WAY	Travis Co	467E	MN-36	78660	800-899
BETHEL CHURCH RD	San Leanna	703J	ME-11	78652	11901-11999 O
	Travis Co	703J	ME-11	78652	11900-11998 E
	Travis Co	703J	ME-11	78652	12000-12399
BETHESDA CT	Pflugerville	409S	MS-40	78660	2100-2299
BETHPAGE DR	Travis Co	408H	MR-42	78634	1000-1299
	Williamson Co	408H	MR-42	78634	900-999
BETHUNE AVE	Austin	556A	ML-27	78752	6900-7499
	Austin	526X	ML-28	78752	7500-7699
BETTERMAN CV	Pflugerville	437D	MP-39	78660	17900-17999
BETTERMAN DR	Pflugerville	437D	MP-39	78660	200-899
BETTIS BLVD	Rollingwood	584T	MG-22	78746	2300-2699
BETTIS TROPHY DR	Austin	641W	MA-16	78739	7600-7999
BETTY BAKER CV	Travis Co	437T	MN-37	78660	1000-1099
BETTY COOK DR	Austin	556R	MM-26	78723	6200-6699
BETTY JO DR	Austin	615P	MJ-20	78704	1500-1599
BETULA DR	Lakeway	489U	WX-31	78734	100-199
BEVERLY CV	Williamson Co	343S	ME-46	78641	2500-2599
BEVERLY LN	Williamson Co	342Z	MD-46	78641	400-699
BEVERLY RD	Austin	554V	MH-25	78703	3000-3399
BEVERLY HILLS DR	Austin	524Y	MH-28	78731	4900-5299
BEVERLY SKYLINE	Austin	524Y	MH-28	78731	4900-5199
BEVERLY VILLAS CT	Travis Co	491Y	MB-31	78732	12200-12499
BEVIN CV	Austin	645T	MJ-16	78744	5500-5599
BEVIN CV	Round Rock	407H	MP-42	78665	2400-2499
BEXAR FOREST CV	Elgin	533F	EA-30	78621	None
BEXLEY CT	Austin	671G	MB-15	78739	5700-5799
BEXLEY LN	Austin	671G	MB-15	78739	10900-11199
BEXTON CIR	Austin	643K	ME-17	78745	6300-6399
BICKLER RD	Austin	615E	MJ-21	78704	1200-1399
BIDENS PL	Travis Co	551P	MA-26	78733	10900-10999
BIDERMANN WAY	Travis Co	409T	MS-40	78660	2500-2599
BIDWELL DR	Williamson Co	434Q	MH-38	78729	13100-13199
BIENVILLE ST	Austin	466K	ML-35	78727	1900-1999
BIERCE ST	Austin	615A	MJ-21	78701	1-99
BIG DR	Georgetown	226P	ML-59	78628	1300-1399
BIG TRL	Austin	465S	MJ-34	78759	11500-11799
BIG BEND DR	Austin	554C	MH-27	78731	3300-3399
BIG BEND DR	Cedar Park	373J	ME-44	78613	1400-1999
	Cedar Park	373K	ME-44	78613	None
BIG BEND RD	West Lake Hills	553X	ME-25	78746	None
BIG BEND TRL	Georgetown	225U	MK-58	78628	4800-5099
BIG BEND TRL	Taylor	322M	MZ-50	76574	500-4499
BIG BILL CT	Lakeway	519R	WX-29	78734	1100-1299
BIG BOGGY TRL	Austin	704A	MG-12	78747	9900-9999
BIG CANYON DR	Travis Co	582R	MD-23	78746	1800-2099
BIG CAT CV	Austin	494S	MG-31	78750	6300-6399
BIG EAGLE CV	Elgin	503T	EA-31	78621	None
BIGELOW DR	Travis Co	619E	MS-21	78724	15000-15199
BIG FALLS DR	Williamson Co	343W	ME-46	78641	14900-15199
BIGGS DR	Austin	615X	MJ-19	78741	2500-2599
BIG HOLLOW DR	Travis Co	436U	MM-37	78728	2100-2399
BIG HORN	Leander	342W	MC-46	78641	2100-2199
BIG HORN CIR	Austin	611M	MB-20	78735	6100-6299
BIG HORN CIR	Lago Vista	399L	WX-41	78645	8600-8699
BIG HORN DR	Travis Co	491W	MA-31	78734	1900-2699
BIG HORN LN	Caldwell Co	767P	MN-5	78616	None
BIG HORN PASS	Bastrop	744K	EC-8	78602	100-199
BIG MEADOW DR	Cedar Park	433A	ME-39	78613	2600-2799
	Williamson Co	433A	ME-39	78613	1500-1599
BIG OAK CIR	Travis Co	310L	WZ-50	78641	16100-16499
BIG OAK HOLLOW	Austin	494S	MG-31	78750	6200-6299
BIG OAKS	Williamson Co	192L	MD-62	78633	1-199
BIG OAKS TRL N	Williamson Co	192G	MD-63	78633	1-199
BIG OAKS TRL S	Williamson Co	192L	MD-62	78633	200-299
BIG ROCK TRL	Travis Co	486V	WR-31	78669	4700-4799
BIG SANDY CV	Travis Co	339D	WX-48	78641	14000-14099
BIG SANDY DR	Hays Co	794N	MG-2	78610	100-499
BIG SANDY DR	Travis Co	340E	WY-48	78641	22700-23399
BIG SKY CV	Hays Co	668M	WV-14	78737	100-199
BIG SKY DR	Travis Co	560F	MU-27	78653	11800-11999
BIG SKY TRL	Georgetown	225C	MK-60	78633	100-199
BIG SPRING DR	Cedar Park	373J	ME-44	78613	600-1099
BIG SUR TRL	Taylor	322M	MZ-50	76574	500-899
BIG THICKET DR	Austin	704A	MG-12	78747	10100-10699
BIG THICKET DR	Cedar Park	373F	ME-45	78613	1500-1699
BIG THICKET ST	Georgetown	225V	MK-58	78628	900-999
BIG TIMBER DR	Austin	611C	MB-21	78735	8400-8499
BIG TRAIL CIR	Austin	465T	MJ-34	78759	4900-5099
BIG TRAIL CV	Austin	465S	MJ-34	78759	11500-11599
BIG VALLEY DR	Travis Co	702T	MC-10	78652	2000-2299
BIG VALLEY SPUR	Williamson Co	192U	MD-61	78633	100-499
BIG VIEW DR	Austin	522J	MC-29	78732	7900-9399
	Travis Co	522C	MD-30	78730	9400-9699
	Travis Co	492U	MD-31	78730	9700-10599
BILBOA DR	Austin	465W	MJ-34	78759	4000-4699
BILBROOK DR	Bastrop Co	743S	EA-7	78602	100-299
BILBROOK PL	Austin	673X	ME-13	78748	9600-10699
BILL ST	Elgin	534J	EC-29	78621	100-199
BILL BAKER DR	Austin	702H	MD-12	78748	1800-1899
BILL HICKCOCK PASS	Austin	673K	ME-14	78748	8900-9199
BILL HUGHES RD	Austin	644W	MG-16	78745	6700-7299
BILLIE CIR	Pflugerville	438T	MQ-37	78660	None
BILLIEM DR	Austin	466L	MM-35	78727	13100-13299
BILLINGHAM TRL	Austin	375W	MJ-43	78717	9300-9699
BILLINGS LN	Travis Co	552L	MD-26	78733	100-299
BILLINGSLEY HEIGHTS	Bastrop Co	741P	MW-8	78612	100-199
BILL PRICE RD	Travis Co	647T	MN-16	78617	3400-3799
BILLS CIR	Bastrop	744C	ED-9	78602	700-799
BILLY BONNEY CT	Austin	641H	MB-18	78749	8100-8199
BILLY BONNEY PASS	Austin	641H	MB-18	78749	6400-6599
BILLY FISKE LN	Austin	702D	MD-12	78748	2200-2399
BILLY MILLS LN	Austin	702D	MD-12	78748	2200-2999
BIMINA LN	Travis Co	467H	MP-36	78660	1200-1299
BINDON DR	Travis Co	432C	MD-39	78613	2100-2299
BING CHERRY LN	Austin	463D	MF-36	78750	9400-9499
BINGHAM CREEK RD	Travis Co	280W	WY-52	78641	24200-25099
	Travis Co	279Z	WX-52	78641	None
BINTLIFF DR	Austin	464J	MG-35	78759	10300-10599
BIRCH DR	Georgetown	225Z	MK-58	78628	1200-1299
	Georgetown	226W	ML-58	78628	1300-1499
BIRCH DR	Williamson Co	433E	ME-39	78613	3000-3299
BIRCH ST	Austin	614X	MG-19	78704	3700-3799
BIRCHBARK TRL	Williamson Co	433P	ME-38	78750	11600-11799
BIRCH BROOK LN	Leander	342M	MD-47	78641	700-899
BIRCH CREEK RD	Austin	645X	MJ-16	78744	4900-5299
BIRCH FOREST DR	Bastrop Co	745U	EF-7	78602	100-199
BIRCHINGTON DR	Travis Co	432C	MD-39	78613	2300-2399
BIRCHLEAF TRL	Austin	702C	MD-12	78748	2600-2699
BIRCHOVER LN	Austin	528J	MQ-29	78754	11400-11499
BIRCHWOOD CT	Austin	644A	MG-18	78745	1400-1499
BIRD BROOK LN	Austin	705E	MJ-12	78747	9000-9099
BIRD CALL PASS	Austin	497X	MN-31	78754	1900-1999
BIRD CREEK DR	Austin	496X	ML-31	78758	900-1099
BIRD DOG LN	Cedar Park	373Z	MF-43	78613	1500-1699
BIRD DOG BEND	Bastrop	744P	EC-8	78602	300-399
BIRD HOUSE DR	Round Rock	346R	MM-47	78665	3600-3799
BRIRDIE CV	Cedar Park	372U	MD-43	78613	1200-1299
BIRDIE DR	Village of the Hills	519K	WW-29	78738	100-199
BIRDLIP CIR	Travis Co	551D	MB-27	78733	10200-10299
BIRDS NEST CT	Williamson Co	433E	ME-39	78613	1900-1999
BIRDSTONE LN	Williamson Co	284A	MG-54	78628	100-299
BIRDWELL LN	Buda	732T	MC-7	78610	100-199
BIRDWOOD CIR	Austin	614P	MG-20	78704	3000-3199
BIRMINGHAM DR	Austin	673G	MF-15	78748	8400-8799
BIRNAM WOOD CT	Austin	583H	MF-24	78746	100-299
BIRRELL ST	Lakeway	519Q	WX-29	78734	15500-15799
BIRSAY DR	Briarcliff	487D	WT-33	78669	22100-22199
BISBEE CT	Austin	642Z	MD-16	78745	8500-8699
BISCAY DR	Austin	465X	MJ-34	78759	3900-4099
BISCAYNE	Lakeway	519B	WW-30	78734	800-999
BISCAYNE CV	Lakeway	519B	WW-30	78734	1000-1099
BISHOPSGATE DR	Travis Co	437G	MP-39	78660	17000-17599
BISMARK CV	Austin	643W	ME-16	78745	8500-8599
BISMARK DR	Austin	702F	MC-12	78748	12500-12899
	Austin	702L	MD-11	78748	13100-13299
BISON CV	Georgetown	257L	MP-56	78626	1700-1799
BISON DR	Georgetown	257L	MP-56	78626	1700-1899
BISON PATH	Round Rock	378F	MQ-45	78626	1000-1099
BISON TRL	Lago Vista	399L	WX-41	78645	21100-21599
BISSEL CIR	Austin	643U	MF-16	78745	6800-6899
BISSEL LN	Austin	643Q	MF-17	78745	1700-1999
BISSET CT	Lakeway	518M	WV-29	78738	100-399
BISSONET LN	Austin	525V	MK-28	78752	600-799
BIT LN	Cedar Park	402Q	MD-41	78613	1100-1199
BITTER CREEK DR	Austin	674G	MH-15	78744	1700-2599
BITTERN CIR	Hays Co	732E	MC-9	78610	400-499
BITTERN HOLLOW	Austin	496J	ML-32	78758	11300-12099
BITTERNUT CV	Austin	464X	MG-34	78759	9600-9699
BITTEROOT CIR	Travis Co	433X	ME-37	78750	11000-11099
BITTEROOT TRL	Austin	674G	MH-15	78744	6800-7099
BITTERROOT LN	Hays Co	669B	WW-15	78737	100-199
BITTERWOOD DR	Travis Co	588N	MQ-23	78724	5500-5899
BITTING SCHOOL RD	Travis Co	591D	MX-24	78653	10900-11099
	Travis Co	561Z	MX-25	78653	11100-11299
	Travis Co	562N	MY-26	78653	11300-11799
BIVINS CT	Travis Co	491Q	MB-32	78732	12800-12899
BIXLER DR	Austin	675S	MJ-13	78744	7700-8099
B. J. MAYES RD	Bastrop Co	715B	EE-12	78602	100-399
BLACK ST N	Round Rock	376Z	MM-43	78664	100-399
BLACK ST S	Round Rock	376Z	MM-43	78664	100-199
BLACKACRE TRL	West Lake Hills	583B	ME-24	78746	1100-1199
BLACK ANGUS CV	Austin	465K	MJ-35	78727	4900-4999
BLACK ANGUS DR	Austin	465K	MJ-35	78727	12000-12399
BLACK BEAR CT	Dripping Springs	636P	WQ-17	78620	100-199
BLACK BEAR DR	Travis Co	702Q	MD-11	78652	1200-1699
BLACKBERRY DR	Austin	674A	MG-15	78745	300-699
BLACKBIRD CT	Cedar Park	403J	ME-41	78613	1100-1199
BLACKBURN PL	Williamson Co	377K	MN-44	78665	1000-1199
BLACK CANYON DR	Williamson Co	434R	MH-38	78729	13300-13399
BLACK CANYON ST	Pflugerville	438F	MQ-39	78660	900-1199
BLACK CHERRY DR	Williamson Co	433E	ME-39	78613	1300-1599
BLACKEYED SUSAN TRL	Travis Co	532L	MZ-29	78621	13000-13199
BLACKFOOT	Lago Vista	428R	WV-38	78654	21100-21199
BLACKFOOT TRL	Austin	434Z	MH-37	78729	12600-12799
	Williamson Co	434Z	MH-37	78729	12800-12899
BLACKFOOT DAISY DR	Travis Co	517J	WS-29	78669	None
BLACK GAP PASS	Austin	557P	MN-26	78724	7500-7599
BLACK HAWK CT	Dripping Springs	636Q	WR-17	78620	100-199
BLACKHAWK DR	Austin	465T	MJ-34	78759	11600-11799
BLACK HILLS DR	Austin	702G	MD-12	78748	12400-12499
BLACK ISLE DR	Pflugerville	437G	MP-39	78660	700-799
	Travis Co	437G	MP-39	78660	800-899
BLACKJACK CV	Austin	675B	MJ-15	78744	5400-5499
BLACK JACK CV	Bastrop	715U	EF-10	78602	100-199
BLACKJACK CV	Round Rock	376J	ML-44	78681	1900-1999
BLACKJACK DR	Round Rock	376J	ML-44	78681	1500-1899
BLACK JACK LN	Bastrop Co	715Q	EF-11	78602	100-299
BLACKJACK PASS	Cedar Park	403A	ME-42	78613	600-799
BLACK KETTLE DR	Williamson Co	343S	ME-46	78641	16500-16999
BLACKLAND DR	Taylor	322Y	MZ-49	76574	1300-1599
BLACK LOCUST DR E	Pflugerville	438J	MQ-38	78660	900-1099
	Pflugerville	437M	MP-38	78660	1100-1699
BLACK LOCUST DR W	Travis Co	437G	MP-39	78660	400-1399
BLACKMAN CT	Hutto	379H	MT-45	78634	1000-1199
BLACKMAN TRL	Hutto	379H	MT-45	78634	100-499
BLACK MESA CV	Travis Co	702A	MC-12	78739	12500-12599
BLACK MESA HOLLOW	Travis Co	702A	MC-12	78739	3500-3699
BLACKMOOR DR	Austin	464F	MG-36	78759	11100-11499
BLACK MOUNTAIN DR	Austin	611T	MA-19	78736	7300-7799
BLACKMULE DR	Austin	674D	MH-15	78744	6100-6199
BLACK OAK ST	Williamson Co	434K	MG-38	78729	8600-8899
BLACK PANDA TRL	Travis Co	707C	MP-12	78617	7200-7299
BLACK ROCK BEND	Williamson Co	375P	MJ-44	78681	7100-7199
BLACKSMITH CV	Travis Co	517M	WT-29	78669	4400-4799
BLACKSMITH LN	Travis Co	672T	MC-13	78748	3000-3099
BLACKSMITHS CIR	Georgetown	225H	MK-60	78633	100-199
BLACKSMITHS DR	Georgetown	225H	MK-60	78633	100-199
BLACKSON AVE	Austin	526W	ML-28	78752	300-1099
BLACKSTONE CV	Round Rock	377Z	MP-43	78665	2700-2799
BLACKTHORN DR	Travis Co	437L	MP-38	78660	1000-1299
BLACKVIREO DR	Travis Co	434G	MH-39	78729	8700-8899
BLACK WALNUT CIR	Georgetown	195Z	MK-61	78633	100-199
BLACKWELL DR	Travis Co	733B	ME-9	78652	600-799
BLACK WILLOW ST	Pflugerville	437M	MP-38	78660	1600-1699
BLACK WOLF RUN	Lakeway	519W	WW-28	78738	100-599
BLADEN SPRINGS CV					
	Williamson Co	375W	MJ-43	78717	9200-9299
BLAINE RD	Austin	497B	MN-33	78753	12600-12899
BLAINE ST N	Weir	258H	MR-57	78626	200-299
BLAINE ST S	Weir	258H	MR-57	78626	100-199
BLAIR AVE	Bastrop	744D	ED-9	78602	600-799
BLAIR ST N	Round Rock	376Y	MM-43	78664	100-399
BLAIR ST S	Round Rock	406C	MM-42	78664	100-299
BLAIR WAY	Austin	614T	MG-19	78704	1100-1299
BLAIR CASTLE CT	Pflugerville	408X	MQ-40	78660	19000-19099
BLAIRVIEW LN	Austin	672Z	MD-13	78748	11200-11499
BLAKE ST	Austin	672R	MD-14	78748	2600-2899
BLAKE-MANOR RD	Manor	529Z	MT-28	78653	16700-16999
	Manor	559D	MT-28	78653	17000-17099
	Travis Co	590V	MV-22	78653	9900-20299
	Travis Co	559D	MT-27	78653	17100-17499
	Travis Co	560J	MU-26	78653	17500-18499
	Travis Co	590L	MV-23	78653	18500-19899
	Travis Co	591W	MW-22	78653	20300-20899
	Webberville	621N	MW-20	78653	20900-21499
BLAKENEY LN	Austin	497N	MN-32	78753	1300-1499
BLAKEY LN	Bastrop	744B	EC-9	78602	None
BLALOCK DR	Austin	466N	ML-35	78758	2100-2399
BLANCHARD DR	Round Rock	406E	ML-42	78681	1500-1699
BLANCHARD DR	Travis Co	490G	WZ-33	78734	15000-15499
BLANCO CIR	Travis Co	429Q	WX-38	78645	6200-6399
BLANCO CV	Georgetown	196W	ML-61	78628	100-199
BLANCO DR	Travis Co	429Q	WX-38	78645	19500-19999
BLANCO DR	Williamson Co	349H	MT-48	78634	100-299
BLANCO ST	Austin	584R	MH-23	78703	600-1199
BLANCO RIVER PASS	Austin	642E	MC-18	78749	5800-6299
BLANCO VISTA CV	Bastrop Co	738W	MQ-7	78617	100-199
BLANCO WOODS BLVD	Elgin	533F	EA-30	78621	100-599
BLAND ST	Austin	554Y	MH-25	78703	2600-2699
BLAND ST	Taylor	353J	EA-47	76574	200-799
	Taylor	353N	EA-47	76574	900-1099
BLANTON DR	Austin	556T	ML-25	78723	5400-5499
BLARWOOD DR	Austin	643K	ME-17	78745	6100-6799
BLAZEWOOD DR	Travis Co	588N	MQ-23	78724	5600-5899
BLAZING STAR DR	Georgetown	225P	MJ-59	78633	100-199
BLAZING STAR DR	Hays Co	668R	WV-14	78737	100-499
BLAZING STAR TRL	Williamson Co	432H	MD-39	78613	3000-3399
BLAZYK DR	Travis Co	640R	WZ-17	78737	8300-8999
BLEICH LN	Austin	527C	MP-30	78754	1100-11199

B

STREET NAME	CITY or COUNTY	MAPSCO GRID	AUSTIN GRID	ZIP CODE	BLOCK RANGE O/E
BLESSING AVE	Austin	556B	ML-27	78752	6900-7499
	Austin	526X	ML-28	78752	7500-7699
BLESSING ST	Williamson Co	406P	ML-41	78681	2500-2699
BLEWETT DR	Hutto	379L	MT-44	78634	1100-2099
BLINN CIR	Austin	556G	MM-27	78723	7300-7399
BLISSFIELD CV	Austin	671B	MA-15	78739	11000-11199
BLISSFIELD DR	Austin	641X	MA-16	78739	6700-6899
BLISS SPILLAR RD	Hays Co	702J	MC-11	78652	2600-3399
	Hays Co	701G	MB-12	78652	4000-4599
	Travis Co	702P	MC-11	78652	2100-2599
	Travis Co	702J	MC-11	78652	3400-3499
	Travis Co	701G	MB-12	78652	3500-3999
BLOCKER LN	Travis Co	736M	MM-8	78719	9000-9899
BLOCK HOUSE DR	Williamson Co	342Z	MD-46	78641	100-699
	Williamson Co	343S	ME-46	78641	700-2499
BLOCK HOUSE DR S	Cedar Park	373A	ME-45	78641	1900-2399
	Williamson Co	372D	MD-45	78641	2400-2799
BLOOMFIELD DR	Austin	643N	ME-17	78745	7500-7699
BLOOMFIELD HILLS LN	Travis Co	491W	MA-31	78732	12900-13099
BLOOMFIELD HILLS PASS	Travis Co	491W	MA-31	78732	2200-2299
BLOOR RD	Austin	558V	MR-25	78724	10500-11399
	Austin	559W	MS-25	78724	11400-12499
	Travis Co	559W	MS-25	78724	12500-12899
BLOSSOMBELL DR	Austin	496K	ML-32	78758	10900-11299
BLOSSOM VALLEY STREAM	Hays Co	762V	MD-4	78610	100-399
BLOSSOMWOOD DR	Austin	465L	MK-35	78727	12400-12499
BLUBELLA CV	Travis Co	432G	MD-39	78613	None
BLUBONNET DR	Williamson Co	377F	MN-45	78664	1800-2199
BLUE CV	Austin	643P	ME-17	78745	2600-2699
BLUE BEACH CV	Austin	464P	MG-35	78759	7400-7599
BLUEBELL CIR	Austin	616W	ML-19	78741	6000-6099
BLUE BELL DR	Cedar Park	402Y	MD-40	78613	1700-1899
BLUEBELL DR	Georgetown	226A	ML-60	78633	100-199
BLUEBELL BEND CV	Round Rock	378W	MQ-43	78665	3200-3299
BLUEBERRY CIR	Lago Vista	399L	WX-41	78645	8500-8599
BLUEBERRY TRL	Austin	586C	MM-24	78723	4700-4999
BLUEBERRY HILL	Austin	644S	MG-16	78745	300-699
BLUE BIRD CT	Round Rock	375V	MK-43	78681	1000-1099
BLUEBIRD DR	Hays Co	701Q	MB-11	78652	900-1099
BLUE BIRD LN	Austin	644P	MG-17	78745	5300-5599
BLUEBIRD LN	Travis Co	428A	WU-39	78654	24000-24099
BLUE BLUFF RD	Austin	559E	MS-27	78653	10400-10999
	Austin	529X	MS-28	78653	11000-11899
	Travis Co	618A	MQ-21	78725	3900-4699
	Travis Co	588P	MQ-23	78724	4700-6799
	Travis Co	558R	MR-26	78653	8900-10599
	Travis Co	529X	MS-28	78653	11900-12199
	Travis Co	617D	MP-21	78725	None
BLUEBONNET CIR	Lago Vista	399Q	WX-41	78645	21100-21199
BLUEBONNET CT	Leander	342K	MC-47	78641	1000-1099
BLUEBONNET DR	Cedar Park	372Z	MD-43	78613	1000-1299
BLUEBONNET DR	Williamson Co	377K	MN-44	78664	2200-2299
BLUEBONNET LN	Austin	614C	MH-21	78704	900-1299
	Austin	614F	MG-21	78704	1500-2599
BLUE BONNET LN	San Leanna	703K	ME-11	78652	11900-12199
BLUEBONNET TRL	Georgetown	256F	ML-57	78628	3400-3599
BLUEBONNET TRL	Leander	342B	MC-48	78641	100-299
BLUEBONNET VALLEY DR	Georgetown	286Z	MM-52	78626	2600-2699
BLUE CANYON CV	Jonestown	371Y	MB-43	78641	None
BLUE CAT LN	Travis Co	489M	WX-32	78734	1600-1899
BLUECAT WAY	Round Rock	347S	MN-46	78665	3700-3799
BLUE CLEARING WAY	Lakeway	518M	WV-29	78738	None
BLUE COVE RD	Travis Co	397S	WS-40	78654	26300-26899
BLUECREEK CV	Travis Co	582J	MC-23	78735	8700-8799
BLUE CREEK LN	Austin	496W	ML-31	78758	9500-9699
BLUE CREST DR	Austin	614F	MG-21	78704	1800-1999
BLUE DAWN TRL	Austin	674G	MH-15	78744	6800-7099
BLUE FLAME RD	Bastrop Co	742C	MZ-9	78612	100-299
	Bastrop Co	712U	MZ-10	78612	300-399
BLUE FLAX LN	Travis Co	467J	MN-35	78660	100-199
BLUE FOX DR	Austin	467X	MN-34	78753	1000-1299
BLUE GOOSE RD	Austin	528N	MQ-29	78754	6200-7299
	Austin	528T	MQ-28	78653	7300-8299
	Travis Co	527L	MP-29	78754	4700-6199
BLUE GRASS CV	Bastrop Co	711C	MX-12	78612	100-199
BLUEGRASS DR	Austin	494G	MH-33	78759	8500-9699
BLUEHAW DR	Georgetown	225V	MK-58	78628	100-599
BLUE HERON CV	Village of Volente	461F	MA-36	78641	7200-7299
BLUE HERON CV	Williamson Co	375K	MJ-44	78681	1700-1799
BLUE HERON LN	Williamson Co	284E	MG-54	78628	100-199
BLUE HILL CT	Travis Co	610Q	WZ-20	78736	9000-9099
BLUE HILL DR	Travis Co	581W	MA-22	78736	9600-9999
	Travis Co	580Z	WZ-22	78736	10000-10199
BLUE HILLS DR	Hays Co	638F	WU-18	78620	100-899
BLUE HOLE PARK RD	Georgetown	286C	MM-54	78626	300-599
BLUEJACK PL	Cedar Park	402D	MD-42	78613	100-199
BLUEJAY BLVD	Lago Vista	458K	WU-35	78645	21300-21899
BLUE JAY CT	Georgetown	227J	MN-59	78628	7600-7699
BLUE JAY CT	Lakeway	519J	WW-29	78734	100-199
BLUEJAY CV	Hutto	350S	MU-46	78634	100-199
BLUEJAY DR	Cedar Park	433A	ME-39	78613	2800-2899
BLUE JAY DR	Lakeway	519J	WW-29	78734	100-199
BLUE JAY LN	Travis Co	491J	MA-32	78732	3300-3499
BLUE JAY PT	Travis Co	490Y	WZ-31	78734	14500-14599
BLUE JAY ST	Hays Co	794E	MG-3	78610	100-199
BLUE JAY WAY	Round Rock	406F	ML-42	78681	800-999
BLUE LAKE CT	Lakeway	519G	WX-30	78734	100-199
BLUE LAKE CV	Lakeway	519G	WX-30	78734	100-199
BLUE LAKE DR	Lago Vista	458J	WU-35	78645	21900-21999
BLUE LILLY DR	Austin	464P	MG-35	78759	7700-7898 E
BLUELINE DR	Cedar Park	372C	MD-45	78613	600-699
	Leander	372C	MD-45	78641	700-899
BLUE MARTIN DR	Williamson Co	433R	MF-38	78750	10000-10099
BLUE MEADOW DR	Austin	674G	MH-15	78744	1900-4799
BLUE MONSTER CV	Round Rock	408C	MR-42	78664	3900-3999
BLUE MOUNTAIN PATH	Round Rock	345J	MJ-47	78681	3800-3899
BLUE OAK CIR	Cedar Park	372V	MD-43	78613	600-799
BLUE OAKS DR	Bastrop Co	742F	MY-9	78612	100-199
BLUE POND DR	Travis Co	439T	MS-37	78660	18500-18699
BLUE QUAIL DR	Austin	526A	ML-30	78758	9000-9099
BLUE QUAIL DR	Williamson Co	284D	MH-54	78628	100-199
BLUE RIDGE DR	Williamson Co	316G	MM-51	78626	100-299
BLUERIDGE CT	Austin	524A	MG-30	78731	5500-5699
BLUE RIDGE DR	Austin	526G	MM-30	78753	1100-1199

STREET NAME	CITY or COUNTY	MAPSCO GRID	AUSTIN GRID	ZIP CODE	BLOCK RANGE O/E
BLUE RIDGE DR	Cedar Park	433B	ME-39	78613	2800-2899
	Williamson Co	433B	ME-39	78613	1500-2799
BLUE RIDGE DR	Dripping Springs	666M	WR-14	78620	100-399
	Dripping Springs	667J	WS-14	78620	400-699
BLUE RIDGE DR	Round Rock	345J	MJ-47	78681	3100-3999
BLUE RIDGE DR	Travis Co	468P	MQ-35	78660	None
BLUE RIDGE PKWY N	Cedar Park	373T	ME-43	78613	100-599
BLUE RIDGE PKWY S	Cedar Park	373X	ME-43	78613	100-299
	Cedar Park	403B	ME-42	78613	300-599
BLUE RIDGE TRL	Elgin	533F	EA-30	78621	100-199
BLUE RIDGE TRL	Travis Co	583Q	MF-23	78746	100-399
BLUE SAGE DR	Cedar Park	402U	MD-40	78613	2000-2099
BLUE SKY CT	Georgetown	225H	MK-60	78633	100-199
BLUE SKY LN	Lago Vista	399L	WX-41	78645	8600-8799
BLUE SKY PL	Round Rock	378W	MQ-43	78665	3000-3099
BLUESKY WAY	Austin	644X	MG-16	78745	6400-6699
BLUE SPRING CIR	Round Rock	376S	ML-43	78681	800-999
BLUE SPRING CV	Round Rock	376S	ML-43	78681	800-899
BLUE SPRING WAY	Austin	496R	MM-32	78753	11500-11699
BLUE SPRINGS BLVD	Georgetown	316G	MM-51	78626	100-899
BLUE SPRUCE CIR	Austin	556Y	MM-25	78723	5000-5099
BLUESTAR CV	Austin	672A	MC-15	78739	10300-10399
BLUESTAR DR	Austin	672A	MC-15	78739	4900-5099
	Austin	642W	MC-16	78739	5100-5399
BLUESTEIN DR	Austin	586R	MM-23	78721	3600-3799
BLUESTEM CV	Williamson Co	193B	ME-63	78633	200-299
BLUESTEM DR	Georgetown	225P	MJ-59	78633	100-199
BLUESTEM LN	Williamson Co	193B	ME-63	78633	100-199
BLUE STEM TRL	Austin	611M	MB-20	78735	6100-6299
BLUESTONE CIR	Austin	466Y	MM-34	78758	12400-12499
BLUESTONE LN	Williamson Co	347E	MN-48	78665	4000-4099
BLUESTONE ST	Austin	674H	MH-15	78744	6600-6699
BLUE VALLEY DR	Austin	673H	MF-15	78748	400-699
BLUE WATER CIR	Austin	466U	MM-34	78758	12400-12499
BLUE WATER DR	Austin	466Y	MM-34	78758	12300-12399
BLUE WILLOW CT	Pflugerville	437M	MP-38	78660	1500-1599
BLUEWOOD LN	Austin	673K	ME-14	78748	1600-1699
BLUFF DR	Round Rock	406K	ML-41	78681	600-1899
BLUFF RD	Burnet Co	426F	WQ-39	78669	100-499
BLUFF ST	Austin	614D	MH-21	78704	1300-1399
BLUFF ST	Buda	762C	MD-6	78610	100-399
BLUFF TRL	Hays Co	700A	WY-12	78610	8000-8299
BLUFF BEND DR	Travis Co	526C	MM-30	78753	10100-10499
	Travis Co	496Z	MM-31	78753	10500-11299
BLUFF CANYON DR	Austin	497W	MN-31	78754	11100-11299
BLUFF MEADOW CV	Georgetown	287M	MP-53	78626	1000-1099
BLUFF PARK CIR	West Lake Hills	583F	ME-24	78746	100-199
BLUFF POINT BEND	Cedar Park	374L	MH-44	78613	300-499
BLUFFRIDGE CIR	Austin	495J	MJ-32	78759	4000-4099
BLUFF RIDGE CV	Lago Vista	399L	WX-41	78645	21200-21299
BLUFFRIDGE DR	Austin	495J	MJ-32	78759	4100-4299
	Austin	494M	MH-32	78759	4300-4399
BLUFF RIDGE TRL	Lago Vista	399L	WX-41	78645	8600-8799
BLUFFSIDE DR	Austin	494L	MH-32	78759	5100-5299
BLUFFSIDE LN	Williamson Co	347E	MN-48	78665	4000-4199
BLUFFS LANDING WAY	Williamson Co	347X	MN-46	78665	None
BLUFF SPRINGS RD	Travis Co	674L	MH-14	78744	6300-7499
	Travis Co	674Y	MH-13	78744	7500-9199
BLUFFSTONE CV	Austin	494L	MH-32	78759	8500-8799
BLUFFSTONE DR	Round Rock	347U	MP-46	78665	2100-2799
	Round Rock	348S	MQ-46	78665	2800-2899
BLUFFSTONE LN	Austin	494L	MH-32	78759	5300-5799
BLUFFTON CV	Travis Co	492Y	MD-31	78730	5000-5099
BLUFFTOP CIR	Round Rock	406J	ML-41	78681	1700-1799
BLUFF VIEW	Round Rock	378P	MQ-44	78664	1-99
BLUFFVIEW DR	Austin	614J	MG-20	78704	2400-2599
BLUFF VIEW RD	Cedar Park	374L	MH-44	78613	400-498 E
BLUFFWATER WAY	Travis Co	489E	WW-33	78645	None
BLUFFWOOD PL	Round Rock	408A	MQ-42	78665	1800-1899
BLUMIE ST	Austin	642R	MD-17	78745	3300-3499
BLUNTLEAF CV	Austin	493U	MF-31	78750	7300-7399
BLYTHEWOOD DR	Austin	644N	MG-17	78745	5700-6099
BMC DR	Cedar Park	403H	MF-42	78613	1200-1299
BOARDMAN LN	Travis Co	553J	ME-26	78746	1-99
BOARDWALK DR	Austin	434S	MG-37	78729	12100-12299
BOAT DOCK RD	Travis Co	459R	WX-35	78645	3700-3999
BOATWRIGHT CV	Travis Co	618R	MR-20	78725	4200-4299
BOB WAY	Austin	616C	MM-21	78721	None
BOBBY LN	Austin	673A	ME-15	78745	2700-2899
BOBBY JONES WAY	Round Rock	378T	MQ-43	78664	3800-3899
BOBBY'S CV	Williamson Co	224R	MH-59	78633	200-299
BOBCAT CV	Lago Vista	399L	WX-41	78645	8500-8599
BOBCAT DR	Williamson Co	375X	MJ-43	78681	8500-8799
BOBCAT TRL	Bastrop Co	744X	EC-7	78602	100-199
BOBCAT TRL	Williamson Co	433K	ME-38	78750	11900-12099
BOB CAT RUN	Austin	524B	MG-30	78731	4900-4999
BOB ESTES CV	Williamson Co	408C	MR-42	78664	100-199
BOB HARRISON	Austin	585Q	MK-23	78702	1200-1499
BOB JOHNSON RD	Travis Co	702Q	MD-11	78652	12800-12899
BOBOLINK DR	Williamson Co	433Q	MF-38	78750	11900-11999
BOBTAIL CV	Austin	702B	MC-12	78739	12200-12299
BOB TEMPLE	Travis Co	619S	MS-19	78725	None
BOB WAR ST	Austin	498W	MQ-31	78653	5200-5299
	Travis Co	498W	MQ-31	78653	5100-5199
BOB WENTZ PARK RD	Travis Co	461P	MA-35	78732	6300-6599
BOBWHITE CT	Round Rock	375R	MK-44	78681	1200-1299
BOB WHITE CV	Dripping Springs	667J	WS-14	78620	100-199
BOB WHITE DR	Austin	526A	ML-30	78758	1000-1099
BOB WHITE LN	Georgetown	256T	ML-55	78628	2600-2799
BOB WIRE CV	Travis Co	517D	WT-30	78669	3800-3899
BOB WIRE RD	Travis Co	517H	WT-30	78669	3700-5299
BOCA CHICA CIR	Travis Co	409T	MS-40	78660	2700-2799
BOCA CHICA DR	Cedar Park	373E	ME-45	78613	600-699
BOCA RATON DR	Pflugerville	439E	MS-39	78660	2100-2299
BOCA RIO CT	Pflugerville	409S	MS-40	78660	2100-2199
BOCK RD	Mustang Ridge	766R	MM-5	78610	9400-9999
	Mustang Ridge	767N	MN-5	78610	10000-10299
BODARK LN	Austin	643Z	MF-16	78745	900-1099
BODEGA CV	Williamson Co	377B	MN-45	78665	2000-2099
BODGERS DR	Austin	497J	MN-32	78753	900-1099
BOECHER LN	Travis Co	439R	MT-38	78634	17100-17299
BOERNE DR	Williamson Co	403W	ME-40	78613	1100-1299
BOFFI CIR	Austin	496J	ML-32	78758	1500-1599
BOGART RD	Cedar Park	373U	MF-43	78613	800-999
BOGEY CT	Austin	645W	MJ-16	78744	5200-5299
BOGGY CREEK DR	Austin	674B	MG-15	78744	1600-1899

STREET NAME	CITY or COUNTY	MAPSCO GRID	AUSTIN GRID	ZIP CODE	BLOCK RANGE O/E
BOGGY FORD RD	Lago Vista	459B	WW-36	78645	19300-20499
	Lago Vista	458G	WV-36	78645	20500-21699
BOGGY RIDGE DR	Austin	673H	MF-15	78748	8000-8199
BOHICA WAY	Cedar Park	372Q	MD-44	78613	1000-1499
BOHLS ST	Pflugerville	468A	MQ-36	78660	200-299
BOIS D'ARC LN	Cedar Park	372D	MD-45	78613	1900-2799
BOIS D'ARC RD	Manor	530G	MV-30	78653	13201-13799 O
	Manor	530G	MV-30	78653	13800-14199
	Travis Co	530G	MV-30	78653	13000-13199
	Travis Co	530G	MV-30	78653	13200-13798 E
	Travis Co	500Z	MV-31	78653	14200-14699
	Travis Co	501P	MW-32	78653	14700-15699
BOLD RULER WAY	Austin	553F	ME-27	78746	5900-6199
BOLEYNWOOD DR	Austin	643Q	MF-17	78745	6500-6799
BOLING DR	Travis Co	611X	MA-19	78736	8200-8299
BOLIVIA DR	Williamson Co	434M	MH-38	78729	13400-13599
BOLLES CIR	Austin	526J	ML-29	78753	100-199
BOLM RD	Austin	616B	ML-21	78702	4600-4999
	Austin	616C	MM-21	78721	5000-6799
BOLTON DR	Hays Co	639X	WW-16	78737	100-299
BOLTON ST	Austin	672R	MD-14	78748	2600-2799
BON AIR DR	Austin	525L	MK-29	78757	8000-8099
BONANZA	Lago Vista	429N	WW-38	78645	20500-20899
BONANZA CIR	Burnet Co	396W	WQ-40	78669	100-298 E
BONAPARTE BEND	Austin	463C	MF-36	78750	10800-10899
BONAVENTURE DR	Austin	492G	MD-33	78730	10700-10799
BOND DR	Austin	645A	MJ-18	78741	2700-3099
BONDICK RD	Cedar Park	372Q	MD-44	78613	1400-1599
BONESET TRL	Williamson Co	377B	MN-45	78665	2100-2399
BONETA CV	Austin	434Y	MH-37	78729	12300-12399
BONETA TRL	Austin	434Y	MH-37	78729	8000-8099
BONHAM LN	Travis Co	608R	WV-20	78736	11000-11699
BONHAM LOOP	Georgetown	195U	MK-61	78633	100-499
BONHAM RANCH RD	Hays Co	608E	WU-21	78620	11200-12199
	Travis Co	578W	WU-22	78620	11000-11199
BONHAM TERRACE	Austin	615J	MJ-20	78704	900-1399
BONIFACE LN	Williamson Co	434V	MH-37	78729	7100-7299
BONITA CT	Leander	342E	MC-48	78641	300-399
BONITA ST	Austin	554Y	MH-25	78703	2200-2399
BONITA VERDE DR	Leander	342P	MC-47	78641	500-1099
BONITA VISTA DR	Buda	762M	MD-5	78610	300-599
BONNELL CT	Austin	554K	MG-26	78731	3500-3599
BONNELL DR	Austin	554K	MG-26	78731	3700-3999
BONNELL VISTA CV	Austin	524T	MG-28	78731	4300-4399
BONNELL VISTA ST	Austin	524T	MG-28	78731	5600-5699
BONNER LN	Bastrop Co	715K	EE-11	78602	100-199
BONNET BLVD	Williamson Co	283L	MF-53	78628	100-299
BONNET LN	Williamson Co	196T	ML-61	78628	1-1199
BONNETT ST	Austin	616P	ML-20	78741	200-299
BONNIE DR	Dripping Springs	636X	WQ-16	78620	100-399
BONNIE LN	Round Rock	347J	MN-47	78665	3900-3999
BONNIE RD	Austin	584B	MG-24	78703	2700-3799
BONNIE BRAE	Austin	526G	MM-30	78753	1200-1399
BONNIEBROOK DR	Austin	612J	MC-20	78735	7400-7599
BONNIE ROSE	Williamson Co	225N	MJ-59	78633	100-199
BONNIEVIEW	Austin	615E	MJ-21	78704	200-299
BONNYRIGG CT	Travis Co	432G	MD-39	78613	2600-2699
BON TERRA DR	Austin	524L	MH-29	78731	6000-6399
BON WINDE RD	Williamson Co	192F	MC-63	78633	1-399
BONWOOD DR	Round Rock	406B	ML-42	78681	100-199
BOOKER AVE	Austin	556A	ML-27	78752	900-1199
BOOMER LN	Williamson Co	434R	MH-38	78729	13100-13199
BOOMER'S CIR	Bastrop Co	738L	MR-8	78617	100-199
BOONE DR	Lago Vista	459E	WW-36	78645	2800-3899
BOONE VALLEY DR	Travis Co	408P	MQ-41	78664	None
BOOTH CIR	Village of Volente	431W	MA-37	78641	15700-15799
	Village of Volente	461A	MA-36	78641	15800-15999
BOOTH ST	Taylor	353J	EA-47	76574	300-899
BOOTHHILL DR	Travis Co	672T	MC-13	78748	11200-11499
BOOTY'S CROSSING RD	Georgetown	256N	ML-56	78628	500-799
	Georgetown	255R	MK-56	78628	1700-2499
	Williamson Co	256N	ML-56	78628	800-1099
BOQUILLA TRL	Georgetown	225Z	MK-58	78628	800-999
BOQUILLAS CANYON DR	Austin	403M	MF-41	78717	14000-15099
BORAGE DR	Austin	674M	MH-14	78744	4600-4899
BORDEAUX DR	Williamson Co	343N	ME-47	78641	900-1199
BORDEAUX LN	Austin	463G	MF-36	78750	9700-9899
BORDEN RD	Austin	525N	MJ-29	78757	3100-3199
BORDEN SPRINGS CV	Williamson Co	375S	MJ-43	78717	8000-8099
BORDER ST	Jonestown	430Q	WZ-38	78645	17400-17699
BORDITT WAY	Lakeway	518M	WV-29	78738	None
BORDLEY CT	Austin	673E	ME-15	78748	9300-9399
BORDLEY DR	Austin	673E	ME-15	78748	2200-2299
BORELLO DR	Lakeway	519T	WW-28	78738	1-99
BORGER	Austin	584P	MG-23	78703	None
BORHO	Williamson Co	344Q	MH-47	78628	1-699
BORICCO LN	Travis Co	466C	MM-36	78727	2100-2199
BO'S BEND	Williamson Co	224R	MH-59	78633	100-199
BOSQUE DR	Williamson Co	350E	MU-48	78634	100-299
BOSQUE LN	Travis Co	527W	MN-28	78754	3300-3399
BOSQUE TRL	Williamson Co	226Y	MM-58	78628	700-999
BOSSWOOD DR	Austin	466L	MM-35	78727	13300-13399
BOSTON LN	Austin	613N	ME-20	78735	4500-4799
BOTANY BAY CIR	Pflugerville	468A	MQ-36	78660	700-799
BOTTLEBRUSH DR	Austin	493H	MF-33	78750	8000-8199
BOTTLE SPRINGS LN	Williamson Co	343W	ME-46	78641	17400-17599
BOULDER BLVD	Travis Co	468P	MQ-35	78660	None
BOULDER DR	Travis Co	468P	MQ-35	78660	None
BOULDER LN	Austin	462H	MD-36	78726	10200-10799
	Austin	463A	ME-36	78726	10800-10999
	Austin	433W	ME-37	78726	11000-11799
BOULDER LN	Bastrop Co	621H	MX-21	78621	100-199
BOULDER PASS	Travis Co	468P	MQ-35	78660	None
BOULDER CREEK	Austin	557T	MN-25	78724	5700-5899
BOULDER CREST DR	Pflugerville	439E	MS-39	78660	18900-19299
BOULDER HEIGHTS	Bee Cave	549K	WW-26	78738	15500-15599
BOULDER RUN	Georgetown	287K	MN-53	78626	2300-2399
BOULDIN AVE	Austin	614D	MH-21	78704	500-1799
	Austin	614L	MH-20	78704	1800-2199
BOULEWARE DR	Austin	646P	ML-17	78744	3200-3399
BOUNDLESS VALLEY DR	Austin	527C	MP-30	78754	11000-11199
BOUNTY TRL	Austin	642E	MC-18	78749	8000-8199
BOURBON ST	Austin	466K	ML-35	78727	13100-13299
BOURG CV	Austin	674H	MH-15	78744	6600-6699
BOUVET CT	Austin	465L	MK-35	78727	4400-4499
BOW CT	Austin	672U	MD-13	78748	11300-11399
BOWDITCH DR	Travis Co	523S	ME-28	78730	7100-7299

B

STREET NAME	CITY or COUNTY	MAPSCO GRID	AUSTIN GRID	ZIP CODE	BLOCK RANGE O/E
BOWER DR	Williamson Co	433B	ME-39	78613	1700-1799
BOWERTON DR	Austin	497S	MN-31	78754	1600-1899
BOWHILL DR	Austin	524U	MH-28	78731	3900-3999
BOWIE CIR	Georgetown	195U	MK-61	78633	100-199
BOWIE CV	Lago Vista	459E	WW-36	78645	20200-20399
BOWIE LN	Hutto	380N	MU-44	78634	100-199
BOWIE RD	Travis Co	552B	MC-27	78733	1100-1499
BOWIE ST	Austin	584V	MH-22	78703	300-599
BOWLIN CV	Hays Co	608E	WU-21	78620	200-299
BOWLING CT	Cedar Park	403E	ME-42	78613	600-699
BOWLING LN	Lakeway	490X	WY-31	78734	15300-15499
	Travis Co	520B	WY-30	78734	15000-15299
BOWLING GREEN DR	Austin	525C	MK-30	78757	8200-8699
BOWMAN AVE	Austin	554X	MG-25	78703	2000-3399
BOWMAN RD E	Round Rock	376M	MM-44	78664	100-1199
	Round Rock	377F	MN-45	78664	1200-1999
	Williamson Co	377F	MN-45	78664	2000-2199
BOWMAN RD W	Round Rock	376P	ML-44	78664	100-499
BOW RIDGE CV	Williamson Co	402V	MD-40	78613	1800-1899
BOW RIDGE DR	Williamson Co	402V	MD-40	78613	1700-1799
BOWSTRING CV	Austin	613E	ME-21	78735	4200-4299
BOWSTRING BEND	Bastrop	744K	EC-8	78602	100-199
BOWSTRING BEND	Cedar Park	374Q	MH-44	78613	3900-3999
BOX CANYON TERRACE	Williamson Co	375U	MK-43	78681	17700-17999
BOXCAR RUN	Austin	643R	MF-17	78745	6000-6299
BOXDALE DR	Austin	525B	MJ-30	78757	3000-3199
BOXELDER CV	Travis Co	582J	MC-23	78735	8500-8599
BOXWOOD CT	Austin	643L	MF-17	78745	1900-1999
BOXWOOD LOOP	Georgetown	225V	MK-58	78628	1000-1199
BOXWOOD PATH	Round Rock	407B	MN-42	78664	2000-2299
BOYCE LN	Austin	528B	MQ-30	78653	5900-6499
	Travis Co	528G	MR-30	78653	6500-7599
	Travis Co	529N	MS-29	78653	9500-9699
BOYCE ST E	Manor	529U	MT-28	78653	100-599
BOYCE ST W	Manor	529U	MT-28	78653	100-399
BOYD LN	Travis Co	550C	WZ-27	78732	1600-1799
BOYDS WAY	Austin	672Z	MD-13	78748	2000-2299
BOYER BLVD	Austin	495R	MK-32	78758	10500-10599
BOYER CT	Austin	495R	MK-32	78758	10500-10599
BOYER DR	Taylor	322Y	MZ-49	76574	2100-2298 E
BOYLE DR	Austin	557U	MP-25	78724	7000-7299
BOYSENBERRY LN	Pflugerville	438Y	MR-37	78660	1401-1599 O
BRACKEN CT	Austin	524D	MH-30	78731	7900-7999
BRACKENRIDGE ST	Austin	615N	MJ-20	78704	1500-2099
	Austin	614R	MH-20	78704	2100-2199
BRAD DR	Travis Co	436U	MM-37	78728	2700-2799
BRADBURY LN	Austin	497B	MN-33	78753	1100-1699
BRADDOCK LN	Round Rock	376K	ML-44	78664	200-299
BRADEL CV	Austin	433W	ME-37	78726	10600-10699
BRADENTON CT	Village of the Hills	519T	WW-28	78738	1-99
BRADFIELD DR	Buda	733W	ME-7	78610	100-499
BRADFORD DR	Austin	525H	MK-30	78758	8500-8599
BRADFORD ST	Hays Co	763J	ME-5	78610	100-199
BRADFORD EDWARD CV	Austin	495S	MJ-31	78759	8300-8399
BRADFORD PARK	Round Rock	408J	MQ-41	78664	3000-3299
BRADLEY CV	Lago Vista	459E	WW-36	78645	20300-20399
BRADLEY DR	Austin	556L	MM-26	78723	6500-6699
BRADLEY LN	Round Rock	377E	MN-45	78664	2400-2599
	Round Rock	376H	MM-45	78664	2600-2699
BRADLEY RANCH RD	Leander	283X	ME-52	78628	1-599
BRADLEY RIDGE LN	Travis Co	704G	MH-12	78747	None
BRADMORE DR	Round Rock	376L	MM-44	78664	1800-1999
BRADNER DR	Austin	672D	MD-15	78748	9200-9499
BRADSHAW DR	Hays Co	669B	WW-15	78737	100-299
BRADSHAW RD	Austin	704P	MG-11	78747	10600-11299
	Travis Co	704P	MG-11	78747	10000-10599
	Travis Co	704X	MG-10	78747	11300-11699
	Travis Co	734B	MG-9	78747	11700-12499
BRADSHER DR	Austin	644S	MG-16	78745	6400-6599
BRADWOOD RD	Austin	555Z	MK-25	78722	1300-4299
BRADY LN	Austin	584N	MG-23	78746	None
	West Lake Hills	584N	MG-23	78746	400-499
BRADY PASS	Hays Co	668F	WU-15	78620	100-399
BRAEBURN GLEN ST	Williamson Co	434F	MG-39	78729	9300-9699
BRAEMAR CV	Austin	704E	MG-12	78747	2400-2599
BRAEMAR DR	Austin	704E	MG-12	78747	10200-10299
BRAESGATE CV	Williamson Co	405E	MJ-42	78717	9000-9099
BRAESGATE DR	Williamson Co	405E	MJ-42	78717	15900-16299
BRAESGREEN DR	Round Rock	376M	MM-44	78664	700-899
BRAES RIDGE DR	Austin	556J	ML-26	78723	1400-1599
BRAES VALLEY ST	Williamson Co	434B	MG-39	78729	9500-9799
BRAESWOOD RD	Austin	614Z	MH-19	78704	200-399
BRAEWOOD DR	Austin	496A	ML-33	78758	11900-11999
BRAHMA TRL	Lago Vista	399Q	WX-41	78645	None
BRAIDED ROPE DR	Austin	466U	MM-34	78727	1300-1599
BRAKER LN E	Austin	496V	MM-31	78753	100-799
	Austin	497S	MN-31	78754	1400-1999
	Austin	527D	MP-30	78754	3400-3599
	Austin	528T	MQ-28	78754	6900-7099
	Travis Co	496V	MM-31	78753	800-1399
BRAKER LN W	Austin	496Q	MM-32	78753	100-799
	Austin	496J	ML-32	78758	800-1999
	Austin	495G	ML-33	78758	2000-3499
	Austin	495A	MJ-33	78759	3500-4999
BRAM CV	Round Rock	345N	MJ-47	78681	3800-3899
BRAMBER LN	Austin	528K	MQ-29	78754	6500-6799
BRAMBLE DR	Austin	644P	MG-17	78745	300-699
BRAMBLE DR	Cedar Park	373Y	MF-43	78613	300-399
BRAMBLE BUSH CIR	Lago Vista	399Q	WX-41	78645	8300-8399
BRAMBLE BUSH DR	Austin	675W	MJ-13	78747	7900-8199
BRAMBLECREST DR	Austin	433X	ME-37	78726	10600-10699
	Austin	463B	ME-36	78726	10700-10799
BRAMBLEWOOD CIR	Austin	524D	MH-30	78731	7700-7799
BRAMHALL DR	Austin	404L	MH-41	78717	15300-15399
BRANCH ST	Austin	585T	MJ-22	78702	1100-1199
BRANCH ST	Taylor	353E	EA-48	76574	100-599
BRANCHING OAK CT	Austin	464L	MH-35	78759	6600-6699
BRANCH LIGHT LN	Travis Co	529H	MT-30	78653	None
BRANCHWOOD DR	Austin	674H	MH-15	78744	6500-6999
BRANDI CT	Austin	494V	MH-31	78759	4000-4099
BRANDI LN	Round Rock	376S	ML-43	78681	1400-1699
BRANDING CHASE	Austin	465K	MJ-35	78727	5100-5499
BRANDING IRON	Lago Vista	429S	WW-37	78645	20600-20799
BRANDING IRON CV	Georgetown	225C	MK-60	78633	100-199
BRANDING IRON LN	Leander	372B	MC-45	78641	2400-2699
BRANDING IRON PASS	Travis Co	490U	WZ-31	78734	14600-14899

STREET NAME	CITY or COUNTY	MAPSCO GRID	AUSTIN GRID	ZIP CODE	BLOCK RANGE O/E
BRANDING IRON TRL	Pflugerville	467C	MP-36	78660	None
BRANDON WAY	Travis Co	552F	MC-27	78733	100-799
BRANDON KELLER CT	Pflugerville	408Z	MR-40	78660	None
BRANDON PARKE TRL	Williamson Co	433P	ME-38	78750	11500-11699
BRANDT DR	Austin	646D	MM-18	78742	1300-1599
BRANDT RD	Austin	674X	MG-13	78744	1800-2499
	Travis Co	674X	MG-13	78747	2500-4599
BRANDTS WOOD ST	Austin	674X	MG-13	78744	9200-9499
BRANDY LN	Georgetown	256P	ML-56	78628	2800-3099
BRANDYWINE CIR	Austin	463C	MF-36	78750	9800-10099
BRANDYWINE CT	Austin	466P	ML-35	78727	12500-12599
BRANDYWINE DR	Bastrop Co	709G	MT-12	78612	None
BRANDYWINE LN	Austin	466P	ML-35	78727	2100-2199
BRANGUS RD	Williamson Co	226Q	MM-59	78628	3000-3899
BRANIGAN LN	Austin	495W	MJ-31	78759	3600-3799
BRANNON CV	Austin	464U	MH-34	78759	10500-10599
BRANSFORD CV	Austin	497G	MP-33	78753	12700-12799
BRANSTON DR	Austin	497K	MN-32	78753	12200-12299
BRANT DR	Williamson Co	224L	MH-59	78633	100-299
BRANTLEY CV	Austin	672M	MD-14	78748	10200-10299
BRANTLEY BEND	Austin	672M	MD-14	78748	10000-10299
BRANUM CV	Cedar Park	372J	MC-44	78613	2100-2199
BRANUM DR	Cedar Park	372J	MC-44	78613	2400-2499
BRASADA LN	Travis Co	427H	WT-39	78654	3100-5199
	Travis Co	428A	WU-39	78654	5200-5599
BRASHEAR LN	Cedar Park	372Q	MD-44	78613	1000-1299
BRASHER DR	Austin	672M	MD-14	78748	9800-9999
BRASS ST	Austin	586W	ML-22	78702	900-1199
BRASS BUTTONS TRL	Travis Co	490M	WZ-32	78734	2800-3299
BRASSIE ST	Austin	616W	ML-19	78741	1600-1999
BRASSIEWOOD DR	Austin	674H	MH-15	78744	4600-4799
	Austin	675E	MJ-15	78744	4800-5199
BRATTON LN	Travis Co	436Q	MM-38	78728	14700-16799
BRATTON HEIGHTS DR	Travis Co	436G	MM-39	78728	3200-3799
BRATTON RIDGE CROSSING	Travis Co	436G	MM-39	78728	3200-3699
BRAXTON CV	Austin	615X	MJ-19	78741	2400-2499
BRAXTON VALLEY CV	Austin	497W	MN-31	78754	1500-1599
BRAYDEN CV	Georgetown	286Z	MM-52	78626	1000-1099
BRAYLEN CV	Austin	673V	MF-13	78748	300-399
BRAYTON PARK DR	Austin	375W	MJ-43	78717	16600-16999
BRAZIL DR	Cedar Park	372C	MD-45	78613	600-699
BRAZOS DR	Williamson Co	255M	MK-56	78628	100-499
BRAZOS DR	Williamson Co	349H	MT-48	78634	100-199
	Williamson Co	350E	MU-48	78634	None
BRAZOS ST	Austin	585S	MJ-22	78701	1-1099
	Austin	585P	MJ-23	78701	1200-1499
	Austin	585K	MJ-23	78701	1700-1899
BRAZOS BEND DR	Cedar Park	373E	ME-45	78613	500-899
BREA DR	Austin	641W	MA-16	78739	7400-7499
BREAKAWAY RD	Cedar Park	374N	MG-44	78613	100-199
	Williamson Co	374S	MG-43	78613	200-1399
BREAKWATER DR	Jonestown	430X	WY-37	78645	17400-17499
BREAUX LN	Round Rock	407X	MN-40	78664	1900-1999
BRECCIA CV	Hays Co	763S	ME-4	78610	100-199
BRECKENRIDGE ST	Georgetown	195V	MK-61	78633	100-199
BRECON LN	Austin	673G	MF-15	78748	1100-1199
BRECOURT MANOR WAY	Austin	641W	MA-16	78739	7300-7699
BREED RD	Hays Co	636B	WQ-18	78620	100-199
BREEDLOVE CT	Austin	586P	ML-23	78721	3300-3399
BREEDS CV	Lago Vista	459J	WW-35	78645	20100-20199
BREEDS HILL DR	Travis Co	527T	MN-28	78754	4600-4699
BREEZE WAY	Austin	556Q	MM-26	78723	6200-6299
	Jonestown	400X	WY-40	78645	8400-8499
	Travis Co	430A	WY-39	78645	8100-8399
BREEZE HOLLOW	Austin	615T	MJ-19	78741	2000-2099
BREEZEKNOLL CIR	Austin	583Z	MF-22	78746	1500-1599
BREEZE POINT CV	Austin	494G	MH-33	78759	9100-9199
BREEZE TERRACE	Austin	585H	MK-24	78722	2800-3299
BREEZEWAY LN	Georgetown	195P	MJ-62	78633	100-799
BREEZEWOOD DR	Austin	644P	MG-17	78745	5700-5999
BREEZY CT	Round Rock	407J	MN-41	78664	1500-1799
BREEZY CV	Round Rock	407J	MN-41	78664	1600-1699
BREEZY PASS	Austin	611Z	MB-19	78749	6600-6999
BREEZY HILL DR	Travis Co	557Q	MP-26	78724	6600-6999
BREEZY MEADOW LN	Travis Co	529H	MT-30	78653	13400-13499
BREEZY PASS CV	Austin	611Z	MB-19	78749	7200-7299
BREEZY POINT CV	Round Rock	347V	MP-46	78665	2700-2799
BREMEN ST	Austin	584C	MH-24	78703	1800-2099
BREMNER DR	Austin	642X	MC-16	78749	4400-4599
BRENDA DR	Austin	525Z	MK-28	78752	6700-6999
BRENDA LN	Williamson Co	347Y	MP-46	78665	1-99
	Williamson Co	377C	MP-45	78665	None
BRENDA ST	Travis Co	436R	MM-38	78728	15200-15799
BRENDON LEE LN	Georgetown	286D	MM-54	78626	1000-1299
BRENHAM ST	Manor	529U	MT-28	78653	100-15199
BRENHAM ST E	Elgin	534N	EC-29	78621	None
BRENHAM ST E	Manor	529Y	MT-28	78653	100-599
BRENHAM ST W	Elgin	533V	EB-28	78621	None
	Elgin	534N	EC-29	78621	None
BRENT KNOLL DR	Travis Co	439F	MS-39	78660	19400-19599
BRENT'S CV	Bastrop Co	738G	MR-9	78617	100-199
BRENTS ELM DR	Austin	674X	MG-13	78744	9200-9499
BRENTWOOD DR	Georgetown	226G	MM-60	78628	100-299
BRENTWOOD DR	Leander	342R	MD-47	78641	100-1999
BRENTWOOD ST	Austin	525Y	MK-28	78757	300-799
	Austin	525T	MJ-28	78757	800-2099
BRENTWOOD ST	Round Rock	376X	ML-43	78681	300-499
BRET LN	Austin	616B	ML-21	78721	900-999
BRETT CV	Rollingwood	584J	MG-23	78746	1-99
BRETTON WOODS DR	Cedar Park	373Y	MF-43	78613	1000-1099
BRETTONWOODS LN	Austin	526T	ML-28	78753	8100-8299
BREUER ST	Austin	467U	MP-34	78660	1100-1199
BREWER CV	Lago Vista	429B	WW-39	78645	6800-6899
BREWER LN	Lago Vista	429F	WW-39	78645	21000-21199
BREWER BLACKBIRD DR	Travis Co	438N	MQ-38	78660	16700-17099
BREWERS PL	Taylor	322U	MZ-49	76574	1900-2299
BREWSTER ST	Austin	614V	MH-19	78704	200-299
BREYFOGLE TRL	Austin	673B	ME-15	78745	1900-1999
BRIAN CIR	Williamson Co	318E	MQ-51	78626	100-199
BRIANA SHAY DR	Austin	466B	ML-36	78727	2600-2699
BRIANNA CT	Cedar Park	402D	MD-42	78613	1300-1399
BRIANS MEADOW CV	Austin	583U	MF-22	78746	1300-1399
BRIAN WOOD CT	Cedar Park	433E	ME-39	78613	2900-2999
BRIAN WOOD DR	Cedar Park	433A	ME-39	78613	1300-1499
BRIAR CV	Cedar Park	372H	MD-45	78613	2000-2199
BRIAR ST	Austin	614L	MH-20	78704	1700-1799

STREET NAME	CITY or COUNTY	MAPSCO GRID	AUSTIN GRID	ZIP CODE	BLOCK RANGE O/E
BRIARCLIFF BLVD	Austin	556K	ML-26	78723	1300-1999
BRIARCLIFF CV	Briarcliff	458N	WU-35	78669	21800-21899
BRIARCLIFF DR	Briarcliff	457R	WT-35	78669	21600-21699
	Briarcliff	458N	WU-35	78669	21700-21899
	Briarcliff	487D	WT-33	78669	21900-21999
BRIARCREEK LOOP	Travis Co	560J	MU-26	78653	11300-14499
BRIARCREST CT	Georgetown	227E	MP-60	78628	30100-30199
BRIARCREST DR	Austin	614A	MG-21	78704	2600-2699
BRIARCREST DR	Georgetown	227J	MN-59	78628	29000-30399
BRIARDALE DR	Austin	525D	MK-30	78758	8900-9099
BRIARDEN DR	Austin	524D	MH-30	78731	7500-7599
BRIAR FOREST DR	Bastrop	746S	EG-7	78602	100-199
	Bastrop Co	745V	EF-7	78602	200-299
BRIARGATE DR	Austin	467X	MN-34	78753	1000-1299
BRIARGROVE DR	Austin	614B	MG-21	78704	2400-2599
BRIAR HILL DR	Austin	615T	MJ-19	78741	1800-1899
BRIAR HILL DR	Georgetown	287K	MN-53	78626	1400-1699
BRIAR HOLLOW DR	Williamson Co	434F	MG-39	78729	13100-13499
	Williamson Co	434B	MG-39	78729	13400-13699
BRIAR OAK LN	Round Rock	375C	MK-45	78681	3000-3199
BRIARPATCH CT	Hays Co	669N	WW-14	78737	100-199
BRIAR PATCH CV	Georgetown	225L	MK-59	78633	100-199
BRIARPATCH DR	Austin	466X	ML-34	78758	1700-1799
BRIAR RIDGE DR	Austin	673J	ME-14	78748	9800-9899
BRIARSTONE DR	Buda	763E	ME-6	78610	200-399
BRIARTON DR	Austin	675X	MJ-13	78747	7900-8099
BRIARTON DR	Round Rock	407G	MP-42	78665	1700-1799
BRIARTON LN	Round Rock	407G	MP-42	78665	1800N-1899N
	Round Rock	407G	MP-42	78665	1700S-1799S
BRIARVIEW DR	Briarcliff	457V	WT-34	78669	22300-22499
BRIARWICK DR	Williamson Co	404Y	MH-40	78729	13400-13599
	Williamson Co	434C	MH-39	78729	13600-13799
BRIAR WOOD CIR	Lago Vista	399Q	WX-41	78645	8400-8499
BRIARWOOD DR	Cedar Park	373U	MF-43	78613	100-199
BRIARWOOD DR	Georgetown	256F	ML-57	78628	100-299
BRIARWOOD DR	Leander	341H	MB-48	78641	200-399
BRIARWOOD LN	Austin	525B	MJ-30	78757	8000-8499
BRIARWOOD ST	Round Rock	376X	ML-43	78681	300-499
BRIARWOOD TRL	Travis Co	583L	MF-23	78746	300-399
BRICK LN	Austin	615W	MJ-19	78741	1800-1899
BRICKFORD CV	Austin	643K	ME-17	78745	2600-2699
BRICKLEBUSH CV	Austin	493M	MF-32	78750	7900-7999
BRIDAL PATH	Cedar Park	372T	MC-43	78613	2000-2199
BRIDAL PATH CV	Cedar Park	372P	MC-44	78613	1500-1599
BRIDAL PATH DR	Lago Vista	429S	WW-37	78645	20600-20799
BRIDGE ST	Georgetown	286L	MM-53	78626	700-999
	Georgetown	286Q	MM-53	78626	1700-1899
BRIDGE HILL CV	Austin	523U	MF-28	78746	6700-6799
BRIDGE POINT PKWY	Austin	523M	MF-29	78730	6000-6599
	Austin	523C	MF-30	78730	7400-7499
	Travis Co	523C	MF-30	78730	7300-7399
BRIDGEPORT DR	Austin	526E	ML-30	78758	8600-8899
BRIDGERFARMER BLVD	Travis Co	439Q	MT-38	78634	16600-17899
BRIDGETOWN DR	Austin	526T	ML-28	78753	8300-8499
BRIDGEWATER CV	Austin	557S	MN-25	78723	6500-6599
BRIDGEWATER DR	Austin	557S	MN-25	78723	6400-6499
BRIDGEWAY CT	Austin	614P	MG-20	78704	2600-2699
BRIDGEWAY DR	Austin	614P	MG-20	78704	1400-1799
BRIDGEWOOD TRL	Williamson Co	434K	MG-38	78729	8900-9099
BRIDIE PATH	Travis Co	439F	MS-39	78660	19200-19299
BRIDLE PATH	Austin	584B	MG-24	78703	2000-3599
	Austin	554W	MG-25	78703	3600-3799
BRIDLE PATH	Hays Co	795K	MJ-2	78610	100-199
BRIDLE PATH	Hays Co	577N	WS-23	78620	400-499
BRIDLEWOOD DR	Austin	465D	MK-36	78727	4400-4699
BRIDLINGTON CIR	Austin	643F	ME-18	78745	6100-6299
BRIENNE DR	Williamson Co	405C	MK-42	78681	8000-8099
BRIGADOON CV	Austin	463H	MF-36	78750	9200-9299
BRIGADOON LN	Austin	465Q	MK-35	78727	12200-12399
BRIGGS DR	Travis Co	703J	ME-11	78652	900-1199
BRIGHAM CT	Travis Co	491T	MA-31	78732	3100-3199
BRIGHAM DR	Travis Co	491T	MA-31	78732	12900-13099
BRIGHT CV	Travis Co	518C	WV-30	78669	2200-2298 E
BRIGHTEN BEND LN	Williamson Co	403W	ME-40	78613	900-1599
BRIGHT LEAF TRL	Georgetown	195K	MJ-62	78633	100-499
BRIGHT LEAF TERRACE	Austin	673W	ME-13	78748	11100-11299
BRIGHTLING LN	Austin	463G	MF-36	78750	9900-10199
BRIGHTMAN LN	Travis Co	552L	MD-26	78733	7800-7999
BRIGHTON CIR	Austin	526L	MM-29	78753	1400-1499
BRIGHTON LN	Austin	526M	MM-29	78753	1400-1499
BRIGHTON LN	Hays Co	639Y	WX-16	78737	100-299
BRIGHTON PL	Round Rock	377L	MP-44	78665	900-1099
BRIGHTON RD	Austin	644E	MG-18	78745	4800-5099
BRIGHTSIDE ST	Williamson Co	434N	MG-38	78729	12600-12699
BRIGHT SKY OVERLOOK	Travis Co	521J	MA-29	78732	12500-12799
	Travis Co	521E	MA-30	78732	12800-13399
BRIGHT STAR LN	Travis Co	611J	MA-20	78736	6700-7199
BRIGHTWATER BLVD	Williamson Co	375U	MK-43	78681	8200-9099
BRIGHTWOOD DR	Austin	583U	MF-22	78746	3100-3199
BRIGSTOCK DR	Austin	497J	MN-32	78753	1200-1299
BRILEY ST	Georgetown	226W	ML-58	78628	1000-1099
BRIMFIELD CT	Austin	463B	ME-36	78726	10500-10599
BRIMFIELD DR	Austin	463B	ME-36	78726	10100-10499
BRIMSTONE LN	Williamson Co	405A	MJ-42	78717	9000-9199
BRINDISI WAY	Travis Co	432L	MD-38	78613	2700-2799
BRINER PASS	Travis Co	551Y	MB-25	78733	2800-2899
BRINKLEY DR	Cedar Park	372Q	MD-44	78613	1100-1199
BRINWOOD AVE	Austin	614U	MH-19	78704	2800-3199
BRIONA WOOD LN	Travis Co	432H	MD-39	78613	2900-3099
BRISBANE RD	Austin	643T	ME-16	78745	2600-2699
BRISCOE CV	Hutto	379G	MT-45	78634	1100-1199
BRISTA WAY	Austin	463A	ME-36	78726	11100-11299
BRISTLECONE LN	Austin	464L	MH-35	78759	11600-11699
BRISTLE OAK TRL	Travis Co	433P	ME-38	78750	11400-11499
	Williamson Co	433P	ME-38	78750	11300-11399
BRISTLEWOOD CV	Cedar Park	403J	ME-41	78613	600-799
BRISTLEWOOD CV	Travis Co	521L	MB-29	78732	11900-11999
BRISTOL CIR	Austin	556Q	MM-26	78723	6300-6399
BRISTOL DR	Austin	556L	MM-26	78723	2100-2299
	Austin	556Q	MM-26	78723	2600-2799
BRISTOL RD	Buda	733W	ME-7	78610	200-299
BRISTOL PARK CT	Austin	587F	MN-24	78724	7000-7199
BRISTOL RIDGE CT	Austin	463E	ME-36	78726	10900-10999
BRITANNIA BLVD	Georgetown	287S	MN-52	78626	100-199
BRITTANY BLVD	Austin	643H	MF-18	78745	1700-1899
BRITTANY LN	Bastrop Co	744Z	ED-7	78602	100-199
BRITTANY POINT LN	Travis Co	550L	WZ-26	78733	2900-3099

STREET NAME	CITY or COUNTY	MAPSCO GRID	AUSTIN GRID	ZIP CODE	BLOCK RANGE O/E
BRITTA OLSON RD	Travis Co	471J	MW-35	78653	12000-12999
	Travis Co	470M	MV-35	78653	None
BRITTLYNS CT	Austin	492Q	MD-32	78730	5700-5899
BRITTWAY LN	Cedar Park	372J	MC-44	78613	2200-2399
BRIXEY CV	Austin	497W	MN-31	78754	1400-1499
BRIXEY LN	Austin	497W	MN-31	78754	11300-11399
BRIXHAM CV	Austin	497J	MN-32	78753	1400-1499
BROAD ST N	Williamson Co	443L	EB-38	78615	100-599
BROAD ST S	Williamson Co	443L	EB-38	78615	100-599
BROADBAY CV	Austin	374Z	MH-43	78717	9700-9799
BROADBAY DR	Austin	374Z	MH-43	78717	16400-16599
BROAD BROOK DR	Austin	705B	MJ-12	78747	6700-6999
BROADE ST E	Leander	312Y	MD-49	78641	100-299
	See.. RM Rd 2243				
BROADE ST W	Leander	312X	MC-49	78641	100-599
	See.. RM Rd 2243				
BROADHILL DR	Austin	586H	MM-24	78723	4600-4999
BROAD LEAF CV	Williamson Co	433K	ME-38	78750	11900-11999
BROADMEADE AVE	Williamson Co	434K	MG-38	78729	12800-13599
BROADMOOR DR	Austin	556S	ML-25	78723	1200-1899
BROAD OAKS DR	Austin	464L	MH-35	78759	11600-11999
BROAD PEAK RD	Georgetown	317F	MN-51	78626	400-499
BROADVIEW ST	Austin	556E	ML-27	78723	1000-1099
BROAD VISTA CT	Georgetown	286W	ML-52	78628	100-199
BROADWAY ST	Austin	615H	MK-21	78702	100-499
BROCK CIR	Austin	673B	ME-15	78745	8500-8699
BROCK CV	Hutto	379C	MT-45	78634	100-199
BROCKMAN LN	Travis Co	674T	MG-13	78744	2000-2299
BROCKMAN ST	Austin	525F	MJ-30	78757	7900-8099
BROCKTON DR	Austin	495G	MK-33	78758	2500-2699
BRODICK DR	Austin	404G	MH-42	78717	15400-15599
BRODIE LN	Austin	643J	ME-17	78745	6500-7299
	Austin	642R	MD-17	78745	7300-8799
	Austin	642Y	MD-16	78748	8800-9299
	Austin	672C	MD-15	78748	9300-10899
	Austin	702B	MC-12	78748	11900-12699
	Sunset Valley	613X	ME-19	78745	5000-5299
	Sunset Valley	643J	ME-17	78745	5301-6499 O
	Travis Co	643J	ME-17	78745	5300-6498 E
	Travis Co	672T	MC-13	78748	10900-11899
BRODIE ST	Austin	614L	MH-20	78704	1000-1099
BRODIE SPRINGS TRL	Austin	672L	MD-14	78748	10400-10599
BROKEN ARROW	Lago Vista	429N	WW-38	78645	20700-20999
BROKEN ARROW DR	Cedar Park	374L	MH-44	78613	200-299
BROKEN ARROW LN	Austin	674A	MG-15	78745	7200-7499
BROKEN BOW CV	Lago Vista	429A	WW-39	78645	21300-21499
BROKEN BOW DR	Round Rock	406Q	MM-41	78681	600-899
BROKEN BOW PASS	Austin	643D	MF-18	78745	4800-5099
BROKEN BOW TRL	Travis Co	490M	WZ-32	78734	14500-15099
BROKEN BRANCH DR	Williamson Co	375Y	MK-43	78681	8000-8399
BROKEN BROOK CV	Austin	433X	ME-37	78726	10800-10899
BROKEN FEATHER TRL	Pflugerville	437Y	MP-37	78660	500-799
	Pflugerville	467C	MP-36	78660	800-899
BROKEN LANCE DR	Dripping Springs	636P	WQ-17	78620	100-799
BROKEN LANCE DR	Travis Co	641B	MA-18	78737	7800-7899
BROKEN OAK DR	Austin	643T	ME-16	78745	2400-2699
BROKENSHOE CV	Round Rock	375M	MK-44	78681	1800-1899
BROKENSHOE DR	Round Rock	375R	MK-44	78681	1700-1799
BROKEN SHOE TRL	Williamson Co	433Q	MF-38	78750	10400-10499
BROKEN SPOKE TRL	Austin	644Z	MH-16	78744	5900-6199
BROKEN SPOKE TRL	Georgetown	256K	ML-56	78628	3200-3499
BROKEN TRACE CT	Williamson Co	346L	MM-47	78665	800-899
BROMLEY DR	Austin	464K	MG-35	78759	7800-7899
BROMPTON CIR	Austin	644J	MG-17	78745	5400-5499
BROMSGROVE DR	Austin	404M	MH-41	78717	9500-9599
BRONC DR	Travis Co	464J	MG-35	78759	8200-8299
BRONCO CIR	Georgetown	226E	ML-60	78633	100-199
BRONCO CIR	Mustang Ridge	766N	ML-5	78610	11900-12099
BRONCO CT	Mustang Ridge	765V	MK-4	78610	100-7099
BRONCO CV	Lago Vista	399L	WX-41	78645	21300-21399
BRONCO DR	Georgetown	226E	ML-60	78633	100-199
BRONCO LN	Lago Vista	399Y	WX-40	78645	7800-8699
BRONCO BEND LOOP	Austin	646T	ML-16	78744	3500-4099
BRONCO BUSTER TRL	Lago Vista	399Q	WX-41	78645	8400-8599
BRONTE DR	Austin	556C	MM-27	78752	2100-2199
BRONZE LN	Williamson Co	281J	MA-53	78641	100-199
BRONZEWOOD DR	Travis Co	610T	WY-19	78736	9500-9699
BROOK CV	Hays Co	763Y	MF-4	78610	None
BROOK WAY	Cedar Park	402M	MD-41	78613	1400-1499
BROOK BEND	Cedar Park	402M	MD-41	78613	800-899
BROOK CREEK CV	Austin	645X	MJ-16	78744	4800-4899
BROOK CREST RD	Austin	645X	MJ-16	78744	4700-4999
BROOKDALE LN	Austin	556X	ML-25	78723	5100-5399
BROOKE ST	Hutto	379L	MT-44	78634	100-299
BROOKE ANN LN	Travis Co	437K	MN-38	78660	16600-16699
BROOKFIELD CV	Cedar Park	372P	MC-44	78613	1900-1999
BROOKFIELD DR	Austin	525H	MK-30	78758	8500-8899
BROOKHAVEN DR	Austin	614A	MG-21	78704	1700-1899
BROOKHAVEN TRL	Travis Co	583M	MF-23	78746	400-699
BROOKHILL DR	Austin	643G	MF-18	78745	2000-2399
BROOK HOLLOW	Cedar Park	372H	MD-45	78613	2000-2199
BROOKHOLLOW CV	Austin	556C	MM-27	78752	7600-7699
BROOKHOLLOW DR	Austin	556G	MM-27	78752	7300-7599
BROOKHOLLOW DR	Bastrop Co	745V	EF-7	78602	100-199
BROOKHOLLOW DR	Pflugerville	438N	MQ-38	78660	400-1099
BROOKHOLLOW TERRACE					
	Georgetown	287K	MN-53	78626	2300-2499
BROOKHURST CV	Travis Co	552F	MC-27	78733	9100-9199
BROOKLYN ST	Austin	615N	MJ-20	78704	2100-2199
BROOK MEADOW CV	Georgetown	287M	MP-53	78626	900-999
BROOK MEADOW TRL	Cedar Park	402M	MD-41	78613	800-999
BROOKS CIR	Georgetown	195U	MK-61	78633	100-199
BROOKS LN	Bastrop Co	743R	EB-8	78602	100-199
BROOKS HOLLOW DR	Lakeway	489Q	WX-32	78734	100-799
	Travis Co	489Q	WX-32	78734	800-1299
BROOKSIDE CT	Round Rock	375V	MK-43	78681	900-999
BROOKSIDE CV	Cedar Park	402H	MD-42	78613	1100-1199
BROOKSIDE DR	Austin	556K	ML-26	78723	6200-6499
BROOKSIDE PASS	Cedar Park	403E	ME-42	78613	500-899
BROOKSIDE ST	Dripping Springs	636V	WR-16	78620	100-499
BROOKSTONE CT	Round Rock	375Z	MK-43	78681	500-598 E
BROOKSWOOD AVE	Austin	586X	ML-22	78721	1100-1199
BROOK VALLEY CIR	Austin	557T	MN-25	78724	7000-7099
BROOK VALLEY DR	Austin	557T	MN-25	78724	5700-5899
BROOK VIEW CT	Williamson Co	346M	MM-47	78665	4000-4099
BROOKVIEW RD	Austin	585D	MK-24	78722	3800-4399
BROOKWOOD CIR	Austin	434W	MG-37	78750	11900-11999
BROOKWOOD CIR	Taylor	322V	MZ-49	76574	700-799
BROOKWOOD CV	Austin	434S	MG-37	78750	11900-11999
BROOKWOOD RD	Austin	434W	MG-37	78750	11700-11999
BROOMFLOWER DR	Austin	672A	MC-15	78739	10200-10399
BROPHY DR	Pflugerville	438P	MQ-38	78660	1200-1299
BROTEN ST	Austin	702H	MD-12	78748	12000-12299
BROUGHAM WAY	Austin	498W	MQ-31	78653	5600-5799
BROUGHTON CT	Austin	466K	ML-35	78727	2200-2399
BROUGHTON WAY	Austin	466K	ML-35	78727	12800-13199
BROWN DR	Pflugerville	467D	MP-36	78660	600-1199
BROWN LN	Austin	526R	MM-29	78754	9000-9599
	Travis Co	526M	MM-29	78754	9600-9999
BROWN LN	Bastrop Co	740J	MU-8	78612	100-199
BROWN ST	Elgin	534X	EC-28	78621	100-299
BROWN ST	Hutto	349H	MT-48	78634	100-399
BROWN ST N	Round Rock	376Y	MM-43	78664	100-399
BROWN ST S	Round Rock	406C	MM-42	78664	100-299
BROWN BARK PL	Austin	465P	MJ-35	78727	4500-4699
BROWN BEAR LN	Travis Co	702L	MD-11	78652	1500-1799
BROWN BLUFF CIR	Travis Co	341T	MA-46	78641	14800-15099
BROWN CEMETERY RD	Travis Co	590V	MV-22	78653	7800-8299
BROWNIE DR	Austin	526C	MM-30	78753	10000-10199
	Austin	496Y	MM-31	78753	10200-10799
BROWNING CV	Lago Vista	399L	WX-41	78645	8700-8799
BROWNING DR	Austin	556G	MM-27	78752	1900-2099
BROWNING DR	Bastrop	744P	EC-8	78602	None
BROWNING ST E	Manor	529Q	MT-29	78653	100-799
BROWNING ST W	Manor	529Q	MT-29	78653	100-399
BROWNLEE CIR	Austin	584R	MH-23	78703	700-799
BROWN PHEASANT CIR	Austin	496E	ML-33	78758	11500-11599
BROWN ROCK TRL	Austin	642E	MC-18	78749	5800-6099
BROWNSBORO CT	Manor	529T	MS-28	78653	11300-11399
BROWNSTONE CV	Round Rock	345N	MJ-47	78681	3700-3899
BROWNSTONE LN	Cedar Park	372T	MC-43	78613	2300-2399
BROWNWOOD CT	Austin	524A	MG-30	78731	6500-6599
BROWNWOOD DR	Austin	525A	MJ-30	78759	3600-3699
B R REYNOLDS DR	Austin	584Z	MH-22	78703	100-299
BRUBECK BEND	Travis Co	402P	MC-41	78613	2700-2899
BRUCE DR	Austin	613U	MF-19	78735	3200-3299
BRUCE JENNER LN	Austin	702C	MD-12	78748	11400-11799
BRUE ST	Travis Co	439F	MS-39	78660	19400-19599
BRUNING AVE	Austin	555L	MK-26	78751	5100-5299
BRUNO CIR	Travis Co	467R	MP-35	78660	14700-14799
BRUNSTON CT	Round Rock	376E	ML-45	78681	2600-2699
BRUNSWICK DR	Austin	556L	MM-26	78723	2100-2199
BRUNT DR	Austin	496J	ML-32	78758	11200-11299
BRUSH COUNTRY RD	Austin	612Z	MD-19	78749	5800-6299
	Austin	642G	MD-18	78749	6300-7299
BRUSHFIELD WAY	Travis Co	529M	MT-29	78653	13800-13899
BRUSHY ST	Austin	585C	MK-24	78702	100-699
BRUSHY ST	Georgetown	286Q	MM-53	78626	1800-2099
BRUSHY ST N	Leander	312X	MC-49	78641	100-499
BRUSHY ST S	Hutto	379D	MT-45	78634	200-299
BRUSHY ST S	Leander	342C	MD-48	78641	100-399
BRUSHY BEND DR	Williamson Co	375N	MJ-44	78681	900-1999
BRUSHY CREEK TRL	Williamson Co	410J	MU-41	78634	100-399
BRUSHY CREEK DR	Round Rock	376V	MM-43	78664	800-1299
BRUSHY CREEK RD	Austin	374Z	MH-43	78613	3900-3998 E
	Cedar Park	403B	ME-42	78613	1-1999
	Cedar Park	374W	MG-43	78613	2000-3899
	Cedar Park	375S	MJ-43	78613	4001-4099 O
	Williamson Co	375S	MJ-43	78613	4000-4098 E
	Williamson Co	375P	MJ-44	78717	4100-4399
BRUSHY CREEK RD	Williamson Co	378F	MQ-45	78634	2000-2099
BRUSHYGATE CV	Williamson Co	405A	MJ-42	78717	8900-8999
BRUSHY GLEN DR	Travis Co	496Z	MM-31	78753	11100-11299
BRUSHY HILL RD	Burnet Co	426K	WQ-38	78669	100-598 E
BRUSHY HOLLOW	Williamson Co	433G	MF-39	78750	12400-12499
BRUSHY RIDGE CV	Austin	674H	MH-15	78744	6500-6599
BRUSHY RIDGE DR	Austin	674H	MH-15	78744	4700-5099
BRUSHY VIEW CV	Austin	527A	MN-30	78754	1500-1699
BRUTIS ST	Travis Co	587H	MP-24	78724	6100-6299
BRUTON SPRINGS RD	Travis Co	521V	MB-28	78733	900-1699
BRYAN CV	Lago Vista	459E	WW-36	78645	20100-20299
BRYAN ST	Austin	585Z	MK-22	78702	2400-2599
BRYANT CV	Cedar Park	372R	MD-44	78613	200-299
BRYANT DR	Bastrop	744D	ED-9	78602	200-299
BRYANT DR	Round Rock	407K	MN-41	78664	1600-1799
BRYANT RD	Williamson Co	381L	MX-44	76574	100-199
BRYCE CANYON DR	Cedar Park	373S	ME-43	78613	200-499
BRYCO CV	Round Rock	346W	ML-46	78681	2900-2999
BRYER CREEK TRL	Williamson Co	405J	MJ-41	78717	8600-8699
BRYKER DR	Austin	554V	MH-25	78703	3000-3399
BRYN MAWR CV	Austin	556M	MM-26	78723	7000-7099
BRYN MAWR DR	Austin	556M	MM-26	78723	6700-6999
BRYONHALL DR	Austin	643P	ME-17	78745	2700-2799
BRYONWOOD DR	Austin	557U	MP-25	78724	6800-6899
BRYONY DR	Austin	670D	WZ-15	78739	11900-12199
BUBBA'S BLUFF	Hays Co	577U	WT-22	78720	10800-10999
	Travis Co	577U	WT-22	78720	10700-10799
BUBBLING BROOK DR	Hutto	379H	MT-45	78634	100-399
BUBBLING SPRINGS TRL					
	Williamson Co	434P	MG-38	78729	8900-9099
BUBBLING WELL LN	Bee Cave	549R	WX-26	78738	4100-4299
BUCCANEER TRL	Williamson Co	434V	MH-37	78729	7000-7199
BUCHANAN CV	Lago Vista	459E	WW-36	78645	20100-20299
BUCHANAN ST	Bastrop	745B	EE-9	78602	None
BUCK LN	Travis Co	650W	MU-16	78617	3100-4099
	Travis Co	680A	MU-15	78617	4100-4899
BUCK LN	Williamson Co	344D	MH-48	78628	100-199
BUCKAROO TRL	Buda	732F	MC-9	78610	500-599
BUCK BEND	Williamson Co	314V	MH-49	78628	200-399
BUCKBOARD BLVD	Round Rock	406L	MM-41	78681	300-699
BUCKBOARD CV	Lago Vista	429A	WW-39	78645	6800-6999
BUCK BOARD DR	Bastrop Co	712R	MZ-11	78602	100-199
BUCKEYE CT	Austin	525H	MK-30	78758	1200-1299
BUCKEYE DR	Lago Vista	458D	WV-36	78645	3700-3799
BUCKEYE LN	Williamson Co	377J	MN-44	78664	1800-2199
BUCKEYE TRL	Travis Co	461Q	MB-35	78732	6600-6699
BUCKEYE TRL	West Lake Hills	583C	MF-24	78746	100-899
BUCKEYE TRL	Williamson Co	432H	MD-39	78613	2600-2999
BUCKHAVEN CV	Cedar Park	374U	MH-43	78613	4000-4099
BUCKHORN	Williamson Co	345W	MJ-46	78681	4300-4399
BUCKHORN CIR	Point Venture	489J	WW-32	78645	18600-18699
BUCKHORN DR	Point Venture	489J	WW-32	78645	200-499
BUCKINGHAM CIR	Austin	615S	MJ-19	78704	700-799
BUCKINGHAM DR	Bastrop Co	709L	MT-11	78612	None
BUCKINGHAM PL	Austin	644W	MG-16	78745	700-899
BUCKINGHAM RD	Austin	464F	MG-36	78759	11500-11999
BUCKINGHAM GATE RD	Austin	702C	MD-12	78748	12000-12199
BUCKINHAM GATE TERRACE	Austin	702C	MD-12	78748	2600-2699
BUCKLEY LN	Round Rock	377E	MN-45	78664	2000-3099
BUCKMAN MOUNTAIN RD	Travis Co	553H	MF-27	78746	5100-5499
BUCK MEADOW DR	Georgetown	227J	MN-59	78626	7600-7999
BUCKMINSTER CT	Travis Co	554N	MG-26	78746	2600-2699
BUCKNELL DR	Austin	556H	MM-27	78723	7200-7499
BUCKNER RD	Travis Co	432V	MD-37	78726	11800-12099
BUCKPASSER CV	Austin	523Y	MF-28	78746	5800-5899
BUCK RACE	Travis Co	672P	MC-14	78748	3400-3499
BUCK RIDGE RD	Cedar Park	374U	MH-43	78613	400-599
BUCK RUN	Travis Co	371Q	MB-44	78641	13100-13499
BUCK RUN CV	Williamson Co	283L	MF-53	78628	100-199
BUCK RUN RD	Travis Co	400E	WY-42	78645	20200-20499
BUCK SHOT CT	Bastrop	744K	EC-8	78602	100-199
BUCKSHOT TRL	Austin	434U	MH-37	78729	7800-8099
BUCKSHOT WAY	Cedar Park	374Q	MH-44	78613	100-199
BUCKSKIN	Williamson Co	375Y	MK-43	78681	400-499
BUCKSKIN CT	Williamson Co	314Q	MH-50	78628	100-199
BUCKSKIN DR	Round Rock	406L	MM-41	78681	500-799
BUCKSKIN PASS	Austin	643D	MF-18	78745	4800-5099
BUCKSKIN TRL	Hays Co	640W	WY-16	78737	9800-9899
BUCKSKIN TRL	Pflugerville	467C	MP-36	78660	None
BUCKSKIN RIDGE	Lago Vista	429K	WW-38	78645	20400-20799
BUCKS RUN	Austin	674H	MH-15	78744	2400-4799
BUCKTHORN DR	Austin	464Q	MH-35	78759	10700-10999
BUCKWHEAT PASS	Hays Co	732F	MC-9	78610	12900-12999
BUDDY AVE	Village of Volente	431W	MA-37	78641	15700-15799
BUDLEY S. DEGROOT LN	Austin	702C	MD-12	78748	11700-11799
BUELL AVE	Austin	525B	MJ-30	78757	2400-2799
BUENA SUERTE DR	Austin	641G	MB-18	78749	7200-7399
BUENA VISTA	Lago Vista	429F	WW-39	78645	20800-21199
BUENA VISTA CIR	West Lake Hills	583H	MF-24	78746	400-499
BUENA VISTA CT	Williamson Co	196J	ML-62	78628	600-699
BUENA VISTA DR	Williamson Co	196J	ML-62	78628	100-499
	Williamson Co	195M	MK-62	78633	500-599
BUENA VISTA LN	Round Rock	407D	MP-42	78665	2200-2299
	Round Rock	408A	MQ-42	78665	None
BUENOS AIRES PKWY	Austin	678N	MQ-14	78617	12800-13099
BUFF ST N	Dripping Springs	636Z	WR-16	78620	100-299
BUFF ST S	Dripping Springs	636Z	WR-16	78620	100-299
BUFFALO AVE N	Cedar Park	373T	ME-43	78613	100-399
BUFFALO AVE S	Cedar Park	373X	ME-43	78613	100-499
	Cedar Park	403C	MF-42	78613	500-899
BUFFALO PASS	Austin	643G	MF-18	78745	5000-5999
	Austin	643L	MF-17	78745	6100-6399
BUFFALO PASS	Round Rock	406G	MM-42	78681	500-799
BUFFALO PASS N	Williamson Co	193C	MF-63	78633	100-199
BUFFALO PASS S	Williamson Co	193C	MF-63	78633	200-299
BUFFALO TRL	Lago Vista	399L	WX-41	78645	8600-8699
BUFFALO TRL	Travis Co	490R	WZ-32	78734	2900-3099
BUFFALO GAP	Austin	465P	MJ-35	78727	5100-5199
BUFFALO GAP	Leander	342W	MC-46	78641	2200-2299
BUFFALO GAP RD	Lakeway	490N	WY-32	78734	1400-1499
	Travis Co	490N	WY-32	78734	1000-1399
	Travis Co	490J	WY-32	78734	1500-1899
BUFFALO GROVE CV	Travis Co	702A	MC-12	78739	12300-12399
BUFFALO LAKE LN	Austin	704A	MG-12	78747	9900-10099
BUFFALO SPRINGS TRL	Georgetown	256F	ML-57	78628	3200-3799
BUFFALO TUNDRA DR	Austin	497X	MN-31	78754	2100-2299
BUFFLEHEAD LN	Cedar Park	373Z	MF-43	78613	500-699
BUFFLEHEAD LN	Williamson Co	282J	MC-53	78641	100-199
BUFFY CV	Hays Co	576C	WR-24	78620	100-299
BUGGY WHIP TRL	Williamson Co	433P	ME-38	78750	11700-11899
BULIAN LN	Travis Co	583R	MF-23	78746	100-599
	West Lake Hills	583R	MF-23	78746	600-799
BULLACE ST	Travis Co	619A	MS-21	78724	15100-15299
BULLARD DR	Austin	525S	MJ-28	78757	3000-5799
BULLBRIER RD	Travis Co	619A	MS-21	78724	15200-15299
BULL CREEK PKWY	Cedar Park	373E	ME-45	78613	500-899
BULL CREEK RD	Austin	554R	MH-26	78731	3600-5099
	Austin	525W	MJ-28	78756	5600-5899
	Austin	525W	MJ-28	78757	5900-6299
BULLET CV	Lago Vista	399L	WX-41	78645	21400-21599
BULLET PASS	Travis Co	766G	MM-6	78610	12900-13099
BULLHILL CV	Cedar Park	372P	MC-44	78613	1400-1499
BULL HOLLOW DR	Austin	464A	MG-36	78750	8800-8899
BULL HORN LOOP	Round Rock	346V	MM-46	78665	1300-1499
BULLICK BLUFF	Travis Co	461V	MB-34	78732	6900-6999
BULLICK HOLLOW RD	Austin	462J	MC-35	78726	11500-12599
	Travis Co	462J	MC-35	78726	12600-13799
BULL MOUNTAIN CV	Travis Co	553H	MF-27	78746	4800-4999
BULL RIDGE DR	Austin	464U	MH-34	78759	10600-10799
BULL RUN	Austin	465J	MJ-35	78727	5200-5399
BULL RUN	Taylor	322R	MZ-50	76574	2800-3099
BULL RUN	Travis Co	590D	MV-24	78653	None
BULL RUN CIR	Austin	465J	MJ-35	78727	5400-5499
BULL RUN RD	Bastrop Co	741M	MX-8	78612	100-199
BULLWHIP PASS	Buda	732P	MC-8	78610	16200-16299
BULLY HILL CV	Austin	464X	MG-34	78759	9500-9599
BUMBLE BEE DR	Georgetown	227E	MP-60	78628	30000-30399
BUMBLEBEE DR	Travis Co	468N	MQ-35	78660	1800-1999
BUMBLE BEE DR	Travis Co	488W	WU-31	78669	2700-2899
	Travis Co	487Z	WT-31	78669	2900-3299
BUMPSTEAD DR	Austin	705A	MJ-12	78747	6200-6599
BUNCHE RD	Austin	586M	MM-23	78721	1700-1799
BUNDORAN DR	Williamson Co	404C	MH-42	78717	9600-9999
BUNDY CREST CIR	Austin	586H	MM-24	78723	4900-4999
BUNDYHILL CIR	Austin	586G	MM-24	78723	5100-5199
BUNDYHILL DR	Austin	586G	MM-24	78723	4600-5099
BUNGALOW LN	Austin	641Q	MB-17	78749	9500-9599
BUNKER CV	Lago Vista	459J	WW-35	78645	20100-20199
BUNKERHILL CV	Williamson Co	375S	MJ-43	78717	9000-9099
BUNNY HOP TRL	Travis Co	489V	WX-31	78734	300-499
BUNNY RUN	Austin	523U	MF-28	78746	2900-4499
	Travis Co	523Q	MF-29	78746	4500-4799
	Travis Co	553B	ME-27	78746	None
BUNRATTY CIR	Pflugerville	407Y	MP-40	78660	1200-1399
BUNTING DR	Austin	464Q	MH-35	78759	11200-11499
BUNYON CIR	Lago Vista	459E	WW-36	78645	3600-3799
BUOY CIR	Williamson Co	224L	MH-59	78633	400-499
BUOY DR	Williamson Co	224G	MH-60	78633	100-399
BURBA LN	Williamson Co	282F	MC-54	78641	3300-3499
BURBANK ST	Austin	525T	MJ-28	78757	1800-2099
BURCH DR	Travis Co	678B	MQ-15	78617	3900-4499

STREET NAME	CITY or COUNTY	MAPSCO GRID	AUSTIN GRID	ZIP CODE	BLOCK RANGE O/E
BURDOCK DR	Lago Vista	429G	WX-39	78645	20000-20099
	Travis Co	429G	WX-39	78645	20100-20499
BURFORD PL	Austin	614B	MG-21	78704	1400-1499
BURGESS CV	Lakeway	520W	WY-28	78734	100-199
BURGESS DR	Leander	312S	MC-49	78641	1000-1299
BURGESS LN	Lakeway	520W	WY-28	78734	100-199
BURGUNDY CV	Austin	466K	ML-35	78727	1900-1999
BURGUNDY DR	Austin	557K	MN-26	78724	5400-5599
BURK BURNETT CT	Austin	642A	MC-18	78749	6200-6299
BURKE BLVD	Point Venture	488R	WV-32	78654	18800-18899
BURKETT ST	Taylor	353B	EA-48	76574	200-1199
BURKS CV	Travis Co	491U	MB-31	78732	12700-12799
BURKS LN	Travis Co	491U	MB-31	78732	3000-3399
BURKWOOD CV	Travis Co	582N	MC-23	78735	8400-8499
BURLESON CT	Austin	615X	MJ-19	78741	2400-2499
BURLESON CV	Round Rock	376M	MM-44	78664	600-699
BURLESON RD	Austin	615X	MJ-19	78741	2300-2699
	Austin	645B	MJ-18	78741	2700-3699
	Austin	645L	MK-17	78744	4400-6899
	Austin	646W	ML-16	78744	6900-7599
	Austin	676B	ML-15	78744	7600-8299
	Austin	676M	MM-14	78719	8300-9999
	Austin	677N	MN-14	78617	10000-10199
BURLESON-MANOR RD	Travis Co	620B	MU-21	78653	6900-7499
	Travis Co	590P	MU-23	78653	7500-8999
BURLEY CV	Austin	643S	ME-16	78745	3200-3299
BURLEY BEND	Austin	643S	ME-16	78745	8000-8099
BURLIEGH CV	Austin	642V	MD-16	78745	3400-3499
BURLINGTON CT	Austin	464H	MH-36	78727	5900-5999
BURLWOOD CT	Round Rock	376M	MM-44	78664	400-599
BURLY OAK CIR	Austin	643T	ME-16	78745	7500-7699
BURLY OAK DR	Austin	643T	ME-16	78745	2300-2699
BURLYWOOD TRL	Williamson Co	433G	MF-39	78750	12300-12599
BURMASTER LN	Williamson Co	433U	MF-37	78750	10300-10499
BURNAM RD	Hays Co	732W	MC-7	78610	1-99
BURNAP ST E	Weir	258H	MR-57	78626	100-199
BURNAP ST W	Weir	258H	MR-57	78626	100-399
BURNELL DR	Austin	556M	MM-26	78723	6900-7099
BURNET LN	Austin	525T	MJ-28	78757	6200-6999
BURNET RD	Austin	555A	MJ-27	78756	4000-5899
	Austin	525T	MJ-28	78757	5900-8599
	Austin	495Y	MK-31	78757	8600-8999
	Austin	495Y	MK-31	78758	9000-11599
	Austin	465Z	MK-34	78758	11600-12099
	Austin	466A	ML-36	78758	12100-12499
	Austin	466A	ML-36	78727	12500-13799
	Travis Co	436X	ML-37	78728	13800-14599
	Travis Co	436K	ML-38	78728	14600-15299
	Williamson Co	436K	ML-38	78728	15300-15799
BURNET ST N	Manor	529Q	MT-29	78653	100-999
BURNET ST N	Round Rock	376Z	MM-43	78664	100-699
BURNET ST S	Manor	529Y	MT-28	78653	100-399
BURNET ST S	Round Rock	376Z	MM-43	78664	100-499
BURNET FOREST CV	Elgin	533E	EA-30	78621	None
BURNEY DR	Austin	494Y	MH-31	78731	4100-4399
BURNHILL DR	Austin	643G	MF-18	78745	5700-5999
BURNIE BISHOP PL	Cedar Park	402L	MD-41	78613	2000-2199
BURNING OAK DR	Austin	614P	MG-20	78704	2900-3099
BURNING TREE CIR	Point Venture	489J	WW-32	78645	200-299
BURNING TREE CV	Lakeway	519G	WX-30	78734	100-199
BURNING TREE DR	Georgetown	286X	ML-52	78628	200-399
BURNS BLVD	Taylor	352D	MZ-48	76574	1300-1499
BURNS ST	Austin	555C	MK-27	78752	6200-6499
BURNS ST	Taylor	322Z	MZ-49	76574	700-799
BURNSALL GATES DR	Travis Co	467P	MN-35	78660	800-999
BURNSIDE CIR	Lago Vista	458J	WU-35	78645	3100-3299
BURNSIDE RD	Austin	643S	ME-16	78745	8100-8199
BURNT CIR	Austin	611Q	MB-20	78736	8200-8299
BURNT OAK CT	Cedar Park	403E	ME-42	78613	900-999
BURNT OAK DR	Hays Co	669C	WX-15	78737	10700-11099
BURNWOOD DR	Austin	496N	ML-32	78758	10800-10899
BUR OAK CV	Cedar Park	433E	ME-39	78613	1400-1499
BUR OAK LN	Georgetown	225K	MJ-59	78633	100-199
BURRELL DR	Austin	525L	MK-29	78757	7900-8599
BURRIS CIR	Austin	614K	MG-20	78704	1800-1999
BURRIS ST E	Weir	258H	MR-57	78626	100-199
BURRIS ST W	Weir	258H	MR-57	78626	100-199
BURR OAK DR	Travis Co	441G	MX-39	78615	20100-20399
	Williamson Co	441C	MX-39	78615	20400-20699
BURR OAK LN	Austin	465H	MK-36	78727	3800-4099
BURROUGH CV	Austin	643G	MF-18	78745	5600-5699
BURROUGH DR	Austin	643G	MF-18	78745	5700-5999
BURROWS PL	Dripping Springs	636Y	WR-16	78620	100-199
BURR RIDGE DR	Williamson Co	434P	MG-38	78729	12300-12499
BURSON DR	Travis Co	702L	MD-11	78652	12700-12799
BURTON DR	Austin	615T	MJ-19	78741	1500-2299
BURTON ST E	Manor	529U	MT-28	78653	100-599
BURTON ST W	Manor	529U	MT-28	78653	100-11599
BUSBY DR	Travis Co	560N	MU-26	78653	18100-18199
BUSBY CROSSING	Williamson Co	258X	MQ-55	78626	1-599
BUSH CV	Bastrop	745A	EE-9	78602	100-199
BUSH COAT LN	Austin	497T	MN-31	78754	1600-1799
BUSHMASTER BEND	Bastrop	744K	EC-8	78602	None
BUSHMILLS CT	Travis Co	437G	MP-39	78660	800-899
BUSHMILLS RD	Travis Co	437G	MP-39	78660	17200-17399
BUSHNELL DR	Austin	643K	ME-17	78745	2800-3099
BUSINESS DR	Austin	495P	MJ-32	78758	9400-9599
BUSINESS CENTER DR	Austin	645K	MJ-17	78744	2300-2599
BUSINESS PARK DR	Austin	495S	MJ-31	78759	8800-8999
BUSINESS PARK DR	Bastrop	745Q	EF-8	78602	1400-1699
BUSLEIGH CASTLE WAY	Pflugerville	408T	MQ-40	78660	600-999
BUTCH GAP CV	Cedar Park	372T	MC-43	78613	1300-1399
BUTE DR	Briarcliff	457Z	WT-34	78669	22300-22399
BUTEO ST	Travis Co	409T	MS-40	78660	20500-20699
BUTLER CIR	Travis Co	610Z	WZ-19	78737	8900-8999
BUTLER CV	Lago Vista	459E	WW-36	78645	3400-3499
BUTLER LN	Bastrop Co	534F	EC-30	78621	100-199
BUTLER RD	Austin	584Z	MH-22	78704	1300-1499
BUTLER WAY	Round Rock	348W	MQ-46	78665	2200-2699
BUTLER NATIONAL DR	Pflugerville	409W	MS-40	78660	2300-2899
BUTLER RANCH RD	Dripping Springs	666M	WR-14	78620	100-1199
	Hays Co	667E	WS-15	78620	None
BUTTE BLVD	Austin	524S	MG-28	78731	5600-5699
BUTTERCUP CT	Leander	342K	MC-47	78641	1000-1099
BUTTERCUP RD	Travis Co	467M	MP-35	78660	1600-1699
	Travis Co	468N	MQ-35	78660	1700-1899
BUTTERCUP RD	Williamson Co	382D	MZ-45	76574	1-499

STREET NAME	CITY or COUNTY	MAPSCO GRID	AUSTIN GRID	ZIP CODE	BLOCK RANGE O/E
BUTTERCUP TRL	Georgetown	226A	ML-60	78633	100-199
BUTTERCUP TRL	Hays Co	732K	MC-8	78610	200-399
BUTTERCUP CREEK BLVD					
	Cedar Park	403A	ME-42	78613	100-999
	Cedar Park	402L	MD-41	78613	1000-1799
BUTTERFLY CV	Georgetown	195P	MJ-62	78633	100-199
BUTTERFLY PL	Village of the Hills	519K	WW-29	78738	1-99
BUTTERMILK GAP	Georgetown	256K	ML-56	78628	400-499
BUTTERNUT PL	Williamson Co	433E	ME-39	78613	1300-1499
BUTTON BEND CIR	Austin	645S	MJ-16	78744	4400-4499
BUTTON BEND RD	Austin	645S	MJ-16	78744	4600-4799
BUTTONBUSH DR	Austin	674R	MH-14	78744	7300-7499
BUTTON QUAIL CV	Austin	496S	ML-31	78758	10300-10399
BUTTON QUAIL DR	Austin	496S	ML-31	78758	10400-10499
BUTTONWOOD DR	Austin	464M	MH-35	78759	11500-11699
BUTTONWOOD ST	Bastrop	745F	EE-9	78602	500-1299
BUVANA DR	Austin	670M	WZ-14	78739	12200-12499
BUZZ SCHNEIDER LN	Austin	702H	MD-12	78748	11800-12299
BYERLY TURK DR	Pflugerville	409E	MS-42	78660	21100-21399
BYERS CV	Austin	497N	MN-32	78753	11800-11899
BYERS LN	Austin	497N	MN-32	78753	1000-1499
BYFIELD DR	Cedar Park	372C	MD-45	78613	2400-2699
BYPASS	Travis Co	459R	WX-35	78645	17800-17899
BYRD AVE	Lago Vista	459J	WW-35	78645	20100-20299
BYRDHILL LN	Austin	674E	MG-15	78748	7700-7799
BYRDS NEST DR	Bee Cave	579D	WX-24	78738	13400-13599
BYRON CIR	Williamson Co	281Y	MB-52	78641	4100-4199
BYRON DR	Austin	614S	MG-19	78704	3800-3899
BYZANTIUM LN	Pflugerville	437F	MN-39	78664	1400-1499

C

STREET NAME	CITY or COUNTY	MAPSCO GRID	AUSTIN GRID	ZIP CODE	BLOCK RANGE O/E
CABALLERO CV	Austin	466F	ML-36	78727	13400-13499
CABALLERO RD	Leander	312W	MC-49	78641	600-699
CABALLO RD	Bastrop Co	739F	MS-9	78617	100-199
CABALLO RANCH RD	Cedar Park	343Z	MF-46	78641	2800-2899
	Cedar Park	344W	MG-46	78641	2900-3199
CABANA LN	Austin	465Q	MK-35	78727	12000-12399
CABELAS DR	Buda	763A	ME-6	78610	1000-1599
	Buda	733W	ME-7	78610	None
CABERNET WAY	Williamson Co	343N	ME-47	78641	1300-1399
CABIN RD	Travis Co	582C	MD-24	78746	1-99
CABINWOOD CV	Austin	583P	ME-23	78746	1600-1699
CABOB ST	Austin	645W	MJ-16	78744	4700-4999
CABO DEL SOL CT	Lakeway	519X	WW-28	78738	100-199
CABO DEL SOL CV	Lakeway	519X	WW-28	78738	100-199
CABOT CV	Lago Vista	459J	WW-35	78645	19800-19899
CABOT VALLEY CV	Travis Co	497G	MP-33	78754	13100-13199
CABRIOLE DR	Pflugerville	468B	MQ-36	78660	900-999
CACHE DR	Austin	642Q	MD-17	78749	8100-8299
CACTUS DR	Round Rock	406K	ML-41	78681	700-999
CACTUS LN	Austin	614W	MG-19	78745	4400-4499
	Austin	613Z	MF-19	78745	4500-4799
CACTUS TRL	Georgetown	256F	ML-57	78628	100-199
CACTUS BEND	Austin	465J	MJ-35	78727	11900-12199
CACTUS BEND CV	Lago Vista	399P	WW-41	78645	8300-8499
CACTUS BEND CV	Williamson Co	194Z	MH-61	78633	100-199
CACTUS BEND DR	Pflugerville	437Y	MP-37	78660	600-899
CACTUS BLOSSOM DR	Pflugerville	437L	MP-38	78660	1400-1699
	Travis Co	437L	MP-38	78660	16800-17099
CACTUS CROSSING	Hays Co	670P	WY-14	78737	6800-6899
CACTUS FLOWER DR	Cedar Park	402H	MD-42	78613	500-699
CACTUS VALLEY DR	Leander	343L	MF-47	78641	2000-2199
CACTUS WREN WAY	Austin	583U	MF-22	78746	3400-3599
CADDIE ST	Austin	616W	ML-19	78741	6100-6299
CADDO ST E	Austin	496Q	MM-32	78753	100-399
CADDO ST W	Austin	496L	MM-32	78753	400-799
CADDO LAKE DR	Williamson Co	344B	MG-48	78628	100-499
CADDO LAKE TRL	Georgetown	195N	MJ-62	78633	100-199
CADE CIR	Travis Co	433T	ME-37	78750	10900-10999
CADENCE DR	Austin	467Q	MP-35	78660	1000-1399
CADILLAC CV	Cedar Park	373U	MF-43	78613	200-299
CADILLAC DR	Travis Co	619E	MS-21	78724	5100-5599
CADIZ CIR	Austin	645F	MJ-18	78741	2200-2299
CADOZ CT	Travis Co	436K	ML-38	78728	3900-3999
CADOZ DR	Travis Co	436K	ML-38	78728	15300-15899
CAFFEY LN	Travis Co	560S	MU-25	78653	10900-10999
CAHILL DR	Williamson Co	434T	MG-37	78729	7900-8599
CAHIR GLEN CV	Pflugerville	437C	MP-39	78660	17700-17799
CAHONE TRL	Austin	434Y	MH-37	78729	12300-12399
CAICOS CV	Lakeway	488Z	WV-31	78734	None
CAIN HARVEST CV	Austin	527C	MP-30	78754	3000-3099
CAIN HARVEST DR	Austin	527C	MP-30	78754	11000-11199
CAINWOOD LN	Williamson Co	434K	MG-38	78729	8700-8899
CAIRA CV	Austin	463H	MF-36	78750	9100-9199
CAISSON CIR	Austin	643X	ME-16	78745	8100-8199
CAISTEAL CASTLE PATH	Pflugerville	408X	MQ-40	78660	18600-18899
CAJUILES CT	Pflugerville	439B	MS-39	78660	19500-19899
CAJUILES DR	Pflugerville	439B	MS-39	78660	2900-3099
CAL CV	Austin	556M	MM-26	78723	6900-6999
CALABASH CV	Austin	643W	ME-16	78745	2700-2799
CALABRIA CT	Travis Co	580G	WZ-24	78738	5000-5099
CALADENDRA DR	Austin	616W	ML-19	78741	1400-1499
CALADIUM CIR	Austin	672K	MC-14	78758	3400-3499
CALADIUM CT	Williamson Co	257F	MN-57	78626	300-399
CALADIUM DR	Williamson Co	257F	MN-57	78626	200-499
CALAIS CT	Austin	644E	MG-18	78745	5200-5299
CALAVAR DR	Austin	463A	ME-36	78726	11000-11199
CALAVERAS DR	Austin	464M	MH-41	78717	14700-15299
CALAW CV	Travis Co	554J	MG-26	78746	2800-2899
CALCITE CV	Round Rock	345P	MJ-47	78681	400-599
CALCITE TRL	Williamson Co	433Q	MF-38	78750	10800-10899
CALCUTTA RUN DR	Jonestown	430Q	WZ-38	78645	7500-7799
CALDER RD	Caldwell Co	767X	MN-4	78616	1-1699
	Mustang Ridge	767N	MN-5	78610	12000-12099
CALDERON ST	Hays Co	794A	MG-3	78610	100-199
CALDVIS RD	Mustang Ridge	766V	MM-4	78610	12000-12099
	Travis Co	766V	MM-4	78610	12100-12399
CALDWELL DR	Austin	433R	MF-38	78750	13600-13699
	Williamson Co	433R	MF-38	78750	13500-13599
CALDWELL LN	Travis Co	650E	MU-18	78617	1800-2599
	Travis Co	649V	MT-16	78617	2600-3899
	Travis Co	679C	MT-15	78617	3900-4399
CALDWELL ST N	Manor	529U	MT-28	78653	100-999
CALDWELL ST S	Manor	529U	MT-28	78653	100-299
CALDWELL RANCH RD	Bastrop Co	711B	MW-12	78612	100-199
CALDWELLS LN	Pflugerville	437V	MP-37	78660	100-399

STREET NAME	CITY or COUNTY	MAPSCO GRID	AUSTIN GRID	ZIP CODE	BLOCK RANGE O/E
CALEB DR	Travis Co	618Z	MR-19	78725	2900-3499
CALEDONIA DR	Williamson Co	405N	MJ-41	78717	8300-8499
CALERA CV	Travis Co	529M	MT-29	78653	13800-13899
CALERA DR	Travis Co	582N	MC-23	78735	8300-8399
	Travis Co	581R	MB-23	78735	8400-9299
CALF ROPING TRL	Williamson Co	466F	ML-36	78727	13200-13299
CALHOUN AVE	Lago Vista	459E	WW-36	78645	19900-20099
CALHOUN LN	Travis Co	309N	WW-50	78641	25900-26599
CALHOUN PASS	Travis Co	309N	WW-50	78641	14200-14399
CALHOUN CANYON LOOP	Austin	612M	MD-20	78735	4800-5199
CALIBER CV	Bastrop	744K	EC-8	78602	200-299
CALICHE LN	Travis Co	460R	WZ-35	78734	5500-5599
CALICO DR	Austin	673L	MF-14	78748	800-999
CALICO BUSH LN	Williamson Co	408J	MQ-41	78664	100-499
CALICO KID	Travis Co	460L	WZ-35	78734	None
CALIDAD DR	Austin	556E	ML-27	78752	6300-6599
CALIFORNIA CV	Austin	641T	MA-16	78739	10600-10699
CALISTOGA CT	Travis Co	521N	MA-29	78732	300-399
CALISTOGA DR	Leander	343N	ME-47	78641	1100-1299
CALISTOGA WAY	Travis Co	521N	MA-29	78732	12400-12699
CALITHEA RD	West Lake Hills	553U	MF-25	78746	900-999
CALLABERO CV	Williamson Co	344V	MH-46	78681	4000-4099
CALLANISH PARK DR	Austin	464E	MG-36	78750	10700-11099
	Austin	463D	MF-36	78750	11100-11199
CALLAWAY GARDEN CT	Travis Co	409S	MS-40	78660	2200-2299
CALLBRAM LN	Austin	611U	MB-19	78736	7300-7899
CALLE ST	Leander	342Q	MD-47	78641	400-499
CALLE ALTA RD	Buda	763K	ME-5	78610	None
CALLE CALICHE	Travis Co	522Y	MD-28	78733	1900-2099
CALLE LIMON	Austin	616B	ML-21	78702	900-999
CALLES ST	Austin	615D	MK-21	78702	500-799
CALLE VERDE CV	Austin	465X	MJ-34	78759	11400-11499
CALLE VERDE DR	Austin	495B	MJ-33	78759	11000-11499
CALLIE'S CT	Bastrop Co	738L	MR-8	78617	100-199
CALLINE MAYES RUN	Buda	732T	MC-7	78610	100-299
CALLINGWOOD DR	Austin	497T	MN-31	78754	2100-2199
CALLISTO TERRACE	Austin	465G	MK-36	78727	4600-4799
CALLOWAY CV	Williamson Co	405E	MJ-42	78717	16100-16199
CALMAR CV	Austin	616C	MM-21	78721	6100-6199
CALM HARBOR DR	Travis Co	439S	MS-37	78660	17900-18099
CALMING CT	Jonestown	430J	WY-38	78645	7400-7499
CALPLY DR	Pflugerville	437A	MN-39	78664	16800-16899
CAL RODGERS ST	Austin	586E	ML-24	78723	3800-3999
CALUMET CV	Austin	643N	ME-17	78745	7500-7599
CALVIN ST	Weir	258H	MR-57	78626	100-399
CALYPSO DR	Lakeway	519E	WW-30	78734	100-199
CAMACHO ST	Austin	586A	ML-24	78723	4000-4499
CAMARGO CT	Travis Co	409S	MS-40	78660	20200-20299
CAMAS DR	Travis Co	436V	MM-37	78728	1700-1899
CAMA VALLEY CV	Austin	672A	MC-15	78739	10200-10299
CAMBOURNE DR	Travis Co	467T	MN-34	78660	13600-14099
CAMBRAY DR	Austin	557Z	MP-25	78724	8100-8199
CAMBRIA CV	Williamson Co	405N	MJ-41	78717	15400-15499
CAMBRIA DR	Buda	763K	ME-5	78610	2000-2199
CAMBRIA DR	Williamson Co	405N	MJ-41	78717	8300-8499
CAMBRIDGE CT	Austin	586J	ML-23	78723	3400-3499
CAMBRIDGE DR	Round Rock	406M	MM-41	78664	500-899
CAMBRIDGE HEIGHTS DR					
	Pflugerville	437C	MP-39	78664	1300-1399
CAMDEN CV	Cedar Park	373Y	MF-43	78613	1100-1199
CAMDEN DR	Austin	525G	MK-30	78757	8000-8099
CAMEL BACK	Lago Vista	429N	WW-38	78645	20500-20799
CAMEL BACK	Leander	371C	MB-45	78641	1400-1499
CAMELBACK DR	Travis Co	522X	MC-28	78733	9000-9299
CAMELIA LN	Austin	495S	MJ-31	78759	8600-8899
CAMELLIA CV	Manor	530T	MU-28	78653	None
CAMELLIA DR	Hutto	379M	MT-44	78634	None
	Hutto	380J	MU-44	78634	None
CAMELOT CIR	Austin	644E	MG-18	78745	1400-1499
CAMEO DR	Round Rock	376L	MM-44	78664	1800-1999
CAMEO LN	Austin	704L	MH-11	78747	10300-10499
CAMERON CV	Cedar Park	374R	MH-44	78613	500-599
CAMERON LOOP	Austin	643W	ME-16	78745	2600-3199
	Austin	642Z	MD-16	78745	3200-8899
CAMERON RD	Austin	556J	ML-26	78723	5000-6599
	Austin	556B	ML-27	78752	6600-7799
	Austin	526Y	MM-28	78754	7800-9399
	Austin	528A	MQ-30	78653	11900-13099
	Travis Co	527H	MP-30	78754	10500-11799
	Travis Co	527D	MP-30	78653	11800-11898 E
	Travis Co	527D	MP-30	78754	11801-11899 O
	Travis Co	498P	MQ-32	78653	13100-14099
	Travis Co	498D	MR-33	78660	14100-14598 E
	Travis Co	498D	MR-33	78653	14101-14999 O
	Travis Co	469T	MS-34	78660	15400-16799
	Travis Co	470N	MU-35	78660	16800-17799
	Travis Co	470F	MU-36	78653	17800-18599
	Travis Co	440X	MU-37	78653	18600-19899
	Travis Co	440Y	MV-37	78615	19900-20299
	Travis Co	441N	MW-38	78615	20300-21199
CAMERON JULIA DR	Travis Co	436K	ML-38	78728	15100-15399
CAMI PATH	Round Rock	347V	MP-46	78665	2600-2699
CAMILLE CT	Lago Vista	429J	WW-38	78645	6000-6499
CAMILLE CT	Pflugerville	438S	MQ-37	78660	200-399
CAMILLIA BLOSSOM LN	Austin	672L	MD-14	78758	10600-10699
CAMINITA CV	Austin	640V	WZ-16	78739	8000-8099
CAMINO ALEMEDA	Cedar Park	344W	MG-46	78641	1700-2099
CAMINO ALTO	Travis Co	553R	MF-26	78746	2200-2599
	Travis Co	554J	MG-26	78746	2600-2699
CAMINO ALTO DR	Leander	312S	MC-49	78641	600-799
CAMINO ARBOLAGO	Lakeway	490S	WY-31	78734	100-399
CAMINO BARRANCA	Travis Co	515Y	WP-28	78620	None
CAMINO DEL SOL	Bastrop Co	738Y	MR-7	78617	100-199
CAMINO DEL VERDES PL					
	Round Rock	375H	MK-45	78681	2200-2399
CAMINO LA COSTA	Austin	556A	ML-27	78752	800-1399
CAMINO PAISANO	Travis Co	515Y	WP-28	78620	None
CAMINO REAL	Austin	525X	MJ-28	78757	5900-6399
CAMINO REAL DR	Leander	312W	MC-49	78641	700-899
CAMINO SECO	Austin	524U	MH-28	78731	5900-5999
CAMINO VIEJO	Austin	466X	ML-34	78758	1700-1999
CAMP CV	Austin	642B	MC-18	78749	7300-7399
CAMP DR	Georgetown	225C	MK-60	78633	100-199
CAMPANA DR	Austin	677R	MP-14	78617	12400-12699
CAMPANELLA CV	Round Rock	378E	MQ-45	78665	1500-1599
CAMPANELLA DR	Round Rock	378A	MQ-45	78665	3400-3499
CAMPANELLO WAY	Travis Co	432G	MD-39	78613	None

STREET NAME	CITY or COUNTY	MAPSCO GRID	AUSTIN GRID	ZIP CODE	BLOCK RANGE O/E
CAMPANULA CT	Pflugerville	468B	MQ-36	78660	1500-1599
CAMPBELL ST	Austin	584Q	MH-23	78703	500-599
CAMP CHAUTAUQUA RD	Travis Co	457D	WT-36	78669	2300-2399
	Travis Co	458A	WU-36	78669	2400-2999
CAMP CRAFT RD	Austin	583N	ME-23	78746	1700-1799
	Travis Co	583K	ME-23	78746	600-699
	Travis Co	583P	ME-23	78746	1300-1699
	West Lake Hills	583K	ME-23	78746	100-599
CAMP CREEK CT	Buda	732X	MC-7	78610	100-199
CAMPDEN DR	Austin	643Q	MF-17	78745	2300-2699
CAMPECHE BAY PL	Williamson Co	405C	MK-42	78681	8100-8399
CAMPERDOWN ELM DR	Austin	703C	MF-12	78748	100-399
CAMPESINA DR	Austin	466F	ML-36	78727	13400-13699
CAMPFIELD PKWY	Austin	673B	ME-15	78745	2000-2199
	Austin	643X	ME-16	78745	2200-2699
CAMPFIRE DR	Cedar Park	374Q	MH-44	78613	3800-3899
CAMP FIRE TRL	Austin	642B	MC-18	78749	5500-5699
CAMP FIRE TRL	Pflugerville	437Z	MP-37	78660	600-799
CAMPINA CROSSING	Travis Co	677Y	MP-13	78617	6700-6999
CAMPOBASSO PL	Travis Co	432Q	MD-38	78613	2700-2799
CAMPOS DR	Austin	435W	MJ-37	78727	12900-13099
CAMPOS DR	Hutto	379H	MT-45	78634	100-199
CAMPO VERDE CT	Austin	642T	MC-16	78749	8900-8999
CAMPO VERDE DR	Austin	642T	MC-16	78749	4300-4499
CAMPO VIEJO CV	Austin	583T	ME-22	78746	4000-4099
CAMP SPRINGS RD	Williamson Co	223R	MF-59	78633	1-899
CAMWOOD TRL	Village of the Hills	519S	WW-28	78738	1-99
CANA CV	Austin	612Y	MD-19	78749	4900-5099
CANADA ST	Elgin	534J	EC-29	78621	100-199
	Elgin	533M	EB-29	78621	None
CANADIAN CV	Hutto	350S	MU-46	78634	400-499
CANADIAN CV	Leander	342L	MD-47	78641	1100-1299
CANAL ST	Austin	616X	ML-19	78741	6700-6899
CANARD CIR	Travis Co	490J	WY-32	78734	16000-16099
CANARY CT	Round Rock	375R	MK-44	78681	1200-1299
CANARY ST	Elgin	533M	EB-29	78621	100-199
CANARY ST	Travis Co	520E	WY-30	78734	15100-15299
CANARY WAY	Lago Vista	458P	WU-35	78645	1700-1799
CANBY DR	Williamson Co	343X	ME-46	78641	1400-1499
CANCELO CV	Williamson Co	375B	MJ-45	78681	3000-3099
CANCELO WAY	Williamson Co	345X	MJ-46	78681	4200-4499
CANCUN CT	Bastrop Co	738X	MQ-7	78617	None
CANDACE LOOP	Pflugerville	408S	MQ-40	78660	18700-18799
CANDEE ST	Georgetown	286Q	MM-53	78626	1700-1799
CANDELARIA DR	Travis Co	641B	MA-18	78737	8300-8999
CANDELARIA MESA DR	Pflugerville	407X	MN-40	78664	1600-1699
CANDLEBERRY CIR	Pflugerville	468F	MQ-36	78660	600-699
CANDLELEAF CT	Village of the Hills	519S	WW-28	78738	1-99
CANDLELEAF CV	Hays Co	667F	WS-15	78620	100-299
CANDLELIGHT CT	Austin	495X	MJ-31	78757	3100-3199
CANDLELIGHT DR	Leander	341H	MB-48	78641	1500-1999
CANDLELITE CIR	Williamson Co	255R	MK-56	78628	100-199
CANDLE RIDGE CV	Austin	524F	MG-30	78731	6600-6699
CANDLE RIDGE DR	Austin	524F	MG-30	78731	4600-4699
CANDLE RIDGE TRL	Georgetown	287K	MN-53	78626	2300-2499
CANDLESTICK PL	Austin	466K	ML-35	78727	12900-13999
CANDLETREE LN	Austin	675A	MJ-15	78744	4500-4899
CANDLEWOOD CT	Austin	615W	MJ-19	78741	2500-2599
CANDO CT	Lakeway	519H	WX-30	78734	1800-1899
CANELLA DR	Austin	674R	MH-14	78744	4900-5299
CANE PACE	Austin	523Z	MF-28	78746	5900-5999
CANERA CT	Travis Co	702G	MD-12	78748	12300-12399
CANE RIVER RD	Pflugerville	408W	MQ-40	78660	200-299
CANEY ST	Austin	615C	MK-21	78702	100-299
CANEY CREEK RD	Travis Co	491Q	MB-32	78732	3900-3999
CANFIELD DR	Austin	641W	MA-16	78739	10700-10999
CANION ST	Austin	525Z	MK-28	78752	300-699
CANJA CT	Lakeway	490X	WY-31	78734	15200-15299
CANNA CV	Austin	464P	MG-35	78759	7500-7599
CANNA LILY LN	Pflugerville	438X	MQ-37	78660	1200-1399
CANNERY CV	Leander	342V	MD-46	78641	100-199
CANNES CIR	Austin	643K	ME-17	78745	6200-6399
CANNES DR	Cedar Park	403T	ME-40	78613	2100-2399
	Cedar Park	403X	ME-40	78613	2400-2599
CANNONADE CT	Austin	553C	MF-27	78746	5800-5899
CANNON LEAGUE DR	Austin	643Q	MF-17	78745	6200-7199
CANNON MOUNTAIN DR	Austin	642A	MC-18	78749	5800-6099
CANNON MOUNTAIN PL	Austin	642A	MC-18	78749	7400-7599
CANNON RANCH RD	Hays Co	637W	WS-16	78620	100-499
CANNONWOOD LN	Austin	643M	MF-17	78745	1700-1999
CANOA HILLS TRL N	Austin	404E	MG-42	78717	10700-10999
CANOA HILLS TRL S	Austin	404E	MG-42	78717	10400-10699
CANOAS DR	Travis Co	522B	MC-30	78730	4000-4499
CANOE CV	Hutto	380E	MU-45	78634	1100-1199
CANOE BROOK DR	Travis Co	582M	MD-23	78746	1300-1599
CANOGA AVE	Austin	587M	MP-23	78724	7900-7999
	Travis Co	587M	MP-23	78724	8000-8499
CANOLA BEND	Williamson Co	434Q	MH-38	78729	8200-8399
CANONADE	Hays Co	638V	WV-16	78737	13800-14399
CANONERO DR	Austin	553L	MF-26	78746	1700-2599
CANON WREN DR	Travis Co	552Z	MD-25	78746	6400-6999
CANON YEOMANS CT	Austin	673W	ME-13	78748	11000-11099
CANON YEOMANS TRL	Austin	703A	ME-12	78748	1100-1899
CANOPY LN	Manor	530K	MU-29	78653	18000-18299
CANOPY CREEK WAY	Travis Co	673T	ME-13	78748	1300-1499
CANTARRA DR	Austin	498J	MQ-32	78660	13000-13699
CANTATA LN	Austin	467Q	MP-35	78660	1100-1299
CANTEEN CIR	Austin	642B	MC-18	78749	7300-7399
CANTER LN	Austin	465V	MK-34	78759	3000-3299
CANTERA CV	Williamson Co	345T	MJ-46	78681	3000-3199
CANTERA WAY	Round Rock	345K	MJ-47	78681	3300-3399
CANTERBURY CV	Williamson Co	402U	MD-40	78613	2200-2299
CANTERBURY DR	Hays Co	639S	WW-16	78737	None
CANTERBURY ST	Austin	615B	MJ-21	78702	1200-1599
	Austin	615G	MK-21	78702	1600-2799
CANTERBURY TRL	Georgetown	287S	MN-52	78626	1000-1099
CANTERBURY TALES LN	Austin	673W	ME-13	78748	11000-11399
CANTERFIELD LN	Cedar Park	403E	ME-42	78613	900-1099
CANTERWOOD LN	Pflugerville	409S	MS-40	78660	19900-20199
CANTLE TRL	Austin	466J	ML-35	78727	12600-12999
CANTON	Manor	529X	MS-28	78653	None
CANUS CV	Austin	672H	MD-15	78748	2800-2899
CANUS DR	Austin	672H	MD-15	78748	9300-9499
CANVASBACK DR	Hays Co	732A	MC-9	78610	200-399
CANVAS BACK DR	Taylor	322U	MZ-49	76574	1900-2299
CANVASBACK TRL	Cedar Park	373Z	MF-43	78613	1500-1599
CANVASBACK CREEK CV	Leander	342K	MC-47	78641	1000-1099
CANVASBACK CREEK DR	Leander	342K	MC-47	78641	900-999
CANYON CIR E	Austin	584J	MG-23	78746	100-199
CANYON CIR W	Austin	584J	MG-23	78746	100-199
CANYON DR	Lago Vista	429N	WW-38	78645	5600-5999
CANYON DR	Travis Co	468P	MQ-35	78660	None
CANYON RD	Georgetown	256G	MM-57	78628	100-199
CANYON ST	Jonestown	400M	WZ-41	78645	10600-10699
CANYON TRL	Austin	403M	MF-41	78717	14100-14299
CANYON BEND CIR	Austin	613N	ME-20	78735	4800-4899
CANYON BEND DR	Hays Co	638X	WU-16	78620	1000-1099
CANYON BEND DR	Pflugerville	467D	MP-36	78660	700-899
CANYON CREEK	West Lake Hills	553V	MF-25	78746	800-899
CANYON CREST CT	Austin	613N	ME-20	78735	4900-4999
CANYON CROSSING	Travis Co	554A	MG-27	78746	4000-4199
CANYON EDGE DR	Travis Co	522T	MC-28	78733	1000-1999
CANYON GLEN CIR	Travis Co	491Q	MB-32	78732	3900-4399
CANYON GLEN DR	Travis Co	491Q	MB-32	78732	12400-12599
CANYON HOLLOW	Lago Vista	429V	WX-37	78645	18700-19199
CANYONLANDS LN	Pflugerville	438E	MQ-39	78660	600-699
CANYON LEDGE CV	Round Rock	345K	MJ-47	78681	3200-3299
CANYON LOOKOUT LN					
	Williamson Co	225A	MJ-60	78633	100-299
CANYON MAPLE RD	Pflugerville	437M	MP-38	78660	1000-1299
CANYON OAK LOOP	Williamson Co	225E	MJ-60	78633	100-199
CANYON OAKS CV	Lago Vista	429J	WW-38	78645	None
CANYON OAKS DR	Lago Vista	428R	WV-38	78645	None
	Lago Vista	429N	WW-38	78645	None
CANYON PARKE CT	Austin	462P	MC-35	78726	8000-8099
CANYON RANCH TRL	Travis Co	486Z	WR-31	78669	4900-5499
	Travis Co	516D	WR-30	78620	None
CANYON RIDGE DR	Austin	496D	MM-33	78753	100-699
CANYON RIM DR	Hays Co	637M	WT-17	78620	600-699
CANYON RIM DR	Travis Co	552Y	MD-25	78746	100-899
CANYON SAGE LN	Pflugerville	439E	MS-39	78660	18900-18999
CANYON SAGE PATH	Williamson Co	317W	MN-49	78665	1900-1999
CANYONSIDE TRL	Austin	524F	MG-30	78731	4200-4399
CANYON SPRINGS DR	Travis Co	402P	MC-41	78613	700-1199
CANYON TRAIL CT	Round Rock	407F	MN-42	78664	600-699
CANYON TURN TRL	Lakeway	518H	WV-30	78734	100-299
CANYON VALLEY RUN	Pflugerville	439J	MS-38	78660	2800-2999
CANYON VIEW	Travis Co	371Y	MB-43	78641	13100-13199
CANYON VIEW	West Lake Hills	553U	MF-25	78746	1500-1699
CANYON VIEW RD	Hays Co	668G	WV-15	78620	1000-1199
CANYON VISTA	Blanco Co	455L	WP-35	78620	100-499
CANYON VISTA LN	Williamson Co	225E	MJ-60	78633	100-299
CANYON VISTA WAY	Austin	463B	ME-36	78726	10300-10599
CANYONWOOD DR	Austin	613N	ME-20	78735	4600-4999
CANYONWOOD DR N	Hays Co	638N	WU-17	78620	100-1099
	Hays Co	637H	WT-18	78620	1100-1299
CANYONWOOD DR S	Hays Co	638X	WU-16	78620	100-499
CANYON WREN DR	Hays Co	732E	MC-9	78610	300-999
CAPADOCIA CV	Austin	466F	ML-36	78727	13400-13499
CAPARZO DR	Travis Co	402U	MD-40	78613	2500-2599
CAPE COD DR	Travis Co	467P	MN-35	78660	None
CAPE CORAL DR	Travis Co	582M	MD-23	78746	5900-6299
CAPEHART CV	Travis Co	552K	MC-26	78733	8700-8899
CAPE HORN DR	Travis Co	467P	MN-35	78660	None
CAPELLA TRL	Travis Co	521F	MA-30	78732	12000-12499
	Travis Co	521E	MA-30	78732	12500-12899
CAPE VERDE CV	Austin	645W	MJ-16	78744	5000-5099
CAPILANO CV	Round Rock	378X	MQ-43	78664	1000-1099
CAPISTAN LN	Williamson Co	224K	MG-59	78633	800-899
CAPISTRANO TRL	Travis Co	672P	MC-14	78739	3500-4199
CAPITAL PKWY	Austin	613D	MF-21	78746	1800-1999
CAPITAL OF TEXAS HWY N	Austin	523U	MF-28	78746	3400-4999
	Austin	524A	MG-30	78731	6100-6599
	Austin	494P	MG-32	78731	6600-8399
	Austin	494P	MG-32	78759	8400-9299
	Austin	495J	MJ-32	78759	9300-10099
	Travis Co	553C	MF-27	78746	100-3399
	Travis Co	523U	MF-28	78731	5000-6099
CAPITAL OF TEXAS HWY S	Austin	613C	MF-21	78746	3300-3699
	Austin	613C	MF-21	78704	3700-4299
	Travis Co	553W	ME-25	78746	100-599
	Travis Co	583E	ME-24	78746	600-2599
	Travis Co	613C	MF-21	78746	2600-3299
CAPITOL AVE	Lago Vista	459A	WW-36	78645	3800-3899
CAPITOL CT	Austin	555K	MJ-26	78756	800-999
CAPITOL DR	Austin	526F	ML-30	78753	400-9199
CAPITOL SADDLERY TRL	Travis Co	521F	MA-30	78732	12100-12699
CAPITOL VIEW DR	Austin	705E	MJ-12	78747	8800-8899
	Travis Co	705J	MJ-11	78747	9000-9599
	Travis Co	704R	MH-11	78747	9600-10399
CAPOTE PEAK DR	Georgetown	195S	MJ-61	78633	200-499
CAPRI	Lakeway	489W	WW-31	78734	100-299
CAPRICE DR	Austin	524U	MH-28	78731	5500-5699
CAPRI ISLE LN	Williamson Co	375W	MJ-43	78717	16900-17099
CAPRIOLA DR	Austin	643R	MF-17	78745	6300-6799
CAP ROCK DR	Austin	613E	ME-21	78735	4600-4899
CAP ROCK LN	Cedar Park	372N	MC-44	78613	1900-1999
CAPROCK PL	Georgetown	287K	MN-53	78626	2200-2499
CAP ROCK TRL	Round Rock	345J	MJ-47	78681	3700-3799
CAPSICUM CV	Travis Co	672T	MC-13	78748	3200-3299
CAP STONE DR	Austin	641X	MA-16	78739	10700-11299
CAPTAIN BAILY'S CT	Austin	497N	MN-32	78753	12000-12099
CAPTAIN HOPKINS CV	Austin	497E	MN-33	78753	12400-12499
CAPTAIN LADD CT	Round Rock	378B	MQ-45	78665	3300-3499
CAPULIN MOUNTAIN	Cedar Park	373X	ME-43	78613	200-399
CARACARA DR	Hays Co	732E	MC-9	78610	200-399
CARACARA DR	Williamson Co	433U	MF-37	78750	10300-10499
CARACAS DR	Travis Co	522X	MC-28	78733	9300-9499
CARA'S CV	Travis Co	437W	MN-37	78660	1300-1399
CARAVAN CIR	West Lake Hills	553Y	MF-25	78746	800-1199
CARAWAY ST	Austin	646B	ML-18	78741	7200-7299
CARBINE CIR	Bee Cave	549Z	WX-25	78738	5400-5499
CARBONDALE AVE	Austin	646W	ML-16	78744	3800-3999
CARDIFF DR	Austin	644F	MG-18	78745	800-999
CARDIGAN ST	Cedar Park	373U	MF-43	78613	1200-1299
CARDIN DR	Austin	494Z	MH-31	78759	8000-8199
CARDINAL AVE	Lago Vista	458K	WU-35	78645	21300-21999
CARDINAL DR	Hays Co	701Q	MB-11	78652	2500-2899
CARDINAL LN	Austin	614U	MH-19	78704	600-999
CARDINAL LN	Cedar Park	373W	ME-43	78613	100-399
CARDINAL LN	Round Rock	375V	MK-43	78681	1200-1399
CARDINAL LOOP	Austin	647J	MN-17	78617	2300-2699
CARDINAL ST	Elgin	533M	EB-29	78621	600-799
CARDINAL HILL	Hays Co	670S	WY-13	78737	13200-13299
CARDINAL HILL CIR	Austin	466U	MM-34	78758	1300-1399
CARDINAL HILL DR	Austin	466U	MM-34	78758	1300-1499
CARDINAL MEADOW WAY					
	Pflugerville	409W	MS-40	78660	None
CARDIZ	Williamson Co	226V	MM-58	78628	5400-5499
CAREFREE CIR	Lakeway	489Z	WX-31	78734	100-199
CARENTAN DR	Austin	641W	MA-16	78739	7700-7799
CAREW CV	Austin	464G	MH-36	78759	7200-7299
CAREY AVE	Taylor	352Q	MZ-47	76574	1700-1999
CARGILL DR	Briarcliff	457V	WT-34	78669	200-799
CARGILL DR	Williamson Co	405G	MK-42	78681	4000-4099
CARGO AVE	Austin	646H	MM-18	78719	9100-9699
	Austin	647J	MN-17	78719	None
CARIBOU DR	Georgetown	257K	MN-56	78626	2200-2399
CARIBOU TRL	Travis Co	582P	MC-23	78735	3300-3599
CARIBOU PARKE CV	Austin	462P	MC-35	78726	8000-8099
CARIBOU RIDGE TRL	Pflugerville	437Y	MP-37	78660	15400-15799
CARILLON WAY	Manor	530T	MU-28	78653	12700-13099
CARISBROOKE LN	Austin	528K	MQ-29	78754	6500-6899
CARISMATIC LN	Austin	703B	ME-12	78748	300-699
CARISSA CV	Austin	464P	MG-35	78759	7400-7499
CARL PL	Travis Co	503K	EA-32	78621	None
CARL RD	Travis Co	734M	MH-8	78747	11400-12399
CARLA DR	Travis Co	527X	MN-28	78754	3600-3699
CARLEEN DR	Austin	524V	MH-28	78757	5900-5999
CARLIN CV	Round Rock	406K	ML-41	78681	1000-1199
CARLISLE DR	Austin	525N	MJ-29	78757	3000-3199
CARLISLE CASTLE CT	Pflugerville	408X	MQ-40	78660	18900-18999
CARLOS G. PARKER BLVD NW					
	Taylor	322L	MZ-50	76574	100-899
	Taylor	352B	MY-48	76574	900-1299
CARLOS G. PARKER BLVD SE					
	Taylor	353L	EB-47	76574	100-1499
.......See.. Carlos Parker Loop Bypass E					
CARLOS G. PARKER BLVD SW					
	Taylor	353S	EA-46	76574	100-399
.... See.. US Hwy 79					
	Taylor	352Q	MZ-47	76574	400-1499
CARLOTTA CV	Travis Co	522S	MC-28	78733	10200-10299
CARLOTTA LN	Travis Co	522N	MC-29	78733	1000-1899
CARLOW DR	Austin	643L	MF-17	78745	2500-2699
CARLSBAD DR	Travis Co	550R	WZ-26	78733	12100-12499
CARLSON CV	Georgetown	287U	MP-52	78626	1-999
CARLSON DR	Austin	615X	MJ-19	78741	1800-1999
CARLSON LN	Travis Co	502M	MZ-32	78621	16300-17299
	Travis Co	503N	EA-32	78621	17300-18899
CARLSON RD	Travis Co	503K	EA-32	78621	17300-18799
CARL STERN DR	Hutto	379G	MT-45	78634	100-1299
	Hutto	380E	MU-45	78634	1300-1399
CARLTON RD	Austin	554Q	MH-26	78703	2700-2899
CARLTON RIDGE CV	Travis Co	548W	WU-25	78738	8000-8099
CARLWOOD DR	Austin	464K	MG-35	78759	7100-7399
CARMEL DR	Austin	586K	ML-23	78721	3900-3999
CARMEL DR	Williamson Co	345X	MJ-46	78681	2700-3999
CARMEL BAY ST	Georgetown	226H	MM-60	78628	30100-30199
CARMEL CREEKSIDE DR					
	Williamson Co	348H	MR-48	78634	1-699
CARMEL PARK LN	Austin	465Q	MK-35	78727	12000-12199
CARMEN CT	Austin	526W	ML-28	78752	300-399
CARNARVON LN	Austin	614V	MH-19	78704	2600-2799
CARNATION TERRACE	Austin	616W	ML-19	78741	6000-6299
CARNEGE CV	Lago Vista	459E	WW-36	78645	20000-20099
CARNELIAN DR	Travis Co	672N	MC-14	78739	11400-11499
CARNFORTH DR	Austin	497J	MN-32	78753	12100-12199
CARNOUSTY CV	Round Rock	378V	MR-43	78664	3600-3699
CARNOUSTY ST	Round Rock	378V	MR-43	78664	3100-3199
CAROL AVE	Leander	342B	MC-48	78641	100-399
CAROL CT	Georgetown	287P	MN-53	78626	200-299
CAROL CV	Bastrop	744H	ED-9	78602	600-699
CAROL CV	Burnet Co	426B	WQ-39	78669	100-199
CAROL DR	Hutto	350N	MU-47	78634	100-599
CAROL ANN DR	Austin	556R	MM-26	78723	3100-3499
CAROL ANN DR	Hays Co	608Z	WV-19	78737	1-99
CAROLINA ST	Elgin	534E	EC-30	78621	800-899
CAROLINA ST	Taylor	353K	EA-47	76574	1100-1199
CAROLINE LN	Travis Co	619A	MS-21	78724	5700-6399
CAROL MICHELLE CV	Cedar Park	402R	MD-41	78613	1400-1499
CAROLYN AVE	Austin	555X	MJ-25	78705	500-799
CAROLYN CV	Taylor	323S	EA-49	76574	2300-2399
CAROLYN DR	Taylor	323S	EA-49	76574	2200-2299
	Taylor	322V	MZ-49	76574	2300-2399
CAROLYNS WAY	Buda	732Q	MD-8	78610	100-399
CAROVILLI DR	Austin	673X	ME-13	78748	10600-10799
CARPENTER AVE	Austin	526E	ML-30	78753	200-799
CARPENTER DR	Williamson Co	381F	MW-45	76574	1-599
CARPENTER LN	Hays Co	701R	MB-11	78652	13500-13899
CARRANZO DR	Travis Co	581R	MB-23	78735	8300-9099
CARRARA	West Lake Hills	583G	MF-24	78746	200-299
CARRERA DR	Austin	465A	MJ-36	78727	12800-12899
CARRIAGE CT	Bastrop Co	712R	MZ-11	78602	100-199
CARRIAGE DR	Austin	525V	MK-28	78752	7500-7699
CARRIAGE CLUB DR	Cedar Park	372T	MC-43	78613	1700-2099
CARRIAGE HILLS CV	Cedar Park	372P	MC-44	78613	2000-2099
CARRIAGE HILLS DR	Manor	530T	MU-28	78653	None
CARRIAGE HILLS DR N	Georgetown	287L	MP-53	78626	300-399
CARRIAGE HILLS DR S	Georgetown	287L	MP-53	78626	100-199
CARRIAGE HILLS TRL	Cedar Park	372P	MC-44	78613	1300-1999
CARRIAGE HOUSE LN	Hays Co	639N	WW-17	78737	1-99
	Hays Co	638R	WV-17	78737	None
CARRIAGE PARK LN	Austin	466P	ML-35	78727	2000-2199
CARRICK LN	Williamson Co	405B	MJ-42	78681	8200-8299
CARRIE MANOR ST E	Manor	529U	MT-28	78653	100-599
CARRIE MANOR ST W	Manor	529U	MT-28	78653	100-699
CARRINGTON DR	Austin	641R	MB-17	78749	6200-6699
CARRINGTON LN	Buda	732T	MC-7	78610	100-399
CARRIZO TERRACE	Austin	525D	MK-30	78758	1200-1299
CARROL LN	Hays Co	636F	WQ-18	78620	100-399
CARRY BACK LN	Austin	523Y	MF-28	78746	5700-6199
CARSHALTON DR	Austin	496F	ML-33	78758	11700-11899
CARSON CREEK BLVD	Austin	646D	MM-18	78742	9300-9599
	Austin	647A	MN-18	78617	9600-9799
CARSONHILL DR	Austin	586D	MM-24	78723	4700-4999
CARSON RIDGE	Austin	646E	ML-18	78741	6300-6599
CARTER LN	Austin	645P	MJ-17	78744	4700-4899
CARTER ST	Bastrop	745A	EE-9	78602	1600-1899
	Bastrop	715W	EE-10	78602	1900-2299
CARTIER CV	Lago Vista	459E	WW-36	78645	20100-20199

STREET NAME	CITY or COUNTY	MAPSCO GRID	AUSTIN GRID	ZIP CODE	BLOCK RANGE O/E
CARTMAN OVERLOOK	Hays Co	607D	WT-21	78720	100-299
CARTO ST	Leander	342P	MC-47	78641	1600-1699
CARTWRIGHT CV	Austin	524E	MG-30	78731	5900-5999
CARVER AVE	Austin	556A	ML-27	78752	6900-7399
	Austin	526X	ML-28	78752	7400-7699
CARVER ST	Elgin	534X	EC-28	78621	100-299
CARWILL DR	Austin	557Y	MP-25	78724	6900-7199
CARY DR	Austin	525S	MJ-28	78757	5800-6499
CARYA CT	Round Rock	375B	MJ-45	78681	3400-3499
CASA BLANCA CV	Round Rock	347S	MN-46	78665	1300-1399
CASA BLANCA DR	Georgetown	226U	MM-58	78628	4300-4399
CASABLANCA LN	Travis Co	489R	WX-32	78734	800-999
CASA GRANDE DR	Travis Co	522T	MC-28	78733	1800-2199
CASA LINDA CV	Round Rock	375H	MK-45	78681	2000-2199
CASA LOMA DR	Williamson Co	225N	MJ-59	78633	100-199
CASA LOMA ST	Buda	762M	MD-5	78610	300-499
CASA NAVARRO DR	Travis Co	409T	MS-40	78660	20500-20599
CASA PIEDRA PL	Pflugerville	407X	MN-40	78664	17300-17499
CASA VERDE	Lakeway	489U	WX-31	78734	1-99
CASA VERDE CV	Williamson Co	194B	MG-63	78633	100-199
CASA VERDE DR	Bastrop Co	738X	MQ-7	78617	None
CASA VERDE DR	Williamson Co	194B	MG-63	78633	200-299
CASCADA CV	Williamson Co	195R	ML-62	78633	100-199
CASCADA DR	Austin	494S	MG-31	78750	6400-6599
CASCADE CIR	Point Venture	488M	WV-32	78654	400-499
CASCADE DR	Austin	525K	MJ-29	78757	2500-2799
CASCADE BLUFF	Bee Cave	549K	WW-26	78738	15200-15299
CASCADE CAVERNS TRL	Austin	702B	MC-12	78739	11900-12499
CASCADE FALLS DR	Travis Co	550R	WZ-26	78733	2600-2899
CASCADERA DR	Austin	554K	MG-26	78731	3400-3499
CASCADES CV	Round Rock	378X	MQ-43	78664	2900-2999
CASEY CV	Williamson Co	403W	ME-40	78613	2300-2399
CASEY LN	Round Rock	377W	MN-43	78664	1500-1599
CASEY ST	Austin	644B	MG-18	78745	1000-1499
CASH CT	Travis Co	490G	WZ-33	78734	3200-3299
CASHELL WOOD CV	Travis Co	432G	MD-39	78613	2700-2799
CASHEL WOOD DR	Travis Co	432L	MD-38	78613	2300-3199
CASHEW LN	Cedar Park	403C	MF-42	78613	800-1099
CASHION CT	Lakeway	490X	WY-31	78734	15200-15299
CASIMIR CV	Austin	671B	MA-15	78739	6600-6699
CASITAS CT	Leander	312W	MC-49	78641	800-899
CASITAS DR	Austin	404F	MG-42	78717	10700-11199
CASPER CV	Round Rock	378U	MR-43	78664	2200-2298 E
CASPIAN CV	Williamson Co	377B	MN-45	78665	2000-2099
CASPIAN DR	Austin	642V	MD-16	78749	8300-8599
CASSADY DR	Austin	465L	MK-35	78727	12200-12499
CASSANDRA DR	Austin	404K	MG-41	78717	9900-10299
CASSANDRA DR	Hutto	379X	MS-43	78634	100-299
CASSAT CV	Austin	467X	MN-34	78753	1000-1099
CASSAVA DR	Travis Co	553D	MF-27	78746	3500-3899
CASSIA CV	Austin	464P	MG-35	78759	10400-10499
CASSIA DR	Austin	464P	MG-35	78759	10300-10799
CASSIDY CT	Williamson Co	285H	MK-54	78628	200-299
CASSIDY DR	Williamson Co	285H	MK-54	78628	200-399
CASSIOPEIA WAY	Travis Co	521E	MA-30	78732	1200-1599
CASSYE CV	Austin	464L	MH-35	78759	7000-7099
CASTEBAR DR	Travis Co	408L	MR-41	78664	500-599
CASTELLAN LN	Williamson Co	348N	MQ-47	78665	None
CASTELLANO WAY	Travis Co	432L	MD-38	78613	3100-3199
CASTILE RD	Travis Co	522W	MC-28	78733	1000-1399
CASTLE CT	Austin	584R	MH-23	78703	1100-1199
CASTLE DR	Hutto	379H	MT-45	78634	100-199
CASTLE PATH	Round Rock	346W	ML-46	78681	1100-1199
CASTLE ARCH CT	Austin	642N	MC-17	78749	8900-8999
CASTLEBAY DR	Briarcliff	457Y	WT-34	78669	500-699
CASTLE CREEK	Williamson Co	344Z	MH-46	78681	4000-4099
CASTLE CREEK CV	Williamson Co	344V	MH-46	78681	4000-4099
CASTLEDALE DR	Austin	673E	ME-15	78748	2400-2599
CASTLEGUARD WAY	Cedar Park	372K	MC-44	78613	1800-1899
CASTLE HILL ST	Austin	584R	MH-23	78703	1200-1299
CASTLEKEEP WAY	Austin	644W	MG-16	78745	6800-7099
CASTLEMAN DR	Travis Co	618M	MR-20	78725	4600-4799
CASTLE PEAK TRL	Austin	462F	MC-36	78726	7900-8199
CASTLE PINES CV	Georgetown	226T	ML-58	78628	4600-4699
CASTLE PINES DR	Austin	404G	MH-42	78717	9100-9899
CASTLE RIDGE RD	Travis Co	583A	ME-24	78746	700-799
	Travis Co	582D	MD-24	78746	800-1199
CASTLE ROCK CT	Austin	464A	MG-36	78750	11600-11699
CASTLE ROCK CV	Round Rock	345N	MJ-47	78681	3800-3899
CASTLE ROCK DR	Round Rock	345J	MJ-47	78681	3700-3899
CASTLETON DR	Travis Co	467P	MN-35	78660	900-999
CASTLETROY DR	Austin	375W	MJ-43	78717	16200-16599
CASTLEVIEW DR	Travis Co	436V	MM-37	78728	2000-2199
CASTLEWOOD CT	Taylor	322Z	MZ-49	76574	1600-1699
CASTLEWOOD DR	Austin	673E	ME-15	78748	9300-9599
CASTLEWOOD TRL	Leander	342Y	MD-46	78641	2200-3599
CASTRO ST	Austin	586W	ML-22	78702	2700-3199
CASWELL AVE	Austin	555R	MK-26	78751	4200-5199
CATALINA DR	Austin	645F	MJ-18	78741	2700-3699
CATALINA DR	Williamson Co	343T	ME-46	78641	1400-1599
CATALONIA DR	Austin	465S	MJ-34	78759	11300-11599
CATALPA CV	Round Rock	378S	MQ-43	78665	900-999
CATALPA ST	Austin	585T	MJ-22	78702	900-1199
CATALPA ST	Bastrop	745B	EE-9	78602	1200-1299
CATAMARAN CT	Travis Co	426C	WR-39	78669	2800-2899
CATAMARAN CV	Travis Co	402Y	MD-40	78613	2400-2499
CATAMARAN DR	Travis Co	426C	WR-39	78669	27000-27099
CATCHFLY CV	Travis Co	402Y	MD-40	78613	1700-1799
CATCLAW CT	Austin	675N	MJ-14	78744	6900-6999
CAT CLAW CV	Williamson Co	433E	ME-39	78613	3000-3099
CAT CREEK TRL	Austin	524B	MG-30	78731	6500-6699
CAT CREEK RUN	Austin	524B	MG-30	78731	4900-4999
CATER DR	Austin	584Y	MH-22	78704	500-599
CATERPILLER LN	Georgetown	195T	MJ-61	78633	100-199
CATES LAKE DR	Travis Co	560K	MU-26	78653	11700-11799
CATFISH CV	Hays Co	668D	WV-15	78620	100-199
CATHEDRAL MOUNTAIN PASS					
	Georgetown	225B	MJ-60	78633	100-399
CATHERINE CT	Round Rock	407J	MN-41	78664	1500-1699
CATHERINE DR	Travis Co	588S	MQ-22	78724	10200-10599
CAT HOLLOW DR	Austin	524C	MH-30	78731	4100-4399
CAT HOLLOW DR	Williamson Co	405G	MK-42	78681	7400-7799
CAT HOLLOW CLUB DR	Briarcliff	457R	WT-35	78669	600-1499
CATLIN CV	Williamson Co	343X	ME-46	78641	1300-1399
CAT MOUNTAIN CV	Austin	524K	MG-29	78731	6200-6399
CAT MOUNTAIN DR	Austin	524K	MG-29	78731	4100-4799
CATSBY CT	Travis Co	619E	MS-21	78724	5500-5599
CATS-EYE LN	Austin	675S	MJ-13	78747	7500-7599
CATSKILL TRL	Travis Co	433T	ME-37	78750	10800-10999
CAT TAIL CV	Austin	493R	MF-32	78750	7600-7699
CATTAIL CV	Williamson Co	379X	MS-43	78634	100-199
CATTHORN CV	Austin	464Q	MH-35	78759	10800-10999
CATTLE CV	Austin	673F	ME-15	78748	1600-1699
CATTLE DR	Austin	642Q	MD-17	78749	8000-8399
CATTLE DR	Cedar Park	402Q	MD-41	78613	1700-1899
CATTLE TRL	Austin	673F	ME-15	78748	1300-1699
CATTLEMAN DR	Hays Co	701H	MB-12	78652	3600-3999
	Travis Co	701H	MB-12	78652	3400-3599
CATTLE TRAIL DR	Hays Co	668P	WU-14	78620	100-799
CATTLE TRAIL WAY	Georgetown	225D	MK-60	78633	100-199
CATUMET DR	Pflugerville	437D	MP-39	78660	200-899
	Pflugerville	438A	MQ-39	78660	None
CAUDILL LN	Travis Co	548Z	WV-25	78738	6700-6999
CAVA PL	Travis Co	582W	MC-22	78735	7800-7999
CAVALCADE CT	Austin	553C	MF-27	78746	3100-3199
CAVALIER CANYON DR	Lakeway	490W	WY-31	78734	15300-15499
	Travis Co	520B	WY-30	78734	15000-15299
CAVALRY CT	Austin	524D	MH-30	78731	7900-7999
CAVALRY TRL	Elgin	533F	EA-30	78621	100-299
CAVALRY RIDE TRL	Travis Co	521K	MA-29	78732	900-1099
CAVE DOME PATH	Round Rock	345P	MJ-47	78681	3300-3399
CAVE HOLLOW	Austin	494S	MG-31	78750	7300-7398 E
CAVEN RD	Austin	645P	MJ-17	78744	3800-4199
CAVERN MIST LN	Austin	702F	MC-12	78739	2800-2999
CAVERN SPRINGS RD	Austin	465L	MK-35	78727	4300-4499
CAVES VALLEY DR	Austin	404M	MH-41	78717	9400-9499
CAVILEER AVE	Austin	525S	MJ-28	78757	2600-2799
CAVU RD	Georgetown	226Y	MM-58	78628	700-799
	Williamson Co	226Y	MM-58	78628	800-899
	Williamson Co	226U	MM-58	78628	3000-3899
CAYENNE LN	Austin	646B	ML-18	78741	7100-7699
CAYLOR CV	Bastrop	744G	ED-9	78602	700-799
CAYMEN PL	Austin	642Q	MD-17	78749	4600-4699
CAYUGA DR	Austin	642V	MD-16	78749	8300-8499
CAYUSE CV	Austin	673Y	MF-13	78748	10400-10499
C-BAR RANCH TRL	Cedar Park	373L	MF-44	78613	1000-1299
CEBERRY DR	Austin	525A	MJ-30	78759	7800-8099
	Austin	494Z	MH-31	78759	8100-8199
CEBO CV	Austin	643P	ME-17	78745	2600-2699
CECELIA ST	Taylor	352D	MZ-48	76574	800-1899
CECIL DR	Travis Co	674T	MG-13	78744	2400-2599
CECIL ROSETTA	Travis Co	735K	MJ-8	78747	None
CEDAR AVE	Austin	585R	MK-23	78702	1200-1899
	Austin	585M	MK-23	78722	1900-2099
CEDAR CIR	Elgin	534P	EC-29	78621	200-299
CEDAR CIR	Point Venture	488R	WV-32	78654	18900-18999
CEDAR CV	Cedar Park	403E	ME-42	78613	800-899
CEDAR CV	Pflugerville	438T	MQ-37	78660	1000-1099
CEDAR CV	Village of Bear Creek	670G	WZ-15	78737	8200-8399
CEDAR DR	Georgetown	256Y	MM-55	78628	500-599
CEDAR DR	Point Venture	488R	WV-32	78654	700-799
CEDAR LN	Bastrop Co	712W	MY-10	78612	100-299
	Bastrop Co	711U	MX-10	78612	300-399
CEDAR LN	Pflugerville	438T	MQ-37	78660	500-799
CEDAR LN	Travis Co	458T	WU-34	78669	20800-21099
CEDAR ST	Austin	585B	MJ-24	78705	3000-3199
	Austin	555X	MJ-25	78705	3400-3799
CEDAR ST	Austin	523U	MF-28	78746	6300-6899
CEDAR ST	Bastrop	745B	EE-9	78602	100-1699
	Bastrop	745C	EF-9	78602	1700-2299
CEDAR ST	Jonestown	400M	WZ-41	78645	18200-18299
CEDAR ST	Travis Co	491H	MB-33	78732	12400-12899
CEDAR ST N	Buda	762D	MD-6	78610	100-399
CEDAR ST S	Buda	762H	MD-6	78610	100-299
CEDAR BEND CV	Austin	466X	ML-34	78758	12300-12399
CEDAR BEND DR	Austin	466S	ML-34	78758	1500-2599
CEDAR BEND DR	Round Rock	376J	ML-44	78681	1800-2099
CEDAR BLUFF CT	Travis Co	400W	WY-40	78645	8100-8199
CEDAR BRANCH DR	Austin	466K	ML-35	78727	2200-2399
CEDAR BRANCH DR	Williamson Co	285G	MK-54	78628	100-199
CEDAR BREAKS RD	Williamson Co	255U	MK-55	78628	800-2199
CEDARBROOK CT	Austin	496L	MM-32	78753	300-399
CEDAR BROOK DR	Cedar Park	372L	MD-44	78613	1100-1499
CEDAR CLIFF DR	Austin	464U	MH-34	78759	5800-5999
CEDAR CLIFFE DR	Austin	464A	MG-36	78750	11200-11599
CEDAR CREEK CV	Round Rock	406J	ML-41	78681	1700-1799
CEDAR CREST CIR	Round Rock	378S	MQ-43	78665	2900-2999
CEDAR CREST CV	Austin	433V	MF-37	78750	11900-11999
CEDAR CREST CV	Round Rock	378W	MQ-43	78665	1000-1099
CEDAR CREST DR	Austin	433Z	MF-37	78750	9100-9599
CEDAR CREST DR	Cedar Park	372Q	MD-44	78613	900-1599
CEDARDALE DR	Austin	644P	MG-17	78745	5700-5999
CEDAR EDGE DR	Austin	646X	ML-16	78744	7400-7599
CEDAR ELM LN	Georgetown	225R	MK-59	78633	1000-1199
CEDAR ELM LN	Round Rock	375M	MK-44	78681	3000-3099
CEDAR ELM TRL	Austin	611H	MB-21	78735	8000-8499
CEDAR FALLS ST	Round Rock	406E	ML-42	78681	1000-1199
CEDAR FOREST DR	Austin	433Z	MF-37	78750	9200-9499
CEDAR GLEN	Austin	644J	MG-17	78745	800-1099
CEDAR GLEN	Lago Vista	458D	WV-36	78645	3800-3899
CEDAR GLEN CV	Lago Vista	399P	WW-41	78645	8200-8499
CEDAR GLEN CV	Lakeway	489Q	WX-32	78734	100-199
CEDAR GLEN CV	Round Rock	375M	MK-44	78681	2000-2098 E
CEDARGROVE DR	Austin	645S	MJ-16	78744	4600-4799
CEDAR HILLS BLVD	Cedar Park	372L	MD-44	78613	1100-1899
CEDAR HOLLOW	Travis Co	340J	WY-47	78641	22700-22799
CEDAR HOLLOW RD	Williamson Co	284L	MH-53	78628	2000-2799
	Williamson Co	254T	MG-55	78628	2800-2999
CEDARHURST CIR	Williamson Co	434K	MG-38	78729	13000-13099
CEDAR HURST LN	Travis Co	489V	WX-31	78734	200-499
CEDAR LAKE BLVD	Georgetown	225Y	MK-58	78633	200-499
CEDARLAWN CIR	Austin	556V	MM-25	78723	3000-3099
CEDARLAWN ST	Taylor	322U	MZ-49	76574	1800-1899
CEDAR LEDGE	Travis Co	460R	WZ-35	78734	15500-15699
CEDAR LIME RD	Travis Co	372W	MC-43	78641	13200-13499
CEDAR MOUND PASS	Travis Co	403A	ME-42	78613	300-499
CEDAR OAK DR	West Lake Hills	583C	MF-24	78746	300-499
CEDAR OAKS DR	Cedar Park	372L	MD-44	78613	1100-1399
CEDAR PARK DR	Cedar Park	373W	ME-43	78613	200-599
	Cedar Park	372Z	MD-43	78613	600-1599
CEDAR PARK DR	West Lake Hills	583H	MF-24	78746	800-899
CEDAR PASS RD	Hays Co	668W	WU-13	78620	1100-1599
CEDAR PAW LN	Hays Co	669D	WX-15	78737	10600-10699
CEDAR POINT DR	Austin	586G	MM-24	78723	4600-4699
CEDAR RIDGE	Travis Co	340E	WY-48	78641	13700-14199
CEDAR RIDGE CIR	Lago Vista	429F	WW-39	78645	6800-6899
CEDAR RIDGE CT	Lago Vista	429B	WW-39	78645	7000-7099
CEDARRIDGE CT	Leander	342H	MD-48	78641	1000-1099
CEDAR RIDGE CV	Lago Vista	429F	WW-39	78645	20800-20899
CEDAR RIDGE DR	Austin	615T	MJ-19	78741	1800-1999
CEDAR RIDGE DR	Lago Vista	429F	WW-39	78645	6800-6999
CEDAR RIDGE DR	Pflugerville	438W	MQ-37	78660	400-799
CEDAR RIDGE DR	Williamson Co	285H	MK-54	78628	200-299
CEDAR ROCK CT	Lakeway	519L	WX-29	78734	700-799
CEDAR SAGE CT	Travis Co	489F	WW-33	78645	None
CEDAR SPRINGS CIR	Travis Co	641C	MB-18	78737	8500-8599
CEDAR SPRINGS PL	Round Rock	375G	MK-45	78681	2700-2799
CEDARSPUR RD	Austin	466N	ML-35	78758	12300-12499
CEDAR VALLEY CV	Austin	496L	MM-32	78753	11800-11899
CEDARVIEW DR	Austin	614J	MG-20	78704	2500-3099
CEDER	Travis Co	530P	MU-29	78653	12700-13099
CEDRICK CV	Austin	673J	ME-14	78748	2300-2399
CEDRO CV	Austin	524E	MG-30	78731	6400-6499
CEDRO TRL	Austin	524E	MG-30	78731	5000-5699
C. E. KELLEY DR	Austin	676M	MM-14	78617	9400-9699
CELANOVA CT	Travis Co	580G	WZ-24	78738	4900-4999
CELE RD	Pflugerville	439R	MT-38	78653	6400-7099
	Pflugerville	440T	MU-37	78653	7100-7799
	Travis Co	439R	MT-38	78660	5700-6399
	Travis Co	440T	MU-37	78653	7800-9099
CELEBRATION CT	Lago Vista	429M	WX-38	78645	7200-7299
CELENDINE DR	Austin	670D	WZ-16	78739	8100-8199
CELERY LOOP	Austin	674J	MG-14	78748	300-599
CELESTE CIR	Austin	586L	MM-23	78721	1800-1899
CELESTIAL LN	Travis Co	467R	MP-35	78660	14300-14699
CELESTIAL ST	Cedar Park	372G	MD-45	78613	600-699
CELETA LN	Austin	495A	MJ-33	78759	4500-4599
CELIA DR	Cedar Park	403T	ME-40	78613	2100-2399
	Cedar Park	403X	ME-40	78613	2400-2599
CELLUS LN	Bastrop Co	744S	EC-7	78602	100-199
CELTIC CT	Austin	528P	MQ-29	78754	6900-6999
CELTIC CV	Round Rock	376A	ML-45	78681	1100-1199
CEMENT PLANT RD	Hays Co	762V	MD-4	78610	100-499
CENIZO PATH	Cedar Park	373P	ME-44	78613	600-699
CENTENNIAL TRL	Austin	433T	ME-37	78726	10700-10999
	Travis Co	433T	ME-37	78750	11000-11499
CENTENNIAL OLYMPIC PARK					
	Travis Co	491Y	MB-31	78732	2800-3099
CENTER ST	Jonestown	400H	WZ-42	78645	18100-18399
CENTER ST	Taylor	353F	EA-48	76574	800-999
CENTERBROOK PL	Williamson Co	346C	MM-48	78665	500-899
CENTER LAKE DR	Austin	466Z	MM-34	78753	12700-13399
	Austin	467S	MN-34	78753	None
CENTER LINE PASS	Austin	467N	MN-35	78753	13300-13799
CENTER POINT LN	Travis Co	489M	WX-32	78734	1500-1899
CENTER RIDGE DR	Austin	466R	MM-35	78753	400-1199
CENTIMETER CIR	Austin	495R	MK-32	78758	2000-2099
CENTRAL AVE	Elgin	534N	EC-29	78621	100-899
CENTRAL DR	Cedar Park	372R	MD-44	78613	100-499
CENTRAL DR E	Georgetown	256U	MM-55	78628	100-899
CENTRAL DR W	Georgetown	256U	MM-55	78628	100-299
CENTRAL COMMERCE CIR					
	Pflugerville	437N	MN-38	78660	1400-1599
CENTRAL COMMERCE CT					
	Pflugerville	437E	MN-39	78664	1800-1899
CENTRAL COMMERCE DR					
	Pflugerville	437J	MN-38	78660	None
	Travis Co	437J	MN-38	78660	15800-16499
	Travis Co	437E	MN-39	78664	16500-16799
CENTRALIA CV	Austin	643N	ME-17	78745	3200-3299
CENTRAL PARK	Travis Co	491Y	MB-31	78732	12300-12799
CENTRAL PARK CT	Austin	644J	MG-17	78745	1200-1399
CENTRE DR	Georgetown	285P	MJ-53	78628	12000-12999
CENTRE ST	Weir	258H	MR-57	78626	100-199
CENTRE CREEK DR	Austin	526Y	MM-28	78754	1600-1899
CENTRE PARK DR	Austin	526Y	MM-28	78754	7900-8199
CENTRE PLAZA	Austin	526Z	MM-28	78754	2100-2399
CENTRUM DR	Austin	527C	MP-30	78754	2900-3299
CENTURY LN	Cedar Park	372R	MD-44	78613	1100-1399
CENTURY ST	Pflugerville	437N	MN-38	78660	1500-1799
CENTURY OAKS TERRACE	Austin	465Y	MK-34	78758	11400-11499
CENTURY PARK BLVD	Austin	466B	ML-36	78727	2300-3399
CENTURY PARK CV	Austin	466A	ML-36	78727	13600-13699
CERCA VIEJO WAY	Austin	583T	ME-22	78746	2000-2299
CERCIS CV	Austin	464P	MG-35	78759	7200-7299
CERES LN	Georgetown	314B	MG-51	78628	100-199
CERRO CT	Leander	341M	MB-47	78641	1800-1899
CERRO CV	Austin	524E	MG-30	78731	6400-6499
CERRO ALTO CV	Travis Co	522W	MC-28	78733	9900-10099
CERULEAN WAY	Round Rock	345S	MJ-46	78681	3600-3799
CERVIN BLVD	Travis Co	436Z	MM-37	78728	1800-2199
CERVIN CV	Travis Co	436Z	MM-37	78728	14800-14899
CERVINIA DR	Williamson Co	316Z	MM-49	78665	4400-4599
CERVINUS RUN	Austin	612C	MD-21	78735	6000-6099
CESAR CHAVEZ ST E	Austin	615B	MJ-21	78702	100-3199
	Austin	616E	ML-21	78702	3200-5299
CESAR CHAVEZ ST W	Austin	585W	MJ-22	78701	100-699
	Austin	584Q	MH-23	78703	700-2399
CESSAL AVE	Austin	586U	MM-22	78721	1100-1199
CESSNA LN	Burnet Co	396W	WQ-40	78669	100-299
CESSNA LN	Williamson Co	375W	MJ-43	78717	9100-9299
CETONA CT	Austin	583Y	MF-22	78746	1900-1999
CEYLON CT	Austin	642M	MD-17	78749	7400-7499
CEYLON TEA CIR	Travis Co	467Q	MP-35	78660	13800-14299
CEZANNE CT	Austin	433P	ME-38	78726	11400-11499
CEZANNE ST	Austin	433P	ME-38	78726	11100-11399
CHACO CANYON	Cedar Park	373X	ME-43	78613	200-399
CHADBURY CV	Austin	465P	MJ-35	78727	4800-4899
CHADSFORD RIDGE	Travis Co	468T	MQ-34	78660	None
CHADWICK DR	Williamson Co	314F	MG-51	78628	100-499
CHADWOOD CT	Williamson Co	375S	MJ-43	78717	17200-17299
CHADWYCK DR	Austin	556Z	MM-25	78723	5500-5699
CHAINFIRE CV	Williamson Co	434U	MH-37	78729	8100-8199
CHALET CIR	Travis Co	401N	MA-41	78641	17700-17799
CHALET DR	Travis Co	708P	MQ-11	78617	14600-14999
CHALICE CV	Round Rock	347W	MN-46	78665	1700-1799
CHALICE WAY	Round Rock	347W	MN-46	78665	1-99
CHALK CV	Williamson Co	402Q	MD-41	78613	1700-1799
CHALK LN	Williamson Co	402Q	MD-41	78613	1300-1499
CHALK DRAW CT	Buda	732X	MC-7	78610	100-199
CHALK HILL CV	Round Rock	407H	MP-42	78665	2100-2199

C

C

STREET NAME	CITY or COUNTY	MAPSCO GRID	AUSTIN GRID	ZIP CODE	BLOCK RANGE O/E
CHALK HILL DR	Austin	464X	MG-34	78759	6800-6999
CHALK KNOLL CV	Travis Co	582E	MC-24	78735	2600-2699
CHALK KNOLL DR	Travis Co	582A	MC-24	78735	8000-8999
CHALK ROCK CV	Travis Co	582A	MC-24	78735	1700-1999
CHALKSTONE CV	Travis Co	522L	MD-29	78730	3600-3699
CHALKSTONE LN	Round Rock	345S	MJ-46	78681	3500-3599
CHALLA DR	Travis Co	402P	MC-41	78613	1100-1199
CHALLENGER	Lakeway	489X	WW-31	78734	800-1299
CHALLENGER CV	Lakeway	489T	WW-31	78734	100-199
CHALLSBURY DR	Austin	643T	ME-16	78745	7600-7699
CHALMERS AVE	Austin	615C	MK-21	78702	1-399
	Austin	585Y	MK-22	78702	400-1099
CHAMA CIR	Travis Co	433X	ME-37	78750	10800-10899
CHAMA TRACE	Hays Co	668J	WU-14	78620	100-799
CHAMBERLAIN CT	Travis Co	619E	MS-21	78724	15200-15399
CHAMBERLAIN DR	Round Rock	348W	MQ-46	78665	2100-2399
CHAMBERS ST	Bastrop	745G	EF-9	78602	1200-1299
	Bastrop	745C	EF-9	78602	1600-1899
CHAMBERS PEAK CV	Travis Co	677Y	MP-13	78617	11800-11899
CHAMBLEY CV	Travis Co	493N	ME-32	78730	6300-6399
CHAMBRAY CT	Travis Co	702G	MD-12	78748	2400-2499
CHAMELEON CT	Village of the Hills	519P	WW-29	78738	1-99
CHAMISA DR	Travis Co	522G	MD-30	78730	3900-4099
CHAMOIS KNOLL	Pflugerville	437B	MN-39	78664	1700-1899
CHAMOMILE CV	Travis Co	467G	MP-36	78660	14900-14999
CHAMONIX TERRACE	Williamson Co	405B	MJ-42	78681	16700-16799
CHAMPAGNE CT	Williamson Co	343N	ME-47	78641	3300-3399
CHAMPION CV	Point Venture	489J	WW-32	78645	200-299
CHAMPION DR	Austin	464A	MG-36	78750	11500-11599
CHAMPION DR	Lakeway	519E	WW-30	78734	100-399
CHAMPION DR	Round Rock	377A	MN-45	78664	1400-1499
	Williamson Co	377A	MN-45	78664	1100-1399
CHAMPION LN	Lakeway	519F	WW-30	78734	1-99
CHAMPION WAY	Bee Cave	549M	WX-26	78738	14200-14499
CHAMPION GRANDVIEW WAY	Austin	523D	MF-30	78750	6400-6599
	Austin	524A	MG-30	78750	None
CHAMPIONS CIR	Point Venture	489J	WW-32	78645	18400-18699
CHAMPIONS CT	Georgetown	226M	MM-59	78628	100-199
CHAMPIONS DR	Georgetown	226M	MM-59	78628	200-799
CHAMPIONS LN	Austin	704S	MG-10	78747	1100-11199
CHAMPIONSHIP DR	Village of the Hills	519P	WW-29	78738	1-99
CHAMPIONS POINT DR	Pflugerville	437Y	MP-37	78660	600-999
CHAMPLAIN CV	Lago Vista	459J	WW-35	78645	20100-20199
CHANCE CV	Cedar Park	372G	MD-45	78613	2200-2299
CHANCE TRL	Georgetown	257K	MN-56	78626	None
CHANCELLROY DR	Austin	464F	MG-36	78759	11400-11599
CHANCERY CT	Hays Co	639X	WW-16	78737	100-199
CHANCERY CT	Round Rock	344R	MH-47	78681	4000-4099
CHANCES WAY	Buda	732R	MD-8	78610	100-199
CHANCOCK CV	Georgetown	285P	MJ-53	78628	100-199
CHANDLER RD	Williamson Co	318R	MR-50	78634	5600-5999
CHANDLER BRANCH DR	Williamson Co	343W	ME-46	78641	500-699
CHANDLER CREEK BLVD	Round Rock	377L	MP-44	78665	2600-2799
	Williamson Co	377F	MN-45	78665	2000-2599
CHANDLER CROSSING CV	Williamson Co	377B	MN-45	78665	300-399
CHANDLER CROSSING TRL	Williamson Co	377B	MN-45	78665	100-299
CHANDLER POINTE LOOP	Williamson Co	377F	MN-45	78665	100-199
CHANDLER VIEW TRL	Williamson Co	377C	MP-45	78665	100-299
CHANDON LN	Lakeway	519F	WW-30	78734	1-99
CHANINGCROSS DR	Travis Co	558J	MQ-26	78724	None
CHANNEL RD	Austin	524S	MG-28	78746	1700-1799
CHANNEL WAY	Jonestown	400H	WZ-42	78645	11000-11099
CHANNEL ISLAND DR	Austin	704A	MG-12	78747	10000-10599
CHANNING CIR	Austin	643K	ME-17	78745	2700-2799
CHANNING DR	Austin	703E	ME-12	78748	11700-11799
CHANOCK DR	Georgetown	285P	MJ-53	78628	1000-2199
CHANTILLY LN	Austin	526P	ML-29	78753	900-999
CHANTILY CV	Lago Vista	399T	WW-40	78645	8100-8199
CHANTILY TRL	Lago Vista	399T	WW-40	78645	8100-8199
CHANTSONG CT	Austin	587M	MP-23	78724	5900-5999
CHAPARRAL DR	Leander	342J	MC-47	78641	400-599
CHAPARRAL DR	Round Rock	376J	ML-44	78681	1800-2199
CHAPARRAL DR	Travis Co	309R	WX-50	78641	14700-15599
CHAPARRAL LN	Hays Co	667H	WT-15	78620	1200-1399
	Hays Co	668E	WU-15	78620	1400-1599
CHAPARRAL RD	Austin	674B	MG-15	78745	200-799
CHAPARRAL RD	Hays Co	701Q	MB-11	78652	1800-2999
CHAPARRAL RD	Williamson Co	284F	MG-54	78628	1-699
CHAPARRAL TRL	Austin	645W	MJ-16	78744	2500-2599
CHAPARRAL HEIGHTS CROSSING	Travis Co	619N	MS-20	78725	15300-15799
CHAPEL LN	San Leanna	703F	ME-12	78748	11400-11699
CHAPEL DOWN ST	Williamson Co	434B	MG-39	78729	9400-9599
CHAPELWOOD DR	Travis Co	557M	MP-26	78724	None
CHAPIN LN	Travis Co	553E	ME-27	78746	1-99
CHAPIN RIDGE	Travis Co	468T	MQ-34	78660	None
CHAPMAN LN	Austin	645L	MK-17	78744	3500-3699
CHAPPELL LN	Travis Co	703B	ME-12	78748	800-999
	Travis Co	703A	ME-12	78748	1000-1699
CHARDON CT	Village of the Hills	519T	WW-28	78738	1-99
CHARDONNAY CV	Austin	493H	MF-33	78750	8100-8199
CHARDONNAY CROSSING	Williamson Co	343N	ME-47	78641	1000-1499
CHARETTE CV	Austin	464U	MH-34	78759	10400-10499
CHARING CROSS RD	Austin	464G	MH-36	78759	11700-12099
CHARIS CT	Austin	612D	MD-21	78735	6100-6199
CHARLA CIR	Travis Co	436Y	MM-37	78728	2500-2599
CHARLEMAGNE CT	Austin	465L	MK-35	78727	4300-4399
CHARLES AVE	Travis Co	523Q	MF-29	78746	4100-4699
CHARLES BLVD	Bastrop	744D	ED-9	78602	600-799
CHARLES ST	Austin	586S	ML-22	78702	3400-3599
CHARLES DICKENS DR	Travis Co	467K	MN-35	78660	14400-14599
CHARLES GOODNIGHT TRL	Travis Co	676A	ML-15	78744	4500-4699
CHARLES M DANIELS DR	Austin	702C	MD-12	78748	2700-2799
CHARLES SHREINER TRL	Austin	642A	MC-18	78749	5800-5999
CHARLESTON PL	Austin	524D	MH-30	78731	7900-7999
CHARLESTOWN CV	Lago Vista	459E	WW-36	78645	20000-20099
CHARLESWORTH DR	Austin	643P	ME-17	78745	2600-2799
CHARLEY HARLEY DR	Williamson Co	343X	ME-46	78641	2400-2499
CHARLOTTE ST	Austin	584L	MH-23	78703	1000-1299
CHARLOTTE WAY	Round Rock	407R	MP-41	78664	2000-2099
CHARLOTTE ESTATES DR	Austin	674W	MG-13	78744	2000-2199
CHARLTON DR	Austin	556H	MM-27	78723	7300-7599
CHARLWOOD DR	Austin	495X	MJ-31	78757	3000-3199
CHARM CIR	Austin	465P	MJ-35	78727	11900-12099
CHARMING HILL DR	Travis Co	497M	MP-32	78754	12800-12999
CHARMING VALLEY DR	Travis Co	497M	MP-32	78754	12800-13299
CHARMSTONE LN	Williamson Co	284E	MG-54	78628	100-199
CHARNWOOD CT	Williamson Co	434K	MG-38	78729	9000-9099
CHAROLAIS CT	Round Rock	375G	MK-45	78681	2500-2599
CHAROLAIS CV	Austin	496K	ML-32	78758	11400-11499
CHAROLAIS DR	Austin	496J	ML-32	78758	1400-1699
CHARPIOT DR	Round Rock	376N	ML-44	78681	1400-1499
CHARRED OAK DR	Austin	464F	MG-36	78759	11400-11599
CHARRINGTON DR	Round Rock	377S	MN-43	78664	1100-1299
CHARTHOUSE CV	Travis Co	492Y	MD-31	78730	9900-9999
CHARTRE DR	Austin	526Z	MM-28	78754	8500-8599
CHARTWELL DR	Austin	586B	ML-24	78723	4600-4699
CHASE CIR	Austin	586K	ML-23	78721	3900-3999
CHASEVIEW DR	Travis Co	557M	MP-26	78724	None
CHASEWIND LN	Travis Co	558J	MQ-26	78724	None
CHASEWOOD CV	Austin	466L	MM-35	78727	13300-13399
CHASEWOOD DR	Austin	466L	MM-35	78727	1500-1999
CHASEWYCH DR	Austin	643H	MF-18	78745	2100-2399
CHASKA CV	Austin	672A	MC-15	78739	10200-10299
CHASM LAKE DR	Austin	587G	MP-24	78724	7600-7699
CHAT LN	Williamson Co	405B	MJ-42	78681	8500-8599
CHATAM BERRY LN	Austin	672Y	MD-13	78748	11100-11599
CHATEAU AVE	Travis Co	490K	WY-32	78734	15800-16199
CHATEAU HILL	Austin	463D	MF-36	78750	10800-11199
CHATEAU VILLAGE WAY	Austin	674Q	MH-14	78744	2300-4699
CHATELAINE CV	Austin	583V	MF-22	78746	1100-1199
CHATELAINE DR	Austin	583Z	MF-22	78746	2800-3099
CHATELLE DR	Round Rock	376A	ML-45	78681	2800-2899
CHATHAM AVE	Austin	556K	ML-26	78723	1600-1699
CHATHAM PL	Austin	556K	ML-26	78723	2000-2099
CHATHAM WOOD DR	Williamson Co	405J	MJ-41	78717	15800-15899
CHATSWORTH CIR	Austin	615S	MJ-19	78704	900-999
CHATTERTON CT	Williamson Co	434F	MG-39	78729	9300-9399
CHAUNCY ST	Travis Co	522C	MD-30	78730	None
CHAYTON CIR	Travis Co	409Y	MT-40	78660	19100-20399
CHECKER DR	Travis Co	402P	MC-41	78613	2700-2899
CHECOTAH DR	Travis Co	460V	WZ-34	78734	15400-15699
CHEERFUL CT	Lakeway	519H	WX-30	78734	100-199
CHEETAH CV	Pflugerville	437B	MN-39	78664	1700-1799
CHELMSFORD DR	Austin	611T	MA-19	78736	7500-7799
CHELSEA DR	Georgetown	195T	MJ-61	78633	100-199
CHELSEA LN	Austin	615P	MJ-20	78704	1500-1699
CHELSEA GLEN PL	Austin	497J	MN-32	78753	12100-12299
CHELSEA MOOR	Austin	464G	MH-36	78759	6800-7599
CHELSEA MOOR CV	Austin	464G	MH-35	78759	11600-11699
CHENEY CV	Austin	673A	ME-15	78745	2700-2899
CHENO CORTINA CV	Austin	641D	MB-18	78749	6500-6599
CHENO CORTINA TRL	Austin	642E	MC-18	78749	7800-8299
CHERICO ST	Austin	616A	ML-21	78702	600-899
	Austin	586W	ML-22	78702	900-1199
CHERIE DR	Austin	496B	ML-33	78758	11900-12099
CHERISE LN	Austin	673E	ME-15	78748	2600-2699
CHERISSE DR	Austin	670D	WZ-15	78739	11000-12199
CHERNOSKY POINT CV	Travis Co	427K	WS-38	78669	None
CHEROKEE LN	Leander	342Y	MD-46	78641	2400-2699
CHEROKEE ST	Austin	496L	MM-32	78753	11700-11899
CHEROKEE TRL	Williamson Co	193Z	MF-61	78633	100-399
CHEROKEE RUN	Pflugerville	437Y	MP-37	78660	1500-1599
CHEROKEE RUN CV	Pflugerville	437Y	MP-37	78660	1501-1599 O
CHERRY CV	Austin	644J	MG-17	78745	5700-5799
CHERRY LN	Austin	584J	MG-24	78703	2700-3499
	Austin	554W	MG-25	78703	3500-3799
CHERRY LN	Cedar Park	372R	MD-44	78613	500-1399
CHERRY LN	Travis Co	460W	WY-34	78645	16900-17199
	Travis Co	459V	WX-34	78645	17200-17799
CHERRY LOOP	Austin	644N	MG-17	78745	5900-5999
CHERRY ST	Buda	762D	MD-6	78610	100-199
CHERRY BARK LN	Hays Co	576T	WQ-22	78620	600-899
CHERRY CREEK DR	Austin	643G	MF-18	78745	5600-6099
CHERRY CREEK DR	Cedar Park	373J	ME-44	78613	601-699 O
CHERRYDALE DR	Austin	643U	MF-16	78745	6900-6999
CHERRY HEARST CT	Austin	464A	MG-36	78750	11500-11599
CHERRY HILL DR	Austin	614Y	MH-19	78704	400-499
CHERRY HOLLOW CT	Travis Co	369V	WX-43	78645	21200-21399
CHERRY HOLLOW CV	Travis Co	369Z	WX-43	78645	21200-21299
CHERRY HOLLOW CV	Travis Co	369V	WX-43	78641	21400-21499
CHERRY HOLLOW DR	Travis Co	369V	WX-43	78641	21500-21799
CHERRY HOLLOW CROSSING	Travis Co	369Z	WX-43	78645	10500-11499
	Travis Co	370S	WY-43	78641	11500-11599
CHERRY LAUREL CIR	Travis Co	409Q	MT-41	78660	21100-21199
CHERRY LAUREL DR	Cedar Park	402D	MD-42	78613	200-299
CHERRY LAUREL TERRACE	Travis Co	580B	WY-24	78738	12400-12499
CHERRYLAWN CIR	Austin	556V	MM-25	78723	6100-6199
CHERRYLAWN DR	Taylor	322T	MY-49	76574	2300-2699
CHERRY MEADOW CIR	Austin	643U	MF-16	78745	1700-1799
CHERRY MEADOW DR	Austin	643U	MF-16	78745	6900-7199
CHERRY ORCHARD DR	Austin	643U	MF-16	78745	1700-1899
CHERRY PARK	Austin	644J	MG-17	78745	5700-5899
CHERRY SAGE LN	Georgetown	314B	MG-51	78628	1700-1799
CHERRY TREE CIR	Austin	554G	MH-27	78731	3300-3399
CHERRYWOOD CIR	Taylor	323S	EA-49	76574	300-399
CHERRY WOOD CT	Williamson Co	196J	ML-62	78628	100-199
CHERRYWOOD DR	Taylor	323N	EA-50	76574	2300-2399
CHERRYWOOD LN	Williamson Co	225E	MJ-60	78633	6600-6699
CHERRYWOOD RD	Austin	585H	MK-24	78722	2900-4099
CHERT CV	Williamson Co	375B	MJ-45	78681	2700-2799
CHERT RD	Williamson Co	375B	MJ-45	78681	3900-4199
CHERVIL CIR	Round Rock	376M	MM-44	78664	800-899
CHERVIL DR	Austin	525A	MJ-30	78759	8000-8099
CHERYL LYNN RD	Travis Co	704G	MH-12	78747	9500-9999
CHESAPEAKE DR	Austin	526E	ML-30	78758	1000-1199
CHESAPEAKE BAY LN N	Williamson Co	375S	MJ-43	78717	200-299
CHESAPEAKE BAY LN S	Williamson Co	375S	MJ-43	78717	300-399
CHESHIRE DR	Austin	556P	ML-26	78723	2000-2099
CHESNEY RIDGE DR	Austin	642T	MC-16	78749	4500-4899
CHESSINGTON DR	Austin	464E	MG-36	78750	11300-11499
CHESTER CV	Austin	463L	MF-35	78750	9900-9999
CHESTER LN	Austin	463G	MF-36	78750	9900-10199
CHESTER BROOK DR	Travis Co	497G	MP-33	78754	2100-2199
CHESTERFIELD AVE	Austin	555L	MK-26	78751	5300-5699
	Austin	555L	MK-26	78752	5700-5899
	Austin	555C	MK-27	78752	6200-6599
CHESTER FOREST ST	Williamson Co	434K	MG-38	78729	8900-9099
CHESTER VALLEY DR	Travis Co	497G	MP-33	78754	13000-13199
CHESTERWOOD CV	Austin	583P	ME-23	78746	1600-1699
CHESTLE CT	Austin	497E	MN-33	78753	12500-12599
CHESTNUT AVE	Austin	585V	MK-22	78702	1100-1899
	Austin	585M	MK-23	78722	1900-2299
CHESTNUT CIR	Round Rock	376J	ML-44	78681	1900-2099
CHESTNUT CT	Georgetown	225R	MK-59	78633	100-199
CHESTNUT CV	Lago Vista	399T	WW-40	78645	8000-8399
CHESTNUT PATH	Round Rock	407B	MN-42	78664	2300-2499
CHESTNUT ST	Bastrop	745G	EF-9	78602	600-1699
CHESTNUT CROSSING	Cedar Park	403E	ME-42	78613	700-799
CHESTNUT HILL	Lakeway	489U	WX-31	78734	100-499
CHESTNUT HILL CV	Lakeway	489Q	WX-32	78734	100-199
CHESTNUT HOLLOW	Austin	494S	MG-31	78750	6100-6199
CHESTNUT RIDGE	Dripping Springs	666H	WR-15	78620	100-199
CHESTNUT RIDGE RD	Austin	463B	ME-36	78726	10000-10999
CHESWICK CT	Travis Co	554N	MG-26	78746	2300-2399
CHEVERLY CT	Village of the Hills	519P	WW-29	78738	1-99
CHEVIOT LN	Austin	647Q	MP-17	78617	3000-3199
CHEVY CIR	Austin	556Y	MM-25	78723	5400-5499
CHEVY CHASE DR	Austin	526S	ML-28	78752	7400-7799
CHEYENNE CIR	Austin	643D	MF-18	78745	2300-2399
CHEYENNE CV	Lago Vista	399W	WW-40	78645	21600-21699
CHEYENNE ST	Leander	342Y	MD-46	78641	2500-2699
CHEYENNE ST	Round Rock	346V	MM-46	78665	3600-3699
	Round Rock	347N	MN-47	78665	3700-3799
CHEYENNE VALLEY CV	Travis Co	408G	MR-42	78660	None
CHEYENNE VALLEY DR	Travis Co	408P	MQ-41	78664	19500-19699
	Travis Co	408L	MR-41	78660	19700-20199
CHIAPPERO TRL	Austin	554H	MH-27	78731	4500-4799
CHICADEE CIR	Travis Co	468N	MQ-35	78660	14800-14899
CHICASAW CT	Austin	642X	MC-16	78749	4400-4499
CHI CHI CV	Round Rock	408C	MR-42	78664	2300-2399
CHI CHI DR	Georgetown	227A	MN-60	78628	30600-30799
CHI CHI'S CV	Round Rock	378Y	MR-43	78664	2300-2399
CHICKADEE CV	Georgetown	225F	MJ-60	78633	100-199
CHICKADEE LN	Lakeway	519M	WX-29	78734	900-999
CHICKORY CT	Round Rock	378S	MQ-43	78665	1000-1099
CHICK PEA LN	Austin	674J	MG-14	78748	8300-8599
CHICO ST	Austin	586U	MM-22	78721	5200-5399
CHICON ST	Austin	615C	MK-21	78702	1-599
	Austin	585Y	MK-22	78702	600-1899
	Austin	585Q	MK-23	78722	1900-2299
CHICORY CT	Leander	342T	MC-46	78641	1100-1199
CHICORY CV	Austin	583Z	MF-22	78746	1300-1399
CHICTORA CV	Austin	494C	MH-33	78759	6000-6199
CHIHUAHUA TRL	Austin	644Q	MH-17	78745	400-599
CHILDERS DR	Bastrop	745N	EE-8	78602	1-299
CHILDRESS	Austin	584K	MG-23	78703	None
CHILDRESS DR	Austin	526H	MM-30	78753	9800-10099
CHILLIP CV	Austin	497E	MN-33	78753	1000-1099
CHILTERN FOREST DR	Williamson Co	404G	MH-42	78717	10100-10199
CHIMAYO CV	Austin	434Y	MH-37	78729	7800-7899
CHIME DR	Manor	530T	MU-28	78653	12800-12899
CHIMNEY CORNERS	Austin	524G	MH-30	78731	7100-7899
CHIMNEY CREEK CIR	Austin	556Q	MM-26	78723	6400-6499
CHIMNEY HILL BLVD	Austin	557B	MN-27	78754	8700-8799
	Travis Co	527X	MN-28	78754	8800-9299
CHIMNEY ROCK DR	Austin	466Y	MM-34	78758	1000-1099
CHIMNEY ROCK RD	Leander	343L	MF-47	78641	2300-2499
CHIMNEY SWIFT TRL	Cedar Park	433F	ME-39	78613	2800-2999
CHINA CV	Elgin	534P	EC-29	78621	300-399
CHINA ST	Buda	762C	MD-6	78610	100-299
CHINABERRY CT	Cedar Park	403E	ME-42	78613	600-699
CHINA BERRY RD	Austin	645X	MJ-16	78744	5300-5799
CHINA GARDEN CV	Travis Co	492U	MD-31	78730	9900-10099
CHINA GARDEN DR	Travis Co	492U	MD-31	78730	3600-5399
CHINA GROVE	Austin	643S	ME-16	78745	3200-3399
CHINA ROSE DR	Austin	587M	MP-23	78724	8900-9199
CHINATI CT	Williamson Co	402V	MD-40	78613	1700-1799
CHINATIMOUNTAIN TRL	Pflugerville	407X	MN-40	78664	1700-1899
CHINCHO DR	Pflugerville	409W	MS-40	78660	None
CHINCOTEAGUE WAY	Round Rock	406N	ML-41	78681	1700-1899
CHINESE ELM CT	Austin	673Y	MF-13	78748	400-499
CHINO CV	Round Rock	407G	MP-42	78665	1700-1799
CHINOOK DR	Austin	611Q	MB-20	78736	6900-7099
CHINO VALLEY TRL	Round Rock	407C	MP-42	78665	1800-1899
CHINQUAPIN CT	Round Rock	376E	ML-45	78681	1200-1299
CHIPMUNK RD	Travis Co	489M	WX-32	78734	1300-1599
CHIPPAWA DR	Travis Co	467P	MN-35	78660	None
CHIPPENDALE AVE	Austin	644L	MH-17	78745	200-499
CHIPPENHOOK CT	Austin	672Q	MD-14	78748	10700-10899
CHIPPEWA	Round Rock	346V	MM-46	78665	1000-1099
CHIPPEWA CV	Lago Vista	429A	WW-39	78645	7100-7199
CHIPPEWAY LN	Austin	643R	MF-17	78745	1400-1699
CHIPSHOT CT	Travis Co	426L	WR-38	78669	2000-2199
CHISELPOINT CV	Round Rock	345N	MJ-47	78681	800-899
CHISHOLM CV	Round Rock	376P	ML-44	78681	300-399
CHISHOLM LN	Austin	673L	MF-14	78748	8700-9399
CHISHOLM PKWY	Round Rock	376K	ML-44	78664	300-399
CHISHOLM TRL	Buda	732Z	MD-7	78610	1-99
CHISHOLM TRL	Pflugerville	467C	MP-36	78660	None
CHISHOLM TRL	Travis Co	488X	WU-31	78669	2100-2499
CHISHOLM TRL	Travis Co	490M	WZ-32	78734	2900-3199
CHISHOLM TRL S	Austin	673Q	MF-14	78748	9400-9799
CHISHOLM TRAIL RD	Round Rock	376T	ML-43	78681	1-99
	Round Rock	406B	ML-42	78681	100-299
	Round Rock	376X	ML-43	78681	300-699
	Round Rock	376P	ML-44	78681	1200-3099
	Round Rock	346X	ML-46	78681	3100-3399
CHISHOLM VALLEY DR	Round Rock	406L	MM-41	78681	400-1199
CHISOS PASS	Austin	557N	MN-26	78724	7200-7499
CHISOS TRL	Austin	403M	MF-41	78717	14000-14099
CHISWICK DR	Austin	526C	MM-30	78753	900-999
CHITINA CT	Williamson Co	374N	MG-44	78613	2600-2699
CHITTIM CIR	Travis Co	491U	MB-31	78732	12600-12699
CHOCTAW CV	Lago Vista	429B	WW-39	78645	21300-21499
CHOCTAW TRL	Austin	613Y	MF-19	78745	2600-2699
CHOKE CANYON LN	Williamson Co	344B	MG-48	78628	100-399
CHOLLA DR	Travis Co	703S	ME-10	78652	12600-12899
CHOQUETTE DR	Austin	525U	MK-28	78757	1200-1599
CHOTE AVE	Austin	616A	ML-21	78702	900-999

C

STREET NAME	CITY or COUNTY	MAPSCO GRID	AUSTIN GRID	ZIP CODE	BLOCK RANGE O/E
CHOWAN CV	Round Rock	406N	ML-41	78681	2600-2699
CHOWAN PL	Round Rock	406N	ML-41	78681	1600-1699
CHOWAN WAY	Round Rock	406N	ML-41	78681	2400-2699
CHRIGHTON CASTLE BEND	Pflugerville	408X	MQ-40	78660	18700-18999
CHRIS CV	Rollingwood	584J	MG-23	78746	1-99
CHRIS LN	Travis Co	408M	MR-41	78660	1400-1499
CHRIS WAY	Travis Co	529T	MS-28	78653	None
CHRISSYS CV	Travis Co	521V	MB-28	78733	800-899
CHRISTENSEN CV	Austin	641W	MA-16	78739	11100-11199
CHRISTENSEN RD	Bastrop Co	564V	ED-25	78621	200-499
CHRISTIAN LN	Travis Co	427E	WS-39	78654	3400-3499
CHRISTIE DR	Austin	586U	MM-22	78721	1100-1199
CHRISTINA DR	Bastrop Co	592J	MY-23	78621	100-199
CHRISTINA GARZA DR	Travis Co	529H	MT-30	78653	16400-16699
	Travis Co	529G	MT-30	78653	16800-16899
CHRISTINE DR	Leander	342W	MC-46	78641	1700-2099
CHRISTINE LN	Williamson Co	192S	MC-61	78642	100-299
CHRISTINE ROSE CT	Round Rock	376E	ML-45	78681	2500-2599
CHRISTMAS MOUNTAIN DR	Georgetown	195X	MJ-61	78633	100-199
CHRISTOFF LOOP	Austin	702G	MD-12	78748	2000-2499
CHRISTOPHER AVE	Round Rock	406K	ML-41	78681	800-1399
CHRISTOPHER DR	Travis Co	553M	MF-26	78746	4500-4799
CHRISTOPHER LN	Williamson Co	312D	MD-51	78641	1-699
CHRISTOPHER ST	Austin	614H	MH-21	78704	800-899
	Austin	614D	MH-21	78704	900-999
CHROMITE ST	Austin	466K	ML-35	78727	12800-12999
CHUCK WAGON TRL	Austin	642B	MC-18	78749	7000-7299
CHUCK WAGON TRL	Georgetown	225L	MK-59	78633	100-199
CHUKAR CIR	Austin	495V	MK-31	78758	9600-9899
	Austin	496S	ML-31	78758	9900-10199
CHUKAR BEND	Austin	496S	ML-31	78758	9900-9999
CHULA VISTA DR	Travis Co	402Y	MD-40	78613	1700-2099
CHURCH LN	Elgin	534S	EC-28	78621	100-199
CHURCH LN	Travis Co	471X	MW-34	78653	16200-16599
	Travis Co	501A	MW-33	78653	None
CHURCH ST	Bastrop	745F	EE-9	78602	1000-1599
	Bastrop	715X	EE-10	78602	1900-1999
CHURCH ST	Elgin	534S	EC-28	78621	100-299
CHURCH ST	Hutto	349Z	MT-46	78634	300-599
CHURCH ST	Weir	258H	MR-57	78626	100-199
CHURCH ST N	Georgetown	256Z	MM-55	78626	600-999
CHURCH ST S	Georgetown	286H	MM-54	78626	200-2399
CHURCH CANYON DR	Austin	527C	MP-30	78754	11200-11599
CHURCHILL CV	Cedar Park	372P	MC-44	78613	1600-1699
CHURCHILL DR	Austin	554V	MH-25	78703	3200-3299
CHURCHILL DOWNS DR	Austin	523V	MF-28	78746	6000-6099
CHURCHILL FARMS DR	Georgetown	287L	MP-53	78626	1-999
CHURCH PARK RD	Cedar Park	374P	MG-44	78613	100-198 E
CHURCHWOOD CV	Austin	583P	ME-23	78746	1600-1699
CIBOLO CREEK DR	Georgetown	195N	MJ-62	78633	100-199
CICERO LN	Travis Co	552M	MD-26	78746	1-99
	Travis Co	553J	ME-26	78746	None
CIDER ORCHARD CV	Georgetown	195P	MJ-62	78633	200-299
CIELO CV	Bastrop Co	738Q	MR-8	78617	100-199
CIELO DR	Williamson Co	226Y	MM-58	78628	600-899
CIELO AZUL PASS	Travis Co	462S	MC-34	78732	6900-7199
CIELO GRANDE ST	Austin	677R	MP-14	78617	12300-12499
CIELO VERDE DR	Bastrop Co	738Q	MR-8	78617	100-199
CIELO VISTA DR	Austin	557Y	MP-25	78724	6600-6699
CIELO VISTA DR	Bastrop Co	738Q	MR-8	78617	100-299
CIERNE CV	Williamson Co	345T	MJ-46	78681	4400-4499
CILANTRO WAY	Austin	646B	ML-18	78741	7300-7399
CIMA CIR	Travis Co	641B	MA-18	78737	8900-8999
CIMA OAK LN	Austin	495S	MJ-31	78759	8400-8699
CIMARRON CV	Leander	342P	MC-47	78641	1300-1399
CIMARRON LN	Williamson Co	226V	MM-58	78628	5300-5599
CIMARRON TRL	Austin	613Z	MF-19	78745	2000-2199
CIMARRON TRL	Lago Vista	429K	WW-38	78645	5900-6399
CIMARRON HILLS TRL E	Williamson Co	283H	MF-54	78628	100-199
	Williamson Co	284E	MG-54	78628	200-399
CIMARRON HILLS TRL W	Williamson Co	283H	MF-54	78628	100-899
CIMARRON PARK LOOP	Buda	732P	MC-8	78610	100-299
CIMA SERENA	Austin	495S	MJ-31	78759	3500-3899
	Austin	494V	MH-31	78759	3900-4099
CIMA SERENA CT	Austin	495S	MJ-31	78759	8400-8499
CINCHRING LN	Austin	466Q	MM-35	78727	12600-12899
CINDER CV	Hays Co	667B	WS-15	78620	None
CINDERELLA DR	Austin	525V	MK-28	78752	200-299
CINDY CT	Round Rock	407J	MN-41	78664	1500-1699
CINDY LN	Austin	466K	ML-35	78727	2100-2499
CINDY LN	Leander	342E	MC-48	78641	900-1099
CINNABAR TRL	Austin	463A	ME-36	78726	9600-9999
CINNAMON PATH	Austin	614P	MG-20	78704	1400-1899
CIRCLE AVE	Round Rock	376Z	MM-43	78664	600-699
CIRCLE CV	Austin	615X	MJ-19	78741	2600-2699
CIRCLE DR	Hays Co	762Z	MD-4	78610	100-299
CIRCLE DR	Round Rock	377W	MN-43	78664	1400-1599
CIRCLE DR	San Leanna	703K	ME-11	78748	11200-11699
CIRCLE DR	Travis Co	611S	MA-19	78736	8800-9199
	Travis Co	610P	WY-20	78736	9200-11099
	Travis Co	640A	WY-18	78736	11100-11199
CIRCLE DR	Travis Co	428A	WU-39	78654	23700-23799
CIRCLE BEND	Taylor	353T	EA-46	76574	None
CIRCLE BEND DR	Austin	496P	ML-32	78758	11300-11599
CIRCLE G RANCH RD	Hays Co	638B	WU-18	78620	100-899
CIRCLE G RANCH RD	Hays Co	608W	WU-19	78620	None
CIRCLE HAVEN	Austin	615T	MJ-19	78741	2000-2099
CIRCLE J LN	Travis Co	398T	WU-40	78654	23500-23899
CIRCLE J LOOP	Travis Co	398X	WU-40	78654	5900-6199
CIRCLE J RD	Travis Co	398W	WU-40	78654	6000-7099
CIRCLE OAK CV	Austin	642G	MD-18	78749	4700-4799
CIRCLE RIDGE DR	West Lake Hills	553X	ME-25	78746	1200-1499
CIRCLE S RD	Austin	644X	MG-16	78745	6400-6799
	Austin	674B	MG-15	78745	6800-8199
CIRCLETREE LOOP	Austin	524C	MH-30	78731	4100-4199
CIRCLEVIEW DR	Travis Co	551Y	MB-25	78733	9800-10099
CIRCULO DR	Lago Vista	429J	WW-38	78645	5800-5999
CIRCULO DE AMISTAD	Austin	616T	ML-19	78741	6300-6599
CISCO DR	Travis Co	426M	WR-38	78669	None
CISCO TRL	Round Rock	347N	MN-47	78665	3500-3599
CISCO TRL	Travis Co	309M	WX-50	78641	24300-24599
CISCO VALLEY CV	Travis Co	408P	MQ-41	78660	None
CISCO VALLEY DR	Travis Co	408K	MQ-41	78660	None
CISSUS CV	Austin	464P	MG-35	78759	7300-7399
CITADEL CV	Austin	556L	MM-26	78723	6800-6899
CITATION AVE	Travis Co	706R	MM-11	78719	8200-8399
CITATION CIR	Travis Co	650B	MU-18	78617	1200-1599
CITATION DR	Travis Co	650K	MU-17	78617	1600-2799
CITRINE PL	Williamson Co	375F	MJ-45	78681	3400-3999
CITRON CV	Travis Co	467V	MP-34	78660	14400-14499
CITRUS CV	Austin	464A	MG-36	78750	11500-11599
CITY HALL DR	Pflugerville	438G	MR-39	78660	18600-18699
CITY PARK RD	Austin	552D	MD-27	78730	1500-1999
	Austin	522R	MD-29	78730	2000-4299
	Austin	523C	MF-30	78730	5500-6499
	Travis Co	523A	ME-30	78730	4300-5499
CITY PARK RD	Pflugerville	438S	MQ-37	78660	300-599
CITY VIEW ST	Travis Co	583N	ME-23	78746	5000-5099
CIVIC DR	Lago Vista	429P	WW-38	78645	6000-6299
CLABURN DR	Austin	495S	MJ-31	78759	3600-3799
CLAIRE AVE	Austin	585A	MJ-24	78703	1000-1299
CLAIRE MORRIS LN	Pflugerville	437C	MP-39	78660	17800-17899
CLAIRMONT CV	Austin	641H	MB-18	78749	8500-8599
CLAIRMONT CV	Bastrop Co	711B	MW-12	78612	100-199
CLAIRMONT DR	Austin	641M	MB-17	78749	6300-6599
CLANCY WAY	Pflugerville	468K	MQ-35	78660	900-999
CLARA ST	Austin	615H	MK-21	78702	1-99
CLARA MARIE CV	Austin	611Z	MB-19	78749	7600-7699
CLARA VAN	Lakeway	520A	WY-30	78734	15500-15599
	Travis Co	490W	WY-31	78734	15600-16099
	Travis Co	489V	WX-31	78734	16100-16499
CLAREDON LN	Travis Co	553E	ME-27	78746	1-99
CLAREMONT CT	Round Rock	377L	MP-44	78665	2700-2799
CLARENCE CT	Buda	732Q	MD-8	78610	100-599
CLARENCE BOHLS LN	Pflugerville	438N	MQ-38	78660	700-999
CLARET CV	Travis Co	702G	MD-12	78748	2400-2499
CLAREWOOD CIR	Austin	525H	MK-30	78758	8600-8699
CLAREWOOD DR	Austin	525D	MK-30	78758	8600-8899
CLARICE CT	Austin	524Z	MH-28	78757	2900-2999
CLARION CT	Austin	641M	MB-17	78749	8700-8799
CLARION CV	Austin	553G	MF-27	78746	5600-5699
CLARION DR	Austin	641M	MB-17	78749	6200-6399
CLARIS LN	Georgetown	257T	MN-55	78626	200-299
CLARK AVE	Lago Vista	459J	WW-35	78645	3000-3099
CLARK ST	Round Rock	376T	ML-43	78681	1200-1399
CLARK BROTHERS DR	Buda	732P	MC-8	78610	1000-1299
CLARKDALE LN	Austin	525B	MJ-30	78757	2600-2799
CLARKE ST	Austin	644C	MH-18	78745	400-599
CLARK-JASON LN	Bastrop Co	742C	MZ-9	78612	100-199
CLARKS WAY	Hutto	350S	MU-46	78634	100-499
CLARKSBURG DR	Austin	643N	ME-17	78745	3300-3499
CLARKS GROVE LN	Williamson Co	409R	MT-41	78634	100-199
CLARKSON AVE	Austin	585H	MK-24	78722	3400-3799
	Austin	555Z	MK-25	78751	4300-4499
	Austin	555R	MK-26	78751	4600-5299
CLARKSVILLE LN	Cedar Park	373E	ME-45	78613	1901-1999 O
CLARMAC DR	Sunset Valley	643C	MF-18	78745	1-99
CLARNO DR	Austin	642L	MD-17	78749	4300-4699
CLARO VISTA CV	Austin	640V	WZ-16	78739	11100-11199
CLARY CT	Buda	763E	ME-6	78610	200-399
CLARY SAGE LOOP	Round Rock	407G	MP-42	78665	1300-1599
CLAUDE CT	Austin	705F	MJ-12	78747	8600-8699
CLAUDIA DR	Hays Co	763J	ME-5	78610	1-99
CLAUDIA DR	Williamson Co	373A	ME-45	78641	2400-2499
	Williamson Co	343W	ME-46	78641	2500-2699
CLAUDIA JUNE AVE	Travis Co	436Y	MM-37	78728	2300-2499
CLAWSON RD	Austin	614S	MG-19	78704	3000-4399
	Austin	644A	MG-18	78745	4400-4799
CLAXTON DR	Travis Co	611J	MA-20	78736	9100-9699
CLAY AVE	Austin	555B	MJ-27	78756	5400-5799
CLAY LN	Cedar Park	432D	MD-39	78613	1700-1999
CLAY LN	Lago Vista	459A	WW-36	78645	3900-3999
CLAY ST	Georgetown	256Y	MM-55	78628	1-1499
CLAY ALLISON PASS	Austin	641H	MB-18	78749	6400-6599
CLAYERA CV	Austin	702B	MC-12	78748	2800-2899
CLAYMOOR DR	Austin	556Y	MM-25	78723	5400-5599
CLAYSTONE CV	Austin	675A	MJ-15	78744	5700-5799
CLAYTON DR	Leander	312S	MC-49	78641	1000-1299
CLAYTON LN	Austin	555H	MK-27	78752	800-899
	Austin	556J	ML-26	78723	900-1199
CLAYTON LN	Taylor	352Q	MZ-47	76574	700-799
CLAYTON WAY	Cedar Park	372J	MC-44	78613	2200-2399
CLAYWOOD DR	Travis Co	496Z	MM-31	78753	10600-11199
CLEAR CV	Austin	613H	MF-21	78704	2600-2699
CLEARBROOK TRL	Williamson Co	434K	MG-38	78729	8700-8899
CLEAR CREEK CV	Cedar Park	373Y	MF-43	78613	400-499
CLEAR CREEK DR	Austin	526U	MM-28	78754	8400-8499
CLEARCREEK DR	Leander	341D	MB-48	78641	500-799
CLEAR CREEK LN	Hays Co	637M	WT-17	78620	500-599
CLEARDAY DR	Austin	644W	MG-16	78745	100-399
CLEARFIELD DR	Austin	525H	MK-30	78758	1200-1499
CLEARLAKE LN	Leander	342H	MD-48	78641	900-1099
CLEAR LAKE PL	Round Rock	408E	MQ-42	78665	2100-2199
CLEAR MEADOW CT	Williamson Co	346G	MM-48	78665	800-899
CLEAR MEADOW PL	Williamson Co	346G	MM-48	78665	4200-4399
CLEAR NIGHT DR	Travis Co	611E	MA-21	78736	9400-9599
CLEAR POND CV	Hays Co	669J	WW-14	78737	100-299
CLEARROCK DR	Austin	433V	MF-37	78750	9100-9499
CLEARSKY CIR	Austin	644W	MG-16	78745	300-399
CLEAR SPRING CT	Travis Co	370N	WY-44	78641	11500-11599
CLEAR SPRING CV	Round Rock	378W	MQ-43	78665	600-799
CLEAR SPRING LN	Leander	341D	MB-48	78641	500-799
CLEAR SPRING RD	Williamson Co	256J	ML-56	78628	100-199
	Williamson Co	255R	MK-56	78628	200-399
CLEAR SPRINGS HOLLOW	Buda	732X	MC-7	78610	100-299
	Buda	732S	MC-7	78610	600-999
CLEARVIEW CV	Round Rock	407A	MN-42	78664	700-799
CLEARVIEW DR	Austin	584B	MG-24	78703	2700-3299
	Austin	554X	MG-25	78703	3300-3599
CLEARVIEW DR	Jonestown	400H	WZ-42	78645	11000-11399
CLEAR VIEW DR	Travis Co	619J	MS-20	78725	4800-5099
CLEARVIEW DR	Williamson Co	316U	MM-49	78626	500-599
	Williamson Co	316Q	MM-50	78626	700-899
CLEARVIEW LOOP	Round Rock	407A	MN-42	78664	1400-1699
CLEARVISTA PATH	Williamson Co	347A	MN-48	78665	4100-4199
CLEARWATER CIR	Austin	497N	MN-32	78753	900-999
CLEARWATER CT	Georgetown	226G	MM-60	78628	31000-31099
CLEARWATER CV	Lago Vista	399P	WW-41	78645	8100-8299
CLEAR WATER DR	Jonestown	400V	WZ-40	78645	None
CLEARWATER DR	Round Rock	376S	ML-43	78681	1900-2299
	Round Rock	375V	MK-43	78681	2200-2299
CLEARWATER TRL	Round Rock	376H	MM-45	78664	800-2499
CLEBURNE PASS	Georgetown	195W	MJ-61	78633	100-199
CLEESE DR	Austin	645A	MJ-18	78741	1900-2099
CLEGG DR	Cedar Park	402L	MD-41	78613	2000-2099
CLEMATIS CV	Austin	493R	MF-32	78750	7500-7599
CLEMENTE CIR	Travis Co	640B	WY-18	78737	10000-10299
CLEMENTINE LN	Austin	645Y	MK-16	78744	5700-5999
CLEM'S CV	Travis Co	437S	MN-37	78660	15400-15499
CLEMSON CV	Pflugerville	467H	MP-36	78660	800-1199
CLENDENIN CT	Travis Co	491Q	MB-32	78732	3700-3799
CLEO BAY DR	Cedar Park	374B	MG-45	78613	None
CLERMONT AVE	Austin	615F	MJ-21	78702	800-1199
	Austin	615F	MJ-21	78701	None
CLEVELAND AVE	Lago Vista	459A	WW-36	78645	4000-4199
CLEVELAND ST W	Elgin	534S	EC-28	78621	100-799
CLEVES ST	Williamson Co	405F	MJ-42	78681	5000-5099
CLICK CV	Austin	496N	ML-32	78758	1400-1499
CLICKETT CV	Austin	497J	MN-32	78753	12100-12199
CLIFF CIR	Travis Co	427J	WS-38	78669	25700-25799
CLIFF CV	Travis Co	427J	WS-38	78669	25800-25899
CLIFF DR	Austin	584Y	MH-22	78704	500-699
CLIFF PT	Travis Co	427J	WS-38	78669	2200-2999
CLIFF ST	Austin	584H	MH-24	78705	1900-1999
CLIFFBROOK CT	Village of the Hills	519T	WW-28	78738	1-99
CLIFFBROOK DR	Travis Co	735L	MK-8	78747	9000-9699
CLIFF CREEK DR	Austin	463B	ME-36	78726	10600-10699
CLIFF CROSSING	Travis Co	427J	WS-38	78669	25200-25699
CLIFFHOUSE BLUFF DR	Bee Cave	549M	WX-26	78738	4200-4299
CLIFFORD AVE	Austin	586J	ML-23	78702	1300-1899
CLIFFORD DR	Austin	644B	MG-18	78745	600-799
CLIFF OVERLOOK	Travis Co	427J	WS-38	78669	2900-3099
CLIFFRIDGE RD	Austin	674M	MH-14	78744	4900-5099
CLIFFSAGE AVE	Travis Co	464F	MG-36	78759	8200-8399
CLIFF'S EDGE DR	Travis Co	551U	MB-25	78733	2000-2499
CLIFFSIDE CV	Lago Vista	399P	WW-41	78645	8300-8399
CLIFFSIDE CV	Round Rock	378S	MQ-43	78665	700-799
CLIFFSIDE DR	Austin	614B	MG-21	78704	1400-1799
CLIFFSTONE CV	Austin	613J	ME-20	78735	4500-4699
CLIFF VIEW DR	Travis Co	457X	WS-34	78669	900-1399
CLIFFVIEW DR	Travis Co	464E	MG-36	78759	8200-8399
CLIFFWOOD CIR	Austin	494M	MH-32	78759	4300-4399
CLIFFWOOD CV	Austin	494M	MH-32	78759	4200-4299
CLIFFWOOD DR	Georgetown	225Y	MK-58	78633	300-399
CLIFFWOOD DR	Travis Co	522N	MC-29	78733	1600-1999
CLIFTON LN	Travis Co	552Z	MD-25	78746	7000-7099
CLIFTON ST	Austin	615N	MJ-20	78704	2100-2199
CLIFTON MOORE ST	Buda	732T	MC-7	78610	100-299
CLINT CT	Round Rock	408J	MQ-41	78664	3300-3399
CLINTON CT	Round Rock	347Z	MP-46	78665	2800-2899
CLINTON LN	Lago Vista	459A	WW-36	78645	3800-4099
CLINTON PL	Round Rock	347Z	MP-46	78665	2900-2999
	Round Rock	348W	MQ-46	78665	3000-3299
CLIPPER CT	Austin	673A	ME-15	78745	8700-8799
CLITHEA CV	Austin	494F	MG-33	78759	9000-9099
CLIVDEN CIR	Austin	464F	MG-36	78759	11700-11799
CLOCK TOWER DR	Austin	526X	ML-28	78752	7800-7899
CLOUD CT	Round Rock	376W	ML-43	78681	600-699
CLOUD RD	Hutto	380N	MU-44	78634	200-299
CLOUDBERRY CIR	Austin	674E	MG-15	78745	7700-7799
CLOUDCROFT DR	Austin	642F	MC-18	78749	5200-5299
CLOUDLAND CT	Burnet Co	426K	WQ-38	78669	100-199
CLOUDMORE LN	Elgin	532H	MZ-30	78621	18300-18499
CLOUD MOUNTAIN CROSSING	Austin	462K	MC-35	78726	12500-12799
CLOUD PEAK CV	Williamson Co	375V	MK-43	78681	200-299
CLOUD PEAK LN	Williamson Co	375U	MK-43	78681	2400-2499
CLOUDS REACH CIR	Austin	677M	MP-14	78617	5200-5499
CLOUDVIEW CV	Cedar Park	403C	MF-42	78613	1000-1099
CLOUDVIEW DR	Austin	674A	MG-15	78745	200-399
	Austin	644W	MG-16	78745	400-499
CLOUDVIEW LN	Cedar Park	403C	MF-42	78613	500-799
CLOUDY RIDGE RD	Travis Co	490M	WZ-32	78734	3500-3599
	Travis Co	491E	MA-33	78734	3600-4199
CLOVE CV	Austin	493R	MF-32	78750	7500-7599
CLOVER CT	Austin	644F	MG-18	78745	400-599
CLOVER LN	Cedar Park	372G	MD-45	78613	1800-2299
CLOVER RD	Bastrop Co	742X	MY-7	78612	100-199
CLOVERBROOK CT	Village of the Hills	519P	WW-29	78738	1-99
CLOVERDALE LN	Austin	556X	ML-25	78723	5100-5399
CLOVERDALE LN	Williamson Co	316Q	MM-50	78626	100-199
CLOVER FLAT RD	Cedar Park	373R	MF-44	78613	500-699
CLOVERLEAF CV	Hays Co	732K	MC-8	78610	100-199
CLOVERLEAF DR	Austin	556N	ML-26	78723	1200-1899
CLOVER RIDGE DR	Williamson Co	403W	ME-40	78613	2200-2399
CLOVER VALLEY LN	Georgetown	286Z	MM-52	78626	2500-2699
CLOVIS DR	Williamson Co	314F	MG-51	78628	200-499
CLOVIS ST	Austin	616P	ML-20	78741	6200-6299
CLUB CT	Austin	495W	MJ-31	78759	8100-8199
CLUB CHASE DR	Pflugerville	437Y	MP-37	78660	1300-1599
CLUB ESTATES PKWY	Village of the Hills	519K	WW-29	78738	1-99
CLUBHOUSE DR	Lago Vista	429N	WW-38	78645	5600-5799
CLUBHOUSE DR	Lakeway	519D	WX-30	78734	100-399
CLUBHOUSE HILL DR	Travis Co	426L	WR-38	78669	1600-1799
CLUBHOUSE TURN DR	Austin	703C	MF-12	78748	10800-10899
CLUB RIDGE CV	Travis Co	582B	MC-24	78735	1400-1499
CLUB RIDGE DR	Travis Co	582B	MC-24	78735	8300-8399
CLUB TERRACE	Austin	616S	ML-19	78741	6000-6299
CLUBVIEW AVE	Austin	616W	ML-19	78741	1600-1899
CLUBWAY LN	Austin	643R	MF-17	78745	6300-6799
CLUCK CREEK TRL	Cedar Park	403E	ME-42	78613	100-999
CLUMPGRASS CV	Travis Co	582J	MC-23	78735	3200-3299
CLYDE LN	Austin	498X	MQ-31	78653	5600-5799
CLYDE BANK CV	Travis Co	437G	MP-39	78660	1100-1199
CLYDE LITTLEFIELD DR	Austin	585K	MJ-23	78705	700-999
CLYDESDALE DR	Austin	643N	ME-17	78745	7600-8099
COACHES CROSSING	Travis Co	437S	MN-37	78660	1100-1299
COACH HOUSE RD	Hays Co	639J	WW-17	78737	1-99
COACHLAMP CV	Cedar Park	372T	MC-43	78613	1500-1599
COACHLAMP DR	Cedar Park	372T	MC-43	78613	1900-2199
COACHWHIP HOLLOW	Austin	494W	MG-31	78750	7100-7199
COALWOOD CV	Austin	671A	MA-15	78739	11600-11699
COALWOOD LN	Austin	671E	MA-15	78739	11500-11599
COASTAL DR	Austin	642U	MD-16	78749	8500-8999
COATBRIDGE DR	Austin	643G	MF-18	78745	2500-2799
COATS CIR	Austin	672Z	MD-13	78748	1900-2299

C

STREET NAME	CITY or COUNTY	MAPSCO GRID	AUSTIN GRID	ZIP CODE	BLOCK RANGE O/E
COATS CV	Austin	672Z	MD-13	78748	2100-2199
COBALT CV	Georgetown	195K	MJ-62	78633	300-399
COBALT CV	Round Rock	345S	MJ-46	78681	3600-3699
COBB CAVERN DR	Georgetown	226A	ML-60	78633	100-199
COBBLER CV	Austin	645S	MJ-16	78744	4600-4699
COBBLESTONE	Austin	611G	MB-21	78735	7900-8799
COBBLESTONE LN	Williamson Co	433L	MF-38	78750	10800-10999
COBRA CROSSING	Round Rock	378Y	MR-43	78664	2300-2399
COCAO CIR	Austin	645S	MJ-16	78744	5200-5299
COCAO LN	Austin	645S	MJ-16	78744	2300-2399
COCHISE TRL	Travis Co	522T	MC-28	78733	2000-2199
COCHISE TRL	Travis Co	490R	WZ-32	78734	14300-14499
COCHRANE CV	Austin	525C	MK-30	78757	8300-8399
COCKBURN DR	Austin	643L	MF-17	78745	2500-2699
COCKLEBUR CV	Travis Co	429G	WX-39	78645	7300-7699
COCKNEY DR	Austin	673H	MF-15	78748	8300-8599
COCKRELL CT	Austin	642X	MC-16	78749	4700-4799
COCKRILL CT	Hutto	349M	MT-47	78634	1000-1199
COCKRILL CV	Hutto	349M	MT-47	78634	2000-2099
COCKRILL ST	Hutto	349M	MT-47	78634	100-299
	Hutto	350J	MU-47	78634	300-399
CODY AVE	Lago Vista	458R	WV-35	78645	2500-2799
CODY CT	Austin	614P	MG-20	78704	2000-2099
COFFEE ST	Georgetown	286R	MM-53	78626	2100-2199
COFFEE BEAN CV	Travis Co	436G	MM-39	78728	3900-3999
COFFEE CUP CV	Austin	645W	MJ-16	78744	5000-5099
COGBILL ST	Austin	643Z	MF-16	78745	1000-1099
COG HILL CT	Lakeway	519W	WW-28	78738	100-199
COGNAC CV	Austin	587C	MP-24	78724	7600-7699
COHOBA DR	Austin	672D	MD-15	78748	2900-3199
COLBERG CT	Austin	641G	MB-18	78749	7000-7099
COLBERG DR	Austin	641L	MB-17	78749	8800-9399
COLBY CV	Austin	556M	MM-26	78723	2500-2599
COLBY LN	Cedar Park	402D	MD-42	78613	200-1699
COLBY HILLS DR	Travis Co	488K	WU-32	78669	19900-20199
COLD SPRING	Hays Co	762Z	MD-4	78610	100-299
COLD SPRING DR	Travis Co	369R	WX-44	78641	21600-22099
COLD SPRINGS DR	Georgetown	225M	MK-59	78633	100-199
COLDSTREAM DR	Austin	673E	MG-15	78748	7800-7999
COLD WATER LN	Lakeway	519H	WX-30	78734	100-199
COLDWATER CANYON DR	Travis Co	523G	MF-30	78730	7300-7499
COLDWATER CREEK CV	Austin	523L	MF-29	78730	None
COLDWATER HOLLOW	Buda	732W	MC-7	78610	1000-1699
COLDWATER LANDING TRL					
	Travis Co	523L	MF-29	78730	None
COLDWATER MOUNTAIN CT	Austin	523C	MF-30	78730	7300-7499
COLE ST	Austin	585G	MK-24	78705	2500-2599
COLE ST	Hays Co	639E	WW-18	78737	100-499
COLEBROOK ST	Austin	641R	MB-17	78749	9500-9599
COLEMAN ST	Austin	614Z	MH-19	78704	100-199
COLEMAN BRANCH CREEK RD					
	Travis Co	621T	MW-19	78653	21000-21099
COLERIDGE LN	Travis Co	553E	ME-27	78746	1-99
COLE SPRINGS RD	Hays Co	762F	MC-6	78610	100-2299
COLETO ST	Austin	585R	MK-23	78702	1100-1499
	Austin	585M	MK-23	78722	1900-2299
COLETO CREEK TRL	Travis Co	491W	MA-31	78732	13200-13699
COLEUS CV	Austin	433U	MF-37	78750	10100-10199
COLFAX AVE	Austin	495Y	MK-31	78757	1900-2399
COLFAX DR	Travis Co	588N	MQ-23	78724	9600-9699
COLGATE LN	Austin	556L	MM-26	78723	2100-2299
COLINA CV	Williamson Co	345X	MJ-46	78681	4000-4199
COLINA DR	Lago Vista	459K	WW-35	78645	19600-19899
COLINA LN	Austin	464Q	MH-35	78759	6000-6799
COLINA VISTA LOOP	Austin	493E	ME-33	78750	7200-7599
COLINTON AVE	Austin	498X	MQ-31	78653	5700-5799
COLLAZO WAY	Austin	642X	MC-16	78749	9400-9499
COLLEGE AVE	Austin	614R	MH-20	78704	2200-2399
COLLEGE ROW	Austin	585Y	MK-22	78702	1900-1999
COLLEGE ST	Bastrop	745K	EE-8	78602	800-1399
COLLEGE ST	Hutto	349Z	MT-46	78634	200-399
COLLEGE ST N	Dripping Springs	636Z	WR-16	78620	100-299
COLLEGE ST N	Georgetown	286D	MM-54	78626	100-399
	Georgetown	257W	MM-55	78626	400-1199
COLLEGE ST N	Round Rock	376Z	MM-43	78664	100-299
COLLEGE ST S	Dripping Springs	636Z	WR-16	78620	100-299
COLLEGE ST S	Georgetown	286H	MM-54	78626	100-1799
COLLEYVILLE DR	Bee Cave	550U	WZ-25	78733	11800-12099
COLLIE PATH	Williamson Co	377A	MN-45	78664	1000-1099
COLLIER LN	Lago Vista	459A	WW-36	78645	20100-20299
COLLIER ST	Austin	614G	MH-21	78704	1100-1999
COLLINDALE CV	Austin	497F	MN-33	78753	12700-12799
COLLINDALE DR	Austin	497B	MN-33	78753	1500-1599
COLLINFIELD DR	Austin	526A	ML-30	78758	8900-9099
COLLINGSWORTH DR	Austin	526G	MM-30	78753	1000-1099
COLLINGWOOD CV	Round Rock	378W	MQ-43	78665	1000-1099
COLLINGWOOD DR	Austin	673E	ME-15	78748	8100-9299
COLLINGWOOD DR	Round Rock	378W	MQ-43	78665	2600-2899
	Round Rock	377V	MP-43	78665	2900-2999
COLLINS ST	Austin	643L	MF-17	78745	2400-2599
COLLINS BLUFF	Bastrop Co	738Q	MR-8	78617	100-199
COLLINS CREEK DR	Austin	645B	MJ-18	78741	2600-3199
COLLINWOOD WEST DR	Travis Co	496Z	MM-31	78753	1000-1399
COLMENERO CIR	Austin	645E	MJ-18	78741	3500-3599
COLOGNE LN	Austin	465Q	MK-35	78727	3800-3999
COLONEL WINN LOOP	Austin	703G	MF-12	78748	10900-11099
COLONIAL DR	Austin	525D	MK-30	78758	8600-8899
COLONIAL DR	Bastrop Co	709G	MT-12	78612	None
COLONIAL DR	Georgetown	226G	MM-60	78628	29000-29099
COLONIAL LN	Lago Vista	459E	WW-36	78645	20000-20199
COLONIAL PKWY	Cedar Park	374J	MG-44	78613	2500-3099
COLONIAL AFFAIR	Hays Co	639S	WW-16	78737	100-399
COLONIAL CLUB DR	Austin	704E	MG-12	78747	10200-10299
COLONIAL MANOR LN	Pflugerville	439E	MS-39	78660	18900-18999
COLONIAL PARK BLVD	Austin	644Q	MH-17	78745	400-1299
COLONY CT	Bastrop Co	712Z	MZ-10	78602	100-199
COLONY CREEK DR	Austin	495Z	MK-31	78758	1700-1899
COLONY LOOP DR	Austin	557Y	MP-25	78724	6700-7199
	Austin	557Z	MP-25	78724	8000-8199
	Austin	587D	MP-24	78724	8200-8599
COLONY NORTH DR	Austin	525H	MK-30	78758	1000-1199
COLONY PARK CV	Austin	557U	MP-25	78724	6700-6799
COLONY PARK DR	Austin	557Y	MP-25	78724	6700-7399
COLORADO CIR	Bastrop Co	712T	MY-10	78612	100-199
COLORADO DR	Bastrop Co	711B	MW-12	78612	100-199
COLORADO DR E	Travis Co	458U	WV-34	78669	20700-20799
COLORADO DR W	Travis Co	458T	WU-34	78669	20800-20999
COLORADO ST	Austin	585S	MJ-22	78701	100-1399
	Austin	585N	MJ-23	78701	1400-1899
COLORADO BEND DR	Cedar Park	373E	ME-45	78613	1400-1799
COLORADO CANYON DR	Travis Co	427M	WT-38	78654	None
COLORADO CROSSING	Austin	524T	MG-28	78731	4500-4799
COLORADO RIVER RD	Georgetown	196W	ML-61	78628	100-499
COLOVISTA DR	Bastrop Co	776F	EG-6	78602	100-399
COLOVISTA PKWY	Bastrop Co	776Q	EH-5	78602	100-699
COLOVISTA RANCH RD	Bastrop Co	776X	EG-4	78602	100-199
COLQUITT CV	Austin	672M	MD-14	78748	2600-2699
COLT CT	Mustang Ridge	765U	MK-4	78610	6900-6999
COLT CV	Lago Vista	458R	WV-35	78645	2700-2799
COLT DR	Mustang Ridge	765Q	MK-5	78610	12100-12399
COLT DR	Travis Co	490U	WZ-31	78734	14600-14799
COLT ST	Cedar Park	373X	ME-43	78613	500-599
COLTEN WAY	Cedar Park	402R	MD-41	78613	1500-1699
COL THORPE LN	Hutto	350J	MU-47	78634	100-299
COLTON RD	Travis Co	676F	ML-15	78719	4800-4899
	Travis Co	676P	ML-14	78719	5100-5899
	Travis Co	676T	ML-13	78744	6100-6499
COLTON-BLUFF SPRINGS RD	Austin	675S	MJ-13	78744	6400-7199
	Travis Co	675X	MJ-13	78744	7200-7599
	Travis Co	705C	MK-12	78744	7600-8299
	Travis Co	706E	ML-12	78744	8300-8999
COLUMBIA CV	Austin	556G	MM-27	78723	2100-2199
COLUMBIA DR	Austin	556L	MM-26	78723	6600-7099
COLUMBIA FALLS CV	Williamson Co	375T	MJ-43	78681	17600-17699
COLUMBIA FALLS DR	Williamson Co	375T	MJ-43	78681	8300-8699
COLUMBIA OAKS CT	Austin	464M	MH-35	78759	6500-6599
COLUMBIA OAKS DR	Austin	464M	MH-35	78759	11800-11899
COLUMBINE AVE	Cedar Park	372H	MD-45	78613	500-699
COLUMBINE CT	Georgetown	225P	MJ-59	78633	100-199
COLUMBINE DR	Austin	465H	MK-36	78727	4100-4599
COLUMBINE LN	Leander	342T	MC-46	78641	1700-1899
COLUMBINE ST	Travis Co	437R	MP-38	78660	16900-17099
COLUMBUS DR	Austin	584X	MG-22	78746	2200-2499
COLUMBUS LN	Lago Vista	459E	WW-36	78645	20000-20099
COLUMBUS LOOP	Williamson Co	348K	MQ-47	78665	None
COLUMBUS ST	Austin	614H	MH-21	78704	800-999
COLUSA CT	Austin	642F	MC-18	78749	5200-5299
COLWYN BAY CV	Travis Co	437K	MN-38	78660	16500-16599
COMAL CV	Elgin	533F	EA-30	78621	None
COMAL ST	Austin	615F	MJ-21	78702	1-399
	Austin	585Y	MK-22	78702	400-1899
	Austin	585Q	MK-23	78722	1900-2299
COMANCHE CIR	Williamson Co	410T	MU-40	78634	100-399
COMANCHE DR	Point Venture	489J	WW-32	78645	100-199
COMANCHE LN	Point Venture	489K	WW-32	78645	200-299
COMANCHE ST	Austin	585G	MK-24	78705	800-899
COMANCHE TRL	Bastrop Co	621Z	MX-19	78621	100-299
COMANCHE TRL	Travis Co	492A	MC-33	78732	5900-6299
	Travis Co	462W	MC-34	78732	6300-6699
	Travis Co	461Q	MB-35	78732	6700-7299
COMANCHE TRL	Travis Co	461C	MB-36	78641	7800-7899
COMANCHE TRL	Williamson Co	223D	MF-60	78633	100-199
COMANCHE CREEK DR	Austin	612M	MD-20	78735	4700-4899
COMBURG DR	Austin	673E	ME-15	78748	9000-9299
COMBURG CASTLE WAY	Austin	673A	ME-15	78748	2200-2699
COMET	Lakeway	489W	WW-31	78734	100-399
COMET CV	Lakeway	489W	WW-31	78734	300-399
COMETA ST	Austin	586K	ML-23	78721	1200-1499
COMFORT CV	Austin	494Z	MH-31	78731	7800-7999
COMFORT LN	Austin	673S	ME-13	78748	1700-1799
COMFORT ST	Cedar Park	372U	MD-43	78613	1100-1499
COMISO PALA PATH	Austin	463A	ME-36	78726	11100-11299
COMMANCHE	Lago Vista	429S	WW-37	78645	4700-4799
COMMANDERS POINT DR	Travis Co	491A	MA-33	78734	4400-4599
COMMELINA DR	Travis Co	401Q	MB-41	78641	16000-16499
COMMERCE BLVD	Georgetown	316U	MM-49	78626	100-499
COMMERCE BLVD	Round Rock	376F	ML-45	78664	100-299
COMMERCE CV	Round Rock	376G	MM-45	78664	200-399
COMMERCE ST	Austin	586K	ML-23	78721	3700-3799
COMMERCE ST N	Williamson Co	443L	EB-38	78615	100-599
COMMERCE ST S	Williamson Co	443Q	EB-38	78615	100-699
COMMERCIAL DR	Bastrop	746N	EG-8	78602	100-199
COMMERCIAL DR	Hays Co	763J	ME-5	78610	100-399
	Hays Co	762M	MD-5	78610	400-699
COMMERCIAL DR	Taylor	323S	EA-49	76574	100-299
COMMERCIAL PKWY	Cedar Park	403A	ME-42	78613	100-199
COMMERCIAL CENTER DR	Austin	645J	MJ-17	78744	3900-4199
COMMERCIAL PARK DR	Austin	557E	MN-27	78724	4600-5199
COMMODORE CIR	Austin	674G	MH-15	78744	6600-6799
COMMON DR	West Lake Hills	583B	ME-24	78746	1100-1199
COMMONS PKWY	Travis Co	409T	MS-40	78660	20500-20799
COMMONS RD	Dripping Springs	636Z	WR-16	78620	100-199
COMMONS FORD RD N	Travis Co	521Z	MB-28	78733	100-999
COMMONS FORD RD S	Travis Co	551D	MB-27	78733	100-399
COMMONWEALTH WAY	Austin	464G	MH-36	78759	11900-12099
COMMUNITY DR	Austin	616S	ML-19	78741	700-1099
COMPANEROS WAY	Austin	642X	MC-16	78749	4300-4499
COMPASS CIR	Travis Co	577L	WT-23	78720	18100-18199
COMPASS DR	Travis Co	557Q	MP-26	78724	7500-7699
COMSOUTH DR	Austin	645L	MK-17	78744	3300-3599
COMSTOCK CV	Lago Vista	429B	WW-39	78645	7100-7299
CONANN CT	Austin	496L	MM-32	78753	11900-11999
CONCAN DR	Hutto	379L	MT-44	78634	1100-2099
CONCHO ST	Austin	615C	MK-21	78702	400-499
	Austin	585Y	MK-22	78702	700-1199
	Austin	585Q	MK-23	78702	1300-1399
	Austin	585L	MK-23	78722	2100-2199
CONCHO TRL	Williamson Co	255M	MK-56	78628	100-199
CONCHO CREEK BEND	Austin	612M	MD-20	78735	5100-5399
CONCHOS CV	Austin	433X	ME-37	78726	11000-11199
CONCHOS TRL	Austin	433X	ME-37	78726	11000-11299
	Travis Co	433X	ME-37	78726	10800-10999
CONCHOS RIVER TRL	Austin	404E	MG-42	78717	11200-11399
CONCHOS VALLEY DR	Williamson Co	405G	MK-42	78681	16200-16599
CONCORD CIR	Hays Co	700J	WY-11	78610	1-99
CONCORD CV	Lago Vista	459N	WW-35	78645	2900-2999
CONCORD DR	Georgetown	225V	MK-58	78628	500-599
CONCORD DR	Round Rock	347N	MN-47	78665	3800-3899
CONCORDIA AVE	Austin	585C	MK-24	78705	1000-1099
	Austin	585C	MK-24	78722	1100-1699
CONCORDIA UNIVERSITY DR	Austin	462M	MD-35	78726	11400-11699
CONE CIR	Austin	524J	MG-29	78731	5900-5999
CONEJO DR	Travis Co	490C	WZ-33	78734	3900-3999
CONESTOGA CV	Lago Vista	458R	WV-35	78645	2700-2799
CONESTOGA PASS	Round Rock	376D	MM-45	78665	1200-1299
CONESTOGA TRL	Austin	644Z	MH-16	78744	1900-2199
CONESTOGA TRL	Pflugerville	467C	MP-36	78660	None
CONFEDERATE ST	Austin	584L	MH-23	78703	1600-1799
CONFERENCE CV	Travis Co	522B	MC-30	78730	3900-3999
CONFERENCE DR	Bastrop	746N	EG-8	78602	100-199
CONFIDENCE CV	Lakeway	519H	WX-30	78734	100-199
CONFLOWER CIR	Travis Co	677R	MP-14	78617	5400-5499
CONGRESS AVE	Austin	585W	MJ-22	78701	100-1099
	Austin	585P	MJ-23	78701	1300-1899
CONGRESS AVE	Lago Vista	459E	WW-36	78645	3400-3899
CONGRESS AVE S	Austin	615E	MJ-21	78704	100-1599
	Austin	614V	MH-19	78704	1600-3699
	Austin	644G	MH-18	78704	3700-3999
	Austin	644T	MG-16	78745	4000-6799
	Austin	674E	MG-15	78745	6800-9099
	See.. Loop 275				
CONGRESSIONAL CIR	Travis Co	582M	MD-23	78746	1800-1899
CONIFER CV	Austin	611E	MA-21	78736	6500-6799
CONNALLY LN	Austin	586D	MM-24	78723	5400-5499
CONN CREEK	Cedar Park	373R	MF-44	78613	2100-2198 E
CONNECTICUT DR	Austin	526E	ML-30	78758	900-999
CONNELLY ST	Austin	555V	MK-25	78751	4600-4699
CONNEMARA LN	Pflugerville	407Y	MP-40	78660	1100-1199
CONNER DOWNS DR	Travis Co	467P	MN-35	78660	13800-14099
CONNIE ST	Travis Co	436R	MM-38	78728	15200-15799
CONNOR LN	Austin	526U	MM-28	78753	8200-8599
CONNORS CV	Cedar Park	372P	MC-44	78613	1800-1899
CONRAD RD	Austin	465J	ML-35	78727	12100-12299
CONRAD ST	Austin	526E	ML-30	78758	900-999
CONROY LN	Travis Co	703L	MF-11	78652	11200-11499
CONSTANTINO CIR	Austin	643Y	MF-16	78745	1600-1899
CONSTANTINOPLE LN	Pflugerville	437F	MN-39	78664	16800-16899
CONSTANT SPRINGS DR	Travis Co	583U	MF-22	78746	1100-1399
CONSTELLATION CIR	Austin	678S	MQ-13	78617	6000-6399
CONSTELLATION DR	Buda	763K	ME-5	78610	2000-2199
CONSTELLATION DR	Manor	530J	MU-29	78653	None
CONSTITUTION CV	Lago Vista	459J	WW-35	78645	19900-19999
CONSTITUTION DR	Lago Vista	459J	WW-35	78645	2900-4199
CONSTITUTION SQUARE	Lago Vista	459J	WW-35	78645	2300-3099
CONTESSA CT	Austin	642T	MC-16	78749	9100-9199
CONTI CT	Austin	675S	MJ-13	78744	6100-6199
CONTINENTAL CV	Lago Vista	459J	WW-35	78645	19900-20099
CONTINENTAL DR	Lago Vista	459J	WW-35	78645	20000-20099
	Lago Vista	458R	WV-35	78645	20100-20499
CONTINENTAL PASS	Cedar Park	372T	MC-43	78613	1400-2199
CONTOUR DR	Austin	525C	MK-30	78757	8500-8599
CONTRAILS WAY	Burnet Co	396S	WQ-40	78669	100-599
CONVICT HILL RD	Austin	642M	MD-17	78749	3500-4599
	Austin	642G	MD-18	78749	4600-6199
	Austin	612W	MC-19	78749	6200-6599
	Austin	611Z	MB-19	78749	6600-6999
CONWAY CV	Round Rock	408C	MR-42	78664	2200-2299
CONWAY SPRINGS CT	Williamson Co	375S	MJ-43	78717	17000-17099
COOING CT	Austin	675A	MJ-15	78744	6000-6099
COOKE ST	Round Rock	377W	MN-43	78664	200-299
COOKSTOWN DR	Austin	465R	MK-35	78759	3500-3799
COOKWOOD CV	Austin	673A	ME-15	78748	9100-9199
COOLBROOK DR	Austin	557T	MN-25	78724	5600-5999
COOL CANYON CV	Williamson Co	375P	MJ-44	78681	7000-7099
COOLIDGE LN	Lago Vista	459A	WW-36	78645	20000-20099
COOL LAKE CV	Round Rock	378W	MQ-43	78665	1100-1199
COOL RIVER LOOP	Round Rock	408E	MQ-42	78665	2800-2899
COOL SHADOW DR	Austin	646D	MM-18	78742	1300-1499
COOL SPRING WAY	Hays Co	668M	WV-14	78737	100-299
	Hays Co	669N	WW-14	78737	300-1899
	Hays Co	668R	WV-14	78737	1900-2599
COOL SPRINGS WAY	Georgetown	195S	MJ-61	78633	1000-1599
COOL WATER DR	Austin	673X	ME-13	78748	700-899
COOMER PATH	Austin	498E	MQ-33	78660	13500-13699
COOMES DR	Austin	678P	MQ-14	78617	13200-13799
COOMES PL	Cedar Park	402L	MD-41	78613	700-799
COOPER CIR	Lago Vista	459B	WW-36	78645	20000-20099
COOPER DR	Austin	526F	ML-30	78753	400-799
COOPER LN	Austin	644S	MG-16	78745	6400-6899
	Austin	643Z	MF-16	78745	6900-7299
	Austin	673D	MF-15	78745	7300-7899
COOPER LN	Lago Vista	459B	WW-36	78645	3900-4399
COOPER WAY	Williamson Co	406P	ML-41	78681	2000-2099
COOPERATIVE WAY	Georgetown	316C	MM-51	78626	100-199
COOPER HILL DR	Austin	496N	ML-32	78758	10500-10799
COOPER LAKE DR	Georgetown	195N	MJ-62	78633	100-499
COOPERS HAWK CV	Bee Cave	549H	WX-27	78738	None
COOPERS HAWK PATH	Pflugerville	437V	MP-37	78660	1100-1199
COPANO CT	Austin	642L	MD-17	78749	4600-4699
COPANO CV	Williamson Co	377E	MN-45	78664	1200-1299
COPANO DR	Austin	642L	MD-17	78749	7700-9099
COPANO DR	Bastrop Co	709G	MT-12	78612	None
COPANO BAY CV	Georgetown	195N	MJ-62	78633	100-199
COPELAND ST	Austin	614H	MH-21	78704	600-799
COPFORD LN	Travis Co	432C	MD-39	78613	2600-2899
COPPER LN	Williamson Co	281J	MA-53	78641	100-399
COPPER PASS	Travis Co	611X	MA-19	78737	8100-8199
COPPERAS DR	Austin	642L	MD-17	78749	7700-7899
COPPERBEND BLVD	Austin	645W	MJ-16	78744	4800-5299
COPPER BREAKS DR	Georgetown	195K	MJ-62	78633	500-599
COPPER BREAKS LN	Cedar Park	373E	ME-45	78613	1800-1899
COPPER CLIFF AVE	Austin	466K	ML-35	78727	12800-12899
COPPER CREEK	Travis Co	468U	MR-34	78660	None
COPPER CREEK DR	Williamson Co	434J	MG-38	78729	9600-9899
COPPERFIELD DR	Austin	497E	MN-33	78753	12300-12599
COPPERHEAD CV	Pflugerville	437B	MN-39	78664	1600-1699
COPPERHEAD DR	Pflugerville	437B	MN-39	78664	16900-17299
COPPER HILLS DR	Hays Co	701M	MB-11	78652	13400-13799
COPPER LAKE LN	Williamson Co	344F	MG-48	78628	100-199
COPPER LEAF CT	Williamson Co	196J	ML-62	78628	100-299
COPPER LEAF LN	Williamson Co	343X	ME-46	78641	16200-16299
COPPERLEAF RD	Lakeway	489U	WX-31	78734	100-599
COPPERLEAF TRAIL DR	Hays Co	701M	MB-11	78652	13600-13799
COPPERLILLY CV	Williamson Co	433J	ME-38	78613	1900-1999
COPPERLILY CV	Austin	494B	MG-33	78759	6400-6499
COPPERMEAD LN	Travis Co	527X	MN-28	78754	5000-5299
COPPER MOUNT CV	Austin	583Z	MF-22	78746	3000-3099
COPPERPLACE DR	Hays Co	701M	MB-11	78652	3600-3799
COPPER POINT CV	Williamson Co	283H	MF-54	78628	100-199
COPPERWOOD DR	Austin	613E	ME-21	78735	4000-4099
COPPERWOOD LOOP	Williamson Co	377C	MP-45	78665	100-199

STREET NAME	CITY or COUNTY	MAPSCO GRID	AUSTIN GRID	ZIP CODE	BLOCK RANGE O/E
COQUINA LN	West Lake Hills	583M	MF-23	78746	500-699
CORA CV	Cedar Park	403N	ME-41	78613	1300-1399
CORA CV	Round Rock	377E	MN-45	78664	2500-2598 E
CORABELLA PL	Travis Co	432G	MD-39	78613	2700-2899
CORAL DR	Cedar Park	402U	MD-40	78613	1700-1899
CORALBERRY CV	Travis Co	491X	MA-31	78732	12700-12799
CORAL CAY LN	Pflugerville	437C	MP-39	78664	1300-1499
CORAL GABLES CT	Travis Co	703R	MF-11	78747	11000-11099
CORAL RIDGE CIR	Austin	704N	MG-11	78747	2400-2499
CORAL STONE TRL	Hays Co	763S	ME-4	78610	100-299
CORALVINE CV	Travis Co	582J	MC-23	78735	3300-3399
CORALVINE WAY	Georgetown	314F	MG-51	78628	400-499
CORA MARIE CV	Pflugerville	437H	MP-39	78660	1400-1499
CORA MARIE DR	Pflugerville	437H	MP-39	78660	1500-1699
CORAZON CV	Williamson Co	345T	MJ-46	78681	4500-4599
CORBE DR	Austin	463E	ME-36	78726	9500-9699
CORBIN LN	Austin	614P	MG-20	78704	2800-3199
CORBIN WAY	Cedar Park	372J	MC-44	78613	2200-2499
CORBIN CREEK CV	Williamson Co	405A	MJ-42	78717	9100-9199
CORDELL LN	Austin	556Y	MM-25	78723	5500-5699
CORDERO DR	Austin	404L	MH-41	78717	14800-15099
CORDILL LN	Travis Co	517G	WT-30	78669	19700-20899
CORDILLERA DR	Williamson Co	405B	MJ-42	78681	16600-16699
CORDOBA CIR E	Georgetown	226U	MM-58	78628	4300-4399
CORDOBA CIR W	Georgetown	226T	ML-58	78628	4300-4499
CORDOBA DR	Austin	587C	MP-24	78724	7200-7499
CORDOVA CV	Cedar Park	373Y	MF-43	78613	300-399
CORDOVA DR	Austin	465X	MJ-34	78759	3900-4299
CORDURA DR	Bastrop	744P	EC-8	78602	None
CORDWOOD	Hays Co	576Q	WR-23	78620	100-299
COREOPSIS DR	Travis Co	551P	MA-26	78733	10500-10699
COREOPSIS WAY	Georgetown	225L	MK-59	78633	100-199
CORIANDER CV	Williamson Co	434Q	MH-38	78729	8300-8399
CORIANDER DR	Austin	646B	ML-18	78741	1300-1799
CORIANDER DR	Williamson Co	434Q	MH-38	78729	12900-13199
CORIDAN DR	Austin	465A	MJ-36	78727	12800-12999
CORINTHIAN	Lakeway	489W	WW-31	78734	200-599
CORK LN	Hays Co	639X	WW-16	78737	100-199
CORK PATH	Austin	643H	MF-18	78745	5500-5599
CORMAC CT	Pflugerville	437C	MP-39	78660	17700-17799
CORMORANT CV	Travis Co	522C	MD-30	78730	10000-10099
CORNELIA DR	Austin	642C	MD-18	78749	5000-5199
CORNELL CV	Lago Vista	459J	WW-35	78645	2300-2899
CORNELL DR	Pflugerville	467D	MP-36	78660	600-899
CORNELL ST	Austin	585V	MK-22	78702	1900-2099
CORNER BROOK CV	Travis Co	672W	MC-13	78739	3500-3599
CORNER BROOK PASS	Travis Co	672W	MC-13	78739	11900-12399
CORNER POST	Williamson Co	375Y	MK-43	78681	100-199
CORNERSTONE	Williamson Co	375X	MJ-43	78681	3500-3799
CORNERWOOD CT	Williamson Co	405K	MJ-41	78717	15900-15999
CORNERWOOD DR	Williamson Co	405K	MJ-41	78717	7600-8499
CORN HILL LN	Round Rock	377W	MN-43	78664	1500-1699
CORNISH CIR	Austin	643K	ME-17	78745	2800-2899
CORNISH HEN CV	Austin	705E	MJ-12	78747	8900-8999
CORNISH HEN LN	Austin	705E	MJ-12	78747	6700-6899
CORNWALL DR	Austin	673M	MF-14	78748	8400-8599
CORONA DR	Austin	556N	ML-26	78723	1200-1999
CORONADO	Leander	371B	MA-45	78641	1600-1699
CORONADO CIR	Austin	556G	MM-27	78752	7200-7299
CORONADO CV	Round Rock	346W	ML-46	78681	1100-1199
CORONADO ST	Austin	585Z	MK-22	78702	2300-2499
CORONADO HILLS DR	Austin	556B	ML-27	78752	1400-2099
CORONATION WAY	Travis Co	467L	MP-35	78660	900-1399
CORONET ST	Austin	465L	MK-35	78727	12400-12499
CORPORATE DR	Bastrop	746N	EG-8	78602	100-199
CORPUS CHRISTI DR	Austin	435S	MJ-37	78729	6700-6799
	Travis Co	435S	MJ-37	78729	6400-6699
CORRAL CV	Lago Vista	399Q	WX-41	78645	8400-8499
CORRAL LN	Austin	674B	MG-15	78745	200-799
CORRAL LN	Lago Vista	399K	WW-41	78645	8400-8499
CORRAL DE TIERRA DR	Travis Co	408G	MR-42	78664	300-599
CORRAN FERRY DR	Austin	642T	MC-16	78749	8700-9099
CORRAN FERRY LOOP	Austin	642T	MC-16	78749	4500-4599
CORRIDA CV	Dripping Springs	636R	WR-17	78620	100-199
CORRIE CV	Austin	611Z	MB-19	78749	7500-7599
CORRIENTES CV	Austin	642W	MC-16	78739	5200-5299
CORRIGAN LN	Round Rock	348W	MQ-46	78665	3100-3299
CORSAIR DR	Georgetown	226Z	MM-58	78628	200-499
CORSAIRE	Lakeway	519B	WW-30	78734	1000-1099
CORSICA PL	Austin	587C	MP-24	78724	7200-7299
CORTA ST	Austin	615D	MK-21	78702	2200-2399
CORTARO CV	Austin	434Y	MH-37	78729	12500-12599
CORTES CT	Williamson Co	348P	MQ-47	78665	2800-2999
CORTES PL	Williamson Co	348P	MQ-47	78665	3300-3499
CORTEZ DR	Travis Co	432H	MD-39	78613	2700-2899
CORTINA DR	Austin	642U	MD-16	78749	3900-4399
CORTINA LN	Williamson Co	345X	MJ-46	78681	3400-3499
CORTO LN	Travis Co	522X	MC-28	78733	1500-1899
CORTO ST	Austin	646G	MM-18	78744	1-99
CORTONA CV	West Lake Hills	583G	MF-24	78746	400-499
CORTONA DR	West Lake Hills	583G	MF-24	78746	300-699
CORUM CV	Travis Co	554A	MG-27	78746	3700-3999
CORUM RIDGE CV	Travis Co	707B	MN-12	78617	11700-11799
CORY LN	Travis Co	488W	WU-31	78669	2700-2799
CORYELL DR	Travis Co	491U	MB-31	78732	12400-12499
COSMOS WAY	Pflugerville	468B	MQ-36	78660	1500-1599
	Travis Co	468B	MQ-36	78660	1600-1699
COSTA AZUL CV	Leander	372F	MC-45	78641	2700-2799
COSTA BELLA CV	Travis Co	490J	WY-32	78734	100-199
COSTA BELLA DR	Travis Co	490J	WY-32	78734	100-299
COSTAKES DR	Austin	433U	MF-37	78750	11400-11499
COSTAS CV	Austin	464Y	MH-34	78759	5700-5799
COSTELLO CT	Travis Co	402T	MC-40	78613	2800-2899
COTTAGE LN	Travis Co	459R	WX-35	78645	17800-17999
COTTAGE GROVE PASS	Williamson Co	375W	MJ-43	78717	9100-9199
COTTESMORE CT	Austin	404F	MG-42	78717	10200-10299
COTTINGHAM DR	Travis Co	618V	MR-19	78725	14200-14599
COTTLE DR	Austin	526G	MM-30	78753	9700-9999
COTTON CV	Hutto	380A	MU-45	78634	100-199
COTTON DR	Travis Co	736M	MM-8	78719	None
COTTON ST	Austin	585U	MK-22	78702	1200-1499
COTTONBOLL DR	Taylor	322R	MZ-50	76574	800-1099
COTTON CREEK WAY	Hutto	380A	MU-45	78634	100-199
COTTONDALE DR	Travis Co	519Q	WX-29	78738	1-99
COTTONMOUTH SCHOOL RD	Travis Co	676N	ML-14	78744	6000-6499

STREET NAME	CITY or COUNTY	MAPSCO GRID	AUSTIN GRID	ZIP CODE	BLOCK RANGE O/E
COTTON PICKING LN	Cedar Park	373J	ME-44	78613	200-399
COTTONTAIL DR	Leander	341H	MB-48	78641	200-2499
	Leander	341G	MB-48	78641	2000-2399
COTTONTAIL LN	Williamson Co	316D	MM-51	78626	200-299
COTTONTAIL TRL	Austin	643V	MF-16	78745	6600-6699
COTTONTAIL TRL	Burnet Co	426F	WQ-39	78669	400-498 E
COTTON TOP DR	Bastrop Co	711C	MX-12	78612	100-199
COTTONWEED TRL	Williamson Co	433E	ME-39	78613	3000-3099
COTTONWOOD CIR	Austin	556Y	MM-25	78723	5000-5099
COTTONWOOD CIR	Lago Vista	429Z	WX-37	78645	5500-5699
COTTONWOOD CT	Bastrop Co	742P	MY-8	78612	100-199
COTTONWOOD CT	Round Rock	407J	MN-41	78664	1600-1699
COTTONWOOD CV	Cedar Park	403E	ME-42	78613	900-999
COTTONWOOD DR	Georgetown	256T	ML-55	78628	1600-2799
COTTONWOOD DR	Hutto	349V	MT-46	78634	100-199
COTTONWOOD DR	Travis Co	309Y	WX-49	78641	24400-24499
COTTONWOOD LN	Pflugerville	438T	MQ-37	78660	300-399
COTTONWOOD ST	Austin	645X	MJ-16	78744	4500-4899
COTTONWOOD CREEK DR	Hays Co	638F	WU-18	78620	100-799
COTTONWOOD CREEK TRL	Cedar Park	373G	MF-45	78613	1100-1499
COTTONWOOD HOLLOW	Lago Vista	459D	WX-36	78645	5300-5699
COTULLA DR	Travis Co	672N	MC-14	78739	11400-11599
COTURNIX DR	Austin	495Z	MK-31	78757	1700-1799
COUGAR AVE N	Cedar Park	373T	ME-43	78613	100-399
COUGAR AVE S	Cedar Park	373X	ME-43	78613	100-399
	Cedar Park	403B	ME-42	78613	400-799
COUGAR CV	Austin	644N	MG-17	78745	900-999
COUGAR CV	Georgetown	257L	MP-56	78626	1700-1799
COUGAR DR	Austin	644N	MG-17	78745	5600-6199
COUGAR DR	Georgetown	257L	MP-56	78626	1700-1799
COUGAR TRL	Caldwell Co	767S	MN-4	78616	1-199
COUGAR COUNTRY DR	Cedar Park	372J	MC-44	78613	1800-2299
COUGAR RUN	Austin	524B	MG-30	78731	6800-6899
COULEE DR	Leander	312S	MC-49	78641	None
COULVER CV	Travis Co	735F	MJ-9	78747	None
COULVER RD	Travis Co	705X	MJ-10	78747	7700-7999
	Travis Co	735C	MK-9	78747	8000-9099
COUNCIL RD	Williamson Co	223D	MF-60	78633	100-299
	Williamson Co	193Z	MF-61	78633	300-399
COUNCIL BLUFF DR	Austin	465D	MK-36	78727	12700-13399
COUNSELOR DR	Austin	642V	MD-16	78749	3600-3899
COUNTRY DR	Williamson Co	378P	MQ-44	78664	1-99
COUNTRY LN	Hays	702W	MC-10	78610	500-599
COUNTRY RD	Williamson Co	256E	ML-57	78628	100-199
	Williamson Co	255H	MK-57	78628	200-599
COUNTRY AIRE DR	Round Rock	376H	MM-45	78664	300-1199
COUNTRY CANYON CV	Austin	494G	MH-33	78759	9100-9199
COUNTRY CLUB DR	Lago Vista	428V	WV-37	78645	4700-4999
	Lago Vista	429N	WW-38	78645	5000-5599
COUNTRY CLUB RD	Austin	615Z	MK-19	78741	1800-1999
COUNTRY CLUB RD	Georgetown	256X	ML-55	78628	600-1599
COUNTRY CREEK DR	Hays Co	669N	WW-14	78737	100-399
COUNTRY ESTATES DR	Hutto	379G	MT-45	78634	100-699
COUNTRY FOLKS LN	Hays Co	763V	MF-4	78610	100-199
COUNTRY KNOLL	Austin	463D	MF-36	78750	10900-11199
COUNTRY LAKE CT	Travis Co	491S	MA-31	78732	3100-3199
COUNTRY LAKE DR	Travis Co	491N	MA-32	78732	13100-13899
COUNTRY MEADOW CIR	Austin	678N	MQ-14	78617	12500-12699
COUNTRY MESA CIR	Austin	678N	MQ-14	78617	5700-5899
COUNTRY RIDGE CIR	Austin	677M	MP-14	78617	11200-11399
COUNTRYSIDE CIR	Travis Co	426H	WR-39	78669	2500-2799
COUNTRY SIDE CT	Williamson Co	197V	MP-61	78626	100-299
COUNTRYSIDE DR	Travis Co	426M	WR-38	78669	26100-26499
COUNTRY SQUIRE DR	Cedar Park	372P	MC-44	78613	1500-1899
COUNTRY TRAILS LN	Travis Co	521B	MA-30	78732	12400-12899
	Travis Co	491W	MA-31	78732	12900-13599
COUNTRY VIEW CIR	Austin	677R	MP-14	78617	5400-5599
COUNTRY VIEW WAY	Cedar Park	374Q	MH-44	78613	100-199
COUNTRY WHITE LN	Travis Co	643A	ME-18	78749	3500-3699
COUNTS CV	Austin	642L	MD-17	78749	4800-4899
COUNTY CORK LN	Leander	342Y	MD-46	78641	500-899
COUNTY DOWN CT	Austin	704S	MG-10	78747	5400-5499
COUNTY DOWN DR	Austin	704T	MG-10	78747	11000-11499
COUNTY GLEN	Leander	342U	MD-46	78641	100-899
COUNTY LINE RD	Elgin	533N	EA-30	78621	12700-13198 E
	Elgin	533E	EA-30	78621	13200-14599
	Travis Co	562G	MZ-27	78621	11900-12199
	Travis Co	532Z	MZ-28	78621	12200-12699
	Travis Co	533N	EA-30	78621	12701-13199 O
	Travis Co	503L	EB-32	78621	14600-16199
	Travis Co	473Z	EB-34	78615	16200-16899
	Travis Co	474S	EC-34	78615	16900-17499
COURAGEOUS	Leander	372E	MC-45	78641	None
COURI PASS	Bee Cave	579D	WX-24	78738	13500-13699
COURMAYEUR CT	Williamson Co	316Z	MM-49	78665	1500-1599
COURT DEL REY	Round Rock	375H	MK-45	78681	2200-2299
COURTLAND CIR	Hays Co	669P	WW-14	78737	100-199
COURTLAND LN	Austin	584B	MG-24	78703	1600-1699
COURTLEIGH CIR	Austin	494D	MH-33	78759	9700-9799
COURTNEY	Georgetown	316L	MM-50	78626	None
COURTNEY CV	Round Rock	407J	MN-41	78664	1800-1899
COURTNEY LN	Williamson Co	402Z	MD-40	78613	1600-1799
COURTNEY ST	Austin	643U	MF-16	78745	2000-2199
COURT OF ST JAMES	Travis Co	522D	MD-30	78730	4500-4599
COURTS	Austin	586N	ML-23	78702	None
COURTSIDE CIR	Burnet Co	396P	WQ-41	78669	100-199
COURTSIDE LN	Burnet Co	396P	WQ-41	78669	100-199
COURTSIDE WAY	Burnet Co	396P	WQ-41	78669	100-199
COURTWAY CV	Williamson Co	197Y	MP-61	78626	100-199
COURTYARD CV	Austin	524E	MG-30	78731	5600-5699
COURTYARD DR	Austin	524J	MG-29	78731	5400-5999
COURTYARD GARDEN LN	Georgetown	195T	MJ-61	78633	100-199
COUSTEAU LN	Travis Co	552R	MD-26	78746	1-99
	Travis Co	553N	ME-26	78746	None
COVALA DR	Cedar Park	402D	MD-42	78613	200-299
COVE DR	Travis Co	426Z	WR-37	78669	25400-25699
COVE CREEK DR	Burnet Co	396P	WQ-41	78669	200-299
COVE CREEK LN	Village of the Hills	519S	WW-28	78738	1-99
COVENANT CANYON TRL	Travis Co	520B	WY-30	78734	300-499
COVENTRY DR	Burnet Co	396S	WQ-40	78669	100-1399
COVENTRY LN	Austin	556U	MM-25	78723	5400-5999
COVERED BRIDGE DR	Austin	611L	MB-20	78736	6600-7799
COVERED WAGON PASS	Austin	644Z	MH-16	78744	2000-2099
COVERED WAGON TRL	Round Rock	378B	MQ-45	78665	3300-3499
COVEY CT	Austin	525D	MK-30	78758	8900-8999

STREET NAME	CITY or COUNTY	MAPSCO GRID	AUSTIN GRID	ZIP CODE	BLOCK RANGE O/E
COVEY LN	Georgetown	287M	MP-53	78626	100-199
	Williamson Co	287M	MP-53	78626	100-199
COVINGTON CV	Williamson Co	314E	MG-51	78628	100-199
COVINGTON DR E	Austin	496R	MM-32	78753	100-799
COVINGTON DR W	Austin	496Q	MM-32	78753	100-399
COVINGTON PL	Round Rock	375C	MK-45	78681	2500-3099
COVINGTON TRL	Austin	465A	MJ-36	78727	12700-12999
COVY RIDGE LN	Austin	496X	ML-31	78758	9600-9699
COWAL DR N	Briarcliff	457V	WT-34	78669	100-499
COWAL DR S	Briarcliff	457Z	WT-34	78669	100-899
COWAN CREEK DR	Georgetown	195X	MJ-61	78633	100-299
COWBOY CV	Lago Vista	399X	WW-40	78645	7300-7399
COW CREEK RD	Burnet Co	307J	WS-50	78654	None
	Travis Co	368E	WU-45	78654	8100-10099
	Travis Co	337V	WT-46	78654	10100-11899
	Travis Co	307Y	WT-49	78654	11900-12599
	Travis Co	367H	WT-45	78654	None
COW CREEK RIDGE	Burnet Co	307F	WS-51	78654	100-799
COWDEN DR	Travis Co	491T	MA-31	78732	3400-3599
COWDRAY PARK	Austin	434A	MG-39	78729	13200-13399
COWHER CT	Austin	641W	MA-16	78739	11200-11299
COWPOKE TRL	Lago Vista	399W	WW-40	78645	7100-7399
COX CV	Cedar Park	372Q	MD-44	78613	1400-1499
COX CROSSING RD	Travis Co	426Z	WR-37	78669	25400-26599
COYOTE CT	Travis Co	490M	WZ-32	78734	3100-3199
COYOTE CT	Travis Co	672P	MC-14	78748	10900-10999
COYOTE LN	Leander	342K	MC-47	78641	800-899
COYOTE TRL	Georgetown	225C	MK-60	78633	100-199
COYOTE TRL	Lago Vista	429B	WW-39	78645	21400-21499
	Lago Vista	399W	WW-40	78645	21500-21699
COYOTE TRL	Williamson Co	379R	MT-44	78634	1-699
COZETTE CT	Travis Co	677X	MN-13	78617	7000-7099
COZETTE DR	Travis Co	677X	MN-13	78617	11400-11499
COZUMEL CT	Bastrop Co	738X	MQ-7	78617	None
CRABAPPLE CT	Village of the Hills	519N	WW-29	78738	1-99
CRABAPPLE CV	Round Rock	375H	MK-45	78681	2000-2098 E
CRABTREE CV	Austin	493H	MF-33	78750	8100-8199
CRABTREE DR	Austin	493H	MF-33	78750	8200-8299
CRACKLING CREEK DR	Austin	611T	MA-19	78736	7600-7799
CRADLEROCK TERRACE	Austin	702C	MD-12	78748	2700-2799
CRAFTON PL	Austin	641R	MB-17	78749	6100-6199
CRAFTS PRAIRIE RD	Bastrop Co	776Z	EH-4	78602	200-399
CRAFTY CV	Austin	642K	MC-17	78749	4800-4899
CRAGGY PT	Austin	524S	MG-28	78731	5600-5699
CRAIG DR	Austin	465P	MJ-35	78727	4700-4999
CRAIG ST	Dripping Springs	636V	WR-16	78620	100-299
CRAIGEN RD	Williamson Co	252C	MD-57	78642	100-399
CRAIGMONT DR	Austin	644T	MG-16	78745	200-399
CRAIG PATRICK WAY	Austin	702G	MD-12	78652	2100-2199
CRAIG'S CREST PATH	Travis Co	437T	MN-37	78660	15300-15499
CRAIGWOOD CIR	Austin	587J	MN-23	78725	6300-6499
CRAIGWOOD DR	Austin	587J	MN-23	78725	4500-4999
CRAINWAY DR	Travis Co	557J	MN-26	78724	None
CRAMPTON CV	Hays Co	639V	WX-16	78737	100-299
CRANBERRY CV	Williamson Co	403W	ME-40	78613	2400-2499
CRANBROOK CV	Austin	673J	ME-14	78748	2600-2699
CRANDALL RD	Austin	640Z	WZ-16	78739	7700-7999
CRANE RD	Travis Co	734Z	MH-7	78610	12900-13599
CRANE ST	Travis Co	520E	WY-30	78734	300-399
CRANE CANYON PL	Round Rock	377Z	MP-43	78665	600-799
CRANE CREEK LOOP	Travis Co	409W	MS-40	78660	19900-20199
CRANFORD CT	Austin	433W	ME-37	78726	10600-10699
CRANSTON CV	Pflugerville	437B	MN-39	78664	1700-1799
CRANSTON DR	Pflugerville	437B	MN-39	78664	16700-17299
CRATER LAKE DR	Pflugerville	438E	MQ-39	78660	400-599
CRATER LAKE PASS	Austin	704A	MG-12	78747	10000-10099
CRATERS OF THE MOON BLVD	Pflugerville	438B	MQ-39	78660	700-1199
CRAVEN LN	Travis Co	529H	MT-30	78653	13100-13299
CRAWFISH LN	Travis Co	458Z	WV-34	78669	1100-1399
CRAWFORD AVE	Austin	555S	MJ-25	78731	3500-3799
CRAWFORD RD	Travis Co	487U	WT-31	78669	3000-4099
	Travis Co	517B	WS-30	78669	4100-4799
CRAYBROUGH CIR	Austin	557T	MN-25	78724	7000-7099
CRAZY CV	Travis Co	487F	WS-33	78669	None
CRAZY DEER RUN	Travis Co	650T	MU-16	78612	None
CRAZY HORSE DR	Travis Co	641B	MA-18	78737	7800-7899
CRAZYHORSE PASS	Travis Co	490Q	WZ-32	78734	1900-2699
CRAZY WELL DR	Austin	404A	MG-42	78717	10900-11299
CREDO LN	Travis Co	619T	MS-19	78725	4500-4699
CREE CIR	Travis Co	460V	WZ-34	78734	15300-15399
CREE LN	Travis Co	460V	WZ-34	78734	5100-5399
CREEDMOOR DR	Travis Co	676X	ML-13	78719	6600-7099
	Travis Co	706B	ML-12	78719	7100-7499
CREEK CV	Round Rock	376P	ML-44	78664	300-499
CREEK CV E	Hays Co	667D	WT-15	78620	2400-2499
CREEK CV W	Hays Co	667L	WT-14	78620	100-199
CREEK DR	Georgetown	256F	ML-57	78628	100-199
CREEK DR E	Hays Co	637Z	WT-16	78620	100-499
	Hays Co	667M	WT-14	78620	500-1899
CREEK DR W	Hays Co	638F	WU-18	78620	600-799
CREEK RD	Dripping Springs	666C	WR-15	78620	100-1199
CREEK RD	Hays Co	666A	WQ-15	78620	1200-3199
CREEK BEND BLVD	Round Rock	375R	MK-44	78681	1700-2099
	Round Rock	345Z	MK-46	78681	None
CREEK BEND BLVD	Williamson Co	375U	MK-43	78681	None
CREEK BEND CIR	Round Rock	375M	MK-44	78681	1700-2499
CREEK BEND CV	Hutto	380E	MU-45	78634	1300-1399
CREEKBEND CV	Pflugerville	438S	MQ-37	78660	900-1099
CREEKBEND CV W	Williamson Co	379Q	MT-44	78634	500-599
CREEKBEND DR	Austin	674H	MH-15	78744	4500-4799
	Austin	675E	MJ-15	78744	4800-5199
CREEKBEND DR	Pflugerville	438N	MQ-38	78660	200-1099
CREEK BEND DR N	Hutto	380E	MU-45	78634	100-299
CREEK BEND DR S	Hutto	379M	MT-44	78634	100-399
CREEK BLUFF CV	Travis Co	370S	WY-43	78641	11500-11599
CREEK BLUFF DR	Austin	494S	MG-31	78750	7300-7799
CREEK BOTTOM	Austin	524T	MG-28	78731	5600-5699
CREEKBRANCH CV	Austin	675A	MJ-15	78744	5700-5799
CREEK CREST WAY	Round Rock	377X	MN-43	78664	1800-1999
CREEK CROSSING CV	Travis Co	577G	WT-24	78720	10200-10299
CREEK FRONT DR	Bee Cave	550S	WY-25	78738	None
CREEK HOLLOW	Austin	527A	MN-30	78754	1500-1699
CREEK LEDGE	Austin	524T	MG-28	78731	4100-4399
CREEK LEDGE DR	Hutto	379R	MT-44	78634	100-399
CREEK LEDGE PL	Round Rock	377X	MN-43	78664	1800-2099
CREEKLINE DR	Austin	644K	MG-17	78745	4900-5299

C

STREET NAME	CITY or COUNTY	MAPSCO GRID	AUSTIN GRID	ZIP CODE	BLOCK RANGE O/E
CREEK MEADOW CV	Travis Co	517R	WT-29	78669	4800-5199
CREEK MEADOW CV	Williamson Co	344A	MG-48	78641	100-199
CREEK MEADOWS	Austin	524T	MG-28	78731	5600-5699
CREEKMERE LN	Austin	674E	MG-15	78748	7800-8099
CREEKMONT CV	Austin	673A	ME-15	78748	8900-8999
CREEK MOUNTAIN	Austin	524T	MG-28	78731	5600-5699
CREEK RIDGE	Austin	613J	ME-20	78735	4600-4699
CREEK RIDGE BLVD	Round Rock	377X	MN-43	78664	1800-1899
CREEK RIDGE DR	Bastrop Co	742U	MZ-7	78602	100-199
CREEK RIDGE LN	Round Rock	377X	MN-43	78664	200-399
CREEK RUN DR	Williamson Co	373A	ME-45	78641	400-599
	Williamson Co	343W	ME-46	78641	15100-15299
CREEK'S EDGE CIR	Travis Co	581C	MB-24	78733	9200-9499
CREEK'S EDGE PKWY	Travis Co	551U	MB-25	78733	1700-2699
	Travis Co	581C	MB-24	78733	2700-3199
CREEKSIDE CIR	Williamson Co	279X	WW-52	78642	1-499
CREEKSIDE CV	Cedar Park	374L	MH-44	78613	300-399
CREEKSIDE CV	Lago Vista	399Q	WX-41	78645	8300-8399
CREEKSIDE DR	Austin	556G	MM-27	78752	7000-7299
CREEKSIDE DR	Hutto	349V	MT-46	78634	100-399
CREEKSIDE DR	Travis Co	369V	WX-43	78645	21100-21499
	Travis Co	370S	WY-43	78645	None
CREEKSIDE DR	Williamson Co	197Y	MP-61	78626	100-299
CREEKSIDE LN	Georgetown	287S	MN-52	78626	2200-2299
CREEKSTONE DR	Cedar Park	403K	ME-41	78613	1300-1399
CREEKVIEW CIR	Leander	313Q	MF-50	78628	100-199
CREEKVIEW DR	Round Rock	406E	ML-42	78681	1100-2399
CREEK VIEW DR	Travis Co	673W	ME-13	78748	10600-10899
CREEK VISTA BLVD	Cedar Park	373V	MF-43	78613	100-499
CREEKWAY CV	Austin	527W	MN-28	78754	None
CREEKWOOD CIR	Travis Co	577V	WT-22	78720	10600-10699
CREEKWOOD CV	Cedar Park	403F	ME-42	78613	300-399
CREEKWOOD DR N	Hays Co	403K	WU-13	78620	100-699
CREEKWOOD PL	Austin	675E	MJ-15	78744	6400-6499
CREEKWOOD RD	Austin	586C	MM-24	78723	4700-4899
CREE LAKE CT	Williamson Co	343S	ME-46	78641	16800-16899
CREIGHTON LN	Austin	556G	MM-27	78723	6900-7199
CRENATA CV	Austin	494C	MH-33	78759	9600-9799
CRENSHAW LN	Round Rock	378U	MR-43	78664	2500-2599
CREOLE CV	Austin	466G	MM-36	78727	13400-13499
CREOLE DR	Austin	466F	ML-36	78727	1800-2099
CREPE MYRTLE DR	Austin	675T	MJ-13	78744	7300-7499
CREPE MYRTLE LN	Georgetown	225D	MK-60	78633	100-199
CRESCENT CT	Burnet Co	426K	WQ-38	78669	100-199
CRESCENT DR	Austin	585D	MK-24	78722	4000-4099
CRESCENT DR	Buda	763A	ME-6	78610	100-199
CRESCENT BLUFF	Lakeway	489Q	WX-32	78734	100-299
CRESCENT HEIGHTS TRL					
	Williamson Co	375S	MJ-43	78717	17000-17299
CRESSWELL DR	Travis Co	437K	MN-38	78660	1000-1299
CREST AVE	Austin	586N	ML-23	78702	2700-2899
CREST CV	Round Rock	344M	MH-47	78681	4000-4099
CREST LN	Round Rock	344R	MH-47	78681	3800-3999
CRESTED BUTTE DR	Austin	583Z	MF-22	78746	1500-1999
CRESTED BUTTE WAY	Georgetown	317J	MN-50	78626	1400-1699
CRESTFIELD PL	Round Rock	375G	MK-45	78681	2600-2699
CRESTHAVEN DR	Austin	614M	MG-21	78704	1700-1999
CRESTHILL DR	Austin	524U	MH-28	78731	3900-3999
CRESTLAND DR E	Austin	525V	MK-28	78752	100-299
CRESTLAND DR W	Austin	525V	MK-28	78752	100-799
CRESTLINE CT	Round Rock	376R	MM-44	78664	1600-1799
CREST MEADOW LN	Austin	672Y	MD-13	78748	11200-11399
CRESTMONT	Travis Co	517F	WS-30	78669	21300-21399
CRESTMONT DR	Austin	555E	MJ-27	78756	4900-5099
CREST OAK RD	Austin	645X	MJ-16	78744	4700-4999
CRESTON CV	Hutto	379Q	MT-44	78634	1000-1099
CRESTON LN	Austin	525V	MK-28	78752	7500-7799
CRESTON ST	Hutto	379U	MT-43	78634	100-399
CREST PARK LOOP	Austin	526H	MM-30	78754	1500-1999
CREST RIDGE CIR	Austin	464A	MG-36	78750	8600-8899
CRESTRIDGE DR	Williamson Co	375N	MJ-44	78681	4300-4599
CRESTVALE DR	Austin	614J	MG-20	78704	3100-3199
CRESTVIEW DR	Cedar Park	373U	MF-43	78613	100-199
CRESTVIEW DR	Jonestown	400M	WZ-41	78645	10600-11099
CREST VIEW DR	Lakeway	519M	WX-29	78734	100-199
CREST VIEW RD	Travis Co	641A	MA-18	78737	8500-8899
CRESTVIEW ST	Round Rock	406E	ML-42	78681	1000-1199
CRESTVIEW ST	Taylor	353C	EB-48	76574	2701-2899 O
CRESTWAY DR	Austin	554C	MH-27	78731	4400-4999
	Austin	524Y	MH-28	78731	5000-5199
CRESTWIND LN	Elgin	532H	MZ-30	78621	18300-18499
CRESTWOOD CT	West Lake Hills	583M	MF-23	78746	100-199
CRESTWOOD CV	Williamson Co	344Z	MH-46	78681	1000-1099
CRESTWOOD LN	Williamson Co	346G	MM-48	78665	700-799
CRESTWOOD RD	Austin	555Z	MK-25	78722	1400-1599
CRETE LN	Travis Co	467M	MP-35	78660	1300-1599
CRETYS CV	Austin	642Z	MD-16	78745	8600-8799
CREWLER CV	Austin	497F	MN-33	78753	1300-1399
CREWS LN	Buda	732P	MC-8	78610	100-199
CRICKET CV	Cedar Park	402H	MD-42	78613	900-999
CRICKET HOLLOW DR	Austin	496J	ML-32	78758	1500-1799
CRIDER LN	Williamson Co	282E	MC-54	78641	100-199
CRIEFF CROSS DR	Travis Co	467P	MN-35	78660	800-999
CRIM LN	Bastrop Co	504V	ED-31	78621	100-199
CRIMSON CLOVER CT	Round Rock	378W	MQ-43	78665	1300-1399
CRIMSON SKY CT	Round Rock	347V	MP-46	78665	2700-2799
CRINIUM CV	Austin	464T	MG-34	78759	10100-10199
CRIPPLE CREEK CV	Austin	496S	ML-31	78758	10200-10299
CRIPPLE CREEK DR	Austin	496S	ML-31	78758	800-1699
CRIPPLE CREEK RD	Cedar Park	402D	MD-42	78613	200-599
CRIPPLE CREEK STAGE RD	Hays Co	546J	WQ-26	78620	1700-2099
CRISPIN HALL LN	Travis Co	439F	MS-39	78660	3200-3299
CRISPIN HALL LN	Travis Co	439F	MS-39	78660	3500-3899
CRISSOM LN	Travis Co	436L	MM-38	78728	15400-15699
CRISWELL RD	Austin	527J	MN-29	78754	9800-10399
	Travis Co	527J	MN-29	78754	9700-9799
CRISWOOD PL	Austin	674E	MG-15	78748	8100-8199
CRITTER CANYON	Travis Co	552T	MC-25	78746	8400-8499
CRIZER CT	Buda	732P	MC-8	78610	100-199
CROCKETT AVE	Lago Vista	459A	WW-36	78645	3800-4199
CROCKETT LOOP	Georgetown	195U	MK-61	78633	100-599
CROCKETT RD	Cedar Park	373U	MF-43	78613	100-299
CROCKETT ST	Austin	614M	MH-20	78704	100-499
CROCUS CV	Cedar Park	402M	MD-41	78613	1300-1399
CROCUS DR	Cedar Park	402H	MD-42	78613	800-899
CROFFORD LN	Travis Co	558A	MQ-27	78754	9700-9999
CROFTWOOD DR	Austin	642R	MD-17	78749	7700-8299
CROMARTY CV	Austin	528F	MQ-30	78754	7000-7099
CROMARTY LN	Austin	528K	MQ-29	78754	6600-6899
CROMWELL CIR	Austin	615Y	MK-19	78741	2200-2499
CROMWELL HILL	Austin	584G	MH-24	78703	1700-1799
CROOKED LN	Austin	615T	MJ-19	78741	1800-1999
CROOKED CREEK	Buda	732X	MC-7	78610	300-599
CROOKED CREEK DR	Travis Co	467Y	MP-34	78660	13500-13799
CROOKED HOLLOW RD	Bastrop Co	563S	EA-25	78621	100-299
CROOKED OAK CV	Austin	642F	MC-18	78749	5200-5299
CROOKED STICK DR	Travis Co	409T	MS-40	78660	20200-20499
CROSBY CIR	Travis Co	582G	MD-24	78746	6900-6999
CROSBY ST	Georgetown	195Z	MK-61	78633	100-199
CROSLIN ST E	Austin	526W	ML-28	78752	100-399
CROSLIN ST W	Austin	525W	MK-28	78752	100-699
CROSS LN	Hays Co	795P	MJ-2	78610	100-399
CROSS ST	Austin	615F	MJ-21	78702	1-99
CROSS ST	Jonestown	401E	MA-42	78645	17700-17999
CROSSBOW TRL	Lago Vista	429A	WW-39	78645	7100-7399
CROSS CREEK	Lakeway	519B	WW-30	78734	100-199
CROSSCREEK DR	Austin	495X	MJ-31	78757	3000-3399
CROSS CREEK DR	Hays Co	667L	WT-14	78620	100-299
CROSSCREEK DR	Hays Co	670X	WY-13	78610	14700-14899
	Hays Co	700A	WY-12	78610	14900-15199
CROSS CREEK LN	Williamson Co	253S	ME-55	78628	1-1799
CROSS CREEK RD	Williamson Co	283H	MF-54	78628	1-499
	Williamson Co	253Q	MF-56	78628	500-2199
CROSS CREEK TRL	Williamson Co	375L	MK-44	78681	1900-2199
CROSS DRAW	Leander	372F	MC-45	78641	1800-2099
CROSSDRAW DR	Austin	494X	MG-31	78731	7500-7599
CROSSFIELD PL	Austin	466U	MM-34	78758	12400-12499
CROSSING PL	Austin	615V	MK-19	78741	1300-1999
CROSSLAND CV	Leander	341D	MB-48	78641	300-399
CROSSLAND DR	Austin	433W	ME-37	78726	11000-11299
CROSSLAND DR	Williamson Co	256W	ML-55	78628	400-499
CROSSLEY ST	Round Rock	407D	MP-42	78665	2400-2599
CROSSLEY CROSSING	Round Rock	407D	MP-42	78665	3200-3299
CROSS MEADOW CV	Williamson Co	318F	MQ-51	78634	100-199
CROSSMEADOW DR	Austin	494S	MG-31	78750	7500-7699
CROSS MEADOW DR	Mustang Ridge	796L	MM-2	78610	100-199
CROSS MEADOW DR	Williamson Co	318G	MR-51	78634	200-399
CROSSOVER LN	Travis Co	370J	WY-44	78641	21500-21799
CROSS PARK DR	Austin	556D	MM-27	78754	8000-8299
	Austin	526V	MM-28	78754	8300-8799
CROSSROAD DR	Caldwell Co	767T	MN-4	78616	1-799
CROSSROADS DR	Hays Co	607F	WS-21	78620	100-499
CROSSTIMBER DR	Williamson Co	433U	MF-37	78750	11600-11799
CROSS TOWN PKWY	Bee Cave	550T	WY-25	78738	None
CROSS VALLEY RUN	Austin	524P	MG-29	78731	4100-4599
CROSSVINE DR	Georgetown	314G	MH-51	78628	1600-1899
CROSSVINE WAY	Pflugerville	438X	MQ-37	78660	1200-1399
CROSSWIND CIR	Travis Co	518F	WU-30	78669	19300-19399
CROSSWIND CT	Cedar Park	374L	MH-44	78613	200-299
CROSSWIND DR	Travis Co	488X	WU-31	78669	2400-2499
	Travis Co	518F	WU-30	78669	2500-3999
CROSSWOOD DR	Austin	643Z	MF-16	78745	7000-7199
CROSSWOOD DR	Round Rock	406J	ML-41	78681	2000-2099
CROTON CV	Austin	464T	MG-34	78759	9700-9799
CROW LN	Austin	644T	MG-16	78745	6200-6299
CROWHEART CV	Travis Co	554K	MG-26	78746	3100-3199
CROWLEY TRL	Travis Co	435W	MJ-37	78729	6300-6599
CROWN CT	Travis Co	588S	MQ-22	78724	10000-10099
CROWN CT	Williamson Co	434L	MH-38	78729	8800-8999
CROWN DR	Austin	644A	MG-18	78745	1700-1899
CROWN ARBOR WAY	Travis Co	529H	MT-30	78653	None
CROWN COLONY DR	Austin	703M	MF-11	78747	10800-10999
CROWNCREST CV	Austin	494Z	MH-31	78758	3700-3899
CROWNCREST DR	Austin	495W	MJ-31	78759	3500-3699
CROWN HILL DR	Bee Cave	549R	WX-26	78738	13900-14299
CROWN KING WAY	Leander	372B	MC-45	78641	1300-1399
CROWN OAKS DR	Austin	526G	MM-30	78753	1100-1199
CROWNOVER ST	Travis Co	618V	MR-19	78725	2700-3799
CROWN POINT CIR	Bastrop Co	776L	EH-5	78602	100-199
CROWN RIDGE PATH	Austin	526G	MM-30	78753	1100-1199
CROWN RIDGE RD	Austin	526G	MM-30	78753	9400-9699
CROWNSPOINT CIR	Austin	673E	ME-15	78748	9400-9499
CROWNSPOINT DR	Austin	673E	ME-15	78748	2000-2999
CROWNSTONE LN	Travis Co	530A	MU-30	78653	12000-12099
CROW RANCH RD	Dripping Springs	667A	WS-15	78620	100-199
CROW WING CV	Travis Co	492Q	MD-32	78730	10500-10599
CROYDON LOOP	Austin	673L	MF-14	78748	8500-8699
CROZIER LN	Austin	647A	MN-18	78617	1500-1799
CRUDEN CV	Georgetown	226P	ML-59	78628	200-299
CRUMLEY LN	Austin	616P	ML-20	78741	6300-6399
CRUMLEY RD	Jonestown	401E	MA-42	78645	11500-11599
CRUMLEY RANCH RD	Hays Co	608K	WU-20	78738	11400-12099
	Travis Co	578P	WU-23	78738	8300-10499
	Travis Co	608B	WU-21	78738	10500-11399
CRUPP CT	Austin	497N	MN-32	78753	1200-1299
CRUZ ST	Austin	616X	ML-19	78741	6600-6899
CRYSTAL CIR	Taylor	322R	MZ-50	76574	2800-3499
CRYSTAL CT	Travis Co	436Y	MM-37	78728	14500-14599
CRYSTAL CV	Jonestown	400V	WZ-40	78645	17900-18099
CRYSTAL CV	Taylor	322Q	MZ-50	76574	3000-3399
CRYSTAL LN	Williamson Co	224M	MH-59	78633	100-199
CRYSTAL WAY	Hays Co	670J	WY-14	78737	13200-13499
CRYSTAL WAY	Lago Vista	458J	WU-35	78645	21700-21999
CRYSTAL BEND DR	Travis Co	467Z	MP-34	78660	1600-2499
	Travis Co	468W	MQ-34	78660	2500-2999
CRYSTALBROOK CV	Austin	557K	MN-26	78724	7600-7699
CRYSTALBROOK DR	Austin	557T	MN-25	78724	6700-7599
CRYSTALBROOK WEST	Austin	557K	MN-26	78724	7500-7799
CRYSTAL CREEK CIR	Travis Co	552X	MC-25	78746	8700-8799
CRYSTAL CREEK DR	Hays Co	702X	MC-10	78610	12500-12599
	Hays Co	732B	MC-9	78610	12600-12799
CRYSTAL CREEK DR	Travis Co	552S	MC-25	78746	100-1399
CRYSTAL DOWNS CV	Austin	375W	MJ-43	78717	16800-16999
CRYSTAL FALLS PKWY	Leander	342Q	MD-47	78641	100-2299
	Leander	341Z	MB-46	78641	2300-2899
	Leander	371H	MB-45	78641	2900-3499
CRYSTAL FALLS PKWY E	Leander	342R	MD-47	78641	10100-10699
	Leander	343J	ME-47	78641	10700-10999
CRYSTAL HILL DR	Travis Co	432K	MC-38	78613	3300-3499
CRYSTAL KNOLL BLVD					
	Williamson Co	257K	MN-56	78626	100-399
CRYSTAL MOUNTAIN DR	Travis Co	552J	MC-26	78733	600-999
CRYSTAL SHORE DR	Travis Co	436Y	MM-37	78728	1900-2099
CRYSTAL SPRING WAY	Hays Co	669N	WW-14	78737	100-199
CRYSTAL SPRINGS CT					
	Village of the Hills	519K	WW-29	78738	1-99
CRYSTAL SPRINGS DR	Georgetown	225M	MK-59	78633	100-199
CRYSTAL TERRACE	Travis Co	551R	MB-26	78733	700-799
CRYSTAL WATER CV	Austin	613E	ME-21	78735	4000-4099
CRYSTAL WATER DR	Austin	613E	ME-21	78735	5000-5299
CUERNAVACA DR N	Travis Co	552A	MC-27	78733	100-699
	Travis Co	522W	MC-28	78733	700-2699
CUERNAVACA DR S	Travis Co	552J	MC-26	78733	100-699
CUERO CV	Round Rock	376A	ML-45	78681	2900-2999
CUESTA CT	Travis Co	493P	ME-32	78730	8500-8599
CUESTA TRL	Travis Co	493Q	MF-32	78730	6400-6799
CUESTA VERDE	Travis Co	554A	MG-27	78746	5100-5299
	Travis Co	553D	MF-27	78746	5300-5599
CUEVA CIR	Bee Cave	549Q	WX-26	78738	5200-5299
CUEVA DR	Bee Cave	549P	WW-26	78738	5100-5499
CUEVA DE ORO CV	Travis Co	583X	ME-22	78746	1900-2099
CULBERSON DR	Travis Co	672Q	MD-14	78748	10700-10899
CULBERTSON ST	Elgin	533R	EB-29	78621	None
CULEBRA CIR	Travis Co	490C	WZ-33	78734	3900-3999
CULEBRA DR	Georgetown	317K	MN-50	78626	200-299
CULLEN AVE	Austin	525U	MK-28	78757	1100-2399
CULLEN BLVD	Buda	732Q	MD-8	78610	100-699
CULLEN LN	Austin	674N	MG-14	78748	8600-9499
CULLERS CV	Austin	643V	MF-16	78745	1200-1299
CULLODEN DR	Austin	528A	MQ-30	78754	6000-6199
CULP ST	Austin	616T	ML-19	78741	700-799
CULPEPPER CV	Travis Co	493S	ME-31	78730	6300-6499
CULPEPPER LN	Cedar Park	402G	MD-42	78613	200-299
CULVER CLIFF LN	Travis Co	432G	MD-39	78613	2700-2799
CUMBERLAND CV	Lago Vista	458R	WV-35	78645	2700-2799
CUMBERLAND RD	Austin	614V	MH-19	78704	100-1299
CUMBERLAND GAP	Williamson Co	403X	ME-40	78613	3500-3599
CUMBRES DR	Georgetown	317E	MN-51	78626	300-399
CUMBRIA LN	Austin	465L	MK-35	78727	4200-4599
CUMMINGS ST	Austin	615A	MJ-21	78701	700-799
CUMMINS WAY	Manor	500Y	MV-31	78653	None
CUMULUS DR	Pflugerville	437P	MN-38	78660	16000-16099
CUPID DR	Austin	613U	MF-19	78735	3200-3299
CUPOLLA MOUNTAIN	Williamson Co	402Q	MD-41	78613	1900-2099
CURACAO CT	Lakeway	518H	WV-30	78738	100-199
CURAHEE DR	Austin	641X	MA-16	78739	10700-10799
CURAMENG CV	Austin	673W	ME-13	78748	1400-1599
CURETON CV	Austin	705E	MJ-12	78747	8600-8699
CURIOSITY CAVE RD	Travis Co	487F	WS-33	78669	1900-1999
CURLEW CV	Austin	673A	ME-15	78748	2700-2799
CURLEW DR	Austin	672M	MD-14	78748	8900-9999
CURLEY MESQUITE CV	Sunset Valley	643B	ME-18	78745	1-99
CURLY LEAF CV	Austin	493V	MF-31	78750	7400-7499
CURPIN CV	Austin	528T	MQ-28	78754	7200-7299
CURRANT CV	Travis Co	702G	MD-12	78748	2700-2799
CURRENT CIR	Austin	611Q	MB-20	78736	8100-8199
CURRIER CV	Williamson Co	405P	MJ-41	78717	7000-7099
CURRIN LN	Austin	672Y	MD-13	78748	11100-11299
CURRY LOOP	Round Rock	376H	MM-45	78664	2400-2499
CURRYWOOD CIR	Austin	495N	MJ-32	78759	4000-4099
CURRYWOOD DR	Austin	495N	MJ-32	78759	8900-9099
CURTIS AVE	Austin	585M	MK-23	78722	2200-2299
CURTIS DR	Travis Co	396C	WR-42	78654	5600-5799
CURTIS DR	Williamson Co	375B	MJ-45	78681	3600-3899
CURVE ST	Austin	585T	MJ-22	78702	1100-1199
CUSHING DR	Round Rock	406H	MM-42	78664	800-1799
CUSHING PARK DR	Round Rock	406M	MM-41	78664	200-1799
CUSSETA CV	Austin	641X	MA-16	78739	7000-7099
CUSSETA LN	Austin	641X	MA-16	78739	10900-11099
	Austin	671B	MA-15	78739	11100-11299
CUSTER CT	Travis Co	490M	WZ-32	78734	14600-14799
CUSTER CV	Lago Vista	459J	WW-35	78645	2300-2899
CUSTER'S CREEK BEND E					
	Pflugerville	468A	MQ-36	78660	100-299
CUSTER'S CREEK BEND W					
	Pflugerville	467D	MP-36	78660	100-799
CUTAWAY	Williamson Co	375Y	MK-43	78681	3000-3199
CUTBACK DR	Travis Co	560J	MU-26	78653	17500-17999
CUT-BACK WAY	Williamson Co	405C	MK-42	78681	3100-3199
CUTLASS	Lakeway	489W	WW-31	78734	600-699
	Lakeway	488Z	WV-31	78734	None
CUTLER RIDGE PL	Austin	642E	MC-18	78749	8000-8199
CUTTING HORSE LN	Austin	466Q	MM-35	78727	1500-1699
CUTTY TRL	Lakeway	489Y	WX-31	78734	500-799
C W RANCH BLVD	Cedar Park	373M	MF-44	78613	1-599
CY LN	Austin	526D	MM-30	78753	10100-10299
CYCLONE RIDGE CV	Williamson Co	377K	MN-44	78665	2000-2099
CYNTHIA CT	Williamson Co	342Z	MD-46	78641	2500-2599
CYPRESS BLVD	Round Rock	346Q	MM-47	78665	1-99
CYPRESS CV	Round Rock	346U	MM-46	78665	1-99
CYPRESS CV	Taylor	322U	MZ-49	76574	1800-1899
CYPRESS DR	Travis Co	467V	MP-34	78660	13900-14199
CYPRESS LN	Cedar Park	372H	MD-45	78613	200-2799
CYPRESS LN	Round Rock	376H	MM-45	78664	400-599
CYPRESS PT E	Travis Co	582M	MD-23	78746	1900-2399
CYPRESS PT N	Travis Co	582L	MD-23	78746	6500-6899
CYPRESS PT W	Travis Co	582L	MD-23	78746	1900-2399
CYPRESS ST	Bastrop	745B	EE-9	78602	600-899
	Bastrop	745C	EF-9	78602	1500-1699
CYPRESS TRL	Taylor	322Q	MZ-50	76574	1200-1499
CYPRESS BEND	Austin	645T	MJ-16	78744	4600-4999
CYPRESS CANYON TRL	Travis Co	486V	WR-31	78669	4100-4399
CYPRESS CREEK DR	Travis Co	462E	MC-36	78726	8100-8299
CYPRESS CREEK RD	Cedar Park	403J	ME-41	78613	100-1399
	Cedar Park	402Z	MD-40	78613	1400-2599
	Travis Co	402Z	MD-40	78613	None
CYPRESS CREEK RD	Travis Co	461C	MB-36	78641	None
CYPRESS CREEK RD E	Leander	403F	ME-42	78613	100-499
CYPRESS KNEE LN	Lakeway	519M	WX-29	78734	1-99
CYPRESS LANDING CV	Austin	375W	MJ-43	78717	16700-16899
CYPRESS MILL CIR	Cedar Park	433A	ME-39	78613	1200-1299
CYPRESS POINT CV	Round Rock	378Z	MR-43	78664	3800-3899
CYPRESS POINT CV	Travis Co	582L	MD-23	78746	6800-6899
CYPRESS RANCH BLVD	Travis Co	517E	WS-30	78669	None
CYPRESS SPRINGS DR	Hays Co	667W	WS-13	78619	100-199
CYRILLA DR	Austin	494G	MH-33	78759	5800-5899
CYRUS AVE	Georgetown	286R	MM-53	78626	100-399
CYRUS CV	Austin	672A	MC-15	78739	10300-10399
CY YOUNG CT	Round Rock	378E	MQ-45	78665	1300-1399

D

STREET NAME	CITY or COUNTY	MAPSCO GRID	AUSTIN GRID	ZIP CODE	BLOCK RANGE O/E
DACY LN	Hays Co	763W	ME-4	78610	5300-5999
DADIVA CT	Travis Co	582S	MC-22	78735	7800-7999
DAFFAN LN	Austin	557H	MP-27	78724	6201-6799 O
	Travis Co	557H	MP-27	78724	6200-6798 E
	Travis Co	557H	MP-27	78724	6800-7599
	Travis Co	558J	MQ-26	78724	7600-8599
DAFFODIL DR	Austin	645M	MK-17	78744	5900-6299
DAFFODIL DR	Cedar Park	402M	MD-41	78613	800-899
DAGAMA CT	Travis Co	432H	MD-39	78613	2700-2799
DAGAMA DR	Travis Co	432H	MD-39	78613	2000-2199
	Williamson Co	432H	MD-39	78613	1900-1999
DAGON DR	Austin	528P	MQ-29	78754	7000-7199
DAHLBERG BLVD	Taylor	323S	EA-49	76574	100-299
DAHLGREEN AVE	Austin	641Z	MB-16	78739	10200-10599
	Austin	671D	MB-15	78739	10600-10799
DAHLIA CT	Pflugerville	438Y	MR-37	78660	1500-1599
DAILEY ST	Austin	584L	MH-23	78703	1200-1299
DAISY DR	Travis Co	466B	ML-36	78727	2200-2699
DAISY LN	Hays Co	636N	WQ-17	78620	100-499
DAISY PATH	Georgetown	225Q	MK-59	78633	100-199
DAISY PATH	Hays Co	668M	WV-14	78737	100-199
DAKOTA CIR	Lago Vista	399T	WW-40	78645	7700-7899
DAKOTA CV	Lago Vista	399X	WW-40	78645	7700-7799
DAKOTA DR	Williamson Co	224E	MG-60	78633	100-199
	Williamson Co	223H	MF-60	78633	None
DAKOTA LN	Austin	434Z	MH-37	78729	12700-12999
DAKOTA DUNES CT	Travis Co	409W	MS-40	78660	2400-2499
DAKOTA MOUNTAIN DR	Hays Co	608A	WU-21	78620	100-199
	Hays Co	607D	WT-21	78720	200-599
DALE CV	Round Rock	376Q	MM-44	78664	1600-1699
DALE DR	Austin	525M	MK-29	78757	1200-1599
DALEA DR	Austin	670D	WZ-15	78739	8200-8299
DALEA DR	Round Rock	375C	MK-45	78681	2500-2699
DALEA BLUFF	Round Rock	378W	MQ-43	78665	1100-1199
DALEA VISTA CT	Austin	641Y	MB-16	78739	10300-10399
DALE RIDGE LN	Travis Co	704F	MG-12	78747	None
DALEVIEW DR	Austin	525B	MJ-30	78757	8200-8299
	Austin	495X	MJ-31	78757	8300-8599
DALEWOOD DR	Williamson Co	434J	MG-38	78729	9500-9799
DALI LN	Austin	554T	MG-25	78703	3600-3699
DALLAS DR	Austin	434V	MH-37	78729	7600-7699
	Williamson Co	435N	MJ-38	78729	6800-6999
	Williamson Co	434V	MH-37	78729	7000-7599
DALLUM DR	Austin	526G	MM-30	78753	9400-9899
DALMAHOY DR	Austin	375W	MJ-43	78717	16600-16699
DALSHANK ST	Pflugerville	408V	MR-40	78660	1700-1799
DALTON LN	Austin	646D	MM-18	78742	1200-1399
	Travis Co	617S	MN-19	78742	500-799
DALTON ST	Austin	642V	MD-16	78745	3300-3499
DALY CV	Austin	704P	MG-11	78747	10900-10999
DALY DR	Austin	704P	MG-11	78747	5500-5799
DAMITA JO DR	Travis Co	591K	MW-23	78653	8500-8999
DAMON RD	Austin	643Y	MF-16	78745	1500-1599
DAMRICH CT	Travis Co	409W	MS-40	78660	19900-19999
DAN PASS	Austin	674L	MH-14	78744	7200-7399
DANA CT	Round Rock	377N	MN-44	78664	1400-1499
DANA CV	Austin	614A	MG-21	78746	2500-2599
DANA DR	Williamson Co	409F	MS-42	78634	100-399
DANBROOK CV	Austin	497B	MN-33	78753	12700-12799
DANBURY SQUARE	Austin	556J	ML-26	78723	1200-1399
DANBURY WOODS CIR	Travis Co	497G	MP-33	78754	13000-13599
DANCIGER LN	Travis Co	432G	MD-39	78613	2400-2599
DANCY ST	Austin	585G	MK-24	78722	2600-3299
DANDELION DR	Georgetown	225P	MJ-59	78633	100-199
DANDELION TRL	Austin	642Z	MD-16	78745	8600-8899
DANDRIDGE DR	Williamson Co	433F	ME-39	78613	1500-1599
DANFORTH CV	Travis Co	552T	MC-25	78746	8000-8199
DANIEL DR	Austin	614D	MH-21	78704	900-1099
DANIEL BOONE DR	Hays Co	639V	WX-16	78737	12600-12899
DANVILLE DR	Williamson Co	433B	ME-39	78613	3400-3499
DAN-JEAN DR	Austin	643U	MF-16	78745	7100-7399
DANLI LN	Austin	642U	MD-16	78749	3900-4099
DAN MOODY TRL	Georgetown	225H	MK-60	78633	100-199
DANNY DR	Austin	465R	MK-35	78759	12300-12399
DANSWORTH CV	Pflugerville	437D	MP-39	78660	900-999
	Pflugerville	437D	MP-39	78660	18000-18099
DANSWORTH DR	Pflugerville	437D	MP-39	78660	17600-18099
DANTE CT	Austin	672Y	MD-13	78748	2600-2699
DANVERS CT	Austin	641Y	MB-16	78739	6400-6499
DANVILLE DR	Austin	526P	ML-29	78753	8400-8699
DANWOOD DR	Austin	464G	MH-36	78759	6000-7799
DANZ BLVD	Travis Co	557E	MN-27	78724	7700-7899
DAPHANE CT	Austin	614T	MG-19	78704	1000-1099
DAPPLEGREY LN	Austin	466Q	MM-35	78727	1300-1999
DARBEY LN	Leander	342U	MD-46	78641	600-699
DARBY ST	Austin	586V	MM-22	78721	3400-3599
DARCUS CV	Austin	464G	MH-36	78759	7100-7199
DARDEN HILL RD	Hays Co	669W	WW-13	78737	10400-10499
	Hays Co	668Z	WV-13	78737	10500-10699
DARJEELING DR	Travis Co	467L	MP-35	78660	1100-1899
DARK LN	Williamson Co	405K	MJ-41	78717	16000-16099
DARK RIDGE CV	Austin	641C	MB-18	78749	8200-8299
DARK SHADOW CV	Austin	641G	MB-18	78749	8600-8699
DARK STAR TERRACE	Austin	463A	ME-36	78726	10000-10099
DARK TREE CV	Travis Co	408L	MR-41	78664	None
DARK TREE LN	Travis Co	408L	MR-41	78664	None
DARK VALLEY CV	Austin	641D	MB-18	78749	8000-8099
DARKWOODS DR	Cedar Park	403C	MF-42	78613	400-799
DARLEEN DR E	Travis Co	401W	MA-40	78641	17000-17599
DARLEEN DR N	Travis Co	401W	MA-40	78641	10000-10399
DARLEEN DR W	Jonestown	401S	MA-40	78641	10300-10599
DARLEEN EXTENSION	Travis Co	401N	MA-41	78641	10400-10599
	Travis Co	400R	WZ-41	78645	10600-10899
DARLESS DR	Cedar Park	372U	MD-43	78613	1200-1299
DARLEY RD	Travis Co	487Y	WT-31	78669	21400-21699
DARLEY ARABIAN DR	Pflugerville	409E	MS-42	78660	1500-1699
DARLINGTON CV	Austin	556Y	MM-25	78723	5300-5399
DARLINGTON LN	Austin	556Y	MM-25	78723	5400-5699
DARNELL DR	Austin	643S	ME-16	78745	3100-3299
DARNELL DR	Cedar Park	372J	MC-44	78613	2200-2399
DAROLD DR	Austin	646D	MM-18	78742	1400-1599
DARRIN LN	Travis Co	677X	MN-13	78617	11400-11499
DARRYL DR	Hays Co	732B	MC-9	78610	12500-12799
DART	Lakeway	489X	WW-31	78734	None
DARTER LN	Austin	583U	MF-22	78746	1300-1399
DARTER LN	Hays Co	606P	WQ-20	78620	100-199
DARTFORD BEND	Travis Co	432C	MD-39	78613	2300-2599
DARTMOOR DR	Travis Co	582H	MD-24	78746	900-999
DARTMOUTH AVE	Austin	525L	MK-29	78757	1500-1899
DARTMOUTH CV	Pflugerville	467D	MP-36	78660	600-699
DARVONE CIR	Austin	673C	MF-15	78745	1100-1199
DARWIN CV	Williamson Co	434Q	MH-38	78729	8100-8199
DARWIN LN	Williamson Co	434Q	MH-38	78729	13200-13299
DARWINS WAY	Lakeway	519V	WX-28	78734	100-499
DARYL CV	Austin	496T	ML-31	78758	10700-10799
DASHER DR	Lakeway	519E	WW-30	78734	100-499
DASHWOOD CT	Village of the Hills	519T	WW-28	78738	1-99
DASHWOOD CREEK CT	Pflugerville	437H	MP-39	78660	700-799
DASHWOOD CREEK DR	Pflugerville	437L	MP-38	78660	17100-17599
	Travis Co	437L	MP-38	78660	16900-17099
DATE PALM TRL	Travis Co	532L	MZ-29	78621	13000-13099
DATURA CT	Travis Co	551Q	MB-26	78733	1700-1799
DAUFUSKIE ISLAND RD	Round Rock	378U	MR-43	78664	3300-3399
DAUGHERTY ST	Austin	525P	MJ-29	78757	6600-7599
DAUPHINE CV	Austin	466L	MM-35	78727	1900-1999
DAUPHINE DR	Austin	465L	MK-35	78727	4100-4299
DAUPHINE ST	Austin	466K	ML-35	78727	13100-13299
DAVE DR	Lakeway	520J	WY-29	78734	15100-15199
	Lakeway	519M	WX-29	78734	15200-15699
DAVENPORT CV	Lago Vista	458M	WV-35	78645	3000-3099
DAVE SILK DR	Austin	702H	MD-12	78748	11800-11999
DAVID CV	Cedar Park	402H	MD-42	78613	1300-1399
DAVID DR	Hutto	379G	MT-45	78634	100-199
DAVID ST	Austin	584M	MH-23	78705	1900-1999
DAVID CURRY DR	Round Rock	376H	MM-45	78664	600-1499
DAVID FERRETTI DR	Georgetown	256R	MM-56	78626	2200-2299
DAVID MOORE DR	Austin	673P	ME-14	78748	9500-10299
DAVIDSON DR	Taylor	323X	EA-49	76574	400-599
DAVID THOMAS RD	Travis Co	553R	MF-26	78746	4700-4799
DAVIOT DR	Briarcliff	487C	WT-33	78669	900-1399
DAVIS CV	Lago Vista	458M	WV-35	78645	2800-2999
DAVIS LN	Austin	673A	ME-15	78745	2000-2699
	Austin	642Z	MD-16	78745	2800-3499
	Austin	642J	MC-17	78749	3500-6199
	Austin	641M	MB-17	78749	6200-6999
DAVIS LN	Williamson Co	224M	MH-59	78633	100-199
DAVIS ST	Austin	615B	MJ-21	78701	600-699
DAVIS ST	Taylor	353E	EA-48	76574	100-599
	Taylor	353A	EA-48	76574	600-1299
	Taylor	322Z	MZ-49	76574	1200-3199
DAVIS MOUNTAIN CIR	Georgetown	225B	MJ-60	78633	100-499
	Georgetown	195X	MJ-61	78633	500-699
DAVIS MOUNTAIN CV	Austin	462K	MC-35	78726	8000-8099
DAVIS MOUNTAIN LOOP	Cedar Park	373J	ME-44	78613	1300-1599
DAVIS MOUNTAIN PASS	Austin	462K	MC-35	78726	7900-8199
DAVIS OAKS TRL	Austin	673G	MF-15	78748	8500-8799
DAVY DR	Village of Volente	461A	MA-36	78641	7500-7699
DAVY CROCKETT DR	Hays Co	640S	WY-16	78737	10100-10499
	Hays Co	639V	WX-16	78737	10500-10599
DAWANA LN	Georgetown	226P	ML-59	78628	100-199
DAWLISH DR	Travis Co	467T	MN-34	78660	800-899
DAWN DR	Georgetown	256U	MM-55	78628	1700-3099
DAWN DR	Lago Vista	429J	WW-38	78645	20200-21199
	Travis Co	429L	WX-38	78645	20100-20199
DAWN DR	Williamson Co	192N	MC-62	78642	100-299
DAWN HILL CIR	Austin	611R	MB-20	78736	7500-7599
DAWNING CT	Travis Co	611E	MA-21	78736	9600-9699
DAWN MESA CT	Round Rock	408B	MQ-42	78665	3100-3299
DAWNRIDGE CIR	Austin	495X	MJ-31	78757	8600-8899
DAWN RIVER CV	Travis Co	520R	WZ-29	78732	100-599
DAWN RIVER PASS	Travis Co	520R	WZ-29	78732	12900-12999
DAWN SONG DR	Austin	613J	ME-20	78735	4800-4899
DAWSON RD	Austin	614D	MH-21	78704	100-999
DAWSON RD	Williamson Co	348X	MQ-46	78665	1-99
DAWSON TRL	Georgetown	195Y	MK-61	78633	100-599
DAWSON CREEK DR	Travis Co	439T	MS-37	78660	18400-18499
DAYBREAK CV	Hays Co	732G	MD-9	78610	200-299
DAYBREAK CV	Travis Co	519U	WX-28	78738	1-99
DAY CAMP LN	Austin	497S	MN-31	78754	11400-11799
DAYFLOWER TRACE	Travis Co	432D	MD-39	78613	2100-2199
	Williamson Co	432D	MD-39	78613	1700-2099
DAYLILY CV	Pflugerville	438Y	MR-37	78660	900-999
DAYMON CT	Hutto	379R	MT-44	78634	5000-5099
DAYNA CV	Williamson Co	372D	MD-45	78613	300-399
DAY STAR CV	Austin	553C	MF-27	78746	3400-3599
DAYTON DR	Round Rock	346R	MM-47	78665	1200-1299
DAYTONA DR	Travis Co	522S	MC-28	78733	1300-1399
DAYWOOD DR	Hays Co	794W	MG-1	78610	100-199
D B WOOD RD	Georgetown	255C	MK-57	78628	2400-3799
	Williamson Co	285H	MK-54	78628	1-1399
	Williamson Co	255Z	MK-55	78628	1400-2399
DEAD END RD	Travis Co	459R	WX-35	78645	3900-3999
DEADOAK LN	Austin	464K	MG-35	78759	11200-11499
DEAD PAN DR	Travis Co	560N	MU-26	78653	18200-18299
DEADWOOD DR	Austin	644V	MH-16	78744	2100-2399
DEADWOOD STAGE RD	Hays Co	546S	WQ-25	78620	3000-3499
DEAF SMITH BLVD	Travis Co	618V	MR-19	78725	14500-14899
DEAN DR	Williamson Co	406P	ML-41	78681	3000-3099
DEANE RD	Travis Co	703N	ME-11	78748	12100-12199
	Travis Co	703N	ME-11	78652	12200-12399
DEAN KEATON ST E	Austin	585E	MJ-24	78705	100-1099
	Austin	585G	MK-24	78722	1100-1499
DEAN KEATON ST W	Austin	585E	MJ-24	78705	100-399
DEARBONNE DR	Austin	678J	MQ-14	78617	13000-13399
DEATONHILL DR	Austin	643L	ME-17	78745	6600-6999
	Austin	643P	ME-17	78745	7000-7099
DEBARR DR	Williamson Co	434V	MH-37	78729	12900-13099
DEBBA CIR	Travis Co	490T	WY-31	78734	1300-1399
DEBBA DR	Lakeway	490T	WY-31	78734	15400-15799
	Travis Co	490Y	WZ-31	78734	14100-15399
	Travis Co	490S	WY-31	78734	15800-15899
DEBBIE DR	Village of Volente	431W	MA-37	78641	7600-7799
DEBBIE ANN DR	Leander	341G	MB-48	78641	200-299
DEBCO LN	Travis Co	488K	WU-32	78669	900-1199
DEBCOE DR	Austin	641D	MB-18	78749	6600-6899
DEBORA DR	Georgetown	316B	ML-51	78628	300-699
DEBORAH DR	Austin	525Z	MK-28	78752	6800-7099
DEBRA DR	Taylor	352G	MZ-48	76574	500-999
DEBUS CIR	Taylor	352G	MZ-48	76574	1-99
DEBUS DR	Taylor	352C	MZ-48	76574	200-1499
DECK CV	Lakeway	519E	WW-30	78738	200-299
DECK DR	Williamson Co	224K	MG-59	78633	100-199
DECKER DR	Hutto	379R	MT-44	78634	100-799
DECKER LN	Austin	587H	MP-24	78724	6500-6999
See.. FM Rd 3177					
	Austin	558W	MQ-25	78724	7000-7399
	Austin	528Y	MR-28	78724	10800-11999
	Travis Co	587H	MP-24	78724	5200-6499
See.. FM Rd 3177					
	Travis Co	558F	MQ-27	78724	7400-10799
DECKER CREEK CV	Travis Co	619Q	MT-20	78653	5600-5699
DECKER CREEK DR	Travis Co	619L	MT-20	78653	16400-16999
DECKER LAKE RD	Austin	588P	MQ-23	78724	10600-11399
	Travis Co	588E	MQ-24	78724	8700-10599
	Travis Co	588P	MQ-23	78724	11400-11599
	Travis Co	589S	MS-22	78653	15100-16199
	Travis Co	619C	MT-21	78653	16200-16699
DECKER PRAIRIE DR	Austin	673X	ME-13	78748	700-799
DECKHOUSE DR	Point Venture	488R	WV-32	78654	500-799
DECLARATION CIR	Lago Vista	458M	WV-35	78645	2800-2999
DECOY CV	Williamson Co	434U	MH-37	78729	12800-12899
DEDHAM CT	Austin	641Y	MB-16	78739	10400-10499
DEDHAM LN	Austin	641Y	MB-16	78739	6100-6299
DEE DR	Travis Co	371U	MB-43	78641	17400-17499
DEE ST	Austin	643Z	MF-16	78745	7200-7299
DEEDE DR	Lago Vista	429F	WW-39	78645	20700-21099
DEE GABRIEL COLLINS RD					
	Travis Co	675M	MK-14	78744	7000-7599
	Travis Co	676N	ML-14	78744	7600-8599
DEEN AVE	Austin	526E	ML-30	78753	100-799
DEEP CIR	Austin	674H	MH-15	78744	6900-7099
DEEP LN	Austin	674M	MH-14	78744	7000-7099
	Austin	674M	MH-14	78744	7200-7299
DEEP BROOK DR	Austin	463E	ME-36	78726	11000-11099
DEEPBROOK PATH	Cedar Park	402M	MD-41	78613	1300-1499
DEEP CREEK	Lago Vista	429W	WW-37	78645	20600-20799
DEEP EDDY AVE	Austin	584P	MG-23	78703	300-699
DEEP FOREST CV	Round Rock	408A	MQ-42	78665	1400-1499
DEEP MEADOW CV	Travis Co	619G	MT-21	78653	16600-16699
DEEP RIVER CIR	Round Rock	408A	MQ-42	78665	2600-2799
DEEP SAND LN	Bastrop Co	564T	EC-25	78621	100-199
DEEP SPRING CV	Travis Co	493X	ME-31	78730	5900-5999
DEEP WATER DR	Travis Co	439K	MS-38	78660	None
DEEPWOOD DR	Georgetown	286T	ML-52	78628	100-499
DEEPWOOD DR	Lago Vista	429B	WW-39	78645	6800-7399
DEEP WOOD DR	Round Rock	376W	ML-43	78681	100-299
	Round Rock	406K	ML-41	78681	300-2099
DEEPWOODS DR	Austin	524C	MH-30	78731	4100-4599
DEEPWOODS TRL	Leander	342T	MC-46	78641	1100-1799
DEER LN	Austin	642Y	MD-16	78749	3500-4399
DEER PASS	Travis Co	553M	MF-26	78746	2400-2499
DEER TRL	Travis Co	486Q	WR-32	78669	3500-4299
DEER TRL	Williamson Co	226Q	MM-59	78628	3300-3599
DEERBROOK TRL	Williamson Co	433G	MF-39	78750	12200-12399
DEER CANYON RD	Travis Co	400L	WZ-41	78645	10400-10999
DEER CHASE CV	Williamson Co	375L	MK-44	78681	1700-1799
DEER CHASE TRL	Austin	704L	MH-11	78747	10200-10699
DEERCREEK CIR	Austin	554U	MH-25	78703	2800-2899
DEER CREEK CIR	Hays Co	577Y	WT-22	78720	100-1399
DEERCREEK LN	Leander	341D	MB-48	78641	100-299
	Leander	341H	MB-48	78641	500-899
DEER CREEK TRL	Williamson Co	377K	MN-44	78665	2000-2199
DEER CREEK SKYVIEW	Travis Co	577R	WT-23	78720	17200-17899
DEER DRAW	Williamson Co	314T	MG-49	78628	100-199
DEER FALLS DR	Williamson Co	434T	MG-37	78729	12300-12699
DEERFERN LN	Round Rock	347V	MP-46	78665	2700-2899
DEERFIELD CV	Lakeway	519B	WW-30	78734	100-199
DEERFIELD DR	Austin	615P	MJ-20	78741	1700-1799
DEER FIELD DR	Williamson Co	224Y	MH-58	78633	20100-20399
DEERFIELD RD	Hays Co	668J	WU-14	78620	1000-1799
DEERFIELD PARK DR	Cedar Park	372M	MD-44	78613	200-399
DEERFOOT CIR	Round Rock	406D	MM-42	78664	400-499
DEERFOOT DR	Round Rock	406D	MM-42	78664	200-799
DEERFOOT TRL	Austin	614B	MG-21	78704	2400-2699
DEERFOOT TRL	Hays Co	670N	WY-14	78737	13200-13299
DEERGROVE DR	Cedar Park	403J	ME-41	78613	900-1199
DEER HAVEN RD	Travis Co	641A	MA-18	78737	8700-9099
DEER HOLLOW LN	Austin	494S	MG-31	78750	6400-6599
DEERHORN CT	Lakeway	519B	WW-30	78734	1-199
DEER HORN CV	Cedar Park	402M	MD-41	78613	1100-1199
DEER HORN DR	Cedar Park	402M	MD-41	78613	1300-1499
DEERHOUND PL	Round Rock	377A	MN-45	78664	1000-1399
DEERINGHILL DR	Austin	643P	ME-17	78745	2600-2899
DEER LEDGE TRL	Cedar Park	402M	MD-41	78613	1400-1599
DEER MEADOW CIR	Georgetown	195P	MJ-62	78633	100-799
DEER RIDGE CIR	Austin	524D	MH-30	78731	7800-7899
DEER RUN	Lago Vista	429K	WW-38	78645	6100-6599
DEER RUN	Round Rock	406F	ML-42	78681	700-1299
DEER RUN DR	Austin	674G	MH-15	78744	1900-2199
DEER RUN DR	Bastrop Co	711A	MW-12	78612	100-199
DEER RUN RD	Travis Co	461C	MB-36	78641	7600-7699
DEER RUN ST	Cedar Park	372Y	MD-43	78613	1300-1599
DEER SHADOW PASS	Travis Co	552N	MC-26	78733	9000-9199
DEER TRACE CV	Cedar Park	402C	MD-42	78613	200-399
DEER TRACE RD	Cedar Park	402D	MD-42	78613	1400-1499
DEER TRACK	Austin	465F	MJ-36	78727	12200-12499
DEER TRACT	Williamson Co	345W	MJ-46	78681	4100-4399
DEER TRAIL CIR	Williamson Co	375A	MJ-45	78681	2400-2699
DEERWOOD CT	Travis Co	492U	MD-31	78730	5200-5299
DEERWOOD LN	Travis Co	492U	MD-31	78730	5300-5399
DEFENDORF DR	Travis Co	439Q	MT-38	78634	16500-16799
DEIDRA DR	Travis Co	591V	MX-22	78621	22500-22799
DEJA AVE	Austin	705F	MJ-12	78747	8500-8699
DELAFIELD LN	Austin	525V	MK-28	78752	7500-7899
DELAHUNTY LN	Travis Co	437X	MN-37	78660	15100-15699
DEL AIRE CT	Georgetown	226G	MM-60	78628	200-299
DELANO ST	Austin	586Q	MM-23	78721	1100-1399
DELANO ST	Bastrop	745C	EF-9	78602	1500-1699
DELAVAN AVE	Williamson Co	405J	MJ-41	78717	8400-8599
DELAVAN CV	Williamson Co	405J	MJ-41	78717	15700-15799
DELAWARE CT	Austin	526E	ML-30	78758	8600-8699
DELBY ST	Hutto	349V	MT-46	78634	100-399
DEL CARMEN CV	Austin	463R	MF-35	78759	8500-8599
DELCOUR DR	Austin	465B	MJ-36	78727	12800-12999
DELCREST DR	Austin	614K	MG-20	78704	2200-2299
DEL CURTO RD	Austin	614P	MG-20	78704	2200-3099
DELEON CT	Travis Co	522T	MC-28	78733	2100-2299
DELGADO WAY	Travis Co	522X	MC-28	78733	9700-9799
DELIA CHAPPA LN	Hutto	379F	MS-45	78634	1100-1499

D

STREET NAME	CITY or COUNTY	MAPSCO GRID	AUSTIN GRID	ZIP CODE	BLOCK RANGE O/E
DELL WAY	Round Rock	406R	MM-41	78664	100-399
	Round Rock	407N	MN-41	78664	400-599
DELLA MAE DR	Bastrop Co	741N	MW-8	78612	100-199
DELLANA LN	Rollingwood	584S	MG-22	78746	2500-2699
DELLA TORRE DR	Austin	433Y	MF-37	78750	11200-11299
DELL CITY DR	Pflugerville	407X	MN-40	78664	17500-17599
DELLINGER ST	Taylor	322V	MZ-49	76574	800-1099
DELLREY DR	Austin	466S	ML-34	78758	12300-12399
DELMAR AVE	Austin	526W	ML-28	78752	300-999
	Austin	556B	ML-27	78752	1100-1199
DELMAR DR	Georgetown	287L	MP-53	78626	700-799
DEL MESA LN	Austin	463R	MF-35	78759	8500-8699
DELMONICO DR	Austin	464X	MG-34	78759	6500-6699
DEL MONTE CV	Round Rock	378Z	MR-43	78664	3700-3799
DEL MONTE RD	Austin	616P	ML-20	78741	6300-6599
DEL NORTE CV	Williamson Co	402V	MD-40	78613	1700-1799
DELONEY ST	Austin	586K	ML-23	78721	1200-1899
DELORES AVE	Austin	466S	MM-32	78721	4700-5399
DELORIO ST	Travis Co	591K	MW-23	78653	20600-20999
DELORIS CT	Travis Co	490L	WZ-32	78734	2700-2799
DEL PARDO LN	Williamson Co	226Y	MM-58	78628	500-699
DEL PASO	Leander	341X	MA-46	78641	1700-1799
DELPHINUS WALK	Travis Co	521A	MA-30	78732	13100-13199
DEL RIO CT	Williamson Co	226U	MM-58	78628	3700-3799
DEL RIO CV	Bastrop Co	738W	MQ-7	78617	100-199
DEL RIO DR	Travis Co	522P	MC-29	78733	2500-2799
DEL ROBLES	Austin	466E	ML-36	78727	3400-3899
	Austin	465D	MK-36	78727	3900-4399
DEL ROY DR	Williamson Co	402Q	MD-41	78613	1000-1299
DELSIE DR	Lakeway	519M	WX-29	78734	800-1399
DELTA DR	Austin	495M	MK-32	78758	10600-10699
DELTA POST DR	Travis Co	619J	MS-20	78724	4900-5599
DEL VALLE ST	Austin	647K	MN-17	78617	2600-2699
DELVIN LN	Travis Co	436Y	MM-37	78728	2000-2199
DELWAU LN	Austin	587W	MN-22	78725	2900-8499
DEL WEBB BLVD	Georgetown	225G	MK-60	78633	300-699
DELWOOD CT	Austin	556P	ML-26	78723	2000-2099
DELWOOD DR	Austin	556P	ML-26	78723	5500-5799
DELWOOD PL	Austin	554Y	MH-25	78703	2600-2699
DEMARET ST	Travis Co	437S	MN-37	78660	1400-1599
DEMARETT DR	Point Venture	488R	WV-32	78654	500-599
DEMOCRACY CV	Lago Vista	458M	WV-35	78645	2700-2799
DEMONA CV	Travis Co	522P	MC-29	78733	9600-9699
DEMONA DR	Travis Co	522P	MC-29	78733	2100-2999
DEMPS ST	Hutto	349H	MT-48	78634	100-199
DEMPSEY LN	Austin	673G	MF-15	78748	8400-8699
DENALI PASS	Cedar Park	374P	MG-44	78613	200-599
DENALI PKWY	Austin	462K	MC-35	78726	8000-8499
DENBAR CT	Travis Co	672P	MC-14	78739	3500-3699
DENEHOE CV	Travis Co	618V	MR-19	78725	3600-3799
DENELL CIR	Travis Co	496Z	MM-31	78753	10600-10699
DENFIELD DR	Round Rock	376L	MM-44	78664	1700-2099
DENFIELD ST	Austin	586T	ML-22	78721	1100-1199
DENIM TRL	Travis Co	672S	MC-13	78739	3900-4199
DENISE CV	Hays Co	670T	WY-13	78610	100-199
DENISE DR	Williamson Co	405A	MJ-42	78717	16500-16699
DENISE ELLEN DR	Hays Co	763W	ME-4	78610	100-499
DENNIS DR	Round Rock	376M	MM-44	78664	400-599
DENNIS LN	Pflugerville	439T	MS-37	78660	4500-4599
DENNY LN	Travis Co	467V	MP-34	78660	14000-14099
DENSON DR	Austin	555C	MK-27	78752	100-799
DENTON DR	Austin	495M	MK-32	78758	2000-2399
DENVER AVE	Austin	586E	ML-24	78723	3300-3499
DENWOOD DR	Austin	525A	MJ-30	78759	3500-3599
DE PAUL CV	Austin	556M	MM-26	78723	6800-6899
DE PEER AVE	Williamson Co	405J	MJ-41	78717	15700-15999
DE PEER CV	Williamson Co	405J	MJ-41	78717	15800-15899
DEPEW AVE	Austin	555V	MK-25	78751	4500-4799
	Austin	555R	MK-26	78751	5100-5399
DEPOT AVE	Elgin	534N	EC-29	78621	1-499
DEPOT AVE W	Elgin	533R	EB-29	78621	None
DEPUTY DR	Travis Co	672U	MD-13	78748	11300-11399
DERBY CV	Austin	556Q	MM-26	78723	6100-6199
DERBY LN	Georgetown	287L	MP-53	78626	300-499
DERBY TRL	Round Rock	344R	MH-47	78681	3600-3899
DERBY DAY AVE	Pflugerville	409J	MS-41	78660	20800-21499
DERBY DOWNS DR	Austin	705A	MJ-12	78747	6700-7599
DERBY HILL LN	Pflugerville	438M	MR-38	78660	18600-18899
DERECHO DR	Travis Co	610Y	WZ-19	78737	9600-9999
	Travis Co	640G	WZ-18	78737	10000-10699
DERECHO BEND	Travis Co	640C	WZ-18	78737	9500-9999
DEREK DR	Cedar Park	402C	MD-42	78613	100-199
DEREN CV	Pflugerville	437D	MP-39	78660	17800-17899
DEREN LN	Pflugerville	437D	MP-39	78660	200-399
DERIDDER CT	Austin	675N	MJ-14	78744	6100-6199
DERRICK CV	Travis Co	518J	WU-29	78669	4300-4399
DERRINGER TRL	Austin	496X	ML-31	78753	10000-10199
DERVINGHAM DR	Travis Co	432C	MD-39	78613	2300-2399
DESCANSO CIR	Austin	677R	MP-14	78617	12400-12599
DESCARTES CV	Austin	497B	MN-33	78753	12700-12799
DESCO DR	Austin	672Z	MD-13	78748	2000-2299
DESERT CANDLE DR	Round Rock	375D	MK-45	78681	2800-2999
DESERT FLOWER	Travis Co	554A	MG-27	78746	3800-3899
DESERT FOREST CT	Lakeway	519S	WW-28	78738	100-199
DESERT HIGHLANDS CT	Lakeway	519X	WW-28	78738	100-199
DESERT HIGHLANDS TRL	Williamson Co	377B	MN-45	78665	100-399
DESERT MOUNTAIN CT	Lakeway	519W	WW-28	78738	100-199
DESERT OAK CIR	Austin	642G	MD-18	78749	5000-5099
DESERT PRIMROSE DR	Austin	703G	MF-12	78748	100-299
DESERT QUAIL LN	Austin	496S	ML-31	78758	1400-1599
DESERT QUAIL LN	Buda	763J	ME-5	78610	None
DESERT ROSE CV	Austin	493V	MF-31	78750	7200-7299
DESERT WILLOW CV	Round Rock	375M	MK-44	78681	3000-3099
DESERT WILLOW CV	Travis Co	582N	MC-23	78735	3200-3399
DESERT WILLOW DR	Round Rock	375M	MK-44	78681	2900-2999
DESERT WILLOW LOOP	Austin	703G	MF-12	78748	10600-11199
DESERT WILLOW PL	Cedar Park	433A	ME-39	78613	1400-1499
DESERT WILLOW WAY	Hays Co	668R	WV-14	78737	100-499
DESIRABLE DR	Austin	586Y	MM-22	78721	1100-1199
DE SOTO CIR	Travis Co	522K	MC-29	78733	2800-2899
DE SOTO DR	Travis Co	522P	MC-29	78733	2400-2899
DESSAU RD	Austin	526M	MM-29	78754	9400-10399
	Austin	497S	MN-31	78754	11600-12299
	Austin	497C	MP-33	78754	12300-13598 E
	Austin	467R	MP-35	78660	13600-14198 E
DESSAU RD (Cont'd)	Pflugerville	467R	MP-35	78660	15000-15399
	Pflugerville	468A	MQ-36	78660	15400-16299
	Travis Co	526D	MM-30	78754	10400-10899
	Travis Co	496Z	MM-31	78753	10900-11199
	Travis Co	497P	MN-32	78754	11200-11599
	Travis Co	497C	MP-33	78754	12301-13599 O
	Travis Co	467R	MP-35	78660	13601-14199 O
	Travis Co	467R	MP-35	78660	14200-14999
DESSAU RIDGE LN	Austin	497C	MP-33	78754	1500-1699
DESTINATION WAY	Jonestown	429H	WX-38	78645	5200-5899
	Lago Vista	430S	WY-37	78645	4500-5199
	Lago Vista	429H	WX-38	78645	5800-8099
DESTINY CV	Travis Co	548U	WV-25	78738	16600-16799
DESTINY HILLS DR	Travis Co	548Y	WV-25	78738	6800-7299
DESTINYS GATE DR	Austin	465H	MK-36	78727	4300-4699
DEUPREE DR	Austin	497N	MN-32	78753	1300-1499
DEURNE DR	Williamson Co	375Y	MK-43	78681	9000-9099
DE VACA DR	Travis Co	522P	MC-29	78733	9700-9799
DEVEREUX DR	Travis Co	522W	MC-28	78733	10100-10299
DE VERNE ST	Austin	614K	MG-20	78704	2000-2299
DEVIL RIDGE	Williamson Co	402Q	MD-41	78613	1200-1399
DEVINE LN	Austin	673G	MF-15	78748	8500-8799
DEVON CIR	Austin	556K	ML-26	78723	1500-1599
DEVONS CV	Buda	732U	MD-7	78610	100-199
DEVONSHIRE CV	Austin	556Q	MM-26	78723	6100-6199
DEVONSHIRE DR	Austin	556Q	MM-26	78723	2300-2599
DEWBERRY CV	Hays Co	732F	MC-9	78610	200-299
DEWBERRY DR	Cedar Park	372Y	MD-43	78613	500-899
DEWBERRY DR	Georgetown	225P	MJ-59	78633	100-199
DEWBERRY DR	Travis Co	467V	MP-34	78660	13800-14499
DEWBERRY HOLLOW	Travis Co	340J	WY-47	78641	22600-22699
DEWDROP CV	Travis Co	519Q	WX-29	78738	1-99
DEW DROP LN	Leander	342F	MC-48	78641	800-899
DEWEY ST	Austin	586T	ML-22	78721	4900-4999
DEWS RD	Williamson Co	280Z	WZ-52	78641	1-799
DEXFORD DR	Austin	497B	MN-33	78753	1100-1499
DEXLER DR	Travis Co	490P	WY-32	78734	15000-15499
DEXMOOR DR	Austin	556P	ML-26	78723	2000-2099
DEXTER DR	Leander	342F	MC-48	78641	900-1099
DEXTER ST	Austin	614C	MH-21	78704	1500-2099
DIABLO CT	Pflugerville	439A	MS-39	78660	2800-2899
DIABLO RD	Pflugerville	439A	MS-39	78660	19400-19999
DIAMOND CV	Lago Vista	399T	WW-40	78645	21200-21299
DIAMOND TRL	Lago Vista	399X	WW-40	78645	7700-7999
DIAMOND TRL	Williamson Co	224R	MH-59	78633	100-399
DIAMONDBACK TRL	Austin	496Y	MM-31	78753	10100-10299
DIAMOND DOVE TRL	Georgetown	227J	MN-59	78628	30000-30299
DIAMOND HEAD CIR	Travis Co	582H	MD-24	78746	6100-6299
DIAMOND HEAD DR	Bastrop Co	775C	EF-6	78602	100-299
DIAMOND HEAD DR	Travis Co	582H	MD-24	78746	6000-6199
DIANA CV	Bastrop Co	709L	MT-11	78612	None
DIANA DR	Round Rock	407R	MP-41	78664	1600-1699
DIANE DR	Austin	644A	MG-18	78745	4400-4499
DIANELLA LN	Austin	464T	MG-34	78759	10000-10399
DIAZ ST	Austin	615D	MK-21	78702	2500-2699
DICKENS CIR	Georgetown	195U	MK-61	78633	100-199
DICKEY ST W	Taylor	353J	EA-47	76574	100-699
DICKSON DR	Austin	614J	MG-20	78704	2000-2299
DIDDLEY CV	Travis Co	402P	MC-41	78613	2800-2899
DIEGO DR	Williamson Co	348N	MQ-47	78665	2600-2699
DIEHL TRL	Austin	465A	MJ-36	78727	5600-5799
DIES RANCH RD	Travis Co	432L	MD-38	78613	11100-12199
DIGBY CT	Williamson Co	343S	ME-46	78641	3200-3299
DIJON DR	Cedar Park	403U	MF-40	78613	2300-2599
DILDY DR	Elgin	533V	EB-28	78621	None
DILL CIR	Travis Co	487R	WT-32	78669	21100-21499
DILLARD CIR	Austin	555D	MK-27	78752	5900-6199
DILLIONHILL DR	Austin	643K	ME-17	78745	2800-2999
DILLMAN ST	Austin	584B	MG-24	78703	1500-1999
DILLO TRL	Williamson Co	222W	MC-58	78642	1-499
DILLON DR	Travis Co	735J	MJ-8	78747	None
DILLON LAKE BEND	Williamson Co	343T	ME-46	78641	1200-1599
DILLWEED DR	Austin	646B	ML-18	78741	7100-7199
DIME CIR	Austin	645R	MK-17	78744	3500-3799
DIME BOX TRL	Travis Co	435S	MJ-37	78729	13200-13299
	Williamson Co	435S	MJ-37	78729	None
DIMITRIOS DR	Austin	704P	MG-11	78747	10500-10599
DIMMIT CT	Travis Co	491U	MB-31	78732	12400-12499
DIMMIT ST	Manor	529Y	MT-28	78653	11300-11599
DINER DR	Cedar Park	373U	MF-43	78613	1300-1399
DINGE BAY DR	Travis Co	408L	MR-41	78664	500-599
DINSDALE LN	Austin	645B	MJ-18	78741	1900-2099
DIONYSUS DR	Austin	497B	MN-33	78753	12800-13099
DIOR DR	Cedar Park	403U	MF-40	78613	2300-2599
DIP CV	Austin	613H	MF-21	78704	2400-2599
DIRECTORS BLVD	Austin	644M	MH-17	78744	1600-1799
	Austin	645J	MJ-17	78744	1800-1899
DI SANTIS PL	Travis Co	432L	MD-38	78613	2700-2799
DISCOVERY BLVD	Cedar Park	373S	ME-43	78613	300-899
	Cedar Park	373K	ME-44	78613	1500-1699
DISCOVERY BLVD S	Cedar Park	373P	ME-44	78613	None
DISCOVERY LN	Austin	646F	ML-18	78741	1700-1999
DISRAELI CIR	Travis Co	437G	MP-39	78660	1000-1299
DISTANT VIEW DR	Travis Co	580Z	WZ-22	78736	6300-6699
DISTRIBUTION CV	Hays Co	762M	MD-5	78610	100-299
DITTMAR RD E	Austin	674F	MG-15	78745	100-199
DITTMAR RD W	Austin	674E	MG-15	78745	200-599
	Austin	673C	MF-15	78745	600-1999
DITTMAR OAKS CV	Austin	673F	ME-15	78748	1600-1699
DITTMAR OAKS DR	Austin	673F	ME-15	78748	8500-8899
DIVERSION CIR	Lago Vista	429R	WX-38	78645	19500-19599
DIVIDE DR	Travis Co	310L	WZ-50	78641	22700-22899
DIVINE MERCY LOOP	Georgetown	287F	MN-54	78626	None
DIXIE DR	Austin	678J	MQ-14	78617	5200-5299
DIXIE DR	Austin	675N	MJ-14	78744	7100-7699
DIXIE LN	Round Rock	406M	MM-41	78664	1800-2199
DIXON DR	Austin	643W	ME-16	78745	8200-8499
D-K RANCH CT	Travis Co	464P	MG-35	78759	7900-7999
D-K RANCH RD	Austin	464P	MG-35	78759	10101-10299 O
	Austin	464P	MG-35	78759	10901-10999 O
	Austin	464F	MG-36	78759	11300-11799
	Travis Co	464P	MG-35	78759	10100-10298 E
	Travis Co	464P	MG-35	78759	10300-10899
	Travis Co	464P	MG-35	78759	10900-10998 E
	Travis Co	464K	MG-35	78759	11000-11299
D MORGAN RD	Travis Co	610B	WY-21	78736	10800-11799
DOAK ST N	Taylor	353E	EA-48	76574	200-599
DOAK ST S	Taylor	353J	EA-47	76574	100-799
DOBBIN DR	Austin	672G	MD-15	78748	10100-10199
DOBIE DR	Austin	526G	MM-30	78753	1200-1399
DOBUSH DR	Travis Co	708S	MQ-10	78617	14800-14999
DOC HOLLIDAY TRL	Austin	496X	ML-31	78753	10200-10499
DOCTOR SCOTT DR	Austin	648Y	MR-16	78617	3700-4098 E
	Austin	678C	MR-15	78617	4100-4398 E
	Travis Co	648Y	MR-16	78617	3701-4099 O
	Travis Co	678C	MR-15	78617	4101-4399 O
DODD ST	Village of Volente	431S	MA-37	78641	16100-16299
DODGE TRL	Lago Vista	399Y	WX-40	78645	20600-21399
DODGE CATTLE CV	Austin	404A	MG-42	78717	15100-15199
DODGE CATTLE DR	Austin	404A	MG-42	78717	10800-11499
DOE TRL	Travis Co	583Q	MF-23	78746	3600-3699
DOEFIELD DR	Cedar Park	372M	MD-44	78613	200-399
DOE MEADOW DR	Austin	642E	MC-18	78749	8000-8399
DOERING LN	Williamson Co	433Q	MF-38	78750	10400-10799
DOE RUN	Travis Co	672P	MC-14	78748	3200-3499
DOE RUN	Williamson Co	344D	MH-48	78628	300-499
	Williamson Co	315W	MJ-49	78628	None
DOE RUN RD	Travis Co	400E	WY-42	78645	20300-20499
DOE VALLEY LN	Austin	494H	MH-33	78759	5100-5399
DOGIE CV	Lago Vista	399X	WW-40	78645	7700-7799
DOGIE TRL	Burnet Co	307E	WS-51	78654	None
DOG LEG DR	Austin	403M	MF-41	78717	11400-11499
DOGWOOD CIR	Taylor	353S	EA-46	76574	200-299
DOGWOOD DR	Bastrop Co	564Z	ED-25	78621	100-199
DOGWOOD DR	Williamson Co	257E	MN-57	78626	100-299
DOGWOOD TRL	Cedar Park	372Z	MD-43	78613	700-1099
DOGWOOD BLOOMS LN	Pflugerville	407Z	MP-40	78660	18300-18399
DOGWOOD CREEK CV	Austin	523U	MF-28	78746	3700-3799
DOGWOOD CREEK DR	Austin	523Y	MF-28	78746	6600-6799
DOGWOOD HOLLOW	Austin	494W	MG-31	78750	6900-6999
DOLAN DR N	Taylor	353F	EA-48	76574	100-399
DOLAN DR S	Taylor	353F	EA-48	76574	100-399
DOLCE VISTA DR	Austin	704L	MH-11	78747	10200-10299
DOLIVER DR	Austin	673J	ME-14	78748	9300-9599
DOLOMITE DR	Hays Co	763S	ME-4	78610	100-299
DOLOMITE TRL	Round Rock	345S	MJ-46	78681	3500-3599
DOLPHIN CV	Austin	614T	MG-19	78704	3300-3399
DOLPHIN DR	Austin	614T	MG-19	78704	3100-3599
DOMAIN BLVD	Austin	465Y	MK-34	78758	11700-11899
DOMAIN DR	Austin	495C	MK-33	78758	10700-11599
	Austin	465Y	MK-34	78758	11600-11999
DOMENICA LN	Austin	674D	MH-15	78744	4500-4599
DOME PEAK LN	Georgetown	225A	MJ-60	78633	900-999
DOMINIC DR	Austin	643S	ME-16	78745	3100-3199
DOMINION CV	Austin	495N	MJ-32	78759	3900-4099
DOMINION HILL	Travis Co	551T	MA-25	78733	2400-2699
DOMINIQUE DR	Austin	497N	MN-32	78753	1300-1499
DONAHUE LN	Austin	644V	MH-16	78744	2100-2299
DONALD DR	Travis Co	436U	MM-37	78728	14500-14599
DON ANN ST	Austin	586T	ML-22	78721	1100-1199
DONA VILLA DR	Austin	462H	MD-36	78726	11400-11499
DONA VILLA PL	Austin	462H	MD-36	78726	9100-9199
DONCASTER DR	Austin	643T	ME-16	78745	7700-7999
DONDALE CIR	Travis Co	583A	ME-24	78746	700-799
DONEGAL RD	Austin	642H	MD-18	78749	6900-6999
DON HILL LN	Taylor	322U	MZ-49	76574	2800-3199
DONINGTON DR	Austin	497J	MN-32	78753	12200-12299
DONLEY DR	Austin	495M	MK-32	78758	2000-2399
DONLEY RIDGE LN	Travis Co	704F	MG-12	78747	None
DONNA DR	Taylor	323S	EA-49	76574	1900-2099
	Taylor	322V	MZ-49	76574	2100-2799
DONNA GAIL DR	Austin	495X	MJ-31	78757	8600-8799
DONNA JANE LOOP	Austin	437W	MN-37	78660	15000-15399
DONNELL DR	Round Rock	407M	MP-41	78664	2900-2999
DONNER CV	Austin	641Q	MB-17	78749	6600-6699
DONNER LN	Austin	641Q	MB-17	78749	9200-9399
DONNER PATH	Round Rock	376A	ML-45	78681	2400-2499
DONOVAN CIR	Austin	497E	MN-33	78753	12300-12399
DOOLEY TRL	Austin	587G	MP-24	78724	6100-6399
DOOLIN DR	Austin	614T	MG-19	78704	3300-3399
DOOLITTLE CV	Lago Vista	458M	WV-35	78645	20300-20499
DOONESBURY CV	Austin	496F	ML-33	78758	11800-11899
DOONESBURY DR	Austin	496F	ML-33	78758	1100-1499
DOONE VALLEY CT	Austin	524P	MG-29	78731	5900-5999
DOOR BELL DR	Manor	530P	MU-29	78653	None
DORADO PASS	Travis Co	488X	WU-31	78669	2000-2399
DORAL CT	Round Rock	378X	MQ-43	78664	1000-1099
DORAL DR	Travis Co	582Q	MD-23	78746	2100-2399
DORA'S DR	Travis Co	437W	MN-37	78660	1000-1199
DORCHESTER DR	Austin	556L	MM-26	78723	6200-6599
DORCHESTER HEIGHTS LN	Travis Co	527T	MN-28	78754	4700-4999
DOREEN CT	Round Rock	377S	MN-43	78664	1200-1299
DORELLA LN	Travis Co	611N	MA-20	78736	8800-9199
DORIA DR	Travis Co	436U	MM-37	78728	14900-15099
DORINE LN	Bastrop Co	715E	EE-12	78602	100-199
DORIS DR	Austin	525C	MK-30	78757	1900-2399
DORIS LN	Cedar Park	372R	MD-44	78613	500-1399
DORIS LN	Round Rock	408B	MQ-42	78664	3800-3999
DORMAN CV	Williamson Co	405E	MJ-42	78717	8700-8799
DORMAN DR E	Williamson Co	405B	MJ-42	78681	16700-16999
DORMAN DR W	Williamson Co	405J	MJ-41	78717	15800-16599
DORMARION LN	Austin	584C	MH-24	78703	2400-2599
DORMAX CIR	Travis Co	341P	MA-47	78641	15200-15399
DORNACH CT	Travis Co	437G	MP-39	78660	800-899
DORNACH DR	Travis Co	437H	MP-39	78660	17400-17499
DORNICK HILLS LN	Travis Co	409W	MS-40	78660	19800-19999
DOROTHA CT	Austin	494V	MH-31	78759	8400-8699
DOROTHY DR	Lakeway	520J	WY-29	78734	14900-15399
DORSEN DR	Austin	670D	WZ-16	78739	12200-12299
DORSET DR	Austin	526H	MM-30	78753	9900-10099
DORSET LN	Hays Co	639T	WW-16	78737	100-199
DORSETT RD	Austin	465U	MK-34	78727	11900-12599
DORSETT OAKS CIR	Austin	465Q	MK-35	78727	4500-4599
DOS AMIGO DR	Travis Co	429Q	WX-38	78645	19800-20099
DOS CABEZAS DR	Austin	642G	MD-18	78749	4200-4399
DOS RIOS WAY	Travis Co	427R	WT-38	78654	None
DOSS RD	Travis Co	460Y	WZ-34	78734	4500-5499
DOSSHILLS DR	Austin	433U	MF-37	78750	11300-11599
DOSWELL CV	Austin	641W	MA-16	78739	10900-10999
DOSWELL LN	Austin	641W	MA-16	78739	7000-7699
DOT DR	Travis Co	436W	ML-37	78727	4200-4299
DOTIE TRL	Travis Co	457X	WS-34	78669	23100-23299
DOUBLE BEND BACK RD	West Lake Hills	553X	ME-25	78746	800-899

Continued on next column

STREET NAME	CITY or COUNTY	MAPSCO GRID	AUSTIN GRID	ZIP CODE	BLOCK RANGE O/E
DOUBLE CANYON DR	Jonestown	400X	WY-40	78645	19000-19299
	Travis Co	400T	WY-40	78645	18700-18999
DOUBLE CREEK DR	Round Rock	407L	MP-41	78664	600-2599
	Round Rock	377Y	MP-43	78665	None
DOUBLE DOME RD	Travis Co	490H	WZ-33	78734	3900-4099
DOUBLE EAGLE DR	Austin	404D	MH-42	78717	15800-16399
DOUBLE EAGLE DR	Travis Co	519K	WW-29	78738	300-599
	Village of the Hills	519K	WW-29	78738	100-299
DOUBLE EAGLE PASS	Austin	404D	MH-42	78717	10200-10299
DOUBLE ELM DR	Travis Co	703P	ME-11	78652	12200-12299
DOUBLE FILE CV	Round Rock	376D	MM-45	78665	900-999
DOUBLE FILE TRL	Round Rock	376D	MM-45	78665	900-1199
DOUBLE FILE TRL	Travis Co	436X	ML-37	78728	14200-14499
DOUBLE FIRE TRL	Georgetown	225L	MK-59	78633	100-199
DOUBLE FORK RD	West Lake Hills	583C	MF-24	78746	100-699
DOUBLE SPUR LOOP	Travis Co	464N	MG-35	78759	10400-10699
DOUBLE TREE	Williamson Co	375A	MJ-45	78681	2500-2799
DOUBLE TREE CV	Williamson Co	433L	MF-38	78750	10600-10699
DOUBLE TREE LN	Williamson Co	433M	MF-38	78750	12200-12399
DOUBLOON CV	Austin	464H	MH-36	78759	11900-11999
DOUGLAS CV	Lago Vista	458M	WV-35	78645	2800-2899
DOUGLAS ST	Austin	615X	MJ-19	78741	2300-2499
	Austin	645B	MJ-18	78741	2500-2699
DOVE CIR	Cedar Park	403W	ME-40	78613	1200-1299
DOVE CT	Austin	674D	MH-15	78744	6200-6299
DOVE CV	Taylor	322R	MZ-50	76574	900-999
DOVE DR	Austin	644Z	MH-16	78744	2300-4499
DOVE DR	Hays Co	701Q	MB-11	78652	800-1199
DOVE DR	Hays Co	732L	MD-8	78610	12700-13999
DOVE LN	Bastrop Co	740H	MV-9	78612	100-199
DOVE RD	Lago Vista	458J	WU-35	78645	1600-1799
DOVE CREEK CV	Austin	645X	MJ-16	78744	4900-4999
DOVE CREEK DR	Austin	674H	MH-15	78744	6200-6299
DOVE CREEK DR	Round Rock	406D	MM-42	78664	300-699
DOVEDALE CV	Village of the Hills	519T	WW-28	78738	1-99
DOVE FLIGHT DR	Travis Co	677X	MN-13	78617	11400-11599
DOVE HAVEN DR	Austin	496M	MM-32	78753	11800-12099
DOVE HAVEN DR	Pflugerville	468F	MQ-36	78660	1200-1799
DOVE HAVEN DR	Round Rock	406D	MM-42	78664	400-699
DOVE HAVEN LOOP	Cedar Park	402M	MD-41	78613	1300-1399
DOVEHILL DR	Austin	674D	MH-15	78744	2200-4599
DOVE HILL DR	Cedar Park	402M	MD-41	78613	1400-1499
DOVE HOLLOW TRL	Georgetown	195Y	MK-61	78633	100-599
DOVE MEADOW CV	Georgetown	287M	MP-53	78626	800-899
DOVEMEADOW DR	Austin	674D	MH-15	78744	2500-4599
DOVER CV	Cedar Park	403J	ME-41	78613	1100-1299
DOVER LN	Round Rock	406M	MM-41	78664	500-899
DOVER PASS	Cedar Park	403J	ME-41	78613	900-1199
DOVER PL	Austin	525J	MJ-29	78757	2900-2999
DOVER CASTLE LN	Pflugerville	408X	MQ-40	78660	800-999
DOVERCLIFFE CV	Travis Co	527X	MN-28	78754	4900-4999
DOVE RIDGE TRL	Leander	342X	MC-46	78641	1900-1999
DOVE SONG DR	Leander	342B	MC-48	78641	100-199
DOVE SPRINGS CIR	Austin	674D	MH-15	78744	6200-6299
DOVE SPRINGS DR	Austin	644Z	MH-16	78744	2100-2199
	Austin	674D	MH-15	78744	2200-4699
	Austin	675A	MJ-15	78744	4700-5099
DOVETAIL CV	Williamson Co	284E	MG-54	78628	200-299
DOVETAIL LN	Williamson Co	284H	MH-54	78628	100-199
DOVETAIL ST	Travis Co	409N	MS-41	78660	2300-2499
DOVE VALLEY CV	Williamson Co	434U	MH-37	78729	8300-8399
DOVE VALLEY DR	Williamson Co	257Z	MP-55	78626	4000-4099
DOVE VALLEY DR	Williamson Co	258W	MQ-55	78626	4000-4099
DOVE VALLEY TRL	Williamson Co	434U	MH-37	78729	12500-12699
DOVEWOOD DR	Austin	674D	MH-15	78744	2500-4599
DOWD LN	Travis Co	436Y	MM-37	78728	2300-2599
DOWITCHER CIR	Hays Co	732E	MC-9	78610	500-599
DOWLING CV	Austin	643X	ME-16	78745	8000-8199
DOWN CV	Austin	613M	MF-20	78704	2800-2899
DOWNHILL LN	Austin	646F	ML-18	78741	None
DOWNIE PL	West Lake Hills	583G	MF-24	78746	1-99
DOWNING LN	Williamson Co	343Y	MF-46	78641	1900-2299
DOWNING ST	Austin	464B	MG-36	78759	7800-8099
DOWNRIDGE CV	Austin	494X	MG-31	78731	4700-4799
DOWNRIDGE DR	Austin	494X	MG-31	78731	7500-7699
DOWNRIDGE DR	Leander	343N	ME-47	78641	900-1199
DOWNS DR	Austin	586L	MM-23	78721	5200-5599
DOWN VALLEY CT	Austin	524P	MG-29	78731	5900-5999
DOYAL DR	Austin	705A	MJ-12	78747	6600-7099
DOYLE RD	Travis Co	738S	MQ-7	78617	10000-10699
DOYLE OVERTON RD	Travis Co	737Z	MP-7	78617	10700-11099
	Travis Co	767K	MN-5	78617	11100-11499
	Travis Co	767K	MN-5	78719	11500-11899
DRAGLINE DR	Travis Co	466C	MM-36	78728	13800-13899
DRAGON	Lakeway	519A	WW-30	78734	500-699
	Lakeway	518D	WV-30	78734	700-799
DRAGON DR	Round Rock	406A	MK-42	78681	1200-1599
DRAGONFLY CT	Austin	674V	MH-13	78744	7400-7499
DRAKE AVE	Austin	615J	MJ-20	78704	1400-1999
DRAKE CV	Lago Vista	458M	WV-35	78645	3000-3099
DRAKE CV	Leander	342L	MD-47	78641	1000-1299
DRAKE DR	Cedar Park	373Z	MF-43	78613	1600-1699
DRAKE LN	Taylor	323S	EA-49	76574	200-499
	Taylor	322V	MZ-49	76574	500-799
DRAKE ELM DR	Pflugerville	438X	MQ-37	78660	1200-1399
DRAPER LN	Williamson Co	282C	MD-54	78628	1-199
DRAPER MOUNTAIN TRL	Travis Co	459J	WW-35	78645	19400-19899
DRAPERS CV	Lago Vista	459F	WW-36	78645	3300-4499
	Travis Co	459J	WW-35	78645	3000-3299
DRAWBRIDGE DR	Travis Co	582D	MD-24	78746	400-599
DRAYTON DR	Austin	496K	ML-32	78758	11700-11799
DREAMTIME LN	Travis Co	467R	MP-35	78660	14500-14699
DRESDEN CV	Austin	556Y	MM-25	78723	2900-2999
DRESDEN CV	Williamson Co	317W	MN-49	78665	1900-1999
DREW LN	Austin	672R	MD-14	78748	None
	Travis Co	672R	MD-14	78748	2400-2699
DREXEL DR	Austin	556M	MM-26	78723	6900-6999
DRIFT DR	Travis Co	609N	WW-20	78736	13000-13199
DRIFTING LEAF DR	Travis Co	402Y	MD-40	78613	2400-2499
DRIFTING MEADOW DR	Georgetown	227J	MN-59	78628	30100-30199
DRIFTING MEADOWS DR	Pflugerville	408Z	MR-40	78660	19500-19599
DRIFTING SANDS DR	Hays Co	667F	WS-15	78620	100-299
DRIFTING WIND RUN	Hays Co	667B	WS-15	78620	100-1399
DRIFTING WIND RUN	Leander	342P	MC-47	78641	1100-1399
DRIFTING WIND RUN					
	Village of the Hills	519N	WW-29	78738	1-99
DRIFTWOOD CT	Dripping Springs	636Q	WR-17	78620	100-199

STREET NAME	CITY or COUNTY	MAPSCO GRID	AUSTIN GRID	ZIP CODE	BLOCK RANGE O/E
DRIFTWOOD DR	Austin	524A	MG-30	78731	5400-5799
DRINGENBERG DR	Williamson Co	434Z	MH-37	78729	12600-12699
DRIPPING SPRINGS RANCH RD					
	Hays Co	668P	WU-14	78620	100-899
DRIP ROCK LN	Travis Co	492U	MD-31	78730	9800-9899
DRISKILL ST	Austin	615B	MJ-21	78701	600-799
DROP TINE DR	Cedar Park	402M	MD-41	78613	1500-1699
DROSSETT DR	Austin	645K	MJ-17	78744	3700-4099
DROVER CIR	Pflugerville	467C	MP-36	78660	None
DROWSY WILLOW TRL	Austin	675A	MJ-15	78744	5900-5999
DRUE LN	Cedar Park	372G	MD-45	78613	2200-2399
DRUMMOND DR	Austin	498X	MQ-31	78653	12300-12499
DRURY LN	Austin	585G	MK-24	78722	2700-2999
DRURY LN	Hays Co	639U	WX-16	78737	100-599
DRUSILLA'S DR	Austin	437W	MN-37	78660	14000-15099
	Travis Co	437W	MN-37	78660	15100-15299
DRY BEAN CV	Cedar Park	373T	ME-43	78613	500-599
DRY BEND CV	Austin	524L	MH-29	78731	6400-6499
DRY BROOK LOOP	Travis Co	439N	MS-38	78660	18300-18699
DRY BROOK CROSSING	Travis Co	439N	MS-38	78660	3500-3599
DRY CLIFF CV	Austin	524L	MH-29	78731	6400-6499
DRY CREEK CT	Round Rock	406Q	MM-41	78681	500-599
DRY CREEK CV	Cedar Park	373Y	MF-43	78613	1100-1199
DRY CREEK CV	Round Rock	406L	MM-41	78681	500-599
DRY CREEK DR	Austin	524P	MG-29	78731	3800-4099
DRY CREEK DR	Round Rock	406Q	MM-41	78681	1900-2399
DRY CREEK RD	Hays Co	669N	WW-14	78737	100-499
DRY CREEK RD	Travis Co	621D	MX-21	78653	100-399
DRYDEN ST	Austin	672R	MD-14	78748	2600-2799
DRYFIELD DR	Austin	525H	MK-30	78758	8500-8599
DRY LAKE LN	Travis Co	439K	MS-38	78660	None
DRY LEDGE CV	Austin	524L	MH-29	78731	3900-3999
DRY OAK TRL	Austin	612Y	MD-19	78749	4800-5099
DRY POND DR	Travis Co	439P	MS-38	78660	18600-18799
DRY RUN CIR	Hays Co	669P	WW-14	78737	100-199
DRY SEASON TRL	Austin	497T	MN-31	78754	1900-2099
DRY TORTUGAS TRL	Austin	704A	MG-12	78747	2100-2299
DRY WELLS RD	Austin	642B	MC-18	78749	5200-5399
DUB DR	Austin	702D	MD-12	78748	11500-11699
DUBER LN	Austin	675W	MJ-13	78747	7800-7899
DUBLIN DR	Austin	643F	ME-18	78745	2800-2999
DUBLIN DR	Leander	342U	MD-46	78641	1700-1999
DUBUQUE LN	Austin	556R	MM-26	78723	6700-6999
	Austin	557J	MN-26	78723	7000-7399
DUCHESS DR	Austin	587E	MN-24	78724	6100-6299
DUCK DR	Taylor	322R	MZ-50	76574	3100-3199
DUCKCREEK CT	Williamson Co	434T	MG-37	78729	12600-12699
DUCK LAKE CT	Lakeway	519G	WX-30	78734	700-799
DUCK LAKE DR	Lakeway	519G	WX-30	78734	1-899
DUDLEY DR	Austin	613U	MF-19	78735	4300-4599
DUDMAR DR	Austin	613U	MF-19	78735	4500-4799
DUELING OAK CIR	Austin	463L	MF-35	78750	9900-9999
DUFF DR	Bastrop	744F	EC-9	78602	100-199
	Bastrop Co	744F	EC-9	78602	200-299
DUGAN DR	Austin	465R	MK-35	78759	3700-3799
DUGOUT BEND	Buda	732W	MC-7	78610	100-199
DUKE AVE	Austin	525L	MK-29	78757	1700-1899
DUKE CV	Pflugerville	467H	MP-36	78660	1000-1099
DUKE RD	Travis Co	557E	MN-27	78724	3200-3599
DULAC CV	Williamson Co	434H	MH-39	78729	13500-13599
DULAC DR	Williamson Co	434H	MH-39	78729	8300-8499
DULCET DR	Austin	673B	ME-15	78745	8300-8899
DULLES AVE	Williamson Co	434M	MH-38	78729	13400-13599
DULLES CV	Williamson Co	434M	MH-38	78729	8300-8399
DULL KNIFE DR	Austin	465N	MJ-35	78759	5000-5199
DULWICH ST	Austin	673H	MF-15	78748	700-899
DUMAINE CIR	Austin	466K	ML-35	78727	1900-1999
DUMAS ST	Austin	584K	MG-23	78703	None
DUMBECK DR	Elgin	534W	EC-28	78621	1-199
DUNBAR CT	Travis Co	432G	MD-39	78613	2900-2999
DUNBARTON DR	Austin	556M	MM-26	78723	2600-2799
DUNBLANE WAY	Austin	528F	MQ-30	78754	11700-11899
DUNBURY DR	Austin	556K	ML-26	78723	5900-6099
DUNCAN DR	Williamson Co	402Q	MD-41	78613	1000-1099
DUNCAN LN	Austin	585C	MK-24	78705	900-999
DUNDALK BAY CV	Pflugerville	467D	MP-36	78660	600-699
DUNDEE CT	Travis Co	488Y	WV-31	78669	2100-2199
DUNDEE DR	Austin	464C	MH-36	78759	12200-12399
DUNES DR	Pflugerville	438D	MR-39	78660	2300-2399
	Pflugerville	439A	MS-39	78660	2400-2799
DUNFRIES LN	Austin	528K	MQ-29	78754	11700-12099
DUNGAN LN	Austin	526M	MM-29	78754	1500-1799
DUNGAN ST	Austin	526J	ML-29	78753	8500-8699
DUNHAM FOREST RD	Austin	404J	MG-41	78717	10400-10599
DUNHILL DR	Leander	311R	MB-50	78641	1200-1299
DUNKELD DR	Briarcliff	457Z	WT-34	78669	100-499
DUNKIRK DR	Austin	611Q	MB-20	78736	7100-7199
DUNLAP RD N	Travis Co	619P	MS-20	78725	4500-5799
DUNLAP RD S	Travis Co	619W	MS-19	78725	1000-1199
	Travis Co	649B	MS-18	78725	1200-1299
DUNLAP ST	Austin	644C	MH-18	78704	100-299
DUNLEIGH DR	Austin	642V	MD-16	78745	3300-3499
DUNLIN DR	Hays Co	732E	MC-9	78610	300-399
DUNMAN DR	Georgetown	256T	ML-55	78628	700-1299
DUNN DR	Briarcliff	487D	WT-33	78669	22200-22299
DUNN ST	Austin	643N	ME-17	78745	7700-7899
	Austin	642V	MD-16	78745	7900-8399
DUNNING LN	Travis Co	554N	MG-26	78746	4000-4399
DUNSMERE CT	Austin	641H	MB-18	78749	6400-6499
DUNSMERE DR	Austin	641H	MB-18	78749	8500-8599
DUNSTAN DR	Austin	643R	MF-17	78745	1100-1299
DUPOINT CV	Austin	673E	ME-15	78748	2700-2799
DUPREE CIR	Austin	672Y	MD-13	78748	2600-2699
DUPREE LN	Austin	672Y	MD-13	78748	2700-2799
DUQUESNE DR	Austin	556L	MM-26	78723	6700-6999
DURANGO CV	Lago Vista	399T	WW-40	78645	7800-7899
DURANGO PASS	Austin	557P	MN-26	78724	5600-5699
DURANGO TRAIL DR	Georgetown	225G	MK-60	78633	100-199
DURANTA CV	Austin	494F	MG-33	78759	6300-6399
DURBAN CT	Round Rock	378X	MQ-43	78664	3000-3099
DURHAM DR	Austin	526P	ML-29	78753	1000-1199
DURLSTON CT	Travis Co	432C	MD-39	78613	2500-2599
DURNBERRY LN	Round Rock	408C	MR-42	78664	3800-3899
DURWOOD RD	Austin	614R	MH-20	78704	2300-2599
DUSIK LN	Austin	583N	ME-23	78746	4500-4699
DUSK CT	Lago Vista	458J	WU-35	78645	1200-1399
DUSK TERRACE CV	Austin	641C	MB-18	78749	8400-8499

STREET NAME	CITY or COUNTY	MAPSCO GRID	AUSTIN GRID	ZIP CODE	BLOCK RANGE O/E
DUSKY THRUSH TRL	Austin	583U	MF-22	78746	1200-1399
DUSTER CV	Cedar Park	402R	MD-41	78613	1400-1499
DUSTY CHISOLM TRL	Pflugerville	439J	MS-39	78660	2800-3199
DUSTY LEATHER CT	Pflugerville	437Y	MP-37	78660	500-599
DUSTY TRAIL CV	Austin	642F	MC-18	78749	5100-5199
DUVAL RD	Austin	465U	MK-34	78759	2800-4399
	Austin	465N	MJ-35	78727	4400-5399
	Austin	465N	MJ-35	78727	5400-5799
DUVAL ST	Austin	585B	MJ-24	78705	2900-3799
	Austin	555M	MK-26	78751	3800-5599
	Austin	555H	MK-27	78752	5700-5899
	Austin	526W	ML-28	78752	7200-7599
DWIGHT EISENHOWER CT	Travis Co	530K	MU-29	78653	13400-13499
DWIGHT EISENHOWER ST	Travis Co	530K	MU-29	78653	12100-12399
	Travis Co	530G	MV-30	78653	12700-12999
DWYCE DR	Austin	525U	MK-28	78757	1200-1499
DYER CREEK PL	Round Rock	407D	MP-42	78665	1000-1199
DYER CROSSING WAY	Round Rock	377Y	MP-43	78665	1000-1099
DYLAN GARRETT CV	Round Rock	376E	ML-45	78681	2400-2499
DYMALOR CIR	Austin	673C	MF-15	78745	1100-1199
DYWER AVE	Austin	614C	MH-21	78704	1600-1899

E

STREET NAME	CITY or COUNTY	MAPSCO GRID	AUSTIN GRID	ZIP CODE	BLOCK RANGE O/E
EAGLE	Lakeway	519A	WW-30	78734	400-699
EAGLE CV	Lakeway	519A	WW-30	78734	100-199
EAGLE DR W	Village of the Hills	519K	WW-29	78738	100-199
EAGLE PASS	Lago Vista	399L	WX-41	78645	8700-8999
EAGLE PT	Travis Co	490V	WZ-31	78734	2400-2499
EAGLE WAY	Williamson Co	375B	MJ-45	78681	3600-3999
EAGLE CLIFF	Austin	523M	MF-29	78731	5700-5799
EAGLECREEK DR	Leander	341D	MB-48	78641	500-899
EAGLE FEATHER DR	Austin	613N	ME-20	78735	4500-4799
	Austin	612M	MD-20	78735	4800-4899
EAGLE FLEDGE TERRACE	Travis Co	439C	MT-39	78660	3600-3799
EAGLE KNOLL DR	Austin	404L	MH-41	78717	9400-9799
EAGLE LOOKOUT DR	Travis Co	521Z	MB-28	78733	300-599
EAGLE MOUNTAIN CV	Georgetown	195S	MJ-61	78633	100-199
EAGLE NEST DR	Hays Co	702X	MC-10	78610	12400-12599
	Hays Co	732B	MC-9	78610	12600-12799
EAGLE PASS RD	Travis Co	701H	MB-12	78652	3600-3699
EAGLE POINT LN	Lago Vista	429G	WX-39	78645	6900-6999
EAGLE RIDGE LN	Travis Co	409Y	MT-40	78660	3300-3399
EAGLE RISING CV	Travis Co	522G	MD-30	78730	9700-9799
EAGLE ROCK CV	Williamson Co	433F	ME-39	78750	12200-12399
EAGLES CT	Travis Co	520B	WY-30	78734	15100-15199
EAGLE'S WAY	Leander	342K	MC-47	78641	800-1099
	Williamson Co	342J	MC-47	78641	1100-1799
	Williamson Co	341R	MB-47	78641	1800-2199
EAGLES FLIGHT LN	Austin	677R	MP-14	78617	5400-5499
EAGLES GLEN CV	Travis Co	521G	MB-30	78732	1800-1899
EAGLES GLEN DR	Travis Co	521L	MB-29	78732	11400-11999
EAGLES LANDING CV	Austin	613J	ME-20	78735	4000-4099
EAGLES LANDING DR	Austin	613E	ME-21	78735	4400-4599
EAGLES NEST ST	Round Rock	346M	MM-47	78665	3300-4099
EAGLE TERRACE	Austin	674B	MG-15	78744	None
EAGLE TRACE DR	Williamson Co	287G	MP-54	78626	50100-50599
EAGLE TRACE TRL	Travis Co	492T	MC-31	78730	5100-5399
EAGLE WING DR	Williamson Co	402V	MD-40	78613	1600-1699
EANES CIR	Austin	583Y	MF-22	78746	3100-3299
EANES CROSSING	Austin	583V	MF-22	78746	3100-3199
EANES SCHOOL RD	Travis Co	583K	ME-23	78746	300-399
	West Lake Hills	583K	ME-23	78746	200-299
EANESWOOD DR	Austin	583V	MF-22	78746	3100-3299
EARHART CV	Lago Vista	458H	WV-36	78645	3100-3199
EARHART LN	Lago Vista	458M	WV-35	78645	20400-20599
EARL CIR	Travis Co	577R	WT-23	78720	17300-17399
EARL LN	Buda	763E	ME-6	78610	100-199
EARL ST	Austin	616U	MM-19	78742	800-899
EARL BRADFORD CT	Pflugerville	437P	MN-38	78660	15900-15999
EARL GREY LN	Travis Co	467L	MP-35	78660	14700-14999
EARLY WAY DR	Austin	612Y	MD-19	78749	6300-6499
EARP WAY	Williamson Co	434M	MH-38	78729	7700-7799
EASINGWOLD LN	Austin	671G	MB-15	78739	5700-5799
EASLEY DR	Travis Co	733B	ME-9	78652	13100-13399
EASON ST	Austin	584R	MH-23	78703	1000-1199
EAST AVE	Austin	615B	MJ-21	78701	1-99
EAST AVE	Jonestown	400R	WZ-41	78645	None
EAST CT	Austin	495W	MJ-31	78759	8100-8199
EAST DR	Austin	585A	MJ-24	78705	2900-3099
EAST DR	Austin	526K	ML-29	78753	8800-9099
EAST DR	Williamson Co	257K	MN-56	78626	1-199
EAST LN	Travis Co	550D	WZ-27	78732	1500-1699
EAST ST	Buda	762H	MD-6	78610	100-499
EAST ST	Hutto	349Z	MT-46	78634	100-799
EAST ST	Leander	312Y	MD-49	78641	301-399 O
EAST ST	Village of Volente	461B	MA-36	78641	7600-7799
EAST BLUFF DR	Austin	674C	MH-15	78744	2000-2299
EAST CAMPUS DR	Austin	585K	MJ-23	78705	1900-2799
See.. Robert Dedman Dr					
EAST CREST DR	Austin	525Z	MK-28	78752	7200-7499
	Austin	526S	ML-28	78752	7500-7799
EASTDALE DR	Austin	586H	MM-24	78723	4800-4999
EASTER CV	Austin	525G	MK-30	78757	8200-8299
EASTFIELD AVE	Austin	586Q	MM-23	78721	1100-1199
EASTGATE RD	Austin	616C	MM-21	78721	6400-6599
EAST GREENWAY	Bastrop Co	712T	MY-10	78612	100-199
EASTHAM CV	Austin	614N	MG-20	78704	1800-1899
EAST HILL DR	Austin	524R	MH-29	78731	6500-6699
EAST HOVE LOOP	Austin	642T	MC-16	78749	4400-4499
EASTLEDGE DR	Austin	554L	MH-26	78731	3700-3899
EAST LESLIE CIR	Austin	616F	ML-21	78721	900-999
EASTMAN CV	Austin	463G	MF-36	78750	10100-10199
EASTON DR	Round Rock	376L	MM-44	78664	1800-2099
EASTON LN	Austin	678E	MQ-15	78617	4900-5099
EASTRIDGE TERRACE	Austin	674C	MH-15	78744	2100-2299
EAST ROCK CV	Williamson Co	407E	MN-42	78664	1000-1499
EAST SIDE DR	Austin	615J	MJ-20	78704	1300-2599
	Austin	614Z	MH-19	78704	2600-2799
EAST VIEW DR	Williamson Co	257Z	MP-55	78626	1-799
EASTVIEW DR	Williamson Co	288A	MQ-54	78626	1-599
	Williamson Co	258W	MQ-55	78626	600-699
EASTWARD LOOK	Hays Co	577U	WT-22	78720	17700-17899
EASTWEND DR	Austin	526B	ML-30	78753	9700-9899
EASTWOOD LN	Round Rock	408J	MQ-41	78664	2500-2699
EASY CV	Hutto	379R	MT-44	78634	1000-1099

D

E

STREET NAME	CITY or COUNTY	MAPSCO GRID	AUSTIN GRID	ZIP CODE	BLOCK RANGE O/E
EASY ST	Austin	703A	ME-12	78748	11700-11899
	Travis Co	703A	ME-12	78748	11500-11699
EASY ST	Hutto	379M	MT-44	78634	100-199
EASY ST	Jonestown	400V	WZ-40	78645	17900-18599
EASY ST	Travis Co	583T	ME-22	78746	1500-1699
EASYBEND DR	Travis Co	619L	MT-20	78653	16500-16899
EASY DAY CV	Austin	644N	MG-17	78745	800-899
EASY JET ST	Travis Co	530Q	MV-29	78653	None
EASY MEADOW CV	Travis Co	619L	MT-20	78653	6000-6199
EASY WIND DR	Austin	525U	MK-28	78757	7000-7299
EASYWOOD WAY	Travis Co	588S	MQ-22	78724	5400-5499
EATON LN	Austin	556Q	MM-26	78723	2000-2099
EATON LN	Hays Co	639U	WX-16	78737	100-199
EATON BROOK AVE	Travis Co	497C	MP-33	78754	1700-2099
EBBSFLEET DR	Travis Co	432C	MD-39	78613	2000-2299
EBERHART LN	Austin	644S	MG-16	78745	100-1099
EBERT AVE	Austin	586U	MM-22	78721	1100-1199
EBONY LN	Williamson Co	433E	ME-39	78613	1900-1999
EBONY ST	Austin	614D	MH-21	78704	900-999
EBONY HOLLOW CV	Travis Co	672W	MC-13	78739	3700-3799
EBONY HOLLOW PASS	Travis Co	672W	MC-13	78739	3600-3899
EBY LN	Austin	524T	MG-28	78731	4500-4799
ECHO CV	Hays Co	702X	MC-10	78610	12500-12599
ECHO LN	Austin	643V	MF-16	78745	900-1299
ECHO LN	Travis Co	491N	MA-32	78732	14000-14099
ECHO BAY CT	Williamson Co	343S	ME-46	78641	3200-3299
ECHO BLUFF	Hays Co	670N	WY-14	78737	14300-14699
ECHO BLUFF CV	Austin	497W	MN-31	78754	1500-1599
ECHO HILLS CT	Austin	404C	MH-42	78717	10000-10099
ECHO HILLS DR	Austin	404C	MH-42	78717	15400-15999
ECHO LAKE DR	Williamson Co	343S	ME-46	78641	1400-1499
ECHO POINT CV	Austin	494G	MH-33	78759	9100-9199
ECHORIDGE DR	Austin	463F	ME-36	78750	10100-10399
ECHO RIDGE LN	Cedar Park	403K	ME-41	78613	1300-1399
ECHO WOOD PL	Round Rock	375G	MK-45	78681	2500-2599
ECK CV	Travis Co	460Y	WZ-34	78734	4400-4499
ECK LN	Travis Co	490C	WZ-33	78734	3700-4199
	Travis Co	460Y	WZ-34	78734	4200-4899
ECKERT ST	Austin	586J	ML-23	78722	2900-2999
ECKHARDT ST	Taylor	352C	MZ-48	76574	1800-1899
ECLIPSE CV	Williamson Co	402U	MD-40	78613	1800-2099
ECLIPSE LN	Austin	641Z	MB-16	78749	10200-10299
ECORIO CT	Travis Co	436G	MM-39	78728	3700-3799
ECORIO DR	Travis Co	436K	ML-38	78728	15300-15799
ED ACKLIN RD	Travis Co	591N	MW-23	78653	20100-20799
ED BLUESTEIN BLVD	Austin	616G	MM-21	78721	200-2799
	Austin	586V	MM-22	78721	2800-4899
	Austin	587E	MN-24	78724	4900-5799
See.. US Hwy 183					
	Austin	557J	MN-26	78723	5800-7499
	Austin	556H	MM-27	78723	7500-7799
ED BURLESON LN	Bastrop	744G	ED-9	78602	None
EDDIE EGAN LN	Austin	702D	MD-12	78748	11400-11499
EDDIE JACKSON BLVD	Austin	464B	MG-36	78750	None
EDDIE ROBINSON RD	Bastrop Co	775U	EF-4	78662	100-299
EDDY CV	Travis Co	582A	MC-24	78735	9200-9299
EDDYSTONE ST	Williamson Co	434N	MG-38	78729	9200-9599
EDELWEISS DR	Cedar Park	402U	MD-40	78613	1500-1899
EDENBOURGH LN	Travis Co	527X	MN-28	78754	4800-5399
EDENDALE CT	Austin	555J	MJ-26	78756	4500-4599
EDENDERRY DR	Austin	404H	MH-42	78717	15700-15899
EDENS DR	Austin	614V	MH-19	78704	2700-2799
EDENVALE PATH	Travis Co	521S	MA-28	78732	12300-12399
EDENWOOD DR	Austin	643P	ME-17	78745	2600-2799
EDGEBROOK DR	Travis Co	702M	MD-11	78748	12300-12399
EDGECLIFF PATH	Georgetown	287K	MN-53	78626	2400-2599
EDGECLIFF ST	Austin	615K	MJ-20	78741	1400-1499
EDGECLIFF TERRACE	Austin	615F	MJ-21	78704	800-1099
EDGECOMB CT	Travis Co	640R	WZ-17	78737	11100-11199
EDGE CREEK DR	Austin	674Q	MH-14	78744	4500-5299
EDGECREEK PL	Round Rock	375C	MK-45	78681	3000-3199
EDGEDALE DR	Austin	556V	MM-25	78723	3000-3199
EDGEFIELD CT	Austin	524G	MH-30	78731	4000-4099
EDGEFIELD DR	Austin	524L	MH-29	78731	6700-7099
EDGEGROVE DR	Rollingwood	584N	MG-23	78746	700-899
EDGEMERE DR	Travis Co	437P	MN-38	78660	16100-16699
EDGEMONT DR	Austin	554L	MH-26	78731	3600-3999
	Austin	554G	MH-27	78731	4000-4699
EDGE MONT DR	Bastrop Co	709T	MS-10	78617	1-199
EDGEMOOR PL	Austin	642P	MC-17	78749	8200-8399
EDGE PARK CIR	Austin	674Q	MH-14	78744	7800-7999
EDGERLY CT	Travis Co	437P	MN-38	78660	16200-16299
EDGERLY LN	Travis Co	437P	MN-38	78660	900-1099
EDGEROCK DR	Austin	524D	MH-30	78731	3900-4099
EDGE ROCK DR	Bastrop Co	709T	MS-10	78617	1-199
EDGERTON ST	Travis Co	522D	MD-30	78730	4800-4899
EDGEWARE DR	Austin	614N	MG-20	78704	1900-1999
EDGEWATER CV	Lakeway	489Q	WX-32	78734	100-199
EDGEWATER DR	Travis Co	459W	WW-34	78669	1000-1499
EDGEWATER DR	Travis Co	522K	MC-29	78733	2500-3199
EDGEWOOD AVE	Austin	585G	MK-24	78722	1100-1699
EDGEWOOD CIR	Cedar Park	403F	ME-42	78613	400-499
EDGEWOOD CV	Leander	341D	MB-48	78641	300-399
EDGEWOOD DR	Georgetown	226G	MM-60	78628	30000-30099
EDGEWOOD DR	Hays Co	732B	MC-9	78610	400-499
EDGEWOOD WAY	Jonestown	430Q	WZ-38	78645	17700-18099
EDINBURCH CV	Austin	642H	MD-18	78749	6800-6999
EDINBURGH CASTLE RD	Pflugerville	408X	MQ-40	78660	18800-18999
EDISON CV	Lago Vista	458M	WV-35	78645	3000-3099
EDISON DR	Hutto	379G	MT-45	78634	100-199
EDMOND ST	Taylor	352H	MZ-48	76574	200-599
	Taylor	352D	MZ-48	76574	700-899
EDMOND ST S	Taylor	352L	MZ-47	76574	100-399
EDMONSON LN	Bastrop Co	711W	MW-10	78612	100-299
EDMUND CT	Austin	642J	MC-17	78749	8700-8799
EDMUNDSBURY DR	Austin	705E	MJ-12	78747	8800-9499
	Austin	705F	MJ-12	78747	9200-9499
EDNA RD	Jonestown	400M	WZ-41	78645	18200-18299
EDS CV	Austin	674L	MH-14	78744	7300-7399
ED SCHMIDT BLVD	Hutto	379C	MT-45	78634	1-299
	Hutto	349Y	MT-46	78634	300-1199
EDVILLE LN	Williamson Co	407U	MP-40	78664	1-99
EDWARD CV	Williamson Co	381Q	MX-44	76574	100-199
EDWARD ST	Travis Co	562F	MY-27	78621	11800-11999
EDWARDS DR	Georgetown	195T	MJ-61	78633	100-199
EDWARDS DR	Round Rock	376H	MM-45	78664	500-699
EDWARDS DR	Travis Co	460H	WZ-36	78734	15900-16299
EDWARDS LN	Bastrop Co	746Z	EH-7	78602	100-199
EDWARDS HOLLOW CV	Travis Co	702B	MC-12	78739	3200-3299
EDWARDS HOLLOW RUN	Travis Co	702B	MC-12	78739	11900-12599
EDWARDS MOUNTAIN CV	Austin	524Q	MH-29	78731	6200-6299
EDWARDS MOUNTAIN DR	Austin	524L	MH-29	78731	3800-4199
EDWARDSON CV	Austin	641M	MB-17	78749	6700-6799
EDWARDSON LN	Austin	641L	MB-17	78749	8900-9399
EDWARDS WALK DR	Cedar Park	374R	MH-44	78613	700-799
EDWIN LN	Travis Co	617J	MN-20	78742	100-499
EDWIN REINHARDT DR	Travis Co	529H	MT-30	78653	16700-16999
EFFINGHAM ST	Williamson Co	434B	MG-39	78729	13300-13499
EGANHILL DR	Austin	643P	ME-17	78745	7100-7499
EGGER AVE	Round Rock	376M	MM-44	78664	1100-2199
EGGER CT	Round Rock	376L	MM-44	78664	500-599
EGGER CV	Round Rock	376M	MM-44	78664	500-599
EGGER ST	Austin	616S	ML-19	78741	700-799
EGGLESTON ST E	Manor	529U	MT-28	78653	100-199
EGGLESTON ST W	Manor	529Q	MT-29	78653	100-399
EGRET CIR	Williamson Co	433R	MF-38	78750	12300-12399
EGRET CV	Georgetown	225F	MJ-60	78633	100-199
EHRLICH RD	Travis Co	552V	MD-25	78746	1-99
EIGER RD	Austin	612P	MC-20	78735	5500-5799
EIGHT OAKS DR	Bastrop Co	712R	MZ-11	78602	100-299
EILERS AVE	Austin	555U	MK-25	78751	4300-4899
	Austin	555R	MK-26	78751	5000-5299
EILERS RD	Travis Co	737X	MN-7	78719	13900-14799
	Travis Co	767C	MP-6	78617	14800-15399
EISENHOWER AVE	Lago Vista	458H	WV-36	78645	3200-3499
EISENHOWER CT	Georgetown	195W	MJ-61	78633	100-199
EITEL LN	Travis Co	610U	WZ-19	78736	9100-9199
E-K LN	Travis Co	527X	MN-28	78754	3500-3699
EKE CT	Bastrop Co	745Z	EF-7	78602	100-199
EKTOM DR	Austin	643C	MF-18	78745	2600-2699
ELANA CT	Austin	645C	MK-18	78741	4500-4599
ELANDER DR	Austin	493G	MF-33	78750	8300-8399
EL CAJON LN	Lago Vista	399L	WX-41	78645	8800-9099
EL CAMINO RD	Austin	466E	ML-36	78727	13000-13399
EL CAMINO RIVER RD	Bastrop Co	775A	EE-6	78602	100-199
EL CIELO	Leander	371B	MA-45	78641	1500-1599
ELDER CIR	Travis Co	552G	MD-27	78733	700-1199
ELDER PL	Round Rock	407B	MN-42	78664	2100-2199
ELDER WAY	Round Rock	407B	MN-42	78664	500-2099
ELDERBERRY	Georgetown	225D	MK-60	78633	100-199
ELDERBERRY CV	Austin	674A	MG-15	78745	600-699
ELDERBERRY CV	Georgetown	195Z	MK-61	78633	100-199
ELDERBERRY DR	Austin	674E	MG-15	78745	7500-7899
ELDERBERRY RD	Hays Co	669P	WW-14	78737	100-399
ELDERBERRY TEA CV	Travis Co	467G	MP-36	78660	900-999
EL DORADO	Lago Vista	429N	WW-38	78645	20600-20899
EL DORADO N	Lakeway	519G	WX-30	78734	200-299
EL DORADO S	Lakeway	519G	WX-30	78734	3300-3399
EL DORADO DR	Travis Co	641B	MA-18	78737	7700-8399
ELDORADO TRL	Travis Co	672S	MC-13	78748	3300-3399
	Travis Co	672S	MC-13	78739	3400-3699
ELEANOR LN	Bastrop Co	744Z	ED-7	78602	100-199
ELEANOR ST	Austin	586Q	MM-23	78721	1100-1299
ELEANOR WAY	Cedar Park	432D	MD-39	78613	2200-2399
ELECTRA	Lakeway	489X	WW-31	78734	800-999
ELECTRIC AVE	Travis Co	517V	WT-28	78669	5200-5299
ELEOS CIR	Austin	582Z	MD-22	78735	6000-6099
ELFCROFT DR	Austin	496B	ML-33	78758	11900-12099
ELFEN CV	Austin	587M	MP-23	78724	9000-9099
ELFEN WAY	Austin	587M	MP-23	78724	6000-6099
ELFLAND DR	Austin	523T	ME-28	78746	6700-6799
EL GALLO DR	Austin	611M	MB-20	78735	6100-6199
ELGIN DR	Briarcliff	457V	WT-34	78669	22200-22399
EL GRECO CV	Austin	554T	MG-25	78703	2400-2599
ELIJA ST	Austin	642R	MD-17	78745	3300-3499
ELIZABETH LN	Bastrop	744D	ED-9	78602	600-699
ELIZABETH ST E	Austin	615J	MJ-20	78704	100-299
ELIZABETH ST W	Austin	614M	MH-20	78704	100-599
	Austin	614H	MH-21	78704	600-999
	Austin	615J	MJ-20	78704	None
ELIZABETH ANNE LN	Round Rock	408J	MQ-41	78664	3200-3299
ELIZABETH JANE CT	Travis Co	492Z	MD-31	78730	4900-4999
ELK DR	Georgetown	257K	MN-56	78626	1600-1699
ELK CROSSING	Austin	587M	MP-23	78724	5700-5799
ELKHART ST	Austin	615C	MK-21	78702	100-299
ELK HERD CV	Georgetown	285P	MJ-53	78628	100-199
ELKHORN MOUNTAIN TRL					
	Williamson Co	434U	MH-37	78729	7600-8199
ELKHORN RANCH RD	Leander	372C	MD-45	78641	2400-2699
ELKINS LN	Cedar Park	402G	MD-42	78613	1500-1799
ELK PARK CIR	Austin	465S	MJ-34	78759	11500-11599
ELK PARK TRL	Austin	465S	MJ-34	78759	11500-11799
ELK PASS DR	Austin	646T	ML-16	78744	7400-7599
ELK RIDGE CV	Williamson Co	377P	MN-44	78664	2000-2099
ELKWATER CV	Travis Co	554E	MG-27	78746	4500-4599
ELLA LN	Austin	646K	ML-17	78744	7800-8299
ELLA LN	Bastrop Co	564A	EC-27	78621	100-199
ELLASON RD	Jonestown	401A	MA-42	78645	18200-18299
ELLAVIEW LN	Austin	464T	MG-34	78759	7200-7399
ELLEN ST	Taylor	352C	MZ-48	76574	1300-1399
ELLINGSON LN	Austin	555U	MK-25	78751	900-1099
ELLINGTON CIR	Austin	557U	MP-25	78724	7100-7299
ELLIOT ST	Taylor	353F	EA-48	76574	100-699
ELLIOT ST	Williamson Co	443L	EB-38	78615	100-199
ELLIOTT ST E	Austin	526K	ML-29	78753	200-299
ELLIOTT ST W	Austin	526J	ML-29	78753	100-799
ELLIOTT RANCH RD	Hays Co	701X	MA-10	78610	1500-1899
ELLIS CV	Georgetown	196K	ML-62	78633	100-199
ELLIS CV	Round Rock	407H	MP-42	78665	1100-1199
ELLIS PL	Elgin	534K	EC-29	78621	300-399
ELLIS RD	Hays Co	607W	WS-19	78620	100-499
ELLISE AVE	Austin	525P	MJ-29	78757	2100-2799
ELLON RD	Austin	647Q	MP-17	78617	2900-3099
ELM CT	Bastrop Co	776U	EH-4	78602	100-199
ELM CT	Cedar Park	403A	ME-42	78613	500-599
ELM CV	Bastrop Co	715R	EF-11	78602	100-199
ELM DR	Bastrop Co	740T	MU-7	78612	100-199
ELM DR	Burnet Co	455A	WN-36	78669	None
ELM DR	Pflugerville	438S	MQ-37	78660	100-199
ELM DR	Travis Co	460H	WZ-36	78734	16200-16399
ELM DR	Travis Co	428A	WU-39	78654	23800-23899
ELM LN	Bastrop Co	712P	MY-11	78612	100-199
ELM ST	Austin	584R	MH-23	78703	1000-1299
ELM ST	Bastrop	745B	EE-9	78602	500-1299
ELM ST	Buda	762D	MD-6	78610	100-399
ELM ST	Jonestown	400H	WZ-42	78645	10900-11299
ELM ST S	Georgetown	286H	MM-54	78626	200-1899
ELM TRL	Williamson Co	345W	MJ-46	78681	2800-3199
EL MALINO DR	Travis Co	437Q	MP-38	78660	400-699
ELM BROOK DR	Austin	496B	ML-33	78758	1400-1499
ELM CREEK CV	Travis Co	610U	WZ-19	78736	9100-9299
ELM CREEK DR	Austin	674C	MH-15	78744	6600-6999
ELM CREST	Leander	342M	MD-47	78641	700-799
ELM FOREST DR	Cedar Park	402M	MD-41	78613	1200-1399
ELM FOREST LOOP	Bastrop Co	739L	MT-8	78612	100-499
ELMFOREST RD	Austin	643Z	MF-16	78745	7200-7699
ELMGLEN DR	Austin	614J	MG-20	78704	2400-2499
ELM GROVE CIR	Travis Co	610U	WZ-19	78736	9300-9399
ELM GROVE CT	Caldwell Co	767Y	MP-4	78616	100-199
ELM GROVE DR	Bastrop Co	742R	MZ-8	78612	100-199
ELM GROVE LN	Hays Co	732N	MC-8	78610	2800-3199
ELM GROVE RD	Travis Co	796E	ML-3	78610	12800-13499
ELMHURST DR	Austin	615P	MJ-20	78741	1500-1799
ELMIRA RD	Austin	586L	MM-23	78721	1600-1899
EL MIRADOR ST	Buda	762H	MD-6	78610	300-399
ELM LEAF LN	Austin	616P	ML-20	78741	6300-6399
EL MOLINO CIR	Austin	677R	MP-14	78617	5400-5599
ELMONT DR	Austin	615Q	MK-20	78741	2100-4699
	Austin	615V	MK-19	78741	4800-5299
ELM RIDGE DR	Bastrop Co	709L	MT-11	78612	None
ELM RIDGE LN	Austin	466B	ML-36	78727	13500-13699
ELMSGROVE DR	Austin	586L	MM-23	78721	4400-4499
ELMSHADE CV	Round Rock	378X	MQ-43	78665	1300-1399
ELM VALLEY DR	Travis Co	703N	ME-11	78652	12300-12499
ELM VIEW WAY	Travis Co	703T	ME-10	78652	400-499
ELMWOOD CV	Cedar Park	402M	MD-41	78613	1000-1099
ELM WOOD DR	Bastrop Co	564Z	ED-25	78621	100-299
ELMWOOD DR	Georgetown	225Z	MK-58	78628	900-1099
ELMWOOD PL	Austin	585B	MJ-24	78705	500-699
ELMWOOD TRL	Cedar Park	403J	ME-41	78613	900-1199
EL NORTE CT	Lakeway	519C	WX-30	78734	100-199
ELOHI DR	Travis Co	554E	MG-27	78746	4400-4699
EL PAISANO LN	Travis Co	703S	ME-10	78652	600-699
EL PASO	Elgin	534S	EC-28	78621	200-299
EL PASO ST	Austin	614U	MH-19	78704	100-599
EL RENO CV	Lakeway	519C	WX-30	78734	100-199
EL REY BLVD	Travis Co	611X	MA-19	78737	8200-8599
	Travis Co	641E	MA-18	78737	8600-9499
EL RIO DR	Lakeway	519C	WX-30	78734	100-399
ELROY RD	Travis Co	677S	MN-13	78617	6300-7099
	Travis Co	707C	MP-12	78617	7100-7799
	Travis Co	708E	MQ-12	78617	7700-8899
	Travis Co	707Z	MP-10	78617	8900-9099
EL SALIDO PKWY	Cedar Park	402Z	MD-40	78613	1500-2299
	Cedar Park	432H	MD-39	78613	2300-2499
	Cedar Park	433E	ME-39	78613	3400-3499
	Williamson Co	432H	MD-39	78613	2500-3099
	Williamson Co	433E	ME-39	78613	3100-3399
	Williamson Co	433P	ME-38	78750	10800-11799
EL SECRETO ST	Buda	762M	MD-5	78610	400-499
EL SOCORRO LN	Travis Co	521N	MA-29	78732	200-399
EL SOL DR	Travis Co	402Y	MD-40	78613	None
	Williamson Co	402Y	MD-40	78613	2300-2399
ELTON LN	Austin	584G	MH-24	78703	1300-1599
	Austin	584C	MH-24	78703	1700-2199
EL TORO CV	Travis Co	554E	MG-27	78746	3200-3299
ELVAS WAY	Austin	496B	ML-33	78758	1500-1699
EL VIEJO CAMINO	Travis Co	522W	MC-28	78733	700-999
ELWOOD RD	Austin	555V	MK-25	78723	4500-4699
ELY CT	Travis Co	402P	MC-41	78613	2800-2899
ELYSIAN FIELDS	Austin	466K	ML-35	78727	1900-2199
ELYSIAN FIELDS CV	Austin	466K	ML-35	78727	13100-13299
EMBASSY DR	Austin	585T	MJ-22	78702	800-899
EMBER GLEN DR	Austin	433W	ME-37	78726	10200-10499
EMBERWOOD DR	Austin	525G	MK-30	78757	8100-8299
EMBLEM CT	Pflugerville	437H	MP-39	78660	1600-1699
EMBLEM DR	Pflugerville	437H	MP-39	78660	1400-1599
EMERALD RD	Lago Vista	458P	WU-35	78645	1300-1799
EMERALD ST	Austin	643R	MF-17	78745	6400-6599
EMERALD FALLS DR	Travis Co	551N	MA-26	78738	11500-11899
EMERALD FOREST CIR	Austin	644J	MG-17	78745	4900-6299
EMERALD FOREST CV	Austin	644E	MG-18	78745	1100-1199
EMERALD FOREST DR	Austin	643V	MF-16	78745	6300-6799
	Austin	644N	MG-17	78745	None
EMERALD HILL DR	Austin	494R	MH-32	78759	8400-8699
EMERALD HILL DR	Williamson Co	345X	MJ-46	78681	2700-3999
EMERALD ISLE DR	Leander	342U	MD-46	78641	1800-2299
EMERALD MEADOW DR	Austin	644E	MG-18	78745	5200-5299
EMERALD OAKS DR	Austin	702B	MC-12	78739	12000-12599
EMERALD RIDGE DR	Travis Co	521S	MA-28	78732	100-699
EMERALD RIDGE DR	Travis Co	704F	MG-12	78747	None
EMERALD VIEW	Lago Vista	459M	WX-35	78645	4600-4799
EMERALD WOOD DR	Austin	644E	MG-18	78745	600-1099
EMERSON CV	Lago Vista	458H	WV-36	78645	3300-3399
EMERY OAKS RD	Austin	466S	ML-34	78758	12300-12499
E M FRANKLIN AVE	Austin	586K	ML-23	78721	1100-1899
	Austin	586F	ML-24	78723	1900-2299
EMILE ST	Bastrop	745K	EE-8	78602	800-1299
	Bastrop	745L	EF-8	78602	1400-1699
EMILIE LN	Austin	555N	MJ-26	78703	1700-1799
EMILY DICKENSON DR	Travis Co	467L	MP-35	78660	800-899
EMMA DR	Williamson Co	342Z	MD-46	78641	100-199
EMMA LOOP	Hays Co	670T	WY-13	78610	100-799
EMMA LEE AVE	Austin	435W	MJ-37	78727	13000-13199
EMMALEIGH'S LN	Travis Co	437S	MN-37	78660	15500-15599
EMMA LONG ST	Austin	586A	ML-24	78723	1900-2199
EMMA LYNN LN	Hutto	379G	MT-45	78634	100-199
EMMANUEL ST	Round Rock	376T	ML-43	78681	800-1099
EMMA ROSE TRL	Leander	342F	MC-48	78641	400-699
EMMETT PKWY	Travis Co	436R	MM-38	78728	2100-2599
EMMITT RUN	Austin	616C	MM-21	78721	1100-1199
EMORY LN	Austin	556R	MM-26	78723	6300-6399
EMORY FARMS AVE	Hutto	349X	MS-46	78634	1000-4099
EMORY FIELDS CV	Hutto	349X	MS-46	78634	1000-1099
EMORY FIELDS DR	Hutto	349T	MS-46	78634	100-199
EMORY OAK LN	Travis Co	580F	WY-24	78738	12300-12399
EMORY PEAK TRL	Georgetown	195S	MJ-61	78633	100-199
EMPEDRADO LN	Bastrop Co	680G	MV-15	78612	100-499
	Bastrop Co	650Z	MV-16	78612	None
	Travis Co	650Z	MV-16	78612	500-599
EMPEROR CT	Pflugerville	437F	MN-39	78664	1500-1599

STREET NAME	CITY or COUNTY	MAPSCO GRID	AUSTIN GRID	ZIP CODE	BLOCK RANGE O/E
EMPIRE CT	Hays Co	639U	WX-16	78737	100-199
EMPLOYEE AVE	Austin	647J	MN-17	78719	2600-3099
EMPRESS BLVD	Austin	673B	ME-15	78745	8300-8599
EMS DR	Dripping Springs	636Y	WR-16	78620	100-199
EMZY TAYLOR DR	Georgetown	285T	MJ-52	78628	100-199
ENCANTO DR	Leander	312W	MC-49	78641	700-899
ENCANTO TRL	Austin	674G	MH-15	78744	7000-7199
ENCHANTED CV	Bastrop Co	711F	MW-12	78612	100-199
ENCHANTED CV	Hays Co	669N	WW-14	78737	100-199
ENCHANTED DR	Georgetown	226E	ML-60	78633	100-199
ENCHANTED LN	Austin	644A	MG-18	78745	4700-4999
ENCHANTED FOREST DR	Austin	465L	MK-35	78727	12400-12599
ENCHANTED ROCK CV	Austin	433X	ME-37	78726	10900-10999
ENCHANTED ROCK CV	Round Rock	345K	MJ-47	78681	4000-4099
ENCHANTED ROCK DR	Cedar Park	373E	ME-45	78613	1800-1899
ENCHANTED ROCK TRL	Georgetown	225U	MK-58	78633	700-799
ENCINAL CV	Austin	644Z	MH-16	78744	5700-5899
ENCINAS ROJAS	Travis Co	553L	MF-26	78746	5400-5499
ENCINITA DR	Leander	312W	MC-49	78641	700-899
ENCINITAS LN	Austin	642F	MC-18	78749	5200-5299
ENCINO CIR	Austin	586J	ML-23	78723	2000-2099
ENCINO DR	Leander	342E	MC-48	78641	1400-1799
ENCINO DR	Travis Co	703X	ME-10	78652	12600-12799
ENCINO VERDE	Travis Co	523W	ME-28	78730	3100-3199
ENCLAVE CV	Austin	524T	MG-28	78731	4400-4499
ENCLAVE TRL	Georgetown	256E	ML-57	78628	100-199
ENCLAVE WAY	Hutto	379L	MT-44	78634	1100-1199
ENCLAVE MESA CIR	Austin	524C	MH-30	78731	4000-4099
ENCLAVE VISTA CV	Austin	492L	MD-32	78730	10800-10899
ENDCLIFFE DR	Austin	494Y	MH-31	78731	4200-4399
ENDEAVOR CIR	Austin	462K	MC-35	78726	8100-8299
ENDER CV	Austin	466L	MM-35	78727	1700-1799
ENDICOTT TRL	Travis Co	436U	MM-37	78728	14800-14899
ENDLESS SHORE DR	Travis Co	439K	MS-38	78660	3400-3499
END OF THE TRL	Travis Co	460G	WZ-36	78734	6100-6199
ENERGY DR	Austin	495R	MK-32	78758	2000-2299
ENFIELD RD	Austin	584B	MG-24	78703	1100-3799
ENGADINA PASS	Williamson Co	346G	MM-48	78665	4100-4299
ENGELKE RD	Hays Co	795P	MJ-2	78610	100-1099
ENGELMANN LN	Travis Co	440U	MV-37	78653	19000-20699
	Travis Co	410Z	MV-40	78615	20700-21199
ENGELWOOD DR	Austin	644F	MG-18	78745	4600-4799
ENGLISH AVE	Travis Co	619E	MS-21	78724	5300-5599
ENGLISH GLADE DR	Austin	587R	MP-23	78724	5100-5399
ENGLISH OAK DR	Austin	703D	MF-13	78748	10200-10399
ENGLISH RIVER LOOP	Williamson Co	343S	ME-46	78641	15200-15399
ENGLISH ROSE DR	Travis Co	467L	MP-35	78660	14700-14799
ENID DR	Travis Co	460V	WZ-34	78734	15400-15699
ENNIS TRL	Austin	375S	MJ-43	78717	16500-17399
ENSIGN-BICKFORD RD	Bastrop Co	738R	MR-8	78617	100-199
ENTERPRISE CT	Austin	556L	MM-26	78723	6800-6999
ENTERPRISE DR	Round Rock	376L	MM-44	78664	2000-2099
ENTRADA CV	Travis Co	493U	MF-31	78730	7900-7999
ENVOY PL	Travis Co	457W	WS-34	78669	1700-1899
EPHRAIM RD	Williamson Co	405N	MJ-41	78717	8100-8699
EPIC CT	Austin	462H	MD-36	78726	9400-9499
EPPERSON TRL	Travis Co	491Q	MB-32	78732	3600-3899
EPPING LN	Austin	643S	ME-16	78745	7800-8099
EPPING FOREST CV	Travis Co	493N	ME-32	78730	6500-6599
EQUESTRIAN CV	Austin	466F	ML-36	78727	13400-13499
EQUESTRIAN TRL	Austin	466F	ML-36	78727	2100-2499
ERIC CIR	Austin	645S	MJ-16	78744	4500-4599
ERICA KAITLIN LN	Cedar Park	402F	MD-42	78613	None
ERICA LEIGH CT	Austin	433W	ME-37	78726	10500-10599
ERICANNA LN	Leander	343L	MF-47	78641	2300-2599
ERIKA CV	Round Rock	407R	MP-41	78664	2000-2099
ERIN CIR	Leander	342Y	MD-46	78641	600-699
ERIN CV	Hutto	379G	MT-45	78634	100-199
ERIN LN	Austin	555J	MJ-26	78756	4500-4599
ERNEST LN	Travis Co	487X	WS-31	78669	21700-21999
ERNEST ROBLES WAY	Sunset Valley	613X	ME-19	78745	4100-4999
EROL DR	Briarcliff	457R	WT-35	78669	200-699
ERUZIONE DR	Austin	702H	MD-12	78748	12000-12299
ESCABOSA DR	Austin	673F	ME-15	78745	8600-8899
ESCALA DR	Travis Co	582T	MC-22	78735	7500-7999
ESCALERA PKWY	Georgetown	314J	MG-50	78628	400-1099
	Williamson Co	314J	MG-50	78628	100-399
ESCARPMENT BLVD	Austin	612W	MC-19	78749	6900-7399
	Austin	642A	MC-18	78749	7400-8599
	Austin	641M	MB-17	78749	8600-10699
	Austin	671F	MA-15	78739	10700-11599
	Austin	671K	MA-14	78739	11700-12199
ESCAVERA CV	Lakeway	519W	WW-28	78738	100-199
ESCONDIDO CV	Austin	554U	MH-25	78703	2600-2699
ESCONDIDO DR	Bastrop Co	739E	MS-9	78617	100-399
ESCONDIDO DR	Leander	312W	MC-49	78641	700-899
ESCONDIDO DR	Williamson Co	195R	ML-62	78633	None
ESCUELITA DR	Austin	675A	MJ-15	78744	5200-5499
ESKEW DR	Austin	642R	MD-17	78749	3500-4499
ESKEW LN N	Bastrop Co	711K	MW-11	78612	100-199
ESKEW LN S	Bastrop Co	711N	MW-11	78612	100-199
ESKEW ST	Bastrop	745J	EE-8	78602	100-299
	Bastrop	745N	EE-8	78602	300-499
ESPANOLA TRL	Travis Co	641B	MA-18	78737	7800-8299
ESPARADA DR E	Williamson Co	226X	ML-58	78628	200-299
ESPARADA DR W	Williamson Co	256A	ML-57	78628	100-599
	Williamson Co	255D	MK-57	78628	600-899
ESPER LN	Travis Co	619S	MS-19	78725	4500-4699
ESPERANZA DR	Travis Co	672N	MC-14	78739	11300-11599
ESPERANZA CROSSING	Austin	495C	MK-33	78758	2900-3499
ESPINA DR	Austin	670H	WZ-15	78739	7400-7999
ESPINO CV	Austin	674G	MH-15	78744	1900-1999
ESPINOSA DR	Austin	646G	MM-18	78744	1-99
ESPLANADE CIR	Austin	466P	ML-35	78727	1900-1999
ESPLANADE ST	Austin	466P	ML-35	78727	12500-13099
ESPRESSO DR	Williamson Co	436F	ML-39	78728	15600-15699
ESQUEL CV	Austin	641Z	MB-16	78739	5500-5599
ESQUIRE ARCES LN	Travis Co	588N	MQ-23	78724	None
ESSEX CV	Travis Co	437K	MN-38	78660	16300-16399
ESSEX LN	Georgetown	195R	MK-62	78633	100-199
ESSEX RIDGE LOOP	Travis Co	704F	MG-12	78747	None
ESTANA LN	Austin	671F	MA-15	78739	6500-6699
ESTANCIA LN	Austin	642W	MC-16	78739	10000-10099
ESTANCIA WAY	Leander	312W	MC-49	78641	700-899
ESTANCIA WAY	Williamson Co	284M	MH-53	78628	100-199
ESTATE CIR	Hays Co	670K	WY-14	78737	13300-13399
ESTATE CV	Williamson Co	409A	MS-42	78634	100-199
ESTATE DR	Williamson Co	409A	MS-42	78634	200-1099
ESTATE ROW	Bastrop Co	711B	MW-12	78612	100-299
ESTATES CV	Austin	644N	MG-17	78745	6100-6199
ESTATES OF BRUSHY CREEK DR	Williamson Co	379L	MT-44	78634	500-699
ESTEFANIA LN	Williamson Co	348N	MQ-47	78665	2600-2699
ESTENCIA REY DR	Austin	404D	MH-42	78717	15800-15999
ESTES AVE	Austin	586U	MM-22	78721	1000-1199
ESTES DR	Hays Co	669B	WW-15	78737	100-399
ESTES PARK	Taylor	322M	MZ-50	76574	500-999
ESTHER DR	Austin	555D	MK-27	78752	6700-6899
ESTRADA CT	Travis Co	491V	MB-31	78732	12100-12199
ESTRELLA CROSSING	Georgetown	256E	ML-57	78628	100-299
ESTRELLAS DR	Austin	646D	MM-18	78742	1400-1599
ETHAN DR	Bastrop Co	592N	MY-23	78621	100-199
ETHEL ST	Austin	614C	MH-21	78704	700-999
ETHEREDGE DR	Travis Co	618Z	MR-19	78725	3000-3499
ETHRIDGE AVE	Austin	584D	MH-24	78703	1400-1699
ETNA DR	Travis Co	550R	WZ-26	78733	2900-2999
ETON DR	Burnet Co	396S	WQ-40	78669	None
ETON LN	Austin	465Q	MK-35	78727	3700-4099
ETTA LN	Travis Co	673X	ME-13	78748	10500-10699
ETTA PL	Austin	496X	ML-31	78753	200-299
ETTA JAMES CV	Travis Co	402P	MC-41	78613	2900-2999
EUBANK DR	Austin	496P	ML-32	78758	11300-11899
EUBANK ST	Georgetown	286R	MM-53	78626	1700-1999
EUCLID AVE	Austin	614R	MH-20	78704	2200-2699
EUDORA CV	Travis Co	675W	MJ-13	78747	6500-6599
EUDORA LN	Travis Co	675W	MJ-13	78747	7900-7999
EUGENE LN	Buda	763E	ME-6	78610	100-199
EULALAH LN	Hays Co	732S	MC-7	78610	100-199
EUNEVA ST	Austin	586S	ML-22	78702	900-999
EUREKA DR	Austin	644N	MG-17	78745	5800-6099
EUROPA LN	Austin	465G	MK-36	78727	12600-12799
EVA DR	Austin	615E	MJ-21	78704	1200-1299
EVA ST	Austin	614M	MH-20	78704	1400-1999
	Austin	614R	MH-20	78704	2100-2199
EVA ST	Austin	647Q	MP-17	78617	3100-3199
EVADEAN CIR	Austin	673C	MF-15	78745	8000-8199
EVALINE LN	Austin	643S	ME-16	78745	7700-8099
EVANGELINE TRL	Austin	434Z	MH-37	78727	6300-6499
EVANS AVE	Austin	555Q	MK-26	78751	4500-4899
	Austin	555M	MK-26	78751	5000-5599
EVANS DR	Williamson Co	405B	MJ-42	78681	7000-7099
EVANS RD	Williamson Co	255Z	MK-55	78628	300-399
EVANS ST	Hutto	379D	MT-45	78634	100-299
EVANS ST E	Leander	312Y	MD-49	78641	100-299
EVANS OAKS RD	Travis Co	310W	WY-49	78641	14600-14999
EVANSTON LN	Austin	643N	ME-17	78745	3100-3299
EVELYN RD	Mustang Ridge	766K	ML-5	78610	8000-9599
	Travis Co	735Z	MK-7	78747	6100-6599
	Travis Co	736W	ML-7	78610	6600-6999
	Travis Co	766A	ML-6	78747	7800-7899
	Travis Co	766R	MM-5	78610	None
EVELYN RD W	Creedmoor	735T	MJ-7	78747	9000-9499
EVENING GROSSBEAK DR	Pflugerville	437V	MP-37	78660	300-599
EVENING MIST LN	Travis Co	467M	MP-35	78660	14800-14999
EVENING PRIMROSE PATH	Austin	464A	MG-36	78750	9000-9099
	Austin	463D	MF-36	78750	9100-9199
EVENING SHADOWS DR	Austin	646D	MM-18	78742	9300-9399
EVENINGSIDE WAY	Bee Cave	549R	WX-26	78738	13900-14099
EVENING SKY CIR	Austin	611M	MB-20	78735	7400-7699
EVENINGSTAR DR	Travis Co	672S	MC-13	78739	11400-11499
EVENTIDE LN	Austin	672X	MC-13	78748	11700-11799
	Travis Co	672X	MC-13	78748	11500-11699
EVEREST CT	Georgetown	195Z	MK-61	78633	100-199
EVEREST LN	Austin	465Q	MK-35	78727	4100-4699
EVERGLADE DR	Austin	644A	MG-18	78745	4700-4899
EVERGREEN AVE	Austin	614L	MH-20	78704	1600-1899
EVERGREEN CIR	Williamson Co	257J	MN-56	78626	100-299
EVERGREEN CT	Austin	524Z	MH-28	78731	5100-5199
EVERGREEN CV	Hays Co	669V	WX-13	78737	14400-14499
EVERGREEN DR	Jonestown	401A	MA-42	78645	11700-11899
EVERGREEN DR	Williamson Co	378K	MQ-44	78664	1-99
EVERGREEN RD	Williamson Co	224E	MG-60	78633	100-199
EVERGREEN WAY	Hays Co	670N	WY-14	78737	13300-13399
	Hays Co	669R	WX-14	78737	13400-13799
EVIDENCE CV	Travis Co	517L	WT-29	78669	4900-5299
EVOLUTIONS PATH	Lakeway	519V	WX-28	78734	100-399
EWA CT	Bastrop Co	746S	EG-7	78602	100-199
EWING CIR	Rollingwood	583V	MF-22	78746	1000-1099
EWING DR	Rollingwood	583V	MF-22	78746	200-299
EXCHANGE BLVD	Hutto	349Y	MT-46	78634	100-199
EXCHANGE DR	Austin	527W	MN-28	78754	8000-8099
	Austin	556D	MM-27	78754	8100-8199
	Austin	526Z	MM-28	78754	8200-8299
EXCURSION FALLS WAY	Jonestown	429R	WX-38	78645	18900-19099
	Jonestown	430N	WY-38	78645	19100-19199
EXECUTIVE CENTER DR	Austin	525A	MJ-30	78731	3400-3799
EXETER DR	Austin	556U	MM-25	78723	5500-5799
EXETER RD	Burnet Co	426A	WQ-39	78669	401-999 O
	Burnet Co	396W	WQ-40	78669	None
EXMOOR DR	Austin	525G	MK-30	78757	8000-8299
EXPEDITION TRL	Jonestown	430S	WY-37	78645	18600-18799
EXPLORER	Lakeway	489U	WX-31	78734	200-799
EXPLORER CV	Lakeway	489U	WX-31	78734	100-199
EXPOSITION BLVD	Austin	584F	MG-24	78703	700-2299
	Austin	554U	MH-25	78703	2300-3499
EXTON CV	Travis Co	552G	MD-27	78733	1100-1199
EYERLEY RD	Travis Co	590Q	MV-23	78653	19100-19799
EZRA CT	Cedar Park	373R	MF-44	78613	2200-2299

F

STREET NAME	CITY or COUNTY	MAPSCO GRID	AUSTIN GRID	ZIP CODE	BLOCK RANGE O/E
FABER DR	Pflugerville	407U	MP-40	78660	1200-1299
	Pflugerville	407U	MP-40	78660	1400-1499
FABER VALLEY CV	Austin	497W	MN-31	78754	11300-11399
FABION DR	Austin	464T	MG-34	78759	7200-7399
FAGERQUIST RD	Bastrop Co	709N	MS-11	78617	17000-17099
	Travis Co	708K	MQ-11	78617	14200-15999
	Travis Co	709N	MS-11	78617	16000-16999
FAINWOOD LN	Austin	641M	MB-17	78749	9100-9199
FAIR LN	Jonestown	400M	WZ-41	78645	18200-18299
FAIRBANKS DR	Austin	556B	ML-27	78752	1200-1399
FAIRBEND LN	Travis Co	557M	MP-26	78724	None
FAIRBLOOM DR	Travis Co	557R	MP-26	78724	None
FAIRBRIDGE DR	Travis Co	557R	MP-26	78724	None
	Travis Co	558J	MQ-26	78724	None
FAIRCHILD DR	Austin	703B	ME-12	78748	700-799
FAIRCREST DR	Austin	467X	MN-34	78753	1100-1299
FAIRCREST DR	Buda	763A	ME-6	78610	400-899
FAIRCROFT DR	Travis Co	558J	MQ-26	78724	None
FAIRFAX RIDGE PL	Travis Co	550Q	WZ-26	78733	12400-12499
FAIRFAX WALK	Austin	585B	MJ-24	78705	3200-3299
FAIRFIELD CT	Georgetown	225V	MK-58	78628	100-199
FAIRFIELD DR	Austin	526E	ML-30	78758	800-1099
	Austin	525H	MK-30	78758	1100-1499
	Austin	525G	MK-30	78757	1500-1599
FAIRFIELD LN	Austin	555Q	MK-26	78751	600-699
FAIRFIELD LOOP	Leander	342V	MD-46	78641	300-499
FAIRGROUND ST	Taylor	352C	MZ-48	76574	1100-1499
FAIRHILL CV	Cedar Park	372J	MC-44	78613	2300-2399
FAIRHILL DR	Austin	643H	MF-18	78745	5300-5499
FAIRLANE DR	Austin	524V	MH-28	78757	5700-5899
	Austin	525S	MJ-28	78757	5900-5999
FAIRLANE DR	Round Rock	406M	MM-41	78664	100-499
FAIRLAWN CV	Williamson Co	407E	MN-42	78664	1000-1299
FAIRLAWN DR	Williamson Co	343X	ME-46	78641	1300-1399
FAIRLAWN LN	Austin	615N	MJ-20	78704	1800-1999
FAIRMEADOW DR	Williamson Co	347A	MN-48	78665	4100-4299
FAIRMONT CIR	Austin	643H	MF-18	78745	5300-5499
FAIRMONT AVE	Austin	615N	MJ-20	78704	700-1299
FAIRMOUNT DR	Georgetown	225Z	MK-58	78628	600-899
FAIR OAKS DR	Austin	643P	MF-18	78745	1600-2399
FAIR OAKS DR	Bastrop Co	742B	MY-9	78612	100-199
FAIR OAKS ST	Williamson Co	343C	MF-48	78641	1-99
FAIRPLAY CT	Austin	586L	MM-23	78721	1600-1699
FAIR VALLEY TRL	Austin	612Y	MD-19	78749	6200-6599
FAIRVIEW CV	Williamson Co	347U	MP-46	78665	700-799
FAIRVIEW DR	Austin	524Z	MH-28	78731	5100-5199
FAIRVIEW DR	Round Rock	347V	MP-46	78665	2700-2799
	Williamson Co	347U	MP-46	78665	1-99
FAIRVIEW RD	Williamson Co	255V	MK-55	78628	700-899
FAIRWAY CIR	Point Venture	489J	WW-32	78645	200-299
FAIRWAY CV	Travis Co	521C	MB-30	78732	12200-12399
FAIRWAY LN	Georgetown	226D	MM-60	78628	700-899
FAIRWAY PATH	Williamson Co	346G	MM-48	78665	4300-4399
FAIRWAY ST	Austin	616W	ML-19	78741	5900-6299
FAIRWAY GREEN CV	Round Rock	406H	MM-42	78664	800-999
FAIRWAY HILL DR	Austin	434W	MG-37	78750	8800-9099
FAIRWEATHER WAY	Cedar Park	372P	MC-44	78613	1700-1899
FAIRWIND DR	Bee Cave	549R	WX-26	78738	14000-14199
FAIRWOOD	Georgetown	226G	MM-60	78628	100-199
FAIRWOOD RD	Austin	555V	MK-25	78723	1200-1499
FALCATA CV	Austin	493V	MF-31	78750	6800-6899
FALCON	Lago Vista	429S	WW-37	78645	20600-20799
FALCON CV	Austin	644E	MG-18	78745	1300-1399
FALCON CV	Georgetown	225D	MK-60	78633	100-199
FALCON DR	Round Rock	375V	MK-43	78681	2200-2599
FALCON DR	Travis Co	520A	WY-30	78734	15100-15299
FALCON LN	Lago Vista	458J	WU-35	78645	21500-21999
FALCON LN	Williamson Co	282E	MC-54	78641	100-699
FALCON ST	Georgetown	225D	MK-60	78633	100-199
FALCONERS WAY	Travis Co	409X	MS-40	78660	3200-3399
FALCON FLIGHT CV	Georgetown	226P	ML-59	78628	100-199
FALCON HEAD BLVD	Bee Cave	549H	WX-27	78738	None
FALCON HILL DR	Austin	643L	MF-17	78745	2100-2399
FALCON LEDGE DR	Travis Co	582D	MD-24	78746	1100-1699
FALCON OAKS DR	Williamson Co	342J	MC-47	78641	1100-1799
	Williamson Co	341R	MB-47	78641	1800-2199
FALCON POINTE BLVD	Pflugerville	439J	MS-38	78660	17900-18199
	Pflugerville	438H	MR-39	78660	18600-18999
	Pflugerville	439E	MS-39	78660	19000-19099
FALCON RIDGE DR	Travis Co	551D	MB-27	78733	10000-10299
FALCON TRAIL CT	Travis Co	529H	MT-30	78653	11600-11699
FALDO CV	Round Rock	408B	MQ-42	78664	2200-2299
FALDO LN	Williamson Co	408C	MR-42	78664	2100-2199
FALKIRK DR	Round Rock	376A	ML-45	78681	2200-2299
FALL TRL	Austin	554K	MG-26	78731	3500-3599
	Austin	554K	MG-26	78731	3600-3699
FALLBROOK CT	Lakeway	519G	WX-30	78734	100-199
FALL CREEK DR	Austin	496R	MM-32	78753	900-1099
FALL CREEK DR	Cedar Park	402R	MD-41	78613	1500-1899
FALL CREEK DR	Leander	342R	MD-47	78641	600-2099
	Leander	343S	ME-46	78641	None
FALL CREEK LOOP	Cedar Park	402R	MD-41	78613	1200-1499
FALL CREEK RD	Blanco Co	455N	WN-35	78620	3400-6099
	Travis Co	455V	WP-34	78669	2300-3399
FALL CREEK ESTATES DR	Travis Co	456T	WQ-34	78669	2700-3299
FALLENASH DR	Travis Co	618M	MR-20	78725	4600-4799
FALLEN LEAF LN	Round Rock	407D	MP-42	78665	1700-1799
FALLEN OAKS DR	Cedar Park	374U	MH-43	78613	500-699
FALLEN TIMBER DR	Travis Co	491E	MA-33	78734	14300-14499
FALLEN TOWER LN	Austin	497A	MN-33	78753	12400-12599
FALLING BROOK CT	Williamson Co	346M	MM-47	78665	4000-4099
FALLINGBROOK CV	Travis Co	554J	MG-26	78746	4400-4499
FALLING LEAVES CT	Cedar Park	374U	MH-43	78613	600-699
FALLING OAKS CV	Village of the Hills	519K	WW-29	78738	1-99
FALLING OAKS TRL	Village of the Hills	519K	WW-29	78738	1-99
FALLING STONE LN	Travis Co	467M	MP-35	78660	14800-14999
FALLING TREE CV	Austin	464Z	MH-34	78759	10700-10799
FALL MEADOW LN	Austin	705A	MJ-12	78747	8400-8599
FALLON CV	Austin	404L	MH-41	78717	9800-9899
FALLS CIR	Georgetown	195Y	MK-61	78633	100-199
FALLSPRINGS WAY	Travis Co	530A	MU-30	78653	13700-13799
FALLWELL LN	Austin	647R	MP-17	78617	3000-3299
	Austin	647R	MP-17	78617	11600-12099
	Austin	648K	MQ-17	78617	12100-14399
FALMER CT	Travis Co	432C	MD-39	78613	2400-2499
FALMOUTH DR	Austin	525G	MK-30	78757	8000-8199
FALSTAFF LN	Travis Co	489M	WX-32	78734	1600-1699
FALSTERBO DR	Pflugerville	439B	MS-39	78660	3000-3099
FAMILY CIR	Williamson Co	318H	MR-51	78634	1-699
FANCY GAP LN	Austin	643X	ME-16	78745	2200-2299
FANDANGO	Leander	371F	MA-45	78641	3600-3699
FANECA DR	Austin	641W	MA-16	78739	11200-11299
FANNIN ST E	Round Rock	376Y	MM-43	78664	100-499
FANNIN FALLS PL	Austin	612M	MD-20	78735	4700-4799
FANNIN RIDGE LN	Travis Co	704F	MG-12	78747	None
FANTAIL LOOP	Lakeway	489Y	WX-31	78734	300-499
FAREAST DR	Austin	587G	MP-24	78724	6200-6499
FAR GALLANT DR	Austin	553L	MF-26	78746	1800-2499
FARGO TERRACE	Travis Co	409W	MS-40	78660	20000-20099

STREET NAME	CITY or COUNTY	MAPSCO GRID	AUSTIN GRID	ZIP CODE	BLOCK RANGE O/E
FARHILLS DR	Austin	524G	MH-30	78731	4100-4399
FARLEIGH LN	Travis Co	432G	MD-39	78613	2500-2699
FARLEY DR	Austin	496U	MM-31	78753	100-799
FARLEY ST	Hutto	349Z	MT-46	78634	100-499
FARLEY TRL	Rollingwood	584T	MG-22	78746	300-499
FARM ST	Bastrop	745F	EE-9	78602	100-1799
FARM DALE CT	Williamson Co	197V	MP-61	78626	100-199
FARMDALE CV	Austin	641M	MB-17	78749	8700-8799
FARMDALE LN	Austin	641M	MB-17	78749	6300-6599
FARMERS CIR	Round Rock	406Z	MM-40	78728	100-199
FARMERS DR	Austin	615S	MJ-19	78704	2000-2099
FARMHAVEN RD	Austin	528K	MQ-29	78754	11400-11799
FARM HILL DR	Georgetown	195P	MJ-62	78633	100-699
FARMINGTON CT	Austin	611Q	MB-20	78736	8200-8399
FARM POND LN	Travis Co	409T	MS-40	78660	19900-20699
FARNISH CV	Austin	497J	MN-32	78753	12200-12399
FARNSWOOD CIR	Austin	614E	MG-21	78704	2100-2399
FARNSWOOD DR	Round Rock	376L	MM-44	78664	1800-2099
FARO DR	Austin	615V	MK-19	78741	1500-2299
FARRAGRET CV	Lago Vista	458M	WV-35	78645	2400-2499
FARRELL PL	Austin	642N	MC-17	78749	8800-8899
FARRELL GLEN DR	Austin	557T	MN-25	78724	6300-6599
FARRINGTON CT	Travis Co	432G	MD-39	78613	2300-2399
FARRINGTON LN	Williamson Co	408D	MR-42	78634	100-199
FARRIOR DR	Austin	641W	MA-16	78739	11100-11299
FARRIS DR	Lakeway	519R	WX-29	78734	800-1399
	Travis Co	519R	WX-29	78734	1400-1499
FARRIS RANCH RD	Williamson Co	192P	MC-62	78633	100-799
FAR VELA LN	Lakeway	519V	WX-28	78734	100-299
FARVIEW CIR	Williamson Co	281Y	MB-52	78641	1100-1399
FAR VIEW CV	Travis Co	522G	MD-30	78730	3400-3599
FAR VIEW DR	Travis Co	522F	MC-30	78730	3300-3899
FAR WEST BLVD	Austin	525J	MJ-29	78731	3300-3499
	Austin	524H	MH-30	78731	3500-4799
FASHER CV	Williamson Co	405B	MJ-42	78681	16700-16799
FAST FILLY AVE	Pflugerville	409J	MS-41	78660	1700-1999
FAST FOX TRL	Travis Co	553M	MF-26	78746	4800-5099
FAST HORSE DR	Austin	465S	MJ-34	78759	11500-11799
FATHOM CIR	Austin	464B	MG-36	78750	8300-8699
FAUBION DR	Williamson Co	314Y	MH-49	78628	100-299
	Williamson Co	344C	MH-48	78628	None
FAUBION TRL	Travis Co	310S	WY-49	78641	14500-15199
	Travis Co	309V	WX-49	78641	15200-15399
FAUNTLEROY TRL	Austin	496T	ML-31	78758	1000-1199
FAUSTINO CV	Williamson Co	343N	ME-47	78641	1400-1499
FAVERO CV	Round Rock	377V	MP-43	78665	2900-2999
FAWN CIR	Lago Vista	429F	WW-39	78645	20500-20799
FAWN CV	Williamson Co	375L	MK-44	78681	1700-1799
FAWN DR	Austin	615T	MJ-19	78741	1700-1799
FAWN DR	Bastrop Co	709L	MT-11	78612	None
FAWN DR	Travis Co	309K	WW-50	78641	24300-25799
FAWN LN	Williamson Co	256W	ML-55	78628	300-399
FAWN TRL	Austin	553D	MF-27	78746	3400-3599
FAWN CREEK PATH	Austin	553D	MF-27	78746	3500-3699
FAWNFIELD DR	Cedar Park	372M	MD-44	78613	200-499
FAWN GLEN	Williamson Co	284D	MH-54	78628	100-199
FAWNHOLLOW CV	Austin	493M	MF-32	78750	7600-7699
FAWN MEADOW DR	Hays Co	668N	WU-14	78620	100-499
FAWN PARK	Lago Vista	458N	WU-35	78645	1200-1399
FAWN RIDGE	Williamson Co	314Z	MH-49	78628	300-399
	Williamson Co	315W	MJ-49	78628	None
FAWNRIDGE CIR	Travis Co	459V	WX-34	78645	17600-17799
FAWN RIDGE DR	Lago Vista	429F	WW-39	78645	20800-21099
FAWNRIDGE DR E	Austin	526F	ML-30	78753	100-599
FAWNRIDGE DR N	Williamson Co	281P	MA-53	78641	1-499
FAWNRIDGE DR W	Austin	526F	ML-30	78753	100-199
FAWN RIDGE RD	Bastrop Co	680Z	MV-13	78612	100-199
	Bastrop Co	710D	MV-12	78612	200-299
FAWN RIDGE TRL	Round Rock	376J	ML-44	78681	1800-1899
FAWN RUN	Austin	613J	ME-20	78735	4700-4899
FAWN RUN DR	Cedar Park	372M	MD-44	78613	500-599
FAWNS CROSSING	Hays Co	577T	WS-22	78720	17900-18199
FAWNVALLEY DR	Travis Co	371V	MB-43	78613	13100-13299
FAWNWOOD CV	Austin	613J	ME-20	78735	4600-4699
FAY DR	Travis Co	396C	WR-42	78654	5700-5799
FAY ST	Austin	498W	MQ-31	78653	12200-12399
FAYETTE ST	Bastrop	745K	EF-8	78602	701-799 O
	Bastrop	745G	EF-9	78602	1001-1599 O
	Bastrop	745F	EE-9	78602	1200-1598 E
FAYLIN DR	Austin	526H	MM-30	78753	9900-10399
FAZIO CV	Round Rock	378Y	MR-43	78664	1000-1999
FEARLESS RD	Travis Co	736E	ML-9	78747	None
FEARLESS TREADWAY	Hays Co	515T	WN-28	78620	2500-3999
FEATHERCREST DR	Travis Co	436Q	MM-38	78728	2800-3199
FEATHERGRASS CT	Austin	495G	MK-33	78758	3200-3299
FEATHERGRASS CT	Travis Co	432K	MC-38	78613	2700-2799
FEATHERGRASS DR	Buda	763T	ME-4	78610	100-499
FEATHERGRASS WAY	Georgetown	314B	MG-51	78628	1600-1899
FEATHERHILL RD	Travis Co	611W	MA-19	78737	8800-9199
FEATHERLITE	Cedar Park	372Y	MD-43	78613	600-699
FEATHER NEST DR	Williamson Co	402V	MD-40	78613	1800-1899
FEATHER ROCK TRL	Travis Co	460K	WY-35	78734	17000-17299
FEBRUARY DR	Austin	497N	MN-32	78753	11400-11699
FEDERAL CIR	Austin	645S	MJ-16	78744	4600-4699
FEIGN LN	Austin	464K	MG-35	78759	7700-7799
FELDER LN	Travis Co	441V	MX-37	78615	12000-12899
	Travis Co	472A	MY-36	78615	12900-13999
FELICIA DR	Briarcliff	458E	WU-36	78669	22400-22699
	Travis Co	457M	WT-35	78669	22700-22899
FELICITY LN	Travis Co	619T	MS-19	78725	4500-4599
FELIPE DR	Austin	705B	MJ-12	78747	6800-6999
FELIX AVE	Austin	616S	ML-19	78741	6000-6299
	Austin	616T	ML-19	78741	6300-6799
FELLER CV	Austin	678J	MQ-14	78617	5200-5299
FELSMERE DR	Pflugerville	438N	MQ-38	78660	1200-1299
FELSPAR DR	Austin	671A	MA-15	78739	7700-7799
FELTER LN	Travis Co	646W	ML-16	78744	4100-4299
FELTS LN	Travis Co	610H	WZ-21	78736	7300-7399
FEN CV	Williamson Co	318B	MQ-51	78634	200-299
FENCE ROW	Austin	645X	MJ-16	78744	5300-5999
FENCE LINE DR	Austin	642C	MD-18	78749	6800-7099
	Austin	642G	MD-18	78749	7100-7299
FENCE POST PASS	Cedar Park	373S	ME-43	78613	600-699
FENCE POST TRL	Travis Co	433P	ME-38	78750	11500-11599
	Williamson Co	433P	ME-38	78750	11600-11799
FENCERAIL RD	Travis Co	701H	MB-12	78652	13100-13299
FENELON DR	Austin	526P	ML-29	78753	800-899
FENNIMORE CV	Williamson Co	405J	MJ-41	78717	15900-15999
FENTON CV	Austin	611T	MA-19	78736	7700-7799
FENTON DR	Austin	611T	MA-19	78736	8400-8899
FENTONRIDGE DR	Austin	643P	ME-17	78745	2600-2799
FENWAY CT	Lakeway	519G	WX-30	78734	100-199
FENWAY PARK	Pflugerville	438N	MQ-38	78660	1200-1299
FENWAY PARK CT	Round Rock	378E	MQ-45	78665	900-999
FENWICK ST	Taylor	353S	EA-46	76574	100-199
FERDINAND ST	Austin	585M	MK-23	78702	1800-1899
FERGUSON DR	Austin	496U	MM-31	78753	100-799
FERGUSON LN	Austin	526R	MM-29	78754	1400-1799
	Austin	527S	MN-28	78754	2200-3399
	Travis Co	527X	MN-28	78754	3400-3699
FERGUSON ST	Taylor	352H	MZ-48	76574	200-699
FERGUSON CUTOFF	Austin	557B	MN-27	78724	8000-8499
FERITTI DR	Lakeway	518H	WV-30	78738	100-199
FERN CT	Cedar Park	402G	MD-42	78613	500-599
FERN CV	Austin	493V	MF-31	78750	7400-7499
FERN BLUFF AVE	Williamson Co	375Q	MK-44	78681	8200-8599
FERNDALE CIR	Austin	674A	MG-15	78745	7300-7499
FERNDALE CV	Austin	674A	MG-15	78745	7300-7399
FERNDALE DR	Round Rock	406H	MM-42	78664	800-999
	Round Rock	407E	MN-42	78664	1000-1299
FERNGLADE LN	Cedar Park	403K	ME-41	78613	1300-1399
FERNHILL DR	Austin	404L	MH-41	78717	14700-15599
FERN HOLLOW	Austin	524N	MG-29	78731	4800-4899
FERN RIDGE LN	Travis Co	467M	MP-35	78660	1500-1599
FERN SPRING CV	Travis Co	493Y	MF-31	78730	6300-6399
FERNSPRING DR	Round Rock	408E	MQ-42	78665	2200-2299
FERNVIEW RD	Austin	643G	MF-18	78745	5400-5599
FERNWOOD CV	Round Rock	406H	MM-42	78664	800-999
FERNWOOD RD	Austin	555Z	MK-25	78723	1100-1399
FERRET PATH	Austin	675A	MJ-15	78744	5500-5599
FERRYSTONE CV	Travis Co	677Y	MP-13	78617	12200-12299
FERRYSTONE PASS	Travis Co	677Y	MP-13	78617	6700-6999
FERRYSTONE GLEN DR	Travis Co	677U	MP-13	78617	12100-12299
FESTUS DR	Travis Co	672T	MC-13	78748	3000-3299
FETA CT	Cedar Park	372K	MC-44	78613	1600-1699
FICKE CV	Williamson Co	405J	MJ-41	78717	8800-8899
FIELD DR	Travis Co	703X	ME-10	78652	400-699
FIELD CREEK RD	Pflugerville	439J	MS-38	78660	None
FIELDCREST DR	Austin	614Q	MH-20	78704	1100-1299
FIELDGATE DR	Austin	467X	MN-34	78753	13000-13399
FIELD LARK DR	Round Rock	375V	MK-43	78681	2500-2599
FIELD SPAR DR	Travis Co	529H	MT-30	78653	13700-13899
FIELDSTONE DR	Austin	613J	ME-20	78735	4600-4899
FIELDSTONE DR	Georgetown	195P	MJ-62	78633	200-699
FIELDSTONE LOOP	Hays Co	669W	WW-13	78737	13000-13299
FIELDSTONE PL	Round Rock	406H	MM-42	78664	800-999
FIELDSTONE ST	Cedar Park	403K	ME-41	78613	1400-1598 E
FIELD STREAM LN	Travis Co	529H	MT-30	78653	13600-13799
FIELD STREAM LN	Travis Co	530E	MU-30	78653	13800-13899
FIELDWOOD DR	Austin	496W	ML-31	78758	900-1099
FIERRO CV	Austin	434U	MH-37	78729	8000-8099
FIESTA ST	Austin	586W	ML-22	78702	900-1199
FIFE DR	Briarcliff	457Z	WT-34	78669	400-599
FIFTH ST	Jonestown	400M	WZ-41	78645	10900-11199
FIG BLUFF LN	Travis Co	518N	WU-29	78669	19700-19799
FIGHTER DR	Austin	646Z	MM-16	78719	3600-3799
FIG VINE CV	Austin	493V	MF-31	78750	7100-7199
FILBERT CV	Austin	493R	MF-32	78750	7400-7499
FILEY CV	Austin	586L	MM-23	78721	4800-4899
FILLMORE CV	Lago Vista	458M	WV-35	78645	2400-2599
FILLY CIR	Mustang Ridge	766N	ML-5	78610	11900-11999
FINCASTLE DR	Austin	404D	MH-42	78717	16200-16399
FINCH LN	Georgetown	287N	MN-53	78626	100-199
FINCH TRL	Austin	643S	ME-16	78745	7700-8099
FINCHER RD	Austin	677F	MN-15	78617	4400-4899
FINE RD	Travis Co	366Y	WR-43	78654	28500-28899
FINKLEA CV	Austin	523C	MF-30	78730	6800-6999
FINLEY DR	Austin	554H	MH-27	78731	4500-4799
	Austin	555E	MJ-27	78731	4800-5099
FINN	Lakeway	489W	WW-31	78734	200-299
FINNEL CV	Hays Co	670T	WY-13	78610	100-199
FINSBURY DR	Austin	672R	MD-14	78748	10600-10799
FIORELLINO PL	Travis Co	432Q	MD-38	78613	3100-3299
FIRE CV	Austin	642B	MC-18	78749	7300-7399
FIRE LN N	Cedar Park	403G	MF-42	78613	1200-1499
FIREBIRD	Lakeway	489U	WX-31	78734	100-199
FIREBIRD CV	Lakeway	489Q	WX-32	78734	100-199
FIREBUSH DR	Pflugerville	438X	MQ-37	78660	1200-1499
	Travis Co	438X	MQ-37	78660	1500-1599
FIREBUSH WAY	Buda	763T	ME-4	78610	100-399
FIRECREST DR	Austin	673E	ME-15	78748	2700-2999
FIREFLY CV	Hays Co	732F	MC-9	78610	12800-12899
FIREFLY DR	Austin	675N	MJ-14	78744	7100-7499
FIRE FLY LN	Cedar Park	402H	MD-42	78613	1000-1099
FIRE GLOW DR	Williamson Co	402V	MD-40	78613	1600-1699
FIREHOUSE RD	Austin	647W	MN-16	78719	10200-10299
FIRE ISLAND DR	Pflugerville	438E	MQ-39	78660	None
FIREMAN'S TRL	Travis Co	459R	WX-35	78645	3700-3899
FIREOAK DR	Austin	464K	MG-35	78759	6700-7699
FIREPLACE CT	Travis Co	309P	WW-50	78641	25600-25699
FIRE RED WAY	Pflugerville	408W	MQ-40	78660	18800-18899
FIRESIDE DR	Austin	525C	MK-30	78757	8600-8699
FIRESTONE CIR	Point Venture	489N	WW-32	78645	200-399
FIRESTONE DR	Austin	524H	MH-30	78731	3800-3899
FIRETHORN CT	Travis Co	521L	MB-29	78732	11500-11599
FIRETHORN LN	Round Rock	407B	MN-42	78664	600-799
FIRETHORN LN	Williamson Co	433R	MF-38	78750	10400-10499
FIREWHEEL HOLLOW	Austin	494W	MG-31	78750	7000-7099
FIROJ DR	Austin	498J	MQ-32	78660	3400-3599
FIRST ST	Bastrop Co	746Z	EH-7	78602	100-199
FIRST ST	Jonestown	400H	WZ-42	78645	10800-11199
FIRST ST W	Travis Co	401S	MA-40	78641	17200-17599
FIRST VIEW	Leander	342W	MC-46	78641	2000-2499
FIRSTVIEW DR	Austin	524Q	MH-29	78731	4000-4199
FIRWOOD CT	Village of the Hills	519T	WW-28	78738	1-99
FIRWOOD DR	Austin	525B	MJ-30	78757	3000-3099
FISET DR	Austin	555E	MJ-27	78731	2600-2699
FISH LN	Austin	467Y	MP-34	78660	1600-1699
FISHBAUGH LN	Hutto	380S	MU-43	78634	100-299
FISHER LN	Travis Co	488X	WU-31	78669	19200-19499
FISHER ST	Elgin	534X	EC-28	78621	100-199
FISHER ST	Taylor	322Z	MZ-49	76574	900-1199
	Taylor	322Y	MZ-49	76574	1400-1499
FISHER HOLLOW TRL	Travis Co	401U	MB-40	78641	15700-16199
FISHER ISLAND DR	Austin	404G	MH-42	78717	15400-15799
FISHERMAN'S WAY	Travis Co	459R	WX-35	78645	17800-18199
FISHSPEAR LN	Williamson Co	284A	MG-54	78628	100-199
FISKVILLE CEMETERY RD	Austin	526L	MM-29	78753	8900-9399
FISTRAL DR	Hutto	379P	MS-44	78634	100-399
FITCHBURG CIR	Pflugerville	437P	MN-38	78660	16000-16199
FITCHWOOD LN	Austin	642J	MC-17	78749	5700-5899
FITTONIA DR	Austin	494B	MG-33	78759	9100-9299
FITZGERALD LN	Pflugerville	437A	MN-39	78664	17000-17199
FITZGIBBON DR	Travis Co	618V	MR-19	78725	14500-14899
FITZHUGH PL	Hays Co	608N	WU-20	78620	12000-12199
FITZHUGH RD	Hays Co	608V	WV-19	78736	13200-15299
	Hays Co	608K	WU-20	78620	15300-15799
	Hays Co	607M	WT-20	78620	15800-16899
	Travis Co	640A	WY-18	78736	10900-10999
	Travis Co	639D	WX-18	78736	11100-11499
	Travis Co	609S	WW-19	78736	11500-13199
FITZHUGH RD W	Hays Co	607E	WS-21	78620	100-1699
	Hays Co	606E	WQ-21	78620	1700-2999
FITZHUGH CORNERS	Hays Co	608K	WU-20	78620	11900-11999
FITZROY AVE	Austin	672Q	MD-14	78748	3500-3599
FITZWILLIAMS LN S	Bastrop Co	744T	EC-7	78602	100-199
FIVE ACRE WOOD	Travis Co	582Q	MD-23	78746	6300-6499
FLAGLER DR	Travis Co	577D	WT-24	78738	17100-17299
	Travis Co	578A	WU-24	78738	17300-17499
	Travis Co	548W	WU-25	78738	17500-17999
	Travis Co	547V	WT-25	78738	18000-18499
FLAGSHIP PARK DR	Jonestown	430P	WY-38	78645	None
FLAGSTAFF CIR	Austin	465X	MJ-34	78759	4300-4399
FLAGSTAFF DR	Austin	465X	MJ-34	78759	4100-4499
FLAGSTONE CT	Cedar Park	374U	MH-43	78613	300-399
FLAGSTONE DR	Austin	495X	MJ-31	78757	8400-8599
FLAGSTONE TRL	Hays Co	763S	ME-4	78610	100-299
FLAHIVE RD	Bastrop Co	743Q	EB-8	78602	100-299
FLAMELEAF CV	Round Rock	377X	MN-43	78664	3100-3199
FLAMELEAF DR	Georgetown	314C	MH-51	78628	100-599
FLAMEVINE CV	Travis Co	582N	MC-23	78735	3600-3699
FLAMINGO BLVD	Lakeway	519A	WW-30	78734	500-599
	Lakeway	518D	WV-30	78734	600-699
FLAMINGO CV	Lakeway	518D	WV-30	78734	600-699
FLAMINGO DR	Travis Co	520F	WY-30	78734	200-399
FLAMINGO DR N	Travis Co	520A	WY-30	78734	15100-15299
FLAMINGO DR S	Lakeway	520E	WY-30	78734	15300-15399
	Travis Co	520E	WY-30	78734	15100-15299
FLAMING OAK CV	Austin	642G	MD-18	78749	4900-5099
FLAMING OAK PL	Austin	642G	MD-18	78749	7400-7499
FLAMINGSWORTH HOLLOW	Austin	494W	MG-31	78750	6900-6999
FLAMING TREE CT	Williamson Co	402U	MD-40	78613	2200-2299
FLANAGAN CV	Austin	614Q	MH-20	78704	1100-1199
FLANAGAN DR	Leander	311R	MB-50	78641	900-1099
FLASHPAN CV	Williamson Co	434U	MH-37	78729	8100-8199
FLASHPOINT CT	Travis Co	609N	WW-20	78736	10800-10899
FLAT BOAT CIR	Hays Co	668C	WV-15	78620	100-199
FLAT CREEK DR	Travis Co	428A	WU-39	78654	23500-23699
FLAT HEAD DR	Travis Co	560N	MU-26	78653	18100-18399
FLAT ROCK CV	Georgetown	285K	MJ-53	78628	100-199
FLAT ROCK DR	Travis Co	641B	MA-18	78737	7800-7899
FLATROCK LN	Austin	612Q	MD-20	78735	6100-6199
FLAT STONE CT	Williamson Co	346G	MM-48	78665	4200-4299
FLATTER'S WAY	Travis Co	467Q	MP-35	78660	800-999
FLAT TOP RANCH RD	Travis Co	491T	MA-31	78732	12800-15099
FLAXEN DR	Austin	705B	MJ-12	78747	8000-8399
FLEECE FLOWER CV	Travis Co	582J	MC-23	78735	3100-3299
FLEENOR DR	Travis Co	641P	MA-17	78739	10000-10299
FLEET DR	Austin	672V	MD-13	78748	2900-3099
FLEETRIDGE DR	Austin	557Y	MP-25	78724	7000-7199
FLEETWOOD DR	Austin	614S	MG-19	78704	3500-3699
FLEISCHER DR	Travis Co	436V	MM-37	78728	1700-1999
FLEMING CT	Austin	645Q	MK-17	78744	5300-5399
FLETCHER LN	Austin	611L	MB-20	78735	6300-6599
FLETCHER ST	Austin	614R	MH-20	78704	200-299
	Austin	614L	MH-20	78704	600-799
FLETCHER HALL LN	Austin	404E	MG-42	78717	11200-11499
	Austin	403H	MF-42	78717	11500-11799
FLICKER CV	Austin	675A	MJ-15	78744	4800-4899
FLICKER LN	Austin	675A	MJ-15	78744	4800-4999
FLIGHT LN	Austin	616Q	MM-20	78742	6500-6699
FLIGHTLINE DR	Austin	646M	MM-17	78719	9300-9499
FLIGHTLINE RD	Lago Vista	399C	WX-42	78645	300-399
FLINDERS REEF LN	Travis Co	436Q	MM-38	78728	3100-3199
FLINN ST	Hutto	349M	MT-47	78634	100-399
FLINNWOOD CIR	Williamson Co	433U	MF-37	78750	11600-11699
FLINT CT	Lakeway	519M	WX-29	78734	1600-1699
FLINT HILL CV	Bastrop Co	741C	MX-9	78612	100-199
FLINTLOCK CIR	Lago Vista	399T	WW-40	78645	7900-8099
FLINTRIDGE RD	West Lake Hills	553W	ME-25	78746	1400-1799
FLINT RIDGE TRL	Williamson Co	254W	MG-55	78628	100-399
FLINT ROCK	Bastrop Co	621M	MX-20	78621	100-199
FLINTROCK CIR	Travis Co	640D	WZ-18	78737	9200-9899
FLINT ROCK CV	Williamson Co	252A	MC-57	78642	1-99
FLINT ROCK DR	Round Rock	406K	ML-41	78681	1900-2099
FLINTROCK DR	Williamson Co	287H	MP-54	78626	50100-50199
FLINT ROCK RD	Travis Co	519Y	WX-28	78738	15300-16199
	Travis Co	549A	WW-27	78738	16200-16899
	Travis Co	518Z	WV-28	78738	16900-17399
FLINTROCK TRACE	Lakeway	519Y	WX-28	78738	2500-3199
FLINTSTONE CV	Austin	611U	MB-19	78736	7900-7999
FLINTWOOD CT	Williamson Co	346H	MM-48	78665	1100-1199
FLINTWOOD LN	Williamson Co	346H	MM-48	78665	4100-4199
FLOATING LEAF DR	Hutto	380E	MU-45	78634	100-399
FLORA CV	Austin	614A	MG-21	78746	2500-2599
FLORADALE DR	Travis Co	526C	MM-30	78753	800-1199
FLORAL PARK DR	Austin	464U	MH-34	78759	10500-10799
	Austin	465W	MJ-34	78759	10800-11099
FLORA VISTA LOOP	Williamson Co	345S	MJ-46	78681	3500-3699
FLORENCE DR	Austin	526K	ML-29	78753	100-499
FLORENCE ST	Round Rock	406C	MM-42	78664	100-299
FLORENCIA LN	Austin	587C	MP-24	78724	5900-6399
FLORES ST	Austin	615F	MJ-21	78702	1100-1199
FLORIBUNDAS LN	Travis Co	532U	MZ-28	78621	17800-17899
FLOURNOY DR	Austin	644N	MG-17	78745	200-699
FLOW LN	Austin	647K	MN-17	78617	2500-2699
FLOWER HILL DR	Round Rock	408J	MQ-41	78664	2900-3099
FLOWERPOT CV	Williamson Co	405G	MK-42	78681	4100-4199
FLOWER SCENT CT	Austin	464A	MG-36	78750	11700-11799
FLOWSTONE LN	Round Rock	345P	MJ-47	78681	3400-3499
FLOYD DR	Austin	526C	MM-30	78753	10000-10199

STREET NAME	CITY or COUNTY	MAPSCO GRID	AUSTIN GRID	ZIP CODE	BLOCK RANGE O/E
FLUSHWING DR	Austin	497T	MN-31	78754	11400-11599
FLYING JIB CT	Lakeway	489Y	WX-31	78734	100-199
FLYING SCOT	Lakeway	519E	WW-30	78734	100-199
FLYNN CIR	Austin	611P	MA-20	78736	7200-7299
FLYWAY LN	Cedar Park	373Z	MF-43	78613	1500-1599
FOAL LN	Austin	466Q	MM-35	78727	1600-1699
FOGGY GLEN CV	Travis Co	522N	MC-29	78733	1700-1799
FOGGY MOUNTAIN DR	Austin	611P	MA-20	78736	8600-8799
FOLEY CIR	Travis Co	428A	WU-39	78654	23600-23699
FOLEY DR	Travis Co	677Q	MP-14	78617	11700-12199
FOLKLORE CIR	Lago Vista	399T	WW-40	78645	7900-7999
FOLKSTONE CV	Austin	463L	MF-35	78750	9600-9699
FOLSOM CT	Williamson Co	314J	MG-50	78628	100-199
FOLSOM CV	Round Rock	346W	ML-46	78681	800-899
FOLTS AVE	Austin	614C	MH-21	78704	1000-1499
FONSO LN	Austin	703G	MF-12	78748	11000-11099
FONTAINE AVE	Travis Co	490K	WY-32	78734	15800-16099
FONTAINE CT	Travis Co	490N	WY-32	78734	1800-1899
FONTANA DR	Austin	614Y	MH-19	78704	3000-3199
FONTENAY DR	Austin	674H	MH-15	78744	4900-5799
FOOTHILL CV	Lago Vista	399T	WW-40	78645	8000-8199
FOOTHILL DR	Austin	554L	MH-26	78731	3300-3399
FOOTHILL PKWY	Austin	554K	MG-26	78731	3400-3499
FOOTHILL FARMS LOOP	Pflugerville	437T	MN-37	78660	15801-15899 O
FOOTHILLS	Leander	342T	MC-46	78641	2000-2099
FOOTHILLS DR	Hays Co	668L	WV-14	78620	1000-1099
FOOTHILLS TRL	Round Rock	345K	MJ-47	78681	3200-3299
FOOTHILL TERRACE	Austin	554L	MH-26	78731	3400-3499
FOPPIANO LOOP	Round Rock	407D	MP-42	78665	1500-1599
FORA CIR	Williamson Co	433Q	MF-38	78750	12000-12099
FORBES DR	Austin	526Z	MM-28	78754	2200-2499
FORBSDALE DR	Austin	675X	MJ-13	78747	7900-8199
FORD CV	Lago Vista	458M	WV-35	78645	2500-2599
FORD ST	Austin	614F	MG-21	78704	1800-2199
FORDHAM CV	Austin	556L	MM-26	78723	2100-2199
FORDHAM LN	Austin	556L	MM-26	78723	2100-2199
FOREMOST DR	Austin	674K	MG-14	78745	100-299
FOREST AVE	Austin	614R	MH-20	78704	2300-2499
FOREST CT	Taylor	322Z	MZ-49	76574	500-599
FOREST CV	Travis Co	460G	WZ-36	78734	16800-16899
FOREST LN	Bastrop Co	746V	EH-7	78602	100-199
FOREST ST	Georgetown	286G	MM-54	78628	200-699
	Georgetown	286L	MM-53	78626	900-1799
FOREST TRL	Austin	584C	MH-24	78703	1500-2299
FOREST TRL	Cedar Park	403A	ME-42	78613	600-899
	Cedar Park	402D	MD-42	78613	900-1299
FOREST TRL	Travis Co	460G	WZ-36	78734	16700-16799
FOREST TRL	Williamson Co	343U	MF-46	78641	100-199
FOREST WAY	Travis Co	460G	WZ-36	78734	16300-16899
FOREST BEND DR	Austin	614E	MG-21	78704	2200-2499
	Austin	613H	MF-21	78704	2500-2699
FOREST BLUFF TRL	Round Rock	378J	MQ-44	78665	1000-1199
FOREST CANYON CV	Round Rock	378W	MQ-43	78665	900-999
FOREST CREEK DR	Round Rock	407C	MP-42	78664	2100-2299
	Round Rock	377Z	MP-43	78665	2300-2899
	Round Rock	378X	MQ-43	78664	2900-3899
FORESTGLADE DR	Austin	644A	MG-18	78745	1700-1999
FOREST GLEN CV	Round Rock	406H	MM-42	78664	800-999
FOREST GLENN CV	Travis Co	708H	MR-12	78617	15700-15999
FOREST GREEN DR	Round Rock	408A	MQ-42	78665	2800-2899
FOREST HEIGHTS LN	Austin	642J	MC-17	78749	8100-8599
FOREST HILL CV	Round Rock	408E	MQ-42	78665	2000-2099
FOREST HILL DR	Austin	644A	MG-18	78745	1600-1999
FOREST HILLS DR	Travis Co	583A	ME-24	78746	6100-6299
	Travis Co	582D	MD-24	78746	6300-6499
FOREST LAKE DR	Bastrop Co	739E	MS-9	78617	100-399
FOREST MEADOW CV	Round Rock	408A	MQ-42	78665	1900-1999
FOREST MEADOW DR	Round Rock	408A	MQ-42	78665	2900-2999
FOREST MESA	Round Rock	378P	MQ-44	78664	1-99
FOREST MESA DR	Austin	495W	MJ-31	78759	8000-8199
FOREST OAKS PATH	Cedar Park	402H	MD-42	78613	1100-1399
FOREST PARKE DR	Austin	462P	MC-35	78726	7900-8099
FOREST RIDGE BLVD	Round Rock	378W	MQ-43	78665	800-1499
	Round Rock	378J	MQ-44	78665	1000-1099
FOREST SAGE ST	Manor	530T	MU-28	78653	None
FOREST VIEW DR	Austin	583H	MF-24	78746	900-1099
	Austin	584A	MG-24	78746	None
	West Lake Hills	583H	MF-24	78746	700-899
FOREST VISTA CV	Round Rock	408A	MQ-42	78665	1600-1699
FOREST WOOD RD	Austin	643Y	MF-16	78745	7200-7599
	Austin	673D	MF-15	78745	7600-8199
FORK RIDGE PATH	Williamson Co	346G	MM-48	78665	800-999
FORMITH ST	Travis Co	560Z	MV-25	78653	10300-10499
FORSMAN RD	Williamson Co	377W	MN-43	78664	1600-1799
FORSYTH CT	Hutto	379R	MT-44	78634	300-399
FORSYTHE DR	Austin	465R	MK-35	78759	12100-12299
FORT BENTON DR	Austin	611H	MB-21	78735	5200-5799
FORT BOGGY DR	Georgetown	195P	MJ-62	78633	400-499
FORT BRANCH BLVD	Austin	586Q	MM-23	78721	1200-1499
FORT CHADBOURNE DR	Austin	703B	ME-12	78748	700-799
FORT CLARK CV	Austin	644L	MH-17	78745	700-799
FORT CLARK DR	Austin	644Q	MH-17	78745	4800-5399
FORT DAVIS CV	Austin	524B	MG-30	78731	6700-6799
FORT DAVIS ST	Georgetown	225U	MK-58	78633	1000-1299
FORT DRUM DR	Austin	644Q	MH-17	78745	400-699
FORT GRANT CV	Round Rock	407G	MP-42	78665	1700-1799
FORT GRANT DR	Round Rock	407G	MP-42	78665	1700-1799
FORT GRIFFIN TRL	Georgetown	195N	MJ-62	78633	400-499
FORT HILL CT	Austin	525J	MJ-29	78757	7000-7099
FORT LEATON DR	Pflugerville	407Y	MP-40	78664	17600-17799
FORT LEXINGTON DR	Austin	678J	MQ-14	78617	12500-12799
FT LLOYD PL	Round Rock	407C	MP-42	78665	1400-1599
FORT MABRY LOOP	Williamson Co	344B	MG-48	78628	100-299
FORT MASON DR	Austin	644Q	MH-17	78745	5100-5399
FORT McGRUDER LN	Austin	614Y	MH-19	78704	300-599
FORT MOULTRIE LN	Travis Co	527X	MN-28	78754	4700-4899
FORT PARK CV	Georgetown	225B	MJ-60	78633	100-199
FORT SMITH TRL	Travis Co	490Y	WZ-31	78734	14100-14399
FORT SUMTER CIR	Austin	643W	ME-16	78745	2700-2799
FORT SUMTER RD	Austin	643W	ME-16	78745	8100-8499
FT THOMAS PL	Round Rock	407C	MP-42	78664	400-699
FORTUNA CV	Travis Co	550R	WZ-26	78733	12000-12099
FORTUNA DR	Travis Co	550R	WZ-26	78733	2700-2899
FORTUNE DR	Austin	614F	MG-21	78704	2300-2399
FORT VIEW RD	Austin	614W	MG-19	78704	1400-2199
FORT WORTH TRL	Travis Co	672T	MC-13	78748	3000-3299
FOSSEWAY DR	Austin	404J	MG-41	78717	10500-10599

STREET NAME	CITY or COUNTY	MAPSCO GRID	AUSTIN GRID	ZIP CODE	BLOCK RANGE O/E
FOSSIL CV	Round Rock	345N	MJ-47	78681	1100-1199
FOSSIL TRL	Leander	342B	MC-48	78641	100-299
FOSSIL TRL	Travis Co	486G	WR-33	78669	24000-24799
FOSSIL RIM CV	Georgetown	225V	MK-58	78633	100-199
FOSSIL RIM RD	Travis Co	553H	MF-27	78746	5100-5499
FOSSILWOOD WAY	Round Rock	345N	MJ-47	78681	3600-3799
FOSSMOOR ST	Austin	404F	MG-42	78717	10200-10299
FOSTER AVE	Austin	584P	MG-23	78703	2200-2499
FOSTER DR	Cedar Park	402C	MD-42	78613	1500-1599
FOSTER LN	Austin	525E	MJ-30	78757	2600-3399
FOSTER RANCH RD	Austin	612L	MD-20	78735	4300-5099
FOUNDATION RD	Travis Co	433S	ME-37	78726	10500-11099
FOUNDER DR	Cedar Park	372F	MC-45	78613	2200-2399
FOUNDERS CIR	Travis Co	426G	WR-39	78669	2300-2499
FOUNDERS PL	Travis Co	426C	WR-39	78669	26700-27199
FOUNDERS OAK WAY	Williamson Co	257M	MP-56	78626	40100-40399
FOUNDERS PARK RD					
	Dripping Springs	636V	WR-16	78620	100-699
	Dripping Springs	637S	WS-16	78620	None
FOUNTAINBLEU CIR	Austin	463C	MF-36	78750	10600-10799
FOUNTAIN FALLS	Travis Co	369R	WX-44	78641	None
FOUNTAIN GROVE CV	Round Rock	377Z	MP-43	78665	2800-2899
FOUNTAINWOOD CIR	Williamson Co	225S	MJ-58	78633	4000-6099
FOUNTAINWOOD DR	Williamson Co	225N	MJ-59	78633	900-1099
	Williamson Co	224R	MH-59	78633	2000-3099
FOUR CABIN CT	Round Rock	378B	MQ-45	78665	1300-1399
FOUR HILLS CT	Pflugerville	409S	MS-40	78660	2200-2299
FOUR HUNDRED AVE	Briarcliff	487D	WT-33	78669	22000-22199
FOUR IRON DR	Austin	464B	MG-36	78750	11600-11899
FOUR OAKS LN	Austin	614E	MG-21	78704	2100-2299
FOUR POINTS DR	Austin	462Y	MD-34	78726	11000-11599
FOURTH ST	Jonestown	400M	WZ-41	78645	10900-11199
FOUR-T RANCH RD	Williamson Co	224C	MH-60	78633	1-599
FOUST TRL	Georgetown	256F	ML-57	78628	3800-3899
FOWLER DR	Travis Co	550U	WZ-25	78733	3600-3699
FOWLER MILL CV	Austin	405A	MJ-42	78717	16500-16699
FOWZER ST	Taylor	353E	EA-48	76574	100-1199
FOX DR	Georgetown	316P	ML-50	78626	100-199
FOXBORO CT	Williamson Co	405P	MJ-41	78717	15700-15799
FOX CHAPEL DR	Travis Co	582M	MD-23	78746	5800-6099
FOX CHASE CIR	Austin	463C	MF-36	78750	9800-9899
FOX CHASE CIR	Williamson Co	224Z	MH-58	78633	20100-20199
FOX CREEK DR	Austin	641Y	MB-16	78739	10400-10499
FOXCROFT PL	Austin	583Z	MF-22	78746	1300-1399
FOXFIRE CV	Round Rock	375M	MK-44	78681	1800-1899
FOXFIRE DR	Austin	583Y	MF-22	78746	3100-3299
FOXFIRE DR	Round Rock	375R	MK-44	78681	1700-1799
FOXGLEN DR	Austin	614A	MG-21	78704	2600-2699
FOXGLOVE CT	Austin	641Y	MB-16	78739	10400-10499
FOXHEAD DR	Travis Co	677L	MP-14	78617	4800-4899
FOX HOLLOW	Hays Co	732F	MC-9	78610	200-399
FOX HOLLOW	Williamson Co	375L	MK-44	78681	3000-3299
FOX HOLLOW CT	Williamson Co	434U	MH-37	78729	12500-12599
FOXHOLLOW DR	Georgetown	285Z	MK-52	78628	100-299
FOX HOME LN	Georgetown	195U	MK-61	78633	100-199
FOXHOUND CV	Williamson Co	434Q	MH-38	78729	12700-12799
FOXHOUND TRL	Williamson Co	434T	MG-37	78729	8100-8599
FOX RUN DR	Hays Co	669Z	WX-13	78737	15400-15699
FOX SPARROW CV	Pflugerville	438J	MQ-38	78660	1100-1199
FOX SPARROW TRL	Cedar Park	433A	ME-39	78613	1200-1399
FOXTAIL CV	Austin	584X	MG-22	78704	1400-1499
FOXTON CV	Austin	672M	MD-14	78748	2800-3099
FOXTREE CV	Austin	493R	MF-32	78750	7100-7399
FOX WAY DR	Austin	464V	MH-34	78759	11100-11199
FOXWOOD CV	Austin	584X	MG-22	78704	1400-1499
FOY CIR	Austin	675N	MJ-14	78744	7100-7199
FOY DR	Travis Co	490X	WY-31	78734	14700-15399
FRAMINGHAM CIR	Travis Co	437K	MN-38	78660	16300-16599
FRANCES DR	Travis Co	554W	MG-25	78746	2000-2099
FRANCIA TRL	Austin	673R	MF-14	78748	8700-8999
FRANCIS AVE	Austin	584Q	MH-23	78703	1700-1799
FRANCISCO ST	Austin	585Z	MK-22	78702	2500-2799
FRANK ST	Taylor	353F	EA-48	76574	600-999
FRANKIE LN	Travis Co	408R	MR-41	78660	20300-20799
FRANKLIN BLVD	Austin	555G	MK-27	78751	100-799
FRANKLIN CV	Lago Vista	458M	WV-35	78645	2600-2699
FRANKLIN ST	Taylor	352G	MZ-48	76574	100-199
FRANKLIN MOUNTAIN DR	Cedar Park	373E	ME-45	78613	1801-1899 O
FRANKLIN PARK DR	Austin	645S	MJ-16	78744	4400-4799
FRANKLINS TALE LOOP	Austin	673W	ME-13	78748	11000-11199
FRANWOOD LN	Austin	525B	MJ-30	78757	8300-8499
FRATE BARKER RD	Austin	702F	MC-12	78748	1800-3099
	Travis Co	702H	MD-12	78748	1400-1799
FRAZELL CV	Williamson Co	375Q	MK-44	78681	9000-9099
FRAZIER AVE	Austin	614K	MG-20	78704	1800-1999
FRED COUPLES DR	Williamson Co	408C	MR-42	78664	100-199
FREDDIE DR	Williamson Co	257N	MN-56	78626	1-299
FREDERICK ST	Austin	614Y	MH-19	78704	100-199
FRED MORSE DR	Austin	556M	MM-26	78723	7000-7399
FREDRICKSON LN	Bastrop Co	474W	EC-34	78621	100-199
FREELAND PATH	Round Rock	377W	MN-43	78664	500-599
FREEMONT	Williamson Co	375Y	MK-43	78681	2900-3299
FREEMONT CIR	Williamson Co	375Y	MK-43	78681	300-399
FREEMONT CV	Williamson Co	375Y	MK-43	78681	300-399
FREESIA CT	Austin	641Y	MB-16	78739	6500-6599
FREESTONE DR	Pflugerville	437K	MN-38	78660	1500-1599
FREEWATER LN	Austin	614T	MG-19	78704	900-999
FREIDRICH LN	Austin	645J	MJ-17	78744	4100-4499
	Austin	644V	MH-16	78744	4500-5499
FREIGHT LN	Austin	646M	MM-17	78719	9100-9499
FREMONT CV	Austin	465Q	MK-35	78727	12000-12099
FRENCH PL	Austin	585G	MK-24	78722	2700-3399
FRENCH HARBOUR CT	Travis Co	460L	WZ-35	78734	16700-16799
FRESCO DR N	Austin	554D	MH-27	78731	5000-5099
FRESCO DR W	Austin	555A	MJ-27	78731	2800-2899
FRESNO SPRINGS	Buda	732W	MC-7	78610	100-299
FRIARCREEK LOOP	Round Rock	407N	MN-41	78664	2300-2399
FRIARS TALE LN	Austin	673W	ME-13	78748	1700-1899
FRIAR TUCK LN	Austin	614V	MH-19	78704	600-699
	Austin	614V	MH-19	78704	2500-2799
FRIAR VILLA DR	Travis Co	640E	WY-18	78737	10900-11199
FRICK LN	Round Rock	377Z	MP-43	78665	2600-2699
FRIEDSAM LN	Travis Co	551U	MB-25	78733	1300-1999
FRIENDLY CIR	Georgetown	225L	MK-59	78633	100-199
FRIENDS CAMP	Williamson Co	257L	MP-56	78626	40100-40199
FRIENDSHIP CV	Leander	342B	MC-48	78641	500-599
FRIENDSHIP DR	Austin	497X	MN-31	78754	11100-11399

STREET NAME	CITY or COUNTY	MAPSCO GRID	AUSTIN GRID	ZIP CODE	BLOCK RANGE O/E
FRIENDSHIP QUILT LN	Travis Co	467G	MP-36	78660	800-1099
FRIENDSWOOD DR	Austin	556U	MM-25	78723	6100-6199
FRIENDSWOOD DR	Georgetown	286W	ML-52	78628	500-699
FRIENDSWOOD LN	Hays Co	670J	WY-14	78737	14300-14699
FRIJOLITA	Travis Co	523X	ME-28	78730	3100-3199
FRINK ST	Taylor	323W	EA-49	76574	1200-1599
FRIO CV	Travis Co	522S	MC-28	78733	10100-10199
FRIO LN	Leander	342E	MC-48	78641	300-399
FRITSCH CV	Williamson Co	405E	MJ-42	78717	16100-16199
FRITSCH DR	Williamson Co	405E	MJ-42	78717	8700-8899
FRITZ FALLS CROSSING	Travis Co	439T	MS-37	78660	4700-4799
FRITZ HUGHES PARK RD	Travis Co	491N	MA-32	78732	3100-3799
FROCK CT	Austin	673F	ME-15	78748	8800-9199
FRODO CV	Travis Co	672S	MC-13	78739	3800-3899
FROG POND LN	Hays Co	638W	WU-16	78620	100-299
FROKE CEDAR TRL	Williamson Co	433G	MF-39	78750	11000-11199
FRONIA WOODWARD	Travis Co	436U	MM-37	78728	14900-14999
FRONT ST	Austin	585B	MJ-24	78705	400-499
FRONT ST E	Hutto	379D	MT-45	78634	100-699
	Hutto	350W	MU-46	78634	200-699
FRONT ST W	Hutto	379C	MT-45	78634	100-999
FRONTERA LN	Austin	616X	ML-19	78741	1200-1299
FRONTERA TRL	Austin	616X	ML-19	78741	6900-7099
FRONTERA RANCH CV	Hays Co	608E	WU-21	78620	100-599
FRONTIER CV	Lago Vista	399T	WW-40	78645	7800-7899
FRONTIER LN N	Cedar Park	374L	MH-44	78613	100-399
FRONTIER LN S	Cedar Park	374U	MH-43	78613	100-999
FRONTIER TRL	Austin	613Z	MF-19	78745	4400-4799
FRONTIER TRL	Hays Co	636A	WQ-18	78620	1000-1099
FRONTIER TRL	Round Rock	406L	MM-41	78681	1500-2499
FRONTIER TRL	Williamson Co	224E	MG-60	78633	100-199
FRONTIER VALLEY DR	Austin	646B	ML-18	78741	1400-1899
FRONT ROYAL DR	Travis Co	582M	MD-23	78746	5900-6099
FROST CIR	Travis Co	437U	MP-37	78660	700-799
FROSTDALE DR	Travis Co	371R	MB-44	78613	13400-13499
FROSTWOOD TRL	Williamson Co	434K	MG-38	78729	9000-9199
FRUITWOOD PL	Austin	496E	ML-33	78758	11600-11699
FRUTH ST	Austin	585A	MJ-24	78705	2800-3099
	Austin	555X	MJ-25	78705	3400-3499
FRYE RYE DR	Austin	675W	MJ-13	78747	8200-8399
FRYMAN HILL DR	Austin	678N	MQ-14	78617	5400-5499
FUCHS GROVE RD	Travis Co	499L	MT-32	78653	13300-15499
FUENTE CV	Austin	643T	ME-16	78745	2300-2399
FULBRIGHT LN	Austin	642J	MC-17	78749	8500-8699
FULKES LN	Travis Co	340A	WY-48	78641	22900-23299
	Travis Co	310W	WY-49	78641	23300-23599
	Travis Co	309Z	WX-49	78641	23600-24299
FULLER LN	Bastrop Co	738H	MR-9	78617	100-199
FULL MOON CV	Williamson Co	375Q	MK-44	78681	9000-9099
FULL MOON TRL	Williamson Co	375Q	MK-44	78681	8100-8399
FULTON AVE	Austin	527E	MN-30	78754	10100-10399
FUNSTON ST	Austin	554V	MH-25	78703	3000-3399
FURLONG DR	Travis Co	552Y	MD-25	78746	500-799
FURNESS CV	Austin	526T	ML-28	78753	8100-8299
FURNESS DR	Austin	526P	ML-29	78753	8100-8899
FURROW CV	Austin	497E	MN-33	78753	12300-12399
FURROW HILL DR	Austin	527G	MP-30	78754	10900-11199
FUTURE DR	Austin	526R	MM-29	78754	1500-1899
FUZZ FAIRWAY	Travis Co	436R	MM-38	78728	2100-2399
FYVIE CASTLE CT	Pflugerville	408X	MQ-40	78660	None

G

STREET NAME	CITY or COUNTY	MAPSCO GRID	AUSTIN GRID	ZIP CODE	BLOCK RANGE O/E
GABION DR	Austin	641L	MB-17	78749	6800-7099
GABLE DR	Austin	465R	MK-35	78759	3400-3799
GABRIAL	Taylor	322Z	MZ-49	76574	1800-1999
GABRIEL ST N	Leander	312Y	MD-49	78641	100-499
GABRIEL FOREST	Williamson Co	285J	MJ-53	78628	1-499
GABRIEL MILLS DR	Round Rock	377W	MN-43	78664	600-799
GABRIEL MILLS DR	Williamson Co	342Z	MD-46	78641	400-699
GABRIELS LOOP	Williamson Co	283L	MF-53	78628	100-199
GABRIEL VIEW DR	Georgetown	256N	ML-56	78628	1600-3099
GABRIEL VISTA E	Williamson Co	194X	MG-61	78633	100-199
GABRIEL VISTA W	Williamson Co	194W	MG-61	78633	200-299
GABRIEL VISTA CT	Williamson Co	194X	MG-61	78633	100-299
GABRIEL WOODS DR	Williamson Co	194X	MG-61	78633	100-199
GADWALL CV	Austin	673E	ME-15	78748	2600-2699
GADWALL LN N	Cedar Park	373V	MF-43	78613	100-199
GADWALL LN S	Cedar Park	373Z	MF-43	78613	100-699
GAELIC CT	Austin	528E	MQ-30	78754	6000-6099
GAELIC DR	Austin	528E	MQ-30	78754	11600-12099
GAIL RD	Austin	673J	ME-14	78748	9900-10199
	Austin	673N	ME-14	78748	10200-10399
GAILLARDIA DR	Travis Co	551K	MA-26	78733	10700-10999
GAILLARDIA WAY	Georgetown	225L	MK-59	78633	100-199
GAINER CT	Hutto	379G	MT-45	78634	4000-4099
GAINER CV	Hutto	379D	MT-45	78634	1100-1199
GAINER DR	Hutto	379H	MT-45	78634	100-399
GAINES CT	Austin	613P	ME-20	78735	3800-4099
GAINES RD N	Bastrop Co	742Q	MZ-8	78612	100-399
GAINES MILL CV	Austin	643T	ME-16	78745	2300-2399
GAINES MILL LN	Austin	643U	MF-16	78745	7300-7899
GAINES RANCH LOOP	Austin	613P	ME-20	78735	4400-4599
GALACIA DR	Austin	465X	MJ-34	78759	3900-4199
GALAHAD DR	Travis Co	582H	MD-24	78746	900-999
GALAPAGOS DR	Austin	642Q	MD-17	78749	4500-4699
GALAXY	Lakeway	519B	WW-30	78734	100-199
GALBRAITH CV	Travis Co	618R	MR-20	78725	4200-4299
GALE RD	Georgetown	314F	MG-51	78628	400-599
GALEANA TRACE CV	Travis Co	552K	MC-26	78733	8400-8599
GALE MEADOW DR	Pflugerville	438D	MR-39	78660	None
GALEN CT	Austin	675A	MJ-15	78744	5000-5199
GALENA DR	Austin	404K	MG-41	78717	14900-15199
GALENA HILLS CV	Williamson Co	344V	MH-46	78681	3700-3799
GALENA HILLS DR	Williamson Co	344Z	MH-46	78681	4000-4099
GALENA HILLS LOOP	Williamson Co	344Z	MH-46	78681	3500-3899
GALESBURG DR	Austin	643N	ME-17	78745	3300-3399
	Austin	642R	MD-17	78745	3400-3499
GALEWOOD DR	Austin	525D	MK-30	78758	8900-9099
GALEWOOD PL	Austin	554Y	MH-25	78703	2500-2599
GALILEE CT	Travis Co	591K	MW-23	78653	20700-20999
GALINDO ST	Austin	616X	ML-19	78741	6600-6899
GALLANT	Manor	530K	MU-29	78653	None
GALLANT FOX RD	Travis Co	641G	MB-18	78737	8700-9299
GALLATIN DR	Austin	611T	MA-19	78736	8200-8499
GALLERIA CIR	Bee Cave	550P	WY-26	78738	12600-13699
GALLERIA CV	Austin	464V	MH-34	78759	10900-11099

F G

STREET NAME	CITY or COUNTY	MAPSCO GRID	AUSTIN GRID	ZIP CODE	BLOCK RANGE O/E
GALLERIA PKWY	Bee Cave	550T	WY-25	78738	3800-4199
GALLERY DR	Bee Cave	549M	WX-26	78738	14000-14399
GALLERY DR	Travis Co	427N	WS-38	78669	25500-25799
GALLIANO CIR	Austin	642G	MD-18	78749	7600-7699
GALLO CIR	Travis Co	490C	WZ-33	78734	4100-4199
GALLOP CV	Austin	643J	ME-17	78745	3300-3399
GALLOPING RD	Round Rock	376T	ML-43	78681	1-99
GALLOWAY LN	Hays Co	669F	WW-15	78737	100-399
GALSTON DR	Briarcliff	457Y	WT-34	78669	600-699
GALSWORTHY CT	Austin	671D	MB-15	78739	5700-5799
GALSWORTHY LN	Austin	671D	MB-15	78739	10500-10899
GALVESTON LN	Austin	642R	MD-17	78745	7600-7699
GALWAY ST	Austin	466N	ML-35	78758	2200-2399
GALWAY BAY CV	Pflugerville	467D	MP-36	78660	600-699
GAMBEL'S QUAIL DR	Austin	496W	ML-31	78758	9500-9699
GAMEZ CV	Austin	614Y	MH-19	78704	700-799
GANN ST	Georgetown	256V	MM-55	78626	200-399
GANNET CV	Lakeway	489X	WW-31	78734	200-299
GANN HILL DR E	Cedar Park	372K	MC-44	78613	2000-2199
GANTON CT	Pflugerville	439A	MS-39	78660	19100-19299
GANTRY DR	Pflugerville	407Z	MP-40	78660	18000-18399
GANTTCREST DR	Austin	642J	MC-17	78749	8100-8799
GANYMEDE CT	Austin	465G	MK-36	78727	12800-12899
GANYMEDE DR	Austin	465G	MK-36	78727	4100-5199
GARBACZ DR	Austin	673W	ME-13	78748	10200-10799
GARCREEK CIR	Austin	587D	MP-24	78724	8300-8499
GARDEN CT	Round Rock	406D	MM-42	78664	300-399
GARDEN PATH	Round Rock	406D	MM-42	78664	400-1199
	Round Rock	407A	MN-42	78664	1200-1499
GARDEN ST	Austin	615B	MJ-21	78702	1200-1599
	Austin	615G	MK-21	78702	1600-2499
GARDENA CANYON DR	Pflugerville	437H	MP-39	78660	1500-1599
GARDEN GATE DR	Travis Co	647D	MP-18	78725	11600-12099
GARDEN GROVE DR	Travis Co	647D	MP-18	78725	11600-12199
GARDENIA CIR	Cedar Park	402H	MD-42	78613	400-499
GARDENIA DR	Travis Co	466B	ML-36	78727	2200-2799
GARDEN MEADOW DR	Georgetown	256Q	MM-56	78628	800-999
GARDEN MEADOW RD	Travis Co	647D	MP-18	78725	11700-12099
GARDEN OAKS DR	Austin	644P	MG-17	78745	5700-5999
GARDEN PATH CV	Round Rock	406D	MM-42	78664	600-699
GARDEN RANCH CT	Austin	642S	MC-16	78749	9200-9299
GARDENRIDGE HOLLOW	Austin	494W	MG-31	78750	6000-6199
GARDEN VALLEY CV	Round Rock	406D	MM-42	78664	800-999
GARDEN VIEW CV	Austin	587E	MN-24	78724	5400-5499
GARDEN VIEW DR	Austin	587E	MN-24	78724	6000-6499
GARDEN VIEW DR	Georgetown	256R	MM-56	78628	900-1099
GARDEN VILLA CIR	Georgetown	256Q	MM-56	78628	700-799
GARDEN VILLA CT	Austin	614U	MH-19	78704	900-999
GARDEN VILLA DR	Georgetown	256Q	MM-56	78628	1600-1999
GARDEN VILLA LN	Austin	614X	MG-19	78704	3000-3899
GARDNER CV	Austin	586Y	MM-22	78721	1100-1199
GARDNER RD	Austin	616C	MM-21	78721	700-1199
GARDNER RD	Hays Co	794Q	MH-2	78610	100-299
GARES RD	Travis Co	366Y	WR-43	78654	28500-28899
GARFIELD LN	Austin	435X	MJ-37	78727	12900-13099
GARFIELD ST	Bastrop	745A	EE-9	78602	1700-1899
GARISON RD	Buda	732Z	MD-7	78610	None
	Hays Co	732Z	MD-7	78610	100-1099
GARLAND AVE	Austin	586U	MM-22	78721	1100-1199
GARLIC CREEK DR	Buda	732T	MC-8	78610	2000-2499
GARNAAS DR	Austin	496B	ML-33	78758	1500-1699
GARNER AVE	Austin	614G	MH-21	78704	700-1799
GARNER CV	Georgetown	195W	MJ-61	78633	100-199
GARNER DR	Cedar Park	373J	ME-44	78613	1700-1899
GARNER PARK DR	Williamson Co	344B	MG-48	78628	100-399
GARNETT LN	Dripping Springs	636V	WR-16	78620	100-199
GARNETT ST	Austin	644G	MH-18	78745	4400-4599
GARRETT CT	Hutto	380N	MU-44	78634	500-599
GARRETT CV	Cedar Park	372G	MD-45	78613	2300-2399
GARRETT ST	Hays Co	639E	WW-18	78737	100-299
GARRETT RUN E	Austin	496X	ML-31	78753	100-399
GARRETT RUN W	Austin	496X	ML-31	78753	100-399
GARRETTSON DR	Austin	672M	MD-14	78748	2600-2699
GARRICK CREEK LN	Austin	672Y	MD-13	78748	11300-11399
GARRISON CIR	Williamson Co	405P	MJ-41	78717	15800-15899
GARRISON DR	Leander	342V	MD-46	78641	2000-2199
GARVEY CV	Austin	672M	MD-14	78748	2900-2999
GARWOOD ST	Austin	616A	ML-21	78702	2800-3199
	Austin	615D	MK-21	78702	None
GARY PLAYER DR	Lago Vista	429Y	WX-37	78645	19000-19999
GASPAR BEND	Cedar Park	402F	MD-42	78613	None
GASTON AVE	Austin	585A	MJ-24	78703	1100-1299
	Austin	554Z	MH-25	78703	1300-1699
GASTON PLACE DR	Austin	556P	ML-26	78723	1800-2199
GATE WAY	Austin	465P	MJ-35	78727	11800-11999
GATECREST	Travis Co	558J	MQ-26	78724	None
GATE DANCER LN	Travis Co	410W	MU-40	78660	4700-5199
GATEHOUSE DR	Austin	497J	MN-32	78753	1100-1199
GATEPOST CT	Cedar Park	374U	MH-43	78613	300-399
GATE RIDGE DR	Austin	702C	MD-12	78748	2500-2699
GATESHEAD CIR	Austin	643G	MF-18	78745	2400-2499
GATESHEAD DR	Austin	643G	MF-18	78745	5800-5999
GATES OF THE ARCTIC AVE					
	Pflugerville	438E	MQ-39	78660	None
GATE TREE LN	Austin	644K	MG-17	78745	400-599
GATEWAY DR	Georgetown	316T	ML-49	78626	100-199
GATEWOOD TRL	Williamson Co	434K	MG-38	78729	13000-13199
GATHRIGHT CV	Austin	614S	MG-19	78704	2000-2099
GATLINBURG DR	Pflugerville	468B	MQ-36	78660	1200-1899
GATLING GUN LN	Austin	672Y	MD-13	78748	11600-11799
	Austin	702B	MC-12	78748	11800-12199
	Austin	702B	MC-12	78739	12200-12499
	Travis Co	672Y	MD-13	78748	11300-11599
GATO PATH	Austin	524E	MG-30	78731	6300-6399
GATOR CREEK DR	Williamson Co	402U	MD-40	78613	1400-1499
GATTIS SCHOOL RD	Round Rock	406M	MM-41	78664	100-1199
	Round Rock	407E	MN-42	78664	1200-3499
	Round Rock	408E	MQ-42	78664	3500-3799
	Travis Co	408G	MR-42	78664	4000-4599
	Williamson Co	408E	MQ-42	78664	3800-3999
	Williamson Co	408H	MR-42	78664	None
GAULT ST	Austin	525Q	MK-29	78757	7600-8099
GAUR CT	Austin	641L	MB-17	78749	9200-9299
GAUR DR	Austin	641L	MB-17	78749	6800-6999
GAVILAN CIR	Travis Co	460Y	WZ-34	78734	15600-15699
GAVIN TRL	Travis Co	409N	MR-36	78660	2300-2499
GAYLOR ST	Austin	525Y	MK-28	78752	500-799

STREET NAME	CITY or COUNTY	MAPSCO GRID	AUSTIN GRID	ZIP CODE	BLOCK RANGE O/E
GAYLORD DR	Travis Co	436Z	MM-37	78728	1600-2099
GAZANIA DR	Pflugerville	437M	MP-38	78660	1000-1299
GAZLEY LN	Travis Co	491Q	MB-32	78732	4100-4199
GEBRON DR	Lakeway	519R	WX-29	78734	15300-15499
	Travis Co	520N	WY-29	78734	15000-15199
	Travis Co	519R	WX-29	78734	15200-15299
GEE ST	Austin	673A	ME-15	78745	2700-2799
GEESE ROUTE	Round Rock	347N	MN-47	78665	3700-3799
GEIR LN	Bastrop Co	743U	EB-7	78602	100-199
GELDING LN	Pflugerville	409J	MS-41	78660	20900-20999
GEM CIR	Austin	614V	MH-19	78704	2900-2999
GEMINI DR	Austin	496K	ML-32	78758	1000-1299
GEMMER ST	Travis Co	677X	MN-13	78617	11500-11799
GEM STONE LN	Bastrop Co	621V	MX-19	78621	100-199
GEMSTONE RD	Austin	642Q	MD-17	78749	3900-4099
GENA CT	Austin	524V	MH-28	78757	6100-6199
GENARD ST	Austin	555L	MK-26	78751	300-699
GENE ALLAN RD	Austin	465D	MK-36	78727	13200-13499
GENE BUTLER DR	Bee Cave	550T	WY-25	78738	None
GENERAL AVIATION AVE	Austin	677A	MN-15	78719	3000-4299
	Austin	676M	MM-14	78617	4300-5199
GENERAL WILLIAMSON DR	Travis Co	490L	WZ-32	78734	14500-15599
GENESSEE CV	Lago Vista	458R	WV-35	78645	20500-20599
GENESTA DR	Buda	763K	ME-5	78610	2000-2099
GENEVA CIR	Austin	556M	MM-26	78723	7100-7299
GENEVA DR	Austin	556H	MM-27	78723	6900-7499
GENEVA DR	Travis Co	708S	MQ-10	78617	14600-14799
GENEVA PKWY	Travis Co	610Y	WZ-19	78736	9300-9399
GENIVEIVE LN	Austin	645A	MJ-18	78741	1900-2099
GENOA DR	Austin	673P	ME-14	78748	1400-1499
GENT DR	Williamson Co	434M	MH-38	78729	13400-13499
GENTILLY CIR	Austin	466P	ML-35	78727	1900-1999
GENTLE BREEZE TERRACE	Austin	524P	MG-29	78731	5800-5899
GENTLEBROOK BEND					
	Village of the Hills	519K	WW-29	78738	1-99
GENTLE OAK DR	Austin	612W	MC-19	78749	6900-7299
GENTLE WINDS LN	Round Rock	345N	MJ-47	78681	3700-3799
GENTRY DR	Leander	311R	MB-50	78641	900-1099
GENTRY DR	Rollingwood	584N	MG-23	78746	3100-3199
	West Lake Hills	583R	MF-23	78746	3200-3399
GEODE DR	Williamson Co	433Q	MF-38	78750	11900-11999
GEOFFS DR	Austin	673S	ME-13	78748	1500-1599
GEORGE ST	Austin	675B	MJ-15	78744	5300-5599
GEORGE ST	Georgetown	286R	MM-53	78626	1600-1699
GEORGE ST	Taylor	322V	MZ-49	76574	800-1099
GEORGE ST	Williamson Co	406P	ML-41	78681	2600-2799
GEORGE BUSH CT	Travis Co	530K	MU-29	78653	12600-12699
GEORGE BUSH ST	Travis Co	530K	MU-29	78653	13200-13799
GEORGE HILL DR	Travis Co	577R	WT-23	78720	9900-10199
GEORGETOWN DR	Jonestown	400M	WZ-41	78645	18400-18599
GEORGETOWN ST	Round Rock	376V	MM-43	78664	100-1499
GEORGETOWN ST N	Round Rock	376V	MM-43	78664	100-1499
GEORGETOWN ST S	Round Rock	376Z	MM-43	78664	100-198 E
GEORGETOWN VIEW LN	Georgetown	286Z	MM-52	78626	100-199
GEORGIA COLEMAN BEND	Austin	672Y	MD-13	78748	2600-11599
GEORGIA LANDING CV	Travis Co	582R	MD-23	78746	1800-1999
GEORGIA MEADOWS DR	Austin	645B	MJ-18	78741	2500-2599
GEORGIAN DR	Austin	526N	ML-29	78753	7900-9099
	Austin	496X	ML-31	78753	10300-10699
	Austin	496U	MM-31	78753	11000-11299
GEORGIAN DR	Bastrop Co	709L	MT-11	78612	None
GEORGIAN DR	Georgetown	286V	MM-52	78626	2200-2299
	Georgetown	287S	MN-52	78626	2300-2799
GEORGIAN ST	Austin	555F	MJ-27	78756	1200-1399
GEORGIAN OAKS DR	Austin	671B	MA-15	78739	11100-11799
GEORGIE TRACE AVE	Austin	705A	MJ-12	78747	8200-8399
GEOSCIENCE DR	Cedar Park	432M	MD-38	78726	2100-2199
GERAD LN	Cedar Park	372J	MC-44	78613	None
GERAGHTY AVE	Austin	525N	MJ-29	78757	2600-2899
GERALD ALLEN LOOP	Austin	672V	MD-13	78748	10800-11099
GERALD FORD ST	Travis Co	530K	MU-29	78653	13500-13599
GERONA DR	Austin	465S	MJ-34	78759	4800-4899
GERONIMO ST	Travis Co	461G	MB-36	78641	14200-14499
GERONIMO TRL	Travis Co	490M	WZ-32	78734	2500-3199
GESSNER DR	Austin	526N	ML-29	78753	7900-8099
GETAWAY DR	Jonestown	430N	WY-38	78645	7200-7399
GETTYSBURG DR	Austin	643W	ME-16	78745	2600-2899
	Austin	643W	ME-16	78745	8700-8799
GETTYSBURG LOOP	Elgin	533G	EB-30	78621	None
GEYSER AVE	Pflugerville	468A	MQ-36	78660	400-799
GHOLSON DR	Travis Co	402T	MC-40	78613	2700-2799
GHOST CREEK	Buda	732W	MC-7	78610	100-299
GIACOMO CV	Travis Co	432L	MD-38	78613	2700-2799
GIANCARLOS LN	Buda	732Q	MD-8	78610	100-199
GIBBS HOLLOW CV	Travis Co	493X	ME-31	78730	5800-5899
GIBERSON WAY	Buda	732P	MC-8	78610	1000-1199
GIBLIN BEND	Travis Co	466H	MM-36	78728	1400-1599
GIBSON ST E	Austin	615E	MJ-21	78704	100-199
GIBSON ST W	Austin	614H	MH-21	78701	100-299
	Austin	614H	MH-21	78704	600-1099
	Austin	614G	MH-21	78704	1100-1299
GIDDENS DR	Cedar Park	372J	MC-44	78613	2300-2399
GIDLEIGH CT	Austin	528E	MQ-30	78754	6300-6399
GIESE LN	Travis Co	501Z	MX-31	78653	14900-16299
	Travis Co	502V	MY-31	78653	16300-16599
	Travis Co	532A	MY-30	78653	None
GIESLA DR	Travis Co	591V	MX-22	78621	22400-22499
GILA PASS	Travis Co	490V	WZ-31	78734	2200-2399
GILA CLIFF DR	Pflugerville	438A	MQ-39	78660	100-299
GILBERT CV	Lago Vista	458R	WV-35	78645	20400-20499
GILBERT RD	Travis Co	618D	MR-21	78724	4700-5699
	Travis Co	588Z	MR-22	78724	5700-6499
	Travis Co	589N	MS-23	78653	7000-7799
GILBERT ST	Austin	554X	MG-25	78703	2700-3799
GILCREST LN	Austin	433X	ME-37	78726	10800-10899
GILES LN	Austin	528W	MQ-28	78754	9700-11199
GILES ST	Austin	585H	MK-24	78722	1600-1799
GILIA DR	Travis Co	551P	MA-26	78733	2200-2399
GILLELAND ST E	Pflugerville	438W	MQ-37	78660	100-199
GILLELAND ST W	Pflugerville	438S	MQ-37	78660	100-399
GILLESPIE LN	Elgin	533F	EA-30	78621	None
GILLESPIE PL	Austin	615N	MJ-20	78704	1100-1199
GILLIAN'S WALK	Bee Cave	550W	WY-25	78738	5100-5199
GILLIS ST	Austin	644A	MG-18	78745	4300-4799
GILLUM CREEK DR	Travis Co	309T	WW-49	78641	13900-14399
GILMORE ST	Taylor	322Z	MZ-49	76574	500-1099
	Taylor	322Y	MZ-49	76574	1400-1599

STREET NAME	CITY or COUNTY	MAPSCO GRID	AUSTIN GRID	ZIP CODE	BLOCK RANGE O/E
GILWELL DR	Austin	678K	MQ-14	78617	12800-13699
GING RD	Williamson Co	443U	EB-37	78615	1-399
GINGER ST	Travis Co	436V	MM-37	78728	15300-15499
GINGERLILY CV	Austin	643V	MF-16	78745	1200-1299
GINGERS CV	Travis Co	464K	MG-35	78759	7800-7899
GINGER SPICE LN	Travis Co	467G	MP-36	78660	1300-1399
GINI LN	Niederwald	794H	MH-3	78610	100-599
GINITA LN	Austin	671C	MB-15	78739	6100-6199
GINKGO CV	Austin	493M	MF-32	78750	7800-7899
GINRE CV	Austin	494G	MH-33	78759	5800-5899
GINSEL LN	Bastrop Co	533S	EA-28	78621	100-199
GINSENG CV	Travis Co	467L	MP-35	78660	14600-14699
GIVENS AVE	Austin	585M	MK-23	78722	2400-2599
GLACIAL STREAM LN	Cedar Park	373R	MF-44	78613	500-598 E
GLACIER DR	Cedar Park	373W	ME-43	78613	200-299
GLACIER BAY ST	Pflugerville	438A	MQ-39	78660	17900-18199
GLACIER FALLS CT	Austin	466L	MM-35	78727	13300-13399
GLACIER PARKE CV	Austin	462K	MC-35	78726	12500-12599
GLACIER PASS LN	Cedar Park	374T	MG-43	78613	3000-3099
GLACIER POINT CV	Taylor	322M	MZ-50	76574	4200-4299
GLACIER POINT TRL	Taylor	322M	MZ-50	76574	500-699
GLADE LINE DR	Austin	674M	MH-14	78744	4500-4699
GLADEVIEW DR	Austin	644E	MG-18	78745	4800-5099
GLADE VIEW DR	Round Rock	406B	ML-42	78681	300-499
GLADIOLA BLVD	Austin	645L	MK-17	78745	3300-3399
GLADNELL ST	Taylor	352C	MZ-48	76574	1500-2499
GLADSTONE DR	Austin	586C	MM-24	78723	5200-5399
GLADSTONE CASTLE TRL					
	Pflugerville	408X	MQ-40	78660	1000-1099
GLASGOW CV	Williamson Co	408D	MR-42	78634	1000-1099
GLASGOW DR	Austin	642H	MD-18	78749	3900-3999
GLASS DR	Leander	342L	MD-47	78641	800-1699
GLASS RD	Mustang Ridge	765V	MK-4	78610	None
	Travis Co	765V	MK-4	78610	12100-12599
GLASS RD	Travis Co	589Z	MT-22	78653	17100-17799
GLASS MOUNTAIN TRL	Austin	433X	ME-37	78750	10500-10599
	Travis Co	433X	ME-37	78750	10600-10799
GLASTONBURY TRL	Travis Co	439F	MS-39	78660	3500-3899
GLAZIER CIR	Austin	526C	MM-30	78753	900-1099
GLEN CV	Round Rock	376P	ML-44	78681	1200-1299
GLEN RD	Austin	496M	MM-32	78753	800-899
GLEN ALLEN	Austin	614N	MG-20	78704	1900-2099
GLENBROOK PATH	Williamson Co	346G	MM-48	78665	100-199
GLEN BURNIE CIR	Williamson Co	433B	ME-39	78613	1500-1598 E
GLEN BURNIE DR	Williamson Co	433B	ME-39	78613	1200-1299
GLEN CANYON DR	Williamson Co	375U	MK-43	78681	8300-9099
GLENCARRIE LN	Austin	463G	MF-36	78750	10000-10199
GLENCLIFF DR	Austin	614A	MG-21	78704	1700-1999
GLENCOE CIR	Austin	644E	MG-18	78745	5000-5099
GLEN CREEK CT	Travis Co	529H	MT-30	78653	13600-13699
GLENCREST DR	Austin	556K	ML-26	78723	1300-1699
GLENDA CT	Austin	496L	MM-32	78753	11900-11999
GLENDA DR	Round Rock	406B	ML-42	78681	1100-1399
GLENDALE LN	Lago Vista	458A	WU-36	78645	4100-4299
GLENDALE PL	Austin	615S	MJ-19	78704	2100-2199
GLENDALOUGH DR	Pflugerville	407Y	MP-40	78660	100-1299
GLENDORA CT	Travis Co	550R	WZ-26	78733	2900-2999
GLENEAGLES CV	Round Rock	408C	MR-42	78664	4000-4099
GLEN ECHO DR	Austin	404L	MH-41	78717	15100-15199
GLENFALLOCH CT	Austin	528P	MQ-29	78754	11400-11599
GLENFIELD CT	Williamson Co	346H	MM-48	78665	1300-1399
GLEN FIELD DR	Cedar Park	372C	MD-45	78613	2400-2699
GLENGARRY DR	Austin	524Q	MH-29	78731	3900-4099
GLEN GROVE WAY	Lakeway	519U	WX-28	78738	None
GLEN HAVEN	Austin	644A	MG-18	78745	4700-4799
GLEN HAVEN PATH	Hays Co	700N	WY-11	78610	7400-7499
GLEN HEATHER CT	Lakeway	519R	WX-29	78734	100-199
GLEN HEATHER DR	Lakeway	519R	WX-29	78734	15000-15799
GLENHILL CV	Austin	556C	MM-27	78752	7600-7699
GLENHILL RD	Austin	556C	MM-27	78752	7300-7599
GLEN HOLLOW DR	Austin	644E	MG-18	78745	5100-5199
GLENHOLLOW PATH	Austin	644N	MG-17	78745	5700-5999
GLEN HOLLOW ST	Cedar Park	403K	ME-41	78613	300-399
GLEN KNOLL DR	Travis Co	529H	MT-30	78653	11500-11699
GLENLAKE DR	Travis Co	522G	MD-30	78730	8700-9899
GLEN MARK DR	Travis Co	529H	MT-30	78653	13400-13799
	Travis Co	530E	MU-30	78653	13800-13899
GLEN MEADOW CV	Georgetown	287M	MP-53	78626	1000-1099
GLEN MEADOW DR	Austin	644P	MG-17	78745	5600-5999
	Austin	644T	MG-16	78745	6000-6299
GLENMEADOWS DR	Round Rock	376S	ML-43	78681	1500-1599
GLENMIST LN	Cedar Park	403J	ME-41	78613	600-699
GLENN CV	Travis Co	582H	MD-24	78746	1200-1299
GLENN DR	Williamson Co	407T	MN-40	78664	200-299
GLENN LN	Austin	526E	ML-30	78753	8800-9399
GLENN ST S	Austin	646X	ML-16	78744	7300-7599
GLEN OAK DR	Austin	644E	MG-18	78745	800-1099
GLEN OAK LN	Williamson Co	282X	MC-52	78641	100-199
GLEN OAKS CT	Austin	585V	MK-22	78702	1000-1099
GLEN OAKS DR	Austin	585V	MK-22	78702	2900-3099
GLEN ORA	Austin	614P	MG-20	78704	3100-3199
GLEN RAE ST	Austin	585Z	MK-22	78702	2900-3099
GLEN RIDGE DR	Austin	524G	MH-30	78731	6800-6999
GLEN ROCK DR	Village of the Hills	519T	WW-28	78738	1-99
GLEN ROSE DR	Austin	554C	MH-27	78731	3300-3399
GLEN ROSE CHASE	Pflugerville	437Y	MP-37	78660	1600-1699
GLEN SPRINGS DR	Lakeway	519Q	WX-29	78734	15700-15999
GLENSPRINGS WAY	Austin	615X	MJ-19	78741	2400-2599
GLEN SUMMER CV	Austin	497J	MN-32	78753	1100-1299
GLEN VALLEY DR	Austin	556K	ML-26	78723	1600-1699
GLEN VALLEY DR	Hays Co	636P	WQ-17	78620	100-199
GLEN VALLEY LN E	Leander	342V	MD-46	78641	100-699
GLENVIEW AVE	Austin	554Z	MH-25	78703	2800-3499
GLENVIEW CIR	Travis Co	577V	WT-22	78720	10800-10899
GLENVIEW LN	Buda	763J	ME-5	78610	None
GLENVILLE CV	Travis Co	548S	WU-25	78738	18000-18099
GLENWAY CT	Village of the Hills	519P	WW-29	78738	1-99
GLENWAY DR	Village of the Hills	519P	WW-29	78738	1-99
GLENWILLOW CV	Round Rock	376N	ML-44	78681	1400-1599
GLENWOOD CV	Round Rock	376T	ML-43	78681	1200-1399
GLENWOOD DR	Austin	556K	ML-26	78723	1300-1499
GLENWOOD DR	Williamson Co	197V	MP-61	78626	100-199
GLENWOOD ST	Round Rock	376X	ML-43	78681	1000-1099
GLENWOOD TRL	Cedar Park	433A	ME-39	78613	2600-2899
GLISSMAN RD	Austin	616A	ML-21	78702	4600-4799
	Austin	616B	ML-21	78702	5100-5399
	Austin	616B	ML-21	78721	5400-5599

STREET NAME	CITY or COUNTY	MAPSCO GRID	AUSTIN GRID	ZIP CODE	BLOCK RANGE O/E
GLOMAR AVE	Austin	586L	MM-23	78721	4200-4599
GLORIOUS LN	Pflugerville	437J	MN-38	78660	16200-16299
GLORY LN	Williamson Co	280Z	WZ-52	78641	1-599
GLOSSON RD	Dripping Springs	636R	WR-17	78620	100-599
GLOUCESTER LN	Austin	556Y	MM-25	78723	5400-5899
GLOWWORM CIR	Austin	675N	MJ-14	78744	7100-7299
GNARL DR	Austin	524C	MH-30	78731	4200-4399
GNARLED OAK CV	Austin	645X	MJ-16	78744	4900-4999
GNU GAP	Pflugerville	437B	MN-39	78664	1700-1899
GOBI DR	Austin	644J	MG-17	78745	1100-1299
GOCHMAN ST	Austin	586A	ML-24	78723	4100-4299
GODDARD BLUFF CV	Austin	497N	MN-32	78754	11700-11799
GODDARD BLUFF DR	Austin	497T	MN-31	78754	1600-1799
GODOLPHIN CT	Pflugerville	409J	MS-41	78660	21000-21099
GOETH CIR	Austin	583Z	MF-22	78746	1300-1399
GOFORTH RD	Creedmoor	795G	MK-3	78610	14601-15499 O
	Travis Co	795G	MK-3	78610	14600-15498 E
GOFORTH RD	Hays Co	794S	MG-1	78610	6300-7299
GOFORTH RD W	Buda	762H	MD-6	78610	100-799
	Buda	763E	ME-6	78610	800-1199
GOLD LN	Lago Vista	458P	WU-35	78645	1300-1399
GOLD WAY	Travis Co	366U	WR-43	78654	None
GOLDBRIDGE DR	Austin	643S	ME-16	78745	2700-2999
GOLD CAVE DR	Austin	403H	MF-42	78717	11500-11599
GOLD CREST CT	Travis Co	492U	MD-31	78730	5100-5199
GOLDDUST PASS	Pflugerville	438M	MR-38	78660	18700-18899
GOLDEN CV	Hays Co	794W	MG-1	78610	100-399
GOLDEN ARROW AVE	Cedar Park	373R	MF-44	78613	1800-2199
GOLDEN BEAR CV	Lakeway	519Y	WX-28	78738	100-199
GOLDEN BEAR CV	Round Rock	378Y	MR-43	78664	900-999
GOLDEN BEAR DR	Georgetown	227A	MN-60	78628	100-199
GOLDEN BEAR DR	Lakeway	519X	WW-28	78738	100-699
GOLDEN BEAR DR	Round Rock	378Y	MR-43	78664	2000-2099
GOLDEN BRIDLE TRL	Leander	372B	MC-45	78641	1200-1299
GOLDEN CREEK CV	Round Rock	377V	MP-43	78665	2900-2999
GOLDEN CREEK DR	Round Rock	377V	MP-43	78665	500-599
GOLDEN CREST DR	Georgetown	256R	MM-56	78628	1600-1699
GOLDEN EAGLE LN	Dripping Springs	636Q	WR-17	78620	100-1199
GOLDEN EAGLE LN	Williamson Co	282J	MC-53	78641	100-599
GOLDEN EAGLE ST	Pflugerville	438J	MQ-38	78660	1200-1399
GOLDEN EAGLE WAY	Elgin	503T	EA-31	78621	None
GOLDENEYE CIR	Hays Co	732B	MC-9	78610	300-399
GOLDEN FLAX TRL	Travis Co	467J	MN-35	78660	13700-14099
GOLDEN GATE DR	Leander	342V	MD-46	78641	100-199
GOLDEN GATE PARK	Travis Co	521B	MA-30	78732	2200-2799
GOLDEN HILLS CIR	Austin	494C	MH-33	78759	9500-9599
GOLDEN MAIZE CV	Georgetown	285T	MJ-52	78628	100-199
GOLDEN MAIZE DR	Travis Co	554E	MG-27	78746	4600-4799
GOLDEN MEADOW DR	Austin	495R	MK-32	78758	10100-10699
GOLDENOAK CIR	Round Rock	375C	MK-45	78681	2800-3399
GOLDEN OAKS DR	Georgetown	256T	ML-55	78628	100-599
	Georgetown	256M	MM-56	78628	900-999
	Williamson Co	256M	MM-56	78628	600-899
GOLDEN OAKS RD	Georgetown	256M	MM-56	78628	600-899
GOLDEN PALOMINO CT	Travis Co	521K	MA-29	78732	900-1099
GOLDEN PHEASANT DR	Austin	496E	ML-33	78758	1700-1999
GOLDEN QUAIL DR	Austin	496S	ML-31	78758	10200-10699
GOLDEN RAIN CV	Travis Co	582J	MC-23	78735	8800-8899
GOLDENROD CV	Austin	493M	MF-32	78750	7900-7999
GOLDENROD WAY	Georgetown	225L	MK-59	78633	100-199
GOLDEN SUNRISE LN	Travis Co	467M	MP-35	78660	1700-2199
GOLDEN VALLEY DR	Travis Co	560J	MU-26	78653	17700-18299
GOLDEN VISTA DR	Georgetown	256Q	MM-56	78628	1600-1899
GOLDFINCH CT	Austin	526J	ML-29	78758	8400-8499
GOLDFINCH CT	Cedar Park	433A	ME-39	78613	1300-1399
GOLDFINCH DR	Cedar Park	433A	ME-39	78613	2400-2699
GOLD FISH POND AVE	Travis Co	436Y	MM-37	78728	14500-14699
GOLD FLOWER HOLLOW	Austin	524N	MG-29	78731	4700-4799
GOLDMOSS CV	Austin	643V	MF-16	78745	6700-6799
GOLDRIDGE CIR	Williamson Co	224V	MH-58	78633	500-599
GOLDRIDGE DR	Williamson Co	224R	MH-59	78633	100-499
GOLD RUN CV	Travis Co	529M	MT-29	78653	11700-11799
GOLD RUSH DR	Cedar Park	372R	MD-44	78613	100-199
GOLD STAR DR	Cedar Park	374N	MG-44	78613	300-398 E
GOLD WING DR	Austin	496E	ML-33	78758	1900-1999
GOLD YARROW DR	Austin	492Q	MD-32	78730	10700-10799
GOLETA CT	Austin	642Q	MD-17	78749	4400-4499
GOLF COURSE RD	Austin	647P	MN-17	78719	10000-10699
GOLF CREST CV	Lakeway	519H	WX-30	78734	100-199
GOLF CREST LN	Lakeway	519D	WX-30	78734	100-799
GOLFLINKS CT	Travis Co	426H	WR-39	78669	2300-2499
GOLFVIEW CIR	Point Venture	489J	WW-32	78645	200-299
GOLF VIEW DR	Georgetown	225K	MJ-59	78633	100-199
GOLF VISTA DR	Travis Co	492X	MC-31	78730	4500-4599
GOLIAD LN	Austin	644F	MG-18	78745	4600-4699
GOMEZ CIR	Bastrop Co	739P	MS-8	78617	100-199
GONZALES ST	Austin	585Z	MK-22	78702	2500-2799
	Austin	615D	MK-21	78702	2800-2899
	Austin	616A	ML-21	78702	2900-4999
GOODALL CT	Austin	641X	MA-16	78739	6500-6599
GOODNIGHT DR	Williamson Co	283D	MF-54	78628	100-399
GOODNIGHT LN	Austin	525X	MJ-28	78757	1700-6599
GOODNIGHT TRL	Dripping Springs	636R	WR-17	78620	100-299
	Dripping Springs	637N	WS-17	78620	300-599
GOOD NIGHT TRL	Leander	371G	MB-45	78641	3500-3799
GOODNIGHT TRL	Pflugerville	467C	MP-36	78660	None
GOODRICH AVE	Austin	614F	MG-21	78704	1700-2299
GOODSON CT	Round Rock	377J	MN-44	78664	1700-1899
GOODSON LN	Round Rock	377J	MN-44	78664	1700-1899
GOODSPEED WAY	Pflugerville	438N	MQ-38	78660	700-899
GOODWATER ST	Georgetown	225H	MK-60	78633	100-199
GOODWIN AVE	Austin	586S	ML-22	78702	2700-3699
	Austin	586S	ML-22	78721	3700-3799
GOOD WOOD DR	Austin	645W	MJ-16	78744	5000-5099
GOOSE ISLAND DR	Georgetown	195N	MJ-62	78633	100-399
GORDON CT	Austin	526F	ML-30	78753	400-499
GORDON ST	Bastrop	745C	EF-9	78602	1500-1699
GORHAM ST	Austin	496F	ML-33	78758	1400-1499
GORHAM GLEN CT	Austin	671G	MB-15	78739	11200-11299
GORHAM GLEN LN	Austin	671G	MB-15	78739	5600-5999
GOSSAMER DR	Austin	497T	MN-31	78754	11400-11599
GOUDA CT	Cedar Park	372K	MC-44	78613	1600-1699
GOULDVILLE CT	Austin	641Y	MB-16	78739	6400-6499
GOVALLE AVE	Austin	586W	ML-22	78702	2700-3799
GOVERNMENT CV	Lago Vista	458R	WV-35	78645	20300-20399
GOVERNORS ROW	Austin	644M	MH-17	78744	4100-4199
GOWER ST	Travis Co	437L	MP-38	78660	16800-17099

STREET NAME	CITY or COUNTY	MAPSCO GRID	AUSTIN GRID	ZIP CODE	BLOCK RANGE O/E
GRACE BLVD	Georgetown	197W	MN-61	78633	100-299
GRACE LN	Taylor	323S	EA-49	76574	100-399
GRACE LN	Travis Co	552P	MC-26	78733	300-599
GRACE ST	Taylor	352C	MZ-48	76574	1100-1499
	Taylor	322Y	MZ-49	76574	1500-2499
GRACEFUL LN	Travis Co	619N	MS-20	78725	4500-4699
GRACELAND TRL	Williamson Co	375M	MJ-43	78717	9400-9599
GRACIOSA CV	Travis Co	583K	ME-23	78746	400-499
GRACY DR	Austin	496F	ML-33	78758	1400-1499
GRACY FARMS LN	Austin	496B	ML-33	78758	1400-2399
	Austin	465Z	MK-34	78758	2400-2799
GRADY DR E	Austin	496Y	MM-31	78753	100-699
GRADY DR W	Austin	496U	MM-31	78753	100-799
GRADY TUCK LN	Bastrop	745J	EE-8	78602	100-199
GRAEF RD	Creedmoor	764M	MH-5	78610	13501-14699 O
	Creedmoor	765S	MJ-4	78610	14700-14799
	Travis Co	764M	MH-5	78610	13500-14698 E
GRAEF RD	Hays Co	794Z	MH-1	78610	100-1599
GRAFTON LN	Hays Co	639X	WW-16	78737	100-399
GRAFTON LN	Pflugerville	407Y	MP-40	78660	1200-1499
GRAFTON GLEN CV	Pflugerville	407Y	MP-40	78660	18100-18199
GRAHAM PL	Austin	585E	MJ-24	78705	700-899
GRAHAM ST	Austin	585R	MK-23	78702	1100-1199
GRAJA TRL	Bastrop Co	738K	MQ-8	78617	100-199
GRAMA CV	Travis Co	580B	WY-24	78738	12600-12699
GRANADA DR	Austin	645B	MJ-18	78741	2200-2399
GRANADA DR	Williamson Co	226X	ML-58	78628	4000-4199
GRANADA HILLS DR	Travis Co	641F	MA-18	78737	8500-9499
GRANBERRY DR	Austin	643U	MF-16	78745	2100-2299
	Austin	643T	ME-16	78745	2300-2499
GRAND CT	Jonestown	430C	WZ-39	78645	None
GRAND ST	Pflugerville	437N	MN-38	78660	15400-15699
GRAND AVENUE PKWY	Pflugerville	437N	MN-38	78660	100-1999
	Pflugerville	436M	MM-38	78728	2000-2699
	Travis Co	436G	MM-39	78728	3000-3399
	Travis Co	436B	ML-39	78728	4100-4199
	Williamson Co	436B	ML-39	78728	4200-4599
GRAND BANKS LN	Travis Co	409X	MS-40	78660	20100-20399
GRAND CANYON DR	Austin	556B	MM-27	78752	6900-7399
GRAND CHAMPION DR	Travis Co	521J	MA-29	78732	1100-1299
GRAND CYPRESS DR	Austin	704E	MG-12	78747	4500-4699
GRANDE BLVD	Austin	466B	ML-36	78727	None
GRANDE CT	Austin	586E	ML-24	78723	3400-3499
GRANDE MESA DR	Georgetown	317J	MN-50	78626	1000-1499
GRANDFALLS DR	Travis Co	402U	MD-40	78613	1400-1499
GRANDFATHER RD	Bastrop Co	742M	MZ-8	78612	100-199
GRANDIFLORAS CV	Travis Co	532Q	MZ-29	78621	12800-12899
GRAND ISLE DR	Williamson Co	377B	MN-45	78665	100-399
GRAND JUNCTION TRL	Georgetown	317K	MN-50	78626	200-399
	Georgetown	317K	MN-50	78626	1600-1799
GRAND LAKE PKWY	Leander	343L	MF-47	78641	2200-2699
GRAND MARSH LN	Williamson Co	377F	MN-45	78665	1000-1099
GRAND MISSION WAY	Pflugerville	438H	MR-39	78660	2500-2599
	Pflugerville	438H	MR-39	78660	2600-3099
GRAND NATIONAL AVE	Pflugerville	409E	MS-42	78660	21100-21499
GRAND OAK CIR	Austin	463G	MF-36	78750	10500-10599
GRAND OAK CV	Austin	463L	MF-35	78750	9300-9399
GRAND OAK DR	Austin	463G	MF-36	78750	9600-10699
GRAND OAKS LN	Williamson Co	284E	MG-54	78628	100-399
GRAND OAKS LOOP	Travis Co	432K	MC-38	78613	2700-2999
GRAND PRAIRIE CIR	Dripping Springs	636V	WR-16	78620	100-899
GRANDRIDGE TRL	Williamson Co	374W	MG-43	78613	900-2599
GRAND SUMMIT BLVD	Hays Co	546K	WQ-26	78620	10000-11699
	Travis Co	546L	WR-26	78620	9200-10099
GRAND TETON CT	Austin	464Y	MH-34	78759	10100-10299
GRAND TETON TRL	Taylor	322R	MZ-50	76574	900-1099
GRANDVIEW DR	Jonestown	400Y	WZ-40	78645	8500-9099
GRANDVIEW ST	Austin	555W	MJ-25	78705	3100-3399
GRAND VISTA CIR	Williamson Co	346H	MM-48	78665	4100-4299
GRAND VISTA CV	Jonestown	400Y	WZ-40	78645	None
GRANGER DR	Austin	674M	MH-14	78744	6800-6899
GRANGER LN	Travis Co	432H	MD-39	78613	2200-2399
GRANITE DR	Williamson Co	288C	MR-54	78626	100-299
GRANITE LN	Hays Co	639Y	WX-16	78737	100-299
GRANITE TRL	Austin	611M	MB-20	78735	6200-6299
GRANITE BASIN CT	Travis Co	432P	MC-38	78613	3400-3499
GRANITE BAY PL	Travis Co	521L	MB-29	78732	11800-11999
GRANITE CREEK DR	Leander	372B	MC-45	78641	1500-1899
GRANITE PEAK CV	Georgetown	196N	ML-62	78628	100-199
GRANITE SPRINGS RD	Leander	343L	MF-47	78641	1900-2199
GRANNY DR	Travis Co	679H	MT-15	78617	4500-4799
GRANT AVE	Pflugerville	437V	MP-37	78660	1200-1399
GRANT CT	Leander	342V	MD-46	78641	100-299
GRANT CV	Hutto	379C	MT-45	78634	100-199
GRANT LN	Lago Vista	458R	WV-35	78645	2300-2499
GRANT ST	Austin	586P	ML-23	78721	3600-3699
GRANT FOREST DR	Austin	674W	MG-13	78744	9200-9399
GRANTMOOR DR	Travis Co	557M	MP-26	78724	None
GRANTON CV	Austin	498W	MQ-31	78653	12300-12499
GRAPE CV	Williamson Co	405E	MJ-42	78717	8800-8899
GRAPEVINE CT	Hays Co	669P	WW-14	78737	100-199
GRAPEVINE DR	Cedar Park	372Y	MD-43	78613	500-899
GRAPEVINE LN	Austin	464Q	MH-35	78759	10900-11199
GRAPEVINE LN	Georgetown	225L	MK-59	78633	100-199
GRAPEVINE CANYON TRL	Leander	372B	MC-45	78641	2400-2599
GRAPEVINE SPRINGS CV					
	Georgetown	256N	ML-56	78628	2600-2699
GRAPEWOOD CT	Village of the Hills	519S	WW-28	78738	1-99
GRASS CV	Austin	464G	MH-36	78759	7300-7399
GRASS HOLLOW	Austin	494S	MG-31	78750	6100-6199
GRASSHOPPER DR	Austin	672D	MD-15	78748	3200-3399
GRASSLAND DR	Leander	341H	MB-48	78641	1800-1999
GRASSLAND LN	Williamson Co	256W	ML-55	78628	400-499
GRASSMERE CT	Austin	671C	MB-15	78739	10900-10999
GRASSY WAY	Bee Cave	549M	WX-26	78738	4100-4199
GRASSY FIELD RD	Hays Co	669N	WW-14	78737	1000-1799
GRASSY KNOLLS DR	Cedar Park	403K	ME-41	78613	1200-1299
GRAVEL PIT RD	Taylor	353C	EB-48	76574	500-899
	Taylor	323Y	EB-49	76574	900-1099
GRAVESEND RD	Travis Co	437G	MP-39	78660	16800-16999
GRAVEYARD POINT RD	Travis Co	489M	WX-32	78734	1400-1899
GRAY BLVD	Austin	495V	MK-31	78758	9600-10099
GRAYBECKER DR	Austin	495V	MK-31	78758	1900-1999
GRAYBUCK RD	Austin	672G	MD-15	78748	3300-3499
GRAY CAMLET CT	Travis Co	702G	MD-12	78748	2600-2699
GRAY CAMLET LN	Travis Co	702G	MD-12	78748	12300-12599
GRAYFORD DR	Austin	614W	MG-19	78704	1500-1699

STREET NAME	CITY or COUNTY	MAPSCO GRID	AUSTIN GRID	ZIP CODE	BLOCK RANGE O/E
GRAY FOX CT	Dripping Springs	636Q	WR-17	78620	100-199
GRAY FOX DR	Austin	465T	MJ-34	78759	4600-4899
GRAYLEDGE DR	Austin	526T	ML-28	78753	8100-8599
GRAYLING LN	Williamson Co	344V	MH-46	78681	3900-3999
GRAY OAK DR	Round Rock	376J	ML-44	78681	1800-1999
GRAYSON CV	Cedar Park	372P	MC-44	78613	1600-1699
GRAYSON LN	Austin	585H	MK-24	78722	3700-3999
GRAYSTONE LN	Williamson Co	194Y	MH-61	78633	100-299
GRAYWOOD CV	Austin	614A	MG-21	78704	1700-1799
GRAZING DEER TRL	Travis Co	580D	WZ-24	78735	11200-11499
GRAZING HORSE LN	Travis Co	703L	MF-11	78652	100-199
GREAT BASIN AVE	Pflugerville	438A	MQ-39	78660	17700-18199
GREAT BASIN DR	Taylor	322R	MZ-50	76574	4000-4099
GREAT BRITAIN BLVD	Austin	673G	MF-15	78748	600-1199
GREAT DIVIDE DR	Bee Cave	550S	WY-25	78738	4700-5299
	Bee Cave	580A	WY-24	78738	5300-5699
GREAT EAGLE TRL	Travis Co	490R	WZ-32	78734	14500-14899
GREATER SCAUP LN	Cedar Park	373V	MF-43	78613	100-199
GREAT FALLS DR	Travis Co	560F	MU-27	78653	18200-18899
GREAT FRONTIER DR	Georgetown	225C	MK-60	78633	100-199
GREAT HILLS TRL	Austin	494H	MH-33	78759	8900-9799
	Austin	495E	MJ-33	78759	9800-10099
GREAT NORTHERN BLVD	Austin	524Z	MH-28	78757	6100-6399
	Austin	525J	MJ-29	78757	6400-7799
	Austin	525A	MJ-30	78757	7900-7999
GREAT OAKS BLVD	Travis Co	310L	WZ-50	78641	22900-23099
GREAT OAKS CV	Williamson Co	375T	MJ-43	78681	900-1199
GREAT OAKS DR	Williamson Co	375K	MJ-44	78681	1700-2199
	Williamson Co	375A	MJ-45	78681	2200-2699
	Williamson Co	345W	MJ-46	78681	2700-3099
	Williamson Co	405K	MJ-41	78681	15900-16699
	Williamson Co	375X	MJ-43	78681	16700-17699
GREAT OAKS PKWY	Austin	555J	MJ-26	78756	2500-2699
GREAT PANDA CV	Travis Co	707C	MP-12	78617	7200-7299
GREAT PLAINS DR	Austin	612H	MD-21	78735	4000-4299
GREAT SAND DUNES AVE	Pflugerville	438E	MQ-39	78660	800-999
GREAT VALLEY DR	Cedar Park	433B	ME-39	78613	2800-2899
	Williamson Co	433B	ME-39	78613	2900-3499
	Williamson Co	403X	ME-40	78613	3500-3599
GREAT VALLEY DR	Travis Co	560F	MU-27	78653	18200-18499
GREATVIEW CT	Williamson Co	346H	MM-48	78665	1200-1299
GREATVIEW DR	Williamson Co	346H	MM-48	78665	4200-4399
GREAT WESTERN DR	Hutto	379P	MS-44	78634	100-299
GREAT WILLOW DR	Travis Co	436U	MM-37	78728	14700-14899
GREELEY CV	Lago Vista	458R	WV-35	78645	20500-20599
GREEN CV	Lago Vista	458M	WV-35	78645	20400-20499
GREEN ACRES	Austin	435W	MJ-37	78727	5900-5999
GREEN ACRES	Williamson Co	197M	MP-62	78626	1-1299
GREEN BRANCH DR	Georgetown	287S	MN-52	78626	1600-1799
GREENBRIAR CT	Austin	555J	MJ-26	78756	4500-4599
GREENBRIAR CT	Round Rock	406H	MM-42	78664	1100-1199
GREENBRIAR CV	Round Rock	406H	MM-42	78664	1000-1099
GREEN BRIAR LOOP	Round Rock	407E	MN-42	78664	900-1299
GREENBRIAR ST	Buda	763P	ME-5	78610	100-199
GREENBROOK PKWY	Austin	556T	ML-25	78723	1700-2099
GREENBROOK PKWY	Pflugerville	438N	MQ-38	78660	1000-1199
GREENBURY DR	Manor	530K	MU-29	78653	None
GREEN CLIFFS RD	Travis Co	524W	MG-28	78746	4000-4499
GREEN DOWNS DR	Round Rock	407E	MN-42	78664	1000-1499
GREEN EMERALD TERRACE					
	Travis Co	672W	MC-13	78739	3300-4099
GREENER DR	Leander	341D	MB-48	78641	300-499
GREEN FALLS CT	Travis Co	524W	MG-28	78746	5200-5299
GREEN FIELD CV	Pflugerville	438S	MQ-37	78660	600-699
GREEN FIELD DR	Cedar Park	402R	MD-41	78613	1200-1399
GREENFIELD DR	Round Rock	376R	MM-44	78664	1400-1599
GREENFIELD PKWY	Austin	615X	MJ-19	78741	2300-2399
GREEN FIELDS DR	Bastrop Co	712Y	MZ-10	78602	100-199
GREENFLINT LN	Austin	494V	MH-31	78759	8400-8599
GREEN FOREST DR	Austin	644E	MG-18	78745	1200-1499
GREEN GRASS TRL	Austin	675S	MJ-13	78744	7300-7399
GREEN GROVE	Georgetown	225V	MK-58	78628	100-199
GREEN GROVE DR	Travis Co	647D	MP-18	78725	11600-11999
GREENHAVEN DR	Austin	525J	MJ-29	78757	7200-7599
GREENHEART DR	Austin	644K	MG-17	78745	5000-5299
GREENHILL DR	Pflugerville	438N	MQ-38	78660	1000-1199
GREENHILL DR	Round Rock	376G	MM-45	78665	500-2399
GREENHILL PL	Austin	494R	MH-32	78759	4000-4099
GREEN HILLS LOOP N	Hays Co	669X	WW-13	78737	14000-14099
GREENING WAY	Leander	342T	MC-46	78641	1500-1899
GREENLAND LN	Austin	643T	ME-16	78745	2500-2699
GREEN LANES	Austin	584D	MH-24	78703	1-99
GREENLAWN BLVD	Round Rock	407J	MN-41	78664	200-2499
	Round Rock	407W	MN-40	78664	3200-3499
	Round Rock	406Z	MM-40	78664	3500-3599
GREENLAWN PKWY	Austin	525J	MJ-29	78757	2400-3399
GREENLAWN ST	Taylor	322U	MZ-49	76574	2800-3199
GREEN LEAF DR	Travis Co	647D	MP-18	78725	12000-12199
GREENLEAF DR	Williamson Co	222W	MC-58	78642	100-699
GREEN LEAF LN	Williamson Co	284E	MG-54	78628	100-299
GREENLEDGE CV	Austin	464Y	MH-34	78759	5700-5799
GREENLEE DR	Austin	554Y	MH-25	78703	2200-3399
GREENLEE DR	Georgetown	286X	ML-52	78628	800-1099
GREENLEE DR	Williamson Co	343T	ME-46	78641	2600-2899
GREEN LODGE CT	Travis Co	529D	MT-30	78653	13500-13599
GREEN MEADOW DR	Georgetown	285P	MJ-53	78628	100-299
GREEN MEADOW DR	Round Rock	376R	MM-44	78664	900-1199
GREENMEADOW DR	Travis Co	733B	ME-9	78652	600-799
GREEN MEADOWS	Pflugerville	437Q	MP-38	78660	200-399
	Travis Co	437Q	MP-38	78660	400-599
GREEN MEADOWS LN	Buda	763P	ME-5	78610	2000-2699
GREENMEER LN	Austin	496X	ML-31	78758	900-999
GREEN MOUNTAIN CV	Round Rock	407E	MN-42	78664	1200-1299
GREENMOUNTAIN LN	Austin	495N	MJ-32	78759	3900-4099
GREEN OAK DR	Hays Co	577Y	WT-22	78720	700-799
GREEN OAKS CIR	Round Rock	377K	MN-44	78665	2100-2199
GREEN OAKS DR	Bastrop Co	715B	EE-12	78602	100-399
GREEN OAKS DR	Travis Co	583A	ME-24	78746	6200-6299
GREENOCK ST	Austin	642M	MD-17	78749	7000-7299
GREENPARK DR	Lago Vista	428Z	WV-37	78645	20700-21299
GREEN PASTURE DR	Williamson Co	378D	MR-45	78634	100-299
	Williamson Co	348Z	MR-46	78634	300-399
GREEN PASTURES CV	Travis Co	647D	MP-18	78725	1400-1499
GREEN PASTURES DR	Travis Co	647D	MP-18	78725	1300-1399
	Travis Co	647H	MP-18	78725	1500-1699
GREENRIDGE DR	Travis Co	409K	MS-41	78660	21100-21399
	Williamson Co	409K	MS-41	78660	21400-21699

G

STREET NAME	CITY or COUNTY	MAPSCO GRID	AUSTIN GRID	ZIP CODE	BLOCK RANGE O/E
GREENRIDGE LN	Hays Co	636K	WQ-17	78620	100-299
GREENRIDGE PL	Austin	494M	MJ-32	78759	4200-4299
GREENRIDGE RD	Williamson Co	255V	MK-55	78628	300-599
GREENRIDGE TERRACE	Austin	644L	MH-17	78745	4600-4799
GREEN RIVER TRL	Travis Co	434V	MH-37	78729	13100-13199
	Williamson Co	434V	MH-37	78729	None
GREENSBORO DR	Austin	556V	MM-25	78723	6400-6499
	Austin	557S	MN-25	78723	6600-6699
GREEN'S CREEK CV	Bastrop Co	742S	MY-7	78612	100-199
GREEN SHORE CIR	Lago Vista	428V	WV-37	78645	4700-5099
GREEN SHORE CV	Lago Vista	428V	WV-37	78645	21200-21299
GREENSHORES DR	Austin	523P	ME-29	78730	6900-7299
GREENSIDE DR	Williamson Co	347A	MN-48	78665	1500-1699
GREENSIDE LN	Georgetown	225V	MK-58	78628	100-699
GREENSIDE TRL	Williamson Co	347E	MN-48	78665	1600-1899
GREENSIDE CROSSING	Georgetown	225R	MK-59	78633	1000-1199
GREENSLOPE CIR	Pflugerville	438N	MQ-38	78660	600-699
GREENSLOPE DR	Austin	494Z	MH-31	78759	7900-8099
	Austin	495W	MJ-31	78759	8100-8399
GREEN SLOPE LN	Georgetown	317F	MN-51	78626	200-499
GREEN TERRACE CV	Lakeway	520J	WY-29	78734	1-99
GREEN TERRACE DR	Round Rock	407A	MN-42	78664	1200-1499
GREEN TRAILS	Austin	524D	MH-30	78731	3700-3799
GREEN TRAILS N	Austin	524D	MH-30	78731	3700-3899
GREEN TRAILS S	Austin	524D	MH-30	78731	3700-3899
GREEN TREE CV	Williamson Co	317X	MN-49	78665	2100-2199
GREEN TREE DR	Williamson Co	317X	MN-48	78665	None
GREENTREE LN	Austin	643M	MF-17	78745	6100-6299
GREEN VALLEY	Austin	494R	MH-32	78759	8600-8699
GREEN VALLEY CV	Pflugerville	438S	MQ-37	78660	500-599
GREEN VALLEY CV	Round Rock	407A	MN-42	78664	1000-1299
GREEN VALLEY DR	Williamson Co	282X	MC-52	78641	100-199
GREEN VISTA CT	Williamson Co	346L	MM-47	78665	700-799
GREEN VISTA PL	Williamson Co	346L	MM-47	78665	4100-4299
GREENWAY	Austin	585C	MK-24	78705	3400-3699
GREENWAY DR	Pflugerville	468F	MQ-36	78660	400-599
GREENWICH DR	Austin	526H	MM-30	78753	1400-1499
GREENWICH PL	Round Rock	406M	MM-41	78664	500-899
GREENWICH MERIDIAN	Austin	464F	MG-36	78759	8100-8199
GREENWILLOW DR	Travis Co	309U	WX-49	78641	14200-14299
GREENWOOD AVE	Austin	586P	ML-23	78721	1100-1199
	Austin	586K	ML-23	78721	1200-1699
	Austin	586E	ML-24	78723	1900-2299
GREENWOOD CT	Georgetown	286S	ML-52	78628	700-799
GREENWOOD DR	Georgetown	286S	ML-52	78628	400-699
GREENWOOD DR	Travis Co	679C	MT-15	78617	16200-16599
GREER DR	Travis Co	402T	MC-40	78613	2500-2599
GREGG DR	Burnet Co	455A	WN-36	78669	None
GREGG LN	Austin	645P	MJ-17	78744	4200-4299
GREGG LN	Austin	498J	MQ-32	78653	5600-5699
	Travis Co	497D	MP-33	78653	1800-3299
	Travis Co	498J	MQ-32	78653	3300-5599
	Travis Co	499G	MT-33	78653	16000-17599
	Travis Co	500N	MU-32	78653	17600-18999
	Travis Co	467Y	MP-34	78660	None
	Travis Co	467Y	MP-34	78754	None
GREGG ST	Manor	529V	MT-28	78653	400-599
GREGG BLUFF RD	Jonestown	400V	WZ-40	78645	17900-18299
GREGG MANOR RD	Manor	529G	MT-30	78653	12500-12799
	Travis Co	529G	MT-30	78653	12800-13299
	Travis Co	499S	MS-31	78653	13300-13699
	Travis Co	498M	MR-32	78653	13700-14499
GREGORY CT	Round Rock	376G	MM-45	78664	500-599
GREGORY CV	Pflugerville	468F	MQ-36	78660	500-599
GREGORY LN	Round Rock	376G	MM-45	78664	1200-2199
GREGORY PL	West Lake Hills	583R	MF-23	78746	5000-5099
GREGORY ST	Austin	585U	MK-22	78702	1500-1799
GREINERT DR	Travis Co	467P	MN-35	78660	13700-13999
GRELLE LN	Travis Co	674Y	MH-13	78744	8500-8999
GRENER CV	Pflugerville	437D	MP-39	78660	17800-17899
GRENNOCK DR	Austin	643P	ME-17	78745	2600-2799
GRETCHEN DR	Cedar Park	372K	MC-44	78613	1500-1699
GREYBULL TRL	Williamson Co	434V	MH-37	78729	13100-13299
GREY CASTLE DR	Travis Co	467L	MP-35	78660	900-1199
GREYCLOUD DR	Austin	644W	MG-16	78745	6800-6999
GREY EAGLE CV	Bastrop Co	711F	MW-12	78612	100-199
GREY FAWN PATH	Williamson Co	433L	MF-38	78750	12000-12199
GREY FEATHER CT	Round Rock	377Y	MP-43	78665	400-499
GREYFEATHER DR	Austin	494F	MG-33	78759	6100-6299
GREY FEATHER DR	Round Rock	407C	MP-42	78664	500-599
GREY FOX TRL	Travis Co	583R	MF-23	78746	600-799
GREYLEAF PATH	Williamson Co	347A	MN-48	78665	1800-1899
GREYMERE CT	Austin	641Y	MB-16	78739	10800-10899
GREY ROCK LN	Williamson Co	433L	MF-38	78750	12000-12199
GREYSON DR	Round Rock	376M	MM-44	78664	1500-1999
GREYSTONE DR	Austin	525E	MJ-30	78731	3400-3599
	Austin	524H	MH-30	78731	3600-4399
	Austin	494X	MG-31	78731	4400-5099
GREYSTONE DR	Bastrop Co	776V	EH-4	78602	100-399
GREYSTONE BLUFF LN	Lago Vista	429L	WX-38	78645	6700-6899
GRIDER PASS	Austin	612Z	MD-19	78749	4500-4699
GRIERSON TRL	Travis Co	491U	MB-31	78732	12600-12799
GRIESENBECK RANCH RD					
	Bastrop Co	744U	ED-7	78602	100-199
GRIFFIN CT	Austin	524D	MH-30	78731	7900-7999
GRIFFIN LN	Bastrop Co	680P	MU-14	78612	100-199
GRIFFITH ST	Austin	555X	MJ-25	78705	3500-3799
GRIGSBY DR	Austin	643U	MF-16	78745	7100-7199
GRIMES RANCH CT	Travis Co	491T	MA-31	78732	12600-12699
GRIMES RANCH RD	Travis Co	491X	MA-31	78732	2700-3599
GRIMSLEY DR	Austin	465R	MK-35	78759	12100-12299
GRISHAM DR	Hutto	379D	MT-45	78634	100-399
GRISHAM TRL	Travis Co	428L	WV-38	78669	2900-5799
GRISSOM CT	Austin	526E	ML-30	78753	500-599
GRIST LN	Travis Co	432H	MD-39	78613	2500-2699
GRISTMILL CV	Williamson Co	433G	MF-39	78750	12500-12699
GRISWOLD LN	Austin	584C	MH-24	78703	2000-2499
GRIZZLY OAK DR	Austin	673Y	MF-13	78748	10000-10299
GROOMS ST	Austin	585B	MJ-24	78705	3100-3299
	Austin	555X	MJ-25	78705	3300-3799
GROSVENER CT	Austin	583V	MF-22	78746	1200-1299
GROUSE MEADOW LN	Austin	496W	ML-31	78758	9400-9499
GROVE BLVD	Austin	616S	ML-19	78741	400-1999
	Austin	646A	ML-18	78741	2000-2499
GROVE CT	Rollingwood	584S	MG-22	78746	1-99
GROVE DR	Austin	616P	ML-20	78741	6100-6299
GROVE DR	Round Rock	375M	MK-44	78681	2100-2399
GROVE LN	Hays Co	732N	MC-8	78610	100-399
GROVE LN	Williamson Co	227R	MP-59	78626	1-1299
GROVE CREST CIR	Austin	611R	MB-20	78736	7600-7699
GROVE CREST DR	Austin	611V	MB-19	78736	6900-7199
GROVEDALE TRL	Williamson Co	434V	MH-37	78729	7500-7799
GROVER AVE	Austin	555F	MJ-27	78756	4700-5899
	Austin	555C	MK-27	78757	5900-6199
	Austin	525Q	MK-29	78757	6200-7699
GROVE RIDGE LN	Travis Co	704F	MG-12	78747	None
GROVETON CV	Travis Co	582M	MD-23	78746	1800-1899
GROW LN	Austin	527E	MN-30	78754	2100-2199
GRUBSTAKE GULCH	Bee Cave	580A	WY-24	78738	12900-13099
GRUETZNER LN	Bastrop Co	564G	ED-27	78621	100-399
GRUNT LN	Travis Co	460F	WY-36	78734	5300-5499
GRUTSCH DR	Bastrop	744P	EC-8	78602	300-399
GUADALAJARA ST	Williamson Co	348P	MQ-47	78665	3300-3499
GUADALUPE DR	Williamson Co	350E	MU-48	78634	100-199
GUADALUPE ST	Austin	585S	MJ-22	78701	100-1899
	Austin	585A	MJ-24	78705	1900-3199
	Austin	555T	MJ-25	78705	3200-3799
	Austin	555K	MJ-26	78751	3800-5599
	Austin	555C	MK-27	78752	5600-6599
	Austin	525Z	MK-28	78752	6600-7599
	Austin	525R	MK-29	78752	7600-7899
	Austin	526J	ML-29	78753	8200-8699
GUADALUPE ST W	Austin	555P	MJ-26	78751	4500-4599
GUADALUPE TRL	Georgetown	196W	ML-61	78628	100-299
GUAJOLOTE CIR	Travis Co	490C	WZ-33	78734	3900-3999
GUANA CAY DR	Pflugerville	437B	MN-39	78660	17200-17399
GUARA CT	Travis Co	432G	MD-39	78613	None
GUARA DR	Travis Co	432C	MD-39	78613	2400-2599
GUARNERE DR	Austin	678P	MQ-14	78617	13300-13499
GUAVA CV	Austin	493V	MF-31	78750	7200-7299
GUERNSEY DR	Austin	496J	ML-32	78758	11400-11599
GUERRERO DR	Austin	647R	MP-17	78617	3000-3099
GUERRERO LN	Travis Co	736E	ML-9	78747	9300-9499
GUFFEY DR	Travis Co	619N	MS-20	78725	15100-15199
GUIDEPOST TRL	Austin	673A	ME-15	78745	2700-2899
GUILDFORD CV	Austin	493N	ME-32	78730	6500-6599
GUINEVERE LN	Travis Co	582C	MD-24	78746	500-599
GUITERREZ CV	Round Rock	406K	ML-41	78681	1100-1199
GULF WAY	Round Rock	346V	MM-46	78665	1000-1099
	Round Rock	347S	MN-46	78665	1100-1599
GULFSTREAM DR	Georgetown	287L	MP-53	78626	300-399
GULLETT ST	Austin	616B	ML-21	78702	800-1099
GUN BOW CT	Austin	523Y	MF-28	78746	6100-6199
GUN FIGHT LN	Travis Co	672U	MD-13	78748	11400-11599
GUNGROVE CIR	Williamson Co	433U	MF-37	78750	11600-11699
GUNGROVE DR	Williamson Co	433Q	MF-38	78750	10600-10799
GUN METAL DR	Austin	702B	MC-12	78739	12300-12599
GUNN LN	Travis Co	530M	MV-29	78653	13100-13399
GUNNISON PASS	Austin	557P	MN-26	78724	7100-7599
GUNNISON SPRINGS DR					
	Williamson Co	375U	MK-43	78681	17500-17599
GUN POWDER CT	Travis Co	672X	MC-13	78748	11600-11699
GUNSIGHT DR	Round Rock	407C	MP-42	78665	1800-1899
GUNSMITH DR	Hays Co	701H	MB-12	78652	13300-13399
	Travis Co	701H	MB-12	78652	13200-13299
GUNSMOKE CIR	Williamson Co	433U	MF-37	78750	11600-11699
GUNSMOKE CT	Mustang Ridge	765R	MK-5	78610	200-7199
GUNSTREAM LN	Travis Co	517M	WT-29	78669	4800-4999
GUNTER ST	Austin	616A	ML-21	78702	600-899
	Austin	586T	ML-22	78721	1100-1199
	Austin	586W	ML-22	78702	None
GURNEY'S EAGLE DR	Elgin	503X	EA-31	78621	None
GUSTINE CV	Williamson Co	405N	MJ-41	78717	15500-15599
GUTHERIE DR	Austin	493H	MF-33	78750	7400-8399
GUTIERREZ ST	Bastrop	745K	EE-8	78602	800-999
GUYAN DR	Lakeway	519L	WX-29	78734	400-499
GWENDOLYN LN	Austin	672M	MD-14	78748	2600-2699
GYM ST	Taylor	353F	EA-48	76574	200-399
GYPSUM CT	Pflugerville	408Z	MR-40	78660	None
GYPSY CV	Austin	465P	MJ-35	78727	4800-4899
GYRFALCON CV	Bee Cave	549H	WX-27	78738	None

H

STREET NAME	CITY or COUNTY	MAPSCO GRID	AUSTIN GRID	ZIP CODE	BLOCK RANGE O/E
HAAS LN	Travis Co	436Y	MM-37	78728	2100-2199
HABANA CT	Bastrop Co	738X	MQ-7	78617	None
HACHITA DR	Austin	641G	MB-18	78749	8900-8999
HACIENDA DR	San Leanna	703F	ME-12	78748	500-599
HACIENDA LN	Georgetown	226H	MM-60	78628	30100-30299
HACIENDA TRL	Bastrop Co	738X	MQ-7	78617	None
HACIENDA RIDGE	Travis Co	550W	WY-25	78738	12800-12999
HACKAMORE DR	Austin	672L	MD-14	78748	3300-3399
HACKBERRY	Williamson Co	432D	MD-39	78613	2500-2599
HACKBERRY DR	Pflugerville	438T	MQ-37	78660	1000-1099
HACKBERRY LN	Austin	526F	ML-30	78753	300-499
HACKBERRY ST	Austin	585U	MK-22	78702	1200-1399
HACKBERRY ST	Taylor	353A	EA-48	76574	700-1199
HACKNEY CV	Austin	466Q	MM-35	78727	1700-1799
HADDICK CIR	Austin	643T	ME-16	78745	7400-7499
HADDINGTON CV	Travis Co	408H	MR-42	78634	None
	Williamson Co	408H	MR-42	78634	21000-21099
HADLE CV	Travis Co	492U	MD-31	78730	5100-5199
HAGEN CT	Georgetown	255X	ML-55	78628	100-199
HAGERTY CROSSING	Travis Co	439S	MS-37	78660	3700-3799
HAGGANS LN	Austin	641W	MA-16	78739	7700-7899
HAGUE ST	Hutto	379D	MT-45	78634	100-199
HAIG POINT CV	Travis Co	409S	MS-40	78660	None
HAILEY LN	Round Rock	408J	MQ-41	78664	3100-3199
HAINSWORTH PARK DR	Austin	404J	MG-41	78717	10500-10599
HAIRY MAN RD	Williamson Co	375R	MK-44	78681	2100-3699
See.. Brushy Creek Rd					
HAISLER LN	Bastrop Co	534E	EC-30	78621	None
	Elgin	534E	EC-30	78621	101-199 O
HALAWA CT	Bastrop Co	775C	EF-6	78602	100-199
HALBERT DR	Austin	493V	MF-31	78750	7200-7399
HALDER CV	Williamson Co	405J	MJ-41	78717	8900-8999
HALE CT	Georgetown	195Z	MK-61	78633	100-199
HALE DR	Austin	642P	MC-17	78749	4800-4899
HALEAKALA DR	Bastrop Co	776A	EG-6	78602	100-199
HALE IRWIN CV	Williamson Co	408C	MR-42	78664	100-199
HALE IRWIN DR	Williamson Co	408C	MR-42	78664	200-299
HALEKALA TRL	Pflugerville	438F	MQ-39	78660	None
HALEY GRAY DR	Pflugerville	437H	MP-39	78660	1300-1499
HALEY HOLLOW	Travis Co	436Q	MM-38	78728	14800-15099
HALEYS CV	Leander	342R	MD-47	78641	600-699
HALEY'S WAY	Cedar Park	372T	MC-43	78613	2200-2299
HALEY'S WAY	Round Rock	346M	MM-47	78665	3700-3999
HALEYS WAY DR	Buda	732Q	MD-8	78610	1000-1299
HALEY'S WAY DR	Leander	342R	MD-47	78641	None
HALF MOON CV	Travis Co	583R	MF-23	78746	600-699
HALF PENNY RD	Austin	585D	MK-24	78722	3800-3899
HALFWAY CV	Williamson Co	344V	MH-46	78681	4000-4099
HALIFAX DR	Austin	526H	MM-30	78753	9700-9899
HALIMILE LN	Bastrop Co	745W	EE-7	78602	100-199
HALL ST	Austin	525X	MJ-28	78757	6300-6599
HALL ST	Cedar Park	372Z	MD-43	78613	800-999
HALL ST	Elgin	534S	EC-28	78621	200-299
HALL ST E	Pflugerville	438W	MQ-37	78660	100-199
HALL ST W	Pflugerville	438W	MQ-37	78660	100-599
HALLBROOK LN	Travis Co	409W	MS-40	78660	20000-21099
HALLIDAY AVE	Travis Co	619N	MS-20	78725	4400-4699
HALLIE CT	Williamson Co	224Q	MH-59	78633	100-199
HALLIE LN	Round Rock	377E	MN-45	78664	2400-2499
HALLSHIRE CT	Austin	672Z	MD-13	78748	2000-2099
HALMAR CV	Georgetown	226Z	MM-58	78628	100-199
HALMARK DR	Austin	556Y	MM-25	78723	5200-5399
HALMIRA ESTATE DR	Travis Co	467R	MP-35	78660	1600-1699
HALO DR	Pflugerville	437P	MN-38	78660	16100-16199
HALSELL CT	Travis Co	491P	MA-32	78732	3400-3499
HALSELL DR	Travis Co	491P	MA-32	78732	13000-13199
HALSEY CT	Austin	671C	MB-15	78739	6500-6599
HALSEY DR	Leander	311R	MB-50	78641	1000-1299
HAL SUTTON CV	Williamson Co	408C	MR-42	78664	100-199
HALTER LN	Cedar Park	402R	MD-41	78613	1700-1799
HALWILL PL	Austin	556N	ML-26	78723	5300-5399
HAMANN LN	Travis Co	440Z	MV-37	78615	10600-10699
	Travis Co	441W	MW-37	78615	10700-11399
HAMBLETONIAN	Austin	523Z	MF-28	78746	4000-4099
HAMDEN CIR	Williamson Co	405P	MJ-41	78717	15700-15899
HAMILTON AVE	Austin	585U	MK-22	78702	1900-2099
HAMILTON AVE	Lago Vista	458H	WV-36	78645	3100-3699
HAMILTON LN	Austin	495A	MJ-33	78759	4600-4899
	Austin	465W	MJ-34	78759	4900-5099
HAMILTON CROSSING					
	Dripping Springs	636X	WQ-16	78620	None
HAMILTON POINT CIR	Manor	529U	MT-28	78653	None
HAMILTON POINT CIRCLE 1	Manor	529Y	MT-28	78653	None
HAMILTON POINT CIRCLE 2	Manor	529Z	MT-28	78653	None
HAMILTON POINT CIRCLE 3	Manor	529Z	MT-28	78653	None
HAMILTON POINT CIRCLE 4	Manor	529V	MT-28	78653	None
HAMILTON POOL RD	Bee Cave	549T	WW-25	78738	14100-15299
	Travis Co	549T	WW-25	78738	15300-15799
	Travis Co	548Z	WV-25	78738	15800-16199
	Travis Co	578A	WU-24	78738	16200-17699
	Travis Co	577F	WS-24	78738	17700-20499
	Travis Co	546R	WR-26	78620	20500-23999
	Travis Co	516W	WQ-28	78620	24000-24299
	Travis Co	515V	WP-28	78620	24300-27199
HAMLET CIR	Georgetown	226H	MM-60	78628	30100-30199
HAMLET CIR	Round Rock	378Z	MR-43	78664	2200-2299
HAMLET CV	Round Rock	378Y	MR-43	78664	3500-3599
HAMMACK DR	Austin	555C	MK-27	78752	300-699
HAMMERMILL RUN	Austin	675A	MJ-15	78744	5700-5999
HAMMERSTONE CV	Williamson Co	283D	MF-54	78628	100-199
HAMMETTS CROSSING	Travis Co	515L	WP-29	78620	None
HAMPSHIRE DR	Austin	526C	MM-30	78753	10000-10099
HAMPSTED CT	Travis Co	554N	MG-26	78746	4200-4299
HAMPTON CIR	Georgetown	195V	MK-61	78633	100-199
HAMPTON CV	Round Rock	407J	MN-41	78664	2200-2299
HAMPTON LN	Round Rock	407J	MN-41	78664	1900-2099
HAMPTON RD	Austin	585F	MJ-24	78705	2900-2999
	Austin	585C	MK-24	78705	3200-3699
HAMPTON ST	Buda	763A	ME-6	78610	400-699
HAMPTON RIDGE CIR	Travis Co	704G	MH-12	78747	None
HAMRICH CT	Austin	464M	MH-35	78759	11900-11999
HANA CT	Bastrop Co	776B	EG-6	78602	100-199
HANAUMA DR	Bastrop Co	775D	EF-6	78602	100-299
HANBRIDGE LN	Austin	611P	MA-20	78736	8200-8599
HANCOCK AVE	Lago Vista	458R	WV-35	78645	2200-3399
HANCOCK DR	Austin	555A	MJ-27	78756	2100-2599
	Austin	555A	MJ-27	78731	2600-2799
	Austin	554D	MH-27	78731	2800-3199
	Austin	524Y	MH-28	78731	3200-3499
HANDSOME DR	Austin	498E	MQ-33	78660	3100-3399
HANEMAN CV	Williamson Co	373D	MF-45	78641	100-199
HANEY DR	Austin	556L	MM-26	78723	6200-6799
HANGAR DR	Austin	646Z	MM-16	78719	10000-10199
HANGER DR	Georgetown	256D	MM-57	78628	100-299
HANGER DR S	Georgetown	256D	MM-57	78628	100-599
HANGING CLIFF CV	Austin	464Z	MH-34	78759	5300-5499
HANGING OAK CIR	Austin	642C	MD-18	78749	7000-7199
HANGING ROCK DR	Pflugerville	438D	MR-39	78660	None
HANGING VALLEY DR	Travis Co	432V	MD-37	78726	12100-12399
HANG TREE CV	Cedar Park	372T	MC-43	78613	1400-1499
HANK AVE	Austin	644B	MG-18	78745	4300-4699
HANK AARON LN	Round Rock	378E	MQ-45	78665	800-899
HANNA CV	Williamson Co	434U	MH-37	78729	12700-12799
HANNAH DR	Hays Co	608J	WU-20	78620	100-499
HANNAH KAY LN	Travis Co	432H	MD-39	78613	2800-2899
HANOVER CT	Georgetown	225V	MK-58	78628	400-498 E
HANOVER LN	Austin	556M	MM-26	78723	6800-6899
HANSA CV	Austin	641T	MA-16	78739	10300-10399
HANSA DR	Austin	641T	MA-16	78739	10400-10599
HANSA LOOP	Austin	641T	MA-16	78739	6600-6999
HANSFORD DR	Austin	526G	MM-30	78753	9300-9999
HANSTROM CT	Hutto	379H	MT-45	78634	3000-3099
HANSTROM DR	Hutto	379H	MT-45	78634	100-299
HANZELL LN	Round Rock	377Z	MP-43	78665	2400-2499
HAOU CT	Bastrop Co	775A	EE-6	78602	100-199
HAPPY TRL	Travis Co	527X	MN-28	78754	9000-9399
HAPPY HOLLOW LN	Austin	554V	MH-25	78703	3400-3499
HAPPY HOLLOW RD	Travis Co	518E	WU-30	78669	19500-19599
HAPPY VALE PATHWAY	Travis Co	487W	WS-31	78669	22200-22499
HARBOR CIR	Williamson Co	224G	MH-60	78633	100-299
HARBOR CV	Burnet Co	396P	WQ-41	78669	None
HARBOR CV	Williamson Co	224G	MH-60	78633	100-199
HARBOR DR	Burnet Co	396T	WQ-40	78669	100-599
HARBOR DR	Jonestown	400Z	WZ-40	78645	9500-9599
HARBOR DR	Williamson Co	224L	MH-59	78633	200-799
HARBOR WAY	Travis Co	518B	WU-30	78669	19200-19299
HARBOR HILL DR	Lakeway	489Z	WX-31	78734	None

STREET NAME	CITY or COUNTY	MAPSCO GRID	AUSTIN GRID	ZIP CODE	BLOCK RANGE O/E
HARBORLIGHT CV	Austin	554F	MG-27	78731	4000-4099
HARBOR POINT CT	Travis Co	439W	MS-37	78660	17700-17799
HARBOR POINT DR	Travis Co	439W	MS-37	78660	3900-4099
HARBOR RIDGE RD	Burnet Co	396P	WQ-41	78669	None
HARBOR VIEW DR	West Lake Hills	553Z	MF-25	78746	1400-1599
HARBOR VILLAGE TRL	Travis Co	554S	MG-25	78746	3800-3899
HARBOUR TOWN CIR	Austin	704E	MG-12	78747	10200-10299
HARCOURT DR	Austin	465Q	MK-35	78727	4100-4399
HARCOURT HOUSE LN	Travis Co	467Q	MP-35	78660	14300-14799
HARDEMAN ST	Austin	614V	MH-19	78704	2800-2899
HARDIN CT	Austin	496T	MM-31	78753	500-599
HARDIN LOOP	Hays Co	732A	MC-9	78610	300-399
HARDING CV	Lago Vista	458H	WV-36	78645	20700-20799
HARDOUIN AVE	Austin	584D	MH-24	78703	1300-1599
HARD ROCK RD	Williamson Co	433P	ME-38	78750	10500-11099
HARDWOOD TRL	Williamson Co	433K	ME-38	78750	11700-12999
HARDWOOD CANYON DR	Lago Vista	459C	WX-36	78645	18700-19199
HARDWOOD GROVES	Georgetown	256J	ML-56	78628	3000-3099
HARDY CIR	Austin	525P	MJ-29	78757	2000-2099
HARDY DR	Austin	525P	MJ-29	78757	6700-7899
HARE TRL	Travis Co	433S	ME-37	78726	11400-11699
HARGIS ST	Austin	586E	ML-24	78723	38000-39999
HARGIS CREEK TRL	Williamson Co	375T	MJ-43	78717	1400-1499
HARGRAVE ST	Austin	585V	MK-22	78702	1000-1099
	Austin	585R	MK-23	78702	1100-1299
HARKEY CV	Travis Co	341Q	MB-47	78641	15100-15199
HARLEY AVE	Austin	672Q	MD-14	78748	10700-10899
HARLEYHILL DR	Austin	643T	ME-16	78745	2600-2899
HARLIQUIN RUN	Austin	495Z	MK-31	78758	1700-1799
HARLOW DR	Austin	641W	MA-16	78739	7500-7599
HARLOW RIDGE	Travis Co	468T	MQ-34	78660	None
HARMON AVE	Austin	585C	MK-24	78705	3500-3899
	Austin	555Z	MK-25	78751	4300-4399
	Austin	555R	MK-26	78751	4600-5499
HARMON RD	Bastrop Co	746R	EH-8	78602	100-399
HARMON HILLS CT	Hays Co	636F	WQ-18	78620	100-199
HARMON HILLS CV	Hays Co	636K	WQ-17	78620	200-699
HARMON HILLS RD	Hays Co	636F	WQ-18	78620	100-1099
	Hays Co	606T	WQ-19	78620	1100-2299
HARMONY LN	Williamson Co	256W	ML-55	78628	300-399
HARMONY FOREST WAY					
	Williamson Co	226V	MM-58	78628	100-199
HARMONY HILL ST	Williamson Co	434N	MG-38	78729	12500-12699
HARMS WAY	Travis Co	472P	MY-35	78653	None
HARNESS LN	Georgetown	225C	MK-60	78633	100-199
HARNESS RACE WAY	Pflugerville	409E	MS-42	78660	1600-1699
HAROLD CT	Austin	586U	MM-22	78721	5500-6599
HAROLD GREEN RD	Travis Co	617Z	MP-19	78725	11600-11999
	Travis Co	618W	MQ-19	78725	12000-13199
HARPER PARK DR	Austin	612U	MD-19	78735	5700-5899
HARPER RANCH RD	Weir	258H	MR-57	78626	1-99
HARPERS FERRY LN	Austin	643N	ME-17	78745	3100-3399
HARPER VILLAGE RD	Hays Co	762A	MC-6	78610	100-299
HARRELL PKWY	Round Rock	377H	MP-45	78665	100-1999
	Round Rock	347Z	MP-46	78665	2000-2399
HARRIER DR	Travis Co	434G	MH-39	78729	8400-8799
HARRIER FLIGHT TRL	Travis Co	439C	MT-39	78660	19800-20399
HARRIER HUNT RD	Travis Co	409T	MS-40	78660	20500-20599
HARRIER MARSH DR	Bee Cave	549F	WW-27	78738	15200-15399
HARRIET CT	Austin	555F	MJ-27	78756	1300-1399
HARRINGTON CV	Austin	524J	MG-29	78731	5800-5899
HARRIS AVE	Austin	585C	MK-24	78705	500-899
HARRIS BLVD	Austin	584D	MH-24	78703	2300-2599
	Austin	554Z	MH-25	78703	2600-3199
HARRIS DR	Hays Co	669B	WW-15	78737	100-799
HARRIS ST	Elgin	534S	EC-28	78621	100-499
HARRIS ST N	Round Rock	376Y	MM-43	78664	100-199
HARRIS ST S	Round Rock	376Y	MM-43	78664	100-199
HARRIS BRANCH PKWY	Austin	528T	MQ-28	78754	10600-12099
	Austin	528E	MQ-30	78653	12100-12299
	Austin	498T	MQ-31	78653	12300-13099
HARRISGLENN DR	Austin	497B	MN-33	78753	12700-13099
	Austin	467X	MN-34	78753	13100-13399
	Travis Co	467X	MN-34	78660	13400-13499
HARRISON CV	Lago Vista	458H	WV-36	78645	20700-20899
HARRISON LN	Austin	646D	MM-18	78742	1200-1399
HARRISON LN	Williamson Co	254N	MG-56	78628	100-299
HARRIS PARK AVE	Austin	585F	MJ-24	78705	2800-3399
HARRIS RIDGE BLVD	Austin	467X	MN-34	78753	12800-13499
	Travis Co	467X	MN-34	78660	13500-14699
HARROGATE DR	Austin	464Q	MH-35	78759	6100-6599
HARROW BLVD	Williamson Co	405G	MK-42	78681	5000-5099
HARROWDEN DR	Austin	466E	ML-36	78727	2400-2799
HARRY LIND RD	Travis Co	502M	MZ-32	78621	15200-15799
	Travis Co	503E	EA-33	78621	15800-16099
	Travis Co	473W	EA-34	78621	16100-16799
HART LN	Austin	524H	MH-30	78731	6400-7999
	Hays Co	636A	WQ-18	78620	100-1099
	Hays Co	606W	WQ-19	78620	None
HART ST	Georgetown	286L	MM-53	78626	1200-1699
	Georgetown	286Q	MM-53	78626	1700-1899
HARTFORD RD	Austin	584H	MH-24	78703	1400-2599
HARTHAN ST	Austin	584R	MH-23	78703	600-799
HART HOLLOW DR	Travis Co	487S	WS-31	78669	3800-4199
HARTKOPF ST	Buda	732U	MD-7	78610	100-199
HARTLEY CV	Austin	703E	ME-12	78748	11800-11899
HARTNELL DR	Austin	556H	MM-27	78723	7200-7399
HARTSHILL DR	Travis Co	493X	ME-31	78730	6100-6199
HARTSMITH DR	Travis Co	618Z	MR-19	78725	14400-14699
HARTUNG CV	Buda	732P	MC-8	78610	100-299
HARTUNG LN	Creedmoor	735X	MJ-7	78610	9100-9299
HARTWICK PL	Austin	557S	MN-25	78723	6400-6499
HARVARD CV	Lago Vista	458M	WV-35	78645	20700-20799
HARVARD DR	Pflugerville	467D	MP-36	78660	800-999
HARVARD ST	Austin	585Z	MK-22	78702	700-1199
HARVEST CIR	Austin	644K	MG-17	78745	5200-5299
HARVEST CV	Cedar Park	372H	MD-45	78613	500-699
HARVEST DR	Williamson Co	378D	MR-45	78634	100-199
HARVEST LN	Austin	644K	MG-17	78745	5300-5499
HARVEST LN	Hutto	380E	MU-45	78634	100-199
HARVEST BEND LN	Cedar Park	403K	ME-41	78613	1400-1899
HARVESTMAN CV	Austin	494Y	MH-31	78731	7800-7899
HARVEST MEADOW CT					
	Village of the Hills	519S	WW-28	78738	1-99
HARVEST MOON DR	Williamson Co	402V	MD-40	78613	2000-2099
HARVEST MOON PL	Williamson Co	402V	MD-40	78613	1600-1699
HARVEST TIME CV	Austin	527C	MP-30	78754	3300-3399
HARVEST TIME DR	Austin	527C	MP-30	78754	11000-11199
HARVEST TRAIL DR	Austin	611Q	MB-20	78736	7100-7199
HARVEY CT	Travis Co	490P	WY-32	78734	15300-15399
HARVEY ST	Austin	586N	ML-23	78702	1100-1199
	Austin	586J	ML-23	78702	1200-1899
HARVEY ST	Elgin	534K	EC-29	78621	100-199
HARVEY PENICK CV	Round Rock	408C	MR-42	78664	3700-3799
HARVEY PENICK DR	Round Rock	378X	MQ-43	78664	3600-3699
	Round Rock	408C	MR-42	78664	3700-3799
	Round Rock	378U	MR-43	78664	3800-4799
HARWAY CT	Austin	644L	MH-17	78745	500-599
HARWICK DR	Austin	643H	MF-18	78745	2100-2399
HARWILL CIR	Austin	556Q	MM-26	78723	5900-5999
HARWIN LN	Austin	643R	MF-17	78745	6100-6299
HARWOOD PL	Austin	615K	MJ-20	78704	1000-1099
HASELWOOD LN	Round Rock	347V	MP-46	78665	2500-2699
HASKEL DR	Travis Co	611T	MA-19	78736	8300-8499
HASKELL ST	Austin	615G	MK-21	78702	1200-2399
HASKIN RIDGE	Travis Co	468T	MQ-34	78660	None
HASLER BLVD N	Bastrop	744M	ED-8	78602	100-199
HASLER BLVD S	Bastrop	744R	ED-8	78602	100-299
HASLER ST	Bastrop	745N	EE-8	78602	200-299
HASLER SHORES DR	Bastrop	744D	ED-9	78602	100-299
HASTINGS LN	Austin	433Y	MF-37	78750	10600-10899
HASWELL LN	Austin	641L	MB-17	78749	6600-6799
HATCH RD	Cedar Park	433E	ME-39	78613	3000-3599
	Williamson Co	433E	ME-39	78613	1500-1899
HATHAWAY DR	Austin	525C	MK-30	78757	8300-8699
HATLEY DR	Rollingwood	584N	MG-23	78746	2400-3299
HATTERAS DR	Austin	467X	MN-34	78753	1000-1299
HATTERY LN	Austin	404E	MG-42	78717	11000-11498 E
HATTON LN	Austin	527E	MN-30	78754	10200-10399
HATTON HILL LN	Travis Co	619S	MS-19	78725	600-699
HAUULA CT	Bastrop Co	775G	EF-6	78602	100-199
HAVANA ST	Austin	614U	MH-19	78704	100-599
HAVELOCK DR	Austin	465R	MK-35	78759	12300-12399
HAVEN LN	Buda	763A	ME-6	78610	None
HAVEN LN	Georgetown	287J	MN-53	78626	1200-1299
HAVENBROOK CV	Austin	464X	MG-34	78759	6700-6799
HAVENSIDE DR	Austin	614Q	MH-20	78704	2400-2499
HAVEN SPRING DR	Austin	583V	MF-22	78746	3000-3099
HAVENWOOD DR	Austin	525A	MJ-30	78759	7900-8099
HAVERCREST CT	Travis Co	558J	MQ-26	78724	None
HAVERFORD DR	Austin	467X	MN-34	78753	1100-1299
HAVERHILL LN	Travis Co	557R	MP-26	78724	None
HAVERLAND DR	Georgetown	257N	MN-56	78626	1-199
	Williamson Co	257N	MN-56	78626	200-299
HAVERSHAM CT	Williamson Co	434F	MG-39	78729	13300-13399
HAVERSTOCK AVE	Travis Co	557R	MP-26	78724	None
HAVERTON DR	Travis Co	558J	MQ-26	78724	None
HAVRE LAFITTE CV	Austin	583V	MF-22	78746	None
HAVRE LAFITTE DR	Austin	583Z	MF-22	78746	1100-1299
HAWEA CT	Bastrop	746S	EG-7	78602	100-199
HAWEA LN	Bastrop Co	745W	EE-7	78602	100-199
HAWICK DR	Williamson Co	405F	MJ-42	78681	8100-8199
HAWK CT	Lakeway	519R	WX-29	78734	1300-1399
HAWK CT	Round Rock	375V	MK-43	78681	1000-1099
HAWK CV	Austin	644E	MG-18	78745	4900-4999
HAWK DR	Cedar Park	372F	MC-45	78613	1400-1699
HAWK DR	Hays Co	701R	MB-11	78652	900-13999
HAWK ST	Lakeway	519R	WX-29	78734	15300-15399
	Travis Co	519R	WX-29	78734	15200-15299
HAWKEYE DR	Austin	642B	MC-18	78749	7600-7699
HAWKEYE PT	Georgetown	317F	MN-50	78626	1100-1299
HAWKHAVEN LN	Austin	465L	MK-35	78727	4600-4999
HAWK HOOD DR	Travis Co	439G	MT-39	78660	20000-20099
HAWKIN'S DR	Williamson Co	312H	MD-51	78641	100-299
HAWKINS LN	Austin	616Z	MM-19	78742	1200-1399
HAWK RIDGE ST	Round Rock	346R	MM-47	78665	3600-3799
HAWKSBURY WAY	Cedar Park	372P	MC-44	78613	1900-2199
HAWKS CANYON CIR	Travis Co	521L	MB-29	78732	1200-1499
HAWKS CANYON PASS	Travis Co	521L	MB-29	78732	11500-11599
HAWKSHEAD DR	Austin	465Q	MK-35	78727	3700-4099
HAWKS NEST CV	Cedar Park	403J	ME-41	78613	1000-1099
HAWKS SWOOP TRL	Travis Co	409T	MS-40	78660	2900-3399
HAWK VIEW CV	Round Rock	347S	MN-46	78665	3500-3699
HAWK VIEW ST	Round Rock	347N	MN-47	78665	3600-3899
HAWTHORN LN	Round Rock	407B	MN-42	78664	500-699
HAWTHORNE CIR	Bastrop Co	776Y	EH-4	78602	100-199
HAWTHORNE CV	Georgetown	256N	ML-56	78628	3000-3099
HAWTHORNE CV	Lago Vista	458H	WV-36	78645	20700-20899
HAWTHORNE CV	Williamson Co	432H	MD-39	78613	1900-1999
HAWTHORNE ST	Bastrop	745B	EE-9	78602	500-599
	Bastrop	715X	EE-10	78602	1000-1599
HAYBARN LN	Williamson Co	348R	MR-47	78634	1-1099
HAYDEN WAY	Round Rock	406H	MM-42	78664	900-1199
HAYDEN BEND	Bee Cave	550V	WZ-25	78733	3100-3299
HAYDEN RIDGE LN	Lakeway	519K	WW-29	78738	None
	Village of the Hills	519K	WW-29	78738	300-399
HAYDEN'S CV	Travis Co	493W	ME-31	78730	5900-5999
HAYES CV	Lago Vista	458H	WV-36	78645	20700-20799
HAYES LN	Austin	494R	MH-32	78759	8300-8499
HAYFIELD SQUARE	Pflugerville	438D	MR-39	78660	None
HAYLEY CT	Williamson Co	318B	MQ-51	78634	400-499
HAY MEADOW RD	Bastrop Co	742S	MY-7	78612	100-199
HAYMOND RD	Williamson Co	402U	MD-40	78613	1500-1599
HAYNIE BEND	Round Rock	347N	MN-47	78665	1500-1599
HAYNIE CREEK LN	Travis Co	427P	WS-38	78669	None
HAYNIE FLAT RD	Burnet Co	426R	WR-38	78669	27200-27399
	Travis Co	457B	WS-36	78669	23700-24399
	Travis Co	427N	WS-38	78669	24400-25799
	Travis Co	426R	WR-38	78669	25800-27199
HAYRIDE CIR	Travis Co	709J	MS-11	78617	16900-17099
HAYRIDE LN	Travis Co	676A	ML-15	78744	4400-4499
HAYRIDE RD	Travis Co	709J	MS-11	78617	7800-8199
HAYS ST	Dripping Springs	666D	WR-15	78620	100-499
HAYS COUNTRY ACRES RD	Hays Co	637Z	WT-16	78620	100-299
	Hays Co	667D	WT-15	78620	300-999
HAYSEL ST	Bastrop	745F	EE-9	78602	1200-1599
HAYS FOREST CV	Elgin	533B	EA-30	78621	None
HAYS HILL DR	Austin	643T	ME-16	78745	7500-7599
HAYSTACK CV	Travis Co	517L	WT-29	78669	20100-20499
HAYS YOUTH DR	Hays Co	762W	MC-4	78610	100-299
HAYWOOD AVE	Austin	615A	MJ-21	78704	400-599
HAYWOOD LN	Elgin	534S	EC-28	78621	100-199
HAYWORTH CV	Pflugerville	437D	MP-39	78660	17900-17999
HAZEL ST	Williamson Co	443G	EB-39	78615	100-299
HAZELHURST DR	Williamson Co	434K	MG-38	78729	8800-9299
HAZELNUT LN	Austin	678J	MQ-14	78617	4900-5099
HAZELTINE CT	Lakeway	519H	WX-30	78734	100-199
HAZELTINE DR	Georgetown	226M	MM-59	78628	100-199
HAZELTINE DR	Lakeway	519H	WX-30	78734	100-499
HAZELTINE LN	Austin	703M	MF-11	78747	2100-2299
HAZELWOOD ST	Leander	342G	MD-48	78641	300-599
HAZEN LN	Austin	673B	ME-15	78745	2200-2299
HAZY HILLS DR	Travis Co	487X	WS-31	78669	4000-4399
HAZY HOLLOW CV	Travis Co	487T	WS-31	78669	22400-22599
HAZY HOLLOW DR	Travis Co	487T	WS-31	78669	22000-22399
HEADLY DR	Austin	643K	ME-17	78745	2900-3099
HEADQUARTERS RD	Bastrop Co	739J	MS-8	78617	100-299
HEADWATER LN	Austin	583Y	MF-22	78746	2000-2199
HEADWAY CIR	Austin	526Y	MM-28	78754	1600-1699
HEARN ST	Austin	584P	MG-23	78703	300-799
HEARTBREAK PASS	Hays Co	763L	MF-5	78610	None
HEARTHSIDE DR	Austin	525C	MK-30	78757	1900-1999
HEARTHSONG LOOP	Round Rock	347V	MP-46	78665	2700-2899
HEARTHSTONE DR	Austin	495Y	MK-31	78757	1900-1999
HEARTWOOD DR	Austin	644K	MG-17	78745	200-599
HEARTWOOD BLUFF LN	Lago Vista	429L	WX-38	78645	6700-6899
HEATHCLIFF DR	Travis Co	522N	MC-29	78733	1600-1699
HEATHER CV	Williamson Co	318C	MR-51	78634	100-199
HEATHER DR	Cedar Park	402Y	MD-40	78613	2000-2299
HEATHER DR	Lago Vista	458P	WU-35	78645	21600-21799
HEATHER DR	Round Rock	376L	MM-44	78664	500-599
HEATHERBLOOM LN					
	Village of the Hills	519S	WW-28	78738	1-99
HEATHERCREST CIR	Austin	524D	MH-30	78731	7800-7899
HEATHERGLEN LN	Austin	496E	ML-33	78758	1800-1999
HEATHER HILL RD	Lakeway	519Q	WX-29	78734	1900-1999
HEATHER HILLS DR	Hays Co	576X	WQ-22	78620	100-899
HEATHERWILDE BLVD	Pflugerville	437M	MP-38	78660	100-1899
	Pflugerville	437D	MP-39	78660	17700-17999
	Pflugerville	438A	MQ-39	78660	18000-18299
	Pflugerville	408W	MQ-40	78660	18300-19199
HEATHERWILDE BLVD S	Pflugerville	437U	MP-37	78660	100-599
	Pflugerville	437X	MN-37	78660	600-1099
	Pflugerville	467B	MN-36	78660	1100-1599
HEATHERWOOD CIR	Round Rock	376L	MM-44	78664	1900-2099
HEATHERWOOD DR	Austin	673E	ME-15	78748	9100-9399
HEATHMOUNT DR	Travis Co	432F	MC-39	78613	2900-3099
HEATHROW DR	Austin	464F	MG-36	78759	11500-11599
HEATON PARK CV	Austin	375W	MJ-43	78717	16500-16599
HEBBE LN	Travis Co	437X	MN-37	78660	15000-15699
HEDDER CIR	Travis Co	341K	MA-47	78641	15100-15199
HEDGE LN	Travis Co	553N	ME-26	78746	1-99
HEDGEBROOK CV	Village of the Hills	519P	WW-29	78738	1-99
HEDGEBROOK WAY	Village of the Hills	519P	WW-29	78738	1-99
HEDGEFIELD CT	Village of the Hills	519P	WW-29	78738	1-99
HEDGEROW PL	Travis Co	677G	MP-15	78617	4600-4899
HEDGEWOOD DR	Austin	644K	MG-17	78745	5000-5299
HEDGEWOOD DR	Georgetown	256F	ML-57	78628	300-999
HEDRA DR	Austin	670D	WZ-15	78739	11800-11899
HEEP RUN	Buda	732T	MC-7	78610	1000-1399
HEES CT	Travis Co	439T	MS-37	78660	4500-4599
HEES LN	Travis Co	439T	MS-37	78660	18300-18499
HEFLIN LN	Austin	586L	MM-23	78721	4600-5199
HEGARTY DR	Cedar Park	402L	MD-41	78613	700-799
HEIDEN LN	Austin	641L	MB-17	78749	9000-9199
HEIDEROSA RUN	Williamson Co	194F	MG-63	78633	1-199
HEIGHTS BLVD	Taylor	322Y	MZ-49	76574	2100-2499
HEIGHTS DR	Austin	583P	ME-23	78746	4300-4599
HEINE FARM RD	Travis Co	677Y	MP-13	78617	6500-7299
HEINEMANN DR	Austin	465A	MJ-36	78727	12600-12899
	Austin	435W	MJ-37	78727	12900-13099
HEKILI DR	Bastrop Co	775D	EF-6	78602	100-299
HELADA CT	Williamson Co	345X	MJ-46	78681	3000-3099
HELEAKALA DR	Bastrop Co	775C	EF-6	78602	100-299
HELECHO CT	Austin	643Y	MF-16	78745	7500-7699
HELEMANO DR	Bastrop Co	775D	EF-6	78602	100-299
HELEN CV	Hutto	379G	MT-45	78634	100-199
HELEN ST	Austin	555M	MK-26	78751	5300-5699
HELENIA DR	Travis Co	672N	MC-14	78739	4500-4599
HELM LN	Williamson Co	224L	MH-59	78633	100-399
HELMS ST	Austin	585B	MJ-24	78705	3100-3499
HELMWAY CIR	Point Venture	488R	WV-32	78654	19000-19099
HEMINGWAY CV	Lago Vista	458H	WV-36	78645	20700-20799
HEMINGWAY ST	Austin	556C	MM-27	78752	7500-7699
HEMLOCK AVE	Austin	585H	MK-24	78722	3200-3399
HEMPHILL PARK	Austin	585A	MJ-24	78705	2700-3099
	Austin	555X	MJ-25	78705	3100-3399
HENDELSON LN	Hutto	350J	MU-47	78634	100-399
HENDERSON DR	Leander	312S	MC-49	78641	1000-1199
HENDERSON PATH	Round Rock	348S	MQ-46	78665	3100-3299
HENDERSON ST	Austin	584V	MH-22	78703	600-799
HENDON ST	Austin	672V	MD-13	78748	10500-10799
HENDRICKS DR	Williamson Co	434Q	MH-38	78729	8000-8199
HENGE DR	Austin	464K	MG-35	78759	11100-11299
HENLEY DR	Round Rock	376A	ML-45	78681	2600-2699
HENNA WAY	Round Rock	407F	MN-42	78665	2100-2199
HENNIG DR	Travis Co	549A	WW-27	78738	4300-4599
HENNINGER ST	Austin	586W	ML-22	78702	1100-1299
HENRY AVE	Lago Vista	458H	WV-36	78645	20600-20899
HENRY KINNEY ROW	Austin	642E	MC-18	78749	7900-8199
HENRY MARX LN	Travis Co	581V	MB-22	78735	8400-8999
HENRY RIFLE RD	Cedar Park	374N	MG-44	78613	2400-2599
HENSLEY CIR	Lakeway	519Z	WX-28	78734	100-199
HENSLEY DR	Lakeway	519Z	WX-28	78734	100-399
HENSLEY DR	Leander	311R	MB-50	78641	1200-1399
HEPPNER DR	Cedar Park	433E	ME-39	78613	1200-1299
HERB CV	Austin	464A	MG-36	78750	11500-11599
HERB BROOKS DR	Austin	702G	MD-12	78652	12000-12099
HERB'S CAVE	Williamson Co	375T	MJ-43	78681	8000-8099
HEREFORD ST	Manor	529X	MS-28	78653	11400-11699
HEREFORD WAY	Austin	465K	MJ-35	78727	5000-5199
HERGOTZ LN	Austin	616P	ML-20	78742	100-399
	Austin	616M	MM-20	78742	6300-6799
	Travis Co	616M	MM-20	78742	6800-7799
	Travis Co	617S	MN-19	78742	7800-9699
HERITAGE DR	Hays Co	639P	WW-17	78737	100-399
HERITAGE WAY	Austin	584F	MG-24	78703	1100-1199
HERITAGE CENTER CIR	Round Rock	376V	MM-43	78664	900-1199
HERITAGE HILL CV	Cedar Park	372G	MD-45	78613	1200-1299
HERITAGE HOLLOW	Williamson Co	257M	MP-56	78626	40000-40299
HERITAGE OAKS DR	Bastrop Co	740X	MU-7	78612	100-499

STREET NAME	CITY or COUNTY	MAPSCO GRID	AUSTIN GRID	ZIP CODE	BLOCK RANGE O/E
HERITAGE OAKS DR	Hays Co	639P	WW-17	78737	1-99
HERITAGE OAKS BEND	Georgetown	225V	MK-58	78628	600-999
HERITAGE PARK DR	Cedar Park	372G	MD-45	78613	1000-1299
HERITAGE SPRINGS TRL	Round Rock	407A	MN-43	78664	900-999
HERITAGE VILLAGE DR	Austin	587E	MN-24	78724	5200-5399
HERITAGE WELL LN	Pflugerville	438D	MR-39	78660	1901-1999 O
HERITAGE WELL LN	Williamson Co	317X	MN-49	78665	4400-4599
HERMALINDA ST	Austin	586E	ML-24	78723	38000-39999
HERMANS SONS RD	Taylor	352N	MY-47	76574	3100-4599
	Williamson Co	351R	MX-47	76574	None
HERMES DR	Travis Co	587Z	MP-22	78725	10000-10199
HERMITAGE DR	Austin	526P	ML-29	78753	800-1199
HERMITAGE DR	Round Rock	376J	ML-44	78681	1300-1999
HERMOSA DR	Travis Co	703W	ME-10	78652	300-399
HERNANDEZ LN	Buda	763E	ME-6	78610	100-199
HERNANDO'S LOOP	Leander	342U	MD-46	78641	100-499
HERNDON LN	Austin	614Q	MH-20	78704	600-1199
HERO CT	Austin	612G	MD-21	78735	4600-4699
HERO DR	Austin	612G	MD-21	78735	5500-5799
HERON CV	Austin	464Q	MH-35	78759	11100-11199
HERON DR	Austin	464Q	MH-35	78759	6200-6599
HERON DR	Travis Co	520E	WY-30	78734	400-599
HERON BAY CV	Bee Cave	549R	WX-26	78738	None
HERON CALL TRL	Travis Co	409T	MS-40	78660	3100-3399
HERON ROOST PASS	Travis Co	439C	MT-39	78660	3600-3899
HERRADURA DR	Cedar Park	344W	MG-46	78641	3100-3299
HERRERA CT	Hutto	379H	MT-45	78634	1000-1099
HERRERA ST	Austin	616P	ML-20	78742	100-199
HERRERA TRL	Hutto	379H	MT-45	78634	100-299
HERRERO PATH	Cedar Park	344W	MG-46	78641	3100-3299
HERRIN ST	Williamson Co	443G	EB-39	78615	100-499
HERRINGTON CV	Round Rock	348S	MQ-46	78665	2600-2799
HERSEE CT	Hutto	380N	MU-44	78634	100-199
HERSHAL LN	Bastrop Co	741N	MW-8	78612	100-299
HESS DR	Austin	673Y	MF-13	78748	10400-10499
HESTER RD	Austin	616D	MM-21	78725	6800-7299
HESTER HOLLOW	Williamson Co	225S	MJ-58	78633	100-499
HESTERS CROSSING RD	Round Rock	406T	ML-40	78681	100-1499
HETHER ST	Austin	614G	MH-21	78704	1400-1999
HEWERS DR	Travis Co	677X	MN-13	78617	6900-7099
HEWITT LN	Travis Co	702G	MD-12	78748	12100-12599
HEWLETT LOOP RD	Georgetown	346B	ML-48	78665	7700-7799
HEYERDAHL DR	Austin	497B	MN-33	78753	12900-12999
HIALEAH DR	Travis Co	677G	MP-15	78617	11100-11399
HIAWATHA RD	Travis Co	461C	MB-36	78641	7700-7899
HIBBETTS RD	Austin	586Z	MM-22	78725	3100-3499
HIBBS LN	Travis Co	561Y	MX-25	78653	10100-11999
HIBISCUS CV	Austin	642W	MC-16	78739	10100-10199
HIBISCUS DR	Austin	557K	MN-26	78724	5400-5599
HIBISCUS DR	Georgetown	314G	MH-51	78628	100-499
HIBISCUS VALLEY DR	Austin	672A	MC-15	78739	4500-5099
	Austin	642W	MC-16	78739	5100-5299
HICKMAN AVE	Austin	556K	ML-26	78723	6200-6599
HICKOK CT	Austin	526C	MM-30	78753	300-399
HICKOK DR	Williamson Co	375X	MJ-43	78681	17000-17099
HICKOK ST	Williamson Co	375X	MJ-43	78681	200-399
HICKORY DR	Austin	675B	MJ-15	78744	5300-5599
HICKORY DR	Williamson Co	374E	ME-39	78613	1600-1799
HICKORY LN	Elgin	534P	EC-29	78621	100-499
HICKORY LN	Georgetown	225V	MK-58	78628	100-199
HICKORY ST	Bastrop	715X	EE-10	78602	500-599
HICKORY BLUFF	Bastrop Co	776Y	EH-4	78602	100-199
HICKORY CREEK CV	Travis Co	582J	MC-23	78735	3300-3399
HICKORY CREEK DR	Travis Co	582J	MC-23	78735	8100-8599
HICKORY GROVE DR	Austin	496V	MM-31	78753	1100-1199
HICKORY GROVE LN	Travis Co	590R	MV-23	78653	20000-20499
HICKORY HOLLOW	Austin	524P	MG-29	78731	4700-4799
HICKORY RIDGE CV	Round Rock	407G	MP-42	78665	1800-1899
HICKORY RIDGE RD	Travis Co	703N	ME-11	78652	400-699
HICKORY RIDGE TRL	Pflugerville	438T	MQ-37	78660	1200-1299
HICKORY RUN DR	Cedar Park	403N	ME-41	78613	500-699
HICKORYSTICK CV	Williamson Co	433M	MF-38	78750	12300-12399
HICKORY TREE DR	Williamson Co	257E	MN-57	78626	100-599
HICKOX DR	Round Rock	346R	MM-47	78665	3800-3899
HIDALGO ST	Austin	615D	MK-21	78702	2400-2699
	Austin	616A	ML-21	78702	3300-3599
HIDATAS CV	Austin	703B	ME-12	78748	700-799
HIDATSA ST	Buda	762D	MD-6	78610	300-499
HIDDEN CV	West Lake Hills	553Z	MF-25	78746	1-99
HIDDEN ACRES DR	Round Rock	377P	MN-44	78664	1-99
	Williamson Co	377P	MN-44	78664	None
HIDDEN BLUFF CV	Round Rock	408A	MQ-42	78665	3000-3099
HIDDEN BLUFF DR	Austin	497W	MN-31	78754	11100-11299
HIDDEN BROOK CT	Austin	674R	MH-14	78744	7600-7799
HIDDEN BROOK LN	Williamson Co	346G	MM-48	78665	300-599
HIDDEN CANYON CV	Travis Co	524W	MG-28	78746	4000-4299
HIDDEN CREEK LN	Travis Co	517R	WT-29	78669	4800-5199
HIDDEN ESTATES DR	Austin	466A	ML-36	78727	3700-3899
HIDDEN GLEN CT	Round Rock	346W	ML-46	78681	700-799
HIDDEN GLEN DR	Round Rock	346W	ML-46	78681	800-999
	Round Rock	345Z	MK-46	78681	1000-1599
HIDDEN HARBOR DR	Travis Co	439S	MS-37	78660	3800-4099
HIDDEN HILL CIR	Austin	643V	MF-16	78745	1200-1299
HIDDEN HILLS CV	Burnet Co	426K	WQ-38	78669	100-299
HIDDEN HILLS DR	Burnet Co	426K	WQ-38	78669	100-399
HIDDEN HILLS DR	Hays Co	638T	WU-16	78620	1000-3899
HIDDEN HILLS LN	Travis Co	432P	MC-38	78613	3100-3399
HIDDEN HOLLOW	Austin	524D	MH-30	78731	3700-3899
HIDDEN LAKE DR	Travis Co	439K	MS-38	78660	None
HIDDEN LAKE CROSSING	Pflugerville	439J	MS-38	78660	3200-3299
	Pflugerville	439U	MT-37	78660	4500-4699
	Travis Co	439J	MS-38	78660	3300-4499
HIDDEN MEADOW DR	Taylor	322Y	MZ-49	76574	1900-2199
HIDDEN MEADOW DR	Williamson Co	433R	MF-38	78750	10000-10199
HIDDEN MESA	Travis Co	340M	WZ-47	78641	100-199
	Williamson Co	340H	WZ-48	78641	200-599
HIDDEN OAK WAY	Cedar Park	374U	MH-43	78613	3500-3599
HIDDEN OAKS CV	Round Rock	375F	MJ-45	78681	3400-3599
HIDDEN OAKS DR	Austin	643P	ME-17	78745	2600-2699
HIDDEN PARK DR	Travis Co	439P	MS-38	78660	4300-4399
HIDDEN QUAIL DR	Austin	496E	ML-33	78758	11400-11799
HIDDEN RIDGE PL	Jonestown	430J	WY-38	78645	18800-18899
HIDDEN SPRINGS CT	Burnet Co	426G	WR-39	78669	100-199
HIDDEN SPRINGS PATH					
	Williamson Co	346H	MM-48	78665	1500-1599
HIDDEN SPRINGS PATH					
	Williamson Co	347E	MN-48	78665	1600-1899

STREET NAME	CITY or COUNTY	MAPSCO GRID	AUSTIN GRID	ZIP CODE	BLOCK RANGE O/E
HIDDEN SPRINGS TRL	Georgetown	225V	MK-58	78628	4800-5199
HIDDEN TRACE	Leander	342H	MD-48	78641	900-999
HIDDEN VALLEY DR	Round Rock	346Q	MM-47	78665	800-1099
HIDDEN VALLEY TRL	Austin	675A	MJ-15	78744	5900-5999
HIDDEN VIEW CIR	Austin	587G	MP-24	78724	7600-8099
HIDDEN VIEW CT	Williamson Co	346H	MM-48	78665	4100-4199
HIDDEN VIEW PL	Austin	587G	MP-24	78724	6000-6099
HIDDEN VIEW PL	Williamson Co	346H	MM-48	78665	900-1199
HIDDEN WEST BLVD	Austin	587G	MP-24	78724	7700-7899
	Travis Co	587G	MP-24	78724	7900-8599
HIDEAWAY CV	Georgetown	316A	ML-51	78628	100-199
HIDEAWAY CV	Hays Co	639P	WW-17	78737	100-199
HIDEAWAY CV	Travis Co	577Q	WT-23	78720	18000-18199
HIDEAWAY LN	Round Rock	407A	MN-42	78664	400-599
HIDEAWAY LN	Travis Co	459R	WX-35	78645	18000-18199
HIDEAWAY LN N	Travis Co	459R	WX-35	78645	3700-3799
HIDEAWAY LN S	Travis Co	459Q	WX-35	78645	3600-3699
HIDEAWAY HOLLOW	Austin	494W	MG-31	78750	6900-6999
HIDEOUT CV	Leander	372B	MC-45	78641	2300-2399
HIGGINS ST	Austin	586J	ML-23	78722	2900-2999
HIGGINS ST	Bastrop	745J	EE-8	78602	100-199
HIGH DR	Lago Vista	459A	WW-36	78645	20200-20499
	Lago Vista	458D	WV-36	78645	20500-21599
	Lago Vista	428Y	WV-37	78645	21600-21699
HIGHALEA CT	Williamson Co	287G	MP-54	78626	100-199
HIGH BLUFF LN	Hays Co	666A	WQ-15	78620	100-499
HIGH BLUFF TRL	Williamson Co	375Q	MK-44	78681	7000-7299
HIGHBURY LN	Austin	586C	MM-24	78723	5100-5199
HIGH CANYON PASS	Bee Cave	549Z	WX-25	78738	4900-5299
HIGH CHAPARRAL CV	Austin	614E	MG-21	78704	2100-2199
HIGH CHAPARRAL DR	Leander	342Q	MD-47	78641	1100-1699
HIGHCLIMB CT	Travis Co	369R	WX-44	78641	21600-21799
HIGH COTTON CV	Round Rock	408J	MQ-41	78664	3300-3399
HIGH COTTON WAY	Round Rock	408J	MQ-41	78664	3300-3399
HIGH COUNTY BLVD	Round Rock	408J	MQ-41	78664	2200-2599
HIGH COUNTY DR	Georgetown	225H	MK-60	78633	100-199
HIGH GABRIEL	Williamson Co	282W	MC-52	78641	100-199
HIGH GABRIEL EAST	Williamson Co	312B	MC-51	78641	1-599
HIGH GATE DR	Travis Co	492Y	MD-31	78730	4600-5099
HIGHGROVE TERRACE	Austin	584L	MH-23	78703	2100-2199
HIGH HOLLOW CV	Austin	493G	MF-33	78750	8000-8099
HIGH HOLLOW DR	Austin	493G	MF-33	78750	7800-8099
HIGH HORSE	Leander	371B	MA-45	78641	3500-3599
HIGHLAND AVE	Austin	584Q	MH-23	78703	600-899
HIGHLAND CT	Austin	554D	MH-27	78731	5000-5099
HIGHLAND CT	Cedar Park	372Q	MD-44	78613	1600-1699
HIGHLAND DR	Cedar Park	372Q	MD-44	78613	1200-1599
HIGHLAND DR	Georgetown	286U	MM-52	78626	2400-2499
HIGHLAND DR	Taylor	323N	EA-50	76574	1-499
HIGHLAND DR	Travis Co	490H	WZ-33	78734	3700-3999
HIGHLAND PASS	Austin	524U	MH-28	78731	5800-5999
HIGHLAND TRL	Leander	372A	MC-45	78641	2500-2799
HIGHLANDALE DR	Austin	524Q	MH-29	78731	6000-6299
HIGHLAND BLUFF CV	Austin	611R	MB-20	78735	7300-7399
HIGHLAND CREST DR	Austin	524Y	MH-28	78731	5400-5699
HIGHLANDER	Lakeway	489W	WW-31	78734	100-599
HIGHLANDER CV	Lakeway	489W	WW-31	78734	100-199
HIGHLAND ESTATES DR	Round Rock	408F	MQ-42	78664	300-399
HIGHLAND HILLS CIR	Austin	524V	MH-28	78731	5700-5799
HIGHLAND HILLS DR	Austin	524V	MH-28	78731	5700-5999
	Austin	524L	MH-29	78731	6000-6399
HIGHLAND HILLS TRL	Austin	524R	MH-29	78731	5900-5999
HIGHLAND HILLS TERRACE	Austin	524U	MH-28	78731	5800-5999
HIGHLAND LAKE DR	Lago Vista	459A	WW-36	78645	20100-20599
	Lago Vista	458H	WV-36	78645	20600-21499
HIGHLAND LAKE LOOP	Lago Vista	458R	WV-35	78645	20600-20699
HIGHLAND MALL BLVD E	Austin	555D	MK-27	78752	100-799
HIGHLAND MALL BLVD W	Austin	555D	MK-27	78752	200-299
HIGHLAND OAKS TRL	Austin	464M	MH-35	78759	11800-11999
HIGHLANDS BLVD	Lakeway	518M	WV-29	78738	None
	Lakeway	519J	WW-29	78738	None
	Travis Co	518Q	WV-29	78669	None
HIGHLANDS DR	Travis Co	488X	WU-31	78669	1900-2099
HIGHLAND SPRINGS LN					
	Williamson Co	224Q	MH-59	78633	300-899
HIGHLAND TERRACE	Austin	554H	MH-27	78731	4500-4699
	Austin	554D	MH-27	78731	4700-4799
HIGHLAND TERRACE	Round Rock	408F	MQ-42	78665	1-99
HIGHLAND TERRACE W	Austin	554D	MH-27	78731	3100-3299
HIGHLAND VIEW DR	Austin	524Q	MH-29	78731	3500-3799
HIGHLINE DR	Travis Co	459R	WX-35	78645	3700-3999
HIGH LONESOME	Leander	371G	MB-45	78641	1100-1899
	Leander	341X	MA-46	78641	1900-2099
HIGH LONESOME TRL	Leander	313F	ME-51	78628	100-1099
HIGH MEADOW	Austin	613E	ME-21	78735	4100-4199
HIGHMEADOWS CV	Round Rock	376P	ML-44	78681	1200-1399
HIGH MOUNTAIN CIR	Lago Vista	458C	WV-36	78645	3500-3599
HIGH NOON	Travis Co	709J	MS-11	78617	16500-16999
HIGH OAK DR	Austin	494V	MH-31	78759	8300-8499
HIGH PLAINS DR	Hays Co	577J	WS-23	78620	100-399
	Travis Co	577J	WS-23	78620	None
HIGH PLAINS CROSSING	Georgetown	314F	MG-51	78628	100-299
HIGH POINT BLVD	Bastrop Co	709M	MT-11	78612	100-199
HIGHPOINT CV	Austin	557S	MN-25	78723	6500-6599
HIGH POINT CV	Round Rock	408N	MQ-41	78664	2800-2899
HIGHPOINT DR	Austin	557S	MN-25	78723	6600-6699
HIGH POINT DR	Travis Co	709P	MS-11	78617	100-199
HIGH POINT DR	Round Rock	408J	MQ-41	78664	2700-2799
HIGH RIDGE DR	Bastrop Co	709P	MS-11	78617	1-199
HIGH RIM RD	Travis Co	487S	WS-31	78669	4000-4199
HIGH RIVER RANCH DR					
	Williamson Co	279K	WW-53	78642	100-299
HIGH SIERRA	Hays Co	638C	WV-18	78737	12600-13999
	Hays Co	608Y	WV-19	78737	None
HIGH SIERRA ST	Manor	530T	MU-28	78653	None
HIGHSMITH ST	Travis Co	618V	MR-19	78725	14200-14799
HIGH TECH DR	Georgetown	286V	MM-52	78626	600-799
HIGHTOWER DR	Williamson Co	375J	MJ-44	78681	4600-4699
	Williamson Co	374M	MH-44	78681	4700-4799
HIGH TRAIL DR	Georgetown	225H	MK-60	78633	100-199
HIGHTRAIL WAY	Village of the Hills	519T	WW-28	78738	1-99
HIGH VALLEY RD	Travis Co	641B	MA-18	78737	8500-8999
HIGHVIEW DR	Austin	464A	MG-36	78750	11500-11599
HIGHVIEW RD	Georgetown	256S	ML-55	78628	100-199
HIGH VISTA CIR	Hays Co	639P	WW-17	78737	100-199
HIGH WATER CV	Travis Co	491J	MA-32	78732	None
HIGINIA RUN	Bastrop Co	738L	MR-8	78617	100-199

STREET NAME	CITY or COUNTY	MAPSCO GRID	AUSTIN GRID	ZIP CODE	BLOCK RANGE O/E
HILCROFT CV	Williamson Co	405P	MJ-41	78717	15700-15799
HILDAGO ST	Austin	615D	MK-21	78702	2200-2699
HILDENE WAY	Austin	587M	MP-23	78724	8800-8899
HILEA CT	Bastrop Co	775G	EF-6	78602	100-199
HILINE RD	Travis Co	460L	WZ-35	78734	5500-5999
HILL CIR N	Williamson Co	282X	MC-52	78641	100-199
HILL CV	Williamson Co	375X	MJ-43	78681	600-699
HILL DR	Travis Co	401J	MA-41	78641	10400-11599
HILL LN	Manor	529F	MS-30	78653	10300-10399
	Travis Co	529F	MS-30	78653	9100-10299
HILL LN	Travis Co	498V	MR-31	78653	7600-7799
HILL ST	Bastrop	745F	EE-9	78602	500-1899
	Bastrop	715X	EE-10	78602	1900-2499
HILL ST	Round Rock	408J	MQ-41	78664	3000-3099
HILL ST	Village of Volente	461B	MA-36	78641	1530015499
HILLANDALE DR	Lakeway	519L	WX-29	78734	None
HILLBILLY LN	Travis Co	523X	ME-28	78746	2900-3299
HILLBROOK	Williamson Co	375T	MJ-43	78681	600-699
HILLBROOK CIR	Austin	524R	MH-29	78731	3500-3599
HILLBROOK DR	Austin	524Q	MH-29	78731	3500-3899
HILL COUNTRY BLVD	Bee Cave	550P	WY-26	78738	12600-12999
HILL COUNTRY DR	Cedar Park	373E	ME-45	78613	1500-1799
HILL COUNTRY DR	Georgetown	225H	MK-60	78633	100-199
HILL COUNTRY DR	Travis Co	310K	WY-50	78641	16300-16599
HILL COUNTRY SKYLINE	Travis Co	577L	WT-23	78720	10000-10599
HILLCREST CIR	Bastrop Co	621U	MX-19	78621	100-199
HILLCREST CT	West Lake Hills	583M	MF-23	78746	200-399
HILLCREST DR	Austin	556K	ML-26	78723	1300-1499
HILLCREST DR	Cedar Park	372Q	MD-44	78613	1700-1799
HILLCREST DR	Taylor	322U	MZ-49	76574	1400-1599
HILLCREST LN	Austin	586Q	MM-23	78721	1700-1799
HILLCROFT DR	Austin	557Y	MP-25	78724	6700-7399
HILLDALE	Travis Co	517F	WS-30	78669	21300-21399
HILLDALE DR	Austin	586H	MM-24	78723	4700-4999
HILLERY CV	Cedar Park	372L	MD-44	78613	900-999
HILL FOREST DR	Austin	612Y	MD-19	78749	6100-6299
HILLHAVEN DR	Austin	672Z	MD-13	78748	11300-11499
HILLHOUSE LN	Travis Co	703L	MF-11	78652	100-199
HILL MEADOW CIR	Austin	611R	MB-20	78736	7500-7599
HILL MEADOW DR	Austin	611R	MB-20	78736	6800-6999
HILLMONT ST	Austin	614C	MH-21	78704	1400-1599
HILLMOORE DR	Travis Co	676P	ML-14	78719	8500-8699
HILL OAKS CT	Austin	584B	MG-24	78703	1900-1999
HILLOAKS DR	Austin	612W	MC-19	78749	6400-6799
HILLRIDGE CT	Williamson Co	346M	MM-47	78665	1100-1199
HILLRIDGE DR	Williamson Co	346H	MM-48	78665	1100-1399
HILL RIDGE DR S	Bastrop Co	746A	EG-9	78602	100-199
HILLRISE DR	Austin	494Z	MH-31	78759	8000-8199
HILL RISE RD	Bastrop Co	621U	MX-19	78621	100-199
HILLROCK CV	Williamson Co	375X	MJ-43	78681	200-299
HILLROCK DR	Williamson Co	375X	MJ-43	78681	8300-8699
HILLSBOROUGH CV	Leander	342R	MD-47	78641	500-599
HILLSIDE AVE	Austin	615E	MJ-21	78704	1000-1499
HILLSIDE CIR	Lago Vista	428Z	WV-37	78645	4100-4199
HILLSIDE CV	Elgin	534P	EC-29	78621	100-199
HILLSIDE CV	Williamson Co	375T	MJ-43	78681	3700-3799
HILLSIDE CT	Travis Co	583K	ME-23	78746	1-99
HILLSIDE DR	Bastrop Co	712P	MY-11	78612	100-199
HILLSIDE DR	Elgin	534P	EC-29	78621	100-199
HILLSIDE DR	Hays Co	636K	WQ-17	78620	100-299
HILLSIDE DR	Hays Co	763W	ME-4	78610	100-399
HILLSIDE DR	Lago Vista	428Z	WV-37	78645	4100-4299
HILLSIDE DR	Travis Co	610W	WY-19	78736	10900-11099
HILLSIDE DR	Williamson Co	406Y	MM-40	78728	16200-16599
HILLSIDE DR	Williamson Co	375X	MJ-43	78681	17000-17399
	Williamson Co	375W	MJ-43	78717	17400-17499
HILLSIDE RD	Jonestown	430B	WY-39	78645	18500-18599
HILLSIDE HOLLOW DR	Austin	494N	MG-32	78750	6500-6599
HILLSIDE NORTH	Travis Co	610W	WY-19	78736	10000-10199
HILLSIDE OAK LN	Williamson Co	433G	MF-39	78750	10900-11099
HILLSIDE OAKS DR	Austin	643Z	MF-16	78745	900-1099
HILLSIDE TERRACE	Hays Co	763S	ME-4	78610	100-2199
HILLSIDE TERRACE CV	Austin	641R	MB-17	78749	9100-9199
HILLSIDE TERRACE DR	Austin	641M	MB-17	78749	6100-6699
HILLS OF TEXAS TRL	Georgetown	225C	MK-60	78633	100-499
HILLS PRAIRIE RD	Bastrop Co	775Y	EF-4	78662	100-499
HILL SPRING CIR	Austin	586G	MM-24	78721	4800-4899
HILL ST CV	Round Rock	408J	MQ-41	78664	2600-2699
HILL STABLE CT	Travis Co	703L	MF-11	78652	11200-11399
HILLSTON DR	Austin	643L	MF-17	78745	6200-6299
HILLSTONE TRL	Williamson Co	253Z	MF-55	78628	100-299
HILLTOP	Williamson Co	375B	MJ-45	78681	2500-2699
HILL TOP DR	Elgin	533M	EB-29	78621	100-199
HILLTOP DR	Hays Co	636L	WR-17	78620	100-299
HILLTOP DR	Leander	342H	MD-48	78641	600-899
HILLTOP DR	Travis Co	489V	WX-31	78734	400-499
HILLTOP DR	Travis Co	577M	WT-23	78720	9900-9999
HILLTOP ST	Austin	496Q	MM-32	78753	11300-11799
HILLTOP TRL	Williamson Co	411X	MW-40	76574	1-299
HILLTOP CANYON CV	Pflugerville	439E	MS-39	78660	18900-18999
HILLTOP COMMERCIAL DR					
	Pflugerville	438G	MR-39	78660	18600-18999
HILLTREE LN	Cedar Park	372L	MD-44	78613	1900-1999
HILL VALLEY CV	Georgetown	226P	ML-59	78628	100-199
HILLVIEW	Round Rock	378P	MQ-44	78664	1-99
HILLVIEW CIR	Travis Co	428A	WU-39	78654	23600-23699
HILL VIEW CV	Round Rock	408N	MQ-41	78664	2900-2999
HILLVIEW DR N	Georgetown	286F	ML-54	78628	100-299
HILLVIEW DR S	Georgetown	286F	ML-54	78628	100-299
HILLVIEW RD	Austin	554Y	MH-25	78703	2400-2699
	Austin	554Q	MH-26	78703	2800-3499
HILLVIEW GREEN LN	Austin	554U	MH-25	78703	2700-2799
HILLVUE RD	Williamson Co	317E	MN-51	78626	1-299
HILLWAY	Round Rock	378P	MQ-44	78664	1-99
HILL WOOD DR	Austin	644E	MG-18	78745	800-999
HILO CT E	Bastrop	746S	EG-7	78602	100-199
HILO CT W	Bastrop	746S	EG-7	78602	100-199
HILTON HEAD DR	Round Rock	378Y	MR-43	78664	2100-2199
HILWIN CIR	Austin	555E	MJ-27	78756	4700-4799
HINDON CT	Austin	673G	MF-15	78748	1100-1199
HINDON LN	Austin	673C	MF-15	78748	8400-8499
HIRIDGE HOLLOW DR	Austin	494N	MG-32	78750	6500-6599
HISPANIA CT	Austin	465P	MJ-35	78727	12000-12199
HITCHCOCK HILL	Cedar Park	373Q	MF-44	78613	400-499
HITCHER BEND	Austin	642J	MC-17	78749	5400-5599
HITCHING POST	Lago Vista	429N	WW-38	78645	5400-5599
HITCHING POST CIR	Austin	642C	MD-18	78749	6800-6899

STREET NAME	CITY or COUNTY	MAPSCO GRID	AUSTIN GRID	ZIP CODE	BLOCK RANGE O/E
HIWAY 40	Bastrop Co	715J	EE-11	78602	100-199
HOBART DR	Cedar Park	372J	MC-44	78613	2400-2499
HOBBITON TRL	Travis Co	672S	MC-13	78739	11500-11999
HOBBS CV	Austin	642V	MD-16	78749	3700-3799
HOBBS CREEK CV	Bastrop Co	741T	MW-7	78612	100-199
HOBBS CREEK LN	Travis Co	497M	MP-32	78754	12800-12899
HOBBY LN	Jonestown	400Y	WZ-40	78645	8900-9099
HOBBY HORSE CT	Austin	465Z	MK-34	78758	11900-11999
HODDE LN	Travis Co	439H	MT-39	78660	19400-20999
	Travis Co	409Z	MT-40	78660	21000-21199
HOEKE LN	Austin	646K	ML-17	78744	2400-2899
HOFFMAN CT	Cedar Park	402L	MD-41	78613	2000-2099
HOFFMAN CV	Austin	642T	MC-16	78749	9100-9199
HOFFMAN DR	Austin	642T	MC-16	78749	4200-4799
HOFFMAN DR	Hays Co	763W	ME-4	78610	100-399
HOFFMAN RD	Bastrop	715Y	EF-10	78602	100-299
HOGAN AVE	Austin	616S	ML-19	78741	5900-6299
HOGAN LN	Round Rock	377J	MN-44	78664	1300-1499
HOG EYE RD	Bastrop Co	592J	MY-23	78621	100-299
	Travis Co	587H	MP-24	78724	8600-9199
	Travis Co	588K	MQ-23	78724	9400-9699
	Travis Co	588H	MR-24	78724	10100-10599
	Travis Co	589E	MS-24	78653	14800-15399
	Travis Co	590C	MV-24	78653	18500-20199
	Travis Co	591A	MW-24	78653	20200-20399
	Travis Co	561W	MW-25	78653	20400-20599
	Travis Co	561X	MW-25	78653	20600-21599
	Travis Co	591C	MX-24	78653	21600-22599
	Travis Co	591H	MX-24	78653	22600-22899
	Travis Co	592J	MY-23	78621	22900-23199
	Travis Co	588J	MQ-23	78724	None
HOGG ST	Georgetown	286R	MM-53	78626	1800-2099
	Austin	703C	MF-12	78748	200-299
HOGG PECAN PASS	Austin	673Y	MF-13	78748	300-499
HOG HOLLOW RD	Hays Co	666Y	WR-13	78620	100-1799
HOKANSON CT	Travis Co	737Z	MP-7	78617	10700-10899
HOKANSON RD	Bastrop Co	738W	MQ-7	78617	100-299
	Travis Co	737Q	MP-8	78617	13400-15899
HOLBROOK ST	Williamson Co	434F	MG-39	78729	9900-9999
HOLBROOKE ST	Hutto	379U	MT-43	78634	100-799
HOLDEN CT	Round Rock	347N	MN-47	78665	3700-3799
HOLDERNESS LN	Pflugerville	437D	MP-39	78660	17900-17999
HOLIDAY HILLS CV	Travis Co	521L	MB-29	78732	1900-1999
HOLLAND AVE	Austin	614F	MG-21	78704	2000-2099
HOLLAND ST	Hutto	349U	MT-46	78634	200-299
HOLLAR SQUARE	Travis Co	497W	MN-31	78754	11400-11499
HOLLIDAY CT	Austin	496Y	MM-31	78753	300-399
HOLLINGSWORTH RD	Burnet Co	426A	WQ-39	78669	100-799
	Travis Co	397W	WS-40	78654	3500-4199
	Travis Co	427A	WS-39	78654	None
HOLLIS LN	Cedar Park	373M	MF-44	78613	2300-2499
HOLLISTER DR	Austin	671A	MA-15	78739	11300-11699
HOLLOW CREEK DR	Austin	614B	MG-21	78704	1100-1399
HOLLOW HOOK	Travis Co	588N	MQ-23	78724	10000-11199
HOLLOW OAK CT	Austin	464L	MH-35	78759	11500-11599
HOLLOW RIDGE DR	Cedar Park	372L	MD-44	78613	1700-1999
HOLLOW TRAIL CT	Round Rock	407F	MN-42	78664	900-999
HOLLOW TREE BLVD	Round Rock	376N	ML-44	78681	1400-1999
HOLLY TRL	Cedar Park	372M	MD-44	78613	1700-1999
HOLLY CT	Hays Co	639Y	WX-16	78737	100-199
HOLLY CT	Pflugerville	438T	MQ-37	78660	700-799
HOLLY LN	Lakeway	490W	WY-31	78734	15300-15499
	Travis Co	520A	WY-30	78734	15000-15299
HOLLY LN	Taylor	322V	MZ-49	76574	2400-2699
HOLLY ST	Austin	615F	MJ-21	78702	900-2499
HOLLY ST S	Georgetown	286H	MM-54	78626	100-799
	Georgetown	286R	MM-53	78626	1800-1999
HOLLYBERRY LN	Georgetown	225L	MK-59	78633	100-199
HOLLYBLUFF ST	Travis Co	496Y	MM-31	78753	800-1199
HOLLYBROOK CV	Cedar Park	373Y	MF-43	78613	1100-1199
HOLLY CREST TERRACE	Travis Co	529H	MT-30	78653	13300-13499
HOLLY FERN CV	Austin	493R	MF-32	78750	7200-7399
HOLLY HILL DR	Austin	613C	MF-21	78746	1800-1999
HOLLY HILL DR	Leander	342X	MC-46	78641	1600-1999
HOLLYHOCK CT	Pflugerville	438X	MQ-37	78660	1500-1599
HOLLY OAK CIR	Austin	674R	MH-14	78744	7600-7699
HOLLY SPRINGS CT	Austin	672H	MD-15	78748	2700-2799
HOLLY SPRINGS CT	Georgetown	225L	MK-59	78633	100-199
HOLLY SPRINGS DR	Taylor	323S	EA-49	76574	1800-2299
HOLLY SPRINGS RD	Austin	672M	MD-14	78748	9600-9799
HOLLYWOOD AVE	Austin	585G	MK-24	78722	3200-3799
HOLMAN LN	Bastrop Co	711A	MW-12	78612	100-199
HOLMAN PATH	Hutto	379H	MT-45	78634	100-299
HOLME LACEY CT	Austin	463B	ME-36	78750	10200-10299
HOLME LACEY LN	Austin	463G	MF-36	78750	10200-10499
HOLMES CT	Austin	585R	MK-23	78702	1100-1199
HOLMES RD	Liberty Hill	252S	MC-55	78642	100-199
	Williamson Co	252S	MC-55	78642	100-199
HOLMSTROM ST	Hutto	349U	MT-46	78634	100-299
HOLSTEIN DR	Austin	496E	ML-33	78758	1500-1699
HOLSTEN HILLS DR	Travis Co	409T	MS-40	78660	2400-2499
HOLSTER CT	Travis Co	672U	MD-13	78748	11200-11299
HOLT DR	Austin	642M	MD-17	78749	3600-3999
HOLTON ST	Austin	616A	ML-21	78702	3100-3299
HOME LN	Austin	555X	MJ-25	78705	3400-3799
HOME PL E	Austin	526F	ML-30	78753	100-399
HOME PL W	Austin	526F	ML-30	78753	100-199
HOMEDALE CIR	Austin	614E	MG-21	78704	2400-2499
HOMEDALE DR	Austin	614E	MG-21	78704	2100-2599
HOME DEPOT BLVD	Bee Cave	550J	WY-26	78738	None
HOME DEPOT BLVD	Travis Co	613W	ME-19	78749	1000-1299
HOME DEPOT WAY	Bastrop Co	744L	ED-8	78602	None
HOMES CV	Lago Vista	458M	WV-35	78645	20700-20799
HOMESTEAD CV	Lago Vista	458M	WV-35	78645	20700-20799
HOMESTEAD DR	Williamson Co	408K	MQ-41	78664	100-199
HOMESTEAD LN	Hays Co	636C	WR-18	78620	100-299
HOMESTEAD TRL	Austin	611M	MB-20	78735	6100-6299
HOMESTEAD VILLAGE CIR	Austin	403M	MF-41	78717	14300-14599
HOMESTEAD VILLAGE TRL	Austin	403M	MF-41	78717	14100-14199
HOMEWOOD CIR	Round Rock	407D	MP-42	78665	1500-2099
HOMONU CT	Bastrop	746N	EG-8	78602	100-199
HONDO LN	Hutto	379L	MT-44	78634	1000-1099
HONDO BEND	Travis Co	435S	MJ-37	78729	6600-6799
HONEY CV	Pflugerville	468K	MQ-35	78660	900-999
HONEY BEAR LOOP	Williamson Co	344V	MH-46	78681	4000-4099
HONEYBEE CT	Travis Co	488W	WU-31	78669	20600-20699
HONEYBEE LN	Hays Co	669N	WW-14	78737	100-299

STREET NAME	CITY or COUNTY	MAPSCO GRID	AUSTIN GRID	ZIP CODE	BLOCK RANGE O/E
HONEYBEE LN	Leander	342T	MC-46	78641	1900-1999
HONEYBEE LN	Travis Co	488W	WU-31	78669	20300-20599
	Travis Co	487Z	WT-31	78669	20600-20699
HONEYBEE BEND	Austin	675N	MJ-14	78744	5600-5799
HONEY BLOSSOM DR	Travis Co	467L	MP-35	78660	1300-1399
HONEYCOMB CIR	Travis Co	340C	WZ-48	78641	22200-22299
HONEYCOMB CT	Travis Co	340C	WZ-48	78641	15000-15199
HONEYCOMB DR	Travis Co	487Z	WT-31	78669	3100-3199
HONEYCOMB DR	Travis Co	640D	WZ-18	78737	9000-9599
HONEYCOMB DR	Travis Co	340C	WZ-48	78641	14500-15199
HONEYCOMB LN	Travis Co	340B	WY-48	78641	22200-22499
HONEYCOMB HOLLOW	Travis Co	340D	WZ-48	78641	15100-22499
HONEYCOMB MESA	Williamson Co	341A	MA-48	78641	1-499
HONEYCOMB RIDGE	Travis Co	583M	MF-23	78746	400-599
HONEYCOMB ROCK CIR	Austin	524C	MH-30	78731	4100-4199
HONEY CREEK LN	Cedar Park	373E	ME-45	78613	1700-1899
HONEY CREEK TRL	Georgetown	195V	MK-61	78633	100-199
HONEY DEW CT	Austin	612Y	MD-19	78749	6200-6299
HONEY DEW TERRACE	Austin	612T	MC-19	78749	5300-5699
HONEY LOCUST LN	Travis Co	532L	MZ-29	78621	17800-17899
HONEYSUCKLE CV	Georgetown	225H	MK-60	78633	100-199
HONEYSUCKLE DR	Cedar Park	403F	ME-42	78613	400-599
HONEYSUCKLE DR	Leander	342P	MC-47	78641	700-1099
HONEYSUCKLE LN	Pflugerville	438X	MQ-37	78660	100-899
	Pflugerville	468B	MQ-36	78660	1200-1399
HONEYSUCKLE LN	Williamson Co	377E	MN-45	78664	1500-1999
HONEYSUCKLE TRL	Austin	495S	MJ-31	78759	8600-8999
HONEY SUCKLE ROSE TRL					
	Travis Co	487F	WS-33	78669	None
HONEY TREE LN	Austin	583V	MF-22	78746	3000-3199
HONEYWEED ST	Williamson Co	433E	ME-39	78613	1500-1799
HONOPU DR	Bastrop	746T	EG-7	78602	100-199
	Bastrop Co	746T	EG-7	78602	None
HONORS DR	Lakeway	519W	WW-28	78738	100-199
HOOD CIR	Austin	643X	ME-16	78745	8000-8299
HOOD ST	Taylor	352D	MZ-48	76574	100-1299
	Taylor	322Z	MZ-49	76574	1300-1899
HOOD HOLLOW	Austin	524N	MG-29	78731	6000-6099
HOOK ST	Elgin	533M	EB-29	78621	100-199
HOOKBILLED KITE DR	Bee Cave	549L	WX-26	78738	None
HOOPES AVE E	Pflugerville	438W	MQ-37	78660	100-299
HOOPES AVE W	Pflugerville	438W	MQ-37	78660	100-299
HOOT OWL CT	Travis Co	309L	WX-50	78641	14900-14999
HOOT OWL LN N	Williamson Co	282N	MC-53	78641	100-499
HOOT OWL LN S	Williamson Co	282N	MC-53	78641	500-599
HOOVER CV	Lago Vista	458M	WV-35	78645	20500-20699
HOPELAND DR	Austin	641R	MB-17	78749	9100-9599
HOPE POND VALLEY	Hays Co	762Y	MD-4	78610	100-199
HOPEWELL CIR	Williamson Co	283D	MF-54	78628	100-199
HOPEWELL CT	Williamson Co	343W	ME-46	78641	2700-2799
HOPI TRL	Austin	584B	MG-24	78703	1500-1999
	Austin	554X	MG-25	78703	2000-2499
HOPKINS CV	Lago Vista	458M	WV-35	78645	2600-2699
HOPKINS DR	Travis Co	460G	WZ-36	78734	6300-6499
HOPPE TRL	Round Rock	376B	ML-45	78681	2500-2999
HOPSACK MILLS RD	Travis Co	702G	MD-12	78748	2500-2599
HORACE DR	Travis Co	526D	MM-30	78753	10300-10399
HORBORNE LN	Travis Co	437X	MN-37	78660	15100-15699
HORIZON CV	Hutto	350N	MU-47	78634	1100-1199
HORIZON CV	Lago Vista	458H	WV-36	78645	3100-3199
HORIZON DR	Bastrop Co	709L	MT-11	78612	None
HORIZON LN	Travis Co	736L	MM-8	78719	9900-9999
HORIZON TRL	Cedar Park	373T	ME-43	78613	600-799
HORIZON PARK BLVD	Leander	342R	MD-47	78641	1800-2099
HORN LN	Austin	584C	MH-24	78703	2300-2399
HORNE DR	Travis Co	402P	MC-41	78613	1000-1099
HORNET DR	Austin	642V	MD-16	78749	8300-8499
HORNSBY LN	Travis Co	518F	WU-30	78669	19100-19399
HORNSBY ST	Austin	496Q	MM-32	78753	11300-11999
HORNSBY TRL	Bastrop Co	712Z	MZ-10	78602	100-199
HORNSBY HILL RD	Travis Co	461W	MA-34	78734	14700-14999
	Travis Co	460Z	WZ-34	78734	15000-15199
HORSEBACK HOLLOW	Travis Co	521J	MA-29	78732	200-1499
HORSEBACK HOLLOW CT	Travis Co	521K	MA-29	78732	12100-12199
HORSEMAN CV	Round Rock	347W	MN-46	78665	1000-1099
HORSEMINT TRL	Travis Co	517J	WS-29	78669	22000-22099
HORSE MOUNTAIN CV	Austin	464N	MG-35	78759	8400-8499
HORSESHOE CIR	Round Rock	375R	MK-44	78681	1700-1799
HORSESHOE DR	Hays Co	577K	WS-23	78620	100-199
	Travis Co	577K	WS-23	78620	None
HORSESHOE DR	Leander	342F	MC-48	78641	400-799
HORSESHOE LOOP	Lago Vista	399W	WW-40	78645	21400-21599
HORSESHOE LOOP	Williamson Co	252S	MC-55	78642	100-499
HORSESHOE TRL	Georgetown	256F	ML-57	78628	100-199
HORSESHOE TRL	Williamson Co	252S	MC-55	78642	500-599
HORSESHOE BEND	Austin	554H	MH-27	78731	4600-4699
HORSESHOE BEND CV	Austin	613M	MF-20	78704	2800-2899
HORSESHOE LEDGE	Travis Co	493T	ME-31	78730	8400-8499
HORSESHOE RANCH DR	Leander	372B	MC-45	78641	1100-1399
HORSETHIEF TRL	Travis Co	733A	ME-9	78652	300-599
HORSE WAGON DR	Austin	497T	MN-31	78754	1800-2199
HORTON TRL	Austin	642Q	MD-17	78749	8300-8499
HOSACK ST	Taylor	323W	EA-49	76574	100-599
HOSKINS LN	Bastrop Co	746V	EH-7	78602	100-199
HOSPITAL DR	Bastrop	745J	EE-8	78602	100-199
HOSTA CV	Austin	433U	MF-37	78750	10100-10199
HOT SPRINGS CT	Austin	641H	MB-18	78749	8300-8399
HOT SPRINGS DR	Austin	641H	MB-18	78749	6600-6799
HOT SPRINGS DR	Taylor	322M	MZ-50	76574	4100-4299
HOT SPRING VALLEY	Hays Co	762Z	MD-4	78610	300-1199
HOUSE CREEK DR	Williamson Co	373A	ME-45	78641	700-999
HOUSEFINCH LOOP	Williamson Co	282J	MC-53	78641	100-499
HOUSE OF LANCASTER	Travis Co	522D	MD-30	78730	4500-4699
HOUSE OF YORK	Travis Co	522C	MD-30	78730	4100-4499
HOUSE WREN LOOP	Travis Co	438N	MQ-38	78660	600-999
HOUSTON CV	Lago Vista	458M	WV-35	78645	20500-20599
HOUSTON LN	Travis Co	649Y	MT-16	78617	3900-4099
	Travis Co	679C	MT-15	78617	4100-4299
HOUSTON ST	Austin	555F	MJ-27	78756	800-1899
HOUSTON ST	Buda	762D	MD-6	78610	100-299
HOUSTON ST	Elgin	534X	EC-28	78621	100-499
HOUSTON ST	Travis Co	490H	WZ-33	78734	3600-3899
HOVENWEEP AVE	Austin	646T	ML-16	78744	3400-3599
HOWARD LN E	Austin	467Y	MP-34	78753	101-999 O
	Austin	467Y	MP-34	78753	1000-1699
	Travis Co	467Y	MP-34	78753	100-998 E

STREET NAME	CITY or COUNTY	MAPSCO GRID	AUSTIN GRID	ZIP CODE	BLOCK RANGE O/E
HOWARD LN W	Austin	467N	MN-35	78753	101-999 O
	Austin	466M	MM-35	78753	1001-1099 O
	Austin	466M	MM-35	78753	1100-1299
	Austin	436W	ML-37	78728	3600-3899
	Travis Co	467N	MN-35	78753	100-998 E
	Travis Co	466M	MM-35	78753	1000-1098 E
	Travis Co	466M	MM-35	78728	1300-2799
	Travis Co	436X	ML-37	78728	2800-3399
	Travis Co	436W	ML-37	78728	3900-4499
	Travis Co	435V	MK-37	78728	4500-5499
HOWARD RD	Austin	616D	MM-21	78725	1901-2499 O
HOWARD ST	Taylor	352H	MZ-48	76574	100-1299
	Taylor	322Z	MZ-49	76574	1300-1499
HOWDEN CIR	Austin	586H	MM-24	78723	4900-4999
HOWELL MOUNTAIN DR	Cedar Park	373R	MF-44	78613	2100-2199
HOWELL TERRACE PL	Round Rock	408J	MQ-41	78664	1000-1099
HOWELLWOOD WAY	Austin	672M	MD-14	78748	2500-2699
HOWE MOUNTAIN DR	Jonestown	400Y	WZ-40	78645	8600-8699
HOWERINGTON CIR	Austin	557U	MP-25	78724	7100-7299
HOWETH CV	Pflugerville	407Z	MP-40	78660	17900-17999
HOWETH DR	Pflugerville	407Y	MP-40	78660	1000-1099
HOWI LN	Bastrop Co	775C	EF-6	78602	100-199
HOWLIN WOLF TRL	Pflugerville	407U	MP-40	78664	1400-1499
HOWRY DR	Georgetown	287P	MN-53	78626	2200-2599
HOXIE ST	Williamson Co	443G	EB-39	78615	100-499
HOYER CV	Williamson Co	345S	MJ-46	78681	4000-4099
HUACO	Lago Vista	429S	WW-37	78645	4700-4799
HUB CV	Austin	494R	MH-32	78759	8400-8499
HUBACH LN	Austin	674J	MG-14	78748	100-599
HUBBARD CIR	Rollingwood	584N	MG-23	78746	2700-2899
HUBBARD ST	Bastrop Co	775Z	EF-4	78662	100-299
HUCKABEE BEND	Travis Co	409N	MS-41	78660	20500-20899
HUCK FINN TRL	Hays Co	668H	WV-15	78620	100-999
HUCKLEBERRY CV	Travis Co	582L	MD-23	78746	6500-6599
HUCKLEBERRY LN	Austin	673K	ME-14	78748	1400-1599
HUCKS HIDEAWAY	Hays Co	668D	WV-15	78620	100-199
HUDDLESTON LN	Austin	673H	MF-15	78748	7700-8199
HUDSON CIR	Travis Co	432Q	MD-38	78726	10501-10699 O
HUDSON CV	Lago Vista	458M	WV-35	78645	20600-20699
HUDSON LN	Hays Co	607H	WT-21	78620	100-499
HUDSON LOOP	Travis Co	611Y	MB-19	78736	7700-7999
HUDSON ST	Austin	586V	MM-22	78721	5400-6599
	Austin	586V	MM-22	78725	6600-6699
HUDSON BEND RD	Travis Co	490C	WZ-33	78734	3700-4299
	Travis Co	460Q	WZ-35	78734	4300-6299
HUDSON HOLLOW	Austin	494G	MH-33	78759	5500-5599
HUEBINGER PASS	Austin	673A	ME-15	78745	8600-8899
HUECO MOUNTAIN TRL	Pflugerville	407X	MN-40	78664	1600-1799
HUELO CT	Bastrop Co	775D	EF-6	78602	100-199
HUERTA ST	Austin	614Q	MH-20	78704	700-799
HUFF LN	Bastrop Co	534D	ED-30	78621	100-199
HUFF ST	Taylor	322Z	MZ-49	76574	700-799
HUGHES DR	Cedar Park	402M	MD-41	78613	1600-1699
HUGHES ST	Travis Co	491H	MB-33	78732	12800-12899
HUGHES PARK RD	Travis Co	491H	MB-33	78732	12700-12899
	Travis Co	492A	MC-33	78732	None
HUGHES RANCH RD	Travis Co	491Q	MB-32	78732	4100-4299
HUGHMONT DR	Pflugerville	437M	MP-38	78660	1000-1299
HUISACHE CT	Georgetown	226S	ML-58	78628	100-199
HUISACHE ST	Austin	555K	MJ-26	78751	5200-5299
HULL CIR	West Lake Hills	553Z	MF-25	78746	1-99
HULSEY RD	Travis Co	498S	MQ-31	78653	12200-12499
HULU CT	Bastrop	746S	EG-7	78602	100-199
HUMBER CV	Travis Co	677X	MN-13	78617	11500-11599
HUMBLE CV	Travis Co	522B	MC-30	78730	3700-3799
HUMBOLDT LN	Travis Co	553E	ME-27	78746	1-99
HUME PL	Austin	585A	MJ-24	78705	2600-2699
HUMINGTON DR	Austin	496P	ML-32	78758	10800-10999
HUMMINGBIRD CIR	Cedar Park	433A	ME-39	78613	2800-2899
HUMMINGBIRD CT	Bastrop Co	709M	MT-11	78612	100-199
HUMMINGBIRD CT	Round Rock	375R	MK-44	78681	1200-1299
HUMMINGBIRD CV	Georgetown	195V	MK-61	78633	100-199
HUMMING BIRD LN	Austin	644P	MG-17	78745	5400-5599
HUMMINGBIRD LN	Travis Co	520E	WY-30	78734	400-599
HUMMINGBIRD LN	Travis Co	491N	MA-32	78732	13900-14099
HUMMINGBIRD LN	Williamson Co	282J	MC-53	78641	100-399
HUMMINGBIRD RD	Hays Co	701Q	MB-11	78652	2800-2999
HUMMINGBIRD WAY	Burnet Co	396T	WQ-40	78669	100-499
HUMPHREY DR	Williamson Co	434L	MH-38	78729	12800-13399
HUNDRED OAKS CIR	Austin	463R	MF-35	78750	9800-9999
HUNDRED YEAR OAK DR	Travis Co	673P	ME-14	78748	9900-10099
	Travis Co	673T	ME-13	78748	10100-10199
HUNGRY HORSE DR	Travis Co	560N	MU-26	78653	11300-11599
HUNLAC CV	Round Rock	406N	ML-41	78681	2600-2699
HUNLAC TRL	Round Rock	406N	ML-41	78681	2600-2799
HUNNICUT CT	Austin	672M	MD-14	78748	2800-2899
HUNT CIR	Williamson Co	342Z	MD-46	78641	2600-2699
HUNT LN	Hays Co	702X	MC-10	78610	400-499
HUNT TRL	Austin	525N	MJ-29	78757	2800-3199
HUNTCLIFF DR	Austin	524L	MH-29	78731	6300-6399
HUNTER ACE WAY	Cedar Park	402R	MD-41	78613	1300-1599
HUNTERS LN	Austin	496Q	MM-32	78753	11300-11599
HUNTERS PASS	Travis Co	490Z	WZ-31	78734	13600-14599
HUNTERS TRL	Round Rock	376N	ML-44	78681	1600-1999
HUNTERS BEND RD	Travis Co	618R	MR-20	78725	14300-14699
	Travis Co	619N	MS-20	78725	14700-15799
HUNTERS CHASE	Bastrop Co	711C	MX-12	78612	100-199
HUNTER'S CHASE DR	Austin	434X	MG-37	78729	12100-12299
	Williamson Co	434Q	MH-38	78729	12300-13199
HUNTERS CREEK	Jonestown	430D	WZ-39	78645	8800-8899
HUNTERS CREEK CV	Williamson Co	403W	ME-40	78613	2400-2499
HUNTERS CREEK DR	Williamson Co	403W	ME-40	78613	900-1199
HUNTERS CROSSING BLVD					
	Bastrop Co	744K	EC-8	78602	100-299
HUNTERS GLEN	Austin	644J	MG-17	78745	5400-5499
HUNTERS GLEN DR	Georgetown	287N	MN-53	78626	2200-2299
HUNTERS GREEN CT	Travis Co	521G	MB-30	78732	None
HUNTERS GREEN TRL	Travis Co	521G	MB-30	78732	None
HUNTERS GROVE CT	Travis Co	426L	WR-38	78669	26600-26699
HUNTERS HOLLOW	Jonestown	430D	WZ-39	78645	17600-17799
HUNTERS LODGE CV	Williamson Co	344U	MH-46	78681	4400-4499
HUNTERS LODGE DR	Williamson Co	344U	MH-46	78681	4400-4499
HUNTER'S POINT CT	Leander	342R	MD-47	78641	400-599
HUNTERS POINT DR	Bastrop	744K	EC-8	78602	100-399
HUNTERS POINT DR	Williamson Co	224Y	MH-58	78633	20100-20399
HUNTERS RIDGE RD	Travis Co	735J	MJ-8	78747	11400-11699

STREET NAME	CITY or COUNTY	MAPSCO GRID	AUSTIN GRID	ZIP CODE	BLOCK RANGE O/E
HUNTERS TRACE	Austin	525D	MK-30	78758	8900-9199
	Austin	495Z	MK-31	78758	9200-9499
HUNTERS TRACE E	Austin	495Z	MK-31	78758	9200-9499
HUNTERWOOD PT	Austin	523U	MF-28	78746	3700-3899
HUNTING CREEK LN	San Leanna	703F	ME-12	78748	11400-11599
HUNTINGDON PL	Austin	644W	MG-16	78745	700-899
HUNTINGTON TRL	Travis Co	408G	MR-42	78664	1400-1499
	Williamson Co	408G	MR-42	78664	1100-1399
HUNTINGTOWER CASTLE BLVD					
	Pflugerville	408X	MQ-40	78660	None
HUNTLAND DR E	Austin	555D	MK-27	78752	100-899
HUNTLAND DR W	Austin	555D	MK-27	78752	100-499
HUNTLEIGH WAY	Austin	587J	MN-23	78725	6300-6499
HUNTRIDGE CIR	Austin	496K	ML-32	78758	1100-1199
HUNTRIDGE DR	Austin	496K	ML-32	78758	900-1199
HUNTSVILLE CV	Georgetown	195W	MJ-61	78633	100-199
HUNTWICK DR	Austin	645C	MK-18	78741	2400-2699
HUNTWOOD CV	Williamson Co	434Q	MH-38	78729	13000-13099
HUPA CIR	Austin	434Z	MH-37	78729	12700-12799
HUR INDUSTRIAL BLVD	Cedar Park	372N	MC-44	78613	1700-1999
HURLBUT RD	Hays Co	636B	WQ-18	78620	100-499
HURLEY CV	Austin	494B	MG-33	78759	9200-9299
HURLOCK DR	Austin	524S	MG-28	78731	5400-5499
HURON DR	Travis Co	467P	MN-35	78660	None
HURON CLUB CT	Travis Co	550L	WZ-26	78733	3000-3099
HURST PL	Lakeway	489X	WW-31	78734	1-99
HURST CREEK CIR	Travis Co	489M	WX-32	78734	16800-16899
HURST CREEK RD	Lakeway	489X	WW-31	78734	100-799
	Travis Co	489R	WX-32	78734	800-1699
HURST HOLLOW	Travis Co	489M	WX-32	78734	1100-1499
HURST VIEW	Travis Co	489M	WX-32	78734	17000-17099
HUTCHINSON DR	Austin	586H	MM-24	78723	5200-5499
HUTTO RD	Georgetown	287N	MN-53	78626	1200-2199
HUTTO ST	Hutto	349Z	MT-46	78634	100-499
HUTTON CT	Williamson Co	343W	ME-46	78641	900-999
HUTTON LN	Williamson Co	343W	ME-46	78641	2400-2699
HUXLEY LN	Pflugerville	407X	MN-40	78664	1900-1999
	Pflugerville	407X	MN-40	78664	2001-2199 O
	Round Rock	407X	MN-40	78664	2000-2198 E
HUXLEY ST	Austin	672R	MD-14	78748	10300-10599
HYACINTH DR	Austin	496F	ML-33	78758	11800-11899
HYATT LOST PINES RD	Bastrop Co	711H	MX-12	78612	100-599
HYCLIMB CIR	Austin	556V	MM-25	78723	3200-3399
HYCREEK DR	Austin	556V	MM-25	78723	3200-3499
HYCREST DR	Austin	494R	MH-32	78759	4100-4299
HYCREST DR	Williamson Co	348Z	MR-46	78634	100-299
HYDE CV	Leander	342R	MD-47	78641	500-599
HYDE PARK CT	Austin	673M	MF-14	78748	700-799
HYDE PARK DR	Round Rock	377L	MP-44	78665	900-1199
HYDE PARK PL	Austin	673M	MF-14	78748	600-799
HYDRO DR	Travis Co	466G	MM-36	78728	1600-1999
HYLAND CIR	Austin	674H	MH-15	78744	6900-6999
HYLAWN DR	Austin	556V	MM-25	78723	6100-6299
HYLTIN ST	Hutto	349U	MT-46	78634	100-299
HYMAN LN	Austin	646D	MM-18	78742	1200-1399
HYMEADOW DR	Austin	433M	MF-38	78750	12500-12599
	Austin	434E	MG-39	78729	12900-13099
	Williamson Co	433M	MF-38	78750	12200-12499
	Williamson Co	434E	MG-39	78729	12600-12899
HYMILL DR	Travis Co	467Z	MP-34	78660	13900-14099
HYRIDGE CIR	Round Rock	406H	MM-42	78664	1400-1499
HYRIDGE DR	Austin	495N	MJ-32	78759	3500-4099
	Austin	494R	MH-32	78759	4100-4599
HYRIDGE ST	Round Rock	406H	MM-42	78664	900-1399
HYSIDE DR	Austin	556V	MM-25	78723	6100-6399
HYSON CROSSING	Travis Co	467L	MP-35	78660	14600-15399
HYTOP DR	Travis Co	467V	MP-34	78660	14000-14299
HY VIEW LN	Williamson Co	348H	MR-48	78634	100-499

I

STREET NAME	CITY or COUNTY	MAPSCO GRID	AUSTIN GRID	ZIP CODE	BLOCK RANGE O/E
IAO CT	Bastrop Co	776B	EG-6	78602	100-199
IBEX TRL	Pflugerville	437B	MN-39	78664	17300-17399
IBIS CV	Austin	643S	ME-16	78745	7900-7999
ICARUS CT	Austin	433X	ME-37	78726	10600-10699
ICE AGE TRAILS ST	Pflugerville	438E	MQ-39	78660	17700-17999
ICEBERG LN	Travis Co	436R	MM-38	78728	15300-15399
ICON ST	Austin	645W	MJ-16	78744	5500-5599
IDAHO FALLS CV	Pflugerville	437K	MN-38	78660	1400-1499
IDAHO FALLS LN	Pflugerville	437K	MN-38	78660	16300-16399
IDALIA DR	Austin	672F	MC-15	78749	3800-4199
IDA RIDGE DR	Austin	466B	ML-36	78727	13600-13699
	Travis Co	466B	ML-36	78727	13700-13899
IDLE HOUR CV	Lakeway	519H	WX-30	78734	1700-1799
IDLEWILD RD	Austin	554R	MH-26	78731	3900-4199
IDLEWILDE RUN DR	Austin	674W	MG-13	78744	1900-2099
IDLEWOOD CV	Austin	644T	MG-16	78745	5900-6299
IGNACIA DR	Georgetown	317F	MN-51	78626	1000-1499
IGUANA CIR	Austin	611M	MB-20	78735	6200-6299
IKEA WAY	Round Rock	346P	ML-47	78665	1-99
ILA ST E	Elgin	534E	EC-30	78621	100-199
ILA ST W	Elgin	534E	EC-30	78621	100-199
IMAGE CV	Austin	493M	MF-32	78750	7700-7899
IMES LN	Travis Co	619N	MS-20	78725	15100-15199
IMMANUEL RD	Pflugerville	468J	MQ-35	78660	100-999
	Travis Co	468J	MQ-35	78660	1000-1399
	Travis Co	497D	MP-33	78660	13300-13599
	Travis Co	467Z	MP-34	78660	13600-14299
	Travis Co	468J	MQ-35	78660	14300-14999
IMOGENE DR	Travis Co	591Z	MX-22	78621	7800-7899
IMPERIAL CT	Travis Co	588S	MQ-22	78724	10000-10099
IMPERIAL DR	Travis Co	587Z	MP-22	78725	4200-4899
IMPERIAL DR N	Travis Co	588S	MQ-22	78724	4900-6599
IMPERIAL EAGLE LN	Elgin	503X	EA-31	78621	None
IMPERIAL JADE DR	Travis Co	436L	MM-38	78728	15500-15699
IMPROVER RD	Travis Co	487E	WS-33	78669	2300-2699
INCA LN	Travis Co	522K	MC-29	78733	9800-9999
INCA DOVE DR	Austin	434G	MH-39	78729	8500-8599
INDEPENDENCE DR	Austin	643G	MF-18	78745	2000-2499
INDEPENDENCE DR	Williamson Co	194E	MG-63	78633	200-299
INDEPENDENCE LOOP	Austin	673K	ME-14	78748	9200-9399
INDEPENDENCE CREEK LN					
	Georgetown	195N	MJ-62	78633	100-499
	Georgetown	194V	MH-61	78633	500-899
INDIAN TRL	Austin	584C	MH-24	78703	2000-2699
INDIAN TRL	Williamson Co	282N	MC-53	78641	100-499
INDIANA DUNES DR	Austin	704A	MG-12	78747	2100-2299
INDIAN BEND DR	Lakeway	489Q	WX-32	78734	100-199
INDIAN BLANKET DR	Travis Co	402Y	MD-40	78613	1900-1999
INDIAN CAMP TRL	Round Rock	376J	ML-44	78681	1700-1799
INDIAN CANYON CV	Travis Co	582H	MD-24	78746	1200-1299
INDIAN CANYON DR	Travis Co	582H	MD-24	78746	6200-6499
INDIAN CHIEF DR	Travis Co	371V	MB-43	78613	16900-17299
INDIAN CREEK CV	Williamson Co	287H	MP-54	78626	50100-50199
INDIAN CREEK DR	Williamson Co	287H	MP-54	78626	50100-50899
INDIAN CREEK RD	Travis Co	490Q	WZ-32	78734	2000-2799
INDIAN DIVIDE CV	Travis Co	487E	WS-33	78669	23500-23699
INDIAN DIVIDE RD	Travis Co	487E	WS-33	78669	2600-2899
INDIANHEAD DR	Austin	496Q	MM-32	78753	11300-11599
	Austin	496L	MM-32	78753	11700-12099
INDIAN HILL	Travis Co	461M	MB-35	78732	13800-13899
INDIAN LODGE DR	Cedar Park	373E	ME-45	78613	1800-1899
INDIAN LODGE ST	Georgetown	225V	MK-58	78628	4600-4799
INDIAN MEADOW DR	Georgetown	287L	MP-53	78626	100-899
INDIAN MEADOWS DR	Williamson Co	346V	MM-46	78665	1-99
INDIAN MOUND DR	Austin	466Y	MM-34	78758	12300-12399
	Austin	466Y	MM-34	78753	None
INDIAN MOUND RD	Burnet Co	396X	WQ-40	78669	100-1199
INDIAN MOUND RD	Williamson Co	226M	MM-59	78628	3000-3599
INDIAN OAK BEND	Manor	530T	MU-28	78653	None
INDIAN OAKS	Williamson Co	344U	MH-46	78681	4300-4399
INDIAN POINT DR	Travis Co	672P	MC-14	78739	3500-3799
INDIAN QUAIL CIR	Austin	526A	ML-30	78758	9200-9299
INDIAN RIDGE DR	Austin	641B	MA-18	78737	7800-7899
INDIAN RUN CT	Pflugerville	437Y	MP-37	78660	801-899 O
INDIAN RUN DR	Pflugerville	437Y	MP-37	78660	600-999
INDIAN SCOUT TRL	Travis Co	610G	WZ-21	78736	10700-10799
INDIAN SHOAL DR	Georgetown	285P	MJ-53	78628	100-399
INDIAN SPRINGS	Travis Co	583M	MF-23	78746	700-799
INDIAN SPRINGS RD	Williamson Co	193T	ME-61	78633	1-2299
INDIAN SUMMER PASS	Round Rock	407C	MP-42	78665	1800-1899
INDIAN SUMMIT	Travis Co	670C	WZ-15	78737	8400-8499
INDIAN TREE TRL	San Leanna	703E	ME-12	78748	700-899
INDIAN WELLS	Leander	342S	MC-46	78641	1700-1799
INDIAN WELLS DR	Austin	704S	MG-10	78747	4600-4799
INDIANWOOD DR	Lakeway	519W	WW-28	78738	100-499
INDICA CV	Austin	464T	MG-34	78759	6900-6999
INDIGO CV	Travis Co	491G	MB-33	78732	13100-13199
INDIGO LN	Williamson Co	284A	MG-54	78628	300-599
INDIGO TRL	Round Rock	378S	MQ-43	78665	3000-3099
INDIGO BROOM LOOP	Travis Co	551P	MA-26	78733	10300-10699
INDIGO BRUSH DR	Austin	463E	ME-36	78726	9500-9899
INDIGO BUNTING CV	Williamson Co	282J	MC-53	78641	100-199
INDIGO RUN CV	Lakeway	519S	WW-28	78738	100-199
INDIGO SKY DR	Austin	587M	MP-23	78724	8901-9199 O
INDIGO WATERS DR	Travis Co	491T	MA-31	78732	3200-3499
INDINA HILLS CV	Austin	404D	MH-42	78717	16100-16199
INDINA HILLS DR	Austin	404D	MH-42	78717	9500-9899
INDIO CIR	Austin	643C	MF-18	78745	5300-5399
INDIO CV	Austin	643C	MF-18	78745	5300-5399
INDIO DR	Austin	643C	MF-18	78745	5300-5399
INDUS CV	Travis Co	522B	MC-30	78730	10100-10199
INDUSTRIAL	Georgetown	286U	MM-52	78626	300-399
INDUSTRIAL BLVD	Austin	644H	MH-18	78745	100-799
INDUSTRIAL BLVD	Bastrop	746J	EG-8	78602	200-399
INDUSTRIAL BLVD	Cedar Park	372M	MD-44	78613	100-299
INDUSTRIAL BLVD N	Round Rock	376P	ML-44	78681	1000-1299
INDUSTRIAL BLVD S	Round Rock	376P	ML-44	78681	1000-1199
INDUSTRIAL BLVD W	Round Rock	376P	ML-44	78681	1300-1599
INDUSTRIAL DR	Taylor	353S	EA-46	76574	1800-1999
INDUSTRIAL OAKS BLVD	Austin	612V	MD-19	78735	5200-5399
INDUSTRIAL PARK CIR	Georgetown	257E	MN-57	78626	10100-40299
INDUSTRIAL TERRACE	Austin	495P	MJ-32	78758	2700-3299
INDUSTRY DR	Bastrop	746N	EG-8	78602	100-199
INGLEWOOD ST	Austin	615K	MJ-20	78741	1400-1599
INGLEWOOD RIDGE LOOP	Travis Co	704F	MG-12	78747	None
INGRAM DR	Travis Co	592E	MY-24	78621	23200-23399
INGRID DR	Travis Co	591M	MX-23	78621	7600-9299
INGRIDS IRIS DR	Pflugerville	407U	MP-40	78664	18100-18299
INICIO LN	Travis Co	619N	MS-20	78725	4500-4699
INKS AVE	Austin	585Y	MK-22	78702	1200-1299
INKS CV	Cedar Park	372G	MD-45	78613	2200-2299
INKS LAKE DR	Travis Co	409T	MS-40	78660	2900-2999
INKS LAKE DR	Williamson Co	344B	MG-48	78628	100-199
INLAND GREENS	Austin	526A	ML-30	78758	1100-1299
INMAN DR	Hutto	379D	MT-45	78634	100-199
INMAN LN	Round Rock	377J	MN-44	78664	1800-1899
INNER LOOP NE	Georgetown	287C	MP-54	78626	100-1099
	Georgetown	257J	MN-56	78626	1100-3299
INNER LOOP SE	Georgetown	316D	MM-51	78626	100-1099
	Georgetown	317A	MN-51	78626	1100-1799
	Georgetown	287L	MP-53	78626	1800-3799
INNER CAMPUS DR	Austin	585E	MJ-24	78705	None
INNES VIEW RD	Austin	528B	MQ-30	78653	12100-12399
INNISBROOK DR	Austin	704E	MG-12	78747	2300-2499
INNWOOD CIR	Georgetown	286S	ML-52	78628	400-499
INNWOOD DR	Georgetown	286S	ML-52	78628	200-699
INRIDGE DR	Austin	643N	ME-17	78745	2600-2999
INSHORE CV	Travis Co	522C	MD-30	78730	10000-10199
INSHORE DR	Travis Co	522C	MD-30	78730	4300-4399
INSPIRATION CIR	Travis Co	459M	WX-35	78645	17800-17899
INSPIRATION DR	Austin	557P	MN-26	78724	7200-7599
	Travis Co	557P	MN-26	78724	7500-7699
INTERCHANGE BLVD	Austin	616G	MM-21	78721	800-899
INTER COUNCIL CV	Austin	524J	MG-29	78731	5900-5999
INTERLACHEN DR	Austin	404F	MG-42	78717	15100-15699
INTERLACHEN LN	Austin	704K	MG-11	78747	4700-5099
INTERPARKE DR	Austin	556D	MM-27	78754	7900-8099
INTERVAIL DR	Austin	583Z	MF-22	78746	1700-1899
INTREPID	Lakeway	489Q	WX-32	78734	None
INTREPID DR	Buda	763K	ME-5	78610	1900-2499
INVERNESS BLVD	Austin	643H	MF-18	78745	1700-1999
INVERNESS DR	Round Rock	376E	ML-45	78681	2000-2099
INVERNESS DR	Travis Co	488Y	WV-31	78669	19300-19699
INVERNESS ST	Leander	342V	MD-46	78641	2101-2299 O
INVERRARY CIR	Travis Co	703R	MF-11	78747	2300-2399
INVESTMENT DR	Travis Co	467Z	MP-34	78660	2200-2499
INVESTMENT LOOP	Williamson Co	378D	MR-45	78634	100-299
INWOOD CIR	Rollingwood	584N	MG-23	78746	1-99
INWOOD CV	Williamson Co	345W	MJ-46	78681	3400-3499
INWOOD DR	Rollingwood	584S	MG-22	78746	200-399
INWOOD PL	Austin	584P	MG-24	78703	2500-2599
IOLA CV	Williamson Co	405N	MJ-41	78717	15300-15399
IOLA DR	Hutto	379C	MT-45	78634	1000-1099
IONIAN CV	Travis Co	523W	ME-28	78730	2500-2599
IOWA ST	Travis Co	490H	WZ-33	78734	14800-15299
IPSWICH BAY DR	Austin	705A	MJ-12	78747	8600-9299
IRA INGRAM DR	Austin	642A	MC-18	78749	6400-6499
IRBY PASS	Williamson Co	434V	MH-37	78729	13000-13099
IRELAND DR	Leander	342U	MD-46	78641	1700-1999
IRENE DR	Cedar Park	372T	MC-43	78613	1300-1399
IRENE ST	Elgin	534E	EC-30	78621	100-199
IRINA CV	Hutto	350N	MU-47	78634	1100-1199
IRINA DR	Hutto	350N	MU-47	78634	100-299
IRIONA BEND	Austin	642U	MD-16	78749	4000-4299
IRIS CV	Round Rock	345N	MJ-47	78681	3800-3899
IRIS DR	Williamson Co	257F	MN-57	78626	900-999
IRIS LN	Austin	612Y	MD-19	78749	5300-5399
IRIS LN	Cedar Park	402U	MD-40	78613	1500-1899
IRISH BEND DR	Austin	643W	ME-16	78745	2700-2799
IRISH MOSS TRL	Round Rock	407G	MP-42	78665	1300-1399
IRMA DR	Austin	555C	MK-27	78752	300-699
IRMA RD	Bastrop Co	740J	MU-8	78612	100-199
IRON BLUFF PL	Travis Co	580F	WY-24	78738	12200-12299
IRONDALE DR	Austin	404Q	MH-41	78717	14700-14899
IRONGATE AVE	Austin	466K	ML-35	78727	12800-13099
IRONGATE CIR	Austin	466K	ML-35	78727	13000-13099
IRON HORSE	Leander	342X	MC-46	78641	1100-1199
IRON HORSE CV	Travis Co	521Q	MB-29	78732	11800-11899
IRON HORSE DR	Williamson Co	378C	MR-45	78634	1-399
IRON HORSE TRL	Williamson Co	287G	MP-54	78626	50100-50399
IRON MUSKET CV	Austin	673K	ME-14	78748	1200-1299
IRON OAK TRL	Williamson Co	433K	ME-38	78750	11200-11299
IRON WEED RUN	Williamson Co	375U	MK-43	78681	8300-8499
IRONWOOD CIR	Austin	464L	MH-35	78759	11600-11699
IRONWOOD CT	Travis Co	432K	MC-38	78613	2900-2999
IRONWOOD CV	Austin	494F	MG-33	78759	6000-6099
IRONWOOD CV	Bastrop Co	564V	ED-25	78621	100-199
IROQUOIS LN	Austin	615X	MJ-19	78741	2000-2099
IRVINE LN	Austin	678J	MQ-14	78617	4900-5099
IRVING CV	Lago Vista	458M	WV-35	78645	2500-2699
IRVING LN	Austin	556B	ML-27	78752	7300-7399
ISAAC PRYOR DR	Austin	642E	MC-18	78749	7900-8299
ISABELLE DR	Austin	525Z	MK-28	78752	6600-7099
ISERNIA DR	Austin	673T	ME-13	78748	900-999
ISLAND AVE	Austin	554B	MG-27	78731	4300-4499
ISLAND CV	Austin	524X	MG-28	78731	4400-4799
ISLAND WAY	Austin	554W	MG-25	78746	3800-3999
ISLANDER DR	Austin	642G	MD-18	78749	7500-7799
ISLAND KNOLL DR	Austin	554N	MG-26	78746	3900-4099
ISLAND LEDGE CV	Travis Co	554N	MG-26	78746	2700-2799
ISLAND OAK DR	Austin	673Y	MF-13	78748	200-499
ISLAND WOOD RD	Travis Co	522U	MD-28	78733	2100-2399
ISLE OF MAN CT	Travis Co	437L	MP-38	78660	900-999
ISLE OF MAN RD	Travis Co	437L	MP-38	78660	16800-16999
ISLE ROYALE WAY	Austin	704A	MG-12	78747	10000-10099
ITASCA DR	Travis Co	467P	MN-35	78660	None
ITO CV	Williamson Co	434Q	MH-38	78729	8200-8299
IVA LN	Austin	614K	MG-20	78704	2200-2299
IVANHOE TRL	Austin	672L	MD-14	78748	10100-10299
IVEAN PEARSON RD	Travis Co	489F	WW-33	78645	600-1399
IVORY KEY CT	Austin	643V	MF-16	78745	7000-7099
IVY CT	Round Rock	376S	ML-43	78681	700-799
IVY DR	Pflugerville	467D	MP-36	78660	700-899
IVY DR	Travis Co	279V	WX-52	78641	1-599
IVY TRL	Austin	614W	MG-19	78704	None
IVYBRIDGE DR	Travis Co	437K	MN-38	78660	1100-1399
IVY HILLS DR	Austin	464Y	MH-34	78759	5900-6099
IVYWOOD CV	Williamson Co	434F	MG-39	78729	13300-13399
IWANNA DR	Travis Co	707B	MN-12	78617	7200-7399
IZORO BEND	Travis Co	432G	MD-39	78613	2600-2799

J

STREET NAME	CITY or COUNTY	MAPSCO GRID	AUSTIN GRID	ZIP CODE	BLOCK RANGE O/E
JABORANDI DR	Austin	670D	WZ-15	78739	7300-7799
JACARANDA DR	Austin	644Z	MH-16	78744	5600-5799
JACKAL DR	Williamson Co	375X	MJ-43	78681	8400-8599
JACK C HAYS TRL	Buda	762G	MD-6	78610	100-499
	Hays Co	762W	MC-4	78610	500-3099
JACK COOK DR	Austin	556R	MM-26	78723	3000-3299
JACKI DR	Round Rock	347V	MP-46	78665	2700-2799
JACKIE ROBINSON PL	Round Rock	378A	MQ-45	78665	1400-1599
JACKIE ROBINSON ST	Austin	586Q	MM-23	78721	5500-5799
JACKIES RANCH BLVD	Travis Co	409Y	MT-40	78660	20200-20599
JACK NICKLAUS BLVD	Williamson Co	283M	MF-53	78628	100-199
JACK NICKLAUS DR	Lakeway	519X	WW-28	78738	100-499
JACK RABBIT TRL	Williamson Co	433K	ME-38	78750	11200-11399
JACKRABBIT RUN	Round Rock	408B	MQ-42	78664	100-199
JACK RYAN LN	Austin	673V	MF-13	78748	300-399
JACKS PASS	Travis Co	490V	WZ-31	78734	2200-2499
JACKSON AVE	Austin	554R	MH-26	78731	3500-4299
JACKSON AVE	Lago Vista	458H	WV-36	78645	20700-20799
JACKSON DR	Williamson Co	433B	ME-39	78613	1500-1799
JACKSON ST	Bastrop	745Q	EF-8	78602	100-499
JACKSON ST	Elgin	534X	EC-28	78621	100-199
JACKSON ST	Travis Co	562E	MY-27	78621	11800-11899
JACKSON ST	Village of Volente	431N	MA-38	78641	16300-16499
	Village of Volente	430R	WZ-38	78645	16500-16699
JACKSON ST S	Bastrop	745Q	EF-8	78602	100-599
JACKSON HOLE CV	Austin	583Z	MF-22	78746	1700-1799
JACKSONVILLE CV	Lago Vista	458M	WV-35	78645	20700-20799
JACK'S POND RD	Travis Co	436Q	MM-38	78728	14800-15099
JACKY ST	Austin	673R	MF-14	78748	200-499
JACOB TRL	Cedar Park	402G	MD-42	78613	600-699
JACOB GLEN	Austin	435W	MJ-37	78727	5900-5999
JACOBS CV	Bastrop Co	744X	EC-7	78602	100-199
JACOBS WAY	Williamson Co	318E	MQ-51	78634	100-299
JACOB'S CREEK CT	Austin	642C	MD-18	78749	5100-5199
JACOBSON RD	Bastrop Co	738D	MR-9	78617	100-299
	Travis Co	471W	MW-34	78653	12200-12799
	Travis Co	501F	MW-33	78653	12800-13999
	Travis Co	708N	MQ-11	78617	14200-16899
	Travis Co	738D	MR-9	78617	16900-17199
JACQUELINE DR	Williamson Co	342Z	MD-46	78641	2500-2599
JACQUELINE LN	Travis Co	619A	MS-21	78724	5700-6399
JADE DR	Williamson Co	405E	MJ-42	78717	9000-9099
JADE LN	Austin	465Y	MK-34	78758	11800-11899
JADESTONE DR	Williamson Co	343W	ME-46	78641	16400-16699
JADEWOOD CT	Austin	672M	MD-14	78748	2800-3099
JAFFNA CV	Austin	642M	MD-17	78749	4000-4099
JAGGED ROCK	Cedar Park	403C	MF-42	78613	700-799

H
I
J

STREET NAME	CITY or COUNTY	MAPSCO GRID	AUSTIN GRID	ZIP CODE	BLOCK RANGE O/E
JAIN LN	Austin	586X	ML-22	78721	5200-5599
	Austin	616C	MM-21	78721	5600-6199
JAIRED DR	Austin	557U	MP-25	78724	6800-6899
JAKES HILL RD	Travis Co	439F	MS-39	78660	19200-19599
JAKES HILL RD	Travis Co	409Y	MT-40	78660	20400-20599
JAKES HILL RD	Travis Co	409U	MT-40	78660	20900-21399
JALISCO CT	Bastrop Co	738X	MQ-7	78617	None
JAMAICA CT	Austin	525N	MJ-29	78757	6600-6699
JAMBOREE CT	Austin	523H	MF-30	78731	5700-5799
JAMES LN	Travis Co	460Y	WZ-34	78734	4200-4399
JAMES PL	Round Rock	376L	MM-44	78664	500-2199
JAMES ST	Georgetown	287J	MN-53	78626	1300-1399
JAMES ST	Taylor	352D	MZ-48	76574	900-1099
JAMES ST W	Austin	615E	MJ-21	78704	100-299
	Austin	614H	MH-21	78704	700-999
JAMES ANDER ST	Austin	642V	MD-16	78745	7700-8099
JAMES BAUSCH LN	Austin	702D	MD-12	78748	2600-2799
JAMES B. CONNOLLY LN	Austin	702D	MD-12	78748	11500-11699
JAMESBOROUGH ST	Austin	554Q	MH-26	78703	2900-3399
JAMES CASEY ST	Austin	644B	MG-18	78745	4000-4399
JAMES GARFIELD ST	Travis Co	530K	MU-29	78653	13500-13699
JAMES HALLER DR	Austin	703A	ME-12	78748	11300-11499
JAMES MADISON ST	Travis Co	530L	MV-29	78653	12800-12999
JAMES MANOR ST	Manor	530L	MV-29	78653	19300-19499
JAMES MONROE ST	Travis Co	530K	MU-29	78653	13300-13499
JAMES PARKER LN	Round Rock	348W	MQ-46	78665	2900-2999
JAMES POLK ST	Travis Co	530K	MU-29	78653	12600-12699
JAMES RYAN WAY	Travis Co	522F	MC-30	78730	10200-10499
JAMESTOWN CV	Lago Vista	458H	WV-36	78645	20800-20899
JAMESTOWN DR	Austin	525M	MK-29	78758	8100-8399
	Austin	526E	ML-30	78758	8400-8899
JAMES VINCENT DR	Travis Co	618V	MR-19	78725	14500-14599
JAMES WHEAT ST	Austin	556W	ML-25	78723	4600-4799
JAMIE CT	Georgetown	287L	MP-53	78626	1000-1099
JAMIE DR	Manor	500Y	MV-31	78653	None
JAMIE GLEN WAY	Travis Co	496Z	MM-31	78753	10900-10999
JAMIESON DR	Austin	433T	ME-37	78750	11600-11699
JAN CT	Austin	526E	ML-30	78753	500-599
JAN DR	Travis Co	409Q	MT-41	78660	2900-3199
JAN LN	Georgetown	287P	MN-53	78626	1-299
JANABYRD CV	Austin	642N	MC-17	78749	9100-9199
JANABYRD LN	Austin	642N	MC-17	78749	5600-5899
JANAE CT	Georgetown	257P	MN-56	78626	1000-1099
JANAK RD	Travis Co	442J	MY-38	78615	19400-19999
	Williamson Co	442J	MY-38	78615	20000-20199
JANA PATRICE DR	Pflugerville	408S	MQ-40	78660	18600-18799
JANCY DR	Austin	493G	MF-33	78750	8300-8399
JANE CV	Cedar Park	372U	MD-43	78613	1700-1799
JANE AUSTEN TRL	Travis Co	467K	MN-35	78660	200-899
JANES RANCH RD	Austin	675T	MJ-13	78744	7100-7199
JANET LOOP	Travis Co	577M	WT-23	78720	10000-10199
JANEY DR	Austin	524V	MH-28	78757	6100-6199
JANICE DR	Austin	554Y	MH-25	78703	2500-2599
JANICE LN	Travis Co	457F	WT-39	78669	700-1299
JANIS DR E	Georgetown	256U	MM-55	78628	100-599
JANIS DR W	Georgetown	256U	MM-55	78628	100-1899
JANIS MAE DR	Hutto	379C	MT-45	78634	100-499
JANUARY DR	Austin	496V	MM-31	78753	11300-11699
JAPONICA CT	Austin	673F	ME-15	78748	9100-9199
JARON DR	Manor	529Z	MT-28	78653	None
JARRATT AVE	Austin	584D	MH-24	78703	2400-2699
JARRETT WAY	Round Rock	406Y	MM-40	78728	3800-3899
JARROD LEE CV	Travis Co	588H	MR-24	78724	12300-12499
JASMINE CT	Pflugerville	438T	MQ-37	78660	700-799
JASMINE PATH	Round Rock	407F	MN-42	78664	2100-2299
JASMINE TRL	Williamson Co	257K	MN-56	78626	800-999
JASMINE WAY	Hutto	379U	MT-43	78634	100-199
JASMINE CREEK DR	Austin	463A	ME-36	78726	9900-9999
JASMINE TEA LN	Travis Co	467L	MP-35	78660	1400-1599
JASON DR	Taylor	322Y	MZ-49	76574	2000-2799
JASPER CT	Georgetown	226L	MM-59	78628	31000-31099
JASPER LN	Williamson Co	402Q	MD-41	78613	2000-2199
JASPER ST	Bastrop	745P	EE-8	78602	800-999
	Bastrop	745Q	EF-8	78602	1300-1999
JASPERWOOD CT	Village of the Hills	519S	WW-28	78738	1-99
JAVA DR	Travis Co	436F	ML-39	78728	4000-4099
JAVELIN DR	Lakeway	519E	WW-30	78734	100-199
JAVELINA CIR	Travis Co	490C	WZ-33	78734	4000-4099
JAVELINA TRL	Bastrop	744K	EC-8	78602	100-299
JAYDEE TERRACE	Georgetown	226P	ML-59	78628	100-299
JAY GOULD WAY	Buda	732T	MC-7	78610	100-199
JAYNE CV	Hays Co	670X	WY-13	78610	100-299
JAY'S LN	Austin	612U	MD-19	78749	6000-6199
JAZZ ST	Round Rock	407T	MN-40	78664	2900-3199
JEAN DR	Austin	496Y	MM-31	78753	10500-10699
JEANETTE CT	Austin	643S	ME-16	78745	3100-3199
JEANNE MARIE CT	Austin	643S	ME-16	78745	3100-3199
JEFFBURN CV	Austin	644J	MG-17	78745	5400-5499
JEFF DAVIS AVE	Austin	555B	MJ-27	78756	5300-5899
JEFFERSON CV	Elgin	533F	EA-30	78621	100-199
JEFFERSON CV	Lago Vista	458M	WV-35	78645	2700-2799
JEFFERSON LN	Williamson Co	257E	MN-57	78626	500-799
JEFFERSON ST	Austin	554Z	MH-25	78703	2600-3499
	Austin	555N	MJ-26	78703	3900-4199
JEFFERSON ST	Bastrop	745P	EE-8	78602	400-499
	Bastrop	745K	EE-8	78602	500-1199
	Bastrop	745B	EE-9	78602	1300-1599
	Bastrop	715X	EE-10	78602	1900-2099
JEFFERSON ST	Bastrop Co	534X	EC-28	78621	None
JEFFERY PL	West Lake Hills	583R	MF-23	78746	5000-5099
JEFFREY DR	Bastrop Co	740X	MU-7	78612	100-299
JEFFREY DR	Cedar Park	402H	MD-42	78613	300-399
JEFFREY PASS	Hays Co	576C	WR-24	78620	100-199
	Hays Co	576G	WR-24	78620	200-399
JEFFREY WAY	Round Rock	376B	ML-45	78665	700-799
JEKEL CIR	Austin	464C	MH-36	78727	12100-12299
JEKINS CV	Travis Co	492Y	MD-31	78730	5100-5199
JELLY PALM TRL	Travis Co	532L	MZ-29	78621	12900-13099
JENARO CT	Austin	462H	MD-36	78726	9400-9499
JENIBETH LN	Austin	674L	MH-14	78744	2300-2599
JENKINS RD	Bastrop Co	740R	MV-8	78612	100-299
	Bastrop Co	741F	MW-9	78612	300-499
JENNA LN	Williamson Co	402Q	MD-41	78613	1400-1499
JENNAVE LN	Travis Co	466D	MM-36	78728	14300-14599
JENNER CV	Williamson Co	434R	MH-38	78729	7800-7899
JENNER LN	Williamson Co	434R	MH-38	78729	13200-13299
JENNIE AVE	Austin	584Q	MH-23	78703	1700-1799
JENNIFER CIR	Williamson Co	318E	MQ-51	78626	100-199
JENNIFER CT	Round Rock	407R	MP-41	78664	1500-1699
JENNIFER LN	Austin	526J	ML-29	78753	100-199
JENNIFER LN	Bastrop	744D	ED-9	78602	200-299
JENNIFER LN	Round Rock	407H	MP-42	78665	1000-1099
JENNIFER LN	Williamson Co	312H	MD-51	78641	1-399
JENNINGS DR	Austin	434Z	MH-37	78727	6300-6599
JENNINGS BRANCH RD					
	Williamson Co	194L	MH-62	78633	1100-1699
JENNYS JUMP DR	Travis Co	521Z	MB-28	78733	10300-10499
JENTSCH CT	Austin	643H	MF-18	78745	1800-1999
JEREMIAH LN	Travis Co	736F	ML-9	78747	9300-9499
JERRY LN	Cedar Park	402Z	MD-40	78613	1900-2199
JERSEY DR	Austin	496E	ML-33	78758	1500-1699
JERUSALEM DR	Pflugerville	437F	MN-39	78664	1500-1799
JESS DR	Travis Co	640Y	WZ-16	78737	11700-12099
JESSAMINE HOLLOW	Austin	524P	MG-29	78731	4400-4499
JESSE ST	Manor	529U	MT-28	78653	400-699
JESSE BOHLS RD	Travis Co	469C	MT-36	78660	5700-8399
	Travis Co	470E	MU-36	78660	8400-8599
JESSE E SEGOVIA ST	Austin	615G	MK-21	78702	1900-2199
JESSE JAMES DR	Austin	673K	ME-14	78748	8800-9199
JESSE OWENS DR	Austin	702D	MD-12	78748	1900-2599
JESSICA DR	Williamson Co	192S	MC-61	78642	100-199
JESSICA LN	Austin	465E	MJ-36	78727	5400-5499
JESSICA PL	Bastrop	744H	ED-9	78602	600-799
JESSIE ST	Austin	584Z	MH-22	78704	300-499
	Austin	614C	MH-21	78704	600-999
JESTER BLVD	Austin	493Z	MF-31	78750	6500-8199
JESTER CIR	Austin	585K	MJ-23	78705	None
JESTER DR	Austin	644A	MG-18	78745	4400-4499
JESTER FARMS RD	Round Rock	377E	MN-45	78664	2100-2199
	Round Rock	376H	MM-45	78664	None
JESTER WILD DR	Austin	494N	MG-32	78750	6800-6999
JET LN	Austin	616U	MM-19	78742	600-999
JETTA CT	Austin	496L	MM-32	78753	600-799
JEWEL CAVE	Cedar Park	373T	ME-43	78613	300-399
JEWELFISH CV	Travis Co	436Q	MM-38	78728	3200-3299
JEWELL ST	Austin	614H	MH-21	78704	600-1199
JEWEL PARK	Lago Vista	458P	WU-35	78645	1300-1399
JFK DR	Travis Co	619B	MS-21	78724	5500-6199
J F NAGLE ST	Manor	529V	MT-28	78653	600-799
J GREGG CV	Austin	464H	MH-36	78759	6500-6599
JIB CIR	Williamson Co	224L	MH-59	78633	300-399
JIB LN	Williamson Co	224L	MH-59	78633	100-299
JIGSAW CV	Pflugerville	437B	MN-39	78664	1600-1699
JIGSAW PATHWAY	Pflugerville	437B	MN-39	78664	17000-17299
JILBUR DR	Williamson Co	405B	MJ-42	78681	8500-8599
JILL SUE CIR	Pflugerville	468F	MQ-36	78660	600-699
JILL SUE CT	Williamson Co	433Q	MF-38	78750	12100-12299
JIM BOWIE DR	Travis Co	456H	WR-36	78669	600-799
JIM BRIDGER DR	Travis Co	640S	WY-16	78737	11900-12099
JIM CAGE LN	Hutto	379D	MT-45	78634	100-199
JIM CRAIG CT	Austin	702H	MD-12	78748	2000-2099
JIM DANDY DR	Elgin	533Q	EB-29	78621	None
JIM DAVIS PL	Travis Co	610Q	WZ-20	78736	8700-8899
JIM HOGG AVE	Austin	555B	MJ-27	78756	5200-5899
JIM HOGG DR	Williamson Co	225J	MJ-59	78633	6600-6699
JIM HOGG RD	Williamson Co	225S	MJ-58	78633	500-1099
	Williamson Co	224R	MH-59	78633	1100-3899
JIMMY CLAY DR	Austin	675B	MJ-15	78744	5300-5499
JIMMY LEE LN	Bastrop Co	715J	EE-11	78602	100-199
JIM RYUN LN	Austin	702D	MD-12	78748	11700-11799
JIM THORPE LN	Austin	702D	MD-12	78748	11100-11899
JINA LN	Round Rock	377J	MN-44	78664	1800-1899
JINGLE DR	Travis Co	487B	WS-33	78669	29900-29999
JINX AVE	Austin	644B	MG-18	78745	4200-4699
J J SEABROOK DR	Austin	586K	ML-23	78721	1600-1899
J M CUBA DR	Taylor	322Q	MZ-50	76574	4200-4399
J M HOLLAWAY LN	Travis Co	588P	MQ-23	78724	5600-6599
JOACHIM LN	Williamson Co	405J	MJ-41	78717	8900-8999
JO ANN DR	Travis Co	521R	MB-29	78733	10400-10499
JOCELYN STRAUS	Travis Co	456F	WQ-36	78669	None
JOCKEY BLUFF CV	Austin	703G	MF-12	78748	200-299
JOCKEY BLUFF DR	Austin	703G	MF-12	78748	11000-11399
JOE BARBEE DR	Pflugerville	437A	MN-39	78664	16700-17099
JOE DIMAGGIO BLVD	Round Rock	377Q	MP-44	78665	2900-3099
JOE HARPER CT	Hays Co	668G	WV-15	78620	100-299
JOE M BOWIE RD	Travis Co	590M	MV-23	78653	19600-19699
JOE'S CV	Leander	341H	MB-48	78641	200-299
JOE SAYERS AVE	Austin	555B	MJ-27	78756	5200-5899
JOE SAYERS ST	Elgin	533R	EB-29	78621	100-299
JOE TANNER LN	Austin	612T	MC-19	78749	6200-6399
JOFFA CT	Pflugerville	437F	MN-39	78664	1400-1499
JOHANNA ST W	Austin	614M	MH-20	78704	100-1199
JOHANNE CT	Austin	494S	MG-31	78750	6400-6499
JOHN ADAMS ST	Travis Co	530L	MV-29	78653	12800-12999
JOHNATHAN WAY	Williamson Co	373A	ME-45	78641	2500-2699
JOHN BLOCKER CT	Austin	642B	MC-18	78749	5800-5899
JOHN BLOCKER DR	Austin	642B	MC-18	78749	7200-7399
JOHN CAMPBELL'S TRL	Austin	613U	MF-19	78735	3200-3299
JOHN CARTER DR	Georgetown	286D	MM-54	78626	100-199
JOHN CHISUM LN	Austin	642A	MC-18	78749	6100-6399
JOHN F KENNEDY ST	Travis Co	530F	MU-30	78653	13500-13699
JOHN GLENN LN	Austin	646B	ML-18	78741	7600-7799
JOHN HAMILTON WAY	Georgetown	346B	ML-48	78665	7700-7899
JOHN MICHAEL DR	Travis Co	529H	MT-30	78653	16800-17099
JOHN NANCE GARNER CIR	Austin	526N	ML-29	78753	300-499
JOHNNY BENCH CT	Round Rock	378E	MQ-45	78665	700-799
JOHNNY MILLER TRL	Travis Co	582G	MD-24	78746	1500-1699
JOHNNY MORRIS CV	Austin	557U	MP-25	78724	6600-6699
JOHNNY MORRIS RD	Austin	587B	MN-24	78724	5100-5999
	Austin	557X	MN-25	78724	6000-7299
	Austin	557Q	MP-26	78724	7300-8898 E
	Travis Co	557Q	MP-26	78724	7301-8899 O
	Travis Co	557Q	MP-26	78724	8900-9499
	Travis Co	558A	MQ-27	78754	9500-9599
JOHNNY WEISMULLER LN	Austin	702C	MC-12	78748	11400-12299
JOHN RECTOR ST	Manor	530L	MV-29	78653	13200-13299
JOHN SIMPSON CT	Travis Co	491Y	MB-31	78732	12400-12499
JOHN SIMPSON TRL	Travis Co	491Q	MB-32	78732	3400-3999
JOHNS LIGHT DR	Travis Co	436W	ML-37	78727	4200-4299
JOHNSON CV	Hutto	349V	MT-46	78634	100-199
JOHNSON LN	Hays Co	608E	WU-21	78620	15500-15599
JOHNSON LN	Round Rock	407D	MP-42	78665	1200-1299
JOHNSON LN	Travis Co	702Q	MD-11	78652	12700-12799
JOHNSON RD	Bastrop Co	712Q	MZ-11	78602	100-299
JOHNSON RD	Manor	500U	MV-31	78653	12001-12299 O
	Manor	500R	MU-31	78653	12600-12999
	Travis Co	500T	MU-31	78653	11700-11999
	Travis Co	500U	MV-31	78653	12000-12298 E
	Travis Co	500U	MV-31	78653	12300-12599
	Travis Co	500R	MU-31	78653	13000-13199
JOHNSON RD	Travis Co	401J	MA-41	78641	10900-11799
JOHNSON ST	Austin	584K	MG-23	78703	2200-2399
JOHNSON TRL	Travis Co	500T	MU-31	78653	14800-15099
JOHNSON WAY	Round Rock	376S	ML-43	78681	1700-1899
JOHNSON WAY	Travis Co	458T	WU-34	78669	800-999
JOHN TEE DR	Cedar Park	372F	MC-45	78613	2200-2399
JOHN THOMAS DR	Georgetown	256N	ML-56	78628	100-299
JOHN TYLER ST	Travis Co	530K	MU-29	78653	13300-13499
JOHN WILSON LN	Round Rock	408J	MQ-41	78664	3000-3099
JOJOBA DR	Travis Co	402Y	MD-40	78613	1800-1999
JOLENA CIR	Austin	586Z	MM-22	78721	1100-1199
JOLIE LN	Cedar Park	372T	MC-43	78613	1100-1299
JOLLY HOLLOW DR	Austin	433Z	MF-37	78750	8900-9099
JOLLYVILLE RD	Austin	495J	MJ-32	78759	9000-9599
	Austin	495A	MJ-33	78759	10000-10899
	Austin	465W	MJ-34	78759	10900-11599
	Austin	464G	MH-36	78759	11600-12299
JOLYNN ST	Travis Co	618Z	MR-19	78725	None
JONAH LN	Travis Co	591J	MW-23	78653	8900-9099
JONATHAN CV	Williamson Co	314K	MG-50	78628	100-199
JONATHAN DR	Austin	555D	MK-27	78752	6500-6699
JONES CV	Lago Vista	458M	WV-35	78645	20800-20899
JONES RD	Austin	643D	MF-18	78745	2000-2699
	Austin	643C	MF-18	78745	2700-2998 E
	Sunset Valley	643C	MF-18	78745	2701-2999 O
	Sunset Valley	613Y	MF-19	78745	3000-3499
JONES RD	Bastrop Co	711Y	MX-10	78612	100-199
	Bastrop Co	741C	MX-9	78612	200-399
JONES RD	Travis Co	561P	MW-26	78653	10400-12099
JONES ST	Bastrop	745J	EE-8	78602	100-199
JONES ST	Taylor	323W	EA-49	76574	1200-1799
JONESTOWN ST	Jonestown	400M	WZ-41	78645	18500-18599
JONQUIL CT	Austin	464A	MG-36	78750	11700-11799
JONSE CT	Travis Co	529H	MT-30	78653	16900-16999
JONWOOD WAY	Travis Co	526D	MM-30	78753	10600-10799
JORDAN CV	Bastrop	744D	ED-9	78602	300-399
JORDAN CV	Williamson Co	343N	ME-47	78641	3400-3499
JORDAN CV N	Bastrop	744D	ED-9	78602	400-499
JORDAN LN	Austin	496N	ML-32	78758	11000-11299
JORDAN LN	Bastrop Co	564Y	ED-25	78621	100-299
JORDAN LN	Round Rock	407H	MP-42	78665	1100-1299
JORGE DR	Austin	524U	MH-28	78731	3600-3699
JORWOODS DR	Austin	643S	ME-16	78745	2700-3099
JOSEPH DR	Lakeway	520J	WY-29	78734	14700-15399
	Lakeway	519M	WX-29	78734	15400-15599
JOSEPH ST	Williamson Co	378A	MQ-45	78665	4600-4699
JOSEPH CLAYTON DR	Travis Co	496Z	MM-31	78753	10600-11299
JOSEPHINE ST	Austin	614D	MH-21	78704	400-499
	Austin	614C	MH-21	78704	600-999
JOSH LN	Travis Co	522B	MC-30	78730	3500-3799
JOSH RIDGE BLVD	Austin	467X	MN-34	78753	1000-1499
JOSHUA CT	Austin	645S	MJ-16	78744	5000-5099
JOSHUA CV	Round Rock	407D	MP-42	78665	2200-2299
JOSHUA DR	Williamson Co	223H	MF-60	78633	100-299
JOSHUA SMITH LN	Bastrop Co	712Z	MZ-10	78602	100-199
JOSHUA TREE CIR	Pflugerville	438A	MQ-39	78660	100-299
JOSIE LN	Bastrop Co	743T	EA-7	78602	100-399
JOTHAN DR	Travis Co	591Y	MX-22	78621	7800-7899
JOURDAN CROSSING BLVD	Austin	497K	MN-32	78753	12200-12399
JOURNEYVILLE CT	Austin	612J	MC-20	78735	5700-5799
JOURNEYVILLE DR	Austin	612J	MC-20	78735	7300-7599
	Austin	611M	MB-20	78735	7600-8099
JOUSTING PL	Travis Co	582D	MD-24	78746	1000-1099
JOY LN	Austin	525C	MK-30	78757	1900-1999
JOY RD	Village of Volente	430R	WZ-38	78645	8100-8199
JOY ST	Travis Co	703A	ME-12	78748	11400-11699
JOYCE DR	Travis Co	309T	WW-49	78641	13900-14299
JOYCE LN	Round Rock	407F	MN-42	78664	1100-1599
JOYCE ST	Austin	525N	MJ-29	78757	6800-6899
JOYCE TURNER DR	Manor	529P	MS-29	78653	12100-12299
JOY LEE LN	Manor	500Y	MV-31	78653	None
JUANITA ST	Austin	614Q	MH-20	78704	800-1299
JUAREZ CV	Bastrop Co	738P	MQ-8	78617	100-199
JUBILEE TRL	Austin	672M	MD-14	78748	2900-3199
JUDSON RD	Austin	645L	MK-17	78744	3400-3699
JUDY DR	Dripping Springs	636X	WQ-16	78620	100-499
JUDY DR	Georgetown	256T	ML-55	78628	700-899
JUDY DR	Travis Co	674S	MG-13	78744	1700-1899
JUDY LYNN DR	Briarcliff	458E	WU-36	78669	1500-1799
JUDY SCHOLL WAY	Williamson Co	375X	MJ-43	78681	16700-16999
JULE'S WALK	Pflugerville	438J	MQ-38	78660	1300-1399
JULIAN ALPS	Bee Cave	549E	WW-27	78738	4900-4999
JULIANAS WAY	Buda	732Q	MD-8	78610	100-199
JULIANA'S WAY	Round Rock	346M	MM-47	78665	3700-3899
JULIANNA'S WAY	Cedar Park	372P	MC-44	78613	1500-1599
JULIAN TERAN ST	Austin	615D	MK-21	78702	300-499
JULIE CV	Taylor	322V	MZ-49	76574	2700-2799
JULIE LN	Travis Co	490H	WZ-33	78734	15000-15199
JULIEANNA CV	Austin	616K	ML-20	78702	1-99
JULIEANNE CV	Hays Co	576G	WR-24	78620	100-699
JULIET ST	Austin	614C	MH-21	78704	1300-1899
JULIETTE WAY	Cedar Park	403N	ME-41	78613	1500-1599
JULIUS ST	Austin	615H	MK-21	78702	1-99
JULY DR	Austin	497S	MN-31	78753	1300-1399
JUMANO LN	Austin	612W	MC-19	78749	6100-6199
JUMPERS DELIGHT LN	Pflugerville	409J	MS-41	78660	20800-20999
JUNE DR	Austin	497S	MN-31	78753	11300-11599
JUNEAU DR	Cedar Park	374P	MG-44	78613	2900-3099
JUNEBERRY CV	Austin	493V	MF-31	78750	7000-7099
JUNIE LN	Taylor	322R	MZ-50	76574	3000-3399
JUNIPER CT	Travis Co	309Z	WX-49	78641	24100-24199
JUNIPER DR	Williamson Co	257K	MN-56	78626	200-399
JUNIPER RD	West Lake Hills	583B	ME-24	78746	400-499
JUNIPER ST	Austin	585U	MK-22	78702	900-1299
JUNIPER ST	Bastrop	715W	EE-10	78602	400-499
JUNIPER TRL	Cedar Park	372M	MD-44	78613	1700-1899
JUNIPER TRL	Round Rock	407F	MN-42	78664	2100-2199
JUNIPER TRL	Travis Co	309Z	WX-49	78641	14300-14599
JUNIPER BERRY TRL	Georgetown	226A	ML-60	78633	100-199
JUNIPER BERRY WAY	Lakeway	519M	WX-29	78734	1-99
JUNIPER HILLS ST	Cedar Park	374U	MH-43	78613	3600-3899

J

STREET NAME	CITY or COUNTY	MAPSCO GRID	AUSTIN GRID	ZIP CODE	BLOCK RANGE O/E
JUNIPER RIDGE DR	Austin	464L	MH-35	78759	11500-11699
JUNIPER RIDGE LOOP	Cedar Park	402V	MD-40	78613	1600-1799
JUNIPER TRACE	Bee Cave	550U	WZ-25	78733	3800-3999
JUNO CIR	Austin	587C	MP-24	78724	6900-6999
JUPITER HILLS DR	Austin	704F	MG-12	78747	10000-10199
JUSTEFORD DR	Pflugerville	437D	MP-39	78660	600-999
JUSTICE DR	Austin	678K	MQ-14	78617	5200-5299
JUSTICE CENTER DR	Pflugerville	438P	MQ-38	78660	600-799
JUSTIN LN	Austin	525U	MK-28	78757	800-2399
JUSTIN LN	Taylor	352A	MY-48	76574	700-999
	Taylor	322T	MY-49	76574	2200-2899
	Williamson Co	352B	MY-48	76574	1000-2199
JUSTIN LEONARD DR	Williamson Co	408G	MR-42	78664	100-199

K

STREET NAME	CITY or COUNTY	MAPSCO GRID	AUSTIN GRID	ZIP CODE	BLOCK RANGE O/E
KAAAWA LN	Bastrop Co	775H	EF-6	78602	100-399
KAALA DR	Bastrop Co	775G	EF-6	78602	100-199
KAANAPALI LN	Bastrop Co	745Z	EF-7	78602	100-199
	Bastrop Co	746X	EG-7	78602	200-599
KAANAPALI LN W	Bastrop Co	745V	EF-7	78602	100-299
KAAPAHU DR	Bastrop Co	746W	EG-7	78602	100-199
KAATZ LN	Williamson Co	409A	MS-42	78634	1-199
	Williamson Co	409B	MS-42	78664	200-499
KABAR TRL	Austin	464N	MG-35	78759	9900-10299
KABAYE CV	Austin	612X	MC-19	78749	5900-5999
KACHINA DR	Austin	612H	MD-21	78735	4100-4299
KADEN WAY	Lakeway	549A	WW-27	78734	None
KAELAN CV	Austin	523G	MF-30	78730	5800-5899
KAELEKU LN	Bastrop Co	745X	EE-7	78602	100-199
KAELEPULU DR	Bastrop Co	775H	EF-6	78602	100-199
	Bastrop Co	776J	EG-5	78602	200-399
KAENA LN	Bastrop Co	776A	EG-6	78602	100-199
KAENAPAPA LN	Bastrop Co	776A	EG-6	78602	100-199
KAFKA CIR	Pflugerville	437B	MN-39	78664	1800-1899
KAHALA SUNSET CT	Travis Co	427J	WS-38	78669	25500-25699
KAHALA SUNSET DR	Travis Co	427K	WS-38	78669	1400-3599
KAHALULU DR	Bastrop Co	776B	EG-6	78602	100-299
KAHANA LN	Bastrop Co	775G	EF-6	78602	100-399
KAHUKU CT	Bastrop Co	745Z	EF-7	78602	100-199
KAI CT	Bastrop Co	776F	EG-6	78602	100-199
KAI DR	Cedar Park	402L	MD-41	78613	600-699
KAILUA LN	Bastrop Co	746S	EG-7	78602	100-199
KAIMUKI CT	Bastrop Co	745Z	EF-7	78602	100-199
KAINALU LN	Bastrop Co	746X	EG-7	78602	100-199
KAISER CV	Austin	672Z	MD-13	78748	11000-11099
KAISER DR	Austin	672Z	MD-13	78748	1900-2299
KAI VISTA DR	Hays Co	794R	MH-2	78610	100-199
	Hays Co	795J	MJ-2	78610	200-599
KAIWI CT	Bastrop Co	775D	EF-6	78602	100-199
KAJON CV	Georgetown	257P	MN-56	78626	1000-1099
KAKI CV	Hutto	379C	MT-45	78634	100-199
KALALEA LN	Bastrop Co	745S	EE-7	78602	100-199
KALAMA DR	Austin	642Q	MD-17	78749	4400-4599
KALAMA DR	Bastrop Co	776E	EG-6	78602	100-199
KALI CV	Travis Co	641E	MA-18	78737	8400-8499
KALINDI RD	Hays Co	700A	WY-12	78610	100-499
KALIS CV	Buda	732U	MD-7	78610	100-199
KALISPEL	Buda	762D	MD-6	78610	300-499
KALIU CT	Bastrop Co	746X	EG-7	78602	100-199
KAMAIKI DR	Bastrop Co	745Z	EF-7	78602	100-199
KAMAKOA LN	Bastrop Co	746W	EG-7	78602	100-199
	Bastrop Co	745V	EF-7	78602	200-299
KAMAR DR	Austin	525G	MK-30	78757	1400-1499
KAMMEY CV	Austin	705A	MJ-12	78747	8600-8699
KAMOI CT E	Bastrop Co	745Z	EF-7	78602	100-199
KAMOI CT W	Bastrop Co	745V	EF-7	78602	100-199
KANAIO DR N	Bastrop Co	776A	EG-6	78602	100-199
KANAIO DR S	Bastrop Co	776A	EG-6	78602	100-199
KANDY DR	Austin	642M	MD-17	78749	3700-4099
KANE CV	Cedar Park	372K	MC-44	78613	2100-2199
KANEOHE LN	Bastrop Co	776E	EG-6	78602	100-199
KANGAROO LN	Austin	672G	MD-15	78748	9600-9699
KANI LN	Bastrop	746N	EG-8	78602	100-199
KANSAS RIVER DR	Austin	673B	ME-15	78745	8400-8599
KAOHIKAIPU DR	Bastrop Co	776E	EG-6	78602	100-199
KAPALUA PL	Travis Co	409S	MS-40	78660	2400-2499
KAPAPA CT	Bastrop Co	745Y	EF-7	78602	100-199
KAPOK LN	Austin	464G	MH-36	78759	7300-7399
KARANKAWA CV	Austin	524J	MG-29	78731	5800-5899
KAREN AVE	Austin	525Y	MK-28	78757	900-2099
KAREN CV	Round Rock	376R	MM-44	78664	1600-1699
KAREN ANN CT	Travis Co	704G	MH-12	78747	5600-5799
KAREN HILL PL	Travis Co	703L	MF-11	78652	100-199
KARIBA CV	Austin	433W	ME-37	78726	10300-10399
KARLING DR	Travis Co	557C	MP-27	78724	8600-8799
KAROLYN DR	Round Rock	376R	MM-44	78664	600-1499
KARST VIEW CV	Williamson Co	405C	MK-42	78681	3100-3199
KASDAN PASS	Cedar Park	373R	MF-44	78613	2200-2299
KASPER ST	Austin	616W	ML-19	78741	6100-6299
KASS CV	Round Rock	377E	MN-45	78664	2000-2099
KASSARINE PASS	Austin	614E	MG-21	78704	2900-2999
KATES CV	Buda	732V	MD-7	78610	100-399
KATES WAY	Hutto	350S	MU-46	78634	100-799
KATHERINE CT	Georgetown	287J	MN-53	78626	1300-1599
KATHERINE WAY	Leander	342A	MC-48	78641	100-399
KATHI LN	Georgetown	256N	ML-56	78628	100-299
KATHLEEN CV	Williamson Co	343S	ME-46	78641	2500-2599
KATHLEEN DR	Travis Co	610R	WZ-20	78736	9200-9299
KATHLEEN LN	Williamson Co	342V	MD-46	78641	300-699
KATHY CV	Austin	614E	MG-21	78704	2400-2499
KATHY LN	Travis Co	487R	WT-32	78669	20900-21599
KATHY RD	Williamson Co	383X	EA-43	76574	1-599
KATHY LYNN CT	Austin	496F	ML-33	78758	1600-1699
KATIE CV	Leander	372B	MC-45	78641	2700-2799
KATIE LN	Cedar Park	374U	MH-43	78613	3700-3899
KATIE LYNCH DR	Pflugerville	437H	MP-39	78660	1300-1499
KATIE MARIE CV	Williamson Co	224M	MH-59	78633	100-199
KATIE'S CORNER LN	Travis Co	437W	MN-37	78660	15100-15299
KATSURA LN	Travis Co	583U	MF-22	78746	3500-3599
KATTER CT	Travis Co	490L	WZ-32	78734	2900-2999
KATY LN	Georgetown	287S	MN-52	78626	2200-2299
KATY LN	San Leanna	703K	ME-11	78748	11400-11599
KATY B LN	Bastrop	744C	ED-9	78602	200-299
KATY CROSSING	Georgetown	257T	MN-55	78626	300-599
KATYDID LN	Austin	674V	MH-13	78744	5600-5699
	Austin	675N	MJ-14	78744	5700-5799
KATZMAN DR	Travis Co	436K	ML-38	78728	3700-3999
KAUAI CT	Bastrop Co	775H	EF-6	78602	100-199
KAUFFMAN RD N	Bastrop Co	775U	EF-4	78662	100-499
KAUFFMAN RD S	Bastrop Co	775Z	EF-4	78662	100-499
KAUKONAHUA LN	Bastrop Co	775M	EF-6	78602	100-199
KAULOO CT	Bastrop Co	745Y	EF-7	78602	100-199
KAUPA CT	Bastrop Co	775H	EF-6	78602	100-199
KAUPO DR N	Bastrop Co	776A	EG-6	78602	100-199
KAUPO DR S	Bastrop Co	776A	EG-6	78602	100-199
KAVANAGH DR	Austin	673G	MF-15	78748	800-1099
KAWAINUI LN	Bastrop Co	775C	EF-6	78602	100-299
KAWELA DR	Bastrop Co	745V	EF-7	78602	100-199
KAWELA LN	Bastrop	746S	EG-7	78602	100-199
KAWNEE DR	Austin	525Z	MK-28	78752	600-699
KAY LN	Pflugerville	438T	MQ-37	78660	600-799
KAY LN	Travis Co	610U	WZ-19	78736	9000-9199
KAY ST	Austin	586S	ML-22	78702	3200-3599
KAYLYN CT	Bastrop Co	744Z	ED-7	78602	100-199
KAYLYNN PL	Austin	642U	MD-16	78749	4000-4099
KAYVIEW DR	Austin	642A	MC-18	78749	5500-5999
KAYWOOD CT	Bee Cave	550Y	WZ-25	78733	4000-4099
KEAAU CT	Bastrop Co	776E	EG-6	78602	100-199
KEAHI CT	Bastrop Co	745X	EE-7	78602	100-199
KEAMUKU CT E	Bastrop Co	746S	EG-7	78602	100-199
KEAMUKU CT W	Bastrop Co	746S	EG-7	78602	100-199
KEANAHALULULU LN	Bastrop Co	745Y	EF-7	78602	100-399
	Bastrop Co	745T	EE-7	78602	300-599
	Bastrop Co	775A	EE-6	78602	600-699
KEARNEY HILL RD	Travis Co	409S	MS-40	78660	20100-20499
KEARSARGE CV	Austin	673A	ME-15	78745	8400-8599
KEARSARGE DR	Austin	643X	ME-16	78745	8200-8499
KEASBEY ST	Austin	555U	MK-25	78751	700-899
KEATING LN	Austin	584C	MH-24	78703	2400-2599
KEATS DR	Austin	614S	MG-19	78704	3800-3999
KEAWAKAPU DR	Bastrop Co	775B	EE-6	78602	100-299
KEDINGTON ST	Austin	705A	MJ-12	78747	6300-6499
KEEGANS DR	Austin	557T	MN-25	78724	6300-6499
KEEGAN'S WAY	Cedar Park	372G	MD-45	78613	2200-2399
KEEHE CT	Bastrop Co	745Y	EF-7	78602	100-199
KEEL CT	Travis Co	426G	WR-39	78669	2700-2799
KEELI LN	Travis Co	439Q	MT-38	78634	18800-19199
KEENE CV	Travis Co	492U	MD-31	78730	5200-5299
KEENLAND DR	Georgetown	287L	MP-53	78626	400-499
KEEPSAKE DR	Austin	673B	ME-15	78745	2000-2599
KEESHOND PL	Williamson Co	377A	MN-45	78664	1000-1299
KEILBAR LN	Austin	643Y	MF-16	78745	1700-1999
KEILMAN LN	Travis Co	408M	MR-41	78660	20000-20599
KEISS DR	Briarcliff	487C	WT-33	78669	900-1099
KEITH LN	Austin	585C	MK-24	78705	900-999
KELI CT	Austin	612J	MC-20	78735	5700-5799
KELLAM RD	Travis Co	708A	MQ-12	78617	6900-7799
KELLEY DR	Georgetown	316X	ML-49	78626	7000-7599
KELLIE'S FARM LN	Austin	466K	ML-35	78727	13000-13199
KELLNER CV	Travis Co	707B	MN-12	78617	7200-7299
KELLOG CT	Austin	642V	MD-16	78745	8200-8299
KELLY CT	Bastrop	744H	ED-9	78602	600-699
KELLY CV	Jonestown	430C	WZ-39	78645	8300-8699
KELLY CV	Taylor	322U	MZ-49	76574	2800-2899
KELLY DR	Point Venture	489J	WW-32	78645	18800-18999
KELLY DR	Taylor	322V	MZ-49	76574	2700-2799
KELLY LN	Hays Co	762E	MC-6	78610	100-199
KELLY LN	Pflugerville	438D	MR-39	78660	1700-2299
	Pflugerville	439E	MS-39	78660	2300-4699
	Travis Co	439Q	MT-38	78660	4700-4799
KELLY RAY'S DR	Travis Co	437W	MN-37	78660	900-999
KELLYWOOD DR	Travis Co	672K	MC-14	78739	3500-4399
KELSEY CV	Round Rock	408J	MQ-41	78664	3400-3499
KELSING CV	Austin	611M	MB-20	78735	6000-6099
KELTON DR	Austin	528B	MQ-30	78653	12200-12399
KEMAH DR	Austin	673N	ME-14	78748	1600-1799
KEMP ST	Austin	616P	ML-20	78741	200-699
KEMPER CV	Travis Co	582R	MD-23	78746	2100-2199
KEMP HILLS DR	Hays Co	670P	WY-14	78737	800-1699
KEMPLER DR	Austin	673J	ME-14	78748	9200-9599
KEMPSON DR	Austin	611M	MB-20	78735	5700-5899
KEMPTON ST	Georgetown	287L	MP-53	78626	2800-2899
KEMPWOOD CT	Williamson Co	347A	MN-48	78665	1900-1999
KEMPWOOD DR	Austin	464A	MG-36	78750	11500-11599
KEMPWOOD LOOP	Williamson Co	317W	MN-49	78665	1900-1999
KEN ST	Austin	496X	ML-31	78758	800-999
KEN AARON CT	Williamson Co	405K	MJ-41	78717	8600-8799
KENAI DR	Cedar Park	374P	MG-44	78613	2800-3199
	Williamson Co	374P	MG-44	78613	16300-16499
KENAI FJORDS DR	Pflugerville	438E	MQ-39	78660	17800-17999
KENBRIDGE DR	Austin	525G	MK-30	78757	2100-2299
KEN CARYL DR	Austin	675W	MJ-13	78747	6200-6499
KENDAL DR	Austin	526H	MM-30	78753	9700-9899
KENDALIA ST	Austin	673S	ME-13	78748	1400-1499
KENDALL CT	Cedar Park	372F	MC-45	78613	1600-1699
KENDALL CV	Elgin	533F	EA-30	78621	None
KENDALL ST	Georgetown	286U	MM-52	78626	1-99
KENDRA CV	Austin	525G	MK-30	78757	1800-1899
KENDRICK BLVD	Austin	671A	MA-15	78739	None
KENESHAW DR	Austin	643X	ME-16	78745	7900-8099
KENILWORTH DR	Austin	556L	MM-26	78723	6300-6499
KENMORE CT	Austin	554X	MG-25	78703	2400-2699
KENNAN RD	West Lake Hills	553Y	MF-25	78746	1000-1299
KENNEDY ST	Elgin	533R	EB-29	78621	None
	Elgin	533V	EB-28	78621	None
KENNELWOOD RD	Austin	554X	MG-25	78703	3700-3899
KENNEMER DR	Pflugerville	438D	MR-39	78660	19100-19299
	Pflugerville	409W	MS-40	78660	19300-19899
	Travis Co	409W	MS-40	78660	19900-20099
KENNETH AVE	Austin	615Z	MK-19	78741	2000-2199
KENNEY FORT TRL	Round Rock	406M	MM-41	78664	1800-1899
KENNEYS WAY	Round Rock	378B	MQ-45	78665	900-1599
KENNISTON DR	Austin	525Z	MK-28	78752	400-699
KENORA CT	Bee Cave	550W	WZ-25	78733	3700-3899
KENOSHA PASS	Austin	612W	MC-19	78749	6700-7299
KENSINGTON LN	Hays Co	639T	WW-16	78737	100-299
KENSINGTON ST	Williamson Co	434E	MG-39	78729	9500-9699
KENSINGTON CASTLE TRL					
	Pflugerville	408X	MQ-40	78660	800-1199
KENSWICK DR	Austin	467Y	MP-34	78753	13000-13299
KENT LN	Austin	584G	MH-24	78703	1300-1499
KENT ST	Taylor	322Z	MZ-49	76574	900-1399
	Taylor	322Y	MZ-49	76574	1400-2199
KENTFIELD RD	Austin	495W	MJ-31	78759	3600-3699
KENTISH CV	Austin	673A	ME-15	78748	8900-8999
KENTISH DR	Austin	673A	ME-15	78748	2700-2899
KENTRA DR	Travis Co	437C	MP-39	78660	1100-1199
KENTSHIRE CIR	Austin	615S	MJ-19	78704	600-699
KENTUCKY DERBY	Austin	523Z	MF-28	78746	5800-5899
KENWOOD AVE	Austin	615J	MJ-20	78704	1100-1699
	Austin	615N	MJ-20	78704	1700-2199
KENYON DR	Austin	643R	MF-17	78745	1100-1299
KEOKEA CT	Bastrop	746P	EG-8	78602	100-199
	Bastrop Co	746P	EG-8	78602	None
KEO KEO DR	Bastrop Co	746W	EG-7	78602	100-199
KEOMUKU LN E	Bastrop Co	775B	EE-6	78602	100-199
KEOMUKU LN W	Bastrop Co	775B	EE-6	78602	100-199
KEOTA DR	Austin	642Q	MD-17	78749	4400-4599
KEPLER CV	Williamson Co	434R	MH-38	78729	13200-13299
KERBEY LN	Austin	554Z	MH-25	78703	2700-3499
	Austin	554V	MH-25	78731	3500-3899
KERBEY HEIGHTS CT	Pflugerville	439E	MS-39	78660	2900-2999
KERLEY CT	Hutto	379H	MT-45	78634	4000-4499
KERLEY DR	Hutto	379H	MT-45	78634	100-299
KERMIT CT	Travis Co	439T	MS-37	78660	18200-18299
KERN RAMBLE ST	Austin	585H	MK-24	78722	1-99
KERR ST	Austin	614C	MH-21	78704	1600-1999
KERR TRL	Travis Co	402U	MD-40	78613	2300-2399
	Williamson Co	402U	MD-40	78613	2200-2299
KERRVILLE FOLKWAY	Travis Co	435S	MJ-37	78729	13200-13299
	Williamson Co	434R	MH-38	78729	None
KERRY CT	Lakeway	519C	WX-30	78734	100-199
KERRYBROOK LN	Austin	495X	MJ-31	78757	2700-2799
KESSLER CV	Pflugerville	437D	MP-39	78660	800-899
KESSLER DR	Pflugerville	437D	MP-39	78660	17500-17799
KESTREL DR	Austin	643S	ME-16	78745	2800-3099
KESWICK DR	Austin	643X	ME-16	78745	7700-7999
KETCH CT	Travis Co	492U	MD-31	78730	5400-5499
KETONA CV	Austin	494C	MH-33	78759	9500-9599
KETTERING DR	Cedar Park	372G	MD-45	78613	700-899
KETTLE CV	Round Rock	378B	MQ-45	78665	3300-3399
KETTLEMAN LN N	Williamson Co	375S	MJ-43	78717	200-299
KETTLEMAN LN S	Williamson Co	375S	MJ-43	78717	300-399
KEVIN LN	Travis Co	490L	WZ-32	78734	15000-15299
KEVIN KELLY PL	Austin	435W	MJ-37	78727	5800-5999
KEVIN TAYLOR DR	Austin	673D	MF-15	78745	800-899
KEY CV	Lago Vista	458M	WV-35	78645	20700-20799
KEY PT	Travis Co	517L	WT-29	78669	None
KEYNES LN	Austin	705A	MJ-12	78747	8600-8799
KEYSTONE CV	Georgetown	195Z	MK-61	78633	100-199
KEYSTONE BEND	Austin	463D	MF-36	78750	10700-10999
KEY VIEW DR	Austin	587G	MP-24	78724	5900-7699
KEY WAY DR	Austin	464V	MH-34	78759	11100-11199
KEY WEST CV	Travis Co	582R	MD-23	78746	1900-2199
KIANA DR	Williamson Co	434R	MH-38	78729	8000-8199
KIAWAH ISLAND CV	Austin	404D	MH-42	78717	10200-10299
KIAWAH ISLAND DR	Austin	404D	MH-42	78717	15800-15999
KICKAPOO CAVERN DR	Travis Co	409T	MS-40	78660	2700-2899
KICKING BIRD DR	Williamson Co	373A	ME-45	78641	16200-16399
KIDD LN	Travis Co	460T	WY-34	78734	16400-16599
KIDNEYWOOD TRL	Austin	611M	MB-20	78735	6000-6199
KIDS CV	Hays Co	669W	WW-13	78737	100-199
KIEFFER CT	Austin	463C	MF-36	78750	10100-10199
KIERAN CV	Georgetown	226P	ML-59	78628	1000-1099
KIEV CV	Austin	671B	MA-15	78739	6700-6799
KIKIPUA LN E	Bastrop Co	775B	EE-6	78602	100-199
KIKIPUA LN W	Bastrop Co	775B	EE-6	78602	100-199
KILBARCHAN DR	Austin	528K	MQ-29	78754	6900-6999
KILDARE CV	Austin	557Y	MP-25	78724	7000-7199
KILDEER ST	Travis Co	520A	WY-30	78734	15200-15299
KILGORE LN	Austin	465Q	MK-35	78727	4100-4399
KILKEE CV	Austin	404F	MG-42	78717	10700-10799
KILKENNY DR	Pflugerville	437C	MP-39	78660	17700-17899
KILKENNY HILL DR	Cedar Park	374R	MH-44	78613	4400-4499
KILLARNEY DR	Leander	342Q	MD-47	78641	1800-1999
KILLDEER DR	Hays Co	732A	MC-9	78610	100-299
KILLDEER LN	Williamson Co	282N	MC-53	78641	100-199
KILLIAN LOOP	Hutto	379U	MT-43	78634	100-299
KILLIANS CV	Cedar Park	372P	MC-44	78613	1800-1899
KILLIANS WAY	Cedar Park	372P	MC-44	78613	1900-2199
KILLINGSWORTH LN	Travis Co	468P	MQ-35	78660	2100-5199
	Travis Co	498C	MR-33	78660	5200-5799
KILMARNOCK DR	Austin	463B	ME-36	78726	10300-10399
KILMARTIN LN	Austin	528B	MQ-30	78653	11900-12399
KILMORY DR	Briarcliff	457V	WT-34	78669	300-399
KILT CT	Austin	528P	MQ-29	78754	6700-6799
KIM CV	Williamson Co	347Y	MP-46	78665	1-99
KIM LN	Austin	585C	MK-24	78705	3300-3499
KIM LN	Travis Co	371Q	MB-44	78641	13300-13399
KIMBERLY CV	Round Rock	407D	MP-42	78665	1000-1099
KIMBERLY DR	Austin	674A	MG-15	78745	200-399
KIMBERLY ST	Georgetown	256P	ML-56	78628	700-899
KIMBERLYN LN	Travis Co	436W	ML-37	78727	4300-4399
KIMBLE CV	Austin	525G	MK-30	78757	8400-8499
KIMBLE LN	Austin	616L	MM-20	78742	100-299
KIMBRO RD	Travis Co	530V	MV-28	78653	12400-13099
KIMBRO ST	Taylor	352D	MZ-48	76574	600-1299
	Taylor	322Z	MZ-49	76574	1300-2399
KIMBROOK DR	Round Rock	375H	MK-45	78681	2000-2099
KIMBRO WEST RD	Travis Co	501T	MW-31	78653	13700-14899
KIMMERLING LN	Austin	496A	ML-33	78758	1600-1799
KIMO CT	Bastrop Co	746W	EG-7	78602	100-199
KIMONO RIDGE DR	Austin	673F	ME-15	78748	8600-9199
KIMRA CV	Georgetown	226Q	MM-59	78628	400-499
KIMRA LN	Travis Co	402U	MD-40	78613	2300-2499
	Williamson Co	402U	MD-40	78613	2100-2299
KIM ZMESKAL PL	Austin	702D	MD-12	78748	11500-11599
KINBRAKE DR	Austin	643G	MF-18	78745	5800-5899
KINCAID CT	Austin	466Q	MM-35	78727	13200-13299
KINCHELOE ST	Travis Co	618M	MR-20	78725	14200-14399
KINCHEON CT	Austin	642F	MC-18	78749	7700-7899
KINCLAVEN CT	Travis Co	432F	MC-39	78613	2500-2599
KIND WAY	Travis Co	619S	MS-19	78725	4500-4699
KINDER PASS	Austin	466L	MM-35	78727	13300-13499
KING LN	Hutto	379R	MT-44	78634	100-199
KING LN	Williamson Co	312D	MD-51	78641	1-499
KING ST	Austin	555W	MJ-25	78705	3100-3799
KING ALBERT	Austin	644N	MG-17	78745	800-1099
KING ARTHUR CT	Travis Co	552Y	MD-25	78746	300-399
KING BEE LN	Travis Co	488W	WU-31	78669	20300-20599

STREET NAME	CITY or COUNTY	MAPSCO GRID	AUSTIN GRID	ZIP CODE	BLOCK RANGE O/E
KING CHARLES DR	Austin	587E	MN-24	78724	5200-5399
KING COTTON LN	Round Rock	407A	MN-42	78664	900-1199
KING EDWARD PL	Austin	644S	MG-16	78745	700-899
KING EIDER LN	Cedar Park	373Z	MF-43	78613	300-699
KING ELDER LN	Williamson Co	282N	MC-53	78641	100-399
KINGFISHER DR	Georgetown	195X	MJ-61	78633	100-199
KINGFISHER LN	Williamson Co	282N	MC-53	78641	None
KINGFISHER CREEK DR	Austin	703B	ME-12	78748	500-799
KINGFISHER RIDGE CV	Travis Co	489C	WX-33	78645	1800-1899
KINGFISHER RIDGE DR	Travis Co	489C	WX-33	78645	17800-18299
KING GEORGE DR	Austin	644S	MG-16	78745	6400-6599
KING HENRY DR	Austin	587E	MN-24	78724	5300-6099
KINGLET CIR	Hays Co	732K	MC-8	78610	1000-1099
KINGLET CT	Austin	675W	MJ-13	78744	6300-6399
KINGMAN DR	Williamson Co	434R	MH-38	78729	13300-13399
KING MONUMENT LN	Travis Co	432Q	MD-38	78613	2900-3398 E
KING RANCH RD	Williamson Co	279B	WW-54	78642	100-399
KING REA	Williamson Co	222F	MC-60	78633	1-699
KING REA SPUR	Williamson Co	222G	MD-60	78633	1-699
KINGS CIR	Travis Co	557E	MN-27	78724	None
KINGS CT	Travis Co	587Z	MP-22	78725	4200-4299
KINGS HWY	Austin	643H	MF-18	78745	5100-5599
KINGS LN	Austin	555W	MJ-25	78705	3100-3399
KINGS PT	Austin	556R	MM-26	78723	6700-6899
	Austin	556R	MM-26	78723	6700W-6899W
KINGS ROW	Travis Co	552Z	MD-25	78746	7000-7199
KINGSBURY DR	Williamson Co	344U	MH-46	78681	4200-4299
KINGSBURY ST	Austin	584M	MH-23	78703	1000-1499
KINGS CANYON DR	Taylor	322M	MZ-50	76574	4000-4499
KINGS CANYON DR N	Cedar Park	373X	ME-43	78613	100-399
KINGS CANYON DR S	Cedar Park	373X	ME-43	78613	100-399
KINGSGATE DR	Austin	672Z	MD-13	78748	11200-11499
KINGSTON CIR	Taylor	322U	MZ-49	76574	1400-1499
KINGSTON DR	Travis Co	610H	WZ-21	78736	7200-7299
KINGSTON WAY	Hays Co	639X	WW-16	78737	None
KINGSTON LACY BLVD	Pflugerville	438E	MQ-39	78660	1200-1899
	Pflugerville	408S	MQ-40	78660	None
KINGS VIEW CT	Austin	464B	MG-36	78750	11700-11799
KINGSWAY RD	Georgetown	226D	MM-60	78628	31000-31199
	Georgetown	227E	MP-60	78628	31200-31499
KINGWOOD CV	Austin	525G	MK-30	78757	1800-1899
KINLOCH CT	Hays Co	669B	WW-15	78737	100-199
KINLOCH DR	Travis Co	432G	MD-39	78613	2900-2999
KINNEY AVE	Austin	614C	MH-21	78704	500-2199
	Austin	614P	MG-20	78704	2900-3099
KINNEY RD	Austin	614K	MG-20	78704	2200-2599
KINNEY OAKS CT	Austin	614P	MG-20	78704	2600-2899
KINNIKINIK LOOP	Hays Co	669Y	WX-13	78737	100-799
KINSER LN	Travis Co	609Y	WX-19	78736	10600-10999
KINSEY CT	Travis Co	490G	WZ-33	78734	15100-15299
KINSHIP CANYON DR	Travis Co	497M	MP-32	78754	12800-13099
KINSINGTON DR	Bastrop Co	709L	MT-11	78612	None
KINTAIL DR	Briarcliff	458W	WU-34	78669	200-399
KIOWA	Lago Vista	428V	WV-37	78645	21200-21299
KIOWA PASS	Austin	613Z	MF-19	78745	4600-4699
KIPAHULU DR	Bastrop Co	776B	EG-6	78602	100-299
KIPAPA CT	Bastrop Co	745X	EE-7	78602	100-199
KIPHEN RD	Round Rock	348W	MQ-46	78665	None
	Williamson Co	347X	MN-46	78665	2400-2699
	Williamson Co	348W	MQ-46	78665	4200-4499
KIPPLING DR	Austin	556G	MM-27	78752	2100-2199
KIRAS CT	Hays Co	669B	WW-15	78737	100-299
KIRBY CV	Austin	464T	MG-34	78759	10300-10399
KIRBY SPRINGS DR	Hays Co	667L	WT-14	78620	1400-1799
KIRK AVE	Austin	586X	ML-22	78702	1100-1199
KIRK ST	Taylor	322Z	MZ-49	76574	600-1099
KIRKEN ST	Travis Co	560Y	MV-25	78653	10300-10499
KIRKGLEN DR	Austin	466L	MM-35	78727	13100-13399
KIRKHAM DR	Austin	611U	MB-19	78736	8100-8199
KIRKLAND CT	Travis Co	580F	WY-24	78738	12000-12099
KIRK RIDGE CV	Travis Co	704G	MH-12	78747	None
KIRKSEY DR	Austin	615Z	MK-19	78741	2000-2199
KIRKWALL CV	Austin	642K	MC-17	78749	8200-8299
KIRKWOOD RD	Austin	585D	MK-24	78722	1300-1599
KIRSCHNER PL	Austin	526E	ML-30	78758	900-999
KIRTOMY LOOP	Travis Co	437G	MP-39	78660	900-1099
KISOBA TERRACE CV	Austin	641Q	MB-17	78749	9400-9499
KISSATCHIE TRL	Round Rock	407S	MN-40	78664	3100-3199
KISSING OAK DR	Austin	673Y	MF-13	78748	200-499
KISSMAN DR	Travis Co	436L	MM-38	78728	3300-3799
KISTLER CV	Austin	464T	MG-34	78759	10100-10199
KIT CARSON DR	Hays Co	639R	WX-17	78737	10600-10999
	See.. Hays Co Rd 355				
KITE	Lakeway	519F	WW-30	78734	100-199
KITE TAIL DR	Travis Co	492Q	MD-32	78730	5100-5599
KITTANSETT CV	Travis Co	583J	ME-23	78746	1300-1399
KITTIWAKE LN	Travis Co	432C	MD-39	78613	2000-2199
KITTOWA CV	Travis Co	554J	MG-26	78746	3100-3299
KITTY AVE	Austin	586L	MM-23	78721	4500-4799
KITTY CIR	Travis Co	609S	WW-19	78736	None
KITTYHAWK CV	Austin	643S	ME-16	78745	3200-3299
KIVA DR	Austin	642F	MC-18	78749	7500-7799
KLAMATH FALLS DR	Williamson Co	375U	MK-43	78681	17500-17699
KLATTENHOFF DR	Travis Co	436Y	MM-37	78728	1900-2399
KLAUS LN	Travis Co	532M	MZ-29	78621	13200-14399
	Travis Co	502Z	MZ-31	78621	14200-14399
KLEBERG LN	Austin	586G	MM-24	78723	4400-4599
KLEBERG TRL	Austin	704L	MH-11	78747	5500-5899
KLEIN CT	Williamson Co	257J	MN-56	78626	100-199
KLONDIKE DR	Georgetown	195Z	MK-61	78633	100-399
KLONDIKE LOOP	Williamson Co	377F	MN-45	78665	1000-1099
KLONDIKE RUSH PT	Austin	462K	MC-35	78726	12200-12399
KNAP HOLLOW	Austin	524P	MG-29	78731	4500-4599
KNAPPLE CV	Travis Co	529H	MT-30	78653	11500-11599
KNARR	Lakeway	489Q	WX-32	78734	100-199
KNIGHT CIR	Austin	556S	ML-25	78723	5200-5299
KNIGHT ST	Georgetown	286R	MM-53	78626	1700-1999
KNIGHTEN LN	Travis Co	619N	MS-20	78725	15200-15299
KNIGHT'S BRIDGE	Austin	464F	MG-36	78759	11700-11999
KNIPP CV	Travis Co	672S	MC-13	78739	11500-11599
KNIPPA CV	Hutto	379K	MS-44	78634	1300-1399
KNOB HILL	Travis Co	577V	WT-22	78720	10600-10699
KNOB OAK LN	Austin	613J	ME-20	78735	4300-4499
KNOLL CREST LOOP	Austin	494G	MH-33	78759	9200-9399
KNOLLPARK CIR	Austin	496K	ML-32	78758	1200-1299
KNOLLPARK DR	Austin	496K	ML-32	78758	11500-11899
KNOLL RIDGE DR	Austin	466Y	MM-34	78758	12300-12499
KNOLL RIDGE DR	Cedar Park	372U	MD-43	78613	1200-1599
KNOLLWOOD CIR	Travis Co	583A	ME-24	78746	700-799
KNOLLWOOD CIR	Williamson Co	374H	MH-45	78681	4700-4799
KNOLLWOOD CV	Austin	524L	MH-29	78731	6600-6699
KNOLLWOOD CV	Round Rock	406E	ML-42	78681	1300-1399
KNOLLWOOD DR	Austin	524L	MH-29	78731	3800-4099
KNOLLWOOD DR	Travis Co	582D	MD-24	78746	700-899
KNOTTINGHAM DR	Travis Co	437P	MN-38	78660	16200-16599
KNOTTINGWOOD CT	Austin	674Q	MH-14	78744	4600-4699
KNOTTY TRL	Austin	466E	ML-36	78727	12800-12899
KNOTTY PINE CV	Austin	463L	MF-35	78750	9800-9899
KNOWELL DR	Austin	497F	MN-33	78753	12600-12699
KNOWLES DR	Hutto	379K	MS-44	78634	1500-1699
KNOX DR	Hays Co	762Z	MD-4	78610	100-499
KNOX DR	Williamson Co	314K	MG-50	78628	100-199
KNOX LN	Austin	524C	MH-30	78731	7300-7399
KOA CT E	Bastrop Co	746W	EG-7	78602	100-199
KOA CT W	Bastrop Co	746W	EG-7	78602	100-199
KOAE CT	Bastrop Co	775D	EF-6	78602	100-199
KOALI DR	Bastrop Co	746X	EG-7	78602	100-199
KOBUK DR	Cedar Park	374J	MG-44	78613	600-699
KODIAK CV	Cedar Park	374T	MG-43	78613	2900-2999
KODIAK DR	Williamson Co	408F	MQ-42	78664	100-199
KODIAK LN	Travis Co	467R	MP-35	78660	14300-14499
KODIAK TRL	Cedar Park	374T	MG-43	78613	400-699
	Williamson Co	374X	MG-43	78613	700-799
KOELE CT	Bastrop Co	745X	EE-7	78602	100-199
KOENIG LN E	Austin	555G	MK-27	78751	100-999
KOENIG LN W	Austin	555B	MJ-27	78756	800-2099
KOERNER LN	Austin	616B	ML-21	78721	900-999
KOHALA LN	Bastrop	746S	EG-7	78602	100-199
KOHLERS TRL	Lakeway	519R	WX-29	78734	1500-1699
KOKO CT	Bastrop Co	775H	EF-6	78602	100-199
KOKO LN	Bastrop	746T	EG-7	78602	100-199
KOKOMO LN	Bastrop Co	745W	EE-7	78602	100-199
KOLACHE CV	Austin	493R	MF-32	78750	7500-7599
KOLEKOLE LN	Bastrop Co	775H	EF-6	78602	100-199
	Bastrop Co	775C	EF-6	78602	200-499
KOLLMEYER CIR	Travis Co	490X	WY-31	78734	100-199
KOLLMEYER DR	Travis Co	520C	WZ-30	78734	13400-14599
	Travis Co	490X	WY-31	78734	14600-15499
KOLO CT	Bastrop Co	746W	EG-7	78602	100-199
KOLOIKI LN	Bastrop Co	776A	EG-6	78602	100-199
KONA DR	Bastrop	746S	EG-7	78602	100-199
	Bastrop Co	746S	EG-7	78602	200-299
KONAHUANUI LN	Bastrop Co	775M	EF-5	78602	100-199
KONSTANTY CIR	West Lake Hills	583K	ME-23	78746	500-599
KOOLUA DR	Bastrop Co	776A	EG-6	78602	100-199
KOPPERL CT	Travis Co	432G	MD-39	78613	2500-2599
KORAT LN	Williamson Co	405B	MJ-42	78681	16900-16999
KORMAN DR	Travis Co	466D	MM-36	78728	1500-1599
KORTH DR	Austin	642N	MC-17	78749	5300-5499
KOTHMAN DR	Hutto	379F	MS-45	78634	1200-1599
KOU CT	Bastrop Co	746X	EG-7	78602	100-199
KOUI CT	Bastrop	746T	EG-7	78602	100-199
KOURI AVE	Round Rock	406U	MM-40	78681	2600-2799
KRAMER LN	Austin	496J	ML-32	78758	800-1999
	Austin	495H	MK-33	78758	2000-2899
KRAUSE LN	Travis Co	580K	WY-23	78738	5600-6099
KREBS LN	Austin	644C	MH-18	78704	100-299
	Austin	614Y	MH-19	78704	400-599
KRINAN CT	Austin	528B	MQ-30	78653	5900-5999
KRISTEN LN	Williamson Co	403W	ME-40	78613	2300-2499
KRISTENCREEK LN	Williamson Co	345S	MJ-46	78681	3900-3999
KRISTINA DR	Georgetown	316B	ML-51	78628	500-799
KRISTY DR	Rollingwood	584J	MG-23	78746	100-199
KRIZAN AVE	Austin	466K	ML-35	78727	1700-2199
KROLLTON DR	Austin	643Q	MF-17	78745	6500-6799
KROMER ST	Austin	525G	MK-30	78757	8200-8699
KRUEGER LN	Austin	586H	MM-24	78723	5200-5399
KRUPA CT	Travis Co	402P	MC-41	78613	2800-2899
KRYSTIN CV	Travis Co	397P	WS-41	78654	None
KUHLMAN AVE	Austin	585Z	MK-22	78702	2900-3099
KUIKUI CT	Bastrop Co	775D	EF-6	78602	100-199
KUKUI CT	Bastrop	746S	EG-7	78602	100-199
KULA CT	Bastrop	746P	EG-8	78602	100-199
	Bastrop Co	746P	EG-8	78602	None
KULUA CT	Bastrop Co	746W	EG-7	78602	100-199
KUMQUAT CT	Austin	644Z	MH-16	78744	2400-2599
KUSKOKWIM RD	Williamson Co	374K	MG-44	78613	3100-3199
KUYKENDALL DR	Georgetown	287P	MN-53	78626	2200-2399
KWAI CV	Leander	342R	MD-47	78641	1800-1899
KYLE DR	Austin	556G	MM-27	78752	7000-7099
KYLE DR	Briarcliff	457Z	WT-34	78669	22000-22299
KYLE LN	Williamson Co	224E	MG-60	78633	100-199
KYLE ST	Hutto	349Q	MT-47	78634	100-299

L

STREET NAME	CITY or COUNTY	MAPSCO GRID	AUSTIN GRID	ZIP CODE	BLOCK RANGE O/E
LAAU CT	Bastrop Co	776A	EG-6	78602	100-199
LA BAHIA RD	Austin	644Q	MH-17	78745	5200-5399
LABRADOR CV	Williamson Co	434T	MG-37	78729	12500-12599
LABRADOR BAY CT	Travis Co	521P	MA-29	78732	12100-12399
LA BARZOLA BEND	Travis Co	580C	WZ-24	78738	11800-12099
LA CALMA DR	Austin	556E	ML-27	78752	6100-6399
LA CANTERA	Leander	341Y	MB-46	78641	1000-1099
LA CARMAN LN	Austin	641M	MB-17	78749	6300-6499
LA CASA DR	Austin	614J	MG-20	78704	2000-2499
LACEVINE LN	Travis Co	581H	MB-24	78735	3100-3299
LACEY AVE	Austin	584J	MG-23	78746	200-299
LACEY RD	Georgetown	314G	MH-51	78628	100-399
LACEY OAK CV	Round Rock	376E	ML-45	78681	2000-2099
LACEY OAK LOOP	Round Rock	376E	ML-45	78681	1200-1299
LACHLAN DR	Austin	404K	MG-41	78717	10000-10199
LA COLINA DR	Bastrop Co	738X	MQ-7	78617	None
LA CONCHA CV	Austin	611Z	MB-19	78749	6800-6899
LA CONCHA PASS	Austin	611Z	MB-19	78749	6600-7699
LA CONTERRA BLVD	Georgetown	317J	MN-50	78626	500-1099
LA COSTA	Leander	341V	MB-46	78641	500-599
LA COSTA CT	Austin	704J	MG-11	78747	2400-2499
LA COSTA DR	Austin	704E	MG-12	78747	10200-10599
LA CREMA CT	Williamson Co	343S	ME-46	78641	800-899
LA CRESADA DR	Austin	642N	MC-17	78749	8600-9199
LA CROSSE AVE	Austin	672A	MC-15	78739	4800-5199
	Austin	641Z	MB-16	78739	5200-7999
LA CROSSE AVE	Austin	640V	WZ-16	78739	8100-8299
LACY DR	Leander	342L	MD-47	78641	800-1699
LADERA TRL	Travis Co	430J	WY-38	78645	7600-8099
LADERA NORTE	Austin	524A	MG-30	78731	6400-7099
LADERA RANCH PKWY	Bee Cave	549M	WX-26	78738	4100-4499
LADERA VERDE DR	Austin	640V	WZ-16	78739	7900-8199
LADERA VISTA DR	Austin	464R	MH-35	78759	11200-11699
LADIN LN	Lakeway	489Z	WX-31	78734	500-699
LADLE LN	Austin	642B	MC-18	78749	7400-7599
LADRIDO LN	Austin	465Q	MK-35	78727	12000-12099
LADYBUG LN	Hutto	380J	MU-44	78634	100-299
LADYBUG ST	Austin	674R	MH-14	78744	7200-7699
LADY DAY CV	Travis Co	402P	MC-41	78613	2900-2999
LADY ELIZABETH'S LN	Travis Co	467G	MP-36	78660	14400-15399
LADY GREY AVE	Travis Co	467L	MP-35	78660	1400-1799
LADY LAURA'S CROSSING	Travis Co	437T	MN-37	78660	15500-15599
LADY SUZANNES CT	Austin	434Y	MH-37	78729	7400-7499
LAE CT	Bastrop	746T	EG-7	78602	100-199
LA ESTRELLA CV	Austin	640V	WZ-16	78739	10900-10999
LA FUANA PATH	Travis Co	641B	MA-18	78737	8800-9299
LA FAUNA VIEW	Travis Co	641A	MA-18	78737	9100-9199
LAFAYETTE AVE	Austin	585G	MK-24	78722	2300-3799
LA FAYETTE LN	Pflugerville	467H	MP-36	78660	1100-1199
LAFAYETTE PARK RD	Jonestown	401E	MA-42	78645	17800-18099
LAFAYETTE SQUARE DR	Leander	342V	MD-46	78641	500-799
LAFITTE LN	Austin	671F	MA-15	78739	11400-11599
LA FRONTERA BLVD	Round Rock	406U	MM-40	78681	2600-2898 E
LAGERWAY CV	Austin	672H	MD-15	78748	2900-2999
LAGOOD DR	Travis Co	522F	MC-30	78730	3700-3799
LAGOONA DR	Round Rock	344R	MH-47	78681	3700-3899
	Round Rock	345N	MJ-47	78681	3900-3999
LAGO SOL CT	Travis Co	461R	MB-35	78732	7100-7199
LAGO VERDE DR	Travis Co	520M	WZ-29	78734	100-499
LAGO VIENTO	Travis Co	490D	WZ-33	78734	4000-4299
	Travis Co	460Z	WZ-34	78734	4300-4599
LAGO VISTA DR	Travis Co	490H	WZ-33	78734	3600-4099
LAGO VISTA WAY	Lago Vista	429J	WW-38	78645	5900-5999
LA GRANGE ST N	Manor	529U	MT-28	78653	100-899
LA GRANGE ST S	Manor	529U	MT-28	78653	100-399
LA GUARDIA LN	Austin	677R	MP-14	78617	12300-12499
LAGUNA CV	Hutto	379K	MS-44	78634	1400-1499
LAGUNA DR	Austin	645F	MJ-18	78741	3100-3499
LAGUNA LN	Austin	523V	MF-28	78746	4700-4899
LAGUNA CLIFF LN	Travis Co	460G	WZ-36	78734	5300-6199
LAGUNA GRANDE	Travis Co	460Z	WZ-34	78734	4200-4399
LAGUNA LOMA CV	Austin	554W	MG-25	78746	1700-1799
LAGUNA SECA LN	Travis Co	408G	MR-42	78664	300-399
LAGUNA VISTA CV	Travis Co	554W	MG-25	78746	3900-3999
LAGUNA VISTA DR	Travis Co	554W	MG-25	78746	100-299
LAGUNA WOODS DR	Austin	404L	MH-41	78717	9100-9299
LA HACIENDA DR	Travis Co	460R	WZ-35	78734	15700-16199
LAI CT E	Bastrop Co	745Z	EF-7	78602	100-199
LAI CT W	Bastrop Co	745Z	EF-7	78602	100-199
LAIRD DR	Austin	525T	MJ-28	78757	5800-6699
LA ISLA CV	Travis Co	488G	WV-33	78669	19700-19799
LA JAITA DR	Cedar Park	373G	MF-45	78613	1600-1899
LAJITAS	Leander	371G	MB-45	78641	3500-3799
LA JOLLA DR	Travis Co	522K	MC-29	78733	9800-9999
LA JOLLA LN	Bastrop Co	743Y	EB-7	78602	100-199
LA JOLLA ST	Buda	762H	MD-6	78610	300-499
LAKE CV	Round Rock	347W	MN-46	78665	3100-3199
LAKE DR	San Leanna	703F	ME-12	78748	11300-11399
LAKE DR	Williamson Co	346Z	MM-46	78665	1-99
LAKE DR E	Taylor	323S	EA-49	76574	100-699
LAKE DR W	Taylor	323W	EA-49	76574	100-399
	Taylor	322Z	MZ-49	76574	400-1699
	Taylor	352C	MZ-48	76574	1700-2499
LAKE LOOP	Travis Co	490N	WY-32	78734	16300-16499
LAKE RD	Williamson Co	443L	EB-38	78615	1-399
LAKE AUSTIN BLVD	Austin	584F	MG-24	78703	2100-3899
LAKE BEACH DR	Travis Co	577V	WT-22	78720	10300-10799
LAKE BLUFF CV	Round Rock	408A	MQ-42	78665	1400-1499
LAKE CHAMPLAIN LN	Travis Co	527T	MN-28	78754	4700-4799
LAKE CHAMPLAIN LN	Travis Co	560L	MV-26	78653	11500-11799
LAKE CHARLES DR	Austin	675N	MJ-14	78744	7200-7399
LAKE CLARK LN	Austin	704A	MG-12	78747	2200-2299
LAKE CLIFF CT	Austin	584E	MG-24	78746	3300-3399
LAKE CLIFF TRL	Austin	584E	MG-24	78746	200-599
LAKECLIFF HILLS LN	Travis Co	521L	MB-29	78732	1600-1999
LAKE COMO DR	Lakeway	489Z	WX-31	78734	100-299
LAKE CREEK CIR	Round Rock	406D	MM-42	78664	300-499
LAKE CREEK CT	Georgetown	225E	MJ-60	78633	900-999
LAKE CREEK DR N	Round Rock	376X	ML-43	78681	100-499
LAKE CREEK DR S	Round Rock	406E	ML-42	78681	100-699
LAKE CREEK PKWY	Austin	434E	MG-39	78729	9900-10199
	Austin	433H	MF-39	78729	10200-10299
	Austin	433H	MF-39	78750	10300-10399
	Williamson Co	433K	ME-38	78750	10400-11499
LAKECREST DR	Travis Co	400D	WZ-42	78645	18700-18999
LAKE DRIVE DR	Travis Co	488W	WU-31	78669	20100-20199
LAKE EDGE CT	Travis Co	439T	MS-37	78660	18300-18399
LAKE EDGE WAY	Travis Co	439T	MS-37	78660	4000-4299
LAKE ESTATES DR	Lakeway	488Z	WV-31	78734	600-699
LAKE FOREST CV	Round Rock	408A	MQ-42	78665	1500-1599
LAKE FOREST DR	Round Rock	408A	MQ-42	78665	2700-2799
LAKEFRONT CIR	Lago Vista	428V	WV-37	78645	4600-4699
LAKEFRONT CV	Lago Vista	428V	WV-37	78645	21600-21699
LAKE FRONT DR	Bastrop Co	711Z	MX-10	78612	100-199
LAKEFRONT DR	Lago Vista	428U	WV-37	78645	21400-21599
LAKEFRONT DR	Point Venture	489J	WW-32	78645	100-199
	Point Venture	488M	WV-32	78645	200-399
LAKE GEORGE CV	Travis Co	560U	MV-25	78653	19000-19099
LAKE GEORGE LN	Travis Co	527T	MN-28	78754	4700-4799
LAKEHEAD CIR	Point Venture	489N	WW-32	78645	18500-18599
LAKE HILLS DR N	Travis Co	552A	MC-27	78733	100-599
LAKE HILLS DR S	Travis Co	551D	MB-27	78733	100-199
LAKE HURON CV	Travis Co	560Q	MV-26	78653	11100-11199
LAKE HURON DR	Travis Co	560Q	MV-26	78653	18800-18999
LAKEHURST DR	Austin	674H	MH-15	78744	2300-2599
LAKEHURST LOOP	Travis Co	518B	WU-30	78669	19500-19599
	Travis Co	488X	WU-31	78669	19600-19999
LAKEHURST RD	Travis Co	488X	WU-31	78669	1800-2399
	Travis Co	518B	WU-30	78669	2400-3999
LAKELAND	Point Venture	488R	WV-32	78654	18600-18899
LAKELAND CIR	Point Venture	489N	WW-32	78645	500-599
LAKELAND DR	Austin	524V	MH-28	78731	3500-3599
LAKELAND DR	Point Venture	489N	WW-32	78645	18400-18599
LAKELAND DR E	Travis Co	550C	WZ-27	78732	1200-1599
LAKELAND DR N	Travis Co	520Y	WZ-28	78732	12900-12999

K
L

STREET NAME	CITY or COUNTY	MAPSCO GRID	AUSTIN GRID	ZIP CODE	BLOCK RANGE O/E
LAKELAND DR W	Travis Co	550C	WZ-27	78732	1200-1599
LAKELINE BLVD	Austin	404P	MG-41	78717	10000-10699
	Austin	403V	MF-40	78717	10700-11499
LAKELINE BLVD N	Cedar Park	402C	MD-42	78613	100-499
	Cedar Park	372Q	MD-44	78613	500-2399
	Leander	372F	MC-45	78641	3000-3399
	Leander	342X	MC-46	78641	3400-3499
	Leander	372B	MC-45	78641	None
LAKELINE BLVD S	Austin	403Y	MF-40	78613	2600-2999
	Cedar Park	402G	MD-42	78613	800-1799
	Cedar Park	403T	ME-40	78613	1800-2599
	Cedar Park	372Y	MD-43	78613	None
LAKELINE MALL DR	Austin	403Z	MF-40	78717	10700-10999
	Austin	433D	MF-39	78717	11000-11099
	Austin	433D	MF-39	78613	11100-11299
LAKELINE OAKS DR	Cedar Park	403S	ME-40	78613	1900-1999
	Williamson Co	403S	ME-40	78613	2000-2099
LAKE LIVINGSTON DR	Williamson Co	314X	MG-49	78628	200-399
LAKE LUCY LOOP	Dripping Springs	636X	WQ-16	78620	None
LAKE MICHIGAN DR	Travis Co	560T	MU-25	78653	18800-18899
LAKE MIST	Travis Co	460V	WZ-34	78734	5300-5399
LAKE MONO CV	Travis Co	560U	MV-25	78653	11000-11099
LAKEMONT DR	Williamson Co	379X	MS-43	78634	100-599
LAKEMOORE DR	Austin	524A	MG-30	78731	5500-5799
LAKE MOUNTAIN LN	Travis Co	461C	MB-36	78641	7900-8199
LAKE OAKS DR	Jonestown	400H	WZ-42	78645	18300-18599
LAKE ONTARIO PL	Travis Co	560P	MU-26	78653	18700-18899
LAKE OVERLOOK RD	Georgetown	255G	MK-57	78633	400-499
	Williamson Co	255G	MK-57	78633	500-599
LAKE PARK CV	Lago Vista	428Y	WV-37	78645	3900-3999
LAKE PARK DR	Lago Vista	428Y	WV-37	78645	21500-21599
LAKE PARK DR	Travis Co	577Q	WT-23	78720	10400-10899
LAKE PINES DR	Williamson Co	375Y	MK-43	78681	17500-17699
LAKEPLACE LN	Travis Co	554A	MG-27	78746	3900-4199
LAKEPOINT CIR	Point Venture	489N	WW-32	78645	18300-18499
LAKEPOINT CV	Point Venture	489N	WW-32	78645	18200-18399
LAKERIDGE CIR	Point Venture	488R	WV-32	78654	19000-19099
LAKE RIDGE DR	Travis Co	522W	MC-28	78733	9800-10099
	Travis Co	521Z	MB-28	78733	10100-10199
LAKESHORE BLVD	Lago Vista	460A	WY-36	78645	17900-18299
LAKESHORE BLVD	Lago Vista	459D	WX-36	78645	18300-18699
	Lago Vista	429Z	WX-37	78645	18700-18999
LAKESHORE BLVD S	Austin	615L	MK-20	78741	1600-2599
LAKESHORE CIR	Point Venture	488M	WV-32	78654	400-599
LAKESHORE DR	Lago Vista	429E	WW-39	78645	6000-6699
LAKESHORE DR	Travis Co	427W	WS-37	78669	600-1299
	Travis Co	426V	WR-37	78669	1300-1399
LAKESHORE DR	Travis Co	554W	MG-25	78746	1700-2299
LAKE SHORE DR	Travis Co	577R	WT-23	78720	17200-17799
LAKESHORE DR E	Hays Co	576L	WR-23	78620	100-299
LAKE SHORE DR E	Travis Co	460H	WZ-36	78734	16200-16399
LAKESHORE DR E	Travis Co	458U	WV-34	78669	20700-20899
LAKESHORE DR W	Hays Co	576F	WQ-24	78620	100-299
LAKESHORE DR W	Travis Co	458T	WU-34	78669	20900-21199
LAKESHORE PT	Travis Co	459H	WX-36	78645	18200-18699
LAKESIDE CIR	Bastrop Co	738L	MR-8	78617	100-299
LAKE SIDE CV	Williamson Co	283Z	MF-52	78628	600-699
LAKESIDE DR	Austin	556R	MM-26	78723	3000-3499
LAKESIDE DR	Bastrop Co	776C	EH-6	78602	100-299
LAKESIDE DR	Jonestown	400M	WZ-41	78645	10300-11499
LAKESIDE DR	Travis Co	428A	WU-39	78654	23500-23999
	Travis Co	398W	WU-40	78654	24000-24399
LAKE SIDE DR	Williamson Co	283Z	MF-52	78628	100-599
LAKESIDE LOOP	Round Rock	347W	MN-46	78665	1300-1399
LAKESIDE TRL	Travis Co	460M	WZ-35	78734	5800-6099
LAKESIDE TRACE	Austin	556R	MM-26	78723	6600-6699
LAKE SOMERVILLE TRL	Georgetown	195T	MJ-61	78633	100-599
LAKE STONE CV	Travis Co	550M	WZ-26	78733	2300-2399
LAKE STONE DR	Travis Co	550M	WZ-26	78733	11700-12299
LAKE SUPERIOR LN	Travis Co	560T	MU-25	78653	10700-11299
LAKE TERRACE DR	Elgin	533M	EB-29	78621	1200-1299
LAKE TERRACE DR	Jonestown	400H	WZ-42	78645	18300-18599
LAKE TERRACE DR W	Jonestown	400H	WZ-42	78645	11000-11299
LAKE TRAVIS DR	Travis Co	460H	WZ-36	78734	16100-16199
LAKE TRAVIS RESORT RD	Travis Co	456D	WR-36	78669	25300-25499
LAKE VICTOR DR	Travis Co	467E	MN-36	78660	14200-14499
LAKE VIEW	Austin	524Y	MH-28	78731	4600-4699
LAKEVIEW AVE	Travis Co	460W	WY-34	78645	3100-3699
LAKEVIEW CIR	Austin	524N	MG-29	78731	5800-5899
LAKE VIEW CV	Round Rock	406F	ML-42	78681	700-799
LAKE VIEW DR	Bastrop Co	741D	MX-9	78612	100-299
LAKEVIEW DR	Bastrop Co	739P	MS-8	78617	100-299
LAKEVIEW DR	Travis Co	491G	MB-33	78732	4700-5099
LAKEVIEW DR	Travis Co	460R	WZ-35	78734	5600-5999
LAKE VIEW DR	Travis Co	371U	MB-43	78641	13000-14099
LAKEVIEW DR	Travis Co	461V	MB-34	78732	13100-13199
	Travis Co	461Q	MB-35	78732	13800-14099
LAKEVIEW DR	Travis Co	401X	MA-40	78641	16700-16899
LAKEVIEW DR	Travis Co	456H	WR-36	78669	24600-25299
LAKEVIEW DR E	Jonestown	400H	WZ-42	78645	18100-18599
LAKEVIEW DR N	Jonestown	400H	WZ-42	78645	11200-11399
LAKEVIEW DR W	Jonestown	400M	WZ-41	78645	10500-11199
	Jonestown	400H	WZ-42	78645	18600-18799
LAKEVIEW LN	Williamson Co	225N	MJ-59	78633	100-199
LAKEVIEW ST	Village of Volente	431S	MA-37	78641	7900-8099
LAKEWAY BLVD	Lakeway	519H	WX-30	78734	1400-4199
	Lakeway	518D	WV-30	78734	4200-4499
LAKEWAY DR	Georgetown	256K	ML-56	78628	100-2199
	Georgetown	257E	MN-57	78628	None
	Lakeway	489W	WW-31	78734	100-499
	Lakeway	519B	WW-30	78734	500-1599
LAKEWAY CENTRE CT	Lakeway	519R	WX-29	78734	1-99
LAKEWAY HILLS CV	Lakeway	518D	WV-30	78734	100-199
LAKE WOOD CIR	Travis Co	577V	WT-22	78720	17200-17499
LAKEWOOD CT	Bastrop Co	776D	EH-6	78602	100-199
LAKEWOOD DR	Austin	524E	MG-30	78731	6200-6899
	Austin	494W	MG-31	78731	6900-7199
	Austin	494N	MG-32	78750	7200-7799
	Austin	493V	MF-31	78750	7800-7899
LAKEWOOD DR	Bastrop Co	776D	EH-6	78602	100-199
LAKEWOOD DR	Hays Co	702X	MC-10	78610	100-699
LAKEWOOD DR	Round Rock	406B	ML-42	78681	1000-1199
LAKEWOOD TRL	Williamson Co	343U	MF-46	78641	100-199
	Williamson Co	373C	MF-45	78641	None
LAKEWOOD HILLS PASS	Travis Co	521J	MA-29	78732	12800-12899
LAKEWOOD HILLS TERRACE	Travis Co	521J	MA-29	78732	700-1199
LAKEWOOD HOLLOW	Austin	494S	MG-31	78750	6300-6399
LAKEWOOD POINT CV	Austin	494N	MG-32	78750	6600-6799
LAKEWOODS DR N	Williamson Co	225E	MJ-60	78633	6500-6999
LAKEWOODS DR S	Williamson Co	225J	MJ-59	78633	6600-6899
LAKOTA CV	Lakeway	519Z	WX-28	78734	101-199 O
LAKOTA PASS	Lakeway	520S	WY-28	78734	100-199
	Lakeway	519Z	WX-28	78734	None
LALEW CV	Austin	675W	MJ-13	78747	8100-8199
LA LLORONA LN	Austin	404A	MG-42	78717	14700-15099
LAMALOA LN	Bastrop Co	745Y	EF-7	78602	100-499
LA MANTILLA CV	Travis Co	554E	MG-27	78746	3200-3299
LAMAR BLVD N	Austin	584R	MH-23	78703	100-1299
	Austin	584H	MH-24	78705	1300-2599
	Austin	585A	MJ-24	78703	2600-2898 E
	Austin	585A	MJ-24	78705	2601-2899 O
	Austin	555N	MJ-26	78705	2900-3799
	Austin	555N	MJ-26	78756	3800-4899
	Austin	555G	MK-27	78751	4900-5699
	Austin	555G	MK-27	78757	5700-6299
	Austin	525Y	MK-28	78752	6300-7999
	Austin	525R	MK-29	78753	8000-8299
	Austin	526J	ML-29	78753	8300-9799
	Austin	496X	ML-31	78753	9800-12299
	Austin	466Q	MM-35	78753	12300-13699
LAMAR BLVD S	Austin	584Z	MH-22	78704	100-499
	Austin	614G	MH-21	78704	500-3999
	Austin	613V	MF-19	78704	4000-4399
	Austin	613V	MF-19	78745	4400-4599
	Sunset Valley	613V	MF-19	78745	4600-4799
LAMAR DR	Round Rock	376L	MM-44	78664	2000-2399
LAMAR PL	Austin	555C	MK-27	78752	700-799
LAMAR SQUARE DR	Austin	614G	MH-21	78704	1300-1399
LAMBERT CIR	Austin	496N	ML-32	78758	10700-10899
LAMBERT LN	Travis Co	736B	ML-9	78719	10500-11199
LAMBETH LN	Austin	673G	MF-15	78748	800-999
LAMBIE ST	Austin	615B	MJ-21	78701	700-899
	Austin	615F	MJ-21	78702	1000-1199
LAMBRUSCO LN	Williamson Co	343N	ME-47	78641	3200-3399
LAMBS LN	Austin	674H	MH-15	78744	4600-4999
	Austin	675J	MJ-14	78744	5000-5199
LAME DEER DR	Travis Co	560P	MU-26	78653	18400-18499
LA MESA	Lago Vista	429K	WW-38	78645	5900-6399
LA MESA DR	Austin	614U	MH-19	78704	2700-2799
LA MESA LN	Williamson Co	285M	MK-53	78628	200-299
LAMONT RIDGE	Travis Co	468T	MQ-34	78660	None
LAMPASAS PASS	Georgetown	195X	MJ-61	78633	100-199
LAMPASAS ST N	Manor	529U	MT-28	78653	200-599
LAMPASAS ST N	Round Rock	376Y	MM-43	78664	100-599
LAMPASAS ST S	Manor	529U	MT-28	78653	100-799
LAMPASAS ST S	Round Rock	376Y	MM-43	78664	100-199
LAMPLIGHT LN	Austin	524G	MH-30	78731	7200-7399
LAMPLIGHT VILLAGE AVE	Austin	466T	ML-34	78758	12300-12499
	Austin	466K	ML-35	78727	12500-13599
LAMPLIGHT VILLAGE CIR	Austin	466P	ML-35	78727	2100-2199
LAMPPOST LN	Austin	466P	ML-35	78727	12500-12899
LAMPTING DR	Travis Co	467P	MN-35	78660	13700-14099
LAMPWICK CIR	Austin	466P	ML-35	78727	2100-2199
LANAI CT	Bastrop Co	746T	EG-7	78602	100-199
LA NARANJA CV	Austin	642E	MC-18	78749	8400-8499
LA NARANJA LN	Austin	642J	MC-17	78749	6000-6299
LANARK LOOP	Travis Co	437G	MP-39	78660	1000-1199
LANCASTER CT	Austin	556S	ML-25	78723	5100-5299
LANCASTER DR	Austin	673E	ME-15	78748	2300-2599
	Austin	555V	MK-25	78723	4800-4899
	Austin	556S	ML-25	78723	4900-5099
LANCASTER DR	Georgetown	226P	ML-59	78628	100-299
LANCASTER DR	Leander	311R	MB-50	78641	1300-1499
LANCASTER GATE CV	Round Rock	406M	MM-41	78664	2100-2199
LANCASTER GATE DR	Round Rock	406M	MM-41	78664	1900-2099
LANCE LN	Round Rock	377S	MN-43	78664	1400-1599
LANCE RD	Travis Co	490Y	WZ-31	78734	1500-1599
LANCE WAY	Austin	496F	ML-33	78758	1400-1499
LANCELOT WAY	Travis Co	582C	MD-24	78746	500-699
LANCER LN	Travis Co	522S	MC-28	78733	1400-1799
LANCRET HILL DR	Austin	643K	ME-17	78745	6500-6799
LAND DR	Williamson Co	434J	MG-38	78729	12800-12899
LAND CREEK CV	Austin	584W	MG-22	78746	1000-1099
LANDER LN	Hays Co	577N	WS-23	78620	400-499
LANDER PASS	Williamson Co	434V	MH-37	78729	13000-13099
LANDMARK INN CT	Georgetown	225B	MJ-60	78633	100-199
LANDON LN	Austin	585B	MJ-24	78705	700-799
LANDONS WAY	Williamson Co	224J	MG-59	78633	100-299
LANDSCAPE DR	Austin	611M	MB-20	78735	6100-6299
LAND'S END	Travis Co	460R	WZ-35	78734	5500-5799
LANDSMAN DR	Austin	611U	MB-19	78736	7900-8399
LANE AVE E	Manor	529Q	MT-29	78653	100-499
LANE AVE W	Manor	529Q	MT-29	78653	100-399
LANES LN	Hays Co	794A	MG-3	78610	100-299
LANGDALE LN	Austin	527E	MN-30	78754	2000-2399
LANGFORD CV	Austin	556Q	MM-26	78723	2200-2299
LANGHAM ST	Austin	616W	ML-19	78741	6100-6299
LANGHOFF CV	Williamson Co	434Y	MH-37	78729	12600-12699
LANGLAND RD	Travis Co	437L	MP-38	78660	16800-16999
LANGSTON DR	Austin	556M	MM-26	78723	6700-7499
LANGTRY LN	Austin	642D	MD-18	78749	4500-4699
LANGWOOD DR	Travis Co	557B	MN-27	78754	5200-5299
LANIER DR	Austin	525G	MK-30	78757	2100-2299
LANIER RANCH RD	Hays Co	668W	WU-13	78620	100-299
LANIKAI CT	Bastrop Co	745Y	EF-7	78602	100-199
LANNA BLUFF LOOP	Austin	642T	MC-16	78749	8800-9099
LANSBURY DR	Austin	556U	MM-25	78723	2500-2699
LANSDOWNE RD	Austin	528F	MQ-30	78754	11500-12099
LANSHIRE DR	Austin	496J	ML-32	78758	10600-10899
LANSING CV	Lago Vista	429W	WW-37	78645	20200-20299
LANSING DR	Austin	644E	MG-18	78745	4800-5099
LANTANA CT	Leander	342K	MC-47	78641	1000-1099
LANTANA DR	Georgetown	225Q	MK-59	78633	100-199
LANTANA DR	Williamson Co	377J	MN-44	78664	1500-2099
LANTANA LN	Leander	342K	MC-47	78641	800-1099
LANTANA LN	Travis Co	617R	MP-20	78725	None
LANTANA LN	Williamson Co	433E	ME-39	78613	1300-1399
LANTANA TRL	Hays Co	732L	MD-8	78610	12900-12999
LANTANA WAY	Austin	641R	MB-17	78749	8800-9299
LANTANA HOLLOW	Austin	524K	MG-29	78731	4600-4699
LANTANA RIDGE CT	Travis Co	491X	MA-31	78732	12800-12899
LANTANA RIDGE DR	Travis Co	491X	MA-31	78732	2800-2999
LANTERN DR	Travis Co	467G	MP-36	78660	14600-15299
LANTERN LIGHT DR	Round Rock	376N	ML-44	78681	1400-1699
LANTERN VIEW DR	Jonestown	430U	WZ-37	78645	6000-7799
LAONA CV	Williamson Co	405J	MJ-41	78717	15600-15699
LA PALMA RANCH RD	Hays Co	701V	MB-10	78652	13700-14399
LA PALOMA DR	Lago Vista	429A	WW-39	78645	21200-21299
LA PALOMA DR	Williamson Co	255D	MK-57	78628	400-799
LA PALOMA LN	Travis Co	429L	WX-38	78645	6000-6499
LA PAZ LN	Austin	677V	MP-13	78617	12500-12799
LA PAZ LN	Bastrop Co	711A	MW-12	78612	100-199
LAPIN CV	Austin	671A	MA-15	78739	7200-7299
LA PLATA CV	Travis Co	641N	MA-17	78737	10600-10699
LA PLATA LOOP	Travis Co	640R	WZ-17	78737	8300-8499
LA POSADA DR	Austin	556E	ML-27	78752	900-1099
LAPOYNOR ST	Manor	529X	MS-28	78653	11300-11799
LA PUENTE DR	Austin	641R	MB-17	78749	9300-9499
LA QUINTA DR	Georgetown	226G	MM-60	78628	30300-31199
LARAMIE TRL	Austin	643D	MF-18	78745	2200-2499
LARAMIE PARKE CV	Austin	462K	MC-35	78726	12500-12599
LARCHBROOK DR	Travis Co	588N	MQ-23	78724	5400-5699
LARCHMONT CV	Austin	614N	MG-20	78704	3500-3599
LARCHMONT DR	Austin	614S	MG-19	78704	1800-1999
LARCH TERRACE	Austin	616S	ML-19	78741	6100-6299
LARCH VALLEY DR	Austin	497T	MN-31	78754	11400-11999
LARCHWOOD CV	Round Rock	376N	ML-44	78681	1400-1499
LAREDO DR	Austin	673S	ME-13	78748	10200-10399
LAREINA DR	Austin	644F	MG-18	78745	200-299
	Austin	644F	MG-18	78745	4400-4599
LARGO CV	Lakeway	518D	WV-30	78734	None
LARIAT CIR S	Hays Co	577P	WS-23	78620	400-599
LARIAT DR	Georgetown	225D	MK-60	78633	100-199
LARIAT LN	Hays Co	577J	WS-23	78620	100-399
LARIAT TRL	Travis Co	490L	WZ-32	78734	2800-15699
LARIAT WAY	Austin	643J	ME-17	78745	3200-3299
LARICAL TRL	Travis Co	558S	MQ-25	78724	8300-8599
LARIOPE LN	Lakeway	519M	WX-29	78734	1-99
LARK CT	Austin	496S	ML-31	78758	10500-10599
LARK CV	Austin	644E	MG-18	78745	5000-5099
LARK LN	Taylor	322Y	MZ-49	76574	2000-2299
LARK ST	Elgin	533R	EB-29	78621	100-199
LARK ST	Williamson Co	282N	MC-53	78641	300-599
LARK CREEK CV	Austin	645X	MJ-16	78744	5000-5099
LARK CREEK DR	Austin	645X	MJ-16	78744	5300-5899
LARKDALE LN	Travis Co	708S	MQ-10	78617	14200-14499
LARK GLEN LN	Austin	672Y	MD-13	78748	2500-2599
LARKHALL DR	Briarcliff	487H	WT-33	78669	900-1399
LARKIN'S LN	Austin	497N	MN-32	78753	1100-1199
LARKSPUR LN	Georgetown	225C	MK-60	78633	100-199
LARKSPUR LN	Hays Co	732F	MC-9	78610	300-399
LARKSPUR RD	Austin	525H	MK-30	78758	1200-1399
LARKSPUR WAY	Williamson Co	433F	ME-39	78613	3400-3499
LARKWOOD CT	Austin	556P	ML-26	78723	1700-1799
LARKWOOD DR	Austin	556N	ML-26	78723	1200-1699
LAROB LN	Travis Co	590C	MV-24	78653	9900-10199
LA ROCA CV	Austin	641S	MA-16	78739	11000-11099
LA ROCHELLE DR	Cedar Park	403U	MF-40	78613	2300-2599
LA RONDE ST	Austin	555J	MJ-26	78731	2600-2699
LARRY LN	Austin	585H	MK-24	78722	3200-3499
LARRY LN	Round Rock	376R	MM-44	78664	1200-1499
LARRY ST	Taylor	353R	EB-47	76574	1900-1999
LARSON CV	Austin	672L	MD-14	78748	3000-3099
LARSON ST	Elgin	534E	EC-30	78621	500-599
	Elgin	534E	EC-30	78621	800-899
LARSTON LN	Cedar Park	372J	MC-44	78613	2200-2399
LARUE BELLE CV	Austin	671B	MA-15	78739	6900-6999
LARUE BELLE LN	Austin	671B	MA-15	78739	11300-11499
LAS ALAS TRL	Austin	677R	MP-14	78617	5600-6099
LA SALLE DR	Austin	556M	MM-26	78723	6700-6999
LA SALLE DR	Austin	465A	MJ-36	78727	12700-12799
LAS BRISAS DR	West Lake Hills	583L	MF-23	78746	1-99
LAS CIMAS PKWY	Travis Co	583E	ME-24	78746	800-1099
LAS COLINAS DR	Austin	524U	MH-28	78731	3600-3699
LAS COLINAS DR	Georgetown	226G	MM-60	78628	100-199
LAS COLINAS DR	Leander	342J	MC-47	78641	400-699
LAS COLINAS WAY	Round Rock	376A	ML-45	78681	3000-3199
LAS CRUCES ST	Buda	762M	MD-5	78610	300-599
LAS ENTRADAS DR	Travis Co	457H	WT-36	78669	1400-1999
LAS FLORES DR	Travis Co	521F	MA-30	78732	12100-12499
LA SIESTA CT	Austin	641M	MB-17	78749	8900-8999
LA SIESTA BEND	Austin	641M	MB-17	78749	8800-9299
LAS LOMAS CT	West Lake Hills	583R	MF-23	78746	100-199
LAS LOMAS DR	West Lake Hills	583M	MF-23	78746	100-799
LAS MADERAS LN	Austin	674D	MH-15	78744	4400-4499
LAS PALMAS DR	Austin	465X	MJ-34	78759	4200-4399
LAS PLUMAS CT	Williamson Co	225Z	MK-58	78628	4300-4399
LAS PLUMAS DR	Williamson Co	225Z	MK-58	78628	300-399
LASS PL	Bee Cave	550S	WY-25	78738	None
LASSANT CV	Austin	642C	MD-18	78749	5100-5199
LASSEN VOLCANIC DR	Pflugerville	438A	MQ-39	78660	700-899
LASSO DR	Round Rock	406P	ML-41	78681	700-2499
LASSO PATH	Austin	643D	MF-18	78745	4600-4799
LAS TERRAZAS DR	Travis Co	517H	WT-30	78669	None
LA STRADA CV	Lakeway	519D	WX-30	78734	100-199
LAS VENTANAS DR	Austin	524B	MG-30	78731	7100-7299
LATCHWOOD LN	Austin	497B	MN-33	78753	12900-12999
LATHAN LN	Taylor	322Y	MZ-49	76574	1900-2399
LATHE CV	Austin	466L	MM-35	78727	13500-13599
LATIGO PASS	Austin	612W	MC-19	78749	6300-6399
LATIGO TRACE	Round Rock	376J	ML-44	78681	1500-1799
LATIMER DR	Travis Co	491U	MB-31	78732	3400-3999
LATING STREAM LN	Travis Co	554J	MG-26	78746	3100-3299
LA TOSCA DR	Travis Co	611X	MA-19	78737	8400-8599
LATTA DR	Austin	642G	MD-18	78749	7500-8799
LATTERIDGE DR	Austin	673H	MF-15	78748	700-899
LAUDER DR	Briarcliff	487C	WT-33	78669	900-1099
LAUGHING WATER	Williamson Co	375U	MK-43	78681	8400-8499
LAUMAIA LN	Bastrop Co	745W	EE-7	78602	100-199
LAURA CT	Round Rock	406K	ML-41	78681	2100-2199
LAURA LN	Bastrop	715U	EF-10	78602	100-299
	Bastrop Co	715L	EF-11	78602	300-499
LAURA LN	Rollingwood	584J	MG-23	78746	100-199
LAURA LN	Williamson Co	192S	MC-61	78642	100-199
LAURA HUNTER LN	Hays Co	636F	WQ-18	78620	100-299
LAURALAN DR	Travis Co	611J	MA-20	78736	9200-9599
LAURANNE LN	Travis Co	522N	MC-29	78733	1900-2199
LAUREL CIR	Austin	554G	MH-27	78731	3300-3399
LAUREL CV	Hays Co	732L	MD-8	78610	100-1099
LAUREL DR	Round Rock	376Q	MM-44	78664	200-299

STREET NAME	CITY or COUNTY	MAPSCO GRID	AUSTIN GRID	ZIP CODE	BLOCK RANGE O/E
LAUREL LN	Austin	555X	MJ-25	78705	100-199
LAUREL LN	Jonestown	400M	WZ-41	78645	10700-10799
LAUREL LN	Leander	342T	MC-46	78641	1700-1899
LAUREL PATH	Hays Co	732B	MC-9	78610	300-399
LAUREL PATH	Williamson Co	377J	MN-44	78664	1600-1999
LAUREL ST	Bastrop	715X	EE-10	78602	400-899
LAUREL ST	Georgetown	287J	MN-53	78626	1200-1799
LAUREL ST	Taylor	323T	EA-49	76574	1500-1799
LAUREL BAY LOOP	Williamson Co	344V	MH-46	78681	3500-3799
LAUREL CANYON DR	Austin	554C	MH-27	78731	4600-4699
LAUREL CREEK CIR	Austin	433T	ME-37	78726	11100-11199
LAUREL CREEK DR	Austin	433S	ME-37	78726	10800-11199
LAUREL GLEN BLVD	Leander	342H	MD-48	78641	900-1699
LAUREL GROVE DR	Austin	526A	ML-30	78758	8900-9099
LAUREL GROVE WAY	Round Rock	376A	ML-45	78681	2900-2999
LAUREL HILL CV	Travis Co	492Q	MD-32	78730	10400-10599
LAUREL HILL ST	Hays Co	639F	WW-18	78737	1-99
LAURELLEAF DR	Pflugerville	437M	MP-38	78660	1000-1299
LAUREL LEDGE LN	Austin	524Q	MH-29	78731	3500-3899
LAUREL OAK LOOP	Round Rock	378W	MQ-43	78665	1400-1599
LAUREL OAK TRL	Pflugerville	437R	MP-38	78660	1000-1299
LAUREL RIDGE CV	Travis Co	521G	MB-30	78732	2000-2099
LAUREL RIDGE DR	Round Rock	346R	MM-47	78665	3800-3899
LAUREL VALLEY DR	Austin	524M	MH-29	78731	6200-6299
LAUREL VALLEY RD	West Lake Hills	583C	MF-24	78746	100-899
LAUREL WOOD DR	Austin	524A	MG-30	78731	6500-6799
LAURELWOOD DR N	Travis Co	551D	MB-27	78733	200-499
LAURELWOOD DR S	Travis Co	551D	MB-27	78733	100-199
LAURELWOOD TRL	Travis Co	583Q	MF-23	78746	200-399
LAUREN CT	Travis Co	426L	WR-38	78669	26500-26599
LAUREN DR	Travis Co	426M	WR-38	78669	1800-2299
LAUREN LN	Williamson Co	224V	MH-58	78633	100-199
LAUREN LOOP	Leander	341G	MB-48	78641	200-2499
LAUREN TRL	Cedar Park	402L	MD-41	78613	300-399
LAURETTAWOOD DR	Cedar Park	433E	ME-39	78613	1200-1299
	Williamson Co	433E	ME-39	78613	1300-1398 E
LAVA LN	Travis Co	705X	MJ-10	78747	10200-10399
LAVA BED DR	Pflugerville	438E	MQ-39	78660	100-399
LAVACA LN	Williamson Co	255M	MK-56	78628	100-199
LAVACA LOOP	Elgin	533F	EA-30	78621	500-999
LAVACA ST	Austin	585W	MJ-22	78701	100-1899
LAVA HILL RD	Travis Co	706A	ML-12	78744	8500-8899
LAVENDALE CT	Austin	672Z	MD-13	78748	2300-2599
LAVENDER CV	Pflugerville	438Y	MR-37	78660	900-999
LAVERA DR	Austin	463A	ME-36	78726	9800-9999
LAVERNE TERRACE	Georgetown	226P	ML-59	78628	100-299
LAVERTY PL	Austin	526K	ML-29	78753	8800-8899
LAVINIA LN	Austin	497J	MN-32	78753	12100-12199
LA VISTA ST	Austin	614V	MH-19	78704	100-299
LAVON HILLS	Travis Co	488K	WU-32	78669	None
LAWHON LN	Georgetown	288S	MQ-52	78626	1200-1799
LAWLESS ST	Austin	586A	ML-24	78723	4100-4199
LAWMAN'S CT	Round Rock	346Z	MM-46	78665	800-899
LAWNDALE DR	Austin	525A	MJ-30	78759	7900-8099
LAWNMONT AVE	Austin	555A	MJ-27	78756	2100-2499
LAWNMONT DR	Round Rock	406H	MM-42	78664	700-1599
LAWRENCE DR	Travis Co	490L	WZ-32	78734	2600-3199
LAWRENCE ST	Austin	616X	ML-19	78741	1200-1499
LAWS RD	Mustang Ridge	766X	MK-4	78610	12100-12799
LAWSON LN	Austin	585U	MK-22	78702	1100-1199
LAWTON AVE	Austin	554R	MH-26	78731	3500-3799
LAYLA DR	Buda	763X	ME-4	78610	100-199
LAYNE LOOP	Travis Co	309T	WW-49	78641	13900-14299
LAYTON LOOP	Travis Co	436W	ML-37	78727	13700-13799
LAYTON WAY	Williamson Co	223H	MF-60	78633	100-199
LAZADA LN	Williamson Co	345X	MJ-46	78681	3100-3299
LAZY LN	Austin	525H	MK-30	78757	7700-8399
LAZY RD	Georgetown	257F	MN-57	78626	1-299
LAZY BROOK	Austin	556T	ML-25	78723	2000-2099
LAZY BROOK CIR	Austin	556T	ML-25	78723	2000-2099
LAZY CREEK DR	Austin	557N	MN-26	78724	7100-7699
LAZYFIELD TRL	Austin	435W	MJ-37	78727	12900-12999
LAZY OAK CV	Hays Co	732F	MC-9	78610	12700-12899
LAZY OAK CV	Round Rock	375F	MJ-45	78681	3300-3499
LAZY OAKS DR	Austin	643P	ME-17	78745	2500-2699
LAZYRIDGE DR	Travis Co	467Z	MP-34	78660	13500-14199
LAZY RIVER CV	Austin	523S	ME-28	78730	7600-7899
LAZY RIVER LN	Bastrop Co	651F	MW-18	78621	100-299
LAZY RIVER RUN	Georgetown	285P	MJ-53	78628	100-699
LEA CV	Austin	494X	MG-31	78731	5000-5199
LEADVILLE DR	Austin	672F	MC-15	78749	3600-3899
LEAF CIR	Austin	465R	MK-35	78759	3100-3199
LEAF LN	Austin	465R	MK-35	78759	3000-3299
LEAFDALE PT	Village of the Hills	519N	WW-29	78738	1-99
LEAFDALE TRL	Hays Co	667B	WS-15	78620	100-399
LEAF HOLLOW DR	Bastrop Co	745U	EF-7	78602	100-199
LEAFIELD DR	Austin	642R	MD-17	78749	3500-3999
LEAFWOOD LN	Austin	463H	MF-36	78750	10600-11199
LEAH CV	Austin	673J	ME-14	78748	2200-2299
LEAH LN	Round Rock	407D	MP-42	78665	1000-1399
LEANDER DR	Leander	342G	MD-48	78641	600-1699
LEANDER RD	Georgetown	286U	MM-52	78626	500-899
	Georgetown	286W	ML-52	78628	900-1799
	Georgetown	316A	ML-51	78628	1800-2099
	Georgetown	315D	MK-51	78628	2100-2299
LEANDER ST	Georgetown	286Q	MM-53	78626	1700-2199
LEANDER ST	Jonestown	401E	MA-42	78645	11400-11499
LEANING OAK CIR	Austin	614T	MG-19	78704	3000-3099
LEANING OAK DR	Lago Vista	458D	WV-36	78645	20700-20899
LEANING ROCK CIR	Travis Co	493N	ME-32	78730	9100-9699
LEANING WILLOW DR	Austin	496N	ML-32	78758	10300-10499
LE ANN LN	Cedar Park	373P	ME-44	78613	700-799
LEANNA OAKS LOOP	San Leanna	703P	ME-11	78652	500-599
LEANNA WOODS CV	San Leanna	703P	ME-11	78652	500-599
LEANNE DR	Georgetown	225Y	MK-58	78633	300-399
LEAPING FROG LN	Pflugerville	407Z	MP-40	78660	600-699
LEAPWOOD PL	Austin	464M	MH-35	78759	11600-11699
LEAR AVE	Buda	732U	MD-7	78610	100-299
LEAR LN	Austin	643T	ME-16	78745	2000-2399
LEATHA LN	Travis Co	456H	WR-36	78669	24700-25099
LEATHER CV	Williamson Co	433L	MF-38	78750	10500-10699
LEATHERLEAF TRL	Austin	675A	MJ-15	78744	4500-4899
LEATHERMAN LN	Travis Co	461G	MB-36	78641	7600-7799
LEATHERWOOD CV	Austin	464M	MH-35	78759	6300-6399
LEBERMAN LN	Austin	554X	MG-25	78703	2000-2099
LECKRONE CV	Austin	611H	MB-21	78735	5800-5899
LECOMPTE RD	Williamson Co	405P	MJ-41	78717	7800-7999

STREET NAME	CITY or COUNTY	MAPSCO GRID	AUSTIN GRID	ZIP CODE	BLOCK RANGE O/E
LE CONTE CV	Austin	641R	MB-17	78749	9300-9399
LEDBETTER ST	Round Rock	376T	ML-43	78681	1100-1599
LEDESMA RD	Austin	586U	MM-22	78721	4600-5799
LEDGE DR	Austin	494S	MG-31	78750	6200-6299
LEDGE ST	Jonestown	400H	WZ-42	78645	18200-18399
LEDGEMONT	Georgetown	226H	MM-60	78628	30300-30399
LEDGE MOUNTAIN DR	Austin	524K	MG-29	78731	6100-6499
LEDGEROCK CIR	Travis Co	582D	MD-24	78746	6500-6699
LEDGESTONE DR	Austin	554B	MG-27	78731	3400-3499
LEDGE STONE DR	Hays Co	639L	WX-17	78737	100-799
LEDGESTONE TERRACE	Travis Co	610Y	WZ-19	78737	9100-9699
	Travis Co	640G	WZ-18	78737	9700-9999
LEDGEWAY E	West Lake Hills	583C	MF-24	78746	400-499
LEDGEWAY W	West Lake Hills	583C	MF-24	78746	500-999
LEDGEWOOD DR	Austin	495V	MK-31	78758	1700-1799
LEE DR	Leander	342B	MC-48	78641	900-999
LEE LN	Lago Vista	458A	WU-36	78645	20000-20299
LEE ST	Taylor	352C	MZ-48	76574	2200-2399
LEE ST N	Round Rock	376Y	MM-43	78664	300-699
LEEANN DR	Austin	466S	ML-34	78758	2000-2099
LEE BARTON DR	Austin	584Z	MH-22	78704	100-399
LEEDS CV	Austin	643F	ME-18	78745	2800-2899
LEEDS WAY	Cedar Park	372P	MC-44	78613	1600-1699
LEEDS CASTLE WALK	Georgetown	287S	MN-52	78626	1000-1099
LEEDS MOUNTAIN CV	Austin	705A	MJ-12	78747	8400-8499
LEE HILL DR	Austin	646K	ML-17	78744	7800-8099
LEE MANOR CV	Travis Co	498H	MR-33	78653	6800-6999
LEE PARK LN	Austin	491X	MA-31	78732	12600-12799
LEE SAGE CIR	Travis Co	366V	WR-43	78654	6700-6799
LEESBURG CIR	Austin	525H	MK-30	78758	8400-8499
LEEWARD CT	Austin	524S	MG-28	78731	4800-4899
LEGENDARY DR	Austin	465B	MJ-36	78727	13000-13599
LEGEND OAKS DR	Williamson Co	285M	MK-53	78628	100-199
LEGEND OAKS DR E	Williamson Co	285M	MK-53	78628	100-199
LEGEND OAKS DR W	Williamson Co	285M	MK-53	78628	200-299
LEGEND OAKS LN	Cedar Park	373K	ME-44	78613	1501-1599 O
LEGENDS LN	Austin	704J	MG-11	78747	10600-11099
LEGENDS OF HUTTO TRL	Hutto	379M	MT-44	78634	100-499
LEGHORN CV	Williamson Co	405F	MJ-42	78681	5100-5199
LE GRANDE AVE	Austin	615E	MJ-21	78704	200-399
LEHIGH DR	Austin	556L	MM-26	78723	2300-2699
LEHMAN LOOP	Austin	704T	MG-10	78747	11100-11199
LEHMAN WAY	Austin	704T	MG-10	78747	10800-11099
LEI CT	Bastrop Co	746W	EG-7	78602	100-199
LEIGH LN	Travis Co	439Q	MT-38	78634	18700-19199
LEIGH ST	Austin	584D	MH-24	78703	1600-1699
LEISHA LEE LN	Williamson Co	343X	ME-46	78641	16100-16199
LEISURE DR	Austin	526V	MM-28	78754	8600-8899
LEISURE LN	Bastrop Co	742B	MY-9	78612	100-199
	Bastrop Co	712S	MY-10	78612	200-599
	Bastrop Co	711V	MX-10	78612	600-699
LEISURE LN	Jonestown	429M	WX-38	78645	18800-19399
	Lago Vista	429M	WX-38	78645	19400-19699
LEISURE RIDGE DR	Travis Co	704K	MG-11	78747	None
LEISURE RUN CV	Austin	644N	MG-17	78745	800-899
LEISURE RUN RD	Austin	644N	MG-17	78745	5900-6099
LEISUREWOODS DR	Hays Co	702W	MC-10	78610	100-299
	Hays Co	732E	MC-9	78610	300-799
LELAND ST	Austin	615J	MH-20	78704	100-299
	Austin	615N	MJ-20	78704	300-599
LEMANS PL	Austin	465K	MJ-35	78727	4800-4899
LEMENS AVE	Williamson Co	348H	MR-48	78634	100-799
LEMENS CIR	Williamson Co	348D	MR-48	78634	100-199
LEMEN'S SPICE CV	Austin	464A	MG-36	78750	11700-11799
LEMEN'S SPICE TRL	Austin	464B	MG-36	78750	8600-8899
LEMEN'S SUGAR CV	Austin	464A	MG-36	78750	11700-11799
LEMON DR	Austin	644Z	MH-16	78744	2100-2199
LEMONGRASS LN	Travis Co	467R	MP-35	78660	14300-14499
LEMON MINT CT	Travis Co	551P	MA-26	78733	1700-1899
LEMONWOOD DR	Austin	524E	MG-30	78731	5500-5699
LEMOS DR	Travis Co	436K	ML-38	78728	3900-3999
LEMUEL LN	Austin	403P	MF-41	78717	11400-11499
LENAPE CV	Travis Co	610M	WZ-20	78736	9900-9999
LENAPE TRL	Travis Co	610G	WZ-21	78736	7300-8099
LEN BAR CT	Williamson Co	312H	MD-51	78641	100-899
LEN BAR LN	Williamson Co	312H	MD-51	78641	1-399
LENDALL LN	Austin	674L	MH-14	78744	2400-4499
LENNOX DR	Austin	644F	MG-18	78745	4600-4699
LENORA DR	Taylor	353B	EA-48	76574	400-599
	Taylor	323X	EA-49	76574	500-599
LENORA ST	Austin	643Z	MF-16	78745	7200-7299
LENTZ ST	Georgetown	286H	MM-54	78626	None
LENWOOD CT	Travis Co	550M	WZ-26	78733	2800-2899
LENZ DR	Williamson Co	375X	MJ-43	78681	17000-17199
LEO ST	Austin	673A	ME-15	78745	8500-8899
LEON LN	Williamson Co	375E	MJ-45	78681	4300-4399
LEON ST	Austin	585E	MJ-24	78705	2200-2599
LEONA ST	Austin	585U	MK-22	78702	1100-1199
	Austin	585L	MK-23	78702	1200-1899
	Austin	585L	MK-23	78722	1900-2299
LEONARD ST	Austin	585F	MJ-24	78705	800-899
LEON GRANDE CV	Austin	464M	MH-35	78759	11500-11599
LEOPOLD LN	Travis Co	552V	MD-25	78746	1-99
LEPPKE CV	Austin	674L	MH-14	78744	7100-7199
LEPRECHAUN DR	Austin	523T	ME-28	78746	6700-6799
LERALYNN ST	Austin	555L	MK-26	78751	5100-5299
LEROY LN	Travis Co	707H	MP-12	78617	None
LERWICK LN	Williamson Co	405B	MJ-42	78681	8100-8199
LES CV	Leander	341H	MB-48	78641	200-299
LES LN	Travis Co	546V	WR-25	78620	None
LESA LN	Williamson Co	288B	MQ-54	78626	100-199
LESLIE AVE	Austin	586L	MM-23	78721	4100-4799
LESLIE CT	Round Rock	406K	ML-41	78681	2300-2399
LESSIN LN	Austin	614Y	MH-19	78704	100-299
LESSMANN LN	Travis Co	649R	MT-17	78617	17200-17399
LETTI LN	Travis Co	467T	MN-34	78660	13600-13899
LEVANDER LOOP	Austin	616F	ML-21	78702	5300-6099
	Austin	616K	ML-20	78725	6100-6399
LEVATA DR	Austin	670D	WZ-15	78739	7900-8099
LEVERING ST	Travis Co	618M	MR-20	78725	14200-14499
LEWIS CV	Lago Vista	459A	WW-36	78645	20200-20299
LEWIS LN	Austin	555N	MJ-26	78756	4000-4199
LEWIS LN	Hays Co	702X	MC-10	78610	400-499
LEWIS LN	Travis Co	457E	WS-36	78669	None
LEWIS RD	Travis Co	279Y	WX-52	78641	1-399
LEWIS ST N	Round Rock	376Z	MM-43	78664	100-699
LEWIS ST S	Round Rock	376Z	MM-43	78664	100-199

STREET NAME	CITY or COUNTY	MAPSCO GRID	AUSTIN GRID	ZIP CODE	BLOCK RANGE O/E
LEWIS CARROLL LN	Travis Co	467L	MP-35	78660	14400-14499
LEWIS MOUNTAIN DR	Travis Co	641N	MA-17	78737	8000-8299
	Travis Co	640R	WZ-17	78737	8300-8599
LEWOOD CIR	Austin	643H	MF-18	78745	2100-2199
LEWOOD DR	Austin	643H	MF-18	78745	5600-5899
LEXFIELD LN	Cedar Park	372K	MC-44	78613	2200-2299
LEXINGTON CV	Lago Vista	429W	WW-37	78645	20300-20399
LEXINGTON DR	Hays Co	639T	WW-16	78737	100-199
LEXINGTON RD	Austin	525N	MJ-29	78757	6600-6899
LEXINGTON RD E	Elgin	534J	EC-29	78621	None
LEXINGTON RD W	Elgin	534J	EC-29	78621	None
LEXINGTON ST	Manor	529L	MT-29	78653	None
	Travis Co	529G	MT-30	78653	13000-13499
LEXINGTON ST	Taylor	352D	MZ-48	76574	800-1199
	Taylor	322Z	MZ-49	76574	1200-1899
LEXINGTON ST N	Manor	529Q	MT-29	78653	100-999
LEXINGTON ST S	Manor	529Y	MT-28	78653	100-399
LEXINGTON HILL LN	Travis Co	497H	MP-33	78754	13000-13299
LEXINGTON MEADOW LN	Austin	678J	MQ-14	78617	4900-5099
LEYTON ST	Williamson Co	434K	MG-38	78729	8900-8999
LIATRIS LN	Georgetown	225P	MJ-59	78633	100-199
LIBBY CT	Taylor	322V	MZ-49	76574	None
LIBERTON LN	Austin	498X	MQ-31	78653	5700-5799
LIBERTY	Manor	529X	MS-28	78653	None
LIBERTY AVE E	Round Rock	376Z	MM-43	78664	100-1199
LIBERTY AVE W	Round Rock	376Y	MM-43	78664	100-499
LIBERTY LN	Lago Vista	429W	WW-37	78645	4200-4699
LIBERTY ST	Austin	585B	MJ-24	78705	3200-3799
LIBERTY ST	Hutto	349Y	MT-46	78634	100-399
LIBERTY FARMS DR	Travis Co	527C	MP-30	78754	11000-11299
LIBERTY GROTTO CT	Lago Vista	429M	WX-38	78645	6700-6799
LIBERTY HILL LN	Williamson Co	280A	WY-54	78642	100-399
LIBERTY OAKS BLVD	Cedar Park	403P	ME-42	78613	1100-1899
LIBERTY PARK DR	Austin	584W	MG-22	78746	1000-1299
LIBERTY WALK	Williamson Co	375Y	MK-43	78681	8000-8399
	Williamson Co	405F	MJ-42	78681	8400-8599
LIBYAN CIR	Austin	644J	MG-17	78745	5600-5699
LIBYAN DR	Austin	644J	MG-17	78745	5600-5899
	Austin	643R	MF-17	78745	5900-6699
LICK CREEK TRL	Travis Co	486H	WR-33	78669	3200-3599
LICORICE LN	Travis Co	436F	ML-39	78728	3900-3999
	Williamson Co	436F	ML-39	78728	4000-4199
LIDELL ST	Hutto	349V	MT-46	78634	100-399
LIDO	Lakeway	519E	WW-30	78734	100-399
LIFFEY CV	Pflugerville	437C	MP-39	78660	17700-17799
LIFFEY DR	Pflugerville	437C	MP-39	78660	1000-1299
LIFFORD CT	Austin	497N	MN-32	78753	1400-1499
LIGHTFOOT CT	Hutto	380N	MU-44	78634	100-199
LIGHTFOOT DR	Round Rock	406S	ML-40	78681	1700-1899
LIGHTFOOT TRL	Austin	643L	MF-17	78745	2400-2699
LIGHTHOUSE LN	Jonestown	430D	WZ-39	78645	None
LIGHTHOUSE LANDING DR					
	Jonestown	430Q	WZ-38	78645	7700-7799
LIGHTNING BUG LN	Austin	702F	MC-12	78739	2700-2799
LIGHTNING RANCH RD	Williamson Co	254N	MG-56	78628	1-599
	Williamson Co	253V	MF-55	78628	600-1299
LIGHTSEY RD	Austin	614Y	MH-19	78704	100-599
	Austin	614P	MG-20	78704	1300-1899
	Austin	614N	MG-20	78704	1900-2199
LIGHTWOOD CV	Austin	672D	MD-15	78748	9400-9499
LIGHTWOOD LOOP	Austin	672D	MD-15	78748	9300-9499
LIGUSTRUM CV	Austin	493V	MF-31	78750	6900-6999
LIKENESS RD	Travis Co	457X	WS-34	78669	1200-1599
LILAC DR	Round Rock	376R	MM-44	78664	600-699
LILAC LN	Austin	643U	MF-16	78745	7100-7299
LILAC LN	Cedar Park	402Y	MD-40	78613	1800-1899
LILLEY BROOK CV	Austin	404J	MG-41	78717	14400-14499
LILLIAN LN	Austin	642Q	MD-17	78749	4000-4099
LILLIE LN	Taylor	352C	MZ-48	76574	2100-2399
LILLIE ROBYN LN	Buda	732X	MC-7	78610	100-299
LILLY ST	Buda	762D	MD-6	78610	100-199
LILY LAKE LOOP	Austin	587G	MP-24	78724	7800-7899
LILY TERRACE	Austin	616S	ML-19	78741	1100-1399
LIMA DR	Travis Co	560J	MU-26	78653	11800-12199
LIME CV	Travis Co	408P	MQ-41	78664	None
LIME CREEK RD	Cedar Park	402N	MC-41	78641	13100-13399
	Travis Co	401X	MA-40	78641	9100-12199
	Travis Co	402N	MC-41	78641	12200-12899
	Village of Volente	431F	MA-39	78641	7700-9099
	Williamson Co	402N	MC-41	78613	12900-13099
LIME KILN DR	Cedar Park	374R	MH-44	78613	None
LIMERICK AVE	Austin	466S	ML-34	78758	12300-12399
	Austin	466N	ML-35	78758	12400-12499
	Austin	466N	ML-35	78727	12500-12699
LIMERICK LN	Leander	342U	MD-46	78641	300-1999
LIMERICK LN	West Lake Hills	583C	MF-24	78746	1-99
LIME ROCK DR	Round Rock	406F	ML-42	78681	600-2099
LIMEROCK HOLLOW	Austin	675A	MJ-15	78744	5700-5799
LIME STONE CIR	Austin	524K	MG-29	78731	4600-4699
LIMESTONE LN	Cedar Park	372U	MD-43	78613	1400-1199
LIMESTONE LN	Williamson Co	285G	MK-54	78628	200-299
LIMESTONE PL	Travis Co	491A	MA-33	78734	4700-4799
LIMESTONE TRL	Hays Co	639L	WX-17	78737	100-599
LIMESTONE COMMERCIAL DR					
	Pflugerville	438C	MR-39	78660	18600-18999
	Pflugerville	408Y	MR-40	78660	19000-19199
LIMESTONE SHOALS CT	Georgetown	196N	ML-62	78628	200-299
LIMEWOOD CT	Austin	465Q	MK-35	78727	4400-4499
LIMMER LOOP	Hutto	349P	MS-47	78634	2900-3399
	Hutto	350U	MV-46	78634	4000-4399
	Williamson Co	348L	MR-47	78665	1-899
	Williamson Co	349J	MS-47	78634	1300-1599
	Williamson Co	349P	MS-47	78634	2000-2899
	Williamson Co	349P	MS-47	78634	3400-3799
	Williamson Co	350U	MV-46	78634	3800-3999
	Williamson Co	350U	MV-46	78634	4400-6099
LIMON LN	Austin	614U	MH-19	78704	700-899
LIMONCILLO CT	Austin	463D	MF-36	78750	11200-11299
LIMONCILLO DR	Austin	463D	MF-36	78750	9200-9399
LIMPIA CREEK DR	Pflugerville	407X	MN-40	78664	17500-17799
LIN LN	Travis Co	486G	WR-33	78669	3400-3699
LINARIA CV	Austin	494C	MH-33	78759	5900-5999
LINARIA LN	Austin	494C	MH-33	78759	5800-5899
LINCOLN AVE	Pflugerville	437V	MP-37	78660	1200-1399
LINCOLN CV	Lago Vista	429W	WW-37	78645	19900-20299
LINCOLN ST	Austin	585Y	MK-22	78702	800-1199
LINCOLN ST	Bastrop	745A	EE-9	78602	100-199

L

STREET NAME	CITY or COUNTY	MAPSCO GRID	AUSTIN GRID	ZIP CODE	BLOCK RANGE O/E
LINCOLNSHIRE DR	Austin	496B	ML-33	78758	11900-12099
LINCOLNS SPARROW CV	Pflugerville	438J	MQ-38	78660	1100-1199
LINDA CT	Georgetown	316A	ML-51	78628	100-199
LINDA LN	Austin	556K	ML-26	78723	6100-6599
LINDA LN	Williamson Co	379E	MS-45	78634	1-1099
LINDA LEE CV	Round Rock	348S	MQ-46	78665	3000-3099
LINDA VISTA	Travis Co	677S	MN-13	78617	10500-11099
LINDBERG LN	Lago Vista	459A	WW-36	78645	4300-4499
LINDELL AVE	Austin	614R	MH-20	78704	2100-2299
LINDELL LN	Travis Co	558H	MR-27	78653	8700-10399
LINDEMAN LN	Travis Co	370T	WY-43	78641	19700-21599
	Travis Co	369M	WX-44	78641	21600-21899
LINDEMAN LOOP	Travis Co	369M	WX-44	78641	11600-11799
LINDEN LOOP	Cedar Park	373U	MF-43	78613	700-1099
LINDEN LOOP	Travis Co	708R	MR-11	78617	8100-8299
	Travis Co	708V	MR-10	78617	8400-8599
LINDEN RD	Travis Co	709J	MS-11	78617	7700-8199
	Travis Co	708U	MR-10	78617	8200-8999
LINDEN ST	Austin	615H	MK-21	78702	100-499
	Austin	586W	ML-22	78702	900-1199
LINDEN ST	Bastrop	715W	EE-10	78602	400-1299
LINDENWOOD CIR	Austin	524D	MH-30	78731	7800-7899
LINDER CT	Austin	645C	MK-18	78741	2500-2599
LINDERO PASS	Georgetown	195K	MJ-62	78633	900-999
LINDO LOOP	Williamson Co	345T	MJ-46	78681	4000-4399
LINDSEY CV	Austin	673E	ME-15	78748	2600-2699
LINDSEY LN	Williamson Co	224V	MH-58	78633	100-199
LINDSEY HILL LN	Travis Co	497H	MP-33	78754	13000-13299
LINDSHIRE LN	Austin	672R	MD-14	78748	9900-10699
LINFORD DR	Austin	497G	MP-33	78753	12600-12799
LINGER LN	Austin	616G	MM-21	78725	700-1099
LINK AVE	Austin	555L	MK-26	78751	5300-5599
	Austin	555G	MK-27	78752	5700-5899
LINK RD	Travis Co	459R	WX-35	78645	17800-17999
LINK ST	Elgin	533M	EB-29	78621	100-199
LINKHILL DR	Travis Co	577M	WT-23	78720	17700-18099
LINKMEADOW DR	Austin	672H	MD-15	78748	9200-9599
LINKS CT	Village of the Hills	519P	WW-29	78738	1-99
LINKS LN	Round Rock	408C	MR-42	78664	3800-3999
	Travis Co	408C	MR-42	78664	4000-4199
	Williamson Co	408C	MR-42	78664	3900-3999
LINKVIEW DR	Travis Co	577M	WT-23	78720	17700-18099
LINKWOOD DR	Travis Co	577M	WT-23	78720	17600-17799
LINNET DR	Austin	643S	ME-16	78745	3000-3199
LINSCOMB AVE	Austin	614C	MH-21	78704	1600-1899
LINSCOMB DR	Travis Co	489R	WX-32	78734	1000-1099
LINTON DR	Austin	673L	MF-14	78748	8800-8899
LINVILLE RIDGE LN	Travis Co	409W	MS-40	78660	2300-2899
LION DR	Leander	342F	MC-48	78641	400-799
LION-HEART DR	Cedar Park	402Y	MD-40	78613	1700-1899
LION'S DEN	Leander	342X	MC-46	78641	1600-1799
LIONS LAIR	Leander	341X	MA-46	78641	1100-1399
	Leander	371B	MA-45	78641	1400-1599
LIPAN TRL	Travis Co	522S	MC-28	78733	900-2099
LIPANES TRL	Travis Co	522N	MC-29	78733	2000-2199
LIPIZZAN CT	Travis Co	491X	MA-31	78732	12700-12799
LIPIZZAN DR	Travis Co	491X	MA-31	78732	2400-2599
LIPOA DR	Bastrop Co	775A	EE-6	78602	100-199
LIPSCOMB ST	Austin	555X	MJ-25	78705	3200-3299
LIPTON LN	Travis Co	467R	MP-35	78660	14600-14999
LIPTON LOOP	Austin	678N	MQ-14	78617	12900-13599
LIRIOPE CV	Austin	433V	MF-37	78750	9900-10099
LIRIOPE LN	Buda	763T	ME-4	78610	100-199
LISA CV	Travis Co	522S	MC-28	78733	10300-10399
LISA DR	Travis Co	521Z	MB-28	78733	200-1599
LISA DR E	Austin	525Z	MK-28	78752	100-299
LISA DR W	Austin	525Z	MK-28	78752	100-299
LISA RAE DR	Round Rock	407G	MP-42	78665	1400-1499
LISCIO CV	Georgetown	226Q	MM-59	78628	400-499
LISCIO LOOP	Georgetown	226P	ML-59	78628	100-399
LISHILL CV	Austin	644K	MG-17	78745	5400-5499
LISI ANNE DR	Austin	404D	MH-42	78717	9400-9699
	Austin	374Z	MH-43	78717	9700-10199
LISMORE LN	Austin	498E	MQ-33	78660	13100-13599
LISSY LN	Hays Co	607R	WT-20	78620	100-599
LIT CANDLE CV	Leander	341D	MB-48	78641	1501-1699 O
LITT RD	Travis Co	366Y	WR-43	78654	28500-28899
LITTIG RD	Bastrop Co	533T	EA-28	78621	100-499
	Bastrop Co	562D	MZ-27	78621	500-699
	Travis Co	530Z	MW-28	78653	14100-14499
	Travis Co	561A	MW-27	78653	14500-17299
	Travis Co	562E	MY-27	78653	17300-18099
	Travis Co	562E	MY-27	78621	18100-19199
LITTLE LN	Lago Vista	429B	WW-39	78645	20900-21099
LITTLE LOOP	Lago Vista	399X	WW-40	78645	21100-21299
LITTLE BARTON DR	Hays Co	636G	WR-18	78620	100-399
LITTLE BARTON LN	Travis Co	550W	WY-25	78738	13000-13099
LITTLE BEAR CV	Travis Co	703P	ME-11	78652	400-499
LITTLE BEAR RD	Hays Co	701X	MA-10	78610	800-1599
LITTLE BEAVER TRL	Travis Co	490V	WZ-31	78734	2000-2399
LITTLE BEND DR	Georgetown	286W	ML-52	78628	100-199
LITTLE BEND RD	West Lake Hills	553X	ME-25	78746	1-99
LITTLE BLUE STEM CV	Travis Co	550W	WY-25	78738	12700-12799
LITTLE BULL CV	Austin	524E	MG-30	78731	6000-6099
LITTLE CREEK CIR	Travis Co	577V	WT-22	78720	9900-10499
LITTLE CREEK CV	Williamson Co	403W	ME-40	78613	2400-2499
LITTLECREEK LN	Leander	341D	MB-48	78641	1600-1999
LITTLE CREEK TRL	Austin	675A	MJ-15	78744	5900-5999
LITTLE CREEK TRL	Travis Co	486V	WR-31	78669	4400-4799
	Travis Co	486Z	WR-31	78669	4800-5299
LITTLE CYPRESS CV	Georgetown	225A	MJ-60	78633	900-999
LITTLE CYPRESS LN	Austin	675J	MJ-14	78744	5500-5799
LITTLE DEER TRL	Georgetown	227J	MN-59	78626	7700-7899
LITTLE DEER CROSSING	Austin	611Q	MB-20	78736	8000-8299
LITTLE DIPPER PATH	Travis Co	521E	MA-30	78732	12700-12999
LITTLE EAGLE CT	Elgin	503X	EA-31	78621	None
LITTLE ELM TRL	Cedar Park	403N	ME-41	78613	1500-1999
	Cedar Park	433F	ME-39	78613	2400-3599
	Williamson Co	403W	ME-40	78613	2000-2399
	Williamson Co	403W	ME-40	78613	2000-2399
LITTLE ELM TRL E	Cedar Park	403L	MF-41	78613	100-399
LITTLE ELM WAY	Williamson Co	349B	MS-48	78634	100-299
LITTLE ELM PARK	Austin	526A	ML-30	78758	1000-1199
LITTLE EMILY WAY	Austin	497E	MN-33	78753	12300-12399
LITTLE FATIMA LN	Austin	497K	MN-32	78753	12200-12399
LITTLEFIELD ST	Austin	586A	ML-24	78723	1900-1999
LITTLE FOX TRL	Travis Co	490M	WZ-32	78734	14700-14799

STREET NAME	CITY or COUNTY	MAPSCO GRID	AUSTIN GRID	ZIP CODE	BLOCK RANGE O/E
LITTLE GABRIEL RIVER DR					
	Williamson Co	279J	WW-53	78642	100-399
LITTLE GULL DR	Travis Co	434G	MH-39	78729	13400-13499
LITTLE HILL CIR	Austin	587J	MN-23	78725	4500-4799
LITTLE JOHN LN	Austin	615S	MJ-19	78704	2400-2699
	Austin	614Z	MH-19	78704	2700-2799
LITTLE LAKE RD	Williamson Co	409A	MS-42	78634	100-299
	Williamson Co	379W	MS-43	78634	300-499
LITTLE LAURA DR	Austin	495X	MJ-31	78757	8600-8899
LITTLE OAK CIR	Lago Vista	429B	WW-39	78645	7400-7499
LITTLE OAK DR	Austin	496L	MM-32	78753	600-799
LITTLE PEBBLE DR	Austin	495R	MK-32	78758	10300-10599
LITTLE POOL RD	Hays Co	762E	MC-6	78610	100-199
LITTLE RIVER RD	Williamson Co	279F	WW-54	78642	1-499
LITTLE SKY DR	Travis Co	560K	MU-26	78653	18400-18599
LITTLE TEXAS LN	Austin	644T	MG-16	78745	100-1199
LITTLE THICKET RD	Travis Co	609J	WW-20	78736	10300-10999
	Travis Co	608R	WV-20	78736	11000-11299
LITTLETON DR	Hays Co	639U	WX-16	78737	100-399
LITTLE TREE BEND	Williamson Co	402U	MD-40	78613	2200-2399
LITTLE VALLEY CV	Austin	615W	MJ-19	78741	2700-2799
LITTLE VALLEY RD	Cedar Park	343Z	MF-46	78641	None
	Williamson Co	344W	MG-46	78641	5000-5099
LITTLE WALNUT DR	Austin	526J	ML-29	78753	100-8999
LITTLE WALNUT PKWY	Austin	526E	ML-30	78758	8900-9199
LITTLE WIND CV	Travis Co	492Q	MD-32	78730	10600-10699
LITTON LN	Bastrop Co	741T	MW-7	78612	100-199
LIVE OAK	Travis Co	370G	WZ-45	78641	20500-20699
LIVE OAK	Williamson Co	222T	MC-58	78642	1-799
LIVE OAK AVE	Travis Co	430Q	WZ-38	78645	7500-7799
LIVE OAK CIR	Austin	554G	MH-27	78731	3300-3399
LIVE OAK CIR	Hays Co	638N	WU-17	78620	400-499
LIVE OAK CIR	Lago Vista	429B	WW-39	78645	6900-6999
LIVE OAK CIR	West Lake Hills	553X	ME-25	78746	800-1099
LIVE OAK CIR	Williamson Co	375E	MJ-45	78681	2100-2399
LIVE OAK CT	Bastrop Co	745V	EF-7	78602	100-199
LIVE OAK CV	Williamson Co	374H	MH-45	78681	5400-5599
LIVE OAK DR	Cedar Park	403E	ME-42	78613	500-899
LIVE OAK DR	Georgetown	286T	ML-52	78628	100-199
LIVE OAK DR	Hays Co	701Q	MB-11	78652	1000-2099
LIVE OAK DR	Lago Vista	429B	WW-39	78645	6800-7099
LIVEOAK DR	Travis Co	523Q	MF-29	78746	6300-6899
LIVE OAK DR	Travis Co	309U	WX-49	78641	14400-14599
LIVE OAK DR	Williamson Co	311B	MA-51	78641	1200-1599
LIVE OAK LN	Burnet Co	455A	WN-36	78669	None
LIVE OAK LN	Hays	702W	MC-10	78610	12600-12699
LIVEOAK LN	Travis Co	591N	MW-23	78653	20700-20899
LIVE OAK RD	Williamson Co	281X	MA-52	78641	900-1399
	Williamson Co	311B	MA-51	78641	1400-1599
LIVE OAK ST	Buda	762C	MD-6	78610	100-799
	Buda	732Y	MD-7	78610	2500-3099
LIVE OAK ST	Williamson Co	345W	MJ-46	78681	2800-3199
LIVE OAK ST E	Austin	614R	MH-20	78704	100-399
	Austin	615S	MJ-19	78704	400-1499
LIVE OAK ST E	Hutto	349Z	MT-46	78634	100-399
LIVE OAK ST W	Austin	614L	MH-20	78704	100-1299
LIVE OAK ST W	Hutto	349Z	MT-46	78634	100-499
LIVE OAK TRL	Williamson Co	192N	MC-62	78642	1-1399
LIVE OAK RIDGE RD	West Lake Hills	583B	ME-24	78746	800-1099
	West Lake Hills	553X	ME-25	78746	1100-1299
LIVE OAK TRAILS	Williamson Co	196C	MM-63	78628	30100-30399
LIVERPOOL DR	Austin	644L	MH-17	78745	100-299
LIVINGSTON CV	Lago Vista	459A	WW-36	78645	20100-20199
LIVONIA DR	Buda	763K	ME-5	78610	2000-2299
LIVORNO CV	Travis Co	432L	MD-38	78613	2900-2999
LIZ LN	Williamson Co	224V	MH-58	78633	100-299
LIZZIE ST	Taylor	352H	MZ-48	76574	200-899
LLANO CV	Georgetown	196W	ML-61	78628	100-199
LLANO ST	Austin	615H	MK-21	78702	1-99
LLANO ST	Manor	529R	MT-29	78653	500-599
LLANO ESTACADO LN	Austin	464X	MG-34	78759	9700-9899
LLIO CT	Bastrop Co	745Z	EF-7	78602	100-199
LLOYD LN	Elgin	534E	EC-30	78621	800-899
LLOYDMINISTER WAY	Cedar Park	372K	MC-44	78613	1600-1899
LLOYD'S LN	Austin	643L	MF-17	78745	5900-5999
LOADSTONE CV	Austin	587A	MN-24	78724	5400-5499
LOASA CV	Travis Co	582P	MC-23	78735	7500-7599
LOB CV	Travis Co	522B	MC-30	78730	4000-4099
LOBELIA DR	Austin	434Y	MH-37	78729	7500-7599
LOBELIA DR	Travis Co	432D	MD-39	78613	2100-2199
	Williamson Co	432D	MD-39	78613	1800-2099
LOBO ST	Cedar Park	373T	ME-43	78613	500-799
LOBO MOUNTAIN LN	Pflugerville	407X	MN-40	78664	1500-1799
LOBOS LN	Bastrop Co	711F	MW-12	78612	100-199
LOCHALINE LOOP	Travis Co	437C	MP-39	78660	1100-1599
LOCHAN ORA DR	Travis Co	489R	WX-32	78734	16900-17099
LOCHINVAR ST	Austin	642M	MD-17	78749	7000-7299
LOCH LINNHE CV	Travis Co	437C	MP-39	78660	1000-1099
LOCH LINNHE LOOP	Travis Co	437C	MP-39	78660	17400-17999
LOCH LOMMOND ST	Austin	642M	MD-17	78749	6900-7299
LOCH NESS CV	Austin	463H	MF-36	78750	10700-10799
LOCH NESS LN	Travis Co	488Y	WV-31	78669	2100-2199
LOCHRIDGE DR	Austin	496E	ML-33	78758	11700-11899
LOCHWOOD BEND CT	Bee Cave	550Y	WZ-25	78733	4000-4099
LOCKE LN	Austin	614U	MH-19	78704	2800-3399
LOCKERBIE CT	Austin	463B	ME-36	78750	10200-10299
LOCKERBIE DR	Austin	463C	MF-36	78750	10400-10699
LOCKHART DR	Austin	615N	MJ-20	78704	300-599
LOCKHART ST N	Manor	529U	MT-28	78653	100-699
LOCKHART ST S	Manor	529U	MT-28	78653	100-199
LOCKLEVEN CV	Austin	463M	MF-35	78750	10200-10299
LOCKLEVEN LOOP	Austin	463M	MF-35	78750	9000-9099
LOCKWOOD CV	Austin	556Q	MM-26	78723	2200-2299
LOCKWOOD RD	Travis Co	560T	MU-25	78653	18100-19999
	Travis Co	561S	MW-25	78653	20000-20499
LOCKWOOD SPRINGS RD	Travis Co	590R	MV-23	78653	8600-8899
	Travis Co	591J	MW-23	78653	8900-9399
LOCUST CV	Williamson Co	433E	ME-39	78613	1800-1898 E
LOCUST ST	Bastrop	715X	EE-10	78602	700-899
LODESTONE CIR	Cedar Park	372R	MD-44	78613	200-299
LODGE CT	Austin	525D	MK-30	78758	9000-9099
LODGE VIEW LN	Austin	524E	MG-30	78731	5000-5199
LODI DR	Williamson Co	405N	MJ-41	78717	8600-8699
LODOSA DR	Cedar Park	402D	MD-42	78613	900-999
LOEFFLER DR	Cedar Park	402G	MD-42	78613	200-298 E
LOESCH DR	Elgin	533H	EB-30	78621	200-299
LOFTON CLIFF DR	Austin	678J	MQ-14	78617	13000-13199

STREET NAME	CITY or COUNTY	MAPSCO GRID	AUSTIN GRID	ZIP CODE	BLOCK RANGE O/E
LOFTY LN	Williamson Co	375P	MJ-44	78681	8200-8499
LOGAN DR	Leander	311R	MB-50	78641	1200-1399
LOGAN DR	Round Rock	407B	MN-42	78664	1800-2299
LOGAN RD	Georgetown	226L	MM-59	78628	400-499
LOGAN ST E	Round Rock	406D	MM-42	78664	100-1199
	Round Rock	407A	MN-42	78664	1200-1499
LOGAN ST W	Round Rock	406C	MM-42	78664	100-299
LOGANBERRY CT	Austin	674E	MG-15	78745	200-399
LOGANBERRY DR	Austin	674A	MG-15	78745	7200-7699
LOGAN RANCH RD	Williamson Co	226L	MM-59	78628	100-399
LOGANS LN	Travis Co	553V	MF-25	78746	600-699
LOGANS WAY	Williamson Co	224J	MG-59	78633	1000-1099
LOGANS HOLLOW DR	Travis Co	553V	MF-25	78746	1800-1899
LOGGERHEAD CV	Williamson Co	282N	MC-53	78641	None
LOGISTICS LN	Austin	647W	MN-16	78719	10100-10599
	Austin	646Z	MM-16	78719	None
LOGUE CV	Leander	342B	MC-48	78641	600-699
LOGWOOD DR	Austin	525F	MJ-30	78757	8000-8199
LOHMAN FORD RD	Lago Vista	459Y	WX-34	78645	2600-3399
	Lago Vista	459G	WX-36	78645	4100-4799
	Lago Vista	429C	WX-39	78645	4800-7899
	Travis Co	489B	WW-33	78645	200-1699
	Travis Co	459Y	WX-34	78645	1700-2599
	Travis Co	459G	WX-36	78645	3400-4099
LOHMANS CROSSING RD	Lakeway	519C	WX-30	78734	800-1599
	Lakeway	519L	WX-29	78734	1600-2499
LOHMANS SPUR	Lakeway	519U	WX-28	78734	1900-2499
LOIRE CT	Austin	674M	MH-14	78744	6800-6899
LOIS LN	Bastrop Co	711P	MW-11	78612	100-199
LOIS LN	Travis Co	486G	WR-33	78669	24200-24799
LOIS LN	Williamson Co	433R	MF-38	78750	13400-13599
LOLA DR E	Austin	526N	ML-29	78753	100-399
LOLA DR W	Austin	526N	ML-29	78753	100-299
LOLLIPOP LN	Cedar Park	373T	ME-43	78613	200-399
LOMA DR	Austin	615P	MJ-20	78741	1200-1399
LOMA LINDA	West Lake Hills	553V	MF-25	78746	700-899
LOMA LINDA ST	Buda	762H	MD-6	78610	300-499
LOMA VERDE ST	Buda	762H	MD-6	78610	300-399
LOMBARD DR	Leander	342V	MD-46	78641	100-299
LOMBARDI WAY	Travis Co	432L	MD-38	78613	3000-3199
LOMBARDIA DR	Lakeway	490W	WY-31	78734	100-299
LOMITA DR	Leander	342J	MC-47	78641	1700-1799
LOMITA DR	Travis Co	550R	WZ-26	78733	3100-3199
LOMITA VERDE CIR	Austin	642J	MC-17	78749	5600-5999
LOMITA VERDE CT	Austin	642N	MC-17	78749	8900-8999
LONCOLA CT	Round Rock	376A	ML-45	78681	2700-2899
LONDON DR	Austin	643F	ME-18	78745	5900-6399
LONDON LN	Georgetown	287S	MN-52	78626	1000-1099
LONDON LN	Travis Co	432H	MD-39	78613	2200-2399
LONDON RD	Round Rock	377N	MN-44	78664	1300-1399
LONDON BRIDGE	Austin	464K	MG-35	78759	7500-7599
LONDONDERRY DR	Leander	342U	MD-46	78641	1800-1999
LONDONSHIRE LN	Austin	671C	MB-15	78739	10600-10899
LONE BUCK PASS	Cedar Park	402M	MD-41	78613	800-1099
LONE CEDAR CT	Lakeway	519L	WX-29	78734	100-199
LONE CYPRESS CV	Hays Co	666V	WR-13	78619	100-199
LONE MESA	Austin	494R	MH-32	78759	8400-8499
LONE MOUNTAIN PASS	Jonestown	371N	MA-44	78641	12300-12899
LONE OAK DR	Austin	615N	MJ-20	78704	300-599
LONE OAK DR	Leander	342Q	MD-47	78641	1700-1999
LONE OAK TRL	Sunset Valley	643C	MF-18	78745	1-99
	Sunset Valley	613Y	MF-19	78745	None
LONE OAKS TRL	Williamson Co	375K	MJ-44	78681	3900-4099
LONE PINE LN	Austin	704L	MH-11	78747	10200-10399
LONE RIDER TRL	Bee Cave	549Z	WX-25	78738	13300-13999
LONESOME CT	Travis Co	370N	WY-44	78641	21400-21499
LONESOME CV	Round Rock	406H	MM-42	78664	900-999
LONESOME CV	Travis Co	370N	WY-44	78641	11700-11799
LONESOME LN	Travis Co	706H	MM-12	78617	7700-7899
LONESOME TRL	Georgetown	256K	ML-56	78628	3200-3499
LONESOME CREEK	Jonestown	371T	MA-43	78641	12800-12999
LONESOME DOVE CV	Austin	434U	MH-37	78729	7800-7899
LONESOME LILLY WAY	Pflugerville	408W	MQ-40	78660	600-699
	Pflugerville	407Z	MP-40	78660	1000-1099
LONESOME VALLEY CT	Austin	524P	MG-29	78731	4200-4299
LONESOME VALLEY TRL	Austin	524P	MG-29	78731	5900-6199
LONE STAR BLVD	Hutto	379H	MT-45	78634	100-599
LONE STAR CIR	Bastrop Co	744S	EC-7	78602	100-299
LONE STAR CT	Hutto	379H	MT-45	78634	6000-6099
LONE STAR DR	Cedar Park	373S	ME-43	78613	300-499
	Cedar Park	372U	MD-43	78613	500-1399
LONE STAR LN	Travis Co	489M	WX-32	78734	17000-17099
LONE STAR WAY	Georgetown	226E	ML-60	78633	100-299
LONE STAR RANCH BLVD					
	Pflugerville	438M	MR-38	78660	18500-18599
LONE TREE CT	Cedar Park	403E	ME-42	78613	700-899
LONE TREE DR	Travis Co	590L	MV-23	78653	8600-9099
LONE TREE PATH	Williamson Co	346G	MM-48	78665	4400-4499
LONE TREE HOLLOW	Hays Co	762Z	MD-4	78610	100-199
LONE WOLF CT	Dripping Springs	636P	WQ-17	78620	100-299
LONE WOLF DR	Williamson Co	343W	ME-46	78641	16300-16599
LONG CT	Austin	523H	MF-30	78730	5700-5999
LONG CV	Round Rock	378X	MQ-43	78664	1000-2099
LONG ARROW CANYON	Bee Cave	549V	WX-25	78738	5100-5199
LONG BAY CV	Travis Co	521C	MB-30	78732	12200-12299
LONG BOW	Leander	342W	MC-46	78641	None
LONG BOW CV	Bastrop Co	743A	EA-9	78602	None
LONG BOW LN	Austin	614V	MH-19	78704	100-699
	Austin	615S	MJ-19	78704	700-899
LONGBOW TRL	Travis Co	490R	WZ-32	78734	2700-2899
LONG BRANCH DR	Georgetown	287S	MN-52	78626	1300-1599
LONG BRANCH DR	Travis Co	609N	WW-20	78736	10900-11499
LONGBRANCH DR	Travis Co	490Y	WZ-31	78734	14700-14999
LONG CANYON DR	Travis Co	493X	ME-31	78730	8000-8799
LONG CHAMP CT	Austin	523Y	MF-28	78746	6000-6099
LONG CHAMP DR	Austin	523Y	MF-28	78746	3700-4499
LONG CREEK RD	Hays Co	639K	WW-17	78737	1-99
LONG DAY CV	Austin	527C	MP-30	78754	10900-10999
LONG DAY DR	Austin	527G	MP-30	78754	2900-3699
LONGDRAW DR	Williamson Co	375U	MK-43	78681	8100-8399
LONGFELLOW CV	Lago Vista	459B	WW-36	78645	4400-4499
LONG HILL CT	Travis Co	370J	WY-44	78641	11900-11999
LONG HILL DR	Travis Co	370J	WY-44	78641	21500-21699
	Travis Co	369M	WX-44	78641	21700-21799
LONG HOLLOW TRL	Travis Co	309U	WX-49	78641	24300-24999
LONG HOLLOW LOOP	Travis Co	309T	WW-49	78641	13800-14299
LONG HOLLOW RD	Bastrop Co	563T	EA-25	78621	100-299

L

STREET NAME	CITY or COUNTY	MAPSCO GRID	AUSTIN GRID	ZIP CODE	BLOCK RANGE O/E
LONGHOLLOW RD	Bastrop Co	767P	MN-5	78616	None
	Caldwell Co	767P	MN-5	78616	1-1199
	Mustang Ridge	767P	MN-5	78616	1400-1599
LONGHORN BLVD	Austin	495P	MJ-32	78758	2600-3399
LONGHORN DR	Austin	466J	ML-35	78727	12700-12899
LONGHORN DR	Pflugerville	467C	MP-36	78660	None
LONGHORN DR	Williamson Co	375A	MJ-45	78681	1-99
LONGHORN LN	Hays Co	638Y	WV-16	78620	100-199
LONGHORN TRL	Georgetown	225C	MK-60	78633	100-199
LONGHORN TRL	Round Rock	346V	MM-46	78665	3400-3699
LONGHORN ACRES ST	Cedar Park	374U	MH-43	78613	3700-3899
LONGHORN CAVERN CV	Georgetown	225V	MK-58	78633	100-199
LONGHORN LANDING	Travis Co	460R	WZ-35	78734	5500-5899
LONGHORN RIDGE RD	Cedar Park	374Q	MH-44	78613	300-398 E
LONGHORN SKYWAY	Travis Co	577L	WT-23	78720	9800-10299
LONG KNIFE CIR	Williamson Co	287H	MP-54	78626	50100-50199
LONG MEADOW DR	Round Rock	376M	MM-44	78664	900-1199
LONG MEADOW DR	Travis Co	467Z	MP-34	78660	13600-13899
LONGMONT LN	Hays Co	639U	WX-16	78737	100-399
LONG POINT CV	Williamson Co	283H	MF-54	78628	100-199
LONG POINT DR	Austin	494Y	MH-31	78731	7500-7799
LONG RIFLE CV	Austin	497N	MN-32	78754	11700-11799
LONG RIFLE DR	Austin	497T	MN-31	78754	1600-1899
LONG SHADOW DR	Travis Co	529H	MT-30	78653	13700-13899
LONG SPUR BLVD E	Austin	526B	ML-30	78753	100-499
LONG SPUR BLVD W	Austin	526B	ML-30	78753	100-799
LONGSPUR DR	Hays Co	732J	MC-8	78610	200-299
LONG SUMMER DR	Austin	527G	MP-30	78754	10800-11299
LONGVALE DR	Williamson Co	434J	MG-38	78729	9300-9599
LONGVIEW RD	Austin	643W	ME-16	78745	7500-8499
LONGVIEW ST	Austin	584H	MH-24	78705	2200-2599
LONG VISTA DR	Pflugerville	436M	MM-38	78728	15400-15899
LONG VOYAGE DR	Austin	527C	MP-30	78754	3400-3499
LONGWEDGE LN	Georgetown	226P	ML-59	78628	100-199
LONG WINTER DR	Austin	497X	MN-31	78754	11000-11399
LONG WOOD AVE	Lakeway	519D	WX-30	78734	100-199
LONG WOOD CV	Lakeway	519H	WX-30	78734	100-199
LONGWOOD LN	Hays Co	639A	WW-18	78737	1-99
LONNIE THOMAS DR	Williamson Co	257K	MN-56	78626	1-199
LONSDALE DR	Williamson Co	434E	MG-39	78729	9800-9899
LOOKOUT CIR	Williamson Co	410P	MU-41	78634	100-599
LOOKOUT CV	Williamson Co	280A	WY-54	78642	300-499
LOOKOUT DR	Williamson Co	280E	WY-54	78642	100-599
LOOKOUT LN	Austin	553C	MF-27	78746	3100-3399
LOOKOUT PT	Lago Vista	428R	WV-38	78654	21600-21699
LOOKOUT BLUFF TERRACE	Austin	611R	MB-20	78735	7200-7399
LOOKOUT HILL CV	Hays Co	638T	WU-16	78620	1000-1099
LOOKOUT MOUNTAIN CV	Austin	524N	MG-29	78731	4700-4799
LOOKOUT MOUNTAIN DR	Austin	524N	MG-29	78731	5800-5999
LOOKOUT RIDGE	Williamson Co	316Q	MM-50	78626	1-199
LOOKOUT RIDGE CV	Travis Co	397N	WS-41	78654	26800-26899
LOOKOUT RIDGE DR	Travis Co	397N	WS-41	78654	4900-5399
LOOKOUT TREE LN	Round Rock	377W	MN-43	78664	400-699
LOOMIS DR	Travis Co	550R	WZ-26	78733	11900-11999
LOON LAKE DR	Travis Co	436Q	MM-38	78728	2600-2699
LOOP CT	Travis Co	553S	ME-25	78746	200-299
LOOP ST	Hays Co	732Z	MD-7	78610	500-599
LOOP ST E	Buda	732Z	MD-7	78610	300-499
	Hays Co	732Z	MD-7	78610	500-599
LOOP ST W	Buda	732Z	MD-7	78610	300-499
LOPA CT	Bastrop Co	775D	EF-6	78602	100-199
LOQUAT LN	Round Rock	377X	MN-43	78664	2300-2399
LORADO DR	Travis Co	617D	MP-21	78725	9900-10199
LORALINDA DR	Austin	526P	ML-29	78753	8100-8699
LORD BYRON CIR	Round Rock	378X	MQ-43	78664	3900-3999
LORD BYRON CIR	Round Rock	408C	MR-42	78664	4000-4099
LORD BYRON CV	Round Rock	408C	MR-42	78664	4000-4199
LORD DERBY DR	Austin	703C	MF-12	78748	10600-10799
LORETO DR	Austin	585J	ML-23	78721	1700-1899
LORI CIR	Bastrop	744D	ED-9	78602	300-399
LORI CIR N	Bastrop	744D	ED-9	78602	400-499
LORI LN	Georgetown	257K	MN-56	78626	None
LORING DR	Austin	433U	MF-37	78750	10400-10699
LORRAIN ST	Austin	584M	MH-23	78703	1000-1599
LORSON LOOP	Round Rock	347J	MN-47	78665	1500-1599
LORYN DR	Hutto	379G	MT-45	78634	100-199
LOS ALAMOS CT	Williamson Co	348N	MQ-47	78665	2800-2899
LOS ALAMOS PASS	Williamson Co	348N	MQ-47	78665	2500-2799
LOS ALTOS DR	Lakeway	519C	WX-30	78734	100-299
LOS ARCOS CV	Austin	641S	MA-16	78739	10900-10999
LOS CIELOS BLVD	Austin	678N	MQ-14	78617	6000-6199
LOS COMANCHEROS RD	Austin	404E	MG-42	78717	11000-11399
LOS DIOS PL	Austin	677R	MP-14	78617	5900-5999
LOS INDIOS CV	Austin	434Y	MH-37	78729	7800-7899
LOS INDIOS TRL	Austin	434Y	MH-37	78729	12200-12499
LOSOYA CT	Hutto	380N	MU-44	78634	600-699
LOS RANCHOS DR	Austin	642Q	MD-17	78749	8000-8599
LOS ROBLES RD	Leander	312S	MC-49	78641	600-799
LOST CV	Travis Co	582L	MD-23	78746	6500-6599
LOST CANYON DR	West Lake Hills	553V	MF-25	78746	700-999
LOST CAVERN CV	Travis Co	672W	MC-13	78739	3800-3899
LOST CEDARS	Williamson Co	225R	MK-59	78633	1-99
LOST CREEK BLVD	Travis Co	583J	ME-23	78746	1100-1299
	Travis Co	582M	MD-23	78746	1300-2599
	Travis Co	582N	MC-23	78735	2600-3799
LOST CREEK CIR	Travis Co	582M	MD-23	78746	6200-6299
LOST CREEK RD	Hays Co	576N	WQ-23	78620	100-1599
LOST HORIZON DR	Austin	494C	MH-33	78759	5600-5999
	Austin	464Y	MH-34	78759	6000-6699
LOST INDIGO TRL	Round Rock	378W	MQ-43	78665	2900-2999
LOST LEDGE PATH	Williamson Co	346H	MM-48	78665	1300-1399
LOST MAPLES LOOP	Cedar Park	373E	ME-45	78613	1700-1899
LOST MAPLES TRL	Austin	703A	ME-12	78748	11100-11499
LOST MAPLES TRL	Georgetown	225V	MK-58	78633	800-899
LOST MEADOW CV	Village of the Hills	519K	WW-29	78738	1-99
LOST MEADOW TRL					
	Village of the Hills	519K	WW-29	78738	1-99
LOST MINE TRL	Leander	372B	MC-45	78641	2400-2699
LOST OAK CV	Williamson Co	254N	MG-56	78628	2800-2899
LOST OASIS HOLLOW	Travis Co	702A	MC-12	78739	3300-3699
	Travis Co	672S	MC-13	78739	3700-4599
LOST PEAK PATH	Georgetown	194V	MH-61	78633	100-299
LOST PINE CV	Travis Co	672W	MC-13	78739	3500-3599
LOST PINES AVE	Bastrop	745M	EF-8	78602	1-99
LOST PINES DR	Bastrop Co	746R	EH-8	78602	200-299
LOST PINES LN	Cedar Park	373E	ME-45	78613	None
LOST RIDGE CIR	Travis Co	401B	MA-42	78641	12900-12999
LOSTRIDGE DR	Austin	494Y	MH-31	78731	4200-4399
LOST RIVER RD	Williamson Co	254U	MH-55	78628	100-399
LOST SPRING	Williamson Co	375L	MK-44	78681	1800-1899
LOST TRAIL CV	Travis Co	493X	ME-31	78730	6000-6099
LOST VALLEY	Austin	643J	ME-17	78745	6700-7099
LOSTWOOD CIR	Austin	702F	MC-12	78748	12200-12499
LOS VISTA DR	Leander	342P	MC-47	78641	500-1099
LOTHIAN DR	Travis Co	432L	MD-38	78613	2700-2899
LOTHIAN DR	Travis Co	467T	MN-34	78660	13600-13999
LOTT AVE	Austin	586U	MM-22	78721	900-1199
	Austin	586Q	MM-23	78721	4800-5199
LOTUS CIR	Hays Co	670W	WY-13	78610	100-399
LOTUS LN	Austin	616C	MM-21	78721	6100-6299
LOU GEHRIG LN	Round Rock	378A	MQ-45	78665	1300-1399
LOUIS AVE	Austin	586Q	MM-23	78721	4700-4999
LOUISE LN	Austin	524Z	MH-28	78757	5600-5799
LOUISE ST	Elgin	534E	EC-30	78621	None
LOUISE ST	Georgetown	287N	MN-53	78626	1600-1899
LOUISE LEE DR	Travis Co	618R	MR-20	78725	3900-4199
LOUIS HENNA BLVD	Round Rock	406V	MM-40	78664	100-599
	Round Rock	407R	MP-41	78664	600-2599
LOUIS HENNA BLVD W	Round Rock	406U	MM-40	78681	100-1499
LOU JOHN ST	Austin	466B	ML-36	78727	2200-2699
LOU NEFF RD	Austin	584U	MH-22	78746	2000-2299
LOUNSBURY PL	Williamson Co	405A	MJ-42	78717	16500-16599
LOURIE ST	Austin	616U	MM-19	78742	800-899
LOVAGE DR	Austin	465H	MK-36	78727	3500-3699
LOVE DR	Hays Co	763S	ME-4	78610	100-599
LOVE BIRD CV	Travis Co	492X	MC-31	78730	10800-10899
LOVE BIRD LN	Travis Co	492X	MC-31	78730	4000-4299
LOVEGRASS LN	Sunset Valley	643B	ME-18	78745	1-99
LOVELAND CV	Austin	583Z	MF-22	78746	3000-3099
LOVELL DR	Austin	586B	ML-24	78723	2600-2999
LOVELY LN	Austin	674M	MH-14	78744	6900-6999
LOVERS LN	Bastrop	745P	EE-8	78602	None
	Bastrop Co	745W	EE-7	78602	1000-1399
	Bastrop Co	775A	EE-6	78602	1400-1499
LOVETT CV	Georgetown	195V	MK-61	78633	100-199
LOVETT LN	Travis Co	402T	MC-40	78613	2500-2799
LOVIE LN	Georgetown	226N	ML-59	78628	100-499
LOVING TRL	Dripping Springs	636R	WR-17	78620	100-399
LOVINGOOD DR	Austin	586J	ML-23	78721	1700-1799
LOVRIDGE CT	Austin	671D	MB-15	78739	10700-10799
LOW BRIDGE LN	Austin	463H	MF-36	78750	10800-11099
LOW BRIM CV	Travis Co	467C	MP-36	78660	900-999
LOWDEN LN	Travis Co	702R	MD-11	78652	12300-13499
LOWDES DR	Austin	643X	ME-16	78745	7700-7999
LOWELL LN N	Travis Co	552L	MD-26	78733	100-499
LOWELL LN S	Travis Co	552Q	MD-26	78733	100-299
LOWER DR	Travis Co	617D	MP-21	78725	3800-4199
LOWER PARK RD	Georgetown	256Z	MM-55	78626	500-699
LOWESWATER LN	Austin	528J	MQ-29	78754	11500-11799
LOW WATER CROSSING RD					
	Travis Co	491J	MA-32	78732	13700-14199
	Travis Co	491J	MA-32	78734	14200-14499
LOXLEY LN	Austin	404C	MH-42	78717	10000-10299
LOYAGA DR	Round Rock	376A	ML-45	78681	2700-2799
LOYOLA DR	Pflugerville	467H	MP-36	78660	100-199
LOYOLA LN	Austin	556L	MM-26	78723	2300-3599
	Austin	557S	MN-25	78723	4600-5499
	Austin	557X	MN-25	78724	5500-7299
	Austin	587D	MP-24	78724	7300-8699
LUA CT E	Bastrop Co	746W	EG-7	78602	100-199
LUA CT W	Bastrop Co	746W	EG-7	78602	100-199
LUBBOCK DR	Georgetown	195Z	MK-61	78633	100-199
LUBBOCK LN	Travis Co	435S	MJ-37	78729	13100-13199
LUCAS DR	Austin	524Y	MH-28	78731	3600-3699
LUCAS LN	Austin	524Y	MH-28	78731	5000-5299
LUCAYAN CV	Lakeway	488Z	WV-31	78734	None
LUCERNE DR	Travis Co	708S	MQ-10	78617	14800-14999
LUCERNE DR	Travis Co	467P	MN-35	78660	None
LUCIAN DR	Travis Co	619N	MS-20	78725	15200-15399
LUCILE RD	Travis Co	550D	WZ-27	78732	10800-10899
LUCINDA DR	Travis Co	592J	MY-23	78621	8400-9099
LUCINDA TERRACE	Georgetown	256A	ML-57	78628	1000-1099
LUCKENBACH LN	Travis Co	435S	MJ-37	78729	6500-6899
LUCKENWALD CV	Williamson Co	405F	MJ-42	78681	8100-8199
LUCKENWALD DR	Williamson Co	405F	MJ-42	78681	16800-16899
LUCKSINGER LN	Austin	644G	MH-18	78745	4400-4599
LUCKY CLOVER LN	Hutto	379M	MT-44	78634	100-299
LUCKY HIT RD	Travis Co	310F	WY-51	78641	16100-16599
LUCY CV	Austin	587B	MN-24	78724	6800-6899
LUCY CV	Hutto	379R	MT-44	78634	100-199
LUCY ST	Round Rock	377E	MN-45	78664	2000-2099
LUDLOW TERRACE	Austin	556N	ML-26	78723	1300-1399
LUEDTKE LN	Pflugerville	439A	MS-39	78660	19100-19299
LUKE LN	Williamson Co	373A	ME-45	78641	700-999
LULING LN	Williamson Co	434M	MH-38	78729	7900-8299
LULLWOOD RD	Austin	555Z	MK-25	78722	4000-4299
LUMBERJACK CT	Bastrop Co	742D	MZ-9	78602	100-199
LUMINOSO LN E	Williamson Co	345T	MJ-46	78681	3000-3399
LUMINOSO LN W	Williamson Co	345W	MJ-46	78681	3400-3699
LUNA DR	Bastrop Co	709L	MT-11	78612	None
LUNA ST	Austin	586K	ML-23	78721	1200-1499
LUNA TRL	Georgetown	226U	MM-58	78628	4000-4499
LUNA MONTANA WAY	Travis Co	462S	MC-34	78732	12900-13199
LUNAR DR	Austin	644W	MG-16	78745	6700-6999
	Austin	674A	MG-15	78745	7000-7699
LUNA VISTA CV	Bastrop Co	737Z	MP-7	78617	100-199
LUNA VISTA DR	Hutto	379M	MT-44	78634	None
	Hutto	380J	MU-44	78634	None
LUNA VISTA DR	Village of the Hills	519K	WW-29	78738	400-599
LUND RD	Bastrop Co	503H	EB-33	78621	100-199
	Bastrop Co	504E	EC-33	78621	200-299
LUND RD N	Travis Co	473Q	EB-35	78615	16600-17999
LUND ST	Austin	614C	MH-21	78704	900-1099
LUNDAY DR	Cedar Park	372Q	MD-44	78613	1500-1599
LUND CARLSON RD	Travis Co	472L	MZ-35	78615	13900-16199
	Travis Co	473T	EA-34	78615	16200-18799
LUNDIE CV	Austin	553A	ME-36	78726	10200-10299
LUPE LN	Travis Co	430A	WY-39	78645	7800-8199
LUPINE LN	Austin	615K	MJ-20	78741	1500-1699
LUPOMONTE CV	Travis Co	523L	MF-29	78730	None
LURA LN	Jonestown	400R	WZ-41	78645	18200-18399
LURAY DR	Williamson Co	403Q	ME-39	78613	1500-1599
LURLYNE CT	Austin	645T	MJ-16	78744	5400-5499
LUTHER DR	Georgetown	286X	ML-52	78628	100-599
	Georgetown	316B	ML-51	78628	600-699
LUTHER LN	Austin	585C	MK-24	78705	900-999
LUTHER PETERSON PL	Round Rock	346Y	MM-46	78665	900-999
LUTON CV	Austin	643F	ME-18	78745	2900-2999
LUVORA CV	Austin	642W	MC-16	78739	9900-9999
LUX ST	Austin	616C	MM-21	78721	5900-5999
LYCKMAN LN	Hays Co	669D	WX-15	78737	10600-10699
LYDIA LN	Round Rock	407H	MP-42	78665	2300-2499
LYDIA ST	Austin	585Y	MK-22	78702	700-1199
LYDIA SPRINGS DR	Travis Co	439T	MS-37	78660	18300-18398 E
LYLE CV	Travis Co	457B	WS-39	78669	24100-24199
LYLE LN	Travis Co	457B	WS-39	78669	800-899
LYLE RD	Austin	647K	MN-17	78617	2600-2899
LYMAN PL	Austin	555F	MJ-27	78756	5100-5299
LYMKO DR	Williamson Co	436F	ML-39	78728	15500-15599
LYNCH LN	Austin	616P	ML-20	78741	6400-6599
LYNCHBURG DR	Travis Co	548S	WU-25	78738	7700-7799
	Travis Co	547V	WT-25	78738	7800-7999
LYNDA SUE ST	Williamson Co	406P	ML-41	78681	1000-1299
LYNDE CV	Pflugerville	437D	MP-39	78660	18000-18099
LYNDHURST ST	Austin	434A	MG-39	78729	13300-13499
LYNDHURST ST	Austin	404S	MG-40	78717	13700-13899
LYNDON DR	Travis Co	491H	MB-33	78732	12500-12699
LYNDON LN	Williamson Co	434L	MH-38	78729	8400-8799
LYNDON B JOHNSON ST	Travis Co	530F	MU-30	78653	13500-13699
LYNN CV	Georgetown	195Z	MK-61	78633	100-199
LYNN CV	Pflugerville	468K	MQ-35	78660	900-999
LYNN LN	Lago Vista	429J	WW-38	78645	6000-6499
LYNN ST	Austin	615G	MK-21	78702	1-99
LYNN ST N	Taylor	322Z	MZ-49	76574	1600-2199
LYNNBROOK DR	Austin	672Q	MD-14	78748	2400-3599
	Travis Co	673S	ME-13	78748	2100-2299
	Travis Co	672V	MD-13	78748	2300-2399
LYNNCREST CV	Austin	433X	ME-37	78726	10600-10699
LYNNDALE DR	Austin	555K	MJ-26	78756	4900-5099
LYNNHAVEN ST	Austin	641Q	MB-17	78749	9500-9599
LYNNVILLE TRL	Austin	466L	MM-35	78727	1600-1799
LYNNWOOD ST	Austin	555E	MJ-27	78756	4900-5099
LYNNWOOD TRL N	Cedar Park	373U	MF-43	78613	100-499
	Cedar Park	373L	MF-44	78613	700-899
LYNNWOOD TRL S	Cedar Park	373Y	MF-43	78613	400-799
LYNRIDGE DR	Austin	556M	MM-26	78723	3000-3199
	Austin	557J	MN-26	78723	3400-3499
LYNSENKO DR	Travis Co	402P	MC-41	78613	1100-1199
LYON CLUB CT	Travis Co	550Q	WZ-26	78733	3400-3499
LYONS RD	Austin	585Z	MK-22	78702	2700-2799
	Austin	586W	ML-22	78702	2800-3699
	Austin	616A	ML-21	78702	3700-4999
LYRA CIR	Austin	645T	MJ-16	78744	4500-4699
LYRIC DR	Austin	674A	MG-15	78745	7100-7199

M

STREET NAME	CITY or COUNTY	MAPSCO GRID	AUSTIN GRID	ZIP CODE	BLOCK RANGE O/E
MAASS LN	Bastrop Co	504G	ED-33	78621	100-199
MABRY CT	Austin	642N	MC-17	78749	5300-5399
MacARTHUR AVE	Lago Vista	458D	WV-36	78645	2300-3499
MACAW DR	Travis Co	432H	MD-39	78613	2200-2399
MACCO RD	Travis Co	489E	WW-33	78645	18600-18699
MACHADO RD	Cedar Park	372Q	MD-44	78613	1200-1399
MACHETE TRL	Williamson Co	434P	MG-38	78729	12700-12799
MACKEN ST	Austin	554T	MG-25	78703	2700-2899
MacKENZIE LN	Williamson Co	432D	MD-39	78613	1600-1799
MacKENZIE WAY	Leander	342F	MC-48	78641	500-599
MACKINAW CROSSING	Jonestown	430T	WY-37	78645	None
MACK'S CANYON DR					
	Village of Volente	461F	MA-36	78641	7200-7599
MACMORA RD	Austin	495R	MK-32	78758	10400-10499
	Austin	496N	ML-32	78758	10500-10899
MACON DR	Williamson Co	402Q	MD-41	78613	2100-2199
MADDEN DR	Pflugerville	407Z	MP-40	78660	17800-17999
MADDUX CT	Travis Co	580G	WZ-24	78738	5300-5399
MADEIRA CV	Williamson Co	343N	ME-47	78641	3300-3399
MADELINE LOOP	Williamson Co	403W	ME-40	78613	2400-2499
MADERA DR	Austin	645E	MJ-18	78741	2200-2299
MADERA LN	Round Rock	377J	MN-44	78664	1600-1699
MADISON AVE	Austin	525Q	MK-29	78757	1200-1999
MADISON CT	Round Rock	344R	MH-47	78681	4000-4099
MADISON CV	Lago Vista	458G	WV-36	78645	20800-20899
MADISON DR	Travis Co	426M	WR-38	78669	None
MADISON DR	Williamson Co	318A	MQ-51	78634	400-699
MADISON LN	Hutto	379R	MT-44	78634	100-299
MADISON ST	Elgin	534P	EC-29	78621	300-899
MADISON MONROE BEND	Travis Co	427X	WS-37	78669	None
MADISON OAKS AVE	Georgetown	286Y	MM-52	78626	100-299
MADISONS CV	Buda	732Q	MD-8	78610	100-199
MADISONS WAY	Buda	732Q	MD-8	78610	100-199
MADISONS WAY	Cedar Park	402L	MD-41	78613	400-599
MA DRAPER LN	Travis Co	459N	WW-35	78645	2900-3099
MADRAS CV	Travis Co	702G	MD-12	78748	2500-2599
MADRID CV	Austin	465X	MJ-34	78759	4000-4099
MADRID DR	Austin	465X	MJ-34	78759	11300-11499
MADRID DR	Georgetown	225V	MK-58	78628	4400-4999
	Williamson Co	226W	ML-58	78628	4100-4199
	Williamson Co	225Z	MK-58	78628	4200-4399
MADRIGAL LN	Austin	467Q	MP-35	78660	13900-13999
MADRONA DR	Austin	554C	MH-27	78731	4600-4699
MADRONE CIR	Village of Bear Creek	670B	WY-15	78737	9200-9399
MADRONE DR	Georgetown	226S	ML-58	78628	900-999
MADRONE RD	West Lake Hills	583B	ME-24	78746	900-1199
MADRONE TRL	Leander	342T	MC-46	78641	1100-1299
MADRONE TRL N					
	Village of Bear Creek	670L	WZ-14	78737	8000-8099
	Village of Bear Creek	670B	WY-15	78737	8100-9399
MADRONE TRL S					
	Village of Bear Creek	670F	WY-15	78737	12700-13199
MADRONE MOUNTAIN WAY	Hays Co	670J	WY-14	78737	13000-13899
MADRONE RANCH TRL	Travis Co	577D	WT-24	78738	8700-9299
MADRONE VISTA DR	Travis Co	577C	WT-24	78738	18500-18699
MADRONO DR	Austin	646G	MM-18	78744	1-99
MAEGAN LN	Bastrop Co	740T	MU-7	78612	100-199
MAELIN CV	Austin	641X	MA-16	78739	6700-6799
MAELIN DR	Austin	641X	MA-16	78739	10700-11299
MAEVES WAY	Hays Co	669B	WW-15	78737	100-399
MAGAZINE CV	Austin	466L	MM-35	78727	13200-13299
MAGAZINE ST	Austin	466F	ML-36	78727	1700-2199

STREET NAME	CITY or COUNTY	MAPSCO GRID	AUSTIN GRID	ZIP CODE	BLOCK RANGE O/E
MAGDELENA DR	Austin	613A	ME-21	78735	5200-5299
	Austin	612D	MD-21	78735	5300-5499
MAGEE BEND	Austin	642J	MC-17	78749	5600-5999
MAGELLAN CV	Lago Vista	458G	WV-36	78645	20900-20999
MAGELLAN DR	Travis Co	522P	MC-29	78733	2700-2799
MAGELLAN WAY	Williamson Co	348P	MQ-47	78665	2900-3099
MAGENTA LN	Austin	671A	MA-15	78739	6400-7599
MAGENTA SKY TRL	Travis Co	491T	MA-31	78732	3200-3299
MAGER LN	Hutto	349V	MT-46	78634	100-299
	Hutto	350S	MU-46	78634	300-999
	Williamson Co	350S	MU-46	78634	1000-1299
MAGIC HILL DR	Travis Co	467R	MP-35	78660	1600-1899
	Travis Co	468N	MQ-35	78660	1900-2099
MAGIC MOUNTAIN CV	Williamson Co	375T	MJ-43	78681	8000-8099
MAGIC MOUNTAIN LN	Williamson Co	375T	MJ-43	78681	9000-9099
MAGIC MOUNTAIN LN W					
	Williamson Co	375T	MJ-43	78681	7000-7499
MAGIN MEADOW DR	Austin	674G	MH-15	78744	2400-4699
MAGNA CT	Austin	671G	MB-15	78739	11400-11499
MAGNA CARTA LOOP	Travis Co	527X	MN-28	78754	8900-9699
MAGNOLIA BLVD	Travis Co	466B	ML-36	78727	13800-13899
MAGNOLIA CT	Cedar Park	373U	MF-43	78613	1200-1299
MAGNOLIA CT	Georgetown	226L	MM-59	78628	31000-31099
MAGNOLIA CV	Hays Co	732L	MD-8	78610	100-1099
MAGNOLIA DR	Round Rock	406M	MM-41	78664	1800-2199
MAGNOLIA ST	Bastrop	715W	EE-10	78602	400-699
	Bastrop	715T	EE-10	78602	700-899
MAGNOLIA MOUND CV	Austin	435W	MJ-37	78727	6200-6299
MAGNOLIA MOUND TRL	Austin	465A	MJ-36	78727	12700-12799
	Austin	434Z	MH-37	78727	12800-12899
MAGNOLIA RANCH CV	Travis Co	470N	MU-35	78653	None
MAGNOLIA RIDGE CV	Travis Co	547Z	WT-25	78738	8000-8199
MAGNUM DR	Travis Co	702G	MD-12	78748	12100-12199
MAGNUM TRL	Bastrop	744K	EC-8	78602	None
MAGNUS ST	Austin	528E	MQ-30	78754	6000-6199
MAGPIE CV	Austin	583U	MF-22	78746	1600-1699
MAHA CIR	Mustang Ridge	736K	ML-8	78747	10700-10799
	Travis Co	736F	ML-9	78747	10500-10699
MAHA CT	Mustang Ridge	766T	ML-4	78610	8400-8799
MAHA DR	Bastrop Co	709P	MS-11	78617	1-199
MAHA RD	Mustang Ridge	767E	MN-6	78719	13600-15299
MAHALO CT	Bastrop	746T	EG-7	78602	100-199
MAHA LOOP RD	Mustang Ridge	767A	MN-6	78719	11000-11199
	Mustang Ridge	766D	MM-6	78719	11200-11299
	Mustang Ridge	736Z	MM-7	78719	11300-11599
	Mustang Ridge	736P	ML-8	78719	11600-11799
	Mustang Ridge	736Z	MM-7	78719	12600-12899
	Travis Co	707Y	MP-10	78617	8800-8999
	Travis Co	737K	MN-8	78617	9000-10499
	Travis Co	737W	MN-7	78719	10700-10999
	Travis Co	736Z	MM-7	78719	None
MAHALUA LN	Bastrop	746S	EG-7	78602	100-199
MAHAN DR	Austin	586Y	MM-22	78721	1100-1199
MAHLOW RD	Travis Co	500B	MU-33	78653	16300-16599
MAHOGANY LN	Cedar Park	402D	MD-42	78613	1100-1299
MAHOGANY LN	Georgetown	257E	MN-57	78626	100-199
MAHOMET DR	Travis Co	467E	MN-36	78660	800-999
MAHONE AVE	Austin	525F	MJ-30	78757	2100-2399
MAHONIA LN	Travis Co	532P	MY-29	78621	17700-17799
MAIDEN LN	Austin	555W	MJ-25	78705	600-699
MAIDENHAIR LN	Travis Co	580B	WY-24	78738	12500-12599
MAIDENHAIR TRL	Travis Co	532L	MZ-29	78621	13000-13199
MAIDENSTONE DR	Austin	464F	MG-36	78759	11300-11499
MAIDSTONE CV	Round Rock	378X	MQ-43	78664	2100-2199
MAIN ST	Bastrop	745F	EE-9	78602	600-1899
	Bastrop	715X	EE-10	78602	1900-2599
MAIN ST	Cedar Park	373J	ME-44	78613	1400-1999
MAIN ST	Hutto	349Z	MT-46	78634	100-799
MAIN ST	Jonestown	401E	MA-42	78645	11500-11699
MAIN ST	Williamson Co	443L	EB-38	78615	100-399
MAIN ST E	Pflugerville	438W	MQ-37	78660	100-199
MAIN ST E	Round Rock	376Z	MM-43	78664	100-1399
	Round Rock	377W	MN-43	78664	1400-1599
MAIN ST N	Bastrop Co	715K	EE-11	78602	2700-2799
MAIN ST N	Buda	762D	MD-6	78610	100-599
	Buda	732Z	MD-7	78610	600-899
	Buda	733W	ME-7	78610	900-1899
MAIN ST N	Elgin	534J	EC-29	78621	100-899
See.. FM Rd 1100					
	Elgin	533H	EB-30	78621	900-1299
MAIN ST N	Georgetown	286C	MM-54	78626	600-799
MAIN ST N	Taylor	353E	EA-48	76574	100-1199
See.. State Hwy 95					
	Taylor	323S	EA-49	76574	1200-3799
	Taylor	322H	MZ-51	76574	3800-4499
MAIN ST N	Weir	258H	MR-57	78626	100-299
MAIN ST S	Buda	762D	MD-6	78610	100-499
MAIN ST S	Elgin	534N	EC-29	78621	100-1099
See.. FM Rd 1704					
MAIN ST S	Georgetown	286H	MM-54	78626	200-2099
MAIN ST S	Taylor	353N	EA-47	76574	100-1999
MAIN ST S	Weir	258H	MR-57	78626	2100-2399
MAIN ST W	Pflugerville	438W	MQ-37	78660	100-499
MAIN ST W	Round Rock	376Y	MM-43	78664	100-499
MAINE DR	Austin	525H	MK-30	78758	8400-8599
MAINTAINANCE BEND	Austin	646Z	MM-16	78719	3600-3699
MAINTAINERS DR	Austin	646Z	MM-16	78719	10100-10199
MAIRO ST	Austin	673H	MF-15	78748	300-699
MAIZE CV	Pflugerville	468F	MQ-36	78660	500-599
MAIZE LN	Travis Co	562L	MZ-26	78621	11500-11899
MAIZE TRL	Cedar Park	402H	MD-42	78613	1200-1299
MAIZE BEND DR	Austin	466G	MM-36	78727	1600-2099
MAJESTIC DR	Austin	644E	MG-18	78745	4900-5199
MAJESTIC ELM LN	Travis Co	532L	MZ-29	78621	17700-18099
MAJESTIC HILLS BLVD	Burnet Co	426K	WQ-38	78669	1100-1399
	Travis Co	426K	WQ-38	78669	1400-1499
MAJESTIC OAK LN E	Williamson Co	224H	MH-60	78633	100-199
MAJESTIC OAK LN W	Georgetown	194Z	MH-61	78633	None
	Williamson Co	224D	MH-60	78633	100-299
	Williamson Co	194Z	MH-61	78633	None
MAJESTIC OAKS DR	Travis Co	491X	MA-31	78732	12700-12999
MAJESTIC OAKS PASS	Travis Co	491X	MA-31	78732	2900-2999
MAJESTIC RIDGE RD	Travis Co	519S	WW-28	78738	17000-17299
MAJORCA DR	Austin	404L	MH-41	78717	9900-10199
MAKAHA DR	Bastrop Co	746T	EG-7	78602	100-399
MAKUA CT	Bastrop Co	745Z	EF-7	78602	100-199
MALA CT	Bastrop Co	776A	EG-6	78602	100-199
MALABAR	Lakeway	518D	WV-30	78734	300-399
	Lakeway	519A	WW-30	78734	400-499
	Lakeway	488Z	WV-31	78734	700-899
MALABAR DR	Georgetown	285P	MJ-53	78628	1000-1499
MALAGA DR	Austin	465T	MJ-34	78759	4300-4599
MALAGA DR	Williamson Co	256A	ML-57	78628	3900-4199
	Williamson Co	226W	ML-58	78628	4200-4399
MALAGA HILLS DR	Williamson Co	405B	MJ-42	78681	16600-16999
MALAQUITA BRANCH	Travis Co	580C	WZ-24	78738	4700-4899
MALARKEY RD	Austin	678N	MQ-14	78617	5600-5899
MALDEN CV	Travis Co	437Q	MP-38	78660	800-899
MALDEN DR	Travis Co	437Q	MP-38	78660	16200-16499
MALDON PL	Austin	585M	MK-23	78722	2100-2199
MALDONADO TRL	Bastrop Co	738L	MR-8	78617	100-299
MALIBU CV	Austin	523T	ME-28	78730	7100-7199
MALINDA DR	Austin	463C	MF-36	78750	9800-9899
MALISH CT	Travis Co	552P	MC-26	78746	8200-8299
MALLARD CV	Hays Co	668R	WV-14	78737	100-199
MALLARD CV	Hutto	350S	MU-46	78634	200-299
MALLARD LN	Georgetown	225L	MK-59	78633	100-199
MALLARD LN	Taylor	323N	EA-50	76574	100-499
	Taylor	322U	MZ-49	76574	500-2899
MALLARD LN	Williamson Co	434T	MG-37	78729	12400-12599
MALLARD GREEN CV	Travis Co	436Q	MM-38	78728	2600-2699
MALLARD GREEN LN	Travis Co	436Q	MM-38	78728	15000-15399
MALLARD LAKE TRL	Leander	342L	MD-47	78641	800-999
MALLARD POND TRL	Pflugerville	409W	MS-40	78660	None
MALLET CT	Hays Co	639S	WW-16	78737	100-299
MALLUS CT	Lakeway	489U	WX-31	78734	100-199
MALONE CT	Austin	672F	MC-15	78749	10200-10299
MALONE DR	Austin	672F	MC-15	78749	3500-3799
MALTESE CROSS DR	Austin	703B	ME-12	78748	700-799
MALVERN HILL CT	Austin	643X	ME-16	78745	7700-7799
MALVERN HILL DR	Austin	643X	ME-16	78745	2000-2199
MALVINAS CV	Austin	641Z	MB-16	78739	10200-10299
MAMALU DR	Bastrop Co	776B	EG-6	78602	100-299
MAMMOTH CT	Round Rock	345N	MJ-47	78681	900-999
MAMMOTH CAVE BLVD	Travis Co	438J	MQ-38	78660	17700-18299
	Pflugerville	438B	MQ-39	78660	18500-18699
MANADA TRL	Cedar Park	344W	MG-46	78641	1800-2099
MANANA CT	Bastrop Co	745Y	EF-7	78602	100-199
MANANA ST	Austin	552H	MD-27	78730	1500-1999
	Travis Co	553A	ME-27	78730	2000-2599
MANANA MOUNTAIN CIR	Travis Co	487X	WS-31	78669	4000-4199
MANASSAS DR	Austin	643X	ME-16	78745	7700-8299
MANAWAINUI DR	Bastrop Co	776B	EG-6	78602	100-299
MANCHACA RD	Austin	614S	MG-19	78704	2800-4399
	Austin	614S	MG-19	78745	4400-4599
	Austin	644A	MG-18	78745	4600-4699
	Austin	643Y	MF-16	78745	4700-8099
	Austin	673F	ME-15	78745	8100-8599
	Austin	673F	ME-15	78748	8600-11299
	Travis Co	703J	ME-11	78748	11300-12299
MANCHACA SPRINGS RD	Hays Co	733T	ME-7	78610	1600-1899
MANCHESTER CIR	Austin	644L	MH-17	78745	4900-4999
MANCHESTER LN	Hays Co	639S	WW-16	78737	None
MANCIAS RD	Caldwell Co	767U	MP-4	78616	101-199 O
MANCINI CV	Travis Co	402T	MC-40	78613	2800-2899
MANCOS DR	Georgetown	317J	MN-50	78626	100-299
MANCUSO BEND	Travis Co	402P	MC-41	78613	2400-2699
MANDA RD	Travis Co	501R	MX-32	78653	14000-14899
MANDA CARLSON RD	Travis Co	501C	MX-33	78653	15600-16399
	Travis Co	471Z	MX-34	78653	16400-17199
	Travis Co	472E	MY-36	78615	17200-18399
	Travis Co	442T	MY-37	78615	18400-20099
MANDAN ST	Buda	762H	MD-6	78610	100-299
MANDARIN CROSSING	Travis Co	467G	MP-36	78660	15000-15299
MANDARIN FLYWAY	Cedar Park	373Z	MF-43	78613	400-799
MANDELL ST S	Round Rock	406G	MM-42	78664	700-999
MANDEVILLE CIR	Austin	433Y	MF-37	78750	9800-10199
MANDRAKE DR	Travis Co	409Q	MT-41	78660	20900-20999
MANFORD HILL DR	Austin	526H	MM-30	78753	1400-1499
MANGAN WAY	Travis Co	439Q	MT-38	78634	18700-19399
MANGO CT	Lakeway	489Y	WX-31	78734	100-199
MANGO GROVE LN	Austin	467X	MN-34	78753	1300-1499
MANGROVE CAVE CT	Round Rock	345P	MJ-47	78681	4200-4299
MANGRUM ST	Travis Co	437S	MN-37	78660	1400-1599
MANHASSET ST	Austin	465H	MK-36	78727	12900-12999
MANHEIM BLVD	Williamson Co	405B	MJ-42	78681	16600-16699
MANIPARI LN	Austin	642S	MC-16	78749	9300-9399
MANISH CT	Travis Co	437C	MP-39	78660	1000-1099
MANISH DR	Travis Co	437G	MP-39	78660	17300-17399
MANITOBA DR	Travis Co	467P	MN-35	78660	None
MANITOU DR	Travis Co	490R	WZ-32	78734	2800-2899
MANITOU SPRINGS CT	Williamson Co	375S	MJ-43	78717	8000-8099
MANITOU SPRINGS LN	Williamson Co	375S	MJ-43	78717	9300-9499
MANJACK CAY DR	Pflugerville	437C	MP-39	78664	1400-1499
MANKATO DR	Austin	673X	ME-13	78748	700-799
MANKINS WAY	Travis Co	436G	MM-39	78728	3800-3899
MANLEY WAY	Cedar Park	372Q	MD-44	78613	1300-1399
MANLOVE CT	Austin	615K	MJ-20	78741	1100-1199
MANLOVE ST	Austin	615K	MJ-20	78741	900-999
MANN CV	Lago Vista	458L	WV-35	78645	20900-21099
MANN LN	Bastrop Co	739R	MT-8	78612	100-199
MANNY CV	Hutto	350S	MU-46	78634	1000-1099
MANOR CIR	Austin	556X	ML-25	78723	2500-2599
MANOR RD	Austin	585L	MK-23	78722	1000-2999
	Austin	586B	ML-24	78723	3000-4999
	Austin	556V	MM-25	78723	5000-6699
	Austin	557N	MN-26	78723	6700-7299
	Travis Co	557N	MN-26	78724	7300-7699
MANOR RIDGE CT	West Lake Hills	583M	MF-23	78746	100-199
MANORWOOD CT	Georgetown	285Z	MK-52	78628	100-199
MANORWOOD RD	Austin	586E	ML-24	78723	3700-3899
MAN O WAR AVE	Travis Co	706Q	MM-11	78719	10500-10699
MAN O WAR DR	Travis Co	650F	MU-18	78617	1300-2399
MANOWAR STRETCH DR	Austin	678P	MQ-14	78617	5400-5699
MANSELL AVE	Austin	616A	ML-21	78702	600-799
	Austin	616B	ML-21	78702	800-1099
	Austin	586Q	MM-23	78721	1100-1199
MANSFIELD CIR	Travis Co	491G	MB-33	78732	13100-13199
MANSFIELD DR	Travis Co	491G	MB-33	78732	13000-13399
MANSFIELD DAM CT	Travis Co	491A	MA-33	78734	14500-14699
MANSFIELD DAM RD	Travis Co	491E	MA-33	78734	4200-4499
MANSFIELD VIEW CT	Travis Co	491H	MB-33	78732	5100-5199
MANTLE DR	Travis Co	554E	MG-27	78746	4500-4899
	Travis Co	553H	MF-27	78746	4900-5099
MANX DR	Williamson Co	405C	MK-42	78681	8000-8299
MANZANILLO DR	Austin	642L	MD-17	78749	4300-4699
MANZANITA DR	Williamson Co	257A	MN-57	78628	4100-4199
MANZANITA ST	Austin	464Q	MH-35	78759	6600-6899
MAP CIR	Austin	586T	ML-22	78721	1100-1199
MAP ST	Austin	586T	ML-22	78721	1100-1199
MAPLE AVE	Austin	585R	MK-23	78702	1200-1899
	Austin	585M	MK-23	78722	1900-2299
MAPLE LN	Cedar Park	372D	MD-45	78613	100-199
MAPLE ST	Bastrop	715T	EE-10	78602	700-899
MAPLE ST	Elgin	534N	EC-29	78621	200-499
MAPLE ST	Georgetown	286H	MM-54	78626	700-1999
	Georgetown	317A	MN-51	78626	3000-3499
	Georgetown	287N	MN-53	78626	None
MAPLE ST	Taylor	353J	EA-47	76574	500-899
MAPLE TRL	Cedar Park	403A	ME-42	78613	500-599
MAPLECREEK DR	Leander	341D	MB-48	78641	500-699
	Leander	311Z	MB-49	78641	700-1099
MAPLE HOLLOW TRL	Travis Co	436U	MM-37	78728	2200-2399
MAPLELAWN CIR	Austin	556U	MM-25	78723	3000-3099
MAPLELAWN ST	Taylor	322U	MZ-49	76574	1800-1899
MAPLELEAF DR	Austin	556P	ML-26	78723	5500-5699
MAPLE LEAF TRL	Bastrop Co	564Z	ED-25	78621	100-299
MAPLERIDGE CIR	Leander	342H	MD-48	78641	1000-1099
MAPLE RUN	Round Rock	377X	MN-43	78664	400-599
MAPLE RUN CV	Round Rock	377X	MN-43	78664	400-499
MAPLE VISTA DR	Travis Co	408Q	MR-41	78660	1700-2199
MAPLEWOOD AVE	Austin	585D	MK-24	78722	3800-4099
MAPLEWOOD CIR	Pflugerville	438T	MQ-37	78660	600-699
MAPLEWOOD DR	Leander	341D	MB-48	78641	2000-2099
MAPLEWOOD DR	Pflugerville	438T	MQ-37	78660	1000-1199
MARATHON BLVD	Austin	555N	MJ-26	78756	3900-4499
MARATHON RD	Austin	403M	MF-41	78717	14000-14399
MARAVILLAS CV	Travis Co	582E	MC-24	78735	2700-2799
MARAVILLAS LOOP	Travis Co	582E	MC-24	78735	2900-3099
MARBLE RD	Williamson Co	433Q	MF-38	78750	10800-11099
MARBLE CREEK LOOP	Austin	675W	MJ-13	78747	6400-6799
MARBLE CREST DR	Austin	675S	MJ-13	78747	7500-7799
MARBLE FALLS CV	Travis Co	435S	MJ-37	78729	13100-13199
MARBLE GLEN LN	Pflugerville	439E	MS-39	78660	18900-19199
MARBLEHEAD DR	Austin	465L	MK-35	78727	4700-4899
MARBLE RIDGE DR	Austin	675S	MJ-13	78747	7300-8099
MARBLE SLAB LN	Leander	343L	MF-47	78641	2500-2599
MARBLEWOOD DR	Austin	524A	MG-30	78731	6500-6699
MARBRY'S RIDGE CV	Austin	524B	MG-30	78731	6800-6899
MARBURY CT	Austin	433W	ME-37	78726	10600-10699
MARCAE CT	Austin	614T	MG-19	78704	3500-3699
MARCARIO DR	Travis Co	619N	MS-20	78725	15000-15099
MARCASITE DR	Williamson Co	375F	MJ-45	78681	3300-3399
MARCEL GRES DR	Austin	587J	MN-23	78725	None
MARCELL ST	Austin	525V	MK-28	78752	7200-7499
MARCH DR	Austin	497S	MN-31	78753	1300-1399
	Austin	497S	MN-31	78753	11400-11599
MARCHMONT LN	Austin	642J	MC-17	78749	5700-5999
MARCOS DR	Williamson Co	314E	MG-51	78628	100-299
MARC TAYLOR DR	Austin	673D	MF-15	78745	700-899
MARCUS PL	Austin	586L	MM-23	78721	1400-1499
MARCUS ABRAMS BLVD	Austin	702D	MD-12	78748	1700-2899
MARCY ST	Austin	644B	MG-18	78745	1100-1299
MARDEN LN	Austin	671C	MB-15	78739	11000-11199
MAREJADA DR	Austin	587F	MN-24	78724	7000-7099
MAREK WAY	Jonestown	400R	WZ-41	78645	None
MARESA PATH	Williamson Co	434M	MH-38	78729	7900-7999
MARESH ST	Taylor	323W	EA-49	76574	400-599
MARFA DR	Austin	673S	ME-13	78748	10500-10599
MARFA LIGHTS TRL	Pflugerville	437B	MN-39	78664	17300-17499
MARFA LIGHTS TRL	Pflugerville	407X	MN-40	78664	17500-17899
MARGALENE WAY	Travis Co	466C	MM-36	78728	1900-2299
MARGARET CIR	Hays Co	670X	WY-13	78610	100-299
MARGARET ST	Austin	614C	MH-21	78704	1600-1899
MARGAY DR	Williamson Co	405B	MJ-42	78681	16900-16999
MARGIE'S WAY	Bastrop Co	744Z	ED-7	78602	None
	Bastrop Co	745W	EE-7	78602	None
MARGIT DR	Williamson Co	434U	MH-37	78729	12700-12999
MARGO CV	Mustang Ridge	766N	ML-5	78610	12100-12199
MARGO DR	Mustang Ridge	766S	ML-4	78610	12000-12399
MARGRA LN	Travis Co	672R	MD-14	78748	10400-10599
MARGRANITA CRESCENT	Austin	554Z	MH-25	78703	1-99
MARIA CT	Georgetown	316A	ML-51	78628	100-199
MARIA ANNA RD	Austin	554U	MH-25	78703	2600-2799
MARIACHI CT	Travis Co	521F	MA-30	78732	1900-1999
MARIAH CV	Austin	404Q	MH-41	78717	9900-9999
MARIAH CV	Williamson Co	377F	MN-45	78665	2000-2099
MARIAS RIVER DR	Austin	673X	ME-13	78748	10600-10699
MARIBEL AVE	Buda	732U	MD-7	78610	100-199
	Buda	732T	MC-7	78610	200-299
MARICELLA LN	Travis Co	467Q	MP-35	78660	13900-14199
MARICOPA CV	Austin	642F	MC-18	78749	7400-7499
MARIE	Bastrop	744M	ED-8	78602	400-499
MARIE LN	Manor	530J	MU-29	78653	None
MARIETTA DR	Austin	673S	ME-13	78748	10300-10499
MARIGOLD LN	Cedar Park	402H	MD-42	78613	300-499
MARIGOLD WAY	Pflugerville	468D	MQ-36	78660	1200-1399
MARIGOLD HEIGHTS CT	Pflugerville	439E	MS-39	78660	2800-2899
MARIGOLD TERRACE	Austin	616W	ML-19	78741	6000-6299
MARILYN DR	Austin	524V	MH-28	78757	5700-6099
MARIMBA TRL	Williamson Co	434U	MH-37	78729	12600-13099
MARIN CT	Travis Co	550R	WZ-26	78733	3300-3399
MARIN CV	Leander	342R	MD-47	78641	100-299
MARINA SHORES DR	Travis Co	426C	WR-39	78669	2700-2999
MARINA VISTA CIR	Travis Co	431Z	MB-37	78641	8100-8299
MARINER	Lakeway	489W	WW-31	78734	700-799
	Lakeway	488Z	WV-31	78734	800-899
MARINERS PT	Point Venture	488M	WV-32	78654	18900-19099
MARINO CT	Bastrop	744C	ED-9	78602	700-799
MARION	Travis Co	487T	WS-31	78669	None
MARIPOSA CIR	Williamson Co	226U	MM-58	78628	700-799
MARIPOSA DR	Austin	615N	MJ-20	78704	700-1399
	Austin	615T	MJ-19	78741	1600-1999
MARIPOSA LN	Bastrop Co	534B	EC-30	78621	100-199
MARIPOSA LN	Taylor	353C	EB-48	76574	400-799
MARIPOSA BONITA CV	Williamson Co	195M	ML-62	78633	None
MARIPOSA RANCH RD	Hays Co	607Q	WT-20	78620	100-599
MARISCAL CANYON DR	Austin	494L	MH-32	78759	8700-8999
MARITIME PASS	Jonestown	430U	WZ-37	78645	7200-7499
MARITIME PT	Jonestown	430P	WY-38	78645	17700-17899
MARITIME ALPS WAY	Bee Cave	549J	WW-26	78738	16100-16299

STREET NAME	CITY or COUNTY	MAPSCO GRID	AUSTIN GRID	ZIP CODE	BLOCK RANGE O/E
MARJESS DR	Bastrop Co	741H	MX-9	78612	100-199
MARJORIE DR	Williamson Co	409A	MS-42	78634	100-299
MARK ST	Austin	586T	ML-22	78721	1100-1199
MARK ADAMS RD	Bastrop Co	739S	MS-7	78612	100-199
MARK BROOKS CV	Williamson Co	408D	MR-42	78664	None
MARKET ST	Bee Cave	550U	WZ-25	78738	3800-4199
MARKET ST	Cedar Park	374E	MG-45	78613	800-999
MARKET ST	Williamson Co	227T	MN-58	78626	100-299
MARKET GARDEN LN	Austin	643W	ME-16	78745	2600-2799
MARKETPLACE DR	Austin	557A	MN-27	78754	8200-8399
	Austin	527W	MN-28	78754	8400-8499
MARKHAM LN	Austin	497E	MN-33	78753	900-1099
MARKLAWN LN	Hutto	350J	MU-47	78634	100-499
MARK RAE	Austin	465D	MK-36	78727	4100-4199
MARK RIDGE LN	Travis Co	704B	MG-12	78747	None
MARKS CIR	Austin	586T	ML-22	78721	1100-1199
MARK'S WAY	Hays Co	795E	MJ-3	78610	100-799
MARKS OVERLOOK	Buda	732U	MD-7	78610	100-399
MARL CT	Austin	675X	MJ-13	78747	7600-7699
MARLBOROUGH CIR	Austin	526L	MM-29	78753	1400-1499
MARLBOROUGH DR	Austin	526H	MM-30	78753	9300-9899
MARLIN CV	Travis Co	646W	ML-16	78744	4400-4599
MARLO DR	Austin	586G	MM-24	78723	4600-4699
MARLOCK RIDGE	Travis Co	468T	MQ-34	78660	None
MARLTON DR	Austin	584F	MG-24	78703	2400-2599
MARLY CV	Travis Co	552B	MC-27	78733	9000-9099
MARLY WAY	Travis Co	552B	MC-27	78733	200-1299
MARLY WAY	Travis Co	522X	MC-28	78733	1100-1299
MARNIE DR	Travis Co	591P	MW-23	78621	8400-8599
MAROGOT RUN	Austin	466N	ML-35	78758	12300-12499
MARQUESA DR	Austin	524Q	MH-29	78731	6000-6199
MARQUESA TRL	Williamson Co	224L	MH-59	78633	100-399
	Williamson Co	224Q	MH-59	78633	600-699
MARQUETTE CV	Lago Vista	458L	WV-35	78645	20900-20999
MARQUETTE LN	Austin	556L	MM-26	78723	2100-2199
MARQUIS LN	Cedar Park	373S	ME-43	78613	300-799
MARR CV	Austin	587C	MP-24	78724	6200-6499
MARRERO DR	Williamson Co	434R	MH-38	78729	13200-13399
MARSALA SPRINGS DR	Williamson Co	405B	MJ-42	78681	16700-16899
MARSEILLES DR	Austin	463C	MF-36	78750	9900-9999
MARSH DR	Austin	673A	ME-15	78748	8900-9699
MARSHA ST	Travis Co	436R	MM-38	78728	15300-15699
MARSHALL	Manor	529X	MS-28	78653	None
MARSHALL AVE	Lago Vista	458G	WV-36	78645	3000-3399
MARSHALL CT	Williamson Co	314E	MG-51	78628	100-199
MARSHALL LN	Austin	584M	MH-23	78703	1200-1599
MARSHALL ST	Taylor	322U	MZ-49	76574	1300-1399
MARSHALL TRL	Round Rock	348S	MQ-46	78665	2300-2499
MARSHALL FORD RD	Travis Co	491G	MB-33	78732	4700-5199
MARSHALLS HARBOR CV	Lago Vista	459H	WX-36	78645	18400-18899
MARSHALLS HARBOR DR	Lago Vista	459D	WX-36	78645	4800-5499
MARSHALL'S POINT CV	Lago Vista	429V	WX-37	78645	6400-6599
	Travis Co	430S	WY-37	78645	6300-6399
MARSHALL'S POINT DR	Lago Vista	429Z	WX-37	78645	18500-18899
	Travis Co	430W	WY-37	78645	17900-18499
MARSH CREEK DR	Austin	494D	MH-33	78759	5300-5499
MARSH HARBOUR CV	Pflugerville	437C	MP-39	78664	1300-1399
MARSH HARBOUR DR	Pflugerville	437C	MP-39	78664	1400-1499
MARSHITAH'S WAY	Austin	673W	ME-13	78748	10400-10799
MARSTON CIR	Austin	526M	MM-29	78753	1400-1499
MARSTON LN	Austin	526M	MM-29	78753	9600-9699
MARTHA ANN DR	Travis Co	371V	MB-43	78641	13100-13199
MARTHA'S CV	Williamson Co	405A	MJ-42	78717	16400-16499
MARTHA'S DR	Williamson Co	405A	MJ-42	78717	8900-9099
MARTIAL EAGLE DR	Elgin	503T	EA-31	78621	None
MARTIN AVE	Austin	555M	MK-26	78751	5000-5399
	Austin	555R	MK-26	78751	5500-5599
MARTIN AVE	Austin	526W	ML-28	78752	7400-7499
MARTIN AVE	Williamson Co	406P	ML-41	78681	800-1299
MARTIN CT	Austin	526J	ML-29	78758	8400-8499
MARTIN CV	Travis Co	546V	WR-25	78620	9800-9899
MARTIN DR	Cedar Park	433A	ME-39	78613	2900-2999
MARTIN LN	Bastrop Co	741M	MX-8	78612	100-199
MARTIN LN	Travis Co	409U	MT-40	78660	20400-21399
	Williamson Co	409L	MT-41	78660	21400-21699
MARTIN LN	Travis Co	456H	WR-36	78669	24700-24999
MARTIN LN	Travis Co	707Z	MP-10	78617	None
MARTIN PL	Georgetown	257S	MN-55	78626	100-299
MARTIN CHURCH RD	Hays Co	794P	MG-2	78610	100-599
MARTIN CROSSING DR	Bastrop Co	742S	MY-7	78612	100-299
MARTINDALE AVE	Williamson Co	192S	MC-61	78642	100-299
MARTINDALE DR	Austin	494R	MH-32	78759	8600-8699
MARTINIQUE PASS	Lakeway	518D	WV-30	78734	None
MARTIN LUTHER KING ST	Georgetown	286L	MM-53	78626	100-1199
MARTIN LUTHER KING JR BLVD E	Austin	585J	MJ-23	78701	100-799
	Austin	585Q	MK-23	78702	800-2899
	Austin	586J	ML-23	78702	2900-3099
	Austin	586H	MM-24	78721	3100-5899
MARTIN LUTHER KING JR BLVD N	Elgin	534J	EC-29	78621	100-199
MARTIN LUTHER KING JR BLVD S	Elgin	534N	EC-29	78621	1-899
MARTIN LUTHER KING JR BLVD W	Austin	585J	MJ-23	78701	100-1099
	Austin	584M	MH-23	78701	1100-1299
MARTIN LUTHER KING JR DR	Bastrop	745Q	EF-8	78602	200-499
	Bastrop	745L	EF-8	78602	500-999
MARTIN MEADOWS	Bastrop Co	741P	MW-8	78612	None
MARTINS CV	Williamson Co	374G	MH-45	78613	100-199
MARVINS CV	Elgin	533H	EB-30	78621	900-999
MARVIN CV	Hutto	379C	MT-45	78634	100-299
MARY ST	Austin	647Q	MP-17	78617	3100-3199
MARY ST	Hays Co	762Z	MD-4	78610	300-499
MARY ST E	Austin	615J	MJ-20	78704	100-299
	Austin	615N	MJ-20	78704	500-599
MARY ST W	Austin	614M	MH-20	78704	100-1399
MARYANNA DR	Travis Co	524S	MG-28	78746	5300-5499
MARYBANK DR	Austin	464E	MG-36	78750	8800-8899
	Austin	463H	MF-36	78750	8900-9199
MARY ELLA DR	Leander	343L	MF-47	78641	1900-2199
MARY HARGROVE LN	Austin	703E	ME-12	78748	11600-11699
MARYLAND DR	Austin	526E	ML-30	78758	800-999

STREET NAME	CITY or COUNTY	MAPSCO GRID	AUSTIN GRID	ZIP CODE	BLOCK RANGE O/E
MARY LOU RETTON LN	Austin	702D	MD-12	78748	2200-2299
MARY MOORE SEARIGHT DR S	Austin	673Q	MF-14	78748	None
MARYMOUNT DR	Austin	556Y	MM-25	78723	5100-5299
MARYSOL TRL	Cedar Park	372T	MC-43	78613	1800-2099
MARYWOOD CIR	Austin	556H	MM-27	78723	7200-7399
MASCHMEIER RD	Travis Co	708V	MR-10	78617	16300-16799
MASHBURN ST	Pflugerville	408V	MR-40	78660	20000-20299
MASHIE CV	Austin	645X	MJ-16	78744	5000-5099
MASI LOOP	Travis Co	439T	MS-37	78660	17700-18599
MASON AVE	Austin	586Q	MM-23	78721	1100-1199
MASON CT	Georgetown	285D	MK-54	78628	301-399 O
MASON ST	Leander	342F	MC-48	78641	700-899
MASON BEND DR	Pflugerville	407Z	MP-40	78660	1100-1299
MASON CREEK BLVD	Leander	342P	MC-47	78641	1300-1499
	Leander	342T	MC-46	78641	1500-1899
MASON DELLS LN	Austin	672Z	MD-13	78748	2300-2799
MASON DIXON CIR	Hays Co	577U	WT-22	78720	17800-17899
	Travis Co	577U	WT-22	78720	None
MASONIC DR	Elgin	534T	EC-28	78621	100-199
MASONIC WAY	Round Rock	377W	MN-43	78664	100-199
MASON RANCH DR	Georgetown	285D	MK-54	78628	400-499
	Williamson Co	285D	MK-54	78628	None
MASON STONE CV	Manor	500Y	MV-31	78653	None
MASONWOOD WAY	Round Rock	375G	MK-45	78681	2300-2399
MASSENGALE ST	Travis Co	437S	MN-37	78660	1300-1599
MASSEY WAY	Round Rock	344R	MH-47	78681	4000-4199
MASTERS CIR	Point Venture	489J	WW-32	78645	18400-18499
MASTERS CV	Point Venture	489J	WW-32	78645	18600-18699
MASTERS PKWY	Travis Co	426L	WR-38	78669	26000-27099
MASTERSON PASS	Austin	496X	ML-31	78753	100-799
MASTHEAD CIR	Point Venture	489N	WW-32	78645	500-599
MASTIFF CV	Williamson Co	377B	MN-45	78664	1100-1199
MATADOR CIR	Travis Co	553M	MF-26	78746	2300-2399
MATADOR DR	Austin	645B	MJ-18	78741	3000-3199
MATADOR LN	Travis Co	553M	MF-26	78746	4900-5099
MATAGORDA DR	Williamson Co	377E	MN-45	78664	1700-1999
MATAGORDA ST	Austin	615T	MJ-19	78741	1800-2099
MATAMOROS ST	Austin	615D	MK-21	78702	300-499
MATCHLOCK CV	Williamson Co	434U	MH-37	78729	8100-8199
MATEO CV	Austin	404Q	MH-41	78717	9900-9999
MATHEW RD	Williamson Co	258Z	MR-55	78626	1100-1399
MATHIAS LN	Hays Co	794W	MG-1	78610	1300-2399
MATHIAS ST	Cedar Park	372L	MD-44	78613	1200-1499
MATHIS CIR	Travis Co	427S	WS-37	78669	25400-25499
MATHRA DR	Austin	678J	MQ-14	78617	5200-5399
MATISSE TRL	Austin	433T	ME-37	78726	11200-11399
MATISSE POINTE DR	Jonestown	430P	WY-38	78645	7300-7399
MATOCA WAY	Austin	433W	ME-37	78726	10200-10299
MATTAPAN DR	Pflugerville	438P	MQ-38	78660	1200-1299
MATTERHORN LN	Austin	614E	MG-21	78704	2100-2399
MATTHEW CV	Hutto	379G	MT-45	78634	100-299
MATTHEW DR	Hutto	379G	MT-45	78634	100-199
MATTHEW LN	Williamson Co	318J	MQ-50	78626	200-299
MATTHEWS DR	Austin	554T	MG-25	78703	1900-2599
MATTHEWS LN	Austin	644U	MF-16	78745	900-2499
MATTIE ST	Austin	586A	ML-24	78723	3800-4299
MATTINGLY ST	Hutto	349U	MT-46	78634	100-299
MAUAI CV	Austin	642Q	MD-17	78749	4300-4399
MAUAI DR	Austin	642Q	MD-17	78749	8100-8599
MAUDE ST	Austin	585Z	MK-22	78702	800-899
MAUFRAIS LN	Austin	645T	MJ-16	78744	4900-5199
MAUFRAIS ST	Austin	584R	MH-23	78703	900-1199
MAUI CT	Bastrop	746S	EG-7	78602	100-199
MAULDING PASS	Austin	612Y	MD-19	78749	5100-5299
MAUNA KEA DR	Travis Co	582Q	MD-23	78746	6300-6499
MAUNA KEA LN	Bastrop	746T	EG-7	78602	100-199
	Bastrop Co	746T	EG-7	78602	200-299
MAUNA LOA LN	Bastrop	746N	EG-8	78602	100-199
	Bastrop	745R	EF-8	78602	200-299
	Bastrop Co	745U	EF-7	78602	300-499
MAUNALUA DR E	Bastrop Co	745X	EE-7	78602	100-199
MAUNALUA DR W	Bastrop Co	745X	EE-7	78602	100-199
MAURICE CV	Cedar Park	402M	MD-41	78613	700-799
MAURICE DR	Cedar Park	402L	MD-41	78613	800-899
MAURY HOLLOW	Austin	494S	MG-31	78750	6300-6399
MAURY'S TRL	Travis Co	493S	ME-31	78730	5900-6299
MAVERICK CT	Mustang Ridge	765R	MK-5	78610	200-7299
MAVERICK DR	Austin	465F	MJ-36	78727	5200-5399
MAVERICK DR	Bastrop	744K	EC-8	78602	None
MAVERICK DR	Mustang Ridge	765U	MK-4	78610	6900-6999
MAX DR	Travis Co	489M	WX-32	78734	17000-17099
MAXA DR	Manor	530J	MU-29	78653	17900-18599
MAXINE'S CV	Travis Co	437W	MN-37	78660	1000-1099
MAXWELL LN	Austin	646E	ML-18	78741	2000-2399
MAY CV	Georgetown	257T	MN-55	78626	100-199
MAY DR	Austin	497S	MN-31	78753	1300-1399
MAY ST	Hutto	379H	MT-45	78634	100-299
MAYAN WAY	Travis Co	522X	MC-28	78733	1100-1299
MAYAPPLE ST	Pflugerville	437M	MP-38	78660	1300-1599
MAYBACH DR	Travis Co	677X	MN-13	78617	11600-11799
MAYBELLE AVE	Austin	555N	MJ-26	78756	4300-4499
MAYDELLE ST	Austin	673S	ME-13	78748	10200-10599
MAYE PL	Travis Co	466H	MM-36	78728	13700-13899
MAYFAIR DR	Austin	525A	MJ-30	78759	3500-3599
MAYFIELD DR	Williamson Co	375J	MJ-44	78681	1600-1999
	Williamson Co	374H	MH-45	78681	2000-2499
MAYFIELD WAY	Cedar Park	372J	MC-44	78613	2200-2399
	Williamson Co	372K	MC-44	78641	None
MAYFIELD CAVE TRL	Round Rock	345P	MJ-47	78681	4000-4099
MAYFIELD RANCH BLVD	Round Rock	345S	MJ-46	78681	3400-3999
MAYFIELD RANCH CV	Round Rock	345S	MJ-46	78681	3200-3299
MAYFLOWER CV	Lago Vista	458L	WV-35	78645	2500-2599
MAYHALL DR	Austin	616C	MM-21	78721	6100-6299
MAYLEAF CV	Travis Co	519Q	WX-29	78738	1-99
MAYNARD ST	Bastrop	745N	EE-8	78602	100-299
MAYO ST	Travis Co	703A	ME-12	78748	11300-11599
MAYS ST N	Round Rock	376Y	MM-43	78664	100-2399
	Round Rock	376B	ML-45	78665	2400-2999
MAYS ST S	Round Rock	406C	MM-42	78664	100-2299
MAYS CROSSING DR	Round Rock	406G	MM-42	78664	100-399
MAYS EXTENSION S	Round Rock	406R	MM-41	78664	2200-2399
MAYVIEW DR	Austin	558W	MQ-25	78724	8400-8599
MAYWOOD AVE	Austin	554Q	MH-26	78703	3100-3399
MAYWOOD CIR	Austin	554Q	MH-26	78703	3000-3099
McALLISTER RD	Bastrop Co	746Y	EH-7	78602	100-199
	Bastrop Co	776C	EH-6	78602	200-799

STREET NAME	CITY or COUNTY	MAPSCO GRID	AUSTIN GRID	ZIP CODE	BLOCK RANGE O/E
McANGUS RD	Travis Co	707G	MP-12	78617	7300-7899
	Travis Co	706D	MM-12	78617	10500-10899
	Travis Co	707E	MN-12	78617	10900-11499
McBAY LN	Travis Co	619N	MS-20	78725	500-599
McBEE DR	Austin	587J	MN-23	78725	None
McBRIDE LN	Cedar Park	374Q	MH-44	78613	100-199
McBRINE PL	Travis Co	554F	MG-27	78746	4100-4199
McCALL LN	Austin	646Q	MM-17	78744	3100-3699
McCALL RD	Austin	584C	MH-24	78703	1600-2499
McCALLEN PASS	Austin	466Z	MN-34	78753	12500-12699
	Austin	467S	MN-34	78753	12700-13799
McCALLUM DR	Austin	584D	MH-24	78703	2500-2699
McCALLUM DR	Leander	311R	MB-50	78641	1100-1299
McCANDLESS ST	Austin	555F	MJ-27	78756	5300-5499
McCANN DR	Austin	495X	MJ-31	78757	8800-8999
McCARTHUR DR	Leander	342V	MD-46	78641	100-699
McCARTHY CIR	Austin	555B	MJ-27	78756	5700-5799
McCARTHY DR	Bastrop Co	776L	EH-5	78602	100-199
McCARTY LN	Austin	612X	MC-19	78749	5200-6199
McCLANNAHAN DR	Austin	702H	MD-12	78748	1700-1899
McCLENDON DR	Elgin	533G	EB-30	78621	300-399
McCLOSKEY ST	Austin	586A	ML-24	78723	1900-2299
McCLURE ST	Taylor	322Z	MZ-49	76574	700-899
McCOMBS ST	Georgetown	287P	MN-53	78626	2200-2399
McCONNELL DR	West Lake Hills	583L	MF-23	78746	100-399
McCOOK DR	Georgetown	287P	MN-53	78626	2300-2499
McCORMICK CV	Lago Vista	458H	WV-36	78645	20800-20899
McCORMICK MOUNTAIN DR	Travis Co	460Z	WZ-34	78734	4300-5199
	Travis Co	461S	MA-34	78734	5200-5299
McCOY LN	Georgetown	256Y	MM-55	78628	1000-1099
McCOY LN	Hutto	380N	MU-44	78634	100-499
McCOY PL	Georgetown	287J	MN-53	78626	1700-1799
McCULLOUGH ST	Austin	554Y	MH-25	78703	2200-2799
McCURRY RD	Travis Co	471C	MX-36	78615	12000-12699
McDADE DR	Austin	613E	ME-21	78735	5000-5299
McDADE RD	Elgin	534P	EC-29	78621	None
McDANIEL DR	Briarcliff	457R	WT-35	78669	22400-22499
McDONALD LN E	Bastrop Co	741V	MX-7	78612	100-199
McDONALD LN W	Bastrop Co	741B	MW-9	78612	100-699
McDOUGLAS CV	Hays Co	668C	WV-15	78620	100-199
McDOWELL RD	Bastrop Co	739N	MS-8	78617	100-299
McDOWELL BEND	Williamson Co	343T	ME-46	78641	1500-1799
McDOW'S HOLE LN	Austin	403H	MF-42	78717	11500-11699
McELROY DR	Austin	525E	MJ-30	78757	2900-3399
McFARLIE CV	Austin	463H	MF-36	78750	10600-10799
McGRATH DR	Travis Co	641N	MA-17	78739	10100-10299
McGREGOR DR	Austin	643L	MF-17	78745	2500-2699
McGREGOR LN	Cedar Park	372G	MD-45	78613	2300-2399
McHALE CT	Austin	495L	MK-32	78758	2500-2699
McILLWAIN CV	Cedar Park	402L	MD-41	78613	2000-2099
McINTYRE CIR	Travis Co	461S	MA-34	78734	5000-5199
McKALLA PL	Austin	495Q	MK-32	78758	10000-10499
McKENDRICK DR	Cedar Park	374N	MG-44	78613	2300-2599
McKENNAS CV	Buda	732Q	MD-8	78610	100-299
McKENZIE DR	Georgetown	286M	MM-53	78626	1000-1099
McKENZIE RD	Travis Co	706E	ML-12	78747	9000-9198 E
	Travis Co	706E	ML-12	78744	9001-9199 O
	Travis Co	706L	MM-11	78719	9200-10499
McKENZIE ST	Round Rock	377E	MN-45	78664	1700-1799
McKIE CV	Austin	556B	ML-27	78752	1300-1399
McKIE DR	Austin	556B	ML-27	78752	1300-1399
McKINLEY AVE	Austin	586N	ML-23	78702	1200-1899
McKINLEY CV	Lago Vista	458H	WV-36	78645	20800-20899
McKINNEY FALLS LN	Georgetown	195N	MJ-62	78633	100-599
McKINNEY FALLS PKWY	Austin	646X	ML-16	78744	3500-4199
	Travis Co	676A	ML-15	78744	4200-5599
	Travis Co	675G	MK-15	78744	5600-7699
McKINNEY SPRING DR	Austin	403M	MF-41	78717	11100-11299
McKINNON LOOP	Hays	702W	MC-10	78610	500-799
McKITTRICK CANYON DR	Austin	494L	MH-32	78759	5101-5199 O
McKITTRICK RIDGE RD	Georgetown	225A	MJ-60	78633	100-599
McKNOWN ST	Travis Co	641K	MA-17	78749	None
McLAIN ST	Taylor	352D	MZ-48	76574	1100-1899
McLEOD PL	Bastrop Co	741T	MW-7	78612	100-199
McLOUGHLIN PT	Austin	462K	MC-35	78726	12500-12599
McMARION LN	Bastrop Co	743V	EB-7	78602	100-199
McMEANS TRL	Travis Co	640U	WZ-16	78737	8300-9399
McMILLIAN DR	Austin	496Y	MM-31	78753	10500-10699
McNEIL DR	Austin	466A	ML-36	78727	3400-4099
	Travis Co	436W	ML-37	78727	4100-4499
McNEIL DR	Austin	435W	MJ-37	78729	6000-6299
	Austin	434Z	MH-37	78729	6300-6899
	Austin	464D	MH-36	78727	6900-7499
	Travis Co	435U	MK-37	78729	5100-5999
McNEIL DR	Austin	493E	ME-33	78750	9400-9999
	Austin	492H	MD-33	78750	10000-10099
McNEIL RD	Austin	495U	MK-31	78758	9200-9699
McNEIL RD	Round Rock	406C	MM-42	78664	100-499
	Round Rock	406G	MM-42	78681	500-1899
	Travis Co	435Q	MK-38	78729	13600-13999
	Travis Co	435Q	MK-38	78729	14100-14299
	Williamson Co	406W	ML-40	78728	1900-3099
	Williamson Co	435D	MK-39	78728	3100-3199
	Williamson Co	435Q	MK-38	78717	3200-5099
McNEIL-MERRILLTOWN RD	Austin	436S	ML-37	78728	13800-14599
	Travis Co	435Z	MK-37	78727	13700-13799
McNELLY TRL	Travis Co	491Q	MB-32	78732	12500-12899
McNUTT RD	Williamson Co	378G	MR-45	78634	100-199
McPHAUL ST	Austin	496T	ML-31	78758	800-999
McVAY LN	Bastrop Co	564E	EC-27	78621	100-299
MEACHAM WAY	Austin	642N	MC-17	78749	9000-9199
MEAD BEND	Travis Co	409P	MS-41	78660	20700-20899
MEADGREEN CIR	Austin	496N	ML-32	78758	1300-1499
MEADGREEN CT	Austin	496P	ML-32	78758	10900-10999
MEADGREEN DR	Austin	496P	ML-32	78758	1200-1399
MEADOR AVE	Austin	556B	ML-27	78752	6900-7399
	Austin	526X	ML-28	78752	7600-7699
MEADOW CIR	Austin	643Q	MF-17	78745	6800-6899
MEADOW CV	Elgin	533H	EB-30	78621	1300-1399
MEADOW DR	Austin	496T	ML-31	78758	900S-1499S
MEADOW DR	Bastrop Co	680C	MV-15	78612	4400-4499
	Travis Co	680C	MV-15	78612	4300-4399
	Travis Co	680C	MV-15	78612	4500-4599
MEADOW DR	Pflugerville	438S	MQ-37	78660	600-899
MEADOW DR	Williamson Co	224C	MH-60	78633	100-299
MEADOW LN	Pflugerville	437V	MP-37	78660	100-399

M

STREET NAME	CITY or COUNTY	MAPSCO GRID	AUSTIN GRID	ZIP CODE	BLOCK RANGE O/E
MEADOW LN	Taylor	322Y	MZ-49	76574	1600-2599
	Taylor	322U	MZ-49	76574	2800-3199
MEADOW WAY	Bastrop Co	742N	MY-8	78612	100-199
MEADOW WAY	Round Rock	378L	MR-44	78664	1-99
MEADOWBANK DR	Austin	554T	MG-25	78703	3700-3799
MEADOW BEND DR E	Austin	557Z	MP-25	78724	7000-7399
MEADOW BLUFF CT	Williamson Co	346L	MM-47	78665	800-899
MEADOW BLUFF WAY	Williamson Co	346G	MM-48	78665	4000-4199
MEADOWBROOK DR	Austin	584B	MG-24	78703	1700-2299
MEADOWBROOK DR	Georgetown	286T	ML-52	78628	500-699
MEADOW BROOK DR	Round Rock	376H	MM-45	78664	2000-2499
MEADOW CREEK CIR	Austin	644E	MG-18	78745	5300-5399
MEADOWCREEK CIR	Round Rock	407A	MN-42	78664	300-799
MEADOW CREEK CV	Austin	644E	MG-18	78745	5100-5199
MEADOWCREEK CV	Round Rock	407A	MN-42	78664	600-699
MEADOW CREEK DR	Austin	644J	MG-17	78745	5100-5299
MEADOW CREEK DR	Hays Co	668M	WV-14	78620	4300-4599
MEADOW CREEK DR	Pflugerville	438S	MQ-37	78660	300-999
MEADOWCREEK DR	Round Rock	407A	MN-42	78664	700-1199
MEADOW CREST	Austin	645X	MJ-16	78744	5300-5899
MEADOW CREST DR	Williamson Co	197V	MP-61	78626	100-399
MEADOW DEW LN	Travis Co	529D	MT-30	78653	13300-13399
MEADOWFIRE DR	Austin	496A	ML-33	78758	11900-11999
MEADOW FORD	Williamson Co	433R	MF-38	78750	10200-10299
MEADOW GOLD DR	Travis Co	529H	MT-30	78653	11600-11699
MEADOW GREEN CT	Travis Co	610U	WZ-19	78736	9100-9199
MEADOWGREENS DR	Georgetown	226G	MM-60	78628	29000-30099
MEADOWHEATH CV	Williamson Co	434E	MG-39	78729	13000-13099
MEADOWHEATH DR	Williamson Co	434F	MG-39	78729	9200-9899
MEADOWILD CV	Williamson Co	408H	MR-42	78664	1400-1499
MEADOWILD DR	Williamson Co	408H	MR-42	78664	1100-1399
MEADOW LAKE BLVD	Austin	674M	MH-14	78744	6600-7399
MEADOWLAND DR	Lakeway	519U	WX-28	78738	100-399
MEADOW LARK AVE	Austin	496R	MM-32	78753	600-799
MEADOW LARK CIR	Cedar Park	433F	ME-39	78613	2900-2999
MEADOWLARK CIR	Georgetown	257T	MN-55	78626	100-299
MEADOW LARK DR	Cedar Park	433E	ME-39	78613	1100-1399
MEADOW LARK LN	Hutto	379R	MT-44	78634	100-299
MEADOWLARK ST	Austin	525M	MK-29	78758	800-999
MEADOWLARK ST N	Lakeway	520A	WY-30	78734	100-499
MEADOWLARK ST S	Lakeway	520A	WY-30	78734	100-299
MEADOWLARK SOUTH ST	Travis Co	520E	WY-30	78734	15100-15299
MEADOW LEA DR	Austin	674A	MG-15	78745	200-699
MEADOWMEAR DR	Austin	526H	MM-30	78753	1300-1499
MEADOWMERE LN E	Austin	496W	ML-31	78758	900-999
MEADOWMERE LN W	Austin	496W	ML-31	78758	900-999
MEADOW OAKS DR	Hays Co	636P	WQ-17	78620	100-999
MEADOWOOD CV	Austin	556H	MM-27	78723	7300-7399
MEADOWOOD DR	Austin	556M	MM-26	78723	7100-7399
MEADOW PARK DR	Georgetown	287M	MP-53	78626	100-599
MEADOW PARK DR	Round Rock	347W	MN-46	78665	3600-3699
MEADOWRIDGE DR	Austin	614F	MG-21	78704	2000-2099
MEADOW RIDGE DR	Hays Co	668R	WV-14	78620	900-1299
MEADOW RIDGE DR	Taylor	322Y	MZ-49	76574	1900-1999
MEADOW RIDGE LOOP	Georgetown	287M	MP-53	78626	900-999
MEADOWRUE CV	Williamson Co	377F	MN-45	78665	1900-1999
MEADOW RUN	Austin	643V	MF-16	78745	6800-7199
MEADOW RUN	Round Rock	378K	MQ-44	78664	1-99
MEADOWS DR	Bastrop Co	651K	MW-17	78621	100-199
MEADOWS DR	Round Rock	376N	ML-44	78681	1000-1699
MEADOWS DR N	Austin	496T	ML-31	78758	800-1199
MEADOWS DR S	Austin	496T	ML-31	78758	900-1199
MEADOWS LN	Hays Co	636P	WQ-17	78620	200-299
MEADOWS END	Georgetown	226L	MM-59	78628	1-99
MEADOWSIDE DR	Hutto	379H	MT-45	78634	100-299
	Hutto	380E	MU-45	78634	300-599
MEADOWSIDE LN	Williamson Co	346G	MM-48	78665	4400-4499
MEADOWSIDE PATH	Williamson Co	346G	MM-48	78665	None
MEADOWSOUTH LN	Travis Co	673P	ME-14	78748	1400-1599
MEADOW TURN	Williamson Co	257L	MP-56	78626	40100-40199
MEADOW VALE	Austin	495Z	MK-31	78758	9100-9499
MEADOW VALE E	Austin	495Z	MK-31	78758	9400-9499
MEADOW VIEW BLVD	Bastrop Co	738L	MR-8	78617	100-299
MEADOW VIEW CV	Bastrop Co	738M	MR-8	78617	100-199
MEADOW VIEW CV	Williamson Co	318C	MR-51	78634	200-299
MEADOW VIEW DR	Leander	342H	MD-48	78641	600-999
MEADOWVIEW LN	Austin	525V	MK-28	78752	7500-7799
MEADOW VISTA LN	Williamson Co	346H	MM-48	78665	4200-4299
MEAD PARKE CV	Austin	462P	MC-35	78726	8000-8099
MEAGAN CV	Hutto	350N	MU-47	78634	1100-1199
MEANDER DR	Austin	586L	MM-23	78721	1400-1799
MEANDERING WAY	Austin	494Z	MH-31	78759	8100-8199
MEANDERING WAY	Round Rock	378P	MQ-44	78664	1-99
MEANDERING CREEK CV	Austin	523U	MF-28	78746	3800-3899
MEANDERING CREEK CV	Georgetown	287M	MP-53	78626	1000-1099
MEANDERING MEADOWS DR	Pflugerville	408Z	MR-40	78660	1800-1899
MEANDERING RIVER CT	Travis Co	554J	MG-26	78746	2900-3099
MEARNS MEADOW BLVD	Austin	526A	ML-30	78758	1000-1099
	Austin	496S	ML-31	78758	1100-1799
	Austin	495R	MK-32	78758	1800-2099
MEARNS MEADOW CV	Austin	496S	ML-31	78758	9900-9999
MECCA CIR	Travis Co	522P	MC-29	78733	9700-9799
MECCA RD	Travis Co	522P	MC-29	78733	2000-3199
MEDA ST	Williamson Co	257N	MN-56	78626	1-299
MEDALIST	Lakeway	489X	WW-31	78734	100-199
MEDALLION LN	Austin	433Y	MF-37	78750	11500-11699
MEDELIN CREEK LOOP	Hays Co	606F	WQ-21	78620	100-1699
MEDERAS DR	Austin	496F	ML-33	78758	1600-1699
MEDFIELD CT	Austin	671C	MB-15	78739	10900-10999
MEDFORD DR	Austin	586C	MM-24	78723	5200-5399
MEDIAN RD	Travis Co	460L	WZ-35	78734	5600-6099
MEDICAL DR	Lakeway	519Q	WX-29	78734	2000-2199
MEDICAL PKWY	Austin	555W	MJ-25	78705	3200-3399
	Austin	555S	MJ-25	78705	3400-3799
	Austin	555N	MJ-26	78756	3800-4499
MEDICAL PKWY	Cedar Park	373K	ME-44	78613	1200-1699
MEDICAL PKWY	Taylor	322R	MZ-50	76574	2700-2799
MEDICAL ARTS ST	Austin	585G	MK-24	78705	2900-3199
MEDICAL ARTS SQUARE	Austin	585G	MK-24	78705	None
MEDICINE CREEK DR	Austin	611H	MB-21	78735	5600-5899
MEDICINE HAT	Leander	341W	MA-46	78641	3700-3999
MEDINA	Austin	585X	MJ-22	78702	100-699
MEDINAH GREENS DR	Austin	404D	MH-42	78717	10200-10699
MEDINA RIDGE	Travis Co	468T	MQ-34	78660	None
MEDINA RIVER WAY	Travis Co	491P	MA-32	78732	12800-13099

STREET NAME	CITY or COUNTY	MAPSCO GRID	AUSTIN GRID	ZIP CODE	BLOCK RANGE O/E
MEDITERRA PL	Travis Co	521S	MA-28	78732	12300-12499
MEDITERRA PT	Travis Co	521S	MA-28	78732	100-499
MEEHAN DR	Austin	466P	ML-35	78727	12700-13099
MEG BRAUER WAY	Austin	642B	MC-18	78749	5400-5599
MEGHAN DR	Cedar Park	372Q	MD-44	78613	1200-1499
MEGHAN LN	Austin	584Y	MH-22	78704	1600-1699
MEINARDUS DR	Austin	644M	MH-17	78744	4300-4799
MEISTER LN	Williamson Co	407R	MP-41	78660	800-1399
	Williamson Co	407L	MP-41	78664	None
MEISTER PL	Round Rock	407Q	MP-41	78664	2700-2799
MEK DR	Austin	524K	MG-29	78731	4100-4199
MELANCHOLY DR	Lakeway	519D	WX-30	78734	200-299
MELANIE CV	Williamson Co	225W	MJ-58	78633	100-499
MELANIE LN	Georgetown	255R	MK-56	78628	None
	Williamson Co	255R	MK-56	78628	100-199
MELANIE'S WALK	Travis Co	437W	MN-37	78660	1000-1099
MELBA PASS	Travis Co	432H	MD-39	78613	2600-2799
MELBER LN	Travis Co	440K	MU-38	78653	19200-20899
	Travis Co	440C	MV-39	78653	21000-21499
	Williamson Co	410X	MU-40	78653	20900-20999
MELBOURNE LN	Round Rock	377N	MN-44	78664	1200-1399
MELBROOK RIDGE	Travis Co	468T	MQ-34	78660	None
MELCHER CT	Austin	641Y	MB-16	78739	10600-10699
MELDRUM RD	Austin	647Q	MP-17	78617	2900-3099
MELEKHIN BEND	Travis Co	402T	MC-40	78613	2400-2699
MELIBEE TRL	Austin	703A	ME-12	78748	1600-1699
MELISSA CIR	Williamson Co	318E	MQ-51	78626	100-199
MELISSA CT	Georgetown	256P	ML-56	78628	100-199
MELISSA LN	Austin	615E	MJ-21	78704	1000-1199
MELISSA OAKS LN	Austin	674X	MG-13	78745	1300-2499
MELLOW LN	Travis Co	464J	MG-35	78759	10700-10999
MELLOW HOLLOW DR	Austin	645U	MK-16	78744	4500-4799
MELLOW MEADOW DR	Williamson Co	433M	MF-38	78750	12300-12599
MELLOW MEADOWS	Williamson Co	433H	MF-39	78750	10500-10699
MELODY	Lakeway	489T	WW-31	78734	100-199
MELODY LN	Travis Co	619E	MS-21	78724	5600-6299
MELONCON CV	Austin	611H	MB-21	78735	7800-7899
MELRIDGE PL	Austin	614B	MG-21	78704	2000-2199
MELROSE CV	Austin	435W	MJ-37	78727	6200-6299
MELROSE TRL	Austin	435W	MJ-37	78727	5900-6599
MELS RD	Travis Co	457A	WS-36	78669	100-399
MELSHIRE DR	Austin	495X	MJ-31	78757	8600-8799
MELSTONE DR	Travis Co	560J	MU-26	78653	11500-11799
MELTED CANDLE CV	Travis Co	467C	MP-36	78660	900-999
MELVILLE CV	Austin	642M	MD-17	78749	7600-7699
MELWAS WAY	Travis Co	439F	MS-39	78660	19400-19599
MELWOOD DR	Austin	587G	MP-24	78724	6000-6199
MEMORIAL DR	Georgetown	286J	ML-53	78628	100-999
MEMORIAL HILL LN	Austin	466H	MM-36	78660	None
MEMORIAL PARK	Travis Co	491X	MA-31	78732	12500-12599
MENDEZ ST	Austin	586A	ML-24	78723	4000-4099
MENDIPS LN	Travis Co	439F	MS-39	78660	3200-3299
MENDOCINO DR	Travis Co	582E	MC-24	78735	8600-8899
MENDOCINO LN	Hays Co	669F	WW-15	78737	100-199
MENDOTA CV	Williamson Co	405K	MJ-41	78717	8300-8399
MENDOZA DR	Austin	586U	MM-22	78721	4800-5099
MENDOZA LN	Buda	763E	ME-6	78610	100-199
MENIFEE ST	Travis Co	618V	MR-19	78725	14500-14799
MENLER DR	Austin	612E	MC-21	78735	7600-7799
	Austin	611H	MB-21	78735	7800-7999
MENLO PARK PL	Williamson Co	405C	MK-42	78681	8100-8399
MENODORA DR	Travis Co	672T	MC-13	78748	11300-11499
MENSARD LN	Austin	645B	MJ-18	78741	2100-2199
MENTEER DR	Cedar Park	402R	MD-41	78613	1500-1699
MENTONE DR	Pflugerville	407X	MN-40	78664	1600-1699
MERCEDES CV	Bastrop	715T	EE-10	78602	100-199
MERCEDES BEND	Austin	464U	MH-34	78759	6200-6399
MERCER DR	Austin	586T	ML-22	78721	1100-1199
MERCER ST E	Dripping Springs	636Z	WR-16	78620	100-199
	See.. State Hwy 64				
MERCER ST W	Dripping Springs	636Z	WR-16	78620	100-599
MERCHANT CV	Austin	466D	MM-36	78728	1600-1799
MERCHANTS TALE LN	Austin	703A	ME-12	78748	1300-1599
MERCURY CV	Williamson Co	281N	MA-53	78641	100-199
MERCURY LN	Austin	465L	MK-35	78727	12400-12499
MEREDITH DR	Travis Co	703J	ME-11	78748	900-1199
MEREDITH LN	Williamson Co	406P	ML-41	78681	1000-2099
MEREDITH ST	Austin	554X	MG-25	78703	3200-3699
MERGANSER LN	Cedar Park	373Z	MF-43	78613	1500-1698 E
MERIDEN LN	Austin	584K	MG-23	78703	700-1199
	Austin	584G	MH-24	78703	1300-1499
MERIDIAN BLVD	Travis Co	409P	MS-41	78660	20600-20899
MERIDIAN PASS	Austin	703A	ME-12	78748	1600-1699
MERIDIAN PATH	Georgetown	195J	MJ-62	78633	100-199
MERIDIAN OAK LN	Austin	674S	MG-13	78744	8700-9199
MERIDIAN PARK BLVD	Austin	670D	WZ-15	78739	11800-12699
MERIMAC	Austin	494Z	MH-31	78731	4000-4099
MERION CIR	Travis Co	557B	MN-27	78754	8700-8899
MERION CV	Round Rock	378X	MQ-43	78664	2500-2599
MERION DR	Hays Co	669F	WW-15	78737	100-299
MERION CRICKET CT	Austin	704N	MG-11	78747	11000-11099
MERION CRICKET DR	Austin	704N	MG-11	78747	4600-4799
MERITAGE BLVD	Williamson Co	343S	ME-46	78641	900-1199
MERKIN CIR	Lakeway	519Q	WX-29	78734	1900-1999
MERLE DR	Austin	614W	MG-19	78745	4400-4599
MERLENE DR	Travis Co	520Z	WZ-28	78732	1000-1099
	Travis Co	550D	WZ-27	78732	1100-1399
MERLIN FALCON TRL	Travis Co	439C	MT-39	78660	20200-20399
MERLOT CV	Williamson Co	343N	ME-47	78641	3400-3499
MERRELL CV	Round Rock	376M	MM-44	78664	1500-1599
MERRIE LYNN AVE	Austin	585H	MK-24	78722	3200-3499
MERRILLTOWN DR	Travis Co	436T	ML-37	78728	14300-14799
MERRITT DR	Austin	644V	MH-16	78744	4900-5199
MERRIWOOD DR	Austin	644S	MG-16	78745	6000-6399
MERRYBROOK CIR	Austin	524D	MH-30	78731	7700-7799
MERRYWING CIR	Austin	492Q	MD-32	78730	5600-5799
	Travis Co	492Q	MD-32	78730	5800-5999
MERRYWING CV	Austin	492Q	MD-32	78730	10600-10699
MERSEYSIDE DR	Travis Co	467P	MN-35	78660	13600-14199
	Travis Co	467T	MN-34	78660	None
MERTZ LN	Cedar Park	373U	MF-43	78613	100-199
MESA CT	Austin	524P	MG-29	78731	4100-4199
MESA CV	Austin	524L	MH-29	78731	4000-4099
MESA DR	Austin	524L	MH-29	78731	5700-7799
	Austin	494Z	MH-31	78731	7800-8099
	Austin	494Z	MH-31	78759	8100-8699
	Austin	495N	MJ-32	78759	8700-9099

STREET NAME	CITY or COUNTY	MAPSCO GRID	AUSTIN GRID	ZIP CODE	BLOCK RANGE O/E
MESA DR	Bastrop Co	738M	MR-8	78617	100-399
	See.. FM Rd 2430				
	Bastrop Co	739E	MS-9	78617	400-799
MESA DR	Blanco Co	455L	WP-35	78620	100-299
MESA DR	Leander	342B	MC-48	78641	100-399
MESA DR	Williamson Co	226W	ML-58	78628	100-299
MESA TRL	Williamson Co	340H	WZ-48	78641	100-299
MESA DOBLE LN	Austin	494R	MH-32	78759	8400-8499
MESA GRANDE DR	Austin	641R	MB-17	78749	6100-6399
MESA GRANDE DR	Williamson Co	310R	WZ-50	78641	400-499
MESA HOLLOW DR	Austin	494N	MG-32	78750	6600-6699
MESA OAKS	Travis Co	340M	WZ-47	78641	100-599
MESA OAKS CIR	Austin	613N	ME-20	78735	4700-4799
MESA PARK CV E	Round Rock	377N	MN-44	78664	1600-1799
MESA PARK DR E	Round Rock	377N	MN-44	78664	1200-1699
MESA PARK DR W	Round Rock	376M	MM-44	78664	1300-1999
	Round Rock	376H	MM-45	78664	2200-2499
MESA PINTO DR	Bastrop Co	776V	EH-4	78602	100-299
MESA RIDGE	Williamson Co	340H	WZ-48	78641	100-299
MESA RIDGE LN	Travis Co	582B	MC-24	78735	1400-1599
MESA SPUR	Williamson Co	226W	ML-58	78628	100-199
MESA TRAILS CIR	Austin	494Z	MH-31	78731	7900-7999
MESA VERDE CIR	Austin	642J	MC-17	78749	5400-6199
MESA VERDE CT	Austin	642J	MC-17	78749	8700-8799
MESA VERDE DR	Bastrop Co	680V	MV-13	78612	100-299
MESA VERDE DR	Hays Co	669F	WW-15	78737	13000-13799
MESA VERDE DR	Round Rock	346W	ML-46	78681	1600-1699
MESA VERDE ST	Cedar Park	373T	ME-43	78613	200-499
MESA VIEW DR N	Bastrop Co	776V	EH-4	78602	100-199
MESA VIEW DR S	Bastrop Co	776V	EH-4	78602	100-199
MESA VILLAGE DR	Austin	613N	ME-20	78735	4100-4199
MESA VISTA DR	Williamson Co	310R	WZ-50	78641	100-299
MESA WOODS DR	Austin	465T	MJ-34	78759	4400-4499
MESCALERO CV	Austin	611L	MB-20	78736	8300-8399
MESCALERO DR	Austin	611Q	MB-20	78736	8100-8299
MESQUITE CV	Austin	643C	MF-18	78745	2600-2699
MESQUITE CV	Bastrop Co	715M	EF-11	78602	100-199
MESQUITE DR	Pflugerville	467C	MP-36	78660	None
MESQUITE DR	Williamson Co	441C	MX-39	78615	20400-20699
MESQUITE LN	Georgetown	256U	MM-55	78628	1600-1999
	Georgetown	256T	ML-55	78628	2200-2299
MESQUITE RD	Cedar Park	433A	ME-39	78613	1200-1699
	Williamson Co	432D	MD-39	78613	1700-1899
MESQUITE ST	Bastrop	715T	EE-10	78602	500-1499
MESQUITE TRL	Travis Co	486L	WR-32	78669	4000-4299
MESQUITE GROVE RD	Austin	645X	MJ-16	78744	5400-5599
	Austin	675B	MJ-15	78744	5600-5799
MESQUITE HOLLOW PL	Williamson Co	346H	MM-47	78665	900-1099
MESQUITE SPRING CV	Austin	613J	ME-20	78735	4400-4499
MESSENGER STAKE	Austin	523U	MF-28	78746	6000-6099
MESSICK LOOP E	Round Rock	406N	ML-41	78681	1500-1899
MESSICK LOOP W	Round Rock	406N	ML-41	78681	1900-2799
MESSICK PL	Round Rock	406N	ML-41	78681	1700-1899
MESTENA TRL	Travis Co	522N	MC-29	78733	2000-2299
METAIRIE CIR	Austin	466P	ML-35	78727	1900-1999
METAL RD	Austin	677A	MN-15	78719	10300-10399
METCALFE RD	Austin	645B	MJ-18	78741	2100-2399
	Austin	615X	MJ-19	78741	2400-2699
METCALFE ST E	Hutto	349Z	MT-46	78634	100-199
METCALFE ST W	Hutto	349Z	MT-46	78634	100-599
METEOR DR	Austin	674B	MG-15	78745	100-199
METLINK DR	Austin	646P	ML-17	78744	7800-8599
METRIC BLVD	Austin	495U	MK-31	78758	9000-11099
	Austin	496A	ML-33	78758	11100-11999
	Austin	466X	ML-34	78758	12000-12499
	Austin	466X	ML-34	78727	12500-13699
METRO CENTER DR	Austin	646F	ML-18	78744	7300-7799
METROPOLIS DR	Austin	645R	MK-17	78744	6500-6799
	Austin	646P	ML-17	78744	6800-8599
METROPOLITAN DR	Austin	495R	MK-32	78758	10100-10599
METTLE DR	Travis Co	519R	WX-29	78734	15000-15299
MEURER LN	Travis Co	679U	MT-13	78617	16000-16699
MEUSE CV	Austin	465L	MK-35	78727	12300-12399
MEXICANA CV	Austin	677R	MP-14	78617	12500-12599
MEXICAN HAT DR	Travis Co	402Y	MD-40	78613	2600-2699
MEXICAN HEATHER CT	Pflugerville	468B	MQ-36	78660	1500-1599
MEXICAN PLUM TRL	Williamson Co	433E	ME-39	78613	1600-1899
MEYERS RD	Hays Co	764W	MG-4	78610	100-199
	Hays Co	763Z	MF-4	78610	200-299
MEYRICK PARK TRL	Austin	405A	MJ-42	78717	9100-9499
MIAMI DR	Travis Co	522W	MC-28	78733	1200-1399
	Travis Co	522S	MC-28	78733	1400-1899
MIA TIA CIR	Austin	524L	MH-29	78731	3700-3899
MICA CV	Austin	642R	MD-17	78749	4000-4099
MICA LN	Leander	342K	MC-47	78641	800-899
MICHAEL CV	Leander	341G	MB-48	78641	200-299
MICHAEL LN	Williamson Co	381Q	MX-44	76574	100-199
MICHAEL ST	Austin	614B	MG-21	78704	1700-1799
MICHAELANGELO WAY	Round Rock	436D	MM-39	78728	100-699
MICHAEL DALE	Travis Co	610U	WZ-19	78736	9900-10099
MICHAEL NEILL DR	Travis Co	522C	MD-30	78730	3900-4199
MICHAEL ROBERT WAY	Cedar Park	402R	MD-41	78613	1600-1699
MICHAELS CV	Travis Co	554E	MG-27	78746	4300-4499
MICHAEL WAYNE DR	Travis Co	466C	MM-36	78728	1800-1899
MICHELE CIR	Rollingwood	584J	MG-23	78746	1-99
MICHELLE CT	Austin	645S	MJ-16	78744	5000-5099
MICHELLE CT	Williamson Co	224D	MH-60	78633	100-199
MICHELLE LYNNE CV	Round Rock	376A	ML-45	78681	2700-2799
MICHIGAN DR	Travis Co	467P	MN-35	78660	None
MICHOACAN DR	Austin	647Q	MP-17	78617	3000-3099
MICKELSON CV	Austin	704T	MG-10	78747	10900-10999
MICKELSON DR	Austin	704T	MG-10	78747	5600-5799
MICKELSON LN	Georgetown	226P	ML-59	78628	200-399
MICKEY DR	Williamson Co	405E	MJ-42	78717	16000-16099
MICKEY MANTLE PL	Round Rock	378E	MQ-45	78665	1300-1999
MIDBURY CT	Austin	672T	MD-13	78748	11000-11499
MIDDALE LN	Austin	556T	ML-25	78723	5200-5399
MIDDLE CT	Austin	495W	MJ-31	78759	8100-8199
MIDDLE LN	Austin	526F	ML-30	78753	300-799
MIDDLEBIE DR	Austin	463H	MF-36	78750	9000-9199
MIDDLE BROOK DR	Leander	312S	MC-49	78641	900-1199
	Leander	311V	MB-49	78641	1000-1199
MIDDLEBURY CV	Austin	556H	MM-27	78723	7300-7399
MIDDLE CREEK DR	Buda	732W	MC-7	78610	100-799
MIDDLE DARLEEN DR	Travis Co	401W	MA-40	78641	10100-10299
MIDDLE EARTH TRL	Travis Co	672S	MC-13	78739	3700-3899

STREET NAME	CITY or COUNTY	MAPSCO GRID	AUSTIN GRID	ZIP CODE	BLOCK RANGE O/E
MIDDLEFIELD CT	Travis Co	673P	ME-14	78748	1400-1499
MIDDLE FISKVILLE RD	Austin	555M	MK-26	78751	5300-5699
	Austin	555H	MK-27	78752	5700-6299
	Austin	556A	ML-27	78752	6300-6899
	Austin	526C	MM-30	78753	9400-10199
	Austin	496Y	MM-31	78753	10600-11299
	Travis Co	526C	MM-30	78753	10200-10599
MIDDLE GROUND CV	Austin	703F	ME-12	78748	300-399
MIDDLEHAM PL	Austin	644S	MG-16	78745	6200-6599
MIDDLEWAY RD	Pflugerville	468F	MQ-36	78660	600-1699
MIDLAND WALK	Austin	465K	MJ-35	78727	12200-12299
MIDMORNING DR	Travis Co	640U	WZ-16	78737	11300-11399
MIDNIGHT LN	Williamson Co	317N	MN-50	78626	1-199
MIDNIGHT STAR DR	Cedar Park	374J	MG-44	78613	2500-2599
MIDOAK CIR	Austin	642G	MD-18	78749	4800-4899
MIDPARK CT	Austin	493R	MF-32	78750	7600-7699
MIDWAY DR	Travis Co	398W	WU-40	78654	23600-23799
MIDWOOD LN	Round Rock	405C	MK-42	78681	3000-3099
MIDWOOD PKWY	Austin	611E	MA-21	78736	6300-6699
	Travis Co	611E	MA-21	78736	6700-7199
MIFFLIN KENEDY CT	Austin	642A	MC-18	78749	6200-6299
MIFFLIN KENEDY TERRACE	Austin	642A	MC-18	78749	7400-7699
MIGHTY TIGER TRL	Dripping Springs	636Y	WR-16	78620	600-1099
MIKE'S WAY	Williamson Co	312H	MD-51	78641	1-299
MIKO DR	Cedar Park	372C	MD-45	78613	600-699
MILAGRO DR	Travis Co	551K	MA-26	78733	1300-1799
MILAM AVE E	Round Rock	376Y	MM-43	78664	100-599
MILAM AVE W	Round Rock	376Y	MM-43	78664	100-199
MILAM LN	Georgetown	196K	ML-62	78633	400-499
MILAM PL	Austin	615J	MJ-20	78704	800-999
	Austin	615K	MJ-20	78704	1000-1099
MILAN DR	Williamson Co	402U	MD-40	78613	2100-2299
MILBANKS DR	Austin	496J	ML-32	78758	11200-11299
MILBURN LN	Austin	616A	ML-21	78702	4600-4799
MILDRED DR	Taylor	323S	EA-49	76574	2100-2399
MILDRED ST	Austin	615G	MK-21	78702	1-199
MILDURA CV	Austin	498E	MQ-33	78660	3200-3299
MILES AVE	Austin	643Q	MF-17	78745	1700-1999
MILESTONE RD	Travis Co	486U	WR-31	78669	23700-23999
MILFOIL CV	Austin	613H	MF-21	78704	2500-2599
MILFORD WAY	Austin	644S	MG-16	78745	900-1099
	Austin	643R	MF-17	78745	1100-1299
MILKWEED CV	Travis Co	532L	MZ-29	78621	17600-17699
MILKY WAY DR	Austin	492L	MD-32	78730	10200-10699
MILL ST	Austin	585Y	MK-22	78702	800-999
MILL ST	Bastrop	745Q	EF-8	78602	1300-1499
MILLAY DR	Austin	556C	MM-27	78752	2000-2099
MILLCREEK LN	Leander	341D	MB-48	78641	500-799
MILL CREEK PATH	Georgetown	195J	MJ-62	78633	100-199
MILL CREEK RD	Travis Co	437Q	MP-38	78660	16300-16499
MILL DAM DR	Williamson Co	434E	MG-39	78729	13100-13199
MILLER LN	Creedmoor	735X	MJ-7	78610	4900-5199
MILLER LN	Hays Co	669D	WX-15	78737	10700-10799
MILLER ST	Taylor	353G	EB-48	76574	1100-2099
MILLER FALLS CV	Williamson Co	375U	MK-43	78681	17700-17799
MILLER FALLS DR	Williamson Co	375U	MK-43	78681	8100-8299
MILL HOLLOW	Williamson Co	433K	ME-38	78750	12100-12199
MILLHOUSE DR	Travis Co	467V	MP-34	78660	1700-2199
MILLIKIN CV	Austin	556M	MM-26	78723	6800-6899
MILLOOK HAVEN	Hutto	379P	MS-44	78634	100-399
MILL POND PATH	Georgetown	196N	ML-62	78628	300-599
MILLRACE DR	Austin	557T	MN-25	78724	6600-7199
MILL REEF CV	Austin	553C	MF-27	78731	2900-2999
MILL RIDGE TRACE	Travis Co	529H	MT-30	78653	11600-11699
MILLS AVE	Austin	555S	MJ-25	78703	3400-3499
	Austin	555S	MJ-25	78731	3500-3699
MILLS RD	Georgetown	193Y	MF-61	78633	None
MILLS ST	Taylor	352D	MZ-48	76574	1100-1499
MILLS CROSSING	Bastrop Co	712Z	MZ-10	78602	100-199
	Bastrop Co	743A	EA-9	78602	None
MILLS MEADOW DR	Round Rock	377N	MN-44	78664	1200-1699
MILL SPRINGS DR	Travis Co	583J	ME-23	78746	1600-1799
MILL STONE DR	Williamson Co	434E	MG-39	78729	13100-13199
MILLSTREAM DR	Travis Co	432K	MC-38	78613	3100-3199
MILLWAY DR	Austin	495X	MJ-31	78757	8200-8899
MILLWRIGHT PKWY	Williamson Co	433Q	MF-38	78750	11800-12299
MILNER PASS	Austin	612W	MC-19	78749	6900-6999
MILO RD	Travis Co	619X	MS-19	78725	15600-15999
	Travis Co	649C	MT-18	78725	16000-16099
MILTON CV	Pflugerville	438P	MQ-38	78660	300-399
MILTON CV	Williamson Co	343S	ME-46	78641	700-799
MILTON ST E	Austin	615J	MJ-20	78704	100-299
MILTON ST W	Austin	614M	MH-20	78704	100-799
	Austin	614G	MH-21	78704	900-1099
MILTON LEASE DR	Austin	705F	MJ-12	78747	8800-8999
MIMEBARK WAY	Travis Co	619A	MS-21	78724	15000-15399
MIMOSA CV	Round Rock	407B	MN-42	78664	2000-2099
MIMOSA DR	Austin	643U	MF-16	78745	2000-2399
MIMOSA LN	Leander	342T	MC-46	78641	1700-1799
MIMOSA PASS	Williamson Co	433E	ME-39	78613	1300-1399
MIMOSA ST	Georgetown	287J	MN-53	78626	1600-1699
MIMOSA TRL	Round Rock	407B	MN-42	78664	2000-2399
MIMS CV	Travis Co	618V	MR-19	78725	3600-3799
MINDA CIR	Austin	496K	ML-32	78758	11600-11699
MINDA DR	Austin	496K	ML-32	78758	900-1199
MINDEN ST	Taylor	353K	EA-47	76574	300-399
MINEOLA CT	Lakeway	519D	WX-30	78734	100-199
MINERAL WELLS DR	Travis Co	409T	MS-40	78660	2900-2999
MINERVA ST	Austin	497B	MN-33	78753	1100-1299
MING TRL	Lago Vista	429L	WX-38	78645	19400-20399
MINGUS DR	Travis Co	432G	MD-39	78613	2600-2799
MINI CIR	Austin	643Q	MF-17	78745	6800-6899
MINIKAHDA CV	Travis Co	582H	MD-24	78746	6500-6599
MINNESOTA LN	Austin	673B	ME-15	78745	8300-8399
MINNIE DR	Travis Co	550D	WZ-27	78732	1100-1599
MINNIE ST	Austin	642R	MD-17	78745	3300-3499
MINNOW CV	Round Rock	347S	MN-46	78665	1200-1298 E
MINOT CIR	Austin	673B	ME-15	78748	8600-8799
MINOW PASS	Hutto	380J	MU-44	78634	100-199
MINT JULEP DR	Austin	703G	MF-12	78748	10800-11099
MINTURN LN	Austin	673L	MF-14	78748	700-1099
MINUTE MAN PASS	Austin	704A	MG-12	78747	2200-2299
MIRA DR	Austin	644U	MH-16	78745	5700-5799
MIRABEAU ST	Austin	466P	ML-35	78727	1900-1999
MIRADOR	Leander	371G	MB-45	78641	1400-1499
MIRADOR CV	Williamson Co	345X	MJ-46	78681	4000-4099
MIRADOR DR	Travis Co	582W	MC-22	78735	4300-4599
	Travis Co	612A	MC-21	78735	4600-5099
MIRAFIELD LN	Hays Co	669F	WW-15	78737	100-499
MIRAGE CV	Austin	404Q	MH-41	78717	10000-10099
MIRA LOMA LN	Austin	556L	MM-26	78723	6600-7099
MIRAMAR CV	Williamson Co	377F	MN-45	78665	2300-2399
MIRAMAR DR	Austin	463A	ME-36	78726	11100-11199
MIRAMAR DR	Williamson Co	255D	MK-57	78628	4300-4399
MIRA MESA DR	Travis Co	491V	MB-31	78732	11800-12099
MIRAMONTE CV	Austin	464R	MH-35	78759	11400-11499
MIRAMONTE DR	Austin	464R	MH-35	78759	5700-5999
MIRANDA DR	Austin	525Z	MK-28	78752	6800-7099
MIRASOL DR	Round Rock	375D	MK-45	78681	2700-2899
MIRASOL LOOP	Round Rock	375C	MK-45	78681	2500-2799
MIRA VISTA	Leander	341V	MB-46	78641	1700-1799
MIRA VISTA DR	Travis Co	491V	MB-31	78732	3600-3999
MIRA VISTA WAY	Austin	462G	MD-36	78726	11800-12099
MIRAWOOD LN	Travis Co	557R	MP-26	78724	None
MIRELA ANN RD	Hays Co	607C	WT-21	78720	31800-32499
MIRIAM AVE	Austin	585M	MK-23	78702	1600-1899
	Austin	585M	MK-23	78722	1900-1999
MIRIQUITA	Williamson Co	255D	MK-57	78628	100-199
MIRROR LAKE LN	Austin	587G	MP-24	78724	5700-5799
MIR WOODS DR	Leander	342V	MD-46	78641	1900-2199
MISS ADRIENNE'S PATH	Travis Co	437S	MN-37	78660	15500-15599
MISS ALLISON'S WAY	Travis Co	437S	MN-37	78660	1200-1599
MISS ASHLEY ST	Hays Co	669B	WW-15	78737	100-199
MISSEL THRUSH CT	Williamson Co	433R	MF-38	78750	12100-12199
MISSEL THRUSH DR	Williamson Co	433U	MF-37	78750	10100-10299
MISSION CREEK CV	Travis Co	581M	MB-23	78735	8900-8999
MISSION CREEK DR	Travis Co	581M	MB-23	78735	3700-3899
MISSION HILL CIR	Austin	645E	MJ-18	78741	2200-2299
MISSION HILL DR	Austin	645F	MJ-18	78741	2200-2599
MISSION HILLS	Leander	341V	MB-46	78641	800-899
MISSION OAKS BLVD	Austin	612R	MD-20	78735	4900-5099
MISSION OAKS DR	Georgetown	285T	MJ-52	78628	100-399
MISSION RIDGE	Austin	615N	MJ-20	78704	1100-1199
MISSION TEJAS DR	Travis Co	409X	MS-40	78660	2700-2999
MISSISSIPPI ST	Taylor	353N	EA-47	76574	100-299
MISS JULIE LN	Austin	465F	MK-36	78727	5000-5099
MISS KIMBERLY'S LN	Travis Co	437T	MN-37	78660	1100-1199
MISTFLOWER	Georgetown	196Q	MK-60	78633	100-199
MIST FLOWER DR	Travis Co	467J	MN-35	78660	100-199
MISTING FALLS TRL	Austin	464Z	MH-34	78759	10700-10799
MISTLETOE TRL	Travis Co	703N	ME-11	78652	12500-12699
MISTLETOE HEIGHTS DR	Austin	404E	MG-42	78717	14800-14999
MISTY CV	Austin	497W	MN-31	78754	1500-1599
MISTY LN	Bastrop Co	740W	MU-7	78612	100-199
MISTY BEND	Travis Co	401D	MB-42	78641	13200-13399
MISTY BROOK CV	Austin	465P	MJ-35	78727	4800-4899
MISTY BROOK DR	Austin	465P	MJ-35	78727	11900-12099
MISTY CREEK DR	Travis Co	581M	MB-23	78735	3400-3799
MISTYGLEN CIR	Austin	583Y	MF-22	78746	3100-3199
MISTYGLEN CV	Bastrop Co	740P	MU-8	78612	100-199
MISTY HARBOR DR	Travis Co	439S	MS-37	78660	17900-18099
MISTY HEIGHTS CV	Pflugerville	439E	MS-39	78660	3000-3199
MISTY HILL CV	Austin	464Y	MH-34	78759	5700-5899
MISTY HOLLOW CV	Austin	434T	MG-34	78759	10400-10499
MISTY MORN LN	Cedar Park	403K	ME-41	78613	400-499
MISTY MORNING WAY	Round Rock	376H	MM-45	78664	600-2399
MISTY OAKS WAY	Round Rock	378W	MQ-43	78665	3200-3299
MISTY RIDGE	Leander	372F	MC-45	78641	1800-1999
MISTY SHORE LN	Travis Co	409X	MS-40	78660	2800-2899
MISTY SLOPE LN	Austin	674M	MH-14	78744	4700-4999
MISTY SLOPE LN	Hays Co	636K	WQ-17	78620	200-299
MISTY VALLEY	Travis Co	402A	MC-42	78641	16200-16299
MISTY WHITE DR	Austin	403H	MF-42	78717	11500-11799
MISTYWOOD CIR	Austin	583Y	MF-22	78746	3100-3199
MISTYWOOD CIR	Cedar Park	403B	ME-42	78613	600-799
MISTYWOOD DR	Austin	583Y	MF-22	78746	1700-2099
MISTY WOODS	Round Rock	378Q	MR-44	78664	1-99
MITCHELL CV	Round Rock	344R	MH-47	78681	3900-3999
MITCHELL DR	Hutto	380N	MU-44	78634	200-699
MITCHELL LN	Austin	672R	MD-14	78748	2500-2599
MITRA DR	Austin	670H	WZ-15	78739	6500-7799
MIXSON DR	Travis Co	550D	WZ-27	78732	12500-12799
MIXTLI CV	Williamson Co	343W	ME-46	78641	16600-16699
MIZZEN ST	Manor	530J	MU-29	78653	None
MOAT CV	Austin	644W	MG-16	78745	7100-7199
MOBIL ST	Williamson Co	406P	ML-41	78681	2600-2699
MOCCASIN PATH	Austin	611Q	MB-20	78736	8300-8499
MOCHA TRL	Travis Co	436G	MM-39	78728	3200-3999
	Williamson Co	436G	MM-39	78728	4000-4299
MOCK CHERRY CV	Austin	673Y	MF-13	78748	400-499
MOCKINGBIRD CIR N	Bastrop Co	709Q	MT-11	78612	100-1099
MOCKINGBIRD CIR S	Bastrop Co	709Q	MT-11	78612	100-2099
MOCKINGBIRD CV	Bastrop Co	709R	MT-11	78612	100-199
MOCKINGBIRD CV	Hutto	350S	MU-46	78634	100-199
MOCKINGBIRD DR	Hays Co	701Q	MB-11	78652	900-1099
MOCKINGBIRD DR	Round Rock	375V	MK-43	78681	2100-2499
MOCKINGBIRD LN	Bastrop Co	709Q	MT-11	78612	100-199
MOCKINGBIRD LN	Leander	342R	MD-47	78641	1700-1999
MOCKINGBIRD LN	Taylor	353C	EB-48	76574	400-899
MOCKING BIRD LN	Travis Co	458T	WU-34	78669	20800-21199
MOCKINGBIRD LN	Williamson Co	224B	MG-60	78633	100-199
MOCKINGBIRD LN E	Austin	644P	MG-17	78745	100-199
MOCKINGBIRD LN W	Austin	644P	MG-17	78745	100-499
MOCKINGBIRD ST	Hays Co	794E	MG-3	78610	100-199
MOCKINGBIRD ST	Lago Vista	458J	WU-35	78645	21700-22099
MOCKINGBIRD HILL	Leander	311G	MB-51	78641	200-299
MODENA TRL	Williamson Co	434U	MH-37	78729	12600-12999
MODESTO ST	Austin	525T	MJ-28	78757	6700-6799
MOETA DR	Travis Co	490Z	WZ-31	78734	1800-1999
MOFFAT DR	Briarcliff	458S	WU-34	78669	21800-21999
	Briarcliff	457V	WT-34	78669	22000-22099
MOGONYE LN	Elgin	533H	EB-30	78621	600-699
MOHAWK	Lago Vista	429N	WW-38	78645	20800-20999
MOHAWK RD	Austin	525N	MJ-29	78757	3000-3199
MOHICAN	Round Rock	346V	MM-46	78665	800-1099
MOHICAN DR	Austin	465T	MJ-34	78759	11700-11799
MOHLE DR	Austin	554Z	MH-25	78703	1400-1899
MOJAVE DR	Austin	644N	MG-17	78745	5700-6099
MOJAVE BEND	Williamson Co	343X	ME-46	78641	1300-1499
MOKALAU DR	Bastrop	746S	EG-7	78602	100-199
MOKOLEA LN	Bastrop Co	775H	EF-6	78602	100-199
MOKOLII CT	Bastrop Co	745Z	EF-7	78602	100-199
MOKU CT	Bastrop Co	746W	EG-7	78602	100-199
MOKUAUIA CT	Bastrop Co	745Z	EF-7	78602	100-199
MOKULEIA CIR	Bastrop Co	775M	EF-5	78602	100-199
MOKULUA LN	Bastrop Co	775C	EF-6	78602	100-299
MOKU MANU DR	Bastrop Co	776E	EG-6	78602	100-299
MOLERA DR	Austin	642Q	MD-17	78749	4600-4799
MOLLIE DR	Hutto	350N	MU-47	78634	100-299
MOLOKAI DR	Austin	642L	MD-17	78749	4200-4499
MOLOKINI DR	Bastrop Co	745Z	EF-7	78602	100-199
MOLSON LAKE DR	Williamson Co	343X	ME-46	78641	1400-1599
MONACO DR	Cedar Park	403U	MF-40	78613	100-2599
MONADALE TRL	Round Rock	407B	MN-42	78664	900-1099
MONAGHAN TRL	Austin	465G	MK-36	78727	12500-12599
MONAHANS DR	Williamson Co	314X	MG-49	78628	200-499
MONAHANS LN	Austin	673W	ME-13	78748	1700-1799
MONARCH AVE	Cedar Park	372Z	MD-43	78613	500-899
MONARCH CV	Cedar Park	372Z	MD-43	78613	300-499
MONARCH DR	Austin	673J	ME-14	78748	2000-2699
MONARCH LN	Hays Co	639U	WX-16	78737	100-299
MONARCH LN	Travis Co	588N	MQ-23	78724	9700-9899
MONARCH TRL	Georgetown	195K	MJ-62	78633	100-799
MONARCH OAKS LN					
	Village of the Hills	519N	WW-29	78738	1-99
MONARCH RIDGE LOOP	Travis Co	704G	MH-12	78747	None
MONDONEDO CV	Travis Co	580C	WZ-24	78738	4800-4899
MONES LN	Williamson Co	343X	ME-46	78641	16200-16299
MONET DR	Austin	433P	ME-38	78726	11300-11499
MONET POINTE DR	Jonestown	430N	WY-38	78645	18300-18599
MONICA LN	Round Rock	407R	MP-41	78664	2000-2099
MONICA ST	Austin	496K	ML-32	78758	1300-1499
MONIKA LN	Taylor	322V	MZ-49	76574	2800-2999
MONITOR DR	Austin	643X	ME-16	78745	2400-2699
MONKEY RD	Bastrop Co	563Q	EB-26	78621	100-299
See.. Bastrop Co Rd 75					
	Bastrop Co	562D	MZ-27	78621	300-699
	Travis Co	562D	MZ-27	78621	700-799
See.. Bastrop Co Rd 75					
MONK'S MOUNTAIN DR	Travis Co	490N	WY-32	78734	16100-16299
MONKS TALE CT	Austin	673W	ME-13	78748	1800-1899
MONMOUTH CIR	Austin	526M	MM-29	78753	9600-9699
MONONA AVE	Williamson Co	405P	MJ-41	78717	7600-8299
MONONA CV	Williamson Co	405P	MJ-41	78717	15700-15799
MONROE CV	Lago Vista	458L	WV-35	78645	20900-20999
MONROE ST	Bastrop Co	534X	EC-28	78621	200-299
	Bastrop Co	534X	EC-28	78621	400-699
MONROE ST E	Austin	615J	MJ-20	78704	100-999
MONROE ST W	Austin	614M	MH-20	78704	100-1199
MONSANTO DR	Austin	616P	ML-20	78741	6300-6399
MONTAGNA CV	Lakeway	519H	WX-30	78734	100-199
MONTALCINO BLVD	Lakeway	489Z	WX-31	78734	100-399
MONTALVO LN	Williamson Co	288B	MQ-54	78626	100-199
MONTANA CT	Leander	341M	MB-47	78641	1800-1899
MONTANA CV	Austin	616X	ML-19	78741	1300-1399
MONTANA ST	Austin	616X	ML-19	78741	6600-7099
MONTANA CREEK CROSSING					
	Burnet Co	307W	WS-49	78654	25000-29999
MONTANA FALLS DR	Williamson Co	375X	MJ-43	78681	17300-17499
MONTANA NORTE	Austin	524G	MH-30	78731	7100-7399
MONTANA RIDGE PASS	Burnet Co	307T	WS-49	78654	29900-29999
	Travis Co	307T	WS-49	78654	29600-29899
MONTANA SKY DR	Austin	466G	MM-36	78727	1800-1999
MONTANA SPRINGS CV	Burnet Co	307W	WS-49	78654	29800-29899
MONTANA SPRINGS DR	Burnet Co	307W	WS-49	78654	11000-11999
	Travis Co	307T	WS-49	78654	12000-12499
MONTAQUE CV	Williamson Co	434R	MH-38	78729	13300-13399
MONTAQUE DR	Williamson Co	434R	MH-38	78729	7500-7799
MONT BLANC DR	Bee Cave	549F	WW-27	78738	4500-4899
MONTCLAIR DR	Round Rock	406M	MM-41	78664	1900-2099
MONTCLAIR BEND	Travis Co	521S	MA-28	78732	11900-12499
MONTCLAIRE ST	Austin	614K	MG-20	78704	2000-2399
MONTEBELLO CT	Austin	583V	MF-22	78746	2900-2999
MONTEBELLO RD	Austin	583V	MF-22	78746	2800-2899
	Rollingwood	583V	MF-22	78746	2900-2999
MONTE CARLO DR	Cedar Park	403U	MF-40	78613	2300-2599
MONTE CARMELO PL	Travis Co	580C	WZ-24	78738	4700-4799
MONTE CASTILLO PKWY	Travis Co	462W	MC-34	78732	12500-12999
MONTECITO BLVD	Hays Co	577Q	WT-23	78720	18000-18399
	Travis Co	577Q	WT-23	78620	None
MONTELL DR	Williamson Co	314F	MG-51	78628	200-299
MONTELL LN	Hutto	379L	MT-44	78634	1100-1299
MONTEREY PATH	Travis Co	521N	MA-29	78732	12600-12799
MONTEREY OAKS BLVD	Austin	612M	MD-19	78749	3900-4999
MONTEREY PINES DR	Round Rock	408G	MR-42	78664	300-399
MONTEROSA LN	Williamson Co	316Z	MM-49	78665	4500-4599
	Williamson Co	317W	MN-49	78665	4600-4699
MONTEROSA LOOP	Williamson Co	316Z	MM-49	78665	1500-1599
MONTERREY CV	Elgin	534W	EC-28	78621	200-299
MONTERREY PL	Austin	496M	MM-32	78753	800-899
MONTERREY ST	Elgin	534W	EC-28	78621	100-299
MONTERREY HILLS DR	Bastrop Co	738X	MQ-7	78617	None
MONTESA DR	Austin	463E	ME-36	78726	11000-11099
MONTEVILLA DR	Austin	463B	ME-36	78726	10500-10599
MONTEVISTA CV	Hays Co	577T	WS-22	78720	18000-18199
MONTE VISTA DR	Austin	554F	MG-27	78731	3400-3499
MONTE VISTA DR	Georgetown	317E	MN-51	78626	300-399
MONTEZUMA ST	Austin	646T	ML-16	78744	7400-7499
MONTGOMERY ST	Georgetown	286L	MM-53	78626	600-799
MONTICELLO CIR	Austin	586K	ML-23	78721	4100-4199
MONTICELLO CT	Williamson Co	317X	MN-49	78665	2100-2199
MONTLEY TRL	Georgetown	195Z	MK-61	78633	100-499
MONTOPOLIS DR	Austin	616P	ML-20	78741	100-1799
	Austin	646A	ML-18	78741	1800-2599
	Austin	645H	MK-18	78741	2600-3099
	Austin	645R	MK-17	78744	3100-3799
MONTORO DR	Travis Co	436T	ML-37	78728	14600-14899
MONTOYA CIR	Williamson Co	405N	MJ-41	78717	8200-8399
MONTOYA CV	Williamson Co	405N	MJ-41	78717	15400-15499
MONTROSE ST	Austin	585B	MJ-24	78705	3400-3799
MONTVIEW DR	Travis Co	491N	MA-32	78732	13300-13899
MONTVIEW ST	Austin	555A	MJ-27	78756	5400-5699
MONTWOOD TRL	Austin	672X	MC-13	78748	3000-3099
	Austin	702B	MC-12	78748	3100-3199
MONTZ PT	Hays Co	794M	MH-2	78610	100-199
MONUMENT DR	Williamson Co	375X	MJ-43	78681	3000-3799
MONUMENT HILL TRL	Georgetown	195K	MJ-62	78633	100-399
MOODY DR	Austin	614Z	MH-19	78704	None
MOON BRAKE RD	Bastrop Co	592R	MZ-23	78621	100-299
MOON DANCE LN	Travis Co	488P	WU-32	78669	19900-20299

STREET NAME	CITY or COUNTY	MAPSCO GRID	AUSTIN GRID	ZIP CODE	BLOCK RANGE O/E
MOONEY CIR	Burnet Co	396W	WQ-40	78669	100-199
MOONFLOWER DR	Austin	493L	MF-32	78750	7800-7999
MOONGLOW DR	Austin	587B	MN-24	78724	6300-6599
	Austin	557X	MN-25	78724	None
MOON GLOW DR	Leander	342K	MC-47	78641	800-1099
MOON LARK CT	Austin	523Y	MF-28	78746	3700-3799
MOONLIGHT DR	Williamson Co	373V	MF-43	78613	1600-1799
MOONLIGHT BAY DR	Travis Co	458Z	WV-34	78669	700-1099
MOONLIGHT BEND	Austin	554T	MG-25	78703	2700-2799
MOONLIGHT TRACE	Travis Co	487F	WS-33	78669	None
MOONMIST CV	Round Rock	347V	MP-46	78665	2700-2799
MOONMONT DR	Austin	674A	MG-15	78745	6800-7099
MOON RISE CV	Jonestown	430L	WZ-38	78645	17800-17899
MOON RISE TRL	Jonestown	430G	WZ-39	78645	8100-8299
MOON RIVER DR	Georgetown	195X	MJ-61	78633	100-199
MOON RIVER RD	Travis Co	583Q	MF-23	78746	3600-3799
MOON ROCK RD	Austin	641X	MA-16	78739	7200-7599
MOONSEED CV	Travis Co	436U	MM-37	78728	14800-14899
MOON SHADOW CV	Austin	612D	MD-21	78735	4000-4099
MOON SHADOW DR	Austin	612D	MD-21	78735	5200-5499
MOONVIEW DR	Austin	645C	MK-18	78741	2400-2499
MOORBERRY ST	Williamson Co	434E	MG-39	78729	9600-9799
MOORCROFT LN	Williamson Co	434V	MH-37	78729	13000-13099
MOORE BLVD	Austin	585B	MJ-24	78705	300-399
MOORE LN	Travis Co	374B	MG-45	78613	1-899
MOORE RD	Travis Co	706Z	MM-10	78719	10500-11599
	Travis Co	737A	MN-9	78719	11600-13299
MOORELAND DR	Austin	703A	ME-12	78748	1100-1199
	Travis Co	703A	ME-12	78748	1200-1299
MOORES BRIDGE RD	Travis Co	677S	MN-13	78617	10200-10598 E
	Travis Co	677S	MN-13	78719	10201-10599 O
MOORE'S CROSSING BLVD	Travis Co	677X	MN-13	78617	6700-7099
MOORING CIR	Lakeway	489Y	WX-31	78734	200-299
MOORLYNCH AVE	Travis Co	439F	MS-39	78660	19300-19799
MOOSE CV	Austin	642P	MC-17	78749	8500-8599
MOOSE DR	Austin	642P	MC-17	78749	4500-4699
MOPAC CIR	Austin	584W	MG-22	78746	1000-1099
MOPAC EXPY N	Austin	584G	MH-24	78703	100-2599
	Austin	554M	MH-26	78703	2600-3499
	Austin	554M	MH-26	78731	3500-5099
	Austin	524V	MH-28	78731	5100-6899
	Austin	525J	MJ-29	78731	6900-7799
	Austin	495P	MJ-32	78759	8200-11499
	Austin	465Y	MK-34	78759	11500-11999
	Austin	465Y	MK-34	78758	12000-12099
	Austin	466N	ML-35	78758	12100-12499
	Austin	466N	ML-35	78727	12500-12799
MOPAC EXPY S	Austin	584W	MG-22	78746	100-1299
	Austin	614A	MG-21	78746	1300-1499
	Austin	613D	MF-21	78746	1500-4099
	Austin	613W	ME-19	78735	4100-5099
	Austin	613W	ME-19	78749	5100-5999
	Austin	643A	ME-18	78749	6000-6299
	Austin	642D	MD-18	78749	6300-9599
	Austin	642N	MC-17	78739	9600-10199
	Austin	671M	MB-14	78739	10200-11999
MOR DR	Travis Co	546V	WR-25	78620	9200-9999
MORADO CIR	Austin	494D	MH-33	78759	10400-10499
	Austin	464Z	MH-34	78759	10500-10699
	Austin	465W	MJ-34	78759	10700-10799
MORADO CV	Austin	494D	MH-33	78759	10300-10399
MORAL PASS	Georgetown	225V	MK-58	78628	100-299
MORAR DR	Briarcliff	458S	WU-34	78669	100-299
MORAVIAN CV	Austin	495W	MJ-31	78759	8000-8099
MORAY LN	Travis Co	432L	MD-38	78613	2500-2699
MORDOR CV	Travis Co	672N	MC-14	78739	3800-3899
MORDRED CT	Austin	671G	MB-15	78739	11400-11499
MORDRED LN	Austin	671G	MB-15	78739	5800-6199
MORELAND DR	Georgetown	225U	MK-58	78633	4800-4899
MORELOS CV	Austin	647Q	MP-17	78617	3000-3099
MORELOS ST	Austin	585Z	MK-22	78702	2200-2399
MORGAN DR	Leander	342K	MC-47	78641	700-799
MORGAN LN	Austin	614W	MG-19	78704	1300-1699
MORGAN LN	Lago Vista	458G	WV-36	78645	3100-3299
MORGANA DR	Travis Co	439F	MS-39	78660	19400-19599
MORGAN CREEK CT	Williamson Co	404G	MH-42	78717	15300-15399
MORGAN CREEK DR	Austin	404G	MH-42	78717	9400-10199
MORGAN FARM RD	Bee Cave	549R	WX-26	78738	None
MORGANHILL DR	Hays Co	636K	WQ-17	78620	700-1099
MORGAN HILL TRL	Williamson Co	375S	MJ-43	78717	16600-17099
MORGAN'S PT	Manor	529X	MS-28	78653	None
MORGANS CHOICE LN	Pflugerville	409J	MS-41	78660	20800-21099
MORIN DR	Travis Co	592J	MY-23	78621	9100-9599
MORITZ LN	Austin	494Z	MH-31	78731	7800-7999
MORLEY DR	Austin	556C	MM-27	78752	2100-2199
MORNEA DR	Travis Co	436Q	MM-38	78728	14900-14999
MORNING CT	Austin	494H	MH-33	78759	9600-9799
MORNING CLOUD	Lakeway	489U	WX-31	78734	100-499
MORNING CLOUD CV	Lakeway	489U	WX-31	78734	100-199
MORNING DEW CV	Round Rock	376H	MM-45	78664	1100-1199
MORNING DEW DR	Austin	612U	MD-19	78749	6000-6399
MORNING DOVE CV	Travis Co	703N	ME-11	78652	700-799
MORNING DOVE DR	Hutto	350N	MU-47	78634	500-699
MORNING GLORY CIR	Georgetown	226A	ML-60	78633	100-199
MORNING GLORY TRL	Travis Co	433P	ME-38	78750	11200-11399
	Williamson Co	433P	ME-38	78750	11400-11499
MORNING HILL DR	Travis Co	640P	WY-17	78737	9400-9499
MORNING MEADOW CV	Round Rock	407J	MN-41	78664	1700-1799
MORNING MIST LN	Travis Co	467M	MP-35	78660	1400-1699
MORNING PRIMROSE CT	Austin	703G	MF-12	78748	100-199
MORNING QUAIL DR	Austin	496E	ML-33	78758	1600-1899
MORNINGSIDE CIR	Williamson Co	409R	MT-41	78634	100-399
MORNING SIDE CV	Round Rock	407N	MN-41	78664	1700-1799
MORNINGSIDE LN	Austin	703E	ME-12	78748	1300-1399
MORNINGSTAR CIR	Travis Co	640P	WY-17	78737	11200-11299
MORNINGSUN DR	Travis Co	640T	WY-16	78737	11500-11599
MORNING SUNRISE CV	Austin	611R	MB-20	78735	7300-7399
MORNING VIEW CT	Travis Co	707B	MN-12	78617	7300-7399
MORNING VIEW DR	Travis Co	707B	MN-12	78617	11600-12099
MORNING VIEW PL	Round Rock	378S	MQ-43	78665	900-999
MORRELL ST S	Round Rock	406G	MM-42	78664	601-999 O
MORRIS DR	Georgetown	256Y	MM-55	78628	500-599
MORRIS RD	Williamson Co	434L	MH-38	78729	13200-13499
MORROW LN	Travis Co	562F	MY-27	78621	11800-12099
MORROW LN	Travis Co	532X	MY-28	78621	12300-12499
MORROW ST	Austin	525V	MK-28	78752	600-799
	Austin	525Q	MK-29	78757	800-1999

STREET NAME	CITY or COUNTY	MAPSCO GRID	AUSTIN GRID	ZIP CODE	BLOCK RANGE O/E
MORROW ST	Cedar Park	372K	MC-44	78613	None
MORROW ST	Travis Co	562F	MY-27	78621	18000-18099
MORROW ST E	Georgetown	286D	MM-54	78626	100-399
	Georgetown	257W	MN-55	78626	None
MORROW ST W	Georgetown	286C	MM-54	78626	1-599
MORSE CV	Georgetown	256T	ML-55	78628	1200-1299
MOSCOW TRL	Williamson Co	434M	MH-38	78729	13400-13499
MOSER RIVER DR	Williamson Co	343S	ME-46	78641	900-1099
MOSES LN	Travis Co	591J	MW-23	78653	20400-20699
MOSLEY LN	Austin	465Q	MK-35	78727	12100-12299
MOSQUERO CIR	Austin	673F	ME-15	78748	8600-8899
MOSS PT	Lago Vista	429S	WW-37	78645	5000-5199
MOSS ST	Austin	586J	ML-23	78722	2900-2999
MOSSBACK CV	Austin	702F	MC-12	78739	12400-12499
MOSSBACK LN	Austin	702B	MC-12	78739	2800-2999
MOSSBROOK CV	Austin	433V	MF-37	78750	12000-12099
MOSS CREEK DR	Leander	342M	MD-47	78641	1400-1599
MOSSHEAD CV	Travis Co	492Q	MD-32	78730	10500-10599
MOSS HOLLOW DR	Williamson Co	344V	MH-46	78681	4100-4199
MOSSROCK DR	Austin	495T	MJ-31	78757	3200-3299
MOSS ROSE CV	Austin	493V	MF-31	78750	6900-6999
MOSSWOOD CIR	Austin	673E	ME-15	78748	9300-9399
MOSSY BARK TRL	Williamson Co	433G	MF-39	78750	12400-12599
MOSSYCUP LN	Travis Co	619E	MS-21	78724	14900-15199
MOSSY GROVE CT	Travis Co	432K	MC-38	78613	3300-3399
MOSSY HOLLOW DR	Lago Vista	429Z	WX-37	78645	5700-6299
MOSSY ROCK CV	Hutto	379M	MT-44	78634	100-199
MOSSY ROCK DR	Hutto	380J	MU-44	78634	200-499
	Hutto	379M	MT-44	78634	None
MOTHERAL DR	Austin	496X	ML-31	78753	10400-10599
	Austin	496T	ML-31	78753	10600-10899
	Austin	496Q	MM-32	78753	11100-11299
MOULIN DR	Briarcliff	487D	WT-33	78669	22000-22099
	Briarcliff	457Z	WT-34	78669	22100-22899
MOULTON LN	Bee Cave	549R	WX-26	78738	13900-14099
MOUNTAIN DR	Lago Vista	458C	WV-36	78645	3600-3699
MOUNTAIN TRL	Taylor	353T	EA-46	76574	1800-2199
MOUNTAIN TRL	Travis Co	461Q	MB-35	78732	6700-7299
MOUNTAIN CEDAR CV	Austin	524X	MG-28	78731	5400-5499
MOUNTAINCLIMB DR	Austin	524Q	MH-29	78731	4000-5999
MOUNTAIN CREEK PASS	Georgetown	194R	MH-62	78633	100-199
MOUNTAIN CREEK RD	Burnet Co	307C	WT-51	78654	100-1399
MOUNTAIN CREST DR	Austin	611C	MB-21	78735	8600-8799
MOUNTAIN LAKE CIR	Austin	433Z	MF-37	78750	9000-9099
MOUNTAIN LAUREL DR	Austin	554U	MH-25	78703	2700-2899
MOUNTAIN LAUREL DR	Cedar Park	403E	ME-42	78613	400-599
MOUNTAIN LAUREL LN	Austin	554U	MH-25	78703	2700-2799
MOUNTAIN LAUREL WAY	Bastrop Co	776Y	EH-4	78602	100-199
MOUNTAIN LAUREL WAY	Hays Co	669J	WW-14	78737	100-399
MOUNTAIN MIST LN	Williamson Co	375T	MJ-43	78681	9000-9099
MOUNTAIN OAKS DR	Travis Co	551D	MB-27	78733	9900-10099
MOUNTAIN PARK CV	Austin	524E	MG-30	78731	6300-6399
MOUNTAIN PATH CIR	Austin	494M	MH-32	78759	8800-8899
MOUNTAIN PATH DR	Austin	494M	MH-32	78759	4300-4599
MOUNTAIN QUAIL RD	Austin	495Z	MK-31	78758	9400-9699
	Austin	496S	ML-31	78758	9700-10199
MOUNTAIN RIDGE CIR	Austin	494M	MH-32	78759	8800-8899
MOUNTAIN RIDGE DR	Austin	494M	MH-32	78759	8700-9199
MOUNTAIN RIDGE DR	Leander	342M	MD-47	78641	700-899
MOUNTAIN SHADOWS CV	Austin	611F	MA-21	78735	8800-8899
MOUNTAIN SHADOWS DR	Austin	611F	MA-21	78735	6000-6299
MOUNTAINSIDE DR	Travis Co	400S	WY-40	78645	19800-25099
	Travis Co	399V	WX-40	78645	None
MOUNTAIN SPRING LN	Leander	311Z	MB-49	78641	1300-1499
MOUNTAIN TOP CIR	Austin	554F	MG-27	78731	3400-3499
MOUNTAIN TOP CIR	Travis Co	400B	WY-42	78645	10700-11499
MOUNTAIN VIEW AVE	Travis Co	490H	WZ-33	78734	3600-3899
MOUNTAIN VIEW CV	Pflugerville	467C	MP-36	78660	800-899
MOUNTAIN VIEW DR	Austin	614J	MG-20	78704	2400-2499
	Austin	613H	MF-21	78704	2500-2599
MOUNTAIN VIEW DR	Pflugerville	467D	MP-36	78660	100-1299
MOUNTAIN VIEW RD	Austin	584B	MG-24	78703	1800-2299
MOUNTAIN VILLA CIR	Austin	524K	MG-29	78731	6100-6199
MOUNTAIN VILLA CV	Austin	524K	MG-29	78731	6100-6199
MOUNTAIN VILLA DR	Austin	524P	MG-29	78731	5900-6299
MOUNTAINWOOD CIR	Austin	495S	MJ-31	78759	8700-8799
MOUNT BARKER DR	Austin	554F	MG-27	78731	3400-3499
MOUNT BARTLETT DR	Austin	494L	MH-32	78759	8900-8999
MOUNTBATTEN CIR	Travis Co	522H	MD-30	78730	8800-9099
MOUNT BONNELL CIR	Austin	554F	MG-27	78731	3400-3499
MOUNT BONNELL CV	Austin	524P	MG-29	78731	6000-6099
MOUNT BONNELL DR	Austin	554F	MG-27	78731	3300-3499
MOUNT BONNELL RD	Austin	554B	MG-27	78731	3300-4699
	Austin	524T	MG-28	78731	4700-5699
	Austin	524P	MG-29	78731	5700-6099
MOUNT BONNELL HOLLOW	Austin	524P	MG-29	78731	6000-6099
MOUNT CARRELL DR	Austin	643Z	MF-16	78745	6800-7199
MOUNT EMORY CV	Austin	494L	MH-32	78759	5200-5299
MOUNT GAINOR RD	Hays Co	666E	WQ-15	78620	100-2099
MOUNT LARSON RD	Travis Co	554S	MG-25	78746	100-1399
	Travis Co	553V	MF-25	78746	1400-1899
MOUNT LAUREL DR	Lago Vista	428Y	WV-37	78645	21500-21699
MOUNT LAUREL RD	Lago Vista	428Y	WV-37	78645	3400-3799
MOUNT LOCKE CT	Georgetown	225A	MJ-60	78633	900-999
MT OLIVE RD	Bastrop Co	742H	MY-8	78612	100-699
MOUNT RAINIER DR	Austin	704A	MG-12	78747	10000-10099
MOUNT RUSHMORE DR N	Cedar Park	373T	ME-43	78613	100-499
MOUNT RUSHMORE DR S	Cedar Park	373X	ME-43	78613	100-599
MOUNT SHASTA CV	Williamson Co	375U	MK-43	78681	8400-8499
MOUNT VERNON AVE	Lago Vista	458D	WV-36	78645	3100-3399
MOUNT VERNON DR	Austin	644F	MG-18	78745	4200-4799
MOUNT VIEW CIR	Lago Vista	458C	WV-36	78645	21200-21299
MOUNT VIEW DR	Lago Vista	428Y	WV-37	78645	21300-21599
MOURA CV	Austin	498E	MQ-33	78660	13500-13599
MOURNING DOVE BLVD	Georgetown	227J	MN-59	78626	30100-30199
MOURNING DOVE CIR	Williamson Co	433Q	MF-38	78750	10300-10399
MOURNING DOVE DR	Williamson Co	433Q	MF-38	78750	10300-10799
MOURNING DOVE LN	Williamson Co	282E	MC-54	78641	100-399
MOURNING DOVE LN	Williamson Co	286Z	MM-52	78626	100-199
	Williamson Co	316D	MM-51	78626	200-299
MOUSE TRAP DR	Williamson Co	405B	MJ-42	78681	16800-16999
MOVING WATER LN	Travis Co	409X	MS-40	78660	2800-2999
MOWINKLE CV	Travis Co	611N	MA-20	78736	7700-7799
MOWINKLE DR	Travis Co	611N	MA-20	78736	7200-8399
MOWSBURY DR	Austin	404E	MG-42	78717	14200-14599
MOYE ST	Round Rock	377W	MN-43	78664	100-199
MOZELLE LN	Travis Co	674T	MG-13	78744	2400-2599

STREET NAME	CITY or COUNTY	MAPSCO GRID	AUSTIN GRID	ZIP CODE	BLOCK RANGE O/E
MUCK DR	Austin	678P	MQ-14	78617	13500-13599
MUCKENDER LN	Austin	528P	MQ-29	78754	7000-7099
MUDDLER CV	Travis Co	551P	MA-26	78733	11100-11199
MUDDY WATERS DR	Pflugerville	407U	MP-40	78664	1400-1499
MUELLER BLVD	Austin	556W	ML-25	78723	4500-5099
MUERY ST	Williamson Co	443Q	EB-38	78615	100-199
MUFFIN DR	Austin	557U	MP-25	78724	7300-7499
MUHLY CV	Travis Co	580B	WY-24	78738	12300-12399
MUIR CT	Georgetown	195V	MK-61	78633	100-199
MUIR LN	Travis Co	552V	MD-25	78746	1-99
MUIRFIELD CIR	Austin	704J	MG-11	78747	2300-2499
MUIRFIELD BEND DR	Travis Co	408D	MR-42	78634	1300-1499
	Williamson Co	408D	MR-42	78634	1500-1599
MUIRFIELD GREENS CV	Lakeway	519K	WW-29	78738	1-99
MUIRFIELD GREENS LN	Lakeway	519J	WW-29	78738	1-99
MUIRLANDS DR	Austin	674Q	MH-14	78744	2400-2599
MUIR PARKE PASS	Austin	462J	MC-35	78726	8000-8099
MULBERRY CIR	Georgetown	225D	MK-60	78633	100-199
MULBERRY DR	Austin	644W	MG-16	78745	400-699
MULBERRY LN	West Lake Hills	583B	ME-24	78746	1-99
MULBERRY WAY	Williamson Co	433E	ME-39	78613	1300-1499
MULBERRY CREEK CT	Travis Co	491U	MB-31	78732	12500-12599
MULBERRY CREEK DR	Travis Co	491U	MB-31	78732	3300-3499
MULDOON DR	Williamson Co	434V	MH-37	78729	12900-13099
MULE DEER CT	Williamson Co	378H	MR-45	78634	100-199
MULEDEER CV	Williamson Co	344D	MH-48	78628	100-199
MULEDEER DR	Austin	642P	MC-17	78749	8600-8699
MULEDEER RUN	Leander	342X	MC-46	78641	1300-1999
MULESHOE TRL	Travis Co	583M	MF-23	78746	3300-3399
MULESHOE BEND TRL	Travis Co	367W	WS-43	78654	6300-7499
MULEY DR	Travis Co	464N	MG-35	78759	8000-8199
MULFORD CV	Austin	615W	MJ-19	78741	2700-2799
MULLEN DR	Austin	525L	MK-29	78757	7600-8199
MULLIGAN DR	Round Rock	378Y	MR-43	78664	1900-1999
MULLIGAN GLEN CT	Austin	497J	MN-32	78753	12200-12299
MULVEY DR	Travis Co	371R	MB-44	78641	13200-13399
MUMRUFFIN LN	Austin	528P	MQ-29	78754	7100-7199
MUNICIPAL DR	Leander	342B	MC-48	78641	400-799
	Leander	342E	MC-48	78641	800-999
MUNSON ST	Austin	586T	ML-22	78721	3600-4899
MURCHISON DR	Bastrop Co	741P	MW-8	78612	100-199
MURCHISON ST	Manor	529Y	MT-28	78653	11400-11799
MURCHISON RIDGE TRL	Pflugerville	438D	MR-39	78660	19100-19399
	Pflugerville	408Z	MR-40	78664	19400-19799
MURCIA DR	Austin	465T	MJ-34	78759	11400-11599
MURFIELD DR	Georgetown	226L	MM-59	78628	1-99
MURFIN RD	Lakeway	520J	WY-29	78734	15400-15499
	Travis Co	520J	WY-29	78734	13500-15399
MURILLO CIR	Austin	554T	MG-25	78703	3600-3699
MURMURING CREEK DR	Travis Co	611E	MA-21	78736	9300-9999
	Travis Co	610H	WZ-21	78736	10000-10199
MUROC ST	Austin	525P	MJ-29	78757	2100-2299
MURPHY ST	Taylor	353F	EA-48	76574	200-599
MURRAY AVE E	Manor	529Q	MT-29	78653	100-399
MURRAY AVE W	Manor	529Q	MT-29	78653	100-399
MURRAY LN	Austin	584M	MH-23	78703	1500-1599
MURRELET WAY	Travis Co	409T	MS-40	78660	2900-3399
MURRON DR	Austin	528E	MQ-30	78754	11600-11699
MUSCOVY CV	Taylor	322Y	MZ-49	76574	1900-2098 E
MUSCOVY LN	Cedar Park	373Y	MF-43	78613	100-399
MUSIC LN	Austin	615E	MJ-21	78704	1000-1199
MUSKBERRY CV	Austin	405A	MJ-42	78717	9300-9499
MUSKDEER DR	Austin	642P	MC-17	78749	4500-4799
MUSKET CV	Travis Co	580G	WZ-24	78738	5200-5299
MUSKET DR	Bastrop Co	712V	MZ-10	78602	100-199
MUSKET RIDGE	Austin	494D	MH-33	78759	5300-5499
MUSKET RIM	Travis Co	580G	WZ-24	78738	11200-12299
MUSKET VALLEY TRL	Austin	497T	MN-31	78754	1600-2299
MUSSELMAN CT	Hutto	380N	MU-44	78634	100-199
MUSSETT ST	Austin	497S	MN-31	78754	1400-1599
MUSTANG	Lago Vista	429W	WW-37	78645	4800-4899
MUSTANG AVE N	Cedar Park	373T	ME-43	78613	100-499
MUSTANG AVE S	Cedar Park	373X	ME-43	78613	100-399
	Cedar Park	403B	ME-42	78613	400-699
MUSTANG CV	Taylor	352L	MZ-47	76574	None
MUSTANG DR	Mustang Ridge	766S	ML-4	78610	12000-12299
MUSTANG ST E	Taylor	353K	EA-47	76574	200-499
MUSTANG ST W	Taylor	353J	EA-47	76574	100-399
MUSTANG TRL	Pflugerville	467C	MP-36	78660	None
MUSTANG WAY	Williamson Co	192P	MC-62	78633	100-599
MUSTANG CHASE	Austin	465K	MJ-35	78727	11800-12499
MUSTANG CROSSING	Bastrop Co	740T	MU-7	78612	100-199
MUSTANG GRAPE CT	Pflugerville	438X	MQ-37	78660	1200-1299
MUSTANG HOLLOW LOOP					
	Caldwell Co	796D	MM-3	78610	700-999
	Mustang Ridge	796H	MM-3	78610	None
MUSTANG ISLAND CIR	Travis Co	409X	MS-40	78660	20200-20299
MUSTANG ISLAND TRAIL DR					
	Georgetown	195J	MJ-62	78633	100-299
MUSTANG MESA DR	Mustang Ridge	765R	MK-5	78610	100-12399
MUSTER CT	Austin	523M	MF-29	78731	5600-5699
MY RD	Travis Co	397Z	WT-40	78654	None
MYRA CT	Austin	642D	MD-18	78749	6200-6299
MYRICK DR	Austin	494Z	MH-31	78731	3900-4099
MY ROAD	Bastrop Co	744D	ED-9	78602	100-199
MYRTLE ST	Austin	585U	MK-22	78702	1100-1199
MYRTLE ST N	Georgetown	286D	MM-54	78626	600-999
MYRTLE ST S	Georgetown	286H	MM-54	78626	100-1599
MYRTLE BEACH DR	Bee Cave	549M	WX-26	78738	None
MYSTIC DR	Travis Co	703X	ME-10	78652	12500-12699
	Travis Co	733B	ME-9	78652	12700-13099
MYSTIC CANYON LN	Georgetown	285P	MJ-53	78628	1000-1099
MYSTIC FOREST LN	Austin	702B	MC-12	78739	12000-12199
MYSTIC HOLLOW	Buda	732W	MC-7	78610	100-299
MYSTIC OAKS CIR	Austin	463L	MF-35	78750	10200-10299
MYSTIC OAKS TRL	Austin	463L	MF-35	78750	9200-9499
MYSTIC SHADOW LN	Buda	732X	MC-7	78610	100-299
MYSTIC SUMMIT DR	Travis Co	432K	MC-38	78613	3200-3399

N

STREET NAME	CITY or COUNTY	MAPSCO GRID	AUSTIN GRID	ZIP CODE	BLOCK RANGE O/E
NACHEZ TRL	Travis Co	490V	WZ-31	78734	2200-2399
NAGEL RIDGE	Travis Co	468T	MQ-34	78660	None
NAIRN DR	Austin	642L	MD-17	78749	7800-8499
NAKALELE LN	Bastrop Co	776B	EG-6	78602	100-199
NAKOMA E	Williamson Co	408D	MR-42	78664	100-399
NAKOMA W	Williamson Co	408C	MR-42	78664	1-99

STREET NAME	CITY or COUNTY	MAPSCO GRID	AUSTIN GRID	ZIP CODE	BLOCK RANGE O/E
NAKOMA DR	Lakeway	519C	WX-30	78734	100-199
NALIDE ST	Austin	644A	MG-18	78745	900-1099
NAMBOCA WAY	Georgetown	225V	MK-58	78628	600-799
NAMELESS RD	Jonestown	371W	MA-43	78641	23700-23799
	Leander	341A	MA-48	78641	14100-14899
	Travis Co	340D	WZ-48	78641	21400-21899
	Travis Co	310Y	WZ-49	78641	21900-22599
	Travis Co	340F	WY-48	78641	22600-23199
	Travis Co	370L	WZ-44	78641	23200-23599
	Travis Co	371W	MA-43	78641	23600-23699
	Williamson Co	340D	WZ-48	78641	14900-15199
NAN LN	Cedar Park	372J	MC-44	78613	2100-2199
NANAKULI DR	Bastrop Co	775H	EF-6	78602	100-199
NANCY DR	Austin	644N	MG-17	78745	5600-6099
NANCY DR	Round Rock	376R	MM-44	78664	800-899
NANCY GALE DR	Austin	613U	MF-19	78735	3200-3299
NANCY JEAN CV	Cedar Park	402H	MD-42	78613	1100-1199
NANCY'S SKYLINE DR	Bee Cave	550W	WY-25	78738	None
NANDAS TRL	Austin	611L	MB-20	78736	8500-8799
NANDINA CV	Austin	463A	ME-36	78726	9800-9899
NANDINA DR	Buda	763T	ME-4	78610	100-199
NANDINA DR	Williamson Co	402U	MD-40	78613	1400-1499
NANDINA TRL	Georgetown	314G	MH-51	78628	100-299
NANTUCKET CV	Lago Vista	458L	WV-35	78645	21000-21099
NAPA CV	Leander	343N	ME-47	78641	1000-1099
NAPA DR	Travis Co	550R	WZ-26	78733	3000-3299
NAPALI CT	Round Rock	346W	ML-46	78681	3200-3299
NAPA VALLEY BEND	Williamson Co	343N	ME-47	78641	3300-3499
NAPIER TRL	Williamson Co	434R	MH-38	78729	7300-7699
NAPLES CV	Austin	671B	MA-15	78739	11300-11499
NAPLES LN	Hays Co	669B	WW-15	78737	100-799
NARANJO DR	Georgetown	226S	ML-58	78628	1000-1699
NARROW GLEN PKWY	Austin	674X	MG-13	78744	2000-2499
NARROW OAK TRL	Austin	464L	MH-35	78759	6900-7199
NARROW RIDGE DR	Travis Co	522C	MD-30	78730	4100-4199
NARROW VALLEY DR	Travis Co	402Y	MD-40	78613	2400-2499
NARSITIN LN	Pflugerville	437D	MP-39	78660	17900-17999
NARUNA WAY	Austin	467E	MN-36	78660	14101-14299 O
	Travis Co	467E	MN-36	78660	14100-14298 E
	Travis Co	467E	MN-36	78660	14300-14699
NARVELLA DR	Travis Co	702R	MD-11	78652	12400-12499
NASCO DR	Austin	525W	MJ-28	78756	5700-5899
	Austin	525S	MJ-28	78757	5900-6699
NASH AVE	Austin	614G	MH-21	78704	1600-1799
NASH ST E	Round Rock	406D	MM-42	78664	100-199
NASH ST W	Round Rock	406C	MM-42	78664	100-299
NASH HERNANDEZ SR RD	Austin	615F	MJ-21	78702	1200-1799
NASHUA CT	Austin	523Y	MF-28	78746	6100-6199
NASHVILLE CV	Lago Vista	458L	WV-35	78645	21000-21099
NASONI CV	Austin	642A	MC-18	78749	6400-6499
NASONI TRL	Williamson Co	223D	MF-60	78633	100-199
NASSAU CIR	Georgetown	195V	MK-61	78633	100-199
NASSAU DR	Austin	556N	ML-26	78723	5400-5999
NATALI ST	Austin	673R	MF-14	78748	200-699
NATALIE CV	Cedar Park	372G	MD-45	78613	2300-2399
NATER LN	Austin	675W	MJ-13	78747	7900-7999
NATHAN DR	Travis Co	436R	MM-38	78728	2100-2399
NATICK LN	Austin	641Y	MB-16	78739	10600-10899
NATIONAL DR	Lago Vista	429W	WW-37	78645	20100-20799
	Lago Vista	428Z	WV-37	78645	20800-21499
NATIONAL PARK BLVD	Austin	704A	MG-12	78747	2000-2699
NATIVE DANCER CV	Austin	553C	MF-27	78746	3500-3599
NATIVE GARDEN CV	Round Rock	346W	ML-46	78681	1100-1199
NATIVE TEXAN TRL	Travis Co	580D	WZ-24	78735	11200-11299
NATRONA CV	Austin	465S	MJ-34	78759	11500-11599
NATRONA DR	Austin	465S	MJ-34	78759	11600-11799
NATURAL BRIDGE CT	Round Rock	345P	MJ-47	78681	4100-4199
NATURAL BRIDGE LN	Pflugerville	437J	MN-38	78660	1500-1699
NATURAL SPRING WAY	Travis Co	436V	MM-37	78728	15000-15299
NATURE CENTER DR	Austin	584T	MG-22	78746	200-599
NATURES WAY	Bastrop Co	534U	ED-28	78621	100-199
NATURES WAY	Jonestown	430N	WY-38	78645	18700-18799
NATURITA DR	Georgetown	317E	MN-51	78626	1000-1499
NAUTILUS AVE	Lakeway	519E	WW-30	78738	100-299
	Lakeway	518H	WV-30	78738	300-399
NAVAJO	Lago Vista	428V	WV-37	78645	4700-4799
NAVAJO PASS	Travis Co	461F	MA-36	78641	7100-8199
	Travis Co	431Y	MB-37	78641	None
NAVAJO PATH	Austin	613Z	MF-19	78745	4500-4599
NAVAJO RD	Travis Co	549A	WW-27	78738	None
NAVAJO TRL	Travis Co	549A	WW-27	78738	4100-4499
NAVAJO TRL	Williamson Co	193Z	MF-61	78633	100-399
NAVARRO BLVD	Bastrop Co	743K	EA-8	78602	100-199
NAVARRO PL	Austin	642L	MD-17	78749	7600-7799
NAVARRO CREEK PASS	Travis Co	678M	MR-14	78617	None
NAVARRO CREEK RD	Travis Co	678H	MR-15	78617	4300-6599
NAVASOTA	Manor	559B	MS-27	78653	None
NAVASOTA CIR	Georgetown	196W	ML-61	78628	101-199 O
NAVASOTA ST	Austin	615F	MJ-21	78702	1-399
	Austin	585Y	MK-22	78702	400-1699
NAVIDAD CV	Travis Co	582K	MC-23	78735	2900-2999
NAVIDAD DR	Travis Co	582E	MC-24	78735	8100-8699
NAVIGATION LN	Jonestown	430T	WY-37	78645	17700-17799
NEAL ST	Austin	585V	MK-22	78702	700-1099
	Austin	586W	ML-22	78702	3000-3599
NEANS DR	Austin	496T	ML-31	78758	800-1399
NEARABOUT RD	Austin	403M	MF-41	78717	11300-11499
NECHES ST	Austin	585T	MJ-22	78701	400-999
NECHES TRL	Williamson Co	223D	MF-60	78633	100-499
NEEDHAM CT	Austin	671C	MB-15	78739	11000-11099
NEEDHAM LN	Austin	641Y	MB-16	78739	6200-6499
	Austin	671C	MB-15	78739	6500-6699
NEEDHAM RD	Dripping Springs	666H	WR-15	78620	100-999
	Hays Co	666H	WR-15	78620	None
NEEDLES CV	Lago Vista	458G	WV-36	78645	21100-21199
NEEDLES DR	Austin	523Y	MF-28	78746	3500-3799
NEELEY DR	Austin	494V	MH-31	78759	8200-8299
NEENAH AVE	Austin	404Q	MH-41	78717	9300-9999
NEENAH AVE	Williamson Co	405E	MJ-42	78717	8400-8899
NEENAH CV	Williamson Co	405J	MJ-41	78717	15900-15999
NEENAH OAK LOOP	Williamson Co	405F	MJ-42	78717	15800-15899
NEIDER DR	Austin	642J	MC-17	78749	8500-8799
NEIDHARDT DR	Travis Co	490G	WZ-33	78734	3100-3299
NEIL KNOLL	Williamson Co	225S	MJ-58	78633	100-499
NEILS THOMPSON DR	Austin	495P	MJ-32	78758	9200-9699
NEILSTON DR	Briarcliff	457Z	WT-34	78669	22300-22499
NELLIE ST	Austin	615E	MJ-21	78704	100-299

STREET NAME	CITY or COUNTY	MAPSCO GRID	AUSTIN GRID	ZIP CODE	BLOCK RANGE O/E
NELMS DR	Austin	644Y	MH-16	78744	1600-1899
NELRAY BLVD	Austin	555G	MK-27	78751	100-799
NELSON ST	Austin	584R	MH-23	78703	800-899
NELSON ST N	Round Rock	376Z	MM-43	78664	100-299
NELSON HOUSER ST	Manor	530L	MV-29	78653	13200-13499
NELSON OAKS DR	Austin	587M	MP-23	78724	5500-6099
NELSON RANCH LOOP	Cedar Park	402G	MD-42	78613	1700-2199
NELSON RANCH RD	Cedar Park	402H	MD-42	78613	700-899
	Cedar Park	403J	ME-41	78613	900-1199
NENE DR	Williamson Co	433V	MF-37	78750	11800-12099
NEPAL CV	Austin	404Q	MH-41	78717	9800-9899
NEPTUNE PL	Georgetown	314F	MG-51	78628	100-399
NESBIT DR	Austin	672H	MD-15	78748	3200-3399
NESTING WAY	Austin	675E	MJ-15	78744	4900-5199
NESTLE CT	Travis Co	467Q	MP-35	78660	14300-14399
NESTLEWOOD DR	Austin	497X	MN-31	78754	2000-2399
NETLEAF RD	Travis Co	619E	MS-21	78724	5600-5799
NETTIE DR	Williamson Co	343T	ME-46	78641	1500-1599
NETTLE LN	Lago Vista	428V	WV-37	78645	2300-4499
NEVADA CV	Lago Vista	458G	WV-36	78645	2900-2999
NEVADA DR	Travis Co	550M	WZ-26	78733	11900-12099
NEVADA PATH	Austin	613Z	MF-19	78745	4600-4699
NEVER BEND CV	Austin	553G	MF-27	78746	2400-2499
NEVILLE WOOD CT	Lakeway	519X	WW-28	78738	100-299
NEVINS CV	Lago Vista	458L	WV-35	78645	2300-2399
NEW CV	Round Rock	376R	MM-44	78664	1600-1699
NEW AIRPORT DR	Austin	647J	MN-17	78719	9500-10399
NEWARK CV	Lago Vista	458G	WV-36	78645	2900-2999
NEWBERRY CV	Lago Vista	458G	WV-36	78645	21200-21299
NEWBERRY DR	Williamson Co	434J	MG-38	78729	9400-9699
NEW BOSTON BEND	Travis Co	435S	MJ-37	78729	13100-13199
NEWBURY ST	Georgetown	287L	MP-53	78626	1300-1499
NEWCASTLE CT	Hays Co	639U	WX-16	78737	100-199
NEWCASTLE DR	Austin	644Q	MH-17	78745	700-899
NEWCASTLE LN	Leander	342Y	MD-46	78641	600-2299
NEWFIELD LN	Austin	584G	MH-24	78703	1300-2399
NEWFOUNDLAND CIR	Austin	496W	ML-31	78758	9600-9699
NEW GRANGE DR	Pflugerville	407Y	MP-40	78660	18000-18099
NEWHALL CV	Travis Co	552U	MD-25	78746	500-599
NEWHALL LN	Travis Co	552U	MD-25	78746	7400-7699
NEW HAMPSHIRE DR	Austin	525H	MK-30	78758	8500-8599
NEW HAVEN CT	Austin	555A	MJ-27	78756	5500-5599
NEW HAVEN CV	Lago Vista	458G	WV-36	78645	21000-21099
NEW HOPE DR W	Cedar Park	372L	MD-44	78613	100-2499
	Cedar Park	372N	MC-44	78613	2500-2699
NEW HOPE RD E	Cedar Park	372H	MD-45	78613	100-499
NEW HORIZONS LN	Austin	642J	MC-17	78749	5500-5699
NEW IBERIA CT	Austin	435W	MJ-37	78727	6100-6199
NEW KATY LN	Travis Co	530P	MU-29	78653	12700-12999
NEWLAND CT	Williamson Co	345N	MJ-47	78681	3800-3898 E
NEWLAND DR	Williamson Co	345N	MJ-47	78681	3700-3899
	Williamson Co	344R	MH-47	78681	3900-3999
NEWLAND PL	Williamson Co	345S	MJ-46	78681	3500-3699
NEW LIDO DR	Lakeway	519F	WW-30	78734	400-499
NEWMAN DR	Austin	584K	MG-23	78703	700-999
NEW MEISTER LN	Pflugerville	408S	MQ-40	78664	100-799
NEW MEISTER LN	Pflugerville	407V	MP-40	78660	800-1399
NEWMONT RD	Austin	496T	ML-31	78758	10500-10899
NEWNING AVE	Austin	615E	MJ-21	78704	1000-1199
	Austin	615J	MJ-20	78704	1200-2099
NEWPORT AVE	Travis Co	526C	MM-30	78753	800-10399
NEWPORT CV	Lago Vista	458G	WV-36	78645	21100-21199
NEWPORT DR	Briarcliff	457Z	WT-34	78669	600-699
	Briarcliff	487D	WT-33	78669	700-899
NEWPORT LN	Travis Co	557B	MN-27	78754	8800-8999
NEWPORT LANDING PL					
	Williamson Co	377F	MN-45	78665	100-299
NEWPORT RIDGE LN	Travis Co	704F	MG-12	78747	None
NEW SWEDEN CHURCH RD	Travis Co	470Z	MV-34	78653	11300-12199
	Travis Co	471S	MW-34	78653	12200-12799
	Travis Co	501C	MX-33	78653	12800-13999
NEWTON DR	Lago Vista	458G	WV-36	78645	2300-3199
NEWTON ST	Austin	614M	MH-20	78704	1200-1999
	Austin	614R	MH-20	78704	2100-2199
	Bastrop	745K	EE-8	78602	800-1399
	Bastrop	745L	EF-8	78602	None
NEW TRAILS	Bastrop Co	504A	EC-33	78621	100-299
	Bastrop Co	474X	EC-34	78621	300-499
NEW YORK AVE	Austin	585U	MK-22	78702	1500-2299
NEW YORK DR	Austin	585V	MK-22	78702	2500-2799
NEY CV	Cedar Park	372Q	MD-44	78613	1200-1299
NEZ PERCE TRACE	Travis Co	589J	MS-23	78653	7000-7799
NIAGARA CV	Lago Vista	458L	WV-35	78645	21000-21099
NIAGARA DR	Travis Co	522K	MC-29	78733	2900-3199
NIAGARA FALLS TERRACE					
	Williamson Co	375U	MK-43	78681	17900-17999
NICHOLAS ZANE DR	Cedar Park	402G	MD-42	78613	1800-1999
NICHOLAUS CV	Round Rock	378T	MQ-43	78664	3600-3699
NICHOLS LN	Bastrop Co	712V	MZ-10	78602	100-199
NICHOLSON BLUFF CV	Travis Co	515F	WN-30	78620	None
NICK CV	Round Rock	408J	MQ-41	78664	3400-3499
NICKERSON ST	Austin	615J	MJ-20	78704	1300-1899
	Austin	614R	MH-20	78704	2100-2199
NICK FALDO TRL	Williamson Co	408C	MR-42	78664	100-299
NICKLAUS DR	Point Venture	488R	WV-32	78654	18800-18999
NICKLAUS PL	Travis Co	582M	MD-23	78746	6300-6399
NICKOLS AVE	Austin	586Q	MM-23	78721	1100-1199
NICK PRICE CV	Williamson Co	408C	MR-42	78664	300-399
NICK PRICE LOOP	Williamson Co	408C	MR-42	78664	100-299
NICOLA TRL	Austin	643W	ME-16	78745	8200-8499
NICOLE CIR	Round Rock	376L	MM-44	78664	1800-1999
NICOLE CV	Austin	496V	MM-31	78753	11300-11399
NICOLE CV	Round Rock	376L	MM-44	78664	100-199
NICOLE LN	Travis Co	439R	MT-38	78634	19100-19499
NICOLE WAY	Bastrop	744D	ED-9	78602	200-399
NICOLE WAY	Williamson Co	224R	MH-59	78633	100-399
NIEDERWALD STRASSE RD					
	Niederwald	794Q	MH-2	78610	5500-7199
	Niederwald	795X	MJ-1	78610	7200-8599
NIEMANN DR	Austin	702C	MD-12	78748	2500-2699
NIGHT CAMP DR	Austin	527G	MP-30	78754	10900-10999
NIGHTHAWK CT	Austin	526J	ML-29	78758	8300-8399
NIGHT HAWK LN	Buda	733W	ME-7	78610	100-299
NIGHTHAWK WAY	Georgetown	226K	MK-60	78633	100-199
NIGHTHAWK DIVE LN	Travis Co	409X	MS-40	78660	3200-3299
NIGHT HERON DR	Travis Co	434G	MH-39	78729	13400-13599
NIGHTINGALE DR	Cedar Park	433A	ME-39	78613	1300-1399

STREET NAME	CITY or COUNTY	MAPSCO GRID	AUSTIN GRID	ZIP CODE	BLOCK RANGE O/E
NIGHTINGALE LN	Lakeway	490W	WY-31	78734	15300-15499
	Travis Co	520A	WY-30	78734	15000-15299
NIGHT JAR DR	Austin	672H	MD-15	78748	9500-9999
NIGHTJAR VIEW TERRACE	Travis Co	439C	MT-39	78660	3700-3799
NIGHT LIFE CV	Travis Co	487B	WS-33	78669	None
NIGHTSHADE DR	Cedar Park	372N	MC-44	78613	2500-2599
NIGHTSHADE LN	Leander	342P	MC-47	78641	1200-1399
NIGHT SKY WAY	Austin	678S	MQ-13	78617	5700-5999
NIGHT STAR DR	Austin	646D	MM-18	78742	9500-9699
NIGHTVIEW DR	Travis Co	467V	MP-34	78660	1600-2199
NIJMEGEN DR	Austin	678N	MQ-14	78617	5600-5899
NILE ST	Austin	585Z	MK-22	78702	800-1199
NILES CV	Village of Bear Creek	670L	WZ-14	78737	8000-8099
NILES RD	Austin	584H	MH-24	78703	1600-1999
NIMBUS DR	Pflugerville	437P	MN-38	78660	1000-1299
NIMITZ AVE	Lago Vista	458G	WV-36	78645	20900-21199
NINA ST	Elgin	534N	EC-28	78621	400-499
NINE OAKS CV	Austin	464P	MG-35	78759	7200-7299
NINOLE CT	Bastrop Co	745X	EE-7	78602	100-199
NIOBRARA RIVER DR	Pflugerville	438B	MQ-39	78660	1000-1199
NIVEA CV	Austin	702B	MC-12	78748	2900-2999
NIXION LN	Austin	587T	MN-22	78725	4100-5199
NIXON DR	Rollingwood	584N	MG-23	78746	300-599
NOACK DR	Travis Co	490L	WZ-32	78734	2900-3099
NOACK HILL	Travis Co	517C	WT-30	78669	21100-21499
NOBEL CIR	Lago Vista	458C	WV-36	78645	3100-3199
NOB HILL CIR	West Lake Hills	553Z	MF-25	78746	1-99
NOBLE HILL CT	Travis Co	522C	MD-30	78730	4500-4599
NOBLEMAN DR	Austin	497X	MN-31	78754	2100-2199
NOCHE CLARA DR	Austin	678N	MQ-14	78617	12800-13199
NOCON CV	Lago Vista	458G	WV-36	78645	21000-21099
NOCONA CV	Round Rock	347N	MN-47	78665	3400-3499
NOCONA TRL	Travis Co	490Q	WZ-32	78734	2600-2699
NOCTURNE CV	Austin	433V	MF-37	78750	9900-10099
NOE LN	Round Rock	345S	MJ-46	78681	3800-3899
NOGALES LN	Leander	342E	MC-48	78641	300-399
NOGALES TRL	Austin	674G	MH-15	78744	2000-2199
NOLAN DR	Georgetown	195Z	MK-61	78633	100-199
NOLAN RYAN BLVD	Round Rock	378E	MQ-45	78665	3600-3699
NOLINA CV	Austin	464P	MG-35	78759	10300-10399
NOLINA DR	Georgetown	314G	MH-51	78628	1800-1999
NOLINA LN	Round Rock	375C	MK-45	78681	2700-2899
NOMA DR	Austin	612W	MC-19	78749	6600-6699
NOMAD DR	Travis Co	456H	WR-36	78669	500-799
NO MOR CV	Austin	496N	ML-32	78758	1500-1599
NOON DAY CV	Travis Co	517H	WT-30	78669	4100-4299
NOPAL CV	Hays Co	732K	MC-8	78610	100-199
NORCHESTER CT	Williamson Co	434K	MG-38	78729	9200-9299
NORCO DR	Travis Co	550R	WZ-26	78733	3000-3099
NORDHAM DR	Austin	643K	ME-17	78745	2700-2899
NORDYKE LN	Travis Co	619N	MS-20	78725	15000-15199
NORFOLK DR	Austin	643S	ME-16	78745	2700-3099
NORMAN LOOP	Williamson Co	408B	MQ-42	78664	3700-3799
NORMAN TRL	Austin	642X	MC-16	78749	4400-4999
NORMANDY ST	Austin	644C	MH-18	78745	400-599
NORMANDY RIDGE LN	Travis Co	550Q	WZ-26	78733	3400-3699
NORMEADOWS CIR	Round Rock	376P	ML-44	78681	1300-1399
NORMEADOWS PL	Round Rock	376N	ML-44	78681	1400-1699
NORRIS CV	Lago Vista	458G	WV-36	78645	21200-21299
NORRIS DR	Austin	614B	MG-21	78704	1500-1799
NORSEMAN TERRACE	Austin	525D	MK-30	78758	1300-1599
NORSHIRE LN	Austin	527J	MN-29	78754	10100-10199
NORTH DR	Austin	526F	ML-30	78753	9100-9399
NORTH DR	Taylor	322Z	MZ-49	76574	1700-4299
NORTH PATH	Austin	494M	MH-32	78759	8800-8899
NORTH PL	Jonestown	400V	WZ-40	78645	9900-9999
NORTH ST	Austin	555F	MJ-27	78756	1200-1599
NORTH ST	Travis Co	430L	WZ-38	78645	17700-17899
NORTH AUSTIN HOSPITAL ACCESS					
	Austin	466S	ML-34	78758	None
NORTHAVENS CV	Travis Co	437G	MP-39	78660	17100-17199
NORTH BEND	Leander	341A	MA-48	78641	1-199
NORTH BEND DR	Austin	496K	ML-32	78758	800-1199
NORTH BLUFF DR	Austin	644X	MG-16	78745	100-899
NORTHCAPE DR	Austin	526G	MM-30	78753	800-1299
NORTH CASCADES AVE	Pflugerville	438E	MQ-39	78660	400-699
NORTH CREEK DR	Austin	526F	ML-30	78753	9300-9799
NORTH CREEK DR	Leander	312W	MC-49	78641	700-1399
	Leander	311Z	MB-49	78641	1400-1499
NORTHCREST BLVD	Austin	525Z	MK-28	78752	7200-7599
	Austin	526S	ML-28	78752	7600-7899
NORTHCREST CIR	Austin	526S	ML-28	78752	200-299
NORTHCROSS DR	Austin	525F	MJ-30	78757	7600-7899
NORTHCROSS RD	Georgetown	256S	ML-55	78628	100-199
	Williamson Co	255V	MK-55	78628	200-299
NORTH CROSSING TRL					
	Williamson Co	377B	MN-45	78665	100-299
NORTHDALE DR	Austin	586H	MM-24	78723	5300-5699
NORTHEAST DR	Austin	556R	MM-26	78723	2400-3599
	Austin	556G	MM-27	78723	6500-7299
NORTHERN TRL	Leander	342B	MC-48	78641	100-399
	Leander	342F	MC-48	78641	400-799
NORTHERN DANCER DR	Austin	553K	ME-26	78746	5900-6299
NORTHFIELD RD	Austin	465H	MK-36	78727	3700-3999
NORTH FIELD ST	Williamson Co	375Y	MK-43	78681	100-399
NORTHFOREST DR	Austin	525A	MJ-30	78759	7900-8099
NORTHGATE BLVD	Austin	495Z	MK-31	78758	8900-9499
NORTHGROVE RD	Austin	524K	MG-29	78731	6300-6399
NORTH HAMPTON DR	Austin	556Q	MM-26	78723	5700-6499
NORTH HEARSEY DR	Austin	645T	MJ-16	78744	5100-5299
NORTH HILLS DR	Austin	524G	MH-30	78731	3400-4399
NORTH LAKE DR	Travis Co	558S	MQ-25	78724	8000-8099
NORTH LAKE CREEK PKWY	Austin	403V	MF-40	78717	9500-9799
	Austin	434A	MG-39	78717	9800-9899
NORTHLAKE HILLS DR	Jonestown	430D	WZ-39	78645	17000-17599
NORTHLAND CIR	Lago Vista	399Y	WX-40	78645	20800-20899
NORTHLAND DR	Austin	525W	MJ-28	78756	2100-2899
	Austin	524Z	MH-28	78757	2900-3199
	Austin	524Z	MH-28	78731	3200-3599
NORTHLAND DR	Lago Vista	429C	WX-39	78645	20600-20899
	Lago Vista	399X	WW-40	78645	20900-21199
NORTHLAWN DR	Taylor	322T	MY-49	76574	2400-2699
NORTHLEDGE DR	Austin	524G	MH-30	78731	7000-7099
NORTH LOOP BLVD E	Austin	555G	MK-27	78751	100-199
NORTH LOOP BLVD W	Austin	555G	MK-27	78751	100-799
	Austin	555E	MJ-27	78756	800-2399
NORTH OAKS DR	Austin	496R	MM-32	78753	11500-12099

STREET NAME	CITY or COUNTY	MAPSCO GRID	AUSTIN GRID	ZIP CODE	BLOCK RANGE O/E
NORTHPARK BLVD	Taylor	322M	MZ-50	76574	4000-4499
NORTH PARK CIR N	Cedar Park	373S	ME-43	78613	100-899
NORTH PARK DR	Austin	525N	MJ-29	78757	6700-6799
NORTH PARK DR	Jonestown	400M	WZ-41	78645	18300-18399
NORTH PLAINS AVE	Austin	525F	MJ-30	78757	2200-2299
NORTH PLATT RIVER DR	Austin	673X	ME-13	78748	10500-10799
NORTH PLAZA	Austin	526K	ML-29	78753	8800-9399
NORTH RIDGE	Lago Vista	429W	WW-37	78645	20600-20899
	Lago Vista	428Z	WV-37	78645	20900-21099
NORTH RIDGE CIR	Travis Co	371Y	MB-43	78641	13100-13299
NORTHRIDGE DR	Austin	556J	ML-26	78723	1200-1699
	Austin	556P	ML-26	78723	1700-2099
NORTHRIDGE RD	Williamson Co	406Y	MM-40	78728	4200-4599
NORTH RIM DR	Austin	494T	MG-31	78731	4900-5199
NORTH RIM DR	Travis Co	401B	MA-42	78641	17500-18299
NORTH SHIELDS DR	Austin	466E	ML-36	78727	2200-3099
NORTHSIDE LN	Bastrop Co	740G	MV-9	78612	100-199
NORTH STAR RD	Travis Co	371Y	MB-43	78641	None
NORTHTOWN BLVD	Travis Co	467E	MN-36	78660	1000-1099
NORTHUMBERLAND RD	Austin	584H	MH-24	78703	1600-1699
NORTHVIEW CV	Travis Co	557Q	MP-26	78724	6800-6899
NORTHVIEW LN	Travis Co	557Q	MP-26	78724	7500-7699
NORTHWAY DR	Austin	525V	MK-28	78752	400-699
NORTHWEST BLVD	Georgetown	256U	MM-55	78628	1200-2199
	Georgetown	256L	MM-56	78628	3100-4199
	Williamson Co	256L	MM-56	78628	2200-3099
NORTHWEST DR	Austin	525L	MK-29	78757	7700-7899
NORTHWEST DR	Round Rock	376U	MM-43	78664	100-1399
NORTH WEST PL	Austin	524N	MG-29	78731	5900-5999
NORTHWESTERN AVE	Austin	615D	MK-21	78702	600-699
	Austin	585V	MK-22	78702	1100-2399
NORTHWOOD CIR	Austin	554U	MH-25	78703	3400-3499
NORTHWOOD DR	Georgetown	256Q	MM-56	78628	300-499
NORTHWOOD RD	Austin	554Z	MH-25	78703	1300-1899
	Austin	554U	MH-25	78703	2700-2999
NORTON AVE	Lago Vista	458G	WV-36	78645	2900-3199
NORWALK LN	Austin	584K	MG-23	78703	700-999
	Austin	584F	MG-24	78703	1000-1499
NORWEGIAN WOOD DR	Austin	496E	ML-33	78758	11600-11799
NORWELL LN	Travis Co	437Q	MP-38	78660	800-999
NORWICH CV	Austin	556Y	MM-25	78723	2900-2999
NORWICH CASTLE DR	Austin	705E	MJ-12	78747	8900-8999
NORWOOD CV	Georgetown	286W	ML-52	78628	200-299
NORWOOD DR	Georgetown	286W	ML-52	78628	100-399
NORWOOD DR	Williamson Co	312H	MD-51	78641	1-299
NORWOOD LN	Austin	676B	ML-15	78744	4300-4699
NORWOOD LN	Bastrop Co	534Z	ED-28	78621	100-299
NORWOOD LN	Travis Co	649S	MS-16	78617	3100-3999
	Travis Co	678D	MR-15	78617	4000-4299
NORWOOD RD	Austin	555V	MK-25	78723	1200-1399
NORWOOD HILL RD	Austin	556Y	MM-25	78723	2900-5099
NORWOOD PARK BLVD	Austin	526T	ML-28	78753	800-1099
NORWOOD WEST	Georgetown	286W	ML-52	78628	100-499
NOTCHES DR	Austin	672H	MD-15	78748	9200-9599
NOTON CT	Pflugerville	437Z	MP-37	78660	1100-1299
NOTON ST E	Pflugerville	468A	MQ-36	78660	100-399
NOTON ST W	Pflugerville	468A	MQ-36	78660	100-399
	Pflugerville	437Z	MP-37	78660	400-1199
NOTRE DAME DR	Austin	556L	MM-26	78723	6700-7099
NOTTAWAY CV	Austin	643S	ME-16	78745	8100-8199
NOTTINGHAM LN	Austin	614V	MH-19	78704	2600-2799
NOTTINGHAM HILL RD	Round Rock	407N	MN-41	78664	1100-1299
NOVA CT	Travis Co	521E	MA-30	78732	1300-1399
NOWOTNY LN	Austin	616A	ML-21	78702	700-799
NOYA DR	Travis Co	436T	ML-37	78728	14600-14799
NOYES LN	Travis Co	491T	MA-31	78732	12800-12999
NUBIAN CV	Austin	641X	MA-16	78739	7200-7299
NUBIAN LN	Austin	641X	MA-16	78739	6900-7099
NUCKOLS CT	Austin	645X	MJ-16	78744	5100-5199
NUCKOLS CROSSING RD	Austin	645T	MJ-16	78744	4300-5499
	Austin	675A	MJ-15	78744	5500-6199
	Austin	674Z	MH-13	78744	8201-9199 O
	Travis Co	674Z	MH-13	78747	8200-9198 E
NUECES LN	Hays Co	669M	WX-14	78737	100-399
NUECES ST	Austin	585J	MJ-23	78701	200-1899
	Austin	585E	MJ-24	78705	1900-2899
NUECES TRL	Georgetown	196W	ML-61	78628	100-299
NUELTIN CT	Round Rock	345Z	MK-46	78681	1900-1999
NUSSER LN	Austin	641X	MA-16	78739	6400-6699
NUTHATCH DR	Hays Co	732E	MC-9	78610	200-299
NUTMEG CV	Austin	493M	MF-32	78750	7800-7899
NUTTALL DR	Travis Co	619E	MS-21	78724	14900-15199
NUTTY BROWN RD	Hays Co	639U	WX-16	78737	12300-12999
See.. Hays Co Rd 163					
	Hays Co	669C	WX-15	78737	13000-14599
	Hays Co	670S	WY-13	78737	14600-14699
NUTWOOD CV	Austin	433W	ME-37	78726	11300-11399
NUU CT	Bastrop Co	776F	EG-6	78602	100-199
NUUANU LN	Bastrop Co	745Y	EF-7	78602	100-199
	Bastrop Co	745Y	EF-7	78602	200-299
NUUPIA CT	Bastrop Co	745Y	EF-7	78602	100-199

O

STREET NAME	CITY or COUNTY	MAPSCO GRID	AUSTIN GRID	ZIP CODE	BLOCK RANGE O/E
OAH CT	Bastrop Co	775H	EF-6	78602	100-199
OAHU CT N	Bastrop	746T	EG-7	78602	100-199
OAHU CT S	Bastrop	746T	EG-7	78602	100-199
OAK BLVD	Austin	612U	MD-19	78735	5600-5799
OAK BLVD E	Austin	612Q	MD-20	78735	5600-5699
OAK BLVD N	Austin	612Q	MD-20	78735	5600-5699
OAK BLVD S	Austin	612U	MD-19	78735	5600-5699
OAK BLVD W	Austin	612U	MD-19	78735	5600-5699
OAK CIR	Hays Co	668F	WU-15	78620	1000-1099
OAK CT	Bastrop Co	776U	EH-4	78602	100-199
OAK CT	Hays Co	576P	WQ-23	78620	100-199
OAK CT	Williamson Co	405N	MJ-41	78717	8000-8199
OAK DR W	Round Rock	376R	MM-44	78664	500E-699E
OAK LN	Bastrop Co	742B	MY-9	78612	100-199
OAK LN	Georgetown	256U	MM-55	78628	1600-1699
	Georgetown	256T	ML-55	78626	2200-2599
OAK LN	Hays Co	576P	WQ-23	78620	100-199
OAK PL	Round Rock	376E	ML-45	78681	2000-2099
OAK ST	Bastrop	715W	EE-10	78602	400-499
OAK ST	Jonestown	400H	WZ-42	78645	10900-11199
OAK ST E	Taylor	353J	EA-47	76574	100-199
OAK TRL	Austin	496R	MM-32	78753	11400-12099

STREET NAME	CITY or COUNTY	MAPSCO GRID	AUSTIN GRID	ZIP CODE	BLOCK RANGE O/E
OAK ALLEY RD	Austin	643S	ME-16	78745	3200-3299
	Austin	642V	MD-16	78745	3300-3399
OAK BEND	Williamson Co	345W	MJ-46	78681	2800-3299
OAK BEND CT	Williamson Co	285M	MK-53	78628	100-299
OAK BEND CV	Austin	465H	MK-36	78727	12800-12899
OAK BEND CV	Williamson Co	345W	MJ-46	78681	4200-4299
OAK BEND DR	Austin	465H	MK-36	78727	12900-12999
OAK BLUFF CV	Lakeway	489Q	WX-32	78734	100-199
OAK BRANCH DR	Hays Co	639G	WX-18	78737	11000-11999
OAK BRANCH DR	Williamson Co	196J	ML-62	78628	100-399
	Williamson Co	195R	MK-62	78633	400-999
OAK BRANCH PL	Round Rock	378W	MQ-43	78665	3100-3199
OAK BREEZE CV	Williamson Co	196J	ML-62	78628	100-199
OAKBROOK DR	Austin	496L	MM-32	78753	11900-11999
OAK CANYON	Travis Co	370C	WZ-45	78641	20500-20699
OAK CANYON RD N	Travis Co	553R	MF-26	78746	2100-2299
OAK CANYON RD S	Travis Co	553R	MF-26	78746	2000-2099
OAKCLAIRE DR	Austin	612T	MC-19	78735	5700-6299
OAKCLAIRE LN	Austin	612Q	MD-20	78735	5900-6099
OAK CLIFF CIR	Travis Co	577V	WT-22	78720	17100-17299
OAK CLIFF DR	Austin	586L	MM-23	78721	4600-4899
OAK CLIFF TRL	Austin	494F	MG-33	78759	None
OAK CREEK CIR	Austin	465H	MK-36	78727	12900-12999
OAK CREEK CV	Austin	465H	MK-36	78727	12800-12899
OAK CREEK DR	Austin	466E	ML-36	78727	3000-3699
	Austin	465D	MK-36	78727	3700-4699
OAK CREEK RD	Williamson Co	281X	MA-52	78641	4200-4499
OAK CREST AVE	Austin	614Q	MH-20	78704	2300-3099
OAKCREST CIR	Cedar Park	403E	ME-42	78613	900-999
OAKCREST DR	Cedar Park	403A	ME-42	78613	300-499
OAK CREST DR	Hays Co	637M	WT-17	78620	500-699
OAK CREST LN	Georgetown	256N	ML-56	78628	100-499
	Williamson Co	255R	MK-56	78628	500-899
OAKDALE CIR	Pflugerville	437V	MP-37	78660	900-999
OAKDALE CT	Austin	554T	MG-25	78703	2600-2699
OAK DALE DR	Cedar Park	372R	MD-44	78613	200-399
OAK DALE DR	Lago Vista	458D	WV-36	78645	20900-21299
OAKDALE DR	Sunset Valley	643F	ME-18	78745	700-899
OAKDALE LN	Pflugerville	437V	MP-37	78660	800-899
OAK FOREST DR	Hays Co	576P	WQ-23	78620	100-199
OAK FOREST DR	Travis Co	460W	WY-34	78645	3100-3599
OAK FOREST DR	Williamson Co	375J	MJ-44	78681	1600-1999
OAK FOREST DR S	Hays Co	576T	WQ-22	78620	200-899
	Hays Co	606B	WQ-21	78620	900-999
OAK FOREST LN	Austin	611U	MB-19	78736	7100-7199
OAK GLEN	Lago Vista	429N	WW-38	78645	20700-20799
OAK GLEN CV	Lakeway	489Q	WX-32	78734	100-199
OAKGLEN DR	Austin	643D	MF-18	78745	2000-2099
OAK GLEN DR	Bastrop Co	709L	MT-11	78612	None
OAK GROVE AVE	Austin	586N	ML-23	78702	1100-1199
OAK GROVE BLVD	Lakeway	490J	WY-32	78734	15600-16199
OAK GROVE CIR	Travis Co	610Y	WZ-19	78736	10200-10299
OAK GROVE DR	Cedar Park	372M	MD-44	78613	1400-1599
OAK GROVE DR	Hays Co	636L	WR-17	78620	100-299
OAK GROVE LN	Williamson Co	255Z	MK-55	78628	600-699
OAK GROVE RD	Williamson Co	312J	MC-50	78641	1-2199
OAK HAVEN CIR	Austin	614J	MG-20	78704	2400-2499
OAK HAVEN CIR	Williamson Co	254X	MG-55	78628	2800-2899
OAK HAVEN CV	Austin	496R	MM-32	78753	11600-11799
OAK HAVEN DR	Austin	614J	MG-20	78704	2600-3099
OAK HAVEN DR	Williamson Co	375Y	MK-43	78681	100-199
OAK HAVEN RD	Austin	496R	MM-32	78753	11700-12099
OAK HEDGE PL	Austin	673D	MF-15	78745	7600-7699
OAK HEIGHTS DR	Austin	615P	MJ-20	78741	1500-1599
OAK HILL LN	Austin	674S	MG-13	78744	1700-1799
	Travis Co	674S	MG-13	78744	1800-1999
OAKHILL LN	Lago Vista	429B	WW-39	78645	20800-20899
OAK HOLLOW CIR	Austin	495V	MK-31	78758	10100-10299
OAK HOLLOW DR	Austin	496S	ML-31	78758	9700-10299
OAK HOLLOW DR	Leander	342X	MC-46	78641	1000-1299
OAK HOLLOW DR	Round Rock	376E	ML-45	78681	1900-1999
OAK HOLLOW RD N	Georgetown	286F	ML-54	78628	100-299
OAK HOLLOW RD S	Georgetown	286F	ML-54	78628	100-299
OAKHURST AVE	Austin	554Z	MH-25	78703	2700-3099
OAK HURST RD	Travis Co	489M	WX-32	78734	1100-1499
OAK KNOLL DR	Austin	464Q	MH-35	78759	11000-12099
OAKLAND AVE	Austin	584Q	MH-23	78703	500-899
OAKLAND DR	Cedar Park	403P	ME-41	78613	1600-1799
OAKLAND DR	Georgetown	286T	ML-52	78628	100-199
OAKLAND DR	Leander	342B	MC-48	78641	100-199
OAKLAND RD	Williamson Co	224C	MH-60	78633	100-199
OAKLAND HILLS DR	Georgetown	226G	MM-60	78628	29000-30099
OAKLANDS DR	Round Rock	376S	ML-43	78681	400-1099
	Round Rock	375V	MK-43	78681	1000-1299
OAKLANE DR	Austin	614J	MG-20	78704	2900-2999
OAKLAWN AVE	Austin	585M	MK-23	78722	2600-2699
OAKLAWN DR	Taylor	322U	MZ-49	76574	1700-2199
OAKLEAF CIR	Austin	556T	ML-25	78723	2000-2099
OAK LEDGE DR	Austin	673A	ME-15	78748	8600-8999
OAKLEY CT	Austin	526E	ML-30	78753	500-599
OAKLYNN CT	Travis Co	530A	MU-30	78653	12000-12099
OAK MEADOW CIR	Austin	611V	MB-19	78736	7000-7099
OAK MEADOW CV	Williamson Co	283R	MF-53	78628	500-599
OAK MEADOW DR	Austin	611V	MB-19	78736	7000-7599
OAK MEADOW DR	Hays Co	638J	WU-17	78620	900-999
	Hays Co	637M	WT-17	78620	1000-1399
OAK MEADOW DR	Round Rock	406N	ML-41	78681	2300-2699
OAK MEADOW DR	Williamson Co	283R	MF-53	78628	100-499
OAK MEADOW DR	Williamson Co	375P	MJ-44	78681	3600-4099
OAK MEADOW LN	Williamson Co	283R	MF-53	78628	600-699
OAK MEADOWS CV	Round Rock	376P	ML-44	78681	1400-1499
OAKMONT BLVD	Austin	554V	MH-25	78703	2800-3499
	Austin	554R	MH-26	78731	3500-3999
	Austin	554H	MH-27	78731	4600-4799
OAKMONT CT	Georgetown	315D	MK-51	78628	100-199
OAKMONT DR	Georgetown	226H	MM-60	78628	30100-30299
OAKMONT DR	Round Rock	346Q	MM-47	78665	2500-3499
	Round Rock	346L	MM-47	78665	2900-3499
OAKMONT LN	Cedar Park	372Q	MD-44	78613	1700-1899
OAKMONT ST	Austin	464C	MH-36	78727	12200-12399
OAKMONT FOREST DR	Cedar Park	402D	MD-42	78613	100-199
OAKMOORE	Round Rock	378Q	MR-44	78664	1-99
OAK MOTTE LN	Austin	674G	MH-15	78744	1900-2199
OAKMOUNTAIN CIR	Austin	495S	MJ-31	78759	8600-8799
OAK PARK DR	Austin	614J	MG-20	78704	2600-3099
OAK PARK DR	Round Rock	376S	ML-43	78681	500-999
OAK PLAZA	Austin	526J	ML-29	78753	200-499

STREET NAME	CITY or COUNTY	MAPSCO GRID	AUSTIN GRID	ZIP CODE	BLOCK RANGE O/E
OAK PLAZA CV	Williamson Co	283M	MF-53	78628	300-399
OAK PLAZA DR	Williamson Co	283M	MF-53	78628	100-299
OAK RIDGE	Lago Vista	429S	WW-37	78645	20500-20999
OAKRIDGE CIR	Georgetown	256N	ML-56	78628	100-199
OAKRIDGE CV	Leander	342H	MD-48	78641	1000-1099
OAK RIDGE CV	Pflugerville	438S	MQ-37	78660	100-199
OAK RIDGE DR	Bastrop Co	742L	MZ-8	78612	100-199
OAK RIDGE DR	Hays Co	576G	WR-24	78620	100-299
OAK RIDGE DR	Pflugerville	438T	MQ-37	78660	200-699
OAKRIDGE DR	Round Rock	406J	ML-41	78681	400-2399
OAK RIDGE DR	Travis Co	488W	WU-31	78669	2600-2999
OAK RIDGE DR	West Lake Hills	583H	MF-24	78746	300-499
OAK RIDGE DR	Williamson Co	375P	MJ-44	78681	3800-3999
OAKRIDGE PASS	Cedar Park	403E	ME-42	78613	300-499
OAK RIDGE RD	Williamson Co	255Z	MK-55	78628	300-499
OAK RIDGE TRL	Travis Co	310L	WZ-50	78641	22600-22899
OAK RIVER DR	Bastrop Co	709M	MT-11	78612	100-299
OAK RUN DR	Austin	496S	ML-31	78758	9800-10199
OAKS RD	Burnet Co	426J	WQ-38	78669	100-399
OAKS ST W	Taylor	353J	EA-47	76574	100-699
OAK SHADOWS CIR	Austin	466Y	MM-34	78758	1200-1399
OAK SHADOWS DR	Bastrop Co	776Q	EH-5	78602	100-199
OAKSHIRE CV	Williamson Co	403W	ME-40	78613	2300-2399
OAK SHORES	Austin	523S	ME-28	78730	7500-8399
	Travis Co	523T	ME-28	78730	6900-7499
OAK SPRINGS CV	Round Rock	375Z	MK-43	78681	2300-2399
OAK SPRINGS DR	Austin	586S	ML-22	78702	2700-3299
	Austin	586S	ML-22	78721	3300-3899
OAK SPRINGS DR	Dripping Springs	667S	WS-13	78620	100-499
OAK TREE DR	Georgetown	226G	MM-60	78628	30100-30499
OAK TREE LN	Cedar Park	403P	ME-41	78613	1500-1599
OAK VALLEY CT	Travis Co	610T	WY-19	78736	10600-10799
OAK VALLEY CT	Williamson Co	194Z	MH-61	78633	100-299
OAK VALLEY DR	Travis Co	583L	MF-23	78746	1-99
	West Lake Hills	583L	MF-23	78746	None
OAK VALLEY RD	Travis Co	673N	ME-14	78748	2100-2399
OAK VALLEY RD	Travis Co	641A	MA-18	78737	8800-9099
OAK VALLEY TRL	Travis Co	610U	WZ-19	78736	10300-10599
OAK VIEW	Round Rock	378Q	MR-44	78664	1-99
OAK VIEW CV	Austin	464K	MG-35	78759	7300-7399
OAK VIEW CV	Williamson Co	283V	MF-52	78628	700-799
OAK VIEW DR	Austin	464Q	MH-35	78759	10500-11599
OAKVIEW DR	Hays Co	636G	WR-18	78620	100-299
OAKVIEW DR	Round Rock	376J	ML-44	78681	1700-1799
OAK VIEW PL	Williamson Co	283Z	MF-52	78628	800-899
OAKVILLE CV	Leander	343N	ME-47	78641	1800-1899
OAK VISTA DR	Travis Co	408Q	MR-41	78660	1900-2199
OAK VISTA LN	Round Rock	405C	MK-42	78681	3000-3099
OAKWOOD BLVD	Round Rock	375Z	MK-43	78681	100-1499
OAKWOOD CIR	Travis Co	577V	WT-22	78720	10800-10899
OAKWOOD CT	Bastrop Co	745V	EF-7	78602	100-199
OAKWOOD CV	Austin	524U	MH-28	78731	5500-5699
OAKWOOD DR	Austin	496L	MM-32	78753	11300-12099
OAKWOOD DR	Georgetown	286S	ML-52	78628	200-299
OAKWOOD DR	Leander	342X	MC-46	78641	900-1299
OAKWOOD LN	Hays Co	638K	WU-17	78620	500-899
OAKWOOD TRL	Williamson Co	343Y	MF-46	78641	100-299
OAKWOOD GLEN CV	Cedar Park	433A	ME-39	78613	1400-1499
OAKWOOD GLEN DR	Cedar Park	433E	ME-39	78613	2600-2999
OASIS DR	Austin	642A	MC-18	78749	6000-6599
	Austin	641H	MB-18	78749	6600-6799
OASIS PASS	Travis Co	462S	MC-34	78732	6700-6999
OASIS BLUFF DR	Travis Co	462S	MC-34	78732	6700-7399
OASIS VIEW	Travis Co	461V	MB-34	78732	6900-6999
OAT MEADOW DR	Pflugerville	468F	MQ-36	78660	400-599
OATMEAL DR	Travis Co	467E	MN-36	78660	800-899
OBAN DR	Briarcliff	457Z	WT-34	78669	22100-22299
OBED RIVER DR	Pflugerville	438B	MQ-39	78660	18800-18999
OBLIQUE DR	Austin	467Q	MP-35	78660	13900-14099
OBSERVATORY LN	Bee Cave	549M	WX-26	78738	4100-4199
OBSERVATORY HILL	Lago Vista	459C	WX-36	78645	4800-4999
OBSIDIAN LN	Williamson Co	375B	MJ-45	78681	3900-3999
O'CALLAHAN DR	Austin	702H	MD-12	78748	1700-2199
OCATILLO LN N	Williamson Co	193B	ME-63	78633	100-199
OCATILLO LN S	Williamson Co	193B	ME-63	78633	200-299
OCEANAIRE BLVD	Austin	434X	MG-37	78750	8600-8699
OCEANNA CT	Travis Co	436Y	MM-37	78728	14400-14499
OCEANS LN	Lago Vista	429G	WX-39	78645	7000-7199
OCELOT CV	Williamson Co	375X	MJ-43	78681	8500-8599
OCELOT WAY	Williamson Co	375X	MJ-43	78681	17000-17099
OCHA LN	Travis Co	467L	MP-35	78660	900-999
OCHILTREE DR	Austin	526G	MM-30	78753	9700-9999
OCHO MESAS CV	Lago Vista	399R	WX-41	78645	9000-9099
O'CONNOR DR	Williamson Co	405G	MK-42	78681	7400-8799
	Williamson Co	405A	MJ-42	78717	8800-9099
OCONTO DR	Williamson Co	405N	MJ-41	78717	15300-15399
OCOTILLO	Leander	342X	MC-46	78641	2000-2099
OCOTILLO DR	Pflugerville	409W	MS-40	78660	19800-19899
	Travis Co	409W	MS-40	78660	None
OCTAVIA LN	Round Rock	345N	MJ-47	78681	3800-3899
ODELL DR	Bastrop Co	709L	MT-11	78612	None
O'DELL ST E	Austin	525V	MK-28	78752	100-199
O'DELL ST W	Austin	525V	MK-28	78752	100-699
ODESSA LN	Austin	524T	MG-28	78731	5400-5499
ODIE LN	Austin	465B	MJ-36	78727	12900-13099
ODOM ST	Austin	585A	MJ-24	78705	800-899
OERTLI LN	Austin	526J	ML-29	78753	100-699
OESTRICK LN	Travis Co	522Q	MD-29	78733	2500-2999
OGDEN DR	Travis Co	522X	MC-28	78733	1000-1399
OGIER DR	Austin	587C	MP-24	78724	6300-6399
OGRIN CV	Round Rock	378V	MR-43	78664	3500-3599
O'HARA LN	Lago Vista	458F	WU-36	78645	21700-21899
O'HENRY AVE	Lago Vista	458F	WU-36	78645	20600-20899
O'HENRY CV	Austin	524B	MG-30	78731	6700-6799
OHLEN RD	Austin	525D	MK-30	78758	1600-1699
	Austin	525D	MK-30	78757	1700-2399
OHMFIELD CT	Austin	671G	MB-15	78739	11400-11499
O K CORRAL	Austin	673G	MF-15	78748	1400-1499
OKLAHOMA ST	Travis Co	490H	WZ-33	78734	14800-15499
OKNER LN	Austin	644N	MG-17	78745	6200-6399
OKOE CT E	Bastrop Co	746W	EG-7	78602	100-199
OKOE CT W	Bastrop Co	746W	EG-7	78602	100-199
OLAA DR	Bastrop	746N	EG-8	78602	100-199
OLAI CT	Bastrop Co	746W	EG-7	78602	100-199
OLANDER ST	Austin	585P	MJ-23	78702	1200-1399
OLD 19TH ST	Austin	584M	MH-23	78705	1100-1399
OLD 51ST ST E	Austin	586B	ML-24	78723	None

STREET NAME	CITY or COUNTY	MAPSCO GRID	AUSTIN GRID	ZIP CODE	BLOCK RANGE O/E
OLD 71	Bastrop Co	711B	MW-12	78612	100-299
	Bastrop Co	680Z	MV-13	78612	300-499
OLD 2243 WEST	Leander	342A	MC-48	78641	400-12199
	Leander	312X	MC-49	78641	11000-11799
	Leander	341D	MB-48	78641	12200-12899
OLD AIRPORT RD	Georgetown	256R	MM-56	78628	2100-2399
OLD ANDERSON MILL RD	Travis Co	436C	MB-36	78641	14500-14899
OLD AUSTIN HWY	Bastrop	744H	ED-9	78602	100-299
	Bastrop	745E	EE-9	78602	100-199
OLD AUSTIN-HUTTO RD	Pflugerville	438X	MQ-37	78660	100-1199
OLD AUSTIN-PFLUGERVILLE RD					
	Pflugerville	437U	MP-37	78660	100-199
	Pflugerville	437T	MN-37	78660	200-999
OLD AUSTIN ROCK RD	Round Rock	406F	ML-42	78681	1300-1599
OLD BAGDAD RD	Leander	342T	MC-46	78641	900-1099
OLD BALDY DR	Austin	374Z	MH-43	78717	16200-16399
OLD BALDY TRL	Hays Co	640S	WY-16	78737	12700-14399
OLD BASTROP RD	Bastrop Co	680J	MU-14	78612	18000-18299
	Travis Co	680J	MU-14	78612	17800-17999
OLD BEE CAVES RD	Austin	612N	MC-20	78735	6700-7099
	Austin	611G	MB-21	78735	7100-9799
OLD BEE CAVES RD	West Lake Hills	583F	ME-24	78746	4800-4999
OLD BISHOP RD	Georgetown	257A	MN-57	78626	1-299
OLD BLACK COLONY RD	Hays Co	762A	MC-6	78610	100-1599
OLD BLISS SPILLAR RD	Hays Co	702N	MC-11	78652	3000-3999
	Travis Co	702N	MC-11	78652	2700-2999
OLD BLUE MOUNTAIN LN					
	Georgetown	225A	MJ-60	78633	100-199
OLD BOWMAN RD E	Round Rock	376Q	MM-44	78664	100-299
OLD BOWMAN RD W	Round Rock	376Q	MM-44	78664	100-299
OLD BRUSHY CREEK RD	Cedar Park	403C	MF-42	78613	600-699
OLD BULL CREEK RD	Austin	524T	MG-28	78731	4100-4399
OLD BURLESON RD	Austin	645R	MK-17	78744	6300-6599
OLD BURNET RD	Jonestown	430P	WY-38	78645	17400-19299
	Lago Vista	429H	WX-39	78645	19300-20199
	Travis Co	430P	WY-38	78645	17200-17399
OLD CASTLE RD	Austin	644Q	MH-17	78745	4600-4999
OLD CEDAR LN	Austin	466Y	MM-34	78758	1000-1499
OLD CHISHOLM TRL	Georgetown	225D	MK-60	78633	100-199
OLD COMANCHE CAMP	Lago Vista	429V	WX-37	78645	18900-19199
OLD COUNTY RD 180 E					
	Williamson Co	373D	MF-45	78641	1-199
OLD COUNTY RD 180 S					
	Williamson Co	373D	MF-45	78641	1-199
OLD COUPLAND RD	Taylor	353T	EA-46	76574	1-2399
OLD COURSE DR	Travis Co	521C	MB-30	78732	2600-2999
OLD CREEKSIDE RD	Williamson Co	284K	MG-53	78628	1-699
OLD EAST RIVERSIDE DR	Austin	615K	MJ-20	78741	1600-1799
OLDE OAK DR	Williamson Co	225T	MJ-58	78633	100-299
OLD FERRY RD	Travis Co	457T	WS-34	78669	23400-24799
	Travis Co	456H	WR-36	78669	24800-25299
OLD FISHER ST	Elgin	534W	EC-28	78621	700-799
OLD FITZHUGH RD	Dripping Springs	636Z	WR-16	78620	100-1099
OLD FM RD 1431	Jonestown	400S	WY-40	78645	19400-19899
	Lago Vista	429D	WX-39	78645	20100-20299
	Travis Co	399Z	WX-40	78645	19900-19999
OLDFORT HILL DR	Austin	586H	MM-24	78723	4700-4999
OLD FREDERICKSBURG RD	Austin	612U	MD-19	78749	5600-6199
OLD GEORGETOWN RD	Taylor	352B	MY-48	76574	1600-3999
	Taylor	322P	MY-50	76574	None
OLD GOFORTH RD	Hays Co	763P	ME-5	78610	700-1799
	Hays Co	763E	ME-6	78610	5000-5099
OLD GRANGER RD	Taylor	323W	EA-49	76574	1500-1699
	Taylor	323S	EA-49	76574	1700-2099
OLD GREGG LN	Travis Co	497C	MP-33	78653	13000-13499
OLD HARBOR LN	Austin	641Y	MB-16	78739	6200-6499
OLD HICKORY CV	Travis Co	521G	MB-30	78732	None
OLD HIGHWAY 81	Austin	466R	MM-35	78753	12500-13699
OLD HUNTERS BEND RD	Travis Co	619J	MS-20	78725	14300-14399
OLD HWY 20	Travis Co	528V	MR-28	78653	9300-9699
	Travis Co	529S	MS-28	78653	9700-11299
	Travis Co	529V	MT-28	78653	17000-17399
	Travis Co	530T	MU-28	78653	17400-18599
	Travis Co	561A	MW-27	78653	None
OLD HWY 290	Dripping Springs	636T	WQ-16	78620	100-699
OLD KIMBRO RD	Manor	530M	MV-29	78653	13100-13199
	Manor	531E	MW-30	78653	13200-13299
	Travis Co	531E	MW-30	78653	13300-13599
OLD KOENIG LN	Austin	555C	MK-27	78756	800-1099
OLD LAMPASAS TRL	Austin	463L	MF-35	78750	8800-9199
	Austin	463L	MF-35	78750	9201-9499 O
	Austin	463L	MF-35	78750	9600-9699
	Travis Co	463L	MF-35	78750	9200-9498 E
	Travis Co	463L	MF-35	78750	9500-9599
OLD LOCKHART HWY	Travis Co	674Y	MH-13	78747	9200-9599
	Travis Co	735A	MJ-9	78747	11000-11399
	Travis Co	735K	MJ-8	78747	11400-11799
OLD LOCKHART RD	Caldwell Co	796G	MM-3	78610	None
	Mustang Ridge	765R	MK-5	78610	6000-7699
	Mustang Ridge	766S	ML-4	78610	7700-8599
	Mustang Ridge	796B	ML-3	78610	8600-8799
	Travis Co	765F	MJ-6	78610	5200-5999
OLD LOCKHART WAY	Travis Co	704L	MH-11	78747	9200-11099
OLD LOCKWOOD RD	Travis Co	560T	MU-25	78653	18400-18699
OLD MAIDS TRL	Travis Co	490N	WY-32	78734	1200-1399
OLD MANCHACA RD	Austin	673S	ME-13	78748	10200-10299
	Austin	673S	ME-13	78748	10700-10999
	Travis Co	673S	ME-13	78748	10300-10699
OLD MANCHACA RD	San Leanna	703K	ME-11	78748	500-699
OLD MANOR RD	Austin	556X	ML-25	78723	4900-5399
OLD MANOR RD	Austin	557G	MP-27	78724	7600-8098 E
	Austin	557G	MP-27	78724	8101-8499 O
	Austin	557G	MP-27	78724	8500-8599
	Austin	557G	MP-27	78724	8601-8999 O
	Travis Co	557G	MP-27	78724	7601-8099 O
	Travis Co	557G	MP-27	78724	8100-8498 E
	Travis Co	557G	MP-27	78724	8600-8998 E
	Travis Co	557G	MP-27	78724	9000-9699
OLD MANOR-TAYLOR RD	Travis Co	500W	MU-31	78653	13900-14399
OLD McDADE RD	Bastrop Co	715P	EE-11	78602	100-499
OLD McDADE RD	Bastrop Co	534U	ED-28	78621	900-1299
OLD MEADOW CT	Williamson Co	346H	MM-48	78665	1300-1399
OLD MILL DR	Hays Co	668H	WV-15	78620	100-499
OLD MILL RD	Cedar Park	403X	ME-40	78613	700-899
	Travis Co	432D	MD-39	78613	2000-2399
	Williamson Co	403W	ME-40	78613	900-1599
	Williamson Co	432D	MD-39	78613	1600-1999

STREET NAME	CITY or COUNTY	MAPSCO GRID	AUSTIN GRID	ZIP CODE	BLOCK RANGE O/E
OLD MILL RD	Georgetown	256F	ML-57	78628	3500-3699
OLD MORMON TRL	Travis Co	554S	MG-25	78746	None
OLD OAKS DR	Williamson Co	378N	MQ-44	78665	1-99
OLD PEAK RD	Georgetown	317F	MN-51	78626	200-699
OLD PERKINS RD	Bastrop Co	715A	EE-12	78602	100-499
OLD POST LOOP	Austin	674M	MH-14	78744	6900-6999
OLD QUARRY LN	Austin	524M	MH-29	78731	6800-6999
OLD QUARRY LN	Cedar Park	374R	MH-44	78613	None
OLD QUARRY RD	Austin	403M	MF-41	78717	11100-11299
OLD QUARRY RD	Leander	342J	MC-47	78641	1-1699
	Leander	342N	MC-47	78641	1700-1899
	Leander	341R	MB-47	78641	1900-2599
OLD RAVINE CT	Williamson Co	346G	MM-48	78665	700-799
OLD SALT TRL	Travis Co	491U	MB-31	78732	12400-12499
OLD SAN ANTONIO RD	Austin	703H	MF-12	78748	10100-11199
	Buda	763A	ME-6	78610	400-699
	Buda	733P	ME-8	78610	700-899
	Hays Co	733P	ME-8	78610	900-1699
	Travis Co	703U	MF-10	78652	11200-12699
	Travis Co	733C	MF-9	78652	12700-13799
OLD SAYERS RD	Bastrop Co	564F	EC-27	78621	100-499
OLD SETTLEMENT RD	Round Rock	377S	MN-43	78664	1600-1699
OLD SETTLER'S BLVD E	Round Rock	376F	ML-45	78664	1-1599
	Round Rock	377A	MN-45	78664	1600-2399
	Round Rock	348W	MQ-46	78665	4200-4499
	Williamson Co	347Y	MP-46	78665	2400-4199
	See.. Kiphen Rd				
OLD SETTLER'S BLVD W	Round Rock	376E	ML-45	78681	1-2199
	See.. FM Rd 3406				
	Round Rock	375H	MK-45	78681	2000-2799
OLD SETTLERS DR	Bastrop Co	712R	MZ-11	78602	100-199
OLD SOUTH BURNET RD	Bee Cave	549Q	WX-26	78738	14100-14599
OLD SPICEWOOD RD	Blanco Co	485A	WN-33	78620	5800-6399
	Blanco Co	455W	WP-34	78620	6400-7699
OLD SPICEWOOD SPRINGS RD					
	Austin	494Q	MH-32	78731	5200-5399
OLD STABLE LN	West Lake Hills	583B	ME-24	78746	1-99
OLD STAGE CV	Williamson Co	433M	MF-38	78750	12300-12399
OLD STAGE TRL	Williamson Co	433R	MF-38	78750	12000-12399
OLD STERLING RD	Cedar Park	373R	MF-44	78613	2100-2299
OLD STONE RD	Austin	644Q	MH-17	78745	600-699
OLD STONE RD	Bastrop Co	711F	MW-12	78612	100-199
OLD STONEHEDGE	West Lake Hills	553Y	MF-25	78746	800-1199
OLD TATUM TRL	Travis Co	457T	WS-34	78669	22900-23499
OLD THORNDALE RD	Taylor	323W	EA-49	76574	200-2599
	Williamson Co	323Y	EB-49	76574	2600-2999
OLD TOWN DR	Austin	556G	MM-27	78752	7300-7599
OLD TRACT RD	Pflugerville	468F	MQ-36	78660	2300-2699
OLD TRAILS CT	Travis Co	366R	WR-44	78654	7200-7299
OLD US HWY 183 N	Cedar Park	373W	ME-43	78613	100-199
OLD US HWY 183 S	Cedar Park	403B	ME-42	78613	200-499
OLD W 38TH ST	Austin	555S	MJ-25	78731	1500-1599
OLD WAGON RD	West Lake Hills	553X	ME-25	78746	1400-1599
OLD WALSH TARLTON	Austin	583V	MF-22	78746	1000-1399
OLD WEST DR	Round Rock	406L	MM-41	78681	200-399
	Round Rock	406Q	MM-41	78681	400-699
OLD WEST PL	Round Rock	406Q	MM-41	78681	2000-2199
OLD WEST TRL	Hays Co	763P	ME-5	78610	100-299
OLD WICK CASTLE WAY	Pflugerville	408X	MQ-40	78660	800-999
OLEANDER LN	Georgetown	314G	MH-51	78628	500-599
OLEANDER LN	Round Rock	407F	MN-42	78664	900-999
OLEANDER TRL	Austin	611H	MB-21	78735	6000-6399
OLGUIN ST	Austin	674A	MG-15	78745	100-199
OLIN CV	Georgetown	287P	MN-53	78626	2000-2199
OLIPHANT ST	Travis Co	618Z	MR-19	78725	14500-14599
OLIVE ST	Austin	585U	MK-22	78702	900-1199
OLIVE ST	Georgetown	286H	MM-54	78626	1200-1799
OLIVE BRANCH	Williamson Co	224V	MH-58	78633	100-199
OLIVE HILL DR	Austin	404Q	MH-41	78717	14400-14799
OLIVER CIR	Travis Co	610X	WY-19	78736	10600-10699
OLIVER DR	Travis Co	610X	WY-19	78736	9900-10099
	Travis Co	640B	WY-18	78737	10100-10299
OLIVER CEMETERY RD	Travis Co	610T	WY-19	78736	11600-11899
OLIVER LOVING CV	Cedar Park	402Q	MD-41	78613	1100-1199
OLIVER LOVING TRL	Austin	642A	MC-18	78749	6100-6599
OLIVIA CT	Williamson Co	318A	MQ-51	78634	500-599
OLLA CERO LN	Austin	581V	MB-22	78735	8500-8599
OLMOS DR	Austin	646G	MM-18	78744	1-99
OLMOS DR	Austin	496M	MM-32	78753	12000-12099
OLMOS DR	Leander	342E	MC-48	78641	300-399
OLOMANA CT	Bastrop Co	745Z	EF-7	78602	100-199
OLSON DR	Austin	433U	MF-37	78750	11500-11799
OLTON'S BLUFF CV	Austin	497T	MN-31	78754	11500-11599
OLTON'S BLUFF DR	Austin	497T	MN-31	78754	2100-2199
OLTORF ST E	Austin	614R	MH-20	78704	100-599
	Austin	615S	MJ-19	78704	600-1599
	Austin	615X	MJ-19	78741	1600-4499
	Austin	645C	MK-18	78741	4500-6299
OLTORF ST W	Austin	614L	MH-20	78704	100-1599
OLYMPIAD DR	Williamson Co	434U	MH-37	78729	12600-12699
OLYMPIA FIELDS LOOP	Austin	704P	MG-11	78747	10800-10999
OLYMPIC CV	Round Rock	378X	MQ-43	78664	2100-2199
OLYMPIC DR	Pflugerville	467H	MP-36	78660	100-799
	Pflugerville	437Y	MP-37	78660	1200-1699
	Travis Co	467H	MP-36	78660	1000-1299
OLYMPIC DR E	Pflugerville	468J	MQ-35	78660	800-1099
OLYMPIC OVERLOOK	Travis Co	582R	MD-23	78746	6200-6299
OLYMPUS DR	Travis Co	522X	MC-28	78733	1100-1899
OMAHA DR	Lago Vista	458F	WU-36	78645	1700-2099
OMAN ST	Hutto	349V	MT-46	78634	100-199
O'MEARA CIR	Austin	704P	MG-11	78747	10800-10899
OMEGA AVE	Austin	586U	MM-22	78721	1100-1199
OMNI PARK	Travis Co	646W	ML-16	78744	None
OMRO CV	Williamson Co	405N	MJ-41	78717	15500-15599
O'NEAL LN	Austin	466N	ML-35	78759	2700-2999
ONE COUNTRY CLUB DR	Bastrop Co	776Y	EH-4	78602	100-199
ONE HOUSE RD	Travis Co	459R	WX-35	78645	3700-3799
ONEIDA DR	Travis Co	467P	MN-35	78660	None
O'NEIL AVE	Lago Vista	458F	WU-36	78645	21700-21899
ONE OAK RD	Austin	642C	MD-18	78749	6700-7099
ONINI CT	Bastrop Co	746W	EG-7	78602	100-199
ONION ST	Austin	615C	MK-21	78702	300-399
	Austin	585Y	MK-22	78702	400-699
ONION BRANCH CV	Round Rock	345P	MJ-47	78681	3200-3299
ONION CREEK CT	Austin	704N	MG-11	78747	11000-11099
ONION CREEK DR	Austin	675J	MJ-14	78744	6800-7099
	Austin	675N	MJ-14	78744	7200-7499
	Austin	674R	MH-14	78744	7400-7499

STREET NAME	CITY or COUNTY	MAPSCO GRID	AUSTIN GRID	ZIP CODE	BLOCK RANGE O/E
ONION CREEK DR	Travis Co	733A	ME-9	78652	13000-13499
ONION CREEK PKWY	Austin	703R	MF-11	78748	1900-2099
	Austin	704N	MG-11	78747	2400-2599
	Travis Co	703R	MF-11	78747	2200-2399
ONION CREEK VILLAGE	Round Rock	376Q	MM-44	78664	1700-1799
ONION CROSSING CT	Austin	675J	MJ-14	78744	6900-6999
ONION CROSSING DR	Austin	675J	MJ-14	78744	6900-7199
	Austin	674R	MH-14	78744	7200-7499
ONION HOLLOW CV	Travis Co	672W	MC-13	78739	3300-3399
ONION HOLLOW RUN	Travis Co	672W	MC-13	78739	11700-12199
ONSLOW DR	Austin	672U	MD-13	78748	2800-3099
ONTARIO DR	Travis Co	467P	MN-35	78660	None
ON THE LAKE RD	Travis Co	550C	WZ-27	78732	12900-13099
ONYX CV	Williamson Co	433U	MF-37	78750	10700-10799
OOLONG LN	Travis Co	467L	MP-35	78660	1300-1399
OPAL TRL	Williamson Co	433Q	MF-38	78750	10800-11099
OPAL FIRE DR	Travis Co	436G	MM-39	78728	15600-15899
OPEN GATE DR	Austin	463B	ME-36	78726	10200-10399
OPEN RANGE TRL	Austin	642A	MC-18	78749	6000-6199
OPEN SKY RD	Hays Co	668R	WV-14	78737	100-399
OPHELIA DR	Austin	556G	MM-27	78752	7400-7499
OPTION AVE	Pflugerville	409S	MS-40	78660	1800-1899
ORA LN	Travis Co	437S	MN-37	78660	15100-15499
ORANGE CV	Georgetown	225L	MK-59	78633	100-199
ORANGE DR	Austin	493G	MF-33	78750	8200-8299
ORANGE BLOSSOM WAY	Austin	675S	MJ-13	78744	6400-6599
ORANGE PEKOE TRL	Travis Co	467L	MP-35	78660	1100-1199
ORANGE SPICE CT	Travis Co	467L	MP-35	78660	1400-1499
ORANGE TREE LN	Georgetown	257E	MN-57	78626	100-199
ORANGEWOOD CIR	Austin	525E	MJ-30	78757	7700-7799
ORANGEWOOD RIDGE LN	Travis Co	704C	MH-12	78747	None
ORBIT RD	Austin	496Q	MM-32	78758	11500-11599
ORCHARD CV	Williamson Co	312D	MD-51	78641	100-199
ORCHARD DR	Williamson Co	282Z	MD-52	78641	1300-1599
ORCHARD RD	Bastrop Co	650Z	MV-16	78612	400-599
	Bastrop Co	680G	MV-15	78612	None
ORCHARD ST	Austin	584V	MH-22	78703	300-499
ORCHARD ST	Cedar Park	372G	MD-45	78613	500-799
ORCHARD WAY	Hutto	380A	MU-45	78634	100-399
ORCHARD FALLS DR	Cedar Park	403K	ME-41	78613	1100-1298 E
ORCHARD FALLS DR	Cedar Park	403P	ME-41	78613	1300-1599
ORCHARD HILL DR	Austin	671B	MA-15	78739	6500-6699
ORCHARD PARK CIR	Travis Co	437P	MN-38	78660	1100-1299
ORCHARD RIDGE BLVD	Travis Co	704C	MH-12	78747	None
ORCHID CIR	Cedar Park	402H	MD-42	78613	300-399
ORCHID LN	Travis Co	466B	ML-36	78727	13700-13899
OREGON LN	Lago Vista	458K	WU-35	78645	21500-21799
OREGON FLAT TRL	Austin	466G	MM-36	78727	13500-13599
O'REILLY CT	Travis Co	490T	WY-31	78734	1300-1699
O'REILLY DR	Lakeway	490T	WY-31	78734	1000-1399
ORGAIN ST	Hutto	379D	MT-45	78634	100-199
ORIGINS LN	Lakeway	519R	WX-29	78734	15200-15399
ORIOLE CV	Bastrop Co	709R	MT-11	78612	100-199
ORIOLE CV	Travis Co	491J	MA-32	78732	3400-3499
ORIOLE DR	Austin	526B	ML-30	78753	900-999
ORION	Lakeway	489U	WX-31	78734	100-199
ORION RD	Georgetown	195T	MJ-61	78633	1-299
ORION ST	Round Rock	346M	MM-47	78665	3900-4099
ORKNEY LN	Austin	528B	MQ-30	78653	12200-12399
ORLAND BLVD	Austin	644F	MG-18	78745	600-899
ORLANDO CIR	Travis Co	522W	MC-28	78733	1100-1499
ORLANDO CV	Lago Vista	458K	WU-35	78645	21600-21699
ORLANDO RD	Travis Co	522W	MC-28	78733	1100-1199
ORLEANS CT	Austin	643H	MF-18	78745	5100-5199
ORLEANS DR	Austin	675N	MJ-14	78744	6100-6399
ORLEANS DR	Cedar Park	403U	MF-40	78613	2300-2599
ORO CT	Williamson Co	226T	ML-58	78628	4200-4299
ORO BELLE WAY	Leander	372C	MD-45	78641	900-1199
O'ROURK LN	Austin	641Y	MB-16	78739	10400-10599
O ROURKE DR	Austin	498E	MQ-33	78660	13300-13499
ORO VALLEY CV	Austin	434Y	MH-37	78729	12600-12699
ORO VALLEY TRL	Austin	434Y	MH-37	78729	12400-12799
ORO VIEJO CV	Travis Co	432B	MC-39	78613	2700-2799
ORO VISTA CV	Lago Vista	399R	WX-41	78645	9000-9099
ORR DR	Austin	673M	MF-14	78748	8300-8399
ORRELL CT	Austin	524D	MH-30	78731	3700-3899
ORRICK DR	Austin	642A	MC-18	78749	7500-7699
ORSINI PL	Austin	463C	MF-36	78750	11100-11199
ORSOBELLO CV	Travis Co	432G	MD-39	78613	2600-2699
ORSOBELLO PL	Travis Co	432G	MD-39	78613	2700-2799
ORTEGA CV	Lago Vista	399M	WX-41	78645	20600-20699
ORTMAN DR	Austin	498E	MQ-33	78660	3500-3599
ORTS LN	Travis Co	439R	MT-38	78634	19300-19499
ORWELL CV	Lago Vista	458K	WU-35	78645	21800-21899
ORWELL LN	Pflugerville	407X	MN-40	78664	17300-17599
OSAGE CT	Williamson Co	257F	MN-57	78626	100-299
OSAGE DR	Leander	342Y	MD-46	78641	100-599
	Leander	372B	MC-45	78641	600-2099
OSAGE LN	Lago Vista	458F	WU-36	78645	21600-21999
OSAGE PT	Travis Co	490U	WZ-31	78734	14800-14899
OSBORNE DR	Williamson Co	434M	MH-38	78729	7800-8399
OSCAR RD	Travis Co	487A	WS-33	78669	23300-23999
	Travis Co	486D	WR-33	78669	24000-24299
OSCAR ST	Taylor	323W	EA-49	76574	200-499
OSCARS ECHO RD	Travis Co	486D	WR-33	78669	1900-2199
OSPREY CIR	Bastrop Co	776L	EH-5	78602	100-199
OSPREY CT	Williamson Co	433R	MF-38	78750	10100-10199
OSPREY DR	Williamson Co	341R	MB-47	78641	600-999
OSPREY RIDGE LOOP	Travis Co	489C	WX-33	78645	1200-2099
OSSEO CV	Williamson Co	405N	MJ-41	78717	15400-15499
OSWEGO CV	Lago Vista	399M	WX-41	78645	20600-20699
OTANI CT	Bastrop Co	776B	EG-6	78602	100-199
OTEKA CV	Austin	611M	MB-20	78735	7800-7899
OTHELLO CV	Austin	612J	MC-20	78735	7200-7299
OTIS ST	Taylor	322Z	MZ-49	76574	400-899
OTOE DR	Travis Co	467P	MN-35	78660	None
OTTAWA ST	Travis Co	522X	MC-28	78733	900-1199
OTTENHOME DR	Bee Cave	579D	WX-24	78738	5800-6099
OTTER CREEK CT	Lakeway	519M	WX-29	78734	200-299
OTTO CT	Lakeway	490X	WY-31	78734	15200-15299
OUIDA DR	Travis Co	436V	MM-37	78728	1700-2099
OUTBACK	Leander	372F	MC-45	78641	None
OUTBACK TRL	Travis Co	486M	WR-32	78669	3600-3899
OUTCROP PATH	Williamson Co	346H	MM-48	78665	900-999
OUTCROP VIEW LN	Lakeway	519U	WX-28	78738	100-199
OUTER AVE	Williamson Co	344P	MG-47	78641	6700-6799
OUTFITTER DR	Bastrop	744P	EC-8	78602	100-399

STREET NAME	CITY or COUNTY	MAPSCO GRID	AUSTIN GRID	ZIP CODE	BLOCK RANGE O/E
OUTLAW CV	Lago Vista	399M	WX-41	78645	9100-9199
OUTLAW COUNTRY DR	Austin	646Z	MM-16	78719	3600-3799
OUTPOST CV	Round Rock	376D	MM-45	78665	1000-1099
OUTPOST TRACE	Lago Vista	428Z	WV-37	78645	3900-4099
	Lago Vista	458A	WU-36	78645	4100-4199
	Lago Vista	429S	WW-37	78645	4200-5199
OUTRIDER PASS	Lago Vista	399M	WX-41	78645	20700-20899
OUTWOOD MILL LN	Austin	674W	MG-13	78744	1900-2099
OVALLA CV	Austin	642U	MD-16	78749	4200-4299
OVALLA DR	Austin	642U	MD-16	78749	8900-9299
OVERBROOK DR	Austin	556Y	MM-25	78723	5100-5699
OVERCUP DR	Round Rock	376J	ML-44	78681	1800-2099
OVERCUP OAK DR	Austin	614T	MG-19	78704	3200-3299
OVERDALE RD	Austin	556Y	MM-25	78723	2900-2999
OVERHILL DR	Austin	586G	MM-24	78721	1700-1899
OVER HILL DR	Lago Vista	458D	WV-36	78645	3800-3899
OVERLAND DR	Leander	342X	MC-46	78641	1900-1999
OVERLAND PASS	Bee Cave	550W	WY-25	78738	13200-13399
	Bee Cave	579D	WX-24	78738	13400-13799
OVERLAND ST	Williamson Co	375Y	MK-43	78681	2900-3199
OVERLAND TRL	Lago Vista	399R	WX-41	78645	20600-20899
OVERLAND HILLS CIR	Travis Co	582G	MD-24	78746	1900-1999
OVERLOOK CIR	Lago Vista	458Z	WV-34	78645	1200-1299
OVERLOOK CT	Georgetown	285H	MK-54	78628	200-299
OVERLOOK CV	Leander	342D	MD-48	78641	None
OVERLOOK DR	Austin	524V	MH-28	78731	5800-5999
OVERLOOK PASS	Travis Co	580G	WZ-24	78738	11500-11999
OVERLOOK BEND	Leander	342D	MD-48	78641	700-1099
OVERLOOK RANCH CIR	Austin	677M	MP-14	78617	12100-12299
OVERPASS RD	Hays Co	763E	ME-6	78610	5000-5099
OVERSTREET CIR	Travis Co	766J	ML-5	78610	12000-12199
OVERTON PASS	Williamson Co	434V	MH-37	78729	13100-13199
OVERTON ST	Round Rock	347V	MP-46	78665	2600-2799
OVERVIEW ST	Williamson Co	375B	MJ-45	78681	2700-2799
OVETA ST	Jonestown	430B	WY-39	78645	8300-8499
OWEN AVE	Austin	555W	MJ-25	78705	3100-3499
OWEN CIR	Austin	555S	MJ-25	78705	3500-3599
OWEN CIR	Williamson Co	287H	MP-54	78626	100-199
OWENS CV	Lago Vista	458K	WU-35	78645	21800-21899
OWENS LN	Lago Vista	458F	WU-36	78645	1900-1999
OWEN-TECH BLVD	Travis Co	466D	MM-36	78728	14000-14499
	Travis Co	436Z	MM-37	78728	14500-14699
OWL CT	Round Rock	375V	MK-43	78681	1200-1299
OWL CV	Williamson Co	433F	ME-39	78750	12300-12399
OWL CREEK DR	Georgetown	227E	MP-60	78626	30400-30499
OWLING WAY	Travis Co	529H	MT-30	78653	11500-11599
OXAUS LN	Austin	464X	MG-34	78759	9700-9899
OXBOW CIR	Lago Vista	399M	WX-41	78645	9300-9399
OXBOW TRL	Buda	732K	MC-8	78610	16100-16299
OXBOW TRL	Lago Vista	399M	WX-41	78645	20600-20699
OXEN CT	Travis Co	491T	MA-31	78732	3400-3499
OXEN WAY	Travis Co	491U	MB-31	78732	12700-12899
OX EYE TRL	West Lake Hills	553U	MF-25	78746	800-899
OXFORD AVE	Austin	614G	MH-21	78704	1300-1599
	Austin	614K	MG-20	78704	2000-2199
OXFORD BLVD	Round Rock	406M	MM-41	78664	1600-2099
	Round Rock	407N	MN-41	78664	2100-2399
OXFORD CT	Hays Co	639X	WW-16	78737	100-199
OXFORD DR	Lago Vista	458F	WU-36	78645	21700-21999
OXFORD DR E	Pflugerville	468A	MQ-36	78660	100-299
	Pflugerville	468E	MQ-36	78660	600-1199
OXFORD DR W	Pflugerville	467D	MP-36	78660	100-499
OXSHEER DR	Travis Co	491T	MA-31	78732	3200-3499
OXSHEER PASS	Travis Co	491T	MA-31	78732	12800-12899
OYSTERCATCHER DR	Travis Co	434G	MH-39	78729	13500-13699
OYSTER CREEK	Buda	732W	MC-7	78610	100-299
	Buda	732T	MC-8	78610	900-1199
OZ RD	Manor	530J	MU-29	78653	17900-17999
OZARK TRL	Travis Co	433X	ME-37	78750	10600-10799
OZARKS PATH	Bee Cave	549E	WW-27	78738	16100-16199
OZONA DR	Austin	673S	ME-13	78748	10200-10299
OZONE PL	Travis Co	436K	ML-38	78728	15300-15599

P

STREET NAME	CITY or COUNTY	MAPSCO GRID	AUSTIN GRID	ZIP CODE	BLOCK RANGE O/E
PACE ST	Austin	615H	MK-21	78702	400-499
PACE BEND S	Travis Co	487J	WS-32	78669	1100-3699
PACE BEND RD N	Travis Co	457H	WT-36	78669	500-1899
	Travis Co	428K	WU-38	78669	1900-5999
PACE BEND RD S	Travis Co	457U	WT-34	78669	100-1099
PACERS GAIT LN	Pflugerville	409J	MS-41	78660	20800-20999
PACES MILL LN	Austin	675W	MJ-13	78744	7700-7899
PACHEA TRL	Austin	463A	ME-36	78726	11300-11399
PACHEA TRL	Williamson Co	377B	MN-45	78665	1900-1999
PACK HORSE DR	Bastrop	744K	EC-8	78602	None
PACK SADDLE PASS	Austin	613Z	MF-19	78745	4400-4799
	Austin	643D	MF-18	78745	4800-5099
PACK SADDLE PASS	Round Rock	406K	ML-41	78681	700-999
PACKSADDLE RD	Travis Co	400L	WZ-41	78645	18600-19499
PACKSADDLE TRL	Lago Vista	399X	WW-40	78645	21100-21299
PADBROOK PARK CV	Austin	404E	MG-42	78717	14300-14399
PADDINGTON CIR	Williamson Co	434B	MG-39	78729	13500-13599
PADDINGTON WAY	Hutto	379M	MT-44	78634	100-399
PADDOCK CV	Lago Vista	429A	WW-39	78645	21300-21399
PADEN CIR	Cedar Park	374N	MG-44	78613	2500-2599
PADEN DR	Cedar Park	374N	MG-44	78613	600-798 E
PADINA CV	Travis Co	522P	MC-29	78733	9600-9699
PADINA DR	Travis Co	522Q	MD-29	78733	2400-2999
PA DRAPER LN	Travis Co	459J	WW-35	78645	19500-19599
PADRE CV	Austin	524E	MG-30	78731	5900-5999
PAGEDALE CV	Cedar Park	402Q	MD-41	78613	1700-1799
PAGEDALE DR	Cedar Park	402R	MD-41	78613	1100-1799
PAGE WHITNEY PKWY	Georgetown	346B	ML-48	78665	100-199
PAGOSA CT	Hays Co	639Y	WX-16	78737	100-199
PAGOSA TRL	Travis Co	433X	ME-37	78726	10700-10799
PAGOSA SPRINGS CT	Williamson Co	375S	MJ-43	78717	17000-17099
PAHALA CT	Bastrop	746N	EG-8	78602	100-199
PAHALAWE LN	Bastrop Co	746W	EG-7	78602	100-199
PAHIHI DR N	Bastrop Co	776A	EG-6	78602	100-199
PAHIHI DR S	Bastrop Co	776A	EG-6	78602	100-199
PAHOA LN	Bastrop Co	745S	EE-7	78602	100-199
PAHOIKI LN	Bastrop Co	746X	EG-7	78602	100-199
PAIA CT	Bastrop Co	745Z	EF-7	78602	100-199
PAIA CT	Bastrop Co	776B	EG-6	78602	100-199
PAIA LN	Bastrop Co	745W	EE-7	78602	100-199
PAIGE CV	Cedar Park	372G	MD-45	78613	2400-2499
PAIGE ST	Georgetown	286R	MM-53	78626	1800-2099

STREET NAME	CITY or COUNTY	MAPSCO GRID	AUSTIN GRID	ZIP CODE	BLOCK RANGE O/E
PAIGE BEND	Hutto	379G	MT-45	78634	100-599
PAINE AVE	Lago Vista	458G	WV-36	78645	21400-21599
PAINT BRUSH CV	Cedar Park	402H	MD-42	78613	400-499
PAINT BRUSH TRL	Cedar Park	402H	MD-42	78613	1000-1299
PAINTBRUSH HOLLOW	Austin	494S	MG-31	78750	6400-6499
PAINTED BUNTING CV	Williamson Co	282E	MC-54	78641	100-199
PAINTED BUNTING DR	Travis Co	432R	MD-38	78726	12200-12599
PAINTED BUNTING LN	Georgetown	225F	MJ-60	78633	100-199
PAINTED PONY CV	Austin	612H	MD-21	78735	4300-4399
PAINTED SHIELD DR	Austin	612D	MD-21	78735	5300-5499
PAINTED SUNSET LN	Travis Co	497C	MP-33	78754	13100-13299
PAINTED VALLEY CV	Austin	464U	MH-34	78759	10500-10599
PAINTED VALLEY DR	Austin	464Z	MH-34	78759	5500-6099
PAINTER PASS	Travis Co	402U	MD-40	78613	None
PAINT ROCK CV	Cedar Park	372N	MC-44	78613	1900-1999
PAINT ROCK DR	Austin	494Y	MH-31	78731	4100-4199
PAIRNOY LN	Austin	641X	MA-16	78739	11000-11199
PAISANO CIR	Hays Co	638G	WV-18	78737	13600-13899
PAISANO PASS	Hays Co	638G	WV-18	78737	13600-13799
PAISANO RD	Travis Co	553Q	MF-26	78746	2000-2299
PAISANO TRL	Austin	643J	ME-17	78745	3100-3499
PAISANO TRL	Hays Co	638C	WV-18	78737	13300-13599
	Hays Co	638G	WV-18	78737	13600-15099
PAISLEY DR	Briarcliff	487C	WT-33	78669	800-999
PALACE PKWY	Austin	673L	MF-14	78748	8200-9199
PALACE GREEN	Austin	524D	MH-30	78731	7900-7999
PALACIOS CV	Austin	642L	MD-17	78749	4200-4299
PALACIOS DR	Austin	642Q	MD-17	78749	7700-7999
PALADIN PL	Austin	408L	MR-41	78664	None
PALAMINO CT	Caldwell Co	767X	MN-4	78616	1-99
PALAZZA ALTO DR	Lakeway	520A	WY-30	78734	100-299
PALCHEFF CT	Travis Co	490L	WZ-32	78734	2700-2799
PALEFACE CT	Travis Co	490R	WZ-32	78734	3000-3099
PALEFACE DR	Georgetown	287B	MP-54	78626	50000-50099
	Williamson Co	287L	MP-53	78626	50100-50199
PALEFACE LAKE DR	Travis Co	456M	WR-35	78669	25200-25299
PALEFACE POINT DR	Travis Co	456D	WR-36	78669	100-499
PALEFACE RANCH RD N	Travis Co	426U	WR-37	78669	100-899
PALEFACE RANCH RD S	Travis Co	456P	WQ-35	78669	100-2599
PALEFACE SHORE DR	Travis Co	426Y	WR-37	78669	25500-26299
PALFREY DR	Austin	466J	ML-35	78727	12500-12899
PALGRAVE CT	Austin	671D	MB-15	78739	10900-10999
PALI CT	Bastrop Co	776F	EG-6	78602	100-199
PALIKEA CIR	Bastrop Co	776J	EG-5	78602	100-199
PALISADE CT	Austin	524S	MG-28	78731	5600-5699
PALISADE DR	Austin	524S	MG-28	78731	4600-4799
PALISADE DR	Hays Co	639U	WX-16	78737	100-399
PALISADES CV	Travis Co	521T	MA-28	78732	100-199
PALISADES PKWY	Travis Co	521N	MA-29	78732	11700-12199
PALISADES POINTE CV	Travis Co	551E	MA-27	78733	12000-12099
PALISADES POINTE LN	Travis Co	551E	MA-27	78733	1400-1799
PALITINE LN	Pflugerville	437D	MP-39	78660	600-999
PALLADIO DR	Austin	524B	MG-30	78731	4300-4399
PALL MALL DR	Austin	672Q	MD-14	78748	10700-10899
PALM CIR	Austin	616S	ML-19	78741	6000-6299
PALM WAY	Austin	465Y	MK-34	78758	2900-3499
PALMA CIR	Austin	646G	MM-18	78744	1-199
PALMA PLAZA	Austin	584M	MH-23	78703	1500-1899
PALMA VERDE DR	Austin	646F	ML-18	78744	7800-8199
PALMBROOK DR	Austin	404D	MH-42	78717	9500-9599
	Austin	374Z	MH-43	78717	9600-10199
PALM DALE CT	Travis Co	550R	WZ-26	78733	2800-2899
PALMER CV	Round Rock	378T	MQ-43	78664	3500-3599
PALMER DR	Point Venture	488R	WV-32	78654	500-599
PALMER DR	Round Rock	378T	MQ-43	78664	3900-3999
PALMER PATH	Hays Co	669Q	WX-14	78737	14000-14099
PALMER RD	Travis Co	734Y	MH-7	78610	12300-13599
PALMERA CV	Austin	644V	MH-16	78744	2200-2299
PALMETTO CIR	Austin	642M	MD-17	78749	7500-7599
PALMETTO DR	Georgetown	195N	MJ-62	78633	100-499
PALMETTO DR	Williamson Co	432D	MD-39	78613	1700-1799
PALM HARBOR WAY	Mustang Ridge	765V	MK-4	78610	500-12399
PALM VALLEY BLVD E	Round Rock	376V	MM-43	78664	100-1199
	See.. US Hwy 79				
	Round Rock	377T	MN-43	78664	1200-4299
	Round Rock	378J	MQ-44	78665	4300-4599
	Williamson Co	378J	MQ-44	78665	4600-4899
	Williamson Co	378J	MQ-44	78665	4900-5699
PALM VALLEY BLVD W	Round Rock	376U	MM-43	78664	100-499
	See.. US Hwy 79				
PALM VALLEY CV	Round Rock	377T	MN-43	78664	100-199
PALM VISTA DR	Travis Co	408Q	MR-41	78660	1900-2199
PALMWOOD CV	Austin	525G	MK-30	78757	1800-1899
PALMWOOD TRL	Pflugerville	438N	MQ-38	78660	100-199
PALMWOOD WAY	Austin	497N	MN-32	78753	11600-11799
PALO ALTO	Leander	341X	MA-46	78641	1800-1899
PALO ALTO LN	Cedar Park	403A	ME-42	78613	600-699
PALO ALTO WAY	Travis Co	521N	MA-29	78732	300-399
PALO BLANCO CT	Austin	645W	MJ-16	78744	5600-5699
PALO BLANCO LN	Austin	645W	MJ-16	78744	5100-5699
	Austin	675A	MJ-15	78744	5700-5799
PALO DURO CT	Williamson Co	226R	MM-59	78628	3200-3299
PALO DURO DR	Cedar Park	373E	ME-45	78613	800-899
PALO DURO DR	Lago Vista	429F	WW-39	78645	20600-20899
PALO DURO RD	Austin	525X	MJ-28	78757	1200-1999
PALOMA CIR	Travis Co	490C	WZ-33	78734	4000-4099
PALOMA DR	Round Rock	376B	ML-45	78665	800-999
PALOMA PT	Williamson Co	284E	MG-54	78628	100-199
PALOMA BLANCA WAY	Travis Co	677V	MP-13	78617	12200-12899
PALOMA LAKE BLVD	Williamson Co	348S	MQ-46	78665	2600-2799
	Williamson Co	348N	MQ-47	78665	None
PALOMAR LN	Austin	465H	MK-36	78727	3400-4099
PALOMINO CV	Lago Vista	429B	WW-39	78645	21200-21399
PALOMINO DR	Travis Co	522P	MC-29	78733	2700-2799
PALOMINO TRL	Austin	646K	ML-17	78744	2800-2899
PALOMINO RIDGE DR	Travis Co	551Q	MB-26	78733	1400-1799
PALO PINTO CV	Round Rock	347N	MN-47	78665	3700-3799
PALO PINTO DR	Austin	586E	ML-24	78723	2100-2299
PALOS VERDES	Leander	341V	MB-46	78641	900-999
	Leander	371C	MB-45	78641	2000-2099
PALOS VERDES DR	Lakeway	519C	WX-30	78734	100-1099
PALO VERDE DR	Austin	645W	MJ-16	78744	2500-2599
PAMELA ST	Travis Co	436R	MM-38	78728	1800-2099
PAMELLA CT	Travis Co	490L	WZ-32	78734	2900-3099
PAMONA DR	Austin	465Q	MK-35	78727	4400-4499
PAMPA DR	Austin	525Z	MK-28	78752	400-599
PAMPAS CV	Austin	493M	MF-32	78750	8100-8199

STREET NAME	CITY or COUNTY	MAPSCO GRID	AUSTIN GRID	ZIP CODE	BLOCK RANGE O/E
PAMPAS RICAS DR	Leander	312W	MC-49	78641	700-899
PAMPLONA VISTA CV	Austin	640Z	WZ-16	78739	8000-8099
PANADERO CV	Austin	705A	MJ-12	78747	6400-6499
PANADERO DR	Austin	675W	MJ-13	78747	8200-8299
	Austin	705A	MJ-12	78747	8300-8999
PANARAMA CT	Travis Co	708H	MR-12	78617	15700-15999
PANDA LN	Travis Co	702Q	MD-11	78652	12800-12899
PANDA ROYALE DR	Travis Co	677Y	MP-13	78617	6700-6999
PANDORA ST	Austin	586N	ML-23	78702	1100-1199
PANHANDLE CV	Lago Vista	399X	WW-40	78645	21000-21199
PANHANDLE PLAINS DR	Georgetown	314K	MG-50	78628	100-499
PANNELL ST	Austin	586J	ML-23	78722	2900-2999
PANNIER LN	Austin	673F	ME-15	78748	1700-1999
PANORAMA DR	Hays Co	577Y	WT-22	78720	500-1099
	Travis Co	577V	WT-22	78720	17200-17699
PANORAMA DR	Travis Co	461Q	MB-35	78732	13800-14199
PANORAMA RIDGE	Lago Vista	429K	WW-38	78645	6600-6799
PANORAMA VISTA DR	Austin	611M	MB-20	78735	6200-6299
PANSY TRL	Travis Co	466C	MM-36	78727	13500-13899
PANTERA RIDGE	Travis Co	464N	MG-35	78759	10200-10499
PANTHER DR	Travis Co	521T	MA-28	78732	11800-11999
PANTHER DR	Travis Co	408V	MR-40	78660	19700-20299
PANTHER LOOP	Travis Co	408V	MR-40	78660	1400-1699
PANTHER TRL	Austin	614N	MG-20	78704	2200-2399
PANTHER HALL	Leander	341W	MA-46	78641	3800-3899
PANTHER JUNCTION TRL	Austin	403M	MF-41	78717	11100-11199
PAPALOA LN	Bastrop Co	746S	EG-7	78602	100-199
PAPAWAI DR	Bastrop Co	775D	EF-6	78602	100-199
PAPER MOON DR	Williamson Co	402V	MD-40	78613	1600-1699
PAPPY'S WAY	Austin	523T	ME-28	78730	3700-3899
PAR CV	Austin	645W	MJ-16	78744	5100-5199
PARADE ST	Dripping Springs	636Y	WR-16	78620	100-299
PARADE RIDGE	Austin	524J	MG-29	78731	5600-5699
PARADISE CT	Travis Co	428E	WU-39	78654	4600-4699
PARADISE CV	Travis Co	428E	WU-39	78654	23500-23799
PARADISE MANOR CIR	Travis Co	366Y	WR-43	78654	6200-6399
PARADISE MANOR DR	Travis Co	366Y	WR-43	78654	6300-28799
PARADISE MOUNTAIN	Hays Co	762Z	MD-4	78610	100-499
PARADISE RIDGE CV	Round Rock	377Z	MP-43	78665	2800-2899
PARADISE RIDGE DR	Round Rock	407D	MP-42	78665	1800-1899
	Round Rock	377Z	MP-43	78665	1900-2399
PARAGON CT	Lakeway	519H	WX-30	78734	100-199
PARAISO PKWY	Travis Co	580G	WZ-24	78738	4700-5099
PARAKEET ST	Travis Co	520E	WY-30	78734	15100-15299
PARALEE COVE CT	Williamson Co	405A	MJ-42	78717	16400-16499
PARAMOUNT AVE	Austin	614F	MG-21	78704	1900-2699
PARCO PATH	Travis Co	468N	MQ-35	78660	14800-14899
PARDONERS TALE LN	Austin	703A	ME-12	78748	11200-11399
PARELL PATH	Austin	645W	MJ-16	78744	4900-5199
PARIS AVE	Austin	466P	ML-35	78727	1800-1899
PARISMINA LN	Travis Co	581V	MB-22	78735	8400-8599
PARIVA TRL	Austin	463B	ME-36	78726	10400-10599
PARK BLVD	Austin	555U	MK-25	78751	500-899
PARK CIR	Lago Vista	428Z	WV-37	78645	21300-21399
PARK CV	Hays Co	668U	WV-13	78620	1200-1399
PARK CV N	Hays Co	762M	MD-5	78610	100-299
PARK DR	Jonestown	400M	WZ-41	78645	18100-18499
PARK DR	Lago Vista	429K	WW-38	78645	20400-21299
PARK DR	Travis Co	459M	WX-35	78645	4100-4399
PARK DR	Travis Co	491H	MB-33	78732	12800-12999
PARK DR	Travis Co	428E	WU-39	78654	23400-23499
PARK DR	Williamson Co	375A	MJ-45	78681	4000-4199
PARK LN	Austin	615J	MJ-20	78704	200-499
PARK LN	Bastrop	746N	EG-8	78602	100-199
PARK LN	Georgetown	256U	MM-55	78628	1400-2099
PARK LN	Lago Vista	428Z	WV-37	78645	4000-4099
PARK LN	Travis Co	491G	MB-33	78732	4800-4899
PARK LN	Webberville	651E	MW-18	78653	2100-2399
PARK PL	Austin	585F	MJ-24	78705	600-699
	Austin	615F	MJ-21	78704	1000-1099
PARK ST	Elgin	533H	EB-30	78621	100-199
PARK ST	Hutto	350W	MU-46	78634	100-499
PARK ST	Taylor	352H	MZ-48	76574	200-399
PARK ST E	Cedar Park	373X	ME-43	78613	100-1699
	Williamson Co	374S	MG-43	78613	None
PARK ST W	Cedar Park	373W	ME-43	78613	300-799
	Cedar Park	402C	MD-42	78613	800-1899
PARK WAY	Round Rock	376Z	MM-43	78664	700-799
PARK 35 CV	Hays Co	762R	MD-5	78610	100S-299S
	Hays Co	763N	ME-5	78610	100S-299S
PARK AT WOODLANDS DR	Austin	587R	MP-23	78724	5000-5499
PARK BEND DR	Austin	466S	ML-34	78758	2000-2699
PARK CENTER DR	Austin	526U	MM-28	78753	1300-1499
PARK CENTRAL BLVD	Georgetown	316U	MM-49	78626	100-199
	Williamson Co	316U	MM-49	78626	None
PARKCREST CT	Pflugerville	438N	MQ-38	78660	900-1099
PARKCREST DR	Austin	524V	MH-28	78731	5400-5699
PARK DALE	Round Rock	407J	MN-41	78664	1600-1699
PARKDALE CV	Austin	525B	MJ-30	78757	8200-8299
PARKDALE DR	Austin	525F	MJ-30	78757	8000-8199
PARKDALE PL	Austin	644A	MG-18	78745	4600-4699
PARKER CIR	Georgetown	256T	ML-55	78628	900-1199
PARKER DR	Georgetown	256T	ML-55	78628	2300-3399
PARKER DR	Round Rock	406Z	MM-40	78728	1-599
	Round Rock	406U	MM-40	78681	2600-2799
PARKER LN	Austin	615P	MJ-20	78741	1200-2899
	Austin	645A	MJ-18	78741	2900-3499
PARKER PL	Cedar Park	372G	MD-45	78613	1200-1299
PARKER BEND	Travis Co	520N	WY-29	78734	1400-1599
PARKFIELD CIR	Round Rock	407N	MN-41	78664	1500-1699
PARKFIELD CV	Round Rock	407N	MN-41	78664	1700-1799
PARKFIELD DR	Austin	525H	MK-30	78758	8500-9199
	Austin	496W	ML-31	78758	9200-11699
PARK GREEN DR	Austin	527E	MN-30	78754	2000-2199
PARKHILL CV	Round Rock	376H	MM-45	78664	400-499
PARK HILLS DR	Rollingwood	584N	MG-23	78746	3200-3399
PARK HOLLOW CT	Travis Co	524W	MG-28	78746	4200-4299
PARK HOLLOW LN	Travis Co	524W	MG-28	78746	5300-5499
PARKHURST DR	Leander	342F	MC-48	78641	900-999
PARKINSON DR	Austin	615K	MJ-20	78704	1400-1499
PARKLAND CV	Round Rock	375V	MK-43	78681	2200-2299
PARKLAND DR	Bastrop Co	741K	MW-8	78612	100-199
PARKLAND DR	Williamson Co	434J	MG-38	78729	12500-12799
PARK MEADOW BLVD	Georgetown	256P	ML-56	78628	300-499
PARK OAK DR	Round Rock	405C	MK-42	78681	2100-2199
PARK ONE BLVD	Leander	342X	MC-46	78641	1800-1999
PARK PLACE CIR	Round Rock	405C	MK-42	78681	2100-2299

STREET NAME	CITY or COUNTY	MAPSCO GRID	AUSTIN GRID	ZIP CODE	BLOCK RANGE O/E
PARK PLACE DR	Williamson Co	283M	MF-53	78628	100-599
PARK PLAZA	Austin	526K	ML-29	78753	800-1099
PARK RD 1A	Bastrop	746E	EG-9	78602	None
PARK RD 1C	Bastrop Co	746G	EH-9	78602	100-399
PARK RIDGE PATH	Williamson Co	346H	MM-48	78665	4100-4199
PARKSIDE CIR	Round Rock	406H	MM-42	78664	1000-1199
	Round Rock	407E	MN-42	78664	1200-1799
PARKSIDE CV	Round Rock	407E	MN-42	78664	1500-1599
PARKSIDE LN	Austin	643M	MF-17	78745	1700-1999
PARKSIDE PKWY	Williamson Co	344B	MG-48	78628	100-799
PARKSIDE RD	Travis Co	519U	WX-28	78738	1-99
PARKSIDE TRL	Leander	342F	MC-48	78641	None
PARKSTONE HEIGHTS DR	Austin	583T	ME-22	78746	4100-4299
PARK STRIP	Lago Vista	429P	WW-38	78645	20100-20299
PARKSVILLE WAY	Cedar Park	372P	MC-44	78613	1900-2199
PARK THIRTY-FIVE CIR	Austin	496H	MM-33	78753	12000-12199
PARK VALLEY DR	Round Rock	375Z	MK-43	78681	16000-16099
	Williamson Co	375U	MK-43	78681	17700-17899
PARKVIEW TRL	Travis Co	460R	WZ-35	78734	5700-5799
PARKVIEW CIR	Austin	494X	MG-31	78731	7500-7699
PARKVIEW CV	Pflugerville	438S	MQ-37	78660	800-899
PARK VIEW DR	Austin	525N	MJ-29	78757	2500-2799
PARKVIEW DR	Georgetown	256V	MM-55	78626	100-299
	Georgetown	257S	MN-55	78626	300-399
PARKVIEW DR	Pflugerville	438S	MQ-37	78660	200-1099
PARKVIEW DR	Round Rock	406B	ML-42	78681	400-799
PARKVIEW DR	Travis Co	436C	MM-39	78728	16400-16599
	Williamson Co	436C	MM-39	78728	16200-16399
PARKVIEW DR	Williamson Co	441C	MX-39	78615	11500-11799
PARKVIEW PL	Austin	494X	MG-31	78731	4800-4899
PARK VILLAGE CV	Austin	496W	ML-31	78758	900-999
PARK VILLAGE DR	Austin	526A	ML-30	78758	9500-9699
PARK VILLAGE DR E	Austin	496X	ML-31	78758	9700-9799
PARK VILLAGE DR W	Austin	496W	ML-31	78758	9700-9799
PARKVISTA TRL	Williamson Co	347A	MN-48	78665	1600-4399
PARKWAY	Austin	584R	MH-23	78703	1200-1599
	Austin	584H	MH-24	78703	1600-2299
PARKWAY DR	Cedar Park	373W	ME-43	78613	100-399
PARKWAY DR	Travis Co	437Q	MP-38	78660	15800-16599
PARKWAY ST	Georgetown	256U	MM-55	78628	500-1699
PARKWAY ST	Pflugerville	438S	MQ-37	78660	800-899
PARK WEST PASS	Austin	641Y	MB-16	78739	10300-10399
PARKWOOD CT	West Lake Hills	583R	MF-23	78746	100-199
PARKWOOD CV	Round Rock	407E	MN-42	78664	100-1199
PARKWOOD DR	Austin	612P	MC-20	78735	5700-6299
PARKWOOD DR	Leander	342T	MC-46	78641	1500-1899
PARKWOOD DR	Travis Co	577Q	WT-23	78720	10300-10499
PARKWOOD RD	Austin	555Z	MK-25	78722	4200-4399
	Austin	555Z	MK-25	78723	4400-4699
PARLIAMENT CV	Austin	587E	MN-24	78724	5300-5399
PARLIAMENT CV	Lago Vista	458B	WU-36	78645	3100-3799
PARLIAMENT DR	Austin	587E	MN-24	78724	6000-6399
PARLIAMENT PL	Austin	464B	MG-36	78759	7800-8099
PARLIAMENT HOUSE RD	Austin	434A	MG-39	78729	9900-10099
	Williamson Co	434A	MG-39	78729	9800-9899
PARMER LN E	Austin	467W	MN-34	78753	100-799
	Austin	497F	MN-33	78753	800-1699
	Austin	497Q	MP-32	78754	1700-4599
	Austin	498W	MQ-31	78653	5200-6799
	Austin	528M	MR-29	78653	8800-9499
	Austin	529N	MS-29	78653	9500-9599
	Travis Co	497Q	MP-32	78754	4600-4799
	Travis Co	498W	MQ-31	78653	4800-5199
	Travis Co	528M	MR-29	78653	6800-8799
PARMER LN W	Austin	466Z	MM-34	78753	100-1099
	Austin	466T	ML-34	78727	1100-3399
	Austin	465B	MJ-36	78727	3400-5599
	Austin	435N	MJ-38	78727	5600-6099
	Austin	435N	MJ-38	78729	6100-7499
	Austin	434M	MH-38	78729	7500-7999
	Austin	404Q	MH-41	78717	9200-10799
	Cedar Park	404Q	MH-41	78613	10800-11099
	Cedar Park	374K	MG-44	78613	11100-13099
	Williamson Co	434M	MH-38	78729	8000-8999
	Williamson Co	404Y	MH-40	78729	9000-9199
	Williamson Co	404Q	MH-41	78717	10500-10999
PARQUE CIR	Georgetown	257S	MN-55	78626	100-199
PARQUE CT	Georgetown	257S	MN-55	78626	100-199
PARQUE CV	Georgetown	257S	MN-55	78626	100-199
PARQUE VISTA	Georgetown	257S	MN-55	78626	100-399
PARRALENA LN	Travis Co	436V	MM-37	78728	1800-1899
PARRISH LN	Travis Co	619N	MS-20	78725	15000-15399
PARROT TRL	Round Rock	375V	MK-43	78681	1000-1299
PARSONS DR	Austin	496P	ML-32	78758	1300-1399
PARSONS RD	Travis Co	560U	MV-25	78653	10200-11999
PARSONS ST E	Manor	529U	MT-28	78653	100-799
PARSONS ST W	Manor	529U	MT-28	78653	100-499
PARTAGE CIR	Austin	704N	MG-11	78747	4700-4799
PARTRIDGE CIR	Austin	495Z	MK-31	78758	9200-9299
PARTRIDGE CT	Round Rock	375V	MK-43	78681	2500-2599
PARTRIDGE BEND CV	Williamson Co	434Q	MH-38	78729	8200-8299
PARTRIDGE BEND DR	Williamson Co	434Q	MH-38	78729	12800-13199
PASADA LN	Williamson Co	345X	MJ-46	78681	4300-4399
PASADENA DR	Austin	525Q	MK-29	78757	1200-2399
PASADERA LN	Travis Co	408G	MR-42	78664	400-499
PASAGUARDA DR	Travis Co	583U	MF-22	78746	1200-1399
PASA TIEMPO	Leander	371C	MB-45	78641	1300-1399
PASATIEMPO CT	Austin	404H	MH-42	78717	15700-15799
PASATIEMPO DR	Austin	404H	MH-42	78717	9400-9899
PASCAL CT	Travis Co	553E	ME-27	78746	6900-6999
PASCAL LN	Travis Co	553E	ME-27	78746	1-199
PASEO DR	Travis Co	672N	MC-14	78739	4100-4299
PASEO LN	Austin	462G	MD-36	78726	8800-8899
PASEO CORTO DR	Travis Co	402X	MC-40	78613	1700-1799
PASEO DEL TORO	Austin	524U	MH-28	78731	5900-5999
PASEO DEL TORO CV	Austin	524Q	MH-29	78731	3800-3899
PASEO DE PRESIDENTE BLVD	Manor	530M	MV-29	78653	13100-13499
PASEO DE VACA	Lago Vista	429F	WW-39	78645	20500-21599
PASEO DE VACA CIR	Lago Vista	429A	WW-39	78645	21200-21399
PASEO GRAND DR	Cedar Park	373R	MF-44	78613	401-599 O
PASEO NUEVO CIR	Austin	677R	MP-14	78617	5400-5599
PASEO VERDE DR	Leander	341M	MB-47	78641	1800-1899
PASO FINO CV	Cedar Park	373S	ME-43	78613	400-499
PASO FINO TRL	Cedar Park	373T	ME-43	78613	500-799
PASQUARELLA DR	Austin	678P	MQ-14	78617	5900-5999
PASSAGE WAY	Round Rock	376N	ML-44	78681	1700-1799
PASSION FLOWER PASS	Travis Co	402X	MC-40	78613	None
PASSION VINE CV	Pflugerville	437H	MP-39	78660	1600-1699
PASTEL PL	Austin	644F	MG-18	78745	4600-4699
PASTERNAK DR	Pflugerville	407X	MN-40	78664	1900-1999
PASTORI CV	Round Rock	407H	MP-42	78665	1700-1799
PASTURE CV S	Hutto	349T	MS-46	78634	1000-1099
PASTURE RD	Austin	612S	MC-19	78749	6900-6999
PATAGONIA PASS	Bee Cave	549J	WW-26	78738	5000-5099
PATCHWAY LN	Austin	673H	MF-15	78748	700-899
PATHFINDER DR	Austin	464X	MG-34	78759	6300-6399
PATHFINDER WAY	Round Rock	346Z	MM-46	78665	1000-1299
PATIO CIR	Travis Co	523X	ME-28	78730	3000-3099
PATRICE DR	Austin	463F	ME-36	78750	9800-9999
PATRICIA RD	Williamson Co	314U	MH-49	78628	100-499
PATRICIA ST	Travis Co	436R	MM-38	78728	15300-15799
PATRICK PL	Travis Co	437X	MN-37	78660	600-799
PATRICKS WAY DR	Hays Co	606U	WR-19	78620	100-199
PATRIOT DR	Lago Vista	458F	WU-36	78645	1900-3299
PATRON DR	Austin	466S	ML-34	78758	12300-12399
PATSY PKWY	Austin	674L	MH-14	78744	2100-4599
PATTERSON AVE	Austin	584Q	MH-23	78703	600-999
PATTERSON RD	Travis Co	551V	MB-25	78733	900-1499
	Travis Co	552S	MC-25	78733	1500-1799
PATTERSON INDUSTRIAL DR					
	Travis Co	467Z	MP-34	78660	2200-2499
PATTI DR	Georgetown	256P	ML-56	78628	2900-2999
PATTI LN	Hays Co	608E	WU-21	78620	100-399
PATTON AVE	Austin	616U	MM-19	78742	600-899
PATTON AVE	Lago Vista	458G	WV-36	78645	21400-21599
PATTON CV	Bastrop	744C	ED-9	78602	400-499
PATTON CV	Lago Vista	458B	WU-36	78645	21900-21999
PATTON DR	Lago Vista	458F	WU-36	78645	21600-21899
PATTON LN	Austin	556K	ML-26	78723	1700-2299
PATTON LN	Bastrop	744C	ED-9	78602	300-399
PATTON RANCH RD	Austin	612T	MC-19	78735	5600-6299
PATTY DR	Travis Co	459V	WX-34	78645	3400-3699
PATTY'S CIR	Bastrop Co	738L	MR-8	78617	100-199
PAUL PASS	Hays Co	764P	MG-5	78610	None
PAUL ST	Austin	584U	MH-22	78703	300-499
PAUL ST	Pflugerville	438W	MQ-37	78660	300-399
	Pflugerville	468A	MQ-36	78660	400-699
PAULA LN	Taylor	322R	MZ-50	76574	2400-2799
PAUL AZINGER CT	Williamson Co	408C	MR-42	78664	200-299
PAUL AZINGER DR	Williamson Co	408C	MR-42	78664	100-199
PAUL C BELL ST	Bastrop	745P	EE-8	78602	100-399
PAUL E ANDERSON DR	Austin	702C	MD-12	78748	11500-11799
PAULETTE DR	Round Rock	375Z	MK-43	78681	400-599
PAULEY DR N	Hutto	379G	MT-45	78634	100-399
PAULEY DR S	Hutto	379G	MT-45	78634	400-899
PAULING LN	Round Rock	348S	MQ-46	78665	3200-3299
PAUL JONES PASS	Austin	703C	MF-12	78748	500-599
PAULS VALLEY RD	Hays Co	608U	WV-19	78737	12300-12799
PAUMA VALLEY WAY	Travis Co	409S	MS-40	78660	2400-2499
PAUWELA LN E	Bastrop Co	775C	EF-6	78602	100-199
PAUWELA LN W	Bastrop Co	775B	EE-6	78602	100-199
PAVELICH PASS	Austin	702H	MD-12	78748	1600-1699
PAVILION BLVD	Austin	464M	MH-35	78759	11800-11999
PAVILION DR	Bastrop Co	711C	MX-12	78612	100-299
PAWNEE	Leander	342W	MC-46	78641	2400-2499
PAWNEE PASS	Travis Co	519W	WW-28	78738	3800-4199
PAWNEE PASS S	Travis Co	549C	WX-27	78738	3400-3799
PAWNEE TRL	Lago Vista	399X	WW-40	78645	21000-21199
PAWNEE PATHWAY	Austin	643D	MF-18	78745	4800-4899
PAW PRINT	Leander	371G	MB-45	78641	1100-1199
PAWTUCKET CT	Pflugerville	409S	MS-40	78660	2200-2299
PAX DR	Austin	611L	MB-20	78736	8200-8299
PAXTON ST	Austin	525V	MK-28	78752	7500-7599
PAYLOAD PASS	Austin	644D	MH-18	78704	3600-4099
PAYNE AVE	Austin	525Y	MK-28	78757	900-2199
PAYNE STEWART DR	Williamson Co	408C	MR-42	78664	100-499
PAYTON FALLS DR	Austin	497S	MN-31	78754	1400-1699
PAYTON GIN RD	Austin	526A	ML-30	78758	800-1299
	Austin	525D	MK-30	78758	1300-1899
PEABODY DR	Williamson Co	434R	MH-38	78729	7400-7799
PEABODY PLACE DR	Hays Co	636T	WQ-16	78620	100-399
PEACEDALE LN	Austin	556T	ML-25	78723	5300-5399
PEACEFUL HAVEN WAY	Hutto	379M	MT-44	78634	100-399
PEACEFUL HILL LN	Austin	674J	MG-14	78748	7700-8699
PEACE HAVEN LN	Bastrop Co	746V	EH-7	78602	100-199
PEACE MAKER ST	Williamson Co	375Y	MK-43	78681	2900-3099
PEACEMAKER TRL	Lago Vista	399Y	WX-40	78645	20700-20999
PEACE ON EARTH PATH	Travis Co	590M	MV-23	78653	19800-19899
PEACE PIPE PATH	Georgetown	285T	MJ-52	78628	1100-1799
	Georgetown	285S	MJ-52	78628	1900-1999
PEACE PIPE PATH	Travis Co	553M	MF-26	78746	4700-4799
PEACH CT	Austin	644Z	MH-16	78744	2300-2399
PEACH ST	Buda	762C	MD-6	78610	100-399
PEACH BLOSSOM CIR	Georgetown	225D	MK-60	78633	100-199
PEACH CREEK LN	Travis Co	427P	WS-38	78669	None
PEACH GROVE CV	Austin	645X	MJ-16	78744	4800-4899
PEACH GROVE RD	Austin	645X	MJ-16	78744	4400-4899
PEACHTREE CV	Round Rock	376P	ML-44	78681	1100-1199
PEACH TREE LN	Cedar Park	372D	MD-45	78613	200-2799
PEACH TREE LN	Georgetown	287J	MN-53	78626	1200-1299
PEACH TREE ST	Austin	614F	MG-21	78704	2000-2199
PEACHTREE VALLEY DR	Round Rock	376N	ML-44	78681	1100-1699
PEACH VISTA DR	Travis Co	408L	MR-41	78660	3500-3799
PEACOCK LN	Austin	614U	MH-19	78704	600-799
PEAHI CT	Bastrop Co	776B	EG-6	78602	100-199
PEA JAY CV	Bastrop	715X	EE-10	78602	500-599
PEAK RD N	West Lake Hills	583R	MF-23	78746	1-99
PEAK RD S	Rollingwood	583V	MF-22	78746	1-99
PEAK LOOKOUT DR	Lakeway	549C	WX-27	78738	None
	Travis Co	549C	WX-27	78738	3500-4199
PEAKRIDGE DR	Travis Co	640C	WX-18	78737	9700-9999
PEALE CT	Austin	463A	ME-36	78726	10900-10999
PEAR CT	Pflugerville	437M	MP-38	78660	1400-1499
PEAR LN	Cedar Park	372D	MD-45	78613	100-299
PEARCE LN	Austin	677M	MP-14	78617	10800-11199
	Austin	677M	MP-14	78617	11200-12699
	Austin	678N	MQ-14	78617	12700-13399
	Austin	678N	MQ-14	78617	13400-14599
	Bastrop Co	740Z	MV-7	78612	100-199
	Bastrop Co	740G	MV-9	78612	5600-6199
	Bastrop Co	710S	MU-10	78612	6200-6499
	Bastrop Co	709Q	MT-11	78612	6500-6799
	Travis Co	708D	MR-12	78617	14600-15899
	Travis Co	709E	MS-12	78617	15900-17499
PEARCE RD	Austin	523W	ME-28	78730	2400-2499
	Austin	523N	ME-29	78730	3500-4299
	Travis Co	523W	ME-28	78730	2500-2599
	Travis Co	553A	ME-27	78730	2600-2999
	Travis Co	523S	ME-28	78730	3000-3499
PEARL CV	Round Rock	376N	ML-44	78681	1400-1599
PEARL ST	Austin	585J	MJ-23	78701	1600-1899
	Austin	585J	MJ-23	78705	1900-2299
	Austin	585E	MJ-24	78705	2400-2599
	Austin	585A	MJ-24	78705	2800-2899
PEARLAND ST	Hutto	350J	MU-47	78634	100-199
PEARLMAN DR	Austin	498E	MQ-33	78660	3100-3299
PEARLSTONE CV	Williamson Co	375S	MJ-43	78717	9400-9499
PEARSALL LN	Hutto	379G	MT-45	78634	1400-1499
PEARSON CV	Round Rock	348S	MQ-46	78665	3000-3099
PEARSON WAY	Round Rock	348S	MQ-46	78665	2200-2699
PEARWOOD PL	Austin	496E	ML-33	78758	11600-11699
PEASE RD	Austin	584H	MH-24	78703	1400-2399
PEAVY DR	Travis Co	618Z	MR-19	78725	3100-3599
PEBBLE CT	Round Rock	378Y	MR-43	78664	3800-3899
PEBBLE CV	Austin	556C	MM-27	78752	7600-7699
PEBBLE LN	Bastrop Co	621D	MX-21	78621	100-199
PEBBLE PATH	Austin	524D	MH-30	78731	3900-4099
PEBBLE PATH	Hutto	380J	MU-44	78634	100-399
	Hutto	380N	MU-44	78634	400-499
PEBBLE TRL	Hays Co	639L	WX-17	78737	100-199
PEBBLE BEACH CV	Austin	704J	MG-11	78747	2400-2499
PEBBLE BEACH DR	Austin	704N	MG-11	78747	2300-2599
PEBBLE BROOK CV	Austin	556C	MM-27	78752	7600-7699
PEBBLE BROOK DR	Austin	556C	MM-27	78752	1700-1799
PEBBLE BROOK DR	Cedar Park	402H	MD-42	78613	1000-1299
PEBBLE CREEK DR	Georgetown	227J	MN-59	78626	7700-8099
PEBBLE GARDEN CT	Austin	671G	MB-15	78739	6100-6199
PEBBLE GARDEN LN	Austin	671G	MB-15	78739	11000-11399
PEBBLE RIDGE CV	Round Rock	345K	MJ-47	78681	4000-4199
PEBBLE RUN PATH	Manor	530B	MU-30	78653	None
PEBBLE STONE CIR	Austin	613E	ME-21	78735	4900-4999
PEBBLESTONE TRL	Williamson Co	347B	MN-48	78665	4100-4199
PEBBLESTONE WALK DR	Cedar Park	403P	ME-41	78613	500-699
PECAN AVE	Round Rock	376V	MM-43	78664	500-799
PECAN CIR	Austin	556Y	MM-25	78723	2900-2999
PECAN DR	Austin	526J	ML-29	78753	100-399
PECAN DR	Elgin	534P	EC-29	78621	100-299
PECAN DR	Jonestown	401A	MA-42	78645	11700-11899
PECAN DR	Travis Co	520L	WZ-29	78734	13200-14099
PECAN DR	Williamson Co	255M	MK-56	78628	100-399
PECAN LN	Round Rock	376V	MM-43	78664	300-399
PECAN PASS	Cedar Park	403J	ME-41	78613	700-799
PECAN ST	Austin	464C	MH-36	78727	12100-12299
PECAN ST	Bastrop	745K	EE-8	78602	300-1899
	Bastrop	715X	EE-10	78602	1900-2899
PECAN ST	Cedar Park	402C	MD-42	78613	1300-1599
PECAN ST	Georgetown	287J	MN-53	78626	1600-1699
PECAN ST E	Hutto	349Z	MT-46	78634	100-299
PECAN ST E	Pflugerville	438W	MQ-37	78660	100-599
	Pflugerville	468W	MQ-36	78660	600-1599
	Pflugerville	468G	MR-36	78660	2700-3199
	Travis Co	468G	MR-36	78660	1600-2699
	Travis Co	469J	MS-35	78660	3200-3799
PECAN ST E	Taylor	353J	EA-47	76574	100-699
PECAN ST W	Hutto	349Z	MT-46	78634	100-499
PECAN ST W	Pflugerville	438W	MQ-37	78660	100-599
	Pflugerville	437V	MP-37	78660	600-1699
	Pflugerville	437T	MN-37	78660	1700-2699
	Travis Co	437T	MN-37	78660	2700-2999
PECAN ST W	Taylor	353J	EA-47	76574	100-699
PECAN BROOK DR	Austin	557P	MN-26	78724	4600-5799
PECAN CHASE	Travis Co	550W	WY-25	78738	4700-4899
PECAN CREEK DR	Pflugerville	438S	MQ-37	78660	1000-1199
PECAN CREEK PKWY	Williamson Co	433Q	MF-38	78750	11500-12199
PECAN CREST CV	Round Rock	375L	MK-44	78681	3100-3199
PECANGATE WAY	Travis Co	530A	MU-30	78653	11900-12399
PECAN GROVE	Leander	312X	MC-49	78641	400-499
PECAN GROVE RD	Austin	615J	MJ-20	78704	500-699
PECAN HILL CV	Manor	530T	MU-28	78653	None
PECAN HOLLOW	Travis Co	340J	WY-47	78641	13600-14199
PECAN PARK BLVD	Austin	434E	MG-39	78729	10200-10399
	Austin	433H	MF-39	78729	10400-10499
	Austin	433H	MF-39	78750	10500-10999
	Austin	433C	MF-39	78613	11000-11099
	Austin	403Y	MF-40	78613	11100-11499
PECAN SPRINGS RD	Austin	556Y	MM-25	78723	2900-3099
	Austin	586C	MM-24	78723	3200-5099
PECAN VALLEY DR	Leander	343L	MF-47	78641	1900-2199
PECAN VISTA CV	Georgetown	257S	MN-55	78626	100-199
PECAN VISTA LN	Georgetown	257S	MN-55	78626	100-199
PECANWOOD LN	Austin	642J	MC-17	78749	5700-5999
PECCARY PASS	Bastrop	744P	EC-8	78602	100-199
PECK AVE	Austin	555Y	MK-25	78751	3800-4099
PECKHAM DR	Point Venture	488M	WV-32	78654	18900-18999
PECOS CT	Georgetown	256F	ML-57	78628	100-199
PECOS CV	Lago Vista	399Y	WX-40	78645	7800-7899
PECOS CV	Leander	311Z	MB-49	78641	900-999
PECOS DR	Travis Co	429Q	WX-38	78645	19600-19899
PECOS DR	Williamson Co	350E	MU-48	78634	100-199
PECOS ST	Austin	584B	MG-24	78703	1500-1899
	Austin	554X	MG-25	78703	1900-3499
PECOS RIVER TRL	Pflugerville	407Y	MP-40	78664	1500-1599
PECOS VALLEY CV	Round Rock	407G	MP-42	78665	1700-1799
PECTORAL DR	Austin	673A	ME-15	78748	2700-2899
PEDDLE PATH	Austin	465R	MK-35	78759	3200-3399
PEDERNALES DR	Travis Co	457B	WS-39	78669	23900-24599
PEDERNALES ST	Austin	615H	MK-21	78702	1-799
PEDERNALES CANYON TRL					
	Travis Co	487S	WS-31	78669	22900-22999
	Travis Co	486V	WR-31	78669	23000-23099
	Travis Co	486Z	WR-31	78669	23100-25299
PEDERNALES CLIFF TRL	Travis Co	457J	WS-35	78669	24100-24699
PEDERNALES FALLS DR	Georgetown	194V	MH-61	78633	200-499
	Georgetown	195W	MJ-61	78633	500-1599
PEDERNALES FALLS DR	Travis Co	409X	MS-40	78660	2700-2999
PEDERNALES POINT DR	Travis Co	456D	WR-36	78669	25300-25699
PEDERNALES SUMMIT PKWY					
	Travis Co	518S	WU-28	78669	None
	Travis Co	548B	WU-27	78669	None
PEDERNALES VISTA DR	Travis Co	486L	WR-32	78669	None
PEDIGREE CV	Austin	703C	MF-12	78748	10700-10799

P

STREET NAME	CITY or COUNTY	MAPSCO GRID	AUSTIN GRID	ZIP CODE	BLOCK RANGE O/E
PEDIGREE DR	Austin	703C	MF-12	78748	200-399
PEEKSTON DR	Austin	463F	ME-36	78726	10200-10499
PEERMAN LN	Travis Co	577F	WS-24	78620	100-199
PEGASUS ST	Austin	466E	ML-36	78727	12900-12999
PEGGOTTY PL	Austin	497J	MN-32	78753	900-1199
PEGGY ST	Austin	556K	ML-26	78723	1800-6399
PEGGY'S CV	Hays Co	794H	MH-3	78610	900-999
PEGGY'S TRL	Hays Co	794H	MH-3	78610	200-299
PEGRAM AVE	Austin	525N	MJ-29	78757	2400-2799
PELE CT	Bastrop Co	746S	EG-7	78602	100-199
PELHAM DR	Austin	465L	MK-35	78727	4500-4999
PELICAN PT	Austin	492P	MC-32	78730	10800-10899
PELICAN BAY CV	Travis Co	521L	MB-29	78732	11600-11699
PEMBERTON PKWY	Austin	584H	MH-24	78703	2400-2499
PEMBERTON PL	Austin	584H	MH-24	78703	2400-2499
PEMBERTON WAY	Hays Co	639S	WW-16	78737	100-599
PEMBROOK TRL	Austin	555E	MJ-27	78731	2600-2699
PENA CV	Round Rock	375R	MK-44	78681	2300-2399
PENA BLANCA DR	Williamson Co	402U	MD-40	78613	2100-2299
PENCEWOOD CT	Austin	433X	ME-37	78750	11000-11099
PENCEWOOD DR	Austin	433Y	MF-37	78750	11200-11599
PENCIL CACTUS DR	Pflugerville	407Z	MP-40	78660	18500-19099
	Pflugerville	408W	MQ-40	78660	19100-19399
PENDLETON DR	Cedar Park	403K	ME-41	78613	1400-1599
PENDLETON LN	Austin	556Y	MM-25	78723	5400-5599
PENDRAGON CASTLE DR	Pflugerville	408X	MQ-40	78660	1000-1099
PENELOPE CIR	Travis Co	464N	MG-35	78759	7700-7799
PENELOPE WAY	Williamson Co	348P	MQ-47	78665	3500-3599
PENICK DR	Austin	615Z	MK-19	78741	5600-5799
PENINSULAR DR N	Travis Co	427B	WS-39	78654	3600-3799
PENINSULAR DR S	Travis Co	427F	WS-39	78654	25500-25699
PENION DR	Travis Co	673X	ME-13	78748	800-1199
PENN CV	Lago Vista	458G	WV-36	78645	21500-21599
PENNINGTON LN	Williamson Co	257M	MP-56	78626	40100-40199
PENNSYLVANIA AVE	Austin	585U	MK-22	78702	1400-2299
PENNSYLVANIA AVE	Austin	586P	ML-23	78721	3300-3699
PENNWOOD LN	Austin	643R	MF-17	78745	6100-6299
PENNY LN	Austin	525B	MJ-30	78757	2400-2999
PENNY LN	Cedar Park	403E	ME-42	78613	600-699
PENNY LN	Georgetown	225U	MK-58	78633	100-199
	Williamson Co	225U	MK-58	78633	None
PENNY LN	Round Rock	406F	ML-42	78681	800-1299
PENNY ST	Austin	586L	MM-23	78721	1400-1499
PENNY CREEK DR	Austin	464V	MH-34	78759	5700-5799
PENNY ROYAL DR	Travis Co	409P	MS-41	78660	20700-21299
PENSTEMON DR	Leander	342P	MC-47	78641	1100-1199
PENTIRE WAY	Hutto	379P	MS-44	78634	100-399
PENWOOD CV	Round Rock	378Y	MR-43	78664	3600-3699
PEONIA CT	Travis Co	551P	MA-26	78733	10400-10499
PEONY CV	Austin	463D	MF-36	78750	11200-11299
PEOPLES ST	Austin	585V	MK-22	78702	1900-2099
PEPPER LN	Austin	644V	MH-16	78744	4800-5199
PEPPERBARK LN	Austin	673K	ME-14	78748	1600-1699
PEPPERELL CT	Austin	526P	ML-29	78753	900-999
PEPPERGRASS CV	Austin	642Z	MD-16	78745	8800-8899
PEPPER GRASS TRL	Williamson Co	433E	ME-39	78613	3000-3299
PEPPERIDGE DR	Austin	670D	WZ-15	78739	12000-12199
PEPPER MILL HOLLOW					
	Williamson Co	433K	ME-38	78750	12200-12299
PEPPERMINT TRL	Travis Co	467G	MP-36	78660	900-1399
PEPPER ROCK CV	Williamson Co	405E	MJ-42	78717	16000-16099
PEPPER ROCK DR	Williamson Co	405E	MJ-42	78717	8600-8999
PEPPER TREE CT	Austin	644Z	MH-16	78744	2300-2399
PEPPER TREE PKWY	Austin	644Z	MH-16	78744	5000-5799
PEPPERVINE CV	Austin	493V	MF-31	78750	6900-6999
PEQUENO ST	Austin	525T	MJ-28	78757	1800-1999
PERALTO CV	Travis Co	493U	MF-31	78730	6600-6699
PERCEVAL LN	Austin	672R	MD-14	78748	2900-2999
PERCH CV	Round Rock	347S	MN-46	78665	3501-3599 O
PERCH CV	Williamson Co	405A	MJ-42	78717	8900-8999
PERCH TRL	Round Rock	347S	MN-46	78665	3400-3599
PERCONTE DR	Austin	678N	MQ-14	78617	12900-13299
PERCY SPRINGS DR	Austin	672V	MD-13	78748	10800-10899
PEREGRINE WAY	Williamson Co	342J	MC-47	78641	700-999
PEREGRINE FALCON DR	Austin	583U	MF-22	78746	3400-3699
PERENNIAL CT	Travis Co	672T	MC-13	78748	11300-11399
PEREZ ST	Austin	586P	ML-23	78721	1200-1499
	Austin	586K	ML-23	78721	1600-1899
PERFORMER RD	Travis Co	487A	WS-33	78669	1700-2099
PERIDOT RD	Travis Co	467R	MP-35	78660	1600-1899
PERIMETER RD	Austin	646Y	MM-16	78719	None
PERIMETER RD E	Austin	677B	MN-15	78719	None
	Austin	647X	MN-16	78719	None
PERIMETER RD W	Austin	676C	MM-15	78719	None
PERIWINKLE PATH	Austin	643D	MF-18	78745	5100-5299
PERKINS DR	Travis Co	674T	MG-13	78744	2400-2599
PERKINS PL	Georgetown	287P	MN-53	78626	2000-2899
PERKINS ST	Bastrop	745J	EE-8	78602	100-799
PERLITA DR	Austin	587C	MP-24	78724	6000-6399
PERPETUATION DR	Lakeway	519V	WX-28	78734	100-199
PERRY AVE	Austin	614L	MH-20	78704	2200-2399
PERRY CV	Lago Vista	458C	WV-36	78645	21500-21599
PERRY LN	Austin	554H	MH-27	78731	2800-3099
	Austin	554C	MH-27	78731	3100-3599
PERRY RD	Austin	616C	MM-21	78721	1100-1199
PERRY MAYFIELD	Williamson Co	344L	MH-47	78628	1-699
PERRYTON DR	Travis Co	520V	WZ-28	78732	12900-13199
PERSHING AVE	Lago Vista	458C	WV-36	78645	21500-21699
PERSHING DR	Austin	586E	ML-24	78723	1900-2299
PERSIMMON LN	Georgetown	195Z	MK-61	78633	100-199
PERSIMMON RD	Williamson Co	433A	ME-39	78613	1700-1799
PERSIMMON ST	Bastrop	715W	EE-10	78602	400-499
PERSIMMON TRL	Austin	673D	MF-15	78745	7800-8099
PERSIMMON GAP DR	Austin	404J	MG-41	78717	11100-11299
PERSIMMON RIDGE CT	Travis Co	491W	MA-31	78732	2200-2299
PERSIMMON SPRINGS DR					
	Williamson Co	375U	MK-43	78681	17800-17899
PERSIMMON VALLEY TRL	Travis Co	491X	MA-31	78732	2900-3199
PERTH PASS	Austin	498E	MQ-33	78660	3500-3599
PERTHSHIRE ST	Williamson Co	434F	MG-39	78729	13300-13499
PERUGA LN	Williamson Co	405C	MK-42	78681	3100-3299
PESCADERO CV	Travis Co	554J	MG-26	78746	3000-3099
PESCADO CIR	Travis Co	460Y	WZ-34	78734	15500-15599
PETACA CV	Austin	434U	MH-37	78729	8000-8099
PETACA TRL	Austin	434Y	MH-37	78729	7800-8099
PETALUMA DR	Cedar Park	402D	MD-42	78613	800-999
PETERSON AVE	Austin	555S	MJ-25	78756	3900-3999
PETERSON CT	Lakeway	489U	WX-31	78734	100-199
PETERSON DR	Cedar Park	374J	MG-44	78613	2500-2599
PETERSON LN	Lakeway	489Z	WX-31	78734	500-699
PETERSON RD	Travis Co	737M	MP-8	78617	9700-10099
	Travis Co	738J	MQ-8	78617	10100-10199
PETERSON ST	Round Rock	406H	MM-42	78664	500-799
PETES PATH	Austin	554R	MH-26	78731	3800-4099
PETIRROJO CT	Bastrop Co	738L	MR-8	78617	100-199
PETITE COVE I	Austin	463G	MF-36	78750	9600-9699
PETITE COVE II	Austin	463G	MF-36	78750	9600-9699
PETRA PATH	Austin	524D	MH-30	78731	3900-4099
PETRA'S CV	Hays Co	794H	MH-3	78610	100-199
PETRA'S WAY	Hays Co	795J	MJ-2	78610	100-699
	Hays Co	794H	MH-3	78610	700-999
PETRIFIED FOREST DR	Austin	704A	MG-12	78747	1800-2299
PETROGLYPH TRL	Pflugerville	438F	MQ-39	78660	None
PETROVE PASS	Travis Co	402T	MC-40	78613	1300-1399
PETTICOAT LN	Travis Co	553Q	MF-26	78746	5300-5499
PETUNIA LN	Pflugerville	468B	MQ-36	78660	1200-1599
PETUNIA ST	Williamson Co	433E	ME-39	78613	1900-1999
PEVENSEY DR	Austin	644S	MG-16	78745	6500-6599
PEVETOE ST	Travis Co	618V	MR-19	78725	3600-3899
PEWTER LN	Austin	645S	MJ-16	78744	4700-4999
PEYTON PL	Cedar Park	373U	MF-43	78613	900-1299
PFENNIG LN E	Pflugerville	437R	MP-38	78660	1100-1799
PFENNIG LN W	Pflugerville	437R	MP-38	78660	100-699
	Pflugerville	438N	MQ-38	78660	700-1699
PFLUGER ST E	Pflugerville	438W	MQ-37	78660	100-299
	Pflugerville	468A	MQ-36	78660	500-799
PFLUGER ST W	Pflugerville	438W	MQ-37	78660	100-499
	Pflugerville	437Z	MP-37	78660	500-1299
PFLUGER-BERKMAN LN	Travis Co	441R	MX-38	78615	12000-13199
	Travis Co	442P	MY-38	78615	13200-14699
PFLUGERVILLE LOOP W	Pflugerville	437P	MN-38	78660	1400-1599
PFLUGERVILLE PKWY E	Pflugerville	438Q	MR-38	78660	100-3499
	Pflugerville	439W	MS-37	78660	3500-4699
PFLUGERVILLE PKWY W	Pflugerville	437D	MP-39	78660	100-799
	Travis Co	437D	MP-39	78660	800-1299
PFLUGERVILLE ESTATES DR					
	Travis Co	467M	MP-35	78660	14900-15099
PHALAROPE DR	Hays Co	702W	MC-10	78610	100-199
PHANTOM CANYON DR	Austin	462F	MC-36	78726	8200-8399
PHANTOM FLIGHT LN	Travis Co	398X	WU-40	78654	5800-5999
PHANTOM HORSE	Leander	342T	MC-46	78641	1900-1999
PHEASANT CV	Hutto	350S	MU-46	78634	300-399
PHEASANT DR E	Austin	526B	ML-30	78753	100-399
PHEASANT DR W	Austin	526B	ML-30	78753	100-199
PHEASANT LN	Lakeway	520A	WY-30	78734	15300-15499
	Travis Co	520A	WY-30	78734	15000-15299
PHEASANT TRL	Bastrop	744P	EC-8	78602	100-299
PHEASANT HOLLOW	Williamson Co	345W	MJ-46	78681	3000-3099
PHEASANT MEADOW CIR	Austin	524D	MH-30	78731	7700-7799
PHEASANT RIDGE	Williamson Co	377F	MN-45	78665	100-699
PHEASANT RIDGE CV	Williamson Co	377G	MP-45	78665	1000-1099
PHEASANT RIDGE DR	Cedar Park	373Q	MF-43	78613	200-299
PHEASANT ROCK RD	Williamson Co	434U	MH-37	78729	7600-8099
PHEASANT ROOST	Austin	496E	ML-33	78758	1700-1799
PHEASANT RUN	Hays Co	732B	MC-9	78610	12600-12799
PHELAN RD	Bastrop Co	715A	EE-12	78602	100-399
PHILCO DR	Austin	644F	MG-18	78745	300-899
	Austin	644B	MG-18	78745	900-999
	Austin	644A	MG-18	78745	1200-1499
	Austin	644A	MG-18	78745	4600-4899
PHILLIP CIR	Dripping Springs	667T	WS-13	78620	100-399
PHILLIP CV	Williamson Co	343W	ME-46	78641	2500-2599
PHILLIPS CIR	Travis Co	460R	WZ-35	78734	5400-5499
PHILLIPS CT	Travis Co	552W	MC-25	78733	1400-1499
PHILLIPS ST	Hutto	349M	MT-47	78634	100-399
PHILOMENA ST	Austin	555V	MK-25	78723	1200-1299
	Austin	556W	ML-25	78723	1300-1499
PHILOX DR	Lakeway	489U	WX-31	78734	100-299
PHLOX CT	Williamson Co	377K	MN-44	78665	2100-2199
PHOEBE CT	Austin	465G	MK-36	78727	12500-12599
PHOEBE DR	Hays Co	732J	MC-8	78610	100-199
PHOENIX CV N	Round Rock	407G	MP-42	78665	2900-2999
PHOENIX CV S	Round Rock	407G	MP-42	78665	2900-2999
PHOENIX PASS	Travis Co	611X	MA-19	78737	7800-7999
PHOENIX WAY	Round Rock	407G	MP-42	78665	2800-2999
PHONES RD	Bastrop Co	745A	EE-9	78602	100-199
PHYLLIS PARK DR	Travis Co	640Y	WZ-16	78737	8600-8699
PIASINO TRL	Lago Vista	399Y	WX-40	78645	7800-7899
PIAZZA VETTA DR	Lakeway	520A	WY-30	78734	100-199
PICADILLY CT	Pflugerville	437E	MN-39	78664	16700-16799
PICADILLY DR	Pflugerville	437A	MN-39	78664	1300-2399
	Pflugerville	436D	MM-39	78664	2400-2699
	Travis Co	437G	MP-39	78660	800-1299
PICASIO LN	Dripping Springs	666C	WR-15	78620	100-599
PICEA DR	Lakeway	489U	WX-31	78734	100-299
PICKARD LN	Austin	672Z	MD-13	78748	11200-11499
PICKET ROPE LN	Austin	466Q	MM-35	78727	12600-12799
PICKETT LN	Travis Co	279U	WX-52	78641	None
	Williamson Co	279Q	WX-53	78642	1-499
PICKFAIR CV	Austin	463C	MF-36	78750	10200-10299
PICKFAIR DR	Austin	463C	MF-36	78750	9700-10899
	Austin	433Y	MF-37	78750	10900-11499
PICKLE DR	Austin	586W	ML-22	78702	3400-3599
PICKLE RD	Austin	614Y	MH-19	78704	100-299
PICKOFF DR	Georgetown	226G	MM-60	78628	30300-30399
PICKWICK LN	Rollingwood	584N	MG-23	78746	2400-2999
	Rollingwood	584N	MG-23	78746	3200-3299
PICNIC CV	Round Rock	407E	MN-42	78664	1600-1699
PICTON CT	Williamson Co	343S	ME-46	78641	3200-3299
PIEDMONT AVE	Austin	525P	MJ-29	78757	1200-1999
PIEDMONT CT	Leander	342V	MD-46	78641	2200-2299
PIEDMONT LN	Georgetown	195T	MJ-61	78633	100-299
PIEDMONT HILLS PASS	Travis Co	521T	MA-28	78732	100-399
PIEDRAS BLANCO DR	Austin	675W	MJ-13	78747	6400-6799
PIER BRANCH RD	Hays Co	638X	WU-16	78620	1000-1099
PIERCE CV	Lago Vista	458C	WV-36	78645	21600-21799
PIERCE ST	Hutto	349M	MT-47	78634	100-699
PIGEONBERRY PASS	Buda	763T	ME-4	78610	100-199
PIGEON FORGE RD	Pflugerville	468K	MQ-35	78660	500-1399
	Pflugerville	468E	MQ-36	78660	900-999
PIGEON VIEW	Round Rock	346R	MM-47	78665	400-1399
PIKE PATH	Round Rock	347S	MN-46	78665	1100-1299
PIKE RD	Travis Co	490Y	WZ-31	78734	1200-1399
PIKE CANYON DR	Travis Co	497H	MP-33	78754	12900-13199
PILAND TRIANGLE	Travis Co	707U	MP-10	78617	12900-13399
PILGRIM CV	Lago Vista	458C	WV-36	78645	3100-3199
PILGRIMS PL	Austin	464F	MG-36	78759	8000-8399
PILLION PL	Travis Co	529M	MT-29	78653	11500-11699
PILLOW RD	Sunset Valley	643C	MF-18	78745	1-99
	Sunset Valley	613Y	MF-19	78745	4900-5099
PILOT PL	Williamson Co	226V	MM-58	78628	100-299
PILOT GROVE CT	Buda	732W	MC-7	78610	100-199
PIMA TRL	Travis Co	490U	WZ-31	78734	14500-14699
PIMLICO CV	Georgetown	287G	MP-54	78626	100-199
PIMLICO DR	Travis Co	677G	MP-15	78617	4600-4899
PINAFORE ST	Hays Co	762H	MD-6	78610	400-499
PINCKNEY ST	Austin	586A	ML-24	78723	4000-4099
PIN CLOVER CT	Travis Co	409T	MS-40	78660	2800-2899
PINE CT	Bastrop Co	776U	EH-4	78602	100-199
PINE PL	Austin	645W	MJ-16	78744	5200-5299
	Austin	644V	MH-16	78744	5300-5499
	Austin	645W	MJ-16	78744	5500-5599
PINE ST	Bastrop	745F	EE-9	78602	700-1699
PINE ST S	Georgetown	286H	MM-54	78626	200-2199
PINE ARBOR TRL	Travis Co	530A	MU-30	78653	13600-13799
PINE BARRENS CT	Lakeway	519W	WW-28	78738	100-199
PINE BLUFFS TRL	Williamson Co	434R	MH-38	78729	7000-7299
PINE CREEK DR	Pflugerville	438T	MQ-37	78660	1000-1099
PINECREST DR	Austin	525J	MJ-29	78757	2900-3399
PINECREST DR	Bastrop Co	776B	EG-6	78602	100-199
PINEDA RD	Caldwell Co	767U	MP-4	78616	2-198 E
PINEDALE CV	Austin	525F	MJ-30	78757	8000-8099
PINE FOREST CIR	Round Rock	408A	MQ-42	78665	1200-1399
PINE FOREST CV	Round Rock	378W	MQ-43	78665	1100-1199
PINE HILL LOOP	Bastrop Co	746V	EH-7	78602	100-399
PINE HOLLOW DR	Bastrop	745R	EF-8	78602	100-299
PINEHURST CIR	Point Venture	489J	WW-32	78645	200-299
PINEHURST CV	Austin	704E	MG-12	78747	2300-2399
PINEHURST DR	Austin	704E	MG-12	78747	10100-10399
	Austin	704N	MG-11	78747	11100-11299
	Travis Co	703R	MF-11	78747	10700-11099
PINEHURST DR	Taylor	322Q	MZ-50	76574	4000-4599
PINEHURST DR S	Austin	704N	MG-11	78747	4600-4799
PINEHURST LN	Round Rock	378V	MR-43	78664	1500-1599
PINE KNOLL DR	Austin	496N	ML-32	78758	1400-1899
PINELAWN DR	Taylor	322T	MY-49	76574	2100-2199
PINELEAF PL	Austin	525K	MJ-29	78757	7500-7599
PINE LODGE DR	Bastrop Co	745V	EF-7	78602	100-299
PINE MEADOW DR	Austin	644J	MG-17	78745	5500-5599
PINE NEEDLE CIR	Round Rock	345N	MJ-47	78681	3300-3799
PINE NEEDLE CV	Round Rock	345N	MJ-47	78681	3200-3299
PINE NEEDLE LN	Round Rock	345S	MJ-46	78681	3800-3899
PINE PORTAGE LOOP	Williamson Co	343S	ME-46	78641	1100-1299
PINERIDGE DR	Williamson Co	434P	MG-38	78729	8700-8999
PINE SHADOWS LN	Bastrop Co	746Z	EH-7	78602	100-199
	Bastrop Co	776D	EH-6	78602	200-299
PINE SISKIN DR	Hays Co	732F	MC-9	78610	400-899
PINE VALLEY DR	Austin	704E	MG-12	78747	2300-2399
PINEVALLEY DR	Austin	704E	MG-12	78747	10200-10299
PINE VISTA DR	Travis Co	408Q	MR-41	78660	3600-3799
PINE WARBLER DR	Travis Co	434G	MH-39	78729	13600-13699
PINEWOOD CV	Leander	342T	MC-46	78641	1400-1499
PINE WOOD DR	Bastrop Co	746B	EG-9	78602	100-199
PINEWOOD TERRACE	Austin	525K	MJ-29	78757	2500-2799
PINEY CREEK LN	Williamson Co	433J	ME-38	78613	1300-1499
PINEY CREEK BEND	Austin	643W	ME-16	78745	8500-8599
	Austin	642Z	MD-16	78745	8600-8899
PINEY POINT DR	Williamson Co	434P	MG-38	78729	8700-8999
PINEY RIDGE DR	Bastrop	715U	EF-10	78602	100-299
PINEYWOODS LN	Williamson Co	344B	MG-48	78628	100-199
PINKNEY LN	Austin	671C	MB-15	78739	10600-10899
PINNACLE CV	Lago Vista	458C	WV-36	78645	3200-3399
PINNACLE DR	Georgetown	317F	MN-51	78626	100-399
PINNACLE RD	Austin	583U	MF-22	78746	3300-3699
	Travis Co	583U	MF-22	78746	3700-3799
PINO LN	Austin	674D	MH-15	78744	6000-6299
PIN OAK	Dripping Springs	667P	WS-14	78620	100-299
PIN OAK CT	Austin	614P	MG-20	78704	3000-3099
PIN OAK CT	Bastrop	745R	EF-8	78602	100-199
PIN OAK DR	Georgetown	286X	ML-52	78628	200-399
PIN OAK LN	Williamson Co	375K	MJ-44	78681	1500-1899
PIN OAK PATH	Austin	643H	MF-18	78745	5200-5299
PIN OAK ST	Hays Co	667P	WS-14	78620	100-299
PIN OAK ST	Hays Co	701P	MA-11	78652	9600-9699
PIN OAK CROSSING	Bastrop Co	564Z	ED-25	78621	100-199
PINON CV	Georgetown	225V	MK-58	78628	500-599
PINON HILLS CT	Travis Co	409N	MS-41	78660	1900-1999
PINON PINE DR	Pflugerville	437H	MP-39	78660	1600-1699
PINON VISTA DR	Austin	587F	MN-24	78724	5600-5999
PIN TAIL CV	Leander	342K	MC-47	78641	None
PINTAIL CV	Williamson Co	434T	MG-37	78729	12500-12599
PINTAIL LN	Taylor	323S	EA-49	76574	200-499
	Taylor	322V	MZ-49	76574	500-6099
PIN TAIL TRL	Leander	342K	MC-47	78641	None
PINTO CIR	Mustang Ridge	766N	ML-5	78610	11800-11899
PINTO CV	Austin	611Q	MB-20	78736	7000-7099
PINTO CV	Lago Vista	429B	WW-39	78645	6800-6999
PINTO PATH	Austin	611Q	MB-20	78736	8000-8199
PINTO CHASE CT	Travis Co	491X	MA-31	78732	12700-12799
PIONEER CV	Lago Vista	458C	WV-36	78645	3100-3199
PIONEER CV	Lago Vista	429A	WW-39	78645	21300-21399
PIONEER PL	Austin	525N	MJ-29	78757	6800-6899
PIONEER TRL	Williamson Co	288G	MR-54	78626	100-299
PIONEER WAY	Round Rock	346Z	MM-46	78665	2800-3099
PIONEER BEND DR	Pflugerville	467D	MP-36	78660	1000-1099
PIONEER CROSSING DR	Round Rock	378F	MQ-45	78665	3300-3499
PIONEER FARMS DR	Austin	497X	MN-31	78754	10700-10899
PIONEER FOREST DR	Austin	674X	MG-13	78744	9200-9499
PIONEER PASSAGE	Bastrop Co	743A	EA-9	78602	200-299
PIPER LN	Burnet Co	396W	WQ-40	78669	100-199
PIPER GLEN DR	Bee Cave	549M	WX-26	78738	None
PIPERS FIELD DR	Austin	466S	ML-34	78758	2000-2199
PIPER SONOMA CT E	Round Rock	378W	MQ-43	78665	2900-2999
PIPER SONOMA CT W	Round Rock	377Z	MP-43	78665	2800-2899
PIPER SONOMA PL	Round Rock	377Z	MP-43	78665	2800-2899
PIPING PLOVER DR	Travis Co	434G	MH-39	78729	13500-13599
PIPING ROCK TRL	Austin	673J	ME-14	78748	2500-2699
PIPIT CT	Travis Co	432C	MD-39	78613	2300-2399
PIRUN CT	Austin	612C	MD-21	78735	6000-6099
PISTACHIO CT	Travis Co	550W	WY-25	78738	12700-12799
PISTOL PASS CIR	Travis Co	766L	MM-5	78610	12900-12999

STREET NAME	CITY or COUNTY	MAPSCO GRID	AUSTIN GRID	ZIP CODE	BLOCK RANGE O/E
PISTON HILL LN	Bastrop Co	534T	EC-28	78621	100-199
PITCAIRN DR	Travis Co	437K	MN-38	78660	1100-1399
PITCHSTONE CV	Williamson Co	254W	MG-55	78628	100-199
PITHER LN	Austin	645B	MJ-18	78741	2700-2799
PIT STOP TRACE	Buda	733X	ME-7	78610	100-299
PITT CV	Lago Vista	458C	WV-36	78645	3200-3299
PITT ST	Bastrop	745G	EF-9	78602	1000-1299
	Bastrop	745L	EF-8	78602	None
PITTER PAT LN	Travis Co	611J	MA-20	78736	7400-8199
	Travis Co	610R	WZ-20	78736	8200-8399
PIUTE TRL	Travis Co	672S	MC-13	78739	3600-3799
PIXIE CV	Austin	523T	ME-28	78746	6700-6799
PIZARRO CV	Austin	641R	MB-17	78749	9200-9299
PIZER ST	Austin	587G	MP-24	78724	6100-6199
PLACID PL	Austin	554H	MH-27	78731	4500-5099
PLACID CREEK CT	Williamson Co	346H	MM-48	78665	1000-1099
PLACID CREEK WAY	Williamson Co	346G	MM-48	78665	4100-4299
PLACID FIELD DR	Travis Co	529H	MT-30	78653	None
PLAINFIELD CT	Travis Co	409S	MS-40	78660	2200-2299
PLAIN ROCK PASS	Travis Co	436U	MM-37	78728	14600-14699
PLAINS TRL	Austin	496T	ML-31	78758	10500-10999
	Austin	496P	ML-32	78758	11100-11299
PLAINS CREST DR	Travis Co	677Y	MP-13	78617	6700-6999
PLAINS VALLEY DR	Travis Co	677U	MP-13	78617	11800-12199
PLAINVIEW DR	Travis Co	676X	ML-13	78719	8700-8799
PLAIN VIEW DR	Travis Co	618M	MR-20	78725	14100-14799
	Travis Co	619J	MS-20	78725	14800-15099
PLANTAIN CV	Travis Co	522H	MD-30	78730	4200-4299
PLANTATION CT	Round Rock	376E	ML-45	78681	1900-1999
PLANTATION CV	Round Rock	376E	ML-45	78681	1900-1999
PLANTATION DR	Round Rock	376A	ML-45	78681	1900-2999
	Round Rock	375M	MK-44	78681	2600-3099
PLANTATION RD	Austin	643S	ME-16	78745	3100-3299
	Austin	642V	MD-16	78745	3300-3499
PLANTERS WOODS DR	Travis Co	492U	MD-31	78730	10000-10499
PLATEAU CIR	Austin	644B	MG-18	78745	900-999
PLATEAU CV	Lago Vista	399X	WW-40	78645	7700-7799
PLATEAU RIDGE	Williamson Co	433B	ME-39	78613	1600-1699
PLATEAU VISTA BLVD	Round Rock	377N	MN-44	78664	1700-1899
PLATINUM LN	Travis Co	366U	WR-43	78654	28700-28999
PLATT LN	Travis Co	617V	MP-19	78725	10000-11599
	Travis Co	647B	MN-18	78725	None
PLATTE PASS	Travis Co	490Z	WZ-31	78734	1900-2099
PLAYERS' PL	Austin	704T	MG-10	78747	11300-11399
PLAZA DR	Austin	496R	MM-32	78753	800-999
PLAZA WAY	Jonestown	400M	WZ-41	78645	None
PLAZA BELLA WAY	Travis Co	432L	MD-38	78613	2700-2799
PLAZA ON THE LAKE	Austin	523R	MF-29	78746	4700-5099
PLEASANT CV	Austin	526V	MM-28	78754	1600-1699
PLEASANT CV	Rollingwood	584N	MG-23	78746	1-99
PLEASANT DR	Rollingwood	584N	MG-23	78746	300-399
PLEASANT LN	Austin	526V	MM-28	78754	8600-8999
PLEASANT GROVE RD	Bastrop Co	534G	ED-30	78621	100-299
	Bastrop Co	504Z	ED-31	78621	300-499
PLEASANT HILL CT	Travis Co	550Q	WZ-26	78733	12300-12399
PLEASANT MEADOW CIR	Austin	524D	MH-30	78731	7700-7799
PLEASANT PANORAMA VIEW					
	Travis Co	551E	MA-27	78733	11800-11899
	Travis Co	550H	WZ-27	78733	11900-12199
PLEASANT RUN PL	Austin	554U	MH-25	78703	3000-3199
PLEASANT VALLEY DR	Georgetown	286Z	MM-52	78626	100-599
PLEASANT VALLEY DR	Pflugerville	437V	MP-37	78660	400-1099
PLEASANT VALLEY RD N	Austin	615D	MK-21	78702	1-799
	Austin	585V	MK-22	78702	800-1199
PLEASANT VALLEY RD S	Austin	615Y	MK-19	78741	1-2499
	Austin	645C	MK-18	78741	2500-3099
	Austin	645F	MJ-18	78741	3100-3599
	Austin	645W	MJ-16	78744	4600-5599
	Austin	675E	MJ-15	78744	5600-6899
	Austin	674R	MH-14	78744	6900-7599
PLOCKTON DR	Briarcliff	487D	WT-33	78669	21900-22099
PLOVER DR	Austin	526B	ML-30	78753	9700-9999
PLOVER PASS	Georgetown	225K	MJ-59	78633	100-199
PLOVER PL	Travis Co	708S	MQ-10	78617	14200-15199
PLOVER RUN TRL	Travis Co	409U	MT-40	78660	3400-3499
PLOVERVILLE LN	Travis Co	436V	MM-37	78728	1700-2099
PLOW HORSE CV	Austin	497T	MN-31	78754	11500-11599
PLOWSHARE DR	Travis Co	467C	MP-36	78660	15000-15299
PLUCHEA CV	Travis Co	551P	MA-26	78733	10600-10699
PLUM CT	Georgetown	225Z	MK-58	78628	300-399
PLUM CV	Lakeway	489U	WX-31	78734	100-199
PLUM DR	Elgin	534P	EC-29	78621	100-199
PLUM DR	Lakeway	489U	WX-31	78734	100-399
PLUMAS LN	Austin	643D	MF-18	78745	5100-5299
PLUMBAGO CV	Buda	763T	ME-4	78610	100-199
PLUMBAGO DR	Pflugerville	468C	MR-36	78660	100-699
	Pflugerville	438Y	MR-37	78660	700-899
PLUMBAGO LN	Georgetown	314G	MH-51	78628	1600-1699
PLUMBROOK DR	Travis Co	583N	ME-23	78746	1800-2299
PLUMCREEK CIR	Austin	554U	MH-25	78703	2600-2699
PLUM CREEK LN	Williamson Co	433J	ME-38	78613	1300-1499
PLUME GRASS PL	Round Rock	407C	MP-42	78665	1500-1699
PLUMEWOOD DR	Austin	463C	MF-36	78750	10500-11199
PLUM HOLLOW OVERLOOK					
	Travis Co	582M	MD-23	78746	6200-6399
PLUMPTON DR	Austin	643Z	MF-16	78745	700-899
PLUTO LN	Austin	465F	MJ-36	78727	12500-12699
PLYMOUTH CV	Lago Vista	458C	WV-36	78645	3200-3299
PLYMOUTH DR	Austin	525H	MK-30	78758	1000-1199
POALSONS PKWY	Travis Co	487X	WS-31	78669	21900-22199
POCMONT TRL	Travis Co	767G	MP-6	78719	15100-15299
POCOHONTAS TRL	Travis Co	461F	MA-36	78641	14500-14999
POCONO CV	Williamson Co	375X	MJ-43	78717	8900-8999
POCONO DR	Williamson Co	405A	MJ-42	78717	16400-16699
	Williamson Co	375W	MJ-43	78717	16700-16999
POE CIR	Travis Co	437U	MP-37	78660	700-799
POE CV	Lago Vista	458C	WV-36	78645	3100-3399
POHAKEA DR N	Bastrop Co	776E	EG-6	78602	100-199
POHAKEA DR S	Bastrop Co	776E	EG-6	78602	100-199
POHAKULOA DR	Bastrop Co	775B	EE-6	78602	100-299
POI CT	Bastrop Co	776F	EG-6	78602	100-199
POINSETTA LN	Austin	674Q	MH-14	78744	7400-7599
POINT CV	Lago Vista	458B	WU-36	78645	3000-3199
POINT DR	Bastrop Co	709T	MS-10	78617	1-199
POINT BLUFF DR	Travis Co	583N	ME-23	78746	1900-2299
POINT CLEAR CT	Travis Co	703R	MF-11	78747	11000-11099
POINTE PL	Round Rock	375C	MK-45	78681	3000-3199
POINTER LN	Austin	525D	MK-30	78758	8900-9099
POINTER LN W	Austin	495Z	MK-31	78758	9000-9099
POINTER LN W	Austin	525D	MK-30	78758	9000-9099
POINT NORTH DR	Travis Co	557U	MP-25	78724	6500-6999
POINT O' WOODS	Travis Co	582P	MC-23	78735	3100-3299
POINT RUN CV	Pflugerville	437Y	MP-37	78660	700-799
POINT RUN DR	Pflugerville	437Y	MP-37	78660	600-999
POINTS EAST RIDGE	Travis Co	577L	WT-23	78720	18000-18099
POINTS WEST RIDGE	Travis Co	577L	WT-23	78720	10200-10299
POINT VIEW DR	Travis Co	550M	WZ-26	78733	10500-10899
POINT VISTA PL	Austin	526G	MM-30	78753	9600-9799
POINT WEST DR	Austin	494R	MH-32	78759	8700-8999
POKEALONG PATH	Lago Vista	429P	WW-38	78645	6100-6499
POKER ALLEY	Round Rock	376T	ML-43	78681	1-99
POLAR DR	Austin	525G	MK-30	78757	8200-8399
POLAR LN	Cedar Park	374T	MG-43	78613	3000-3099
POLARIS AVE	Austin	495Y	MK-31	78757	2000-2399
POLISHED STONE CV	Travis Co	467C	MP-36	78660	900-999
POLK CV	Lago Vista	458C	WV-36	78645	21400-21699
POLK RD	Travis Co	703J	ME-11	78748	11900-12099
POLLARD DR	Austin	435W	MJ-37	78727	13000-13199
POLLO DR	Travis Co	587Z	MP-22	78725	9900-10099
POLLYANNA AVE	Austin	496R	MM-32	78753	11300-12099
POLLYS PT	Hays Co	668D	WV-15	78620	100-199
POLO RD	Austin	584G	MH-24	78703	1800-1899
POLO CLUB DR	Hays Co	639S	WW-16	78737	100-899
POLZIN ST	Williamson Co	443G	EB-39	78615	100-299
POMEGRANATE PASS	Cedar Park	403E	ME-42	78613	500-699
POMMEL CV	Austin	464J	MG-35	78759	8300-8399
POMMEL DR	Austin	464J	MG-35	78759	8200-8399
	Travis Co	464J	MG-35	78759	8100-8199
POMPANO CV	Williamson Co	405N	MJ-41	78717	8300-8399
POMPEY CT	Austin	671G	MB-15	78739	11300-11399
POMPEY SPRINGS CT	Buda	732W	MC-7	78610	100-299
POMPTON DR	Austin	525G	MK-30	78757	1800-2299
PON CT	Pflugerville	437F	MN-39	78664	16700-16799
PONCA ST	Austin	616T	ML-19	78741	6000-6799
PONCHA PASS	Austin	612W	MC-19	78749	6300-6699
	Austin	611Z	MB-19	78749	6700-6999
PONCHO SPRINGS LN	Williamson Co	375S	MJ-43	78717	17000-17299
PONCIANA DR	Austin	644V	MH-16	78744	5100-5799
PONCIANA LOOP	Austin	644V	MH-16	78744	2100-2199
POND WAY	Williamson Co	379T	MS-43	78634	100-199
PONDER LN	Travis Co	706Q	MM-11	78719	10500-10699
PONDEROSA PKWY	Austin	465F	MJ-36	78727	5100-5199
PONDSDALE LN	Travis Co	557Y	MP-25	78724	6800-6999
POND SPRINGS RD	Austin	464C	MH-36	78729	12800-12899
	Austin	434N	MG-38	78729	12900-13699
POND VIEW CIR	Austin	526H	MM-30	78753	10100-10199
POND WOODS DR	Williamson Co	434J	MG-38	78729	12600-12799
PONOMA TRL	Austin	642F	MC-18	78749	7400-7799
PONTEVEDRA PL	Travis Co	580G	WZ-24	78738	16000-16099
PONTIC PASS	Bee Cave	549F	WW-27	78738	15600-15799
PONTON PL	Austin	524L	MH-29	78731	6500-6699
PONY LN	Austin	466U	MM-34	78727	12600-12699
PONY PASS	Bastrop	744K	EC-8	78602	None
PONY TRL	Travis Co	670C	WZ-15	78737	None
PONY CHASE	Austin	465J	MJ-35	78727	4700-5499
POOL CANYON CV	Travis Co	460L	WZ-35	78734	5600-5799
POOL CANYON RD	Travis Co	460M	WZ-35	78734	16000-16399
POPANO CV	Travis Co	554J	MG-26	78746	2900-2999
POPE DR	Lago Vista	458B	WU-36	78645	21600-21899
POPE BEND N	Bastrop Co	711G	MX-12	78612	100-399
POPE BEND S	Bastrop Co	711L	MX-11	78612	100-299
	Bastrop Co	711U	MX-10	78612	300-599
POPLAR CV	Austin	497S	MN-31	78753	11600-11699
POPLAR DR	Georgetown	225Z	MK-58	78628	900-999
POPLAR LN	Cedar Park	372D	MD-45	78613	2200-2799
POPLAR PATH	Pflugerville	437M	MP-38	78660	1300-1399
POPLAR ST	Austin	585A	MJ-24	78705	900-999
POPLAR ST	Bastrop	715P	EE-11	78602	700-899
POPLAR RIDGE CV	Georgetown	226T	ML-58	78628	100-199
POPPY CV	Hays Co	732K	MC-8	78610	300-399
POPPY PASS	Pflugerville	438X	MQ-37	78660	1200-1399
POPPY TRL	Austin	645M	MK-17	78744	3300-3399
POPPY HILLS CV	Georgetown	226M	MM-59	78628	100N-199N
	Georgetown	226M	MM-59	78628	100S-199S
POPPY HILLS CV	Round Rock	378Z	MR-43	78664	3800-3899
POPPY HILLS DR	Georgetown	226M	MM-59	78628	100-199
POPPY HILLS TRL	Travis Co	408G	MR-42	78664	20300-20699
POPPY SEED LN	Austin	646B	ML-18	78741	1400-1799
POPPY WOOD CV	Travis Co	672T	MC-13	78748	11300-11399
POQUITO ST	Austin	585Z	MK-22	78702	1100-1899
	Austin	585L	MK-23	78722	1900-2299
POQUONOCK RD	Austin	584H	MH-24	78703	1600-1699
POQUOSON DR	Austin	465H	MK-36	78727	12700-12899
PORPOISE	Lakeway	519B	WW-30	78734	900-1099
PORSCHE LN	Austin	612U	MD-19	78749	5400-5699
PORTA CIMA CT	Lakeway	519X	WW-28	78738	100-199
PORTAFINO LN	Williamson Co	224U	MH-58	78633	100-199
PORTAGE CV	Williamson Co	405J	MJ-41	78717	8500-8599
PORT ANNE WAY	Williamson Co	343S	ME-46	78641	3100-3299
PORT ARTHUR ST	Travis Co	490H	WZ-33	78734	3700-3899
PORTCHESTER CASTLE PATH					
	Pflugerville	408T	MQ-40	78660	600-1199
	Pflugerville	438B	MQ-39	78660	1200-1599
PORT DANIEL DR	Williamson Co	343S	ME-46	78641	900-1199
PORTER CV	Lago Vista	458C	WV-36	78645	21500-21599
PORTER LN	Williamson Co	280Z	WZ-52	78641	1-399
PORTER ST	Austin	616W	ML-19	78741	6300-6899
PORTER ST	Taylor	353A	EA-48	76574	100-1199
PORTER ST	Taylor	323W	EA-49	76574	1200-1499
PORTER CREEK CV	Round Rock	407H	MP-42	78665	3300-3399
PORTERFIELD DR	Austin	497B	MN-33	78753	1100-1399
PORT HOOD DR	Williamson Co	343W	ME-46	78641	16400-17599
PORTLAND TRL	Williamson Co	434M	MH-38	78729	7700-7999
PORTMARNOCK CT	Austin	704P	MG-11	78747	5100-5199
PORTOBELLA DR	Travis Co	491V	MB-31	78732	11900-12199
PORTOFINO CT	Travis Co	491Z	MB-31	78732	3700-3799
PORTOFINO DR	Travis Co	491V	MB-31	78732	11700-12099
PORTOFINO RIDGE DR	Travis Co	582F	MC-24	78735	2300-2499
PORTOLA CT	Travis Co	550R	WZ-26	78733	3000-3199
PORT ROYAL DR	Travis Co	582R	MD-23	78746	1900-2199
PORTRUSH CT	Austin	704K	MG-11	78747	10300-10399
PORTSMOUTH CV	Lago Vista	458C	WV-36	78645	21200-21399
PORTSMOUTH DR	Georgetown	195R	MK-62	78633	100-399
PORTULACA DR	Round Rock	375C	MK-45	78681	2800-3099
PORTWOOD BEND CV	Williamson Co	403W	ME-40	78613	2200-2399
POSADA CV	Travis Co	461F	MA-36	78641	7200-7299
POSITANO CT	Travis Co	523L	MF-29	78730	None
POSSE TRL	Leander	371F	MA-45	78641	3600-3699
POSSUM TRL	Taylor	322R	MZ-50	76574	2800-2999
POSSUM HOLLOW DR	Williamson Co	434U	MH-37	78729	12700-12799
POSSUM HOLLOW RD	Bastrop Co	742K	MY-8	78612	100-199
POSSUM TROT	Austin	584K	MG-23	78703	800-1499
POSSUM TROT	Williamson Co	252A	MC-57	78642	1-299
POSSUM TROT	Williamson Co	375K	MJ-44	78681	1700-1899
POST RD	Austin	614R	MH-20	78704	2200-2299
POST TRL	Austin	404J	MG-41	78717	14300-14399
POSTEN LN	Austin	646L	MM-17	78744	8100-8199
POST OAK	Williamson Co	222T	MC-58	78642	1-399
POST OAK CIR	Cedar Park	372Y	MD-43	78613	600-899
POST OAK CIR	Point Venture	489J	WW-32	78645	200-299
POST OAK CT	Bastrop Co	745V	EF-7	78602	100-199
POST OAK DR	Dripping Springs	666R	WR-14	78620	100-199
	Dripping Springs	667N	WS-14	78620	200-899
POST OAK DR	Elgin	534P	EC-29	78621	100-199
POST OAK DR	Lago Vista	429B	WW-39	78645	20500-21099
POST OAK LN	Williamson Co	255Z	MK-55	78628	400-499
POST OAK PATH	Hays Co	701P	MA-11	78652	1000-2099
POSTOAK PKWY	Travis Co	591N	MW-23	78653	20600-20799
POST OAK RD	Bastrop Co	709P	MS-11	78617	1-199
POST OAK RD	Webberville	651E	MW-18	78653	1400-2399
	Webberville	650H	MV-18	78653	2400-2799
POST OAK ST	Austin	614D	MH-21	78704	700-1199
POST OAK TRL	Bastrop Co	739M	MT-8	78612	100-299
POST OAK BEND LOOP	Travis Co	397G	WT-42	78654	26200-26299
	Travis Co	397F	WS-42	78654	26500-26999
POST OAK RIM	Bastrop	715Y	EF-10	78602	100-199
POST RIVER RD	Williamson Co	374N	MG-44	78613	2800-3199
POST ROAD DR	Austin	614Y	MH-19	78704	400-599
POSTVINE DR	Austin	587R	MP-23	78724	9000-9199
POSTWOOD RD	Village of the Hills	519T	WW-28	78738	1-99
POTEAU CIR	Travis Co	460Z	WZ-34	78734	4400-4599
POTOMAC CIR	Williamson Co	403W	ME-40	78613	1600-1699
POTOMAC PATH	Austin	526P	ML-29	78753	800-999
POTOMAC ST	Taylor	353N	EA-47	76574	100-699
POTOSI CV	Williamson Co	405J	MJ-41	78717	8500-8599
POTTER CV	Hutto	379M	MT-44	78634	1000-1099
POTTER LN	Georgetown	195X	MJ-61	78633	100-299
POTTERS PT	Hays Co	668G	WV-15	78620	100-199
POTTERS TRL	Williamson Co	434V	MH-37	78729	7300-7499
POWDER CV	Lago Vista	399Y	WX-40	78645	7900-7999
POWDER CREEK CV	Georgetown	225K	MJ-59	78633	300-399
POWDER CREEK DR	Travis Co	560E	MU-27	78653	17600-18099
POWDERHAM LN	Travis Co	432C	MD-39	78613	2400-2599
POWDERHORN CV	Williamson Co	375T	MJ-43	78681	600-799
POWDERHORN DR	Williamson Co	375T	MJ-43	78681	700-3899
POWDER HORN RD	Bastrop Co	712V	MZ-10	78602	100-199
POWDER HORN RD	Williamson Co	192L	MD-62	78633	1-199
POWDERHORN ST	Austin	466K	ML-35	78727	12800-13099
POWDER MILL TRL	Williamson Co	433K	ME-38	78750	11200-11599
POWDER RIVER RD	Austin	465N	MJ-35	78759	4900-5199
POWELL CIR	Austin	614Y	MH-19	78704	400-599
	Austin	614Y	MH-19	78704	3100-3299
POWELL DR	Leander	342F	MC-48	78641	500-599
POWELL LN	Bastrop Co	564W	EC-25	78621	100-399
POWELL LN E	Austin	526N	ML-29	78753	100-799
POWELL LN W	Austin	526N	ML-29	78753	100-799
POWELL ST	Austin	584Q	MH-23	78703	500-599
POWELL ST	Williamson Co	443G	EB-39	78615	100-499
POWER CIR	Georgetown	256T	ML-55	78628	2400-2499
POWER LN	Cedar Park	371Z	MB-43	78613	None
	Travis Co	371Z	MB-43	78613	1200-1599
POWER RD	Georgetown	256T	ML-55	78628	500-1299
POWERS CIR	Caldwell Co	796D	MM-3	78610	100-199
POW WOW	Leander	372A	MC-45	78641	2000-2099
POYNETTE PL	Williamson Co	405P	MJ-41	78717	15600-15699
POZITO CT	Austin	643U	MF-16	78745	7400-7499
PRADERA DR	Austin	464K	MG-35	78759	11300-11599
PRADERA PATH	Cedar Park	344W	MG-46	78641	1800-1999
PRADO ST	Austin	616A	ML-21	78702	2800-3199
PRAIRIE AVE	Buda	762H	MD-6	78610	100-199
PRAIRIE LN	Travis Co	406Y	MM-40	78728	3700-4199
PRAIRIE LN N	Williamson Co	193C	MF-63	78633	100-199
PRAIRIE LN S	Williamson Co	193C	MF-63	78633	200-299
PRAIRIE ST	Jonestown	430Q	WZ-38	78645	7800-8099
	Travis Co	430Q	WZ-38	78645	7900-8099
PRAIRIE TRL	Austin	496P	ML-32	78758	800-1199
PRAIRIE CLOVER PATH	Travis Co	491N	MA-32	78732	3100-3299
PRAIRIE CREEK TRL	Georgetown	194R	MH-62	78633	100-299
PRAIRIE DELL	Austin	526S	ML-28	78752	200-299
	Austin	525V	MK-28	78752	300-499
PRAIRIE DOG TRL	Williamson Co	433K	ME-38	78750	11300-11399
PRAIRIE DOVE CIR	Austin	496J	ML-32	78758	11000-11299
PRAIRIE DUNES DR	Austin	704K	MG-11	78747	4700-5199
PRAIRIE DUNES DR	Georgetown	226P	ML-59	78628	800-1299
PRAIRIE GLEN CT	Travis Co	677Y	MP-13	78617	12200-12299
PRAIRIE GRASS LN	Georgetown	195P	MJ-62	78633	800-899
PRAIRIE HEN CV	Austin	496E	ML-33	78758	1700-1799
PRAIRIE HEN LN	Austin	496E	ML-33	78758	11500-11899
PRAIRIE HILL DR	Caldwell Co	767Y	MP-4	78616	1-499
PRAIRIE KNOLL CT	Austin	496A	ML-33	78758	1800-1999
PRAIRIE MIST CT	Travis Co	432K	MC-38	78613	2800-2899
PRAIRIE POINT DR	Pflugerville	438M	MR-38	78660	None
PRAIRIE RIDGE TRL	Pflugerville	467D	MP-36	78660	1000-1299
PRAIRIE ROCK WAY	Round Rock	407A	MN-42	78664	1800-1999
PRAIRIE SAGE CV	Manor	530T	MU-28	78653	None
PRAIRIE SPRINGS CV	Georgetown	257P	MN-56	78626	100-199
PRAIRIE SPRINGS LN	Georgetown	257P	MN-56	78626	100-299
PRAIRIE SPRINGS LOOP	Georgetown	257P	MN-56	78626	100-299
PRAIRIE STAR CV	Williamson Co	377J	MN-44	78664	1600-1699
PRAIRIE STAR LN	Williamson Co	377J	MN-44	78664	1500-1999
PRAIRIE VERBENA LN	Travis Co	532Q	MZ-29	78621	17600-18099
PRAIRIE WOLF CT	Dripping Springs	636Q	WR-17	78620	100-199
PRATHER LN	Austin	614S	MG-19	78704	2000-2399
PRATHER ST	Taylor	322Z	MZ-49	76574	900-1299
	Taylor	352C	MZ-48	76574	1300-1899
PRATOLINA DR	Austin	670C	WZ-15	78739	12200-12499
PRATT LN	Austin	672Q	MD-14	78748	10700-10999
PRAVADA ST	Austin	495C	MK-33	78758	11400-11699
PREAKNESS DR	Travis Co	677G	MP-15	78617	4600-4799
PREAKNESS PL	Georgetown	287L	MP-53	78626	300-599
PRECIPICE CV	Austin	524S	MG-28	78731	4800-4899

P

STREET NAME	CITY or COUNTY	MAPSCO GRID	AUSTIN GRID	ZIP CODE	BLOCK RANGE O/E
PRECIPICE WAY	Georgetown	317F	MN-51	78626	200-399
PRECISION DR	Buda	762L	MD-5	78610	100-199
PREECE DR	Williamson Co	434P	MG-38	78729	12500-12599
PREMIER PARK ST	Austin	704P	MG-11	78747	10400-10499
PRENTICE LN	Austin	554N	MG-26	78746	3900-4099
PRESA DR	Austin	496M	MM-32	78753	12000-12099
PRESA ABAJO DR	Travis Co	522T	MC-28	78733	9500-9699
PRESA ARRIBA RD	Travis Co	522W	MC-28	78733	800-1099
PRESCOTT DR	Austin	641R	MB-17	78749	9500-9699
PRESERVATION CV	Austin	583T	ME-22	78746	4000-4099
PRESERVE PL	Round Rock	407D	MP-42	78665	1000-1199
PRESERVE TRL	Cedar Park	372N	MC-44	78613	2500-2599
PRESERVE WAY	Travis Co	580D	WZ-24	78735	4400-4499
PRESERVE VISTA TERRACE					
	Travis Co	550M	WZ-26	78733	11900-12099
PRESIDENTIAL BLVD	Austin	647J	MN-17	78719	2500-2899
	Austin	646R	MM-17	78719	2900-3599
	Austin	647N	MN-17	78719	3600-4399
PRESIDIO DR	Leander	342R	MD-47	78641	100-399
PRESIDIO RD	Austin	644Q	MH-17	78745	5300-5399
PRESLAR CIR	Hays Co	608Q	WV-20	78736	100-299
PRESQUE CV	Austin	462K	MC-35	78726	12500-12599
PRESSLER ST	Austin	584R	MH-23	78703	300-899
PRESTANCIA DR	Austin	404C	MH-42	78717	15300-16199
PRESTON AVE	Austin	554Z	MH-25	78703	1400-1699
PRESTON TRAILS CV	Travis Co	703R	MF-11	78747	2300-2399
PRESTON TRAILS DR	Austin	704N	MG-11	78747	1090-1099
PRESTONWOOD CIR	Lakeway	519F	WW-30	78734	1-99
PRESTONWOOD CV	Lakeway	519F	WW-30	78734	1-99
PRESTWICK DR	Travis Co	408H	MR-42	78634	20800-20999
PRESTWOOD PL	Austin	583Z	MF-22	78746	1400-1499
PRESWYCK DR	Austin	556Y	MM-25	78723	5600-5699
PREWITT LN	Round Rock	378B	MQ-45	78664	3500-3599
PREZIA DR	Travis Co	551K	MA-26	78733	10500-10699
PRICE ST	Taylor	353F	EA-48	76574	1000-1199
PRICKLY PEAR DR	Austin	524C	MH-30	78731	4200-4399
PRICKLY PEAR PASS	Hays Co	732L	MD-8	78610	100-699
PRICKLY POPPY CV	Travis Co	551P	MA-26	78733	10500-10599
PRIEM LN	Travis Co	408M	MR-41	78660	1000-1499
PRIEST RIVER CV	Williamson Co	375Y	MK-43	78681	17400-17499
PRIEST RIVER DR	Williamson Co	375X	MJ-43	78681	8300-8899
PRIMROSE	Cedar Park	403E	ME-42	78613	800-899
PRIMROSE LN	Austin	495X	MJ-31	78757	8600-8799
PRIMROSE LN	Leander	342S	MC-46	78641	1700-1799
PRIMROSE ST	Austin	526J	ML-29	78753	400-499
PRIMROSE TRL	Georgetown	256K	ML-56	78628	3200-3499
PRIMROSE TRL	Williamson Co	377E	MN-45	78664	1500-2199
PRIMWOOD PATH	Travis Co	432H	MD-39	78613	2800-2899
PRINCE DR	Austin	526S	ML-28	78752	100-299
PRINCE ANDREW LN	Travis Co	522H	MD-30	78730	4100-4299
PRINCE ARN DR	Austin	643Z	MF-16	78745	700-899
PRINCE CHARLES DR	Travis Co	522H	MD-30	78730	9200-9499
PRINCE PHILLIP WAY	Travis Co	529H	MT-30	78653	11500-11699
PRINCETON AVE	Austin	525L	MK-29	78757	1500-1899
PRINCETON CV	Pflugerville	467D	MP-36	78660	900-999
PRINCETON DR	Austin	645B	MJ-18	78741	2400-2799
PRINCETON DR	Pflugerville	467D	MP-36	78660	600-899
PRINCE VALIANT DR	Austin	643Z	MF-16	78745	600-899
PRINCE WILLIAM	Travis Co	522D	MD-30	78730	9100-9599
PRINCEWOOD PASS	Austin	673J	ME-14	78748	9700-9799
PRINGLE CIR	Austin	646D	MM-18	78742	1300-1499
PRISCILLA DR	Austin	525Z	MK-28	78752	6900-7099
PRISM DR	Austin	463B	ME-36	78726	10200-10399
PRISTINE LN	Georgetown	195X	MJ-61	78633	100-299
PRIVADA DR	Bastrop Co	739F	MS-9	78617	100-299
	Bastrop Co	739L	MT-8	78612	300-399
PRIVATE RD 902	Williamson Co	193D	MF-63	78633	1-499
PRIVATE RD 904	Williamson Co	193B	ME-63	78633	1-499
PRIVATE RD 906	Williamson Co	318M	MR-50	78634	1-199
PRIVATE RD 907	Williamson Co	252F	MC-57	78642	100-499
PRIVATE RD 908	Williamson Co	318M	MR-50	78634	1-799
PRIVATE RD 909	Williamson Co	196H	MM-63	78628	1-799
PRIVATE RD 910	Williamson Co	288G	MR-54	78626	1-499
PRIVATE RD 911	Williamson Co	280T	WY-52	78641	1-299
PRIVATE RD 914	Williamson Co	197J	MN-62	78628	1-699
PRIVATE RD 916	Williamson Co	227C	MP-60	78626	1-399
PRIVATE RD 918	Williamson Co	312G	MD-51	78641	1-399
PRIVATE RD 919	Williamson Co	343Z	MF-46	78641	1-99
PRIVATE RD 920	Williamson Co	343B	ME-48	78641	1-799
PRIVATE RD 921	Williamson Co	343B	ME-48	78641	1-399
PRIVATE RD 929	Williamson Co	383F	EA-45	76574	1-599
PRIVATE RD 931	Weir	258G	MR-57	78626	1-99
PRIVATE RD 932	Weir	258D	MR-57	78626	1-99
PRIVATE RD 933	Weir	258D	MR-57	78626	1-99
PRIVATE RD 934	Weir	258D	MR-57	78626	1-99
PRIVATE RD 945	Williamson Co	318X	MQ-49	78665	1-799
PRIVATE RD 947	Williamson Co	412R	MZ-41	76574	1-299
PRIVATE RD 949	Williamson Co	282W	MC-52	78641	200-499
PRIZE OAKS DR	Cedar Park	402D	MD-42	78613	100-499
	Cedar Park	372Y	MD-43	78613	500-999
PROCK LN	Austin	586T	ML-22	78721	4600-4999
	Austin	586Y	MM-22	78721	5100-5599
PROFIT CENTRE DR	Austin	527W	MN-28	78754	3000-3099
PROMENADE CT	Williamson Co	377G	MP-45	78665	1000-1099
PROMONTORY POINT DR	Austin	645P	MJ-17	78744	3700-4099
PRONGHORN PASS	Bastrop	744P	EC-8	78602	100-199
PROSPECT AVE	Austin	585Z	MK-22	78702	700-1199
PROSPECTOR PASS	Georgetown	225L	MK-59	78633	100-199
PROSPERITY	Leander	372F	MC-45	78641	2700-2798 E
PROSPERITY HILLS DR	Georgetown	226P	ML-59	78628	1000-1399
PROUD PANDA DR	Travis Co	677Y	MP-13	78617	7000-7299
PROVENCIAL CV	Austin	587E	MN-24	78724	6100-6199
PROVENCIAL DR	Austin	587E	MN-24	78724	5100-5299
PROVIDENCE AVE	Austin	526X	ML-28	78752	7400-7699
PROVIDENCE PKWY	Elgin	534W	EC-28	78621	None
PROVIDENCE ST	Georgetown	195R	MK-62	78633	100-199
PROVIDENT LN	Round Rock	377N	MN-44	78664	1100-1999
PROVINES DR	Austin	496U	MM-31	78753	100-799
PRUETT ST	Austin	584K	MG-23	78703	2300-2499
PRUSSIAN LN	Austin	671B	MA-15	78739	6600-6699
PRYOR LN	Travis Co	460V	WZ-34	78734	5000-5299
PTARMIGAN CV	Austin	496E	ML-33	78758	11300-11499
PTARMIGAN DR	Austin	496E	ML-33	78758	10900-11499
PUCCOON CV	Austin	494G	MH-33	78759	5700-5799
PUCKETT CT	Austin	642P	MC-17	78749	8700-8799
PUDDLEBY CV	Austin	583Z	MF-22	78746	1300-1399
PUEBLA DR	Austin	647Q	MP-17	78617	3000-3099
PUEBLO CV	Lago Vista	399X	WW-40	78645	7800-7899
PUERTA VISTA	Austin	494V	MH-31	78759	8300-8399
PUKOO DR	Bastrop Co	746W	EG-7	78602	100-199
PULEHU CT	Bastrop Co	746X	EG-7	78602	100-199
PUMA PASS	Austin	557P	MN-26	78724	5800-5899
PUMA TRL	Austin	524B	MG-30	78731	6800-6899
PUMPKIN RIDGE	Leander	371B	MA-45	78641	3500-3599
PUMPKIN RIDGE CT	Austin	404G	MH-42	78717	9900-9999
PUMPKIN RIDGE CT	Travis Co	409S	MS-40	78660	2500-2699
PUMPKIN RIDGE DR	Austin	404H	MH-42	78717	15600-15899
PUNA LN	Bastrop	746N	EG-8	78602	100-199
PURCELL PL	Dripping Springs	636T	WQ-16	78620	100-399
PURDUE CV	Williamson Co	402U	MD-40	78613	1300-1399
PURE BROOK WAY	Hays Co	669S	WW-13	78737	100-199
PURNELL DR	Austin	526N	ML-29	78753	8000-8099
PURNIMA CV	Austin	670M	WZ-14	78739	7300-7399
PURPLE HERON DR	Austin	583U	MF-22	78746	3500-3699
PURPLE IRIS CV	Pflugerville	437H	MP-39	78660	1600-1699
PURPLE MARTIN CT	Pflugerville	468J	MQ-35	78660	900-999
PURPLE MARTIN CV	Williamson Co	282J	MC-53	78641	100-199
PURPLE MARTIN DR	Pflugerville	468J	MQ-35	78660	800-1199
PURPLE SAGE CIR	Leander	342P	MC-47	78641	1300-1399
PURPLE SAGE CV	Round Rock	406L	MM-41	78681	1900-1999
PURPLE SAGE DR	Austin	557N	MN-26	78724	4900-5799
PURPLE SAGE DR	Bastrop Co	741K	MW-8	78612	100-199
PURPLE SAGE DR	Georgetown	225L	MK-59	78633	100-199
PURPLE SAGE DR	Round Rock	406L	MM-41	78681	400-699
PURPLE SAGE DR	Travis Co	402Y	MD-40	78613	1600-1699
PURPLE SAGE LN	Williamson Co	349B	MS-48	78634	100-199
PURPLE THISTLE DR	Travis Co	409P	MS-41	78660	2600-2899
PURSLANE CV	Travis Co	551K	MA-26	78733	10700-10799
PURSLANE MEADOW TRL	Travis Co	436V	MM-37	78728	14900-15099
PURTIS CREEK LN	Williamson Co	344B	MG-48	78628	100-599
PURYEAR	Hays Co	576P	WQ-23	78620	None
PURYEAR RD	Travis Co	733G	MF-9	78652	2300-2599
PUSCH RIDGE LOOP	Austin	642M	MD-17	78749	7300-7499
PUTNAM DR	Austin	525C	MK-30	78757	8500-8799
PUTT RD	Travis Co	641A	MA-18	78737	9100-9299
PUTTER CV	Round Rock	378Y	MR-43	78664	3900-3999
PUTTERS CV	Austin	645W	MJ-16	78744	4800-4899
PUU CT	Bastrop Co	776E	EG-6	78602	100-199
PUU KAUA CT	Bastrop Co	745Z	EF-7	78602	100-199
PUU WAA WAA LN	Bastrop Co	745Y	EF-7	78602	100-199
PYEGRAVE PL	Austin	497J	MN-32	78753	900-1099
PYRAMID DR	Lakeway	490P	WY-32	78734	1300-1899
	Travis Co	490P	WY-32	78734	1900-2999
PYRENEES PASS	Bee Cave	549F	WW-27	78738	4500-5099
PYRENEESE DR	Austin	465S	MJ-34	78759	11400-11599

Q

STREET NAME	CITY or COUNTY	MAPSCO GRID	AUSTIN GRID	ZIP CODE	BLOCK RANGE O/E
Q RANCH RD	Austin	464M	MH-35	78759	11400-11799
Q S GOINS LN	Elgin	534K	EC-29	78621	200-699
QUADROS PASS	Williamson Co	434R	MH-38	78729	13200-13299
QUAIL BLVD	Austin	496W	ML-31	78758	9800-9999
QUAIL CIR	Cedar Park	433A	ME-39	78613	1200-1299
QUAIL CIR	Hutto	350S	MU-46	78634	100-399
QUAIL CT	Austin	496W	ML-31	78758	9500-9599
QUAIL CT	Travis Co	309U	WX-49	78641	14700-14799
QUAIL CV	Austin	526A	ML-30	78758	9200-9299
QUAIL CV	Hays Co	732C	MD-9	78610	12700-12799
QUAIL CV	Taylor	322Y	MZ-49	76574	2100-2199
QUAIL LN	Round Rock	375V	MK-43	78681	1100-1199
QUAIL LN	Williamson Co	256W	ML-55	78628	200-299
QUAIL PASS	Austin	496E	ML-33	78758	1600-1699
QUAIL PT	Burnet Co	426K	WQ-38	78669	None
QUAIL RD	Hays Co	701Q	MB-11	78652	900-1099
QUAIL COVER CIR	Austin	496S	ML-31	78758	1500-1599
QUAIL CREEK CIR	Round Rock	406D	MM-42	78664	500-599
QUAIL CREEK DR	Austin	526E	ML-30	78758	8900-9199
QUAIL CREEK DR	Round Rock	406D	MM-42	78664	500-699
QUAIL CREEK RD	Burnet Co	307F	WS-51	78654	100-599
QUAIL CREEK TRL	Cedar Park	373Y	MF-43	78613	1300-1399
QUAIL CREST DR	Austin	496N	ML-32	78758	1400-1699
QUAIL FARM DR	Dripping Springs	636T	WQ-16	78620	100-299
QUAILFIELD CIR	Austin	526A	ML-30	78758	1200-1399
QUAIL FIELD DR	Austin	526A	ML-30	78758	9200-9399
QUAIL FOREST CV	Austin	496W	ML-31	78758	900-999
QUAIL HILL CIR	Austin	526A	ML-30	78758	9200-9299
QUAIL HOLLOW	Austin	494S	MG-31	78750	6200-6299
QUAIL HOLLOW DR	Hutto	379R	MT-44	78634	100-499
QUAIL HUTCH DR	Austin	495V	MK-31	78758	10000-10199
QUAIL LODGE CT	Round Rock	378Z	MR-43	78664	3800-3899
QUAIL MEADOW DR	Austin	525D	MK-30	78758	9200-9499
QUAIL MEADOW DR	Georgetown	287N	MN-53	78626	2200-2299
QUAIL PARK DR	Austin	526A	ML-30	78758	1000-1399
QUAIL RAVINE	Travis Co	408G	MR-42	78664	None
	Williamson Co	408G	MR-42	78664	1300-1399
QUAIL RIDGE DR	Austin	496N	ML-32	78758	10300-10499
QUAIL RIDGE DR	Hays Co	668Q	WV-14	78620	1000-1299
QUAIL ROCK CIR	Austin	526A	ML-30	78758	9200-9299
QUAIL RUN	Burnet Co	396P	WQ-41	78669	100-399
QUAIL RUN	Hays Co	794E	MG-3	78610	100-199
QUAIL RUN	Travis Co	553M	MF-26	78746	5100-5199
QUAIL RUN	Travis Co	557C	MP-27	78724	5800-5899
QUAIL RUN	Williamson Co	193B	ME-63	78633	100-299
QUAIL RUN	Williamson Co	345W	MJ-46	78681	2700-3199
QUAIL RUN CT	Burnet Co	396P	WQ-41	78669	200-399
QUAIL RUN CV	Lago Vista	458F	WU-36	78645	2300-2399
QUAIL RUN RD	Pflugerville	468F	MQ-36	78660	600-1599
QUAIL RUN TRL	Cedar Park	372M	MD-44	78613	1700-1799
QUAIL VALLEY BLVD	Austin	495V	MK-31	78758	10000-10199
	Austin	496S	ML-31	78758	10200-10399
QUAIL VALLEY CT	Travis Co	369V	WX-43	78645	21600-21799
QUAIL VALLEY CV	Travis Co	369V	WX-43	78645	21500-21599
QUAIL VALLEY DR	Austin	526A	ML-30	78758	9000-9199
QUAIL VALLEY DR	Georgetown	286V	MM-52	78626	600-1099
	Georgetown	287S	MN-52	78626	1100-2099
QUAIL VALLEY DR	Travis Co	369Z	WX-43	78645	10600-10899
QUAIL VILLAGE LN	Austin	526A	ML-30	78758	9500-9599
QUAIL WOOD DR	Austin	526A	ML-30	78758	9200-9399
QUAKER RIDGE DR	Travis Co	582M	MD-23	78746	1100-1599
QUANAH DR	Round Rock	406S	ML-40	78681	2600-2899
QUANAH PARKER TRL	Travis Co	490U	WZ-31	78734	1800-2499
QUANTICO CT	Pflugerville	408Z	MR-40	78660	None
QUAPAW DR	Travis Co	467K	MN-35	78660	None
QUARRY LOOP	Leander	342S	MC-46	78641	2200-2299
QUARRY RD	Austin	584G	MH-24	78703	2100-2399
	Austin	584F	MG-24	78703	2400-2599
QUARRY CREEK	Williamson Co	375L	MK-44	78681	3200-3299
QUARRY LAKE PKWY	Austin	465W	MJ-34	78759	None
QUARRY OAKS TRL	Austin	404E	MG-42	78717	10600-11099
QUARRY RIDGE	Leander	342W	MC-46	78641	2200-2299
QUARRY RIDGE LN	Travis Co	704C	MH-12	78747	None
QUARTER BOOT CV	Austin	466Q	MM-35	78727	1700-1799
QUARTERHORSE DR	Travis Co	531Q	MX-29	78621	12700-12899
QUARTER HORSE TRL	Williamson Co	433K	ME-38	78750	11500-11699
QUARTZ CIR	Williamson Co	433P	ME-38	78750	11700-11799
QUARTZ CT	Cedar Park	372U	MD-43	78613	900-999
QUARTZ LN	Bastrop Co	621R	MX-20	78621	100-299
QUASSIA DR	Austin	670D	WZ-15	78739	11900-12199
QUEEN CT	Travis Co	588S	MQ-22	78724	10000-10099
QUEEN BEE LN	Travis Co	488W	WU-31	78669	20300-20599
QUEENS WAY	Austin	464F	MG-36	78759	11500-11699
QUEENSBURY CV	Austin	433W	ME-37	78726	10600-10699
QUEENSLAND DR	Williamson Co	434B	MG-39	78729	9700-9999
QUEENS PARK CV	Austin	405A	MJ-42	78717	9300-9399
QUEENSWOOD DR	Austin	673E	ME-15	78748	8900-9599
QUERNUS CV	Austin	612D	MD-21	78735	5900-5999
QUEST PKWY	Cedar Park	373N	ME-44	78613	900-999
QUICK HILL RD	Williamson Co	436B	ML-39	78728	3500-3899
QUICKSILVER BLVD	Austin	674R	MH-14	78744	2100-5199
QUICKSILVER CIR	Austin	674M	MH-14	78744	7300-7399
QUICKSILVER CIR	Round Rock	346M	MM-47	78665	1400-1499
QUICKSILVER DR	Cedar Park	372R	MD-44	78613	200-299
QUICKSILVER ST	Round Rock	346M	MM-47	78665	1300-1499
QUICK STREAM DR	Austin	587M	MP-23	78724	8900-9099
QUICK WATER CV	Austin	613E	ME-21	78735	4900-4999
QUIET BROOK PL	Lago Vista	429M	WX-38	78645	7200-7399
QUIET CREEK DR	Cedar Park	403P	ME-41	78613	1200-1399
QUIET MOON TRL	Travis Co	402Y	MD-40	78613	2600-2799
QUIET MOUNTAIN CV	Travis Co	523F	ME-30	78730	5100-5199
QUIET OAKS LN	Travis Co	561W	MW-25	78653	20400-20699
QUIET POND CT	Travis Co	436Q	MM-38	78728	15200-15299
QUIETTE DR	Travis Co	527X	MN-28	78754	3500-3599
	Travis Co	557B	MN-27	78754	3600-3699
QUIET WATER PASS	Pflugerville	439E	MS-39	78660	2500-2799
QUIET WATER PASS	Williamson Co	317X	MN-49	78665	4400-4499
QUIET WOOD DR	Travis Co	436U	MM-37	78728	2200-2399
QUILBERRY DR	Williamson Co	434B	MG-39	78729	9600-9899
QUILL LEAF CV	Austin	493V	MF-31	78750	7000-7099
QUIMPER LN	Austin	612W	MC-19	78749	7100-7299
QUINCY CV	Austin	671F	MA-15	78739	6600-6799
QUINCY DR	Pflugerville	437G	MP-39	78660	600-699
QUINLAN PARK RD N	Travis Co	521J	MA-29	78732	100-2399
	Travis Co	491R	MB-32	78732	2400-4999
QUINLAN PARK RD S	Travis Co	520R	WZ-29	78732	100-1199
	Travis Co	550D	WZ-27	78732	1200-1799
QUINLEY DR	Travis Co	436L	MM-38	78728	15300-15499
QUINN DR	Hays Co	607M	WT-20	78720	100-599
QUINN TRL	Austin	435W	MJ-37	78727	12900-12999
QUINTON CV	Austin	705A	MJ-12	78747	8600-8699
QUINTON DR	Austin	705B	MJ-12	78747	6400-7099
QUIRIN DR	Austin	678J	MQ-14	78617	12700-12899
QUITMAN PASS	Travis Co	466G	MM-36	78728	13800-13899
QUITMAN MOUNTAIN WAY					
	Pflugerville	407U	MP-40	78664	17700-17999
QUIVIRA RD	Austin	673C	MF-15	78745	1800-1999

R

STREET NAME	CITY or COUNTY	MAPSCO GRID	AUSTIN GRID	ZIP CODE	BLOCK RANGE O/E
RABB RD	Austin	614B	MG-21	78704	1400-2299
RABB GLEN ST	Austin	614F	MG-21	78704	1800-2299
RABBIT HOLLOW LN	Williamson Co	316D	MM-51	78626	100-399
RABBIT RUN	Georgetown	286Z	MM-52	78626	100-199
	Williamson Co	316D	MM-51	78626	200-399
RABBIT RUN	Round Rock	406D	MM-42	78664	700-999
RABBIT RUN CIR	Travis Co	489M	WX-32	78734	1100-1399
RACCOON RUN	Austin	611L	MB-20	78736	6700-6899
RACCOON RUN	Hays Co	732K	MC-8	78610	300-399
RACEBROOK CT	Lakeway	519C	WX-30	78734	100-199
RACERS FORD LN	Pflugerville	409J	MS-41	78660	20800-20999
RACETRACK DR	Austin	703G	MF-12	78748	200-499
RACHAEL CT	Austin	673J	ME-14	78748	2300-2399
RACHEL CT	Round Rock	407K	MN-41	78664	2400-2499
RACHEL LN	Round Rock	407K	MN-41	78664	1800-2199
RACHEL RIDGE	Williamson Co	402Q	MD-41	78613	2000-2299
RACHEL'S CANYON DR	Hays Co	668M	WV-14	78620	100-199
RACINE CV	Williamson Co	405J	MJ-41	78717	15700-15799
RACINE TRL	Williamson Co	405K	MJ-41	78717	8100-8599
RACIN PATTY ST	Travis Co	530U	MV-28	78653	19100-19199
RADAM CIR	Austin	644J	MG-17	78745	1100-1499
RADAM LN	Austin	644C	MH-18	78745	100-799
RADCLIFF DR	Austin	556B	ML-27	78752	1200-1399
RADHOLME CT	Pflugerville	437A	MN-39	78664	16800-16899
RADNOR DR	Village of the Hills	519P	WW-29	78738	1-99
RAE WAY	Travis Co	610V	WZ-19	78736	9800-9899
RAE DELL AVE	Austin	614J	MG-20	78704	2200-3099
RAFFEE CV	Austin	494T	MG-31	78731	4900-5099
RAFINA RD	Bastrop Co	738P	MQ-8	78617	100-199
RAGING RIVER DR	Travis Co	436Q	MM-38	78728	3000-3299
RAGLAN CASTLE PATH	Pflugerville	408X	MQ-40	78660	19000-19099
RAGSDALE ST	Austin	556W	ML-25	78723	1400-1499
RAIL ST	Lakeway	520J	WY-29	78734	15000-15199
RAIL FENCE CV	Austin	673G	MF-15	78748	1300-1399
RAILROAD AVE	Georgetown	286U	MM-52	78626	1000-2299
RAILROAD AVE N	Pflugerville	438W	MQ-37	78660	100-1599
RAILROAD AVE S	Pflugerville	468A	MQ-36	78660	100-699
RAILROAD ST	Leander	312Y	MD-49	78641	100-399
RAILROAD ST N	Buda	762D	MD-6	78610	100-399
RAILROAD ST S	Buda	762D	MD-6	78610	100-199
RAILTON DR	Travis Co	677X	MN-13	78617	11600-11799
RAINBOW CT	Williamson Co	434N	MG-38	78729	12500-12599
RAINBOW CV	Round Rock	378A	MQ-45	78665	1200-1299
RAINBOW CV	West Lake Hills	583M	MF-23	78746	600-699
RAINBOW LN	Bastrop Co	739A	MS-9	78617	100-199
RAINBOW BEND	Austin	584H	MH-24	78703	1500-1599
RAINBOW BRIDGE DR N	Cedar Park	373T	ME-43	78613	100-499
RAINBOW BRIDGE DR S	Cedar Park	373X	ME-43	78613	100-299
RAINBOW CONNECTION SKYWAY					
	Travis Co	487F	WS-33	78669	None
RAINBOW HOLLOW DR	Travis Co	460W	WY-34	78645	3100-3599
RAINBOW ONE	Travis Co	460V	WZ-34	78734	15100-15399
RAINBOW PARKE DR	Round Rock	378E	MQ-45	78665	1200-1599

STREET NAME	CITY or COUNTY	MAPSCO GRID	AUSTIN GRID	ZIP CODE	BLOCK RANGE O/E
RAINBOW RIDGE CIR	Austin	586Q	MM-23	78721	5100-5199
RAINBOW TWO	Travis Co	460V	WZ-34	78734	15200-15399
RAIN CREEK DR	Williamson Co	349A	MS-48	78634	100-399
RAIN CREEK PKWY	Austin	494D	MH-33	78759	5000-5699
	Austin	464P	MG-35	78759	5700-7499
RAINDANCE	Leander	372B	MC-45	78641	2600-2699
RAIN DANCE CV	Travis Co	554J	MG-26	78746	3200-3299
RAINDANCE DR	Williamson Co	287H	MP-54	78626	50100-50399
RAINDROP CV	Austin	464Y	MH-34	78759	5600-5799
RAINEY ST	Austin	615B	MJ-21	78701	1-99
RAINFALL TRL	Travis Co	432D	MD-39	78613	2600-2699
	Williamson Co	432D	MD-39	78613	None
RAIN FOREST CV	Austin	464M	MH-35	78759	11700-11899
RAIN FOREST DR	Austin	583Y	MF-22	78746	3400-3499
RAINIER LN	Austin	527E	MN-30	78754	2300-2499
RAINING OAK CV	Austin	464Z	MH-34	78759	10700-10799
RAINLILLY LN	Austin	464X	MG-34	78759	9600-9799
RAIN LILY LN	Georgetown	225L	MK-59	78633	100-199
RAINMEADOW PATH	Williamson Co	347A	MN-48	78665	4300-4399
RAINTREE BLVD	Austin	644F	MG-18	78745	4600-4699
RAINTREE DR	Georgetown	287P	MN-53	78626	100-399
RAINTREE PATH	Round Rock	377X	MN-43	78664	2100-2499
RAINTREE PL	Austin	494Z	MH-31	78759	8000-8199
RAINWATER CV	Georgetown	195T	MJ-61	78633	100-199
RAIN WATER DR	Travis Co	490V	WZ-31	78734	2000-2499
RAINWOOD CV	Austin	675T	MJ-13	78744	6700-6799
RAINY MEADOWS DR	Austin	496A	ML-33	78758	1800-1999
RAINY RIVER DR	Williamson Co	343T	ME-46	78641	2900-3099
RALEIGH AVE	Austin	584B	MG-24	78703	1500-1699
	Austin	554X	MG-25	78703	1700-2199
RALEIGH CIR	Austin	674H	MH-15	78744	4500-4599
RALEIGH CV	Lago Vista	458D	WV-36	78645	3500-3599
RALEY RD	Travis Co	374C	MH-45	78613	1-199
RALPH ABLANEDO DR	Austin	674J	MG-14	78748	100-299
	Austin	673M	MF-14	78748	300-699
RALPH C CRAIG LN	Austin	702D	MD-12	78748	1800-1999
RALPH COX RD	Austin	702H	MD-12	78748	1800-1999
RALPH RITCHIE RD	Travis Co	530F	MU-30	78653	13500-13899
RAMADA TRL	Williamson Co	226X	ML-58	78628	4000-4199
RAMBLE LN	Austin	644K	MG-17	78745	100-999
RAMBLE CREEK DR	Travis Co	437L	MP-38	78660	800-1399
RAMBLER VALLEY DR	Travis Co	402T	MC-40	78613	2700-2899
RAMBLE THREE ST	Travis Co	640H	WZ-18	78737	9800-9999
RAMBLEWOOD DR	Austin	673J	ME-14	78748	9400-9599
RAMBLING CV	Cedar Park	402M	MD-41	78613	1300-1399
RAMBLING TRL	Cedar Park	403J	ME-41	78613	800-1199
	Cedar Park	402M	MD-41	78613	1200-1399
RAMBLING CREEK LN	Travis Co	409X	MS-40	78660	2900-2999
RAMBLING RANGE	Austin	465J	MJ-35	78727	5200-5499
RAMBLING RAPIDS CV	Georgetown	285K	MJ-53	78628	100-299
RAMBLING RUN	Georgetown	285K	MJ-53	78628	100-199
RAMBOLLET TERRACE	Williamson Co	405B	MJ-42	78681	7000-7099
RAMIES RUN	Austin	642T	MC-16	78749	4500-4799
RAMIREZ LN	Dripping Springs	666C	WR-15	78620	100-599
RAMIREZ LN	Travis Co	617P	MN-20	78742	8400-9399
RAMIREZ RD	Elgin	534W	EC-28	78621	101-199 O
RAMONA ST	Austin	614D	MH-21	78704	900-999
RAMOS ST	Austin	616A	ML-21	78702	600-899
RAMPART CIR	Austin	466P	ML-35	78727	1900-1999
RAMPART ST	Austin	466L	MM-35	78727	12500-13299
RAMROD CV	Lago Vista	399M	WX-41	78645	9400-9499
RAMROD DR	Hays Co	701H	MB-12	78652	13300-13499
RAMROD TRL	Lago Vista	399M	WX-41	78645	20600-20799
RAMSEY AVE	Austin	555N	MJ-26	78756	4000-4899
RAMSGATE CT	Pflugerville	468E	MQ-36	78660	None
RAMS HORN WAY	Round Rock	346R	MM-47	78665	3500-3799
RAN RD	Leander	341H	MB-48	78641	200-499
RANCH CV	Cedar Park	403J	ME-41	78613	1300-1399
RANCH CV	Travis Co	309P	WW-50	78641	14600-14699
RANCH RD	Austin	643K	ME-17	78745	6900-6999
	Austin	643S	ME-16	78745	8000-8099
RANCH RD	Bastrop Co	739J	MS-8	78617	100-399
	Bastrop Co	738H	MR-9	78617	None
RANCH RD	Georgetown	256T	ML-55	78628	500-1199
RANCH RD	Travis Co	309P	WW-50	78641	24800-25799
RANCH CREEK RD	Travis Co	522G	MD-30	78730	3600-3999
RANCHERO DR	Mustang Ridge	796P	ML-2	78610	None
RANCHERO RD	Leander	312W	MC-49	78641	600-799
RANCH HOUSE CV	Georgetown	225C	MK-60	78633	100-199
RANCH HOUSE CV	Travis Co	369M	WX-44	78641	11600-11699
RANCHLAND HILLS BLVD	Jonestown	430C	WZ-39	78645	8800-9699
RANCHLAND HILLS CT	Jonestown	430C	WZ-39	78645	16000-16099
RANCHLAND HILLS CV	Jonestown	430G	WZ-39	78645	8400-8699
RANCHLAND HILLS VISTA	Jonestown	400Y	WZ-40	78645	17700-18499
RANCHO ALTO RD	Travis Co	702H	MD-12	78748	11900-12399
RANCHO BUENO DR	Williamson Co	284G	MH-54	78628	100-299
	Williamson Co	254Z	MH-55	78628	300-399
RANCHO CIELO CT	Travis Co	429X	WW-37	78645	19800-20299
RANCHO MIRAGE	Leander	341Y	MB-46	78641	1200-1299
RANCHO VIEJO LN	Leander	312S	MC-49	78641	700-999
RANCH PARK TRL	Round Rock	375B	MJ-45	78681	3200-3499
RANCH TRAILS	Cedar Park	374P	MG-44	78613	3500-3899
RANCHVIEW CT	Travis Co	521K	MA-29	78732	11800-11899
RANCHVIEW RD	Blanco Co	455J	WN-35	78620	100-699
RANCH VIEW RD	Williamson Co	318P	MQ-50	78665	100-199
RANCHWOOD LN	Bee Cave	549R	WX-26	78738	4100-4199
RANDALL DR	Austin	526C	MM-30	78753	9900-9999
RANDALL ST	Taylor	322V	MZ-49	76574	800-1099
RANDALSTONE DR	Travis Co	467P	MN-35	78660	13800-13999
RANDIG LN	Travis Co	439T	MS-37	78660	4500-4799
RANDLEMAN DR	Austin	678T	MQ-13	78617	6000-6199
RANDLETT CT	Travis Co	491U	MB-31	78732	12700-12799
RANDOLPH PL	Rollingwood	584N	MG-23	78746	1-99
RANDOLPH RD	Austin	585H	MK-24	78722	3300-3499
RANDOLPH RD	Georgetown	256S	ML-55	78628	100-199
RANDOLPH ST	Village of Volente	461B	MA-36	78641	15300-15499
RANDOLPH RIDGE TRL	Austin	583T	ME-22	78746	1600-1899
RANDOM CV	Village of the Hills	519P	WW-29	78738	1-99
RANDY CIR	Austin	644E	MG-18	78745	1400-1499
RANDY RD	Travis Co	433T	ME-37	78726	11200-11599
RANDY ST	Williamson Co	257N	MN-56	78626	1-199
RANEY PL	Caldwell Co	796X	ML-1	78644	1-299
RANFT CV	Austin	678J	MQ-14	78617	12800-12899
RANGE HORSE RD	Austin	466F	ML-36	78727	12300-13399
RANGEL RD	Bastrop Co	740M	MV-8	78612	100-199
RANGELAND DR	Austin	677R	MP-14	78617	5400-5499
RANGE OAK CIR	Austin	642C	MD-18	78749	6900-6999
RANGER DR	Hays Co	732F	MC-9	78610	100-499
RANGER TRL	Lago Vista	399M	WX-41	78645	20800-21199
RANGE VIEW CV	Travis Co	492X	MC-31	78730	4200-4299
RANGE VIEW DR	Travis Co	492X	MC-31	78730	10700-10999
RANGOON RD	Austin	587A	MN-24	78724	5400-5599
RANIER CV	Williamson Co	377F	MN-45	78665	1000-1099
RANIER LN	Georgetown	195V	MK-61	78633	100-299
RANIER LN	Williamson Co	377G	MP-45	78665	100-799
RANKIN TRL	Williamson Co	434V	MH-37	78729	7300-7499
RANNOCH DR	Travis Co	437C	MP-39	78660	17400-17599
RANSOM ST	Travis Co	437S	MN-37	78660	1400-1599
RAPID CREEK TRL	Austin	675A	MJ-15	78744	5900-5999
RAPID SPRINGS CV	Georgetown	285K	MJ-53	78628	100-299
RAPID SPRINGS CV E	Travis Co	554E	MG-27	78746	4500-4599
RAPID SPRINGS CV W	Travis Co	554E	MG-27	78746	4500-4599
RAPTOR ROOST RD	Travis Co	409Y	MT-40	78660	20500-20699
RAPTURE CV	Austin	612Y	MD-19	78749	6400-6499
RARE EAGLE CT	Lakeway	519D	WX-30	78734	100-199
RARITAN CT	Lakeway	519H	WX-30	78734	100-199
RASPBERRY CV	Austin	672L	MD-14	78748	3300-3399
RASPBERRY RD	Austin	672L	MD-14	78758	2900-3299
RATAMA WAY	Round Rock	378W	MQ-43	78665	2900-2999
RATH DR	Williamson Co	193L	MF-62	78633	100-199
RATHDOWNEY CV	Austin	404E	MG-42	78717	10700-10799
RATHERVUE PL	Austin	585B	MJ-24	78705	500-699
RATHLIN DR	Travis Co	432H	MD-39	78613	2800-2899
RATON PASS	Austin	557N	MN-26	78724	5100-5299
RATTAN CIR	Williamson Co	343W	ME-46	78641	2600-2699
RATTLEBUSH CV	Austin	464A	MG-36	78750	8800-8899
RATTLESNAKE HILL RD	Bastrop Co	504G	ED-33	78621	100-199
RATTLING HORN CV	Cedar Park	402R	MD-41	78613	1300-1399
RAVELLO PASS	Austin	642U	MD-16	78749	8800-8999
RAVELLO RIDGE CV	Travis Co	582K	MC-23	78735	8100-8199
RAVELLO RIDGE DR	Travis Co	582K	MC-23	78735	2600-2999
RAVEN DR	Austin	556C	MM-27	78752	1700-1799
RAVEN CAW PASS	Travis Co	439C	MT-39	78660	3600-3799
RAVENS CV	Cedar Park	403J	ME-41	78613	1100-1199
RAVENSBROOK CT	Travis Co	409P	MS-41	78660	2600-2699
RAVENSBROOK BEND	Cedar Park	372T	MC-43	78613	1300-1399
RAVENSCROFT DR	Austin	673W	ME-13	78748	1700-1799
	Austin	672Z	MD-13	78748	1800-2299
RAVENSDALE LN	Austin	556X	ML-25	78723	5100-5399
RAVENWOOD CV	Austin	463L	MF-35	78750	9800-9899
RAVENWOOD DR	Round Rock	377Z	MP-43	78665	2500-2699
RAVEY ST	Austin	614K	MG-20	78704	1600-1799
RAVINE DR	Austin	615E	MJ-21	78704	1200-1299
RAVINE RIDGE CV	Travis Co	523Z	MF-28	78746	5500-5599
RAVINE RIDGE TRL	Travis Co	523Z	MF-28	78746	4100-4399
RAWHIDE DR	Round Rock	406Q	MM-41	78681	1800-2399
RAWHIDE LN	Williamson Co	193C	MF-63	78633	100-499
RAWHIDE LOOP	Round Rock	406L	MM-41	78681	300-1899
RAWHIDE TRL	Cedar Park	373U	MF-43	78613	900-1299
RAWHIDE TRL	Lago Vista	399M	WX-41	78645	20600-21199
RAWHIDE TRL	Travis Co	610G	WZ-21	78736	10200-11399
	Travis Co	580T	WY-22	78736	11400-11999
RAY AVE	Austin	496X	ML-31	78758	10200-10399
RAY BERGLUND BLVD	Round Rock	407F	MN-42	78664	600-1399
RAYBURN LN	Austin	586D	MM-24	78723	5400-5599
RAYMOND C. EWRY LN	Austin	702D	MD-12	78748	11600-11799
RAYNER PL	Travis Co	580F	WY-24	78738	12100-12199
RAYNHAM HILL DR	Travis Co	518V	WV-28	78738	17200-17299
RAYO DE LUNA LN	Travis Co	521F	MA-30	78732	12000-12399
RAY VISTA ST	Village of Volente	461A	MA-36	78641	15800-15899
RAYWOOD DR	Austin	614Q	MH-20	78704	2700-3199
RAZIL CT	Travis Co	673W	ME-13	78748	10600-10799
REABURN ST	Austin	642M	MD-17	78749	7000-7299
READVILL CT	Austin	671C	MB-15	78739	6200-6299
READVILL LN	Austin	671C	MB-15	78739	11000-11299
REAGAN HILL DR	Austin	556B	ML-27	78752	1400-1599
REAGAN TERRACE	Austin	615K	MJ-20	78704	1000-1399
REAGAN WELLS DR	Hutto	379K	MS-44	78634	1100-1599
REAL ST	Austin	585M	MK-23	78722	2800-2899
REAL CATORCE	Austin	583X	ME-22	78746	1800-2299
REAL QUIET CV	Austin	703G	MF-12	78748	200-299
REAL QUIET DR	Austin	703G	MF-12	78748	11100-11299
REAL WIND CV	Austin	553K	ME-26	78746	1700-1899
REARDEN RD	Austin	643J	ME-17	78745	6700-6899
REATA CV	Round Rock	408J	MQ-41	78664	3300-3399
REATA DR	Travis Co	766L	MM-5	78610	11500-11799
REBECCA DR	Austin	496K	ML-32	78758	900-1199
REBECCA LN	Bastrop	744D	ED-9	78602	600-699
REBECCA RD	Williamson Co	224V	MH-58	78633	1-199
REBEL	Lakeway	489W	WW-31	78734	None
REBEL DR	Hays Co	762M	MD-5	78610	1-599
REBEL RD	Austin	615N	MJ-20	78704	2200-2399
RECREATION CT	Williamson Co	375W	MJ-43	78717	8000-8099
RECTOR LOOP	Travis Co	529C	MT-30	78653	13200-13399
	Travis Co	499U	MT-31	78653	13400-13999
RECTOR ST E	Manor	529Q	MT-29	78653	100-499
RECTOR ST W	Manor	529Q	MT-29	78653	100-399
REDBAY DR	Austin	493M	MF-32	78750	7700-7799
RED BAY DR	Williamson Co	433E	ME-39	78613	3000-3299
RED BIRD CT	Austin	462K	MC-35	78726	8100-8199
REDBIRD CV	Lago Vista	458F	WU-36	78645	2300-2399
RED BIRD DR	Cedar Park	433B	ME-39	78613	1000-1199
RED BIRD DR	Hays Co	762R	MG-3	78610	100-199
REDBIRD DR	Lago Vista	458F	WU-36	78645	21700-22099
RED BIRD LN	Austin	644P	MG-17	78745	100-399
RED BIRD TRL	Travis Co	459V	WX-34	78645	3300-4099
REDBIRD TRL	Travis Co	428A	WU-39	78654	23900-23999
RED BIRD TRL	Williamson Co	224G	MH-60	78633	1-199
RED BLUFF RD	Austin	616E	ML-21	78702	4500-5099
RED BLUFF RD	Burnet Co	426J	WQ-38	78669	200-399
RED BRANGUS DR	Travis Co	456Q	WR-36	78669	25400-26199
REDBUD	Hutto	349Z	MT-46	78634	200-299
RED BUD CV	Leander	342B	MC-48	78641	600-699
REDBUD CV	West Lake Hills	583A	ME-24	78746	1-99
RED BUD DR	Cedar Park	372Z	MD-43	78613	1000-1299
REDBUD DR	Hays Co	732L	MD-8	78610	100-199
REDBUD LN	Jonestown	400H	WZ-42	78645	18300-18399
REDBUD LN	Leander	342P	MC-47	78641	1300-1399
RED BUD LN	Round Rock	378T	MQ-43	78664	1-1399
	Round Rock	408B	MQ-42	78664	1400-2899
	Williamson Co	408K	MQ-41	78664	2900-3399
RED BUD LN N	Round Rock	378F	MQ-45	78664	100-699
	Round Rock	348X	MQ-46	78665	700-1599
	Round Rock	348P	MQ-47	78665	1600-1799
REDBUD TRL	Austin	584E	MG-24	78746	3100-3599
	Austin	583D	MF-24	78746	3600-3999
REDBUD TRL	Hays	702W	MC-10	78610	12600-12699
REDBUD TRL	San Leanna	703F	ME-12	78748	500-699
RED BUD TRL	West Lake Hills	583D	MF-24	78746	1-499
	West Lake Hills	553X	ME-25	78746	500-1399
	West Lake Hills	583B	ME-24	78746	1400-1499
RED BUD TRL	Williamson Co	378S	MQ-43	78665	1-99
RED BUD MEADOW E	Williamson Co	224H	MH-60	78633	100-199
RED BUD MEADOW W	Williamson Co	224H	MH-60	78633	100-299
RED CLIFF DR	Austin	496S	ML-31	78758	900-1199
REDCLIFF LN	Williamson Co	317W	MN-49	78665	4400-4499
RED CLOUD DR	Austin	465T	MJ-34	78759	4100-4499
RED CLOUD DR	Round Rock	406N	ML-41	78681	1900-1999
RED CLOVER LN	Austin	465M	MK-35	78727,	12600-12699
REDD ST	Austin	644A	MG-18	78745	900-1699
	Austin	614W	MG-19	78745	1700-2199
RED DEER PASS	Williamson Co	434U	MH-37	78729	12700-12799
REDDEN CV	Cedar Park	402R	MD-41	78613	1400-1499
RED EGRET DR	Travis Co	434G	MH-39	78729	13500-13599
RED ELM PKWY	Travis Co	532L	MZ-29	78621	13000-13199
RED FEATHER TRL	Travis Co	490R	WZ-32	78734	14100-14399
REDFIELD LN	Austin	525D	MK-30	78758	8600-8899
RED FOX LN	Bastrop Co	743K	EA-8	78602	100-199
RED FOX RD	Travis Co	490V	WZ-31	78734	1100-2499
REDGATE CT	Austin	671C	MB-15	78739	6300-6399
REDGATE LN	Austin	671C	MB-15	78739	10800-10999
RED GATE LN	Hays Co	638G	WV-18	78737	13300-13399
RED HAWK CV	Travis Co	672S	MC-13	78739	12000-12099
RED HAWK DR	Leander	341M	MB-47	78641	400-599
	Williamson Co	342J	MC-47	78641	600-999
RED HERON DR	Williamson Co	343W	ME-46	78641	15000-15099
RED HUMP RD	Bastrop Co	651C	MX-18	78621	100-199
RED IVY CV	Travis Co	409P	MS-41	78660	2800-2899
RED LAKE DR	Travis Co	560K	MU-26	78653	18600-18999
REDLANDS ST	Austin	525T	MJ-28	78757	1800-1999
REDLEAF LN	Austin	643T	ME-16	78745	2500-2699
RED MAPLE CV	Austin	464P	MG-35	78759	7100-7199
RED MESA HOLLOW	Travis Co	672W	MC-13	78739	12300-12599
REDMOND CV	Austin	671C	MB-15	78739	10800-10899
REDMOND RD	Austin	641Y	MB-16	78739	10500-10599
	Austin	671C	MB-15	78739	10600-10899
RED OAK	Williamson Co	222Y	MD-58	78642	1-899
RED OAK CIR	Austin	526N	ML-29	78753	100-299
RED OAK CIR	Georgetown	225D	MK-60	78633	100-199
RED OAK CIR	Round Rock	375H	MK-45	78681	2000-2199
RED OAK CIR S	Austin	526N	ML-29	78753	8200-8299
RED OAK CT	Georgetown	316A	ML-51	78628	100-199
RED OAK CV	Hays Co	669V	WX-13	78737	14400-14499
RED OAK LN	Williamson Co	281U	MB-52	78641	4300-4499
RED OAK ST	Cedar Park	372H	MD-45	78613	100-399
RED OAK VALLEY CT	Travis Co	521Q	MB-29	78732	1200-1299
RED OAK VALLEY LN	Travis Co	521L	MB-29	78732	11600-11799
REDONDO DR N	Austin	586L	MM-23	78721	1400-1699
REDONDO DR S	Austin	586L	MM-23	78721	1400-1499
RED PEBBLE RD	Austin	641X	MA-16	78739	7200-7399
RED POPPY TRL	Georgetown	225K	MJ-59	78633	100-199
	Georgetown	225P	MJ-59	78633	200-399
RED RANCH CIR	Cedar Park	402M	MD-41	78613	1100-1299
REDRICK DR	Austin	675S	MJ-13	78747	7500-7599
RED RIDGE DR	Austin	557Y	MP-25	78724	6800-6899
RED RIVER CV	Hays Co	668V	WV-13	78737	100-199
RED RIVER CV	Lago Vista	399M	WX-41	78645	9300-9499
RED RIVER DR	Williamson Co	350E	MU-48	78634	100-599
RED RIVER LN	Leander	311Z	MB-49	78641	700-899
RED RIVER LN	Pflugerville	467C	MP-36	78660	None
RED RIVER ST	Austin	585X	MJ-22	78701	100-1899
	Austin	585K	MJ-23	78705	1900-3899
	Austin	555Y	MK-25	78751	3900-4999
RED ROCK CV	Austin	642E	MC-18	78749	8000-8199
RED ROCK CV	Round Rock	407C	MP-42	78665	1700-1799
RED ROCK DR	Round Rock	407C	MP-42	78665	1800-1999
RED ROCK DR	Travis Co	468T	MQ-34	78660	None
RED STAG PL	Round Rock	346R	MM-47	78665	1300-1399
RED STONE CT	Austin	613J	ME-20	78735	4600-4799
RED STONE LN	Austin	466P	ML-35	78727	2100-2199
RED TAILED HAWK DR	Pflugerville	437V	MP-37	78660	300-599
RED TAILS DR	Travis Co	619S	MS-19	78725	500-699
RED TOWN RD	Bastrop Co	504U	ED-31	78621	900-1699
	Bastrop Co	534B	EC-30	78621	900-999
RED WAGON LN	Travis Co	401L	MB-41	78641	16400-16899
REDWATER DR	Austin	673S	ME-13	78748	1600-1799
RED WILLOW DR	Austin	611Q	MB-20	78736	8000-8599
REDWING WAY	Round Rock	407F	MN-42	78664	2000-2199
REDWOOD DR	Lago Vista	429F	WW-39	78645	6700-7099
REDWOOD LN	Pflugerville	438S	MQ-37	78660	100-199
REDWOOD TRACE	Round Rock	407B	MN-42	78664	2400-2499
RED YUCCA RD	Travis Co	517E	WS-30	78669	22200-22299
REED DR	Village of Volente	461B	MA-36	78641	7300-7699
REEDA LN	Austin	525C	MK-30	78757	8300-8399
REEDERS DR	Travis Co	618R	MR-20	78725	3900-4199
REED PARK RD	Jonestown	400U	WZ-40	78645	17200-17599
	Jonestown	430D	WZ-39	78645	17600-17999
	Jonestown	400X	WY-40	78645	18700-19299
	Travis Co	430D	WZ-39	78645	18000-18699
REED WILL DR	Travis Co	618U	MR-19	78725	14200-14299
REEDY CT	Jonestown	400M	WZ-41	78645	18100-18199
REEF LN	Williamson Co	224K	MG-59	78633	100-499
REESE CV	Travis Co	546V	WR-25	78620	9500-9799
REESE DR	Sunset Valley	643C	MF-18	78745	1-99
REESE LN	Austin	525U	MK-28	78757	6900-7099
REEVES CIR	Austin	615X	MJ-19	78741	2600-2699
REEVES LN	Bastrop Co	739H	MT-9	78612	100-199
REFLECTION BAY CT	Lakeway	519S	WW-28	78738	100-199
REFUGIO CT	Travis Co	491U	MB-31	78732	3500-3599
REGAL CT	Travis Co	587Z	MP-22	78725	9900-9999
REGAL ROW	Travis Co	703E	ME-12	78748	1100-1299
REGAL OAKS DR	Hays Co	669H	WX-15	78737	10700-10799
REGAL PARK LN	Austin	672Z	MD-13	78748	2400-2599
REGATTA CT	Lakeway	489Y	WX-31	78734	300-399
REGATTA VIEW DR	Jonestown	430U	WZ-37	78645	17400-17899
REGENCY CV	Austin	587E	MN-24	78724	5200-5299
REGENCY DR	Austin	587E	MN-24	78724	5000-5499
REGENCY LN	Round Rock	377L	MP-44	78665	1000-1099

STREET NAME	CITY or COUNTY	MAPSCO GRID	AUSTIN GRID	ZIP CODE	BLOCK RANGE O/E
REGENTS PARK	Austin	583Z	MF-22	78746	2700-2999
REGENTS WALK	Travis Co	436Z	MM-37	78728	14500-14599
REGGIE JACKSON TRL	Round Rock	378E	MQ-45	78665	600-699
REGIENE RD	Austin	586Z	MM-22	78725	6500-6799
REGINA CV	Williamson Co	381Q	MX-44	76574	1-399
REGINA DR	Hays Co	763S	ME-4	78610	100-499
REGIS DR	Pflugerville	437D	MP-39	78660	17700-18099
REICHER DR	Austin	556U	MM-25	78723	5700-6299
REID DR	Austin	495U	MK-31	78758	9200-9599
REIDS BEND	Bastrop Co	715S	EE-10	78602	100-399
REIMERS PEACOCK RD	Travis Co	517K	WS-29	78669	5300-5499
REIMS CT	Travis Co	550Q	WZ-26	78733	3400-3499
REINE'S CV	Bastrop Co	738G	MR-9	78617	100-199
REINHARDT BLVD	Georgetown	287L	MP-53	78626	100-599
REINHARDT CT	Georgetown	287L	MP-53	78626	100-199
REINLI ST	Austin	555M	MK-26	78751	900-999
	Austin	556J	ML-26	78723	1000-1199
RELIANCE DR	Buda	763K	ME-5	78610	500-899
RELIANCE CREEK DR	Austin	527G	MP-30	78754	10900-11199
REMINGTON DR	Leander	312S	MC-49	78641	900-1299
REMINGTON LN	Austin	525D	MK-30	78758	8500-8599
REMINGTON RD	Cedar Park	374Q	MH-44	78613	3800-3999
REMINGTON RUN	Bastrop	744K	EC-8	78602	100-299
REMMINGTON RD	Travis Co	490Y	WZ-31	78734	1300-1699
REMUDA CIR	Round Rock	406L	MM-41	78681	1500-1799
REMUDA TRL	Austin	643D	MF-18	78745	2200-2499
REMUDA TRL	Buda	732K	MC-8	78610	16200-16299
RENAISSANCE CT	Travis Co	466C	MM-36	78728	14000-14099
RENAISSANCE TRL	Round Rock	377G	MP-45	78665	1100-1199
RENDEZVOUS CV	Lago Vista	399H	WX-42	78645	21000-21099
RENDOVA LN	Travis Co	467M	MP-35	78660	1500-1699
	Travis Co	468J	MQ-35	78660	1700-2099
RENEGADE RD	Bastrop	715Z	EF-10	78602	100-199
RENEL DR	Austin	496P	ML-32	78758	11100-11299
RENFERT WAY	Austin	466S	ML-34	78758	12100-12299
RENFRENSHIRE DR	Austin	528P	MQ-29	78754	7000-7099
RENNALEE LOOP	Austin	496L	MM-32	78753	11900-11999
RENO DR	Austin	673D	MF-15	78745	900-1199
RENTAL CAR LN	Austin	646M	MM-17	78719	9100-9599
RENTON DR	Austin	525C	MK-30	78757	8200-8399
REPLICA RD	Travis Co	457W	WS-34	78669	23700-23899
REPUBLIC AVE	Lago Vista	429X	WW-37	78645	4600-4699
REPUBLIC OF TEXAS BLVD	Austin	613N	ME-20	78735	4500-4799
	Austin	612H	MD-21	78735	4800-5999
RESACA BLVD	Bee Cave	550R	WZ-26	78733	3000-3099
	Travis Co	551E	MA-27	78733	1500-1899
	Travis Co	550M	WZ-26	78733	1900-2999
RESEARCH BLVD	Austin	525H	MK-30	78758	7900-8799
	Austin	495U	MK-31	78758	8800-9299
	Austin	495J	MJ-32	78759	9300-10899
	Austin	465N	MJ-35	78759	10900-11999
	Austin	464H	MH-36	78759	12000-12799
RESERVE RD	Austin	584U	MH-22	78703	1200-1499
RESERVE CREEK DR	Travis Co	702G	MD-12	78748	12300-12599
RESERVIST RD	Austin	676H	MM-15	78719	3700-4299
	Austin	677A	MN-15	78719	None
RESERVOIR CT	Austin	557D	MP-27	78754	9700-9799
RESNICK DR	Round Rock	376A	ML-45	78681	2500-2599
RESTON CV	Williamson Co	347B	MN-49	78665	2100-2199
RETAMA CT	Georgetown	287G	MP-54	78626	100-199
RETAMA DR	Cedar Park	402D	MD-42	78613	1000-1099
RETAMA DR	Georgetown	287G	MP-54	78626	100-199
RETAMA ST	Austin	614D	MH-21	78704	900-999
RETEMA CT	Lakeway	519F	WW-30	78734	1-99
RETHA DR	Dripping Springs	636X	WQ-16	78620	100-399
RETREAT RD	Travis Co	487W	WS-31	78669	4400-4799
REUNION BLVD	Hays Co	670X	WY-13	78610	1000-2099
REVEILLE RD	West Lake Hills	583L	MF-23	78746	100-399
REVERE CV	Lago Vista	458D	WV-36	78645	3600-3699
REVERE RD	Austin	645S	MJ-16	78744	4400-4599
REVLON	Austin	525E	MJ-30	78757	None
REXFORD DR	Austin	556Y	MM-25	78723	3000-3299
REYES DR	Bastrop Co	680Z	MV-13	78612	100-199
REYES ST	Austin	586P	ML-23	78721	4600-4799
REYNA LN	Buda	762H	MD-6	78610	100-199
REYNA ST	Austin	644C	MH-18	78704	3800-4099
REYNA ST	Elgin	534S	EC-28	78621	100-199
REYNALDO ST	Cedar Park	372Q	MD-44	78613	1000-1099
REYNERO LN	Travis Co	737Y	MP-7	78617	14500-15499
REYNOLDS CT	Travis Co	490L	WZ-32	78734	2700-2799
REYNOLDS RD	Austin	612X	MC-19	78749	5400-5899
REYNOSA DR	Travis Co	672N	MC-14	78739	3900-4599
RHAPSODY RIDGE DR	Williamson Co	402U	MD-40	78613	1500-1599
RHEA CT	Austin	465G	MK-36	78727	12600-12799
RHETT PL	Austin	675N	MJ-14	78744	7300-7399
RHETT BUTLER DR	Austin	641Z	MB-16	78739	10200-10399
RHODES RD	Austin	586L	MM-23	78721	1800-1899
RHONDA CT	Austin	644L	MH-17	78745	500-599
RHONDA CV	Hutto	350N	MU-47	78634	1200-1299
RHONDSTAT RUN	Travis Co	402T	MC-40	78613	1000-1399
RHONE DR	Travis Co	708S	MQ-10	78617	14600-14799
RIALTO BLVD	Austin	612E	MC-21	78735	6300-7699
	Austin	611H	MB-21	78735	7700-7899
RIAS WAY	Austin	374Z	MH-43	78717	9700-9899
RIATA PARK CT	Austin	465B	MJ-36	78727	5200-5399
RIATA TRACE PKWY	Austin	464H	MH-36	78727	12100-12299
	Austin	465E	MJ-36	78727	12300-12599
	Austin	465B	MJ-36	78727	12600-12699
RIATA VISTA CIR	Austin	465B	MJ-36	78727	12500-13099
RIBBECKE AVE	Austin	586L	MM-23	78721	4600-4899
RIBBON REEF LN	Travis Co	436P	ML-38	78728	3400-3599
RIBELIN RANCH CT	Austin	493E	ME-33	78750	9800-9899
RIBELIN RANCH DR	Austin	493E	ME-33	78750	7000-7299
RICE AVE	Cedar Park	372U	MD-43	78613	1200-1299
RICES CROSSING LN	Round Rock	407A	MN-43	78664	1400-1599
RICES CROSSING RD	Taylor	353S	EA-46	76574	100-1099
	Taylor	352V	MZ-46	76574	1100-1599
RICH LN	Hays Co	764P	MG-5	78610	1200-1499
RICH TRL	Travis Co	309Q	WX-50	78641	14900-15099
RICHARD LN	Austin	554Y	MH-25	78703	2900-2999
RICHARD RD	Williamson Co	288K	MQ-53	78626	1-299
RICHARD CARLTON BLVD	Austin	435W	MJ-37	78727	5900-6099
RICHARDINE AVE	Austin	586U	MM-22	78721	1100-1199
RICHARD KING CT	Austin	642E	MC-18	78749	8100-8199
RICHARD KING TRL	Austin	642E	MC-18	78749	7900-8199
RICHARD NIXON ST	Travis Co	530F	MU-30	78653	13500-13699
RICHARDS DR	Hutto	379H	MT-45	78634	100-699
RICHARDS DR	Travis Co	679B	MS-15	78617	15300-16099
RICHARDSON LN	Austin	616S	ML-19	78741	6000-6499
RICHARD WALKER BLVD	Travis Co	466C	MM-36	78728	14300-14499
RICHCREEK RD	Austin	525Q	MK-29	78757	1200-2799
RICHELIEU RD	Austin	463C	MF-36	78750	9800-10099
RICHELLE CV	Pflugerville	437D	MP-39	78660	17800-17899
RICHERSON DR	Travis Co	490H	WZ-33	78734	15000-15299
RICHFIELD LANDING	Pflugerville	439E	MS-39	78660	2800-3199
RICHLAND LN	Williamson Co	256W	ML-55	78628	300-399
RICHLAND RD	Travis Co	441G	MX-39	78615	11400-11899
RICHLAND ST	Austin	644C	MH-18	78745	4100-4199
RICHMOND AVE	Austin	644E	MG-18	78745	4500-5099
RICHMOND ST	Cedar Park	373U	MF-43	78613	200-299
RICHWOOD DR	Austin	525G	MK-30	78757	1800-1899
RICK ST W	Taylor	353J	EA-47	76574	600-699
RICKEM CV	Austin	496B	ML-33	78758	11900-11999
RICKERHILL CT	Austin	671C	MB-15	78739	10900-10999
RICKERHILL LN	Austin	671C	MB-15	78739	5900-6199
RICKEY DR	Austin	525S	MJ-28	78757	5900-5999
	Austin	524V	MH-28	78757	6000-6199
RICK WHINERY DR	Travis Co	436R	MM-38	78728	2000-2499
RICKY CV	Austin	464T	MG-34	78759	None
RICO CV	Austin	494T	MG-31	78731	5200-5299
RIDDLE RD	Austin	673N	ME-14	78748	2100-2699
RIDDLEWOOD DR	Austin	496R	MM-32	78753	800-999
RIDER'S TRL	Travis Co	521V	MB-28	78733	500-699
RIDGE DR	Austin	586N	ML-23	78721	1100-1299
RIDGE DR	San Leanna	703F	ME-12	78748	11300-11599
RIDGE RD	Travis Co	459M	WX-35	78645	18100-18399
RIDGEBACK DR	Austin	524Q	MH-29	78731	6300-6399
RIDGEBEND DR	Williamson Co	347A	MN-48	78665	4200-4399
RIDGEBLUFF CIR	Leander	342M	MD-47	78641	1000-1099
RIDGECREST DR	Round Rock	406D	MM-42	78664	600-799
RIDGECREST DR	Travis Co	553L	MF-26	78746	1100-1599
RIDGE CREST DR	Travis Co	370W	WY-43	78641	21000-21199
RIDGECREST RD	Georgetown	256N	ML-56	78628	100-599
RIDGEFIELD LOOP	Williamson Co	346M	MM-47	78665	1300-1399
RIDGEHAVEN DR	Austin	556N	ML-26	78723	1200-1699
RIDGEHILL DR	Austin	494R	MH-32	78759	8700-8799
	Austin	495N	MJ-32	78759	8800-8899
RIDGE HOLLOW	Austin	494W	MG-31	78750	6900-7099
RIDGELEA DR	Austin	554R	MH-26	78731	3800-4199
RIDGELINE N	Austin	494Y	MH-31	78731	7800-7999
RIDGELINE BLVD	Austin	433C	MF-39	78613	12500-12999
	Austin	403Y	MF-40	78613	13000-13099
RIDGE LINE BLVD E	Georgetown	317F	MN-51	78626	100-499
RIDGE LINE BLVD W	Georgetown	317E	MN-51	78626	100-399
RIDGELINE DR	Austin	494Z	MH-31	78731	4000-4199
RIDGELINE DR	Hays Co	639K	WW-17	78737	100-199
RIDGELINE DR	Round Rock	376M	MM-44	78664	900-1199
RIDGELINE RD	Williamson Co	280T	WY-52	78641	1-499
RIDGELINE TRL	Austin	494Y	MH-31	78731	4100-4199
RIDGEMEADOW WAY	Round Rock	378Q	MR-44	78664	1-99
RIDGEMONT CIR	Leander	342M	MD-47	78641	900-999
RIDGEMONT CT	Georgetown	285Z	MK-52	78628	100-199
RIDGEMONT CT	West Lake Hills	583M	MF-23	78746	100-199
RIDGEMONT DR	Austin	556N	ML-26	78723	1200-1999
RIDGEMONT ST	Round Rock	406H	MM-42	78664	900-1399
RIDGEMOOR DR	Austin	524Y	MH-28	78731	5000-5199
RIDGE OAK DR	Austin	524U	MH-28	78731	4400-5699
RIDGE OAK DR	Georgetown	286S	ML-52	78628	100-599
RIDGE OAK RD	Austin	612X	MC-19	78749	6400-7299
RIDGEPOINT DR	Austin	556D	MM-27	78754	2200-2799
RIDGEPOLE LN	Travis Co	517M	WT-29	78669	4100-4499
RIDGE RIM DR	Travis Co	369Z	WX-43	78645	10500-10699
RIDGEROCK CV	Leander	343J	ME-47	78641	900-999
RIDGE ROCK DR	Round Rock	406J	ML-41	78681	1500-1699
RIDGE RUN	Round Rock	378Q	MR-44	78664	1-99
RIDGE RUN CT	Georgetown	285Z	MK-52	78628	200-299
RIDGE RUN DR	Georgetown	285Z	MK-52	78628	300-399
RIDGESIDE CT	Austin	524P	MG-29	78731	4400-4499
RIDGESTONE DR	Austin	524D	MH-30	78731	7600-7899
RIDGETOP DR	Round Rock	376M	MM-44	78664	1900-2099
RIDGETOP BEND	Cedar Park	374U	MH-43	78613	400-499
RIDGETOP TERRACE	Travis Co	461P	MA-35	78732	14400-14599
RIDGEVIEW CIR	Lago Vista	399X	WW-40	78645	21400-21499
RIDGEVIEW CIR	Travis Co	577Q	WT-23	78720	10400-10599
RIDGE VIEW CV	Williamson Co	283V	MF-52	78628	600-699
RIDGE VIEW DR	Leander	342M	MD-47	78641	600-899
RIDGE VIEW DR	Taylor	353T	EA-46	76574	800-999
RIDGE VIEW DR	Williamson Co	283Q	MF-53	78628	100-599
RIDGEVIEW LOOP	Lago Vista	429B	WW-39	78645	21000-21099
RIDGEVIEW RD	Lago Vista	429B	WW-39	78645	20600-21199
	Lago Vista	399X	WW-40	78645	21200-21499
RIDGEVIEW ST	Austin	614B	MG-21	78704	2300-2599
RIDGE VISTA PATH	Williamson Co	346H	MM-48	78665	4100-4199
RIDGEWAY	Jonestown	400M	WZ-42	78645	10800-10999
RIDGEWAY CV	Lago Vista	458D	WV-36	78645	3500-3599
RIDGEWAY DR	Austin	586S	ML-22	78702	1100-1199
RIDGEWELL PL	Austin	642N	MC-17	78749	9200-9299
RIDGEWOOD CV	Georgetown	286S	ML-52	78628	200-299
RIDGEWOOD CV	Williamson Co	194Y	MH-61	78633	100-199
RIDGEWOOD DR	Cedar Park	403A	ME-42	78613	300-499
RIDGEWOOD DR	Georgetown	286S	ML-52	78628	100-599
RIDGEWOOD DR	Leander	343J	ME-47	78641	1100-1699
RIDGEWOOD RD	Austin	584N	MG-23	78746	200-499
	West Lake Hills	583R	MF-23	78746	200-499
	West Lake Hills	584N	MG-23	78746	500-999
RIDGEWOOD RD E	Williamson Co	224C	MH-60	78633	100-199
	Williamson Co	194Y	MH-61	78633	200-299
RIDGEWOOD RD W	Williamson Co	224E	MG-60	78633	100-699
RIDGMAR RD	Williamson Co	313Y	MF-49	78641	1-399
	Williamson Co	343F	ME-48	78641	400-1199
RIDINGS ST	Elgin	534S	EC-28	78621	100-299
RIFLE BEND	Austin	611Q	MB-20	78736	6900-6999
RIFLE BEND DR	Georgetown	287S	MN-52	78626	2100-2399
RIGEL ST	Round Rock	346R	MM-47	78665	3800-3899
RIGSBEE CT	Austin	641Y	MB-16	78739	10700-10799
RIKER RIDGE TRL	Austin	672Z	MD-13	78748	2200-2499
RILEY CV	Round Rock	376M	MM-44	78664	600-699
RILEY RD	Rollingwood	584P	MG-23	78746	100-699
RILEY TRL	Cedar Park	374U	MH-43	78613	400-699
RIM CV	Austin	494T	MG-31	78731	7600-7799
RIMCREST CV	Austin	611R	MB-20	78735	7300-7399
RIMDALE DR	Austin	494Y	MH-31	78731	4300-4399
RIMFIRE	Leander	372F	MC-45	78641	None
RIMINI TRL	Williamson Co	434M	MH-38	78729	8000-8199
RIMNER CV	Austin	464T	MG-34	78759	6900-6999
RIMROCK CIR	Lago Vista	428V	WV-37	78645	21500-21599
RIMROCK CT	Lago Vista	428U	WV-37	78645	4200-4399
RIMROCK CV	Georgetown	285Z	MK-52	78628	100-199
RIMROCK DR	Georgetown	285Z	MK-52	78628	100-399
RIMROCK DR	Lago Vista	428U	WV-37	78645	4100-4699
RIM ROCK DR	Leander	341H	MB-48	78641	200-299
	Leander	341H	MB-48	78641	2000-2199
RIMROCK DR N	Travis Co	550M	WZ-26	78733	2200-2299
RIMROCK DR S	Travis Co	550M	WZ-26	78733	2300-2399
RIM ROCK PATH	Austin	613Z	MF-19	78745	4500-4599
RIM ROCK RD	Travis Co	366Y	WR-43	78654	28700-28899
RIMROCK TRL	Austin	586G	MM-24	78723	4500-4699
RIM ROCK TRL	Travis Co	640N	WY-17	78737	11200-11699
	Travis Co	639M	WX-17	78737	11700-11899
RIMSTONE DR	Cedar Park	372T	MC-43	78613	1300-1599
RIMSTONE TRL	Travis Co	610U	WZ-19	78736	9900-10199
RINARD RD	Travis Co	704Z	MH-10	78747	10600-11299
RINEHARDT ST	Hutto	349M	MT-47	78634	100-399
RING DR	Manor	530T	MU-28	78653	12600-13499
RING ST	Manor	530T	MU-28	78653	None
RINGSBY CV	Austin	675W	MJ-13	78747	7900-7999
RINGSBY RD	Austin	675W	MJ-13	78747	6200-6399
RINGTAIL CV	Lago Vista	399H	WX-42	78645	21100-21199
RINGTAIL CV	Williamson Co	254W	MG-55	78628	100-199
RINGTAIL RIDGE	Travis Co	582R	MD-23	78746	1800-2199
RINGWOOD RD	Austin	497E	MN-33	78753	900-999
RIO BRAVO LN	Hays Co	670P	WY-14	78737	6800-6899
RIO BRAVO LOOP	Leander	311Z	MB-49	78641	1400-1799
RIO BRAVO RD	Williamson Co	285G	MK-54	78628	100-399
RIO BRISAS CV	Round Rock	375D	MK-45	78681	2200-2299
RIO CONCHO CV	Georgetown	196W	ML-61	78628	100-199
RIO FRIO CV	Bastrop Co	738W	MQ-7	78617	100-199
RIO GABRIEL CV	Williamson Co	280B	WY-54	78642	400-499
RIO GABRIEL DR	Williamson Co	280B	WY-54	78642	100-399
RIO GRANDE AVE	Williamson Co	349H	MT-48	78634	100-399
	Williamson Co	350E	MU-48	78634	400-499
RIO GRANDE LOOP	Georgetown	196W	ML-61	78628	100-999
RIO GRANDE ST	Austin	585J	MJ-23	78701	400-1899
	Austin	585A	MJ-24	78705	1900-2999
RIO GRANDE ST E	Taylor	353J	EA-47	76574	100-999
	Taylor	353K	EA-47	76574	600-999
RIO GRANDE ST S	Taylor	352V	MZ-46	76574	700-1599
RIO GRANDE ST W	Taylor	353J	EA-47	76574	100-799
	Taylor	352R	MZ-47	76574	800-1499
RIO LEON CV	Georgetown	196W	ML-61	78628	100-199
RIO MESA DR	Travis Co	521F	MA-30	78732	1900-2899
RIO ROBLES DR	Travis Co	554J	MG-26	78746	4000-4499
RIOS ST	Hutto	349R	MT-47	78634	100-199
RIO SECO	Leander	341X	MA-46	78641	1900-1999
RIO VISTA	Georgetown	256V	MM-55	78626	100-199
	Georgetown	257S	MN-55	78626	200-299
RIO VISTA CV	Georgetown	256V	MM-55	78626	100-199
RIO VISTA DR	Austin	463A	ME-36	78726	11000-11199
RIPFORD CT	Travis Co	491U	MB-31	78732	3700-3799
RIP FORD DR	Travis Co	491U	MB-31	78732	3500-3799
RIPLEY CASTLE CV	Pflugerville	408X	MQ-40	78660	1000-1099
RIPON CV	Williamson Co	405J	MJ-41	78717	8600-8699
RIPPERTON RUN	Travis Co	402P	MC-41	78613	800-999
RIPPLE CREEK DR	Travis Co	583U	MF-22	78746	3600-3699
RIPPLE ROCK LN	Hays Co	732B	MC-9	78610	300-399
RIPPLE RUN	Austin	674H	MH-15	78744	6600-6799
RIPPLEWOOD DR	Austin	525G	MK-30	78757	8100-8199
RIPPLING CREEK CT	Travis Co	491S	MA-31	78732	3100-3199
RISA CT	Williamson Co	345X	MJ-46	78681	4000-4199
RISING HILLS CIR	Austin	464Y	MH-34	78759	10300-10399
RISING HILLS DR	Austin	464Y	MH-34	78759	5700-5999
RISING SMOKE LOOP	Travis Co	610H	WZ-21	78736	10200-10399
RISING SUN CV	Round Rock	376H	MM-45	78664	2300-2399
RITA BLANCA CIR	Travis Co	409T	MS-40	78660	20400-20499
RITCHIE DR	Austin	557U	MP-25	78724	7100-7399
RITTENHOUSE SHORE DR	Travis Co	460R	WZ-35	78734	5600-6099
RITTER DR	Travis Co	402T	MC-40	78613	1100-1299
RIVA RIDGE	Williamson Co	282Y	MD-52	78641	600-799
RIVA RIDGE RD	Austin	553C	MF-27	78746	2900-3599
RIVENDELL LN	Hays Co	700S	WY-10	78610	16600-16799
RIVER RD	Austin	554T	MG-25	78703	3300-3799
RIVER RD	Georgetown	256N	ML-56	78628	100-199
RIVER RD	Travis Co	520Q	WZ-29	78734	500-999
RIVER RD	Travis Co	650Y	MV-16	78612	3100-3799
	Travis Co	680C	MV-15	78612	3800-4299
RIVER RD	Travis Co	457A	WS-36	78669	24900-25099
	Travis Co	427W	WS-37	78669	25100-25499
RIVER ST	Austin	615B	MJ-21	78701	500-999
RIVERBANK LN	Georgetown	314L	MH-50	78628	1100-1199
RIVERBED PASS	Hutto	380J	MU-44	78634	100-199
RIVER BEND	Travis Co	550C	WZ-27	78732	10700-13099
RIVER BEND RD	Georgetown	256T	ML-55	78628	100-1299
RIVER BIRCH WAY	Pflugerville	437M	MP-38	78660	1400-1499
RIVER BLUFF CIR	Georgetown	257T	MN-55	78626	300-599
	Georgetown	257S	MN-55	78626	600-799
RIVER BOW DR	Georgetown	286W	ML-52	78628	100-299
RIVER CHASE BLVD	Georgetown	286J	ML-53	78628	100-199
	Georgetown	285H	MK-54	78628	200-599
RIVER CHASE CT	Georgetown	285H	MK-54	78628	300-398 E
RIVERCHASE DR	Jonestown	430N	WY-38	78645	18600-18699
RIVERCLIFF CV	Travis Co	456R	WR-35	78669	24400-24699
RIVERCLIFF DR	Travis Co	456Z	WR-34	78669	800-2099
RIVER CREST	Leander	342M	MD-47	78641	600-799
RIVERCREST DR	Austin	523X	ME-28	78746	2700-3799
	Travis Co	523Q	MF-29	78746	4000-4599
RIVER CROSSING CIR	Austin	615Z	MK-19	78741	1800-1899
RIVER CROSSING TRL	Williamson Co	377B	MN-45	78665	100-499
RIVER DOWN RD	Georgetown	315D	MK-51	78628	100-299
	Georgetown	286W	ML-52	78628	300-599
	Georgetown	285Z	MK-52	78628	600-799
RIVER DOWNS CV	Austin	523V	MF-28	78746	6000-6099
RIVER FERN CT	Travis Co	309S	WW-49	78641	25500-25699
RIVER FERN WAY	Georgetown	314G	MH-51	78628	1600-1699
RIVER FOREST CV	Round Rock	408A	MQ-42	78665	1300-1399
RIVER FOREST DR	Bastrop Co	776G	EH-6	78602	100-299
RIVER FOREST DR	Round Rock	408A	MQ-42	78665	1300-1499
RIVER FOREST DR	Travis Co	672P	MC-14	78739	11000-11099
RIVER GARDEN TRL	Travis Co	554S	MG-25	78746	4100-4499
RIVER HAVEN DR	Georgetown	257S	MN-55	78626	900-999
RIVER HILLS DR	Georgetown	286F	ML-54	78628	100-399

R

STREET NAME	CITY or COUNTY	MAPSCO GRID	AUSTIN GRID	ZIP CODE	BLOCK RANGE O/E
RIVER HILLS RD	Travis Co	552C	MD-27	78733	100-1399
	Travis Co	522Q	MD-29	78733	1400-2899
RIVERINE WAY	Cedar Park	373V	MF-43	78613	301-399 O
RIVERLAWN DR	Round Rock	406E	ML-42	78681	600-1199
RIVER OAK DR	Leander	342M	MD-47	78641	1200-1599
RIVER OAKS CV	Georgetown	286F	ML-54	78626	200-299
RIVER OAKS DR	Austin	496M	MM-32	78753	800-999
RIVER OAKS DR	Bastrop Co	712T	MY-10	78612	100-299
RIVER OAKS DR	San Leanna	703F	ME-12	78748	400-799
RIVER OAKS TRL	Austin	496R	MM-32	78753	11600-11699
	Austin	497N	MN-32	78753	11700-11999
RIVER PARK CV	Georgetown	257T	MN-55	78626	100-199
RIVER PARK LN	Georgetown	257S	MN-55	78626	100-199
RIVER PLACE BLVD	Austin	492L	MD-32	78730	5500-6699
	Austin	492C	MD-33	78726	6700-7699
	Travis Co	522B	MC-30	78730	3800-3999
	Travis Co	492X	MC-31	78730	4000-5499
RIVER PLANTATION DR	Austin	704E	MG-12	78747	10200-10299
	Austin	704J	MG-11	78747	10300-11599
RIVER RIDGE DR	Georgetown	286W	ML-52	78628	200-399
RIVER RIDGE DR	Travis Co	550D	WZ-27	78732	1100-1399
RIVER ROCK CT	Travis Co	702E	MC-12	78739	12500-12599
RIVER ROCK DR	Georgetown	195P	MJ-62	78633	100-299
RIVER ROCK DR	Travis Co	468P	MQ-35	78660	None
RIVER RUN	Hays Co	576K	WQ-23	78620	100-299
RIVER RUN	Williamson Co	282S	MC-52	78641	100-799
RIVERSIDE DR	Bastrop Co	775B	EE-6	78602	100-299
	Bastrop Co	775F	EE-6	78602	200-599
	Bastrop Co	776J	EG-5	78602	600-899
RIVERSIDE DR	Georgetown	256Y	MM-55	78628	500-1199
RIVERSIDE DR E	Austin	615A	MJ-21	78704	100-1299
	Austin	615K	MJ-20	78741	1300-5999
	Austin	646B	ML-18	78741	6000-7699
	Austin	646B	ML-18	78744	7700-8299
	Austin	646G	MM-18	78719	8500-8699
RIVERSIDE DR W	Austin	584Z	MH-22	78704	100-1399
	Austin	615A	MJ-21	78704	100-699
RIVERSIDE FARMS RD	Austin	615Z	MK-19	78741	2000-2399
	Austin	645D	MK-18	78741	2400-2499
RIVERSTONE DR	Austin	587D	MP-24	78724	8200-8499
RIVER TERRACE	Travis Co	521V	MB-28	78733	10600-10699
RIVER TIMBER DR	Travis Co	650F	MU-18	78617	17800-18799
RIVERTON DR	Travis Co	434V	MH-37	78729	6900-6999
	Williamson Co	434V	MH-37	78729	7000-7099
RIVER TREE CV	Georgetown	286S	ML-52	78628	100-199
RIVERVIEW CV	Georgetown	285Z	MK-52	78628	100-199
RIVERVIEW DR	Georgetown	285Z	MK-52	78628	100-599
RIVERVIEW DR	Travis Co	456M	WR-35	78669	400-499
RIVERVIEW LN	Williamson Co	441C	MX-39	78615	11300-11399
RIVERVIEW ST	Austin	615G	MK-21	78702	1700-2399
RIVERWALK DR	Hutto	379Q	MT-44	78634	100-399
RIVERWALK LN	Bastrop Co	776U	EH-4	78602	100-299
RIVERWALK TRL	Georgetown	225V	MK-58	78633	800-999
RIVERWAY LN	Leander	341D	MB-48	78641	500-699
	Leander	311Z	MB-49	78641	700-899
RIVER WIND	Blanco Co	455E	WN-35	78620	100-399
RIVER WOOD CT	Austin	524X	MG-28	78731	4500-4599
RIVERWOOD DR	Bastrop Co	745A	EE-9	78602	100-199
RIVERWOOD DR	Cedar Park	403E	ME-42	78613	500-799
RIVERWOOD DR	Georgetown	286W	ML-52	78628	100-199
RIVERY BLVD	Georgetown	286C	MM-54	78628	1100-1499
	Georgetown	256Y	MM-55	78628	1500-1699
RIVIERA CIR N	Cedar Park	403T	ME-40	78613	1000-1199
RIVIERA CIR S	Cedar Park	403X	ME-40	78613	900-1199
RIVIERA DR	Cedar Park	403U	MF-40	78613	100-1199
RIVIERA DR E	Cedar Park	403T	ME-40	78613	2100-2599
RIVIERA DR W	Cedar Park	403T	ME-40	78613	2100-2399
	Cedar Park	403X	ME-40	78613	2400-2699
RIVIERA RD	Travis Co	522P	MC-29	78733	2800-3099
RIVIERA ESTATES DR	Travis Co	461C	MB-36	78641	8000-8099
RIVINA DR	Travis Co	551P	MA-26	78733	2100-2399
RIVKA CV	Austin	645G	MK-18	78741	4600-4699
RIVULET LN	Lakeway	519U	WX-28	78738	100-299
R O DR	Travis Co	488W	WU-31	78669	3000-3099
	Travis Co	517F	WS-30	78669	3100-5099
ROAD 1	Hays Co	667H	WT-15	78620	None
ROAD 2	Hays Co	667H	WT-15	78620	None
ROAD 3	Hays Co	667M	WT-14	78620	None
ROAD 4	Hays Co	667M	WT-14	78620	None
ROAD A	Austin	495L	MK-32	78758	None
ROADRUNNER DR	Cedar Park	433A	ME-39	78613	1300-1399
ROADRUNNER LN	Austin	612V	MD-19	78749	5100-5299
ROADRUNNER RD	West Lake Hills	553U	MF-25	78746	900-999
ROADRUNNER VIEW RD	Travis Co	590M	MV-23	78653	8700-8999
ROAN LN	Austin	611T	MA-19	78736	8200-8499
ROANOAK DR	Dripping Springs	667N	WS-14	78620	100-199
ROANOKE DR	Austin	556L	MM-26	78723	6800-6899
ROANOKE DR	Williamson Co	433B	ME-39	78613	3400-3499
	Williamson Co	403X	ME-40	78613	3500-3599
ROARING FORK	Leander	371L	MB-44	78641	1300-1499
ROARING SPRINGS DR	Austin	611P	MA-20	78736	7200-7699
ROBALO RD	Austin	525L	MK-29	78757	7600-7799
ROBB LN	Round Rock	376Q	MM-44	78664	1500-1899
ROBBIE DR	Austin	495S	MJ-31	78759	8400-8699
ROBBIE CREEK CV	Austin	494S	MG-31	78750	6500-6699
ROBBINS PL	Austin	585J	MJ-23	78705	1900-1999
ROBBINS RD	Travis Co	523T	ME-28	78730	3400-3799
ROBBINS ST	Pflugerville	438W	MQ-37	78660	100-199
ROBBS RUN	Austin	554Y	MH-25	78703	2800-2899
ROBBY LN	Williamson Co	403W	ME-40	78613	2300-2399
ROBERT BROWNING ST	Austin	556W	ML-25	78723	1300-1499
ROBERT BURNS DR	Austin	642H	MD-18	78749	3800-3999
ROBERT DEDMAN DR	Austin	585K	MJ-23	78705	1900-2799
See.. East Campus Dr					
ROBERT DIXON DR	Austin	642C	MD-18	78749	6800-7099
ROBERT E LEE RD	Austin	584Y	MH-22	78704	400-899
	Austin	614B	MG-21	78704	900-1399
ROBERT F MORRISON DR	Austin	642V	MD-16	78745	3400-3499
ROBERT I WALKER BLVD	Travis Co	436U	MM-37	78728	14400-14599
ROBERT KLEBURG LN	Austin	642A	MC-18	78749	7400-7599
ROBERT L JOHNSON RD	Niederwald	795W	MJ-1	78610	100-399
ROBERTO DR	Lakeway	490W	WY-31	78734	None
ROBERTO CLEMENTE LN					
	Round Rock	378E	MQ-45	78665	3500-3599
ROBERTS AVE	Austin	614P	MG-20	78704	1600-1699
ROBERTS CIR	Williamson Co	224R	MH-59	78633	100-299
ROBERTSON ST	Austin	584Q	MH-23	78703	900-999
ROBERT T MARTINEZ JR ST	Austin	615C	MK-21	78702	1-699
ROBERT WEAVER AVE	Austin	615F	MJ-21	78702	1500-1599
ROBERT WOODING DR	Austin	703A	ME-12	78748	11300-11699
ROBIN CT	Austin	525M	MK-29	78758	8300-8399
ROBIN CT	Travis Co	520B	WY-30	78734	15000-15099
ROBIN LN	Taylor	322Y	MZ-49	76574	2000-2299
ROBIN RD	Elgin	533H	EB-30	78621	1100-1199
ROBIN RD	Hays Co	701L	MB-11	78652	2300-2899
ROBIN ST	Elgin	533R	EB-29	78621	100-199
ROBIN TRL	Lago Vista	458P	WU-35	78645	1300-1499
ROBIN TRL	Round Rock	375R	MK-44	78681	1200-1299
ROBINDALE CT	Lakeway	489Q	WX-32	78734	600-699
ROBINDALE DR	Lakeway	489Q	WX-32	78734	600-699
ROBINHOOD RD	Travis Co	459V	WX-34	78645	17200-17799
ROBINHOOD TRL	Austin	584B	MG-24	78703	1500-1799
	Austin	554X	MG-25	78703	1800-2299
ROBIN RIDGE LN	Williamson Co	433R	MF-38	78750	12100-12299
ROBINSDALE LN	Austin	556T	ML-25	78723	5200-5399
ROBINS NEST LN	Williamson Co	434N	MG-38	78729	9200-9399
ROBINSON AVE	Austin	585G	MK-24	78722	2800-3199
	Austin	585C	MK-24	78722	3300-3799
ROBINSON RD	Austin	495C	MK-33	78758	11400-11499
ROBINSON ST N	Taylor	353F	EA-48	76574	100-399
ROBINSON FAMILY RD	Travis Co	577C	WT-24	78738	9000-9199
ROBINS RUN	Hays Co	669Q	WX-14	78737	10400-10499
ROBINWOOD CIR	Austin	495R	MK-32	78758	10400-10599
ROBLE CIR	Williamson Co	226X	ML-58	78628	4000-4099
ROBLE GRANDE CIR	Williamson Co	256B	ML-57	78628	3800-3899
ROBLE ROJA DR	Williamson Co	195M	MK-62	78633	100-299
ROB ROY RD	Travis Co	552V	MD-25	78746	1-99
ROB SCOTT ST	Austin	586L	MM-23	78721	5000-5299
ROCHA DR	Buda	763E	ME-6	78610	100-199
ROCHELLE DR	Austin	672M	MD-14	78748	2900-3099
ROCHESTER LN	Austin	467X	MN-34	78753	13100-13399
ROCHESTER CASTLE WAY					
	Pflugerville	408X	MQ-40	78660	800-999
ROCK RD	Bastrop Co	621M	MX-20	78621	100-199
ROCK ST S	Georgetown	286L	MM-53	78626	200-1199
ROCK WAY	Rollingwood	584N	MG-23	78746	2800-2899
ROCKBERRY CV	Austin	493R	MF-32	78750	7400-7499
ROCK BLUFF DR	Lakeway	489Q	WX-32	78734	500-599
ROCK BLUFF PL	Travis Co	491A	MA-33	78734	4600-4699
ROCKBRIDGE TERRACE	Austin	615S	MJ-19	78741	1700-1799
ROCK CANYON CV	Travis Co	428N	WU-38	78654	3800-4399
ROCK CASTLE CV	Austin	642S	MC-16	78749	9200-9299
ROCK CHALK CT	Williamson Co	408K	MQ-41	78664	100-199
ROCK CLIFF CT	Hays Co	639K	WW-17	78737	100-199
ROCK CLIFF CV	Travis Co	309K	WW-50	78641	14600-14799
ROCK CLIFF DR	Jonestown	430B	WY-39	78645	8300-8399
	Jonestown	400X	WY-40	78645	8400-8499
ROCK CLIFF DR	Travis Co	309K	WW-50	78641	13900-14899
ROCKCLIFF RD	Austin	524W	MG-28	78746	1300-1899
	Travis Co	554A	MG-27	78746	1100-1299
	Travis Co	523Z	MF-28	78746	4600-4799
ROCK CREEK	Travis Co	460R	WZ-35	78734	15300-15699
ROCK CREEK DR	Bastrop Co	709P	MS-11	78617	1-199
ROCK CREEK DR	Round Rock	406J	ML-41	78681	1500-2099
ROCK CREEK DR	West Lake Hills	583H	MF-24	78746	800-899
ROCKCREST CIR	Austin	495J	MJ-32	78759	9100-9199
ROCKCREST DR	Austin	495N	MJ-32	78759	8900-9099
ROCKCREST DR	Georgetown	286X	ML-52	78628	100-899
ROCKDALE CIR	Austin	614T	MG-19	78704	1500-1599
ROCK DOVE LN	Williamson Co	287M	MP-53	78626	100-499
ROCKEFELLER CV	Lago Vista	458D	WV-36	78645	3600-3699
ROCKET	Lakeway	489T	WW-31	78734	100-199
ROCK FACE CT	Round Rock	345P	MJ-47	78681	600-699
ROCKFIELD LN	Bee Cave	549M	WX-26	78738	4100-4199
ROCKFORD LN	Austin	494V	MH-31	78759	4100-4199
ROCKGATE DR	Williamson Co	405A	MJ-42	78717	16300-16499
ROCK HARBOUR DR	Austin	462Q	MD-35	78726	11300-11699
ROCKHILL DR	Travis Co	460W	WY-34	78645	3100-3599
ROCK HILL RD	Williamson Co	344U	MH-46	78681	4300-4399
ROCK HOLLOW LN	Austin	526B	ML-30	78753	300-399
ROCK HOLLOW LN W	Austin	526B	ML-30	78753	300-399
ROCK HOUSE DR	Williamson Co	252A	MC-57	78642	1-499
	Williamson Co	222S	MC-58	78642	500-699
ROCKHURST LN	Austin	557N	MN-26	78723	3200-3599
ROCKHURST ST	Buda	763A	ME-6	78610	500-699
ROCKIES RUN SUMMIT	Bee Cave	549J	WW-26	78738	16100-16399
ROCKING A TRL	Travis Co	487S	WS-31	78669	22300-22899
ROCKING CHAIR RD	Austin	645S	MJ-16	78744	4600-4799
ROCKINGHAM CIR	Austin	614E	MG-21	78704	2400-2499
ROCKINGHAM DR	Austin	614E	MG-21	78704	2500-2899
ROCKING HORSE RD	Austin	672G	MD-15	78748	10000-10299
ROCKING SPUR CV	Travis Co	467D	MP-36	78660	900-999
ROCKIN J RD	Williamson Co	347Z	MP-46	78665	3500-3599
ROCKLAND DR	Austin	673S	ME-13	78748	1500-2199
ROCKLEDGE CV	Austin	524L	MH-29	78731	6800-6899
ROCKLEDGE DR	Austin	524L	MH-29	78731	3800-4099
ROCK LEDGE DR	Georgetown	287K	MN-53	78626	2300-2399
ROCK MIDDEN LN	Williamson Co	346L	MM-47	78665	700-799
ROCK MONT DR	Bastrop Co	709T	MS-10	78617	1-199
ROCKMOOR AVE	Austin	584A	MG-24	78703	1500-1799
	Austin	554X	MG-25	78703	1800-2099
ROCKMOOR DR	Georgetown	286X	ML-52	78628	200-999
ROCKNEY RD	Williamson Co	288K	MQ-53	78626	1-299
ROCKPARK CIR	Lago Vista	459A	WW-36	78645	4000-4099
ROCK PARK DR	Travis Co	583R	MF-23	78746	600-699
ROCKPARK LN	Lago Vista	459A	WW-36	78645	20300-20599
ROCK PIGEON DR	Travis Co	434G	MH-39	78729	8600-8699
ROCKPOINT CIR	Austin	524C	MH-30	78731	7600-7699
ROCKPOINT DR	Austin	524D	MH-30	78731	7500-7699
ROCK POINT DR	Bastrop Co	709P	MS-11	78617	1-199
ROCKRIDGE CT	Austin	674H	MH-15	78744	6600-6799
ROCKRIDGE DR	Austin	674H	MH-15	78744	2300-2599
ROCKRIDGE ST	Round Rock	406E	ML-42	78681	1200-1399
ROCK ROSE AVE	Austin	495C	MK-33	78758	11400-11699
	Austin	465Y	MK-34	78758	11700-11999
ROCKROSE CT	Georgetown	225Q	MK-59	78633	100-199
ROCKROSE CT	Leander	342K	MC-47	78641	1100-1199
ROCK ROSE PL	Round Rock	408A	MQ-42	78665	3000-3099
ROCK SAGE CV	Elgin	532H	MZ-30	78621	18300-18399
ROCK SHELF LN	Round Rock	345P	MJ-47	78681	3500-3699
ROCK SPRING CV	Round Rock	376S	ML-43	78681	900-999
ROCK SPRINGS CV	Williamson Co	434V	MH-37	78729	7100-7199
ROCKSTOP BLVD	Austin	433C	MF-39	78613	11500-11599
ROCK TERRACE CIR	Austin	614E	MG-21	78704	2400-2499
ROCK TERRACE DR	Austin	614E	MG-21	78704	2500-2899
ROCK TERRACE DR	Lago Vista	458D	WV-36	78645	3400-3799
ROCK VISTA RUN	Hays Co	639K	WW-17	78737	100-299
ROCK WAY CV	Rollingwood	584N	MG-23	78746	1-99
ROCK WAY DR	Travis Co	610U	WZ-19	78736	9000-9599
ROCKWELL CT	Austin	433T	ME-37	78726	11300-11399
ROCKWELL PL	Austin	433T	ME-37	78726	11400-11599
ROCKWOOD	Dripping Springs	636R	WR-17	78620	None
ROCKWOOD CIR	Travis Co	610R	WZ-20	78736	7900-8199
ROCKWOOD DR	Lago Vista	459A	WW-36	78645	3900-4099
	Lago Vista	428Z	WV-37	78645	4100-4299
ROCKWOOD LN	Austin	525F	MJ-30	78757	7800-8399
	Austin	495X	MJ-31	78757	8400-8699
ROCKWOOD LN	Cedar Park	372Q	MD-44	78613	1700-1899
ROCKWOOD PASS	Williamson Co	194C	MH-63	78633	100-199
ROCK WREN RD	Travis Co	517E	WS-30	78669	22200-23399
ROCKY DR	Travis Co	520Z	WZ-28	78732	1000-1099
ROCKY WAY	Travis Co	468P	MQ-35	78660	None
ROCKY BROOK CV	Georgetown	285P	MJ-53	78628	1100-1199
ROCKY COAST DR	Lakeway	518H	WV-30	78738	100-499
ROCKY CREEK	Travis Co	468T	MQ-34	78660	None
ROCKY CREEK DR	Pflugerville	438N	MQ-38	78660	700-1399
ROCKY FORD DR	Austin	672F	MC-15	78749	3600-3899
ROCKY HOLLOW TRL	Georgetown	256K	ML-56	78628	3200-3899
ROCKY LEDGE RD	West Lake Hills	583H	MF-24	78746	500-699
ROCKY MOUND LN	Cedar Park	372Y	MD-43	78613	1500-1599
ROCKY MOUNTAIN TRL	Round Rock	345K	MJ-47	78681	4000-4199
ROCKY RIDGE RD	Travis Co	460L	WZ-35	78734	16300-17299
ROCKY RIVER CV	West Lake Hills	583H	MF-24	78746	1-99
ROCKY RIVER RD	West Lake Hills	583G	MF-24	78746	400-1099
ROCKY SHORE LN	Travis Co	439P	MS-38	78660	3900-4099
	Travis Co	439P	MS-38	78660	None
ROCKY SPOT DR	Hays Co	669J	WW-14	78737	100-199
ROCKY SPRING RD	Austin	496R	MM-32	78753	900-1099
ROCKY TOP LN	Travis Co	432K	MC-38	78613	3200-3299
ROD RD	Travis Co	610U	WZ-19	78736	9100-9299
ROD & GUN CLUB RD	Travis Co	488N	WU-32	78669	20000-20399
ROD CAREW DR	Round Rock	378E	MQ-45	78665	3300-3799
RODEO CV	Austin	466F	ML-36	78727	13300-13399
RODEO DR	Austin	466F	ML-36	78727	2000-2499
RODEO DR	Georgetown	225C	MK-60	78633	200-298 E
RODRIGUEZ RD	Travis Co	735D	MK-9	78747	9000-9899
	Travis Co	736A	ML-9	78747	9900-10599
RODRIGUEZ ST	Hays Co	763J	ME-5	78610	100-299
ROEHAMPTON DR	Austin	643X	ME-16	78745	2400-2699
ROEMER RD	Bastrop Co	504Q	ED-32	78621	100-599
ROGART DR	Briarcliff	458N	WU-35	78669	100-799
ROGER HANKS PKWY					
	Dripping Springs	636X	WQ-16	78620	None
	Dripping Springs	666B	WQ-15	78620	None
ROGERS AVE	Austin	585M	MK-23	78722	2600-2699
ROGERS LN	Austin	587L	MP-23	78724	5200-5599
ROGERS LN W	Austin	587L	MP-23	78724	7700-7999
ROGERS LOOP	Austin	587L	MP-23	78724	None
ROGERS RD	Austin	495C	MK-33	78758	2900-3399
ROGGE LN	Austin	556T	ML-25	78723	1700-3599
ROHDE RD	Hays Co	794T	MG-1	78610	100-1799
ROLAND JOHNSON DR	Austin	556A	ML-27	78752	6900-7199
ROLLER CROSSING	Travis Co	436G	MM-39	78728	3300-3699
ROLLING BROOK LN	Cedar Park	403P	ME-41	78613	None
ROLLING CANYON TRL	Round Rock	345K	MJ-47	78681	3900-3999
ROLLING GREEN CIR	Round Rock	376M	MM-44	78664	900-1099
ROLLING GREEN DR	Lakeway	519L	WX-29	78734	200-799
ROLLING HILL	Williamson Co	375W	MJ-43	78681	3800-4099
ROLLING HILL DR	Austin	466Y	MM-34	78758	12300-12499
ROLLING HILLS CV	Lago Vista	399H	WX-42	78645	9300-9499
ROLLING HILLS DR	Williamson Co	280A	WY-54	78642	500-1199
ROLLING HILLS TRL	Lago Vista	399M	WX-41	78645	9100-9399
ROLLING MEADOW DR	Pflugerville	438S	MQ-37	78660	600-899
	Pflugerville	437V	MP-37	78660	900-1099
ROLLING MEADOW RD	Austin	642C	MD-18	78749	7200-7299
ROLLING MEADOW TRL					
	Williamson Co	224L	MH-59	78633	100-199
ROLLING OAK DR	Round Rock	377W	MN-43	78664	500-799
ROLLING OAKS TRL	Austin	463L	MF-35	78750	9200-9599
ROLLING PLAINS CT	Travis Co	432K	MC-38	78613	2600-2699
ROLLING PLAINS DR	Georgetown	314K	MG-50	78628	600-1099
ROLLING RIDGE DR	Round Rock	407H	MP-42	78665	1000-1399
ROLLING STONE CV	Austin	641X	MA-16	78739	7300-7399
ROLLING WATER DR	Pflugerville	439P	MS-38	78660	4400-4799
	Travis Co	439P	MS-38	78660	4100-4399
ROLLINGWAY CV	Williamson Co	375X	MJ-43	78681	8700-8799
ROLLINGWAY DR	Williamson Co	375T	MJ-43	78681	600-799
ROLLINGWOOD DR	Austin	584S	MG-22	78746	2300-2399
	Rollingwood	584N	MG-23	78746	2400-4999
ROLLINGWOOD RD	West Lake Hills	583R	MF-23	78746	5000-5399
ROLLINS DR	Travis Co	578A	WU-24	78738	8600-8899
ROLLS RD	Williamson Co	281T	MA-52	78641	700-899
ROLSTON PL	Travis Co	432R	MD-38	78726	12100-12299
ROMA PL	Austin	586V	MM-22	78721	None
ROMA ST	Austin	614M	MH-20	78704	1600-1699
ROMAYNE LN	Austin	673L	MF-14	78748	8900-8999
ROMEO DR	Cedar Park	372F	MC-45	78613	2200-2499
ROMERIA DR	Austin	525Y	MK-28	78757	800-1699
	Austin	525X	MJ-28	78757	1700-2199
ROMFORD DR	Austin	614T	MG-19	78704	1800-1899
ROMNEY RD	Austin	673M	MF-14	78748	8400-8599
RONALD RD	Williamson Co	288K	MQ-53	78626	1-199
RONALD W REAGAN BLVD					
	Cedar Park	374A	MG-45	78641	13200-13899
	Leander	343C	MF-48	78641	15800-16699
	Leander	313Y	MF-49	78641	16700-18099
	Williamson Co	343C	MF-48	78641	13900-15799
	Williamson Co	283J	ME-53	78628	18100-21899
	Williamson Co	252D	MD-57	78642	21900-23600
	Williamson Co	222G	MD-59	78642	23700-25900
	Williamson Co	192Z	MD-61	78633	26000-26699
	Williamson Co	193S	ME-61	78633	26700-28699
RONAY DR N	Briarcliff	458S	WU-34	78669	100-599
RONAY DR S	Briarcliff	458W	WU-34	78669	100-399
	Briarcliff	457Z	WT-34	78669	400-699
RONCHAMPS DR	Williamson Co	405F	MJ-42	78681	6000-6099
RONSON ST	Austin	555S	MJ-25	78705	3700-3799
RONWOOD DR	Austin	463C	MF-36	78750	10500-10599
ROOKERY LN	Austin	497J	MN-32	78753	None
ROONEY CV	Austin	641W	MA-16	78739	11200-11299
ROOSEVELT AVE	Austin	555F	MJ-27	78756	5300-5699

R

STREET NAME	CITY or COUNTY	MAPSCO GRID	AUSTIN GRID	ZIP CODE	BLOCK RANGE O/E
ROOSEVELT CV	Lago Vista	458D	WV-36	78645	3600-3699
ROOSEVELT ST	Bastrop	745A	EE-9	78602	1700-1899
ROOSTER SPRINGS RD	Hays Co	639N	WW-17	78737	13100-13299
ROPERS DR	Pflugerville	437Z	MP-37	78660	None
ROSALINA LOOP	Williamson Co	348P	MQ-47	78665	3400-3799
ROSANKY ST	Bastrop	745C	EF-9	78602	1500-1599
ROSA WELLS LN	Travis Co	436U	MM-37	78728	15000-15099
ROSE DR	Hays Co	636T	WQ-16	78620	100-299
ROSE LN	Caldwell Co	767U	MP-4	78616	100-298 E
ROSE ST	Austin	584V	MH-22	78703	1100-1199
ROSE ST	Buda	762D	MD-6	78610	100-299
ROSEBERRY ST	Buda	733W	ME-7	78610	400-699
ROSEBROUGH DR	Austin	675X	MJ-13	78747	6200-6799
ROSEBUD LN	Georgetown	225V	MK-58	78628	100-199
ROSEBUD PL	Williamson Co	375Q	MK-44	78681	18000-18099
ROSEBUD SPRING	Hays Co	762F	MD-4	78610	100-199
ROSECLIFF DR	Georgetown	195T	MJ-61	78633	100-399
ROSEDALE AVE	Austin	555N	MJ-26	78756	3900-4799
ROSEDALE BLVD	Georgetown	225Z	MK-58	78628	100-599
	Georgetown	226S	ML-58	78628	600-1199
ROSEDALE TERRACE	Austin	615N	MJ-20	78704	800-999
ROSEFINCH TRL	Austin	583Q	MF-23	78746	3300-3499
ROSEGLEN DR	Cedar Park	372N	MC-44	78613	2400-2499
ROSE GRASS LN	Travis Co	517E	WS-30	78669	22100-22199
ROSE HILL CIR	Austin	643M	MF-17	78745	5400-5599
ROSE HILL RD	Travis Co	500T	MU-31	78653	14400-14699
ROSEHIP LN	Travis Co	467G	MP-36	78660	15200-15299
ROSE MALLOW WAY	Austin	703G	MF-12	78748	100-299
ROSEMARY CV	Georgetown	257T	MN-55	78626	100-199
ROSEMARY LN	Austin	526K	ML-29	78753	8500-8599
ROSEMARY LN	Round Rock	407B	MN-42	78664	2000-2299
ROSEMARY HOLLOW	Buda	732S	MC-7	78610	100-399
ROSEMARY RIDGE DR	Travis Co	704C	MH-12	78747	None
ROSE MAY CV	Williamson Co	345S	MJ-46	78681	4000-4099
ROSEMONT CT	Leander	343J	ME-47	78641	900-999
ROSEMONT ST	Austin	556E	ML-27	78723	1000-1099
ROSEMOUNT CV	Round Rock	377Z	MP-43	78665	2700-2799
ROSEMOUNT DR	Round Rock	377Z	MP-43	78665	600-799
ROSENBERRY DR	Austin	675W	MJ-13	78747	7900-8199
ROSENBOROUGH DR	Austin	675W	MJ-13	78747	6300-6799
ROSENBOROUGH DR	Round Rock	407G	MP-42	78665	1700-1799
ROSENBOROUGH LN	Round Rock	407G	MP-42	78665	1800N-1899N
	Round Rock	407G	MP-42	78665	1700S-1799S
ROSE PAVONIA PL	Travis Co	436Z	MM-37	78728	14900-14999
ROSESPRING	Williamson Co	283D	MF-54	78628	100-399
ROSETHORN DR	Austin	496A	ML-33	78758	11900-12099
ROSEWOOD AVE	Austin	585U	MK-22	78702	1200-2699
ROSEWOOD CT	Round Rock	407N	MN-41	78664	1600-1699
ROSIE LN	Cedar Park	372U	MD-43	78613	1300-1399
ROSITA CT	Austin	702C	MD-12	78748	12100-12199
ROSS CV	Round Rock	408J	MQ-41	78664	3300-3399
ROSS LN	Lago Vista	458D	WV-36	78645	3300-3499
ROSS RD	Austin	678J	MQ-14	78617	5300-5699
	Travis Co	678J	MQ-14	78617	4500-5299
	Travis Co	677R	MP-14	78617	5700-7099
ROSS ST	Elgin	534E	EC-30	78621	800-899
ROSS ST	Hutto	349Z	MT-46	78634	300-399
ROSSEAU ST	Travis Co	618R	MR-20	78725	14200-14499
ROSSELLO DR	Williamson Co	434R	MH-38	78729	13400-13499
ROSSETTI DR	Austin	556G	MM-27	78752	1900-1999
ROSSON DR	Travis Co	611Y	MB-19	78736	7900-8199
ROSSPORT BEND	Williamson Co	343T	ME-46	78641	1500-1799
ROTAN DR	Austin	641D	MB-18	78749	6300-6799
ROTHERHAM DR	Austin	497N	MN-32	78753	11700-12099
ROTUNDA VIEW	Travis Co	705J	MJ-11	78747	6700-6798 E
ROUGES ROOST DR	Lakeway	519L	WX-29	78734	100-199
ROUGH HOLLOW	Lakeway	518H	WV-30	78734	None
	Lakeway	518H	WV-30	78738	None
ROUGHNECK CV	Lago Vista	399H	WX-42	78645	21100-21199
ROUNDABOUT LN	Round Rock	408J	MQ-41	78664	2400-3399
ROUND MOUNTAIN CIR	Travis Co	310K	WY-50	78641	23000-23699
ROUND MOUNTAIN DR N	Travis Co	489V	WX-31	78734	100-499
ROUND MOUNTAIN RD	Travis Co	340A	WY-48	78641	14300-14599
	Travis Co	310B	WY-51	78641	14600-17399
ROUND ROCK AVE	Round Rock	376Y	MM-43	78664	100-699
	Round Rock	376W	ML-43	78681	700-1999
	See.. RM Rd 620				
	Round Rock	375Z	MK-43	78681	2000-2499
ROUNDROCK RD	Jonestown	400D	WZ-42	78645	18300-18599
ROUND ROCK RANCH BLVD					
	Round Rock	407G	MP-42	78665	2900-2999
ROUND ROCK WEST CV	Round Rock	406B	ML-42	78681	1300-1399
ROUND ROCK WEST DR	Round Rock	406B	ML-42	78681	300-899
ROUND TABLE CV	Austin	553C	MF-27	78746	5800-5999
ROUND TABLE RD	Austin	553G	MF-27	78746	2800-2999
ROUNDTOP CIR	Bee Cave	580A	WY-24	78738	13100-13199
ROUNDUP LN	Pflugerville	467C	MP-36	78660	None
ROUNDUP TRL	Austin	613Z	MF-19	78745	4500-4699
	Austin	643D	MF-18	78745	4700-4899
ROUNDUP TRL	Lago Vista	429F	WW-39	78645	20700-20999
ROUNDUP TRL	Pflugerville	467C	MP-36	78660	None
ROUNDUP TRL	Round Rock	406G	MM-42	78681	1300-1799
ROUNDUP WAY	Lago Vista	429P	WW-38	78645	5600-5799
ROUNDVILLE LN	Williamson Co	407T	MN-40	78664	1-99
ROUNTREE DR	Austin	586E	ML-24	78722	2000-2299
ROUNTREE RANCH LN	Austin	403M	MF-41	78717	14000-14499
ROWAN DR	Georgetown	226S	ML-58	78628	1200-1499
ROWE LN	Travis Co	409V	MT-40	78660	1700-3199
	Williamson Co	410S	MU-40	78660	None
ROWE LOOP	Pflugerville	409N	MS-41	78660	1700-2199
ROWEL DR	Austin	464J	MG-35	78759	8100-8199
ROWENA ST	Austin	555U	MK-26	78751	4700-5099
ROWLAND DR	Austin	644L	MH-17	78745	200-499
ROWLANDS SAYLE RD	Austin	674X	MG-13	78745	9200-9499
ROWLEY DR	Travis Co	402P	MC-41	78613	1100-1299
ROWOOD DR	Travis Co	677W	MN-13	78617	6600-6699
ROWOOD RD	Austin	555Z	MK-25	78723	4400-4599
ROXANNA DR	Austin	673J	ME-14	78748	9300-9999
ROXANNE'S RUN	Travis Co	437S	MN-37	78660	1300-1499
ROXBOROUGH ST	Williamson Co	434P	MG-38	78729	8900-9099
ROXBURY LN	Austin	641Y	MB-16	78739	6000-6199
ROXIE DR	Austin	434W	MG-37	78729	12100-12399
ROXMOOR DR	Austin	556U	MM-25	78723	2500-2699
ROYAL CT	Travis Co	588N	MQ-23	78724	9800-9899
ROYAL DR	Georgetown	256V	MM-55	78626	100-299
ROYAL LN	Cedar Park	372V	MD-43	78613	500-1099
ROYAL ST	Taylor	353F	EA-48	76574	100-199
ROYAL WAY	Hays Co	700J	WY-11	78610	100-199
ROYAL APPROACH DR	Austin	523Y	MF-28	78746	6500-6799
ROYAL ASCOT DR	Pflugerville	409J	MS-41	78660	1600-1799
ROYAL ASHDOWN DR	Austin	404D	MH-42	78717	15800-15999
ROYAL BIRKDALE OVERLOOK					
	Travis Co	582M	MD-23	78746	6200-6499
ROYAL BURGESS DR	Williamson Co	408D	MR-42	78634	100-299
	Williamson Co	408C	MR-42	78664	400-999
ROYAL CREST DR	Austin	615P	MJ-20	78741	1400-1799
ROYAL DUBLIN DR	Austin	404H	MH-42	78717	15600-15699
ROYAL HILL DR	Austin	615W	MJ-19	78741	1600-1799
ROYAL LYTHAM DR	Austin	674C	MG-12	78747	2400-2599
ROYAL NEW KENT DR	Austin	404C	MH-42	78717	9800-10199
ROYAL OAK CV	Lakeway	519G	WX-30	78734	100-199
ROYAL OAK LN	Lakeway	519G	WX-30	78734	100-199
ROYAL PALMS DR	Austin	646G	MM-18	78744	1-99
ROYAL PINES DR	Bastrop Co	746U	EH-7	78602	100-199
ROYAL POINTE DR	Pflugerville	408S	MQ-40	78660	18600-18799
ROYAL PORT RUSH DR	Round Rock	378T	MQ-43	78664	3700-3799
ROYAL TARA CV	Austin	404F	MG-42	78717	10600-10699
ROYAL TROON CV	Round Rock	378X	MQ-43	78664	3700-3899
ROYAL TROON DR	Round Rock	378T	MQ-43	78664	3800-3899
ROYAL VISTA BLVD	Williamson Co	344V	MH-46	78681	3400-3599
ROYAL WOOD DR	Austin	464A	MG-36	78750	8700-8899
ROY BUTLER DR	Austin	404C	MH-42	78717	10100-11099
ROYCE LN	Cedar Park	372Q	MD-44	78613	1400-1599
ROYCE LN	Williamson Co	434M	MH-38	78729	7900-8199
ROY CREEK LN	Hays Co	638J	WU-17	78620	400-599
ROY DAVIS RD	Bastrop Co	534Y	ED-28	78621	100-199
ROY RIVERS RD	Elgin	533L	EB-29	78621	100-199
ROYSTER AVE	Austin	647Q	MP-17	78617	3000-3199
ROYSTON LN	Pflugerville	437K	MN-38	78664	1300-1899
ROZNOVAK ST	Hutto	349M	MT-47	78634	100-799
R TREVINO ST	Travis Co	766J	ML-5	78610	None
RUBIO ST	Round Rock	406G	MM-42	78664	500-799
RUBLES CT	Leander	312S	MC-49	78641	700-899
RUBY DR	Travis Co	496Y	MM-31	78753	800-899
RUBY DR	Williamson Co	193L	MF-62	78633	100-299
RUBY ISLE DR	Leander	342Y	MD-46	78641	700-799
RUBY RED DR	Travis Co	436L	MM-38	78728	3400-3699
RUBY SPRINGS TRL	Lago Vista	429L	WX-38	78645	19700-19799
RUCKER ST	Georgetown	286G	MM-54	78626	600-799
RUDDER DR	Lakeway	519E	WW-30	78738	100-199
RUDDINGTON DR	Austin	673M	MF-14	78748	8500-8799
RUDDY DUCK LN	Cedar Park	373Z	MF-43	78613	1500-1599
RUDI CV	Austin	464T	MG-34	78759	6900-6999
RUE ST	Austin	555E	MJ-27	78731	4600-4799
RUE DE ST GERMAINE	Travis Co	554S	MG-25	78746	2000-2199
RUE DE ST RAPHAEL	Travis Co	554S	MG-25	78746	3800-3899
RUE DE ST TROPEZ	Travis Co	554S	MG-25	78746	1800-2099
RUEL CV	Williamson Co	405E	MJ-42	78717	15900-15999
RUE LE FLEUR DR	Austin	674H	MH-15	78744	4700-4899
RUELLIA DR	Georgetown	225D	MK-60	78633	100-199
RUFFED GROUSE CV	Pflugerville	438J	MQ-38	78660	1100-1199
RUFFED GROUSE DR	Austin	496E	ML-33	78758	11400-11799
RUFUS DR	Austin	525Z	MK-28	78752	6900-7199
RUGGED EARTH DR	Hays Co	639W	WW-16	78737	100-399
RUGGIO RD	Travis Co	439Q	MT-38	78634	16700-16899
RUIDOSA ST	Travis Co	706Q	MM-11	78719	10500-10699
RUMFELDT ST	Travis Co	618R	MR-20	78725	14500-14799
RUMMEL RANCH RUN	Cedar Park	402G	MD-42	78613	500-599
RUM RUNNER RD	Travis Co	490D	WZ-33	78734	4300-4499
RUNDBERG LN E	Austin	526B	ML-30	78753	100-1499
RUNDBERG LN W	Austin	526A	ML-30	78758	800-1399
	Austin	495V	MK-31	78758	1400-2399
RUNDELL PL	Austin	614F	MG-21	78704	2000-2399
RUNNEL RIDGE RD	Travis Co	529M	MT-29	78653	11300-11499
RUNNELS CT	Travis Co	491U	MB-31	78732	3700-3799
RUNNERS RIDGE	Pflugerville	437Y	MP-37	78660	600-899
RUNNING BIRD LN	Austin	466X	ML-34	78758	12100-12499
RUNNING BROOK CV	Lago Vista	399M	WX-41	78645	9200-9399
RUNNING BROOK DR	Austin	556T	ML-25	78723	1800-1999
RUNNING BRUSH CV	Austin	403H	MF-42	78717	11700-11799
RUNNING BRUSH LN	Austin	403M	MF-41	78717	11400-11699
RUNNING BUCK LN	Williamson Co	433L	MF-38	78750	10800-10999
RUNNING DEER DR	Austin	465P	MJ-35	78759	4700-4899
RUNNING DEER LN	Dripping Springs	636Q	WR-17	78620	100-399
RUNNING DEER TRL	Travis Co	703W	ME-10	78652	13000-13199
RUNNING DEER TRL	Travis Co	490V	WZ-31	78734	14000-14999
RUNNING DOE LN	Travis Co	371V	MB-43	78613	13100-13299
RUNNING FOX TRL	Austin	465T	MJ-34	78759	11700-11799
RUNNING ROPE	Austin	524C	MH-30	78731	7100-7399
RUNNING ROPE CIR	Austin	524C	MH-30	78731	7200-7299
RUNNING WATER DR	Austin	675W	MJ-13	78744	7200-7499
	Austin	675W	MJ-13	78747	7500-8099
RUNNING WATER ST	Georgetown	226A	ML-60	78633	100-199
RUNNING WATER WAY	Hays Co	668R	WV-14	78737	100-299
RUNNINGWAY DR	Williamson Co	375T	MJ-43	78681	100-199
RUNNING WYLD	Leander	372A	MC-45	78641	2600-2699
RUN OF THE OAKS	Austin	614X	MG-19	78704	3800-4099
RUPEN CT	Lakeway	489Y	WX-31	78734	100-199
RUPEN DR	Lakeway	489Y	WX-31	78734	100-599
RURAL SPACE RD	Williamson Co	280X	WY-52	78641	1-599
RUSH RD	Travis Co	520Z	WZ-28	78732	10800-10899
RUSH CREEK LN	Travis Co	521J	MA-29	78732	12500-12899
RUSHMORE CV	Georgetown	195V	MK-61	78633	100-199
RUSK CT	Austin	586D	MM-24	78723	5400-5499
RUSK CT	Round Rock	377Z	MP-43	78665	2500-2599
RUSK LN	Williamson Co	258N	MQ-56	78626	1-599
RUSK RD	Round Rock	377Z	MP-43	78665	600-999
RUSK RD	Round Rock	407H	MP-42	78665	1000-1499
RUSKIN PASS	Williamson Co	375S	MJ-43	78717	9300-9399
RUSSELL DR	Austin	614W	MG-19	78745	4400-4599
RUSSELL LN	Hays Co	636N	WQ-17	78620	100-199
RUSSELL ST	Pflugerville	437V	MP-37	78660	100-399
RUSSET HILL DR	Austin	586H	MM-24	78723	4700-4999
RUSSET VALLEY DR	Cedar Park	403E	ME-42	78613	400-899
RUSSWOOD CV	Williamson Co	344V	MH-46	78681	1000-1099
RUST RD	Williamson Co	433L	MF-38	78750	11800-11999
RUSTED NAIL CV	Williamson Co	433G	MF-39	78750	12300-12499
RUSTIC CV	Williamson Co	405E	MJ-42	78717	8900-8999
RUSTIC LN	Burnet Co	396T	WQ-40	78669	800-1399
	Burnet Co	426A	WQ-39	78669	None
RUSTIC LN	Williamson Co	405E	MJ-42	78717	15800-16199
RUSTIC CEDAR TRL	Williamson Co	225E	MJ-60	78633	100-199
RUSTIC MANOR CT	Williamson Co	433L	MF-38	78750	12300-12399
RUSTIC MANOR LN	Williamson Co	433L	MF-38	78750	10800-11099
RUSTIC OAK LN	Austin	673A	ME-15	78748	2300-2499
RUSTIC RIVER CV	Travis Co	554J	MG-26	78746	3200-3299
RUSTIC ROCK DR	Austin	464R	MG-36	78750	11400-11799
RUSTLE CV	Williamson Co	255H	MK-57	78628	4100-4199
RUSTLE CV E	Georgetown	255H	MK-57	78628	100-199
RUSTLE LN	Williamson Co	433Q	MF-38	78750	11800-11999
RUSTLERS RD	Round Rock	376J	ML-44	78681	1500-1899
RUSTLERS WAY	Lago Vista	399H	WX-42	78645	21100-21199
RUSTLING CIR	Austin	524C	MH-30	78731	7600-7699
RUSTLING CV	Austin	524C	MH-30	78731	7600-7699
RUSTLING RD	Austin	524C	MH-30	78731	7600-7699
	Austin	494Y	MH-31	78731	7700-7799
RUSTLING OAKS TRL	Austin	464L	MH-35	78759	6700-6899
RUSTOWN DR	Austin	465P	MJ-35	78727	4700-4899
RUSTY DR	Austin	646K	ML-17	78744	2800-2899
RUSTY FIG DR	Austin	493V	MF-31	78750	6900-7299
RUSTY NAIL LOOP	Round Rock	376N	ML-44	78681	1600-1899
RUSTY RIDGE DR	Austin	524L	MH-29	78731	6300-6599
RUTERSVILLE E	Georgetown	287J	MN-53	78626	1000-1199
RUTERSVILLE W	Georgetown	287J	MN-53	78628	1000-1099
RUTGERS AVE	Austin	525L	MK-29	78757	7600-7899
RUTGERS DR	Pflugerville	467H	MP-36	78660	1000-1199
RUTH AVE	Austin	525U	MK-28	78757	900-1599
RUTHERFORD DR	Leander	343J	ME-47	78641	1000-1999
RUTHERFORD LN	Austin	526T	ML-28	78753	800-1499
	Austin	526Y	MM-28	78754	1500-1899
RUTHERFORD PL	Austin	615J	MJ-20	78704	800-899
RUTHERFORD B HAYES ST	Travis Co	530F	MU-29	78653	12300-12699
RUTHERGLEN DR	Austin	642K	MC-17	78749	4800-4899
RUTHIE RUN	Cedar Park	372T	MC-43	78613	1700-1999
RUTLAND DR	Austin	496W	ML-31	78758	800-1499
	Austin	495R	MK-32	78758	1500-2599
RUTLAND VILLAGE EAST	Austin	495V	MK-31	78758	10000-10399
RUTLAND VILLAGE WEST	Austin	495R	MK-32	78758	10200-10299
RUTLEDGE LN	Austin	643G	MF-18	78745	5900-6099
RUTLEDGE SPUR	Austin	404W	MG-40	78717	13500-13899
RUTTER LN	Travis Co	639D	WX-18	78737	10800-11299
RUXTON CV	Austin	641M	MB-17	78749	9000-9099
RUXTON LN	Austin	641M	MB-17	78749	6400-6799
RUZIN LN	Travis Co	619N	MS-20	78725	15100-15199
RYAN CV	Hutto	379G	MT-45	78634	100-199
RYAN DR	Austin	525U	MK-28	78757	6900-7199
RYAN DR	Briarcliff	458W	WU-34	78669	21800-21899
	Briarcliff	457Z	WT-34	78669	21900-21999
RYAN LN	Georgetown	256U	MM-55	78628	200-399
RYAN JORDAN LN	Cedar Park	402F	MC-42	78613	300-399
RYAN MATTHEW DR	Austin	466B	ML-36	78727	13500-13599
RYDALWATER LN	Austin	528F	MQ-30	78754	11600-11899
RYDALWATER BRIDGE	Austin	528F	MQ-30	78754	6400-6499
RYDELL LN	Taylor	322X	MY-49	76574	2500-2599
RYDEN ST	Travis Co	498S	MQ-31	78653	12300-12399
RYDERS RIDGE	Williamson Co	347U	MP-46	78665	700-799
RYE ST N	Round Rock	376V	MM-43	78664	200-399
RYEGATE DR	Travis Co	560N	MU-26	78653	18100-18199
RYOAKS CV	Austin	404Q	MH-41	78717	9600-9699
RYON CV	Round Rock	375M	MK-44	78681	1800-1899
RYON LN	Round Rock	375R	MK-44	78681	1700-1799

S

STREET NAME	CITY or COUNTY	MAPSCO GRID	AUSTIN GRID	ZIP CODE	BLOCK RANGE O/E
SABA CV	Cedar Park	372L	MD-44	78613	900-999
SABAL PALM RD	Travis Co	619A	MS-21	78724	15100-15299
SABER TRL	Williamson Co	433L	MF-38	78750	12200-12399
SABER CREEK CV	Austin	464J	MG-35	78759	10600-10699
SABER CREEK TRL	Austin	464J	MG-35	78759	8300-8599
SABERTOOTH DR	Williamson Co	405B	MJ-42	78681	16700-16999
SABINAL TRL	Williamson Co	432D	MD-39	78613	2500-2999
SABINAL MESA DR	Travis Co	672N	MC-14	78739	11400-11499
SABINAS CT	Williamson Co	226U	MM-58	78628	800-899
SABINAS DR	Leander	312S	MC-49	78641	None
SABINE DR	Williamson Co	255M	MK-56	78628	100-599
SABINE ST	Austin	585X	MJ-22	78701	400-699
	Austin	585T	MJ-22	78701	1100-1299
SABLE OAKS DR	Round Rock	378T	MQ-43	78664	4000-5099
SABLE TRAIL CT	Round Rock	407F	MN-42	78664	800-899
SABRINA CV	Austin	705B	MJ-12	78747	8400-8499
SABRINA DR	Austin	705A	MJ-12	78747	6700-6999
SABRINA DR	Taylor	353B	EA-48	76574	400-499
SACAHUISTA CT	Austin	463D	MF-36	78750	11200-11299
SACBE CV	Austin	643S	ME-16	78745	3100-3199
SACRAMENTO DR	Austin	614U	MH-19	78704	400-599
SACRED ARROW DR	Austin	613J	ME-20	78735	4400-4499
SACRED MOON CV	Travis Co	554E	MG-27	78746	3500-3599
SADDLE CIR	Austin	465K	MJ-35	78727	5100-5199
SADDLE CIR	Travis Co	766L	MM-5	78610	12800-12999
SADDLE DR	Austin	465K	MJ-35	78727	4900-5099
SADDLE TRL	Georgetown	225C	MK-60	78633	100-199
SADDLE BACK PASS	Bee Cave	579H	WX-24	78738	13400-13699
SADDLEBACK RD	Hays Co	669J	WW-14	78737	100-499
	Hays Co	668M	WV-14	78737	500-699
SADDLE BLANKET DR	Hays Co	577J	WS-23	78620	200-399
SADDLE BLANKET PL	Leander	372B	MC-45	78641	2700-2799
SADDLEBLANKET TRL	Hays Co	763P	ME-5	78610	100-199
SADDLEBROOK CIR	Cedar Park	403E	ME-42	78613	900-999
SADDLEBROOK TRL	Williamson Co	434L	MH-38	78729	13300-13499
SADDLEBROOK CANYON CT					
	Travis Co	426L	WR-38	78669	1100-1399
SADDLEGIRTH LN	Travis Co	467G	MP-36	78660	15000-15099
SADDLE HORN CV	Austin	673K	ME-14	78748	1300-1399
SADDLEHORN DR	Hays Co	577K	WS-23	78620	None
	Travis Co	577E	WS-24	78620	100-699
SADDLE MOUNTAIN TRL	Travis Co	672T	MC-13	78739	11300-11799
SADDLER LN	Austin	587G	MP-24	78724	6100-6399
SADDLERIDGE CV	Austin	494H	MH-33	78759	5100-5199
SADDLE RIDGE DR	Cedar Park	374Q	MH-44	78613	100-399
SADDLE RIDGE DR N	Cedar Park	374Q	MH-44	78613	100-199
SADDLESTRING TRL	Travis Co	672T	MC-13	78739	3400-3799
SADDLETREE LN	Hays Co	577J	WS-23	78620	100-699
	Hays Co	576M	WR-23	78620	700-799
SAFFRON ST	Austin	642M	MD-17	78749	7300-7499
SAFFRON SPRINGS	Buda	732S	MC-7	78610	100-199
SAGE CT	Hays Co	700J	WY-11	78610	None
SAGE CT	Pflugerville	438T	MQ-37	78660	700-799
SAGE DR	Travis Co	464K	MG-35	78759	7900-7999
SAGE ST	Jonestown	400H	WZ-42	78645	10900-11099
SAGE BOOT DR	Pflugerville	468F	MQ-36	78660	400-1699
SAGEBRUSH CIR	Austin	613Z	MF-19	78745	4700-4799

STREET NAME	CITY or COUNTY	MAPSCO GRID	AUSTIN GRID	ZIP CODE	BLOCK RANGE O/E
SAGEBRUSH CIR	Hays Co	732F	MC-9	78610	12700-12899
SAGE BRUSH CT	Williamson Co	285H	MK-54	78628	200-299
SAGEBRUSH DR	Austin	496T	ML-31	78758	800-999
SAGEBRUSH DR	Round Rock	406G	MM-42	78681	1200-1699
SAGEBRUSH TRL	Austin	613Z	MF-19	78745	4600-4799
SAGEBRUSH TRL	Lago Vista	399S	WW-40	78645	7600-7799
SAGE CANYON DR	Cedar Park	373R	MF-44	78613	2100-2399
SAGE CREEK LOOP	Austin	615S	MJ-19	78704	2100-2199
SAGE GROUSE DR	Travis Co	434G	MH-39	78729	13400-13799
SAGE HEN CIR	Austin	465K	MJ-35	78727	12100-12199
SAGE HEN CT	Austin	465K	MJ-35	78727	12100-12199
SAGE HEN CV	Austin	465K	MJ-35	78727	12100-12199
SAGE HEN DR	Austin	465K	MJ-35	78727	4800-4999
SAGE HILL PASS	Blanco Co	455L	WP-35	78620	100-299
SAGE HOLLOW CIR	Austin	496J	ML-32	78758	1600-1699
SAGE HOLLOW DR	Austin	496J	ML-32	78758	10900-11299
SAGE MOUNTAIN TRL	Austin	611L	MB-20	78736	8300-8499
SAGE OAK CV	Austin	464P	MG-35	78759	10900-10999
SAGE OAK TRL	Austin	464P	MG-35	78759	7300-7499
SAGER DR	Austin	645A	MJ-18	78741	1900-2099
SAGEWOOD DR	Taylor	322Q	MZ-50	76574	1200-1499
SAGO PALM TRL	Travis Co	532Q	MZ-29	78621	12800-12999
SAGUARO DR	Hays Co	732P	MC-8	78610	100-199
SAGUARO RD	Austin	674R	MH-14	78744	4700-4899
SAHARA AVE	Austin	644N	MG-17	78745	800-1199
	Austin	643M	MF-17	78745	1200-1699
SAHM ST	Austin	586E	ML-24	78723	3900-3999
SAILBOAT PASS	Travis Co	426G	WR-39	78669	2300-2799
SAILFISH	Lakeway	489W	WW-31	78734	100-199
SAILING BREEZE TRL	Austin	675S	MJ-13	78744	6400-6599
SAILMASTER	Lakeway	489Y	WX-31	78734	100-499
	Lakeway	519B	WW-30	78734	1000-1099
SAILOR'S RUN	Lakeway	519C	WX-30	78734	100-299
SAILPOINT CT	Travis Co	426H	WR-39	78669	26400-26499
SAILPOINT DR	Travis Co	426H	WR-39	78669	2400-2599
ST ALBANS BLVD	Austin	643H	MF-18	78745	1600-1999
ST AMANT PL	Austin	642R	MD-17	78749	7500-7699
ST ANDREWS DR	Georgetown	226D	MM-60	78628	30100-30499
	Georgetown	227A	MN-60	78628	30500-30699
ST ANDREWS DR	Round Rock	378X	MQ-43	78664	1900-2199
	Round Rock	378T	MQ-43	78664	None
ST ANDREWS WAY	Travis Co	582G	MD-24	78746	6600-6899
ST ANTHONY ST	Austin	554Y	MH-25	78703	2600-2699
ST CECELIA ST	Austin	525K	MJ-29	78757	7500-7599
ST CHARLES AVE	Austin	466L	MM-35	78727	13300-13399
SAINT CHRISTINA CT	Williamson Co	348P	MQ-47	78665	2900-2999
SAINT CHRISTOPHER CT					
	Williamson Co	348P	MQ-47	78665	3400-3499
ST CLAIR ST	Travis Co	467K	MN-35	78660	None
ST CROIX LN	Travis Co	467M	MP-35	78660	1300-1599
ST EDWARDS CIR	Austin	615W	MJ-19	78704	2700-2899
ST EDWARDS DR	Austin	614V	MH-19	78704	300-799
	Austin	615W	MJ-19	78704	800-1499
SAINT ELIAS ST	Bee Cave	549F	WW-27	78738	4300-4399
ST ELMO RD E	Austin	644G	MH-18	78745	100-699
	Austin	644H	MH-18	78745	700-1299
	Austin	644M	MH-17	78744	1600-1799
	Austin	645J	MJ-17	78744	1800-5099
ST ELMO RD W	Austin	644B	MG-18	78745	100-999
SAINT FEDERICO WAY	Williamson Co	348N	MQ-47	78665	2800-2999
ST FRANCES CT	Williamson Co	348N	MQ-47	78665	2800-2899
ST GENEVIEVE DR	Williamson Co	343N	ME-47	78641	3200-3399
ST GEORGES GREEN	Austin	643H	MF-18	78745	5200-5399
ST HELENA DR	Leander	343J	ME-47	78641	900-1899
ST JAMES PL	Round Rock	377L	MP-44	78665	2500-2599
ST JOHN CT	Pflugerville	467H	MP-36	78660	1100-1199
ST JOHNS AVE E	Austin	526W	ML-28	78752	100-799
	Austin	556B	ML-27	78752	800-1599
ST JOHNS AVE W	Austin	525V	MK-28	78752	100-799
	Austin	525V	MK-28	78757	800-899
	Austin	525P	MJ-29	78757	1000-1999
ST JOHNS CIR	Austin	525U	MK-28	78757	7000-7099
ST JOSEPH BLVD	Austin	525K	MJ-29	78757	2000-2399
ST JOSEPH HILL	Austin	614Z	MH-19	78704	None
ST LEGER ST	Pflugerville	409E	MS-42	78660	1400-1699
ST LOUIS ST	Austin	525K	MJ-29	78757	7500-7599
ST LUCIA CV	Lakeway	518D	WV-30	78734	None
ST MARY DR	Manor	530T	MU-28	78653	12600-12899
ST MARY'S DR	Williamson Co	379X	MS-43	78634	100-299
ST MERRYN RD	Austin	528K	MQ-29	78754	11200-11699
ST PATRICKS PL	Travis Co	467M	MP-35	78660	1700-1799
ST PAUL LN	Bastrop Co	711C	MX-12	78612	100-199
ST PEARL ST	Austin	555W	MJ-25	78705	2900-2999
ST PHILLIP ST	Austin	525P	MJ-29	78757	7500-7599
SAINT RAGUEL RD	Travis Co	470Q	MV-35	78653	18800-19299
SAINT RICHIE LN	Hays Co	669B	WW-15	78737	100-299
SAINT RODRIGO CT	Williamson Co	348N	MQ-47	78665	2800-2899
ST STANISLAWS DR	Austin	703E	ME-12	78748	1100-1399
ST STEPHENS CV	Travis Co	553J	ME-26	78746	6800-6899
ST STEPHENS DR	Travis Co	523X	ME-28	78746	6200-6599
ST STEPHENS SCHOOL RD	Travis Co	553J	ME-26	78746	1-99
	Travis Co	552V	MD-25	78746	None
	Travis Co	553S	ME-25	78746	None
ST STEPHENS SCHOOL RD S					
	Travis Co	552V	MD-25	78746	300-499
SAINT THERESE RD	Travis Co	470Q	MV-35	78653	17000-17399
SAINT THOMAS DR	Austin	678E	MQ-15	78617	11300-12899
ST THOMAS LN	Bastrop Co	711G	MX-12	78612	100-199
ST TROPEZ DR	Austin	554S	MG-25	78746	4000-4099
ST WILLIAMS AVE	Round Rock	406F	ML-42	78681	700-1499
ST WILLIAMS LOOP	Round Rock	406E	ML-42	78681	1400-1599
ST WILLIAMS ST	Round Rock	406K	ML-41	78681	1500-1899
SALADO ST	Austin	585A	MJ-24	78705	2600-2899
SALCON CLIFF DR	Austin	642N	MC-17	78749	5800-5999
	Austin	641R	MB-17	78749	6000-6499
SALDANA DR	Bastrop Co	739H	MT-9	78612	100-199
SALEM DR	Bastrop Co	709L	MT-11	78612	None
SALEM LN	Travis Co	526C	MM-30	78753	800-1099
SALEM HILL DR	Austin	644J	MG-17	78745	5300-5599
SALEM HOUSE WAY	Austin	497J	MN-32	78753	12100-12199
SALEM MEADOW CIR	Austin	644J	MG-17	78745	1400-1499
SALEM OAK CV	Austin	703C	MF-12	78748	10200-10299
SALEM PARK CT	Austin	644J	MG-17	78745	1100-1299
SALEM WALK DR	Austin	644J	MG-17	78745	5400-5599
SALEN CV	Briarcliff	487H	WT-33	78669	1000-1299
SALERNO PL	Travis Co	432G	MD-39	78613	2600-2699
SALES ST	Austin	525G	MK-30	78757	7900-7999
SALIDA DR	Austin	672F	MC-15	78749	10200-10399
SALIDA DEL SOL PASS	Travis Co	521F	MA-30	78732	12200-12399
SALINA ST	Austin	615G	MK-21	78702	1-99
	Austin	615C	MK-21	78702	200-299
	Austin	585U	MK-22	78702	1100-1199
	Austin	585Q	MK-23	78702	1200-1899
	Austin	585L	MK-23	78722	1900-2299
SALLE AVE	Buda	732Q	MD-8	78610	100-199
	Buda	732P	MC-8	78610	200-399
SALLY LUNN WAY	Travis Co	467L	MP-35	78660	900-999
SALMON DR	Austin	672F	MC-15	78749	10300-10399
SALOMA PL	Austin	642L	MD-17	78749	4600-4799
SALORN CV	Round Rock	375G	MK-45	78681	2800-2899
SALORN WAY	Round Rock	375G	MK-45	78681	2400-2799
SALT BLOCK CIR	Williamson Co	433L	MF-38	78750	10500-10599
SALT CEDAR TRL	Williamson Co	433F	ME-39	78750	11200-11399
SALT FLAT LN	Pflugerville	407X	MN-40	78664	17400-17599
SALTILLO CT	Lakeway	519G	WX-30	78734	3300-3499
SALT MILL HOLLOW	Williamson Co	433Q	MF-38	78750	10500-10799
SALTON DR	Austin	464R	MH-35	78759	6000-6099
SALT SPRINGS DR	Austin	675S	MJ-13	78744	7100-8199
SALVIA CT	Leander	342K	MC-47	78641	1000-1099
SALVIA CV	Austin	464X	MG-34	78759	9900-9999
SAM-BEAUX DR	Williamson Co	434F	MG-39	78729	9300-9399
SAMARIPA ST	Manor	529U	MT-28	78653	500-799
SAM BASS CIR	Round Rock	376T	ML-43	78681	1000-1399
SAM BASS RD	Round Rock	376N	ML-44	78681	700-2099
	Round Rock	375M	MK-44	78681	2100-2399
	Round Rock	375M	MK-44	78681	2700-3099
	Williamson Co	375M	MK-44	78681	2400-2699
	Williamson Co	375E	MJ-45	78681	3100-4599
	Williamson Co	374D	MH-45	78681	4600-4799
	Williamson Co	344Z	MH-46	78681	5300-5499
SAMBUCA CIR	Travis Co	436G	MM-39	78728	15600-15899
SAMBUCA CT	Travis Co	436G	MM-39	78728	3900-3999
SAM CARTER DR	Travis Co	611N	MA-20	78736	8800-9199
SAM HOUSTON CIR	Austin	524J	MG-29	78731	5700-5799
SAM HOUSTON DR	Bastrop Co	712V	MZ-10	78602	100-199
SAM MAVERICK PASS	Austin	641D	MB-18	78749	6300-6499
SAMOA CT	Travis Co	467R	MP-35	78660	1600-1799
SAM RAYBURN DR	Austin	526N	ML-29	78753	8200-8299
SAMS CIR	Taylor	323X	EA-49	76574	600-699
SAMS CT	Taylor	323W	EA-49	76574	300-599
SAMSON DR	Hutto	379G	MT-45	78634	1100-1399
SAMSUNG BLVD	Austin	527C	MP-30	78754	10700-11599
	Austin	497V	MP-31	78754	11600-12299
SAMUEL BISHOP DR	Austin	611P	MA-20	78736	8600-8799
SAMUEL HUSTON AVE	Austin	586M	MM-23	78721	5200-5799
SANALOMA DR	Williamson Co	226V	MM-58	78628	3000-3599
SAN ANTONIO RD	Georgetown	196W	ML-61	78628	100-299
SAN ANTONIO ST	Austin	585J	MJ-23	78701	100-1899
	Austin	585E	MJ-24	78705	1900-2599
SAN ANTONIO ST	Buda	762C	MD-6	78610	100-399
SAN ANTONIO ST	Travis Co	490G	WZ-33	78734	3400-3799
SAN ANTONIO RIVER WALK	Hutto	379T	MS-43	78634	100-299
SAN AUGUSTINE DR	Travis Co	522W	MC-28	78733	1100-1199
SANBEL CT	Round Rock	346W	ML-46	78681	3200-3299
SAN BENITO CT	Travis Co	550Q	WZ-26	78733	3300-3599
SAN BERNARD ST	Austin	585U	MK-22	78702	1100-1499
SAN CARLOS DR	Austin	525Y	MK-30	78757	1500-1599
SANCHEZ LN	Bastrop Co	651C	MX-18	78621	100-199
	Bastrop Co	621Y	MX-19	78621	None
SANCHEZ ST	Austin	586J	ML-23	78702	1400-1899
SAN CHISOLM DR	Travis Co	408K	MQ-41	78664	None
SANDALWOOD CV	Austin	525B	MJ-30	78757	8200-8299
SANDALWOOD HOLLOW	Austin	524P	MG-29	78731	5800-5899
SANDBAR DR	Travis Co	557K	MN-26	78724	5500-5699
SANDBERG DR	Austin	556C	MM-27	78752	2000-2099
SANDY BROWN LN	Webberville	621X	MW-19	78653	20800-21099
SANDCASTLE DR	Travis Co	458Z	WV-34	78669	19500-19899
SAND CREEK RD	Cedar Park	373V	MF-43	78613	1900-1999
SAND DOLLAR CT	Travis Co	436Q	MM-38	78728	14900-14999
SAND DOLLAR DR	Travis Co	436Q	MM-38	78728	2800-2999
SAND DUNES AVE	Austin	646T	ML-16	78744	3400-3699
SANDEEN RD	Travis Co	471F	MW-36	78615	12000-13299
	Travis Co	471R	MX-35	78653	13300-13999
SANDERLING TRL	Austin	583Q	MF-23	78746	3200-3499
SANDERS ST	Travis Co	672R	MD-14	78748	2400-2599
SANDERSON AVE	Austin	642D	MD-18	78749	6300-6599
SAND HILL DR	Austin	675J	MJ-14	78744	5300-5499
SAND HILLS CV	Georgetown	226P	ML-59	78628	100-199
SANDHILLS DR	Cedar Park	373E	ME-45	78613	1700-1798 E
SANDHURST CIR	Austin	556U	MM-25	78723	5700-5799
SANDIA LOOP	Travis Co	582P	MC-23	78735	7500-7799
SAN DIEGO RD	Travis Co	641A	MA-18	78737	9000-9599
SANDIFER ST	Travis Co	618V	MR-19	78725	14100-14599
SANDOVAL CT	Travis Co	491U	MB-31	78732	3600-3699
SANDOVAL ST	Buda	763E	ME-6	78610	100-199
SANDPIPER AVE	Austin	496M	MM-32	78753	700-799
SANDPIPER CV	Georgetown	225F	MJ-60	78633	100-199
SANDPIPER CV	Williamson Co	282J	MC-53	78641	100-199
SANDPIPER PERCH CT	Travis Co	409X	MS-40	78660	20100-20199
SANDPIPER PERCH LN	Travis Co	439C	MT-39	78660	3600-3699
SANDPIPER SPOT CT	Travis Co	409X	MS-40	78660	20200-20299
SANDPIPER SPOT TRL	Travis Co	439C	MT-39	78660	20200-20399
SANDPOINT CV	Williamson Co	405E	MJ-42	78717	16100-16199
SANDRA CV	Cedar Park	432D	MD-39	78613	1800-1899
SANDRA DR	Cedar Park	432D	MD-39	78613	2200-2399
SANDRA LN	Travis Co	650H	MV-18	78653	2300-2499
	Webberville	650H	MV-18	78653	2000-2499
SANDRA ST	Austin	644P	MG-17	78745	100-299
SANDRA A MURAIDA WAY	Austin	584Z	MH-22	78703	100-199
SANDRINGHAM CIR	Austin	615S	MJ-19	78704	600-699
SANDSHOF CIR	Austin	557Y	MP-25	78724	6700-6799
SANDSHOF DR	Austin	587B	MN-24	78724	5900-6399
	Austin	557X	MN-25	78724	6400-6899
SANDSTONE ST	Travis Co	640G	WX-18	78737	9100-9599
SANDSTONE TRL	Hays Co	763S	ME-4	78610	100-599
SANDSTONE TRL	Williamson Co	433P	ME-38	78750	11100-11299
SANDUST WAY	Travis Co	676X	ML-13	78719	8901-8999 O
SANDWICK DR	Travis Co	437C	MP-39	78660	17200-17299
SANDY LN	Jonestown	401E	MA-42	78645	17700-17999
SANDY LN	Williamson Co	322D	MZ-51	76574	1-99
SANDY ST	Jonestown	400H	WZ-42	78645	18200-18299
SANDY ACRE LN	Austin	524S	MG-28	78746	4000-4299
SANDY BEACH RD	Travis Co	577R	WT-23	78720	10100-10399
SANDY BEND WAY	Bee Cave	549M	WX-26	78738	4100-4199
SANDY BOTTOM DR	Travis Co	439P	MS-38	78660	18500-18699
SANDY BROOK DR	Round Rock	347J	MN-47	78665	3600-4199
SANDY CREEK TRL	Georgetown	195K	MJ-62	78633	100-199
SANDY HAVEN CV	Williamson Co	344V	MH-46	78681	3500-3599
SANDY HILL RANCH RD	Bastrop Co	564X	EC-25	78621	100-199
SANDY KOUFAX LN	Round Rock	378A	MQ-45	78665	3400-3699
SANDY LOAM TRL	Williamson Co	433T	ME-37	78750	11500-11599
SANDY MEADOW CIR	Travis Co	340F	WY-48	78641	14100-14299
SANDY RIDGE	Travis Co	369M	WX-44	78641	11700-11799
SANDY SHORE DR	Travis Co	439K	MS-38	78660	None
SANDY SIDE DR	Travis Co	436Y	MM-37	78728	14400-14699
SAN FELIPE BLVD	Austin	434Y	MH-37	78729	7600-8199
SAN FERNANDO CT	Williamson Co	348S	MQ-46	78665	2400-2499
SANFORD DR	Austin	672H	MD-15	78748	9200-9599
SANFORD LN	Hays Co	639V	WX-16	78737	100-199
SAN GABRIEL BLVD	Georgetown	286T	ML-52	78628	100-499
SAN GABRIEL PKWY	Leander	311R	MB-50	78641	None
	Leander	312N	MC-50	78641	None
SAN GABRIEL ST	Austin	585J	MJ-23	78701	1700-1899
	Austin	585A	MJ-24	78705	1900-2899
	Austin	555W	MJ-25	78705	2900-2999
SAN GABRIEL ST	Taylor	353N	EA-47	76574	300-399
SAN GABRIEL OAKS DR					
	Williamson Co	222T	MC-58	78642	1-1199
SAN GABRIEL OVERLOOK					
	Georgetown	286T	ML-52	78628	500-799
SAN GABRIEL VILLAGE BLVD					
	Georgetown	286C	MM-54	78626	200-799
SANGER DR	Austin	673F	ME-15	78748	9000-9199
SANGIACOMO CV	Austin	464X	MG-34	78759	6700-6799
SAN GIOVANI CT	Lakeway	519T	WW-28	78738	1-99
SAN GIOVANI CV	Lakeway	519T	WW-28	78738	1-99
SANGREMON WAY	Travis Co	439F	MS-39	78660	19400-19699
SANG SALOON RD	Cedar Park	374N	MG-44	78613	500-599
SAN JACINTO BLVD	Austin	585W	MJ-22	78701	1-1899
	Austin	585K	MJ-23	78705	1900-2999
SAN JACINTO DR	Williamson Co	350E	MU-48	78634	100-399
SAN JOSE AVE	Travis Co	706H	MM-12	78617	10500-10999
SAN JOSE ST	Austin	526J	ML-29	78753	100-599
SAN JOSE ST	Georgetown	286R	MM-53	78626	1500-2299
SAN JUAN DR	Travis Co	522T	MC-28	78733	1500-2899
SAN JUAN PASS	Travis Co	641F	MA-18	78737	9200-9399
SAN LEANNA DR	San Leanna	703F	ME-12	78748	400-699
	Travis Co	703F	ME-12	78748	300-399
SAN LUCAS DR	Travis Co	641A	MA-18	78737	9300-9599
SAN LUIS TRL	Travis Co	522P	MC-29	78733	9800-10099
SAN MARCOS N	Dripping Springs	636Z	WR-16	78620	100-299
SAN MARCOS S	Dripping Springs	636Z	WR-16	78620	100-299
SAN MARCOS ST	Austin	615F	MJ-21	78701	1-99
	Austin	615B	MJ-21	78702	100-199
	Austin	585X	MJ-22	78702	200-1099
SAN MARCOS ST N	Buda	762C	MD-6	78610	100-499
SAN MARCOS ST N	Manor	529U	MT-28	78653	100-899
SAN MARCOS ST S	Buda	762C	MD-6	78610	100-199
SAN MARCOS ST S	Manor	529U	MT-28	78653	100-399
SAN MARCOS WAY	Georgetown	196W	ML-61	78628	100-199
SAN MARINO DR	Austin	645A	MJ-18	78741	3300-3399
SAN MATEO CT	Travis Co	550Q	WZ-26	78733	3500-3599
SAN MATEO DR	Travis Co	550Q	WZ-26	78733	3300-3499
SAN MATEO TERRACE	Cedar Park	403A	ME-42	78613	100-199
SAN MIGUEL LN	Austin	554S	MG-25	78746	1900-2099
SANOSTEE CV	Travis Co	552K	MC-26	78733	200-299
SAN PAUBLO CT	Austin	642J	MC-17	78749	6000-6099
SAN PEDRO ST	Austin	585A	MJ-24	78705	2600-2899
SAN REMO BLVD	Lakeway	520A	WY-30	78734	None
SAN SABA DR	Georgetown	196W	ML-61	78628	100-399
SAN SABA ST	Austin	615H	MK-21	78702	1-499
	Austin	585Z	MK-22	78702	700-999
SAN SABA ST	Round Rock	376Y	MM-43	78664	100-299
SAN SAVIO CT	Lakeway	519X	WW-28	78738	1-99
SAN SAVIO DR	Lakeway	519X	WW-28	78738	1-99
SAN SIMEON DR	Austin	642L	MD-17	78749	4500-4899
SANSIVERA CV	Austin	493V	MF-31	78750	7100-7199
SANSOM RD	Travis Co	527X	MN-28	78754	8600-9299
SANS SOUCI CV	Austin	464Q	MH-35	78759	6500-6599
SANS SOUCI PL	Austin	464Q	MH-35	78759	10500-10999
SANTA ALTO AVE	Lago Vista	458K	WU-35	78645	1800-2299
SANTA ANA CV	Lago Vista	458Q	WV-35	78645	21100-21199
SANTA ANITA WAY	Georgetown	287L	MP-53	78626	300-799
SANTA ANNA ST	Austin	586P	ML-23	78721	4600-4999
SANTA BARBARA LOOP					
	Williamson Co	348S	MQ-46	78665	2400-2699
SANTA BIANCA CV	Lago Vista	458K	WU-35	78645	21300-21399
SANTA CARLO AVE	Lago Vista	458G	WV-36	78645	21100-21399
	Lago Vista	458K	WU-35	78645	21400-21699
SANTA CECELIA CV	Lago Vista	458K	WU-35	78645	21200-21299
SANTA CLARA LN	Williamson Co	348S	MQ-46	78665	2400-2499
SANTA CLARA ST	Austin	525T	MJ-28	78757	1800-1999
SANTA CRUZ CIR	Lago Vista	458K	WU-35	78645	1800-2099
SANTA CRUZ CV	Lago Vista	458K	WU-35	78645	21400-21499
SANTA CRUZ DR	Austin	465X	MJ-34	78759	11100-11799
SANTA DOMINGO LN	Lago Vista	458K	WU-35	78645	21400-21599
SANTA ELENA CIR	Lago Vista	458K	WU-35	78645	21500-21599
SANTA ELENA LN	Austin	403H	MF-42	78717	11700-11799
SANTA FE DR	Austin	645F	MJ-18	78741	3200-3599
SANTA FE TRL	Pflugerville	467C	MP-36	78660	None
SANTA HELENA ST	Austin	646E	ML-18	78741	2100-2299
SANTALUZ LN	Travis Co	520V	WZ-28	78732	200-399
SANTALUZ PATH	Travis Co	520V	WZ-28	78732	400-1099
SANTA MADRINA LN	Lago Vista	458K	WU-35	78645	21300-21399
SANTA MARIA ST	Austin	615D	MK-21	78702	2200-2499
SANTA MARTA CV	Lago Vista	458K	WU-35	78645	21300-21399
SANTA MATEO LN	Lago Vista	458K	WU-35	78645	21200-21399
SANTA MONICA AVE	Lago Vista	458P	WU-35	78645	21100-21299
SANTA MONICA DR	Austin	645F	MJ-18	78741	3100-3599
SANTANA ST	Cedar Park	372Q	MD-44	78613	1400-1599
SANTA PAULA AVE	Lago Vista	458L	WV-35	78645	21000-21199
SANTA RITA ST	Austin	615C	MK-21	78702	2200-2499
SANTA ROSA AVE	Lago Vista	458F	WU-36	78645	21000-21499
SANTA ROSA CV	Lago Vista	458L	WV-35	78645	21000-21099
SANTA ROSA ST	Austin	615D	MK-21	78702	2200-2799
SANTA THERESA DR	Austin	646E	ML-18	78741	6900-6999
SANTA VISTA WAY	Lago Vista	458P	WU-35	78645	1700-1799
SANTEE DR	Travis Co	550R	WZ-26	78733	3200-3399
SANTIAGO ST	Austin	644H	MH-18	78745	4100-4299
SANTOLINA CT	Pflugerville	438Y	MR-37	78660	1500-1599
SANTOLINA CV	Austin	524F	MG-30	78731	6400-6599

S

STREET NAME	CITY or COUNTY	MAPSCO GRID	AUSTIN GRID	ZIP CODE	BLOCK RANGE O/E
SANTOLINA LN	Williamson Co	408K	MQ-41	78664	100-399
SANTOS ST	Austin	616W	ML-19	78741	6300-6899
SAN VINCENTE RD	Leander	312S	MC-49	78641	800-899
SAP CV	Travis Co	408P	MQ-41	78664	None
SAPLING CV	Austin	613J	ME-20	78735	4900-4999
SAPLING CV	Cedar Park	403E	ME-42	78613	600-799
SAPOTE CT	Austin	645W	MJ-16	78744	5500-5599
SAPPHIRE CT	Round Rock	344R	MH-47	78681	3800-3899
SAPPHIRE CV	Williamson Co	402V	MD-40	78613	1800-1899
SAPPHIRE LOOP	Round Rock	344M	MH-47	78681	3800-4199
SARA DR	Austin	586T	ML-22	78721	4600-5199
SARA DR	Round Rock	376L	MM-44	78664	500-599
SARACEN RD	Travis Co	522S	MC-28	78733	1600-1799
SARAH CT	Austin	524V	MH-28	78757	5900-5999
SARAH CV	Taylor	352Q	MZ-47	76574	1900-1999
SARAH LN	Travis Co	736E	ML-9	78747	None
SARAH ANN DR	Travis Co	618R	MR-20	78725	14200-14399
SARAH'S CREEK DR	Travis Co	437S	MN-37	78660	15100-15699
SARALEE TRL	Williamson Co	434Z	MH-37	78729	7300-7399
SARASOTA DR	Austin	642L	MD-17	78749	4300-4599
SARATOGA CV	Austin	523V	MF-28	78746	5900-5999
SARATOGA DR	Travis Co	522K	MC-29	78733	2100-2899
SARATOGA FARMS BLVD	Elgin	533Q	EB-29	78621	None
SARAZEN LOOP N	Georgetown	226L	MM-59	78628	1-99
SARAZEN LOOP S	Georgetown	226Q	MM-59	78628	500-599
SARDUCCI LN	Austin	672Y	MD-13	78748	11600-11899
SARONG WAY	Austin	673F	ME-15	78748	1800-1899
SASKATCHEWAN DR	Travis Co	490Z	WZ-31	78734	13800-14099
SASPARILLA CV	Travis Co	672U	MD-13	78748	3100-3199
SASSAFRAS ST	Hutto	350J	MU-47	78634	100-399
SASSAFRAS TRL	Travis Co	467G	MP-36	78660	14800-15099
SASSMAN RD	Travis Co	705L	MK-11	78747	7700-8999
SATELLITE RD	Austin	496P	ML-32	78758	11500-11599
SATELLITE VIEW	Round Rock	346M	MM-47	78665	700-999
SATICOY DR	Austin	587G	MP-24	78724	5600-5999
SATSUMA CV	Austin	494C	MH-33	78759	6000-6099
SATTERWHITE RD	Hays Co	763V	MF-4	78610	100-599
	Hays Co	764S	MG-4	78610	600-3499
	Hays Co	794C	MH-3	78610	3500-6099
SAUCEDA RANCH RD	Pflugerville	407X	MN-40	78664	1800-1899
SAUCEDO ST	Austin	586X	ML-22	78721	1100-1199
SAUGUS LN	Travis Co	522P	MC-29	78733	9500-9899
SAUL ST	Hutto	349L	MT-47	78634	100-699
SAULS DR	Travis Co	436L	MM-38	78728	2700-3599
SAUNDERS DR	Round Rock	376H	MM-45	78664	600-999
SAUNDERS LN	Austin	495Q	MK-32	78758	9600-9799
SAUSALITO DR	Austin	464Y	MH-34	78759	10200-10499
SAUTELLE LN	Austin	641R	MB-17	78749	9000-9299
SAVAGE SPRINGS DR	Austin	527C	MP-30	78754	3300-3699
SAVANA DR	Austin	643M	MF-17	78745	1300-1399
SAVANNA LN	Cedar Park	403C	MF-42	78613	800-1099
SAVANNA CANYON CT	Travis Co	677Y	MP-13	78617	11800-11899
SAVANNA CANYON DR	Travis Co	677Y	MP-13	78617	6700-6999
SAVANNAH CT	Austin	671C	MB-15	78739	11000-11099
SAVANNAH CT	Round Rock	375M	MK-44	78681	2000-2099
SAVANNAH CV	Elgin	534E	EC-30	78621	None
SAVANNAH DR	Round Rock	375M	MK-44	78681	1900-1999
SAVANNAH HEIGHTS DR	Austin	404K	MG-41	78717	15000-15199
SAVANNAH RIDGE DR	Austin	462H	MD-36	78726	9400-9599
	Austin	463A	ME-36	78726	9800-9999
SAVILLE LOOP	Austin	645A	MJ-18	78741	2700-2999
SAVIN HILL CT	Austin	671G	MB-15	78739	5900-5999
SAVIN HILL LN	Austin	671G	MB-15	78739	11100-11399
SAVIN RISE CT	Pflugerville	438N	MQ-38	78660	100-199
SAVOREY LN	Austin	674R	MH-14	78744	4800-5199
SAVOY CT	Travis Co	550U	WZ-25	78733	3500-3599
SAVOY PL	Austin	525N	MJ-29	78757	3000-3099
SAWATCH CIR	Travis Co	433T	ME-37	78726	11500-11599
SAWDUST CT	Travis Co	521F	MA-30	78732	1300-1399
SAWGRASS CV	Travis Co	583J	ME-23	78746	1300-1399
SAW GRASS CV	Williamson Co	193B	ME-63	78633	300-399
SAWGRASS LN	Round Rock	375D	MK-45	78681	2600-2699
SAW GRASS LN N	Williamson Co	193B	ME-63	78633	100-199
SAW GRASS LN S	Williamson Co	193B	ME-63	78633	200-299
SAW GRASS TRL	Georgetown	226H	MM-60	78628	30100-30199
SAWMILL CT	Bastrop Co	743B	EA-9	78602	100-199
SAWMILL DR	Austin	672F	MC-15	78749	3500-4099
SAWTOOTH LN	Williamson Co	434P	MG-38	78729	9000-9099
SAWYER FAY LN	Austin	673V	MF-13	78748	9500-9799
SAWYER RANCH RD	Hays Co	639W	WW-16	78737	13800-13999
See.. Hays Co Rd 164					
	Hays Co	668H	WV-15	78620	14000-14998 E
	Hays Co	668H	WV-15	78737	14001-14999 O
SAXBY CT	Austin	434A	MG-39	78729	13200-13299
SAXON LN	Austin	616P	ML-20	78741	200-399
SAXONY LN	Austin	465G	MK-35	78727	12000-12199
SAYAN CV	Bee Cave	549F	WW-27	78738	15700-15799
SAYERS RD	Bastrop Co	715E	EE-12	78602	100-299
SAYERS ST	Austin	584V	MH-22	78703	1100-1199
SCALES ST	Austin	586A	ML-24	78723	4100-4299
SCAMPER CV	Lakeway	519E	WW-30	78734	100-199
SCARLET CIR	Travis Co	610Z	WZ-19	78737	8800-8899
SCARLET ST	Travis Co	436R	MM-38	78728	15300-15799
SCARLET MAPLE DR	Cedar Park	403K	ME-41	78613	400-599
SCARLET OAK CV	Round Rock	378W	MQ-43	78665	3100-3199
SCARLET RIDGE	Hays Co	638R	WV-17	78737	1-99
SCARLET SAGE DR	Cedar Park	402U	MD-40	78613	None
SCARLET VIEW DR	Austin	614E	MG-21	78704	2000-2099
SCARSDALE DR	Austin	645S	MJ-16	78744	4800-4999
SCATES CT	Travis Co	491U	MB-31	78732	12500-12599
SCENIC CIR	Hays Co	577Z	WT-22	78720	800-899
SCENIC CIR	Travis Co	458Z	WV-34	78669	1300-1399
SCENIC CV	Austin	671B	MA-15	78739	6500-6599
SCENIC CV	Round Rock	378Q	MR-44	78664	1-99
SCENIC DR	Austin	584A	MG-24	78703	1400-1799
	Austin	554W	MG-25	78703	1900-3199
SCENIC DR	Georgetown	286Q	MM-53	78626	100-2399
SCENIC DR	Jonestown	401S	MA-40	78641	10300-11099
SCENIC DR	Travis Co	459W	WW-34	78669	19400-19599
	Travis Co	458Z	WV-34	78669	19600-19999
SCENIC LOOP	Round Rock	406E	ML-42	78681	1600-1799
SCENIC PATH	Leander	342H	MD-48	78641	600-699
SCENIC BLUFF DR	Travis Co	551D	MB-25	78733	9200-9999
SCENIC BROOK DR	Austin	611V	MB-19	78736	6900-7799
	Travis Co	611T	MA-19	78736	7800-8199
SCENIC HILLS DR	Austin	554T	MG-25	78703	3500-3599
SCENIC LAKE DR	Williamson Co	317W	MN-49	78665	4400-4699
SCENIC LOOK CV	Leander	342D	MD-48	78641	None
SCENIC MEADOW CV	Georgetown	287M	MP-53	78626	900-999
SCENIC OAKS CIR	Austin	643T	ME-16	78745	7200-7399
SCENIC RIDGE CV	Travis Co	582B	MC-24	78735	8200-8299
SCENIC TERRACE	Round Rock	378T	MQ-43	78664	1-99
SCENIC VIEW DR	Travis Co	553Q	MF-26	78746	5100-5399
SCEPTRE CV	Austin	465L	MK-35	78727	12400-12499
SCHAEFER BLVD	Bastrop	744D	ED-9	78602	100-399
SCHAFFER BLVD S	Bastrop	744M	ED-8	78602	100-199
SCHEBLER ST	Travis Co	707B	MN-12	78617	7200-7499
SCHEIDER DR	Austin	497S	MN-31	78754	1400-1499
SCHICK RD	Williamson Co	434T	MG-37	78729	8700-8999
SCHIEFFER AVE	Austin	585D	MK-24	78722	1700-1799
SCHIRRA PL	Austin	526J	ML-29	78753	200-299
SCHLEICHER TRL	Travis Co	491Q	MB-32	78732	12800-12999
SCHMID DR	Village of Volente	431E	MA-39	78641	8700-9099
SCHMIDT LN	Travis Co	470W	MU-34	78653	9400-10499
	Travis Co	500B	MU-33	78653	10500-11499
SCHMIDT LN	Travis Co	610X	WY-19	78737	10000-10299
SCHMIDT LOOP	Travis Co	500G	MV-33	78653	15200-16199
SCHOOL DR	Austin	434A	MG-39	78729	None
SCHOOL RD	Austin	612P	MC-20	78735	6000-6299
SCHOOL DAYS LN	Round Rock	406H	MM-42	78664	300-799
SCHOOL DRIVEWAY	Georgetown	225X	MJ-58	78633	None
SCHOOL HOUSE CT	Williamson Co	433L	MF-38	78750	10900-10999
SCHOOL HOUSE LN	Williamson Co	433L	MF-38	78750	10400-10999
SCHOONER DR	Lakeway	519E	WW-30	78738	100-199
SCHREINER CT	Travis Co	491U	MB-31	78732	12600-12699
SCHRIBER RD	Mustang Ridge	766H	MM-6	78610	11100-11999
SCHRIBER ST	Austin	615S	MJ-19	78704	2200-2299
SCHUBERT LN	Hays Co	795X	MJ-1	78610	100-1799
SCHUG CV	Austin	464X	MG-34	78759	9400-9499
SCHULLE AVE	Austin	584B	MG-24	78703	1500-1899
	Austin	554X	MG-25	78703	1900-2599
SCHULTZ LN	Pflugerville	407Y	MP-40	78660	17500-18399
	Pflugerville	407Y	MP-40	78660	18601-18899 O
	Round Rock	407Y	MP-40	78660	18600-18898 E
	Round Rock	407Y	MP-40	78660	18900-18999
	Travis Co	407Y	MP-40	78660	18400-18599
SCIOTO CT	Austin	704K	MG-11	78747	10700-10799
SCISSORTAIL DR	Travis Co	703S	ME-10	78652	12400-12899
SCISSORTAIL DR	Williamson Co	433R	MF-38	78750	12100-12199
SCISSORTAIL TRL	Georgetown	225F	MJ-60	78633	100-199
	Georgetown	225L	MK-59	78633	200-299
SCOFIELD LN	Austin	466K	ML-35	78727	1700-2199
SCOFIELD FARMS DR	Austin	466T	ML-34	78758	12300-12499
	Austin	466U	MM-34	78727	12500-13099
SCOFIELD RIDGE PKWY	Austin	466F	ML-36	78727	1300-3199
SCONE DR	Briarcliff	458S	WU-34	78669	100-299
SCORPION DR	Lakeway	519J	WW-29	78734	100-199
SCOTCH BROOM DR	Austin	465R	MK-35	78759	3300-3399
SCOTIA BLUFF LOOP	Austin	672Y	MD-13	78748	2800-2899
SCOTLAND WELL CV	Austin	463M	MF-35	78750	9000-9099
SCOTLAND WELL DR	Austin	463H	MF-36	78750	10400-11199
SCOTLAND YARD	Austin	464F	MG-36	78759	7800-8099
SCOTSMAN DR	Austin	464E	MG-36	78750	8800-8899
	Austin	463H	MF-36	78750	8900-9199
SCOTT DR	Travis Co	490G	WZ-33	78734	3100-3499
SCOTT LN	Travis Co	490Q	WZ-32	78734	2100-2299
SCOTT ST	Taylor	353F	EA-48	76574	1000-1199
SCOTT CRESCENT	Austin	554Z	MH-25	78703	1-99
SCOTTISH PASTURES CV	Austin	463H	MF-36	78750	9100-9199
SCOTTISH PASTURES DR	Austin	463M	MF-35	78750	8900-9099
SCOTTISH THISTLE DR	Austin	672A	MC-15	78739	4800-5099
	Austin	642W	MC-16	78739	5100-5299
SCOTTISH WOODS CV	Austin	583P	ME-23	78746	4700-4799
SCOTTISH WOODS TRL	Austin	583N	ME-23	78746	1300-1799
SCOTTSDALE DR	Williamson Co	343T	ME-46	78641	1400-1599
SCOTTSDALE LN	Austin	497K	MN-32	78753	1600-1799
SCOTTSDALE RD	Austin	586L	MM-23	78721	4300-4499
SCOUT CV	Austin	643D	MF-18	78745	None
SCOUT BLUFF	Austin	523M	MF-29	78731	5700-5799
SCOUT ISLAND CIR N	Austin	524E	MG-30	78731	5300-5799
SCOUT ISLAND CIR S	Austin	524J	MG-29	78731	5100-5699
SCOUT ISLAND CV	Austin	524J	MG-29	78731	5700-5799
SCRANTON DR	Austin	467X	MN-34	78753	13400-13499
SCRAPPER'S CV	Bastrop Co	738L	MR-8	78617	100-199
SCRIBE DR	Austin	465R	MK-35	78759	12000-12399
SCRUB OAK LN	Austin	464G	MH-36	78759	6600-6699
SCULL CREEK DR	Travis Co	492U	MD-31	78730	10000-10399
SCURRY PASS	Georgetown	195Z	MK-61	78633	100-299
SCURRY ST E	Austin	496Q	MM-32	78753	200-299
SCURRY ST W	Austin	496Q	MM-32	78753	100-799
SEA ASH CIR	Williamson Co	375Q	MK-44	78681	8400-8799
SEA BISCUIT DR	Austin	678P	MQ-14	78617	13200-13699
SEABROOK ST	Austin	586H	MM-24	78723	5100-5199
SEA EAGLE VIEW	Travis Co	550M	WZ-26	78733	1800-2199
SEA EAGLE VIEW CV	Travis Co	550M	WZ-26	78733	11900-11999
SEAFARER	Lakeway	518D	WV-30	78734	None
SEAGULL LN	Williamson Co	282N	MC-53	78641	200-399
SEA HERO CT	Austin	703C	MF-12	78748	10800-10899
SEA HERO LN	Austin	703C	MF-12	78748	10700-11199
SEA ISLAND DR	Pflugerville	439A	MS-39	78660	19100-19699
SEA JAY DR	Austin	643W	ME-16	78745	3000-3099
SEAN AVERY PATH	Travis Co	518N	WU-29	78669	18900-19599
SEA RIM CV	Georgetown	195T	MJ-61	78633	100-199
SEA SHELL	Lakeway	489X	WW-31	78734	300-399
SEATTLE SLEW DR	Austin	678P	MQ-14	78617	5800-5899
SEAWIND	Lakeway	519A	WW-30	78734	200-499
SEAY ST	Austin	528P	MQ-29	78754	11100-11399
SEBASTAPOL CV	Austin	462K	MC-35	78726	8100-8199
SEBASTIAN CV	Round Rock	345S	MJ-46	78681	3800-3899
SEBASTIAN LN	Williamson Co	223H	MF-60	78633	100-399
SEBASTIAN BEND	Travis Co	467L	MP-35	78660	800-999
SEBASTIANS RUN	Lakeway	519Z	WX-28	78734	100-299
SEBRITE DR	Austin	463A	ME-36	78726	11000-11099
SECLUDED HOLLOW	Austin	465D	MK-36	78727	4400-4699
SECLUDED WILLOW CV	Pflugerville	438D	MR-39	78660	None
SECOND ST	Bastrop Co	746V	EH-7	78602	100-199
SECOND ST	Jonestown	400M	WZ-41	78645	10800-11199
SECOND ST W	Weir	258H	MR-57	78626	100-399
SECREST DR	Austin	464M	MH-35	78759	5800-5899
SECRETARIAT	Hays Co	639S	WW-16	78737	100-399
SECRETARIAT RIDGE LN	Pflugerville	409E	MS-42	78660	21000-21399
SECTION HOUSE RD	Travis Co	733A	ME-9	78652	None
SECURE LN	Travis Co	619T	MS-19	78725	4500-4599
SEDALIA ST	Cedar Park	373U	MF-43	78613	900-1099
SEDBURY WAY	Cedar Park	372T	MC-43	78613	1500-1599
SEDGEFIELD DR	Travis Co	582M	MD-23	78746	5600-5999
SEDGEMOOR TRL	Austin	673F	ME-15	78748	9000-9299
SEDGEWICK LN	Round Rock	407J	MN-41	78664	2200-2299
SEDONA	Leander	342T	MC-46	78641	1100-1299
SEDONA DR	Austin	494C	MH-33	78759	5600-5699
SEDRO TRL	Georgetown	225Q	MK-59	78633	200-299
	Williamson Co	225Q	MK-59	78633	300-399
SEED CV	Travis Co	408L	MR-41	78664	None
SEELING DR	Austin	646P	ML-17	78744	8000-8199
SEGER DR	Travis Co	679C	MT-15	78617	None
SEGOVIA WAY	Travis Co	467N	MN-35	78660	100-499
SEGUNDO DR	Williamson Co	226Q	MM-59	78628	1000-1199
SEIDERS AVE	Austin	555N	MJ-26	78756	3900-3999
SELDALIA TRL	Travis Co	491Q	MB-32	78732	4100-4199
SELLERS ST	Austin	616A	ML-21	78702	3400-3499
SELMA DR	Austin	496P	ML-32	78758	11100-11299
SELMA HUGHES PARK RD	Travis Co	521W	MA-28	78732	11800-12499
	Travis Co	520V	WZ-28	78732	12500-12699
SELWAY DR	Austin	611P	MA-20	78736	8400-8599
SEMINARY RIDGE DR	Austin	643W	ME-16	78745	7700-8599
SEMINOLE	Lago Vista	429N	WW-38	78645	21000-21199
SEMINOLE DR	Austin	644L	MH-17	78745	400-599
SEMINOLE RD	Leander	342Y	MD-46	78641	200-699
SEMINOLE CANYON DR					
	Williamson Co	344B	MG-48	78628	100-299
SENDA LN	Travis Co	619S	MS-19	78725	4500-4699
SENDERA BONITA	Lakeway	490S	WY-31	78734	100-299
SENDERA MESA DR	Austin	642T	MC-16	78749	8800-9299
SENDERO DR	Austin	612D	MD-21	78735	3800-3899
	Austin	613A	ME-21	78735	3900-4399
SENDERO LN	Leander	342E	MC-48	78641	300-399
SENDERO HILLS PKWY	Austin	587F	MN-24	78724	5200-6699
SENDERO SPRINGS DR					
	Williamson Co	345T	MJ-46	78681	1000-5199
SENDERO VERDE	Travis Co	703W	ME-10	78652	500-599
SENECA CIR	Austin	611P	MA-20	78736	7100-7199
SENECA DR	Austin	465D	MK-36	78727	4700-4799
SENECA FALLS DR	Austin	641X	MA-16	78739	10600-10699
SENECA FALLS LN	Austin	641T	MA-16	78739	6800-6999
SENECA FALLS LOOP	Austin	641T	MA-16	78739	7100-7799
SENECIO CV	Austin	494F	MG-33	78759	6300-6399
SENNA HILLS DR	Travis Co	551P	MA-26	78733	10400-10999
SENNA RIDGE TRL	Round Rock	378W	MQ-43	78665	3000-3099
SENORA CREEK CT	Austin	612M	MD-20	78735	4800-4899
SENTENAL DR	Austin	673X	ME-13	78748	10400-10499
SENTINEL HILL	Hays Co	639J	WW-17	78737	1-99
SENTRY PT	Williamson Co	410N	MU-41	78634	100-199
SEPTEMBER DR	Austin	497S	MN-31	78753	1300-1399
SEPTEMBER SONG DR	Hays Co	701G	MB-12	78652	4000-4299
SEQUOIA CV	Leander	342T	MC-46	78641	1400-1499
SEQUOIA DR	Austin	525H	MK-30	78758	8400-8499
SEQUOIA DR	Leander	342T	MC-46	78641	1700-1899
SEQUOIA TRL E	Williamson Co	226T	ML-58	78628	4000-4199
SEQUOIA TRL W	Williamson Co	257B	MN-57	78628	3900-4099
	Williamson Co	226W	ML-58	78628	4100-4199
SEQUOIA SPUR E	Williamson Co	226W	ML-58	78628	100-199
SEQUOIA SPUR W	Georgetown	225Z	MK-58	78628	None
	Williamson Co	225Z	MK-58	78628	200-799
SEQUOYAH ST	Buda	762D	MD-6	78610	100-299
SERAFY CT	Austin	497F	MN-33	78753	12700-12899
SERENA CV	Travis Co	493U	MF-31	78730	6600-6699
SERENADA DR	Georgetown	256F	ML-57	78628	100-199
	Williamson Co	256F	ML-57	78628	200-399
	Williamson Co	226U	MM-58	78628	900-1199
SERENA WOODS CT	Austin	495S	MJ-31	78759	3600-3699
SERENDIPITY PL	Travis Co	487X	WS-31	78669	21500-21699
SERENE HILLS CT	Travis Co	519N	WW-29	78738	3400-3499
SERENE HILLS DR	Lakeway	548H	WV-27	78738	None
	Travis Co	519W	WW-28	78738	3400-4299
SERENE HILLS PASS	Travis Co	519N	WW-29	78738	17700-17899
SERENE HOLLOW	Buda	732X	MC-7	78610	100-299
SERENE OAK DR	Cedar Park	372M	MD-44	78613	1400-1599
SERENITY CT	Hays Co	639U	WX-16	78737	100-199
SERENITY DR	Travis Co	467R	MP-35	78660	1600-1899
	Travis Co	468N	MQ-35	78660	1900-2099
SERENITY PL	Lago Vista	429M	WX-38	78645	19400-19699
SERENITY SPRINGS CV					
	Williamson Co	402U	MD-40	78613	1600-1699
SERIA WAY	Leander	372C	MD-48	78641	2900-2999
SERRANO TRL	Travis Co	460K	WY-35	78734	4900-5299
SERVICE AVE	Austin	647N	MN-17	78719	9700-9999
SERVICE DR	Georgetown	256D	MM-57	78628	100-499
SERVICE RD	Austin	646M	MM-17	78719	None
SERVICE RD	Georgetown	287E	MN-54	78626	1300-1399
SESBANIA DR	Austin	672T	MC-13	78748	3000-3099
	Travis Co	672T	MC-13	78748	3100-3399
SESQUICENTENNIAL BLVD	Austin	494F	MG-33	78759	6200-6299
SETON AVE	Austin	585E	MJ-24	78705	2400-2599
SETON PKWY	Round Rock	347K	MN-47	78665	1-399
SETON CENTER PKWY	Austin	465W	MJ-34	78759	4500-4899
SETON HALL LN	Pflugerville	467H	MP-36	78660	1100-1199
SETTING SUN	Pflugerville	438S	MQ-37	78660	800-899
SETTLEMENT CV	Cedar Park	373P	ME-44	78613	900-999
SETTLEMENT DR	Bastrop	744G	ED-9	78602	100-199
SETTLEMENT DR	Round Rock	347S	MN-46	78665	2700-3499
SETTLEMENT ST	Cedar Park	373P	ME-44	78613	500-899
SETTLER'S DR	Cedar Park	402D	MD-42	78613	100-399
SETTLERS PATH	Williamson Co	257L	MP-56	78626	40000-40399
SETTLERS TRL	Hays Co	636A	WQ-18	78620	2000-13099
SETTLERS TRL	Williamson Co	433Q	MF-38	78750	10500-10699
SETTLERS BLUFF CIR	Austin	677M	MP-14	78617	11200-11399
SETTLERS HOME DR	Cedar Park	373V	MF-43	78613	301-399 O
SETTLERS PARK LOOP	Round Rock	347V	MP-46	78665	2100-2199
	Round Rock	348W	MQ-46	78665	2200-3099
SETTLERS VALLEY CV	Pflugerville	437Z	MP-37	78660	600-699
SETTLERS VALLEY DR	Pflugerville	467D	MP-36	78660	100-999
	Pflugerville	437Y	MP-37	78660	1000-1699
SEVAN CIR	Austin	494X	MG-31	78731	5100-5199
SEVAN CV	Austin	494X	MG-31	78731	5000-5099
SEVAN DR	Austin	494X	MG-31	78731	5100-5199
SEVEN BRIDGES CT	Travis Co	409S	MS-40	78660	None
SEVEN OAKS CV	Austin	464Q	MH-35	78759	10700-10799
SEVENTH ST	Jonestown	400M	WZ-41	78645	10900-11099
SEVEN WINS CT	Travis Co	522U	MD-28	78733	2000-2099
SEVEN WINS DR	Travis Co	522Y	MD-28	78733	2100-2499

S

STREET NAME	CITY or COUNTY	MAPSCO GRID	AUSTIN GRID	ZIP CODE	BLOCK RANGE O/E
SEVILLA DR	Austin	556C	MM-27	78752	7300-7599
	Williamson Co	226W	ML-58	78628	4000-4299
SEVILLE DR	Austin	587C	MP-24	78724	6000-6299
SEWARD VIEW RD	Williamson Co	281T	MA-52	78641	1200-1299
SEXSON RIDGE CV	Austin	678J	MQ-14	78617	12800-12999
SHACKLEFORD DR	Travis Co	672Q	MD-14	78748	10700-10899
SHADED WAY	Round Rock	378Q	MR-44	78664	1-99
SHADESTONE TERRACE	Travis Co	521Q	MB-29	78732	11400-11599
SHADE TREE CV	Austin	464M	MH-35	78759	11500-11599
SHADE TREE DR	Austin	673X	ME-13	78748	700-899
SHADOW LN	Austin	554C	MH-27	78731	4700-4799
SHADOW LN	Hays Co	732B	MC-9	78610	300-399
SHADOW BEND	Austin	644T	MG-16	78745	6100-6399
SHADOW BEND CV	Austin	644S	MG-16	78745	300-399
SHADOWBROOK CIR	Round Rock	406N	ML-41	78681	1800-2099
SHADOW CANYON DR	Georgetown	285P	MJ-53	78628	10000-10399
SHADOW CANYON DR	Travis Co	432P	MC-38	78613	3100-3199
SHADOW CREEK DR	Travis Co	529H	MT-30	78653	11500-11699
SHADOWGLADE PL	Travis Co	529M	MT-29	78653	None
SHADOWGLEN BLVD	Manor	529M	MT-29	78653	13900-13999
	Travis Co	529M	MT-29	78653	13500-13899
SHADOWGLEN TRACE	Travis Co	529H	MT-30	78653	11500-11999
	Travis Co	530A	MU-30	78653	12000-12599
SHADOW HILL DR	Austin	525E	MJ-30	78731	7400-7499
SHADOWLAWN TRACE	Travis Co	529M	MT-29	78653	13700-13899
SHADOW MOUNTAIN CV	Austin	524Q	MH-29	78731	6200-6299
SHADOW MOUNTAIN DR	Austin	524L	MH-29	78731	6100-6399
SHADOW OAK LN	Travis Co	524W	MG-28	78746	4000-4399
SHADOW OAKS DR	Bastrop Co	621Y	MX-19	78621	100-299
SHADOW OAKS LN	Bastrop Co	715B	EE-12	78602	100-199
SHADOWOOD DR	Austin	525G	MK-30	78757	8100-8299
SHADOWPOINT CV	Round Rock	347V	MP-46	78665	2800-2899
SHADOW RIDGE	Leander	342X	MC-46	78641	2000-2099
SHADOWRIDGE RUN	Austin	612W	MC-19	78749	7400-7699
SHADOW VALLEY CV	Austin	524R	MH-29	78731	6000-6099
SHADOW VALLEY CV	Cedar Park	373Y	MF-43	78613	1000-1099
SHADOW VALLEY DR	Austin	524L	MH-29	78731	6000-6699
SHADOWVIEW DR	Austin	466T	ML-34	78758	1700-1799
SHADOW WATER LN	Georgetown	285T	MJ-52	78628	100-299
SHADOWOOD TRL	Bastrop Co	709M	MT-11	78612	100-199
SHADY CT	Hays Co	732N	MC-8	78610	100-199
SHADY LN	Austin	616F	ML-21	78721	100-999
	Austin	616B	ML-21	78721	1000-1099
	Austin	586X	ML-22	78721	1100-1199
SHADY LN	Lago Vista	429F	WW-39	78645	6300-6699
SHADY LN	Williamson Co	405N	MJ-41	78717	15300-15499
SHADY LOOP	Round Rock	376V	MM-43	78664	100-199
SHADY ACRES DR	Hays Co	702X	MC-10	78610	12400-12499
	Hays Co	732B	MC-9	78610	12500-12799
SHADY BLUFF CV	Round Rock	378W	MQ-43	78665	800-899
SHADYBROOK CV	Travis Co	553V	MF-25	78746	1-99
SHADY BROOK LN	Austin	556T	ML-25	78723	1900-2099
SHADY BROOK LN	Cedar Park	372Q	MD-44	78613	1700-1899
SHADY CEDAR DR	Austin	675J	MJ-14	78744	6700-6999
SHADY CREEK	Burnet Co	426E	WQ-39	78669	100-1299
SHADY CREEK CV	Austin	523Y	MF-28	78746	6600-6699
SHADY CREEK TRL	Travis Co	402U	MD-40	78613	1500-1699
SHADY ELM DR	Williamson Co	224H	MH-60	78633	100-199
	Williamson Co	225A	MJ-60	78633	200-299
SHADY GLADE CT	Austin	555E	MJ-27	78756	4900-4999
SHADY GROVE	Williamson Co	224H	MH-60	78633	100-199
SHADY GROVE PATH	Cedar Park	402M	MD-41	78613	1200-1399
SHADY HILLSIDE PASS	Round Rock	408A	MQ-42	78665	1500-1699
SHADY HOLLOW DR	Travis Co	672P	MC-14	78748	10900-11199
SHADY HOLLOW DR	Williamson Co	256L	MM-56	78628	600-899
SHADY HOLLOW LN	Bastrop Co	564R	ED-26	78621	100-199
SHADY MEADOW WAY	Travis Co	529H	MT-30	78653	11500-11599
SHADY MOUNTAIN RD	Travis Co	370G	WZ-45	78641	12700-13299
SHADY OAK CIR	Williamson Co	374G	MH-45	78681	5300-5499
SHADY OAK CT	Austin	525W	MJ-28	78756	5600-5699
SHADY OAK DR	Bastrop Co	745V	EF-7	78602	100-199
SHADY OAK DR	Georgetown	286T	ML-52	78628	100-499
SHADY OAKS DR	Williamson Co	434J	MG-38	78729	9200-9699
SHADY OAKS LOOP	Bastrop Co	740N	MU-8	78612	100-399
SHADY OAK TERRACE	Williamson Co	434N	MG-38	78729	12500-12599
SHADY PARK DR	Austin	586C	MM-24	78723	3000-3099
SHADY PATH CV	Round Rock	407A	MN-42	78664	400-499
SHADY RIDGE LN	Travis Co	529M	MT-29	78653	None
SHADY ROCK CT	Williamson Co	378N	MQ-44	78665	1-99
SHADY ROCK CV	Lago Vista	399S	WW-40	78645	21700-21799
SHADYROCK DR	Austin	524C	MH-30	78731	7600-7899
SHADY SPRINGS RD	Austin	496B	ML-33	78758	11900-12099
SHADY TRAILS PASS	Cedar Park	402D	MD-42	78613	100-199
SHADY VALLEY DR	Travis Co	672P	MC-14	78748	3300-3499
	Travis Co	672P	MC-14	78739	3500-3799
SHADYVIEW DR	Austin	466T	ML-34	78758	12300-12499
SHADYWOOD DR	Austin	644W	MG-16	78745	6800-7099
	Austin	674A	MG-15	78745	7000-7599
SHADYWOOD LN	Hays Co	636P	WQ-17	78620	100-899
SHAG BARK TRL	Austin	466Y	MM-34	78758	1400-1499
	Austin	466T	ML-34	78758	1600-1799
SHAKER LN	Williamson Co	344V	MH-46	78681	3900-3999
SHAKER TRL	Austin	497T	MN-31	78754	1800-2099
SHAKESPEAREAN WAY	Austin	464F	MG-36	78759	11500-11699
SHALE ST	Austin	642M	MD-17	78749	7700-7799
	Austin	642R	MD-17	78749	7800-7999
SHALLOT WAY	Austin	674J	MG-14	78748	8300-8599
SHALLOWBROOK TRL	Travis Co	646W	ML-16	78744	4200-4499
SHALLOWFORD DR	Travis Co	610X	WY-19	78736	9600-9899
SHALLOW POOL DR	Travis Co	439N	MS-38	78660	18200-18499
SHALLOW STREAM CV	Travis Co	582A	MC-24	78735	2000-2099
SHALLOW WATER CV	Austin	404E	MG-42	78717	14700-14799
SHALLOW WATER RD	Austin	404E	MG-42	78717	11000-11499
SHAMITAS CT	Leander	342E	MC-48	78641	1400-1499
SHAMROCK AVE	Austin	525C	MK-30	78757	2200-2399
SHAMROCK RD	Leander	342U	MD-46	78641	700-899
SHANE LN	Dripping Springs	636U	WR-18	78620	300-399
SHANE LANDON CT	Travis Co	549A	WW-27	78738	16400-16499
SHANGHAI PIERCE RD	Austin	642A	MC-18	78749	5900-6099
SHANKEL DR	Travis Co	641N	MA-17	78739	10100-10299
SHANNON CIR	Leander	342Y	MD-46	78641	600-699
SHANNON DR	Austin	557Y	MP-25	78724	6700-7299
SHANNON LN	Georgetown	256U	MM-55	78628	100-399
SHANNON MEADOW CV	Williamson Co	403S	ME-40	78613	2100-2199
SHANNON MEADOW TRL	Williamson Co	403W	ME-40	78613	900-999

STREET NAME	CITY or COUNTY	MAPSCO GRID	AUSTIN GRID	ZIP CODE	BLOCK RANGE O/E
SHANNON OAKS TRL	Austin	583N	ME-23	78746	1200-1699
SHANNONS WAY	Buda	732Q	MD-8	78610	100-199
SHANT ST	Austin	673R	MF-14	78748	200-599
SHANTY CREEK PL	Travis Co	409T	MS-40	78660	2600-2699
SHAPARD LN	Austin	647K	MN-17	78617	2400-2699
SHARDICK DR	Austin	556C	MM-27	78752	None
SHARI LN	Cedar Park	372T	MC-43	78613	1300-1399
SHARK LOOP	Round Rock	378U	MR-43	78664	2200-2299
SHARL CV	Travis Co	640Y	WZ-16	78737	8300-8399
SHARON CT	Williamson Co	347V	MP-46	78665	700-799
SHARON DR	Cedar Park	402Z	MD-40	78613	2100-2499
SHARON LN	Austin	584C	MH-24	78703	1600-2499
SHARON LN	Williamson Co	288K	MQ-53	78626	1-199
SHARON PL	Cedar Park	402Z	MD-40	78613	1600-1799
SHARON RD	Village of Volente	430R	WZ-38	78645	8000-8199
SHARPER MENS LN	Austin	645A	MJ-18	78741	1900-2099
SHARPS RD	Travis Co	490X	WY-31	78734	1100-1599
SHARPSHINED HAWK	Bee Cave	549L	WX-26	78738	None
SHARPSTONE TRL	Williamson Co	405A	MJ-42	78717	8900-9099
SHASTA CV	Austin	464P	MG-35	78759	7300-7399
SHASTA CV	Georgetown	195Z	MK-61	78633	100-199
SHASTA LN	Williamson Co	434J	MG-38	78729	12500-12699
SHATTUCK CV	Williamson Co	375W	MJ-43	78717	8900-8999
SHAUN DR	Cedar Park	372R	MD-44	78613	1200-1299
SHAVANO CV	Austin	672F	MC-15	78749	10200-10299
SHAVANO DR	Austin	672F	MC-15	78749	3900-4099
SHAW DR	Travis Co	396B	WQ-42	78654	4000-5699
	Travis Co	366V	WR-43	78654	5700-7499
SHAW LN	Travis Co	676A	ML-15	78744	4600-5399
SHAW ST	Taylor	352H	MZ-48	76574	200-499
SHAWNA DNAY DR	Austin	466B	ML-36	78727	13501-13599 O
SHAWNEE	Leander	342T	MC-46	78641	1900-1999
SHAWNEE CIR	Travis Co	490Y	WZ-31	78734	1400-1499
SHAWNEE DR	Travis Co	733B	ME-9	78652	12900-13299
SHAWNEE TRL	Dripping Springs	637N	WS-17	78620	100-199
SHAWNEE MISSION TRL	Austin	673B	ME-15	78745	1900-1999
SHAWN LEE CV	Travis Co	496Z	MM-31	78753	10900-10999
SHEA CV	Cedar Park	402L	MD-41	78613	2000-2099
SHEA DR	Cedar Park	402L	MD-41	78613	300-399
SHEBA CV	Austin	464K	MG-35	78759	11100-11199
SHEEP HOLLOW TRL	Travis Co	309U	WX-49	78641	24200-24999
SHEFFIELD DR	Austin	644L	MH-17	78745	200-399
SHEFFIELD WAY	Round Rock	377G	MP-45	78665	1300-1399
SHEILA DR	Cedar Park	402L	MD-41	78613	700-799
SHEILA DR	Leander	342L	MD-47	78641	100-399
SHELBOURNE DR	Austin	556C	MM-27	78752	1700-1799
SHELBY LN	Austin	644M	MH-17	78745	700-1299
SHELBY OAK LN	Austin	673A	ME-15	78748	2300-2499
SHELDON CV	Austin	526Q	MM-29	78753	1200-1299
SHELDON LAKE DR	Georgetown	195W	MJ-61	78633	100-399
	Georgetown	194V	MH-61	78633	400-699
SHELF LAKE LN	Austin	587G	MP-24	78724	5700-5799
SHELL RD	Williamson Co	225Z	MK-58	78628	100-1199
	Williamson Co	226F	ML-60	78633	1200-3799
	Williamson Co	196Z	MM-61	78628	3800-4299
SHELLCASTLE LN	Round Rock	345S	MJ-46	78681	3500-3599
SHELLEY AVE	Austin	584R	MH-23	78703	900-1299
SHELL HILL CV	Travis Co	309L	WX-50	78641	14900-14999
SHELL SPUR	Georgetown	226K	ML-59	78628	400-499
	Williamson Co	226K	ML-59	78633	300-399
SHELLSTONE TRL	Hays Co	763S	ME-4	78610	100-199
SHELL STONE TRL	Williamson Co	196Y	MM-61	78628	1-799
SHELTER CV	Travis Co	492U	MD-31	78730	5100-5199
SHELTIE CV	Williamson Co	377A	MN-45	78664	1000-1099
SHELTIE LN	Williamson Co	377B	MN-45	78664	1100-1499
SHELTON LN	Dripping Springs	667A	WS-15	78620	600-1099
SHELTON RD	Austin	586Z	MM-22	78725	6600-7799
SHELTON RANCH RD	Hays Co	607W	WS-19	78620	100-1499
	Hays Co	606Z	WR-19	78620	None
SHEMYA CV	Williamson Co	434Z	MH-37	78729	12700-12799
SHENANDOAH DR	Austin	526T	ML-28	78753	8100-8599
SHENANDOAH DR	Cedar Park	403X	ME-40	78613	1200-1399
	Williamson Co	433B	ME-39	78613	1400-3499
SHENANDOAH TRL	Elgin	533F	EA-30	78621	100-299
SHEP ST	Austin	673M	MF-14	78748	200-699
SHEPARD DR	Austin	526E	ML-30	78753	8900-9199
SHEPHERD RD	Williamson Co	256S	ML-55	78628	500-699
	Williamson Co	255V	MK-55	78628	700-999
SHEPHERD MOUNTAIN CV	Austin	523H	MF-30	78730	5900-6099
SHEPHERDS CORRAL	Travis Co	577Q	WT-23	78720	18200-18399
SHEPPARD ST N	Round Rock	376Z	MM-43	78664	100-599
SHEPPARD ST S	Round Rock	376Z	MM-43	78664	100-199
SHERATON AVE	Austin	644L	MH-17	78745	100-899
SHERBOURNE ST	Williamson Co	434K	MG-38	78729	12700-13099
SHERBROOKE ST	Williamson Co	434J	MG-38	78729	9400-9599
SHERIDAN AVE	Austin	556J	ML-26	78723	5800-6299
SHERIDAN TRL	Williamson Co	433B	ME-39	78613	1500-1599
SHERIFF CT	Travis Co	672U	MD-13	78748	12200-12299
SHERINGHAM DR	Austin	615Y	MK-19	78741	2500-4699
SHERI OAK LN	Austin	673A	ME-15	78748	2300-2499
SHERMAN CT	Travis Co	490L	WZ-32	78734	2700-2799
SHERMAN RD	Austin	616Z	MM-19	78742	9000-9399
	Austin	617W	MN-19	78742	9400-9599
SHERMAN ST	Village of Volente	431N	MA-38	78641	16400-16699
SHERRY DR	Leander	342B	MC-48	78641	600-899
SHERRY DR	Taylor	322L	MZ-50	76574	1200-1599
SHERRY LEE CV	Travis Co	496Z	MM-31	78753	10900-10999
SHERWOOD CT	Georgetown	225Z	MK-58	78628	4400-4499
SHERWOOD LN	Austin	614V	MH-19	78704	2400-2799
SHERWOOD RD	Austin	643Y	MF-16	78745	7300-7699
SHERWOOD FOREST	Austin	464B	MG-36	78759	11500-11699
SHERWYN DR	Austin	587J	MN-23	78725	4500-4699
SHERYL ANN CV	Williamson Co	194Y	MH-61	78633	100-199
SHETLAND RD	Dripping Springs	667J	WS-14	78620	100-399
SHETLAND CHASE	Austin	465K	MJ-35	78727	12100-12199
SHIER CV	Austin	643Q	MF-17	78745	6800-6899
SHILOH CT	Austin	643X	ME-16	78745	8100-8199
SHILOH DR	Austin	643X	ME-16	78745	2000-2699
SHILOH RD	Bastrop Co	744S	EC-7	78602	100-299
	Bastrop Co	743U	EB-7	78602	300-799
	Bastrop Co	742T	MY-7	78602	800-1099
	Bastrop Co	742T	MY-7	78612	1100-1199
SHILOH ST	Cedar Park	373Y	MF-43	78613	1100-1299
SHIMMERING CV	Austin	554F	MG-27	78731	4100-4199
SHINER ST	Travis Co	435S	MJ-37	78729	6500-6799
SHINNECOCK HILLS DR	Austin	704E	MG-12	78747	10000-10399
SHINNECOCK HILLS DR	Georgetown	226P	ML-59	78628	900-1799

STREET NAME	CITY or COUNTY	MAPSCO GRID	AUSTIN GRID	ZIP CODE	BLOCK RANGE O/E
SHINOAK DR	Austin	554G	MH-27	78731	3400-3499
SHINY ROCK DR	Austin	673X	ME-13	78748	700-799
SHIPSHAW RIVER CV	Williamson Co	343S	ME-46	78641	16700-16799
SHIPSHAW RIVER DR	Williamson Co	343S	ME-46	78641	16600-16899
SHIRAZ LN E	Round Rock	408E	MQ-42	78665	3400-3499
SHIRAZ LN W	Round Rock	407H	MP-42	78665	3400-3499
SHIRAZ LOOP	Round Rock	407H	MP-42	78665	3400-3599
SHIRE ST	Pflugerville	409J	MS-41	78660	1700-1799
SHIRE RIDGE DR	Travis Co	491X	MA-31	78732	2400-2799
SHIRE RIDGE DR	Travis Co	704F	MG-12	78747	None
SHIRLEY AVE	Austin	525Y	MK-28	78752	6500-6799
	Austin	525Z	MK-28	78752	6900-6999
SHIRLEY DR	Travis Co	396C	WR-42	78654	5600-5799
SHIRLEY LN	Williamson Co	224E	MG-60	78633	100-299
SHIRO LN	Travis Co	432G	MD-39	78613	None
SHIVELY LN	Travis Co	736A	ML-9	78747	9800-10399
SHOAL DR	Williamson Co	224L	MH-59	78633	100-299
SHOAL CLIFF CT	Austin	585A	MJ-24	78705	900-999
SHOAL CREEK BLVD	Austin	584R	MH-23	78701	1100-1399
	Austin	584M	MH-23	78701	1400-1699
	Austin	584H	MH-24	78705	2100-2399
	Austin	585A	MJ-24	78703	2600-2799
	Austin	555A	MJ-27	78756	3800-5699
	Austin	525A	MJ-30	78757	5700-8299
	Austin	495X	MJ-31	78757	8300-8999
SHOAL CREEK WEST DR	Austin	525S	MJ-28	78757	6200-6499
SHOAL CREST AVE	Austin	585A	MJ-24	78705	2800-2899
SHOAL EDGE CT	Austin	525W	MJ-28	78756	5600-5699
SHOALMONT DR	Austin	555A	MJ-27	78756	2100-2499
SHOALWOOD AVE	Austin	555J	MJ-26	78756	4200-5099
	Austin	525W	MJ-28	78756	5400-5899
	Austin	525W	MJ-28	78757	5900-6299
SHOECROSS	Williamson Co	252S	MC-55	78642	100-199
SHOETOP	Williamson Co	252S	MC-55	78642	100-198 E
SHOMITA WAY	Travis Co	552A	MC-27	78733	200-299
SHOOTING STAR CV	Williamson Co	402U	MD-40	78613	1800-1899
SHOOTING STAR WAY	Bee Cave	549M	WX-26	78738	4100-4199
SHOOT OUT CT	Travis Co	672X	MC-13	78748	3000-3099
SHOPS PKWY	Bee Cave	550T	WY-25	78738	12400-13099
SHORELESS DR	Travis Co	439J	MS-38	78660	18700-18799
SHORELINE DR	Bastrop Co	744D	ED-9	78602	100-199
SHORELINE DR	Travis Co	436Q	MM-38	78728	2800-4399
SHORELINE RANCH DR	Lago Vista	459C	WX-36	78645	4500-5399
	Lago Vista	429Z	WX-37	78645	5400-6099
SHORE OAKS CT	Lakeway	519X	WW-28	78738	100-199
SHOREVIEW CV	Travis Co	521Q	MB-29	78732	1400-1699
SHOREVIEW OVERLOOK	Travis Co	521Q	MB-29	78732	11400-11799
SHORE VISTA DR	Travis Co	520Y	WZ-28	78732	12800-13499
SHORT RD	Williamson Co	281X	MA-52	78641	1-199
SHORT ST	Georgetown	287P	MN-53	78626	2300-2399
SHORT ST	Hutto	349Z	MT-46	78634	100-199
SHORT HACKBERRY	Austin	585U	MK-22	78702	1200-1299
SHORT HORN CV	Round Rock	346R	MM-47	78665	1400-1499
SHORT HORN LN	Round Rock	346R	MM-46	78665	3600-3699
SHORT KEMP	Austin	616T	ML-19	78741	700-799
SHORT SPRINGS DR	Austin	527C	MP-30	78754	10900-11099
SHORT SUMMER DR	Austin	497X	MN-31	78754	1900-2099
SHOSHONE DR	Austin	465T	MJ-34	78759	11600-11799
SHOSHONI TRL	Hays Co	638D	WV-18	78737	12600-12999
SHOTGUN CT	Pflugerville	438N	MQ-38	78660	1300-1399
SHOTGUN LN	Travis Co	672Y	MD-13	78748	2900-2999
SHOTTS DR	Briarcliff	457Z	WT-34	78669	21900-22399
SHOTWELL LN	Round Rock	377J	MN-44	78664	1500-1699
SHOW BARN CV	Williamson Co	433N	ME-38	78750	11600-11699
SHOWBOAT CV	Travis Co	492Q	MD-32	78730	10600-10699
SHOWDOWN LN	Austin	403H	MF-42	78717	14400-14499
SHOWERS DR	Travis Co	591R	MX-23	78621	8600-8799
SHOW LOW CT	Lakeway	519L	WX-29	78734	700-799
SHOWPLACE LN	Austin	526B	ML-30	78753	700-799
SHREVEPORT DR	Austin	435W	MJ-37	78727	5500-5999
SHRIKE DR	Hays Co	732E	MC-9	78610	300-399
SHROPSHIRE BLVD	Austin	497J	MN-32	78753	11800-12399
SHUBERG ST	Austin	586U	MM-22	78721	1100-1199
SHUMARD CIR	Austin	464L	MH-35	78759	6900-7199
SHUMARD OAK TRL	Austin	611G	MB-21	78735	6100-6299
SIDE CV	Austin	613H	MF-21	78704	2500-2599
SIDE CV	Williamson Co	375X	MJ-43	78681	500-599
SIDEHILL PATH	Austin	524D	MH-30	78731	3900-4099
SIDE OATS DR	Travis Co	580A	WY-24	78738	12600-12699
SIDEREAL DR	Austin	465G	MK-36	78727	4500-4699
SIDESADDLE ST	Austin	643E	ME-18	78745	6700-6899
SIDEWINDER	Leander	371B	MA-45	78641	1100-1299
SIDEWINDER CV	Lago Vista	399T	WW-40	78645	21500-21599
SIENNA DR	Travis Co	402Y	MD-40	78613	1600-1699
SIEPEL DR	Austin	557Y	MP-25	78724	7100-7299
SIERRA ROSE LOOP	Georgetown	286D	MM-54	78626	100-199
SIERRA CV	Round Rock	376M	MM-44	78664	500-599
SIERRA DR	Austin	524L	MH-29	78731	3900-4099
SIERRA DR	Williamson Co	226U	MM-58	78628	3200-3899
SIERRA TRL	Lago Vista	399T	WW-40	78645	21400-21799
SIERRA WAY	Georgetown	316K	ML-50	78626	1-99
SIERRA ARBOR CT	Austin	464U	MH-34	78759	6000-6199
SIERRA BLANCA	Travis Co	433T	ME-37	78726	10800-11499
SIERRA COLORADO	Austin	464Q	MH-35	78759	10900-10999
SIERRA GRANDE	Austin	464V	MH-34	78759	5900-6099
SIERRA LEON	Austin	464R	MH-35	78759	5800-6199
SIERRA MADRE	Austin	464R	MH-35	78759	5700-5999
SIERRA MONTANA	Austin	464Q	MH-35	78759	11100-11199
SIERRA NEVADA	Austin	464Q	MH-35	78759	10800-11299
	Austin	464R	MH-35	78759	11400-11799
SIERRA NEVADA CT	Austin	464M	MH-35	78759	5900-5999
SIERRA OAKS	Austin	464Q	MH-35	78759	10600-10999
SIERRA RIDGE CT	Austin	641X	MA-16	78739	11000-11099
SIERRA TAHOE	Austin	464U	MH-34	78759	6300-6399
SIERRA VERDE TRL	Austin	464Q	MH-35	78759	10900-11099
SIERRA VISTA DR	Travis Co	429Q	WX-38	78645	6300-6599
SIERRA WIND CV	Elgin	532M	MZ-29	78621	None
SIERRA WIND LN	Elgin	532H	MZ-30	78621	13500-13799
SIESTA SHORES DR	Travis Co	488K	WU-32	78669	19900-20999
SIGNAL PT	Austin	587F	MN-24	78724	5600-6099
SIGNAL HILL DR	Travis Co	639M	WX-17	78737	11000-11099
SIGNAL HILL DR	Williamson Co	282W	MC-52	78641	100-199
SIGNAL HILL RD	Hays Co	669D	WX-15	78737	10100-11199
SIGNAL HILL VIEW	Hays Co	669D	WX-15	78737	10400-10499
	Hays Co	670E	WY-15	78737	10500-10699
SIGRID DR	Travis Co	591U	MX-22	78621	8100-8399
SIKA WAY	Austin	642P	MC-17	78749	4700-4899

STREET NAME	CITY or COUNTY	MAPSCO GRID	AUSTIN GRID	ZIP CODE	BLOCK RANGE O/E
SIL CV	Leander	341H	MB-48	78641	200-299
SILBURY DR	Austin	496L	MM-32	78758	900-1099
SILCANTU DR	Austin	673T	ME-13	78748	800-999
SILENE CT	Pflugerville	437M	MP-38	78660	1500-1599
SILENT TRL	Travis Co	554E	MG-27	78746	4400-4499
SILENT BROOK TRL	Round Rock	408E	MQ-42	78665	2400-2499
SILENT HARBOR LOOP	Travis Co	439P	MS-38	78660	17300-18499
SILENT OAKS DR	Georgetown	285P	MJ-53	78628	100-199
SILENT SPRING DR	Cedar Park	403K	ME-41	78613	300-499
SILENT WATER WAY	Travis Co	439P	MS-38	78660	18500-18799
SILICON DR	Austin	498X	MQ-31	78653	5800-6199
SILKGRASS BEND	Austin	672D	MD-15	78748	3100-3399
SILK OAK CV	Austin	672D	MD-15	78748	9300-9399
SILK OAK DR	Austin	672D	MD-15	78748	3200-3499
SILKTAIL CV	Travis Co	492Q	MD-32	78730	10500-10599
SILK TREE LN	Williamson Co	408K	MQ-41	78664	100-199
SILKWOOD CV	Travis Co	672S	MC-13	78739	11800-11899
SILMARILLION TRL	Travis Co	672S	MC-13	78739	11400-11899
SILONE CIR	Pflugerville	437B	MN-39	78664	1800-1899
SILO VALLEY DR	Austin	527C	MP-30	78754	11000-11299
SILVER CIR	Travis Co	490U	WZ-31	78734	1900-2099
SILVER TRL	Williamson Co	408F	MQ-42	78664	100-499
SILVERADO CIR	Travis Co	582G	MD-24	78746	1500-1599
SILVERADO LOOP	Williamson Co	195R	MK-62	78633	None
SILVERADO TRL	Cedar Park	373U	MF-43	78613	1300-1399
SILVER ARROW CIR	Austin	495N	MJ-32	78759	8800-8899
SILVER ARROW CT	Austin	495N	MJ-32	78759	8800-8899
SILVER BELL CIR	Georgetown	225L	MK-59	78633	100-199
SILVER BELL LN	Hays Co	668R	WV-14	78737	100-199
SILVERBELL LN	Travis Co	409T	MS-40	78660	20700-20899
SILVER BONNET DR	Georgetown	195P	MJ-62	78633	100-199
SILVERBROOK LOOP	Austin	557T	MN-25	78724	5900-5999
SILVER CHARM	Hays Co	638V	WV-16	78737	100-299
SILVER CREEK DR	Austin	465H	MK-36	78727	12600-13199
SILVER CREEK DR	Williamson Co	281J	MA-53	78641	100-799
SILVER CREEK RD	Hays Co	607R	WT-20	78620	12400-13099
SILVERCREST CIR	Austin	525K	MJ-29	78757	7600-7699
SILVERCREST DR	Austin	525K	MJ-29	78757	7500-7599
SILVER DALE CIR	Austin	611V	MB-19	78736	7000-7099
SILVER DALE DR	Austin	611V	MB-19	78736	7100-7199
SILVER DOLLAR CIR	Austin	645R	MK-17	78744	3600-3699
SILVER HAWK CT	Dripping Springs	636T	WQ-16	78620	100-199
SILVERHILL CIR	Lago Vista	429W	WW-37	78645	4500-4599
SILVER HILL CIR	Travis Co	583Q	MF-23	78746	3600-3699
SILVERHILL CV	Austin	495N	MJ-32	78759	8800-8899
SILVERHILL DR	Lago Vista	429W	WW-37	78645	4300-4599
SILVER HILL DR	Travis Co	583Q	MF-23	78746	1100-1399
SILVERHILL LN	Austin	495N	MJ-32	78759	8700-8899
SILVER LACE LN	Williamson Co	408K	MQ-41	78664	100-299
SILVER LAKE CT	Travis Co	521L	MB-29	78732	11500-11599
SILVERLEAF CIR	Austin	525J	MJ-29	78757	2800-2899
SILVER LEAF CV	Leander	342M	MD-47	78641	700-799
SILVERLEAF CV	Round Rock	377X	MN-43	78664	2300-2399
SILVERLEAF DR	Austin	525E	MJ-30	78757	2900-3399
SILVERLEAF DR	Georgetown	256Q	MM-56	78628	1900-1999
SILVER LEAF DR	Williamson Co	195M	ML-62	78628	100-199
SILVERLEAF LN	Round Rock	377X	MN-43	78664	2200-2299
SILVER MAPLE CV	Williamson Co	408K	MQ-41	78664	100-199
SILVER MAPLE DR	Travis Co	489E	WW-33	78645	None
SILVERMAPLE TRL	Cedar Park	402D	MD-42	78613	100-199
SILVERMINE DR	Austin	611Q	MB-20	78736	6600-7299
SILVER MOUNTAIN CV	Travis Co	641J	MA-17	78737	8300-8499
SILVER MOUNTAIN DR	Travis Co	641J	MA-17	78737	9900-10299
SILVER OAK DR	Williamson Co	408C	MR-42	78664	1-299
SILVER OAK TRL	Cedar Park	373Z	MF-43	78613	1500-1599
SILVER PINE CV	Travis Co	552N	MC-26	78733	9200-9299
SILVERPLUME CIR	Austin	525K	MJ-29	78757	7600-7699
SILVER QUAIL LN	Austin	496W	ML-31	78758	900-999
SILVER RIDGE DR	Austin	494V	MH-31	78759	8300-8699
SILVER SCREEN DR	Austin	704L	MH-11	78747	5600-5999
SILVERSPRING DR	Austin	495N	MJ-32	78759	3900-4099
SILVER SPUR	Austin	466N	ML-35	78727	12500-12699
SILVER SPUR CV	Leander	372B	MC-45	78641	1800-1899
SILVER SPUR DR	Round Rock	406Q	MM-41	78681	2000-2499
SILVER SPUR LN	Leander	372B	MC-45	78641	2400-2799
SILVERSTONE DR	Austin	674L	MH-14	78744	4400-4699
SILVERSTONE DR	Williamson Co	224R	MH-59	78633	100-199
SILVERSTONE LN	Cedar Park	372R	MD-44	78613	200-1099
SILVERTON CT	Austin	497J	MN-32	78753	1100-1299
SILVER VALLEY LN	Georgetown	286Z	MM-52	78626	2600-2699
SILVERWAY DR	Austin	525K	MJ-29	78757	2700-2799
	Austin	525J	MJ-29	78757	2800-2899
SILVER WING DR	Travis Co	619S	MS-19	78725	600-699
SILVERWOOD CT	Austin	495N	MJ-32	78759	8800-8899
SILVIA DR	Travis Co	591U	MX-22	78621	21900-22199
SIMBRAH CV	Travis Co	402Y	MD-40	78613	2000-2099
SIMBRAH DR	Travis Co	402Y	MD-40	78613	2100-2199
	Williamson Co	402Y	MD-40	78613	2000-2099
SIMMONS DR	Cedar Park	402F	MD-41	78613	None
SIMMONS RD	Austin	494C	MH-33	78759	9100-9399
SIMON RD	Georgetown	286K	ML-53	78628	100-199
SIMON ST	Taylor	353J	EA-47	76574	400-599
SIMOND AVE	Austin	586A	ML-24	78723	1800-2099
SIMONETTI DR	Austin	673L	MF-14	78748	700-799
SIMON RIDGE CT	Cedar Park	374U	MH-43	78613	3900-3999
SIMPSON AVE	Bastrop Co	711P	MW-11	78612	100-399
SIMPSON VALLEY DR	Travis Co	497G	MP-33	78754	12900-13099
SIMSBROOK DR	Pflugerville	437L	MP-38	78660	17100-17199
	Travis Co	437L	MP-38	78660	16900-17099
SINCLAIR AVE	Austin	555J	MJ-26	78756	4000-4899
SINCLAIR DR	Briarcliff	458S	WU-34	78669	100-699
SINCLAIR ST	Williamson Co	406P	ML-41	78681	2600-2699
SINGING BROOK	Austin	556T	ML-25	78723	2000-2099
SINGING HILLS	Leander	342X	MC-46	78641	2000-2099
SINGING QUAIL DR	Austin	495Z	MK-31	78758	9200-9499
SINGING WOOD DR	Bee Cave	549R	WX-26	78738	14000-14099
SINGLEFOOT LN	Austin	646P	ML-17	78744	2700-2899
SINGLE OAK CV	Travis Co	583A	ME-24	78746	800-899
SINGLE OAK CROSSING	Bastrop Co	742S	MY-7	78612	100-199
SINGLE PEAK CV	Travis Co	517R	WT-29	78669	19500-19799
SINGLE SHOT CIR	Austin	586D	MM-24	78723	4800-5199
SINGLETON AVE	Austin	585R	MK-23	78702	1200-1899
SINGLETON DR	Travis Co	427F	WS-39	78654	25500-25899
SINGLETON RD	Travis Co	397X	WS-40	78654	4300-4599
	Travis Co	427B	WS-39	78654	None
SINGLETON BEND RD	Travis Co	427A	WS-39	78654	3600-4199
	Travis Co	397P	WS-41	78654	4200-7699
	Travis Co	368W	WU-43	78654	None
SINGLETON BEND RD E	Travis Co	397Q	WT-41	78654	24400-26099
SINGLE TRACE	Travis Co	436X	ML-37	78728	14300-14899
SINGLE TRACE CT	Travis Co	436T	ML-37	78728	2800-2999
SINGLETREE AVE	Austin	466J	ML-35	78727	2100-2499
SINTON LN	Travis Co	435S	MJ-37	78729	13000-13199
SINUSO DR	Georgetown	226U	MM-58	78628	500-599
	Williamson Co	226X	ML-58	78628	200-499
SIOUX	Lago Vista	429S	WW-37	78645	4700-4799
SIOUX LN	Travis Co	460V	WZ-34	78734	5100-5299
SIOUX TRL	Leander	342Y	MD-46	78641	200-699
SIOUX TRL N	Austin	434Z	MH-37	78729	7100-7299
SIOUX TRL S	Austin	434Z	MH-37	78729	7000-7199
SIR CHRISTOPHER'S CV	Austin	434Y	MH-37	78729	12500-12599
SIR GAWAIN DR	Austin	643Z	MF-16	78745	7000-7399
SIRINGO PASS	Austin	641D	MB-18	78749	7300-8399
SIRIUS CV	Travis Co	521E	MA-30	78732	1500-1599
SIR IVOR CV	Austin	553L	MF-26	78746	5900-5999
SIROCCO DR	Austin	644N	MG-17	78745	800-999
SIR THOPAS TRL	Austin	703A	ME-12	78748	1300-1699
SIRUS ST	Round Rock	346M	MM-47	78665	3800-3899
SISK LN	Travis Co	547S	WS-25	78620	9100-9699
SISKIN CV	Austin	643W	ME-16	78745	8400-8499
SISKIN DR	Austin	643W	ME-16	78745	3000-3199
SISSINGHURST DR	Austin	643K	ME-17	78745	2800-2999
SISTERDALE LN	Austin	527E	MN-30	78754	2500-2699
SITIO DEL RIO BLVD	Austin	492H	MD-33	78730	6600-6699
SITTING BULL LN	Travis Co	487T	WS-31	78669	22300-22399
SIX FLAGS DR	Georgetown	225H	MK-60	78633	100-199
SIX GUN TRL	Travis Co	672Y	MD-13	78748	2900-3099
SIXTH ST	Jonestown	400M	WZ-41	78645	10900-10999
SKAHAN LN	Austin	671C	MB-15	78739	6100-6299
SKALA CIR	Austin	525Z	MK-28	78752	None
SKILLET CV	Travis Co	517H	WT-30	78669	4000-4099
SKIMINO DR	Austin	465H	MK-36	78727	13000-13099
SKINNER CV	Austin	464U	MH-34	78759	6500-6599
SKINNERS LN	Georgetown	256N	ML-56	78628	1-599
SKIPSTONE LN	Travis Co	470T	MU-34	78653	None
SKIPTON DR	Austin	465Q	MK-35	78727	3700-3999
SKIP TYLER DR	Travis Co	402U	MD-40	78613	1500-1599
SKI SHORES TERRACE	Austin	523W	ME-28	78730	3100-3199
SKI SLOPE DR	Travis Co	522N	MC-29	78733	1600-1999
SKOG RD	Travis Co	473J	EA-35	78615	17000-18299
SKY LN	Round Rock	345N	MJ-47	78681	3800-3899
SKY CORRAL RD	Leander	372B	MC-45	78641	1500-1599
SKYCREST DR	Austin	644W	MG-16	78745	6400-6699
SKYE CV	Austin	463M	MF-35	78750	9100-9199
SKYFLOWER CV	Austin	464T	MG-34	78759	7400-7499
SKYFLOWER DR	Austin	464T	MG-34	78759	10200-10699
SKY HARBOR DR	Austin	677R	MP-14	78617	12200-12899
SKY KISS	Leander	341X	MA-46	78641	3500-3599
SKYLARK DR	Austin	525J	MJ-29	78757	2900-3399
SKYLARK HILL LN	Pflugerville	468J	MQ-35	78660	900-1099
SKYLERS CIR	Williamson Co	347U	MP-46	78665	700-799
SKYLIGHT CV	Bee Cave	549M	WX-26	78738	4100-4199
SKYLINE DR	Travis Co	458U	WV-34	78669	700-1199
SKYLINE DR	Travis Co	461Q	MB-35	78732	13800-14099
SKYLINE DR	West Lake Hills	583D	MF-24	78746	100-299
	West Lake Hills	553Z	MF-25	78746	300-499
SKYLINE RD	Caldwell Co	767T	MN-4	78616	1-1499
SKYLINE RD	Williamson Co	255Z	MK-55	78628	100-499
SKYLINE SPUR	Williamson Co	255Z	MK-55	78628	101-199 O
SKYLOOP DR	Austin	644S	MG-16	78745	100-399
SKY MOUNTAIN DR	Austin	611G	MB-21	78735	8700-8899
SKYNOOK DR	Austin	644W	MG-16	78745	6700-7099
SKY PARK ST	Austin	677V	MP-13	78617	6200-6499
SKY RIDGE LN	Travis Co	432P	MC-38	78613	3200-3399
SKY ROCK DR	Austin	641T	MA-16	78739	10800-10999
SKYSAIL	Manor	530J	MU-29	78653	None
SKYVIEW	Williamson Co	373Q	MF-44	78613	500-699
SKYVIEW CV	Williamson Co	280A	WY-54	78642	100-199
SKYVIEW LN	Williamson Co	280A	WY-54	78642	100-399
SKYVIEW RD E	Austin	555G	MK-27	78752	100-399
SKYVIEW RD W	Austin	555G	MK-27	78752	100-299
SKYVIEW TERRACE	Leander	342B	MC-48	78641	100-199
SKYVIEW TERRACE	Williamson Co	312A	MC-51	78641	100-199
SKYWAY CIR	Austin	614J	MG-20	78704	2800-2899
SKY WEST DR	Austin	496B	ML-33	78758	11900-12099
SLANT OAK DR	Austin	434L	MH-38	78729	8400-8599
SLATE CREEK CT	Williamson Co	375W	MJ-43	78717	8000-8099
SLATE CREEK DR	Cedar Park	373V	MF-43	78613	1800-1899
SLATE CREEK TRL	Williamson Co	375W	MJ-43	78717	9200-9699
SLAUGHTER LN E	Austin	674T	MG-13	78744	100-599
	Austin	674T	MG-13	78744	600-899
	Travis Co	674T	MG-13	78747	900-999
	Travis Co	704B	MG-12	78747	1000-1899
SLAUGHTER LN W	Austin	674S	MG-13	78748	100-199
	Austin	673J	ME-14	78748	200-2599
	Austin	672M	MD-14	78748	2600-3499
	Austin	672B	MC-15	78749	3500-4299
	Austin	642T	MC-16	78749	4300-5799
	Austin	641L	MB-17	78749	5800-7599
SLAUGHTER CREEK DR	Austin	673T	ME-13	78748	9700-9899
	Travis Co	673T	ME-13	78748	9900-10899
	Travis Co	703B	ME-12	78748	10800-11299
SLAYTON DR	Austin	526F	ML-30	78753	8800-9399
S L DAVIS AVE	Austin	585V	MK-22	78702	1800-2299
SLEAT DR	Travis Co	457R	WT-35	78669	100-599
SLEDGE DR	Lakeway	519M	WX-29	78734	1100-1399
SLEEPY DAISY CV	Travis Co	409P	MS-41	78660	20900-20999
SLEEPY HOLLOW DR	Travis Co	467V	MP-34	78660	13900-14199
SLEEPY HOLLOW DR	Travis Co	460S	WY-34	78645	17000-17499
SLEEPY HOLLOW LN	Lago Vista	399W	WW-40	78645	7600-7699
SLEEPY HOLLOW RD	San Leanna	703K	ME-11	78652	11800-12199
SLEEPY HOLLOW RD	Travis Co	609J	WW-20	78736	13300-13399
SLEEPYTIME TRL	Travis Co	467Q	MP-35	78660	1200-1599
SLEEPY VALLEY	Austin	435W	MJ-37	78727	13000-13099
SLICKROCK CV	Austin	704F	MG-12	78747	4500-4699
SLIDELL CT	Austin	435W	MJ-37	78727	12700-12799
SLINGSHOT RD	Austin	404E	MG-42	78717	14800-14899
SLIPPERY ELM TRL	Williamson Co	433K	ME-38	78750	11200-11399
SLIPPERY ROCK DR	Hays Co	702X	MC-10	78610	12300-12499
SLOAN ST	Taylor	352C	MZ-48	76574	100-1699
SLOWPOKE DR	Austin	466F	ML-36	78727	13300-13399
SLOW TURTLE CV	Travis Co	553M	MF-26	78746	2500-2799
SLY PASS	Austin	673X	ME-13	78748	700-799
SMALL DR	Austin	524T	MG-28	78731	4300-4699
SMALLWOOD DR	Austin	558W	MQ-25	78724	7400-7499
SMITH AVE	Pflugerville	438W	MQ-37	78660	100-199
SMITH AVE	Taylor	322Y	MZ-49	76574	2000-2599
SMITH RD	Austin	616C	MM-21	78721	1000-1999
SMITH RD	Bastrop Co	715A	EE-12	78602	100-499
SMITH ST	Bastrop	745J	EE-8	78602	100-199
SMITH BRANCH BLVD	Georgetown	287S	MN-52	78626	2100-2499
SMITH CREEK RD	Georgetown	287F	MN-54	78626	100-499
SMITHFIELD DR	Williamson Co	343S	ME-46	78641	3200-3399
SMITH GIN ST	Manor	530L	MV-29	78653	19300-19499
SMITH OAK TRL	Austin	612Y	MD-19	78749	6000-6399
SMITH SCHOOL RD	Austin	645V	MK-16	78744	4000-4299
SMOKEHOUSE TRL	Austin	642B	MC-18	78749	7200-7299
SMOKE SIGNAL PASS	Pflugerville	437Y	MP-37	78660	600-799
	Pflugerville	467C	MP-36	78660	800-899
SMOKETREE CV	Travis Co	581M	MB-23	78735	8700-8899
SMOKE TREE TRL	Round Rock	375M	MK-44	78681	2100-2199
SMOKEY HILL RD	Austin	611Q	MB-20	78736	6800-7299
SMOKEY MOUNTAIN DR	Austin	465K	MJ-35	78727	4900-5099
SMOKEY ROCK LN	Hays Co	732B	MC-9	78610	300-399
SMOKEY VALLEY	Austin	524A	MG-30	78731	4900-5199
SMOKY RIDGE	Travis Co	523X	ME-28	78730	3100-3299
SMOOTHING IRON DR	Travis Co	467C	MP-36	78660	900-999
SMOOTH OAK DR	Austin	494M	MH-32	78759	4500-4599
SMYERS LN	Williamson Co	405C	MK-42	78681	17000-17699
SNAKE EAGLE CV	Bee Cave	549L	WX-26	78738	4700-4799
SNAPDRAGON DR	Austin	672A	MC-15	78739	10200-10499
SNAPPER	Lakeway	489X	WW-31	78734	100-199
SNAPPER CV	Williamson Co	255H	MK-57	78628	100-199
SNEAD DR	Georgetown	286Y	MM-52	78626	3500-3599
	Georgetown	316C	MM-51	78626	3600-3899
SNEAD PATH	Round Rock	378U	MR-43	78664	3300-3499
SNEED CV	Austin	644Y	MH-16	78744	6100-6299
SNELLING CV	Williamson Co	373A	ME-45	78641	16300-16399
SNELLING DR	Williamson Co	343W	ME-46	78641	14800-15099
SNIPE CT	Lakeway	519E	WW-30	78734	100-199
SNOOK HOOK TRL	Williamson Co	434M	MH-38	78729	7900-8099
SNOW LN	Manor	530T	MU-28	78653	12800-12999
SNOWBERRY ST	Pflugerville	437H	MP-39	78660	1400-1499
SNOWBIRD PASS	Austin	641D	MB-18	78749	7800-7899
SNOWDEN CV	Williamson Co	434L	MH-38	78729	8600-8699
SNOWDONIA CV	Bee Cave	549E	WW-27	78738	16000-16099
SNOWDRIFT TRL	Williamson Co	408F	MQ-42	78664	100-199
SNOW FALL DR	Austin	466L	MM-35	78727	13400-13499
SNOW FINCH RD	Austin	496A	ML-33	78758	11900-11999
SNOWFLAKE DR	Williamson Co	408F	MQ-42	78664	100-199
SNOW GOOSE	Leander	342K	MC-47	78641	1100-1299
SNOW GOOSE RD	Austin	496A	ML-33	78758	11900-12099
SNOWMASS CV	Austin	642F	MC-18	78749	5200-5299
SNOWMASS HEIGHTS	Bee Cave	549F	WW-27	78738	15300-15399
SNOW OWL HOLLOW	Hays Co	762Z	MD-4	78610	100-199
SNOWY OWL CT	Austin	583Q	MF-23	78746	1100-1199
SOAP BERRY CV	Travis Co	532Q	MZ-29	78621	17600-17699
SOARING CLIFF CV	Georgetown	285T	MJ-52	78628	100-199
SOARING EAGLE	Travis Co	554E	MG-27	78746	3700-3799
SOCORRO CIR	Travis Co	672T	MC-13	78739	3400-3499
SOCORRO DR	Travis Co	490Y	WZ-31	78734	1200-1399
SOCORRO TRL	Travis Co	672S	MC-13	78739	3400-3699
SOCORRO BEND	Williamson Co	343X	ME-46	78641	2400-2699
SOFTCLOUD CV	Williamson Co	375T	MJ-43	78717	400-499
SOFT WIND CIR	Austin	644N	MG-17	78745	6200-6299
SOFTWOOD DR	Austin	675A	MJ-15	78744	6000-6399
SOHO DR	Austin	673M	MF-14	78748	8500-8799
SOJOURNER ST	Travis Co	618R	MR-20	78725	3700-4799
SOLANA VISTA LOOP	Austin	493E	ME-33	78750	9400-9799
SOLANO CV	Leander	343N	ME-47	78641	1800-1899
SOLANO DR	Williamson Co	433L	MF-38	78750	1000-1099
SOLEDAD CT	Travis Co	491V	MB-31	78732	3700-3799
SOLEIL CT	Travis Co	490K	WY-32	78734	15900-15999
SOLERA DR	Austin	404Q	MH-41	78717	14900-15099
SOLITARE	Round Rock	347J	MN-47	78665	1300-1399
SOLITARY FAWN TRL	Travis Co	550Z	WZ-25	78735	11200-11299
SOLITUDE CV	Round Rock	408A	MQ-42	78665	2000-2099
SOLOMON LN	Bastrop Co	743R	EB-8	78602	100-199
SOLONA CIR	Williamson Co	256B	ML-57	78628	200-299
SOL WILSON AVE	Austin	585V	MK-22	78702	1100-2499
	Austin	586N	ML-23	78702	2500-2899
SOMBRA CV	Austin	674G	MH-15	78744	2100-2199
SOMBRERO CV	Lago Vista	399S	WW-40	78645	21900-21999
SOMBRERO DR	San Leanna	703K	ME-11	78748	11400-11599
SOMERSET AVE	Travis Co	526D	MM-30	78753	1100-1299
SOMERSET DR	Round Rock	376N	ML-44	78681	1300-1899
SOMERSET RD	Buda	763A	ME-6	78610	500-599
SOMERSET CANYON LN	Travis Co	402U	MD-40	78613	1500-1599
	Williamson Co	402U	MD-40	78613	1600-1699
SOMMERLAND WAY	Austin	641R	MB-17	78749	8900-9299
SONGBIRD CT	Bastrop Co	709M	MT-11	78612	100-199
SONGBIRD CV	Williamson Co	433K	ME-38	78750	11200-11399
SONNET AVE	Austin	525A	MJ-30	78759	8000-8199
SONNY DR	Leander	342G	MD-48	78641	100-599
	Leander	342K	MC-47	78641	800-1099
	Williamson Co	342K	MC-47	78641	None
SONNY RD	Bastrop Co	712D	MZ-12	78602	100-299
SONOMA CV	Leander	342R	MD-47	78641	1800-1899
SONOMA CV	Travis Co	550R	WZ-26	78733	2500-2599
SONOMA DR	Travis Co	550Q	WZ-26	78733	11600-12599
SONORA CT	Austin	555A	MJ-27	78756	2400-2499
SONORA CV	Austin	464P	MG-35	78759	10500-10599
SONORA TRACE	Georgetown	225V	MK-58	78628	4600-5099
SOONER ST	Travis Co	460Y	WZ-34	78734	4400-4599
SOOTA LN	Travis Co	550D	WZ-27	78732	10700-10799
SOPHIE CT	Pflugerville	438S	MQ-37	78660	400-599
SOPHIE DR	Pflugerville	438S	MQ-37	78660	400-499
SOPHIE DR	Travis Co	490P	WY-32	78734	15100-15299
SOPHORA CT	Round Rock	375B	MJ-45	78681	3400-3499
SOPHORA CV	Austin	464X	MG-34	78759	9700-9799
SOPHORA PL	Cedar Park	402D	MD-42	78613	100-299
SORDELLO DR	Austin	556G	MM-27	78752	7400-7499
SORGHUM HILL CV	Austin	497W	MN-31	78754	10700-10799
SORGHUM HILL DR	Austin	497W	MN-31	78754	1900-2099
SORREL CT	Leander	342K	MC-47	78641	1100-1199
SORREL CV	Travis Co	522G	MD-30	78730	3900-3999
SORRENTO CT	Austin	494D	MH-33	78759	9700-9799
SORRET TREE CT	Austin	644V	MH-16	78744	2200-2399
SOSA CV	Round Rock	378A	MQ-45	78665	1300-1399
SOSEBEE PKWY	Hays Co	762A	MC-6	78610	100-199
SOTER PKWY	Austin	612D	MD-21	78735	600-6199
	Austin	582Z	MD-22	78735	6200-6699

STREET NAME	CITY or COUNTY	MAPSCO GRID	AUSTIN GRID	ZIP CODE	BLOCK RANGE O/E
SOTOGRANDE DR	Pflugerville	439E	MS-39	78660	19100-19399
SOTOL CV	Austin	494B	MG-33	78759	6200-6299
SOTOL PASS	Georgetown	225L	MK-59	78633	100-199
SOULE DR	Georgetown	286M	MM-53	78626	1000-1099
SOUTH DR	Austin	495W	MJ-31	78759	3700-3899
SOUTH PATH	Austin	494R	MH-32	78759	8700-8799
SOUTH ST	Bastrop	745Q	EF-8	78602	1500-1999
SOUTH ST E	Leander	312Y	MD-49	78641	100-299
SOUTH ST W	Leander	342B	MC-48	78641	100-1099
SOUTHAMPTON WAY	Round Rock	408J	MQ-41	78664	2800-2899
SOUTH BAY LN	Austin	671B	MA-15	78739	11000-11499
SOUTH BEND AVE	Travis Co	611S	MA-19	78736	8500-8599
SOUTHBEND ST	Lago Vista	459A	WW-36	78645	20400-20599
SOUTHBROOK DR	Austin	611U	MB-19	78736	7100-7299
SOUTH BROOK DR	Leander	312S	MC-49	78641	500-1199
SOUTH CENTER ST	Austin	614X	MG-19	78704	600-1099
SOUTHCREEK DR	Leander	341D	MB-48	78641	1500-2099
SOUTH CREEK DR	Round Rock	407B	MN-42	78664	600-1399
SOUTHCREST DR	Rollingwood	584S	MG-22	78746	4900-4999
SOUTHCROSS RD	Georgetown	256W	ML-55	78628	100-299
	Williamson Co	256W	ML-55	78628	300-399
	Williamson Co	255Z	MK-55	78628	400-499
SOUTH CROSSING DR	Round Rock	407F	MN-42	78664	2300-2399
SOUTHEAST DR	Austin	645W	MJ-16	78744	4600-4699
SOUTHEASTERN TRL	Round Rock	407J	MN-41	78664	1600-2299
SOUTHERN DR	Buda	732J	MC-8	78610	100-1199
SOUTHERN PL	Round Rock	378J	MQ-44	78665	1100-1199
SOUTHERN HILLS PL	Travis Co	582M	MD-23	78746	6300-6399
SOUTHERN OAKS DR	Austin	643D	MF-18	78745	2000-2399
SOUTH FOREST DR	Austin	644A	MG-18	78745	4600-4799
SOUTHFORK DR	Georgetown	286T	ML-52	78626	2200-2299
SOUTH GABRIEL DR	Williamson Co	282T	MC-52	78641	500-1299
SOUTHGATE	Travis Co	646W	ML-16	78744	7400-7599
SOUTHGATE CIR	Austin	614T	MG-19	78704	1600-1699
SOUTH GLEN CV	Williamson Co	318G	MR-51	78634	100-199
SOUTH HEARSEY DR	Austin	645T	MJ-16	78744	5400-5599
SOUTHHILL CIR	Austin	554T	MG-25	78703	3300-3499
SOUTH INDUSTRIAL DR	Austin	645J	MJ-17	78744	3800-4299
SOUTHLAND DR	Austin	614P	MG-20	78704	2400-2599
SOUTH MEADOWS BLVD	Austin	644S	MG-16	78745	6400-6499
SOUTH OAK DR	Austin	614T	MG-19	78704	3100-3499
SOUTHPARK BLVD	Taylor	353W	EA-46	76574	100-199
SOUTH PARK DR	Austin	614U	MH-19	78704	400-599
SOUTHPARK MEADOWS DR	Austin	673V	MF-13	78748	9200-9699
SOUTHPORT DR	Austin	614X	MG-19	78704	1200-1599
SOUTH RIDGE	Lago Vista	429W	WW-37	78645	20700-20799
	Lago Vista	428Z	WV-37	78645	20800-21099
SOUTH RIDGE CIR	Georgetown	286W	ML-52	78628	100-499
SOUTH RIDGE CIR	Travis Co	401C	MB-42	78641	13100-13199
SOUTH RIDGE CT	Georgetown	286W	ML-52	78628	100-199
SOUTHRIDGE DR	Austin	614T	MG-19	78704	3500-3899
SOUTH RIDGE DR	Bastrop Co	742Q	MZ-8	78612	100-199
SOUTH RIDGE LN	Travis Co	460P	WY-35	78734	16800-17099
SOUTH SHORE RD	Bastrop Co	746B	EG-9	78602	100-199
SOUTH TRACE DR	Austin	643R	MF-17	78745	1100-1299
SOUTH VALLEY DR	Williamson Co	192U	MD-61	78633	100-199
SOUTHVIEW	Austin	644F	MG-18	78745	300-399
SOUTHVIEW PT	Travis Co	427Y	WT-37	78654	None
SOUTH VIEW RD	Travis Co	611W	MA-19	78737	8300-8799
SOUTHVIEW HILLS CIR	Travis Co	706X	ML-10	78719	None
SOUTHWALK ST	Georgetown	287S	MN-52	78626	1000-1299
SOUTHWARD CV	Travis Co	552A	MC-27	78733	9600-9699
SOUTHWAY DR	Austin	614X	MG-19	78704	3800-3899
SOUTHWEST DR	Austin	645W	MJ-16	78744	4500-4599
SOUTHWEST PKWY	Austin	613N	ME-20	78735	4000-4699
	Austin	612A	MC-21	78735	4700-7599
	Austin	611D	MB-21	78735	7600-8599
	Travis Co	581P	MA-23	78735	8600-10299
SOUTHWESTERN BLVD	Georgetown	287E	MN-54	78626	1600-1699
SOUTHWESTERN TRL	Round Rock	407J	MN-41	78664	1600-1899
SOUTH WEST OAKS	Travis Co	639G	WX-18	78737	11000-11599
SOUTHWICK DR	Austin	587R	MP-23	78724	8700-9199
SOUTHWICK DR	Travis Co	588N	MQ-23	78724	9600-9699
SOUTHWIND DR	Austin	643T	ME-16	78745	7200-7399
SOUTHWIND RD	Point Venture	489J	WW-32	78645	200-499
SOUTHWOOD RD	Austin	614L	MH-20	78704	1100-1299
SOUTHWOOD HILLS DR	Taylor	353Q	EB-47	76574	1100-2399
SOVRAN LN	Williamson Co	433Q	MF-38	78750	12000-12099
SPACE LN	Austin	496K	ML-32	78758	1000-1299
SPANCREEK CIR	Austin	524Q	MH-29	78731	6000-6099
SPANDERA CV	Austin	494Z	MH-31	78759	8000-8099
SPANIEL DR	Austin	465R	MK-35	78759	3300-3399
SPANISH BAY CT	Round Rock	378Y	MR-43	78664	3800-3899
SPANISH BAY CV	Travis Co	521L	MB-29	78732	1900-1999
SPANISH DAGGER TRL	Travis Co	487S	WS-31	78669	22400-22799
SPANISH DOVE CT	Georgetown	227J	MP-60	78628	7600-7699
SPANISH GOLD LN	Cedar Park	374V	MH-43	78613	4400-4498 E
SPANISH OAK	Travis Co	370G	WZ-45	78641	20500-20699
SPANISH OAK CIR	Georgetown	286T	ML-52	78628	100-199
SPANISH OAK CIR	Lago Vista	429B	WW-39	78645	20600-20699
SPANISH OAK DR	Austin	554C	MH-27	78731	3400-3499
SPANISH OAK DR	Georgetown	256N	ML-56	78628	100-199
	Williamson Co	255R	MK-56	78628	200-299
SPANISH OAK DR	Lago Vista	429B	WW-39	78645	7200-7499
SPANISH OAK DR	Williamson Co	375N	MJ-44	78681	4000-4199
SPANISH OAK LN	Hays Co	638U	WV-16	78620	4000-4099
SPANISH OAK TRL	Austin	554C	MH-27	78731	4500-4599
SPANISH OAK TRL	Bastrop Co	564Z	ED-25	78621	100-199
SPANISH OAK TRL	Burnet Co	455A	WN-36	78669	None
SPANISH OAK TRL	Dripping Springs	667N	WS-14	78620	100-499
SPANISH OAK TRL	Hays Co	701P	MA-11	78652	1000-2099
SPANISH OAK TRL	Travis Co	340J	WY-47	78641	46800-48299
	Travis Co	339H	WX-48	78641	None
SPANISH OAK TRL	Williamson Co	374H	MH-45	78681	1600-3099
SPANISH OAK ESTATES DR					
	Cedar Park	373P	ME-44	78613	400-499
	Cedar Park	373Q	MF-44	78613	500-1599
SPANISH OAK ESTATES LN					
	Cedar Park	373Q	MF-44	78613	1300-1599
SPANISH OAKS CIR	Hays Co	700A	WY-12	78610	8200-8399
SPANISH OAKS TRL	Hays Co	702X	MC-10	78610	100-199
SPANISH OAKS CLUB BLVD					
	Bee Cave	550S	WY-25	78738	6900-7199
	Travis Co	580C	WZ-24	78738	4300-6299
	Travis Co	550S	WY-25	78738	6300-6899
SPANISH OAKS CLUB DR	Travis Co	550S	WY-25	78738	12900-13099
SPANISH OAK TERRACE	Austin	554C	MH-27	78731	4500-4599

STREET NAME	CITY or COUNTY	MAPSCO GRID	AUSTIN GRID	ZIP CODE	BLOCK RANGE O/E
SPANISH OAK TERRACE					
	Williamson Co	375Y	MK-43	78681	600-699
SPANISH RIDGE CV	Pflugerville	437Z	MP-37	78660	500-599
SPANISH WELLS DR	Austin	404L	MH-41	78717	9600-9899
SPARKLE DR	Travis Co	703N	ME-11	78652	600-699
SPARKLING BROOK LN	Leander	311Z	MB-49	78641	500-899
SPARKLING BROOK LN	Travis Co	554J	MG-26	78746	2900-3099
SPARKLING CREEK CIR					
	Williamson Co	434T	MG-37	78729	12400-12499
SPARKLING CREEK DR					
	Williamson Co	434T	MG-37	78729	8800-9099
SPARKS AVE	Austin	585B	MJ-24	78705	700-799
SPARKS RD	Travis Co	500H	MV-33	78653	11600-12799
SPARKSWOOD LN	Cedar Park	372P	MC-44	78613	1700-1799
SPARROW CV	Georgetown	287M	MP-53	78626	800-899
SPARROW DR	Hays Co	701R	MB-11	78652	2200-2399
SPARROW DR	Round Rock	375V	MK-43	78681	2400-2499
SPARROW LN	Lakeway	520N	WY-29	78734	1100-1199
	Travis Co	520N	WY-29	78734	1200-1299
SPARROW RD	Hutto	379M	MT-44	78634	100-299
SPARROW TRL	Travis Co	439Q	MT-38	78634	19100-19199
SPARROWGLEN LN	Village of the Hills	519S	WW-28	78738	1-99
SPARROW HAWK DR	Williamson Co	341R	MB-47	78641	3000-3099
SPARTA LN	Williamson Co	434L	MH-38	78729	8700-8799
SPARTAN CV	Austin	494C	MH-33	78759	5900-5999
SPARTANBURG CV	Travis Co	492Y	MD-31	78730	5000-5099
SPEAKING ROCK	Leander	371L	MB-44	78641	1100-1199
SPEARFISH CANYON	Travis Co	580H	WZ-24	78738	11100-11399
SPEARHEAD CV	Williamson Co	405E	MJ-42	78717	8900-8999
SPEARMAN DR	Austin	525C	MK-30	78757	8500-8599
SPEARMINT TEA TRL	Travis Co	467L	MP-35	78660	14400-14599
SPEAR OAK CV	Austin	464P	MG-35	78759	11000-11199
SPEARPOINT CV	Williamson Co	284A	MG-54	78628	100-199
SPEARSON LN	Austin	643V	MF-16	78745	1100-1399
SPECTRUM DR	Austin	404U	MH-40	78717	9400-10199
SPEEDWAY	Austin	585F	MJ-24	78705	1900-3099
	Austin	555X	MJ-25	78705	3100-3799
	Austin	555T	MJ-25	78751	3800-4699
SPEEGLE CT	Bastrop Co	741P	MW-8	78612	100-199
SPEEGLE ST	Taylor	322Z	MZ-49	76574	1000-1299
SPEER LN	Austin	644S	MG-16	78745	900-1099
	Austin	643R	MF-17	78745	1100-1399
SPEIDEL DR	Travis Co	409S	MS-40	78660	2000-3799
SPELLBROOK LN	Lakeway	519D	WX-30	78734	100-199
SPENCE ST	Austin	615B	MJ-21	78702	800-1199
SPENCER LN	Austin	616E	ML-21	78702	400-499
SPENCEWOOD DR	Bastrop Co	743P	EA-8	78602	100-199
SPEYSIDE DR	Austin	528B	MQ-30	78653	5800-6299
SPICE BERRY CV	Travis Co	436Y	MM-37	78728	2200-2299
SPICEBERRY PATH	Williamson Co	347A	MN-48	78665	4200-4299
SPICEBRUSH CV	Austin	494F	MG-33	78759	6200-6299
SPICEBRUSH DR	Austin	494B	MG-33	78759	8800-9299
SPICELAND CIR	Austin	587R	MP-23	78724	9000-9099
SPICEWOOD LN	Austin	494Z	MH-31	78759	8000-8199
SPICEWOOD PKWY	Austin	463G	MF-36	78750	10200-11299
	Austin	433Y	MF-37	78750	11300-11699
SPICEWOOD CLUB DR	Austin	463C	MF-36	78750	10600-11099
	Austin	433Y	MF-37	78750	11100-11399
SPICEWOOD MESA	Austin	464N	MG-35	78759	9700-10399
	Travis Co	464N	MG-35	78759	10400-10599
SPICEWOOD MESA CV	Austin	464N	MG-35	78759	8500-8599
SPICEWOOD SPRINGS CV	Austin	464J	MG-35	78759	8300-8399
SPICEWOOD SPRINGS RD	Austin	525A	MJ-30	78759	3400-3899
	Austin	494Q	MH-32	78759	3900-5099
	Austin	494A	MG-33	78759	5400-5899
	Austin	494A	MG-33	78759	5900-6298 E
	Austin	464B	MG-36	78759	7000-7399
	Austin	463R	MF-35	78759	7400-7998 E
	Austin	463R	MF-35	78759	8000-8099
	Austin	464B	MG-36	78750	8100-8699
	Travis Co	494A	MG-33	78759	5901-6299 O
	Travis Co	494A	MG-33	78759	6300-6999
	Travis Co	463R	MF-35	78759	7401-7999 O
SPIDERLILLY VIEW	Cedar Park	433A	ME-39	78613	1400-1499
	Williamson Co	433E	ME-39	78613	1500-1899
SPIDERLING CIR	Travis Co	551K	MA-26	78733	10700-10799
SPIDERWORT DR	Travis Co	402Y	MD-40	78613	2000-2099
SPIERS WAY	Austin	678N	MQ-14	78617	12800-13199
SPILLAR RANCH RD	Hays Co	701B	MA-12	78652	4600-4699
SPILLER LN	West Lake Hills	583G	MF-24	78746	400-599
SPILLMAN LOOP	Lakeway	549C	WX-27	78738	3300-3999
	Travis Co	549C	WX-27	78738	None
SPILLMAN ST	Austin	614C	MH-21	78704	1800-1899
SPILLMAN RANCH LOOP	Bee Cave	549L	WX-26	78738	14600-16399
SPILLWAY DR	Williamson Co	434J	MG-38	78729	12800-12899
SPINDLETOP TERRACE					
	Williamson Co	375Q	MK-44	78681	6000-6099
SPINEL RD	Travis Co	467V	MP-34	78660	1600-2099
SPINNAKER CV	Austin	554B	MG-27	78731	4200-4299
SPINNING LEAF CV	Travis Co	582A	MC-24	78735	9100-9199
SPIREA CV	Austin	642N	MC-17	78749	5300-5399
SPIRIT LAKE CV	Travis Co	554A	MG-27	78746	3800-3899
SPIRIT OF TEXAS DR	Austin	647E	MN-18	78617	2300-2499
	Austin	647J	MN-17	78719	2500-2799
	Austin	646M	MM-17	78719	2800-3499
SPIRIT SPRINGS LN	Georgetown	285P	MJ-53	78628	100-299
SPIVEY DR	Austin	642F	MC-18	78749	7400-7599
SPIVEY RD	Williamson Co	281T	MA-52	78641	1000-1499
SPLENDOR CT	Jonestown	429R	WX-38	78645	19300-19599
SPLENDOR PASS	Travis Co	519W	WW-28	78738	17000-17099
SPLIT RAIL TRL	West Lake Hills	583M	MF-23	78746	700-799
SPLITARROW DR	Williamson Co	405E	MJ-42	78717	8800-8999
SPLIT CEDAR CV	Austin	612M	MD-20	78735	5100-5199
SPLIT OAK CIR	Austin	495N	MJ-32	78759	8900-8999
SPLIT OAK CV	Pflugerville	438T	MQ-37	78660	1100-1199
SPLIT OAK TRL	Pflugerville	438T	MQ-37	78660	100-799
SPLIT RAIL CV	Williamson Co	433G	MF-39	78750	12400-12499
SPLIT RAIL PKWY	Williamson Co	433G	MF-39	78750	12300-12599
SPLITROCK	Williamson Co	375X	MJ-43	78681	200-699
SPLIT ROCK TRL	Travis Co	672T	MC-13	78748	3300-3399
	Travis Co	672T	MC-13	78739	3400-3499
SPLIT STONE WAY	Austin	641X	MA-16	78739	10800-10999
SPOFFORD ST	Austin	614C	MH-21	78704	700-899
SPOKE CT	Austin	644Z	MH-16	78744	5700-5799
SPONBERG DR	Austin	644R	MH-17	78744	1700-1899
SPOONBILL CT	Travis Co	432C	MD-39	78613	2000-2099
SPOONEMORE DR	Pflugerville	438J	MQ-38	78660	1300-1399

STREET NAME	CITY or COUNTY	MAPSCO GRID	AUSTIN GRID	ZIP CODE	BLOCK RANGE O/E
SPORTS PARK RD	Dripping Springs	666H	WR-15	78620	None
	Hays Co	667A	WS-15	78620	None
SPORTSPLEX ST	Dripping Springs	636Y	WR-16	78620	100-999
SPOTTED EAGLE DR	Williamson Co	343W	ME-46	78641	16300-16799
SPOTTED EAGLE LN	Elgin	503T	EA-31	78621	None
SPOTTED FAWN CIR	Travis Co	522S	MC-28	78733	10200-10299
SPOTTED FAWN CIR	Williamson Co	378H	MR-45	78634	4300-4399
SPOTTED FAWN CV	Cedar Park	402R	MD-41	78613	1300-1399
SPOTTED FAWN DR	Williamson Co	378H	MR-45	78634	100-399
SPOTTED HORSE DR	Austin	465T	MJ-34	78759	11600-11799
SPOTTED HORSE TRL	Travis Co	672S	MC-13	78748	3300-3399
	Travis Co	672S	MC-13	78739	3400-3699
SPOTTED OAK CV	Austin	464L	MH-35	78759	11300-11399
SPOTTED OWL CIR	Pflugerville	409W	MS-40	78660	None
SPOTTED OWL LN	Pflugerville	409W	MS-40	78660	None
SPOTTED WOLF TRL	Travis Co	490R	WZ-32	78734	3000-3099
SPRAGUE LN	West Lake Hills	583B	ME-24	78746	1100-1299
SPRAY LN	Williamson Co	224K	MG-59	78633	100-299
SPREADING OAK RD	Travis Co	340A	WY-48	78641	14100-14299
SPRING CIR	Austin	556Y	MM-25	78723	2900-2999
SPRING CIR	Travis Co	610U	WZ-19	78736	10200-10399
SPRING CT	Georgetown	225R	MK-59	78633	100-198 E
SPRING LN	Austin	554Y	MH-25	78703	2400-2699
SPRING LN	Jonestown	400M	WZ-41	78645	18200-18399
SPRING PL	Leander	342B	MC-48	78641	None
SPRING ST	Bastrop	745F	EE-9	78602	500-1299
	Bastrop	745G	EF-9	78602	1700-1799
SPRING ST	Round Rock	376Z	MM-43	78664	400-699
SPRING ST E	Georgetown	286D	MM-54	78626	100-399
SPRING ST W	Georgetown	286C	MM-54	78626	100-199
SPRING ARBOR LN	Cedar Park	403J	ME-41	78613	500-698 E
SPRINGBOK DR	Williamson Co	375Y	MK-43	78681	500-599
SPRING BRANCH	Bastrop Co	744X	EC-7	78602	100-199
SPRING BRANCH	Williamson Co	375T	MJ-43	78681	3700-3899
SPRING BRANCH TRL	Travis Co	490N	WY-32	78734	16000-16399
SPRING BREEZE CV	Round Rock	376M	MM-44	78664	1100-1199
SPRING BREEZE DR	Round Rock	376H	MM-45	78664	2100-2399
SPRINGBROOK DR	Pflugerville	407Z	MP-40	78660	100-1299
SPRINGBROOK LN	Leander	342H	MD-48	78641	600-899
SPRING CANYON TRL	Round Rock	345J	MJ-47	78681	3600-3699
SPRING CREEK	Williamson Co	375T	MJ-43	78681	3800-3899
SPRING CREEK DR	Austin	614B	MG-21	78704	2200-2599
SPRING CREEK DR	Williamson Co	279T	WW-52	78642	100-599
SPRING CREEK DR	Williamson Co	375K	MJ-44	78681	3000-3599
SPRINGDALE RD	Austin	616E	ML-21	78702	100-899
	Austin	586X	ML-22	78702	900-999
	Austin	586X	ML-22	78721	1000-1899
	Austin	586G	MM-24	78723	4300-5399
	Austin	556Z	MM-25	78723	5400-6599
	Austin	557B	MN-27	78724	8400-8499
	Austin	557B	MN-27	78754	8500-8599
	Travis Co	557E	MN-27	78724	7700-8399
	Travis Co	527X	MN-28	78754	8600-10699
SPRINGER LN	Austin	495V	MK-31	78759	1600-1699
SPRING FEVER TRL	Austin	675T	MJ-13	78744	6400-6599
SPRINGFIELD DR	Austin	675U	MK-13	78744	7100-7199
SPRINGFIELD GORGE DR					
	Williamson Co	375Q	MK-44	78681	8400-8599
SPRING GARDEN DR	Williamson Co	378D	MR-45	78634	100-299
	Williamson Co	348Z	MR-46	78634	None
SPRING GARDEN RD	Austin	583U	MF-22	78746	1400-1599
SPRING HEATH RD	Travis Co	467N	MN-35	78660	13700-13999
SPRING HILL DR	Austin	496R	MM-32	78753	11500-11999
SPRING HILL LN	Travis Co	437X	MN-37	78660	15100-15699
SPRING HOLLOW	Georgetown	286F	ML-54	78628	100-199
SPRING HOLLOW CIR	Austin	433Z	MF-37	78750	9100-9499
SPRING HOLLOW DR	Leander	342M	MD-47	78641	600-1099
SPRING HOLLOW PATH	Round Rock	376W	ML-43	78681	1900-2299
SPRINGLAKE CIR	Hays Co	636L	WR-17	78620	100-299
SPRING LAKE DR	Austin	464A	MG-36	78750	8800-8899
	Austin	463D	MF-36	78750	8900-8999
	Austin	433Z	MF-37	78750	9000-9199
	Dripping Springs	636R	WR-17	78620	100-799
	Hays Co	636C	WR-18	78620	800-1699
	Hays Co	606Y	WR-19	78620	1700-1999
SPRINGMAIL CIR	Williamson Co	434K	MG-38	78729	8800-8899
SPRING MEADOW	Bastrop Co	744X	EC-7	78602	100-199
SPRING MEADOW CV	Austin	645X	MJ-16	78744	4800-4899
SPRING MEADOW CV	Williamson Co	193B	ME-63	78633	100-199
SPRING MEADOW RD	Austin	645X	MJ-16	78744	5200-5899
SPRING PEONY CT	Pflugerville	468B	MQ-36	78660	1500-1599
SPRINGS LN	Hays Co	636N	WQ-17	78620	100-499
SPRINGS EDGE DR	Austin	404E	MG-42	78717	14600-14799
SPRINGS HEAD LOOP	Austin	403H	MF-42	78717	11700-12099
SPRINGTIME TRL	Austin	675X	MJ-13	78744	7400-7499
	Austin	675X	MJ-13	78747	7500-7599
SPRING TREE ST	Williamson Co	375T	MJ-43	78681	800-1099
SPRINGVALE DR	Williamson Co	434K	MG-38	78729	12800-13099
SPRING VALLEY DR	Austin	611P	MA-20	78736	8200-8699
SPRING VALLEY DR	Hays Co	606U	WR-19	78620	1700-2599
SPRING VALLEY RD	Georgetown	256S	ML-55	78628	400-699
	Williamson Co	256S	ML-55	78628	100-399
SPRING VALLEY RD	Travis Co	640E	WY-18	78737	10300-10899
SPRING VALLEY ST	Williamson Co	409G	MT-42	78634	1-599
SPRINGVILLE LN	Austin	674M	MH-14	78744	5300-5499
	Austin	675N	MJ-14	78744	5500-5899
SPRING WAGON LN	Travis Co	436U	MM-37	78728	2300-2599
SPRINGWATER CIR	Austin	496M	MM-32	78753	11900-11999
SPRINGWATER DR	Round Rock	376S	ML-43	78681	1700-1999
SPRINGWATER LN	Williamson Co	225Q	MK-59	78633	1-199
SPRINGWILLOW LN	Williamson Co	345S	MJ-46	78681	4000-4199
SPRINGWOOD DR	Austin	433Z	MF-37	78750	9200-9499
SPRINGWOOD LN	Georgetown	256J	ML-56	78628	2500-2999
SPRINGWOOD RD	Dripping Springs	666V	WR-13	78620	100-299
	Dripping Springs	667S	WS-13	78620	300-599
SPRINKLE RD	Travis Co	527N	MN-29	78754	9100-10499
SPRINKLE CUTOFF RD	Austin	527B	MN-30	78754	10500-10799
	Austin	497X	MN-31	78754	11300-11499
	Travis Co	527B	MN-30	78754	10800-11299
SPRUCE CV	Austin	645S	MJ-16	78744	5100-5199
SPRUCE CV	Round Rock	377X	MN-43	78664	3100-3199
SPRUCE LN	Austin	645S	MJ-16	78744	5000-5099
SPRUCE CANYON DR	Austin	640V	WZ-16	78739	10000-10199
	Austin	641W	MA-16	78739	10200-11699
SPRUCE GUM LN	Austin	674G	MH-15	78744	6800-6899
SPRUCELEAF CIR	Austin	525K	MJ-29	78757	2300-2599
SPRUCEWOOD CV	Austin	524E	MG-30	78731	6300-6399

S

STREET NAME	CITY or COUNTY	MAPSCO GRID	AUSTIN GRID	ZIP CODE	BLOCK RANGE O/E
SPRUCEWOOD DR	Austin	524E	MG-30	78731	6300-6399
SPUMANTI LN	Williamson Co	343P	ME-47	78641	3300-3499
SPUR ST	Austin	586T	ML-22	78721	1100-1199
SPUR TRL	Travis Co	486G	WR-33	78669	24200-24699
SPURFLOWER CV	Austin	494G	MH-33	78759	8900-8999
SPURFLOWER DR	Austin	494G	MH-33	78759	5600-5799
SPURLOCK DR	Austin	524G	MH-30	78731	7100-7399
SPURLOCK VALLEY	West Lake Hills	553V	MF-25	78746	600-699
SPY CV	Williamson Co	342Z	MD-46	78641	2600-2799
SPYGLASS CIR	Georgetown	226H	MM-60	78628	30100-30199
SPYGLASS CV	Round Rock	378Y	MR-43	78664	3800-3899
SPYGLASS DR	Austin	584W	MG-22	78746	1000-1399
	Austin	614U	MG-21	78746	1400-1799
	Austin	613D	MF-21	78746	1800-1899
SPYGLASS HILL	Leander	341Y	MB-46	78641	2000-2099
SQUAW VALLEY	Leander	341Y	MB-46	78641	1100-1199
SQUAW VALLEY LN	Williamson Co	375W	MJ-43	78717	16800-16999
SQUIRES DR	Lakeway	519D	WX-30	78734	100-199
SQUIRREL HOLLOW	Austin	672Q	MD-14	78748	3100-3499
SQUIRREL HOLLOW DR	Georgetown	227E	MP-60	78626	7700-7899
SQUIRREL OAK CIR	Austin	642G	MD-18	78749	7100-7299
STABENO ST	Elgin	534J	EC-29	78621	500-599
STABLE LN	Lago Vista	399X	WW-40	78645	7500-7599
STABLEFORD CIR	Travis Co	427K	WS-38	78669	None
STABLEFORD CT	Travis Co	427P	WS-38	78669	None
STABLEFORD CV	Travis Co	427P	WS-38	78669	None
STABLESTONE DR	Austin	524D	MH-30	78731	3800-3899
STACEY LN	Georgetown	256P	ML-56	78628	100-199
STACEY LN	Travis Co	459V	WX-34	78645	17600-17899
STACEY ANN CV	Hays Co	576C	WR-24	78620	100-499
STACH DR	Elgin	534S	EC-28	78621	100-199
STACIA'S WAY	Travis Co	437W	MN-37	78660	1000-1099
STACY DR	Taylor	353B	EA-48	76574	400-599
STACY LN	Austin	614U	MH-19	78704	2600-2799
STADIUM DR	Georgetown	256Z	MM-55	78626	100-299
STADLER CV	Round Rock	378V	MR-43	78664	3400-3499
STAFFORD ST	Austin	585M	MK-23	78722	2100-2299
STAFFORDSHIRE LN	Williamson Co	405P	MJ-41	78717	15600-15899
STAGE COACH CV	Bastrop Co	712R	MZ-11	78602	100-199
STAGECOACH CV	Lago Vista	399X	WW-40	78645	7600-7699
STAGECOACH CV	Leander	372B	MC-45	78641	1200-1299
STAGECOACH DR	Georgetown	256F	ML-57	78628	800-999
STAGE COACH TRL	Austin	643J	ME-17	78745	6700-7099
STAGECOACH TRL	Round Rock	376J	ML-44	78681	1700-1899
STAGECOACH WAY	Travis Co	703W	ME-10	78652	13000-13099
STAGECOACH RANCH LOOP					
	Hays Co	546S	WQ-25	78620	2000-3799
STAGECOACH RANCH RD	Hays Co	546S	WQ-25	78620	2200-2999
STAGECOACH RANCH RD	Travis Co	515Z	WP-28	78620	100-599
STAGE LINE TRL	Pflugerville	408Z	MR-40	78660	None
STAGE STOP CIR	Bee Cave	579D	WX-24	78738	5600-5799
STAGGERBRUSH RD	Austin	613S	ME-19	78749	4100-4399
	Austin	612V	MD-19	78749	4400-4899
STAGHORN CV	Austin	464X	MG-34	78759	6500-6599
STAGHORN DR	Point Venture	489J	WW-32	78645	18500-18699
STAHL CV	Austin	524F	MG-30	78731	6900-6999
STAKED PLAINS DR	Austin	404J	MG-41	78717	11100-11399
	Austin	403H	MF-42	78717	11400-11699
STAKED PLAINS LOOP	Austin	403M	MF-41	78717	14300-14499
	Austin	404E	MG-42	78717	14500-14899
	Austin	403H	MF-42	78717	14900-15599
STALLION DR	Cedar Park	373T	ME-43	78613	500-699
STALLION DR	Mustang Ridge	766N	ML-5	78610	12000-12199
STALLION DR	Travis Co	552E	MC-27	78733	9200-9399
STAMBOURNE ST	Austin	705E	MJ-12	78747	8800-8899
STAMFORD LN	Austin	584C	MH-24	78703	1700-2299
STAMFORD WAY	Austin	584C	MH-24	78703	2500-2599
STAMPEDE TRL	Lago Vista	399T	WW-40	78645	21400-21799
STANDING OAK DR	Williamson Co	224D	MH-60	78633	100-299
	Williamson Co	194Z	MH-61	78633	None
STANDING OAKS LN	Travis Co	524W	MG-28	78746	5100-5199
STANDING ROCK DR	Travis Co	493S	ME-31	78730	5600-5999
STANDISH DR	Austin	643G	MF-18	78745	2300-2399
STANFIELD CT	Travis Co	491Q	MB-32	78732	3800-3899
STANFORD CT	Leander	342R	MD-47	78641	100-499
STANLEY AVE	Austin	643R	MF-17	78745	1700-1999
STANSTED MANOR DR	Pflugerville	468E	MQ-36	78660	700-799
	Pflugerville	468E	MQ-36	78660	None
STANWICH DR	Austin	404M	MH-41	78717	9500-9599
STANWOOD DR	Austin	495X	MJ-31	78757	3000-3199
STANZEL DR	Williamson Co	434Q	MH-38	78729	12900-12999
STAPLE CV	Travis Co	467C	MP-36	78660	1200-1299
STAPLEFORD DR	Cedar Park	372C	MD-45	78613	2500-2599
STAPP CT	Travis Co	491U	MB-31	78732	12500-12599
STAR	Lakeway	489X	WW-31	78734	100-199
STAR DR	Austin	674A	MG-15	78745	6800-6999
STARBOARD CIR	Jonestown	430T	WY-37	78645	None
STARBRIGHT DR	Austin	644W	MG-16	78745	100-399
STARBRIMSON TRL	Travis Co	532Q	MZ-29	78621	12800-12999
STAR CANYON RD	Travis Co	486U	WR-31	78669	4800-4999
STARCREST LN	Travis Co	557Q	MP-26	78724	6600-6899
STARDUST DR	Austin	525J	MJ-29	78757	2900-3399
STARDUST DR	Williamson Co	373Q	MF-44	78613	1600-1899
STARDUST LN	Georgetown	195T	MJ-61	78633	100-399
STAR FLOWER WAY	Travis Co	467J	MN-35	78660	100-199
STARGAZER CV	Bee Cave	549M	WX-26	78738	4100-4199
STAR GAZER WAY	Pflugerville	407V	MP-40	78660	18300-18499
	Pflugerville	407Z	MP-40	78660	18600-18899
STAR GRASS CIR	Austin	673A	ME-15	78745	2500-2599
STARK PL	Austin	584D	MH-24	78703	2400-2499
STARK ST	Austin	555C	MK-27	78756	800-999
STAR LIGHT CIR	Williamson Co	402V	MD-40	78613	1700-1799
STAR LIGHT CV	Williamson Co	402V	MD-40	78613	1500-1599
STARLIGHT TRL	Williamson Co	224M	MH-59	78633	100-299
STARLIGHT CANYON CT	Travis Co	426P	WQ-38	78669	1000-1199
STARLIGHT TERRACE	Austin	586Q	MM-23	78721	5100-5299
STARLIGHT VISTA	Round Rock	378W	MQ-43	78665	3200-3399
STARLINE DR	Austin	525A	MJ-30	78759	3500-3699
STARLING DR	Round Rock	375V	MK-43	78681	2600-2699
STARLING DR E	Austin	526B	ML-30	78753	200-299
STARLING DR W	Austin	526B	ML-30	78753	100-199
STARR PASS	Leander	342X	MC-46	78641	2000-2099
STARRY NIGHT WAY	Bee Cave	549M	WX-26	78738	14100-14199
STARSTREAK DR	Austin	644X	MG-16	78745	6400-6699
STARVIEW DR	Williamson Co	256W	ML-55	78628	200-499
STAR VIEW TRL	Travis Co	433P	ME-38	78750	11500-11599
	Williamson Co	433P	ME-38	78750	11600-11799
STARWOOD DR	Cedar Park	373L	MF-44	78613	700-999
	Williamson Co	373L	MF-44	78613	1600-1899
STASNEY ST	Taylor	322Z	MZ-49	76574	1800-2599
STASSNEY LN E	Austin	644U	MH-16	78745	100-1199
	Austin	644Z	MH-16	78744	1500-2399
	Austin	645W	MJ-16	78744	2400-6399
STASSNEY LN W	Austin	644P	MG-17	78745	100-1599
	Austin	643H	MF-18	78745	1600-2699
STATLER BEND DR	Pflugerville	407V	MP-40	78660	1000-1299
STATON CV	Austin	466P	ML-35	78727	1800-1899
STATON DR	Austin	466L	MM-35	78727	12800-13199
STATUS KNOLL	Georgetown	314L	MH-50	78628	900-999
STAUNTON DR	Austin	525H	MK-30	78758	8400-8599
STAVE OAK LN	Travis Co	619E	MS-21	78724	15000-15199
STAYE WAY	Travis Co	795G	MK-3	78610	None
STEAMBOAT DR	Austin	672K	MC-14	78749	10200-10499
STEAMBOAT CROSSING	Hays Co	668D	WV-15	78620	100-399
STEAMBOAT SPRINGS CV	Austin	613D	MF-21	78746	1900-1999
STEAMLINE CIR	Austin	673B	ME-15	78745	8300-8599
STEARMAN DR	Georgetown	256D	MM-57	78628	200-299
STEARN'S LN	Austin	613U	MF-19	78735	4200-4899
STECK AVE	Austin	525A	MJ-30	78757	2500-3399
	Austin	495W	MJ-31	78759	3400-3899
	Austin	494V	MH-31	78759	3900-4499
STECK RD	Travis Co	520L	WZ-29	78734	None
STEED DR	Austin	642X	MC-16	78749	4500-4699
STEEDS CROSSING	Pflugerville	409J	MS-41	78660	1500-2099
STEELE RUN	Austin	612Y	MD-19	78749	6200-6299
STEEPLECHASE DR	Georgetown	287L	MP-53	78626	300-499
STEEPLE-CHASE DR	Williamson Co	434U	MH-37	78729	12800-13099
STEER TRL	Austin	612Y	MD-19	78749	6300-6499
STEER ACRES CT	Cedar Park	374U	MH-43	78613	300-399
STEER CREEK CT	Cedar Park	374U	MH-43	78613	3700-3799
STEGER LN	Travis Co	470F	MU-36	78653	16900-18199
STEGNER LN	Travis Co	553E	ME-27	78746	1-99
STEINER RANCH BLVD	Travis Co	491Y	MB-31	78732	2900-4599
	Travis Co	492J	MC-32	78732	4600-5999
STELLAR CV	Austin	641Z	MB-16	78739	10200-10299
STENSON DR	Travis Co	432D	MD-39	78613	2500-2699
STEP DOWN CV	Austin	494Y	MH-31	78731	7500-7599
STEPHANIE LN	Lakeway	549A	WW-27	78734	None
STEPHANIE LEE LN	Travis Co	496Z	MM-31	78753	1100-1199
STEPHANIE'S TRL	Hays Co	795J	MJ-2	78610	100-299
STEPHANIE ST. JOHN ST	Austin	466F	ML-36	78727	13500-13599
STEPHANNE CREEK CV	Austin	674W	MG-13	78744	2000-2099
STEPHANS ST	Austin	498E	MQ-33	78660	3300-3599
STEPHANY TAYLOR DR	Austin	673D	MF-15	78745	7700-7799
STEPHEN DR	Williamson Co	378A	MQ-45	78665	2600-2699
STEPHEN LN	Georgetown	257T	MN-55	78626	100-299
STEPHEN F AUSTIN BLVD					
	Bastrop Co	712Z	MZ-10	78602	100-499
STEPHEN F AUSTIN DR	Austin	584U	MH-22	78703	None
STEPP CV	Cedar Park	403J	ME-41	78613	1100-1199
STEPP BEND	Cedar Park	403N	ME-41	78613	1200-1299
STEPPING STONE CV	Austin	465H	MK-36	78727	12800-12899
STERLING DR	Austin	494Y	MH-31	78731	7800-7899
STERLING HEIGHTS CT	Travis Co	432P	MC-38	78613	3400-3499
STERLINGHILL DR	Austin	496K	ML-32	78758	11500-11899
STERLING PANORAMA CT	Travis Co	550R	WZ-26	78733	2600-2699
STERLING PANORAMA TERRACE					
	Travis Co	550R	WZ-26	78733	11700-11899
STERZING ST	Austin	584Y	MH-22	78704	400-499
STETSON CIR	Georgetown	226A	ML-60	78633	100-199
STETSON CV	Lago Vista	399S	WW-40	78645	21900-21999
STETSON TRL	Georgetown	226A	ML-60	78633	100-199
STEVEN ST	Hutto	379G	MT-45	78634	100-199
STEVENAGE DR	Pflugerville	468E	MQ-36	78660	600-899
STEVEN CREEK WAY	Austin	616C	MM-21	78721	5500-5899
STEVENS CV	Austin	556G	MM-27	78723	2400-2499
STEVENSON AVE	Austin	554X	MG-25	78703	3000-3899
STEVEN WAYNE CT	Travis Co	549A	WW-27	78738	16200-16399
STEVE SCARBOROUGH DR	Austin	465T	MJ-34	78759	4200-4399
STEVIE RAY DR	Pflugerville	407U	MP-40	78664	18200-18399
STEWART CV	Travis Co	489R	WX-32	78734	1000-1099
STEWART DR	Hutto	379R	MT-44	78634	200-599
	Hutto	380N	MU-44	78634	600-899
STEWART RD	Lakeway	490S	WY-31	78734	15600-15699
	Travis Co	490S	WY-31	78734	15700-16299
	Travis Co	489R	WX-32	78734	16300-16599
STILES CV	Austin	586Y	MM-22	78721	6200-6299
STILES LN	Cedar Park	374V	MH-43	78613	4400-4499
STILL FOREST DR	Bastrop Co	711V	MX-10	78612	100-299
STILL FOREST ST	Williamson Co	434K	MG-38	78729	13000-13299
STILL HOLLOW CREEK	Buda	732X	MC-7	78610	100-199
STILLHOUSE SPRING	Williamson Co	375T	MJ-43	78681	800-1199
STILLMEADOW	Round Rock	378L	MR-44	78664	1-99
STILLMEADOW CT	Village of the Hills	519N	WW-29	78738	1-99
STILL MEADOW CV	Georgetown	287M	MP-53	78626	1000-1099
STILL MEADOW CV	Williamson Co	375L	MK-44	78681	1700-1799
STILL MEADOW DR	Leander	342P	MC-47	78641	1100-1399
STILLMEADOW DR	Village of the Hills	519N	WW-29	78738	1-99
STILLRIDGE DR	Austin	611V	MB-19	78736	7600-7699
STILLWATER CT	Georgetown	226G	MM-60	78628	31000-31099
STILLWATER LN	Williamson Co	434L	MH-38	78729	8800-8999
STILLWELL RIDGE	Williamson Co	402Q	MD-41	78613	1100-1299
STILLWOOD CT	Lago Vista	458D	WV-36	78645	21000-21199
STILLWOOD DR	Lago Vista	458D	WV-36	78645	3600-3799
STILLWOOD LN	Austin	525B	MJ-30	78757	7900-8599
	Austin	495X	MJ-31	78757	8600-8799
STIPPLING LN	Austin	467Q	MP-35	78660	1100-1199
STIRLING CASTLE CT	Pflugerville	408X	MQ-40	78660	18900-18999
STIRRAT ST	Austin	498E	MQ-33	78660	3100-3299
STIRRUP CIR	Hays Co	577J	WS-23	78620	400-499
STIRRUP CV	Lago Vista	399S	WW-40	78645	21900-21999
STIRRUP CV	Leander	372C	MD-45	78641	2800-2899
STIRRUP DR	Hays Co	577J	WS-23	78620	200-399
	Travis Co	577J	WS-23	78738	None
STIRRUP DR	Round Rock	406Q	MM-41	78681	2100-2499
STIRRUP LN	Leander	372B	MC-45	78641	None
STOBAUGH ST	Austin	525R	MK-29	78757	800-1299
STOCK LN	Austin	645A	MJ-18	78741	2800-3099
STOCKMAN TRL	Georgetown	225G	MK-60	78633	100-199
STOCK TANK CV	Austin	403H	MF-42	78717	14600-14699
STOCKTON DR	Williamson Co	343S	ME-46	78641	16800-16999
STOCKTON LN	Austin	678E	MQ-15	78617	4900-5199
STOKES DR	Austin	586W	ML-22	78702	2900-3199
STOKES LN	Travis Co	439R	MT-38	78634	19300-19399
STOKESAY CASTLE PATH	Pflugerville	408T	MQ-40	78660	600-799
STONE CIR	Georgetown	286Q	MM-53	78626	600-699
STONE PASS	Austin	643L	MF-17	78745	6000-6099
STONE ST N	Round Rock	376Z	MM-43	78664	100-299
STONE ST S	Round Rock	376Z	MM-43	78664	101-199 O
STONE WAY	Round Rock	408A	MQ-42	78665	1400-1499
STONEBRIDGE DR	Austin	496W	ML-31	78758	9500-9699
STONEBRIDGE DR	Williamson Co	375W	MJ-43	78681	500-3899
STONEBRIDGE MEADOW DR					
	Travis Co	530A	MU-30	78653	13700-13799
STONE CANYON DR	Travis Co	553R	MF-26	78746	900-999
STONECLIFF CIR	Austin	524H	MH-30	78731	7500-7599
STONECLIFF CV	Austin	524H	MH-30	78731	7400-7499
STONECLIFF DR	Austin	524D	MH-30	78731	7500-7599
STONE CLIFF DR	Lago Vista	428V	WV-37	78645	20900-21199
STONECREEK DR	Round Rock	375G	MK-45	78681	2800-3099
STONECREEK PL	Round Rock	375G	MK-45	78681	2800-2899
STONE CREST BLVD	Buda	763N	ME-5	78610	100-299
STONE CREST DR	Austin	614Q	MH-20	78704	2400-2499
STONE CREST DR	Travis Co	468P	MQ-35	78660	None
STONECROFT DR	Austin	642M	MD-17	78749	3800-4199
STONEFIELD TRL	Hays Co	763S	ME-4	78610	100-499
STONE FOREST TRL	Round Rock	345N	MJ-47	78681	1100-1199
STONE GATE CIR	Austin	586M	MM-23	78721	4400-4499
STONE GATE DR	Austin	586M	MM-23	78721	5100-5299
STONEHAM CIR	Pflugerville	437P	MN-38	78660	16001-16199 O
STONEHAVEN CIR	Austin	524D	MH-30	78731	7700-7799
STONEHAVEN LN	Williamson Co	347E	MN-48	78665	1600-1799
STONEHEDGE BLVD	Georgetown	287L	MP-53	78626	1-499
STONEHENGE CV	Cedar Park	372P	MC-44	78613	1900-1999
STONEHENGE PATH	Round Rock	345K	MJ-47	78681	3900-3999
STONE HILL DR	Pflugerville	438C	MR-39	78660	1500-1699
STONEHOLLOW DR	Austin	496E	ML-33	78758	11500-11599
	Austin	495D	MK-33	78758	11600-11799
	Austin	496A	ML-33	78758	11800-11999
STONELAKE BLVD	Austin	495F	MJ-33	78759	9400-10699
	Austin	495B	MJ-33	78759	10700-10999
STONE LEDGE CIR	Austin	611U	MB-19	78736	7100-7199
STONE MANOR TRL	Round Rock	377G	MP-45	78665	1300-1399
STONE MOUNTAIN DR	Jonestown	400Z	WZ-40	78645	9201-9399 O
STONE OAK DR	Round Rock	345P	MJ-47	78681	3400-4499
STONEOAK LN	Austin	643V	MF-16	78745	900-1299
STONE RIDGE CIR	Austin	583Y	MF-22	78746	1800-1899
STONE RIDGE DR	Taylor	322Q	MZ-50	76574	1200-1499
STONE RIDGE DR	Travis Co	489V	WX-31	78734	200-499
STONERIDGE RD	Austin	583Y	MF-22	78746	1700-1999
	Travis Co	583X	ME-22	78746	3200-3699
STONERIDGE GAP LN	Manor	530B	MU-30	78653	None
STONERIDGE TERRACE	Travis Co	583X	ME-22	78746	1700-2099
STONE RIM LOOP	Buda	763J	ME-5	78610	1000-1899
STONE RIVER DR	Austin	643X	ME-16	78745	2100-2499
STONE SHADOW CV	Lakeway	518H	WV-30	78734	100-199
STONE SLOPE CT	Williamson Co	346H	MM-48	78665	1100-1199
STONESTOP BLVD	Austin	403Y	MF-40	78613	13100-13199
STONE TERRACE DR	Lakeway	520J	WY-29	78734	1-99
STONETHROW WAY	Austin	673W	ME-13	78748	1400-1499
STONE VIEW TRL	Hays Co	639L	WX-17	78737	100-699
STONEWALL DR	Round Rock	345J	MJ-47	78681	3300-3399
STONEWALL LN	Travis Co	583R	MF-23	78746	300-399
STONEWALL BEND CV	Pflugerville	439J	MS-38	78660	2800-2899
STONEWALL RIDGE LN	Travis Co	552Z	MD-25	78746	700-899
STONEWATER BLVD	Manor	530B	MU-30	78653	None
STONEWAY DR	Austin	525J	MJ-29	78757	2900-3199
STONEWREATH DR	Williamson Co	375K	MJ-44	78681	1900-1999
STONEY BROOK	Williamson Co	375T	MJ-43	78681	600-799
STONEY BROOK DR	Bastrop Co	712S	MY-10	78612	100-199
STONEY BROOK DR	Williamson Co	409C	MT-42	78634	100-499
STONEY CREEK CV	Lakeway	519F	WW-30	78734	100-199
STONEY HILL	Williamson Co	375W	MJ-43	78681	3900-4099
STONEY HILL WAY	Travis Co	468P	MQ-35	78660	None
STONEY MEADOW DR	Travis Co	677Y	MP-13	78617	11800-12299
STONEY POINT RD	Hays Co	669N	WW-14	78737	100-399
STONEYWOOD DR	Austin	524D	MH-30	78731	7600-7899
STONLEIGH PL	Austin	674G	MH-15	78744	6500-7399
STONY DR	Austin	465V	MK-34	78759	3100-3199
STONYBROOK DR	Travis Co	460W	WY-34	78645	17000-17299
STONY CREEK DR	Bastrop Co	709P	MS-11	78617	1-199
STONY MEADOW LN	Austin	524F	MG-30	78731	4400-4499
STONY MONT DR	Bastrop Co	709P	MS-11	78617	1-99
STONY POINT DR	Bastrop Co	709P	MS-11	78617	1-299
STONY RIDGE DR	Bastrop Co	709P	MS-11	78617	1-199
STORK RD	Bastrop Co	738X	MQ-7	78617	100-399
STORM DR	Travis Co	490Q	WZ-32	78734	15100-15699
STORMY RIDGE RD	Travis Co	672N	MC-14	78739	11000-11399
STOUT OAK TRL	Williamson Co	433K	ME-38	78750	11900-12099
STOUTWOOD CIR	Austin	643G	MF-18	78745	2500-2799
STOW CIR	Briarcliff	487C	WT-33	78669	22200-22299
STOW DR	Briarcliff	487D	WT-33	78669	800-999
STOWAWAY CV	Lakeway	519C	WX-30	78734	200-299
STRADER CIR	Lakeway	519R	WX-29	78734	15000-15099
	Travis Co	519R	WX-29	78734	15100-15299
STRAHLE LN	Lakeway	489Z	WX-31	78734	500-599
STRAIT WAY	Travis Co	619F	MS-21	78724	None
STRAND ST	Austin	672U	MD-13	78748	10700-10999
STRANDTMAN CV	Austin	616K	ML-20	78702	1-99
STRASS DR	Austin	555E	MJ-27	78731	4600-5099
STRATFORD CT	Round Rock	407N	MN-41	78664	1100-1199
STRATFORD CV	Round Rock	407N	MN-41	78664	1100-1199
STRATFORD DR	Austin	584E	MG-24	78746	2200-3499
STRATFORD DR	Round Rock	407J	MN-41	78664	1200-1799
STRATFORD GREEN LN	Austin	584E	MG-24	78746	None
STRATFORD HILLS LN	Austin	584E	MG-24	78746	3200-3499
STRATHERN DR	Travis Co	587L	MP-23	78724	5600-5999
STRATTON CT	Hays Co	639T	WW-16	78737	100-199
STRAWBERRY CV	Austin	644W	MG-16	78745	500-599
STRAW FLOWER DR	Travis Co	551K	MA-26	78733	10600-10899
STRAY CV	Williamson Co	375X	MJ-43	78681	16900-16999
STREAMSIDE DR	Travis Co	611E	MA-21	78736	9600-9699
STRICHEN DR	Briarcliff	458N	WU-35	78669	400-599
STRICKLAND DR	Austin	673G	MF-15	78748	1100-1699
STRIDER DR	Travis Co	672S	MC-13	78739	3900-3999
STROBEL LN	Austin	702H	MD-12	78748	1700-1799
STRONTIAN PASS	Travis Co	437C	MP-39	78660	17500-17699
STROUP CIR	Travis Co	490P	WY-32	78734	15400-15599
STRUIE LN	Austin	642T	MC-16	78749	9200-9399
STRUTTON CV	Austin	464U	MH-34	78759	6600-6699
STUART CIR	Austin	616C	MM-21	78721	5400-5699

S

STREET NAME	CITY or COUNTY	MAPSCO GRID	AUSTIN GRID	ZIP CODE	BLOCK RANGE O/E
STUART CT	Austin	586Y	MM-22	78721	5500-5599
STUART CV	Williamson Co	343W	ME-46	78641	700-799
STUBBLEFIELD DR	Elgin	533H	EB-30	78621	100-199
STUBBLE QUAIL CIR	Austin	496N	ML-32	78758	10300-10399
STUBBLE QUAIL DR	Austin	496N	ML-32	78758	10300-10399
STURGIS LN	Austin	702G	MD-12	78748	2400-2499
STURGIS ST	Taylor	353J	EA-47	76574	300-799
	Taylor	353N	EA-47	76574	1000-1199
STURMER ST	Austin	705A	MJ-12	78747	8600-8799
SUBURBAN DR	Austin	644Q	MH-17	78745	4600-5399
SUCCESSOR RD	Travis Co	457W	WS-34	78669	1300-1599
SUDBURY CV	Austin	702C	MD-12	78748	11900-11999
SUDDUTH DR	Georgetown	257E	MN-57	78626	100-199
SUEDE TRL	Cedar Park	373Q	MF-44	78613	400-499
SUENA DR	Austin	616X	ML-19	78741	6800-6899
SUFFIELD DR	Hays Co	762Z	MD-4	78610	100-199
	Hays Co	763W	ME-4	78610	100-499
SUFFOLK CT	Cedar Park	373U	MF-43	78613	1000-1099
SUFFOLK DR	Austin	556N	ML-26	78723	1300-1699
SUGAR BERRY CV	Round Rock	377X	MN-43	78664	3000-3099
SUGARBERRY DR	Cedar Park	402D	MD-42	78613	1100-1299
SUGARBERRY LN	Austin	673K	ME-14	78748	1400-1699
SUGAR CREEK DR	West Lake Hills	583R	MF-23	78746	1-99
SUGAR HILL DR	Austin	672H	MD-15	78748	9600-9799
SUGAR LEAF PL	Austin	702B	MC-12	78748	12300-12399
SUGARLOAF DR	Bee Cave	549M	WX-26	78738	None
SUGAR MAPLE CT	Austin	644Z	MH-16	78744	5400-5499
SUGAR MAPLE CT	Travis Co	432K	MC-38	78613	2800-2899
SUGAR MAPLE DR	Travis Co	489E	WW-33	78645	None
SUGAR SHACK DR	Austin	584J	MG-23	78746	3000-3199
	West Lake Hills	584J	MG-23	78746	1-99
SULLIVAN ST	Pflugerville	408V	MR-40	78660	1700-1799
SULLIVAN RIDGE	Hays Co	606T	WQ-19	78620	100-399
SULLY CREEK DR	Austin	702G	MD-12	78748	2300-2499
SULTANA CT	Williamson Co	408K	MQ-41	78664	100-199
SUMAC CT	Round Rock	375C	MK-45	78681	3000-3099
SUMAC CV	Williamson Co	193B	ME-63	78633	100-199
SUMAC DR	Austin	524L	MH-29	78731	6400-6699
SUMAC LN	Cedar Park	372D	MD-45	78613	200-2799
SUMAC LN N	Williamson Co	193C	MF-63	78633	100-199
SUMAC LN S	Williamson Co	193C	MF-63	78633	200-299
SUMATRA LN	Travis Co	467Q	MP-35	78660	14100-14299
SUMMER CIR	Austin	615Z	MK-19	78741	5300-5499
SUMMER DR	Austin	615Z	MK-19	78741	5200-5399
SUMMER RD	Georgetown	195V	MK-61	78633	100-399
SUMMER ALCOVE WAY	Travis Co	521S	MA-28	78732	200-599
SUMMER CANYON DR	Travis Co	491P	MA-32	78732	3200-3399
SUMMER CREEK CT	Austin	614P	MG-20	78704	1600-1699
SUMMER CREEK DR	Austin	614P	MG-20	78704	1400-1599
SUMMERCREST BLVD	Georgetown	287K	MN-53	78626	1200-1899
SUMMERCREST CV	Williamson Co	344Z	MH-46	78681	2000-2099
SUMMERCREST LOOP N	Williamson Co	344Y	MH-46	78681	4100-4299
SUMMERCREST LOOP S	Williamson Co	344Z	MH-46	78681	4300-4499
SUMMERHILL CV	Austin	494H	MH-33	78759	9200-9299
SUMMER LAKE DR	Travis Co	560L	MV-26	78653	18600-18999
SUMMER OAK CT	Williamson Co	283Q	MF-53	78628	100-199
SUMMER OAKS DR	Austin	614X	MG-19	78704	1300-1399
SUMMER PLACE DR	Austin	495W	MJ-31	78759	8200-8399
SUMMER RAIN DR	Williamson Co	402V	MD-40	78613	1800-1999
SUMMER RIDGE LN	Georgetown	195T	MJ-61	78633	100-199
SUMMERS	Austin	586N	ML-23	78702	1100-1199
SUMMERSET TRL	Austin	612Y	MD-19	78749	4700-5399
SUMMERS GREEN	Georgetown	225V	MK-58	78628	101-399 O
SUMMER SIDE DR	Austin	495W	MJ-31	78759	8200-8399
SUMMER SKY DR	Travis Co	611E	MA-21	78736	9300-9599
SUMMERSTONE DR	Austin	614X	MG-19	78704	1500-1599
SUMMERSWEET CV	Austin	434Y	MH-37	78729	12400-12499
SUMMER TREE CT	Austin	495S	MJ-31	78759	8400-8499
SUMMERVALE DR	Travis Co	641C	MB-18	78737	7600-7899
SUMMERWALK PL	Round Rock	347V	MP-46	78665	2600-2799
SUMMER WIND CIR	Austin	674Q	MH-14	78744	7700-7799
SUMMERWOOD CT	Cedar Park	373Y	MF-43	78613	1300-1399
SUMMER WOOD CT	Williamson Co	283Q	MF-53	78628	200-299
SUMMERWOOD DR	Austin	495S	MJ-31	78759	8200-8399
SUMMIT PASS	Hays Co	608Z	WV-19	78737	12400-12599
SUMMIT DR	Dripping Springs	636R	WR-17	78620	100-399
SUMMIT DR	Travis Co	436X	ML-37	78728	14000-14199
SUMMIT DR	Travis Co	436C	MM-39	78728	16300-16499
	Williamson Co	436C	MM-39	78728	16200-16299
SUMMIT DR E	Briarcliff	487D	WT-33	78669	700-799
SUMMIT DR W	Briarcliff	487D	WT-33	78669	22100-22199
SUMMIT ST	Austin	615P	MJ-20	78741	1000-1799
SUMMIT ST	Georgetown	195T	MJ-61	78633	100-399
SUMMIT ST	Round Rock	376U	MM-43	78664	700-999
SUMMIT BEND	Austin	525A	MJ-30	78759	3600-3699
SUMMIT EDGE DR	Travis Co	550D	WZ-27	78732	1200-1499
SUMMIT HEIGHTS CT	Pflugerville	439E	MS-39	78660	2800-2899
SUMMIT RIDGE DR	Lago Vista	429V	WX-37	78645	5900-6199
SUMMIT RIDGE DR N	Point Venture	489J	WW-32	78645	100-499
SUMMIT RIDGE DR S	Point Venture	489J	WW-32	78645	100-199
SUMMITT CIR	Taylor	322U	MZ-49	76574	1400-1499
SUMMIT VIEW	Austin	584G	MH-24	78703	1700-1799
SUMMIT VIEW DR	Travis Co	309U	WX-49	78641	14200-14599
SUMMONERS TALE CT	Austin	703A	ME-12	78748	1300-1399
SUMNER CT	Travis Co	552L	MD-26	78733	8300-8399
SUNBEAM CV	Round Rock	376M	MM-44	78664	1100-1199
SUNBIRD CT	Georgetown	195V	MK-61	78633	100-199
SUN BIRD LN	Travis Co	520A	WY-30	78734	15100-15299
SUNBONNET CV	Travis Co	736M	MM-8	78719	11900-12099
SUN BONNET DR	Hays Co	762M	MD-5	78610	400-499
SUNBURST PKWY	Williamson Co	375Q	MK-44	78681	8000-8399
SUNBURST TERRACE	Williamson Co	375P	MJ-44	78681	9000-9099
SUN CHASE BLVD	Cedar Park	402V	MD-40	78613	1900-2299
	Williamson Co	402V	MD-40	78613	1400-1899
	Williamson Co	432D	MD-39	78613	2300-2499
SUN CITY BLVD	Georgetown	196S	ML-61	78628	500-799
	Georgetown	196Z	MK-61	78633	800-1099
	Georgetown	225C	MK-60	78633	1100-1899
	Georgetown	195P	MJ-62	78633	1900-3199
	Williamson Co	196P	ML-62	78628	1-499
	Williamson Co	225C	MK-60	78633	None
SUNCREST RD	Travis Co	530B	MU-30	78653	13500-14199
	Travis Co	500X	MU-31	78653	14200-14299
SUN DANCE CV	Lago Vista	399S	WW-40	78645	21600-21699
SUNDANCE DR	Round Rock	376D	MM-45	78665	1500-1599
	Round Rock	377A	MN-45	78665	1600-1699
SUNDANCE LN	Georgetown	195V	MK-61	78633	100-599
SUNDANCE PKWY	Round Rock	406T	ML-40	78681	100-499
SUNDANCE TRL	Hays Co	576M	WR-23	78620	100-299
	Hays Co	577E	WS-24	78620	300-399
SUNDANCER CIR	Jonestown	430T	WY-37	78645	None
SUNDANCE RIDGE DR	Hays Co	668B	WU-15	78620	1000-1099
SUN DAPPLE CT	Travis Co	529M	MT-29	78653	None
SUNDARA DR	Austin	670H	WZ-15	78739	12300-12399
SUNDAY SCHOOL DR	Georgetown	225X	MJ-58	78633	200-299
SUNDAY SILENCE DR	Austin	678P	MQ-14	78617	5500-5699
SUNDERLAND DR	Austin	497J	MN-32	78753	12100-12199
SUNDEW PASS	Austin	672A	MC-15	78739	10100-10299
SUNDIAL CV	Austin	673H	MF-15	78748	600-699
SUNDOWN	Lago Vista	429S	WW-37	78645	5000-5199
SUNDOWN DR	Travis Co	551N	MA-26	78738	1600-1699
SUNDOWN PKWY	Travis Co	583F	ME-24	78746	1-199
	West Lake Hills	583F	ME-24	78746	None
SUNDOWN TRL	Travis Co	672S	MC-13	78748	11400-11699
SUNDOWN RIDGE	Hays Co	638M	WV-17	78737	100-499
SUN DRENCHED PATH	Travis Co	491N	MA-32	78732	3100-3199
SUNDROP CV	Round Rock	407G	MP-42	78665	1200-1399
SUNDROP PL	Round Rock	407C	MP-42	78665	1100-1299
SUNDROP VALLEY DR	Austin	672A	MC-15	78739	10200-10399
SUNFISH	Lakeway	519B	WW-30	78734	300-599
	Lakeway	489X	WW-31	78734	600-899
SUNFLOWER CT	Leander	342P	MC-47	78641	1100-1199
SUNFLOWER DR	Pflugerville	468B	MQ-36	78660	100-499
	Pflugerville	438X	MQ-37	78660	500-999
SUNFLOWER DR	Travis Co	736M	MM-8	78719	9700-9999
SUNFLOWER ST	Georgetown	225H	MK-60	78633	100-199
SUNFLOWER TRL	Sunset Valley	613X	ME-19	78745	None
SUNGATE DR	Austin	524G	MH-30	78731	7100-7299
SUN GLASS DR	Travis Co	530E	MU-30	78653	11500-11799
SUN GLIDE LN	Travis Co	529H	MT-30	78653	None
SUNHAVEN CV	Elgin	532M	MZ-29	78621	None
SUN HILL DR	Austin	496S	ML-31	78758	10200-10299
SUNHILLOW BEND	Austin	496A	ML-33	78758	11900-11999
SUNKEN CREEK PASS	Pflugerville	408Z	MR-40	78660	None
SUNKIST DR	Caldwell Co	796Z	MM-1	78644	1-299
SUNKIST LN	Austin	612Z	MD-19	78749	6200-6299
SUN LAKE	Williamson Co	375K	MJ-44	78681	1800-1899
SUNLAND DR	Austin	672X	MC-13	78748	3000-3299
SUN MOUNTAIN	Leander	372E	MC-45	78641	2700-2799
SUNNINGDALE CV	Austin	404F	MG-42	78717	10200-10299
SUNNINGDALE ST	Austin	404F	MG-42	78717	15100-15399
SUNNY LN	Austin	615E	MJ-21	78704	500-599
SUNNY LN	Austin	554D	MH-27	78731	3200-3299
SUNNY LN	Cedar Park	403E	ME-42	78613	700-999
SUNNY LN	Jonestown	400M	WZ-41	78645	10500-10899
SUNNY LN	Taylor	322V	MZ-49	76574	2700-2799
SUNNY BROOK DR	Austin	556T	ML-25	78723	1900-2099
SUNNY BROOK DR	Leander	341D	MB-48	78641	200-799
SUNNY CREEK DR	Williamson Co	288D	MR-54	78626	100-199
SUNNY CREEK LN	Travis Co	529H	MT-30	78653	11500-11699
SUNNY GROVE LN	Williamson Co	224D	MH-60	78633	100-199
SUNNY HILLS DR	Austin	674L	MH-14	78744	2200-2599
SUNNYLAWN CIR	Austin	556V	MM-25	78723	3100-3199
SUNNY OAK LN	Travis Co	340E	WY-48	78641	23000-23299
	Travis Co	339H	WX-48	78641	None
SUNNY OAKS	Pflugerville	438N	MQ-38	78660	800-899
SUNNY SIDE BEND	Georgetown	195P	MJ-62	78633	100-199
SUNNYSKY WAY	Austin	644X	MG-16	78745	6400-6599
SUNNY SLOPE DR	Austin	554Y	MH-25	78703	2200-2399
SUNNY SLOPE DR	Williamson Co	252B	MC-57	78642	100-399
	Williamson Co	222X	MC-58	78642	400-999
SUNNYVALE	Williamson Co	197Z	MP-61	78626	100-599
SUNNY VALE ST	Austin	615P	MJ-20	78741	1500-1699
SUNNY VISTA DR	Austin	642N	MC-17	78749	5500-5899
SUNRIDGE CT	Austin	645G	MK-18	78741	4700-4799
SUNRIDGE DR	Austin	645C	MK-18	78741	2600-3099
SUNRISE CIR	Austin	614R	MH-20	78704	500-599
SUNRISE LN	Bastrop Co	564T	EC-25	78621	100-199
SUNRISE RD	Round Rock	376M	MM-44	78664	1000-2699
	Round Rock	376D	MM-45	78665	2700-2799
	Round Rock	346V	MM-46	78665	2800-4399
	Williamson Co	346L	MM-47	78665	4400-4499
SUNRISE TRL	Hays Co	576M	WR-23	78620	100-599
SUNRISE RIDGE CV	Lakeway	549D	WX-27	78734	100-299
SUNRISE RIDGE LOOP	Lakeway	549D	WX-27	78734	100-299
SUNRISE TERRACE	Williamson Co	373R	MF-44	78613	100-599
SUNRISE VALLEY LN	Georgetown	286Z	MM-52	78626	2400-2999
SUNSET CIR	Austin	614R	MH-20	78704	500-599
SUNSET DR	Round Rock	376U	MM-43	78664	100-499
	Round Rock	376T	ML-43	78681	600-699
SUNSET DR	San Leanna	703F	ME-12	78748	11400-11599
SUNSET DR	Williamson Co	256W	ML-55	78628	400-499
SUNSET DR W	San Leanna	703K	ME-11	78748	11600-11699
SUNSET LN	Austin	615J	MJ-20	78704	1400-1999
SUNSET LN	Lago Vista	429W	WW-37	78645	20300-20599
SUNSET RD	Williamson Co	224E	MG-60	78633	100-299
SUNSET TRL	Austin	613Y	MF-19	78745	4600-5099
	Sunset Valley	643C	MF-18	78745	1-99
SUNSET BLUFF	Jonestown	429M	WX-38	78645	6800-7099
SUNSET CANYON DR N	Hays Co	638P	WU-17	78620	1000-1099
SUNSET CANYON DR S	Hays Co	638Y	WV-16	78720	1000-1099
	Hays Co	668G	WV-15	78620	None
SUNSET HEIGHTS CIR	Austin	612J	MC-20	78735	7300-7499
SUNSET HOLLOW	Travis Co	340J	WY-47	78641	22400-22799
SUNSET PARK CV	Lakeway	489V	WX-31	78734	1-99
SUNSET RIDGE	Austin	611C	MB-21	78735	5500-5999
SUNSET RIDGE	Hays Co	576M	WR-23	78620	100-299
SUNSET RIDGE	Williamson Co	224D	MH-60	78633	100-299
	Williamson Co	194Z	MH-61	78633	300-499
SUNSET RIDGE	Williamson Co	252E	MC-57	78642	100-599
SUNSET RIVER CIR	Travis Co	427W	WS-37	78669	25200-25299
SUNSET STRIP	Lago Vista	429K	WW-38	78645	20400-20599
SUNSET TERRACE	Cedar Park	373V	MF-43	78613	None
	Williamson Co	373U	MF-43	78613	200-599
SUNSET VIEW	Austin	584Y	MH-22	78704	1800-1899
SUNSHINE DR	Austin	555C	MK-27	78756	4800-5799
	Austin	555C	MK-27	78757	5800-5999
SUNSHINE DR	Georgetown	286T	ML-52	78628	100-299
SUN SHOWER BEND	Austin	587R	MP-23	78724	8900-9099
SUN SPIRIT DR	Austin	613E	ME-21	78735	4100-4299
SUNSTRIP DR	Austin	644S	MG-16	78745	6400-6699
SUNSWEPT DR	Jonestown	430J	WY-38	78645	7200-7299
SUNTERRO DR	Austin	466L	MM-35	78727	1600-1799
SUN TREE CV	Travis Co	492T	MC-31	78730	10500-10799
SUN VALLEY CT	Lakeway	519M	WX-29	78734	1600-1699
SUNVIEW RD	Travis Co	519Q	WX-29	78738	1-99
SUN VISTA DR	Austin	612Y	MD-19	78749	6000-6299
SUPERIOR DR	Travis Co	467K	MN-35	78660	None
SUPERVIEW DR	Travis Co	610G	WZ-21	78736	10500-10899
SURRENDER AVE	Travis Co	436Y	MM-37	78728	2000-2199
SURREY DR	Austin	644L	MH-17	78745	4700-4899
SURREY DR	Round Rock	406M	MM-41	78664	1400-2299
SURREY LN	Cedar Park	372P	MC-44	78613	1800-1899
SURREY LN	Lago Vista	399S	WW-40	78645	21400-21899
SURREY HILL DR	Austin	583S	ME-22	78746	1500-1999
SURVEYORS CROSSING	Travis Co	577L	WT-23	78720	18200-18699
SURVIVAL RD	Austin	646Z	MM-16	78719	3500-3599
SUSAN DR	Hays Co	763S	ME-4	78610	100-499
SUSAN DR	Travis Co	490T	WY-31	78734	1400-1799
SUSAN LN	Williamson Co	342Z	MD-46	78641	300-699
	Williamson Co	343S	ME-46	78641	2200-2499
SUSANA CT	Georgetown	286X	ML-52	78628	100-199
SUSANA DR	Georgetown	286X	ML-52	78628	100-399
	Georgetown	316A	ML-51	78628	400-599
SUSETTE DR	Bastrop Co	592N	MY-23	78621	8600-9099
SUSIE CT	Austin	524Z	MH-28	78757	5700-5799
SUSIE ST	Travis Co	703A	ME-12	78748	11300-11699
SUSQUEHANNA LN	Austin	556M	MM-26	78723	2900-3199
	Austin	557J	MN-26	78723	3200-3599
SUSSEX GARDENS LN	Austin	702B	MC-12	78748	2900-3099
SUSSEX DR	Austin	644Q	MH-17	78745	800-899
SUSSEX PL	Round Rock	377G	MP-45	78665	None
SUSSEX WAY	Round Rock	377L	MP-44	78665	900-1199
SUSSMAN CT	Travis Co	466C	MM-36	78728	14200-14299
SUTER ST	Austin	702M	MD-11	78748	1700-1899
SUTHERLIN RD	Austin	556U	MM-25	78723	5700-5799
SUTTER CREEK TRL	Williamson Co	375S	MJ-43	78717	1200-1299
SUTTERVILLE CV	Williamson Co	375S	MJ-43	78717	200-299
SUTTON DR	Travis Co	490L	WZ-32	78734	15000-15599
SUTTON PL	Austin	464K	MG-35	78759	7700-7799
SUTTON PL	Georgetown	255H	MK-57	78628	200-399
SUTTON LEIGH'S LN	Travis Co	437S	MN-37	78660	15500-15599
SUZI CV	Pflugerville	437J	MN-38	78660	16300-16399
SUZI LN	Pflugerville	437J	MN-38	78660	1400-1699
SUZZANE RD	Pflugerville	468F	MQ-36	78660	400-599
SVENSKA RD	Travis Co	472D	MZ-36	78615	14900-15599
SWALLOW CT	Austin	525M	MK-29	78758	8300-8399
SWALLOW CV	Williamson Co	282J	MC-53	78641	100-199
SWALLOW DR	Hays Co	701Q	MB-11	78652	1000-1099
SWALLOW DR	Williamson Co	433V	MF-37	78750	11900-12199
SWALLOW RIDGE CV	Pflugerville	468E	MQ-36	78660	900-999
SWALLOWTAIL CIR	Georgetown	225D	MK-60	78633	100-199
SWALLOWTAILED KITE CV	Bee Cave	549L	WX-26	78738	14900-14999
SWAN DR	Austin	433V	MF-37	78750	11500-11899
	Williamson Co	433V	MF-37	78750	11900-12099
SWANEE DR	Austin	525Z	MK-28	78752	300-699
SWANSON CV	Austin	673R	MF-14	78748	600-699
SWANSON LN	Austin	673M	MF-14	78748	8600-9199
SWANSON'S RANCH RD	Austin	673P	ME-14	78748	9600-9899
SWAN VALLEY LN	Austin	464T	MG-34	78759	10000-10199
SWEARINGEN DR	Austin	496K	ML-32	78758	11300-12099
SWEENEY CIR	Austin	556U	MM-25	78723	5800-5899
SWEENEY LN	Austin	556U	MM-25	78723	2500-2999
SWEET AUTUMN CV	Travis Co	582J	MC-23	78735	3100-3299
SWEET BASIL CT	Austin	433W	ME-37	78726	11400-11699
SWEET BASIL DR	Austin	433W	ME-37	78726	10400-10499
SWEETBRIAR AVE	Austin	556P	ML-26	78723	1600-1699
SWEETBRUSH DR	Austin	554X	MG-25	78703	2300-2499
SWEET CADDIE'S DR	Travis Co	437W	MN-37	78660	15100-15399
SWEET CHERRY DR	Austin	464J	MG-35	78750	8400-8599
SWEET CLOVER DR	Austin	673B	ME-15	78745	2000-2699
SWEETGUM CT	Austin	673K	ME-14	78748	1400-1499
SWEETGUM CV	Round Rock	407B	MN-42	78664	500-599
SWEETGUM CV	Travis Co	582J	MC-23	78735	3100-3199
SWEETGUM DR	Austin	673K	ME-14	78748	9100-9699
SWEETGUM LN	Round Rock	407B	MN-42	78664	600-999
SWEETGUM TRACE	Williamson Co	433E	ME-39	78613	3301-3499 O
SWEET LEAF LN	Travis Co	467L	MP-35	78660	200-1699
SWEET MELISSA DR	Austin	437W	MN-37	78660	1000-1099
SWEETNESS LN	Austin	464J	MG-35	78750	8400-8599
SWEETSHADE LN	Austin	464F	MG-36	78759	11500-11699
SWEET SPRING CT	Travis Co	370S	WY-43	78641	11400-11499
SWEET SUMMER DR	Travis Co	340B	WY-48	78641	22400-22699
SWEETWATER CV	Round Rock	375V	MK-43	78681	900-999
SWEETWATER CV	Austin	433P	ME-38	78750	None
	Williamson Co	433P	ME-38	78750	11300-11399
SWEETWATER TRL	Austin	433P	ME-38	78750	11500-11599
	Williamson Co	433P	ME-38	78750	11600-11799
SWEETWATER RIVER CV	Austin	673T	ME-13	78748	10200-10299
SWEETWATER RIVER DR	Austin	673T	ME-13	78748	800-999
SWEET WILLIAM LN	Pflugerville	438X	MQ-37	78660	1200-1499
SWEETWOOD TRL	Hays Co	700N	WY-11	78610	16200-16399
SWEETWOOD SONG DR	Pflugerville	437M	MP-38	78660	1500-1699
SWELFLING TERRACE	Travis Co	640V	WZ-16	78737	11000-11099
SWENSON AVE	Austin	585Z	MK-22	78702	700-1199
SWENSON BLVD	Elgin	533V	EB-28	78621	100-999
SWENSON DR	Hutto	379D	MT-45	78634	100-499
SWENSON FARMS BLVD	Pflugerville	437V	MP-37	78660	100-999
	Pflugerville	437M	MP-38	78660	1000-1299
SWIFTCURRENT TRL	West Lake Hills	583F	ME-24	78746	100-199
SWIFTWATER	Hays Co	667B	WS-15	78620	100-299
SWIFTWATER CV	Village of the Hills	519S	WW-28	78738	1-99
SWIFTWATER TRL	Village of the Hills	519S	WW-28	78738	1-99
SWINDOLL LN	Hutto	380S	MU-43	78634	1-299
SWINDON LN	Austin	643T	ME-16	78745	7800-8099
SWING LN	Travis Co	490K	WY-32	78734	15600-15799
SWINLEY FOREST CV	Austin	404F	MG-42	78717	14600-14699
SWIRLING WIND CV	Travis Co	581D	MB-24	78735	2300-2499
SWISHER ST	Austin	585G	MK-24	78705	2700-2999
SWISS DR	Travis Co	708T	MQ-10	78617	14800-15099
SWISS ALPS CT	Bee Cave	549K	WW-26	78738	15200-15499
SWITCHGRASS CV	Austin	464A	MG-36	78750	11700-11799
SWITCH WILLO	Austin	465P	MJ-35	78727	4400-4899
SYBERT LN	Georgetown	227A	MN-60	78628	30800-30899
SYCAMORE CV	Round Rock	377X	MN-43	78664	3200-3299
SYCAMORE DR	Austin	585D	MK-24	78722	3800-3999
SYCAMORE DR	Cedar Park	402D	MD-42	78613	100-499
SYCAMORE ST	Cedar Park	433A	ME-39	78613	1600-1699

STREET NAME	CITY or COUNTY	MAPSCO GRID	AUSTIN GRID	ZIP CODE	BLOCK RANGE O/E
SYCAMORE ST	Georgetown	225R	MK-59	78633	100-399
SYCAMORE ST	Taylor	353A	EA-48	76574	1000-1199
SYCAMORE TRL	Round Rock	377X	MN-43	78664	2100-2499
SYCAMORE TRL	Sunset Valley	613X	ME-19	78745	None
SYCAMORE HILLS RD	Austin	404E	MG-42	78717	10700-10799
SYDNEE DR	Leander	341H	MB-48	78641	2000-2199
SYDNEY DR	Travis Co	436U	MM-37	78728	2800-2999
SYDNEY MARILYN LN	Austin	673V	MF-13	78748	9500-9799
SYDNEYS WAY	Buda	732U	MD-7	78610	100-199
SYKES CT	Pflugerville	468E	MQ-36	78660	800-899
SYLVAN DR	Austin	615P	MJ-20	78741	1600-1899
SYLVAN ST	Hutto	349M	MT-47	78634	100-399
SYLVAN WAY	Travis Co	430Q	WZ-38	78645	17400-17499
SYLVANDALE DR	Austin	644A	MG-18	78745	4700-4999
SYLVAN GLADE	Austin	644A	MG-18	78745	1500-1699
SYLVESTER FORD RD	Lago Vista	459U	WX-34	78645	17801-18599 O
	Travis Co	459U	WX-34	78645	17800-18598 E
SYLVIA LN	Pflugerville	468K	MQ-35	78660	800-899
SYLVIA LN	Round Rock	376N	ML-44	78681	1400-1899
SYMES ST	Taylor	353J	EA-47	76574	300-799
	Taylor	353N	EA-47	76574	1000-1199
SYRACUSE CV	Austin	556R	MM-26	78723	6800-6899

T

STREET NAME	CITY or COUNTY	MAPSCO GRID	AUSTIN GRID	ZIP CODE	BLOCK RANGE O/E
TABBY CV	Austin	678N	MQ-14	78617	5500-5599
TABITHA CV	Austin	678P	MQ-14	78617	5400-5499
TABLEROCK CIR	Leander	342F	MC-48	78641	500-599
TABLEROCK DR	Austin	494Y	MH-31	78731	4000-4199
TABLE TOP TRL	Austin	645W	MJ-16	78744	5000-5099
TABLETOP MOUNTAIN DR	Travis Co	487T	WS-31	78669	3100-3799
TABOR CT	Austin	673J	ME-14	78748	2200-2299
TABOR OAKS DR	Austin	702F	MC-12	78739	12400-12599
TACON LN	Travis Co	437X	MN-37	78660	15100-15699
TAD PARK CV	Williamson Co	375T	MJ-43	78681	8500-8599
TAEBAEK DR	Austin	527C	MP-30	78754	2800-3699
TAFFY CT	Austin	614T	MG-19	78704	1000-1099
TAHITIAN DR	Bastrop	746S	EG-7	78602	100-199
	Bastrop Co	746S	EG-7	78602	200-299
	Bastrop Co	776E	EG-6	78602	300-599
TAHOE LN	Lago Vista	399R	WX-41	78645	20700-20799
TAHOE TRL	Austin	643C	MF-18	78745	4900-5299
TAHOE PARKE CIR	Austin	462K	MC-35	78726	8000-8199
TAHOKA DAISY DR	Travis Co	402Y	MD-40	78613	1500-1699
TAHOMA PL	Austin	464V	MH-34	78759	5700-5799
TAILFEATHER DR	Round Rock	345T	MJ-46	78681	3800-3899
TAILS END	Hays Co	638D	WV-18	78737	12900-13699
TAKU RD	Williamson Co	374J	MG-44	78613	2800-3199
TALAMORE RD	Pflugerville	409S	MS-40	78660	2100-2199
TALBOT CV	Travis Co	552T	MC-25	78746	8200-8299
TALBOT LN	Travis Co	552T	MC-25	78746	8100-8399
TALBOT ST	Taylor	353A	EA-48	76574	100-1199
TALINE CIR	Austin	673R	MF-14	78748	8700-8999
TALKEETNA LN	Cedar Park	374P	MG-44	78613	400-499
TALKING STICK	Leander	342X	MC-46	78641	2000-2099
TALLAHASSEE AVE	Lago Vista	458B	WU-36	78645	21800-21899
TALL CEDARS RD	Cedar Park	374Q	MH-44	78613	3700-3799
TALL CHIEF	Leander	372F	MC-45	78641	None
TALLEY LOOP	Buda	732P	MC-8	78610	1000-1099
	Buda	732T	MC-7	78610	1300-1499
TALLEY ST	Taylor	353K	EA-47	76574	100-599
TALLEYRAN CV	Austin	463G	MF-36	78750	9700-9799
TALLEYRAN DR	Austin	463G	MF-36	78750	9800-10699
TALL FOREST DR	Bastrop Co	746Y	EH-7	78602	100-199
	Bastrop Co	776F	EG-6	78602	200-399
TALLGRASS PRAIRIE DR	Pflugerville	438F	MQ-39	78660	18500-18599
	Pflugerville	438F	MQ-39	78660	None
TALLISON TERRACE	Austin	614Y	MH-19	78704	3600-3699
TALL OAK DR	Williamson Co	349A	MS-48	78634	100-399
TALL OAK TRL	Williamson Co	433P	ME-38	78750	10800-10999
TALL OAKS TRL	Hays Co	639E	WW-18	78737	1-99
TALLOW CT	Austin	644Z	MH-16	78744	2200-2299
TALLOW TRL	Cedar Park	403C	MF-42	78613	800-1099
TALLOWFIELD WAY	Austin	496E	ML-33	78758	11600-11799
TALLOWOOD DR	Austin	494Y	MH-31	78731	4200-4399
TALLOWOOD RIDGE DR	Travis Co	704G	MH-12	78747	None
TALLOW TREE DR	Austin	644Z	MH-16	78744	5400-5799
TALL SHADOWS DR	Austin	646D	MH-18	78742	1400-1599
TALL SKY TRACE	Austin	587R	MP-22	78724	9000-9299
TALLSTAR DR	Lakeway	519A	WW-30	78734	100-199
TALL WITHERS CV	Austin	497X	MN-31	78754	2100-2199
TALLWOOD DR	Austin	495S	MJ-31	78759	8400-8899
	Austin	494V	MH-31	78759	None
TALLWOOD DR	Georgetown	286S	ML-52	78628	100-399
TALLYHO TRL	Williamson Co	434Q	MH-38	78729	8000-8199
TALOGA CT	Austin	642Q	MD-17	78749	4300-4399
TALON CIR	Lago Vista	399Q	WX-41	78645	8500-8599
TALYNE CHAISE CIR	Williamson Co	434L	MH-38	78729	8600-8799
TAM CT	Austin	528P	MQ-29	78754	6900-6999
TAMANGO WAY	Austin	642N	MC-17	78749	5300-5399
TAMAR CT	Austin	466Q	MM-35	78727	13100-13199
TAMAR LN	Austin	466L	MM-35	78727	1400-1699
TAMARA CT	Georgetown	316B	ML-51	78628	100-199
TAMARA DR	Georgetown	316B	ML-51	78628	200-599
TAMARAC CT	Lakeway	519D	WX-30	78734	100-199
TAMARAC TRL	Leander	342P	MC-47	78641	1100-1499
TAMARACK TRL	Austin	465H	MK-36	78727	3600-4699
TAMARISK CIR	Austin	644Z	MH-16	78744	2300-2399
TAMARISK CV	Austin	704N	MG-11	78747	4600-4699
TAMARRON BLVD	Austin	613C	MF-21	78746	2900-3299
TAMAYO DR	Williamson Co	434M	MH-38	78729	13000-13499
TAMIL ST	Austin	642M	MD-17	78749	3700-3999
TAMMI LN	Taylor	352C	MZ-48	76574	1600-1799
TAMMY LN	Williamson Co	347Y	MP-46	78665	1-99
TAMMYE LN	Travis Co	459V	WX-34	78645	17600-17899
TAMPA CV	Austin	556R	MM-26	78723	6700-6799
TAMRA CT	Round Rock	406K	ML-41	78681	1700-1899
TAMRA CV	Round Rock	406K	ML-41	78681	1000-1099
TAMRANAE CT	Austin	583Z	MF-22	78746	1200-1299
TAMWORTH AVE	Austin	644L	MH-17	78745	300-599
TANAGER CIR	Hays Co	668R	WV-14	78737	100-199
TANAGER TRL	Georgetown	225G	MK-60	78633	100-199
TANAK CV	Austin	641M	MB-17	78749	6200-6299
TANAK LN	Austin	641R	MB-17	78749	9000-9099
TANAQUA CV	Austin	671B	MA-15	78739	6700-6799
TANAQUA LN	Austin	671B	MA-15	78739	6800-7399
TANBARK CV	Austin	464G	MH-36	78759	7300-7399

STREET NAME	CITY or COUNTY	MAPSCO GRID	AUSTIN GRID	ZIP CODE	BLOCK RANGE O/E
TANDEM BLVD	Travis Co	436T	ML-37	78728	14200-14399
TANDI TRL	Round Rock	408J	MQ-41	78664	2500-2699
TANDI TRAIL CV	Round Rock	408E	MQ-42	78664	2500-2599
TANGLEBRIAR CT E	Bastrop Co	776L	EH-5	78602	100-199
TANGLEBRIAR CT W	Bastrop Co	776L	EH-5	78602	100-199
TANGLEBRIAR CV	Williamson Co	433K	ME-38	78750	12100-12199
TANGLEBRIAR TRL	Travis Co	433K	ME-38	78750	11500-11599
	Williamson Co	433K	ME-38	78750	11600-12199
TANGLERIDGE CIR	Travis Co	610W	WY-19	78736	10900-11099
TANGLEVINE DR	Austin	673J	ME-14	78748	2200-2299
TANGLEWILD DR	Austin	466X	ML-34	78758	12100-12299
TANGLEWOOD DR	Bastrop Co	745U	EF-7	78602	100-199
TANGLEWOOD DR	Georgetown	256U	MM-55	78628	400-599
TANGLEWOOD DR	Leander	342H	MD-48	78641	900-1199
TANGLEWOOD LN	Hutto	380E	MU-45	78634	100-199
TANGLEWOOD ST	Round Rock	376X	ML-43	78681	1000-1099
TANGLEWOOD TRL	Austin	554T	MG-25	78703	2600-2699
TANGLEWOOD TRL	Hays	702W	MC-10	78610	500-599
TANKSLEY CIR	Georgetown	285D	MK-54	78628	100-199
TANNEHILL LN	Austin	586R	MM-23	78721	3800-4799
	Austin	586H	MM-24	78723	4800-4999
	Austin	586Z	MM-22	78721	None
TANNER CIR	Georgetown	257T	MN-55	78626	100-299
TANNER LOOP	Taylor	352R	MZ-47	76574	1700-1899
TANNER TRL	Pflugerville	437Y	MP-37	78660	500-599
TANNEY ST	Austin	586T	ML-22	78721	4600-4899
TANTALLON CT	Lakeway	519D	WX-30	78734	100-199
TANTARA CT	Williamson Co	434U	MH-37	78729	8000-8099
TANTARA DR	Williamson Co	434U	MH-37	78729	12700-12999
TANTIVY DR	Williamson Co	434Q	MH-38	78729	13000-13099
TANYA TRL	Austin	433S	ME-37	78726	11200-11399
TANZA CT	Georgetown	316A	ML-51	78628	100-199
TAOS BLVD	Austin	613Z	MF-19	78745	2400-2499
TAOS CT	Williamson Co	226U	MM-58	78628	5200-5299
TAPADERA TRACE LN	Austin	465E	MJ-36	78727	5600-5799
TAPADERO CT	Austin	466Q	MM-35	78727	1500-1599
TAPADERO DR	Austin	466Q	MM-35	78727	12900-13099
TAPADO CANYON TRL	Round Rock	345N	MJ-47	78681	3900-3999
TAPESTRY CV	Travis Co	467G	MP-36	78660	800-899
TAPO LN	Austin	587G	MP-24	78724	7900-7999
	Travis Co	587G	MP-24	78724	8000-8199
TAPPAN LN	Austin	496J	ML-32	78758	1800-1899
TARA DR	Austin	675S	MJ-13	78744	6100-6399
	Austin	675S	MJ-13	78747	6400-6799
TARA LN	Travis Co	610Z	WZ-19	78737	8800-9299
TARAHILL DR	Pflugerville	407V	MP-40	78660	None
TARANTO DR	Williamson Co	434Q	MH-38	78729	7800-8099
TARANTULA CT	Travis Co	369Z	WX-43	78645	10500-10699
TARBET DR	Briarcliff	458N	WU-35	78669	300-699
TARBOX BROWN DR	Buda	732T	MC-7	78610	100-299
TARGA CT	Austin	612Y	MD-19	78749	6500-6599
TARLETON CT	Round Rock	375M	MK-44	78681	2000-2099
TARLETON LN	Round Rock	375M	MK-44	78681	1900-1999
TARLTON CV	Austin	583Y	MF-22	78746	2200-2299
TARLTON LN	Austin	583Y	MF-22	78746	3200-3499
TARON CV	Round Rock	376N	ML-44	78681	1800-1899
TARON DR	Round Rock	376P	ML-44	78681	1500-1799
TARRAGONA LN	Austin	465Q	MK-35	78727	3700-3999
TARRAZA CT	Travis Co	491V	MB-31	78732	12000-12099
TARRY TRL	Austin	554U	MH-25	78703	2900-2999
TARRYHOLLOW DR	Austin	554U	MH-25	78703	3200-3299
TARTAN	Lakeway	519E	WW-30	78734	500-599
TARTAN LN	Austin	526G	MM-30	78753	1200-1299
TARTAR WAY	Travis Co	522T	MC-28	78733	1700-1899
TASAJILLO CV	Austin	641Y	MB-16	78739	10400-10499
TASAJILLO TRL	Austin	641Y	MB-16	78739	6000-6699
TASCATE ST	Georgetown	226S	ML-58	78628	100-599
TASHA CT	Cedar Park	402L	MD-41	78613	800-899
TASHA TRAILS RD	Travis Co	396F	WQ-42	78654	None
TASSEY ST	Round Rock	406D	MM-42	78664	600-799
TASUS WAY	Georgetown	286U	MM-52	78626	200-299
TATE LN	Williamson Co	347R	MP-47	78665	1-299
TATERWOOD DR	Austin	433U	MF-37	78750	11200-11599
TATTERSHALL LN	Austin	465Q	MK-35	78727	3700-3999
TATTLER DR	Travis Co	432C	MD-39	78613	2000-2299
TAULBEE LN	Austin	525R	MK-29	78757	800-1299
TAURUS WALK	Bee Cave	549E	WW-27	78738	4800-4899
TAVARES CV	Travis Co	522P	MC-29	78733	9600-9699
TAVERN RD	Travis Co	518E	WU-30	78669	19500-19799
TAVIA CV	Travis Co	522P	MC-29	78733	9500-9599
TAVIA LN	Travis Co	522Q	MD-29	78733	9400-9499
TAVISTOCK DR	Austin	672Q	MD-14	78748	3300-3599
TAWNY CIR	Austin	674A	MG-15	78745	7100-7199
TAWNY CV	Lago Vista	399Q	WX-41	78645	8400-8499
TAWNY DR	Austin	674A	MG-15	78745	300-499
TAWNY FARMS RD	Travis Co	702G	MD-12	78748	12200-12299
TAYLOR AVE	Pflugerville	437V	MP-37	78660	1200-1399
TAYLOR DR	Hays Co	702X	MC-10	78610	12500-12599
	Hays Co	732B	MC-9	78610	12600-12799
TAYLOR LN	Bastrop Co	742H	MZ-9	78612	100-299
TAYLOR LN	Bastrop Co	534K	EC-29	78621	None
	Elgin	534K	EC-29	78621	None
TAYLOR LN	Austin	619C	MT-21	78653	6600-6899
	Travis Co	589V	MT-22	78653	6900-8499
	Travis Co	590J	MU-23	78653	8500-9999
	Travis Co	560X	MU-25	78653	10000-10799
	Travis Co	560U	MV-25	78653	10800-11099
TAYLOR RD	Elgin	533M	EB-29	78621	None
	Elgin	534J	EC-29	78621	None
TAYLOR RD	Georgetown	287J	MN-53	78626	1-1899
TAYLOR RD	Travis Co	522Y	MD-28	78733	8700-8899
TAYLOR ST	Austin	615B	MJ-21	78702	900-1399
TAYLOR ST	Hutto	349Z	MT-46	78634	100-399
TAYLOR ST	Williamson Co	443G	EB-39	78615	300-399
TAYLORCREST CV	Austin	641M	MB-17	78749	9100-9199
TAYLORCREST DR	Austin	642N	MC-17	78749	5600-5999
	Austin	641M	MB-17	78749	6000-6599
TAYLOR DRAPER CV	Austin	464R	MH-35	78759	5600-5999
TAYLOR DRAPER LN	Austin	465S	MJ-34	78759	11200-11299
	Austin	464V	MH-34	78759	11300-11399
TAYLOR FALLS DR	Travis Co	439J	MS-38	78660	3200-3499
TAYLOR GAINES ST	Austin	615P	MJ-20	78741	1500-1799
TAYLORS CV	Buda	732Q	MD-8	78610	100-199
TAYLORS DR	Austin	554P	MG-26	78703	3400-3799
TAYLOR-SIMONETTI AVE	Travis Co	436Y	MM-37	78728	2100-2299
TAYSHAS ST	Manor	530M	MV-29	78653	19400-19499
TAYSIDE DR	Travis Co	467T	MN-34	78660	900-1099

STREET NAME	CITY or COUNTY	MAPSCO GRID	AUSTIN GRID	ZIP CODE	BLOCK RANGE O/E
TAY TERRACE	Austin	498W	MQ-31	78653	12400-12499
TAZA TRL	Austin	587G	MP-24	78724	7800-7999
	Travis Co	587G	MP-24	78724	8000-8199
T-BAR TRL	Travis Co	464P	MG-35	78759	7700-7799
T C OATTS LN	Round Rock	348W	MQ-46	78665	3200-3299
TEABERRY CIR	Austin	644W	MG-16	78745	500-599
TEABERRY DR	Austin	644W	MG-16	78745	7000-7299
TEACUP CV	Georgetown	225L	MK-59	78633	100-199
TEACUP LN	Travis Co	467Q	MP-35	78660	14300-14399
TEAGLE DR	Austin	645A	MJ-18	78741	1900-2099
TEAGUE TRL	Williamson Co	434P	MG-38	78729	12600-12799
TEAK CV	Austin	493R	MF-32	78750	7400-7499
TEAK HAWK CV	Travis Co	554J	MG-26	78746	3000-3099
TEAKWOOD DR	Austin	525G	MK-30	78757	1900-2399
TEAKWOOD TRL	Pflugerville	438S	MQ-37	78660	1100-1199
TEAL	Lakeway	489W	WW-31	78734	400-499
TEAL LN	Leander	342F	MC-48	78641	700-899
TEAL TRL	Austin	674R	MH-14	78744	7500-7599
TEAL TRL	Cedar Park	373V	MF-43	78613	1600-1699
TEA LEAF DR	Travis Co	467L	MP-35	78660	1200-1799
TEALWOOD	Austin	494Z	MH-31	78731	4000-4199
TEALWOOD TRL	Austin	494Z	MH-31	78731	7900-7999
TEAPOT DR	Travis Co	467L	MP-35	78660	1000-1199
TEA ROOM CV	Travis Co	467Q	MP-35	78660	14200-14299
TEA ROSE TRL	Austin	672C	MD-15	78748	9300-9699
TEASDALE TERRACE	Austin	526L	MM-29	78753	9300-9899
TEA TREE CV	Georgetown	195P	MJ-62	78633	800-899
TECATE TRL	Travis Co	672N	MC-14	78739	4000-4299
TECHNI CENTER DR	Austin	586R	MM-23	78721	5800-6199
TECHNOLOGY BLVD	Austin	464C	MH-36	78727	12000-12599
TECHNOLOGY DR	Bastrop	745Q	EF-8	78602	None
TECH RIDGE BLVD	Austin	496D	MN-33	78753	12100-12799
TECK CIR	Travis Co	490N	WY-32	78734	1200-1399
TECON CV	Hays Co	762M	MD-5	78610	100-199
TECUMSEH DR	Austin	526P	ML-29	78753	8300-8499
TED BURGER RD	Hays Co	606H	WR-21	78620	100-1099
TEDFORD ST	Austin	496L	MM-32	78753	11300-11499
TEE DR	Austin	675W	MJ-13	78747	7800-8099
TEEWOOD DR	Austin	674H	MH-15	78744	4700-4799
TEGUA CV	Lago Vista	399Q	WX-41	78645	8600-8799
TEHAMA CT	Travis Co	550R	WZ-26	78733	3200-3299
TEJANO CT	Williamson Co	226U	MM-58	78628	3800-3899
TEJAS DR	Round Rock	406K	ML-41	78681	2000-2299
TEJAS TRL	Austin	613Z	MF-19	78745	4500-4699
TEJAS TRL	Lago Vista	399R	WX-41	78645	3300-3999
TEJAS TRL	Leander	342Y	MD-46	78641	2400-2699
TEJAS TRL	Williamson Co	193Z	MF-61	78633	100-199
TEJON CIR	Travis Co	490C	WZ-33	78734	4000-4099
TEKOA CV	Georgetown	285P	MJ-53	78628	100-199
TEKOA CV	Travis Co	554E	MG-27	78746	3600-3799
TELANDER DR	Round Rock	377M	MP-44	78665	1-99
TELEGRAPH PASS	Lago Vista	399R	WX-41	78645	20500-20699
TELLO PATH	Austin	642X	MC-16	78749	4400-4799
TELLURIDE DR	Georgetown	317K	MN-50	78626	200-299
TELLURIDE TRL	Austin	641D	MB-18	78749	6700-6999
TELLUS	Lakeway	489U	WX-31	78734	100-399
TEMECULA PASS	Williamson Co	375W	MJ-43	78717	9300-9499
TEMPLE DR	Austin	586K	ML-23	78721	1800-1899
TEMPLEMORE CV	Austin	404E	MG-42	78717	14500-14599
TENAVA CT	Austin	463B	ME-36	78726	10200-10299
TENAZA CV	Round Rock	377X	MN-43	78664	3200-3299
TENDERFOOT CV	Lago Vista	399Q	WX-41	78645	20800-20899
TENISON CT	Austin	494U	MH-31	78731	4900-4999
TENNESSEE ST	Taylor	353K	EA-47	76574	100-299
TENNISON HILL DR	Bee Cave	550U	WZ-25	78733	3600-3799
TEN OAKS CIR	Austin	674M	MH-14	78744	6900-7099
TEN OAKS DR	Williamson Co	196J	ML-62	78628	100-499
TENSLEY TRL	Austin	673L	MF-14	78748	800-1099
TEPEE CV	Lago Vista	399R	WX-41	78645	8700-8799
TEQUESTA BLVD	Travis Co	497M	MP-32	78754	2200-3999
TERAVISTA PKWY	Williamson Co	346H	MM-48	78665	100-1399
TERAVISTA CLUB DR	Williamson Co	346H	MM-48	78665	4000-4399
	Williamson Co	347A	MN-48	78665	4400-4899
	Williamson Co	317W	MN-49	78665	4900-6899
TERCELLO LN	Austin	465B	MJ-36	78727	5400-5599
TERCEL TRACE	Travis Co	529H	MT-30	78653	13600-13899
TERESA LN	Bastrop Co	740T	MU-7	78612	100-199
TERESINA DR	Austin	642U	MD-16	78749	8800-8999
TERI CT	Georgetown	225U	MK-58	78633	100-199
TERI RD	Austin	644V	MH-17	78744	1600-2199
	Austin	645S	MJ-16	78744	2200-5899
TERISU CV	Travis Co	436Y	MM-37	78728	1900-1999
TERISU LN	Travis Co	466C	MM-36	78728	14200-14499
TERJO LN	Travis Co	520Z	WZ-28	78732	1100-1199
TERLINGUA DR	Travis Co	432G	MD-39	78613	2500-2699
TERLINGUA TRL	Williamson Co	255M	MK-56	78628	100-199
TERMINAL DR	Georgetown	256D	MM-57	78628	100-599
TERN CIR	Austin	645S	MJ-16	78744	2300-2399
TERRA DR	Elgin	534W	EC-28	78621	100-199
TERRA ST	Round Rock	346M	MM-47	78665	900-1499
TERRACE CT	Hays Co	639K	WW-17	78737	100-199
TERRACE DR	Austin	615N	MJ-20	78704	300-599
TERRACE DR	Jonestown	401E	MA-42	78645	18100-18299
TERRACE DR	Leander	342E	MC-48	78641	900-1099
TERRACE DR	Williamson Co	406X	ML-40	78728	16200-16599
TERRACE BLUFF DR	Austin	497W	MN-31	78754	11100-11299
TERRACE CANYON DR	Hays Co	637M	WT-17	78620	500-699
TERRACE MEADOW WAY	Travis Co	529M	MT-29	78653	11300-11499
TERRACE MOUNTAIN CV					
	West Lake Hills	553Z	MF-25	78746	1-99
TERRACE MOUNTAIN DR	Travis Co	400C	WZ-42	78645	18700-19499
TERRACE MOUNTAIN DR					
	West Lake Hills	553Y	MF-25	78746	200-999
TERRACE PARKE TRL	Williamson Co	433P	ME-38	78750	11500-11699
TERRACE VIEW DR	Cedar Park	372T	MC-43	78613	1300-1599
TERRADYNE DR	Pflugerville	409W	MS-40	78660	2100-2299
TERRAIN LN	Austin	554H	MH-27	78731	2900-2999
TERRANOVA CV	Austin	670H	WZ-15	78739	12300-12399
TERRA NOVA LN	Austin	465L	MK-35	78727	12500-12699
TERRA OAK CIR	Austin	642C	MD-18	78749	6800-6899
TERRAPIN CT	Austin	583U	MF-22	78746	1400-1599
TERRA VERDE DR	Austin	404K	MG-41	78717	15000-15199
TERRAVISTA DR	Austin	612J	MC-20	78735	5500-5999
	Austin	611H	MB-21	78735	6000-6699
TERRAZA CIR	Austin	462G	MD-36	78726	11800-12399
TERRELL HILL DR	Austin	614U	MH-19	78704	600-1099
TERRENCE PL	Georgetown	314F	MG-51	78628	100-199

STREET NAME	CITY or COUNTY	MAPSCO GRID	AUSTIN GRID	ZIP CODE	BLOCK RANGE O/E
TERRI TRL	Bastrop Co	651C	MX-18	78621	100-199
TERRIER CV	Williamson Co	377B	MN-45	78664	1100-1199
TERRILANCE DR	Austin	645F	MJ-18	78741	4400-4499
TERRINA ST	Austin	495W	MJ-31	78759	3700-3799
TERRITORY CV	Cedar Park	373S	ME-43	78613	600-699
TERRITORY DR	Bastrop Co	712R	MZ-11	78602	100-199
TERRITORY TRL	Cedar Park	373S	ME-43	78613	400-599
TERRY DR	Austin	586U	MM-22	78721	1100-1199
TERRY LN	Austin	647Q	MP-17	78617	2900-2999
TERRY LN	Georgetown	256U	MM-55	78628	1800-2299
TERRY LN	Williamson Co	311B	MA-51	78641	300-399
TERRY-O LN	Austin	644H	MH-18	78745	4100-4599
TESORO TRL	Williamson Co	434V	MH-37	78729	6900-7199
TESSA CV	Austin	678N	MQ-14	78617	5400-5599
TESSA HEIGHTS LN	Travis Co	518J	WU-29	78669	19400-19699
TETBURY CV	Austin	673G	MF-15	78748	8400-8499
TETBURY LN	Austin	673G	MF-15	78748	1100-1499
TETHER TRL	Austin	613M	MF-20	78704	2700-2799
TETON DR	Austin	525C	MK-30	78757	1800-1999
TETON PASS	Lago Vista	399R	WX-41	78645	8500-8799
TETON RIDGE CV	Austin	466L	MM-35	78727	13300-13399
TETONS CT	Bee Cave	549F	WW-27	78738	15800-15899
TEXALLA CV	Round Rock	345P	MJ-47	78681	4000-4099
TEXAN DR	Travis Co	402Y	MD-40	78613	2400-2599
TEXANA CT	Round Rock	375G	MK-45	78681	3200-3399
TEXANA LOOP	Round Rock	347N	MN-47	78665	3500-3699
TEXAS AVE	Austin	555X	MJ-25	78705	500-799
TEXAS AVE	Round Rock	376L	MM-44	78664	100-499
	Round Rock	376G	MM-45	78664	500-599
TEXAS AVE W	Round Rock	376K	ML-44	78664	100-199
TEXAS DR	Georgetown	225D	MK-60	78633	1-199
TEXAS DR	Georgetown	195Z	MK-61	78633	200-1299
TEXAS ST	Travis Co	490H	WZ-33	78734	14900-15199
	Travis Co	490C	WZ-33	78734	15300-15499
TEXAS TRL	Hays Co	670P	WY-14	78737	800-999
TEXAS ASH CV	Travis Co	703L	MF-11	78652	100-199
TEXAS BLUEBELL DR	Travis Co	517E	WS-30	78669	5100-5699
TEXAS MEADOWS DR	Travis Co	409T	MS-40	78660	20700-20999
TEXAS OAK WAY	Williamson Co	433E	ME-39	78613	1300-1699
TEXAS OAKS CV	Austin	673K	ME-14	78748	1300-1399
TEXAS OAKS DR	Austin	673K	ME-14	78748	8700-9499
TEXAS PLUME RD	Austin	464J	MG-35	78759	7801-7999 O
	Travis Co	464J	MG-35	78759	7800-7998 E
	Travis Co	464J	MG-35	78759	8000-8299
TEXAS SAGE CT	Travis Co	491X	MA-31	78732	12800-12899
TEXAS STAR LN	Austin	583Y	MF-22	78746	3300-3399
TEXAS SUN DR	Austin	673K	ME-14	78748	8700-9199
TEXAS TOPAZ DR	Travis Co	436L	MM-38	78728	3200-3699
TEXAS TRADITIONS	Williamson Co	255M	MK-56	78628	1-299
TEXAS WILDLIFE TRL	Travis Co	580D	WZ-24	78735	3900-4399
TEXOMA DR	Travis Co	467K	MN-35	78660	None
TEXSTAR DR	Georgetown	286V	MM-52	78626	2200-2399
TEYA CT	Austin	612X	MC-19	78749	7100-7199
THACKERAY LN	Travis Co	437G	MP-39	78660	800-1299
THACKERY CT	Lakeway	489Q	WX-32	78734	100-199
THADDEUS CV	Travis Co	583J	ME-23	78746	1300-1499
THAMES CIR	Austin	556Q	MM-26	78723	2100-2199
THAMES DR	Austin	556Q	MM-26	78723	5700-6199
THANNA'S WAY	Austin	674M	MH-14	78744	7000-7499
THATCH CT	Austin	675N	MJ-14	78744	6900-6999
THATCH LN	Austin	675N	MJ-14	78744	6800-7099
THATCHER DR	Austin	404L	MH-41	78717	14700-15299
THATCHERS CT	Hays Co	668D	WV-15	78620	100-299
THAXTON RD	Austin	675W	MJ-13	78744	7800-7899
	Austin	675W	MJ-13	78747	7900-8099
	Austin	705B	MJ-12	78747	8000-8099
	Travis Co	705B	MJ-12	78747	8100-8999
	Travis Co	705T	MJ-10	78747	9000-10799
	Travis Co	735A	MJ-9	78747	10800-11399
THAYER CV	Travis Co	467G	MP-36	78660	900-999
THEATER PASS	Austin	614Z	MH-19	78704	None
THE CIRCLE	Austin	615J	MJ-20	78704	100-299
	Austin	615E	MJ-21	78704	1200-1399
THECKLA TERRACE	Austin	555B	MJ-27	78756	1400-1699
THE ENTRANCE RD	Travis Co	577K	WS-23	78720	18500-18699
THE HIGH RD	Travis Co	553Q	MF-26	78746	100-5599
THE HILLS DR	Village of the Hills	519K	WW-29	78738	1-399
THE LAKES BLVD	Austin	467E	MN-36	78660	13800-14299
	Austin	466H	MM-36	78660	14300-14499
THE LIVING END	Travis Co	582D	MD-24	78746	800-899
THELMA DR	Austin	644W	MG-16	78745	300-699
THEO DR	Austin	586E	ML-24	78723	2100-2199
THEODORA CV	Austin	497S	MN-31	78753	1400-1499
THEODORE ROOSEVELT ST					
	Travis Co	530G	MV-30	78653	13500-13799
THE PIER RD	Travis Co	552C	MD-27	78733	None
THERESA AVE	Austin	584Q	MH-23	78703	600-999
THERESA CV	Cedar Park	402M	MD-41	78613	700-799
THERESA BLANCHARD LN	Austin	702C	MD-12	78748	2600-2699
THERIOT TRL	Austin	435W	MJ-37	78727	12700-12799
THERMAL DR	Travis Co	466D	MM-36	78728	13700-14199
THIBODEAUX DR	Round Rock	407T	MN-40	78664	1400-1699
THICKET TRL	Williamson Co	433P	ME-38	78750	10800-10999
THICKWOODS CV	Travis Co	582A	MC-24	78735	9000-9099
THINLEAF CV	Austin	464Y	MH-34	78759	9800-9899
THIRD ST	Bastrop Co	746V	EH-7	78602	100-199
THIRD ST	Jonestown	400M	WZ-41	78645	10800-11199
THIRLMARE CT	Austin	528E	MQ-30	78754	6300-6399
THISTLE CIR	Cedar Park	402H	MD-42	78613	1100-1199
THISTLE CT	Travis Co	551D	MB-27	78733	100-199
THISTLE TRL	Cedar Park	402D	MD-42	78613	1000-1299
THISTLE TRL	Georgetown	225P	MJ-59	78633	200-299
THISTLE HILL WAY	Austin	528P	MQ-29	78754	6800-7099
THISTLE MOSS CV	Austin	672A	MC-15	78739	10300-10399
THISTLE MOUND CV	Round Rock	378S	MQ-43	78665	800-899
THISTLE RIDGE	Travis Co	521Z	MB-28	78733	10100-10299
THISTLEWOOD DR	Austin	644K	MG-17	78745	300-599
T H JOHNSON DR	Taylor	323J	EA-50	76574	100-199
	Taylor	322R	MZ-50	76574	200-1599
THOMAS CT	Georgetown	286D	MM-54	78626	100-399
THOMAS CV	Lago Vista	458F	WU-36	78645	21600-21699
THOMAS CV	Leander	341G	MB-48	78641	200-299
THOMAS DR	Austin	554Y	MH-25	78703	2600-2699
THOMAS LN	Travis Co	577R	WT-23	78720	10000-10299
THOMAS LN	Weir	258D	MR-57	78626	100-399
THOMAS ST	Elgin	534X	EC-28	78621	101-199 O
THOMAS ST	Taylor	352G	MZ-48	76574	2300-2499
THOMAS ST	Travis Co	491H	MB-33	78732	12800-12899
THOMAS JEFFERSON ST	Travis Co	530K	MU-29	78653	12700-12999
THOMAS KINCHEON ST	Austin	642V	MD-16	78745	3300-3499
THOMAS SINCLAIR BLVD	Travis Co	466B	ML-36	78728	13900-13999
	Travis Co	436X	ML-37	78728	14000-14299
THOMAS SPRINGS RD	Travis Co	611E	MA-21	78736	6300-7099
	Travis Co	610M	WZ-20	78736	7100-8199
THOMASWOOD LN	Travis Co	610H	WZ-21	78736	10200-10699
THOME VALLEY DR	Austin	678P	MQ-14	78617	12700-13399
THOMPKINS DR	Austin	497F	MN-33	78753	11900-12499
THOMPSON LN	Austin	616U	MM-19	78742	100-699
THOMPSON ST	Austin	585V	MK-22	78702	700-999
	Austin	586X	ML-22	78702	3200-3799
THOMPSON ST	Cedar Park	372M	MD-44	78613	100-299
THOMPSON ST	Taylor	352D	MZ-48	76574	1100-1299
	Taylor	322Z	MZ-49	76574	1300-1499
THOMPSON TRL	Bastrop	744K	EC-8	78602	None
THOMPSON TRL	Round Rock	407E	MN-42	78664	1700-1899
THOREAU LN	Lago Vista	458F	WU-36	78645	21500-21599
THOREAU LN	Travis Co	552R	MD-26	78746	1-99
THORNBERRY RD	Austin	647A	MN-18	78617	1300-1499
	Austin	647A	MN-18	78742	1500-1699
	Austin	646H	MM-18	78742	1700-1999
THORNBLADE CT	Travis Co	409T	MS-40	78660	2600-2699
THORNCLIFFE DR	Austin	524M	MH-29	78731	6800-6999
THORN CREEK PL	Williamson Co	377E	MN-45	78664	1100-1199
THORNE RD	Bastrop Co	742L	MZ-8	78612	100-199
THORNHILL DR	Austin	675J	MJ-14	78744	5500-5799
THORNRIDGE RD	Austin	496W	ML-31	78758	1300-1599
	Austin	495V	MK-31	78758	1600-1699
THORNTON CV	Georgetown	256Q	MM-56	78628	300-399
THORNTON LN	Georgetown	256Q	MM-56	78628	400-1899
THORNTON RD	Austin	614K	MG-20	78704	2100-2799
THORNWILD PASS	Austin	466S	ML-34	78758	2100-2399
THORNWOOD CT	Austin	675N	MJ-14	78744	6900-6999
THORNWOOD DR	Austin	675J	MJ-14	78744	5300-5499
THORNWOOD RD	Georgetown	256F	ML-57	78628	100-199
THORNY BROOK TRL	Williamson Co	433F	ME-39	78750	11200-11499
THOROUGHBRED DR	Austin	703C	MF-12	78748	10500-10799
THORPE CIR	Lago Vista	458B	WU-36	78645	21700-21899
THORPE CV	Lago Vista	458F	WU-36	78645	2700-2799
THORPE CV	Lago Vista	458B	WU-36	78645	2900-2999
THOUSAND OAKS BLVD	Georgetown	286X	ML-52	78628	100-1099
THOUSAND OAKS CIR	Austin	583Y	MF-22	78746	1700-1799
THOUSAND OAKS CV	Austin	583U	MF-22	78746	3300-3399
THOUSAND OAKS DR	Austin	583Y	MF-22	78746	2900-3299
THOUSAND OAKS DR	Bastrop Co	740K	MU-8	78612	100-599
	Bastrop Co	739H	MT-9	78612	600-699
THRASHER LN	Austin	616T	ML-19	78741	500-699
	Austin	646E	ML-18	78741	2000-2599
THREADBO ST	Williamson Co	434B	MG-39	78729	9600-9699
THREADGILL ST	Austin	586A	ML-24	78723	4000-4299
THREADGILL ST	Taylor	353F	EA-48	76574	300-399
THREADWELL ST	Austin	614C	MH-21	78704	1100-1899
THREE ARROWS CT	Cedar Park	374V	MH-43	78613	4500-4599
THREE CREEK TRL	Travis Co	486R	WR-32	78669	4000-4499
THREE G RANCH RD	Hays Co	794L	MH-2	78610	100-599
THREE LOT RD	Bastrop Co	776F	EG-6	78602	100-199
THREE OAKS CIR	Austin	464G	MH-36	78759	6600-6699
THREE OAKS LN	Bastrop Co	743N	EA-8	78602	100-199
THREE OAKS TRL	Austin	464L	MH-35	78759	11500-11899
THREE POINTS RD	Pflugerville	437N	MN-38	78660	1400-1899
	Pflugerville	436M	MM-38	78728	1900-2099
THREE RIVERS DR	Travis Co	554E	MG-27	78746	3200-3499
THRUSH AVE	Austin	496V	MM-31	78753	600-799
THRUSH DR	Leander	342H	MD-48	78641	600-799
THRUSHWOOD DR	Austin	495X	MJ-31	78757	2700-3099
THUNDER TRL	Travis Co	490S	WY-31	78734	16000-16099
THUNDERBAY DR	Georgetown	287L	MP-53	78626	300-499
THUNDERBIRD	Lago Vista	429P	WW-38	78645	4600-5999
THUNDERBIRD CV	Travis Co	611S	MA-19	78736	8800-8899
THUNDERBIRD LN	Williamson Co	287H	MP-54	78626	50100-50599
THUNDERBIRD RD	Travis Co	611T	MA-19	78736	8200-8899
THUNDERCLOUD CV	Williamson Co	405J	MJ-41	78717	15900-15999
THUNDER CREEK RD	Austin	465N	MJ-35	78759	5100-5399
THUNDER GULCH DR	Austin	678P	MQ-14	78617	5500-5699
THUNDER HEAD CV	Georgetown	314L	MH-50	78628	1100-1399
THUNDERHEAD RD	Travis Co	490Y	WZ-31	78734	14500-14899
THUNDER VALLEY TRL	Georgetown	286Z	MM-52	78626	100-399
THURBER LN	Lago Vista	458F	WU-36	78645	2100-2599
THURGOOD AVE	Austin	586Y	MM-22	78721	6200-6499
THURGOOD CIR	Austin	616D	MM-21	78721	1100-1199
THURMAN RD	Travis Co	459T	WW-34	78645	2700-3199
THURMAN BEND RD	Travis Co	458Z	WV-34	78669	19400-21399
	Travis Co	488A	WU-33	78669	21400-21499
	Travis Co	487H	WT-33	78669	21500-21699
THURMAN BLUFF DR	Travis Co	458U	WV-34	78669	1000-1299
THURMOND ST	Austin	526J	ML-29	78758	800-999
THYME SPRINGS	Buda	732S	MC-7	78610	100-199
THYONE DR	Travis Co	647G	MP-18	78725	11800-11999
TIBEE DR	Austin	462H	MD-36	78726	11400-11599
TIBER CIR	Travis Co	522X	MC-28	78733	9300-9399
TIBURON CT	Village of the Hills	519P	WW-29	78738	1-99
TIBURON DR	Village of the Hills	519T	WW-28	78738	1-99
TICHESTER CT	Williamson Co	434F	MG-39	78729	13300-13399
TICKFORD DR	Travis Co	677X	MN-13	78617	11400-11699
TICONDEROGA AVE	Lago Vista	458B	WU-36	78645	21700-21899
TICONDEROGA CV	Lago Vista	458B	WU-36	78645	2900-2999
TIDDLE LN	Pflugerville	439P	MS-38	78660	4500-4699
TIDELAND CV	Travis Co	522C	MD-30	78730	10000-10099
TIDEWATER CV	Williamson Co	375W	MJ-43	78717	16900-16999
TIERRA DR	Austin	466A	ML-36	78727	13400-13599
TIERRA ALTO ST	Leander	342Q	MD-47	78641	1500-1699
TIERRA BLANCO CV	Williamson Co	433A	ME-39	78613	1700-1799
TIERRA BLANCO TRL	Williamson Co	432D	MD-39	78613	2400-2599
	Williamson Co	433A	ME-39	78613	2600-2999
TIERRA GRANDE CT	Travis Co	521N	MA-29	78732	200-299
TIERRA GRANDE TRL	Travis Co	521N	MA-29	78732	12500-12799
	Travis Co	520R	WZ-29	78732	12800-12999
TIERRA LINDA LN	Austin	640V	WZ-16	78739	8100-8299
TIFFANY CIR	Georgetown	256T	ML-55	78628	800-899
TIFFANY DR	Austin	642L	MD-17	78749	7900-8199
TIFFANY LN	Georgetown	256T	ML-55	78628	900-1099
TIFFANY TRL	Mustang Ridge	736Q	MM-8	78719	None
TIFFANY TRL	Williamson Co	375L	MK-44	78681	1-99
TIFFANY NICOLE DR	Williamson Co	378A	MQ-45	78665	4500-4699
TIFFER LN	Travis Co	436Y	MM-37	78728	14400-14499
TIGER LN	Hays Co	636N	WQ-17	78620	100-599
TIGER CITY LN	Leander	372B	MC-45	78641	1200-1299
TIGER EYE CV	Austin	642R	MD-17	78749	7900-7999
TIGER LILY WAY	Austin	672A	MC-15	78739	4900-5099
TIGER VALLEY LN	Georgetown	226P	ML-59	78628	100-299
TIGER WOODS DR	Georgetown	227A	MN-60	78628	30200-30499
TILBURY LN	Austin	644L	MH-17	78745	300-599
TILDEN AVE	Austin	527E	MN-30	78754	10100-10599
TILDER DR	Williamson Co	434Q	MH-38	78729	13100-13199
TILGHMAN TRL	Williamson Co	434K	MG-38	78729	12900-13099
TILLER DR	Williamson Co	224L	MH-59	78633	100-299
TILLERFIELD TRL	Travis Co	673P	ME-14	78748	1300-1399
TILLERY ST	Austin	616E	ML-21	78702	100-899
	Austin	586W	ML-22	78702	900-1199
	Austin	586J	ML-23	78721	1300-1899
	Austin	586J	ML-23	78723	1900-2299
TILLERY SQUARE	Austin	615H	MK-21	78702	200-399
TILLMAN DR	Cedar Park	402G	MD-42	78613	2001-2099 O
TILLOTSON AVE	Austin	585Y	MK-22	78702	1900-2099
TIM LN	Travis Co	371U	MB-43	78641	17300-17399
TIMAROU TERRACE	Austin	528P	MQ-29	78754	7000-7099
TIMARRON	Leander	341V	MB-46	78641	700-799
TIMBER CIR	Travis Co	577V	WT-22	78720	10800-10899
TIMBER CT	Bastrop Co	743B	EA-9	78602	100-199
TIMBER LN	Austin	645A	MJ-18	78741	2900-3099
TIMBER LN	Bastrop Co	776F	EG-6	78602	100-199
TIMBER PASS	Austin	645A	MJ-18	78741	2900-3099
TIMBER ST	Georgetown	286L	MM-53	78626	1200-1599
TIMBER TRL	Austin	524V	MH-28	78731	5800-5899
TIMBER TRL	Cedar Park	403A	ME-42	78613	500-899
	Cedar Park	402D	MD-42	78613	900-1199
TIMBER TRL	Lago Vista	399R	WX-41	78645	8300-9399
TIMBER BEND DR	Pflugerville	438N	MQ-38	78660	1000-1299
TIMBER BRUSH TRL	Austin	615W	MJ-19	78741	1700-1799
TIMBER CREEK CIR	Travis Co	677G	MP-15	78617	4600-4699
TIMBER CREEK CV	Round Rock	378W	MQ-43	78665	700-799
TIMBER CREEK CV	Travis Co	677G	MP-15	78617	4600-4699
TIMBER CREEK DR	Travis Co	677G	MP-15	78617	4600-4899
TIMBER CREST DR	Taylor	322Q	MZ-50	76574	4000-4599
TIMBERCREST DR	Travis Co	468P	MQ-35	78660	None
TIMBERCREST LN	Williamson Co	433Q	MF-38	78750	10300-10599
TIMBERGROVE CT	Cedar Park	402H	MD-42	78613	600-699
TIMBER HEIGHTS DR	Austin	497T	MN-31	78754	11400-12699
TIMBER HILLS DR	Travis Co	708M	MR-11	78617	7500-8099
TIMBER HITCH CT	Williamson Co	196S	ML-61	78628	100-199
TIMBERLINE DR	Dripping Springs	636V	WR-16	78620	100-199
TIMBERLINE DR	Rollingwood	584N	MG-23	78746	2500-4999
	Rollingwood	583V	MF-22	78746	5000-5099
TIMBERLINE DR	Round Rock	377K	MN-44	78665	1-99
TIMBERLINE DR	Travis Co	459W	WW-34	78669	19400-19499
	Travis Co	458Z	WV-34	78669	19500-19699
TIMBER LINE RD	Williamson Co	194Y	MH-61	78633	100-299
TIMBERLINE TRL	Hays Co	638F	WU-18	78737	14000-14099
TIMBERLINE RIDGE	Rollingwood	584S	MG-22	78746	1-99
TIMBER RIDGE CV	Travis Co	552A	MC-27	78733	100-199
TIMBER RIDGE DR	Austin	615W	MJ-19	78741	1600-1799
TIMBER RIDGE DR	Cedar Park	372Q	MD-44	78613	1700-1899
TIMBER RIDGE PASS	Travis Co	552A	MC-27	78733	9700-9899
TIMBER RIDGE RD	Austin	645A	MJ-18	78741	1600-1699
TIMBERSIDE DR	Austin	465H	MK-36	78727	12800-12899
TIMBER VIEW LN	Cedar Park	372L	MD-44	78613	1800-1999
TIMBER WOLF CIR	Austin	465K	MJ-35	78727	5000-5099
TIMBER WOLF TRL	Austin	465P	MJ-35	78727	12000-12199
TIMBERWOOD CIR	Austin	554Q	MH-26	78703	3400-3499
TIMBERWOOD DR	Austin	615W	MJ-19	78741	1700-1799
TIMBERWOOD DR	Cedar Park	372L	MD-44	78613	1500-1999
TIMBERWOOD DR	Round Rock	376V	MM-43	78664	800-1099
TIMBERWOOD ST	Austin	611U	MB-19	78736	7100-7199
TIMBROOK TRL	Williamson Co	433K	ME-38	78750	11200-11399
TIMOTHY CIR	Travis Co	460V	WZ-34	78734	5000-5199
TIMOTHY LN	Travis Co	460V	WZ-34	78734	15200-15299
TIMOTHY JOHN DR	Pflugerville	408S	MQ-40	78660	200-799
TIMPANAGOS DR	Lakeway	519C	WX-30	78734	100-399
TIMSON CT	Austin	524D	MH-30	78731	3700-3799
TINA CT	Austin	526E	ML-30	78758	8900-8999
TIN BARN ALLEY	Georgetown	286L	MM-53	78626	1-99
TIN CAN DR	Austin	497X	MN-31	78754	2100-2299
TIN CUP DR	Austin	433U	MF-37	78750	11500-11599
TINER TRL	Austin	587G	MP-24	78724	6100-6499
TINITA CT	Austin	671G	MB-15	78739	5800-5899
TINMOUTH ST	Austin	672R	MD-14	78748	2600-2899
TINNIN FORD RD	Austin	615Q	MK-20	78741	1100-1699
TIN ROOF CV	Williamson Co	405B	MJ-42	78681	8700-8799
TINY TRL	Williamson Co	375T	MJ-43	78681	9000-9099
TINY SEED CV	Travis Co	408K	MQ-41	78660	None
TIOMBE BEND	Austin	642N	MC-17	78749	8700-9099
TIP CV	Austin	613H	MF-21	78704	2600-2699
TIPPERARY CV	Austin	465M	MK-35	78759	12300-12399
TIPPERARY DR	Leander	342U	MD-46	78641	1900-1999
TIPPS CT	Georgetown	195Y	MK-61	78633	100-199
TIPTON DR	Austin	556Y	MM-25	78723	5400-5599
TIP TOP DR	Jonestown	430C	WZ-39	78645	800-899
TIRADO ST	Austin	555H	MK-27	78752	800-899
TIS AUTUMN CT	Hays Co	701L	MB-11	78652	4901-4999 O
TISDALE DR	Austin	525Q	MK-29	78757	7600-8099
TISHOMINGO TRL	Travis Co	490U	WZ-31	78734	2100-2199
TITANIUM ST	Austin	498T	MQ-31	78653	12400-12899
TITIAN DR	Austin	496K	ML-32	78758	11300-11599
TITUS CT	Austin	491T	MA-31	78732	13000-13099
TIVOLI DR	Travis Co	432G	MD-39	78613	2400-2599
TOBAGO CV	Austin	642L	MD-17	78749	4600-4799
TOBERMORY DR	Travis Co	437D	MP-39	78660	17100-17699
TOBIN DR	Buda	763A	ME-6	78610	200-699
TOBLER TRL	Austin	497N	MN-32	78753	11800-11999
TOBRINA LN	Austin	464X	MG-34	78759	9500-9699
TOBY TRL	Hutto	379X	MS-43	78634	100-199
TOCKINGTON WAY	Austin	673H	MF-15	78748	8100-8199
TODD LN	Austin	645K	MJ-17	78744	3700-4999
TODD LN	Cedar Park	402Z	MD-40	78613	1700-1899
TODD TRL	Bastrop Co	651B	MW-18	78621	100-199
TODD TRL	Round Rock	347V	MP-46	78665	2900-2999
TOFINO CV	Round Rock	378S	MQ-43	78665	700-799
TOLCARNE DR	Hutto	379T	MS-43	78634	100-299
TOLEDO DR	Austin	465T	MJ-34	78759	11200-11599
TOLEDO TRL	Georgetown	226Y	MM-58	78628	400-599
	Williamson Co	226Y	MM-58	78628	600-899
TOLIVER ST	Bastrop	745L	EF-8	78602	500-599

T

STREET NAME	CITY or COUNTY	MAPSCO GRID	AUSTIN GRID	ZIP CODE	BLOCK RANGE O/E
TOLLARD LN	Austin	528K	MQ-29	78754	11500-11599
TOLLESBORO CV	Austin	641X	MA-16	78739	10600-10899
TOLSTOY CIR	Pflugerville	437B	MN-39	78664	1800-1999
TOLTEC TRL	Georgetown	317K	MN-50	78626	1000-1299
TOM ADAMS DR	Travis Co	496Z	MM-31	78753	11100-11299
TOMAH DR	Williamson Co	405J	MJ-41	78717	8600-8699
TOMAHAWK	Lago Vista	429S	WW-37	78645	20800-20999
TOMAHAWK TRL	Austin	643D	MF-18	78745	4900-4999
TOMAHAWK TRL	Williamson Co	287G	MP-54	78626	50100-50299
TOMANET TRL	Austin	466N	ML-35	78758	12200-12499
	Austin	466N	ML-35	78727	12500-12899
TOMBSTONE CV	Lago Vista	399U	WX-40	78645	8300-8399
TOMCAT CV	Williamson Co	405B	MJ-42	78681	8600-8699
TOMCAT DR	Williamson Co	405B	MJ-42	78681	16700-16999
TOM GARY CV	Round Rock	346X	ML-46	78665	3000-3099
TOM GREEN ST	Austin	585B	MJ-24	78705	3100-3799
TOM GREEN SCHOOL RD	Buda	763P	ME-5	78610	400-499
TOM KEMP LN	Austin	404Y	MH-40	78717	13800-14099
TOM KITE CIR	Travis Co	582H	MD-24	78746	6500-6599
TOM KITE DR	Williamson Co	408G	MR-42	78664	100-199
	Williamson Co	408C	MR-42	78664	300-799
TOM McDANIELS PKWY					
	Williamson Co	227Y	MP-58	78626	400-599
TOM MILLER ST	Austin	586A	ML-24	78723	1900-2899
TOM SASSMAN RD	Mustang Ridge	736W	ML-7	78747	11400-11599
	Travis Co	736W	ML-7	78747	11200-11399
	Travis Co	766A	ML-6	78747	None
TOM SAWYER RD	Hays Co	668D	WV-15	78620	100-1499
TOM SEAVER PL	Round Rock	378E	MQ-45	78665	1000-1099
TOM WOOTEN CV	Austin	524J	MG-29	78731	5800-5899
TOM WOOTEN DR	Austin	524J	MG-29	78731	5800-5999
TONIA LOOP	Round Rock	347J	MN-47	78665	1500-1599
TONKAWA TRL	Austin	555S	MJ-25	78756	3800-3999
TONKAWA TRL	Williamson Co	375L	MK-44	78681	1800-2099
TONKAWA TRL E	Lakeway	519X	WW-28	78738	3900-3999
TONKAWA TRL W	Lakeway	519W	WW-28	78738	16500-16699
TONKAWA HILLS DR	Bastrop	715Z	EF-10	78602	100-199
TONKAWA RIDGE	Williamson Co	410N	MU-41	78634	100-299
TONKINESE DR	Williamson Co	405C	MK-42	78681	8000-8099
	Williamson Co	405B	MJ-42	78681	8100-8299
TONKOWA TRL	Williamson Co	226R	MM-59	78628	6000-6099
TONOPA LN	Austin	587L	MP-23	78724	7900-7999
	Travis Co	587L	MP-23	78724	8000-8199
TONQUIN DR	Williamson Co	343T	ME-46	78641	2800-2899
TONTO LN	Travis Co	522S	MC-28	78733	1800-2199
TONY DR	Round Rock	406G	MM-42	78664	800-899
TOOLWRICH LN	Austin	671B	MA-15	78739	6600-6699
TOOMEY RD	Austin	584Y	MH-22	78704	1300-1799
TOP CT	Travis Co	366R	WR-44	78654	28400-28599
TOP CV	Austin	613H	MF-21	78704	2600-2699
TOPANGA LN	Austin	587G	MP-24	78724	7900-7999
	Travis Co	587G	MP-24	78724	8000-8199
TOPAWA CV	Austin	434Y	MH-37	78729	7800-7899
TOPAZ LN	Leander	342K	MC-47	78641	700-899
TOPAZ RD	Travis Co	467V	MP-34	78660	1900-2099
TOPHILL CIR	Travis Co	467Z	MP-34	78660	13900-13999
TOP OF TEXAS TRL	Travis Co	580D	WZ-24	78735	4100-4399
TOP OF THE TRAIL CV	Travis Co	460K	WY-35	78734	5400-5499
TOP O THE LAKE DR	Lakeway	519L	WX-29	78734	100-299
TOPPEL CV	Travis Co	492Y	MD-31	78730	9800-9899
TOPPER LN	Travis Co	702R	MD-11	78652	12600-12899
TOPPERWEIN DR	Austin	496N	ML-32	78758	10600-10899
TOPRIDGE DR	Austin	463D	MF-36	78750	9100-9599
TOP ROCK LN	Round Rock	345T	MJ-46	78681	3700-3899
TOPSAIL	Manor	530K	MU-29	78653	None
TOREADOR DR	Travis Co	553M	MF-26	78746	4600-4899
TORI DR	Hays Co	763X	ME-4	78610	100-199
TORNASOL LN	Austin	641S	MA-16	78739	10900-11099
TORO CANYON RD	Travis Co	553R	MF-26	78746	1800-3499
	Travis Co	554A	MG-27	78746	3500-3999
TORO CREEK CV	Austin	464J	MG-35	78759	8600-8699
TORO GRANDE BLVD	Cedar Park	374B	MG-45	78613	1000-1398 E
	Cedar Park	344X	MG-46	78613	1400-1698 E
TORO RING	Travis Co	553H	MF-27	78746	3000-3199
TORRAN CV	Austin	642T	MC-16	78749	9100-9199
TORRANCE CT	Travis Co	550U	WZ-25	78733	12300-12399
TORRES LN	Hays Co	669H	WX-15	78737	100-199
TORRES ST	Austin	616P	ML-20	78741	6300-6499
TORREY PINE CIR	Georgetown	226M	MM-59	78628	30100-30199
TORREY PINES CV	Travis Co	582H	MD-24	78746	6500-6699
TORRINGTON CT	Village of the Hills	519T	WW-28	78738	1-99
TORRINGTON DR	Hays Co	639X	WW-16	78737	100-499
TORRINGTON LN	Village of the Hills	519T	WW-28	78738	1-99
TORRINGTON ST	Buda	763A	ME-6	78610	500-699
TORTILLA FLAT	Travis Co	550Y	WZ-25	78738	4300-4499
TORTOISE LN	Williamson Co	255M	MK-56	78628	100-199
TORTOISE ST	Pflugerville	437B	MN-39	78664	16800-17199
TORTOSA PATH	Williamson Co	434V	MH-37	78729	13200-13299
TORTUGA CV	Austin	524T	MG-28	78731	4500-4599
TORTUGA PL	Austin	524X	MG-28	78731	4900-4999
TORTUGA TRL	Austin	524X	MG-28	78731	5200-5499
TORTUGA RACING LN	Hays Co	577U	WT-22	78720	10900-10999
TOSCA CV	Travis Co	402Y	MD-40	78613	1900-1999
TOSCANA AVE	Austin	587F	MN-24	78724	5400-6399
TOSSA LN	Williamson Co	434R	MH-38	78729	13400-13499
TOTOVIA DR	Bastrop Co	738L	MR-8	78617	100-199
TOTTENHAM CT	Williamson Co	434K	MG-38	78729	9300-9399
TOUCHSTONE ST	Austin	586G	MM-24	78723	3300-3599
TOULOUSE DR	Austin	673E	ME-15	78748	2100-2699
TOUR DE FRANCE CV	Travis Co	522U	MD-28	78733	2000-2099
TOURMALINE TRL	Williamson Co	375B	MJ-45	78681	3400-3499
TOURNAMENT CV	Village of the Hills	519J	WW-29	78738	1-99
TOURNAMENT WAY					
	Village of the Hills	519J	WW-29	78738	1-99
TOURNEY CV	Village of the Hills	519J	WW-29	78738	1-99
TOURNEY LN	Village of the Hills	519J	WW-29	78738	1-99
TOURNUS TRL	Austin	674M	MH-14	78744	4800-4899
TOVAR DR	Williamson Co	434R	MH-38	78729	7400-7799
TOWAN WAY	Hutto	379P	MS-44	78634	100-199
TOWANA CIR	Travis Co	611N	MA-20	78736	7600-7699
TOWANA TRL	Austin	611N	MA-20	78736	8700-8999
	Travis Co	611N	MA-20	78736	9000-9599
TOWBRIDGE CIR	Austin	556Q	MM-26	78723	2200-2499
TOWER DR	Austin	554Y	MH-25	78703	2000-2599
TOWER DR	Georgetown	286V	MM-52	78626	2300-2499
TOWER DR	Round Rock	406M	MM-41	78664	100-199

STREET NAME	CITY or COUNTY	MAPSCO GRID	AUSTIN GRID	ZIP CODE	BLOCK RANGE O/E
TOWER RD	Manor	501B	MW-33	78653	12200-12998 E
	Travis Co	501B	MW-33	78653	11900-12199
	Travis Co	501B	MW-33	78653	12201-12999 O
	Travis Co	530B	MU-30	78653	13000-13099
TOWER RD	Williamson Co	222Z	MD-58	78642	1-2199
TOWER TRL	Austin	586D	MM-24	78723	5200-5399
TOWERING OAKS DR	Austin	643P	ME-17	78745	7000-7299
TOWER VIEW CT	Austin	586E	ML-24	78723	3700-3899
TOWERY LN	Travis Co	707E	MN-12	78617	7400-7699
TOWHEE DR	Hays Co	732J	MC-8	78610	200-399
TOWN BLUFF DR	Travis Co	520Y	WZ-28	78732	900-1099
TOWN CENTER DR	Pflugerville	438G	MR-39	78660	1400-1699
TOWN CENTRE DR	Round Rock	407K	MN-41	78664	2000-2199
TOWN CREEK DR	Austin	615Q	MK-20	78741	1100-1599
TOWN CROSSING	Pflugerville	438C	MR-39	78660	1300-1399
TOWNE PARK TRL	Austin	555Y	MK-25	78751	400-499
TOWNES LN	Austin	584D	MH-24	78703	1800-1899
	Austin	554Y	MH-25	78703	2100-2999
TOWNES ST E	Manor	529Q	MT-29	78653	100-499
TOWNES ST W	Manor	529Q	MT-29	78653	100-399
TOWNESOUTH CIR	Austin	615X	MJ-19	78741	1900-1999
TOWN HILL DR	Travis Co	436U	MM-37	78728	14000-14699
TOWN LAKE CIR	Austin	615Q	MK-20	78741	2200-2499
TOWNS ST N	Weir	258H	MR-57	78626	100-399
TOWNSBOROUGH DR	Austin	557Y	MP-25	78724	6900-7199
TOWNSHIP CV	Austin	464Q	MH-35	78759	11100-11199
TOWNSHIP TRL	Austin	464Q	MH-35	78759	6700-6899
TOWNSMILL RD N	Weir	258C	MR-57	78626	1-399
	Williamson Co	258C	MR-57	78626	400-599
TOWNSMILL RD S	Weir	258L	MR-56	78626	1-499
TOWNVIEW CV	Austin	645D	MK-18	78741	5200-5299
TOWSER CT	Austin	645T	MJ-16	78744	5300-5399
TOYAHVILLE TRL	Pflugerville	407X	MN-40	78664	17300-17499
TOYATH ST	Austin	584L	MH-23	78703	1000-1199
TOYE DR	Austin	678P	MQ-14	78617	6000-6199
TRABADORA CV	Austin	464V	MH-34	78759	5900-5999
TRACE CHAIN DR	Austin	642B	MC-18	78749	7200-7399
TRACE CREEK PASS	Austin	587R	MP-23	78724	5500-5699
TRACI MICHELLE DR	Austin	437W	MN-37	78660	1000-1199
TRACOR LN	Austin	586M	MM-23	78721	5700-6199
	Austin	587J	MN-23	78725	6200-6599
TRACTON CT	Austin	671B	MA-15	78739	6400-6499
TRACTON LN	Austin	671B	MA-15	78739	11200-11399
TRACY CV	Williamson Co	342Z	MD-46	78641	2500-2599
TRACY TRL	Travis Co	436U	MM-37	78728	2500-2699
TRACY LYNN LN	Austin	616G	MM-21	78721	5700-6099
TRACY MILLER LN	Cedar Park	402Z	MD-40	78613	1700-1899
TRADE CENTER DR	Austin	645M	MK-17	78744	5800-6299
TRADEMARK DR	Hays Co	762R	MD-5	78610	None
TRADESMAN DR	Williamson Co	378D	MR-45	78634	100-299
TRADESMEN'S PARK DR					
	Williamson Co	378D	MR-45	78634	100-599
TRADESMEN'S PARK LOOP					
	Williamson Co	378C	MR-45	78634	600-999
TRADEWIND DR	Travis Co	518B	WU-30	78669	2700-3099
TRADE WINDS LOOP	Georgetown	314K	MG-50	78628	100-199
TRADEWIND VIEW DR	Jonestown	430T	WY-37	78645	None
TRADING BEND	Austin	613E	ME-21	78735	5000-5299
TRAFALGAR CV	Cedar Park	372P	MC-44	78613	1900-1999
TRAFALGAR DR	Austin	556U	MM-25	78723	2300-2499
TRAIL CV	Travis Co	582H	MD-24	78746	1100-1199
TRAIL CREST CIR	Austin	613E	ME-21	78735	4500-4899
TRAIL DRIVE CIR	Bastrop	744G	ED-9	78602	100-199
TRAIL DRIVER	Hays Co	608Z	WV-19	78737	12300-12599
	Hays Co	638D	WV-18	78737	12600-14099
	Hays Co	608Z	WV-19	78737	14100-14299
TRAIL DUST DR	Cedar Park	374N	MG-44	78613	500-699
TRAILHEAD CT	Cedar Park	374Q	MH-44	78613	3700-3799
TRAILING VINE WAY	Round Rock	408A	MQ-42	78665	2500-2599
TRAILMASTER DR	Travis Co	640Y	WZ-16	78737	12100-12299
TRAIL OF MADRONES	Travis Co	553R	MF-26	78746	1800-2999
TRAIL OF THE FLOWERS	Georgetown	225K	MJ-59	78633	100-399
TRAIL OF THE WOODS	Travis Co	460K	WY-35	78734	16800-17299
TRAIL RIDER PASS	Hays Co	669N	WW-14	78737	100-199
TRAIL RIDER WAY	Georgetown	226E	ML-60	78633	100-299
TRAILRIDER'S CV	Travis Co	531H	MX-30	78621	22300-22499
TRAIL RIDGE CIR	Austin	524V	MH-28	78731	5800-5899
TRAILRIDGE DR	Austin	524V	MH-28	78731	5700-5899
TRAILRIDGE DR	Cedar Park	373Y	MF-43	78613	100-499
TRAILRIDGE RD	Williamson Co	224F	MG-60	78633	100-199
TRAILS END	Hays Co	638D	WV-18	78737	12900-13199
	Hays Co	639E	WW-18	78737	13200-13699
TRAILS END CV	Travis Co	401G	MB-42	78641	16700-17099
TRAILS END DR	Georgetown	287N	MN-53	78626	2200-2499
TRAILS END RD	Travis Co	401C	MB-42	78641	9800-12699
	Travis Co	371Y	MB-43	78641	12700-12999
TRAILSIDE DR	Austin	614B	MG-21	78704	2200-2699
TRAILSIDE ESTATES BLVD	Travis Co	588H	MR-24	78724	7600-7799
TRAIL VIEW CV	Travis Co	460F	WY-36	78734	16900-16999
TRAILVIEW MESA CV	Travis Co	554N	MG-26	78746	2800-2899
TRAILVIEW MESA DR	Travis Co	554J	MG-26	78746	4000-4399
TRAILVIEW MESA TERRACE					
	Travis Co	554J	MG-26	78746	2900-2999
TRAILWAY ST	Round Rock	376V	MM-43	78664	100-199
TRAIL WEARY DR	Austin	497W	MN-31	78754	10800-10899
TRAIL WEST DR	Austin	613J	ME-20	78735	4500-5199
TRAILWOOD RD	Austin	465H	MK-36	78727	12800-13099
TRALAGON TRL	Austin	498J	MQ-32	78660	3400-3599
TRAMSON DR	Austin	645B	MJ-18	78741	1900-2099
TRANQUILITY FALLS CV	Lago Vista	429M	WX-38	78645	19600-19699
TRANQUILITY MOUNTAIN	Hays Co	762V	MD-4	78610	100-599
TRANQUILO TRL	Austin	674G	MH-15	78744	1900-2199
TRANQUIL OAKS DR	Travis Co	672N	MC-14	78739	11200-11299
TRANSIT CIR	Austin	465G	MK-36	78727	4800-4999
TRANSIT CV	Austin	465G	MK-36	78727	12700-12799
TRAPINI PL	Travis Co	432G	MD-39	78613	None
TRAPPER LN	Lago Vista	399Q	WX-41	78645	20700-20899
TRAPPER TRL	Bastrop	744P	EC-8	78602	100-199
TRAPPERS TRL	Travis Co	591J	MW-23	78653	20300-21099
TRAUTWEIN RD	Hays Co	608P	WU-20	78737	12000-12699
	Hays Co	638U	WV-16	78620	12700-14198 E
	Hays Co	638U	WV-16	78737	12701-14199 O
TRAVERTINE CV	Travis Co	581D	MB-24	78735	9300-9399
TRAVIS CIR	Travis Co	459M	WX-35	78645	18100-18199
TRAVIS DR	Georgetown	195X	MJ-61	78633	100-199
TRAVIS DR	Jonestown	400H	WZ-42	78645	10900-11299
TRAVIS DR	Lago Vista	429P	WW-38	78645	20000-20299

STREET NAME	CITY or COUNTY	MAPSCO GRID	AUSTIN GRID	ZIP CODE	BLOCK RANGE O/E
TRAVIS DR	Travis Co	459M	WX-35	78645	18100-18299
TRAVIS RD	Travis Co	460R	WZ-35	78734	15600-15699
TRAVIS ST	Jonestown	401A	MA-42	78645	11500-11699
TRAVIS ST	Taylor	352G	MZ-48	76574	100-199
TRAVIS BEND LN	Travis Co	397Z	WT-40	78654	None
TRAVIS BLUFF WAY	Travis Co	427X	WS-36	78669	1200-1299
TRAVIS COOK RD	Austin	611C	MB-21	78735	5500-5899
	Travis Co	611C	MB-21	78735	5400-5499
TRAVIS COUNTRY BLVD	Austin	613N	ME-20	78735	4900-4999
TRAVIS COUNTRY CIR	Austin	612D	MD-21	78735	3200-4099
	Austin	613N	ME-20	78735	4100-5099
TRAVIS COUNTRY DR	Austin	612D	MD-21	78735	3200-4199
TRAVIS GREEN LN	Austin	612G	MD-21	78735	5400-5899
TRAVIS HEIGHTS BLVD	Austin	615N	MJ-20	78704	1100-2199
TRAVIS HILLS DR	Austin	611C	MB-21	78735	8700-8899
TRAVIS LAKESIDE CV	Travis Co	427L	WT-38	78669	24700-24799
TRAVIS LAKESIDE DR	Travis Co	427P	WS-38	78669	2000-3099
TRAVIS LOOKOUT	Travis Co	427Z	WT-37	78654	None
TRAVIS OAKS DR	Travis Co	428E	WU-39	78654	4800-5399
	Travis Co	398W	WU-40	78654	5400-5699
TRAVIS PEAK TRL	Travis Co	397V	WT-40	78654	None
TRAVIS T TRL	Austin	498T	MQ-31	78653	None
TRAVISTA DR	Travis Co	401X	MA-40	78641	16700-16899
TRAVIS VIEW CT	Travis Co	491G	MB-33	78732	4700-4799
TRAVIS VIEW LOOP	Travis Co	491G	MB-33	78732	13000-13199
TRAVIS VISTA DR	Travis Co	518Z	WV-28	78738	4300-4499
TRAVIS WOODS CV	Travis Co	460G	WZ-36	78734	5900-6099
TRAWELL RD	Mustang Ridge	767N	MN-5	78616	12100-12199
TRAWOOD PATH	Austin	672X	MC-13	78748	11800-11899
TREADSOFT CV	Travis Co	672P	MC-14	78748	3300-3499
TREADWELL BLVD	Austin	525S	MJ-28	78757	6200-6699
TREADWELL ST	Austin	614C	MH-21	78704	1100-1899
TREASURE CV	Austin	643V	MF-16	78745	7000-7199
TREASURE ISLAND DR	Travis Co	492U	MD-31	78730	10100-10499
TREASURE OAKS DR	Leander	342B	MC-48	78641	100-299
TREAT TRL	Travis Co	459K	WW-35	78645	19300-19399
TREATY OAK CIR	Austin	642C	MD-18	78749	6900-7099
TREBBLED WATERS TRL	Hays Co	666Z	WR-13	78619	1100-1899
TREDE CV	Austin	643U	MF-16	78745	7400-7499
TREDE DR	Austin	643T	ME-16	78745	2000-2299
TREE BEND CV	Austin	463L	MF-35	78750	9800-10099
TREE BEND DR	Austin	463G	MF-36	78750	9500-9899
TREE FERN LN	Austin	493V	MF-31	78750	6700-6899
TREEHAVEN LN	Village of the Hills	519S	WW-28	78738	1-99
TREEHOUSE LN	Austin	642U	MD-16	78749	8000-8499
TREELINE DR	Cedar Park	372U	MD-43	78613	1400-1799
TREE LINE DR	Williamson Co	434P	MG-38	78729	12400-12699
TREEMONT DR	Rollingwood	583V	MF-22	78746	1-99
TREE SAP WAY	Williamson Co	408L	MR-41	78664	None
TREE TOP DR	Travis Co	590L	MV-23	78653	18900-18999
TREETOP WAY	Hays Co	732K	MC-8	78610	200-599
TRELAWNEY LN	Austin	671D	MB-15	78739	5600-5799
TREMOLO PASS	Travis Co	702G	MD-12	78748	2500-2599
TREMONT DR	Cedar Park	372L	MD-44	78613	1000-1399
TREMONT ST	Austin	584R	MH-23	78703	1400-1499
TRENDAL LN	Austin	674G	MH-15	78744	6800-7099
TRENT DR	Austin	465X	MJ-34	78759	11100-11199
TRENTON DR	Travis Co	611E	MA-21	78736	7300-7399
TRES CORONAS RD	Travis Co	457W	WS-34	78669	23300-23799
	Travis Co	486D	WR-33	78669	23800-23999
TREVIN CV	Manor	529Z	MT-28	78653	None
TREVINO DR	Round Rock	378T	MQ-43	78664	3800-3899
TREVINO DR	Travis Co	582M	MD-23	78746	1700-2099
TREY CT	Williamson Co	318F	MQ-51	78634	200-299
TREY DR	Taylor	322V	MZ-49	76574	1300-1499
TREY ST	Round Rock	406F	ML-42	78681	1300-1399
TREYBURN LN	Travis Co	409W	MS-40	78660	20100-20499
TREYS WAY	Austin	644S	MG-16	78745	300-699
TRIANGLE AVE	Austin	555P	MJ-26	78756	4500-4699
TRIANGLE ACRES	Bastrop Co	711F	MW-12	78612	100-299
TRIANON LN	Austin	465Q	MK-35	78727	12000-12099
TRIBORO TRL	Austin	642H	MD-18	78749	4200-4399
TRIBUTARY RIDGE CT	Austin	464U	MH-34	78759	6000-6099
TRIBUTARY RIDGE DR	Austin	464U	MH-34	78759	5800-6099
TRICIA CV	Hutto	350N	MU-47	78634	1200-1299
TRICIA LN	Hutto	350N	MU-47	78634	100-299
TRICKLE TRACE TRL	Williamson Co	375X	MJ-43	78681	9100-9199
TRICKLING SPRINGS WAY	Travis Co	439N	MS-38	78660	3400-3599
TRIDENS CT	Austin	464B	MG-36	78750	11600-11699
TRIDENT LN	Jonestown	430J	WY-38	78645	7200-7299
TRIGG RD	Bastrop Co	744X	EC-7	78602	100-299
TRIGO LN	Williamson Co	345X	MJ-46	78681	3100-3199
TRILLUM CV	Travis Co	551P	MA-26	78733	1900-1999
TRIMARAN CIR	Jonestown	430T	WY-37	78645	None
TRIMBLE AVE	Hays Co	762R	MD-5	78610	1000-1999
TRINIDAD LN	Travis Co	468J	MQ-35	78660	15000-15099
TRINITY CV	Lago Vista	399R	WX-41	78645	20600-20699
TRINITY ST	Austin	585W	MJ-22	78701	1-1999
	Austin	585F	MJ-24	78705	2300-2499
TRINITY HILL DR	Austin	496R	MM-32	78753	11500-11599
TRINITY HILLS DR	Hays Co	639T	WW-16	78737	100-1599
TRIPLE CREEK CIR	Hays Co	608J	WU-20	78620	12200-12399
TRIPLE CREEK DR	Hays Co	608N	WU-20	78620	12100-12599
TRIPLE CROWN	Austin	523V	MF-28	78746	4100-4199
TRIPOD DR	Austin	675W	MJ-13	78747	8301-8399 O
TRIPSHAW LN	Austin	615W	MJ-19	78741	1900-2199
TRISTAM DR	Travis Co	591L	MX-23	78621	8700-9399
TRISTANS WAY	Buda	732U	MD-7	78610	100-299
TRISTANS WAY	Cedar Park	372K	MC-44	78613	1600-1699
TRITON CT	Lakeway	519J	WW-29	78734	100-199
TROGON CT	Williamson Co	433Q	MF-38	78750	10300-10399
TROLLEY CV	Leander	342V	MD-46	78641	2200-2299
TROLL HAVEN	Austin	523X	ME-28	78746	6700-6799
TRONE CIR	Austin	525D	MK-30	78758	8900-8999
TRONEWOOD DR	Austin	525D	MK-30	78758	8900-8999
TROON DR	Lakeway	519J	WW-29	78738	1-99
TROOPS TRL	Austin	466F	ML-36	78727	13100-13199
TROPHY CT	Bastrop	744K	EC-8	78602	300-399
TROPHY CV	Austin	703C	MF-12	78748	10700-10799
TROPHY DR	Lakeway	519J	WW-29	78738	100-199
TROPHY PASS	Austin	703C	MF-12	78748	200-299
TROTTER DR	Georgetown	287G	MP-54	78626	100-199
TROTTERS LN	Pflugerville	409J	MS-41	78660	20800-20999
TROTWOOD DR	Austin	497J	MN-32	78753	12000-12199
TROUT CV	Austin	672F	MC-15	78749	10300-10399
TROUT DR	Austin	672F	MC-15	78749	3900-4099
TROUT LN	Georgetown	195V	MK-61	78633	100-199

T

STREET NAME	CITY or COUNTY	MAPSCO GRID	AUSTIN GRID	ZIP CODE	BLOCK RANGE O/E
TROWBRIDGE CV	Williamson Co	375W	MJ-43	78717	9200-9299
TROY LN	Round Rock	377J	MN-44	78664	1200-1499
TRUE CV	Austin	673S	ME-13	78748	1800-1899
TRUMAN CV	Lago Vista	458B	WU-36	78645	2700-2899
TRUMAN CV	Williamson Co	434Q	MH-38	78729	7900-7999
TRUMAN DR	Lago Vista	458F	WU-36	78645	2200-2899
TRUMAN LN	Cedar Park	373U	MF-43	78613	800-999
TRUMAN OAK CV	Travis Co	619J	MS-20	78724	14900-14999
TRUMPET DR	Travis Co	619E	MS-21	78724	15400-15499
TRUMPET VINE TRL	Cedar Park	403A	ME-42	78613	300-499
TRUNSTONE DR	Austin	674D	MH-15	78744	4500-4599
TRUSTWORTHY	Leander	372F	MC-45	78641	None
TRUTH WAY	Travis Co	619N	MS-20	78725	4500-4699
TUCK ST	Bastrop Co	741C	MX-9	78612	100-399
TUCKER HILL LN	Bastrop Co	680K	MU-14	78612	4600-5499
	Travis Co	650Y	MV-16	78612	3800-4099
	Travis Co	680C	MV-15	78612	4500-4599
TUCUMCARI TRL	Travis Co	490Y	WZ-31	78734	14400-14699
TUDOR BLVD	Austin	495K	MJ-32	78759	3600-3799
TUDOR HOUSE RD	Travis Co	467Q	MP-35	78660	200-1599
TUFFIT LN	Austin	497N	MN-32	78753	1100-1499
TULANE DR	Austin	556R	MM-26	78723	6700-6999
TULARE DR	Travis Co	550R	WZ-26	78733	12000-12099
TULAROSA PASS	Austin	463F	ME-36	78726	10100-10499
TULE CV	Austin	642Q	MD-17	78749	4200-4299
TULIP TRAIL BEND	Cedar Park	373U	MF-43	78613	100-299
TULLOCH WAY	Austin	528K	MQ-29	78754	6700-6899
TULSA CV	Austin	556R	MM-26	78723	6700-6799
TUMBLEWEED DR	Austin	557P	MN-26	78724	7100-7599
TUMBLEWEED TRL	Austin	613S	ME-19	78749	None
TUMBLEWEED TRL N	Travis Co	552E	MC-27	78733	100-899
TUMBLEWEED TRL S	Travis Co	552E	MC-27	78733	100-299
	Travis Co	551H	MB-27	78733	300-399
TUMBLING CIR	Austin	524R	MH-29	78731	5900-5999
TUMBLING CREEK TRL	Austin	702C	MD-12	78748	12100-12199
TUMBLING RIVER DR	Leander	372B	MC-45	78641	2500-2799
TUMLINSON FORT DR	Williamson Co	342Z	MD-46	78641	400-699
	Williamson Co	343W	ME-46	78641	2600-2899
TUNNEL TRL	San Leanna	703K	ME-11	78652	11700-11998 E
	Travis Co	703K	ME-11	78653	11701-11999 O
	Travis Co	703K	ME-11	78652	12000-12199
TUPELO DR	Austin	675S	MJ-13	78744	6200-6399
TURA LN	Austin	586U	MM-22	78721	5600-5799
TURBINE DR	Travis Co	466G	MM-36	78728	13700-13999
TURETELLA DR	Round Rock	345N	MJ-47	78681	3700-3799
TURF CV	Austin	703C	MF-12	78748	200-299
TURK LN	Austin	674S	MG-13	78748	100-299
TURKEY CV	Hays Co	732B	MC-9	78610	12700-12799
TURKEY BEND	Jonestown	400L	WZ-41	78645	10500-10999
TURKEY CREEK DR	Travis Co	522M	MD-29	78730	3600-4399
TURKEY HOLLOW	Austin	494S	MG-31	78750	6200-6299
TURKEY HOLLOW TRL	Austin	403M	MF-41	78717	14000-14099
TURKEY PATH BEND	Cedar Park	374U	MH-43	78613	3500-3899
TURKEY RIDGE CT	Williamson Co	434U	MH-37	78729	12500-12599
TURKEY ROOST RD	Travis Co	701H	MB-12	78652	13100-13299
TURKEY RUN	Austin	466K	ML-35	78727	12800-13099
TURKEY TREE RD	Burnet Co	396T	WQ-40	78669	100-899
TURKEY TROT	Williamson Co	224Y	MH-58	78633	20100-20199
TURKEY TROT TRL	Travis Co	577Q	WT-23	78720	17900-18099
TURKOMAN DR	Austin	523Y	MF-28	78746	None
TURK'S CAP CT	Austin	464A	MG-36	78750	8900-8999
TURLEY DR	Travis Co	733B	ME-9	78652	100-699
TURMAN CV	Travis Co	492U	MD-31	78730	9900-9999
TURNABOUT LN	Austin	555A	MJ-27	78731	5100-5399
TURNABOUT ST	Elgin	533M	EB-29	78621	100-199
TURNBACK	Lago Vista	428V	WV-37	78645	4700-4999
TURNBERRY CT	Georgetown	226L	MM-59	78628	29000-29099
TURNBERRY DR	Round Rock	378X	MQ-43	78664	3000-3099
TURNBOW TRL	Cedar Park	373T	ME-43	78613	600-699
TURNBUOY DR	Austin	523T	ME-28	78730	7200-7499
TURNER DR	Austin	496Y	MM-31	78753	10500-10899
TURNER LN	Austin	557N	MN-26	78723	4600-4799
TURNER RD	Taylor	323P	EA-50	76574	1600-2599
TURNER RANCH RD	Travis Co	367W	WS-43	78654	27500-28099
	Travis Co	366Z	WR-43	78654	28100-28399
TURNERSVILLE RD	Creedmoor	765F	MJ-6	78610	1800-2299
	Creedmoor	765E	MJ-6	78610	4300-5299
	Creedmoor	735X	MJ-7	78610	12400-12499
See.. FM Rd 1625					
	Hays Co	733V	MF-7	78610	1300-1499
	Travis Co	734X	MG-7	78610	2700-3099
	Travis Co	764D	MH-6	78610	3100-4299
	Travis Co	765E	MJ-6	78610	5300-5599
	Travis Co	765P	MJ-5	78610	5600-6299
	Travis Co	733V	MF-7	78610	None
TURNERSVILLE RD N	Travis Co	734N	MG-8	78610	12400-13599
TURNERSVILLE RD S	Hays Co	794A	MG-3	78610	100-599
	Hays Co	764W	MG-4	78610	600-1199
	Hays Co	764J	MG-5	78610	1200-1799
	Travis Co	734W	MG-7	78610	13500-14599
	Travis Co	764J	MG-5	78610	13900-14599
TURNING LIZARD CT	Travis Co	702G	MD-12	78748	12300-12399
TURNSTONE CT	Austin	675A	MJ-15	78744	6000-6099
TURNSTONE DR	Hays Co	732E	MC-9	78610	300-399
TURQUOISE CV	Austin	642R	MD-17	78749	4000-4099
TURQUOISE TRL	Austin	642Q	MD-17	78749	7700-7999
TURTLE CV	Williamson Co	255M	MK-56	78628	100-199
TURTLE LN	Travis Co	433S	ME-37	78726	11500-11699
TURTLEBACK LN	Austin	465L	MK-35	78727	12300-12499
TURTLE BEND	Williamson Co	255M	MK-56	78628	100-399
TURTLE CREEK BLVD	Austin	644N	MG-17	78745	700-1199
	Austin	643R	MF-17	78745	1200-1699
TURTLE DOVE DR	Austin	674D	MH-15	78744	6000-6299
TURTLE MOUNTAIN BEND	Austin	702L	MD-11	78748	2100-2499
TURTLE POINT DR	Travis Co	582R	MD-23	78746	6100-6299
TURTLE RIVER DR	Williamson Co	343X	ME-46	78641	2500-2899
TURTLE ROCK RD	Williamson Co	434T	MG-37	78729	12300-13199
TUSCAN TERRACE	Austin	613H	MF-21	78746	2800-2899
TUSCANY WAY	Austin	557A	MN-27	78754	8200-8899
	Austin	527W	MN-28	78754	8900-9199
TUSCANY WAY	Williamson Co	224L	MH-59	78633	100-199
TUSCARORA TRL	Austin	434Y	MH-37	78729	8000-8199
TUSCOLA CIR	Travis Co	490Y	WZ-31	78734	14400-14499
TUSMAN DR	Austin	611M	MB-21	78735	7800-7999
TUTT LN	Caldwell Co	767Z	MP-4	78616	1-99
TUXFORD CV	Austin	497J	MN-32	78753	1300-1399
TWAIN CV	Lago Vista	458F	WU-36	78645	21500-21599
TWEED CT	Austin	465E	MJ-36	78727	12000-12199
TWEED BERWICK DR	Austin	464E	MG-36	78750	8800-8999
	Austin	463H	MF-36	78750	9000-9199
TWEEDSMUIR DR	Austin	463H	MF-36	78750	10400-10699
TWELVE OAKS LN	Austin	614U	MH-19	78704	600-699
TWIGGY LN	Austin	675W	MJ-13	78747	8400-8499
TWILIGHT CV	Lago Vista	399R	WX-41	78645	20600-20699
TWILIGHT CV	Round Rock	344R	MH-47	78681	4100-4199
TWILIGHT TRL	Travis Co	672X	MC-13	78748	3100-3299
TWILIGHT WAY	Hutto	380A	MU-45	78634	100-199
TWILIGHT BLUFF LN	Bee Cave	549M	WX-26	78738	14100-14199
TWILIGHT MESA DR	Austin	641C	MB-18	78749	6900-7599
TWILIGHT RIDGE DR	Travis Co	553Q	MF-26	78746	1500-1699
TWILIGHT SHADOW DR	Austin	641G	MB-18	78749	7300-7599
TWILIGHT TERRACE DR	Austin	641C	MB-18	78749	8000-8399
TWILIGHT VISTA	Travis Co	610T	WY-19	78736	10500-10799
TWIN ACRES LN	Bee Cave	549V	WX-25	78738	4600-5299
TWINBERRY CV	Austin	583Y	MF-22	78746	3200-3299
TWINBERRY TRL	Williamson Co	375Q	MK-44	78681	6000-6099
TWIN BRANCH DR	Cedar Park	374U	MH-43	78613	3500-3699
TWIN CEDAR DR	Williamson Co	196J	ML-62	78628	100-199
TWIN CEDARS RD	Williamson Co	280U	WZ-52	78641	1-699
TWIN CREEK CIR	Hays Co	577Z	WT-22	78720	100-499
TWIN CREEK CV	Travis Co	703P	ME-11	78652	400-499
TWIN CREEK DR	Pflugerville	438S	MQ-37	78660	1000-1199
TWIN CREEK DR	Travis Co	703S	ME-10	78652	12200-12599
TWIN CREEK HOLLOW	Austin	493V	MF-31	78750	6500-6599
TWIN CREEK MEADOWS DR					
	Travis Co	619L	MT-20	78653	16600-16799
TWIN CREEK PARK DR	Travis Co	703T	ME-10	78652	12200-12599
TWIN CREEKS CIR	Travis Co	703N	ME-11	78652	12300-12499
TWIN CREEKS RD	Travis Co	703X	ME-10	78652	100-599
	Travis Co	703N	ME-11	78652	12100-12799
TWIN CREEKS CLUB DR	Travis Co	432G	MD-39	78613	2300-3299
TWIN CREST DR	Austin	525Z	MK-28	78752	6800-7199
	Austin	526W	ML-28	78752	7200-7399
TWIN HILLS CT	Lakeway	519L	WX-29	78734	700-799
TWIN LAKE CIR	Travis Co	577Q	WT-23	78720	10300-10399
TWIN LAKE LOOP	Travis Co	577L	WT-23	78720	10000-10299
TWIN LEDGE CIR	Austin	524K	MG-29	78731	6100-6199
TWIN LEDGE CV	Austin	524K	MG-29	78731	6100-6199
TWIN LEDGE DR	Austin	524K	MG-29	78731	6100-6199
TWIN MESA DR	Bee Cave	550W	WY-25	78738	None
TWIN OAKS DR	Austin	525S	MJ-28	78757	2400-2899
TWIN OAKS LN	Bastrop Co	564R	ED-26	78621	100-199
TWIN OAK TRAIL DR	Cedar Park	403A	ME-42	78613	200-899
TWIN PEAKS CV	Leander	342V	MD-46	78641	2200-2299
TWIN RIDGE DR	Round Rock	406H	MM-42	78664	200-499
TWIN RIDGE PKWY	Round Rock	378L	MR-44	78664	1-99
TWIN SADDLES	Travis Co	577K	WS-23	78620	100-199
TWIN SPRINGS RD	Williamson Co	224N	MG-59	78633	1-599
TWIN TERRACE CT	Round Rock	378W	MQ-43	78665	1000-1099
TWIN VALLEY CIR	Austin	524K	MG-29	78731	4500-4699
TWIN VALLEY CV	Austin	524K	MG-29	78731	6000-6099
TWIN VALLEY DR	Austin	524J	MG-29	78731	4500-4899
TWISTED BRIAR LN	Williamson Co	434P	MG-38	78729	12600-12799
TWISTED FENCE DR	Travis Co	467C	MP-36	78660	800-999
TWISTED OAK DR	Leander	342T	MC-46	78641	1800-1899
TWISTED OAKS DR	Austin	643T	ME-16	78745	7000-7299
TWISTED TREE CV	Austin	613J	ME-20	78735	4500-4599
TWISTED TREE DR	Austin	613J	ME-20	78735	4300-4599
TWISTING TRL	Lago Vista	429W	WW-37	78645	20600-20799
	Lago Vista	428Z	WV-37	78645	20800-21299
TWO COVES DR	Travis Co	523B	ME-30	78730	8000-8299
TWO HOUSE RD	Travis Co	459R	WX-35	78645	18000-18099
TWO IRON ST	Austin	645W	MJ-16	78744	5100-5399
TWO JACKS TRL	Williamson Co	375P	MJ-44	78681	7200-7499
TWO RIVERS CV	Williamson Co	405K	MJ-41	78717	15900-15999
TY COBB PL	Round Rock	378A	MQ-45	78665	1300-1599
TYDINGS CV	Travis Co	553A	ME-27	78730	2500-2599
TYHURST DR	Austin	642J	MC-17	78749	8400-8599
TYLER CT	Round Rock	408J	MQ-41	78664	3300-3399
TYLER CT	Williamson Co	318A	MQ-51	78634	300-399
TYLER LN	Taylor	322U	MZ-49	76574	2800-3199
TYLER ST	Austin	555E	MJ-27	78756	4900-4999
TYLER TRL	Travis Co	430A	WY-39	78645	19200-19399
	Travis Co	400W	WY-40	78645	19400-19799
TYNDALE CV	Travis Co	552G	MD-27	78733	8200-8399
TYRAH LN	Bastrop Co	744Z	ED-7	78602	100-199
TYREE RD	Cedar Park	373R	MF-44	78613	400-599
TYRONE DR	Austin	465R	MK-35	78759	3400-3699
TYRONE DR	Leander	342Q	MD-47	78641	400-699
TYSON CV	Austin	466S	ML-34	78758	12200-12299
TYX TRL	Travis Co	486M	WR-32	78669	3900-4299

U

STREET NAME	CITY or COUNTY	MAPSCO GRID	AUSTIN GRID	ZIP CODE	BLOCK RANGE O/E
ULIT AVE	Austin	585M	MK-23	78702	1400-1899
ULLMAN DR	Travis Co	490K	WY-32	78734	15400-15599
ULLRICH AVE	Austin	555B	MJ-27	78756	1500-1599
	Austin	525X	MJ-28	78756	1600-1999
ULLSWATER CV	Austin	463G	MF-36	78750	10100-10199
ULLSWATER LN	Austin	463G	MF-36	78750	9800-10099
ULUPAU CIR	Bastrop Co	776F	EG-6	78602	100-299
ULYSSES S GRANT ST	Travis Co	530K	MU-29	78653	13500-13599
UMBRIA ST	Lakeway	490W	WY-31	78734	None
UMIPAA LN	Bastrop Co	775D	EF-6	78602	100-199
UNA MAS	Lago Vista	429F	WW-39	78645	6600-6699
UNBRIDLED	Hays Co	639S	WW-16	78737	100-299
UNDERHILL RD	Travis Co	520M	WZ-29	78734	100-399
UNDERWOOD DR	Travis Co	766J	ML-5	78610	11600-12099
UNICE DR	Travis Co	591K	MW-23	78621	8800-9099
UNION CIR	Austin	645S	MJ-16	78744	4500-4599
UNION ST	Leander	342R	MD-47	78641	1700-2299
UNION CHAPEL RD	Bastrop Co	742G	MZ-9	78612	100-299
	Bastrop Co	712S	MY-10	78612	300-699
	Bastrop Co	711L	MX-11	78612	700-999
UNION CHAPEL RD E	Bastrop Co	743E	EA-9	78602	100-199
	Bastrop Co	742H	MZ-9	78602	None
UNION LEE CHURCH RD	Travis Co	621G	MX-21	78653	21200-22299
UNITED DR	Austin	495T	MJ-31	78758	9000-9499
UNITED KINGDOM DR	Austin	673L	MF-14	78748	8500-9299
UNIVERSE CIR	Austin	678N	MQ-14	78617	12700-12799
UNIVERSITY AVE	Austin	585K	MJ-23	78705	1900-2099
	Austin	585F	MJ-24	78705	2300-2699
	Austin	585B	MJ-24	78705	2900-3099
UNIVERSITY AVE E	Georgetown	286L	MM-53	78626	100-1099
	Georgetown	287F	MN-54	78626	1100-3099
UNIVERSITY AVE W	Georgetown	286L	MM-53	78626	100-999
	Georgetown	286L	MM-53	78628	1000-1399
	Georgetown	285M	MK-53	78628	1400-1599
UNIVERSITY BLVD	Round Rock	346L	MM-47	78665	100-499
	Round Rock	347E	MN-48	78665	800-2099
	Round Rock	317Z	MP-49	78665	None
	Williamson Co	346L	MM-47	78665	500-799
	Williamson Co	318T	MQ-49	78665	None
	Williamson Co	318T	MQ-49	78665	None
	Williamson Co	347E	MN-48	78665	None
UNIVERSITY CIR	Austin	614Z	MH-19	78704	None
UNIVERSITY DR	Bastrop Co	741C	MX-9	78612	100-199
UNIVERSITY CLUB DR	Travis Co	521G	MB-30	78732	1400-3099
	Travis Co	491Y	MB-31	78732	3100-3299
UNIVERSITY OAKS BLVD					
	Round Rock	346P	ML-47	78665	100-299
UNIVERSITY PARK DR	Georgetown	287P	MN-53	78626	2000-2199
UNNAMED ST 252	Travis Co	441E	MW-39	78615	None
UPHILL LN	Austin	646F	ML-18	78741	2000-2299
UPLAND DR	Austin	615K	MJ-20	78741	1100-1299
UPLAND DR	Hays Co	638F	WU-18	78620	700-799
UPLANDS BEND	Georgetown	314K	MG-50	78628	1000-1299
UPLANDS RIDGE DR	Bee Cave	550U	WZ-25	78733	11600-12199
UPOLA CT	Bastrop Co	775A	EE-6	78602	100-199
UPOLU CT	Bastrop Co	746W	EG-7	78602	100-199
UPPER BRANCH CV	Hays Co	667C	WT-15	78620	2100-2299
UPPER ELGIN RIVER RD	Bastrop Co	533Y	EB-28	78621	100-299
See.. Bastrop Co Rd 127					
	Bastrop Co	563N	EA-26	78621	300-799
	Bastrop Co	562Z	MZ-25	78621	800-1199
	Bastrop Co	592K	MY-23	78621	1200-1699
	Bastrop Co	621Z	MX-19	78621	2100-2199
	Bastrop Co	651D	MX-18	78621	2200-2299
UPPER PASSAGE LN	Round Rock	345P	MJ-47	78681	3900-3999
UPPER WOODS CV	Travis Co	460F	WY-36	78734	16900-16999
UPSLOPE DR	Austin	612W	MC-19	78749	7200-7299
UPSON ST	Austin	584P	MG-23	78703	500-699
	Austin	584L	MH-23	78703	700-799
UPVALLEY CT	Austin	524P	MG-29	78731	4500-4599
UPVALLEY RUN	Austin	524P	MG-29	78731	5800-6099
URAY DR	Austin	557K	MN-26	78724	7500-7699
URBANEK FARM RD	Williamson Co	382N	MY-44	76574	1-599
URIAH DR	Bastrop Co	592N	MY-23	78621	100-199
URSA MAJOR PATH	Travis Co	521E	MA-30	78732	12800-12999
UTAH CIR	Travis Co	702M	MD-11	78652	12500-12599
UTAH FLATS DR	Austin	466G	MM-36	78727	13500-13599
UTE DR	Austin	557P	MN-26	78724	5800-5899
UTE TRL N	Austin	434Z	MH-37	78729	7100-7399
UTE TRL S	Austin	434Z	MH-37	78729	7000-7399
UTICA CV	Austin	671C	MB-15	78739	6100-6199
UTICA LN	Austin	463B	ME-36	78726	10300-10399
UTOPIA CT	Austin	556K	ML-26	78723	1900-1999
UTOPIA LN	Hutto	379G	MT-45	78634	1200-1299
UTTIMER LN	Austin	497E	MN-33	78753	12300-12499
UVALDE CV	Travis Co	672N	MC-14	78739	11200-11299
UVALDE DR	Hutto	379G	MT-45	78634	1400-1699
UVALDE CREEK DR	Travis Co	521E	MA-30	78732	12500-12699

V

STREET NAME	CITY or COUNTY	MAPSCO GRID	AUSTIN GRID	ZIP CODE	BLOCK RANGE O/E
VAIL CT	Georgetown	195Z	MK-61	78633	100-199
VAIL LN	Hays Co	732B	MC-9	78610	400-499
VAILCO LN	Lakeway	520W	WY-28	78734	100-299
VAIL DIVIDE	Bee Cave	549F	WW-27	78738	3900-5199
VAIL VALLEY DR	Austin	642F	MC-18	78749	7500-7899
VAILVIEW CV	Austin	493H	MF-33	78750	8100-8199
VAL DR	Austin	556M	MM-26	78723	3000-3199
	Austin	557J	MN-26	78723	3200-3499
VALBURN CIR	Austin	494T	MG-31	78731	5200-5399
VALBURN CT	Austin	494U	MH-31	78731	5000-5199
VALBURN DR	Austin	494T	MG-31	78731	6700-7999
VALCOUR BAY LN	Travis Co	527X	MN-28	78754	4700-4899
VALDERRAMA CT	Austin	404G	MH-42	78717	15300-15399
VALDERRAMA DR	Austin	404G	MH-42	78717	9800-10199
VALDEZ ST	Austin	616X	ML-19	78741	700-1299
VALE DR	Cedar Park	373S	ME-43	78613	200-299
VALE ST	Rollingwood	584T	MG-22	78746	100-599
VALENCIA CIR	Austin	465W	MJ-34	78759	11100-11199
VALENCIA CT	Williamson Co	226U	MM-58	78628	5400-5499
VALENTINE DR	Pflugerville	407X	MN-40	78664	17300-17499
VALERIA ST	Austin	614F	MG-21	78704	1600-1799
VALERIAN TRL	Round Rock	407C	MP-42	78665	2000-2199
VALERIAN TEA DR	Travis Co	467G	MP-36	78660	14900-15299
VALERIE'S CV	Travis Co	437N	MN-38	78660	15600-15699
VALHALLA CT	Village of the Hills	519P	WW-29	78738	1-99
VALIANT CIR	Austin	612U	MD-19	78749	6000-6199
VALIANT CV	Austin	612T	MC-19	78749	5600-5699
VALJEAN DR	Pflugerville	408W	MQ-40	78660	300-599
VALK ST	Cedar Park	372M	MD-44	78613	100-299
VALLARTA LN	Round Rock	345N	MJ-47	78681	3800-3999
VALLARTA LN	Travis Co	522K	MC-29	78733	2700-2999
VALLECITO CV	Austin	464L	MH-35	78759	11300-11399
VALLECITO DR	Austin	464L	MH-35	78759	6600-7199
VALLECITO DR	Georgetown	317J	MN-50	78626	100-299
VALLEJO ST	Austin	525T	MJ-28	78757	1800-2099
VALLE VERDE DR	Cedar Park	344W	MG-46	78641	1800-1899
VALLEY CIR	Austin	524T	MG-28	78731	5800-5899
VALLEY DR	Travis Co	400X	WY-40	78645	8500-8599
VALLEY LN	Georgetown	286Z	MM-52	78626	200-399
VALLEY RD	Travis Co	366Y	WR-43	78654	28700-28899
VALLEY ST E	Georgetown	286C	MM-54	78626	100-399
VALLEY ST W	Georgetown	286C	MM-54	78626	100-199
VALLEY TRL	Williamson Co	408B	MQ-42	78664	1-99
VALLEYCREEK DR	Williamson Co	408F	MQ-42	78664	1-99
VALLEYCREST CV	Williamson Co	197Z	MP-61	78626	300-399
VALLEYCREST LOOP	Williamson Co	197Z	MP-61	78626	100-299
VALLEYDALE CV	Austin	525B	MJ-30	78757	8200-8299
VALLEY DALE DR	Austin	494Y	MH-31	78731	7500-7799
VALLEYFIELD DR	Austin	557Z	MP-25	78724	8000-8199
	Austin	558W	MQ-25	78724	8300-8599
VALLEY FORGE CV	Lago Vista	458L	WV-35	78645	2100-2199
VALLEY FORGE DR	Austin	526P	ML-29	78753	800-999
VALLEY GLEN CV	Travis Co	437G	MP-39	78660	900-999
VALLEY GLEN RD	Travis Co	437G	MP-39	78660	17100-17299
VALLEY HIGH CIR	Austin	644Z	MH-16	78744	2300-2399

T U V

STREET NAME	CITY or COUNTY	MAPSCO GRID	AUSTIN GRID	ZIP CODE	BLOCK RANGE O/E
VALLEY HILL CIR	Austin	615T	MJ-19	78741	1900-1999
VALLEY HILL DR	Point Venture	489J	WW-32	78645	200-499
	Travis Co	489J	WW-32	78645	500-599
VALLEY HILL LN	Point Venture	489J	WW-32	78645	18400-18499
VALLEY MEADOW DR	Pflugerville	438S	MQ-37	78660	600-899
VALLEY OAK DR	Austin	554D	MH-27	78731	4700-5299
VALLEY OAKS LOOP	Georgetown	286Z	MM-52	78626	100-499
VALLEY PIKE RD	Williamson Co	433B	ME-39	78613	3100-3499
	Williamson Co	403X	ME-40	78613	3500-3599
VALLEYRIDGE CIR	Austin	614T	MG-19	78704	1400-1499
VALLEY RIDGE CT	Travis Co	582D	MD-24	78746	6500-6599
VALLEY RIDGE DR	Austin	614T	MG-19	78704	1400-1699
VALLEY RIDGE DR	Hays Co	606U	WR-19	78620	100-299
VALLEY RUN TRL	Elgin	533F	EC-30	78621	100-299
VALLEYSIDE RD	Austin	524R	MH-29	78731	6500-6699
VALLEY SPRING RD	Austin	584J	MG-23	78746	2700-2799
VALLEY VIEW	Travis Co	578J	WU-23	78620	9800-9999
VALLEY VIEW	Williamson Co	375B	MJ-45	78681	3800-3999
VALLEY VIEW CIR	Williamson Co	343H	MF-48	78641	1-99
VALLEY VIEW CV	Williamson Co	375B	MJ-45	78681	2600-2799
VALLEY VIEW DR	Bastrop Co	712Z	MZ-10	78602	100-199
VALLEYVIEW DR	Lago Vista	429J	WW-38	78645	5900-6399
VALLEY VIEW DR	Pflugerville	438X	MQ-37	78660	600-999
VALLEY VIEW DR	Travis Co	522W	MC-28	78733	600-999
VALLEYVIEW DR	Williamson Co	408F	MQ-42	78664	1-99
VALLEY VIEW DR	Williamson Co	343H	MF-48	78641	100-199
VALLEY VIEW RD	Austin	614S	MG-19	78704	3700-3799
	Austin	614W	MG-19	78704	3800-4299
VALLEY VIEW RD	Williamson Co	224A	MG-60	78633	100-299
VALLEY VIEW RD	Williamson Co	281T	MA-52	78641	4400-4699
VALLEY VISTA	Travis Co	640A	WY-18	78737	10600-10799
VALLEY WOODS DR	Taylor	353T	EA-46	76574	None
VALONA DR	Austin	404K	MG-41	78717	10000-10099
VALONA DR	Williamson Co	375Y	MK-43	78681	201-399 O
VALONA LOOP	Williamson Co	375Y	MK-43	78681	200-499
VALORIE CT	Cedar Park	402H	MD-42	78613	1200-1299
VAL VERDE DR	Travis Co	521F	MA-30	78732	1800-2099
VAL VERDE DR	Williamson Co	226W	ML-58	78628	4000-4299
VAN ALLEN CV	Lago Vista	458L	WV-35	78645	20900-20999
VAN BUREN ST	Elgin	534X	EC-29	78621	100-199
VANCE CIR	Austin	585J	MJ-23	78701	1800-1899
VANCE LN	Rollingwood	584P	MG-23	78746	2400-2499
	Rollingwood	584N	MG-23	78746	2800-2899
VANCE ST	Taylor	353E	EA-48	76574	100-1199
	Taylor	323W	EA-49	76574	1200-1299
VANCE CIRCLE RD	Travis Co	400F	WY-42	78645	10300-10399
VANCOUVER CV	Lago Vista	458L	WV-35	78645	2000-2099
VANDAGRIFF DR	Lakeway	490X	WY-31	78734	500-899
VANDERBILT CIR	Austin	556L	MM-26	78723	2300-2399
VANDERBILT CIR	Pflugerville	467H	MP-36	78660	1000-1199
VANDERBILT LN	Austin	556G	MM-27	78723	2100-2299
VANDERHILL CV	Cedar Park	372K	MC-44	78613	1800-1899
VANDEVER ST	Travis Co	618R	MR-20	78725	14100-14499
VAN DYKE DR	Williamson Co	434V	MH-37	78729	7700-7899
VANESSAS WAY	Buda	732U	MD-7	78610	100-199
VANGUARD	Lakeway	519F	WW-30	78734	600-1099
VAN HORN CT	Pflugerville	407Y	MP-40	78664	17600-17699
VAN HORN CV	Williamson Co	402Q	MD-41	78613	2100-2199
VAN HORN DR	Pflugerville	407Y	MP-40	78664	1500-1599
VAN HORN WAY	Williamson Co	402Q	MD-41	78613	1100-1299
VANILLA BEAN DR	Travis Co	467R	MP-35	78660	1400-1699
VANSHIRE DR	Bee Cave	550V	WZ-25	78733	3400-3599
VAN WINKLE CT	Austin	641Z	MB-16	78739	10300-10399
VAN WINKLE LN	Austin	641Z	MB-16	78739	5500-5899
VAPOR DR	Pflugerville	437P	MN-38	78660	1000-1299
VAQUERA CT	Round Rock	375D	MK-45	78681	2600-2799
VAQUERO CV	Austin	464N	MG-35	78759	8400-8499
VAQUERO TRL	Austin	464N	MG-35	78759	10100-10299
VARA DR	Travis Co	527X	MN-28	78754	3500-3699
VARCELLA TRL	Williamson Co	434M	MH-38	78729	7800-7999
VARCO DR	Lakeway	520W	WY-28	78734	100-299
VARGAS RD	Austin	616T	ML-19	78741	300-1599
	Austin	646A	ML-18	78741	1600-1999
VARNER CT	Travis Co	491Q	MB-32	78732	4000-4099
VARNER DR	Travis Co	428E	WU-39	78654	23500-23599
VARRELMAN ST	Travis Co	618V	MR-19	78725	14200-14899
VASEY BLVD	Travis Co	619A	MS-21	78724	5800-6099
VASQUEZ ST	Austin	616X	ML-19	78741	900-1199
VASSAL DR	Austin	673E	ME-15	78748	2300-2599
VASSAR DR	Austin	556M	MM-26	78723	6900-6999
VASSAR RD	Travis Co	400K	WY-41	78645	10000-10299
VAUGHTER LN	Cedar Park	372U	MD-43	78613	1400-1599
VAUGHT RANCH RD	Travis Co	493U	MF-31	78730	6500-6799
VEGA AVE	Austin	612P	MC-20	78735	5000-5999
VEILED FALLS DR	Travis Co	439P	MS-38	78660	4100-4399
VELARDE CV	Austin	434U	MH-37	78729	12600-12699
VELASCO PL	Austin	642Q	MD-17	78749	4500-4799
VELASQUEZ DR	Austin	554T	MG-25	78703	2500-2699
VELDT DR	Travis Co	617D	MP-21	78725	3800-4099
VELETTA PL	Travis Co	581G	MB-24	78735	9500-9699
VELIA'S WAY	Travis Co	437S	MN-37	78660	15300-15399
VELMA DR	Taylor	323S	EA-49	76574	200-499
VENADA TRL	Williamson Co	226X	ML-58	78628	4100-4199
VENADO DR	Austin	524C	MH-30	78731	4200-4299
VENADO DR	Travis Co	490C	WZ-33	78734	15400-15499
VENDRELL DR	Williamson Co	434R	MH-38	78729	13200-13299
VENEER DR	Austin	673F	ME-15	78748	1800-1899
VENETIAN CV	Austin	703F	ME-12	78748	300-399
VENITA CV	Travis Co	522S	MC-28	78733	10200-10299
VENTANA CT	Pflugerville	439E	MS-39	78660	19100-19299
VENTANA CANYON	Leander	371C	MB-45	78641	1300-1399
VENTURA DR	Austin	645F	MJ-18	78741	2200-2499
VENTURA RIDGE RD	Travis Co	704G	MH-12	78747	None
VENTURE	Williamson Co	378D	MR-45	78634	100-199
VENTURE BLVD N	Point Venture	489K	WW-32	78645	200-399
VENTURE BLVD S	Point Venture	489N	WW-32	78645	100-599
VENTURE DR	Point Venture	489J	WW-32	78645	18400-18899
	Point Venture	488R	WV-32	78645	18900-19099
VENTUS ST	Austin	616C	MM-21	78721	5900-5999
VENUS LN	Georgetown	195T	MJ-61	78633	100-199
VERA LN	Austin	616P	ML-20	78741	6200-6299
VERA WAY	Round Rock	377E	MN-45	78664	1600-1699
VERA CRUZ RD	Travis Co	641A	MA-18	78737	9300-9599
VERANDAH CT	Austin	462F	MC-36	78726	12500-12599
VERANO DR	Travis Co	581M	MB-23	78735	3600-4399
VERBANK VILLA DR	Austin	675W	MJ-13	78747	7900-8199
VERBENA CT	Leander	342K	MC-47	78641	1100-1199
VERBENA DR	Georgetown	225C	MK-60	78633	100-199
VERBENA DR	Williamson Co	433L	MF-38	78750	1000-2099
VERBENA WAY	Williamson Co	377J	MN-44	78664	1600-1999
VERCHOTA DR	Austin	702H	MD-12	78748	12000-12199
VERDANT WAY	Austin	583V	MF-22	78746	1200-1399
VERDE CT	Mustang Ridge	765R	MK-5	78610	100-7199
VERDE CT	Williamson Co	226W	ML-58	78628	100-199
VERDE BANK CIR	Austin	554U	MH-25	78703	2700-2799
VERDE KNOLL CV	Travis Co	487N	WS-32	78669	3200-3399
VERDE KNOLL DR	Travis Co	487N	WS-32	78669	3500-4099
VERDE MESA CV	Travis Co	547Z	WT-25	78738	8300-8399
VERDE RANCH LOOP	Leander	372C	MD-45	78641	1-199
VERDE VISTA	Austin	554Y	MH-25	78703	2700-2799
VERDE VISTA	Georgetown	225Z	MK-58	78628	4600-4699
VERDE VISTA	Williamson Co	256A	ML-57	78628	4100-4299
	Williamson Co	225Z	MK-58	78628	4300-4399
VERDE VISTA DR	Lago Vista	429F	WW-39	78645	6600-6699
VERDI PL	Austin	584J	MG-23	78746	200-299
VERDIN DR	Hays Co	732J	MC-8	78610	100-399
VERMILLON DR	Austin	642L	MD-17	78749	7300-7399
VERMONT RD	Austin	616E	ML-21	78702	500-699
VERNA ST	Travis Co	591K	MW-23	78653	20800-20999
VERNA SPUR	Georgetown	256F	ML-57	78628	100-199
VERNELL WAY	Round Rock	377E	MN-45	78664	1800-2599
VERNON AVE	Austin	556Q	MM-26	78723	2800-2899
VERNON ST	Taylor	352H	MZ-48	76574	200-699
VERONA CV	Austin	642U	MD-16	78749	4000-4099
VERONA TRL	Austin	642U	MD-16	78749	8500-8999
VERRENA WAY	Georgetown	226P	ML-59	78628	100-199
VERSAILLES DR	Cedar Park	403U	MF-40	78613	2300-2599
VERSANTE CIR	Austin	462G	MD-36	78726	11900-12099
VERTEX BLVD	Austin	674Z	MH-13	78747	8600-8699
VERVAIN CT	Travis Co	551P	MA-26	78733	2000-2099
VERVER LN	Buda	762H	MD-6	78610	100-199
VESPER LN	Travis Co	518B	WU-30	78669	19200-19399
VESPERS TRL	Travis Co	553Q	MF-26	78746	1700-1799
VESTAVIA RIDGE LN	Travis Co	432L	MD-38	78613	2400-2599
VESTAVIO CT	Travis Co	704J	MG-11	78747	10800-10899
VETERANS DR	Austin	584P	MG-23	78703	2100-2399
VEVEY DR	Travis Co	708S	MQ-10	78617	14600-14999
VFW RD	Austin	496H	MM-33	78753	400-599
VFW RD	Bastrop Co	564A	EC-27	78621	100-299
VIA DR	Austin	612D	MD-21	78735	5800-5899
VIA COLINA DR	Travis Co	491V	MB-31	78732	4100-4199
VIA CORDOVA CT	Travis Co	521F	MA-30	78732	2300-2399
VIA CORRETO DR	Austin	641H	MB-18	78749	6400-7399
VIA DONO DR	Austin	641G	MB-18	78749	7000-7299
VIA FORTUNA	Austin	613H	MF-21	78746	2500-3199
VIA GRANDE DR	Austin	641S	MA-16	78739	11000-11099
	Austin	640V	WZ-16	78739	11100-11899
VIA MEDIA	Travis Co	553M	MF-26	78746	4600-4799
VIA MIA DR	Austin	641G	MB-18	78749	8700-8799
VIAMONTE LN	Austin	642W	MC-16	78739	5300-5399
VIA RICCO DR	Austin	641H	MB-18	78749	6800-6999
VIA SONOMA TRL	Round Rock	407D	MP-42	78665	1000-1699
	Round Rock	408E	MQ-42	78665	1700-2799
VIA VERDE DR	Austin	641S	MA-16	78739	7800-8099
	Austin	640V	WZ-16	78739	8100-8299
VIBAR CV	Round Rock	345Z	MK-46	78681	1300-1499
VICINITY TRL	Travis Co	456H	WR-36	78669	100-399
VICKEY LN	Travis Co	557E	MN-27	78724	3200-3299
VICKSBURG CV	Elgin	533G	EB-30	78621	None
VICKSBURG CV	Lago Vista	458L	WV-35	78645	2200-2299
VICKSBURG LOOP	Elgin	533G	EB-30	78621	None
VICTOR ST	Austin	496U	MM-31	78753	100-799
VICTORIA CT	Hays Co	639T	WW-16	78737	100-199
VICTORIA CV	Cedar Park	402L	MD-41	78613	600-699
VICTORIA CV	Round Rock	378T	MQ-43	78664	2900-2999
VICTORIA DR	Austin	586F	ML-24	78721	1700-1899
VICTORIA DR	Cedar Park	402L	MD-41	78613	400-699
VICTORIA ST	Taylor	352D	MZ-48	76574	100-1299
	Taylor	322Z	MZ-49	76574	1300-1499
VICTORIA CHASE	Lago Vista	429X	WW-37	78645	19900-20199
VICTORIAN OAKS LN	Hays Co	638J	WU-17	78620	100-199
VICTORIA PEAK	Georgetown	225K	MJ-59	78633	100-299
VICTORIA RIDGE DR	Pflugerville	468E	MQ-36	78660	800-1099
VICTORIA STATION BLVD	Pflugerville	437B	MN-39	78664	1300-1899
	Pflugerville	407W	MN-40	78664	1900-2399
VICTORINE LN	Travis Co	649Y	MT-16	78617	3400-3899
VICTORY DR	Austin	614S	MG-19	78704	3800-4399
VICTORY GALLOP DR	Austin	678P	MQ-14	78617	5500-5699
VIDA NUEVA AVE	Austin	677V	MP-13	78617	6200-6399
VIENTO DEL SUR	Travis Co	703W	ME-10	78652	13000-13299
VIEWING PL	Travis Co	676X	ML-13	78719	6700-7099
VIEWPOINT DR	Austin	645T	MJ-16	78744	5200-5499
VIEW RIDGE	Hays Co	670N	WY-14	78737	13300-13399
VIEW RIDGE DR	Austin	557Z	MP-25	78724	8100-8399
VIEW WEST	Austin	613J	ME-20	78735	4500-4699
VIGEN CIR	Austin	673R	MF-14	78748	8900-9299
VIKI LYNN CT	Pflugerville	437J	MN-38	78660	1600-1699
VIKI LYNN PL	Pflugerville	437J	MN-38	78660	16200-16499
VIKING DR	Austin	526A	ML-30	78758	8900-9099
VIKING JACK ST	Travis Co	530Q	MV-29	78653	19100-19199
VIKKI TERRACE	Travis Co	610Y	WZ-19	78736	9800-10099
VILAMOURA ST	Pflugerville	439B	MS-39	78660	19200-19999
VILLA CT	Austin	614Y	MH-19	78704	3600-3699
VILLA CV	Round Rock	376Q	MM-44	78664	1500-1599
VILLA ACUNA CT	Austin	675W	MJ-13	78744	6300-6399
VILLACLIFF CIR	Austin	495J	MJ-32	78759	4100-4199
VILLAGE CIR	Austin	643G	MF-18	78745	2300-2399
VILLAGE CT E	Austin	645W	MJ-16	78744	4600-4699
VILLAGE CT W	Austin	645W	MJ-16	78744	4500-4599
VILLAGE CV	Austin	645W	MJ-16	78744	5300-5399
VILLAGE DR	Austin	554H	MH-27	78731	2900-3099
VILLAGE DR	Georgetown	256P	ML-56	78628	1-299
VILLAGE DR	Travis Co	577R	WT-23	78720	17400-17899
VILLAGE LN	Austin	645W	MJ-16	78744	5400-5699
VILLAGE LN	Buda	762M	MD-5	78610	400-499
VILLAGE LN E	Austin	496X	ML-31	78758	900-999
VILLAGE LN W	Austin	496W	ML-31	78758	900-999
VILLAGE PATH	Austin	645W	MJ-16	78744	5200-5299
VILLAGE TRL	Austin	645W	MJ-16	78744	5200-5499
VILLAGE CENTER DR	Austin	524M	MH-29	78731	7000-7099
VILLAGE COMMONS BLVD					
	Georgetown	225R	MK-59	78633	100-499
VILLAGE CREEK CIR	Austin	674R	MH-14	78744	7700-7799
VILLAGE GLEN	Georgetown	225R	MK-59	78633	101-199 O
VILLAGE GLEN CV	Travis Co	437G	MP-39	78660	17200-17299
VILLAGE GLEN RD	Travis Co	437G	MP-39	78660	17100-17299
VILLAGE GREEN DR	Austin	526G	MM-30	78753	1100-1199
VILLAGE GREEN PKWY	Georgetown	225R	MK-59	78633	100-299
VILLAGE OAK CT	Austin	614P	MG-20	78704	1800-1899
VILLAGE OAK LOOP	Williamson Co	375W	MJ-43	78717	16700-16999
VILLAGE PARK DR	Georgetown	225R	MK-59	78633	101-299 O
VILLAGE SQUARE DR	Austin	675A	MJ-15	78744	4900-5199
VILLAGE TRAIL CIR	Austin	645W	MJ-16	78744	2500-2599
VILLAGE VIEW LOOP	Pflugerville	438H	MR-39	78660	2100-2499
VILLAGE WALK	Austin	645W	MJ-16	78744	2400-2599
VILLAGE WAY CT	Austin	643H	MF-18	78745	5400-5499
VILLAGE WAY DR	Austin	643D	MF-18	78745	2100-2399
VILLAGE WEST DR	Travis Co	522S	MC-28	78733	1000-1599
VILLA HILL DR	Travis Co	401C	MB-42	78641	1000-1099
VILLA MARIA CT	Austin	464T	MG-34	78759	7000-7099
VILLA MARIA CV	Austin	464X	MG-34	78759	9800-9899
VILLA MARIA LN	Austin	464T	MG-34	78759	7100-7299
VILLA MONTANA WAY	Travis Co	462S	MC-34	78732	12800-13299
VILLA NORTE DR	Austin	462G	MD-36	78726	8900-9399
VILLANOVA DR	Austin	525G	MK-30	78757	1500-1599
VILLA OAKS CIR	Austin	644S	MG-16	78745	300-399
VILLA PARK DR	Williamson Co	434F	MG-39	78729	13100-13399
VILLITA CV	Austin	616X	ML-19	78741	6900-6999
VILLITA AVENIDA	Austin	616X	ML-19	78741	6800-7199
VINCA CIR	Austin	674R	MH-14	78744	7400-7499
VINCA DR	Georgetown	225P	MJ-59	78633	100-199
VINCA DR	Lakeway	489Y	WX-31	78734	100-199
VINCAS SHADOW CT	Hays Co	666V	WR-13	78619	100-299
VINCENT PL	Travis Co	437T	MN-37	78660	800-1299
VINE ST	Austin	525N	MJ-29	78757	6500-6899
VINE ST	Georgetown	287N	MN-53	78626	1500-1999
VINE HILL DR	Austin	675N	MJ-14	78744	5400-5899
VINELAND DR	Austin	585D	MK-24	78722	3500-4099
VINEMONT DR	Austin	641U	MB-16	78749	9600-9699
VINEWOOD CV	Austin	525B	MJ-30	78757	3000-3099
VINEWOOD LN	Austin	525B	MJ-30	78757	7900-8199
VINEYARD CV	Leander	343N	ME-47	78641	1900-1999
VINEYARD WAY	Bee Cave	549R	WX-26	78738	4100-4199
VINEYARD VIEW	Lago Vista	459H	WX-36	78645	4900-4999
VINSON CT	Round Rock	408J	MQ-41	78664	2700-2799
VINSON DR	Austin	644F	MG-18	78745	4400-4899
VINTAGE DR	Leander	343J	ME-47	78641	900-1999
	Williamson Co	343N	ME-47	78641	2000-2099
VINTAGE DR	Round Rock	378P	MQ-44	78664	3300-3499
VINTAGE HILLS CV	Austin	557J	MN-26	78723	3300-3399
VINTAGE HILLS DR	Austin	556H	MM-27	78723	7400-7499
VINTAGE STAVE RD	Travis Co	702G	MD-12	78748	2400-2599
VINWOOD CV	Round Rock	377V	MP-43	78665	2700-2799
VINYARD DR	Travis Co	733B	ME-9	78652	12900-13099
VIOITHA DR	Austin	556R	MM-26	78723	6300-6499
VIOLA DR	Travis Co	592J	MY-23	78621	22800-22899
VIOLET LN	Travis Co	532Q	MZ-29	78621	17800-17899
VIOLET BLUE DR	Pflugerville	407U	MP-40	78664	1500-1599
VIREO CV	Travis Co	552Z	MD-25	78746	6700-6799
VIREO DR	Hays Co	732A	MC-9	78610	100-199
VIRGINIA AVE	Austin	584Y	MH-22	78704	1600-1799
VIRGINIA DR	Round Rock	376R	MM-44	78664	500-999
VIRGINIA ST	Georgetown	287N	MN-53	78626	1600-1899
VIRGINIA DARE LN	Travis Co	527X	MN-28	78754	4700-4899
VIRGINIA WOLF BEND	Travis Co	467L	MP-35	78660	14300-14399
VIRGO LN	Austin	587B	MN-24	78724	6300-6599
VIRIDIAN LN	Austin	671A	MA-15	78739	7000-7199
VIRIDIAN WAY	Austin	671A	MA-15	78739	11300-11599
VISALIA LN	Austin	466Q	MM-35	78727	1500-1599
VISA ROSE DR	Austin	703G	MF-12	78748	11100-11199
VISION DR	Pflugerville	437N	MN-38	78660	15500-15999
VISTA AVE	Round Rock	376U	MM-43	78664	100-399
VISTA DR	Bastrop Co	564L	ED-26	78621	100-199
VISTA LN	Austin	584C	MH-24	78703	1700-2499
VISTA LN	Williamson Co	194X	MG-61	78633	100-199
VISTA CORTA	Lago Vista	429W	WW-37	78645	4200-4299
VISTA DEL SOL	Travis Co	522N	MC-29	78733	10100-10199
VISTA DEL VERDE DR	Bee Cave	549R	WX-26	78738	4300-4499
VISTA ESTATES CT	Travis Co	517F	WS-30	78669	4500-4799
VISTA ESTATES DR	Travis Co	517B	WS-30	78669	21300-21499
VISTA HILLS BLVD	Williamson Co	345S	MJ-46	78681	3400-4199
VISTA ISLE DR	Williamson Co	344V	MH-46	78681	3900-4199
VISTA MOUNTAIN DR	Austin	494X	MG-31	78731	7300-7399
VISTAO ST	Travis Co	427V	WT-37	78654	None
VISTA OAKS DR	Cedar Park	372W	MC-43	78641	13500-13599
	Travis Co	372W	MC-43	78641	13400-13499
VISTA OAKS DR	Hays Co	576H	WR-24	78620	100-199
VISTA PARKE DR	Austin	462P	MC-35	78726	11600-12099
VISTA RIDGE	Bee Cave	550P	WY-26	78738	3800-4199
VISTA RIDGE	Williamson Co	197Y	MP-61	78626	100-199
VISTA RIDGE BLVD N	Cedar Park	374N	MG-44	78613	100-999
VISTA RIDGE BLVD S	Williamson Co	374S	MG-43	78613	100-799
VISTA RIDGE CV	Austin	497W	MN-31	78754	1400-1499
VISTA RIDGE CV	Williamson Co	197U	MP-61	78626	200-299
VISTA RIDGE DR	Leander	342E	MC-48	78641	1100-1899
	Leander	341M	MB-47	78641	1900-1999
VISTA ROCK DR	Travis Co	371Q	MB-44	78641	13100-13399
VISTA VERDE PATH	Williamson Co	347A	MN-48	78665	4300-4399
VISTA VIEW CIR	Austin	463G	MF-36	78750	10200-10299
VISTA VIEW DR	Austin	463G	MF-36	78750	9600-9899
VISTA VILLAS DR	Lago Vista	458L	WV-35	78645	1900-2099
VISTA WEST CT	Bastrop	715W	EE-10	78602	400-499
VISTA WEST CV	Austin	494T	MG-31	78731	5200-5299
VITEX DR	Lakeway	489U	WX-31	78734	100-299
VIVAS LN	Austin	612C	MD-21	78735	4000-4099
VIVIAN DR	Travis Co	592N	MY-23	78621	22800-22899
VIVIAN DR	Williamson Co	374M	MH-44	78681	1900-2199
VIVION LN	Georgetown	287N	MN-53	78626	100-199
VIXEN CT	Lakeway	519E	WW-30	78734	100-199
VIZQUEL LOOP	Austin	678J	MQ-14	78617	13000-13499
VOELKER LN	Travis Co	531K	MW-29	78653	14900-15399
	Travis Co	531Q	MX-29	78621	15400-16299
VOELKER REINHARDT WAY					
	Travis Co	529D	MT-30	78653	11700-11899
VOGUE CV	Pflugerville	468A	MQ-36	78660	600-699
	Cedar Park	432M	MD-38	78726	12700-12799
	Cedar Park	433J	ME-38	78726	None
	Travis Co	432T	MC-37	78641	12800-13899
	Travis Co	461D	MB-36	78641	13900-14999
	Village of Volente	461B	MA-36	78641	15000-15399
	Village of Volente	431X	MA-37	78641	15400-16099

STREET NAME	CITY or COUNTY	MAPSCO GRID	AUSTIN GRID	ZIP CODE	BLOCK RANGE O/E
VOLTAIRE DR	Austin	556G	MM-27	78752	1900-2099
VOLTERRA ST	Lakeway	490W	WY-31	78734	None
VOL WALKER CV	Austin	642F	MC-18	78749	5600-5699
VOL WALKER DR	Austin	642F	MC-18	78749	7400-7699
VON HERFF CT	Travis Co	491Q	MB-32	78732	12400-12499
VONNEGUT CT	Round Rock	347N	MN-47	78665	3800-3899
VON QUINTUS RD	Mustang Ridge	736Q	MM-8	78719	11600-11899
	Travis Co	736Q	MM-8	78719	11900-11999
	Travis Co	736M	MM-8	78719	12000-12899
	Travis Co	737N	MN-8	78719	12900-13399
	Travis Co	737N	MN-8	78719	13400-13899
VORTAC LN	Williamson Co	226V	MM-58	78628	3200-3399
VORWERK RD	Travis Co	440S	MU-37	78653	17600-18099
VOSS PKWY	Bastrop Co	741U	MX-7	78612	100-199
VOUGEOT DR	Austin	675J	MJ-14	78744	6600-6799
VOYAGEURS LN	Austin	704A	MG-12	78747	2200-2299
VP RANCH DR	Williamson Co	314E	MG-51	78628	100-499
W					
WABASH AVE	Austin	555W	MJ-25	78705	3100-3199
WABASH ST	Taylor	353N	EA-47	76574	100-499
WACO ST	Travis Co	490G	WZ-33	78734	3500-3799
WADE AVE	Austin	554Q	MH-26	78703	2800-3299
WADFORD ST	Austin	644C	MH-18	78704	3800-4099
WADING POOL PATH	Travis Co	673P	ME-14	78748	9900-10199
WADLEY PL	Round Rock	406Z	MM-40	78728	3500-3799
WADSWORTH WAY	Austin	672M	MD-14	78748	2900-3099
WAFER ASH WAY	Austin	464E	MG-36	78750	8700-8799
WAGNER WAY	Taylor	353C	EB-48	76574	100-199
WAGON RD W	Travis Co	609T	WW-19	78736	10200-10999
WAGON TRL	Austin	496P	ML-32	78758	800-1199
WAGON WAY	Bastrop Co	712M	MZ-11	78602	100-299
WAGON WAY	Travis Co	371R	MB-44	78613	13400-13599
WAGON BEND TRL	Austin	644Z	MH-16	78744	5900-6099
WAGON CROSSING PATH	Austin	644Z	MH-16	78744	1900-2499
WAGONER CV	Lago Vista	399G	WX-42	78645	8900-8999
WAGON GAP CT	Bastrop Co	712M	MZ-11	78602	None
WAGONGAP DR	Round Rock	406L	MM-41	78681	1500-2299
WAGON GAP DR	Williamson Co	433U	MF-37	78750	10400-10699
WAGON HITCH CV	Austin	642C	MD-18	78749	5100-5199
WAGON TRAIN CV	Austin	642B	MC-18	78749	5600-5699
WAGON TRAIN RD	Austin	642B	MC-18	78749	5500-5899
WAGON WHEEL	Lago Vista	429N	WW-38	78645	5600-5799
WAGON WHEEL CIR	Bastrop	744G	ED-9	78602	100-199
WAGONWHEEL DR	Round Rock	406L	MM-41	78681	600-799
WAGON WHEEL TRL	Georgetown	256K	ML-56	78628	100-899
WAGON WHEEL TRL	Pflugerville	437Z	MP-37	78660	600-799
WAGTAIL CV	Austin	673A	ME-15	78748	8900-8999
WAGTAIL DR	Austin	673A	ME-15	78748	9000-9199
WAHANE LN	Bastrop Co	776A	EG-6	78602	100-199
	Bastrop Co	775D	EF-6	78602	200-399
WAIALEE CT	Bastrop Co	745Z	EF-7	78602	100-199
WAIALUA CT	Bastrop Co	745Z	EF-7	78602	100-199
WAIANAE CT	Bastrop Co	745X	EE-7	78602	100-199
WAIEHU LN E	Bastrop Co	775G	EF-6	78602	100-199
WAIEHU LN W	Bastrop Co	775G	EF-6	78602	100-199
WAIHI CT	Bastrop Co	775D	EF-6	78602	100-199
WAIKAKAAUA DR	Bastrop Co	745X	EE-7	78602	100-199
	Bastrop Co	775B	EE-6	78602	200-299
WAIKIKI DR	Bastrop Co	775G	EF-6	78602	100-199
WAILUPE CIR	Bastrop Co	775M	EF-5	78602	100-199
WAIMALU CT	Bastrop Co	745Y	EF-7	78602	100-199
WAIMALU CV	Bastrop Co	745Y	EF-7	78602	100-199
WAIMANALO LN	Bastrop Co	775C	EF-6	78602	100-199
WAIMEA CT	Round Rock	346W	ML-46	78681	1000-1099
WAIMEA BEND	Round Rock	346W	ML-46	78681	1100-1199
WAINEE DR	Bastrop Co	745Z	EF-7	78602	100-199
WAIPAHOEHOE DR	Bastrop Co	775B	EE-6	78602	100-299
WAIPIO CT	Bastrop Co	745Y	EF-7	78602	100-199
WAIZEL WAY	Georgetown	287P	MN-53	78626	2100-2699
WAKASHAN CV	Lago Vista	399L	WX-41	78645	21200-21299
WAKEFIELD DR	Austin	642R	MD-17	78749	7700-8099
WAKE FOREST LN	Austin	556R	MM-26	78723	6800-6899
WAKONDA CT	Travis Co	409T	MS-40	78660	2500-2599
WALDEN CIR	Austin	586G	MM-24	78723	4700-4999
WALDON DR	Austin	494W	MG-31	78750	7200-7799
WALDON HOLLOW	Austin	494S	MG-31	78750	6100-6199
WALDORF AVE	Austin	586K	ML-23	78721	1400-1499
WALDROP CV	Austin	673G	MF-15	78748	1400-1499
WALEBRIDGE CT	Austin	641Y	MB-16	78739	10700-10799
WALEBRIDGE LN	Austin	641X	MA-16	78739	6300-6999
WALES WAY	Austin	673H	MF-15	78748	700-799
WALHILL CV	Austin	494R	MH-32	78759	8500-8599
WALHILL LN	Austin	494R	MH-32	78759	4100-4499
WALKER DR	Bastrop Co	741G	MX-9	78612	100-199
WALKER DR N	Williamson Co	343W	ME-46	78641	2600-2799
WALKER DR S	Williamson Co	343W	ME-46	78641	2600-2899
WALKER LN	Austin	616P	ML-20	78741	6200-6299
WALKER ST	Hutto	379D	MT-45	78634	100-199
WALKER WAY	Williamson Co	345S	MJ-46	78681	4000-4099
WALKING STICK LN	Austin	675N	MJ-14	78744	7200-7399
WALKUP LN	Austin	705F	MJ-12	78747	6700-7199
WALL ST	Austin	526V	MM-28	78754	8400-9299
WALLACE	Dripping Springs	636Z	WR-16	78620	100-399
WALLACE CV	Austin	494S	MG-31	78750	6300-6499
WALLACE DR	Austin	494W	MG-31	78750	6900-7199
WALLACE ST	Taylor	322Z	MZ-49	76574	900-1199
	Taylor	322Y	MZ-49	76574	1300-1499
WALLER CT	Georgetown	195Y	MK-61	78633	100-199
WALLER ST	Austin	615B	MJ-21	78702	1-299
	Austin	585X	MJ-22	78702	300-1099
	Austin	585U	MK-22	78702	1100-1199
	Austin	585Q	MK-23	78702	1200-1599
WALLEYE CV	Round Rock	347N	MN-47	78665	3600-3699
WALLEYE WAY	Round Rock	347S	MN-46	78665	3200-3799
WALLIN LOOP	Round Rock	377E	MN-45	78664	1800-1999
WALLIN PATH	Round Rock	377E	MN-45	78664	1800-1899
WALLIN ST	Hutto	349V	MT-46	78634	100-199
WALLIN FARMS CV	Hutto	349X	MS-46	78634	1000-1099
WALLING DR	Austin	585B	MJ-24	78705	3100-3199
WALLINGFORD BEND DR	Austin	525Y	MK-28	78752	700-799
WALLING FORGE DR	Austin	465H	MK-36	78727	4200-4499
WALLINGSTONE LN	Williamson Co	433R	MF-38	78750	12200-12399
WALLINGWOOD DR	Austin	584W	MG-22	78746	2200-2599
WALLIS DR	Rollingwood	584N	MG-23	78746	1-599
WALLY AVE	Austin	586L	MM-23	78721	4600-4799

STREET NAME	CITY or COUNTY	MAPSCO GRID	AUSTIN GRID	ZIP CODE	BLOCK RANGE O/E
WALNUT AVE	Austin	585V	MK-22	78702	1100-1199
	Austin	585R	MK-23	78702	1200-1899
	Austin	585H	MK-24	78722	2100-3299
WALNUT CV	Cedar Park	373U	MF-43	78613	1300-1399
WALNUT DR E	Austin	526J	ML-29	78753	100-399
WALNUT DR W	Austin	526J	ML-29	78753	100-199
WALNUT ST	Bastrop	745K	EE-8	78602	700-1399
	Bastrop	745L	EF-8	78602	None
WALNUT ST E	Pflugerville	438W	MQ-37	78660	100-199
WALNUT ST E	Taylor	353J	EA-47	76574	100-1799
WALNUT ST S	Georgetown	286H	MM-54	78626	200-1899
WALNUT ST W	Pflugerville	438W	MQ-37	78660	100-799
WALNUT ST W	Taylor	353J	EA-47	76574	100-699
WALNUT BEND DR	Travis Co	526D	MM-30	78753	10300-10699
WALNUT CANYON BLVD	Pflugerville	438E	MQ-39	78660	700-899
	Pflugerville	438F	MQ-39	78660	1000-1199
WALNUT CLAY DR	Austin	524L	MH-29	78731	3800-4099
WALNUT CREEK DR	Austin	496M	MM-32	78753	800-899
WALNUT CREEK DR	Cedar Park	373U	MF-43	78613	100-299
WALNUT CREEK DR	Cedar Park	373J	ME-44	78613	None
WALNUT CREEK PARK RD	Austin	496C	MM-33	78758	None
WALNUT GROVE CT	Austin	675B	MJ-15	78744	5200-5299
WALNUT GROVE DR	Austin	675B	MJ-15	78744	5300-5499
WALNUT HILLS DR	Austin	556R	MM-26	78723	5900-6499
WALNUT HOLLOW CV	Austin	645X	MJ-16	78744	5800-5899
WALNUT PARK CROSSING	Austin	496G	MM-33	78753	12100-12599
WALNUT RIDGE DR	Austin	496V	MM-31	78753	11300-11699
WALNUT TREE LOOP	Williamson Co	224H	MH-60	78633	100-199
	Williamson Co	225E	MJ-60	78633	None
WALPOLE LN	Austin	641Y	MB-16	78739	10400-10699
WALSALL CV	Austin	642T	MC-16	78749	9200-9299
WALSALL LOOP	Austin	642T	MC-16	78749	4300-4799
WALSER CV	Austin	612E	MC-21	78735	5700-5799
WALSH DR	Williamson Co	375J	MJ-44	78681	1300-2499
WALSH LN	Round Rock	406F	ML-42	78681	800-1299
WALSH ST	Austin	584V	MH-22	78703	400-599
WALSH HILL TRL	Cedar Park	374V	MH-43	78613	400-1199
WALSH RANCH BLVD	Williamson Co	375F	MJ-45	78681	3900-4099
WALSH TARLTON LN	Austin	583U	MF-22	78746	1000-1099
	Austin	583U	MF-22	78746	1400-2299
	Austin	613C	MF-21	78746	2300-2799
	Travis Co	583U	MF-22	78746	1100-1399
WALTER AVE E	Pflugerville	468A	MQ-36	78660	100-299
WALTER AVE W	Pflugerville	468A	MQ-36	78660	100-399
	Pflugerville	437Z	MP-37	78660	400-999
WALTER CT	Pflugerville	437Z	MP-37	78660	1000-1099
WALTER ST	Austin	585V	MK-22	78702	900-1099
	Austin	585V	MK-22	78702	2500-2599
WALTHEN ST	Williamson Co	443L	EB-38	78615	100-199
WALTON LN	Austin	616B	ML-21	78721	1100-1199
WALTON WAY	Cedar Park	373N	ME-44	78613	1-299
WALTON HEATH CIR	Austin	704N	MG-11	78747	4500-4599
WALTON HILL PASS	Travis Co	471A	MW-36	78615	11400-12299
WALTONS LN	Bastrop Co	534U	ED-28	78621	100-199
WALT WHITMAN TRL	Travis Co	467L	MP-35	78660	14600-14699
WALWORTH ST	Austin	586H	MM-24	78723	5200-5299
WAMEL WAY	Bastrop Co	741T	MW-7	78612	100-199
WAMPTON WAY	Austin	641R	MB-17	78749	8900-9299
WANAKAH CT	Lakeway	519H	WX-30	78734	100-199
WANAKAH RIDGE CV	Travis Co	432G	MD-39	78613	2900-2999
WANAKAH RIDGE DR	Travis Co	432L	MD-38	78613	2500-2599
WANDER LN	Williamson Co	433K	ME-38	78750	11900-12199
WANDERING WAY	Austin	527A	MN-30	78754	10800-11199
	Travis Co	496Z	MM-31	78753	11100-11199
WANDERING MEADOWS	Travis Co	554E	MG-27	78746	3400-3499
WANDERING OAK RD	Austin	612W	MC-19	78749	7000-7199
WANDERING VINE CV	Pflugerville	439E	MS-39	78660	18900-19099
WANDERING VINE TRL	Williamson Co	317W	MN-49	78665	4400-4599
WAPATO CV	Williamson Co	377B	MN-45	78665	2000-2099
WAR PATH	Austin	465H	MK-36	78727	12700-12999
WAR ADMIRAL DR	Austin	678P	MQ-14	78617	5500-5899
WARBLER CT	Austin	525M	MK-29	78758	8300-8399
WARBLER CV	Hutto	379M	MT-44	78634	1000-1099
WARBLER DR	Lakeway	520J	WY-29	78734	1000-1099
	Lakeway	520J	WY-29	78734	15000-15199
	Travis Co	520J	WY-29	78734	1200-1299
WARBLER WAY	Georgetown	225F	MJ-60	78633	100-199
WARBLER WAY	Travis Co	582A	MC-24	78735	2200-2299
WARBLER LEDGE	Travis Co	580G	WZ-24	78738	11500-11599
WARBONNET	Williamson Co	287G	MP-54	78626	50100-50199
WAR BONNET CV	Lago Vista	399L	WX-41	78645	21200-21299
WAR BONNET DR	Travis Co	521V	MB-28	78733	10500-10599
WAR BONNET WAY	Lago Vista	399G	WX-42	78645	21100-21199
WARDMAN DR	Travis Co	707B	MN-12	78617	7100-7299
WARDOUR LN	Austin	672V	MD-13	78748	2900-3099
WARE RD	Austin	645B	MJ-18	78741	2400-2899
WAREHAM CT	Austin	671C	MB-15	78739	10900-10999
WAREHAM LN	Austin	671C	MB-15	78739	6400-6499
WAREHOUSE DR	Hays Co	762R	MD-5	78610	100-199
WAREHOUSE ROW	Austin	644D	MH-18	78704	3600-4099
WARELY LN	Austin	645B	MJ-18	78741	1900-2099
WARFIELD RD	Williamson Co	343C	MF-48	78641	1-99
WARFIELD WAY	Travis Co	436Y	MM-37	78728	2100-2299
WAR HORSE LN	Pflugerville	437F	MN-39	78664	1600-1699
WARM BREEZE CV	Williamson Co	375S	MJ-43	78717	400-499
WARM MIST CV	Williamson Co	375S	MJ-43	78717	400-499
WARM MOON CV	Williamson Co	375T	MJ-43	78717	400-499
WARNER DR	Elgin	533M	EB-29	78621	200-299
WARNER BEND	Hutto	379G	MT-45	78634	100-399
WARNER RANCH DR	Pflugerville	407X	MN-40	78664	2000-2099
WARNER RANCH DR	Round Rock	407T	MN-40	78664	1800-1899
	Round Rock	407X	MN-40	78664	1900-1999
WARPATH LN	Hays Co	732B	MC-9	78610	300-399
WARREN CV	Cedar Park	402R	MD-41	78613	1500-1599
WARREN CV	Lago Vista	458G	WV-36	78645	2600-2899
WARREN ST	Austin	554Q	MH-26	78703	2700-2899
	Austin	554Q	MH-26	78703	3200-3299
WARRINGTON CV	Austin	526H	MM-30	78753	10100-10199
WARRINGTON DR	Austin	526C	MM-30	78753	900-1399
WARRIOR LN	Austin	647A	MN-18	78617	1400-1599
WARRIOR TRL	Lago Vista	399G	WX-42	78645	21400-21599
WARWICK CV	Cedar Park	372P	MC-44	78613	1800-1899
WARWICK WAY	Austin	702B	MC-12	78748	2800-3099
WARWICK WAY	Cedar Park	372P	MC-44	78613	1700-1799
WASHAM DR	Georgetown	256U	MM-55	78628	400-499
WASHBURN DR	Leander	311R	MB-50	78641	900-1099
WASHBURN ST	Taylor	353A	EA-48	76574	100-1099

STREET NAME	CITY or COUNTY	MAPSCO GRID	AUSTIN GRID	ZIP CODE	BLOCK RANGE O/E
WASHINGTON CV	Lago Vista	458L	WV-35	78645	2300-2399
WASHINGTON ST	Elgin	534X	EC-28	78621	100-499
WASHINGTON CUT OFF	West Lake Hills	583B	ME-24	78746	400-499
WASHINGTON SQUARE	Austin	555W	MJ-25	78705	3000-3099
WASHINGTON SQUARE DR	Leander	342V	MD-46	78641	100-799
WASHITA CV	Lago Vista	399G	WX-42	78645	21400-21599
WASHITA DR	Austin	642Q	MD-17	78749	8100-8499
WASHOE CIR	Travis Co	490Z	WZ-31	78734	14000-14199
WASSAIL ST	Austin	675A	MJ-15	78744	5500-5599
WASSON RD	Austin	644P	MG-17	78745	5000-5599
WATCHFUL FOX DR	Austin	703B	ME-12	78748	10500-11099
WATCHHILL RD	Austin	584H	MH-24	78703	1600-1999
WATCHWOOD DR	Austin	643P	ME-17	78745	7000-7099
WATER LN	Travis Co	491G	MB-33	78732	13000-13199
WATER ST	Bastrop	745B	EE-9	78602	300-1899
	Bastrop	715X	EE-10	78602	2000-2099
	Bastrop	715T	EE-10	78602	2200-2399
WATER ST	Webberville	620Y	MV-19	78653	900-1099
WATER BANK CV	Austin	553G	MF-27	78746	2800-2999
WATER BIRCH	Round Rock	346R	MM-47	78665	1100-1199
WATERBROOK DR	Austin	556X	ML-25	78723	5100-5499
WATER BROOK DR	Pflugerville	468F	MQ-36	78660	1600-1699
WATERCLIFFE DR	Travis Co	489B	WW-33	78645	1000-1599
WATERCREST CT	Travis Co	550M	WZ-26	78733	11800-11899
WATERCREST DR	Georgetown	287K	MN-53	78626	1500-1799
WATERCREST DR	Travis Co	550R	WZ-26	78733	2400-2599
WATERFALL AVE	Leander	311Z	MB-49	78641	1200-1899
WATERFALL DR	Village of the Hills	519T	WW-28	78738	1-99
WATERFALL HILL CV	Burnet Co	426F	WQ-39	78669	100-199
WATERFALL HILL PKWY	Burnet Co	426K	WQ-38	78669	27200-27599
	Travis Co	426K	WQ-38	78669	27000-27199
WATERFORD LN	Williamson Co	283Z	MF-52	78628	100-199
WATERFORD PL	Austin	524X	MG-28	78731	4300-4599
WATERFORD CENTRE BLVD	Austin	495T	MJ-31	78758	9000-9299
WATERFORD RUN WAY	Manor	530B	MU-30	78653	None
WATERFOWL RD	Austin	678E	MQ-15	78617	12400-12499
WATER FRONT AVE	Lakeway	488Z	WV-31	78734	1-99
WATERGATE WAY	Hutto	379P	MS-44	78634	200-399
WATER HOLE TRL	Williamson Co	402Q	MD-41	78613	1000-1199
WATERING ROCK LN	Austin	464Z	MH-34	78759	10700-10799
WATERLILLY CIR	Georgetown	225H	MK-60	78633	100-199
WATERLILLY LN	Georgetown	225H	MK-60	78633	100-199
WATER LILY WAY	Hays Co	669N	WW-14	78737	100-299
WATERLILY WAY	Hutto	379H	MT-45	78634	100-299
	Hutto	380E	MU-45	78634	300-399
WATER LINE RD	Austin	524C	MH-30	78731	7100-7499
WATERLOO TRL	Austin	614P	MG-20	78704	1400-1799
WATERMELON WAY	Travis Co	647D	MP-18	78725	1200-1399
WATER MILL CV	Williamson Co	434J	MG-38	78729	12900-12999
WATER OAK CV	Williamson Co	408K	MQ-41	78664	100-199
WATER OAK DR	Cedar Park	373Y	MF-43	78613	200-499
WATER OAK LN	Williamson Co	434G	MH-39	78729	13300-13399
WATER OAK PKWY	Georgetown	314K	MG-50	78628	1000-1899
WATER RACE CT	Williamson Co	434J	MG-38	78729	13000-13099
WATERS WAY	Austin	641D	MB-18	78749	6800-6899
WATERS EDGE CIR	Georgetown	286G	MM-54	78626	1-99
WATERSEDGE CV	Austin	554B	MG-27	78731	4200-4299
WATERSEDGE DR	Austin	554B	MG-27	78731	3900-4499
WATERSEDGE TERRACE DR	Bastrop Co	651T	MW-16	78621	100-499
WATERSIDE DR	Lago Vista	458Q	WV-35	78645	20900-20999
WATERSIDE TRL	Williamson Co	433L	MF-38	78750	12200-12599
WATER SONG	Williamson Co	283D	MF-54	78628	100-299
WATER SPANIEL WAY	Williamson Co	377A	MN-45	78664	1000-1699
WATERS PARK RD	Austin	465R	MK-35	78759	12100-12299
	Austin	466N	ML-35	78759	12300-12799
WATERSTON AVE	Austin	584L	MH-23	78703	1600-1899
WATERSTONE CV	Williamson Co	283D	MF-54	78628	100-199
WATERTON PARKE CIR	Austin	462P	MC-35	78726	12200-12499
WATERTON PARKE CV	Austin	462K	MC-35	78726	12400-12499
WATERWAY CV	Travis Co	436U	MM-37	78728	2300-2399
WATERWAY BEND	Travis Co	436U	MM-37	78728	2100-2399
WATER WELL LN	Travis Co	436U	MM-37	78728	2300-2699
WATER WHEEL CV	Williamson Co	434E	MG-39	78729	12900-12999
WATHEN AVE	Austin	584D	MH-24	78703	1400-1499
WATSON ST	Austin	525R	MK-29	78757	7600-7899
WATSON WAY	Travis Co	467E	MN-36	78660	700-999
WATT DR	Elgin	533H	EB-30	78621	100-199
WATTS LN	Bastrop Co	740W	MU-7	78612	100-199
WATUMBA RD	Travis Co	460Z	WZ-34	78734	15400-15599
WAUKESHA DR	Travis Co	437E	MN-39	78660	1800-2099
WAVECREST BLVD	Travis Co	436Q	MM-38	78728	2900-3499
WAVERLY CT	Austin	434A	MG-39	78729	13300-13399
WAVER TREE CT	Austin	642V	MD-16	78745	8200-8299
WAXBERRY LN	Austin	673K	ME-14	78748	1500-1699
WAXLER CT	Austin	497S	MN-31	78754	11500-15599
WAXWING CIR	Williamson Co	433R	MF-38	78750	12200-12299
WAXWING CT	Austin	526J	ML-29	78758	8400-8499
WAX WING DR	Hays Co	732A	MC-9	78610	200-299
WAY LN	Austin	671B	MA-15	78739	6500-6599
WAYBORNE HILL DR	Austin	556Y	MM-25	78723	5100-5299
WAYCROSS DR	Austin	644T	MG-16	78745	6000-6299
WAYCROSS DR	Williamson Co	284C	MH-54	78628	100-199
WAYMAKER CV	Austin	553G	MF-27	78746	5900-5999
WAYMAKER WAY	Austin	553G	MF-27	78746	2400-2899
WAYNE DR	Round Rock	376M	MM-44	78664	800-1199
	Round Rock	377J	MN-44	78664	1200-1499
WAYNE RIDDELL LOOP	Austin	703G	MF-12	78748	10800-11399
WAYNEROY DR	Austin	586T	ML-22	78721	1100-1199
WAYNESBOROUGH DR	Austin	557Y	MP-25	78724	6800-6999
WAYNESBURG CV	Austin	557W	MN-25	78723	6300-6399
WAYNESPUR LN	Travis Co	532Q	MZ-29	78621	12600-12999
WAYSIDE BLVD	Travis Co	588N	MQ-23	78724	9600-10099
WAYSIDE CT	Bastrop Co	564X	EC-25	78621	100-299
WAYSIDE DR	Austin	584K	MG-23	78703	700-1199
WAYSIDE DR	Bastrop Co	564X	EC-25	78621	100-299
WAYWARD SUN DR	Austin	497X	MN-31	78754	1900-2199
WAYWOOD DR	Travis Co	588N	MQ-23	78724	5600-5999
WAYZATA CT	Travis Co	409S	MS-40	78660	20300-20399
WEATHERBY PASS	Bastrop	744K	EC-8	78602	None
WEATHERFORD DR	Austin	467X	MN-34	78753	1000-1699
WEATHERHILL CV	Travis Co	522M	MD-29	78730	3700-3799
WEATHERS LN	Austin	614Q	MH-20	78704	1000-1199
WEATHERWOOD CV	Travis Co	582Q	MD-23	78746	6400-6499
WEBB LN	Travis Co	460H	WZ-36	78734	15700-16199
WEBBER LN	Bastrop Co	712Z	MZ-10	78602	100-199

V W

STREET NAME	CITY or COUNTY	MAPSCO GRID	AUSTIN GRID	ZIP CODE	BLOCK RANGE O/E
WEBBER ST	Webberville	620Y	MV-19	78653	1200-1399
WEBBER OAKS CV	Travis Co	621L	MX-20	78653	21400-21499
WEBBERVILLE RD	Austin	586L	MM-23	78721	1100-1999
	Austin	615D	MK-21	78702	2200-2299
	Austin	585Z	MK-22	78702	2300-2899
	Austin	586S	ML-22	78702	2900-3699
	Bastrop Co	533R	EB-29	78621	None
	Elgin	533R	EB-29	78621	None
	Elgin	534N	EC-29	78621	None
WEBBERWOOD DR	Webberville	651E	MW-18	78653	1600-2399
WEBBERWOOD WAY N	Travis Co	621Q	MX-20	78653	100-299
WEBBERWOOD WAY S	Travis Co	621X	MX-20	78653	100-799
	Webberville	621X	MW-19	78653	800-1099
	Webberville	651B	MW-18	78653	1100-1599
WEBBERWOOD RIDGE DR					
	Travis Co	621P	MW-20	78653	21400-21499
WEBBWOOD WAY	Travis Co	588S	MQ-22	78724	10000-10099
WEBER AVE	Austin	585M	MK-23	78722	2500-2599
WEBSTER LN	Lago Vista	458G	WV-36	78645	2600-2699
WEDDING DR	Manor	530P	MU-29	78653	12700-13099
WEDDINGTON DR	Round Rock	376R	MM-44	78664	500-599
WEDGEWOOD DR	Austin	496V	MM-31	78753	11300-11699
WEEKS CV	Austin	435W	MJ-37	78727	6300-6399
WEEPING WILLOW DR	Austin	526P	ML-29	78753	1000-1099
WEE SCOT CV	Lakeway	489W	WW-31	78734	100-199
WEGSTROM ST	Hutto	349M	MT-47	78634	100-399
WEIDEMAR LN	Austin	644M	MH-17	78745	4500-5199
WEIR LOOP CIR	Travis Co	610V	WZ-19	78736	9800-10199
WEIR RANCH RD	Williamson Co	315C	MK-51	78628	300-1899
WEISER DR	Williamson Co	434T	MG-37	78729	8700-8799
WEISKOPF LOOP	Round Rock	378U	MR-43	78664	1500-1599
WEISS LN	Georgetown	287P	MN-53	78626	2200-2299
WEISS LN	Travis Co	469F	MS-36	78660	16200-17799
	Travis Co	439U	MT-37	78660	17800-19199
WELCH ST	Taylor	352L	MZ-47	76574	700-2499
WELCH WAY	Cedar Park	372U	MD-43	78613	1100-1199
WELCOME GLEN	Austin	494D	MH-33	78759	5200-5399
WELDON LN	Travis Co	436Y	MM-37	78728	14200-14499
WELDON SPRINGS CT	Austin	462P	MC-35	78726	8000-8099
WELETKA DR	Travis Co	460V	WZ-34	78734	4400-5199
WELLAND CIR	Austin	465X	MJ-34	78759	4300-4399
WELLER DR	Austin	433U	MF-37	78750	10400-10599
WELLESLEY DR	Travis Co	527X	MN-28	78754	9000-9299
WELLINGTON DR	Austin	556Y	MM-25	78723	5300-5999
WELLS LN	Travis Co	501M	MX-32	78621	15100-15799
	Travis Co	502A	MY-33	78653	15800-16499
	Travis Co	472T	MY-34	78653	16500-17699
WELLS RD	Travis Co	502P	MY-32	78621	14800-15399
	Travis Co	502G	MZ-33	78653	15400-16299
	Travis Co	472V	MZ-34	78653	16300-17199
WELLS BEND	Hutto	379L	MT-44	78634	100-399
WELLS BEND CT	Hutto	379L	MT-44	78634	2000-2099
WELLS BRANCH PKWY E					
	Pflugerville	467G	MP-36	78660	1000-1699
	Travis Co	467G	MP-36	78660	700-999
	Travis Co	468J	MQ-35	78660	2100-2999
WELLS BRANCH PKWY W	Austin	437W	MN-37	78660	500-1599
	Travis Co	466C	MM-36	78728	1600-2199
	Travis Co	436X	ML-37	78728	2200-3599
WELLS FARGO TRL	Hays Co	638D	WV-18	78737	12900-13299
WELLS POINT PASS	Pflugerville	437Y	MP-37	78660	600-699
WELLS PORT CV	Travis Co	436U	MM-37	78728	2200-2299
WELLS PORT DR	Pflugerville	436Q	MM-38	78728	15300-15699
	Travis Co	436Q	MM-38	78728	14300-15299
WELLSPRING DR	Bee Cave	550V	WZ-25	78733	3500-3699
WELLS SCHOOL RD	Travis Co	501D	MX-33	78653	14000-15099
	Travis Co	502K	MY-32	78653	15100-16299
WELLS TRACE	Travis Co	589P	MS-23	78653	7000-7699
WELSH WAY	Austin	678N	MQ-14	78617	5700-5999
WELTON CLIFF DR	Travis Co	432F	MC-39	78613	2800-3199
WENDE RD	Travis Co	705Y	MK-10	78747	8200-8999
WENDEL CV	Austin	524R	MH-29	78731	3500-3599
WENDI'S WAY	Williamson Co	433Q	MF-38	78750	10500-10599
WENTWORTH DR	Austin	587D	MP-24	78724	6700-6999
WERCHAN LN	Travis Co	472H	MZ-36	78615	17400-18699
WERNER AVE	Austin	585G	MK-24	78722	3300-3799
WERNER HILL DR	Austin	526H	MM-30	78753	1400-1499
WESAL DR	Austin	674Z	MH-13	78747	8300-8398 E
WESCOTT DR	Round Rock	377N	MN-44	78664	1200-1499
WESLEY ST	Travis Co	562E	MY-27	78621	11800-11999
WESLEYAN DR	Georgetown	286H	MM-54	78626	900-999
WESLEY RIDGE DR	Burnet Co	396Q	WR-41	78669	100-1099
WESSEX WAY	Austin	673G	MF-15	78748	900-1099
WESSON CV	Cedar Park	402R	MD-41	78613	1400-1499
WEST AVE	Austin	584V	MH-22	78703	100-599
	Austin	585J	MJ-23	78701	600-1899
	Austin	555W	MJ-25	78705	2900-3799
WEST CT	Austin	495W	MJ-31	78759	8100-8199
WEST DR	Austin	585A	MJ-24	78705	2900-2999
WEST DR	Village of Volente	430M	WZ-38	78645	8200-8399
WEST DR N	Leander	342B	MC-48	78641	100-299
WEST DR S	Leander	342Q	MD-47	78641	100-1999
WEST LN	Travis Co	550D	WZ-27	78732	1500-1699
WEST LOOP	Austin	495Y	MK-31	78758	1900-2099
WEST PASS	Travis Co	522S	MC-28	78733	10100-10199
WEST ST	Georgetown	286L	MM-53	78626	200-1099
WEST ST	Hutto	349Z	MT-46	78634	100-599
WEST ST	Taylor	352C	MZ-48	76574	2300-2499
WEST ST	Travis Co	430P	WY-38	78645	7400-7699
WESTALL ST	Travis Co	618R	MR-20	78725	14000-14499
WESTBANK DR	Travis Co	583P	ME-23	78746	1100-4399
	West Lake Hills	583P	ME-23	78746	900-1099
WEST BEACH CIR	Travis Co	460F	WY-36	78734	5500-5599
WEST BEACH RD	Travis Co	460F	WY-36	78734	17100-17399
WESTBLUFF CIR	Austin	494R	MH-32	78759	8800-8899
WESTBROOK DR	Travis Co	583M	MF-23	78746	200-699
	West Lake Hills	583Q	MF-23	78746	100-199
	West Lake Hills	583M	MF-23	78746	600-899
WESTBROOK DR W	Travis Co	583L	MF-23	78746	100-299
WESTBROOK LN N	Bastrop Co	534K	EC-29	78621	100-599
WESTBROOK LN S	Bastrop Co	534L	ED-29	78621	100-399
WESTBURY LN	Georgetown	225V	MK-58	78628	100-899
WESTBURY TRL	Austin	525D	MK-30	78758	1400-1599
WEST CAVE BLVD	Hays Co	577Q	WT-23	78720	10900-11299
	Travis Co	577Q	WT-23	78720	None
WEST CAVE CIR	Hays Co	577T	WS-22	78720	11100-11299
WEST CAVE CV	Hays Co	577T	WS-22	78720	18200-18299
WEST CAVE LOOP	Hays Co	577Q	WT-23	78720	None
	Travis Co	577L	WT-23	78720	10000-10899
WEST CAVE CROSSING	Hays Co	577P	WS-23	78720	10800-10999
WESTCHESTER AVE	Austin	525A	MJ-30	78759	3400-3599
WESTCHESTER RD	Taylor	353S	EA-46	76574	500-699
	Taylor	352V	MZ-46	76574	700-799
WESTCLIFF PL	Travis Co	523B	ME-30	78730	5400-5499
WEST COURTYARD DR	Austin	523G	MF-30	78730	5900-6999
WEST COW PATH	Austin	465J	MJ-35	78727	11800-12599
WESTCREEK DR	Austin	612Y	MD-19	78749	5700-6099
WEST CREEK LOOP	Round Rock	406J	ML-41	78681	1100-1999
WEST CREEKVIEW DR	Travis Co	581W	MA-22	78736	6400-6699
WEST CREST LN	Travis Co	558S	MQ-25	78724	8300-8599
WEST END PL	Round Rock	345Z	MK-46	78681	1600-1699
	Round Rock	346W	ML-46	78681	1700-1799
WESTERKIRK DR	Austin	464E	MG-36	78750	8800-8999
	Austin	463H	MF-36	78750	9000-9199
WESTERN DR	Austin	643J	ME-17	78745	3200-3399
WESTERN TRL	Georgetown	256K	ML-56	78628	100-699
WESTERN TRL	Lago Vista	399G	WX-42	78645	8800-9399
WESTERN HILLS DR	Austin	524U	MH-28	78731	5300-5499
	Austin	524U	MH-28	78731	5500-5599
WESTERN LAKE DR	Williamson Co	317X	MN-49	78665	4500-4599
WESTERN OAKS BLVD	Austin	642C	MD-18	78749	6700-7099
WESTERN SKY BLVD	Elgin	532M	MZ-29	78621	13400-13799
WESTERN TRAILS BLVD	Austin	613Z	MF-19	78745	2200-2799
WESTFALIAN TRL	Travis Co	521F	MA-30	78732	None
WESTFIELD DR	Austin	554H	MH-27	78731	4800-5099
WESTFIELD DR	Williamson Co	344B	MG-48	78628	100-199
WESTFOREST DR	Austin	614N	MG-20	78704	2300-2399
WEST FRANCES PL	Austin	554H	MH-27	78731	4800-5099
WEST GATE BLVD	Austin	613V	MF-19	78735	4400-4499
	Austin	613Z	MF-19	78745	4500-4999
	Austin	643C	MF-18	78745	5000-8899
	Austin	672H	MD-15	78748	9100-9999
WESTGATE CIR	Rollingwood	583V	MF-22	78746	1-99
WESTGATE WAY	Travis Co	409P	MS-41	78660	2600-2699
WESTHAMPTON CT	Round Rock	408N	MQ-41	78664	2700-2799
WESTHAVEN DR	West Lake Hills	583L	MF-23	78746	100-399
WESTHEIMER DR	Austin	556F	ML-27	78752	1200-1399
WESTHILL DR	Austin	614J	MG-20	78704	2700-3399
WEST HOVE LOOP	Austin	642T	MC-16	78749	8900-8999
WESTINGHOUSE DR	Round Rock	346F	ML-48	78664	100-199
WESTINGHOUSE RD	Georgetown	316X	ML-49	78626	1-899
	Georgetown	346B	ML-48	78665	None
WESTLAKE CV	Travis Co	554P	MG-26	78746	2900-2999
WESTLAKE DR	Austin	554W	MG-25	78746	2200-2999
	Austin	523Y	MF-28	78746	4200-4799
	Travis Co	553Z	MF-25	78746	1900-1999
	Travis Co	554W	MG-25	78746	2000-2199
	Travis Co	554A	MG-27	78746	3000-3999
	Travis Co	523Z	MF-28	78746	4000-4199
WESTLAKE DR	Travis Co	577Q	WT-23	78720	17600-17899
WESTLAKE DR	West Lake Hills	583G	MF-24	78746	100-1199
	West Lake Hills	553Z	MF-25	78746	1200-1899
WESTLAKE PASS	Travis Co	554S	MG-25	78746	1900-2499
WEST LAKE PKWY	Williamson Co	254P	MG-56	78628	20100-20199
WESTLAKE CUT OFF	Travis Co	554N	MG-26	78746	None
WESTLAND DR	Austin	614N	MG-20	78704	3300-3399
WESTLAND RIDGE RD	Hays Co	668F	WU-15	78620	1000-1099
WESTLEDGE CIR	Austin	554L	MH-26	78731	3400-3499
WEST LYNN ST	Austin	584Q	MH-23	78703	500-1699
WEST MARKET DR	Austin	554D	MH-27	78731	4800-5099
WESTMEADOW TRL	Williamson Co	347A	MN-48	78665	1600-1799
WESTMINISTER PL	Round Rock	406M	MM-41	78664	500-899
WESTMINSTER DR	Austin	556P	ML-26	78723	5300-5999
WESTMINSTER WAY	Cedar Park	372P	MC-44	78613	1700-1899
WESTMINSTER GLEN AVE	Travis Co	523E	ME-30	78730	8800-8999
	Travis Co	522D	MD-30	78730	9000-9999
WESTMONT DR	Austin	524U	MH-28	78731	5800-5899
WESTMOOR DR	Austin	556N	ML-26	78723	1200-1899
WESTMORLAND DR	Austin	644Q	MH-17	78745	300-699
WESTOAK DR	Austin	614N	MG-20	78704	2300-2399
WEST OAK DR	Bastrop Co	711S	MW-10	78612	100-199
WEST OAK LOOP	Bastrop Co	711S	MW-10	78612	100-299
WESTON LN N	Travis Co	552H	MD-27	78733	100-1499
WESTON LN S	Travis Co	552Q	MD-26	78733	100-299
WESTONBIRT LN	Travis Co	439F	MS-39	78660	3100-3199
WESTOVER RD	Austin	554Z	MH-25	78703	1300-1799
	Austin	554Y	MH-25	78703	2100-2699
WESTOVER CLUB DR	Austin	494R	MH-32	78759	8700-8899
WEST PARK DR	Austin	554H	MH-27	78731	4700-5099
WESTRIDGE DR	Austin	614F	MG-21	78704	1800-1999
	Austin	614F	MG-21	78704	2000-2099
WEST RIDGE DR	Bastrop Co	742P	MY-8	78612	100-199
WEST RIDGE LN	Williamson Co	193B	ME-63	78633	100-299
WEST RIM CV	Austin	494Y	MH-31	78731	4600-4699
WEST RIM DR	Austin	524C	MH-30	78731	7100-7499
	Austin	494Y	MH-31	78731	7500-7999
WEST RIM DR	Jonestown	400R	WZ-41	78645	18100-18499
WESTROCK DR	Austin	614N	MG-20	78704	2300-2399
WESTSIDE CV	Austin	524R	MH-29	78731	3400-3499
WESTSIDE DR	Austin	524R	MH-29	78731	6000-6499
WESTSIDE LN	Round Rock	376S	ML-43	78681	1100-1199
WESTSLOPE CIR	Austin	524S	MG-28	78731	4700-4799
WESTSLOPE CV	Austin	524N	MG-29	78731	5800-5899
WESTSLOPE DR	Austin	524N	MG-29	78731	5700-5999
WEST SPRING DR	West Lake Hills	583G	MF-24	78746	100-399
WEST TERRACE DR	Austin	525N	MJ-29	78757	3000-3199
WESTVALLEY PL	Williamson Co	347A	MN-48	78665	1900-2099
WEST VALLEY SPUR	Williamson Co	192T	MC-61	78633	100-199
WESTVIEW DR	Austin	524Z	MH-28	78731	4900-5199
WESTVIEW DR	Williamson Co	407M	MP-41	78664	1-99
WEST VIEW DR	Williamson Co	283Z	MF-52	78628	100-199
WESTVIEW RD	Austin	612X	MC-19	78749	5400-5899
WEST VIEW RD	Travis Co	611W	MA-19	78737	8700-9399
WESTWARD CV	Travis Co	552A	MC-27	78733	100-199
WESTWARD DR	Travis Co	552A	MC-27	78733	9700-9999
WESTWARD HO PASS	Lago Vista	399L	WX-41	78645	21200-21599
WESTWARD HO TRL	Travis Co	490U	WZ-31	78734	1500-1999
WESTWARD LOOK	Hays Co	577U	WT-22	78720	17800-17999
WESTWATER CT	Travis Co	489E	WW-33	78645	None
WESTWAY CIR	Austin	614N	MG-20	78704	2300-2399
WESTWAY DR W	Buda	732E	MC-9	78610	100-199
WESTWIND AVE	Round Rock	406K	ML-41	78681	2300-2399
WEST WIND TRL	Austin	643C	MF-18	78745	4800-5099
WESTWOOD CIR	Austin	674C	MH-15	78744	6600-6799
WESTWOOD DR	Round Rock	376X	ML-43	78681	900-1199
WESTWOOD LN	Georgetown	256U	MM-55	78628	1600-1699
	Georgetown	256Q	MM-56	78628	1700-2399
WESTWOOD TERRACE	Travis Co	583L	MF-23	78746	300-699
	West Lake Hills	583L	MF-23	78746	200-299
WESTWORTH CIR	Austin	614N	MG-20	78704	2300-2399
WETHERSBY WAY	Austin	497A	MN-33	78753	12500-12599
WETHERSFIELD RD	Austin	584H	MH-24	78703	1500-1799
WETMORE LN	Hays Co	639U	WX-16	78737	100-199
WET SEASON DR	Austin	497T	MN-31	78754	11100-11399
WEXFORD DR	Austin	464F	MG-36	78759	8100-8399
WEYBURN DR	Austin	525C	MK-30	78757	8300-8399
WEYFORD DR	Austin	525G	MK-30	78757	1500-1599
WHARF CV	Village of Volente	431W	MA-37	78641	16100-16199
WHARTON CT	Travis Co	491Q	MB-32	78732	3900-3999
WHARTON PARK TRL	Austin	404E	MG-42	78717	14400-14599
WHEAT AVE	Austin	586N	ML-23	78702	2400-2499
WHEATFALL LN	Austin	673G	MF-15	78748	1400-1499
WHEATLAND DR	Travis Co	550Q	WZ-26	78733	12500-12599
WHEATLEY AVE	Austin	526X	ML-28	78752	900-1199
WHEATON TRL	Cedar Park	372J	MC-44	78613	1900-2399
WHEELER ST	Austin	555W	MJ-25	78705	3100-3199
WHEELER ST E	Manor	529U	MT-28	78653	100-799
WHEELER ST W	Manor	529Q	MT-29	78653	100-399
WHEELER BRANCH CIR	Austin	642B	MC-18	78749	5200-5399
WHEELER BRANCH TRL	Austin	642B	MC-18	78749	7000-7299
WHEELESS ST	Austin	585Y	MK-22	78702	1000-1099
WHEEL RIM CIR	Austin	642E	MC-18	78749	7800-7999
WHELESS CV	Austin	556Q	MM-26	78723	6100-6199
WHELESS LN	Austin	556K	ML-26	78723	1300-1699
	Austin	556P	ML-26	78723	1700-2199
	Austin	556Q	MM-26	78723	2200-2899
WHETSTONE	Williamson Co	375Y	MK-43	78681	17100-17199
WHETSTONE ST	Williamson Co	375Y	MK-43	78681	200-399
WHIFFLEWIND WAY	Austin	528P	MQ-29	78754	7000-7199
WHIG WAY	Georgetown	287S	MN-52	78626	2500-2599
WHIP-O-WILL	Williamson Co	375L	MK-44	78681	1800-1899
WHIPPLE WAY	Austin	643G	MF-18	78745	6100-6199
WHIPPOORWILL CIR	Williamson Co	282W	MC-52	78641	100-199
WHIPPOORWILL CV	Georgetown	225K	MJ-59	78633	100-199
WHIPPOORWILL DR	Cedar Park	433A	ME-39	78613	1300-1399
WHIPPOORWILL ST N	Lakeway	520A	WY-30	78734	100-299
WHIPPOORWILL ST S	Lakeway	520A	WY-30	78734	100-299
WHIPPOORWILL TRL	Travis Co	582D	MD-24	78746	400-499
	Travis Co	582C	MD-24	78746	500-599
WHIPPOORWILL TRL	Travis Co	460S	WY-34	78645	17200-17599
WHIPPOORWILL WAY	Georgetown	225K	MJ-59	78633	100-199
WHIRLAWAY	Hays Co	638V	WV-16	78737	100-599
WHIRLAWAY DR	Travis Co	650L	MV-17	78617	2000-2899
WHIRLAWAY DR	Travis Co	677G	MP-15	78617	4600-4899
WHIRLING EDDY CV	Hutto	379M	MT-44	78634	100-199
WHIRLWIND CV	Georgetown	195T	MJ-61	78633	100-199
WHIRLWIND CV	Travis Co	517M	WT-29	78669	4400-4599
WHIRLWIND TRL	Round Rock	407J	MN-41	78664	1600-1899
WHISENANT LN	Dripping Springs	636M	WR-17	78620	1-399
WHISKEY RIVER DR	Travis Co	672U	MD-13	78748	11000-11399
WHISPER LN	Williamson Co	314P	MG-50	78628	1-799
WHISPERING DR	Round Rock	376H	MM-45	78664	1000-2299
WHISPERING CREEK CIR	Austin	611V	MB-19	78736	7300-7399
WHISPERING CREEK CT	Austin	611V	MB-19	78736	7100-7199
WHISPERING CREEK DR	Austin	611V	MB-19	78736	6900-7099
WHISPERING HOLLOW CIR					
	Point Venture	488R	WV-32	78654	600-699
WHISPERING HOLLOW DR					
	Point Venture	488R	WV-32	78654	18900-19099
WHISPERING OAKS CV	Lago Vista	399L	WX-41	78645	8800-8899
WHISPERING OAKS DR	Austin	643T	ME-16	78745	6900-7699
WHISPERING OAKS LN					
	Williamson Co	375J	MJ-44	78681	1800-1999
WHISPERING SPRING LN					
	Williamson Co	224Q	MH-59	78633	100-299
WHISPERING VALLEY	Hays Co	668K	WU-14	78620	100-299
WHISPERING VALLEY DR	Austin	465P	MJ-35	78727	4400-4999
WHISPERING WIND DR	Georgetown	225G	MK-60	78633	1-299
	Georgetown	195V	MK-61	78633	300-999
WHISPERING WINDS DR	Austin	643T	ME-16	78745	7100-7799
WHISPERING WOODS CT					
	Round Rock	375G	MK-45	78681	3200-3299
WHISPERING WOODS CV					
	Georgetown	285P	MJ-53	78628	1100-1199
WHISPER OAKS LN	Georgetown	256K	ML-56	78628	2900-3199
WHISPER RIDGE DR	Austin	494P	MG-32	78750	5800-6199
WHISTLERS WALK TRL	Cedar Park	374N	MG-44	78613	500-799
WHISTLESTOP CV	Austin	642A	MC-18	78749	6000-6099
WHISTLESTOP DR	Austin	642A	MC-18	78749	7400-7599
WHISTLING WAY	Taylor	322Y	MZ-49	76574	2000-2299
WHISTLING STRAITS DR	Austin	404G	MH-42	78717	15300-15599
WHITAKER DR	Leander	311R	MB-50	78641	800-899
WHITE CIR	Williamson Co	433F	ME-39	78613	1500-1599
WHITEBEAD TRL	Travis Co	490U	WZ-31	78734	1900-2499
WHITEBROOK DR	Austin	557T	MN-25	78724	5700-5899
WHITEBRUSH LOOP	Williamson Co	405A	MJ-42	78717	16700-16999
WHITE CHAPEL CT	Cedar Park	402D	MD-42	78613	100-199
WHITE CLIFF DR	Travis Co	494F	MG-33	78759	8500-8899
WHITE CLOUD CV	Lago Vista	399G	WX-42	78645	21300-21399
WHITE CREEK CV	Williamson Co	405E	MJ-42	78717	16200-16299
WHITE CREEK DR	Williamson Co	405E	MJ-42	78717	8700-8799
WHITECREST CV	Round Rock	345K	MJ-47	78681	4000-4199
WHITECROWE TRL	Austin	613U	MF-19	78735	4400-4799
WHITE DOVE CV	Cedar Park	403N	ME-41	78613	1300-1399
WHITE DOVE PASS	Travis Co	490V	WZ-31	78734	2000-2499
WHITE EAGLE PASS	Williamson Co	287H	MP-54	78626	2-398 E
WHITE EAGLE RD	Austin	702G	MD-12	78748	12400-12499
WHITE ELM CT	Austin	612Z	MD-19	78749	4700-4799
WHITE ELM CV	Cedar Park	433A	ME-39	78613	1400-1499
WHITE ELM DR	Austin	612Y	MD-19	78749	4600-4999
WHITEHALL CV	Travis Co	522C	MD-30	78730	4500-4599
WHITEHALL DR	Travis Co	437D	MP-39	78660	800-999
WHITE HAWK CIR	Hays Co	670X	WY-13	78610	8000-8099
WHITE HILLS CIR	Travis Co	366Q	WR-44	78654	6800-6899
WHITE HILLS LN	Travis Co	366R	WR-44	78654	6700-7399
WHITE HORSE CV	Travis Co	518J	WU-29	78669	19100-19499
WHITE HORSE TRL	Austin	525S	MJ-28	78757	2100-2799
WHITE HOUSE ST	Travis Co	530L	MV-29	78653	12800-12999
WHITEHURST CV	Round Rock	376A	ML-45	78681	3000-3099
WHITEHURST DR	Round Rock	376A	ML-45	78681	2500-2699
WHITE IBIS DR	Travis Co	434G	MH-39	78729	8500-8899

W

STREET NAME	CITY or COUNTY	MAPSCO GRID	AUSTIN GRID	ZIP CODE	BLOCK RANGE O/E
WHITE INDIGO TRL	Williamson Co	377B	MN-45	78665	1800-1899
WHITE MAGNOLIA CIR	Lakeway	519M	WX-29	78734	1-99
WHITEMARSH VALLEY WALK					
	Travis Co	582H	MD-24	78746	6300-6699
WHITEMOSS DR	Travis Co	408M	MR-41	78634	1100-1299
WHITE OAK CIR	Round Rock	375M	MK-44	78681	1900-1999
WHITE OAK CV	Round Rock	375M	MK-44	78681	1800-1899
WHITE OAK DR	Austin	526N	ML-29	78753	100-399
WHITE OAK DR	Lago Vista	429B	WW-39	78645	7200-7499
	Lago Vista	399X	WW-40	78645	7500-7699
WHITE OAK LOOP	Round Rock	375M	MK-44	78681	1500-1999
WHITE PANDA RUN	Travis Co	707C	MP-12	78617	7200-7299
WHITEPINE DR	Austin	525E	MJ-30	78757	3000-3399
WHITE POST DR	Williamson Co	433B	ME-39	78613	1500-3099
WHITE RIM CV	Travis Co	400D	WZ-42	78645	11500-11599
WHITE RIM TRL	Travis Co	400D	WZ-42	78645	18600-19099
WHITE RIM TERRACE	Travis Co	370Z	WZ-43	78645	11500-12199
WHITE RIVER BLVD	Pflugerville	437P	MN-38	78660	16000-16299
WHITE RIVER DR	Georgetown	317J	MN-50	78626	300-399
WHITE ROCK BLVD	Williamson Co	288G	MR-54	78626	100-299
WHITE ROCK DR	Austin	525W	MJ-28	78756	2200-2899
	Austin	524V	MH-28	78757	2900-3199
WHITEROCK DR	Lago Vista	429W	WW-37	78645	20400-20499
WHITES DR	Austin	613U	MF-19	78735	3200-3299
WHITE SANDS DR	Lakeway	519G	WX-30	78734	100-199
WHITE STALLION WAY	Leander	372C	MD-45	78641	2400-2699
WHITESTONE BLVD E	Cedar Park	373P	ME-44	78613	100-1699
	Cedar Park	374E	MG-45	78613	1700-4399
WHITESTONE BLVD W	Cedar Park	372V	MD-43	78613	100-2999
	Leander	371V	MB-43	78613	3000-3699
WHITESTONE DR	Austin	643H	MF-18	78745	2000-2399
WHITESTONE DR	Williamson Co	256W	ML-55	78628	300-399
WHITESTONE LN	Cedar Park	373N	ME-44	78613	1000-1199
WHITETAIL CV	Williamson Co	378H	MR-45	78634	4700-4799
WHITETAIL DR	Travis Co	703W	ME-10	78652	300-599
WHITETAIL DR	Williamson Co	314Z	MH-49	78628	400-599
	Williamson Co	344D	MH-48	78628	600-699
WHITETAIL LN	Williamson Co	378H	MR-45	78634	100-499
WHITE TAIL PASS	Cedar Park	371R	MB-44	78613	17000-17199
	Leander	371R	MB-44	78641	None
	Travis Co	371R	MB-44	78641	1100-1199
WHITE TAIL RD	Bastrop Co	710D	MV-12	78612	100-299
WHITE TAIL TRL	Travis Co	609N	WW-20	78736	13300-13499
	Travis Co	608R	WV-20	78736	13500-13699
WHITETAIL RIDGE RD	Hays Co	638Y	WV-16	78620	100-999
WHITETHORN CT	Travis Co	554A	MG-27	78746	4900-4999
WHITE WASH WAY	Hays Co	668H	WV-15	78620	100-199
WHITE WATER CV	Travis Co	439P	MS-38	78660	None
WHITEWATER CV	Williamson Co	375Q	MK-44	78681	18100-18299
WHITEWATER DR	Burnet Co	307A	WS-51	78654	100-2199
WHITE WATER WAY	Travis Co	439P	MS-38	78660	None
WHITEWAY DR	Austin	525E	MJ-30	78757	2900-3399
WHITEWING AVE	Austin	496Q	MM-32	78753	11300-11599
WHITEWING DR	Bastrop Co	709L	MT-11	78612	None
WHITEWING DR	Cedar Park	402M	MD-41	78613	900-999
WHITEWING DR	Williamson Co	282N	MC-53	78641	100-299
WHITEWING WAY	Georgetown	225K	MJ-59	78633	100-199
WHITE WING WAY	Round Rock	406D	MM-42	78664	300-699
WHITEWORTH LOOP	Austin	642T	MC-16	78749	8800-9099
WHITEY FORD WAY	Round Rock	378A	MQ-45	78665	3900-3999
WHITFIELD ST	Hutto	349Z	MT-46	78634	100-399
WHITIS AVE	Austin	585J	MJ-23	78705	1900-2099
	Austin	585E	MJ-24	78705	2400-2699
	Austin	585A	MJ-24	78705	2700-2899
	Austin	585B	MJ-24	78705	3000-3199
WHITLEY DR	Lakeway	520W	WY-28	78734	100-199
WHITLEY DR	Leander	312S	MC-49	78641	900-1199
WHITLEY BAY DR	Austin	404D	MH-42	78717	9800-10199
WHITLOW CV	Round Rock	375R	MK-44	78681	2300-2399
WHITNEY CV	Lago Vista	458L	WV-35	78645	2300-2399
WHITNEY DR	Travis Co	456H	WR-36	78669	24700-25199
WHITNEY WAY	Austin	615Z	MK-19	78741	1600-1899
WHITNEY WOODS CIR	Williamson Co	224P	MG-59	78633	100-299
WHITSUN DR	Austin	642R	MD-17	78749	7700-7999
WHITT LOOP	Austin	672F	MC-15	78749	3600-3799
WHITTARD OF CHELSEA LN					
	Travis Co	467M	MP-35	78660	1500-1999
WHITTIER CV	Lago Vista	458G	WV-36	78645	2500-2799
WHITTMAN CV	Austin	525C	MK-30	78757	8400-8499
WHITWORTH LN	Williamson Co	375T	MJ-43	78681	8000-8099
WIAMEA CT E	Bastrop Co	746S	EG-7	78602	100-199
WIAMEA CT W	Bastrop Co	746S	EG-7	78602	100-199
WICHITA CV	Lago Vista	399G	WX-42	78645	21600-21699
WICHITA ST	Austin	585F	MJ-24	78705	2500-2699
WICHITA TRL	Williamson Co	223D	MF-60	78633	100-199
WICKERSHAM LN	Austin	615Y	MK-19	78741	1400-2399
	Austin	645C	MK-18	78741	2400-2999
WICKETT WAY	Travis Co	402Y	MD-40	78613	1900-1999
WICKFIELD LN	Austin	497J	MN-32	78753	900-1099
WICKFORD CIR	Austin	615N	MJ-20	78704	700-799
WICKHAM LN	Travis Co	618V	MR-19	78725	2900-3599
WICKLOW DR	Leander	342U	MD-46	78641	600-699
WICKLOW MOUNTAIN TRL					
	Cedar Park	374R	MH-44	78613	4400-4599
WICKSHIRE LN	Austin	645A	MJ-18	78741	1800-2199
WIDE ANTLER CV	Cedar Park	402R	MD-41	78613	1300-1399
WIDELEAF CV	Travis Co	619A	MS-21	78724	15200-15299
WIDELEAF DR	Travis Co	619A	MS-21	78724	5800-6299
WIDGE DR	Austin	466Q	MM-35	78727	12800-13099
WIER HILLS RD	Austin	611M	MB-20	78735	5100-6399
WIER LOOP RD	Travis Co	610M	WZ-20	78736	9400-9699
WIGEON CV	Cedar Park	373V	MF-43	78613	100-299
WIGHT CV	Austin	556U	MM-25	78723	5700-5799
WIGHTMAN DR	Travis Co	557B	MN-27	78754	8900-8999
WIGINTON DR	Austin	496K	ML-32	78758	11500-11799
WIGWAM	Leander	342X	MC-46	78641	1000-1699
WIGWAM CIR	Lago Vista	399G	WX-42	78645	21500-21599
WILBARGER PT	Georgetown	287F	MN-54	78626	100-499
WILBARGER ST E	Pflugerville	438W	MQ-37	78660	100-199
WILBARGER ST W	Pflugerville	438W	MQ-37	78660	100-499
WILBUR DR	Austin	525S	MJ-28	78757	6300-6499
WILCAB RD	Austin	586V	MM-22	78721	5700-6599
WILCOTT CT	Austin	643L	MF-17	78745	6000-6099
WILCOX AVE	Austin	586X	ML-22	78721	5100-5199
WILCREST DR	Austin	673E	ME-15	78748	2700-2899
WILD ST	Austin	525Y	MK-28	78757	6300-6799
WILD BASIN S	West Lake Hills	553V	MF-25	78746	1400-1699

STREET NAME	CITY or COUNTY	MAPSCO GRID	AUSTIN GRID	ZIP CODE	BLOCK RANGE O/E
WILD BASIN RD	Travis Co	553S	ME-25	78746	100-299
WILD BASIN LEDGE	Travis Co	553U	MF-25	78746	800-1399
	Travis Co	553Q	MF-26	78746	1400-1799
WILD BEAR PATH	Lago Vista	399G	WX-42	78645	21400-21599
WILD BRIAR CT	Cedar Park	403E	ME-42	78613	600-699
WILD BRIAR PASS	Austin	583N	ME-23	78746	4600-4899
WILD CANYON LOOP	Travis Co	491S	MA-31	78732	3100-3299
WILD CAT DR	Bastrop	744K	EC-8	78602	100-199
WILDCAT DR	Elgin	533H	EB-30	78621	100-199
WILDCAT DRAW	Buda	732W	MC-7	78610	100-299
WILD CAT HOLLOW	West Lake Hills	583D	MF-24	78746	100-299
	West Lake Hills	553Z	MF-25	78746	1400-1899
WILD CHERRY DR	Lakeway	519Y	WX-28	78738	2900-3799
WILD COW CV	Travis Co	518N	WU-29	78669	4600-4699
WILD DUNES CT	Austin	704F	MG-12	78747	4500-4599
WILD DUNES DR	Austin	704F	MG-12	78747	10000-10199
WILDERNESS CV	Austin	583V	MF-22	78746	1200-1299
WILDERNESS DR	Austin	583V	MF-22	78746	1200-1399
WILDERNESS PATH	Round Rock	376D	MM-45	78665	800-1299
WILDERNESS TRL	Elgin	533G	EB-30	78621	100-299
WILDERNESS TRL	Lago Vista	399L	WX-41	78645	21500-21599
WILDERNESS TRL	Williamson Co	223X	MG-58	78633	100-199
WILDERNESS WAY	Round Rock	378P	MQ-44	78664	1-99
WILDERNESS PATH BEND					
	Cedar Park	374U	MH-43	78613	3900-4099
WILDER RIDGE	Austin	494C	MH-33	78759	5700-5799
WILDFIRE	Leander	342X	MC-46	78641	1900-1999
WILDFLOWER CV	Bastrop Co	741L	MX-8	78612	100-199
WILDFLOWER DR	Round Rock	376R	MM-44	78664	1500-1699
WILDFLOWER LN	Georgetown	257T	MN-55	78626	300-699
WILDFLOWER LN	Travis Co	522W	MC-28	78733	10000-10099
	Travis Co	521Z	MB-28	78733	10100-10299
WILDFLOWER TRL	Williamson Co	378T	MQ-43	78664	1-99
WILD FOXGLOVE RD	Travis Co	517J	WS-29	78669	5400-5699
WILDGROVE DR	Austin	614B	MG-21	78704	2400-2599
WILD HORSE CV	Travis Co	518N	WU-29	78669	4700-4899
WILD HORSE LN	Round Rock	375R	MK-44	78681	1700-1799
WILD HORSE WAY	Georgetown	226E	ML-60	78633	100-199
WILDHORSE CREEK	Buda	732W	MC-7	78610	100-399
WILD IRIS LN	Travis Co	436W	ML-37	78727	4200-4299
WILDLIFE RUN	Williamson Co	374W	MG-43	78613	2300-2699
WILD LILY CV	Travis Co	532Q	MZ-29	78621	17700-17799
WILD OAK CIR	Austin	464G	MH-36	78759	6600-6699
WILD ONION DR	Austin	674R	MH-14	78744	7200-7799
WILD ORCHARD DR	Pflugerville	437M	MP-38	78660	1600-1699
WILD ORCHARD DR	Williamson Co	343W	ME-46	78641	2600-2699
WILD PETUNIA WAY	Pflugerville	438X	MQ-37	78660	800-999
WILD PLUM CIR	Georgetown	196W	ML-61	78628	100-199
WILD PLUM CT	Austin	524P	MG-29	78731	4300-4399
WILD PLUM WAY	Hays Co	669N	WW-14	78737	100-199
WILDRIDGE CIR	Austin	494R	MH-32	78759	4300-4399
WILDRIDGE DR	Austin	494R	MH-32	78759	8700-9199
WILD ROCK CV	Travis Co	491T	MA-31	78732	3100-3199
WILDROSE DR	Austin	586F	ML-24	78721	1800-1899
WILD ROSE DR	Georgetown	225H	MK-60	78633	100-199
WILD ROSE DR	Hays Co	669P	WW-14	78737	100-999
WILD ROSE TRL	Cedar Park	403E	ME-42	78613	600-899
WILD SENNA DR E	Travis Co	467N	MN-35	78660	100-399
WILD SENNA DR W	Travis Co	467J	MN-35	78660	100-399
WILD TURKEY CV	Hays Co	669N	WW-14	78737	100-199
WILD TURKEY DR	Travis Co	733B	ME-9	78652	13100-13299
WILD TURKEY LN	Georgetown	225F	MJ-60	78633	100-199
WILD TURKEY PASS	Travis Co	490Z	WZ-31	78734	13700-13999
WILD VINE CV	Round Rock	378W	MQ-43	78665	1400-1499
WILDWATER WAY	Williamson Co	375T	MJ-43	78681	9000-9099
WILD WIND CV	Buda	732X	MC-7	78610	100-199
WILDWIND PT	Travis Co	554N	MG-26	78746	1-99
WILDWOOD CIR	Travis Co	577V	WT-22	78720	10800-10899
WILDWOOD CV	Lago Vista	399K	WW-41	78645	21500-21599
WILDWOOD DR	Georgetown	225Y	MK-58	78633	100-499
WILDWOOD DR	Round Rock	406J	ML-41	78681	1500-1799
WILDWOOD RD	Austin	555Z	MK-25	78722	4100-4299
WILDWOOD TRL	Travis Co	460R	WZ-35	78734	15700-15899
WILDWOOD CROSSING					
	Williamson Co	194G	MH-63	78633	1000-1199
WILDWOOD HILLS LN	Hays Co	669Q	WX-14	78737	9700-10599
WILEY ST	Hutto	349M	MT-47	78634	100-799
WILEY WAY	Austin	705A	MJ-12	78747	8600-9099
WILHELM ST	Bastrop	745B	EE-9	78602	600-699
WILKE DR	Austin	614F	MG-21	78704	2300-2599
WILKE LN	Pflugerville	408Y	MR-40	78660	19100-19599
WILKE RIDGE LN	Pflugerville	437H	MP-39	78660	17600-17699
	Pflugerville	438A	MQ-39	78660	17700-18099
WILKIE LN	Weir	258C	MR-57	78626	1-199
WILKS AVE	Austin	556B	ML-27	78752	900-1199
WILL LN	Hutto	379G	MT-45	78634	100-399
WILLAMETTE DR	Austin	556M	MM-26	78723	6500-6899
WILLBERT RD	Austin	555Y	MK-25	78751	3900-3999
WILLERS WAY	Austin	673J	ME-14	78748	9700-9999
WILLET DR	Hays Co	732E	MC-9	78610	200-399
WILLET TRL	Austin	643W	ME-16	78745	7900-8199
WILLFIELD DR	Austin	526H	MM-30	78753	10100-10299
WILLHEATHER GLEN	Austin	493G	MF-33	78750	8300-8399
WILLIAM ANDERSON DR	Pflugerville	408S	MQ-40	78660	18500-18799
WILLIAM BARTON DR	Austin	584X	MG-22	78746	2100-2299
WILLIAM CANNON DR E	Austin	644X	MG-16	78745	100-699
	Austin	674H	MH-15	78744	1600-4899
	Austin	675J	MJ-14	78744	4900-7099
WILLIAM CANNON DR W	Austin	644S	MG-16	78745	100-899
	Austin	643V	MF-16	78745	900-3499
	Austin	643J	ME-17	78749	3500-3799
	Austin	642B	MC-18	78749	3800-5699
	Austin	612Y	MC-19	78749	5700-6399
	Austin	612J	MC-20	78735	6400-7499
WILLIAM HARRISON CT	Travis Co	530K	MU-29	78653	13300-13399
WILLIAM HARRISON ST	Travis Co	530K	MU-29	78653	12600-12799
WILLIAM HIGGINS DR	Bastrop Co	776R	EH-5	78602	100-199
WILLIAM KENNEDY DR	Austin	466F	ML-36	78727	13500-13598 E
WILLIAMS DR	Georgetown	256U	MM-55	78628	1100-3499
	Georgetown	256E	ML-57	78628	3501-3999 O
	Georgetown	225T	MJ-58	78633	4500-4899
	Williamson Co	256E	ML-57	78628	3500-3998 E
	Williamson Co	256E	ML-57	78628	4000-4099
	Williamson Co	255D	MK-57	78628	4100-4499
	Williamson Co	225T	MJ-58	78633	4900-5899
WILLIAMS LN	Bastrop Co	711K	MW-11	78612	100-299
WILLIAMS ST	Austin	525Y	MK-28	78752	600-799

STREET NAME	CITY or COUNTY	MAPSCO GRID	AUSTIN GRID	ZIP CODE	BLOCK RANGE O/E
WILLIAMS ST	Elgin	534S	EC-28	78621	300-499
WILLIAMS WAY	Cedar Park	374V	MH-43	78613	400-1199
WILLIAMS WAY	Williamson Co	379X	MS-43	78634	100-199
WILLIAMSBURG CIR	Austin	524D	MH-30	78731	3700-3899
WILLIAM SCOTSMAN	Georgetown	227X	MN-58	78626	None
WILLIAMSON CV	Elgin	533F	EA-30	78621	100-199
WILLIAMSON RD	Caldwell Co	796X	ML-1	78610	None
	Creedmoor	765S	MJ-4	78610	5300-6899
	Creedmoor	795C	MK-3	78610	6900-7499
	Hays Co	794H	MH-3	78610	100-1199
	Hays Co	764Z	MH-4	78610	1200-1799
	Mustang Ridge	795C	MK-3	78610	7500-8598 E
	Mustang Ridge	796X	ML-1	78610	None
	Niederwald	794Q	MH-2	78610	None
	Travis Co	795C	MK-3	78610	7501-8599 O
	Travis Co	796J	ML-2	78610	8600-9399
WILLIAMSON CREEK DR	Travis Co	610R	WZ-20	78736	7400-8399
WILLIAMS RIDGE WAY	Austin	524K	MG-29	78731	6400-6499
WILLIAM WALLACE WAY	Austin	528K	MQ-29	78754	6800-7099
WILLIE DR	Pflugerville	439T	MS-37	78660	18600-18699
WILLIE MAY WAY	Bastrop Co	621Y	MX-19	78621	100-199
WILLIE MAYS LN	Round Rock	378E	MQ-45	78665	3800-3899
WILLIFORD LN	Travis Co	738A	MQ-9	78617	9300-9599
WILLIS ST E	Leander	312Y	MD-49	78641	100-299
WILLIS ST W	Leander	312X	MC-49	78641	100-399
WILLIS CREEK CT	Georgetown	195X	MJ-60	78633	100-199
WILLOW CV	Lago Vista	399L	WX-41	78645	8800-8899
WILLOW CV	Round Rock	377T	MN-43	78664	3100-3199
WILLOW CV	Williamson Co	318F	MQ-51	78634	200-299
WILLOW DR	Williamson Co	318B	MQ-51	76574	100-199
WILLOW LN	Cedar Park	372H	MD-45	78613	1900-1999
WILLOW LN	Georgetown	256T	ML-55	78628	1600-2099
WILLOW LN	Taylor	352C	MZ-48	76574	2200-2399
WILLOW ST	Austin	615A	MJ-21	78701	500-599
	Austin	615B	MJ-21	78702	800-1599
	Austin	615G	MK-21	78702	1600-2799
WILLOW ST	Pflugerville	468A	MQ-36	78660	100-699
WILLOW WAY	Austin	674H	MH-15	78744	6600-6699
WILLOW WAY	Round Rock	377W	MN-43	78664	1500-1799
	Round Rock	377X	MN-43	78664	2000-2699
WILLOW BAY RD	Austin	678E	MQ-15	78617	12400-12499
WILLOWBEND CV	Round Rock	376M	MM-44	78664	500-599
WILLOW BEND DR	Austin	466Y	MM-34	78758	12300-12499
WILLOWBEND DR	Round Rock	376H	MM-45	78664	1900-2099
WILLOW BLUFF DR	Pflugerville	437H	MP-39	78660	1300-1799
WILLOWBRIDGE CIR	Austin	554Q	MH-26	78703	2900-2999
WILLOWBROOK DR	Austin	585D	MK-24	78722	3800-3999
WILLOWBROOK DR	Cedar Park	373U	MF-43	78613	1100-1299
WILLOWBROOK DR	Hutto	379H	MT-45	78634	100-499
WILLOW BROOK TRL	Taylor	322Q	MZ-50	76574	1200-1499
WILLOW CITY VALLEY	Hays Co	762Z	MD-4	78610	100-299
WILLOW CREEK DR	Austin	615X	MJ-19	78741	1600-2299
WILLOW CREEK DR	Leander	342H	MD-48	78641	1100-1499
WILLOW HILL DR	Austin	615U	MK-19	78741	2400-2599
WILLOWICK DR	Austin	495S	MJ-31	78759	8600-8899
WILLOWMOUNT CT	Travis Co	552Q	MD-26	78746	300-399
WILLOW OAK LN	Williamson Co	375Q	MK-44	78681	16700-16999
WILLOWOOD CIR	Austin	554Q	MH-26	78703	3000-3099
WILLOW RUN	Williamson Co	194Z	MH-61	78633	100-199
WILLOWRUN CV	Austin	644D	MH-18	78704	3400-3499
WILLOWRUN DR	Austin	644D	MH-18	78704	3400-3499
WILLOW SPRINGS RD	Austin	644D	MH-18	78704	3400-3699
	Austin	644G	MH-18	78745	4100-4399
WILLOW TANK DR	Austin	404J	MF-41	78717	14100-14299
WILLOW TRAIL CT	Round Rock	407F	MN-42	78664	1100-1199
WILLOW VISTA DR	Travis Co	408Q	MR-41	78660	3700-3799
WILLOW WALK CV	Hays Co	669T	WW-13	78737	100-299
WILLOW WALK DR	Pflugerville	407Z	MP-40	78660	400-799
WILLOWWICK CIR	Pflugerville	438N	MQ-38	78660	1100-1199
WILLOW WILD DR	Austin	466U	MM-34	78758	12300-12499
WILLOW WOOD DR	Pflugerville	438S	MQ-37	78660	300-699
WILL ROGERS LN	Austin	466G	MM-36	78727	13400-13799
WILL SMITH CIR	Williamson Co	348R	MR-47	78634	500-599
WILL SMITH DR	Williamson Co	348R	MR-47	78634	100-199
WILMA RUDOLPH RD	Austin	702D	MD-12	78748	2000-2599
WILMES DR	Austin	555C	MK-27	78752	300-699
WILMINGTON DR	Austin	557Z	MP-25	78724	6900-6999
WILMONT CV	Williamson Co	405P	MJ-41	78717	15500-15599
WILSHIRE BLVD	Austin	555Z	MK-25	78722	1100-1799
WILSHIRE PKWY	Austin	555Z	MK-25	78722	4200-4299
WILSON AVE	Lago Vista	458L	WV-35	78645	2400-2999
WILSON RD	Travis Co	441C	MX-39	78615	20400-20499
WILSON ST	Austin	614R	MH-20	78704	2000-2799
	Austin	614U	MH-19	78704	2800-2999
	Austin	644C	MH-18	78704	3600-3899
WILSON ST	Bastrop	745B	EE-9	78602	1200-1899
	Bastrop	715X	EE-10	78602	1900-2099
WILSON ST	Taylor	322Z	MZ-49	76574	700-799
WILSON WAY	Cedar Park	402Z	MD-40	78613	1900-1999
WILSON HEIGHTS DR	Travis Co	583J	ME-23	78746	1200-1599
WILSON PARKE AVE	Austin	462P	MC-35	78726	11400-12699
WILTON CIR	Austin	643L	MF-17	78745	6600-6699
WILTSHIRE CV	Williamson Co	408D	MR-42	78634	1000-1099
WILTSHIRE DR	Travis Co	467P	MN-35	78660	800-899
WILTSHIRE DR	Williamson Co	408D	MR-42	78634	100-699
WIMBERLEY ST	Hutto	349U	MT-46	78634	100-499
WIMBERLY CV	Travis Co	582A	MC-24	78735	8900-9099
WIMBERLY LN	Travis Co	581D	MB-24	78735	1900-1999
	Travis Co	582A	MC-24	78735	2000-2799
WIMBLEDON DR	Travis Co	557B	MN-27	78754	4800-5299
WINCHELSEA CT	Austin	463B	ME-36	78750	10600-10699
WINCHELSEA DR	Austin	463B	ME-36	78750	10600-10899
WINCHESTER CT	Austin	644L	MH-17	78745	200-399
WINCHESTER CV	Lago Vista	399G	WX-42	78645	21600-21699
WINCHESTER DR	Cedar Park	374Q	MH-44	78613	3801-3899 O
WINCHESTER DR	Georgetown	287S	MN-52	78626	2200-2399
WINCHESTER DR	Hays Co	577J	WS-23	78620	100-299
WINCHESTER DR	Hays Co	577E	WS-24	78620	400-699
WINCHESTER DR	Round Rock	407G	MP-42	78665	2900-2999
WINCHESTER DR	Travis Co	577E	WS-24	78620	300-399
WINCHESTER RD	Travis Co	522X	MC-28	78733	9300-9599
WINDBERRY CT	Williamson Co	347A	MN-48	78665	4100-4299
WINDBERRY PATH	Williamson Co	347A	MN-48	78665	1800-1999
WINDBORNE WAY	Buda	763E	ME-6	78610	700-799
WINDBOURNE WAY	Cedar Park	372K	MC-44	78613	1900-1999
WIND CAVE DR	Taylor	322R	MZ-50	76574	4100-4299
WIND CAVE TRL	Austin	704A	MG-12	78747	10000-10299

STREET NAME	CITY or COUNTY	MAPSCO GRID	AUSTIN GRID	ZIP CODE	BLOCK RANGE O/E
WINDCLIFF WAY	Austin	672Y	MD-13	78748	2900-2999
WINDCREST CV	Travis Co	408G	MR-42	78664	100-199
WINDCREST DR	Travis Co	408C	MR-42	78664	1400-1499
	Williamson Co	408C	MR-42	78664	1300-1399
WINDEMERE EAST	Williamson Co	313Y	MF-49	78641	1-99
WINDEMERE WEST	Williamson Co	313X	ME-49	78641	100-199
WINDERMERE DR	Pflugerville	437T	MN-37	78660	15800-16299
	Travis Co	437T	MN-37	78660	16300-16399
WINDERMERE MEADOWS	Austin	464F	MG-36	78759	11200-11799
WINDFLOWER LN	Williamson Co	255H	MK-57	78628	4100-4199
WINDHILL LOOP	Round Rock	345T	MJ-46	78681	3600-3699
WIND HOLLOW DR	Georgetown	225Y	MK-58	78633	300-399
WINDING TRL	Austin	643C	MF-18	78745	4900-5099
WINDING WAY	Round Rock	408J	MQ-41	78664	3200-3399
	Travis Co	408K	MQ-41	78660	None
	Williamson Co	408J	MQ-41	78664	3400-3699
WINDING BROOK DR	Austin	702B	MC-12	78748	2600-2899
WINDING CREEK CV	Travis Co	581H	MB-24	78735	3200-3299
WINDING CREEK DR	Travis Co	581H	MB-24	78735	3200-3599
	Travis Co	582J	MC-23	78735	3600-3799
WINDING CREEK PL	Williamson Co	346G	MM-48	78665	900-1199
WINDING CREEK RD	Travis Co	609N	WW-20	78736	12700-13399
WINDING OAK CIR	Austin	463L	MF-35	78750	9900-9999
WINDING OAK DR	Williamson Co	313P	ME-50	78641	100-699
WINDING OAK TRL	Austin	463L	MF-35	78750	9400-9599
WINDING RIDGE BLVD	Austin	494P	MG-32	78750	8000-8099
WINDING RIVER TRL	Round Rock	345K	MJ-47	78681	3200-3499
WINDING SHORE LN	Travis Co	409T	MS-40	78660	3000-3599
	Travis Co	409X	MS-40	78660	None
WINDING WALK	Austin	495X	MJ-31	78757	8600-8699
WINDLEDGE DR	Austin	644L	MH-17	78745	600-799
WINDLESS WAY	Travis Co	439P	MS-38	78660	None
WINDMILL	Lakeway	519B	WW-30	78734	None
WINDMILL CIR	Leander	312X	MC-49	78641	100-299
WINDMILL CIR	Travis Co	467Z	MP-34	78660	13800-13899
WINDMILL CV	Georgetown	256L	MM-56	78628	100-199
WINDMILL DR	Bastrop Co	709Q	MT-11	78612	None
WINDMILL RD	Hays Co	638P	WU-17	78620	1000-1099
WINDMILL WAY	Hays Co	762M	MD-5	78610	1-599
WINDMILL RANCH AVE	Travis Co	409P	MS-41	78660	20800-20999
WINDMILL RIDGE ST	Travis Co	409P	MS-41	78660	20700-20999
WINDOAK DR	Austin	615T	MJ-19	78741	1700-1799
WINDRIDGE CV	Austin	464P	MG-35	78759	7000-7099
WIND RIDGE CV	Williamson Co	254T	MG-55	78628	100-299
WINDRIDGE DR	Austin	464P	MG-35	78759	10700-10899
WINDRIDGE DR	Niederwald	795X	MJ-1	78610	200-299
WINDRIDGE VILLAGE CV					
	Georgetown	286H	MM-54	78626	300-399
WINDRIFT WAY	Austin	643V	MF-16	78745	6600-7199
WINDRIFT WAY	Round Rock	407J	MN-41	78664	1600-2499
WIND RIVER RD	Austin	465T	MJ-34	78759	4600-5299
WINDRUSH DR	Williamson Co	434R	MH-38	78729	7500-7799
WINDSHILL CIR	Austin	554Q	MH-26	78703	2900-2999
WINDSLOW CT	Austin	556Q	MM-26	78723	6300-6399
WIND SONG CV	Williamson Co	433P	ME-38	78750	11700-11799
WINDSONG DR	Bastrop Co	709L	MT-11	78612	None
WINDSONG TRL	Round Rock	407J	MN-41	78664	1500-2099
WINDSONG TRL	West Lake Hills	553Y	MF-25	78746	600-899
WINDSOR RD	Austin	584H	MH-24	78703	1200-3199
	Austin	554X	MG-25	78703	3200-3799
WINDSOR RD	Round Rock	406M	MM-41	78664	500-899
WINDSOR RD E	Austin	584H	MH-24	78703	2200-2399
WINDSOR CASTLE DR	Pflugerville	408X	MQ-40	78660	600-999
WINDSOR HILL DR	Pflugerville	468E	MQ-36	78660	800-999
WIND SPIRIT	Williamson Co	375K	MJ-44	78681	1800-1899
WINDSTONE CT	Travis Co	529D	MT-30	78653	13500-13599
WINDSWEPT CV	Austin	613Y	MF-19	78745	2700-2799
WINDSWEPT DR	Travis Co	550M	WZ-26	78733	2200-2399
WIND TREE LN	Elgin	532H	MZ-30	78621	18300-18499
WIND VALLEY WAY	Pflugerville	439J	MS-38	78660	18600-18899
WINDVIEW LN	Travis Co	409P	MS-41	78660	2700-2799
WINDWARD DR	Austin	556T	ML-25	78723	5500-5699
WINDWOOD CT	Village of the Hills	519T	WW-28	78738	1-99
WINDY CV	Round Rock	406E	ML-42	78681	1400-1499
WINDY CV	Travis Co	523V	MF-28	78746	4400-4499
WINDY LN	Williamson Co	413F	EA-42	76574	1-399
WINDY TRL	Austin	496P	ML-32	78758	900-1199
WINDY BROOK DR	Austin	586C	MM-24	78723	4600-4699
WINDY HARBOR DR	Travis Co	490M	WZ-32	78734	3300-3599
WINDY HILL RD	Williamson Co	288A	MQ-54	78626	1-899
WINDY OAKS CV	Williamson Co	403S	ME-40	78613	2100-2199
WINDY PARK CIR	Round Rock	407J	MN-41	78664	1700-1799
WINDY PARK CT	Round Rock	407J	MN-41	78664	1600-1699
WINDY PARK DR	Round Rock	407J	MN-41	78664	1600-1999
WINDY RIDGE RD	Travis Co	433S	ME-37	78726	11800-11899
	Travis Co	432R	MD-38	78726	11900-12199
	Travis Co	433N	ME-38	78726	12200-12299
WINDY SHORES LOOP	Travis Co	488P	WU-32	78669	800-1099
WINDY TERRACE	Cedar Park	432M	MD-38	78613	2000-2099
WINDY TRAIL CIR	Austin	496P	ML-32	78758	10700-10799
WINDY VALLEY DR	Travis Co	340A	WY-48	78641	22900-24099
	Travis Co	309Z	WX-49	78641	None
WINDY WALK CV	Travis Co	487M	WT-32	78669	1700-1899
WINECUP CT	Leander	342K	MC-47	78641	1100-1199
WINECUP DR	Leander	342P	MC-47	78641	1200-1299
WINECUP PATH	Bastrop Co	709M	MT-11	78612	100-199
WINECUP TRL N	Cedar Park	373W	ME-43	78613	100-199
WINECUP TRL S	Cedar Park	403A	ME-42	78613	100-499
WINECUP WAY	Georgetown	225M	MK-59	78633	100-199
WINECUP WAY	Hays Co	669N	WW-14	78737	100-399
WINECUP HOLLOW	Austin	494S	MG-31	78750	7200-7299
WINECUP MALLOW TRL	Travis Co	532K	MY-29	78621	13000-13299
WINEDALE DR	Austin	464G	MH-36	78759	6900-7099
WINFIELD CV	Austin	614S	MG-19	78704	3600-3699
WINFIELD DR	Austin	614P	MG-20	78704	3400-3599
WINFIELD RIDGE DR	Travis Co	704G	MH-12	78747	None
WINFLO DR	Austin	584R	MH-23	78703	600-899
WING RD	Austin	612Y	MD-19	78749	4900-5099
WINGATE WAY	Austin	466E	ML-36	78727	13000-13199
WINGED ELM DR	Travis Co	432P	MC-38	78613	3200-3299
WINGFEATHER DR	Austin	675A	MJ-15	78744	6000-6299
WINGFOOT CV	Georgetown	226M	MM-59	78628	30100-30199
WINGREEN LOOP	Travis Co	519Q	WX-29	78738	1-99
WINNEBAGO LN	Austin	645P	MJ-17	78744	4700-5299
WINNERS RIBBON CIR	Pflugerville	409J	MS-41	78660	1700-1799
WINNING COLORS	Hays Co	638V	WV-16	78737	100-499
WINNIPEG CV	Austin	464U	MH-34	78759	6700-6799

STREET NAME	CITY or COUNTY	MAPSCO GRID	AUSTIN GRID	ZIP CODE	BLOCK RANGE O/E
WINSLOW CV	Lago Vista	458L	WV-35	78645	21100-21299
WINSLOW DR	Williamson Co	343X	ME-46	78641	2500-2899
WINSOME CT	Austin	554F	MG-27	78731	3500-3599
WINSTEAD AVE	Round Rock	376U	MM-43	78664	100-199
WINSTED LN	Austin	584L	MH-23	78703	700-2599
WINSTON CT	Austin	554H	MH-27	78731	2800-2899
WINTER DR	Georgetown	195V	MK-61	78633	100-299
WINTERBERRY DR	Austin	493V	MF-31	78750	6500-7199
WINTERBORNE CT	Austin	528K	MQ-29	78754	11600-11699
WINTERCREEPER CV	Travis Co	581M	MB-23	78735	9000-9099
WINTERFIELD DR	Williamson Co	408D	MR-42	78634	100-699
WINTERGREEN HILL	Austin	463D	MF-36	78750	10800-11199
WINTER HAVEN RD	Austin	705A	MJ-12	78747	8400-8999
WINTER PARK RD	Austin	613D	MF-21	78746	1800-1999
WINTERS CV	Austin	678N	MQ-14	78617	13100-13199
WINTERSTEIN DR	Austin	673B	ME-15	78745	8300-8699
WINTHROP CV	Lago Vista	458G	WV-36	78645	2500-2699
WINWICK WAY	Austin	466K	ML-35	78727	13000-13199
	Austin	466F	ML-36	78727	13200-13399
WIPPLE TREE CV	Williamson Co	433L	MF-38	78750	12300-12399
WIRE RD	Travis Co	401H	MB-42	78641	12200-12499
	Travis Co	402A	MC-42	78641	12500-13299
	Travis Co	372X	MC-43	78641	13300-13599
WIRTH RD	Travis Co	703N	ME-11	78748	11900-12199
	Travis Co	703N	ME-11	78652	12200-12499
WIRTZ AVE	Austin	614L	MH-20	78704	2100-2399
WISEMAN DR	Pflugerville	437H	MP-39	78660	17400-17799
WISHBONE DR	Lago Vista	429N	WW-38	78645	20800-20999
WISHEK CV	Travis Co	492U	MD-31	78730	5300-5399
WISHING WELL DR	Austin	674A	MG-15	78745	7100-7299
WISTERIA CIR	Austin	526P	ML-29	78753	1000-1099
WISTERIA DR	Williamson Co	257F	MN-57	78626	100-299
WISTERIA TRL	Austin	526P	ML-29	78753	1000-1099
WISTERIA WAY	Round Rock	377X	MN-43	78664	2400-2499
WISTERIA VALLEY DR	Austin	670D	WZ-15	78739	7400-7999
WISTERWOOD ST	Williamson Co	434B	MG-39	78729	13300-13499
WISTFUL CV	Williamson Co	434P	MG-38	78729	12500-12599
WITHAM LN	Austin	644L	MH-17	78745	4500-4599
WITHERS WAY	Austin	466Q	MM-35	78727	12700-13099
WITSOME LOOP	Austin	615X	MJ-19	78741	2600-2699
WITTE CV	Williamson Co	345S	MJ-46	78681	4000-4099
WITTMER DR	Williamson Co	434Z	MH-37	78729	12600-12799
W L WALDEN DR	Georgetown	257W	MN-55	78626	100-399
WOLD DR	Hutto	379M	MT-44	78634	None
WOLF CT	Austin	523M	MF-29	78731	5600-5698 E
WOLF LN	Bastrop Co	709P	MS-11	78617	7900-8399
	Travis Co	679M	MT-14	78617	4900-6899
	Travis Co	709G	MT-12	78617	6900-7899
WOLF RD	Georgetown	286E	ML-54	78628	1-599
WOLFCREEK PASS	Austin	612S	MC-19	78749	6400-6999
WOLF CREEK WAY	Williamson Co	408F	MQ-42	78664	100-499
WOLF JAW CV	Williamson Co	434U	MH-37	78729	8100-8199
WOLF RANCH PKWY	Georgetown	256X	ML-55	78628	300-499
	Georgetown	286B	ML-54	78628	500-2399
WOLF RANCH RD	Travis Co	552E	MC-27	78733	300-499
WOLF RUN	Austin	612Y	MD-19	78749	5300-5599
WOLFTRAP DR	Austin	672F	MC-15	78749	10000-10499
WOLKIN CV	Round Rock	376A	ML-45	78681	2700-2799
WOLLE LN	Round Rock	376B	ML-45	78681	100-199
WOLVERINE CV	Georgetown	257K	MN-56	78626	1700-1799
WOLVERINE PASS	Bastrop	744K	EC-8	78602	301-399 O
WOLVERTON DR	Austin	644L	MH-17	78745	400-599
WOMACK DR	Travis Co	401S	MA-40	78641	10100-10299
WOMMACK RD	Austin	673N	ME-14	78748	10200-10499
WONDER DR	Round Rock	376T	ML-43	78681	700-1099
	Round Rock	376T	ML-43	78681	1100-1299
WONSLEY DR E	Austin	526N	ML-29	78753	100-799
WONSLEY DR W	Austin	526N	ML-29	78753	100-299
WOOD CT	Georgetown	285M	MK-53	78628	100-199
WOOD CV	Williamson Co	196K	ML-62	78628	200-299
WOOD ST	Austin	584V	MH-22	78703	600-799
WOOD TRL	West Lake Hills	583F	ME-24	78746	100-199
WOOD ACRE LN	Travis Co	522T	MC-28	78733	1400-2199
WOODALL DR	Georgetown	226Q	MM-59	78628	100-199
WOODBAY PARKE DR	Austin	462Q	MD-35	78726	8000-8099
WOODBINE CIR	Georgetown	256N	ML-56	78628	2500-2599
WOOD BINE DR	Austin	644K	MG-17	78745	300-599
WOODBRIAR LN	Austin	556Z	MM-25	78723	3300-3499
WOODBRIDGE DR	Austin	554Q	MH-26	78703	3100-3199
WOODBROOK CIR	Austin	495S	MJ-31	78759	3800-3899
WOODBROOK TRL	Hays Co	763Y	MF-4	78610	100-399
WOODBURY DR	Austin	644C	MH-18	78704	3700-4099
WOOD CHASE TRL	Travis Co	436U	MM-37	78728	2400-2599
WOODCHESTER LN	Austin	465H	MK-36	78727	3700-3999
WOOD CLIFF DR	Austin	643Z	MF-16	78745	7400-7699
WOOD CREEK DR	Cedar Park	372Q	MD-44	78613	1000-1499
WOODCREEK RD	Austin	642C	MD-18	78749	4700-5199
WOODCREST CT	Georgetown	285Z	MK-52	78628	100-199
WOODCREST DR	Austin	464L	MH-35	78759	6000-6899
WOODCREST RD	Williamson Co	224F	MG-60	78633	1-199
WOODCROFT DR	Austin	642R	MD-17	78749	7700-7999
WOODCUTTER CT	Bastrop Co	743A	EA-9	78602	100-199
WOODCUTTERS WAY	Travis Co	554E	MG-27	78746	3400-3999
WOODDUCK CV	Leander	342K	MC-47	78641	1000-1099
WOODDUCK TRL	Leander	342K	MC-47	78641	900-999
WOODED WAY	Round Rock	378P	MQ-44	78664	1-99
WOODED LAKE CT	Travis Co	521J	MA-29	78732	12800-12899
WOODFIELD DR	Austin	526A	ML-30	78758	1200-1299
WOODFORD DR	Cedar Park	372C	MD-45	78613	400-599
WOODGLEN CV	Austin	526D	MM-30	78753	10200-10299
WOODGLEN DR	Austin	526D	MM-30	78753	10000-10199
WOOD GLEN DR	Round Rock	375H	MK-45	78681	1900-1999
	Round Rock	376E	ML-45	78681	2000-2099
WOODGREEN CV	Austin	643D	MF-18	78745	5100-5199
WOODGREEN DR	Round Rock	406N	ML-41	78681	1500-1799
WOODHALL CV	Williamson Co	405P	MJ-41	78717	8000-8099
WOODHAVEN CT	Williamson Co	347A	MN-48	78665	1900-1999
WOODHAVEN DR	Austin	526G	MM-30	78753	10000-10199
WOODHAVEN PATH	Williamson Co	346H	MM-48	78665	1500-1599
WOODHAVEN TRL	Williamson Co	347A	MN-48	78665	4100-4299
WOODHILL DR	Round Rock	406N	ML-41	78681	1500-1699
WOODHILL PATH	Austin	674C	MH-15	78744	6600-6699
	Austin	674G	MH-15	78744	6700-6799
WOOD HOLLOW CT	Bastrop Co	743A	EA-9	78602	100-199
WOODHOLLOW CV	Cedar Park	403N	ME-41	78613	1200-1299
WOOD HOLLOW DR	Austin	524H	MH-30	78731	6700-7499
	Austin	525E	MJ-30	78731	7500-7799

STREET NAME	CITY or COUNTY	MAPSCO GRID	AUSTIN GRID	ZIP CODE	BLOCK RANGE O/E
WOODHOLLOW LN	Cedar Park	403J	ME-41	78613	800-1199
WOODHOLLOW LN	Georgetown	195J	MJ-62	78633	100-799
WOODHOLLOW TRL	Williamson Co	378N	MQ-44	78665	1-99
WOODHUE CT	Austin	643U	MF-16	78745	7100-7199
WOODHUE DR	Austin	643V	MF-16	78745	6100-7199
WOOD IBIS CIR	Williamson Co	433R	MF-38	78750	12200-12399
WOODLAKE CIR	Travis Co	551H	MB-27	78733	300-399
WOODLAKE CV	Travis Co	551D	MB-27	78733	9900-9999
WOODLAKE DR	Georgetown	225Y	MK-58	78633	100-299
WOODLAKE TRL	Travis Co	551D	MB-27	78733	9900-9999
WOODLAND AVE	Austin	615N	MJ-20	78704	600-1499
	Austin	615U	MK-19	78741	1500-2299
WOODLAND CT	Bastrop Co	776G	EH-6	78602	100-199
WOODLAND DR	Cedar Park	372L	MD-44	78613	1700-1999
WOODLAND LN	Round Rock	378P	MQ-44	78664	1-99
WOODLAND LOOP	Round Rock	378P	MQ-44	78664	1-99
WOODLAND RD	Georgetown	256N	ML-56	78628	100-199
WOODLAND TRL	Williamson Co	343U	MF-46	78641	100-199
	Williamson Co	373C	MF-45	78641	None
WOODLAND HILLS CV	Travis Co	521C	MB-30	78732	None
WOODLAND HILLS TRL	Travis Co	521G	MB-30	78732	None
WOODLAND OAKS CT	Austin	645W	MJ-16	78744	5300-5399
WOODLAND PARK	Williamson Co	224H	MH-60	78633	100-599
	Williamson Co	225E	MJ-60	78633	None
WOODLANDS DR	Bastrop Co	743A	EA-9	78602	100-499
WOODLAND VILLAGE DR	Austin	433R	MF-38	78750	9900-9999
	Williamson Co	433R	MF-38	78750	10000-10299
WOODLAWN BLVD	Austin	584L	MH-23	78703	1300-1799
	Austin	584H	MH-24	78703	2300-2399
WOODLAWN DR	Pflugerville	438P	MQ-38	78660	1200-1299
WOODLAWN ST	Taylor	322U	MZ-49	76574	2800-3199
WOODLEIGH ST	Austin	614Z	MH-19	78704	3400-3499
WOODLEY RD	Leander	342B	MC-48	78641	100-399
WOODLIEF TRL	Round Rock	376H	MM-45	78664	900-1199
WOOD LILY TRL	Travis Co	532Q	MZ-29	78621	12600-12999
WOODMERE ST	Williamson Co	434K	MG-38	78729	12800-12899
WOOD MESA CT	Williamson Co	346L	MM-47	78665	700-799
WOOD MESA DR	Williamson Co	346L	MM-47	78665	800-1099
WOODMONT AVE	Austin	584C	MH-24	78703	2000-2699
WOODMONT DR	Georgetown	286X	ML-52	78628	100-399
WOODMOOR CIR	Austin	586M	MM-23	78721	4500-4599
WOODMOOR DR	Austin	586M	MM-23	78721	5100-5399
WOODPECKER TRL	Travis Co	426L	WR-38	78669	26600-26799
WOOD RANCH RD	Williamson Co	285L	MK-53	78628	1-799
WOOD RIDGE CV	Williamson Co	403S	ME-40	78613	2100-2199
WOOD RIDGE LN	Williamson Co	403S	ME-40	78613	900-999
WOOD ROCK DR	Round Rock	406E	ML-42	78681	1200-1699
WOODROW AVE	Austin	555F	MJ-27	78756	4800-5999
	Austin	525L	MK-29	78757	6000-7899
WOODROW ST	Austin	585C	MK-24	78705	3400-3599
WOODS BLVD	Round Rock	376J	ML-44	78681	1300-1899
WOODS CV	Round Rock	376J	ML-44	78681	2000-2099
WOODS LN	Cedar Park	342Z	MD-46	78613	1-399
WOODS LOOP	Dripping Springs	667T	WS-13	78620	100-2299
WOODSHIRE DR	Austin	673J	ME-14	78748	9500-9999
WOODSIDE DR	Austin	613N	ME-20	78735	4700-4899
WOODSORREL WAY	Round Rock	407C	MP-42	78665	400-599
WOOD SPRINGS LN	Round Rock	405C	MK-42	78681	3000-3099
WOODSTOCK DR	Austin	526G	MM-30	78753	9900-10199
WOODSTOCK DR	Georgetown	225Y	MK-58	78633	4900-4999
WOODSTON DR	Round Rock	375H	MK-45	78681	2100-2199
WOODSTONE N	Cedar Park	372Q	MD-44	78613	1500-1599
WOODSTONE S	Cedar Park	372Q	MD-44	78613	1500-1599
WOODSTONE CT	Cedar Park	372Q	MD-44	78613	1800-1899
WOODSTONE CV	Austin	642R	MD-17	78749	7600-7699
WOODSTONE DR	Austin	525C	MK-30	78757	8500-8699
WOODSTONE DR	Georgetown	286X	ML-52	78628	200-399
WOODSTONE SQUARE	Austin	554Q	MH-26	78703	1-199
WOOD STORK DR	Travis Co	434G	MH-39	78729	8500-8899
WOODTHORPE ST	Williamson Co	434E	MG-39	78729	13200-13299
WOODVALE DR	Williamson Co	434J	MG-38	78729	9500-9699
WOODVIEW AVE	Austin	555A	MJ-27	78756	4700-5899
	Austin	525W	MJ-28	78757	5900-6299
WOODVIEW CT	West Lake Hills	583R	MF-23	78746	100-199
WOODVIEW DR	Georgetown	286X	ML-52	78628	500-1099
WOODVIEW DR	Leander	342H	MD-48	78641	800-1199
WOODVIEW LN	Bastrop Co	743S	EA-7	78602	100-199
WOODVISTA PL	Williamson Co	347E	MN-48	78665	1700-1899
WOODWARD ST	Austin	614Z	MH-19	78704	100-499
	Austin	644D	MH-18	78704	500-799
	Austin	645A	MJ-18	78741	800-1199
	Austin	645A	MJ-18	78741	1200-2099
	Austin	645J	MJ-17	78744	2100-2299
WOODWAY	Round Rock	375V	MK-43	78681	2300-2399
WOODWAY N	Round Rock	375V	MK-43	78681	2300-2399
WOODWAY S	Round Rock	375V	MK-43	78681	2300-2399
WOODWAY DR	Austin	524C	MH-30	78731	4200-4399
WOODWAY DR	Bastrop Co	621Y	MX-19	78621	100-399
WOODWAY DR	Leander	341D	MB-48	78641	2000-2199
WOODWAY DR	Williamson Co	255Z	MK-55	78628	300-599
WOODWIND LN	Austin	496F	ML-33	78758	1600-1699
	Austin	496A	ML-33	78758	1700-1799
WOODY CV	Round Rock	378W	MQ-43	78665	3000-3099
WOODY WAY	Williamson Co	318P	MQ-50	78634	100-199
WOODY RIDGE VIEW	Travis Co	492Y	MD-31	78730	9500-9799
WOOLDRIDGE DR	Austin	584D	MH-24	78703	1400-2599
	Austin	554Z	MH-25	78703	2600-2899
WOOLY BUCKET CV	Travis Co	532Q	MZ-29	78621	12800-12899
WOOTEN DR	Austin	525L	MK-29	78757	1300-1699
	Austin	525G	MK-30	78757	1700-2199
WOOTEN ST	Cedar Park	372Z	MD-43	78613	800-999
WOOTEN PARK DR	Austin	525L	MK-29	78757	1700-1899
WORCESTER CV	Austin	463G	MF-36	78750	10200-10299
WORCHESTER CV	Travis Co	582H	MD-24	78746	6000-6099
WORDHAM DR	Austin	642R	MD-17	78749	7600-7799
WORDSWORTH DR	Austin	614S	MG-19	78704	2100-2199
WORLD OF TENNIS SQUARE					
	Lakeway	519J	WW-29	78738	1-299
WORLEY DR	Pflugerville	437D	MP-39	78660	17700-18099
WORN SOLE DR	Austin	497X	MN-31	78754	10800-11199
WRAGLER CV	Lago Vista	399G	WX-42	78645	21600-21699
WREN AVE	Austin	496M	MM-32	78753	700-799
WREN AVE	Pflugerville	468A	MQ-36	78660	100-299
WREN CIR	Cedar Park	433B	ME-39	78613	2900-2999
WREN CT	Round Rock	375V	MK-43	78681	1000-1099
WREN CV	Hutto	379R	MT-44	78634	100-199
WREN RD	Hays Co	701Q	MB-11	78652	2800-2999

STREET NAME	CITY or COUNTY	MAPSCO GRID	AUSTIN GRID	ZIP CODE	BLOCK RANGE O/E
WREN WAY	Taylor	322Y	MZ-49	76574	2000-2099
WREN VALLEY CV	West Lake Hills	553X	ME-25	78746	1-99
WRIGHT CIR	Round Rock	376G	MM-45	78664	2300-2399
WRIGHT DR	Bastrop Co	740W	MU-7	78612	100-299
WRIGHT RD	Creedmoor	734V	MH-7	78610	12300-12599
	Travis Co	734V	MH-7	78610	12600-12999
	Travis Co	764D	MH-6	78610	13000-13599
WRIGHT ST	Austin	614B	MG-21	78704	2000-2199
WRIGHT BROTHERS DR	Georgetown	256H	MM-57	78628	100-599
WRIGHTWOOD RD	Austin	585D	MK-24	78722	3900-4099
WRIGLEY LN	Round Rock	378A	MQ-45	78665	3500-3599
WROUGHT IRON DR	Austin	466K	ML-35	78727	2100-2199
WROXTON WAY	Round Rock	377N	MN-44	78664	1200-1599
WT GALLAWAY ST	Manor	530L	MV-29	78653	19300-19499
WUNN WAY	Travis Co	561C	MX-27	78621	None
WYATT CV	Lago Vista	399G	WX-42	78645	8900-8999
WYCHWOOD DR	Austin	583Y	MF-22	78746	1900-2199
WYCLIFF LN	Austin	465Q	MK-35	78727	12000-12499
WYCOMBE DR	Austin	642R	MD-17	78749	7700-7899
WYE OAK ST	Austin	673V	MF-13	78748	300-499
WYERS PL	Bastrop Co	740W	MU-7	78612	100-199
WYETH ST	Taylor	352G	MZ-48	76574	200-899
WYKEHAM DR	Austin	642R	MD-17	78749	7700-8099
WYLDWOOD RD	Travis Co	672K	MC-14	78739	3500-4399
WYLIE DR	Austin	673S	ME-13	78748	10400-10599
WYMAN CV	Williamson Co	344Z	MH-46	78681	4000-4099
WYNDEN CV	Austin	673J	ME-14	78748	9500-9599
WYNNE LN	Austin	673C	MF-15	78745	7500-8199
WYNONA AVE	Austin	525W	MJ-28	78756	5700-5899
	Austin	525W	MJ-28	78757	5900-6299
WYNSTONE LN	Austin	374Z	MH-43	78717	16200-16399
WYOMING PASS	Lago Vista	399L	WX-41	78645	21300-21699
WYOMING SPRINGS DR	Round Rock	375Z	MK-43	78681	7000-7299
	Round Rock	375C	MK-45	78681	9000-9899
	Round Rock	345K	MJ-47	78681	10900-10999
	Williamson Co	375U	MK-43	78681	7300-7399
WYOMING VALLEY DR	Austin	466L	MM-35	78727	13400-13599

No "X" Streets

Y

STREET NAME	CITY or COUNTY	MAPSCO GRID	AUSTIN GRID	ZIP CODE	BLOCK RANGE O/E
YABERS CT	Travis Co	619S	MS-19	78725	701-799 O
YACHT CT	Lakeway	519E	WW-30	78734	100-199
YACHT CLUB CV	Lakeway	518D	WV-30	78734	100-199
YACHT HARBOR DR	Travis Co	456M	WR-35	78669	800-999
YAGER LN E	Austin	496D	MM-33	78753	100-399
	Austin	497E	MN-33	78753	400-1699
	Austin	497Q	MP-32	78754	3000-4599
	Travis Co	497Q	MP-32	78754	1700-2999
	Travis Co	497Z	MP-31	78653	4600-4799
	Travis Co	527D	MP-30	78653	4800-4999
YAGER LN W	Austin	496C	MM-33	78753	200-999
YALDING DR	Travis Co	432G	MD-39	78613	2700-2799
YALE DR	Pflugerville	467D	MP-36	78660	700-899
YALE ST	Austin	585V	MK-22	78702	1900-1999
YANDALL DR	Austin	672X	MC-13	78748	2600-3199
YARBOROUGH AVE	Austin	646X	ML-16	78744	3800-3999
YARBROUGH DR	Austin	672X	MC-13	78748	11800-12099
YARMONT WAY	Austin	497F	MN-33	78753	12300-12399
YARROW CT	Travis Co	551P	MA-26	78733	10500-10599
YARROW BEND	Georgetown	314G	MH-51	78628	1400-1899
YARSA BLVD	Austin	673L	MF-14	78748	600-799
YATES AVE	Austin	525Q	MK-29	78757	6500-7699
YAUPON CIR	Lakeway	519R	WX-29	78734	1900-1999
YAUPON CV	Cedar Park	372H	MD-45	78613	500-599
YAUPON DR	Austin	494F	MG-33	78759	6200-6699
	Austin	464P	MG-35	78759	6700-7799
	Austin	464F	MG-36	78759	7900-7999
	Travis Co	464P	MG-35	78759	7800-7899
	Travis Co	464F	MG-36	78759	8000-8399
YAUPON DR	Williamson Co	349A	MS-48	78634	100-199
YAUPON LN	Georgetown	195Z	MK-61	78633	100-199
YAUPON TRL	Cedar Park	372H	MD-45	78613	1700-2399
YAUPON TRL	Round Rock	407F	MN-42	78664	2000-2099
YAUPON TRL	Travis Co	309Z	WX-49	78641	24100-24299
YAUPON CREEK DR	Lakeway	519R	WX-29	78734	1800-1899
YAUPON HOLLOW	Round Rock	407F	MN-42	78664	2100-2199
YAUPON SPRINGS CIR	Travis Co	641C	MB-18	78737	8500-8599
YAUPON VALLEY	Williamson Co	194Z	MH-61	78633	None
YAUPON VALLEY RD	West Lake Hills	583B	ME-24	78746	100-1299
	West Lake Hills	553W	ME-25	78746	1300-2099
YEARLING CV	Austin	466P	ML-35	78727	12700-12799
YEARLING LN	Pflugerville	467C	MP-36	78660	None
YEGUA CREEK RD	Williamson Co	433E	ME-39	78613	3300-3399
YELLOW BELLS PL	Georgetown	314G	MH-51	78628	200-299
YELLOW BIRD TRL	Travis Co	490V	WZ-31	78734	2100-2399
YELLOW JACKET LN	Austin	646F	ML-18	78741	2000-2399
YELLOWLEAF TRL	Travis Co	436U	MM-37	78728	14800-14999
YELLOW OAK ST	Williamson Co	434L	MH-38	78729	8500-8699
YELLOWPINE TERRACE	Austin	525E	MJ-30	78757	3000-3399
YELLOW ROSE CV	Austin	612Z	MD-19	78749	6100-6199
YELLOW ROSE TRL	Austin	612Z	MD-19	78749	4200-4699
YELLOW ROSE TRL	Cedar Park	402H	MD-42	78613	1200-1399
YELLOW ROSE TRL	Georgetown	225K	MJ-59	78633	1-199
YELLOW SAGE	Pflugerville	437U	MP-37	78660	16000-16399
	Pflugerville	437Q	MP-38	78660	16500-16599
YELLOWSTONE DR	Austin	704E	MG-12	78747	10300-10499
YELLOWSTONE DR	Taylor	322R	MZ-50	76574	800-4399
YELLOWSTONE RD	Georgetown	195V	MK-61	78633	100-199
YELLOW TAIL CV	Sunset Valley	643B	ME-18	78745	1-99
YEOMAN ST	Austin	498J	MQ-32	78660	3600-3699
YOAKUM ST	Austin	673S	ME-13	78748	1600-1699
YOGI BERRA CV	Round Rock	378E	MQ-45	78665	1400-1499
YOGI BERRA WAY	Round Rock	378E	MQ-45	78665	3400-3499
YORA DR	Travis Co	436P	ML-38	78728	14600-14799
YORK BLVD	Austin	495K	MJ-32	78759	3600-3799
YORK BRIDGE CIR	Austin	642S	MC-16	78749	5600-6599
YORK CASTLE DR	Travis Co	437K	MN-38	78660	1000-1399
YORK HILL DR	Austin	586H	MM-24	78723	4700-4999
YORKSHIRE DR	Austin	556J	ML-26	78723	1300-1499
YORKSHIRE LN	Round Rock	377N	MN-44	78664	1200-1399
YORKSHIRE ST	Pflugerville	438S	MQ-37	78660	1000-1099
YORKTOWN CV	Austin	463A	ME-36	78726	10900-10999
YORKTOWN TRL	Austin	463B	ME-36	78726	10700-10999
YOSEMITE DR	Travis Co	522P	MC-29	78733	2300-2599
YOSEMITE RD	Georgetown	195V	MK-61	78633	100-299
YOSEMITE TRL	Taylor	322R	MZ-50	76574	500-999
YOUNG LN	Travis Co	641J	MA-17	78737	8100-8999
YOUNGER CT	Austin	496Y	MM-31	78753	300-399
YOUNG RANCH RD	Williamson Co	223C	MF-60	78633	100-799
	Williamson Co	193Y	MF-61	78633	None
YOUNGS PRAIRIE RD	Bastrop Co	562Z	MZ-25	78621	300-499
	Bastrop Co	563W	EA-25	78621	None
YOUNTVILLE DR	Leander	343N	ME-47	78641	1300-1399
YOUTH SPORTS ASSOCIATION RD					
	Dripping Springs	636U	WR-16	78620	None
YUCATAN LN	Austin	465Q	MK-35	78727	4200-4399
YUCCA CV	Georgetown	225H	MK-60	78633	100-199
YUCCA CV	Hays Co	669S	WW-13	78737	100-199
YUCCA DR	Austin	646G	MM-18	78744	1-99
YUCCA DR	Austin	464J	MG-35	78759	10300-10399
	Travis Co	464J	MG-35	78759	10400-11399
YUCCA DR	Lago Vista	428Z	WV-37	78645	21100-21299
YUCCA DR	Round Rock	406L	MM-41	78681	400-699
YUCCA LN	Cedar Park	433A	ME-39	78613	1600-1699
	Williamson Co	433A	ME-39	78613	1700-1899
YUCCA HILL DR	Austin	674M	MH-14	78744	4700-4899
YUCCA HOUSE DR	Pflugerville	438E	MQ-39	78660	300-499
YUCCA MOUNTAIN RD	Travis Co	494A	MG-33	78759	8900-9199
	Travis Co	464W	MG-34	78759	9200-10099
YUKON CIR	Williamson Co	374N	MG-44	78613	2800-3199
YUKON TERRACE	Georgetown	195V	MK-61	78633	200-399
YUMA DR	Travis Co	467K	MN-35	78660	None

Z

STREET NAME	CITY or COUNTY	MAPSCO GRID	AUSTIN GRID	ZIP CODE	BLOCK RANGE O/E
ZACHARY DR	Austin	557T	MN-25	78724	7000-7299
ZACHARY LN	Taylor	322U	MZ-49	76574	2800-3199
ZACHARYS WAY	Austin	703E	ME-12	78748	1101-1399 O
ZACHARY SCOTT ST	Austin	704K	MG-11	78747	5500-5899
ZACH RUSSELL DR	Cedar Park	402G	MD-42	78613	1800-1899
ZACH SCOTT ST	Austin	586A	ML-24	78723	1800-2299
ZADOCK WOODS DR	Austin	642A	MC-18	78749	6300-6499
ZAGROS WAY	Bee Cave	549E	WW-27	78738	15900-16299
ZAMBIA DR	Travis Co	402X	MC-40	78613	2500-2999
ZANZIBAR LN	Travis Co	467R	MP-35	78660	14600-14999
ZAPPA DR	Travis Co	402P	MC-41	78613	700-899
ZARAGOSA ST	Austin	585Z	MK-22	78702	2600-2799
ZARAGOZA ST	Elgin	534W	EC-28	78621	100-199
ZEBECCA CREEK DR	Travis Co	491T	MA-31	78732	3200-3499
ZEKE BEND	Austin	673A	ME-15	78745	2800-2999
ZELLER LN	Austin	497E	MN-33	78753	12300-12599
ZEN GARDENS WAY	Travis Co	520R	WZ-29	78732	12800-13299
ZEN GARDENS TERRACE	Travis Co	520V	WZ-28	78732	700-799
ZENITH CV	Austin	464Q	MH-35	78759	6700-6799
ZENITH RD	Georgetown	317F	MN-51	78626	400-499
ZENNIA ST	Austin	555L	MK-26	78751	300-799
ZENNOR CT	Travis Co	432G	MD-39	78613	2500-2599
ZEPHYR	Lakeway	519E	WW-30	78734	500-599
ZEPHYR LN	Round Rock	407J	MN-41	78664	1300-2199
ZEPPELIN DR	Travis Co	402Q	MD-41	78613	2300-2799
	Williamson Co	402Q	MD-41	78613	2100-2299
ZEQUIEL CT	Austin	675T	MJ-13	78744	7400-7499
ZEQUIEL DR	Austin	675T	MJ-13	78744	6600-6799
ZEUS CIR	Round Rock	346V	MM-46	78665	1000-1099
ZEUS CV	Austin	464U	MH-34	78759	10600-10699
ZIESCHANG LN	Travis Co	430H	WZ-39	78645	None
ZILKER CLUBHOUSE RD	Austin	584T	MG-22	78746	200-699
ZILLER CV	Travis Co	618V	MR-19	78725	3900-3999
ZIMMERMAN CV	Round Rock	375M	MK-44	78681	1800-1899
ZIMMERMAN LN	Austin	462U	MD-34	78726	11000-11599
ZIMMERMAN LN	Round Rock	375R	MK-44	78681	1700-1799
ZINFANDEL LN	Williamson Co	343N	ME-47	78641	3300-3399
ZION AVE	Taylor	322M	MZ-50	76574	4100-4299
ZION WAY	Travis Co	522P	MC-29	78733	9700-9899
ZIRCON CV	Travis Co	467R	MP-35	78660	1800-1899
ZOA DR	Cedar Park	372J	MC-44	78613	2100-2399
ZOELLER DR	Austin	704T	MG-10	78747	None
ZOLA LN	Pflugerville	407X	MN-40	78664	17100-17499
ZOPILOTE CIR	Travis Co	490C	WZ-33	78734	4100-4199
ZUNI DR	Austin	465T	MJ-34	78759	4200-4499
ZUNIGA DR	Austin	642X	MC-16	78749	9400-9699
ZUNKER CV	Round Rock	347W	MN-46	78665	1600-1699
ZURGA RD	Williamson Co	280N	WY-53	78641	1-199
ZURICK DR	Travis Co	708S	MQ-10	78617	14600-14999
ZYANYA CV	Williamson Co	343W	ME-46	78641	15100-15199
ZYDECO DR	Round Rock	407S	MN-40	78664	1700-1799
ZYLE LN	Travis Co	640U	WZ-16	78737	11300-11399
ZYLE RD	Travis Co	640V	WZ-16	78737	8400-9499

W X Y Z

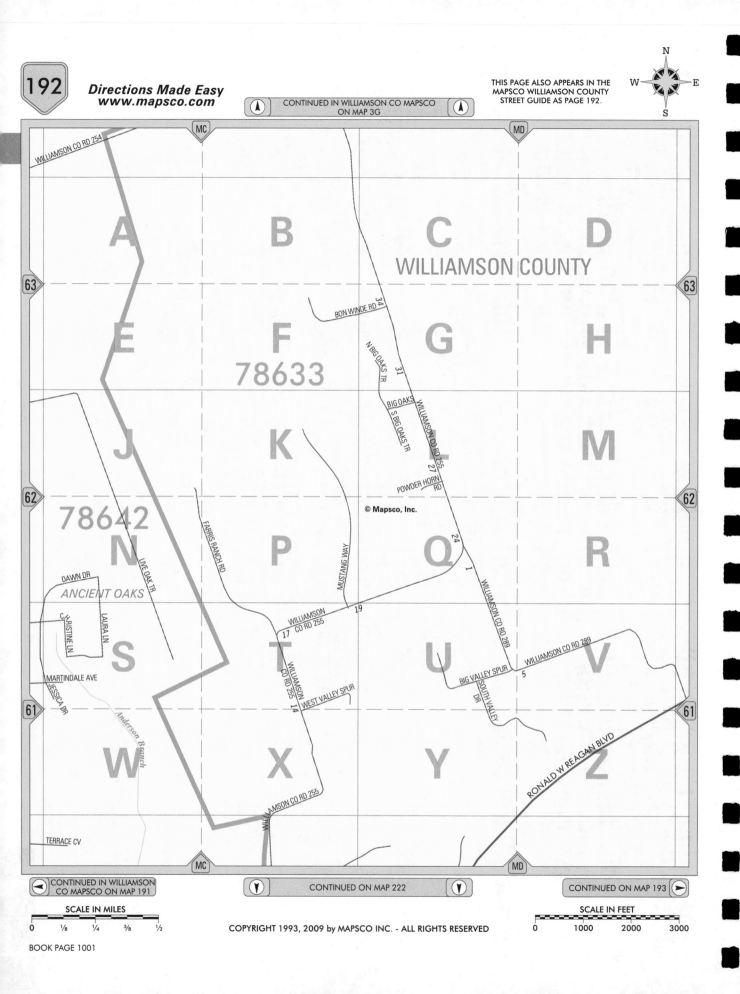

Directions Made Easy
www.mapsco.com

CONTINUED IN WILLIAMSON CO MAPSCO ON MAP 3G

THIS PAGE ALSO APPEARS IN THE MAPSCO WILLIAMSON COUNTY STREET GUIDE AS PAGE 192.

N
W E
S

MC
MD

WILLIAMSON CO RD 254

63   63

A   B   C   D

WILLIAMSON COUNTY

BON WINDE RD   34

E   F   G   H

78633

N BIG OAKS TR   31

BIG OAKS

S BIG OAKS TR

WILLIAMSON CO RD 255

J   K   L   M

27

POWDER HORN RD

62   © Mapsco, Inc.   62

78642

24

N   P   Q   R

FARRIS RANCH RD   1

WILLIAMSON CO RD 289

MUSTANG WAY

LIVE OAK TR

DAWN DR

ANCIENT OAKS

LAURA LN

CHRISTINE LN

19

WILLIAMSON CO RD 255

17

S   T   U   V

BIG VALLEY SPUR   WILLIAMSON CO RD 289   5

MARTINDALE AVE

WILLIAMSON CO RD 255

SOUTH VALLEY DR

JESSICA DR

61   61

Anderson Branch

WEST VALLEY SPUR

14

W   X   Y   Z

WILLIAMSON CO RD 255

RONALD W REAGAN BLVD

TERRACE CV

MC   MD

CONTINUED IN WILLIAMSON CO MAPSCO ON MAP 191

CONTINUED ON MAP 222

CONTINUED ON MAP 193

SCALE IN MILES

0   ⅛   ¼   ⅜   ½

SCALE IN FEET

0   1000   2000   3000

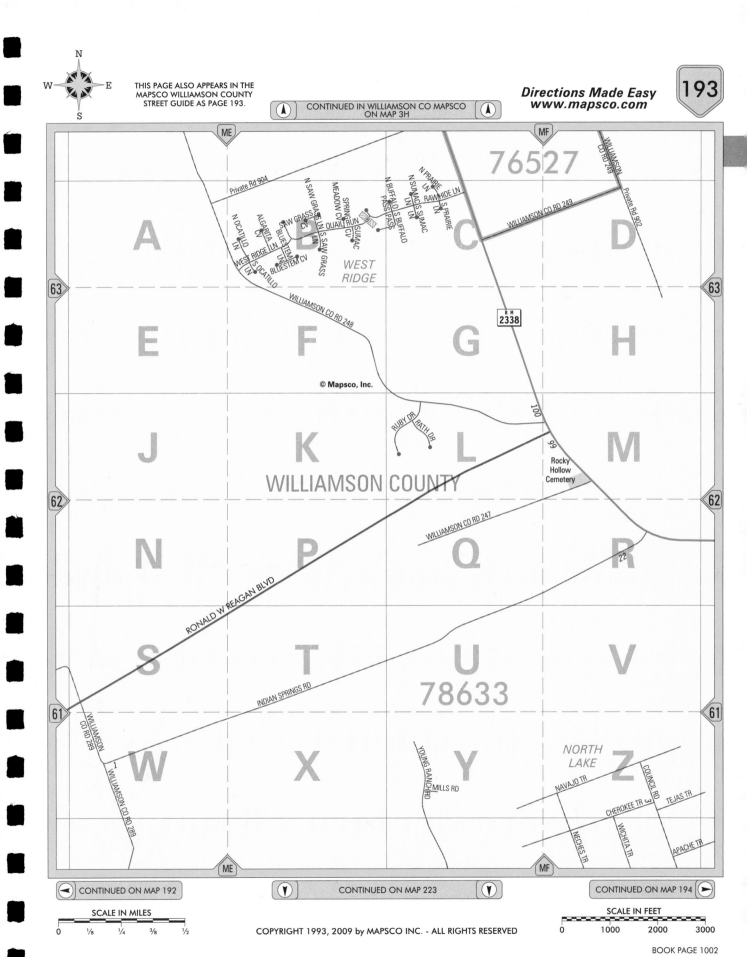

N W E S

THIS PAGE ALSO APPEARS IN THE
MAPSCO WILLIAMSON COUNTY
STREET GUIDE AS PAGE 193.

Directions Made Easy
www.mapsco.com

CONTINUED IN WILLIAMSON CO MAPSCO
ON MAP 3H

ME   MF

76527

Private Rd 904

N OCATILLO LN
ALGARITA LN
S BLUESTEM LN
WEST RIDGE LN
S OCATILLO LN
BLUESTEM CV
N SAW GRASS LN
SAW GRASS CV
MEADOW CV
N SAW GRASS LN
SPRING RUN
QUAIL RUN
SUMAC CV
S SAW GRASS
N BUFFALO PASS
S BUFFALO PASS
N SUMAC LN
S SUMAC LN
N PRAIRIE LN
RAWHIDE LN
S PRAIRIE

A   B   C   D

63   63

WEST
RIDGE

WILLIAMSON CO RD 249

Private Rd 902

WILLIAMSON CO RD 249

WILLIAMSON CO RD 248

RM 2338

E   F   G   H

© Mapsco, Inc.

RUBY DR   RATH DR

100

99

J   K   L   M

WILLIAMSON COUNTY

Rocky
Hollow
Cemetery

62   62

WILLIAMSON CO RD 247

N   P   Q   R

22

RONALD W REAGAN BLVD

S   T   U   V

78633

61   61

INDIAN SPRINGS RD

WILLIAMSON CO RD 289

1

W   X   Y   Z

NORTH
LAKE

YOUNG RANCH RD
MILLS RD

NAVAJO TR

COUNCIL RD
3
CHEROKEE TR   TEJAS TR

WILLIAMSON CO RD 289

NECHES TR
WICHITA TR
APACHE TR

ME   MF

CONTINUED ON MAP 192   CONTINUED ON MAP 223   CONTINUED ON MAP 194

SCALE IN MILES
0   1/8   1/4   3/8   1/2

SCALE IN FEET
0   1000   2000   3000

BOOK PAGE 1002

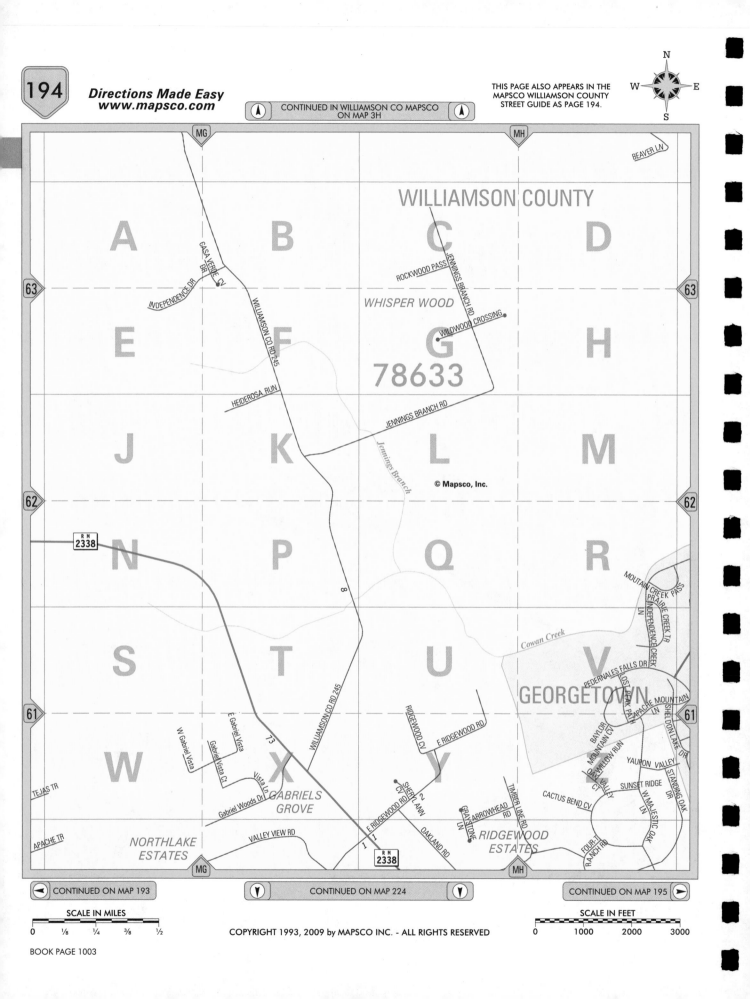

CONTINUED IN WILLIAMSON CO MAPSCO
ON MAP 3H

THIS PAGE ALSO APPEARS IN THE
MAPSCO WILLIAMSON COUNTY
STREET GUIDE AS PAGE 194.

N
W E
S

MG   MH

BEAVER LN

WILLIAMSON COUNTY

A   B   C   D

CASA VERDE CV DR

ROCKWOOD PASS

JENNINGS BRANCH RD

63   63

INDEPENDENCE DR

WHISPER WOOD

WILLIAMSON CO RD 245

WILDWOOD CROSSING

E   F   G   H

78633

HEIDEROSA RUN

JENNINGS BRANCH RD

J   K   L   M

Jennings Branch

© Mapsco, Inc.

62   62

RM 2338

N   P   Q   R

MOUNTAIN CREEK PASS

PRAIRIE CREEK TR

INDEPENDENCE CREEK LN

8

Cowan Creek

PEDERNALES FALLS DR

LOST PEAK PATH

APACHE MOUNTAIN LN

SHELDON LAKE DR

S   T   U   V

GEORGETOWN

WILLIAMSON CO RD 245

61   61

RIDGEWOOD CV

E RIDGEWOOD RD

BAYLOR MOUNTAIN CV

OAK WILLOW RUN

YAUPON VALLEY LN

STANDING OAK

W GABRIEL VISTA

E GABRIEL VISTA

73

SUNSET RIDGE

W MAJESTIC OAK

W   X   Y   Z

Gabriel Vista Ct

Vista Ln

Gabriels Grove

Gabriel Woods Dr

SHERN ANN CV

2

E RIDGEWOOD RD

GRAY STONE LN

ARROWHEAD RD

TIMBER LINE RD

CACTUS BEND CV

DEL VALLE CT

FOUR T RANCH RD

RIDGEWOOD ESTATES

TEJAS TR

APACHE TR

NORTHLAKE ESTATES

VALLEY VIEW RD

1
1

RM 2338

OAKLAND RD

MG   MH

◄ CONTINUED ON MAP 193   ▼ CONTINUED ON MAP 224   ▼   CONTINUED ON MAP 195 ►

SCALE IN MILES
0   1/8   1/4   3/8   1/2

SCALE IN FEET
0   1000   2000   3000

THIS PAGE ALSO APPEARS IN THE
MAPSCO WILLIAMSON COUNTY
STREET GUIDE AS PAGE 195.

Directions Made Easy
www.mapsco.com

195

CONTINUED IN WILLIAMSON CO MAPSCO
ON MAP 3H

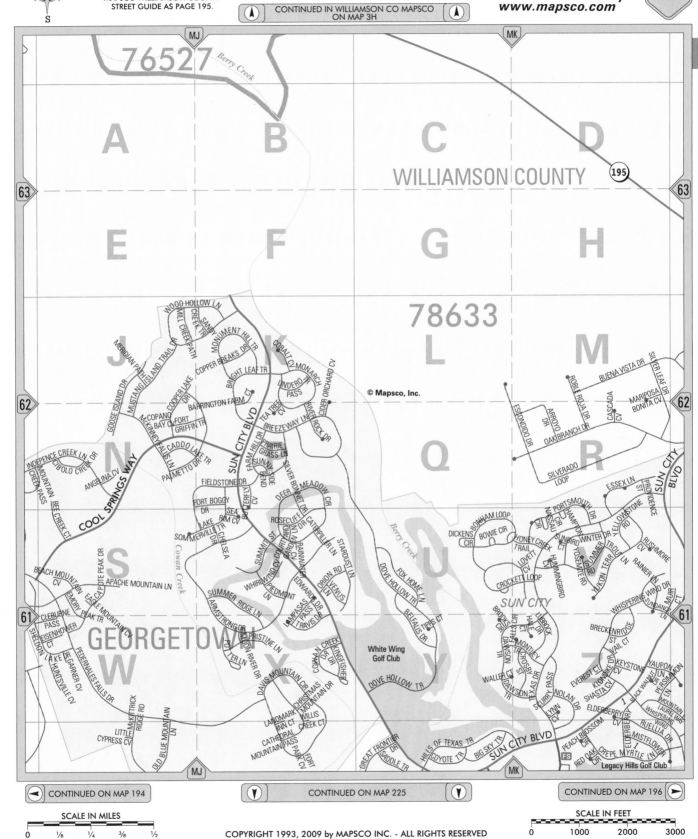

CONTINUED ON MAP 194

CONTINUED ON MAP 225

CONTINUED ON MAP 196

SCALE IN MILES

0   1/8   1/4   3/8   1/2

SCALE IN FEET

0   1000   2000   3000

BOOK PAGE 1004

CONTINUED IN WILLIAMSON CO MAPSCO
ON MAP 3H

THIS PAGE ALSO APPEARS IN THE
MAPSCO WILLIAMSON COUNTY
STREET GUIDE AS PAGE 196.

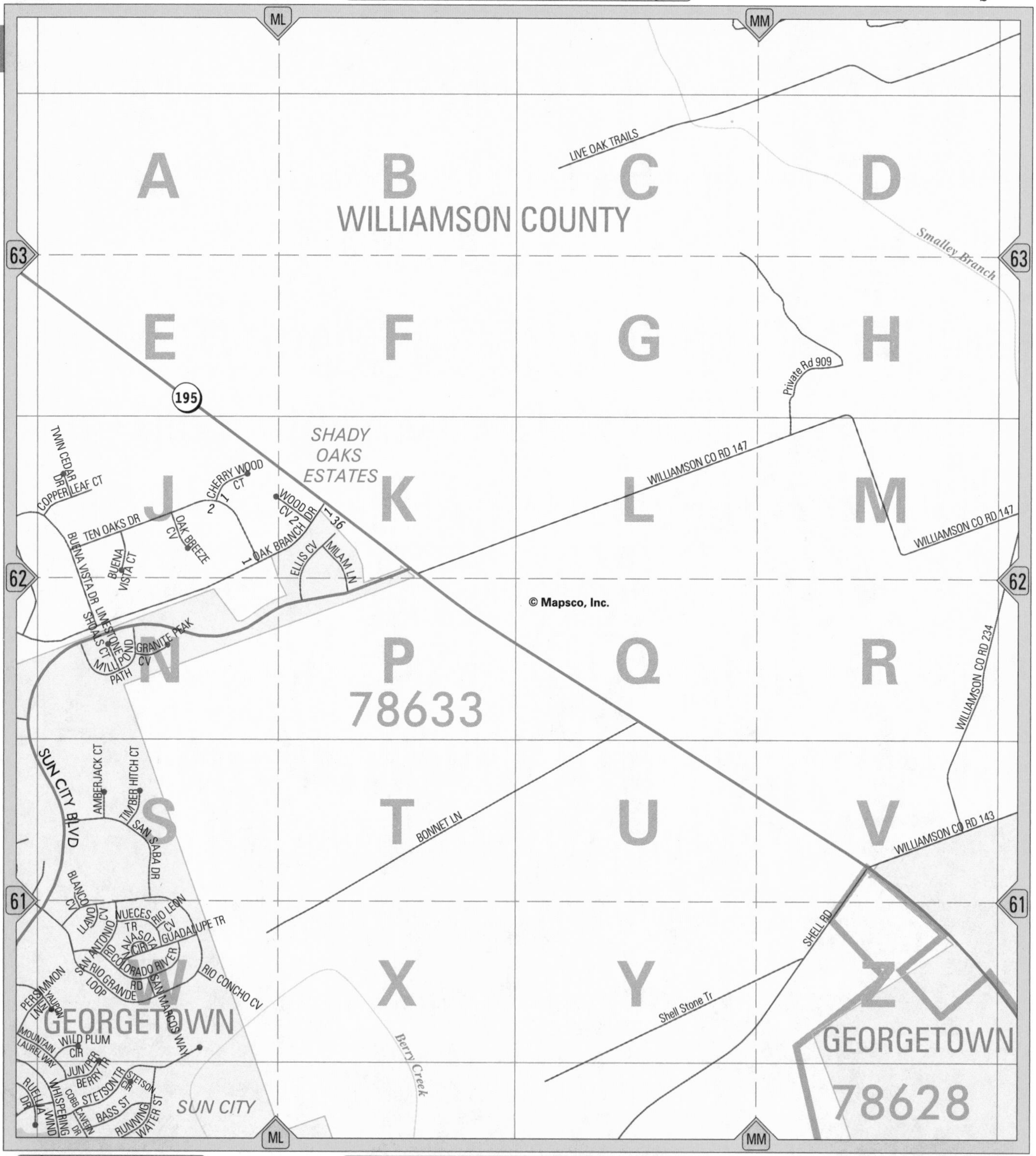

N
W E
S

ML MM

A B C D

63 63

WILLIAMSON COUNTY

LIVE OAK TRAILS

Smalley Branch

E F G H

195

Private Rd 909

SHADY OAKS ESTATES

J K L M

WILLIAMSON CO RD 147

TWIN CEDAR DR
COPPER LEAF CT
CHERRY WOOD CT
WOOD DR CV 2H
TEN OAKS DR
OAK BREEZE CV
ELLIS CV
OAK BRANCH RD
MILAM LN
WILLIAMSON CO RD 147

62 62

BUENA VISTA DR
BUENA VISTA CT
LIMESTONE
SHOALS CT
MILLPOND
GRANITE PEAK CV
PATH

© Mapsco, Inc.

N P Q R

78633

WILLIAMSON CO RD 234

SUN CITY BLVD
AMBERJACK CT
TIMBER HITCH CT
SAN SABA DR
S T U V

BONNET LN

WILLIAMSON CO RD 143

BLANCO CV
NUECES CIR
RIO LEON CV
SAN ANTONIO CV
VASOTA CIR
GUADALUPE TR

61 61

SHELL RD

PERSIMMON
AUDUBON LN
COLORADO RIVER RD
SAN RIO GRANDE LOOP
SAN MARCOS WAY
RIO CONCHO CV

W X Y Z

MOUNTAIN LAUREL WAY
WILD PLUM CIR
JUNIPER BERRY
STETSON CIR
STETSON TR
SHELL STONE TR

GEORGETOWN

GEORGETOWN
78628

RUELLA WIND DR
WHISPERING OAKS DR
COBB LAVEN
BASS ST
RUNNING ST
WATER ST

Berry Creek

SUN CITY

ML MM

CONTINUED ON MAP 195
CONTINUED ON MAP 226
CONTINUED ON MAP 197

SCALE IN MILES
0 1/8 1/4 3/8 1/2

SCALE IN FEET
0 1000 2000 3000

COPYRIGHT 1993, 2009 by MAPSCO INC. - ALL RIGHTS RESERVED

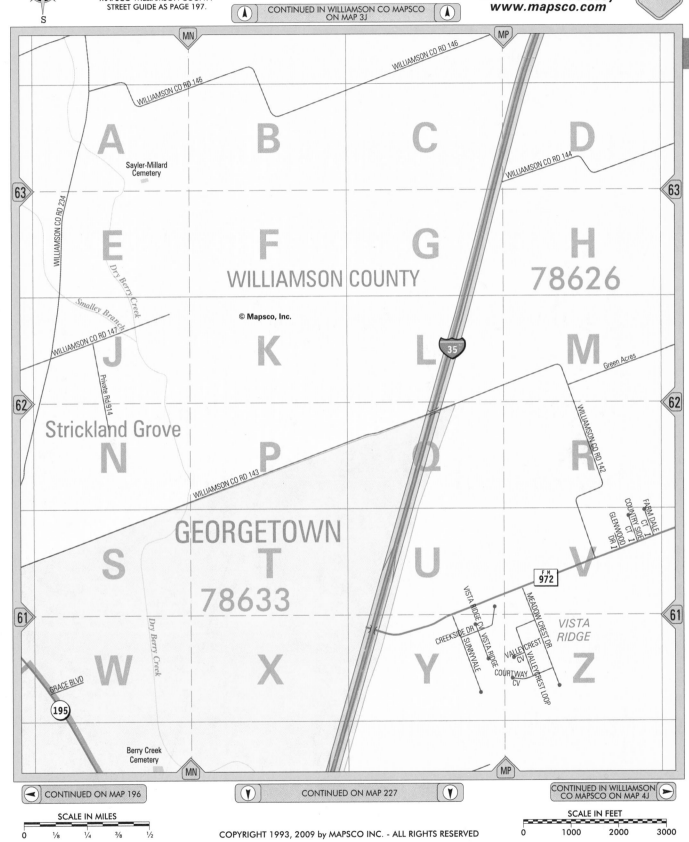

THIS PAGE ALSO APPEARS IN THE
MAPSCO WILLIAMSON COUNTY
STREET GUIDE AS PAGE 197.

CONTINUED IN WILLIAMSON CO MAPSCO
ON MAP 3J

Directions Made Easy
www.mapsco.com

MN

WILLIAMSON CO RD 146

MP

WILLIAMSON CO RD 146

A   B   C   D

Sayler-Millard
Cemetery

WILLIAMSON CO RD 144

63   63

WILLIAMSON CO RD 234

E   F   G   H

WILLIAMSON COUNTY   78626

Dry Berry Creek

© Mapsco, Inc.

Smalley Branch

35

WILLIAMSON CO RD 147

J   K   L   M

Green Acres

Private Rd 914

WILLIAMSON CO RD 142

62   62

Strickland Grove

N   P   Q   R

WILLIAMSON CO RD 143

FARM DALE CT
COUNTRY SIDE CT 1
GLENWOOD DR 1

GEORGETOWN

S   T   U   V

FM 972

78633

VISTA
RIDGE

61   61

VISTA RIDGE CV

CREEKSIDE DR

MEADOW CREST DR

W   X   Y   Z

SUNNYVALE
VISTA RIDGE
VALLEY CREST CV
VALLEY CREST LOOP

GRACE BLVD

COURTWAY CV

195

Dry Berry Creek

Berry Creek
Cemetery

MN   MP

CONTINUED ON MAP 196

CONTINUED ON MAP 227

CONTINUED IN WILLIAMSON
CO MAPSCO ON MAP 4J

SCALE IN MILES

0   1/8   1/4   3/8   1/2

COPYRIGHT 1993, 2009 by MAPSCO INC. - ALL RIGHTS RESERVED

SCALE IN FEET

0   1000   2000   3000

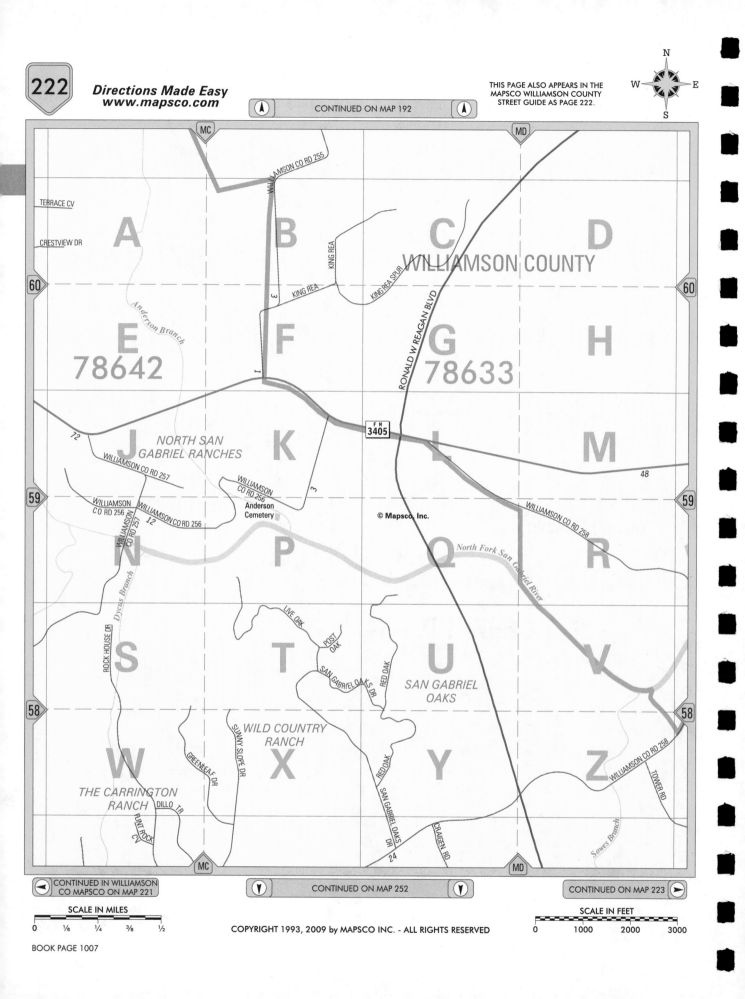

Directions Made Easy
www.mapsco.com

N
W E
S

CONTINUED ON MAP 192

MC

MD

TERRACE CV

CRESTVIEW DR

A

B

WILLIAMSON CO RD 255

KING REA

KING REA

C

WILLIAMSON COUNTY

KING REA SPUR

D

60

60

Anderson Branch

KING REA

3

RONALD W REAGAN BLVD

E

78642

F

1

G

78633

H

72

J

NORTH SAN
GABRIEL RANCHES

WILLIAMSON CO RD 257

K

FM
3405

L

M

48

59

WILLIAMSON
CO RD 256

WILLIAMSON CO RD 256

WILLIAMSON
CO RD 257

12

WILLIAMSON
CO RD 256

3

Anderson
Cemetery

© Mapsco, Inc.

WILLIAMSON CO RD 258

59

Dycus Branch

N

ROCK HOUSE DR

P

Q

North Fork San Gabriel River

R

S

LIVE OAK

POST OAK

SAN GABRIEL OAKS DR

RED OAK

T

U

SAN GABRIEL
OAKS

V

58

GREENLEAF DR

SUNNY SLOPE DR

WILD COUNTRY
RANCH

X

RED OAK

SAN GABRIEL OAKS DR

Y

CRAIGEN RD

WILLIAMSON CO RD 258

TOWER RD

Z

58

W

THE CARRINGTON
RANCH

DILLO TR

FLINT ROCK CV

24

Sowes Branch

MC

MD

CONTINUED IN WILLIAMSON
CO MAPSCO ON MAP 221

CONTINUED ON MAP 252

CONTINUED ON MAP 223

SCALE IN MILES

0   ⅛   ¼   ⅜   ½

SCALE IN FEET

0   1000   2000   3000

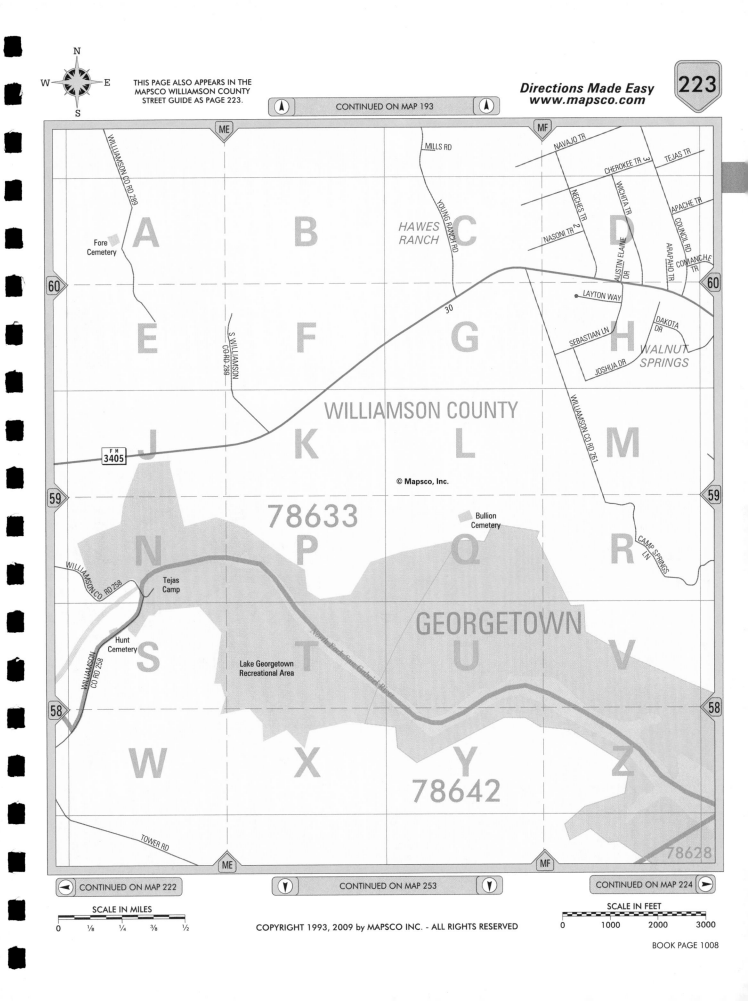

N
W E
S

THIS PAGE ALSO APPEARS IN THE
MAPSCO WILLIAMSON COUNTY
STREET GUIDE AS PAGE 223.

Directions Made Easy
www.mapsco.com

CONTINUED ON MAP 193

ME

MF

WILLIAMSON CO RD 289

Fore
Cemetery

A

B

MILLS RD

HAWES
RANCH

C

NAVAJO TR

CHEROKEE TR 3

TEJAS TR

NECHES TR 2

WICHITA TR

APACHE TR

NASONI TR 2

AUSTIN ELAINE DR

ARAPAHO TR

COUNCIL RD

COMANCHE TR

YOUNG RANCH RD

60

60

E

S WILLIAMSON CO RD 289

F

30

G

LAYTON WAY

SEBASTIAN LN

H

DAKOTA DR

WALNUT
SPRINGS

JOSHUA DR

WILLIAMSON COUNTY

J

K

L

WILLIAMSON CO RD 261

M

FM
3405

59

© Mapsco, Inc.

59

78633

Bullion
Cemetery

N

P

Q

R

CAMP SPRINGS LN

WILLIAMSON CO RD 258

Tejas
Camp

GEORGETOWN

Hunt
Cemetery

WILLIAMSON CO RD 258

S

Lake Georgetown
Recreational Area

T

North Fork San Gabriel River

U

V

58

58

W

X

Y

Z

78642

TOWER RD

78628

ME

MF

CONTINUED ON MAP 222

CONTINUED ON MAP 253

CONTINUED ON MAP 224

SCALE IN MILES

0   1/8   1/4   3/8   1/2

SCALE IN FEET

0   1000   2000   3000

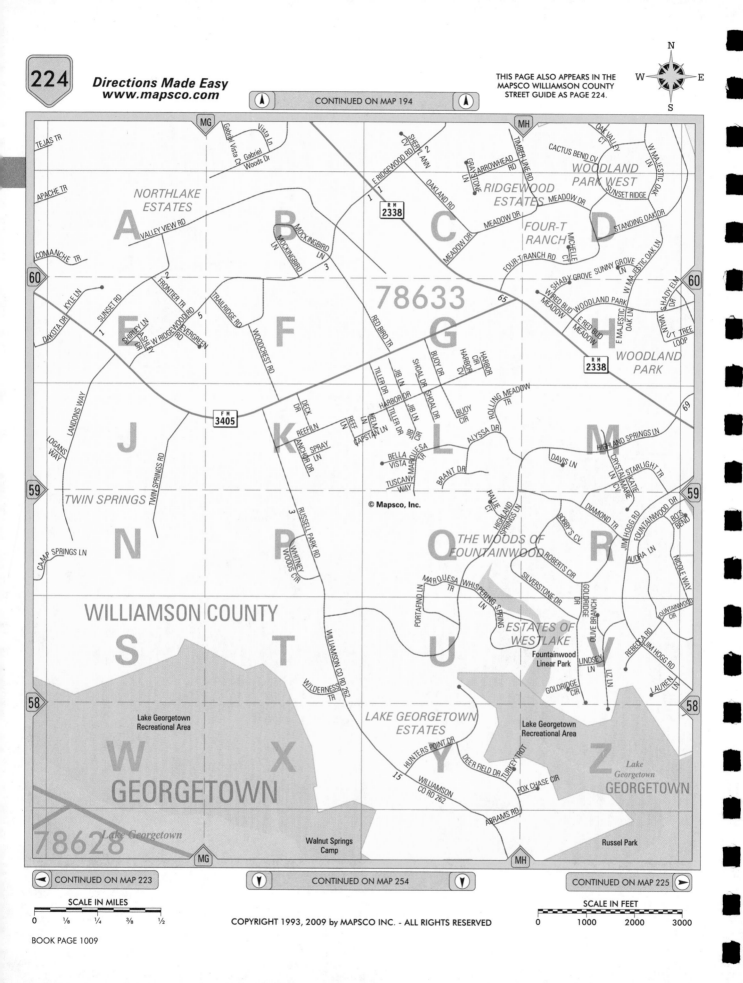

THIS PAGE ALSO APPEARS IN THE
MAPSCO WILLIAMSON COUNTY
STREET GUIDE AS PAGE 224.

N
W E
S

CONTINUED ON MAP 194

MG
MH

TEJAS TR

Vista Ln

Gabriel Vista Ct
Gabriel Woods Dr

SHERI ANN CV

E RIDGEWOOD RD

OAKLAND RD

GRAYSTONE LN

ARROWHEAD RD

TIMBERLINE RD

OAK VALLEY CT

CACTUS BEND CV

W MAJESTIC OAK LN

WOODLAND PARK WEST

NORTHLAKE ESTATES

APACHE TR

VALLEY VIEW RD

A

B

C

RM 2338

RIDGEWOOD ESTATES

MEADOW DR

SUNSET RIDGE

D

STANDING OAK DR

MEADOW DR

MEADOW DR

COMANCHE TR

MOCKINGBIRD LN

MOCKINGBIRD LN

78633

FOUR-T RANCH

FOUR-T RANCH RD

MICHELLE CT

SHADY GROVE

SUNNY GROVE LN

W MAJESTIC OAK LN

SHADY ELM DR

60

60

65

WIRED BUD MEADOW

WOODLAND PARK

E RED BUD MEADOW

E MAJESTIC OAK LN

WALNUT TREE LOOP

DAKOTA DR

KYLE LN

SUNSET RD

FRONTIER TR

TRAILRIDGE RD

SHIRLEY LN

E

EASHLEY DR

W RIDGEWOOD RD

EVERGREEN

F

WOODCREST RD

RED BIRD TR

RM 2338

WOODLAND PARK

H

G

69

LANDONS WAY

FM 3405

DECK DR

REEF LN

ANCHOR DR

SPRAY

TILLER LN

JIB LN

SHOAL DR

HARBOR DR

BUOY DR

HELM ST

TILLER DR

JIB LN

SHOAL DR

HARBOR CIR

HARBOR CV

BUOY CIR

HARBOR LN

ROLLING MEADOW TR

HIGHLAND SPRINGS LN

J

K

REEF LN

CAPSTAN LN

BELLA VISTA

MARQUESA TR

ALYSSA DR

L

DAVIS LN

CRYSTAL MARIE LN

KATIE CV

STARLIGHT TR

M

LOGANS WAY

TWIN SPRINGS RD

TUSCANY WAY

BRANT DR

59

DIAMOND TR

JIM HOGG RD

FOUNTAINWOOD DR

BO'S BEND

59

TWIN SPRINGS

N

CAMP SPRINGS LN

RUSSELL PARK RD

WHITNEY WOODS CIR

HALLIE CT

HIGHLAND SPRINGS LN

BOBBY'S CV

ROBERTS CIR

Q

THE WOODS OF FOUNTAINWOOD

SILVERSTONE DR

GOLDRIDGE DR

OLIVE BRANCH

R

AUDRA LN

NICOLE WAY

REBECCA RD

JIM HOGG RD

WILLIAMSON COUNTY

3

MARQUESA TR

PORTAFINO LN

WHISPERING SPRING LN

ESTATES OF WESTLAKE

Fountainwood Linear Park

LINDSEY LN

LIZ LN

FOUNTAINWOOD CIR

S

T

WILLIAMSON CO RD 262

U

V

GOLDRIDGE CIR

LAUREN LN

WILDERNESS TR

58

58

Lake Georgetown
Recreational Area

LAKE GEORGETOWN ESTATES

HUNTERS POINT DR

DEER FIELD DR

TURKEY TROT

Lake Georgetown
Recreational Area

Lake Georgetown

Z

GEORGETOWN

W

X

15

WILLIAMSON CO RD 262

Y

FOX CHASE CIR

ARRAMS RD

78628

Lake Georgetown

Walnut Springs
Camp

Russel Park

GEORGETOWN

© Mapsco, Inc.

MG

MH

CONTINUED ON MAP 223
CONTINUED ON MAP 254
CONTINUED ON MAP 225

SCALE IN MILES

0   1/8   1/4   3/8   1/2

SCALE IN FEET

0   1000   2000   3000

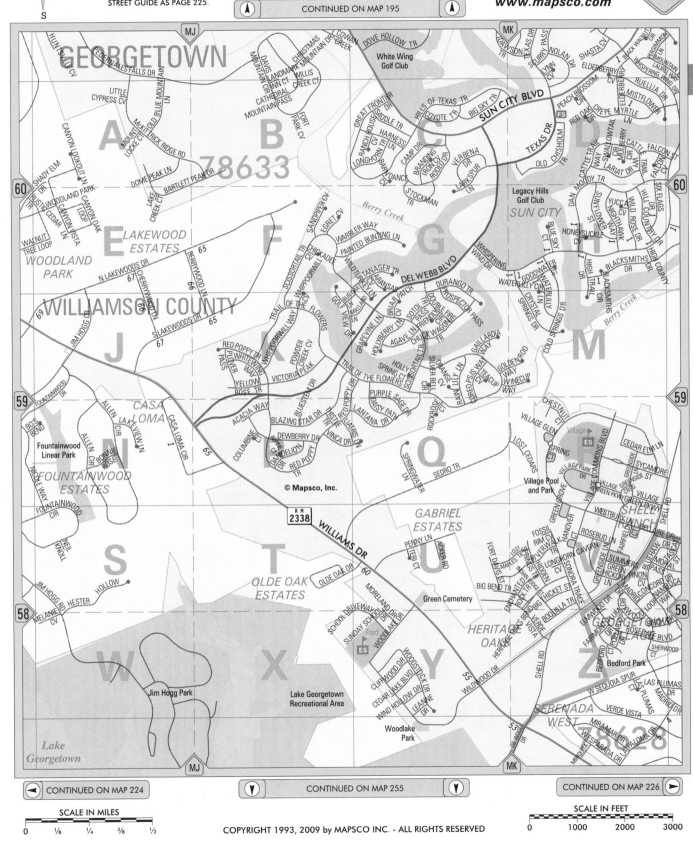

THIS PAGE ALSO APPEARS IN THE
MAPSCO WILLIAMSON COUNTY
STREET GUIDE AS PAGE 225.

N
W E
S

GEORGETOWN

78633

A B C D

E F G H

WILLIAMSON COUNTY

J K L M

N Q

S T U V

W X Y Z

LAKEWOOD
ESTATES

WOODLAND
PARK

CASA
LOMA

FOUNTAINWOOD
ESTATES
Fountainwood
Linear Park

SUN CITY
Legacy Hills
Golf Club
White Wing
Golf Club

DEL WEBB BLVD

SUN CITY BLVD

GABRIEL
ESTATES

SHELL
RANCH
Village Pool
and Park

HERITAGE
OAKS

OLDE OAK
ESTATES
Green Cemetery

Bedford Park

SERENADA
WEST

WILLIAMS DR

RM 2338

Jim Hogg Park

Lake Georgetown
Recreational Area

Woodlake
Park

Lake
Georgetown

© Mapsco, Inc.

78628

60 60

59 59

58 58

CONTINUED ON MAP 224
CONTINUED ON MAP 255
CONTINUED ON MAP 226

SCALE IN MILES
0   1/8   1/4   3/8   1/2

SCALE IN FEET
0   1000   2000   3000

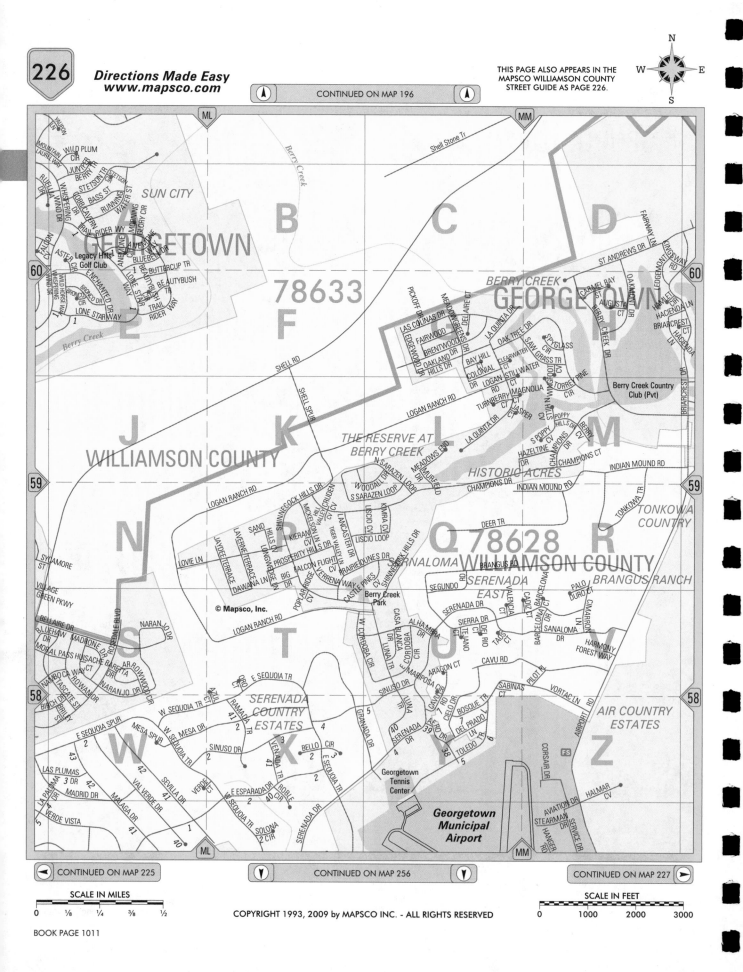

Directions Made Easy
www.mapsco.com

CONTINUED ON MAP 196

THIS PAGE ALSO APPEARS IN THE
MAPSCO WILLIAMSON COUNTY
STREET GUIDE AS PAGE 226.

N
W E
S

SUN CITY

GEORGETOWN

Legacy Hills
Golf Club

60

Berry Creek

78633

BERRY CREEK

GEORGETOWN

St Andrews Dr

Berry Creek Country
Club (Pvt)

60

Shell Rd

Shell Spur

WILLIAMSON COUNTY

THE RESERVE AT
BERRY CREEK

Logan Ranch Rd

HISTORIC ACRES

INDIAN MOUND RD

59   59

TONKOWA
COUNTRY

Logan Ranch Rd

Q 78628 R

SERNALOMA WILLIAMSON COUNTY

BRANGUS RANCH

SYCAMORE
ST

VILLAGE
GREEN PKWY

SERENADA
EAST

Berry Creek
Park

Logan Ranch Rd

58   58

AIR COUNTRY
ESTATES

SERENADA
COUNTRY
ESTATES

W   X   Y

Z

Georgetown
Tennis
Center

**Georgetown
Municipal
Airport**

© Mapsco, Inc.

CONTINUED ON MAP 225

CONTINUED ON MAP 256

CONTINUED ON MAP 227

SCALE IN MILES

0   ⅛   ¼   ⅜   ½

SCALE IN FEET

0   1000   2000   3000

CONTINUED ON MAP 197

THIS PAGE ALSO APPEARS IN THE MAPSCO WILLIAMSON COUNTY STREET GUIDE AS PAGE 227.

Directions Made Easy
www.mapsco.com

N
W E
S

MN

MP

GRACE BLVD

78633

A

B

C

D

Berry Creek Cemetery

SYBERT LN
ST ANDREWS DR
TIGER WOODS
CHI CHI DR

BERRY CREEK

ANIKA CV
GOLDEN BEAR DR
KINGSWAY RD

60

60

SUNNYVALE

MEADOW CREST DR
VALLEYCREST LOOP

WILLIAMSON CO RD 196

Private Road

g16

WILLIAMSON COUNTY

HAMLET CIR

BRIARCREST CT
HACIENDA LN

Berry Creek Country Club (Pvt)

E

F

G

H

195

Dry Berry Creek

78626

SPANISH DOVE CT
BRIARCREST DR
LITTLE DEER TR
OWL CREEK DR
SQUIRREL HOLLOW DR
MOURNING DOVE
BUCK MEADOW DR
DRIFTING MEADOW DR
DIAMOND DOVE TR
RUMBLE BEE
BLUE JAY CT
Villages of Berry Creek Park
PEBBLE CREEK DR

WILLIAMSON CO RD 150

L

M

J

K

BERRY CREEK DR

Berry Creek

INDIAN MOUND RD

59

59

GEORGETOWN

© Mapsco, Inc.

N

P

Q

R

78628

Dry Berry Creek

GROVE LN

3

31

Berry Springs Park and Preserve

35

MARKET ST

S

T

U

V

58

58

WILLIAM SCOTSMAN

W

X

Y

Berry Springs Park and Preserve

TOM McDANIELS PKWY

WILLIAMSON CO RD 152

Z

OLD BISHOP RD

OLD BISHOP PLACE

130

Berry Creek

MN

MP

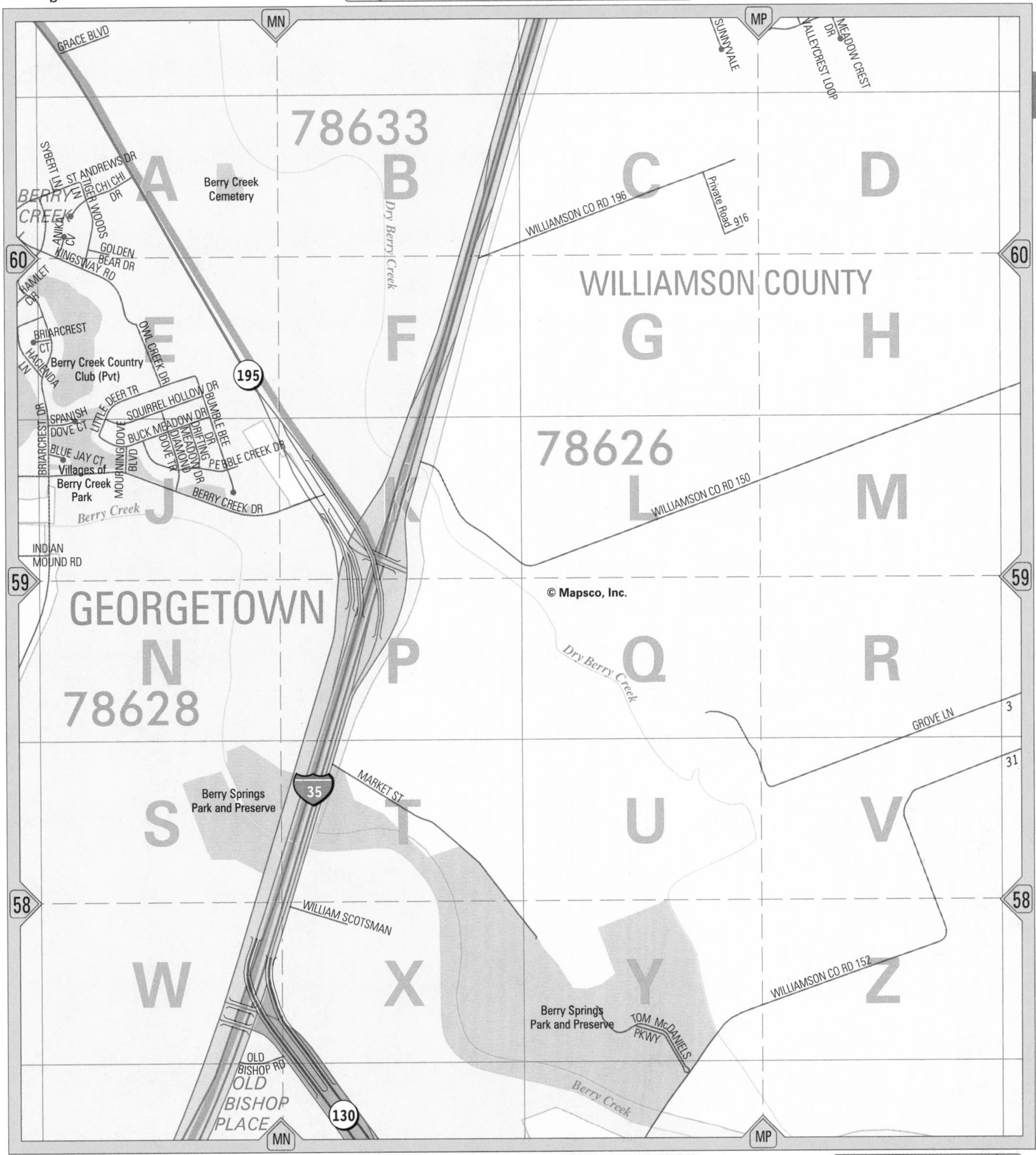

CONTINUED ON MAP 226

CONTINUED ON MAP 257

CONTINUED IN WILLIAMSON CO MAPSCO ON MAP 228

SCALE IN MILES
0   ⅛   ¼   ⅜   ½

SCALE IN FEET
0   1000   2000   3000

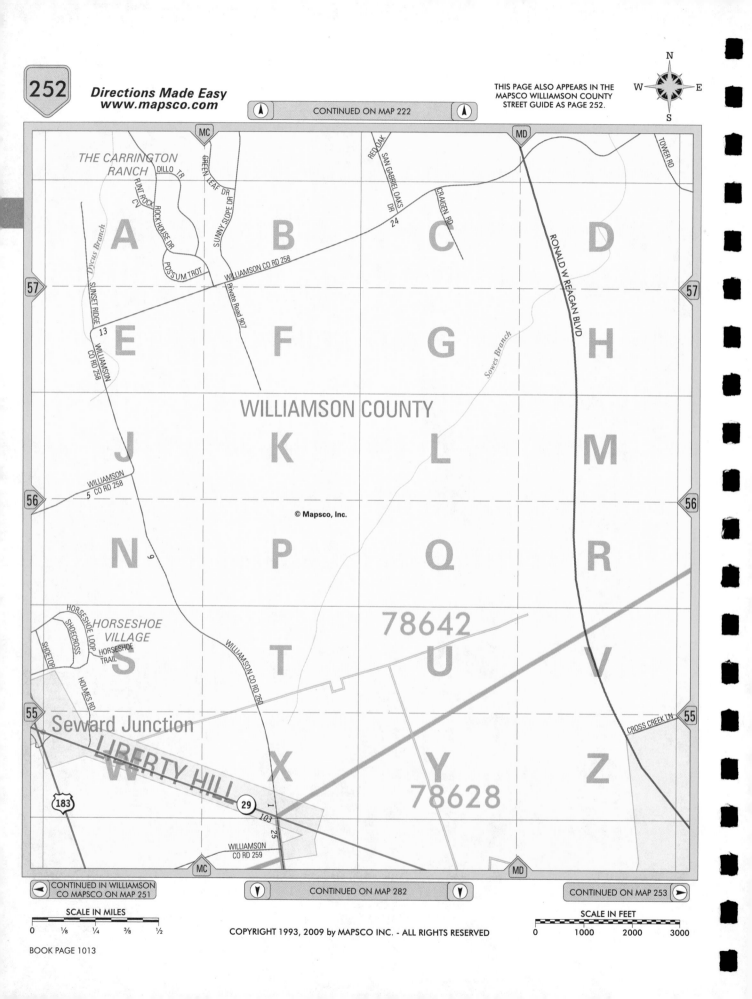

Directions Made Easy
www.mapsco.com

CONTINUED ON MAP 222

THIS PAGE ALSO APPEARS IN THE
MAPSCO WILLIAMSON COUNTY
STREET GUIDE AS PAGE 252.

N
W E
S

THE CARRINGTON RANCH

DILLO TR

GREEN LEAF DR

REDOAK

SAN GABRIEL OAKS DR

CRAIGEN RD

MC

MD

TOWER RD

FLINT ROCK CV

ROCKHOUSE DR

SUNNY SLOPE DR

A   B   C   D

POSSUM TROT

Dycus Branch

WILLIAMSON CO RD 258

24

RONALD W REAGAN BLVD

57   57

SUNSET RIDGE

Private Road 907

E   F   G   H

13

WILLIAMSON CO RD 258

Sowes Branch

WILLIAMSON COUNTY

J   K   L   M

WILLIAMSON CO RD 258

5

56   56

© Mapsco, Inc.

N   P   Q   R

9

HORSESHOE LOOP

SHOECROSS

HORSESHOE VILLAGE

HORSESHOE TRAIL

78642

SHOETOP

S   T   U   V

WILLIAMSON CO RD 260

HOLMES RD

55   Seward Junction   CROSS CREEK LN   55

LIBERTY HILL

W   X   Y   Z

183

29

1

78628

103

25

WILLIAMSON CO RD 259

MC

MD

CONTINUED IN WILLIAMSON CO MAPSCO ON MAP 251

CONTINUED ON MAP 282

CONTINUED ON MAP 253

SCALE IN MILES

0   ⅛   ¼   ⅜   ½

SCALE IN FEET

0   1000   2000   3000

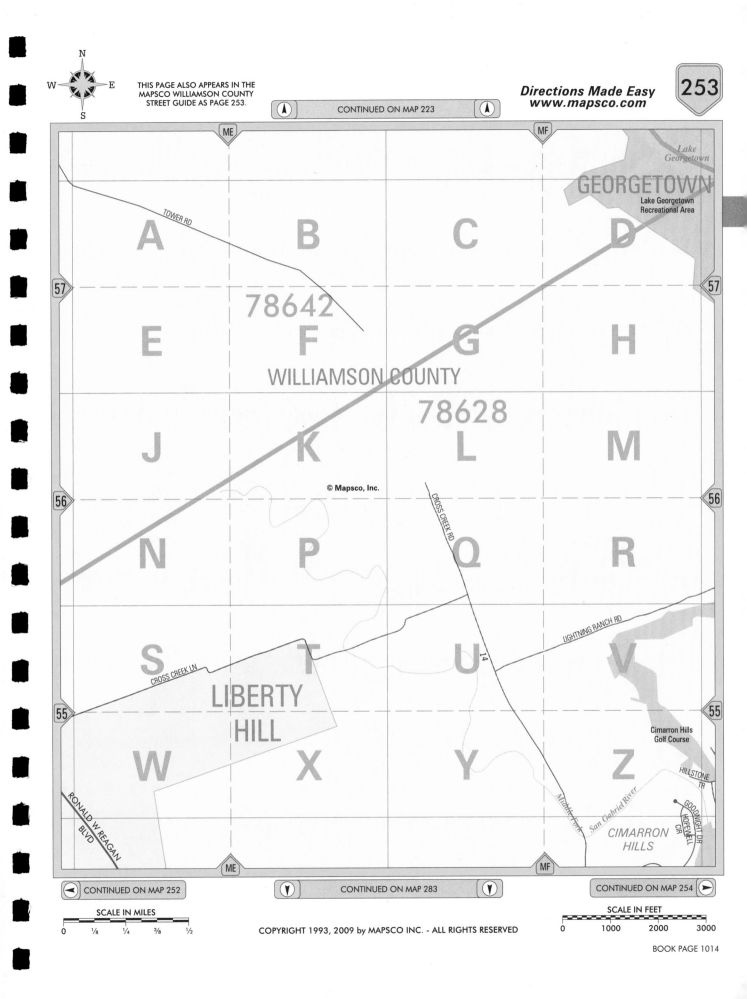

CONTINUED ON MAP 223

THIS PAGE ALSO APPEARS IN THE
MAPSCO WILLIAMSON COUNTY
STREET GUIDE AS PAGE 253.

N
W E
S

ME

MF

Lake Georgetown

GEORGETOWN

Lake Georgetown
Recreational Area

TOWER RD

A   B   C   D

57   57

78642

E   F   G   H

WILLIAMSON COUNTY

78628

J   K   L   M

56   56

© Mapsco, Inc.

CROSS CREEK RD

N   P   Q   R

LIGHTNING RANCH RD

CROSS CREEK LN

S   T   U   V

14

Cimarron Hills
Golf Course

55   55

**LIBERTY
HILL**

W   X   Y   Z

HILLSTONE TR

RONALD W REAGAN BLVD

Middle Fork
San Gabriel River

GOODNIGHT DR
HOPEWELL CIR

*CIMARRON
HILLS*

ME

MF

CONTINUED ON MAP 252

CONTINUED ON MAP 283

CONTINUED ON MAP 254

SCALE IN MILES

0   ⅛   ¼   ⅜   ½

SCALE IN FEET

0   1000   2000   3000

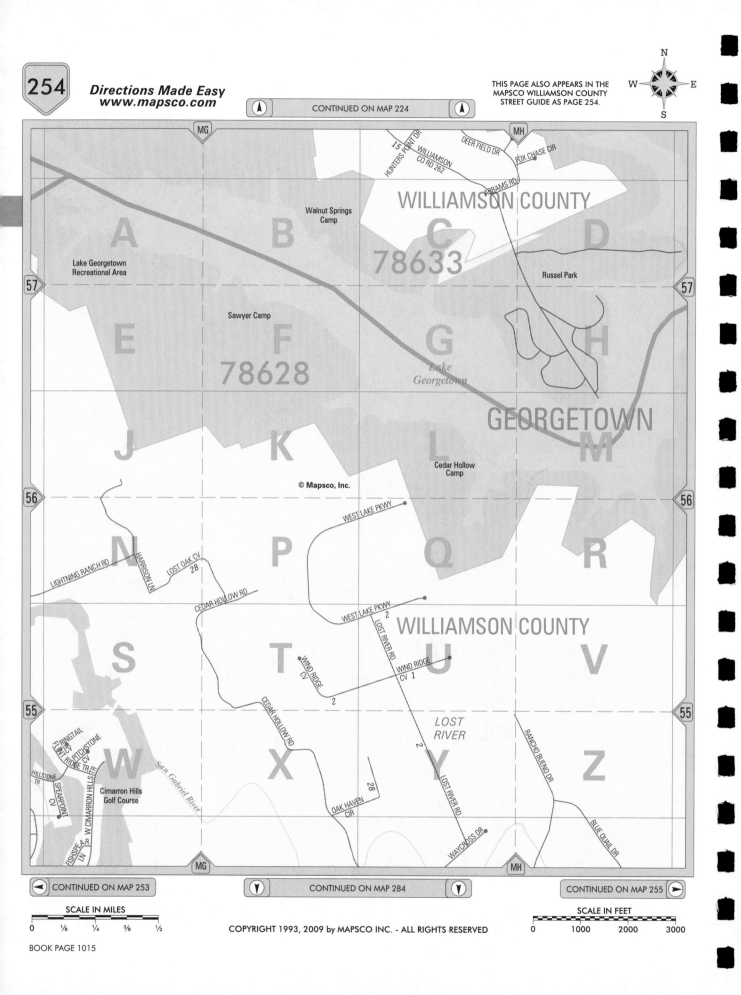

254

Directions Made Easy
www.mapsco.com

THIS PAGE ALSO APPEARS IN THE
MAPSCO WILLIAMSON COUNTY
STREET GUIDE AS PAGE 254.

N
W E
S

CONTINUED ON MAP 224

MG

MH

DEER FIELD DR

HUNTERS POINT DR

15

WILLIAMSON
CO RD 262

FOX CHASE CIR

ABRAMS RD

WILLIAMSON COUNTY

A

B

Walnut Springs
Camp

C

78633

D

Lake Georgetown
Recreational Area

57

Russel Park

57

E

Sawyer Camp

F

78628

G

H

Lake
Georgetown

GEORGETOWN

J

K

L

Cedar Hollow
Camp

M

© Mapsco, Inc.

56

56

WEST LAKE PKWY

N

P

Q

R

LIGHTNING RANCH RD

HARRISON LN

LOST OAK CV

28

CEDAR HOLLOW RD

WEST LAKE PKWY

LOST RIVER RD

WILLIAMSON COUNTY

S

T

WIND RIDGE CV

WIND RIDGE
CV 1

U

V

2

55

CEDAR HOLLOW RD

*LOST
RIVER*

RANCHO BUENO DR

55

RINGTAIL CV

PITCHSTONE CV

FLINT RIDGE TR

HILLSTONE TR

SPEARPOINT CV

W CIMARRON HILLS TR

W

Cimarron Hills
Golf Course

San Gabriel River

X

Y

2

28

LOST RIVER RD

Z

BLUE QUAIL DR

FISHSPEAR LN

OAK HAVEN
CIR

WAYCROSS DR

MG

MH

CONTINUED ON MAP 253

CONTINUED ON MAP 284

CONTINUED ON MAP 255

SCALE IN MILES

0   1/8   1/4   3/8   1/2

SCALE IN FEET

0   1000   2000   3000

THIS PAGE ALSO APPEARS IN THE
MAPSCO WILLIAMSON COUNTY
STREET GUIDE AS PAGE 255.

N
W E
S

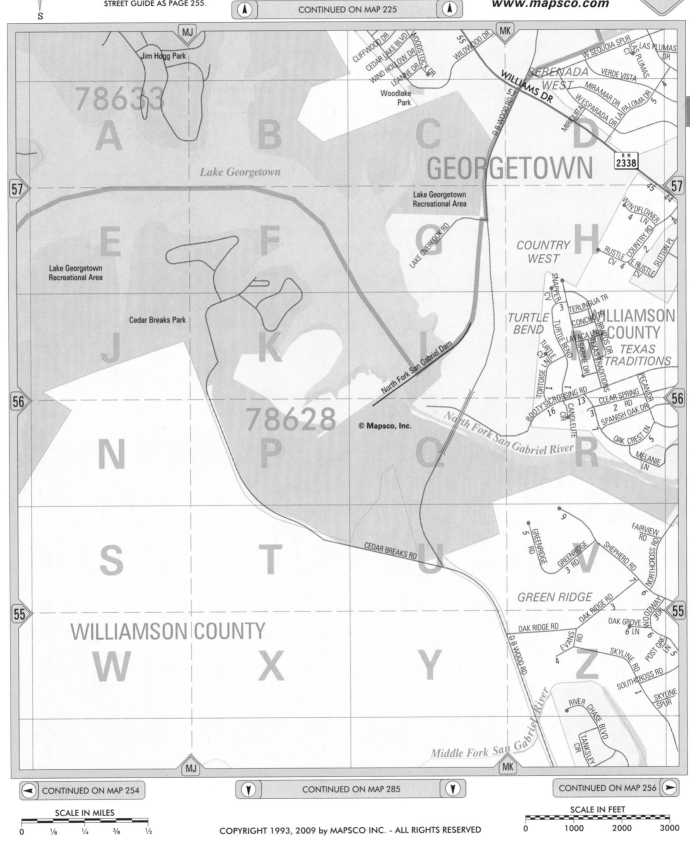

CONTINUED ON MAP 225

MJ

Jim Hogg Park

78633

A

B

CLIFFWOOD DR
CEDAR LAKE BLVD
WIND HOLLOW DR
WOODSTOCK DR
LEANNE DR
WILDWOOD DR

Woodlake
Park

C

WILLIAMS DR

MK

W SEQUOIA SPUR
CT
LAS PLUMAS
DR
LAS PLUMAS
VERDE VISTA

SERENADA
WEST

D.B. WOOD RD

55
53

GEORGETOWN

MIRAMAR DR
LA PALOMA DR
MIRQUITA
WESPARADA DR

R M
2338

D

45
44

57

Lake Georgetown

Lake Georgetown
Recreational Area

G

Lake Overlook Rd

WINDFLOWER
LN
OE RUSTLE
CV
COUNTRY RD
SUTTON PL

COUNTRY
WEST

H

RUSTLE
CV

57

E

F

Lake Georgetown
Recreational Area

Cedar Breaks Park

J

K

North Fork San Gabriel Dam

I

© Mapsco, Inc.

78628

SNAPPER
CV
TERLINGUA TR
CONCHO
TURTLE BEND
BRAZOS DR
LAVACA LN
SABINE DR
TEXAS TRADITIONS
TORTOISE
TURTLE
CV

TURTLE
BEND

WILLIAMSON
COUNTY

TEXAS
TRADITIONS

PECAN DR
CLEAR SPRING
RD
SPANISH OAK DR

56

P

N

Q

BOOTY'S CROSSING RD
CANDLELITE
CIR

North Fork San Gabriel River

R

OAK CREST LN

MELANIE
LN

56

CEDAR BREAKS RD

U

GREENRIDGE
RD
GREENRIDGE
RD
NORTHCROSS RD
SHEPHERD RD
FAIRVIEW
RD

V

55

S

T

Y

GREEN RIDGE

OAK RIDGE RD

OAK RIDGE RD

D.B. WOOD RD

WOODWAY
DR
OAK GROVE
LN
POST OAK
LN

WILLIAMSON COUNTY

W

X

EVANS
RD
SKYLINE RD
SOUTHCROSS RD
SKYLINE
SPUR

Z

RIVER CHASE BLVD
TANKSLEY
CIR

Middle Fork San Gabriel River

MJ

MK

CONTINUED ON MAP 254

CONTINUED ON MAP 285

CONTINUED ON MAP 256

SCALE IN MILES

0   ⅛   ¼   ⅜   ½

SCALE IN FEET

0   1000   2000   3000

BOOK PAGE 1016

Directions Made Easy
www.mapsco.com

CONTINUED ON MAP 226

THIS PAGE ALSO APPEARS IN THE
MAPSCO WILLIAMSON COUNTY
STREET GUIDE AS PAGE 256.

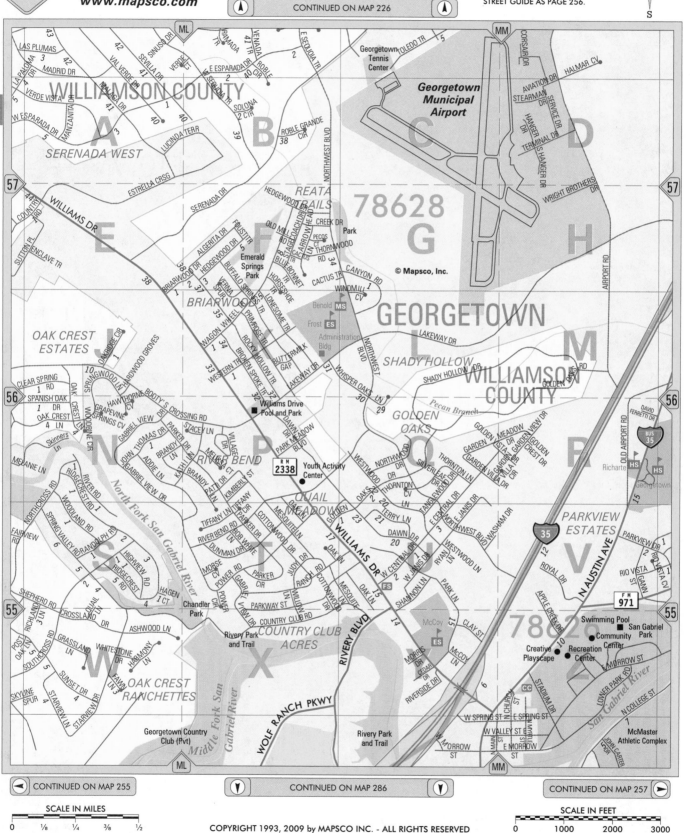

CONTINUED ON MAP 255
CONTINUED ON MAP 286
CONTINUED ON MAP 257

SCALE IN MILES

0   1/8   1/4   3/8   1/2

SCALE IN FEET

0   1000   2000   3000

CONTINUED ON MAP 227

Directions Made Easy
www.mapsco.com

257

THIS PAGE ALSO APPEARS IN THE
MAPSCO WILLIAMSON COUNTY
STREET GUIDE AS PAGE 257.

78628

OLD BISHOP PLACE

CRYSTAL KNOLL TERRACE

78626

WILLIAMSON COUNTY

Berry Springs Park and Preserve

Berry Creek

LAKEWAY DR

INDUSTRIAL PARK CIR

INDUSTRIAL PARK CIR

WILLIAMSON CO RD 152

Lazy Rd

N AUSTIN AVE

WILLIAMSON CO RD 151

Crystal Knoll Park

PECAN BRANCH NORTH

CHANCE TRAIL

EAST DR

LORI LN

WILLIAMSON CO RD 152

LONNIE THOMAS DR

WOLVERINE CV

COUGAR DR

BISON DR

CARIBOU DR

ELK DR

FRIENDS CAMP

SETTLERS PATH

MEADOW TURN

PENNINGTON LN

HERITAGE HWY

FOUNDERS OAK WAY

Pennington Cemetery

PENNINGTON PLACE

David Ferretti Dr

Georgetown Ninth Grade Campus

Georgetown

Pecan Branch

MEDA ST

RANDY ST

FREDDIE DR

HAVERLAND DR

Georgetown Memorial Cemetery

FM 971

© Mapsco, Inc.

Cooper

Forbes

KATON CV

PRAIRIE SPRINGS LN

JANAE CV

PRAIRIE SPRINGS CV

KATY CROSSING

PECAN VISTA LN

PARQUE VISTA

BENCHMARK

RIO VISTA

PARQUE VISTA

PARQUE CV

PARQUE CIR

PARKVIEW ESTATES

MARTIN PL

BASTIAN LN

RIVER PARK CV

Katy Crossing Park

Old Oak Park

KATY CROSSING BLVD

ROSEMARY

ADKINS CV

MEADOWLARK CIR

CLARIS LN

TANNER

E MAY

STEPHEN CV

RIVER PARK LN

RIVER BLUFF LN

RIVER BLUFF CIR

WILDFLOWER LN

Katy Crossing Trail Park

Guadalupe City Cemetery

GEORGETOWN RR CO

130

San Gabriel River

Berry Ln

EAST VIEW DR

DOVE VALLEY DR

River Haven Dr

E MORROW ST

San Gabriel Park

Parks and Recreation Admin

N COLLEGE ST

W L WALDEN DR

GEORGETOWN

Smith Branch

McMaster Athletic Complex

CONTINUED ON MAP 256
CONTINUED ON MAP 287
CONTINUED ON MAP 258

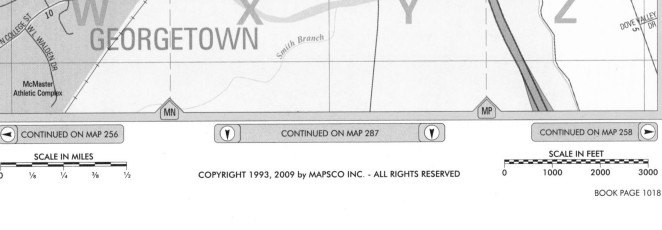

SCALE IN MILES

0   1/8   1/4   3/8   1/2

SCALE IN FEET

0   1000   2000   3000

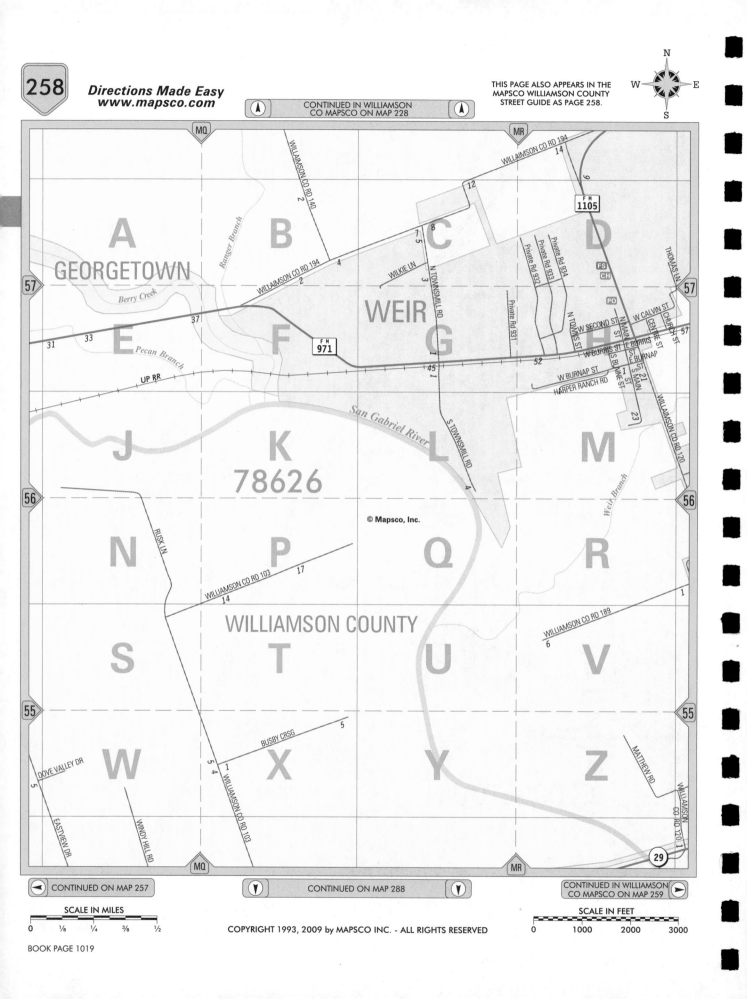

Directions Made Easy
www.mapsco.com

CONTINUED IN WILLIAMSON CO MAPSCO ON MAP 228

THIS PAGE ALSO APPEARS IN THE MAPSCO WILLIAMSON COUNTY STREET GUIDE AS PAGE 258.

N
W   E
S

MQ   MR

WILLIAMSON CO RD 194
14
9
12
F M 1105

A   B   C   D
GEORGETOWN

Ranger Branch
WILLIAMSON CO RD 140 2
WILLIAMSON CO RD 194 4
WILKIE LN
2
7 8
5
3
N TOWNSMILL RD

Private Rd 934
Private Rd 933
Private Rd 932
Private Rd 931

FS CH
PO
THOMAS LN

57   **WEIR**   57

Berry Creek

E   F   G   H
Pecan Branch
FM 971
W SECOND ST
N TOWNS ST
W CALVIN ST
CENTRE ST
CHURCH ST
57
W BURRIS ST
E BURRIS ST
52
W BURNAP ST
E BURNAP
S BLAINE ST
N MAIN ST
S MAIN ST
1 ST
21
23

31   33
37
45
1

UP RR
W BURNAP ST
HARPER RANCH RD

San Gabriel River

J   K   L   M
78626
© Mapsco, Inc.
S TOWNSMILL RD
4
Weir Branch
WILLIAMSON CO RD 120

56   56

RUSK LN

N   P   Q   R
WILLIAMSON CO RD 103
17
14
WILLIAMSON CO RD 189
6
1

WILLIAMSON COUNTY

S   T   U   V

55   55

DOVE VALLEY DR
BUSBY CRSG
5
5
MATTHEW RD

W   X   Y   Z
5
5 4 1
WILLIAMSON CO RD 103

EASTVIEW DR
WINDY HILL RD
WILLIAMSON CO RD 120 1

MQ   MR   29

CONTINUED ON MAP 257

CONTINUED ON MAP 288

CONTINUED IN WILLIAMSON CO MAPSCO ON MAP 259

SCALE IN MILES
0   ⅛   ¼   ⅜   ½

SCALE IN FEET
0   1000   2000   3000

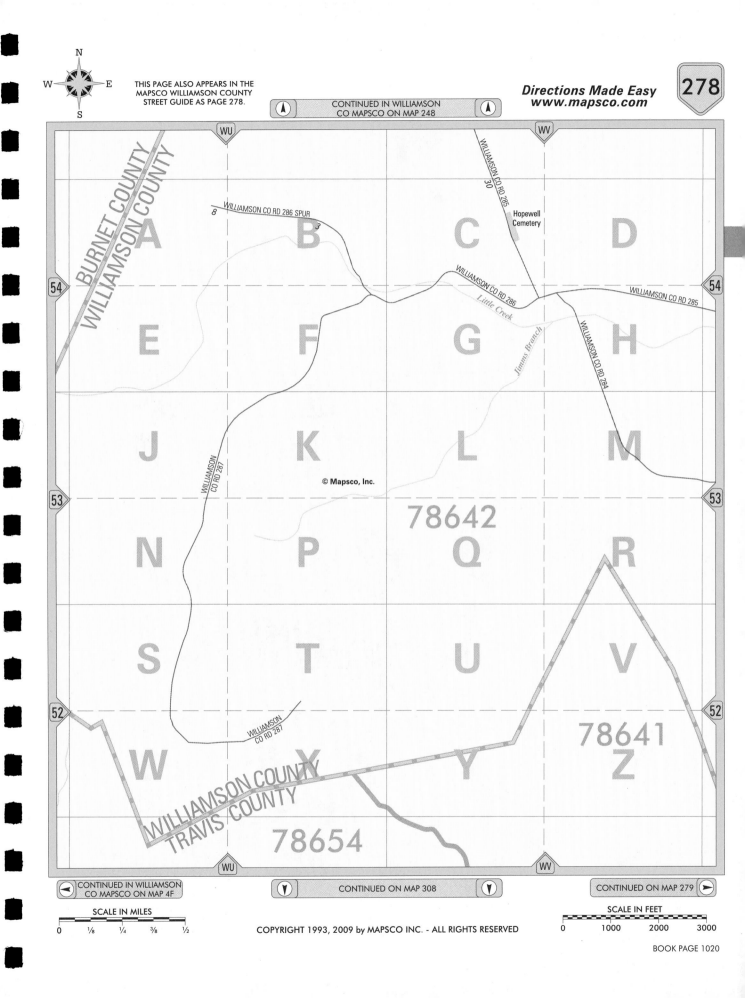

CONTINUED IN WILLIAMSON
CO MAPSCO ON MAP 248

Directions Made Easy
www.mapsco.com

278

N
W · E
S

WU

WV

BURNET COUNTY
WILLIAMSON COUNTY

WILLIAMSON CO RD 285
30

A

WILLIAMSON CO RD 286 SPUR
8

B
3

C

Hopewell
Cemetery

D

54

WILLIAMSON CO RD 286

Little Creek

WILLIAMSON CO RD 285

54

E

F

G

Jimms Branch

WILLIAMSON CO RD 284

H

J

WILLIAMSON
CO RD 287

K

© Mapsco, Inc.

L

M

53

N

P

78642

Q

R

53

S

T

U

V

52

WILLIAMSON
CO RD 287

78641

Z

52

W

X

WILLIAMSON COUNTY
TRAVIS COUNTY

Y

78654

WU

WV

CONTINUED IN WILLIAMSON
CO MAPSCO ON MAP 4F

CONTINUED ON MAP 308

CONTINUED ON MAP 279

SCALE IN MILES

0   1/8   1/4   3/8   1/2

SCALE IN FEET

0   1000   2000   3000

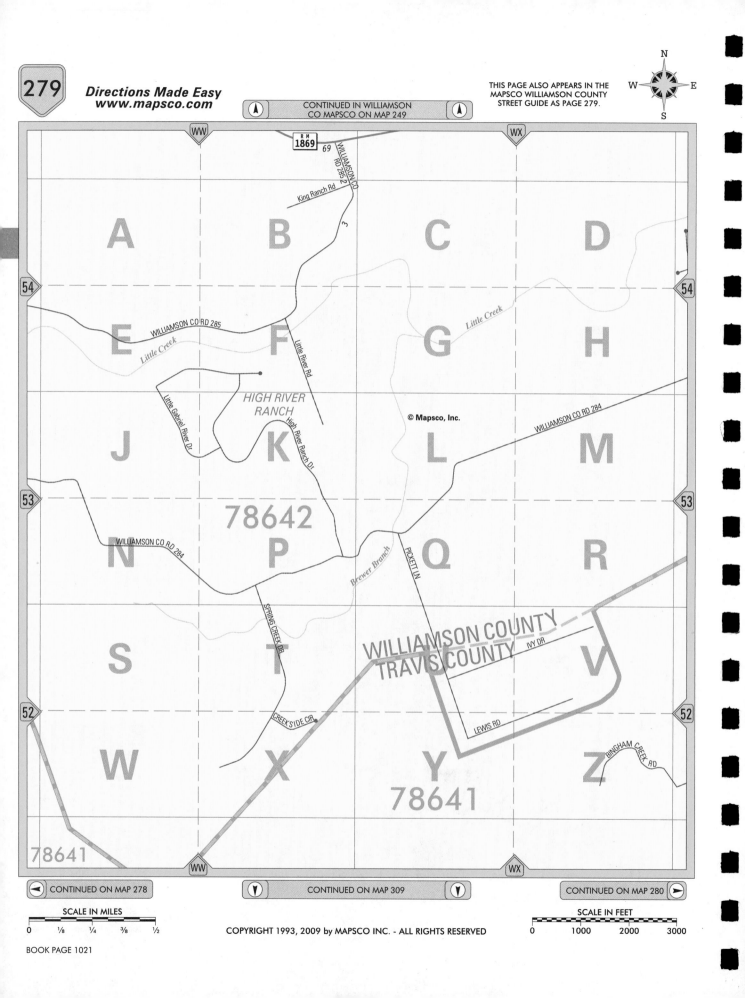

THIS PAGE ALSO APPEARS IN THE
MAPSCO WILLIAMSON COUNTY
STREET GUIDE AS PAGE 279.

N
W · E
S

CONTINUED IN WILLIAMSON
CO MAPSCO ON MAP 249

WW

WX

R M
1869
69

WILLIAMSON CO RD 285 2

King Ranch Rd

3

A

B

C

D

54

54

WILLIAMSON CO RD 285

Little Creek

Little Creek

E

F

G

H

Little River Rd

Little Gabriel River Dr

HIGH RIVER RANCH

High River Ranch Dr

© Mapsco, Inc.

WILLIAMSON CO RD 284

J

K

L

M

53

53

WILLIAMSON CO RD 284

Brewer Branch

PICKETT LN

N

P

Q

R

Spring Creek Dr

WILLIAMSON COUNTY
TRAVIS COUNTY

IVY DR

S

T

V

52

52

Creek's Ide Cir

LEWIS RD

BINGHAM CREEK RD

78642

W

X

Y

Z

78641

78641

WW

WX

CONTINUED ON MAP 278

CONTINUED ON MAP 309

CONTINUED ON MAP 280

SCALE IN MILES

0   1/8   1/4   3/8   1/2

SCALE IN FEET

0   1000   2000   3000

BOOK PAGE 1021

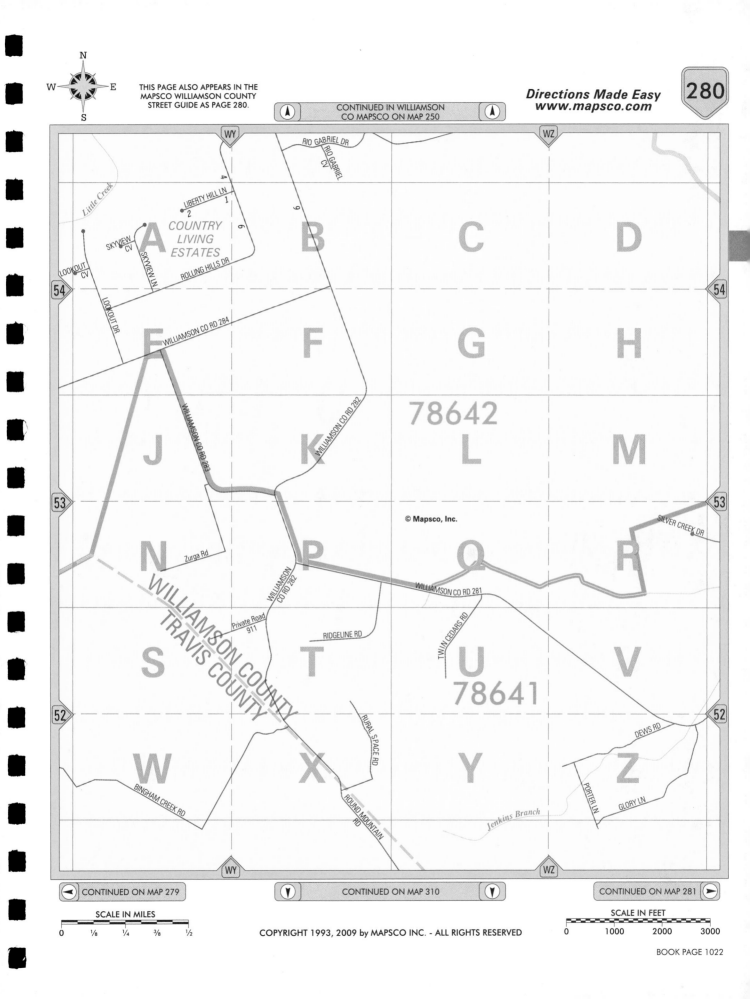

THIS PAGE ALSO APPEARS IN THE
MAPSCO WILLIAMSON COUNTY
STREET GUIDE AS PAGE 280.

Directions Made Easy
www.mapsco.com

CONTINUED IN WILLIAMSON
CO MAPSCO ON MAP 250

WY

WZ

RIO GABRIEL DR

RIO GABRIEL CV

Little Creek

LIBERTY HILL LN

COUNTRY
LIVING
ESTATES

A

SKYVIEW CV

SKYVIEW LN

ROLLING HILLS DR

LOOKOUT CV

54

LOOKOUT DR

WILLIAMSON CO RD 284

54

E

B

C

D

F

G

H

WILLIAMSON CO RD 282

78642

WILLIAMSON CO RD 283

J

K

L

M

53

© Mapsco, Inc.

53

SILVER CREEK DR

Zurga Rd

N

P

WILLIAMSON CO RD 282

WILLIAMSON CO RD 281

Q

R

Private Road 911

Ridgeline Rd

TWIN CEDARS RD

WILLIAMSON COUNTY

TRAVIS COUNTY

S

T

U

V

78641

52

RURAL SPACE RD

DEWS RD

52

W

X

Y

Z

PORTER LN

GLORY LN

BINGHAM CREEK RD

ROUND MOUNTAIN RD

Jenkins Branch

WY

WZ

CONTINUED ON MAP 279

CONTINUED ON MAP 310

CONTINUED ON MAP 281

SCALE IN MILES

0   ⅛   ¼   ⅜   ½

SCALE IN FEET

0   1000   2000   3000

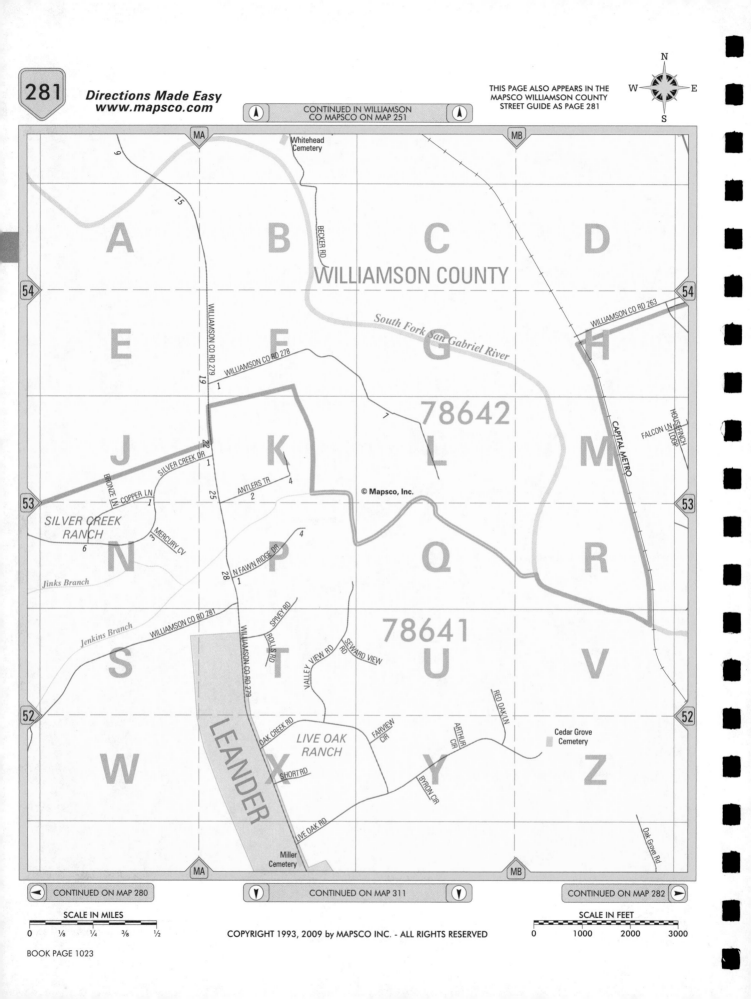

281

Directions Made Easy
www.mapsco.com

CONTINUED IN WILLIAMSON CO MAPSCO ON MAP 251

THIS PAGE ALSO APPEARS IN THE
MAPSCO WILLIAMSON COUNTY
STREET GUIDE AS PAGE 281

N
W E
S

MA
MB

Whitehead Cemetery

9

15

BECKER RD

A

B

WILLIAMSON COUNTY

C

D

54

54

WILLIAMSON CO RD 263

South Fork San Gabriel River

WILLIAMSON CO RD 279

E

WILLIAMSON CO RD 278

F

G

78642

H

HOUSEFINCH LOOP

FALCON LN

CAPITAL METRO

19

1

7

J

SILVER CREEK DR

22

K

ANTLERS TR

L

© Mapsco, Inc.

M

53

BRONZE LN

COPPER LN

1

25

1

2

4

53

SILVER CREEK RANCH

MERCURY CV

3

6

N

Jinks Branch

N FAWN RIDGE DR

28

1

4

P

Q

R

Jenkins Branch

WILLIAMSON CO RD 281

SPIVEY RD

ROLLS RD

VALLEY VIEW RD

SEWARD VIEW RD

78641

52

WILLIAMSON CO RD 279

S

T

U

V

52

LEANER

W

OAK CREEK RD

LIVE OAK RANCH

X

SHORT RD

FARVIEW CIR

ARTHUR CIR

RED OAK LN

Cedar Grove Cemetery

Y

BYRON CIR

Z

LIVE OAK RD

Miller Cemetery

Oak Grove Rd

MA
MB

CONTINUED ON MAP 280

CONTINUED ON MAP 311

CONTINUED ON MAP 282

SCALE IN MILES

0   1/8   1/4   3/8   1/2

SCALE IN FEET

0   1000   2000   3000

COPYRIGHT 1993, 2009 by MAPSCO INC. - ALL RIGHTS RESERVED

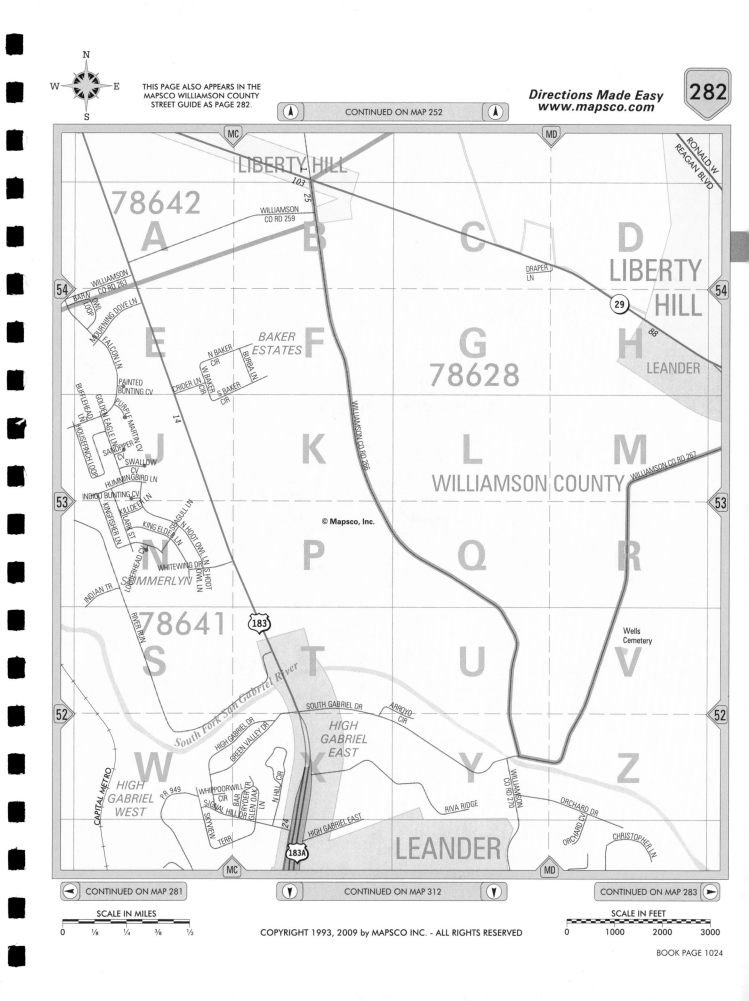

CONTINUED ON MAP 252

THIS PAGE ALSO APPEARS IN THE MAPSCO WILLIAMSON COUNTY STREET GUIDE AS PAGE 282.

Directions Made Easy
www.mapsco.com

282

LIBERTY HILL

RONALD W REAGAN BLVD

78642

A

WILLIAMSON CO RD 259

B

C

DRAPER LN

D

LIBERTY HILL

29

54

WILLIAMSON CO RD 263

BARN OWL LOOP

MOURNING DOVE LN

54

88

H

LEANDER

FALCON LN

E

BAKER ESTATES

F

N BAKER CIR

W BAKER CIR

BURBA LN

G

78628

PAINTED BUNTING CV

CRIDER LN CIR

S BAKER CIR

BUFFLEHEAD LN

GOLDEN EAGLE LN

HOUSEFINCH LOOP

PURPLE MARTIN CV

SANDPIPER CV

SWALLOW CV

14

J

K

L

WILLIAMSON CO RD 266

M

WILLIAMSON CO RD 267

HUMMINGBIRD LN

INDIGO BUNTING CV

KINGFISHER LN

KILLDEER LN

SEAGULL LN

N HOOT OWL LN

S HOOT OWL LN

WILLIAMSON COUNTY

53

53

LARK ST

KING ELDER LN

LOGGERHEAD CV

N

SUMMERLYN

WHITEWING DR

P

Q

R

© Mapsco, Inc.

Wells Cemetery

INDIAN TR

RIVER RUN

78641

S

T

U

V

183

SOUTH GABRIEL DR

ARROYO CIR

HIGH GABRIEL EAST

52

HIGH GABRIEL DR

GREEN VALLEY DR

N HILL CIR

52

W

HIGH GABRIEL WEST

CAPITAL METRO

P.R. 949

WHIPPOORWILL CIR

BAR RYDER TR

GLEN OAK LN

SIGNAL HILL DR

SKYVIEW TERR

X

24

Y

RIVA RIDGE

WILLIAMSON CO RD 270

Z

ORCHARD DR

ORCHARD CV

CHRISTOPHER LN

HIGH GABRIEL EAST

183A

LEANDER

CONTINUED ON MAP 281

CONTINUED ON MAP 312

CONTINUED ON MAP 283

SCALE IN MILES

0 1/8 1/4 3/8 1/2

SCALE IN FEET

0 1000 2000 3000

COPYRIGHT 1993, 2009 by MAPSCO INC. - ALL RIGHTS RESERVED

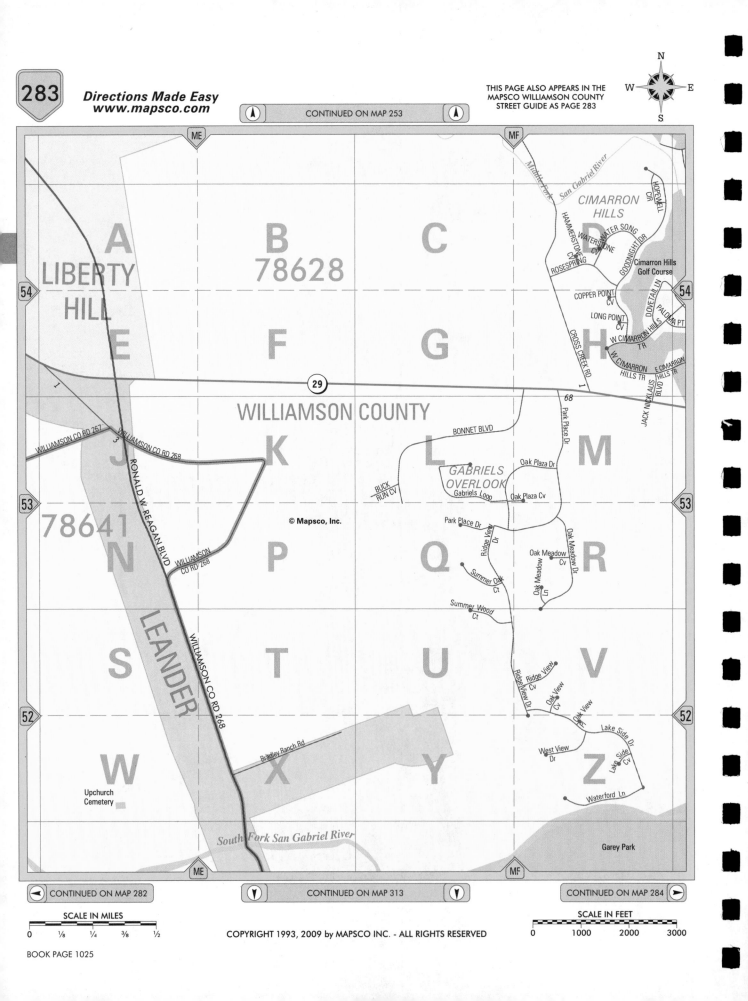

283

Directions Made Easy
www.mapsco.com

THIS PAGE ALSO APPEARS IN THE
MAPSCO WILLIAMSON COUNTY
STREET GUIDE AS PAGE 283

N
W E
S

CONTINUED ON MAP 253

ME

MF

Middle Fork
San Gabriel River

A
LIBERTY
HILL

B
78628

C

CIMARRON
HILLS

HOPEWELL CIR

HAMMERSTONE
WATERSTONE CV
WATER SONG CV
GOODNIGHT DR
ROSESPRING

Cimarron Hills
Golf Course

54

E

F

G

COPPER POINT CV

LONG POINT CV

W CIMARRON HILLS TR

W CIMARRON HILLS TR

D

DOVETAIL LN
PALOMA PT

H

E CIMARRON HILLS TR

54

1

29

1

WILLIAMSON COUNTY

CROSS CREEK RD

Park Place Dr

JACK NICKLAUS BLVD

68

BONNET BLVD

J

K

L

GABRIELS
OVERLOOK

Oak Plaza Dr

M

WILLIAMSON CO RD 257

WILLIAMSON CO RD 268

RONALD W REAGAN BLVD

53

BUCK
RUN CV

Gabriels Loop

Oak Plaza Cv

53

78641

N

Park Place Dr

P

WILLIAMSON CO RD 268

Q

Ridge View Dr

Oak Meadow Cv

Oak Meadow Dr

R

© Mapsco, Inc.

Summer Oak Ct

Oak Meadow Ln

Summer Wood Ct

S

LEANDER

T

U

Ridge View Dr

Ridge View Cv

V

Oak View Cv

Oak View Pt

52

52

Lake Side Dr

W

Bradley Ranch Rd

X

Y

West View Dr

Z

Lake Side Cv

Upchurch
Cemetery

Waterford Ln

Garey Park

South Fork San Gabriel River

ME

MF

CONTINUED ON MAP 282

CONTINUED ON MAP 313

CONTINUED ON MAP 284

SCALE IN MILES

0   1/8   1/4   3/8   1/2

SCALE IN FEET

0   1000   2000   3000

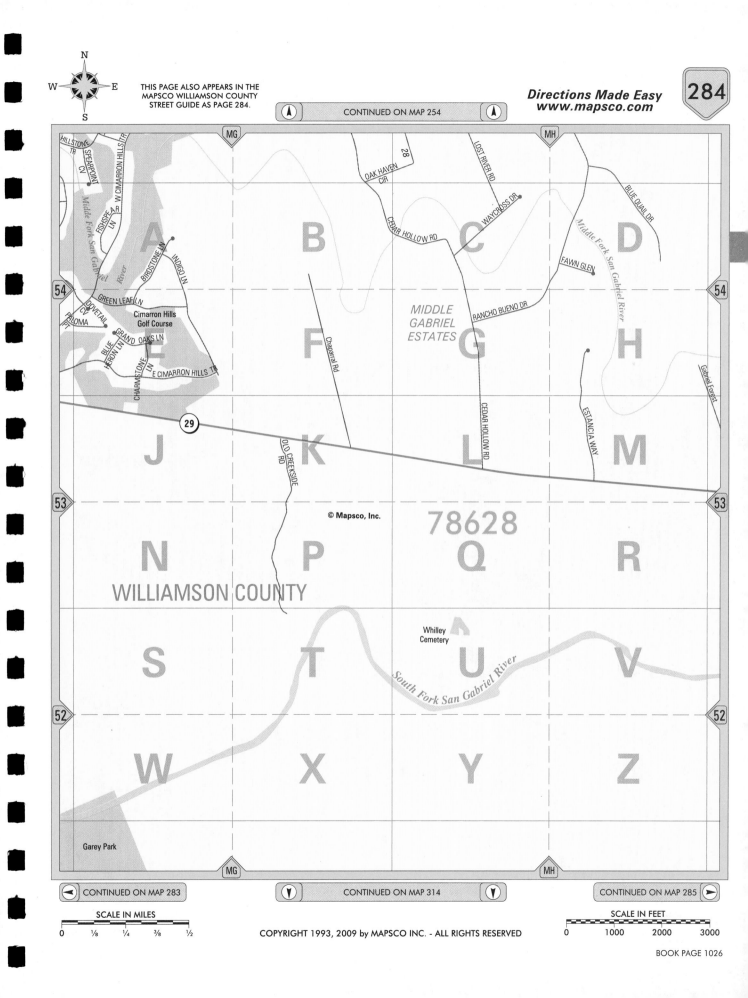

THIS PAGE ALSO APPEARS IN THE
MAPSCO WILLIAMSON COUNTY
STREET GUIDE AS PAGE 284.

Directions Made Easy
www.mapsco.com

CONTINUED ON MAP 254

N
W E
S

HILLSTONE TR
SPEARPOINT CV
W CIMARRON HILLS TR
FISHSPEAR LN
BIRDSTONE LN
INDIGO LN
GREEN LEAF LN
DOVETAIL CV
PALOMA PST
BLUE HERON LN
CHARMSTONE LN
GRAN'D OAKS LN
E CIMARRON HILLS TR

Middle Fork San Gabriel River

Cimarron Hills
Golf Course

54   54

OAK HAVEN CIR
28
LOST RIVER RD
CEDAR HOLLOW RD
WAYCROSS DR
BLUE QUAIL DR
Middle Fork San Gabriel River
FAWN GLEN

A   B   C   D

MIDDLE
GABRIEL
ESTATES

RANCHO BUENO DR

F   G   H

Gabriel Forest

CHAPARRAL RD

CEDAR HOLLOW RD

ESTANCIA WAY

29

J   K   L   M

OLD CREEKSIDE RD

53   53

© Mapsco, Inc.

78628

N   P   Q   R

WILLIAMSON COUNTY

Whilley
Cemetery

S   T   U   V

South Fork San Gabriel River

52   52

W   X   Y   Z

Garey Park

CONTINUED ON MAP 283

CONTINUED ON MAP 314

CONTINUED ON MAP 285

SCALE IN MILES
0   ⅛   ¼   ⅜   ½

SCALE IN FEET
0   1000   2000   3000

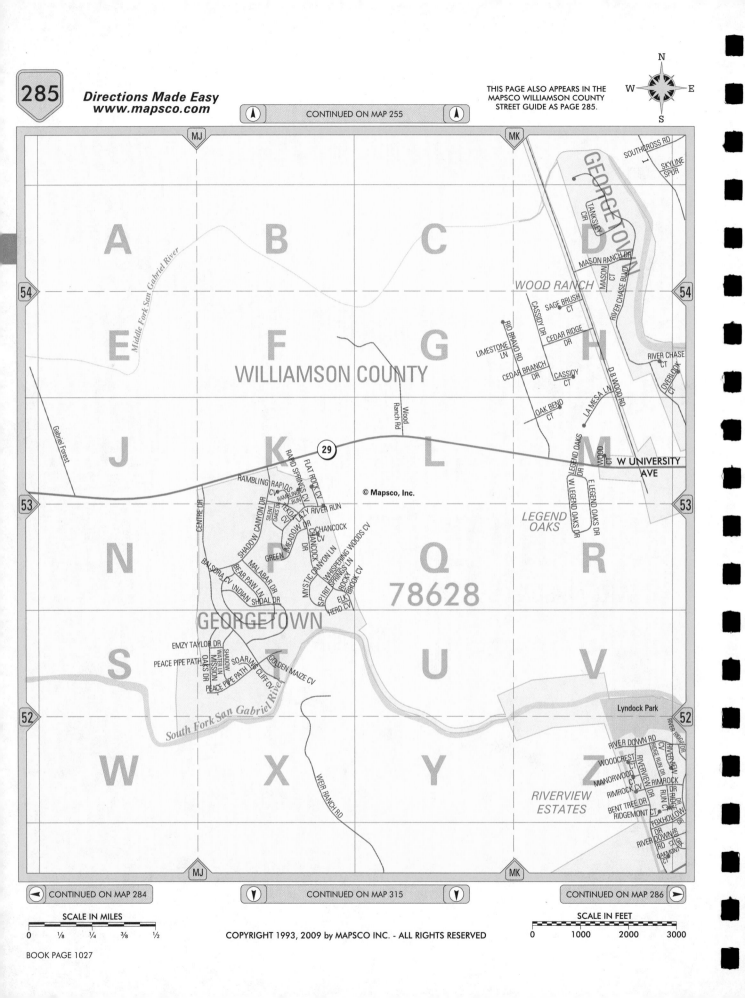

285

Directions Made Easy
www.mapsco.com

N
W E
S

CONTINUED ON MAP 255

MJ   MK

GEORGETOWN

SOUTHCROSS RD

SKYLINE SPUR

A   B   C   D

TANKSLEY CIR

MASON RANCH DR

54   54

MASON CT

RIVER CHASE BLVD

WOOD RANCH

SAGE BRUSH CT

CASSIDY DR

CEDAR RIDGE DR

E   F   G   H

RIVER CHASE CT

LIMESTONE LN

RIO BRAVO RD

CEDAR BRANCH DR

CASSIDY CT

D.B. WOOD RD

OVERLOOK CT

WILLIAMSON COUNTY

OAK BEND CT

LA MESA LN

Wood Ranch Rd

29

W University Ave

RAMBLING RAPIDS

FLAT ROCK CV

RAPID SPRINGS CV

J   K   L   M

53   53

CENTRE DR

RAMBLING RAPIDS CV

RAMBLING RUN

SILENT OAKS DR

TEKOLA CV

LAZY RIVER RUN

W LEGEND OAKS DR

E LEGEND OAKS DR

LEGEND OAKS

© Mapsco, Inc.

SHADOW CANYON DR

MEADOW DR

CHANCOCK CV

CHANCOCK CV

WHISPERING WOODS CV

N   P   Q   R

GREEN

MALABAR DR

MYSTIC CANYON LN

SPIRIT SPRINGS LN

ROCKY BROOK CV

BALSORA CV

BEAR PAW LN

INDIAN SHOAL DR

ELK HERD CV

78628

GEORGETOWN

EMZY TAYLOR DR

PEACE PIPE PATH

WATER LN

SHADOW MISSION

SOARING CLIFF CV

GOLDEN MAIZE CV

S   T   U   V

OAKS DR

PEACE PIPE PATH

Lyndock Park

52   52

RIVER DOWN RD

River Ridge Cv

South Fork San Gabriel River

WEIR RANCH RD

W   X   Y   Z

RIVERVIEW

WOODCREST CT

MANORWOOD

RIVERVIEW DR

RIMROCK RUN

RIVERVIEW ESTATES

RIMROCK CV

BENT TREE DR

RIDGEMONT CT

BED OAK RIDGE DR

FOXHOLLOW DR

RIVER DOWN RD

RED OAK CT

OAKMONT CT

MJ   MK

CONTINUED ON MAP 284

CONTINUED ON MAP 315

CONTINUED ON MAP 286

SCALE IN MILES
0   1/8   1/4   3/8   1/2

SCALE IN FEET
0   1000   2000   3000

BOOK PAGE 1027

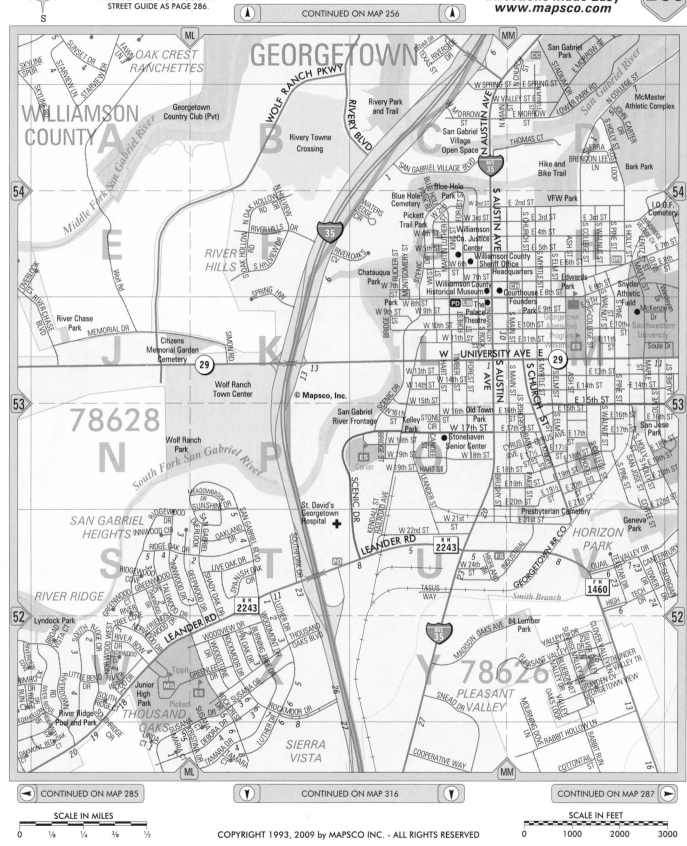

THIS PAGE ALSO APPEARS IN THE
MAPSCO WILLIAMSON COUNTY
STREET GUIDE AS PAGE 286.

Directions Made Easy
www.mapsco.com

CONTINUED ON MAP 256

GEORGETOWN

WILLIAMSON
COUNTY

OAK CREST
RANCHETTES

San Gabriel
Park

McMaster
Athletic Complex

Georgetown
Country Club (Pvt)

Rivery Park
and Trail

Rivery Towne
Crossing

Hike and
Bike Trail

Bark Park

I.O.O.F.
Cemetery

San Gabriel
Village Open Space

VFW Park

Blue Hole
Park

RIVER
HILLS

Blue Hole
Cemetery

Pickett
Trail Park

Williamson
Co. Justice
Center

Williamson County
Sheriff Office
Headquarters

Edwards
Park

Snyder
Athletic
Field

Chatauqua
Park

Williamson County
Historical Museum

Courthouse

McKenzie
Dr

River Chase
Park

Park

Founders
Park

The
Palace
Theatre

Georgetown
Alternative
Program

Southwestern
University

Citizens
Memorial Garden
Cemetery

Soule Dr

UNIVERSITY AVE

78628

Wolf Ranch
Town Center

Old Town
Park

San Gabriel
River Frontage

Kelley
Park

Wolf Ranch
Park

Stonehaven
Senior Center

San Jose
Park

SAN GABRIEL
HEIGHTS

Carver

St. David's
Georgetown
Hospital

Presbyterian Cemetery

Geneva
Park

HORIZON
PARK

RIVER RIDGE

LEANDER RD

Smith Branch

Lyndock Park

84 Lumber
Park

Junior
High
Park

78626

River Ridge
Pool and Park

THOUSAND
OAKS

SIERRA
VISTA

PLEASANT
VALLEY

CONTINUED ON MAP 285

CONTINUED ON MAP 316

CONTINUED ON MAP 287

SCALE IN MILES

0   ⅛   ¼   ⅜   ½

COPYRIGHT 1993, 2009 by MAPSCO INC. - ALL RIGHTS RESERVED

SCALE IN FEET

0   1000   2000   3000

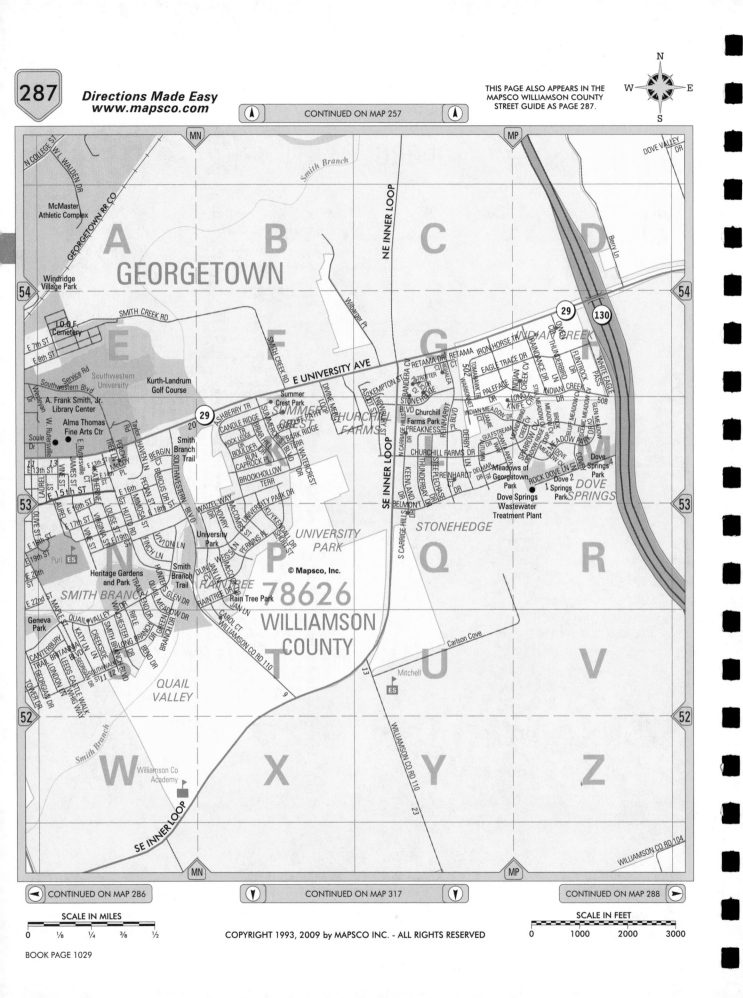

Directions Made Easy
www.mapsco.com

THIS PAGE ALSO APPEARS IN THE
MAPSCO WILLIAMSON COUNTY
STREET GUIDE AS PAGE 287.

N
W E
S

CONTINUED ON MAP 257

GEORGETOWN

A   B   C   D

54   54

E   F   G

29 130

© Mapsco, Inc.

78626

**WILLIAMSON
COUNTY**

N   P   Q   R

53   53

S   T   U   V

52   52

W   X   Y   Z

CONTINUED ON MAP 286

CONTINUED ON MAP 317

CONTINUED ON MAP 288

SCALE IN MILES

0   ⅛   ¼   ⅜   ½

SCALE IN FEET

0   1000   2000   3000

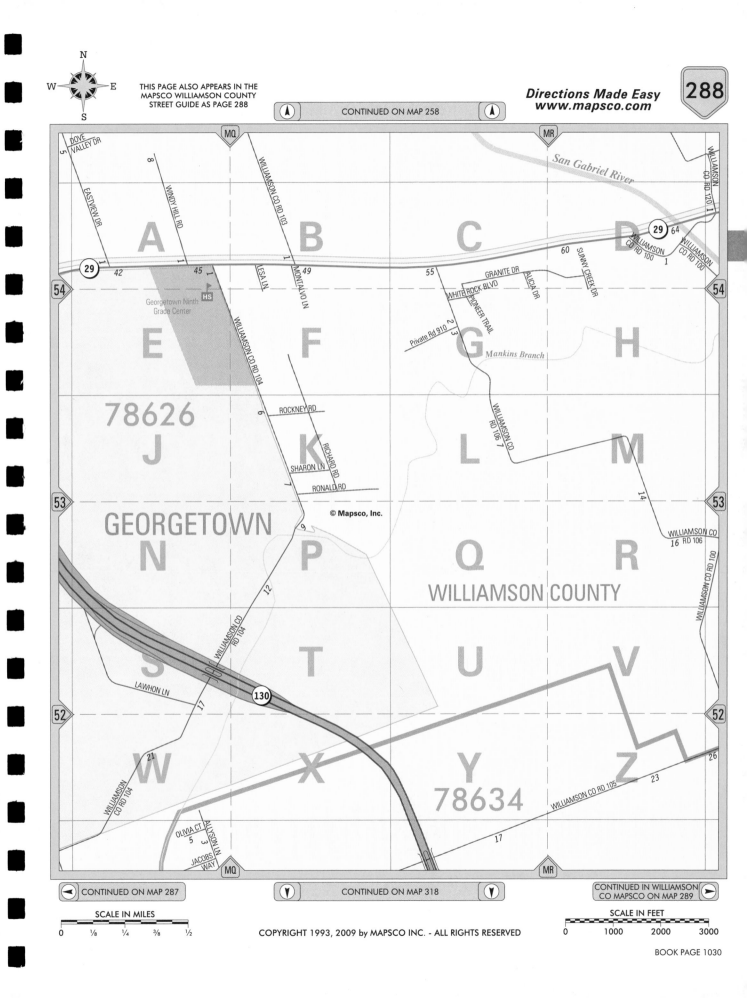

288

THIS PAGE ALSO APPEARS IN THE
MAPSCO WILLIAMSON COUNTY
STREET GUIDE AS PAGE 288

Directions Made Easy
www.mapsco.com

N
W · E
S

CONTINUED ON MAP 258

San Gabriel River

MQ   MR

DOVE VALLEY DR
5
EASTVIEW DR
8
WINDY HILL RD
WILLIAMSON CO RD 103

WILLIAMSON CO RD 120   1

A   B   C   D   29   64

29
42   45   1
LESA LN
MONTALVO LN   49
55
WHITE ROCK BLVD
GRANITE DR
PIONEER TRAIL
ALICIA DR
60
SUNNY CREEK DR
WILLIAMSON CO RD 100   1
WILLIAMSON CO RD 100

54   54

HS
Georgetown Ninth
Grade Center

E   F   G   H

Pivate Rd 910   2
3
Mankins Branch

WILLIAMSON CO RD 104

78626

ROCKNEY RD
6
WILLIAMSON CO RD 106   7

J   K   L   M

RICHARD RD
SHARON LN
RONALD RD
7
14

GEORGETOWN

53   53

9
WILLIAMSON CO RD 106   16

N   P   Q   R

WILLIAMSON COUNTY
WILLIAMSON CO RD 100

© Mapsco, Inc.

12

WILLIAMSON CO RD 104

S   T   U   V

LAWHON LN
17
130

52   52

21   26
23

W   X   Y   Z

OLIVIA CT   5
ALLYSON LN   3
JACOBS WAY
17
WILLIAMSON CO RD 105
WILLIAMSON CO RD 104

78634

MQ   MR

CONTINUED ON MAP 287

CONTINUED ON MAP 318

CONTINUED IN WILLIAMSON
CO MAPSCO ON MAP 289

SCALE IN MILES
0   ⅛   ¼   ⅜   ½

SCALE IN FEET
0   1000   2000   3000

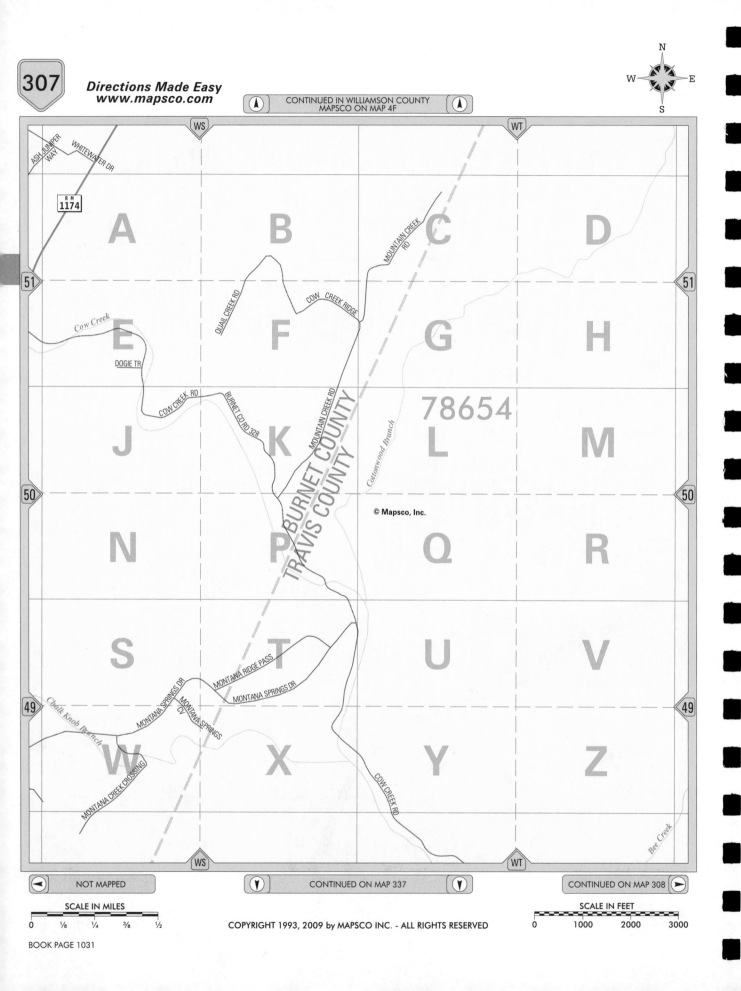

307

Directions Made Easy
www.mapsco.com

CONTINUED IN WILLIAMSON COUNTY
MAPSCO ON MAP 4F

ASH JUNIPER WAY
WHITEWATER DR

R M 1174

WS · WT

A · B · C · D

51 · 51

Cow Creek

QUAIL CREEK RD

E · F · COW CREEK RIDGE · G · H

MOUNTAIN CREEK RD

DOGIE TR

COW CREEK RD

BURNET CO RD 328

MOUNTAIN CREEK RD

78654

J · K · L · M

BURNET COUNTY
TRAVIS COUNTY

Cottonwood Branch

50 · 50

© Mapsco, Inc.

N · P · Q · R

Montana Ridge Pass

S · T · MONTANA SPRINGS DR · U · V

MONTANA SPRINGS DR

49 · 49

Chalk Knob Branch

MONTANA SPRINGS DR

MONTANA SPRINGS CV

MONTANA SPRINGS

W · X · Y · Z

MONTANA CREEK CROSSING

COW CREEK RD

Bee Creek

WS · WT

◄ NOT MAPPED | ▼ CONTINUED ON MAP 337 | CONTINUED ON MAP 308 ►

SCALE IN MILES
0 · 1/8 · 1/4 · 3/8 · 1/2

SCALE IN FEET
0 · 1000 · 2000 · 3000

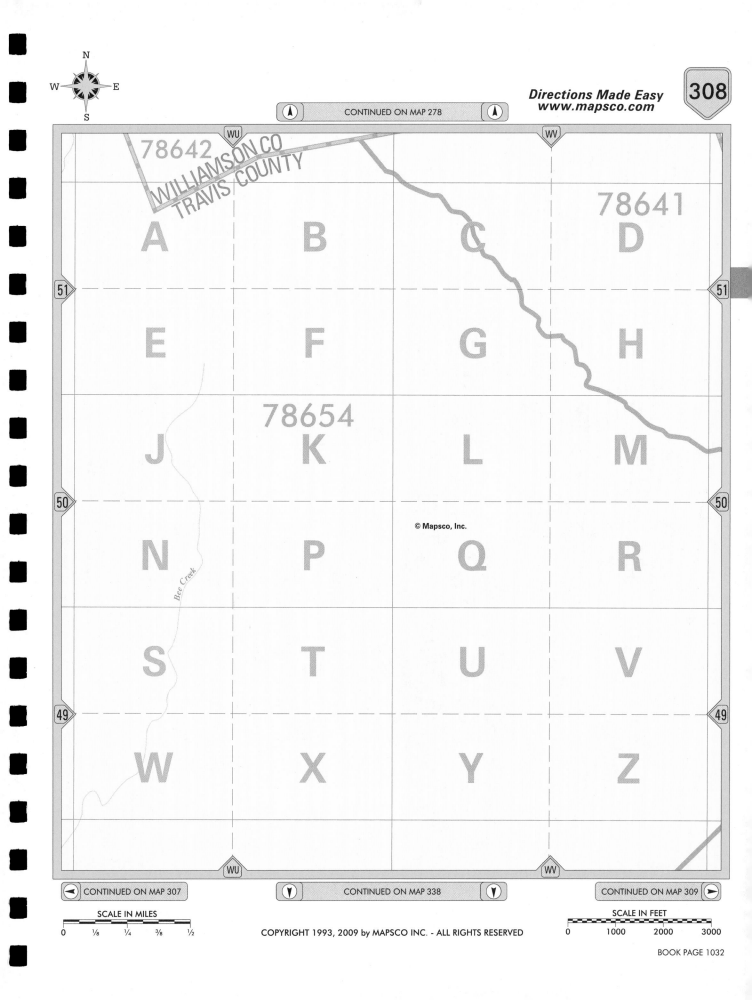

W N E S

CONTINUED ON MAP 278

WU

WV

78642

WILLIAMSON CO
TRAVIS COUNTY

78641

A   B   C   D

51   51

E   F   G   H

78654

J   K   L   M

50   50

© Mapsco, Inc.

N   P   Q   R

Bee Creek

S   T   U   V

49   49

W   X   Y   Z

WU

WV

CONTINUED ON MAP 307

CONTINUED ON MAP 338

CONTINUED ON MAP 309

SCALE IN MILES

0   ⅛   ¼   ⅜   ½

SCALE IN FEET

0   1000   2000   3000

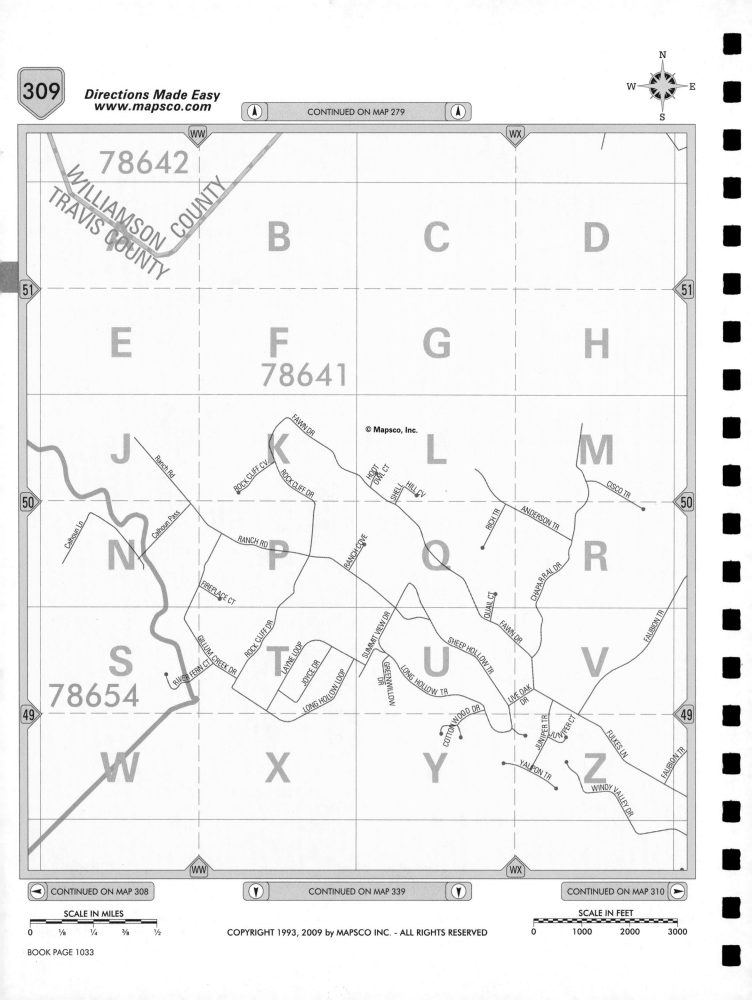

CONTINUED ON MAP 279

N
W E
S

78642

WILLIAMSON COUNTY
TRAVIS COUNTY

51

B   C   D

51

E   F   G   H

78641

© Mapsco, Inc.

J   K   L   M

Ranch Rd
FAWN DR
ROCK CLIFF CV
ROCK CLIFF DR
HOOT OWL CT
SHELL
HILL CV
CISCO TR
RICH TR
ANDERSON TR

50   50

Calhoun Ln
Calhoun Pass

N   RANCH RD   P   RANCH COVE   Q   R

QUAIL CT
FAWN DR
CHAPARRAL DR

FIREPLACE CT

FAUBION TR

S   T   U   V

78654

GILLUM CREEK DR
ROCK CLIFF DR
LAYNE LOOP
JOYCE DR
LONG HOLLOW LOOP
SUMMIT VIEW DR
GREENWILLOW DR
LONG HOLLOW TR
SHEEP HOLLOW TR
LIVE OAK DR
River Fern Ct

49   49

COTTONWOOD DR
JUNIPER TR
JUNIPER CT
FULKES LN
FAUBION TR

W   X   Y   Z

YAUPON TR
WINDY VALLEY DR

CONTINUED ON MAP 308
CONTINUED ON MAP 339
CONTINUED ON MAP 310

SCALE IN MILES
0   1/8   1/4   3/8   1/2

SCALE IN FEET
0   1000   2000   3000

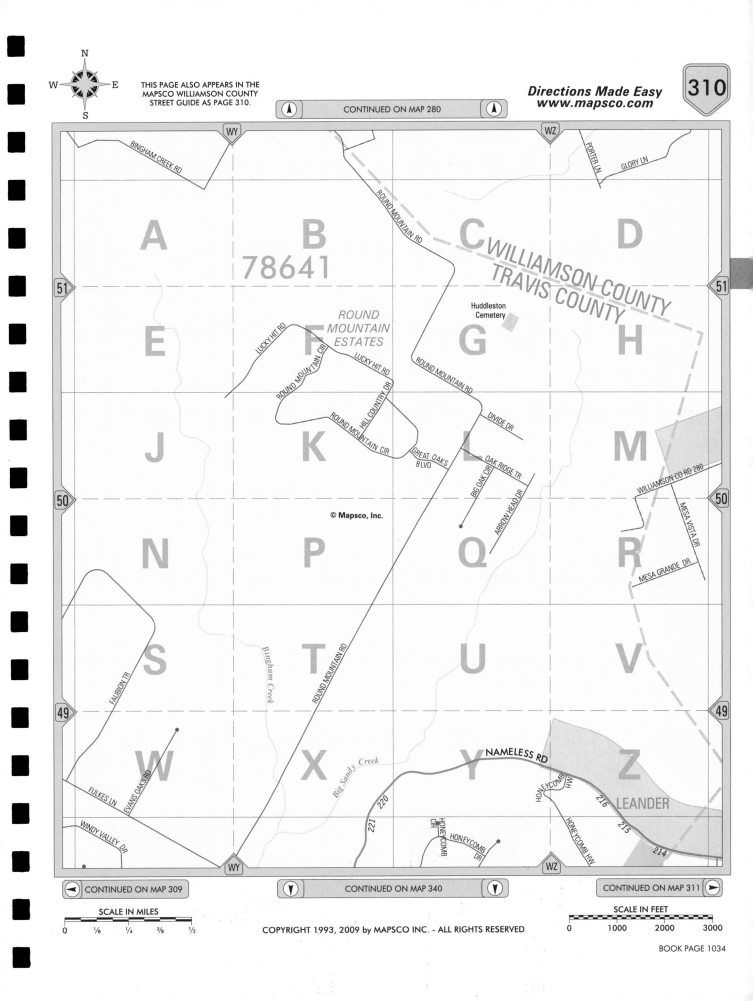

CONTINUED ON MAP 280

Directions Made Easy
www.mapsco.com

310

N
W E
S

WY
WZ

PORTER LN
GLORY LN

BINGHAM CREEK RD

ROUND MOUNTAIN RD

A
B
78641
C
WILLIAMSON COUNTY
TRAVIS COUNTY
D

51
51

Huddleston
Cemetery

E
ROUND
MOUNTAIN
ESTATES
F
G
H

LUCKY HIT RD
LUCKY HIT RD
ROUND MOUNTAIN CIRL
ROUND MOUNTAIN RD

HILL COUNTRY DR
DIVIDE DR

J
K
ROUND MOUNTAIN CIR
L
M

GREAT OAKS BLVD
OAK RIDGE TR
BIG OAK CIR
ARROW HEAD DR

WILLIAMSON CO RD 280

© Mapsco, Inc.

MESA VISTA DR

50
50

N
P
Q
R

MESA GRANDE DR

Bingham Creek

S
T
ROUND MOUNTAIN RD
U
V

FAUBION TR

49
49

WINDY VALLEY DR
FULKES LN
EVANS OAKS RD

W
X
Big Sandy Creek
Y
NAMELESS RD
Z
LEANDER

HONEYCOMB HW
216
215
214

221
220

HONEYCOMB CIR
HONEYCOMB DR

HONEYCOMB HW

WY
WZ

CONTINUED ON MAP 309
CONTINUED ON MAP 340
CONTINUED ON MAP 311

SCALE IN MILES
0   ⅛   ¼   ⅜   ½

SCALE IN FEET
0   1000   2000   3000

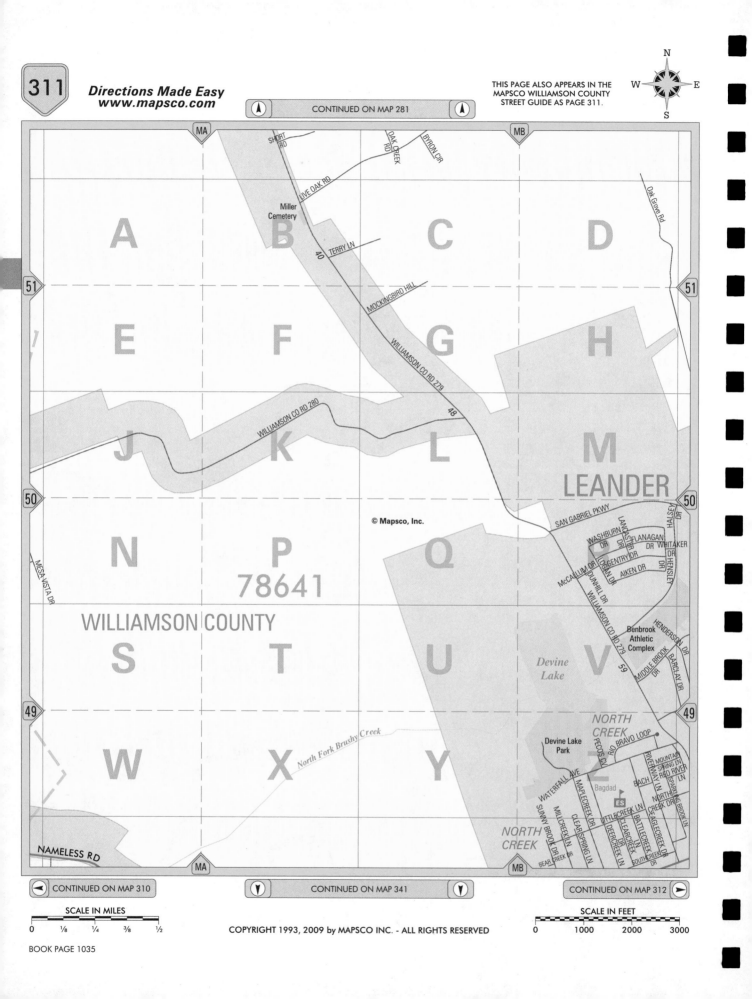

THIS PAGE ALSO APPEARS IN THE MAPSCO WILLIAMSON COUNTY STREET GUIDE AS PAGE 312.

N W E S

Directions Made Easy
www.mapsco.com

CONTINUED ON MAP 282

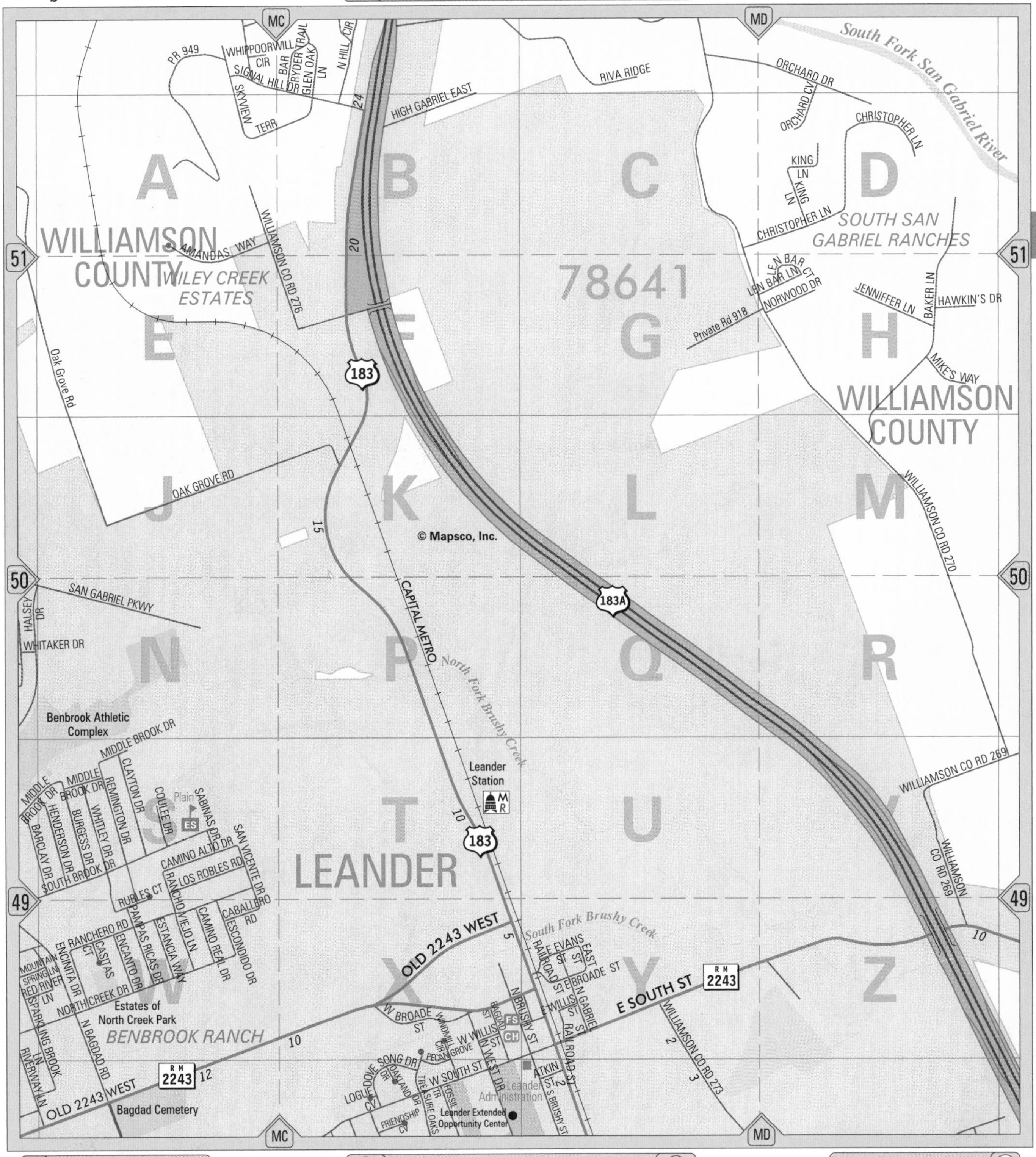

MC

MD

South Fork San Gabriel River

PR 949
WHIPPOORWILL CIR
BAR
RYDER TRAIL
GLEN OAK LN
N HILL CIR
SIGNAL HILL DR
SKYVIEW TERR
24
HIGH GABRIEL EAST

RIVA RIDGE

ORCHARD DR
ORCHARD CV
CHRISTOPHER LN

A

B

C

D

KING LN
KING LN
CHRISTOPHER LN

SOUTH SAN GABRIEL RANCHES

51

WILLIAMSON COUNTY
WILEY CREEK ESTATES
AMANDAS WAY
WILLIAMSON COUNTY RD 276

20

78641

GLEN BAR LN
GLEN BAR CT
NORWOOD DR
Private Rd 918

JENNIFFER LN
BAKER LN
HAWKIN'S DR

51

E

F

G

H

183

MIKE'S WAY

WILLIAMSON COUNTY

Oak Grove Rd

OAK GROVE RD

15

J

K

CAPITAL METRO

© Mapsco, Inc.

North Fork Brushy Creek

L

183A

M

WILLIAMSON CO RD 270

50

San Gabriel Pkwy
SAN GABRIEL PKWY
Halsey DR
WHITAKER DR

50

N

P

Q

R

WILLIAMSON CO RD 269

Benbrook Athletic Complex

MIDDLE BROOK DR

MIDDLE BROOK DR
MIDDLE BROOK DR
CLAYTON DR
REMINGTON DR
Coulee Dr
Plain
Sabinas Dr
ES

Leander Station
M R

HENDERSON DR
BARCLAY DR
BURGESS DR
WHITLEY DR
SOUTH BROOK DR
CAMINO ALTO DR
LOS ROBLES RD
SAN VICENTE DR
RANCHO ALTO DR

S

T

U

WILLIAMSON CO RD 269

49

RUBLES CT
PAMPAS RICAS DR
CABALLERO RD
SAN BRO RD
CAMINO REAL DR
ESCONDIDO DR
CAMINO MEJO LN
ESTANCIA WAY

183

LEANDER

49

RANCHERO RD
ENCINITA DR
CASITAS
ENCANTO DR
NORTHCREEK DR
10

OLD 2243 WEST
South Fork Brushy Creek
E EVANS ST
RAILROAD ST
EAST ST
E BROADE ST
E WILLIS ST
GARRIEL ST
RAILROAD ST

E SOUTH ST

RM 2243

V

W

X

Y

Z

MOUNTAIN SPRING LN
RED RIVER
N SPARKLING BROOK
N BAGDAD RD
RIVERVAN LN

Estates of North Creek Park

BENBROOK RANCH

10

W BROADE ST
LOGUE COVE SONG DR
GRAND DR
PECAN GROVE
WINDMILL
W WILLIS ST
N BRISTY ST
FS
CH
ATKIN
WILLIAMSON CO RD 273

N BRISTY ST
S BRISHY ST

W SOUTH ST
TREASURE OAKS TR
Leander Administration

RM 2243

OLD 2243 WEST

12

FRIENDSHIP CV
Leander Extended Opportunity Center

Bagdad Cemetery

2

3

MC

MD

CONTINUED ON MAP 311

CONTINUED ON MAP 342

CONTINUED ON MAP 313

SCALE IN MILES
0   1/8   1/4   3/8   1/2

SCALE IN FEET
0   1000   2000   3000

COPYRIGHT 1993, 2009 by MAPSCO INC. - ALL RIGHTS RESERVED

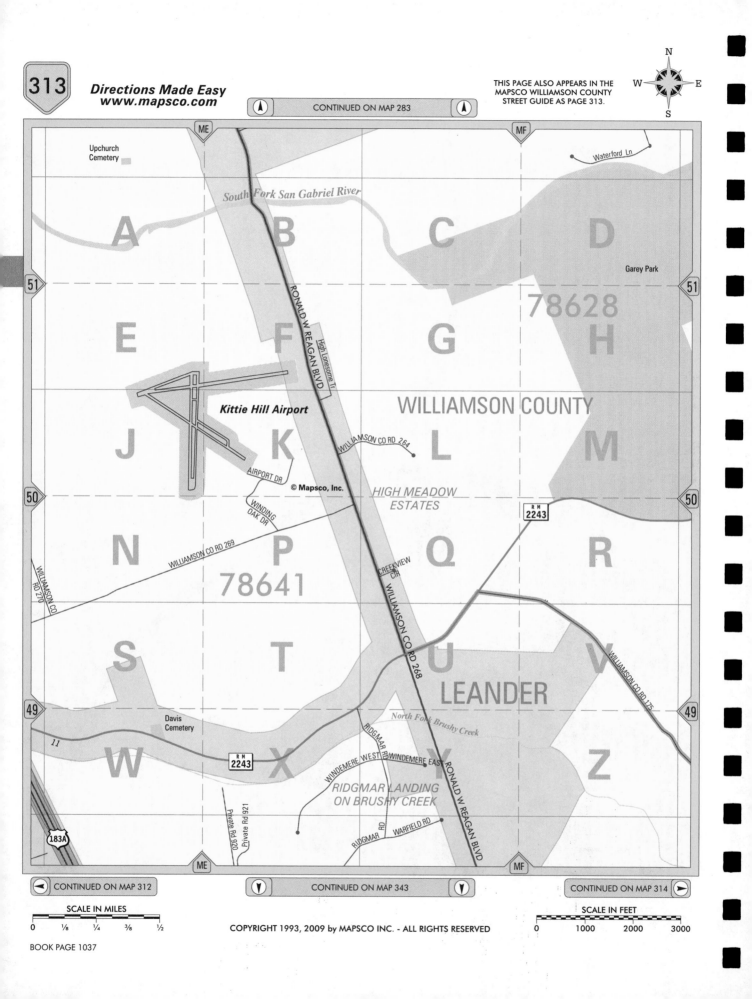

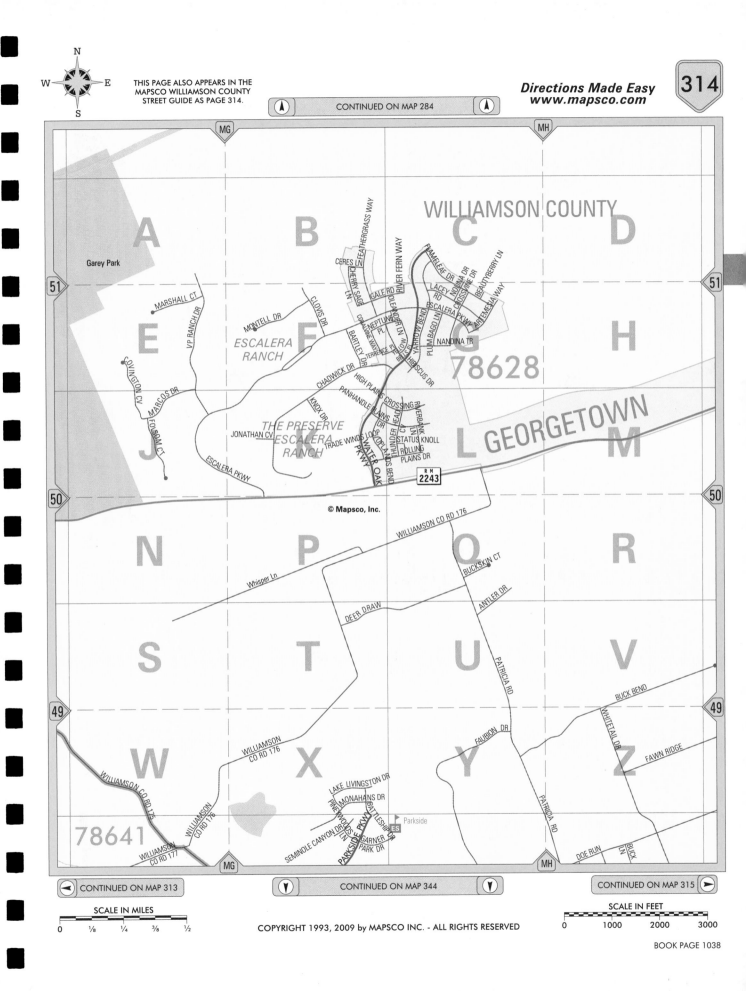

THIS PAGE ALSO APPEARS IN THE
MAPSCO WILLIAMSON COUNTY
STREET GUIDE AS PAGE 314.

Directions Made Easy
www.mapsco.com

314

N
W E
S

CONTINUED ON MAP 284

MG   MH

A   B   WILLIAMSON COUNTY C   D

Garey Park

51   51

FEATHERGRASS WAY
CERES LN
RIVER FERN WAY
FLAMELEAF DR
NANDINA DR
BEAUTYBERRY LN
CHERRY SAGE LN
GALE RD
OLEANDER LN
LACEY RD
CROSSVINE DR
ARTEMESIA WAY

MARSHALL CT
CLOVIS DR
MONTELL DR
NEPTUNE PL
CORALVINE WAY
BARTLEY DR
ESCALERA PKWY
PLUMBAGO LN
YARROW BEND

VP RANCH DR

E   ESCALERA RANCH   F   G   H

78628

COVINGTON CV
CHADWICK DR
HIGH PLAINS CROSSING
HIBISCUS DR

MARCOS DR
KNOX DR
PANHANDLE PLAINS DR
RIVERBANK LN
STATUS KNOLL

FOLSOM CT
JONATHAN CV
THE PRESERVE ESCALERA RANCH
TRADE WINDS LOOP
THUNDER HEAD LN
COPLANDS BEND
ROLLING PLAINS DR

J   WATER OAK PKWY   L   GEORGETOWN   M

ESCALERA PKWY

R M 2243

© Mapsco, Inc.

50   50

WILLIAMSON CO RD 176

N   P   Q   R

BUCKSKIN CT

Whisper Ln
DEER DRAW
ANTLER DR
PATRICIA RD

S   T   U   V

BUCK BEND

49   49

FAUBION DR
WHITETAIL DR
FAWN RIDGE

WILLIAMSON CO RD 175
WILLIAMSON CO RD 176

W   X   Y   Z

LAKE LIVINGSTON DR
MONAHANS DR
PATRICIA RD

78641

PINE WOODS DR
BATTLESHIP DR
Parkside
ES

SEMINOLE CANYON DR
PARKSIDE PKWY
GARNER PARK DR

WILLIAMSON CO RD 177

DOE RUN
BUCK LN

MG   MH

CONTINUED ON MAP 313
CONTINUED ON MAP 344
CONTINUED ON MAP 315

SCALE IN MILES
0   1/8   1/4   3/8   1/2

SCALE IN FEET
0   1000   2000   3000

BOOK PAGE 1038

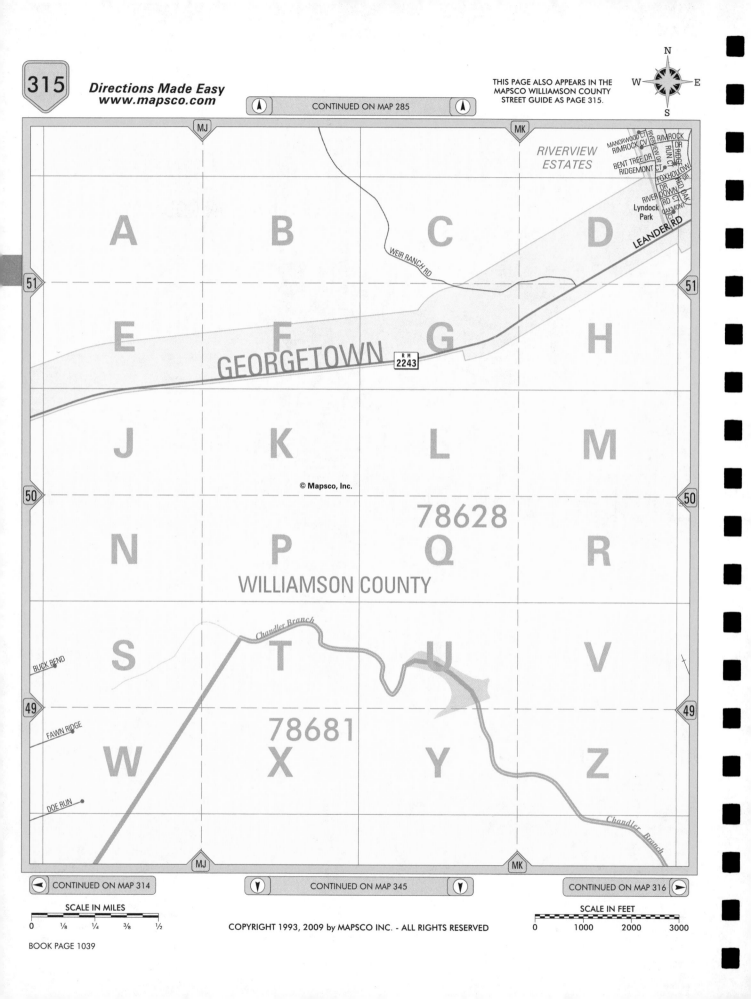

315

Directions Made Easy
www.mapsco.com

N
W · E
S

CONTINUED ON MAP 285

MJ

MK

A

B

C

D

RIVERVIEW
ESTATES

MANORWOOD CT
RIMROCK CV
RIMROCK

BENT TREE DR
RIDGEMONT CT

RIVERVIEW DR
RIMROCK
RUN CT
RIDGE DR

FOXHOLLOW

RIVER
DOWN
RD CT

RED OAK

OAKMONT

Lyndock
Park

LEANDER RD

WEIR RANCH RD

51

51

E

F

G

H

GEORGETOWN

RM
2243

J

K

L

M

© Mapsco, Inc.

50

50

78628

N

P

Q

R

WILLIAMSON COUNTY

Chandler Branch

S

T

U

V

BUCK BEND

49

49

78681

FAWN RIDGE

W

X

Y

Z

DOE RUN

Chandler Branch

MJ

MK

CONTINUED ON MAP 314

CONTINUED ON MAP 345

CONTINUED ON MAP 316

SCALE IN MILES

0   ⅛   ¼   ⅜   ½

SCALE IN FEET

0   1000   2000   3000

THIS PAGE ALSO APPEARS IN THE
MAPSCO WILLIAMSON COUNTY
STREET GUIDE AS PAGE 316.

Directions Made Easy
www.mapsco.com

316

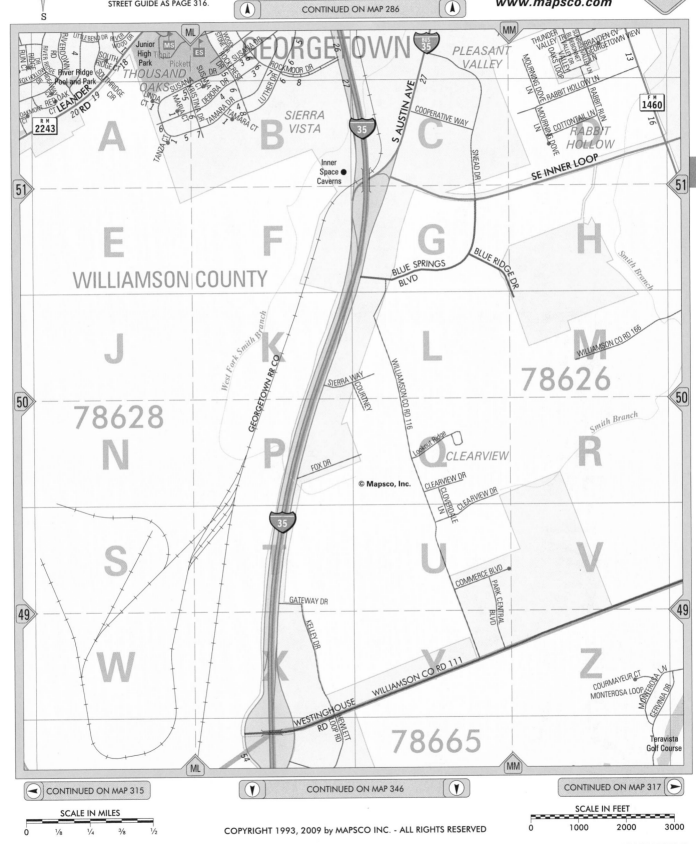

CONTINUED ON MAP 286

GEORGETOWN

PLEASANT VALLEY

THUNDER VALLEY TR

GEORGETOWN VIEW

RABBIT HOLLOW

LITTLEBEND DR
RIVERDOWN
RIVER WOOD DR
SOUTH RIDGE
RIVER RIDGE
FOX HOLLOW
RED OAK
OAKMONT CT
LEANDER
RD 19

THOUSAND OAKS

STONE ROCK CREST
WOOD
SUSANA DR
ROCKMOOR DR
LUTHER DR
DEBORA DR
KRISTINA DR
LINDA CT
SUSANA CT
MAYA CT
TAMARA DR
TAMARA CT
TANZA CT

Junior High Park
Tippit
Pickett
River Ridge Pool and Park

S AUSTIN AVE

SIERRA VISTA

COOPERATIVE WAY

SNEAD DR

MOURNING DOVE LN
RABBIT HOLLOW LN
RABBIT RUN
OAKS LOOP
COTTONTAIL LN

FM 1460

A   B   C   MM

Inner Space Caverns

SE INNER LOOP

51   51

E   F   G   H

WILLIAMSON COUNTY

BLUE SPRINGS BLVD

BLUE RIDGE DR

Smith Branch

WILLIAMSON CO RD 166

J   K   L   M

West Fork Smith Branch

Georgetown RR Co

SIERRA WAY
COURTNEY

WILLIAMSON CO RD 116

78626

50   50

78628

N   P   Q   R

Lookout Ridge

CLEARVIEW

Smith Branch

© Mapsco, Inc.

FOX DR

CLEARVIEW DR
CLOVERDALE LN
CLEARVIEW DR

35

S   T   U   V

COMMERCE BLVD
PARK CENTRAL BLVD

49   49

GATEWAY DR

KELLEY DR

W   K   V   Z

COURMAYEUR CT
MONTEROSA LOOP
MONTEROSA LN
CERVINIA DR

WESTINGHOUSE RD
HEWLETT LOOP RD

WILLIAMSON CO RD 111

78665

Teravista Golf Course

ML   MM

CONTINUED ON MAP 315   CONTINUED ON MAP 346   CONTINUED ON MAP 317

SCALE IN MILES
0   1/8   1/4   3/8   1/2

SCALE IN FEET
0   1000   2000   3000

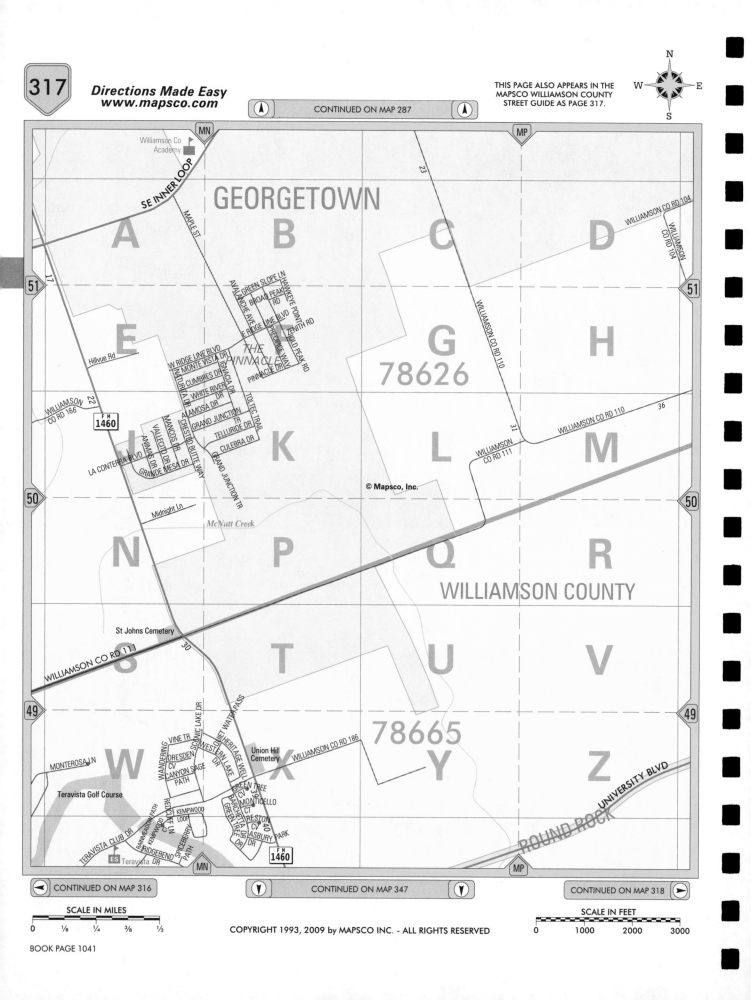

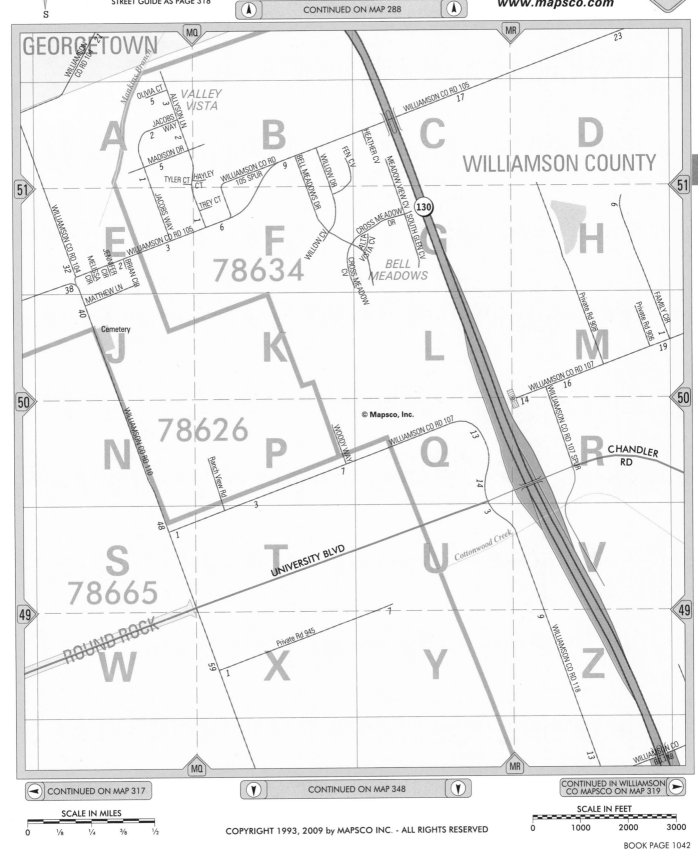

THIS PAGE ALSO APPEARS IN THE
MAPSCO WILLIAMSON COUNTY
STREET GUIDE AS PAGE 318

Directions Made Easy
www.mapsco.com

N
W E
S

CONTINUED ON MAP 288

MQ

MR

GEORGETOWN

WILLIAMSON CO RD 104

21

23

OLIVIA CT
5
ALLYSON LN
3

VALLEY
VISTA

JACOBS
WAY
2
2

WILLIAMSON CO RD 105
17

MADISON DR
5

A

B

C

WILLIAMSON COUNTY

D

HEATHER CV

51

TYLER CT
HAYLEY
CT
1

WILLIAMSON CO RD
105 SPUR

FEN CV

WILLOW DR

BELL MEADOWS DR

9

130

51

TREY CT
1

JACOBS WAY

9

WILLIAMSON CO RD 105
6

MEADOW VIEW CV / SOUTH GLEN CV

CROSS MEADOW
DR

ALTA
VISTA CV

E

F
78634

WILLOW CV

G

BELL
MEADOWS

H

WILLIAMSON CO RD 104

JENNIFER
CIR
2
MELISSA
CIR

BRIAN CIR

WILLIAMSON CO RD 105
3

32

CROSS MEADOW
CV

Private Rd 906

Private Rd 906

FAMILY CIR

1
19

38

MATTHEW LN

40

J

Cemetery

K

L

M

50

WILLIAMSON CO RD 110

78626

WILLIAMSON CO RD 107
16

50

WILLIAMSON CO RD 107 SPUR

14

N

Ranch View Rd

P

WOODY WAY

© Mapsco, Inc.

WILLIAMSON CO RD 107

13

Q

R

CHANDLER
RD

7

3

14

48

1

3

S
78665

T

U

Cottonwood Creek

V

UNIVERSITY BLVD

3

49

49

ROUND ROCK

Private Rd 945

7

9

WILLIAMSON CO RD 118

W

59

1

X

Y

Z

WILLIAMSON CO
RD 118

13

MQ

CONTINUED ON MAP 317

MR

CONTINUED ON MAP 348

CONTINUED IN WILLIAMSON
CO MAPSCO ON MAP 319

SCALE IN MILES

0   1/8   1/4   3/8   1/2

SCALE IN FEET

0   1000   2000   3000

BOOK PAGE 1042

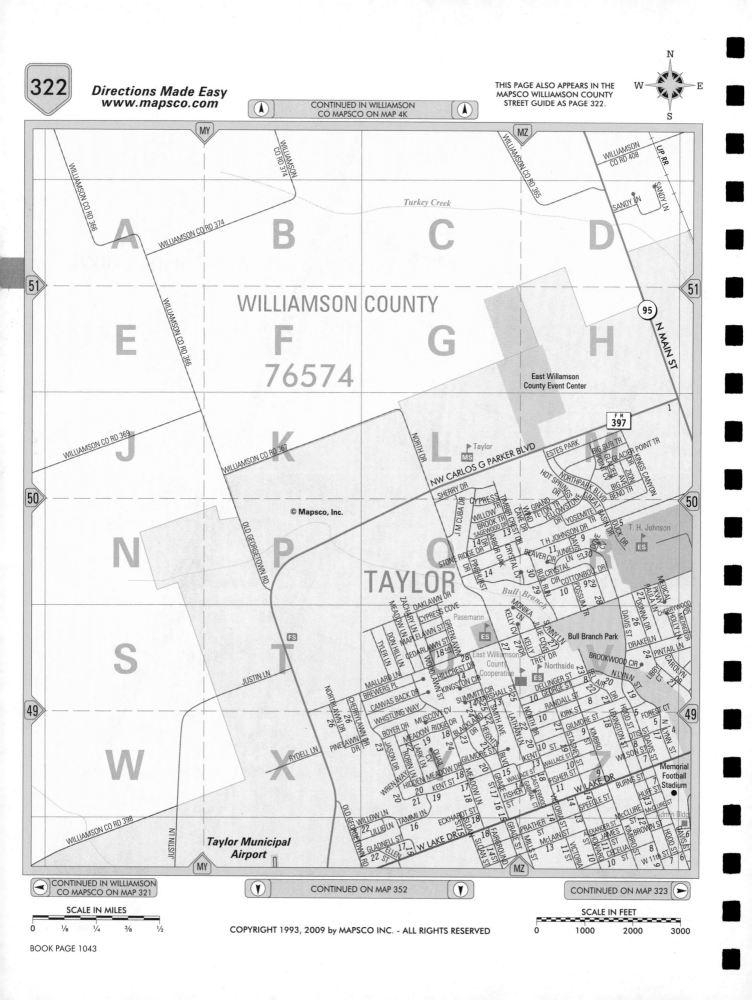

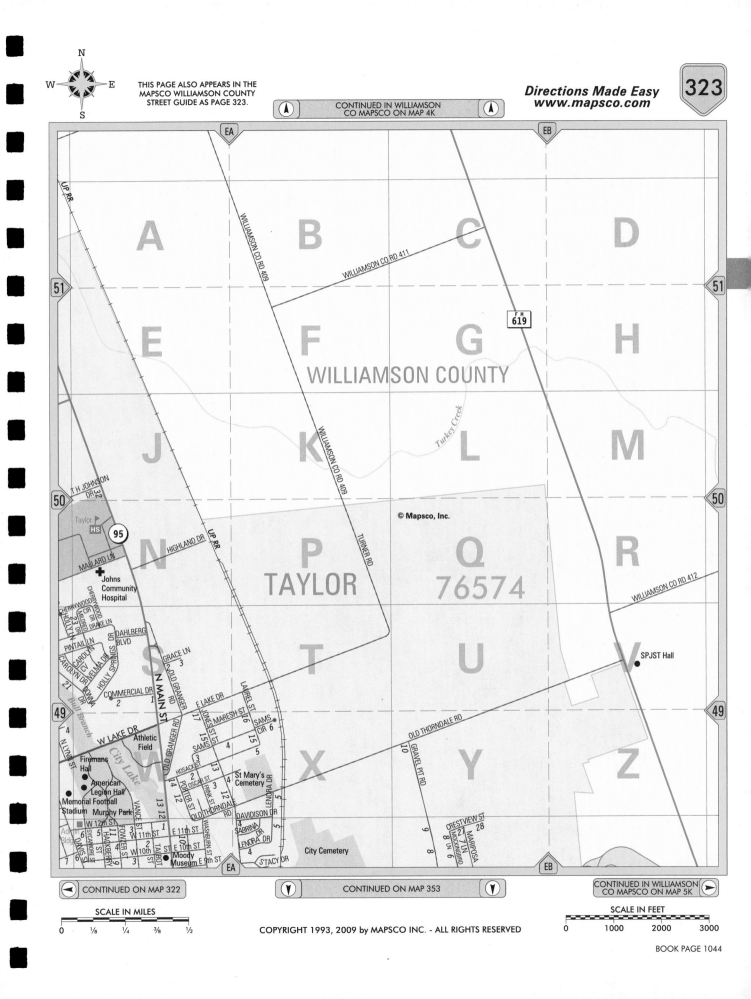

N
W E
S

THIS PAGE ALSO APPEARS IN THE
MAPSCO WILLIAMSON COUNTY
STREET GUIDE AS PAGE 323.

Directions Made Easy
www.mapsco.com

CONTINUED IN WILLIAMSON
CO MAPSCO ON MAP 4K

EA   EB

UP RR

A   B   C   D

51   51

WILLIAMSON CO RD 411

WILLIAMSON CO RD 409

FM 619

E   F   G   H

WILLIAMSON COUNTY

Turkey Creek

WILLIAMSON CO RD 409

J   K   L   M

T H JOHNSON DR 32

50   50

Taylor HS

95

© Mapsco, Inc.

MALLARD LN

HIGHLAND DR

UP RR

TURNER RD

N   P   Q   R

Johns Community Hospital

TAYLOR   76574   WILLIAMSON CO RD 412

CHERRYWOOD CIR DR MILDRED DR DRAKE LN
HOLLY LN
PINTAIL LN   DAHLBERG BLVD
CAROLYN CV   GRACE LN
CAROLYN DR DONNA VELMA DR   3
HOLLY SPRINGS DR

SPJST Hall
V

COMMERCIAL DR 2   N MAIN ST   S   T   U

21   OLD GRANGER RD

49   49

WOOD GRANGER RD   E LAKE DR   LAUREL ST   SAMS CIR 6

W LAKE DR   MARESH ST 16   JONES ST 17   SAMS CIR 6   OLD THORNDALE RD

Athletic Field   15   SAMS ST   4   15   5   GRAVEL PIT RD

N LYNN ST   Firemans Hall   HOSACK ST 13   12   W   X   Y   Z

American Legion Hall   OSCAR ST   FRINK ST   12   LENORA DR 5

Memorial Football Stadium   Murphy Park   13 12   VANCE ST   14 12   PORTER ST   OLD THORNDALE RD   DAVIDISON DR   10   8   Z

Admin Bldg   W 12th ST   1   E 11th ST   SABRINA DR   9   CRESTVIEW ST 28

SYCAMORE ST   11   W 11th ST   WASHBURN ST   LENORA DR   City Cemetery   8 LN 7 IN   MARIPOSA   MOCKINGBIRD

DAVIS ST 6   HACKBERRY ST 9   W 10th ST   3   TALBOT ST   E 10th ST   4   8 7 IN

7   FOWLER ST   Moody Museum   E 9th ST   STACY DR   8

EA

CONTINUED ON MAP 322   CONTINUED ON MAP 353   CONTINUED IN WILLIAMSON CO MAPSCO ON MAP 5K

SCALE IN MILES
0   ⅛   ¼   ⅜   ½

SCALE IN FEET
0   1000   2000   3000

Directions Made Easy
www.mapsco.com

NOT MAPPED

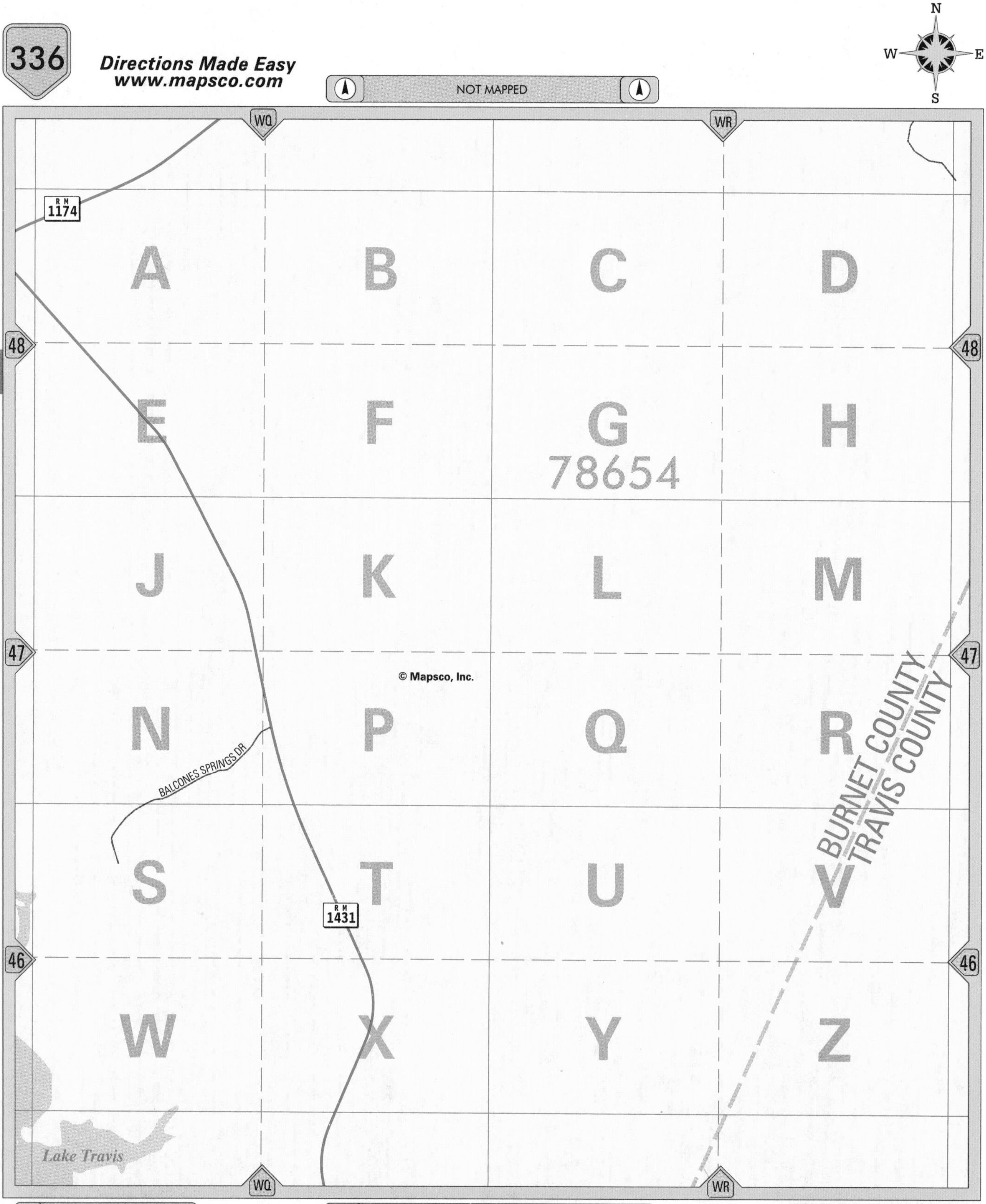

N
W E
S

RM 1174

A B C D

48 48

E F G H

78654

J K L M

47 47

© Mapsco, Inc.

N P Q R

BALCONES SPRINGS DR

BURNET COUNTY
TRAVIS COUNTY

S T U V

RM 1431

46 46

W X Y Z

Lake Travis

WQ WR

NOT MAPPED

CONTINUED ON MAP 366

CONTINUED ON MAP 337

SCALE IN MILES
0   ⅛   ¼   ⅜   ½

SCALE IN FEET
0   1000   2000   3000

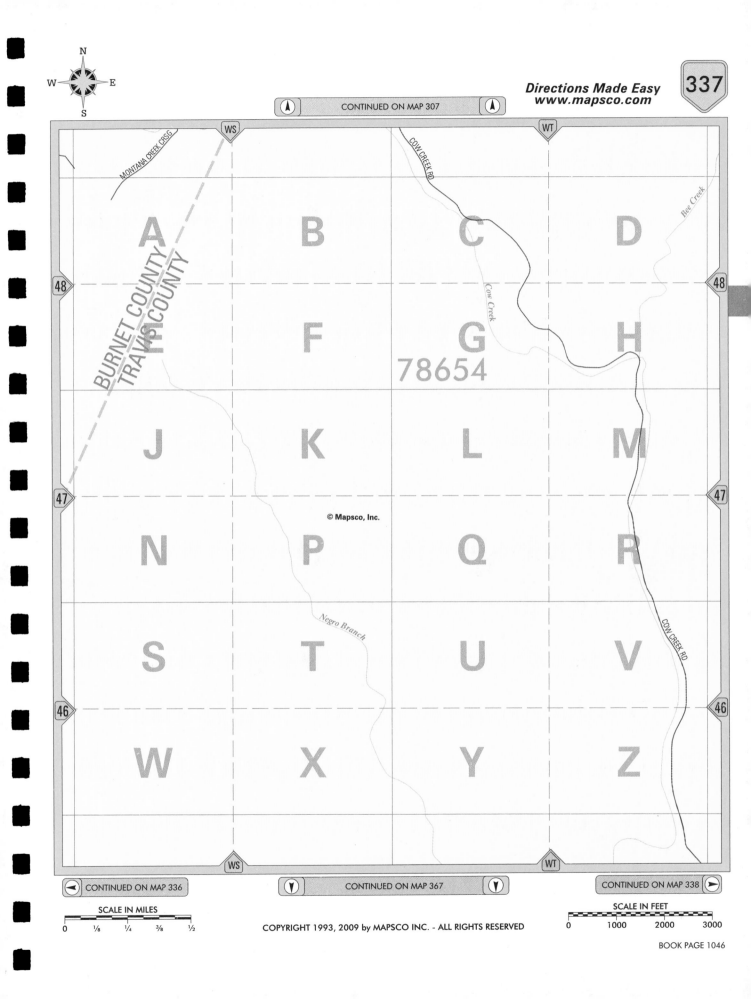

CONTINUED ON MAP 307

N
W   E
S

WS

WT

COW CREEK RD

Bee Creek

MONTANA CREEK CRSG

48

A

BURNET COUNTY
TRAVIS COUNTY

B

Cow Creek

C

D

48

E

F

G
78654

H

J

K

L

M

47

© Mapsco, Inc.

N

P

Q

R

47

Negro Branch

S

T

U

V

COW CREEK RD

46

W

X

Y

Z

46

WS

WT

CONTINUED ON MAP 336

CONTINUED ON MAP 367

CONTINUED ON MAP 338

SCALE IN MILES
0   1/8   1/4   3/8   1/2

SCALE IN FEET
0   1000   2000   3000

Directions Made Easy
www.mapsco.com

CONTINUED ON MAP 308

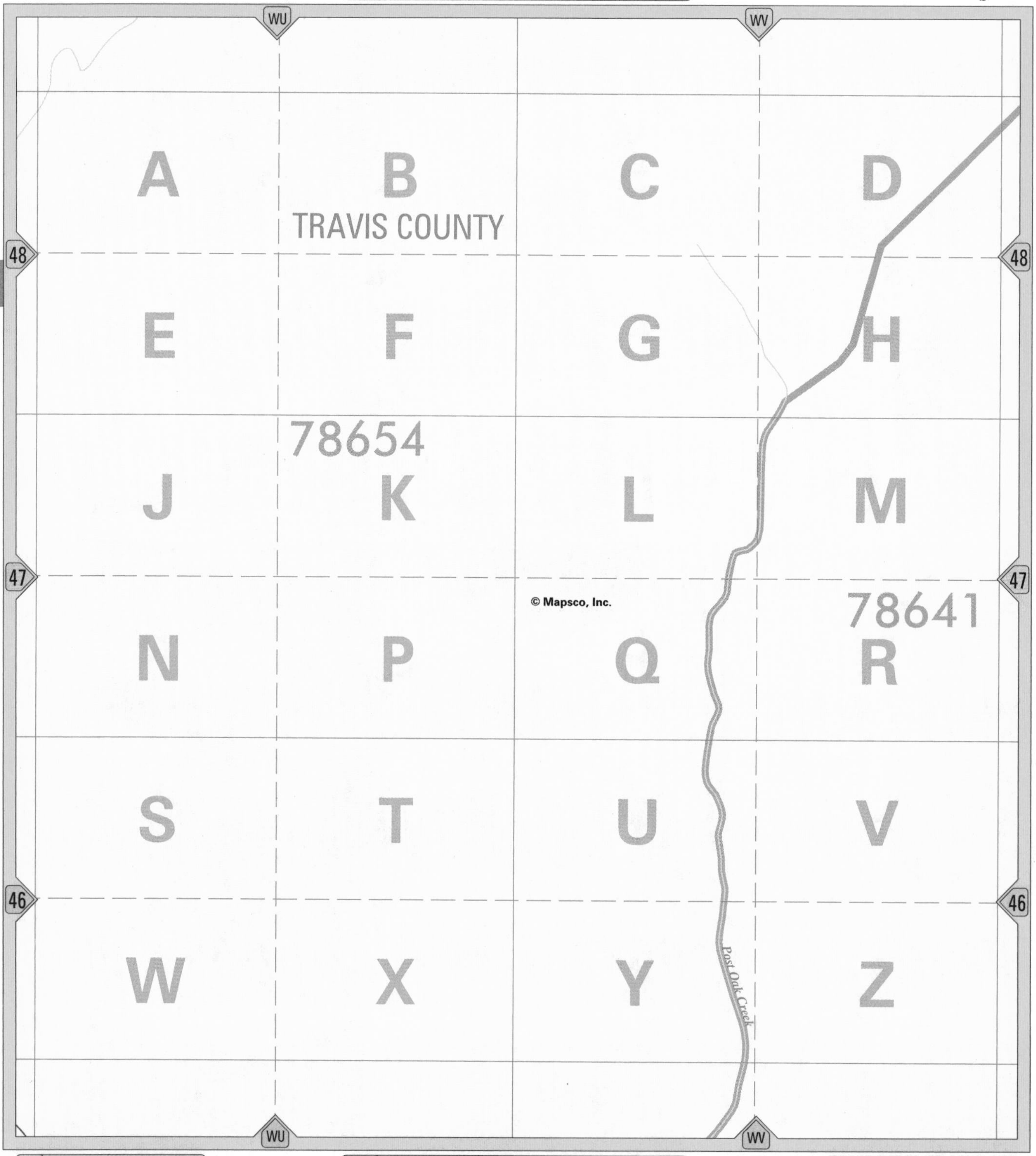

N
W E
S

WU WV

A B C D

TRAVIS COUNTY

48 48

E F G H

78654

J K L M

47 47

© Mapsco, Inc.

78641

N P Q R

S T U V

46 46

W X Y Z

Post Oak Creek

WU WV

CONTINUED ON MAP 337

CONTINUED ON MAP 368

CONTINUED ON MAP 339

SCALE IN MILES

0 ⅛ ¼ ⅜ ½

SCALE IN FEET

0 1000 2000 3000

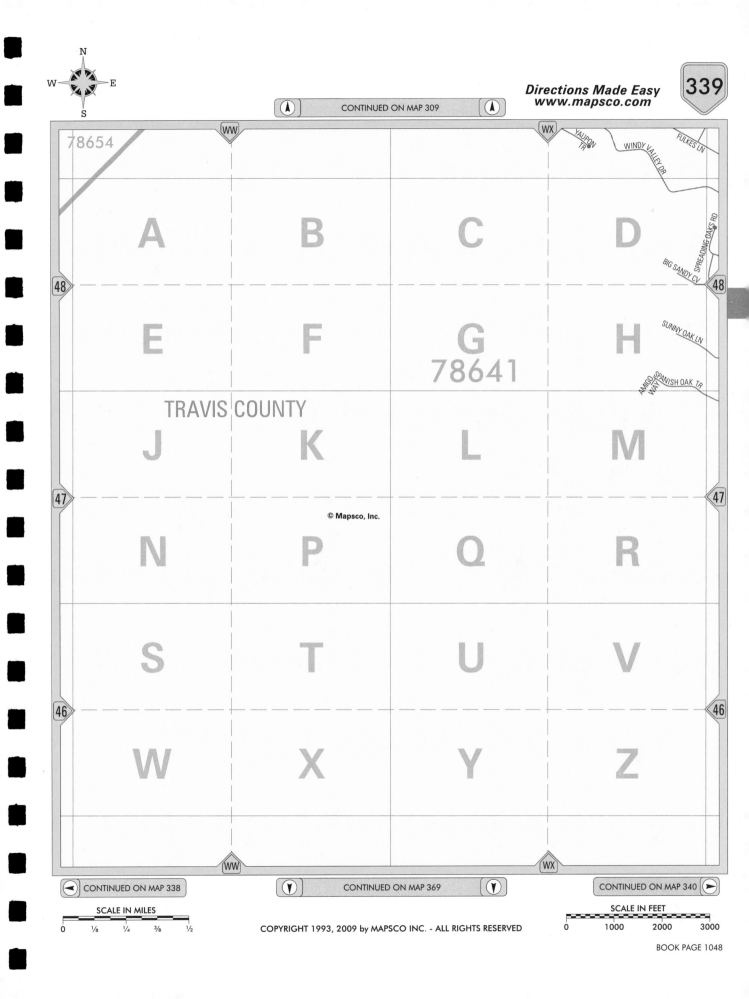

CONTINUED ON MAP 309

339

78654

N
W E
S

WW

WX

YAUPON TR

WINDY VALLEY DR

FULKES LN

A

B

C

D

SPREADING OAKS RD

48

48

BIG SANDY CV

E

F

G

H

SUNNY OAK LN

78641

AMIGO WAY

SPANISH OAK TR

TRAVIS COUNTY

J

K

L

M

47

47

© Mapsco, Inc.

N

P

Q

R

S

T

U

V

46

46

W

X

Y

Z

WW

WX

CONTINUED ON MAP 338

CONTINUED ON MAP 369

CONTINUED ON MAP 340

SCALE IN MILES

0   1/8   1/4   3/8   1/2

SCALE IN FEET

0   1000   2000   3000

BOOK PAGE 1048

Directions Made Easy
www.mapsco.com

N
W · E
S

CONTINUED ON MAP 310

WY
WZ

LEANDER

EVANS OAKS RD
FULKES LN
SPREADING OAKS RD
ROUND MOUNTAIN RD
220
221
HONEYCOMB CIR
216
215
NAMELESS RD
214
Honeycomb
Hills Park
HONEYCOMB MESA

A
SWEET SUMMER DR
HONEYCOMB LN
B
C
HONEYCOMB HW
HONEYCOMB CT
D

WINDY VALLEY DR
HONEYCOMB DR
HONEYCOMB HW

48
48

BIG SANDY DR
NAMELESS RD
TRAVIS COUNTY
WILLIAMSON COUNTY

E
SANDY MEADOW CIR
F
G
H
MESA RIDGE

SUNNY OAK LN
CEDAR RIDGE
Round Mountain
MESA TRI
HIDDEN MESA

SPANISH
OAK TR
PECAN HW
CEDAR HW
J
K
L
M
MESA OAKS
HIDDEN MESA
TRAVIS CO RD 290

DEWBERRY HW
78641

SUNSET HW
225
© Mapsco, Inc.

47
47

N
P
Q
R

LEANDER

S
T
U
V

Big Sandy Creek

46
46

NAMELESS RD

W
X
228
Y
Z

229

WY
WZ

CONTINUED ON MAP 339
CONTINUED ON MAP 370
CONTINUED ON MAP 341

SCALE IN MILES
0   1/8   1/4   3/8   1/2

SCALE IN FEET
0   1000   2000   3000

THIS PAGE ALSO APPEARS IN THE
MAPSCO WILLIAMSON COUNTY
STREET GUIDE AS PAGE 341.

Directions Made Easy
www.mapsco.com

341

CONTINUED ON MAP 311

N
W E
S

MA

MB

Devine
Lake
Park
WATERFALL
AVE
Bagdad
ES
BACH
RED RIVER LN
SPARKING BROOK

LEANDER

NORTH CREEK

NORTH CREEK DR
RIVERWAY LN
EAGLECREEK

LITTLACREEK LN
CLEARCREEK LN
BATTLECREEK LN
EAGLECREEK LN

A

B

C

CLEAR SPRING LN
MAPLECREEK DR
DEERCREEK LN

HONEYCOMB MESA

North Fork Brushy Creek

SUNNY BROOK DR
MILLCREEK LN
SOUTHCREEK LN

BEAR CREEK DR
MAPLEWOOD DR

LIT CANDLE
CV

NORTH
BEND

NAMELESS RD

OLD 2243 WEST
20

BELLO DR
GREENER
DR

48

WOODWAY DR
25

CROSSLAND
DR
EDGEWOOD
CV

DEERCREEK LN
JOE'S CV
LES CV
SIL CT
CANDLELIGHT

48

141

E

F

2243

G

SYDNEE
DR
BRIARWOOD DR
RIM ROCK
CIR
RIM ROCK DR
COTTONTAIL DR
CANDLELIGHT DR

GRASSLAND DR

South Fork Brushy Creek

30

BAN RD

LAUREN
LOOP

MICHAEL CV

DEBBIE
ANN DR

COTTONTAIL
DR

THOMAS CV

WESTWOOD

RIO LN

BARANCO WAY

APPLE SPRINGS DR

APPLE
SPRINGS CIR

*APPLE
SPRINGS*

APPLE
SPRINGS CIR

VISTA RIDGE DR
MONTANA
ALTA VISTA DR
EL CERRO
LI CT
PASEO VERDE DR
RED HAWK DR

J

78641

K

HEDDER CIR

APPLE SPRINGS HW

DORMAX CIR

© Mapsco, Inc.

L

WILLIAMSON COUNTY
TRAVIS COUNTY

M

47

47

EAGLE'S WAY

N

P

HARVEY
73

APPLE SPRINGS DR

Q

SPARROW HAWK
DR
OSPREY CIR
FALCON OAKS DR
OLD QUARRY RD

R

BROWN BLUFF CIR

46

Mira Vista

Timarron

La Costa

46

S

T

Palos Verdes

U

Mission Hills

V

25

LEANDER

Medicine Hat

Sky
Kiss

Rio Seco

La Cantera

Squaw Valley

W

X

High Lonesome
Del Paso

Palo Alto

Crystal Falls
Golf Course

Z

Panther Hall

Lions Lair

Sidewinder

High Horse

Bear Claw

Coronado

El Cielo

Spyglass Hill

*GRAND
MESA*

Rancho Mirage

Palos Verdes

Ventana Canyon

CRYSTAL FALLS PKWY

28

Y

MA

MB

CONTINUED ON MAP 340

CONTINUED ON MAP 371

CONTINUED ON MAP 342

SCALE IN MILES
0   1/8   1/4   3/8   1/2

SCALE IN FEET
0   1000   2000   3000

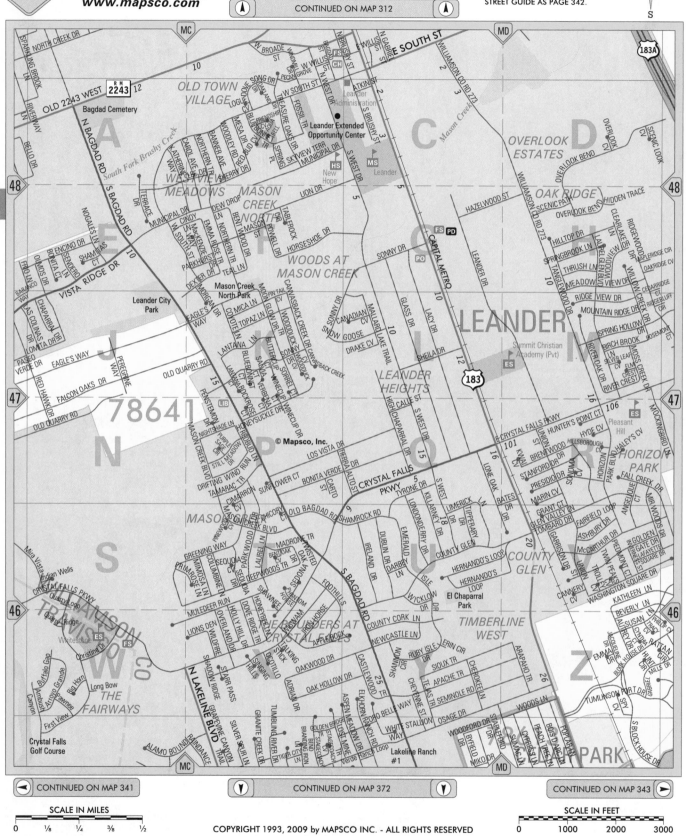

CONTINUED ON MAP 312

CONTINUED ON MAP 341
CONTINUED ON MAP 372
CONTINUED ON MAP 343

SCALE IN MILES

0   1/8   1/4   3/8   1/2

SCALE IN FEET

0   1000   2000   3000

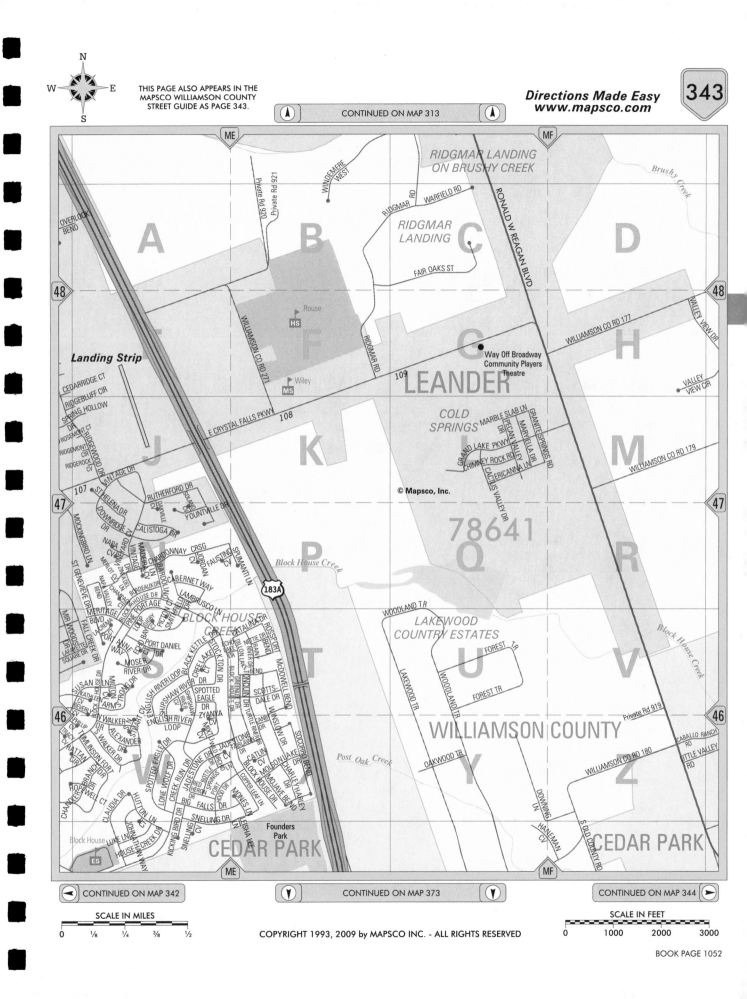

THIS PAGE ALSO APPEARS IN THE MAPSCO WILLIAMSON COUNTY STREET GUIDE AS PAGE 343.

Directions Made Easy
www.mapsco.com

CONTINUED ON MAP 313

RIDGMAR LANDING ON BRUSHY CREEK

Brushy Creek

RIDGMAR RD
WARFIELD RD

RIDGMAR LANDING

RONALD W REAGAN BLVD

FAIR OAKS ST

OVERLOOK BEND

WILLIAMSON CO RD 177

VALLEY VIEW DR

A B C D

48 48

Rouse
HS

Way Off Broadway Community Players Theatre

WILLIAMSON CO RD 271

RIDGMAR RD

Landing Strip

CEDARRIDGE CT
RIDGEBLUFF CIR
SPRING HOLLOW
ROSEMONT CT
RIDGEMONT CIR
RIDGEWOOD DR
RIDGEROCK CV

E CRYSTAL FALLS PKWY

109

LEANER

VALLEY VIEW CIR

F G H

Wiley
MS

COLD SPRINGS

MARBLE SLAB LN
PECAN VALLEY DR
MARVELLA DR
GRANITE SPRINGS RD

GRAND LAKE PKWY
CHIMNEY ROCK RD
AMERICANNA LN
CACTUS VALLEY DR

J K L M

108

© Mapsco, Inc.

WILLIAMSON CO RD 179

47 47

VINTAGE DR
107
ST HELENA DR
DOWNRIDGE DR
RUTHERFORD DR
OAKVILLE
YOUNTVILLE DR
CALISTOGA DR

78641

MOCKINGBIRD LN
ST GENEVIEVE DR
NARA
CV
VINEYARD CV
VINTAGE LN
CHARDONNAY
MADERA LN
CRSG
JORDAN CV
FAUSTINO
CV
SPUMANTI LN

Block House Creek

N P Q R

MERLOT CT
NAPA VALLEY BEND
ZINFANDEL CT
BORDEAUX DR
BAROLO LN
CABERNET WAY
LAMBRUSCO LN

183A

MERITAGE BLVD
ECHO BAY
PINE PORTAGE LOOP
PICTON DR
SMITHFIELD
PORTAGE
CATALINA DR

BLOCK HOUSE CREEK

WOODLAND TR

LAKEWOOD COUNTRY ESTATES

Block House Creek

MIR WOODS DR
LAFAYETTE SQUARE DR
FALL CREEK DR
ANNE WAY
PORT DANIEL DR
MOSER RIVER DR

ROSSPORT BEND
McDOWELL BEND
ECHO
NETTIE DR
NALON LN
RIVER DR
GREENLEE DR
BLOCK HOUSE DR

DIXON DR
TURTLE RIVER
WINSLOW DR

FOREST TR

LAKEWOOD TR
WOODLAND TR
FOREST TR

S T U V

SUSAN LN
ROSELLE LN
STRONG DR
KATHLEEN LN
ENGLISH RIVER LOOP
SHIPSHAW RIVER DR
CREEK KETTLE LN
BLACK KETTLE LN
STOCKTON DR
SHIPSHAW RIVER
SCOTTSDALE DR
CANB DR
SOCORRO BEND

SPOTTED EAGLE DR
ZYANYA CV

46 46

BEVERLY
BLOCK ARMS
N WALKER LN
ALEXANDER
ENGLISH RIVER LOOP
JADESTONE DR
FAIRLAWN
CATLIN CV
CHARLEY HARLEY

WILLIAMSON COUNTY

Private Rd 919

CABALLO RANCH
LITTLE VALLEY RD

PHILLIP DR
TIMLINSON FORT
W WALKER DR
JADESTONE DR
RED HERON
BOTTLE CV
MIDNIS LN
COPPER LEAF LN
MOLSON LAKE BEND
CHARLEY HARLEY

Post Oak Creek

OAKWOOD TR

WILLIAMSON CO RD 180

W

CHANDLER BRANCH DR
GRATTAN CIR
HOPEWELL CT
SPOTTED EAGLE DR
CREEK RUN DR
LONE WOLF DR
BIG FALLS DR
SPRINGS LN
DOCTOR LN
BLOCK HOUSE DR

DOWNING LN
HANEMAN CV
S OLD COUNTY RD

WILLIAMSON CO RD 180

X Y Z

CLAUDIA DR
HUTTON LN
KICKING BIRD RD
SNELLING CV
SNELLING
SNELLING DR
LEISHA LEE

Block House
LUKE LN
JOHNATHAN WAY
HOUSE CREEK DR

Founders Park

CEDAR PARK

CEDAR PARK

ES

CONTINUED ON MAP 342

CONTINUED ON MAP 373

CONTINUED ON MAP 344

SCALE IN MILES
0 1/8 1/4 3/8 1/2

COPYRIGHT 1993, 2009 by MAPSCO INC. - ALL RIGHTS RESERVED

SCALE IN FEET
0 1000 2000 3000

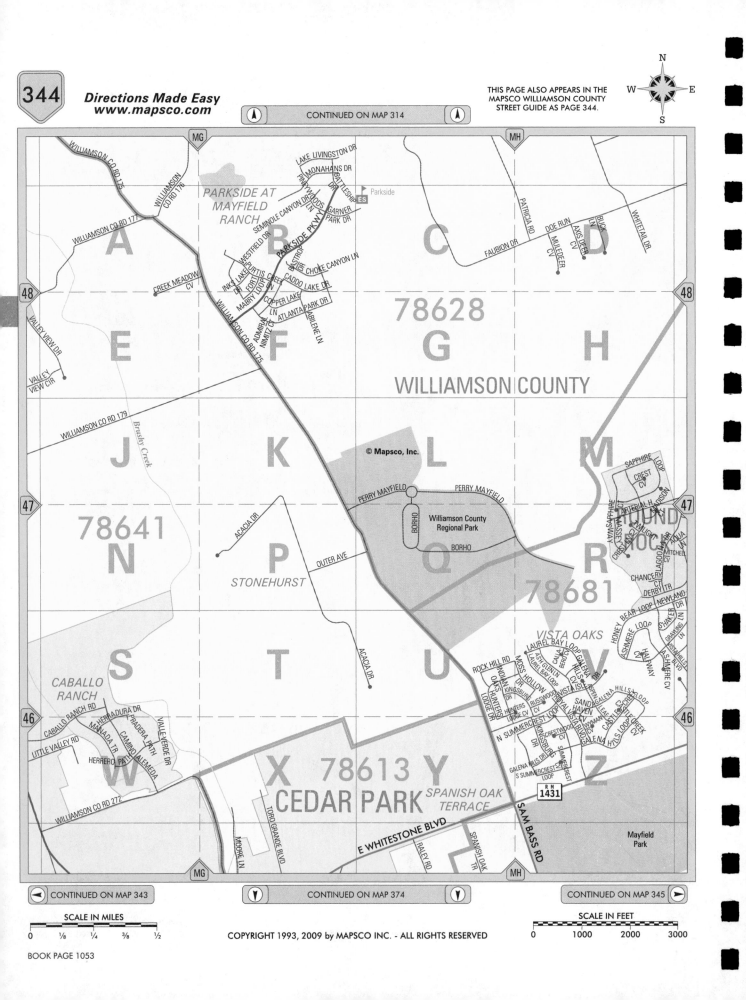

344

Directions Made Easy
www.mapsco.com

THIS PAGE ALSO APPEARS IN THE
MAPSCO WILLIAMSON COUNTY
STREET GUIDE AS PAGE 344.

N
W   E
S

CONTINUED ON MAP 314

MG   MH

WILLIAMSON CO RD 175
WILLIAMSON CO RD 176
WILLIAMSON CO RD 177

A

CREEK MEADOW CV

PARKSIDE AT MAYFIELD RANCH

LAKE LIVINGSTON DR
MONAHANS DR
PINEYWOODS DR
SEMINOLE CANYON DR
BATTLESHIP
GARNER PARK DR
WESTFIELD DR

B

Parkside
ES

INKS LAKE DR
CURTIS CREEK
BASTROP
FORT
MABRY LOOP
COPPER LAKE LN
ADMIRAL NIMITZ CT
ATLANTA PARK DR
ABILENE LN
CADDO LAKE DR
CHOKE CANYON LN

F

PATRICIA RD
DOE RUN
AXIS DEER
MULEDEER CV
FAUBION DR

C

BUCK LN
WHITETAIL DR

D

48   48

E

VALLEY VIEW DR
VALLEY VIEW CIR

78628

G

H

WILLIAMSON CO RD 175

WILLIAMSON COUNTY

WILLIAMSON CO RD 179

Brushy Creek

J

K

© Mapsco, Inc.

L

SAPPHIRE LOOP
CREST CV

M

47   47

78641

N

ACACIA DR

P

STONEHURST

OUTER AVE

PERRY MAYFIELD
PERRY MAYFIELD

BORHO

Williamson County Regional Park

BORHO

Q

ROUND ROCK

SAPPHIRE LOOP
MASSEY
ARTERIAL H
ADDISON
MOONLIGHT
AQUA
MITCHELL
CHANCERY
CT
DERBY TR

R

78681

HONEY BEAR LOOP
NEWLAND DR
ASHMERE LOOP
STACKER
GRAYLING LN
ASHMERE CV
HALFWAY

S

CABALLO RANCH

CABALLO RANCH RD
HERRADURA DR
MANADA TR
PRADERA PATH
VALLEVERDE DR
CAMINO ALEMEDA
LITTLE VALLEY RD
HERRERO PATH

T

ACACIA DR

U

ROCK HILL RD
INDIAN OAKS DR
HUNTERS LODGE DR
HUNTERS LODGE CV
MOSS HOLLOW
KINGSBURG CV
RUSSWOOD CV
N SUMMERCREST LOOP
KINGSBURG

VISTA OAKS

LAUREL BAY LOOP
CALLA
BERG
LAUREL BAY LOOP
ASH GLEN LN
GALENA
HILLS CV
ROYAL VISTA BLVD
VISTA ISLE
SANDY HAVEN
CRESTWOOD CV
GALENA HILLS X
ASPEN
WYMAN
EAST
SUMMERCREST LOOP
GALENA HILLS LOOP
CASTLE CREEK CV
CASTLE CREEK

V

48   46
46

GALENA HILLS LOOP
N SUMMERCREST LOOP
S SUMMERCREST LOOP

W

WILLIAMSON CO RD 272

TORO GRANDE BLVD
MOORE LN

X

78613
CEDAR PARK

E WHITESTONE BLVD

RALEY RD

Y
SPANISH OAK TERRACE

SPANISH OAK TR

SAM BASS RD

RM 1431

Z

Mayfield Park

MG   MH

CONTINUED ON MAP 343
CONTINUED ON MAP 374
CONTINUED ON MAP 345

SCALE IN MILES
0   1/8   1/4   3/8   1/2

SCALE IN FEET
0   1000   2000   3000

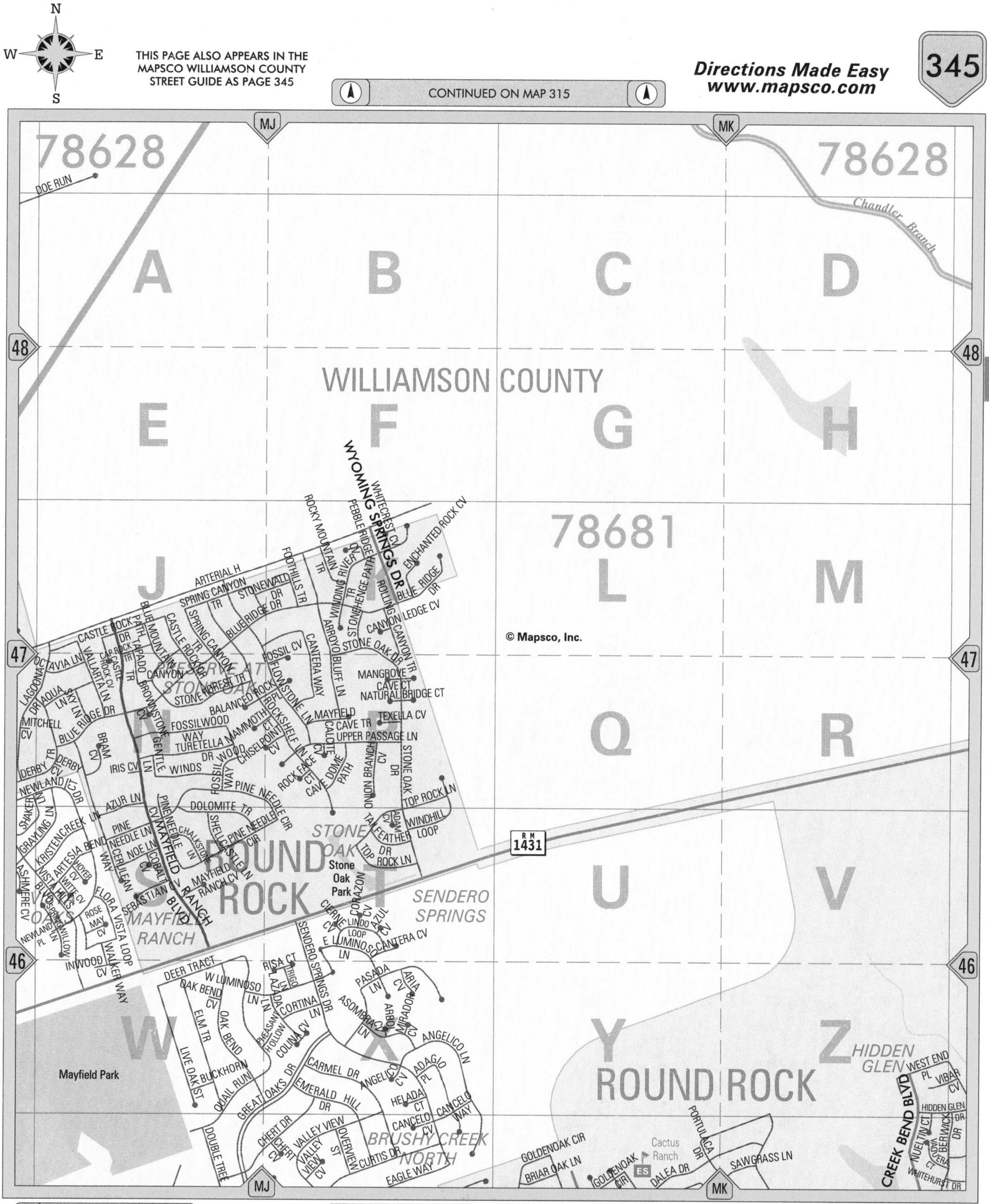

THIS PAGE ALSO APPEARS IN THE
MAPSCO WILLIAMSON COUNTY
STREET GUIDE AS PAGE 345

Directions Made Easy
www.mapsco.com

345

CONTINUED ON MAP 315

N
W E
S

78628

78628

Chandler Branch

MJ

MK

A

B

C

D

48

48

WILLIAMSON COUNTY

E

F

G

H

78681

J

L

M

© Mapsco, Inc.

WYOMING SPRINGS DR

WHITECREST CT
PEBBLE RIDGE
ROCKY MOUNTAIN TR
FOOTHILLS TR
STONEHENGE PATH
WINDOM RIVER TR
ENCHANTED ROCK CV
BLUE RIDGE DR

ARTERIAL H
SPRING CANYON TR
STONEWALL DR
BLUE RIDGE DR
ROLLING CANYON TR
CANYON LEDGE CV

47

47

OCTAVIA LN
CASTLE ROCK DR
BLUE MOUNTAIN PATH
PRADO
CASTLE ROCK
SPRING CANYON
RED ROCK TR
CANYON FOREST TR
ARROYO BLUFF LN
STONE OAK DR
CANTERA WAY
MANGROVE
CAVE CT
NATURAL BRIDGE CT

LAGONA LN
DRIAQUA LN
VALARTA LN
BROWNSTON GENTLE
FOSSIL CV
FLOWSTONE LN
MANGAROCK
ROCKSHELF LN
MAYFIELD
CALCITE CV
TEXELLA CV

MITCHELL CV
BLUE RIDGE DR
BRAM
FOSSILWOOD
WAY
TURETELLA LN
MAMMOTH DR
CHISEL POINT
ROCK FACE
CAVE TR
UPPER PASSAGE LN

DERBY TR
DERBY
IRIS CV
WA WOOD
WINDS
PINE NEEDLE LN
ROCK DOME
CAVE PATH
NONG BRANCH
STONE OAK

NEWLAND CR
DOLOMITE TR
CHALKSTONE
TOP ROCK LN
TALL FEATHER DR

SHAKER
GRAYLING IN
KRISTEN CREEK LN
AZUR LN
PINE NEEDLE CIR
PINE NEEDLE LN
SHELL
COBALT DR
CERULEAN
PINE
NEEDLE LN
NOE LN
WINDHILL LOOP

N
O
S
T

ARTESIA BEND
HOVER
MAYFIELD RANCH BLVD
MAYFIELD
RANCH CT
Q
R
RM 1431

ASHMERE CV
NEWLAND
FLORA VISTA LOOP
ROSE MAY LN
SEBASTIAN DR
ROUND
ROCK
CUERNE LINDO
CORAZON
JUL
E LUMINOSO
CANTERA CV
Stone
Oak
Park
U
V

46
INWOOD
WILLOW
WALKER WAY
MAYFIELD
RANCH
LOOP
SENDERO SPRINGS DR
SENDERO
SPRINGS
46

DEER TRACT
W LUMINOSO
RISA CT
AZALEA LN
Bridge
PASADA LN
ARIA CV
ARBOR

W
OAK BEND CV
ELM TR
OAK BEND
PHEASANT
CORTINA
COLINA CV
LN
ASOMBRA LN
AMAPOLA
ANGELICO LN
X

LIVE OAK ST
BUCKHORN
GREAT OAKS DR
CARMEL DR
ANGELICO CV
HELADA LN
ADAGIO PL
Y

ROUND ROCK

Z
HIDDEN GLEN
WEST END
VIBAR CV

Mayfield Park
QUAIL RUN
EMERALD HILL DR
ANGELICO CV
CANCELO LN
CANCELO WAY

HIDDEN GLEN DR
BERWICK DR

DOUBLE TREE
CHERT DR
CHERT CV
VALLEY VIEW ST
VALLEY VIEW CV
CURTIS DR
EAGLE WAY
OVERVIEW
BRUSHY CREEK
NORTH

GOLDENOAK CIR
BRIAR OAK LN
GOLDENOAK CIR
ES
Cactus
Ranch
DALEA DR
PORTULACA DR
SAWGRASS LN

CREEK BEND BLVD
NUELTIN CT
WHITEHURST DR

MK

SCALE IN MILES
0   ⅛   ¼   ⅜   ½

SCALE IN FEET
0   1000   2000   3000

BOOK PAGE 1054

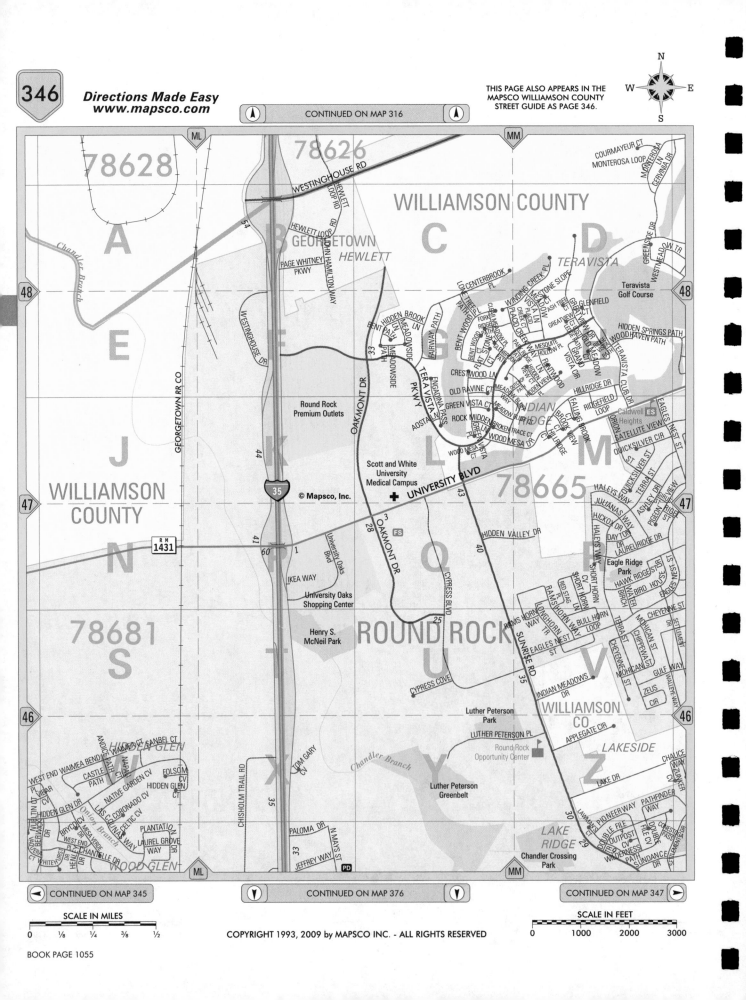

THIS PAGE ALSO APPEARS IN THE MAPSCO WILLIAMSON COUNTY STREET GUIDE AS PAGE 347.

Directions Made Easy
www.mapsco.com

347

CONTINUED ON MAP 317

N
W E
S

WILLIAMSON COUNTY

ROUND ROCK

78665

University Blvd
N A W Grimes Blvd
Seton Pkwy
Williamson Co Rd 112
FM 1460

Union Hill Cemetery
Williamson Co Rd 186
McNutt Creek

Teravista
Teravista Golf Course
Texas State University-Round Rock Higher Education Center
Seton Medical Center Williamson

Indian Ridge

Canyon Sage Path
Wandering Vine Tr
Green Tree Cv
Monticello
Barchetta Dr
Reston Cv
Asbury Park
Kempwood Loop
Spiceberry Path
Pebblestone Pl
Ridgebend Dr
Windberry Dr
Woodhaven Tr
Westvalley Ln
Terravista Club Dr
Vista Verde Dr
Parkvista Trail
Fairmeadow Dr
Greyleaf Path
Clearvista Path
Greenside Dr
Woodvista Pl
Westmeadow Trail
Greenside Tr
Stonehaven Ln
Bluffside Int
Hidden Springs Path
Bluestone

Satellite View
Lorson Loop
Tonia Loop
Eagles Nest St
Bonnie Ln
Terra Loop
Ashley Dr
Pigeon View
Rigel St
Solitaire Rd
Wayne Dr
Bend Cv
Holden Cv
Haynie Bend
Amistad Way
Sandy Brook Dr
Nocona Ln
Texana Loop
Casa Blanca Cv
Palo Pinto Cv
Hawk View
Concord Dr
Geese Route
Cheyenne St
Walleye Way
Pike Path
Perch Tr
Settlement Dr
Minnow Bass Loop
Bluecat Way
Perch Cv
Lakeside Loop

ROUND ROCK

MEADOW LAKE

LAKESIDE
Meadow Lake Park

Chalice Way
Chalice Cv
Zuhner Cv
Meadow Park
Pathfinder Way
Horseman Cove
Conestoga Pass
Saddle Pack Way
Trading Post Tr
Settlement Tr

Meadow Lake
Meadow Lake Park

Bluffs Landing Way
Water Spaniel Way
Mastiff Cv
Sheltie Ln
Kiphen Rd
North Crossing Tr
Chandler View Tr
Tammy Ln
Brenda Ln
Kim Cv

Union Hill
Hopewell
ES MS

SADDLEBROOK ESTATES
Skylers Dr
Ryders Ridge
Fairview
Deer Fern Ln
Summerwalk Pl
Haselwood Ln
Shadowpoint Cv
Sharon
Woodmere
Breezy Point
Fairview Dr
Bluffstone Dr
Crimson Sky Ct
Amberglow Ct
Rockin J Rd
E Old Settlers Blvd

SETTLERS OVERLOOK

ESTATES AT SETTLERS PARK
Tate Ln
Herrington Cv
Overton St
Jack Nicklaus Dr
Aaron Ross
Settlers Park Loop
Todd Dr
Clinton Ct
Aaron Ross
Hearthsong Loop
Parker Ln

ROUND ROCK
YMCA Complex
Old Settlers at Palm Valley Park
Soccer Fields
Harrell Pkwy
Aten Loop
CHANDLER CREEK
Rod Carew Dr

© Mapsco, Inc.

48 47 46

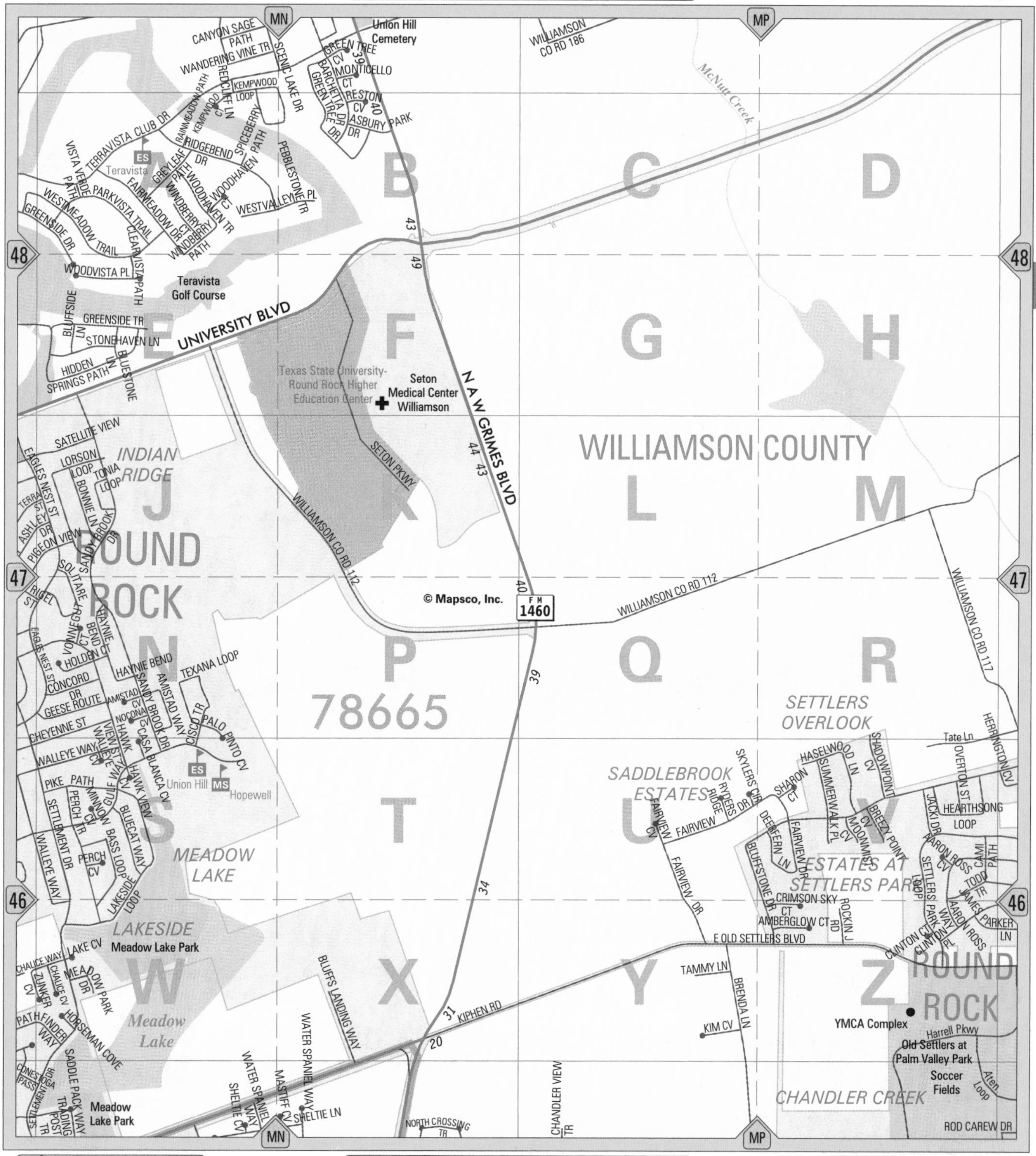

CONTINUED ON MAP 346
CONTINUED ON MAP 377
CONTINUED ON MAP 348

SCALE IN MILES
0 1/8 1/4 3/8 1/2

SCALE IN FEET
0 1000 2000 3000

N
W E
S

CONTINUED ON MAP 318

130

WILLIAMSON CO RD 110

WILLIAMSON CO RD 118

A   B   C   D

48   48

LEMENS CIR

CARMEL CREEKSIDE DR

HY VIEW LN

E   F   G   H

LEMENS AVE

WILLIAMSON CO RD 112

78634

Veterans Hill
ES

J   K   L   M

LIMMER LOOP

McNutt Creek

1   13

47   47

PALOMA LAKE BLVD

LOS ALAMOS PASS

CASTELLAN LN

ST FEDERICO WAY

ESTEFANIA LN

COLUMBUS LOOP

ST CHRISTOPHER CT

ST CHRISTOPHER CT

MEGELLAN WAY

CORTES CT

CORTES CT

ANGELINA DR

GUADALAJARA ST

ROSALINA LOOP

PENELOPE WAY

ROSALINA LOOP

WILL SMITH CIR

WILL SMITH DR

HAYBARN LN

WILLIAMS DR

COUNTRY VIEW ESTATES

DIEGO DR

ST FRANCES CT

ST RODRIGO CT

ST CHRISTOPHER CT

N   P   Q   R

LOS ALAMOS PASS

LOS ALAMOS CT

N RED BUD LN

PALOMA LAKE

WILL SMITH CIR

WILLIAMSON COUNTY

N WILLIAMSON CO RD 122

PALOMA LAKE BLVD

Tate Ln

BLUFFSTONE DR

WILLIAMSON CO RD 117

HERRINGTON CT

SANTA BARBARA LOOP

SANTA CLARA LN

SAN FERNANDO CT

WILLIAMSON CO RD 110

S   T   U   V

78665

46   46

ESTATES

SETTLERS PARK

AARON WAY

TODD TR

LINDA LEE LN

ROSS ST

PEARSON ST

PEARSON ST

MARSHALL TRAIL

HENDERSON PATH

PAULING LN

JAMES PARKER LN

SETTLERS PARK LOOP

CLINTON LN

BUTLER WAY

CORRIGAN LN

CHAMBERLAIN DR

E OLD SETTLERS BLVD

DAWSON RD

W   X   Y   Z

HARTELL PKWY

Old Settlers at Palm Valley Park

T C OATTS LN

N RED BUD LN

ROUND ROCK

Baseball Complex

Aten Loop

ROD CAREW DR

HYCREST DR

SPRING GARDEN DR

GREEN PASTURE DR

TRADESMEN'S PARK DR

TRADESMEN'S PARK LOOP

TRADESMAN DR

© Mapsco, Inc.

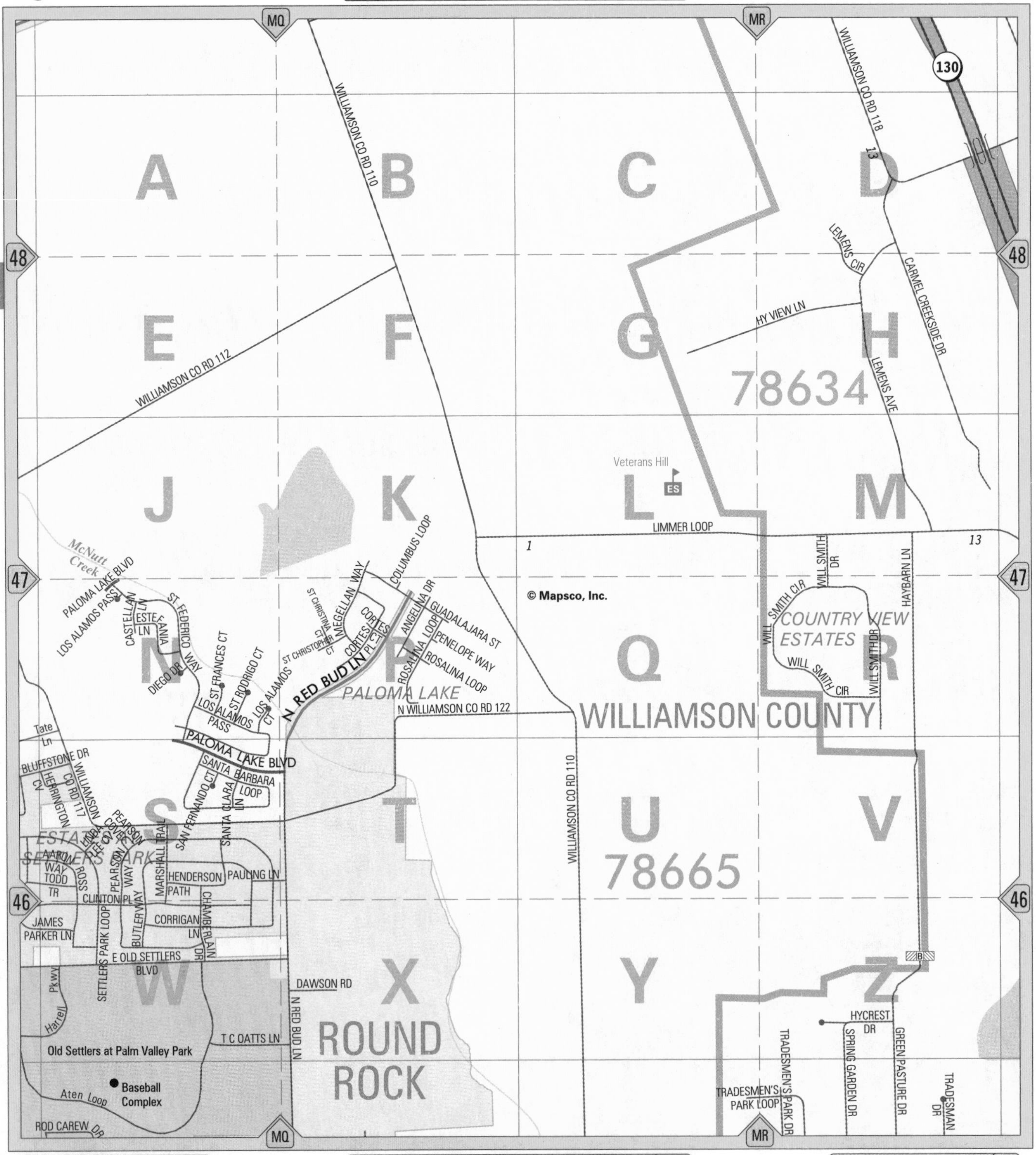

CONTINUED ON MAP 347

CONTINUED ON MAP 378

CONTINUED ON MAP 349

SCALE IN MILES
0   ⅛   ¼   ⅜   ½

SCALE IN FEET
0   1000   2000   3000

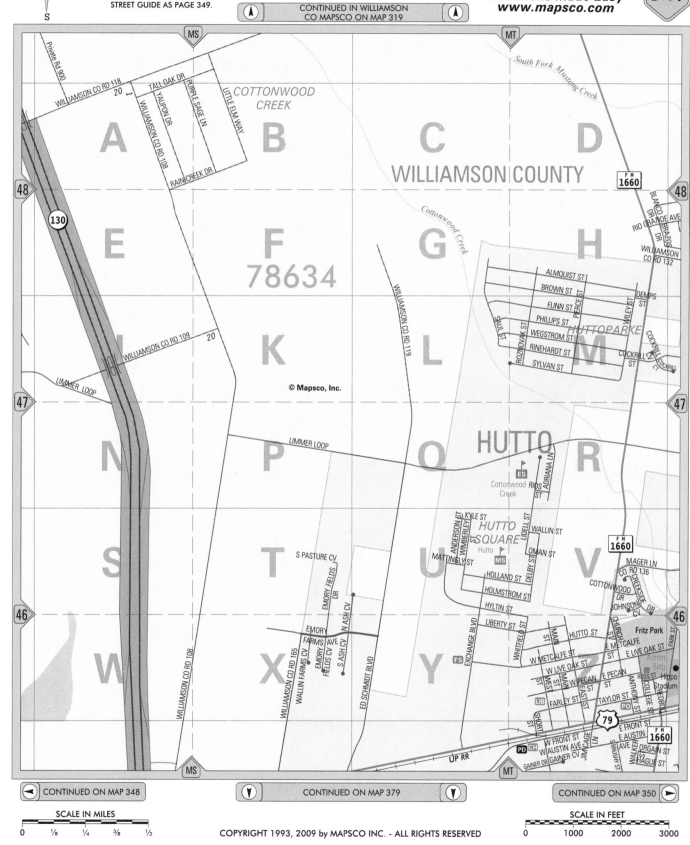

THIS PAGE ALSO APPEARS IN THE
MAPSCO WILLIAMSON COUNTY
STREET GUIDE AS PAGE 349.

Directions Made Easy
www.mapsco.com

CONTINUED IN WILLIAMSON
CO MAPSCO ON MAP 319

N
W ·|· E
S

Private Rd 900

WILLIAMSON CO RD 118
20
TALL OAK DR
YAUPON DR
WILLIAMSON CO RD 108
PURPLE SAGE LN
LITTLE ELM WAY
RAIN CREEK DR

COTTONWOOD
CREEK

A

B

C

D

WILLIAMSON COUNTY

FM 1660

48
130
48

RIO GRANDE AVE
BLANCO DR
BRAZOS DR
WILLIAMSON CO RD 132

E

F
78634

G

Cottonwood Creek

H

ALMQUIST ST
BROWN ST
FLINN ST
PHILLIPS ST
WEGSTROM ST
RINEHARDT ST
SYLVAN ST
PIERCE ST
WILEY ST
DEMPS
SAUL ST
ROZNOVAK ST
HUTTOPARKE
COCKRILL ST
COCKRILL ST
COCKRILL CT

47
47

I

WILLIAMSON CO RD 109
20
WILLIAMSON CO RD 119

K

L

M

LIMMER LOOP

© Mapsco, Inc.

LIMMER LOOP

N

P

Q

HUTTO

R

ES
Cottonwood
Creek
RIOS ST
ADRIANA LN

S

T

S PASTURE CV

ANDERSON ST
WIMBERLEY
KYLE ST
HUTTO
SQUARE
Hutto
MS
MATTINGLY ST
LIDELL ST
WALLIN ST
LOMAN ST
DELBY ST
HOLLAND ST
HOLMSTROM ST
HYLTIN ST
LIBERTY ST

U

FM 1660

V

MAGER LN
CO RD 136
COTTONWOOD DR
CREEKSIDE DR
JOHNSON ST

46

EMORY FIELDS DR
N ASH CV
EMORY FARMS AVE
EMORY FIELDS CV
S ASH CV
WILLIAMSON CO RD 165
WALLIN FARMS CV
ED SCHMIDT BLVD

W

X

Y

EXCHANGE BLVD
FS
WHITFIELD ST
MAIN ST
HUTTO ST
W METCALFE ST
E METCALFE ST
W LIVE OAK ST
W PECAN ST
E PECAN ST
MAIN ST
WEST ST
E CAST ST
FARLEY ST
TAYLOR ST
SHORT ST
LIB
Z
CHURCH ST
E LIVE OAK ST
ANTHONY ST
COLLEGE ST
ROSS ST
ADMIN Bldg
Hippo Stadium
PARK ST
Fritz Park
PO
79
FM 1660

46

W FRONT ST
W AUSTIN AVE
GAINER DR
GAINER CV
UP RR
PD CH
JIM CAGE
BRUSHY ST
WALKER
E FRONT ST
E AUSTIN ST
ORGAIN ST
HAGUE ST
DOBIE DR

CONTINUED ON MAP 348

CONTINUED ON MAP 379

CONTINUED ON MAP 350

SCALE IN MILES
0   1/8   1/4   3/8   1/2

SCALE IN FEET
0   1000   2000   3000

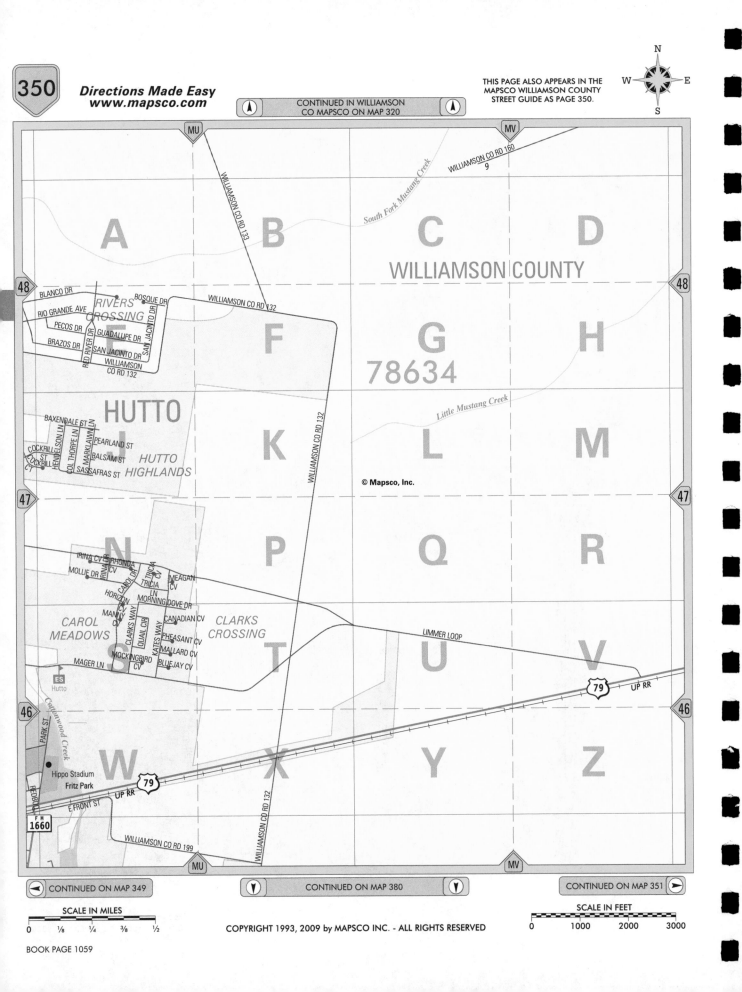

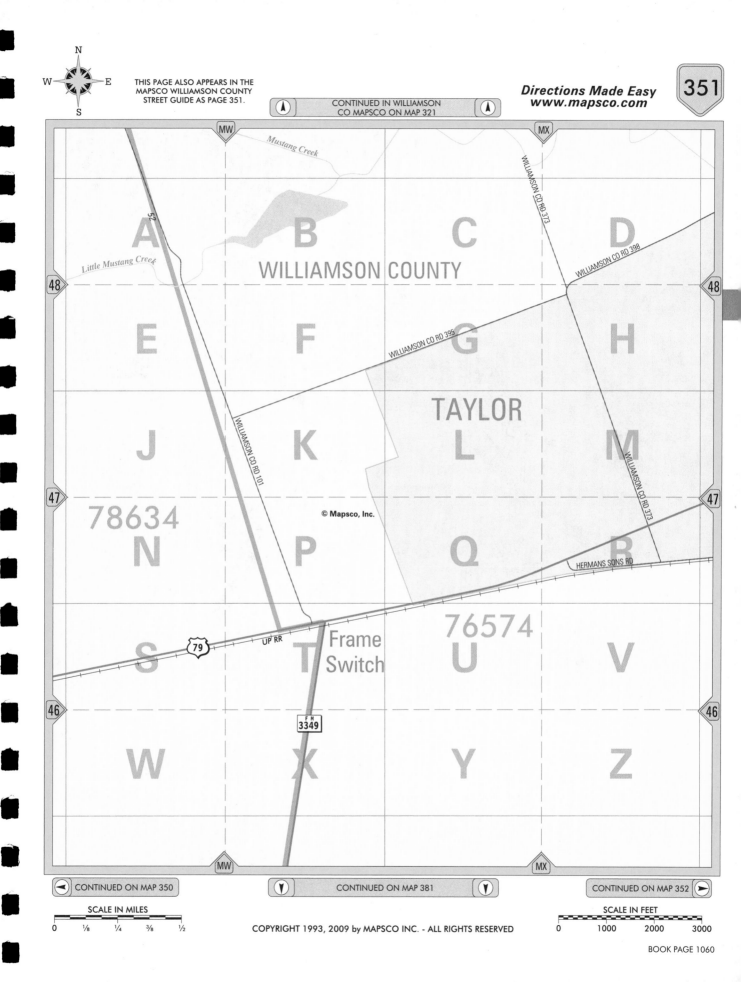

Directions Made Easy
www.mapsco.com

THIS PAGE ALSO APPEARS IN THE
MAPSCO WILLIAMSON COUNTY
STREET GUIDE AS PAGE 351.

N
W E
S

CONTINUED IN WILLIAMSON
CO MAPSCO ON MAP 321

MW

Mustang Creek

MX

WILLIAMSON CO RD 373

A

B

C

D

WILLIAMSON CO RD 398

WILLIAMSON COUNTY

Little Mustang Creek

48

48

E

F

WILLIAMSON CO RD 395

G

H

52

TAYLOR

J

WILLIAMSON CO RD 101

K

L

M

WILLIAMSON CO RD 373

47

47

78634

© Mapsco, Inc.

N

P

Q

R

HERMANS SONS RD

76574

S

79

UP RR

T

Frame
Switch

U

V

46

46

W

X

FM
3349

Y

Z

MW

MX

CONTINUED ON MAP 350

CONTINUED ON MAP 381

CONTINUED ON MAP 352

SCALE IN MILES

0   ⅛   ¼   ⅜   ½

COPYRIGHT 1993, 2009 by MAPSCO INC. - ALL RIGHTS RESERVED

SCALE IN FEET

0   1000   2000   3000

BOOK PAGE 1060

Directions Made Easy
www.mapsco.com

THIS PAGE ALSO APPEARS IN THE
MAPSCO WILLIAMSON COUNTY
STREET GUIDE AS PAGE 352.

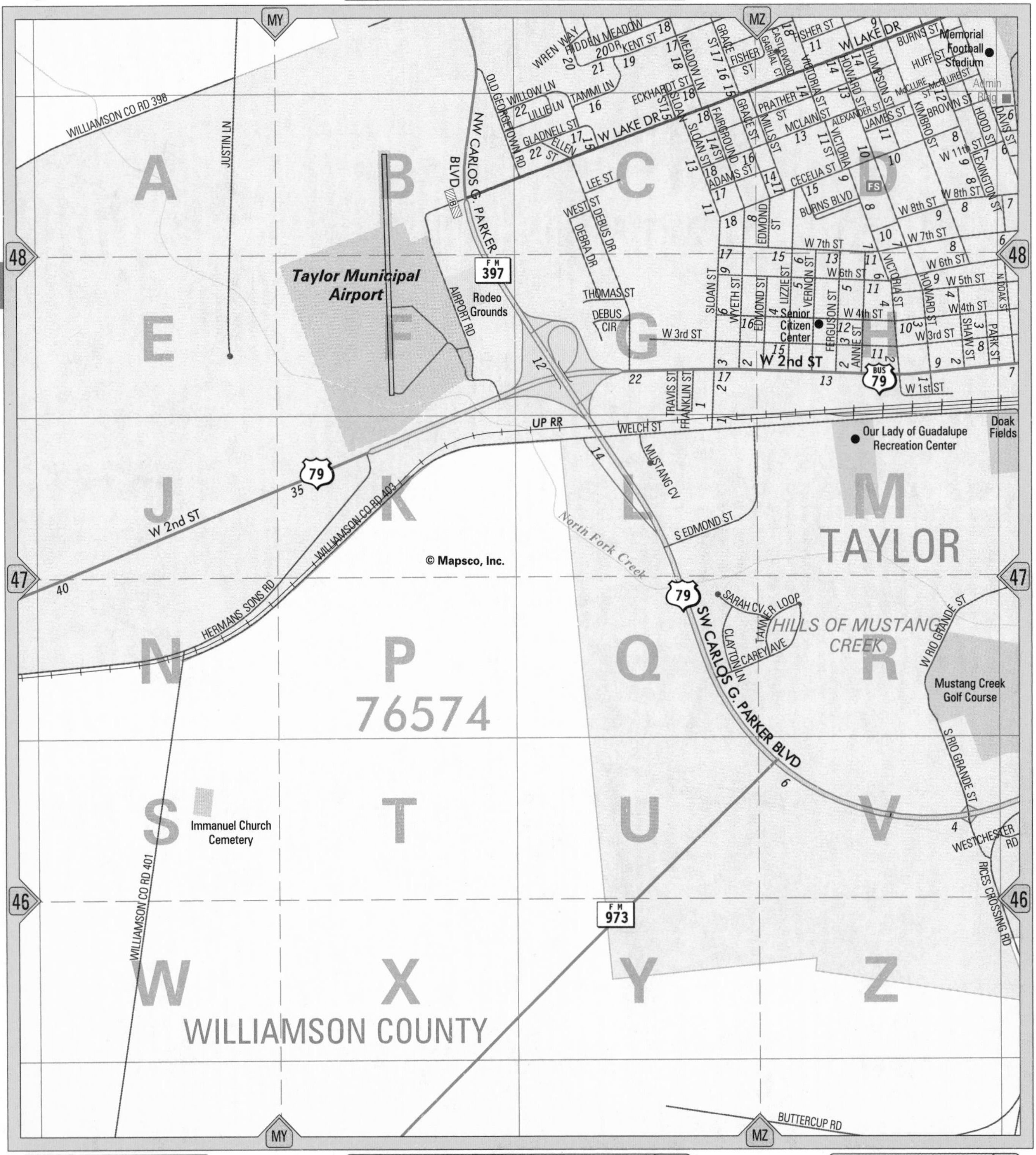

N W E S

CONTINUED ON MAP 322

MY

WREN WAY
HIDDEN MEADOW
20 DR KENT ST 18
WILLOW LN
LILLIE LN
GLADNELL ST
TAMMI LN
MEADOW LN
FISHER ST
GRACE ST
FISHER ST
W LAKE DR
BURNS ST
HUFF ST
Memorial
Football
Stadium
Admin
Bldg

WILLIAMSON CO RD 398

A B C D

NW CARLOS G. PARKER BLVD

FM 397

W LAKE DR
ECKHARDT ST
GABRIEL CT
EASTWOOD
VICTORIA ST
CASTLEWOOD
THOMPSON ST
HOWARD ST
McCLURE
McCLURE ST
BROWN ST
HOOD ST
DAVIS ST
PRATHER ST
McLAIN ST
ALEXANDER ST
JAMES ST
KIMBRO ST
W 11th ST
LEXINGTON ST
GRACE ST
MILLS ST
ADAMS ST
VICTORIA ST
CECELIA ST
BURNS BLVD
FS
W 8th ST
W 8th ST
EDMOND ST
W 7th ST
W 7th ST
SLOANS ST
WYETH ST
W 6th ST
VERNON ST
VICTORIA ST
HOWARD ST
W 6th ST
W 5th ST
N OAK ST
PARK ST
LIZZIE ST
EDMOND ST
FERGUSON ST
W 4th ST
W 4th ST
SHAW ST
ANNIE ST
Senior
Citizen
Center
W 3rd ST
W 3rd ST

48 48

A B C D

Taylor Municipal
Airport

Airport RD

Rodeo
Grounds

12

E F G H

WEST ST
S DEBUS ST
DEBRA DR
THOMAS ST
DEBUS
CIR
W 3rd ST
LEE ST

TRAVIS ST
FRANKLIN ST
22
17
13
W 2nd ST
BUS 79
W 1st ST
7

UP RR
WELCH ST
N MUSTANG CV
14
Our Lady of Guadalupe
Recreation Center
Doak
Fields

79
35
J K L

W 2nd ST

S EDMOND ST
M
TAYLOR

47 47

40

© Mapsco, Inc.

North Fork Creek

79
SARAH CV
TANNER LOOP
CLAYTON LN
CAREY AVE
HILLS OF MUSTANG
CREEK
W RIO GRANDE ST
S RIO GRANDE ST
Mustang Creek
Golf Course

N P Q R

76574

SW CARLOS G. PARKER BLVD
6

HERMANS SONS RD
WILLIAMSON CO RD 403

WILLIAMSON CO RD 401

S T U V

Immanuel Church
Cemetery

4
WESTCHESTER RD
RICES CROSSING RD

46 46

FM 973

W X Y Z

WILLIAMSON COUNTY

BUTTERCUP RD

MY MZ

CONTINUED ON MAP 351
CONTINUED ON MAP 382
CONTINUED ON MAP 353

SCALE IN MILES

0   1/8   1/4   3/8   1/2

COPYRIGHT 1993, 2009 by MAPSCO INC. - ALL RIGHTS RESERVED

SCALE IN FEET

0   1000   2000   3000

THIS PAGE ALSO APPEARS IN THE
MAPSCO WILLIAMSON COUNTY
STREET GUIDE AS PAGE 353.

Directions Made Easy
www.mapsco.com

353

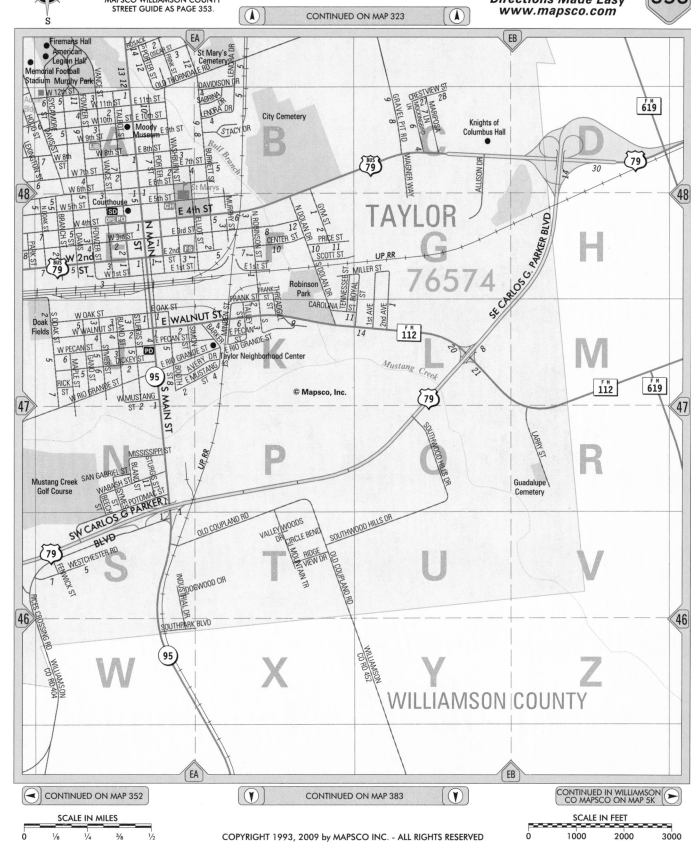

CONTINUED ON MAP 323

CONTINUED ON MAP 352

CONTINUED ON MAP 383

CONTINUED IN WILLIAMSON
CO MAPSCO ON MAP 5K

© Mapsco, Inc.

SCALE IN MILES

0   1/8   1/4   3/8   1/2

SCALE IN FEET

0   1000   2000   3000

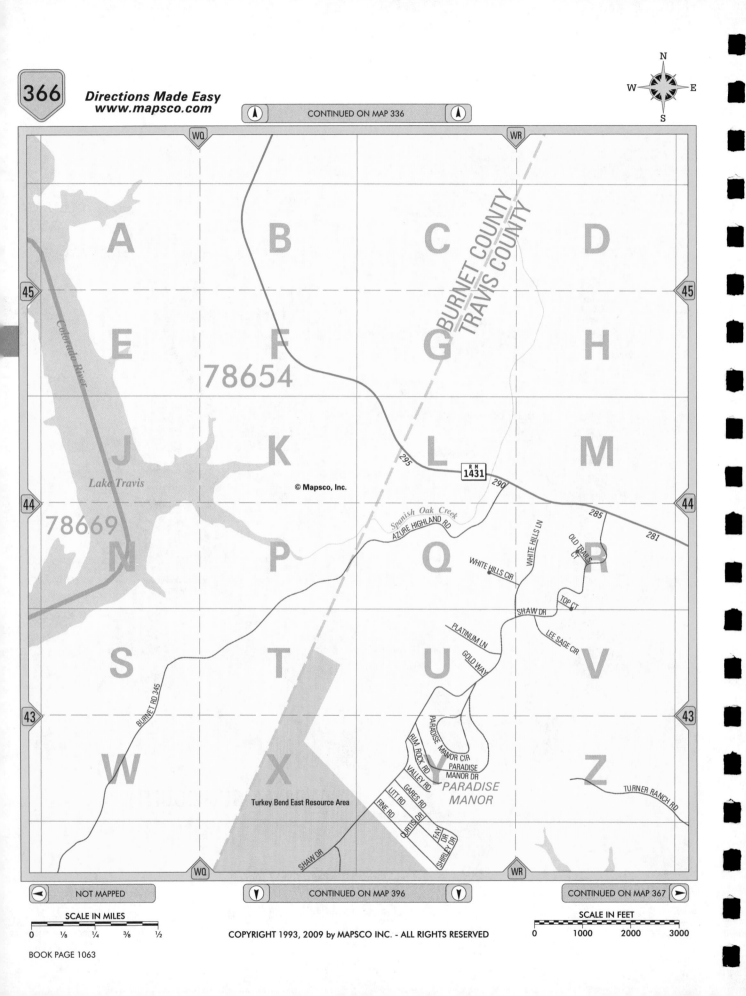

366

Directions Made Easy
www.mapsco.com

N
W E
S

CONTINUED ON MAP 336

WQ   WR

45   45

A   B   BURNET COUNTY   C   D
                      TRAVIS COUNTY

E   F   G   H
     78654

44   44

J   K   L   M
                      295 RM 1431

     Lake Travis   290   285

     78669   281

N   P   Spanish Oak Creek Q   R
                      AZURE HIGHLAND RD
© Mapsco, Inc.
                           WHITE HILLS CIR   WHITE HILLS LN   OLD TRAILS CT

                                             TOP CT
                                        SHAW DR
                                   PLATINUM LN   LEE SAGE CIR
43   43
S   T   U   GOLD WAY   V

     BURNET RD 345

W   X   PARADISE MANOR CIR Z
                      RIM ROCK RD
                      VALLEY RD   PARADISE
     Turkey Bend East Resource Area MANOR DR   TURNER RANCH RD
                      GABES RD   PARADISE
                      LITT RD   MANOR
                      FINE RD
                           CURTIS DR FAY DR
                      SHAW DR   SHIRLEY DR

WQ   WR

NOT MAPPED   CONTINUED ON MAP 396   CONTINUED ON MAP 367

SCALE IN MILES
0   1/8   1/4   3/8   1/2

SCALE IN FEET
0   1000   2000   3000

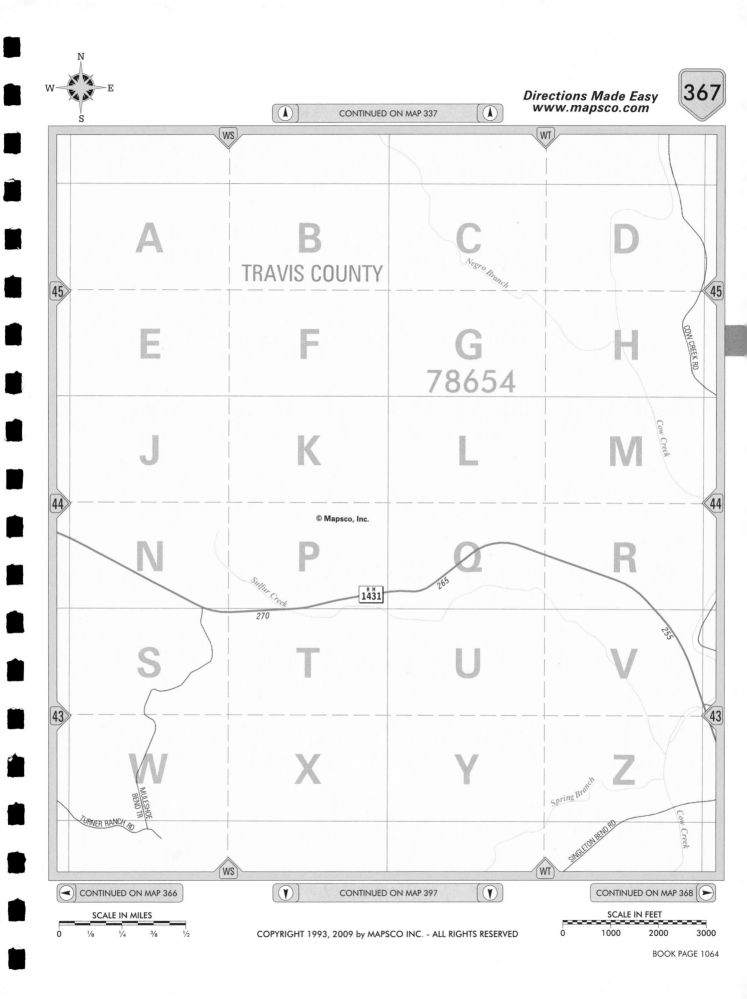

CONTINUED ON MAP 337

Directions Made Easy
www.mapsco.com

367

WS

WT

A

B

TRAVIS COUNTY

C

Negro Branch

D

45

E

F

G

78654

H

COW CREEK RD

45

J

K

L

M

Cow Creek

44

N

© Mapsco, Inc.

P

Q

R

44

Sulfur Creek

RM 1431

265

270

255

S

T

U

V

43

W

X

Y

Z

43

MULESHOE BEND TR.

TURNER RANCH RD

Spring Branch

SINGLETON BEND RD

Cow Creek

WS

WT

CONTINUED ON MAP 366

CONTINUED ON MAP 397

CONTINUED ON MAP 368

SCALE IN MILES

0   ⅛   ¼   ⅜   ½

SCALE IN FEET

0   1000   2000   3000

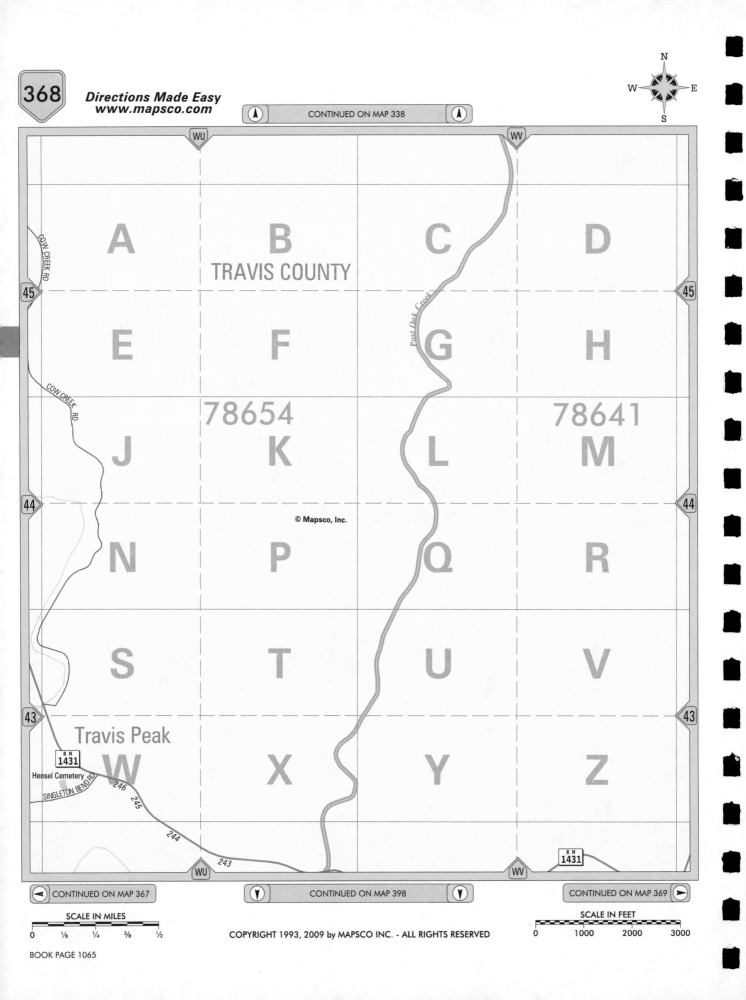

N
W E
S

CONTINUED ON MAP 338

WU

WV

A　　B　　C　　D

TRAVIS COUNTY

COW CREEK RD

45　　　　　　　　　　　　　　　45

E　　F　　G　　H

Post Oak Creek

COW CREEK RD

78654　　　　　　78641

J　　K　　L　　M

44　　　　　　　　　　　　　　　44

© Mapsco, Inc.

N　　P　　Q　　R

S　　T　　U　　V

43　　　　　　　　　　　　　　　43

Travis Peak

R M
1431

W　　X　　Y　　Z

Hensel Cemetery

SINGLETON BEND RD

246

245

244

243

R M
1431

WU

WV

◄ CONTINUED ON MAP 367

▼ CONTINUED ON MAP 398

CONTINUED ON MAP 369 ►

SCALE IN MILES

0　1/8　1/4　3/8　1/2

SCALE IN FEET

0　1000　2000　3000

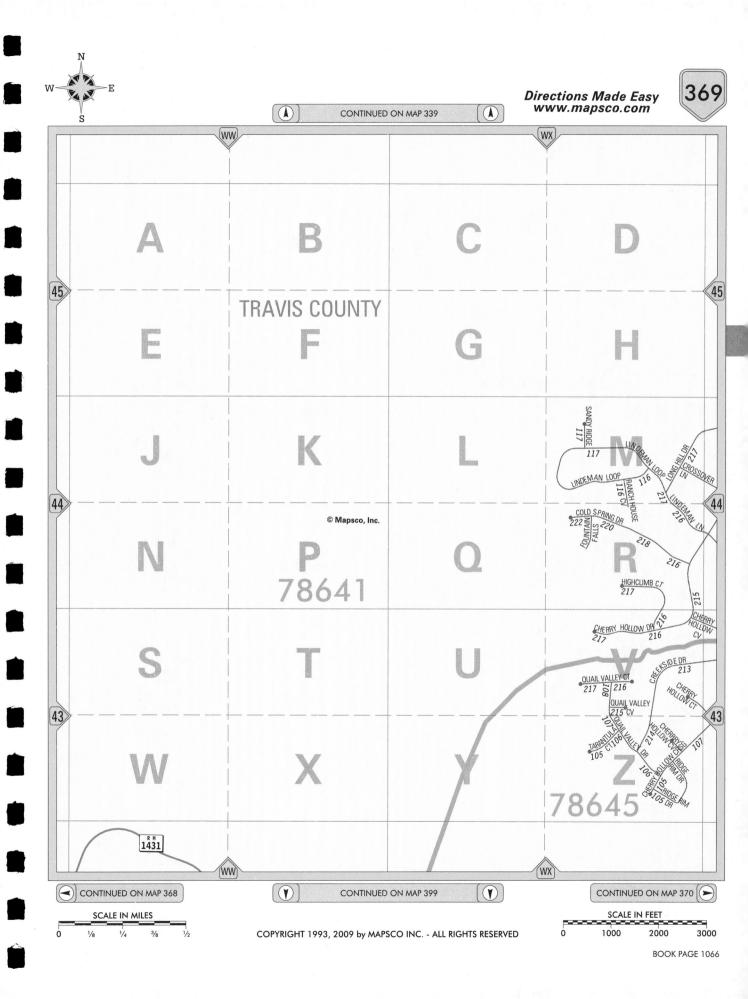

CONTINUED ON MAP 339

WW

WX

A

B

C

D

45

45

TRAVIS COUNTY

E

F

G

H

J

K

L

M

SANDY RIDGE
117

117

LINDEMAN LOOP

LONG HILL DR

LINDEMAN LOOP

LIN DEMAN LOOP

CROSSOVER

217

116

116 CV

RANCH HOUSE

217

LINDEMAN LN

44

44

© Mapsco, Inc.

N

P

Q

R

COLD SPRING DR

222

220

218

216

FOUNTAIN FALLS

216

78641

HIGHCLIMB CT
217

215

CHERRY HOLLOW CV

CHERRY HOLLOW DR
217

216

216

S

T

U

V

CREEKSIDE DR
213

QUAIL VALLEY CT
217

216

708

CHERRY HOLLOW CT

QUAIL VALLEY
215 CV

43

43

107 LN

QUAIL VALLEY DR
106 CT

106

214

CHERRY HOLLOW CV RIDGE

CHERRY HOLLOW CV RIDGE
107

TARANTULA
105

W

X

Y

Z

106

CHERRY HOLLOW RIM DR

RIDGE RIM
105

105 DR

78645

◄ CONTINUED ON MAP 368

▼ CONTINUED ON MAP 399 ▼

CONTINUED ON MAP 370 ►

WW

WX

R M
1431

SCALE IN MILES

0   ⅛   ¼   ⅜   ½

SCALE IN FEET

0   1000   2000   3000

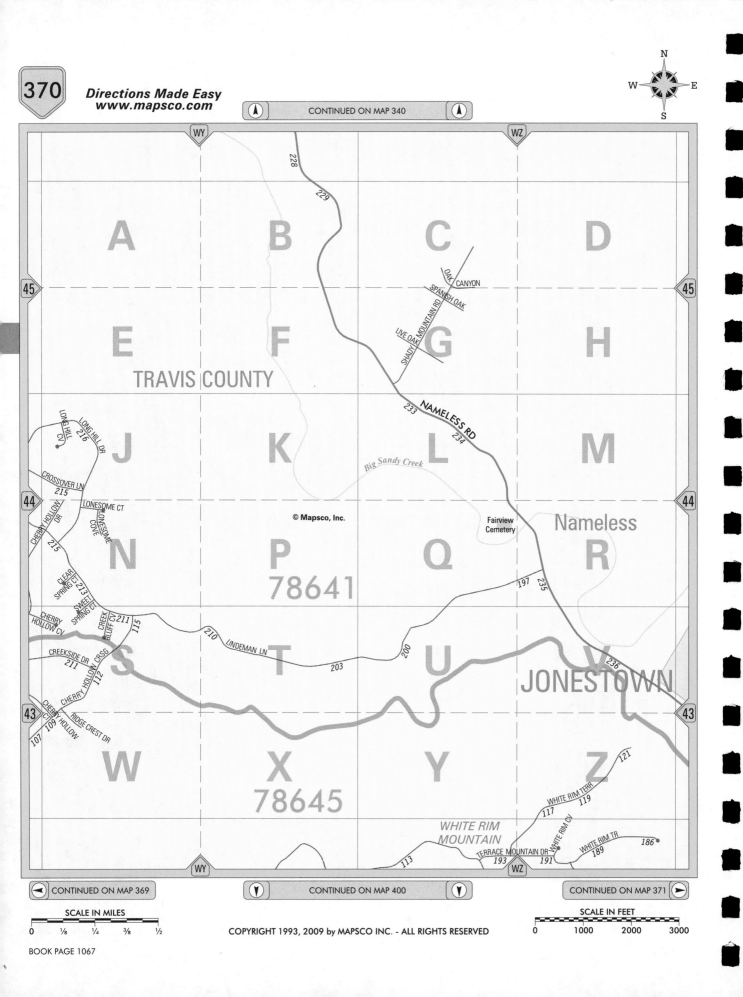

Directions Made Easy
www.mapsco.com

CONTINUED ON MAP 340

N
W E
S

WY

WZ

228

229

A

B

C

D

45

45

OAK CANYON

SPANISH OAK

SHADY MOUNTAIN RD

LIVE OAK

E

F

G

H

TRAVIS COUNTY

233

NAMELESS RD

234

J

K

L

M

LONG HILL DR

LONG HILL CV

216

Big Sandy Creek

CROSSOVER LN

215

LONESOME CT

44

44

© Mapsco, Inc.

Fairview Cemetery

Nameless

CHERRY HOLLOW DR

LONESOME COVE

215

N

P

Q

R

CLEAR SPRING CT 213

78641

197

235

CHERRY HOLLOW CV

SWEET SPRING CT

CREEK BLUFF CV 211

115

210

LINDEMAN LN

200

236

CREEKSIDE DR

CHERRY HOLLOW CRSG 112

211

S

203

T

U

V

JONESTOWN

43

CHERRY HOLLOW CT

RIDGE CREST DR

43

107

109

W

X

Y

Z

121

78645

WHITE RIM TERR

119

117

WHITE RIM MOUNTAIN

WHITE RIM CV

WHITE RIM TR

186

113

TERRACE MOUNTAIN DR

193

191

189

WY

WZ

CONTINUED ON MAP 369

CONTINUED ON MAP 400

CONTINUED ON MAP 371

SCALE IN MILES

0   1/8   1/4   3/8   1/2

SCALE IN FEET

0   1000   2000   3000

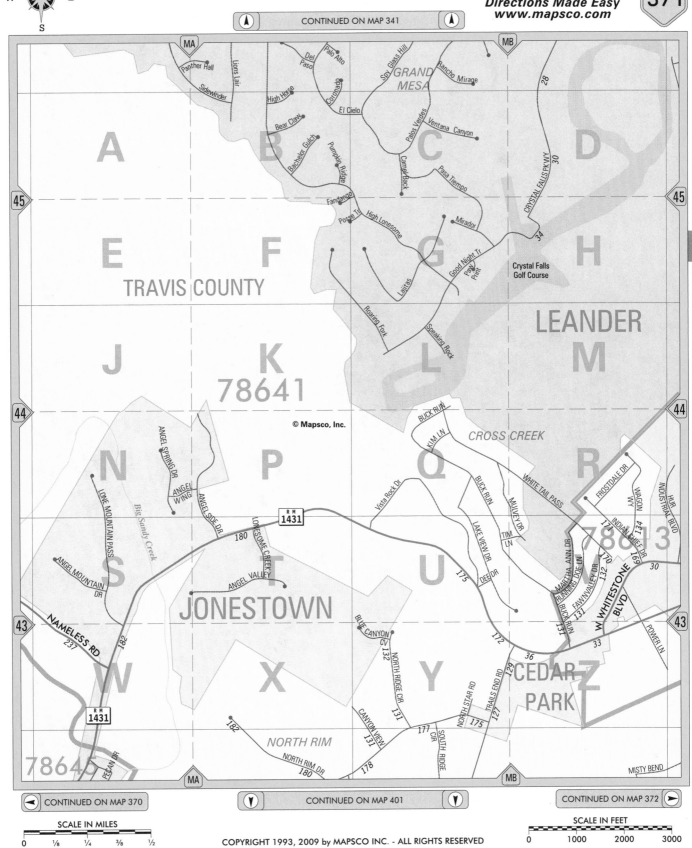

CONTINUED ON MAP 341

CONTINUED ON MAP 370

CONTINUED ON MAP 401

CONTINUED ON MAP 372

N
W E
S

MA

MB

Panther Hall
Lions Lair
Sidewinder
Del Paso
Palo Alto
High Horse
Coronado
El Cielo
Bear Claw
Bachelor Gulch
Pumpkin Ridge
Fandango
Posse Tr
High Lonesome
Laiitas
Roaring Fork
Speaking Rock

Soy Glass Hill
GRAND MESA
Rancho Mirage
Palos Verdes
Ventana Canyon
Camelback
Pasa Tiempo
Mirador
Good Night Tr
Paw Print

28
30
34

CRYSTAL FALLS PKWY

Crystal Falls
Golf Course

A B C D

45
45

E F G H

TRAVIS COUNTY

LEANDER

J K L M

78641

© Mapsco, Inc.

44
44

Angel Spring Dr
Angel Wing
Angel Side Dr
Lone Mountain Pass
Big Sandy Creek
Angel Mountain Dr
Lonesome Creek
Angel Valley

BUCK RUN
KIM LN
CROSS CREEK
Vista Rock Dr
Buck Run
WHITE TAIL PASS
Mulvey Dr
Lake View Dr
Tim Ln
Dee Dr
Frostdale Dr
Wagon Wy
Indian Whee Dr
Industrial Blvd
Hub
Martha Ann Dr
Running Doe Ln
Fawn Valley Dr
Buck Run
W WHITESTONE BLVD
Power Ln

N P Q R

78613

S T U

175
172

172
134
169
132
30
131
131
33
36

RM 1431
180

JONESTOWN

CEDAR PARK

W X Y Z

Blue Canyon
CV 132
North Ridge Cir
131
Canyon View
131
North Rim Dr
180
NORTH RIM
182

North Star Rd
Trails End Rd
127
175
South Ridge
177
Cir
178

129
127

MISTY BEND

Nameless Rd
237
182

43
43

RM 1431

78645
Pecan Dr

MA

MB

SCALE IN MILES
0   ⅛   ¼   ⅜   ½

SCALE IN FEET
0   1000   2000   3000

CONTINUED ON MAP 342

THIS PAGE ALSO APPEARS IN THE
MAPSCO WILLIAMSON COUNTY
STREET GUIDE AS PAGE 372.

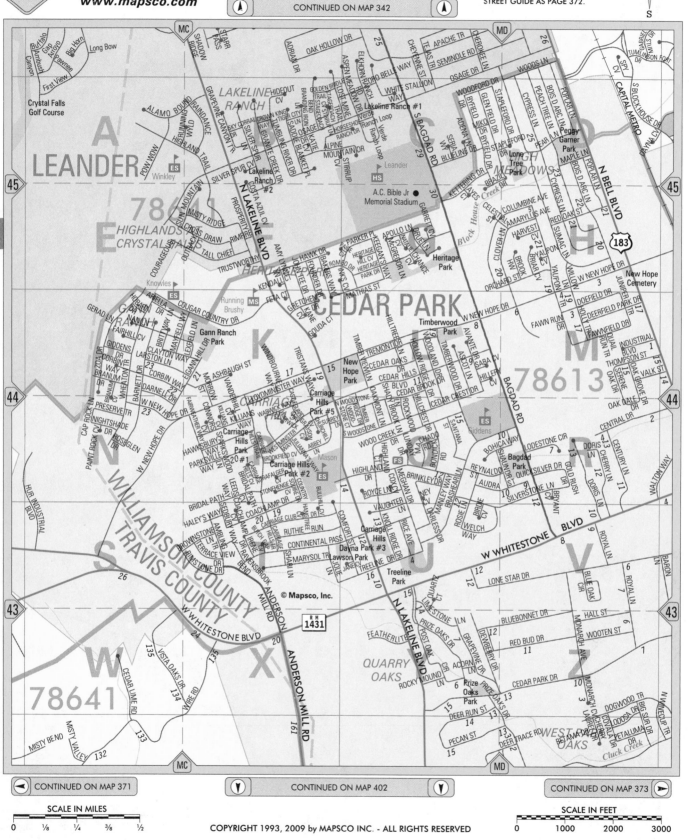

CONTINUED ON MAP 371

CONTINUED ON MAP 402

CONTINUED ON MAP 373

SCALE IN MILES

0   1/8   1/4   3/8   1/2

SCALE IN FEET

0   1000   2000   3000

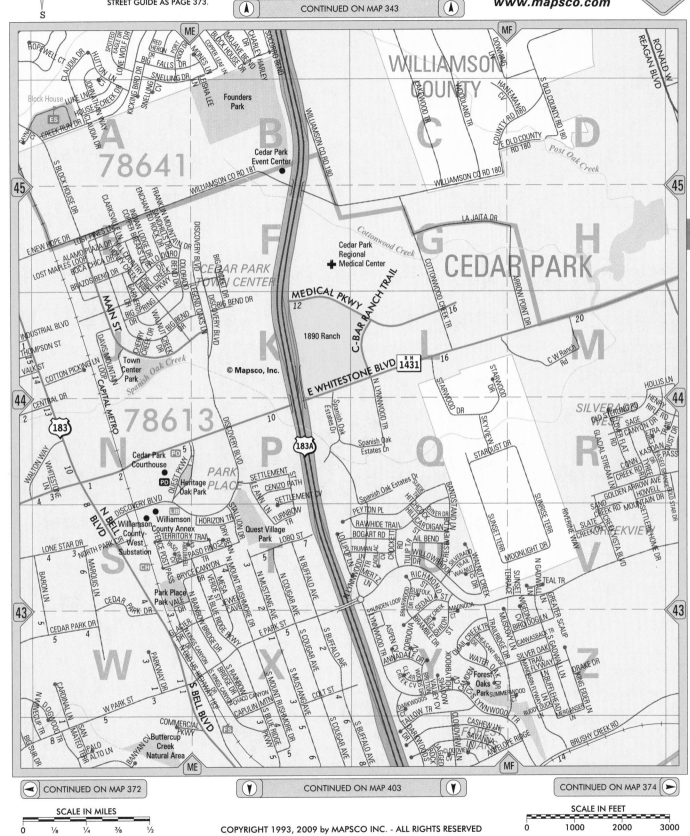

THIS PAGE ALSO APPEARS IN THE
MAPSCO WILLIAMSON COUNTY
STREET GUIDE AS PAGE 373.

CONTINUED ON MAP 343

WILLIAMSON COUNTY

CEDAR PARK

78641

78613

Founders Park

Cedar Park Event Center

Cedar Park Regional Medical Center

1890 Ranch

Post Oak Creek

Cottonwood Creek

MEDICAL PKWY

E WHITESTONE BLVD

RM 1431

Cedar Park Town Center

Town Center Park

Spanish Oak Creek

Cedar Park Courthouse

PARK PLACE

Heritage Oak Park

Williamson County-West Substation

Quest Village Park

Park Place Park

Buttercup Creek Natural Area

SILVERA WEST

Forest Oaks Park

© Mapsco, Inc.

CONTINUED ON MAP 372

CONTINUED ON MAP 403

CONTINUED ON MAP 374

SCALE IN MILES
0   1/8   1/4   3/8   1/2

SCALE IN FEET
0   1000   2000   3000

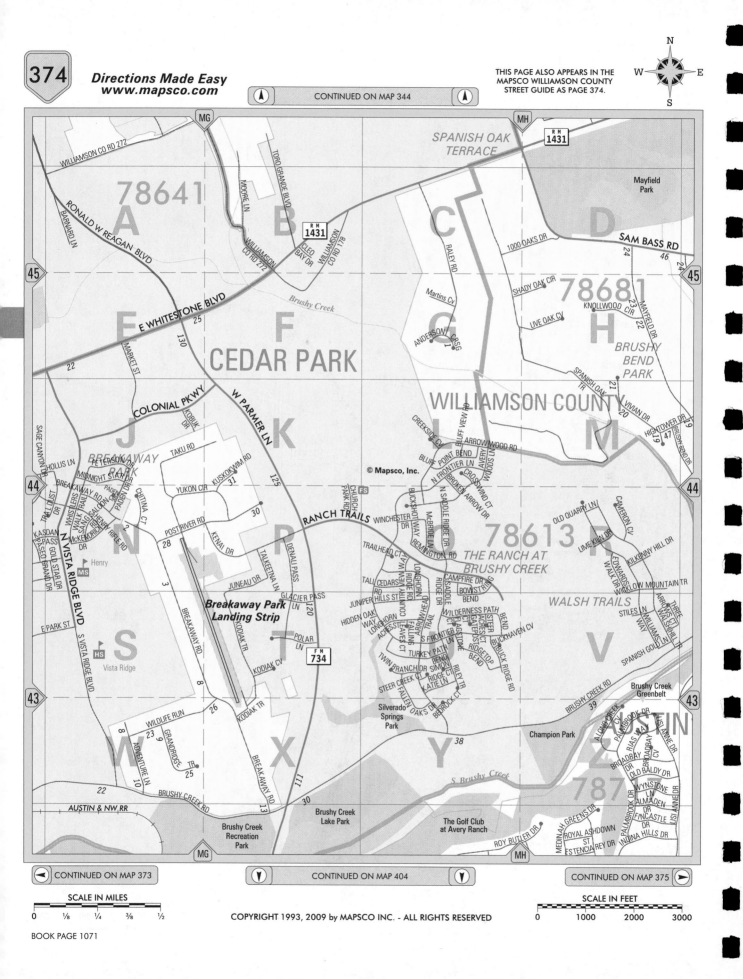

THIS PAGE ALSO APPEARS IN THE
MAPSCO WILLIAMSON COUNTY
STREET GUIDE AS PAGE 374.

N
W E
S

CONTINUED ON MAP 344

MG
MH

SPANISH OAK
TERRACE

R M
1431

Mayfield
Park

78641

WILLIAMSON CO RD 272

RONALD W REAGAN BLVD

BARNARD LN

TORO GRANDE BLVD

MOORE LN

R M
1431

WILLIAMSON CO RD 272

CLEO BAY DR

WILLIAMSON CO RD 178

SAM BASS RD

A
B
C
D

45
45

1000 OAKS DR
24
46
24

78681

SHADY OAK CIR

RALEY RD

KNOLLWOOD CIR
23
22

MAYFIELD DR

Martins Cv

E WHITESTONE BLVD
25

Brushy Creek

LIVE OAK CV

E
F
G
H

130

ANDERSON CR5G
I

BRUSHY
BEND
PARK

MARKET ST

22

CEDAR PARK

SPANISH OAK TR
21

VIVIAN DR
20

HIGHTOWER DR
19
47
19

BRUSHY BEND DR

COLONIAL PKWY

W PARMER LN

WILLIAMSON COUNTY

KOBUK DR

CREEKSIDE CV

BLUFF VIEW IN

ARROWWOOD RD

J
K
L
M

TAKU RD

BREAKAWAY
PARK

PETERSON DR

MIDNIGHT STAR DR

KUSKOKWIM RD
31

BLUFF POINT BEND

N FRONTIER LN

BROKEN ARROW DR

CROSSWIND CT

AVERY WOODS LN

SAGE CANYON DR

HOLLIS LN

44
44

BREAKAWAY RD

PADEN DR

CHITINA CT

YUKON CIR

125

CHURCH
PARK RD
FS

WINCHESTER DR

BUCKSHOT WAY

N SADDLE RIDGE DR

McBRIDE LN

OLD QUARRY LN

CAMERON CV

78613

LIME KILN DR

WALK DR

EDWARDS DR

KILKENNY HILL DR

WHISLERS
DR

SAAG SALOON DR

RILEY
DR

RIFLE RD
30

POST RIVER RD

KENAI DR

RANCH TRAILS

TRAILHEAD CT

BEMINGTON

REMINGTON RD

THE RANCH AT
BRUSHY CREEK

WICKLOW MOUNTAIN TR

TRAIL DIST
DR

McKENZIE
DR

28

TALKEETNA LN

DENALI PASS

N
P
Q
R

KASDAN
PASS

N VISTA RIDGE BLVD

GOLD STAR DR

PASEO GRAND DR

2

JUNEAU DR

TALL CEDARS RD

LONGHORN RIDGE RD

CAMPFIRE DR

BOWSTRING BEND

ISADDLE RIDGE DR

WALSH TRAILS

STILES LN

WILLIAMSON WAY

THREE ARROWS TR

WALSH HILL

Henry
MS

3

GLACIER PASS

1120

JUNIPER HILLS ST

HIDDEN OAK WAY

LONGHORN

ACHES CT

WILDERNESS PATH

SISTER BEND

GATEPOST CT

ACHES CT

RIDGETOP

BUCKHAVEN CV

BUCK RIDGE RD

SPANISH GOLD LN

E PARK ST

S VISTA RIDGE BLVD

HS

Vista Ridge

S

Breakaway Park
Landing Strip

KODIAK TR

KODIAK CV

POLAR LN

FM
734

FALLING LEAVES CT

TURKEY PATH

S FRONTIER BEND

FLAGSTONE

RIDGETOP BEND

T
U
V

TWIN BRANCH LN

SIMON BEND

STEER CREEK CT

RIDGE CT

KATIE LN

RILEY TR

43
43

KODIAK TR

8

BREAKAWAY RD

26

WILDLIFE RUN

23
8

GRANDRIDGE

FALLEN OAKS DR

BEDROCK CT

Silverado
Springs
Park

Brushy Creek
Greenbelt

ALONG CREEK

PALMBROOK DR

RIAS WAY

BROADWAY DR

LISIANNE DR

AUSTIN

ADVENTURE LN

10

TR
25

W
X
Y
Z

22

BRUSHY CREEK RD

13

30

Brushy Creek
Lake Park

38

S Brushy Creek

Champion Park

Brushy Creek Rd
39

OLD BALDY DR

WYNSTONE LN

ALMADEN DR

787

AUSTIN & NW RR

Brushy Creek
Recreation
Park

The Golf Club
at Avery Ranch

ROY BUTLER DR

MEDINAH GREENS DR

ROYAL ASHDOWN ST

ESTENCIA

REY DR

PALMBROOK DR

FINCASTLE DR

INDINA HILLS DR

MG
MH

CONTINUED ON MAP 373
CONTINUED ON MAP 404
CONTINUED ON MAP 375

© Mapsco, Inc.

SCALE IN MILES

0   1/8   1/4   3/8   1/2

SCALE IN FEET

0   1000   2000   3000

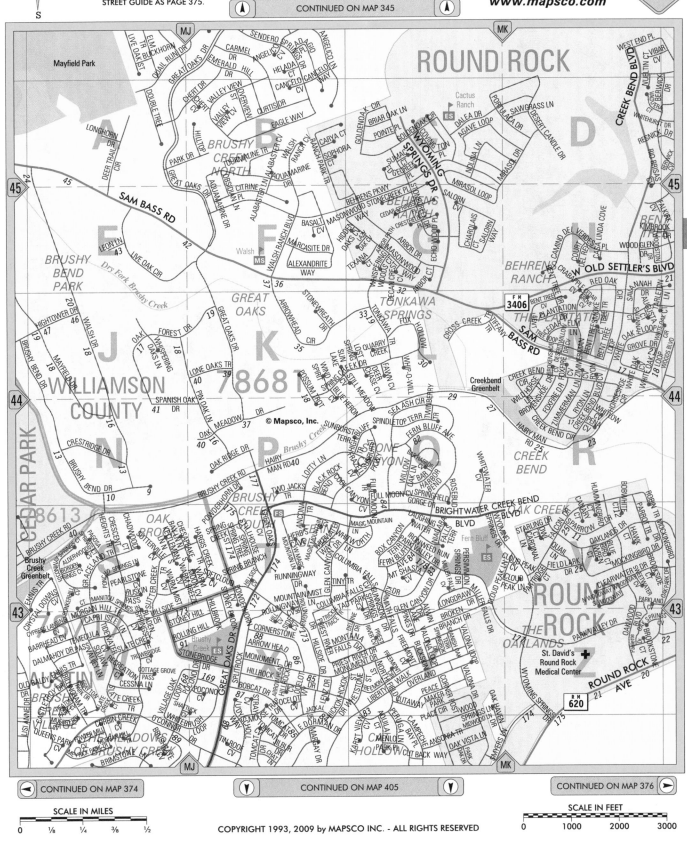

THIS PAGE ALSO APPEARS IN THE
MAPSCO WILLIAMSON COUNTY
STREET GUIDE AS PAGE 375.

Directions Made Easy
www.mapsco.com

375

CONTINUED ON MAP 345

ROUND ROCK

Mayfield Park

SAM BASS RD

BRUSHY
BEND
PARK

WILLIAMSON
COUNTY

78681

© Mapsco, Inc.

GREAT
OAKS

TONKAWA
SPRINGS

BEHRENS
RANCH

OLD SETTLER'S BLVD

FM
3406

SAM
BASS
RD

THE PLANTATION

CREEK
BEND

CREEK BEND BLVD

CEDAR PARK

78613

Brushy
Creek
Greenbelt

OAK
BROOK

BRUSHY
CREEK
SOUTH

BRIGHTWATER CREEK BEND
BLVD

OAK CREEK

ROUND
ROCK

THE
OAKLANDS

St. David's
Round Rock
Medical Center

ROUND ROCK AVE

AUSTIN

BRUSHY

MEADOWS OF
BRUSHY CREEK

MENLO
HOLLOW

RM
620

CONTINUED ON MAP 374

CONTINUED ON MAP 405

CONTINUED ON MAP 376

SCALE IN MILES

0   1/8   1/4   3/8   1/2

SCALE IN FEET

0   1000   2000   3000

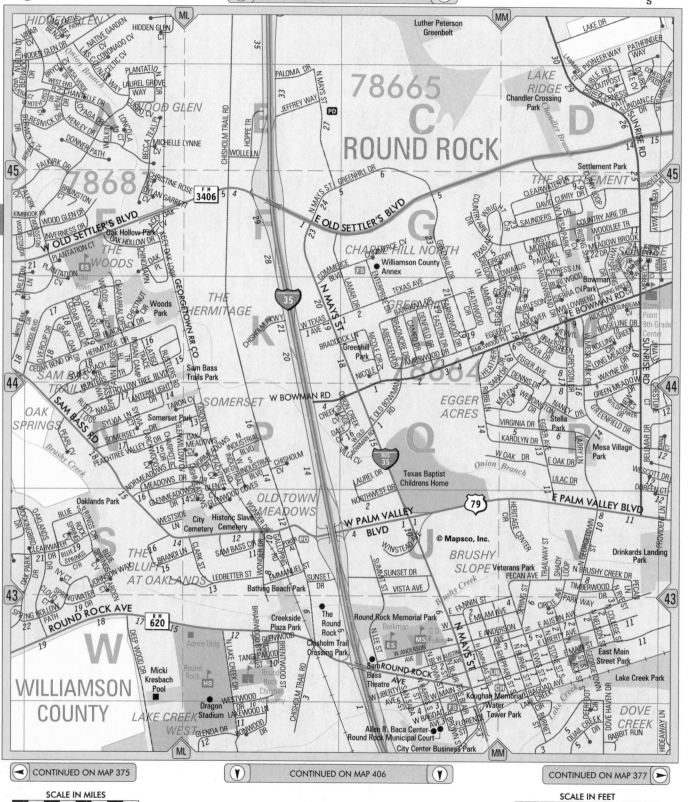

CONTINUED ON MAP 346

78665
C
ROUND ROCK

78681

78664

WILLIAMSON
COUNTY

© Mapsco, Inc.

CONTINUED ON MAP 375

CONTINUED ON MAP 406

CONTINUED ON MAP 377

SCALE IN MILES

0   1/8   1/4   3/8   1/2

SCALE IN FEET

0   1000   2000   3000

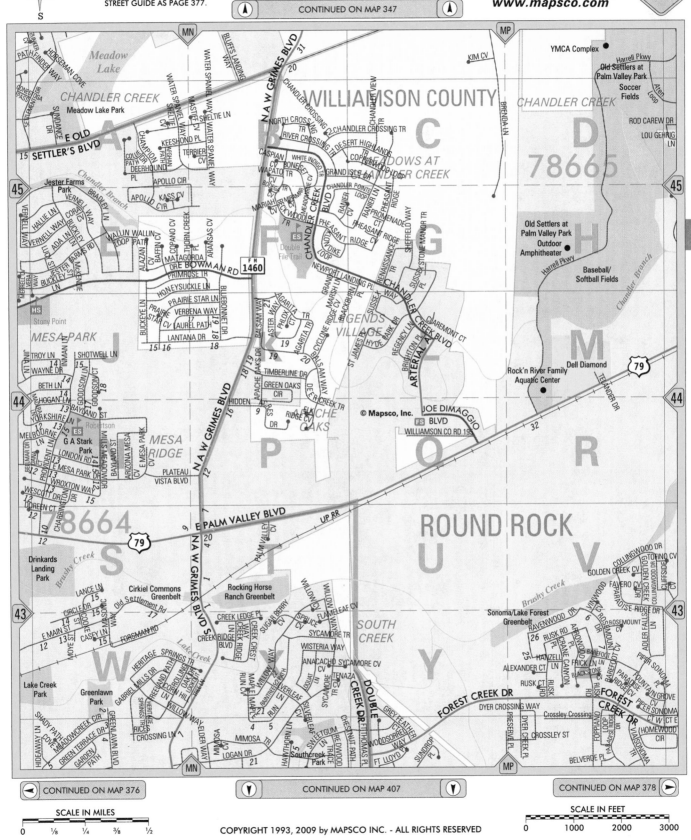

THIS PAGE ALSO APPEARS IN THE
MAPSCO WILLIAMSON COUNTY
STREET GUIDE AS PAGE 377.

CONTINUED ON MAP 347

WILLIAMSON COUNTY

78665

ROUND ROCK

78664

CONTINUED ON MAP 376

CONTINUED ON MAP 407

CONTINUED ON MAP 378

SCALE IN MILES

0   ⅛   ¼   ⅜   ½

SCALE IN FEET

0   1000   2000   3000

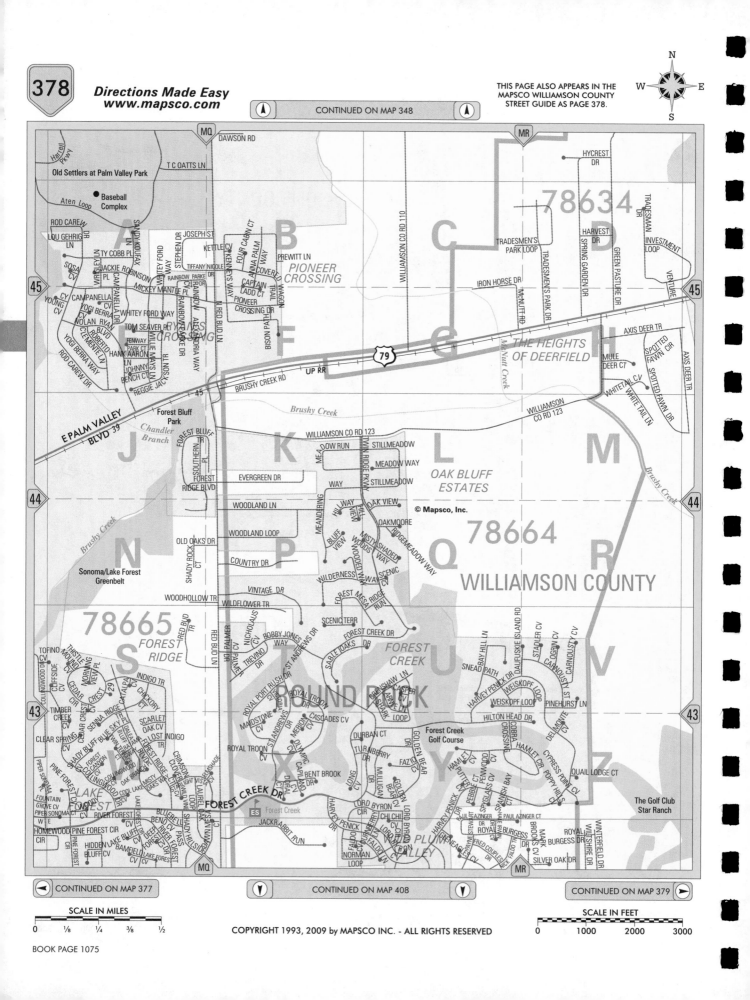

THIS PAGE ALSO APPEARS IN THE MAPSCO WILLIAMSON COUNTY STREET GUIDE AS PAGE 379.

Directions Made Easy
www.mapsco.com

379

N
W E
S

CONTINUED ON MAP 349

MS
MT

Country Estates

W PECAN ST · E PECAN ST · ANTHONY ST
WEST ST · W MAIN ST · EAST ST · TAYLOR ST · COLLEGE ST · REDBUD
FARLEY ST · LIB · E MAIN ST
SHORT ST · PO

US 79 · UP RR

FM 1660

PD CH · W AUSTIN AVE · JIM CAGE · E FRONT ST · E AUSTIN AVE
GAINER GAINER DR · WALKER · ORGAN ST
GAINER CV · SWENSON DR · EVANS ST · ORCHARD · HAGUE ST

A · B · C · D

45 · 45

INVESTMENT LOOP

130

LINDA LN

ED SCHMIDT BLVD

WILLIAMSON CO RD 165

WILLIAMSON CO RD 108

EXCHANGE BLVD

HS · Hutto

MARVIN CV · IOLA DR · KAKI CV · GRISHAM DR
GBANT CV · BENNETT CV · INMAN DR
EMMA LYNN LN · JANIS MAE DR · MAY ST · CASTLE DR · AGUILAR DR · WILLOWBROOK DR
WARNER BEND · EDISON DR · RICHARDS DR · TANGLEWOOD LN
ERIN CV · GAINER CV · HANSTROM JR · CAMPOS DR · MEADOWSIDE DR

THE ENCLAVE AT BRUSHY CREEK

78634

HUTTO

Johnson ES

CARL STERN DR

LEGENDS OF HUTTO

E · F · G · H

DELIA CHAPPA LN · PAIGE DR · WARNER BEND · PRARSAL
RYAN CV · S PAULEY DR · N PAULEY DR · LONE STAR BLVD
WILL LN · LORYN DR · DANIEL · HANSTROM CT · KERLEY CT · HERRERA CT · BLACKMAN · BLAC TR
COUNTRY ESTATES · GAINER CV · LONE STAR CT · KERLEY DR · HOLMAN PATH · BUBBLING BROOK DR
K KOTHMAN DR · BRISCOE CV · SAMSON DR · Country Estates Park · MATTHEW DR · LEGENDS DR · HUTTO TR · PEACEFUL HAVEN WAY
UVALDE DR · CONCAN DR · STEVEN ST · WARBLER CV · LUCKY CLOVER LN · MOSSY CREEK BEND DR · WHIRLING EDDY
UTOPIA LN · BLEWET DR · BROOKE ST · PADDINGTON WAY · LUNA VISTA DR · ROCK CV · WATERLILY WAY
LAGUNA CV · KNOWLES DR · CAMELLIA DR

CREEK BEND

J · K · L · M

FM 685

Brushy Creek Greenbelt

KNIPPA CV · WELLS BEND · HONDO LN · MONTELL LN
REAGAN WELLS DR · ENCLAVE WAY · WELLS BEND CT · ESTATES OF BRUSHY CREEK DR

Brushy Creek

ADAMAE LN · POTTER CV
BAKERS LN · BAKERS CV · EASY ST
SPARROW CV · MEADOW LARK LN · WREN CV · KING LN
COYOTE TR · EASY CIR · QUAIL HOLLOW · MADISON LN · DECKER CT · LUCY CV · DAYMON CT · BALLENTINE CT
WILLIAMSON EDGE DR · FORSYTH CT · STEWART DR · GARRETT CT
WILLIAMSON CO RD 135

44 · 44

© Mapsco, Inc.

W CREEKBEND CV

Brushy Creek Meadows

Hutto City Cemetery

FM 1660

N · Q

TOWAN WAY · WATERGATE WAY
BEACON CV · FISTRAL DR · MILLOOK HAVEN · PENTIRE WAY · ALTAMONT ST · RIVERWALK DR · CRESTON CV · HOLBROOKE ST
GREAT WESTERN DR · TOLCARNE DR · KILLIAN LOOP · CRESTON ST · JASMINE WAY
PARK AT BRUSHY CREEK · BALDWIN ST · KILLIAN LOOP
SAN ANTONIO RIVER WALK

MS · Farley

S · T · U · V

43 · 43

POND WAY

LAKEMONT DR

Hutto Lake Park

CATTAIL CV · ST MARY'S DR · CASSANDRA ST

WILLIAMSON COUNTY

W · Y · Z

WILLIAMS WAY · ESTATE DR · TOBY TR · LAKESIDE ESTATES

LITTLE LAKE RD

The Golf Club Star Ranch

KAATZ LN · KAATZ LN

WILLIAMSON CO RD 197 · WILLIAMSON CO RD 137

STONEY BROOK DR

St. Mary's Cemetery

MS · MT

CONTINUED ON MAP 378 · CONTINUED ON MAP 409 · CONTINUED ON MAP 380

SCALE IN MILES
0 · 1/8 · 1/4 · 3/8 · 1/2

SCALE IN FEET
0 · 1000 · 2000 · 3000

Directions Made Easy
www.mapsco.com

CONTINUED ON MAP 350

THIS PAGE ALSO APPEARS IN THE
MAPSCO WILLIAMSON COUNTY
STREET GUIDE AS PAGE 380.

N
W E
S

79
UP RR
E FRONT ST

FM
1660

MU

MV

WILLIAMSON COUNTY

WILLIAMSON CO RD 199

WILLIAMSON CO RD 132

Creekside Park

MEADOWSIDE DR
WILLOWBROOK DR
COTTON CV

A

B

C

D

ORCHARD WAY

CREEKSIDE
ESTATES

COTTON CREEK WAY

45

TWILIGHT WAY

45

HARVEST LN

TANGLEWOOD LN

MEADOWSIDE DR

SAGE CV

CREEK BEND

E

F

G

H

FLOATING LEAF DR

IN CREEK BEND DR

WATERLILY WAY

CARL STERN DR

RIVER BEND PASS

S CREEK BEND DR

BUBBLING BROOK DR

Cottonwood Creek

HUTTO

MINNOW PASS

PEACEFUL HAVEN WAY

J

K

L

M

CREEK BEND

MOSSY ROCK DR

LADYBUG LN

LUNA VISTA DR

PEBBLE PATH

© Mapsco, Inc.

CAMELLIA DR

BOWIE LN

44

PEBBLE PATH

HERSEE CT

MUSSELMAN CT

44

LOSOYA CT

HERSEE CT

GLENWOOD

ANDROSS CT

ABAMILLO CT

LIGHTFOOT

N

P

Q

R

BALLENTINE CT

GARRETT LN

STEWART DR

MITCHELL DR

CLOUD RD

MCCOY LN

FISHBAUGH LN

FM
1660

BAYLISS ST

S

Ray
ES

SWINDOLL LN

T

78634

U

V

76574

43

43

WILLIAMSON CO RD 163

W

X

WILLIAMSON CO RD 134

Y

WILLIAMSON CO RD 134

Z

MU

MV

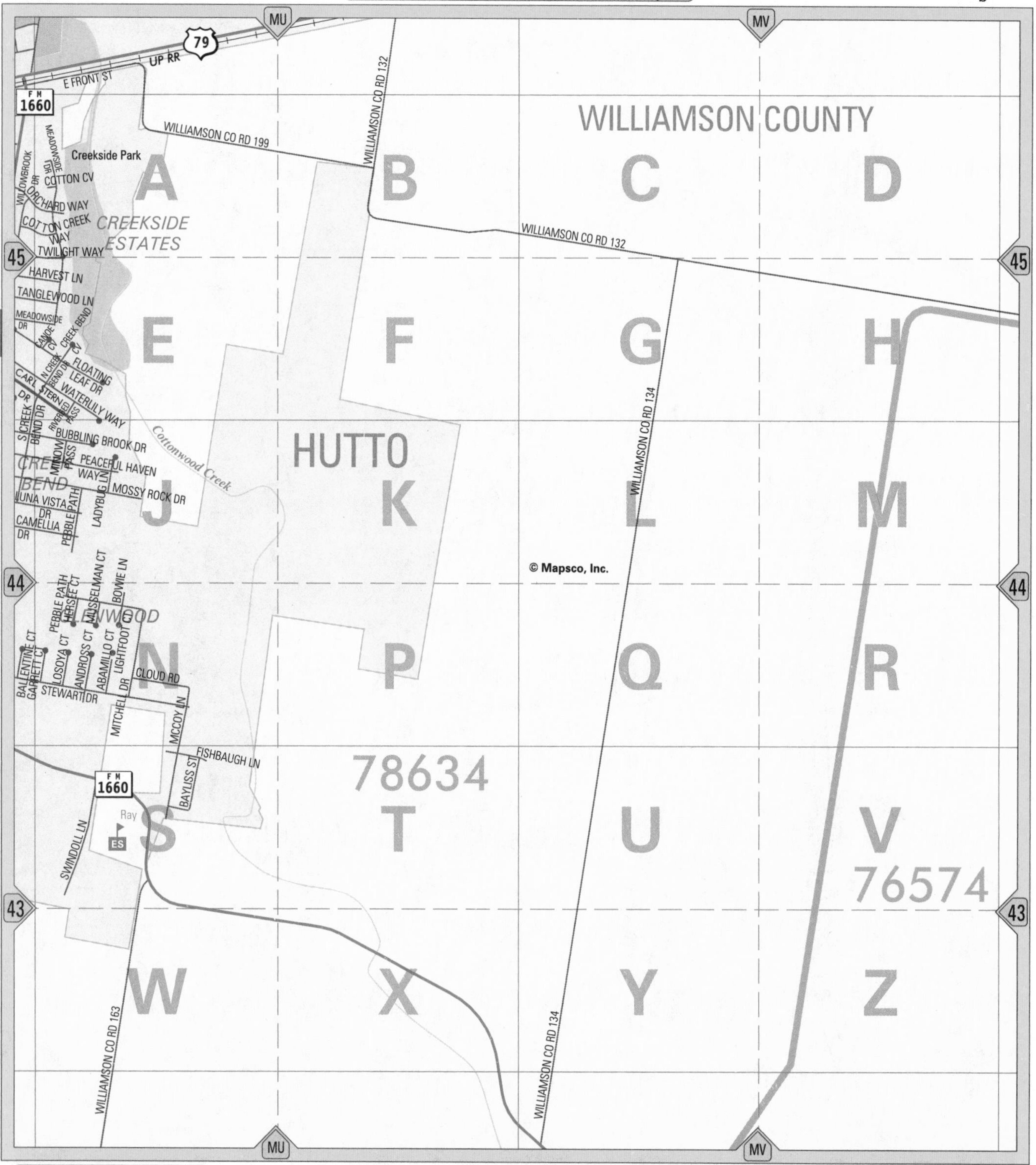

CONTINUED ON MAP 379

CONTINUED ON MAP 410

CONTINUED ON MAP 381

SCALE IN MILES

0   1/8   1/4   3/8   1/2

SCALE IN FEET

0   1000   2000   3000

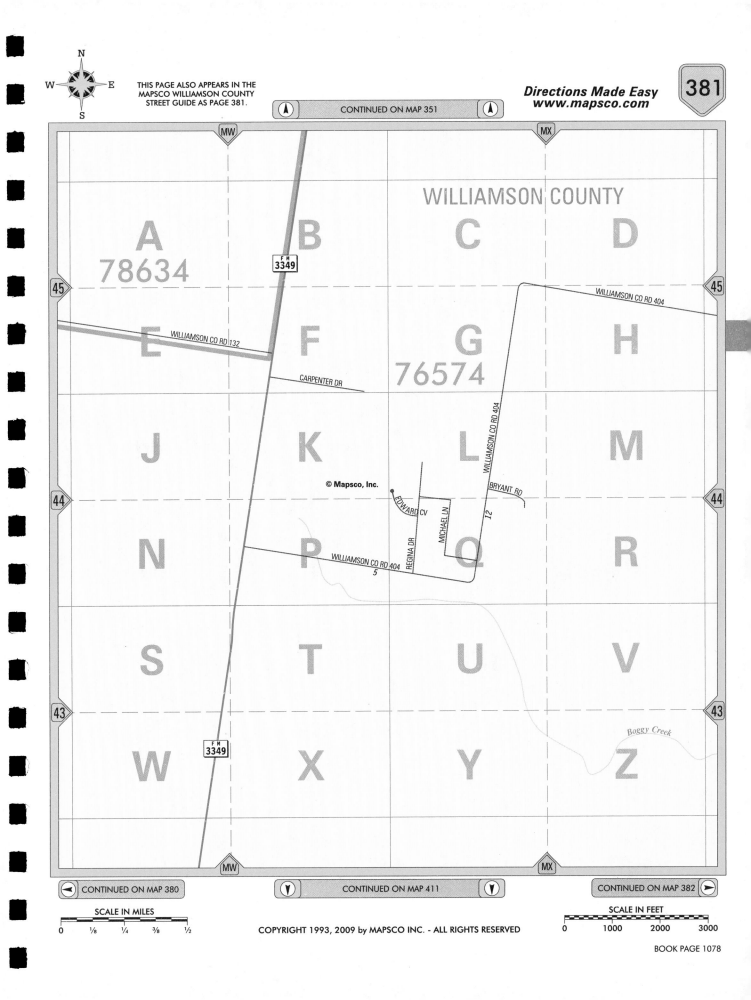

THIS PAGE ALSO APPEARS IN THE MAPSCO WILLIAMSON COUNTY STREET GUIDE AS PAGE 381.

CONTINUED ON MAP 351

Directions Made Easy
www.mapsco.com

381

WILLIAMSON COUNTY

A
78634

B
FM 3349

C

D

45

WILLIAMSON CO RD 404

45

E
WILLIAMSON CO RD 132

F
CARPENTER DR

G
76574

H

J

K

© Mapsco, Inc.

L

WILLIAMSON CO RD 404

M

44

N

EDWARD CV
REGINA DR

P
WILLIAMSON CO RD 404
5

MICHAEL LN

Q

BRYANT RD

12

R

44

S

T

U

V

43

W
FM 3349

X

Y

Z
Boggy Creek

43

CONTINUED ON MAP 380

CONTINUED ON MAP 411

CONTINUED ON MAP 382

SCALE IN MILES
0   ⅛   ¼   ⅜   ½

SCALE IN FEET
0   1000   2000   3000

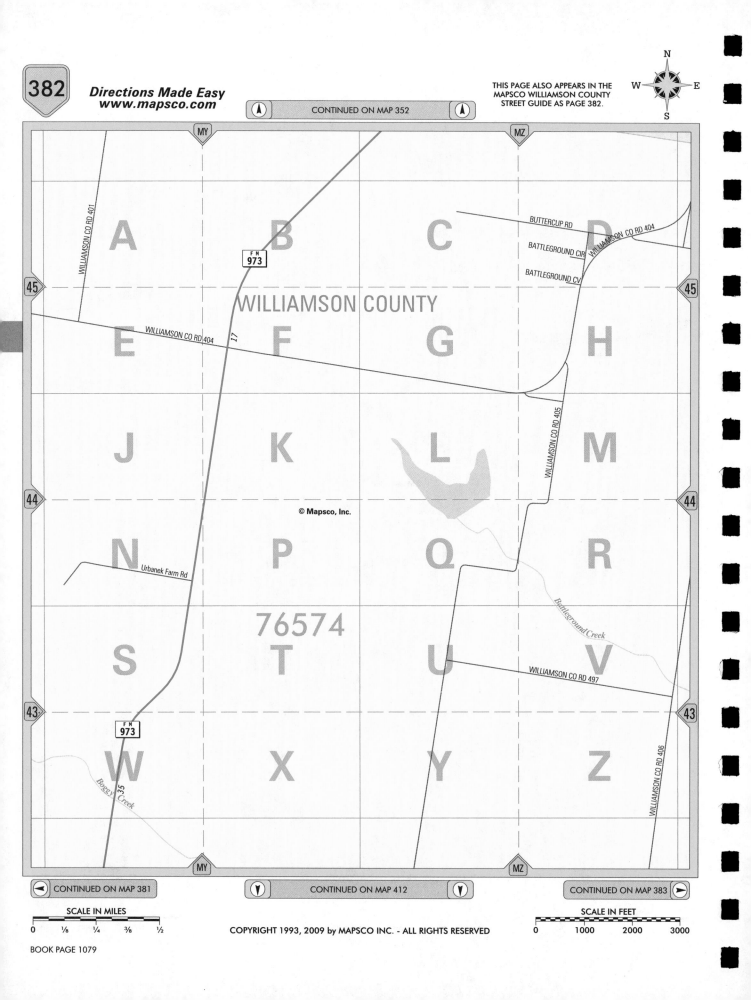

THIS PAGE ALSO APPEARS IN THE
MAPSCO WILLIAMSON COUNTY
STREET GUIDE AS PAGE 382.

N
W E
S

CONTINUED ON MAP 352

MY
MZ

WILLIAMSON CO RD 401

A
B
C
D

FM 973

BUTTERCUP RD
BATTLEGROUND CIR
WILLIAMSON CO RD 404
BATTLEGROUND CV

45
45

WILLIAMSON COUNTY

E
F
G
H

WILLIAMSON CO RD 404
17

WILLIAMSON CO RD 405

J
K
L
M

44
44

© Mapsco, Inc.

N
P
Q
R

Urbanek Farm Rd

Battleground Creek

76574

S
T
U
V

WILLIAMSON CO RD 497

43
43

FM 973

W
X
Y
Z

WILLIAMSON CO RD 406

Boggy Creek
35

MY
MZ

CONTINUED ON MAP 381
CONTINUED ON MAP 412
CONTINUED ON MAP 383

SCALE IN MILES
0   1/8   1/4   3/8   1/2

SCALE IN FEET
0   1000   2000   3000

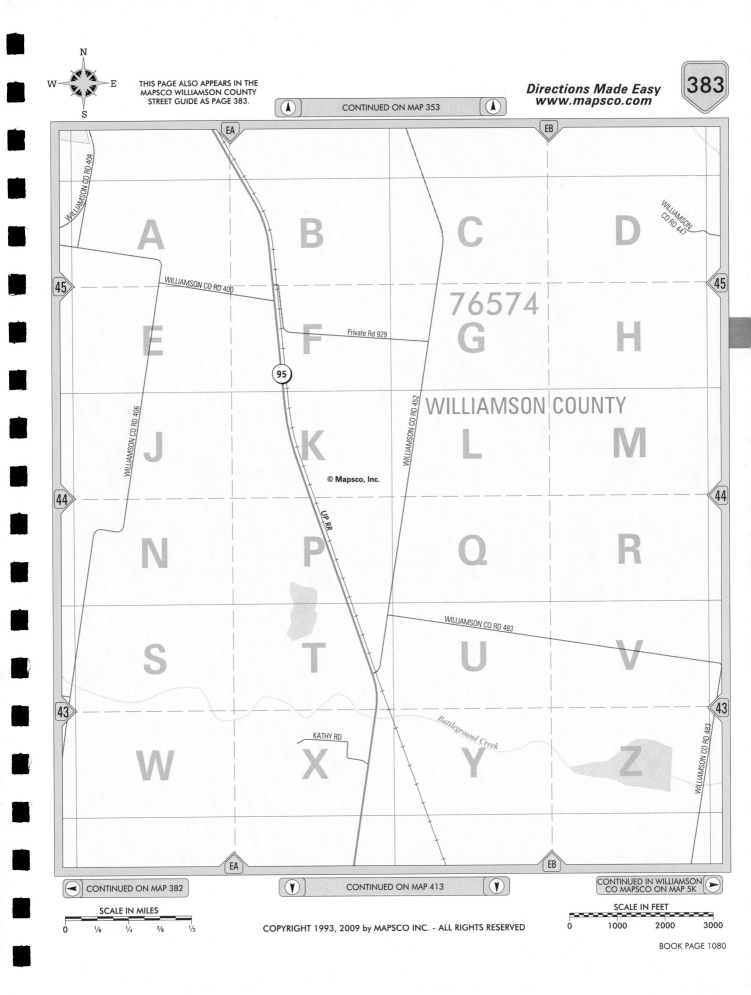

N
W E
S

THIS PAGE ALSO APPEARS IN THE
MAPSCO WILLIAMSON COUNTY
STREET GUIDE AS PAGE 383.

Directions Made Easy
www.mapsco.com

383

CONTINUED ON MAP 353

EA

EB

WILLIAMSON CO RD 404

WILLIAMSON CO RD 447

A

B

C

D

45

45

WILLIAMSON CO RD 400

76574

E

F

Private Rd 929

G

H

95

WILLIAMSON CO RD 406

WILLIAMSON CO RD 452

WILLIAMSON COUNTY

J

K

L

M

© Mapsco, Inc.

44

44

U.P. RR

N

P

Q

R

WILLIAMSON CO RD 483

S

T

U

V

43

43

Battleground Creek

KATHY RD

WILLIAMSON CO RD 483

W

X

Y

Z

EA

EB

CONTINUED ON MAP 382

CONTINUED ON MAP 413

CONTINUED IN WILLIAMSON
CO MAPSCO ON MAP 5K

SCALE IN MILES

0   1/8   1/4   3/8   1/2

SCALE IN FEET

0   1000   2000   3000

BOOK PAGE 1080

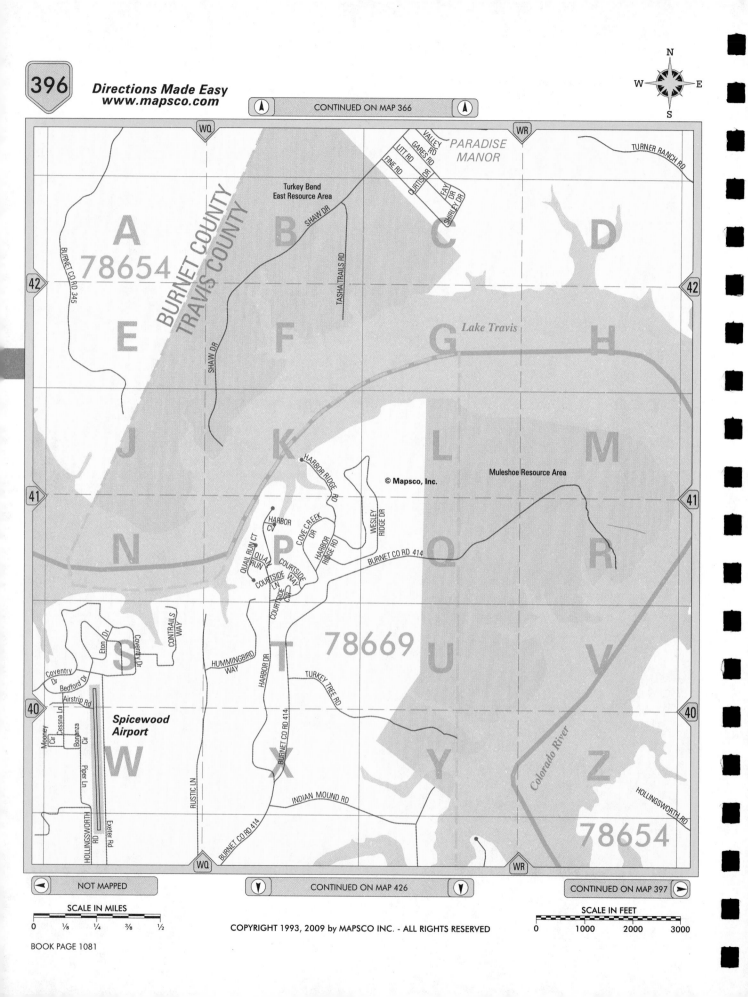

Directions Made Easy
www.mapsco.com

CONTINUED ON MAP 366

N
W E
S

WQ

WR

PARADISE MANOR

VALLEY RD
GABES RD
LITT RD
FINE RD
CURTIS DR
FAY DR
SHIRLEY DR

TURNER RANCH RD

Turkey Bend
East Resource Area

SHAW DR

BURNET COUNTY
TRAVIS COUNTY

42

A
78654

B

C

D

42

BURNET CO RD 345

SHAW DR

TASHA TRAILS RD

E

F

G

Lake Travis

H

41

J

K

HARBOR RIDGE RD

© Mapsco, Inc.

L

Muleshoe Resource Area

M

41

N

HARBOR CV

P

COVE CREEK DR

HARBOR RIDGE RD

WESLEY RIDGE DR

BURNET CO RD 414

Q

R

QUAIL RUN CT

QUAIL RUN

COURTSIDE WAY

COURTSIDE LN

COURTSIDE CIR

CONTRAILS WAY

Eton Dr

Coventry Dr

S

HUMMINGBIRD WAY

HARBOR DR

T
78669

TURKEY TREE RD

U

V

Coventry Dr

Bedford Dr

Airstrip Rd

Mooney Cir

Cessna Ln

Bonanza Cir

**Spicewood
Airport**

W

BURNET CO RD 414

X

Y

Colorado River

Z
78654

Piper Ln

RUSTIC LN

INDIAN MOUND RD

HOLLINGSWORTH RD

HOLLINGSWORTH RD

Exeter Rd

BURNET CO RD 414

WQ

WR

40

40

NOT MAPPED

CONTINUED ON MAP 426

CONTINUED ON MAP 397

SCALE IN MILES
0   1/8   1/4   3/8   1/2

SCALE IN FEET
0   1000   2000   3000

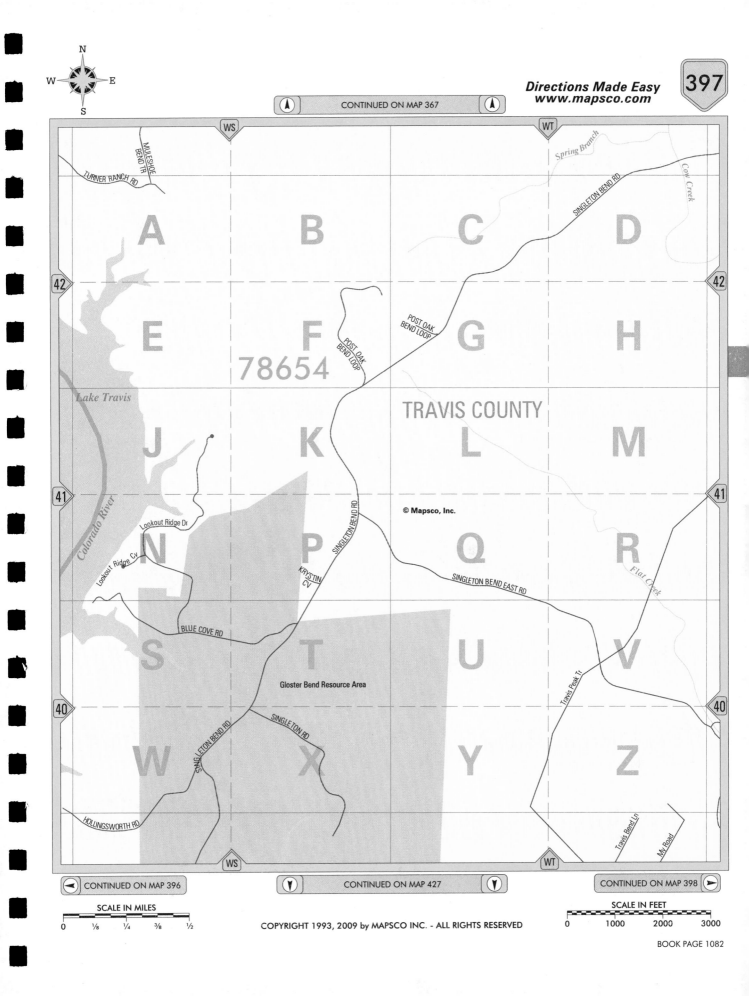

N
W — E
S

CONTINUED ON MAP 367

WS

WT

MULESHOE BEND TR

Spring Branch

TURNER RANCH RD

SINGLETON BEND RD

Cow Creek

A

B

C

D

42

42

POST OAK BEND LOOP

E

F

G

H

POST OAK BEND LOOP

78654

Lake Travis

TRAVIS COUNTY

J

K

L

M

41

Colorado River

41

Lookout Ridge Dr

© Mapsco, Inc.

N

P

Q

R

Flat Creek

Lookout Ridge Cv

SINGLETON BEND RD

KRYSTIN CV

SINGLETON BEND EAST RD

BLUE COVE RD

S

T

U

V

Travis Peak Tr

Gloster Bend Resource Area

40

40

SINGLETON BEND RD

SINGLETON RD

W

X

Y

Z

Travis Bend Ln

Mt. Road

HOLLINGSWORTH RD

WS

WT

CONTINUED ON MAP 396

CONTINUED ON MAP 427

CONTINUED ON MAP 398

SCALE IN MILES

0   1/8   1/4   3/8   1/2

SCALE IN FEET

0   1000   2000   3000

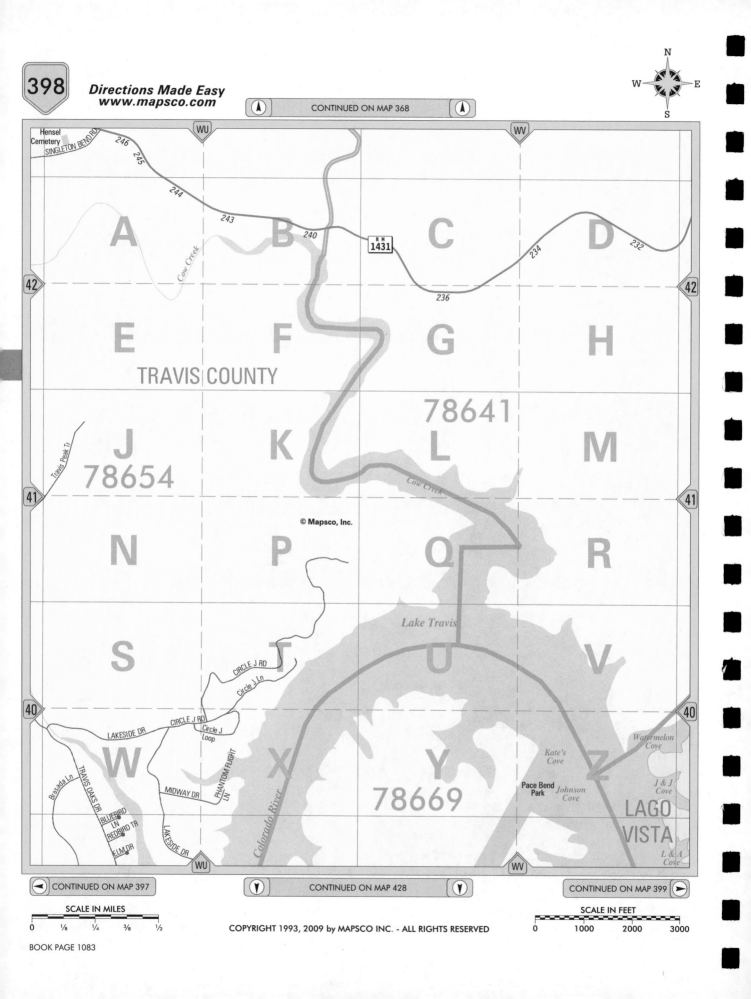

N
W E
S

CONTINUED ON MAP 368

WU

Hensel Cemetery
SINGLETON BEND RD
246
245
244
243

WV

A
B
240
R M 1431
C
234
D
232

Cow Creek

42
42

E
F
G
H

TRAVIS COUNTY

78641

J
78654
K
L
M

Travis Peak Tr

Cow Creek

41
41

© Mapsco, Inc.

N
P
Q
R

Lake Travis

S
T
CIRCLE J RD
Circle J Ln
U
V

40
40

LAKESIDE DR
CIRCLE J RD
Circle J Loop
PHANTOM FLIGHT LN
Watermelon Cove

Kate's Cove

W
X
Y
Z
J & J Cove

Brasada Ln
Travis Oaks Dr
MIDWAY DR
Colorado River
78669
Pace Bend Park
Johnson Cove
LAGO VISTA

BLUEBIRD LN
REDBIRD TR
LAKESIDE DR
L & A Cove

ELM DR

WU

WV

◄ CONTINUED ON MAP 397
▼ CONTINUED ON MAP 428 ▼
CONTINUED ON MAP 399 ►

SCALE IN MILES
0   1/8   1/4   3/8   1/2

SCALE IN FEET
0   1000   2000   3000

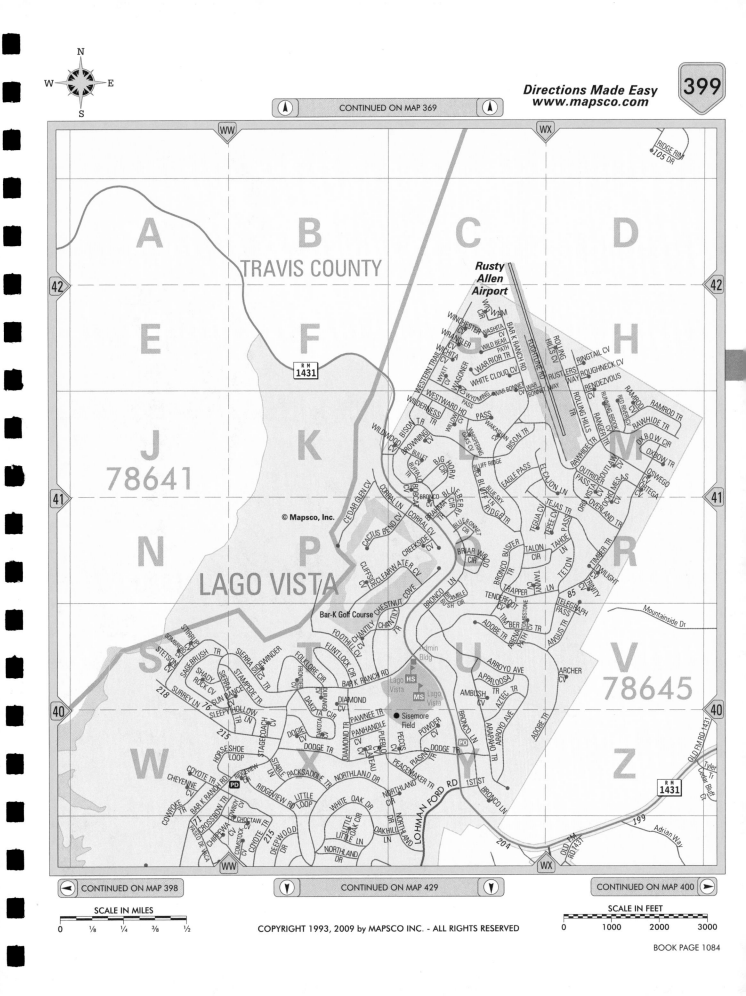

CONTINUED ON MAP 369

Directions Made Easy
www.mapsco.com

399

CONTINUED ON MAP 398

CONTINUED ON MAP 429

CONTINUED ON MAP 400

TRAVIS COUNTY

78641

LAGO VISTA

78645

Rusty Allen Airport

Bar-K Golf Course

© Mapsco, Inc.

SCALE IN MILES

0   ⅛   ¼   ⅜   ½

SCALE IN FEET

0   1000   2000   3000

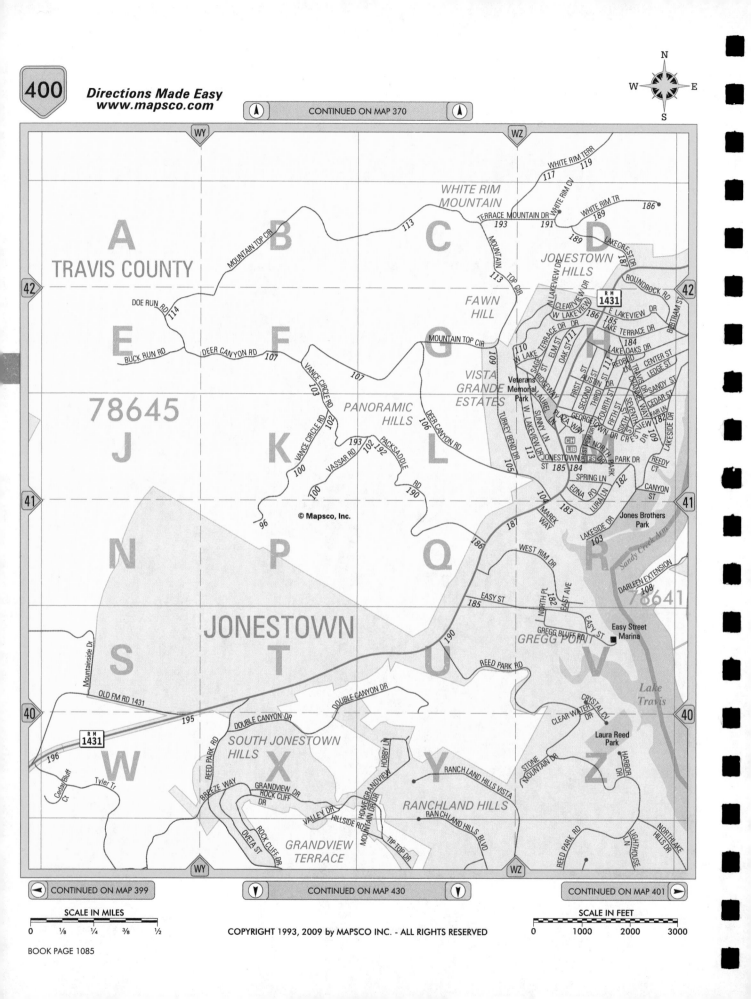

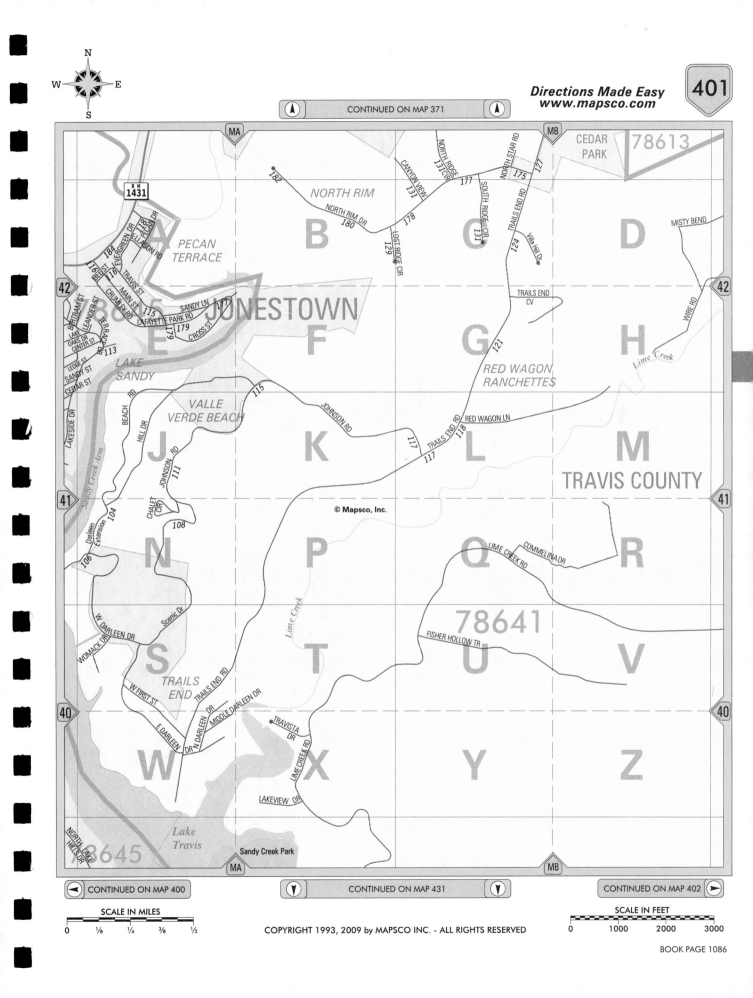

CONTINUED ON MAP 371

N
W E
S

MA

MB

CEDAR PARK

78613

NORTH STAR RD

NORTH RIDGE

131 CIR

CANYON VIEW

131

177

175

127

MISTY BEND

182

NORTH RIM

NORTH RIM DR

180

178

129

LOST RIDGE CIR

SOUTH RIDGE CIR

131

TRAILS END RD

124

Villa Hill Dr

B

C

D

R M
1431

PECAN
TERRACE

A

118
PECAN DR

EVERGREEN DR

EL LASON DR

184

EVERGREEN ST

116 BEE ST

116

TRAVIS ST

MAIN ST

CRUMLEY RD

115

SANDY LN

177

LAFAYETTE PARK RD

JONESTOWN

TRAILS END
CV

42

42

WIRE RD

78065

BERTRAM ST

LEANDER ST

TERRACE DR

179

179

LAFAYETTE PARK RD

CROSS ST

E

F

G

121

H

Lime Creek

LAKE
OAKS DR

CENTER ST

113

LEDGE ST

SANDY ST

CEDAR ST

LAKE
SANDY

RED WAGON
RANCHETTES

LAKESIDE DR

BEACH RD

VALLE
VERDE BEACH

115

JOHNSON RD

TRAILS END RD

117

117

118

RED WAGON LN

HILL DR

JOHNSON RD

111

J

K

L

M

Sandy Creek Arm

41

41

CHALET CIR

108

Darleen Extension

104

106

N

P

Q

COMMELINA DR

R

LIME CREEK RD

TRAVIS COUNTY

© Mapsco, Inc.

Scenic Dr

W DARLEEN DR

WOMACK DR

S

Lime Creek

78641

FISHER HOLLOW TR

T

U

V

TRAILS
END

W FIRST ST

TRAILS END RD

MIDDLE DARLEEN DR

N DARLEEN DR

40

40

E DARLEEN DR

TRAVISTA DR

LIME CREEK RD

W

X

Y

Z

LAKEVIEW DR

NORTH LAKE HILLS DR

78645

Lake
Travis

Sandy Creek Park

MA

MB

CONTINUED ON MAP 400

CONTINUED ON MAP 431

CONTINUED ON MAP 402

SCALE IN MILES

0   1/8   1/4   3/8   1/2

SCALE IN FEET

0   1000   2000   3000

COPYRIGHT 1993, 2009 by MAPSCO INC. - ALL RIGHTS RESERVED

Directions Made Easy
www.mapsco.com

THIS PAGE ALSO APPEARS IN THE
MAPSCO WILLIAMSON COUNTY
STREET GUIDE AS PAGE 402.

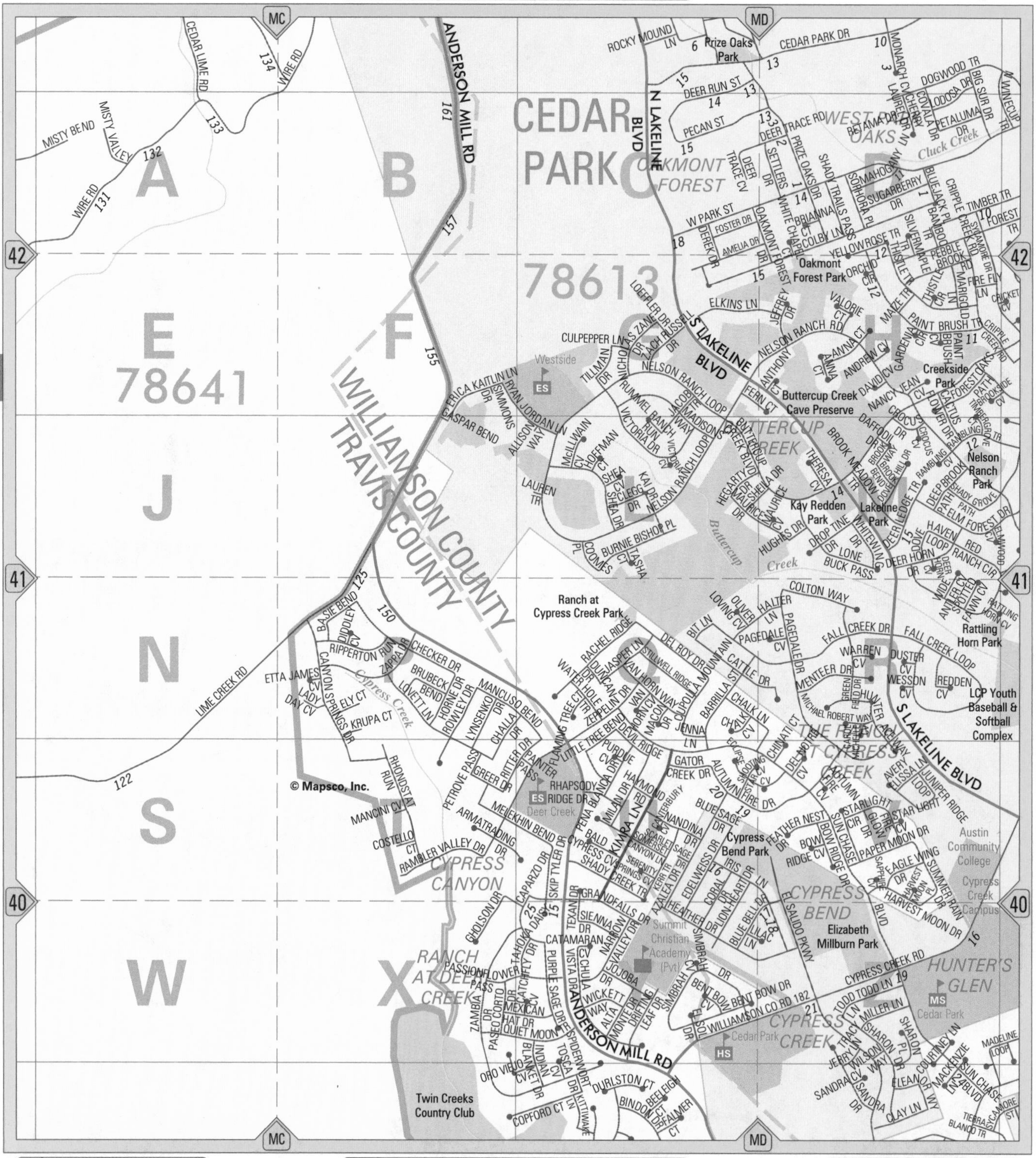

N
W · E
S

CEDAR PARK

OAKMONT FOREST

WEST OAKS

Cluck Creek

78613

78641

WILLIAMSON COUNTY
TRAVIS COUNTY

Westside ES

Buttercup Creek Cave Preserve

BUTTERCUP CREEK

Creekside Park

Nelson Ranch Park

Kay Redden Park

Lakeline Park

Buttercup Creek

Haven Loop Ranch Cir

Rattling Horn Park

Ranch at Cypress Creek Park

Colton Way

Fall Creek Dr

Fall Creek Loop

LCP Youth Baseball & Softball Complex

THE RANCH AT CYPRESS CREEK

Deer Creek ES

Cypress Bend Park

Austin Community College Cypress Creek Campus

CYPRESS BEND

Elizabeth Millburn Park

CYPRESS CANYON

RANCH AT DEER PASS CREEK

Summit Christian Academy (Pvt)

HUNTER'S GLEN

Cedar Park MS

CYPRESS CREEK

HS

ANDERSON MILL RD

WILLIAMSON CO RD 182

Twin Creeks Country Club

© Mapsco, Inc.

S LAKELINE BLVD

N LAKELINE BLVD

ANDERSON MILL RD

LIME CREEK RD

CEDAR LIME RD

WIRE RD

◄ CONTINUED ON MAP 401

▼ CONTINUED ON MAP 432

CONTINUED ON MAP 403 ►

SCALE IN MILES
0   ⅛   ¼   ⅜   ½

SCALE IN FEET
0   1000   2000   3000

COPYRIGHT 1993, 2009 by MAPSCO INC. - ALL RIGHTS RESERVED

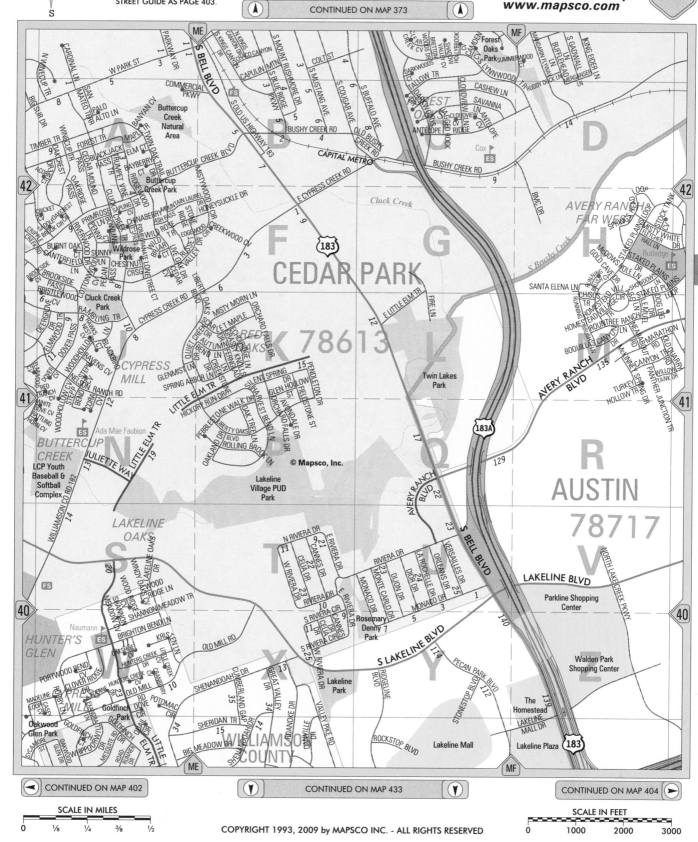

THIS PAGE ALSO APPEARS IN THE
MAPSCO WILLIAMSON COUNTY
STREET GUIDE AS PAGE 403.

Directions Made Easy
www.mapsco.com

403

CONTINUED ON MAP 373

N
W E
S

42

41

40

CEDAR PARK

78613

AUSTIN
78717

AVERY RANCH
FAR WEST

Avery Ranch Blvd

S BELL BLVD

© Mapsco, Inc.

Cluck Creek

Buttercup
Creek
Natural
Area

Buttercup
Creek Park

Cypress
Mill

Cluck Creek
Park

Wildrose
Park

BUTTERCUP
CREEK
LCP Youth
Baseball &
Softball
Complex

LAKELINE
OAKS

HUNTER'S
GLEN

Naumann

Oakwood
Glen Park

Goldfinch
Park

Lakeline
Village PUD
Park

Twin Lakes
Park

Lakeline
Park

Rosemary
Denny
Park

WILLIAMSON
COUNTY

LAKELINE BLVD

S LAKELINE BLVD

Parkline Shopping
Center

Walden Park
Shopping Center

The
Homestead

Lakeline Mall

Lakeline Plaza

Forest
Oaks
Park

FOREST
OAKS

Cox
ES

42

41

40

CAPITAL METRO

BUSHY CREEK RD

BUSHY CREEK RD

183

183A

183

CONTINUED ON MAP 402
CONTINUED ON MAP 433
CONTINUED ON MAP 404

SCALE IN MILES
0   1/8   1/4   3/8   1/2

SCALE IN FEET
0   1000   2000   3000

Directions Made Easy
www.mapsco.com

THIS PAGE ALSO APPEARS IN THE
MAPSCO WILLIAMSON COUNTY
STREET GUIDE AS PAGE 404.

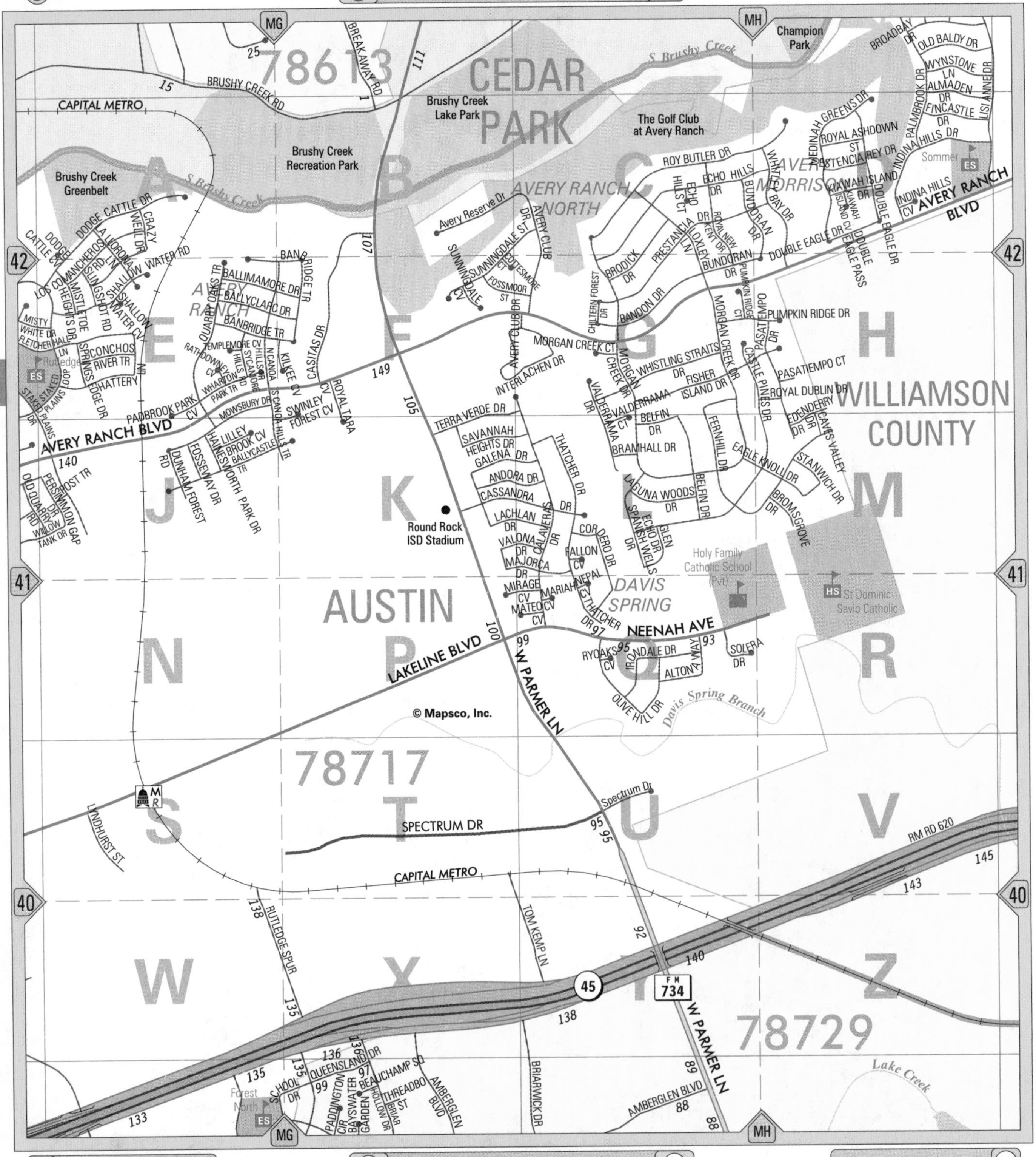

N
W E
S

CONTINUED ON MAP 374

CEDAR PARK

78613

S Brushy Creek

Champion Park

Broadbay Dr
Old Baldy Dr

CAPITAL METRO

Brushy Creek Lake Park

The Golf Club at Avery Ranch

Wynstone Ln
Almaden Dr
Fincastle Dr
Lisl Anne Dr

Brushy Creek Recreation Park

Brushy Creek Greenbelt

Medina Dr
Greens Dr
Royal Ashdown St
Indian Palmbrook Dr
Indian Hills Dr

Roy Butler Dr

Echo Hills Dr
White Morris

Avery Ranch North

Avery Reserve Dr
Avery Club

AVERY RANCH BLVD

42

AVERY RANCH

Sunningdale St
Sunningdale St

Sunningdale

Rossmoor St

Brodick Dr
Bandon Dr
Chilten Forest

Prestancia Dr
Loxley Dr
Bundoran
Pumpkin Ridge

Pumpkin Ridge Dr
Pasatiempo Ct

E

Misti Toe
Crazy
Well Dr
Water Rd
Shallow
Water Cv

WILLIAMSON COUNTY

Ballimamore Dr
Ban Bridge Tr
Ballyclare Dr
Banbridge Tr

Morgan Creek Ct
Morgan Creek Dr
Whistling Straits Dr
Fisher Island Dr
Castle Pines Dr

Royal Dublin Dr
Edenderry Dr
Camas Valley

F
G
H

149

105

Templemore Cv
Kilgee Cv
Casitas Dr
Royal Tara
Swinley Forest Cv

Interlachen Dr

Terra Verde Dr

Valderrama Ct
Valderrama Dr
Belfin Dr
Bramhall Dr

Fernhill Dr
Belfin Dr

Eagle Knoll Dr
Stanwich Dr
Bromsgrove

AVERY RANCH BLVD

140

Lilley Brook Cv
Ballycastle

Savannah Heights Dr
Galena Dr

Thatcher Dr

Laguna Woods Dr

J
K
L
M

Dunham Forest
Fosseway Dr
Hainesworth Park Dr

Andora Dr
Cassandra Dr

Glen
Echo Dr
Spanish Wells

41

Round Rock ISD Stadium

Lachlan Dr
Valona Dr
Majorca Dr
Mirage Cv
Mateo Cv

La Javera Cv
Cor Derio Dr
Fallon Cv
Nepal
Mariah Cv
Thatcher Dr

Holy Family Catholic School (Pvt)

St Dominic Savio Catholic

41

AUSTIN

DAVIS SPRING

NEENAH AVE

N
P
R

LAKELINE BLVD

100
99

W PARMER LN

97
95
93

Ry Oaks Cv
Irondale Dr
Alton Way
Solera Dr

78717

© Mapsco, Inc.

Olive Hill Dr
Davis Spring Branch

Spectrum Dr

S
T
U
V

Lyndhurst St

SPECTRUM DR
95
95

RM RD 620
145
143

CAPITAL METRO

40
40

W
X
Y
Z

Rutledge Spur

Tom Kemp Ln

45

FM 734

W PARMER LN

78729

Lake Creek

138
135
136
135
135
133

School Dr
Queensland Dr
Bayswater
Paddington
Beauchamp Sq
Threadbo
Amberglen Blvd
Briarwick Dr

Forest North

Amberglen Blvd
88
89

CONTINUED ON MAP 403

CONTINUED ON MAP 434

CONTINUED ON MAP 405

SCALE IN MILES
0   1/8   1/4   3/8   1/2

SCALE IN FEET
0   1000   2000   3000

COPYRIGHT 1993, 2009 by MAPSCO INC. - ALL RIGHTS RESERVED

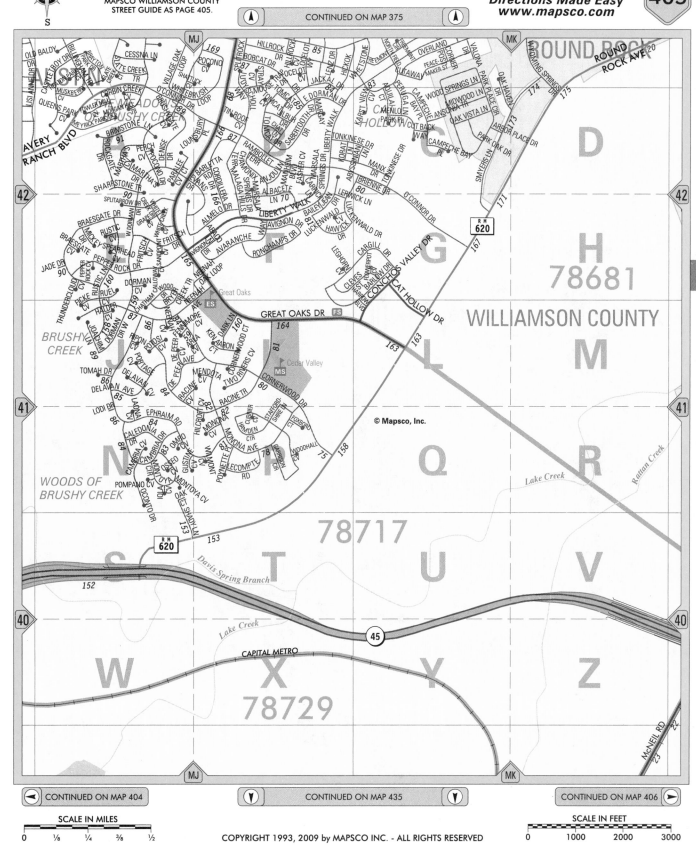

405

THIS PAGE ALSO APPEARS IN THE
MAPSCO WILLIAMSON COUNTY
STREET GUIDE AS PAGE 405.

Directions Made Easy
www.mapsco.com

N
W · E
S

CONTINUED ON MAP 375

ROUND ROCK
ROUND ROCK AVE

RM 620

78681

WILLIAMSON COUNTY

BRUSHY CREEK

GREAT OAKS DR

Cedar Valley

WOODS OF
BRUSHY CREEK

RM 620

Davis Spring Branch

Lake Creek

45

CAPITAL METRO

78717

78729

McNEIL RD

© Mapsco, Inc.

CONTINUED ON MAP 404
CONTINUED ON MAP 435
CONTINUED ON MAP 406

SCALE IN MILES
0   ⅛   ¼   ⅜   ½

SCALE IN FEET
0   1000   2000   3000

Directions Made Easy
www.mapsco.com

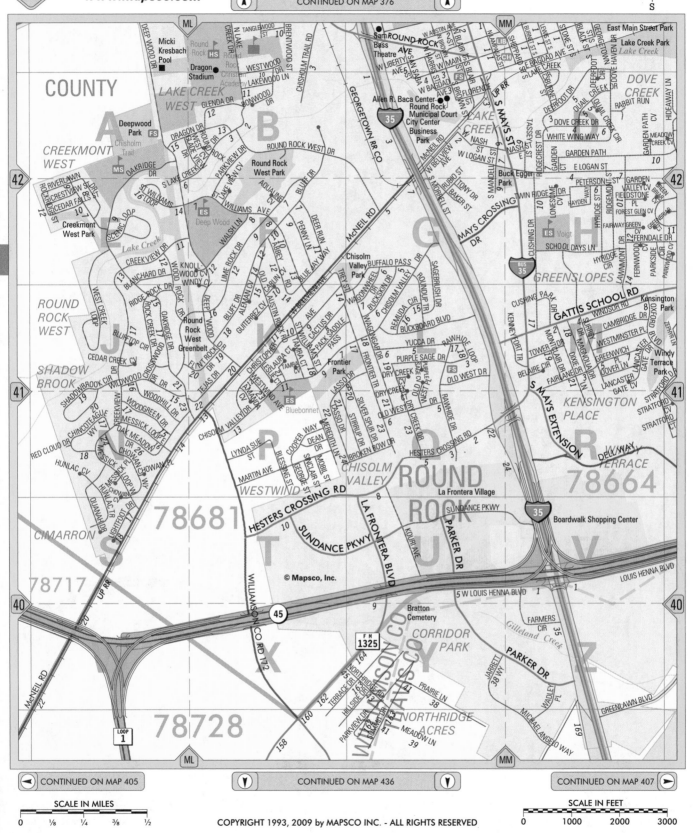

CONTINUED ON MAP 376

CONTINUED ON MAP 405

CONTINUED ON MAP 436

CONTINUED ON MAP 407

SCALE IN MILES

0   ⅛   ¼   ⅜   ½

SCALE IN FEET

0   1000   2000   3000

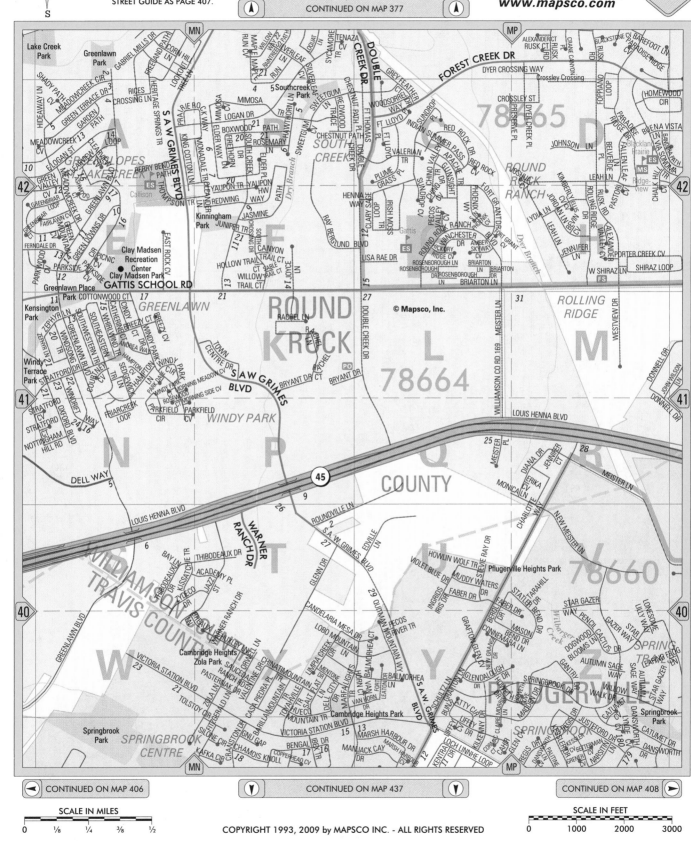

THIS PAGE ALSO APPEARS IN THE
MAPSCO WILLIAMSON COUNTY
STREET GUIDE AS PAGE 407.

Directions Made Easy
www.mapsco.com

CONTINUED ON MAP 377

CONTINUED ON MAP 406

CONTINUED ON MAP 437

CONTINUED ON MAP 408

SCALE IN MILES
0   ⅛   ¼   ⅜   ½

SCALE IN FEET
0   1000   2000   3000

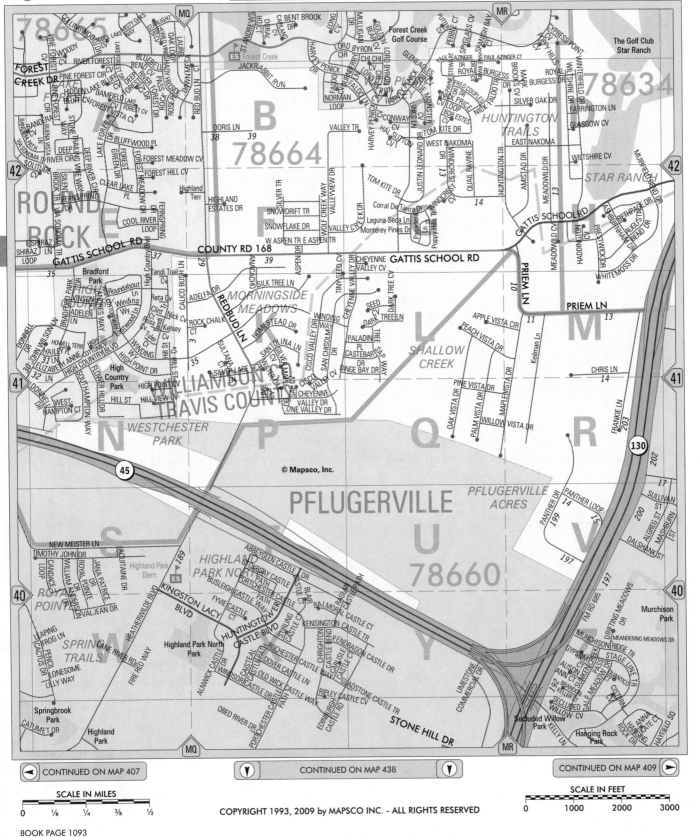

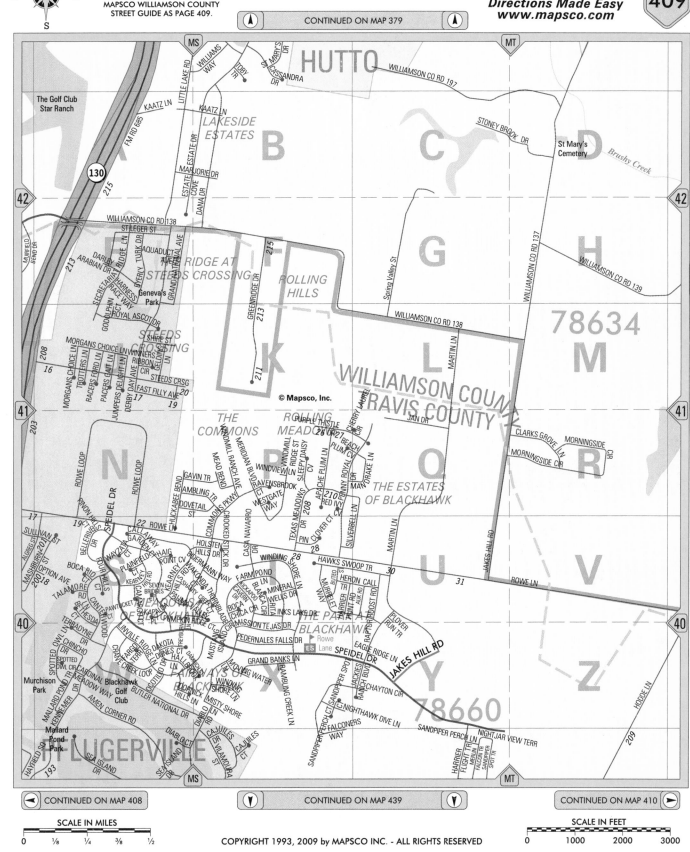

THIS PAGE ALSO APPEARS IN THE
MAPSCO WILLIAMSON COUNTY
STREET GUIDE AS PAGE 409.

Directions Made Easy
www.mapsco.com

N
W E
S

CONTINUED ON MAP 379

MS

MT

HUTTO

WILLIAMSON CO RD 197

The Golf Club
Star Ranch

KAATZ LN

WILLIAMS WAY
LITTLE LAKE RD
ST MARY'S DR
TOBY TR
CASSANDRA DR

KAATZ LN

LAKESIDE
ESTATES

B

STONEY BROOK DR

St Mary's
Cemetery

C

D

Brushy Creek

130
215

42   42

MARJORIE DR
ESTATE COVE
DANA DR

WILLIAMSON CO RD 138

MUIRFIELD BEND DR

213

E

ST LEGER ST
RIDGE LN
AQUADUCTAL AVE
GRANDMAE AVE
DARLEY DR
BYERLY TURK DR
ARABIAN DR
SECRETARIAT DR
HARNESS RACE WAY

215

F

WILLIAMSON CO RD 137

G

Spring Valley St

H

WILLIAMSON CO RD 139

RIDGE AT
STEEDS CROSSING

Geneva's
Park

GREENRIDGE DR

213

ROLLING
HILLS

WILLIAMSON CO RD 138

78634

M

DOLPHIN CT
GODOLPHIN
ROYAL ASCOT DR

SHIRE ST
WINNERS CIR

STEEDS
CROSSING

K

MORGANS CHOICE LN
TROTTERS LN
RACERS FORD LN
PACERS GAIT LN
JUMPERS DELIGHT LN
DERBY DAY AVE
FAST FILLY AVE

RIBBON CIR
GELDING
STEEDS CRSG

211

© Mapsco, Inc.

MARTIN LN

L

WILLIAMSON COUNTY
TRAVIS COUNTY

208
16

41

203

20
19

41

THE
COMMONS

N

ROLLING
MEADOWS

PURPLE THISTLE
26 OR 27

CHERRY LAUREL
BEACH
PLUM CV
DRAKE LN

JAN DR

Q

CLARKS GROVE LN

MORNINGSIDE CIR

MORNINGSIDE CIR

R

ROWE LOOP
ROWE LOOP

SPEIDEL DR

MERIDIAN BLVD
MEAD BEND
WINDMILL RANCH AVE
GAVIN TR
RAMBLING TR
DOVETAIL ST

WINDVIEW
WINDMILL
RIDGE ST
SLEEPY DAISY CV
RAVENSBROOK CT
WESTGATE WAY

APACHE PLUM LN
PENNY ROYAL DR

SILVERBELL LN

210
RED IVY
CLOVER CT
PIN

TEXAS MEADOWS
208

THE ESTATES
OF BLACKHAWK

MARTIN LN

17
19
18

22 ROWE LN

RINON HILLS

BELLERIVER

FOUR HILLS
BOCA RIO

WAYZATA CT
GARDEN CT

PLAINFIELDS
POINT CV
BIDERMANN WAY

HOLSTEN HILLS DR
CASA NAVARRO DR
STICK DR
CROOKED STICK DR

FARMIPOND
WINDING SHORE LN

28
28

HAWKS SWOOP TR

30

BUTED
HERON CALL
MURRELET WAY
FARRIER TR

31

ROWE LN

U

V

SULLIVAN ST
AGREED ST
MASHBURN
OPTION AVE
201

HAIG
KEARVEY
KEARNEY
TALAMORE RD
BETHESDA RD
CANTERBURY RD

WAKONDA
SEVEN BRIDGES
CITY CREEK DR
PHILLS

BLANCA DR
KICKAPOO CAVERN
BOCA
CHICA DR
MINERAL WELLS DR
WRITA

LINKS LAKE DR

ANT RD
AUK RD

RAPFORD ROST RD

CLOVER RUN TR

40   40

TERRADYNE
CHINCHO
SPOTTED OWL CIR

OWL DR
SPOTTED OWL DR

CARDINAL
MEADOW WAY

KENNEMER

CHAPARRAL
PAWTUCKET
PUMPKIN RIDGE CT

LINVILLE RIDGE DR
FARGO
CRANE CREEK LOOP
OCOTILLO

BLVD

DUNES CT
HALL DR
DAKOTA
MUSTANG ISLAND
WINDING SHORE LN

DAMISHANA CT
FEATHER TRIBE DR

MISSION TEJAS DR

PEDERNALES FALLS DR
ES
Rowe Lane

THE PARK AT
BLACKHAWK

EAGLE RIDGE LN
RANCH BLVD

SPEIDEL DR

JAKES HILL RD

X

CAJUILES DR
VILAMOURA LN
DIABLO CT
SEA ISLAND DR

CAJUILES CT

MOVING WATER
GRAND BANKS LN
RAMBLING CREEK LN
MISTY SHORE

Murchison
Park

Mallard Pond

Blackhawk
Golf Club

MALLARD POND TR
AMEN CORNER RD

BUTLER NATIONAL DR
ROANOK HILLS LN
DIABLO DR

FAIRWAYS OF
BLACKHAWK

JACKIES
RANCH CHAYTON CIR
SANDPIPER SPOT

NIGHTHAWK DIVE LN

78660

Mallard
Pond
Park

HAYFIELD SQ

193

PFLUGERVILLE

MS

SANDPIPER PERCH CT
FALCONERS WAY
SANDPIPER PERCH LN

HARRIER FLIGHT TRL
MERLIN TR
FALCON TR
SANDPIPER SPOT TR

NIGHTJAR VIEW TERR

209

MT

CONTINUED ON MAP 408

CONTINUED ON MAP 439

CONTINUED ON MAP 410

SCALE IN MILES
0   ⅛   ¼   ⅜   ½

SCALE IN FEET
0   1000   2000   3000

COPYRIGHT 1993, 2009 by MAPSCO INC. - ALL RIGHTS RESERVED

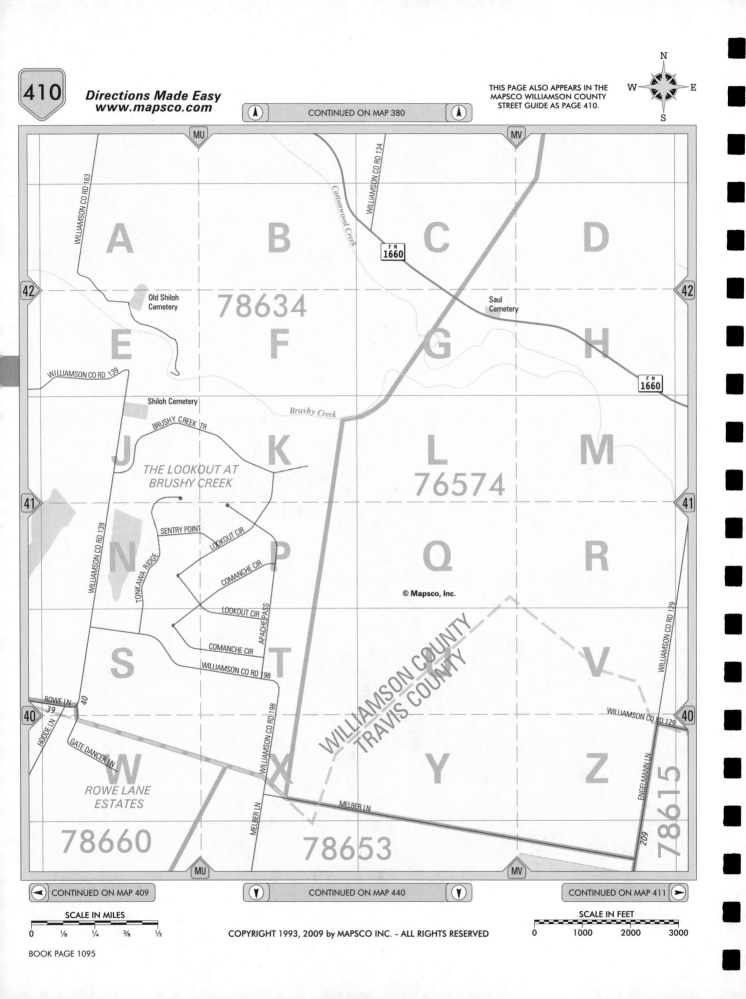

410

Directions Made Easy
www.mapsco.com

N
W E
S

CONTINUED ON MAP 380

42   42

WILLIAMSON CO RD 163

WILLIAMSON CO RD 134

Cottonwood Creek

FM 1660

A   B   C   D

Old Shiloh
Cemetery

78634

Saul
Cemetery

E   F   G   H

WILLIAMSON CO RD 139

FM 1660

Shiloh Cemetery

Brushy Creek

BRUSHY CREEK TR

J   K   L   M

76574

THE LOOKOUT AT
BRUSHY CREEK

41   41

SENTRY POINT

LOOKOUT CIR

WILLIAMSON CO RD 139

TONKAWA RIDGE

N   P   Q   R

COMANCHE CIR

WILLIAMSON CO RD 129

LOOKOUT CIR

APACHE PASS

© Mapsco, Inc.

COMANCHE CIR

WILLIAMSON CO RD 198

S   T   V

WILLIAMSON COUNTY
TRAVIS COUNTY

WILLIAMSON CO RD 198

ROWE LN
39   40

40   40

HODDE LN

GATE DANCER LN

WILLIAMSON CO RD 129

ENGELMANN LN

W   X   Y   Z

MELBER LN

ROWE LANE
ESTATES

MELBER LN

209

78615

78660   78653

CONTINUED ON MAP 409
CONTINUED ON MAP 440
CONTINUED ON MAP 411

SCALE IN MILES
0   1/8   1/4   3/8   1/2

SCALE IN FEET
0   1000   2000   3000

BOOK PAGE 1095

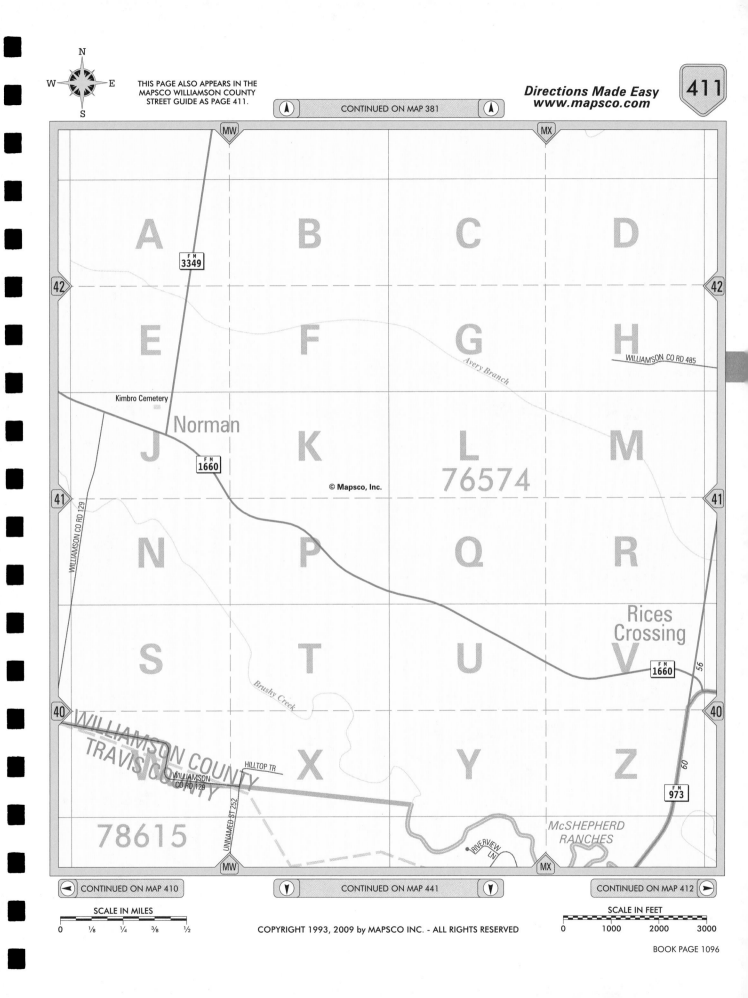

THIS PAGE ALSO APPEARS IN THE
MAPSCO WILLIAMSON COUNTY
STREET GUIDE AS PAGE 411.

Directions Made Easy
www.mapsco.com

411

CONTINUED ON MAP 381

A B C D

42 42

FM 3349

E F G H

WILLIAMSON CO RD 485

Avery Branch

Kimbro Cemetery

Norman

J K L M

76574

FM 1660

© Mapsco, Inc.

41 41

WILLIAMSON CO RD 129

N P Q R

Rices
Crossing

S T U V

56

FM 1660

Brushy Creek

40 40

WILLIAMSON COUNTY
TRAVIS COUNTY

HILLTOP TR

60

WILLIAMSON
CO RD 129

X Y Z

FM 973

UNNAMED ST 252

78615

McSHEPHERD
RANCHES

RIVERVIEW LN

CONTINUED ON MAP 410

CONTINUED ON MAP 441

CONTINUED ON MAP 412

SCALE IN MILES

0   ⅛   ¼   ⅜   ½

SCALE IN FEET

0   1000   2000   3000

BOOK PAGE 1096

Directions Made Easy
www.mapsco.com

⬆ CONTINUED ON MAP 382 ⬆

THIS PAGE ALSO APPEARS IN THE
MAPSCO WILLIAMSON COUNTY
STREET GUIDE AS PAGE 412.

N
W E
S

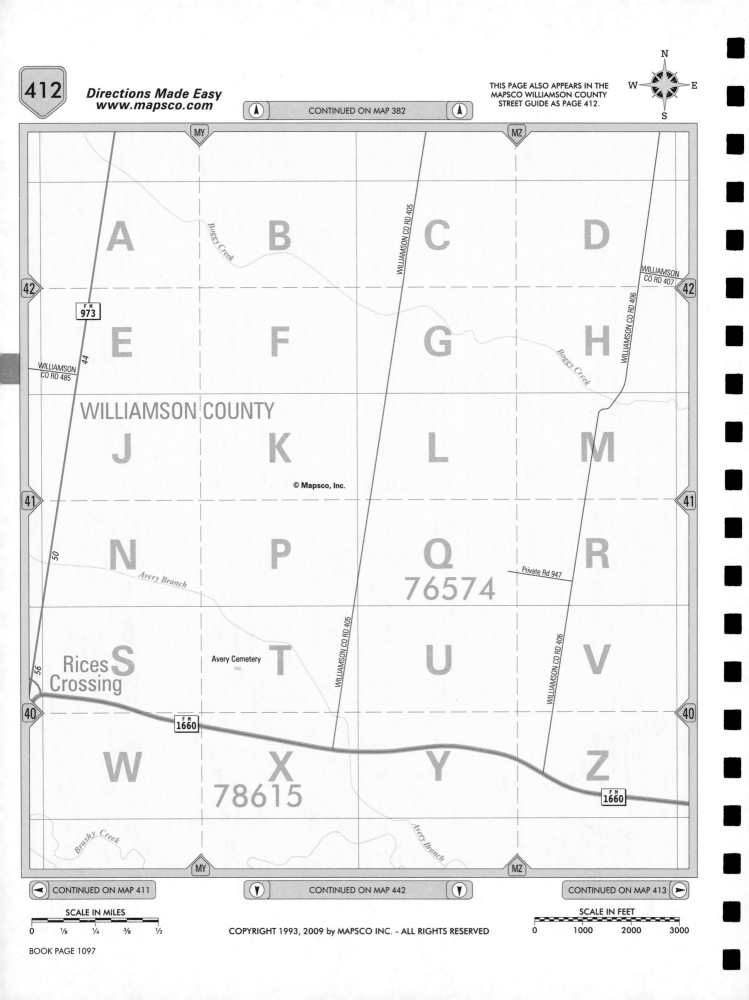

MY

MZ

A

Boggy Creek

B

WILLIAMSON CO RD 405

C

D

WILLIAMSON CO RD 407

42

FM 973

E

F

G

H

WILLIAMSON CO RD 406

42

44

WILLIAMSON CO RD 485

Boggy Creek

WILLIAMSON COUNTY

J

K

L

M

© Mapsco, Inc.

41

41

N

Avery Branch

P

Q

76574

R

Private Rd 947

50

WILLIAMSON CO RD 405

S

Rices Crossing

Avery Cemetery

T

U

WILLIAMSON CO RD 406

V

56

40

FM 1660

40

W

X

78615

Y

Z

FM 1660

Brushy Creek

Avery Branch

MY

MZ

◀ CONTINUED ON MAP 411
▼ CONTINUED ON MAP 442 ▼
CONTINUED ON MAP 413 ▶

SCALE IN MILES

0   ⅛   ¼   ⅜   ½

SCALE IN FEET

0   1000   2000   3000

BOOK PAGE 1097

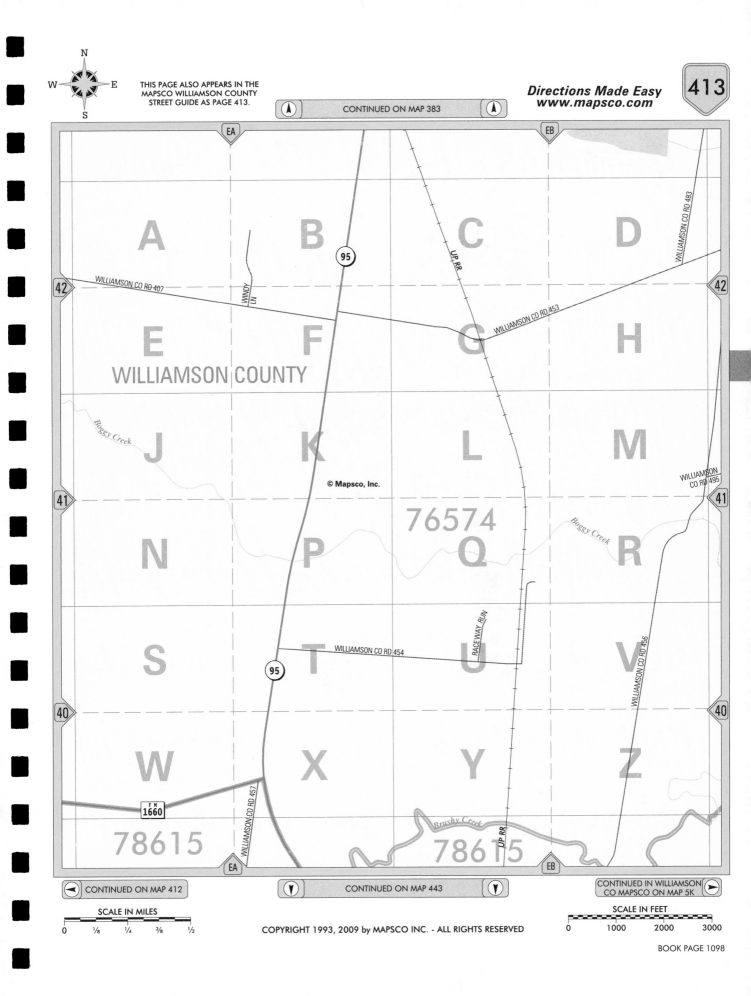

CONTINUED ON MAP 396

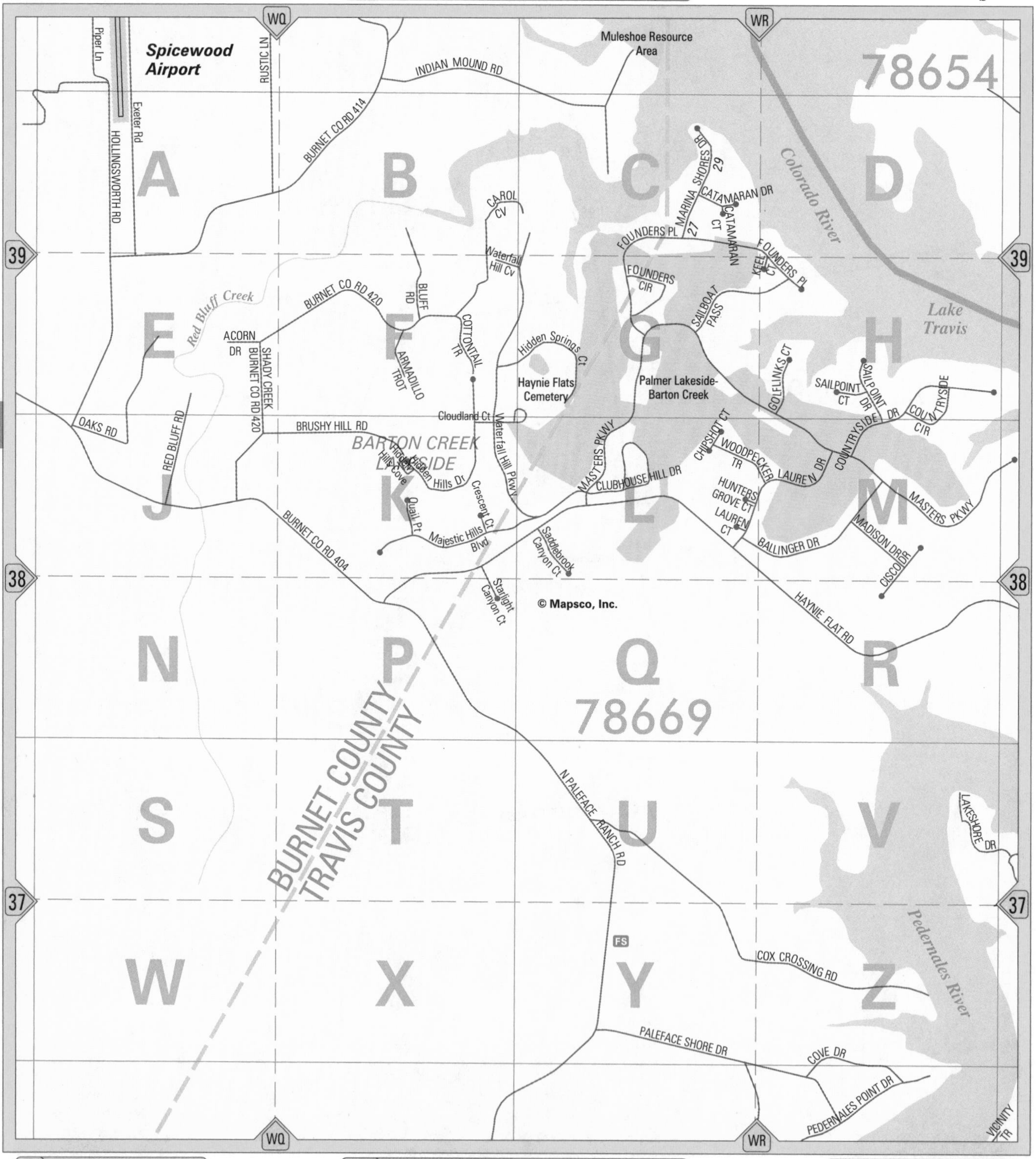

N
W E
S

Spicewood Airport

Piper Ln
Exeter Rd
HOLLINGSWORTH RD
RUSTIC LN
WQ

INDIAN MOUND RD

Muleshoe Resource Area

WR

78654

BURNET CO RD 414

A
B
C
D

CAROL CV

MARINA SHORES DR
29
CATAMARAN CT
CATAMARAN DR
27
FOUNDERS PL
FOUNDERS PL

Colorado River

39
39

Waterfall Hill Cv

FOUNDERS CIR

SAILBOAT PASS

Lake Travis

Red Bluff Creek

BURNET CO RD 420

BLUFF RD

ACORN DR

COTTONTAIL TR

ARMADILLO TROT

Hidden Springs Ct

Haynie Flats Cemetery

Palmer Lakeside- Barton Creek

GOLFLINKS CT

SAILPOINT CT

SAILPOINT DR
SAILPOINT DR
COUNTRYSIDE DR
COUNTRYSIDE CIR

E
F
G
H

SHADY CREEK
BURNET CO RD 420

OAKS RD

RED BLUFF RD

Cloudland Ct

BRUSHY HILL RD

Waterfall Hill Pkwy

BARTON CREEK LAKESIDE

Hidden Hills Dr
Lk Cove

CHIPSHOT CT

WOODPECKER TR

COUNTRYSIDE DR
LAUREN

J
K
L
M

MASTERS PKWY

Crescent Ct

Quail Pt
Majestic Hills Blvd

Saddlebrook Canyon Ct

CLUBHOUSE HILL DR

HUNTERS GROVE CT
LAUREN CT

LAUREN

BALLINGER DR

MADISON DR
OSCO DR

MASTERS PKWY

BURNET CO RD 404

Starlight Canyon Ct

© Mapsco, Inc.

38
38

HAYNIE FLAT RD

N
P
Q
R

BURNET COUNTY
TRAVIS COUNTY

78669

N PALEFACE RANCH RD

S
T
U
V

LAKESHORE DR

37
37

Pedernales River

FS

COX CROSSING RD

W
X
Y
Z

PALEFACE SHORE DR

COVE DR

PEDERNALES POINT DR

VICINITY TR

WQ

CONTINUED ON MAP 456

WR

CONTINUED ON MAP 427

NOT MAPPED

SCALE IN MILES
0   1/8   1/4   3/8   1/2

SCALE IN FEET
0   1000   2000   3000

COPYRIGHT 1993, 2009 by MAPSCO INC. - ALL RIGHTS RESERVED

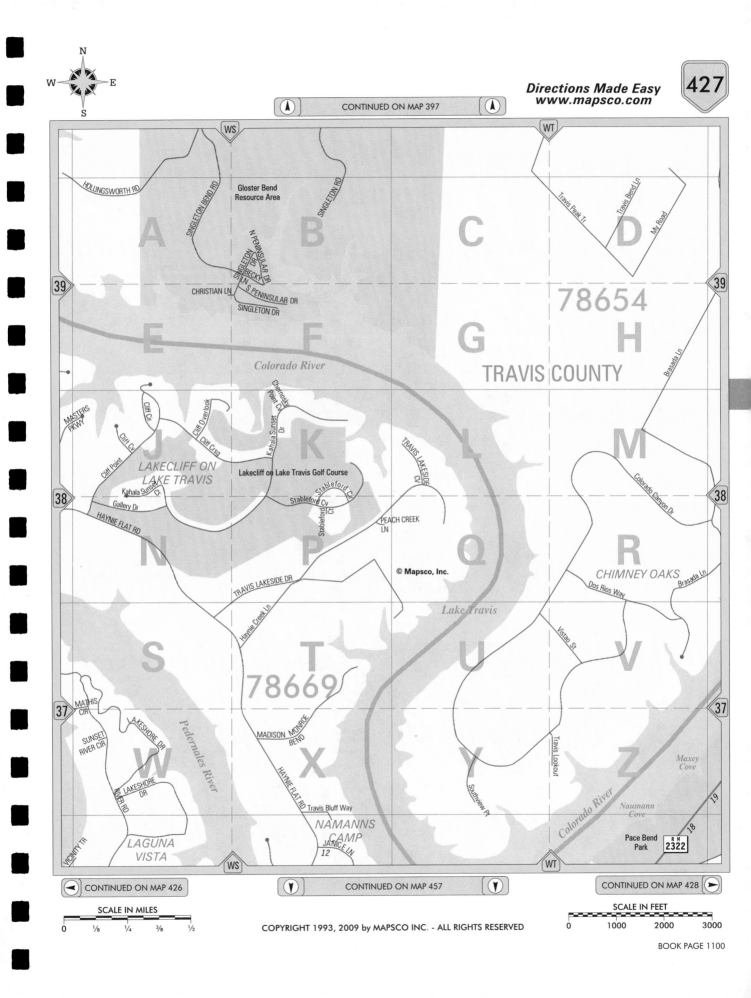

N
W E
S

CONTINUED ON MAP 397

WS

WT

HOLLINGSWORTH RD

SINGLETON BEND RD

Gloster Bend
Resource Area

SINGLETON RD

A

B

C

Travis Peak Tr.

Travis Bend Ln

My. Road

D

N PENINSULAR DR

SINGLETON DR

BECKY LN

CHRISTIAN LN

S PENINSULAR DR

SINGLETON DR

39

39

E

F

G

78654

H

Brasada Ln

Colorado River

TRAVIS COUNTY

MASTERS PKWY

Cliff Cir.

Cliff Cv.

Cliff Overlook

Cliff Ct sq.

Chernosky Point Cv.

Kahala Sunset Dr

J

K

TRAVIS LAKESIDE CV

L

M

Cliff Point

**LAKECLIFF ON
LAKE TRAVIS**

Lakecliff on Lake Travis Golf Course

Stableford Cir

Colorado Canyon Dr.

Kahala Sunset Ct.

Gallery Dr

Stableford Cv

Stableford Ct

PEACH CREEK LN

38

38

HAYNIE FLAT RD

N

P

Q

R

CHIMNEY OAKS

TRAVIS LAKESIDE DR

Dos Rios Way

Brasada Ln

© Mapsco, Inc.

Lake Travis

Haynie Creek Ln

Vistao St.

MATHIS CIR

S

T
78669

U

V

37

37

LAKESHORE DR

SUNSET RIVER CIR

MADISON MONROE BEND

Travis Lookout

Maxey Cove

19

LAKESHORE RIVER RD

W

HAYNIE FLAT RD

X

Y

Z

Colorado River

Naumann Cove

18

VICINITY TR

LAGUNA VISTA

Travis Bluff Way

NAMANNS CAMP

JANICE LN
12

Southview Pt

Pace Bend Park

R M 2322

WS

WT

CONTINUED ON MAP 426
CONTINUED ON MAP 457
CONTINUED ON MAP 428

SCALE IN MILES
0   1/8   1/4   3/8   1/2

SCALE IN FEET
0   1000   2000   3000

CONTINUED ON MAP 398

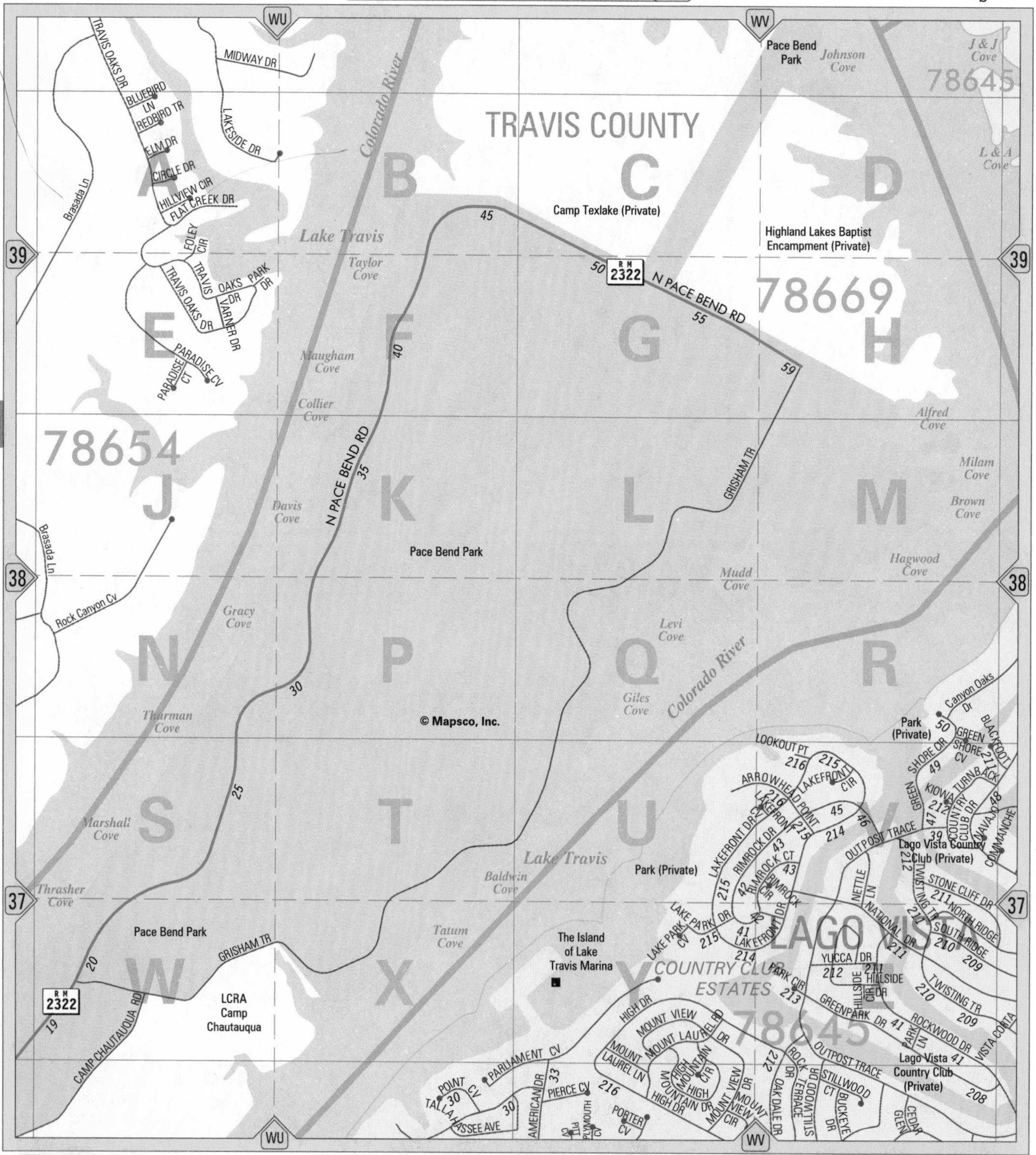

N
W E
S

WU

WV

Pace Bend Park

Johnson Cove

J & J Cove

MIDWAY DR

TRAVIS OAKS DR
BLUEBIRD LN
REDBIRD TR
ELM DR
CIRCLE DR
HILLVIEW CIR
FLAT CREEK DR
FOLEY CIR
TRAVIS OAKS DR
OAKS PARK DR
WARNER DR
PARADISE CT
PARADISE CV

LAKESIDE DR

Brasada Ln

Colorado River

TRAVIS COUNTY

Camp Texlake (Private)

Highland Lakes Baptist
Encampment (Private)

78645

L & A Cove

39

39

A

B

C

D

78669

45

50

R M
2322

N PACE BEND RD

55

59

Lake Travis

Taylor Cove

E

F

G

H

Maugham Cove

40

Collier Cove

Alfred Cove

78654

35

Davis Cove

J

K

L

M

Milam Cove

Brown Cove

N PACE BEND RD

Pace Bend Park

GRISHAM TR

Mudd Cove

Hagwood Cove

Brasada Ln

Rock Canyon Cv

Gracy Cove

N

P

Q

R

Levi Cove

Colorado River

Giles Cove

© Mapsco, Inc.

30

Thurman Cove

Canyon Oaks Dr

Park (Private)

50

GREEN SHORE CIR
SHORE CR
GREEN SHORE CV
BLACKFOOT
TURNBACK
KIOWA
COUNTRY CLUB DR
NAVAJO
COMMANCHE

25

Marshall Cove

S

T

U

LOOKOUT PT
216
215
ARROWHEAD POINT
216
215
LAKEFRONT CIR

49
48
47

Lago Vista Country Club (Private)

212

STONE CLIFF DR
211
NORTH RIDGE
SOUTH RIDGE
210
209

Lake Travis

Park (Private)

45
46
214

OUTPOST TRACE

LAKEFRONT DR
43
RIMROCK CT
43
RIMROCK
42
LAKE PARK CT
41
LAKEFRONT DR
LAKE PARK CV
215
215
215

NETTLE LN
NATIONAL DR

TWISTING TR
TWISTING TR
210
210
209

37

37

Thrasher Cove

Baldwin Cove

Tatum Cove

The Island of Lake Travis Marina

LAGO VISTA

COUNTRY CLUB ESTATES

78645

YUCCA DR
HILLSIDE DR
THISTLE CIR
212
211
PARK CIR
213
GREENPARK DR
41
212

ROCKWOOD DR
41
VISTA CORTA

CEDAR GLEN
208

Pace Bend Park

GRISHAM TR

CAMP CHAUTAUQUA RD

20

19

R M
2322

LCRA Camp Chautauqua

W

X

Y

HIGH DR
MOUNT VIEW DR
MOUNT LAUREL DR
MOUNT LAUREL
LAUREL LN
MOUNT MOUNTAIN DR
HIGH
MOUNTAIN CIR
HIGH DR
MOUNT VIEW CIR
MOUNT VIEW DR
HIGH DR

PARLIAMENT CV

POINT CV
30
TALLAHASSEE AVE

AMERICANDR
PIERCE CV
33
30
216

PLYMOUTH

PORTER CV

OUTPOST TRACE
ROCK TERRACE
LOOM HILLS DR
STILLWOOD CT
OAK DALE DR
BUCKEYE DR

Lago Vista Country Club (Private)

WU

WV

CONTINUED ON MAP 427

CONTINUED ON MAP 458

CONTINUED ON MAP 429

SCALE IN MILES
0 1/8 1/4 3/8 1/2

SCALE IN FEET
0 1000 2000 3000

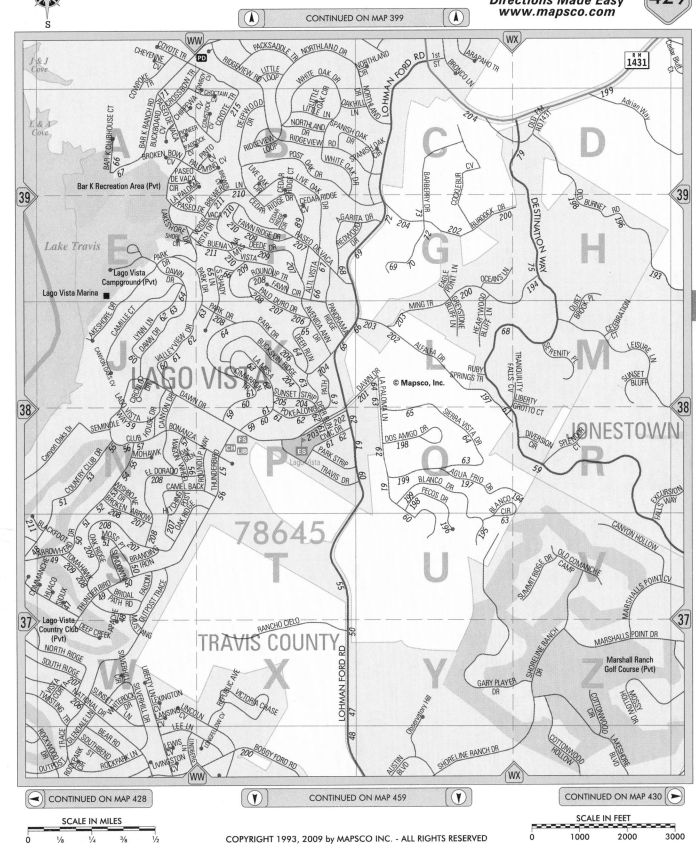

N
W E
S

CONTINUED ON MAP 399

RM 1431

CONTINUED ON MAP 428

CONTINUED ON MAP 459

CONTINUED ON MAP 430

LAGO VISTA

78645

TRAVIS COUNTY

JONESTOWN

Lake Travis

J & J Cove

L & A Cove

Bar K Recreation Area (Pvt)

Lago Vista Campground (Pvt)

Lago Vista Marina

Lago Vista Country Club (Pvt)

Marshall Ranch Golf Course (Pvt)

© Mapsco, Inc.

SCALE IN MILES
0   1/8   1/4   3/8   1/2

SCALE IN FEET
0   1000   2000   3000

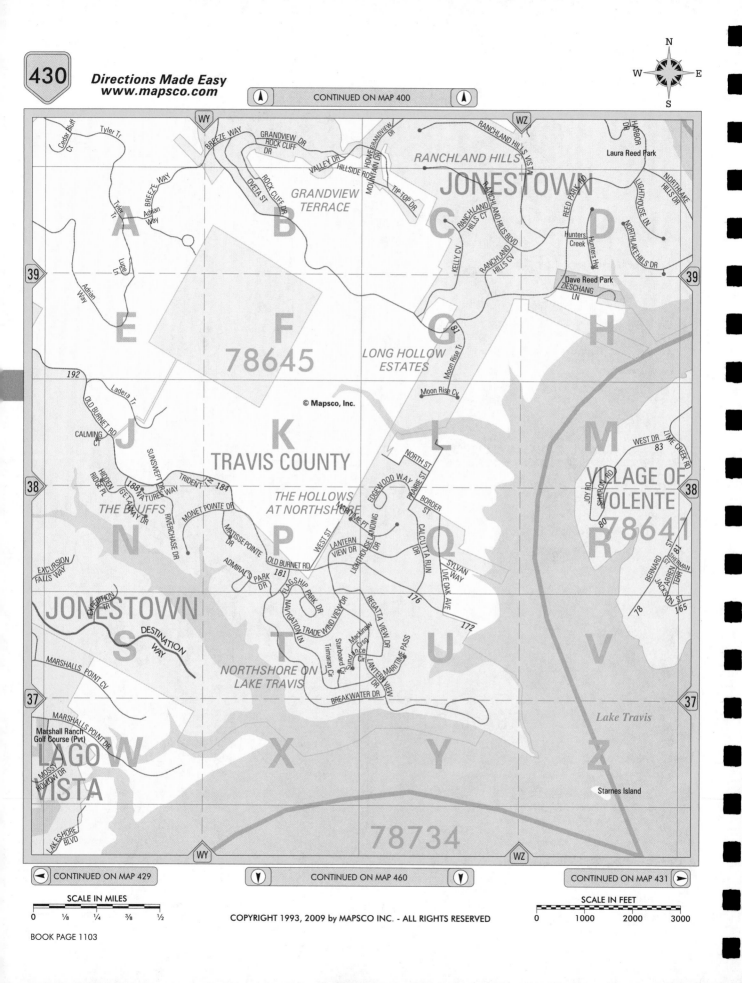

430

Directions Made Easy
www.mapsco.com

CONTINUED ON MAP 400

JONESTOWN

RANCHLAND HILLS

Laura Reed Park

Cedar Bluff Ct
Tyler Tr
Tyler Tr
BREEZE WAY
BREEZE WAY
WY
Adrian Way
Lupe Ln
Adrian Way
Grandview Dr
Rock Cliff Dr
Valley Dr
Hillside Dr
Oveta St
Rock Cliff Dr
GRANDVIEW TERRACE
Home Grandview Dr
Mountain Dr
Tip Top Dr

A
B
C

Ranchland Hills Vista
WZ
Ranchland Hills Ct
Ranchland Hills Blvd
Kelly Cv
Ranchland Hills Cv
Reed Park Rd
Hunters Creek
Hunters Hwy
Dave Reed Park
ZIESCHANG LN

Harbor Dr
Lighthouse Ln
Northlake Hills Dr
Northlake Hills Dr

D

39

39

E
F
78645

LONG HOLLOW ESTATES

Moon Rise Tr
Moon Rise Cv

G
81
H

192
Ladera Tr
Old Burnet Rd
CALMING CT

© Mapsco, Inc.

J
K
TRAVIS COUNTY
L

North St
Prairie St

M
WEST DR
LIME CREEK RD
83
VILLAGE OF VOLENTE
78641

38

Hidden Ridge Pl
188
Sunswept Dr
Natures Way
Getaway Dr
Trident Tr
184
Monet Pointe Dr
Riverchase Dr
THE BLUFFS

N

THE HOLLOWS AT NORTHSHORE

Matisse Pointe Dr
Admiral's Park Dr
Old Burnet Rd
181

West St
Moore
Maritime Pt
Lantern View Dr
Lighthouse Landing Dr
Edgewood Way
Border St
Calcutta Run
Sylvan Way
Live Oak Ave

P
Q
176
172

Joy Rd
Sharon St
80
Bernard St
Warren St
Jackson St
Sherman Terr
78
165
81

R

EXCURSION FALLS WAY

JONESTOWN

Expedition Tr
DESTINATION WAY
MARSHALLS POINT CV

S

Flagship Park Dr
Navigation Ln
Tradewind View Dr
Starboard Dr
Trimaran Cir
Mackinaw Cir
Lance Cir
Lantern View Dr
Regatta View Dr
Maritime Pass
BREAKWATER DR
NORTHSHORE ON LAKE TRAVIS

T
U
V

Lake Travis

37

MARSHALLS POINT DR

Marshall Ranch Golf Course (Pvt)
Mossy Hollow Dr
LAGO VISTA
LAKESHORE BLVD

W
X
Y
Z

Starnes Island

78734

CONTINUED ON MAP 429
CONTINUED ON MAP 460
CONTINUED ON MAP 431

SCALE IN MILES
0   1/8   1/4   3/8   1/2

COPYRIGHT 1993, 2009 by MAPSCO INC. - ALL RIGHTS RESERVED

SCALE IN FEET
0   1000   2000   3000

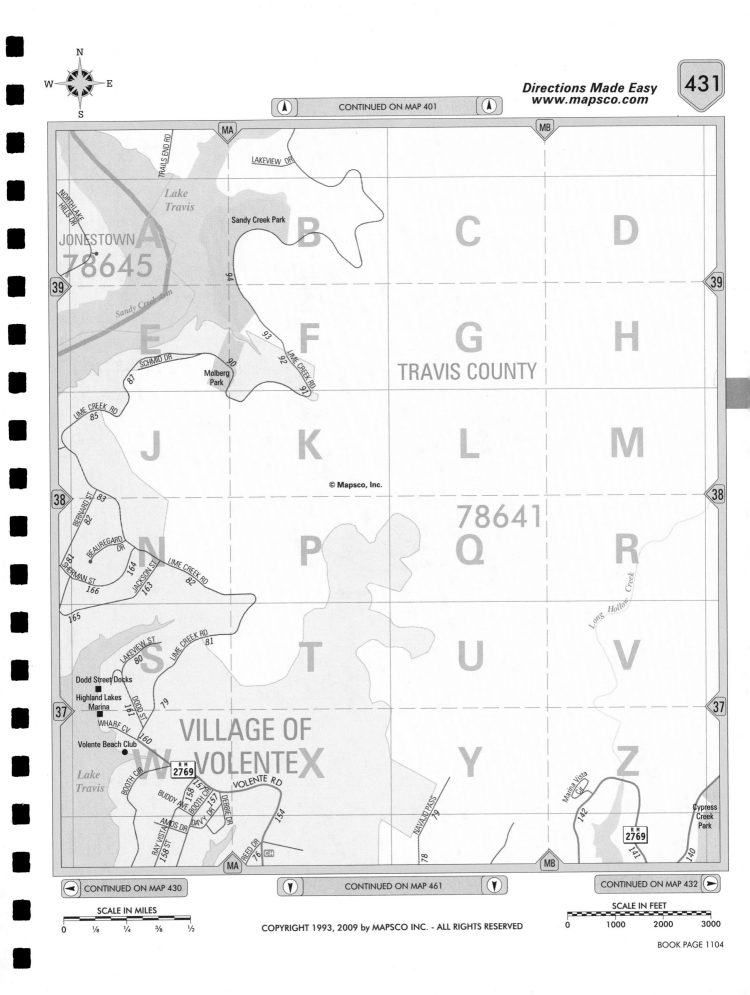

CONTINUED ON MAP 401

MA

MB

TRAILS END RD

LAKEVIEW DR

NORTHLAKE HILLS DR

Lake Travis

Sandy Creek Park

JONESTOWN
78645

A

B

C

D

39

39

Sandy Creek Arm

94

E

F

G

H

SCHMID DR

93

90

92

LIME CREEK RD

TRAVIS COUNTY

87

Molberg Park

91

LIME CREEK RD

85

J

K

L

M

© Mapsco, Inc.

38

38

BERNARD ST

83

82

N

P

Q

78641

R

BEAUREGARD DR

81

164

JACKSON ST

LIME CREEK RD

SHERMAN ST

166

163

82

165

Long Hollow Creek

LAKEVIEW ST

LIME CREEK RD

80

81

S

T

U

V

Dodd Street Docks

Highland Lakes Marina

DODD ST

79

37

161

37

WHARF CV

160

Volente Beach Club

W

VILLAGE OF
VOLENTE

X

Y

Z

Lake Travis

BOOTH CIR

RM
2769

VOLENTE RD

Marina Vista Cir

BUDDY AVE

158

157 ST

BOOTH CIR

157

DEBBIE DR

NAVAJO PASS

79

142

Cypress Creek Park

AMOS DR

RAY VISTA

158 ST

DAVY DR

154

RM
2769

141

140

REED DR

76

CH

MA

78

MB

CONTINUED ON MAP 430

CONTINUED ON MAP 461

CONTINUED ON MAP 432

SCALE IN MILES

0   ⅛   ¼   ⅜   ½

SCALE IN FEET

0   1000   2000   3000

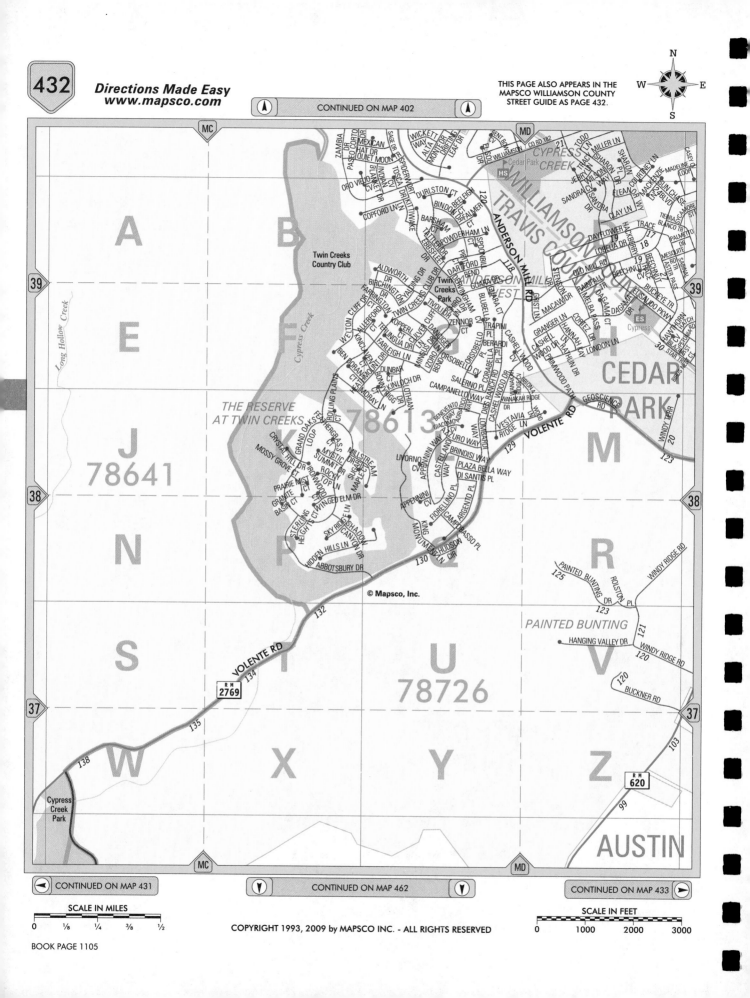

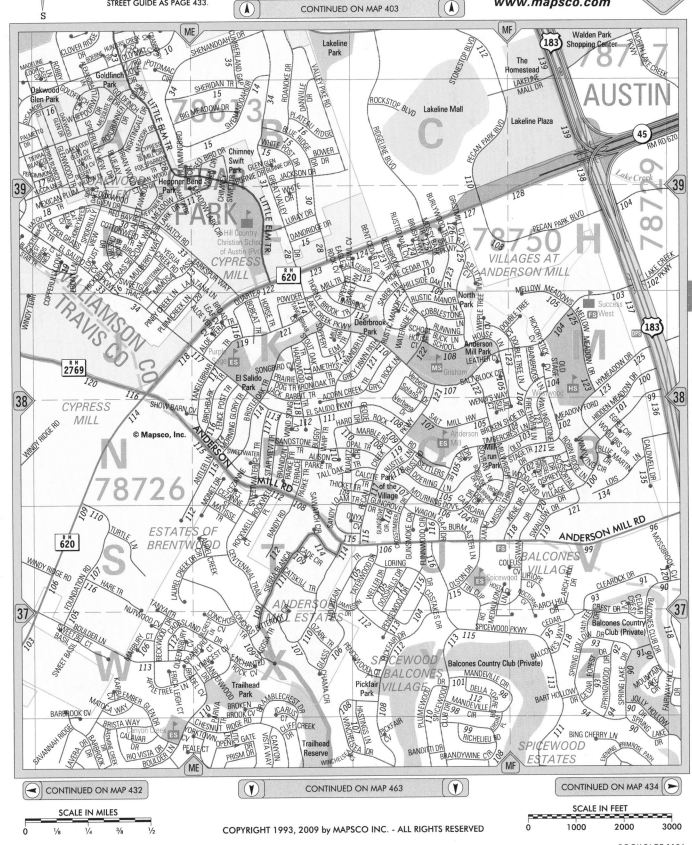

Directions Made Easy
www.mapsco.com

CONTINUED ON MAP 403

CONTINUED ON MAP 432

CONTINUED ON MAP 463

CONTINUED ON MAP 434

SCALE IN MILES

0   1/8   1/4   3/8   1/2

SCALE IN FEET

0   1000   2000   3000

© Mapsco, Inc.

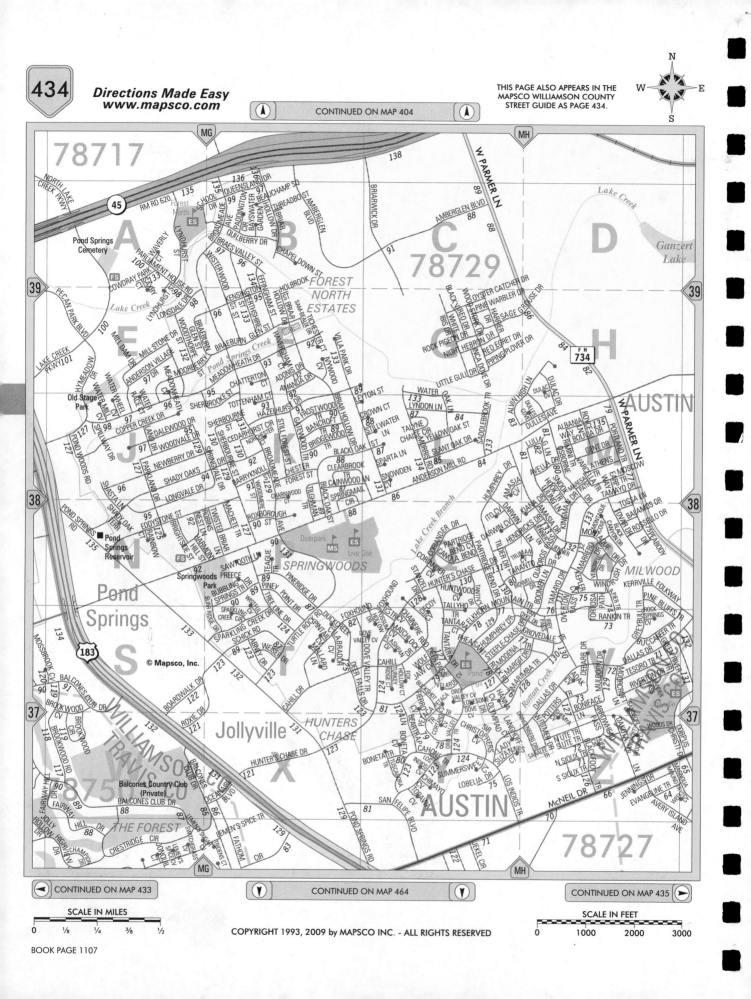

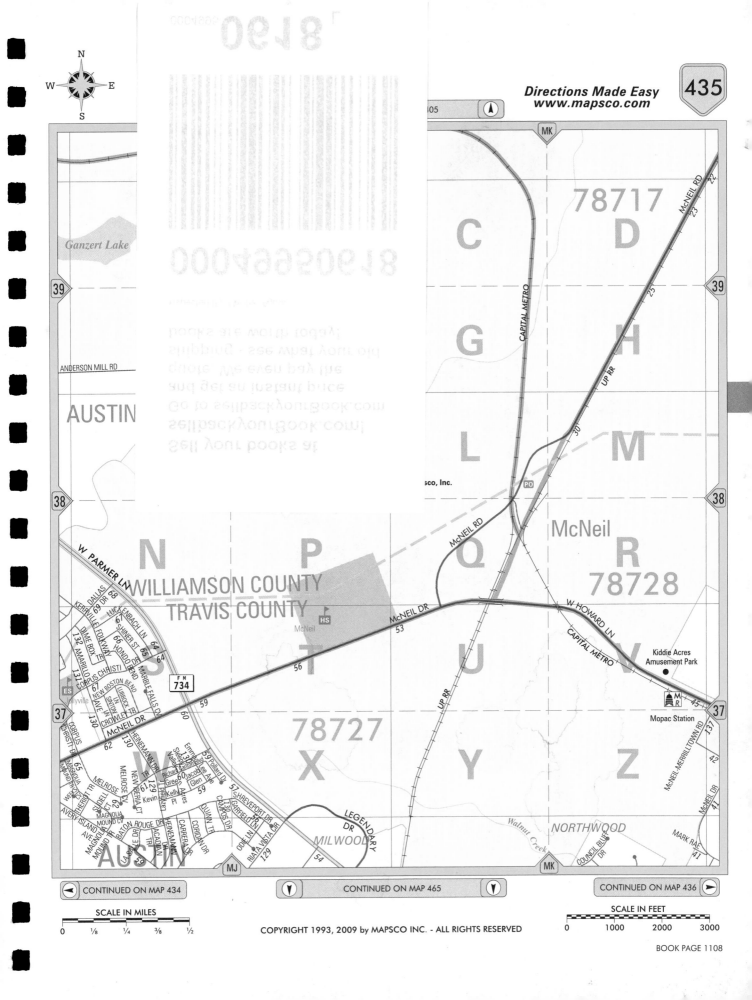

N
↑
W · E
S

Ganzert Lake

39

ANDERSON MILL RD

AUSTIN

38

37

78717

C
D

39

CAPITAL METRO

G
H

UP RR

L
M

PO

McNeil

McNEIL RD

N
P
Q
R
78728

WILLIAMSON COUNTY

TRAVIS COUNTY

McNeil
HS

McNEIL DR
53

38

W HOWARD LN

CAPITAL METRO

Kiddie Acres
Amusement Park

W PARMER LN

DALLAS
KERRVILLE FOLKWAY
LUCKENBACH LN
SHINER ST
HONDO BEND
MARBLE FALLS CV
DIME BOX
AMARILLO
CORPUS CHRISTI
NEW BOSTON BEND
CROWLEY TR
LUBBOCK
UN
SINTON

S
T
U
V

FM
734

56

78727

UP RR

Y

Z

McNEIL DR

CORPUS CHRISTI DR
HEINEMANN DR

MELROSE

W

X

SHREVEPORT DR
GABRIELD DR
Pollard Dr

NORTHWOOD

Mopac Station

37

McNEIL-MERRILLTOWN RD
MARK RAE

MAGNOLIA
SLIDELL
THERIOT TR
AVERY ISLAND
MOUND CV
MAGNOLIA
AVE
MOUND TR
NEW IBERIA CT

MELROSE
Kevin Pl
Kelly Pl
CORIDAN DR
CARRERA DR
ACADIAN
HEINEMANN
BIATA VISTA DR
ODELL LN

QUINN TR
CAMPOS DR

LEGENDARY
DR
MILWOOD

54

Walnut Creek

COUNCIL BLUFF DR

AUSTIN

MJ

MK

◀ CONTINUED ON MAP 434

CONTINUED ON MAP 465

CONTINUED ON MAP 436 ▶

SCALE IN MILES

0   ⅛   ¼   ⅜   ½

SCALE IN FEET

0   1000   2000   3000

BOOK PAGE 1108

Directions Made Easy
www.mapsco.com

CONTINUED ON MAP 406

THIS PAGE ALSO APPEARS IN THE
MAPSCO WILLIAMSON COUNTY
STREET GUIDE AS PAGE 436.

N W E S

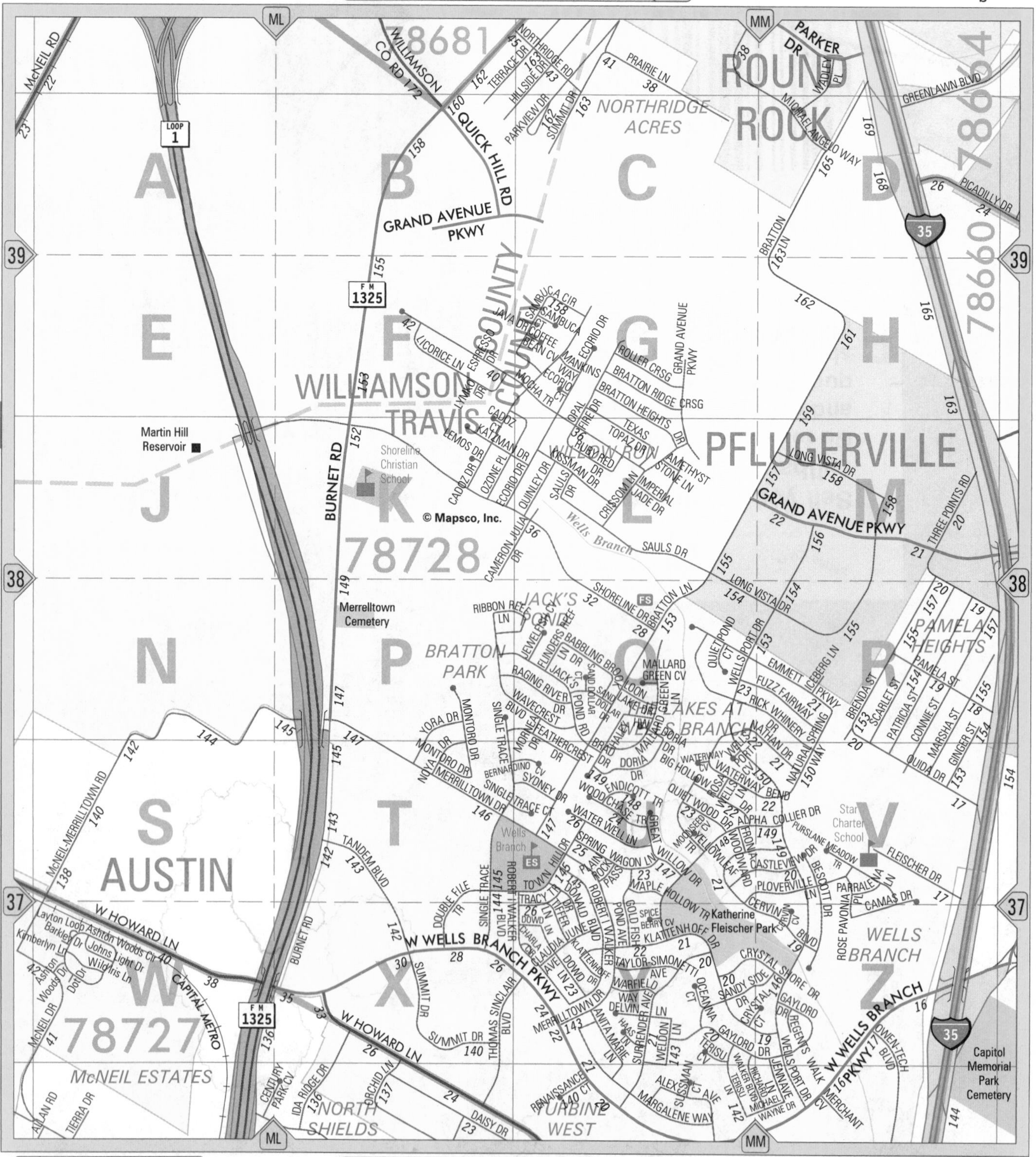

ROUND ROCK

PFLUGERVILLE

WILLIAMSON
TRAVIS

AUSTIN

78681
78664
78660
78728
78727

McNEIL ESTATES

Martin Hill Reservoir

Shoreline Christian School

© Mapsco, Inc.

Merrelltown Cemetery

Bratton Park

Jack's Pond

Wells Branch

THE LAKES AT WELLS BRANCH

PAMELA HEIGHTS

Star Charter School

Katherine Fleischer Park

WELLS BRANCH

Capitol Memorial Park Cemetery

NORTH SHIELDS

TURBINE WEST

GRAND AVENUE PKWY

QUICK HILL RD

BURNET RD

CAPITAL METRO

W HOWARD LN

W WELLS BRANCH PKWY

CONTINUED ON MAP 435

CONTINUED ON MAP 466

CONTINUED ON MAP 437

SCALE IN MILES
0   1/8   1/4   3/8   1/2

SCALE IN FEET
0   1000   2000   3000

COPYRIGHT 1993, 2009 by MAPSCO INC. - ALL RIGHTS RESERVED

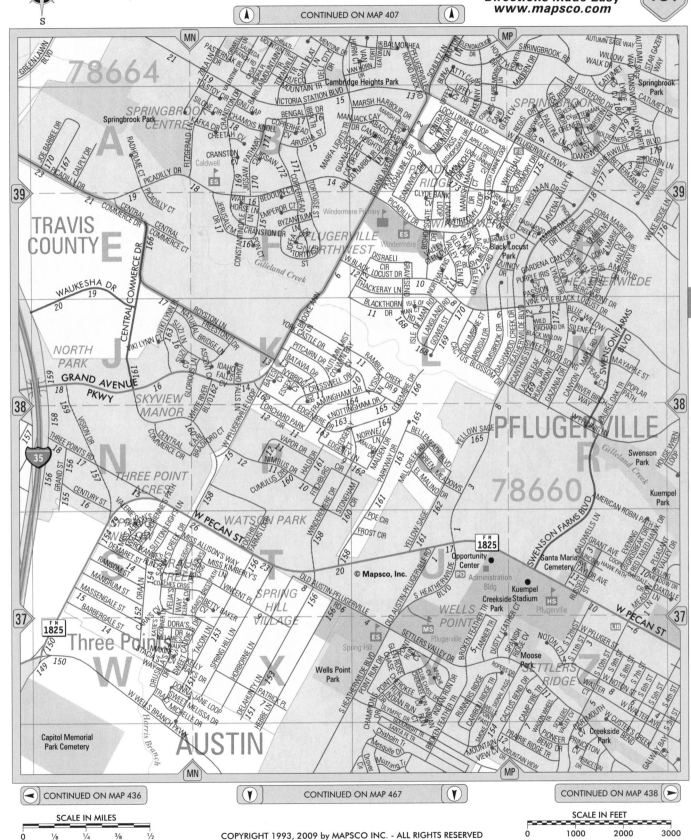

CONTINUED ON MAP 407
CONTINUED ON MAP 436
CONTINUED ON MAP 467
CONTINUED ON MAP 438

SCALE IN MILES
0   1/8   1/4   3/8   1/2

SCALE IN FEET
0   1000   2000   3000

BOOK PAGE 1110

CONTINUED ON MAP 408

438

Directions Made Easy
www.mapsco.com

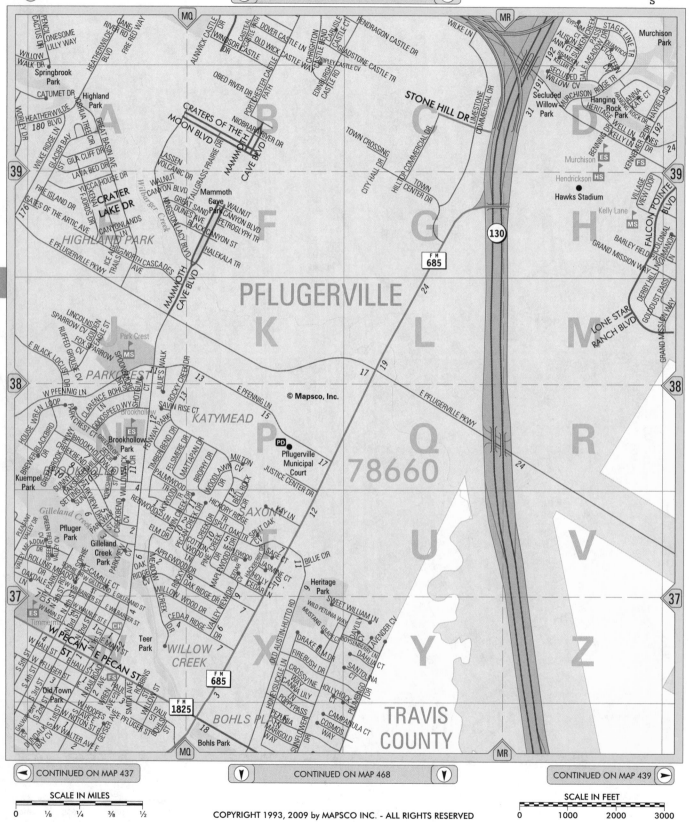

PFLUGERVILLE

78660

TRAVIS COUNTY

CONTINUED ON MAP 437
CONTINUED ON MAP 468
CONTINUED ON MAP 439

SCALE IN MILES

0   1/8   1/4   3/8   1/2

SCALE IN FEET

0   1000   2000   3000

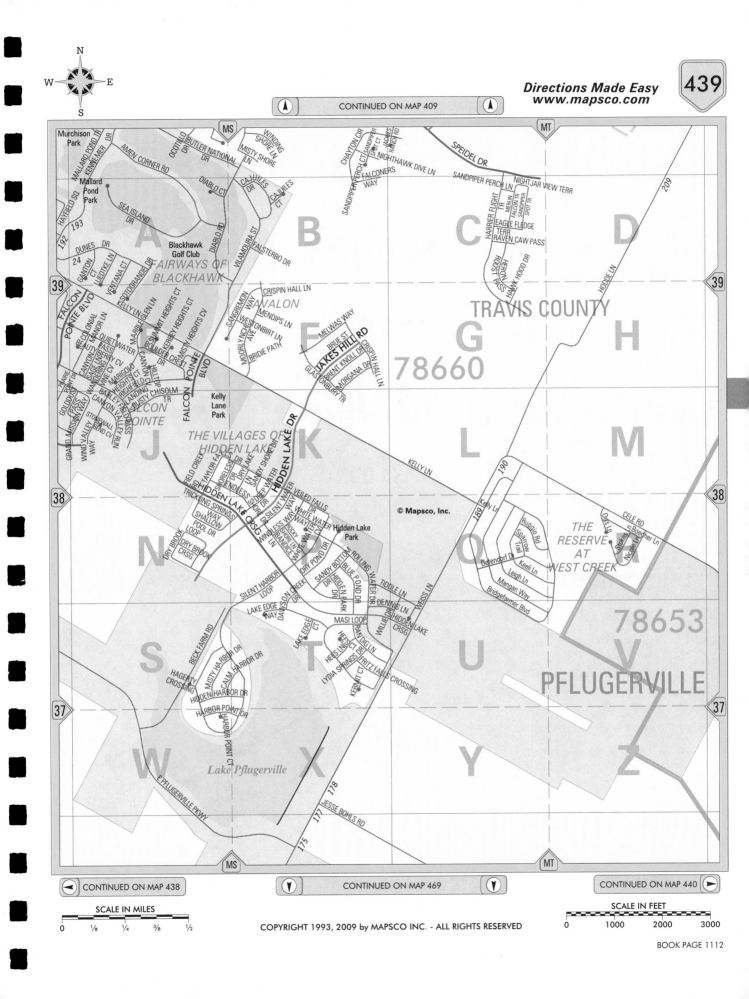

N
W E
S

CONTINUED ON MAP 409

MS
MT

Murchison Park

MALLARD POND TR
KENNEMER DR
OCOTILLO DR
BUTLER NATIONAL DR
AMEN CORNER RD
WINDING SHORE LN
MISTY SHORE LN
CHAYTON CIR
SANDPIPER PERCH CT
SANDPIPER CT
JACKS RANCH RD
NIGHTHAWK DIVE LN
SPEIDEL DR
NIGHTJAR VIEW TERR
209

DIABLO CT
CAJUILES DR
CAJUILES CT
FALCONERS WAY
SANDPIPER PERCH LN
HARRIER FLIGHT TR
MERLIN FALCON TR
SANDPIPER SPOT TR
EAGLE FLEDGE TERR
RAVEN CAW PASS

Mallard Pond Park

HAYFIELD SQ
192 193
SEA ISLAND DR

Blackhawk Golf Club

A
B
C
D

FAIRWAYS OF BLACKHAWK

DUNES DR
24
GANTON CT
WEDTKE LN
VENTANA CT

VILAMOURA ST
FALSTERBO DR

CRISPIN HALL LN
AVALON
MENDIPS WAY
WESTONBIRT LN
BRIDLE PATH
MELWAS WAY
BRUE ST

SANGREMON

HERON ROOST PASS
HAWK HOOD DR
HODDE LN

TRAVIS COUNTY

39
39

39
FALCON POINTE BLVD
COLONIAL PASS
KELLY LN
GLEN LN
SUTTOGRANDE DR
SUMMIT HEIGHTS CT
KERBEY HEIGHTS CT
MISTY HEIGHTS CV

E
F
G
H

BEAUTY LIBERTY CV
QUIETWATER
MARBLE PASS
MARICOND HEIGHTS
CANYON CT
BOULDER CREST DR
HILLTOP
JAKES HILL RD
LAKES HILL RD
78660

WANDERING LN
RICHFIELD
ISLANDING
DUSTY CHISOLM TR
FALCON POINTE BLVD
GLASTONBURY TR
BRENT KNOLL DR
MORGANA DR
CRISPIN HALL LN

PRAIRIE POINT DR
GOLDDUST PASS
GRAND MISSION WAY
WIND VALLEY WAY
STONEWALL BEND CV
CANYON VALLEY RUN
BARLEY FIELD PASS

Kelly Lane Park

J
K
L
M

FALCON POINTE

THE VILLAGES OF HIDDEN LAKE

HIDDEN LAKE DR
KELLY LN
KELLY LN

190
189
Kelly Ln

© Mapsco, Inc.

38
HIDDEN LAKE CRSG
TAYLOR FALLS
SHORELESS DR
SHORELINE DR
SANDY SHORE DR
DEEP WATER
SILENT WATER
VEILED FALLS
WHITE WATER
WATER WAY
38

FIELD CREEK
TRICKLING SPRINGS
WINDLESS WAY
SHORELESS

N
Q
R

DEFENDORF DR
RUGGIO RD
SPARROW TRAIL
KEELI LN
LEIGH LN
MANGAN WAY
STORRS
OTIS LG
L.A. BOETHER LN
NICELLE LN
CELE RD

THE RESERVE AT WEST CREEK

SHALLOW POOL DR
DRY BROOK LOOP
DRY BROOK CRSG

DAWSON CREEK DR
SILENT WATER WAY
ROCKY SHORE LN
BANDICE LN
WHITE WATER
ROLLING WATER DR
SANDY BOTTOM DR
DRY POND DR
HIDDEN PARK DR
BLUE POND DR
TIDDLE LN
WEISS LN

Hidden Lake Park

SILENT HARBOR LOOP
LAKE EDGE WAY
LAKE EDGE CT
MASI LOOP
IRAN DIG LN
DENNIS LN
HIDDEN LAKE CRSG

BRIDGEFARMER BLVD

S
T
U
Y

BECK FARM RD
HAGERTY CROSSING
MISTY HARBOR DR
CALM HARBOR DR
HIDDEN HARBOR DR
HARBOR POINT DR
HARBOR POINT CT

HEISS LN
HESS CT
LYDIA SPRINGS
KEERMIT CT
DEFRITZ FALLS CROSSING

78653

PFLUGERVILLE

V

37
W
X
Z
37

Lake Pflugerville

E PFLUGERVILLE PKWY

178
177
JESSE BOHLS RD
175

MS
MT

CONTINUED ON MAP 438
CONTINUED ON MAP 469
CONTINUED ON MAP 440

SCALE IN MILES
0 1/8 1/4 3/8 1/2

SCALE IN FEET
0 1000 2000 3000

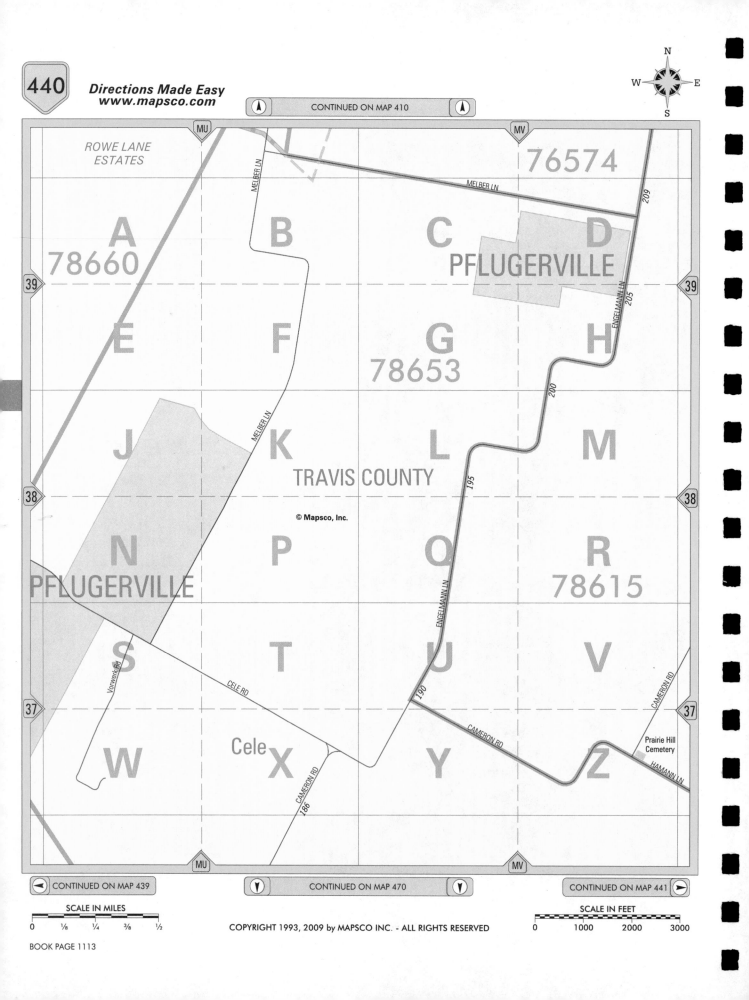

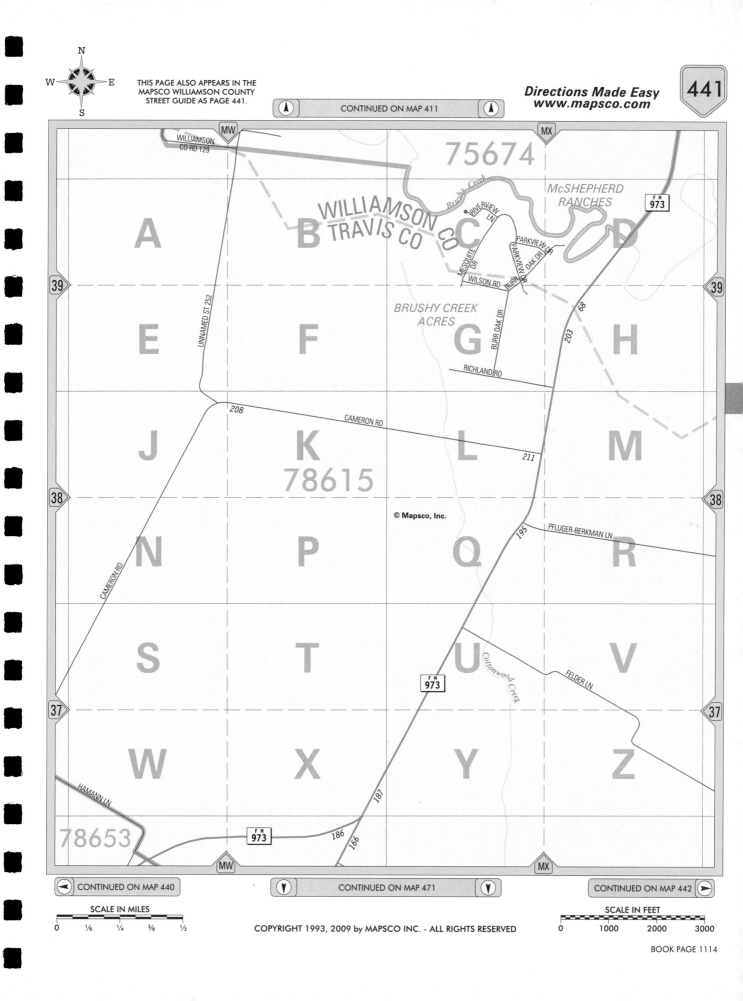

THIS PAGE ALSO APPEARS IN THE
MAPSCO WILLIAMSON COUNTY
STREET GUIDE AS PAGE 441.

Directions Made Easy
www.mapsco.com

CONTINUED ON MAP 411

75674

WILLIAMSON CO RD 129

McSHEPHERD RANCHES

FM 973

WILLIAMSON CO
TRAVIS CO

A   B   C   D

Brushy Creek

RIVERVIEW LN

PARKVIEW DR
PARKVIEW DR
BURR OAK DR
MESQUITE DR

39   39

E   F   G   H

UNNAMED ST 252

WILSON RD

BRUSHY CREEK ACRES

BURR OAK DR

68

203

RICHLAND RD

208

CAMERON RD

211

J   K   L   M

78615

© Mapsco, Inc.

38   38

N   P   Q   R

195

PFLUGER-BERKMAN LN

CAMERON RD

S   T   U   V

FM 973

Cottonwood Creek

FELDER LN

37   37

W   X   Y   Z

HAMANN LN

187

78653

FM 973

186
166

CONTINUED ON MAP 440
CONTINUED ON MAP 471
CONTINUED ON MAP 442

SCALE IN MILES
0   ⅛   ¼   ⅜   ½

SCALE IN FEET
0   1000   2000   3000

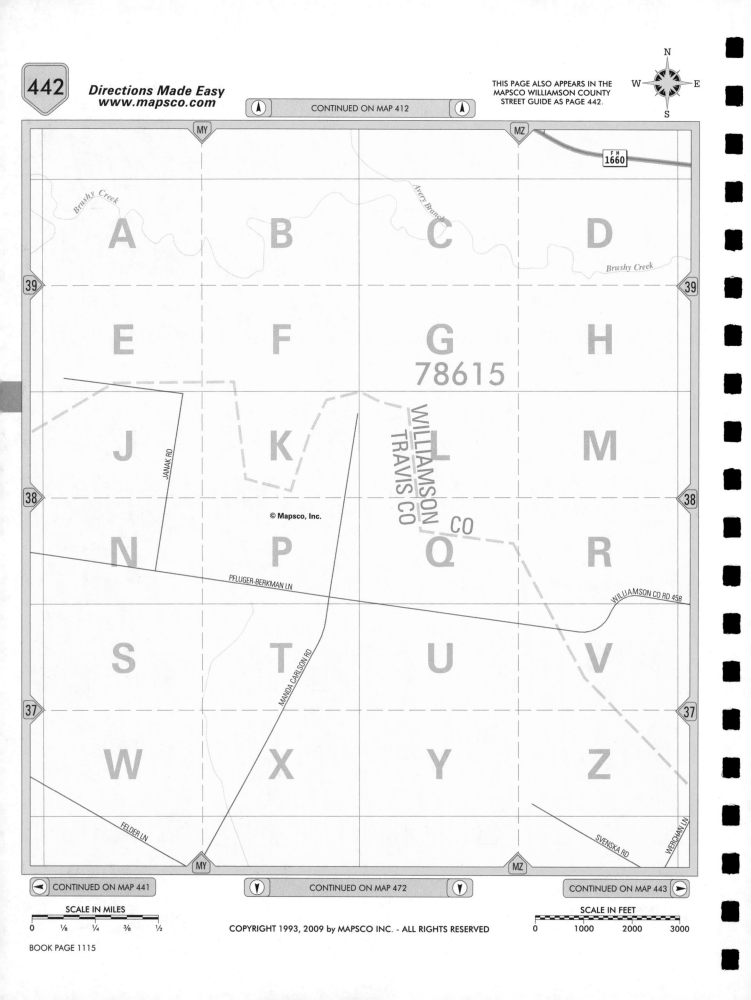

CONTINUED ON MAP 412

N
W E
S

MY

MZ

F M
1660

Brushy Creek

Avery Branch

A B C D

Brushy Creek

39 39

E F G H

78615

J K L M

WILLIAMSON
TRAVIS CO

JANAK RD

38 38

© Mapsco, Inc.

N P Q CO R

PFLUGER-BERKMAN LN

WILLIAMSON CO RD 458

S T U V

MANDA CARLSON RD

37 37

W X Y Z

FELDER LN

SVENSKA RD

WERCHAN LN

MY MZ

CONTINUED ON MAP 441

CONTINUED ON MAP 472

CONTINUED ON MAP 443

SCALE IN MILES

0   1/8   1/4   3/8   1/2

SCALE IN FEET

0   1000   2000   3000

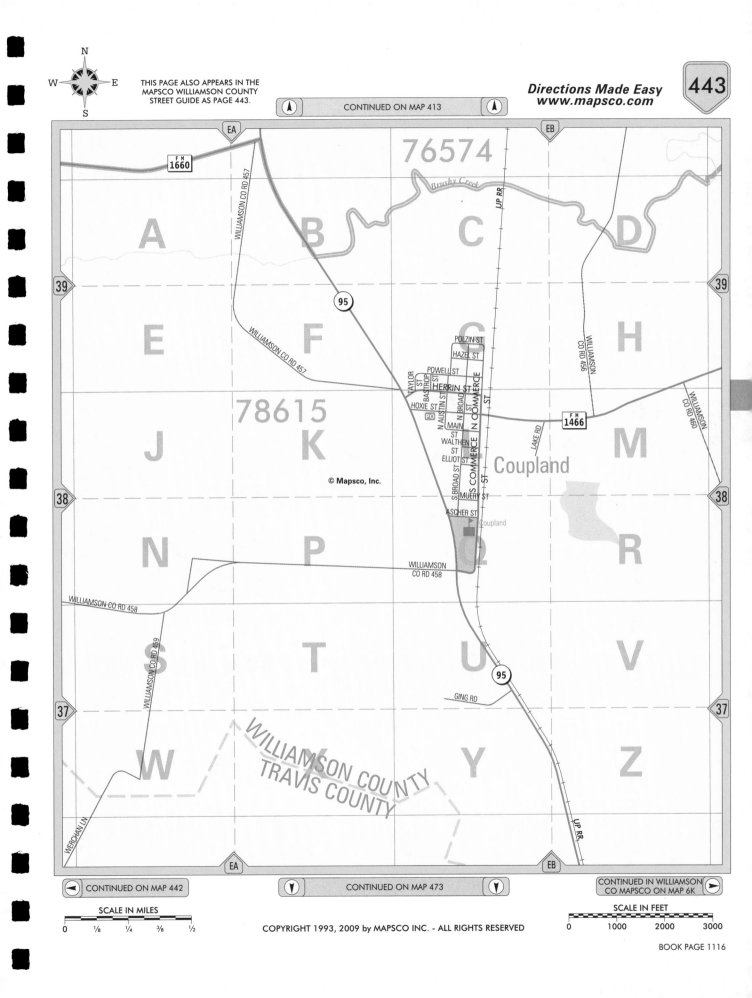

CONTINUED ON MAP 413

443

Directions Made Easy
www.mapsco.com

N
W E
S

THIS PAGE ALSO APPEARS IN THE
MAPSCO WILLIAMSON COUNTY
STREET GUIDE AS PAGE 443.

EA

EB

FM 1660

76574

Brushy Creek

WILLIAMSON CO RD 457

39

39

A

B

C

D

95

E

F

G

H

WILLIAMSON CO RD 456

WILLIAMSON CO RD 457

POLZIN ST

HAZEL ST

POWELL ST

78615

TAYLOR ST

BASTROP ST

HERRIN ST

HOXIE ST

N AUSTIN ST

N BROAD ST

N COMMERCE ST

PO

MAIN ST

FM 1466

LAKE RD

WILLIAMSON CO RD 460

J

K

WALTHEN ST

Coupland

M

© Mapsco, Inc.

ELLIOT ST

S COMMERCE ST

S BROAD ST

38

38

MUERY ST

ASCHER ST

Coupland

N

P

Q

R

WILLIAMSON CO RD 458

WILLIAMSON CO RD 458

WILLIAMSON CO RD 459

S

T

U

V

95

37

37

GING RD

W

WILLIAMSON COUNTY

Y

Z

TRAVIS COUNTY

UP RR

WERCHAN LN

EA

EB

CONTINUED ON MAP 442

CONTINUED ON MAP 473

CONTINUED IN WILLIAMSON
CO MAPSCO ON MAP 6K

SCALE IN MILES

0   ⅛   ¼   ⅜   ½

SCALE IN FEET

0   1000   2000   3000

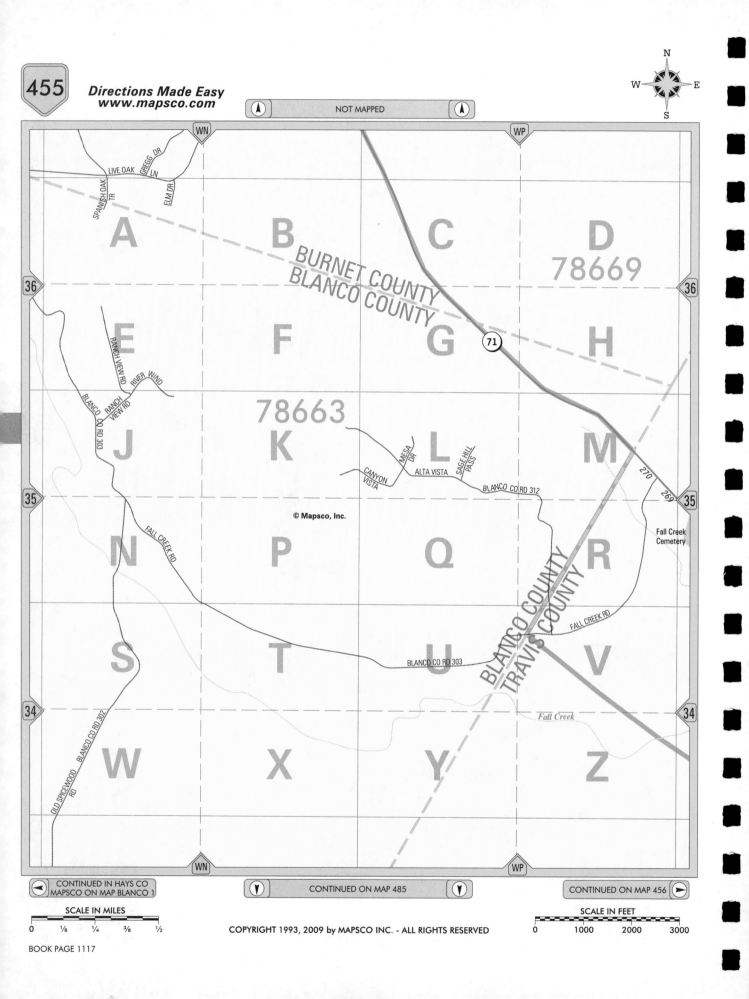

N
W E
S

NOT MAPPED

WN

WP

WN

A

LIVE OAK
GREGG DR
ELM DR
SPANISH OAK TR
LN

B

C

D
78669

BURNET COUNTY
BLANCO COUNTY

36

36

71

E
RANCH VIEW RD
RIVER WIND

F

G

H

BLANCO CO RD 303
RANCH VIEW RD

78663

J

K

L
MESA DR
ALTA VISTA
SAGE HILL PASS
CANYON VISTA
BLANCO CO RD 312

M

270

269

35

35

© Mapsco, Inc.

Fall Creek
Cemetery

FALL CREEK RD

N

P

Q

R

BLANCO COUNTY
TRAVIS COUNTY

Fall Creek Rd

34

S

BLANCO CO RD 302

T

BLANCO CO RD 303

U

V

34

OLD SPICEWOOD RD

Fall Creek

W

X

Y

Z

WN

WP

CONTINUED IN HAYS CO
MAPSCO ON MAP BLANCO 1

CONTINUED ON MAP 485

CONTINUED ON MAP 456

SCALE IN MILES
0   ⅛   ¼   ⅜   ½

SCALE IN FEET
0   1000   2000   3000

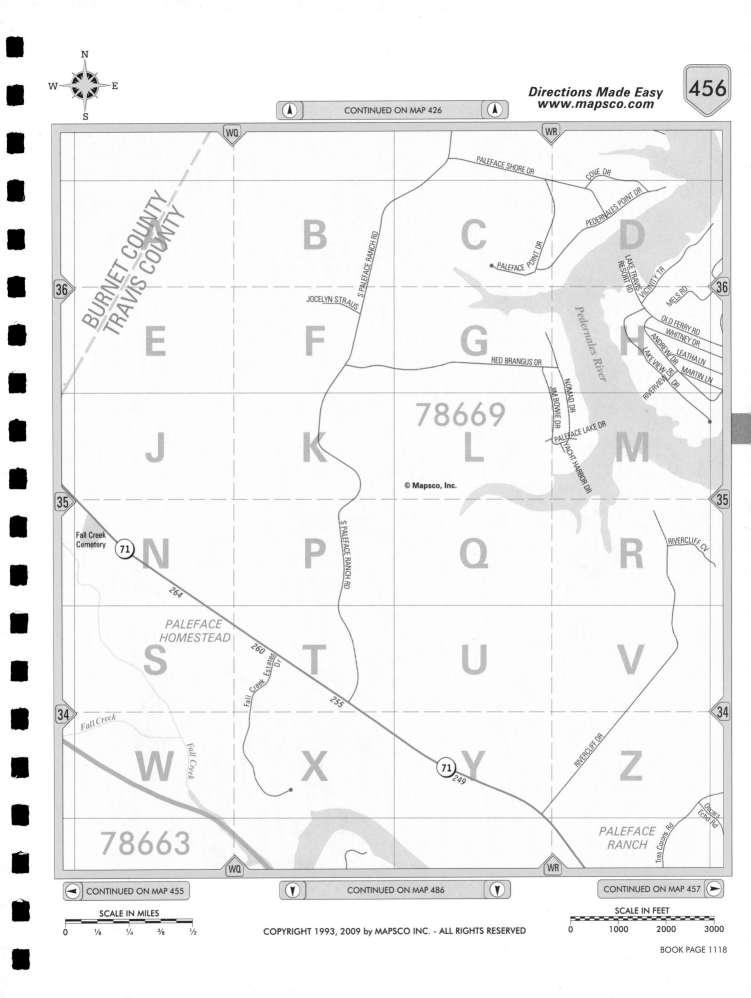

N
W E
S

CONTINUED ON MAP 426

WQ
WR

PALEFACE SHORE DR

COVE DR

PEDERNALES POINT DR

B

C

D

BURNET COUNTY
TRAVIS COUNTY

S PALEFACE RANCH RD

PALEFACE POINT DR

PALEFACE POINT DR

36

LAKE TRAVIS RESORT RD

VICINITY TR

MELS RD

36

JOCELYN STRAUS

E

F

G

Pedernales River

H

OLD FERRY RD

WHITNEY DR

ANDREW DR

LEATHA LN

RED BRANGUS DR

MARTIN LN

LAKE VIEW DR

RIVERVIEW DR

78669

JIM BOWIE DR

NOMAD DR

J

K

L

PALEFACE LAKE DR

YNACHT HARBOR DR

M

© Mapsco, Inc.

35

35

RIVERCLIFF CV

Fall Creek
Cemetery

71

N

P

Q

R

264

PALEFACE
HOMESTEAD

260

S

Fall Creek Estates Dr

T

U

V

255

34

Fall Creek

34

Fall Creek

RIVERCLIFF DR

W

X

71
249

Y

Z

Oscars Echo Rd

78663

PALEFACE
RANCH

Tres Corons Rd

WQ

WR

CONTINUED ON MAP 455

CONTINUED ON MAP 486

CONTINUED ON MAP 457

SCALE IN MILES

0   ⅛   ¼   ⅜   ½

SCALE IN FEET

0   1000   2000   3000

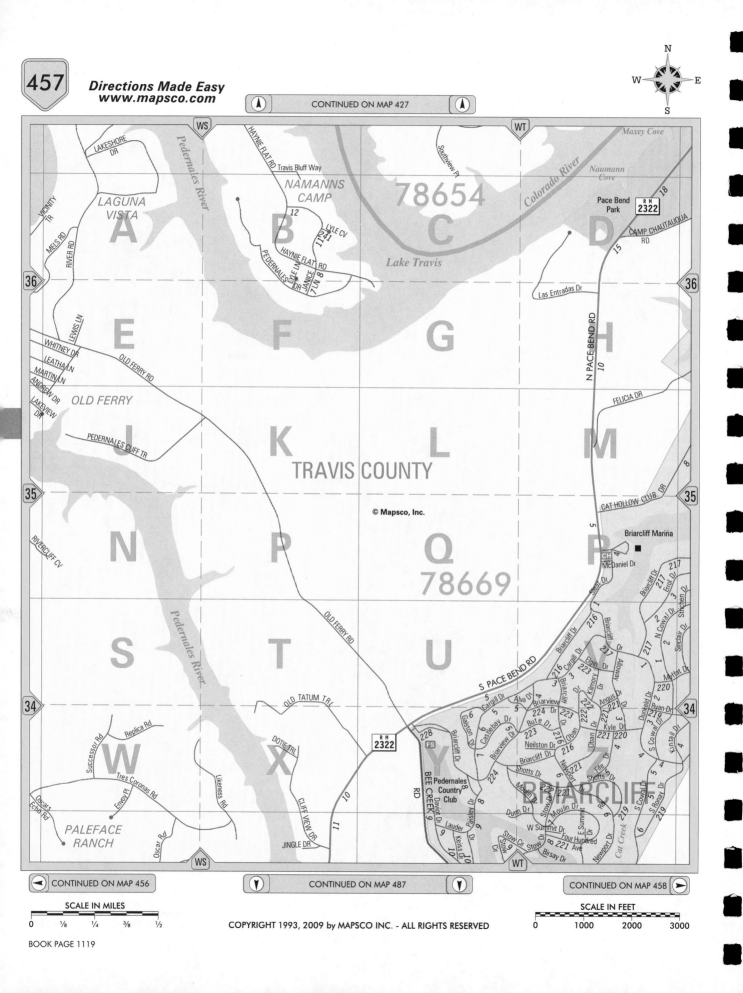

457

Directions Made Easy
www.mapsco.com

CONTINUED ON MAP 427

CONTINUED ON MAP 456

CONTINUED ON MAP 487

CONTINUED ON MAP 458

SCALE IN MILES

0   1/8   1/4   3/8   1/2

COPYRIGHT 1993, 2009 by MAPSCO INC. - ALL RIGHTS RESERVED

SCALE IN FEET

0   1000   2000   3000

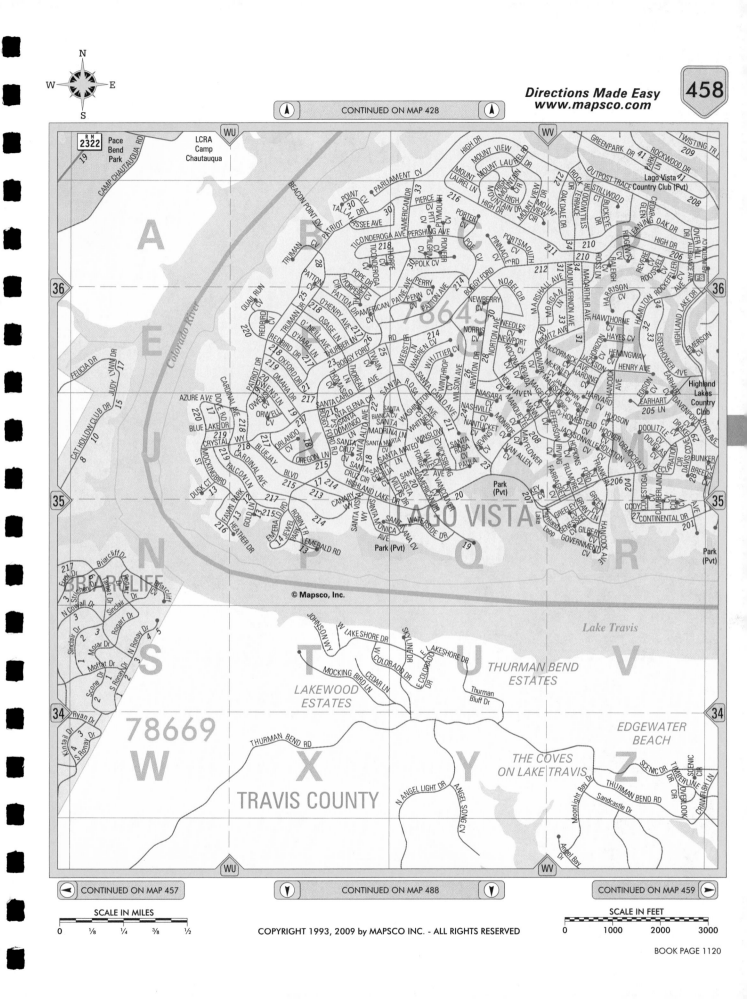

CONTINUED ON MAP 428

LCRA
Camp
Chautauqua

Pace
Bend
Park

RM 2322

LAGO VISTA

78645

Lago Vista
Country Club (Pvt)

Highland
Lakes
Country
Club

Colorado River

Lake Travis

BRIARCLIFF

THURMAN BEND
ESTATES

LAKEWOOD
ESTATES

EDGEWATER
BEACH

THE COVES
ON LAKE TRAVIS

78669

TRAVIS COUNTY

Park (Pvt)

© Mapsco, Inc.

CONTINUED ON MAP 457

CONTINUED ON MAP 488

CONTINUED ON MAP 459

SCALE IN MILES

0   ⅛   ¼   ⅜   ½

SCALE IN FEET

0   1000   2000   3000

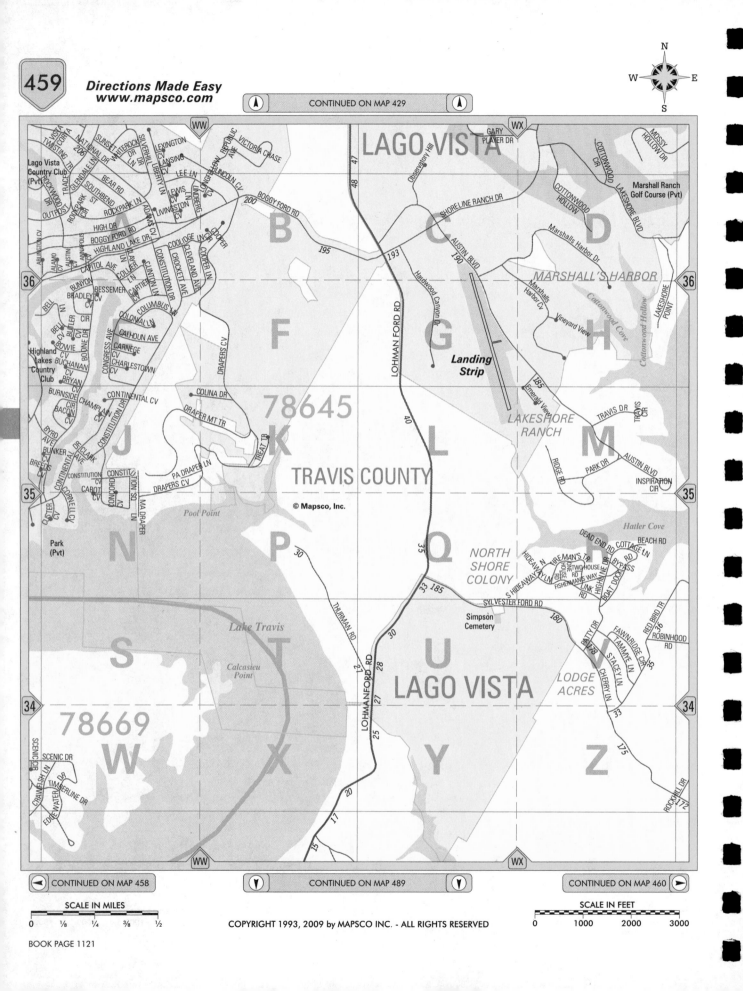

Directions Made Easy
www.mapsco.com

CONTINUED ON MAP 429

N
W   E
S

LAGO VISTA

GARY PLAYER DR

WX

MOSSY HOLLOW DR

COTTONWOOD CIR

Lago Vista Country Club (Pvt)

VISTA CT A
VISTA CT B
TWISTING TR
NATIONAL DR
SUNSET DR
WHITEROCK DR
SILVERHILL CV
LEXINGTON
CV
LANSING
LIBERTY LN
GLENDALE LN
SOUTHBEND
BEAR RD
TRACER
ROCKWOOD DR
OUTPOST
ROCKPARK ST
ROCKPARK LN
ADAMS LN
LONGFELLOW
REPUBLIC AVE
VICTORIA CHASE
LEE LN
LEWIS CV
LINDBERG
CV

206

Shoreline Ranch Dr

Marshall Ranch Golf Course (Pvt)

COTTONWOOD HOLLOW

LAKESHORE BLVD

B

47

C

48

193

D

36

Obsession Hill

Marshalls Harbor Dr

36

BOGGY FORD RD

200

195

AUSTIN BLVD

190

MARSHALL'S HARBOR

ABINGTON CV
ALAMO CV
AUSTIN CV
ANNAPOLIS
HIGH DR
BOGGY FORD RD
HIGHLAND LAKE DR
CAPITOL AVE
COOLIDGE LN
COLLIER LN
CLINTON CV
CONSTITUTION DR
CROCKETT AVE
CLEVELAND AVE
COOPER CV
CROPER
COOPER LN

BUNYON
BRADLEY CV
BELL N1
BELL CV
BESSEMER
CARTIER LN
COLUMBUS LN

F

LOHMAN FORD RD

HARDWOOD CANYON DR

G

Marshalls Harbor Cv
Vineyard View

Cottonwood Cove

LAKESHORE POINT

Cottonwood Hollow

BUTLER CV
BOWIE
BOONE DR
COLONIAL LN
CALHOUN AVE
CARNEGE
CONGRESS AVE
CHARLESTOWN
CV

DRAPERS CV

H

185

Emerald View

TRAVIS DR
TRAVIS CIR

Highland Lakes Country Club

BUCHANAN CV
BRYAN

BURNSIDE
CHAMPLAIN CV
CIR
BACON CV

CONTINENTAL CV

COLINA DR

78645

Landing Strip

LAKESHORE RANCH

M

PARK DR

AUSTIN BLVD

BYRD AVE
BUNKER AVE
BREEDS CV
CUSTER CV
CONSTITUTION DR CLARK
CONTINENTAL DR
CONSTITUTION
CAROT CV
CORNELL CY

DRAPER MT TR

J

TREAT TR

K

40

L

RIDGE RD

INSPIRATION CIR

35

35

CONSTIT
CONCORD CV
CONSTITUTION SQ LN
MA DRAPER
PA DRAPER LN
DRAPERS CV

© Mapsco, Inc.

TRAVIS COUNTY

Pool Point

N

P

30

35

Q

185

33

North Shore Colony

Hatler Cove

BEACH RD

DEAD END RD
COTTAGE LN
BYPASS
HIDEAWAY DR
FIRE MAN'S TR
LONE HOUSE RD
TWO HOUSE RD
FISHERMANS WAY
BOAT DOCK
LINK RD
S HIDEAWAY LN

Park (Pvt)

Lake Travis

SYLVESTER FORD RD

THURMAN RD

180

Simpson Cemetery

RED BIRD TR
36
ROBINHOOD RD

S

Calcasieu Point

T

30

U

LAGO VISTA

35

LODGE ACRES

FAWNRIDGE CIR
TAMMYE LN
STACEY LN
CHERRY LN
178
KATY DR

34

27
28
21

LOHMANFORD RD

25

Y

34

78669

W

X

20

17

15

SCENIC CIR
SCENIC DR
CRAWFISH LN
TIMBERLINE DR
EDGEWATER

Z

175

ROCKHILL DR
172

CONTINUED ON MAP 458
CONTINUED ON MAP 489
CONTINUED ON MAP 460

WW

WX

SCALE IN MILES

0   ⅛   ¼   ⅜   ½

SCALE IN FEET

0   1000   2000   3000

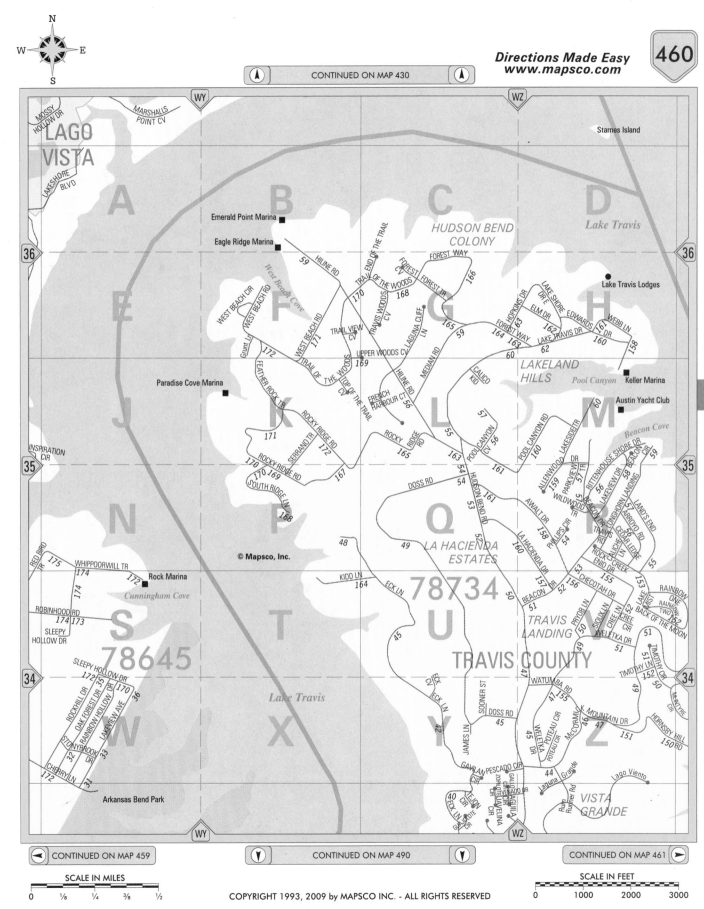

CONTINUED ON MAP 430

N
W E
S

LAGO VISTA

MOSSY HOLLOW DR
MARSHALLS POINT CV
LAKESHORE BLVD

Starnes Island

A B C D

HUDSON BEND COLONY

Lake Travis

Emerald Point Marina
Eagle Ridge Marina

Lake Travis Lodges

36 36

West Beach Cove

HILINE RD
59
TRAIL END OF THE TRAIL
170
168
FOREST CV
FOREST TR
FOREST WAY
166

E F G H

WEST BEACH CIR
WEST BEACH RD
WEST BEACH RD
Grant Ln
171
TRAIL VIEW CV
TRAVIS WOODS CV
LAGUNA CLIFF
MEDIAN RD
165
59
HOPKINS DR
LAKE SHORE DR E
63
ELM DR
162
FOREST WAY
164
163
EDWARDS
LAKE TRAVIS DR
62
60
WEBB LN
161
DR
160
158

172
TRAIL OF THE WOODS CV
UPPER WOODS CV
169
FEATHER ROCK TR
HILINE RD
FRENCH HARBOUR CT
56

J K L M

Paradise Cove Marina

CALICO KID
57
55
163
54
POOL CANYON CV
56
161
160

LAKELAND HILLS
Pool Canyon
Keller Marina
Austin Yacht Club

Beacon Cove

M

ROCKY RIDGE RD
SERRANO TR
171
172
ROCKY RIDGE RD
170 169
ROCKY RIDGE RD
167
SOUTH RIDGE LN
168
ROCKY RIDGE RD
165

INSPIRATION CIR
35 35

DOSS RD
54
HUDSON BEND RD
53

ALLENWOOD DR
159
PARKVIEW DR
57 TR
WILDWOOD
LAKESIDE TR
RITTENHOUSE SHORE DR
56
58
BEACON DR
LONGHORN LANDING
57
59
ARROYO RD
CEDAR LEDGE
LAND'S END
55

N P Q R

RED BIRD TR
175
WHIPPOORWILL TR
174
174
172
Rock Marina
Cunningham Cove

48
49
LA HACIENDA ESTATES
52
160
LA HACIENDA DR
158
PHILLIPS CIR
54
AWALT DR
161
157
156
TRAVIS RD
ROCK CREEK
153
ENID DR
155
CHECOTAH DR

ROBINHOOD RD
174 173
SLEEPY HOLLOW DR

S 78645
KIDD LN
164
ECK LN
78734
50
BEACON DR
51
52
PRYOR LN
SIOUX LN
CREEL CIR
CREE
WELETKA DR
51
RAINBOW ONE
RAINBOW TWO 152
BACK OF THE MOON
152
51

SLEEPY HOLLOW DR
172
170
36
ROCKHILL DR
35
OAK FOREST DR
RAINBOW HOLLOW DR
LAKEVIEW AVE
STONYBROOK DR
32
33
CHERRY LN
172
31

T U
TRAVIS LANDING
TRAVIS COUNTY
47
49
TIMOTHY LN
152
50
51 49
MCINTYRE
34 34

ECK LN
45
ECK CV
ECK LN
42
JAMES LN
SOONER ST
DOSS RD
45
WATUMBA RD
47
55
POTEAU CIR
WELETKA DR
45
POTEAU CIR
MCCORMICK MOUNTAIN DR
46
47
151
HORNSBY HILL
150 RD

W X Y Z

Lake Travis

Arkansas Bend Park

GAVILAN CIR
PESCADO CIR
44
GALLO
AGUILA
VENADO DR
GREBE CIR
ZOPILOTE
LAGUNA GRANDE
Lago Viento
Rumer Rd

VISTA GRANDE

LEON CIR
40
ECK LN
COYOTE CIR
LAVELINA CIR

© Mapsco, Inc.

SCALE IN MILES
0 ⅛ ¼ ⅜ ½

COPYRIGHT 1993, 2009 by MAPSCO INC. - ALL RIGHTS RESERVED

SCALE IN FEET
0 1000 2000 3000

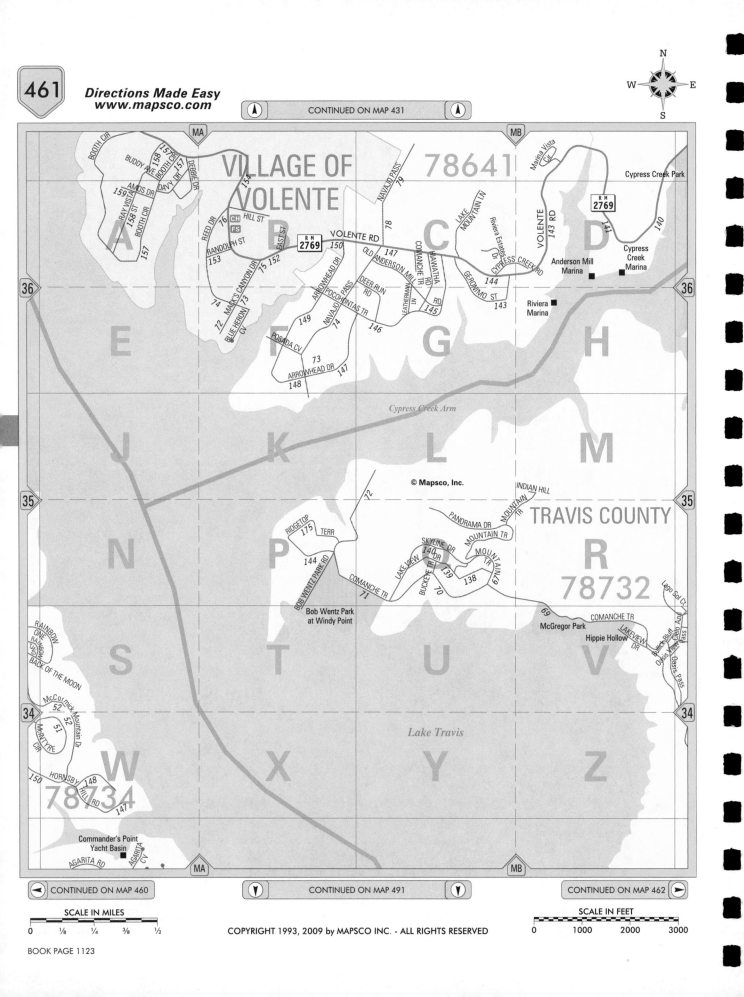

Directions Made Easy
www.mapsco.com

N
W E
S

CONTINUED ON MAP 431

MA

MB

VILLAGE OF VOLENTE

78641

Marina Vista Cir

Cypress Creek Park

RM 2769

BOOTH CIR

BUDDY AVE 158

158 BOOTH CIR 157

DAVY DR 157 DEBBIE DR

154

AMOS DR

RAY VISTA DR 159

158 ST

BOOTH CIR 157

A

HILL ST

CH FS

REED DR 76

RANDOLPH ST

EAST ST

RM 2769 150

NAVAJO PASS 79

78

VOLENTE RD 147

B

Lake Mountain Ln

Riviera Estates Dr

VOLENTE 143 RD

C

141

D

140

Cypress Creek Marina

Anderson Mill Marina

36

153

75 152

74 MARK'S CANYON DR 73

72

BLUE HERON CV

ARROWHEAD DR

POCOHONTAS TR

NAVAJO PASS

OLD ANDERSON MILL

DEER RUN RD

COMANCHE TR

LEATHERMAN LN

HIAWATHA RD 145

RD 143

GERONIMO ST

CYPRESS CREEK RD 144

Riviera Marina

36

E

149

74

146

POSADA CV

73

ARROWHEAD DR 147

148

F

G

H

Cypress Creek Arm

J

K

L

M

© Mapsco, Inc.

INDIAN HILL

72

35

RIDGETOP 175

TERR

144

BOB WENTZ PARK RD

Panorama Dr

Mountain Tr

SKYLINE DR

LAKE VIEW

140 DR

BUCKEYE TR

139

70

138

MOUNTAIN TR

TRAVIS COUNTY

R

78732

Lago Sol Cv

35

N

P

COMANCHE TR 71

Bob Wentz Park at Windy Point

69

McGregor Park

Hippie Hollow

COMANCHE TR

LAKEVIEW DR

Cielo Azul Pass

Oasis View

Oasis Pass

Bunica Bluff

S

T

U

V

34

RAINBOW ONE

RAINBOW

BACK OF THE MOON

McCormick Mountain Dr

52

52

MCINTYRE CIR

51

150

HORNSBY 148

HILL RD

141

Lake Travis

34

W

78734

X

Y

Z

Commander's Point Yacht Basin

AGARITA RD

AGARITA CV

MA

MB

CONTINUED ON MAP 460
CONTINUED ON MAP 491
CONTINUED ON MAP 462

SCALE IN MILES

0 1/8 1/4 3/8 1/2

SCALE IN FEET

0 1000 2000 3000

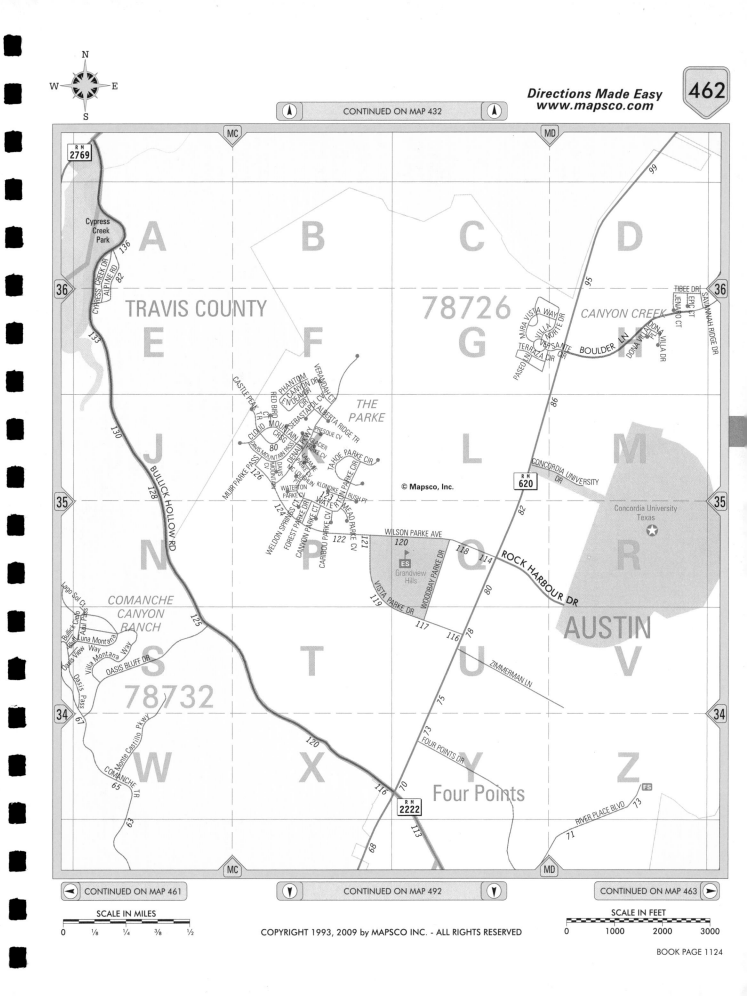

CONTINUED ON MAP 432

N
W E
S

MC
MD

RM 2769

Cypress
Creek
Park

A
B
C
D

36

CYPRESS CREEK DR
ALPINE RD
136
82

TIBEE DR
JENARO CT
EPIC CT
SAVANNAH RIDGE DR

36

TRAVIS COUNTY

78726

NURA VISTA WAY
VILLA NORTE DR
VERSANTE DR
TERRAZA CIR
PASEO LN
DONA VILLA CT
DONA VILLA DR

CANYON CREEK

95

E
F
G
H

133

BOULDER LN

86

PHANTOM CANYON DR
VERANDAH CT
VIDEMOR CIR
CASTLE PEAK TR
RED BIRD CT
SEBASTAPOL
ALBERTA RIDGE TR

THE
PARKE

130

CLOUD MOUNTAIN CRG
DENALI PKWY
PRESQUE CV
GLACIER PARKE CV
TAHOE PARKE CIR

J
K
L
M

DAVIS MOUNTAIN PASS
MUIR PARKE PASS
MOONJAK CV
MCLOUGHLIN PARKE CT
KLONDIKE CV
RUSH PT
TAHOE PARKE CIR

80
126

35

BULLICK HOLLOW RD
128

WATERTON PARKE CV
WELDON SPRINGS CT
FOREST PARKE DR
CANYON PARKE CT
WATERTON PARKE CV
CARIBOU PARKE CV
MEAD PARKE CV

RM 620

CONCORDIA UNIVERSITY DR

82

Concordia University
Texas

35

© Mapsco, Inc.

124

122

121

WILSON PARKE AVE
120

ES
Grandview
Hills

118

114

ROCK HARBOUR DR

N
P
Q
R

COMANCHE
CANYON
RANCH

125

VISTA PARKE DR

119

117

116

80

78

AUSTIN

Lago Sol Ct
Bullick Cielo
Luna Montana
Oasis View Way
Villa Montana Way
OASIS BLUFF DR
Oasis Pass

S
T
U
V

78732

34

67

Monte Castillo Pkwy

120

COMANCHE TR
65

116

70

ZIMMERMAN LN

75

73

FOUR POINTS DR

34

W
X
Y
Z

63

RM 2222

113

Four Points

69

FS

RIVER PLACE BLVD
73
71

MC
MD

CONTINUED ON MAP 461
CONTINUED ON MAP 492
CONTINUED ON MAP 463

SCALE IN MILES
0 1/8 1/4 3/8 1/2

SCALE IN FEET
0 1000 2000 3000

BOOK PAGE 1124

CONTINUED ON MAP 433

N
W E
S

Trailhead Park

Pickfair Park

SPICEWOOD AT BALCONES VILLAGE

SPICEWOOD ESTATES

Balcones Country Club (Pvt)

Canyon Creek

Trailhead Reserve

SPICEWOOD AT BULL CREEK

AUSTIN
J
78726

© Mapsco, Inc.

Northwest Balcones Park

Bull Creek Greenbelt Upper

Concordia University Texas

Upper Bull Creek Preserve

Oak Grove Cemetery

78750
TRAVIS COUNTY

CANYON MESA

78759

St Edwards Park

Bull Creek

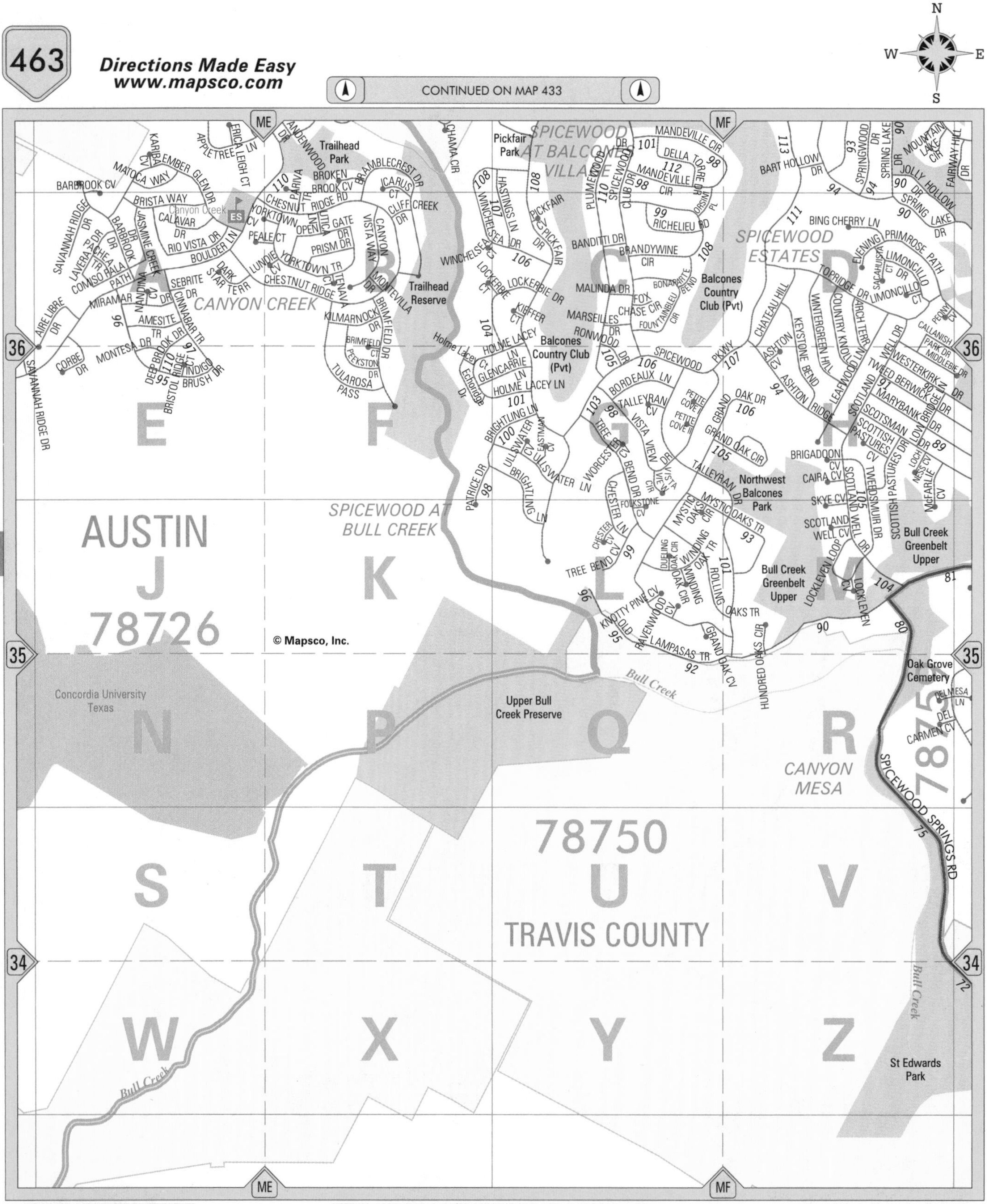

CONTINUED ON MAP 462
CONTINUED ON MAP 493
CONTINUED ON MAP 464

SCALE IN MILES
0   1/8   1/4   3/8   1/2

SCALE IN FEET
0   1000   2000   3000

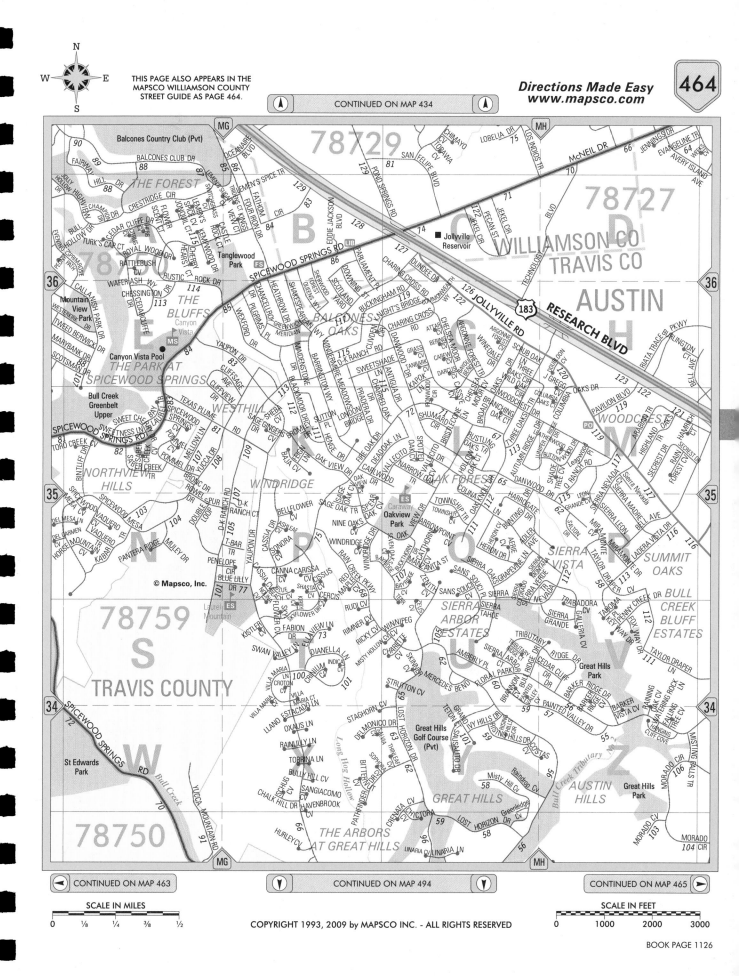

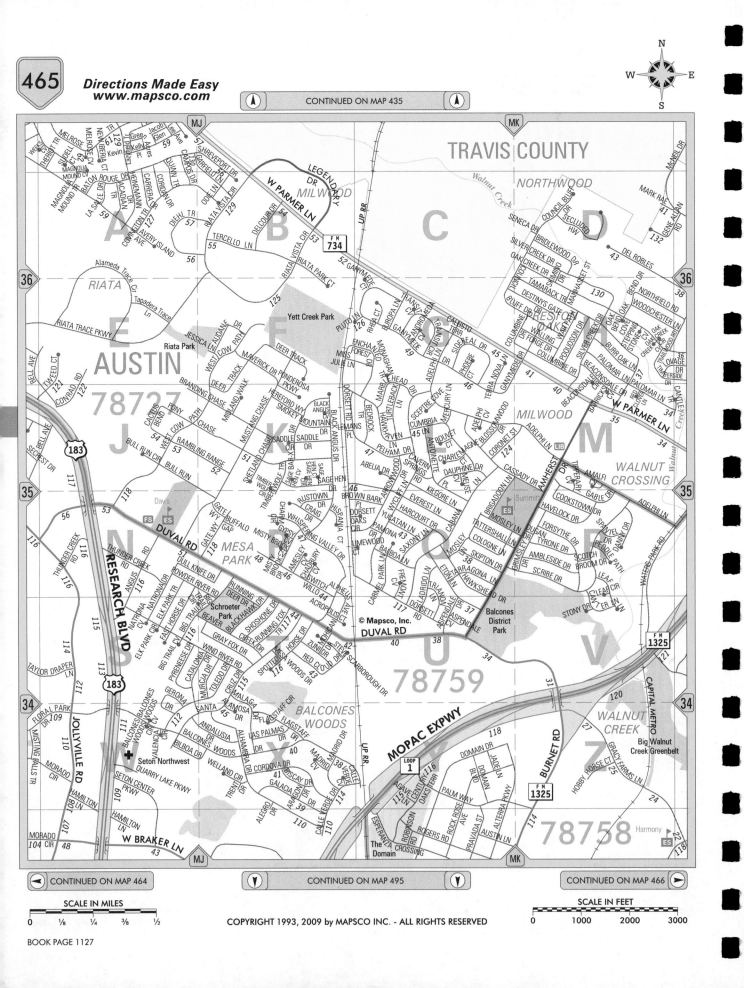

CONTINUED ON MAP 435

TRAVIS COUNTY

NORTHWOOD

AUSTIN
78727

RIATA

Yett Creek Park

MILWOOD

W PARMER LN

WALNUT
CROSSING

MESA
PARK

RESEARCH BLVD

DUVAL RD

DUVAL RD

© Mapsco, Inc.

Balcones
District
Park

78759

BALCONES
WOODS

MOPAC EXPWY

BURNET RD

WALNUT
CREEK

Big Walnut
Creek Greenbelt

78758

The
Domain

W BRAKER LN

◄ CONTINUED ON MAP 464   ▼ CONTINUED ON MAP 495   ▼   CONTINUED ON MAP 466 ►

SCALE IN MILES
0   ⅛   ¼   ⅜   ½

SCALE IN FEET
0   1000   2000   3000

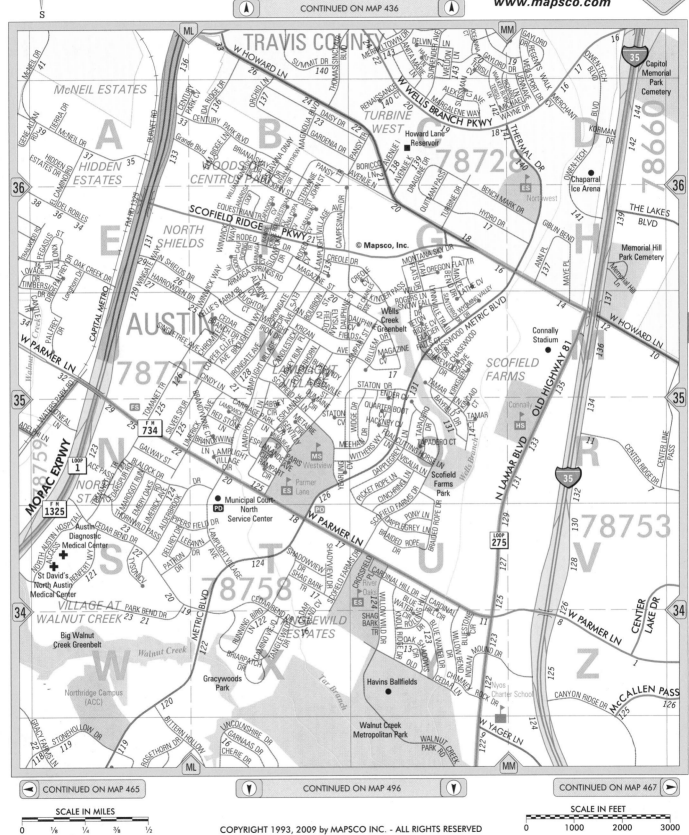

CONTINUED ON MAP 436

TRAVIS COUNTY

AUSTIN

78728
78727
78753
78758
78759
78660

McNEIL ESTATES

HIDDEN ESTATES

WOODS OF CENTRUM PARK

NORTH SHIELDS

SCOFIELD RIDGE PKWY

Wells Creek Greenbelt

SCOFIELD FARMS

Capitol Memorial Park Cemetery

Chaparral Ice Arena

Memorial Hill Park Cemetery

Connally Stadium

Scofield Farms Park

MOPAC EXPWY

NORTH ST

VILLAGE AT WALNUT CREEK

Big Walnut Creek Greenbelt

Gracywoods Park

Northridge Campus (ACC)

Walnut Creek

RIDGEWILD ESTATES

Havins Ballfields

Walnut Creek Metropolitan Park

Austin Diagnostic Medical Center

St David's North Austin Medical Center

North Austin Hospital

Municipal Court - North Service Center

Westview

Parmer Lane

River Oaks

Nyos Charter School

Walnut Park Rd

SCALE IN MILES

0   ⅛   ¼   ⅜   ½

SCALE IN FEET

0   1000   2000   3000

© Mapsco, Inc.

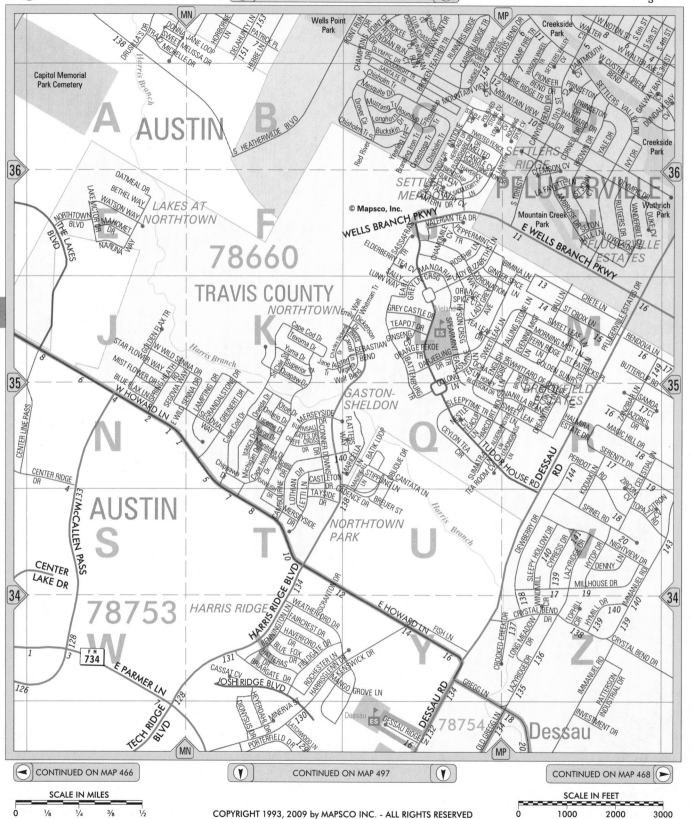

CONTINUED ON MAP 437

AUSTIN

PFLUGERVILLE

78660

TRAVIS COUNTY

NORTHTOWN

© Mapsco, Inc.

Capitol Memorial Park Cemetery

LAKES AT NORTHTOWN

Harris Branch

WELLS BRANCH PKWY

E WELLS BRANCH PKWY

GASTON-SHELDON

AUSTIN

78753

HARRIS RIDGE

NORTHTOWN PARK

HARRIS RIDGE BLVD

E HOWARD LN

DESSAU RD

78754

Dessau

E PARMER LN

TECH RIDGE BLVD

FM 734

JOSH RIDGE BLVD

BRECKFIELD ESTATES

CONTINUED ON MAP 466

CONTINUED ON MAP 497

CONTINUED ON MAP 468

SCALE IN MILES

0   ⅛   ¼   ⅜   ½

SCALE IN FEET

0   1000   2000   3000

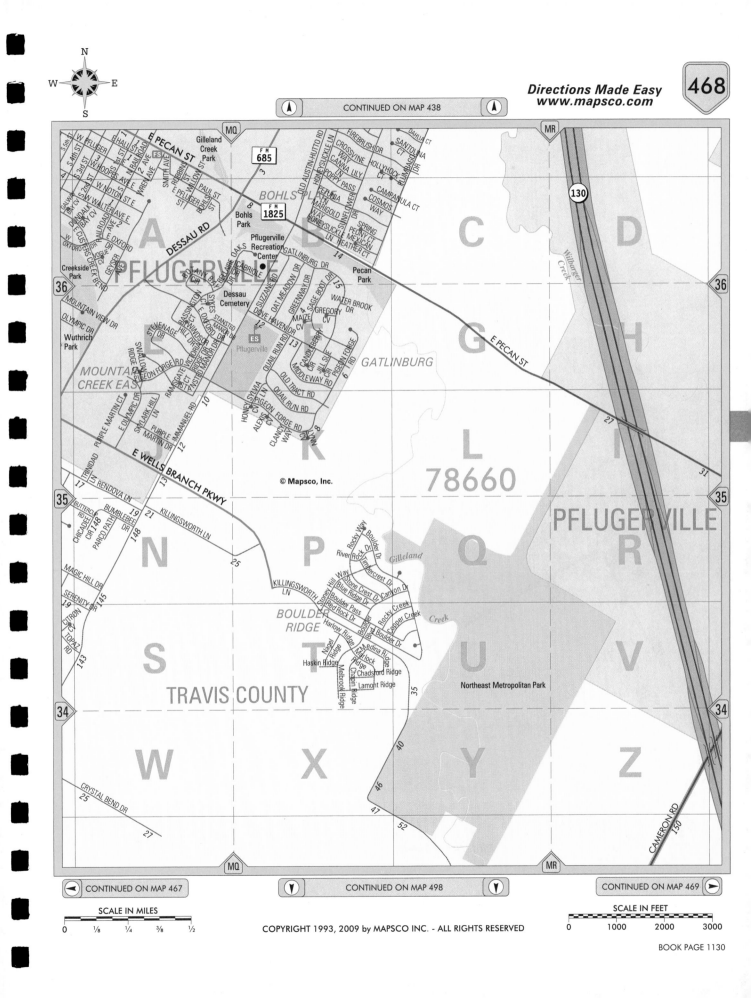

CONTINUED ON MAP 438

PFLUGERVILLE

BOHLS PL

C

D

36

130

E PECAN ST

Gilleland Creek Park

Bohls Park

Pflugerville Recreation Center

Dessau Cemetery

ES Pflugerville

Pecan Park

Water Brook

GATLINBURG

G

H

36

Wilbarger Creek

35

Creekside Park

Wuthrich Park

MOUNTAIN CREEK EAST

© Mapsco, Inc.

L

78660

E WELLS BRANCH PKWY

N

P

Q

PFLUGERVILLE

R

KILLINGSWORTH LN

BOULDER RIDGE

Gilleland

Creek

U

Northeast Metropolitan Park

V

S

T

TRAVIS COUNTY

W

X

Y

Z

CAMERON RD

34

34

150

CONTINUED ON MAP 467

CONTINUED ON MAP 498

CONTINUED ON MAP 469

SCALE IN MILES

0   ⅛   ¼   ⅜   ½

SCALE IN FEET

0   1000   2000   3000

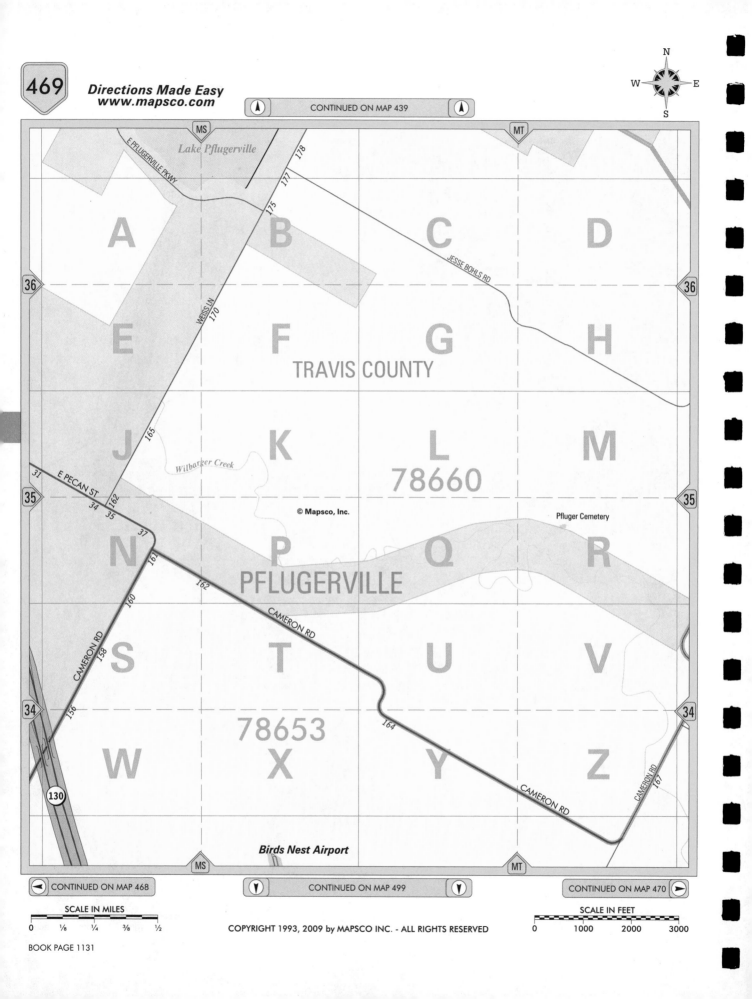

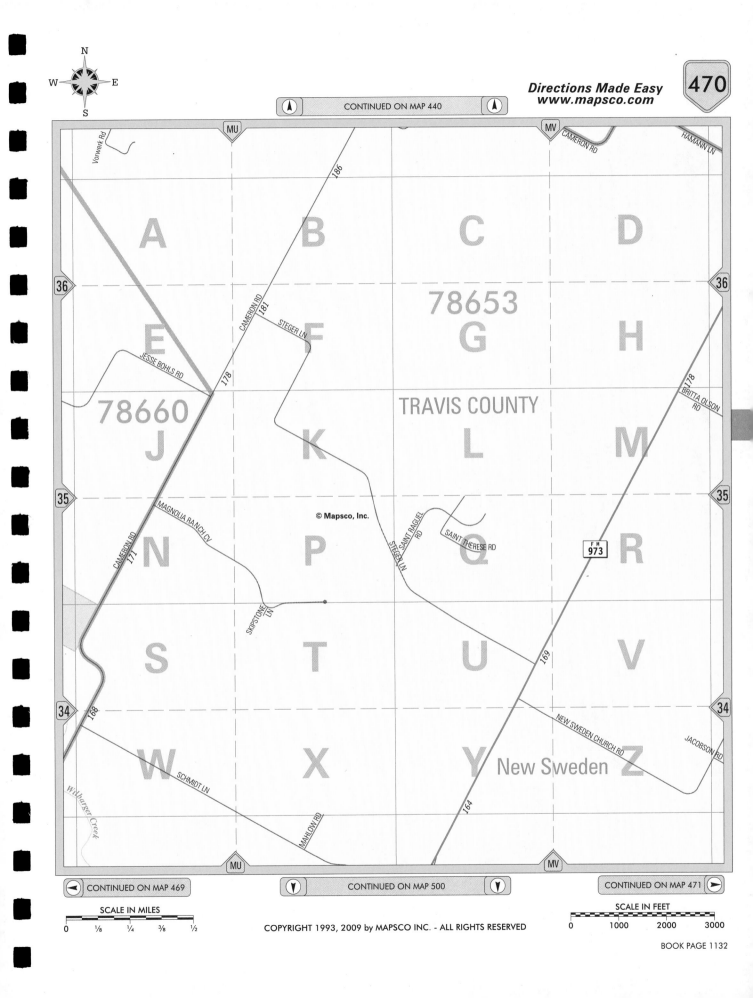

CONTINUED ON MAP 440

MU

MV

CAMERON RD

HAMANN LN

Vorwerk Rd

186

A

B

C

D

36

36

CAMERON RD

STEGER LN

E

F

G

H

181

JESSE BOHLS RD

178

178

BRITTA OLSON RD

78660

TRAVIS COUNTY

78653

J

K

L

M

© Mapsco, Inc.

35

35

SAINT RAGUEL RD

MAGNOLIA RANCH CV

SAINT THERESE RD

FM 973

CAMERON RD

171

N

P

STEGER LN

Q

R

SKIPSTONE LN

169

S

T

U

V

34

168

34

NEW SWEDEN CHURCH RD

JACOBSON RD

W

SCHMIDT LN

X

Y

New Sweden

Z

Wilbarger Creek

MAHLOW RD

164

MU

MV

CONTINUED ON MAP 469

CONTINUED ON MAP 500

CONTINUED ON MAP 471

SCALE IN MILES

0   1/8   1/4   3/8   1/2

SCALE IN FEET

0   1000   2000   3000

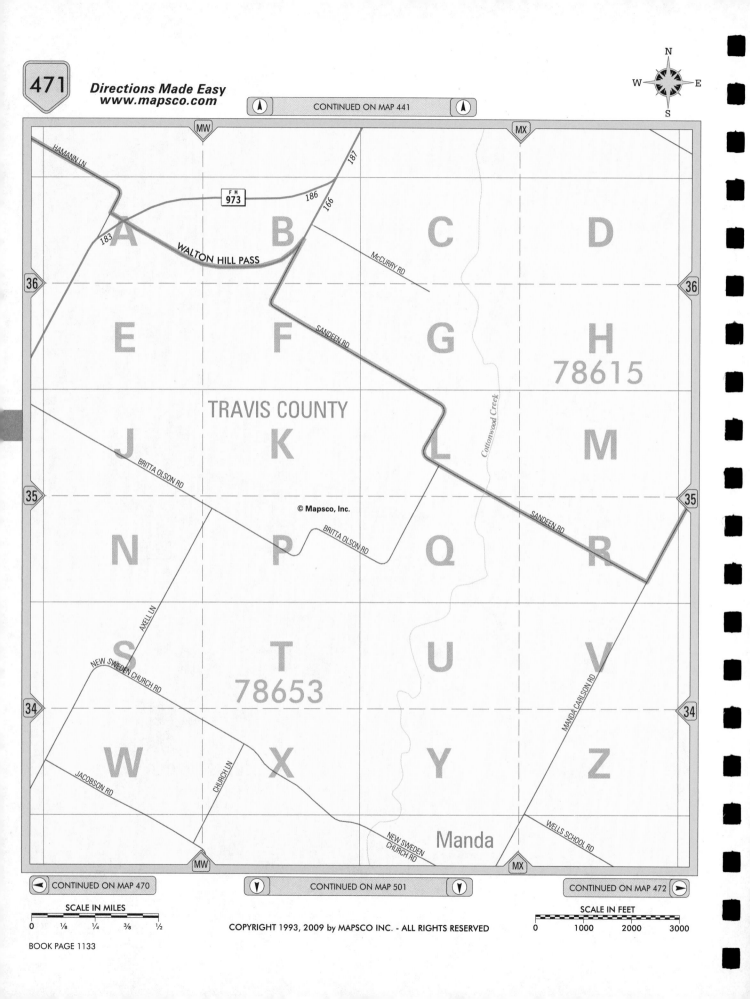

471

Directions Made Easy
www.mapsco.com

CONTINUED ON MAP 441

N
W · E
S

HAMANN LN

FM 973

183

WALTON HILL PASS

186
187
166

McCURRY RD

A
B
C
D

36
36

SANDEEN RD

E
F
G
H
78615

Cottonwood Creek

TRAVIS COUNTY

J
K
L
M

BRITTA OLSON RD

35
35

© Mapsco, Inc.

SANDEEN RD

BRITTA OLSON RD

N
P
Q
R

AXELL LN

NEW SWEDEN CHURCH RD

MANDA CARLSON RD

S
T
78653
U
V

34
34

W
X
Y
Z

JACOBSON RD

CHURCH LN

NEW SWEDEN CHURCH RD

WELLS SCHOOL RD

Manda

CONTINUED ON MAP 470
CONTINUED ON MAP 501
CONTINUED ON MAP 472

SCALE IN MILES

0   1/8   1/4   3/8   1/2

SCALE IN FEET

0   1000   2000   3000

BOOK PAGE 1133

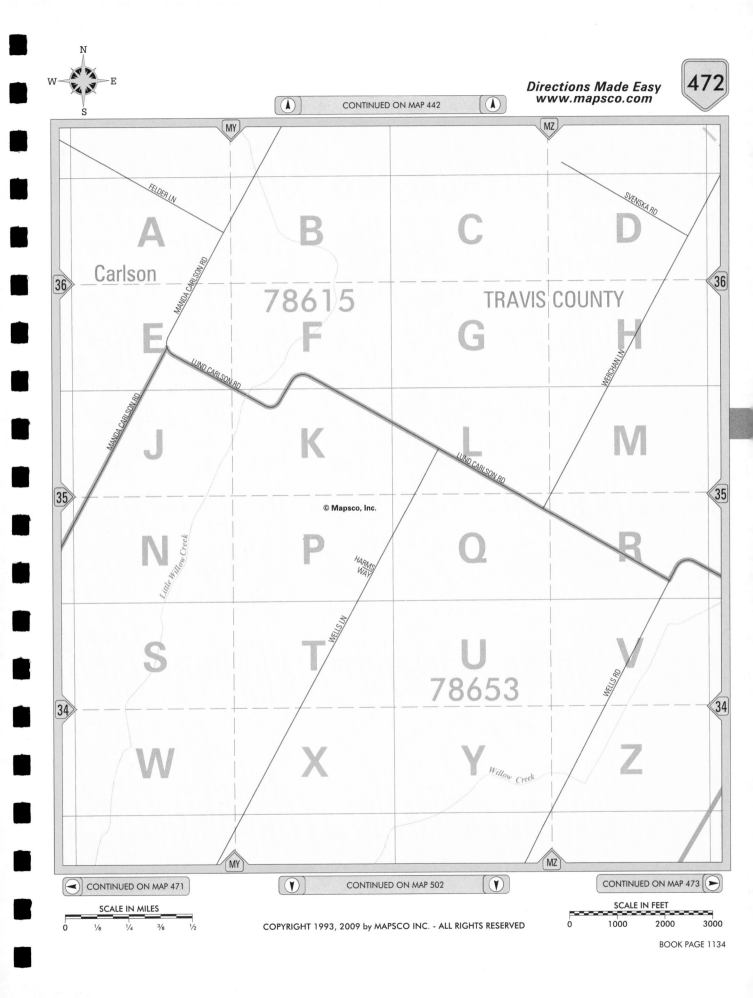

473

Directions Made Easy
www.mapsco.com

CONTINUED ON MAP 443

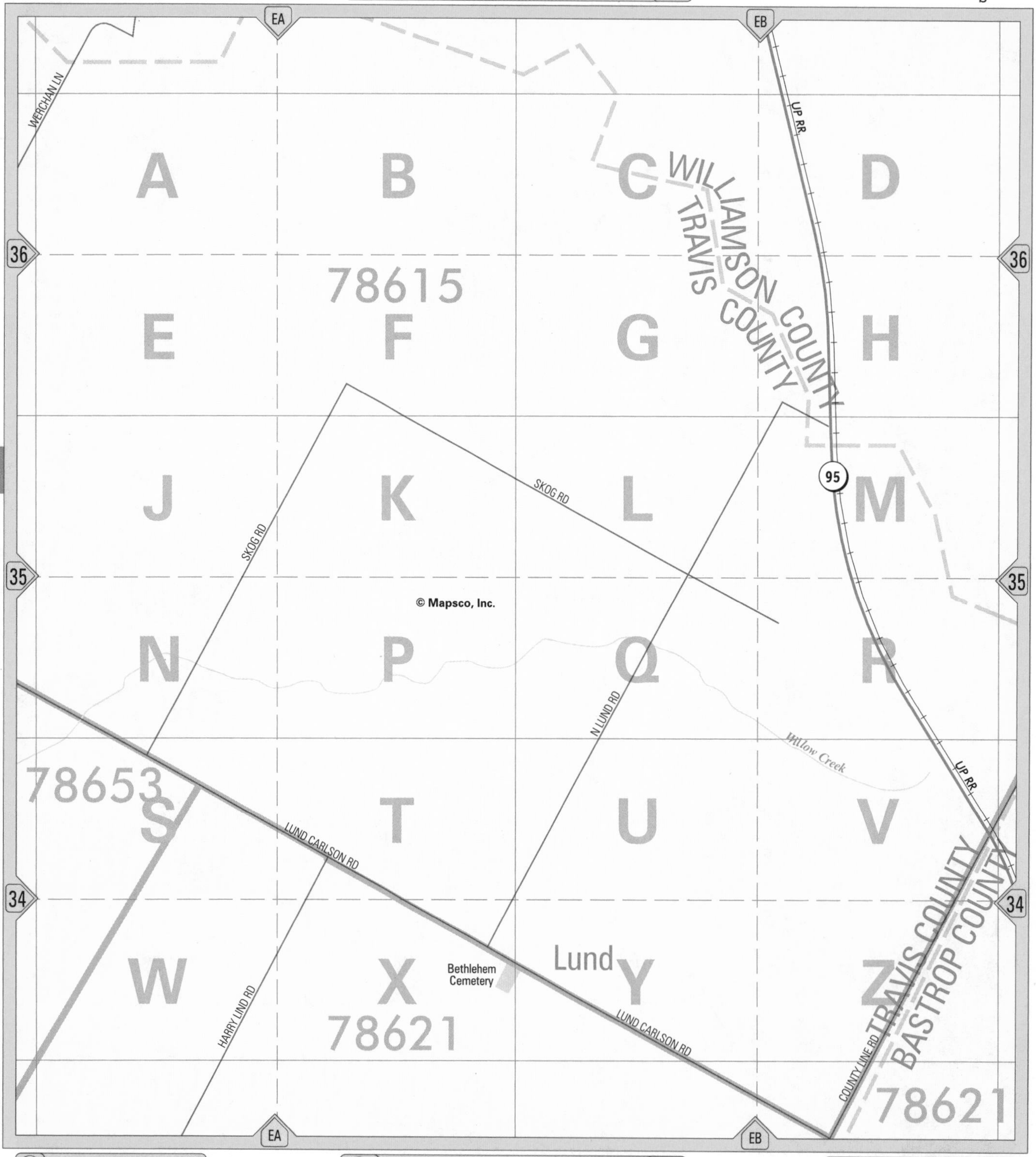

N
W   E
S

EA   EB

A   B   C   D

WILLIAMSON COUNTY
TRAVIS COUNTY

UP RR

36   36

78615

E   F   G   H

SKOG RD

95

J   K   L   M

SKOG RD

35   35

© Mapsco, Inc.

N   P   Q   R

N LUND RD

Willow Creek

UP RR

78653

S   T   U   V

LUND CARLSON RD

34   34

TRAVIS COUNTY
BASTROP COUNTY

W   X   Y   Z

Lund

Bethlehem
Cemetery

78621

HARRY LIND RD

LUND CARLSON RD

COUNTY LINE RD

78621

EA   EB

CONTINUED ON MAP 472

CONTINUED ON MAP 503

CONTINUED ON MAP 474

SCALE IN MILES

0   1/8   1/4   3/8   1/2

SCALE IN FEET

0   1000   2000   3000

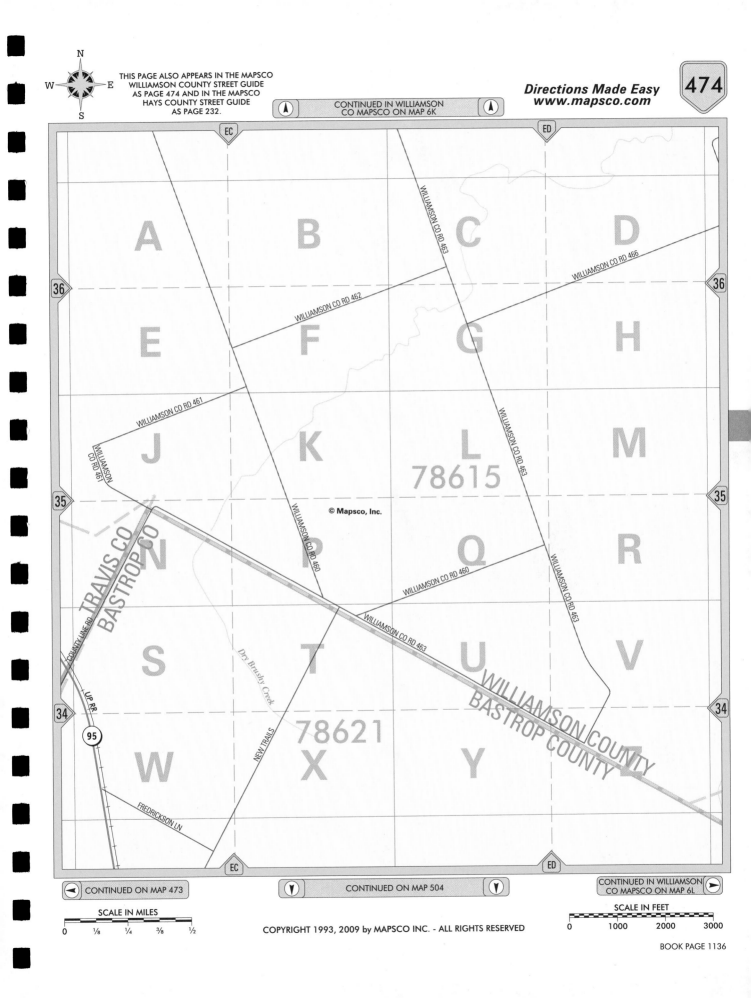

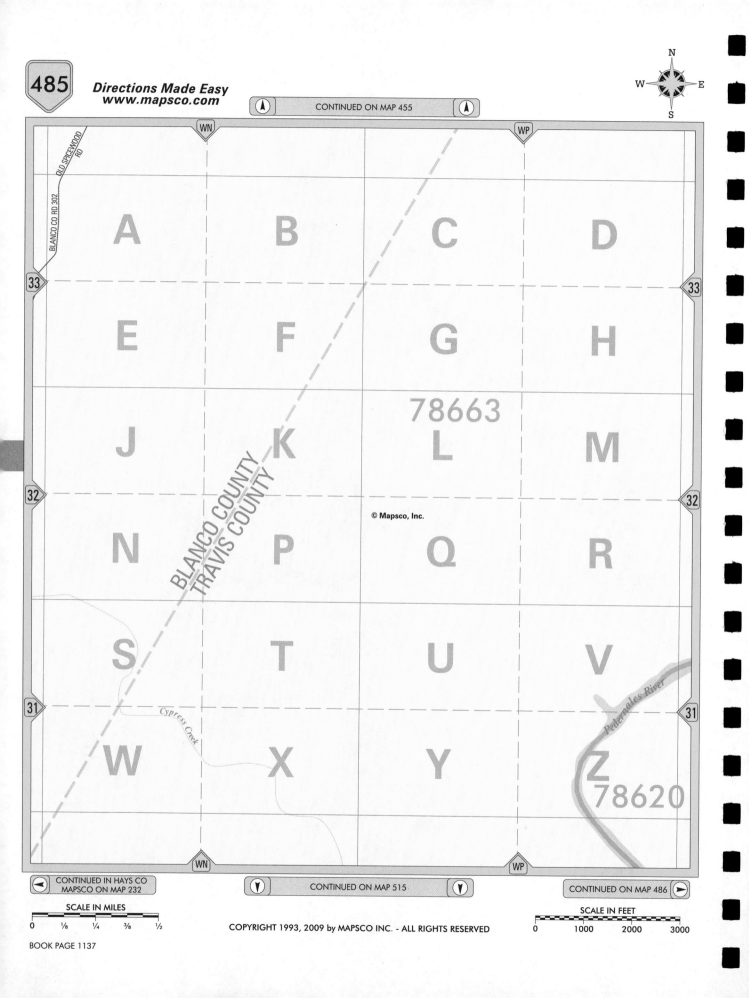

485 **Directions Made Easy**
www.mapsco.com

CONTINUED ON MAP 455

WN   WP

OLD SPICEWOOD RD

BLANCO CO RD 302

| A | B | C | D |

33

| E | F | G | H |

78663

| J | K | L | M |

BLANCO COUNTY
TRAVIS COUNTY

32

© Mapsco, Inc.

| N | P | Q | R |

| S | T | U | V |

Pedernales River

31

Cypress Creek

| W | X | Y | Z |
78620

WN   WP

CONTINUED IN HAYS CO
MAPSCO ON MAP 232

CONTINUED ON MAP 515

CONTINUED ON MAP 486

SCALE IN MILES

0   ⅛   ¼   ⅜   ½

SCALE IN FEET

0   1000   2000   3000

BOOK PAGE 1137

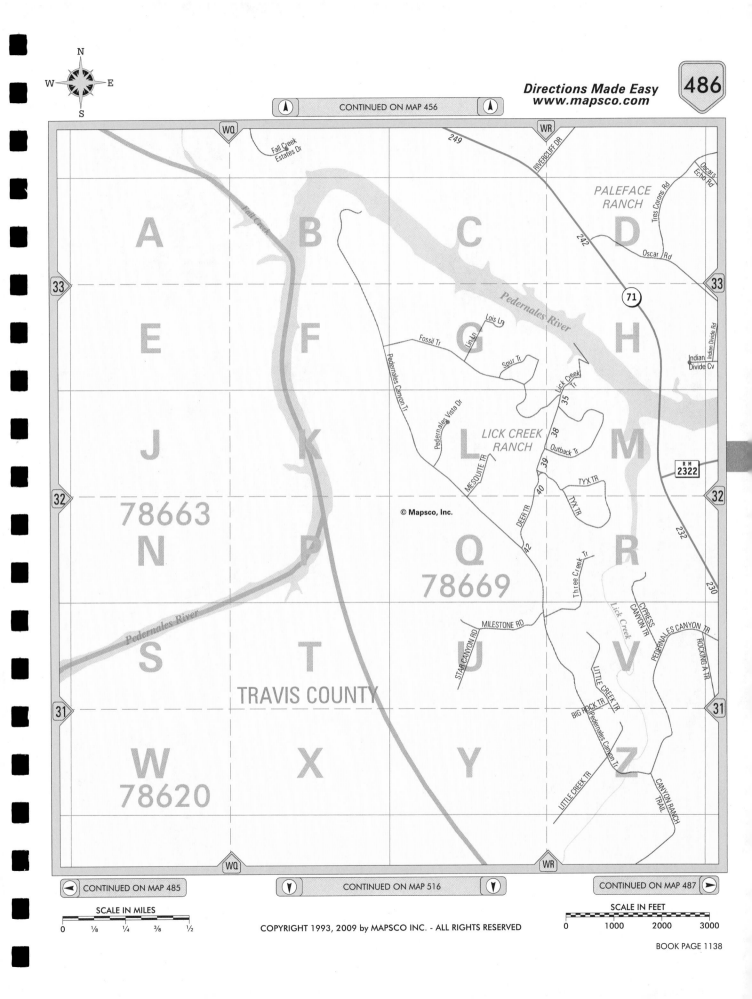

N
W E
S

CONTINUED ON MAP 456

WQ

WR

249

RIVERCLIFF DR

Oscars Echo Rd

PALEFACE RANCH

Tres Coconis Rd

A   B   C   D

33   33

Fall Creek Estates Dr

Fall Creek

Pedernales River

242

71

Oscar Rd

Indian Divide Rd

E   F   G   H

Lois Ln

Lin Ln

Fossil Tr

Spur Tr

Pedernales Canyon Tr

Lick Creek Tr

Indian Divide Cv

Pedernales Vista Dr

35

J   K   L   M

78663

Mesquite Tr

38

Outback Tr

39

LICK CREEK RANCH

© Mapsco, Inc.

RM 2322

32   32

40

TYX TR

TYX TR

DEER TR

232

N   P   Q   R

78669

42

Three Creek Tr

Lick Creek

CYPRESS CANYON TR

230

PEDERNALES CANYON TR

Pedernales River

MILESTONE RD

ROCKING A TR

S   T   U   V

STAR CANYON RD

TRAVIS COUNTY

31   31

LITTLE CREEK TR

BIG ROCK TR

Pedernales Canyon Tr

W   X   Y   Z

78620

LITTLE CREEK TR

CANYON RANCH TRAIL

WQ

WR

CONTINUED ON MAP 485

CONTINUED ON MAP 516

CONTINUED ON MAP 487

SCALE IN MILES

0   1/8   1/4   3/8   1/2

SCALE IN FEET

0   1000   2000   3000

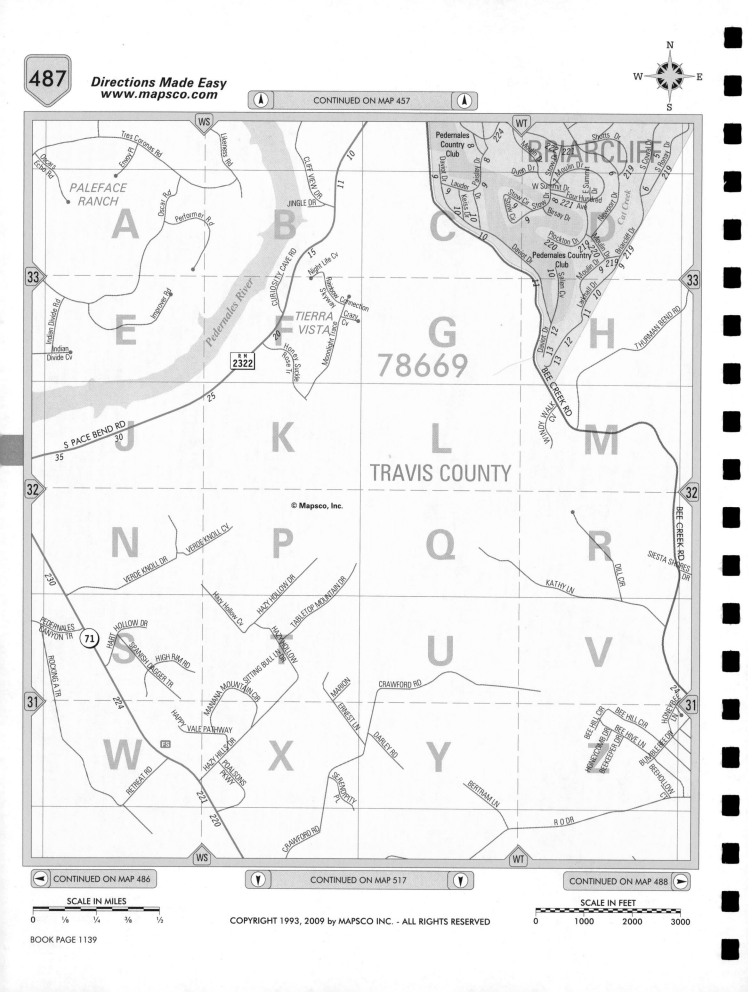

CONTINUED ON MAP 457

N
W E
S

PALEFACE RANCH

Tres Coronas Rd
Envoy Pl
Oscar's
Echo Rd
Oscar Rd
Performer Rd
Improver Rd

Likeness Rd

WS

CLIFF VIEW DR
JINGLE DR

11
10
15

A
B

Pedernales Country Club
WT
BRIARCLIFF
Shotts Dr
224
222
Moulin Dr
Stow
S Cowall Dr
S Rotary Dr
219
219
Dunn Dr
Daviot Dr
Paisley Dr
Lauder
Keiss Dr
W Summit Dr
E Summit
Four Hundred
221 Ave
Newport Dr
9
6
Stow Cir
Stow
Stow Cir
Stow
Birsay Dr
Plockton Dr
220
Pedernales Country Club
Moulin Dr
Briarcliff
219
Daviot Dr
Salen Cv
Lawhall Dr
10
11
9 219

C
D

Indian Divide Rd
Indian Divide Cv

E
F

Pedernales River

Curiosity Cave Rd

TIERRA VISTA

Night Life Cv
Rainbow Connection
Skyway
Crazy Cv
Honey Suckle
Rose Tr
Moonlight Trace

15
20

R M 2322

G

78669

H

Daviot Dr
Windy Walk Cv
BEE CREEK RD
Thurman Bend Rd
Cat Creek
12
13
12
13

25
S PACE BEND RD
30
35

33
33

J
K
L

TRAVIS COUNTY

M

© Mapsco, Inc.

32
32

230

N
Verde Knoll Cv
Verde Knoll Dr
Verde Knoll Dr

P
Hazy Hollow Dr
Hazy Hollow Cv
Hazy Hollow Dr
Tabletop Mountain Dr

Q

R
Kathy Ln
Dill Cir
Siesta Shores Dr

Pedernales Canyon Tr
71
Hart Hollow Dr
Spanish Dagger Tr
High Rim Rd
Rocking A Tr
224

S
Manana Mountain Cir
Sitting Bull Ln Dr
Hazy Hollow Dr

T
Marion
Ernest Ln
Crawford Rd
Darley Rd

U

V

224

31
31

Retreat Rd
Happy Vale Pathway
Hazy Hills Dr
Poalsons Pkwy
221
220
FS

W
X
Serendipity Pl
Crawford Rd

Y
Bertram Ln
R O Dr

Bee Hill Cir
Bee Hill Cir
Honeycomb Dr
Bee Hive Ln
Beekeeper Dr
Honeybee Ln
Bumblebee Dr
Beehollow Cv
Z

WS
WT

CONTINUED ON MAP 486
CONTINUED ON MAP 517
CONTINUED ON MAP 488

SCALE IN MILES
0   1/8   1/4   3/8   1/2

SCALE IN FEET
0   1000   2000   3000

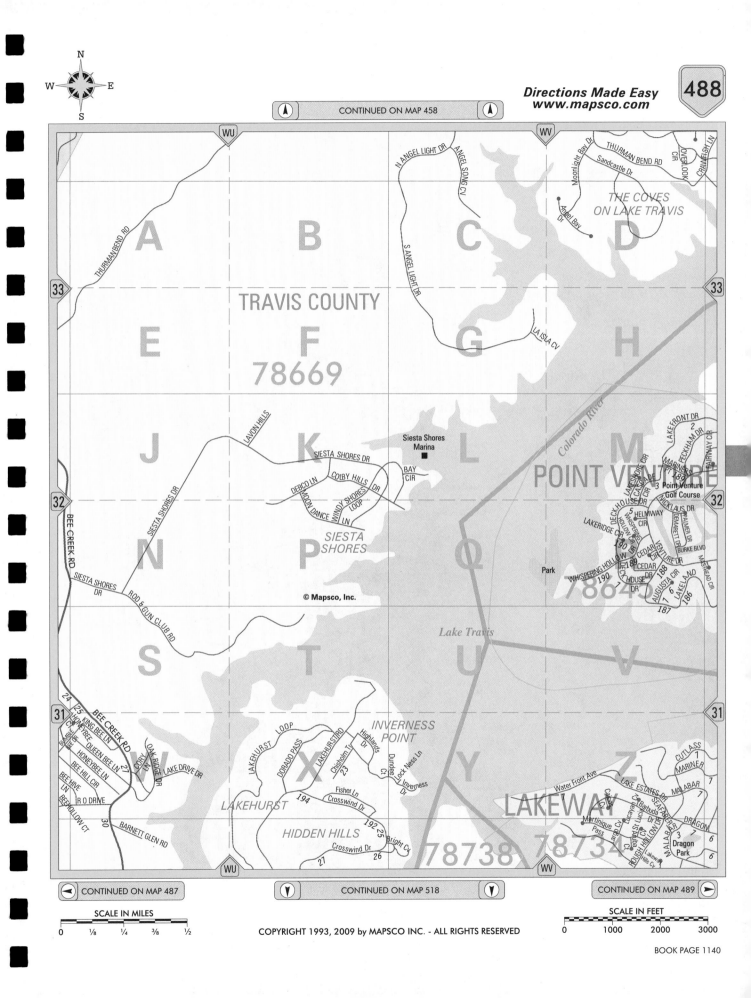

N
W E
S

CONTINUED ON MAP 458

WU

WV

THURMAN BEND RD

N ANGEL LIGHT DR

ANGEL SONG CV

Moonlight Bay Dr

Sandcastle Dr

THURMAN BEND RD

OVERLOOK CIR

CRAWFISH LN

THE COVES
ON LAKE TRAVIS

Angel Bay Dr

A   B   C   D

33   33

TRAVIS COUNTY

E   F   G   H

78669

S ANGEL LIGHT DR

LA ISLA CV

Colorado River

LAVON HILLS

Siesta Shores
Marina

LAKEFRONT DR

PECKHAM DR

FAIRWAY CIR

J   K   SIESTA SHORES DR   L   M

COLBY HILLS DR

DEBCO LN

MOON DANCE LN

WINDY SHORES LOOP

BAY CIR

POINT VENTURE

MARINERS CIR

LAKESHORE CIR

CASCADE DR

Point Venture
Golf Course

DECK HOUSE DR

HELMWAY CIR

WHISPERING HOLLOW DR

NICKLAUS DR

PALMER DR

DEMARET DR

BURKE BLVD

VENTURE DR

32   32

LAKERIDGE CIR

CEDAR

CEDAR

MASTHEAD CIR

AUGUSTA CIR

LAKELAND

N   SIESTA SHORES DR

Park

WHISPERING HOLLOW DR

DECK HOUSE DR

78645

ROD & GUN CLUB RD

BEE CREEK RD

SIESTA SHORES DR

© Mapsco, Inc.

SIESTA
SHORES

P

Lake Travis

S   T   U   V

Q

BEE CREEK RD

31   31

24

25

KING BEE LN

HONEYBEE

QUEEN BEE LN

BUMBLE BEE

HONEYBEE LN

BEE HILL CIR

CORY LN

OAK RIDGE DR

LAKE DRIVE DR

LAKEHURST LOOP

DORADO PASS

LAKEHURST RD

CHISHOLM TR

Highlands

INVERNESS
POINT

Dundee

Lock Ness Ln

J Inverness Dr

Water Front Ave

CUTLASS

MARINER

MALABAR

LAKE ESTATES DR

DRAGON

W   X   Y   Z

BEE HIVE LN

R O DRIVE

BEE HOLLOW CT

BARNETT GLEN RD

LAKEHURST

194

Fisher Ln

Crosswind Dr

HIDDEN HILLS

192

25

Bright Cv

LAKEWAY

78738   78734

Martinique
Pass

ROUGH HOLLOW CV

MALABAR

Lakeway Hills Cv

Dragon
Park

Crosswind Dr

27   26

SELF

CONTINUED ON MAP 487

CONTINUED ON MAP 518

CONTINUED ON MAP 489

WU

WV

SCALE IN MILES

0   ⅛   ¼   ⅜   ½

SCALE IN FEET

0   1000   2000   3000

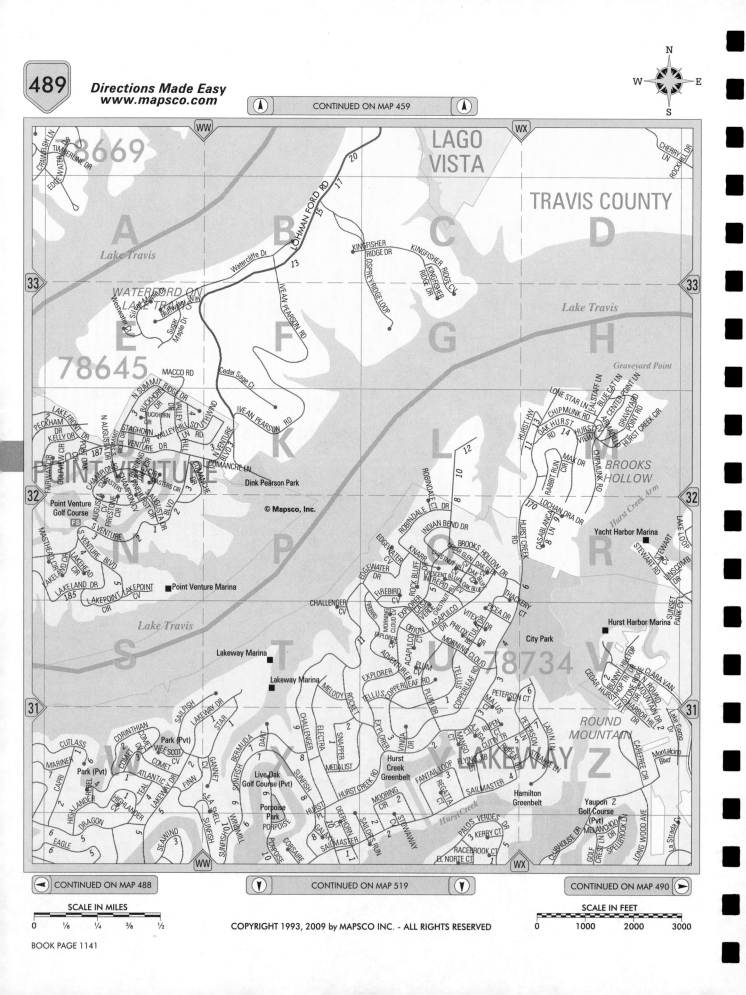

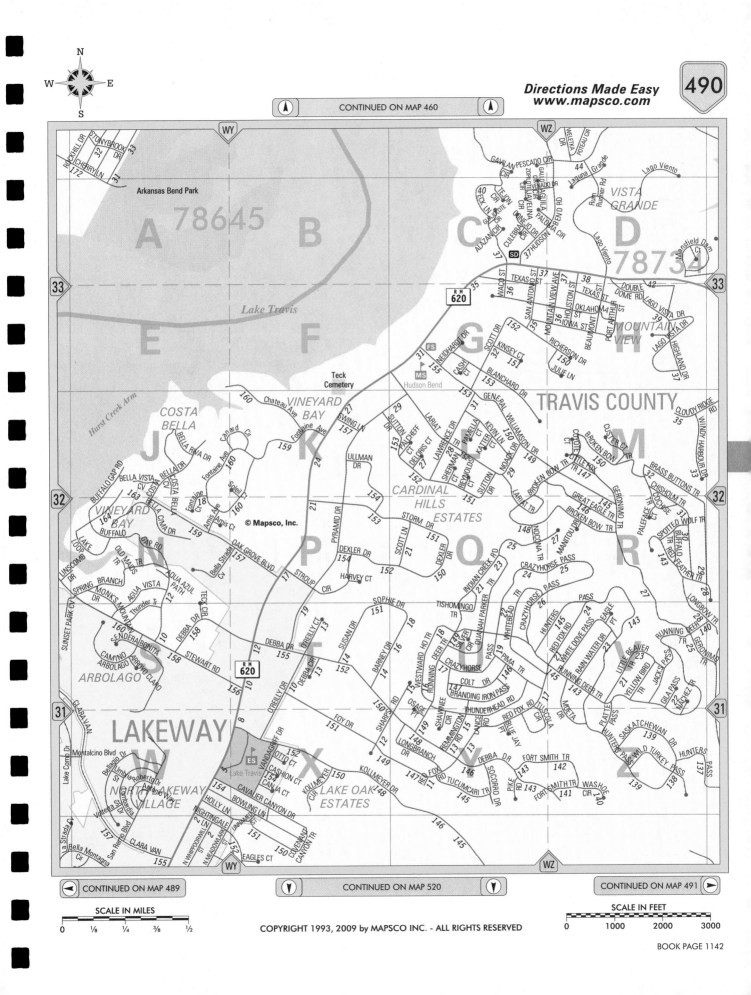

CONTINUED ON MAP 460

N
W E
S

Arkansas Bend Park

A 78645 B

Lake Travis

E F

TRAVIS COUNTY

Teck Cemetery

VINEYARD BAY

COSTA BELLA

Hurst Creek Arm

J K L M

78734

VISTA GRANDE

MOUNTAIN VIEW

Mansfield Dam

Hudson Bend

CARDINAL HILLS ESTATES

VINEYARD BAY

ARBOLAGO

N P Q R

LAKEWAY

S T U V

NORTH LAKEWAY VILLAGE

LAKE OAK ESTATES

W X Y Z

© Mapsco, Inc.

CONTINUED ON MAP 489
CONTINUED ON MAP 520
CONTINUED ON MAP 491

SCALE IN MILES
0   1/8   1/4   3/8   1/2

SCALE IN FEET
0   1000   2000   3000

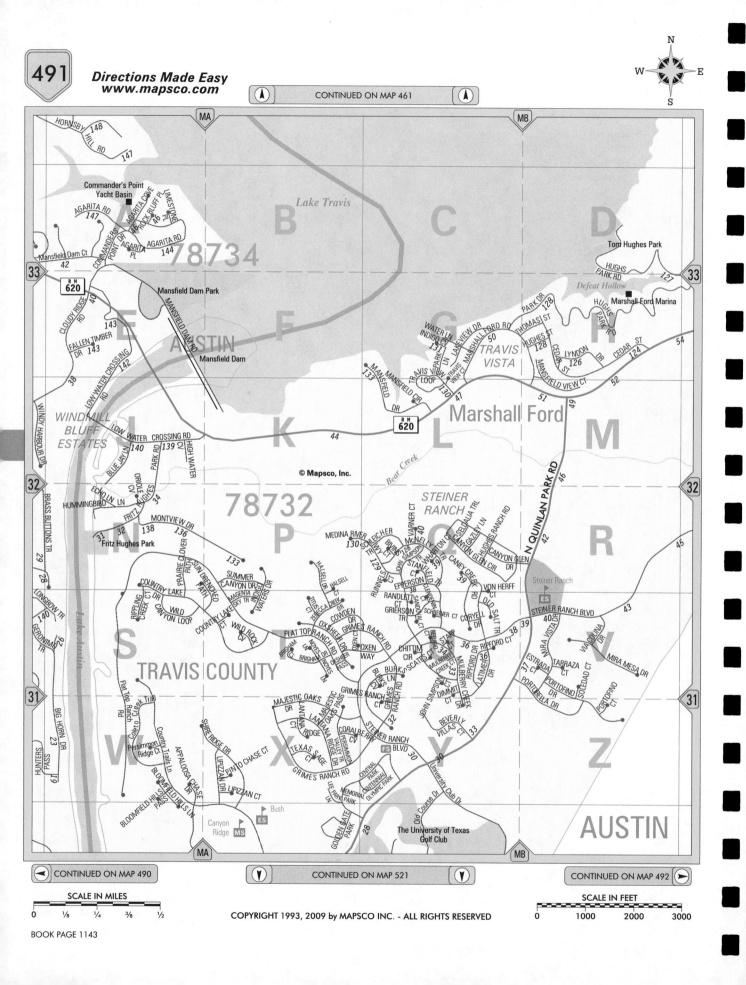

Directions Made Easy
www.mapsco.com

N
W · E
S

CONTINUED ON MAP 461

MA   MB

HORNSBY HILL RD 148 147

Commander's Point Yacht Basin

Lake Travis

B   C   D

Tom Hughes Park

AGARITA RD 147

LIMESTONE
ROCK BLUFF PL
AGARITA COVE

COMMANDERS POINT AGARITA PL

AGARITA RD 144

78734

HUGHS PARK RD 127

33   33

Mansfield Dam Ct 42

R M 620

Mansfield Dam Park

Defeat Hollow

PARK DR 128

Marshall Ford Marina

HUGHS PARK RD

CLOUDY RIDGE RD 40

E   F   G   H

WATER LN
INDIGO CT

LAKEVIEW DR
MARSHALL FORD RD 50

THOMASI ST

HUGHS ST

CEDAR ST 54

FALLEN TIMBER DR 143 143

AUSTIN

Mansfield Dam

MANSFIELD DAM RD

LOW WATER CROSSING RD 142

38

MANSFIELD DR 133

MANSFIELD CIR

TRAVIS VIEW LOOP

TRAVIS VIEW CT 130

MARSHALL FORD RD 47

TRAVIS VISTA

HUGHS ST 128

LYNDON DR 126

CEDAR ST 124

MANSFIELD VIEW CT 52

WINDMILL BLUFF ESTATES

WINDY HARBOUR DR

LOW WATER CROSSING RD

PARK RD 139

HIGH WATER CT

BLUE JAY LN

Bear Creek

R M 620

44

51

49

Marshall Ford

L   M

N QUINLAN PARK RD

46

32   32

BRASS BUTTONS TR 29

28

ECHO LN
HUMMINGBIRD

ORIOLE
HUGHES 34

FRITZ

78732

MEDINA RIVER 130

SCHLEICHER TRL
IRVING

VARNER CT

STEINER RANCH

SELJALIA TRL

GAZELEY LN

HUGHS RANCH RD

CANYON GLEN CIR

CANYON GLEN DR

42

45

R

MONTVIEW DR 138 136

FRITZ 32

Fritz Hughes Park 31

133

PRAIRIE CLOVER PATH

SUN DRENCHED PATH

SUMMER CANYON DR

MAGENTA
SKY TR INDIGO

WATERS DR

HALSELL CT

HALSELL

ZEBECCA CREEK DR

JOHN SIMPSON

RUNNING WATER CT

McNELLY

WHARTON CT

STANFIELD TR

EPPERSON

CANEY CREEK RD 39

VON HERFF

LEWDEN

RANDLETT

SANDOVAL CT

SCHLEGENER CT

OLD SALT TR

CORYELL

Steiner Ranch

ES

STEINER RANCH BLVD

MIRA VISTA DR

VIA COLINA

40

43

LONGBOW TR 140

GERONIMO TR 26

S

RIPPLING CREEK CT

COUNTRY LAKE DR

CANYON LOOP

WILD CANYON CV

WILD ROCK CV

COUNTRY LAKE CT

FLAT TOP RANCH RD

T

BRIGHAM LN
NOYES DR

OXSHEER DR

COWDEN DR

GRIMES

DIVEN CT

GRIMES RANCH RD

OXEN WAY

CHITTIM CIR

BURK SCATES CT

GRIERSON TR

RIPFORD CT

STAR

RIPFORD CT 38 39

37 36

MULBERRY CT

DIMMIT CT

TARRAZA CT

PORTOFINO CT

PORTOFINO

MIRA MESA DR

SOLEDAD CT

PORTOBELLA DR

V

BIG HORN DR 23

HUNTERS PASS 19

FLAT TOP RANCH RD

Coleto Creek Trail

Country Trails Ln

Persimmon Ridge Ct

TRAVIS COUNTY

SHIRE RIDGE DR

MAJESTIC OAKS DR

LANTANA RIDGE

MAJESTIC OAKS PASS

CORALBERRY CV

PERSIMMON VALLEY TR

STEINER RANCH BLVD 30

BURK RD

GRIMES RANCH CT

GRIMES RANCH RD 32

JOHN SIMPSON CT

LATIMER CT

MULBERRY CREEK

BEVERLY VILLAS CT 33

ESTRADA

X   Y

TEXAS SAGE CT

GRIMES RANCH RD

LE PARK LN

CENTRAL PARK CENTENNIAL OLYMPIC PARK

University Club Dr

Old Course Dr

Z

AUSTIN

APALOOSA CHASE

LIPIZZAN DR

PINTO CHASE CT

LIPIZZAN CT

Bush
ES

Canyon Ridge MS

MEMORIAL PARK

GOLDEN GATE PARK 28

The University of Texas Golf Club

BLOOMFIELD HILLS LN
BLOOMFIELD HILLS PASS

MA   MB

CONTINUED ON MAP 490   CONTINUED ON MAP 521   CONTINUED ON MAP 492

© Mapsco, Inc.

SCALE IN MILES
0   1/8   1/4   3/8   1/2

SCALE IN FEET
0   1000   2000   3000

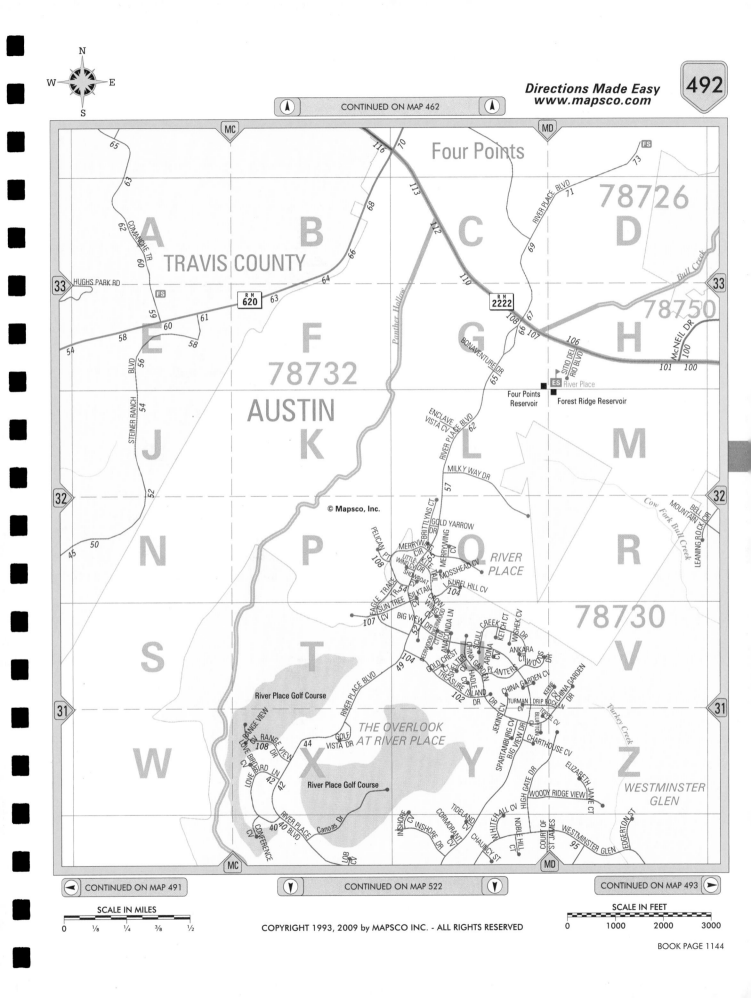

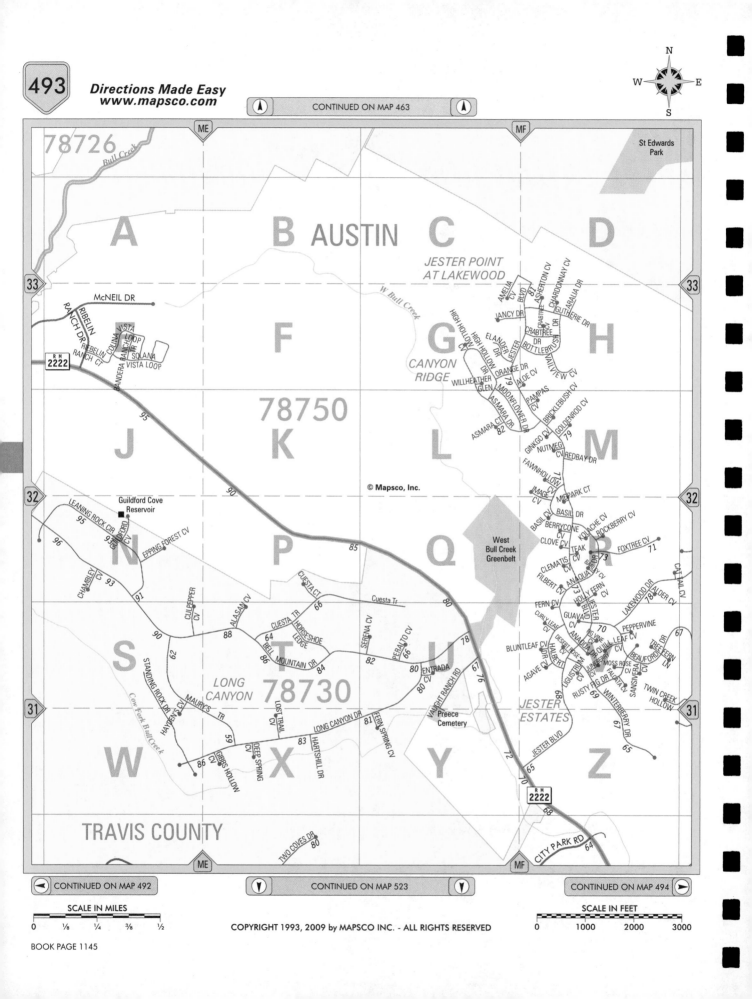

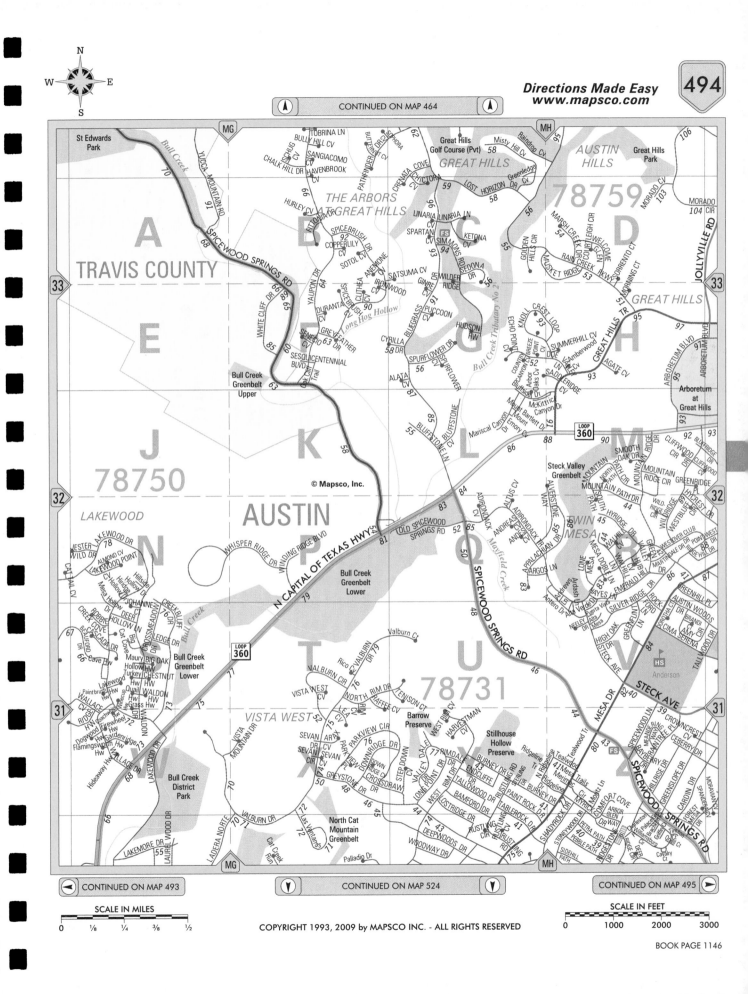

CONTINUED ON MAP 465

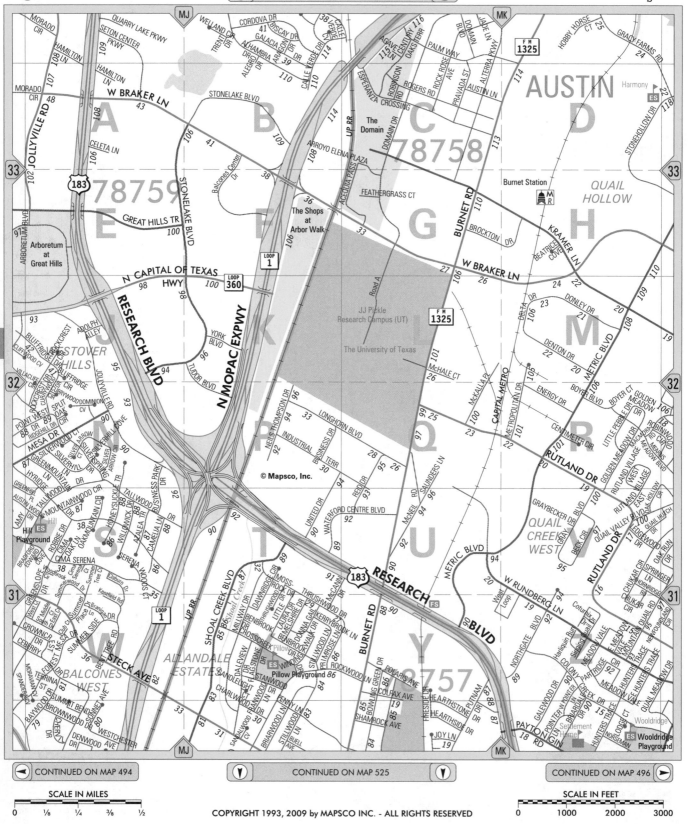

CONTINUED ON MAP 494
CONTINUED ON MAP 525
CONTINUED ON MAP 496

SCALE IN MILES

0   1/8   1/4   3/8   1/2

SCALE IN FEET

0   1000   2000   3000

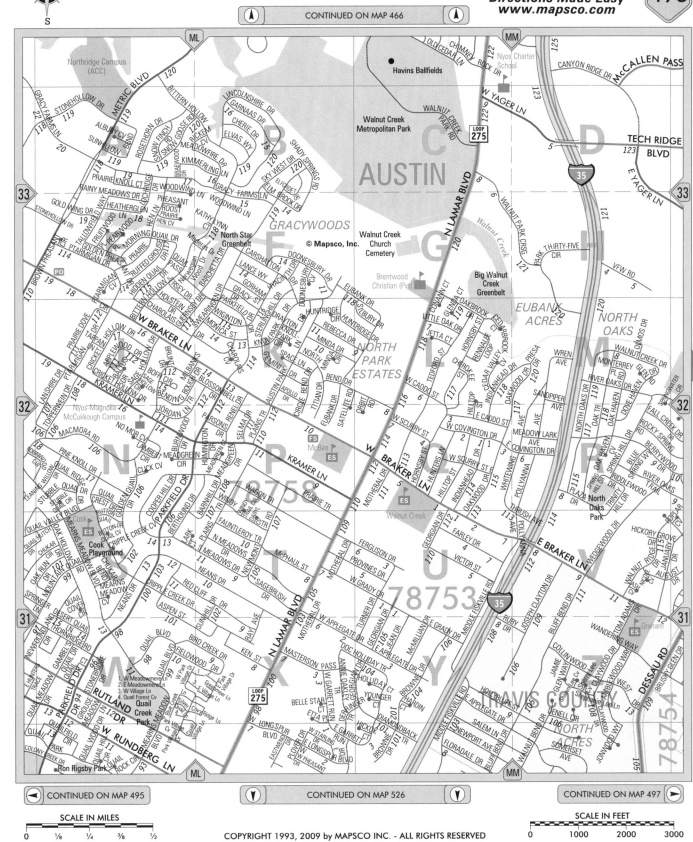

CONTINUED ON MAP 466

SCALE IN MILES

0   1/8   1/4   3/8   1/2

SCALE IN FEET

0   1000   2000   3000

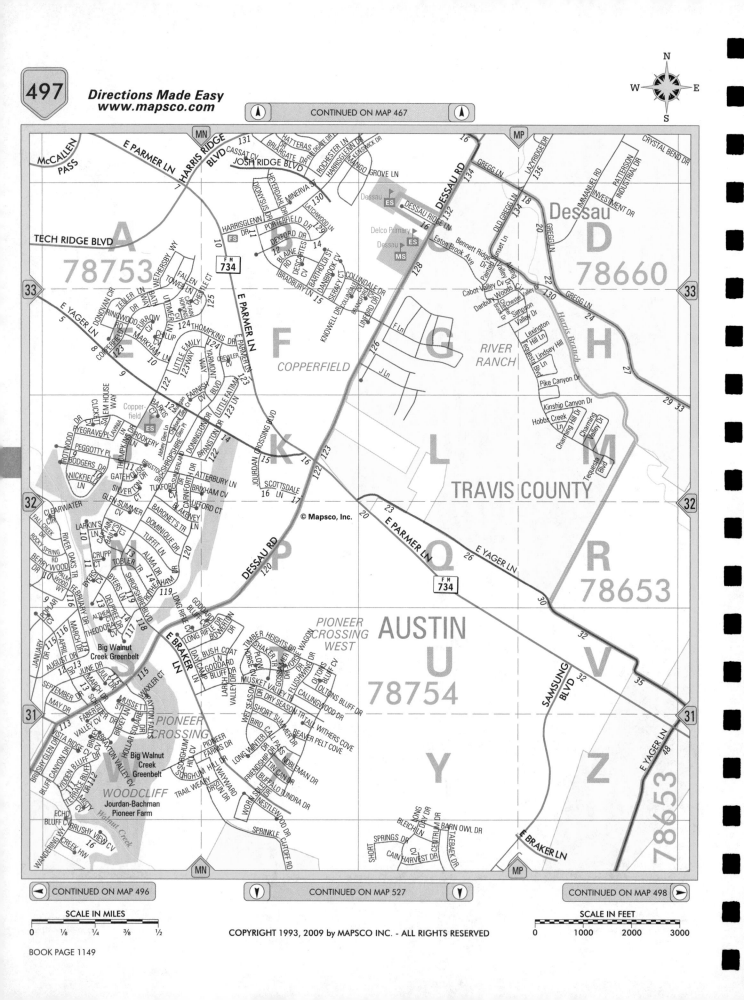

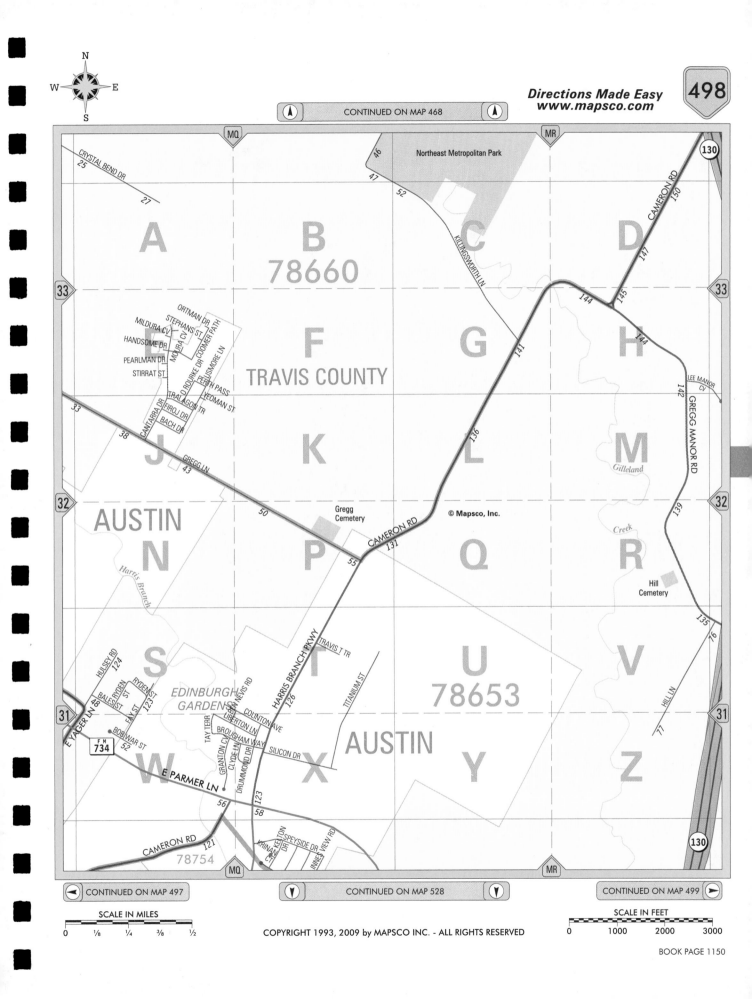

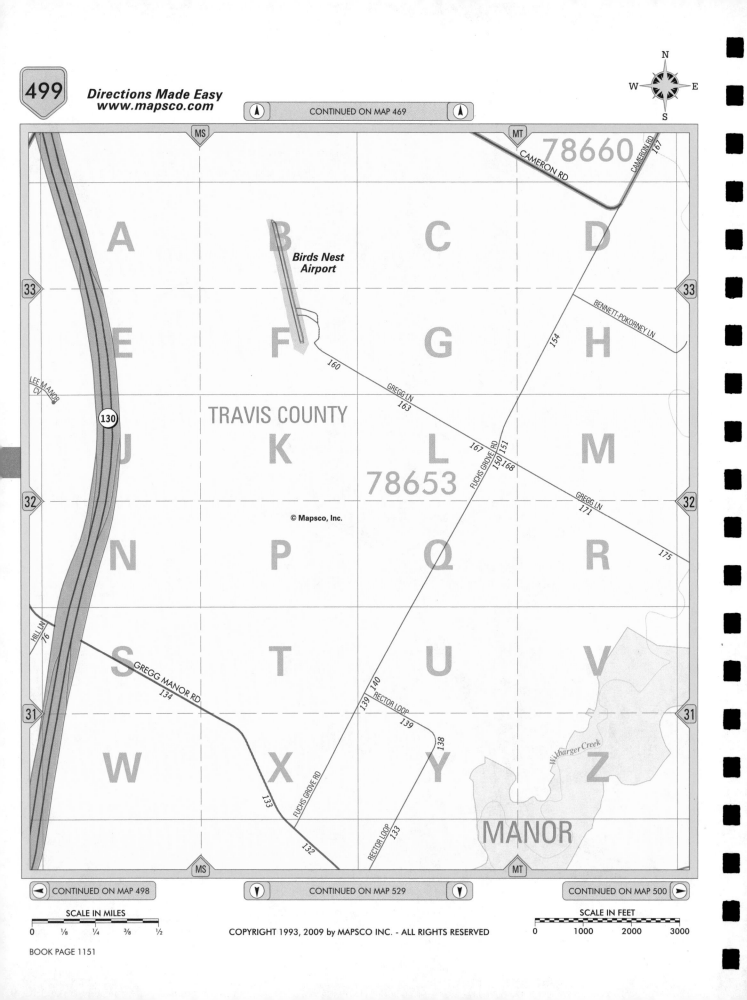

499

Directions Made Easy
www.mapsco.com

CONTINUED ON MAP 469

N
W — E
S

MS

MT

78660

CAMERON RD

CAMERON RD
167

A   B   C   D

Birds Nest
Airport

33   33

BENNETT-POKORNEY LN

E   F   G   H

154

160

GREGG LN
163

LEE MANOR
CV

130

TRAVIS COUNTY

J   K   L   M

78653

167   150 151
FUCHS GROVE RD
168

GREGG LN
171

© Mapsco, Inc.

32   32

175

N   P   Q   R

HILL LN
76

S   GREGG MANOR RD   T   U   V   Willbarger Creek
134

RECTOR LOOP
140

139

31   31
139   138

FUCHS GROVE RD

W   X   Y   Z

133

RECTOR LOOP
132   133

MANOR

MS   MT

CONTINUED ON MAP 498
CONTINUED ON MAP 529
CONTINUED ON MAP 500

SCALE IN MILES

0   ⅛   ¼   ⅜   ½

SCALE IN FEET

0   1000   2000   3000

COPYRIGHT 1993, 2009 by MAPSCO INC. - ALL RIGHTS RESERVED

BOOK PAGE 1151

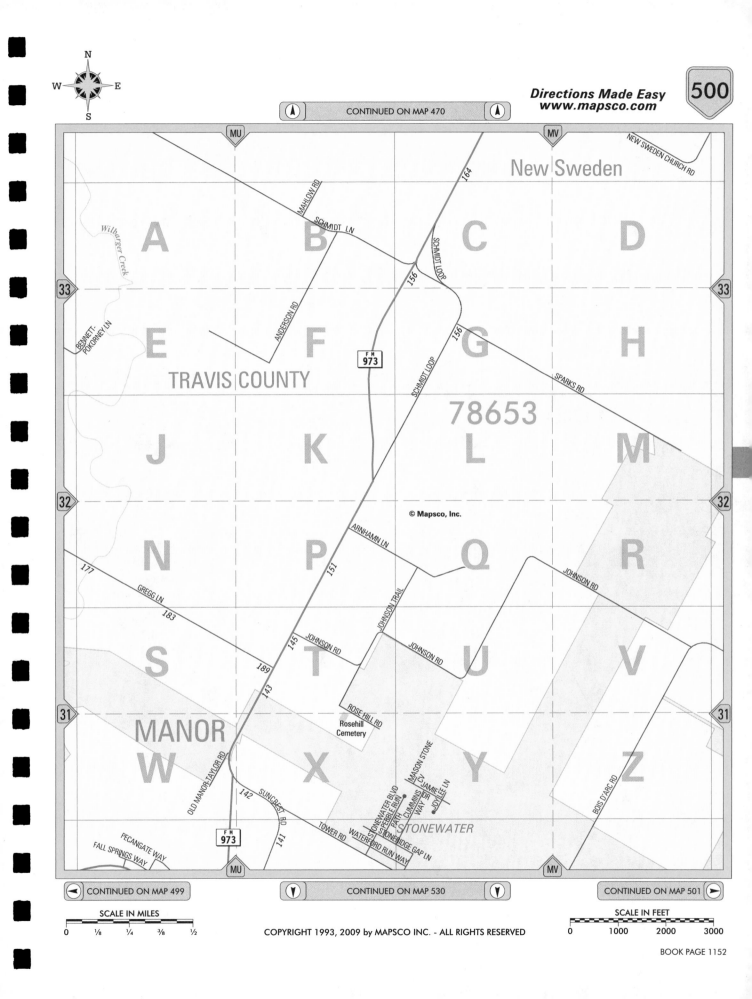

CONTINUED ON MAP 470

Directions Made Easy
www.mapsco.com

500

N
W E
S

New Sweden

NEW SWEDEN CHURCH RD

33

A

B

C

D

MU

MV

164

MAHLOW RD

SCHMIDT LN

SCHMIDT LOOP

156

33

E

F

G

H

Wilbarger Creek

BENNETT-POKORNEY LN

ANDERSON RD

FM 973

SCHMIDT LOOP

156

SPARKS RD

TRAVIS COUNTY

J

K

78653

L

M

© Mapsco, Inc.

32

32

N

P

Q

R

177

GREGG LN

183

ARNHAMN LN

151

JOHNSON TRAIL

JOHNSON RD

JOHNSON RD

S

T

U

V

145

JOHNSON RD

189

143

JOHNSON RD

31

31

MANOR

ROSE HILL RD

Rosehill Cemetery

W

X

Y

Z

OLD MANOR-TAYLOR RD

142

SUNCREST RD

141

TOWER RD

FM 973

PECANGATE WAY

FALL SPRINGS WAY

STONEWATER BLVD

PEBBLE RUN

PATH

MASON STONE CV

CUMMINS WAY

JAMIE DR

JOYLEE LN

STONERIDGE GAP LN

WATERFORD RUN WAY

STONEWATER

BOIS D'ARC RD

MU

MV

CONTINUED ON MAP 499

CONTINUED ON MAP 530

CONTINUED ON MAP 501

SCALE IN MILES

0   ⅛   ¼   ⅜   ½

SCALE IN FEET

0   1000   2000   3000

BOOK PAGE 1152

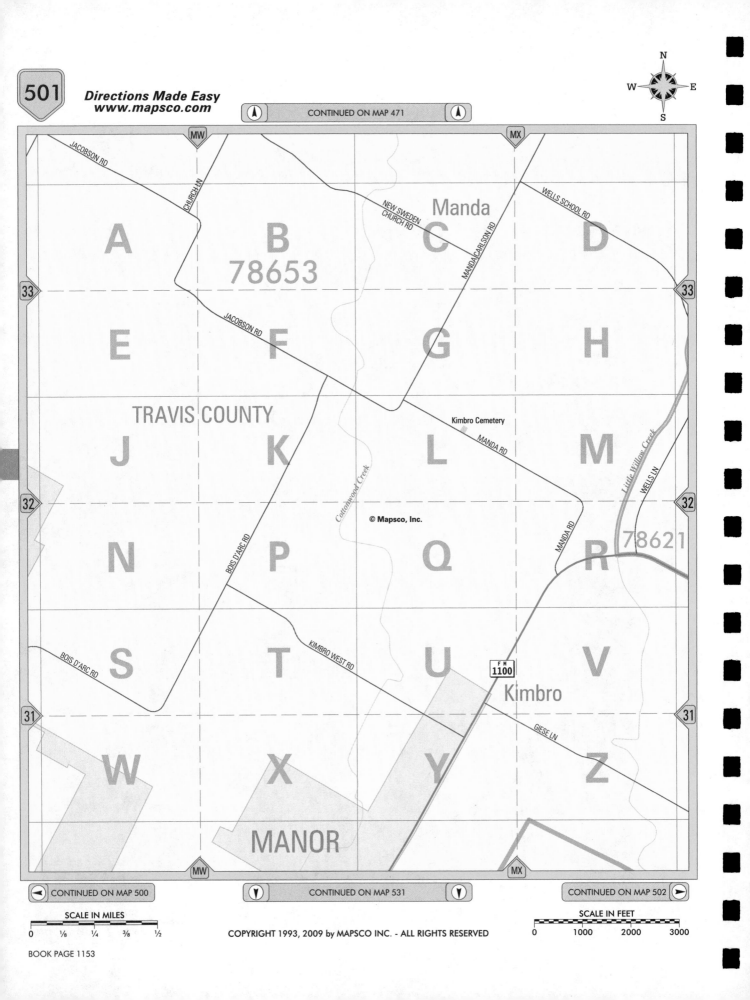

501

Directions Made Easy
www.mapsco.com

CONTINUED ON MAP 471

N
W E
S

JACOBSON RD

CHURCH LN

MW

MX

NEW SWEDEN CHURCH RD

Manda

WELLS SCHOOL RD

MANDA CARLSON RD

A

B
78653

C

D

33

33

JACOBSON RD

E

F

G

H

TRAVIS COUNTY

Kimbro Cemetery

J

K

MANDA RD

L

M

Little Willow Creek

WELLS LN

32

32

Cottonwood Creek

© Mapsco, Inc.

BOIS D'ARC RD

MANDA RD

78621

N

P

Q

R

KIMBRO WEST RD

BOIS D'ARC RD

S

T

U

F M 1100

V

Kimbro

Z

31

31

GIESE LN

W

X

Y

MX

MW

MANOR

CONTINUED ON MAP 500

CONTINUED ON MAP 531

CONTINUED ON MAP 502

SCALE IN MILES

0   ⅛   ¼   ⅜   ½

SCALE IN FEET

0   1000   2000   3000

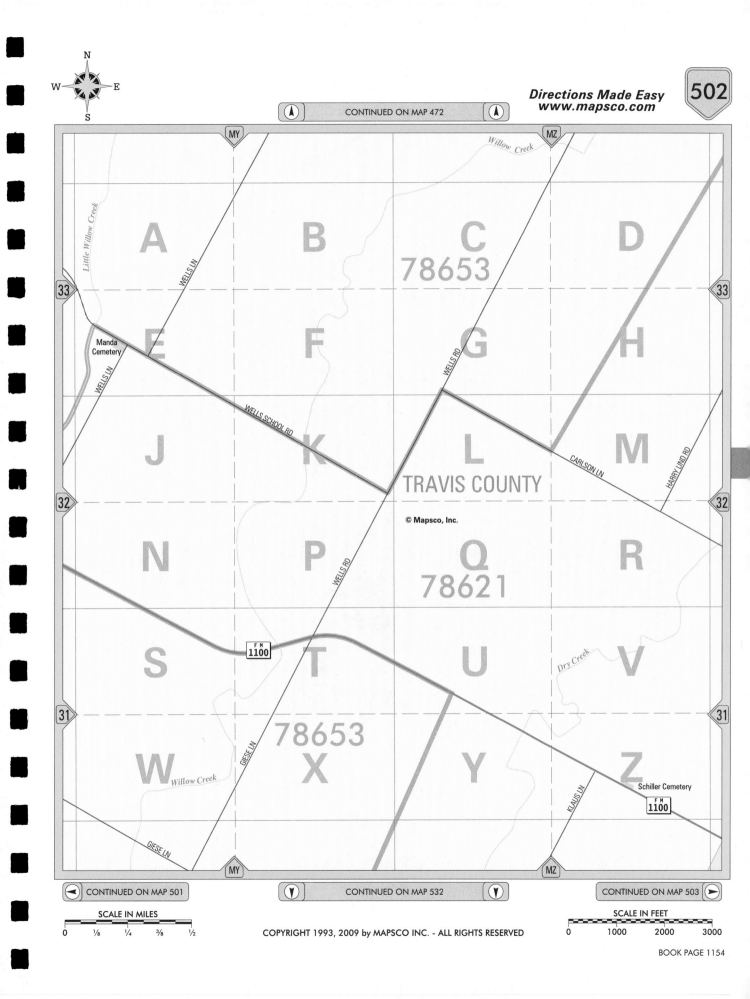

CONTINUED ON MAP 472

N
W E
S

MY

MZ

Willow Creek

Little Willow Creek

A

B

C
78653

D

33

33

Manda
Cemetery

E

WELLS LN

F

WELLS RD

G

H

WELLS LN

WELLS SCHOOL RD

J

K

L

CARLSON LN

M

HARRY LIND RD

TRAVIS COUNTY

© Mapsco, Inc.

32

32

N

P

WELLS RD

Q
78621

R

FM
1100

S

T

U

Dry Creek

V

31

31

W

Willow Creek

GIESE LN

X
78653

Y

KLAUS LN

Z

Schiller Cemetery

FM
1100

GIESE LN

MY

MZ

CONTINUED ON MAP 501

CONTINUED ON MAP 532

CONTINUED ON MAP 503

SCALE IN MILES

0   ⅛   ¼   ⅜   ½

SCALE IN FEET

0   1000   2000   3000

BOOK PAGE 1154

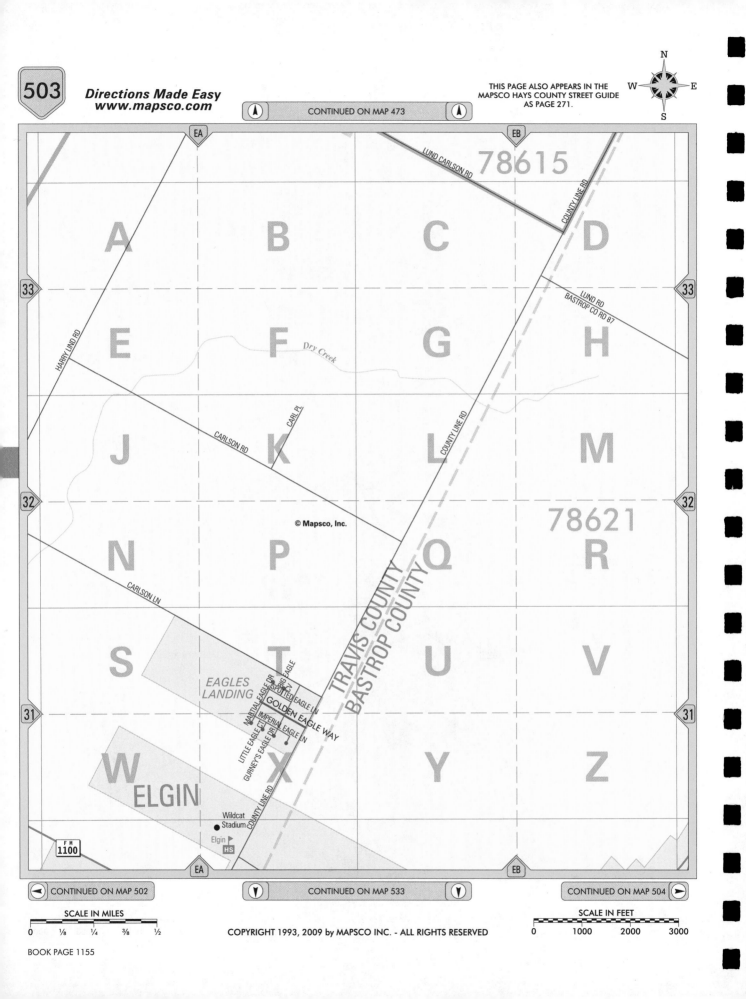

503

Directions Made Easy
www.mapsco.com

CONTINUED ON MAP 473

THIS PAGE ALSO APPEARS IN THE
MAPSCO HAYS COUNTY STREET GUIDE
AS PAGE 271.

N
W E
S

EA

EB

LUND CARLSON RD

78615

COUNTY LINE RD

A   B   C   D

33   33

LUND RD
BASTROP CO RD 87

HARRY LUND RD

E   F   Dry Creek   G   H

CARL PL

CARLSON RD

J   K   L   COUNTY LINE RD   M

32   32

© Mapsco, Inc.

78621

N   P   Q   R

CARLSON LN

TRAVIS COUNTY
BASTROP COUNTY

S   T   U   V

EAGLES
LANDING

BIG EAGLE

SPOTTED EAGLE LN

MARTIAL EAGLE DR

GOLDEN EAGLE WAY

31   IMPERIAL EAGLE LN   31

LITTLE EAGLE CT

GURNEY'S EAGLE DR

W   X   Y   Z

ELGIN

COUNTY LINE RD

Wildcat
Stadium

Elgin
HS

FM
1100

EA   EB

CONTINUED ON MAP 502   CONTINUED ON MAP 533   CONTINUED ON MAP 504

SCALE IN MILES

0   ⅛   ¼   ⅜   ½

COPYRIGHT 1993, 2009 by MAPSCO INC. - ALL RIGHTS RESERVED

SCALE IN FEET

0   1000   2000   3000

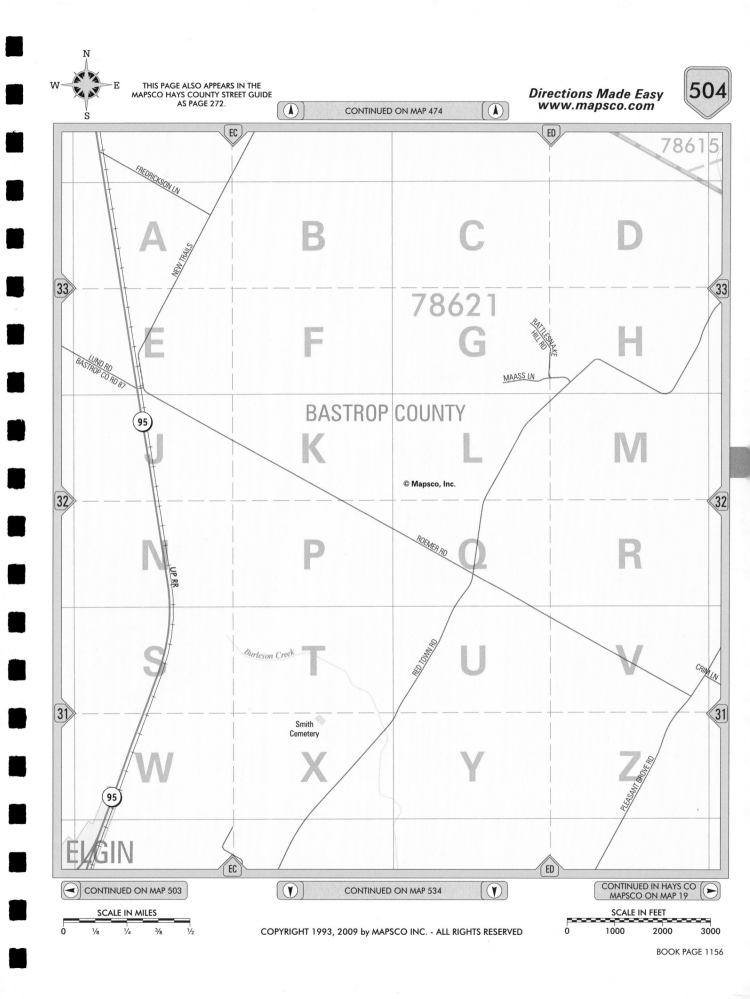

N
W E
S

THIS PAGE ALSO APPEARS IN THE
MAPSCO HAYS COUNTY STREET GUIDE
AS PAGE 272.

Directions Made Easy
www.mapsco.com

CONTINUED ON MAP 474

78615

FREDRICKSON LN

NEW TRAILS

A

B

C

D

33   33

78621

LUND RD
BASTROP CO RD 87

E

F

G

RATTLESNAKE HILL RD

H

MAASS LN

95

BASTROP COUNTY

J

K

L

© Mapsco, Inc.

M

32   32

ROEMER RD

N

UP RR

P

Q

R

Burleson Creek

S

T

RED TOWN RD

U

V

CRIM LN

31   31

Smith
Cemetery

95

W

X

Y

Z

PLEASANT GROVE RD

ELGIN

CONTINUED ON MAP 503

CONTINUED ON MAP 534

CONTINUED IN HAYS CO
MAPSCO ON MAP 19

SCALE IN MILES

0   ⅛   ¼   ⅜   ½

SCALE IN FEET

0   1000   2000   3000

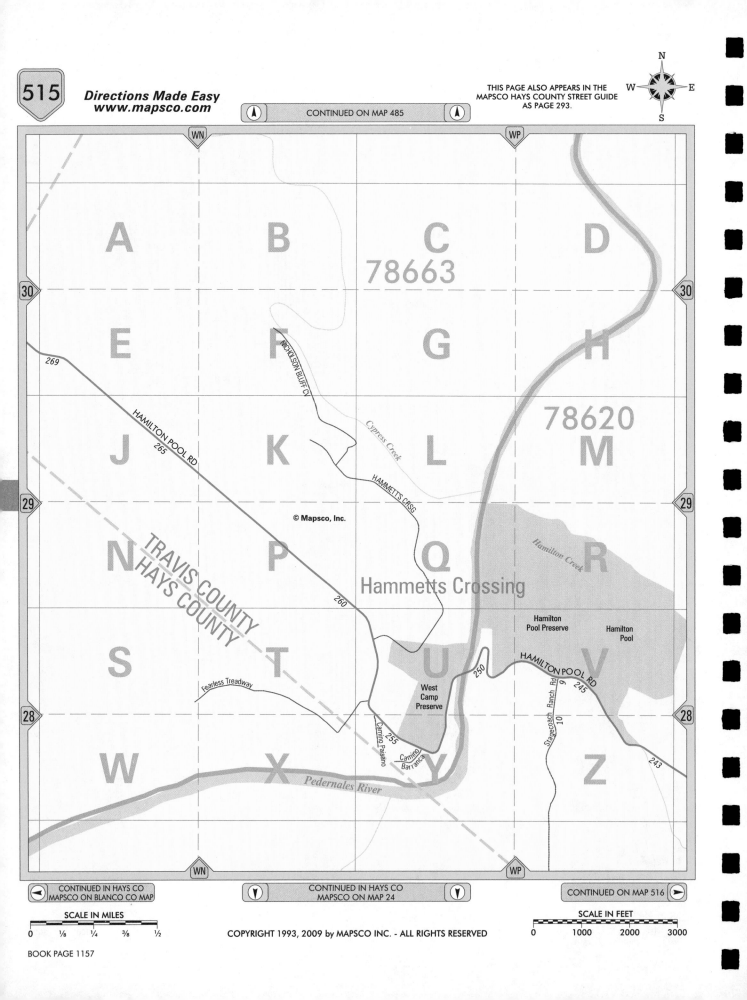

Directions Made Easy
www.mapsco.com

THIS PAGE ALSO APPEARS IN THE
MAPSCO HAYS COUNTY STREET GUIDE
AS PAGE 293.

N
W   E
S

CONTINUED ON MAP 485

WN   WP

30   30

A   B   C   D

78663

E   F   G   H

269

NICHOLSON BLUFF CV

Cypress Creek

HAMILTON POOL RD

265

J   K   L   M

78620

HAMMETTS CRSG

29   29

© Mapsco, Inc.

Hamilton Creek

N   P   Q   R

TRAVIS COUNTY
HAYS COUNTY

260

Hammetts Crossing

Hamilton
Pool Preserve

Hamilton
Pool

S   T   U   V

Fearless Treadway

West
Camp
Preserve

250

HAMILTON POOL RD

Stagecoach Ranch Rd

9

245

28   28

Camino Paisano

255

Camino
Barranca

10

W   X   Y   Z

Pedernales River

243

WN   WP

CONTINUED IN HAYS CO
MAPSCO ON BLANCO CO MAP

CONTINUED IN HAYS CO
MAPSCO ON MAP 24

CONTINUED ON MAP 516

SCALE IN MILES
0   ⅛   ¼   ⅜   ½

SCALE IN FEET
0   1000   2000   3000

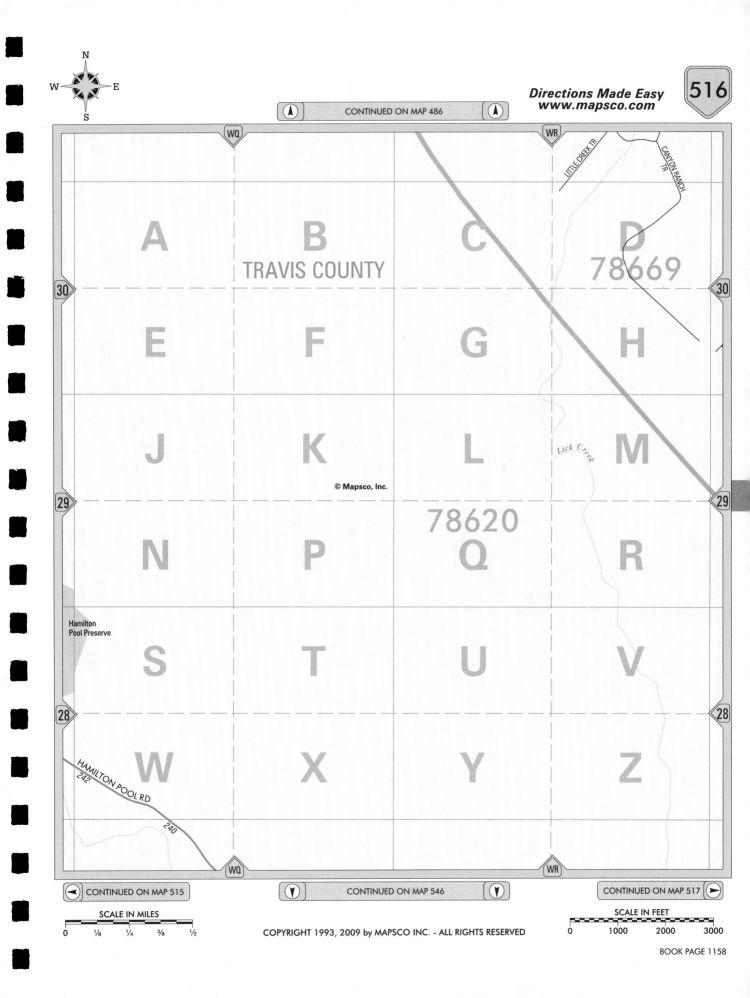

CONTINUED ON MAP 486

N
W E
S

WQ

WR

LITTLE CREEK TR.

CANYON RANCH TR.

A

B

TRAVIS COUNTY

C

D

78669

30

E

F

G

H

30

J

K

L

M

Lick Creek

© Mapsco, Inc.

29

N

P

78620

Q

R

29

Hamilton
Pool Preserve

S

T

U

V

28

W

X

Y

Z

28

HAMILTON POOL RD
242

240

WQ

WR

CONTINUED ON MAP 515

CONTINUED ON MAP 546

CONTINUED ON MAP 517

SCALE IN MILES

0   ⅛   ¼   ⅜   ½

SCALE IN FEET

0   1000   2000   3000

Directions Made Easy
www.mapsco.com

CONTINUED ON MAP 487

N
W E
S

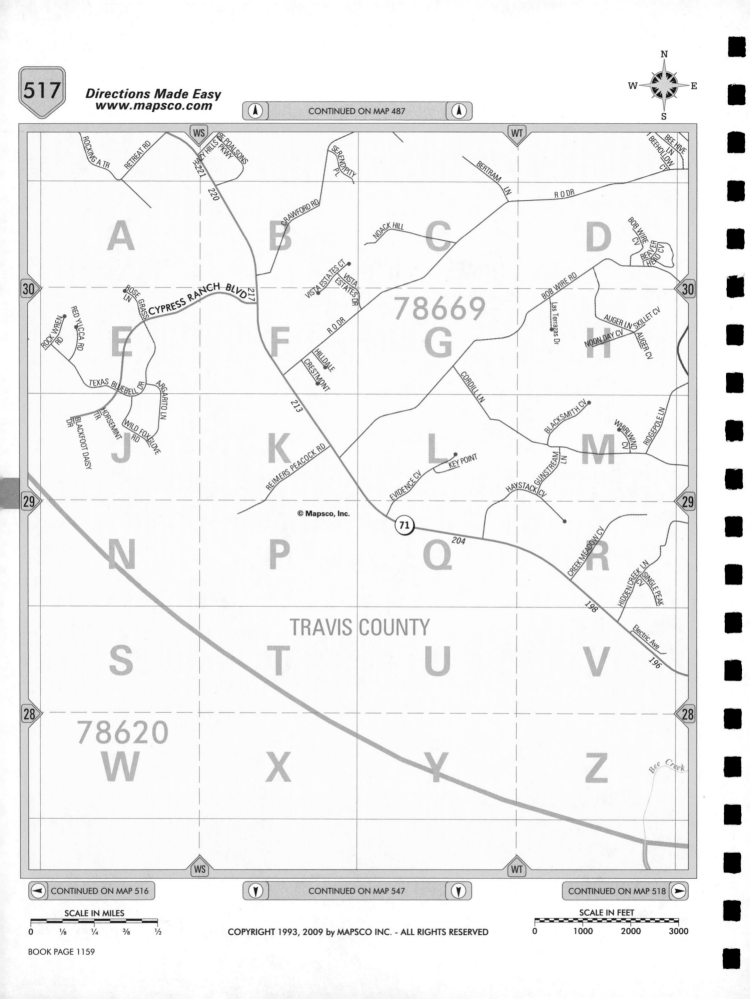

ROCKING A TR

RETREAT RD

WS

BE POALSONS

HAZY HILLS PKWY

221

220

CRAWFORD RD

SERENDIPITY PL

NOACK HILL

BERTRAM LN

R O DR

WT

BEE HIVE LN

BEEHOLLOW CT

A

B

C

D

BOB WIRE CV

BEAVER HERD CV

30

ROSE GRASS LN

CYPRESS RANCH BLVD

217

VISTA ESTATES CT

VISTA ESTATES DR

78669

BOB WIRE RD

30

RED YUCCA RD

ROCK WREN RD

E

R O DR

F

G

Las Terrazas Dr

AUGER LN SKILLET CV

NOON DAY CV

AUGER CV

H

TEXAS BLUEBELL DR

ARGARITO LN

HILLDALE

CRESTMONT

CORDILL LN

BLACKSMITH CV

WHIRLWIND CV

RIDGEPOLE LN

HORSEMINT RD

WILD FOXGLOVE

BLACKFOOT DAISY DR

J

213

K

REIMERS PEACOCK RD

L

KEY POINT

EVIDENCE CV

GUNSTREAM LN

HAYSTACK CV

M

© Mapsco, Inc.

71

204

N

P

Q

R

CREEK MEADOW CV

198

HIDDEN CREEK LN

SINGLE PEAK

29

29

Electric Ave

196

TRAVIS COUNTY

S

T

U

V

28

28

78620

W

X

Y

Z

Bee Creek

WS

CONTINUED ON MAP 547

WT

CONTINUED ON MAP 516

CONTINUED ON MAP 518

SCALE IN MILES

0   ⅛   ¼   ⅜   ½

SCALE IN FEET

0   1000   2000   3000

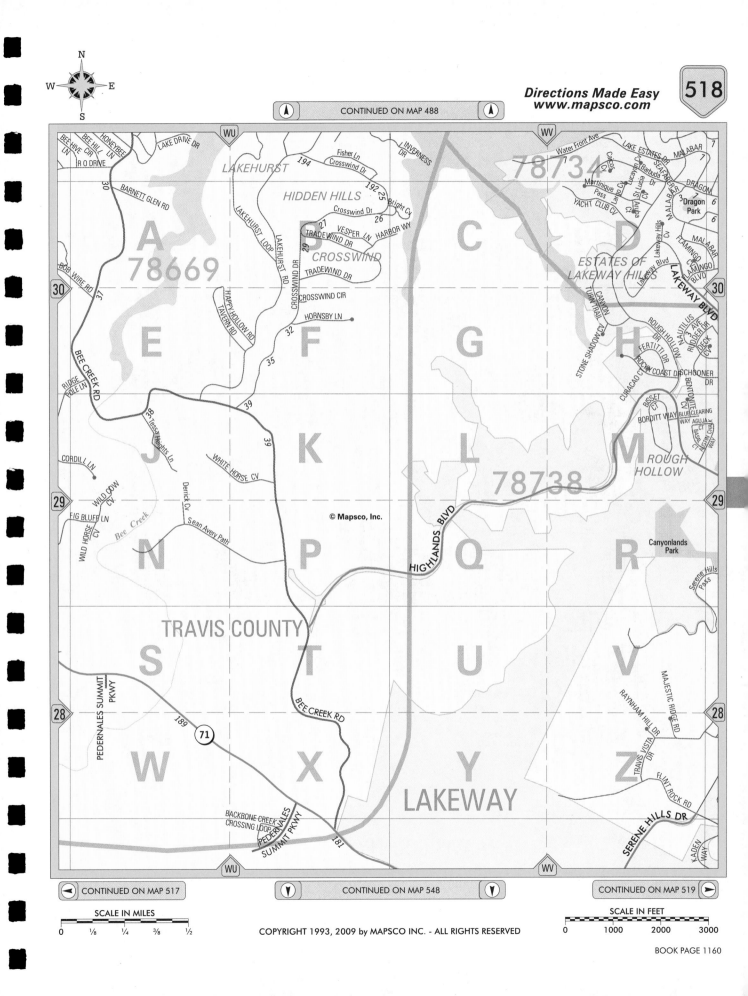

LAKEWAY

GLEN HEATHER

VILLAGE OF THE HILLS

THE HILLS OF LAKEWAY

MAJESTIC HILLS RANCHETTES

Live Oak Golf Course (Pvt)

Yaupon Golf Course (Pvt)

Hills of Lakeway Golf Course (Pvt)

Flint Rock at Hurst Creek Golf Course

FLINT ROCK AT HURST CREEK

THE RIDGE AT ALTA VISTA

Dragon Park

Park (Pvt)

Porpoise Park

Lakeway Activity Center

Lakeway Justice Center

Smith Greenbelt

Hurst Creek Greenbelt

Hamilton Greenbelt

Bella Montana

Lakeway World of Tennis

Lakeway Air Park

Lakeway Skate Park

Swim Center

Village of the Hills Offices

Swim Center Park

Serene Hills ES

Canyonlands Park

Park (Pvt)

Crystal Springs

Yaupon Creek

Hurst Creek

Yaupon Creek

LAKEWAY BLVD

HIGHLANDS BLVD

RM 620

TRAVIS COUNTY

78738   78734

© Mapsco, Inc.

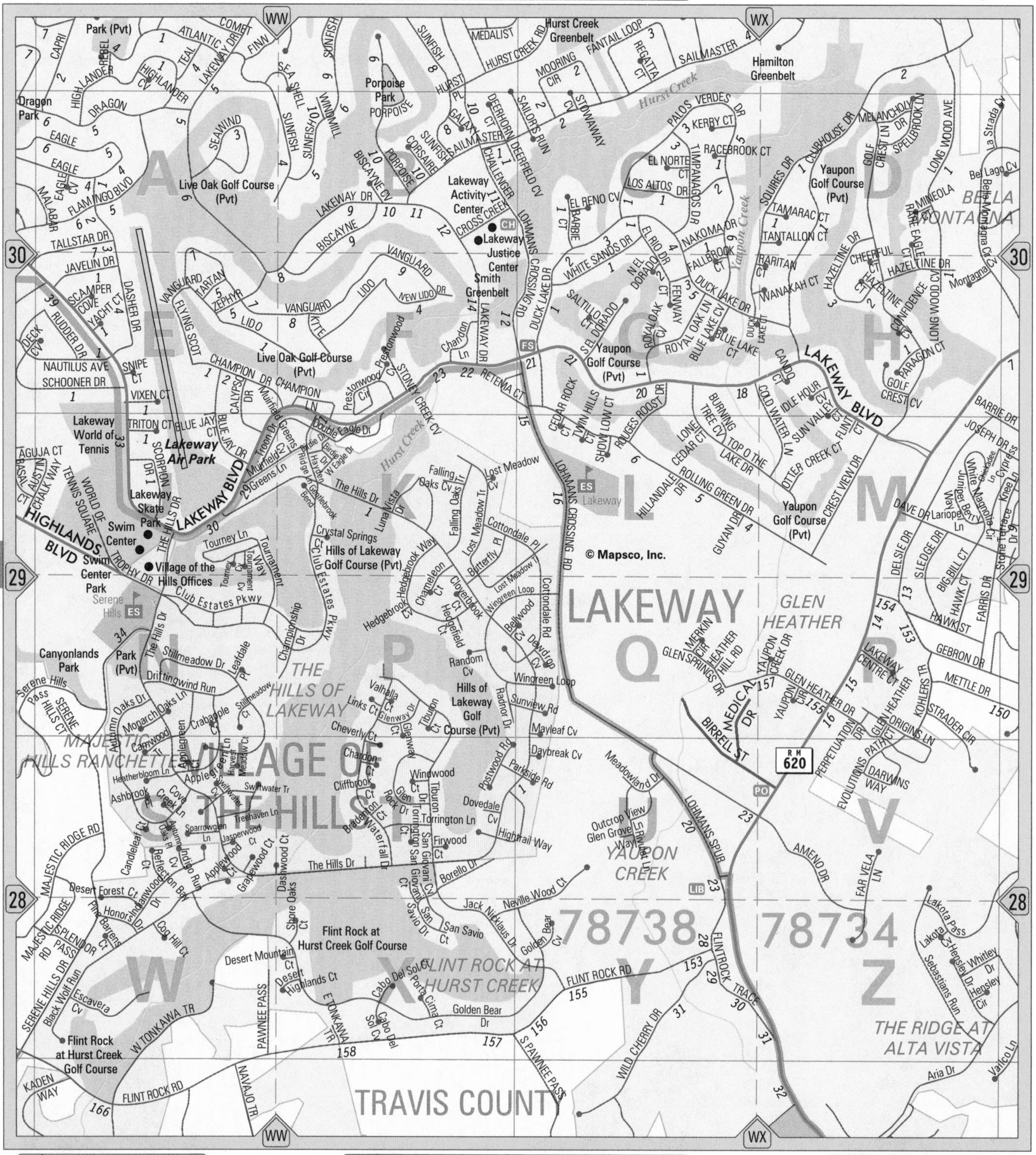

CONTINUED ON MAP 518
CONTINUED ON MAP 549
CONTINUED ON MAP 520

SCALE IN MILES
0   1/8   1/4   3/8   1/2

SCALE IN FEET
0   1000   2000   3000

CONTINUED ON MAP 490

CONTINUED ON MAP 519

CONTINUED ON MAP 550

CONTINUED ON MAP 521

SCALE IN MILES

0   ⅛   ¼   ⅜   ½

SCALE IN FEET

0   1000   2000   3000

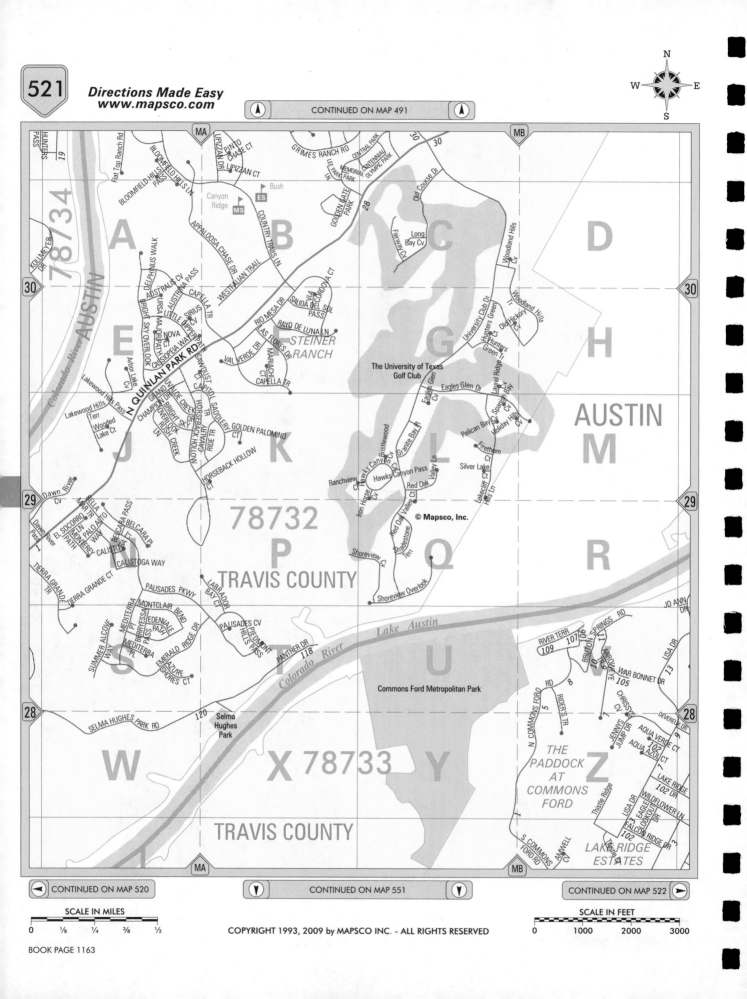

Directions Made Easy
www.mapsco.com

CONTINUED ON MAP 491

N
W   E
S

AUSTIN

78734

© Mapsco, Inc.

78732

TRAVIS COUNTY

AUSTIN

Lake Austin

Colorado River

Commons Ford Metropolitan Park

THE PADDOCK AT COMMONS FORD

LAKE RIDGE ESTATES

W   X 78733   Y   Z

TRAVIS COUNTY

CONTINUED ON MAP 520   CONTINUED ON MAP 551   CONTINUED ON MAP 522

SCALE IN MILES

0   ⅛   ¼   ⅜   ½

SCALE IN FEET

0   1000   2000   3000

COPYRIGHT 1993, 2009 by MAPSCO INC. - ALL RIGHTS RESERVED

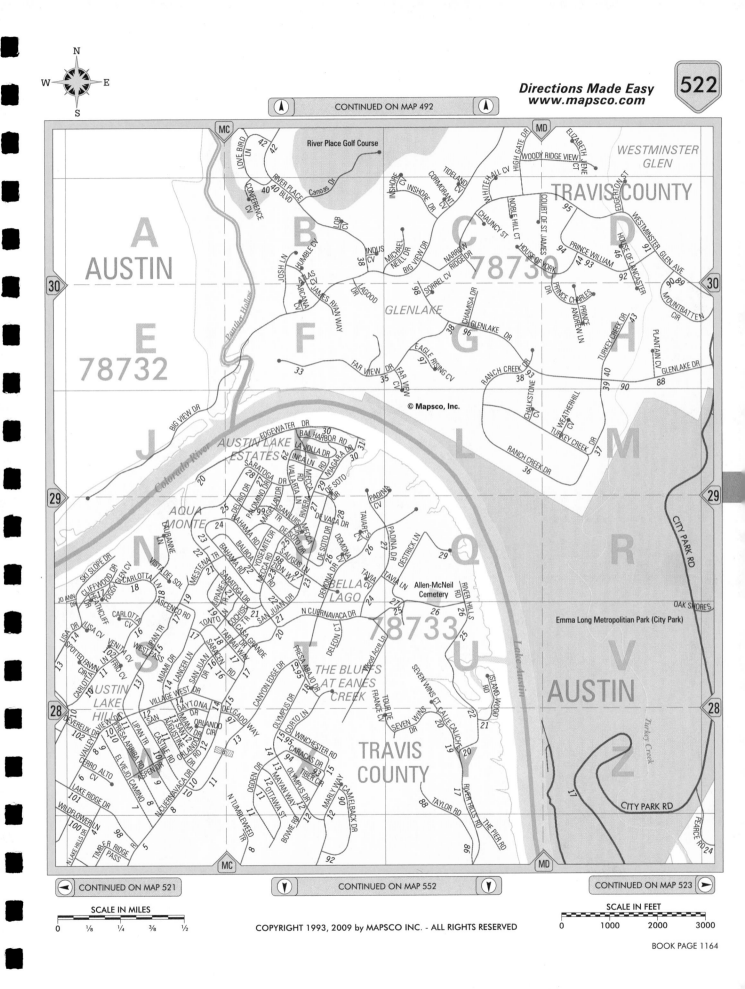

CONTINUED ON MAP 492

Directions Made Easy
www.mapsco.com

522

N
W E
S

MC

River Place Golf Course

WESTMINSTER GLEN

MD

Elizabeth Jene Ct

Woody Ridge View

High Gate Dr

TRAVIS COUNTY

Lone Bird Ln

42 42

River Place Blvd

40 40

Conference Cv

Canoas Dr

Inshore Cv

Inshore Dr

Cormorant Cv

Tideland Cv

Whitehall Cv

Court De St James

Edgerton Ct

95

Westminster Glen Ave

House De Lancaster

A
AUSTIN

B

Josh Ln

Humble Cv

Atlas Cv

Arcana Cv

James Ryan Way

Indus Cv

38

Lob Cv

Michael Neill Dr

Big View Dr

Narrow Ridge Dr

Noble Hill Ct

House of York

Prince William

C
78730

94

44 93

46 91

92

D

Mountbatten Cir

90 89

30

30

E
78732

Pantha Hollow

Lagood Dr

Glenlake

Sorrel Cv

Chamisa Dr

Glenlake Dr

98

38 96

Eagle Rising Cv

97

Prince Charles Dr

Prince Andrew Ln

G

Ranch Creek

93

38

Chalkstone Cv

Weatherhill Dr

Turkey Creek Dr

Turkey Creek

37

Turkey Creek Dr

39 40

90 88

Plantain Cv

Glenlake Dr

43

H

Far View Dr

35

Far View Cv

33

© Mapsco, Inc.

Ranch Creek Dr

36

L

M

Big View Dr

Colorado River

J

Austin Lake Estates

Edgewater Dr

Bal Harbor Rd

La Jolla Dr

Inca Ln

Valaria Ln

Mecca Rd

Niagara Rd

De Soto Dr

30

29

30 31

Saratoga Dr

Del Rio Dr

Palomino Dr

Paomino Dr

Bahama Rd

Magellan Dr

San Luis Dr

De Soto Dr

Yosemite Dr

Mecca Rd

San Juan Wy

Demona Dr

Padina Cv

Tavaris Dr

Padina Dr

Destrick Ln

Tavia Ln

26 27

29

Q

Aqua Monte

Laurianne Ln

Vista Del Sol

20

25

24

23

22

21

Mestena Ln

Saratoga Dr

Balboa Dr

Bahama Rd

Mecca Rd

22

De Soto Dr

98

25

Uranie Dr

San Juan Dr

Tavia Cv

24

26

Demona Dr

Bella Lago

Allen-McNeil Cemetery

River Hills Rd

26

25

26

78733

R

City Park Rd

Oak Shores

Emma Long Metropolitan Park (City Park)

N

Ski Slope Dr

Cliffwood Dr

Heathcliff

Jo Ann Dr

Foggy Glen Cv

Carlotta Ln

17

18

Ascengo Rd

Tonto Ln

19

Pan Tr

West Pass

Lisa Dr

Ilsa Cv

14

Spotted Fawn Ln

Venita Cv

Frio Cv

102

Carlotta Cv

16

15

S

Carlotta Ln

13

11

Miami Dr

Lancer Ln

San Juan Dr

Cochise Tr

Casa Grande

Tartar Win

Saracen Rd

17

21

19

21

20

N Cuernavaca Dr

Deleon Ct

Presa Abajo Dr

19 95

18

T

The Bluffs at Eanes Creek

Canyon Edge Dr

Olympus Dr

Wood Ace Ln

France Cv

Seven Wins Ct

Seven Wins Rd

Seven Wins Dr

Calle Caliche

22

Island Wood Rd

U

V
AUSTIN

Lake Austin

Turkey Creek

28

28

Deverux Dr

Valley View Dr

10

12

San

Lipan Tr

Presa Arriba Rd

Castle Rd

Aspen Dr

Augustine

Orlando Dr

Orlando Cir

Daytona Dr

Miami Dr

Village West

13

14

Delgado Way

Winchester Rd

Coreto Ln

Caracas Dr

Tiber Cv

95 97

93

91

15

16

17

M

Cerro Alto Cv

6

El Viejo Camino

9

N Cuernavaca Dr

7

8

10

11

Ogden Dr

Bowie Rd

Ottawa St

Mayan Way

Olympus Dr

12

13

14

11

12

Marly Way

Camelback Dr

Taylor Rd

15

Z

Pearce Rd

24

17

Lake Ridge Dr

101

Wildflower Ln

100

98

Lake Hills Dr

Timber Ridge Pass

5

8

92

88

River Hills Rd

The Pier Rd

MD

CONTINUED ON MAP 521

CONTINUED ON MAP 552

CONTINUED ON MAP 523

Austin Lake Hills

TRAVIS COUNTY

SCALE IN MILES
0   1/8   1/4   3/8   1/2

SCALE IN FEET
0   1000   2000   3000

BOOK PAGE 1164

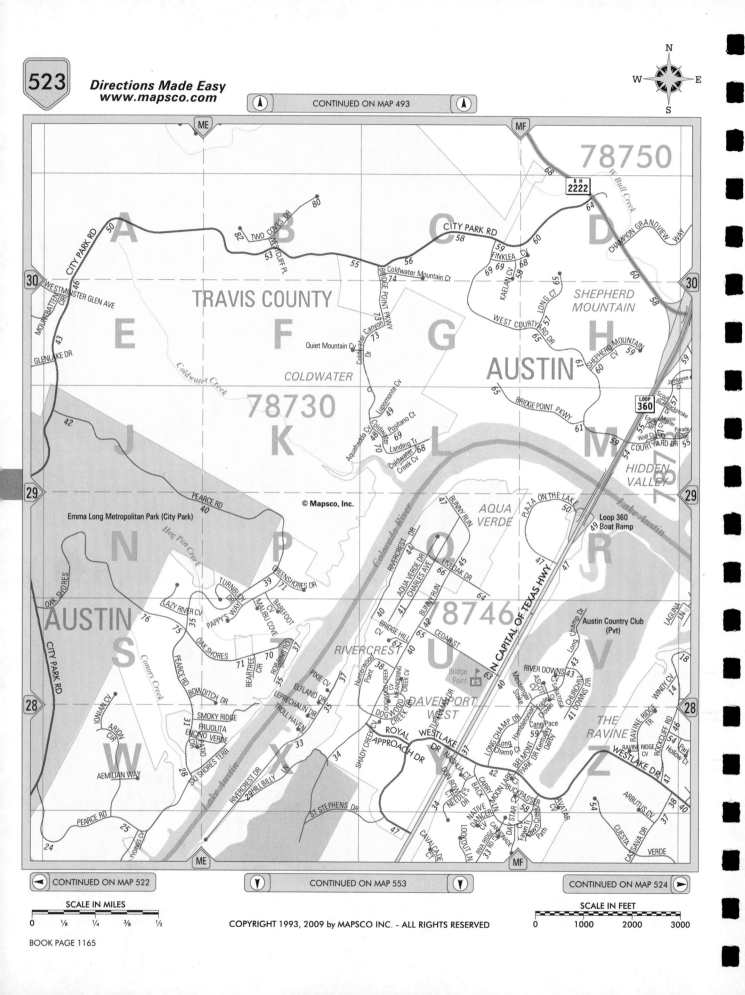

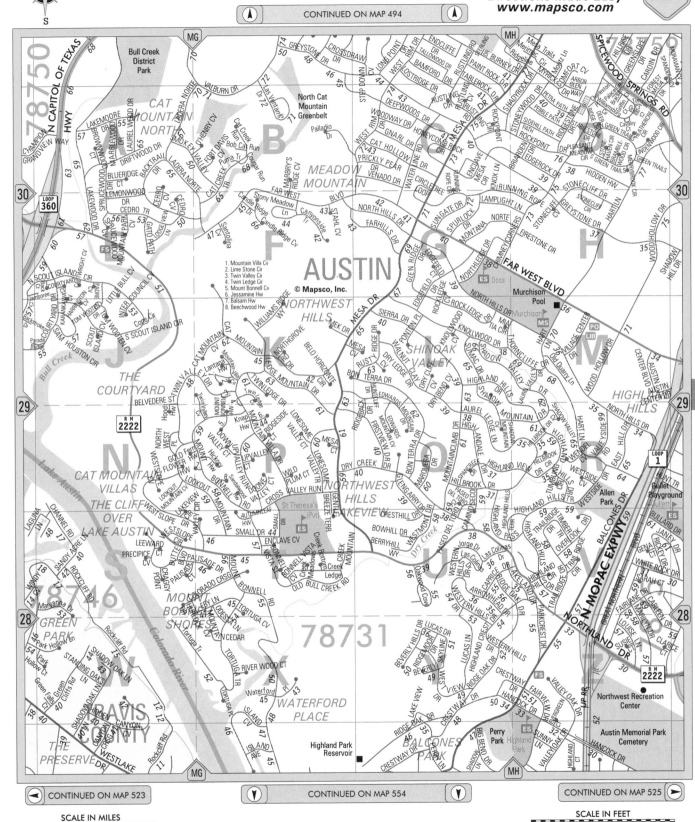

CONTINUED ON MAP 494

CONTINUED ON MAP 523
CONTINUED ON MAP 554
CONTINUED ON MAP 525

AUSTIN

© Mapsco, Inc.

78731

78750

78746

1. Mountain Villa Cv
2. Lime Stone Cir
3. Twin Valley Cir
4. Twin Ledge Cir
5. Mount Bonnell Cv
6. Jessamine Hw
7. Balsam Hw
8. Beechwood Hw

SCALE IN MILES
0   1/8   1/4   3/8   1/2

SCALE IN FEET
0   1000   2000   3000

BOOK PAGE 1166

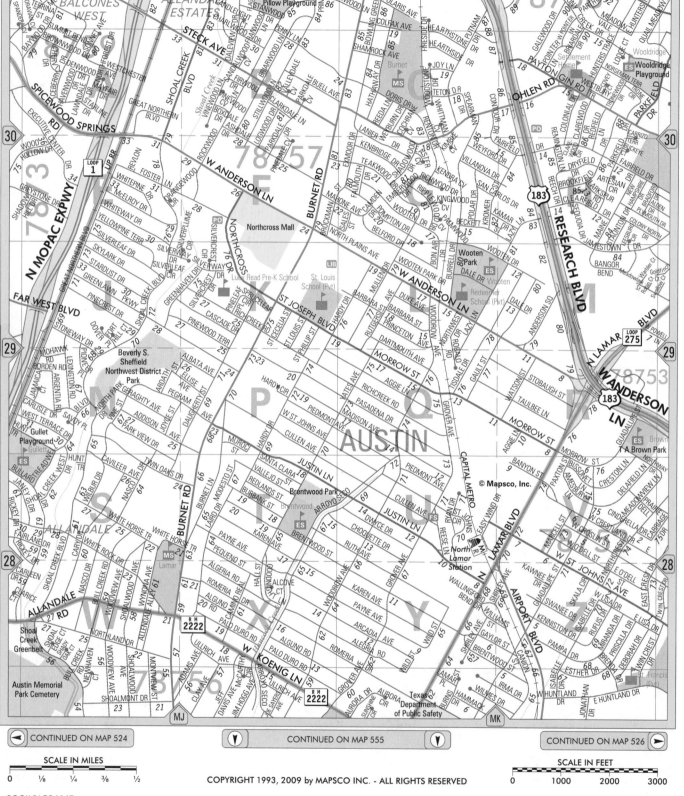

CONTINUED ON MAP 495

CONTINUED ON MAP 524

CONTINUED ON MAP 555

CONTINUED ON MAP 526

SCALE IN MILES

0   1/8   1/4   3/8   1/2

SCALE IN FEET

0   1000   2000   3000

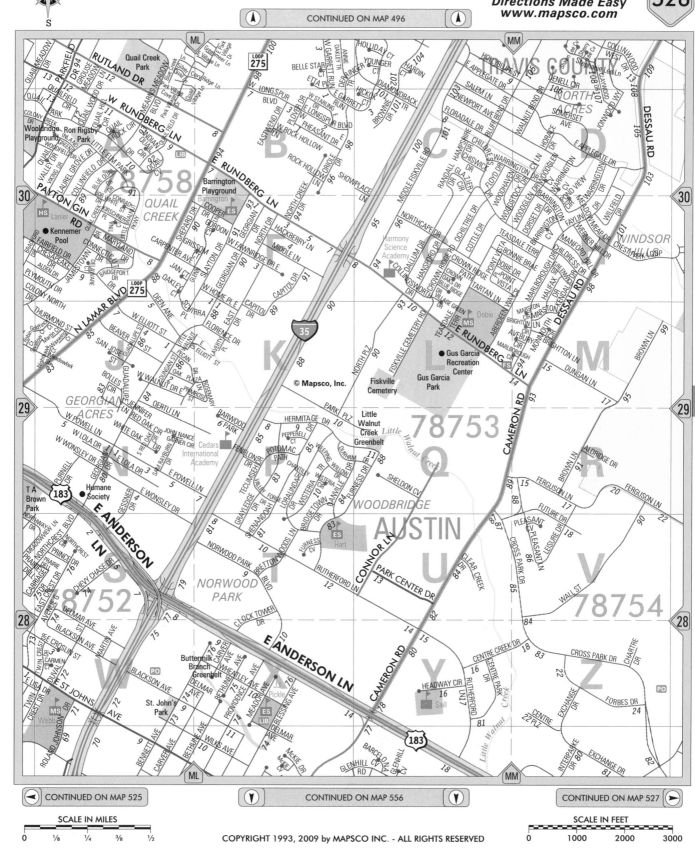

CONTINUED ON MAP 496

CONTINUED ON MAP 525
CONTINUED ON MAP 556
CONTINUED ON MAP 527

© Mapsco, Inc.

SCALE IN MILES
0   1/8   1/4   3/8   1/2

SCALE IN FEET
0   1000   2000   3000

CONTINUED ON MAP 497

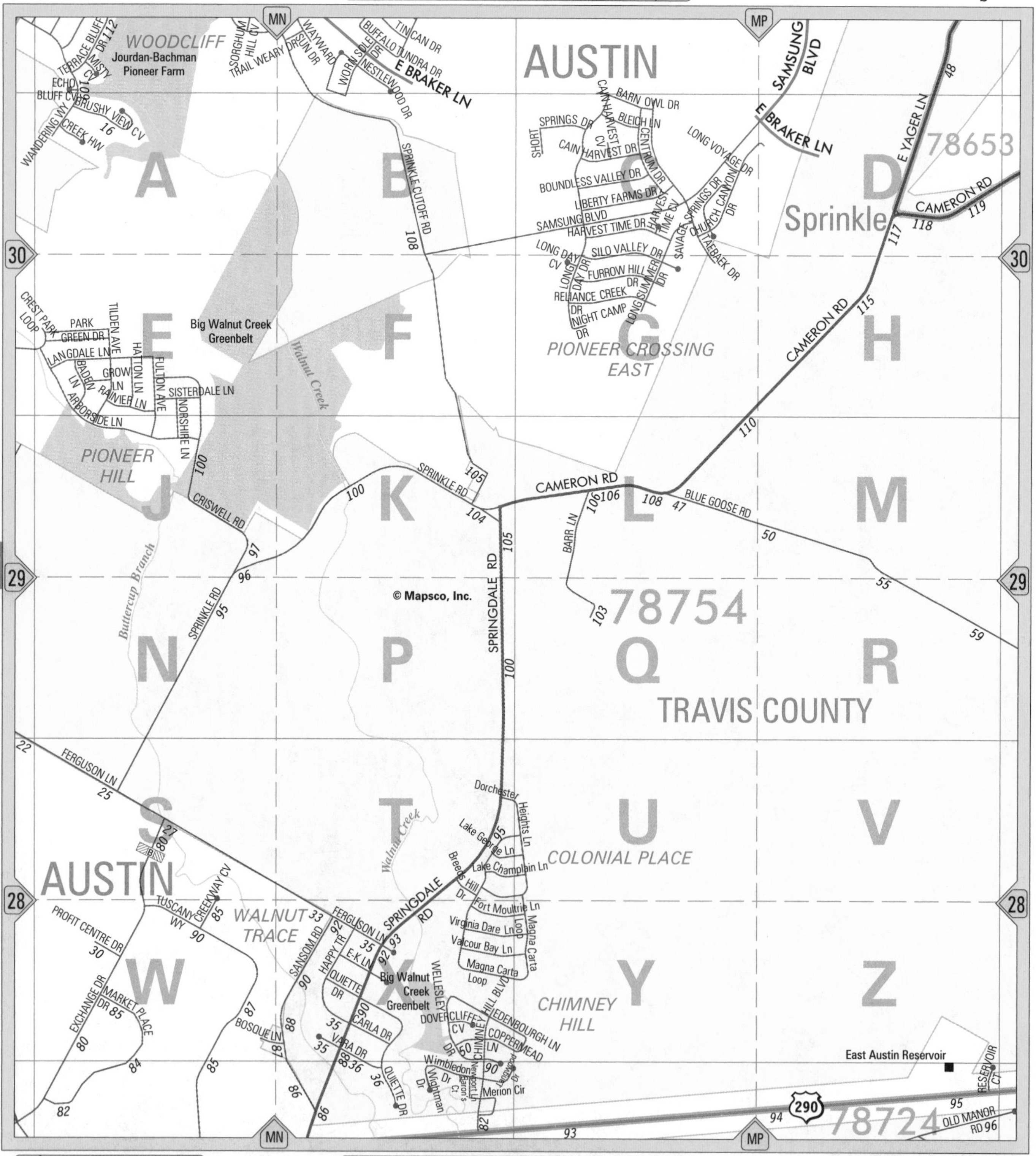

N W E S

AUSTIN

WOODCLIFF

Jourdan-Bachman Pioneer Farm

E BRAKER LN

SAMSUNG BLVD

E BRAKER LN

78653

Sprinkle

CAMERON RD

30 30

Big Walnut Creek Greenbelt

PIONEER CROSSING EAST

PIONEER HILL

Walnut Creek

Buttercup Branch

SPRINKLE RD

CAMERON RD

BLUE GOOSE RD

29 29

© Mapsco, Inc.

SPRINGDALE RD

78754

TRAVIS COUNTY

Walnut Creek

FERGUSON LN

Dorchester

COLONIAL PLACE

28 28

AUSTIN

WALNUT TRACE

SPRINGDALE RD

Big Walnut Creek Greenbelt

CHIMNEY HILL

East Austin Reservoir

290 **78724** OLD MANOR RD

MN MP

CONTINUED ON MAP 526

CONTINUED ON MAP 557

CONTINUED ON MAP 528

SCALE IN MILES

0 1/8 1/4 3/8 1/2

COPYRIGHT 1993, 2009 by MAPSCO INC. - ALL RIGHTS RESERVED

SCALE IN FEET

0 1000 2000 3000

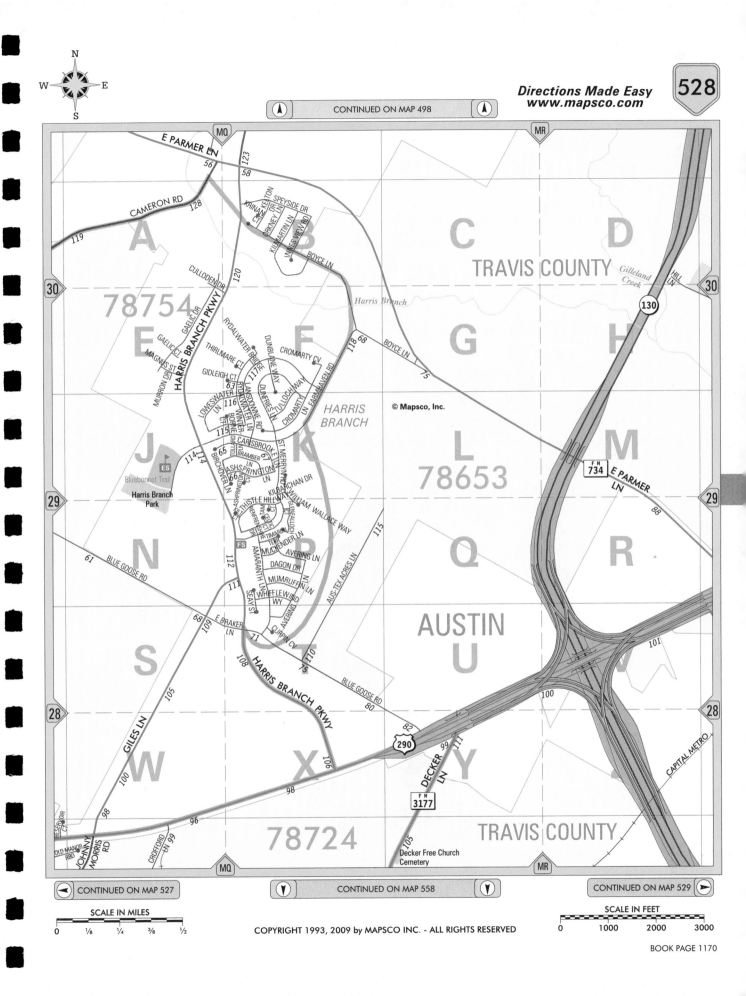

N
W E
S

CONTINUED ON MAP 498

E PARMER LN

MQ

MR

CAMERON RD

123

56

58

128

KRINAN CT

ORKNEY DR

KELTON

SPEYSIDE DR

KILMARTIN LN

INNES VIEW RD

A

119

B

BOYCE LN

TRAVIS COUNTY

Gilleland Creek

C

D

HILL LN

30

30

CULLODEN DR

78754

120

Harris Branch

130

GAELIC DR

HARRIS BRANCH PKWY

RYDALWATER BRIDGE

DUNBLANE WAY

CROMARTY CV

118

68

BOYCE LN

GAELIC CT

THIRLMARE CT

E

F

G

H

MAGNUS ST

GIDLEIGH CT

RYDALWATER LN

LANSDOWNE LN

TULLOCH WAY

FARMHAVEN RD

75

MURRON DR

117

63

WINTER LN

DUNFRIES LN

CROMARTY LN

Harris Branch

116

BOYNE LN

LOWESWATER LN

115

CARISBROOK LN

ST MERRYN RD

© Mapsco, Inc.

78653

114

J

K

L

M

BIRCHOVER LN

GRAMBER CT

ASHPRINGTON LN

KILBARCHAN DR

GLENALLOCH

WILLIAM WALLACE WAY

FM 734

E PARMER LN

88

Bluebonnet Trail

ES

66

66

66

THISTLE HILL WAY

115

29

29

Harris Branch Park

BRENTHOPE

AVERING LN

MUCKENDER LN

TIMABOU

DAGON DR

AUS-TEX ACRES LN

N

112

FS

AMARANTH LN

P

Q

R

61

BLUE GOOSE RD

111

MUMRUFFIN LN

WHIFFLE WIND WY

SEAY ST

AVERING LN

AUSTIN

S

U

V

28

68

109

E BRAKER LN

71

CURPIN CV

110

108

HARRIS BRANCH PKWY

75

BLUE GOOSE RD

80

100

101

28

GILES LN

105

100

82

290

99

111

DECKER LN

CAPITAL METRO

98

96

W

X

106

Y

98

RESERVOIR CT

OLD MANOR RBD

JOHNNY MORRIS RD

CRAFORD LN 99

78724

FM 3177

105

TRAVIS COUNTY

Decker Free Church Cemetery

MQ

MR

CONTINUED ON MAP 527

CONTINUED ON MAP 558

CONTINUED ON MAP 529

SCALE IN MILES

0   ⅛   ¼   ⅜   ½

SCALE IN FEET

0   1000   2000   3000

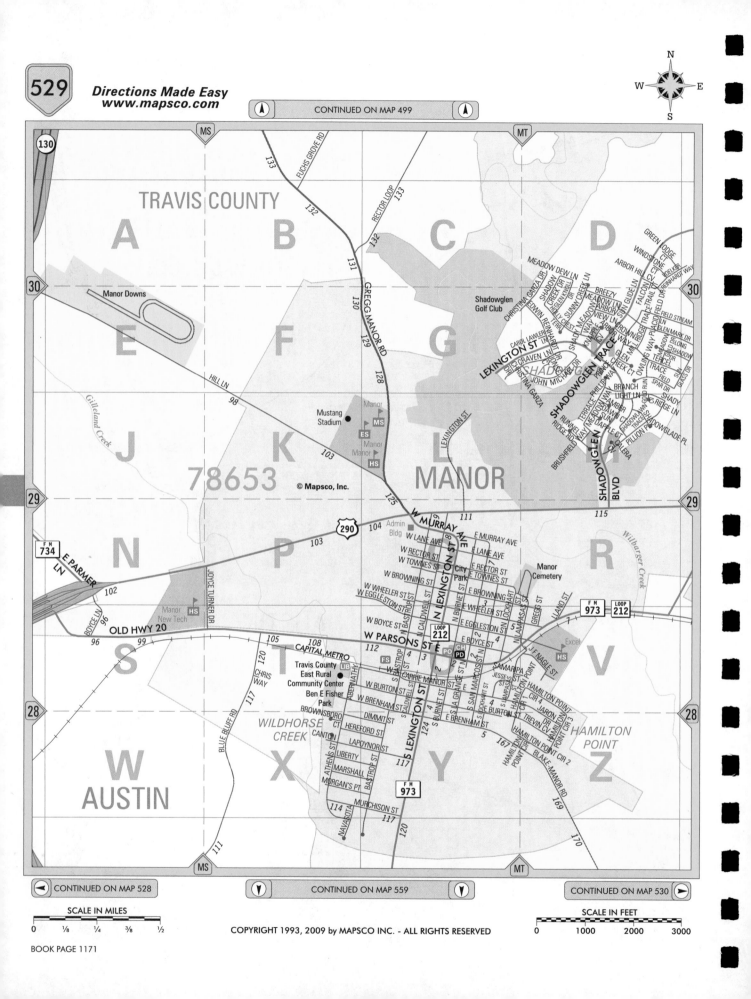

529

Directions Made Easy
www.mapsco.com

CONTINUED ON MAP 499

130

TRAVIS COUNTY

A   B   C   D

Green Lodge
Windstone
Arbor Hill CV

30   30

Manor Downs

Shadowglen Golf Club

Meadow Dew Ln
Shadow Creek Dr
Sunny Creek Ln
Breezy Way
Falconhead

E   F   G

Lexington St
John Michael Dr
Christina Garza Dr
Edwin Reinhardt Dr

HILL LN
98

GREGG MANOR RD
129
128

SHADOWGLEN

Mustang Stadium
Manor
MS
ES
Manor
HS

78653

© Mapsco, Inc.
125

J   K   L

MANOR

Lexington St

SHADOWGLEN BLVD

Branch
Shady Glen

29   29
115

E PARMER LN
FM 734
102

JOYCE TURNER DR

290
103   104
Admin Bldg

W MURRAY AVE
9   8
111

E MURRAY AVE
E LANE AVE

Manor Cemetery

N   P   R

Wilbarger Creek

Boyce Ln
96
OLD HWY 20
99

Manor New Tech
HS

W LANE AVE
W RECTOR ST
W TOWNES ST
W BROWNING ST

City Park

E RECTOR ST
E TOWNES ST

E BROWNING ST

FM 973
LOOP 212

N LEXINGTON ST
N BURNET ST
N CALDWELL ST

W WHEELER ST
W EGGLESTON ST

E WHEELER ST
E EGGLESTON ST

N LOCKHART ST
GREGG ST
LAND ST
7

S   LOOP 212
105   108
CAPITAL METRO
112

W PARSONS ST E
W BOYCE ST

CH
PO
PD

E BOYCE ST

J F NAGLE ST

Excel
HS

CHRIS WAY

Travis County East Rural Community Center
Ben E Fisher Park

FS
LIB

CARRIE MANOR
BASTROP ST
CALDWELL ST

W BURTON ST
W BRENHAM ST

S BURNET ST
S LEXINGTON ST
LA GRANGE ST
S SAN MARCOS ST
S LOCKHART ST

SAMARIPA
JESSE
HAMPTON
HAMILTON POINT

HAMILTON POINT CIR 1
JARON DR
TREVIN CV

V

ABERNATHY
BROWNSBORO CT
DIMMIT ST
HEREFORD ST
CANTON
LAPOYNOR ST
LIBERTY
ATHENS ST
MARSHALL
MORGAN'S PT

28   28

WILDHORSE CREEK

W   X   Y   Z

AUSTIN

FM 973

MURCHISON ST
114
117
120

NAVASOTA

124
117

S COCKRELL ST
E BURTON ST
E BRENHAM ST
5
167

HAMILTON POINT CIR 2
HAMILTON POINT CIR 3
BLAKE MANOR RD

HAMILTON POINT

169
170

CONTINUED ON MAP 528

CONTINUED ON MAP 559

CONTINUED ON MAP 530

SCALE IN MILES
0   1/8   1/4   3/8   1/2

SCALE IN FEET
0   1000   2000   3000

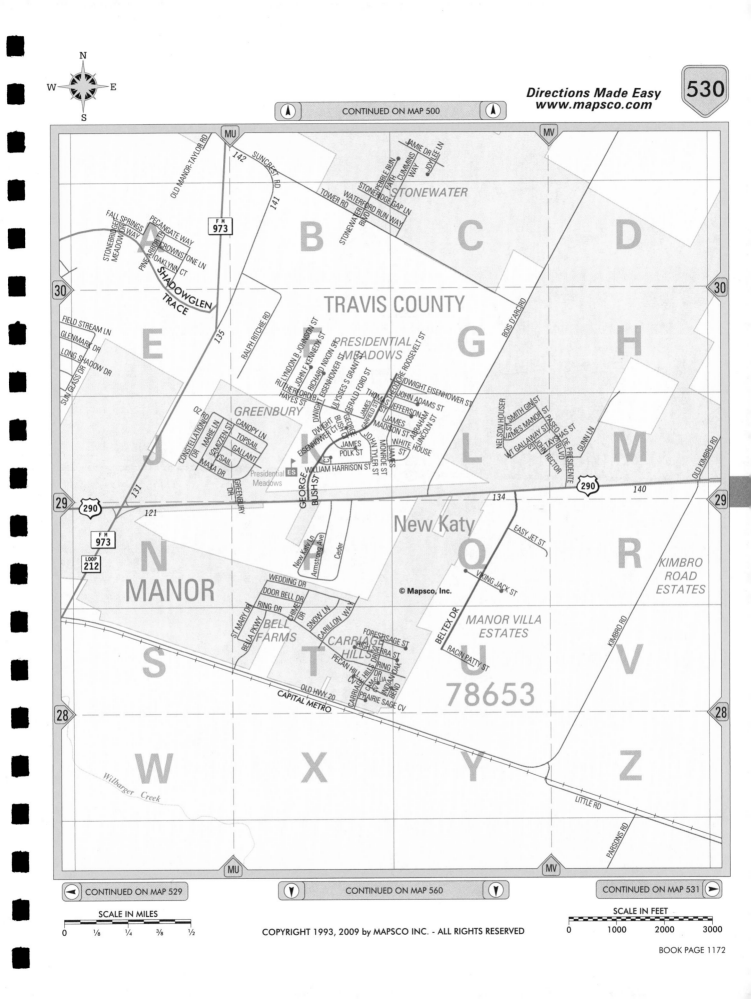

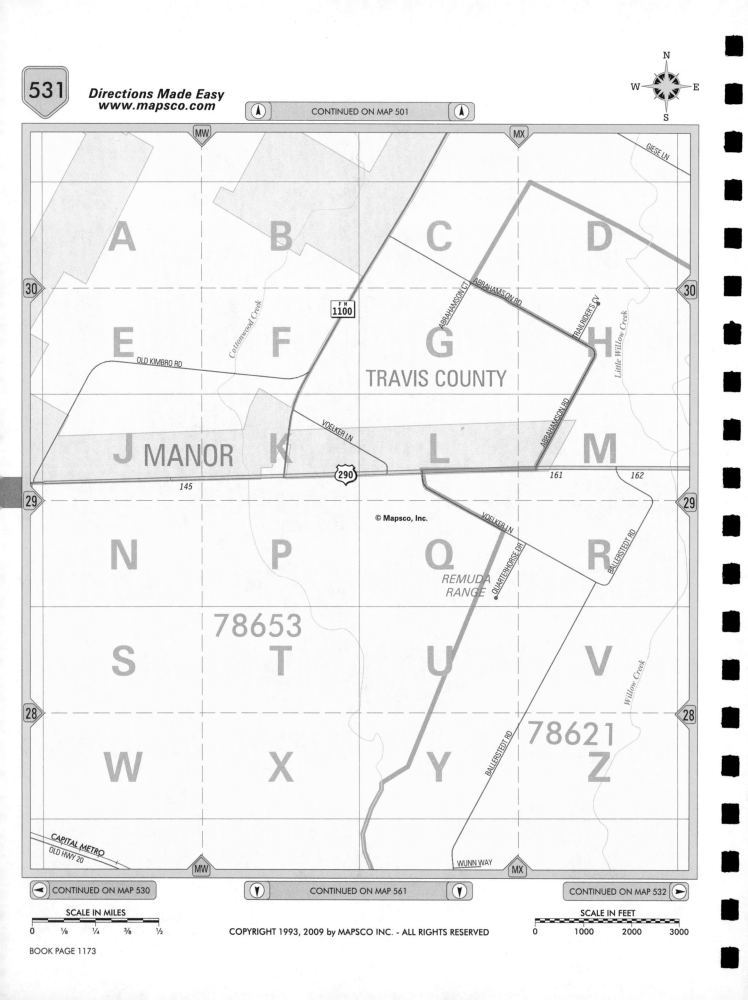

531

Directions Made Easy
www.mapsco.com

CONTINUED ON MAP 501

N
W · E
S

A | B | C | D

30 | 30

Cottonwood Creek

FM
1100

E | F | G | H

GIESE LN

ABRAHAMSON CT

ABRAHAMSON RD

TRAILRIDER'S CV

Little Willow Creek

OLD KIMBRO RD

TRAVIS COUNTY

VOELKER LN

ABRAHAMSON RD

J | K | L | M

MANOR

290

145 | 161 | 162

29 | 29

© Mapsco, Inc.

N | P | Q | R

VOELKER LN

QUARTERHORSE DR

BALLERSTEDT RD

REMUDA
RANGE

78653

S | T | U | V

Willow Creek

28 | 28

BALLERSTEDT RD

78621

W | X | Y | Z

CAPITAL METRO
OLD HWY 20

WUNN WAY

CONTINUED ON MAP 530
CONTINUED ON MAP 561
CONTINUED ON MAP 532

SCALE IN MILES

0 | ⅛ | ¼ | ⅜ | ½

SCALE IN FEET

0 | 1000 | 2000 | 3000

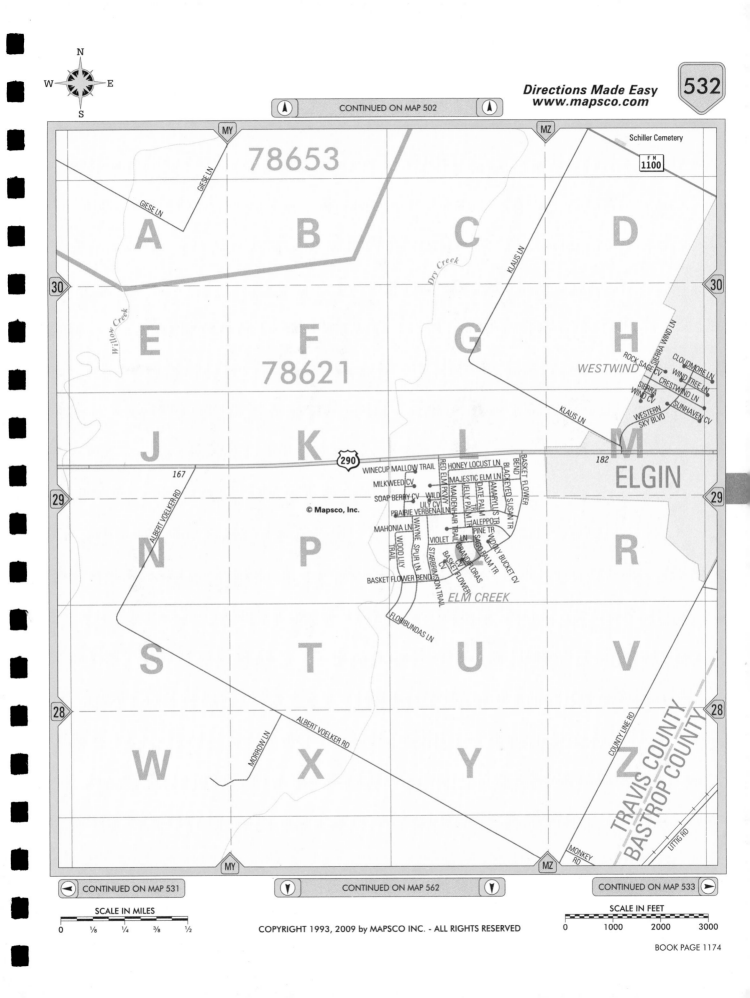

N

W E

S

CONTINUED ON MAP 502

MY

MZ

Schiller Cemetery

FM 1100

78653

A   B   C   D

GIESE LN

GIESE LN

30   30

Willow Creek

Dry Creek

KLAUS LN

E   F   G   H

WESTWIND

ROCK SAGE CV

SIERRA WIND LN

CLOUDMORE LN

WIND TREE LN

CRESTWIND LN

SIERRA WIND CV

SUNHAVEN CV

WESTERN SKY BLVD

78621

KLAUS LN

J   K   L   182   M

290   ELGIN

WINECUP MALLOW TRAIL

167   MILKWEED CV

SOAP BERRY CV   WILD

PRAIRIE VERBENA LN

RED ELM PKWY

HONEY LOCUST LN

MAJESTIC ELM LN

JELLY PALM

DATE PALM

MAIDENHAIR TRAIL

AMARYLLIS TR

BLACKEYED SUSAN TR

BASKET FLOWER BEND

29   29

© Mapsco, Inc.

MAHONIA LN

WOOD LILY TRAIL

WAYNE SPUR LN

LILY CV

VIOLET LN

ALEPPO

PINE TR

SAGO PALM TR

GRAND FLORAS

WOOLLY BUCKET CV

N   P   L   R

BASKET FLOWER BEND

STARBRIMASON TRAIL

BASKET FLOWER

ELM CREEK

FLORIBUNDAS LN

S   T   U   V

28   28

COUNTY LINE RD

MORROW LN

ALBERT VOELKER RD

W   X   Y   Z

TRAVIS COUNTY

BASTROP COUNTY

LITTIG RD

MY   MZ   MONKEY RD

CONTINUED ON MAP 531   CONTINUED ON MAP 562   CONTINUED ON MAP 533

SCALE IN MILES

0   1/8   1/4   3/8   1/2

SCALE IN FEET

0   1000   2000   3000

COPYRIGHT 1993, 2009 by MAPSCO INC. - ALL RIGHTS RESERVED

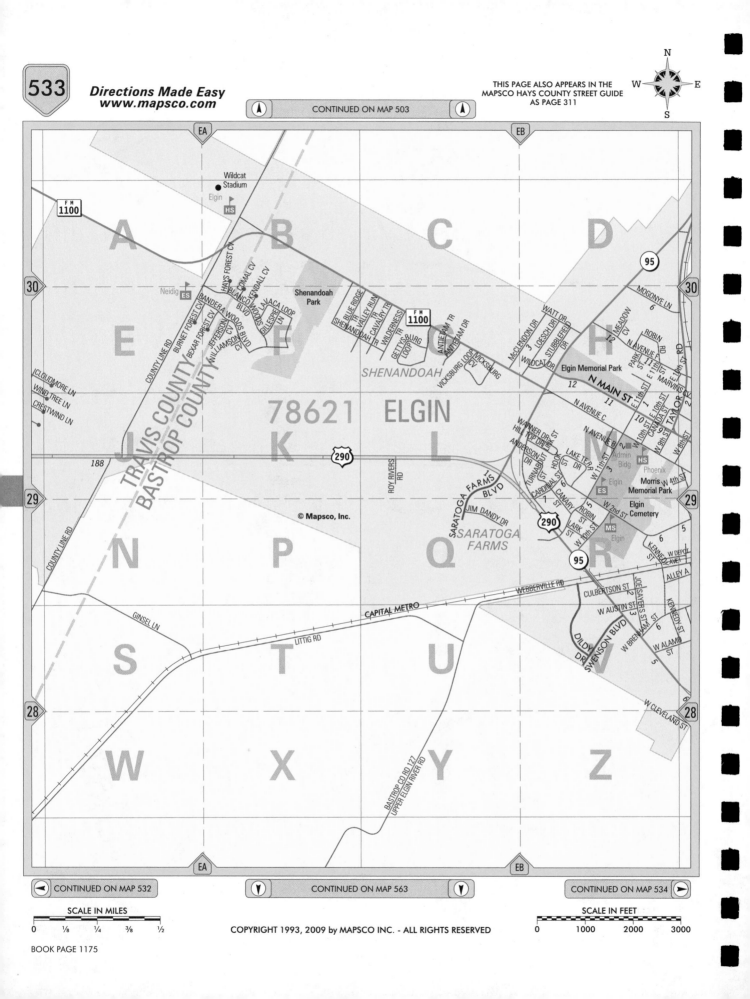

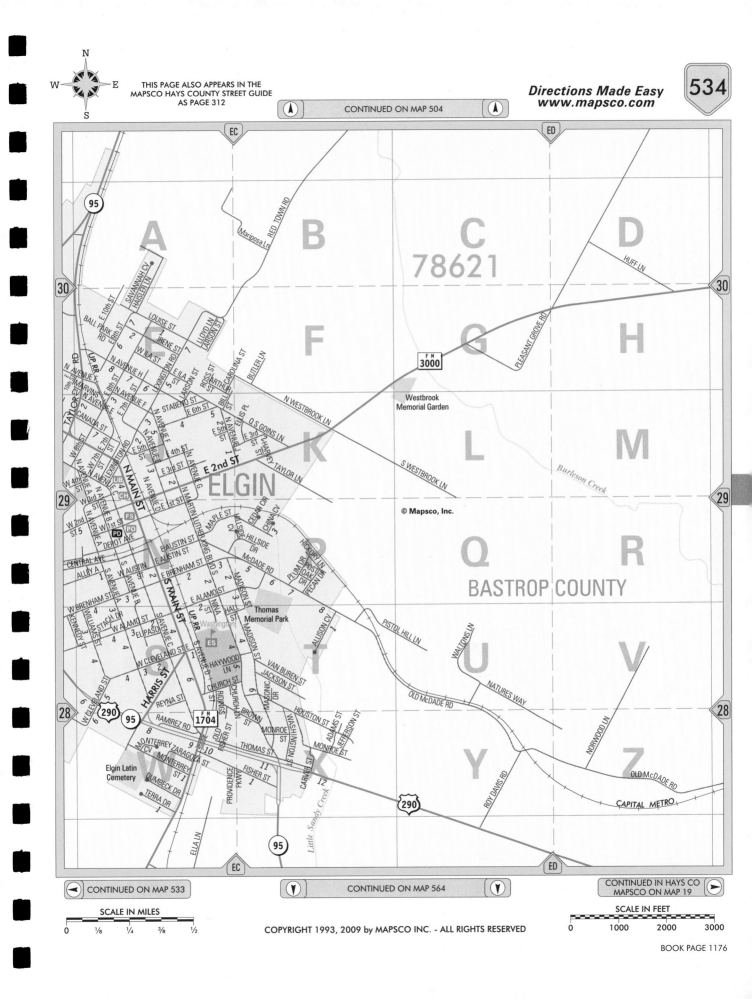

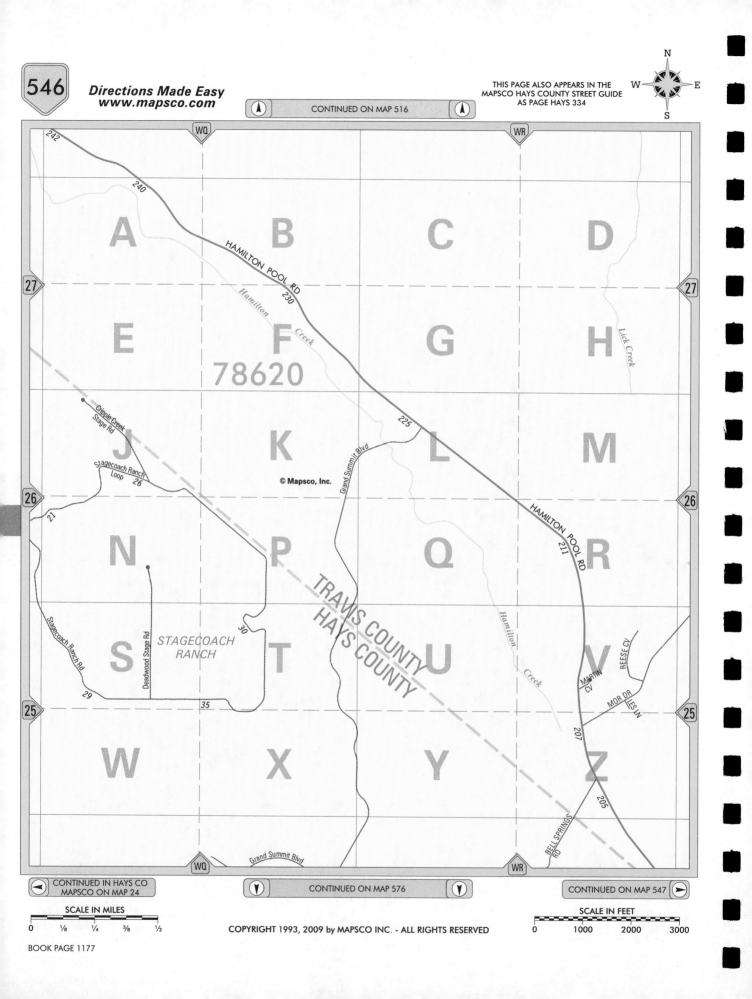

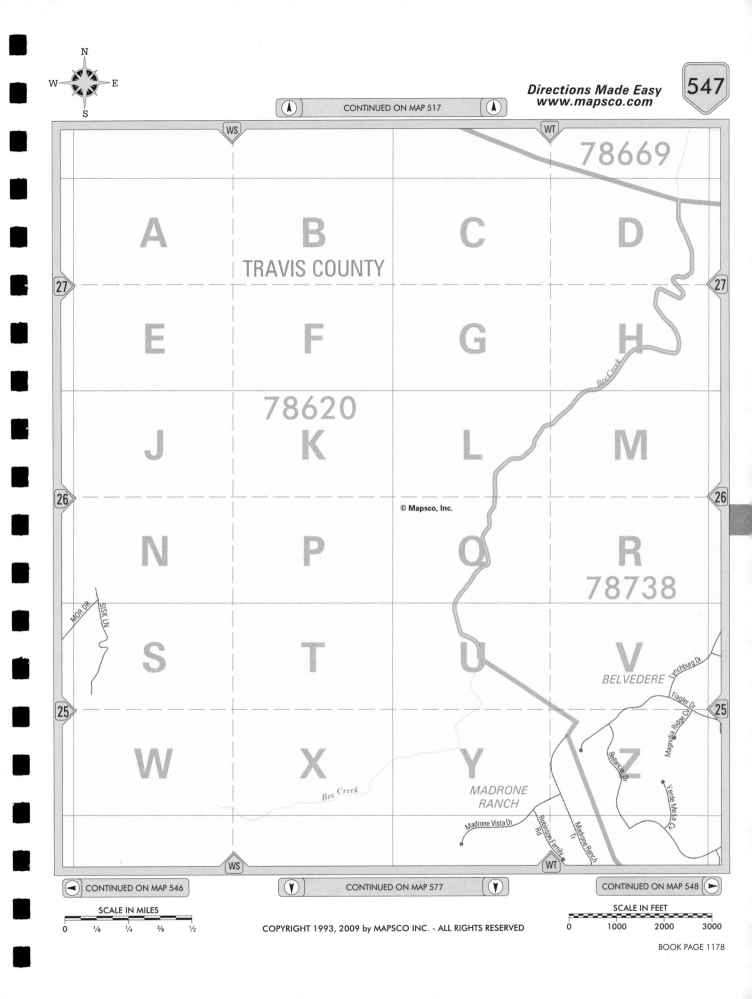

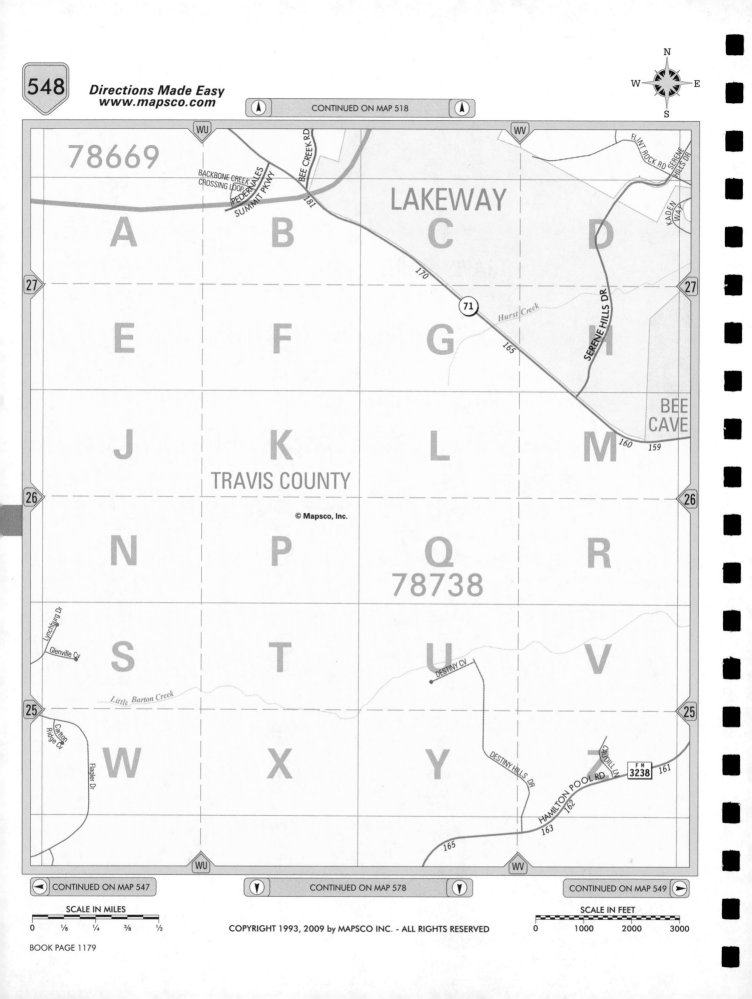

CONTINUED ON MAP 518

N
W E
S

78669

WU

Backbone Creek
Crossing Loop

Bee Creek Rd

Pedernales
Summit Pkwy

181

WV

Flint Rock Rd

Serene Hills Dr

LAKEWAY

Kaden Way

A B C D

170

71

Hurst Creek

Serene Hills Dr

27 27

E F G H

165

BEE
CAVE

160

159

J K L M

TRAVIS COUNTY

© Mapsco, Inc.

26 26

N P Q R

78738

Lynchburg Dr

Glenville Cv

S T U V

Destiny Cv

Little Barton Creek

25 25

Canton
Ridge Cv

Flagler Dr

W X Y Z

Destiny Hills Dr

Hamilton Pool Rd

Caudill Ln

FM 3238

161

162

163

165

WU

WV

◄ CONTINUED ON MAP 547
▼ CONTINUED ON MAP 578 ▼
CONTINUED ON MAP 549 ►

SCALE IN MILES
0   ⅛   ¼   ⅜   ½

SCALE IN FEET
0   1000   2000   3000

BOOK PAGE 1179

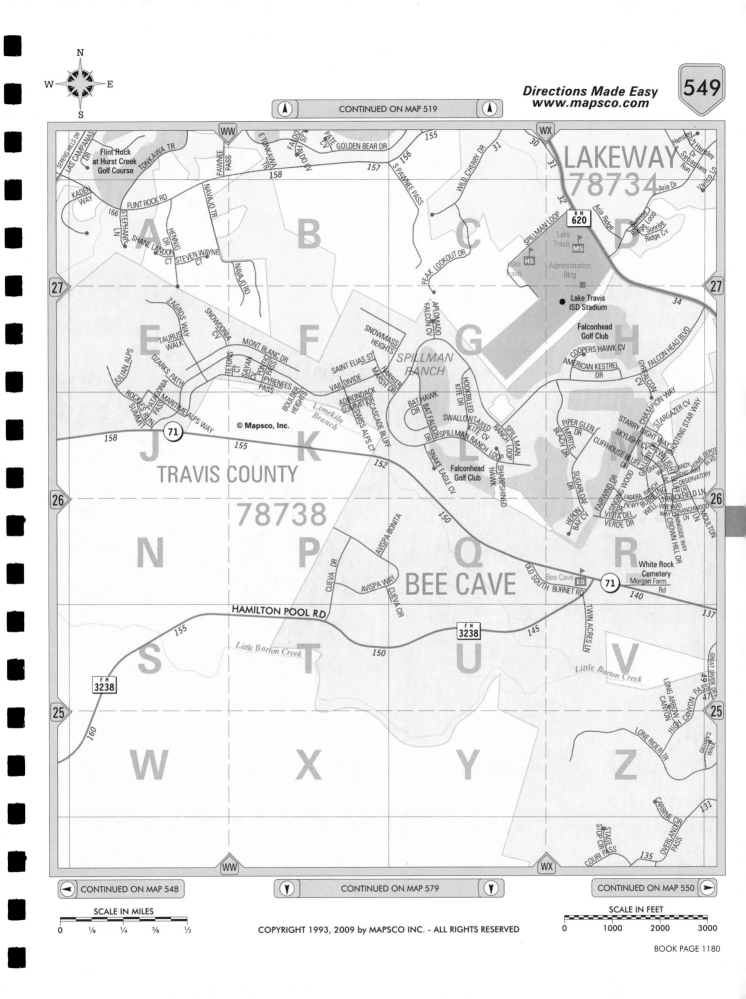

CONTINUED ON MAP 519

LAKEWAY
78734

N
W E
S

Flint Rock
at Hurst Creek
Golf Course

SERENS HILLS DR
LAS CAMPANAS
DR

TONKAWA TR

KADEN
WAY

FLINT ROCK RD

166

STEPHANS
LN

SHANE LANDON
CT

HENING
DR

STEVEN WAYNE
CT

NAVAJO TR

NAVAJO RD

E TONKAWA
TR

PAWNEE
PASS

FALDO ST
FALDO CV

PATE
CV

GOLDEN BEAR DR

158

157

156

155

S PAWNEE PASS

WILD CHERRY DR

31

30

31

32

AREA DR

ARIA DR

HENSLEY
DR

E HENSLEY

SEBASTIANS
Run

SUNRISE
Ridge LOOP

SUNRISE
Ridge CV

VALICO LN

RM
620

Lake
Travis
MS

Lake
Travis
HS

Administration
Bldg

PEAK LOOKOUT DR

Lake Travis
ISD Stadium

Falconhead
Golf Club

34

FALCON HEAD BLVD

A

B

C

D

27

27

ZAGROS WAY

SNOWDONIA
CV

TAURUS
WALK

MONT BLANC DR

OZARKS PATH

JULIAN ALPS

SAYAN
CT

TETONS
CT

PONTIC
PASS

PYRENEES
PASS

SAINT ELIAS ST

VAIL DIVIDE

ADIRONDACK

SUMMIT DR

SWISS ALPS CT

BOULDER
HEIGHTS

CASCADE BLUFF

Limekiln
Branch

SNOWMASS
HEIGHTS

APLOMADO
FALCON CV

HARRIER
MARSH DR

HOOKBILLED
KITE CV

KITE DR

BAT HAWK
CIR

BAT FALCON
DR

SWALLOWTAILED
KITE CV

SPILLMAN
RANCH

SPILLMAN
RANCH LOOP

SPILLMAN
LOOP

COOPERS HAWK CV

AMERICAN KESTREL
DR

GYRFALCON
CV

PIPER GLEN
DR

MYRTLE
BEACH DR

CLIFFHOUSE BLUFF
DR

SKYLIGHT
CV

CHAMPION Way

STARRY NIGHT Way

STARGAZER CV

SHOOTING STAR Way

TWILIGHT
Way

GALLERY
CV

E

F

G

H

© Mapsco, Inc.

71

158

155

152

150

SNAKE EAGLE CV

Falconhead
Golf Club

SHARPSHINED
HAWK

FAIRWIND DR

SINGING WOOD

GRASS
CV

LADERA RANCH
PKWY

SUGARLOAF
DR

HERON
BAY CV

VISTA DEL
VERDE DR

BUBBLING
WELL LN

VINEYARD
WAY

CROWN HILL DR

ROCKFIELD LN

Home Depot

BEND WAY

OBSERVATORY

SANDY
BLUFF LN

BRANCHWOOD

MORNINGSIDE WAY

MOULTON

J

K

L

Q

R

White Rock
Cemetery

Morgan Farm
Rd

TRAVIS COUNTY

78738

26

26

BEE CAVE

AVISPA BONITA

CUEVA
DR

AVISPA WAY

CUEVA CIR

OLD SOUTH
BURNET RD

Bee Cave
ES

71

140

137

TWIN ACRES LN

N

P

Q

R

HAMILTON POOL RD

155

Little Barton Creek

FM
3238

150

FM
3238

145

Little Barton Creek

LONG ARROW
CANYON

HIGH CANYON

GREAT DIVIDE DR

PASS
49

47

S

T

U

V

FM
3238

160

25

25

LONE RIDER TR

GILLIAN'S
WALK

CARBINE CIR

STAGE
STOP CIR

OVERLAND
PASS

COURI PASS

131

135

W

X

Y

Z

WW

WX

WW

WX

◄ CONTINUED ON MAP 548

CONTINUED ON MAP 579

CONTINUED ON MAP 550 ►

SCALE IN MILES

0   ⅛   ¼   ⅜   ½

SCALE IN FEET

0   1000   2000   3000

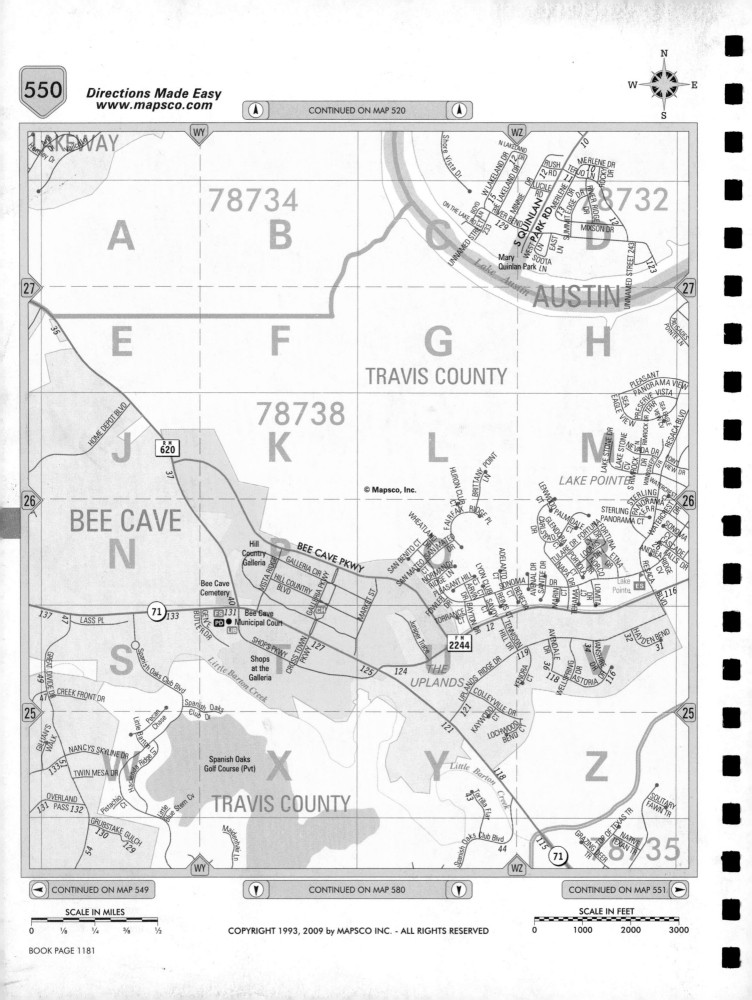

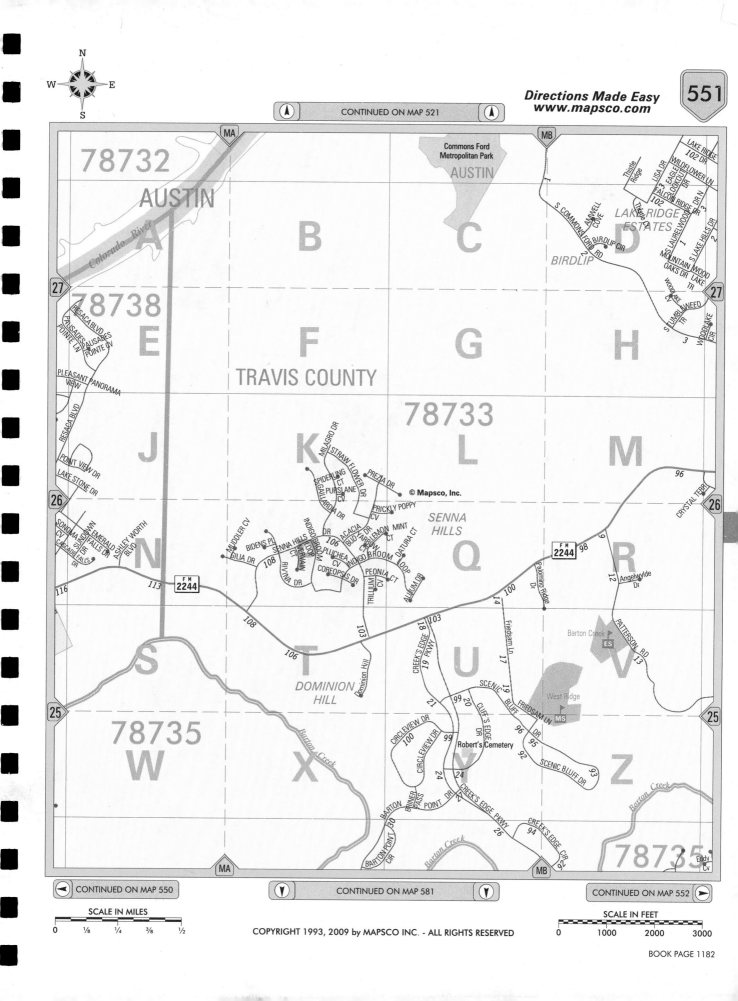

CONTINUED ON MAP 521

Directions Made Easy
www.mapsco.com

551

78732
AUSTIN

Commons Ford
Metropolitan Park
AUSTIN

LAKE RIDGE
ESTATES

BIRDLIP

78738

TRAVIS COUNTY

78733

SENNA
HILLS

© Mapsco, Inc.

DOMINION
HILL

Barton Creek

West Ridge

Robert's Cemetery

78735

78735

CONTINUED ON MAP 550

CONTINUED ON MAP 581

CONTINUED ON MAP 552

SCALE IN MILES

0   ⅛   ¼   ⅜   ½

SCALE IN FEET

0   1000   2000   3000

BOOK PAGE 1182

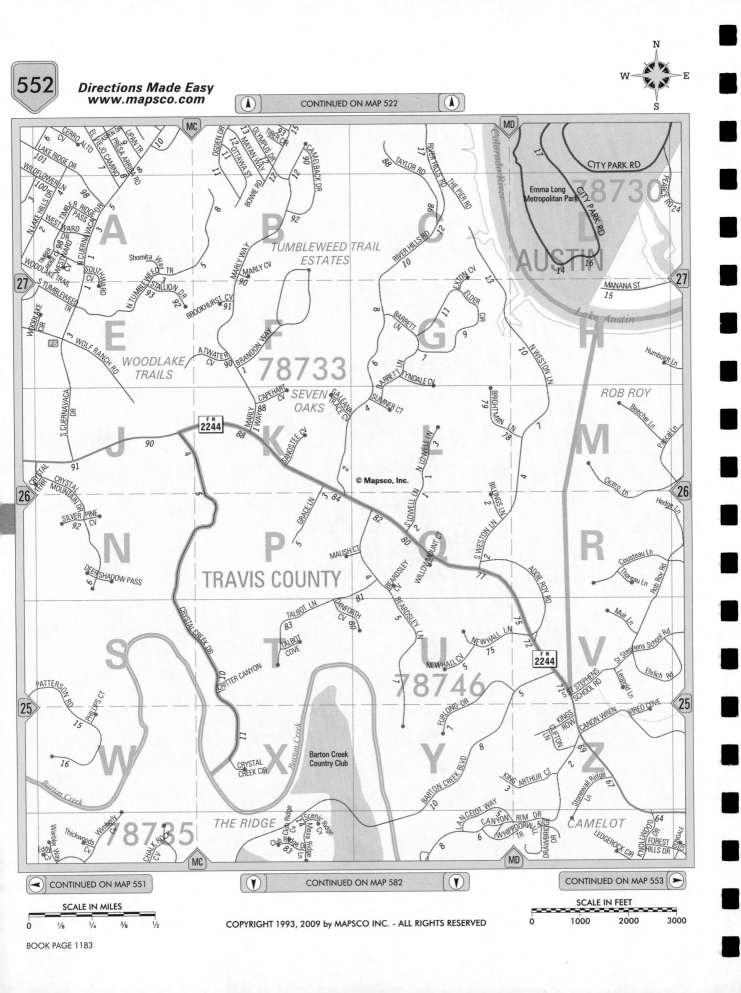

CONTINUED ON MAP 522

N
W E
S

CITY PARK RD

Emma Long
Metropolitan Park

78730

AUSTIN

MANANA ST
15

Lake Austin

ROB ROY

Beecher Ln

Humboldt Ln

Pascal Ln

Cicero Ln

Hedge Ln

Cousteau Ln

Thoreau Ln

Rob Roy Rd

Muir Ln

TUMBLEWEED TRAIL
ESTATES

78733

Woodlake
Trails

SEVEN
OAKS

S Cuernavaca Dr

FM 2244

TRAVIS COUNTY

78746

DEER SHADOW PASS

CRITTER CANYON

CRYSTAL
CREEK CIR

Barton Creek
Country Club

© Mapsco, Inc.

St Stephens School Rd

St Stephens
School Rd

Leopold Ln

Ehrlich Rd

Vireo Cove

FM 2244

Canon Wren

KINGS
ROW

CLIFTON
LN

KING ARTHUR CT

LANCELOT WAY

CANYON
RIM DR

WHIPPOORWILL
TR

DRAWBRIDGE DR

CAMELOT

Stonewall Ridge
Ln

LEDGEROCK CIR

KNOLLWOOD DR

FOREST
HILLS DR

PATTERSON RD

PHILLIPS CT

Barton Creek

78735

Warbler
Way

Thickwoods
Cv

Wimberly
Cv

CHALK ROCK
CV

Eddy
Cv

Club Ridge

Scenic Ridge

Mesa Ridge

Club Ridge Dr

THE RIDGE

BARTON CREEK BLVD

CONTINUED ON MAP 551

CONTINUED ON MAP 582

CONTINUED ON MAP 553

SCALE IN MILES
0   ⅛   ¼   ⅜   ½

SCALE IN FEET
0   1000   2000   3000

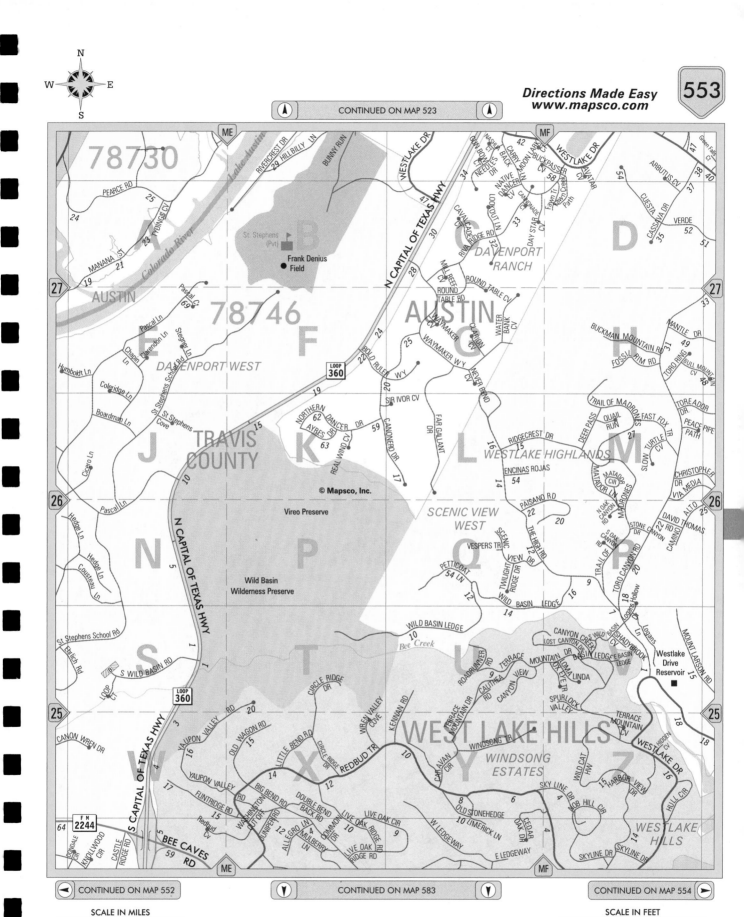

CONTINUED ON MAP 523

CONTINUED ON MAP 552

CONTINUED ON MAP 583

CONTINUED ON MAP 554

SCALE IN MILES

0   ⅛   ¼   ⅜   ½

SCALE IN FEET

0   1000   2000   3000

Directions Made Easy
www.mapsco.com

CONTINUED ON MAP 524

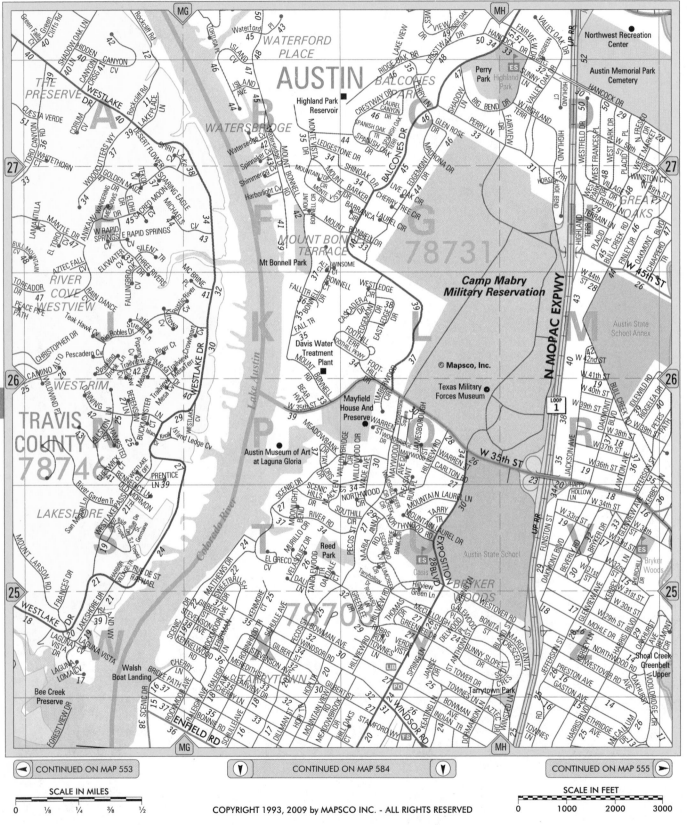

AUSTIN

WATERFORD PLACE

Highland Park Reservoir

WATERSBRIDGE

THE PRESERVE

BALCONES

Northwest Recreation Center

Austin Memorial Park Cemetery

Perry Park

GREAT OAKS

MOUNT BONNELL TERRACE

Mt Bonnell Park

78731

Camp Mabry Military Reservation

Austin State School Annex

© Mapsco, Inc.

Davis Water Treatment Plant

Texas Military Forces Museum

LOOP 1

RIVER COVE WESTVIEW

WEST RIM

Mayfield House and Preserve

TRAVIS COUNTY
78746

Austin Museum of Art at Laguna Gloria

Reed Park

LAKESHORE

W 35TH ST

Austin State School

BRYKER WOODS

Bryker Woods

Tarrytown Park

Shoal Creek Greenbelt Upper

78703

Walsh Boat Landing

Bee Creek Preserve

ENFIELD RD

N. MOPAC EXPWY

W 45th ST

◄ CONTINUED ON MAP 553

▼ CONTINUED ON MAP 584

CONTINUED ON MAP 555 ►

SCALE IN MILES

0   ⅛   ¼   ⅜   ½

SCALE IN FEET

0   1000   2000   3000

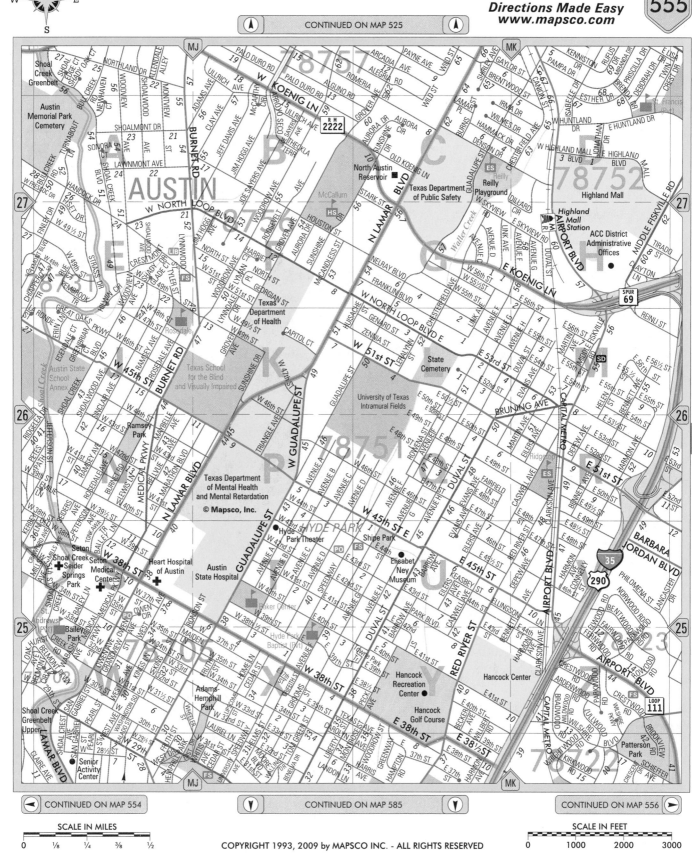

CONTINUED ON MAP 525

78757

MK

Shoal Creek Greenbelt

Austin Memorial Park Cemetery

AUSTIN

78752

Highland Mall

St. Francis (Prt)

W KOENIG LN

RM 2222

North Austin Reservoir

Texas Department of Public Safety

Reilly Playground

Highland Mall Station

ACC District Administrative Offices

McCallum

W NORTH LOOP BLVD

87361

Texas Department of Health

E KOENIG LN

SPUR 69

78751

W NORTH LOOP BLVD E

W 51st ST

State Cemetery

University of Texas Intramural Fields

BRUNING AVE

Texas School for the Blind and Visually Impaired

Austin State School Annex

W 45th ST

BURNET RD

Rosedale

Ramsey Park

Texas Department of Mental Health and Mental Retardation

© Mapsco, Inc.

W 45th ST E

BARBARA JORDAN BLVD

I-35

290

Seton Medical Center

Heart Hospital of Austin

Shoal Creek Seider Springs Park

W 38th ST

Hyde Park Theater

Shipe Park

Elisabet Ney Museum

W 45th ST E

Austin State Hospital

Baker Center

Hyde Park Baptist (Prt)

Hancock Recreation Center

Hancock Center

LOOP 111

Bailey Park

Adams-Hemphill Park

E 38th ST

Hancock Golf Course

78723

78722

Patterson Park

Shoal Creek Greenbelt Upper

78703

Senior Activity Center

E 38½ ST

CONTINUED ON MAP 554

CONTINUED ON MAP 585

CONTINUED ON MAP 556

CONTINUED ON MAP 526

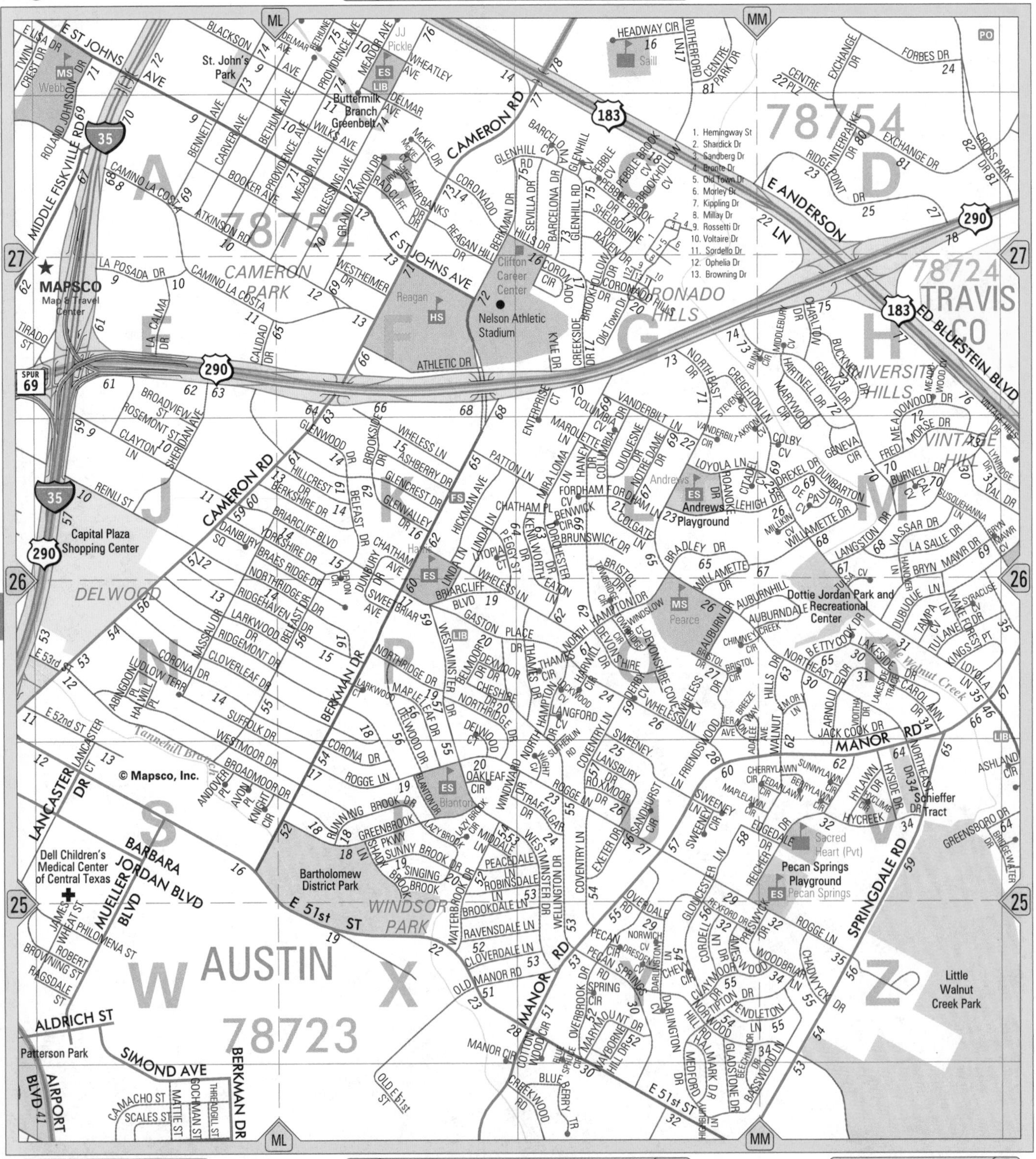

N W E S

MM   PO

1. Hemingway St
2. Shardick Dr
3. Sandberg Dr
4. Brunte Dr
5. Old Town Dr
6. Morley Dr
7. Kippling Dr
8. Millay Dr
9. Rossetti Dr
10. Voltaire Dr
11. Sordello Dr
12. Ophelia Dr
13. Browning Dr

78754

78752

78724

TRAVIS CO

78723

★ **MAPSCO**
Map & Travel
Center

CAMERON PARK

St. John's Park

Buttermilk Branch Greenbelt

Clifton Career Center

Nelson Athletic Stadium

Coronado Hills

University Hills

Vintage Hills

Capital Plaza Shopping Center

DELWOOD

Andrews Playground

Dottie Jordan Park and E Recreational Center

Pearce

© Mapsco, Inc.

Dell Children's Medical Center of Central Texas

Bartholomew District Park

WINDSOR PARK

Blanton

Sacred Heart (Pvt)

Pecan Springs Playground
Pecan Springs

Schieffer Tract

Little Walnut Creek Park

AUSTIN

Patterson Park

ALDRICH ST

SIMOND AVE

AIRPORT BLVD

MANOR RD

SPRINGDALE RD

E 51st ST

CAMERON RD

E ANDERSON LN

FED BLUESTEIN BLVD

ML   MM

◄ CONTINUED ON MAP 555   ▼ CONTINUED ON MAP 586 ▼   CONTINUED ON MAP 557 ►

SCALE IN MILES
0   1/8   1/4   3/8   1/2

SCALE IN FEET
0   1000   2000   3000

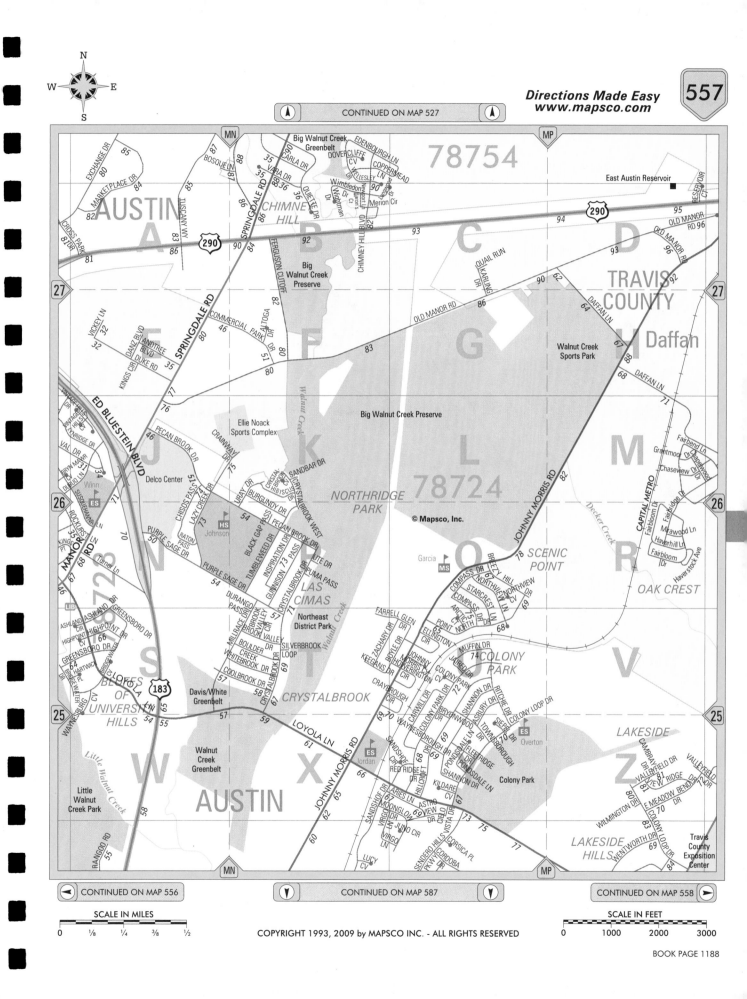

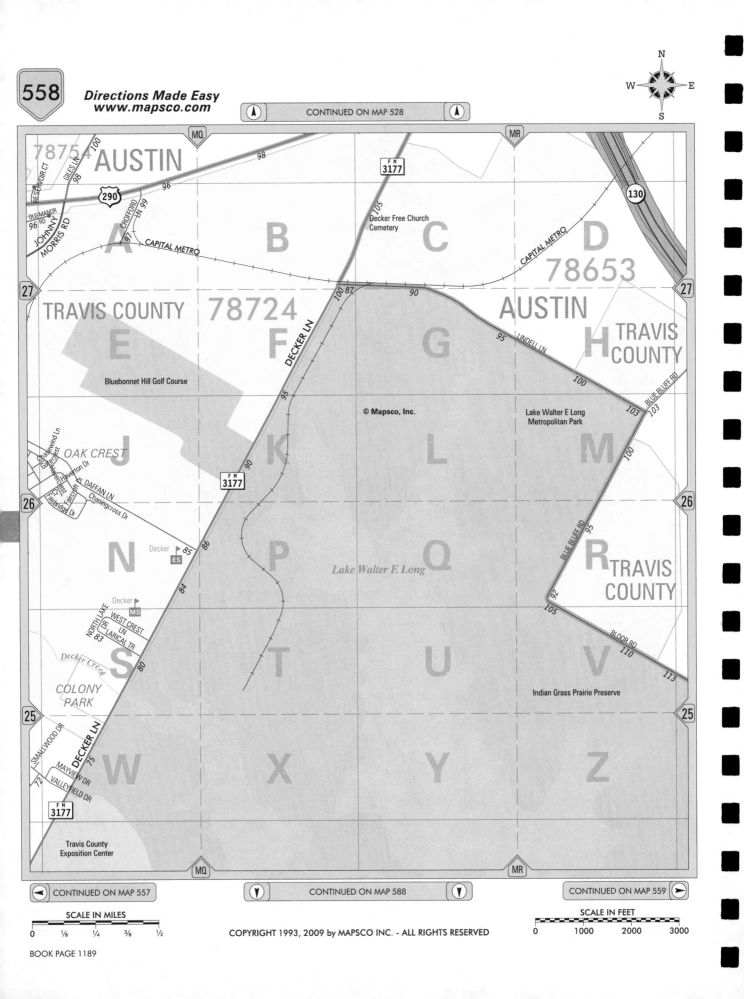

558

Directions Made Easy
www.mapsco.com

CONTINUED ON MAP 528

N
W E
S

78754

AUSTIN

290

98

96

FM
3177

105

130

Decker Free Church
Cemetery

A   B   C   D

CAPITAL METRO   CAPITAL METRO

78653

27   27

TRAVIS COUNTY   78724   AUSTIN   TRAVIS
COUNTY

E   F   G   H

DECKER LN

100 87

90

95

LINDELL LN

Bluebonnet Hill Golf Course

100

95

© Mapsco, Inc.

103

BLUE BLUFF RD

103

Lake Walter E Long
Metropolitan Park

J   K   L   M

100

OAK CREST

DAFFAN LN

26   26

Chaningcross Dr

90

95

BLUE BLUFF RD

Decker   85

N   P   Q   R   TRAVIS
COUNTY

86

Lake Walter E Long

92

84

105

Decker
MS

NORTH LAKE
DR   WEST CREST
LN   LARICAL TR
83

S   T   U   V

80

BLOOR RD

110

Decker Creek

COLONY
PARK

Indian Grass Prairie Preserve

113

25   25

SMALLWOOD DR

DECKER LN   75

MAYVIEW DR

W   X   Y   Z

72   VALLEYFIELD DR

FM
3177

Travis County
Exposition Center

CONTINUED ON MAP 557   CONTINUED ON MAP 588   CONTINUED ON MAP 559

SCALE IN MILES
0   1/8   1/4   3/8   1/2

SCALE IN FEET
0   1000   2000   3000

BOOK PAGE 1189

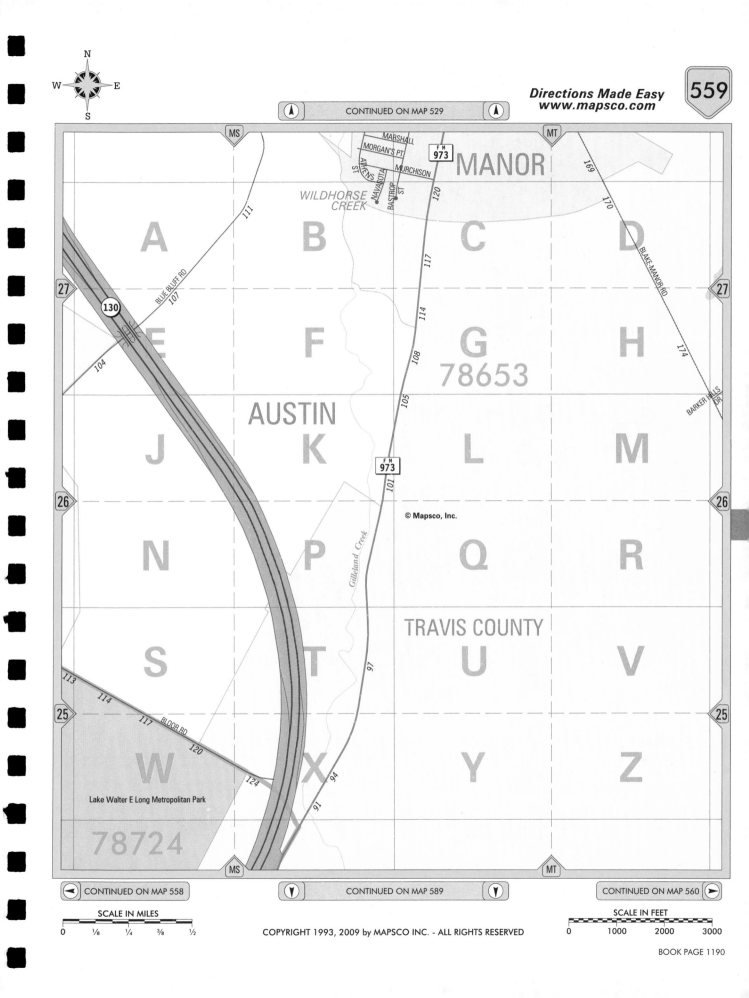

CONTINUED ON MAP 529

MS

MT

MARSHALL

MORGAN'S PT

MURCHISON

ATHENS ST

NAVASOTA

BASTROP ST

FM 973

MANOR

169

170

WILDHORSE CREEK

A

B

120

C

D

111

BLAKE-MANOR RD

27

27

130

BLUE BLUFF RD

107

117

E

F

G

H

174

104

114

108

78653

BARKER HILLS DR

AUSTIN

J

K

105

L

M

FM 973

26

26

101

N

P

© Mapsco, Inc.

Q

R

Gilleland Creek

TRAVIS COUNTY

S

T

97

U

V

113

25

25

114

BLOOR RD

117

120

W

X

94

Y

Z

124

Lake Walter E Long Metropolitan Park

91

78724

MS

MT

CONTINUED ON MAP 558

CONTINUED ON MAP 589

CONTINUED ON MAP 560

SCALE IN MILES

0   ⅛   ¼   ⅜   ½

SCALE IN FEET

0   1000   2000   3000

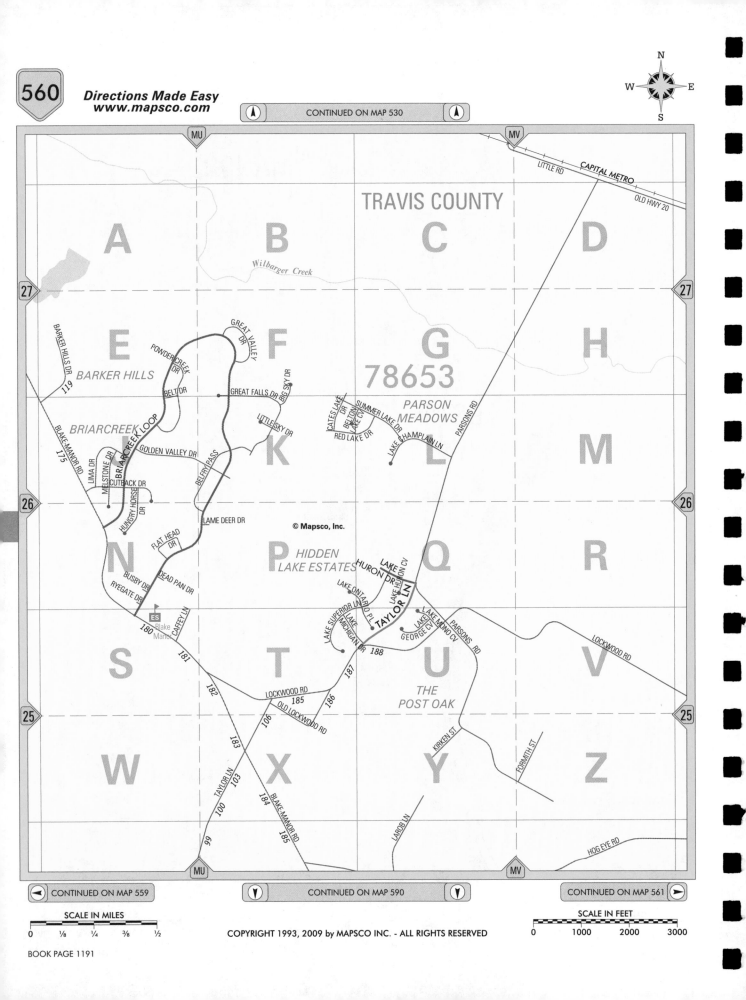

560

Directions Made Easy
www.mapsco.com

CONTINUED ON MAP 530

TRAVIS COUNTY

A   B   C   D

Wilbarger Creek

27

E   F   G   H

78653

BARKER HILLS

GREAT VALLEY DR
POWDER CREEK DR
BELT DR
GREAT FALLS DR
BIG SKY DR
LITTLE SKY DR

CATES LAKE DR
BELTON LAKE CV
SUMMER LAKE DR
RED LAKE DR
LAKE CHAMPLAIN LN

PARSON MEADOWS

PARSONS RD

BRIARCREEK
BRIARCREEK LOOP

BLAKE MANOR RD
175
LIMA DR
MELSTONE DR
CUTBACK DR
GOLDEN VALLEY DR
BELFRY PASS

J   K   L

M

26

HUNGRY HORSE DR
LAME DEER DR

© Mapsco, Inc.

N   P   Q   R

FLAT HEAD DR
HIDDEN LAKE ESTATES
LAKE HURON DR
LAKE HURON CV

BUSBY DR
DEAD PAN DR
RYEGATE DR
LAKE ONTARIO PL
TAYLOR LN
LAKE MONO CV
PARSONS RD

ES Blake Manor
CAFFEY LN
180
181
LAKE SUPERIOR LN
LAKE MICHIGAN DR
LAKE GEORGE CV
188
LOCKWOOD RD

S   T   U   V

182
LOCKWOOD RD
185
186
187
THE POST OAK

25

106
OLD LOCKWOOD RD
183
KIRKEN ST
FORMITH ST

W   X   Y   Z

TAYLOR LN
103
100
184
BLAKE MANOR RD
185
99
LAROB LN
HOG EYE RD

LITTLE RD
CAPITAL METRO
OLD HWY 20

BARKER HILLS DR
119
BLAKE MANOR RD

CONTINUED ON MAP 559

CONTINUED ON MAP 590

CONTINUED ON MAP 561

SCALE IN MILES
0 ⅛ ¼ ⅜ ½

SCALE IN FEET
0 1000 2000 3000

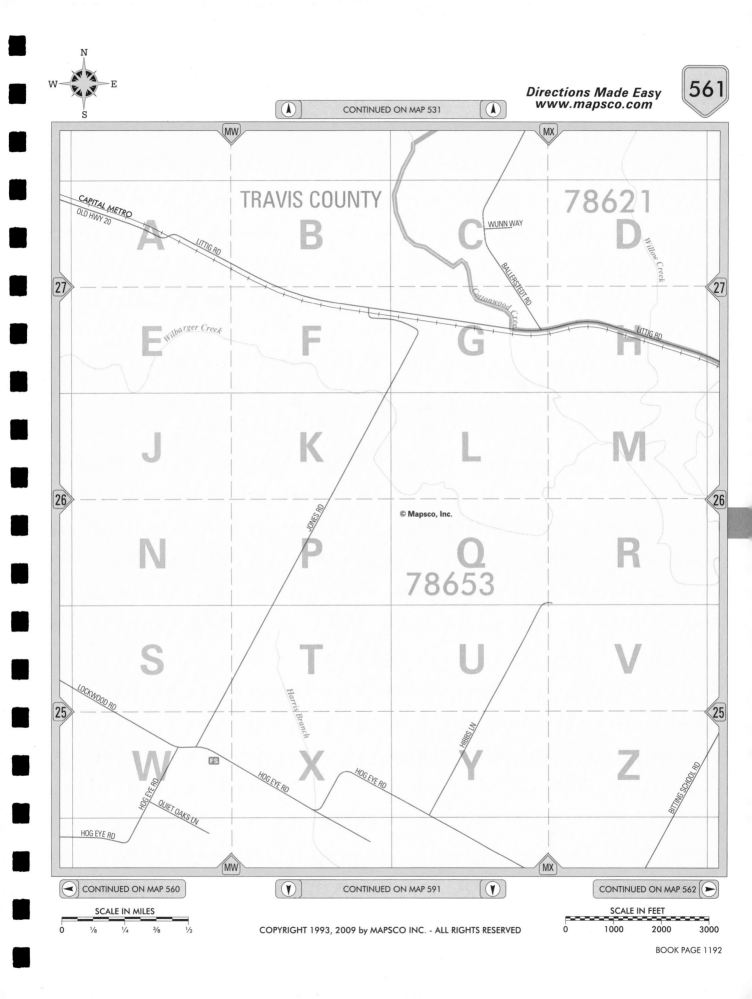

CONTINUED ON MAP 531

Directions Made Easy
www.mapsco.com

561

N
W E
S

TRAVIS COUNTY

78621

CAPITAL METRO
OLD HWY 20

A   B   C   D

WUNN WAY

BALLERSTEDT RD

Cottonwood Creek

Willow Creek

27   27

E   F   G   H

Wilbarger Creek

LITTIG RD

LITTIG RD

J   K   L   M

JONES RD

26   26

© Mapsco, Inc.

N   P   Q   R

78653

S   T   U   V

Harris Branch

LOCKWOOD RD

HIBBS LN

25   25

W   X   Y   Z

FS

HOG EYE RD

HOG EYE RD

BITTING SCHOOL RD

QUIET OAKS LN

HOG EYE RD

CONTINUED ON MAP 560
CONTINUED ON MAP 591
CONTINUED ON MAP 562

SCALE IN MILES
0   ⅛   ¼   ⅜   ½

SCALE IN FEET
0   1000   2000   3000

BOOK PAGE 1192

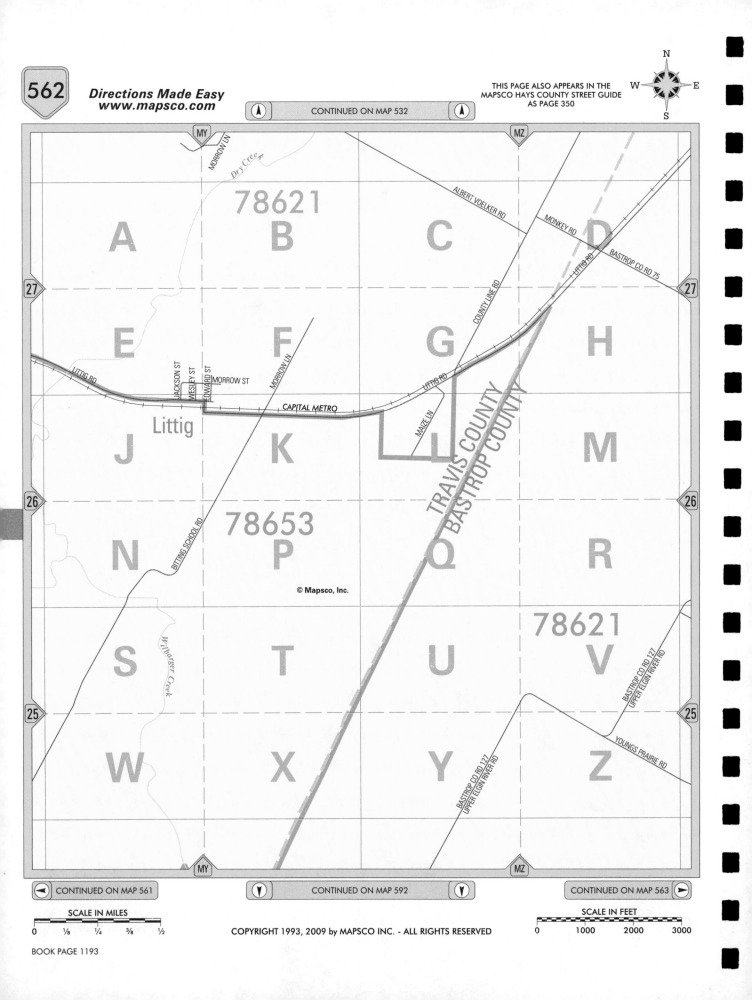

THIS PAGE ALSO APPEARS IN THE
MAPSCO HAYS COUNTY STREET GUIDE
AS PAGE 351

Directions Made Easy
www.mapsco.com

563

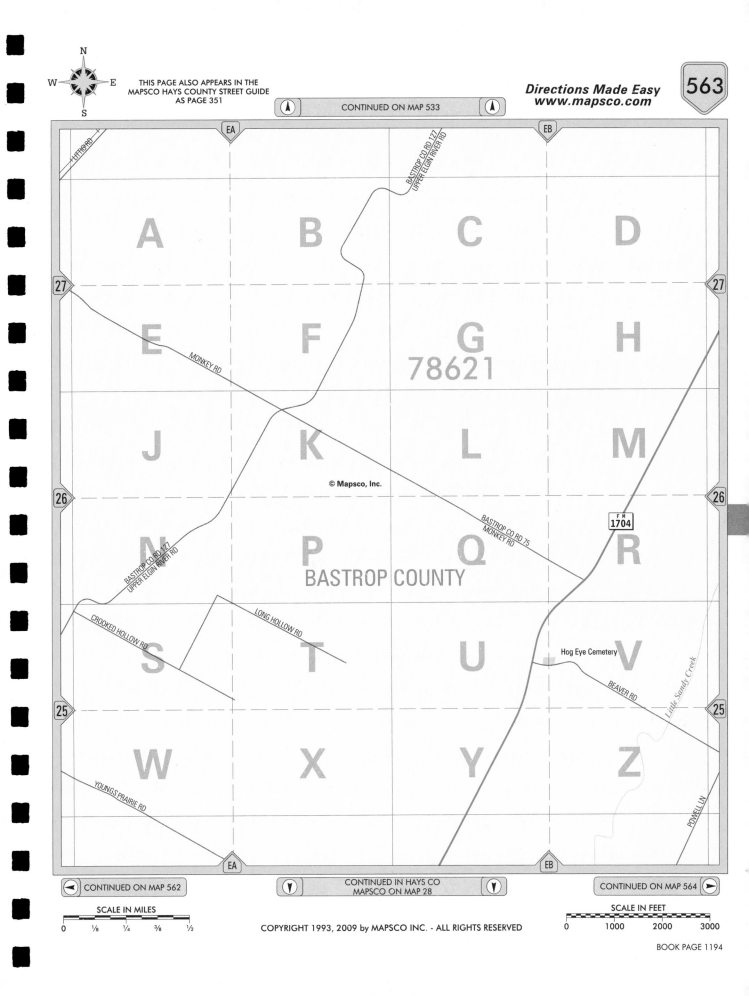

CONTINUED ON MAP 533
CONTINUED ON MAP 562
CONTINUED IN HAYS CO
MAPSCO ON MAP 28
CONTINUED ON MAP 564

N
W E
S

EA

BASTROP CO RD 127
UPPER ELGIN RIVER RD

EB

A   B   C   D

27   27

E   F   G   H
78621

MONKEY RD

J   K   L   M

© Mapsco, Inc.

26   26

FM 1704

N   P   Q   R

BASTROP CO RD 75
MONKEY RD

BASTROP CO RD 127
UPPER ELGIN RIVER RD

BASTROP COUNTY

LONG HOLLOW RD

CROOKED HOLLOW RD

S   T   U   V

Hog Eye Cemetery

BEAVER RD

Little Sandy Creek

25   25

W   X   Y   Z

YOUNGS PRAIRIE RD

POWELL LN

EA

EB

SCALE IN MILES
0   1/8   1/4   3/8   1/2

SCALE IN FEET
0   1000   2000   3000

Directions Made Easy
www.mapsco.com

THIS PAGE ALSO APPEARS IN THE
MAPSCO HAYS COUNTY STREET GUIDE
AS PAGE 352

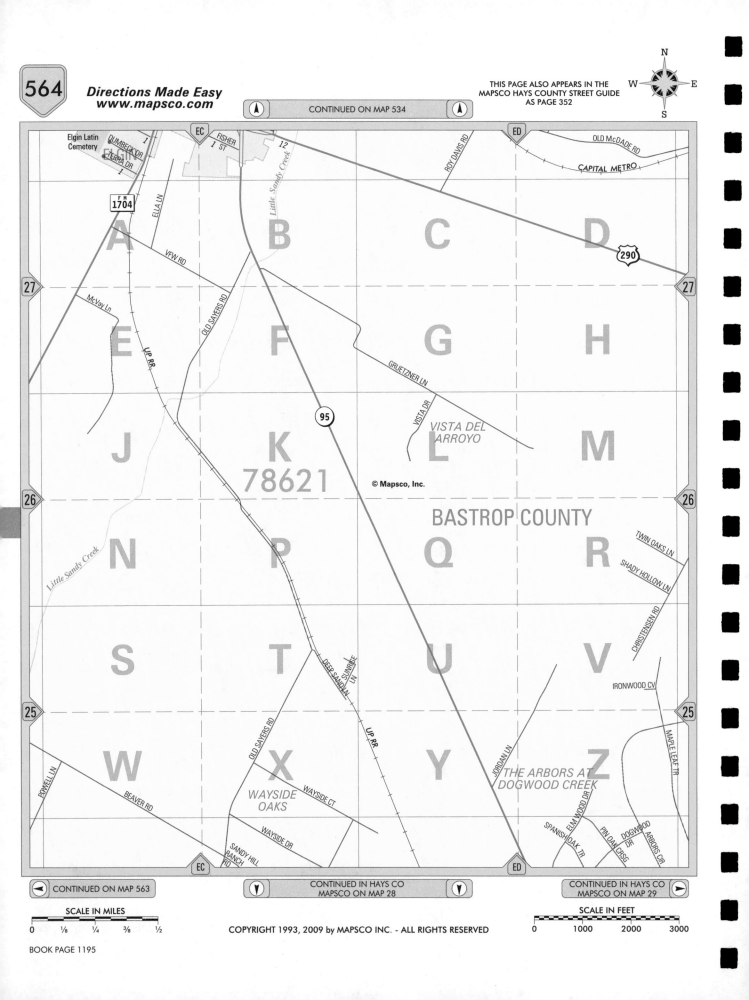

CONTINUED ON MAP 534

Elgin Latin Cemetery

DUMBECK DR
TERRA DR
ELGIN
FM 1704

FISHER 1 ST
EC

ROY DAVIS RD
ED
OLD McDADE RD
CAPITAL METRO

A
B
C
D
290

27
27

ELLA LN
VFW RD
OLD SAYERS RD

McVay Ln
UP RR

E
F
G
H

GRUETZNER LN

95
VISTA DR
VISTA DEL ARROYO

J
K
78621
L
M

© Mapsco, Inc.

BASTROP COUNTY

26
26

Little Sandy Creek

TWIN OAKS LN
SHADY HOLLOW LN

N
P
Q
R

CHRISTENSEN RD

S
T
U
V

IRONWOOD CV

DEEP SANDY LN
SUNRISE LN
UP RR

25
25

OLD SAYERS RD
JORDAN LN

MAPLE LEAF TR

POWELL LN
BEAVER RD

W
X
Y
Z
THE ARBORS AT DOGWOOD CREEK

WAYSIDE OAKS
WAYSIDE CT

WAYSIDE DR

SANDY HILL RANCH RD
EC

SPANISH OAK TR
ELM WOOD DR
PIN OAK CRSG
DOGWOOD DR
ARBORS CIR

ED

Little Sandy Creek

CONTINUED ON MAP 563

CONTINUED IN HAYS CO MAPSCO ON MAP 28

CONTINUED IN HAYS CO MAPSCO ON MAP 29

SCALE IN MILES
0   ⅛   ¼   ⅜   ½

SCALE IN FEET
0   1000   2000   3000

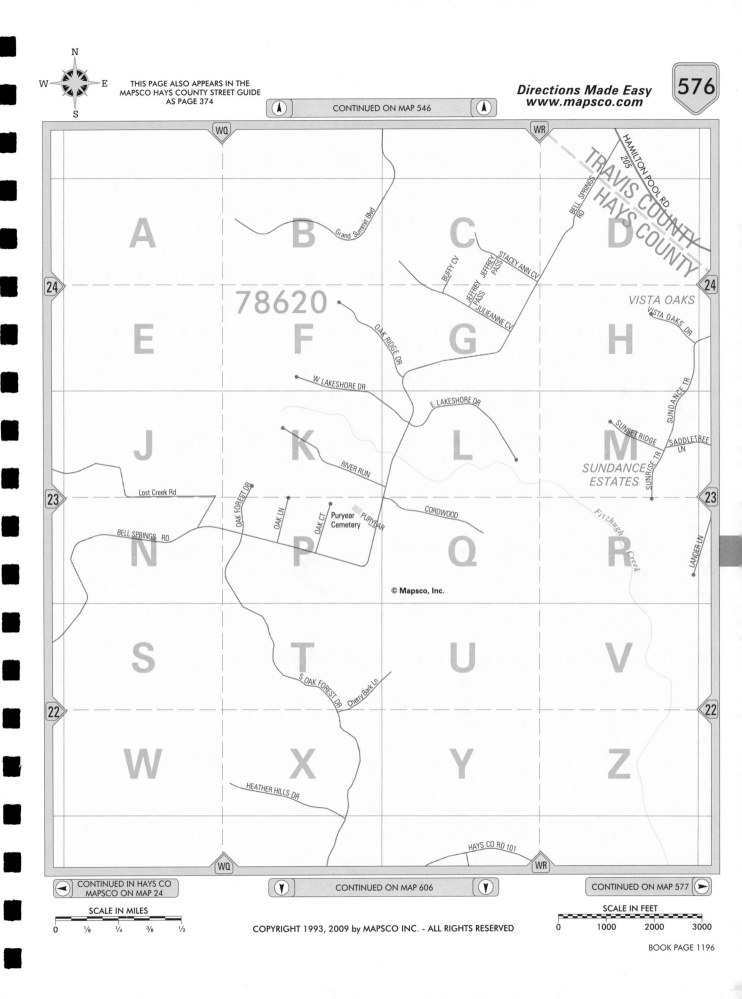

THIS PAGE ALSO APPEARS IN THE
MAPSCO HAYS COUNTY STREET GUIDE
AS PAGE 374

Directions Made Easy
www.mapsco.com

CONTINUED ON MAP 546

TRAVIS COUNTY
HAYS COUNTY

HAMILTON POOL RD
205

Grand Summit Blvd

BELL SPRINGS RD

Buffy Cv

Jeffrey Pass

Jeffrey Pass

Stacey Ann Cv

Julieanne Cv

VISTA OAKS

VISTA OAKS DR

78620

OAK RIDGE DR

W LAKESHORE DR

E LAKESHORE DR

SUNDANCE TR

SUNSET RIDGE

SADDLETREE LN

SUNRISE TR

SUNDANCE ESTATES

RIVER RUN

Lost Creek Rd

OAK FOREST DR

OAK LN

OAK CT

Puryear Cemetery

PURYEAR

CORDWOOD

Fitzhugh Creek

LANDER LN

© Mapsco, Inc.

BELL SPRINGS RD

S OAK FOREST DR

Cherry Bark Ln

HEATHER HILLS DR

HAYS CO RD 101

24
24
23
23
22
22

A B C D
E F G H
J K L M
N P Q R
S T U V
W X Y Z

CONTINUED IN HAYS CO
MAPSCO ON MAP 24

CONTINUED ON MAP 606

CONTINUED ON MAP 577

SCALE IN MILES
0   1/8   1/4   3/8   1/2

SCALE IN FEET
0   1000   2000   3000

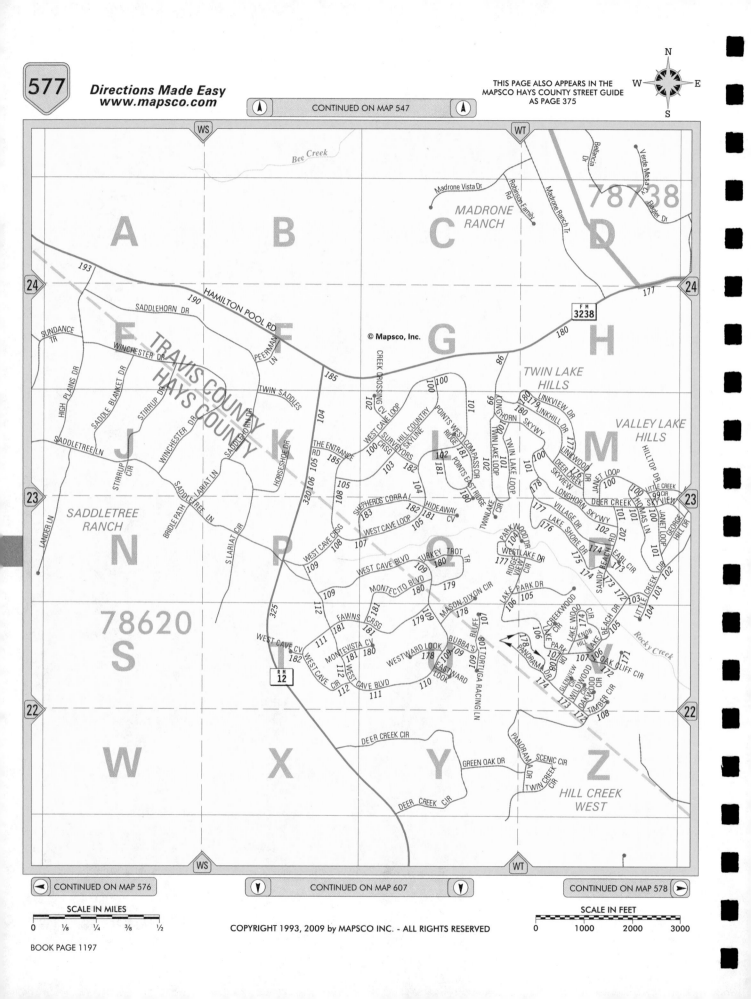

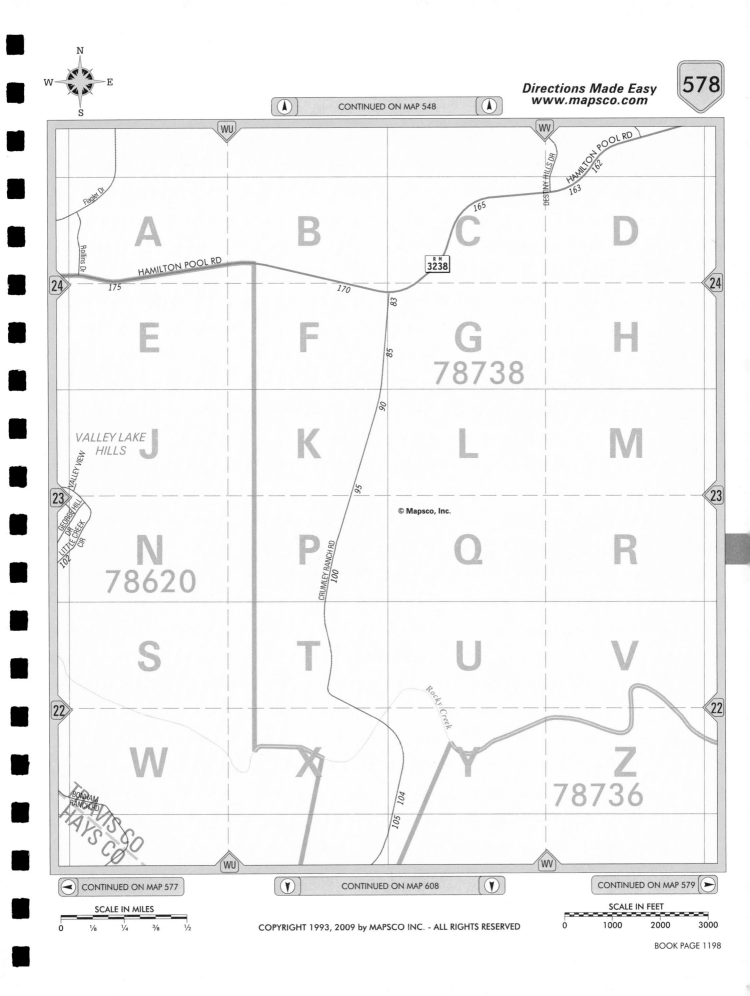

CONTINUED ON MAP 548

WU WV

Flagler Dr
Rollins Dr

HAMILTON POOL RD
DESTINY HILLS DR
163
162
165

A B C D

24 24
175
HAMILTON POOL RD
170
83
R M
3238

E F G H
85
78738

90

VALLEY LAKE
HILLS
J K L M
VALLEY VIEW
23 23
GEORGE HILL DR
LITTLE CREEK CIR
102
95
© Mapsco, Inc.

N P Q R
78620
CRUMLEY RANCH RD
100

S T U V

Rocky Creek
22 22

W X Y Z
BONHAM RANCH RD
104 78736
TRAVIS CO
HAYS CO
105

WU WV

CONTINUED ON MAP 577

CONTINUED ON MAP 608

CONTINUED ON MAP 579

SCALE IN MILES
0 1/8 1/4 3/8 1/2

SCALE IN FEET
0 1000 2000 3000

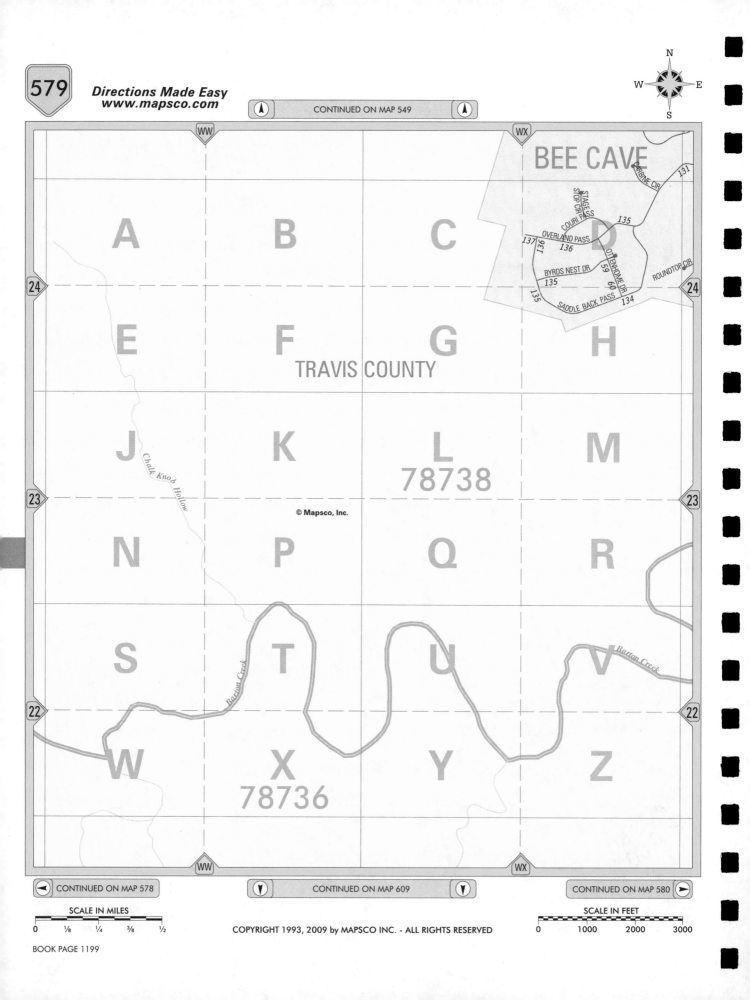

CONTINUED ON MAP 549

N
W E
S

BEE CAVE

CARBINE CIR
131
STAGE STOP CIR
COURI PASS
135
OVERLAND PASS
137
136
136
D
OTTENHOME DR
59
BYRDS NEST DR
60
ROUNDTOP CIR
135
135
SADDLE BACK PASS
134

A   B   C   D

24   24

E   F   G   H

TRAVIS COUNTY

J   K   L   M
78738

© Mapsco, Inc.

23   23

N   P   Q   R

S   T   U   V
Barton Creek

22   22

W   X   Y   Z
78736

Chalk Knob Hollow

Barton Creek

CONTINUED ON MAP 578   CONTINUED ON MAP 609   CONTINUED ON MAP 580

SCALE IN MILES
0   ⅛   ¼   ⅜   ½

SCALE IN FEET
0   1000   2000   3000

COPYRIGHT 1993, 2009 by MAPSCO INC. - ALL RIGHTS RESERVED

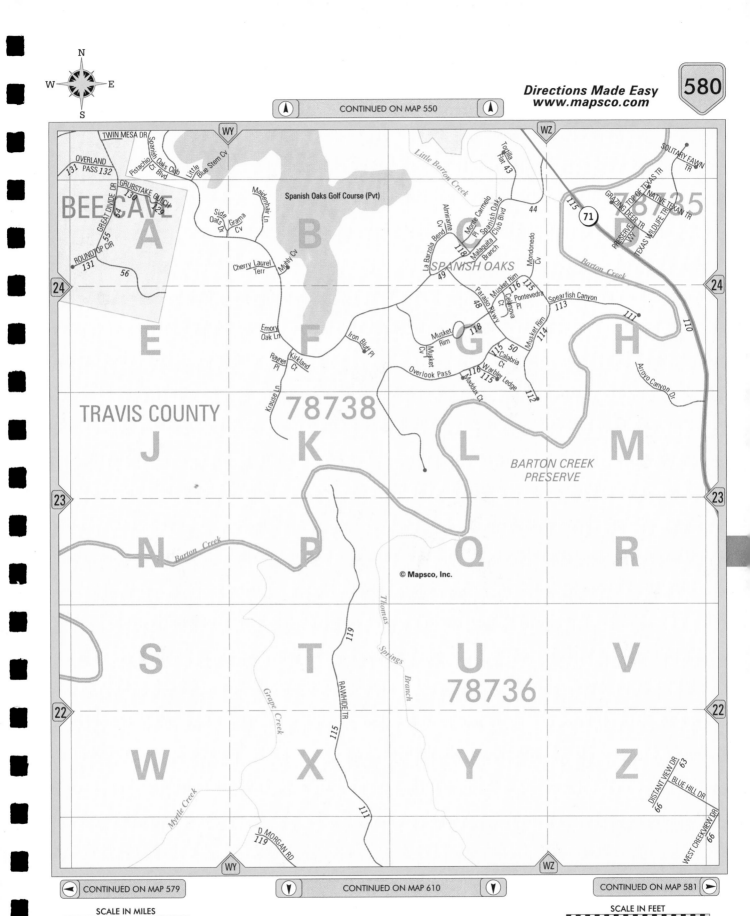

CONTINUED ON MAP 550

N
W · E
S

WY

WZ

TWIN MESA DR

OVERLAND
131 PASS 132

Spanish Oaks Club Blvd

Pistachio Cir

GRUBSTAKE GULCH
130 129

GREAT DIVIDE DR

BEE CAVE
A
54

ROUNDTOP CIR
131

55

56

Little Blue Stem Cv

Maidenhair Ln

Side Oats Dr

Grama Cv

Muhly Cv

Cherry Laurel Terr

Spanish Oaks Golf Course (Pvt)

B

Little Barton Creek

Toquilla Flat 43

44

115

71

SOLITARY FAWN TR

TOP OF TEXAS TR

GRAZING DEER TR

NATIVE TEXAN TR

78735

D

TEXAS WILDLIFE TR

PRESERVE WY

24

24

Almirante Cv

La Barrola Bend

Monte Carmelo Pl

Malaquita Branch

Spanish Oaks Club Blvd

Mondonedo Cv

118

49

SPANISH OAKS

C

Barton Creek

E

Emory Oak Ln

Rayner Pl

Kirkland Ct

Iron Bluff Pl

F

Paraiso Pkwy

48

Musket Rim Ct

Cordova

116

115

Pontevedra Pl

Spearfish Canyon

113

111

G

110

H

Krause Ln

Musket Rim Cv

Musket

118

115

Calabria Ct

50

Musket Rim

114

Arroyo Canyon Dr

TRAVIS COUNTY

78738

Overlook Pass

Warbler Ledge

116

115

112

Maddox Ct

J

K

L

BARTON CREEK PRESERVE

M

23

23

N

Barton Creek

P

Q

© Mapsco, Inc.

R

Thomas Springs Branch

S

T

611

115

RAWHIDE TR

U

78736

V

Grape Creek

22

22

W

X

Y

Z

DISTANT VIEW DR 63

BLUE HILL DR

66

Myrtle Creek

D MORGAN RD
119

111

WEST CREEKVIEW DR 66

WY

WZ

CONTINUED ON MAP 579

CONTINUED ON MAP 610

CONTINUED ON MAP 581

SCALE IN MILES

0   ⅛   ¼   ⅜   ½

SCALE IN FEET

0   1000   2000   3000

BOOK PAGE 1200

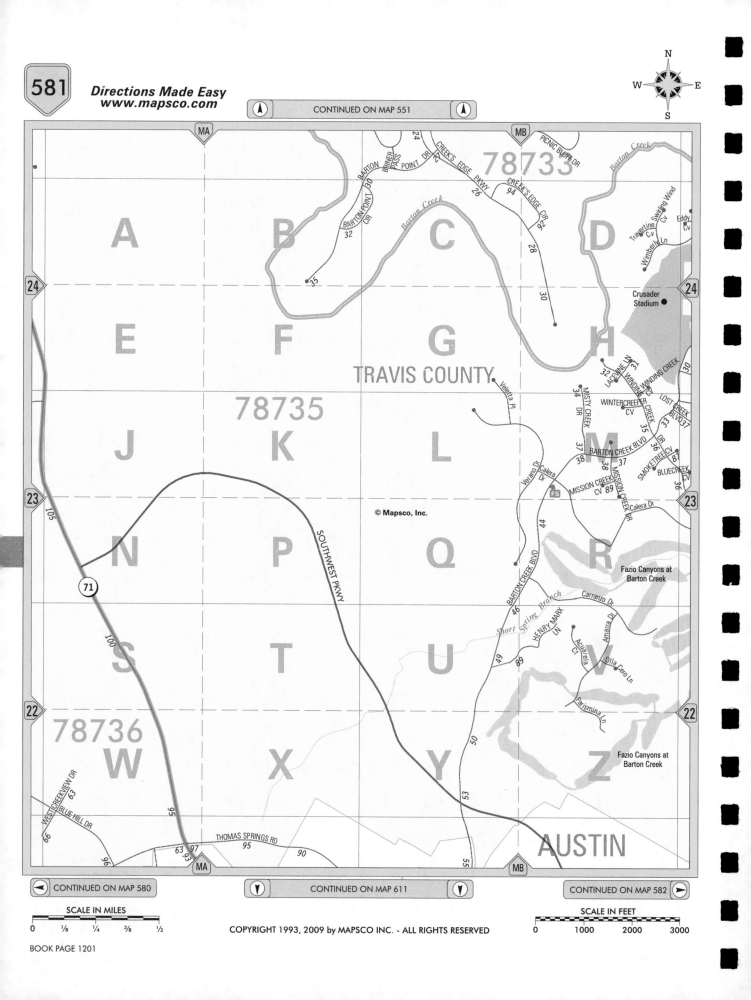

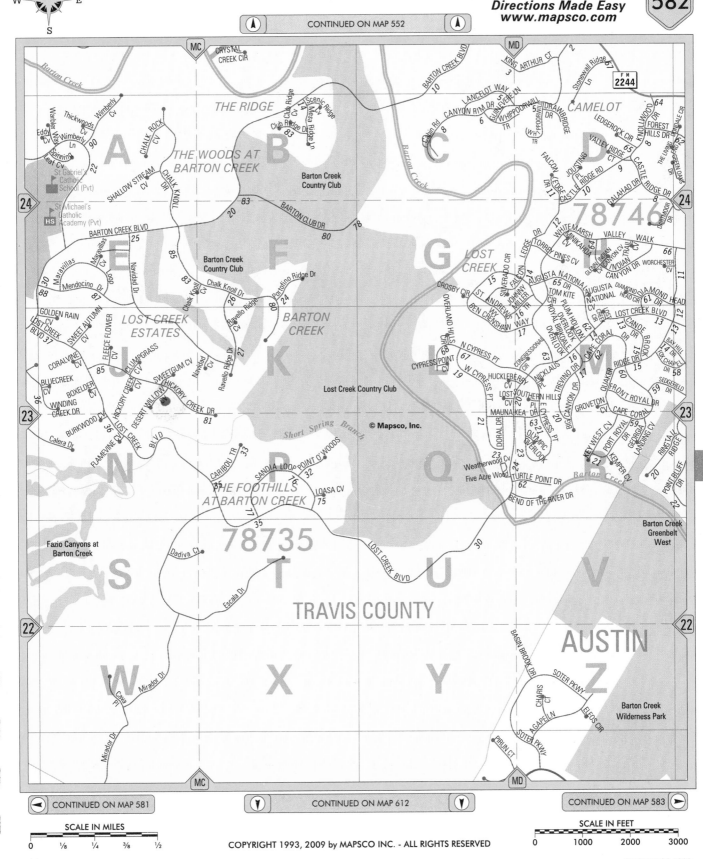

CONTINUED ON MAP 552

THE RIDGE

THE WOODS AT BARTON CREEK

Barton Creek Country Club

CAMELOT

78746

LOST CREEK

Barton Creek Country Club

BARTON CREEK

LOST CREEK ESTATES

Lost Creek Country Club

© Mapsco, Inc.

THE FOOTHILLS AT BARTON CREEK

78735

Fazio Canyons at Barton Creek

Barton Creek Greenbelt West

TRAVIS COUNTY

AUSTIN

Barton Creek Wilderness Park

St Gabriel's Catholic School (Pvt)

St Michael's Catholic Academy (Pvt)

CONTINUED ON MAP 581
CONTINUED ON MAP 612
CONTINUED ON MAP 583

SCALE IN MILES
0   ⅛   ¼   ⅜   ½

SCALE IN FEET
0   1000   2000   3000

BOOK PAGE 1202

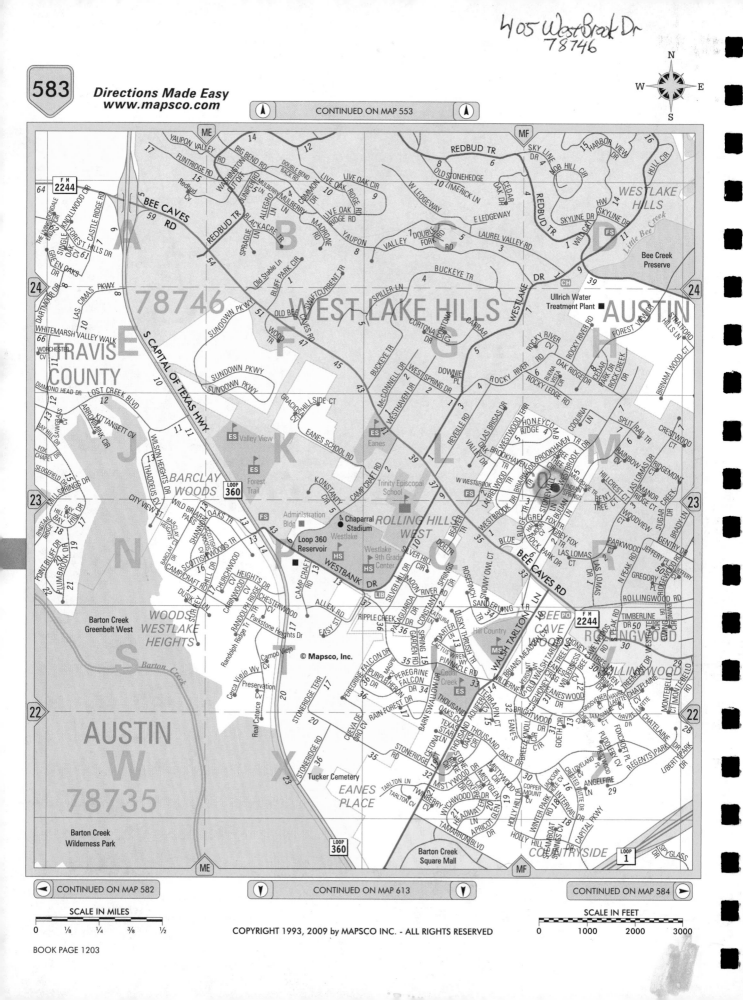

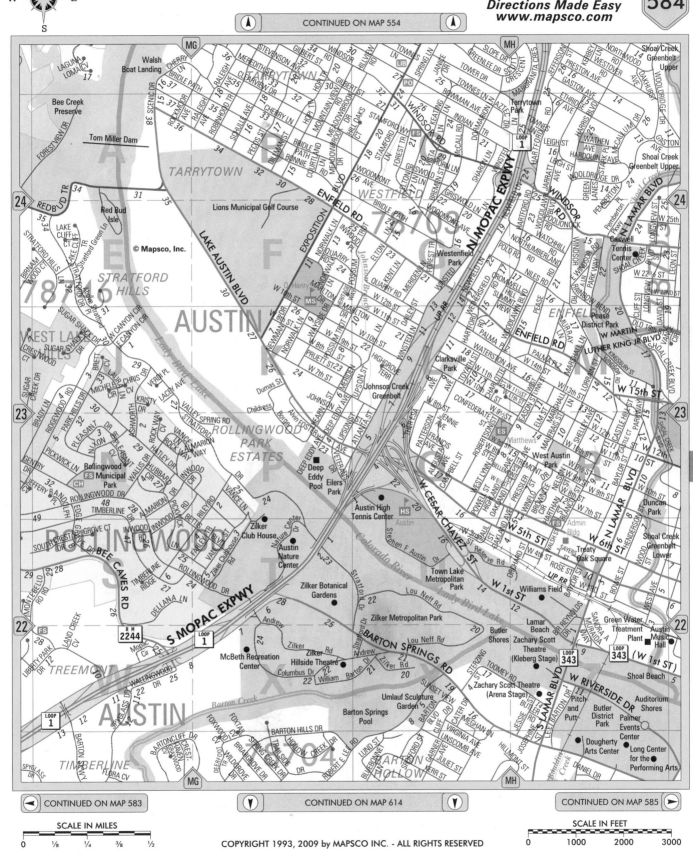

CONTINUED ON MAP 554

CONTINUED ON MAP 583

CONTINUED ON MAP 614

CONTINUED ON MAP 585

SCALE IN MILES

0   ⅛   ¼   ⅜   ½

SCALE IN FEET

0   1000   2000   3000

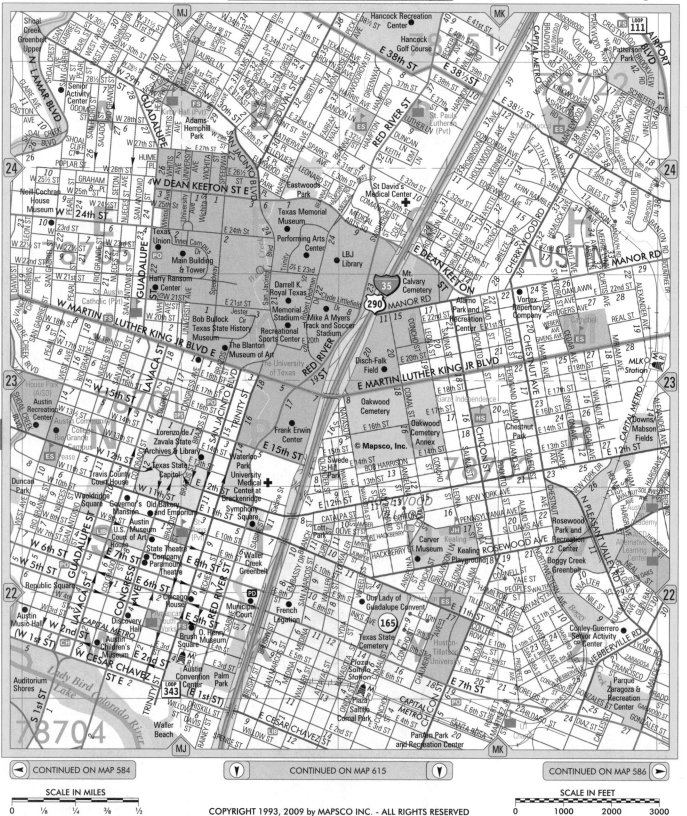

CONTINUED ON MAP 555

CONTINUED ON MAP 584
CONTINUED ON MAP 615
CONTINUED ON MAP 586

SCALE IN MILES

0   1/8   1/4   3/8   1/2

SCALE IN FEET

0   1000   2000   3000

COPYRIGHT 1993, 2009 by MAPSCO INC. - ALL RIGHTS RESERVED

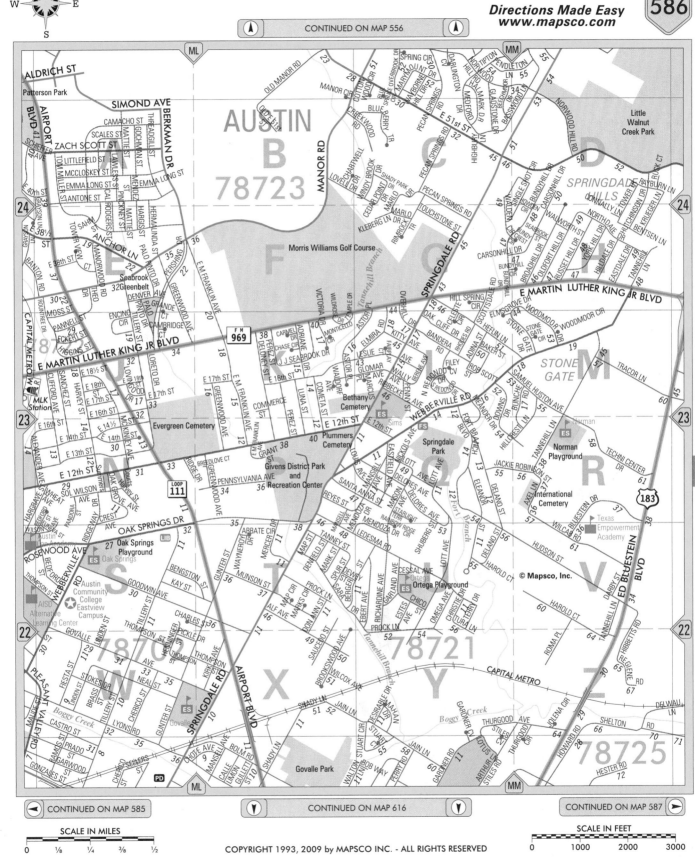

CONTINUED ON MAP 556

AUSTIN
B
78723

Morris Williams Golf Course

SPRINGDALE HILLS

Little Walnut Creek Park

E MARTIN LUTHER KING JR BLVD

STONE GATE

Evergreen Cemetery

Bethany's Cemetery

Plummers Cemetery

Springdale Park

Norman Playground

International Cemetery

Givens District Park and Recreation Center

Texas Empowerment Academy

Oak Springs Playground

Ortega Playground

Austin Community College Eastview Campus

AISD Alternative Learning Center

78702

78721

78725

Boggy Creek

Govalle Park

Patterson Park

E MARTIN LUTHER KING JR BLVD

◄ CONTINUED ON MAP 585

▼ CONTINUED ON MAP 616

CONTINUED ON MAP 587 ►

© Mapsco, Inc.

SCALE IN MILES
0   1/8   1/4   3/8   1/2

SCALE IN FEET
0   1000   2000   3000

N
W E
S

CONTINUED ON MAP 557

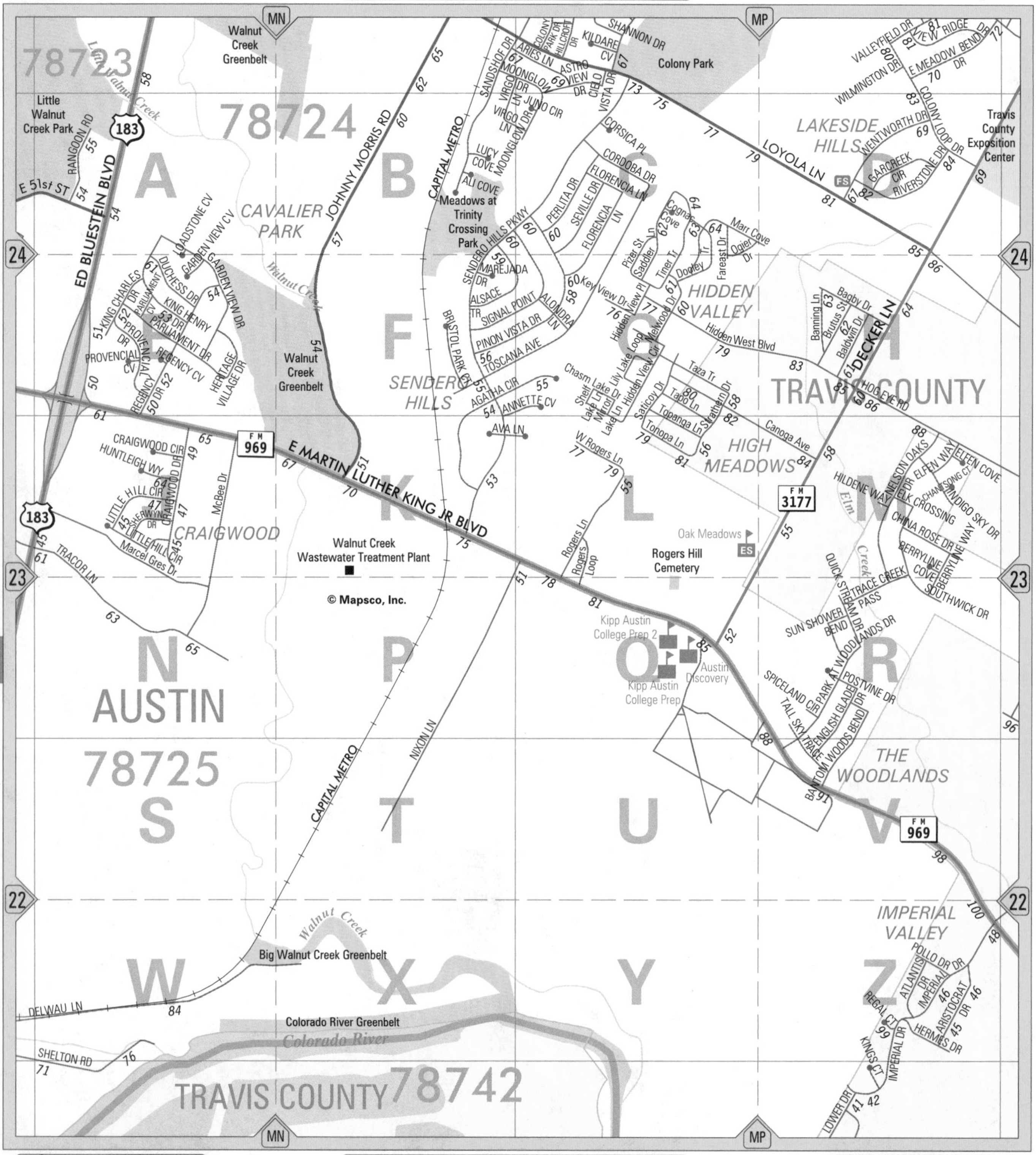

MN
MP

78723

Walnut Creek Greenbelt

78724

Little Walnut Creek Park

Shannon Dr

Colony Park Dr
Hillcroft Dr
Colony Park
Aries Ln
Sandshof Dr
Kildare Cv
Valleyfield Dr
Kew Ridge Dr
E Meadow Bend Dr

Wilmington Dr
Colony Loop Dr
Wentworth Dr

Lakeside Hills

Travis County Exposition Center

Garcreek Cir
Riverstone Dr

US 183

E 51st ST

Loadstone Cv
Garden View Cv
Garden View Dr

Duchess Dr
King Charles
King Henry Dr
Parliament Dr
Parmer
Regency Cv
Provincial Cv
Provincial
Regency Dr
Heritage Village Dr

Cavalier Park

Johnny Morris Rd
Capital Metro

Walnut Creek

Walnut Creek Greenbelt

Walnut Creek Greenbelt

Sendero Hills

A B C D

Astro View Dr
Virgo Dr
Moonglow Dr
Cielo
Virgo Ln
E Juno Cir
Moonglow Ln
Virgo Ln

Corsica Pl

Cordoba Dr
Florencia Ln
Florencia Dr
Perlita Dr
Seville Dr
Florencia

Lucy Cove
Ali Cove

Meadows at Trinity Crossing Park

Sendero Hills Pkwy
Marejada
Alsace
Signal Point
Pinon Vista Dr
Toscana Ave

Bristol Park Ct

Agatha Cir
Annette Cv
Ava Ln

Loyola Ln

FS

Cognac Cove
Marr Cove
Fareast Dr
Ogier Dr

Key View Dr
Pribri St
Sadler St
Tinel Tr
Dooley

Hidden View Pl
Melwood Dr
Hidden West Blvd
Hidden Valley

Banning Dr
Bagby Dr
Brutus St
Baldwin Dr
Decker Ln

Tara Tr
Tada Tr
Saltcoy Dr
Topanga Ln
Topopa Ln

Chasm Lake Dr
Steel Lake Dr
Mirror Lake Dr
Land Ln
Hidden Lake Dr

Canoga Ave

Hoeye Rd

TRAVIS COUNTY

High Meadows

FM 969

E MARTIN LUTHER KING JR BLVD

Craigwood Cir
Huntleigh Wy
Craigwood Dr
Little Hill Cir
Kenwyn Dr
Little Hill Cir
Marcel Gres Dr

McBee Dr

Craigwood

US 183

Tracor Ln

W Rogers Ln
Rogers Ln
Rogers Loop

F G H
J K L M
N P Q R
S T U V W

Nixon Ln

Capital Metro

AUSTIN

78725

Walnut Creek Wastewater Treatment Plant

© Mapsco, Inc.

Oak Meadows
ES

Rogers Hill Cemetery

Kipp Austin College Prep 2

Kipp Austin College Prep

Austin Discovery

FM 3177

Hildene Way
Elk Crossing
Chamisong Dr
Nelson Oaks
Elfen Way
Elfen Cove
Indigo Sky Dr
China Rose Dr
Berryline Way
Berryline Cove
Southwick Dr

Sun Shower
Quick Stream Dr
Trace Creek Pass
Spiceland Cir
English Glade Dr
Tall Skytrail
Bantom Woods Bend Dr
Postvine Dr
Woodlands Dr
Spiceland Cir Park at Woodlands

THE WOODLANDS

FM 969

Big Walnut Creek Greenbelt

Delwau Ln

Walnut Creek

Colorado River Greenbelt
Colorado River

Shelton Rd

TRAVIS COUNTY 78742

X Y Z

IMPERIAL VALLEY

Pollo Dr
Atlantis Dr
Imperial Dr
Aristocrat Dr
Regal Ct
Kings Ct
Hermes Dr
Imperial Dr
Lower Dr

MN
MP

CONTINUED ON MAP 586

CONTINUED ON MAP 617

CONTINUED ON MAP 588

SCALE IN MILES

0 1/8 1/4 3/8 1/2

SCALE IN FEET

0 1000 2000 3000

COPYRIGHT 1993, 2009 by MAPSCO INC. - ALL RIGHTS RESERVED

BOOK PAGE 1207

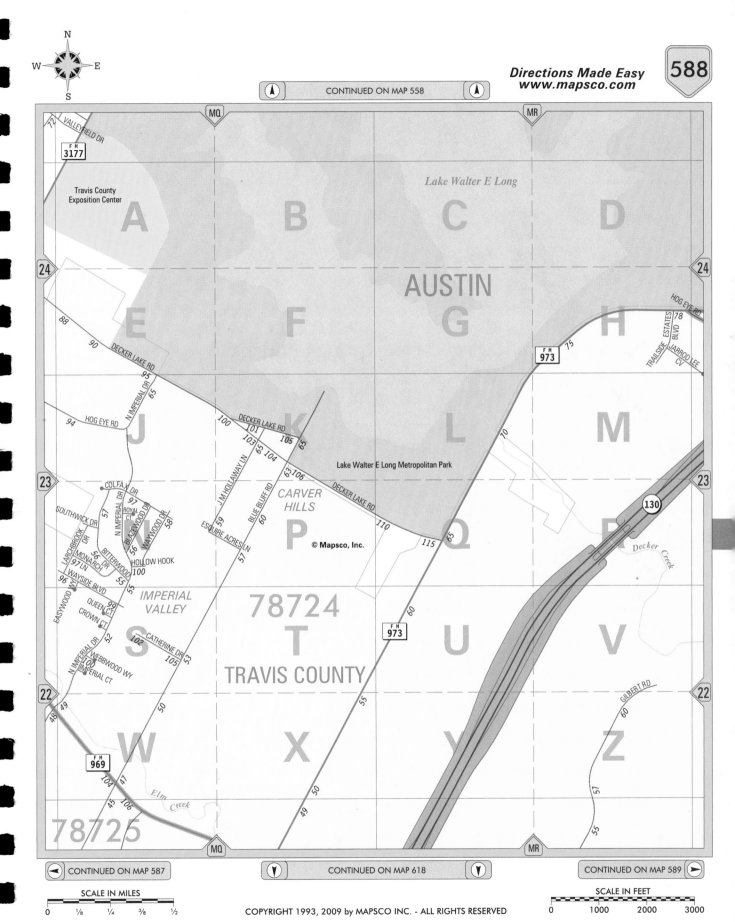

CONTINUED ON MAP 558

MQ

MR

FM 3177

VALLEYFIELD DR

72

Travis County
Exposition Center

A

B

Lake Walter E Long

C

D

24

24

E

F

AUSTIN

G

HOG EYE RD

H

78

TRAILSIDE ESTATES BLVD

JARROD LEE CV

FM 973

75

88

90

DECKER LAKE RD

95

N IMPERIAL DR

65

94

HOG EYE RD

J

DECKER LAKE RD

100

101

105

65

103 104

55

K

65

63 106

CARVER
HILLS

L

Lake Walter E Long Metropolitan Park

70

M

23

COLFAX DR

97

ROYAL CT

57

BLAZEWOOD DR

N IMPERIAL DR

56

WAYWOOD DR

58

JM HOLLAWAY LN

59

ESQUIRE ACRES LN

BLUE BLUFF RD

60

N

P

© Mapsco, Inc.

DECKER LAKE RD

110

115

65

Q

DECKER CREEK

130

R

23

SOUTHWICK DR

LARCHBROOK DR

97 LN

MONARCH

96

WAYSIDE BLVD

BITTERWOOD DR

36

55

HOLLOW HOOK

100

55

IMPERIAL
VALLEY

57

78724

T

FM 973

U

60

V

EASWOOD WY

QUEEN CT

99

CROWN CT

52

S

102

CATHERINE DR

105

53

N IMPERIAL DR

WEBBWOOD WY

100

IMPERIAL CT

TRAVIS COUNTY

973

55

GILBERT RD

60

22

22

48

49

50

W

FM 969

104

47

45

106

Elm Creek

X

50

49

Y

57

55

Z

MQ

MR

SCALE IN MILES

0   1/8   1/4   3/8   1/2

SCALE IN FEET

0   1000   2000   3000

78725

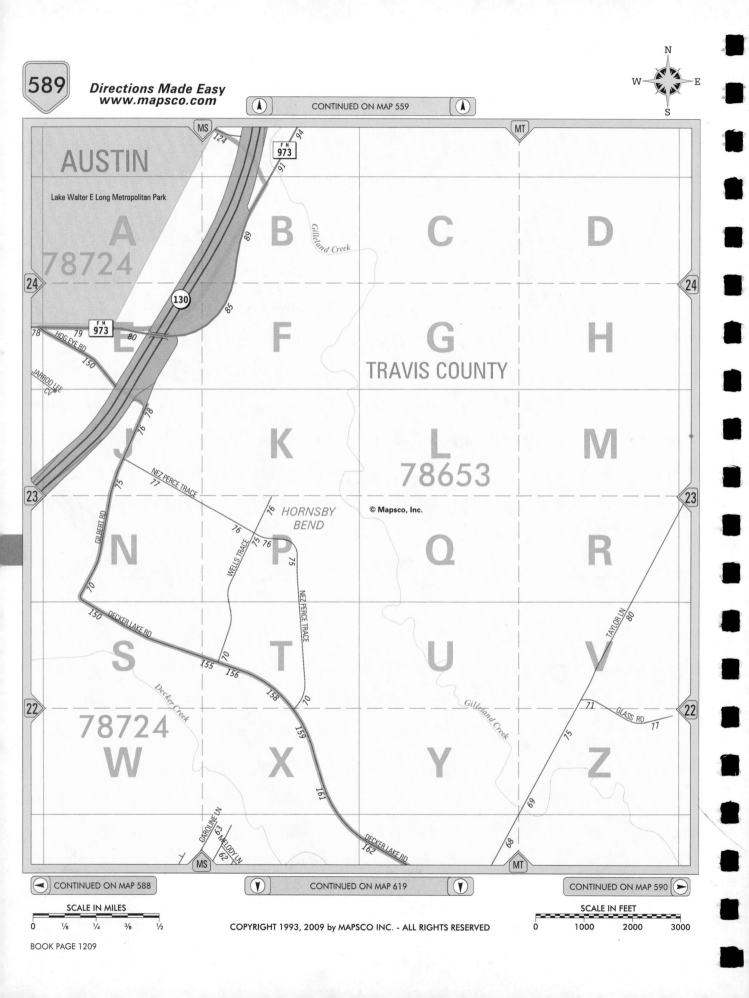

589

Directions Made Easy
www.mapsco.com

CONTINUED ON MAP 559

AUSTIN

Lake Walter E Long Metropolitan Park

A
78724

24

B

Gilleland Creek

C

D

24

MS

FM 973

94

91

89

130

85

E

FM 973

78   79   80

HOG EYE RD

150

F

G

TRAVIS COUNTY

H

JARROD LEE CV

76   78

J

75

NEZ PERCE TRACE   77

K

76

HORNSBY BEND

76

L
78653

© Mapsco, Inc.

M

23

GILBERT RD

70

75   76

WELLS TRACE

N

P

75

NEZ PERCE TRACE

Q

R

23

150

DECKER LAKE RD

S

70

155   156

T

158

70

U

Gilleland Creek

TAYLOR LN   80

V

71

75

GLASS RD   77

22

Decker Creek

78724

W

X

159

161

Y

69

68

Z

22

CAROLINE LN   63

MELODY LN   62

DECKER LAKE RD

162

MS

MT

CONTINUED ON MAP 588

CONTINUED ON MAP 619

CONTINUED ON MAP 590

SCALE IN MILES

0   1/8   1/4   3/8   1/2

SCALE IN FEET

0   1000   2000   3000

BOOK PAGE 1209

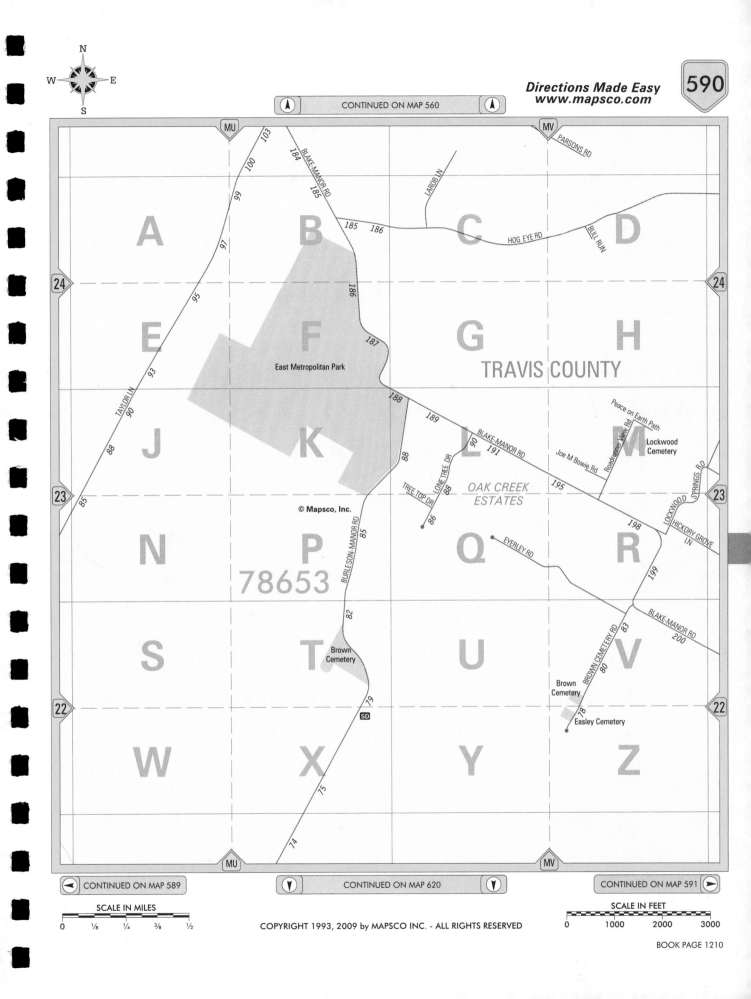

CONTINUED ON MAP 560

Directions Made Easy
www.mapsco.com

590

MU

MV

PARSONS RD

103

100

99

97

184

BLAKE-MANOR RD

185

185   186

LAROB LN

HOG EYE RD

BULL RUN

A

B

C

D

24   24

95

186

E

F

G

H

187

TRAVIS COUNTY

East Metropolitan Park

Peace on Earth Path

93

TAYLOR LN

90

188

Roadrunner View Rd

189

Lockwood Cemetery

M

J

K

L

190

BLAKE-MANOR RD

191

Joe M Bowie Rd

88

85

88

88

OAK CREEK ESTATES

195

198

LOCKWOOD SPRINGS RD

23   23

© Mapsco, Inc.

TREE TOP DR

LONE TREE DR

86

HICKORY GROVE LN

N

P

Q

EYERLEY RD

R

BURLESON-MANOR RD

85

199

78653

82

200

BLAKE-MANOR RD

BROWN CEMETERY RD

80   83

S

T

Brown Cemetery

U

V

Brown Cemetery

79

78

Easley Cemetery

Z

22   22

SD

W

X

Y

MU

MV

75

74

CONTINUED ON MAP 589

CONTINUED ON MAP 620

CONTINUED ON MAP 591

SCALE IN MILES

0   ⅛   ¼   ⅜   ½

SCALE IN FEET

0   1000   2000   3000

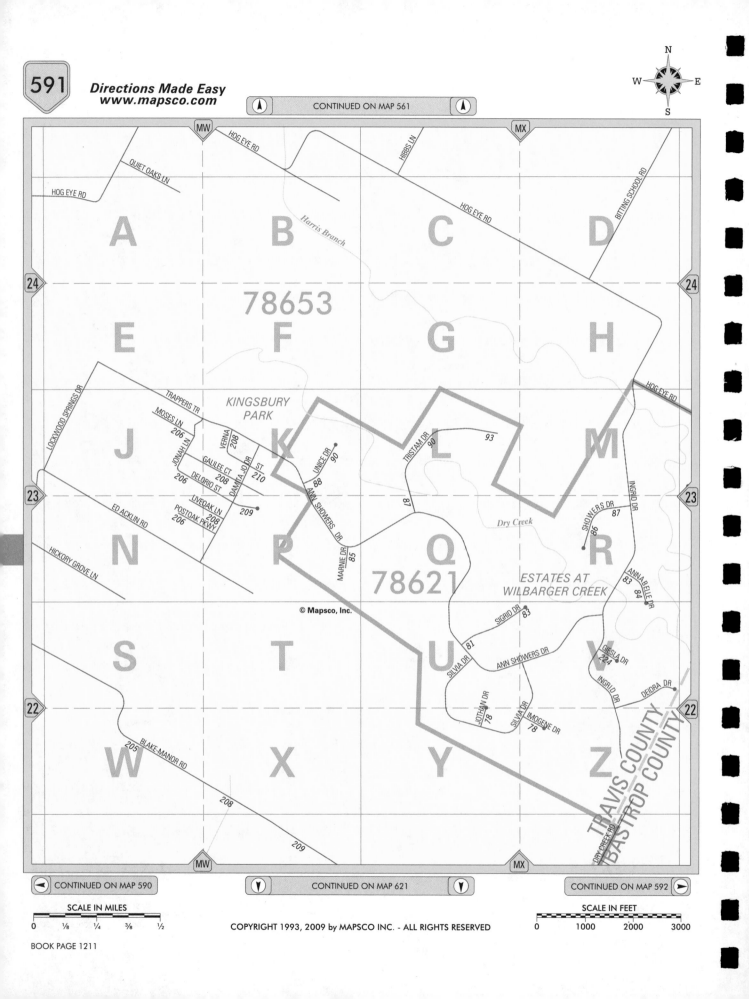

591 Directions Made Easy
www.mapsco.com

CONTINUED ON MAP 561

N
W E
S

A   B   C   D

24   24

78653

E   F   G   H

LOCKWOOD SPRINGS DR
TRAPPERS TR
KINGSBURY PARK
MOSES LN 206
VERNA 208
JONAH LN 206
GALILEE CT 208
DELORIO ST
DAMITA JO DR
ST 210
LINICE DR 90
TRISTAM DR 90   93

J   K   L   M

HOG EYE RD

23   23

ED ACKLIN RD
LIVEOAK LN 208
POSTOAK PKWY 206
209
ANN SHOWERS DR 88
87
SHOWERS DR 87
INGRID DR
86

HICKORY GROVE LN
MARNIE DR 85
Dry Creek

N   P   Q   R

© Mapsco, Inc.

78621
ESTATES AT WILBARGER CREEK
ANNA BELLE DR 83 84

S   T   U   V

SIGRID DR 83
SILVIA DR 81
ANN SHOWERS DR
GIESLA DR 224
INGRID DR
DEIDRA DR

22   22

BLAKE-MANOR RD 205
208
209
JOTHAN DR 78
SILVIA DR
IMOGENE DR 78
DRY CREEK RD
TRAVIS COUNTY
BASTROP COUNTY

W   X   Y   Z

CONTINUED ON MAP 590   CONTINUED ON MAP 621   CONTINUED ON MAP 592

SCALE IN MILES
0   1/8   1/4   3/8   1/2

COPYRIGHT 1993, 2009 by MAPSCO INC. - ALL RIGHTS RESERVED

SCALE IN FEET
0   1000   2000   3000

BOOK PAGE 1211

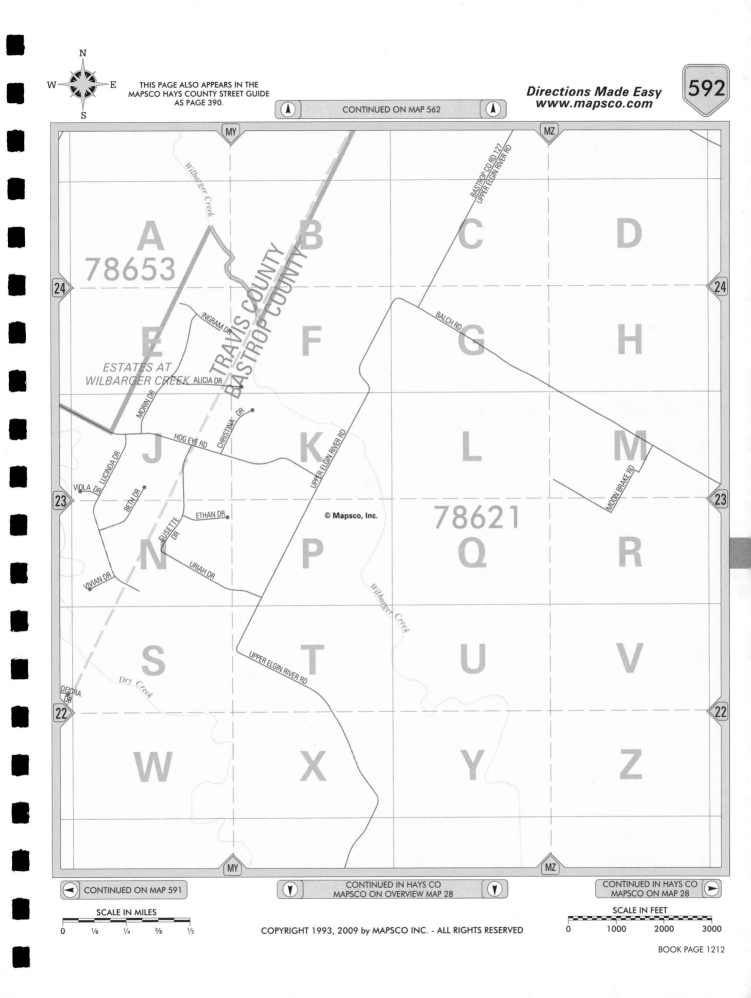

N
W E
S

THIS PAGE ALSO APPEARS IN THE
MAPSCO HAYS COUNTY STREET GUIDE
AS PAGE 390.

Directions Made Easy
www.mapsco.com

CONTINUED ON MAP 562

24

MY

MZ

BASTROP CO RD 127
UPPER ELGIN RIVER RD

A
78653

B

TRAVIS COUNTY
BASTROP COUNTY

C

D

24

24

INGRAM DR

E

F

BALCH RD

G

H

ESTATES AT
WILBARGER CREEK ALICIA DR

MORIN DR

Wilbarger Creek

HOG EYE RD

CHRISTINA DR

UPPER ELGIN RIVER RD

J

LUCINDA DR

K

L

M

MOON BRAKE RD

23

VIOLA DR

BETH DR

ETHAN DR

© Mapsco, Inc.

78621

23

SUSETTE DR

N

URIAH DR

P

Q

R

VIVIAN DR

S

T

Wilbarger Creek

U

V

Dry Creek

UPPER ELGIN RIVER RD

DEIDRA DR

22

22

W

MY

X

MZ

Y

Z

CONTINUED ON MAP 591

CONTINUED IN HAYS CO
MAPSCO ON OVERVIEW MAP 28

CONTINUED IN HAYS CO
MAPSCO ON MAP 28

SCALE IN MILES
0   ⅛   ¼   ⅜   ½

SCALE IN FEET
0   1000   2000   3000

BOOK PAGE 1212

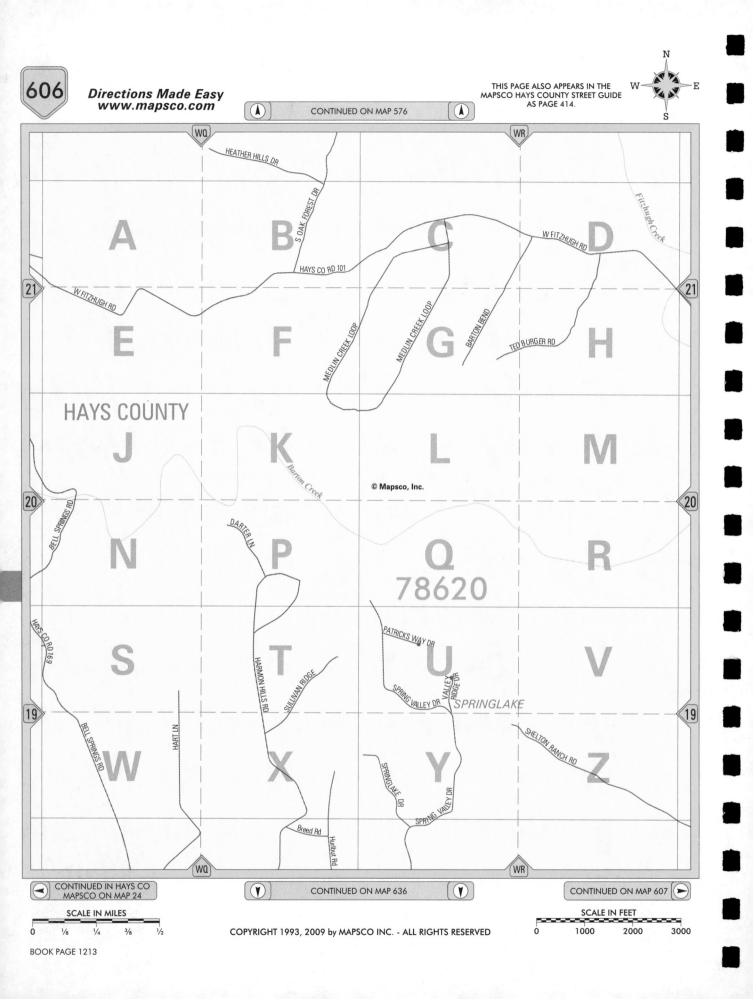

Directions Made Easy
www.mapsco.com

THIS PAGE ALSO APPEARS IN THE
MAPSCO HAYS COUNTY STREET GUIDE
AS PAGE 414.

N
W · E
S

CONTINUED ON MAP 576

WQ

HEATHER HILLS DR

S OAK FOREST DR

WR

Fitzhugh Creek

A   B   C   W FITZHUGH RD   D

HAYS CO RD 101

21   W FITZHUGH RD   21

E   F   G   H
MEDLIN CREEK LOOP   MEDLIN CREEK LOOP   BARTON BEND   TED BURGER RD

HAYS COUNTY

J   K   L   M
Barton Creek

© Mapsco, Inc.

20   20

BELL SPRINGS RD   DARTER LN

N   P   Q   R
78620

HAYS CO RD 169   PATRICKS WAY DR

S   T   U   V
HARMON HILLS RD   SULLIVAN RIDGE   SPRING VALLEY DR   VALLEY RIDGE DR

HART LN

19   BELL SPRINGS RD   SPRINGLAKE   SHELTON RANCH RD   19

W   X   Y   Z
SPRINGLAKE DR   SPRING VALLEY DR

BREED RD   Hulbut Rd

WQ   WR

CONTINUED IN HAYS CO
MAPSCO ON MAP 24

CONTINUED ON MAP 636

CONTINUED ON MAP 607

SCALE IN MILES
0   ⅛   ¼   ⅜   ½

SCALE IN FEET
0   1000   2000   3000

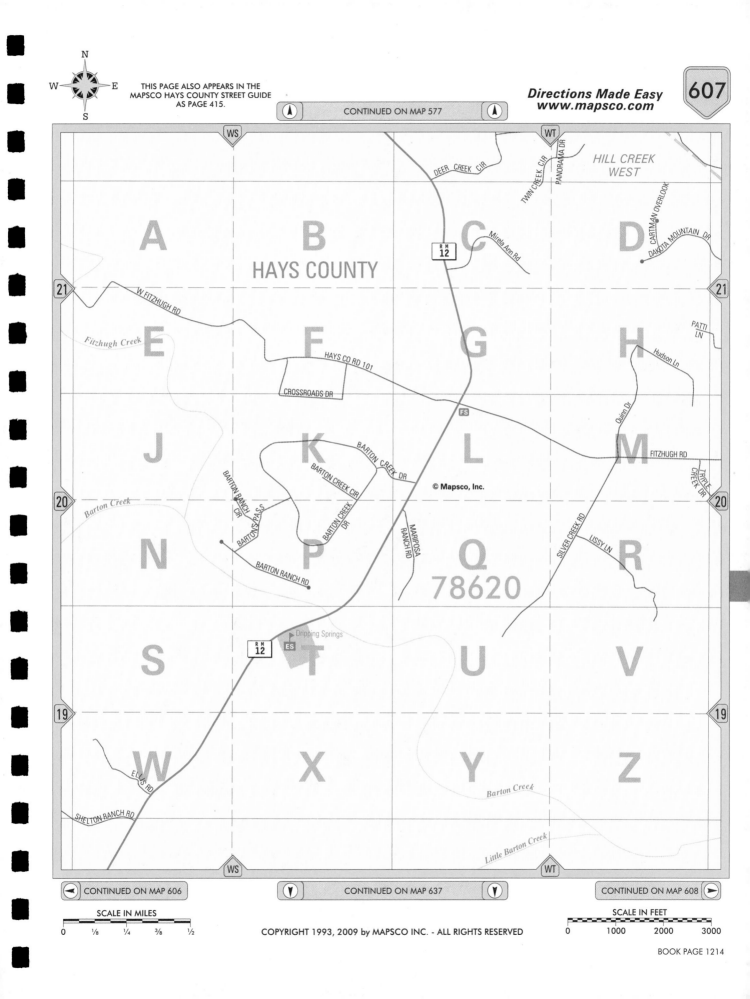

Directions Made Easy
www.mapsco.com

THIS PAGE ALSO APPEARS IN THE
MAPSCO HAYS COUNTY STREET GUIDE
AS PAGE 415.

N W E S

CONTINUED ON MAP 577

WS

WT

DEER CREEK CIR

HILL CREEK WEST

TWIN CREEK CIR

PANORAMA DR

A

B

HAYS COUNTY

C

R M 12

Mirela Am Rd

D

CARTMAN OVERLOOK

DAKOTA MOUNTAIN DR

21

21

W FITZHUGH RD

E

Fitzhugh Creek

F

HAYS CO RD 101

G

H

PATTI LN

Hudson Ln

CROSSROADS DR

FS

Quinn Dr

J

K

BARTON CREEK DR

BARTON CREEK CIR

L

© Mapsco, Inc.

M

FITZHUGH RD

TRIPLE CREEK DR

20

Barton Creek

BARTON RANCH CIR

BARTONS PASS

BARTON CREEK DR

MARIPOSA RANCH RD

SILVER CREEK RD

LISSY LN

20

N

P

BARTON RANCH RD

Q

78620

R

S

R M 12

ES

Dripping Springs

T

U

V

19

19

W

ELLIS RD

X

Y

Barton Creek

Z

SHELTON RANCH RD

Little Barton Creek

WS

WT

CONTINUED ON MAP 606

CONTINUED ON MAP 637

CONTINUED ON MAP 608

SCALE IN MILES

0   ⅛   ¼   ⅜   ½

COPYRIGHT 1993, 2009 by MAPSCO INC. - ALL RIGHTS RESERVED

SCALE IN FEET

0   1000   2000   3000

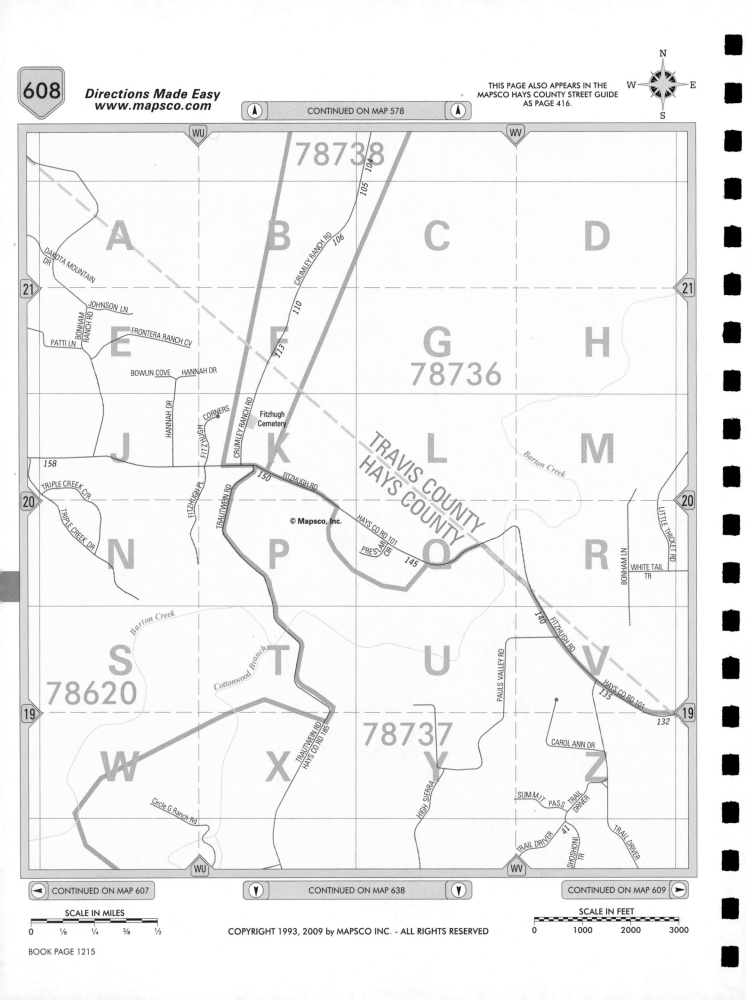

608

Directions Made Easy
www.mapsco.com

CONTINUED ON MAP 578

THIS PAGE ALSO APPEARS IN THE
MAPSCO HAYS COUNTY STREET GUIDE
AS PAGE 416.

N
W E
S

WU

78738

WV

105 104

CRUMLEY RANCH RD

106

A   B   C   D

21   21

DAKOTA MOUNTAIN DR

JOHNSON LN

110

BONHAM RANCH RD
FRONTERA RANCH CV

E   F   G   H

PATTI LN   78736

113

BOWLIN COVE   HANNAH DR

HANNAH DR

FITZHUGH CORNERS

CRUMLEY RANCH RD

Fitzhugh
Cemetery

Barton Creek

J   K   L   M

158

150   FITZHUGH RD

TRAVIS COUNTY
HAYS COUNTY

TRIPLE CREEK CIR

FITZHUGH PL

TRAUTWEIN RD

© Mapsco, Inc.

HAYS CO RD 101

BONHAM LN

LITTLE THICKET RD

20   20

TRIPLE CREEK DR

PRES LAB CIR

145

WHITE TAIL TR

N   P   Q   R

Barton Creek

FITZHUGH RD

140

Cottonwood Branch

PAULS VALLEY RD

HAYS CO RD 101

135

S   T   U   V

78620

19   19

132

TRAUTWEIN RD
HAYS CO RD 185

78737

CAROL ANN DR

HIGH SIERRA

SUMMIT PASS
TRAIL DRIVER

W   X   Y   Z

CIRCLE G RANCH RD

TRAIL DRIVER
41
SHOSHONI TR

TRAIL DRIVER

WU   WV

CONTINUED ON MAP 607   CONTINUED ON MAP 638   CONTINUED ON MAP 609

SCALE IN MILES

0   1/8   1/4   3/8   1/2

SCALE IN FEET

0   1000   2000   3000

COPYRIGHT 1993, 2009 by MAPSCO INC. - ALL RIGHTS RESERVED

BOOK PAGE 1215

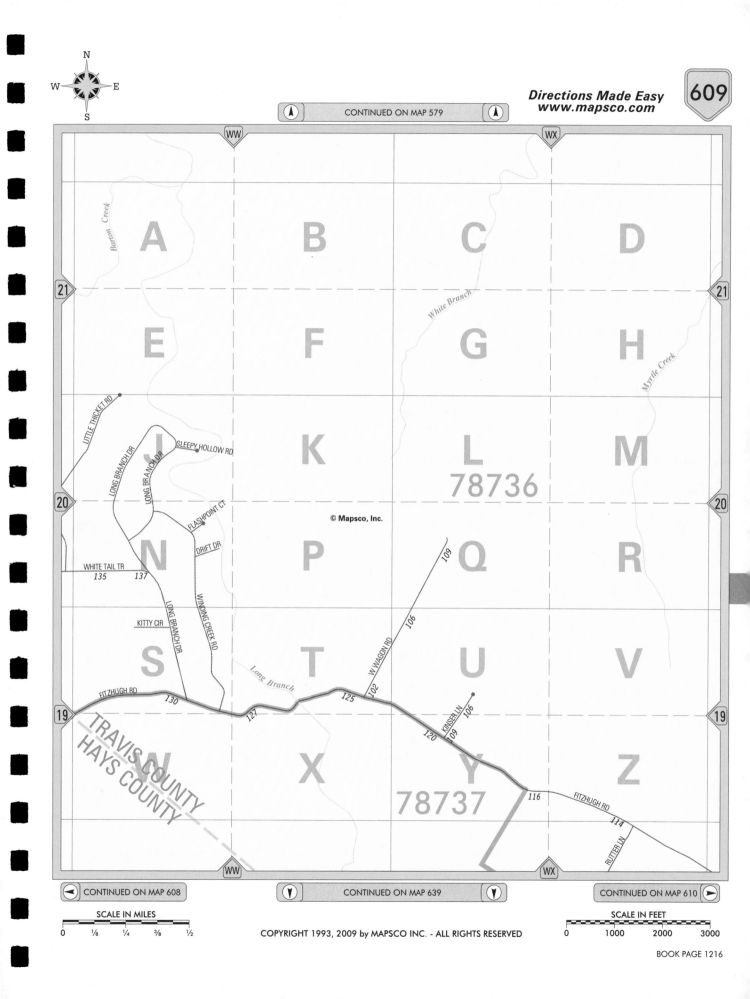

Directions Made Easy
www.mapsco.com

CONTINUED ON MAP 579

WW

WX

N
W E
S

A   B   C   D

21   21

E   F   G   H

Barton Creek

White Branch

Myrtle Creek

LITTLE THICKET RD

J   SLEEPY HOLLOW RD   K   L

LONG BRANCH DR

78736

LONG BRANCH DR

20   20

© Mapsco, Inc.

FLASHPOINT CT

N   DRIFT DR   P   Q   109

WHITE TAIL TR

135   137

WINDING CREEK RD

106

KITTY CIR

LONG BRANCH DR

S   T   U   V

Long Branch

W WAGON RD

102

FITZHUGH RD   125

130   127

19   120   09   106   19

TRAVIS COUNTY   KINSER LN

HAYS COUNTY   W   X   Y   Z   116   FITZHUGH RD

78737   114

RUTTER LN

WW   WX

CONTINUED ON MAP 608

CONTINUED ON MAP 639

CONTINUED ON MAP 610

SCALE IN MILES

0   ⅛   ¼   ⅜   ½

SCALE IN FEET

0   1000   2000   3000

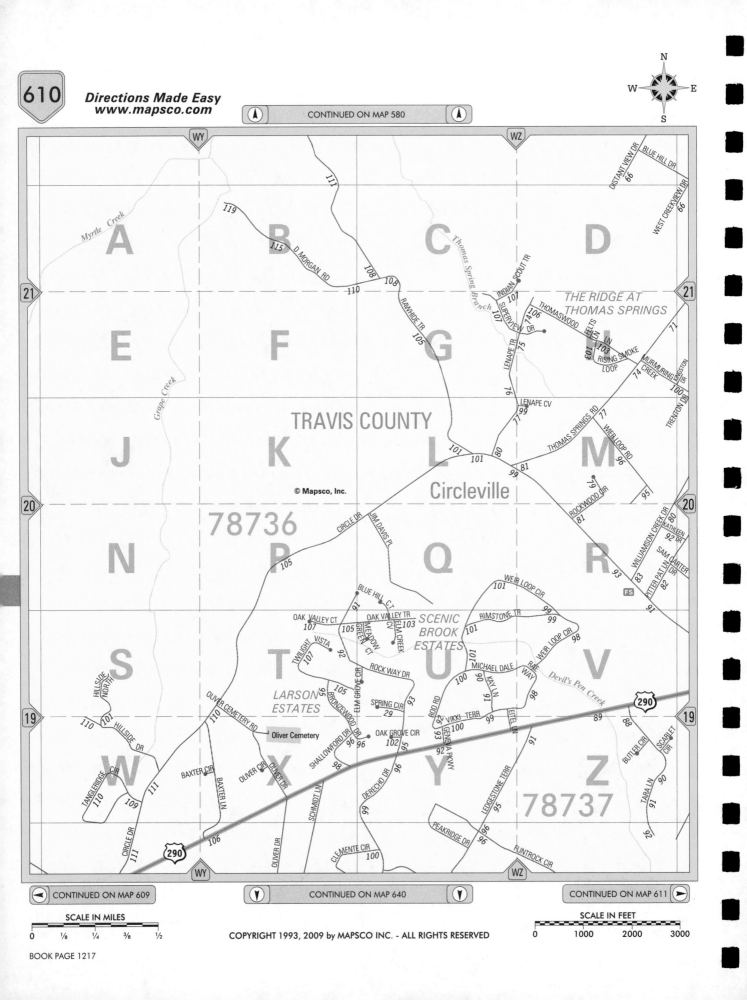

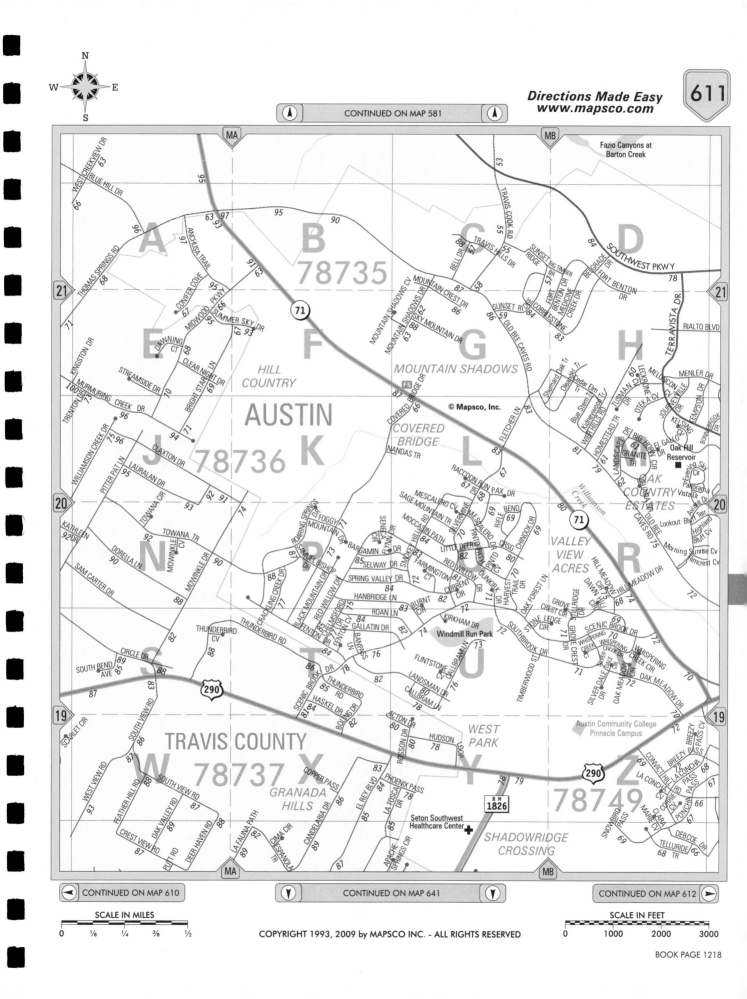

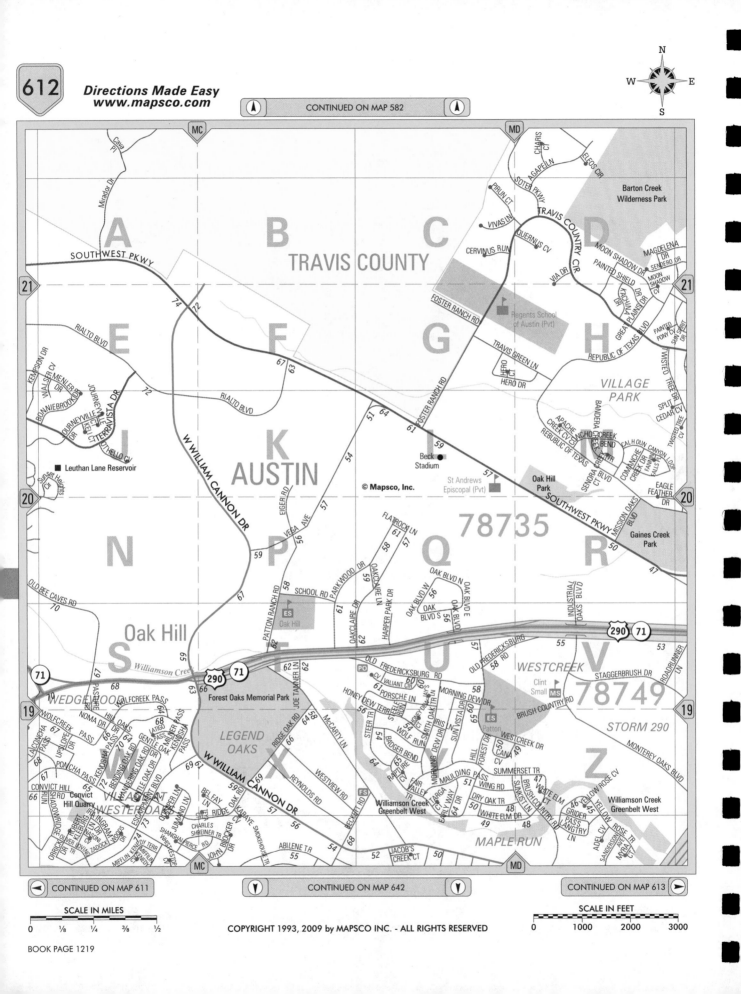

Directions Made Easy
www.mapsco.com

CONTINUED ON MAP 582

N
W   E
S

TRAVIS COUNTY

Barton Creek
Wilderness Park

A   B   C   D

SOUTHWEST PKWY

21   21

E   F   G   H

VILLAGE
PARK

AUSTIN

Leuthan Lane Reservoir

I   J   K

© Mapsco, Inc.

Beck
Stadium

St Andrews
Episcopal (Pvt)

Oak Hill
Park

Regents School
of Austin (Pvt)

20   N   P   Q   78735   R   20

SOUTHWEST PKWY

Gaines Creek
Park

Oak Hill

Williamson Creek

71   290   71

S   290   71   Forest Oaks Memorial Park   U   290   71   V

WESTCREEK   78749

Clint
Small
MS

19   Legend   Oaks   Storm 290   19
WEDGEWOOD   Patton
W   X   Z

W WILLIAM CANNON DR

Williamson Creek
Greenbelt West   Williamson Creek
Greenbelt West

MAPLE RUN

MC   MD

CONTINUED ON MAP 611
CONTINUED ON MAP 642
CONTINUED ON MAP 613

SCALE IN MILES
0   1/8   1/4   3/8   1/2

SCALE IN FEET
0   1000   2000   3000

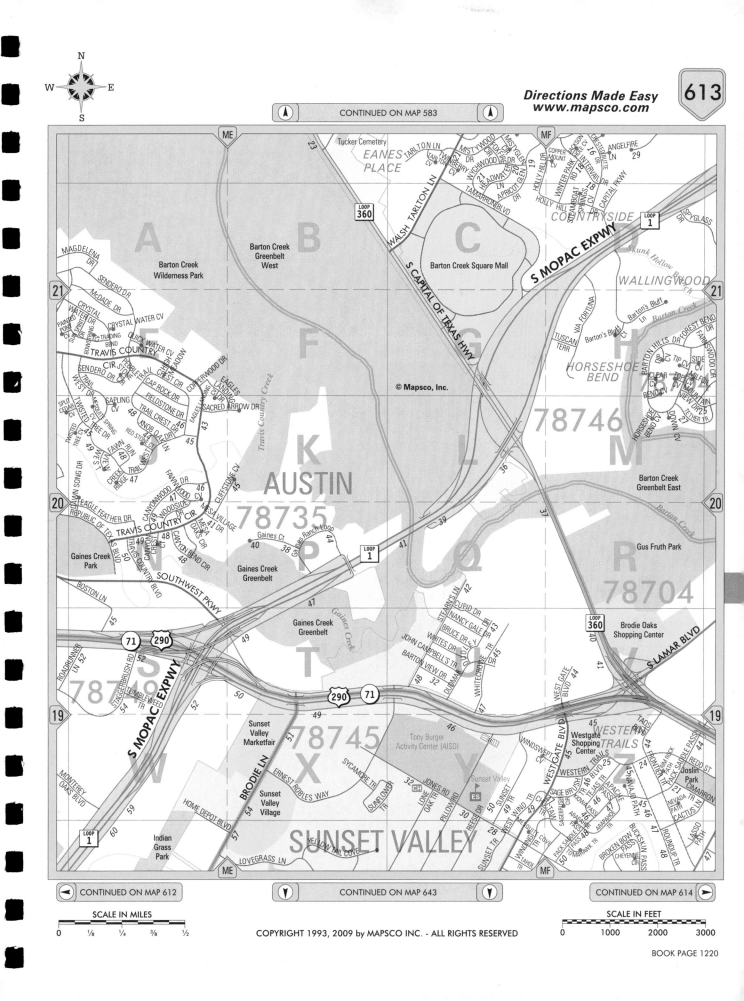

CONTINUED ON MAP 583

N
W E
S

ME

Tucker Cemetery

EANES PLACE

23

COUNTRYSIDE

21

LOOP 360

A

Barton Creek Wilderness Park

B

Barton Creek Greenbelt West

C

Barton Creek Square Mall

MF

MISTYWOOD

ANGELFIRE
29

SPYGLASS

S MOPAC EXPWY

LOOP 1

WALLINGWOOD

21

MAGDELENA DR

SENDERO DR

McDADE DR

CRYSTAL WATER DR

CRYSTAL WATER CV

E

QUICK WATER CV

HIGH MEADOW

COPPERWOOD DR

EAGLES LANDING

F

G

S CAPITAL OF TEXAS HWY

Barton's Bluff Ln

Barton Creek

Via Fortuna

TUSCAN TERR

Barton's Bluff Ct

HORSESHOE BEND

H

BARTON HILLS DR

FOREST BEND DR

FARNSWOOD DR

PAINTED POND

TRADING BEND

PEBBLE TRAIL

CAP ROCK DR

FIELDSTONE DR

EAGLES LANDING

SACRED ARROW DR

© Mapsco, Inc.

78746

DIP

CLEAR BEND

TIP CV

TOP CV

MILFON

MOUNTAIN VIEW DR

SIDE

25

TETHER TR

TRAVIS COUNTRY CIR

SENDERO TRAIL

WEST DR

SAPLING CV

48

TRAIL CREST DR

46

TRAIL CREST CIR

KNOB OAK LN

RED STONE CV

43

45

J

K

45

CLIFFSTONE CV

45

CANYONWOOD DR

47

WOODSIDE DR

46

MESA VILLAGE

AUSTIN

78735

L

36

HORSESHOE BEND DR

DOWN CV

M

Barton Creek Greenbelt East

SPLIT CEDAR CV

TWISTED TREE 45

49

TWISTED TREE CV

MESQUITE SPRING

FAWN CREEK RIDGE 47

48

WEST

TRAIL

20

DAWN SONG DR

EAGLE FEATHER DR

REPUBLIC OF TEXAS BLVD

TRAVIS COUNTRY CIR

CANYON

48

CANYON BEND CIR

48

MESA OAKS CIR

41

Gaines Ct

40

38

Gaines Ranch Loop

44

N

P

41

39

LOOP 1

37

Barton Creek

20

Gaines Creek Park

Gaines Creek Greenbelt

SOUTHWEST PKWY

Travis Country Blvd

49

50

BOSTON LN

45

Q

Gus Fruth Park

R

78704

Gaines Creek Greenbelt

47

Gaines Creek

LOOP 360

40

Brodie Oaks Shopping Center

49

71

290

ROADRUNNER LN 52

52

STAGGERBRUSH RD

TUMBLEWEED TR

S MOPAC EXPWY

78749

54

52

50

T

STEARN'S LN

CUPID DR

42

NANCY GALE DR

43

BRUCE DR

WHITES DR

DUDLEY

45

JOHN CAMPBELL'S TR

BARTON VIEW DR

48

32

WHITECHAPEL

47

WEST GATE BLVD

44

S LAMAR BLVD

41

Y

19

MONTEREY OAKS BLVD

19

290

71

49

78745

50

49

46

Tony Burger Activity Center (AISD)

Sunset Valley

WINDSWEPT DR

WEST GATE BLVD

45

Western Trails

Westgate Shopping Center

WESTERN TRAILS

25

45

TAOS BLVD

44

24

TACK SADDLE PASS

REDD ST

NAVAJO PATH

44

WESTERN TRAILS

Z

Sunset Valley Marketfair

BRODIE LN

ERNEST ROBLES WAY

51

Sunset Valley Village

54

HOME DEPOT BLVD

57

W

59

60

LOOP 1

Indian Grass Park

X

SYCAMORE TR

SUNFLOWER TR

32

LONE OAK TR

JONES RD

CH

PILLOW RD

30

ES

28

SUNSET TR

SUNSET VALLEY

YELLOW TAIL COVE

LOVEGRASS LN

ME

WEST WIND DR

49

WEST WIND DR

CHESTNUT

SUNSET

SUNSET TR

50

46

47

48

SAGEBRUSH

TEXAS TR

APACHE

ARAPAHOE

21

CACTUS LN

NEVADA PATH

LASSO PATH

ROUNDUP TR

BUCKSKIN PASS

BROKEN BOW PASS

CHEYENNE

TOMAHAWK TR

Joslin Park

CIMARRON

47

48

MF

CONTINUED ON MAP 612

CONTINUED ON MAP 643

CONTINUED ON MAP 614

SCALE IN MILES

0   ⅛   ¼   ⅜   ½

SCALE IN FEET

0   1000   2000   3000

Directions Made Easy
www.mapsco.com

CONTINUED ON MAP 584

N
W · E
S

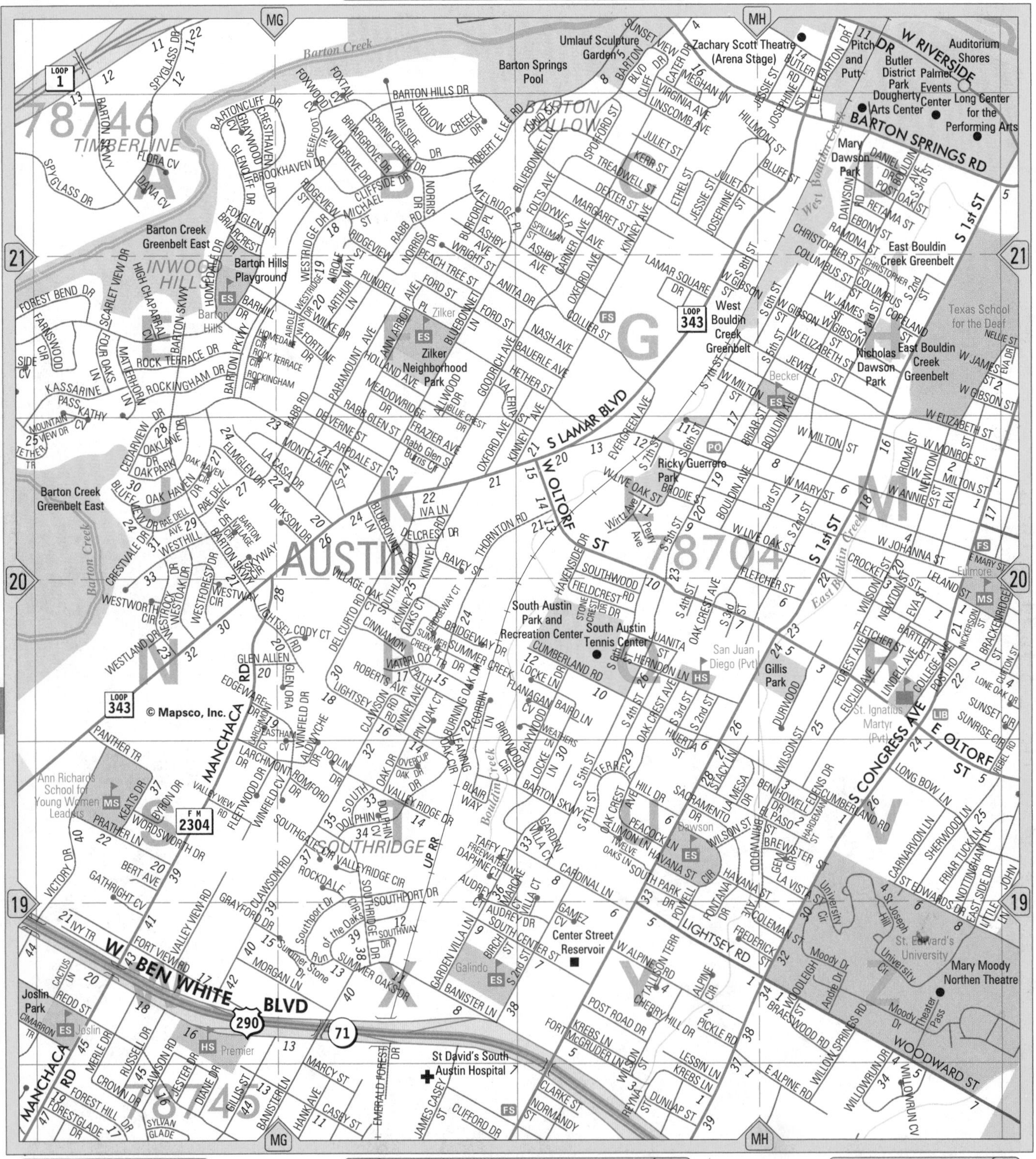

◄ CONTINUED ON MAP 613

CONTINUED ON MAP 644

CONTINUED ON MAP 615 ►

SCALE IN MILES
0 ⅛ ¼ ⅜ ½

SCALE IN FEET
0 1000 2000 3000

COPYRIGHT 1993, 2009 by MAPSCO INC. - ALL RIGHTS RESERVED

© Mapsco, Inc.

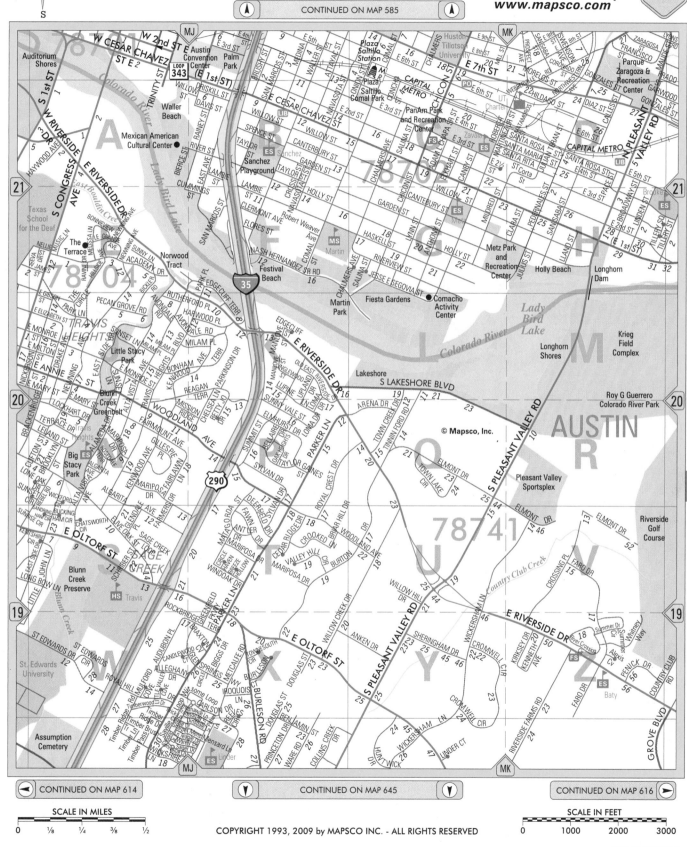

CONTINUED ON MAP 585

MJ

MK

CONTINUED ON MAP 614

CONTINUED ON MAP 645

CONTINUED ON MAP 616

© Mapsco, Inc.

AUSTIN

78741

SCALE IN MILES

0   ⅛   ¼   ⅜   ½

SCALE IN FEET

0   1000   2000   3000

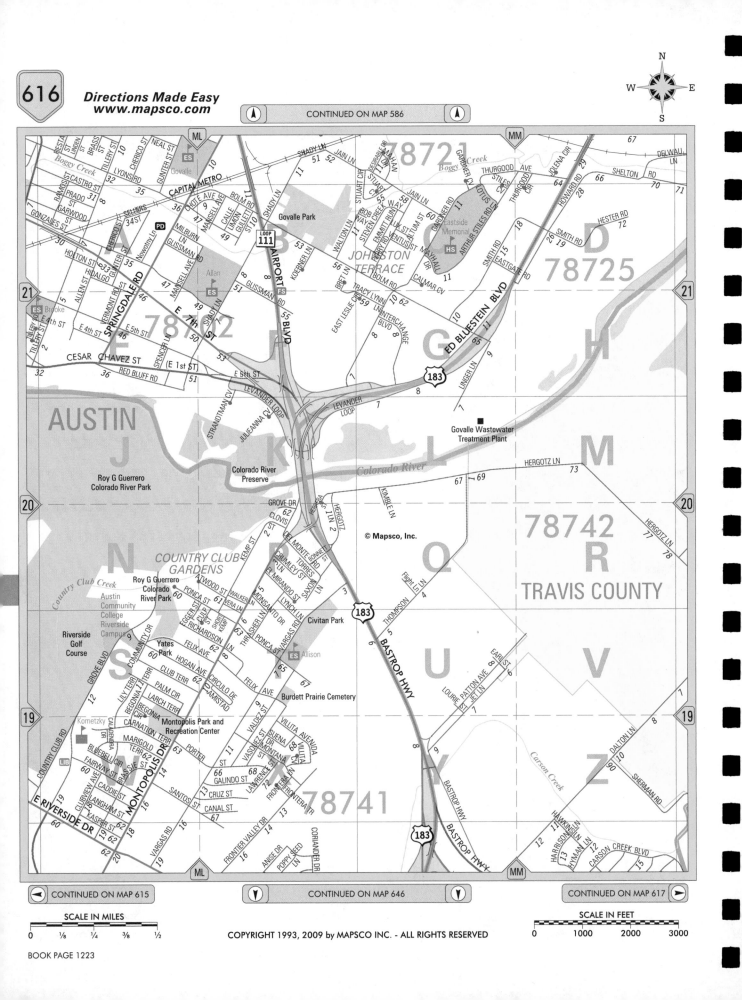

Directions Made Easy
www.mapsco.com

N
W E
S

CONTINUED ON MAP 586

ML
MM

Boggy Creek

78721

ES Govalle

CAPITAL METRO

Govalle Park

LOOP 111

Boggy Creek

Gardner Creek

Eastside Memorial HS

78725

JOHNSTON TERRACE

SPRINGDALE RD

E 7th ST

78702

AIRPORT BLVD

ED BLUESTEIN BLVD

CESAR CHAVEZ ST (E 1st ST)

RED BLUFF RD

E 5th ST

LEVANDER LOOP

183

LEVANDER LOOP

AUSTIN

J

Roy G Guerrero
Colorado River Park

Colorado River
Preserve

Colorado River

Govalle Wastewater
Treatment Plant

HERGOTZ LN

M

78742

R

TRAVIS COUNTY

COUNTRY CLUB
GARDENS

Roy G Guerrero
Colorado
River Park

Austin
Community
College
Riverside
Campus

Riverside
Golf
Course

Country Club Creek

GROVE DR

Civitan Park

ES Allison

183

BASTROP HWY

Burdett Prairie Cemetery

U

V

Yates
Park

Kometzky

LIB

Montopolis Park and
Recreation Center

MONTOPOLIS DR

78741

Z

Carson Creek

183

BASTROP HWY

Carson Creek

E RIVERSIDE DR

ML

MM

© Mapsco, Inc.

CONTINUED ON MAP 615

CONTINUED ON MAP 646

CONTINUED ON MAP 617

SCALE IN MILES
0   1/8   1/4   3/8   1/2

SCALE IN FEET
0   1000   2000   3000

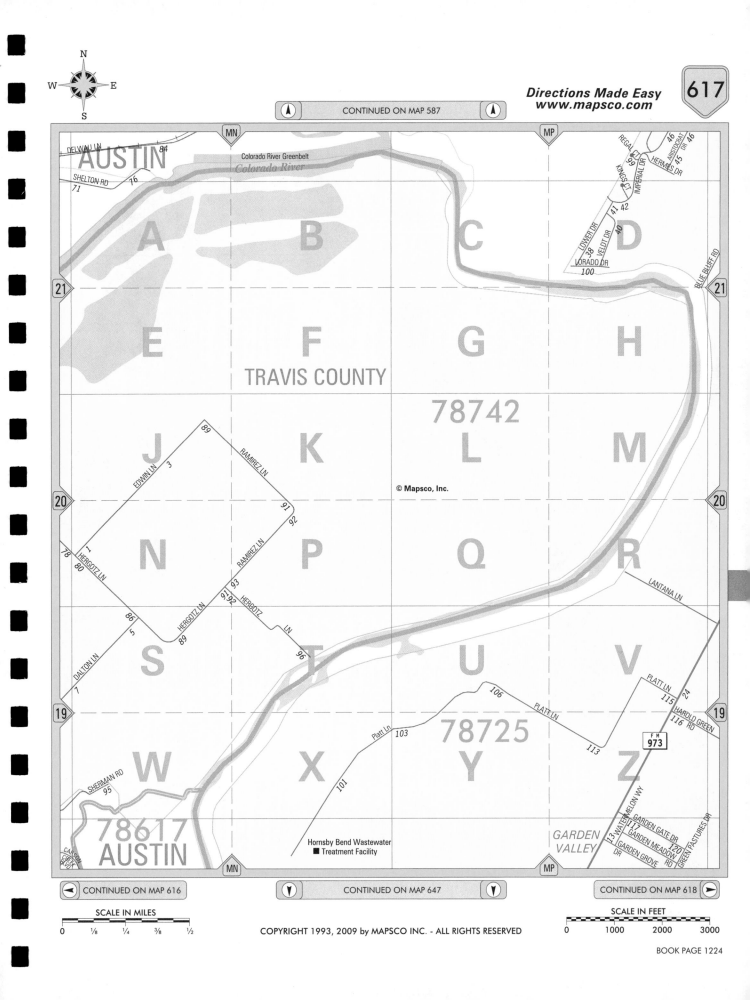

N
W E
S

CONTINUED ON MAP 587

MN

MP

AUSTIN
DELWAU LN 84
Colorado River Greenbelt
Colorado River
SHELTON RD 76
71

A

B

C

D
REGAL CT
KINGS CT
ARISTOCRAT DR 46
HERMES DR 45
IMPERIAL DR 99
41 42
LOWER DR
VELDT DR 40
38
LORADO DR
100
BLUE BLUFF RD

21

21

E

F

G

H

TRAVIS COUNTY

78742

J
89
RAMIREZ LN
EDWIN LN 3

K

L

© Mapsco, Inc.

M

20

91
92

20

78
HERGOTZ LN
80
1

N

RAMIREZ LN

P

Q

R
LANTANA LN

86
5
HERGOTZ LN
89
93
91 92
HERGOTZ LN
96

S

T

U

V
PLATT LN
115 24
HAROLD GREEN RD
116

DALTON LN
7

106
PLATT LN
113

19

19

PLATT LN 103

78725

FM 973

Platt Ln
101

W
SHERMAN RD
95

X

Hornsby Bend Wastewater
■ Treatment Facility

Y

Z
WATERMELON WY
117 GARDEN GATE DR
120 GARDEN MEADOW DR
13
GARDEN GROVE DR
GREEN PASTURES DR

78617
AUSTIN
CARSON CREEK

GARDEN VALLEY

MN

MP

◄ CONTINUED ON MAP 616

▼ CONTINUED ON MAP 647

CONTINUED ON MAP 618 ►

SCALE IN MILES
0   ⅛   ¼   ⅜   ½

SCALE IN FEET
0   1000   2000   3000

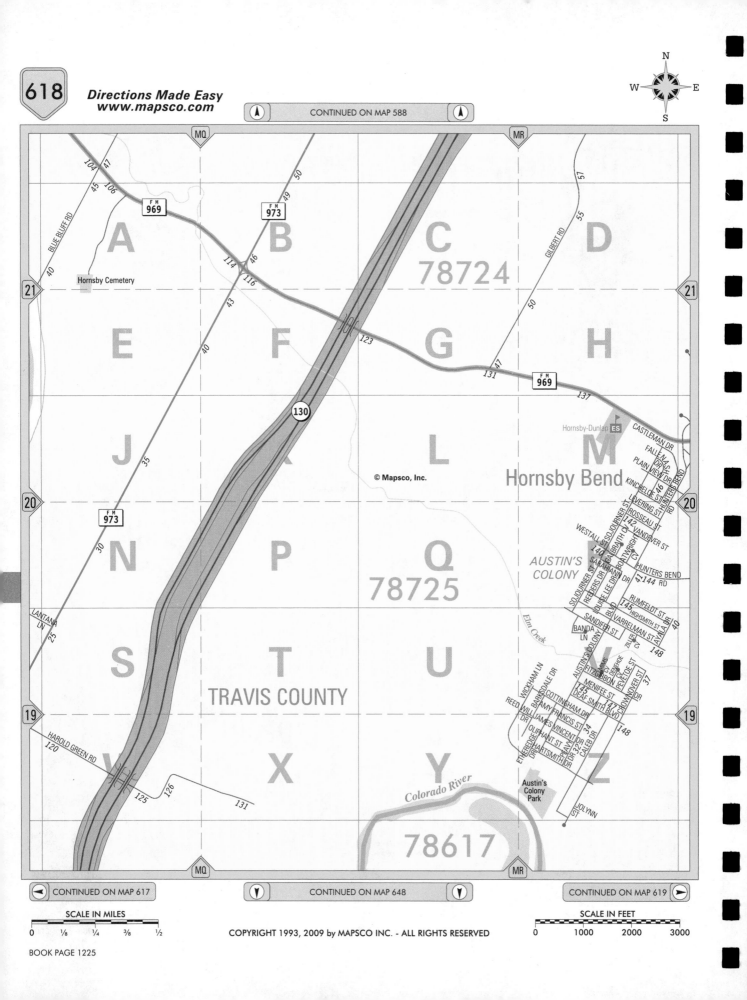

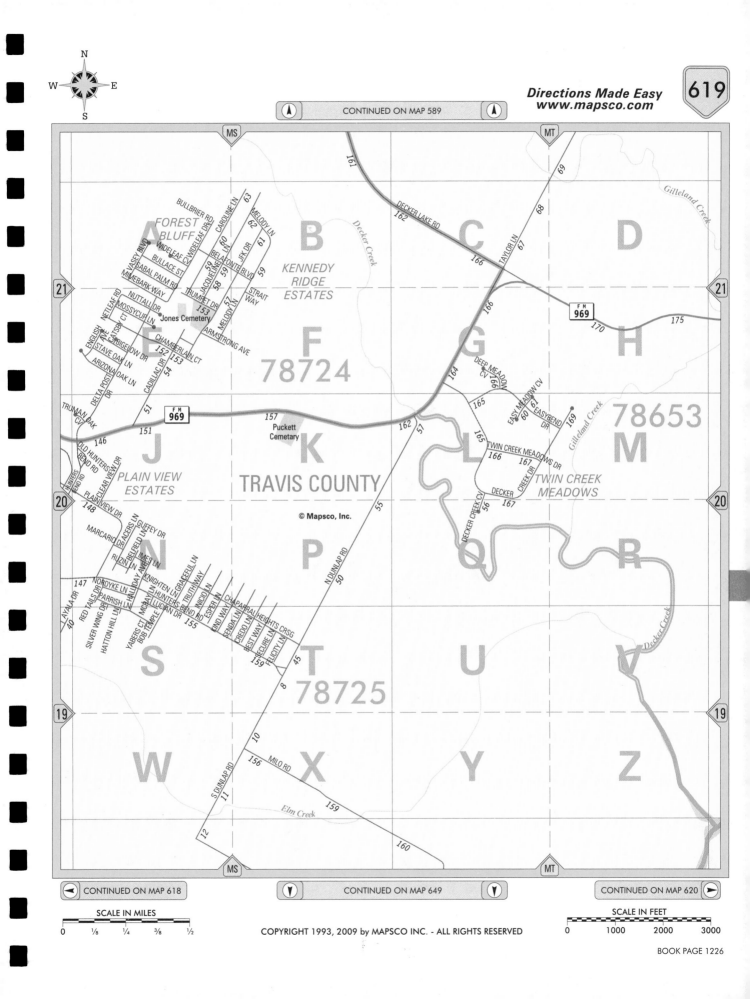

CONTINUED ON MAP 589

MS

MT

161

Gilleland Creek

162 DECKER LAKE RD

69

68

67

Decker Creek

A FOREST BLUFF

BULLBRIER RD.
WIDELEAF DR
CAROLINE LN
63
MELODY LN
62
61
W WIDELEAF CV
WIDELEAF CV
VASEY BLVD
BULLACE ST
SABAL PALM RD
60
BELAFONTE BLVD
59
JFK DR
59
JACQUELINE LN
58 59
TRUMPET DR 57
STRAIT WAY
MINEBARK WAY
153

B

C

D

21

TAYLOR LN

166

FM 969

21

175

170

KENNEDY RIDGE ESTATES

E
NETLEAF RD
NUTTALL DR
MOSSYCUP LN
CATSPAW CT
ENGLISH OAK LN
C BIGELOW DR
STAVE OAK LN
ARIZONA OAK LN
CHAMBERLAIN CT
152 153
CADILLAC DR
54
DELTA POST OAK DR
Jones Cemetery
MELODY LN
ARMSTRONG AVE

F
78724

G

H
78653

166

164

DEEP MEADOW CV 166

165

EASY MEADOW CV
60 61
EASYBEND DR
169

TRUMAN OAK CV
51
146
FM 969
151
157
Puckett Cemetery
162 57

J

K

L
TWIN CREEK MEADOWS DR
166 167
DECKER CREEK DR
DECKER CREEK CV
56
DECKER 167

M

OLD HUNTERS BEND RD
CLEAR VIEW DR
PLAIN VIEW ESTATES
PLAINVIEW DR
148
HUNTERS BEND RD

N

P

Q

R

20

HUNTERS BEND RD

20

55

TRAVIS COUNTY

© Mapsco, Inc.

MARCARIO DR
PLACERS LN
GUFFEY DR
BELFIELD LN
RUZIN LN
IMES LN
NORDYKE LN
RED TAILS DR
HALLIDAY AVE
KNIGHTEN LN
PARRISH LN
SILVER WING DR
MCRANY LN
HUNTERS BEND RD
LUCIAN DR 155
HATTON HILL LN
YABERS CT
BOB TEMPLE LN
GRACEFUL LN
TRUTH WAY
INICIO LN
ESPER LN
CHAPARRAL HEIGHTS CRSG
KIND WAY
RENDAL LN
CREDO LN
BEST WAY
SECURE LN
FELICITY LN
159

N DUNLAP RD
50

S

LAYALA DR
40
147

T
78725
45
8

U

V

Decker Creek

19

19

S DUNLAP RD
10
11

MILO RD
156

Elm Creek
159

12

160

W

X

Y

Z

MS

MT

CONTINUED ON MAP 618

CONTINUED ON MAP 649

CONTINUED ON MAP 620

SCALE IN MILES
0 1/8 1/4 3/8 1/2

SCALE IN FEET
0 1000 2000 3000

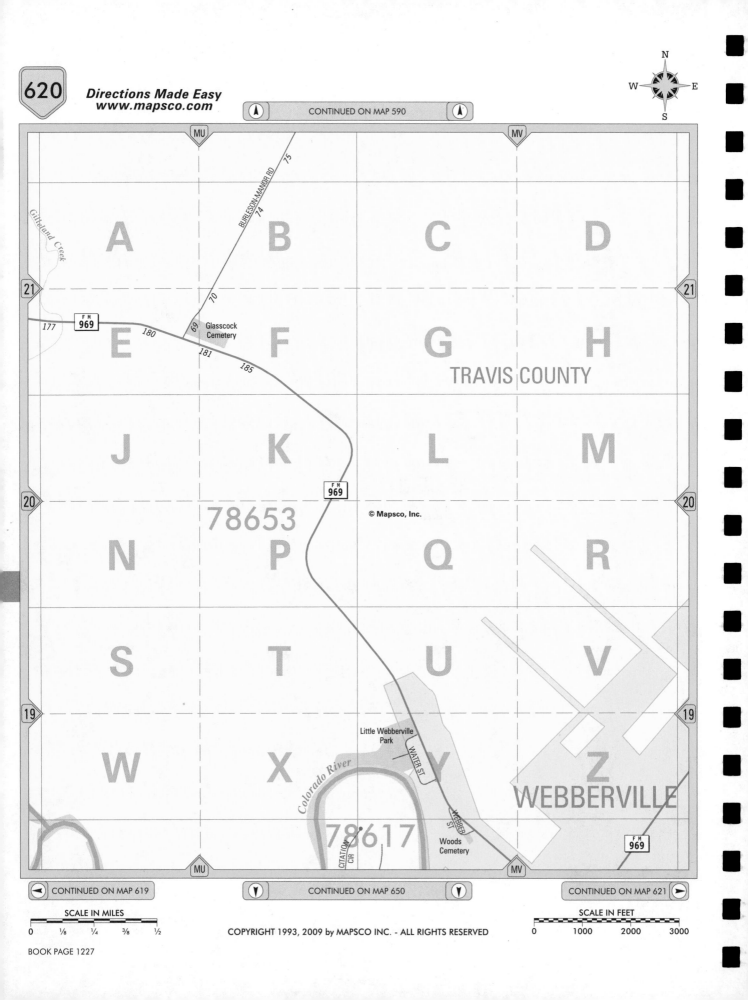

620

Directions Made Easy
www.mapsco.com

CONTINUED ON MAP 590

N
W · E
S

MU

MV

BURLESON-MANOR RD

75
74
70
69

21

FM 969

177
180
181
185

Glasscock
Cemetery

A

B

C

D

E

F

G

H

TRAVIS COUNTY

Gilleland Creek

J

K

L

M

FM 969

20

78653

© Mapsco, Inc.

N

P

Q

R

20

S

T

U

V

19

19

Little Webberville
Park

WATER ST

WEBBER ST

CITATION CIR

Colorado River

78617

Woods
Cemetery

W

X

Y

Z

WEBBERVILLE

FM 969

MU

MV

CONTINUED ON MAP 619

CONTINUED ON MAP 650

CONTINUED ON MAP 621

SCALE IN MILES

0   ⅛   ¼   ⅜   ½

SCALE IN FEET

0   1000   2000   3000

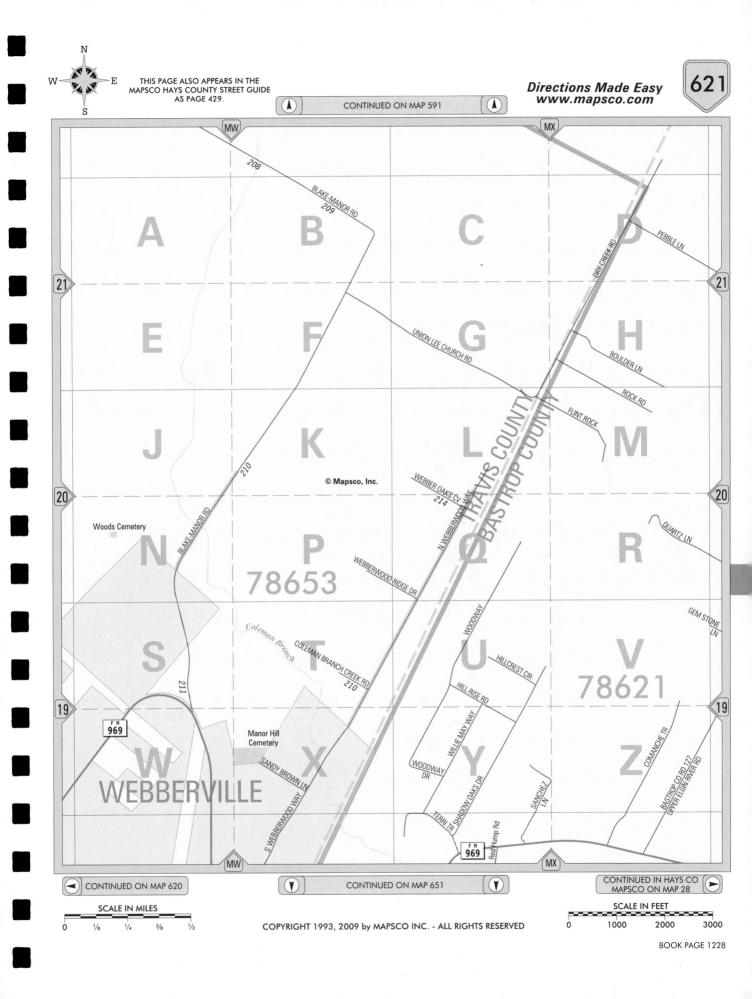

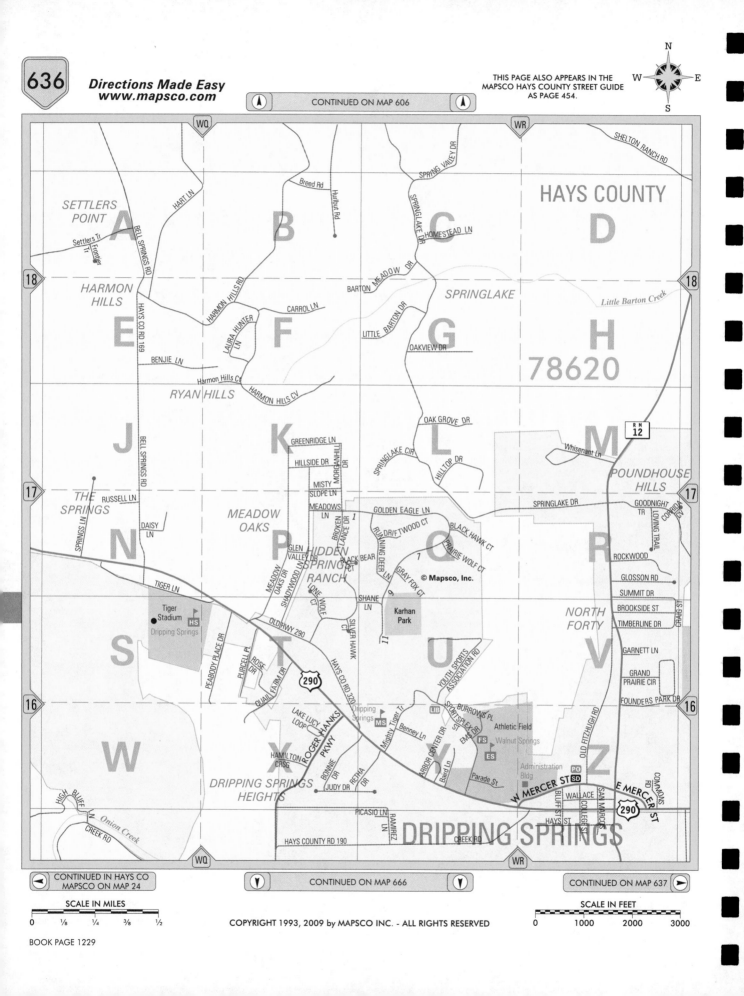

Directions Made Easy
www.mapsco.com

THIS PAGE ALSO APPEARS IN THE
MAPSCO HAYS COUNTY STREET GUIDE
AS PAGE 454.

N
W   E
S

CONTINUED ON MAP 606

WQ   WR

SHELTON RANCH RD

SETTLERS
POINT

A

HART LN

Breed Rd

Hurlbut Rd

B

SPRING VALLEY DR

C

SPRING LAKE DR

Homestead LN

HAYS COUNTY

D

18   18

BELL SPRINGS RD

HARMON
HILLS

HARMON HILLS RD

BARTON MEADOW DR

CARROL LN

SPRINGLAKE

Little Barton Creek

E

HAYS CO RD 169

LAURA HUNTER LN

F

LITTLE BARTON DR

OAKVIEW DR

G

H

78620

BENJIE LN

Harmon Hills Ct

RYAN HILLS

HARMON HILLS CV

OAK GROVE DR

RM
12

J

BELL SPRINGS RD

GREENRIDGE LN

HILLSIDE DR

K

MORGANHILL DR

SPRINGLAKE CIR

HILLTOP DR

L

Whisenant Ln

M

*POUNDHOUSE
HILLS*

17   17

*THE
SPRINGS*

RUSSELL LN

SPRINGS LN

DAISY LN

*MEADOW
OAKS*

N

MISTY SLOPE LN

MEADOWS LN

GLEN VALLEY DR

P

BROKEN LANCE DR

GOLDEN EAGLE LN

RUNNING DEER LN

DRIFTWOOD CT

Q

BLACK HAWK CT

PRAIRIE WOLF CT

GRAY FOX CT

© Mapsco, Inc.

SPRINGLAKE DR

GOODNIGHT TR

LOVING TRAIL

CORRIDA CV

ROCKWOOD

R

GLOSSON RD

SUMMIT DR

TIGER LN

Tiger
Stadium
HS
Dripping Springs

MEADOW OAKS DR

SHADYWOOD LN

LONE WOLF CT

HIDDEN
SPRINGS
RANCH

Black Bear Ct

SHANE LN

SILVER HAWK CT

Karhan
Park

*NORTH
FORTY*

BROOKSIDE ST

TIMBERLINE DR

GARNETT LN

S

PEABODY PLACE DR

PURCELL PL

ROSE DR

QUAIL FARM DR

T

HAYS CO RD 320

OLD HWY 290

U

YOUTH SPORTS ASSOCIATION RD

V

GRAND PRAIRIE CIR

FOUNDERS PARK DR

OLD FITZHUGH RD

CRAIG ST

16   16

290

LAKE LUCY LOOP

ROGER HANKS PKWY

Dripping
Springs
MS

MIGHTY TIGER TR

Benney Ln

LIB

SPORTSPLEX DR

BURROWS PL

EMS ST

Athletic Field

FS

Walnut Springs

ES

PO

SD

W

HAMILTON CRSG

BONNIE DR

RETHA DR

X

JUDY DR

*DRIPPING SPRINGS
HEIGHTS*

ARBOR CENTER DR

Baird Ln

Parade St

Administration
Bldg

Y

W MERCER ST

BLUFF ST

HAYS ST

WALLACE

COLLEGE ST

SAN MARCOS

E MERCER ST

COMMONS RD

Z

290

HIGH BLUFF LN

Onion Creek

CREEK RD

PICASIO LN

RAMIREZ

HAYS COUNTY RD 190

CREEK RD

DRIPPING SPRINGS

WQ   WR

CONTINUED IN HAYS CO
MAPSCO ON MAP 24

CONTINUED ON MAP 666

CONTINUED ON MAP 637

SCALE IN MILES

0   ⅛   ¼   ⅜   ½

SCALE IN FEET

0   1000   2000   3000

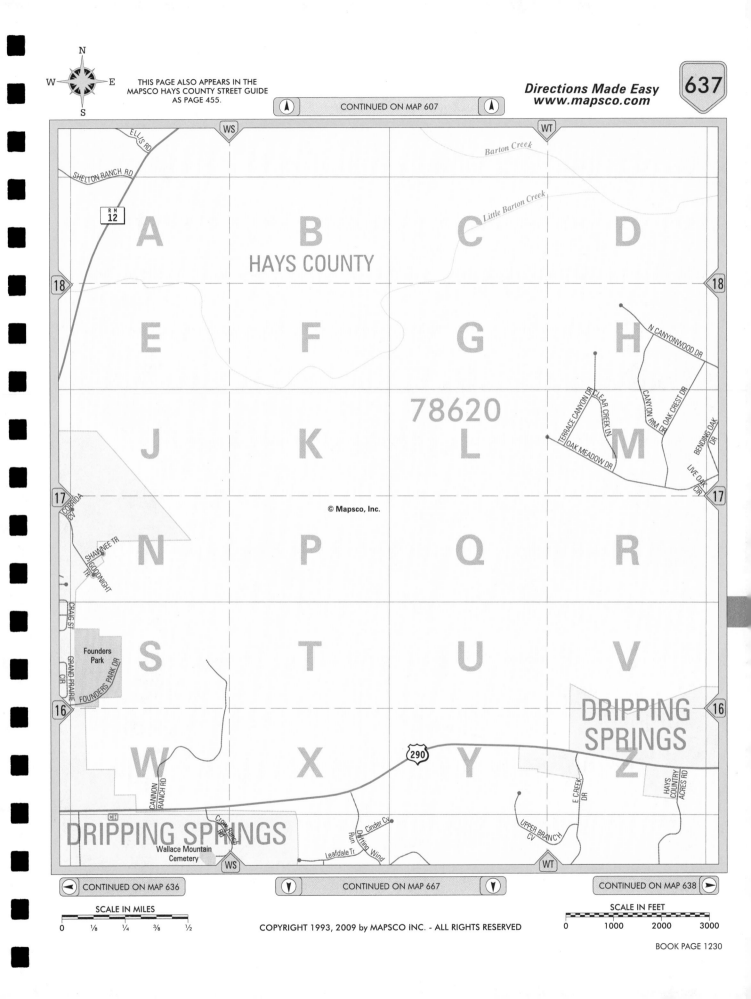

N
W E
S

THIS PAGE ALSO APPEARS IN THE
MAPSCO HAYS COUNTY STREET GUIDE
AS PAGE 455.

Directions Made Easy
www.mapsco.com

CONTINUED ON MAP 607

WS
WT

Barton Creek

ELLIS RD

SHELTON RANCH RD

R M 12

18

A   B   C   D

HAYS COUNTY

Little Barton Creek

18

E   F   G   H

N CANYONWOOD DR

78620

J   K   L   M

TERRACE CANYON DR
CLEAR CREEK LN
OAK MEADOW DR
CANYON RIM DR
OAK CREST DR
BENDING OAK DR
LIVE OAK CIR

17   17

© Mapsco, Inc.

CORRIDA CV

N   P   Q   R

SHAWNEE TR
GOODNIGHT TR

CRAIG ST

Founders
Park

GRAND PRAIRIE CIR
FOUNDERS PARK DR

S   T   U   V

16   16

**DRIPPING
SPRINGS**

W   X   Y   Z

CANNON RANCH RD

290

E CREEK DR

HAYS COUNTRY ACRES RD

DRIPPING SPRINGS

CH

CROW RANCH RD

Cinder Cv

UPPER BRANCH CV

Wallace Mountain
Cemetery

Run
Drifting Wind

Leafdale Tr

WS
WT

CONTINUED ON MAP 636
CONTINUED ON MAP 667
CONTINUED ON MAP 638

SCALE IN MILES
0   1/8   1/4   3/8   1/2

SCALE IN FEET
0   1000   2000   3000

BOOK PAGE 1230

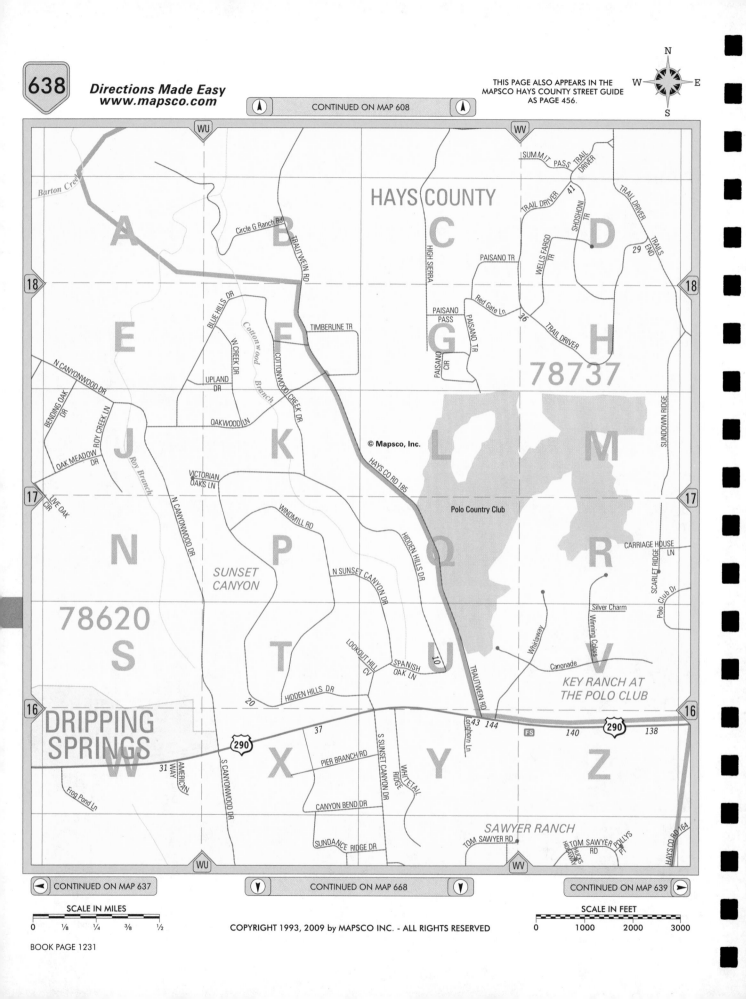

Directions Made Easy
www.mapsco.com

CONTINUED ON MAP 608

THIS PAGE ALSO APPEARS IN THE
MAPSCO HAYS COUNTY STREET GUIDE
AS PAGE 456.

N
W E
S

WU

WV

Barton Creek

HAYS COUNTY

Circle G Ranch Rd

TRAUTWEIN RD

A

B

C

D

SUMMIT PASS TRAIL DRIVER
TRAIL DRIVER 41
WELLS FARGO TR
SHOSHONI TR
TRAIL DRIVER TRAILS END
29

18

18

High Sierra

Paisano Tr

E

BLUE HILLS DR

Cottonwood Branch

F

Timberline Tr

G

Paisano Pass

Red Gate Ln

Paisano Tr

36

Trail Driver

H

78737

W CREEK DR

UPLAND DR

COTTONWOOD CREEK DR

N CANYONWOOD DR

BENDING OAK DR

ROY CREEK LN

OAKWOOD LN

OAK MEADOW DR

J

Roy Branch

VICTORIAN OAKS LN

K

L

© Mapsco, Inc.

HAYS CO RD 185

Paisano Cir

M

Sundown Ridge

17

LIVE OAK CIR

N

N CANYONWOOD DR

WINDMILL RD

P

SUNSET CANYON

N SUNSET CANYON DR

Polo Country Club

Q

HIDDEN HILLS DR

R

CARRIAGE HOUSE LN

SCARLET RIDGE

Polo Club Dr

17

78620

S

T

LOOKOUT HILL CV

SPANISH OAK LN

U

TRAUTWEIN RD

Whitlaway

Silver Charm

Winning Colors

Canonade

V

KEY RANCH AT
THE POLO CLUB

10

16

DRIPPING
SPRINGS

W

31 AMERICAN WAY

Frog Pond Ln

20

S CANYONWOOD DR

37

HIDDEN HILLS DR

290

X

PIER BRANCH RD

CANYON BEND DR

SUNDANCE RIDGE DR

S SUNSET CANYON DR

WHITETAIL RIDGE

Y

Longhorn Ln

43 144

FS

140

290

138

Z

SAWYER RANCH

TOM SAWYER RD

CHUCKS HIGHWAY

TOM SAWYER RD

POLLYS PT

HAYS CO RD 164

16

WU

WV

CONTINUED ON MAP 637

CONTINUED ON MAP 668

CONTINUED ON MAP 639

SCALE IN MILES

0   1/8   1/4   3/8   1/2

SCALE IN FEET

0   1000   2000   3000

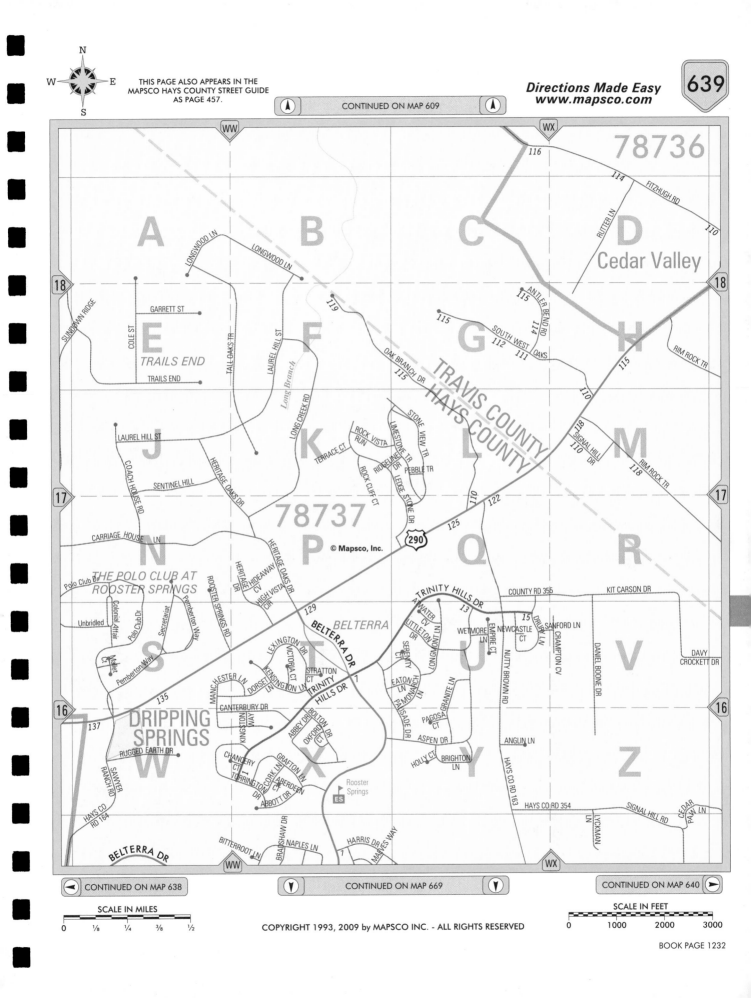

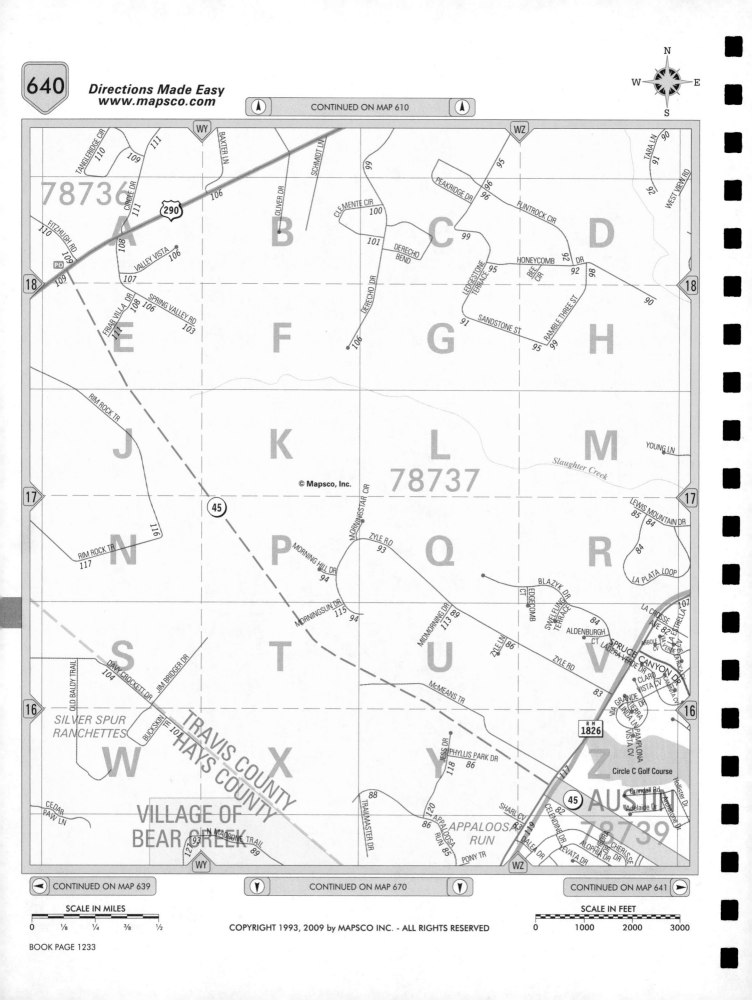

N
W E
S

MA   MB

R M 1826

GRANADA HILLS

AUSTIN
78874

SHADOWRIDGE CROSSING

Seton Southwest Healthcare Center

D

COPPER PASS   PHOENIX PASS   LA CONCLAVA   CONVICT HILL RD   PASS
SOUTH VIEW RD   EL REY BLVD   LA TOSCANA DR   CLARA   CORRIE   PONCHA   PASS
WEST VIEW RD   FEATHER HILL RD   CIMA CIR   APACHE SPRINGS CIR   SNOWBIRD PASS   MARK CV   DEBCOE DR
CREST VIEW RD   OAK VALLEY RD   ESPANOLA TR   SUMMERVALE CIR   TWILIGHT MESA DR   WATERS WAY   TELLURIDE TR
PUTT RD   DEER HAVEN RD   CANDELARIA DR   FLAT ROCK DR   CEDAR SPRINGS   DUSK TERRACE CV   DARK VALLEY CV   SAM MAVERICK   SIRINGO PASS
SAN LUCAS DR   LA FAUNA PATH   DEL DORADO DR   INDIAN RIDGE DR   HIGH VALLEY DR   GALLANT FOX RD   DARK SHADOW CV   TWILIGHT TERRACE DR   HOT SPRINGS DR   ROTAN CV   CHEINO CORTINA
VERA CRUZ RD   LA FAUNA VIEW   CRAZY HORSE DR   BROKEN LANCE DR   TWILIGHT SHADOW DR   BUENA SUERTE   HOT SPRINGS CT   BILLY BONNEY   CLAY ALLISON   OASIS
SAN DIEGO RD   SAN JUAN   ADOBE TR   VIA CORRETO DR   VIA MIA DR   BUDA CORTINA
18   18

GRANADA ESTATES
78737

EL REY BLVD   SAN JUAN PASS   VIA DONO DR   OAKLAND VILLAGE   Latta Branch Greenbelt
SAN DIEGO RD   VIA CORRETO DR   VIA RICCO DR
EL DORADO DR   ■ Slaughter Lane Reservoir   COLBERG CT   COLBERG DR   DUNSMORE DR   CLAIRMONT   Latta Branch Greenbelt
KALI CV   CIRCLE C RANCH   ALLERTON AVE   BEATTY   ABILENE TR   FARMDALE
SILVER MOUNTAIN CV   BELLA VISTA TR   GARION DR   HEIGERTON   BEATTY CV   CLARION   MESA VERDE CIR
SILVER MOUNTAIN DR   LOOKOUT POINT   AXTELLON   AUCKLAND   FAINWOOD   RUXTON   TAYLORCREST DR   SALCON CLIFF DR
YOUNG LN   LEWIS MOUNTAIN RANCH   AUCK END   BARSTOW AVE   HILLSIDE   LA SIESTA   TAYLORCREST WAY
J   K   McKNOWN ST   HASWELL DR   TERRACE TERR   ES Mills   MESA GRANDE DR   SALCON CLIFF DR   MEACHAM
17   DONNER LN   DONNER CV   LA PUENTE DR   SUMMERLAND WAY   17
Lewis Mountain Ranch Park   Shankel Dr   KISORA   SALCON CLIFF DR   RIDGEWAY LN
LEWIS MOUNTAIN DR   Mc Grath Dr   N   P   Q   BUNGALOW LN   HOPELAND DR   WAMPTON WAY   SALCON CLIFF DR
LA PLATA LOOP   Fleenor Dr   © Mapsco, Inc.   ARGYLE LN   COLEBROOK DR   GRAFTON DR
LA PLATA CV   PRESCOTT DR   CARRINGTON LN
R M 1826   McKNOWNVILLE   Slaughter Creek   LYNN HAVEN ST   VINEMONT LN   W SLAUGHTER LN

TRAVIS COUNTY
78739

ALTA MIRA   S   T   U   Southwest Soccer Complex   V
ALTA CROSSE AVE   VIA VERDE DR   SENECA FALLS LOOP   Circle C Ranch Metropolitan Park
RIO GRANDE DR   TORINSOL   SENECA FALLS LN   HANSA LOOP   Circle C Ranch Metropolitan Park
LOS ARCOS   CALIFORNIA CV   HANSA LN   59   58
16   Bastrone Loop   SENECA FALLS CV   LA CROSSE AVE   CIRCLE C RANCH   97   16
Bettis Trophy Dr   Brecourt Manor Way   RED PEBBLE RD   NUBAN CV   Tasajillo Tr   ESQUEL
Faxton Rd   Haggans Dr   MOON   ROCKIRDSTONE WAY   ROLLING STONE   NUBAN CV   TOLLESBORO CV   DEDHAM LN   VAN WINKLE LN   AUSTRAL
Colyber Ct   Carltron Dr   Christensen Cv   SPLIT   NUSSERG LN   ESCARPMENT BLVD   RHETT BUTLER DR   ECLIPSE LN   AUSTRAL LOOP
THOR   ES Clayton   W   X   GOODALL   GOULDVILLE   FRESIA   DALEA VISTA   LA CROSSE AVE   AUSTRAL ESTANCIA
HIELSCHER   Rponey   DOSWELL LN   PAIRNOY   NEEDHAM LN   PARK WEST PASS   ROXBURY LN   BANKS LN   DAHLGREN LN   STEWART CV
SPRUCE CANYON DR   VIRIDIAN WAY   SIERRA RIDGE CT   MAELIN DR   WALBRIDGE LN   LONDONBERRY LN   ES Kiker   TRELAWNEY LN
Circle C Golf Course   MAGENTA LN   LAPIN CV   BLISSFIELD   HALSEY CT   REDGATE LN   GINITA LN   AYLFORD LN   GALSWORTHY LN
Archshire Dr   Felspar Dr   Hollister Dr   VIRIDIAN LN   LARUE BELLE LN   TANAQUA LN   NAPLES   BACK BAY LN   WAREHAM   GRASSMERE LN   PINKNEY LN   GALSWORTHY LN

MA   MB   **LOOP 1**

SCALE IN MILES
0   1/8   1/4   3/8   1/2

SCALE IN FEET
0   1000   2000   3000

BOOK PAGE 1234

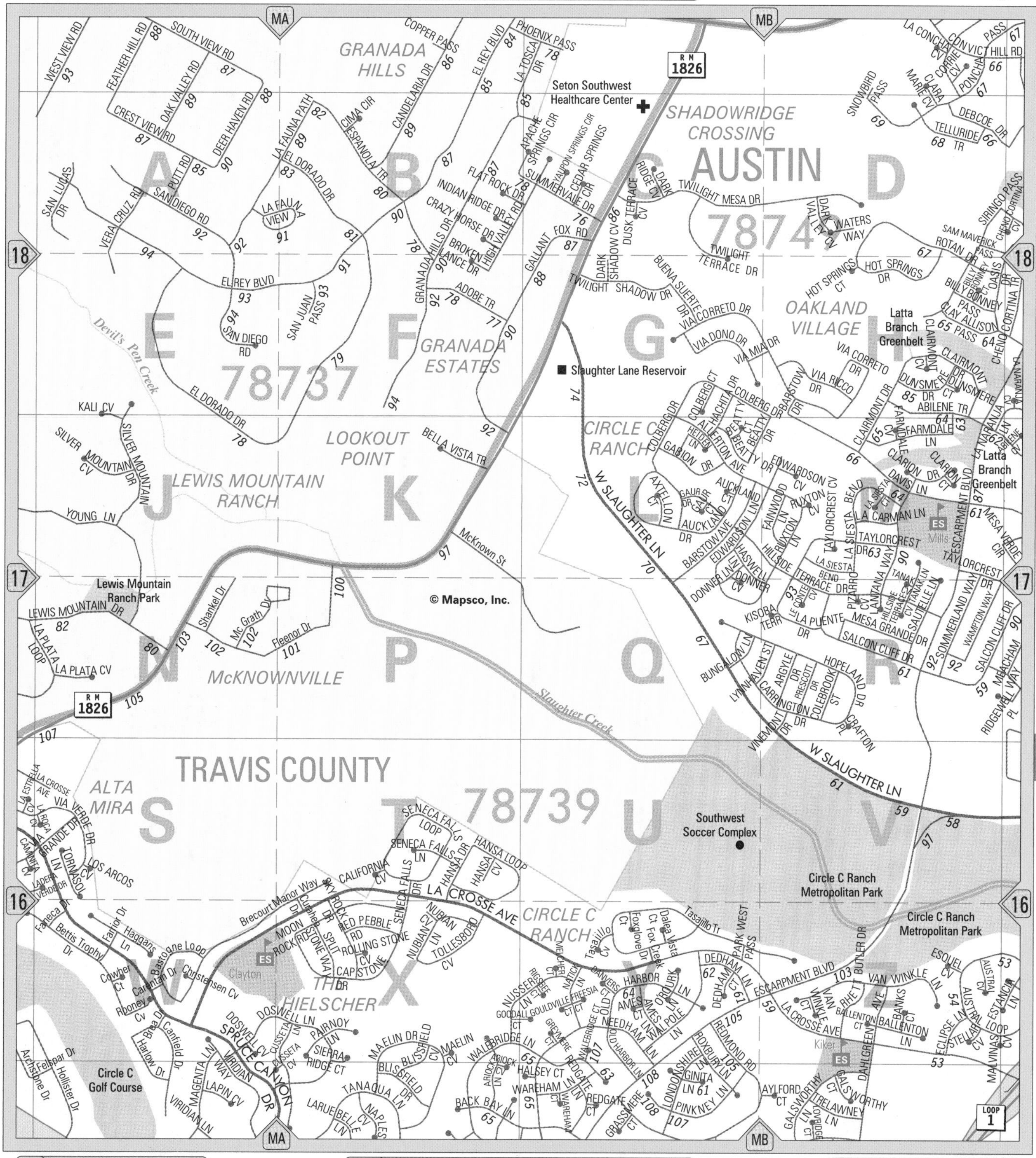

CONTINUED ON MAP 612

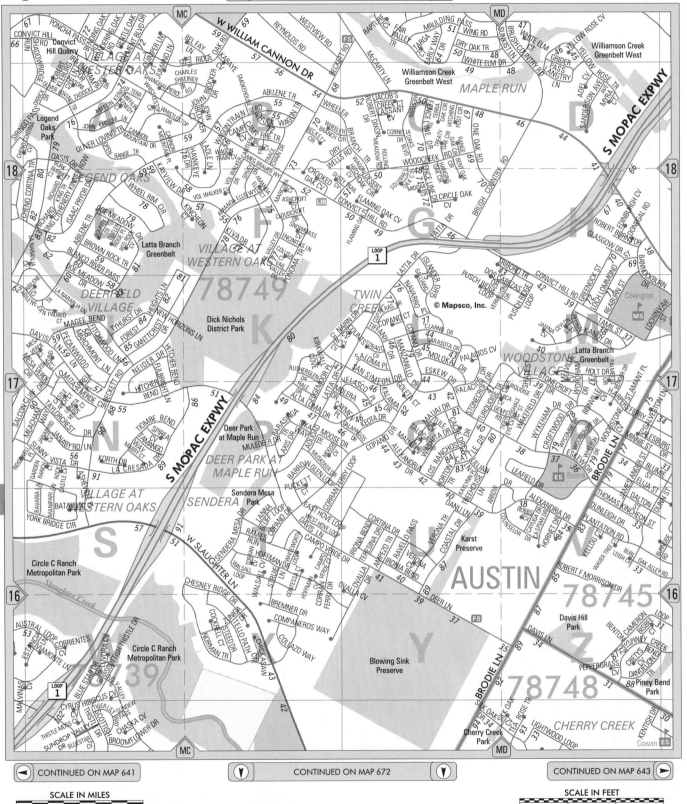

◄ CONTINUED ON MAP 641

▼ CONTINUED ON MAP 672 ▼

CONTINUED ON MAP 643 ►

SCALE IN MILES

0   ⅛   ¼   ⅜   ½

SCALE IN FEET

0   1000   2000   3000

COPYRIGHT 1993, 2009 by MAPSCO INC. - ALL RIGHTS RESERVED

CONTINUED ON MAP 613

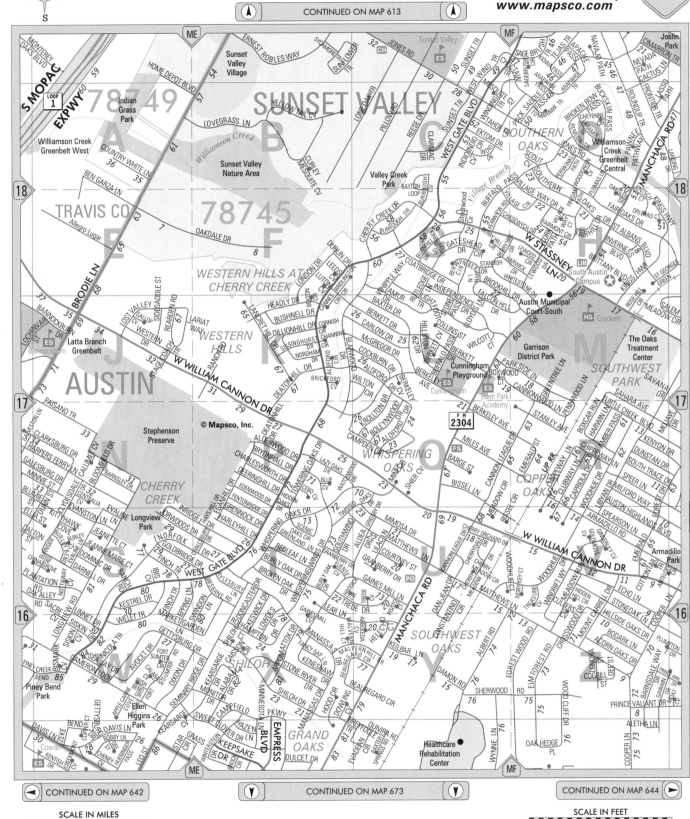

CONTINUED ON MAP 642

CONTINUED ON MAP 673

CONTINUED ON MAP 644

SCALE IN MILES

0   1/8   1/4   3/8   1/2

SCALE IN FEET

0   1000   2000   3000

MG

MH

Joslin Park
REDD ST
ES Joslin

Mary Moody Northen Theatre
Moody Theatre
St. Edward's University

WOODWARD ST

MANCHACA RD

St David's South Austin Hospital

290
71

E BEN WHITE BLVD

Blunn Creek

78704

Assumption Cemetery

18   18

Williamson Creek Greenbelt Central

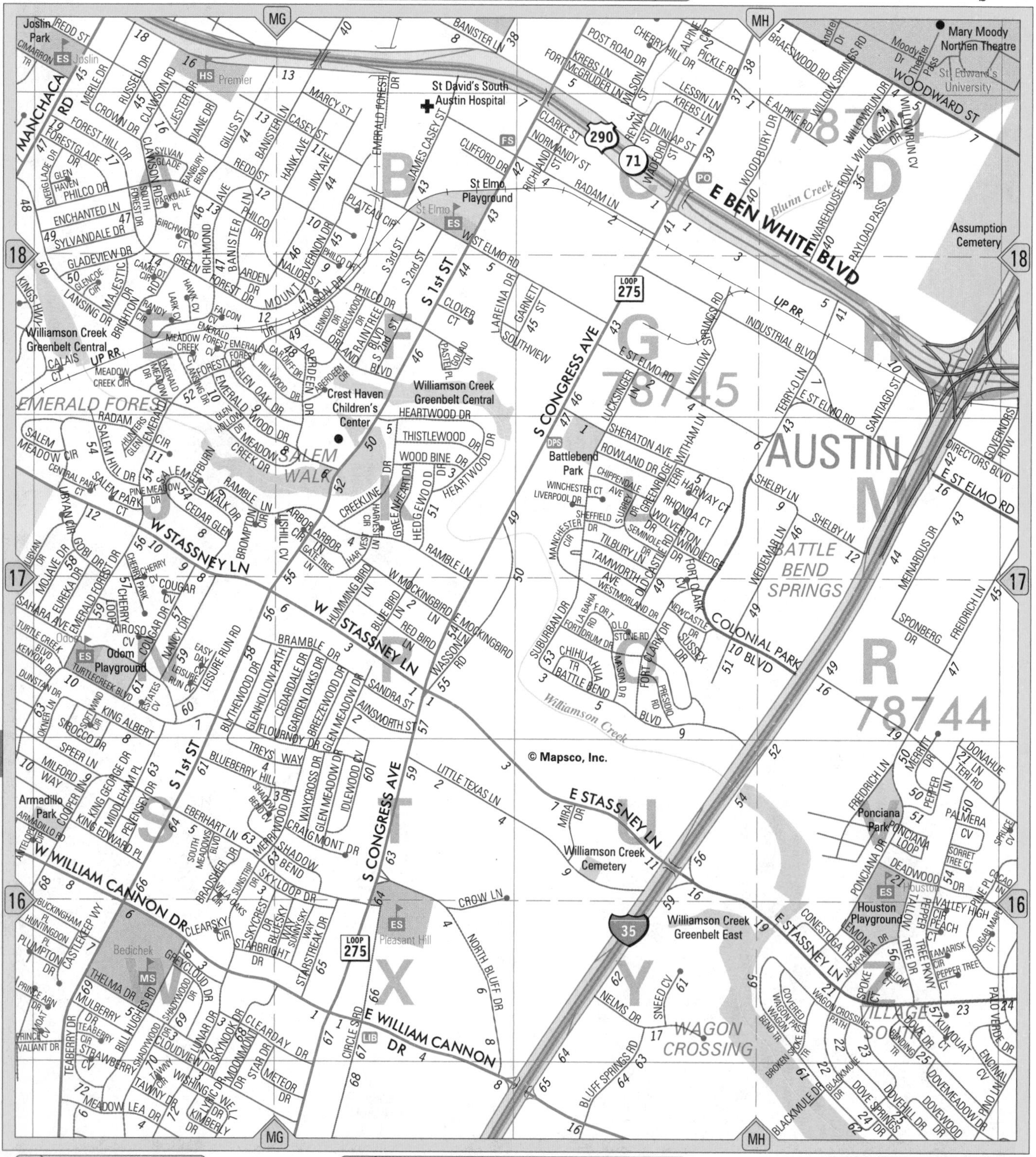

LOOP 275

St Elmo Playground
ES

Crest Haven Children's Center

Williamson Creek Greenbelt Central

S CONGRESS AVE

78745

INDUSTRIAL BLVD

UP RR

Emerald Forest

SALEM WALK

Battlebend Park

AUSTIN

BATTLE BEND SPRINGS

Battle Bend

W STASSNEY LN

17   17

Odom Playground

W STASSNEY LN

COLONIAL PARK BLVD

78744

Williamson Creek

© Mapsco, Inc.

Armadillo Park

E STASSNEY LN

Williamson Creek Cemetery

Ponciana Park

Houston Playground
ES

16   16

S CONGRESS AVE

35

Williamson Creek Greenbelt East

VILLAGE SOUTH

Bedichek
MS

LOOP 275

Pleasant Hill
ES

E WILLIAM CANNON DR

LIB

WAGON CROSSING

MG

MH

SCALE IN MILES
0   1/8   1/4   3/8   1/2

SCALE IN FEET
0   1000   2000   3000

COPYRIGHT 1993, 2009 by MAPSCO INC. - ALL RIGHTS RESERVED

BOOK PAGE 1237

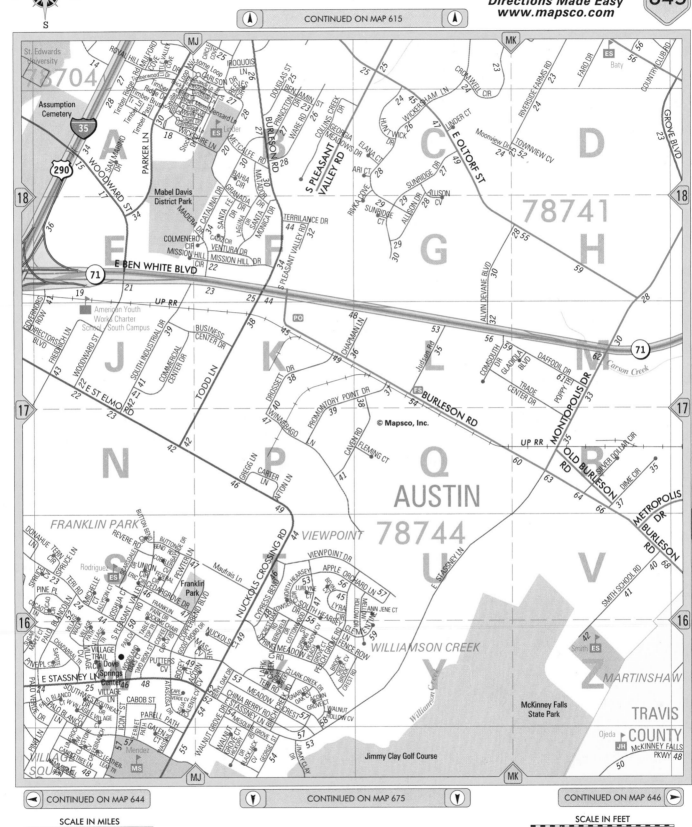

CONTINUED ON MAP 615

CONTINUED ON MAP 644

CONTINUED ON MAP 675

CONTINUED ON MAP 646

AUSTIN
78744

78704

78741

TRAVIS COUNTY

SCALE IN MILES

0   ⅛   ¼   ⅜   ½

SCALE IN FEET

0   1000   2000   3000

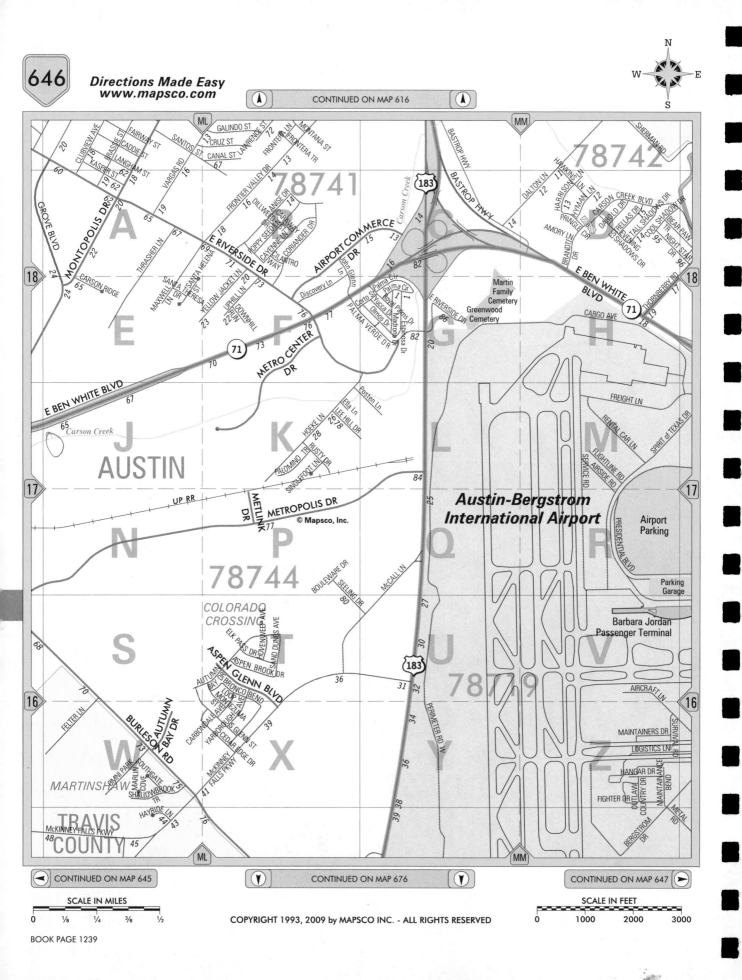

Directions Made Easy
www.mapsco.com

CONTINUED ON MAP 616

N
W   E
S

78741

78742

78744

AUSTIN

Carson Creek

Austin-Bergstrom International Airport

Airport Parking

Parking Garage

Barbara Jordan Passenger Terminal

78719

Martin Family Cemetery
Greenwood Cemetery

© Mapsco, Inc.

TRAVIS COUNTY

MARTINSHAW

COLORADO CROSSING

CONTINUED ON MAP 645
CONTINUED ON MAP 676
CONTINUED ON MAP 647

SCALE IN MILES
0   1/8   1/4   3/8   1/2

SCALE IN FEET
0   1000   2000   3000

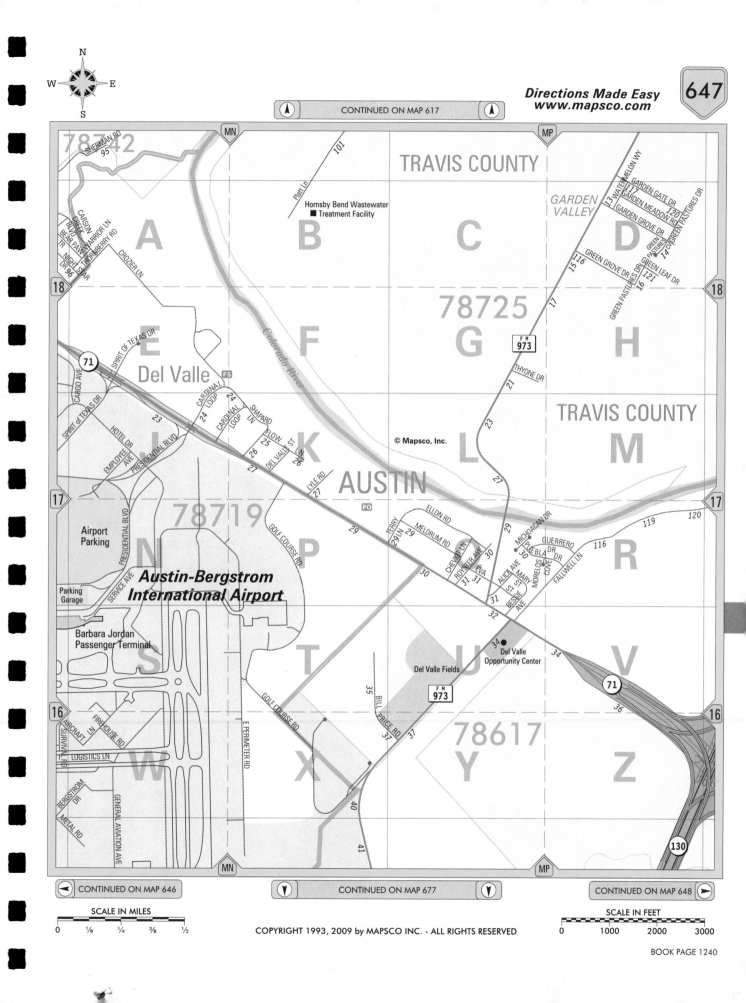

CONTINUED ON MAP 617

TRAVIS COUNTY

GARDEN VALLEY

Hornsby Bend Wastewater Treatment Facility

78725

78719

Del Valle

Austin-Bergstrom International Airport

Airport Parking

Parking Garage

Barbara Jordan Passenger Terminal

© Mapsco, Inc.

AUSTIN

TRAVIS COUNTY

Del Valle Opportunity Center

Del Valle Fields

78617

CONTINUED ON MAP 646

CONTINUED ON MAP 677

CONTINUED ON MAP 648

SCALE IN MILES

0   1/8   1/4   3/8   1/2

SCALE IN FEET

0   1000   2000   3000

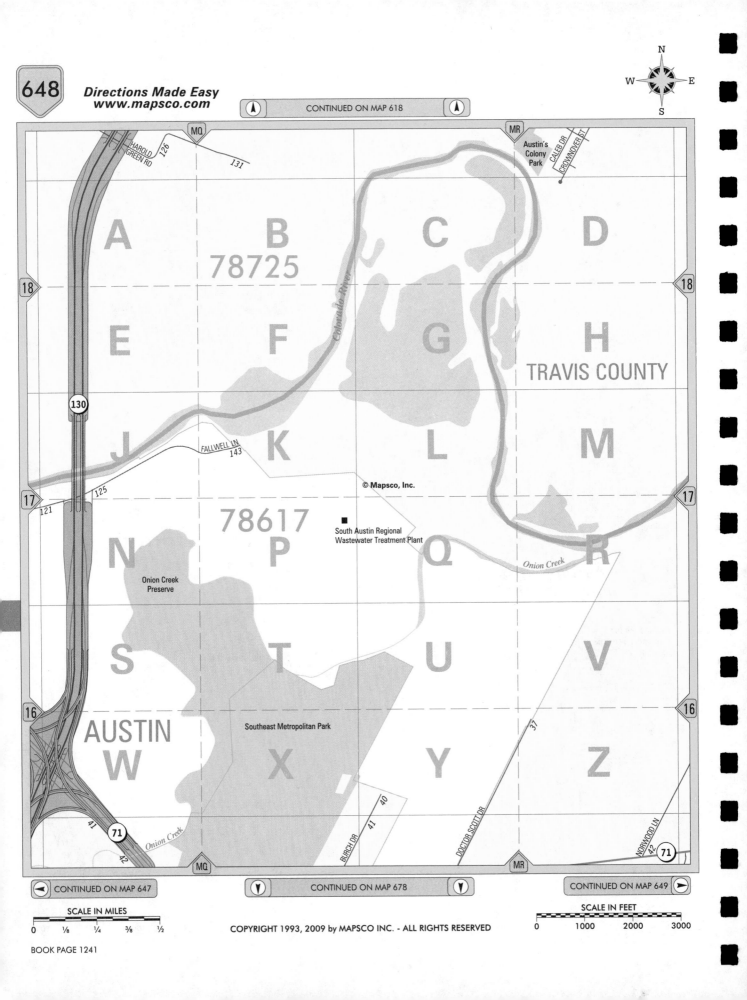

648

Directions Made Easy
www.mapsco.com

CONTINUED ON MAP 618

N
W E
S

MQ

HAROLD GREEN RD
126
131

MR

Austin's Colony Park

CALEB DR
CROWNOVER ST

A

B

78725

C

D

18

18

E

F

Colorado River

G

H

TRAVIS COUNTY

130

J

K

FALLWELL LN
143

L

M

© Mapsco, Inc.

17

125

121

78617

South Austin Regional
Wastewater Treatment Plant

Onion Creek

17

N

P

Q

R

Onion Creek
Preserve

S

T

U

V

16

16

AUSTIN

W

Southeast Metropolitan Park

X

Y

37

Z

BURCH DR
40
41

DOCTOR SCOTT DR

NORWOOD LN
42

71

41

71

Onion Creek

42

MQ

MR

CONTINUED ON MAP 647

CONTINUED ON MAP 678

CONTINUED ON MAP 649

SCALE IN MILES

0   1/8   1/4   3/8   1/2

SCALE IN FEET

0   1000   2000   3000

BOOK PAGE 1241

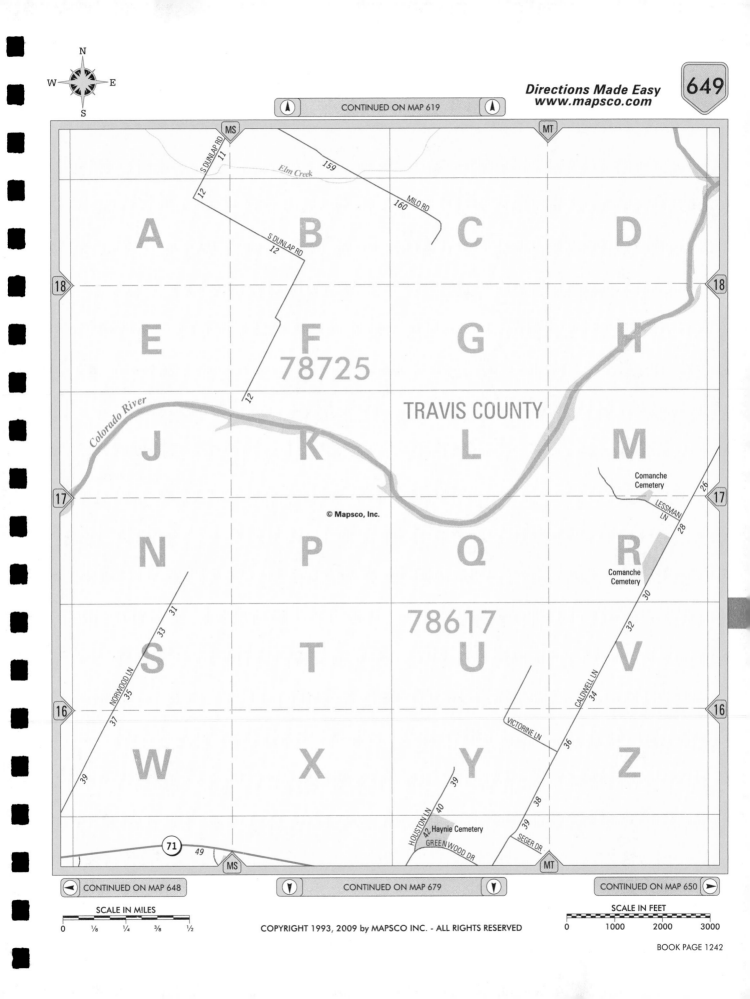

CONTINUED ON MAP 619

MS

S DUNLAP RD

11

12

Elm Creek

159

MILO RD

160

MT

A

B

S DUNLAP RD

12

C

D

18

18

E

F

78725

12

G

H

Colorado River

J

K

TRAVIS COUNTY

L

M

Comanche
Cemetery

26

LESSMAN LN

17

17

© Mapsco, Inc.

N

P

Q

R

Comanche
Cemetery

28

30

NORWOOD LN

31

33

32

78617

S

T

U

CALDWELL LN

V

34

35

16

16

37

VICTORINE LN

36

W

X

Y

Z

39

HOUSTON LN

40

38

42

Haynie Cemetery

39

71

49

GREENWOOD DR

SEGER DR

MS

MT

CONTINUED ON MAP 648

CONTINUED ON MAP 679

CONTINUED ON MAP 650

SCALE IN MILES

0   ⅛   ¼   ⅜   ½

SCALE IN FEET

0   1000   2000   3000

Directions Made Easy
www.mapsco.com

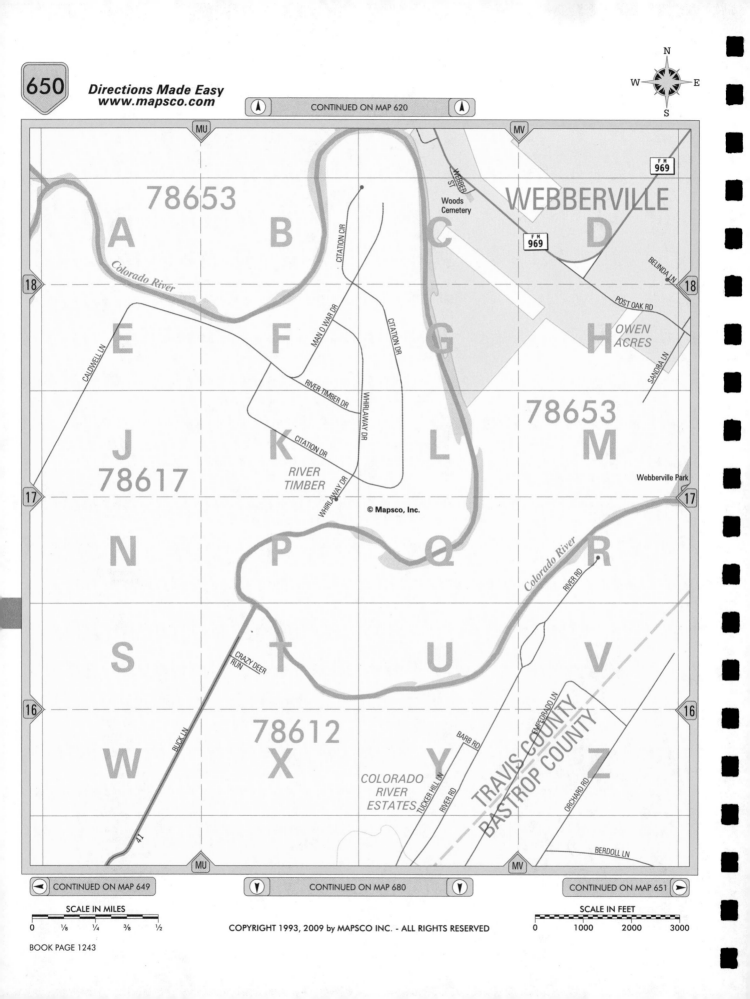

CONTINUED ON MAP 620

MU

MV

78653

A

B

CITATION CIR

Colorado River

WEBBERVILLE

WEBBER ST

Woods Cemetery

F M 969

F M 969

C

D

BELINDA LN

18

18

E

F

MAN O WAR DR

CITATION DR

G

H

POST OAK RD

OWEN ACRES

SANDRA LN

CALDWELL LN

RIVER TIMBER DR

WHIRLAWAY DR

78653

J

78617

K

CITATION DR

RIVER TIMBER

L

M

17

WHIRLAWAY DR

© Mapsco, Inc.

Webberville Park

17

N

P

Q

Colorado River

RIVER RD

R

S

T

CRAZY DEER RUN

U

V

16

16

BUCK LN

78612

X

COLORADO RIVER ESTATES

TUCKER HILL LN

BARB RD

RIVER RD

Y

EMPEDRADO LN

TRAVIS COUNTY
BASTROP COUNTY

ORCHARD RD

Z

W

41

BERDOLL LN

MU

MV

CONTINUED ON MAP 649

CONTINUED ON MAP 680

CONTINUED ON MAP 651

SCALE IN MILES

0   1/8   1/4   3/8   1/2

SCALE IN FEET

0   1000   2000   3000

COPYRIGHT 1993, 2009 by MAPSCO INC. - ALL RIGHTS RESERVED

BOOK PAGE 1243

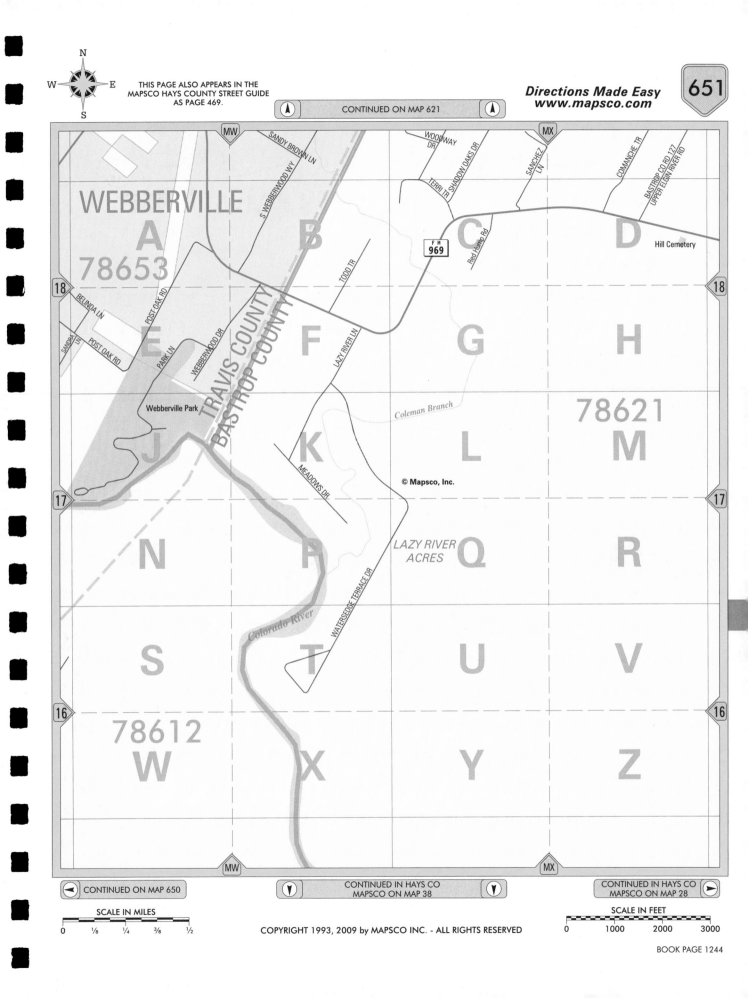

THIS PAGE ALSO APPEARS IN THE
MAPSCO HAYS COUNTY STREET GUIDE
AS PAGE 469.

Directions Made Easy
www.mapsco.com

CONTINUED ON MAP 621

MW

MX

WOODWAY DR

SANDY BROWN LN

S WEBBERWOOD WY

TERRI TR

SHADOW OAKS DR

SANCHEZ LN

COMANCHE TR

BASTROP CO RD 127
UPPER ELGIN RIVER RD

WEBBERVILLE

A
78653

B

FM 969

C

Red Hump Rd

D

Hill Cemetery

18

18

BELINDA LN

POST OAK RD

SANDRA LN

POST OAK RD

PARK LN

WEBBERWOOD DR

TRAVIS COUNTY
BASTROP COUNTY

TODD TR

LAZY RIVER LN

E

F

G

H

Webberville Park

Coleman Branch

78621

J

MEADOWS DR

K

L

© Mapsco, Inc.

M

17

17

Colorado River

N

P

WATERSEDGE TERRACE DR

*LAZY RIVER
ACRES*

Q

R

16

16

78612

S

T

U

V

W

X

Y

Z

MW

MX

CONTINUED ON MAP 650

CONTINUED IN HAYS CO
MAPSCO ON MAP 38

CONTINUED IN HAYS CO
MAPSCO ON MAP 28

SCALE IN MILES

0   1/8   1/4   3/8   1/2

SCALE IN FEET

0   1000   2000   3000

Directions Made Easy
www.mapsco.com

CONTINUED ON MAP 636

THIS PAGE ALSO APPEARS IN THE
MAPSCO HAYS COUNTY STREET GUIDE
AS PAGE 494.

N W E S

WQ

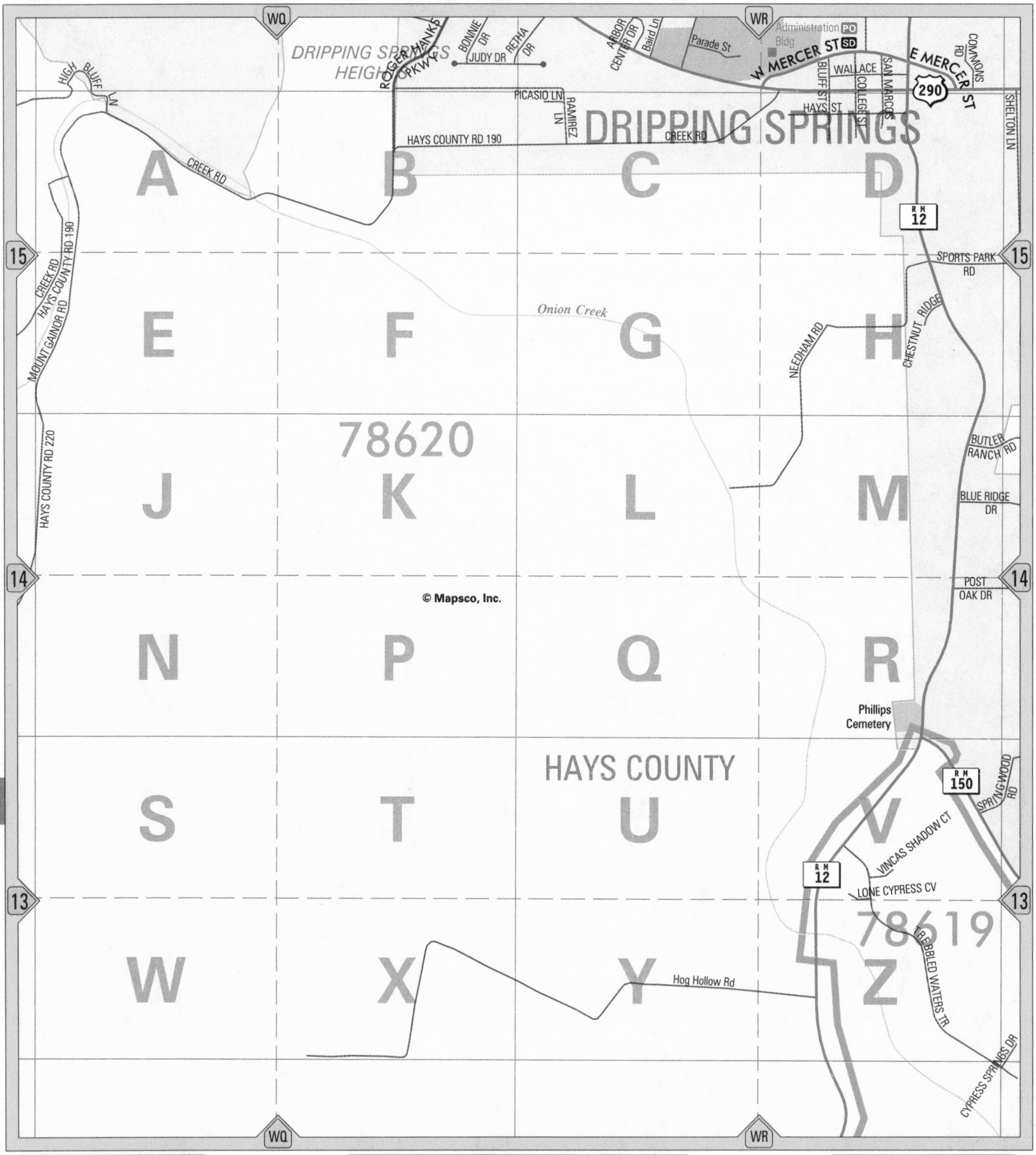

DRIPPING SPRINGS HEIGHTS

BONNIE DR
ROGER HANKS PKWY
JUDY DR
RETHA DR

ARBOR CENTER DR
BAIRD LN
Parade St

WR
Administration Bldg PO
W MERCER ST SD
E MERCER ST
WALLACE
COMMONS RD
BLUFF ST
COLLEGE ST
SAN MARCOS
290

PICASIO LN
RAMIREZ LN
HAYS ST
SHELTON LN

HAYS COUNTY RD 190
CREEK RD

DRIPPING SPRINGS

HIGH BLUFF LN
CREEK RD

A B C D

RM 12

15 SPORTS PARK RD 15

Onion Creek

E F G H

CREEK RD
HAYS COUNTY RD 190
MOUNT GAINOR RD

NEEDHAM RD
CHESTNUT RIDGE

BUTLER RANCH RD

78620

HAYS COUNTY RD 220

J K L M

BLUE RIDGE DR

14 POST OAK DR 14

© Mapsco, Inc.

N P Q R

Phillips Cemetery

HAYS COUNTY

RM 150

S T U V

SPRINGWOOD RD

VINCAS SHADOW CT

RM 12
LONE CYPRESS CV

13 13

78619

W X Y Z

Hog Hollow Rd

TREBBLED WATERS TR

CYPRESS SPRINGS DR

WQ WR

CONTINUED IN HAYS CO MAPSCO ON MAP 34 | CONTINUED IN HAYS CO MAPSCO ON MAP 34 | CONTINUED ON MAP 667

SCALE IN MILES
0 1/8 1/4 3/8 1/2

SCALE IN FEET
0 1000 2000 3000

COPYRIGHT 1993, 2009 by MAPSCO INC. - ALL RIGHTS RESERVED

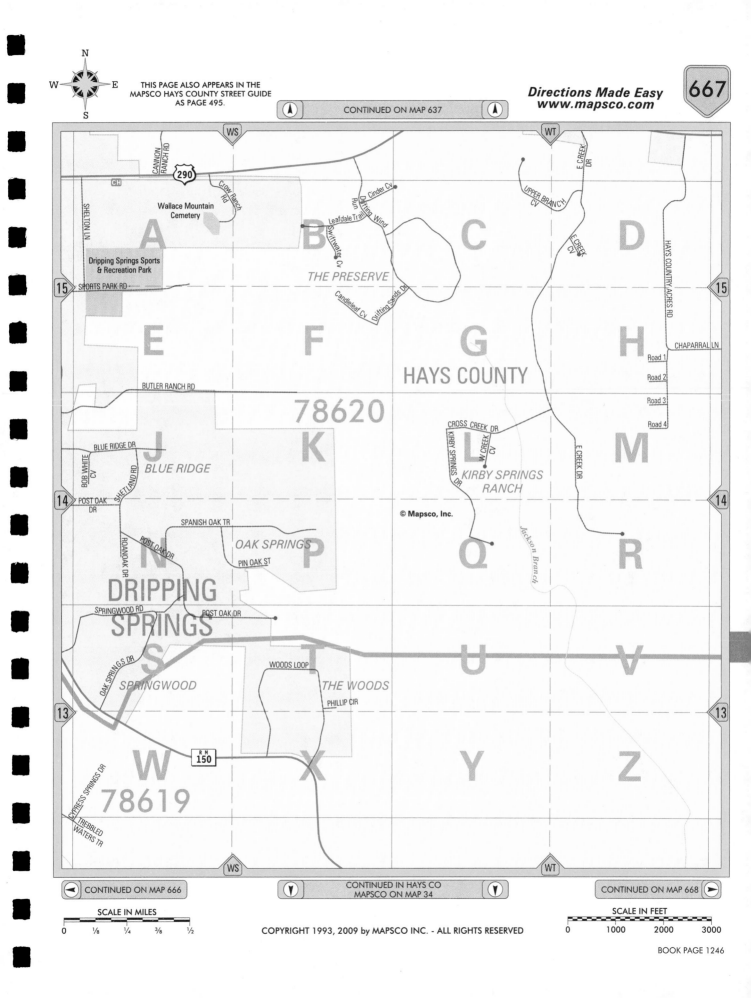

CONTINUED ON MAP 638

THIS PAGE ALSO APPEARS IN THE
MAPSCO HAYS COUNTY STREET GUIDE
AS PAGE 496.

N
W   E
S

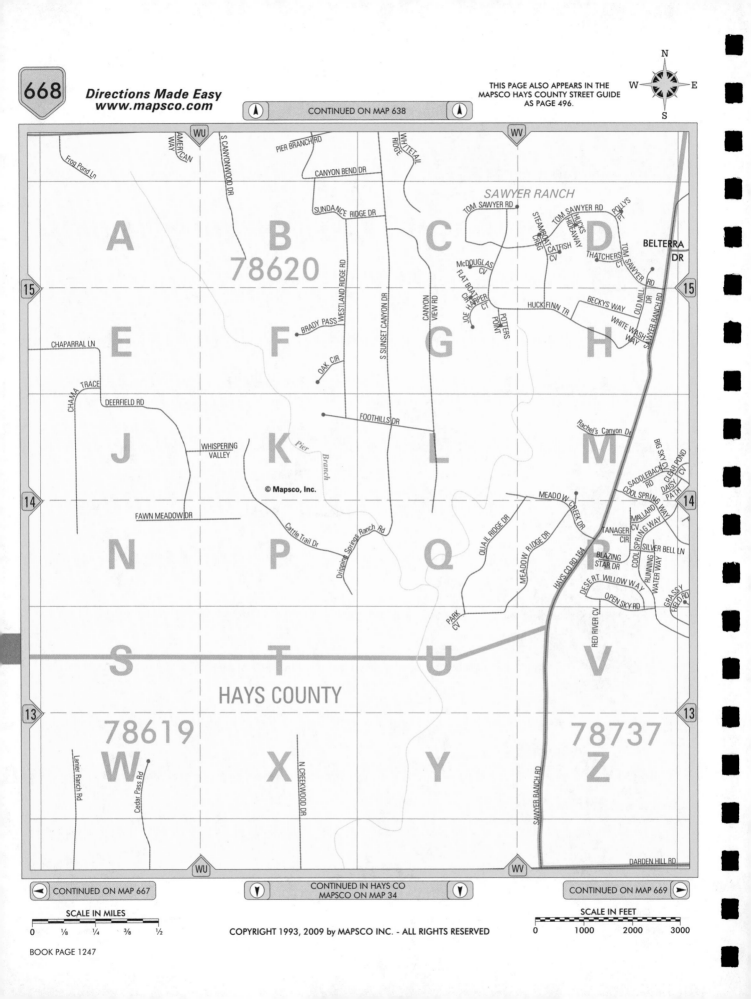

WU

WV

AMERICAN WAY

Frog Pond Ln

S CANYONWOOD DR

PIER BRANCH RD

CANYON BEND DR

WHITETAIL RIDGE

WV

SAWYER RANCH

SUNDANCE RIDGE DR

TOM SAWYER RD

TOM SAWYER RD

POLLYS PT

A

B
78620

C

STEAMBOAT CRSG

HUCKS HIDEAWAY

D

BELTERRA DR

CATFISH CV

THATCHERS CT

15

WESTLAND RIDGE RD

CANYON VIEW RD

McDOUGLAS CV

TOM SAWYER RD

15

BRADY PASS

S SUNSET CANYON DR

FLAT BOAT CIR

HARPER CT

OLD MILL DR

SAWYER RANCH RD

E

Chaparral Ln

F

G

JOE

HUCK FINN TR

BECKYS WAY

WHITE WASH WAY

H

OAK CIR

POTTERS POINT

CHAMA TRACE

DEERFIELD RD

FOOTHILLS DR

Rachel's Canyon Dr

J

WHISPERING VALLEY

K

Pier Branch

L

M

BIG SKY CV

CLEAR POND CV

© Mapsco, Inc.

SADDLEBACK RD

DAISY PATH

14

MEADOW CREEK DR

COOL SPRING WAY

14

FAWN MEADOW DR

MALLARD CV

SILVER BELL LN

N

P

Cattle Trail Dr

Dripping Springs Ranch Rd

Q

QUAIL RIDGE DR

MEADOW RIDGE DR

TANAGER CIR

R

BLAZING STAR DR

COOL SPRING WAY

RUNNING WATER WAY

GRASSY FIELD RD

HAYS CO RD 164

DESERT WILLOW WAY

OPEN SKY RD

PARK CV

RED RIVER CV

S

T

HAYS COUNTY

U

V

13

78619

W

Lanier Ranch Rd

Cedar Pass Rd

X

N CREEKWOOD DR

Y

78737

Z

SAWYER RANCH RD

WU

WV

DARDEN HILL RD

CONTINUED ON MAP 667

CONTINUED IN HAYS CO
MAPSCO ON MAP 34

CONTINUED ON MAP 669

SCALE IN MILES

0   ⅛   ¼   ⅜   ½

SCALE IN FEET

0   1000   2000   3000

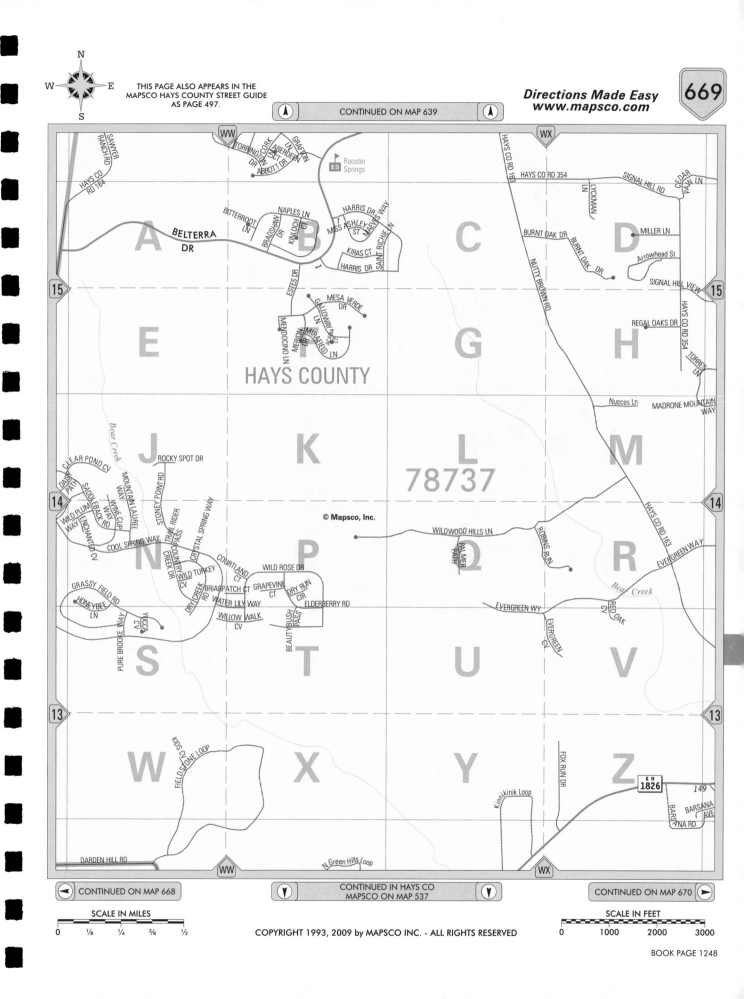

THIS PAGE ALSO APPEARS IN THE
MAPSCO HAYS COUNTY STREET GUIDE
AS PAGE 497.

Directions Made Easy
www.mapsco.com

CONTINUED ON MAP 639

WW WX

A BELTERRA DR

SAWYER RANCH RD

HAYS CO RD 164

BITTERROOT LN

NAPLES LN

BRADSHAW DR

KINLOCH

TORRINGTON DR

CORK CT

ABERDEEN CT

ABBOTT DR

GRAFTON LN

ES Rooster Springs

HARRIS DR S WAY

MISS ASHLEY ST

MAEVES WAY

SAINT RICHIE LN

KIRAS CT

HARRIS DR

HAYS CO RD 163

HAYS CO RD 354

LYCKMAN LN

SIGNAL HILL RD

CEDAR PAWL LN

BURNT OAK DR

BURNT OAK DR

MILLER LN

Arrowhead St

SIGNAL HILL VIEW

15 15

B C D

ESTES DR

MENDOCINO LN

MERION RD

GALLOWAY PASS LN

MIRAFIELD LN

MESA VERDE DR

NUTTY BROWN RD

REGAL OAKS DR

HAYS CO RD 354

TORRES LN

E F G H

HAYS COUNTY

Nueces Ln

MADRONE MOUNTAIN WAY

Bear Creek

CLEAR POND CV

DAISY PATH

MOUNTAIN LAUREL WAY

WINE CUP WAY

SADDLEBACK RD

WILD PLUM WAY

ENCHANTED CV

COOL SPRING WAY

ROCKY SPOT DR

STONEY POINT RD

TRAIL RIDER

CRYSTAL SPRING WAY

COMPASS

COUNTRY CREEK DR

78737

© Mapsco, Inc.

WILDWOOD HILLS LN

ROBINS RUN

PALMER PATH

HAYS CO RD 163

EVERGREEN WAY

J K L M

14 14

GRASSY FIELD RD

HONEYBEE LN

PURE BROOKE WAY

YUCCA CV

WILD TURKEY CV

DRY CREEK RD

COURTLAND

BRIARPATCH CT

WATER LILY WAY

WILLOW WALK CV

WILD ROSE DR

GRAPEVINE CT

DRY RUN CIR

ELDERBERRY RD

BEAUTYBUSH PASS

EVERGREEN WY

EVERGREEN CV

Bear Creek

RED OAK CV

N P Q R

S T U V

13 13

FIELDSTONE LOOP

FOX RUN DR

Kinnikinik Loop

RM 1826

149

BARSANA AVE

BARSANA RD

W X Y Z

DARDEN HILL RD

N Green Hills Loop

WW WX

CONTINUED ON MAP 668

CONTINUED IN HAYS CO
MAPSCO ON MAP 537

CONTINUED ON MAP 670

SCALE IN MILES

0   ⅛   ¼   ⅜   ½

SCALE IN FEET

0   1000   2000   3000

COPYRIGHT 1993, 2009 by MAPSCO INC. - ALL RIGHTS RESERVED

BOOK PAGE 1248

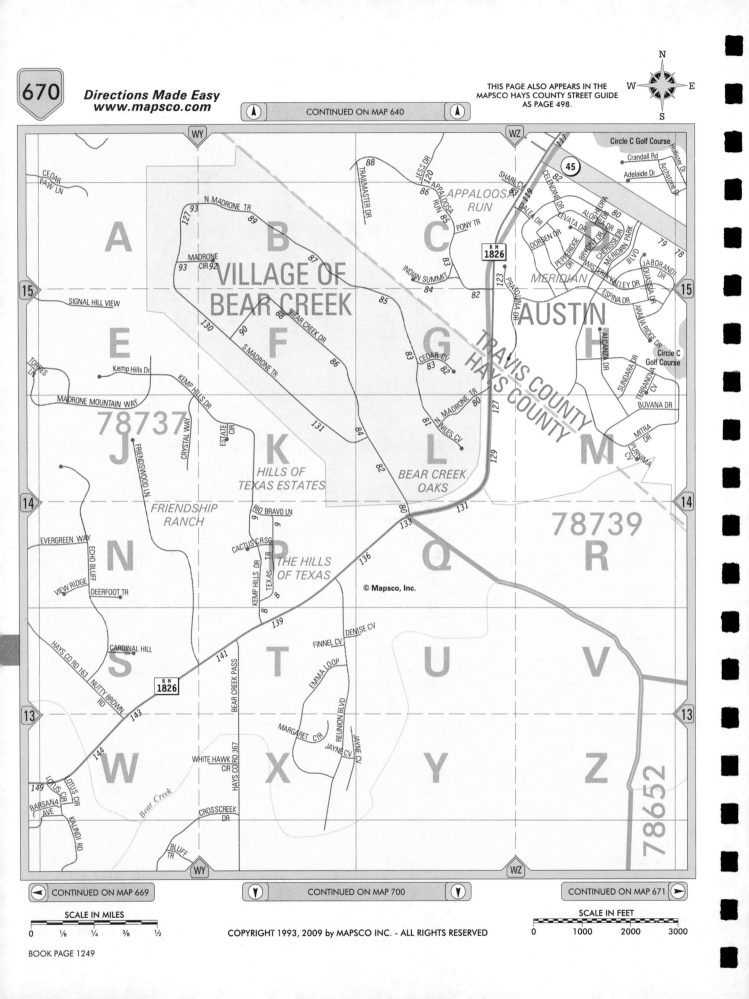

N W E S

THIS PAGE ALSO APPEARS IN THE
MAPSCO HAYS COUNTY STREET GUIDE
AS PAGE 499.

Directions Made Easy
www.mapsco.com

671

CONTINUED ON MAP 641

MA

MB

ES

Circle C
Golf Course

THE HIELSCHER

SPRUCE CANYON DR

Achstone Dr
Felsgar Dr
Hollister Dr
Bear Dr
Harlow Dr
Canfield Dr
Doswell Cv
Doswell Dr
Cusseta Ln
Cusseta Ln
Doswell Ln
Fairnoy Ln
Sierra Ridge Ct
Maelin Dr
Maelin Cv
Blissfield Dr
Blissfield Dr
Wallbridge Ln
Nisser Ln
Gouldville Ct
Freesia Ct
Needham Ln
Ames Ct
Ames Ln
Inval Pole
105
59
La Crosse Ave
Van Ln
Ballenton Ln
Ballenton Ln
Banks Ln
Austral Loop
Austral Loop
Stelley Cv
Mavina Ct
54
53

Magenta Ln
Lapin Way
Viridian Way
Cusseta Ln
Larue Belle
Larue Belle Cv
Tanaqua Ln
Naples Ln
Napils Ct
Toolwrich Way
Scenic Hill Dr
Orchard Aden Ln
Back Bay Ln
South Bay Ln
Halsey Ct
Wareham Ln
Wareham
Ariock Ln
Ariock Cv
Redgate Ct
Grassmere Ct
Grenmere Ct
Redgate
Odharbor Ln
Londashire Ct
Ginta
Pinkney Ct
107
108
107
Roxburn
Redmond Rd
Redmond Rd
103
Aylford Ct
Galsworthy Ct
Trelawney Ln
Galsworthy Ln
Lovridge Ln
Palgrave Ln
Beachmont Ct
Beachmont Cv
Beachmont Ln
Dahlgreen Ln
Eclipse Ct
Kiker

Magenta Ln
Viridian Ln
Coalwood Ln
Coalhill Cv
Bastian Ln
Quincy Ln
Oaks Dr
Lafitte Ln
Alberta Dr
Alberta Ln
Basminti Ln
Georgian Ln
Prussian Cv
Antigo Ln
Estana Ln
Escarpment Blvd
Escarpment Blvd
Readvill Ln
Skahan Ln
Utica Cv
Utica Ln
Savin Hill
Savin Hill
Readvill
Readvill Ln
Rickerhill Ln
Rickerhill Ct
Medfeld Ct
Medfeld
Beacham Ct
Savannah Ln
Easingwold
Tinita Ct
Anselm Ln
Gorham Glen
Gorham Ln
Bexley Ln
Bexley Ct
Glen Ct
62 Ln
59
110
108
59
Pebble Gardens Ct
Pebble Gardens
Pompey Ct
Mabna Ct
Morired Ct
Morired
Ohmfeld Ct
Savin Hill
Back Bay Ct
Back Bay Ct

78
75
15
45
70
66
65
65
64
65
61
63
108
105

Circle C Golf Course
Mitra Dr
Buvana Dr
Helenia Dr

LOOP 1
S MOPAC EXPWY
110

AUSTIN
CIRCLE C RANCH

A B C D
E F G H
J K L M
N P Q R
S T U V
W X Y Z

78739
© Mapsco, Inc.

15
14
13

15
14
13

60
55
117
53

45

TRAVIS COUNTY
HAYS COUNTY

Spillar Ranch Rd
Bear Creek

78652

MA

MB

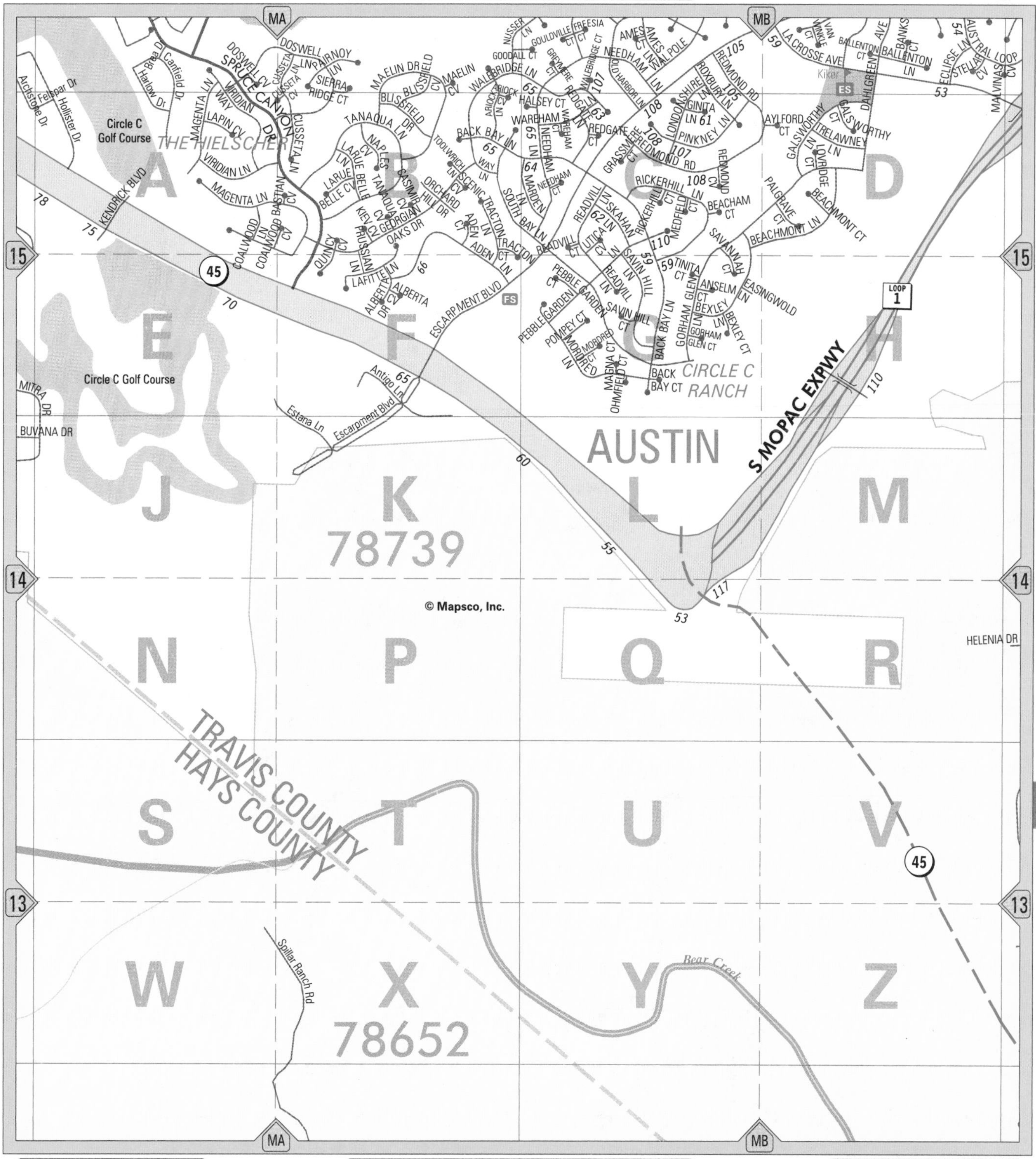

CONTINUED ON MAP 670

CONTINUED ON MAP 701

CONTINUED ON MAP 672

SCALE IN MILES
0   1/8   1/4   3/8   1/2

SCALE IN FEET
0   1000   2000   3000

BOOK PAGE 1250

Directions Made Easy
www.mapsco.com

CONTINUED ON MAP 642

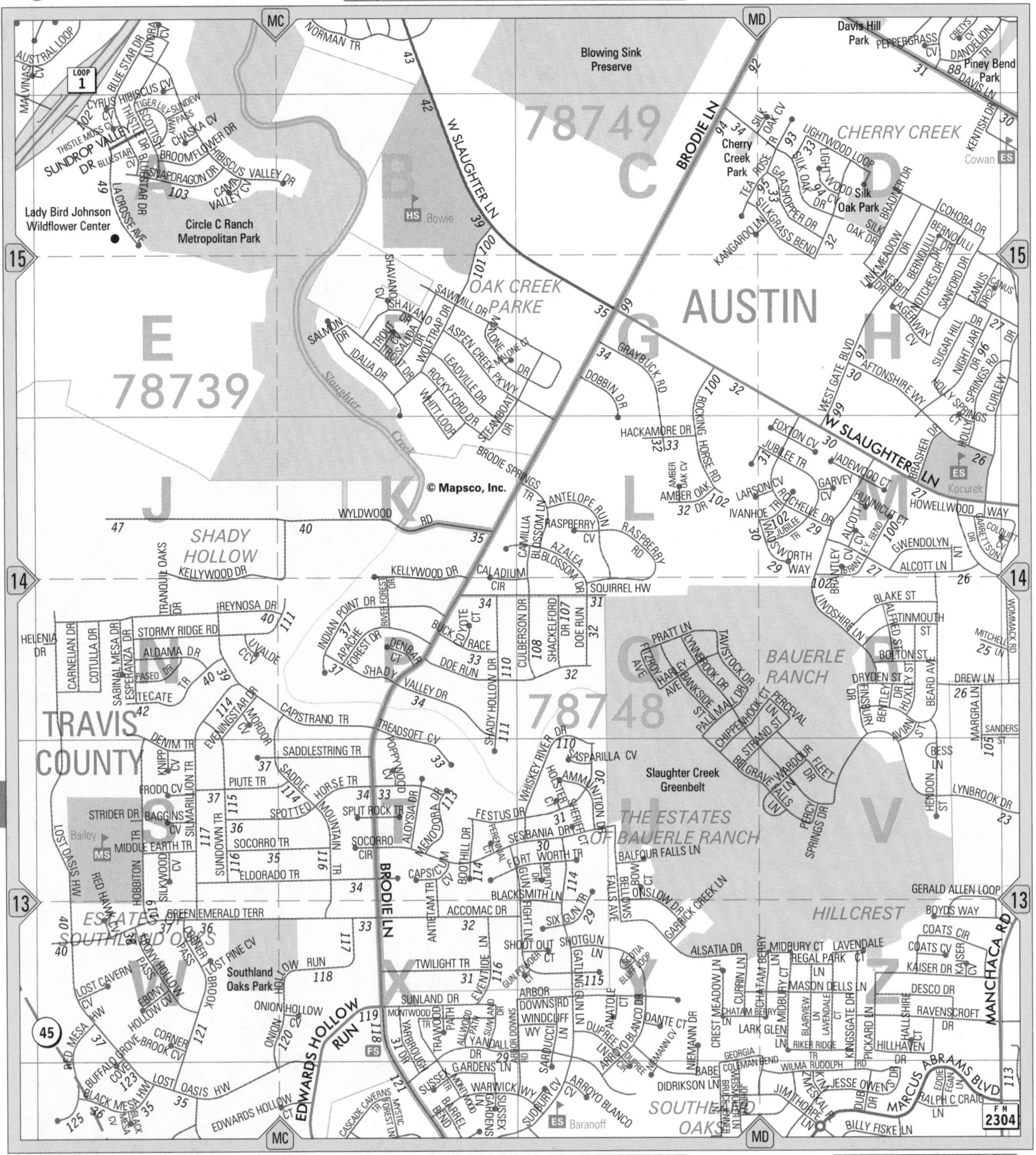

N W E S

78749

AUSTIN

CHERRY CREEK

Davis Hill Park

Blowing Sink Preserve

Cherry Creek Park

Silk Oak Park

BRODIE LN

W SLAUGHTER LN

Piney Bend Park

Lady Bird Johnson Wildflower Center

Circle C Ranch Metropolitan Park

LOOP 1

Sundrop Valley

Bowie HS

OAK CREEK PARKE

78739

E

© Mapsco, Inc.

SHADY HOLLOW

W SLAUGHTER LN

Kocurek ES

Cowan ES

BAUERLE RANCH

78748

THE ESTATES OF BAUERLE RANCH

Slaughter Creek Greenbelt

TRAVIS COUNTY

Bailey MS

HILLCREST

ESTATES OF SOUTHLAND OAKS

Southland Oaks Park

45

SOUTHLAND OAKS

Baranoff ES

MANCHACA RD

MARCUS ABRAMS BLVD

FM 2304

EDWARDS HOLLOW RUN

CONTINUED ON MAP 671

CONTINUED ON MAP 702

CONTINUED ON MAP 673

SCALE IN MILES
0   1/8   1/4   3/8   1/2

SCALE IN FEET
0   1000   2000   3000

COPYRIGHT 1993, 2009 by MAPSCO INC. - ALL RIGHTS RESERVED

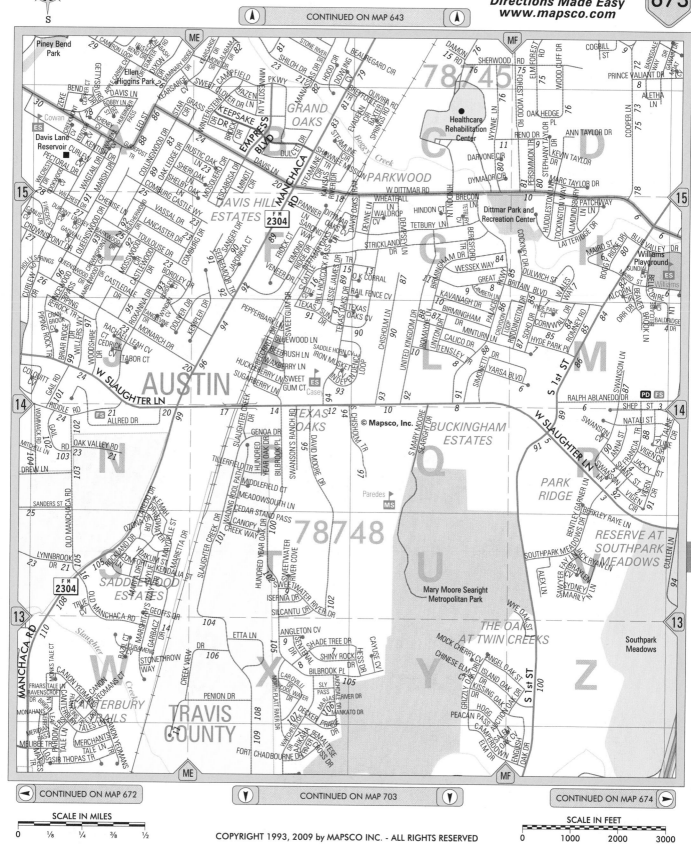

CONTINUED ON MAP 643

CONTINUED ON MAP 672

CONTINUED ON MAP 703

CONTINUED ON MAP 674

SCALE IN MILES

0   ⅛   ¼   ⅜   ½

SCALE IN FEET

0   1000   2000   3000

BOOK PAGE 1252

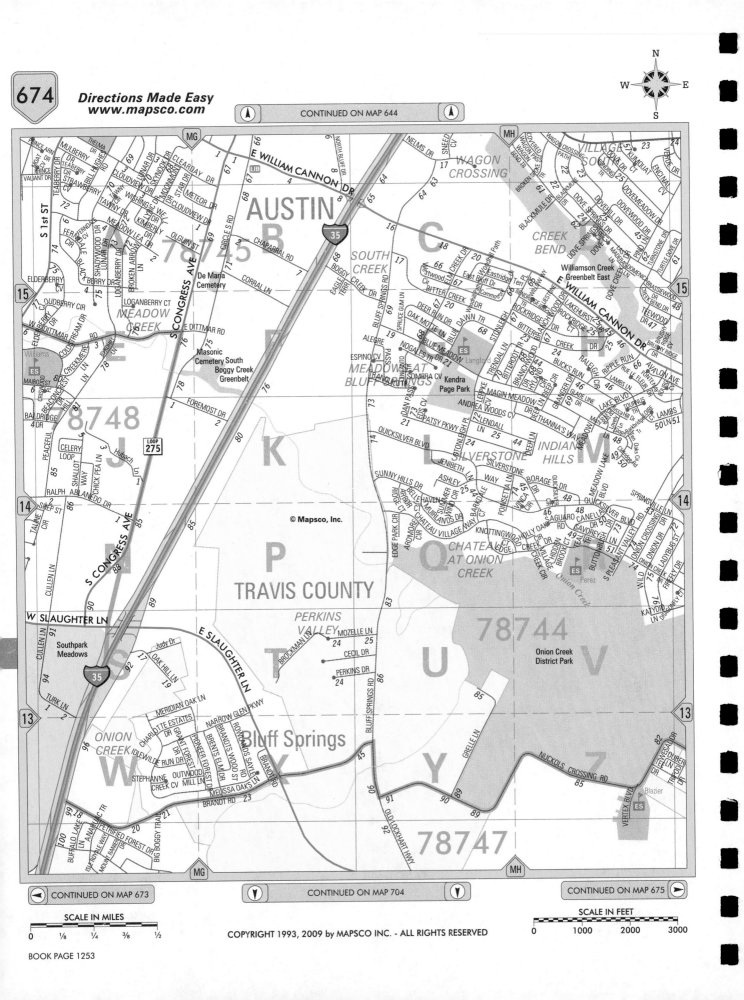

674

Directions Made Easy
www.mapsco.com

CONTINUED ON MAP 644

AUSTIN

TRAVIS COUNTY

© Mapsco, Inc.

78748

78745

78744

78747

CONTINUED ON MAP 673

CONTINUED ON MAP 704

CONTINUED ON MAP 675

SCALE IN MILES

0   1/8   1/4   3/8   1/2

SCALE IN FEET

0   1000   2000   3000

BOOK PAGE 1253

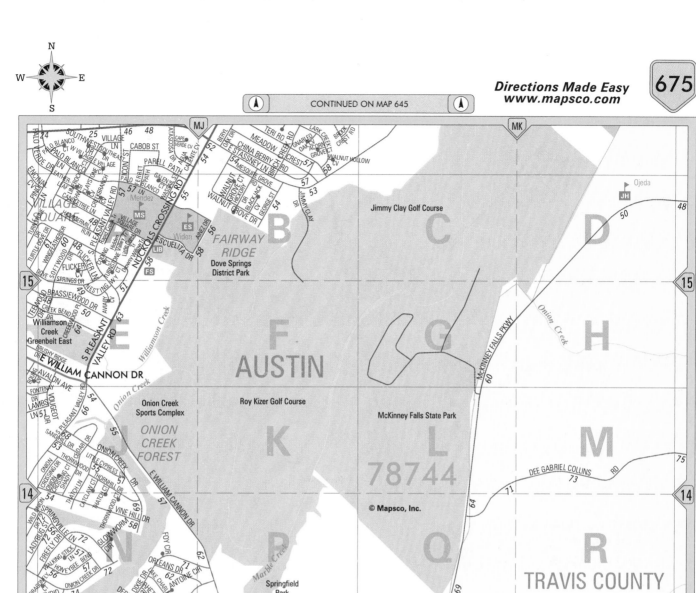

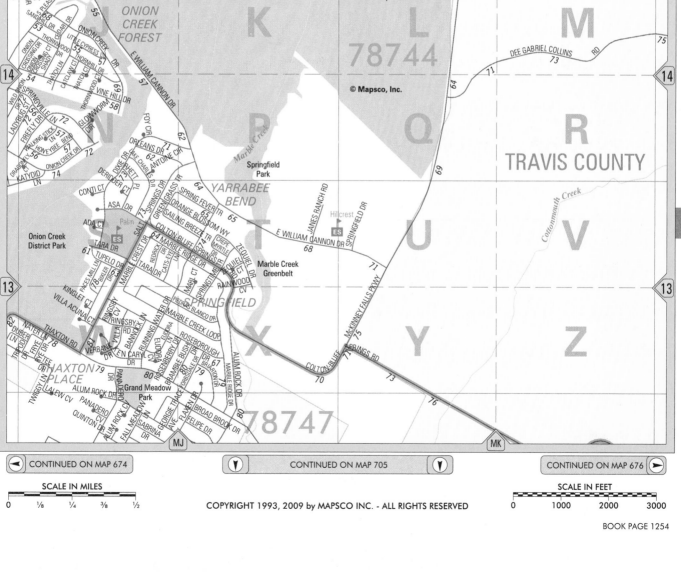

CONTINUED ON MAP 645

CONTINUED ON MAP 674

CONTINUED ON MAP 705

CONTINUED ON MAP 676

SCALE IN MILES

0   ⅛   ¼   ⅜   ½

SCALE IN FEET

0   1000   2000   3000

BOOK PAGE 1254

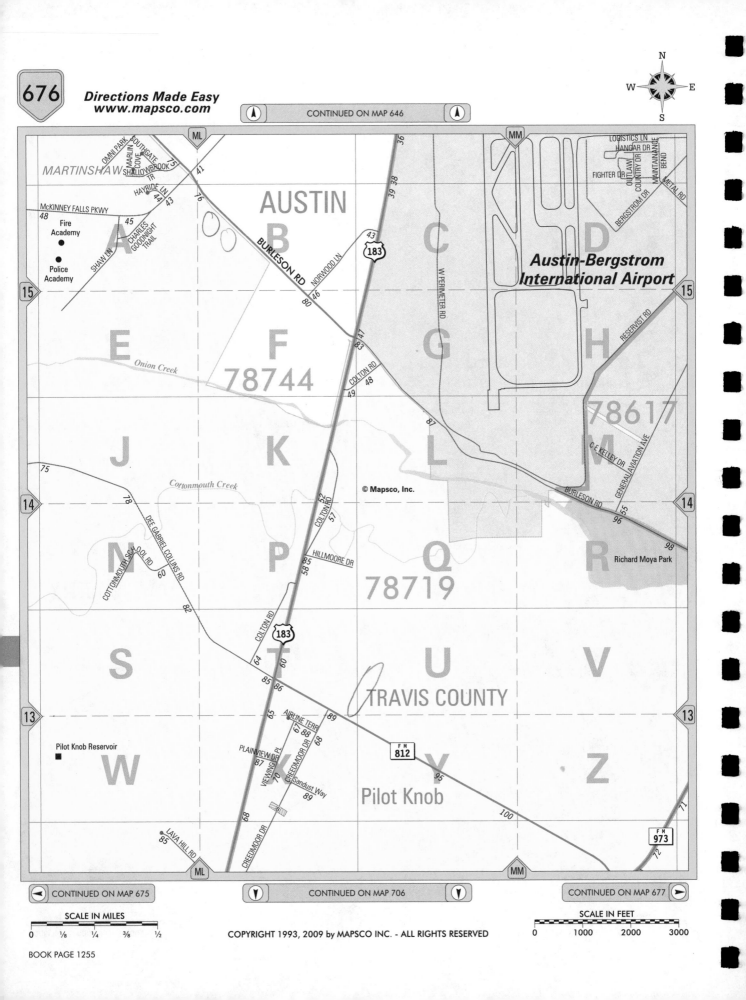

N
W E
S

CONTINUED ON MAP 646

ML
MM

OMNI PARK
SOUTHGATE
MARLIN
SHALLOWBROOK
COVE
TR
75
41
76

MARTINSHAW

HAYRIDE LN
44 43
43

AUSTIN

LOGISTICS LN
HANGAR DR

FIGHTER DR
OUTLAW
COUNTRY DR
MAINTAINANCE
BEND
BERGSTROM DR
METAL RD

McKINNEY FALLS PKWY
48
45

Fire
Academy

CHARLES GOODNIGHT TRAIL

SHAW LN

Police
Academy

A

45

B

BURLESON RD

NORWOOD LN

80 46

C

W PERIMETER RD

D

**Austin-Bergstrom
International Airport**

43
183

15
15

E

Onion Creek

F
78744

83
41

COLTON RD
48
49

G

H

RESERVIST RD

87

78617

75

Cottonmouth Creek

J

78

K

52
COLTON RD
57

L

© Mapsco, Inc.

M

C.E. KELLEY DR
GENERAL AVIATION AVE

14
14

DEE GABRIEL COLLINS RD

COTTONMOUTH SCHOOL RD

M
60

P
HILLMOORE DR
85
58

Q
78719

BURLESON RD
55
96

R
Richard Moya Park

82

98

13
13

COLTON RD
64 60
85 86

183

S

T

U

TRAVIS COUNTY

V

AIRLINE TERR
65
67 88
68

PLAINVIEW DR
87

VIEWING PL
70

CREEDMOOR DR
89
68

Sandust Way
89

FM
812

95

Y

100

Z

71

FM
973

W

Pilot Knob Reservoir

Pilot Knob

72

LAVA HILL RD
85

CREEDMOOR DR
68

ML

MM

CONTINUED ON MAP 675   CONTINUED ON MAP 706   CONTINUED ON MAP 677

SCALE IN MILES

0   1/8   1/4   3/8   1/2

SCALE IN FEET

0   1000   2000   3000

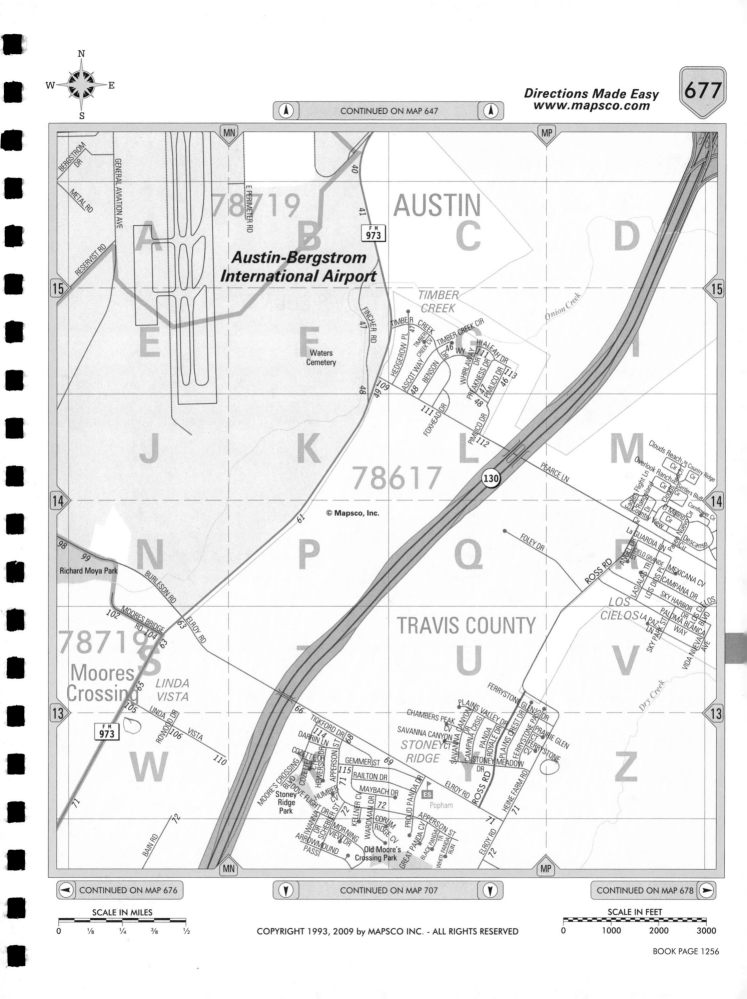

N
W · E
S

CONTINUED ON MAP 647

MN

MP

BERGSTROM DR

METAL RD

GENERAL AVIATION AVE

RESERVIST RD

15

78719

A

B

40

41

FM 973

AUSTIN

C

D

15

Austin-Bergstrom International Airport

E PERIMETER RD

FINCHER RD

47

TIMBER CREEK

Onion Creek

E

F

Waters Cemetery

48

109

TIMBER CREEK PL

HEDGEROW PL

ASCOT WAY

TIMBER CREEK CV

BENSON

46

WHIRLAWAY DR

HIALEAH DR

PREAKNESS DR

PIMLICO DR

111

113

46

48

FOXHEAD DR

111

PIMLICO DR

112

I

14

J

K

78617

© Mapsco, Inc.

130

PEARCE LN

M

Clouds Reach Cir

Country Ridge Cir

Overlook Ranch Ln

Settlers Bluff

Eagles Flight Ln

Cobors Cir

El Molino Cir

Cornflower Cir

14

61

N

P

Q

FOLEY DR

La Guardia Ln

ANGELITA CV

CIELO GRANDE

Paseo Nuevo

Descanso

R

MEXICANA CV

CAMPANA DR

Richard Moya Park

98

99

BURLESON RD

MOORES BRIDGE

102

RD 104

63

ELROY RD

LASALA TRL

LOS DIAS PL

SKY HARBOR DR

LOS CIELOS

PALOMA BLANCA

La Paz St

VIDA NUEVA

ROSS RD

TRAVIS COUNTY

78719

S

Moores Crossing

13

65

105

63

LINDA VISTA

FM 973

LINDA VISTA DR

ROWOOD DR

106

110

T

U

FERRYSTONE GLEN

PLAINS VALLEY DR

STONEY MEADOW

FERRYSTONE

SKY PARK ST

PALOMA BLANCA WAY

AVE

V

Dry Creek

13

71

72

66

W

TICKFORD DR

DARRIN LN

68

114

COZETTE DR

MOORE'S CROSSING BLVD

HUMBER ST

HEMERS DR

APPERSON ST

GEMMER ST

RAILTON DR

115

71

MAYBACH DR

CORUM RIDGE CV

KELLNER CV

WARDMAN DR

SCHEBER DR

MORNING VIEW

IAWANNA

ARROWMOUND PASS

72

Old Moore's Crossing Park

Stoney Ridge Park

CHAMBERS PEAK CV

SAVANNA CANYON CV

CAMPINA CRSG

SAVANNA CANYON DR

PANDA ROYALE DR

PLAINS CREST DR

69

72

PROUD PANDA DR

GREAT PANDA CV

BLACK PANDA TRL

WHITE PANDA RUN

ES

Popham

APPERSON ST

STONEY RIDGE

PRAIRIE GLEN

FERRYSTONE CT

FERRYSTONE CV

Y

ELROY RD

ROSS RD

71

HEINE FARM RD

ELROY RD

71

72

Z

CONTINUED ON MAP 676

MN

CONTINUED ON MAP 707

MP

CONTINUED ON MAP 678

SCALE IN MILES

0   ⅛   ¼   ⅜   ½

SCALE IN FEET

0   1000   2000   3000

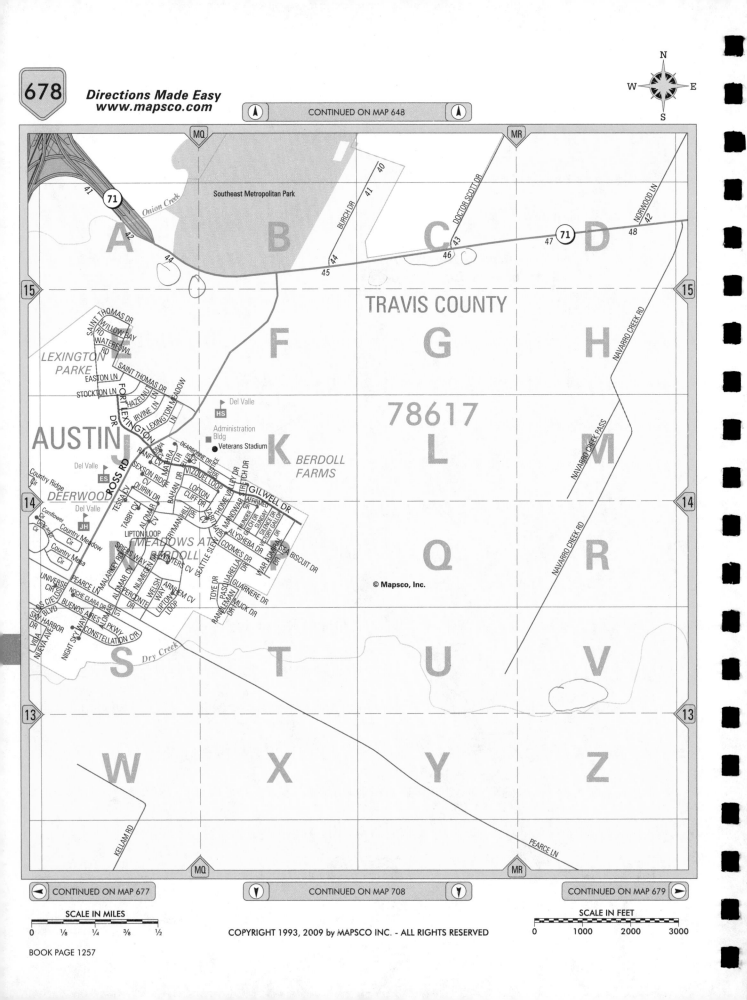

678

Directions Made Easy
www.mapsco.com

CONTINUED ON MAP 648

N
W ✦ E
S

MQ   MR

71

40

41

41   BURCH DR   DOCTOR SCOTT DR   NORWOOD LN

42   42

44   43   47 71   48

45   44   46

15   15

TRAVIS COUNTY

SAINT THOMAS DR
WILLOW BAY
RD
WATERFOWL
RD   F   G   H

*LEXINGTON
PARKE*   SAINT THOMAS DR

EASTON LN

STOCKTON LN   HAZELNUT LN
                    IRVINE LN
                    LEXINGTON MEADOW
                    LN

FORT LEXINGTON DR

Del Valle
HS

78617

Administration
Bldg
Veterans Stadium

AUSTIN   J   RANFT CV   K   *BERDOLL
                    MATHA   FARMS*   L
Del Valle   SEXTON RIDGE   DEARBONNIE DR
ES   QUIRIN DR   VIZQUEL LOOP
Country Ridge   BAHAN DR   THORNE VALLEY DR
Cir   TESSA CV   LOFTON   GILWELL DR
14   ALOMAR   CLIFF DR   AFFIRMED   M   14
DEERWOOD   CV   BERRYMANHILL MANOWAR STRETCH DR
Del Valle   TABBY CV   LIPTON LOOP HUNTER
Cornflower   ALOMAR CV   SILENCE DR
Cir   JH   SPIERS WAY   SEATTLE SLEW ALYSHEBA DR SEA BISCUIT DR
Dea-ster Country Meadow BEYWATERS CV   WAR ADMIRAL DR
Cir   Cir   NIJMEGEN   COOMES DR
Country Mesa   WELSH   TOYE DR   GUARNERE DR
Cir   PERDONTE DR   PASQUARELLA DR
UNIVERSE   PEARCE LN   RANDLEMAN DR MUCK DR
CIR   NOCHE CLARA DR LIPTON
DOS CIELOS BLVD   BUENOS AIRES   LOOP   ARNHEM CV
SAN HARBOR   SOMAR   Q   R
DR   NIGHT SKY WAY
VIDA   CONSTELLATION CIR
NUEVA AVE   A PKWY
                    Dry Creek
S   T   U   V

13   13

W   X   Y   Z

MQ   MR

© Mapsco, Inc.

CONTINUED ON MAP 677   CONTINUED ON MAP 708   CONTINUED ON MAP 679

SCALE IN MILES   SCALE IN FEET
0   1/8   1/4   3/8   1/2   0   1000   2000   3000

COPYRIGHT 1993, 2009 by MAPSCO INC. - ALL RIGHTS RESERVED

BOOK PAGE 1257

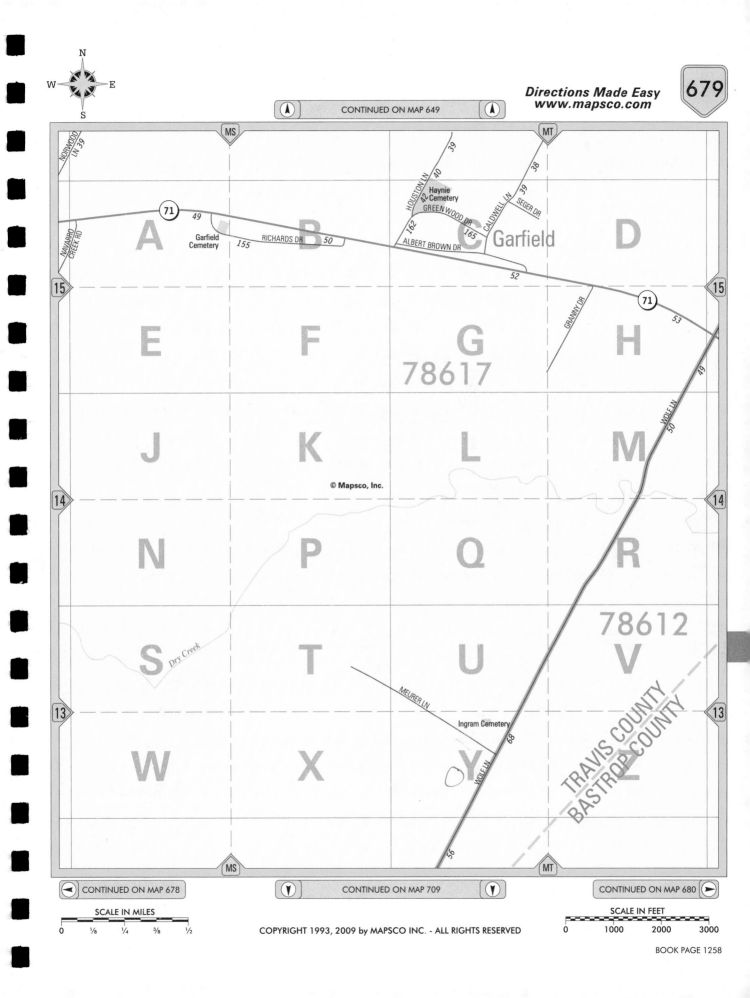

CONTINUED ON MAP 649

N
W · E
S

MS

NORWOOD LN 39

71
49

NAVARRO CREEK RD

A

Garfield
Cemetery

RICHARDS DR
155 50

B

162

HOUSTON LN

Haynie
42 Cemetery
40

GREENWOOD DR
165

ALBERT BROWN DR

39

CALDWELL LN

C

Garfield

MT

39
38

SEGER DR

D

15

52

GRANNY DR

71
53

15

E

F

G

78617

H

WOLF LN
49
50

J

K

L

© Mapsco, Inc.

M

14

14

N

P

Q

R

78612

S

Dry Creek

T

MEURER LN

Ingram Cemetery

U

V

TRAVIS COUNTY
BASTROP COUNTY

13

W

X

68

WOLF LN

Y

56

MT

Z

13

MS

CONTINUED ON MAP 678

CONTINUED ON MAP 709

CONTINUED ON MAP 680

SCALE IN MILES
0   1/8   1/4   3/8   1/2

SCALE IN FEET
0   1000   2000   3000

BOOK PAGE 1258

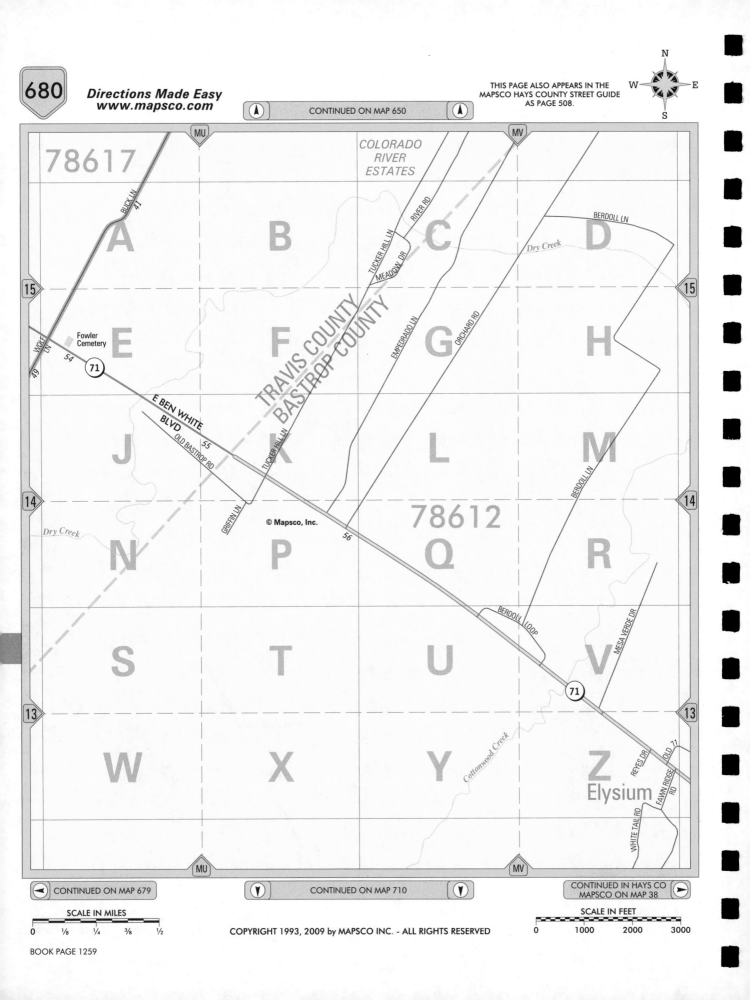

680

Directions Made Easy
www.mapsco.com

N
W • E
S

CONTINUED ON MAP 650

78617

COLORADO
RIVER
ESTATES

BUCK LN
41

A

B

BERDOLL LN

TUCKER HILL LN

RIVER RD

C

Dry Creek

D

MEADOW DR

15

15

Fowler
Cemetery

WOLF LN

49   54

E

F

EMPEDRADO LN

ORCHARD RD

G

H

71

E BEN WHITE
BLVD

OLD BASTROP RD

55

TUCKER HILL LN

TRAVIS COUNTY
BASTROP COUNTY

J

K

L

BERDOLL LN

M

14

GRIFFIN LN

© Mapsco, Inc.

56

78612

14

Dry Creek

N

P

Q

R

BERDOLL LOOP

MESA VERDE DR

S

T

U

71

V

13

13

W

X

Cottonwood Creek

Y

Z

Elysium

REYES DR

OLD 71

FAWN RIDGE RD

WHITE TAIL RD

CONTINUED ON MAP 679

CONTINUED ON MAP 710

CONTINUED IN HAYS CO
MAPSCO ON MAP 38

SCALE IN MILES

0   1/8   1/4   3/8   1/2

SCALE IN FEET

0   1000   2000   3000

N

W E

S

THIS PAGE ALSO APPEARS IN THE
MAPSCO HAYS COUNTY STREET GUIDE
AS PAGE 538.

Directions Made Easy
www.mapsco.com

700

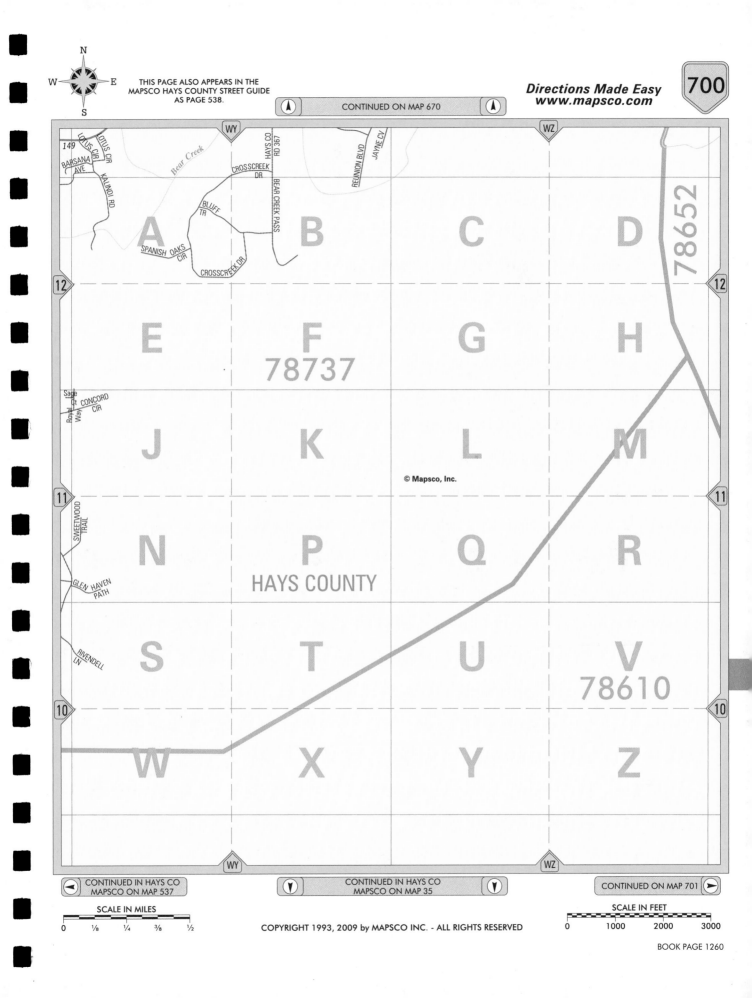

CONTINUED ON MAP 670

149
LOTUS CIR
LOTUS CIR
BARSANA AVE
KALINDI RD

Bear Creek

WY

CROSSCREEK DR

HAYS CO RD 367

BEAR CREEK PASS

REUNION BLVD

JAYNE CV

WZ

78652

BLUFF TR

SPANISH OAKS CIR

CROSSCREEK DR

A B C D

12 12

E F G H

78737

Sage Ct
Royal Way
CONCORD CIR

J K L M

© Mapsco, Inc.

11 11

SWEETWOOD TRAIL

N P Q R

HAYS COUNTY

GLEN HAVEN PATH

RIVENDELL LN

S T U V

78610

10 10

W X Y Z

WY WZ

CONTINUED IN HAYS CO
MAPSCO ON MAP 537

CONTINUED IN HAYS CO
MAPSCO ON MAP 35

CONTINUED ON MAP 701

SCALE IN MILES

0   1/8   1/4   3/8   1/2

SCALE IN FEET

0   1000   2000   3000

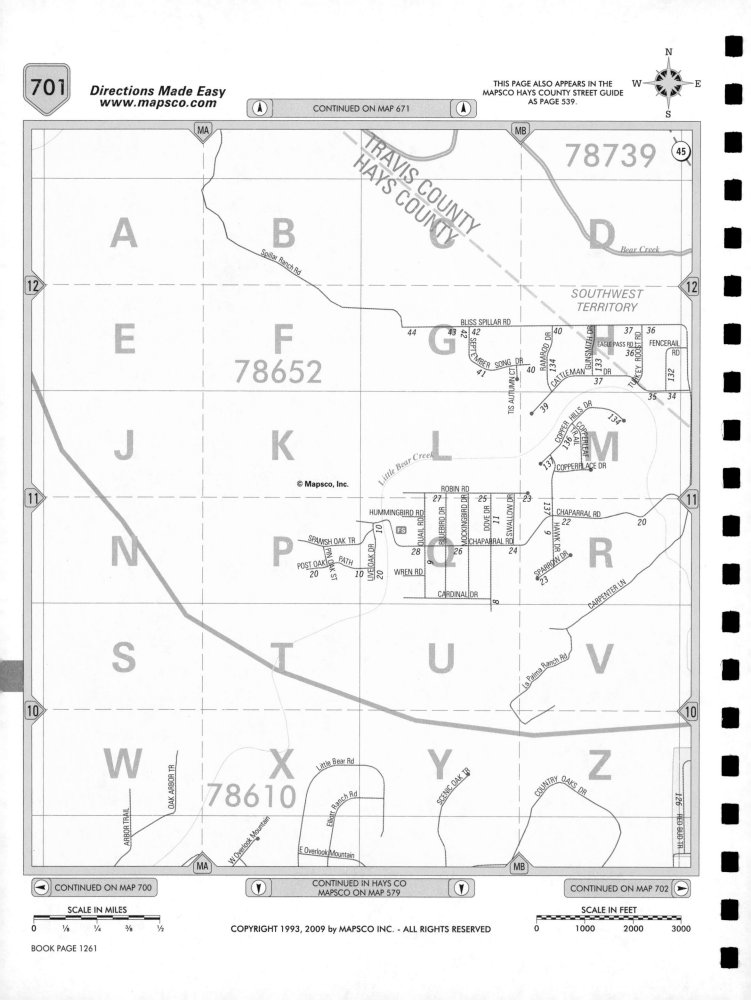

Directions Made Easy
www.mapsco.com

CONTINUED ON MAP 671

THIS PAGE ALSO APPEARS IN THE
MAPSCO HAYS COUNTY STREET GUIDE
AS PAGE 539.

N
W E
S

MA   MB

78739   45

TRAVIS COUNTY
HAYS COUNTY

A   B   C   D
                                    Bear Creek

Spillar Ranch Rd

12   12

SOUTHWEST
TERRITORY

E   F   G   H

78652   BLISS SPILLAR RD
                    44   43 42 42 40   37 36
                                            EAGLE PASS RD   FENCERAIL
                    SEPTEMBER SONG DR   36   RD
                    41   RAMROD DR   133
                              40   CATTLEMAN 134 GUNSMITH DR DR 132
                    TIS AUTUMN CT   DR   37
                                              37   35 34
                              39

J   K   L   M
                                    COPPER HILLS DR   134
                                    136 COPPERLEAF TRAIL
Little Bear Creek   137   COPPERPLACE DR

© Mapsco, Inc.

                    ROBIN RD   137
                    27   25   23   CHAPARRAL RD
11   HUMMINGBIRD RD   22   20   11
                    QUAIL RD BLUEBIRD DR MOCKINGBIRD DR DOVE DR SWALLOW DR
      SPANISH OAK TR 10 FS   9 HAWK DR
M   POST OAK PIN OAK ST PATH 28 26 CHAPARRAL RD 24   SPARROW DR   R
      20   10   LIVEOAK DR 9   23
              10   20   WREN RD   8
                    CARDINAL DR

S   T   U   V
                                    La Palma Ranch Rd   CARPENTER LN

10   10

W   X   Y   Z
78610   Little Bear Rd   Scenic Oak Tr   Country Oaks Dr
ARBOR TRAIL OAK ARBOR TR
              Elliott Ranch Rd   126 RED BUD TR
      W Overlook Mountain
              E Overlook Mountain

MA   MB

CONTINUED ON MAP 700   CONTINUED IN HAYS CO
                              MAPSCO ON MAP 579   CONTINUED ON MAP 702

SCALE IN MILES   SCALE IN FEET
0   1/8   1/4   3/8   1/2   0   1000   2000   3000

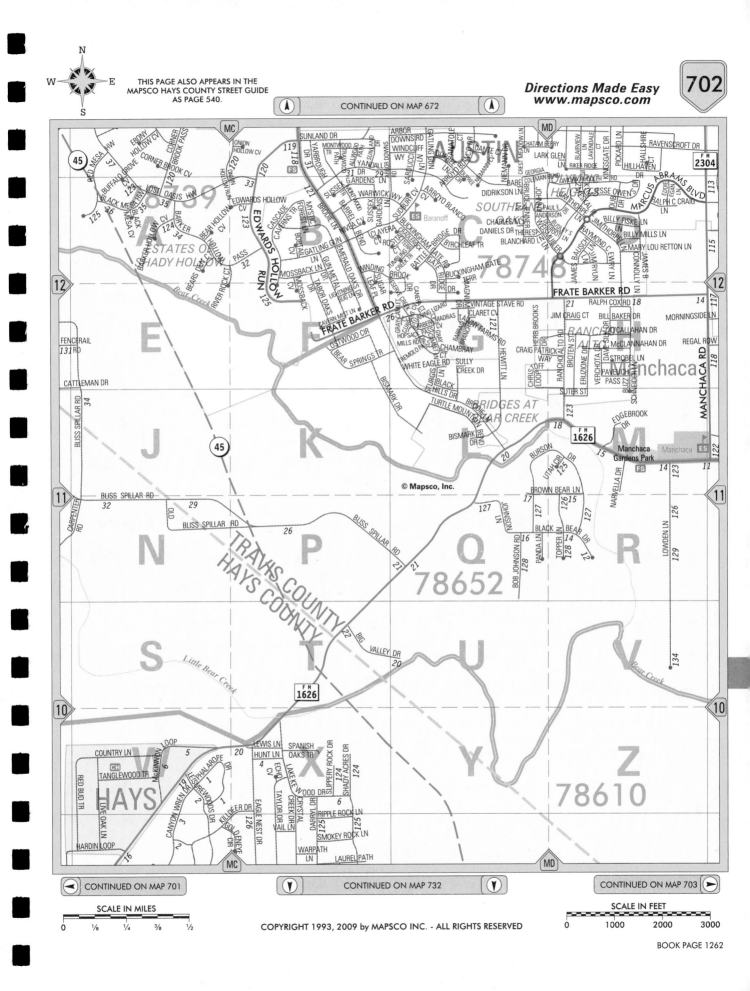

CONTINUED ON MAP 673

N
W E
S

AUSTIN

Mary Moore Searight
Metropolitan Park

Southpark
Meadows

THE KNOLLS

78748

CANTERBURY
TRAILS

SAN LEANNA

Chapel Hill
Memorial
Park

Rex Kitchens
Youth Athletic Complex

MANCHACA RD

Manchaca

FM 2304

FM 1626

78652

Onion Creek
Club (Pvt)

Onion Creek

Brown Cemetery

Live Oak
Cemetery

TRAVIS COUNTY

I-35

78747

78610

© Mapsco, Inc.

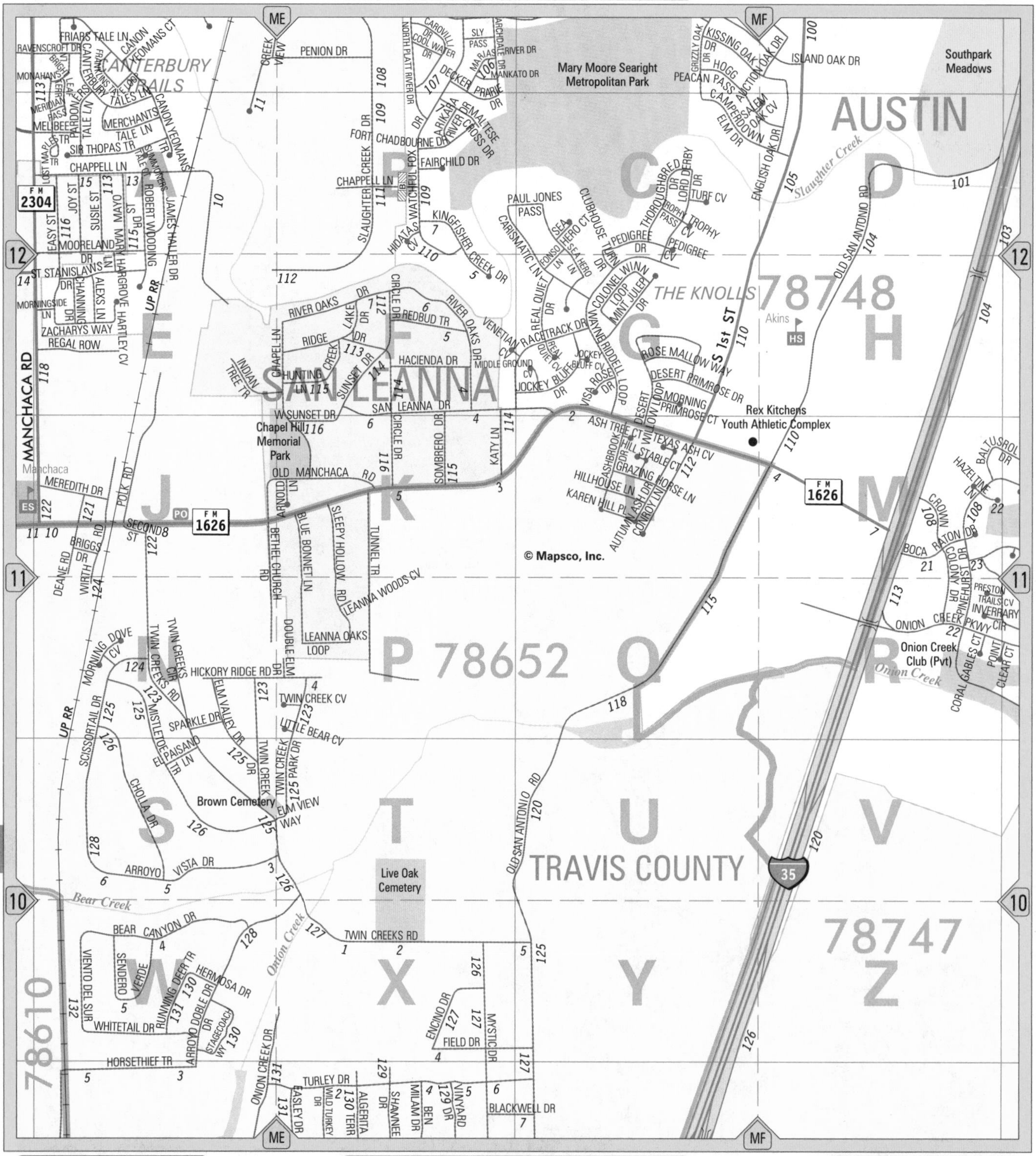

CONTINUED ON MAP 702

CONTINUED ON MAP 733

CONTINUED ON MAP 704

SCALE IN MILES
0 1/8 1/4 3/8 1/2

SCALE IN FEET
0 1000 2000 3000

COPYRIGHT 1993, 2009 by MAPSCO INC. - ALL RIGHTS RESERVED

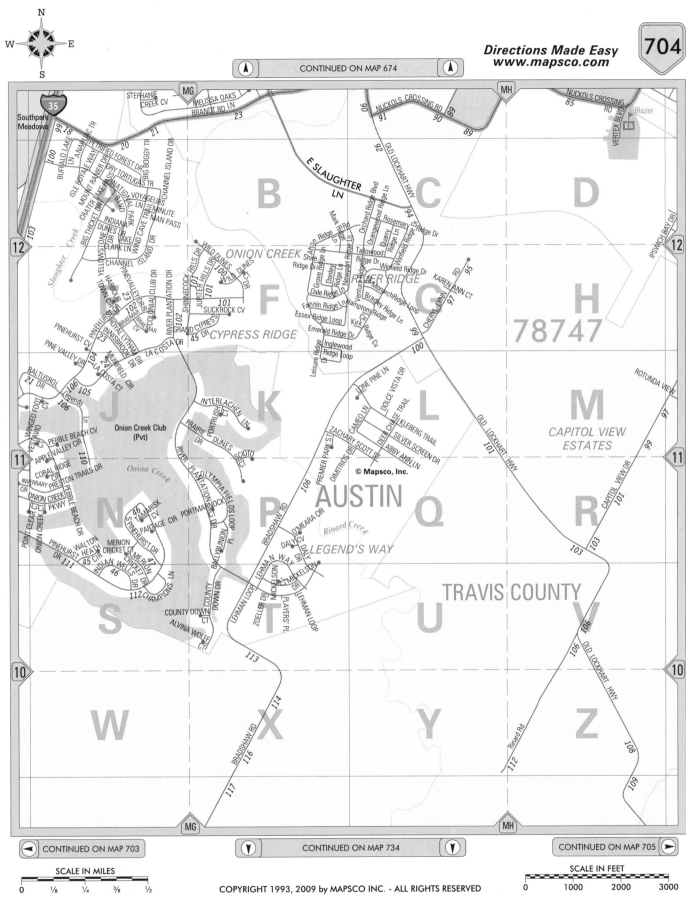

N
W E
S

CONTINUED ON MAP 674

MG   MH   Nuckols Crossing   Vertex Blvd   Blazier   ES

Southpark Meadows

Stephanie Creek CV   Melissa Oaks   Brandt Rd LN

35

99 18
100
Buffalo Lakes LN
Isle Royale Way
Mount Ranier Dr
Crater Lake Dr
Petrified Forest Dr
Dry Tortugas Tr
Big Boggy Tr
20   21
23
Channel Island Dr
Voyageurs LN
Minute Man Pass
National Park Blvd

E SLAUGHTER LN

Nuckols Crossing RD
90   91   92   89   89   85
90
94

Indiana Dunes Dr
Clark LN
Channel Island Dr
Lake Clark LN
Wind Cave Trail Dr

ONION CREEK   B   Mak Rd   Afton Ridge LN   Shire Ridge Dr   Orchard Ridge Blvd   Orangewood Ridge Ln   Rosemary Dr   Ridge Ln   Ridge Dr   C   D

12   103   Slaughter Creek
Yellowstone Cir
Town Cir
Big Thicket Tr
Haboub Dr
23
102
Pinehurst Cv
Colonial Club Dr
River Plantation Dr
Wild Dunes Dr
Shinnecock Hills Dr
Jupiter Hills Dr
100
101
Wild Dunes Dr
101
Slickrock CV
La Costa Dr
45 Dr
Grand Cypress
Braemar Dr
Braemar Cv
Royal Lytham Dr
Innisbrook Dr
Pinehurst Cv
104
24
23
Muirfield Cir
La Costa Ct

F   Dale Ridge Ln   Donley Ridge Ln   Grove Ridge Ln   Venture Dr   MonarchRidge Loop   Bradley Ridge Ln   Hampton Ridge Cir   Kirk   G   Karen Ann Ct   95   97   H   12
    Fannin Ridge Ln   Essex Ridge Loop   Emerald Ridge Dr   Inglewood Ridge Loop   Ridge Cv   99   Cheryl Lynn Rd
    Leisure Ridge Ln   Cheryl Lynn Dr
    CYPRESS RIDGE   100
    78747

Pine Valley Dr
Baltusrol Dr
21
Winged Foot Cv
David Cir
106   105
106
Legends

J   Interlachen Ln   K   Lone Pine Ln   Cameo Ln   Dolce Vista Dr   L   Rotunda View
    Prairie Dunes Dr   Zachary Scott St   Chase Trail   Kleberg Trail   Old Lockhart Hwy   CAPITOL VIEW ESTATES   M   97   99   101
    Portrush Ln   Deer Chase   Silver Screen Dr   101
    Scioto Ct   Abby Ann Ln   11

11   Pebble Beach Cv   Premier Park St   © Mapsco, Inc.
    Apple Valley Cir   River Plantation Dr   Bradshaw Rd   Dimitrios Dr   106
    Coral Ridge Cir   Olympia Fields Loop   AUSTIN   Q   Capitol View Dr   R   101
    Preston Trails Dr   110   N   Tamarisk Cv   Partage Cir   Portmarnock Cir   P   O'Meara Cir   Rinard Creek   103   103
    Inverrary Cir   46   Sinclair Dr   Daly CV   LEGEND'S WAY   106
    Onion Creek Pkwy   Pinehurst Dr   Ballyjunion   Daly Dr   V
    Point Clear Cir   Pinehurst Heath Dr   Merion Cricket Ct   Lehman N Way   Mickelson   TRAVIS COUNTY   106
    Pebble Beach Dr   45 Cir   Merion Cricket Dr   Lehman Loop   Mickelson Dr   Players' Pl   Old Lockhart Hwy
    Onion Creek Cir   Walton Heath Dr   Indian Wells Dr   46   Lehman Loop   108
    111   112   Champions Ln   County Down Dr   Zoeller Dr   T   U   103
    S   County Down Ct   X   Y   112   Z
    Alvina Wolfe Cir   113   W   Rinard Rd   106
    114   116   117   109

10   Onion Creek   Onion Creek Club (Pvt)   10

SCALE IN MILES
0   1/8   1/4   3/8   1/2

CONTINUED ON MAP 703
CONTINUED ON MAP 734
CONTINUED ON MAP 705

SCALE IN FEET
0   1000   2000   3000

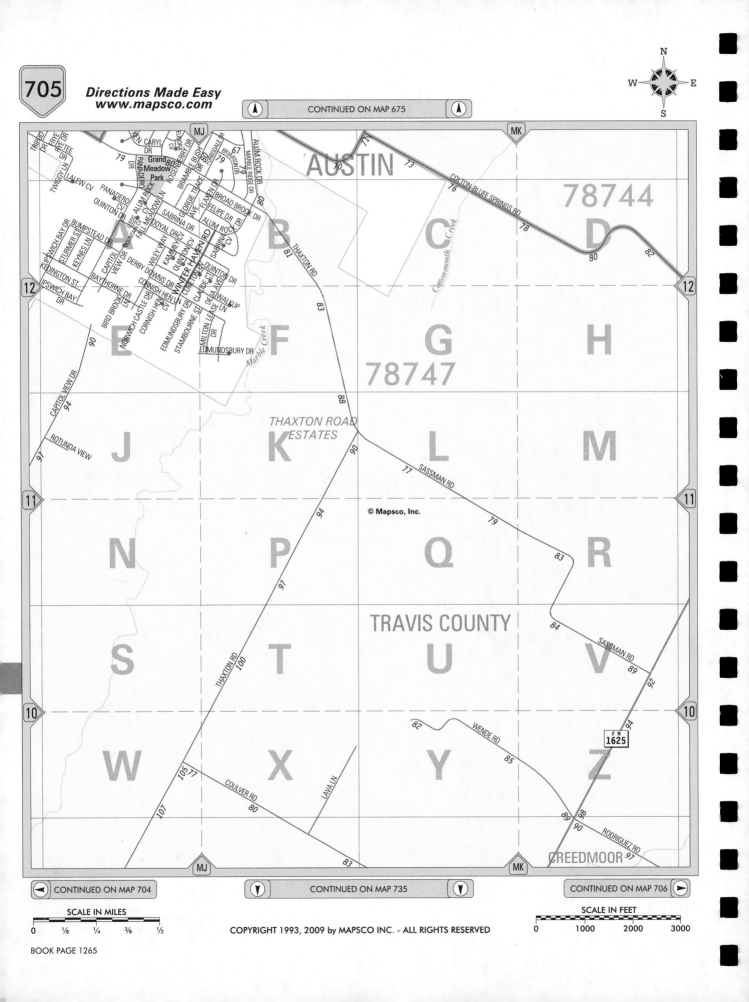

CONTINUED ON MAP 675

CONTINUED ON MAP 704

CONTINUED ON MAP 735

CONTINUED ON MAP 706

AUSTIN

78744

78747

THAXTON ROAD ESTATES

© Mapsco, Inc.

TRAVIS COUNTY

CREEDMOOR

COLTON-BLUFF SPRINGS RD

SASSMAN RD

SASSMAN RD

WENDE RD

FM 1625

RODRIGUEZ RD

COULVER RD

THAXTON RD

LAVA LN

SCALE IN MILES

0   1/8   1/4   3/8   1/2

SCALE IN FEET

0   1000   2000   3000

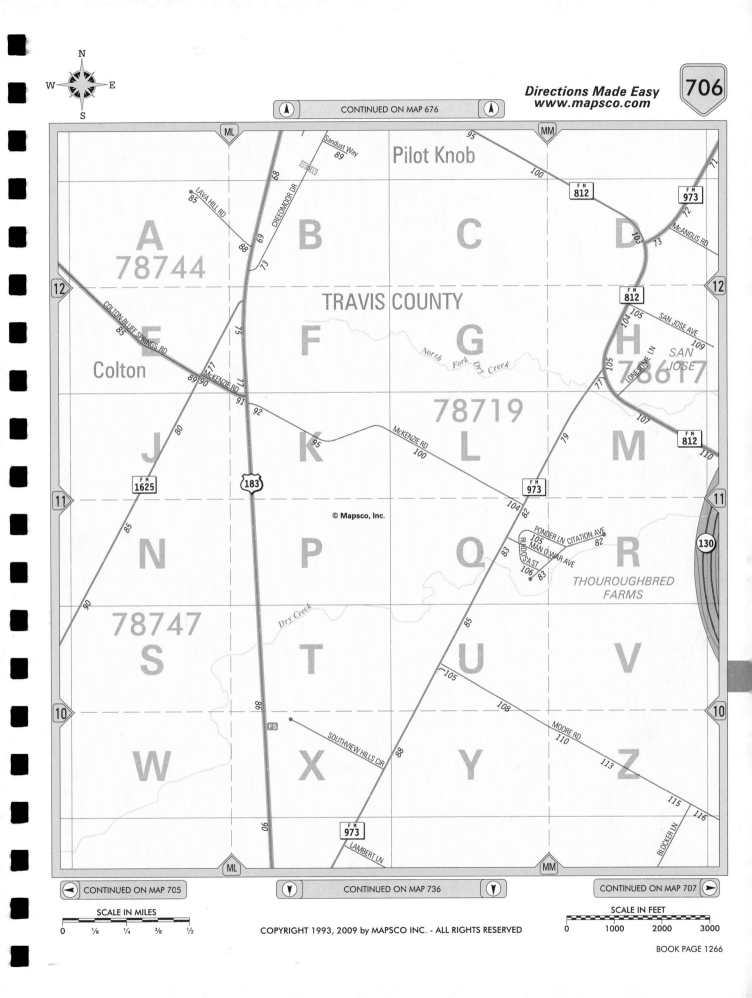

Directions Made Easy
www.mapsco.com

CONTINUED ON MAP 676

N
W E
S

ML

MM

Sandust Way
89

Pilot Knob

95

100

FM 812

FM 973

11

72

McANGUS RD

68

CREEDMOOR DR

LAVA HILL RD
85

A
78744

B

C

D

103

73

12

12

69

88

73

TRAVIS COUNTY

FM 812

104 105

San Jose Ave
109

75

COLTON-BLUFF SPRINGS RD
85

E

F

North Fork

Dry Creek

G

105

77

H
78617

LONESOME LN

SAN JOSE

Colton

89 90

McKENZIE RD

77

91

92

McKENZIE RD
100

95

79

107

FM 812

110

78719

80

J

K

L

104 82

M

FM 1625

US 183

FM 973

11

11

85

PONDER LN CITATION AVE
105   82

130

MAN O WAR AVE

RUIDOSA ST

N

P

83

Q

106 83

R

THOUROUGHBRED FARMS

90

78747

Dry Creek

© Mapsco, Inc.

85

105

S

T

U

108

MOORE RD
110

V

98

SOUTHVIEW HILLS CIR

88

113

10

FS

115

W

X

FM 973

Y

BLOCKER LN

116

Z

90

LAMBERT LN

ML

MM

CONTINUED ON MAP 705

CONTINUED ON MAP 736

CONTINUED ON MAP 707

SCALE IN MILES
0   ⅛   ¼   ⅜   ½

SCALE IN FEET
0   1000   2000   3000

BOOK PAGE 1266

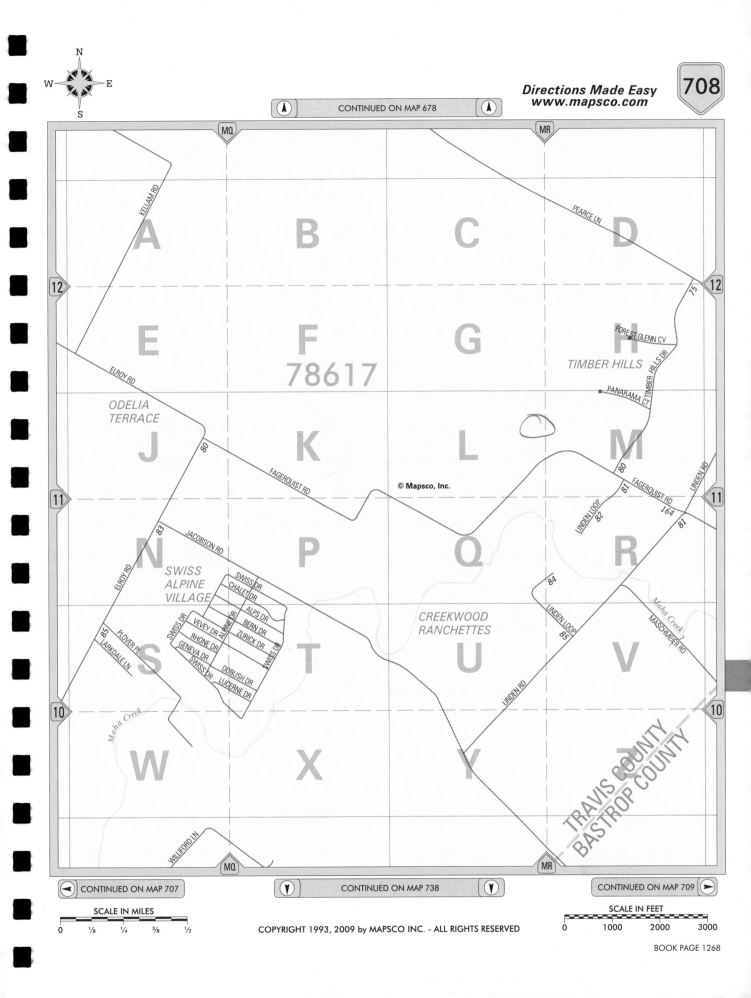

Directions Made Easy
www.mapsco.com

CONTINUED ON MAP 678

N
W · E
S

MQ
MR

KELLAM RD

PEARCE LN

A

B

C

D

12

12

75

E

F

G

H

FOREST GLENN CV
TIMBER HILLS DR
TIMBER HILLS

ELROY RD

78617

PANARAMA CT

ODELIA
TERRACE

J

80

K

L

M

80

FAGERQUIST RD

© Mapsco, Inc.

LINDEN LOOP

81

FAGERQUIST RD

LINDEN RD

82

164

11

11

81

83

JACOBSON RD

N

P

Q

R

ELROY RD

SWISS
ALPINE
VILLAGE

SWISS DR
CHALET DR

84

LINDEN LOOP

85

Maha Creek

MASCHMEIER RD

SWISS DR
VEVEY DR
RHONE DR
GENEVA DR
SWISS DR

ALPINE DR
ALPS DR
BERN DR
ZURICK DR
DOBUSH DR
LUCERNE DR

SWISS DR

CREEKWOOD
RANCHETTES

PLOVER PL

85

LARKDALE LN

S

T

U

V

10

Maha Creek

10

LINDEN RD

W

X

Y

TRAVIS COUNTY
BASTROP COUNTY

Z

WILLIFORD LN

MQ

MR

CONTINUED ON MAP 707

CONTINUED ON MAP 738

CONTINUED ON MAP 709

SCALE IN MILES
0   ⅛   ¼   ⅜   ½

SCALE IN FEET
0   1000   2000   3000

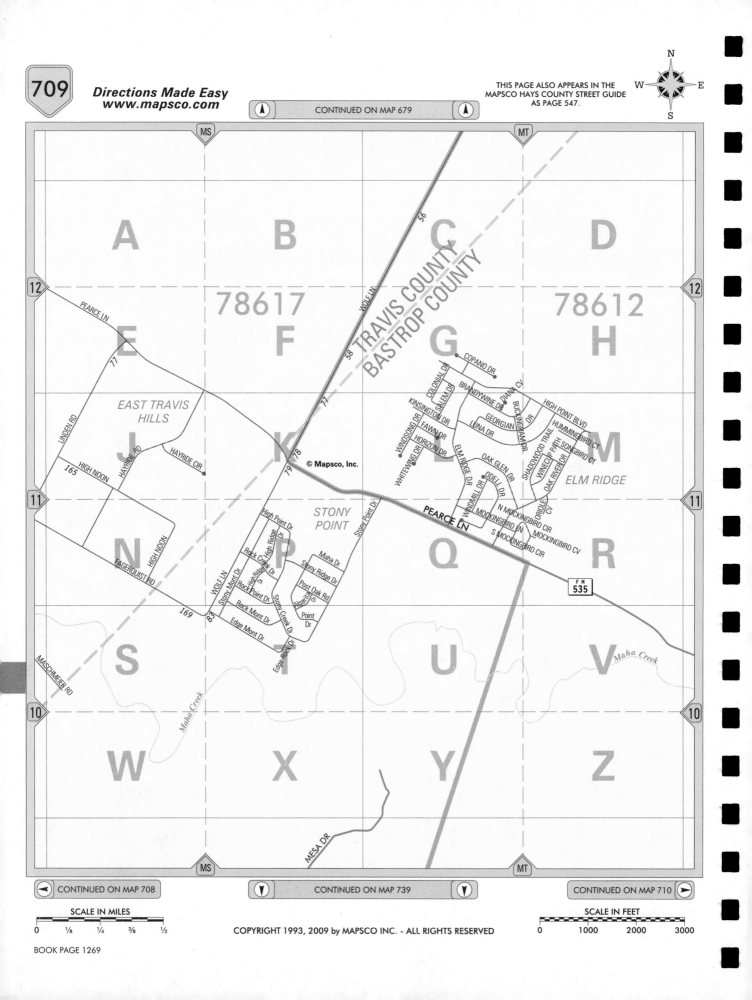

709

Directions Made Easy
www.mapsco.com

THIS PAGE ALSO APPEARS IN THE
MAPSCO HAYS COUNTY STREET GUIDE
AS PAGE 547.

N
W E
S

CONTINUED ON MAP 679

MS

MT

A   B   C   D

12   12

78617   78612

E   F   G   H

WOLF LN

TRAVIS COUNTY
BASTROP COUNTY

56

58

77

PEARCE LN

77

LINDEN RD

EAST TRAVIS
HILLS

COPANO DR

COLONIAL DR

BRANDYWINE DR

DIANA CV

SALEM DR

HIGH POINT BLVD

KINSINGTON DR

GEORGIAN

BUCKINGHAM DR

HUMMINGBIRD CT

J   K   L   M

WINDSONG DR

FAWN DR

LUNA DR

SHADOWWOOD TRAIL

SONGBIRD CT

HAYRIDE RD

HIGH NOON

HAYRIDE CIR

HORIZON DR

WINECUP PATH

165

78

WHITEWING DR

ELM RIDGE DR

OAK GLEN DR

OAK RIVER DR

ELM RIDGE

79

© Mapsco, Inc.

WINMILL DR

ODELL DR

ORIOLE CV

MOCKINGBIRD CIR

11   11

STONY
POINT

Stony Point Dr

PEARCE LN

N MOCKINGBIRD LN

MOCKINGBIRD CV

S MOCKINGBIRD CIR

High Point Dr

MOCKINGBIRD LN

N   P   Q   R

High Ridge Dr

Maha Dr

Rock Creek Dr

Stony Ridge Dr

FAGERQUIST RD

HIGH NOON

WOLF LN

High Sidney Dr

Post Oak Rd

FM 535

Rock Point Dr

Stony Creek Dr

Algarita Dr

Rock Mont Dr

169   83

Point
Dr

Rock Mont Dr

Edge Mont Dr

S   T   U   V

Maha Creek

Edge Rock Dr

MASCHMEIER RD

Maha Creek

10   10

W   X   Y   Z

MESA DR

CONTINUED ON MAP 708
CONTINUED ON MAP 739
CONTINUED ON MAP 710

MS   MT

SCALE IN MILES

0   ⅛   ¼   ⅜   ½

SCALE IN FEET

0   1000   2000   3000

BOOK PAGE 1269

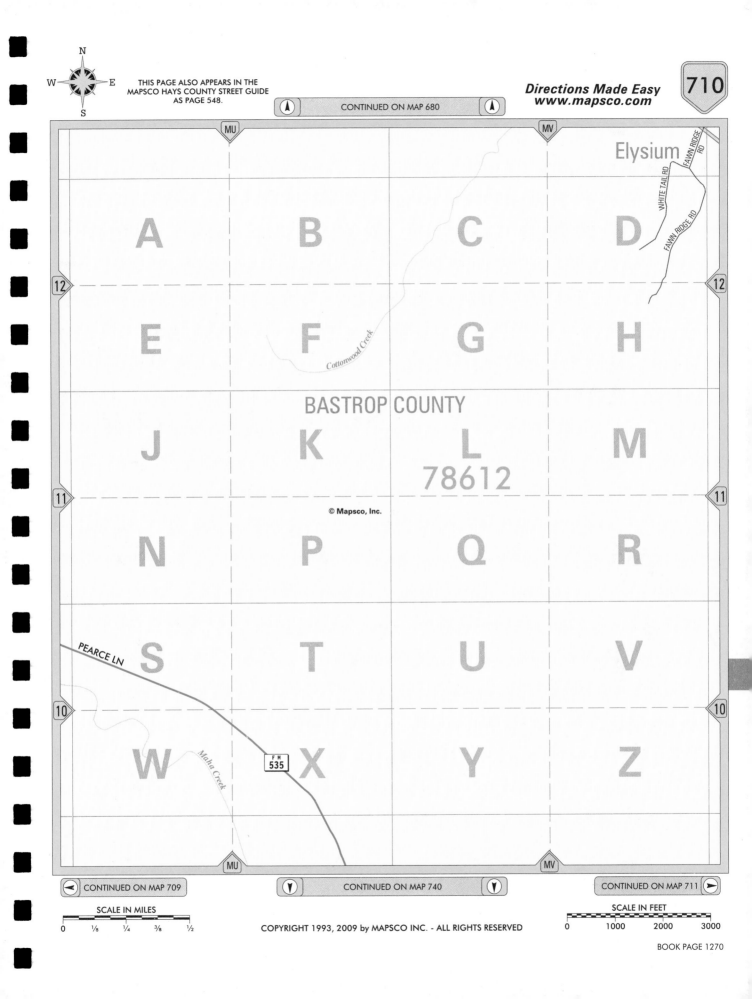

N
W E
S

THIS PAGE ALSO APPEARS IN THE
MAPSCO HAYS COUNTY STREET GUIDE
AS PAGE 548.

Directions Made Easy
www.mapsco.com

CONTINUED ON MAP 680

MU

MV

Elysium

WHITE TAIL RD

FAWN RIDGE RD

FAWN RIDGE RD

A   B   C   D

12   12

E   F   G   H

Cottonwood Creek

BASTROP COUNTY

J   K   L   M

78612

© Mapsco, Inc.

11   11

N   P   Q   R

PEARCE LN

S   T   U   V

10   10

W   X   Y   Z

Maha Creek

FM 535

MU   MV

CONTINUED ON MAP 709

CONTINUED ON MAP 740

CONTINUED ON MAP 711

SCALE IN MILES
0   ⅛   ¼   ⅜   ½

SCALE IN FEET
0   1000   2000   3000

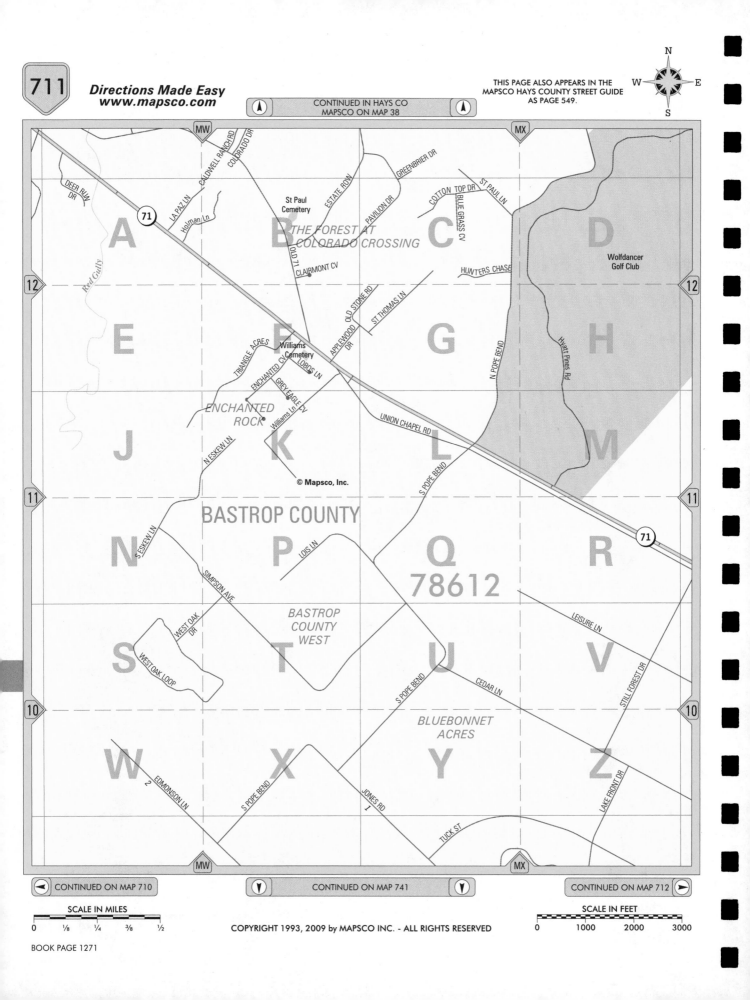

THIS PAGE ALSO APPEARS IN THE
MAPSCO HAYS COUNTY STREET GUIDE
AS PAGE 550.

Directions Made Easy
www.mapsco.com

712

N
W E
S

CONTINUED IN HAYS CO
MAPSCO ON MAP 38

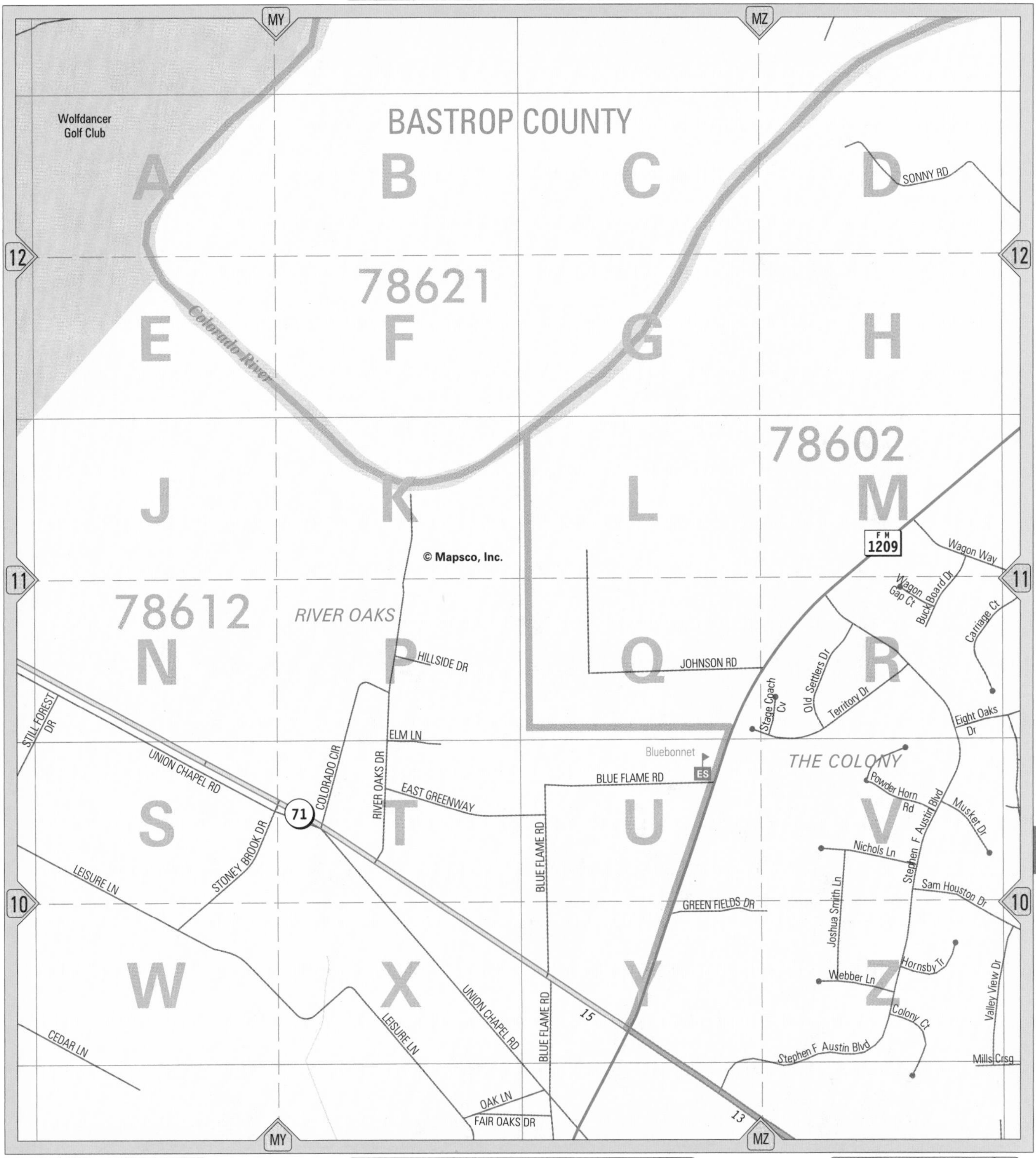

MY

MZ

Wolfdancer
Golf Club

BASTROP COUNTY

A   B   C   D   SONNY RD

12   12

78621

E   F   G   H

Colorado River

J   K   L   M   78602

© Mapsco, Inc.

FM 1209

Wagon Way

11   Wagon Gap Ct   Buckboard Dr   11
Carriage Ct

78612   RIVER OAKS

N   HILLSIDE DR   P   Q   JOHNSON RD   R   Eight Oaks Dr

Old Settlers Dr
Stage Coach Cv   Territory Dr

Still Forest Dr   ELM LN   THE COLONY

UNION CHAPEL RD   Bluebonnet   Powder Horn Rd   Musket Dr
COLORADO CIR   RIVER OAKS DR   ES   BLUE FLAME RD

S   EAST GREENWAY   T   U   V   Nichols Ln   Sam Houston Dr
71   BLUE FLAME RD   Joshua Smith Ln   Stephen F Austin Blvd
Stoney Brook Dr   BLUE FLAME RD   Hornsby Tr

LEISURE LN   GREEN FIELDS DR
10   10

W   X   Y   Z   Webber Ln   Colony Ct   Valley View Dr

CEDAR LN   LEISURE LN   15   Stephen F Austin Blvd   Mills Crsg
UNION CHAPEL RD

OAK LN
FAIR OAKS DR   13

MY   MZ

CONTINUED ON MAP 711

CONTINUED ON MAP 742

CONTINUED IN HAYS CO
MAPSCO ON MAP 551

SCALE IN MILES
0   ⅛   ¼   ⅜   ½

SCALE IN FEET
0   1000   2000   3000

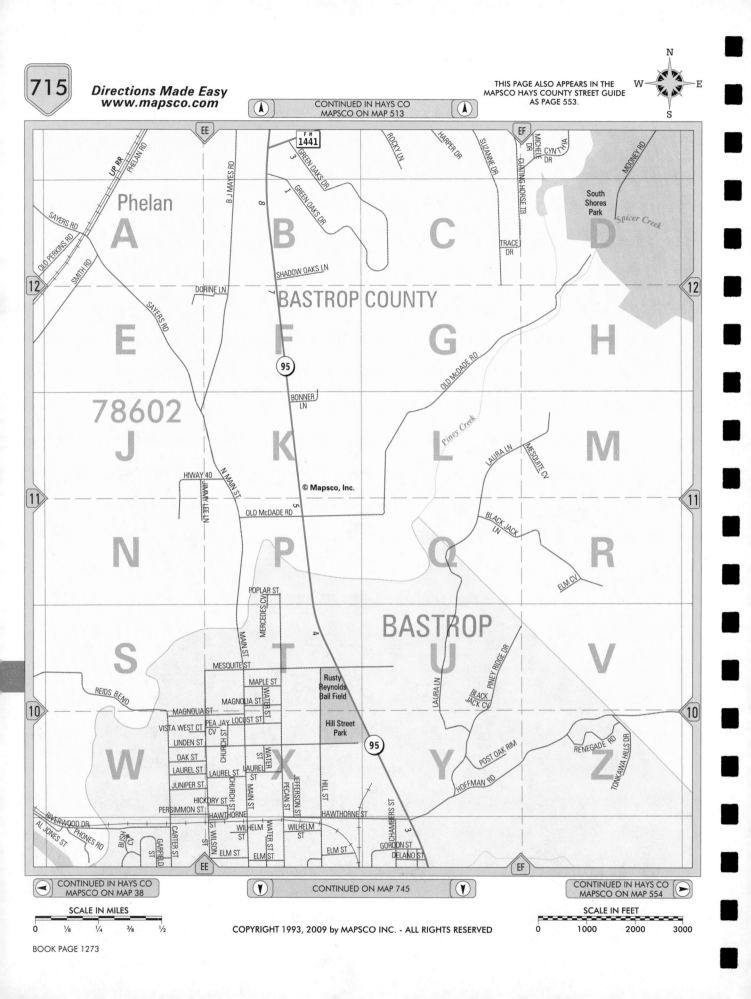

Directions Made Easy
www.mapsco.com

THIS PAGE ALSO APPEARS IN THE
MAPSCO HAYS COUNTY STREET GUIDE
AS PAGE 553.

N
W E
S

CONTINUED IN HAYS CO
MAPSCO ON MAP 513

EE

FM 1441

EF

Phelan

UP RR
PHELAN RD

SAYERS RD

OLD PERKINS RD

SMITH RD

B J MAYES RD

GREEN OAKS DR

8

GREEN OAKS DR

ROCKY LN

HARPER DR

SUZANNE DR

CUTTING HORSE TB

MICHELE DR

CYNTHIA DR

MODNEY RD

South Shores Park

Spicer Creek

A

B

C

D

12

SAYERS RD

DORINE LN

SHADOW OAKS LN

7

BASTROP COUNTY

TRACE DR

12

E

F

G

H

95

78602

BONNER LN

OLD McDADE RD

Piney Creek

LAURA LN

MESQUITE CV

J

K

L

M

11

HIWAY 40

N MAIN ST

JIMMY LEE LN

OLD McDADE RD

5

© Mapsco, Inc.

BLACK JACK LN

ELM CV

11

N

P

Q

R

POPLAR ST

MERCEDES CV

MAIN ST

BASTROP

S

T

U

V

REIDS BEND

MESQUITE ST

MAPLE ST

WATER ST

MAGNOLIA ST

Rusty Reynolds Ball Field

LAURA LN

PINEY RIDGE DR

BLACK JACK CV

10

MAGNOLIA ST

PEA JAY CV

LOCUST ST

Hill Street Park

95

POST OAK RIM

RENEGADE RD

TONKAWA HILLS DR

10

VISTA WEST CT

LINDEN ST

CHURCH ST

WATER ST

W

OAK ST

LAUREL ST

LAUREL ST

LAUREL ST

X

JEFFERSON ST

PECAN ST

HILL ST

Y

HOFFMAN RD

Z

JUNIPER ST

HICKORY ST

CHURCH ST

MAIN ST

PERSIMMON ST

HAWTHORNE

HAWTHORNE ST

CHAMBERS ST

RIVERWOOD DR

AL JONES ST

PHONES RD

BUSH CT

CARTER ST

GARFIELD ST

WILSON ST

WILHELM ST

ELM ST

WATER ST

ELM ST

WILHELM ST

ELM ST

GORDON ST

DELANO ST

3

4

EE

EF

CONTINUED IN HAYS CO
MAPSCO ON MAP 38

CONTINUED ON MAP 745

CONTINUED IN HAYS CO
MAPSCO ON MAP 554

SCALE IN MILES

0   1/8   1/4   3/8   1/2

SCALE IN FEET

0   1000   2000   3000

COPYRIGHT 1993, 2009 by MAPSCO INC. - ALL RIGHTS RESERVED

N W E S

THIS PAGE ALSO APPEARS IN THE
MAPSCO HAYS COUNTY STREET GUIDE
AS PAGE 580.

CONTINUED ON MAP 702

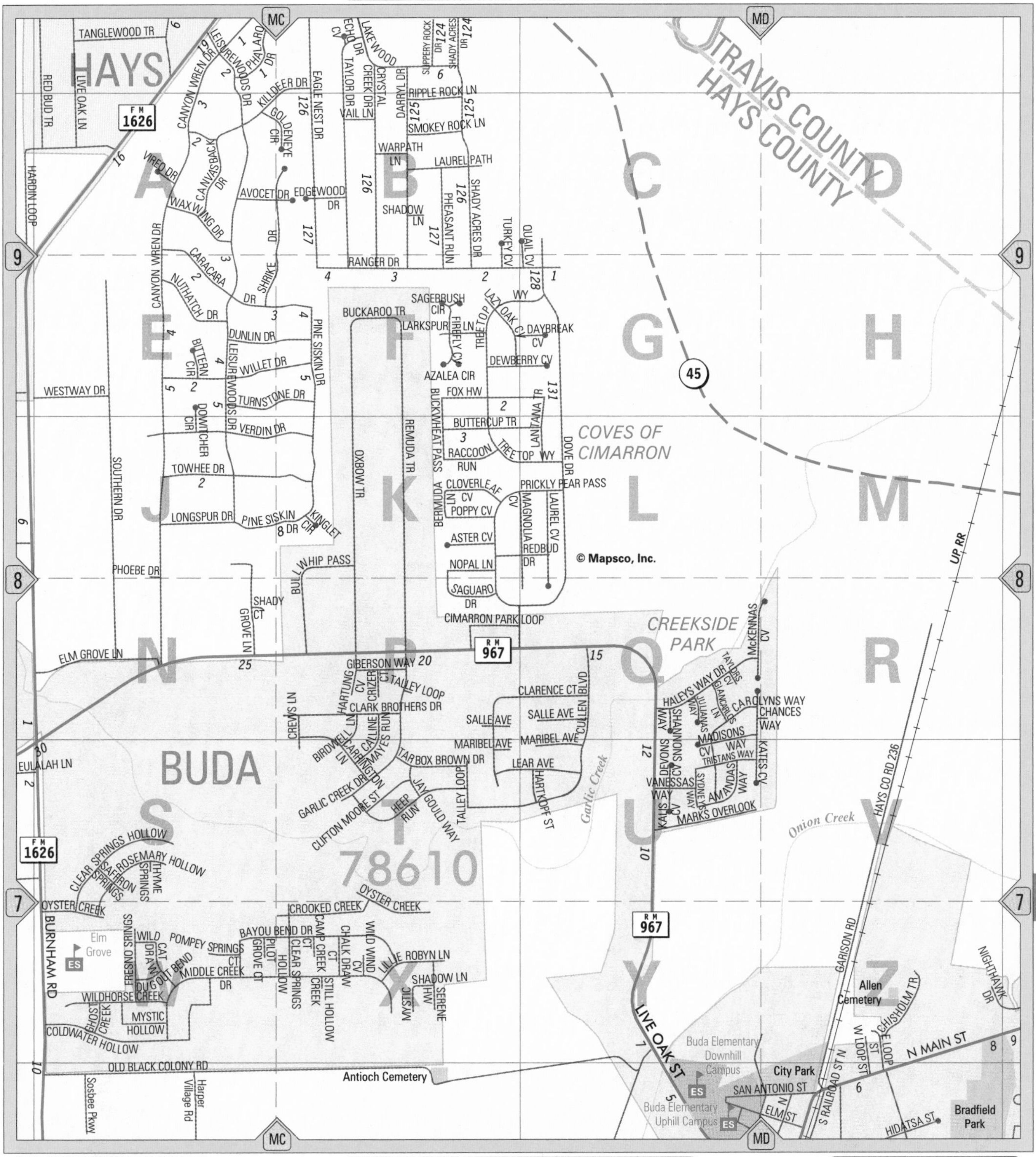

HAYS

TANGLEWOOD TR

RED BUD TR
LIVE OAK LN

FM 1626

HARDIN LOOP

9

CANYON WREN DR
LEISUREWOODS DR
PHALAROPE DR
KILLDEER DR
GOLDENEYE CIR
DENEYE

VIREO DR
CANVASBACK DR
WAX WING DR

EAGLE NEST DR
TAYLOR DR
VAIL LN

ECHO CREEK DR
LAKEWOOD DR
CRYSTAL DR
DAR DR

SLIPPERY ROCK
DR 124
SHADY ACRES
DR 124

RIPPLE ROCK LN

SMOKEY ROCK LN

AVOCET DR
EDGEWOOD DR

CARACARA DR
SHRIKE DR
NUTHATCH DR

CANYON WREN DR

WARPATH LN
SHADOW LN

LAUREL PATH
PHEASANT RUN
SHADY ACRES DR

RANGER DR

QUAIL CV
TURKEY CV

BUCKAROO TR
SAGEBRUSH CIR
LARKSPUR
FIREFLY CV
LAZY OAK CV
TREE TOP
DAYBREAK CV
DEWBERRY CV

DUNLIN DR
WILLET DR
BITTERN CIR
PINE SISKIN DR
LEISUREWOODS DR

WESTWAY DR

TURNSTONE DR
VERDIN DR
DOWITCHER CIR

AZALEA CIR
FOX HW
BUTTERCUP TR

VAN ZANDT
LANTANA TR

G

COVES OF CIMARRON

45

H

SOUTHERN DR

TOWHEE DR

LONGSPUR DR
PINE SISKIN DR
KINGLET CIR

REMUDA TR
OXBOW TR

BUCKWHEAT PASS
RACCOON RUN
CLOVERLEAF CV
POPPY CV
BOMADILLA CV
ASTER CV
NOPAL LN
SAGUARO DR
MAGNOLIA CV
REDBUD DR
PRICKLY PEAR PASS
LAUREL CV
DOVE DR
TREE TOP WY

© Mapsco, Inc.

M

UP RR

PHOEBE DR

BULL WHIP PASS
GROVE LN
SHADY CT

CIMARRON PARK LOOP

CREEKSIDE PARK

McKENNAS CV

8

ELM GROVE LN

GIBERSON WAY 20
TALLEY LOOP
CLARK BROTHERS DR
HARTLING CV
BIRDWELL LN
CLEARING LN
CREWS LN
SALLE AVE
MARIBEL AVE

RM 967

CLARENCE CT
SALLE AVE
MARIBEL AVE
LEAR AVE

CULLEN BLVD

15

HALEYS WAY
SHANNONS CV
TAYLORS CV
BLANCARDS
WILLIAMS WAY
MADISONS CV
CAROLYNS WAY
CHANCES WAY
TRISTANS WAY
SYDNEYS WAY
AMANDAS WAY
KATES CV

BUDA

78610

GARLIC CREEK DR
CLIFTON MOORE ST
JAY GOULD WAY
JEEP RUN
TALLEY LOOP
TARBOX BROWN DR
HARTKOPF ST

GARLIC CREEK

VANESSAS WAY
KAYS WAY
MARKS OVERLOOK

12

10

Onion Creek

HAYS CO RD 236

EULALAH LN

FM 1626

CLEAR SPRINGS HOLLOW
ROSEMARY HOLLOW
SAFFRON SPRINGS
THYME SPRINGS

OYSTER CREEK
CLEAR SPRINGS

7

BURNHAM RD

Elm Grove
ES

WILD CAT DRAW
POMPEY SPRINGS
DUG OUT BEND
MIDDLE CREEK DR
STONES THROW
WILDHORSE CREEK
MYSTIC HOLLOW
COLDWATER HOLLOW
SPROSE CREEK

BAYOU BEND DR
PILOT GROVE CT
CAMP CREEK CT
CLEAR SPRINGS CT
CHALK DRAW CV
WILD WIND CV
ROBYN LN
SHADOW LN
STILL HOLLOW
SERENE HW
MYSTIC HW
CROOKED CREEK
OYSTER CREEK

RM 967

LIVE OAK ST

Allen Cemetery

GARISON RD
CHISHOLM TRL

NIGHTHAWK DR

Z

OLD BLACK COLONY RD

Antioch Cemetery

Sosbee Pkwy
Harper Village Rd

Buda Elementary Downhill Campus
ES

Buda Elementary Uphill Campus
ES

City Park

SAN ANTONIO ST
ELM ST

S RAILROAD ST
N RAILROAD ST
W LOOP ST

N MAIN ST
HIDATSA ST

Bradfield Park

TRAVIS COUNTY
HAYS COUNTY

CONTINUED IN HAYS CO MAPSCO ON MAP 579

CONTINUED ON MAP 762

CONTINUED ON MAP 733

SCALE IN MILES
0   1/8   1/4   3/8   1/2

SCALE IN FEET
0   1000   2000   3000

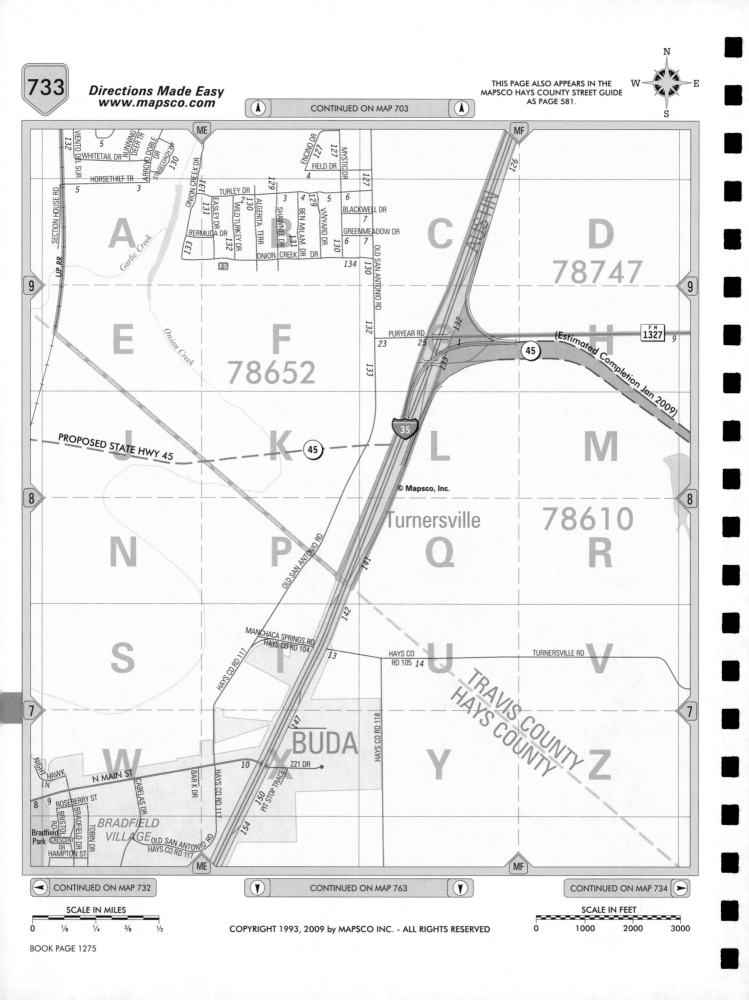

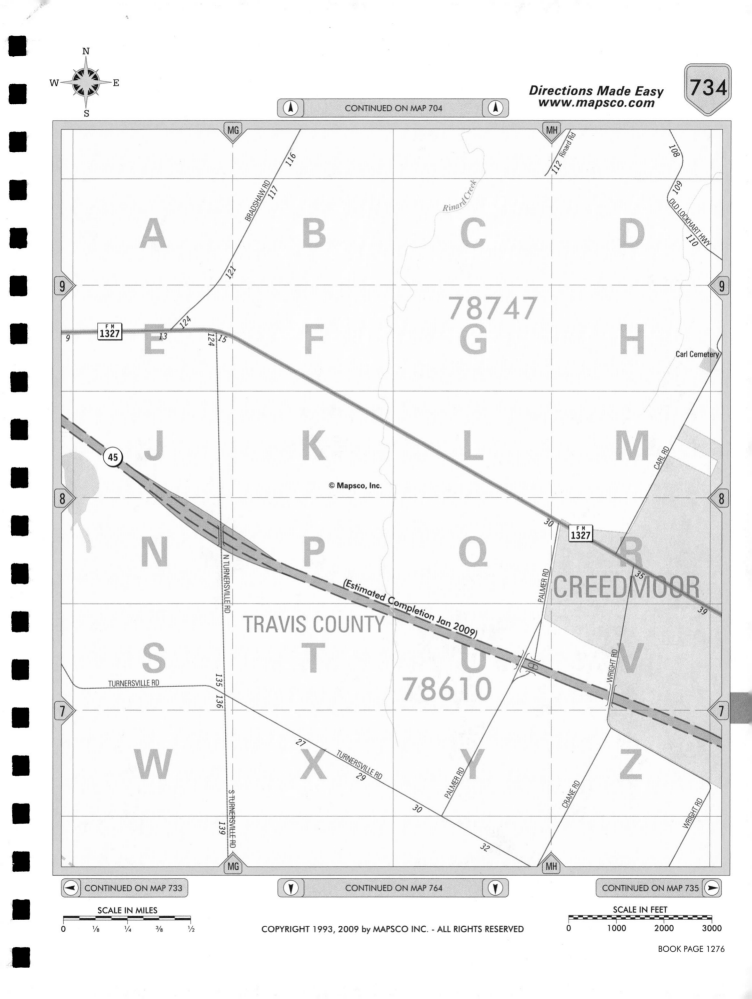

CONTINUED ON MAP 704

MG   MH

BRADSHAW RD
116
117

Rinard Rd
112
108

Rinard Creek

OLD LOCKHART HWY
101
110

A   B   C   D

78747

9   9

121

F M
1327
9   13   124   15   124

E   F   G   H

Carl Cemetery

45   J   K   L   M   CARL RD

© Mapsco, Inc.

8   8

30
F M
1327

N   P   Q   R   35
                                        CREEDMOOR

N TURNERSVILLE RD

PALMER RD
(Estimated Completion Jan 2009)

TRAVIS COUNTY

S   T   U   V   39

WRIGHT RD

TURNERSVILLE RD   78610

135 136

7   7

27
TURNERSVILLE RD
29

W   X   Y   Z

PALMER RD
CRANE RD
WRIGHT RD

S TURNERSVILLE RD
139

30

32

MG   MH

CONTINUED ON MAP 733   CONTINUED ON MAP 764   CONTINUED ON MAP 735

SCALE IN MILES
0   ⅛   ¼   ⅜   ½

SCALE IN FEET
0   1000   2000   3000

BOOK PAGE 1276

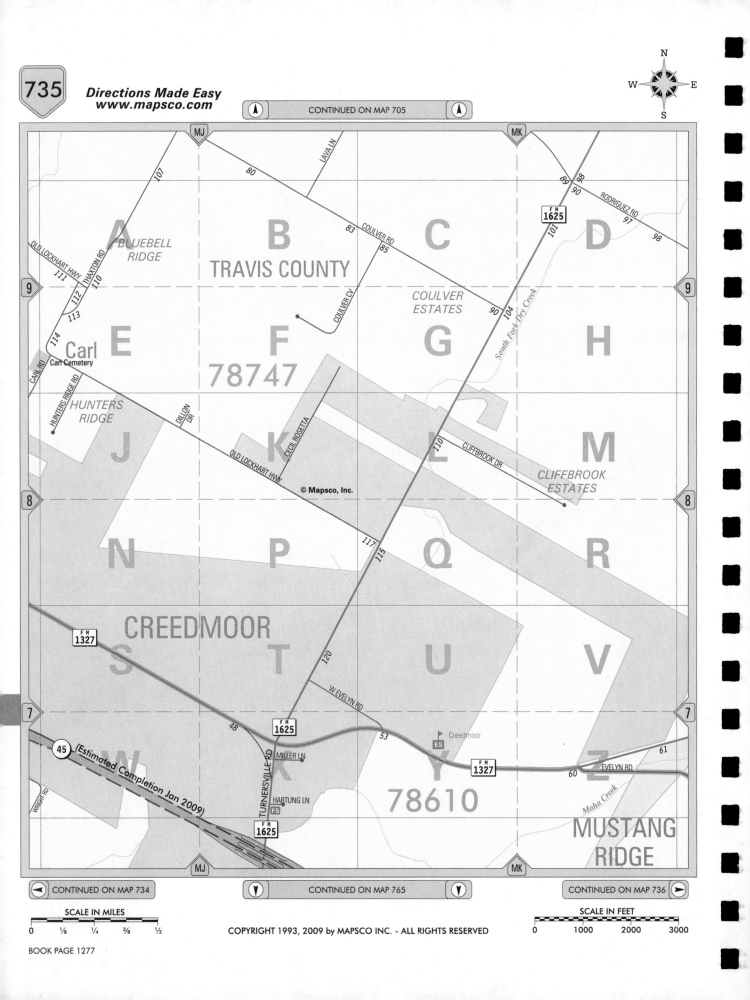

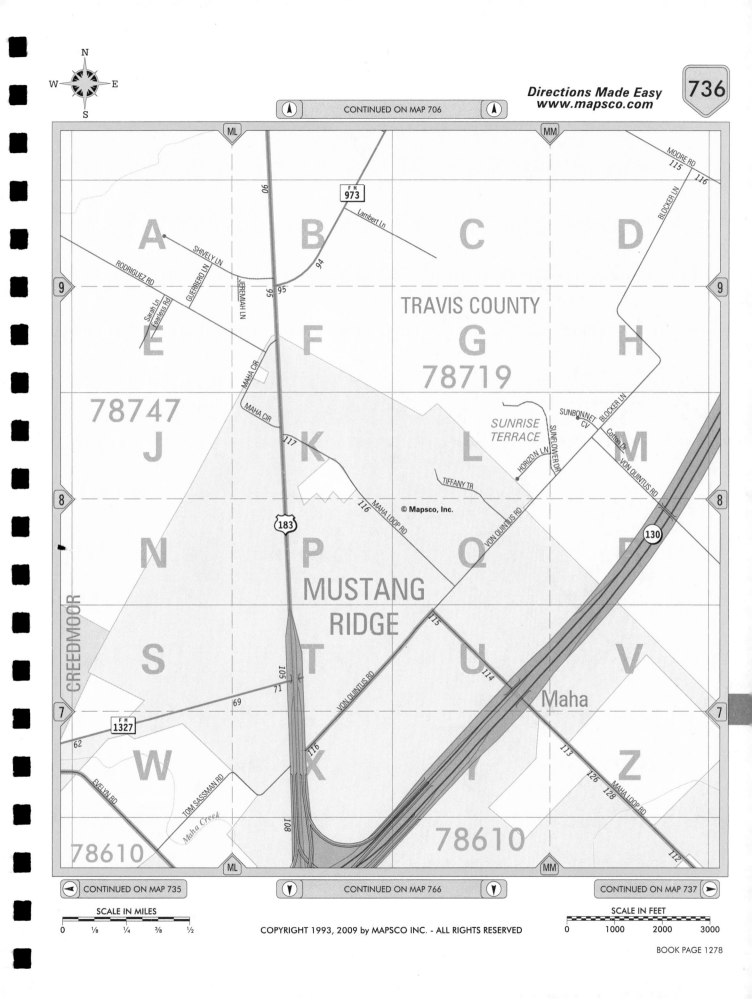

N
W E
S

CONTINUED ON MAP 706

ML

MM

MOORE RD
115
116

FM 973

Lambert Ln

A

B

C

D

BLOCKER LN

SHIVELY LN

94

TRAVIS COUNTY

9

RODRIGUEZ RD

GUERRERO LN

JEREMIAH LN

95
95

9

Sarah Ln

Fearless Rd

E

F

G
78719

H

MAHA CIR

78747

MAHA CIR

117

J

K

SUNRISE
TERRACE

SUNBONNET
CV

BLOCKER LN

HORIZON LN

SUNFLOWER DR

Cotton Dr

M

VON QUINTUS RD

TIFFANY TR

L

116

MAHA LOOP RD

© Mapsco, Inc.

VON QUINTUS RD

8

183

N

P

Q

R

130

8

MUSTANG
RIDGE

115

CREEDMOOR

S

T

VON QUINTUS RD

105

71

69

U

114

Maha

V

113

7

FM 1327

7

62

W

X

Y

116

Z

126

128

MAHA LOOP RD

112

EVELYN RD

TOM SASSMAN RD

Maha Creek

108

78610

78610

ML

MM

CONTINUED ON MAP 735

CONTINUED ON MAP 766

CONTINUED ON MAP 737

SCALE IN MILES

0   ⅛   ¼   ⅜   ½

SCALE IN FEET

0   1000   2000   3000

Directions Made Easy
www.mapsco.com

CONTINUED ON MAP 707

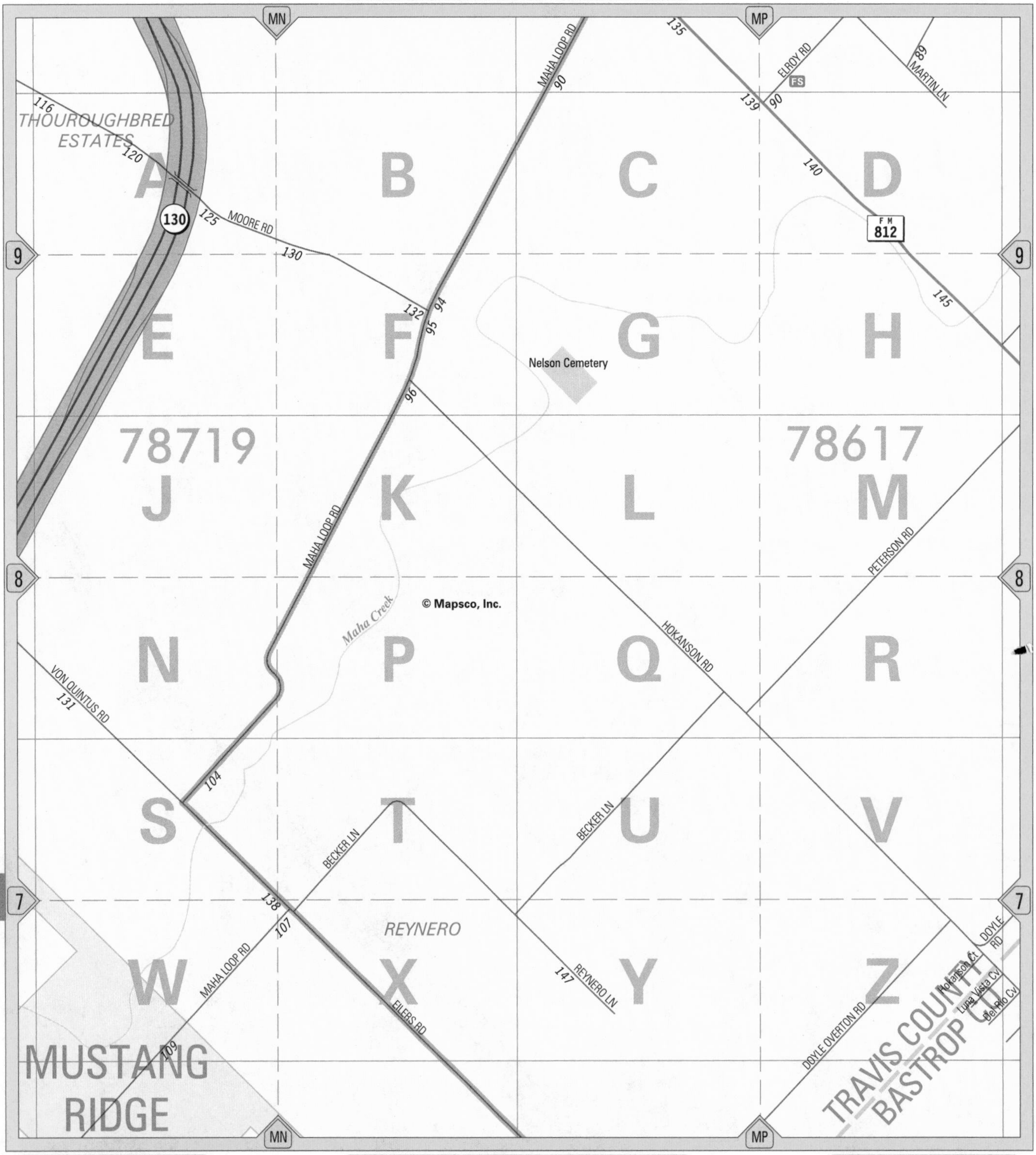

N
W ⊕ E
S

MN

116
THOUROUGHBRED ESTATES
120

A

MAHA LOOP RD
90

135

MP

ELROY RD
FS

89
MARTIN LN

139
90

B

C

140

D

130
125
MOORE RD
130

9

FM
812

9

132 94
95 94

E

F

G

H

96

Nelson Cemetery

145

78719

J

MAHA LOOP RD

K

L

78617

M

PETERSON RD

© Mapsco, Inc.

8

8

Maha Creek

VON QUINTUS RD
131

N

P

Q

HOKANSON RD

R

104

S

T

BECKER LN

U

BECKER LN

V

7

7

138
107

REYNERO

REYNERO LN
147

Y

DOYLE OVERTON RD

DOYLE RD

Z

Luna Vista Cv

MAHA LOOP RD

W

109

X

EILERS RD

MUSTANG RIDGE

TRAVIS COUNTY
BASTROP CO.

MN

MP

CONTINUED ON MAP 736
CONTINUED ON MAP 767
CONTINUED ON MAP 738

SCALE IN MILES
0   ⅛   ¼   ⅜   ½

SCALE IN FEET
0   1000   2000   3000

BOOK PAGE 1279

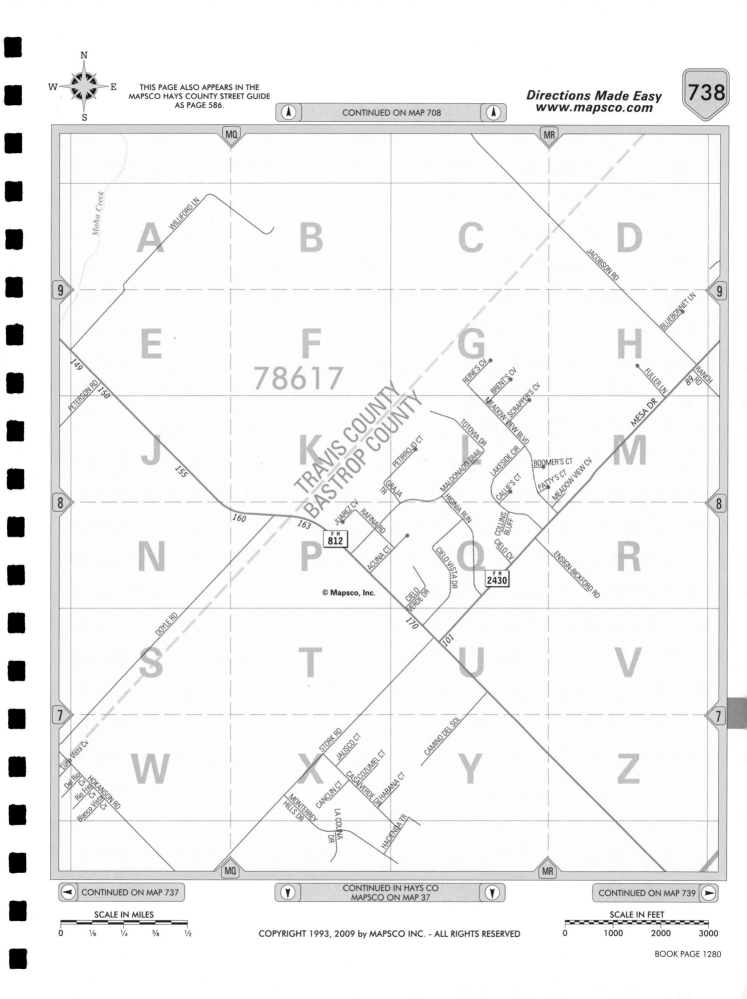

THIS PAGE ALSO APPEARS IN THE
MAPSCO HAYS COUNTY STREET GUIDE
AS PAGE 586.

Directions Made Easy
www.mapsco.com

738

CONTINUED ON MAP 708

MQ MR

A B C D

9 9

Maha Creek

WILLIFORD LN

JACOBSON RD

BLUEBONNET LN

E F G H

78617

149

150

PETERSON RD

RANCH 89 RD

REINE'S CV
BRENT'S CV
SCRAPPER'S CV
MEADOW VIEW BLVD

FULLER LN

MESA DR

TRAVIS COUNTY
BASTROP COUNTY

J K L M

155

PETIRROJO CT

TOTOVIA DR

MALDONADO TRAIL

LAKESIDE CIR

BOOMER'S CT

PATTY'S CT

MEADOW VIEW CV

8 8

160 163

GRAJA TR

JUAREZ CV RAFINARD

HIGINIA RUN

CALLIE'S CT

COLLINS BLUFF

ACUNA CT

FM 812

N P Q R

© Mapsco, Inc.

CIELO VISTA DR

CIELO CV

ENSIGN-BICKFORD RD

FM 2430

CIELO VERDE DR

170 101

DOYLE RD

S T U V

7 7

Luta Vista Cv

Del Rio Cv
Rio Frio Cv
HOKANSON RD
Blanco Vista Cv

W X Y Z

STORK RD

JALISCO CT

CAMINO DEL SOL

CANCUN CT

CASA COZUMEL CT

VERDE DR

HABANA CT

MONTERREY HILLS DR

LA COLINA DR

HACIENDA TR

MQ MR

CONTINUED ON MAP 737

CONTINUED IN HAYS CO
MAPSCO ON MAP 37

CONTINUED ON MAP 739

SCALE IN MILES

0 ⅛ ¼ ⅜ ½

SCALE IN FEET

0 1000 2000 3000

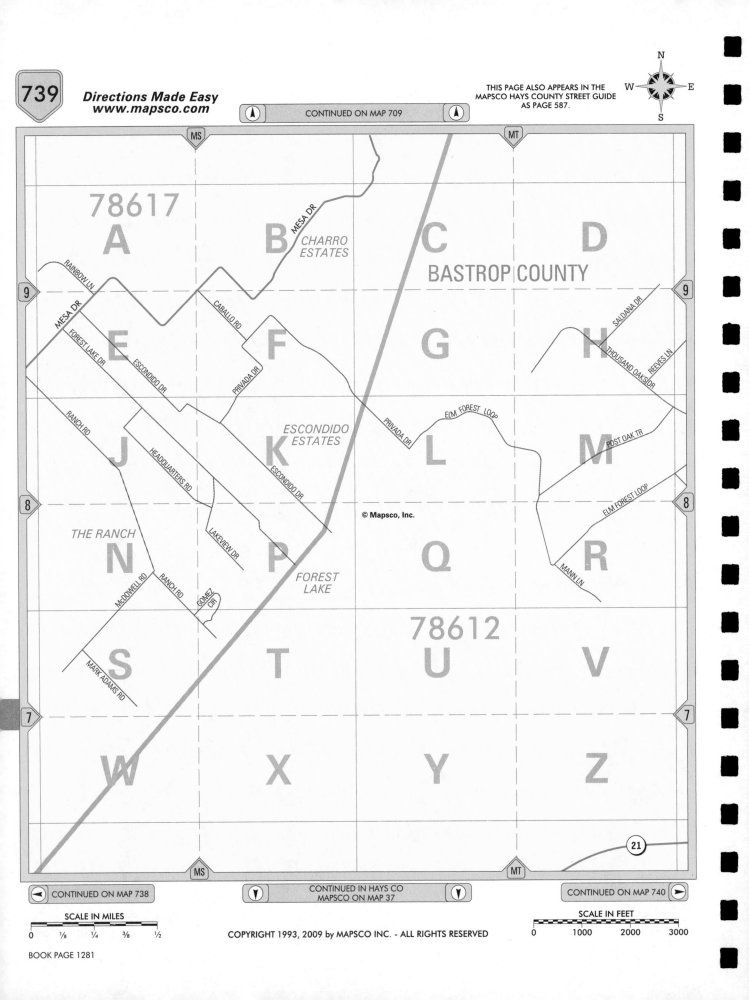

739

Directions Made Easy
www.mapsco.com

THIS PAGE ALSO APPEARS IN THE
MAPSCO HAYS COUNTY STREET GUIDE
AS PAGE 587.

N
W · E
S

CONTINUED ON MAP 709

MS   MT

78617

A   B   CHARRO   C   D
                ESTATES
                               BASTROP COUNTY
9   9
        MESA DR

        RAINBOW LN
MESA DR
                CABALLO RD   SALDANA DR
        FOREST LAKE DR
E   F   G   H
                                                    THOUSAND OAKS DR
        ESCONDIDO DR   REEVES LN
                PRIVADA DR
        RANCH RD
                                        PRIVADA DR   ELM FOREST LOOP
                                                              POST OAK TR
J   K   L   M
        HEADQUARTERS RD   ESCONDIDO
                           ESTATES
8   ESCONDIDO DR   8
                                        © Mapsco, Inc.   ELM FOREST LOOP

        LAKEVIEW DR
THE RANCH
N   P   Q   R
                                                    MANN LN
        McDOWELL RD RANCH RD
                    GOMEZ   FOREST
                    CIR   LAKE
                                        78612
S   T   U   V

        MARK ADAMS RD

7   7

W   X   Y   Z

                                                         21

CONTINUED ON MAP 738

CONTINUED IN HAYS CO
MAPSCO ON MAP 37

CONTINUED ON MAP 740

SCALE IN MILES
0   1/8   1/4   3/8   1/2

SCALE IN FEET
0   1000   2000   3000

BOOK PAGE 1281

THIS PAGE ALSO APPEARS IN THE
MAPSCO HAYS COUNTY STREET GUIDE
AS PAGE 588.

Directions Made Easy
www.mapsco.com

740

N
W E
S

CONTINUED ON MAP 710

A   B   C   D

BASTROP COUNTY

9   9

REEVES LN

E   F   G   H

NORTHSIDE LN

PEARCE LN

Dove Ln

RANGEL RD

THOUSAND
OAKS

78612

J   K   L   M

ELM FOREST LOOP

IRMA RD

MISTYGLEN CV

THOUSAND OAKS DR

© Mapsco, Inc.

F M
535

BROWN LN

8   8

SHADY OAKS LOOP

N   P   Q   R

JENKINS RD

S   T   U   V

MUSTANG CRSG

ELM DR

MAEGAN LN

TERESA LN

HERITAGE
OAKS

PEARCE LN

7   7

MISTY LN

W   X   Y   Z

HERITAGE OAKS DR

JEFFREY DR

Lower
Cedar Creek
Cemetery

WRIGHT DR

WYERS PL

BARTON LN

BARTON LN

PEARCE LN

21

WATTS LN

Cedar
Creek

ES

MU

MV

Upper
Cedar Creek
Cemetery

F M
535

CONTINUED ON MAP 739

CONTINUED IN HAYS CO
MAPSCO ON MAP 37

CONTINUED ON MAP 741

SCALE IN MILES

0   1/8   1/4   3/8   1/2

SCALE IN FEET

0   1000   2000   3000

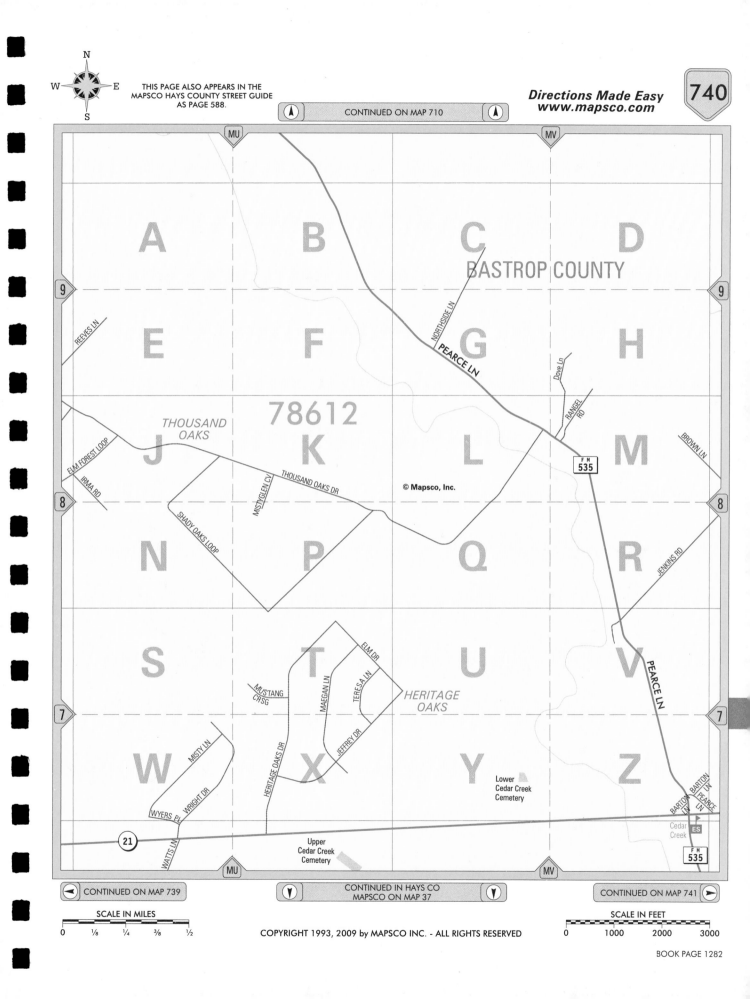

741

Directions Made Easy
www.mapsco.com

THIS PAGE ALSO APPEARS IN THE
MAPSCO HAYS COUNTY STREET GUIDE
AS PAGE 589.

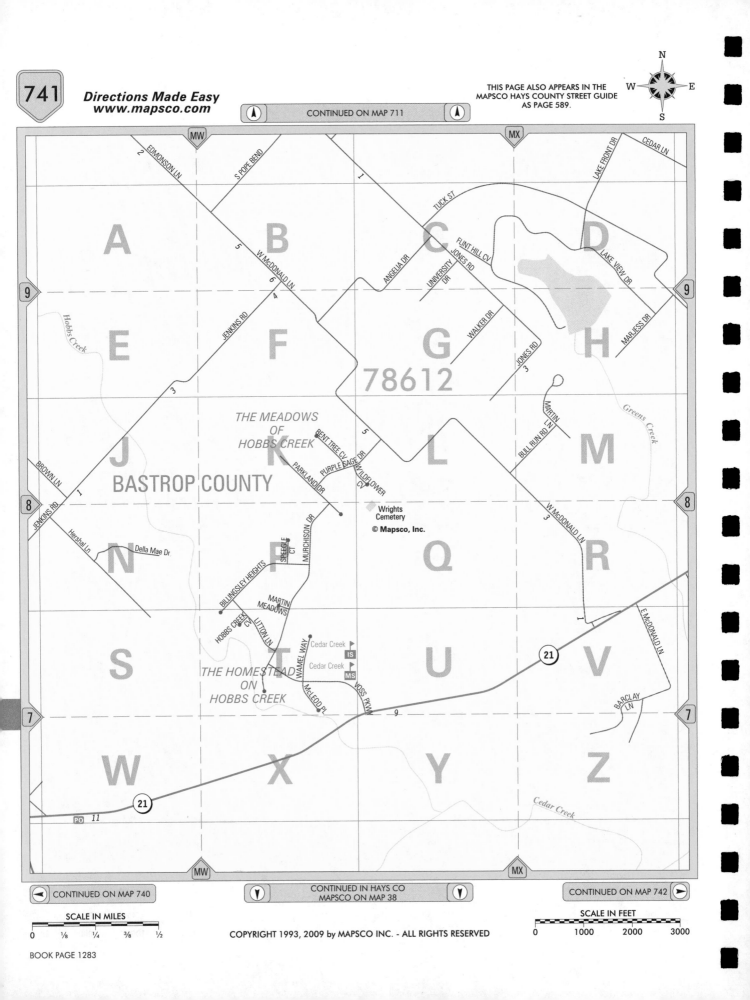

CONTINUED ON MAP 711

CONTINUED ON MAP 740

CONTINUED IN HAYS CO
MAPSCO ON MAP 38

CONTINUED ON MAP 742

78612

THE MEADOWS
OF
HOBBS CREEK

BASTROP COUNTY

Wrights
Cemetery

© Mapsco, Inc.

BILLINGSLEY HEIGHTS

MARTIN
MEADOWS

THE HOMESTEAD
ON
HOBBS CREEK

SCALE IN MILES

0   1/8   1/4   3/8   1/2

SCALE IN FEET

0   1000   2000   3000

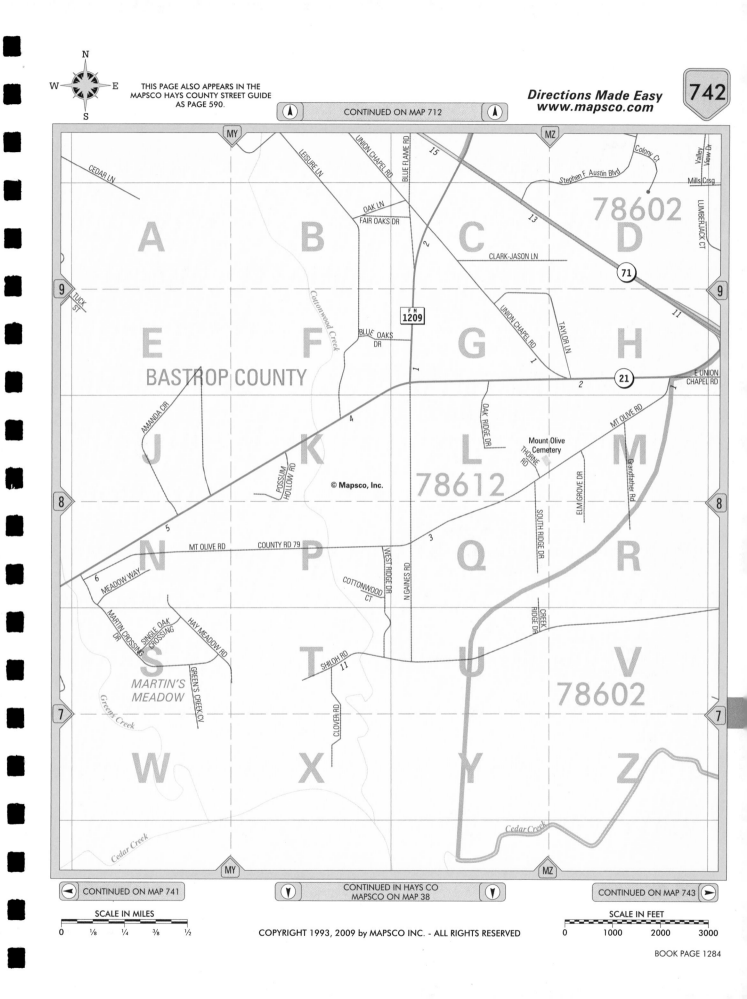

Directions Made Easy
www.mapsco.com

THIS PAGE ALSO APPEARS IN THE
MAPSCO HAYS COUNTY STREET GUIDE
AS PAGE 590.

N
W E
S

CONTINUED ON MAP 712

MY

MZ

CEDAR LN

LEISURE LN

UNION CHAPEL RD

BLUE FLAME RD

15

Stephen F. Austin Blvd

Colony Ct

Valley View Dr

Mills Crsg

78602

A

OAK LN
FAIR OAKS DR

B

13

C

CLARK-JASON LN

D

LUMBERJACK CT

9

TUCK ST

9

2

UNION CHAPEL RD

TAYLOR LN

71

11

F M
1209

E

Cottonwood Creek

BLUE OAKS DR

F

G

1

H

BASTROP COUNTY

1

2

21

E UNION
CHAPEL RD

AMANDA CIR

4

OAK RIDGE DR

Mount Olive
Cemetery

MT OLIVE RD

THORNE RD

ELM GROVE DR

Grandfather Rd

J

POSSUM HOLLOW RD

K

© Mapsco, Inc.

L

78612

M

8

SOUTH RIDGE DR

8

5

3

N

MT OLIVE RD

COUNTY RD 79

WEST RIDGE DR

N GAINES RD

P

Q

R

CREEK RIDGE DR

6

MEADOW WAY

COTTONWOOD CT

MARTIN CROSSING DR

SINGLE OAK CROSSING

HAY MEADOW RD

S

GREEN'S CREEK CV

T

SHILOH RD

11

U

V

78602

MARTIN'S
MEADOW

Greens Creek

CLOVER RD

7

7

W

X

Y

Z

Cedar Creek

Cedar Creek

MY

MZ

CONTINUED ON MAP 741

CONTINUED IN HAYS CO
MAPSCO ON MAP 38

CONTINUED ON MAP 743

SCALE IN MILES

0   1/8   1/4   3/8   1/2

SCALE IN FEET

0   1000   2000   3000

BOOK PAGE 1284

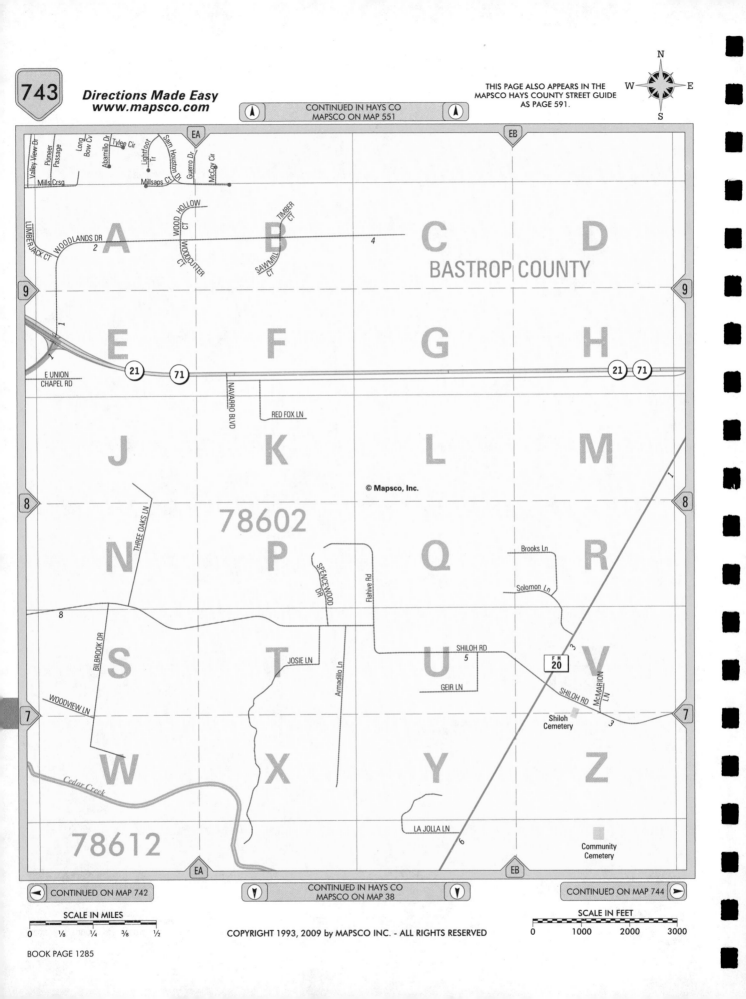

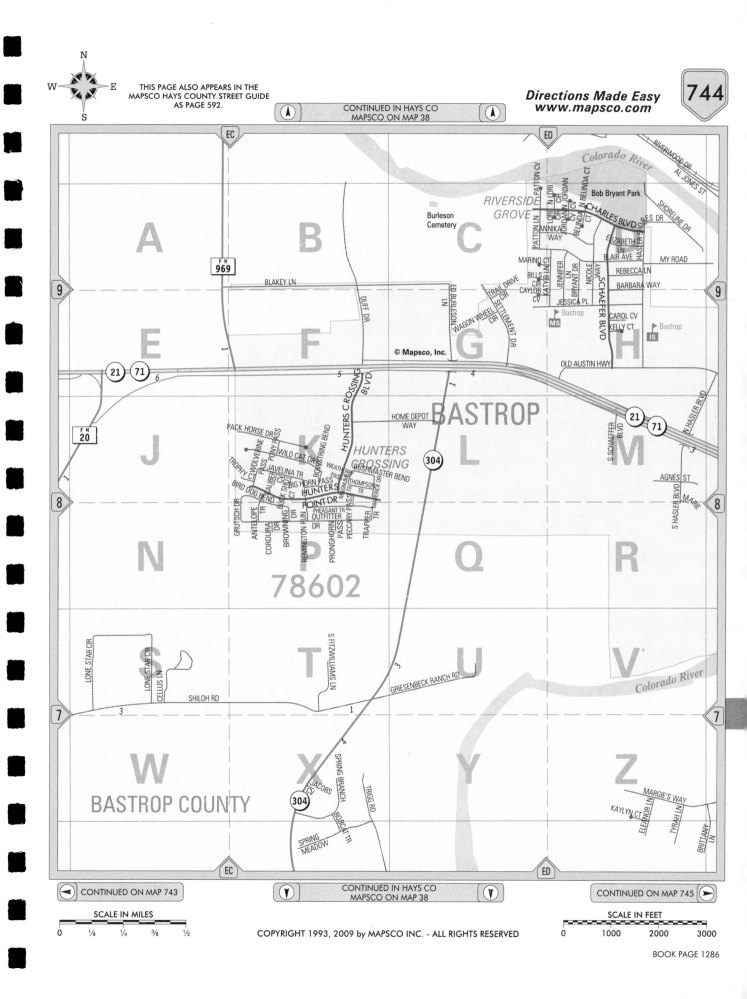

N
W E
S

THIS PAGE ALSO APPEARS IN THE
MAPSCO HAYS COUNTY STREET GUIDE
AS PAGE 592.

Directions Made Easy
www.mapsco.com

CONTINUED IN HAYS CO
MAPSCO ON MAP 38

EC

ED

Colorado River

RIVERWOOD DR

AL JONES ST

Bob Bryant Park

RIVERSIDE
GROVE

Burleson
Cemetery

A

B

C

SHORELINE DR

PATTON CV
PATTON LN
LORI N LORI CIR
JORDAN JORDAN
CIR CV
ANNIKA WAY
BELINDA N BELINDA CT
CHARLES BLVD
ELIZABETH LN
BLAIR AVE

FM 969

BLAKEY LN

DUFF DR

ED BURLESON LN

MARINO CT
BILLS CIR
CAYLOR CV
KATY LN

JENNIFER LN
BRYANT DR
NICOLE WAY
SCHAEFER BLVD

MY ROAD
REBECCA LN
BARBARA WAY

9

9

E

F

G

H

WAGON WHEEL CIR
SETTLEMENT DR
TRAIL DRIVE

JESSICA PL

Bastrop
MS

CAROL CV
KELLY CT

Bastrop
IS

© Mapsco, Inc.

OLD AUSTIN HWY

21 71

6

1

5

HUNTERS CROSSING BLVD

1

4

BASTROP

21 71

3

N HASLER BLVD

FM 20

HOME DEPOT WAY

HUNTERS
CROSSING

S SCHAEFER BLVD

J

PACK HORSE DR
WILD CAT DR
TWO WOLVERINE PASS
PONY PASS
BOWSTRING BEND

K

BUSHMASTER BEND
WEATHERBY PASS
MAGNUM PASS
THOMPSON TR

L

M

8

TROPHY CT
JAVELINA TR
CALIBER CV
BIG HORN PASS
BUCK SHOT CT
HUNTERS POINT DR

304

AGNES ST
S HASLER BLVD MARIE

8

BIRD DOG BEND
ANTELOPE TR
CORDURA DR
BROWNING DR
REMINGTON RUN
PRONGHORN
PHEASANT TR
OUTFITTER DR
PECCARY PASS TR
MAVERICK DR
TRAPPER TR

GRUTSCH DR

N

P

Q

R

78602

LONE STAR CIR
LONE STAR CIR
CELLUS LN

S

S FITZWILLIAMS LN

T

U

V

Colorado River

GRIESENBECK RANCH RD

SHILOH RD

3

1

3

7

7

W

X

Y

Z

BASTROP COUNTY

JACOBS CV
304
SPRING BRANCH
BOBCAT TR
SPRING MEADOW

TRIGG RD

4

MARGIE'S WAY
KAYLYN CT
ELEANOR CT
TYRAH LN
BRITTANY LN

EC

ED

CONTINUED ON MAP 743

CONTINUED IN HAYS CO
MAPSCO ON MAP 38

CONTINUED ON MAP 745

SCALE IN MILES

0   ⅛   ¼   ⅜   ½

SCALE IN FEET

0   1000   2000   3000

THIS PAGE ALSO APPEARS IN THE MAPSCO HAYS COUNTY STREET GUIDE AS PAGE 593.

N W E S

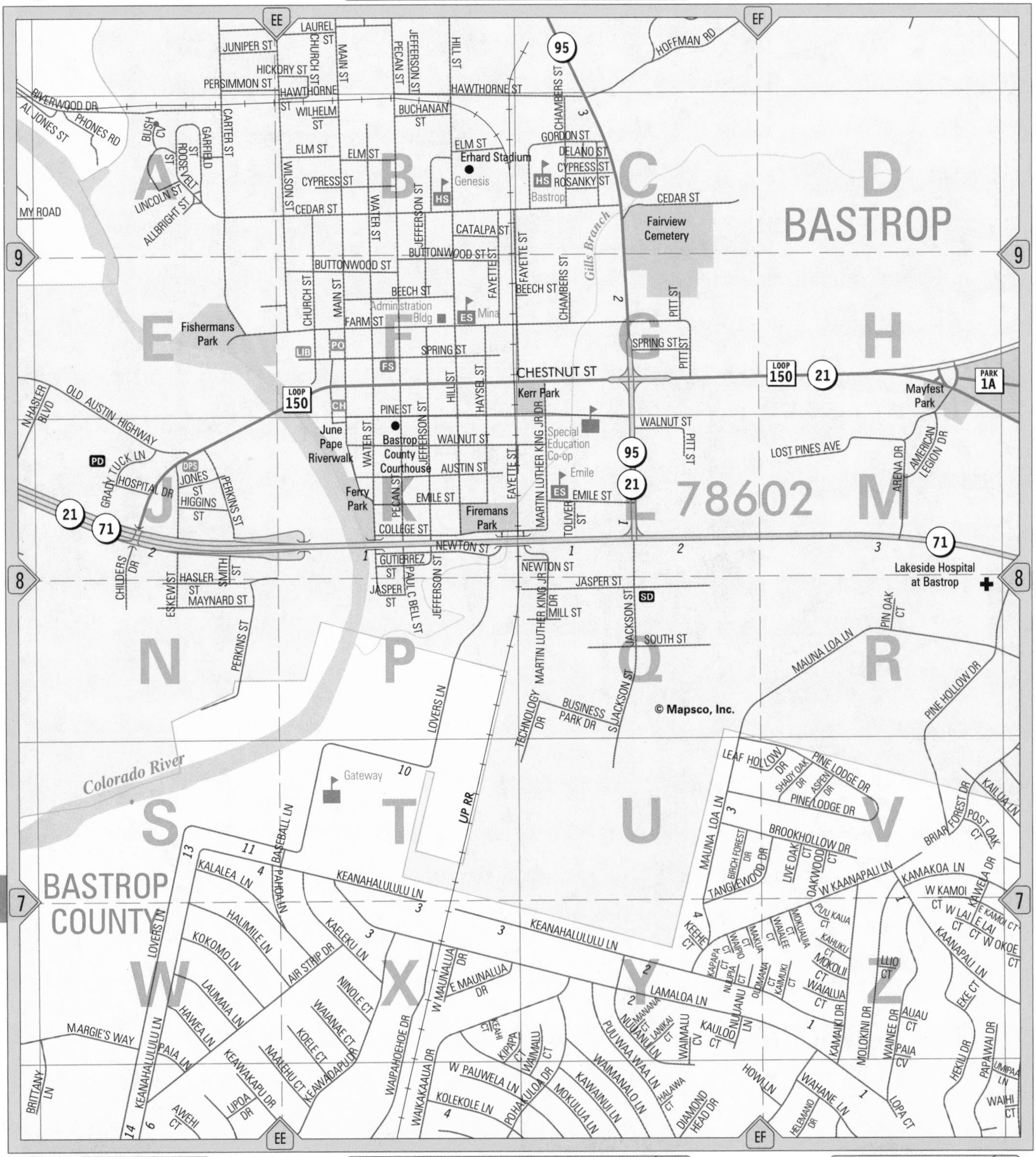

CONTINUED ON MAP 715

EE
EF

JUNIPER ST
LAUREL
HICKORY ST
CHURCH ST
MAIN ST
PECAN ST
JEFFERSON ST
HILL ST
95
HOFFMAN RD
PERSIMMON ST
HAWTHORNE ST
HAWTHORNE ST
CHAMBERS ST
RIVERWOOD DR
PHONES RD
BUSH CV
GARFIELD ST
CARTER ST
WILHELM ST
BUCHANAN ST
AL JONES ST
ROOSEVELT ST
ELM ST
ELM ST
ELM ST
GORDON ST
LINCOLN ST
DELANO ST
A
B
CYPRESS ST
C
CEDAR ST
D
BASTROP
MY ROAD
ALLBRIGHT ST
WILSON ST
CYPRESS ST
Erhard Stadium
Genesis
ROSANKY ST
HS Bastrop
CEDAR ST
CATALPA ST
WATER ST
CEDAR ST
BUTTONWOOD ST
BUTTONWOOD ST
FAYETTE ST
Fairview Cemetery
9
9
CHAMBERS ST
PITT ST
E
Fishermans Park
CHURCH ST
MAIN ST
FARM ST
BEECH ST
Administration Bldg
ES Mina
F
BEECH ST
SPRING ST
G
SPRING ST
H
LIB
PO
FS
HILL ST
HAYSEL ST
CHESTNUT ST
Kerr Park
LOOP 150
21
PARK 1A
LOOP 150
CH
PINE ST
WATER ST
JEFFERSON ST
June Pape Riverwalk
Bastrop County Courthouse
WALNUT ST
Special Education Co-op
WALNUT ST
Mayfest Park
LOST PINES AVE
ARENA DR
AMERICAN LEGION DR
95
78602
AUSTIN ST
FAYETTE ST
MARTIN LUTHER KING JR DR
Emile
21
I
J
Ferry Park
K
EMILE ST
ES EMILE ST
L
M
COLLEGE ST
Firemans Park
TOLIVER ST
21
71
71
Lakeside Hospital at Bastrop
8
8
N HASLER BLVD
OLD AUSTIN HIGHWAY
GRADY TUCK LN
HOSPITAL DR
JONES ST
HIGGINS ST
PERKINS ST
NEWTON ST
NEWTON ST
PD
DPS
GUTIERREZ ST
JASPER ST
JASPER ST
CHILDERS DR
ESKEW ST
HASLER ST
SMITH ST
MAYNARD ST
PAUL C BELL ST
JEFFERSON ST
MILL ST
JACKSON ST
SD
PIN OAK CT
MAUNA LOA LN
N
PERKINS ST
P
SOUTH ST
Q
R
PINE HOLLOW DR
Business Park Dr
© Mapsco, Inc.
TECHNOLOGY DR
BUSINESS PARK DR
JACKSON ST
LEAF HOLLOW DR
SHADY OAK
PINE LODGE DR
Colorado River
Gateway
10
LOVERS LN
UP RR
S
T
U
PINE LODGE DR
BIRCH FOREST DR
BROOKHOLLOW DR
BRIAR FOREST DR
POST OAK
KAILUA LN
MAUNA LOA LN
TANGLEWOOD DR
LIVE OAK
OAKWOOD
W KAANAPALI DR
KAMAKOA LN
V
BASTROP COUNTY
13
11
BASEBALL LN
PAPOHAIN
KEANAHALULULU LN
KEANAHALULULU LN
KEEHE CT
W KAMOI CT
W LAI E LAI CT
W OKOE CT
KAANAPALI LN
KALALEA LN
HALIMILE LN
KAELEKU LN
W MAUNALUA DR
E MAUNALUA DR
LAMALOA LN
PUU KAUA
KAHUKU
MOKUALIA
WAIALEE
PUU KAUA
MOKOLII
LLIO CT
EKE CT
KOKOMO LN
NINOLE CT
LAMALOA LN
MANANA
NIUPAA CT
NIUPAA CT
WAIALUA CT
KAMAIKI CT
AUAU CT
W
LAUMAIA LN
AIR STRIP DR
WAIANAE CT
KOELE CT
WAIPAHOEHOE DR
X
KIPAPA
WAIMALU
WAIMALU DR
KIPAPA
WAIMANALO LN
NUUANU LN
LANIKAI
WAIMANU CT
KAULOO CT
Y
Z
KAMANA
WAIAHA
WAIALUA
WAINEE DR
PAIA CV
MOLOKINI DR
WAINEE DR
MARGIE'S WAY
HAWEA LN
KEAWAKAPU DR
NAALEHU CT
KEANAADAPU DR
WAIKAKAUA DR
W PAUWELA LN
POHAKULOA DR
KAWAINUI LN
MOKUUA LN
HALAWA CT
HOWLN
WAHANE LN
LOPA CT
KAPAUA
AWEHI CT
LIPOA DR
KOLEKOLE LN
DIAMOND HEAD DR
HELEMANO DR
KAMAIKI DR
HEKILI DR
UMIPAA LN
PAPAWAI DR
WAIHI
BRITTANY LN
KEANAHALULULU LN
LIPAA LN
LOVERS LN
14
6
EE
EF

CONTINUED ON MAP 744
CONTINUED ON MAP 775
CONTINUED ON MAP 746

7
7

SCALE IN MILES
0   1/8   1/4   3/8   1/2

SCALE IN FEET
0   1000   2000   3000

COPYRIGHT 1993, 2009 by MAPSCO INC. - ALL RIGHTS RESERVED

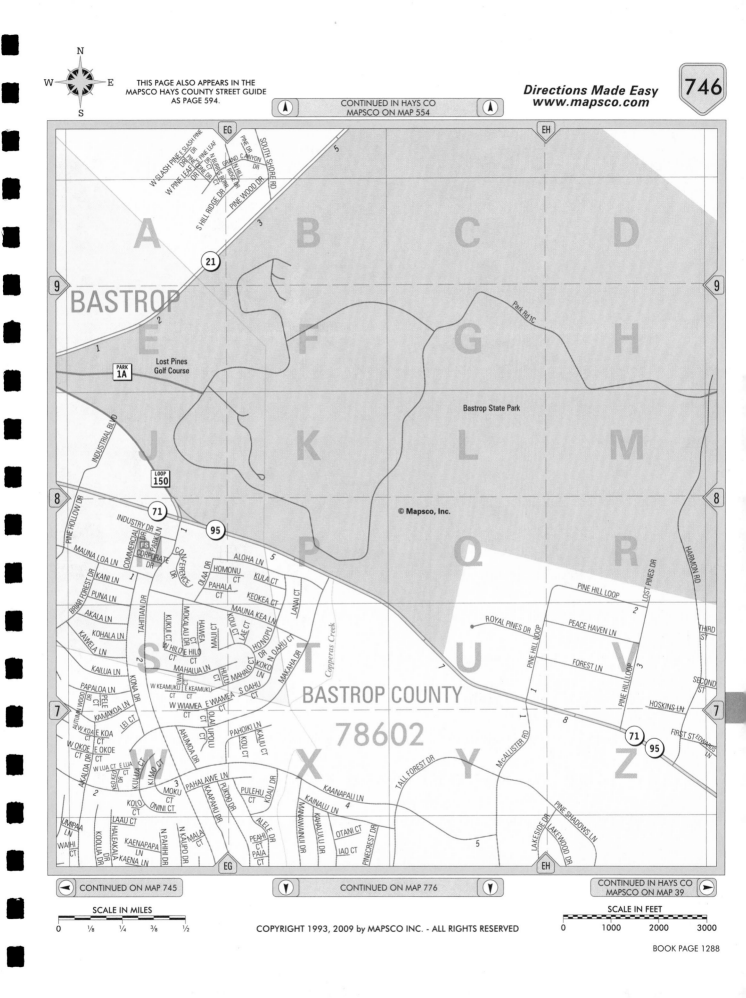

Directions Made Easy
www.mapsco.com

CONTINUED ON MAP 732

THIS PAGE ALSO APPEARS IN THE
MAPSCO HAYS COUNTY STREET GUIDE
AS PAGE 620.

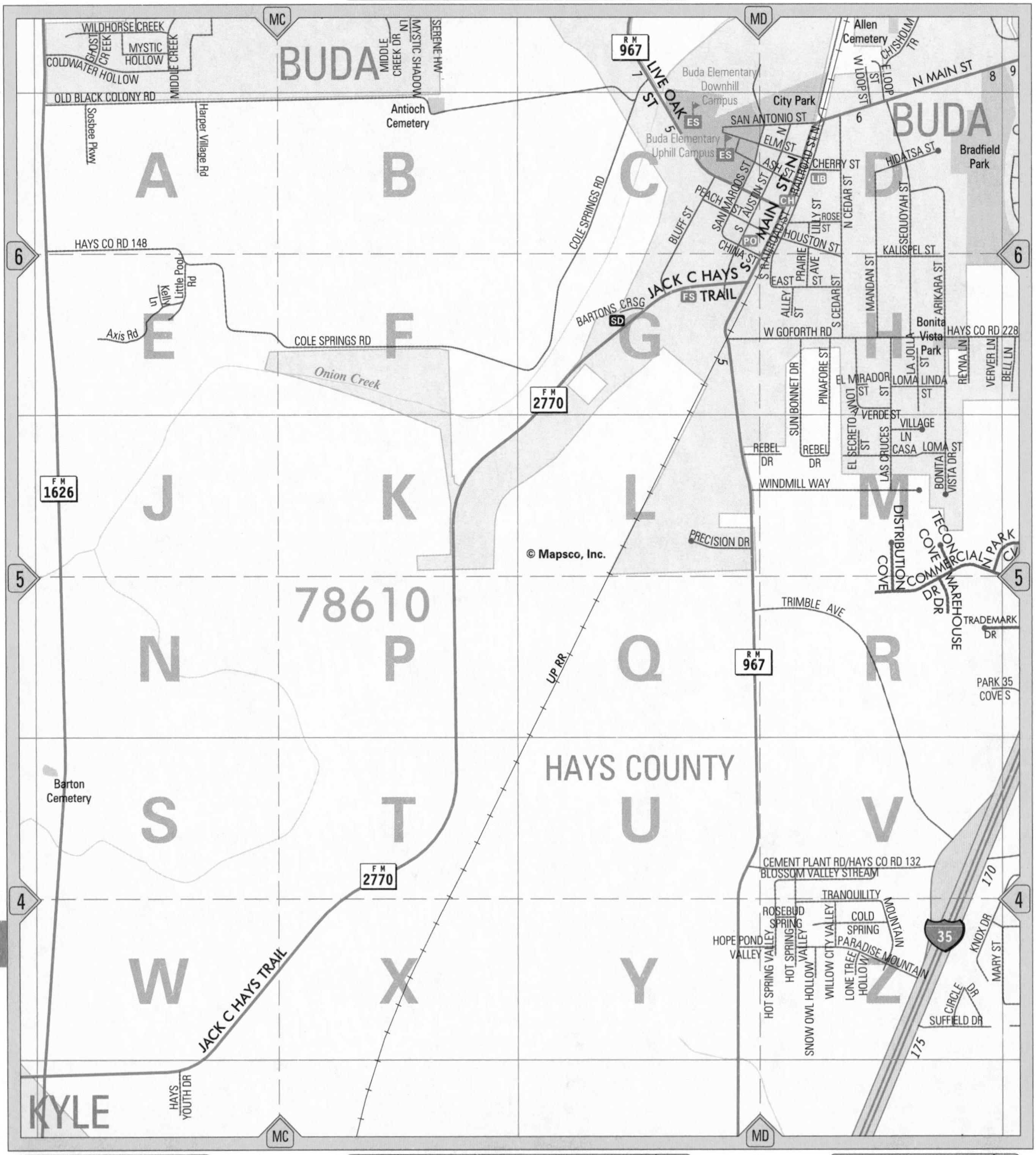

N W E S

MC

BUDA

MD

WILDHORSE CREEK
GHOST CREEK
MYSTIC HOLLOW
COLDWATER HOLLOW
MIDDLE CREEK
MIDDLE CREEK DR
MYSTIC SHADOW
SERENE HW

RM 967

Allen Cemetery
CHISHOLM TR
W LOOP ST
E LOOP ST
N MAIN ST

9

OLD BLACK COLONY RD

ANTIOCH Cemetery

LIVE OAK ST

Buda Elementary Downhill Campus

City Park

San Antonio St

BUDA

8

Bradfield Park

HARPER VILLAGE RD
SOSBEE PKWY

A

B

C

Buda Elementary Uphill Campus
ES

ELM ST
ASH ST
CHERRY ST
HIDATSA ST

D

6

HAYS CO RD 148

Little Pool Rd
KELLY

Axis Rd

E

COLE SPRINGS RD

F

BLUFF ST
SAN MARCOS ST
PEACH ST
CHINA ST
S MAIN ST
AUSTIN ST
HOUSTON ST
PRAIRIE
EAST AVE
S CEDAR ST
N CEDAR ST
LILY ST
ROSE
MANDAN ST
KALISPEL ST
SEQUOYAH ST
ARIKARA ST
REYNA LN
VERVER LN
BELL LN

PO
CH
LIB

JACK C HAYS TRAIL
FS

BARTONS CRSG
SD

W GOFORTH RD

Bonita Vista Park
HAYS CO RD 228

6

Onion Creek

G

SUN BONNET DR
PINAFORE LN
EL MIRADOR
LOMA LINDA ST
LA JOLLA
VERDE ST

Loma Linda ST

H

FM 2770

J

K

L

REBEL DR
REBEL DR
EL SECRETO
LAS CRUCES
VILLAGE LN
CASA
LOMA ST
Bonita Vista DR

WINDMILL WAY

M

DISTRIBUTION COVE
TECONIC PARK
COMMERCIAL PARK
WAREHOUSE COVE DR
DR

FM 1626

© Mapsco, Inc.

PRECISION DR

78610

UP RR

N

P

Q

RM 967

R

TRIMBLE AVE

5

TRADEMARK DR

PARK 35 COVE S

Barton Cemetery

HAYS COUNTY

S

T

U

V

W

4

FM 2770

CEMENT PLANT RD/HAYS CO RD 132
BLOSSOM VALLEY STREAM

TRANQUILITY

ROSEBUD SPRING
COLD SPRING

MOUNTAIN

170

HOPE POND VALLEY

WILLOW CITY VALLEY
PARADISE MOUNTAIN

35

KNOX DR
MARY ST

JACK C HAYS TRAIL

HAYS YOUTH DR

HOT SPRING VALLEY
HOT SPRING VALLEY
SNOW OWL HOLLOW
LONE TREE HOLLOW

X

Y

Z

CIRCLE DR
SUFFIELD DR

175

KYLE

MC

MD

CONTINUED IN HAYS CO MAPSCO ON MAP 35

CONTINUED IN HAYS CO MAPSCO ON MAP 660

CONTINUED ON MAP 763

SCALE IN MILES

0   1/8   1/4   3/8   1/2

SCALE IN FEET

0   1000   2000   3000

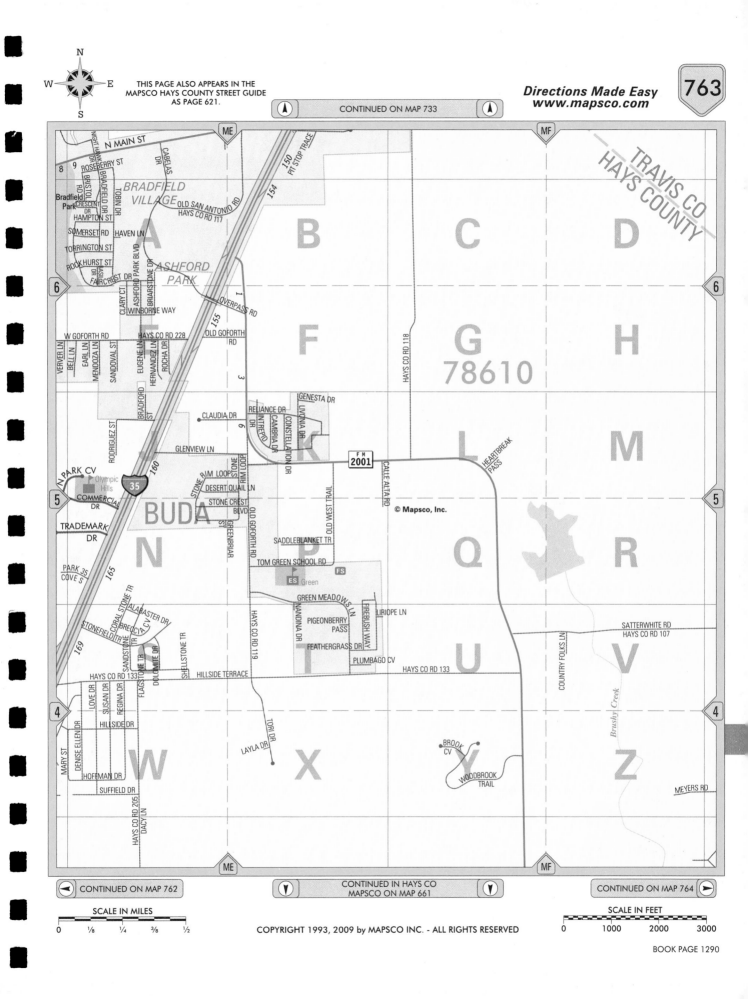

THIS PAGE ALSO APPEARS IN THE
MAPSCO HAYS COUNTY STREET GUIDE
AS PAGE 621.

Directions Made Easy
www.mapsco.com

CONTINUED ON MAP 733

TRAVIS CO
HAYS COUNTY

N MAIN ST
ME
MF

NIGHT HAWK
ROSEBERRY ST
CABELAS DR
PIT STOP TRACE
150

BRISTOL
BRADFIELD DR
TOBIN DR
154

BRADFIELD
VILLAGE

Bradfield
Park
CRESCENT DR
HAMPTON ST
OLD SAN ANTONIO RD
HAYS CO RD 117

A
B
C
D

SOMERSET RD
HAVEN LN

TORRINGTON ST

ROOKHURST ST
OASIS DR
FAIRCREST DR
ASHFORD PARK BLVD
ASHFORD
PARK
BRIARSTONE DR

6
6

CLARY CT
WINBORNE WAY
1
OVERPASS RD
155

W GOFORTH RD
HAYS CO RD 228
OLD GOFORTH
RD

VERVER LN
BELL LN
EARL LN
MENDOZA LN
EUGENE LN
HERNANDEZ LN
ROCHA DR
SANDOVAL ST

E
F
G
H

3

78610

BRADFORD ST

RODRIGUEZ ST
CLAUDIA DR
RELIANCE DR
GENESTA DR
LIVONIA DR

6
INTREPID
CAMBRIA DR
CONSTELLATION DR

GLENVIEW LN

I
J
K
L
M

N PARK CV
160
35
Olympic
Hills
COMMERCIAL DR

STONE RIM LOOP
DESERT QUAIL LN
WALLINGTON

STONE CREST BLVD
CALLE ALTA RD
HEARTBREAK PASS

FM
2001

© Mapsco, Inc.

5
5

TRADEMARK DR

BUDA

GREENBRIAR ST
OLD GOFORTH RD
OLD WEST TRAIL
SADDLEBLANKET TR

N
Q
R

PARK 35
COVE S
165

TOM GREEN SCHOOL RD
FS
ES   Green

GREEN MEADOWS LN
LIRIOPE LN

SATTERWHITE RD
HAYS CO RD 107

ALABASTER DR
CORAL STONE TR
BRECCIA CV
PIGEONBERRY PASS
NANDINA DR
FIREBUSH WAY

STONEFIELD TR
SANDSTONE TR
SHELLSTONE TR
HAYS CO RD 119
FEATHERGRASS DR

COUNTRY FOLKS LN

Brushy Creek

169
DOLOMITE DR
FLAGSTONE TR
PLUMBAGO CV
HAYS CO RD 133

S
T
U
V

HAYS CO RD 133
HILLSIDE TERRACE
HAYS CO RD 133

LOVE DR
SUSAN DR
REGINA DR

4
4

MARY ST
DENISE ELLEN DR
HILLSIDE DR
TORI DR

HOFFMAN DR
LAYLA DR
BROOK CV

W
X
Y
Z

SUFFIELD DR
WOODBROOK TRAIL

HAYS CO RD 205
DACY LN
MEYERS RD

ME
MF

CONTINUED ON MAP 762

CONTINUED IN HAYS CO
MAPSCO ON MAP 661

CONTINUED ON MAP 764

SCALE IN MILES
0   1/8   1/4   3/8   1/2

SCALE IN FEET
0   1000   2000   3000

COPYRIGHT 1993, 2009 by MAPSCO INC. - ALL RIGHTS RESERVED

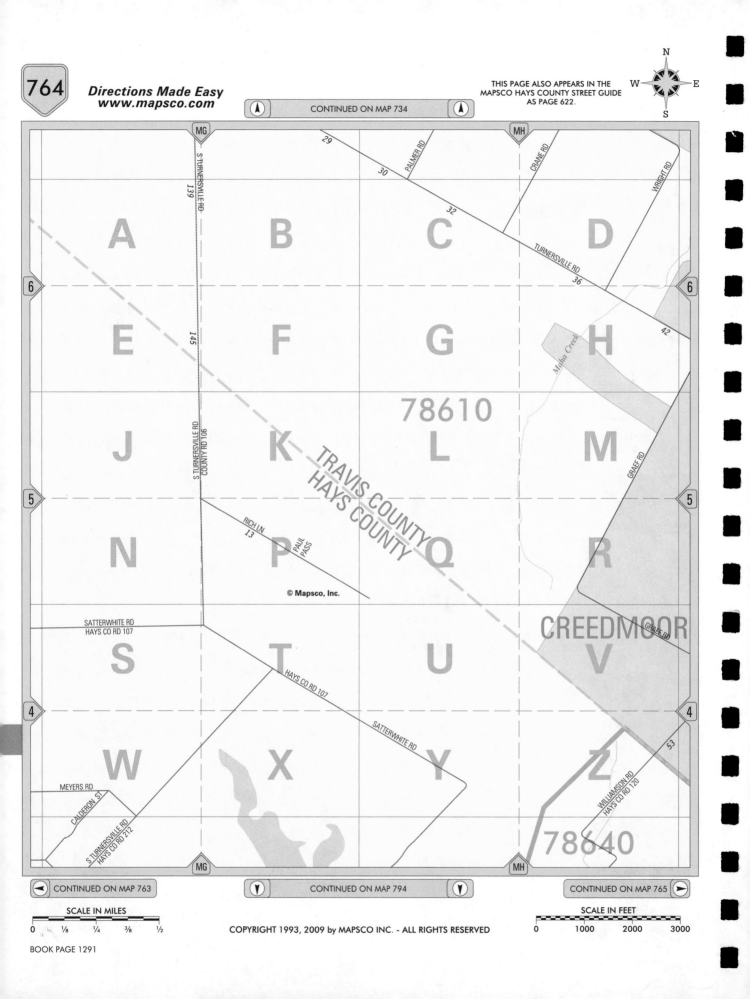

764

Directions Made Easy
www.mapsco.com

THIS PAGE ALSO APPEARS IN THE
MAPSCO HAYS COUNTY STREET GUIDE
AS PAGE 622.

CONTINUED ON MAP 734

MG

MH

29
30
PALMER RD
CRANE RD
WRIGHT RD
32

S TURNERSVILLE RD
139

A
B
C
D

TURNERSVILLE RD
36

6
6

E
F
G
H
42

Maha Creek

145

78610

J
K
L
M

S TURNERSVILLE RD
COUNTY RD 106

GRAFF RD

5
5

RICH LN
13

PAUL PASS

N
P
Q
R

TRAVIS COUNTY
HAYS COUNTY

© Mapsco, Inc.

CREEDMOOR

SATTERWHITE RD
HAYS CO RD 107

GRAFF RD

S
T
U
V

HAYS CO RD 107

SATTERWHITE RD

4
4
53

MEYERS RD

W
X
Y
Z

CALDERON ST

WILLIAMSON RD
HAYS CO RD 120

S TURNERSVILLE RD
HAYS CO RD 212

78640

MG

MH

CONTINUED ON MAP 763

CONTINUED ON MAP 794

CONTINUED ON MAP 765

SCALE IN MILES

0   ⅛   ¼   ⅜   ½

SCALE IN FEET

0   1000   2000   3000

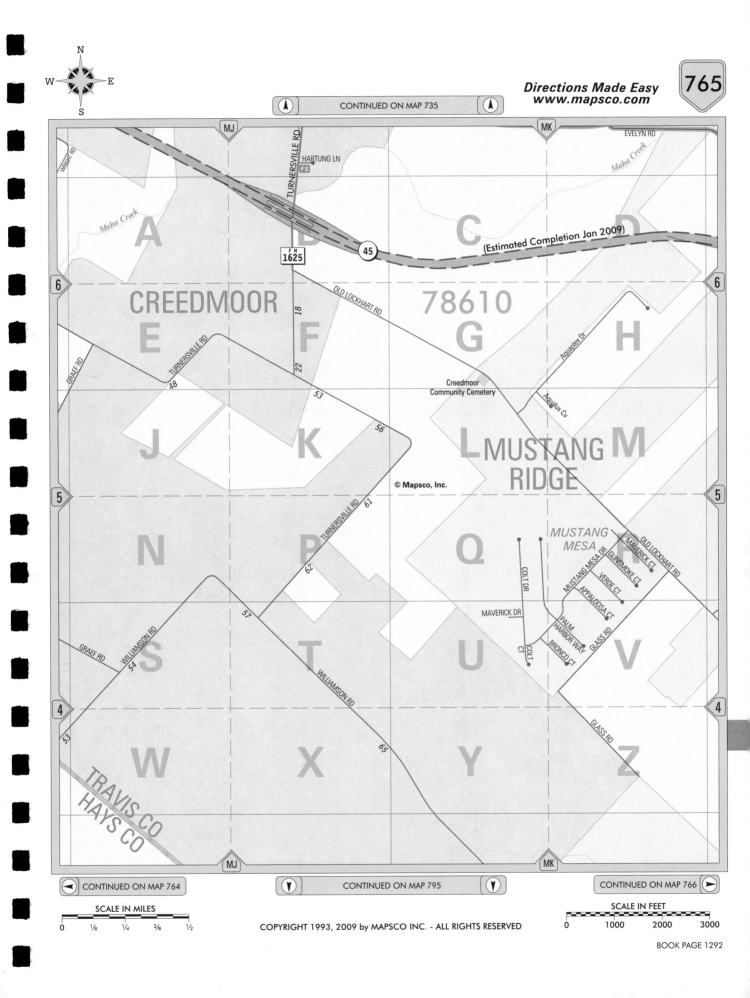

CONTINUED ON MAP 735

N
W E
S

MJ

MK

EVELYN RD

Maha Creek

WRIGHT RD

TURNERSVILLE RD

HARTUNG LN
FS

Maha Creek

A

D

C

(Estimated Completion Jan 2009)

45

6

6

FM
1625

CREEDMOOR

OLD LOCKHART RD

78610

18

E

F

G

H

Aquaplex Dr

GRAEF RD

TURNERSVILLE RD

48

22

53

Creedmoor
Community Cemetery

Aquilux Cv

56

J

K

© Mapsco, Inc.

L MUSTANG M
RIDGE

5

5

N

TURNERSVILLE RD

61

P

Q

MUSTANG
MESA

OLD LOCKHART RD

MAVERICK CT

MUSTANG MESA DR

GUNSMOKE CT

62

COLT DR

VERDE CT

APPALOOSA CT

MAVERICK DR

GLASS RD

57

PALM
HARBOR WAY

GRAEF RD

WILLIAMSON RD

S

T

U

COLT
CT

BRONCO CT

V

54

WILLIAMSON RD

4

4

65

53

W

X

Y

GLASS RD

Z

TRAVIS CO

HAYS CO

MJ

MK

CONTINUED ON MAP 764

CONTINUED ON MAP 795

CONTINUED ON MAP 766

SCALE IN MILES
0   1/8   1/4   3/8   1/2

SCALE IN FEET
0   1000   2000   3000

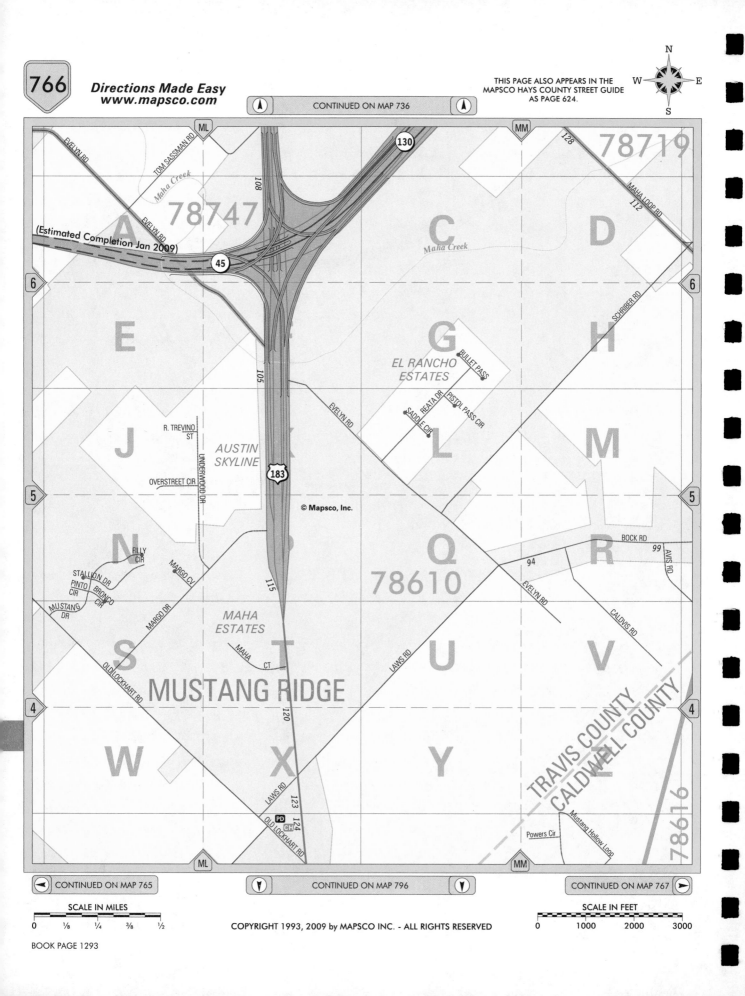

766

Directions Made Easy
www.mapsco.com

THIS PAGE ALSO APPEARS IN THE
MAPSCO HAYS COUNTY STREET GUIDE
AS PAGE 624.

CONTINUED ON MAP 736

78719

78747

C

D

A

(Estimated Completion Jan 2009)

45

6

6

E

G

H

EL RANCHO
ESTATES

Bullet Pass

Evelyn Rd

Reata Dr

Pistol Pass Cir

J

AUSTIN
SKYLINE

Saddle Cir

R. TREVINO ST

UNDERWOOD DR

K

L

M

OVERSTREET CIR

183

5

5

© Mapsco, Inc.

N

Filly Cir

Margo Cv

Q

Bock Rd

99

Avis Rd

78610

94

R

Stallion Dr

Evelyn Rd

Pinto Cir

Bronco Cir

Mustang Dr

Margo Dr

MAHA
ESTATES

Caldvis Rd

S

Maha Ct

T

Laws Rd

U

V

MUSTANG RIDGE

Old Lockhart Rd

115

120

4

4

TRAVIS COUNTY
CALDWELL COUNTY

W

X

Y

78616

Laws Rd

123

124

PD

CH

Powers Cir

Mustang Hollow Loop

Old Lockhart Rd

CONTINUED ON MAP 765

CONTINUED ON MAP 796

CONTINUED ON MAP 767

SCALE IN MILES

0   ⅛   ¼   ⅜   ½

SCALE IN FEET

0   1000   2000   3000

BOOK PAGE 1293

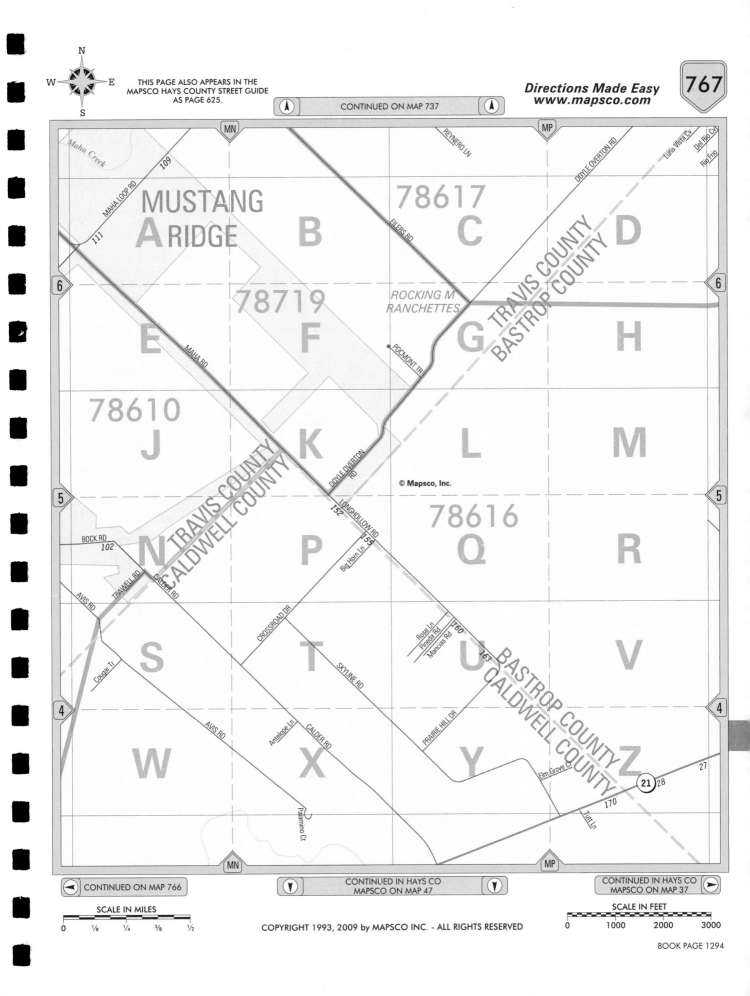

THIS PAGE ALSO APPEARS IN THE
MAPSCO HAYS COUNTY STREET GUIDE
AS PAGE 625.

Directions Made Easy
www.mapsco.com

767

CONTINUED ON MAP 737

MN

MP

Maha Creek

109

MAHA LOOP RD

MUSTANG
A RIDGE

B

REYNERO LN

78617

C

DOYLE OVERTON RD

Luna Vista Cv

Del Rio Cir

Rio Frio

TRAVIS COUNTY

BASTROP COUNTY

D

111

6

6

EILERS RD

78719

E

MAHA RD

F

ROCKING M
RANCHETTES

POCMONT TR

G

H

78610

J

K

DOYLE OVERTON RD

© Mapsco, Inc.

L

M

TRAVIS COUNTY

CALDWELL COUNTY

152

LONGHOLLOW RD

153

78616

5

5

BOCK RD

102

N

TRAWELL RD

CALDER RD

P

Big Horn Ln

Q

R

AVIS RD

CROSSROAD DR

Rose Ln

Pineda Rd

Mancias Rd

160

163

S

Cougar Tr

T

SKYLINE RD

PRAIRIE HILL DR

U

BASTROP COUNTY

CALDWELL COUNTY

V

4

4

AVIS RD

Antelope Ln

CALDER RD

W

X

Y

Elm Grove Ct

Z

21

28

27

Palamino Ct

Tuff Ln

170

MN

MP

CONTINUED ON MAP 766

CONTINUED IN HAYS CO
MAPSCO ON MAP 47

CONTINUED IN HAYS CO
MAPSCO ON MAP 37

SCALE IN MILES

0   1/8   1/4   3/8   1/2

SCALE IN FEET

0   1000   2000   3000

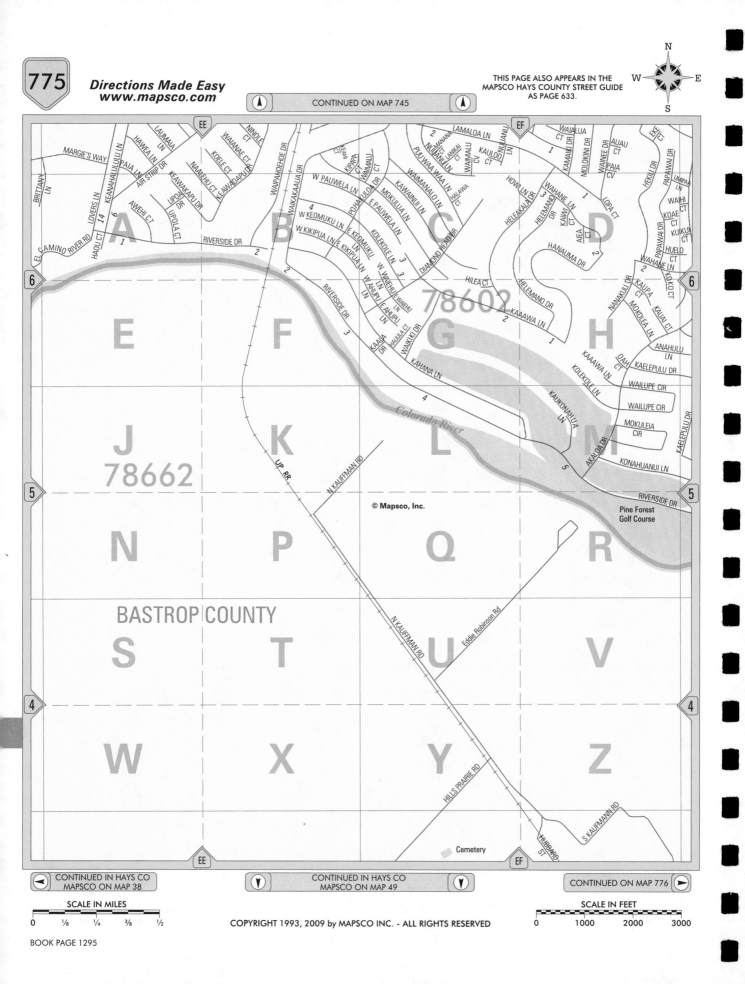

775

Directions Made Easy
www.mapsco.com

THIS PAGE ALSO APPEARS IN THE
MAPSCO HAYS COUNTY STREET GUIDE
AS PAGE 633.

N
W E
S

CONTINUED ON MAP 745

EE
EF

MARGIE'S WAY

BRITTANY LN

HAWEA LN
PAIA LN
KEANAHALULULU LN
LAUMAIA LN
AIR STRIP DR
KEAWAKAPU DR
NAAEHU CT
KOELE CT
NINOLE CT
WANANAE CT

LOVERS LN
HAOU CT
AWEHI CT
LIPOA DR
UPOLA CT

EL CAMINO REAL RD
RIVERSIDE DR

14
6
1

WAIKAKAAUA DR
WAIPAHOEHOE DR

A
B

KIEAHI
KIPAPA CT
WAIMALU CT

W PAUWELA LN

W KEOMUKU LN
POHAKULOA DR
E KEOMUKU LN
E PAUWELA LN
MOKULUA LN

W KIKIPUA LN
E KIKIPUA LN
KOLEKOLE LN
W WAIENUE
E AHUPU LN
W AHUPU LN
KAAUA DR
WAIKIKI DR
HAUULA CT

RIVERSIDE DR

KAWAINUI LN
WAIMANALO LN
PUU WAA WAA LN
NUUANU LN
MANANA CT
LAIWAI
WAIMALU
KAULOO CT
HALAWA

LAMALOA LN
NUUANU LN

HOWLI LN
HELEAKALA DR
WAHANE LN
KAWI CT
AIEA LN

HILEA CT
DIAMOND HEAD DR

HANAUMA DR
HELEMANO DR

KAAAWA LN

78602

HELEAKALA DR

WAIALUA CT
KAMAIKI DR
MOLOKINI DR
WAINEE DR
AUAU DR
PAIA CV
EKE CT
HEKILI DR
PAPAWAI DR
UMIPAA LN
WAIHI
KOAE CT
KUIKUI
PAPAWAI DR
HUELO CT
WAHANE LN
KOKO CT

LOPA CT

NANAKULI LN
KAUPA CT
KAUAI CT
MOKOLEA LN

ANAHULU LN
OAH CT
KAELEPULU DR
WAILUPE CIR

KOLEKOLE LN
KAAAWA LN

WAILUPE CIR

MOKULEIA CIR

KAELEPULU DR

KAUKONAHUA LN

AKALOA DR
KONAHUANUI LN

RIVERSIDE DR

Colorado River

Pine Forest
Golf Course

C
D
6
E
F
G
H
5

J
78662
K
N
P
Q
R

UP RR
N KAUFFMAN RD

© Mapsco, Inc.

BASTROP COUNTY

S
T
U
V
4
W
X
Y
Z

N KAUFFMAN RD
Eddie Robinson Rd

HILLS PRAIRIE RD

S KAUFMANN RD

HUBBARD ST

Cemetery

EE
EF

CONTINUED IN HAYS CO
MAPSCO ON MAP 38

CONTINUED IN HAYS CO
MAPSCO ON MAP 49

CONTINUED ON MAP 776

SCALE IN MILES
0   1/8   1/4   3/8   1/2

SCALE IN FEET
0   1000   2000   3000

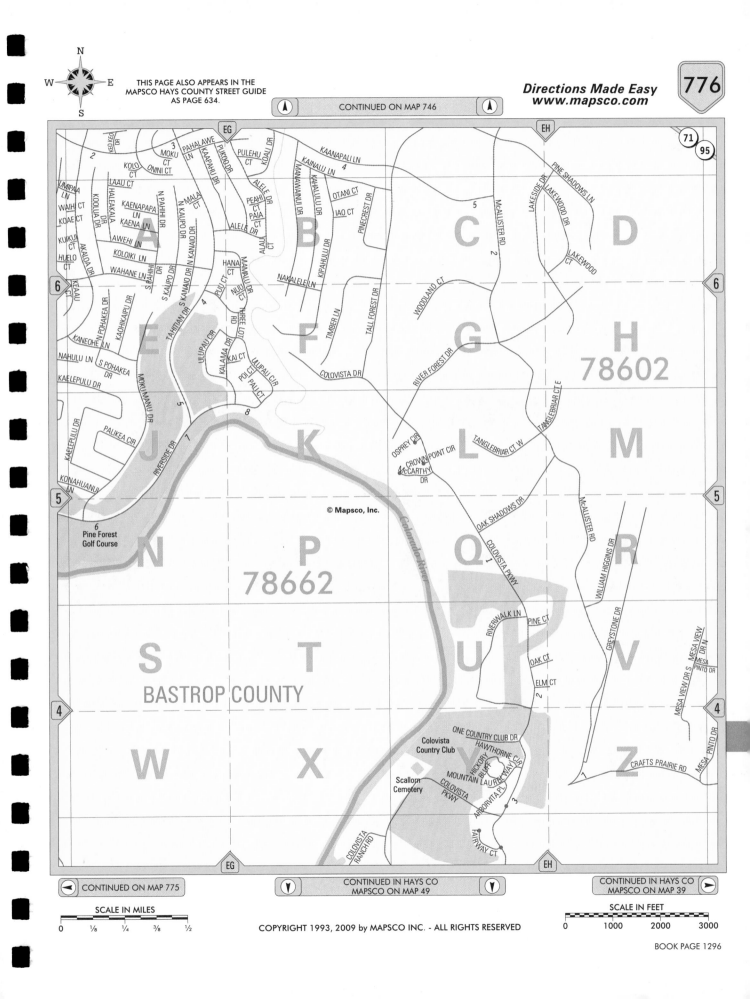

794 **Directions Made Easy**
www.mapsco.com

THIS PAGE ALSO APPEARS IN THE
MAPSCO HAYS COUNTY STREET GUIDE
AS PAGE 662.

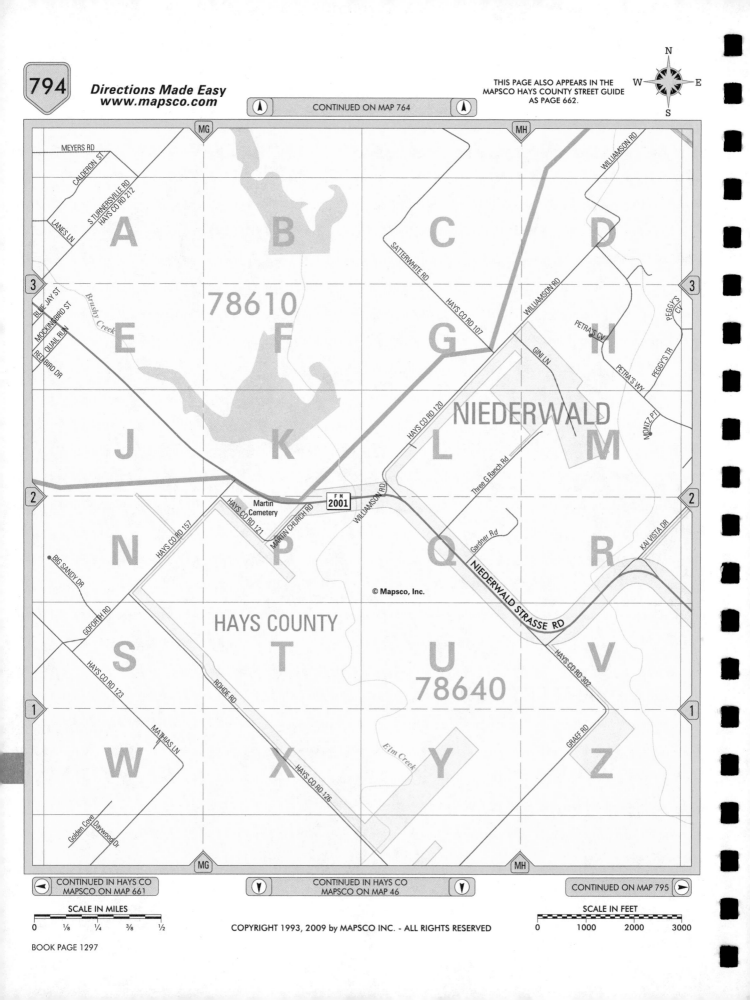

CONTINUED ON MAP 764

MEYERS RD
CALDERON ST
S TURNERSVILLE RD
HAYS CO RD 212
LANES LN
WILLIAMSON RD
SATTERWHITE RD
HAYS CO RD 107
WILLIAMSON RD
PEGGY'S CV

A   B   C   D

78610

BLUE JAY ST
MOCKINGBIRD ST
QUAIL RUN
RED BIRD DR
Brushy Creek
GINI LN
PETRA'S CV
PETRA'S WY
PEGGY'S TR
MONTZ PT

E   F   G   H

HAYS CO RD 120
NIEDERWALD

J   K   L   M

Three G Ranch Rd

HAYS CO RD 121
Martin
Cemetery
MARTIN CHURCH RD
FM 2001
WILLIAMSON RD
Gardner Rd
KAI VISTA DR

N   P   Q   R

HAYS CO RD 157
© Mapsco, Inc.
NIEDERWALD STRASSE RD
HAYS CO RD 302

BIG SANDY DR
GOFORTH RD
HAYS COUNTY
HAYS CO RD 123
ROHDE RD
78640

S   T   U   V

MATHIAS LN
Elm Creek
HAYS CO RD 126
GRAEF RD

W   X   Y   Z

GOLDEN COVE
DAYWOOD DR

CONTINUED IN HAYS CO
MAPSCO ON MAP 661

CONTINUED IN HAYS CO
MAPSCO ON MAP 46

CONTINUED ON MAP 795

SCALE IN MILES
0   1/8   1/4   3/8   1/2

SCALE IN FEET
0   1000   2000   3000

BOOK PAGE 1297

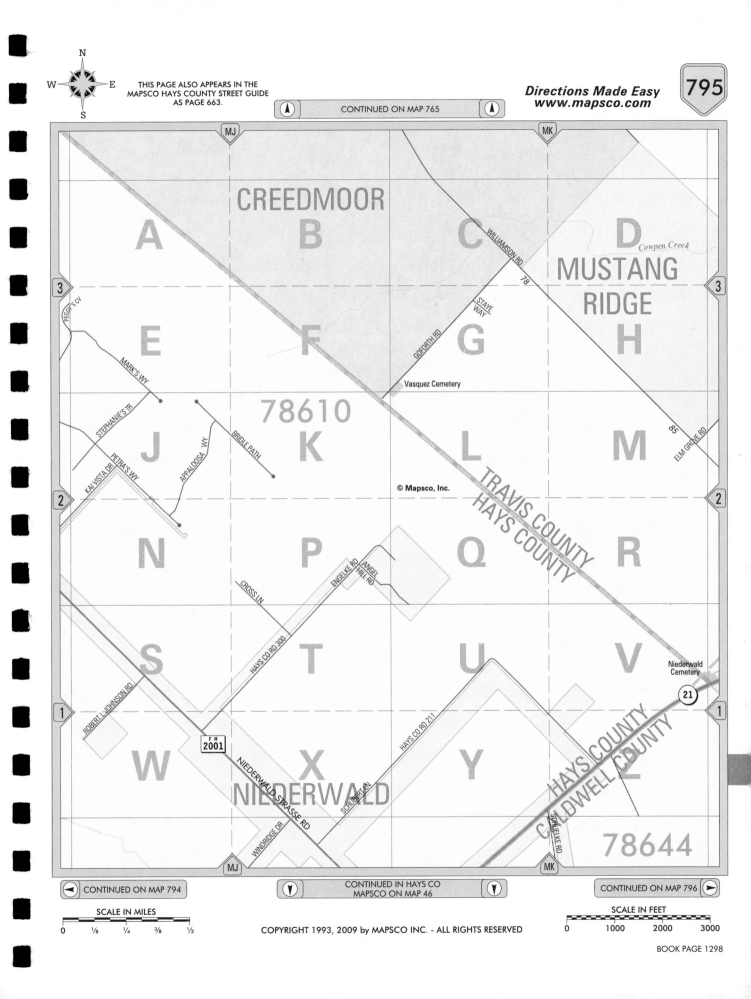

N
W E
S

THIS PAGE ALSO APPEARS IN THE
MAPSCO HAYS COUNTY STREET GUIDE
AS PAGE 663.

Directions Made Easy
www.mapsco.com

CONTINUED ON MAP 765

MJ   MK

CREEDMOOR

A   B   C   D   *Cowpen Creek*

WILLIAMSON RD

3   MUSTANG   3
                                      RIDGE

E   F   G   H

STAVE WAY

78   85

GOFORTH RD

Vasquez Cemetery

78610

J   K   L   M

ELM GROVE RD

MARK'S WY

STEPHANIE'S TR

APPALOOSA WY

BRIDLE PATH

KAI VISTA DR

PETRA'S WY

© Mapsco, Inc.

TRAVIS COUNTY
HAYS COUNTY

2   N   P   Q   R   2

ENGELKE RD
ANGEL HILL RD

CROSS LN

HAYS CO RD 300

S   T   U   V

Niederwald
Cemetery

ROBERT L JOHNSON RD

HAYS CO RD 211

21

1   1

FM 2001

W   X   Y   Z

NIEDERWALD
NIEDERWALD STRASSE RD

SCHLUERTON

HAYS COUNTY
CALDWELL COUNTY

SCHUELKE RD

WINDRIDGE DR

78644

MJ   MK

CONTINUED ON MAP 794

CONTINUED IN HAYS CO
MAPSCO ON MAP 46

CONTINUED ON MAP 796

SCALE IN MILES

0   1/8   1/4   3/8   1/2

SCALE IN FEET

0   1000   2000   3000

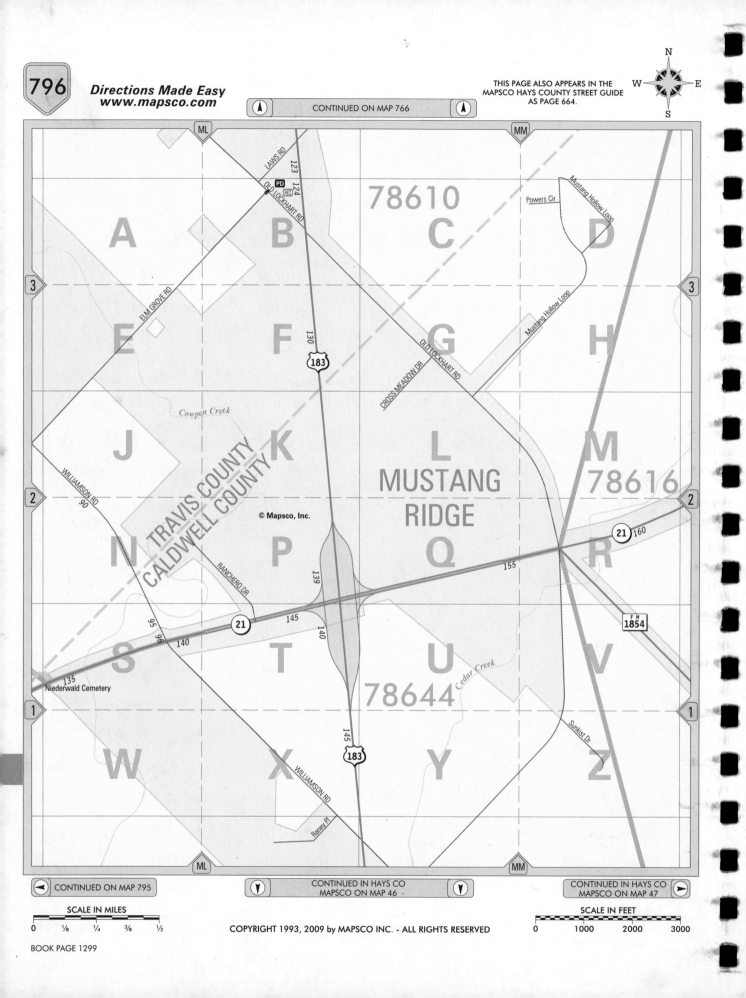

CONTINUED ON MAP 766

N
W E
S

ML MM

LAWS RD

123
124

78610

PD
CH

OLD LOCKHART RD

A B C Powers Cir Mustang Hollow Loop D

3 3

ELM GROVE RD

130

E F 183 G OLD LOCKHART RD H

Mustang Hollow Loop

CROSS MEADOW DR

Cowpen Creek

J TRAVIS COUNTY K CALDWELL COUNTY L M 78616

MUSTANG
RIDGE

© Mapsco, Inc.

WILLIAMSON RD

90

2 2
21 160

N RANCHERO DR P 139 Q 155 R

FM
1854

95 96 21 145

S 140 T 140 U Cedar Creek V

135
Niederwald Cemetery

1 78644 1

Sunkist Dr

145

W X 183 Y Z

WILLIAMSON RD

Raney Pl

ML MM

CONTINUED ON MAP 795

CONTINUED IN HAYS CO MAPSCO ON MAP 46

CONTINUED IN HAYS CO MAPSCO ON MAP 47

SCALE IN MILES
0 1/8 1/4 3/8 1/2

SCALE IN FEET
0 1000 2000 3000